Discover the New World with us

Amerindia offers a style of travel in Latin America where comfort, beauty and style go hand in hand with a discovery - or rediscovery - of the many varied and often unique charms, attractions and elements of the New World.

We can organise high quality tours and circuits for groups and individuals which are tailored according to particular interest in soft adventure, history, culture, art and artifacts, natural history, and sheer beauty. We will be covering the whole of Latin America, but right away have offices in the following countries:

• Ecuador • Perú • Bolivia • Central America •

Amerindia
The Undiscovered World

Contact the following offices for more information

Amerindia UK • Steeple Cottage / Easton, Winchester / Hampshire SO21 1EH England •
Tel: 01962-779317 • Fax: 01962-779458 • e-mail: pkellie@yachtors.u-net.com

Amerindia USA • 7855 N.W. 12th Street / Suite 115 / Miami, FL 33126 USA
Tel: (305) 599-9008 • 1-800-247-2925 • Fax: (305) 592-7060 • e-mail: tumbaco@gate.net

Mexico & Central America
Handbook

Sarah Cameron

with Ben Box

Footprint Handbooks

Oh I must hurry, I must hurry out
To the unspoiled savannahs of El Cayo
Where the flat grass rolls out into the haze
And the primenta flare their fans
In protest of the sun's insistence.

Raymond Barrow, *Oh I must Hurry*

2

Footprint Handbooks

TM

6 Riverside Court, Lower Bristol Road
Bath BA2 3DZ England
T 01225 469141 F 01225 469461
E mail handbooks@footprint.cix.co.uk

ISBN 1 900949 03 2 ISSN 0965-5492
CIP DATA: A catalogue record for this book is
available from the British Library

In North America, published by

PASSPORT BOOKS
NTC/Contemporary Publishing Company

4255 West Touhy Avenue, Lincolnwood
(Chicago), Illinois 60646-1975, USA
T 847 679 5500 F 847 679 24941
E mail NTCPUB2@AOL.COM

ISBN 0-8442-4784-7
Library of Congress Catalog Card
Number: on file
Passport Books and colophon are registered
trademarks of NTC Publishing group

Every effort has been made to ensure that
the facts in this Handbook are accurate.
However travellers should still obtain
advice from consulates, airlines etc about
current travel and visa requirements and
conditions before travelling. The editors
and publishers cannot accept responsibilty
for any loss, injury or inconvenience,
however caused.

Maps - the black and white text maps are
not intended to have any political
significance.

Title page quotation taken from *West Indian
Poetry*, edited by Kenneth Ramchand & Cecil
Gray, Longman 1989

Cover design by Newell and Sorrell;
photography by Jamie Marshall and Exodus

Production: Design by Mytton Williams;
Secretarial assistance Rhoda Williams;
Typesetting by Jo Morgan and Ann Griffiths;
Maps by Sebastian Ballard, Kevin Feeney and
Aldous George; Proofread by Rod Gray.

Printed and bound in Great Britain by
Clays Ltd., Bungay, Suffolk

Contents

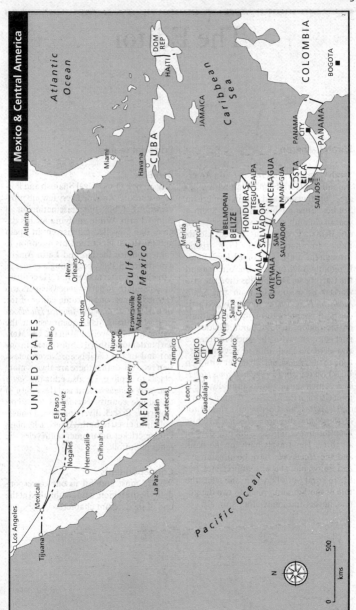

Mexico & Central America

Atlantic Ocean

COLOMBIA

BOGOTA

DOM REP
HAITI

Caribbean Sea

JAMAICA

CUBA

PANAMA CITY

PANAMA

Havana

COSTA RICA

SAN JOSE

NICARAGUA

MANAGUA

HONDURAS

TEGUCIGALPA

EL SALVADOR

SAN SALVADOR

BELMOPAN

BELIZE

GUATEMALA

GUATEMALA CITY

Merida

Cancun

Miami

Atlanta

New Orleans

Gulf of Mexico

Houston

Dallas

Brownsville/Matamoros

Nuevo Laredo

Tampico

Veracruz

Salina Cruz

MEXICO CITY

Puebla

Acapulco

UNITED STATES

El Paso/Cd Juárez

Monterrey

Zacatecas

Leon

Guadalajara

Mazatlán

Chihuahua

MEXICO

Hermosillo

Nogales

Mexicali

Los Angeles

Tijuana

La Paz

Pacific Ocean

N

500

kms

0

The Editor

Sarah Cameron

Sarah Cameron's interest in Latin America and the Caribbean began with a degree in Iberian and Latin American Studies, during which time she spent a year in Colombia. Following a spell with the British Council she joined Lloyds Bank International in 1977 rising through the ranks to become Lloyds Bank Economic Advisor on Latin America and the Caribbean. During this time she also worked as a sub-editor on the *South American Handbook* and contributed articles and chapters to many publications on the region. In 1990 Sarah decided to part company with the world of finance and debt rescheduling to devote more time to the *Handbooks*. Together with Ben Box she wrote the *Caribbean Islands Handbook*, which she now edits annually, she is joint editor of the *Mexico & Central American Handbook* and occasional sub-editor of the *South American Handbook*, while keeping an eye on the economic data in all three. Her travels both for the bank and the *Handbooks* have been extensive and enjoyable; she also appreciates her life in rural Suffolk, where she takes the role of mother and groom to two daughters, horses and many other animals.

Editorial team

Ben Box

A doctorate in medieval Spanish and Portugese studies provided very few job prospects for Ben Box, but a fascination for all things Latin. While studying for his degree, Ben travelled extensively in Spain and Portugal. He turned his attention to contemporary Iberian and Latin American affairs in 1980, beginning a career as a freelance writer at that time. He contributed regularly to national newspapers and learned tomes, and became editor of the first *Mexico & Central America Handbook* in 1991. During his frequent visits to the region he has travelled from the US/Mexico border to southern Chile (not all in one go) and in the Caribbean. Nevertheless, Ben recognises that there are always more places to explore. He also edits the *South American Handbook* and is series editor of the single country *Handbooks* for South America. To seek diversion from a household immersed in Latin America, he plays village cricket in summer and cycles the lanes of Suffolk.

Correspondents

We are most grateful to our correspondents in the region, who are thanked at the end of the relevant chapters.

Specialist contributors
Kate Hennessy and Huw Clough, subeditors of the Mexico, Belize and Honduras chapters; Peter Pollard, subeditor of the Guatemala, El Salvador and Panama chapters; Rachel Rogers, subeditor of the Costa Rica and Nicaragua chapters; Nigel Gallop for music and dance; Paul Davies of Journey Latin America for details of air transport; John Lewis for information on business travel; Richard Robinson for hotel and other information; Binka and Robin le Breton for motoring; Ashley Rawlings for motorcycling; Hallam Murray for cycling; Hilary Bradt for hiking and trekking; Mark Eckstein of David Bellamy Associates for responsible tourism and Dr David Snashall for health.

Acknowledgements
Much additional help has been received during the preparation of this edition All contributions have been tremendously helpful and are duly acknowledged on page 1231.

We try as hard as we can to make each Footprint Handbook as up-to-date and accurate as possible but, of course, things always change. Many people write to us with new information, amendments or simply comments. Please do get in touch. In return we will send you details of our special guidebook offer.

See page 1233 for more information

Mexico and Central America

THINKING of visiting Latin America? Press reports, travel articles and TV holiday programmes cite Latin America as full of promise for 'adventurous' holidays. The pictures are clear to see: ancient Mayan pyramids, Spanish colonial splendours, the flora and fauna of a vast array of habitats, Indian markets, adventure sports, or just lazing on the beach. If the correspondence we receive about Mexico and Central America is anything to go by, the popularity of the countries in the region is already great. These are by no means secret hideaways, although each year pioneering travellers find new routes and uncover new treasures. Behind the publicity, the reality is as magnificent as the images suggest. Part of their appeal lies in contrasts: the juxtaposition of traditional and modern (in architecture, agriculture, transport, music), dry savannah or sodden cloud forest, flat wetlands or majestic volcanoes, rich or poor...

It is undeniable that some aspects of Latin America have received a negative press. The stereotyped 'bandido' has become the drug trafficker, the guerrilla, the urban criminal. However, no country in all of Latin America can be categorized as politically unstable, a health risk, or dangerous to visit. The signing of the peace accord in Guatemala in late 1996 marked the official end to the last civil war in Central America. This is expected to boost investment, social improvement, and ultimately tourism, already a significant contributor to the economy. Elections are due in several counties and the increase in political activity is based on democracy, not the prospect of coups and violence. Even those rare parts of the region which still host guerrilla movements may be travelled without peril – provided you seek local advice. As for crime, we now live in a world where crime is a fact of life. Travellers are always vulnerable but Central America is no worse than many other places.

Tour operators are quoting Peru, Chile, Mexico, Cuba, Costa Rica and Belize as among the top new destinations for adventure holidays. Four of those countries feature in this *Handbook*. Cuba is increasingly attracting independent travellers and many of those visit the island from Mexico as an excursion from the Yucatán. This year Sarah Cameron visited to check out the new resort developments, while our researcher, Gavin Clark travelled the length of the Sierra Maestra, Hilary Emberton toured colonial cities, our resident correspondent, Angie Todd, thoroughly revised the Havana section, and our secretarial assistant, Rhoda Williams, tested the sun loungers. All the team reported favourably, as have all the travellers who have written to the *Handbook*. Go with an open mind, don't expect miracles of a country starved of foreign exchange and imports, and you will discover its major asset: the Cuban people, whose warmth and vibrancy have produced a fascinating culture with its music, theatre, dance, cinema, art, architecture. Some of the beaches are pretty good too.

We hope that we can inspire you to travel the length and breadth of the region, or just take a short break, and that this, our 8th edition of the *Mexico & Central America Handbook*, will provide you with all the necessary materials for a successful trip.

Sarah Cameron, The Editor

Responsible tourism

Much has been written about the adverse impacts of tourism on the environment and local communities. It is usually assumed that this only applies to the more excessive end of the travel industry such as the Spanish Costas and Bali. However it now seems that travellers can have an impact at almost any density and this is especially true in areas 'off the beaten track' where local people may not be used to western conventions and lifestyles, and natural environments may be very sensitive.

Of course, tourism can have a beneficial impact and this is something to which every traveller can contribute. Many National Parks are part funded by receipts from people who travel to see exotic plants and animals, Barro Colorado (Panama) and the Cockscomb Jaguar Sanctuary (Belize) are good examples of such sites. Similarly, travellers can promote patronage and protection of valuable archaeological sites and heritages through their interest and entrance fees.

However, where visitor pressure is high and/or poorly regulated, damage can occur. This is especially so in parts of the Caribbean where some tour operators are expanding their activities with scant regard for the environment or local communities. It is also unfortunately true that many of the most popular destinations are in ecologically sensitive areas easily disturbed by extra human pressures. The desire to visit sites and communities that are off the beaten track is a driving force for many travellers. However, these are the areas that are often most sensitive to change as a result of increased pressure from visitors. Eventually the very features that tourists travel so far to see may become degraded and so we seek out new sites, discarding the old, and leaving someone else to deal with the plight of local communities and the damaged environment.

Fortunately, there are signs of a new awareness of the responsibilities that the travel industry and its clients need to endorse. For example, some tour operators fund local conservation projects and travellers are now more aware of the impact they may have on host cultures and environments. We can all contribute to the success of what is variously described as responsible, green or alternative tourism. All that is required is a little forethought and consideration. It would be impossible to identify all the possible impacts that might need to be addressed by travellers, but it is worthwhile noting the major areas in which we can all take a more responsible attitude in the countries we visit. These include, changes to natural ecosystems (air, water, land, ecology and wildlife), cultural values (beliefs and behaviour) and the built environment (sites of antiquity and archaeological significance). At an individual level, travellers can reduce their impact if greater consideration is given to their activities. Backpacking along the Maya trade routes makes for great stories, but how do local communities cope with the sudden invasive interest in their lives? Will the availability of easy tourist money and gauche behaviour affect them for the worse, possibly diluting the significance of culture and customs? Similarly, have the environmental implications of increased visitor pressure been considered? Litter and disturbance of wildlife might seem to be small issues and, on an individual scale they probably are, however multiplied several fold they become more serious (as the Inca Trail in Peru can attest).

Some of these impacts are caused by factors beyond the direct control of travellers, such as the management and operation of a hotel chain. Even here it is possible to voice concern about damaging activities and an increasing number of hotels and travel operators are taking 'green concerns' seriously, even if it is only to protect their share of the market.

Environmental Legislation Legislation is increasingly being enacted to control damage to the environment, and in some cases this can have a bearing on travellers. The establishment of National Parks may involve rules and guidelines for visitors and these should always be followed. In addition there may be local or national laws controlling behaviour and use of natural resources (especially wildlife) that are being increasingly enforced. If in doubt, ask. Finally, international legislation, principally the Convention on International Trade in Endangered Species of Wild Fauna and Flora (CITES), may affect travellers.

CITES aims to control the trade in live specimens of endangered plants and animals and also 'recognizable parts or derivatives' of protected species. Sale of Black Coral, Turtle Shells, Protected Orchids and other wildlife is strictly controlled by signatories of the convention. The full list of protected wildlife varies, so if you feel the need to purchase souvenirs and trinkets derived from wildlife, it would be prudent to check whether they are protected. Every country included in this Handbook is a signatory of CITES. In addition, most European countries, the USA and Canada are all signatories of CITES. Importation of CITES protected species into these countries can lead to heavy fines, confiscation of goods and even imprisonment. Information on the status of legislation and protective measures can be obtained from Traffic International, UK office T (01223) 277427, F (01223) 277237, e-mail traffic @wcmc.org.uk.

Green Travel Companies and Information The increasing awareness of the environmental impact of travel and tourism has led to a range of advice and information services as well as spawning specialist travel companies who claim to provide 'responsible travel' for clients. This is an expanding field and the veracity of claims needs to be substantiated in some cases. The following organizations and publications can provide useful information for those with an interest in pursuing responsible travel opportunities.

Organizations Green Flag International Aims to work with travel industry and conservation bodies to improve environments at travel destinations and also to promote conservation programmes at resort destinations. Provides a travellers guide for 'green' tourism as well as advice on destinations, T (UK 01223) 890250. Tourism Concern Aims to promote a greater understanding of the impact of tourism on host communities and environments; Southlands College, Wimbledon Parkside, London SW19 5NN, T (UK 0181) 944-0464, e-mail tourconcern@gn.apc.org. Centre for Responsible Tourism CRT coordinates a North American network and advises on N American sources of information on responsible tourism. CRT, PO Box 827, San Anselmo, California 94979, USA. Centre for the Advancement of Responsive Travel CART has a range of publications available as well as information on alternative holiday destinations, T (UK-01732) 352757.

La Ruta Maya
Integrated tourism and conservation

THE RUTA MAYA

This ambitious project aims to tap the tourist potential of that region of southern Mexico and Central America once dominated by the Maya. It involves the cooperation of public and private tourist bodies of Mexico, Guatemala, Belize, El Salvador and Honduras. It is one of the regions of the world with the greatest variety of tourist attractions. As well as archaeological sites, the various countries share to a greater or lesser degree modern Maya culture, national parks, beaches, lakes, volcanoes and various types of forest. There is still a long way to go before the fully-integrated tourist circuit envisaged in the *National Geographic* magazine of October 1989 comes to fruition. To date, a regional Ruta Maya headquarters has been inaugurated just outside Belize City, tour operators have been meeting regularly to plan cross-border routes, etc, and the concept has become well established.

Many archaeological sites are already popular tourist attractions, with the accompanying infrastructure (eg Tikal, Guatemala page 667; Palenque, Chichén Itzá, Mexico page 411 and page 443; Copán, Honduras page 938). Others, while thoroughly excavated, are less well-known and yet others, still under excavation, are becoming part of the tourist route (eg Caracol, Belize page 777; Calakmul, Mexico page 482; Joya del Cerén, El Salvador page 829). As present-day knowledge of the historical Maya grows, so efforts are being made to safeguard the traditions of the Maya peoples living now,

traditions which are both centuries old and enmeshed with Catholicism. In the context of the Ruta Maya, such safeguards must include the avoidance of the worst aspects of voyeuristic tourism. Both people and their environment face economic and population pressures. The expansion of natural parks, for instance the recent enlargement by 55,000 hectares of the Montes Azules biological reserve in Lacandonia to include Bonampak and Yaxchilán (Mexico page 417), have been welcomed. Parks in existence cover rainforest and cloud forest, Belize's diverse environments, including marine, the *biotopos* in Guatemala and the waterbird sanctuaries in northern Yucatán, Mexico. Of the landscapes, one can mention the chain of volcanoes extending through Mexico, Guatemala and El Salvador, associated with which are some beautiful lakes, or, offshore, the cayes and reefs of Belize.

The Ruta Maya should prove beneficial in terms of road building, flight links, hotel construction and ease of access between neighbouring countries. One major question surrounds this development, though; is there a danger that the Ruta Maya will isolate this region as a tourist 'hot spot', to the detriment of the region itself (ie as an extension of what is generally accepted to be overdevelopment at Cancún, Mexico page 451), and to the detriment of other parts of Mexico and the rest of Central America through a lack of comparable funding? It is to be hoped that this danger will not arise. Mexican tourism projects are spread over many areas in the country, taking in a wide array of archaeological heritage, both pre-conquest and colonial. Beach developments, such as Huatulco (Mexico see page 361), are taking place concurrently with whatever progress is being made on the Ruta Maya. A colonial cities programme, covering 51 places, has been developed. For both Guatemala and Belize, the Ruta Maya will build on the attractions to which visitors are already drawn. While Copán, Honduras' main Maya connection may act as an enticement for people to travel to other parts of the country, El Salvador will expect the Ruta Maya to encourage the reemergence of a tourist industry as the country rebuilds after the civil war. Much depends upon how great a percentage of Ruta Maya tourism is concentrated in the package tour market.

The Mundo Maya is a sister project to the Ruta Maya in that it covers the same area, but is operated by Central American and Mexican representatives (the Ruta Maya was founded in the USA).

● **Contacts**: Wilbur Garrett, Ruta Maya Foundation, 209 Seneca Road, Great Falls, VA 22066, USA, T (703) 450-4160.

● **Maps** in this volume which refer to areas discussed in the Ruta Maya: Mexico (page 67), Regional South (page 342) and Yucatán (page 405); Guatemala, Country Map (page 605) and El Petén and Alta Verapaz (page 663); Belize, Country Map (page 736) and Cuyes Map (page 753); El Salvador, Country Map (page 798); Honduras, Western Honduras and Copán (page 936).

Precolumbian civilizations

The Aztec empire which Hernán Cortés encountered in 1519 and subsequently destroyed was the third major power to have dominated what is now known as Mexico. Before it, the empires of Teotihuacan and Tula each unified what had essentially been an area of separate Indian groups. All 3, together with their neighbours such as the Maya (dealt with below) and their predecessors, belong to a more-or-less common culture called Mesoamerica.

Despite the wide variety of climates and terrains that fall within Mesoamerica's boundaries, from northern Mexico to El Salvador and Honduras, the civilizations that developed there were interdependent, sharing the same agriculture (based on maize, beans and squash) and many sociological features. These included an enormous pantheon, with the god of rain and the feathered serpent hero predominant; the offering of blood to the gods, from oneself and from sacrificial victims usually taken in war; pyramid-building; a game played with a rubber ball; trade in feathers, jade and other valuable objects, possibly from as far away as the Andean region of South America; hieroglyphic writing; astronomy; an elaborate calendar.

The Mesoamerican calendar was a combination of a 260-day almanac year and the 365-day solar year. A given day in one of the years would only coincide with that in the other every 52 years, a cycle called the Calendar Round. In order to give the Calendar Round a context within a larger timescale, a starting date for both years was devised; the date chosen by the Classic Maya was equivalent to 3113 BC in Christian time. Dates measured from this point are called Long Count dates.

Historians divide Mesoamerican civilizations into 3 periods, the Pre-classic, which lasted until about AD 300, the Classic, until AD 900, and the Post-classic, from 900 until the Spanish conquest. An alternative delineation is: Olmec, Teotihuacan and Aztec, named after the dominant civilizations within each of those periods.

The Olmecs

Who precisely the Olmecs were, where they came from and why they disappeared, is a matter of debate. It is known that they flourished from about 1400 to 400 BC, that they lived in the Mexican Gulf Coast region between Veracruz and Tabasco, and that all later civilizations have their roots ultimately in Olmec culture. They carved colossal heads, stelae (tall, flat monuments), jade figures and altars; they gave great importance to the jaguar and the serpent in their imagery; they built large ceremonial centres, such as San Lorenzo and La Venta. Possibly derived from the Olmecs and gaining importance in the first millenium BC was the centre in the Valley of Oaxaca at Monte Albán. This was a major city, with certain changes of influence, right through until the end of the Classic period. Also derived from the Olmecs was the Izapa civilization, on the Pacific border of present day Mexico and Guatemala. Here seems to have taken place the progression from the Olmec to the Maya civilization, with obvious connections in artistic style, calendar-use, ceremonial architecture and the transformation of the Izapa Long-lipped God into the Maya Long-nosed God.

Teotihuacan

Almost as much mystery surrounds the origins of Teotihuacan as those of the Olmecs. Teotihuacan, 'the place where men become gods', was a great urban state, holding in its power most of the central highlands of Mexico. Its influence can be detected in the Maya area, Oaxaca and the civilizations on the Gulf Coast which succeeded the Olmecs. The monuments in the city itself are enormous, the planning precise; it is estimated that by the 7th century AD some 125,000 people were living in its immediate vicinity. Early evidence did not suggest that Teotihuacan's power was gained by force, but research now indicates both human sacrifice and sacred warfare. Again for reasons unknown, Teotihuacan's influence over its neighbours ended around 600 AD. Its glory coincided with that of the Classic Maya, but the latter's decline occurred some 300 years later, at which time a major change affected all Mesoamerica.

The Toltecs

The start of the Post-classic period, between the Teotihuacan and Aztec horizons, was marked by an upsurge in militarism. In the semi-deserts to the N of the settled societies of central Mexico and Veracruz lived groups of nomadic hunters. These people, who were given the general name of Chichimecs, began to invade the central region and were quick to adopt the urban characteristics of the groups they overthrew. The Toltecs of Tula were one such invading force, rapidly building up an empire stretching from the Gulf of Mexico to the Pacific in central Mexico. Infighting by factions within the Toltecs split the rulers and probably hastened the empire's demise sometime after 1150. The exiled leader Topíltzin Quetzalcóatl (Feathered Serpent) is possibly the founder of the Maya-Toltec rule in the Yucatán (the Maya spoke of a Mexican invader named Kukulcán – Feathered Serpent). He is certainly the mythical figure the Aztec ruler, Moctezuma II, took Cortés to be, returning by sea from the E.

The Mixtecs

Another important culture which developed in the first millenium AD was the Mixtec, in western Oaxaca. They infiltrated all the territory held by the Zapotecs, who had ruled Monte Albán during the Classic period and had built many other sites in the Valley of Oaxaca, including Mitla. The Mixtecs, in alliance with the Zapotecs successfully withstood invasion by the Aztecs.

The Aztecs

The process of transition from semi-nomadic hunter-gatherer to city and empire-builder continued with the Aztecs, who bludgeoned their way into the midst of rival city states in the vacuum left by the destruction of Tula. They rose from practically nothing to a power almost as great as Teotihuacan in about 200 years. From their base at Tenochtitlán in Lake Texcoco in the Valley of Mexico they extended through aggression their sphere of influence from the Tarascan Kingdom in the N to the Maya lands in the S. Not only did the conquered pay heavy tribute to their Aztec overlords, but they also supplied the constant flow of sacrificial victims needed to satisfy the deities, at whose head was Huitzilopochtli, the warrior god of the Sun. The speed with which the Aztecs adapted to a settled existence and fashioned a highly effective political state is remarkable. Their ability in sculpting stone, in pottery, in writing books, and in architecture (what we can gather from what the Spaniards did not destroy), was great. Surrounding all this activity was a strictly ritual existence, with ceremonies and feasts dictated by the 2 enmeshing calendars.

It is impossible to say whether the Aztec empire would have gone the way of its predecessors had not the Spaniards arrived to precipitate its collapse. Undoubtedly, the Europeans received much assistance from people who had been oppressed by the Aztecs and who wished to be rid of them. Needless to say, Cortés, with his horses and an unknown array of military equipment in relatively few hands, brought to an end in 2 years an extraordinary culture.

The Maya

The best known of the pre-Conquest Indian civilizations of the present Central American area was the Maya, which is thought to have evolved in a formative period in the Pacific highlands of Guatemala and El Salvador between 1500 BC and about AD 100. After 200 years of growth it entered what is known today as its Classic period when the civilization flourished in Guatemala, Belize and Honduras, and in Chiapas, Campeche and Yucatán (Mexico).

The Maya civilization was based on independent and antagonistic city states, including Tikal, Uaxactún, Kaminaljuyú, Iximché, Zaculeu and Quiriguá in Guatemala; Copán in Honduras; Altún Ha, Caracol, Lamanai in Belize; Tazumal and San Andrés in El Salvador; and Palenque, Bonampak (both in Chiapas), Uxmal, Mayapán, Tulum and the Puuc hill cities of Sayil, Labná and Kabah (all on the Yucatán peninsula) in Mexico. Recent research has revealed that these cities, far from being the peaceful ceremonial centres as once imagined, were warring adversaries, striving to capture victims for sacrifice. Furthermore, much of the cultural activity, controlled by a theocratic minority of priests and nobles, involved blood-letting, by even the highest members of society. Royal blood was the most precious offering that could be made to the gods. This change in perception of the Maya was the result of the discovery of defended cities and of a greater understanding of the Maya's hieroglyphic writing. Although John Lloyd Stephens' prophecy that 'a key surer than that of the Rosetta stone will be discovered' has not been fulfilled, the painstaking decipherment of the glyphs has uncovered many of the secrets of Maya society (see *Breaking the Maya Code* by Michael D Coe, Thames and Hudson).

Alongside the preoccupation with blood was an artistic tradition rich in ceremony, folklore and dance. They achieved paper codices and glyphic writing, which also appears on stone monuments and their fine ceramics; they were skilful weavers and traded over wide areas, though they did not use the wheel and had no beasts of burden. The cities were all meticulously dated. Mayan art is a mathematical art: each column, figure, face, animal, frieze, stairway and temple expresses a date or a time relationship. When, for example, an ornament on the ramp of the Hieroglyphic Stairway at Copán was repeated some 15 times, it was to express that number of elapsed 'leap' years. The 75 steps stand for the number of elapsed intercalary days. The Mayan calendar was a nearer approximation to sidereal time than either the Julian or the Gregorian calendars of Europe; it was only .000069 of a day out of true in a year. They used the zero centuries in advance of the Old World, plotted the movements of the sun, moon, Venus and other planets, and conceived a cycle of more than 1,800 million days.

Their tools and weapons were flint and hard stone, obsidian and fire-hardened wood, and yet with these they hewed out and transported great monoliths over miles of difficult country, and carved them over with intricate glyphs and figures which would be difficult enough with modern chisels. Also with those tools they grew lavish crops. To support urban populations now believed to number tens of thousands, and a population density of 150 per sq km (compared with less than 1 per sq km today), an agricultural system was developed of raised fields, fertilized by fish and vegetable matter from surrounding canals.

The height of the Classic period lasted until AD 900-1000, after which time the Maya concentrated into Yucatán after a successful invasion of their other lands by non-Maya people (this is only one theory: another is that they were forced to flee because of drought and a peasant rebellion). They then came under the influence of the Toltecs who invaded Yucatán; Chichén Itzá is considered to be an example of a Maya city which displays a great many Toltec features. From that time their culture declined. The Toltecs, who had firm control in Yucatán in the 10th century, gradually spread their empire as far as the southern borders of Guatemala. They in turn, however, were conquered by the Aztecs, who did not penetrate into Central America.

The music of the region

MEXICO

Mexican Music is particularly attractive and vibrant and a vigorous radio, film and recording industry has helped make it highly popular throughout Latin America. There can be no more representative an image of Mexico than the Mariachi musician and his *charro* costume. The Spanish conquistadores and the churchmen that followed them imposed European musical culture on the defeated natives with a heavy hand and it is this influence that remains predominant. Nobody knows what precolumbian music sounded like and even the music played today in the Indian communities is basically Spanish in origin. African slaves introduced a third ingredient, but there is no Afro-Mexican music as such and indeed there are few black Mexicans. The music brought from Europe has over the centuries acquired a highly distinctive sound and style of which every Mexican is justly proud, even if many of the young now prefer to listen to Anglo-American rock and pop, like their counterparts the world over.

There is a basic distinction between Indian and Mestizo music. The former is largely limited to the Indians' own festive rituals and dances, religious in nature and solemn in expression. The commonest instruments are flute and drum, with harp and violin also widely used. Some of the most spectacular dances are those of the Concheros (mainly urban), the Quetzales (from the Sierra de Puebla), the Voladores (flying pole – also Sierra de Puebla), the Tarascan dances from around Lake Pátzcuaro and the Yaqui deer dance (Sonora).

Mestizo music clearly has more mass appeal in what is an overwhelmingly mixed population. The basic form is the *son* (also called *huapango* in eastern areas), featuring a driving rhythm overlaid with dazzling instrumentals. Each region has its own style of *son*, such as the *son huasteco* (Northeast), *son calentano* (Michoacán/Guerrero), *chilena* (Guerrero coast), *son mariachi* (Jalisco), *jarana* (Yucatán) and *son jarocho* (Veracruz). One *son jarocho* that has achieved world status is 'La Bamba'. Instrumental backing is provided in almost all these areas by a combination of large and small guitars, with the violin as virtuoso lead in the *huasteca* and the harp in Veracruz. The *chilena* of Guerrero is said to have been introduced by Chilean seamen and miners on their way to the California gold rush, while Yucatán features a version of the Colombian *bambuco*. The *son* is a dance form for flirtation between couples, as befits a land of passionate men and women, and often involves spectacular heel-and-toe stamping by the man. Another widespread dance rhythm is the *jarabe*, including the patriotic 'Jarabe Tapatío', better known to the English-speaking world as the 'Mexican Hat Dance'. Certain regions are known for more sedate rhythms and a quite different choice of instruments. In the N, the Conjunto Norteño leads with an accordion and favours the polka as a rhythm. In Yucatán they prefer wind and brass instruments, while the Isthmus of Tehuantepec is the home of the *marimba* (xylophone), which it shares with neighbouring Guatemala.

For singing, as opposed to dancing, there are 3 extremely popular genres.

First is the *corrido*, a narrative form derived from old Spanish ballads, which swept across the country with the armies of the Revolution and has remained a potent vehicle for popular expression ever since. A second is the *canción* (literally 'Song'), which gives full rein to the romantic, sentimental aspect of the Mexican character and is naturally slow and languid. 'Las Mañanitas' is a celebrated song for serenading people on their birthdays. The third form is the *ranchera*, a sort of Mexican Country and Western, associated originally with the cattle-men of the Bajío region. Featured in a whole series of Mexican films of the 1930s and 1940s, *rancheras* became known all over the Spanish-speaking world as the typical Mexican music. The film and recording industry turned a number of Mexican artists into household names throughout Latin America. The 'immortals' are Pedro Infante, Jorge Negrete, Pedro Vargas, Miguel Aceves Mejía and the Trio Los Panchos, with Agustín Lara as an equally celebrated and prolific songwriter and composer, particularly of romantic *boleros*. To all outsiders and most Mexicans however there is nothing more musically Mexican than *mariachi*, a word said to be derived from the French 'mariage', introduced at the time of Maximilian and Carlota.

Originating in the state of Jalisco, *mariachi* bands arrived in Mexico City in the 1920s and have never looked back. Trumpets now take the lead, backed by violins and guitars and the players all wear *charro* (cowboy) costume, including the characteristic hat. They play all the major musical forms and can can be found almost every evening in Mexico City's Plaza Garibaldi, where they congregate to be seen, heard and, they hope, hired. This is the very soul of Mexico.

Finally, there are a number of distinguished 20th century composers who have produced symphonies and other orchestral works based on indigenous and folk themes. Carlos Chávez is the giant and his 'Sinfonía India' a particularly fine example. Other notable names are Silvestre Revueltas ('Sensemayá'), Pablo Moncayo ('Huapango'), Blas Galindo ('Sones de Mariachi') and Luis Sandi ('Yaqui Music').

CENTRAL AMERICA

Native music is at its most vigorous and flourishing at either end of the region, in Guatemala and Panama. In the intervening 4 republics its presence is more localized and indeed elusive. From Guatemala southwards a rich musical tradition based largely on the *marimba* (xylophone) as an instrument and the *son* as a song/dance genre fades fast but continues tenuously all the way down to Costa Rica, while Panama has its own very distinctive vein of traditional music, with a combination of Spanish and African elements. While the influence of Mexican music is all pervasive in the northern 5 republics, Panama is more closely linked with the Caribbean coasts of Colombia and Venezuela in its musical idioms.

Guatemala

This is the heartland of the *marimba*, which it shares with parts of southern Mexico. How this came about has been much debated between adherents of a native precolumbian origin and those who believe the *marimba* came from Africa with colonial slavery. Whatever its origins, it is now regarded as the national instrument in Guatemala, belonging equally to Indian and *ladino*. Among the Indians the more rustic *marimba de tecomate* with gourds as resonators is still to be found, whereas most instruments now have the box resonator. The manufacture and playing of *marimbas* has developed to the point where a number of them are now combined to form an orchestra, as with the Pans of Trinidad. Among the best known *marimba* orchestras are the Marimba Tecún Umán, Marimba Antigua and highly sophisticated Marimba Nacional de Concierto. Every village has its *marimba* players and no wedding or other secular celebration would be complete without them. The music played is generally either a fast or slow *son*, but the modern repertoire is likely to include many Mexican numbers.

Although the *marimba* is basic to the Indians as well as to the *ladinos*, the former have other instruments for their religious rituals and processions, such as the *tun* (a precolumbian drum), *tzicolaj* (flute), *chirimía* (oboe) and violin. These are the instruments that accompany the colourful vernacular dances of the 'Culebra' (snake), 'Venado' (deer) and 'Palo Volador' (flying pole), as also the 'Baile de las Canastas' and 'Rabinal Achí', 2 precolombian historical dramas that have amazingly survived the conquest and colonial period and are still performed at Chajul and Rabinal (Alta Verapaz) respectively.

El Salvador and Honduras

Two countries that tend to 'hide their light under a bushel' as regards native music. It is here above all that the Mexican music industry seems to exert an overwhelming cultural influence, while the virtual absence of an Indian population may also be partly responsible, since it is so often they who maintain traditions and hold to the past, as in Guatemala. Whatever the reason, the visitor who is seeking specifically Salvadorean or Honduran native music will find little to satisfy him or her. El Salvador is an extension of 'marimba country', but in both republics popular songs and dances are often accompanied by the guitar and seem to lack a rhythm or style that can be pinpointed as specifically local. An exception in El Salvador is the music played on the *pito de caña* and *tambor* which accompanies the traditional dances called 'Danza de los Historiantes', 'La Historia' or 'Los Moros y Cristianos'. Over 30 types of dance have been identified, mostly in the W and centre of the country, although there are a few in the E. The main theme is the conflict between christianized *indígenos* and 'heretic' *indígenos* and the dances are performed as a ritual on the local saint's day. Honduras shares with Belize and Guatemala the presence of Garífuna or Black Caribs on the Caribbean coast. These descendants of Carib Indians and escaped black slaves were deported to the area from St Vincent in the late 18th century and continue to maintain a very separate identity, including their own religious observances, music and dances, profoundly African in spirit and style.

Nicaragua

Here we again find ourselves in 'marimba country' and here again the basic musical genre is the *son*, here called the 'Son Nica'. There are a number of popular dances for couples with the names of animals, like 'La Vaca' (cow), 'La Yeguita' (mare) and 'El Toro' (bull). The folklore capital of Nicaragua is the city of Masaya and the musical heart of Masaya is the Indian quarter of Monimbó. Here the *marimba* is king, but on increasingly rare occasions may be supported by the *chirimía* (oboe), *quijada de asno* (asses jaw) and *quijongo*, a single-string bow with gourd resonator. Some of the most traditional Sones are 'El Zañate', 'Los Novios' and 'La Perra Renca', while the more popular dances still to be found are 'Las Inditas', 'Las Negras', 'Los Diablitos' and 'El Torovenado', all involving masked characters. Diriamba is another centre of tradition, notable for the folk play known as 'El Güeguense', accompanied by violin, fife and drum and the dance called 'Toro Guaco'. The Caribbean coast is a totally different cultural region, home to the Miskito Indians and English speaking black people of Jamaican origin concentrated around Bluefields. The latter have a maypole dance and their music is typically Afro-Caribbean, with banjos, accordeons, guitars and of course drums as the preferred instruments.

Costa Rica

This is the southernmost in our string of 'marimba culture' countries. The guitar is also a popular instrument for accompanying folk dances, while the *chirimía* and *quijongo*, already encountered further N, have not yet totally died out in the Chorotega region of Guanacaste Province. This province is indeed the heartland of Costa Rican folklore and the 'Punto Guanacasteco', a heel-and-toe dance for couples, has been officially decreed to be the 'typical national dance', although it is not in fact traditional, but was composed at the turn of the century by Leandro Cabalceta Brau during a brief sojourn in gaol. There are other dances too, such as the 'Botijuela Tamborito' and 'Cambute', but it must honestly be said that they will not be found in the countryside as a tradition, but are performed on stage when outsiders need to be shown some native culture. Among the country's most popular native performers are the duet Los Talolingas, authors of 'La Guaria Morada', regarded as the 'second national anthem' and Lorenzo 'Lencho' Salazar, whose humorous songs in the vernacular style are considered quintessentially 'tico'.

Some of the republic's rapidly deculturizing Indian groups have dances of their own, like the 'Danza de los Diablitos' of the Borucas, the 'Danza del Sol' and 'Danza de la Luna' of the Chorotegas and the 'Danza de los Huesos' of the Talamancas. A curious ocarina made of beeswax, the *dru mugata* is still played by the Guaymí Indians and is said to be the only truly precolumbian instrument still to be found. The drum and flute are traditional among various groups, but the guitar and accordeon are moving in to replace them. As in the case of Nicaragua, the Caribbean coast of Costa Rica, centred on Puerto Limón, is inhabited by black people who came originally from the English speaking islands and whose music reflects this origin. The *sinkit* seems to be a strictly local rhythm, but the *calypso* is popular and the *cuadrille*, square dance and maypole dance are also found. There is too a kind of popular hymn called the *saki*. Brass, percussion and string instruments are played, as also the accordeon.

Panama

Panama is the crossroads of the Americas, where Central America meets South America and the Caribbean backs onto the Pacific. One of the smallest Latin American republics and the last to achieve independence, from Colombia, it nonetheless possesses an outstandingly rich and attractive musical culture. Albeit related to that of the Caribbean coast of Colombia and Venezuela, it is extremely distinctive. The classic Panamanian folk dances are the *tambor* or *tamborito*, *cumbia*, *punto* and *mejorana*, largely centred on the central provinces of Coclé and Veraguas and those of Herrera and Los Santos on the Azuero Peninsula. Towns that are particularly noted for their musical traditions are Los Santos, Ocú, Las Tablas, Tonosí and Chorrera. The dances are for couples and groups of couples and the rhythms are lively and graceful, the man often dancing close to his partner without touching her, moving his hat in rhythmic imitation of fanning. The woman's *pollera* costume is arguably the most beautiful in Latin America and her handling of the voluminous skirt is an important element of the dance. The *tamborito* is considered to be Panama's national dance and is accompanied by 3 tall drums. The *cumbia*, which has a common origin with the better known Colombian dance of the same name, has a fast variant called the *atravesado*, while the *punto* is slower and more stately. The name *mejorana* is shared by a small native guitar, a dance, a song form and a specific tune. The commonest instruments to be found today are the tall drums that provide the basic beat, the violin, the guitar and the accordeon, with the last named rapidly becoming predominant. The *tuna* is a highly rhythmic musical procession with womens' chorus and massed hand-clapping.

Turning to song, there are 2 traditional forms, both of Spanish origin, the *copla*, sung by women and accompanying the *tamborito*, and the *mejorana*, which is a male solo preserve, with the lyrics in the form of *décimas*, a verse form used by the great Spanish poets of the Golden Age. It is accompanied by the ukulele-like guitar of the same name. Quite unique to Panama are the *salomas* and *gritos*, the former between 2 or more men. The yodelling and falsetto of the *salomas* are in fact carried over into the singing style and it is this element, more than any other, that gives Panamanian folk song its unique and instantly recognizable sound. There are other traditional masked street dances of a carnavalesque nature, such as the very African 'Congos', the 'Diablicos Sucios' (dirty little devils) and the 'Grandiablos' (big devils). In the area of the Canal there is a significant English speaking black population, similar to those in Nicaragua and Costa Rica, who also sing *calypso*, while the Guaymí Indians in the W and the Cuna and Chocó of the San Blas islands and Darién isthmus possess their own song, rituals and very attractive flute music.

David M Fishlow adds: when travelling in rural areas during working hours, listen for the distinctive yodelling call of Panamanian farm workers, who greet each other in the fields over long distances with the *saloma*, a cry that slides from a rumble in the throat to a falsetto and back into a rumble, usually rendered in Spanish as '*Ajuuúa*'. Folk tradition says the custom was adopted from the Indians, who are certainly among its most expert and frequent practitioners. Psychologists say letting fly with such a yelp releases the fatigue and heat-induced tension built up by long hours swinging a machete to eliminate weeds from pastures, or to prepare fields for planting. Complex *saloma* based calls have heavily influenced Panamanian traditional song and the chanting that accompanies much dance. The '*Ajuuúa*' can also be heard as an expression of approval at baseball games, football matches, and anywhere high spirits provide the occasion for whoops of delight.

Section 2

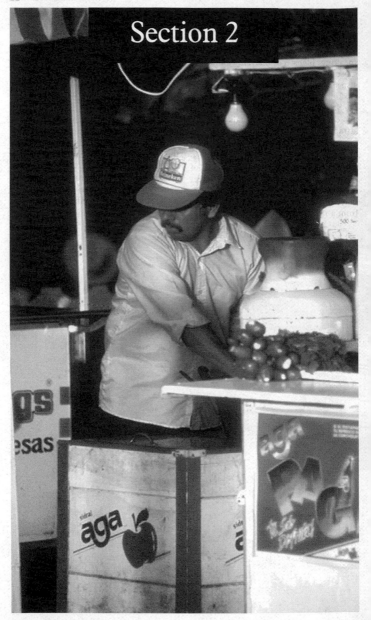

Introduction and hints

GETTING THERE

AIR

All the main airlines plying to each country are given in the 'Information for travellers' sections. Weight allowances if going direct from Europe are 20 kg for economy and business class or 30 kg for first class. If you have special baggage requirements, check with an agency about anomalies which exist on different weight allowances one way, for example. Many people travel to Mexico and Central America via the USA, and this usually means a luggage allowance of 2 pieces. This varies from airline to airline, but allows you more than 20 kg. However, weight limits for internal flights are often lower; best to enquire beforehand.

Prices and discounts

1 It is generally cheaper to fly from London rather than a point in Europe to Latin American destinations; fares vary from airline to airline, destination to destination and according to time of year. Check with an agency for the best deal for when you wish to travel.

2 Most airlines offer discounted (cheaper than official) fares of one sort or another on scheduled flights. These are not offered by the airlines direct to the public, but through agencies who specialize in this type of fare. In UK, these include Journey Latin America, 14-16 Devonshire Rd, Chiswick, London, W4 2HD (T 0181-747 3115) and 28-30 Barton Arcade, 51-63 Deansgate, Manchester, M3 2BH (T 0161-832 1441); Trailfinders, 194 Kensington High St, London, W8 7RG (T 0171-938 3939); Encounter Overland, 267 Old Brompton Rd, London, SW5 9JA (T 0171-370 6845); Hayes & Jarvis, 152 King St, London, W6 0QU (T 0181-222 7844), South American Experience, 47 Causton St, Pimlico, London, SW1P 4AT (T 0171-976 5511); Passage to South America, Fovant Mews, 12 Noyna Rd, London, SW17 7PH (T 0181-767 8989); STA Travel, Priory House, 6 Wrights Lane, London, W8 6TA (T 0171-361 6166). The very busy seasons are as follows: 7 December–15 January and July to mid September. If you intend travelling during those times, book as far ahead as possible.

3 With the promotion of Cancún as a gateway from Europe, there has been an increase in the number of scheduled flights to Mexico, at the expense of charter flights from Britain (eg Iberia flies daily in summer Madrid-Miami-Cancún, 5 times a week at other periods; Air Europa Madrid to Cancún, twice a week; Air France/AeroMéxico twice weekly Paris-Cancún; Condor Flugdienst from Frankfurt to Cancún, Acapulco and Puerto Vallarta – also to San José, Costa Rica). At the same time, British Airways operates three scheduled services a week from

London to Mexico City. British Airways' flights link with AeroMéxico and, to a lesser extent, Mexicana for access to the rest of the country. If you do not stop over in Mexico City, low-cost add-ons are available to Mexican domestic destinations through British Airways' link with the main national airlines. Between Feb and June scheduled airfares from Europe to Mexico City can be very low, commensurate with some transatlantic fares (the same does not apply to holiday destinations like Cancún or Acapulco). It is therefore worth considering Mexico City as an entry/exit point for a Mexican trip. For the widest range of options and keenest prices Mexico City is best, but Continental and American Airlines serve a wide range of provincial cities via their hubs, Houston and Dallas/Miami; their prices are similar to those for Mexico City. If flexible on time, you can seek promotional fares on smaller Mexican carriers not represented in Europe when you arrive.

4 Other fares fall into 3 groups, and are all on scheduled services:

● **Excursion** (return) fares with restricted validity either 7-90 days, or 7-180 days (Mexico), depending on the airline; 7-90 days (Central America). These are fixed date tickets where the dates of travel cannot be changed after issue of ticket.

● **Yearly fares**: these may be bought on a one-way or return basis, and usually the returns can be issued with the return date left open. You must, however, fix the route.

● **Student (or Under 26) fares** (there is a wider range of these to Mexico than elsewhere). Some airlines are flexible on the age limit, others strict. One way and returns available, or 'Open Jaws' (see below). There is also a wider range of cheap one-way student fares originating in Latin America than can be bought outside the continent. **NB** There is less availability in the busy seasons (see above).

5 For people intending to travel a linear route and return from a different point from that which they entered, there are 'Open Jaw' fares, which are available on student, yearly, or excursion fares. Iberia and KLM are good for 'Open Jaw' fares within Mexico, or to Mexico and elsewhere. Continental and American have a wide range of 'Open Jaw' fares within Mexico, but not regionally.

6 Many of these fares require a change of plane at an intermediate point, and a stopover may be permitted, or even obligatory, depending on schedules. Simply because a flight stops at a given airport does not mean you can break your journey there – the airline must have traffic rights to pick up or set down passengers between points A and B before it will be permitted. This is where dealing with a specialized agency (like Journey Latin America!) will really pay dividends. On multi-stop itineraries, the specialized agencies can often save clients hundreds of pounds.

7 Although it's a little more complicated, it's possible to sell tickets in London for travel originating in Latin America at substantially cheaper fares

than those available locally. This is useful for the traveller who doesn't know where he or she will end up, or who plans to travel for more than a year. But a oneway ticket from Latin America is more expensive than a oneway in the other direction, so it's always best to buy a return (but see **Student fares**, above).

8 Certain Central American countries impose local tax on flights originating there. Among these are Guatemala, Costa Rica and Mexico.

9 There are several cheap French charters to Mexico and Guatemala, but no-one in the UK sells them. There are a number of 'packages' that include flights from Mexico to Cuba which can be bought locally in Mexico, or in advance from London.

Travellers starting their journey in continental Europe should make local enquiries about charters and agencies offering the best deals.

10 If you buy discounted air tickets *always* check the reservation with the airline concerned to make sure the flight still exists. Also remember the IATA airlines' schedules change in March and October each year, so if you're going to be away a long time it's best to leave return flight coupons open. **NB** If you know that you will be returning at the very busy seasons (see paragraph **2**, above), you should make a reservation.

In addition, it is vital to check in advance whether you are entitled to any refund or re-issued ticket if you lose, or have stolen, a discounted air ticket.

Air passes

Aviateca, Taca, Lacsa, Nica and Copa operate a Visit Central America Pass (VICA), which uses a complex zoning system and incorporates the USA and South America. Fares range from US$307-US$1,363. Under IATA mileage fare principles, it is worth investigating the incorporation of stopovers into a linear route, say Guatemala City-Panama City, at no extra cost. AeroPerú, AeroMéxico and Mexicana have the Mexi-AmeriPass, available until end-1997, which covers the whole of Latin America; the region is divided into 10 zones

and a minimum of 3 flights must be purchased (domestic or international); fares start at US$50-70 for single domestic coupons, rising to US$400 for the longest legs (validity 3-90 days). Details of AeroMéxico and Mexicana's Mexiplan are given in Mexico, **Information for travellers**.

If you buy internal airline tickets in Latin American countries you may find cash refunds difficult to get if you change your plans: better to change your ticket for a different one. Overbooking by Latin American airlines is very common (largely due to repeated block bookings by travel agents, which everyone knows will not be used), so always reconfirm the next stage of your flight within 72 hrs of your intended departure. And it does no harm to reconfirm yet again in the last 24 hrs, just to show them you mean it, and turn up for the flight in good time (at least 2 hrs before departure). Also provide the airline with a contact phone number for the week prior to departure.

We advise people who travel the cheap way in Latin America to pay for all transport as they go along, and not in advance. This advice does not apply to people on a tight schedule: paying as you go along may save money, but it is likely to waste your time somewhat. The one exception to this general principle is in transatlantic flights; here money is saved by booking as far as possible in one operation. International air tickets are very expensive if purchased in Latin America. If buying airline tickets routed through the USA, check that US taxes are included in the price.

The Amerbuspass covers the whole of Latin America, from Mexico City to Ushuaia, and entitles the holder to 15-20% discounts on tickets with participating operators; bookable in all Latin American capitals, Europe, Asia, Africa, Oceania, it is valid for 9,999 miles, up to 180 days. Unlimited stopovers, travel with either a confirmed or open itinerary. Contact TISA Internacional, B Irigoyen 1370, Oficina 25/26, 1138 Buenos Aires, Argentina, T 307-1956/631-1108, F 300-5591, PO Box 40 Suc 1 (B), 1401 Buenos Aires.

TRAVEL TO THE USA

Although visa requirements for British air travellers with round-trip tickets to the USA have been relaxed, it is advisable to have a visa to allow entry by land, or on airlines from South and Central America which are not 'participating carriers' on the Visa Waiver scheme. If you are thinking of travelling via the USA, or of visiting the USA after Latin America, you are strongly advised to get your visa and find out about any other requirements from a US Consulate in your own country, not while travelling.

The US Department of Agriculture places restrictions on agricultural items brought to the United States from foreign countries as well as those brought to the mainland from Hawaii, Puerto Rico, and the US Virgin Islands. Prohibited items can harbour foreign animal and plant pests and diseases that could seriously damage America's crops, livestock, pets and the environment.

Because of this threat, travellers are required to list on the Customs' declaration form any meats, fruits, vegetables, plants, animals, and plant and animal products they are bringing into the country. The declaration must list all agricultural items carried in baggage, hand luggage and in vehicles coming across the border.

USDA inspectors will confiscate illegal items for destruction. Travellers who fail to declare items can be fined up to US$100 on the spot, and their exit from the airport will be delayed. Some items are permitted. Call 301-436-5908 for a copy of the helpful pamphlet, 'Travelers Tips'. The best advice is to check before purchasing an agricultural item and trying to bring it back to the United States.

SEA

There are few shipping services which carry passengers to Central America from Europe, the USA or elsewhere. The only regular service that does is Horn Line, sailing from Dover, Antwerp, Hamburg, Felixstowe and Le Havre, via the French Antilles to Moín in Costa Rica before returning to Europe: £1,400-1,550 one way, £2,000-2,200 round trip from Felixstowe, £2,300-2,500 from Dover. On some voyages, the ship calls at Bridgetown, Barbados, and Castries, St Lucia. Polish Ocean Line has a very flexible service from Gdynia to La Guaira and Puerto Cabello (Venezuela), Cartagena (Colombia), Puerto Limón, Puerto Cortés, Santo Tomás de Castilla, New Orleans, Houston, and back to Gdynia, 2½-3 months, £2,650 pp in a double cabin, £2,800 single.

Our thanks are due to John Alton of Strand Cruise and Travel Centre, Charing Cross Shopping Concourse, The Strand, London WC2N 4HZ, T 0171-836 6363, F 0171-497 0078, for the above information. Enquiries regarding passages should be made through agencies in your own country, or through Strand Cruise and Travel Centre, who also have information on occasional one-way services to the Gulf of Mexico from Europe. Also in the UK, information can be obtained from Cargo Ship Voyages Ltd, Hemley, Woodbridge, Suffolk, IP12 4QF, T/F 01473-736265. In Europe, contact Wagner Frachtschiffreisen, Stadlerstrasse 48, CH-8404, Winterthur, Switzerland, T (052) 242-1442, F 242-1487. In the USA, contact Freighter World Cruises, 180 South Lake Ave, Pasadena, CA 91101, T (818) 449-3106, or Travltips Cruise and Freighter Travel Association, 163-07 Depot Rd, PO Box 188, Flushing, NY11358, T (800) 872-8584.

Details on shipping cars are given in **Motoring**, below, and in the relevant country sections.

NB Some countries in Latin America officially require travellers who enter their territory to have an onward or return ticket. (Look under 'Information for travellers' sections for the countries you intend to visit.) In 1995-96 this regulation was rarely enforced by any country. (It does not apply to travellers with their own vehicles.) In lieu of an onward ticket out of the country you are entering, any ticket out of another Latin American country may suffice, or proof that you have sufficient funds to buy a ticket (a credit card will do).

MIAMI

Miami is a good place for connections between Europe and Central and South America. A 5 hr transfer, whether by choice or out of necessity, may seem like a daunting prospect, but Miami airport is surprisingly user-friendly and there is quite a lot to do in the city if you have a longer stopover.

The airport is rather like a big, horse-shoe-shaped suburban shopping mall. The upper level has shops and airline check-in counters; the lower level has other services like car rentals and baggage claim. The airport is divided into a series of concourses labelled B to H.

On arrival

Immigration queues are long, and can take 30-50 mins. Heavy hand luggage is more of a nuisance than at most airports, both in the queues and because of the long walk up and down the fingers which lead to the planes. Customs is crowded, but the queue moves faster. Through booking of baggage is now possible for Miami airport; ask for a suitable label at your point of departure.

Baggage There are baggage carts in customs, but these must be left behind when you have been cleared. From this point on there are *skycaps* (tip around US$1-2 per large bag). Skycaps can also be called from the paging phones which are thick on the ground in the concourses and entrances.

There are luggage lockers at all entrances to the airport and at various other points. They cost US$1 in quarters (25 cents – look for change machines, or ask information counters). After 24 hrs, bags are taken to a storage facility next to the *lost and found* office in concourse E. The charge for storage here is US$2 per day.

For very large items there is a left luggage office (baggage service office) on the lower level of concourse G and on the second level of concourse B. Charges are US$2-6 per day, depending on the size of the item.

Filling in time

The concourses are chocabloc with snack-bars, duty free shops, and gift shops selling overpriced junk. Once through Customs and into the duty free area there is one newsagent selling a limited amount of confectionery and newspapers, magazines, etc, and one poorly-stocked, over-priced Duty Free shop. Some items, such as cosmetics and perfumes, are better value in town. Drinking fountains only become plentiful once you get near the bus stops. **NB** A 6% sales tax is added to the marked price. Watch out if you are fine-tuning your US currency before departure.

The best place to pass the time and relax is probably the *Hotel MIA*, in the middle of the horseshoe on concourse E. The Lobby Lounge, open 1000-0100, is on the same floor as flight check in. The upper floors have a sundeck (free), an open air swimming pool, gym and sauna area (US$5 per day), racquetball courts (US$8 per hour), snackbar, lounge bar (the happy hour, 1700-1900, has drinks on special and complimentary snacks). There is also the *Top of The Port* restaurant, with pleasant surroundings and much better food than on the concourses (open 0700-2300; full breakfast US$7.75, lunch specials from US$8, dinner specials from US$15).

The hotel has special day rates between 0800 and 1800.

Information There are very helpful information counters in concourse E and just outside customs. They can also be contacted from any paging phone. (Counters open 0630-2230, paging phone service 24 hrs.) They will advise on ground transport, airport services, and the Miami area generally. They also have information on the full calendar of events in the city throughout the year.

Nursery Mainly for changing or feeding babies, on concourse E. If locked, the information office in this concourse has a key.

Banking Barnett Bank on concourse C, Monday to Friday 0900-1600, Saturday 0900-1200. Visa and Mastercard cash advances (US$25 minimum, US$2,000 maximum) on production of passport and one other piece of identification. 24-hr cashpoint on concourse outside the bank. Several foreign exchange counters, including a 24-hr one on concourse E.

Service Centre between concourses B and C has stamp machines, credit card phones, TDD phone for deaf or mute passengers, and another cashpoint.

Post Office Leave the building at the lower level of concourse B and walk a couple of metres along the airport road. Open Monday to Friday 0830-2100 and 0930-1330 on Saturday. Also sells bubble packing, padded envelopes, mailing tubes for posters etc. Express mail service in the post office is open 24 hrs.

Leaving the Airport

If you want to venture into the real world, you can use:

Rental Cars This works out at around US$30 per day for a small car. Many companies have offices on the lower level concourses. It can take an hour or more to book a car, take the company bus to its main office, fill out all the forms, and pick up a car. Leaving the car can take just as long. The information counters have a full list of companies. Some car hire firms may offer lower rates to passengers flying with certain airlines. Check in advance.

Drive Away Look for agencies, under D in the phone book, who handle cars belonging to people who have flown to their destination, but need their car driven there by someone else. It can be a quick, uncomplicated way to leave Miami if you have your passport and an international driving licence; sometimes accommodation and fuel may be included.

Buses Miami has a good bus service. Fare is US$1.25, with US$0.25 for a transfer to another route. Buses stop outside concourse E. Route 37 runs N-S every 30 mins in the day, every hour late evenings and weekends; Route 42 also runs N-S, every hour. Route J runs every 20-30 mins or every hour on Sundays to Miami Beach; Route 7 runs every 20-40 mins. Eastbound buses go downtown, westbound buses go to the Mall of the Americas and the International Mall, 2 big shopping complexes.

Routes J and 42 connect with the *Greyhound* bus terminal at Coral Gables.

Metrorail All of the airport bus routes connect with stations on the Metrorail line. This gives a quick service every 15 mins from 0600 to 2400 between downtown Miami and many suburban areas.

Metromover Metrorail tickets give a free connection to Metromover, a 1.9 mile (3 km) elevated track which whizzes round downtown Miami. The connection is at Government Center station.

Tri-Rail is another rail system which connects Miami and points N. The full journey to West Palm Beach takes 1 hr 52 mins. Connecting buses leave from outside concourse E; it is an 18 min ride to the station. Departures between 0430 and 2220 on weekdays, fewer at weekends. T 1-800-TRI-RAIL/1-800-874-7245.

Supershuttle is a minibus running to and from the airport. You can book ahead to be picked up from a hotel or private house. The Super Shuttle at the airport can be found at several locations on the lower concourse, look for the "Van Service" signs. The attendant will ask you where you are going, using the zip code as a reference. Zip codes are classified into zones which will determine which van can take you to your destination as well as fix cost (T 305-871-2000). The fare is US$8-12 for downtown, US$10-20 for South Miami Beach, US$20 to Fort Lauderdale airport.

Taxis are more expensive. A flat rate taxi service operates from the airport, with fares fixed according to zone, eg US$22 to South Miami Beach.

Hotels

Rooms at the *Miami International Airport Hotel (MIA)* in the airport start at **L2** plus 12.5% tax for a double, **L3** corporate rate. Rooms are quite small but double glazing keeps out aircraft noise, very impersonal, T 1-800-327-1276 from within the USA, or 305-871-4100 from elsewhere, F 305-871-0800. Quick access from airport: **L2** *Sheraton River House*, 3900 NW 21st St, T 305-871-3800, travel industry and senior discount available. Information has a good listing of downtown hotels, starting from the cheapest (*Bayman International*,

Flagler Street, T 266-5098 and *Miami Springs Hotel*, 661 E Drive, T 888-8421) and ending with the most expensive (*Miami Airport Hilton*, 5101 Blue Lagoon Drive, T 262-1000, and *Marriott Hotel*, 1202 NW LeJeune Road, T 649-5000). One minute from the terminal is **A1** *Ramada Hotel Miami International Airport*, 3941 NW 22nd St, T 871-1700, F 871-4830, courtesy van from airport, shuttle buses to various points in the city. **B** *Miami Airways Motel*, T 883-4700, F 888-8072, free airport shuttle, pool, breakfast, good value.

Information also has a separate listing of Miami Beach hotels (alphabetical, not by price). Best value in Miami Beach are: *Miami Beach International Hostel*, 236 9th St, Miami Beach, T 305-534-0268, F 305-534-5862, **D** hostel accommodation, **B** for private room; take bus J from airport to 41st St and Indian Creek Rd, transfer to bus C to 9th and Washington. *Clay Hotel*, 1438 Washington Avenue, which has a youth hostel attached, is reached by the same buses, but get off bus C at 14th and Washington. Single rooms are **C**, hostel accommodation is **D** (cheaper with ISIC or IYHA card), T 305-534-2980, F 305-673-0346. *Clay Hotel* has young and friendly staff and caters for many young European tourists; it has a kitchen but no utensils. *The Tropics*, 1550 Collins Ave, Miami Beach, Fl 33139, T 305-531-0361, F 305-531-8676, **D** in a 4-bedded room, swimming pool, rec. There are direct free phone lines to several hotels next to the baggage check in on lower level concourse E.

There are also reservations services which will make reservations for you. Try CRS (Toll free 1-800-683-3311), Express Reservation (Toll free 1-800-627-1356), or Room with a View (305-433-4343).

Shopping For bargains, try Flagler Street in downtown Miami, it's crowded and full of action. The suburban malls are more expensive and more relaxed: Mall of the Americas and International Mall are easiest to reach by bus.

Things to see in Miami

This guide is not the place for a full listing. Two 90-minute tours are offered by the Old Town Trolley Bus: Miami Magic City Tour and Miami Beach Tour. Both allow you to stay on board or to disembark at any stop to sightsee, shop or eat. You can reboard free and make as many stops as you like. No reservations necessary. Miami Beach Tour (US$14 adults, US$5 children 3-12) stops at Ocean Drive, 11th Street in the wonderful Art Deco district, the Holocaust Memorial (very powerful and interesting), Collins Avenue and 46th Street and Lincold Road Mall. It runs every two hours 1045-1645 (last at 1645). Miami Magic City Tour includes stops at the Seaquarium, Coconut Grove, Coral Gables, including the Venetian Pool on Desoto Boulevard (historic landmark with lagoon-style pool, caves, bridges all carved out of coral rock and a sandy beach; small café, admission US$4 adults, US$3.50 13-17 year-olds, US$1.50 under 12s; Monday-Friday 1100-1930, weekends 1000-1630). The airport information office has a useful booklet, *Destination Miami*, which gives details of a wide range of cultural events.

Miami is about the nearest that the continental USA gets to a tropical environment. Many attractions are designed for visitors from the N. The Monkey Jungle, Orchid Jungle, Parrot Jungle, etc may not be that exciting if you have just seen the real thing. With half a day to spare, however, you should be able to visit any of these, or the Metrozoo, or the Seaquarium. Museums include Vizcaya, a Renaissance-style villa with formal gardens, and the Spanish Monastery in North Miami Beach, brought to America in pieces by William Randolph Hearst from Segovia in Spain, where it was first built in 1141.

Miami Beach is probably the best place for a short stay. There are plenty of interesting Art Deco buildings, with restaurants and cafes along the sea front. Shops, hotels, nightclubs, etc are all within walking distance. Moreover, you can walk around at night without getting mugged. It also has the Bass Museum, with a good collection of European paintings. N of the Haulover channel is a section of beach where nude bathing is tolerated.

If you have a full day in Miami, there would be time to rent a car and drive to the *Everglades National Park*, a huge freshwater swamp with interesting wildlife and an excellent network of interpretative centres and nature trails. The nearer Florida Keys would be an alternative, but are probably not too exciting if you have just been to any of the Central American islands in the Caribbean.

NB Non-US citizens should remember that US immigration will not permit entry to the USA without an onward ticket (ie you cannot enter for the sole purpose of buying a cheap ticket to a third country). Moreover, while agencies in Miami can sell cheap tickets (eg Getaway Travel, Le Jeune Rd, Coral Gables), it is very difficult to check air tickets purchased outside the USA through a Miami agency. Recommended travel agents are Jorge Domínguez (Uruguayan) at *Bestway*, 420 Lincoln Rd, Suite 359, Miami Beach, FL 33139, T (305) 672-3035, F 672-2580; *Carmen* at *The Cruise and Travel Center*, 1600 Collins Ave, Miami Beach, FL 33139, T (305) 532-7273, F (305) 532-7638; *Florida Best Travel Services*, 1905 Collins Ave, Miami Beach, FL 33139, T (305) 673-0909, F (305) 673-2600.

Note also that Houston, Continental's hub, is another good place for connections to the region.

ON ARRIVAL

APPEARANCE

There is a natural prejudice in all countries against travellers who ignore personal hygiene and have a generally dirty and unkempt appearance. Most Latin Americans, if they can afford it, devote great care to their clothes and appearance; it is appreciated if visitors do likewise. How you dress is mostly how people will judge you. Buying clothing locally can help you look less like a tourist. It may be advantageous to carry a letter from someone in an official position testifying to one's good character, on official-looking notepaper.

Men wearing earrings are liable to be ridiculed in more 'macho' communities (ie in some rural areas). A medium weight shawl with some wool content is recommended for women: it can double as pillow, light blanket, bathrobe or sunscreen as required. For men, a smart jacket can be very useful.

COURTESY

Remember that politeness – even a little ceremoniousness – is much appreciated. In this connection professional or business cards are useful. Men should always remove any headgear and say 'con permiso' when entering offices, and be prepared to shake hands (this is much commoner in Latin America than in Europe or North America); always say 'Buenos días' before midday, or 'Buenas tardes' and wait for a reply before proceeding further. Always remember that the traveller from abroad has enjoyed greater advantages in life than most Latin American minor officials, and should be friendly and courteous in consequence. Never be impatient; do not criticize situations in public: the officials may know more English than you think and they can certainly interpret gestures and facial expressions. Be judicious about discussing politics with strangers (especially in Guatemala, Honduras, Nicaragua and El Salvador). Politeness can be a liability, however, in some situations; most Latin Americans are disorderly queuers. In Mexico, though, orderly queuing is common. On the other hand, Mexicans rarely respect punctuality. In commercial transactions (buying a meal, goods in a shop, etc) politeness should be accompanied by firmness, and always ask the price first.

Politeness should also be extended to street traders; saying "No, gracias" with a smile is better than an arrogant dismissal. Whether you give money to beggars is a personal matter, but your decision should be influenced by whether a person is begging out of need or trying to cash in on the tourist trail. In the former case, local people giving may provide an indication. Giving money to children is a separate issue, upon which most agree: don't do it. There are occasions where giving food in a restaurant may be appropriate, but first inform yourself of local practice.

Moira Chubb, from New Zealand, suggests that if you are a guest and are offered food that arouses your suspicions, the only courteous way out is to feign an allergy or a stomach ailment. If worried about the purity of ice for drinks, ask for a beer.

DOCUMENTS

Passports

Latin Americans, especially officials, are very document-minded. You should always carry your passport in a safe place about your person, or if not going far, leave it in the hotel safe. If staying in a country for several weeks, it is worthwhile registering at your Embassy or Consulate. Then, if your passport is stolen, the process of replacing it is simplified and speeded up. Keeping photocopies of essential documents, including your flight ticket, and some additional passport-sized photographs, is recommended.

It is your responsibility to ensure that your passport is stamped in and out when you cross frontiers. The absence of entry and exit stamps can cause serious difficulties: seek out the proper migration offices if the stamping process is not carried out as you cross. Also, do not lose your entry card; replacing one causes a lot of trouble, and possibly expense. Citizens of countries which oblige visitors to have a visa (eg France) can expect more delays and problems at border crossings.

If planning to study in Latin America for a long period, make every effort to get a student visa in advance.

Identity and Membership Cards

Membership cards of British, European and US motoring organizations can be useful for discounts off hotel charges, car rentals, maps, towing charges, etc. Student cards must carry a photograph if they are to be of any use in Latin America for discounts. Business people should carry a good supply of visiting cards, which are essential for good business relations in Latin America. Identity, membership or business cards in Spanish (or a translation) and an official letter of introduction in Spanish are also useful.

If you are in full-time education you will be entitled to an International Student Identity Card, which is distributed by student travel offices and travel agencies in 77 countries. The ISIC gives you special prices on all forms of transport (air, sea, rail etc), and access to a variety of other concessions and services. If you need to find the location of your nearest ISIC office contact: The ISIC Association, Box 9048, 1000 Copenhagen, Denmark T (+45) 33 93 93 03.

KEEPING IN TOUCH

Mail

Postal services in most countries are not very efficient, and pilfering is frequent. All mail, especially packages, should be registered. Check before leaving home if your Embassy will hold mail, and for how long, in preference to the Poste Restante/General Delivery (*Lista de Correos*) department of a country's Post Office. (Cardholders can use American Express agencies.) If there seems to be no mail at the Lista under the initial letter of your surname, ask them to look under the initial of your forename or your middle name. Remember there is no W in Spanish, look for letters under V, or ask. For the smallest risk of misunderstanding, use title, initial and surname only.

Phones

AT&T's 'USA Direct', Sprint and MCI are all available for calls to the USA. It is much cheaper than operator-assisted calls. Other countries have similar systems, eg UK, Canada; obtain details before leaving home.

Communicating by fax is a convenient way of sending messages home. Many places with public fax machines (post offices, telephone companies or shops) will receive messages as well as send. Fax machines are often switched off; you may have to phone to confirm receipt.

E-mail

E-mail is becoming more common and public access to the internet is fairly widespread with cybercafés opening in both large and small towns. There is usually a charge per page sent or received, which compares favourably with fax charges.

World Band Radio

South America has more local and community radio stations than practically anywhere else in the world; a shortwave (world band) radio offers a practical means to brush up on the language, sample popular culture and absorb some of the richly varied regional music. International broadcasters such as the BBC World Service, the Voice of America, Boston (Mass)-based Monitor Radio International (operated by *Christian Science Monitor*), and the Quito-based Evangelical station, HCJB, keep the traveller abreast of news and events, in both English and Spanish.

Compact or miniature portables are recommended, with digital tuning and a full range of shortwave bands, as well as FM, long and medium wave. Detailed advice on radio models (£150 for a decent one) and wavelengths can be found in the annual publication, *Passport to World Band Radio* (Box 300, Penn's Park, PA 18943, USA). Details of local stations are listed in *World TV and Radio Handbook* (WRTH), PO Box 9027, 1006 AA Amsterdam, The Netherlands, US$19.95. Both of these, free wavelength guides and selected radio sets, are available from the BBC World Service Bookshop, Bush House Arcade, Bush House, Strand, London WC2B 4PH, UK, T 0171-257 2576.

LANGUAGE AND LITERATURE

Without some knowledge of Spanish you can become very frustrated and feel helpless in many situations. English, or any other language, is absolutely useless off the beaten track. Some initial study, to get you up to a basic Spanish vocabulary of 500 words or so, and a pocket dictionary and phrase-book, are most strongly recommended: your pleasure will be doubled if you can talk to the locals. Not all the locals speak Spanish, of course; you will find that some Indians in the more remote highland parts of Guatemala speak only their indigenous languages, though there will usually be at least 1 person in each village who can speak Spanish.

The basic Spanish of Hispanic America is that of south-western Spain, with soft 'c's' and 'z's' pronounced as 's', and not as 'th' as in the other parts of Spain. Castilian Spanish is readily understood, but is not appreciated when spoken by non-Spaniards; try and learn the basic Latin American pronunciation. Differences in vocabulary also exist, both between peninsular Spanish and Latin American Spanish, and between the usages of the different countries. Language classes are available at a number of centres in Mexico and Central America, for instance Cuernavaca, Antigua, Quezaltenango, San José, and others. See the text for details, under **Language Courses**.

AmeriSpan, PO Box 40007, Philadelphia, PA 19106, T 800-879-6640, offers Spanish immersion programs, volunteer and internship positions throughout Latin America. Language programs are offered in Costa Rica (San José, Escazú, Alajuda, Heredia, Manuel Antonio, Monte Verde), El Salvador, Guatemala (Antigua, Quetzaltenango), Honduras (La Ceiba, Trujillo, Copán), Mexico (Cuernavaca, Guanajuato, Oaxaca, Mazatlán, Mérida, Morelia, San Miguel de Allende), Panama City as well as throughout South America. Contact AmeriSpan at above address or Web http://www.amerispan.com for details.

Literature

This Handbook does not at present have space to contain sections on Latin American literature. Interested readers are recommended to see Jason Wilson, *Traveller's Literary Companion, South and Central America* (Brighton, UK: In Print, 1993), which has extracts from works by Latin American writers and by non-Latin Americans about the various countries and has very useful bibliographies.

MONEY

The three main ways of keeping in funds while travelling are with US dollars cash, US dollars travellers' cheques (TCs), or plastic.

Cash

Sterling and other currencies are not recommended. Though the risk of loss is

greater, the chief benefit of US dollar notes is that better rates and lower commissions can usually be obtained for them. In many countries, US dollar notes are only accepted if they are in excellent, if not perfect condition (likewise, do not accept local currency notes in poor condition). Low-value US dollar bills should be carried for changing into local currency if arriving in a country when banks or *casas de cambio* are closed (US$5 or US$10 bills). They are very useful for shopping: shopkeepers and exchange shops (*casas de cambio*) tend to give better exchange rates than hotels or banks (but see below). The better hotels will normally change travellers' cheques for their guests (often at a rather poor rate), but if you are travelling on the cheap it is essential to keep in funds; watch weekends and public holidays carefully and never run out of local currency. Take plenty of local currency, in small denominations, when making trips into the interior.

Travellers' cheques

These are convenient but they attract thieves (though refunds can of course be arranged) and you will find that they are more difficult than dollar bills to change in small towns (denominations of US$50 and US$100 are preferable, though one does need a few of US$20). American Express, Visa or Thomas Cook US$ TCs are recommended, but less commission is often charged on Citibank or Bank of America TCs, if they are cashed at Latin American branches of those banks. These TCs are always accepted by banks, even though they may not be as well known outside banks as those of American Express, Visa or Thomas Cook. (It is also easier to obtain refunds for stolen TCs with the last three than with Citicorp cheques.) It is a good idea to take 2 kinds of cheque: if large numbers of one kind have recently been forged or stolen, making people suspicious, it is unlikely to have happened simultaneously with the other kind. Several banks charge a high fixed commission for changing TCs – sometimes as much as US$5-10 a cheque – because they don't really want to be bothered. Exchange houses (*casas de cambio*)

are usually much better for this service. Some establishments may ask to see the customer's record of purchase before accepting. **NB** In Mexico, *casas de cambio* may be open longer hours than banks, but they do not offer better exchange rates.

Plastic

It is straightfoward to obtain a cash advance against a credit card and, in the text, we give the names of banks that do this.

There are two international **ATM** (automatic telling machine) acceptance systems, Plus and Cirrus. Many issuers of debit and credit cards are linked to one, or both (eg Visa is Plus, Mastercard is Cirrus). Look for the relevant symbol on an ATM and draw cash using your PIN. Frequently, the rates of exchange on ATM withdrawals are the best available. Find out before you leave what ATM coverage there is in the countries you will visit and what international 'functionality' your card has. Check if your bank or credit card company imposes handling charges. Obviously you must ensure that the account to which your debit card refers contains sufficient funds. With a credit card, obtain a credit limit sufficient for your needs, or pay money in to put the account in credit. If travelling for a long time, consider a direct debit to clear your account regularly. Do not rely on one card, in case of loss. If you do lose a card, immediately contact the 24-hr helpline of the issuer in your home country (keep this number in a safe place). (With thanks to Nigel Baker, Debit Card Manager, Natwest Bank plc, London.)

For purchases, credit cards of the Visa and Mastercard (Eurocard, Access) groups, American Express (Amex), Carte Blanche and Diners Club can be used. Make sure you know the correct procedure if they are lost or stolen. Credit card transactions are normally at an officially recognized rate of exchange; they are often subject to tax. Many establishments in Latin America charge a fee of about 5% on credit card transactions; although forbidden by credit card company rules there is not a lot you can do about this, except get the charge itemized on the receipt and complain to the card company. For credit card security, insist that imprints are made in your presence and that any imprints incorrectly completed should be torn into tiny pieces. Also destroy the carbon papers after the form is completed (signatures can be copied from them).

NB In general terms, Mastercard ATMs are available throughout Mexico, but only in Central American capitals. The Mastercard/Cirrus connection is poorly represented in Guatemala; check with your card issuer before leaving home. Visa is of greater use in Central America than Mastercard.

NB also Money can be transferred between banks. A recommended method is, before leaving, to find out which local bank is correspondent to your bank at home, then when you need funds, telex your own bank and ask them to telex the money to the local bank (confirming by fax). Give exact information to your bank of the routing number of the receiving bank. Cash in dollars, or local currency depending on the country can be received within 48 banking hours.

Exchange

There is a parallel market in local currency in some countries. Before changing money on the street, check whether exchange rates are significantly better than in a bank or *casa de cambio*. If changing money on the street, do not do so alone. If unsure of the currency of the country you are about to enter, check rates with more than one changer at the border, or ask locals or any traveller who may be leaving that country.

Whenever you leave a country, sell any local currency before leaving, because the further away you get, the less the value of a country's money. **NB** When departing by air, never forget that you have to pay airport departure tax; do not leave yourself short of money.

Americans (we are told) should know that if they run out of funds they can usually expect no help from the US Embassy or Consul other than a referral to some welfare organization. In this regard, find out before you go precisely what services and assistance your embassy or consulate can provide if you find yourself in difficulties.

Exchange rates	
COUNTRY	Exchange rate/US$
BELIZE (Belize dollar)	2.00
COSTA RICA (colón)	233.09
CUBA (Cuban peso) *casa de cambio*	1.00 21.00
EL SALVADOR (colón)	8.75
GUATEMALA (quetzal)	5.90
HONDURAS (lempira)	13.00
MEXICO (Mexican peso)	7.64
NICARAGUA (córdoba oro)	7.96
PANAMA (balboa)	1.00

Correct at 4 July 1997

PHOTOGRAPHY

Always ask permission before photographing people. Film prices vary but are not much different from Europe. Film can be bought cheaply in the USA or in the Colón Tax Free Zone (Panama). Slide film is difficult to find. Kodachrome is almost impossible to buy, and Fuji Film is less easy to find than Kodak in Central America. Some travellers (but not all) have advised against mailing exposed films home; either take them with you, or have them developed, but not printed, once you have checked the laboratory's quality. Note that postal authorities may use less sensitive equipment for X-ray screening than the airports do. Modern controlled X-ray machines are supposed to be safe for any speed of film, but it is worth trying to avoid X-ray as the doses are cumulative. Many airport officials will allow film to be passed outside X-ray arches; they may also hand-check a suitcase with a large quantity of film if asked politely.

Dan Buck and Anne Meadows write: A note on developing film in Latin America. Black and white is a problem. Often it is shoddily machine-processed and the negatives are ruined. Ask the store if you can see an example of their laboratory's work and if they hand-develop.

Jeremy Till and Sarah Wigglesworth suggest that exposed film can be protected in humid areas by putting it in a balloon and tying a knot. Similarly, keeping your camera in a plastic bag may reduce the effects of humidity.

SAFETY

Drugs

Users of drugs, even of soft ones, without medical prescription should be particularly careful, as some countries impose heavy penalties – up to 10 years' imprisonment – for even the simple possession of such substances. In this connection, the planting of drugs on travellers, by traffickers or the police, is not unknown. If offered drugs on the street, make no response at all and keep walking. Note that people who roll their own cigarettes are often suspected of carrying drugs and subjected to intensive searches. Advisable to stick to commercial brands of cigarettes – but better still not to smoke at all.

Keeping safe

Generally speaking, most places in Latin America are no more dangerous than any major city in Europe or North America. In provincial towns, main places of interest, on day time buses and in ordinary restaurants the visitor should be quite safe. Nevertheless, in large cities (particularly in crowded places such as markets and bus stations), crime exists, most of which is opportunistic. If you are aware of the dangers, act confidently and use your common sense you will lessen many of the risks. The following tips, all endorsed by travellers, are meant to forewarn, but not alarm, you. Keep all documents secure; hide your main cash supply in different places or under your clothes (extra pockets sewn inside shirts and trousers, pockets closed with a zip or safety pin, moneybelts – best worn below the waist rather than at it or around the neck, neck or leg pouches, and elasticated support bandages for keeping money and cheques above the elbow or below the knee have been repeatedly recommended – the last by John Hatt in *The Tropical Traveller*). Waist packs worn outside the clothes are not safe. Keep cameras in bags (preferably with a chain or wire in the strap to defeat the slasher) or briefcases; take spare spectacles (eyeglasses); don't wear wrist-watches or jewellery. If you wear a shoulder-bag in a market, carry it in front of you. Backpacks are vulnerable to slashers: a good idea is to cover the pack with a sack (a plastic one will also keep out rain and dust) with maybe a layer of wire netting between, or make an inner frame of chicken wire. Use a pack which is lockable at its base.

Ignore mustard smearers and paint or shampoo sprayers, and strangers' remarks like 'what's that on your shoulder?' or 'have you seen that dirt on your shoe?'. Furthermore, don't bend over to pick up money or other items in the street. These are all ruses intended to distract your attention and make you easy for an accomplice to steal from. If someone follows you when you're in the street, let him catch up with you and 'give him the eye'. While you should take local advice about being out at night, do not assume that daytime is safer than nighttime. If walking after dark, walk in the road, not on the pavement/sidewalk.

Be wary of 'plainclothes policemen'; insist on seeing identification and on going to the police station by main roads. Do not hand over your identification (or money – which he should not need to see anyway) until you are at the station. On no account take them directly back to your lodgings. Be even more suspicious if he seeks confirmation of his status from a passer-by. If someone tries to bribe you, insist on a receipt. If attacked, remember your assailants may well be armed, and try not to resist.

It is best, if you can trust your hotel, to leave any valuables you don't need in safe-deposit there, when sightseeing locally. Always keep an inventory of what you have deposited. If you don't trust the hotel, lock everything in your pack and secure that in your room (some people take eyelet-screws for padlocking cupboards or drawers). If you lose valuables, always report to the police and note details of the report – for insurance purposes.

When you have all your luggage with you at a bus or railway station, be especially careful: don't get into arguments with any locals if you can help it, and lock all the items together with a chain or cable if you are waiting for some time. Take a taxi between airport/bus station/railway station and hotel, if you can possibly afford it. Keep your bags with you in the taxi and pay only when you and your luggage are safely out of the vehicle. Make sure the taxi has inner door handles, in case a quick exit is needed. Avoid night buses; never arrive at night; and watch your belongings whether they are stowed inside or outside the cabin (rooftop luggage racks create extra problems, which are sometimes unavoidable – make sure your bag is waterproof). Major bus lines often issue a luggage ticket when bags are stored in the bus' hold, generally a safe system. When getting on a bus, keep your ticket handy; someone sitting in your seat may be a distraction for an accomplice to rob you while you are sorting out the problem. Finally, never accept food, drink, sweets or cigarettes from unknown fellow-travellers on buses or trains. They may be drugged, and you would wake up hours later without your belongings. In this connection, never accept a bar drink from an opened bottle (unless you can see that that bottle is in general use): always have it uncapped in front of you.

For specific local problems, see under the individual countries in the text.

Rape This can happen anywhere in the world. If you are the victim of a sexual assault, you are advised in the first instance to contact a doctor (this can be your home doctor if you prefer). You will need tests to determine whether you have contracted any sexually-transmitted diseases; you may also need advice on post-coital contraception. You should also contact your embassy, where consular staff are very willing to help in cases of assault.

Police

Whereas in Europe and North America we are accustomed to law enforcement on a systematic basis, in general, enforcement in Latin America is achieved by periodic campaigns. The most typical is a round-up of criminals in the cities just before Christmas. In December, therefore, you may well be asked for identification at any time, and if you cannot produce it, you will be jailed. If a visitor is jailed his/her friends should provide food every day. This is especially important for people on a diet, such as diabetics. In the event of a vehicle accident in which anyone is injured, all drivers involved are automatically detained until blame has been established, and this does not usually take less than 2 weeks.

Never offer a bribe unless you are fully conversant with the customs of the country. Wait until the official makes the suggestion, or offer money in some form which is apparently not bribery, eg 'In our country we have a system of on-the-spot fines (*multas de immediato*). Is there a similar system here?' Do not assume that an official who accepts a bribe is prepared to do anything else that is illegal. You bribe him to persuade him to do his job, or to persuade him not to do it, or to do it more quickly, or more slowly. You do not bribe him to do something which is against the law. The mere suggestion would make him very upset. If an official suggests that a bribe must be paid before you can proceed on your way, be patient (assuming you have the time) and he may relent.

SOUVENIRS

Remember that these can almost invariably be bought more cheaply away from the capital, though the choice may be less wide. Bargaining seems to be the general rule in most countries' street markets, but don't make a fool of yourself by bargaining over what, to you, is a small amount of money.

If British travellers have no space in their luggage, they might like to remember Tumi, the Latin American Craft Centre, who specialize in Mexican and Andean products and who produce cultural and educational videos for schools: at 23/2A Chalk Farm Road, London NW1 8AG (F 0171-485 4152), 8/9 New Bond Street Place, Bath BA1 1BH (T 01225 462367, F 01225 444870), 1/2 Little Clarendon St, Oxford OX1 2HJ (T/F 01865-512307), 82 Park St, Bristol BS1 5LA (T/F 0117 929 0391). Tumi (Music) Ltd specializes in different rhythms of Latin America. See *Arts and Crafts of South America*, by Lucy Davies and Mo Fini, published by Tumi (1994), for a fine introduction to the subject. There are similar shops in the USA.

TRAVELLING ALONE

Many points of security, dress and language have been covered already. First time exposure to countries where sections of the population live in extreme poverty or squalor and may even be starving can cause distress to travellers. So can the exceptional curiosity extended to visitors, especially women. Simply be prepared for this and try not to over-react. These additional hints have mainly been supplied by women, but most apply to any single traveller. When you set out, err on the side of caution until your instincts have adjusted to the customs of a new culture. If, as a single woman, you can befriend a local woman, you will learn much more about the country you are visiting. Unless actively avoiding foreigners like yourself, don't go too far from the beaten track; there is a very definite 'gringo trail' which you can join, or follow, if seeking company. This can be helpful when seeking safe accommodation, especially if arriving after dark (which is best avoided). Remember that for a single woman a taxi at night can be as dangerous as wandering around on her own. At borders dress as smartly as possible. Travelling by train is a good way to meet locals, but buses are much easier for a person alone; on major routes your seat is often reserved and your luggage can

usually be locked in the hold. It is easier for men to take the friendliness of locals at face value; women may be subject to much unwanted attention. To help minimize this, do not wear suggestive clothing and, advises Alex Rossi of Jawa Timur, Indonesia, do not flirt. By wearing a wedding ring, carrying a photograph of your 'husband' and 'children', and saying that your 'husband' is close at hand, you may dissuade an aspiring suitor. If politeness fails, and a man persists, specially mentioning sex or being obnoxious, do not feel bad about showing offence and departing. When accepting a social invitation, make sure that someone knows the address and the time you left. Ask if you can bring a friend (even if you do not intend to do so). A good rule is always to act with confidence, as though you know where you are going, even if you do not. Someone who looks lost is more likely to attract unwanted attention. Do not disclose to strangers where you are staying. (Much of this information was supplied by Alex Rossi, and by Deirdre Mortell of Carrigaline, Co Cork).

WHAT TO TAKE

Everybody has his/her own list. In addition to items already suggested in other sections above, those most often mentioned include air cushions for slatted seats, inflatable travel pillow for neck support, strong shoes (and remember that footwear over 9½ English size, or 42 European size, is difficult to obtain in Latin America except Argentina and Brazil); a small first-aid kit and handbook, fully waterproof top clothing, waterproof treatment for leather footwear, wax earplugs (which are impossible to find outside large cities) and airline-type eye mask to help you sleep in noisy and poorly curtained hotel rooms, sandals (rubber-thong Japanese-type, or other – can be worn in showers to avoid athlete's foot), a polyethylene sheet 2 x 1m to cover possibly infested beds and shelter your luggage, polyethylene bags of varying sizes (up to heavy duty rubbish bag size) with ties, a toilet bag you can tie round your waist, a sheet sleeping-bag and pillow-case or a separate pillow-case – in some countries they are not changed often in cheap hotels; a 1½-2m piece of 100% cotton can be used instead of a towel (dries quicker, is lighter), as a bedsheet, beach towel, makeshift curtain and wrap; a mosquito net (or a hammock with a fitted net), a straw hat which can be rolled or flattened and reconstituted after 15 mins soaking in water, a clothes line, a nailbrush (useful for scrubbing dirt off clothes as well as off oneself), a vacuum flask, a water bottle, a small dual-voltage immersion heater, a small dual-voltage (or battery-driven) electric fan, a light nylon waterproof shopping bag, a universal bath- and basin plug of the flanged type that will fit any wastepipe (or improvise one from a sheet of thick rubber), string, velcro, electrical insulating tape, large penknife preferably with tin and bottle openers, scissors and corkscrew – the famous Swiss Army range has been repeatedly recommended (for knife sharpening, go to a butcher's shop), alarm clock or watch, candle, torch (flashlight) – especially one that will clip on to a pocket or belt, pocket mirror, pocket calculator, an adaptor and flex to enable you to take power from an electric-light socket (the Edison screw type is the most commonly used), a padlock for the doors of the cheapest and most casual hotels (or for tent zip if camping), spare chain-lengths and padlock for securing luggage to bed or bus/train seat. Remember not to throw away spent batteries containing mercury or cadmium; take them home to be disposed of, or recycled properly.

Useful medicaments are given at the end of the 'Health' section (page 54); to these might be added some lip salve with sun protection, and pre-moistened wipes (such as 'Wet Ones'). Always carry toilet paper. Natural fabric sticking plasters, as well as being long-lasting, are much appreciated as gifts. Dental floss can be used for backpack repairs, in addition to its original purpose. **Never** carry firearms. Their possession could land you in serious trouble.

A note for **contact lens wearers**: the availability of products for the care of lenses varies from country to country (throughout Central America, but not Mexico, it is hard to find). In any country, lens solutions can be difficult to find outside major cities. Where available, it is expensive. Practice also varies as to whether it is stocked by chemists/pharmacies or opticians.

Be careful when asking directions. Women probably know more about the neighbourhood; men about more distant locations. Policemen are often helpful. However, many Latin Americans will give you the wrong answer rather than admit they do not know.

Lastly, a good principle is to take half the clothes and twice the money, that you think you will need.

WHERE TO STAY

HOTELS

A cheap but not bad hotel might be US$7 a night upwards in Mexico, less in some, but not all of, the Central American countries. For those on a really tight budget, it is a good idea to ask for a boarding house – *casa de huéspedes*, *hospedaje*, *pensión*, *casa familial* or *residencial*, according to country; they are normally to be found in abundance near bus and railway stations and markets. Good value hotels can also be found near truckers' stops/service stations; they are usually secure. There are often great seasonal variations in hotel prices in resorts. In Mexico, couples should ask for a room with *cama matrimonial* (double bed), normally cheaper than a room with two beds. Note that in the text the term 'with bath' usually means 'with shower and toilet', not 'with bath tub'. Remember, cheaper hotels don't always supply soap, towels and toilet paper. Useful tips: book even cheap hotels in advance by registered mail, if you receive no reply, don't worry. In any class, hotel rooms facing the street may be noisy; always ask for the best, quietest room. To avoid price hikes for gringos, ask if there is a cheaper room.

Hotel prices					

Our hotel price ranges, including taxes and service charges but without meals unless stated, are as follows:

L1	Over US$200	**L2**	US$151-200	**L3**	US$101-150
A1	US$81-100	**A2**	US$61-80	**A3**	US$46-60
B	US$31-45	**C**	US$21-30	**D**	US$12-20
E	US$7-11	**F**	US$4-6	**G**	Up to US$3

NB Prices are for double rooms, except in **F** and **G** ranges where the price is almost always per person.

Other abbreviations used in the book (apart from pp = per person; a/c = air conditioned; rec = recommended; T = telephone; TCs = travellers' cheques; s/n = "sin número", no street number; p = piso – floor, in Spanish-speaking countries) should be self-explanatory.

Cockroaches

These are ubiquitous and unpleasant, but not dangerous. Take some insecticide powder if staying in cheap hotels, trailer parks, etc; Baygon (Bayer) has been recommended. Stuff toilet paper in any holes in walls that you may suspect of being parts of cockroach runs.

Toilets

Many hotels, restaurants and bars have inadequate water supplies. **Almost without exception, used toilet paper should not be flushed down the pan, but placed in the receptacle provided.** This applies even in quite expensive hotels. Failing to observe this custom will block the pan or drain, a considerable health risk.

NB The electric showers used in innumerable hotels should be checked for obvious flaws in the wiring; try not to touch the rose while it is producing hot water.

CAMPING

Organized campsites are referred to in the text immediately below hotel lists, under each town. If there is no organized site in town, a football pitch or gravel pit might serve. Obey the following rules for 'wild' camping: (1) arrive in daylight and pitch your tent as it gets dark; (2) ask permission to camp from the parish priest, or the fire chief, or the police, or a farmer regarding his own property; (3) never ask a group of people – especially young people; (4) never camp on a beach (because of sandflies and thieves). If you can't get information from anyone, camp in a spot where you can't be seen from the nearest inhabited place and make sure no one saw you go there.

If taking a cooker, the most frequent recommendation is a multifuel stove (eg MSR International, Coleman Peak 1), which will burn unleaded petrol or, if that is not available, kerosene, *benzina blanca*, etc. Alcohol-burning stoves are simple, reliable, but slow and you have to carry a lot of fuel: for a methylated spirit-burning stove, the following fuels apply, *alcohol desnaturalizado, alcohol metílico, alcohol puro (de caña)* or *alcohol para quemar* (avoid this in Honduras as it does not burn). Ask for 95%, but 70% will suffice. In Mexico fuel is sold in supermarkets; in all countries it can be found in chemists/pharmacies. Gas cylinders and bottles are usually exchangeable, but if not can be recharged; specify whether you use butane or propane. Gas canisters are not always available. Camping supplies are usually only available in larger cities, so stock up when possible.

Hammocks

A hammock can be an invaluable piece of equipment, especially if travelling on the cheap. It will be of more use than a tent because many places have hammock-hooks, or you can sling a hammock between trees, etc. Bryan Crawford, of Beauly, Inverness-shire, Scotland, recommends carrying a 10m rope and some plastic sheeting. 'The rope gives a good choice of tree distances and the excess provides a hanging frame for the plastic sheeting to keep the rain off. Metal S-hooks can be very useful, especially under lorries'. Don't forget a mosquito net if travelling in insect-infected areas. Tips on buying a hammock are given in the Mérida (Yucatán) **Shopping** section. Good hammocks are also sold in Guatamala. If in any doubt about quality or size, seek advice before buying. And as Remo Bulgheroni of Killroergen (Switzerland) says: 'don't make a mess with your end strings because it makes your hammock useless and only the sellers can help you fast.'

YOUTH HOSTELS

Organizations affiliated to the Youth Hostels movement exist in Mexico, Costa Rica and Guatemala. Further information in the country sections and from the IYHA.

FOOD

There is a paragraph on each nation's food under 'Information for travellers'. Most restaurants serve a daily special meal, usually at lunchtime, which is cheaper than other dishes and good. Vegetarians should be able to list all the foods they cannot eat; saying 'Soy vegetariano/a' (I'm a vegetarian) or 'no como carne' (I don't eat meat) is often not enough.

GETTING AROUND

NB See above for details of air passes within the region.

BUSES AND TRAINS

There is an extensive road system for motor traffic, with frequent bus services. Some bus services in Mexico and Central America are excellent. In mountainous country, however, do not expect buses to get to their destination, after long journeys, anywhere near on time. Do not turn up for a bus at the last minute; if it is full it may depart early. Tall travellers are advised to take aisle, not window seats on long journeys as this allows more leg room. When the journey takes more than 3 or 4 hrs, meal stops at country inns or bars,

good and bad, are the rule. Often no announcement is made on the duration of the stop: follow the driver, if he eats, eat. See what the locals are eating – and buy likewise, or make sure you're stocked up well on food and drink at the start. For drinks, stick to bottled water or soft drinks or coffee (black). The food sold by vendors at bus stops may be all right: watch if locals are buying, though unpeeled fruit is of course reliable. (See above on **Security** in buses.)

In the few countries where **trains** run, they are slower than buses. They tend to provide finer scenery and you can normally see much more wildlife than from the road – it is less disturbed by 1 or 2 trains a day than by the more frequent road traffic. Moreover, so many buses now show video films that you can't see the countryside because the curtains are drawn. Complaining loudly to the conductor that you cannot see the beautiful landscape may persuade him to give you his seat at the front.

MOTORING

The machine

What kind of motoring you do will depend on what kind of car you set out with. Four-wheel drive is not necessary, although it does give you greater flexibility in mountain and jungle territory. Wherever you travel you should expect from time to time to find roads that are badly maintained, damaged or closed during the wet season, and delays because of floods, landslides and huge potholes. Don't plan your schedules too tightly.

Diesel cars are much cheaper to run than petrol ones, and the fuel is easily available. Most towns can supply a mechanic of sorts, and probably parts for Bosch fuel injection equipment. Watch the mechanics like a hawk, since there's always a brisk market in spares, and some of yours may be highly desirable. That apart, they enjoy a challenge, and can fix most things, eventually.

The electronic ignition and fuel metering systems on modern emission controlled cars are allergic to humidity, heat and dust, and cannot be repaired by bush mechanics. Standard European and Japanese cars run on fuel with a higher octane rating than is commonly available in North, South or Central America. Unleaded fuel is now available nearly everywhere. The most easily maintained petrol engined cars, then, are the types manufactured in Latin American countries, ie pre-emission control models such as the VW Kombi with carburettors and conventional (non-electronic) ignition, or the old type Toyota Landcruisers common in Central America. Older model American cars, especially Ford or GM pickups, are easily maintained, but high fuel consumption offsets this advantage. Isuzu, Mitsubishi and Datsun/Nissan are present throughout the region. Toyota is not represented to any degree in Mexico, so it is best to bring any little Toyota spares at the outset. American makes – Ford, Chevrolet, Dodge – are mostly popular in Mexico and Costa Rica. Volkswagen is also present in the region, notably Mexico.)

Preparation

Preparing the car for the journey is largely a matter of common sense: obviously any part that is not in first class condition should be replaced. It's well worth installing extra heavy-duty shock-absorbers (such as Spax or Koni) before starting out, because a long trip on rough roads in a heavily laden car will give heavy wear. Fit tubes on 'tubeless' tyres, since air plugs for tubeless tyres are hard to find, and if you bend the rim on a pothole, the tyre will not hold air. Take spare tubes, and an extra spare tyre. Also take spare plugs, fan-belts, radiator hoses and headlamp bulbs; even though local equivalents can be found in cities, it is wise to take spares for those occasions late at night or in remote areas when you might need them. You can also change the fanbelt after a stretch of long, hot driving to prevent wear (eg after 15,000 km/10,000 miles). If your vehicle has more than one fan belt, never replace one, replace all at the same time (make sure you have the necessary tools if doing it yourself). If your car has sophisticated

electrics, spare 'black boxes' for the ignition and fuel injection are advisable, plus a spare voltage regulator or the appropriate diodes for the alternator, and elements for the fuel, air and oil filters if these are not a common type. (Some drivers take a spare alternator of the correct amps, especially if the regulator is incorporated into the alternator.) Dirty fuel is a frequent problem, so be prepared to change filters more often than you would at home: in a diesel car you will need to check the sediment bowl often, too. An extra in-line fuel filter is a good idea if feasible (although harder to find, metal canister type is preferable to plastic), and for travel on dusty roads an oil bath air filter is best for a diesel car. (Fuel filters are not available in Mexico.) It is wise to carry a spade, jumper cables, tow rope and an air pump. Fix tow hooks to both sides of the vehicle frame. A 12 volt neon light for camping and repairs will be invaluable. Spare fuel containers should be steel and not plastic, and a siphon pipe is essential for those places where fuel is sold right out of the drum. Take a 10 litre water container for self and vehicle. Note that in some areas gas stations are few and far between. Fill up when you see one: the next one may be out of fuel. Some countries have periodic fuel conservation strategies which means you can't get any after a certain hour in the evening, and often not at weekends either.

Security

Apart from the mechanical aspects, spare no ingenuity in making your car secure. Your model should be the Brink's armoured van: anything less secure can be broken into by the determined and skilled thief. Use heavy chain and padlocks to chain doors shut, fit security catches on windows, remove interior window winders (so that a hand reaching in from a forced vent cannot open the window). All these will help, but none is foolproof. Anything on the outside – wing mirrors, spot lamps, motifs etc – is likely to be stolen too. So are wheels if not secured by locking nuts. Try never to leave the car unattended except in a locked garage or guarded parking space. Remove all belongings and leave the empty glove compartment open when the car is unattended. Also lock the clutch or accelerator to the steering wheel with a heavy, obvious chain or lock. Street children will generally protect your car fiercely in exchange for a tip. Don't wash your car: smart cars attract thieves. Be sure to note down key numbers and carry spares of the most important ones (but don't keep all spares inside the vehicle).

Documents

A 'carnet de passage' is no longer accepted in any country. Land entry procedures for all countries are simple, though time-consuming, as the car has to be checked by customs, police and agriculture officials (see, however, Mexico, **Automobiles** in **Information for travellers**, on regulations). All you need is the registration document in the name of the driver, or, in the case of a car registered in someone else's name, a notarized letter of authorisation. Note that Costa Rica does not recognize the International Driving Licence, which is otherwise useful. In Guatemala, Honduras and Costa Rica, the car's entry is stamped into the passport so you may not leave the country even temporarily without it. A written undertaking that the vehicle will be re-exported after temporary importation is useful and may be requested in Nicaragua, Costa Rica and Panama. Most countries give a limited period of stay, but allow an extension if requested in advance. Of course, do be very careful to keep **all** the papers you are given when you enter, to produce when you leave. (An army of 'helpers' loiters at each border crossing, waiting to guide motorists to each official in the correct order, for a tip. They can be very useful, but don't give them your papers.) Bringing a car in by sea or air is much more complicated and expensive: generally you will have to hire an agent to clear it through, expensive and slow. Insurance for the vehicle against accident, damage or theft is best arranged in the country of origin: in Latin American countries it is very expensive to insure against accident and theft, especially as you should take into account the value of the car increased by duties calculated in real (ie non devaluing) terms. If the car is stolen or written off, you will be required to pay very high duty on its value. A few countries (eg Costa Rica) insist on compulsory third party insurance, to be bought at the border: in other countries it's technically required, but not checked up on (again, see Mexico, **Automobiles**, for details on Sanborns and other insurers, who will insure vehicles for driving in Mexico and Central America). Get the legally required minimum cover – not expensive – as soon as you can, because if you should be involved in an accident and are uninsured, your car could be confiscated. If anyone is hurt, do not pick them up (you become liable). Seek assistance from the nearest police station or hospital if you are able to do so. You may find yourself facing a hostile crowd, even if you are not to blame. Expect frequent road checks by police, military (especially Honduras, where there is a check point on entering and leaving every town), agricultural and forestry produce inspectors, and any other curious official (or guerrilla) who wants to know what a foreigner is doing driving around in his domain. Smiling simple-minded patience is the best tactic to avoid harassment by zealous, often not very well educated officials on these occasions.

From Central To South America – how to avoid the Darién Gap

Shipping from Panama to mainland South America is expensive; you must shop around to find the cheapest way. The shipping lines and agents, and the prices for the services from Panama and elsewhere change frequently. Current details will be found in the Panama chapter under **Shipping a Vehicle**, page 1220.

Car Hire

The main international car hire companies operate in all countries, but tend to be very expensive, reflecting the high costs and accident rates. Hotels and tourist agencies will tell you where to find cheaper rates, but you will need to check that you have such basics as spare wheel and toolkit and functioning lights etc. You'll probably have more fun if you drive yourself, although it's always possible to hire a car with driver. If you plan to do a lot of driving and will have time at the end to dispose of it, investigate the possibility of buying a second hand car locally: since hiring is so expensive it may well work out cheaper and will probably do you just as well. For visiting Mexico and beyond, investigate the cost of buying a vehicle in the USA and selling it there at the end of a round trip (do not try to sell a car illegally in Mexico or Central America).

Car Hire Insurance Check exactly what the hirer's insurance policy covers. In many cases it will only protect you against minor bumps and scrapes, not major accidents, nor 'natural' damage (eg flooding). Ask if extra cover is available. Also find out, if using a credit card, whether the card automatically includes insurance. Beware of being billed for scratches which were on the vehicle before you hired it.

NB For RV/motorhome users, a surge protector is recommended to prevent damage to electrical equipment. Ground your trailer with a rod and jumper cable/jump lead.

MOTORCYCLING

People are generally very friendly to motorcyclists and you can make many friends by returning friendship to those who show an interest in you.

The Machine

It should be off road capable: my choice would be the BMW R80/100/GS for its rugged and simple design and reliable shaft drive, but a Kawasaki KLR 650s, Honda Transalp/Dominator, or the ubiquitous Yamaha XT600 Tenere would also be suitable. Buying a bike in the States and driving down works out cheaper than buying one in the UK. A road bike can go most places an off road bike can go at the cost of greater effort.

Preparations

Many roads in Latin America are rough. Fit heavy duty front fork springs and the best quality rebuildable shock absorber you can afford (Ohlins, White Power). Fit lockable luggage such as Krausers (reinforce luggage frames) or make some detachable aluminium panniers. Fit a tank bag and tank panniers for better weight distribution. A large capacity fuel tank (Acerbis), +300 mile/480 km range is essential if going off the beaten track. A washable air filter is a good idea (K&N), also fuel filters, fueltap rubber seals and smaller jets for high altitude motoring. A good set of trails-type tyres as well as a high mudguard are useful. Get to know the bike before you go, ask the dealers in your country what goes wrong with it and arrange a link whereby you can get parts flown out to you. If riding a chain driven bike, a fully enclosed chaincase is useful. A hefty bash plate/sump guard is invaluable.

Spares

Reduce service intervals by half if driving in severe conditions. A spare rear tyre is useful but you can buy modern tyres in most capital cities. Take oil filters, fork and shock seals, tubes, a good manual, spare cables (taped into position) a plug cap and spare plug lead. A spare electronic ignition is a good idea, try and buy a second hand one and make arrangements to have parts sent out to you. A first class tool kit is a must and if riding a bike with a chain then a spare set of sprockets and an 'o' ring chain should be carried. Spare brake and clutch levers should also be taken as these break easily in a fall. Parts are few and far between, but mechanics are skilled at making do and can usually repair things. Castrol oil can be bought everywhere and relied upon.

Take a puncture repair kit and tyre levers. Find out about any weak spots on the bike and improve them. Get the book for international dealer coverage from your manufacturer, but don't rely on it. They frequently have few or no parts for modern, large machinery.

Clothes and Equipment

A tough waterproof jacket, comfortable strong boots, gloves and a helmet with which you can use glass goggles (Halycon) which will not scratch and wear out like a plastic visor. The best quality tent and camping gear that you can afford and a petrol stove which runs on bike fuel are helpful.

Security

Not a problem in most countries. Try not to leave a fully laden bike on its own. An Abus D or chain will keep the bike secure. A cheap alarm gives you peace of mind if you leave the bike outside a hotel at night. Most hotels will allow you to bring the bike inside. Look for hotels that have a court-yard or more secure parking and never leave luggage on the bike overnight or whilst unattended.

Documents

Passport, International Driving Licence, bike registration document are necessary. In Mexico and Central America, a *carnet de passages* is not required.

Shipping

Bikes may be sent from Panama to Colom-bia by cargo flight (eg CAC). You must drain the fuel and oil and remove the battery, but it is easier to disconnect and seal the overflow tube. Tape cardboard over fragile bits and insist on loading the bike yourself. The Darién Gap is impossi-ble unless you carry the bike.

Border Crossings

All borders in Central America seem to work out at about US$20 per vehicle. The exceptions to this are Mexico (see **Auto-mobiles** in Mexico **Information for trav-ellers**) and Panama (approx US$4.50). All borders are free on exit, or should be on most occasions. Do not try to cross borders on a Sunday or a holiday anywhere as you are charged double the rate in Central America countries. It is sometimes very difficult to find out exactly what is being paid for. If in doubt ask to see the boss and/or the rule book.

HITCHHIKING

This custom is quite common in Latin America, and travellers have reported suc-cess in virtually all countries. Neatness of appearance certainly helps. See **Informa-tion for travellers** sections for local condi-tions. If trying to hitchhike away from main roads and in sparsely-populated ar-eas, however, allow plenty of time.

Hitchhiking in Latin America is rea-sonably safe and straightforward for males and couples, provided one speaks some Spanish. It is a most enjoyable mode of transport – a good way to meet the local people, to improve one's languages and to learn about the country. Truck drivers in particular are often well versed in things of interest one is passing, eg crops and industries. Some trucking compa-nies, though, do not allow their drivers to take hitchhikers.

A few general hints: in remoter parts, make enquiries first about the volume of traffic on the road. On long journeys, set out at crack of dawn, which is when trucks usually leave. They tend to go longer distances than cars.

CYCLING

Hallam Murray writes (with recent addi-tions from other cyclists): Since the early 1980s, bicycle technology has improved in leaps and bounds. With the advent of Kevlar tyres and puncture-resistant inner tubes it is now theoretically possible to cycle from Alaska to Tierra del Fuego with-out so much as a single puncture. For the traveller with a zest for adventure and a limited budget there is unlikely to be a finer way to explore. At first glance a bi-cycle may not appear to be the most obvi-ous vehicle for a major journey, but given ample time and reasonable energy it most certainly is the best. It can be ridden, carried by almost every form of transport from an aeroplane to a canoe, and can even be lifted across one's shoulders over short distances. Cyclists can be the envy of trav-ellers using more orthodox transport, since they can travel at their own pace, explore more remote regions and meet people who are not normally in contact with tourists.

Choosing a Bicycle

The choice of bicycle depends on the type and length of expedition being under-taken and on the terrain and road surfaces likely to be encountered. Unless you are planning a journey almost exclusively on paved roads – when a high quality touring bike such as a Dawes Super Galaxy would probably suffice – a mountain bike is strongly recommended. The good quality ones (and the cast iron rule is **never** to skimp on quality) are incredibly tough and rugged, with low gear ratios for difficult terrain, wide tyres with plenty of tread for good road-holding, cantilever brakes, and a low centre of gravity for improved stability. Although touring bikes, and to a lesser extent mountain bikes, and spares are available in the larger Latin American cities, remember that in the developing world most indigenous manufactured goods are shoddy and rarely last. In some countries, such as Mexico, imported components can be found but they tend to be extremely expensive. (Shimano parts are generally the easiest to find.) Buy everything you possibly can before you leave home.

Bicycle Equipment

A small but comprehensive tool kit (to include chain rivet and crank removers, a spoke key and possibly a block remover), a spare tyre and inner tubes, a puncture repair kit with plenty of extra patches and glue, a set of brake blocks, brake and gear cables and all types of nuts and bolts, at least 12 spokes (best taped to the chain stay), a light oil for the chain (eg Finish-Line Teflon Dry-Lube), tube of waterproof grease, a pump secured by a pump lock, a Blackburn parking block (a most invaluable accessory, cheap and virtually weightless), a cyclometer, a loud bell, and a secure lock and chain. *Richard's Bicycle Book* makes useful reading for even the most mechanically minded.

Luggage and equipment

Strong and waterproof front and back panniers are a must. When packed these are likely to be heavy and should be carried on the strongest racks available. Poor quality racks have ruined many a journey for they take incredible strain on unpaved roads. A top bag cum rucksack (eg Carradice) makes a good addition for use on and off the bike. A Cannondale front bag is good for maps, camera, compass, altimeter, notebook and small tape-recorder. (Other rec panniers are Ortlieb luggage – front and back – which is waterproof and almost 'sandproof', Mac-Pac, Madden, Karimoor.) 'Gaffa' tape is excellent for protecting vulnerable parts of panniers and for carrying out all manner of repairs. My most vital equipment included a light and waterproof tent, a 3 season sleeping bag, an Optimus petrol stove (recommended as it is light and efficient and petrol can be found almost everywhere; see also **Camping**, see page 42), a plastic survival bag for storing luggage at night when camping, 4 elastic straps, 4 one-litre water bottles, Swiss Army knife, torch, candle, comprehensive medical kit, money belts, a hat and sunglasses to protect against hours of ferocious tropical sun and small presents such as postcards of home, balloons and plastic badges. A rubber mouse can do wonders for making contact with children in isolated villages.

All equipment and clothes should be packed in plastic bags to give extra protection against dust and rain. (Also protect documents etc carried close to the body from sweat.) Always take the minimum clothing. It's better to buy extra items en route when you find you need them. Naturally the choice will depend on whether you are planning a journey through tropical lowlands, deserts, high mountains or a combination, and whether rain is to be expected. Generally it is best to carry several layers of thin light clothes than fewer bulky, heavy ones. Always keep one set of dry clothes, including long trousers, to put on at the end of the day. The incredibly light, strong, waterproof and wind resistant goretex jacket and overtrousers are invaluable. Training shoes can be used for both cycling and walking.

Useful Tips

Wind, not hills is the enemy of the cyclist. Try to make the best use of the times of day when there is little; mornings tend to be best but there is no steadfast rule. Take care to avoid dehydration, by drinking regularly. In hot, dry areas with limited supplies of water, be sure to carry an ample supply. For food, carry the staples (sugar, salt, dried milk, tea, coffee, porridge oats, raisins, dried soups, etc) and supplement these with whatever local foods can be found in the markets. Give your bicycle a thorough daily check for loose nuts or bolts or bearings. See that all parts run smoothly. A good chain should last 2,000 miles, 3,200 km or more but be sure to keep it as clean as possible – an old toothbrush is good for this – and to oil it lightly from time to time. Always camp out of sight of a road. Remember that thieves are attracted to towns and cities, so when sightseeing, try to leave your bicycle with someone such as a café owner or a priest. Country people tend to be more honest and are usually friendly and very inquisitive. However, don't take unnecessary risks; always see that your bicycle is secure (most hotels will allow bikes to be kept in rooms). In more remote regions dogs can be vicious; carry a stick or some small stones to frighten them off. Traffic on main roads can be a nightmare; it is usually far more rewarding to keep to the smaller roads or to paths if they exist. Most towns have a bicycle shop of some description, but it is best to do your own repairs and adjustments whenever possible. In an emergency it is amazing how one can improvise with wire, string, dental floss, nuts and bolts, odd pieces of tin or 'Gaffa' tape!

The Expedition Advisory Centre, administered by the Royal Geographical Society, 1, Kensington Gore, London SW7 2AR has published a useful monograph entitled *Bicycle Expeditions*, by Paul Vickers. Published in March 1990, it is available direct from the Centre, price £6.50 (postage extra if outside the UK). In the UK there is also the Cyclists' Touring Club, CTC, Cotterell House, 69 Meadrow, Godalming, Surrey, GU7 3HS, T 01483-417217, e-mail: cycling@ctc.org.uk, for touring and technical information.

Matthias Müller of Berlin 31 adds: From Guatemala to Panama, border officials ask for a document of ownership and a frame number for your bicycle. Without these you will have a lot of trouble crossing frontiers. Most cyclists agree that the main danger comes from other traffic. A rear view mirror has frequently been recommended to forewarn you of trucks or cars which are too close behind. You also need to watch out for oncoming, overtaking vehicles, unstable loads on trucks, protruding loads, etc. In Mexico most roads have a good gravel shoulder to cycle on. Make yourself conspicuous by wearing bright clothing and a helmet; also, displaying a Mexican flag helps to keep the truckers patient and prompts encouragement.

Ryan Flegal of Los Angeles, California, says that, instead of taking your own expensive bicycle from home with the attendant need for specialized tools and high risks of loss, one can buy a bike in Latin America. 'Affix a sturdy rear rack, improvise securing luggage to the bicycle, and go. Carry only a patch kit and wrench to remove the wheel, and rely on the many bike mechanics in the area to do the rest'. Another cyclist, Andy Walter (Swindon UK), agrees that local mechanics, of whom there are plenty in Mexico (usually in every town), are competent and inventive. If undertaking maintenance of your own bike though, make sure you know how to do it, and research what tyres you will need, before you go. Paul Olai-Olssen of Oslo, Norway, recommends a steel frame, rather than aluminium, because it is more durable when heavily laden over long periods and can be welded if damaged (aluminium cannot).

Recommended reading: *Latin America by Bike - A Complete Touring Guide*, Walter Sienko (The Mountaineers, 1993); *Bicycling Mexico*, Erick Weisbroth and Eric Ellman (Hunter Publishing Inc, 1990); *Bicycling Baja*, Bonnie Wong (Sunbelt Publications, 1988).

HIKING AND TREKKING

A network of paths and tracks covers much of Central America and is in constant use by the local people. In Guatemala, which has a large Indian population, you can walk just about anywhere, but in the more European countries, particularly Costa Rica you must usually limit yourself to the many excellent national parks with hiking trails. Most Central American countries have an Instituto Geográfico Militar which sells topographical maps, scale 1:100,000 or 1:50,000. The physical features shown on these are usually accurate; the trails and place names less so. National Parks offices also sell maps.

Hiking and backpacking should not be approached casually. Even if you only plan to be out a couple of hours you should have comfortable, safe footwear (which can cope with the wet) and a day-pack to carry your sweater and waterproof (which must be more than showerproof – Ed). At high altitudes the difference in temperature between sun and shade is remarkable. The longer trips mentioned in this book require basic backpacking equipment. Essential items are: backpack with frame, sleeping bag, closed cell foam mat for insulation, stove, tent or tarpaulin, dried food (not tins), water

bottle, compass. Some but not all of these things are available locally.

Hikers have little to fear from the animal kingdom apart from insects (although it's best to avoid actually stepping on a snake), and robbery and assault are very rare. You are much more of a threat to the environment than vice versa. Leave no evidence of your passing; don't litter and don't give gratuitous presents of sweets or money to rural villagers. Respect their system of reciprocity; if they give you hospitality or food, then is the time to reciprocate with presents.

Maps and Guide Books

Those from the Institutos Geográficos Militares in the capitals (see above) are often the only good maps available in Latin America. It is therefore wise to get as many as possible in your home country before leaving, especially if travelling by land. A recommended series of general maps is that published by International Travel Maps (ITM), 345 West Broadway, Vancouver BC, V5Y 1P8, Canada, T (604) 8789-3621, F (604) 879-4521, compiled with historical notes, by the late Kevin Healey. Available are South America South, North East and North West (1:4M), Ecuador (1:1M), The Galapagos Islands (1:500,000), Easter Island (1:30,000), Argentina (1:4M), Rio de Janeiro (1:20,000), Venezuela (1:1.75M), Central America (1:1.8M), Panama (1:800,000), Guatemala and El Salvador (1:500,000), El Salvador (1:375,000), Nicaragua (1:750,000), Honduras (1:750,000), Costa Rica (1:500,000), Belize (1:350,000), Mexico (1:3.3M), Mexico City (1:10,000), Mexico South (1:1M), the Yucatán (1:1M) and Baja California (1:1M). Another map series that has been mentioned is that of New World Edition, Bertelsmann, Neumarkter Strasse 18, 81673 München, Germany, *Mittelamerika, Südamerika Nord, Südamerika Sud, Brasilien* (all 1:4,000,000). For information on Bradt Publications' titles (eg on Belize, Cuba and several South American destinations) and imported maps and guides, contact 41 Nortoft Road, Chalfont St Peter, Bucks, SL9 0LA, UK, T/F 01494 873478. Worthy of mention here are *Backpacking in Central America*, by Tim Burford, and *Central and South America by Road*, by Pam Ascanio, both published by Bradt Publications in 1996.

A very useful book, highly recommended, aimed specifically at the budget traveller is *The Tropical Traveller*, by John Hatt (Penguin Books, 3rd edition, 1993). **The South American Explorers' Club** is at Avenida Portugal 146 (Casilla 3714), Lima, Peru (T 425-0142), Jorge Washington y Leonidas Plaza, Apartado 17-21-431, Eloy Alfaro, Quito, Ecuador (T 225-228), and 126 Indian Creek Road, Ithaca, NY 14850, USA T (607) 277-0488, v mail explorer@samexplo.org. Books, maps and travel planning services are available at the US office. The South American Explorers Club is represented in the UK by Bradt Publications.

The Latin American Travel Advisor is a quarterly news bulletin with up-to-date detailed and reliable information on countries throughout South and Central America. The publication focuses on public safety, health, weather and natural phenomena, travel costs, economics and politics in each country. Annual airmail subscriptions cost US$39, a single current issue US$15, electronically transmitted information (fax or e-mail) US$10 per country. Payment by US$ cheque, MasterCard or VISA (no money orders, credit card payments by mail or fax with card number, expiry date, cardholder's name and signature). Free sample available, contact PO Box 17-17-908, Quito, Ecuador, international F 593-2-562-566, USA and Canada toll free F (888) 215-9511, e-mail LATA@pi.pro.ec, World Wide Web http://www.amerispan.com/latc/.

AmeriSpan, 6 Av Norte No 40, Antigua, Guatemala, T/F 832-0164, e-mail amspan.ibm.net, has information about language schools (in Guatemala and elsewhere in Latin America), tours, hotels, bars, restaurants, etc; competitive T/F service; friendly English/Spanish speaking staff. In USA, PO Box 40513, Philadelphia, PA 19106-0513, T (USA and Canada) 800-879-6640, worldwide 215-985-4522, F 215-985-4524; e-mail info@amerispan.com, or on internet http://www.amerispan.com.

Another website worth visiting for information, especially on ecotourism and language schools, is Ron Mader's *El Planeta Platica*: http://www.planeta.com.

TRAVELLING WITH CHILDREN

People contemplating overland travel in Latin America with children should remember that a lot of time can be spent waiting for buses, trains, and especially for aeroplanes. On bus journeys, if the children are good at amusing themselves, or can readily sleep while travelling, the problems can be considerably lessened. If your child is of an early reading age, take reading material with you as it is difficult, and expensive, to find. A bag of, say 30 pieces, of Duplo or Lego can keep young children occupied for hours. Travel on trains, while not as fast or at times as comfortable as buses, allows more scope for moving about. Some trains provide tables between seats, so that games can be played. (Beware of doors left open for ventilation, especially if air-conditioning is not working – Ed.)

Food

Food can be a problem if the children are not adaptable. It is easier to take biscuits, drinks, bread etc with you on longer trips than to rely on meal stops where the food may not be to taste. Avocados are safe, easy to eat and nutritious; they can be fed to babies as young as 6 months and most older children like them. A small immersion heater and jug for making hot drinks is invaluable, but remember that electric current varies. Try and get a dual-voltage one (110v and 220v).

Fares

On all long-distance buses you pay for each seat, and there are no half-fares if the children occupy a seat each. For shorter trips it is cheaper, if less comfortable, to seat small children on your knee. Often there are spare seats which children can occupy after tickets have been collected. In city and local excursion buses, small children generally do not pay a fare, but are not entitled to a seat when paying customers are standing. On sightseeing tours you should *always* bargain for a family rate – often children can go free. (In trains, reductions for children are general, but not universal.)

All civil airlines charge half for children under 12, but some military services don't have half-fares, or have younger age limits. Note that a child travelling free on a long excursion is not always covered by the operator's travel insurance; it is advisable to pay a small premium to arrange cover.

Hotels

In all hotels, try to negotiate family rates. If charges are per person, always insist that 2 children will occupy 1 bed only, therefore counting as 1 tariff. If rates are per bed, the same applies. In either case you can almost always get a reduced rate at cheaper hotels. Occasionally when travelling with a child you will be refused a room in a hotel that is 'unsuitable'. (In restaurants, you can normally buy children's helpings, or divide 1 full-size helping between 2 children.)

Travel with children can bring you into closer contact with Latin American families, and generally, presents no special problems – in fact the path is often smoother for family groups. Officials tend to be more amenable where children are concerned and they are pleased if your child knows a little Spanish. Moreover, even thieves and pickpockets seem to have some of the traditional respect for families, and may leave you alone because of it! Always carry a copy of your child's birth certificate and passport-size photos.

Health in Latin America

WITH the following advice and precautions you should keep as healthy as you do at home. Most visitors return home having experienced no problems at all apart from some travellers' diarrhoea. In Latin America the health risks, especially in the lowland tropical areas, are different from those encountered in Europe or the USA. It also depends on where and how you travel. There are clear health differences between the countries of Latin America and in risks for the business traveller, who stays in international class hotels in large cities, the backpacker trekking from country to country and the tourist who heads for the beach. There is huge variation in climate, vegetation and wildlife from the semi-desert of northern Mexico to the rain forests of Costa Rica and from smouldering volcano cones, to the teeming capital cities. There are no hard and fast rules to follow; you will often have to make your own judgment on the healthiness or otherwise of your surroundings. There are English (or other foreign language) speaking doctors in most major cities who have particular experience in dealing with locally-occurring diseases. Your Embassy representative will often be able to give you the name of local reputable doctors and most of the better hotels have a doctor on standby. If you do fall ill and cannot find a recommended doctor, try the Outpatient Department of a hospital – private hospitals are usually less crowded and offer a more acceptable standard of care to foreigners.

BEFORE TRAVELLING

Take out medical insurance. Make sure it covers all eventualities especially evacuation to your home country by a medically equipped plane, if necessary. You should have a dental check up, obtain a spare glasses prescription, a spare oral contraceptive prescription (or enought pills to last) and, if you suffer from a chronic illness (such as diabetes, high blood pressure, ear or sinus troubles, cardio-pulmonary disease or nervous disorder) arrange for a check up with your doctor, who can at the same time provide you with a letter explaining the details of your disability in English and if possible Spanish and/or Portuguese. Check the current practice in countries you are visiting for malaria prophylaxis (prevention). If you are on regular medication, make sure you have enough to cover the period of your travel.

Children

More preparation is probably necessary for babies and children than for an adult and perhaps a little more care should be taken when travelling to remote areas where health services are primitive. This is because children can be become more rapidly ill than adults (on the other hand they often recover more quickly). Diarrhoea and vomiting are the most common problems, so take the usual precautions, but more intensively. Breastfeeding is best and most convenient for babies, but powdered milk is generally available and so are baby foods in most countries. Papaya, bananas and avocados are all nutritious and can be cleanly prepared. The treatment of diarrhoea is the same for adults, except that it should start earlier and be continued with more persistence. Children get dehydrated very quickly in hot countries and can become drowsy and uncooperative unless cajoled to drink water or juice plus salts. Upper respiratory infections, such as colds, catarrh and middle ear infections are also common and if your child suffers from these normally take some antibiotics against the possibility. Outer ear infections after swimming are also common and antibiotic eardrops will help. Wet wipes are always useful and sometimes difficult to find in some countries, as, in some places are disposable nappies.

MEDICINES AND WHAT TO TAKE

There is very little control on the sale of drugs and medicines. You can buy any and every drug in the numerous pharmacies without a prescription. Be wary of this because pharmacists can be poorly trained and might sell you drugs that are unsuitable, dangerous or old. Many drugs and medicines are manufactured under licence from American or European companies, so the trade names may be familiar to you. This means you do not have to carry a whole chest of medicines with you, but remember that the shelf life of some items, especially vaccines and antibiotics, is markedly reduced in hot conditions. Buy your supplies at the better outlets where there are refrigerators, even though they are more expensive and check the expiry date of all preparations you buy. Immigration officials occasionally confiscate scheduled drugs (Lomotil is an example) if they are not accompanied by a doctor's prescription.

Self-medication may be forced on you by circumstances so the following text contains the names of drugs and medicines which you may find useful in an emergency or in out-of-the-way places. You may like to take some of the following items with you from home:

Sunglasses
  ones designed for intense sunlight

Earplugs
  for sleeping on aeroplanes and in noisy hotels

Suntan cream
  with a high protection factor

Insect repellent
  containing DET for preference

Mosquito net
  lightweight, permethrin-impregnated for choice

Tablets
for travel sickness

Tampons
can be expensive in some countries in Latin America

Condoms

Contraceptives

Water sterilising tablets

Antimalarial tablets

Anti-infective ointment eg Cetrimide

Dusting powder for feet etc containing fungicide

Antacid tablets
for indigestion

Sachets of rehydration salts
plus anti-diarrhoea preparations

Painkillers
such as Paracetamol or Aspirin

Antibiotics
for diarrhoea etc

First Aid kit
Small pack containing a few sterile syringes and needles and disposable gloves. The risk of catching hepatitis etc from a dirty needle used for injection is now negligible in Latin America, but some may be reassured by carrying their own supplies – available from camping shops and airport shops.

Vaccination and immunisation

Smallpox vaccination is no longer required anywhere in the world. Neither is cholera vaccination recognized as necessary for international travel by the World Health Organisation – it is not very effective either. Nevertheless, some immigration officials are demanding proof of vaccination against cholera in Latin America and in some countries outside Latin America, following the outbreak of the disease which originated in Peru in 1990-91 and subsequently affected most surrounding countries. Although very unlikely to affect visitors to Latin America, the cholera epidemic continues making its greatest impact in poor areas where water supplies are polluted and food hygiene practices are insanitary.

Vaccination against the following diseases are recommended:

Yellow Fever
This is a live vaccination not to be given to children under 9 months of age or persons allergic to eggs. Immunity lasts for 10 years, an International Certificate of Yellow Fever Vaccination will be given and should be kept because it is sometimes asked for. Yellow fever is very rare in Latin America, but the vaccination is practically without side effects and almost totally protective.

Typhoid
A disease spread by the insanitary preparation of food. A number of new vaccines against this condition are now available; the older TAB and monovalent typhoid vaccines are being phased out. The newer, eg Typhim Vi, cause less side effects, but are more expensive. For those who do not like injections, there are now oral vaccines.

Poliomyelitis
Despite its decline in the world this remains a serious disease if caught and is easy to protect against. There are live oral vaccines and in some countries injected vaccines. Whichever one you choose it is a good idea to have booster every 3-5 years if visiting developing countries regularly.

Tetanus
One dose should be given with a booster at 6 weeks and another at 6 months and 10 yearly boosters thereafter are recommended. Children should already be properly protected against diphtheria, poliomyelitis and pertussis (whooping cough), measles and HIB all of which can be more serious infections in Latin America than at home. Measles, mumps and rubella vaccine is also given to children throughout the world, but those teenage girls who have not had rubella (german measles) should be tested and vaccinated. Hepatitis B vaccination for babies is now routine in some countries. Consult your doctor for advice on tuberculosis inoculation: the disease is still widespread in Latin America.

Infectious Hepatitis
Is less of a problem for travellers than it used to be because of the development of two extremely effective vaccines against

the A and B form of the disease. It remains common, however, in Latin America. A combined hepatitis A & B vaccine is now licensed and will be available in 1997 – one jab covers both diseases.

Other vaccinations:
Might be considered in the case of epidemics eg meningitis. There is an effective vaccination against rabies which should be considered by all travellers, especially those going through remote areas or if there is a particular occupational risk, eg for zoologists or veterinarians.

FURTHER INFORMATION

Further information on health risks abroad, vaccinations etc may be available from a local travel clinic. If you wish to take specific drugs with you such as antibiotics these are best prescribed by your own doctor. Beware, however, that not all doctors can be experts on the health problems of remote countries. More detailed or more up-to-date information than local doctors can provide are available from various sources. In the UK there are hospital departments specialising in tropical diseases in London, Liverpool, Birmingham and Glasgow and the Malaria Reference Laboratory at the London School of Hygiene and Tropical Medicine provides free advice about malaria, T 0891 600350. In the USA the local Public Health Services can give such information and information is available centrally from the Centre for Disease Control (CDC) in Atlanta, T (404) 3324559.

There are additional computerized databases which can be assessed for destination-specific up-to-the-minute information. In the UK there is MASTA (Medical Advisory Service to Travellers Abroad), T 0171 631 4408, F 0171 436 5389, Tx 8953473 and Travax (Glasgow, T 0141 946 7120, ext 247). Other information on medical problems overseas can be obtained from the book by Dawood, Richard (Editor) (1992) *Travellers' Health: How to stay healthy abroad*, Oxford University Press 1992, £7.99. We strongly recommend this revised and updated edition, especially to the intrepid traveller heading for the more out of the way places. General advice is also available in the UK in *Health Information for Overseas Travel* published by the Department of Health and available from HMSO, and *International Travel and Health* published by WHO, Geneva.

STAYING HEALTHY

INTESTINAL UPSETS

The thought of catching a stomach bug worries visitors to Latin America but there have been great improvements in food hygiene and most such infections are preventable. Travellers' diarrhoea and vomiting is due, most of the time, to food poisoning, usually passed on by the insanitary habits of food handlers. As a general rule the cleaner your surroundings and the smarter the restaurant, the less likely you are to suffer.

Foods to avoid: uncooked, undercooked, partially cooked or reheated meat, fish, eggs, raw vegetables and salads, especially when they have been left out exposed to flies. Stick to fresh food that has been cooked from raw just before eating and make sure you peel fruit yourself. Wash and dry your hands before eating – disposable wet-wipe tissues are useful for this.

Shellfish eaten raw are risky and at certain times of the year some fish and shellfish concentrate toxins from their environment and cause various kinds of food poisoning. The local authorities notify the public not to eat these foods. Do not ignore the warning. **Heat treated milk** (UHT) pasteurized or sterilized is becoming more available in Latin America as is pasteurized cheese. On the whole matured or processed cheeses are safer than the fresh varieties and fresh unpasteurized milk from whatever animal can be a source of food poisoning germs, tuberculosis and brucellosis. This applies equally to icecream, yoghurt and cheese made from unpasteurized milk, so avoid these homemade products – the factory made ones are probably safer.

Tap water is rarely safe outside the major cities, especially in the rainy season. Stream water, if you are in the countryside, is often contaminated by communities living surprisingly high in the mountains. Filtered or bottled water is usually available and safe, although you must make sure that somebody is not filling bottles from the tap and hammering on a new crown cap. If your hotel has a central hot water supply this water is safe to drink after cooling. Ice for drinks should be made from boiled water, but rarely is so stand your glass on the ice cubes, rather than putting them in the drink. The better hotels have water purifying systems.

TRAVELLERS' DIARRHOEA

This is usually caused by eating food which has been contaminated by food poisoning germs. Drinking water is rarely the culprit. Sea water or river water is more likely to be contaminated by sewage and so swimming in such dilute effluent can also be a cause.

Infection with various organisms can give rise to travellers' diarrhoea. They may be viruses, bacteria, eg Escherichia

Water purification

There are a number of ways of purifying water in order to make it safe to drink. Dirty water should first be strained through a filter bag (camping shops) and then boiled or treated. Bringing water to a rolling boil at sea level is sufficient to make the water safe for drinking, but at higher altitudes you have to boil the water for longer to ensure that all the microbes are killed.

There are sterilising methods that can be used and there are proprietary preparations containing chlorine (eg Puritabs) or iodine (eg Pota Aqua) compounds. Chlorine compounds generally do not kill protozoa (eg giardia).

There are a number of water filters now on the market available in personal and expedition size. They work either on mechanical or chemical principles, or may do both. Make sure you take the spare parts or spare chemicals with you and do not believe *everything* the manufacturers say.

coli (probably the most common cause worldwide), protozoal (such as amoebas and giardia), salmonella and cholera. The diarrhoea may come on suddenly or rather slowly. It may or may not be accompanied by vomiting or by severe abdominal pain and the passage of blood or mucus when it is called dysentery.

How do you know which type you have caught and how to treat it?

If you can time the onset of the diarrhoea to the minute ('acute') then it is probably due to a virus or a bacterium and/or the onset of dysentery. The treatment in addition to rehydration is Ciprofloxacin 500 mg every 12 hrs; the drug is now widely available and there are many similar ones.

If the diarrhoea comes on slowly or intermittently ('sub-acute') then it is more likely to be protozoal, ie caused by an amoeba or giardia. Antibiotics such as Ciprofloxacin will have little effect. These cases are best treated by a doctor as is any outbreak of diarrhoea continuing for more than 3 days. Sometimes blood is passed in amoebic dysentery and for this you should certainly seek medical help. If this is not available then the best treatment is probably Tinidazole (Fasigyn) 1 tablet four times a day for 3 days. If there are severe stomach cramps, the following drugs may help but are not very useful in the management of acute diarrhoea: Loperamide (Imodium) and Diphenoxylate with Atropine (Lomotil) They should not be given to children.

Any kind of diarrhoea, whether or not accompanied by vomiting, responds well to the replacement of water and salts, taken as frequent small sips, of some kind of rehydration solution. There are proprietary preparations consisting of sachets of powder which you dissolve in boiled water or you can make your own by adding half a teaspoonful of salt (3.5 gms) and 4 tablespoonsful of sugar (40 gms) to a litre of boiled water.

Thus the lynch pins of treatment for diarrhoea are rest, fluid and salt replacement, antibiotics such as Ciprofloxacin for the bacterial types and special diagnostic tests and medical treatment for the amoeba and giardia infections. Salmonella infections and cholera, although rare, can be devastating diseases and it would be wise to get to a hospital as soon as possible if these were suspected.

Fasting, peculiar diets and the consumption of large quantities of yoghurt have not been found useful in calming travellers' diarrhoea or in rehabilitating inflamed bowels. Oral rehydration has on the other hand, especially in children, been a life saving technique and should always be practised, whatever other treatment you use. As there is some evidence that alcohol and milk might prolong diarrhoea they should be avoided during and immediately after an attack.

Diarrhoea occurring day after day for long periods of time (chronic diarrhoea) is notoriously resistent to amateur attempts at treatment and again warrants proper diagnostic tests (most towns with reasonable sized hospitals have laboratories for stool samples). There are ways of preventing travellers' diarrhoea for short periods of time by taking antibiotics, but this is not a foolproof technique and should not be used other than in exceptional circumstances. Doxycycline is possibly the best drug. Some preventatives such as Enterovioform can have serious side effects if taken for long periods.

Paradoxically **constipation** is also common, probably induced by dietary change, inadequate fluid intake in hot places and long bus journeys. Simple laxatives are useful in the short-term and bulky foods such as maize, beans and plenty of fruit are also useful.

HIGH ALTITUDE

Spending time at high altitude, especially in the tropics, is usually a pleasure – it is not so hot, there are no insects and the air is clear and spring like. Travelling to high altitudes, however, can cause medical problems, all of which can be prevented if care is taken.

On reaching heights above about 3,000m, heart pounding and shortness of breath, especially on exertion are a normal response to the lack of oxygen in the air. A condition called acute mountain sickness can also affect visitors. It is more likely to affect those who ascend rapidly, eg by plane and those who over-exert themselves (teenagers for example). The condition takes a few hours or days to come on and presents with a bad headache, extreme tiredness, sometimes dizziness, loss of appetite and frequently nausea and vomiting. Insomnia is common and is often associated with a suffocating feeling when lying in bed. Keen observers may note their breathing tends to wax and wane at night and their face tends to be puffy in the mornings – this is all part of the syndrome. Anyone can get this condition and past experience is not always a good guide: the author, having spent years in Peru travelling constantly between sea level and very high altitude never suffered symptoms, then was severely affected whilst climbing Kilimanjaro in Tanzania.

The treatment of acute mountain sickness is simple – rest, painkillers, (preferably not aspirin based) for the headache and anti sickness pills for vomiting. Oxygen is actually not much help, except at very high altitude. Various local panaceas – Coramina glucosada, Effortil, Micoren are popular in Latin America and mate de coca (an infusion of coca leaves widely available and perfectly legal) will alleviate some of the symptoms.

To **prevent** the condition: on arrival at places over 3,000m have a few hours rest in a chair and avoid alcohol, cigarettes and heavy food. If the symptoms are severe and prolonged, it is best to descend to a lower altitude and to reascend slowly or in stages. If this is impossible because of shortage of time or if you are going so high that acute mountain sickness is very likely, then the drug Acetazolamide (Diamox) can be used as a preventative and continued during the ascent. There is good evidence of the value of this drug as a preventative, but some people do experience peculiar side effects. The usual dose is 500 mg of the slow release preparation each night, starting the night before ascending above 3,000m.

Watch out for **sunburn** at high altitude. The ultraviolet rays are extremely powerful. The air is also excessively dry at high altitude and you might find that your skin dries out and the inside of your nose becomes crusted. Use a moisturiser for the skin and some vaseline wiped into the nostrils. Some people find contact lenses irritate because of the dry air. It is unwise to ascend to high altitude if you are pregnant, especially in the first 3 months, or if you have a history of heart, lung or blood disease, including sickle cell.

A more unusual condition can affect mountaineers who ascend rapidly to high altitude – **acute pulmonary oedema**. Residents at altitude sometimes experience this when returning to the mountains from time spent at the coast. This condition is often preceded by acute mountain sickness and comes on quite rapidly with severe breathlessness, noisy breathing, cough, blueness of the lips and frothing at the mouth. Anybody who develops this must be brought down as soon as possible, given oxygen and taken to hospital.

A rapid descent from high places will make sinus problems and middle ear infections worse and might make your teeth ache. Lastly, don't fly to altitude within 24 hrs of SCUBA diving. You might suffer from 'the bends'.

HEAT AND COLD

Full acclimatisation to high temperatures takes about 2 weeks. During this period it is normal to feel a bit apathetic, especially if the relative humidity is high. Drink plenty of water (up to 15 litres a day are required when working physically hard in the tropics), use salt on your food and avoid extreme exertion. Tepid showers are more cooling than hot or cold ones. Large hats do not cool you down, but do prevent sunburn. Remember that, especially in the highlands, there can be a large and sudden drop in temperature between sun and shade and between night and day, so dress accordingly. Warm jackets or woollens are essential after dark at high altitude. Loose cotton is still the best material when the weather is hot.

INSECTS

These are mostly more of a nuisance than a serious hazard and if you try, you can prevent yourself entirely from being bitten. Some, such as mosquitos are, of course, carriers of potentially serious diseases, so it is sensible to avoid being bitten as much as possible. Sleep off the ground and use a mosquito net or some kind of insecticide. Preparations containing Pyrethrum or synthetic pyrethroids are safe. They are available as aerosols or pumps and the best way to use these is to spray the room thoroughly in all areas (follow the instructions rather than the insects) and then shut the door for a while, re-entering when the smell has dispersed. Mosquito coils release insecticide as they burn slowly. They are widely available and useful out of doors. Tablets of insecticide which are placed on a heated mat plugged into a wall socket are probably the most effective. They fill the room with insecticidal fumes in the same way as aerosols or coils.

You can also use insect repellents, most of which are effective against a wide range of pests. The most common and effective is diethyl metatoluamide (DET). DET liquid is best for arms and face (care around eyes and with spectacles – DET dissolves plastic). Aerosol spray is good for clothes and ankles and liquid DET can be dissolved in water and used to impregnate cotton clothes and mosquito nets. Some repellents now contain DET and Permethrin, insecticide. Impregnated wrist and ankle bands can also be useful.

If you are bitten or stung, itching may be relieved by cool baths, antihistamine tablets (care with alcohol or driving) or mild corticosteroid creams, eg. hydrocortisone (great care: never use if any hint of infection). Careful scratching of all your bites once a day can be surprisingly effective. Calamine lotion and cream have limited effectiveness and antihistamine creams are not recommended – they can cause allergies themselves.

Bites which become infected should be treated with a local antiseptic or antibiotic cream such as Cetrimide, as should any infected sores or scratches.

When living rough, skin infestations with body lice (crabs) and scabies are easy to pick up. Use whatever local commercial preparation is recommended for lice and scabies.

Crotamiton cream (Eurax) alleviates itching and also kills a number of skin parasites. Malathion lotion 5% (Prioderm) kills lice effectively, but avoid the use of the toxic agricultural preparation of Malathion, more often used to commit suicide.

TICKS

They attach themselves usually to the lower parts of the body often after walking in areas where cattle have grazed. They take a while to attach themselves strongly, but swell up as they start to suck blood. The important thing is to remove them gently, so that they do not leave their head parts in your skin because this can cause a nasty allergic reaction some days later. Do not use petrol, vaseline, lighted cigarettes etc to remove the tick, but, with a pair of tweezers remove the beast gently by gripping it at the attached (head) end and rock it out in very much the same way that a tooth is extracted. Certain tropical flies which lay their eggs under the skin of sheep and cattle also occasionally do the same thing to humans with the unpleasant result that a maggot grows under the skin and pops up as a boil or pimple. The best way to remove these is to cover the boil with oil, vaseline or nail varnish so as to stop the maggot breathing, then to squeeze it out gently the next day.

SUNBURN

The burning power of the tropical sun, especially at high altitude, is phenomenal.

Always wear a wide brimmed hat and use some form of suncream lotion on untanned skin. Normal temperate zone suntan lotions (protection factor up to 7) are not much good; you need to use the types designed specifically for the tropics or for mountaineers or skiers with protection factors up to 15 or above. These are often not available in Latin America. Glare from the sun can cause conjunctivitis, so wear sunglasses

especially on tropical beaches, where high protection factor sunscreen should also be used.

PRICKLY HEAT

A very common intensely itchy rash is avoided by frequent washing and by wearing loose clothing. Cured by allowing skin to dry off through use of powder and spending two nights in an airconditioned hotel!

ATHLETES FOOT

This and other fungal skin infections are best treated with Tolnaftate or Clotrimazole.

OTHER RISKS AND MORE SERIOUS DISEASES

Remember that rabies is endemic throughout Latin America, so avoid dogs that are behaving strangely and cover your toes at night from the vampire bats, which also carry the disease. If you are bitten by a domestic or wild animal, do not leave things to chance: scrub the wound with soap and water and/or disinfectant, try to have the animal captured (within limits) or at least determine its ownership, where possible, and seek medical assistance at once. The course of treatment depends on whether you have already been satisfactorily vaccinated against rabies. If you have (this is worthwile if you are spending lengths of time in developing countries) then some further doses of vaccine are all that is required. Human diploid vaccine is the best, but expensive: other, older kinds of vaccine, such as that derived from duck embryos may be the only types available. These are effective, much cheaper and interchangeable generally with the human derived types. If not already vaccinated then anti rabies serum (immunoglobulin) may be required in addition. It is important to finish the course of treatment whether the animal survives or not.

AIDS

AIDS in the region is increasing but is not wholly confined to the well known high risk sections of the population, ie homosexual men, intravenous drug abusers and children of infected mothers. Heterosexual transmission is now the dominant mode and so the main risk to travellers is from casual sex. The same precautions should be taken as with any sexually transmitted disease. The Aids virus (HIV) can be passed by unsterilized needles which have been previously used to inject an HIV positive patient, but the risk of this is negligible. It would, however, be sensible to check that needles have been properly sterilized or disposable needles have been used. If you wish to take your own disposable needles, be prepared to explain what they are for. The risk of receiving a blood transfusion with blood infected with the HIV virus is greater than from dirty needles because of the amount of fluid exchanged. Supplies of blood for transfusion should now be screened for HIV in all reputable hospitals, so again the risk is very small indeed. Catching the AIDS virus does not always produce an illness in itself (although it may do). The only way to be sure if you feel you have been put at risk is to have a blood test for HIV antibodies on your return to a place where there are reliable laboratory facilities. The test does not become positive for some weeks.

MALARIA

Malaria is theoretically confined to coastal and jungle zones, but is now on the increase again. Mosquitos do not thrive above 2,500m, so you are safe at altitude. There are different varieties of malaria, some resistant to the normal drugs. Make local enquiries if you intend to visit possibly infected zones and use a prophylactic regime. Start taking the tablets a few days before exposure and continue to take them for 6 weeks after leaving the malarial zone. Remember to give the drugs to babies and children also. Opinion varies on the precise drugs and dosage to be used for protection. All the drugs may have some side effects and it is important to balance the risk of catching the disease against the albeit rare side effects. The increasing complexity of the subject is such that as the malarial parasite becomes immune to the new generation of drugs it has made

concentration on the physical prevention from being bitten by mosquitos more important. This involves the use of long sleeved shirts or blouses and long trousers, repellants and nets. Clothes are now available impregnated with the insecticide Permethrin or Deltamethrin or it is possible to impregnate the clothes yourself. Wide meshed nets impregnated with Permethrin are also available, are lighter to carry and less claustrophobic to sleep in.

Prophylaxis and treatment

If your itinerary takes you into a malarial area, seek expert advice before you go on a suitable prophylactic regime. This is especially true for pregnant women who are particularly prone to catch malaria. You can still catch the disease even when sticking to a proper regime, although it is unlikely. If you do develop symptoms (high fever, shivering, headache, sometimes diarrhoea), seek medical advice immediately. If this is not possible and there is a great likelihood of malaria, the treatment is:

Chloroquine, a single dose of 4 tablets (600 mg) followed by 2 tablets (300 mg) in 6 hrs and 300 mg each day following.

Falciparum type of malaria or type in doubt: take local advice. Various combinations of drugs are being used such as Quinine, Tetracycline or Halofantrine. If falciparum type malaria is definitely diagnosed, it is wise to get to a good hospital as treatment can be complex and the illness very serious.

INFECTIOUS HEPATITIS (JAUNDICE)

The main symptoms are pains in the stomach, lack of appetite, lassitude and yellowness of the eyes and skin. Medically speaking there are two main types. The less serious, but more common is Hepatitis A for which the best protection os the careful preparation of food, the avoidance of contaminated drinking water and scrupulous attention to toilet hygiene. The other, more serious, version is Hepatitis B which is acquired usually as a sexually transmitted disease or by blood transfusions. It can less commonly be transmitted by injections with unclean needles and possibly by insect bites. The symptoms are the same as for Hepatitis A. The incubation period is much longer (up to 6 months compared with 6 weeks) and there are more likely to be complications.

Hepatitis A can be protected against with gamma globulin. It should be obtained from a reputable source and is certainly useful for travellers who intend to live rough. You should have a shot before leaving and have it repeated every 6 months. The dose of gamma globulin depends on the concentration of the particular preparation used, so the manufacturer's advice should be taken. The injection should be given as close as possible to your departure and as the dose depends on the likely time you are to spend in potentially affected areas, the manufacturer's instructions should be followed. Gamma globulin has really been superceded now by a proper vaccination against Hepatitis A (Havrix) which gives immunity lasting up to 10 years. After that boosters are required. Havrix monodose is now widely available as is Junior Havrix. The vaccination has negligible side effects and is extremely effective. Gamma globulin injections can be a bit painful, but it is much cheaper than Havrix and may be more available in some places.

Hepatitis B can be effectively prevented by a specific vaccine (Engerix) – 3 shots over 6 months before travelling. If you have had jaundice in the past it would be worthwhile having a blood test to see if you are immune to either of these two types, because this might avoid the necessity and costs of vaccination or gamma globulin. There are other kinds of viral hepatitis (C, E etc) which are fairly similar to A and B, but vaccines are not available as yet.

TYPHUS

Can still occur carried by ticks. There is usually a reaction at the site of the bite and a fever. Seek medical advice.

INTESTINAL WORMS

These are common and the more serious ones such as hookworm can be contracted from walking barefoot on infested earth or beaches.

Various other tropical diseases can be caught in jungle areas, usually transmitted by biting insects. They are often related to African diseases and were probably introduced by the slave labour trade. Onchocerciasis (river blindness) carried by black flies is found in parts of Mexico and Venezuela. Leishmaniasis (Espundia) is carried by sandflies and causes a sore that will not heal or a severe nasal infection. Wearing long trousers and a long sleeved shirt in infected areas protects against these flies. DET is also effective. Epidemics of meningitis occur from time-to-time. Be careful about swimming in piranha or caribe infested rivers. It is a good idea not to swim naked: the Candiru fish can follow urine currents and become lodged in body orifices. Swimwear offers some protection.

LEPTOSPIROSIS

Various forms of leptospirosis occur throughout Latin America, transmitted by a bacterium which is excreted in rodent urine. Fresh water and moist soil harbour the organisms which enter the body through cuts and scratches. If you suffer from any form of prolonged fever consult a doctor.

SNAKE BITE

This is a very rare event indeed for travellers. If you are unlucky (or careless) enough to be bitten by a venomous snake, spider, scorpion or sea creature, try to identify the creature, but do not put yourself in further danger. Snake bites in particular are very frightening, but in fact rarely poisonous – even venomous snakes bite without injecting venom. What you might expect if bitten are: fright, swelling, pain and bruising around the bite and soreness of the regional lymph glands, perhaps nausea, vomiting and a fever. Signs of serious poisoning would be the following symptoms: numbness and tingling of the face, muscular spasms, convulsions, shortness of breath and bleeding. Victims should be got to a hospital or a doctor without delay. Commercial snake bite and scorpion kits are available, but usually only useful for the specific type of snake or scorpion for which they are designed. Most serum has to be given intravenously so it is not much good equipping yourself with it unless you are used to making injections into veins. It is best to rely on local practice in these cases, because the particular creatures will be known about locally and appropriate treatment can be given.

Treatment of snake bite Reassure and comfort the victim frequently. Immobilize the limb by a bandage or a splint or by getting the person to lie still. Do not slash the bite area and try to suck out the poison because this sort of heroism does more harm than good. If you know how to use a tourniquet in these circumstances, you will not need this advice. If you are not experienced do not apply a tourniquet.

Precautions

Avoid walking in snake territory in bare feet or sandals – wear proper shoes or boots. If you encounter a snake stay put until it slithers away, and do not investigate a wounded snake. Spiders and scorpions may be found in the more basic hotels. The sting of some species of Mexican scorpion can be quite dangerous. If stung, rest and take plenty of fluids and call a doctor. The best precaution is to keep beds away from the walls and look inside your shoes and under the toilet seat every morning. Certain tropical sea fish when trodden upon inject venom into bathers' feet. This can be exceptionally painful. Wear plastic shoes when you go bathing if such creatures are reported. The pain can be relieved by immersing the foot in extremely hot water for as long as the pain persists.

DENGUE FEVER

This is increasing worldwide including in South and Central American countries and the Caribbean. It can be completely prevented by avoiding mosquito bites in

the same way as malaria. No vaccine is available. Dengue is an unpleasant and painful disease, presenting with a high temperature and body pains, but at least visitors are spared the more serious forms (haemorrhagic types) which are more of a problem for local people who have been exposed to the disease more than once. There is no specific treatment for dengue – just pain killers and rest.

DANGEROUS ANIMALS

Apart from mosquitos the most dangerous animals are men, be they bandits or behind steering wheels. Think carefully about violent confrontations and wear a seat belt if you are lucky enough to have one available to you.

WHEN YOU RETURN HOME

Remember to take your antimalarial tablets for 6 weeks after leaving the malarial area. If you have had attacks of diarrhoea it is worth having a stool specimen tested in case you have picked up amoebas. If you have been living rough, blood tests may be worthwhile to detect worms and other parasites. If you have been exposed to bilharzia (*schistosomiasis*) by swimming in lakes etc, check by means of a blood test when you get home, but leave it for 6 weeks because the test is slow to become positive. Report any untowards symptoms to your doctor and tell the doctor exactly where you have been and, if you know, what the likelihood of disease is to which you were exposed.

The above information has been compiled for us by Dr David Snashall, who is presently Senior Lecturer in Occupational Health at the United Medical Schools of Guy's and St Thomas' Hospitals in London and Chief Medical Adviser to the British Foreign and Commonwealth Office. He has travelled extensively in Central and South America, worked in Peru and in East Africa and keeps in close touch with developments in preventative and tropical medicine.

Section 3
The region

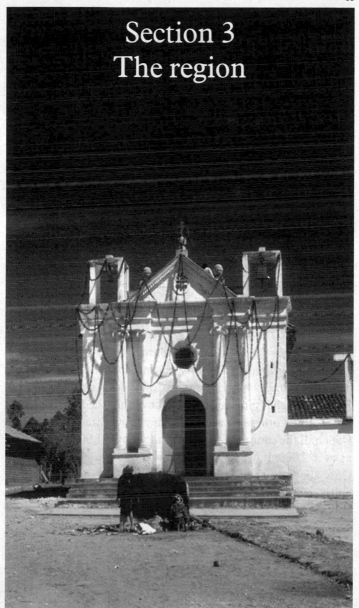

Mexico

CORTES, asked what the country looked like, crushed a piece of parchment in his fist, released it and said: "That is the map of Mexico." This crumpled land is so splendid to the eye, and so exotic to the other senses, that millions visit it each year.

Mexico is the third largest country in Latin America and the most populous Spanish-speaking country anywhere. Its geography ranges from swamp to desert, from tropical lowland jungle to high alpine vegetation above the tree line, from thin arid soils to others so rich that they grow three crops a year. Over half the country is at an altitude of over 1,000m and much at over 2,000m; over half is arid and another 30% semi-arid. Only about 30 million ha (16% of the total land area) can be cultivated.

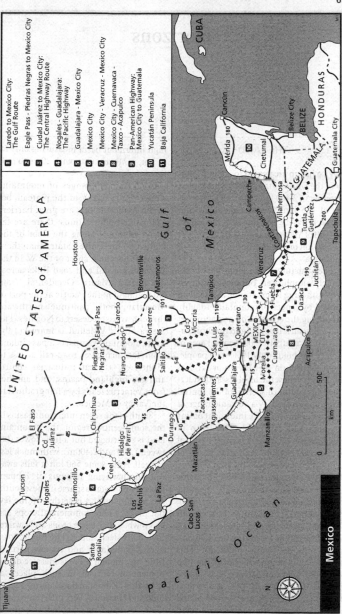

Mexico

1. Laredo to Mexico City:
   The Gulf Route
2. Eagle Pass - Piedras Negras to Mexico City
3. Ciudad Juárez to Mexico City:
   The Central Highway Route
4. Nogales - Guadalajara:
   The Pacific Highway
5. Guadalajara - Mexico City
6. Mexico City
7. Mexico City - Veracruz - Mexico City
8. Mexico City - Cuernavaca -
   Taxco - Acapulco
9. Pan-American Highway:
   Mexico City to Guatemala
10. Yucatán Peninsula
11. Baja California

Horizons

THE LAND

Mexico has an area equal to about a quarter of the United States, with which it has a frontier of 2,400 km. The southern frontier of 885 km is with Guatemala and Belize. It has a coast line of 2,780 km on the Gulf of Mexico and the Caribbean, and of 7,360 km on the Pacific and the Gulf of California.

The structure of the land mass is extremely complicated, but may be simplified (with large reservations) as a plateau flanked by ranges of mountains roughly paralleling the coasts. The northern part of the plateau is low, arid and thinly populated; it takes up 40% of the total area of Mexico but holds only 19% of its people. From the Bolsón de Mayrán as far S as the Balsas valley, the level rises considerably; this southern section of the central plateau is crossed by a volcanic range of mountains in which the intermont basins are high and separated. The basin of Guadalajara is at 1,500m, the basin of México at 2,300m, and the basin of Toluca, W of Mexico City, is at 2,600m. Above the lakes and valley bottoms of this contorted middle-land rise the magnificent volcano cones of Orizaba (5,700m), Popocatépetl (5,452m), Ixtaccíhuatl (5,286m), Nevado de Toluca (4,583m), Matlalcueyetl or La Malinche (4,461m), and Cofre de Perote (4,282m). This mountainous southern end of the plateau, the heart of Mexico, has ample rainfall. Though only 14% of the area of Mexico, it holds nearly half of the country's people. Its centre, in a small high intermont basin measuring only 50 sq km, is Mexico City, with 20 or so million inhabitants.

The two high ranges of mountains which rise E and W of the plateau, between it and the sea, are great barriers against communications: there are far easier routes N along the floor of the plateau to the United States than there are to either the E coast or the W. In the W there are rail and road links across the Sierra Madre Occidental from Guadalajara to the Pacific at the port of Mazatlán; both continue northward through a coastal desert to Nogales. The Sierra Madre Oriental is more kindly; in its mountain ramparts a pass inland from Tampico gives road-rail access to Monterrey, a great industrial centre, and the highland basins; and another from Veracruz leads by a fair gradient to the Valley of México.

South of the seven intermont basins in the south-central region the mountain-land is still rugged but a little lower (between 1,800 and 2,400m), with much less rainfall. After some 560 km it falls away into the low-lying Isthmus of Tehuantepec. Population is sparse in these southern mountains and is settled on the few flat places where commercial crops can be grown. Subsistence crops are sown on incredibly steep slopes. The Pacific coast here is forbidding and its few ports of little use, though there is massive development of tourism in such places as Acapulco, Zihuatanejo, Puerto Escondido and Huatulco. Very different are the Gulf Coast and Yucatán; half this area is classed as flat, and much of it gets enough rain the year round, leading to its becoming one of the most important agricultural and cattle raising areas in the country. The Gulf Coast also provides most of Mexico's oil and sulphur. Geographically, North America may be said to come to an end in the Isthmus of Tehuantepec. South of the Isthmus the land rises again into the thinly populated highlands of Chiapas.

CLIMATE

Climate and vegetation depend upon altitude. The *tierra caliente* takes in the coastlands and plateau lands below 750m. The *tierra templada*, or temperate zone is at 750 to 2,000m. The *tierra fría*, or cold zone, is from 2,000m upwards. Above the tree line at 4,000m are high moorlands (*páramos*).

The climate of the inland highlands is mostly mild, but with sharp changes of temperature between day and night, sunshine and shade. Generally, winter is the dry season and summer the wet season. There are only two areas where rain falls the year round: S of Tampico along the lower slopes of the Sierra Madre Oriental and across the Isthmus of Tehuantepec into Tabasco state; and along the Pacific coast of the state of Chiapas. Both areas together cover only 12% of Mexico. These wetter parts get most of their rain between June and Sept, when the skies are so full of clouds that the temperature is lowered: May is a hotter month than July. Apart from these favoured regions, the rest of the country suffers from a climate in which the rainy season hardly lives up to its name and the dry season almost always does.

NATIONAL PARKS

Mexico is the world's third most biologically diverse country, behind only Brazil and Colombia. It boasts between 21,600 and 33,000 of the 250,000-odd known species of higher plants (including 150 conifers, and around a thousand each of ferns, orchids, and cacti), 693-717 reptiles (more than any other country), 436-455 mammals (second only to Indonesia), 283-289 amphibians (fourth in the world), 1,018 birds, 2,000 fish, and hundreds of thousands of insect species. Five Mexican vertebrates (all birds) have become extinct in the 20th century, and about 35 species are now only found in other countries; 1,066 of around 2,370 vertebrates are listed as threatened.

This is of course an immense country, with an immense range of habitats and wildlife; the far S is in the Neotropical kingdom, with a wealth of tropical forest species, while the far N is very much part of the Nearctic kingdom, with typically North American species, and huge expanses of desert with unique ecosystems. The greater part of the country is a transition zone between the two kingdoms, with many strange juxtapositions of species that provide invaluable information to scientists, as well as many endemic species. Many of these sites are now protected, but these are often of little interest except to specialists; what's more Mexico's National Parks per se were set up a long time ago primarily to provide green recreation areas for city dwellers; they are generally small and often now planted with imported species such as eucalyptus, and thus of no biological value. However the country does also have a good number of Biosphere Reserves, which are both of great biological value and suitable for tourism.

Starting in the far S, in Chiapas, **El Triunfo Biosphere Reserve** protects Mexico's only cloud forest, on the mountains (up to 2,750m) above the Pacific coast; the main hiking route runs from Jaltenango (reached by bus from Tuxtla) to Mapastepec on the coastal highway. Groups need to book in advance through the state's Institute of Natural History, on Calzada de Hombres de la Revolución, by the botanical garden and Regional Museum (Apdo 391, Tuxtla 29000; T 23663, F 29943, e-mail: ihnreservas@laneta.apc.org).

From Jaltenango you need to hike or hitch a ride about 29 km to Finca Prusia and then follow a good muletrack for 3 hrs to the El Triunfo campamento (1,650m). There are endemic species here, including the very rare azure-rumped tanager; the horned guan is found only here and across the border in the adjacent mountains of Guatemala. Other wildlife includes the quetzal, harpy eagles, jaguars, tapirs, and white-lipped peccary.

Turn left in the clearing for the route down to Tres de Mayo, 25 km away; this is an easy descent of 5 hrs to a pedestrian suspension bridge on the dirt road to Loma Bonita. From here you should take a pick-up to Mapastepec, 25 km away.

Also in Chiapas is the immense **Lacandón Forest**, supposedly protected by the **Azules Biosphere Reserve** but in reality still being eaten away by colonization and logging. New plant species and even families are still being discovered in this rainforest, best visited either from the Bonampak and Yaxchilán ruins, or by the road/boat route via Pico de Oro and Flor de Café to Montebello.

In Yucatán the **Sian Ka'an Biosphere Reserve** is one of the most visited in Mexico, being just S of Cancún; it's a mixture of forest, savanna and mangrove swamp, best visited on a day-trip run by Los Amigos de Sian Ka'an at Av Cobá 5, 3rd floor, offices 48-50, Apdo 770, Cancún (T 849 583, F 873 080, e-mail: sian@cancun.rce.com.mx). It is also well worth visiting the **Río Lagartos** and **Río Celestún** reserves on the N and W coasts of Yucatán, well known for their flamingos. The **Calakmul Biosphere Reserve** is important mainly for its Mayan ruins, seeming to the layman more like scrub than forest.

Across the country's centre is the Transversal Volcanic Belt, one of the main barriers to Nearctic and Neotropic species; it's easiest to head for the **Ixta-Popo National Park** (from Amecameca), the **Zoquiapan National Park** (on the main road to Puebla) or the **El Tepozteco National Park** (on the main road to Cuernavaca), and naturally the volcanoes themselves are well worth climbing.

Only small areas of the northern deserts and sierras are formally protected. The most accessible areas are in Durango state, including **La Michilía Biosphere Reserve**, with pine, oak and red-trunked Arbutus and Arctostaphylus trees typical of the Sierra Madre Occidental. A daily bus runs to San Juan de Michis, and you should get off at a T-junction 2 km before the village and walk W, first getting permission from the Jefe de Unidad Administrativo, Instituto de Ecología, Apdo 632, 34000 Durango (T 121483); their offices are at Km 5 on the Mazatlán highway. The **Mapimí Biosphere Reserve** covers an area of desert matorral (scrub) which receives just 200 mm of rain a year; it lies to the E of Ceballos, on the Gómez Palacio-Ciudad Jiménez highway. In addition to many highly specialized bushes and cacti, this is home to giant turtles, now in enclosures at the Laboratory of the Desert.

There is a great variety of protected areas in Baja California, all of considerable biological value: the highest point (3,000m) is the **Sierra de San Pedro Mártir**, in the N, which receives plenty of precipitation and has largely Californian fauna and flora. A dirt road starts at the Puente San Telmo, on the main road down the W coast, and leads almost 100 km to an astronomical observatory. Desert environments are, of course, unavoidable here, with 80 endemic cacti: the **Gran Desierto del Altar** is a dry lunar landscape, best seen from the main road along the US border, while the **El Vizcaíno Biosphere Reserve** protects a huge area of central Baja, characterized by agaves and drought-resistant scrub. However the main reason for stopping here is to see the migration of the grey whale to its breeding grounds. In the far S, the **Sierra de La Laguna** actually boasts a unique type of cloud forest, with several endemic species; to get here you have to cross about 20 km of desert from just S of Todos Santos to La Burrera, and then follow a trail for 11 km to a rangers' campamento at about 1,750m.

Limited information on National Parks and Biosphere Reserves can be had from SEDESOL (Ministry of Social Development), Av Revolución 1425, Mexico DF (Barranca del Muerto metro), where you'll also find the National Institute of Ecology (INE), for more general information on conservation; their publications are stocked by the Librería Bonilla, nearby at Francia 17.

Non-governmental conservation organizations include Naturalia (Apdo Postal 21-541, 04021 México DF; T 674-6678, F 674-5294), and Pronatura (Asociación Mexicano por la Conservación de la Naturaleza, Av Nuevo León 144, Col Hipódromo Condesa, México DF, T 286-9642).

HISTORY

PRE-CONQUEST

Of the many Indian nations in the vast territory of Mexico, the two most important before the Conquest were the Aztecs of Tenochtitlán (now Mexico City) and the Maya of Yucatán. The Aztecs, a militarist, theocratic culture, had obtained absolute control over the whole Valley of México and a loose control of some other regions. The Maya were already in decline by the time the Spaniards arrived. A brief history of these and other pre-Conquest, Mexican people is given in **Precolumbian civilizations**, page 14.

SPANISH RULE

The 34-year-old **Hernán Cortés** disembarked near the present Veracruz with about 500 men, some horses and cannon, on 21 April 1519. They marched into the interior; their passage was not contested; they arrived at Tenochtitlán in Nov and were admitted into the city as guests of the reigning monarch, Moctezuma. There they remained until June of the next year, when Pedro de Alvarado, in the absence of Cortés, murdered hundreds of Indians to quell his own fear of a rising. At this treacherous act the Indians did in fact rise, and it was only by good luck that the Spanish troops, with heavy losses, were able to fight their way out of the city on the Noche Triste (the Night of Sorrows) of 30 June. Next year Cortés came back with reinforcements and besieged the city. It fell on 30 August 1521, and was utterly razed. Cortés then turned to the conquest of the rest of the country. One of the main factors in his success was his alliance with the Tlaxcalans, old rivals of the Aztecs. The fight was ruthless, and the Aztecs were soon mastered.

There followed 300 years of Spanish rule. In the early years all the main sources of gold and silver were discovered. Spanish grandees stepped into the shoes of dead Aztec lords and inherited their great estates and their wealth of savable could with little disturbance, for Aztec and Spanish ways of holding land were not unlike: the *ejido* (or agrarian community holding lands in common), the *rancho*, or small private property worked by the owner; and that usually huge area which paid tribute to its master, the Spanish *encomienda*, soon to be converted into the *hacienda*, with its absolute title to the land and its almost feudal way of life. Within the first 50 years all the Indians in the populous southern valleys of the plateau had been christianized and harnessed to Spanish wealth-getting from mine and soil. The more scattered and less profitable Indians of the N and S had to await the coming of the missionizing Jesuits in 1571, a year behind the Inquisition. Too often, alas, the crowded Jesuit missions proved as fruitful a source of smallpox or measles as of salvation, with the unhappy result that large numbers of Indians died; their deserted communal lands were promptly filched by some neighbouring *encomendero*: a thieving of public lands by private interests which continued for 400 years.

By the end of the 16th century the Spaniards had founded most of the towns which are still important, tapped great wealth in mining, stock raising and sugar-growing, and firmly imposed their way of life and belief. Government was by a Spanish-born upper class, based on the subordination of the Indian and *mestizo* populations and a strict dependence on Spain for all things. As throughout all Hispanic America, Spain built up resistance to itself by excluding from government both Spaniards born in Mexico and the small body of educated *mestizos*.

REVOLUTION AND CIVIL WAR

The standard of revolt was raised in 1810 by the curate of Dolores, **Miguel Hidalgo**. The Grito de Dolores: "Perish the Spaniards" (*"Mueran los gachupines"*), collected 80,000 armed supporters, and had it not been for Hidalgo's loss of nerve and failure to engage the Spaniards, the capital might have been captured in the first month and a government created not differing much from the royal Spanish government. But 11 years of fighting created bitter differences.

A loyalist general, **Agustín de Iturbide**, joined the rebels and proclaimed an independent Mexico in 1821. His Plan of Iguala proposed an independent monarchy with a ruler from the Spanish royal family, but on second thoughts Iturbide proclaimed himself Emperor in 1822: a fantasy which lasted a year. A federal republic was created on 4 October 1824, with General Guadalupe Victoria as President. Conservatives stood for a highly centralized government; Liberals favoured federated sovereign states. The tussle of interests expressed itself in endemic civil war. In 1836, Texas, whose cotton-growers and cattle-ranchers had been infuriated by the abolition of slavery in 1829, rebelled against the dictator,

Santa Ana, and declared its independence. It was annexed by the United States in 1845. War broke out and US troops occupied Mexico City in 1847. Next year, under the terms of the treaty of Guadalupe Hidalgo, the US acquired half Mexico's territory: all the land from Texas to California and from the Río Grande to Oregon.

Benito Juárez

A period of reform dominated by independent Mexico's great hero, the Zapotec Indian, Benito Juárez, began in 1857. The church, in alliance with the conservatives, hotly contested by civil war his liberal programme of popular education, freedom of the press and of speech, civil marriage and the separation of church and state. Juárez won, but the constant civil strife wrecked the economy, and Juárez was forced to suspend payment on the national debt. Promptly, Spain, France and Britain landed a joint force at Veracruz to protect their financial rights. The British and the Spanish soon withdrew, but the French force pushed inland and occupied Mexico City in 1863. Juárez took to guerrilla warfare against the invaders.

The **Archduke Maximilian of Austria** became Emperor of Mexico with Napoleon III's help, but United States insistence and the gathering strength of Prussia led to the withdrawal of the French troops in 1867. Maximilian, betrayed and deserted, was captured by the Juaristas at Querétaro, tried, and shot on 19 June. Juárez resumed control and died in July 1872. He was the first Mexican leader of any note who had died naturally since 1810.

General Porfirio Díaz

Sebastián Lerdo de Tejada, the distinguished scholar who followed Juárez, was soon tricked out of office by Gen Porfirio Díaz, who ruled Mexico from 1876 to 1910. Díaz's paternal, though often ruthless, central authority did introduce a period of 35 years of peace. A superficial prosperity followed upon peace; a civil service was created, finances put on a sound basis, banditry put down, industries started, railways built, international relations improved, and foreign capital protected. But the main mass of peasants had never been so wretched; their lands were stolen from them, their personal liberties curtailed, and many were sold into forced labour on tobacco and henequen plantations from which death was the only release. It was this open contradiction between dazzling prosperity and hideous distress which led to the upheaval of Nov 1910 and to Porfirio Díaz's self-exile in Paris.

A new leader, **Francisco Madero**, who came from a landowning family in Coahuila, championed a programme of political and social reform, including the restoration of stolen lands.

Madero was initially supported by revolutionary leaders such as **Emiliano Zapata** in Morelos, **Pascual Orozco** in Chihuahua and **Pancho Villa** in the N During his presidency (1911-13), Madero neither satisfied his revolutionary supporters, nor pacified his reactionary enemies. After a coup in Feb 1913, led by Gen Victoriano Huerta, Madero was brutally murdered, but the great new cry, *Tierra y Libertad* (Land and Liberty) was not to be quieted until the revolution was made safe by the election of Alvaro Obregón to the Presidency in 1920. Before then, Mexico was in a state of civil war, leading first to the exile of Huerta in 1914, then the dominance of Venustiano Carranza's revolutionary faction over that of Zapata (assassinated in 1919) and Villa.

Later, **President Lázaro Cárdenas** fulfilled some of the more important economic objectives of the revolution; it was his regime (1934-40) that brought about the division of the great estates into *ejidos* (or communal lands), irrigation, the raising of wages, the spread of education, the beginnings of industrialization, the nationalization of the oil wells and the railways. Later presidents nationalized electric power, the main airlines and parts of industry, but at the same time encouraged both Mexican and foreign (mainly US) entrepreneurs to develop the private sector. All presidents have pursued an independent and non-aligned foreign policy.

RECENT POLITICS

In 1946, the official party assumed the name **Partido Revolucionario Institucional (PRI)**, since when it held a virtual monopoly over all political activity. Having comfortably won all elections against small opposition parties, in the 1980s electoral majorities were cut as opposition to dictatorship by the Party grew. Corruption and fraud were claimed to be keeping the PRI in power. The PRI candidate in 1988, Carlos Salinas de Gortari, saw his majority dramatically reduced when Cuauhtémoc Cárdenas (son of the former president), at the head of a breakaway PRI faction, stood in opposition to him. The disaffected PRI members and others subsequently joined the **Partido de la Revolución Democrática (PRD)**, which rapidly gained support as liberalization of many of the PRI's long-held political and economic traditions became inevitable. In 1989, for the first time, a state governorship was conceded by the PRI, to the right wing party, Partido de Acción Nacional (PAN).

On New Year's Day of the election year, 1994, at the moment when the North American Free Trade Agreement (NAFTA – Mexico, USA and Canada) came into force, a guerrilla group briefly took control of several towns in Chiapas. The Ejército Zapatista de Liberación Nacional (EZLN) demanded social justice, indigenous people's rights, democracy at all levels of Mexican politics, an end to government corruption, and land reform for the peasantry. Peace talks were overshadowed by the assassination in Tijuana on 23 March of the PRI's appointed presidential candidate, Luis Donaldo Colosio. Further disquiet was caused by the murder of the Tijuana police chief and the kidnapping of several prominent businessmen and other linked killings in subsequent months. To replace Colosio, President Salinas nominated Ernesto Zedillo Ponce de León, a US-trained economist and former education minister. Despite continued unrest in Chiapas, Zedillo won a comfortable majority in the August elections, as did the PRI in Congress. Zedillo's opponents, Cuauhtémoc Cárdenas of PRD and Diego Fernández Cevallos of PAN claimed fraud, to no effect.

On 28 September, the PRI general secretary, José Francisco Ruiz Massieu, was shot dead. In Nov, his brother Mario, deputy attorney general and chief investigator into the murder, resigned, claiming a high-level cover-up by PRI officials. The ensuing row within the PRI overshadowed Zedillo's inauguration on 1 December. Zedillo appointed a reformist cabinet and announced a judicial review. However, the Chiapas state governorship elections had been won dubiously by the PRI candidate and the governorship of Tabasco was also disputed. On 20 December, Zedillo devalued the peso, claiming that political unrest was causing capital outflows and putting pressure on the currency. In fact, devaluation was necessary for a variety of economic reasons, but Zedillo linked the economic necessity with the political situation in the South. On 22 December, however, a precipitate decision to allow the peso to float against the dollar caused an immediate crisis of confidence and investors in Mexico lost billions of dollars as the peso's value plummetted.

Economic problems mounted in the first half of 1995 and Mexicans were hard hit by the recession. The PRI was heavily defeated by the PAN in state elections in Jalisco (Feb) and in Guanajuato (May). In the same month, a narrow PRI victory in Yucatán was hotly disputed. In Aug the PAN retained the state governorship of Baja California Norte, first won in 1989. In Chiapas, Zedillo suspended the

controversial PRI governor, but the tension between EZLN and the army continued. A 72-hr campaign to apprehend the EZLN leader, Subcomandante Marcos, was a failure. Talks recommenced in April, with the EZLN calling a ceasefire but the first peace accord was not signed until Feb 1996.

Zedillo appointed as attorney general Antonio Lozano of PAN, who uncovered PRI involvement in Colosio's murder and ordered the arrest of Raúl Salinas, brother of ex-president Carlos Salinas, for masterminding the murder of Ruiz Massieu. This broke the convention granted former presidents and their families of immunity from criticism or prosecution. Carlos Salinas acrimoniously left Mexico for an undisclosed destination. Meanwhile, scandal within the PRI continued: Mario Ruiz Massieu was arrested in the USA on suspicion of covering up Raúl Salinas' involvement in the Ruiz Massieu murder and of receiving money from drugs cartels when he was in charge of anti-narcotics operations. Raul Salinas was also investigated for alleged money laundering and illicit enrichment after his wife was arrested in Switzerland trying to withdraw US$84mn from an account opened in a false name. Stories of his massive fortune in land and investment filled the Mexican newspapers.

Political reform advanced in 1996. Despite a boycott of talks by the PAN, the other major parties agreed to introduce direct elections for the mayoralty of Mexico City; abolish government control of the Federal Electoral Institute, which will become independent; introduce constitutional reforms to allow referenda and guarantee fairer access to the media for party broadcasts during elections. The President's campaign to clean up government was strengthened when he sacked the governor of Guerrero for his alleged involvement in a peasant massacre. Midterm congressional elections were due in July 1997 and presidential elections in 2000. At stake in the 1997 elections were six state governorships, the entire 500-seat Congress and one third of the Senate, as well as the mayoralty of Mexico City. There was a wave of defections from the PRI by disaffected members who failed to get chosen as candidates, while Mexico City was expected to be won by an opposition party. In 1997, Manuel Camacho, a PRI outcast, founded a new party, Partido del Centro Democrático, to contest the presidential elections. A former Foreign Minister, Mayor of Mexico City and peace negotiator in Chiapas, Camacho was expelled from the PRI after he complained at not being chosen as the presidential candidate for the PRI in the 1994 elections.

CULTURE

PEOPLE

About 9% are considered white and about 30% Indian; about 60% are *mestizos*, a mixture in varying proportions of Spanish and Indian; a small percentage (mostly in the coastal zones of Veracruz, Guerrero and Chiapas) are a mixture of black and white or black and Indian or *mestizo*. Mexico also has infusions of other European peoples, Arab and Chinese. There is a national cultural prejudice in favour of the Indian rather than the Spanish element, though this does not prevent Indians from being looked down on by the more hispanic elements. There is hardly a single statue of Cortés in the whole of Mexico, but he does figure, pejoratively, in the frescoes of Diego Rivera and his contemporaries. On the other hand the two last Aztec emperors, Moctezuma and Cuauhtémoc, are national heroes.

Indians

Among the estimated 24 million Indians there are 54 groups or sub-divisions, each with its own language. The Indians are far from evenly distributed; 36% live on the Central Plateau (mostly Hidalgo, and México); 35% are along the southern Pacific coast (Oaxaca, Chiapas, Guerrero), and 23% along the Gulf coast (mostly Yucatán and Veracruz): 94% of them, that is, live in these three regions. There are also sizable concentrations in Nayarit and Durango, Michoacán, and Chihuahua, Sinoloa and Sonora. The main groups are: Pápago (Sonora); Yaqui (Sonora); Mayo (Sonora and Sinaloa); Tarahumara (Chihuahua); Huastec and Otomí in San Luis Potosí; Cora and Huichol (Nayarit); Purépecha/Tarasco (Michoacán); scattered groups of Nahua in Michoacán, Guerrero, Jalisco, Veracruz and other central states; Totonac (Veracruz); Tlapaneco (Guerrero); in Oaxaca state, Mixtec, Mixe and Zapotec; in Chiapas, Lacandón, Tzoltzil, Tzeltal, Chol and others; Maya in Campeche, Yucatán and Quintano Roo.

Land ownership

The issue of access to the land has always been the country's fundamental problem, and it was a despairing landless peasantry that rose in the Revolution of 1910 and swept away Porfirio Díaz and the old system of huge estates. The accomplishments of successive PRI governments have been mixed. Life for the peasant is still hard. The minimum wage barely allows a simple diet of beans, rice, and *tortillas*. The home is still, possibly, a shack with no windows, no water, no sanitation, and the peasant may still not be able to read or write, but something was done to redistribute the land in the so-called *ejido* system, which gave either communal or personal control of the land. The peasant was freed from the landowner, and his family received some basic health and educational facilities from the state. In 1992 new legislation was approved which radically overhauled the outdated agricultural sector with far-reaching political and economic consequences. Farmers now have the right to become private property owners, if two-thirds of the *ejido* votes in favour; to form joint ventures with private businessmen; and to use their land as collateral for loans. Private property owners may form joint stock companies, thereby avoiding the constitutional limits on the size of farms and helping them to raise capital. The failure of any agricultural reforms to benefit the peasants of Chiapas was one of the roots of the EZLN uprising in early 1994.

RELIGION

Roman Catholicism is the principal religion, but the State is determinedly secular. Because of its identification firstly with Spain, then with the Emperor Maximilian and finally with Porfirio Díaz, the Church has been severely persecuted in the past by reform-minded administrations, and priests are still not supposed to wear ecclesiastical dress (see *The Lawless Roads* and *The Power and the Glory*, by Graham Greene). Rapprochement between State and Church was sought in the early 1990s.

GOVERNMENT

Under the 1917 Constitution Mexico is a federal republic of 31 states and a Federal District containing the capital, Mexico City. The President, who appoints the Ministers, is elected for 6 years and can never be re-elected. Congress consists of the 128-seat Senate, half elected every 3 years on a rotational basis, and the 500-seat Chamber of Deputies, elected every 3 years. There is universal suffrage.

Local administration

The States enjoy local autonomy and can levy their own taxes, and each State has its Governor, legislature and judicature. The President has traditionally appointed the Chief of the Federal District but direct elections are expected for 1997 for the first time.

THE ECONOMY

Structure of production

Mexico has been an oil producer since the 1880s and was the world's leading producer in 1921, but by 1971 had become a net importer. This position was reversed in the mid-1970s with the discovery in 1972 of major new oil reserves. Mexico is the world's sixth largest producer at 2.9 million barrels a day of crude petroleum, 65% of this coming from offshore wells in the Gulf of Campeche, and 28% from onshore fields in the Chiapas-Tabasco area in the SE. Proven reserves stood at 51 billion barrels of crude oil in 1995 (giving 52 years until exhaustion) and 1,973 trillion cu metres of natural gas. Natural gas production in 1994 was 37.5 billion cu metres. Mexico depends on fossil fuels to generate 100% of its electricity and exports of crude oil, oil products and natural gas account for a third of exports and about 20% of government revenues.

Mexico's mineral resources are legendary. Precious metals make up about 36% of non-oil mineral output. The country is the world's leading producer of silver (although low prices have forced the closure of hundreds of mines), fluorite and arsenic, and is among the world's major producers of strontium, graphite, copper, iron ore, sulphur, mercury, lead and zinc. Mexico also produces gold, molybdenum, antimony, bismuth, cadmium, selenium, tungsten, magnesium, common salt, celestite, fuller's earth and gypsum. It is estimated that although 60% of Mexico's land mass has mineral potential, only 25% is known, and only 5% explored in detail.

Agriculture has been losing importance since the beginning of the 1970s and now contributes only 5.8% of gdp. About 13% of the land surface is under cultivation, of which only about one-quarter is irrigated. Over half of the developed cropland lies in the interior highlands. Mexico's agricultural success is almost always related to rainfall and available water for irrigation. On average, 4 out of every 10 years are good, while 4 are drought years.

Manufacturing, including oil refining and petrochemicals, contributes 17.6% of gdp. Mexico City is the focal point for manufacturing activity and the metropolitan area holds about 45% of the employment in manufacturing and 30% of the country's industrial establishments. The government offers tax incentives to companies relocating away from Mexico City and the other major industrial centres of Guadalajara and Monterrey; target cities are Tampico, Coatzacoalcos, Salina Cruz and Lázaro Cárdenas, while much of the manufacturing export activity takes place in the in-bond centres along the border with the USA. There are now over 2,000 *maquiladoras* (in-bond), employing about 518,000 people. Several large industrial plants have been ordered closed to control pollution in Mexico City.

Tourism is a large source of foreign exchange and the largest employer, with about a third of the workforce. About 6.7 million tourists visit Mexico every year, of whom about 85% come from the USA. The Government is actively encouraging new investment in tourism and foreign investment is being welcomed in hotel construction projects.

Recent trends

During 1978-81 the current account of the balance of payments registered increasing deficits because of domestic expansion and world recession. Mounting public sector deficits were covered by foreign borrowing of increasingly shorter terms until a bunching of short term maturities and a loss of foreign exchange reserves caused Mexico to declare its inability to service its debts in Aug 1982, thus triggering what became known as the international debt crisis. Under the guidance of an IMF programme and helped by commercial bank debt rescheduling agreements, Mexico was able to improve its position largely because of a 40% drop in imports in both 1982 and 1983. In 1986, however, the country was hit by the sharp fall in oil prices, which reduced export revenues by 28%, despite a rapid growth of 37% in non-oil exports through vigorous promotion and exchange rate depreciation policies. Several debt rescheduling and new money agreements were negotiated during the 1980s with the IMF, the World Bank and the commercial banks. Mexico managed to secure progressively easier terms, helped by the US administration's concern for geopolitical reasons, and debt

growth was contained. Prepayment of private debt and debt/equity conversions even reduced the overall level of foreign debt. In 1989, Mexico negotiated the first debt reduction package with commercial banks, which was designed to cut debt servicing and restructure debt over a 30-year period supported by collateral from multinational creditors and governments. As a result of this agreement and higher oil prices during the Gulf crisis, foreign exchange reserves rose sharply and the Government was able to curb the rate of currency depreciation and reduce interest rates. Large capital inflows financed a growing trade and current account deficit caused by strong demand for imports as the economy picked up.

The economic improvement allowed President Salinas to open negotiations with the USA on a free trade agreement which, including Canada, would open up the whole of North America (NAFTA). Major economic reforms were introduced to encourage private investment, including the privatization of many state-owned industries, banks and basic public services, such as telephones, motorways, water treatment, electricity generation, railways and ports. New legislation made it easier to invest in mining (except uranium) and foreign investment was permitted in several previously restricted areas. The Government's tight fiscal and monetary policies led to low inflation and a budget surplus, but at the cost of high real interest rates to attract capital from overseas to finance the massive current account deficit.

The political unrest in the first half of 1994 threatened the stability of the peso against the dollar, so interest rates remained high to protect the currency. Rising US interest rates further increased the cost of financing the current account deficit (US$29.5bn in 1994), dampened confidence and jeopardized a rapid return to economic growth, already depressed by the high cost to the private sector of restructuring to compete within NAFTA.

Mexico: fact file

Geographic

Land area	1,958,201 sq km
forested	25.5%
pastures	39.0%
cultivated	13.0%

Demographic

Population (1996)	92,711,000
annual growth rate (1985-94)	2.2%
urban	71.3%
rural	28.7%
density	49.6 per sq km
Religious affiliation	
Roman Catholic	89.7%
Birth rate per 1,000 (1995)	27.6
	(world av 25.0)

Education and Health

Life expectancy at birth,	
male	69.0 years
female	75.0 years
Infant mortality rate	
per 1,000 live births (1993)	17.5
Physicians (1994)	1 per 613 persons
Hospital beds	
	1 per 1,196 persons
Calorie intake as %	
of FAO requirement	135%
Population age 15 and over	
with no formal schooling	14.1%
Literate males (over 15)	88.7%
Literate females (over 15)	83.5%

Economic

GNP (1994)	US$368,679mn
GNP per capita	US$4,010
Public external	
debt (1994)	US$92,843mn
Tourism receipts (1994)	US$6,318mn
Inflation (annual av 1990-95)	7.1%
Radio	1 per 4.3 persons
Television	1 per 6.6 persons
Telephone	1 per 10.0 persons

Employment

Population economically active (1993)	
	33,651,812
Unemployment rate (official)	2.4%
% of labour force in	
agriculture	26.3
mining	0.5
manufacturing	15.1
construction	5.6
Military forces	175,000

Source *Encyclopaedia Britannica*

Partly for political reasons, the Salinas government refused to devalue the peso and increased domestic credit, despite the dangerous accumulation of public and private short term debt and an excess supply of pesos. Poor debt management led to a bunching of maturities at the end of the year of the dollar-linked *tesobonos* issued by the Government. Soon after Zedillo had succeeded Salinas, the peso was devalued and then floated (see above, **History**) after US$4bn of reserves were lost in 2 days.

The subsequent financial crisis had severe repercussions on other Latin American economies (the 'Tequila effect'). Its swiftness, and the scale of capital flight, prompted large-scale international emergency funding to help the country honour its short term debts. The IMF pledged US$17.8bn, while a US$20bn credit line was offered by President Clinton. On 9 March 1995 an austerity programme was imposed despite opposition from Mexican industry and the middle classes. It cut government spending by 10%, reduced subsidies on basic items such as tortillas, raised VAT from 10 to 15% and increased tariffs on electricity, petrol and telephone calls by up to 35%. Real incomes were forecast to fall by 50%; many businesses faced bankruptcy as they could not service bank loans. This in turn led to a banking crisis; bank deposits fell by 18.5% while non-performing loans trebled to 18% of banks' total loan portfolio. Of the 18 banks privatized in 1992, seven collapsed. They and others had to be taken over by foreigners. Emergency schemes to keep banks solvent and provide interest relief for small debtors cost the Government about 5.5% of gdp.

Inflation soared to 52% in 1995 (compared with 8% in 1994), while gdp fell by 6.9%. On the plus side, the policies did stabilize the peso at about 6.15 to the dollar by June, compared with 7.45=US$1 in Mar although it fell back again in the autumn. The US and IMF funds helped the government to redeem almost US$17bn of *tesobonos*. While imports fell, exports grew significantly to turn a trade deficit throughout 1994 into a surplus of US$7.4bn in 1995. Moreover, international reserves began to recover. Interest rates started to fall and the stock market showed signs of recovery, but the middle and lower classes felt betrayed by the inappropriateness of Zedillo's election slogan, "Well-being for the whole family." The recession continued to threaten jobs and real wages, with pay settlements averaging only half the rate of inflation. The trade union movement split in 1996 with the traditional faction supporting the government and a rebel wing seeking an independent labour movement, which contributed to the erosion of the traditionally close ties between the government, labour and employers.

By the end of 1996 economic improvement was apparent and inflation was halved. At the beginning of 1997 Mexico was able to settle its debts with the USA, paying off the emergency loan, and confidence surged. The Finance Minister responsible for the turnaround, Guillermo Ortiz, forecast a 1997 growth rate of 4.5% and inflation rate of 15%. Private savings are to be encouraged with the launch of private pension funds in 1997, while planned tax reforms should encourage companies to reinvest profits. Nevertheless, although the export-oriented economy was booming, the domestic economy remained in the doldrums, taking much longer to recover from the 1995 recession.

Laredo to Mexico City: the Gulf Route

THE FIRST FOUR sections describe the four great road routes from the US border towards Mexico City. First, the 1,226 km Gulf Route from **Laredo** (by Pan-American Highway), which takes in the major industrial centre of **Monterrey** and the port of **Tampico**. The route passes through the coastal state of Tamaulipas before entering Huastec and Otomí Indian regions and then leads to the old silver-mining centre of Pachuca.

The first route to be opened was the Gulf Route. Traffic from the central and eastern parts of the United States can enter NE Mexico through four gateways along the Río Bravo; at **Matamoros** (see below), opposite Brownsville; at **Reynosa** opposite McAllen; at **Ciudad Miguel Alemán**, opposite Roma; and at **Nuevo Laredo**, opposite Laredo. The roads from these places all converge upon Monterrey (a new toll road from Nuevo Laredo is the quickest route, US$12). There are alternative roads from Reynosa and Matamoros which join the Nuevo Laredo-Mexico City highway at Montemorelos and Ciudad Victoria, respectively: the latter runs along the tropical Gulf coastal plain and then climbs sharply through the Sierra Madre Oriental to Ciudad Victoria, at 333m.

CROSSING INTO MEXICO

By **car**, the best way is by the **Colombia Bridge**: on Interstate 35, take the exit to Milo (the first exit N of the Tourist Bureau and is signed, take Farm Road 1472 W),

little traffic and friendly staff, but it does involve a 40 km detour (it is well signposted on the Mexican side). The toll on the international bridge is US$1.25/N$6). Once in Mexico you can either go back to Nuevo Laredo, or continue to Monterrey either on Route 85 or following the railway line via Ciudad Anáhuac and Lampazos.

The direct route is on San Bernardo parallel to I 35 on the W; turn W at Washington, S at Salinas, cross about 10 traffic lights and turn E to the **International bridge**. Do not be directed into the narrow columns: after verbal processing, go 2 miles to the full processing location at Av Cesar López de Lara 1200, opposite train station. This entails six steps, including photocopying of documents (keep copies), US$2-3, and the bureaucracy described under **Automobiles** in Information for travellers.

If pressed for time, avoid 20 Nov and other national holidays as there are delays at customs owing to Mexicans visiting the USA in large numbers. Border formalities can take 2 hrs or more.

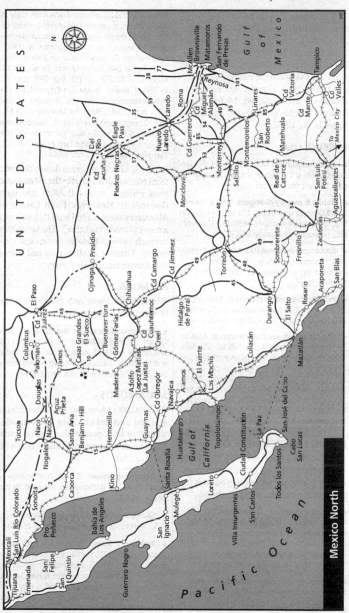

Mexico North

The Nuevo Laredo **bus** station is not near the border; take a bus to the border, then walk across. It is not possible to get a bus from the Laredo Greyhound terminal to the Nuevo Laredo terminal unless you have a ticket to the interior. Connecting tickets from Houston via Laredo to Monterrey are available, 14 hrs. Some buses to Laredo connect with Greyhound buses in the US.

LAREDO, USA

● **Accommodation** Two trailer parks, the better of the two is E side of Route I 35, Main St exit, 10 mins from border.

● **Banks & money changers** UNB Convent and **Matamoros** charges 1% commission on TCs, it charges pesos, open 0830-1600 Mon-Fri; **IBC**, no commission under US$500.

● **Embassies & consulates** Mexican Consulate, Farragut and Maine, 4th light on the right after leaving Interstate 35, open 0800-1400 Mon-Fri, helpful.

● **Post & telecommunications Fax**: and to receive letter, TCR, Martin and Sandra Resendez, 820 Juarez, nr post office, international service.

● **Useful addresses Car insurance**: AAA on San Bernardo Av (exit 4 on Interstate 35); Sanborns on Santa Ursula (exit 16 on Interstate 35), a bit more expensive, open 24 hrs a day; Johnson's Mexico Insurance, Tepeyac Agent, Lafayette and Santa Ursula (59 and Interstate 35), US$2.60/day, open 24 hrs, rec. **Car tyres**: Tire Center of Laredo Inc, 815 Park, at San Bernardo Av.

NUEVO LAREDO, MEXICO

(*Pop* 400,000; *Phone code* 871) This is the most important town of the border crossings. It is a bit of a tourist trap but it is fun to stroll through the souvenir shops.

● **Accommodation** C *Alameda*, on plaza; C *Dos Laredos*, Matamoros y 15 de Junio; E *Calderón*, with bath, hot water, fan, run down, friendly; many F hotels, none of which have been rec. **Motels**: A3 *Hacienda*, Prol Reforma 5530; B *Reforma*, Av Guerrero 822.

● **Shopping** Centro Artesanal Nuevo Laredo, Maclovio Herrera 3030, T 26399.

● **Transport Trains** To Mexico City, US$12 2nd class, US$22 *primera preferente*, daily at 1855, 24 hrs, it can get cold at night, meals on train poor, take your own food, or buy at stations (leaves Mexico City for the border at 0900). Information: Av López César de Lara y Mina, Apdo Postal 248, Nuevo Laredo, Tamps, 88000 Mexico, T 28097; or PO Box 595, Laredo, Tx 78042. **Buses** To **Mexico City** with Estrella Blanca/Transportes del Nte 9 buses a day, 16½ hrs, US$42. Buses for **Monterrey** (4 hrs, US$10, departures every hour), **Guadalajara** (18 hrs, US$46.50, 9 a day, Transportes del Nte or Estrella Blanca), to **San Luis Potosí**, US$38, **Tampico**, **Morelia** (17 hrs, US$43).

After 130 km of grey-green desert, the road from Nuevo Laredo climbs the Mamulique Pass, which it crosses at 700m, and then descends to Monterrey. From Laredo to Monterrey there is a toll road ('cuota') and a non-toll road ('vía Libre'). The latter goes through Sabinas Hidalgo (hotels and museum). There is a toll bypass and a free truck route around Monterrey.

REYNOSA

(*Pop* 300,000; *Phone code* 892) This is the border town opposite McAllen.

● **Accommodation On** the Zócalo: D *San Carlos*, rec, and E *Plaza*. In McAllen on the US side of the border, E *Arcade*, corner of Cedar and N 12th St, 2 blocks from Greyhound terminal, S from Valley Transit bus terminal.

MATAMOROS

(*Pop* 400,000; *Phone code* 891) A town with a bright and unforbidding museum, designed to let a prospective tourist know what he can expect in Mexico. It is well worth a visit.

● **Accommodation** C *Ritz*, Matamoros y Siete. There are 4 motels on the road to the beach, all C/B.

● **Shopping** Centro Artesanal Matamoros, C 5a Hurtado and Alvaro Obregón (T 20384).

● **Transport Trains** Tamaulipeco train leaves Matamoros at 0920 for Reynosa (opp McAllen, Texas, arrives 1125) and Monterrey (arrives 1600, US$9 *primera preferente*). **Buses** Several lines run first-class buses to **Mexico City** in 14 hrs for US$38. Transportes del Nte to **Ciudad Victoria** for US$10.75 (4 hrs).

Visas can be obtained in Brownsville on the US side of the border from the Mexican Consulate at 940, E Washington. Crossing the border by car here is quick and easy; permission is granted for 6 months (multiple entry) for passengers and vehicle, paperwork takes only about 10 mins if everything is in order. The return journey is equally easy.

110 km S of Matamoros is **San Fernando de Presas**, a convenient distance from the border, especially if driving to the USA. **B** *Hotel Las Palomas*, on highway, quite good; excellent pizza place, serving more than pizza, near the *Hotel América*.

MONTERREY

(*Pop* 3,000,000; *State pop 1995* 3,549,273; *Alt* 538m; *Phone code* 83) Capital of Nuevo León state, third largest city in Mexico, 253 km S of the border and 915 km from Mexico City. The city is dominated by the Cerro de la Silla from the E and evenings are cool. Its population is still growing in spite of its unattractive climate: too hot in summer, too cold in winter, dusty at most times and a shortage of water. It now turns out (using cheap gas from near the Texas border and increasingly from the new gas fields in the S), over 75% of Mexico's iron and steel, and many other products accompanied by an almost permanent industrial smog. Its people are highly skilled and educated, but its architecture is drab, its layout seems unplanned and its streets are congested. In its main centre, Plaza Zaragoza, there is a pleasant 18th century Cathedral badly damaged in the war against the US in 1846-47, when it was used by Mexican troops as a powder magazine. Plaza Zaragoza, Plaza 5 de Mayo and many surrounding blocks now form the Gran Plaza, claimed to be the biggest civic square in the world; its centrepiece is the Laser Beam Tower. (There is a clean public convenience beneath the Gran Plaza, on Matamoros between Avs Zua Zua and Zaragoza, near the Neptune Fountain.)

Museums

C Morelos is a pedestrians-only shopping centre. Its famous Instituto Tecnológico (Av Garza Sada 2501) has valuable collections of books on 16th century Mexican history, of rare books printed in Indian tongues, and 2,000 editions of Don Quixote in all languages. The new Mexican History Museum, off N end of plaza, is an excellent interactive museum, good for children, opens 1000.

Students of architecture should see the remarkable church of San José Obrero built in a working-class district by Enrique de la Mora and his team. The Monterrey Museum is in the grounds of the Cuauhtémoc Brewery, Av Universidad (beer – in small bottles – is handed out free in the gardens). The Mexican Baseball Hall of Fame is in part of the museum, as is a museum of Modern Art; open Tues-Fri 0930-1800, Sat-Sun 1030-1730. The Alfa Cultural Centre, in the Garza García suburb, has a fine planetarium and an astronomy and physics section with do-it-yourself illustrations of mechanical principles, etc. In a separate building is a Rufino Tamayo stained-glass window. Reached by special bus from W end of Alameda, hourly on the hour 1500-2000, the centre is open 1500-1920, closed Mon. The Alameda Gardens, between Avs Aremberri and Washington, on Av Pino Suárez, are a pleasant place to sit (open 1000-1700, closed Tues). The Cerro del Obispado affords good views, smog permitting. The Palace (1787) is a regional museum (open Tues-Sat 1000-1300, 1500-1800, Sun 1000-1700); it served as HQ for both Pancho Villa and Gen Zachary Taylor. Take No 1 bus which stops at the foot of the hill.

Excursions

In the hills around are the bathing resort of **Topo Chico**, 6½ km to the NW; water from its hot springs is bottled and sold throughout Mexico; and 18 km away Chipinque Mesa, at 1,280m in the Sierra Madre, with magnificent views of the Monterrey area.

West of Monterrey, off the Saltillo road are the **García Caves** (about 10 km from Villa García, which is 40 km from Monterrey). The entrance is 800m up, by cable car, and inside are beautiful stalagmites and stalactites. At the foot of the cable car are a pool and recreational centre. A tour of the caves takes 1½ hrs, and it is compulsory to go in a group with a guide. You can take a bus to Villa García, but it is a dusty walk to the caves. On Sun Transportes Saltillo-Monterrey run a bus to the caves at 0900, 1000 and 1100. Otherwise, take an agency tour, eg Osetur (details from Infotur); book at *Hotel Ancira* (on Tues, US$3.50).

Local information
● Accommodation
It is difficult to obtain accommodation because of the constant movement of people travelling N/S.

L3 *Holiday Inn*, Av Universidad 101, T 766555, also at Av Eugenio Garza Sada 3680 S, T 762400, F 320565; **L3** *Holiday Inn Crowne Plaza*, Av Constitución 300 Ote, nr Plaza Zaragoza, best, T 196000.

A1 *Ambassador*, Hidalgo y Galeana, T 422040; **A1** *Ancira*, Hidalgo y Escobedo, T 432060; **A1** *Colonial*, Escobedo y Hidalgo, T 436791; **A1** *Río*, Padre Mier 194 Pte, T 449510; **A1** *Royal Courts* (Best Western), Av Universidad 314, T/F 762017.

C *Yamallel*, Zaragoza 912, Nte Madero, T 753400, good.

D *Estación*, Guadalupe Victoria 1450, opp train station, bath; **D** *Nuevo León*, Amado Nervo 1007 Nte con Av Madero, T 741900, with bath (hot water), dark, seedy, poor value, close to bus station; **D** *Posada*, Juan Méndez 1515, Nte, with bath, rec. Many hotels between Colón and Reforma, 2 blocks from the bus station, nothing below US$15; **D** *Victoria*, Bernardo Reyes 1205 Nte, T 756919, with bath, parking, a bit noisy.

Motels: **A3** *El Paso Autel*, Zaragoza y Martínez, T 400690; **D** *Motel/Trailerpark Nueva Castilla*, on Highway 85 before Saltillo bypass, 12 spaces for RVs with hook-up, pool, hot showers, reasonable restaurant, clean but drab, US$17 for vehicle and 2 people; several on Nuevo Laredo highway.

Youth hostel: Av Madero Ote s/n, Parque Fundidora, CP64000, T 557360.

● Places to eat
23 eating places around the 'Zona Rosa' and Plaza Zaragoza in the heart of town.

Vegetarian: *Los Girasoles* on Juan Ignacio Ramón (number not known), possibly best, good value; *Señor Natural*, Escobedo 713, similar; *Superbom*, Padre Mier, upstairs, good *menú*.

● Airline offices
AeroMéxico, T 435560; American Airlines, T 403031; Mexicana, T 405511; Taesa, T 433077; Continental, T 95-800-537-9222.

● Banks & money changers
If stuck without pesos on Sun, the red hotel/restaurant just opp the bus station changes TCs if you buy something in the restaurant.

● Embassies & consulates
British Consulate (Honorary) Mr Edward Lawrence, Privada de Tamazunchale 104, Colonia del Valle, Garza García, T 782565/569114.

Canadian Consul, T 443200.

● Tourist offices
Infotur on Gran Plaza (W side). Large city maps available at bookshops. Office by an airport on highway from Nuevo Laredo, helpful.

● Transport
Air Gen Mariano Escobedo airport (MTY), 24 km from centre. Daily flights from Mexico City take 1 hr 20 mins. Many flights to US (Chicago, Dallas, Detroit, Houston, Las Vegas, Los Angeles, Minneapolis, Nashville, New York, Phoenix, San Antonio, Tulsa, Wichita), and Mexican cities (Aguascalientes, Cancún, Chihuahua, Ciudad Juárez, Cuernavaca, Culiacán, Durango, Guadalajara, Hermosillo, Huatulco, Ixtapa, La Paz, León, Manzanillo, Matamoros, Mazatlán, Monclova, Piedras Negras, Puebla, Puerto Vallarta, Querétaro, San Luis Potosí, Tampico, Tijuana, Torreón, Veracruz, Villahermosa.

Trains Nuevo Regiomontano leaves for **Mexico City** at 1950; it leaves Mexico City at 1800, 15 hrs (from US$73 for a sleeper, *primera preferente* US$25). Tamaulipeco leaves at 1030 for **Reynosa** (arr 1440, US$6.60) and **Matamoros** (arr 1710, US$9).

Buses Terminal on Av Colón, between Calzada B Reyes and Av Pino Suárez. Monterrey-**Mexico City**, US$33, 12½ hrs. A more scenic trip is from Mexico City (northern bus terminal) to **Ciudad Valles**, 10 hrs, from where there are many connecting buses to Monterrey. To **San Luis Potosí**, US$14.80. To

Nuevo Laredo, departures every hour, 4 hrs, US$10. To Matamoros, Transportes del Nte, 4 hrs, US$10. To Chihuahua with Transportes del Nte, 8 a day, 12 hrs, US$30. Frequent buses to Saltillo, but long queues for tickets. To Guadalajara, US$36.50. To Santiago for Cola de Caballo falls, US$1.65.

NB Motorists: if driving Monterrey-Saltillo, there is nothing to indicate you are on the toll road until it is too late. The toll is US$7. Look for the old road.

MONTERREY TO CIUDAD VICTORIA

Leaving Monterrey, the road threads the narrow and lovely Huajuco canyon; from Santiago village a road runs to within 2 km of the Cola de Caballo, or Horsetail, Falls, in the **Cumbres de Monterrey** national park. (First-class hotel on the way, and you can get a colectivo, US$1.65, from the bus stop to the falls, and a horse, US$1.65, to take you to the top of the falls, entrance US$2.40; cost of guide US$5.) The road drops gradually into lower and warmer regions, passing through a succession of subtropical valleys with orange groves, banana plantations and vegetable gardens.

At **Montemorelos**, just off the highway, 79 km S of Monterrey, a branch road from the Matamoros Monterrey highway comes in. On 53 km is **Linares** (*Pop* 100,000), a fast-expanding town.

● **Accommodation** B *Escondido Court*, motel, clean, a/c, pool and restaurant, rec, 1½ km N of Linares on Route 855; B *Hotel Guidi*, nr the plaza.

● **Transport Buses** Linares to San Luis Potosí, US$14.80.

A most picturesque 96 km highway runs W from Linares up the lovely Santa Rosa canyon, up and over the Sierra Madre. After Iturbide, turn S on top of the Sierra Madre and continue on a good road through the unspoilt Sierra via La Escondida and Dr Arroyo. Alternatively, stay on the main road for San Roberto, N of Matehuala (see page 94) and join the Highway 57 route from Eagle Pass to Mexico City.

CIUDAD VICTORIA

(Km 706; *Pop* 300,000; *State pop 1995* 2,526,387; *Alt* 336m; *Phone code* 131) Capital of Tamaulipas state, a quiet, clean, unhurried city with a shaded plaza. Here Route 85 from Monterrey and Route 101 from Matamoros meet. It is often used as a stop-over. The N-S streets (parallel to the Sierra) have names and numbers, the E-W streets have only names.

Places of interest

The Parque Siglo 21 is the same end of town as the bus station. The centrepiece is a planetarium which looks like a huge red ball that landed on the banks of the Río San Marcos. Good view of the sierra from behind the planetarium where there is a large Rosa de los Vientos. Across the river is the Government Plaza, a 12-storey glass tower, the tallest thing in town. Also the state library in a green, tiled, Aztec-style building. The Centro Cultural Tamaulipas, 15 y Hidalgo, opposite the Palacio del Gobierno is a functional, modern building with a library and various cultural functions. The Museo de la Universidad Autónoma de Tamaulipas on the plaza has a good section on the Huasteca culture. On top of a hill is a tiny church: the temple of Nuestra Señora de Guadalupe, the patron saint of Mexico. (With thanks to Dan Golopentia, Seattle.)

Excursions

Tamatán, a suburb (plenty of colectivos), has a large park with a zoo and a small lake, popular with Mexicans at leisure. Take a colectivo to Ejido Libertad for the **Parque Ecológico Los Troncones**, where you can walk along the river and in the hills; good swimming holes.

Northeast of Ciudad Victoria is Nueva Ciudad Padilla; nearby is Viejo Padilla, where Agustín de Iturbide was shot in 1824. Also nearby is Presa Vicente Guerrero, a large lake with good fishing and many tourist facilities.

East of Ciudad Victoria sits the quiet town of **Soto La Marina**, with several

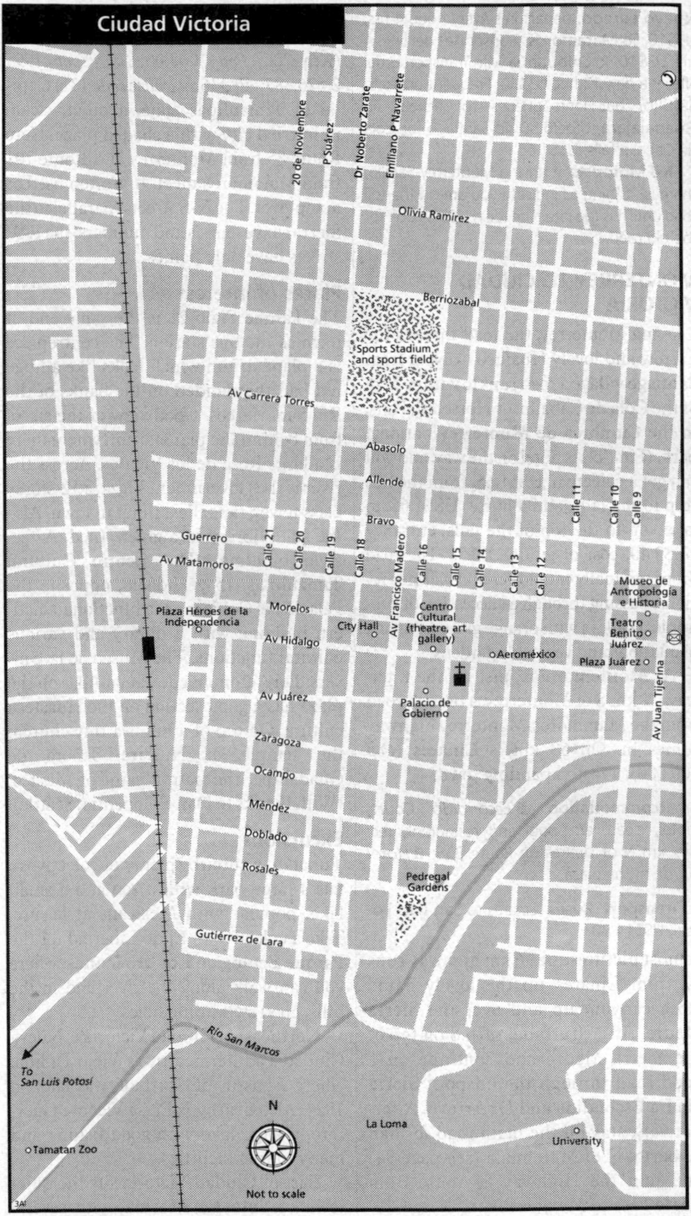

Ciudad Victoria

20 de Noviembre
P Suárez
Dr Noberto Zarate
Emiliano P Navarrete
Olivia Ramirez
Berriozabal
Sports Stadium and sports field
Av Carrera Torres
Abasolo
Allende
Bravo
Calle 11
Calle 10
Calle 9
Guerrero
Av Matamoros
Calle 21
Calle 20
Calle 19
Calle 18
Av Francisco Madero
Calle 16
Calle 15
Calle 14
Calle 13
Calle 12
Museo de Antropología e Historia
Morelos
Plaza Heroes de la Independencia
City Hall
Centro Cultural (theatre, art gallery)
Teatro Benito Juárez
Av Hidalgo
Plaza Juárez
Aeroméxico
Av Juárez
Palacio de Gobierno
Zaragoza
Ocampo
Av Juan Tijerina
Méndez
Doblado
Rosales
Pedregal Gardens
Gutiérrez de Lara
Río San Marcos
To San Luis Potosí
N
La Loma
Tamatan Zoo
University
Not to scale

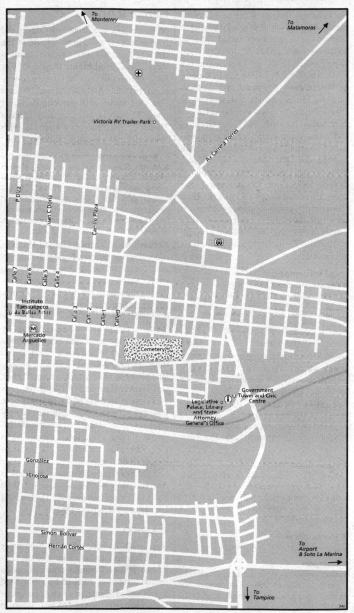

To Monterrey

To Matamoras

Av Carrera Torres

Victoria RV Trailer Park

P Díez

Juan C Doria

Camilo Plaza

Calle 7

Calle 6

Calle 5

Calle 4

Instituto
Tamaulipeco
de Bellas Artes

Mercado
Arguelles

Calle 3

Calle 2

Calle 1

Callejo

Cemetery

Government
Tower and Civic
Centre

Legislative
Palace, Library
and State
Attorney
General's Office

González

Hinojosa

Simón Bolívar

Hernán Cortés

To
Airport
& Soto La Marina

To
Tampico

places to stay including the new **D** *Hotel Maná Christina*, which is good if you want to avoid the large city of Ciudad Victoria. Southwest of Ciudad Victoria, 20 km along Route 101 (direction Jamuave) is a sign to the Zona Arqueológica **El Balcón de Moctezuma**. The site consists of circular buildings and staircases, showing Huastec influence. It is similar to Chicomostoc, La Quemada and Casas Grandes and was a commercial centre with contacts with tribes in present day USA. Ask for the guide Don Gabino, who took part in the excavations, which were completed in June 1990. From the signpost to the Zona Arqueológica it's a 4 km walk, then 100m uphill (a high clearance vehicle can get within 100m and you can park at Altas Cumbres near the site). We are grateful to Helmut Zettl, Ebergassing, for this information.

Local information
● **Accommodation**

A2 *Santorín* (Best Western), Cristóbal Colón Nte 349, T 128938, F 128342, a/c, TV, parking, restaurant.

B *Sierra Gorda*, Hidalgo 990 Ote, T 32280, garage US$0.70 a night.

Several **E** hotels by bus station and in the centre.

Motels: **D** *Los Monteros*, Plaza Hidalgo, T 20300, downtown; **B** *Panorámica*, Lomas de Santuario, T 25506.

Trailer Park: *Victoria RV Trailer Park*, Libramiento 101-85, T/F 24824, follow signs, good service, electricity, hot showers; owner (Rosie) has travel information, US$10 for 2 plus vehicle.

● **Places to eat**

Chavos, C 12, Hidalgo y Juárez, all you can eat buffet; *Daddy's* on the plaza, sort of a *Denny's*, with a Mexican touch for the homesick American; locals congregate at *Café Cantón*, half a block from the plaza on C 9.

● **Tourist offices**

C 16 y Rosales nr Parque Alameda.

● **Transport**

Buses Terminal is on the outskirts. Omnibuses Blancos to Ciudad Valles (see below) for US$8.50. Bus Ciudad Victoria-Mexico City 10 hrs, US$26.65.

CIUDAD MANTE

After crossing the Tropic of Cancer the road enters the solid green jungle of the tropical lowlands. 137 km S of Ciudad Victoria is **Ciudad Mante** (Route 85, Km 570), which is almost exactly the mid-way point between Matamoros and Mexico City and makes a convenient stop-over place. The city is, however, dirty. It has a Museo de Antropología e Historia, with objects from the Huastec culture.

● **Accommodation** Best hotel is probably the **B** *Mante*, Guerrero 500 Nte, T 20990, shaded grounds at N edge of business sector; **D** *Monterrey*, Av Juárez 503, Ote, T 21512, in old section, with bath, hot water, a/c, cable TV, helpful manager speaks English, safe parking, rec, new annex at back, restaurant not so good; several hotels a few blocks S of Zócalo.

Excursions 45 km N of Ciudad Mante is the village of **Gómez Farías**, an important centre for ornithological research: the highlands above the village represent the northernmost extent of several tropical vegetation formations. Many tropical bird species reach the northern limit of their range. Gómez Farías is reached by turning off the main highway, 14 km over a paved road to the town plaza. From there, an easy 2-km walk provides excellent views of bird habitats. (Jim Turner, Oak Grove, Missouri.) A 1-hr drive, plus 5 hrs' walk, leads to **El Cielo Biosphere Reserve** which has four different ecosystems at various altitudes, including tropical jungle and cloud forest (about 200m to 2,500m). In the reserve is Canindo Research Station.

South of Ciudad Mante at Km 548 is Antiguo Morelos. A road turns off W to San Luis Potosí (see page 96) 314 km, and Guadalajara (see page 196).

TAMPICO

(*Pop* 560,000; *Phone code* 121) Monterrey trains run via Ciudad Victoria to the Caribbean port of **Tampico**, definitely not a tourist attraction, reached by a fine road from Ciudad Mante, in a rich sugar-growing area, a deviation of 156 km. Tampico is on the northern bank of the Río Pánuco, not far from a large oilfield: there are storage tanks and refineries for miles along the southern bank. The summer heat, rarely above 35°C, is tempered by sea breezes, but June and July are trying. Cold northerlies blow now and again during the winter. There are two pleasant plazas, Plaza de Armas at Colón y Carranza, with squirrels in the trees, and Plaza de la Libertad, Madero y Juárez. Fishing (both sea and river) is excellent. Huge, interesting market, but watch your possessions carefully. The Playa de Miramar, a beach resort, is a tram or bus-ride from the city, but is reported dirty. If walking there, go along the breakwater (Escollera Norte) on N side of Río Pánuco, for views of the shipping and to see the monument to Mexican merchant seamen killed in WW2. The Museo de la Cultura Huasteca in **Ciudad Madero**, an adjacent town, is worth visiting (Instituto Tecnológico, Av 1 de Mayo y Sor Juana Inés de la Cruz – in poor condition); take a colectivo, 'Madero', from the centre of Tampico to the Zócalo in Ciudad Madero, then another to the Instituto; open 1000-1500, except Mon, small but select collection. Ciudad Madero claims to be Mexico's petroleum capital, with a huge oil refinery.

A second 145-km paved road W from Tampico through the oil camp of Ebano joins the Nuevo Laredo-México highway further S at Ciudad Valles. There are direct buses to Brownsville (Texas). A splendid new bridge was opened at the end of 1988 to replace the ferry to Villa Cuauhtémoc, S of Tampico. Further S, the coast road, Route 180, enters Veracruz state, leading to Túxpan, Poza Rica and Veracruz (the northern towns of that state are described on page 326).

● **Accommodation A1** *Camino Real*, Av Hidalgo 2000, T 38811; **A1** *Impala*, Mirón 220 Pte, T 20990; **A1** *Inglaterra*, Mirón y Olmos; **B** *Imperial*, Aurora Sur 201, T 25678, clean, shower, fan, but noisy; **B** *Nuevo León*, Aduana N 107, T 24370, a/c, shower, clean; **B** *Tampico*, Carranza 513, T 24970; **C** *Ritz*, on Miramar

beach, beautiful beach, deserted at night. Several cheap hotels nr Plaza de la Libertad: eg *Sevilla* (always full), **E** *América*, nr market on Olmos, dirty but safe; **E** *Rex*, dirty, no hot water. All hotels downtown nr market should be treated with discretion; many have a rapid turnover. RVs can stay in the parking lot of the airport, which has rest rooms, US$15/vehicle, noisy from traffic.

● **Places to eat** *El Diligencias*, Héroes del Canonero Tampico 415 Ote y Gral López de Lara, excellent seafood; *Emir*, FA Olmos between Díaz Mirón y Madero, good; for breakfast, *El Selecto*, opp market.

● **Airline offices** AeroMéxico, T 170939, Mexicana, T 139600.

● **Embassies & consulates** German Consul, 2 de Enero, 102 Sur-A, Hon Consul Dieter Schulze. Postal Address: Apdo 775, T 129784/129817. Also deals with British affairs.

● **Tourist offices** Plaza de Armas, above *Chantal* ice cream parlour on C FA Olmos, helpful.

● **Transport Air** The Gen F Javier Mina airport (TAM) is 8 km from the centre. Mexicana has daily flights to Mexico City and Seroliteral flies to Durango, Guadalajara, Ixtapa, Monclova, Monterrey, Piedras Negras, Torreón, Veracruz and Villahermosa.

CIUDAD VALLES

(Km 476; *Pop* 320,000) **Ciudad Valles** is on a winding river and a popular stop-over with many hotels. **Museo Regional Huasteco**, C Rotarios y C Artes (or Peñaloza), open 1000-1200, 1400-1800, Mon-Fri, centre of archaeological and ethnographic research for the Huastec region. Visit the market, which is very busy. There are many cheap places to eat tacos.

● **Accommodation A3** *Valles*, T 20050, with trailer park, full hook-up, hot shower, a bit run-down, US$10 for 2 in car, on Carretera México-Laredo; **B** *San Fernando*, T 20184, on main highway, clean, large rooms, a/c, TV, parking; **D** *Condesa*, Av Juárez 109, T 20015, clean, basic, fan, friendly, OK. 11 km S of town is campground *El Banito*, warm sulphur pools, good restaurant, a bit run down.

● **Transport Buses** Omnibus Oriente to San Luis Potosí for US$6.60 (4 hrs); Mexico City 10 hrs.

TAMAZUNCHALE

(Km 370; *Pop* 150,000; *Alt* 206m)
Tamazunchale, with riotous tropical vegetation, is perhaps the most popular of all the overnight stops. (*San Antonio Hotel*; **B** *Mirador*, good, but passing traffic by night is noisy; **E** *Hotel OK*, cheapest but not rec.) The potholed road S of here begins a spectacular climb to the highland, winding over the rugged terrain cut by the Río Moctezuma and its tributaries. The highest point on the road is 2,502m. From (Km 279) **Jacala** (two very basic hotels, erratic water supply) there is a dizzying view into a chasm. **Zimapán** (*Posada del Rey*, fascinating but very run down, out on the highway), with a charming market place and a small old church in the plaza, is as good a place as any to stay the night. From (Km 178) **Portezuelo** a paved road runs W to Querétaro (see page 99), 140 km.

IXMIQUILPAN

In an area of 23,300 sq km N and S of (Km 169) **Ixmiquilpan**, just off the highway, 65,000 Otomí Indians 'live the bitterest and saddest life'. The beautifully worked Otomí belts and bags may sometimes be bought at the Mon market, and also in the Artesanía shop in the main street almost opposite the government aid offices.

See early Indian frescoes in the main church, which is one of the 16th century battlemented Augustinian monastery-churches; the monastery is open to the public. John Streather writes: "At sunset each day white egrets come to roost in the trees outside the church; it's worth going up on to the battlements to see them swoop down. The church of El Carmen is worth a visit too, lovely W façade and gilded altars inside. There is also a 16th century bridge over the river; beautiful walk along the ahuehuete-lined banks."

Excursions Near Ixmiquilpan are several warm swimming pools, both natural and man-made: San Antonio, Dios Padre, Las Humedades, and near Tephé (the only warm-water bath, clean, entry

US$0.40) and Tzindejé (this is about 20 mins from town). The Otomí villages of La Lagunita, La Pechuga and La Bonanza, in a beautiful valley, have no modern conveniences.

The Barranca de Tolantongo, 37 km NE of Ixmiquilpan, is about 1,500m deep with a waterfall and thermal spring; at weekends there is a small eating place. Entry US$2, car parking US$2 at entrance to recreational area; camping permitted. To get there take the road towards El Cardonal, then an unpaved turn-off about 3 km before El Cardonal (there is a bus from Pachuca).

● **Accommodation C** *Hotel Diana*, rear buildings slightly dearer rooms but much cleaner, rec, safe parking; **E** *Hotel/Restaurant Los Portales*, 1 block from main square, clean, safe parking, mediocre food.

ACTOPAN TO TULA

Actopán (Km 119) has another fine 16th century Augustinian church and convent (**B** *Hotel Rira*). From Actopán a 56 km branch road runs to one of Mexico's great archaeological sites: Tula, capital of the Toltecs (see page 292).

On the way to Tula there is an interesting cooperative village, **Cruz Azul**. Free concerts on Sun mornings at 1000 in front of main market. At (Km 85) Colonia, a road runs left for 8 km to Pachuca.

PACHUCA

(*Pop* 320,000; *State pop 1995* 2,111,782; *Alt* 2,445m) This is one of the oldest silvermining centres in Mexico and capital of Hidalgo state. The Aztecs mined here before the Spaniards came and the hills are honeycombed with old workings and terraced with tailings.

Places of interest

Although the centre is largely modern, there are a number of colonial buildings among its narrow, steep and crooked streets. These include the treasury for the royal tribute, **Las Cajas Reales**, Venustiano Carranza 106 (1670), now used as offices; **Las Casas Coloradas** (1785), on Plaza Pedro María Anaya, now the Tribunal Superior Justicia; and a former **Franciscan convent** (1596) on Arista y Hidalgo next to Parque Hidalgo. **Casa de las Artesanías** for Hidalgo state is at the junction of Av Revolución y Av Juárez. In the Plaza Independencia is a huge clock with four Carrara marble figures. The modern buildings include a notable **theatre**, the **Palacio de Gobierno** (which has a mural depicting ex-President Echeverría's dream of becoming Secretary-General of the UN), and the **Banco de Hidalgo**. The town centre is partly pedestrianized. Colectivos run from Julián Carrillo (very frequent, US$40) to the large silver-mining camp of Real (or Mineral) del Monte, picturesque and with steep streets.

Museums

The **Museo de la Minería** at Mina 110 has an excellent display of the history of mining in Pachuca, free entry, open Tues-Sun 1000-1400, 1500-1800. An outstanding **photographic museum** (free, open Tues-Sun 1000-1800) is in the large cloister on the far side of the convent. The **Museo Regional de Hidalgo**, displaying chronological exhibits of the state's history, is known as the Centro Cultural Hidalgo (open Tues-Sun, 0900-1800 – may close early on Sun pm). In the complex there is a souvenir shop with reproductions of ceramic and metal anthropological items and recordings of indigenous music, a library and exhibition hall.

Excursions

Cornish miners settled at **Real del Monte** in the 19th century; their blue-eyed descendants may be seen among the local inhabitants. Note also the Flemish-style gable roofs. At each entry to the town is a mural commemorating the first strike in the Americas, by silver miners in 1776. The Panteón Inglés (English cemetery) is on a wooded hill opposite the town (ask the caretaker for the key). Mineral del Chico is a beautiful little town 30 km from Pachuca in **El Chico National Park**. The

Park has many campsites (mostly dirty with no facilities). There is no information/maps at the Park headquarters. The town is full of weekend homes for the wealthy of Mexico City. There are huge rock formations covered in pine forests; splendid walks. Bus from Pachuca bus station.

Local information
● Accommodation
B *Ciro's* Independencia, rec.

C *El Dorado*, Guerrero 721, T 42831, clean, friendly; **C** *Motel San Antonio*, 6 km from Pachuca on road to Mexico City (ask repeatedly for directions), spacious rooms, good value, clean, quiet, restaurant.

D *De los Baños*, on Plaza Independencia, rooms not up to standard of entrance, good, friendly and helpful, rec; **D** *Grenfell*, Plaza Independencia 116, T 50277, with bath, clean, friendly, pleasant, good value (cheaper without bath, but communal toilets are filthy), bus from bus station passes the door; **D** *Hidalgo*, Matamoras 503, rec; **D** *Juárez*, Barreda 107, with bath, some rooms without windows, just before Real del Monte, in superb wooded surroundings.

F *Colonial*, Guerrero 505, central.

● Places to eat
Casino Español, Everardo Márquez, old-time favourite; *La Blanca*, next to *Hotel de los Baños*, local dishes, rec; *El Buen Gusto*, Arista y Viaducto Nuevo Hidalgo, clean, good value *comida corrida*; *Palacio*, Av Juárez 200D, excellent breakfast, central; *El Rinconcito*, on Juárez, good cheap food. 'Paste' is the local survivor from Cornish miners' days; a good approximation of the real pasty, but a bit peppery! Eg at *Pastes Pachuqueños*, Arista 1023, rec.

● Tourist offices
In clock tower, Plaza Independencia, opp *Hotel Grenfell*.

● Transport
Buses Terminal is outside town; take any bus marked 'Central'.

NORTH AND EAST OF PACHUCA

North of Pachuca via Atotonilco el Grande, where there are a chapel and convent half-way down a beautiful canyon, is the impressive **Barranca de Metztitlán** which has a wealth of different varieties of cacti, including the 'hairy old man' cactus, and a huge 17th century monastery. Farther N (difficult road) is Molango, where there is a restored convent, Nuestra Señora de Loreto. 34 km NE of Pachuca is **San Miguel Regla**, a mid-18th century *hacienda* built by the Conde de Regla, and now run as a resort, fine atmosphere, excellent service; pool, lush gardens, tennis, horse-riding, log fires, highly recommended: T (91 771) 54311, or 680-0448/651-6369 (Mexico City) for reservations (**A1** full board). A road continues to **Tulancingo**, on the Pachuca-Poza Rica road, Route 130. 17 km from Pachuca, and a further 4 km off Route 130 to the right is **Epazoyucan**, a village with an interesting convent of San Andrés. After Tulancingo, Route 119 branches off to the right to **Zacatlán**, famous for its apple orchards and now also producing plums, pears and cider. Its alpine surroundings include an impressive national park, **Valle de las Piedras Encimadas** (stacked rocks), camping possible. Nearby is *Posada Campestre al Final de la Senda*, a ranch with weekend accommodation, horse riding, walks, B pp full board, T Puebla 413 821 for reservations. Some 16 km S of Zacatlán is **Chignahuapan** (about 1½ hrs from Puebla), a leading producer of *sarapes*, surrounded by several curative spas.

30 km from Tulancingo on Route 130 is *La Cabaña* restaurant, of log-cabin construction; thereafter, the road descends with many bends and slow lorries, and in winter there may be fog. At **Huachinango**, an annual flower fair is held in Mar; 22 km from here is **Xicotepec de Juárez** (*Mi Ranchito*, one of the nicest small hotels in Mexico; **D** *Italia*, near main square). Along the route are the villages of **Pahuatlan** and **San Pablito**, where sequined headbands are made, and paintings are done on flattened *amate* bark. The entire route from desert to jungle is 190 km, taking 5 hrs.

PACHUCA TO MEXICO CITY

A 4-lane highway now runs from Pachuca to Mexico City via (Km 27) Venta de Carpio, from which a road runs E to Acolman, 12 km, and Teotihuacan, another 10 km. Neither of these places should be missed (see page 290); buses are available from Pachuca; get them at the tollbooth on the highway to Mexico City.

At Santa Clara, 13 km short of the Capital, the road forks. The right-hand fork (easy driving) goes direct to the City; the left fork goes through Villa Madero, where you can see the shrine of Guadalupe.

Eagle Pass – Piedras Negras to Mexico City

A POPULAR ROUTE which goes through various mining centres (for silver and gemstones): Real de Catorce is now a ghost town; San Luis Potosí has many historical features, as does Querétaro, now an industrial city retaining a well-kept colonial centre.

This route, 1,328 km (825 miles), is 102 km longer than the Laredo route, but is very wide, very fast and much easier to drive. Take in enough gasoline at Monclova to cover the 205 km to Saltillo. Hotel, restaurant and camping prices have risen rapidly.

Piedras Negras (*Pop* 150,000; *Alt* 220m), is across the Río Bravo from Eagle Pass, Texas. (Artesanía shop – Centro Artesanal Piedras Negras, Edif la Estrella, Puerta México, T 21087.) Beyond Hermanas (137 km) the highway begins to climb gradually up to the plateau country.

● **Transport Trains** Coahuilense train leaves for **Saltillo** at 0915 (arr 1855), US$5.75 2nd class, US$12 *primera preferente*.

Monclova (243 km from border) has one of the largest steel mills in Mexico, and 250,000 people.

SALTILLO

(Km 448; *Pop* 650,000; *State pop 1995* 2,172,136; *Alt* 1,600m; *Phone code* 841) The capital of Coahuila state is a cool, dry popular resort noted for the excellence of its *sarapes*. Its 18th century cathedral, a mixture of romanesque, churrigueresque, baroque and plateresque styles, is the best in northern Mexico and it has a grand market. Good golf, tennis, swimming. College students from the US attend the popular Summer School at the Universidad Interamericana. **Museo de los Aves** (the Bird Museum), on Hidalgo (a few blocks N of Sarape factory) contains hundreds of stuffed birds, cafe, small admission charge, guides available. On Blvd Nazario Ortiz Garza, the house of the artist Juan Antonio Villarreal Ríos (Casa 1, Manzana 1, Colonia Saltillo 400, T 152707/151206 – home) has an exhibition in every room of Dali-esque work, entry is free and visitors are welcome, phone first. Good views from El Cerro del Pueblo overlooking city. An 87-km road runs E to Monterrey, both toll (US$7) and *vía libre*. You turn right for Mexico City.

A short bus ride away is the quaint village of **Arteaga**, shady parks and beautiful stream. Three restaurants at entrance to village. Many buses from Saltillo.

Local festivals

Local *feria* in first half of Aug; cheap accommodation impossible to find at this time. Indian dances during 30 May and 30 Aug; picturesque ceremonies and bull-fights during Oct *fiestas*. *Pastorelas*, the story of the Nativity, are performed in the neighbourhood in Christmas week.

Local information
● **Accommodation**
Several hotels a short distance from the plaza at the intersection of Allende and Aldama, the main streets.

A1 *San Jorge*, Manuel Acuña Nte 240, T 22222, F 29400.

B *Rancho El Marillo*, Prol Obregón Sur, T 174078, converted hacienda, excellent value, meals available; **B** *Saade*, Aldama 397, T 33400; **B** *Urdiñola*, Victoria 211, T 40940, reasonable.

C *De Avila*, Padre Flores 211, T 37272, basic, cold water, safe motorcycle parking. **C** *Metropolí*, Allende 436, basic, with shower, a little dark but adequate, quiet.

D *Hidalgo*, on Padre Flores, without bath, not worth paying for bath in room, cold water only (hot baths open to public and guests for small fee).

E *Zamora*, Ramos Arzipe (Pte) 552, cheap, noisy, clean, tepid water; **E** *El Conde*, Pérez Treviño y Acuña. Several hotels in front of the bus station, eg **D** *Saltillo*; **E** *Central*, with bath, ample safe parking, clean, comfy.

Several good motels: **A1** *Camino Real*, Blvd Los Fundadores 2000, T 52525, F 53813; **A1** *Eurotel Plaza*, 2 km N of centre, Blvd V Carranza Nte 4100, T and F 151000, parking, a/c, TV, restaurant, etc, AAA rec; **A3** *Huizache*, Blvd Carranza 1746, T 28112; **A3** *La Fuente*, Blvd Fundadores, T 22090.

Trailer park: turn right on road into town from Monterrey between *Hotel del Norte* and *Kentucky Fried Chicken*, hook-ups, toilets, basic.

● **Places to eat**
Viena, Acuña 519, rec; *Victoria*, Padre Flores 221, by *Hotel Hidalgo* has reasonable *comida*; *Café Plaza*, off Plaza de Armas, good breakfasts; *Café Bagdad*, Hidalgo 849 y Castillo, excellent snacks, live music or theatre at weekends. Excellent *licuados* (milkshakes) upstairs in the market. Many restaurants and bars in front of the bus station. Drinks and night-time view can be had at the *Rodeway Inn* on the N side of town.

● **Post & telecommunications**
Telephones: long-distance calls from *Café Victoria*, Padre Flores 221, nr market.

● **Tourist offices**
Near crossroads of Allende and Blvd Francisco Coss in old railway station, long way from centre. Map with all useful addresses, inc hotels.

● **Transport**
Air The airport (SLW) is 16 km from town. Flights to Mexico City daily with Mexicana.

Trains Regiomontano calls here en route to Mexico City at 2200, and to Monterrey and Nuevo Laredo at 0545. *Primera preferente* Saltillo-Mexico City, 12 hrs, US$22, sleepers from US$65. To Monterrey US$2.80 *primera preferente*. Coahuilense connects with Regiomontano for Piedras Negras 0815 (7½ hrs).

Buses Terminal is a long way from centre; minibuses to Pérez Treviño y Allende (for centre) will take luggage. Bus to **Mexico City**, 1st class, US$29.50, 11 hrs. To **Ciudad Acuña**, 2nd class, US$14.30, 8 hrs. To **Monterrey** and **Nuevo Laredo** with Transportes del Nte. For **Torreón**, all buses originate in Monterrey and tickets only sold when bus arrives; be prepared to stand.

SALTILLO TO MATEHUALA

Chris and Miyuki Kerfoot write: From Saltillo to Matehuala by 2nd class bus, Estrella Blanca, 1½ hrs, US$3.75 to San Roberto, which is no more than a road junction (a 96-km road runs E over the Sierra Madre to Linares, on the Gulf Route (see page 85) with a Pemex petrol station, hitch to the junction of Highways 58 and 68 and catch a bus (Transportes Tamaulipas) to Matehuala (US$5, 4½ hrs). From these junctions near Caleana to La Soledad the scenery is worthwhile, as the road winds its way up and down through wooded valleys. The final section to Matehuala passes through undulating scrub country.

There are three Pemex stations between Saltillo and Matehuala, the most northerly one being also a police checkpoint for traffic heading N. Between Matehuala and San Luis Potosí there are frequent Pemex stations. The 'vía libre' from Saltillo to San Luis Potosí is good all the way; the turn-off to the 'custa' road is well signposted.

Matehuala is an important road junction. Fiesta, 6-20 January.

● **Accommodation A3** *Motel Trailerpark Las Palmas*, on the N edge of town (Km 617), T 20001, clean, English spoken and paperbacks sold, bowling alley and miniature golf, tours to Real de Catorce (see below) arranged; *El Dorado* nearby, T 20174, cheaper, rec; *E Alamo*, C Guerrero 116, T 20017, hot showers, clean and very pleasant rooms, safe motorcycle parking, friendly, rec. *Restaurant La Fontella* in the centre, good regional food.

● **Transport Buses** To Real de Catorce, US$2; **San Luis Potosí**, with Estrella Blanca, 2½ hrs, US$6.25; **Mexico City** (US$22), Monterrey and Querétaro.

REAL DE CATORCE

56 km W of Matehuala is one of Mexico's most interesting old mining towns, **Real de Catorce** (*Alt* 2,765m), founded in 1772. This remarkable city, clustering around the sides of a valley, used to be so quiet that you could hear the river in the canyon, 1,000m below. It is becoming increasingly popular as a tourist destination, with new hotels being built.

To get there, turn left along the Zacatecas road through Cedral. After 27 km turn left off the paved road, on to a cobblestone one. The road passes through Potrero, a big centre for nopal cactus. Some people live in the old mine workings and old buildings. Huichol Indians are seen here occasionally. A silver mine is still being worked at Santana.

Real de Catorce is approached through Ogarrio, an old mine gallery widened (only just) to allow trucks through (US$1.65 toll to drive through). It is 2½ km long, and very eerie, with the odd tunnel leading off into the gloom on either side. There is an overtaking bay half way through. A small chapel to the Virgen de los Dolores is by the entrance. The tunnel opens out abruptly into the old city, originally called Real d'Alamos de la Purísima Concepción de los Catorce. Legend has it that 14 bandits hid in nearby caves until the

silver was discovered and the town founded. Engineers came from Ireland, Germany and France.

Places of interest

The first church was the **Virgen del Guadalupe** (1779), a little way out of town (beautiful ceiling paintings remain, as well as the black coffin used for the Mass of the Cuerpo Presente). Many of the images from this church were moved to the **Church of San Francisco** (1817), which is believed to be miraculous. The floor of the church is made of wooden panels, which can be lifted up to see the catacombs below. In a room to one side of the main altar are *retablos*, touchingly simple paintings on tin, as votive offerings to the Saint for his intercession. Next to the church is a small museum (entry US$0.10) showing mining equipment, etc, worth a visit. In the early 19th century, when the population was about 40,000, Real minted its own coins, which circulated only within the city limits (they are now collectors' items). After WW2 the population fell dramatically to 400, but it has risen now to about 1,200, since silver is being worked again and tourism is growing. Guided tours are available from the **Casa de la Moneda**, in front of the Cathedral; they include the **Palenque**, an 8-sided amphitheatre built in 1863, which seated 500-600 people (this is otherwise closed to the public). In the Casa de la Moneda you can see silversmiths at work.

There are good hikes in the surrounding mountains. Very peaceful. Take good footwear, sun protection and a jumper. A 30-min walk takes you to the ghost town 'pueblo fantasmo' from where there are fine views over the town.

Local festivals

There is a pilgrimage here for San Francisco (whose day is 4 Oct), on foot from Matehuala, overnight on 3 Oct (take local bus from Matehuala to La Paz and join the groups of pilgrims who set out from early evening onwards; walk takes about 7 hrs, be prepared for rain). It is possible to walk from Matehuala to Real de Catorce, other than on the San Francisco pilgrimage, with the aid of the 1:50,000 map from INEGI (see **Information for travellers**, page 520). On Good Friday, thousands of visitors gather to watch a lively passion play 'with almost real Roman soldiers and very colourful Jews and apostles'.

Local information

● Accommodation

One in the main street, very comfortable with restaurant and bar, expensive, another, **D** *Hotel Real*, in a side street, clean, nice atmosphere, friendly Italian owner, good restaurant, rec; **D** *La Posada del Sol*, on way to cemetery from main square, with bath, TV, beautiful views, poor restaurant, rec; **E** *Providencia*, on main street, hot water, clean, restaurant. Several other hotels, and various restaurants. Accommodation is easy to find: boys greet new arrivals and will guide motorists through the peculiar one-way system (or face a police fine). Basic rooms F pp.

● Places to eat

El Eucalyptus, on way to Bócalo, Italian-Swiss run, excellent homemade pasta, vegetarian food, cakes, pricey but rec; many cheap restaurants on main street and stalls selling tacos and hot drinks.

● Transport

Trains Real de Catorce can also be reached from Saltillo or San Luis Potosí by train, but schedules are awkward (US$3.35, 5 hrs). Station, called Catorce, is 13 km away. Jeeps collect passengers from the station (US$16.50/jeep) and follow a more spectacular route than the minibuses.

No fuel on sale in Real de Catorce; the Pemex Station before Cedral does not have *magna sin*, the one before Matehuala does.

Buses Many buses a day to Matehuala with Transportes Tamaulipas, from the corner of C del Guerrero and Mendiz, US$2 one-way. A taxi can be hired nearby for US$25, economic for 4 people; local buses from office 1 block N of the Zócalo.

Huizache (785 km from Eagle Pass) is the junction with the Guadalajara-Antiguo Morelos-Tampico highway. At 901 km we come to San Luis Potosí.

SAN LUIS POTOSI

(*Pop* 850,000; *State pop 1995* 2,191,712; *Alt* 1,880m; *Phone code* 481) 423 km from Mexico City, the capital of its state is the centre of a rich mining and agricultural area, which has expanded industrially in recent years. Glazed, many-coloured tiles are a feature of the city: one of its shopping streets, the main plaza, and the domes of many of its churches are covered with them. It became an important centre after the discovery of the famous San Pedro silver mine in the 16th century, and a city in 1658.

Places of interest

The **Cathedral** is on **Plaza Hidalgo**. See the churches of **San Francisco**, with its white and blue tiled dome and suspended glass boat in the transept (try and get into the magnificent sacristy); **El Carmen**, in **Plaza Morelos**, with a grand tiled dome, an intricate façade, and a fine pulpit and altar inside (the **Teatro de la Paz** is next door); the baroque **Capilla de Aránzazu**, behind San Francisco inside the regional museum (see below); the **Capilla de Loreto** with a baroque façade; **Iglesia de San Miguelito**, in the oldest part of the city; **San Agustín**, with its ornate baroque tower; and the startling modern **Templo de la Santa Cruz**, in the Industria Aviación district, designed by Enrique de la Mora. The **Palacio de Gobierno**, begun 1770, contains oil-paintings of past governors, and the colonial treasury, **Antigua Real Caja**, built 1767. Other points of interest are the pedestrian precinct in C Hidalgo and the **Caja del Agua** fountain (1835) in Av Juárez. **Plaza de San Francisco** is very pleasant. The modern railway station has frescoes by Fernando Leal. The **Teatro Alarcón** is by Tresguerras (see under Celaya, page 150). Locally made *rebozos* (the best are from Santa María del Río) are for sale in the markets. The **University** was founded in 1804. A scenic road leads to Aguascalientes airport.

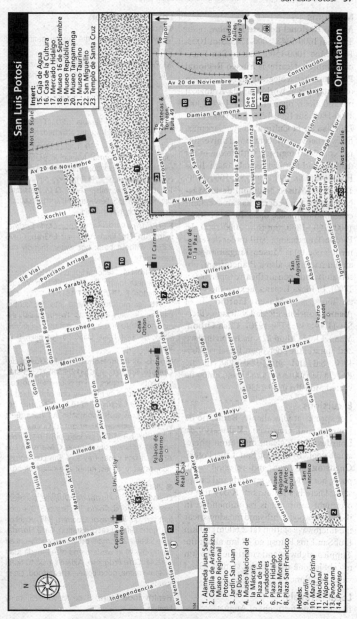

San Luis Potosí

Not to Scale

Insert:
15. Caja de Agua
16. Casa de la Cultura
17. Mercado Hidalgo
18. Museo 16 de Septiembre
19. Museo Republica
20. Museo Tangamanga
21. Museo Taurino
22. San Miguelito
23. Templo de Santa Cruz

Orientation

To Airport

To Ciudad Valles, Ruta 49

Av 20 de Noviembre

Constitución

Av Juárez

5 de Mayo

Damian Carmona

See Detail

To Zacatecas & Torreón, Ruta 49

Av Ferrocarril

Av José O. santiago

Av Muñoz

Nicolas Zapata

Mariano Carranza

Av Venustiano Carranza

Av Cuauhtémoc

Al Himno

Nacional

Blvd Diagonal Sur

Guacalajar

Parque Recreativo Tangamanga

Not to Scale

Av 20 de Noviembre

Otrhegu

Xochitl

Manuel José Othon

Eje Vial

Ponciano Arriaga

Juan Sarabia

Escohedo

Morelos

Hidalgo

Allende

González Bocanegra

Gonz Ortega

Julián de los Reyes

Mariano Arista

Damián Carmona

Av Venustiano Carranza

Independencia

Av Alvarc Obregón

Los Bravo

Capilla de Loreto

University

Palacio de Gobierno

Antigua Real Caja

Francisco I Madero

Diaz de León

Guerrero

El Carmen

Casa Othon

Cathedral

Manuel José Othon

Aldama

Museo Regional de Artec Popular

San Francisco

Galeana

Teatro de O la Paz

Villerias

Escobedo

Iturbide

5 de Mayu

Gral Vicente Guerrero

Universidad

Morelos

Zaragoza

Teatro A Alaçón

San Agustín

Abasolo

Ignacio Comonfort

Vallejo

Galeana

N

1. Alameda Juan Sarabia
2. Capilla de Aránzazu, Museo Regional Potosino
3. Jardín San Juan de Dios
4. Museo Nacional de la Máscara
5. Plaza de los Fundadores
6. Plaza Hidalgo
7. Plaza Morelos
8. Plaza San Francisco

Hotels:
9. Jardín
10. María Cristina
11. Nacional
12. Nápoles
13. Panorama
14. Progreso

Museums

Museo Regional de Arte Popular, open Tues-Sat 1000-1345, 1600-1745; Sun 1000-1400, Mon 1000-1500, next to San Francisco church. Nearby is **Museo Regional Potosino**, archaeological, and a collection of wrought iron work, Capilla Aránzazu on 2nd floor, open Tues-Fri 1000-1300, 1500-1800, Sat 1000-1200, Sun 1000-1300. **La Casa de la Cultura** on Av Carranza, halfway between the centre and university, is a converted mansion with frequent art displays and musical recitals, open Tues-Fri, 1000-1400, 1600-1800, Sat 1000-1400, 1800-2100. **Museo Nacional de la Máscara**, in Palacio Federal, has an excellent collection of masks, open Tues-Fri 1000-1400, 1600-1800, Sat-Sun 1000-1400. In Parque Tangamanga (still under development S of city) is **Museo Tangamanga** in an old hacienda, also a Planetarium, observatory and open air theatre (open 0600-1800). In Plaza España, next to the Plaza de Toros, is a **Museo Taurino** (E of Alameda on Universidad y Triana, Tues-Sat 1100-1330, 1730-1930). **Casa Othon**, Manuel José Othon 225, is the birthplace and home of the poet, open Tues-Fri 0800-1900, Sat and Sun 1000-1300; in the Palacio de Gobierno some rooms may be visited Mon-Fri 0930-1330.

Excursions

Hot springs at Ojocaliente, Balneario de Lourdes and Gogorrón. **Balneario de Lourdes** (hotel, clean, nice atmosphere, small pool, B) is S of San Luis Potosí. **Gogorrón** is clean and relaxing, with pools, hot tubs, picnic grounds and campsites. There is a restaurant. A day trip or overnight camp-out is recommended in the lightly wooded hills and meadows near the microwave station (at 2,600m) 40 km E of San Luis Potosí: go 35 km along the Tampico highway and continue up 5 km of cobblestone road to the station. Good views and flora.

Local festivals

In the second fortnight of August.

Local information

● **Accommodation**

Many hotels between the railway station and the cathedral.

A1 *Panorama*, Av Venustiano Carranza 315, T 121777, F 124591; **A3** *María Cristina*, Juan Sarabia 110, Altos, T 129408, F 186417, with swimming pool on roof, modern, clean, with restaurant, good value.

C *Nápoles*, Juan Sarabia 120, T 128418, F 142104, good restaurant attached, rec.

D *Jardín*, Los Bravo 530, T 123152, good, restaurant rec; **D** *Nacional*, Manuel José Othon, on the Alameda, 1 block from train station, with bath, cheaper without, basic; **D** *Progreso*, Aldama 415, T 120366, dark, rather seedy; **D** *Universidad*, Universidad 1435, between train and bus station, clean, friendly, hot showers.

E *El Principal*, Juan Sarabia opp *María Cristina*, with bath, OK, loud TV in hall; **E** *Gran*, Bravo 235, F without bath, hot water, friendly but basic, dirty.

Youth hostel: Diagonal Sur, on the SW side of the Glorieta Juárez, 5 mins' walk from central bus station, F, CP 78000, T 181617.

NB For motorists driving into the centre, parking is very difficult. There is an *estacionamiento* nr the police station on Eje Vial, US$1 for first hour, US$0.65 for each subsequent hour.

Motels: all along Highway 57: **L3** *Hostal del Quijote*, Km 420, T 181312, F 185105, 5-star, convention facilities, 6 km S on the San Luis Potosí-Mexico City highway, one of the best in Mexico; **A3** *Cactus*, T 121871; **A3** *Santa Fe*, T 125109; all with pools. Also **A1** *Tuna* (Best Western), Highway 80, nr exit to Guadalajara, T 131207, F 111415, parking, pool, restaurant and bar, nr University campus; **C** *Mansión Los Arcos*, a few kilometres S of San Luis Potosí, signposted, with restaurant and safe parking.

● **Places to eat**

Los Molinos, in *Hostal del Quijote*, excellent well-served food; *Tokio*, Los Bravo 510, excellent *comida*. *El Girasol*, Guerrero 345, vegetarian; good cafetería at bus station. *Café Florida*, Juan Sarabia 230; many other reasonably-priced eating places at western end of Alameda Juan Sarabia. *Café Progreso*, Aldama, next to hotel of same name, good coffee, cheap food, clean toilets.

Health food store: 5 de Mayo 325, fairly limited.

● **Airline offices**
Aeromar, T 77936; AeroMéxico, T 91-800-
36202; Mexicana, T 78836; United, T 91-800-
00307 (English), 800-426-5561 (Spanish).

● **Post & telecommunications**
Post Office: Morelos y González Ortega.

● **Shopping**
Local sweets and craftwork at Plaza del Carmen
325, Los Bravo 546 and Escobedo 1030. The
famous local painter, Vicente Guerrero, lives in
a modest neighbourhood at Plata 407, Colonia
Morales (T 38057) where he also has his studio.

Markets: head N on Hidalgo and you come to
Mercado Hidalgo, then Mercado República, and
Mercado 16 de Septiembre. 3-storey hypermar-
ket, *Chalita*, on Jardín San Juan de Dios between
Av Alavaro Obregón and Los Bravo.

● **Tourist offices**
Dirección Estatal de Turismo, Carranza 325;
Coordinación Regional de Turismo, Jardín
Guerrero 14 (Plaza San Francisco), both helpful.

● **Transport**
Air The airport (SLP) is nearly 6 km from the
centre. Flights to San Antonio in Texas. Many daily
to Mexico City, also flights to Aguascalientes,
Colima, Durango, Guadalajara, Monclova, Monterrey, Puerto Vallarta, Tampico and Tijuana.

Trains To **Querétaro**, US$4 1st class, US$2.35
2nd, supposed to leave at 1005 but arrives full
and late from Nuevo Laredo; to **Mexico City**,
10-11 hrs, US$12 *primera preferente*, sleepers
from US$34 (6¼ hrs on Regiomontano, leaves
0345, arrives Mexico City 1000), to **San Miguel
de Allende**, 3-4 hrs.

Buses Bus station on outskirts of town 1½ km
from centre. Bus to centre US$0.20. Flecha
Amarilla to **Querétaro**, US$7, 2 hrs, US$13.25
(ETN luxury service) (88 km of 4-lane highway
have been built N of Querétaro, about half the
way, and 40 km have also been completed to
the S of San Luis Potosí); to **San Miguel de
Allende**, 2nd class, daily, with Flecha Amarilla;
to **Nuevo Laredo**, US$42. To **Linares**,
US$14.80. To **Matehuala**, 2½ hrs, US$6.25,
with Estrella Blanca. To **Monterrey**, US$14.80.
To **Mexico City**, US$6.25, 5 hrs non-stop,
US$28 with ETN.

(1,021 km from border) **San Luis De La
Paz**, the junction with Route 110 leading
W to three of the most attractive towns
in Mexico: Dolores Hidalgo, Guanajuato, and San Miguel de Allende. (See

page 143-155). No one who yields to the
temptation of this detour can expect to
get back to the main route for 3 or 4 days.

POZOS

Near San Luis de la Paz is another of
Mexico's mining ghost-towns, **Pozos** (*Alt*
2,305m), once one of the most important
mining centres of Mexico. First you come
to the ruins. It's very silent and a complete
contrast to Real de Catorce. Many of the
mining shafts still remain pristine and
very deep. Drive on and you reach the
town, where several workshops have pre-
hispanic musical instruments and artefacts for show and sale, all handmade
mostly in Pozos; *Camino de Piedra* on Plaza
Zaragozo also sells CDs, T-shirts and souvenirs. Particularly helpful is the lady at *Cal-
mecac* (near the square, open Mon-Sat
1000-1900), who demonstrates how many of
the not-so-obvious instruments work. There
is a Museo Cultural (open 1000-1600) with
a modest display and workshop.

Pozos was founded in 1576 when silver
was discovered. Last century the population reached 80,000 but following the
Revolution most of the foreign (French
and Spanish) owners left and the workforce migrated to the capital. After the
1985 earthquake there, people who had
lost their homes drifted back. The men
now work in Querétaro and the women
work at home making clothes to sell in
local markets. The population has slowly
risen to 2,000. The town is very quiet and
the whole area was decreed a historical
monument in 1982. (Francesca Pagnacco,
Exeter, Devon.) There are no rooms to let.
Pozos can be reached by bus from San
Miguel de Allende (change at San Luis
de la Paz) or San José de Iturbe.

QUERETARO

(*Pop* 550,000; *State pop 1995* 1,248,844; *Alt*
1,865m) Route 57 from San Luis Potosí to
Querétaro is divided dual carriageway.
Querétaro is 215 km from the capital and
1,105 km from Eagle Pass. Because of the

altitude it can be quite cold at night. The city was founded in 1531 and the name means 'Place of Rocks' in Tarascan. It is now an important industrial centre and capital of Querétaro state, an old and beautiful city, dotted with attractive squares. (No buses in the centre.) Hidalgo's rising in 1810 was plotted here, and it was also here that Emperor Maximilian surrendered after defeat, was tried, and was shot, on 19 June 1867, on the Cerro de las Campanas (the Hill of Bells), outside the city.

La Corregidora (Doña Josefa Ortiz de Domínguez, wife of the Corregidor, or Mayor), a member of the group of plotters for independence masquerading as a society for the study of the fine arts, was able, in 1810, to get word to Father Hidalgo that their plans for revolt had been discovered. Hidalgo immediately gave the cry (*grito*) for independence. Today, the Corregidor gives the Grito from the balcony of the **Palacio Municipal** (on Plaza Independencia) every 15 Sept at 1100 (it is echoed on every civic balcony thoughout Mexico on this date). La Corregidora's home may be visited.

Places of interest

The **Santa Rosa de Viterbo** church and monastery, remodelled by Francisco Tresguerras (tours in English); his reconstruction of **Santa Clara**, one of the loveliest churches in Mexico, and that is saying much; the church and monastery of **Santa Cruz**, which served as the HQ of Maximilian and his forces (view from the bell tower); the church of **San Felipe**, now being restored for use as the Cathedral; the splendid **Palacio Federal**, once an Augustinian convent with exceptionally fine cloisters, now restored with an art gallery containing some beautiful works; the **Teatro de la República**, where Maximilian and his generals were tried, and where the Constitution of 1917 (still in force) was drafted; the **aqueduct**, built in 1726 and very impressive. Several *andadores* (pedestrian walkways) have been developed, greatly adding to the amenities

of the city. The *andadores* replace particular roads in places, eg Av 16 de Septiembre becomes Andador de la Corregidora in the centre, and then reverts to its original name. Walking tours can be arranged through the Tourist Office, daily at 1030 and 1800, 2½ hrs, in Spanish but you can ask if an English-speaking guide is available, US$1.80, rec. There are local opals, amethysts and topazes for sale; remarkable mineral specimens are shaped into spheres, eggs, mushrooms, and then polished until they shine like jewels (US$10-30, cheaper than San Juan del Río, but more expensive than Taxco). Recommended is Joyería Villalón, Andador Libertad 24a, for fine opals at good prices. City tour plus execution site and Juárez monument, excellent value, from J Guadalupe Velásquez 5, Jardines de Oro, Santa Cruz, T 21298, daily at 1130, US$12. On Sun, family excursions leave the Plaza de Armas at 1000. La Cruz market, 10 mins walk from centre is very well stocked, busy and clean.

Museums

The important and elegant **Museo Regional** is on the main plaza, known as the Plaza de Armas or as Plaza Obregón (not all its galleries are always open). It contains much material on the revolution of 1810 and the 1864-67 period (entry free).

Local festivals

There is a *feria agrícola* from 2nd week of Dec until Christmas; bull fights and cock fights. On New Year's Eve there is a special market and special performances are given in the main street.

Local information

● **Accommodation**

L3 *Mesón de la Merced*, 16 de Septiembre Ote 95, Centro, T 141498, F 145198 (in Mexico City T 514-2728/207-5666), small, elegant, restaurant with Mexican cuisine.

A1 *HolidayInn*, Av 5 de Febrero y Pino Suárez, on Highway 57, T 60202, F 168902, 5-star, restaurant, bars; also 5-star, *Antigua Hacienda Galindo*, Km 5 on road to Amealco, Apdo Postal 16, T 20050, F 20100; **A1** *Mirabel*, Constituyentes 2, T 143585, good, garage, restaurant; **A2** *Mesón de Santa Rosa*, Pasteur Sur 17, Centro, T 145623/5781, F 125522 (in Mexico City 514-2728), small-300-year old inn, tastefully modernized, good restaurant with international and Mexican cuisine; *Casa Blanca*, 4-star, Constituyentes 69 Pte, T 160102, F 160100; *Real de Minas*, Constituyentes 124, T 60444/60257, 4-star.

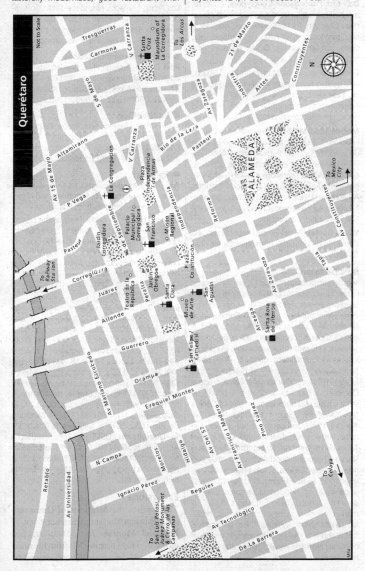

B *Corregidora*, Corregidora 138, T 140406, reasonable but noisy; **B** *Del Marqués*, Juárez Nte 104, T 20414, clean.

D *El Cid*, Prolongación Corregidora, T 23518, more of a motel, clean, good value; **D** *Plaza*, Plaza Obregón, T 21138, with bath, good location, airy, lovely inner patio, modernized, safe, clean, comfortable, rec; **D** *San Agustín*, Pino Suárez 12, T 23919, small.

E *Hidalgo*, nr Zócalo, Madero 11 Pte, T 20081, with bath, quiet, friendly, excellent value for two or more, not so for singles (English owner, Adrian Leece). On the whole, it is difficult to find good, cheap accommodation in Querétaro.

Motels: *Posada Campestre*, Madero y Circunvalación, T 162728; **A1** *Jurica*, edge of town on road to San Luis Potosí, former *hacienda*, with gardens, squash, golf-course, opulent, T 21081; **A1** *La Mansión*, 6½ km S of town, excellent dining facilities, gorgeous grounds; **A3** *Azteca*, 15 km N on road to San Luis Potosí, T 22060; **A3** *Flamingo*, on Constituyentes Pte 138, T 162093, comfortable.

Youth hostel: Av del Ejército Republicano, ex-Convento de la Cruz, **E**, running water am only, T 143050.

● **Places to eat**
Mesón Santa Rosa, Pasteur 17, in hotel of same name, good but expensive, restored colonial building; *Fonda del Refugio*, Jardín Corregidora, pretty but food is poor; *La Corregidora*, on the other side of the street, is reported as greatly superior; *Lonergan's*, Plaza de Armas, pleasant café with small art gallery, magazines in English, French and German; *Don Juan*, Jardín Corregidora, rec (*Pizza Piazza* at same location is not rec); *Flor de Querétaro*, on Plaza Obregón, Juárez Nte 5, good but pricey; on same square, *Manolo*, good *paella*; *La Cocina Mexicana*, Pino Suárez 17, opp *Hotel San Agustín*, cheap and good but rather dark, à la carte better value than *comida corrida*; *Los Tacos de mi General*, Av Reforma y Manuel G Najera, cheap and good 4-course *comida corrida*; *Arcangel*, Plaza Chica, pleasant setting, good food; *Le Bon Vivant*, Pino Suárez, cheap, good value, rec; *Ostionería Tampico*, Corregidora Nte 3, good cheap fish; *Leo's*, at La Cruz market, excellent tacos and quesadillas, popular; *La Mariposa*, A Peralta 7, excellent coffee, *tortas* and fruit shakes; *Bisquetes*, in arcade of old *Gran Hotel* on Zócalo, good value. Try local Hidalgo Pinot Noir wine.

● **Entertainment**
Corral de Comedias, Carranza 39, T 20765, an original theatre company, colonial surroundings and suppers; *JBJ Disco*, Blvd Zona Dorada, Fracc Los Arcos. Mariachis play in the Jardín Corregidora, 16 de Septiembre y Corregidora, in the evenings. The town band plays in the Jardín Obregón on Sun evening, lovely atmosphere.

● **Post & telecommunications**
Post Office: Arteaga Pte 5 (inadequate). DHL, International courier service, Blvd Zona Dorada 37, Fracc Los Arcos, T 142526 or 145256, open Mon-Fri 0900-1800, Sat 0900-1200.

● **Tourist offices**
State office, Pasteur Nte 4, on Plaza Independencia at junction with Libertad, T 121412, F 121094; federal office Av Constituyentes Ote 102 (away from centre T 138483/138511).

● **Transport**
Air There are daily flights from Guadalajara, Mexico City (except Sat), Monterrey and Morelia, and weekday flights from Puebla.

Trains The station is not far N of the centre, close to Prolongación Corregidora. División del Nte train (for Ciudad Juárez) leaves Mexico City at 0800, arrives Querétaro 1130, US$6.60 *primera preferente*; the Mexico City-Nuevo Laredo train leaves the capital at 0900, passing Querétaro 1300, 2nd class US$3.70, also *primera preferente*.

Buses Bus station SE of city, nr Estado Corregidora, Terminal A, modules 1 and 2, 1st class and plus, Terminal B, modules 3, 4 and 5, 2nd class. Bus US$0.25, fixed price taxis to centre, about US$1.25. To **Mexico City**, frequent 1st and 2nd class buses, 2½ hrs, US$7.15, several companies, US$15.50 ETN; 9 buses a day to Mexico City airport with Primera Plus; to **Nuevo Laredo**, US$51, to **San Miguel de Allende**, 1 hr, hourly with Flecha Amarilla, US$2.20. To **Guadalajara**, US$12 (US$22 ETN). To **San Juan del Río**, US$2, 30 mins, frequent. To **Tula** US$5. To **Guanajuato**, US$5.75, 2½ hrs (Flecha Amarilla), 1030, 1230, 1430; to **San Luis Potosí**, Flecha Amarilla, US$7, ETN, US$13.25, 2 hrs; to **Pachuca**, US$4.50, 4½ hrs (Estrella Blanca, poor buses).

Excursions

The road to the **Missions of Querétaro** goes through the small market town of **Ezequiel Montes** (*Pop* 5,000), reached either by a road turning NE from the main highway 21 km from Querétaro, or by

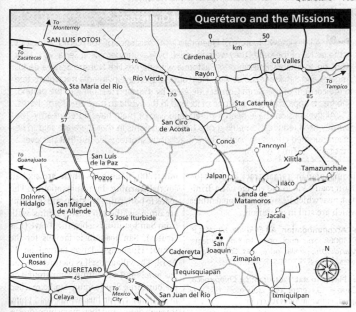

Querétaro and the Missions

Route 120 from San Juan del Río (see below). Two places of interest off the first-mentioned road are the town of Colón (14 km off the road, with 17th century Templo de Nuestra Señora de los Dolores de Soriana) and **Bernal**, 75 km from Querétaro, a centre for clothing, blankets, wall hangings and carpets made by cottage industry. Near Bernal is the remarkable **Peñón de Bernal**, a massive rocky outcrop 350m high. On the night before and the day of the Spring equinox (21 April) there is a festival held here. Local indigenous people believe the mountain is an energy point, because of its distinctive shape, and come to get energy for the coming year from the first sun of the year.

48 km from Querétaro is **San Juan del Río**, near where the best fighting bulls are raised; the town is a centre for handicrafts, and also for polishing gemstones: opals and amethysts. There is one friendly and reasonable shop: La Guadalupana, 16 de Septiembre 5; others are expensive and less friendly. Several *balnearios* in San Juan (try *Venecia*, cold water, very quiet mid-week, US$1.30).

● **Accommodation A1** *Hotel Mansión Galindo*, T 20050, restored hacienda; apparently given by Cortés to his mistress Malinche, beautiful building; **D** *Hotel Layseca*, Av Juárez 9 Ote, colonial building, large rooms, nice furniture, excellent, car parking, no restaurant; several picturesque hotels, **D**; **E** *Estancia*, good, enclosed parking.

A branch road runs NE from San Juan to the picturesque town of **Tequisquiapán**, with thermal baths, fine climate, watersports, weekend residences, expensive, good hotels, *Artesanías Bugambilia*, on the main square, recommended. Note that town is deserted from Mon to Thur and big reductions in hotel prices can be found. On the other hand, there is nothing other than the resort: a good cheap Mexican meal is hard to find. The dam near the town is worth a visit. There is a geyser, at Tecozautla, 1¼ hrs from Tequisquiapán. Between San Juan del Río and

The missions of Querétaro

🌑 A little-known feature of Querétaro is the existence of 18th century missions in the far NE of the state. They were founded by Fray Junípero de la Serra, who later went on to establish missions in California with names like Nuestra Señora de los Angeles and San Francisco de Asís. He is also said to have planted a miraculous tree in the convent of the Santa Cruz in Querétaro by thrusting his staff into the ground. The tree is apparently the only one of its kind in the world to have cruciform thorns.

All five missions have been restored, and two of them have hotels nearby. The journey itself requires something of a head for heights in that there are said to be seven hundred curves en route. There is a slightly shorter way, but that has over a thousand ... (Tim Connell)

Tequisquiapán, a small track leads off the main road 4 km to the village of La Trinidad, near which lie some of the opal mines which are still in operation.

● **Accommodation A3** *El Relox*, Morelos 8, T 30066, spa pool open to non-residents; *Maridelphi*, similar price; *Las Cavas*, Paseo Media Luna 8, T 30804, F 30671.

● **Places to eat** Restaurant *La Chiapaneca*, Carrizal 19, centre, opp craft market, is very good, reasonably priced, clean.

● **Transport Buses** San Juan del Río-Tequisquiapán US$1, 20 mins.

Beyond Tequisquiapán is **Cadereyta** (Km 75), colonial in style, with two noteworthy churches in the main square, one dedicated to St Peter, the other St Paul. The latter houses an important collection of colonial religious art. Nearby is the Casa de los Alemanes, which houses an enormous collection of cacti. There is a petrol station at Cadereyta and another at Vizarrón, a local centre for marble.

East of Route 120, there are ruins at **San Joaquín** (Km 138): Ranas and Toluquilla which have both been only partially excavated. The former receives about 200 visitors a month, the latter only 40 visitors a month. You must register upon arriving. A donation is requested. The sites have been attributed to the Toltecs and the Chichimecs. Ranas is a 30-min walk from the village and has stupendous views; Toluquilla lies 45 mins from the village (poorly marked road). Although there were only, at

most, 200 inhabitants, there are six ball courts! **Warning** Tarantulas abound. The roads to both ruins are steep and the ruins are often swathed in mist. 15 mins' walk from San Joaquín is a beautiful cave (Las Grutas). San Joaquín is famous for the annual Huapango dance festival on 15 April. The village itself is picturesque and has hotels and a beautiful campground on the outskirts. San Joaquín can be reached in 3 hrs by car or bus, windy road going through desert and then misty pine forests.

The bends really start after Vizarrón. Much of the journey from here on is through rather arid and yet dramatic terrain with gorges and panoramic views. The high point (aptly enough) is called la Puerta del Cielo, as you can actually look down on the clouds. As the road begins to descend so the vegetation becomes more tropical and the weather gets much warmer. (Jalpan is at only 700m above sea level, Concá 500). There is a petrol station at Ahuacatlán (Km 166), before Jalpan.

JALPAN

Jalpan, the first of the missions, becomes visible way below in a broad lush valley. It is the largest of the missions, which are located in valleys that spread out from here. Jalpan was the first to be founded in 1774 and has cloisters as well as the main church. The town itself is picturesque without being spoilt. It makes a good base for day trips to the other missions. Also there are pleasant walks along tree-lined river banks. There is a nice museum in town, worth a visit, open 1000-1500, 5 pesos. All the churches are distinguished by the profusion of baroque carving, their superb location and the care with which they have been conserved. They are all different and all worth the trip: **Landa de Matamoros**, 18 km E of Jalpan, **Tilaco**, 25 km beyond Landa to the E, and **Tancoyol**, 37 km to the N of Landa. (The roads are good apart from the last 15 km into Tilaco).

● **Accommodation** **D** *Posada Fray Junípero*, Ezequiel Montes 124, T 121241, opp church, with bath and TV, clean, friendly, credit cards, colonial style, pool, restaurant, good value but noisy because of bus station; **E** *Posada Aurora*, with bath, hot water, fan, clean, friendly, rec.

● **Places to eat** *Las Cazuelas*, to right of church, delicious tacos, very clean; *Las Jacarandas*, next to bus station, good *comida corrida*, reasonably priced, clean. Shrimp cocktails at stalls on plaza.

● **Transport Buses** Three buses direct from Mexico City, US$11, 6 hrs, beautiful trip. Hourly buses from Jalpan to Landa de Matamoros, US$0.50, 20 mins. Buses to Tilaco and Tancoyol involve a 40-min journey to La Lagunita, hourly, then combis (on market day, Sat) or hitchhike. To Querétaro every hour, 5 hrs, US$3.50, 2nd class, Flecha Amarilla. To Ciudad del Valle, frequent, via Matamoros and Xilitla, 2nd class, Transp Vencedor.

38 km NNW of Jalpan is **Concá**. There is a large hotel in its own grounds a few kilometres from the village and mission, again in colonial style with a pool fed by warm spring water. *Acamaya*, freshwater crayfish, is a local speciality. At the bridge of Concá nearby a hot water river flows into one with cold water. The church itself

is built on a ridge, creating a dramatic skyline when viewed from below. The village is very small. Two restaurants and a general store. Hourly bus to Concá from Jalpan, US$1.30.

It is possible to drive from Concá to San Luis Potosí, which is about 3 hrs further on. The journey to Jalpan from Querétaro takes about 6 hrs. At least 3 days should be allowed to see everything properly.

Between Jalpan and Ciudad Valles is the charming village of **Xilitla**, overlooking a lush tropical valley. Famous for the house (*El Castillo*) and garden (*Las Pozas*) of the late Edward James, born 1907, millionaire heir to the Phelps Dodge copper fortune, with connections to the British royal family. Las Pozas is 30 mins' walk from Xilitla and is fascinating with extravagant concrete structures intertwined with exuberant vegetation, waterfalls, birds and butterflies. Accommodation at **A3-B** *El Castillo*, includes breakfast, pool, fine views, run by Avery and Leonore Danzinger, T 52136, 50038, F 50055. Several smaller hotels too. At *Restaurant Los Cayos* (good view), try *enchiladas huastecas* and local coffee. Buses from Jalpan every hour, US$2.30, 2½ hrs.

QUERETARO TO MEXICO CITY

There is a 4-lane motorway (US$3 a car) from Irapuato past Querétaro to Mexico City. The Mexico City motorway passes close to Tula and Tepozotlán (see page 292). There are various country clubs along the road. In the state park of El Ocotal is a Swiss-chalet style hotel with excellent restaurant, **B**.

Ciudad Juárez to Mexico City

A ROUTE OF much historical interest: **Chihuahua** has strong links with the revolutionary and independence movements, besides being the starting point for a magnificent rail journey to the Pacific, through Tarahumara Indian country: **Zacatecas** is a mining centre. **Aguascalientes** is colonial, but of far greater colonial significance are **Guanajuato** and **San Miguel de Allende**, while **Dolores Hidalgo** is the birthplace of Mexican independence.

CIUDAD JUAREZ

(*Pop* 1,100,000; *Alt* 1,150m; *Phone code* 16) Opposite El Paso, Texas; to Mexico City: 1,866 km. Juárez and El Paso have over 1.1 million people each; the cross border industry has made Ciudad Juárez the largest *maquiladora* city in the world. Twin plant assembly and manufacturing operations now supersede tourism and agriculture in the city. **NB** El Paso is on Mountain Standard Time, which is 1 hr behind Central Standard Time and General Mexican Time.

The Spanish conquistador Cabeza de Vaca discovered the Paso del Norte on the Camino Real. The name was retained until 1888 when Porfirio Díaz renamed the city after Benito Juárez. Today four bridges link the two cities: Santa Fe, for pedestrians, and cars leaving Mexico; Stanton Street, for pedestrians and cars leaving USA; Cordova bridge (2-way traffic); and the new Zaragosa toll bridge to the E. The Río Bravo/Grande, which divides the cities and forms the border, has been canalized and is used for irrigation upstream, so often it has little or no water.

Places of interest

In Ciudad Juárez, the **Nuestra Señora de Guadalupe de El Paso del Norte** mission was the first established in the region; the building was completed in 1668. It, and the nearby **Cathedral**, are 2 blocks W of Av Juárez on 16 de Septiembre. At the junction of Av Juárez and 16 de Septiembre is the Aduana, the former customs building, now the **Museo Histórico**. In Parque Chamizal, just across the Cordova bridge, are the **Museo de Arte Prehispánica** with exhibits from each Mexican state, **Botanic Gardens** and a memorial to Benito Juárez. Continuing S down Av Lincoln, you come to the Pronaf area with the **Museo de Arte Historia**. The University Cultural Centre and the **Fonart** artisan centre, which acts as a Mexican 'shop window' is well worth it for the uninitiated tourist. There are a number of markets, the racetrack is very popular (with dog races in spring and summer), the **Plaza Monumental de Toros** (López

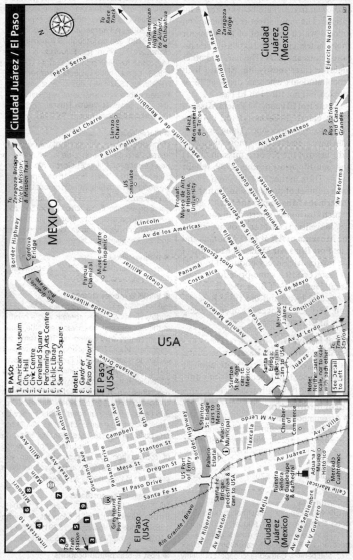

Ciudad Juárez / El Paso

EL PASO:
1. Americana Museum
2. City Hall
3. Civic Centre
4. Cleveland Square
5. Performing Arts Centre
6. Public Library
7. San Jacinto Square

Hotels:
8. Gardner
9. El Paso del Norte

MEXICO

USA

El Paso
(USA)

Ciudad
Juárez
(Mexico)

Note:
Neither part to
scale, nor to scale
with each other

See Detail
to Left

Mateos y Triunfo de la República) holds bullfights between April and Aug, and *charreadas* (rodeos) are held at various locations. The main street is Av Juárez, on or near which are most of the souvenir shops, hotels, cheap and expensive restaurants, clubs and bars. The bars and other nightlife cater mostly for El Paso high school students who can drink at 18 in Mexico, but not till 21 in El Paso.

To the E of **El Paso**, the **Ysleta Mission** is the oldest in Texas (1680), built by Franciscan monks and Tigua Indians, who have a 'reservation' (more like a suburb) nearby; the Socorro mission (1681) and San Elizario Presidio (1789, rebuilt 1877-87) are in the same direction. There are a number of museums, including the **Americana Museum** in the Civic Centre (which also houses a performing arts centre, convention centre and tourist office), the **Museum of Art** at 1211 Montana and The **Fort Bliss Air Defence Museum** of the nearby Air Base. Conducted tours of El Paso (US$10 – same price for Juárez) usually take in Fort Bliss, the University, the Scenic Drive and the Tigua Reservation. Very few services are open at weekends in El Paso.

Local festivals

2-5 May, Festival de la Raza; music, dance, cultural events. 5 May celebrations on Av Juárez. 15 Sept, Independence. June-July, Feria Juárez in Parque Chamizal.

Local information

● **Accommodation**

A1 *Calinda Quality Inn*, Calz Hermanos Escobar 3515, T 137250; *Holiday Inn Express*, Paseo Triunfo de la República 8745, T 296000, F 296020.

B *Impala*, Lerdo Nte 670, T 91160431/0491, clean, OK.

C *Continental*, Lerdo Sur 112 (downtown), T 150084, clean, TV, noisy, friendly, restaurant good; **C** *Parador Juárez*, Miguel Ahumada 615 Sur, T 159184; and many others in the upper price ranges. **F** *San Luis*, Mcal y Morelos, 1 block S of, and behind, Cathedral, cheapest but filthy and insecure; better is **D** *Correo*, Lerdo Sur 250, just across 16 de Septiembre.

In El Paso there are many places to stay, inc *Westin Paso del Norte Hotel*, with its Tiffany glass dome, black and pink marble lobby and European chandeliers (the most expensive), T 534-3000; **A3** *Ramada*, on Oregon, rec, T 544-3300; also on Oregon, **B** *International Hotel*, a/c, TV, clean, rec; **E** *Juárez*, Lerdo Nte 143, close to Stanton Street bridge, comfortable, hot water, good value; **D** *Gardner*, 311 E Franklin Av, T 532-3661, hot water, shared bath, TV and phone in room, rooms with bath available, also serves as **Youth Hostel**, US$12 for members only. Many motels.

● **Places to eat**

Many eating places either side of the border. In Juárez, *Taco Cabaña* on C de la Peña, next to *Hotel Continental*, and *El Gordo No 2*, Francisco Madero, ½ block from 16 de Septiembre, are good for tacos and burritos (about US$2-3); *Plaza Lerdo Café*, Lerdo Sur 285 at Galeana, good breakfasts; *El Saucito*, Lerdo Sur 263, popular, good breakfasts; *Florida*, Juárez 301, 2 blocks from *Hotel Impala*, clean, good food and service; plenty of Chinese restaurants.

● **Airline offices**

Aero California, T 183399; AeroMéxico, T 138719; Taesa, T 292370.

● **Banks & money changers**

In Ciudad Juárez most *cambios* are on Av Juárez and Av de las Américas; there is also a *cambio* at the bus terminal. Rates vary very little, some places charge commission on TCs; some are safer than others. The best and most convenient exchange houses are in El Paso: Valuta Corp, 301 Paisano Drive, buys and sells all foreign currencies but poor rates, wires money transfers, open 24 hrs inc holidays, commission charged on all TCs except Amex; Melek Corp, 306 Paisano Drive, not open 24 hrs, otherwise offers most of the same services as Valuta but only dollars and pesos; Loren Inc, 1611 Paisano Drive, much the same, but rates slightly worse (if coming from US immigration, when you reach Paisano Drive/Highway 62, turn E for these places). In El Paso, banks are closed on Sat.

● **Embassies & consulates**

US, López Mateos 924, Cd Juárez, T 134048. British (Honorary) Mr CR Maingot, C Fresno 185, Campestre Juárez, T 75791. Mexican, 910, E San Antonio, El Paso, T 533-4082.

● **Post & telecommunications**

Post Office: on corner of Lerdo Sur and C Ignacio de la Pena.

● **Shopping**

Tourist market on Av 16 de Septiembre, 3 blocks past *Hotel Continental* (on opp side) away from Juárez.

● **Tourist offices**

In Ciudad Juárez, on ground floor of the Presidencia (City Hall, at Malecón y Francisco Villa), on left as you cross Santa Fe bridge, T 152301/140837; in El Paso T 5340536. El Paso Tourist Office in Civic Centre Plaza, T 5340686; also at airport.

● **Transport**

Local Taxis: in Juárez, charge by zone, from US$2.75 to US$7.25.

Air Ciudad Juárez's airport, Abraham González (CJS), is 19 km S of the city (T 190731/161363); flights with AeroMéxico, Serolitoral, Taesa and/or Aero California to **Mexico City**, and, among others, Chihuahua, Culiacán, Guadalajara, Monterrey, Mazatlán, Hermosillo, La Paz, Los Mochis, Puerto Vallarta, Torreón, Tijuana and Zacatecas. El Paso's airport is nr Fort Bliss and Biggs Field military airbase with flights by American, Delta, America West Airlines and Southwest Airlines to all parts of the USA. There are also flights to El Paso from Chihuahua and Culiacán. Colectivo Ciudad Juárez airport to El Paso, or El Paso airport, US$15.50.

Trains División del Nte leaves Ciudad Juárez for **Mexico City** (1,970 km), at 2200, 36 hrs, fare one way is US$29.50 2nd class, US$53 *primera preferente*. Reverse journey leaves at 2000 from Mexico City. The route is through Chihuahua, Torreon, Zacatecas, Aguascalientes, León, Silao (for Guanajuato), Celaya and Querétaro. At 0800, Mon, Wed and Fri and train leaves Ciudad Juárez for **La Junta** (W of Ciudad Cuauhtémoc, see below, page 127), via **Nuevo Casas Grandes** and **Madera**; on Tues, Thur and Sat at 0800 a train goes as far as Madera. Journey times (very approximately): 5½ hrs to Nuevo Casas Grandes (240 km), 12 hrs to Madera (432 km) and 14 hrs to La Junta (572 km). Station in Ciudad Juárez is at Eje Vial Juan Gabriel e Insurgentes, a couple of blocks S of junction of Av Juárez and 16 de Septiembre. Information: T 122557 149717 (Nacionales de México) or 545-2247 (Amtrak in El Paso).

Road Sanborns, for insurance and information, 440 Raynolds, El Paso, T (915) 779-3538, F 772-1795, open Mon-Fri 0830-1700. AAA office: 916 Mesa Avenue, El Paso. **Buses** Terminal is at Blvd Oscar Flores 4010, T 132083, S of the centre. There is a taxi information booth which

can give you estimated fares before you approach a driver. From the terminal to centre or Santa Fe bridge, taxi fare is about US$8. If you walk from the terminal to the highway, take any bus going to the right marked *centro* for US$0.30. Shuttle bus to **El Paso** US$5, hourly, to Greyhound Terminal. From Ciudad Juárez, several bus companies run to **Chihuahua** (4 hrs, US$17.50) and on to **Mexico City** (26 hrs, eg Omnibus de Mexico, US$66, good service), via all the major cities en route, eg **Torreón** (US$27), **Zacatecas** (US$43.75), **Aguascalientes** (US$46.25), or **San Luis Potosí** (US$46.25). **Querétaro** (US$56). Services also to **Monterrey** (US$44), eg Trans del Nte, 8 a day, **Hermosillo** (US$26.50) and **Tijuana** (US$44 1st class, Caballero Azteca), **Guadalajara** (US$50), **Mazatlán** (US$53), and other Pacific coast destinations. **Express Limousine service**: El Paso-Los Angeles, US$40, El Paso-Albuquerque US$27; the El Paso office is just across the Juárez bridge at 6th and Oregon. Greyhound, El Paso, T 532-2365. **Turismos Rápidos**, 828 S El Paso, off Santa Fe Bridge, to many US destinations.

CROSSING THE BORDER

From El Paso you can get on a bus outside Gate 9 of the Greyhound terminal and pay the driver (US$5); as you cross the border he should stop and wait for your documents to be processed. On entry you are automatically given 30 days to stay in Mexico, unless you ask for longer. Trolley buses cross the border for short trips. Alternatively you can walk across (US$0.35 toll pp). Walking from Mexico to the USA costs US$0.35 (toll for cars leaving Mexico US$2.05). Border formalities are minimal, although you are likely to have your bags searched on entering the USA on foot because most pedestrians do not carry luggage. If you cross into the USA with a view to leaving the USA by plane, as a non-US citizen you must ask for an immigration card for when you do leave; you may have problems without one. Remember, also, to have your US visa if you require one. The US Embassy charges US$20 to make an enquiry so make sure you have everything you need.

There is a new border crossing at Santa Teresa, New Mexico, just W of El Paso.

For trucks and southbound travellers by car, this will avoid the congestion of Ciudad Juárez.

CIUDAD JUAREZ TO CHIHUAHUA

The road is wide, mostly flat, easy to drive, and not as interesting as the Gulf and Pacific routes. From Ciudad Juárez, for some 50 km along the Río Bravo, there is an oasis which grows cotton of an exceptionally high grade. The next 160 km of the road to Mexico City are through desert; towns en route are Salamayuca (restaurant), at Km 58; **Villa Ahumada** (Km 131, *Hotel Cactus*, T 42250; **D** *Casa Blanca*, with bath and hot water, room heater, clean, opposite train depot on main street, ½ block S of bus terminal). At Km 180 is Moctezuma (restaurant). The road leads into grazing lands and the valley of Chihuahua. The road Chihuahua-Ciudad Juárez is being made into an *autopista*; toll 30 km N of Chihuahua, US$6.30 for cars or pick-ups (the alternative is a long 2-sides-of-a-triangle detour to avoid the toll).

This is the country of the long-haired, fleet-footed Tarahumara Indians, able, it is said, to outstrip a galloping horse and to run down birds. A few Indians can be seen in Chihuahua and Nuevo Casas Grandes, mostly women and children and most, sadly, begging. Tarahumara can be seen in much less unfortunate conditions and in greater numbers in Creel and beyond, but note that the Indians are shy, living in remote ranchos rather than the towns. 12 Dec is a festival for the Tarahumara.

PALOMAS

Mexico Route 2 runs W from Ciudad Juárez, roughly parallel with the Mexico-US border. Between Juárez and Janos, at the northern end of lateral Mexico 24, is the dusty border town of **Palomas**, Chihuahua, opposite Columbus, New Mexico. The modern border facilities are open 24 hrs. Palomas itself has few attractions apart from limited duty-free shopping for liquor and pharmaceuticals, but Columbus was the site of Pancho Villa's 1916 incursion into New Mexico, which led to reprisals by the forces of American Gen John J Pershing. The Columbus Historical Museum (open daily from 1000 to 1600), 3 miles N of the border, offers exhibits on Villa's sacking and burning of Columbus.

• **Accommodation** Reasonable accommodation at **D** *Hotel Restaurant San Francisco*, also *Motel Santa Cruz Hotel Regis*. On the Columbus side, **A3** *Martha's Place* (T 531-2467), an attractive bed and breakfast, and **C** *Motel Columbus*. **Camping**: excellent, well-maintained sites at Pancho Villa State Park, opp the Columbus Historical Museum, for US$7/night, additional charge for electrical hook-up.

• **Transport** There is no public transport on the US side, but hourly buses connect Palomas with Tres Caminos, where travellers can board buses from Juárez to Nuevo Casas Grandes (see below).

JANOS

At the intersection of Mexico Route 2 and Chihuahua Route 10 to Nuevo Casas Grandes is **Janos** (*Restaurant Durango*, de facto bus station at the intersection, has good inexpensive food; several others at junction, plus **D** *Hotel Restaurant La Fuente*). The landscape between Ciudad Juárez and Nuevo Casas Grandes is quite barren and, in the winter months, it can be cold.

Near Janos are the northernmost Mennonite colonies in Mexico; numerous vendors sell Mennonite cheese, which also has a market in upscale restaurants across the border in New Mexico. The German-speaking Mennonites are very conspicuous, the men in starched overalls and the women in long dresses and leggings, their heads covered with scarves.

AGUA PRIETA

Northwest of Janos, via the border route of Mexico 2, are the border crossings of **Agua Prieta** (opposite Douglas, Arizona) and **Naco** (adjacent to its Arizona namesake and a short distance S of the historic, picturesque copper mining town of Bisbee).

Agua Prieta (*Pop* 80,000) is growing rapidly with the proliferation of *maquiladoras* on both sides of the border. If possible, avoid crossing in late afternoon, when traffic across the border can be very congested as Mexican labourers return home from Douglas.

Agua Prieta is 162 km from Janos via Route 2, which crosses the scenic Sierra San Luís, covered by dense oak-juniper woodland, to the continental divide (elevation 1,820m) at Puerto San Luís, the border between the states of Sonora and Chihuahua. There are outstanding views of the sprawling rangelands to the W. Southbound motorists from the United States must present their papers to Mexican customs at La Joya, a lonely outpost 70 km NW of Janos.

● **Accommodation** Unusually for Mexican cities, Agua Prieta lacks true budget accommodation in the centre and nr the border; the main alternatives are **B** *Motel La Hacienda*, 2 blocks from the border; **B** *Hotel El Greco*; **B** *Motel Ruiz*; in Naco, the only formal accommodation is **D** *Motel Colonial*, which is often full, but the manager may tolerate a night's auto camping within the motel compound. Accommodation is cheaper in Douglas, on the Arizona side: **C** *Border Motel*; the venerable **B** *Gadsden Hotel*, a registered historical landmark, has been used as a location for Western films. **C** *Motel 6*. Rates are higher in Bisbee, a very popular tourist destination, but the town offers good value for money. **Camping**: RV parks on the Arizona side charge about US$10/night for vehicle, US$5 for tent camping: *Double Adobe Trailer Park* off Highway 80, *Copper Horse Shoe R V Park* on Highway 666.

● **Places to eat** In Agua Prieta, *El Pollo Loco*, nr the plaza, for roasted chicken; in Naco, *Restaurant Juárez*. On the Douglas side, restaurant at *Hotel Gadsden* is good and reasonable, but the best selection in the area is at Bisbee, 10 miles N of Naco.

● **Useful services** On the Douglas side, the Chamber of Commerce (T 364-2477) at 1125 Pan American has good information on Mexico as well as Arizona, with a wealth of maps (inc Agua Prieta) and brochures. Librolandia del Centro, a bookstore, has a good selection of material on local and regional history.

● **Transport** Buses from Agua Prieta, Tres Estrellas and Transportes Nte de Sonora offer service to **Ciudad Juárez** (4 daily, US$13.25), **Chihuahua** (9 daily, US$20), **Nogales** (4 daily, US$8.25), **Tijuana** (6 daily, US$33), **Hermosillo** (8 daily, US$13.25), **Guaymas** (4 daily, US$18), **Navojoa** (3 daily, US$24.75), **Los Mochis** (4 daily, US$30), and **Mexico City** (daily, US$82.50). Bridgewater Transport (T 364-2233) connects Douglas with Tucson twice daily (US$30), with connections to Los Angeles (US$92, but more expensive if purchased in California).

CROSSING THE BORDER

Both the Agua Prieta and Naco ports of entry are open 24 hrs. There is no public transport other than taxi to Naco, Arizona, but there are buses from Naco, Sonora, to Agua Prieta and Nogales. Mexican automobile insurance is not available in Naco, Sonora, but readily obtained at Douglas. Mexican consulate in Douglas, helpful.

WARNING Drug smuggling, auto theft, and other illegal activities are common knowledge along the southeastern Arizona border. Watch your belongings and money closely even during 'routine' searches by US Customs officials, whose reputation has been sullied by reports of corruption in recent years. Moreover, the police in Agua Prieta have a bad reputation for stopping drivers for no good reason and trying to extract bribes on the threat of jail.

CASAS GRANDES

The archaeological site of Casas Grandes, or Paquimé, can be reached from Chihuahua, Ciudad Juárez or Agua Prieta. Nuevo Casas Grandes is a town built around the railway; it is very dusty when dry, the wind blowing clouds of dust down the streets, and when wet the main street becomes a river. There is not much to do, but there are cinemas which show US and Mexican films (don't be put off by people standing at the back, there are usually seats free).

Casas Grandes/Paquimé was probably a trading centre, which reached its peak between 1210 and 1261 AD. The city was destroyed by fire in 1340. Its commercial influence is said to have reached as far as

Colorado in the N and into southern Mexico. At its height, it had multi-storeyed buildings; the niches that held the beams for the upper floors are still visible in some buildings. A water system, also visible, carried hot water from thermal springs to the N, and acted as drainage. Most of the buildings are of a type of adobe, but some are faced with stone. You can see a ball court and various plazas among the buildings. The site is well-tended. Significant archaeological reconstruction is under way at Casas Grandes. About 2 hrs is sufficient to see it all; open 1000-1700, entry US$3.50. To get there take a yellow bus from outside the furniture shop at 16 de Septiembre y Constitución Pte in Nuevo Casas Grandes, US$0.20, 15 mins. From the square in Casas Grandes village either take C Constitución S out of the square past the school, walk to the end of the road, cross a gulley, then straight on for a bit, turn right and you will see the site, or take Av Juárez W out of the square and turn left at the sign to Paquimé, 1 km.

Paquimé ceramics, copying the original patterns, either black on black, or beige with intricate red and grey designs, are made in the village of Mata Ortiz, 21 km from Nuevo Casas Grandes. Either take a bus from C Jesus Urueta, W of the railway track, at 1630 (return at 0800), US$2.40, take the train which is supposed to pass through Nuevo Casas Grandes on Tues, Thur and Sat at 1300, arriving 1400 (return Mon, Wed, Fri 1225), or hitch.

Local information
● Accommodation
Accommodation can only be found in Nuevo Casas Grandes: **B** *Motel Hacienda*, Av Juárez 2603, T 41046/7/8/9/50, the best, sometimes has Paquimé ceramics on sale; **C** *California*, Constitución Pte 209, reasonable, takes credit cards, hot water takes a while to come through; **C** *Motel Piñón*, Juárez 605, T 41066, helpful; **C** *Paquimé*, with fan and a/c, clean, large, pleasant, rec; **C** *Parque*, Av Juárez, just past main square heading N, with TV and phone; **D** *Juárez*, A Obregón 110, between bus companies, supposedly hot water, some English

spoken, friendly, safe parking, basic bathroom (take your key with you when you go out); *Suites Victoria*, Guadalupe Victoria, 1 block W of Constitución Pte, off 5 de Mayo.

● Places to eat
Café de la Esquina, 5 de Mayo y A Obregón, nr bus offices, cheap, clean, friendly, popular; *Tacos El Brasero*, Obregón opp *Hotel Juárez*, open 24 hrs; *Dinno's Pizza*, Minerva y Constitución Ote, fair, takes credit cards, opp Ciné Variedades; *Alameda*, next to *Hotel California*, for breakfast and *comida corrida*, average; *Denni's*, Juárez y Jesús Urueta, mostly steaks, quite good, good service.

● Banks & money changers
Banks on 5 de Mayo and Constitución Ote; *Casa de Cambio California* next to hotel of that name.

● Post & telecommunications
Long-distance telephone: at Rivera bus office, on Alvaro Obregón.

● Transport
Trains The station, between Constitución Pte and Ote (as is the railway), is at 1,454m, 240 km from Ciudad Juárez. In theory trains call daily, except Sun, en route to Ciudad Juárez and La Junta or Madera.

Buses All bus offices are on Alvaro Obregón. Several daily to **Ciudad Juárez**, 3 companies, 4 hrs, US$10.60; 3 companies to **Chihuahua**, 5 hrs, US$12.10; Omnibús de México to **Mexico City** once a day via El Sueco, once via Cuauhtémoc, also to **Monterrey**; Chihuahua Madera to **Cuauhtémoc** and **Madera**; Caballero Azteca to **Agua Prieta** (3 a day), **Hermosillo**, **Tijuana** and **Nogales** (once each).

From Chihuahua, the turn-off from the road to Ciudad Juárez is near El Sueco (157 km from Chihuahua, 219 from Ciudad Juárez); from here State Highway 10 to Nuevo Casas Grandes (198 km) passes through Constitución (bus stop), Flores Magón (hotel) and Buenaventura (114 km, a pleasant-looking place). About 100 km from El Sueco a brief section of 'camino sinuoso' affords views of the plains you have just crossed; from Buenaventura the road passes through different valleys, of varying degrees of fertility, the most productive being Buenaventura itself and Lagunillas. Buses from Chihuahua to

Nuevo Casas Grandes go either via El Sueco or via Ciudad Cuauhtémoc (see below) and Madera (the Sierra route, see also below), which has some pleasant landscapes (if heading S from the USA, via Casas Grandes, you can continue on the Sierra route to Creel on the Chihuahua-Los Mochis railway).

MADERA

(*Pop* 13,000; *Alt* 2,100m) **Madera** is in the Sierra Madre, surrounded by rugged mountain scenery. It is high enough to receive snow in winter (rainy season Sept-Mar, best time to visit May-Aug). The region around Madera has ample scope for tourism: archaeological sites, birdwatching, hunting, fine landscapes and good infrastructure. It can be reached by 2nd class train from Nuevo Casas Grandes. By road from the N is via Buenaventura and Gómez Farías. From Chihuahua either turn off Ruta 16 at La Junta (see below) and take Ruta 37 via Guerrero (*Posada Alicia*; Pemex magna sin), or turn off at Ciudad Cuauhtémoc onto Ruta 65 via Alvaro Obregón (restaurants, Pemex magna sin), Bachiniva (restaurants, Pemex) and Soto Maynes (Pemex magna sin). Before Gómez Farías, turn W onto Ruta 180; this takes you through Bavícora, site of George Hearst's ranch (Pemex, nova only) and on to Madera.

Local information
● Accommodation
A3 *Motel Real del Bosque*, Carretera Chihuahua, Barrio Americano, on main road into town, T (157) 20066, F 20538, 3-star, clean, friendly, parking, bar, disco, restaurant, English spoken, director Angel Leal Estrada is also president of local Comité Pro Turismo, very enthusiastic, tours organized from the hotel (see **Excursions** below); he is planning to build a backpackers' hostel.

C *Parador de la Sierra*, C 3 y Independencia, T 20277, clean, heating, discount for more than 1 night, off-street parking, restaurant; **C** *María*, C 5 y 5 de Mayo, cheaper rooms available, heating, clean, limited parking, restaurant open 24 hrs, good; **C** *Mirmay*, C 3 y Guerrero, T 20944, next to *Café Los Lobos*, not too clean.

F *Motel Maras*, C5 (one block S of *Mirmay*), hot water, noisy, clean apart from dusty rooms.

● Places to eat
Several restaurants in town.

● Banks & money changers
Banamex, only place for Visa and Mastercard advances, **Bancomer** and **Banrural** will change dollars (possibly TCs).

● Transport
Local Madera has an **airstrip**; call *Motel Real del Bosque* to arrange a landing (Unicom 122.8 and ADF 1300 service). Estrella Blanca **bus** (T 20431) to/from Chihuahua every hour, takes 5 hrs, bus stop on C 5.

Madera's prosperous past

During the Porfirio Díaz era, two US financiers were granted rights to exploit the area: George Hearst (of the famous newspaper family), who farmed cattle between Madera and Gómez Farias, and William Green. In exchange for building the railway, which now runs between Chihuahua, Nuevo Casas Grandes and Ciudad Juárez, Green was allowed to extract timber from the forests. He wished to extend the railway to Cananea (northern Sonora), to take lumber to the mine he owned there, but this section was never built. In 1904 the first saw mills were in operation. The town developed, with a 66-room hotel, a casino and the largest wooden box-making factory in the world at the time. Green went bankrupt in 1908. During the Revolution, the factories casting iron for the railway turned to making cannon; Pancho Villa ordered two and also permitted the workers to take over management of the factories since the US managers had left. Eventually the North Americans returned following the workers' lack of success.
(Francesca Pagnacco)

Excursions

Madera is on an important waterfowl migratory route, with white-fronted, blue and snow geese, mallard, pintail, teal, widgeon and redhead duck, and sandhill crane passing through. This does mean that it has become a popular centre for shooting (season mid-Nov-Feb), but bird-watching expeditions can be arranged at *Motel Real del Bosque*.

Taking C 3 in a northerly direction out of town, the road soon becomes dirt (stony, potholed, good suspension advisable). It parallels the railway to Casas Grandes, passing through pine forest and cultivated fields and heads into the plateau of the Sierra Madre. 12 km from town, after a signpost to Nuevo Madera, is a lake at Presa Penitentes, to the right. At the water's edge, the clockwise track takes you to the far side where you can fish for rainbow trout. Anticlockwise takes you to a picnic area with restaurant and toilets, children's play area and volley ball pitch. Camping possible; the restaurant is always staffed. Behind the dammed part of the lake is a rainbow trout farm, open 0900-1700 every day, fish can be bought. Waterskiing on the lake (4 hrs' tour from *Motel Real del Bosque*, US$30, min 4 people, alternatively hitch-hiking is possible). Another trout farm and trailer park is under construction near Nuevo Madera.

Back on the main road, you come to a signed turning right to Las Varas, which leads to Casas Grandes (there is another, unsigned turning to Las Varas further on). Straight on is El Salto, a 35m waterfall, best seen after the spring thaw (Mar-April). The fall is along a track to the left; to see it you have to walk round the rim of a little canyon. It is possible to hike down to the river below (about 1 hr). Ask at the house on the track to the fall if you want to camp (no facilities). 4 km from the turn-off to El Salto is the entrance to **Cuarenta (40) Casas**, with a visitors' hut (1 hr 15 mins from Madera). 40 Casas is a series of cave dwellings, inhabited

originally by Indians of the Paquimé culture. Some of the houses have the palet-shaped windows/doorways also seen at Casas Grandes (called here La Cueva de las Ventanas); some are of 2 storeys. There is a good view of the cave houses from the visitors' hut. A trail descends to the river before climbing steeply to the cave, 45 mins-1 hr one way. 40 Casas is open 0900-1600 every day (except 16 Sept), entry free. Camping is possible only when personnel are staying the night, no facilities other than water. (Tour from *Motel Real del Bosque*, 6 hrs, US$65, min 4 people, alternatively hitchhiking is possible.)

South of Madera is the **Misión Tres Ojitos**, where the Spanish priest, Padre Espronceda, makes ham. Fiesta 7 Oct, Virgen del Rosario, with rodeos and other activities. Take the road to La Junta from Madera and at the signpost, turn off right. On the dirt road, take the left fork through the village. Go past the church and on the right the Mission is signed (10 km from Madera).

In Madera there is a sign indicating Zona Arqueológica Huapoca, going W on Independencia. At Km 13 on this good dirt road is Lago Campo 3, shallow and marshy, with wildlife. Camping and picnicing possible. (The lake's name comes from a logging camp.) At 18 km from town you reach 2,500m, with stunning views of the Sierra Madre. Plenty of birdlife can be seen from the road. The Huapoca Ranch, a US-owned experimental horse-breeding centre at Km 30, does not take visitors. At Km 41 is the entrance to the Zona Arqueológica **Anasazi**, which contains the Nido del Aguila cave dwellings and the Cueva del Serpiente. The 2 km road to the site is terrible; about 300m are impassable (you have to find somewhere to park before the 'estacionamiento'). There is no path to the Nido del Aguila, but if you keep to the left slope from the 'car park', you reach first a mirador, then the cave around a big bluff. There is another mirador further on. A guide is necessary. On the righthand hillcrest

from the 'car park' is the Cueva del Serpiente: a path leads to a sign on a tree,
behind which to the left is a crevasse. 10
mins into the crevasse (steep in places) is
a set of three chambers and the remains
of two others. Follow round on a narrow
ledge to 11 more complete chambers and
three ruins. All the rooms (covered in
graffiti, unfortunately) can be entered;
the rows of rooms interconnect and have
the typical palet-shaped windows. A
strong torch is useful for locating the
inner rooms. If you jump up and down,
the ground sounds hollow, suggesting
that there are more rooms below. The
views are magnificent.

At Km 44 is a brightly-painted house
where, in Nov-Dec, they sell cheese. The
beautiful valley of the Río Huapoca becomes visible at Km 51. A sign to Aguas
Termales at Km 53 leads on to another
terrible track, to hot springs with a small
pool under a waterfall and a cooler section
nearer the river (2 toilets). The main road
then crosses the Puente Huapoca suspension bridge, built in 1950 (a tour this far,
including lunch, fishing, and swimming
in the rapids, from *Motel Real del Bosque*,
10 hrs, costs US$65). **NB** In this area,
close any gates that you go through; farm
ers graze cows and horses on the land,
which is private.

58 km from Madera is the turn-off to
Cueva Grande. A clear trail leads in 15
mins to a waterfall, behind which is the
50m cave with two complete 2-storey
houses and some ruins. Visitors can climb
to the upper storey and in the ruins see
exactly how the constructions were made.
Behind the house on the right is a circular
trough which was used to store grain. The
cave was inhabited from 1060 AD. There
are rock pools for swimming by the fall
(best Mar-April) and it is possible, but
difficult, to climb to the head of the fall.
At the car park you can camp or have a
barbecue (but remember if lighting a fire
to encircle it with stones; forest fires are
a real danger).

OJINAGA TO CHIHUAHUA

Chihuahua may also be reached from the
border at **Ojinaga**: this route is recommended not only for the ease of crossing
(it is used only by cattle ranchers, no hassles), but also for the spectacular scenery
either side of the border.

From Interstate 10 (San Antonio-El
Paso), turn SW after Fort Stockton on
Highway 67. This goes to Alpine, 67
miles, no gas en route, where there are 8
motels, most on Highway 90. From Alpine it is 26 miles to Marfa, where the film
'Giant' was made in 1955 with James
Dean, Elizabeth Taylor, Rock Hudson. In
Motel El Paisano there are signed photos
of the film crew on display, T 915-729-
3145; 2 other motels. 9 miles E of Marfa
on Highway 90 is a viewing point for the
Marfa 'Ghost Lights', an unexplained
natural phenomenon. At Marfa Highway
67 head S 60 miles to **Presidio**. On the
way, look out for two bizarre rock formations, a kneeling elephant with its
back to the road, and a profile of Abraham Lincoln. 20 miles from Marfa,
Shafter is passed, a silver mining ghost
town; no gas on this stretch. In Presidio
(*Pop* 3,500) is **C** *Motel Siesta*, clean, TV,
pool; **B** *Three Palms Inn*, with bath, a/c,
clean, friendly, takes credit cards, pool,
open 0700-2200; *Rose's Café*, opposite,
has good meals for US$6, open 0600-
2130, try the 'hot chocolate', good
breakfasts; 2 other restaurants. Also
bank, post office (*Presidio Information
Center* next door, T 915-229-4478, 0900-
1800), fuel, shops. Southeast of Presidio
is Big Bend National Park; to the NW is
Pinto Canyon.

Crossing the border

Follow signs to Ojinaga; pass US immigration on left (if you need to, surrender US
visa waiver form here). On the Mexican
side, a guard will check your passport.
Those with vehicles then park before doing paperwork. Boys selling chiclets will
look after your car/bike, but you can see it
through the office windows. There are

separate desks for personal and vehicle papers. Photocopying can be done for US$1. Get insurance before Presidio, no one sells it there, but you could ask Stella McKeel Agency, T (915) 229-3221/5. Full details of entry requirement for drivers is given in **Information for travellers**, page 528. The border is open 24 hrs.

Leaving Mexico, note that the bus station is 2 km from the border. Make sure all your papers are stamped correctly.

Local festivals
1-4 June.

Local information
● **Accommodation**
In Ojinaga: 5 hotels in all, inc **D** *Armendariz*, Zaragoza nr Zócalo, T 31198/32241, clean, safe parking; *Casa de Huéspedes*. Cheaper to stay in Ojinaga than Presidio.

● **Places to eat**
Cheap meals at *Lonchería Avenida* opp bus station.

● **Banks & money changers**
Bancomer on Zócalo, changes TCs, no commission; opp is *Casa de Cambio Allende*, cash only, poorer rates.

● **Transport**
Local Daily buses to/from Chihuahua, US$6; also daily train service.

42 km from Ojinaga on Route 16 towards Chihuahua is **El Peguis**, overlooking an extraordinary canyon. Also here is *garita*, where vehicle papers are checked (in the middle of nowhere). A further 46 km is **Coyame**, a village with caves 1 km away; ask for a guide (tourist complex, thermal springs, *balneario*, no hotel). Pemex with magna sin in Coyame. The road continues in good condition SW, with no fuel stations until **Aldama**, 26 km from Chihuahua. This pleasant town has tree-lined avenues, a shady central square and a church (1876) of pink sandstone (hotels, 2 motels on road to Chihuahua, restaurant *Campestre* opposite the motels, clean, friendly). After Aldama the traffic increases on the way to the state capital.

CHIHUAHUA

(*Pop* 800,000; *State pop 1995* 2,792,989; *Alt* 1,420m; *Phone code* 14) Capital of Chihuahua state; centre of a mining and cattle area (375 km from the border, 1,479 km from the capital). It is mostly a modern and rather rundown industrial city, but has strong historical connections, especially with the Mexican Revolution. Pancho Villa operated in the country around, and once captured the city by disguising his men as peasants going to market. Summer temperatures often reach 40°C but be prepared for ice at night as late as November. Rain falls from July to September. The local hairless small dog has a constant body temperature of 40°C (104°F), the world's only authentic 'hot dog'.

Places of interest
There are also associations with the last days of Padre Hidalgo: the old tower of the **Capilla Real** in which he awaited his execution is now in the **Palacio Federal** (Libertad y Guerrero). The dungeon (calabozo) is quite unremarkable and the Palacio itself is very neglected. The **Palacio de Gobierno**, on the other hand, is in fine condition, with a dramatic set of murals by Aaron Piña Morales depicting Chihuahua's history. There are a number of old mansions (see **Museums** below) and the Paseo Bolívar area is pleasant. Calle Libertad is for pedestrians only from Plaza Constitución to the Palacios de Gobierno and Federal. Calle Cuarta (4a) and streets that cross it NW of Juárez are bustling with market stalls and restaurants. Worth looking at is the **Cathedral** on Plaza Constitución, begun 1717, finished 1789; its Baroque façade dates from 1738, the interior is mostly unadorned, with square columns, glass chandeliers and a carved altar piece. In the SE of the town near C Zarco are ancient aqueducts. Walk N along Ocampo and over the river for fine views of the city at sunset.

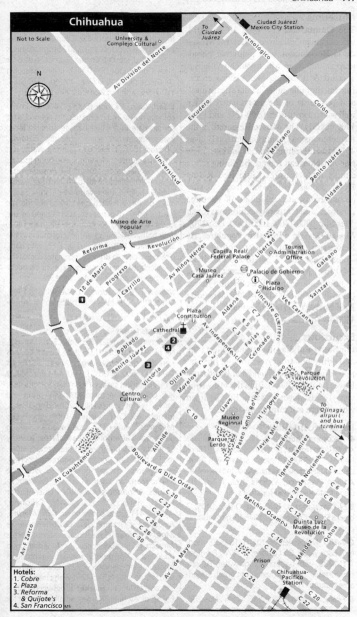

Chihuahua

Not to Scale

N

To Ciudad Juárez

Ciudad Juárez/
Mexico City Station

Tecnológico

University &
Complejo Cultural

Av División del Norte

Escudero

Colón

Universidad

El Mexicano

Benito Juárez

Aldama

Museo de Arte
Popular

Reforma

Revolución

Capilla Real/
Federal Palace

Libertad

Tourist
Administration
Office

Galeano

12 de Marzo

Progreso

J Carrillo

Av Niños Héroes

Museo
Casa Juárez

Palacio de Gobierno

Plaza
Hidalgo

Salazar

Plaza
Constitución

Aldama

Vincente Guerrero

Vet Carranza

Cathedral

Av Independencia

Farias

Coronado

Doblado

Benito Juárez

Victoria

Ojinaga

Morelos

Gómez

C 2

C 4

C 7

Parque
Revolución

N 6 avo

Centro
Cultural

C 10

Llave

Museo
Regional

Paseo Señor Bolívar

Hinojosa

Javier Mira

To
Ojinaga,
airport
and bus
terminal

Jiménez

Parque
Lerdo

Ignacio Ramírez

C 2

Boulevard G Díaz Ordaz

Allende

C 20

C 22

C 24

C 26

C 28

C 30

Av F Zarco

Av Cuauhtémoc

Melchor Ocampo

Av 20 de Noviembre

C 10

C 12

C 16

Quinta Luz/
Museo de la
Revolución

Méndez

Ochoa

C 4

C 6

C 8

Av 1 de Mayo

Prison

C 18

C 24

Chihuahua-
Pacífico
Station

C 20

C 22

Hotels:
1. Cobre
2. Plaza
3. Reforma
   & Quijote's
4. San Francisco

Museums

The **Quinta Luz** (1914), C 10 No 3014, where Pancho Villa lived, is now the **Museo de la Revolución**, with many old photographs, the car in which Pancho Villa was assasinated ("looking like a Swiss cheese from all the bullet holes"), Villa's death mask and postcards of the assassinated leader, well worth a visit, open 0900-1300 and 1500-1900 (US$1). The **Museo Regional**, in the former mansion Quinta Gameros at Bolívar 401, with interesting exhibits and extremely fine Art-Nouveau rooms: the dining room, child's room features Little Red Riding Hood scenes; bathroom, frogs playing among reeds, etc, exhibition of Paquimé ceramics, and temporary exhibitions (open Tues-Sun 0900-1300, 1600-1900, US$0.70). **Museo de Arte e Industria Populares**, Av Reforma 5 (Tarahumara art and lifestyle; shops; open Tues – Sat 0900-1300, 1600-1900, free); **Museo de Casa Juárez**, C Juárez y Quinta, house and office of Benito Juárez (Mon-Fri 0900-1500, 1600-1800). **Museo de Arte Sacro**, Libertad y Segunda, Mon-Fri 1400-1800.

Excursions

For **Santa Eulalia** silver mine, take a blue and white bus from near the old bus station. Bus is marked *Chihuahua Postillo* and leaves hourly. After visiting the mine (fine views) walk down to Santa Eulalia town where there is a mining museum.

Local information
● **Accommodation**

A1 *Palacio del Sol*, Independencia 500 y Niños Héroes, T 166000, F 159947, smart, with Torres del Sol travel agency and Número Uno car rental; **A1** *San Francisco*, Victoria 409, T 167770, *Degá* restaurant good for steaks.

B *El Campanario*, Blvd Díaz Ordaz 1405, 2 blocks SW of Cathedral, T 154545, good rooms, clean, TV, rec.

C *Balflo*, Niños Héroes 702, T 160300, modern, poor value; **C** *El Cobre*, C 10A y Progreso T 151730, with bathroom, hot water, TV, very comfortable, *Bejarano* restaurant good, reasonable laundry.

D *Plaza*, behind cathedral, C 4, No 206, T 155833, noisy, quite clean, cold shower, fair,

run down; **D** *Reforma*, C Victoria 809, T 106848, also colonial (inc rooms, some floors look unsafe), friendly, clean, fan, hot water, TV in reception, safe, parking next door for cars (US$0.25) or motorbikes in courtyard, rec; **D-E** *Cortez*, Gómez Farías 6 (nr Plaza Constitución, T 100471, clean, quiet, big courtyard, pleasant; **D** *Del Carmen*, C 10 No 4, T 157096, with hot water, a/c, OK.

E *San Juan*, Victoria 823, T 100035, in old colonial house, but rooms (repairs needed, a bit sombre) are in another part, reasonable food, water sometimes scarce, friendly; **E** *Roma*, Libertad 1015, T 102363, with hot water, run down (taxi drivers on commission bring tourists here), neither has restaurant; **E-F** *Posada Aida*, C 10 y Av Juárez, with bath and hot water, friendly, helpful, three yappy chihuahua dogs!, night porter will watch cars parked outside, rec (*Cabral* on C 10 is not rec, rooms hired by the hour); **E** *Casa de Huéspedes*, Libertad 1405, with bath, basic but clean, several others in the same street; **E** *Turista*, Juárez 817, with bath, dirty beds, clean bathroom, noisy and damp. The cheaper hotels are in C Juárez and its cross-streets; the cheapest are behind the cathedral.

Motels: **B** *Mirador*, Universidad 1309, T 132205; **C** *Nieves*, Tecnológico y Ahuehuetes, T 132516.

● **Places to eat**
The smartest and best are in the 'Zona Dorada', NE of the centre on Juárez, nr Colón, eg: *Los Parados de Tomy Vega*, Juárez 3316, *La Calesa*, Juárez y Colón, and *La Olla*, Juárez 3331, excellent steaks. *La Parilla*, Victoria 450, rec; *Quijote's*, Victoria 807, good food and value, buffet meals till 1700, dinner also, friendly; *Mi Café*, Victoria 1000, good; *Los Milagros*, Victoria 812, young people's meeting place, good atmosphere; *La Galatea*, Juárez y Segunda, restaurant within department store, rec for breakfast, cheap; *El Gallo*, on Libertad, good and cheap breakfasts; *Flor de Michoacán*, on Libertad, serves excellent licuados; *Armando's*, Aldama y V Guerrero, for snacks, refrescos, coffee; *Café Calicanto*, Aldama 411, good coffee shop; *Café Merino*, Av Juárez y Ocampo, rec; *Ostionería de la Monja*, nr main Plaza, good seafood; *Tortas Mexico*, on Independencia, nr cathedral, good breakfasts; *Kosmovita* for natural products (shop), at Independencia 725. Corn (maize) is sold on the streets, excellent with cheese, lime, salt and chile. The **market** is between C 2a y 6a, SE of Av Niños Heroes, small but good for fruit and vegetables.

● **Airline offices**

AeroMéxico, T 156303; **Lone Star Airlines,** T 800-817-1932.

● **Banks & money changers**

Bancomer on Plaza Constitución offers better rates than **Multibanco Comermex** on same square. *Casa de cambio Rachasa,* Independencia y Guadelupe Victoria, on Plaza, poorer rates, no commission on cash, 2% on TCs, open Mon-Sat 0900-2100 (also at Aldama 711); *Hernández,* Aldama 410, T 162399, Mon-Fri 0900-1400, 1600-1900, Sat 0900-1500. Exchange is available in the bus terminal, but rates are slightly better downtown.

● **Entertainment**

Cinema: on Universidad nr Post Office, shows films from the USA.

● **Laundry**

Ocampo 1412. Julián Carrillo 402.

● **Post & telecommunications**

Calle Libertad in the Palacio Federal. Also in Central Camionera. Credit card phone outside AeroMéxico office on Guadalupe Victoria, $\frac{1}{2}$ block from Plaza Constitución (towards Carranza). Main phone office on Av Universidad.

● **Shopping**

Artesanías Tarahumaras, C5 y Doblado 312, T 130627, crafts, baskets, wood carvings, jewellery.

● **Tour companies & travel agents**

Guillermo Bochman, T 30253, arranges stays at cabins above Bahuichivo, nr Copper Canyon. *Viajes Flamingo, Santa Anita Hotel,* T 91 (681) 21613, F 83393, will book train tickets in advance, no commission charged, English spoken. *Turismo Al Mar,* T 16 5950, accommodation and rail packages to Copper Canyon, 5 nights and some meals, US$500 for 2 people.

● **Tourist offices**

Ground floor of Palacio de Gobierno T 151526, F 160032, for general information, maps, pamphlets, etc, open Mon-Fri 0900-1900, Sat-Sun 0900-1400. Administration office at Departmento de Comercio y Turismo, Libertad 1300 y C 13, 10th floor, Mon-Fri 0900-1500, T 162436.

● **Transport**

Local Taxi: work on a zone system. Agree price before boarding, to avoid unpleasant surprises. **Town buses**: cost US$0.15, go everywhere, ask which one to take. **Bicycle spares**: Independencia 807, open 0900-2000.

Air Airport Gen Fierro Villalobos (CUU) on Blvd Juan Pablo II, 18 km from centre on road to Ojinaga, T 200676, airport buses collect passengers from hotels, fare US$1.10. Also minibuses. Taxi US$16 (no other transport at night). AeroMéxico or Serolitoral to Ciudad Juárez, Ciudad Obregón, Culiacán, Durango, Guadalajara, Guerrero Negro, Hermosillo, La Paz, León, Los Cabos, Los Mochis, Manzanillo, Matamoros, Mexico City, Monterrey, Tijuana and Torreón. Aeroméxico to Los Angeles daily, and Serolitoral or Lone Star Airlines to Dallas and El Paso in the USA.

Trains There are two railway stations in Chihuahua: the station for Ciudad Juárez and Mexico City is 3 km walk along Av Niños Heroes, left at Av Colón, which becomes Av Tecnológico, past the river and right along Av División Nte, T 130714. If looking for a taxi, take care of your luggage. Train División del Nte to **Mexico City**, daily at 0315, 30 hrs, no food provided, soft drinks available, fares 2nd class, US$24, US$43 *primera preferente,* book in advance if you can. **Zacatecas** about 22 hrs. División del Nte for **Ciudad Juárez** leaves 0120 (5 hrs 25 mins), US$8. The station for the 631 km Chihuahua-Pacífico railway is 1 block behind the prison (nr Av 20 de Noviembre and Blvd Díaz Ordaz – take bus marked C Rosario, or walk up Av Independencia, then right along Paseo Bolívar or Av 20 de Noviembre); in the early morning you may have to take a taxi. Taxi fare between the 2 stations US$6.65, negotiate price. Information and tickets by post: Departamento Regional de Pasajeros, Apdo Postal 46, Chihuahua, CHIH, Mexico, T 157756, F 109059.

Buses Bus terminal on Blvd Juan Pablo II, 8 km from centre on way to airport, SE of town, T 202286, 20 mins by bus to centre (US$0.30), or taxi US$4 (fixed price). There is an exchange office (beware shortchanging), cafeteria and left luggage. To **Mexico City** and intermediate destinations, frequent services with several companies: **Mexico City**, 20 hrs, US$53; **Querétaro,** US$45.50; **San Luis Potosí**, US$36.50; **Aguascalientes**, US$33.50; **Zacatecas**, US$33, 12 hrs; **Durango**, US$32; **Torreón**, US$16.50. 2nd class bus, to **Hidalgo del Parral**, US$7, 1st class US$10.50, 2$\frac{1}{2}$ hrs. To **Mazatlán**, 2 companies, US$38, 19 hrs, heart-stopping view. To **Creel**, US$11, 4-5 hrs, 9 a day 0700-1730, paved all the way; to **Nuevo Casas Grandes**, see above (note that Chihuahua-Madera buses go either via El Sueco, or via the Sierra). At busy times allow several hours to buy tickets for buses

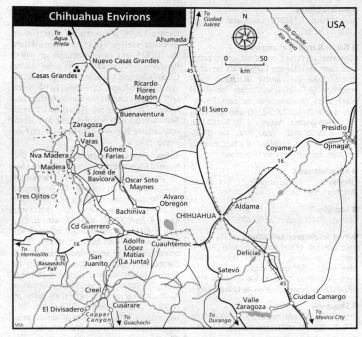

Chihuahua Environs

going N, often full as they start elsewhere: to **Ciudad Juárez**, many buses, US$17.50. To other border points: Caballero Azteca to **Tijuana**, US$55, 3 a day, or with Tres Estrellas de Oro at 2400, 1st class express, US$50, and to **Agua Prieta**, US$20, 4 a day; also to **Hermosillo**, US$31, twice. Trans del Nte to **Nuevo Laredo** at 2030, US$36; also to **Monterrey**, US$30, and **Saltillo**, US$25 (other companies also to Monterrey). To **Guadalajara**, several, US$41, inc Estrella Blanca which also goes to **Acapulco**, US$63, and **Puerto Vallarta**, US$53.

CHIHUAHUA TO LOS MOCHIS

The train journey to **Los Mochis** is very spectacular and exciting on the descent to the coast beyond Creel: book seats in advance. Sit on left hand side of carriage going to Los Mochis. The *primera especial* leaves daily at 0700, supposedly arriving at Creel at about 1225, Divisadero at 1345 and Los Mochis at 2050, local time, but delays are common (land slides and accidents may cause delays of two days and more). Reserved seat US$36, restaurant, snacks are reasonably priced, bring your own drinking water and toilet paper; fare to Creel US$15.50; double check all details as they are subject to frequent change. Do not take large amounts of cash or jewellery, there are security problems on the railway. There is food at 2-3 stations along the way (eg Divisadero). An ordinary train ('mixto') to Los Mochis leaves at 0800, but often late, tickets are not sold until the 1st class train has left (2nd class only, carriages are good, a/c and comfortable, most windows do not open, mixed reports on cleanliness, US$8.60; fare to Creel US$3.85, arrives 1400), reaching Divisadero at 1530 and Los Mochis at 2225. As the most interesting part of the journey is between Creel and Los Mochis it is better to travel from Los Mochis; that section of the line is described under Los Mochis. If wishing to see the best scenery, there is little point in taking the train Chihuahua-Creel-Chihuahua (on this stretch, the cheaper train is just as good as the *primera especial*). If planning to spend a few days in Creel, there are frequent buses Chihuahua-Creel. If taking the train from Creel to the Pacific with a view to connecting with a train to the N or S buy a ticket to Sufragio (US$17.50 in *primera especial*, US$4.30 on ordinary train, both arrive after dark, see page 487) not Los Mochis. Delays are possible in the rainy season.

A US company, DRC Rail Tours (PO Box 671107, Houston, TX 77267-1107, T 713-659-7602, or 800-659-7602) sells deluxe rail trips on The South Orient Express, a private train running through the Copper Canyon, using restored vintage carriages. From 3 to 9 day tours, fares from US$995 pp, double occupancy, to US$2,299; service does not operate beginning Jan to mid-Feb, or end-April to end-September.

West of Chihuahua are high plains, windy and sparsely populated. This is a large apple-growing zone; diesel stoves next to the trunks of some varieties provide the fruit with sufficient heat to ripen. From Chihuahua, the railway and road (Route 16, *cuota* and *libre* after Km 45, latter good) cross the Sierra of the Tarahumara Indians, who call themselves the Raramuri ('those who run fast'). They were originally cave-dwellers and nomads, but now work as day-labourers in the logging stations and have settled around the mission churches built by the Spanish in the 17th century. Soon after La Junta/López Matías, where the railway divides to Nuevo Casas Grandes and Creel, a road branches S while Route 16 continues to Hermosillo. The southerly road goes through beautiful scenery to Creel, 90 km from the turning.

CREEL

Creel (*Pop* 5,000; *Alt* 2,356m) (very cold in winter) is the commercial centre of the Tarahumara region, important for its timber and as a tourist centre. Creel is easily reached by car from El Paso or Arizona. The town is named after Enrique Creel (1854-1931), economist and entrepreneur, governor of Chihuahua state in 1907, who built the railway and planned to improve the Tarahumara's lives by establishing a colony here. His statue stands in the central square, just below the railway. Around the square are two churches (one of which broadcasts classical music in the evening), the Presidencia Municipal containing the post office (second door inside on right), the Banco Serfín and the Misión Tarahumara, which sells maps of the region (US$3.10 for topographical sheets, US$1.35 for simpler ones), description of the train ride and other good buys (such as excellent photographs of Indians, wood carvings, baskets, books). The Misión acts as a quasi-tourist office; open Mon-Sat 0900-1300. There are several souvenir shops selling Tarahumara weavings, musical instruments, pine-needle baskets, etc. Also on sale are books such as *The National Parks of NW Mexico* (also obtainable from R Fisher, PO Box 40092, Tucson, Arizona 85717). Look also for *Tarahumara of the Sierra Madre* by John Kennedy (published by AHM, ISBN 0-88295-614-0).

Local information
● **Accommodation**
Make hotel reservations in advance as not many rooms are available.

A2 *Motel Parador La Montaña*, Av López Mateos 44, T (145) 60075 F 60085 (full board available), will exchange foreign currency at reasonable rates, TV, clean, quiet, restaurant, bar, organizes excursions, safe parking; **A3** *Motel Cascada Inn*, López Mateos 49, T 60253, F 60151 (L3 for full board), clean, parking, restaurant; *Parador* and *Cascada* have live music most evenings; **A3** *Pension Creel*, Av López Mateos 61, about 1 km from the plaza and railway station, T (145) 60071, F (145) 60200, breakfast inc, shared bath, kitchen and living

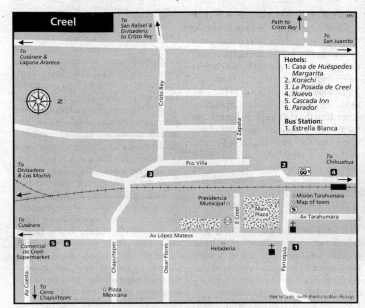

Creel

Hotels:
1. Casa de Huéspedes Margarita
2. Korachi
3. La Posada de Creel
4. Nuevo
5. Cascada Inn
6. Parador

Bus Station:
1. Estrella Blanca

room, cabins with kitchen for rent (same price), cabins renovated in 1996, very nice, dormitory annex out of town, tourist information, mountain bikes for hire and tours organized.

C *Cabañas Berti's*, Av López Mateos 31, heating, soap and towels, parking, one kitchenette, excursions; **C** *Korachi*, in cabin, **E** in room, neither helpful nor clean; **C** *Posada de Creel*, 1½ blocks S of station on opp side of the tracks, T/F (145) 60142, Apdo Postal 7, remodelled building, gas fires in rooms, very clean, **F** pp without bath, hot water, helpful, English-speaking managers, coffee served from 0630, rec.

D *Nuevo*, other side of railway from station, meals overpriced, but nice and clean, some inside rooms dark.

F pp *Casa de Huéspedes Margarita*, López Mateos 11, T 60045, between the two churches on corner of square, cheapest in dormitory rising to **D**, double with bath, breakfast and dinner, good communal meals, very popular meeting place (book in advance in high season), Margarita's reps meet arriving passengers, quite pushy, organizes tours (see below), horses can be hired (US$2.50/hr with guide, lazy horses), highly rec (if full, Margarita's sister will put you up for **E** with dinner and breakfast, enjoyable).

A few kilometres out of town, 40 mins' drive from station set in high grassland nr Cusárare waterfall, is **L** pp *Copper Canyon Sierra Lodge* (Apdo 3, 33200 Creel, Chihuahua, full board, US reservation, 2741 Paldan St, Auburn Hills, MI48326, T 800-776 3942, or T 810-340-7230, F 810-340-7212, minimum stay 3 days, closed in June, reservations cannot be made direct at the hotel), which has a minibus to collect travellers, rustic woodstoves and oil-lamps, 8-day packages available; Jesús Manuel is a guide based here, highly rec for excellent burro hiking trips.

● **Places to eat**

There are plenty of eating places in the town, on López Mateos, eg *Veronica*, good *comida corrida*, and *Estela*, also good, open 0800-2100 and on Sun. *Café El Manzano*, beside railway line, good food. Also many shops selling food (inc Mennonite cheese), but few open on Sun. *Panadería* next to *Estela* will sell to individuals. There are bars in town, but ask which are the better ones (many are for Mexican men only); beers are expensive. *Bar Plaza Mexicana*, on Chapultepec, owned by *Margarita's* (see hotels), is rec. Good ice cream shop on López Mateos between Parroquia and Oscar Flores. Next door is *Mi Café*, good food, cheap, try the apple empanadas, friendly. Water shortages are common.

● **Banks & money changers**
Banco Serfín, on the square, very friendly, open 0900-1300, changes dollars cash no commission, but commission charged on TCs (US$1 per cheque), TCs must be authorized by manager, Visa and Mastercard advances, no commission; on Sat and Sun exchange at shops, but at poor rates; some places accept dollars, also at poor rates.

● **Laundry**
Pink house opp side of tracks from square, US$3/load, 2 hrs, good, Mon-Sat 0900-2000, restricted hours on Sun. General stores also on López Mateos.

● **Post & telecommunications**
Post Office: on W side of main square, Presidencia Municipal, no sign. Long-distance phone office in *Hotel Nuevo*.

● **Tour companies & travel agents**
Tours and rentals: many people hang around the square offering tours in a variety of vehicles, or other means of transport. **Horses**: for rent at several locations, US$5/hr/horse. **Bicycle hire**, ask for Arturo at shop to left of *Margarita's*, US$3/hr, US$11/4 hrs, US$20 all day, good bikes, guided tours available. Also from *Complejo Turístico Arareko*, López Mateos, opp *Berlis*, US$5/hr, US$11/day, poor bikes. Map of town on the wall between Banco Serfín and Misión Jarahumara.

● **Transport**
Trains Schedules given above and under Los Mochis: station office is open Mon 0800-1000, 1100-1600; Tues-Fri 1000-1600, Sat 1000-1300.

Buses To Chihuahua with Estrella Blanca from 0700-1700, 9 a day, US$11, 4-5 hrs. To Guachochi, 0700, 1600, US$3. Buses also to surrounding villages. All leave from outside *Hotel Korachi*, across railway track from square. To Cusárare (see below), at 0700, US$1.75, or lift in *Margarita's* transport US$4.50, or hitchhike.

NB There is a time change between Creel (GMT − 6 hrs) and Los Mochis (GMT − 7 hrs).

Excursions

Creel is an excellent centre for trekking and horse riding. It is also a good centre for reaching several deep canyons, including that of the Río Urique, known as the

Barranca del Urique, or **del Cobre** (the Urique, or Copper Canyon − see below).

From the town footpaths lead to the Cristo Rey statue, to a viewpoint on Cerro Chapultepec and into the hills around. To see inhabited Tarahumara caves, turn right off the main road S out of town, about 5 mins (by car) after the turn off signed to San Rafael. The woman and her daughters welcome visitors. Further to the S, walk to San Ignacio mission, passing the Valle de Hongos (mushrooms), entry fee charged by local community US$3.25; continue to **Laguna Arareco** (8 km from Creel), around which one can walk (the lake is just off the Creel-Guachochi/Batopilas road), entry fee US$3.25. 20 km away, on the same road, is **Cusárare** ('place of the eagles'), with a Jesuit church (1767) painted by Indians and a 30m waterfall, entry fee US$1. To get to the falls: 100m after the junction to Cusárare there is a hotel sign on the right; turn right, pass the hotel and then the bridge, at the junction turn right, about 45 mins' walk; it is not well-signposted. There is very good hiking around Cusárare, but as the Misión in Creel does not stock the Creel/Cusárare topographical map, a guide may be necessary. Sr Reyes Ramírez and his son have been recommended for tours to the canyon, US$20 per day for 2 people, including guide and two pack donkeys. Allow 4 days to see the canyon properly, tough hiking. The canyon is hot by day and cold by night. Accommodation is extra. The American Cristóbal, at *Margarita's* has also been recommended.

Just past Laguna Arareco is an unsigned right turn onto a bumpy track which leads, in 1½ hrs in a hardy vehicle, to the top of the **Recohuata canyon**. A clear path descends in an hour or so to first a dry river, then the Río Tararécua. Follow the path along the river to where hot springs come out of the canyon's side. A pool has been made. In heavy rain many paths are flooded. The climb back up to the top also takes about an hour (loose scree on the

Creel Environs

N

To Chihuahua
La Junta

To Hermosillo
Yepachic

Cuauhtémoc

Basaseáchi Fall

San Juanito

Creel

R Conchas

Cusárare

El Divisadero
San Rafael

Copper Canyon

Bachuichivo

R Urique

Samachique
La Bufa

Batópilas

Buenavista

Satevo

R Fuerte

R Batopilas

Nachacachi

Sinforosa Canyon

Guachochi

To Los Mochis

0   50
km

MSd

path), or you can continue to other hot springs, several hours' walk, camping equipment essential (look out for the green arrows). Backpacking in the canyon is beautiful and, with a topographical map, original walks are easy to do. There are more trails than shown on maps: if the one you are on leads to a river or house it is not too difficult to find another, but many are vague and some lead to cliff edges. Do not add to the litter in the canyon.

At Cusárare, the road bifurcates. One branch heads SE to **Norogachi**, 75 km from Cusárare, with Tarahumara school and authentic costumes worn on Sun, typical fiestas. This road continues to join the more usual route to Guachochi, which is the southern fork out of Cusárare.

GUACHOCHI

156 km from Creel Guachochi has a wild west appearance, buses to Creel twice daily, US$3 (check at *Korachi Hotel* for schedule from Creel); also reached from Hidalgo del Parral, bus leaves for Parral at 0800 and 1200, now paved, but not spectacular. Hotels of questionable quality; **E** *Chaparre*, overpriced but good restaurant; **E** *Orpimel*, in same building as bus station. There is a bank. From Guachochi one can walk 4 hrs to the impressive **Barranca de Sinforosa**. Outside the town take road to the left of a wooden hut, after 6 km take another left turn just after crossing a viaduct, carry on until you come to a gate on the left side of the road before it veers off to the right. Beyond the gate there is an orchard with a tower in the middle. It seems that you have to cross several sets of barbed wire to get to the canyon. The Canyon is not visible until you reach the edge of it. Marlen Wolf and Markus Tobler of Switzerland write: "You will reach a point several hundred metres above the Río Verde where you can see an unforgettable extended system of immense canyons, grander than you can see from El Divisadero or on crossing the Barranca del Cobre. You can descend to the river on a path". This is not advisable for women alone.

The road S out of Cusárare leads eventually to Batópilas, passing a turn-off to El Tejabán in the Barranca del Urique/Cobre; **Basíhuare** ('Sash') village, surrounded by pink and white rock formations (40 km from Creel); Puente del Río Urique, spanning the Urique canyon, ideal camping climate. At the T junction Creel-Guachochi-Bufa is a small restaurant/hotel, **F** *La Casita*, very primitive and romantic. The road is paved as far as the junction but is bumpy from then on. Just after the junction is **Samachique**, where the *rari-pame* race, consisting of kicking a wooden ball in a foot-race of 241 km without rest, often takes 2-3 days and nights in September. Stranded travellers can find a room and food at the bus stop (no more than a shack) in Samachique. **Quírare**, 65 km from Creel offers sights of Batópilas canyon, of great beauty. After Quírare there is an awesome 14 km descent at La Bufa into Batópilas Canyon.

BATOPILAS

Batópilas, 120 km from Creel, is a little town of 600 inhabitants, quiet, palm-fringed, sub-tropical and delightful, hemmed in by the swirling river and the cactus-studded canyon walls. There are good parties in the Plaza at Christmas and New Year. It is a good centre for walking – the Urique canyon can be reached. Horses, pigs, goats and chickens wander freely along the cobblestone streets. Europeans arrived here in 1690. The Mina de Guadalupe was discovered in 1780 by Pedro de la Cruz. Batópilas became a thriving silver-mining centre, with mines owned by the Shepard family. Their mansion, abandoned during Pancho Villa's campaign, is now overgrown and dilapidated. Apparently, Batópilas was the second place in Mexico, after the capital, to receive electricity (Joe Bowbeer, Rio Rancho, NM). The town only has electricity from 1800 to midnight, although a new generator is expected.

● **Accommodation** The owners of the *Copper Canyon Sierra Lodge* (Creel) have opened the **L2** *Copper Canyon Riverside Lodge* (US reservations, T 800-776-3942, F 810-340-7212), same prices for full board, closed in June, renovated 19th century hacienda, with gardens, luxurious. **C** *Mari*, reservations as for *Parador de la Montaña* in Creel; **E** *Batópilas*, clean, also *Parador Batópilas*, more expensive, but not too much; **E** *Don Mario*, close to the bridge, where the bus driver stays, is popular; **E** *Chulavista*, also nr bridge at entrance to village, clean, hot water. Basic rooms also at **F** *Restaurant Clarita* (basic accommodation) and Sra Monsé, **E** – ask prices first – at plaza (she sells Tarahumara violins), rooms with gas lamps. She can give information in English (which she likes to practice on tourists). *Carmen's Youth Hostel*, basic accommodation, good food, friendly.

● **Places to eat** *Restaurant El Puente Colgante*, new, pleasant and friendly. Meals at the private house of Sra Enedina Caraveo de Hernández on the Plaza Constitución are good and cheap, large portions. In the village there are only basic supplies in shops, no bread or alcohol. The store on the corner of the plaza, *Tienda Grande*, can change TCs at a poor rate. (Bring insect repellent against locally-nicknamed 'assassin bug' or bloodsucking insect.)

● **Tour companies & travel agents** Several people in Creel offer trips to Batópilas. A rec guide is Pedro Estrada Pérez (limited English but patient), T 560079. An overnight trip for 4 (min) costs US$60 pp, plus lodging and meals, inc trip to Jesuit mission at Satevo (see below). Many hotels arrange tours to some of the places mentioned in this section; prices vary from hotel to hotel, some require a minimum number of people, some provide lunch. Some examples, to Cusárare (US$12-15), mission and falls, and Basíhuare; Recohauta hot springs (US$8 plus US$1.50 entrance); San Ignacio, Valle de Hongos and Laguna Arareco; to Basaseachi (US$58 inc lunch, min 4 from *Parador La Montaña*); Batópilas; Divisadero (US$20, min 5, from *Margarita's*). These tours are pricey, but good fun and may involve more walking or climbing than advertised. Recommended for guided tours deep into the Urique Canyon is Adventure Specialists, Inc (president Gary Ziegler), Bear Basin Ranch, Westcliffe, CO 81252 (303/783-2519, 800/621-8385, ext 648), US$700-800 for 11-day tours from El Paso, vigorous, knowledgeable.

● **Transport** Buses from Creel, Tues, Thur, and Sat at 0700, 6-10 hrs depending on weather, US$7.50, buy ticket the day before, very crowded. Tickets are sold from *Restaurant La Herradura* in the main street; the best time to try is when the bus (white with 'Batópilas' in blue on the side) stands outside from about 1225 having just arrived on its return to Creel, Mon, Wed, and Fri, leaves Batópilas at 0400 (have a torch handy as it is very dark).

The Porfirio Díaz mine above the bridge into town can be explored to about 3 km into the mountain (take torch); as you get into the mine there is the sickly, sweet smell of bat droppings, after about 1 km the air is thick with disturbed bats. **Satevo**, a 7 km walk from Batópilas along the river, a poor place with 15 houses, 2 of which sell drinks, has a 350-year-old Jesuit Mission whose dome has been re-painted and whose interior is under repair. The family next door has the key (US$ donation appreciated). The route to Satevo can be driven on a rough jeep track. The surrounding area, but not the town, is inhabited by the Tarahumaras known as Gentiles (women don't look at, or talk to, men). If you go 'off road' here, beware of drug cultivation areas. It is possible to walk in the other direction to **Cerro Colorado** and back in a day. In this tiny village some people still mine for gold, carrying the ore down to the river by donkey where it is ground up in water-powered stone mills. You can camp in the schoolyard, or on a small beach 15 mins before the town. At **Cerro Yerbanis** there are amazing views of Batópilas Canyon. With luck you can hitch to Cerro Colorado, then walk 2 hrs to Munérache, a remote village, to meet Tarahumara Indians (best to arrange a local guide through Sra Monsé on the plaza in Batópilas as drug cultivation in this part of the canyon means some areas are unsafe). A 2-3 day hike goes from Batópilas Canyon via Urique Canyon, then get a ride to Bahuichivo for a train to Creel or Las Mochis.

DIVISADERO

The Barranca del Urique/del Cobre is a long way from Creel. Apart from the access from Batópilas (see above), or from Bahuichivo (see rail description from Los Mochis), the simplest way to see the canyon is to go to **Divisadero** or *Posada Barrancas* by rough road, paved halfway from Creel by mid-1996 (hitch, no public transport), or by train. The *primera especial* leaves Creel at 1225, US$5, the ordinary train at 1320, US$1, 1½ hrs, *Posada Barrancas* is 5 mins further on, same fare. To hitch, walk along López Mateos out of Creel to the paved main road; continue for 1 km to the turning to San Rafael and wait for a lift there. Single women should only accept a ride if other women are in the vehicle and ask the women how far they are going. Return to Creel on the slow train at 1700 (or by hitching back); alternatively nip out for 10-15 mins and continue to Los Mochis, or stay overnight.

- **Accommodation At Divisadero**: A *Hotel Divisadero Barrancas*, PO Box 661, 31238 Chihuahua, T 103330, F 156575, full board and inc 2 tours (to Balancing Rock, see below, and San Luis de Majuachic). 2-3 km by road, 5 mins by train from Divisadero is **A** *Posada Barrancas Mirador*, across the tracks from the old *Posada*

Barrancas, new hotel has views from every room, full board, free lemonade on arrival and free margarita later, rec, book through *Hotel Santa Anita*, Los Mochis, T (681) 57046, F (681) 20046, tours arranged, inc hike or horseback trip to a Tarahumara village. **A** *Hotel Mansión Tarahumara* (reservations, Av Juárez 1602-A, Chihuahua, T 154721, F 165444), reached from *Posada Barrancas* station, full board, good food, lovely rooms, clean, friendly. In all cases full board is the only option because there is nowhere to buy food. Reservations are advisable. If you want the train to stop at *Posada Barrancas*, tell a railway official. To stay cheaply at Divisadero, walk 1½ km down the road, past the 'camping' sign to a hamlet of three houses. First house on left has a rustic room with earth floor and lantern with a double and a single bed, **F**. Breakfast and dinner available with the friendly Gutiérrez family. To hike into canyon, take path at the back of their house to a stone wall and stream that leads down into the canyon. Follow trails down to Tarahumara Indian dwellings and interesting mushroom-shaped rocks. Ask locals for 'piedras como hongos'. From the canyon rim, best views are in the late afternoon.

Excursions

The Balancing Rock is at the edge of the canyon; it wobbles in a stomach-churning way as you stand on it. Reached by *camioneta* from *Hotel Divisadero Barrancas*, or walk 1-2 km from Divisadero (away from Creel) and on the left you will see the wooden entrance gate. From there it is 45 mins to the rock with stops at the canyon viewing points. Guides available at hotel. Car drivers can park outside the entrance, or ask at the hotel for the key to open the gate. Also here is a marked trail for mountain bikes.

From *Posada Barrancas Mirador* you can hike down 5 mins to a Tarahumara cave dwelling, souvenirs sometimes on sale. You can also hike around the rim to the village.

The canyon can also be reached on foot from Divisadero or *Posada Barrancas*; from the former it is 6 km (walk or hitch) along the dirt road that runs beside the railway to the house of Florencio Manzinas (at the first group of houses you come to). He will hire out donkeys, give directions to the canyon (for a small tip), or will accompany you as guide (more expensive). He also provides food and accommodation in his house, or may let you camp free. From there it's a day's hike along narrow, slippery, often steep and sometimes overgrown trails into the canyon, descending from cool pine forest into gradually more sub-tropical vegetation as you approach the river and the canyon floor. At this point there are mango, orange and banana trees. Take plenty of water for the hike as, after descending the first section following a stream, you have to go over another hill before getting down to the river, which means several hours without access to water.

30 km NE of Creel is **San Juanito**, a little larger than Creel, with cobblestone streets which are less dusty than other towns in the region. It has an annual *fiesta* on 20-24 June (**C** *Motel Cobre*, very nice rooms). It is on the main road to Chihuahua, which continues to La Junta, a road and rail junction between Chihuahua and Madera, on one of the routes to Nuevo Casas Grandes and Ciudad Juárez.

East of La Junta, some 105 km W of Chihuahua, is **Ciudad Cuauhtémoc**, a town surrounded by 20 or so Mennonite villages (*campos*), self-sufficient agricultural communities (**A3** *Motel Tarahumara Inn*, corner of Allende and C 5a, T 22801/24865, comfortable, plenty of hot water, good restaurant, travel agency, safe parking, popular, worth booking ahead, recommended; **E** *Hotel del Norte*, C Reforma, basic, sometimes no hot water). The Mexican Mennonites, originally from Belgium, Holland and Germany, arrived from Canada early in the 20th century. Many are blond, blue-eyed and speak old German; they can be seen in town (also in Chihuahua and Nuevo Casas Grandes) selling cheese and vegetables and buying supplies. Bus from

Chihuahua US$3.80 every 30 mins after 0700 (hourly 0500-0700); also from Creel. Toll between Ciudad Cuauhtémoc and Chihuahua, US$5.50.

A very rough road NW from San Juanito goes 75 km to the **Basaseachi** falls, the highest single-jump waterfall in North America, 311m (low-bodied cars would be wise to take the longer route via La Junta, on the Cuauhtémoc road). They are at their best in July-September. The top of the falls are 3 km from town (2 km by dirt road, 1 km by signed trail); a better viewpoint is 3 km from the trailhead (can be driven to/from S of town). Hitching is difficult here, better to take a tour (US$16). Free camping at trailhead, no water, and near the lookout on the other side of the canyon. Hotels: **C** *Alma Rosa*, 1 km towards Hermosillo, some new rooms with fire places and oil lamps, TV, electricity 0800-2000, hot water; **E** *Nena*, 'downtown', bathroom in room, but no door, no electricity after dark, provides oil lamps; *Deny* also 'downtown', has own generator. From there the road goes on through beautiful mountains and forest to **Yepachic**, winding its way though Maicova, Yécora and **San Nicolás** into Sonora. From San Nicolás the road continues to the Pacific highway at Ciudad Obregón (it is paved from San Juanito to Hermosillo, but watch out for rock and mud slides in the rainy season on the older section in the mountains, it is heavily potholed from San Nicolás to Ciudad Obregón). The scenery is beautiful, the services in the villages limited, but you will probably not meet another tourist.

NB Unleaded fuel is only available for 320 km until 1.5 km before *Hotel Alma Rosa* (coming from Hermosillo), and the next is at La Junta, 80 km from *Alma Rosa*, on the Cd Cuauhtémoc road. It is available in Anáhuac, on Route 16 libre, near Cd Cuauhtémoc. There is also *magna sin* in Creel.

SOUTH FROM CHIHUAHUA

CIUDAD DELICIAS

The first major town is on Route 45; it is the centre of a major agricultural area. There is a Museo de Paleontología, with fossils from the Zona de Silencio (see below) and from the inland sea that covered the area 80 million years ago (Av Río Chuvíscar Norte y Círculo de la Plaza de la República). At the same address is a cultural centre, open 0900-2000, Mon-Sat, T 28513.

● **Accommodation** *Casa Grande*, Av 6 Ote 601, T 40404, 5-star; *del Norte*, Av Agricultura Nte 5, T 20200, 4-star; *Baeza*, C 2 Nte 309, T 21000, 3-star; *Delicias*, nr market, several others of similar quality nearby.

● **Shopping** **Markets**: Mercado Juárez, Av del Parque y 3 Nte, local produce and handicrafts, Mon-Sat 0900-2000, Sun 0900-1500. Mercado Morelos, C 4 Sur 600.

● **Transport** **Train Station**: 7 Av Ote, T 2-08-34. **Buses** To/from Chihuahua hourly, US$3; Omnibus de México, 6 Av y 2 C Nte, T 21020; Estrella Blanca, 6 Av Nte 300, T 21509; Rápidos Delicias, 5 Av Nte 301, T 21030.

CIUDAD CAMARGO

(Km 1,332), a small cattle town in a green valley, quiet save for its 8 days of *fiesta* for Santa Rosalía beginning on 4 Sept, when there are cockfights, horse racing and dancing. Black bass fishing at the dam lake, and warm sulphur springs 5 km away.

● **Accommodation** **B** *Siesta Inn*, S edge of town on highway. **Motel**: **D** *Victoria*, Comonfort y Jiménez, clean and cheap.

From **Ciudad Jiménez** (1,263 km from Mexico City; **B** *Motel Florido*, hot water) there are two routes to Fresnillo and Zacatecas: the Central Highway through Durango or a more direct route via Torreón (237 km from Ciudad Jiménez), passing Escalón (restaurant), **Ceballos** (**E** *Hotel San José*, basic), Yermo (restaurants) and Bermejillo (restaurant), on Route 49.

Between Escalón and Ceballos is the Zona del Silencio (the Silent Zone), a highly magnetic area where, it is claimed, electrical appliances fall silent, aircraft radar goes haywire, and so on. It inspires much interest and research but as yet no proof.

TORREON

(*Pop* 700,000; *Alt* 1,137m; *Phone code* 17)
Torreón is the principal industrial city of La Laguna cotton and wheat district. It is reported hot, polluted, without colonial atmosphere. Here is the Bolsón de Mayrán, an oasis of about 28,500 sq km which might be irrigated, but only about 2,000 sq km have been developed and much of that is stricken with drought. On the opposite side of the mostly dry Nazas River are the two towns of **Gómez Palacio** (*feria* first half of Aug) and Lerdo.

● **Accommodation** **In Torreón**: **A3** *Palacio Real*, Morelos 1280, T 60000; **A3** *Paraíso del Desierto*, Independencia y Jiménez, T 61122, resort; **A3** *Río Nazas*, highrise, very good, on Av Morelos y Treviño. **A3/D** *Posada de Sol*, Bulevar Revolucionario, opp La Unidad de Deportes sports complex, modern motel, secure parking, small restaurant, bar, hot showers, rooms range from basic, windowless, plain *cabañas* to large, North American-style rooms with TV, good value. **D** *Galicia*, Cepeda 273, good; **D** *Laguna*, Carrillo 333; **D** *Princesa*, Av Morelos nr Parque Central. Few decent places to eat in the centre. **In Gómez Palacio**: **C** *Motel La Siesta*, Av Madero 320 Nte, T 140291/142840, clean, hot water, safe parking, good; **D** *Motel La Cabaña*, hot water; **E** *Colonial*, 3 blocks S of train station, hot water, bath, only internal locks on doors, basic.

● **Transport** **Air** Torreón airport is 14.5 km from the centre. Serolitoral (T AeroMéxico 62-122989) has services to Chihuahua, Ciudad Juárez, Culiacán, Durango, El Paso (Texas), Guadalajara, Guerrero Negro, Hermosillo, León, Manzanillo, Matamoros, Mazatlán, Monterrey, Puerto Vallarta and San Antonio (Texas). Aero California (T 17-221888) flies to Ciudad Juárez, Durango, Guadalajara, Mexico City and Tijuana, and also to Los Angeles, California. AeroMéxico also flies to Mexico City. Lone Star Airlines fly to Dallas and Del Río in Texas. **Buses** Local buses on Bulevar Revolucionario go to all parts of the city. The new Torreón bus station is 5 km S of the city; if coming from the N, drivers allow you to leave the bus in the centre. There is a shuttle service between the centre and the bus station; taxis to centre operate a fixed-fare system. To **Chihuahua**, 6 hrs, US$16.50; to **Tepic**, US$30; to **Ciudad Juárez**, US$30; about 6 a day to **Durango**, 4½ hrs 2nd class. There is also an airport. Note that Gómez Palacio has its own bus station, without a shuttle to the centre. City buses outside have frequent services to all three city centres, US$0.33. When leaving either bus terminal, make sure that your bus does not stop at the other terminal; this can cause long delays.

Between Gómez Palacio and Zacatecas are **Cuencamé** (**D** *Motel la Posta*, hot water, N of town; hotel S of town, D, not recommended, damp, dirty, but has parking; just N of Cuencamé, as you turn off Ruta 49 onto Ruta 40 to Durango is *Menudo El Zancas*, 100m on left, a truckers' meal stop open 24 hrs, which is excellent, set meal US$3.45), **Río Grande** (**D** *Hotel Río*) and **Fresnillo** (**C** *Motel La Fortuna*, comfortable, hot water; **D** *Hotel Cuauhtémoc*, basic)

HIDALGO DEL PARRAL

From Ciudad Jiménez it is 77 km to (Km 1,138) **Hidalgo del Parral**, an old mining town of 100,000 people with narrow streets. The city's history is split between its mining heritage and the fact that Pancho Villa was assassinated here. In 1629, Juan Rangel de Viezma discovered 'La Negrita' the first mine in the area. Now known as 'La Prieta', it overlooks the city from the top of Cerro la Prieta. Rangel founded the town in 1631 under the name of San Juan del Parral; it was renamed Hidalgo in honour of the father of the Revolution in 1833. When Parral was founded, the population consisted of Spaniards, mestizos, black slaves from Cuba and Africa, and Indians (who became the workforce for the mining industry). The mine owners were generous benefactors to the city, leaving many beautiful buildings which still stand. On 8 September 1944, severe damage was caused by a flood. The decrease in population, either through drowning or flight, led to a recession.

Hidalgo del Parral is now a pleasant, safe, affluent city. It has a compact centre with a string of shaded plazas, many bridges over the sinuous, and often dry, Río del Parral and several churches. A one-way system operates in the centre, with pedestrian crossings marked with faded yellow lines; drivers should proceed with extreme caution and be wary of obscurely placed traffic lights.

Places of Interest

On the Plaza Principal is the **Parroquia/Templo de San José**, with a beautiful interior. Following Av Maclovio Herrera you reach **Plaza G Baca**, in which there is a statue to El Buscador de Ilusiones, a naked man panning for gold. The **cathedral** is on this square and, on the opposite side, is the **Templo San Juan de Dios** with an exuberant altar piece, painted gold. Across the road from the cathedral is the former *Hotel Hidalgo* (not in use), built in 1905 by mine owner Pedro Alvarado and given to Pancho Villa in the 1920s. Next door is **Casa Stallforth** (1908), the shop and house of a German family who supplied everything imaginable to the city. It is still a shop, with the original interior. Continuing on Maclovio Herrera, before the bridge, is **Casa Griensen**, now the Colegio Angloamericano Isaac Newton. Griensen, another German, married Alvarado's sister. Behind this house is **Casa Alvarado**, still a private residence, only for viewing from the outside. Crossing the bridge at the end of Maclovio Herrera, you come to the site of Villa's death, on the corner of Plaza Juárez. Also worth seeing is the façade of the **Teatro Hidalgo** on Plazuela Independencia. Just off Av Independencia is the **Templo de la Virgen del Rayo** (the Virgin of the Lightning). There is no tourist office in Hidalgo del Parral.

Excursions

21 km N of Parral on Route 45 is the turning for Talamantes, which is a further

The assassination of Pancho Villa

🐾 The infamous assassination of Pancho Villa took place in the town centre on 20 July 1923. Villa owned a house on Calle Zaragoza (now a shop called *Almacenes Real de Villa*, painted bright pink) and was making his way from there to the *Hotel Hidalgo*, which he also owned, when he was ambushed on Av Juárez. The house chosen by the assassins is now the Museo Pancho Villa (open Mon-Fri 0900-2000, Sat 0900-1300). Twelve of the 100 bullets fired hit Villa, who was taken immediately to the *Hotel Hidalgo*. The death mask taken there can be seen in the museum and also in the museum in Chihuahua. His funeral took place the next day and he was buried in the Panteón Municipal; his tomb is still there even though the body has been transferred to Mexico City.

11 km down a dirt road in good condition. Turn right at the square and continue 3 km out of town to the **Ojo de Talamantes**, a warm, natural pool of clear spring water, 2m deep (open daily 0900-1800, US$1). There is also a man-made swimming pool, picnic areas, changing rooms and toilets. Boats, in poor shape, can be rented, US$6/hr. Bring your own food, not much on sale. The village itself is virtually a ghost town, with the remains of what must have been great estates. No public transport runs to Talamantes.

26 km N of Parral a well-signed road leads 5 km to **Valle de Allende** (*Pop* 4,000). Originally called Valle de San Bartolomé, it was the site of the first Franciscan mission in Chihuahua, founded in the late 16th century by Fray Agustín Rodríguez. The original monastery building still stands on the main square, but it is unused (it has also been used as a *refrigeradora* to store apples). Also on the square is the Parroquia de San Bartolomé and an unsightly Pepsi plant (no longer in production), which replaced the building in which the heads of the Independence leaders Hidalgo, Allende, Aldama and Jiménez were deposited for a night on their parade around the country after their execution. The town was renamed after Allende in 1825. Valle de Allende is a beautiful little town with a shaded central square, many colonial-style houses and a number of orchards which produce fruit and walnuts. During Semana Santa there is a reenactment of Christ carrying the Cross to Calvary; all the villagers take part. The painter of the murals in the Palacio de Gobierno, Chihuahua, lives here and is setting up an art school and ceramics workshop.

Outside town is the ruined Hacienda San Gregorio, dating from the 19th century. Among the visible features is the Rebote court, in which a type of squash/rackets was played, using a hard leather bat and a stone ball wrapped in metal (there were a lot of injuries; a gentler form of Rebote is played in town using a tennis ball and bare hands). The Balneario El Trébol is open April-Sept: swimming pools for adults and children, toilets, changing rooms, entry US$1; picnic areas. Behind the Balneario you can swim or fish in the Río Allende.

● **Accommodation** Rooms to let at *Almacén La Norteña*, C Cuauhtémoc 40, basic but clean, family atmosphere. There is a scheme for private house owners to rent rooms to visitors.

● **Transport** Buses from Parral leave between 0530-2000 from the Central Camionera, returning 0625-2000, US$1, 30 mins. There is a Pemex station with magna sin.

Southwest of Parral are the mining towns of Santa Bárbara and San Francisco el Oro. **Santa Bárbara** was founded in 1567 and a Franciscan mission was set up in 1571. The church on the town square dates from this time. The Museo Comunitario El Minero, C Allende (free), has many items relating to mining and other objects. The town is quite pretty and you can walk to the mine. Buses from Parral (C Jesús García) take 30 mins, US$0.50, half hourly. The bus stops at the Mercado, from where buses go to **San Francisco el Oro** (every hour on the hour, 20 mins, US$0.30, also to Parral). The mine dominates the town; it was discovered in 1658. The town has little to offer the visitor and the church (20th century) is ugly.

Local information
● Accommodation
B *Adriana*, Colegio 2, between Plaza Principal and Plaza Baca, T 22570, F 24770, a/c, restaurant, bar, parking.

C *Acosta*, Agustín Barbachano 3, T 20221, F 29555, off Plaza Principal, quiet, parking for car or motorbike, rooftop terrace with fine view, laundry facilities, very clean, central, friendly, helpful, hot water, excellent value, rec; **C** *Moreira*, Jesús García 2, nr cathedral, unwelcoming; **C** *San José*, Santiago Méndez 5, nr Plaza Principal, with bath, safe parking, clean, central; **C** *Turista*, Plazuela Independencia 12, T 24489, F 24704, clean, nice.

D *Chihuahua*, Colón 1, off Jesús García, clean, simple; **D** *Fuentes*, nr Plaza Baca, dirty, dour rooms, restaurant has cheap *comida corrida*.

E *Margarita*, nr bus station, rec

F *Internacional*, Flores Magón, basic, friendly, parking, dirty, **F** *La Fe*, Flores Magón 57, shared bath, dirty.

● Places to eat
La Parroquia in *Hotel San José*, good value meals, inc breakfast. *Morelos*, Plazuela Morelos 22, off Plaza Principal, clean, rather expensive, open 0700-2300, Fri and Sat open 24 hrs. On Independencia: *Nutripan*, No 221, cakes, pastries and bread, inc brown; sliced brown bread at *La Patita*, No 60; wide choice of bread and cakes at *El Parralense*, off Independencia on C Los Ojitos.

● Banks & money changers
Banco Unión, in *Hotel Adriana* complex, exchange until 1200, poor rates, similarly at *Banamex* opp; good rates at *Bancomer*, Plaza Principal until 1200. Opposite is *Cambios de Oro*, no commission, good rates, open Mon-Fri 0900-1900, Sat until 1400; *Cambios Palmilla*, Maclovio Herrera 97, Plaza Baca, good rates, open daily 0900-2100. Also at Gasolinera Palmilla on road to Santa Bárbara, 3 km out of town.

● Shopping
Mercado Hidalgo on the corner of Plaza Principal, *comedores*, fruit, vegetables, shoes, etc. Boutiques on Independencia. *Centro Naturista El Vergel*, in front of Casa Alvarado, massage, physiotherapy, natural medicines, herbs and vitamins for sale, etc.

● Transport
Buses The bus station is outside the town; 20 mins' walk, taxi about US$2. To Durango, Transportes Chihuahuenses US$18, 6 hrs. To Zacatecas, Omnibuses de México, US$30, 9 hrs. To Chihuahua, frequent departures, 2½ hrs, US$7 2nd class, US$10.50 1st. Also to Guachochi (see page 124). Few bus lines start here so it is difficult to reserve seats.

ROUTES An alternative route to Parral from Chihuahua is by Ruta 24, which turns S from Ruta 16, 38 km W of Chihuahua. It is a lonely road, if shorter than the major road, and in good condition. After 50 km there is a restaurant and Pemex station with magna sin at the turning to Satevó. At Km 110 is *Centro Trailer El Chamuco*, restaurant, rooms to let (C), clean, hot water. A few kilometres further is Valle Zaragoza, lots of *comedores*, Pemex magna sin. Then nothing until Parral.

PARRAL TO DURANGO
Ruta 45, S of Parral, is in good condition all the way to Durango. Pemex magna sin is available at Villa de Nieve, just before Caunutillo. Here, 3 km down a winding road, well signed, is Pancho Villa's hacienda, with an excellent museum (give a donation to the man who opens the door). Villa was given the hacienda in exchange for promising to lay down his arms and retire to private life (28 July 1920). After Revolución the road becomes dead straight for many km. Pemex magna sin (and a federal document check) at the big cross roads for Torreón. Between Rodeo and Durango, is the 'Western landscape' beloved of Hollywood film-makers. Cinema enthusiasts can visit the Western sets of Villa del Oriente (9 km from Durango) and Chupaderos (10.5 km), both decaying (especially the latter) but smelling authentically of horse (Cía San Juan del Río buses go there or take a taxi, US$14,

which takes you to both sets with a 15-min stay at each). Also after Rodeo there are some beautiful villages along the river. 4 km off the road, at San Juan del Río, is a Pemex station with magna sin. Half-way down the side road to San Juan is a signed road to Coyotada, off which is a 4 km road to Pancho Villa's birthplace and museum (modest, a few artefacts and photos, free, donation welcome). For extensive new information on this region we are grateful to Francesca Pagnacco (Exeter, UK).

DURANGO

(*Pop* 600,000; *State pop 1995* 1,430,964; *Alt* 1,924m; *Phone code* 181) Victoria de Durango, capital of Durango state: founded in 1563 (Km 926 – some 260 km SW of Torreón). It is a pleasant city, with parks, many beautiful old buildings (see the Casa de los Condes de Suchill, now Bancomer, on 5 de Febrero), a Cathedral (1695) and a famous iron-water spring. The main street is Av 20 de Noviembre. Parque Guadiana at W edge of town, with huge eucalyptus trees, is a nice place to relax. Good views of the city from Cerro de Los Remedios; many flights of steps up to a chapel.

Excursions

Presa Victoria can be reached by bus from Durango; one can swim in the lake enclosed by the dam. Balneario La Florida on the outskirts is pleasant (take green 'Potreros' bus on C Pasteur). Take a bus from Plaza Boca Ortiz to the big *hacienda* in Ferreria, a 7 km walk along mostly deserted roads leads to the Mirador la Ventana with great views. **Santiago Papasquiaro** is 3 hrs N on Ruta 23 (on the way, in Canatlán, are Mennonite colonies), **D** *Hotel División del Norte*, Madero 35, in a former convent; the owner's husband was in Pancho Villa's División del Norte. *Restaurant Mirador*, across from the market, good food. There are a number of hot springs in the area, Hervideros is the most popular, take the bus to Herreras, then 30 mins' walk. **Tepehuanes**, 1 hr further on, is a small pleasant town with two hotels. Walk to Purísima and then to a small, spectacular canyon. A dirt road continues to **Guanacevi**, a mining town in the Sierra.

Durango is on the Coast-to-Coast Highway from Mazatlán to Matamoros. The 320 km stretch of road from Durango W to Mazatlán is through splendid mountain scenery. 60 km from Durango is El Tecuán Parque Recreativo, nice forest location, no facilities but camping free. For a day trip, go as far as **El Salto** (96 km), 7 buses a day, but go early to get ticket. The town is dirty and uninviting, but the people are very friendly (**D** *Hotel Diamante*, Fco 1 Madero, T 60700, clean, basic, friendly, no running water in room, rec).

Between Durango and Zacatecas is **Sombrerete**, a small, lively and pretty colonial mining town with 10 good churches and a superbly, partially restored Franciscan convent. (Hotels: **E** *Real de Minas*, clean, comfortable, enclosed parking; **E** *Villa de Llerena*, on main square, clean but dark rooms; *La Calera* restaurant, good).

Durango Environs

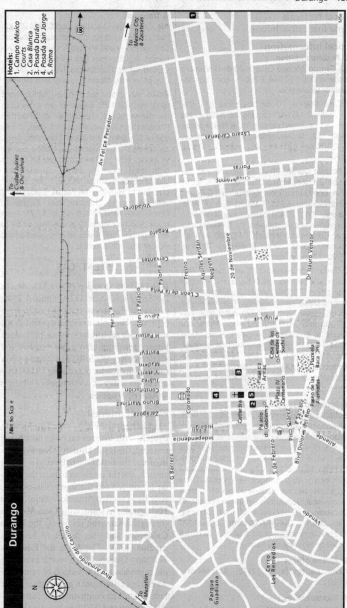

Durango

N

Hotels:
1. Campo México
   Courts
2. Casa Blanca
3. Posada Durán
4. Posada San Jorge
5. Roma

To Ciudad Juárez
& Chihuahua

To México City
& Zacatecas

Blvd Armando del Castillo

To Mazatlan

Parque
Guadiana

Cerro
Los Remedios

Av Felipe Pescador

Voladores

Regaio

Cervantes

Fresno

Aquiles Serdán

Negrete

León de la Peña

Paloma

Zarco

Gómez Palacio

Perilla

Pino

H Patoni

Pasteur

Madero

Victoria

Juárez

Constitución

Bruno Martínez

Zaragoza

Coronado

Cathedral

Independencia

Hidalgo

Palacio
d Gobierno

5 de Febrero

Pino Suárez

F Sarabia

Blvd Dolores del Río

Paseo de las Alamedas

Allende

Venazo

Lázaro Cárdenas

Porras

20 de Noviembre

Dr Isauro Venzor

Laguna

Casa de los
Condes de
Sudini

Plaza de
Armas

Plaza IV
Centenario

Plazuela
Baca Ortiz

Mile

Local festivals

Feria first half of July.

Local information

● **Accommodation**

A2 *Campo México Courts*, 20 de Noviembre extremo Ote, T 87744, F 83015, good but restaurant service poor.

B *Casa Blanca*, 20 de Noviembre 811 Pte, T 13599, F 14704, nice, big old hotel in the centre, unguarded parking lot; **B** *Fiesta Mexicana*, 20 de Noviembre y Independencia, T 121050, F 121511, very pleasant, lots of plants.

C *Posada Durán*, 20 de Noviembre 506 Pte, T 12412, colonial inn on Plaza de Armas, rec by AAA, good atmosphere, helpful staff; **C** *Reyes*, 20 de Noviembre 220, T 15050, clean; **C** *Villa*, P Juárez 206, T 23491, across roundabout from bus station, clean, pleasant, TV; **C** *Plaza Catedral*, Constitución 216 Sur, T 132480, well-appointed; *Roma*, 20 de Noviembre 705 Pte, T/F 20122, clean, comfortable.

D *Gallo*, 5 de Febrero 117, with bath, clean, motorcycle parking, rec; **D** *Karla*, P Juárez opp bus station, T 16348, small, clean, friendly but noisy; **E** *Oasis*, Zarco between 20 de Noviembre y 5 de Febrero, with bath, hot water, rooms on the top floor have a good view; *Motel Los Arcos*, nr bus station, Heroica Colegio/Militar 2204, T 72216, good restaurant; **D** *Buenos Aires*, Constitución 126 Nte, fairly clean; **D-E** *Posada San Jorge*, Constitución 102 Sur, old colonial building, patio, large rooms, friendly, parking, rec.

● **Places to eat**

Buho's Bar/Restaurant, on Zócalo, 1st floor, overlooking cathedral, reasonably-priced food, good pancakes; good breakfasts at *Café Salum*, 5 de Febrero y Progreso, nice; *Mariscos Ramírez*, in front of the market, good sea food. *La Peña*, Hidalgo 120 N, Fri night is fiesta night with local music and singing, very popular. There is a good food store on the first block of Progreso where local foodstuffs are displayed in bulk. *El Zocabón*, on 5 de Febrero, off main plaza opp Cathedral, rec. *Gorditas Gabino*, Constitución 112 Nte, very cheap, good. Also rec is *La Unica* on 20 de Noviembre y Pasteur.

● **Airline offices**

Aero California, T 77177; AeroMéxico, T 12813.

● **Tourist offices**

Hidalgo 408 Sur, helpful.

● **Transport**

Air Guadalupe Victoria Airport (DGO) is 5 km from centre. There are international flights from Chicago (Mexicana) and Los Angeles (Aero California), and domestic flights from Chihuahua, Ciudad Juárez, Guadalajara, Mazatlán, Mexico City, Monterrey, Morelia, Tijuana and Torreón.

Buses Bus station out of town: minibus No 2 to centre, US$0.25. Several buses a day cross the Sierra Madre Occidental to **Mazatlán** (Transportes Chihuahuenses, 1st class, 7 hrs, US$14.80), 0400 and 1000. This is rec if you cannot do the Los Mochis-Chihuahua journey, sit on left side. Second class buses for camera buffs stop more frequently. **Guadalajara**, US$22.25; **Chihuahua**, US$32, 10 hrs. Second class bus to **Hidalgo del Parral**, 7 hrs, US$18 with Transportes Chihuahuenses. **Zacatecas**, Omnibus de México, 4½ hrs, US$7.75. Town buses stop running early in evening, so try to arrive before dark if you wish to avoid a long walk or taxi ride to centre.

ZACATECAS

(*Pop* 150,000; *State pop 1995* 1,336,348; *Alt* 2,495m; *Phone code* 492) Founded 1548, capital of Zacatecas state (Km 636 from capital). This picturesque up-and-down mining city is built in a ravine, pink stone houses towering above one another and scattered over the hills. The largest silver mine in the world, processing 10,000 tonnes of ore a day or 220 tonnes of silver, is at **Real de Angeles**.

Places of interest

The **Cathedral** (1730-52); the **San Agustín** church, with interior carvings now being restored; the Jesuit church of **Santo Domingo** and the little houses behind it (in the church, ask the sacristan to turn the lights on so you can see the frescoes in the sacristy by Francisco Antonio Vallejo). **Plaza Hidalgo** and its statues; the **Casa Moneda** (better known as the Tesorería); the **Teatro Calderón**, and the chapel of **Los Remedios** (1728). The **Mina del Edén**, Av Torreón y Quebradilla, is worth a visit, the old mine has a short section of mine railway in operation (not a proper train), tour lasts about 1 hr, commentary in fast Spanish, admission US$2 (see below); there is also a disco in the mine, entry US$10, buy ticket before 2030, varied music. On the way to the mine note the interesting façade (1738) brought from the hacienda of Los Condes de San Mateo, which now adorns the main offices of the local cattle-breeding association.

Zacatecas is famous for its *sarapes* and has two delicacies: the local cheese, and *queso de tuna*, a candy made from the fruit of the nopal cactus (do not eat too much, it has laxative properties). Visit the small *tortilla* factories near the station, on the main road. Several good silverware shops around the Cathedral area. Zacatecas is reckoned by many travellers to be the most pleasant town in this part of Mexico.

Museums

The **Museo Pedro Coronel** on Plaza Santo Domingo, admission US$4.35 (1000-1400, 1600-1900; closed Thur), which houses an excellent collection of European and modern art (including Goya, Hogarth, Miró, Tapié) as well as folk art from Mexico and around the world (take a guide to make the most of the collections). The **Rafael Coronel Museum**, housed in the ex-Convento de San Francisco, has a vast collection of masks and puppets, primarily Mexican, nice garden, entry US$4.35, students US$1.75. The **Cerro de La Bufa** (cablecar, US$0.80 one way, starts at 1000, finishes 1800 (cancelled when windy), recommended for the views, best light in early mornings, nice walk, crowded Sun) which dominates the city, contains the **Museo de la Toma de Zacatecas**, commemorating Pancho Villa's victory over Huerta's forces in 1914 (entry US$1.65). There is also a statue of Villa, an observatory, and the Mausoleo de Los Hombres Ilustres, on the hill. The **Museo Francisco Goitia**, housed in what was once the governor's mansion, is by the Parque General on Enrique Estrada, Col Sierra de Alicia near the old **Acueducto del Cubo**, with modern paintings by Zacatecans, admission US$0.80.

Excursions

Beyond Zacatecas to the E lies the Convento de Guadalupe, a national monument, with a fine church and convent, which now houses a museum of colonial religious art; admission US$3.45 (Tues-Sun 1000-1700). Next door is Museo Regional de Historia, under development. Frequent buses, No 13, from López Mateos y Salazar, near old terminal, US$0.15, 20 mins. Visit also the **Chicomostoc** ruins 56 km S by taking the 0800 or 1100 Línea Verde bus from main terminal to Adjuntas (about 45 mins, US$0.60), on the Villanueva road. Then walk 30 mins through beautiful, silent, nopal-cactus scenery to the ruins, which offer an impressive view. There is the Palace of the Eleven Columns, a pyramid of the Sun and other remains on a rocky outcrop, in various stages of restoration. In themselves the ruins are not spectacular, but together with the setting they are worth the trip. Take water. Admission US$3.35; no information on site, so ask for explanations. A museum is being built. Women are advised to keep at a distance from the caretaker. For the return from the junction at Adjuntas wait for a bus (possibly a long wait), or hitch back to Zacatecas. **Jerez** is an old colonial town about 65 km from Zacatecas, where the wide brimmed *sombrero charro* is still worn, worth a visit, becoming popular with tourists; **C** *Hotel Leo*, short walk from bus station, good; **D** *Hotel Félix*, recommended; frequent buses to Zacatecas from new bus terminal.

Local festivals

Spreads over most of Sept, a rainy month here. There are bullfights on Sun.

Local information

● Accommodation

A1 *Galería*, López Mateos s/n, T 23311, nr old bus station, very comfortable; **A1** *Mesón de Jobito*, Jardín Juárez 143, Centro, T/F 241722 (in Mexico City T 514-2728/207-5666), in heart of Centro Histórico, small, select hotel, attractive restaurant with international and Mexican cuisine; **A1** *Quinta Real*, Av González Ortega, T 29104, beautiful, built around old bull ring

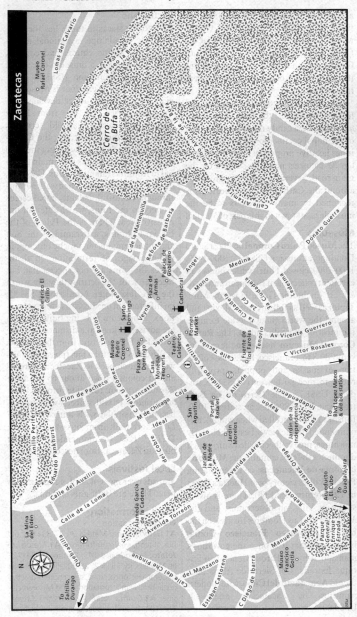

Zacatecas

Museo Rafael Coronel

Lomas del Calvario

Paseo la Bufa

Cerro de la Bufa

Calle Altamira

Juan Tolsa

Teleférica El Grillo

Genaro Codina

Los Bolos

C de la Mantequilla

Rebote de Barbosa

Palacio de Gobierno

Plaza de Armas

Veyna

Santo Domingo

Museo Pedro Coronel

Plaza Santo Domingo

Santero

Casa Moneda Tesorería

Teatro Calderón

Cathedral

Angel

Mono

Medina

Donato Guerra

3a Ciudadela

24 Cd

1a Ciudadela

Ledesma

Av Vicente Guerrero

Former Market

Calle Tacuba

Fuente de los Faroles

Tenorio

C Victor Rosales

Cjon de Pacheco

C Felix U Gomez

Lancaster

Caja

M de Chicago

San Agustin

Portal Rosales

Hidalgo y Costilla

C Allende

To Blvd López Mateos & old bus station

Anillo Periférico

Eduardo Pankhurst

Ideal

del Cobre

Lazo

Jardin Morelos

Rayon

Jardin de la Independencia

J Rosas

Independencia

Avenida Juárez

González Ortega

Rebote

Acueducto El Cubo

To Guadalajara

la Mina del Edén

Quebradilla

Calle del Auxilio

Calle de la Loma

Alameda García de la Cadena

Jardin de la Madre

Avenida Torreón

Calle del Che Pinbue

Manuel M Ponce

Parque General Enrique Estrada

Museo Francisco Goitia

N

To Saltillo Durango

Calle del Manzano

Esteban Castorena

C Diego de Ibarra

(said to be the 2nd oldest in Latin America), aqueduct goes past the front door. **A2** *Paraíso Radisson*, opp Cathedral, on Av Hidalgo, T 26183; **A2** *Aristos*, Lomas de Soledad, T 21788; **A2** *María Bonita*, Av López Velarde 319, T 24545, F 26645, hot water, heating, very good.

B *Posada de La Moneda*, nr Cathedral, Av Hidalgo 413, T 20881, F 23693, nice and clean, but a bit noisy.

C *Condesa*, opp *Posada de los Condes*, Av Juárez, T 21160, OK, helpful, some rooms quiet with good views of Cerro de la Bufa, cheap restaurant.

D *Posada de los Condes*, Juárez 107, T 21093, F 21650, a bit noisy, rooms darkish. **D** *Barranca*, opp old bus terminal, Blvd López Mateos 401, T 21494, poor value, and noisy traffic; **D** *Colón*, Av López Velarde 508, T 20464, clean, showers; **D** *Gami*, Av López Mateos 309, T 28005, rooms with TV, OK; **D** *Insurgentes*, Insurgentes 114, T 23419, off Plaza del Vivar, without bath, hot showers extra.

E *Conde de Villarreal* (was *Zamora*), Plaza de Zamora 303, T 21200, with bath, central, very basic; **E** *Del Parque*, González Ortega 302, clean, good value; **E** *Morelos*, Morelos 825, T 22505, economical, very basic, shared bath; **E** *Río Grande*, Calzada de la Paz 217, T 25349, with bath (F without), ask for quiet room on the patio, beautiful view from one side, clean, friendly, hot water, good value; the cheap hotels (very few) are all within 5 mins' walk of the old bus station, towards Av Hidalgo.

Motels: **B-C** *Hacienda Del Bosque*, T 46666, Fortín de la Peña, close to centre so may be noisy, attractive rooms, good food, has camping facilities and hook-ups, showers and toilets, only for small cars and vans; **C** *Parador Zacatecas*, excellent, Pan-American Highway.

Youth hostel: Parque del Encantado 103, T 21151/21891, CP 98000, on bus route to centre from bus station, **F** (no singles); also Av de los Deportes beside Estadio Fco Villa, CP 98064, T 29377.

Trailer park at Morelos junction, about 20 mins NW of the city, where Route 54 Saltillo-Guadalajara crosses Route 49. Hook-ups, basic, US$8, behind Pemex.

● **Places to eat**

La Cuija, in old Centro Comercial on Av Tacuba, good food, music, atmosphere; *El Jacalito*, Juárez 18, excellent *comida corrida* and breakfast; *La Cabana*, Jardín de la Independencia,

cheap, excellent set meals; *Dragón de Oro*, González Ortega, 2 blocks from *Hotel del Parque*, cheap, good Chinese, slow service; *Burgerlandia*, beside Teatro Calderón; good; *El Carnerito*, Av Juárez 110, cheap. *Pizzería Fugazetta*, Av Guerrero 136, charming, good pizzas; *Mr Laberinto*, Av Hidalgo 342344, luxury atmosphere, 1970s décor, quite cheap, good breakfast and dinners, rec; *El Paraíso*, Av Hidalgo y P Goytta, corner of market, bar/restaurant, nice atmosphere, closed Sun; opp is *Nueva España*, bar with loud music, closed Sun; *Chapa Rosa*, Plaza Genaro Codina 112, good, moderate prices; *La Unica*, Aldana 243, good food, cheap; *La Cantera Musical*, Av Tacuba, Mexican, good atmosphere, poor a/c, good food but drinks limited after 2000. Good cafés inc: *Cafetería La Terazza*, in market on a balcony, very pleasant, good *malteadas*; *Café Arús*, Centro Comercial, Av Hidalgo y Costilla, serves breakfast; *Acrópolis*, opp Cathedral, 50 year old, café and diner, good breakfast, slow service; *Café Zaz*, Av Hidalgo y Costillo 201. Several cheap restaurants along Av Independencia. *El Quixote* (at *María Bonita Hotel*), Av López Velarde, good breakfasts. *Helder*, nr old bus station, excellent breakfasts. Plenty of good coffee shops selling real *expresso* coffee. Many good *tamales* sold on the streets.

Health food: store at Rayón 413, excellent food at reasonable prices.

● **Airline offices**

Mexicana, T 27429; Taesa, T 20050.

● **Banks & money changers**

Banamex rec. Bancomer has a Visa cash dispenser and gives cash (pesos) on Visa cards. Both on Av Hidalgo.

● **Cultural centres**

Alianza Francesa, Callejón del Santero 111, T 40348, French film every Tues at 1900 (free).

● **Hospitals & medical services**

Santa Elena Clinic, Av Guerrero, many specialists, consultation, US$15.

● **Post & telecommunications**

Fax: service at *Telégrafos*, Av Hidalgo y Juárez.
Post Office: C Allende 111.

● **Shopping**

Interesting shops on Independencia selling hats, riding equipment, fruit and other produce, not touristy. Cheap postcards for sale in the toy shop and stationers on Hidalgo on the right if coming from the Cathedral. Between Hidalgo and

Tacuba the elegant 19th century market building has been converted into a pleasant shopping centre (popular café on balcony, reasonable). The market is now dispersed in various locations a few blocks to the SW.

● **Tour companies & travel agents**
Cantera Tours, Centro Comercial El Mercado, Local A-21, T 29065, tour to Chicomostoc and Jérez at 0930, US$10.

● **Tourist offices**
On Av Hidalgo y Costilla, T 28467/26683, friendly, helpful, free maps, good hotel information, inc cheaper hotels. Ask here about language classes at the University.

● **Transport**
Air La Calera airport (ZCL) 27 km N of city, flights daily with Mexicana or Taesa to Mexico City, Tijuana, Guadalajara, Ciudad Juárez, Morelia, Aguascalientes. Direct flights to several US cities: Chicago, Denver, Los Angeles, Oakland, California with both airlines.

Trains To Mexico City (according to timetables) 2005, arrives 0930, US$10.50 2nd class, US$19 *primera preferente*, a very cold trip, wear warm clothes; from Mexico City at 2000, arrives 0930; to **Querétaro**, 10 hrs, US$5, 2nd class; to **Chihuahua** 0930.

Buses New terminal 4 km N of town; red No 8 buses from Plaza Independencia, or white camionetas from Av González Artegú (old bus station on Blvd A López Mateos only serves local destinations). To Durango with Estrella Blanca, 5 hrs, US$7.75 (if continuing to Mazatlán, stay the night in Durango in order not to miss the views on the way to the coast). To Chihuahua via Torreón, 12 hrs, 1st class US$33; Jiménez, US$26.50; to Hidalgo del Parral with Chihuahuenses and Omnibus de México, US$30, 10 hrs; San Luis Potosí with Estrella Blanca; Ciudad Juárez 1st class with Omnibus de México at 1930, 11 hrs, US$43.75; to Guadalajara, 6½ hrs, several companies, US$14.50, but shop around for different journey times (road windy and in poor condition in parts). Aguascalientes, every 30 mins, 2½ hrs, US$2.80. To León, 4½ hrs, US$8.80. To Mexico City, 8 hrs, US$23.50. Apart from buses to Mexico City, Chihuahua and a few other major towns, most routes do not have bookable seats. As the majority of buses pass through Zacatecas and don't start their journey there, long waits are probable.

AGUASCALIENTES

(Km 508; *Pop* 750,000; *State pop 1995* 862,335; *Alt* 1,987m; *Phone code* 491) Founded in 1575, capital of its state, the name comes from its hot mineral springs. An oddity is that the city is built over a network of tunnels dug out by a forgotten people. It has pretty parks, a pleasant climate, delicious fruits, and specializes in drawn linen threadwork, pottery, and leather goods.

Places of interest
Palacio de Gobierno (once the castle home, started in 1698, of the Marqués de Guadalupe: splendid courtyard, with decorated arches on two levels; the grand staircase in the centre, built in the 1940s, blends in magnificently with the earlier structure; also colourful murals), and the Palacio Municipal. Among the churches **San Antonio**, on Zaragoza, should not be missed, neither should the **Carmelite Temple of San Marcos**, built 1733-65 on the site of a chapel which had existed since the mid-16th century, in the barrio of San Marcos. Beyond the church of San Marcos is an enormous concrete commercial and leisure complex known as Expo-Plaza which includes the *Fiesta Americana* hotel and new bull-ring. There is much industrial development on the outskirts.

  Teatro Morelos next to the Cathedral; T 50097. The **University** is 30 mins from the city centre. Its administrative offices are in the ex-Convento de San Diego, by the attractive Jardín del Estudiante, and the Parián, a shopping centre. The market is not far away. There is carp fishing at El Jocoqui and Abelardo Rodríguez. The bull ring is on Av López Mateos.

Museums
Museo de Aguascalientes, C Zaragoza 505, is by the Church of San Antonio; it has a collection of contemporary art, including fine paintings by Saturnino Herrán, and works by Orozco, Angel, Montenegro and others (open from 1030

daily, except Sun and Mon). The **José Guadalupe Posada** museum is in a gallery, by the Templo del Cristo Negro, close to a pleasant garden – Díaz de León (known locally as the Jardín del Encino); it has a remarkable collection of prints by the lithographer Posada, best known for his *calaveras*, macabre skeletal figures illustrating and satirizing the Revolution and events leading up to it. Admission US$1, Tues-Sun 1000-1400, 1700-2100, shut Mon; cultural events in the courtyard on Sat and Sun. The **Casa de las Artesanías** is near the main square. The **Casa de la Cultura**, on Venustiano Carranza and Galeana Norte, is a fine colonial building. It holds a display of *artesanía* during the *feria*.

Excursions

Hacienda de San Blas, 34 km away, contains the **Museo de la Insurgencia**, with murals by Alfredo Zermeño.

Thermal Baths Balneario Ojo Caliente, E end of town beyond train station, at end of Calzada Revolución (Alameda), claims to have been founded in 1808, some private hot baths and 2 excellent public pools (US$0.75), take bus marked 'Alameda'; saunas, squash and tennis courts on the site. At end of Alameda fork right to Deportivo Ojocaliente, a large complex with several pools (not so warm water), US$0.65. 20 km N is a thermal swimming pool at Valladolid (camping is permitted in the grounds, secure, night watchman in attendance).

Encarnación de Díaz (**C** *Hotel Casa Blanca*, Anguiano 107 on the plaza, hot water, secure parking nearby, reasonable restaurant) is halfway to **Lagos de Moreno** (Km 425), a charming old town with fine baroque churches; the entry over the bridge, with domes and towers visible on the other side, is particularly impressive. See the ex-convent of the Capuchins and the Teatro Rosas Moreno. *Feria* last week of July and first of August. Lagos de Moreno has several hotels (on main plaza: **C** *La Traje*; **D** *París*; **D** *Plaza*, best rooms facing the front, small and

dark at the back; just off the plaza is **C** *Colonial*; **C** *Victoria*, 2 blocks away, near river) and restaurants (recommended is *La Rinconada*, colonial building, old photos, on plaza 2 blocks behind Municipalidad, which is on main plaza, good *enchiladas*). A road (Route 80) turns off right to Guadalajara, 197 km away; the same road leads, left, to Antiguo Morelos via San Luis Potosí. 42 km SW on Route 80 is the colonial town of **San Juan de los Lagos**, a major pilgrimage centre, crowded during Mexican holidays, famous for glazed fruit; many hotels. There is also a fine view on entering this town: as the road descends you see the twin-towered church with its red, blue and yellow tiled dome.

Local festivals

The area is famous for viticulture; the local wine is called after San Marcos, and the *feria* in his honour lasts for 3 weeks, starting in the middle of April, with processions, cockfights (in Mexico's largest *palenque*, seating 4,000), bullfights, agricultural shows etc. The Plaza de Armas is lavishly decorated. The *feria*, covered by national TV networks, is said to be the biggest in Mexico. Accommodation can be very difficult and prices double during the *feria*. Bullfight also on New Year's day.

Local information

● Accommodation

L3 *Fiesta Americana*, on Expo Plaza, Col Flores, T 186010, F 186118; **L3** *Gran Hotel Hacienda de la Noria*, Av Héroe de Nacozari Sur 1315, Col La Salud, T 184343, F 185259 (in Mexico City T 5142728/2075666), very comfortable, jacuzzi in all rooms, Mexican, Japanese and international cuisine, gardens, swimming pool.

A1 *Francia*, Plaza Principal, T 56080, airy, colonial style; good restaurant (*El Fausto*) for breakfast and lunch.

B *Hotel Suites Alamo*, Alameda 129, T 56885, pool.

D *Praga*, with TV, Zaragoza 214, T 52357, OK. On main square, **D** *Señorial*, Colón 104, T 52179, helpful lady speaks English. **D** *Don Jesús*, Juárez 427, T 55598, cold water, good value; **D** *Reforma*, Av Guerrero, 1 block W of main square, friendly, clean, piano show Mon-Fri at 2000 to 2200; **D** *Maser*, 3 blocks from Cathedral on Montaro, T 53562, *comedor* for breakfast; **D** *Casa de Oro*, on Hidalgo 1, good; **D** *San José*, Hidalgo 207, T 51431, friendly. At Rep de Brasil 403, **E** *Casa de Huéspedes*, nr main square, and at No 602, **D** *Gómez*, T 70409. Cheap hotels around Juárez market (Av Guadalupe y C Guadalupe Victoria), eg **E** *Brasil*, Guadalupe 110, with bath, quiet, and **D** *Bahía*, No 144, with bath, **E** *México*, no bath or hot water; **E** *Casa Belén*, López Mateos y Galeana, T 158593, central, hot water, clean, friendly.

Motel: A3 *El Medrano*, Chávez 904, T 55500, F 68076; **B** *La Cascada*, Chávez 1501, T 61411.

Youth hostel: Av de la Convención y Jaime Nuno s/n, CP 20190, T 700873.

● **Places to eat**
Lack of conventional facilities, except in some of the more expensive hotels. Try the area around 5 de Mayo for *pollo rostizado*. Good *comida corrida* at *Sanfer*, Guadalupe Victoria 204, also at **Woolworth** restaurant 1 block away. *Jacalito*, López Mateos, also nr Plaza Crystal, cheap *tortas*, clean; *Mexicali Rose*, López Mateos, US$10 *comida corrida*. Also *Freeday* video bar and restaurant, nr Benito Juárez statue, lively at weekends. *Café Parroquia* on Hidalgo, 1 block W off Madero, good, cheap.

● **Airline offices**
Aero California, T 72310; **AeroMéxico**, T 70252; **Taesa**, T 82698.

● **Post & telecommunications**
Post Office: Hospitalidad, nr El Porián shopping centre.

● **Shopping**
Bookshop: Librería Universal, Madero 427.

Market: main one at 5 de Mayo y Unión, large and clean, with toilet on upper floor.

● **Tourist offices**
Federal tourist office in Palacio de Gobierno, T 60123.

● **Transport**
Local Taxis: there is a ticket system for taxis from the Central Camionera, with the city divided into different fare zones. There is no need to pay extra; a phone number for complaints is on the ticket.

Air The airport (AGU) is 21 km from the town centre. Domestic flights to Culiacán, Mexico City, Monclova, Monterrey, Puerto Vallarta, San Luis Potosí, Tampico, Tijuana and Zacatecas with a variety of airlines. US flights to Houston and Los Angeles with AeroMéxico and San Antonio, Texas with Serolitoral.

Trains Twice a day to **Mexico City**, en route from Ciudad Juárez and Torreón. Train station at E end of Av Madero. Bus 17 goes there from C Hornedo, 1 block behind *Hotel Reforma*.

Buses Bus station about 1 km S of centre on Av Circunvalación Sur. Bus: to **Guadalajara**, 5 hrs, US$8.25 1st, US$15.50 ETN (2 hrs direct with Estrella Blanca). To **Guanajuato** US$4.50 with Flecha Amarilla, 3½ hrs. To **Zacatecas**: US$2.80, every 30 mins, 2½ hrs. To **Ciudad Juárez**, US$46.25. ETN (luxury service) to **Mexico City** US$31.50, 7 hrs, ordinary fare US$14. Some 170 km to the E is San Luis Potosí (see page 96).

LEON

(*Pop* 1,200,000; *Alt* 1,885m; *Phone code* 47)
After about 1,600 km of desert or semi-arid country, we now enter, surprisingly, the basin of Guanajuato, known as the Bajío, greener, more fertile, higher (on average over 1,800m), and wetter, though the rainfall is still not more than 635 to 740 mm a year. The Bajío is the granary of central Mexico, growing maize, wheat, and fruit. The towns we pass through, León, Irapuato, and Celaya, have grown enormously in population and importance. 50 km before León there are some impressive buttes (isolated, steep hills).

(Km 382) **León** (de los Aldamas), in the fertile plain of the Gómez River, is now said to be Mexico's fifth city. Nuño de Guzmán reached the area that is now León on 2 December 1530. Local farms and estates were granted to the Spaniards until eventually Don Martín Enríquez de Almanza decreed on 12 December 1575 that a city, called León, would be founded if 100 volunteers could be persuaded to live there for 10 years, or a town if only 50 could be found. On 20 January 1576 a town was founded by Dr Juan Bautista de Orozco but León did not become a city

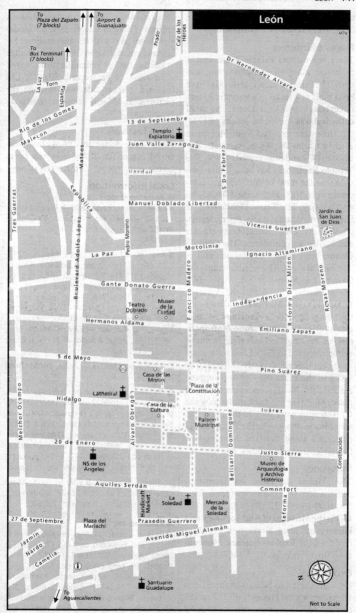

until 1830. The business centre is the delightful **Plaza de Constitución**.

Places of interest

There is a striking **Palacio Municipal**, a cathedral, many shaded plazas and gardens. The Palacio Municipal is said to have been built as a result of a winning lottery ticket bought by a local doctor! The small **cathedral** was started by Jesuits in 1744, but they were expelled from Mexico in 1767 by Carlos III. It was eventually finished in 1837 and consecrated in 1866. The **Templo Expiatorio** has been under construction for most of this century, catacombs open 1000-1200 (closed Wed), well worth seeing. The **Teatro Doblado** on Av Hermanos Aldama stages opera, ballet, classical concerts, contemporary theatre and houses art exhibitions. The **Casa de Cultura** also houses exhibitions and is 'buzzing' at night. Also worth seeing is the **Casa de Las Monas** on 5 de Mayo 127/9 where Pancho Villa issued the Agrarian Reform law on 24 May 1915, and the beautiful **Santuario de Guadelupe**. A new tourist attraction, the **Parque Metropolitano** on Prolongación Morelos, Camino a la Presa, opened in 1995. León is the main shoe centre of the country (high quality shoes in the Plaza del Zapato shopping mall, Hilario Medina, and cheaper ones in places round the bus station), and is noted for its leather work (buy in the Plaza Piel shopping mall opposite the Plaza del Zapato, and along Belisario Domínguez), fine silver-trimmed saddles, and *rebozos*.

Museums

The **Museo de León** on Hermanos Aldama has art exhibitions (open Tues-Sat, 1000-1400 and 1630-1930, Sun 1000-1400); the **Museum of Anthropology and History** on Justo Sierra is a beautiful building; the **Explora Science Museum** is on Blvd Fco Villa 202, T 116711.

Excursions

Between León and **Silao** (bus from León US$0.70), left off Highway 45 at Km 387 (going S) are the famous swimming pools of Comanjilla fed by hot sulphurous springs. There is a luxurious, hacienda-style hotel (**A1**) with restaurant. From Silao take micro to León Centro and change at Los Sauces for Comanjilla turn-off, well signposted. 11 km beyond Silao, at Los Infantes, a short side road through the picturesque Marfil canyon leads to Guanajuato.

Local festivals

Fiesta: San Sebastián, 19-24 Jan, very crowded, good fun (if staying outside León, take an early bus out of town when leaving).

Local information

● **Accommodation**

A2 *Fiesta Americana*, Blvd A López Mateos 1102 Ote, T 136040, F 135380; **A3** *Camino Real*, Blvd A López Mateos 1311 Ote, T 163939, F 163940.

B *Real de Minas*, A López Mateos 2211, T 710660, F 712400, rec; **B** *Estancia*, A López Mateos 1317 Pte, T/F 169900, restaurant rec; **B** *Condesa*, on Plaza, Portal Bravo 14, T 131120, F 148210, 3-star, restaurant rec; **B** *León*, Madero 113, T 141050, F 132262, 3-star; **B** *Robert*, Blvd L Mateos Ote 1503, T 167213; **B** *Roma*, Nuevo Vallarta 202, T/F 161500, 3-star; **B** *Señorial*, nr Plaza, Juárez 221, T 145959.

C *Fénix*, Comonfort 338, 2-star; *Colón*, 20 de Enero 131, 1-star.

D *Fundadores*, J Ortiz de Domínguez 218, T 161727, F 166612, better than similarly-priced hotels in centre; **D** *Posada de Fátima*, Belisario Domínguez 205, clean, central; **D** *Rex*, 5 de Febrero 104, nr Plaza, rec; **D** *Monte Carlo*, Justo Sierra 432, clean, friendly, central; **D** *Tepeyac*, Av Obregón 727, 1-star, OK, rooms a bit dark. Also several cheaper ones nr market.

At **Silao** (for airport): **B** *Villa Victoria*, Alvaro Obregón 245, T 21831, F 22422; *San Javier*, C Coecillo y Libramiento de Silao, T 20642.

● **Places to eat**

Several in Colonia Jardines del Moral area in centre, inc: *El Jardín de Ling Choy*, Blvd A López Mateos 2105 Pte, T 177507, also *La Pagoda de Ling Choy*, López Mateos 1501 Ote, T 149026, both Chinese; *Kamakura*, Rocío 114, T 184383, Japanese; *Lupillos*, Blvd A López Mateos 2003 Ote, opp stadium, T 711868, pasta and pizza; also several branches of the US fast food chains. Many restaurants in the Gran Plaza complex next to Macdonalds. Vegetarian snacks at **GFU**, on López Mateos, nr IMSS building. *Cadillac*, ½ block from cathedral on Hidalgo, good *comida corrida* US$5. *Panteón Taurino*, Calzado de Los Héroes 408, T 134969, expensive but worth visiting to see the incredible decor. Look for listings in local guides; lots of places offering seafood, pizzas, Spanish, Oriental, Arab, Argentine, Brazilian and Mexican food.

● **Airline offices**
AeroMéxico, Madero 410, T 166226, 149667; **Mexicana**, Blvd A López Mateos 401 Ote, T 149500, 134550; **Taesa**, Pedro Moreno 510 Centro, T 143660, 143532, 143621; **Continental**, Blvd A López Mateos 2307 Pte, T 135199, 143937, 91-800-90050.

● **Banks & money changers**
Bancomer, Belisario Domínguez 322, and Banco Internacional on the plaza.

● **Entertainment**
Bars: lots of bars inc *JJ Sport*, Rocío 115-A, Jardines del Moral; *Pepe's Pub*, Madero 120, Zona Centro; *Fut-bol Bar*, Blvd Hidalgo 923-B, T 178020.

Discos: inc *Domus*, Blvd López Mateos 2611 Ote, T 116614; *Ossy's*, Salida a Lagos por Av Paseo de los Insurgentes, T 176880; *La Iguana*, C Comercial Insurgentes Local 4 y 5B, T 181416.

Nightclubs: *Piano Bar Maya*, Prolongación Calzada 112, T 169734.

● **Post & telecommunications**
Post Office: on Obregón y 5 de Mayo, open Mon-Fri 0800-1900.

● **Shopping**
Several shopping centres: *La Gran Plaza*, Blvd López Mateos 1902 Pte; *Plaza Mayor*, Av de las Torres, Esq Prolongación Morelos; *Plaza León*, Blvd López Mateos 1102 Ote; *Centro Comercial Insurgentes*, Blvd López Mateos y Alud, Jardines del Moral; *Plaza del Zapato*, Hilario Medina y Blvd López Mateos, T 146442; *Plaza Piel*, Hilario Medina y López Mateos.

● **Tour companies & travel agents**
Viajes Sindy de León, 20 de enero 319, T 131224, F 165080, rec; *Jovi de León*, Madero 319 Centro, T 145094, F 166217, rec.

● **Tourist offices**
In Edif Cielo 501 on López Mateos Pte y M Alemán. Helpful but limited information (good city map available free at Palacio Municipal).

● **Transport**
Air New international airport, del Bajío (BJX), 18 km from León, 6 km from Silao: American Airlines to Dallas; Mexicana de Aviación to Chicago; Continental (T 185254), AeroMéxico (T 131807) and American Airlines to Houston; AeroMéxico and Mexicana de Aviación to Los Angeles; Continental to Nashville, Tennessee; Taesa to Oakland, California; Serolitoral to San Antonio, Texas; Mexicana de Aviación to San José, California. Several airlines fly to Mexico City (with connections to external and internal destinations), Puerto Vallarta, Tijuana, Monterrey, Chihuahua, Zacatecas, Guadalajara, Morelia. Taxis are expensive to León; either take one to Silao, US$10, and then take a bus to León or Guanajuato, or walk 1½ km to the main road and take a bus from there.

Buses Terminal has post office, long distance phones, restaurant and shops (street plan on sale, US$2.75). Plenty of buses to **Mexico City**, US$13.50 (US$27.50 ETN, T 131410), **Querétaro**, US$6. Irapuato and Celaya. Frequent services to **Guanajuato**, 40 mins, US$3 ETN. To **Zacatecas**, 4½ hrs, US$8.80. To **Poza Rica**, Omnibús de México, T 135798, US$21. Same company to **Monterrey**, US$25, and **Guadalajara**, every 30 mins, first at 0600, 4 hrs, US$7.75, US$15.50 ETN. Many buses run to **Ciudad Juárez**, US$50, passing through the cities mentioned above (eg Durango US$16.50, Chihuahua, US$38.50). Primera Plus, T 146000; Elite, T 169879; Futura, T 145451; Turistar Ejecutivo, T 145451; Turistar Plus y Estrella Blanca, T 145451, 133216; Tres Estrellas de Oro, T 169879, 169932.

The highway from León to Mexico City is dual carriageway all the way.

GUANAJUATO

(*Pop* 150,000; *State pop 1995* 4,393,160; *Alt* 2,010m; *Phone code* 473) The beautiful capital of Guanajuato state and a university city, now declared a national monument and Unesco World Heritage Zone, has been important for its silver since 1548. Its name derives from the Tarascan Quanax-Huato, place of frogs. It stands in a narrow gorge amid wild and striking scenery; the Guanajuato River cutting through it has been covered over and several underground streets opened – an unusual and effective attraction. Some, like Padre Belaunzarán, are not entirely enclosed; others, such as Hidalgo, are, so they fill with traffic fumes (as does much of the city). The Túnel Los Angeles leads from the old subterranean streets to the modern roadway which connects with the Carretera Panorámica and the monument to Pipila (see below). Taking traffic underground has not relieved the congestion of the surface streets, which are steep, twisted and narrow, following the contours of the hills. Some are steps cut into the rock: one, the **Callejón del Beso** (Street of the Kiss), is so narrow that kisses can be – and are – exchanged from opposite balconies. Over the city looms the shoulder of La Bufa mountain (you can hike to the summit up a trail which takes 1 hr: from the Pipila monument (see below), follow the main road for about 1 km to the hospital. Walk past the hospital to a power station where the main trail starts; if you pass the quarry, note the quality of the stone masonry on the mason's shelter).

Places of interest

Guanajuato contains a series of fine museums (see below) as well as the most elegant marble-lined public lavatories in Mexico. The best of many colonial churches are **La Compañía** (Jesuit, 1765, note the brick ceiling, by the University); **San Diego** (1663) on the Jardín de la Unión; the **Parroquia del Inmaculado Corazón de María**, on Juárez, opposite Mercado Hidalgo, has interesting statues on the altar; the **Basílica** (Cathedral, 1693, on Plaza de la Paz), **San Roque** (1726) on a small park between Juárez and Pocitos, and **San Francisco** (1671).

When Father Hidalgo took the city in 1810, the Alhóndiga was the last place to surrender, and there was a wanton slaughter of Spanish soldiers and royalist prisoners. When Hidalgo was himself caught and executed, along with three other leaders, at Chihuahua, their heads, in revenge, were fixed at the four corners of the Alhóndiga. There is a fine view from the **monument to Pipila**, the man who fired the door of the Alhóndiga so that the patriots could take it, which crowns the high hill of Hormiguera. Look for the 'Al Pipila' sign. Local buses go from *Hotel Central*, on the hour, to the Pipila, otherwise it's a steep but short climb up (about 15 mins); a number of cobbled stairways through picturesque terraces go up (or down) eg Callejón del Calvario, leading off Sopeña. Take a camera for fine panoramic views of the city. The Carretera Panorámica which encircles the city passes the Pipila monument. At its eastern end the Panorámica goes by the **Presa de la Olla**, a favourite picnic spot; good cheap meals available from roadside stalls. From the dam, Paseo de la Olla runs to the city centre, passing mansions of the wealthy silver barons and the **Palacio de Gobierno** (note the use of local stone). Also on the E side of the Panorámica is Casa de las Leyendas, with entertainment for children. Local pottery can be bought in the **Mercado Hidalgo** (1910), in the centre; there is also a Casa de Artesanías behind the **Teatro Juárez** (see **Entertainment** below).

Museums

A most interesting building is the massive **Alhóndiga de Granadita**, built as a granary, turned into a fortress, and now a museum with artefacts from the pre-Colombian and colonial periods (US$1.80). An unusual sight shown to visitors is of mummified bodies in the small **Museo de las Momias** in the Panteón Municipal, above the city off Tepetapa; buses go there ('Momias', sign-posted Panteón Municipal, US$0.10, 10 mins, along Av Juárez), but you can walk. It's a gruesome and disturbing spectacle, glass cases of naturally mummified bodies, their mouths gaping from skin contraction, some bodies with shoes and socks on, and, it is claimed, the smallest mummy in the world (entry US$2, US$0.75 to take photos, tip the Spanish-speaking guide, open 0900-1800, large queues on Sun). The **Museo Iconográfico del Quijote**, opened

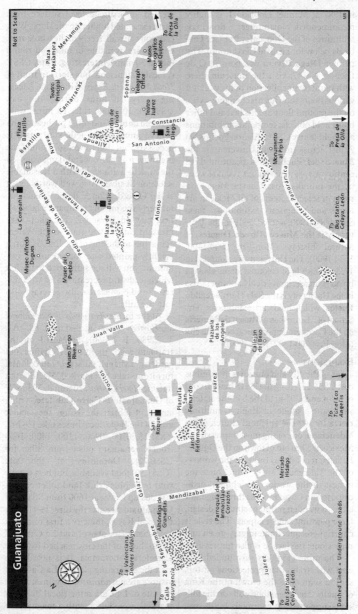

Dashed Lines = Underground Roads

in 1987 at Manuel Doblado 1, is highly recommended: paintings, drawings, sculptures of the Don, entry free (see **Festivals** below for Festival Cervantino). The painter **Diego Rivera** was born in C de Pocitos, No 47; visit the **museum** there with permanent collection of his work on various floors showing his changing styles; on the ground floor are his bed and other household objects; temporary exhibitions also held (entry US$1). Also on Pocitos No 7, just across from the University is the **Museo del Pueblo** in a beautiful 17th century mansion; it has one room of work by the muralist José Chávez Morado, a room of selected items of all Mexican art forms and temporary exhibitions, Tues-Sun, 0900-1900, entry US$1. In the University is the **Museo Alfredo Dugues**, of natural history (Mon-Fri, 0900-1400, 1630-1900). The University was founded in 1732; its façade of coloured stone, above a broad staircase, glows richly at sunset. Also in the University is the **Sala Hermenegildo Bustos**, which holds art exhibitions. The School of Mining has a **Museo de Minería** on the Carretera Panorámica, N of the city (Mon-Fri 0900-1300, 1630-1900).

Excursions

Tours of the city and outskirts by minibus cost US$6.15, rising to US$18 for tours out of town and US$40 to the S of the state; if you want a guide in English, multiply prices by 10. The splendid church of **La Valenciana**, one of the most impressive in Mexico, is 5 km out of town on the Dolores Hidalgo road; it was built for the workers of the Valenciana silver mine, once the richest in the world. The church, dedicated to San Cayetano, has three huge, gilt altars, a wooden pulpit of sinuous design, large paintings and a cupola. The style is churrigueresque, done in grey-green and pink stone; the façade is also impressive.

The mine (1548) is surrounded by a wall with triangular projections on top, said to symbolize the crown of the King of Spain. The huge stone walls on the hillside, supported by enormous buttresses, created an artificial level surface from earth excavated higher up the slope. With care you can walk freely in the whole area. Guides are available to take you round (about 30 mins), interesting. Entry US$1. A local 'Valenciana' bus starts in front of *Hotel Mineral de Rayas*, Alhóndiga 7, leaving every 30 mins during the day, US$0.10, 10 mins' ride; 10 mins' walk between church and mine pit-head; don't believe anyone who tells you a taxi is necessary, but don't walk to it along the highway, it is narrow and dangerous. At the mine is a gift shop with a reasonable selection of silver. Also well worth a visit is the Casa de Conde de la Valenciana, formerly the mining company's head office, now an attractive craft shop with pleasant café. If you stay on the 'Valenciana' bus to the end of the line, a church brightly-painted and turned into a restaurant, you will see a dirt road to the left which leads to a recreation area with reservoir and picnic area, also several walks into the hills.

At the former *Hacienda de San Gabriel de Barrera* (now a 4-star hotel, A1, T 23980, F 27460), at Marfil on the Irapuato road, there are 15 patios and gardens, a chapel, museum and colonial furniture (take bus marked 'Marfil' from outside *Hotel Central*, 10 mins). 30 km W of Guanajuato is **Cerro Cubilete**, with a statue of Christ the King, spectacular view of the Bajío, local buses take 1½ hrs, US$1.15, 0700, 0900, 1100, 1400, 1600 from Guanajuato (also from Silao for US$0.75). Dormitory at the site (US$1.50) food available, but best to take your own, plus drink (and toilet paper); last bus up leaves at 1600 from Silao and Guanajuato. See also the three local silver mines of Rayas, the city's first mine, La Valenciana (see above) and La Cata. All are to the N of the city, reached from the Carretera Panorámica. It is possible to visit the separating plant at **La Cata**, but visitors are not admitted to mines. At the old site of La Cata mine (local bus near market), is a church with a magnificent baroque façade and the shrine of El Señor de Villa Seca (the patron of adulterers) with *retablos* and crude drawings of miraculous escapes from harm, mostly due to poor shooting by husbands.

Presa de Insurgentes, a few kilometres up the mountain highway, has a parking area and a couple of tables for picnics; it is a nursery for plants to be planted around the countryside. 4 km up a narrow road from Presa de la Olla is Panifiel, a village with an old church. Children will take visitors into the mission whose doors are held shut against stray animals by a large, round stone just inside the doors (a child's arm is small enough to fit beneath to move the stone). Take lunch.

Local festivals

Arts festival, the Festival Cervantino de Guanajuato (in honour of Cervantes), is an important cultural event in the Spanish-speaking world, encompassing theatre, song and dance. There is a mixture of free, open-air events, and paying events. Internationally famous artists from around the world perform. The festival lasts 2 weeks, is highly recommended and is very crowded; accommodation must be booked in advance (usually held the last 2 weeks in Oct, check dates). For information T Guanajuato (473) 20959, or Mexico City (5) 533-4121, The International Cervantino Festival, Alvaro Obregón 273, p 4, Colonia Roma, 06700 México DF. Viernes de las Flores is held on the Fri before Good Friday, starting with the Dance of the Flowers on Thur night at about 2200 right through the night, adjourning at Jardín de la Unión to exchange flowers. Very colourful and crowded. During the Christmas period, students dress up in traditional costumes and wander the streets singing carols and playing music. Groups leave from in front of the theatre at 2030.

Local information
● **Accommodation**

At the bus station you will probably be met by a tour guide who will suggest a hotel, perhaps arrange a discount, and then try to persuade you to buy a tour of the city. The guides have a hotel price list, which is higher than the official price list, which in turn differs from what hoteliers actually charge, but not by much. Most hotels charge in advance. Some also try to insist on a room with two beds, which is more expensive than with a double bed. Hotel rooms can be hard to find after 1400. Book ahead during holidays and weekends. There are frequent water shortages, so that hotels with no reservoirs of their own have no water on certain days; when there is water, do not drink it.

On Dolores Hidalgo road exit: A1 *Castillo de Santa Cecilia*, tourist-bus haven, T 20485, F 20153; **A1** *Parador San Javier*, Plaza Aldama 92, opp side of Dolores road, T 20626, F 23114, genuine hacienda style; and Motels given below. On exit to Irapuato, **A1** *Real de Minas*, Nejayote 17 at city entrance, T 21460, F 21508; on the Panorámica, not far from Pipila, **A1** *Paseo de la Presa*, T 23761, F 23224, quiet, good value, fantastic views, small pool, tennis courts. On Jardín de la Unión, **A1** *Posada Santa Fe*, No 12, T 20084, F 24653, good restaurant on open terrace with excellent service, and **B** *San Diego*, No 1, T 21321, F 25626, good bar and restaurant but slow, colonial style, very pleasant; **A2** *La Casa de Los Espíritus Alegres*, ex-Hacienda La Trinidad No 1, Marfil, 3 km from Guanajuato, T/F (473) 31013, 18th century hacienda house now owned by US artists, bed and breakfast, library, parking, bus stop close by, no children, pets or smoking, in USA contact Joan Summers, 2817 Smith Grade, Santa Cruz, CA 95060, T (408) 423-0181; **B** *Hostería del Frayle*, Sopeña 3, next door to Teatro Juárez, T 21179, rooms next to the Teatro are noisy, otherwise excellent, highly rec; **B** *La Abadía*, San Matías 50, T/F 22464; **C** *Central*, Juárez 111, T 20080, nr old bus station, restaurant noisy; **C** *El Insurgente*, Juárez 226, T 22294, pleasant, clean, avoid rooms on 4th floor where there is a disco, good breakfasts; **D** *Posada San Francisco*, Av Juárez y Gavira, T 22084, on Zócalo, good value but noisy on outside rooms, no hot water, lovely inner patio; **D** *Reforma*, Av Juárez 113, T 20469, with bath, overpriced, little hot water. **D** *Alhóndiga*, Insurgentes 49, T 20525, good, clean, quiet, restaurant *La Estancia*. Also on Insurgentes, **C** *del Conde* (No 1, T 21465), with excellent and reasonable restaurant *Mesa de los Reyes*, and **D** *Murillo Plaza* (No 9, T 21884), hot water; **D** *Posada La Condesa*, Plaza de La Paz, small, basic rooms, clean, hot water, drinking water available; **D** *El Minero*, Alhóndiga 12A, T 25251, restaurant.

D *Mineral de Rayas*, Alhóndiga 7, T 21967, with bath, clean linen, pool, garage, restaurant, bar and *Danny's Bar*; **D** *Molino del Rey*, Campañero 15, T 22223, simple and quaint. **E-F** *Casa Kloster*, Alonso 32, T 20088, book ahead, good location, very friendly, rooms for 4 (although few with private bath, D, some without windows), clean, very good value, repeatedly rec, often full, gardens, no parking (touts in town will say it is shut, but it is not). On Juárez, **E** *Granaditos* (No 109), with bath, hot showers, clean, friendly, run down but good value; **E** *Posada Juárez*, T 22559, rec; **D/E** *Posada del Carmen*, No 111A, T 29330, rec, nr Cine Reforma, bath, TV; and **E** *del Comercio*, T 22065. Other hotels are mostly in our C range. Accommodation in private home, **F** pp *Marilu Ordaz*, private home on Barranca 34, T 24705, friendly, 5 mins' walk from market.

Motels: many on Dolores Hidalgo road exit: **A3** *Villa de Plata*, T 21173. Trailer Park 1 km N of *Mineral de Rayas*, there is a sign on the Ruta Panorámica, hot showers. **B** *De Los Embajadores*, Paseo Embajadores, T 20081, Mexican décor, restaurant, famous Sun lunch; **B** *El Carruaje*, T 22140, F 21179. **B** *Guanajuato*, T 20689, good pool and food, quiet, rec; **B** *Valenciana*, T 20799.

● **Places to eat**
Tourists are given the à la carte menu; ask for the *menú de día* or *comida corrida* (but they stop serving them early). Reasonable food, *comida corrida* very good value, at *El Retiro*, Sopeña 12, nr Jardín de la Unión; also on Sopeña, *Pizzería Mamma Fan* and *La Colmena*. Pizza *Piazza*, Plaza San Fernando and several other locations, cheap and good; *Cuatro Ranas*, in *Hotel San Diego*, Jardín Unión 1, good location but loud US music and overpriced, reasonable *menú del día*, US$3; *Valadez* on Jardín de la Unión y Sopeña, excellent *menú del día*; also on Jardín de la Unión, *Bar Luna* and *El Gallo*, popular with travellers, good; *La Lonja*, on the corner of the Jardín opp *Hotel San Diego*, is a pleasant and lively bar, beers come with complimentary dish of tacos with salsa; meals at *Casino de Guanajuato* on Jardín de la Unión. *La Bohemia*, C Alonso, opp *Casa Kloster*, overpriced and uninspiring; *Mesón de Marco*, Juárez 25, 'rare' Mexican food, flights in balloon offered at US$100, T 27040; *La Carreta*, mostly chicken, fair, on Av Juárez about 200m up from Mercado Hidalgo; also on Juárez, *Tasca de los Santos*, on Plaza de la Paz, smart; *El Zaguán*, Plaza de la Paz No 48, very good

and cheap food, entertainment inside courtyard; *Café Truco 7*, Callejón Truco, off Plaza de la Paz, menu of the day US$2-3, relaxed family atmosphere, rec, theatre in back room Fri and Sat pm; *La Flor Alegre* (*casa de pan pizza*), Plazuela de San Fernando 37, good, clean and cheap; *El Mexicano*, Juárez 214, good *comida corrida* with dessert and drink; *El Granero*, Juárez 25, good *comida*, until 1700; *La Mancha*, C Galarza 7, rec for *comida corrida*, reasonable price; *Cafetería Neverria*, opp University, good, inexpensive; *Vegetariano*, Callejón Calixto 20, inexpensive, sells wholewheat bread; *Jelly Shot Bar*, below *Hostería del Frayle*, lovely atmosphere, cheap drinks, rec; *El Unicornio Azul* on Plaza Baratillo is a good health food shop, *pan integral*, also sells cosmetic products. You can eat well and cheaply in the market (eg *bolillos* – sandwiches, fresh fruit juices) and in the *locales* behind Mercado Hidalgo (some open till 2200; better value on 1st floor; the ladies have been forbidden by their rivals in the covered market to shout the merits of their menus, but their mime is just as engaging). Good *panaderías* also, eg *Panadería Internacional*, Contarranas y Sopena, sells wholewheat bread. Dairy products are safe, all coming from the pasteurizing plant at Silao. Also from Silao come strawberries in December.

● **Banks & money changers**
At banks, **Bancomer, Banca Serfín, Banamex**, 0900-1100.

● **Entertainment**
Sketches from classical authors out of doors in lovely old plazas from April to August. Teatro Juárez on Sopeña (a magnificent French-type Second Empire building, US$0.50 to view, US$0.35 to take photos), shows art films and has symphony concerts, US$1.50. A band plays in Jardín de la Unión (next to the theatre) three times a week. The Teatro Principal is on Cantarranas, by Plaza Mexiamora. Two nightclubs have been rec: *Disco El Grill* on Alonso (100m from *Casa Kloster*) and *Disco Los Comerciales* on C Juan Valle.

● **Language schools**
Spanish courses: for foreigners at the University and at *Instituto Falcon*, Sostenes Rocha 9, T 23694, e-mail: infalcon@redes.int.com.mx, web: http://www.Infonet.com.mx/falcon, good quality instruction. Also at the University are many US exchange students so you can usually find someone who speaks English. See also *AmeriSpan*, under **Learning Spanish** in Information for travellers.

● **Laundry**
Lavandería Internacional, Alhóndiga 35A, self or service wash (US$3.45); *La Burbuja Express*, Plazuela Baratillo; *Lavandería Automática Internacional*, Manuel Doblado 28, US$3.50; *Lavandería del Centro*, Sopeña 26, US$3.60.

● **Post & telecommunications**
Post Office: corner of Subida San José, by La Compañía church.

Telephone: international phone calls from phone booths with coins, or collect. Long-distance offices in Miscelánea Unión shop, by Teatro Principal and on Pocitos, opp Alhóndiga de Granaditas.

● **Shopping**
Fonart shop opp La Valenciana church (see above). Excellent selection of handicrafts. High prices but superb quality.

● **Tourist offices**
Plaza de la Paz; they have all hotel rates (except the cheapest) and give away folders. Map on sale US$1.35, compared with US$2.70 for state map with town plans at bus station. Federal representative office, Juárez 250 (opp old bus station).

● **Transport**
Trains Station is off Tepetapa (continuation of Juárez), W of centre. Passenger service no longer runs, although a high speed trainline linking the whole State of Guanajuato is under construction (due to open in 1998).

Buses A clean, new bus terminal has opened on the road to Silao, nr toll gate, 20 mins from centre by bus, US$0.30, pick up from outside Mercado Hidalgo. Taxi to centre, US$1.50. At the terminal is a tourist office (reported permanently closed but with notice-board listing

hotels, addresses and phone numbers, when open has free town map), post office, long-distance phone (not international; 0700-2200), restaurant, left-luggage and shops. To **Mexico City**, US$11, 5 hrs, about 3 companies, each with 3-4 buses daily, ETN US$24.25, 3 Estrellas de Oro at 0700 and 1500 via Dolores Hidalgo (US$2.25), San Miguel Allende (US$3.30 – also Flecha Amarilla, 1½ hrs) and Querétaro, 3½ hrs (US$5.75); super express at 1700; also Omnibús de México (T 27702/20438), Estrella Blanca and Chihuahuenses (book in advance). Bus Guanajuato-Dolores Hidalgo, Flecha Amarilla, US$2, 1 hr 25 mins (of which the first 20 mins is from bus station back into Guanjajuato, so catch bus outside Hotel Mineral de Rayas – same applies to buses for San Miguel De Allende). Similarly, alight from buses coming from Dolores Hidalgo in the town centre; don't wait for the bus station.

To **Guadalajara** 5 hrs, US$10.15, several companies, via León and Lagos de Moreno. To **Zacatecas**, with Omnibús de México 1st class, at 2100, US$10, 5½ hrs. Half hourly service to **Morelia** Flecha Amarilla, 2nd class, 4-5 hrs, US$4.50). To **San Luis Potosí**, US$7.75 en route to Tampico (US$20 with Omnibús de México). Buses also to Monterrey, Ciudad Juárez and Nuevo Laredo, but some involve a change in León. In fact, to many destinations it is better to go to León and pick up the more frequent services that go from there (buses every 10 mins Guanajuato-León, US$1.30). Flecha Amarilla have more buses, to more destinations, than other companies in this area; it is not the most reliable company and buses tend to leave when full. Set fare for city buses, US$0.25.

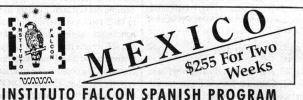

IRAPUATO

(Route 45, Km 315; *Pop* 475,000) **Irapuato** is noted for delicious strawberries, which should on no account be eaten unwashed. It is a prosperous industrial and agricultural town and an important distribution centre.

In the town centre, around the **Plaza de los Fundadores** and the **Jardín Hidalgo**, there is a cluster of historic buildings. The **Templo del Hospital** built around 1550, rebuilt 1617, façade completed 1733, said to have the country's largest chandelier. Outside, the **Cruz Monolítica** commemorates the visit of San Sebastian of Aparicio. The façade of the **Templo de San Francisco**, also known as El Convento (1799), is a mixture of baroque and neo-classical. The huge **Parroquia** (parish church) was rebuilt mid-18th century. The **Presidencia Municipal**, 19th century, incorporates a former 18th century school, the **Colegio de Enseñanza para Niños**. The fountain, **Fuente de los Delfines** was given to the town by Emperor Maximilian.

Unfortunately, the centre has been invaded by unsightly and incongruous modern buildings. Just off the centre is the 16th century church of **San José**, with fine examples of American indigenous art. Also the **Templo of Nuestra Señora de Guadalupe** (1890), with its striking late neo-classical gold-leaf-decorated interior.

● **Accommodation & places to eat** *Hotel Real de Minas*, T 62380, overpriced, with equally overpriced restaurant, on Portal Carrillo Puerto, quiet rooms on church side; *Restaurant El Gaucho*, Díaz Ordaz y Lago.

CELAYA

(Km 265; *Pop* 420,000; *Alt* 1,800m; *Phone code* 461) **Celaya** is famous for its confectionery, especially a caramel spread called *cajeta*, and its churches, built by Mexico's great architect Francisco Eduardo Tresguerras (1759-1833), a native of the town. His best is considered to be El Carmen, with a fine tower and dome. He also built

a fine bridge over the Río de la Laja. On 12 October 1570 the royal cedula was granted to found a town, the Villa de la Purísima Concepción de Zalaya, close to an Otomí settlement known as Nat Tah Hi. Zalaya, or Celaya, was in fact founded on 1 January 1571, but both dates are celebrated locally. Its status was elevated to that of city on 20 October 1655 by King Felipe IV of Spain. The city was located in a productive agricultural region and soon became important as a supply centre for the mines, thereby boosting commerce and making it prosperous. It was an important trading post on the route to Guanajuato, Zacatecas and Guadalajara as well as the transport of metals to the capital. The 17th and 18th centuries saw the construction of many great houses and religious buildings and in 1725 a university was founded. Don Miguel Hidalgo y Costilla arrived in Celaya with 40,000 men on 21 September 1810 in his quest for independence. He lodged in the Mesón de Guadalupe (now the *Hotel Guadalupe*) and received the support of the city, being proclaimed Captain General of the rebel army. He left with 50,000 fighters. Industrialization dates from 1836, when the first factory was built to produce thread and cloth. The railway arrived in 1878, the same year in which the first *cajeta* factory was started. Nowadays industrial enterprises include food processing, mechanical engineering, chemical products and others.

Places of interest

Templo del Carmen, built by Tresguerras in 1802-1807, the interior and exterior are neoclassical with a simple elegance, you can see Tresguerras' own paintings inside. **Convento de San Francisco**, one of the largest in the country, the interior is 17th century baroque. The façade of the cloisters was rebuilt by Tresguerras. **Templo de San Francisco** was rebuilt in 1683 after the original chapel was demolished. The façade is neoclassical and was rebuilt, together with the altars, by Tresguerras between 1810-1820. **Claustro Agustino**

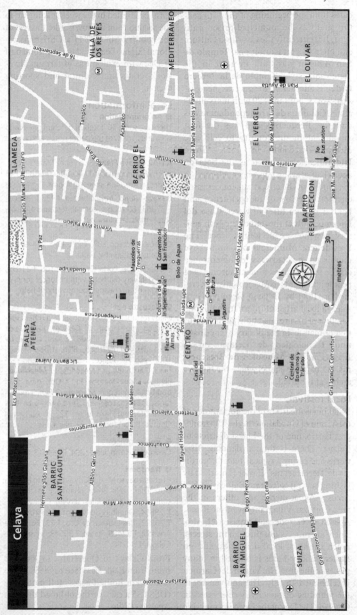

Celaya

16 de septiembre

VILLA DE LOS REYES

MEDITERRANEO

Tampico

Acapulco

EL OLIVAR

Plan de Ayuda

Río Bravo

BARRIO EL ZAPOTE

Tenochtitlan

José María Morelos y Pavón

Dr. José María Luis Mora

EL VERGEL

ALAMEDA

Ignacio Manuel Altamirano

To
Bus station

Antonio Plaza

José Ma. Lía Pino Suárez

Alameda

La Paz

Vicente Riva Palacio

BARRIO RESURRECCION

Guadalupe

Mausoleo de Tresguerras

Convento de San Francisco

Bolo de Agua

Blvd Adolfo López Mateos

5 de Mayo

Independencia

Columa a la
In-dependencia

Casa de la
cultura

N

30

PALAS ATENEA

El Carmen

Lic Benito Juárez

Plaza de Armas

Portal Guadalupe

Allende

San Agustín

metres

0

Los Aztecas

Hermanos Aldama

Casa del
Diezmo

Gral Ignacio Comonfort

Francisco Madero

Emeterio Valencia

Central de
Bomberos y
Tránsito

Av Insurgentes

Cuauhtémoc

Miguel Hidalgo

BARRIC SANTIAGUITO

Hermenejildo Galeana

Albino García

Melchor Ocampo

Diego Rivera

Río Lema

Francisco Javier Mina

Gral Antonio Rabago

Mariano Abasolo

BARRIO SAN MIGUEL

SUIZA

CENTRO

dates from the beginning of the 17th century and was the municipal prison until 1961. It is currently the Casa de la Cultura and often has art exhibitions. **Templo de San Agustín** was built in 1609 in the plateresque style. **Templo de la Tercera Orden** is another of Tresguerras' neoclassical works, built in 1820 with marvellous altars. **Columna de la Independencia** was built by Tresguerras and was the first monument in the country to celebrate Mexico's freedom in 1828. **Torre Hidráulica**, also known as the **bola de agua** (ball of water), has been adopted as the symbol of the city; it was inaugurated on the centenary of independence and holds 1 million litres of water. **Casa del Diezmo**, built at the end of the 17th century, now houses the tourist office. The **Presidencia Municipal** has impressive murals up the stairways in the entrance off the main square, a metamorphosis of people and events in Mexico's history, created in 1980 by Octavio Ocampo González, a local artist of international fame. Another of his murals, showing the evolution of man, is in the library of the **Instituto Tecnológico de Celaya**, on C Irrigación. The **Mausoleo de Tresguerras**, is a baroque chapel where the famous architect is buried.

Local festivals

10-20 Jan is the fiesta of the appearance of the Virgin of Guadalupe in the Tierrasnegras barrio, one of the oldest districts of Celaya. There is drama, dancing, fireworks and eating a typical *antojito*, 'gorditas de Tierrasnegras'. Easter is marked by visiting several *balnearios*: Balnearios Los Arcos y Aguacaliente and others in the area, Cortázar, Villagrán, Juventino Rosas, Apaseo el Grande and Apaseo el Alto. There are processions through the streets, much eating of local delicacies, and on Easter Sunday Judas is burned in many places in the city. The Virgen del Carmen is celebrated 16 July. The anniversary of the founding of the city is celebrated in October. The Day of the Dead is a movable feast, celebrated in the week leading up to the second Mon in Nov, unlike the rest of the country. Since 1844 a Christmas regional fair has been held in the second half of Dec with exhibitions of farming, livestock, crafts and cultural and sporting events.

Local information

● **Accommodation**

There are some 30 hotels of different prices and standards; many of the better hotels are outside the centre.

A1-A2 *Celaya Plaza*, Blvd López Mateos y Carretera Panamericana, T 46260, F 46889, 143 rooms, tennis, spa, meeting rooms.

B *Plaza Bajío Inn*, Libertad 133, T 38603, F 37353, 80 rooms, central, restaurant, disco, convention facilities, parking, medical service, laundry.

C *Isabel*, Hidalgo 207, T 22096, F 33449, restaurant, bar, laundry, parking.

E *Guadalupe*, Portal Guadalupe 108, T 21839, F 29514, very old hotel with historical connections, central, cheaper rooms without bath.

● **Places to eat**

Many restaurants serving steak and others specializing in seafood. *El Caserío*, Blvd López Mateos 1302 Pte, T 55608, Spanish cuisine; *La Mansión del Marisco*, Blvd López Mateos 1000, esq Fco Juárez, T 55262, fish and seafood, live music at weekends; *El Mezquital*, Blvd A López Mateos 1113 Ote, meat and traditional barbeque; *Mamma O'Fan*, 3 restaurants, at Benito León 203, Blvd A López Mateos 1008 Ote, and Plaza Juárez 127, in Apaseo el Grande, Italian food, pizza, pasta, etc.

● **Tourist offices**

Casa del Diezmo, Juárez 204, T/F 34313, helpful.

● **Transport**

6 buses a day to Mexico City airport with Primera Plus. There is a 24-hr pharmacy at the bus station. Bus companies serving Celaya: ETN, T 28664; Omnibus de México, T 23614; Elite, T 20533; Tres Estrellas de Oro, T 23776; Flecha Amarilla, T 22489; Tucán, T 36543; Turismos de Celaya, T 34280.

From Celaya to Querétaro, to join the route from Eagle Pass (see page 99), there is a 56-km limited-access toll motorway (US$4.35 a car), or the old road through Apaseo el Alto.

From Guanajuato, Celaya can be reached via the historic towns of Dolores Hidalgo, Atotonilco and San Miguel Allende. 15 km from Guanajuato on the road to Dolores is **Santa Rosa**; in a story book setting in the forest is *Hotel El Crag*, **D**, clean; *Restaurant La Sierra* next door (the Flecha Amarilla bus stops here on the way to Dolores Hidalgo). There are two or three other places, including *Rancho de Enmiedo*, good dried meat specialities and beautiful scenery. The road corkscrews up in spectacular fashion before winding down through impressive rocky outcrops and ravines to the plain on which Dolores Hidalgo stands. The last 10 km or so are very arid.

DOLORES HIDALGO

(*Pop* 135,000) The home of Father Hidalgo, is 54 km from Guanajuato, a most attractive, tranquil small town; celebrations are held on 15 and 16 September. The main square, or Jardín, is lovely, dominated by a statue of Hidalgo. On one side is the church of **Nuestra Señora de los Dolores** (1712-1778) in which Hidalgo gave the Grito, the façade is impressive,

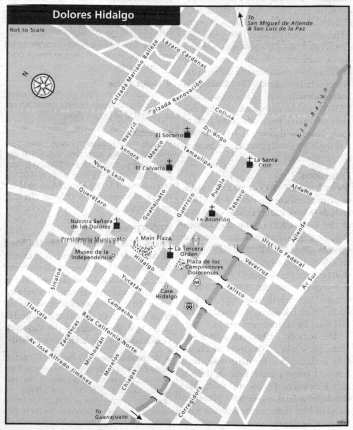

and the churrigueresque side altar pieces, one of gold leaf, one of wood are more ornate than the main altar. It is not always open. In an arcade beside the church is the tourist office (limited). Also on the Jardín are many restaurants and cafés, and banks.

Places of interest

La Asunción, Puebla y Sonora, has a large tower at one end, a dome at the other, with large murals and a tiled floor inside. Two blocks away, at Puebla y Jalisco, is Plaza de los Compositores Dolorenses with a bandstand. Between these 2 sites on Puebla is the post and telegraph office. Visit Hidalgo's house, **Casa Hidalgo**, Morelos y Hidalgo, open Tues-Sat 1000-1800, Sun 1000-1700, US$4.35; a beautiful building with a courtyard and wells, many memorabilia and one room almost a shrine to the Father of Independence. The **Museo de la Independencia**, on Zacatecas, entry US$0.70, was formerly a jail, now has displays of striking paintings of the path of Independence. Traditional Talavera tiles still made here and ceramics can be seen all over the town.

Excursions

About 5 km SE of town on a dirt track (walk or hitch) are the ruins of the **Hacienda de la Erre**, Padre Hidalgo's first stop on the independence route after leaving Dolores (free entrance to the untended ruins and grounds). The standing walls are only 3-4m high; there are about 4 rooms with ceilings; the patio, with a lot of litter is overgrown, but the chapel has been rebuilt. Outside is the huge mezquite tree under which Hidalgo is supposed to have said mass for his insurgent troops.

The walk (1½-2 hrs) starts from the plaza, then take C Guerrero to the E, take Tamaulipas to the main road. Turn left for 1 km to a gravel road on the left on a long curve. Follow this to the Hacienda in a fertile area with plenty of trees; in May there is much colour with the cacti in flower.

Local information

● **Accommodation**

Hotel María Dolores, Av de los Héroes 13, T 20517, 2-star.

C *Posada Las Campanas*, Guerrero 15, T 20427.

D *Posada Cocomacan*, on the plaza, T 20018, pleasant colonial house where Juárez stayed, comfortable, good value, good food, rec.

E *Posada Dolores*, on Yucatán, with bath, clean, OK, small room.

● **Places to eat**

Caballo Blanco, on Jardín by corner of Hidalgo and Guerrero, good value. Excellent ice cream at *Helado Torres*, SW corner of Jardín. *Fruti-Yoghurt*, Hidalgo y Guerrero, just off Jardín, delicious yoghurt, wholefood cakes and biscuits, also sells homeopathic medicines, etc.

Market: is on Tabasco, S side, between Jalisco and Hidalgo. Another market, nr *Posada Dolores*, on Yucatán.

● **Tourist offices**

On the Zócalo. They can direct you to places making the traditional talavera tiles which can be bought at very good prices.

● **Transport**

Bus station is at Hidalgo y Chiapas, 5 mins from main square; has restaurant, toilets, left luggage, local phones. Frequent buses to Guanajuato, León (US$3.65), Mexico City (US$10.50), San Luis Potosí (US$5) and San Luis de la Paz (US$2). To Aguascalientes, US$6.50, 2nd class, via San Felipe.

ATOTONILCO

About 20 km further on is the small town of **Atotonilco**, where there is a church built around 1740 whose inside walls and ceiling are covered with frescoes done in black, red and grey earth: unrivalled anywhere for sheer native exuberance. It was from Atotonilco's church that Padre Hidalgo took the banner of the Virgen de Guadalupe to act as his battle standard.

● **Accommodation A3** *Parador El Cortijo*, Apdo Postal 585, San Miguel de Allende, T 91-465-21700, very good, pool open to non-residents US$3.30, below the hotel on Querétaro-Dolores Hidalgo road are Las Grutas thermal baths, which belong to the hotel. Take Dolores Hidalgo bus from San Miguel de Allende bus station, or 'Santuario' hourly bus from covered market off Plaza Allende nr top of San Miguel: either passes the door.

Across the river from Atotonilco is the tiny village of San Miguelito. A short distance beyond, natural thermal waters rise from the river bed; local women construct hot tubs, called *arenas*, by piling sand around the springs in which to wash clothes and themselves. There is a spa, the Balneario Taboada (admission US$2, open Wed-Sun), between Atotonilco and San Miguel (about 20 mins bus ride direct from San Miguel market, it is a long walk from the main road, better to go by car or taxi). The Spa has a small hot pool, a fine swimming pool and good fishing in a nearby lake – very popular (café open only Sat and Sun). Near the Spa is *Hacienda Taboada* hotel (5-star, large thermal pool, swimming pool, prior booking necessary – open only to residents). Another spa is close by, Santa Verónica, with huge clean pool, open 0900-1800, US$2.50, bus stops outside, recommended. From San Miguel de Allende, for either spa, catch bus from Mesones by the market.

SAN MIGUEL DE ALLENDE

(*Pop* 150,000; *Alt* 1,850m; *Phone code* 415)
A charming old town on a steep hillside facing the broad sweep of the Río Laja and the distant blue of the Guanajuato mountains, is 50 km N of Querétaro by paved road, 90 km from Guanajuato. The city was founded as San Miguel in 1542, and Allende added in honour of the independence patriot born there. Its twisting cobbled streets rise in terraces to the mineral spring of El Chorro, from which the blue and yellow tiled cupolas of some 20 churches can be seen. It has been declared a national monument and all changes in the town are strictly controlled. The area around Parque Juárez and El Chorro is very picturesque with steep alleyways and women washing clothes in the springs. In recent years there has been a large influx of American residents (now numbering

over a thousand) and tourists, with a consequent rise in prices. See **Shopping**, below.

Places of interest
Social life revolves around the market and the Jardín, or central plaza, an open-air living room for the whole town. Around it are the colonial **Palacio Municipal**, several hotels, and the **Iglesia Parroquial** (parish church), adorned by an Indian mastermason in the late 19th century, Zeferino Gutiérrez, who provided the austere Franciscan front with a beautiful façade and a Gothic tower; see also the mural in the chapel. The church of **San Felipe Neri**, with its fine baroque façade, is at the SW end of the market. Notable among the baroque façades and doors rich in churrigueresque details is the **Casa del Mayorazgo de Canal**, and **San Francisco** church, designed by Tresguerras. The convent of **La Concepción**, built in 1734, now houses an art school, the **Centro Cultural Nigromonte**, locally known as Bellas Artes (good cafetería in its courtyard), one of the rooms off the courtyard contains a large mural by Siqueiros, locked up because of vandalism, but you can get the key from the secretary at the entrance; the summer residence of the Condes del Canal, on San Antonio, contains an art school and a language school, the Instituto Allende, started in the 1940s by Stirling Dickinson (which has an English-language library and runs Spanish courses, usually without accommodation, but some rooms can be rented – for others, see below). Tours of old houses and gardens start from the public library, Sun 1215, 4 hrs (US$8). A magnificent view of the city can be gained from the mirador on the Querétaro road (the views are also good before you get to the Mirador).

Excursions
A good all-day hike can be made to the Palo Huérfano mountain on the S side of town. Take the road to just before the radio pylon then take the trails to the summit, where there are oaks and pines. Between San Miguel de Allende and

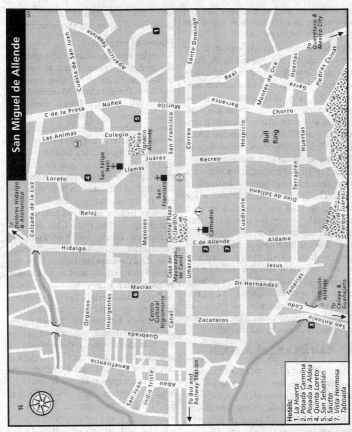

San Miguel de Allende

Hotels:
1. La Huerta
2. Posada Carmina
3. Posada la Aldea
4. Quinta Loreto
5. San Sebastián
6. Sautto
7. Vista Hermosa
   Taboada

Celaya is **Comonfort** (25 km); from there go 3 km N to Rancho Arias: on a hilltop to the W are precolumbian pyramids. Cross the river N of the church and climb to ruins via goat-tracks. **El Charco del Ingenio** Botanical Gardens (reached by taking a bus to El Gigante shopping centre, turn left and continue for 15 mins, or go up C Homobono, a more interesting and attractive route) cover an area of 64 ha with lovely views, a deep canyon, an artificial lake and cacti. Admission US$1 (free on Wed).

Local festivals

End-July to mid-Aug, classical chamber music festival, information from Bellas Artes. Main ones are Independence Day (15-16 Sept); Fiesta of San Miguel (28 Sept-1 Oct, with Conchero dancers from many places); Day of the Dead (2 Nov); the Christmas Posadas, celebrated in the traditional colonial manner (16-24 Dec); the pre-Lenten carnival, Easter Week, and Corpus Christi (June). There is a Christmas season musical celebration, started in 1987, which attracts musicians of international level, T 20025.

Local information

● **Accommodation**

Many weekend visitors from Mexico City: book ahead if you can. A good source of information on inexpensive accommodation is the English language paper published weekly by the Anglo-Mexican Library on Insurgentes.

A1 *Mansión del Bosque*, Aldama 65, T 20277, half-board; **A1** *Villa Jacaranda*, Aldama 53, T 21015, central, a couple of blocks behind cathedral, very good restaurant; **A2** *Misión de los Angeles*, de luxe, 2 km out on Celaya road, T 21026, colonial style, swimming pool, convenient facilities; **A3** *Posada de San Francisco*, main square, T 20072, pleasant restaurant; **A3** *Posada La Aldea*, C Ancha de San Antonio, T 21022, colonial style, clean, quiet, swimming pool, gardens.

B *Parador San Miguel Aristos*, at Instituto Allende, Ancha de San Antonio 30, T 20149, students given priority, large rooms, some with a fireplace and kitchen, parking US$2; **B** *Rancho-Hotel El Atascadero*, T 20206, Querétaro road entrance, in an old colonial hacienda, very satisfactory; **B** *Vista Hermosa Taboada*, Allende 11, very popular, nice old colonial building, some ground floor rooms dark and noisy.

Near Jardín, on C Viñarón **C** *Posada La Fuente*, has a few rooms, good food (by arrangement), Ancha de San Antonio 95, T 20629, **C** *Posada de las Monjas*, Canal 37, T 20171, with shower, excellent set meals in restaurant, clean and attractive, very good value, a converted convent, also has a few D rooms at back if you ask; **C** *Mesón San Antonio*, Mesones 80, T 20580, renovated mansion, clean, friendly, quiet, **C** *Monteverdi*, T 21814, clean, hot water; **C** *Posada Carmina*, Cuña de Allende 7, T 20485, colonial building, courtyard for meals, rec; **C-D** *Quinta Loreto*, Loreto 13, T 22380, TV, clean, quiet, swimming pool, pleasant garden, next to Mercado de Artesanías, hot water problems, good, cheap food, restaurant closed in evening (but beware of mosquitoes).

D *Casa de Huéspedes*, Mesones 27, T 21378, family atmosphere, clean, hot water, popular, roof garden, nice location, good value; **D** *Sautto*, Dr Macías 59, T 20072, for room with fridge, fireplace and bath, new rooms best, rustic, garden, hot water, parking, rec; **D** *Hidalgo*, Hidalgo 22, hot water (but not all day), rooms not always cleaned and vary in quality; **D** *San Sebastián*, Mesones 7, T 20707, nr market, rec, with bath, charming, large rooms with fireplace, clean, car park, noisy at front (most rooms at the back), courtyard.

E *San Miguel International Hostal*, Organos 34, T 20674, 4 blocks from the central plaza, shared bath, double with breakfast, or F pp in dormitory, bed linen US$2 extra, 15 mins of chores each day, friendly, cosy, clean, kitchen and laundry facilities available, free tea and coffee, book exchange, Spanish classes Mon-Thur, 1700-1900, US$1.75/hr, US owners; **E** unnamed *Casa de Huéspedes* on C Mesones, 150m E of Plaza Allende, clean, quiet, hot shower; **E** *Vianey*, del Fccolo; another cheap *casa de huéspedes* on Animas, just past the market building; **E-F** *La Huerta*, bath, clean, well-furnished, quiet, at the bottom of a dead-end street 4 blocks from the market in woodland, dark and unpleasant at night for lone females walking back, free parking, but watch your valuables, no phone.

Motels: **A1** *Villa del Molino*, Mexico City road entrance; **B** *Siesta*, road to Guanajuato, with trailer park, gardens; KAO campgrounds further out on same road, quiet, grassy site, all facilities, pleasant, Dutch owner.

● **Places to eat**

Mesón de San José, Mesones 38, Mexican and international cuisine, vegetarian dishes excellent breakfasts, nice setting, German/Mexican owners, open 0800-2200, live music Sun, gift shop, rec; *Mama Mía*, C Umaran W of main square, main meals good but not cheap, free live folk music or films in pm, excellent cheap breakfasts; *Café de la Parroquia*, Jesus 11, good, French owner speaks English; *Andale Pizza*, Hidalgo 1 /, good and economical pizzas, salad and *comida corrida*, rec, rec; *Casa Mexas*, Canal 15, good American food, clean, popular with gringos, English TV; *Matador*, Hernández Macías 76, clean, excellent food, not too expensive, rec; *Italia*, hotel/restaurant, on Dr Hernández, pasta, nice; *Rincón Español*, opp Correos, good *comida corrida*, rec, flamenco at weekends; *El Jardín*, C San Francisco, close to Plaza, friendly service, good food, also vegetarian, violinist plays upstairs at weekends for price of a drink; *Flamingos*, Juárez, good set lunch US$4.50; *La Princesa*, Recreo 5, set menu 1300-2000, inc glass of wine, live music from 2100, cosy cellar atmosphere; *La Guarida del Zorro*, Recreo 16 entre Correo y Hospicio, excellent steaks and *parrillada*, good value, pleasant atmosphere; *La Vianda*, Zacateros 56, good for cheap *comida corrida* at lunchtime; *La Vendimie*, C Hidalgo, English proprietor, poetry readings Mon pm (must book), occasional fish and chips; *La Pirata*, Jesús, excellent, cheap, popular with Mexicans and tourists in the know; *Doña Anita*, Mesones 23, good; *Café Delante*, through *Remo's* on C Mesones, patio, fountain, homemade cakes, coffee; *El Infierno*, Mesones, just below Plaza Allende, excellent *sopa azteca*, good value, *menú del día*, US$2.50; *El Tomate*, vegetarian restaurant on Mesones, attractive, spotless, excellent food, generous helpings, not cheap; *Tentenpié*, C Allende, pleasant café/taquería. Good cheap chicken restaurant on C San Francisco between Juárez and Reloj (roast chicken in windows). *El Otro Café*, Mesones 95, quiet wholefood café, sells *The News*, English book and magazine exchange, free refills of coffee, excellent pecan pie, friendly. Try the *licuados* (fruit-shakes) in the market; ask for a *campechana*!

● **Banks & money changers**
Casas de Cambio Deal on Correo, opp Post Office, and on Juárez.

● **Embassies & consulates**
Consulate: US Consular Agent, Plaza Colondrinas arcade, C Hernandes Macías, T 22357, emergencies 20068/20980, Mon and Wed 0900-1300, 1600-1900, Tues and Thur 1600-1900.

● **Entertainment**
English language films at *Villa Jacarandá* hotel video bar. US$5 inc alcoholic drink and popcorn.

● **Language schools**
Many of the schools demand payment in US dollars (technically illegal) and you may prefer to arrange private tuition for US$3-4/hr. Academía Hispanoamericana, rec for language lessons and sessions on Mexican history, folklore, literature, singing and dancing; very helpful; accommodation with families. The Academia América-Española offers full time Spanish courses; Casa de la Luna teaches Spanish less formally. *Inter/Idiomas*, 20 de Enero Sur 42, Col San Antonio 37750, T 24115, F 20135, small classes, 2-4 hrs a day of classes, fees from US$10/day, accommodation list available, also Mexican history and cookery classes, rec. *Card Game Spanish*, Pilancón 19, T 21758, F 20135, intensive courses for beginners or intermediate, run by Warren Hardy, the inventor of the Card Game method. See also **Learning Spanish** in Information for travellers. The library arranges 'amigo' sessions where Mexicans and foreigners can practice English and Spanish for free. Many activities arranged here.

● **Laundry**
On Pasaje de Allende, US$3 wash and dry, same day service; unnamed laundry at Correo 42, good.

● **Libraries**
English language library on Insurgentes has an excellent selection on Mexico; very extensive bilingual library, with computer centre and English-speaking staff.

● **Shopping**
Bookshop: *El Colibrí*, Díez de Sollano 30, good selection of French and English books. The English-language *The News* is sold on the Jardín.

Handicrafts: pottery, cotton cloth and brasswork. In the Mercado de Artesanías the merchandise tends to be souvenirs rather than real handicrafts; prices are high and the selection poor. Tues is the best day for bargains. The shops on Canal have a good selection and quality is high, but so are the prices; bargaining is next to impossible. It may be better to try elsewhere for genuine handicrafts (eg the Ciudadela handicraft market in the capital). *La Casa del Vidrio*, Correo 11, offers an excellent selection of brown-glass items at fair prices (sale prices in the summer, 40% off). *Joyería Rubí*, Correo 7, good value, jewellery made to order, rec.

● **Tour companies & travel agents**
Viajes Vertiz, on Hidalgo, American Express agent, mail collection and cheque cashing available. Excursions organized by the friends of the local school for handicapped children are US$10 pp, interesting destinations to local ranch or artesans or houses not normally open to the public.

● **Tourist offices**
On Plaza next to the church, helpful with finding hotels, English spoken, US$2 for city map.

● **Useful addresses**
Immigration: for tourist card extensions, etc, at Shopping Centre *Gigante* above the town. Take 2 copies of passport, tourist card and credit card or TCs.

● **Transport**
Trains The railway station is a long way from the centre, beyond the bus terminal. Both are served by bus. Train leaves 1309 for **Mexico City** (via Querétaro); leaves the capital 0900, arrives San Miguel 1435, US$8.75 *primera preferente*, US$5 2nd class; T 20007 for reservations. Train N to San Luis Potosí, with connections for Piedras Negras or Monterrey, at 1435 daily.

Buses The bus station is on the outskirts, regular bus to the centre US$0.25, returns from the market or outside *Posada San Francisco* on the Jardín. Frequent buses to **Guanajuato** (2 hrs) with Flecha Amarilla and Estrella Blanca, via Dolores Hidalgo, US$3.30. To **Dolores Hidalgo**, US$1.50. Buses to **Mexico City** via Querétaro (US$2.20) 4 a day before 1200, US$12, 2nd class with Flecha Amarilla, crowded but interesting. Bus at 0530 to Mexico City airport with Primera Plus. Buses to **Morelia** until 2040 daily, 4 hrs, US$6.25, 2nd class. Bus to **Atotonilco** US$1, plus short walk. **NB** There are two routes between San Miguel de Allende and Guanajuato: the southerly route is faster than the northerly route through Dolores Hidalgo.

Nogales-Guadalajara: the Pacific Highway

THE ROAD ALONG the Pacific Coast gives access to several resorts (eg **Guaymas**, **Mazatlán**, **Puerto Vallarta**), to ferry terminals for Baja California, and to the Los Mochis end of the railway to **Chihuahua**. It heads inland, through **Tepic**, towards **Guadalajara**.

In summer, W coast drivers prefer the Central Route from El Paso, Texas, unless they love heat. It is dangerous to drive on retread tyres over the hot desert. Do not drive at night and never park or sleep along the road.

The Pacific Highway down the coast to Acapulco and Salina Cruz is completely paved but has military searches in the State of Guerrero (for narcotics and arms). There are many motels along the whole route, so that each town of any importance has one or more nearby.

From Nogales to Guaymas on the Gulf, the road runs along the western slopes of the Sierra Madre, whose summits rise to 3,000m. From Guaymas on to Mazatlán it threads along the lowland, with the Sierra Madre Occidental's bold and commanding escarpment to the E. Like the W coasts of all continents between latitudes 20° and 30°, the whole area is desert, but fruitful wherever irrigated by water flowing from the mountains. Summers are very hot, sometimes rainy, but winters are mild and very dry. Within the Sierra Madre nomadic people hunt the many wild animals; along the coasts available water determines the spots of concentrated settlement and of agriculture. Mexico gets most of its wheat from the southern part of Sonora state, and the irrigated valley bottoms (around Hermosillo) are also used for maize, cotton and beans. Farther S, in frost-free Sinaloa and Nayarit, sugar, rice, winter vegetables, tomatoes, and tobacco are grown. The three coastal states the route passes through make up 21% of Mexico's area, but include only 6% of its population.

NOGALES

(Km 2,403; *Phone code* 631) **Nogales** lies astride a mountain pass at 1,120m across from Nogales, Arizona. Population estimates range from 180,000 to 240,000, with another 20,000 on the Arizona side. Nogales is the largest town in the Pimería Alta, the area of southern Arizona and northern Sonora occupied by the Pima Indians at the arrival of the Spaniards. The Pimería Alta Historical Society, a block from the border in Nogales, Arizona, is open weekdays 0900 to 1700, Sat 1000 to 1600, and Sun from 1300 to 1600; no admission charge. It has excellent exhibits

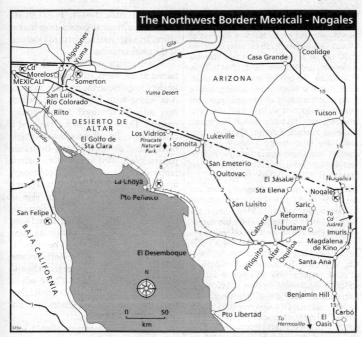

The Northwest Border: Mexicali - Nogales

on the history of the region, a valuable library and archives, and also organizes tours to the Sonoran missions. The staff are a good source of information on the Mexican side. The city's commercial centre is squeezed into a few narrow blocks centred on Av Obregón. The town is a mining area and a busy trans-shipment point for fruit and vegetables destined for US supermarkets; walnut groves (*nogales*) and cattle ranches surround it, and the bordertown flavour is that of a miniature Tijuana: liquor stores, glass, silver and leather goods, cheap bars and colourful markets.

Local festivals

Cinco de Mayo festival, lasting 4 days, celebrates the defeat of the French army at Puebla on 5 May 1862.

Local information
● **Accommodation**

B *Fray Marcos de Niza*, Campillo 91, gaudy but none too good.

C *Granada*, López Mateos y González, T 22911; **C** *Motel Miami*, Campillo and Ingenieros, basic but friendly and good; **C** *Olivia*, Obregón 125, T 22200, a/c, TV, reasonable; there is a wide selection of cheaper hotels on Juárez, a 1-block extension of Av López Mateos between Campillo and the border, 2 blocks from the Mexican port of entry.

● **Places to eat**

El Greco, upstairs at Obregón and Pierson, has attractive, reasonably priced international menu. Other rec restaurants on or nr Obregón, inc *El Cid* (No 124, good but dear), *Olivia*, *Casa de Maria*, *El Toro Steakhouse*. *Café Olga*, Juárez 37 next to bus station, open all hours.

● **Tourist offices**

Tourist office at the border closed 1991, but small brochures and a basic map of Nogales are available.

● **Transport**

Trains Pacific Railway Nogales-Benjamín Hill-Guadalajara, and on by National Railways of Mexico. Guadalajara, 1,759 km away, is reached in 30 hrs, at a speed of 60 km/hr (*primera preferente*, dep Nogales 1530, US$41). From Guadalajara, the *primera preferente* leaves at 0930, divides at Benjamín Hill, arriving Nogales 1 day later. Conditions vary, several unpleasant experiences reported, eg lack of a/c, dirt, overcrowding, etc. The trains stop at Hermosillo, Guaymas, Navojoa, Sufragio, Mazatlán, Tepic and many other towns. Luggage must be checked, except hand luggage, and then must be kept an eye on. Ticket office at border immigration office open 0800-1100, 1400-1600.

Buses Nogales, new bus terminal is 8 km S of the city centre, along the highway to Magdalena and Hermosillo; parking US$1/hr. Taxis at the border ask US$5 to take you to the bus station, but on the return journey the booth selling taxi vouchers charges less than US$4. A local bus, 1 peso, leaves 1 block from the border. To Mexico City, 42 hrs with Transportes de Pacífico, daily at 2030, or twice daily with Nte de Sonora, US$88. To Guadalajara, 1st class, US$60, 4 daily with Transportes del Pacífico. Other destinations inc Hermosillo (US$10), Guaymas (US$10), Los Mochis (US$24), Mazatlán (US$43), Tepic (US$53), Agua Prieta (US$8.25), Tecate (US$25), Tijuana (US$25), and Chihuahua (US$28). On the Arizona side 1 block from the port of entry, Citizen Auto Stage Company (T 287-5628) runs 10 buses daily between Tucson and Nogales (US$6.50); stops at Tucson airport en route. Stopovers (no additional charge) are possible to visit Tumacacori mission, N of Nogales. US Greyhound is about ¼ block from the border.

CROSSING THE BORDER

The Nogales crossing is open 24 hrs. To avoid the congestion of the downtown route, motorists are generally advised to use the truck crossing (open 0600 to 2000, currency exchange available), which is reached by the Mariposa Avenue exit from Interstate 19, 2½ miles N of downtown Nogales, Arizona. Returning from Mexico to the US, follow the sign to the 'Periférico' which avoids the downtown area. Get a tourist card before crossing the border, at an insurance agent (Jones Associates, linked to International Gateway Insurance, 2981 N Grand Ave,

Nogales, T 602-281-9141, F 281-0430), border town Mexican consulate or tourist office. Try to get your tourist card validated at the truck crossing.

Motor vehicle documents can be obtained at the Mexican Customs post 21 km S of Nogales, on the highway to Santa Ana, along with US insurance (which may also be obtained at the border proper). There is a tourist office and a cambio here. Two photocopies of vehicle registration, driver's licence, insurance papers, credit card and visitor's permit (approved), are required; a photocopy machine is available. Drivers leaving Mexico are advised by a large sign to surrender papers here; this involves crossing the southbound traffic and joining the queues of drivers entering Mexico. It can be chaotic. The post is poorly-equipped and has few officers who speak English; high vehicles should avoid the low inspection shed. Those whose destination lies within Sonora State may find these entry procedures are not needed. Check locally.

Bus and rail passengers should seek out the tourist office at the border to obtain a tourist card. Customs agents at the bus station will turn a blind eye if you get on a bus without a tourist card, but if the bus is stopped for routine checks (frequent) you may get sent back to the border.

ROAD TOLLS

If driving from Nogales to Mazatlán by the 4-lane, divided toll road (Route 15), there are 12 toll gates, The first is 88 km S of Nogales. No motorcycles, bicycles (but see page 404), pedestrians or animals are allowed on the highway, which is fenced and patrolled. The toll stations are well-lit, have good bathrooms, fuel and food. Total distance Nogales-Mazatlán is 1,118 km; the road is being extended beyond Mazatlán so that about 70% of the entire Nogales-Guadalajara route is now 4-lane. The *autopista* sections beyond Mazatlán, eg the sections before and after Tepic, are worth taking for the time they save. It is not possible to list in this guide every toll location and every deviation to avoid it. Most deviations are dirt roads and should not be taken in the rainy season. The high toll cost on this route has contributed to a decline in tourism in Sonora and in Sinaloa. On toll routes and their avoidance, seek advice from US motoring associations and clubs (see page 530) as costs and conditions change rapidly.

MAGDALENA VALLEY

The highway passes through the Magdalena Valley. The Cocóspera mines are near Imuris and there are famous gold and silver mines near **Magdalena** (*Hotel El Cuervo*, near plaza, C without TV, B with) which has a great Indian *fiesta* in the first week of October. On the Magdalena bypass is a toll, US$5, avoidable by driving through town (at N of town heading S, 95 km S of Nogales, keep left to avoid the backstreets). The free road S to Hermosillo becomes 'speed bump alley'. See also page 163. Beyond, the cactus-strewn desert begins. At 120 km from Nogales is Santa Ana, where the road from Tijuana and Mexicali comes in.

From Imuris, a major highway junction with numerous inexpensive restaurants, Mexico 2 heads E (to Naco and Agua Prieta) through the scenic Sierra de Pintos to the historic and still important copper mining centre of **Cananea**, where a 1906 miners' strike against the American-owned Cananea Consolidated Copper Company was one of the critical events in the last years of the Porfirio Díaz dictatorship. Hundreds of Arizona Rangers crossed the border to join the Sonora militia in putting down the strike, which is commemorated at the Museo de La Lucha Obrera, the former city jail, on Av Juárez. There are several motels along the highway.

THE NORTHWEST BORDER

From Baja California Route 2 from Tijuana (see page 490) runs close to the border, going through Mexicali (see page 486), San Luis Río Colorado, Sonoita, and Caborca to Santa Ana, where it joins the West Coast Highway (Route 15) to Mexico City. Route 15 is a divided 4-lane motorway from Nogales to Guaymas. East of Mexicali the fast 4-lane highway crosses the fertile Mexicali valley to a toll bridge over the diminished Colorado River, and continues to **San Luís Río Colorado** (*Pop* 134,000), a cheerfully tourist-oriented border town in the 'free zone' and serving cotton country: summer bullfights, small night-life district like those of the Old West, including a so-called 'zona de tolerancia'. Americans cross the border to purchase eyeglasses, prescription pharmaceuticals and have dental work done at much lower prices than in the USA. The port of entry is open 24 hrs, but there is no public transport from Yuma.

The Kino missions

Padre Eusebio Francisco Kino was the foremost pioneer missionary of NW Mexico and Baja California. He attempted the first major settlement of the Baja peninsula (San Bruno, 1683); after its failure he was assigned to the mainland, where he blazed a *ruta de misiones* as far as present-day Tucson. Kino was a versatile and hardy Jesuit of Italian origin – astronomer, cartographer, farmer, physician, navigator, explorer and a man of unlimited faith. Most of his adobe mission buildings were later replaced by substantial Franciscan churches, such as at Pitiquito, Oquitoa and at Magdalena, where his grave was discovered in 1966; the remains are enclosed in glass *in situ* and the site is a colonial monument. The church of San Ignacio, between Magdalena and Imuris (see page 163) is in excellent repair, with a wooden spiral staircase of mesquite.

● **Accommodation A1** *Hotel San Angel; El Reuy* and others on Av Obregón, en route to Sonoita. Budget hotel: *Capra*.

North of San Luis (35 km) is Baja's last international border crossing point, the farming town of **Algodones** (*Pop* 12,000). Border open 0600-2000, but motor vehicle documents are processed weekdays only, 0800-1500. The road N from San Luis skirts the Algodones dunes, the longest in North America. Algodones has one hotel, the rather misnamed **E** *Motel Olímpico*, dozens of souvenir stands, and several decent restaurants. Mexican car insurance is readily available, and there are several *casas de cambio*.

At Andrade, on the California side, the Quechan Indians operate an RV park and campground (US$12 per site with electricity, US$8 without; including hot showers, access to laundry room). Winter is the peak season, as the town is nearly deserted during the unbearably hot summer. From the W bank of the river, notice the abandoned Hanlon headgate for the Alamo Canal, which burst in 1905 and poured water into California's Imperial Valley for 8 months, creating the enormous 'Salton Sea'.

There is public transportation hourly between Algodones and Mexicali but, other than taxi, there is none from Yuma, Arizona, to Andrade (although the road has recently been paved and the number of visitors is rapidly increasing). Most visitors park at the lot operated by Quechan Indians from the nearby Fort Yuma Reservation (US$1, but there is plenty of free parking with easy disposal of the border, except on the busiest days).

9 km S of San Luis is **Pozos**, which 40 years ago had 60,000 inhabitants, now only 2,500. It has ruins of large buildings, churches, but no hotels. State highway 40 runs S to Riíto (gas and a few stores) then follows the railway across the edge of the barren Gran Desierto to **El Golfo de Santa Clara**, a good-sized fishing town which has a fish-processing plant, supermarket, general store, church and a couple of eating places. The tidal range at the head of the Gulf is wide but there are good sandy beaches nearby at high tide. Public camping area (no facilities) at the end of a 3 km sandy track past the town. The highway is paved, a round-trip from San Luís of 230 km.

After leaving San Luís Rio Colorado, Highway 2 crosses the sandy wastes of the **Desierto de Altar** – Mexico's own mini-Sahara. The road is very narrow in places, watch out for overloaded Mexican trucks. For 150 km there are no facilities (gas at Los Vidrios), only three houses and an enveloping landscape of sand dunes, cinder cones and a dark lava flow from the Cerro del Pinacate, so extensive that it stands out vividly on photographs from space. All the area around the central range is protected by the **Pinacate Natural Park**; a gravel road 10 km E of Los Vidrios gives access to the northern sector of the park, which contains much wildlife: eg puma, deer, antelope, wild boar, Gila monster, wild sheep, quail, red-tailed eagle. Several volcanic craters, the treacherous lava fields and an interesting cinder mine may also be visited (the area was used to train US astronauts during the Moon missions). Visitors must register at the entrance and are restricted to the Cerro Colorado and Elegante Crater area.

SONOITA

After a hot and monotonous 200 km from San Luís, Route 2 reaches the sunbleached bordertown of **Sonoita**, a short distance from Lukeville, Arizona. (**NB** If coming from Lukeville to San Luís Río Colorado, make sure you turn right (W) at Sonoita and not left (S) to San Luisito; they are both on Highway 2 but 320 km apart in opposite directions!). Sonoita has little of interest itself, but there are several American-style accommodations: **C** *Motel Sol de Desierto*, a/c but no heat in some rooms (request extra blankets); **C/B** *Motel San Antonio*; **B** *Motel Excelsior*. Restaurants are few and mediocre at best – the coffee shop at Lukeville is a better alternative. Transportes Norte de Sonora and Tres Estrellas de Oro both run first-class bus services. Water and snacks should be carried anywhere in this very arid region, and, if driving your own vehicle, the tank should be kept full and replenished wherever possible. Arizona's picturesque Organ Pipe Cactus National Monument is just across the border from Sonoita.

The border crossing between Lukeville and Sonoita is open from 0800 to 2400. Camping is possible at developed sites near visitor centre at Organ Pipe National Monument for US$8 (US$3 visitor permit is valid for 15 days).

Highway 8 goes SW from Sonoita through 100 km of sand dunes; a sign, 'Dunas – 10 km', at Km 80, points to a sandy road to dramatic, desolate inland dunes through mountain-rimmed black lava fields, 4WD recommended.

PUERTO PEÑASCO

(*Pop* 60,000) One of the most important shrimping ports on the Gulf; the huge shrimp are too expensive for the US market and are mostly exported to Japan. It is very popular with Arizona and California RV drivers for fishing, surfing and the beach. It lies on the Mexicali railway and also has a regular air service. On the N side of the bay, 12 km, is La Choya, largely a gringo place, sandy streets, full of trailers and beach cottages, and several fine beaches. Fishing tournaments are held in the Bahía La Choya; Playa de Oro has good surf but Playa Hermosa now suffers from pollution. South of the town is the elite community of Las Conchas, security gate, US-owned beach chalets, self-contained. Souvenirs are the mirrors, necklaces and figurines locally made from coral, seashells and snail shells.

Local festivals

Navy Day is held in Puerto Peñasco, 29 May-1 June, with a colourful parade, dancing and a widely-attended sporting contest.

Local information
● **Accommodation**
C *Viña del Mar*, C 1 de Junio y Blvd Malecón Kino, T 33600, modern resort, cliffside jacuzzi, video-disco, etc, attractive rooms, good value.

D *Motel Mar y Sol*, Km 94 on Sonoita road, pleasant gardens, restaurant, a/c, friendly; **D** *Motel Señorial*, T 32065, C Tercera 81, 1 block from main beach, good restaurant, dearer upstairs rooms are a/c.

E *Motel Davis*, Emiliano Zapata 100, T 34314, pleasant.

Camping: *Playa de Oro Trailer Resort*, Mata moros 36, T 32668, 2 km E, laundry, boat ramp, 200 sites, US$12 for 2; *Playa Bonita RV Park*, on lovely Playa Bonita, T 32596, 245 spaces, restaurant, shop, laundry; *Playa Miramar*, C Matamoros y Final Av Campeche, T 32351, 105 spaces, laundry, boat ramp, satellite hook-ups; *Pitahaya Trailer Park*, beachfront at *Hotel Villa Granada*, E of town, 25 spaces, full hook-ups, toilets, no showers. Nominal camping fee at La Choya, showers.

● **Places to eat**
Costa Brava Restaurant, Kino y 1 de Junio, best in town, modest prices, exotic menu, pleasant; *Café La Cita*, 1 de Junio nr the gas station, authentic Mexican, budget; *La Curva*, Kino y C Comonfort, T 33470, Americanized menu, popular, budget prices, little atmosphere; *La Gaviota* coffee shop at *Hotel Viña del Mar*, good breakfasts and views.

● **Banks & money changers**
2 banks.

● **Shopping**
Jim-Bur Shopping Center, Benito Juárez nr railway crossing, is the main commercial hub and has a tourist office. Try *El Vaquero* or *El Gift Shop* for souvenirs and camping supplies. Fresh fish from open-air fish market on the Malecón (old town). Laundromat Liz, C Altamirano y C Simón Morua.

● **Transport**
Air Great Lakes Aviation flies from Albuquerque via Tucson and from Phoenix several times a week.

Recently-paved state highway 37 continues on S and E, roughly following the rail line to Caborca (180 km) – an alternative to the inland Highway 2 route.

CABORCA

(*Pop* 38,000; *Alt* 286m) Route 2 continues from Sonoita to Caborca (150 km), passing through a number of small towns (San Emeterio, San Luisito) and a more mountainous but still arid land. Customs and Immigration station near Quitovac (28 km S of Sonoita), where tourist cards and vehicle papers are validated as you enter the Mexican 'mainland'.

Caborca lies on the Mexicali-Benjamín Hill railway in the midst of a gently sloping plain. A 'Grape Fair' is held 21-26 June, with wine exhibitions and industrial and agricultural show. Caborca's restored Church of Nuestra Señora de la Concepción was one of the 25 missions founded by Padre Kino in Sonora and Arizona between 1687 and 1711. (It was also used in 1857 as a fortress during a raid by US renegades under self-styled 'General' Crabb; their defeat is still commemorated by a fair held each 6 April.) Caborca is the best base for exploring the Kino missions.

● **Accommodation** *Motel Posada San Cristóbal;* **A3** *Motel El Camino;* **C** *Motel San Carlos;* **D** *Hotel San Francisco;* **D** *Hotel Yaqui,* clean, a/c, TV; service station and general facilities.

ALTAR TO ARIZONA BORDER

Highway 2 continues E through **Altar** (café, gas station) to join Highway 15 at **Santa Ana** (*Pop* 12,500; *Alt* 690m), a small town of little note. The Fiesta of Santa Ana is held 17-26 July: horse racing, fireworks, etc. **B** *Motel San Francisco,* a/c, shower baths, restaurant; motel across the road not so nice, also **B**. There is a Canadian-Mexican trailer park S of town, on the right going S, space for 9-10 trailers, rustic, useful overnight stop. 2 km W is San Francisco, with another Kino mission.

From Altar, there is a little-travelled alternative route to El Sásabe, Sonora/Arizona, 68 miles SW of Tucson via Arizona Routes 86 and 286, perhaps the most isolated, forlorn and least frequented legal border crossing between the United States and Mexico. The 98-km dirt road from Altar, which passes W of the Sierra del Carrizal and Sierra de San Juan, is passable for any ordinary vehicle except after the heaviest rains (**NB** Mexican maps for Sonora tend to be inaccurate in this area). From Altar, drive 3 km NE toward Saric and bear left at the clearly signed junction; do not continue on the more inviting paved route unless you wish to visit the Kino mission sites and churches at Oquitoa and Tubutama – although maps show an equivalent dirt road beyond Saric to El Sásabe, there are numerous closed gates, some of them locked, over *ejido* (community) lands. Keep an eye out for semi-wild longhorn cattle along the road to Sásabe.

The border at **El Sásabe** is open from 0800 to 2000, but there is no public transportation on either side, nor is there any Mexican automobile insurance agency. For information as to road conditions, phone US Customs (T 602-823-4231); although they appear not to encourage traffic over this route, they will tell you whether vehicles have entered recently from Mexico and what drivers have said about the road.

42 km S the Pacific Highway reaches **Benjamín Hill**, where the Mexicali railway joins the main Nogales-Guadalajara track; brightening up this forgettable junction is the Children's Park, with an amusement park, lake, zoo, and a delightful scaled-down children's railway (motel, cheaper than those in Santa Ana, but only 10 mins away if not preferable). For northbound drivers there is a drug search at Benjamín Hill.

There is little of note on the straight run S to Hermosillo through semi-arid farming and rangeland, apart from the little towns of El Oasis and nearby Carbó (on the rail line) – both have gasoline supplies. 158 km from Santa Ana the land becomes greener and the irrigated fields and citrus groves begin to enclose.

HERMOSILLO

(*Pop* 698,300; *State pop 1995* 2,083,630; *Alt* 237m; *Phone code* 62) Capital of Sonora state, Hermosillo is a modern city, resort town and centre of a rich orchard area. Just E, the Rodríguez Dam captures the fickle flow of the Río Sonora, producing a rich strip of cotton fields, vegetables, melons, oranges and grapes. The local farmers are also big exporters of turkey and beef. Hermosillo's expanding industries draw many people from the hinterland, especially the new Ford assembly plant (manufacturing cars for the US market) as well as electronics and clothing manufacturers.

Places of interest

Reminders of an illustrious colonial past can be found around the central Plaza Zaragoza (invaded by noisy blackbirds at sunset): the imposing **Catedral de La Asunción** (1779, neoclassical, baroque dome, three naves) and the **Palacio de Gobierno**, with its intricately-carved pillars and pediment, historical murals and grandiose statues amid landscaped gardens. Highway 15 sweeps into Hermosillo from the N as a wide boulevard, vibrant in summer with orange-flowering trees, becoming Búlevar Rosales through the commercial centre before exiting S across the ring road (Periférico) for Guaymas (toll at Hermosillo US$5.35). The old traditional quarter is to the E of it, a few blocks SE of Plaza Zaragoza, where delightful houses and narrow streets wind around the base of Cerro de la Campana (fine views). On the eastern slope is the **Museo de Sonora** (Wed-Sat 1000-1730, Sun 1000-1530, free).

Not far N of downtown (Rosales y Transversal) is **University City**, with its modern buildings of Mexican architecture blended tastefully with Moorish and Mission influences. The main building contains a large library auditorium and interesting museum, open daily 0900-1300, closed holidays. There is an active fine arts and cultural life, with many events throughout the year open to visitors (check at Tourist Office for details). 2 km S of Plaza Zaragoza, near the Periférico Sur, is the wonderful **Centro Ecológico de Sonora**, a botanical garden and zoo displaying Sonoran and other desert flora and fauna in well-cared-for surroundings.

Local information
● **Accommodation**

Generally poor standard of hotels, although there are **A1** *Señorial*, Blvd E Kino y Guillermo Carpena, T 155155, F 155093, a/c, pool, parking, restaurant, bar; **A1** *Holiday Inn* on Blvd Eusebio Kino 368 (NE entry highway), T 151112, with restaurant, bars, entertainment, etc.

C *Motel El Encanto*, Blvd E Kino 901, a/c, phone, TV, comfortable; **C** *San Alberto*, Serdán y Rosales, T 121800, with breakfast, a/c, cable TV, pool, good value; **C/D** *Kino*, Pino Suárez 151, Sur (base of Campana hill), T 124599, popular business hotel, a/c, TV, fridge.

D *Guaymas Inn*, 5½ km N, a/c rooms with shower; **D** *Monte Carlo*, Juárez y Sonora, T 123354, a/c, old, clean, very popular, as is adjoining restaurant; **D** *Washington*, Dr Noriega Pte 68, T 131183, clean, a/c, basic rooms off narrow courts, with bath, best budget hotel, parking for motorbikes.

E *Casa de los Amigos*, contact the Asociación Sonorense de los Amigos, Felipe Salido 32, Col Centro Hermosillo, T/F 170142, dormitories, living room, library, garden, laundry and kitchen; **E** *Royal*, in centre, a/c but grubby. A/c desirable in summer; check that it works before taking room. Cheap hotels and *casas de huéspedes* can be found around Plaza Zaragoza and along Sonora nr Matamoros (red-light activity, choose carefully).

Motels: **C** *Bugambilia*, Padre Kino 712, T 145050. Two close to railway station.

● **Places to eat**

Jardín Xochimilco, Obregón 51, Villa de Seris, very good beef, not cheap; *Mariscos Los Arcos de Hermosillo*, Michel y Ocampo (4 blocks S of Plaza), fresh seafood, attractive and expensive; *Henry's Restaurant*, across the road from Motel Encanto, Blvd Kino Nte, nice old house, good; *La Huerta*, San Luis Potosí 109, seafood; *René's Café*, Rosales y Moreno, good value lunches, pleasant; *El Rodeo Rosticería*, Dr Noriega Pte 92, rec; *San César*, P Elías C 71 Pnte, excellent chop sueys, seafood and expensive 'gringo' food. Mexican specialities better value, open for breakfast.

● **Airline offices**
AeroMéxico, T 168206; **Mexicana**, T 171103; **Great Lakes**, T 91-800-00307; **Taesa**, T 173606.

● **Tourist offices**
Palacio de Gobierno, ground floor, T 172964.

● **Transport**
Air The Gen Pesquira/García airport (HMO) is 12 km from town. Daily to Mexico City, AeroMéxico, Mexicana, Aero California and Taesa. Other domestic flights to Chihuahua, Ciudad Juárez, Ciudad Obregón, Cuernavaca, Culiacán, Guadalajara, Guerrero Negro, La Paz, Los Mochis, Matamoros, Mazatlán, Mexicali, Monterrey, Tijuana and Torreón. International flights to Los Angeles (Aero California, AeroMéxico), Tucson (Serolitoral, Aero California and Great Lakes Aviation) and Phoenix (Great Lakes Aviation and Serolitoral).

Trains Station just off Highway 15, 2½ km N of downtown; overnight to Mazatlán; southbound departures at 1945 1st class, 1220 2nd class, northbound for Nogales leaves 0745 1st class, 1540 2nd class. Hermosillo-Guadalajara 2nd class, US$19.60.

Buses Bus station on Búlevar Transversal 400, N of University; to **Nogales** US$10, 4 hrs, hourly 0230-1830 (Tres Estrellas de Oro, 1st class); to **Agua Prieta**, 7 hrs, US$13.25, 6 a day (2nd class); to **Mexicali**; **Guaymas**, hourly round the clock, US$6, 2½ hrs; to **Los Mochis**, 1st class, US$22, 7½ hrs through scrubland and wheat fields. Bus to **Tijuana**, US$35 1st class, 11 hrs, there can be long queues, especially nr Christmas. Bus to **Mazatlán** 10-12 hrs, US$30. To **Kino**, US$3.35, 4 a day, 2 hrs (2nd class).

BAHIA KINO

A paved 118-km road runs W past the airport to **Bahía Kino** (*Phone code* 624), divided into the old, somnolent and somewhat down-at-heel fishing village, and the new **Kino Nuevo**, a 'winter gringoland' of condos, trailer parks and expensive hotels. Although the public beaches are good, most American visitors come for the sportfishing (International Sportfishing Tournament in June). There is no bank in the area. The nearest is in Miguel Alemán, between Kino and Hermosillo, 48 km away (Bancomer). The Seri Indians, who used to live across El Canal del Infiernillo

(Little Hell Strait) from the port on the mountainous Isla del Tiburón (Shark Island), have been displaced by the navy to the mainland, down a dirt road from Bahía Kino in a settlement at Punta Chueca (no E access). They come into Kino on Sat and Sun to sell their ironwood animal sculptures (non-traditional) and traditional basketware (not cheap). They may usually be found at the *Posada del Mar Hotel*. A fine Museo Regional de Arte Seri has opened in new Kino, C Puerto Peñasco, 3 blocks from the main beach road.

● **Accommodation** **A2** Gloria McDonagh has a beautiful bed and breakfast house on the beach, American-run, PO Box 80-83340, T 20141; *Hotel Posada del Mar*, T 181205, F 181237, quality declining; *Hotel Saro*, 5 rooms, on beach. **Camping**: on the beaches is possible with or without tent. Camping at one of the trailer parks costs about US$12 a night (eg *Kino Bay RV Park*, Av Mar de Cortez, PO Box 857, Hermosillo, T (624) 20216/(621)53197). *Islandia Marina Trailer Park*, Puerto Peñasco y Guaymas, US$10, English spoken, hospitable. June Ellen Hayna runs an RV Park, PO Box 50, T 20615, also cabins, **B**.

● **Places to eat** Reasonably-priced meals are available in old Kino at *La Palapa* and *Marlin* restaurants (latter next to *Islandia Marina Trailer Park*), extremely fresh seafood and snacks. *El Pargo Rojo*, really good seafood, rec.

GUAYMAS AND BAHIA SAN CARLOS

At Km 1,867 (from Mexico City) the road reaches the Gulf at the port of **Guaymas** (*Pop* 200,000), on a lovely bay backed by desert mountains; excellent deep-sea fishing, and sea-food for the gourmet. Miramar beach, on Bocachibampo bay with its blue sea sprinkled with green islets, is the resort section. Watersports on 10 May. The climate is ideal in winter but unpleasant in summer. The 18th century church of San Fernando is worth a visit; so also, outside the town, is the 17th century church of San José de Guaymas. Excursions to the cactus forests.

● **Accommodation** **B** *Ana*, C 25 No 135, T 20593, nr cathedral, a/c; **B** *Santa Rita*, Serdán and C 9, with bath, a/c, clean, good; **E** *América*, Alemán (C 20) y Av 18, T 21120, a/c, dirty, noisy; **F** *Casa de Huéspedes Martha*, C 13, with bath, fan, hot water, clean, garden, rec. **Motels**: **B** *Flamingos*, Carretera Internacional, T 20960; **C** *Malibu*, T 22244, Carretera Internacional N. **At Miramar Beach**: **A1** *Playa de Cortés*, T 11224, F 10135, also has excellent RV park (US$12.50/day), hot showers, clean, hotel has private beach, pool, restaurant and bar, etc; **A3** *Leo's Inn*, at end of the beach, T 29490, PO Box 430, Guaymas.

● **Places to eat** *Todos Comen*, on Serdán, good food at reasonable prices.

● **Transport** The Gen José M Yanez airport (GYM) is 5 km from Guaymas on the way to San Carlos. AeroMéxico (T 622 20123) has flights to La Paz, Mexico City and Tucson. Great Lakes/Arizona Air Express (T 91-800-00307) flies from Phoenix.

SAN CARLOS

15 km N of Guaymas (or 12 km from Highway 15) is the **Bahía San Carlos**, very Americanized and touristy, where 'Catch 22' was filmed; above the bay a twin peaked hill, the Tetas de Cabra, is a significant landmark; good fishing with an international tournament each July. North of San Carlos further development is taking place on Sonora Bay. Both Miramar and San Carlos beaches are easily reached by bus. The free beaches are dirty.

● **Accommodation & services** *Condominio Pilar*, check office for rentals, good camp area; **A3/B** *Hotel Fiesta San Carlos*, T 60229, PO Box 828, clean, good food (US$10-15); pool; **A2** *Tetakawi Hotel, Suites and RV Park* (Best Western), T 60220, F 60248, PO Box 71, San Carlos, Guaymas, by beach, swimming pool, bar, snack bar, disco, a/c, cable TV, trailer park rates US$14/day; just over 1 km up a dirt track is *Restaurant Norsa*, good limited menu, no alcohol; *La Roca Restaurant*. 7 km from the Highway, behind the shops, are the post office and police station; the beer depository will sell by the half case. Next, after 10 km, is **B/C** *Creston Motel*, beach side, clean, good value. Then the gas station and bank opp the phone and fax centre. *The Country Club*, with hotel and tennis, is extensive. **A2-B** *La Posada de San Carlos*, on the beach, very nice. After 10 km from the Highway a road branches to **C** *Dorada*

Rental Units, T 60307, PO Box 48, on beach, pleasant, and **C** *Ferrer Apartments*, cooking facilities, hot water, pleasant patio, good value. At Km 13 the road forks: left 1 km to two secluded bays with limited trailer camping, and right to the new Marina Real, the *Howard Johnson Hotel*, *Club Mediterranée*, T (622) 60176, F 60070, all on Sonora Bay, and beyond a beach with open camping.

● **Places to eat** *Cantón*, Serdán between 20 and 21, Guaymas, good Chinese. *Piccolo*, good pasta, salads, good value. Generally, restaurants are overpriced.

● **Tourist offices** Av Serdán, lots of pamphlets.

● **Transport Trains** *Autovía* from Guaymas to Nogales leaves daily except Sat; book in advance. Trains to **Guadalajara**, and intermediate stops, and Nogales, both 1st and 2nd class, daily. All trains leave from station at Empalme, a US$4 taxi ride from Guaymas. The station is very run down and basic. Bus to **Empalme** will allow you to take the train at 1500 (very full at times) coming from Nogales to **Sufragio** (often delays and breakdowns), to catch the Los Mochis-Chihuahua train the next morning. Empalme-Guadalajara US$52.70 *primera preferente*, US$20.25 2nd class. **Buses** 1st class bus to **Hermosillo** (2½ hrs, US$6); **Mazatlán**, frequent, 12 hrs, US$30; **Tijuana**, 18 hrs, US$47. To **Culiacán**, 9 hrs, US$16.50. Buses from Empalme to Los Mochis/Sufragio with Autotransportes Tufesa US$9.50, 5½ hrs, T 32770. **Ferry** Sematur sail from Guaymas to **Santa Rosalía**, Baja California, 7-hr trip, see schedule, page 532 for details.

CIUDAD OBREGON

From Guaymas to Mazatlán is 784 km. There is a toll 8 km W of Empalme, US$5; this is on the toll road which skirts Guaymas completely. An alternative route goes into Guaymas, but forks to avoid the centre from both N and S. A third route goes into the centre of Guaymas which should be avoided unless you have business there. Toll at Esperanza, US$5. First comes **Ciudad Obregón** (*Pop* 180,000), mainly important as the centre of an agricultural region. It is a good place for buying leather goods, such as western boots and saddles.

● **Accommodation** **A3** *Motel Valle Grande*, M Alemán y Tetabiate, T 40940;

A3 *Costa de Oro*, M Alemán 210, T 41765, well-kept and pleasant; **C** *Dora*, California 1016 Sur; **C** *San Jorge*, M Alemán 929 Nte, T 6414 9514, F 6414 4353, a/c, TV, restaurant, bar, pool, safe parking, clean, friendly, with colonial Spanish decor; also 2 hotels on street of main bus station (turn right on leaving), 1 block to **D** *La Aduana*, dirty, cold water, and further down, *Gema*. **Youth hostel**: Laguna de Nainari s/n, CP 85000, US$2 pp, ask for bus to Seguro Social – state hospital – and walk round lake to hostal from there Villas Deportivas Juveniles campsite, T 641-41359.

● **Places to eat** Expensive but good local food at *Café Bibi*, behind cathedral.

● **Transport** The airport (CEN) is 16 km from town. Flights to Chihuahua, Culiacán, Guadalajara, Hermosillo, La Paz, Loreto, Los Mochis, Mexicali, Mexico City, Tijuana and Veracruz. Flights to US cities: El Paso, Phoenix and Tucson. Airlines: AeroMéxico, T 641-32190; Great Lakes, T 91-800-00307; Taesa, T 641-39525.

From Ciudad Obregón to **Navajoa** (*Pop* 200,000) is a 4-lane highway in poor condition (toll at Navajoa, US$7). Navajoa has the *Motel El Rancho* (T 20004) and *Motel del Río* (T 20331) and a trailer park in the N of town on Route 15 (run down, shaded, US$10 for full hook-up, US$5 for car or small jeep, dollars preferred to pesos). West of Navajoa, on Huatabampo bay, are the survivors of the Mayo Indians; their festivals are in May.

ALAMOS

52 km into the hills is the delightful old colonial town of **Alamos**, now declared a national monument. It is set in a once famous mining area fascinating for rock enthusiasts. Although the area was explored by the Spanish in the 1530s, development did not begin for another 100 years when the Jesuits built a mission nearby. In 1683 silver mines were discovered near the village of **Aduana** and the population began to rise. By the 1780s there were over 30,000 people and the town had provided emigrants to settle new towns such as San Francisco and Los Angeles. At the end of the 18th century silver production was at its peak and Alamos was

the world's greatest producer. Political recognition followed and in 1827 it was made capital of Occidente (Sonora and Sinaloa). However, the mining industry declined in the 19th century and by 1909 most of the mines had closed because of rising costs and revolutions. In 1933 the railroad was abandoned and the population declined to only 1,000 inhabitants. This has since recovered to about 6,200, largely because of US immigration, attracted by the sunny climate, attractive architecture and surroundings, and the proximity of the US border. You can visit the very photogenic old mine site of Aduana, near the village of Minas Nuevas on the road between Navajoa and Alamos, bus US$0.25. There is a good, unnamed restaurant there, American-run, reservations essential, ask in Alamos. Several walking tours of Alamos are offered by the local US community, including a tour of the historical colonial town, and one of the homes and gardens, proceeds are reported to support school children's scholarships. The **Museo Costumbrista** has good explanations of the history of Alamos. The Alamos Music Festival is an annual event held for 7 days at the end of January.

● **Accommodation L3-A1** *Casa Encantada*, Juárez 20, T 642-80482, F 642-80221, in USA F (714) 752-2331, courtyard rooms to luxury suites, bed and breakfast, charming, small pool, will find rooms elsewhere if town is 'full'; **A2-A3** *Mansión de la Condesa Magdalena*, same ownership, beautifully renovated, clean, quiet, relaxing, colonial rooms, beautiful gardens, excellent food, rec; also *Posada La Hacienda*, on edge of town; **B** *Los Portales Hotel*, T 80111, with beautiful frescoes, on plaza; **D** *Somar*, on the road into Alamos, T 80125, Madero 110. *El Caracol Trailer Park*, US$8.50, rustic, good pool; 2 other trailer parks, *Real de los Alamos*, US$10, with pool (too far to walk from town) and *Dolisa*, C Madero 72, T (642) 80131, US$13, also **B-C** motel, small rooms, a/c, fireplace, with bath, TV.

● **Transport Air** There is a paved, 1,190m landing strip but no scheduled services. **Buses** Navajoa-Alamos every hour on the 30 mins from 0630, US$2, until 1830, 1 hr, good road. Bus station for Alamos is about 8 blocks from main bus station, but you must ask directions because it is a confusing route. **NB** For drivers heading N, there is a fruit and vegetable checkpoint on entering Sonora state. Toll at Sinaloa border US$5.35. Further toll and drug search 16 km N of Los Mochis, US$3.35.

LOS MOCHIS

(*Pop* 200,000) **Los Mochis**, in a sugar-cane area, is a fishing resort 25 km from the sea with a US colony. The name is derived either from a local word meaning 'hill like a turtle', or possibly, from 'mocho', meaning one-armed, perhaps after a cowboy thus mutilated. The city was founded in 1904 around a sugar mill built by the American, Benjamin Johnson. His wife built the Sagrado Corazón church. The family lost everything in the Revolution. There are plenty of night spots and bars visited by roaming mariachis, who play excellent music. A stairway leads up the hillside behind La Pérgola, a pleasant public park near the city reservoir, for an excellent view of Los Mochis. Toll at Los Mochis US$3.65.

Local information
● **Accommodation**

A1 *Santa Anita*, Leyva y Hidalgo, T (681) 87046, F 20046, comfortable, clean dining room (good), noisy a/c, stores luggage, mixed reports about Flamengo travel agency attached, has own bus service to station, safe garage to leave car whilst visiting Copper Canyon, US$4/day; it is usually possible to change dollars.

Under same ownership is *Plaza Inn*, on Leyva, the main street; also on this street, **B** *El Dorado*, 20 mins from centre, a/c, pool, friendly, very good, and *Florida*. **C** *Fénix*, A Flores 365 Sur, T 22623, safe, clean, very good; **D** *América*, Allende Sur 655, T 21355, no hot water in early am, noisy, a/c, has restaurant with good, cheap sandwiches, enclosed parking; **D** *Beltrán*, Hidalgo 281 Pte, T 20688, a bit run-down, rooms facing street very noisy, a/c, TV, rec, has all travel time-tables and will make reservations; **D** *del Valle*, Guillermo Prieto y Independencia, T 20105, a/c, bath, OK but pricey; **D** *El Parque*,

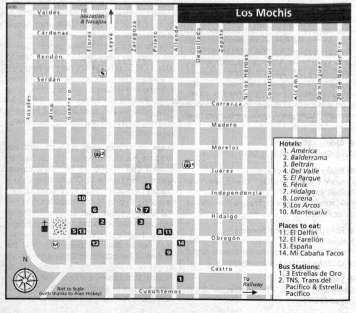

Los Mochis

Hotels:
1. América
2. Balderrama
3. Beltrán
4. Del Valle
5. El Parque
6. Fénix
7. Hidalgo
8. Lorena
9. Los Arcos
10. Montecarlo

Places to eat:
11. El Delfín
12. El Farellón
13. España
14. Mi Cabaña Tacos

Bus Stations:
1. 3 Estrellas de Oro
2. TNS, Trans del Pacífico & Estrella Pacífico

Not to Scale (with thanks to Alan Hickey)

across from Parque Sinaloa; **D** *Hidalgo*, opp *Beltrán* at No 260 Pte, T 23456, cheap cafetería, friendly, sometimes no hot water; **D** *Lorena*, Prieto y Obregón, T 20958, with bath, TV, gloomy, poor value but good cafetería; **F** *Los Arcos*, Allende, without bath, clean but dingy, fills up quickly, some rooms noisy.

Motel: **D** *Santa Rosa*, López Mateos 1051 N, modest.

Trailer Park: *Río Fuerte Trailer Resort*, 16 km N of Los Mochis on Route 15, good, heated swimming pool, rec, US$10/car and 2 people, US$12 motor home, offers hunting, shooting, fishing expeditions. **NB** The Pemex Station 1.5 km S of here has a very bad reputation and bad pumps. Ask at *Río Fuerte* which service stations are best, eg the one 16 km S on the right. There is another *Hotel Resort y Trailer Park* on Highway 15 at the turn-off to Topolobampo, sophisticated, with disco.

● **Places to eat**
El Farellón, Flores and Obregón, good seafood and service, reasonably priced; opp, on Obregón, is *España*, very good; *Café Panamá León*, Obregón 419, good meals, inc breakfast, cakes, inexpensive; *El Vaquero* in *Hotel Montecarlo*, rec; *El Delfín*, on Allende Sur nr Obregón, restaurant and bar, nice atmosphere (owner's husband is a mariachi musician); *El Taquito*, Leyva, 1 block from Santa Anita, is open 24 hrs; *Tay-Pak*, nr Independencia, Chinese, good clean, reasonably priced; *Chispa*, Leyva Sur 117, nr Morelos, art deco design, clean, good; *Mi Cabaña Tacos*, corner of Obregón y Allende, popular with locals, friendly, rec; *Las Palmeras*, excellent, reasonably priced; good seafood at *El Bucanero*. *Birria* is a local beef dish; many places to eat are referred to as a *birriería*.

● **Airline offices**
Aero California, T 681-52250.

● **Banks & money changers**
Casa de Cambio Rocha, T 25500, opp *Hotel Beltrán*; others, and banks, on Leyva. American Express at *Viajes Krystal*, Av Obregón, all services.

● **Hospitals & medical services**
Hospital: *Fátima*, Loaizo 606 Pte, T 55703/23312, private, English spoken, maybe a good place to start in an emergency.

● **Laundry**
Lavamatic, Allende 218; another laundry at Juárez 225.

● **Transport**
Air Airport Federal (LMM) is $6^{1}/_{2}$ km from town. Flights to Chihuahua, Ciudad Obregón, Culiacán, Guadalajara, Hermosillo, La Paz, León, Los Cabos, Mazatlán, Mexico City, Monterrey and Tijuana with a variety of airlines. Flights to Los Angeles, Phoenix and Tucson with AeroMéxico and/or Aero California.

Trains Connections with the Nogales-Guadalajara train are made at **Sufragio**, 37 km from Los Mochis (see also page 487). The *servicio estrella* passes Sufragio about 0215 going S, 0045 going N, the second class train goes through at a more civilized hour (2015 going S, 0710 going N). For **Creel and Chihuahua**, see below. **NB** If coming from Chihuahua and you don't want to stay in Los Mochis, assuming the train is not overdelayed, you can take a night bus to Mazatlán at 2200, arriving 0630. Sufragio station is open 24 hrs, including its restaurant and waiting room; warm to sleep in, guards will wake you if asked; handy for those with late-night connections but recent reports of poor security here. Los Mochis station has toilets and local phones; ticket office is open 1 hr before train leaves. The station is 8 km from town; do not walk there or back in the dark. There is a bus service from 0500, US$0.15 from corner of hotels *Hidalgo* and *Beltrán*, otherwise take the 0500 bus from *Hotel Santa Anita*, US$3.50 (for house guests only), or taxi, of which there is any number going into town after the arrival of the Chihuahua train. Taxis in the centre go from Hidalgo y Leiva; fare to station US$5/car, bargaining not possible, make sure price quoted is not pp, rip-offs are common. If driving and looking for secure parking while taking the train, ask for Sr Carlos at the station ticket office, he will guard the car at his home for a modest fee. There is more expensive parking downtown.

Buses Unlike most cities in Mexico, each bus company has its own terminal in Los Mochis. **Mexico City**, US$60, 25 hrs. **Guadalajara**, frequent, Tres Estrellas de Oro, 1st class, US$31. **Ciudad Obregón**, US$16.50. **Tijuana**, US$53, several daily up to 24 hrs. **Mazatlán**, $5^{1}/_{2}$ hrs, US$16.50, 1st class, Tres Estrellas de Oro or Transportes Nte de Sonora, hourly, also Estrella Blanca. **Nogales**, US$27, 12 hrs. No reservations can be made for buses N or S at the terminal of Tres Estrellas de Oro and it is difficult to get on buses. Try instead Transportes de Pacífico, 3 blocks away and next to TNS terminal. First class bus to **Guaymas** $5^{1}/_{2}$ hrs, US$9.50 with Tufesa. To **Tepic**, Tres Estrellas de Oro, 1st class, US$25, 13 hrs. To **Topolobampo**, US$1, buses leave from Mercado Cuauhtémoc, Marcial Ordóñez y Cuauhtémoc.

TOPOLOBAMPO

A side road, running SW from Los Mochis crosses the salt flats to **Topolobampo** (20 km, 30 mins). The town is built on a number of hills facing the beautiful bay-and-lagoon-indented coast. In the bay, which has many outlets, there are a number of islands; sunsets here are lovely. Boats can be hired, and fishing trips are available from the jetty. It is difficult to find a beach unless one pays for a private launch. Pemex has a storage facility here and Topolobampo is being developed as a deep-water port. This is as a consequence of the full operation of the Ojinaga (see page 115) – Pacific railway (of which the Los Mochis-Creel-Chihuahua route forms part). Originally conceived in 1872 as an outlet for US goods from Kansas and the S to Japan, the line across the Mexican Sierra was not completed until 1961.

- **Accommodation B** *Yacht Hotel*, 3-4 km S of town, modern, a/c, clean and good food, quiet, good views, but seems to close for the winter; **E** *Estilo Europeo Poama*, at the ferry terminal, 10 mins' walk from Los Mochis bus; for other accommodation go to Los Mochis.

- **Transport Ferry** Topolobampo-La Paz, Baja California Sur. For schedule and fares, see page 532, book ticket before 1800 on previous day (not Sun) or from 0600 on day of travel, T (686) 20141, F 20035. Travel agency *Viajes Paotán*, Rendón y Angel Flores, can book tickets for you on day of departure. See also page 513.

TO CREEL AND CHIHUAHUA BY TRAIN

The journey (see page 121) shows the spectacular scenery of the Sierra Madre and the Barranca del Urique/Cobre (Urique, or Copper Canyon). The *servicio estrella* train leaves daily at 0600, US$21 to Creel (about 9 hrs), US$26 to Chihuahua (about 14 hrs, but expect delays). Bring your own toilet paper, food and drinking water. Tickets must be bought in advance, not on

the train, either on morning of departure or, in high season (July-Aug, New Year, Holy Week) a day or more before. Return tickets are valid for 30 days. Tickets can be bought at Flamingo Travel (mixed reports) in *Hotel Santa Anita*, but they will try to persuade you to book into their preferred (expensive) hotels. It may be worth buying tickets from them to avoid long queues at the station. Buy return tickets as it is impossible to reserve seats from Creel back to Los Mochis. A local bus (US$0.10) leaves from the crossroads near *Hotel Beltrán* for train station. Departs 0530, arriving 0555. The ordinary train, *Tarahumara*, leaves at 0700, US$4.60 to Creel, US$8.60 to Chihuahua, not possible to reserve seats. 2nd class is reasonably comfortable and it is possible to open the windows, many stops. On either train, sit on the right for the best views, except when approaching Temoris, then return to the right until the first tunnel after Temoris; thereafter good views can be seen on either side. On the *primera especial* the windows do not open so, to take photos, stand between the carriages. Motorists taking the train to Creel have been advised to park in front of the station as there are lights and people at all times.

To begin with the journey is through flat country; Sufragio is reached after 40 mins, **El Fuerte** *(Pop 120,000)* after 1½ hrs. This town has recently been renovated and has interesting colonial architecture (it was founded in 1564). The station is 10 km from the town; taxis US$4 pp. *Posada del Hidalgo* in historical mansion, details from *Hotel Santa Anita* in Los Mochis; **D** *Hotel Oasis*, ½ block from C Benito Juárez in centre, not very clean, some rooms better than others, a/c; *Hotel San Francisco*, good value. Good restaurants, nice plaza.

The high, long bridge over the Río Fuerte heralds the beginning of more interesting scenery (this is the first of 37 major bridges); 3 hrs from Los Mochis the first, and longest, of the 86 tunnels is passed, then, 10 mins later the Chinapas bridge (this is approximately the Sinaloa/Chihuahua border, where clocks go forward an hour). Before Temoris (4 hrs) the track loops round to the left, goes through Temoris, then enters a tunnel in which the railway turns through 180°. **Bahuichivo** (5 hrs) has a simple hotel and a few shops; if you don't want to go all the way you can return from here (Bahuichivo-Creel, 1st class, US$4). From Bahuichivo, pick-ups make the 5-hr journey to **Urique**, in the heart of the Barranca del Urique (not Sun); 2 simple hotels in Urique, the one on the main street (F) is good value, bus leaves from here to return to Bahuichivo at 0800.

Cuiteco (5½ hrs) has the **B** *Hotel Cuiteco*, delightful, with a patio which has an unimpeded view of the mountains, quiet, oil lamps, gas stove in courtyard; **San Rafael** (20 mins later), where there is a 10-mins stop, is just after the La Laja bridge and tunnel; in a further 25 mins *Hotel Posada Barrancas* is reached, followed in 5 mins by **El Divisadero**, where there is an all-too-brief, 10-mins stop to view the Barranca del Urique, buy souvenirs from the Tarahumara women, and let the down train pass. 17 km beyond Pitorreal (7 hrs) is the Lazo loop, in which the track does a 360° turn; soon afterwards the highest point, Los Ojitos, is passed. Creel is reached in 8 hrs. Creel, its surroundings, and the various accommodations in the area are described under Creel, page 121.

CULIACAN

(*Km 1,429*; *Pop 950,000*; *State pop 1995 2,424,745*; *Phone code 671*) Some 210 km beyond Los Mochis is the capital of Sinaloa state **Culiacán**, chief centre for winter vegetables. No longer a colonial city, but attractive and prosperous; it has a university.

The highway is widened and divided for 90 km S of Los Mochis to Guamúchil, where the old freeway continues to Culiacán. North of the city, the N and southbound carriageways are on different levels with no divide (very dangerous). A new toll section of freeway heads nearer to the coast, past Navolata, bypasses Culiacán and rejoins Highway 15 a few kilometres S of that city. Note, though that this is a very isolated stretch of road and there have been robberies on it at times. Do not drive at night. The area around Culiacán is also a drugs-growing region.

Excursions

The safe beaches of **Altata** are 30 mins by paved road. 18 km W of Altata on gravel, then sand (passable) is Tambor Beach, wind and waves, and fewer people than Altata.

Local information
● **Accommodation**

A3 *Executivo*, Madero y Obregón, T 39370.

C *Del Valle*, Solano 180, T 39026, noisy, not rec.

D *San Francisco*, Hidalgo 227, with bath, clean, friendly, free parking.

E *Louisiana*.

Motels: A3 *Los Tres Ríos*, 1 km N of town on highway 15, trailer park, US$10, pool, resort style, good restaurant. *Pizzería Tivoli*, good, friendly. **C** *Los Caminos*, Carretera Internacional y Blvd Leyva Solano, T 153300, a/c, phone, satellite TV, restaurant, pool, nightclub, safe parking, clean rooms.

● **Transport**

Air Airport Federal de Bachigualato (CUL) 10 km from centre. Airlines: Aero California, T 60250; AeroMéxico, T 53772; Taesa, T 68899. Flights to Aguascalientes, Chihuahua, Ciudad Juárez, Ciudad Obregón, Cuernavaca, El Paso (Texas), Guadalajara, Hermosillo, La Paz, Los Angeles (California), Los Cabos, Los Mochis, Mexicali, Mexico City, Monterrey, San Antonio (Texas), Tijuana, Torreón and Tucson (Arizona).

Buses To Tepic, 8¼ hrs, US$12; to Guaymas, 9 hrs, US$16.50.

MAZATLAN

Another 208 km along Highway 15 (good condition) bring us to a roadside monument marking the Tropic of Cancer. Toll 27 km N of Mazatlán, US$11.35. Beyond the Tropic, 13 km is (Km 1,089) **Mazatlán** (*Pop 800,000*; *Phone code 678*), spread along a peninsula at the foot of the Sierra

Madre. It is the largest Mexican port on the Pacific Ocean and the main industrial and commercial centre in the W. The beauty of its setting and its warm winters have made it a popular resort, but unfortunately with expansion it has lost some of its attraction. It overlooks Olas Altas (High Waves) bay, which has a very strong current. Tourism is now concentrated in the Zona Dorada, which includes the beaches of Gaviotas, Los Sabalos, Escondida, Delfin, Cerritos, Cangrejo and Brujas; the area is built up and accommodation is expensive. From Olas Altas the promenade, lined by hotels with a long beach at its foot, curves around the bay, first as Paseo Claussen, then Av del Mar which leads to Av Camarón Sabalo in the Zona Dorada. The sunsets are superb seen from this side of the peninsula; at this time of day high divers can be watched and the fishermen return to the N beach. There are many good beach bars from which to view the setting sun. Buses from C Arriba go to Zona Dorada for US$0.50. On the other side of the peninsula the Av del Puerto promenade overlooks a number of islands. From the ferry terminal at the southern end of Av del Puerto, a boat can be taken to Isla de los Chivos for US$1; there you can stroll along the beaches and eat at the beach bars. There are more islands in the nearby lagoons, which teem with wild life. The best beaches, 3 to 5 km from the city, are easily reached by taxi. The lighthouse,

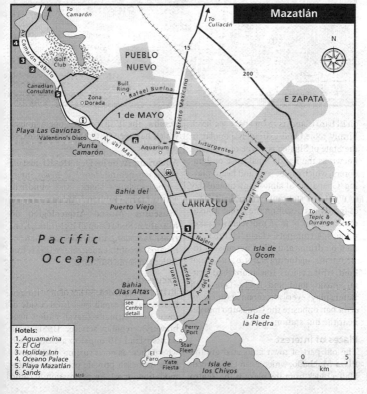

Mazatlán Centre

on El Faro island, is 157m above sea-level. Firmly rooted and extremely popular in the State of Sinaloa is a type of orchestra known as the Banda Sinaloense or Tamborera, which can be seen and heard playing 'Chaparral' at almost any time of day or night in restaurants, dance halls, bars, at family parties or on the street. It usually has from 14 to 16 musicians: 4 saxophones, 4 trumpets, clarinets, tuba, 3-4 men on drums and other percussion instruments, including *maracas*, *guiro*, and loud, strong voices. It is unabashed, brutal music, loud and lively. One such Banda plays every afternoon at the *Chaparral* bar, opposite the Conasupo market near the bus station.

Places of interest

The old part of town is located around **Plaza Machado**, which is on C Carnival. Half a block from the plaza is the **Teatro Peralta**, the 17th century opera house, which has been restored and reopened to the public.

Aquarium Av de los Deportes III, just off the beach, behind *Hotel Las Arenas*, interesting, includes sharks and blindfish, adults US$3, children US$1.50.

Museums **Museo Arqueológico de Mazatlán**, Sixto Osuna 115, ½ block from *Hotel Freeman*, small, covering state of Sinaloa, recommended, entry US$1, free gallery in same building.

Excursions

To **Isla de la Piedra**, 30 km of now littered beach. Take a small boat from S side of town from Armada (naval station near brewery), regular service, US$1, walk across island (10 mins) to a clean beach where there is good surfing. Local *comedores* on beach provide primitive accommodation, or ask for permission to camp on the beach. Try smoked fish sold on a stick. Beware of sandflies. Star Fleet boats may be rented at the sports fishing docks for a cruise round the Dos Hermanos rocks, where boobies and many other birds can be seen. A boat excursion on the *Yate Fiesta* cruises out at 1000 or 2000 (with dancing), from second last bus stop in the direction of Playa del Sur. Refreshments included, and you can see the wildlife in the day time.

About 100 km N of Mazatlán is a turn-off to the town of **La Cruz**, with two hotels, including: **D** *Las Palmitas*, off the main street, quiet. Few tourists.

At the foot of the Sierra Madre, 30 mins from Mazatlán is **L1** *Rancho Las Moras*, a converted tequila ranch, now with 6 hotel rooms and 5 villas, tennis courts, pool, laundry service, children's summer camp, restaurant and riding for all abilities (daytime activities for non-residents available), reservations T (69) 165044, F 165045, highly recommended (address of office Av Camarón Sabalo 204, Suite 6, Zona Dorada 82110, Mazatlán, or 9297 Siempre Viva Rd, Suite 15-474, San Diego, CA 92173, USA), from Route 15, take the road towards La Noria for 9 km, then turn left up dirt road at sign.

Local festivals

The local Shrovetide carnival is almost as good as at Veracruz.

Local information

● **Accommodation**

The expensive hotels are in the area known as the Zona Dorada; budget hotels can be found around Cerro de la Nevería and on C Angel Flores, C Aquiles Serdán and C José Azueta. Ask taxi drivers for the cheaper places.

Along the northern beach, Av Camarón Sabalo or just off it, are: *Los Sábalos*, RT Loaiza 100, T 835333, Health Club facilities; *Playa Mazatlán*, same street, T 134455, good atmosphere; *El Cid*, Camarón Sabalo, with *El Caracol* nightclub and *Club 21*, T 133333; *Camino Real* (T 131111), *Oceano Palace* (Best Western, T 130666), *Holiday Inn*, Camarón Sabalo 696 (T 132222, F 841287, resort facilities) all in our **A2-L2** ranges. **A3** *Las Palmas*, Camarón Sabalo 305, Zona Dorada, PO Box 135, T 134255, good value, rec.

Along Av del Mar beach (front rooms in all are likely to be noisy) are: **A1-3** *Aguamarina*, No 110, T 817080, F 824624; **A1** *De Cima* (T 827300); **A1** *El Dorado* (T 817418); **A1** *Hacienda* (T 827000); **C** *Amigos Plaza*, T 830333, before *Las Brisas*, some rooms a/c, noisy at weekends, otherwise OK; **D** *The Sands (Las Arenas)*, pool, a/c, TV, fridge, garden, good restaurant, rec, on beach; **C** *Don Pelayo/Days Inn*, Av del Mar IIII, T 831888, TV, a/c, pool, parking off street, bar (may be noisy late at night); **C** *Tropicana*, RT Loaiza 27, T 838000, a/c, shower, large rooms, rec.

Along Olas Altas beach are: **C** *Belmar*, T 820799, modernized but old; **D** *La Siesta*, T 812640, a/c, clean, friendly, safe, very good, nice patio, restaurant: *Shrimp Bucket*

On Paseo Centenario is: **C** *Olas Altas*, T 813192, with fan, efficiently run and clean, good views, restaurant. Most of the others are in the downtown area away from the beach front: **C** *Del Centro*, JM Canizales 705 Pte, T 821673, behind main church; **D** *Económico*, with bath and fan, noisy, dark but very clean, next to bus station, 500m from main beach; **E** *San Fernando*, 21 de Marzo 926, T 815980, with bath, hot water eventually, very basic, very friendly, rec, car park outside; **D** *Posada Familiar Sarita*, Mariano Escobedo, colonial, nr beach; **E** *Casa de huéspedes El Castillo*, José Azueta 1612, 2 blocks from market, clean, family atmosphere, big rooms; **E** *Lerma*, Simón Bolívar 5, nr beach, with fan and hot showers, friendly, clean, simple, but quiet and cool, highly rec, **E** *Roma*, Av Juan Carrasco 127, T 823685, 2 blocks from beach, with bath but some rooms noisy, clean; **E** *Vialta*, Azueta 2006, 3 blocks from market, with bath and fan, friendly, helpful, comfortable; **E** *Zaragoza*, Zaragoza 18, old and pretty, with bath, cheap cold drinks, free drinking water, parking for motorbikes.

North of the city there are undeveloped beaches with free overnight camping; some have camped alone, but it is safer in a group (take bus to Sabalos and get out where it turns round). At least 10 trailer parks on Playa del Nte/Zona Dorada and on towards the N, inc **D** *Casa Blanca Disco*, cheapest, on beach side, dirty. Big hotels rapidly expanding all along N beach seashore to Mármol.

Motels: are strung all along the ocean front: **B** *Marley*, RT Loaiza 226, T 135533, rec, reservations necessary; **C** *Del Sol*, Av del Mar 200, T 814712, big rooms, with a/c and TV, clean, bright, nice pool, English spoken, motorcyclists allowed to park in front of room, close to aquarium, also have some apartments with kitchen. **C** *Papagayo*, Papagayo 712, T 816489. *La Posta Trailer Park* (turn inland at *Valentino's Disco* from northern beach road), busy, hook-ups at most sites, ½ block off beach, with swimming pool and tent space, lots of shade. *Mar Rosa Trailer Park*, 2½ km N of *La Posta* T 836187, hot water, safe, own beach, rec. 4 km N of *Mar Rosa* is **Playa Escondida**, Av Sábalo-Cerritos 999, T 88-00-77, laid back, 236 spaces for RV park, not all have water and electricity, OK, US$13 (**B-D** in bungalows), pool, volleyball, TV. Beware of theft from trailer parks. If driving to trailer parks N of the city, pass airport on Route 15, avoid left fork 'Centro y Playas'; follow route signed 'Culiacán' but do not go onto the toll road to Culiacán which starts at the Carta Blanca agency. Keep left and 10 km further turn left at sign 'Playa Cerritos', at beach road turn left again. This leads to **Maravilla Trailer Park**, next to Edif DIF, PO Box 1470, Mazatlán, T 40400, 35 spaces, US$10 daily, hot showers, clean, quiet; *Holliday*, opp beach, and *Canoa*, private club, nice, expensive. If coming to Mazatlán from the N turn right at 'Playas Mazatlán Nte' sign on Highway 15; after about 14 km you reach the junction with the Av Camarón Sabalo.

● **Places to eat**
Doney's, M Escobedo 610, downtown, charming old building, good home cooking; *Mamucas*, Bolívar 73, seafood expensive. *Shrimp Bucket* and *Señor Frog*, Olas Altas 11 and Av del Mar, same owners, very famous, popular, good; *Beach Boys Club*, on Malecón nr fishermans' monument, good value meals, US owned; *El Paraíso*, on beach in Zona Dorada is rec; *Balneario Playa Norte*, Av del Mar, nr Monument, friendly, reasonable prices, rec; also on Ave del Mar, Playa Nte, *Bella Mar*, good, comparatively cheap; *Lobster Trap*, Camarón Sabalo, good chicken(!). *Joncol's*, Flores 254, a/c, downtown, popular; *Los Comales*, Angel Flores, 2 blocks from Correo, good. Best value fish meals, US$4, above the markets nr Plaza de la República (bring beer with you from supermarket opp – not sold in cheap restaurants). Try mixed fish dish, US$15 for 2, very good. *Bar Pacífico*, on main plaza, excellent guacamole and chicken wings, pleasant atmosphere; *Las Cazuelas*, Canizales 273, good cheap comedor, friendly; *Canaduria el Tunel*, opp theatre, excellent chicken enchiladas; *Pastelería y Cafetería Panamá*, several branches for reasonable meals, pastries, coffee. *Casa del Naturista*, Zaragoza 809, sells good wholegrain bread. US fast food places, eg *McDonald's*, *Pizza Hut*, are more expensive than in North America.

● **Airline offices**
Aero California, T (69) 132042; **AeroMéxico**, T (69) 841111; **Alaska Airlines**, T 95-800-426-0333; **Delta** (69) 8327 09; **Mexicana**, T (69) 827722.

● **Banks & money changers**
American Express, Av Camarón Sabalo 310, Zona Dorada, all services. **Banamex**, Benito Juárez and Angel Flores, also Av Camarón Sabalo 434, 0900-1330, 1530-1730. *Casas de Cambio* on same avenida, Nos 109, 1009 and at junction with Rodolfo T Loaiza; also at R T Loaiza 309.

● **Embassies & consulates**
Consulates: Canada, *Hotel Playa Mazatlán*, Rodolfo T Loaiza 202, T 137320/F 146655; **US** Consulate, T 134455 ext 285; **France**, Jacarandas 6, T 828552; **Netherlands**, Av Sabalo Cerritos 6, T 135155; **Germany**, Jacarandas 10, T 822809; **Italy**, Av Olas Altas 66-105, T 814855; **Norway**, F Alcalde 4, T 813237.

● **Language schools**
See *AmeriSpan* under **Learning Spanish** in **Information for travellers**.

● **Laundry**
On Av del Mar, between bus station and *Hotel Aguamarina*.

● **Post & telecommunications**
Post Office: Benito Juárez y 21 de Marzo, opp Government Palace, T 812121. **Mail Boxes etc**: Av Camarón Sabalo 310, T 164009, F 164011, mail boxes, courier service, fax service. Sending faxes from private offices is much cheaper than from the Post Office.

Telephones: 1 block from American Express; also 21 de Marzo y B Juárez, T 05. Computel phone and fax service, T (69) 160267/69, F 160268. Phone rental, Accetel, Calz Camarón Sabalo 310-4, T 165056.

● **Sports**
Fishing is the main sport (sailfish, tarpon, marlin, etc). Shrimp from the Gulf are sent, frozen, to all parts of Mexico. Its famous fishing tournament follows Acapulco's and precedes the one at Guaymas. In the mangrove swamps are egrets, flamingoes, pelicans, cranes, herons, and duck. Nearby at Camarones

there is 'parachute flying', drawn by motor-boats. The northern beach tourist strip offers boat trips to nearby deserted islands, snorkel hire and paragliding. For riding, see *Rancho Las Moras* in **Excursions** below. **NB** Always check with the locals whether swimming is safe, since there are strong rip currents in the Pacific which run out to sea and are extremely dangerous. There is a free Red Cross treatment station 9 blocks along the avenue opp the Beach Man on the right. There are bull-fights at Mazatlán, good view from general seats in the shade (*sombra*), although you can pay much more to get seats in the first 7 rows – Sun at 1600, very touristy.

● **Tour companies & travel agents**
Travel agents: *Explora Tours*, Centro Comercial Lomas, *segunda* at Camarón Sabalo 204-L-10, T 139020, F 161322, very helpful, rec; *Zafari Tours*, Paseo Claussen 25, ferry bookings, helpful.

● **Tourist offices**
Rodolfo T Loaizo 100, Local N6, T 132545; on road to northern beach, opp *Hotel Los Sabalos*. Also Av Olas Altas 1300, Edif Bancen, Col Centro, T 851222/851847.

● **Useful telephone numbers**
Emergency: call 06; Red Cross 8136901; Ambulance 851451; Police 821867.

● **Transport**
Local Green and white express buses on the 'Sabalo centro' route run from Playa Cerritos to the city centre along the seafront road, US$0.35. Taxis charge an average US$3.50-5 between Zona Dorada and city centre. From Bahía del Puerto Viejo to centre, taxi US$1, bus US$0.20.

Air Airport Gen Rafael Buelna (MZT) 19 km from centre. Taxi, fixed fare US$24 airport-Mazatlán; micro bus US$6 pp Daily flights to Mexico City, Guadalajara, La Paz, Durango, Ciudad Juárez, Hermosillo, León, Los Cabos, Los Mochis, Monterrey, Puerto Vallarta, Tijuana and Torreón. US destinations: Atlanta, Greenville, Los Angeles, San Francisco, Houston, Milwaukee, Denver, Las Vegas, Seattle, Tucson, San Antonio and Phoenix.

Trains Take 'Insurgentes' bus out to Morelos railway station. Train to **Mexicali**, *primera* departs 2000, *segunda* at 2330; to **Guadalajara**, 9 hrs, US$32.25 *primera preferente*, departs 0815, but is usually late, air-conditioned (if working), scenic trip with a variety of topography and agriculture; 2nd class at 0435, 11 hrs, US$8.85. From Tepic (5½ hrs) it climbs gradually through the hills to 1,650m at Guadalajara,

passing through some 30 or 40 tunnels. To Sufragio at 1830 1st class, 2230 2nd, 9 hrs (US$4.35, take torch). For Creel train, spend the night at San Blas, from where there are many buses to Sufragio or take 2nd class train to Sufragio and connect to 2nd class train to Creel. Buy tickets at agency in Pasaje Linguna in the Zona Dorada, close to Tourist Office or queue at 0730, seat numbers are not observed so sit in the first empty seat.

Buses Terminal at Chachalaco y Ferrusquilla s/n, T 812335/815381; take 'Insurgentes' bus from terminal to Av Ejército Mexicano for the centre, via market at C Serdán; if you cross the boulevard and take bus in the other direction it goes to the railway station (US$0.60); taxi US$3. Bus fare to **Mexico City** about US$55, 18 hrs. (Tres Estrellas de Oro, T 813680, 1st class, express at 2100 a little more expensive; Transportes del Pacífico hourly 1st class slightly cheaper but over 20 hrs, via Irapuato and Querétaro). **Mexicali** US$50, Pullman, 21 hrs. **Guadalajara**, several companies, several times a day, US$19.25 (10 hrs). To **Chihuahua**, US$38 1st class, 19 hrs. To crossroads for **San Blas**, US$8; **Tepic** US$8 (5¼ hrs, Tepic is the best place to make connections to Puerto Vallarta); bus (frequent) to **Los Mochis** (5½ hrs), US$16.50 with Transportes Nte de Sonora, Estrella Blanca or Transportes del Pacífico, tickets available only 45 mins before departure. To **Navajoa**, US$11 1st class; 1st class Transportes del Nte bus to **Durango**, US$14.80, take an am bus to see the scenery; **Guaymas**, 12 hrs, US$30. Bus to **Rosario** US$1.65, can then with difficulty catch bus to Caimanero beach, nearly deserted. Terminal Alamos, Av Ote Guerrero 102, 2 blocks from market, buses to **Alamos** every hour on the half hour. **Tolls**: Mazatlán to Culiacán US$65. **Cycling**: beware, the road Mazatlán-Tepic-Guadalajara has been described as 'the most dangerous in the world for cyclists'.

Ferry La Paz (Baja California Sur), see schedule, page 532, for other information see under La Paz, Baja California section. Allow plenty of time for booking and customs procedure. Tickets from *Hotel Aguamarina*, Av del Mar 110, with 10% commission, also from travel agents. Ferry terminal is at the southern end of Av del Puerto, quite a way from centre (take bus marked 'Playa Sur', which will also go from street corner opp ferry terminal to Av Ejército Méxicano nr bus station). **NB** Ticket office for La Paz ferry opens

0830-1300 only, on day of departure, arrive before 0800, unclaimed reservations on sale at 1100. Don't expect to get vehicle space for same-day departure.

MAZATLAN TO DURANGO

24 km beyond Mazatlán, the Coast-to-Coast Highway to Durango (a spectacular stretch), Torreón, Monterrey and Matamoros turns off left at Villa Unión. Heading E, the road reaches **Concordia**, a delightful colonial town with a well-kept plaza and a splendid church (hotel on main road, only one, D, old-world atmosphere, swimming pool), then climbs the mountains past **Copalá**, another mining ghost-town (basic hotel); *Daniel's Restaurant*, open 0900-1700. Copalá can be reached by tour bus from Mazatlán or by Auriga pick-up truck from Concordia. On this road, 40 km from Concordia, 3 km before **Santa Lucía**, at La Capilla del Taxte, 1,240m, there is a good German hotel and restaurant, D, *Villa Blanca*, T 21628. Before reaching La Ciudad (no accommodation) and the plains the road goes through a spectacular section with vertical drops on both sides, called the Devil's Spine; superb views. After reaching the high plateau the road passes through pine forests to Durango. **NB** Cyclists will find this road narrow, dangerous and hard work: there are many bends and hills, many of which are steep.

ROUTE TO TEPIC

The road to Tepic continues S from Villa Unión. At **Rosario**, 68 km S of Mazatlán, an old mining town riddled with underground workings, the church is worth a visit (D *Hotel Los Morales*, with a/c, E with fan, on main highway opposite Pemex, clean, quiet, good bathrooms; there is a very good *palapa* and hilltop restaurant with limited access, 360° view). South of Rosario is **Escuinapa** (several kilometres N of Escuinapa is **B** *Motel Virginia*, Carretera Internacional Km 1107-1108, T 695-32755, good clean, *palapa* restaurant next door, possible trailer parking).

There is a good seafood restaurant on the left at the entrance of Escuinapa coming from Mazatlán. In Escuinapa a good road turns off 30 km to the coast at **Teacapán**. The Boca de Teacapán, an inlet from the sea opening into lagoons and the mangrove swamps, is the border between Sinaloa and Nayarit. The area has palm trees, much bird and animal life, cattle ranches, and is an exporter of shrimp and mangoes. The fishing is excellent and you can buy fresh fish directly from the fishermen on Teacapán beach. There are fine beaches such as Las Cabras, La Tambora and Los Angeles. Dolphins can be seen at certain times of year. Buses from Escuinapa; tours from Mazatlán US$45 (eg Marlin Tours, T 135301/142690, F 164616); **B** *Rancho Los Angeles*, Teacapán Ecológico (Las Palmas 1-B, Col Los Pinos, Mazatlán, T/F 817867), former home of a drug baron (deceased), 16 km S from Teacapán towards Escuinapa, on beach, good value, swimming pool, trailer park, US$12; **D** *Hotel Denisse*, on square, T/F 695-45266, José Morales and Carol Snobel, clean, next to phone office, noisy, local trips arranged; you can also rent houses with kitchen facilities a few kilometres before Teacapán on the road at Hacienda Los Angeles; three trailer parks (*Oregon*, US$8, no signs, on beach in town, run down but one of better places to stay, new Mexican hotel next door; *Las Lupitas*, US$8, rustic, run down; another on bay, take road next to *Las Lupitas*, US$3, primitive, pretty setting). *SR Wayne's Restaurant*, on beach behind *Palmeras Hotel*, recommended. Quaint little towns just off the highway between Mazatlán and Tepic: **Acaponeta** (turnoff for El Novillero beach, large waves and many sandflies), Rosamorada, Tuxpan and Santiago Ixcuintla, all with colonial religious buildings and archaeological museums. From Highway 15, the island of **Mexcaltitán** can be reached. Turn off to Sentispac, from where a dirt road leads to La Batanga on Laguna Mexcaltitán. Boats go to the small island, which is only

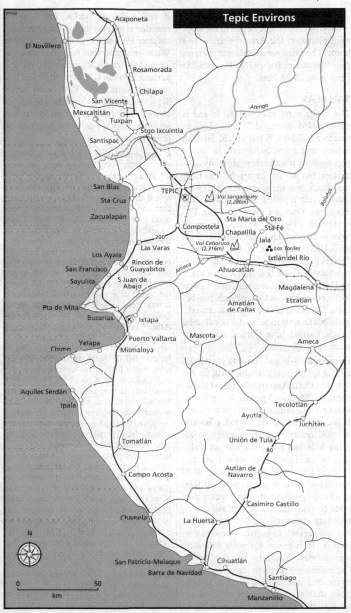

Tepic Environs

about 350m in diameter, now a fishing village, but reputed to be one of the stopping places on the Aztecs' search for a home. The name means 'place of the temple of the moon'. Its *fiesta*, St Peter and St Paul, is on 28-29 June.

SAN BLAS

The resort is 69 km from Tepic and is overcrowded during US and Mexican summer holidays. It has an old Spanish fortress and a smelly harbour. In Aug it becomes very hot and there are many mosquitoes, but not on the beach 2 km from the village (but there are other biting insects, so take repellent anyway); few tourists at this time or early in the year. The best beach is Playa de las Islas (the one in town is dirty). 7 km from San Blas (bus, taxi US$3 per car) is the beach of Matanchén, good swimming but many mosquitoes. Good homemade fruit cakes and bread sold here. 16 km S from San Blas is the beautiful Los Cocos beach (see below). The beach is empty except at weekends. **NB** Don't wander too far from public beach; tourists have warned against attacks and robberies.

Excursions 4-hr boat trips to see whales and dolphins are available. Ask at the Tourist Office. Armando is a good guide, charges US$52 for 3 people. It is possible to take a 3-hr jungle trip in a boat (bus to launching point, US$1.50) to **La Tovara**, a small resort with fresh-water swimming hole and not much else, or walking, to do. Tour buses leave from the bridge 1 km out of town and cost US$30 for canoe with 6 passengers. Official prices are posted but it still seems possible to shop around. There are coatis, raccoons, iguanas, turtles, boat-billed herons, egrets and parrots. Avoid motorized boats as the motor noise will scare any animals. Tours by foot are better. Crocodiles are kept in caves along the route. You have to pay US$2 to see the poor, shabby creatures, not rec. Twilight tours enable naturalists to see pottos and,

if very lucky, an ocelot. La Tovara is crowded at midday during the summer. A cheaper 1½-2 hrs' cruise is also possible. When arranging your trip make sure you are told the length of journey and route in advance. You can take a bus from San Blas towards Santa Cruz (see below under Tepic) and get off at Matanchén beach (see above). From here, a boat for ½-day hire includes the best part of the jungle cruise from San Blas.

- **Accommodation A1** *Marino Inn*, Batail-lon, T 50340, a/c, friendly, pool, fair food; **A1** *Garza-Canela*, Cuauhtémoc Sur 106, T 50112, very clean, highly rec, excellent restaurant; **B** *Bucanero*, Juárez Pte 75, T 50101, with bath and fan, frequented by Americans, food good, pool, lizards abound, noisy discos 3 times a week and bar is open till 0100 with loud music; **B** *Posada del Rey*, very clean, swimming pool, excellent value, on Campeche, T 50123; *Posada de Morales* also has a swimming pool, more expensive, ½ block from *Posada del Rey*, T 50023; **C** *San Blas Motel*, nr Zócalo, patio, fans, good value, swimming pool, safe parking; **D** *Flamingos*, Juárez Pte 105, huge rooms, ceiling fans, colonial, clean, friendly; **D** *Posada Azul*, 4 blocks from plaza towards beach, 3-bedded rooms with fan and hot water, **F** for simple 1-bedded rooms without bath, cooking facilities; **D/E** *El Tesoro de San Blas*, 50m S of dock, 5 mins from centre, rooms and villas, hot water, satellite TV, US owners; **E** *María's*, fairly clean with cooking, washing and fridge facilities, without bath, **D** with bath and fan, a bit noisy, friendly, rec. No camping or sleeping permitted on beaches but several pay camp-sites available. Sometimes free camping possible behind **E** *Playa Hermosa Hotel*, old house, only partly occupied, rooms in use clean, 2 km from town. **Trailer park** at town beach; all trailer parks in the centre are plagued by mosquitoes. The best trailer park is on Los Cocos beach: *Playa Amor*, good beach, on a narrow strip of land between road to Santa Cruz and cliff, good, popular, 16 km S of town, US$7-10. Next S is **E** *Hotel Delfín*, with bath, balcony, good view, good value; then *Raffles Restaurant* with trailer and camping area attached (no facilities). Last on Los Cocos beach is *Hotel y Restaurante Casa Mañana*, T (324) 80610 or Tepic T/F (321) 33565, Austrian run, good food. Many apartments for rent.

• **Places to eat** *La Familia*, try the *mere-quetengue* dishes, rec; *Amparo*, on main square, cheap and good; *MacDonald* just off Zócalo, good breakfast. Plenty of seafood restaurants on the beach; eg *Las Olas*, good and cheap.

• **Banks & money changers** Banamex just off Zócalo, exchange 0830-1000 only. **Comercial de San Blas** on the main square will change money, plus commission.

• **Transport** Buses to Tepic, frequent US$2.20, 1½ hrs. To **Guadalajara**, US$10, 8½ hrs.

Before reaching Tepic both road and railway begin the long climb from the lowland level over the Sierra Madre to the basin of Jalisco, 1,500m above sea-level. The Mirador El Aguila is on Highway 15, 11 km after the junction to San Blas; it overlooks a canyon where many birds can be seen in the morning and the late afternoon.

TEPIC

(Km 807; *Pop* 200,000; *State pop 1995* 895,975; *Alt* 900m) Capital of Nayarit state, Tepic was founded in 1531 at the foot of the extinct volcano of Sangagüey. It is a slightly scruffy town with much rebuilding going on but clean. There are many little squares, all filled with trees and flowers.

The landscape around Tepic is wild and mountainous; access is very difficult. Here live the Huichol and Cora Indians. Their dress is very picturesque; their craftwork – bags (carried only by men), scarves woven in colourful designs and necklaces (*chaquira*) of tiny beads and wall-hangings of brightly coloured wool – is available from souvenir shops (these handicrafts are reported to be cheaper in Guadalajara, at the Casa de Artesanías). You may see some in Tepic but it is best to let Indians approach you when they come to town if you want to purchase any items.

Places of interest

The **Cathedral** (1891), with two fine Gothic towers, in Plaza Principal, has been restored; it is painted primrose yellow,

adorned with gold. Worth seeing are the **Palacio Municipal**; the **Casa de Amado Nervo** (the poet and diplomat), Zacatecas 281; the **Museo Regional de Antropología e Historia**, Av México 91 Nte (open 1000-1400 and 1700-2000 hrs, closed Mon); **Emilia Ortez Museum of Art**, C Lerdo 192; **Plaza de los Constituyentes** (México y Juárez) with, on one side, the **Palacio de Gobierno**; and the **Convento de la Cruz**, on the summit of a hill close to the centre. The tombs in the cemetery are worth seeing.

Local information
● **Accommodation**

B-C *Bugain Villas*, Av Insurgentes y Libramiento Pte, T 180225, very comfy rooms with a/c, TV, pool, garden, restaurant with great food and good wine list; **C** *Fray Junipero Serra*, Lerdo Pte 23, T 22525, main square, comfortable, big rooms, clean, a/c, good restaurant, friendly, good service, rec; **C** *Ibarra*, Durango 297 A Nte, T 23870, luxurious rooms, with bath and fan (some rooms noisy), and slightly spartan, cheaper rooms without bath, very clean, DHL collection point. **C** *San Jorge*, Lerdo 124, T 21324, very comfortable, good value; **C** *Villa de las Rosas*, Insurgentes 100, T 31800, fans, friendly, noisy in front, good food, but not too clean.

D *Altamirano*, Mina 19 Ote, T 27131, nr Palacio del Gobierno, noisy but good value; **D** *Santa Fe*, Calzada de la Cruz 85, nr La Loma park, a few minutes from centre, with TV, clean, comfortable, good restaurant; **D** *Sierra de Alicia*, Av México 180 Nte, with fan, tiled stairways, friendly.

E *Camarena*, 4 blocks from Zocalo on San Luis Nte, without bath; **E** *Juárez*, nr Palacio de Gobierno, on Juárez 116, T 22112, clean room with bath, locks on room doors not very effective, limited parking in courtyard; **E** *México*, México 116 Nte, T 22354. **E** *Nayarit*, E Zapata 190 Pte, T 22183; **E** *Pensión Morales*, Insurgentes y Sánchez, 4 blocks from bus station, clean and friendly. **E** *Sarita*, Bravo 112 Pte, T 21333, clean, good; **E** *Tepic*, Dr Martínez 438, T 31377, nr bus station outside town, with bath, clean, friendly but noisy.

Motels: B *La Loma*, Paseo la Loma 301 (swimming pool), T 32222, run down; *Bungalows and Trailer Park Koala*, La Laguna, Santa María del Oro, has bungalows at US$20, each accommodating up to 4, several trailer sites and a large campground. Good cheap meals available. Fishing and waterskiing on nearby lagoon.

● **Places to eat**
El Apacho, opp *Hotel Ibarra*, good *sopes*, cheap; *El Tripol*, in mall, nr plaza, excellent vegetarian; *Danny O* ice cream shop next door; *Roberto's* and *Chante Clair*, both good food and nr La Loma Park, closed Sun; *La Terraza*, Mexican and American food, pies, cakes; good vegetarian restaurant at Veracruz 16 Nte, try the granola yoghurts; *Tiki Room*, San Luis Nte opp *Hotel Camarena*, restaurant, art gallery, video bar, fun. Restaurant in bus terminal, overpriced. Lots of fish stalls by market on Puebla Nte. The local *huevos rancheros* are extremely picante.

● **Banks & money changers**
Casas de cambio at México 91 and 140 Nte, Mon-Sat 0900-1400, 1600-2000.

● **Post & telecommunications**
Telephones: credit card phone at Veracruz Nte y Zapata Pte.

● **Tour companies & travel agents**
Viajes Regina, tours to San Blas, 8 hrs, US$22.50; Playas de Ensueño, Fri, 8 hrs, US$15.50; Tepic city tour, Mon and Sat, 3 hrs, US$7. *Tovara*, Ignacio Allende 30.

● **Tourist offices**
México 30 Nte, 1 block from cathedral, T 29546, English spoken, helpful.

● **Transport**
Air Airport (TPQ) with flights to Los Angeles, Manzanillo, Mexico City and Tijuana daily with Aero California (T 321-61636) or AeroMéxico.

Trains To **Guadalajara**, 2nd class leaves at 1025, arrives at 1755, sit on left-hand side for best views. Train to **Mexicali**, 28 hrs on Tren del Pacífico, departs 1335, to **Nogales**, 21 hrs (same train to Benjamín Hill, where it divides); 2nd class train at 1645 to Mexicali and Nogales via Benjamín Hill.

Buses Bus station is a fairly short walk into town; bus from centre to terminal from Puebla Nte by market. At bus station there are phones, inc credit card, post office, left luggage and tourist information (not always open). Bus to **San Blas** from Central Camionera: US$2.20, 0600-1600, frequent. To **Guadalajara**, US$7.50, frequent departures, several companies; **Mazatlán**, 4½ hrs, US$8; to **Puerto Vallarta**, 3 hrs, US$6; **Mexico City**, US$30.25.

Excursions

One can visit Huichol villages only by air,

as there are no real roads, and it takes at least 2 days. About 50 km from Tepic is an attractive volcanic lagoon, take the bus to Santa María del Oro. To various beaches along the coast, some of them off the Nogales highway, eg, **Santa Cruz**, about 37 km from Tepic (rocky beach). No hotels, but there are rental apartments, a camping area and accommodation at *Peter's Shop*, E, basic but pleasant and friendly. Simple food available, *Restaurant Belmar*, fish and rice, all reminiscent of the South Seas. There is a shrimp farm nearby. (2 buses a day from San Blas to Santa Cruz, US$1.10, or 2½ hrs' ride by open-sided lorry, US$0.75.) A road runs S from Tepic through **Compostela** (**F** *Hotel Naryt*, with bath, basic but clean, a pleasant small town with an old church, El Señor de la Misericordia, built 1539. From Compostela one can catch an old bus to **Zacualapán**, 1½ hrs over a paved road, to visit a small enclosed park with sculptures that have been found in the area, 2 blocks from main square. Gate to the park must be unlocked by caretaker: inside there is a small museum. Zacualapán is a pleasant village, knock on a door to ask for the caretaker.

A road from Compostela reaches the coast at **Las Varas** (**E** *Hotel Contreras*, with fan and bath, clean, small rooms). Las Varas is connected also by good road to San Blas, N up the coast. Beaches on the coast road S to Puerto Vallarta include Chacala, nice free beach lined with coconut palms, good swimming, cold showers (restaurant *Delfín*, delicious smoked fish), and reached by an unsurfaced road through jungle; **Rincón de Guayabitos**, which is being developed as a tourist resort with hotels, holiday village and trailer park (**C** *Coca*, among several hotels and restaurants on a rocky peninsula to the S of the beach); Los Ayala, Lo de Marcos, San Francisco (*Costa Azul Resort*, on beach, delightful, pool, apartments, restaurant), Sayulita (*Trailer Park* highly recommended, on beautiful beach, German owner, very friendly, US$10/day, also has bungalows, Apdo 5-585, CP 06500, Mexico DF, T Mexico City 572-1335, F 390-2750, also bungalows, turn off Route 200 at Km 123, 2½ km), **Punta de Mita**, a fishing village at the tip of a peninsula (nearby **A3** *Hotel and Trailer Park Piedras Blancas*, good, also camping, US$10, hook-ups US$12-14, restaurants; excellent restaurant at Playa Desileteros not cheap but delicious food, bus from Puerto Vallarta), Cruz de Huanacaxtle, **Bucerías** (*Hotel Playa de Bucerías*, Km 154, and **B** *Marlyn*), **Peñita de Jaltemba** (**C** bungalows at N end of town, with clean rooms and kitchen; **C-D** *Hotel Mar Azul*) and others.

PUERTO VALLARTA

(*Pop* 100,000) The road S from Tepic, through Compostela, enters Jalisco state just before **Puerto Vallarta**. This is the second largest resort in Mexico, Greater Puerto Vallarta is drawn-out along some 25 km of the W-facing curve of the deeply-incised Banderas Bay. For ease of reference, it can be split into five sections: **N central**, the oldest, with the main plaza, cathedral and seafront Malecón as well as an uninviting strip of pebble/sand beach; **S central**, across the Río Cuale, is newer but similarly packed with shops and restaurants and bordered by the fine, deep sand of Playa de los Muertos, **S shore**, where the mountains come to the sea, several cove beaches and a scattering of big hotels; **N hotel zone**, a long stretch from town towards the cruise ship terminal and the airport, with mediocre beaches, many big hotels, several commercial centres; **Marina Vallarta**, further N, with a dazzling array of craft, a golf course, smart hotels and poor quality beach; **Nuevo Vallarta**, 18 km N of centre, with golf course and marina, in the neighbouring state of Nayarit (time difference), modern, all-inclusive hotels are strung along miles of white sand beach, far from amenities.

A highly commercialized sun-and-sand holiday resort marred by congestion and widespread condominium developments, Puerto Vallarta also has its advantages. The stepped and cobbled streets of the old centre are picturesque, accommodations and restaurants are varied enough to suit everybody; there is much good hiking in the surrounding hills and watersports and diving are easily accessible. Increasingly it has become a base for excursions and for special interest trips including ornithology and whale watching.

Most travellers will find the central area the most convenient to stay in; its two halves are divided by the Río Cuale and a narrow island where souvenir shops, cafés and the museum are located. The most dramatic beach in the centre is Playa de los Muertos, apparently named after the murderous activities of pirates in the late 16th century, although the 'dead' tag could apply equally to the fierce undertow or possibly to the pollution which affects this corner of the bay. The authorities are trying to get people to use a sunnier sobriquet: 'Playa del Sol'. Conchas Chinas is probably the best beach close to town, being quiet and clean (at any holiday time, though, every beach is packed); a cobblestone road leads to Conchas Chinas from route 200, just after *Club Alexandra*.

NB Those confined to wheelchairs are warned that parts of Puerto Vallarta are bad, with high kerbs, steps and cobblestone streets. North Central and S Central are both difficult, but the northern area and the Marina are flatter and more accessible.

Excursions

During the rainy season, June-Sept, some trips are not possible. From Nov-April, humpback whale watching is organized. A recommended trip including snorkelling is with John Pegueros, who owns the schooner *Elias Mann*. Contact him at Lázaro Cárdenas 27, Apdo Postal 73, Bucerías, Nayarit, CP63732, T 329-80060, F 80061. Tickets from Marina Vallarta, US$60 inc some meals, starts 0800.

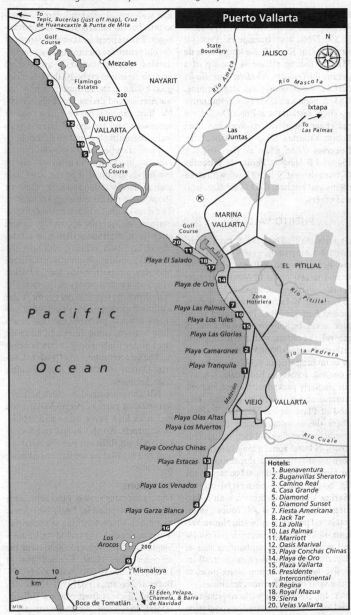

Puerto Vallarta

To Tepic, Bucerías (just off map), Cruz de Huanacaxtle & Punta de Mita

Golf Course

Mezcales

Flamingo Estates

200

NUEVO VALLARTA

Golf Course

State Boundary

JALISCO

NAYARIT

Rio Ameca

Rio Mascota

Las Juntas

Ixtapa

To Las Palmas

Golf Course

MARINA VALLARTA

EL PITILLAL

Rio Pitillal

Playa El Salado

Playa de Oro

Zona Hotelera

Playa Las Palmas

Playa Los Tules

Playa Las Glorias

Rio la Pedrera

Playa Camarones

Playa Tranquila

Malecón

VIEJO VALLARTA

Rio Cuale

Playa Olas Altas

Playa Los Muertos

Playa Conchas Chinas

Playa Estacas

Playa Los Venados

Playa Garza Blanca

Los Arocos

200

Mismaloya

To El Eden, Yelapa, Chamela, & Barra de Navidad

Boca de Tomatlán

P a c i f i c

O c e a n

0   10
km

M10c

N

Hotels:
1. Buenaventura
2. Buganvillas Sheraton
3. Camino Real
4. Casa Grande
5. Diamond
6. Diamond Sunset
7. Fiesta Americana
8. Jack Tar
9. La Jolla
10. Las Palmas
11. Marriott
12. Oasis Marival
13. Playa Conchas Chinas
14. Playa de Oro
15. Plaza Vallarta
16. Presidente Intercontinental
17. Regina
18. Royal Mazua
19. Sierra
20. Velas Vallarta

Sayulita, 40 km N, is a beach resort, with accommodation and restaurants, but the beach is said to be badly littered. **Punta de Mita**, 45 km N (by Medina or Pacífico buses, every 15 mins), is a small fishing and beach resort with fish restaurants, miles of beach, abundant birdlife. There are boat trips to the nearby **Islas Marietas**, where there are caves and birds. Camping is possible on the beach. Simple accommodation available or stay at the attractive **C** *Quinta del Sol*. 40 km NE of Puerto Vallarta is the inland village of **Las Palmas**, a typical though unremarkable *pueblo* (buses every 30 mins, 1 hr 10 mins). On the way is the workers' *pueblo* of **Ixtapa**,

Puerto Vallarta Centre

Bahía de Banderas

N

Hotels:
1. *Cuatro Vientos*
2. *Eloísa*
3. *Fontana del Mar*
4. *Molino de Agua*
5. *San Marino Plaza*
6. *Paraíso*
7. *Playa Los Arcos*
8. *Posada Río Cuale*
9. *Rosita*

Plaza Hidalgo

Allende
Pipila
Leona Vicario
Josefa de Domínguez
Abasolo
Aldama
Corona
Galeana
Mina

Paseo Díaz Ordaz
Malecón
Morelos
Juárez
Hidalgo
Matamoros
Miramar
Iturbide
Zaragoza

Plaza de Armas
Cathedral
Government Offices
Libertad
Guerrero
A. Rodríguez
Plaza

Río Cuale
Museum
Isla Cuale
Cultural Centre

Playa de Los Muertos

Olas Altas
Plaza Lázaro Cárdenas
Ignacio Vallarta
Pino Suárez
Constitución
Insurgentes
Serdán
Madero
Cárdenas
Carranza
Badillo
Restaurant Puerto Nuevo
Aguacate
Naranjo
Jacarandas

Dieguez
Rodríguez
Gómez
Pulpito

Not to Scale

established by the Montgomery Fruit Co in 1925. Near here are postclassic stone mounds scattered over a wide area. 10 km S of Puerto Vallarta, along the coast road is **Mismaloya**, where John Huston made *Night of the Iguana* with Richard Burton. A lovely beach backed by a steep sub-tropical valley, even though the *La Jolla Mismaloya* hotel looms over the sands. The film set has been developed as 'Iguana Park', and the ruins on a pier were being converted to a restaurant by the hotel in 1997. There are many condominiums on the N side. You can go horse riding up the valley with Victor, of Rancho Manolo, beside the road bridge, T 80018. **Boca de Tomatlán**, 4 km further S, is a quaint and rather down at heel fishing village at the river estuary. There are apartments to rent, simple restaurants, a dirty beach and a footbridge across the river. To **Yelapa**, an Indian village with a waterfall, now commercialized with entertainment ranging from live music to rodeo. Tourist water taxi from pier (Los Muertos) US$12 return, leaves 1030, 1100. From fisherman's quay on Malecón (by *Hotel Rosita*, opp *McDonald's*) US$5 one way, leaves 1130. From Boca de Tomatlán (bus, US$0.30) water taxi is US$3.50 one way, from beach, leaves 1030. Organized tours may be better value for anyone wanting to combine such activities as snorkelling at Los Arcos en route. B *Lagunitas*, cabina hotel with pool. *Tino's Oasis* is an excellent place to stay, American owned, cheap. Alternatively stay with Mateo and Elenita, **C**, inc breakfast, visit their waterfall. Camping available 30 mins' walk up valley, US$4 pp, in beautiful setting, owners Beto and Felicidad (ask for Felicidad's home-made tortillas "the best in Mexico").

Walk or mountain bike up valley of Río Cuale, through magnificent hills with dense sub-tropical vegetation, some bathing pools, many birds, a few *ranchitos* and *pueblecitos*. To begin, walk to eastern extremity of Lázaro Cárdenas, cross wide bridge and turn sharp right; walk along cobbled street with river on right. Pass

colonia of Buenos Aires and water purification plant; later cross suspension footbridge and continue up rough track with river on left. 2 km later, recross the now crystalline Río Cuale via stepping stones. Go as far as you like. 54 km onward is the ex-mining (silver, gold) village of **Cuale**; cobbled streets, rustic.

Local information
● Accommodation
North Central: L3 *Casa Kimberley*, Zaragoza 445, T 21336, former home of Richard Burton and Elizabeth Taylor, 10 rooms full of memorabilia of the actors, breakfast inc, much cheaper in low season; **A2** *Casa Del Puente*, by bridge opp market, T 20749, suites with kitchen in a private villa suspended above river, delightful, book months ahead; **B** *Cuatro Vientos*, Matamoros 520, T 20161, up steep cobbled street from church, lots of steps, great views, restaurant, plunge pool, breakfast inc; **C** *Rosita*, Paseo Díaz Ordaz 901, at N end of Malecón, T 32000, F 32142, resort's original holiday hotel (est 1948) with pool, on town beach, excellent value and location, rec; **D** *Hotel Escuela*, Hidalgo 300, corner Guerrero, T 24910, F 30294, is where they teach trainee hotel personnel, a bit clinical, with street noise, but said to be good value; **E** unmarked *hospedaje* at Allende 257, esq Guadalupe, T 20986, US owner, Isabel Jordan also has rooms and *cabañas* in Yelapa, more expensive.

South Central: **L3** *Meza Del Mar*, Amapas 380, T 24888, F 22308, perched high above Los Muertos beach with slow lifts, balconies remain in shade, small pool, all-inclusive packages; **L3** *Playa Los Arcos*, Olas Altas 380, T 20583, F 22418, good location for restaurants, undersized pool terrace overflows to Los Muertos beach; **A1** *Buenaventura*, Mexico 1301, T 23737, F 23546, on shore, fringe of centre, lively holiday hotel; **A1** *Molina de Agua*, Ignacio L Vallarta 130, T 21957, F 26056, cabins in pleasant wooded glade on bank of river, a/c, good service, 2 pools, rec; **A1** *San Marino Plaza* (formerly the *Oro Verde*, Rodolfo Gómez 111, T 21553, F 22431, a/c, pleasant, friendly, standard holiday package, compact pool terrace adjoins los Muertos beach; **A3** *Casa Corazón*, Amapas 326, T/F 21371, hard to find US-owned hideaway on steep slope down to Los Muertos beach, overpriced but 3 big rooms on top terrace with spectacular views worth the premium, inc big breakfast; **B** *Eloisa*, Lázaro Cárdenas 179,

T 26465, F 20286, on square by Playa de los Muertos, a holiday hotel with small pool, most rooms face dim hallways; **B** *Gaviotas*, behind *Eloisa*, Madero 154, Parque Lázaro Cárdenas, T 21500, F 25516, faintly colonial, balcony access, glimpses of sea; **B** *Posada de Roger*, Basilio Badillo 237, T 20639, F 30482, courtyard arrangement, neat rooms off narrow access balconies, tiny and overpriced, splash pool; **B** *Posada Río Cuale*, Aquiles Serdán 242, nr new bridge, T/F 20450, small pool in front garden, not very private, nice, colonial-style rooms; **C** *Gloria del Mar*, Amapas 115, T 25143, by Playa de los Muertos, charmless but clean, convenient holiday base, small rooms; **D** *Belmar*, Insurgentes 161, T/F 20572, spartan, ill-lit but friendly, on main road nr buses; **D** *Yasmín*, B Badillo 168, T 20087, a claustrophobic courtyard arrangement behind *Café Olla*, good value, noisy till at least 2300. There are several cheaper hotels grouped in C Francisco y Madero, W of Insurgentes: **E** *Azteca*, No 473, T 22750, probably best of this group; **E** *Villa del Mar*, No 440, T 20785, also satisfactory; **E-F**, and within a few doors are: *Cartagena*, No 428, *Lina*, No 376, T 21661, with bath, no hot water, run down, rooms on street noisy. *Analiz* and *Bernal*, No 423, T 23605, friendly, large rooms, fan, good showers, nee, all convenient for restaurants, a few blocks from long distance buses.

North Hotel Zone: **L1** *Fiesta Americana*, T 42010, F 42108, maintains high service standards in Disneyesque jungly theme; **L1** *Krystal Vallarta*, T 40202, F 40222, has suites, apartments, flanking cobbled lanes in Mexican pueblo style, amid greenery, fountains, wrought iron streetlights; **L1** *Sheraton Bouganvilias*, T 30404, F 20500, dated block on good patch of beach close to downtown, vast but unexciting expanse of grounds; **L2** *Continental Plaza*, Playa Las Glorias, T 40123, F 45236, in overly-cute 'Old Mexico' style; **L2** *Holiday Inn*, T 61700, F 45683, unmissable deep mustard edifice shares undersized pool with hulking condominium next door; **L2** *Moranda Casa Grande*, T 30916, F 24601, all-inclusive, tasteless; **L2** *Qualton Spa*, T 44446, F 44445, blocky atrium hotel with crowded pool area extending to beach; **L3** *Las Palmas*, Blvd Medina Ascencio, Km 2.5, T 40650, F 40543, castaway-on-a-desert-island theme, all rooms with sea view; **A1** *Hacienda Buenaventura*, Paseo de la Marina, T 46667, F 46242, modern, with colonial influence, pleasant pool, is nicest in zone but 100m to beach and on main road, discounts out of season; **A1** *Los Pélicanos*,

T 41010, F 41111, small-scale, rooms enclose central quadrangle with pool, 100m to beach; **A1** *Plaza Las Glorias*, T 44444, F 46559, attractive white low-rise, breezy beachfront location; **A1** *Suites del Sol*, Francia y Liverpool, T 42541, F 42213, above offices at busy junction on wrong side of road for beach, jumbled open-plan public rooms, tiny pool, large rooms; *Vista Club Playa de Oro*, Av Las Garzas, T 46868, F 40348, nr cruise ship terminal, a predictable all-inclusive with much manufactured fun, many activities. Cheap hotels are scarce here: **C** *Motel Costa del Sol*, 300m N of *Sheraton*, opp side, T 22055.

Marina Vallarta: **L1** *Marriott Casa Magna*, T 10004, F 10760, grandiose interiors, superb pool, upmarket restaurants; **L1** *Westin Regina*, T 11100, F 11141, vibrant colours, imaginative lighting, much cascading water, lush gardens; **L2** *Royal Maeva*, T 10200, big, brassy all-inclusive packages; **L2** *Velas Vallarta*, T 10751, F 10755, Moorish touches to big, part timeshare hotel with verdant gardens; **A1** *Plaza Iguana*, T 10880, F 10889, small pool adjoins marina promenade, 10 mins walk to beach.

Nuevo Vallarta: **L2** *Diamond Resort*, T 329-70400, F 329-70626, gaudy, raucous all-inclusive; **L2** *Sierra*, T 329-71300, F 329-70800, colourful building-block hotel, smart, modern, all-inclusive; **L3** *Oasis Marival*, T 329-70100, F 70160, more established and sedate than competitors here, all-inclusive.

Southern shore: **L1** *Camino Real*, Playa de las Estacas, T 15000, F 16000 on lovely beach 3 km S of centre; **L1** *La Jolla de Mismaloya*, Km 11.5, T 80660, F 80500, romantic though over-developed setting on film-set beach, **L1** *Presidente Intercontinental*, Km 8.5 Carretera a Barra de Navidad, T 80507, F 80116, stylish luxury on quiet sandy cove; **L3** *Majahuitas Resort*, between Quimixto and Yelapa beaches, T 322-15808, run by Margot and Lirio González, inc breakfast and dinner, 3 guesthouses, more planned, on cove, sandy beach, rustic furniture, solar energy, riding and snorkelling available, 30% of profits go to indigenous community of Chacala; **A1** *Casa Grande*, Playa Palo María, T 21023, hulking twin towers of all-inclusive fun on crummy beach, 4 km S of centre; **A2** *Playa Conchas Chinas*, Km 2.5 Carretera a Barra de Navidad, T/F 15770, about 1 km before *Camino Real*, on W side of road, spacious rooms with kitchenettes and ocean views.

Camping: 2 trailer parks: *Tacho*, on road to Pipala, opp Marina, 60 spaces but spacious (treat the police at the traffic lights/turn off to the trailer park with caution and respect); *Puerto Vallarta*, N of centre, just N of bypass then E 2 blocks, popular. Also at fishing village of Yelapa, best reached by boat from *Hotel Rosita* at 1130: camp under shelters (*palapas*), about US$4 pp.

● **Places to eat**
South Centre: *Posada de Roger*, Basilio Badillo 237, good courtyard dining, mainly Mexican menu, cheapish; *Café Olla*, lower end Basilio Badillo, good-value Mexican and barbecue in cramped open-fronted dining room, queues wait for more than an hour in high season, demonstrating a lack of imagination rather than discerning palate; *Puerto Nuevo*, on Badillo, expensive but good food; *Buengusto*, Rodríguez, excellent home cooked Mexican meals; *A Page in the Sun* (café), Olas Altas opp *Los Arcos* hotel on corner, coffee is excellent, cakes home-made, second-hand bookshop; *Los Arbolitos*, E end of Lazaro Cardenas, 3 balconied floors above river, Mexican, good atmosphere, moderate prices; *El Dorado*, palapa restaurant on Playa de los Muertos, inexpensive and attractive surroundings but touristy and besieged by belligerent chiclet vendors, third-rate musicians etc; *La Fuente del Puente*, riverfront at old bridge, opp market, Mexican, colourful, good music, good value meals but drinks expensive; *Jazz Café/Le Bistro*, by the bridge on Insurgentes, garden, bamboo, beside river, pleasant for coffee and classical music (piano or harp) in morning, crowded and expensive in evening, many vegetarian dishes, clean; *Café Maximilian*, Olas Altas 380-B, rear part of *Playa Los Arcos*, open 1600-2300, closed Sun, huge Austrian owner, food rec, about US$22 pp meal with wine, clean, efficient, busy, some tables on pavement.

North Centre: *Pepe's Tacos*, on Honduras, opp Pemex at northern end of downtown, cheap, ethnic and delicious in spartan pink/white dining room, open all night; *Juanita's*, Av Mexico 1067, attracts locals as well as value-seeking gringos, good; *Las Margaritas*, Juárez 512, forget the queues at the popular gringo restaurants, this one is excellent, moderately-priced, cosmopolitan and curiously under-patronized, colonial-style courtyard, rec; *Café Amadeus*, Miramar 271, up steps from Guerrero, classical music, books, board games in delightful whitewashed rooms or balcony perched above old town, coffee, delectable cakes, rec; *La Dolce Vita*, midway along Malecón, is hugely popular

(queues) Italian and pizza place favoured by package tourists; *Rico Mac Taco*, Av Mexico, corner Uruguay, busy, cheap and widely popular eatery.

● **Bars**
Carlos O'Brian's, Malecón and *Andale*, Olas Altas, attract a motley crowd of revellers and start hopping after 2200. Martini types head for *Christine*, at *Hotel Krystal*, for spectacular light show, disco, expensive drinks and cover. Many clubs and late bars throughout central area.

● **Airline offices**
AeroMéxico, T 42777; Alaska Airlines, T 95-800-426-0333; American Airlines, T 91-800-90460; America West, T 800-235-9292, 800-533-6862; Continental, T 91-800-90050; Delta, T 91-800-90221; Mexicana, T 48900; United, T 911-800-00307, 800-426-5561.

● **Banks & money changers**
Cambios on nearly every street in tourist areas. Rates inferior to Guadalajara. Check **Bancomer's** *cambio* at Juárez 450, for best rates. Like most, it is open every day until late. Numerous banks offer slightly better rates (but slower service) and ATMs for Visa, Mastercard.

● **Embassies & consulates**
Consulates: Canada, Edif Vallarta Plaza, Zaragoza 160, 1st floor, interior 10, T 25398, F 23517, open 1000-1400.

● **Hospitals & medical services**
Doctor: *Dra Irma Gittelson*, Juárez 479, speaks French and English, very helpful. **Emergency**: T 915-724-7900.

● **Laundry**
Practically one on every block in S central; numerous throughout resort.

● **Post & telecommunications**
Post Office: on Juárez 628.

Long distance **phone** (*casetas*) and **fax** at Lázaro Cárdenas 267, open daily to 2300, also in lobby of *Hotel Eloisa*, both US$3/min to Europe. Many shops bear *Larga distancia* sign, check tariffs.

● **Shopping**
Endless opportunities, including armies of non-aggressive beach vendors. The flea market is grossly overpriced; the many shops often better value, but not to any great degree. Guadalajara is cheaper for practically everything. The market is by the bridge at the end of Insurgentes, sells silver, clothes, souvenirs as well as meat and fish. Large, well-stocked supermarket nearby.

Jewellery at *Olas de Plata*, Francisco Rodríguez 132. Plaza Malecón has 28 curio shops, restaurant, music etc. *GR* supermarket, Constitución 136, reasonable for basics. Second-hand books, English and some in German, at *Rosas Expresso*, Olas Altas 399.

● **Tour companies & travel agents**
American Express, Morelos 660, esq Abasolo, T 32955, F 32926, town guide available; *Open Air Expeditions*, Guerrero 339, T 23310, e-mail: openair@vivamexico.com, Oscar and Isabel run hiking trips (mountain or waterfall), whale watching (winter), kayaking, birdwatching and other trips from US$40, knowledgeable guides; *Mountain Bike Adventures*, Guerrero 361, T 31834, offer trips for cyclists of varying grades of competence, from local environs up to 3-4 days in old silver towns of Sierra Madre, all equipment provided inc good, front-suspension bikes, from US$36; *Sierra Madre*, facing the Malecón nr Domínguez, are agents for many tours and some of their own, inc a long, all-day truck safari to Sierra Madre mountains; *Rancho El Charro*, T 40114, horseback expeditions to jungle villages, Sierra Madre silver towns. Independent horse riding guides and horses congregate at lower end of Basilio Badillo, also occasionally at fisherman's wharf, by *Hotel Rosital*, for short beach and mountain trips, agree price beforehand. Many agents and hotel tour desks offer boat trips, car hire and tours at big discounts if you accept a timeshare presentation. Worthwhile savings are to be made for those prepared to brazen out the sales pitch, and many do.

● **Tourist offices**
Morelos 28-A; in the government building on the main square, very helpful.

● **Useful addresses**
Immigration: Morelos 600, T 21478.

● **Transport**
Local Buses: Mismaloya to Marina, US$0.22, but complicated routing. The main southbound artery through town is México-Morelos-Vallarta, the main northbound is Juárez-Insurgentes. Plaza Lázaro Cárdenas is the main terminal in S of town and starting point for Mismaloya-Boca buses going S. Buses marked 'Olas Altas' go to S Central, those marked 'Hoteles' or 'Aeropuerto' to N hotel zone and beyond. Buses are also marked for 'Marina' and 'Mismaloya/Boca' (Boca de Tomatlán). The ones marked 'Centro' go through town, those with 'Tunel' take the bypass. Buses to outlying villages

with Medina bus line, terminal at Brasil, between Brasilia and Guatemala, regular (15-20 mins) service to Nuevo Vallarta, San José, San Juan, Bucerías, L Manzanilla, Punta de Mita and others. Fares from US$0.75-US$1.50. **Car hire**: widely available. **Scooter hire**: opp *Sheraton*, T 21765.

Air International Ordaz airport (PVR) 6 km from centre. If you walk 100m to the highway and catch a local bus to town, it will cost far less than the US$10 taxi fare. Mexicana to Chicago, Denver, Los Angeles (also Air Alaska, Delta), New York (also AeroMéxico); American to Dallas (also AeroMéxico); TWA to Kansas City and St Louis; Continental to Houston (also AeroMéxico); Air Alaska to Phoenix, Portland, San Francisco, San José and Seattle; AeroMéxico to San Diego. Mexican destinations served inc Mexico City, Guadalajara, Aguascalientes, León, Los Cabos, Mazatlán and Monterrey.

Buses Elite terminal is on Basilio Badillo, esq Insurgentes. Transportes del Pacífico runs from an office around the corner on Insurgentes. ETN and Primera Plus share same terminal on Lázaro Cárdenas, 2 blocks NW. Frequent service to **Guadalajara**, ETN 8 a day, US$21.25, Transportes del Pacífico, 1st class, US$16.25. Elite runs to Guadalajara, Mexico City, Tijuana, Mazatlán, Cd Juárez, Monterrey, Zihuatanejo, Acapulco, Aguascalientes, Tecoman. Primera Plus to Guadalajara, León, Querétaro, Metaque, Manzanillo (US$9.50, dep 0300, 4½ hrs), Cd Guzmán, Colima, and Barra de Navidad, 4 hrs, 0800 and 1300.

SOUTH OF PUERTO VALLARTA

South of Puerto Vallarta paved Route 200 continues down the coast to Melaque, Barra de Navidad and Manzanillo. Beaches and hotels on this route: 103 km S of Puerto Vallarta and 12 km inland, at the town of **Tomatlán** (not to be confused with Boca de Tomatlán, on the coast), are a few modest hotels (eg **E** *Posada Carmelita*, with bath, clean); at **Chamela**, Perula village at N end of Chamela beach; **C** *Hotel Punta Perula*, T (333) 70190, on beach, Mexican style; *Villa Polonesia Trailer Park*, US$12 for car and two people, recommended, full hook-ups, hot showers, on lovely beach (follow signs from Route 200 on unmade road); restaurant on road to trailer park, clean, good food. Pemex at

Chamela is closed, no other for miles. 2 hrs S of Puerto Vallarta is the luxury resort **L1** *Las Alamandas*, T (328) 55500, beautiful beach, health club, horse riding, tennis etc. The resort is 1 km S of Puente San Nicolas on Route 200, turn right towards coast at sign to Quemaro. Owned by Isobel Goldsmith, it is very exclusive, has been featured in several magazines for the clientèle it attracts and reservations should be made in advance. In the UK (0171) 373-1762. The excellent **A1** *Hotel Careyes* is en route, and several others, **A3-B** *El Tecuán*, Carretera 200, Km 32.5, T (333) 70132 (lovely hotel, gorgeous beach, mediocre bar/restaurant, pool, highly rec), and, 8 km further S, **A3** *Hotel Tenacatita* near the village of the same name (see page 223). The road continues to Zihuatanejo and Acapulco, and finally to Salina Cruz. The road from 40 km S of Chamela to Melaque is very poor.

TEPIC TO GUADALAJARA

Route 15 leaves Tepic for Guadalajara. At Chapalilla is a turn-off to Compostela and Puerto Vallarta. At **Ahuacatlán**, 75 km from Tepic, the 17th century ex-convent of San Juan Evangelista stands on the Plaza Principal; handicrafts on sale here. Nearby, the village of **Jala** has a festival mid-August. **E** *Hotel Cambero*, From here the **Ceboruco** volcano can be reached in a day. On the main road a lava flow from Ceboruco is visible (*El Ceboruco*, *parador turístico*, with restaurant, information, toilets and shop; buses do not stop here). 84 km (1¼ hrs by bus) from Tepic is **Ixtlán del Río** (**D** *Hotel Colonial*, Hidalgo 45 Pte, very friendly, recommended; *Motel Colón*; cheaper hotels round the Zócalo are *Roma* and *Turista*). 2 km out of town along this road are the ruins of **Los Toriles**, a Toltec ceremonial centre on a warm, wind-swept plain. The main structure is the Temple of Quetzalcoatl, noted for its cruciform windows and circular shape. The ruins have been largely restored, admission US$2.35, some explanatory notes posted around the site. There is a caretaker but no real facilities. The journey from Tepic to Guadalajara cannot easily be broken at Ixtlán for sightseeing since buses passing through in either direction tend to be full; bus on to Guadalajara 3 hrs, US$4.25. There are a few souvenir shops, a Museo Arqueológico in the Palacio Municipal, a *casa de cambio* and a railway station. Harvest (maize) festival mid-September. 2 km beyond the Los Toriles site is *Motel Hacienda*, with pool. The road climbs out of the valley through uncultivated land, trees intermixed with prickly pear and chaparral cactus. Jalisco state is entered (see below) and 19 km before Tequila is Magdalena (hotel, *Restaurant Magdalena*), congested with traffic, small lake nearby. As the bus approaches Tequila there may be opportunities to buy the drink of the same name on board. The blue agave, from which it is distilled, can be seen growing in the pleasant, hilly countryside.

TEQUILA

Tequila (*Pop* 33,000; *Alt* 1,300m; *Phone code* 374), 58 km from Guadalajara, is the main place where the famous Mexican drink is distilled. Tours of the distilleries are available (see box) and stores will let you sample different tequilas before you buy. Often around 20 bottles are open for tasting. The town is attractive and a mix of colonial and more modern architecture. It is a pleasant place to stay but there is not much to do other than tour the distilleries and there is little in the way of nightlife. A day trip from Guadalajara is possible. Coming into town from Guadalajara, the road forks at the Pemex station, the right fork is the main highway and the left fork continues into town as C Sixto Gorjón, the main commercial street. Buses will let you off here, from where it is 5-7 blocks to the main plaza. Along C Sixto Gorjón there are several liquor stores selling tequila, restaurants where you can eat for under US$5, pharmacies, doctors, dentists and the Rojo de los Altos bus ticket office at No 126A. There are two plazas next to each other. On one is the

"A field of upright swords" – the making of tequila

The quote from Paul Theroux's *The Old Patagonian Express* describes the swathes of blue agave grown in the dry highlands of the state of Jalisco and a few neighbouring areas. Agave is the raw material for the firewater, tequila, and although there are some 400 varieties of agave, only one, the blue agave is suitable. The spiky leaves are hacked off and the central core, weighing around 45 kg, is crushed and roasted to give the characteristic smell and flavour to the drink. The syrup extracted is then mixed with liquid sugar, fermented for 30-32 hrs and then distilled twice. White tequila is the product of a further 4 months in wooden or stainless steel vats. It can be drunk neat, with a pinch of salt on the back of your hand, followed by a suck on a wedge of lime, or mixed into cocktails such as the famous Margarita. Gold tequila is a blend of white tequila and tequila which has been aged in wooden casks. Añejo, or aged, tequila, is a golden brown from spending at least 2 years in oak casks. As it ages it becomes smoother and is drunk like a fine brandy or aged rum. Special premium tequila has no sugar added, it is pure agave aged in wooden casks.

In pre-conquest times, the Indians used the agave sap to brew a mildly alcoholic drink, pulque, which is still drunk today. The Spaniards, however, wanted something more refined and stronger. They developed mescal and set up distilleries to produce what later became tequila. The first of these was established in 1795 by royal decree of King Charles IV of Spain. It is still in existence today: La Rojena, the distillery of José Cuervo, known by its black crow logo, is the biggest in the country. Around the town of Tequila there are 12 distilleries, of which 10 produce 75% of the country's tequila. Tours of the distilleries can be arranged with free samples and of course shopping opportunities. Tequila Cuervo, T 634-4170, F 634-8893, in Guadalajara, or T 20070 in Tequila (contact Srta Clara Martínez for tours); Tequila Sauza, T 679-0600, F 679-0690, dating from 1873, see the famous fresco illustrating the joys of drinking tequila; Herradura, T 614-9657, 658-4717, F 614-0175, in Amatitlán, 8 km from Tequila in an old hacienda outside the village, which has adobe walls and cobblestone streets, worth a visit.

Templo de Santiago Apóstol, a large, pretty old stone building, with a 1930s municipal market next to it. Behind the church is the *Elypsis* discotheque, open at weekends. Also on this plaza is the Post Office and Banamex. About a block behind Banamex where Sixto Gorjón ends, is the entrance to the Cuervo tequila distillery. On the other square is the **Sauza Museo de Tequila** at C Albino Rojas at 22, open until 1400, and the **Presidencia Municipal** with tourist office.

● **Accommodation** D *Motel Delicias*, Carretera Internacional 595, on the highway from Guadalajara about 1 km before Tequila, best available, TV, off-street parking; **E** *Abasolo*, Abasolo 80, parts under construction, rooms have TV; **F** *Colonial*, Morelos 52, corner of Sixto Gorjón, characterless, but central, clean and not run down, some rooms with private bath; **F** *Morelos*, corner of Morelos and Veracruz, a few blocks from the plaza, above a billiard hall, basic, ask in bar downstairs if there is no one at the hotel desk. Half-way between Tequila and Guadalajara, in the mountains, is the British-run **L3** *Rancho Rio Caliente*, 8 km from the highway, a vegetarian thermal resort (room rates vary accordingly to location), excursions, massages and other personal services extra, taxi from Guadalajara 1 hr, US$55, for reservations in USA, Spa Vacations, PO Box 897, Millbrae, CA 94030, T 415-615-9543.

● **Places to eat** *El Callejón*, C Sixto Gorjón 105, rustic Mexican decor, main courses for under US$5, *antojitos* for less than US$3, hamburgers also available; *El Marinero*, C Albino

Rojas 16B, nice seafood restaurant with strolling musicians; *El Sauza*, Juárez 45, beside Banamex, restaurant/bar, Mexican atmosphere.

● **Banks & money changers** Banamex, corner of Sixto Gorjón and Juárez, 24-hr ATM accepts Visa, Mastercard, and cards from the Cirrus and Plus networks. *Casa de cambio*, C Sixto Gorjón 73, open 0900-1400, 1600-2000, change cash and TCs.

● **Transport Buses** 2nd class from the old terminal, Sala B, in Guadalajara, Rojo de los Altos, up to 2 hrs, US$2. Return from outside Rojo de los Altos ticket office, C Sixto Gorjón, 126A, every 20 mins, 0500-1600, then every 30 mins until 2000. **Taxi**: to Guadalajara US$19, plus US$7 in tolls if you take the expressway.

NB There is a time change between Nayarit and Jalisco; the latter is 6 hrs behind GMT, the former, as with all the Pacific coast N of Jalisco, 7 hrs behind.

Guadalajara to Mexico City

FROM the second city, Guadalajara, with its fine historical centre, to the capital, an area rich in crafts and traditions, especially the music and dance of Jalisco and Michoacán. There are lakes to visit (Chapala and Pátzcuaro), volcanoes (Colima, Paricutín, Toluca), the colonial city of Morelia, and worthwhile detours to the Pacific coast and to the towns S of Toluca.

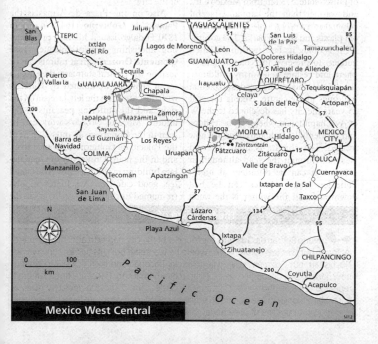

Mexico West Central

The cultural life of Jalisco state has been helped by an economy based on crafts, agriculture, and livestock, with fewer pockets of abject poverty than elsewhere in Mexico. Many villages have traditional skills such as pottery, blown glass, shoemaking, and a curious and beautiful form of filigree weaving in which miniature flower baskets, fruit and religious images are shaped from *chilte* (chicle, the raw substance from which chewing-gum is made). The state is the original home of Mexico's *mariachis*: roving musical groups dressed in the gala suits and *sombreros* of early 19th century rural gentry.

GUADALAJARA

(*Pop* 5,000,000 in metropolitan area; *State pop 1995* 5,990,054; *Alt* 1,650m; *Phone code* 03) **Guadalajara**, Mexico's second city founded on 14 February 1542 and capital of Jalisco state, 573 km from Mexico City, and warmer than the capital. Graceful colonial arcades, or *portales*, flank scores of old plazas and shaded parks. The government is doing its best (within a limited budget) to preserve the colonial atmosphere and restore noteworthy buildings. It is illegal to modify the façades of colonial buildings in the centre. During the past 25 years the city has developed to the W of Av Chapultepec, where the best shops and residential neighbourhoods are now located. The climate is mild, dry and clear all through the year, although in summer it can be thundery at night. Pollution from vehicles can be bad downtown and the winter is the worst time for smog. However, afternoons are usually clear and sunny and during the rainy summer season smog is no problem.

Places of interest

The heart of the city is the Plaza de Armas. On its N side is the **Cathedral**, begun in 1561, finished in 1618, in rather a medley of styles; its two spires are covered in blue and yellow tiles. There is a reputed Murillo Virgin inside (painted 1650), and the famous La Virgen del Carmen, painted by Miguel de Cabrera, a Zapotec Indian from Oaxaca. In the dome are frescoes of the four gospel writers and in the Capilla del Santísimo are more frescoes and paintings of the Last Supper. From outside you can see the sunset's rays streaming through the dome's stained glass. The Cathedral's W façade is on Plaza de los Laureles, on the N side of which is the **Palacio Municipal** (1952), which contains murals by Gabriel Flores of the founding of the city.

Also on the Plaza de Armas is the **Palacio de Gobierno** (1643) where in 1810 Hidalgo issued his first proclamation abolishing slavery (plaque). **José Clemente Orozco's** great murals can be seen on the central staircase; they depict social struggle, dominated by Hidalgo, with the church on the left, fascism on the right and the suffering peasants in the middle. More of Orozco's work can be seen in the **Congreso**, an integral part of the Palacio de Gobierno (entrance free), and in the main **University of Guadalajara** building in the Museo de Arte (small fee, good café), on Avs Juárez y Tolsá (re-named Enrique Díaz de León), in the

The founding of a city

Nuno Beltrán de Guzmán, the founder of the city, named it after his birthplace in Spain, but was less certain about where he wanted it built. Its first location was at Nochistlán, but Guzmán ordered it moved to Tlacotlán and then in 1533 to what is now Tonalá. Still dissatisfied, in 1535 he moved it back to Tlacotlán, but it suffered repeated attacks from the Cazcanes, Tecuejes and Zapoteco Indians. After a particularly bloody massacre, the 26 survivors abandoned what was left of their village and moved to the site of present day Guadalajara.

The Cristero War

The 1917 Constitution contained many provisions to curtail the political and economic power of the Catholic Church and the governments of the 1920s were decidedly anti-clerical in their efforts to implement it. Many, including President Plutarco Elías Calles (1924-28), who consolidated the Sonoran Dynasty in power for 15 years after the Revolution, sought to extirpate the Church. Catholic resistance turned to civil war (1926-29), which was most virulent in west-central parts of the country where many clergy and others lost their lives. The war cry of the Catholic rebels was 'Viva Cristo Rey' (long live Christ the King), which became shortened to Cristero as a nickname for the rebels and their war. The rebels were eventually betrayed by the vatican and the bishops, who reached a compromise peace settlement with the Government.

dome of which is portrayed man asleep, man meditating, and man creating: lie on your back or look in a mirror. Other works by this artist can be seen at the University's main Library, at Glorieta Normal, and at the massive Cabañas Orphanage near the Mercado de la Libertad, now known as **Instituto Cultural Cabañas**. The Orphanage is a beautiful building with 22 patios, which is floodlit at night (open Tues-Sat 1015-1800, Sun 1015-1445, entry US$1, US$15 to take photos). The contents of the former Orozco museum in Mexico City have been transferred here. Look for 'Man of Fire' painted in the dome. Also in the Instituto Cabañas, exhibitions of Mexican art are shown and other events are held, listed under **Entertainment** below.

Going E from the Cathedral is the Plaza de la Liberación, with a statue of Hidalgo, where the national flag is raised and lowered daily (with much ceremony). On the N side are the **Museo Regional** (see **Museums** below) and the **Palacio Legislativo** (neo-classical, remodelled in 1982, open to the public 0900 to 1800); it has a list of the names of all the Constituyentes, from Hidalgo to Otero (1824-57 and 1917). At the eastern end of this plaza is the enormous and fantastically decorated **Teatro Degollado** (1866, see **Entertainment** below), open 1000-1400, well worth seeing even if you do not go to a performance.

A pedestrian mall, **Plaza Tapatía**, has been installed between the Teatro Degollado and the Instituto Cultural Cabañas, crossing the Calzada Independencia, covering 16 square blocks. It has beautiful plants, fountains, statuary, a tourist office, and is designed in colonial style. Facing Cabañas, on Morelos, is a sculpture by Rafael Zamarripa of Jalisco's symbol: 2 lions (in bronze) supporting a tree. The **Mercado Libertad** (San Juan de Dios, see **Shopping**), is S of Plaza Tapatía and between the market and Cabañas is a park, with a fine modern sculpture 'The Stampede', by Jorge de la Peña (1982).

Churches include **Santa Mónica** (1718), Santa Mónica y Reforma, small, but very elaborate with impressive arches full of gold under a clear atrium and a richly carved façade; **La Merced**, Hidalgo y Pedro Loza, beautiful interior with a remarkable number of confessional booths; **El Carmen**, Av Juárez 638, with a main altar surrounded by gilded Corinthian columns; **San José**, Alcalde y Reforma, a 19th century church with a fine gilded rococo pulpit, eight pillars in a semicircle around the altar, painted deep red and ochre behind, give an unusual effect, the overall light blue gives an airy feel; in the plaza outside is a statue of Núñez, defender of the Reforma, who was killed in 1858; **San Miguel de Belén**, Hospital 290, enclosed in the Hospital Civil Viejo which contains three fine late

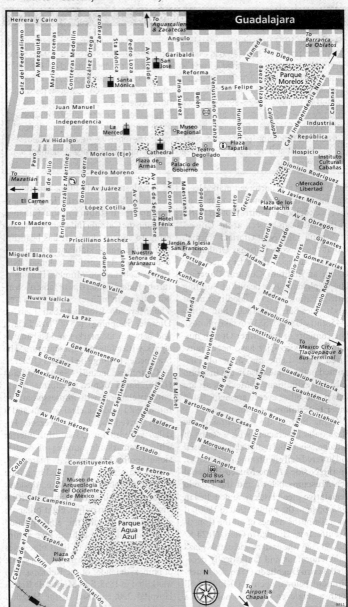

Guadalajara

Herrera y Cairo

Calz del Federalismo
Av Mezquitán
Mariano Bárcenas
Contreras Medellín
González Ortega
Zaragoza
Sta Mónica
Pedro Loza
Av Alcalde

To Aguascalien & Zacatecas

Angulo

Garibaldi
San José

Reforma

Alameda
San Diego

To Barranca de Oblatos

Baeza Alzaga

Parque Morelos

Cabañas

Santa Mónica

Pino Suárez
Belén

Venustiano Carranza
San Felipe

Humboldt
Calzada Independencia Norte
Calzadulpan

Juan Manuel

Independencia

Industria
República

Av Hidalgo

La Merced

Museo Regional

Plaza Tapatía

Hospicio
Instituto Cultural Cabañas

Pavo
8 de Julio

Donato Guerra
Enrique González Martínez

Morelos (Eje)

Plaza de Armas

Cathedral

Teatro Degollado

Dionisio Rodríguez
Av Javier Mina

To Mazatlán

Pedro Moreno

Palacio de Gobierno

Av 16 de Septiembre
Av Colón
Av Corona
Maestranza
Degollado
Molina
Huerto
Grecia

Mercado Libertad

Av Juárez

El Carmen

López Cotilla

Plaza de los Mariachis

Av A Obregón

Fco I Madero

Hotel Fénix

Priciliano Sánchez

Ocampo
Galeana

Jardín & Iglesia San Francisco

Nuestra Señora de Aránzazu

Gigantes

Lic Verdía
J M Mercado
J Antonio Torres
Gómez Farías
Antonio Rosales

Miguel Blanco

Libertad

Portugal

Aldama

Leandro Valle

Ferrocarri

Kunhardt

Holanda

Medrano

Nueva Galicia

Av Revolución

Av La Paz

Constitución

To Mexico City, Tlaquepaque & Bus Terminal

J Gpe Montenegro

8 de Julio
E González

Mexicaltzingo

Comercio
D R Michel
20 de Noviembre
28 de Enero
5 de Mayo

Guadalupe Victoria
Cuauhtémoc

Av Niños Héroes

Manzano
Av 16 de Septiembre Sur
Calz Independencia Sur

Bartolomé de las Casas

Antonio Bravo

Analco
Nicolás Bravo

Cuitlahuac

Balderas

Gante

N Morquecho

Los Angeles

Estadio

Constituyentes
Regules

5 de Febrero

Old Bus Terminal

Colón
Calzada de el Aguila
Cartero

Museo de Arqueología del Occidente de México

G Gallo

Calz Campesino

Parque Agua Azul

España

Plaza Juárez

Turín

Circunvalación

N

To Airport & Chapala

M11

18th century *retablos*; behind the hospital is the **Panteón de Belén**, a beautiful old cemetery closed to new burials for many years, entrance at C Belén 684 at corner of C Eulogio Parra, open until 1500; **San Agustín**, Morelos y Degollado (16th century), quite plain, with carved stones, musical school next door; and **San Francisco** (1550) with a 3-tiered altar with columns, a feature repeated on the façade. To the N of this last church is the **Jardín San Francisco** (pleasantly shaded, starting point for horse-drawn carriages), and to the W the old church of **Nuestra Señora de Aránzazu**, with three fantastic churrigueresque altarpieces; equally impressive are the coloured ceilings and the finely carved dado, the only light comes from high-up windows and from the open E door. In the shadow of San Francisco is a modern statue to teachers. **María de Gracia**, V Carranza y Hidalgo, is beautiful. The **Santuario de Guadalupe**, on the corner of Av Alcalde and Juan Alvarez, is lovely inside; outside, in the Jardín del Santuario, fireworks are let off on 12 Dec, the day of the Virgin of Guadalupe, with musicians, vendors, games and people celebrating in the plaza.

Other sights worth seeing are the **Parque Alcalde**, Jesús García y Av de los Maestros, to the N of the centre; the **Plaza de Los Mariachis**, Obregón and Leonardo Vicario, near Mercado Libertad, and the **Templo Expiatorio**, Av Enrique Díaz de León y Madero, with fine stained glass and intricate ceiling, gothic style, still unfinished after most of a century. There is a large park, zoological garden with plenty of Central American animals and aviaries in a delightful atmosphere (entry US$1) and planetarium just past the bullring going out on Calzada Independencia Norte. **Selva Mágica** amusement park is inside the zoo; it has a dolphin and seal show 3-4 times a day.

On Calzada Independencia Sur, at the intersection of Constituyentes and González Gallo is **Parque Agua Azul** (open 0800-1900, Tues to Sun, US$0.20). A park with a good aviary, trees, flowers and fountains; it contains the **Auditorio González Cano**, an outdoor concert bowl with portraits of famous Jalisco musicians, the **Teatro Experimental** and the **Casa de las Artesanías de Jalisco** (see **Crafts** below). On the other side of Calzada Independencia Sur is **Plaza Juárez** with an impressive monument ringed by the flags of other Latin American countries (take bus 52 or 54 up Av 16 de Septiembre or 60 or 62 up Calzada Independencia back to centre).

There are three universities (visit architectural faculty near Parque Mirador, 20 mins by car from centre; or take bus (see local **Transport** below), overlooking Barranca de Oblatos, a huge canyon).

Museums

Museo de Arqueología del Occidente de México, Calzada Independencia Sur y Calzada del Campesino (Plaza Juárez), open Mon-Fri 1000-1400, 1600-1800, Sat-Sun 1100-1430, 2 pesos: objects from Jalisco, Colima and Nayarit, pottery, ornaments, weapons, figures, illustrations

Tapatío

The word 'tapatío' is used to describe the people of Guadalajara and sometimes of the State of Jalisco but it is believed to derive from the Indian word 'tlapatiotl', used in the valley of Atemajac to describe a monetary and commercial unit, equivalent to 'three'. In Guadalajara everything was sold in groups of three. The first known reference to the word 'tlapatiotl' was in the work of Fray Francisco Jiménez, *Cuatro libros de la naturaleza y virtudes medicinales de las plantas y animales de la Nueva España*, published in 1615, where the word referred to a commercial unit.

of tombs, very comprehensive, small booklet in English. **Museo Regional de Guadalajara**, Liceo 60, between Hidalgo y C Independencia (NE of Cathedral), T 614-2227. In an old seminary (1710) with a good prehistoric section (including the complete skeleton of a mammoth found in Jalisco), an interesting display of shaft tombs, excellent display of Colima, Nayarit, and Jalisco terracotta figures (but less extensive than Museo Arqueológico), possibly the finest display of 17th-18th century colonial art in Mexico outside the Museo Virreinal in Mexico City, musical instruments, Indian art and one room devoted to the history of Jalisco from the Conquistadores to Iturbide (highly recommended). Open Mon-Fri 0900-1900, Sat 0900-1800, Sun 0900-1500, US$2, free Sun and holidays, over 60s and students with ID. **Museo de Periodismo y Artes Gráficas**, Av Alcalde 225, between San Felipe and Reforma, T 613-9285/6, restored and opened 1994, the building is known as the Casa de los Perros because of two large dog statues on the roof. The first printing shop in Guadalajara was here and the first '*periódico insurgente*' in the Americas, *El Despertador Americano* was published here in 1810. The museum contains old printing presses, newspapers, etc. When Av Alcalde was widened in 1950, the building's façade was moved back 9m. Open Tues-Sat 1000-1800, Sun 1100-1500, entrance 5 pesos, students with ID half price, over 60s free, Sun free. **Museo de la Ciudad**, C Independencia 684, in pretty colonial building with two columned patios, with information on the city from its founding to the present day, including maps and population statistics. Open Wed-Sat 1000-1730, Sun 1000-1430, 3 pesos, free Sun and for over 60s. **Albarrán Hunting Museum**, Paseo de los Parques 3530, Colinas de San Javier, Sat and Sun 1000-1400, with a collection of rare animals from all over the world. **Casa Museo López Portillo**, C Liceo 177, T 613-2411/2435, formerly the family home of the ex-President, restored 1982

when he was in office. It is a colonial house with a large tiled courtyard, and surrounding rooms furnished with 18th and 19th century Italian and French furniture. It is also used as a cultural centre with classes in music, dance, literature, children's literature, chess, Indian culture and languages. Across the street at Liceo 166 in another nice colonial building are the offices of the **Instituto Nacional de Antropología e Historia** (INAH), where there is a library with books on Guadalajara, open 1000-1600. **Casa José Clemente Orozco**, Aurelio Aceves 29, pedestrian street half a block from Los Arcos, built in 1940s and donated to the state of Jalisco by the family on his death in 1951, open 1000-1600. Two other museums are the **Museo de Cera**, Libertad 1872 entre Colonias y Hemerson and the **Museo del Juguete**, Hidalgo 1291, esq General Coronado. The **Casa de la Cultura**, Av 16 de Septiembre y Constituyentes, holds contemporary art exhibitions and lectures.

Excursions

In a NW suburb of Guadalajara are the Basílica de **Zapopán**, with a miraculous image of Nuestra Señora on the main altar, given to the Indians in 1542, and a museum of Huichol Indian art (agricultural fair in Nov). Zapopán is reached by bus 275 along Av Alcalde, or take line 1 of the metro to Avila Camacho stop and pick up bus 175 to Zapopán. (**NB** There are several different 175s, check with driver that bus goes all the way to Zapapán.)

8 km (NE) to the canyon of **Barranca de Oblatos**, 600m deep, reached by bus 42 and others from the market to end of line (admission US$0.10), with the Río Grande de Santiago cascading at the bottom (except in dry season). Guides to the bottom. Once described as a stupendous site; now spoilt by littering and sewage. See especially the Cola de Caballo waterfall and the Parque Mirador Dr Atl. The park is crowded on Sun; Balneario Los Comachos, a large swimming pool with diving boards set on one side of the Barranca

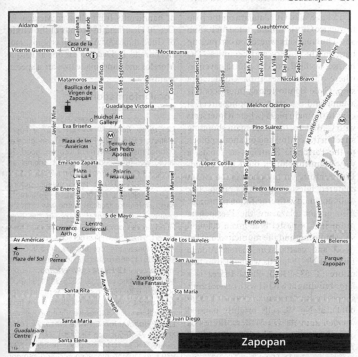

Zapopan

de Oblatos, has many terraces with tables
and chairs and barbecue pits under mango
trees; drinks and snacks on sale; now described as dirty. Entry US$1.50. Also to
Barranca de Huentitán, access via the Mirador de Huentitán at the end of Calzada
Independencia Norte, interesting flora,
tremendous natural site. 1 hr to the bottom
(no guide needed) and the river which is
straddled by the historic bridge of Huentitán. Buses to Huentitán: 42 'Jouilla Centro' from city centre; 44 'Sevilo C Médico',
stops 100m short. All buses cost US$0.25.

En route for Tepic is the Bosque de
Primavera, reached by town buses. Pine
forests ideal for picnics, although increasingly littered; US$0.50 for a swim. Good
restaurant, *Los Pioneros*, Carretera a
Tesistán 2005, esq Av Hospital Angel
Leaño, with bar, live music, attractions
and US 'Wild West' atmosphere.

4 hrs N of Guadalajara on the road from
Zapopán through San Cristóbal de la Barranca is the small town of **Totatiche** near
the Río Tlatenango, founded by the Caxcan
Indians but taken over by the Spaniards
between 1592-1600. Both Totatiche and
neighbouring Temastián were evangelized
by Franciscans and the church is in the
classical Franciscan style, with a 3-tiered
tower. In the church is the urn containing
the remains of the recently beatified Father
Cristóbal Magallanes, who was killed in the
Cristero War (see box). Next to the church
is the Museo Cristero containing personal
effects and furniture. At **Temastián**, 12 km
away, the Basílica houses an image of Christ
venerated for escaping a lightening bolt
which destroyed the cross it was on, known
as 'el Señor de los Rayos'. Its fiesta is 11 Jan
and is celebrated with dancing, parades
and rodeos.

15 km SW of Guadalajara on the road to Mexico City is **Tonalá**, noted for its Sun and Thur markets, where you can pick up bargains in pottery and ceramics. The market is held on the central avenue, where all the buses from Guadalajara stop. Calle Benito Juárez intersects this avenue and is a main shopping street. It runs to the main plaza (where it intersects with C Madero, the other main shopping street in the centre) and on another block to the Parroquia Santiago de Tonalá, a very beautiful church built in the mid-17th century. On the plaza is the cream coloured Iglesia Sagrado Corazón. The walls are lined with crucifixion paintings. Also on the plaza are the Presidencia Municipal, a pastel blue-green colonial style building, and the municipal market (food and crafts). On Juárez: Aldana Luna, at No 194, sells wrought iron furniture (T 683-0302); Plaza Juárez is a large building at No 141 with several craft shops in it; Artesanías Nuño (T 683-0011), at No 59, sells brightly painted wooden animals. On Madero: there is a *casa de cambio* at No 122; *Restaurant Jalapeños* at No 23 serves pizza, beer and regular meals; **D** *Hotel Tonalá*, opposite, at No 22, is plain but in good shape, some rooms with TV. Another attractive restaurant is *El Rincón del Sol*, at 16 de Septiembre 61, serving steaks and Mexican food.

Local festivals

21 Mar commemorates Benito Juárez' birthday and everything is closed for the day. Ceremonies around his monument at the Agua Azul park. In June the Virgin of Zapopán (see **Excursions** above), leaves her home to spend each night in a different church where fireworks are let off. The virgin has a new car each year but the engine is not started, men pull it through the streets with ropes, the streets are decorated. The climax is 12 Oct when the virgin leaves the Cathedral for home, there are great crowds along the route. Throughout the month of Oct there is a great *fiesta* with concerts, bullfights, sports and exhibitions of handicrafts from all over Mexico. 28 Oct-20 Dec, *fiesta* in honour of the Virgin of Guadalupe; Av Alcalde has stalls, music, fair etc. In Dec there is one at Parque Morelos and hand-made toys are a special feature.

Local information

● Accommodation

Many in our price ranges A3 and up, inc: **L2** *Quinta Real*, Av México 2727 y López Mateos, T 615-0000, F 300-1797, designed as colonial manor, convenient location, good, 78 large, well-furnished rooms, but original art work; **L3** *Camino Real*, Vallarta 5005, T 121-8000, F 121-8070, 5 pools, tennis, putting green, children's playground, 3 restaurants, bars, conference facilities, some way from the centre; **L3** *Continental Plaza*, in the Expo Guadalajara Convention Centre, 20 mins from airport, 5 mins from Plaza del Sol, Av de las Rosas 2933, Rinconada del Bosque, T 678-0505, F 678-0511, 466 rooms, 22 storeys high, luxury, impressive; **L3** *Fiesta Americana*, López Mateos at Minerva circle, T 825-3434, 91 (800) 50450, F 630-3725, rooms not as grand as the price might suggest, but excellent views from upper floors, and impressive towering hallway; **L3-A1** *Holiday Inn Crowne Plaza*, Av López Mateos 2500 Sur, opp Plaza del Sol, shopping centre, T 634-1034, 91 (800) 36555, F 631-9393, restaurant, nightclub, etc, and also opp Plaza del Sol, is **L3** *Presidente Intercontinental*, López Mateos Sur and Av Moctezuma, T 678-1237, F 678-1222, some deluxe suites with private patio, high rise tower with built-in shopping centre, cavernous lobby.

A1-A3 *La Villa del Ensueño*, Florida 305, Tlaquepaque, in USA F (818) 597-0637, e-mail: aldez@soca.com, 8 rooms, 2 suites, pool, inc breakfast, no smoking, English and Spanish spoken; **A3** *Plaza Génova* (Best Western), Juárez 123, T 613-7500, F 614-8253, inc continental breakfast and welcome cocktail, clean, good service, good restaurant, rec; **A3-A2** *Fénix*, Av Corona 160, just off López Cotilla, T 614-5714, F 613-4005, high rise block, roof garden with drinks, good restaurant; **A3-A1** *Calinda Roma*, Juárez 170, T 614-8650, F 614-2629; **A2-A1** *Aranzazú*, Av Revolución 110 Pte, T 613-3232, F 613-3232 ext 1369, central, very good; **A2-A1** *El Tapatío*, Blvd Aeropuerto 4275, T 635-6050, F 635-6664, in Tlaquepaque, nearest hotel to airport, fine view of city, extensive grounds, very attractive and comfortable rooms; **A3-B de Mendoza**, Venustiano Carranza 16, T 613-4646, 91 (800) 36126, F 613-7310, just off Plaza Tapatía, pleasant, small rooms but pretty colonial-style lobby and restaurant, small pool, rec; **A3-C Francés**, Maestranza 35, T 613-0917, F 658-2831, colonial building with central patio, oldest hotel in the city, built in 1610, have a drink there at 'happy hour' 1800-1900, to enjoy the bygone atmosphere, disco and bar music noisy at night, some rooms small but very good value penthouse suite for 4, with 2 very large bedrooms, living room and kitchen, expensive parking underneath adjoining Plaza de la Liberación; **A1 Holiday Inn**, Guadalajara-Airport, Av Providencia 2848, T 678-9000, F 678-9002.

B del Parque, Av Juárez 845, T 825-2800, clean, friendly, courteous, nr Parque Revolución, *tren ligero*, University administration; **B Internacional**, Pedro Moreno 570, T 613-0330, F 613-2866, clean, comfortable, safe, rec; **B Nueva Galicia**, Av Corona 610, T 614-8780, F 613-3892, older style; **B Posada del Sol**, López Mateos Sur 4205, T 631-5205, F 631-5731; **B Rotonda**, Liceo 130, T 614-1017, central, nr Cathedral, remodelled 19th century building, attractive, dining area in courtyard, cheap set lunches, nice public areas, rooms OK, with TV, phones, covered parking; **B-C Plaza Diana**, Av Circunvalación Agustín Yañez 2760, T 615-5510, F 630-3685, 126 rooms, many refurbished 1995, a/c, TV, restaurant with low-cal menu; **B-C San Francisco Plaza**, Degollado 267, T 613-8954/8971, T 613-3257, threadbare, many rooms face inwards, street rooms noisy, several patios, hot water, TV, pleasant.

C El Parador at new bus terminal, T 600-0910, F 600-0015, overpriced because of location (does not take Amex), spartan rooms with TV, expensive laundry, clean, noisy, pool, 24-hr café *El Jardín*; **C Hotel Plaza Los Arcos**, Av Vallarta 2456, T 616-3816, F 616-3817, 1-bedroom suites, huge hard bed, sitting room, kitchen, good bathroom, very clean, 2-weekly and monthly rates available.

D Sevilla, Prisciliano Sánchez 413, T 614-9037, good, clean (4 blocks S of cathedral), owner speaks English, good restaurant (not always open); **D-E Estación**, Calzada Independencia Sur 1297, T 619-0051, across the main boulevard beside train station, quiet, clean, safe, luggage store, hot water, rec, small, limited restaurant, station porters will carry luggage there US$0.50-1.

There are cheap hotels along Calzada Independencia (very noisy), on 5 de Febrero and in the 2 blocks N of the old bus station, C 28 de Enero and C 20 de Noviembre (where there is a small market, good for breakfasts) and the side streets (although rooms can sometimes be filthy, so check); they inc **D Nueva York**, Independencia Sur 43, T 617-3398, with bath, hot water; **D-E Canadá**, Estadio, ½ block from old bus station, all rooms with bath, hot water, some with TV, clean, good value; **E Casa de Huéspedes Norteña**, basic; **E Lincoln**, good, clean, helpful; **E Royal**, C Los Angeles, nr old bus terminal, clean; **F León**, Calz Independencia Sur 557, bath, towel, hot water, clean, staff friendly and helpful; on 5 de Febrero, **D San José** (No 116), T 619-1153, **Emperador** (No 530), T 619-2246, remodelled, adequate, all rooms have TV and phone, enclosed parking, good public areas, and **Monaco** (No 152); on 20 de Noviembre, **San Carlos** (No 728B), **Praga Central** (No 733A) and **Madrid** (No 775), all **D/E**, rec, but rooms on street are noisy.

Cheaper hotels in the centre, and nr Mercado Libertad: several on Javier Mina, eg **D Ana Isabel**, Javier Mina 184, central, TV, clean, tiny rooms but very good value, tell them when you are checking out or room may be relet before you have gone. **D Azteca**, 1½ blocks from Mercado Libertad, clean, parking around the corner (ask at the desk); **D Continental**, on C Corona, rec; **F González**, behind Mercado Corona, 4 blocks W of cathedral, González Ortega 77, basic, often full, very friendly, not too clean; **D-E Posada Tapatía**, López Cotilla 619, T 614-9146, colonial style house, 2-3 blocks from Federalismo, one of the better budget places, traffic can be a problem; **D Maya**, López Cotilla 39, T 614-4654, with private bath, blankets, pleasant atmosphere, rec; **D-E México 70**, Javier Mina, opp Mercado Libertad, with bath, clean, TV available, rec; **D Imperio**, next door, clean and popular, noisy, other hotels on Corona of similar quality but cheaper; **D Posada San Pablo**, Madero 268, shared bath, hot water, family run, rec; **D Janeiro**, Obregón 93, by market, very clean, good value, cheap laundry service, noisy from Mariachi music in nearby square, rec; **E Hamilton**, Madero 381, with bath, clean, friendly, good value; **F del Maestro**, Herrera y Cayro No 666, between Mariano Barcenas and Contreras Medellín, buses from Cathedral 52, 54, 231, from bus station 275), no sign, not very clean, friendly, OK; **F Lisboa**, on corner of Grecia and Juárez in precinct, noisy, shared bath, but cheap.

Motels: **A1** *Las Américas*, López Mateos Sur 2400, T 613-7548, F 631-4415, opp Plaza del Sol shopping centre, a/c, pool, good; **C** *El Bosque*, L Mateos Sur 265, T 121-4700, F 122-1955, TV and phone in all rooms; **C** *Isabel*, Montenegro 1572, sector Hidalgo, T 826-2630, pleasant, pool. There are additional ones at the end of Vallarta, and along López Mateos nr the edge of town, before the *periférico* road.

Trailer Parks: *La Hacienda*, Circunvalación Pte 66, 16 km out of town, in Col Cd Granja, off Av Vallarta on left before you reach periférico and head to Tepic, T 627-1724, F 627-1724 ext 117, US$10 for 2, US$14 for 4, shaded, pool, clubhouse, hook-ups, rec. Also *San José del Tajo*, 25 km from city on Route 15/80 towards Manzanillo, about 1 km from city boundary, full hook-up, hot showers, pool, laundry facilities, US$13.35 for vehicle and 2 people, reported in need of repair.

Youth hostel: at Prolongación Alcalde 1360, Sector Hidalgo, T 653-0044, away from centre, US$5, inc pillow and blanket, fairly clean, many mosquitoes. Bus from Cathedral 52, 54 or 231; from bus terminal No 275 (alight just after it leaves Av Alcalde to Av Camacho, then 5 mins' walk). Also at Prolongación Federalismo y Lázaro Cárdenas, Unidad Deportiva, CP 44940.

● **Places to eat**
As can be expected in a city of this size there is a wide variety of restaurants on offer, look in local tourist literature for the latest in International, Mexican, Spanish, Italian, Argentine, Arab, Chinese, Japanese or German cooking. There are also fast food outlets, pizzerías and Mexican cafeterías and bars. *Carnes Asadas Tolsa*, Enrique Díaz de León 540 and Chapultepec, T 825-6875, rec. *Piaf*, Marsella 126, excellent, French cuisine, live music, friendly, closed Sun; *Búfalo*, Calderón de la Barca y Av Vallarta, tacos and cheap *comida corrida*, very friendly; *La Banderillas*, Av Alcalde 831, excellent food at reasonable prices; *El Mexicano*, Plaza Tapatía, Morelos 81, rustic Mexican decor, rec; *Madrid*, Juárez 264 y Corona, good breakfast, excellent coffee and fruit salad, very smoky (from cigarettes); *La Catedral del Antojito*, Pedro Moreno 130, a pedestrian street, colonial style house, restaurant upstairs above bridal gown shops, serves tacos, etc, good meal for under US$2; *Café Madoka*, Enrique González, Martínez 78, T 613-3134, just S of Hidalgo, excellent very early breakfasts, well known for the men who play dominoes there. Many cheap restaurants in the streets nr the old bus station, especially in C de Los Angeles, and upstairs in the large Mercado Libertad (San Juan de Dios) in centre, but not very hygienic here. *La Trattoria*, Niños Héroes 3051, very good, reasonably priced Italian, very popular (queues form for lunch from 1400). Delicious *carne en su jugo* (beef stew with potatoes, beans, bacon, sausage, onion and avocado, garnished with salsa, onion and coriander) from *Carnes Asadas El Tapatío* in Libertad market (there are 3), or *Carnes Asadas Rigo's*, C Independencia 584A, popular. Goat is a speciality, roasted each day and served with radish, onion and chilli. *Karne Garibaldi*, Garibaldi 1306, esq J Clemente Orozco, Col Sta Teresita, nice place, serves *carne en su jugo*. For those so inclined, *Lido*, Colón 294 y Miguel Blanco (Plaza San Francisco), serves *criadillas*, bull's testicles; *Cortijo La Venta*, Federación 725, T 617-1675, open daily 1300-0100, invites customers to fight small bulls (calves) after their meal (the animals are not harmed, guests might be), restaurant serves meat, soups, salads. *El Ganadero*, on Av Américas, excellent beef, reasonable prices; *Café Pablo Picasso*, Av Américas 1939, T 636-1996/6141, breakfast, lunch, dinner and tapas, galería, boutique, smart clientèle, pricey, decorated with photos of Picasso and his work; *El Asadero*, opp the basilica in Zapopán suburb (see **Excursions** above), is very good. *La Calle*, Autlán 2, nr Galería de Calzado and bus terminal, expensive but good, with garden. Good *Lonchería* at Morelos 99 y Gerardo Juárez, by Tourist Office, try *tortas de lomo doble carne con aguacate*. *La Bombilla*, López Cotilla y Penitenciaría, very good for *churros* and hot chocolate. In the cloister of La Merced is a fast food place, popular with young people; *La Chata*, Francisco Zarco 2277, and *Gemma*, López Mateos Sur 1800, 2 chains serving Mexican food, are usually quite good (*Gemma* has 8 branches in the city and does Guadalajaran 'lonches', *tortas ahogadas*). *La Pianola*, Av México 3220 and several locations, good, reasonable prices, serves *chiles en nogada*, excellent. A good place for fish is *El Delfín Sonriente*, Niños Héroes 2293, T 616-0216/7441, nice, attractive; a good Mexican restaurant is *La Gorda*, C Juan Alvarez 1336, esq Gral Coronado, Col Sta Teresita; *La Rinconada*, Morelos 86 on Plaza Tapatía, is in a beautiful colonial building, columned courtyard, carved wood doors, entrées at US$4-8 range, open until 2130, separate bar. Plenty of US fast food places: *Pizza Hut*, *McDonald's*, *Burger King*, *Carl's Junior*, with several outlets.

In **Tlaquepaque** (see **Shopping** below), *Restaurante Sin Nombre*, Madero 80, in colonial house, seating in courtyard, tropical plants and birds, inc peacocks. Nearby, same owner, is *El Portico*, also in colonial house on corner of Obregón and Independencia. Other attractive restaurants in colonial houses are *El Patio*, Independencia 186, and *Casa Fuerte*, Independencia 224.

● **Bars**

La Fuente, Pino Suárez 78, very popular, mixed clientèle, live music, lots of atmosphere. Many bars serve snacks, *botanas*, with drinks between 1300 and 1500, free. Most of these bars are for men only, though. **NB** The bars in the centre are popular with the city's gay population, eg *Rotanero el Ciervo* is a gay bar, 20 de Noviembre 797, corner of C Los Angeles, opp old bus station.

● **Airline offices**

Mexicana, reservations T 678-7676, arrival and departure information T 688-5775, ticket offices: Av Mariano Otero 2353, by Plaza del Sol, T 112-0011, Av 16 de Septiembre 495, T 614-8195, Plaza Patria, local 8H, T 641-5352, López Cotilla 1552, T 615-3099/3480, between Av Chapultepec and Américas; **AeroMéxico**, reservations T 669-0202, airport information T 688-5098, ticket offices, Av Corona 196 and Plaza del Sol, local 30, Zona A; **Delta**, López Cotilla 1701, T 630-3130; **Aero California**, López Cotilla 1423 (T 826-8850); on Av Vallarta: **Air France**, No 1540 103 (T 630-3707). **American**, No 2440 (T 616-4090 for reservations, T 688-5518 at airport), **KLM**, No 1390-1005 (T 825-3261), **Continental**, ticket office Astral Plaza, Galerías del *Hotel Presidente Intercontinental*, locales 8-9, T 647-4251 reservations, T 688-5141 airport; **Saro**, Av 16 de Septiembre 334, T 91-800-83224; **Taesa**, López Cotilla 1531B, just past Av Chapultepec, reservations T 91 (800) 90463; **United**, Plaza Los Arcos, Av Vallarta 2440, local A13, T 616-9489.

● **Banks & money changers**

There are many *casas de cambio* on López Cotilla between Independencia and 16 de Septiembre and one in Plaza del Sol. Despite what they say, *casas de cambio* close 1400 or 1500 till 1600, not continuously open 0900-1900. **American Express**, Plaza los Arcos, Local 1-A, Av Vallarta 2440, esq Fco García de Quevedo, about 5 blocks E of Minerva roundabout, T 630-0200, F 615-7665, open 0900-1800 for the travel agency and 0900-1430, 1600-1800 to change money. Across Prisciliano Sánchez from the

Jardín San Francisco is a **Banco Inverlat** with a 24-hr ATM which gives cash on American Express cards if you are enrolled in their Express Cash programme.

● **Cultural centres**

Goethe Institute, Morelos 2080 y Calderón de la Barca, T 615-6147, 616-0495, F 615-9717, library, nice garden, newspapers. **Alliance Française**, López Cotilla 1199, Sector Juárez, T 825-2140, 825-5595. The **Instituto Cultural Mexicano-Norteamericano de Jalisco** (see below, **Language schools**). US at Enrique Díaz de León 300.

● **Embassies & consulates**

Australia, López Cotilla 2030, T 615-7418, F 630-3479, open 0800-1330, 1500-1800; **Austria**, Montevideo 2695, Col Providencia, T 641-1834, open 0900-1330; **Belgium**, Metalúrgica 2818, Parque Industrial El Alamo, T 670-4825, F 670-0346, open Mon-Fri 0900-1400; **Brazil**, Cincinati 130, esq Nueva Orleans, Col La Aurora, next to train station, T 619-2102, open 0900-1700; **Canada**, *Hotel Fiesta Americana*, local 31, T 615-6215, open 0830-1700; **Denmark**, Calz Lázaro Cárdenas 601, 6° piso, T 669-5515, F 678-5997, open 0900-1300, 1600-1800; **Dominican Republic**, Colón 632, T 613-5478, F 614-5019, open 0900 1400, 1600-1900; **Ecuador**, C Morelos 685, esq Pavo, T 613-1666, F 613-1729, open 1700-2000; **El Salvador**, C Fermín Riestra 1628, entre Bélgica y Argentina, Col Moderna, T 810-1061, hours for visas 1230-1400, normally visas will be received the same day; **Finland**, Justo Sierra 2562, 5th Floor, T 616-3623, F 616-1501, open 0830-1330; **France**, López Mateos Nte 484 entre Herrera y Cairo y Manuel Acuña, T 616-5516, open 0930-1400; **Germany**, Corona 202, T 613-9623, F 613-2609, open 1130-1400; **Great Britain**, Eulogio Parra 2539, T 616-0629, F 615-0197, 0900-1500, 1700-2000; **Guatemala**, Mango 1440, Col del Fresno, T 811-1503, open 1000-1400; **Honduras**, Ottawa 1139, Col Providencia, T 817-4998, F 817-5007, open 1000-1400, 1700-1900; **Israel**, Av Vallarta 2482 Altos SJ, T 616-4554, open 0930-1500; **Italy**, López Mateos Nte 790-1, T 616-1700, F 616-2092, open 1100-1400, Tues-Fri; **Netherlands**, Calz Lázaro Cárdenas 601, 6th Floor, Zona Industrial, T 811-2641, F 811-5386, open 0900-1400, 1630-1900; **Nicaragua**, Eje Central 1024, esq Toreros, Col Guadalupe Jardín, behind Club Atlas Chapalita, T 628-2919, open 1600-1800; **Norway**, Km 5 Antigua Carretera a Chapala 2801, Col La

Nogalera, T 812-1411, F 812-1074, in the building Aceite El Gallo, open 0900-1800; **Perú**, Bogotá 2923, entre Terranova y Alberta, Col Providencia, T 642-3009, open 0800-1600; **Spain**, Av Vallarta 2185 SJ, T 630-0450, F 616-0396, open 0830-1330; **Portugal**, Colimán 277 Cd del Sol, T 121-7714, F 684-3925; **Sweden**, J Gpe Montenegro 1691, T 825-6767, F 825-5559, open 0900-1400, 1600-1900; **Switzerland**, Av Revolución 707, Sector Reforma, T 617-5900, F 617-3208, open 0800-1400, 1600-1900; **USA**, Progreso 175, T 825-2700, F 626-6549.

● **Entertainment**

Cinema: average cost of a ticket is US$2. Good quality films, some in English, are shown in the evenings at 1600, 1800, 2000, US$1.25 at the ciné-teatro in the *Instituto Cultural Cabañas* (see **Places of interest** above), which also has a good cafetería.

Discos: two gay discos are *SOS*, Av La Paz 1413, and *Monica's* in Sector Libertad, to the E of the centre, both well known locally.

Music: concerts and theatre in the ex-Convento del Carmen. A band plays every Thur at 1800 in the Plaza de Armas, in front of the Palacio de Gobierno, free. Organ recitals in the Cathedral. *Peña Curicacalli*, Av Niños Héroes almost at corner of Av Chapultepec, T 825-4690, opens 2000, US$5 cover charge, food and drink available, fills up fast; local groups perform variety of music inc Latin American folk music Fri, Sat.

Theatre: *Ballet Folklórico de la Universidad de Guadalajara*, every Sun at 1000 in the Degollado Theatre, superb, highly rec, prehispanic and Mexican-wide dances, and other cultural shows, US$2-10, T 658-3812, 614-4773 (check before you go, if there is another function in the theatre they may perform elsewhere). The *Grupo Folklórico Ciudad de Guadalajara* performs here every Thur at 2000. The *Ballet Folklórico del Instituto Cultural Cabañas* performs Wed 2030 at the Instituto Cultural Cabañas, US$3. The Instituto is also an art school, with classes in photography, sculpture, ceramics, literature, music, theatre and dance.

● **Hospitals & medical services**

Dentist: *Dr Abraham Waxtein*, Av México 2309, T 615-1041, speaks English.

Doctor: *Dr Daniel Gil Sánchez*, Pablo Neruda 3265, 2nd floor, T 642-0213, speaks English.

Hospitals: good private hospitals are *Hospital del Carmen*, Tarascos 3435, Fracc Monraz (behind Plaza México, a shopping centre), T 813-0042 (take credit cards); *Hospital San Javier*, Pablo Casals 640 (on the corner of Eulogio Parra and Aquaducto), Colonia Providencia, T 669-0222 (take credit cards); *Hospital Angel Leaño*, off the road to Tesistán, T 834-3434, affiliated with the University (UAG); a less well-equipped but good hospital nr the centre that is also affiliated with the UAG is the *Hospital Ramón Garibay*, Enrique Díaz de León 238, across the street from the Templo Expiatorio, T 825-5313, 825-5159, 825-5115, 825-5050, inexpensive out-patient clinic with various specialists. Probably the best private laboratory is the *Unidad de Patología*, Av México 2341, T 616-5410, takes credit cards. For those who cannot afford anything else there are the *Hospital Civil*, T 614-5501, and the *Nuevo Hospital Civil*, F 617-7177; *Antirrábico* (rabies), T 643-1917, you have to go to Clinic 3 of the Sector Salud to receive the vaccine, T 823-3262, at the corner of Circunvalación Division del Nte and Calzada Federalismo, across the street from a Telmex office, nr the División Nte Station, Line 1, *tren ligero*, you can also get an AIDS blood test here; *Sidatel* (AIDS), T 613-7546.

Infectologist: *Dr J Manuel Ramírez R*, Dom Ermita 1031-26, Col Chapalita, by the intersection of Lázaro Cárdenas and López Mateos, T 647-7161.

Ophthalmologist: *Dr Virginia Rivera*, Eulogia Parra 2432, nr López Mateos, T 616-6637, 616-4046, English speaking.

Pharmacies: three big chains of pharmacies are *Farmacias Guadalajara*, *Benavides* and *ABC*. The *Farmacia Guadalajara* at Av Américas and Morelos has vaccines and harder to find drugs, T 615-5094. Other good pharmacies for hard to find drugs are the *Farmacia Especializada*, Av Américas 124, just S of Av México, T 616-9388, and *Farmacia Géminis*, across the street from the *Hospital del Carmen*, T 813-2874.

● **Language schools**

Centro de Estudios para Extranjeros de la Universidad de Guadalajara, Tomás de Gómez 125, between Justo Sierra and Av México, T 616-4399, 616-4382, registration US$85 pa, US$585 for 5 weeks of 4 hrs/day instruction, US$490 for 5 weeks living with a Mexican family with 3 meals a day. *The Universidad Autónoma de Guadalajara (UAG)*, a private university, offers Spanish classes through their Centro Internacional de Idiomas, T 641-7051, ext 32251, 0800-1800, at Edif Humanidades (1st floor), on the main campus on Av Patria 1201, Col Lomas del Valle 3a sección, US$350 for 4 weeks of 4 hrs/day instruction,

5 days a week, 7 levels of instruction, each lasting 4 weeks, US$13/day accommodation and 3 meals with Mexican family. *The Instituto Cultural Mexicano-Norteamericano de Jalisco*, at Enrique Díaz de León 300, T 825-5838, 825-2666, US$440 for 6 weeks of 3 hrs/day plus 30 mins conversation, 5 days a week, 5 levels of instruction, cultural lectures on Fri, US$18/day to live with Mexican family with 3 meals. *Spanish Language School AC*, Ermita 1443 entre 12 de Diciembre y Av Las Rosas, Col Chapalita, Apdo Postal 5-959, T/F 121-4774. For German and French lessons see **Cultural centres**, above. See also National Registration Center for Study Abroad under **Learning Spanish** Information for travellers.

● Laundry
Aldama 125, US$3.30/3 kg load (walk along Independencia towards train station, turn left into Aldama).

● Post & telecommunications
Post Office: V Carranza, just behind Hall of Justice, open Mon-Fri 0800-1900, Sat 0900-1300. There are also branches at the Mercado Libertad and at the old bus station, convenient for the cheap hotels. To send parcels abroad go to Aduana Postal in same building as main post office, open Mon-Fri 0800-1300, T 614-9002. Federal Express has 3 outlets: Av Américas 1395, Plaza del Sol locales 51 and 55, Av Washington 1129, next to Bolerana 2000, T 817-2502, F 817-2374 United Parcel Service at Av Américas 981, local 19, T 91 (800) 90292.

Telecommunications: international collect calls can be made from any coin-box phone kiosk and direct dial calls can be made from LADA pay phones, of which there are many all over the city. You can also make long-distance calls and send faxes from Computel outlets: one in front of old bus station, one on Corona y Madero, opp *Hotel Fénix*. Another chain, Copyroyal, charges 3 times as much for a fax to USA. Mayahuel, Paseo Degollado 55 has long distance service, fax, sells Ladatel cards, postcards and maps. There is a credit card phone at Ramón Corona y Av Juárez, by Cathedral. 2 USA Direct phones, one within and one beyond the customs barrier at the airport.

E-mail: Cyber café with Internet access at López Cotilla 773-203, primer piso, SW corner of Parque Revolución, T 826-3771, 826-3286, F 826-5610, http://www.internet-cafe.com.mx, or http://www.i-set.com.mx/cybercafe. They charge 20 pesos/hr for Internet access and give free course in its use; 1 peso/page to print; they receive your e-mail, 5 pesos/page to print out; will notify you when any messages come in; also serve pizza, snacks, beer and soft drinks. Another cyber café is *Arrobba*, Av Lázaro Cárdenas 3286, just W of intersection with López Mateos, open Mon-Sat 1000-2200, Internet access 25 pesos/hr, printouts 2 pesos, http://www.arrobba.com.mx, drinks, snacks, salads.

● Security
Guadalajara is generally a safe city. The centre is not deserted at night and people wander the streets in sociable groups. Normal precautions required against pickpockets but little more. Much safer than many US cities.

● Shopping
The best shops are no longer in the centre, although a couple of department stores have branches there. The best stores are in the shopping centres, of which there are many, small and large, mainly on the W side. The newest and biggest is La Gran Plaza, 3 floors, Sears, Salinas and Roche, 12-screen cinema, many smaller shops, between Av Lázaro Cárdenas and Av Vallarta, nr where they merge. Plaza México is another large centre, and nearby, with smaller boutiques, Plaza Bonito. The Plaza del Sol shopping centre, with over 100 shops, is located at Chapalita in the S of the city, while the equally modern Plaza Patria, with as many shops, is at the N end nr the Zapopán suburb. There are many other shopping malls such as the Galeriá del Calzado (on Av México, several blocks W of Av López Mateos), selling, as the name implies, only shoes. *El Toro Loco*, and *Botas Los Potrillos*, on Morelos by Plaza Tapatía, sell good boots.

The markets, in particular the Libertad (San Juan de Dios) which has colourful items for souvenirs with lots of Michoacán crafts inc Paracho guitars and Sahuayo hats, leather jackets, and delicious food upstairs on the 1st level (particularly goat meat, *birria*, also *cocada*), fruit juices and other soft drinks; the *tianguis* (Indian market) on Av Guadalupe, Colonia Chapalita, on Fri is of little interest to foreigners, bus 50 gets you there; the *tianguis* nr the University Sports Centre on Calzada Tlaquepaque on Sun.

Bookshops: English books available at a reasonable mark up, at *Sanborns*, Av Vallarta 1600 y Gen San Martín, Juárez y 16 de Septiembre, Plaza Bonita and López Mateos Sur 2718 (nr Plaza de Sol), also English language magazines in all stores, pharmacy section, mid-priced restaurants with good food. German journals at *Sanborns*, Av Vallarta branch. *Librería*

Británica, Av Hidalgo 1796-B, Sector Hidalgo, T 615-5803, 615-5807, F 615-0935. *Sandi's*, Av Tepeyac 718, Colonia Chapalita, T 121-0863, F 647-4600, has a good selection of English-language books, inc medical textbooks and cards. *Librería México* in Plaza del Sol, local 14, area D, on Av López Mateos side, T 121-0114, has US magazines and newspapers. *El Libro Antiguo*, Pino Suárez 86, open 1000-2000, mostly Spanish but large selection of English paperbacks. *Librería La Fuente*, C Medellín 140, nr C Juan Manuel in the centre, T 613-5238, sells used books and magazines in English and Spanish, interesting to browse in, some items quite old, from 1940s and 1950s. Bookshops can be found on López Cotilla, from González Martínez towards 16 de Septiembre.

Crafts: two glass factories at **Tlaquepaque** where the blue, green, amber and amethyst blown-glass articles are made (bus 275 from the centre goes through Tlaquepaque en route to bus station). Calle Independencia is the main shopping street and closed to traffic. The **Museo Regional de la Cerámica** is at Independencia 237. For beautiful, expensive furniture go to *Antigua de Mexico*, No 255, lovely building, used to be a convent, the family has branches in Nogales and Tucson so furniture can be shipped to their shops there. *La Casa Canela*, opp, sells furniture and crafts, don't miss the colonial kitchen at the back of the house. *Adobe Diseño*, also in a colonial house, sells expensive leather furniture. Visit the shop of **Sergio Bustamante**, who sells his own work (good modern jewellery): expensive but well worth a look, a stream runs through this house with a colonial façade on C Independencia 236. Some way from the main shopping area is the **Casa de los Telares** (C de Hidalgo 1378), where Indian textiles are woven on hand looms. Potters can be watched at work both in Guadalajara and at Tlaquepaque; you may find better bargains at **Tonalá** (pottery and ceramics, some glass), see **Excursions**, above, on market days Thur and Sun; take bus 275 (see local **Transport** below), bumpy 45 mins' journey. Overall, Tlaquepaque is the cheapest and most varied source of the local crafts, with attractive shops set in old colonial villas; best buys: glass, papier mâché goods, leather (cheapest in Mexico), and ceramics. See also the **Tienda Tlaquepaque**, at Av Juárez 267-B, in Tlaquepaque, T 635-5663. **Casa de Artesanías de Jalisco**, González Gallo 20, T 619-4664, open 1000-1900 (1400 Sun), free, in Parque Agua Azul: high quality display (and

sale) of handicrafts, ceramics, paintings, hand-blown glass, dresses, etc (state-subsidized to preserve local culture, reasonably priced but not cheap – a percentage goes to the artisan). There is another shop-cum-exhibition at the **Instituto de Artesanía Jaliscense, Casa de Las Artesanías Normal**, Av Alcalde 1221, T 624-4624. Calle Independencia runs from Blvd Tlaquepaque (the main avenue into Guadalajara) to the main plaza (where you can see the restored Parroquia de San Pedro Tlaquepaque and the Basílica La Teranensis) and then to the **Parián**, another plaza on the SE corner. The Parián is a very large, square building occupying most of the plaza, with bars (pretty woodwork and tiling) and kitchens around the perimeter. The rest is an open courtyard with tables and mariachis, who play Fri, Sat, Sun, 1530 and 2130, also roving mariachis play on demand for a fee.

● **Sports**
Bullfights: Oct to Mar; football throughout year; *charreadas* (cowboy shows) are held in mid-Sept at Unión de San Antonio; *charreada* nr Agua Azul Park at Aceves Calindo Lienzo, Sun at 1200. Baseball, April-September.

Golf: at Santa Anita, 16 km out on Morelia road, championship course; Rancho Contento, 10 km out on Nogales road; San Isidro, 10 km out on Saltillo road, noted for water hazards; Areas, 8 km out on Chapala road (US$13 during the week, US$20 at weekends is the average price for a round). The *Guadalajara Country Club*, has a beautiful clubhouse and golf course in the middle of the city, nr the Plaza Patria shopping centre, Mar Caribe 260, T 817-3502, phone ahead for start time and to check green fee.

Hiking: club *Colli*, bulletin board Av Juárez 460, details from *Café Madrid*, Juárez 264 or T 623-3318, 617-9248.

● **Tourist offices**
Federal tourist office (**Sectur**), Morelos 102, Plaza Tapatía, T 614-8686 (Mon-Fri 0900-2000), has information in German and English inc good walking tour map of the historic centre, helpful but often understaffed; Jalisco state offices at Paseo Degollado 105/Morelos 102, Plaza Tapatía, T 614-8686, open Mon-Sat 0900-2000, and a booth in capitol building. There are several booths staffed by Tourist Police nr many of the main attractions. Municipal office at Pedro Moreno 1590, just W of Av Chapultépec and Los Arcos, over Av Vallarta, T 616-3332. *Siglo 21* newspaper has a good entertainments

section, *Tentaciones* on Fri, every day it has good music, film and art listings. **Instituto Nacional de Estadística**, Geografía e Informática, 16 de Septiembre 670, T 614-9461, F 658-3969, new, fully computerized office, for maps and information, open 0800-2000.

● **Useful services**

Immigration: Mexican tourist cards can be renewed at the immigration office (primer piso) in the Palacio Federal on Av Alcalde between Calles Juan Alvarez and Hospital, across the avenue from the Santuario de Guadalupe. The Palacio Federal also contains a post and telegraph office and fax service.

● **Transport**

Local Horse-drawn carriages US$5 for a short ride or US$7.50/hr from the Museo Regional de Guadalajara at the corner of Liceo and Hidalgo. Tourist Office in Plaza Tapatía has a full list of local buses. If in doubt ask bus driver. Regular buses cost 1.50 pesos, Línea Azul 'luxury' bus 3.50 pesos, Feb 1997. Some useful lines: No 275, from Zapopán-Plaza Patria-Glorieta Normal-Av Alcalde-Av 16 de Septiembre-Av Revolución-Tlaquepaque-new bus station-Tonalá (there are different 275s, from A to T, most follow this route, check with driver); route 707 also goes to Tonalá (silver-blue bus with Tur on the side); bus 60 goes along Calzada Independencia from zoo, passing Estadio Jalisco, Plaza de Toros, Mercado Libertad and Parque Agua Azul to the old bus terminal and the railway station (note, if you are going to Parque Mirador, take bus 62 northbound, otherwise 62 has the same route as 60); there is also a new trolley bus that runs along the Calzada to the N terminus of the Calzada at the entrance to the Mirador, better than 60 or 62; to train station take 60 or 62 S along Calz Independencia or 52 or 54 S along Av Alcalde/16 de Septiembre; to the old bus station, minibus 174 S along Calz Independencia from Mercado Libertad, or bus 110 S along Av Alcalde; bus 102 runs from the new bus terminal along Av Revolución, 16 de Septiembre and Prisciliano Sánchez to Mercado Libertad; No 258 or 258A from San Felipe (N of Cathedral) or 258D along Madero to Plaza del Sol; No 371 from Tonalá to Plaza del Sol. A shuttle bus runs between the two bus stations. The Metro, or *Tren Ligero*, has Línea 1 running under Federalismo from Periférico Sur to Periférico Nte. Línea 2, runs from Juárez station westbound and passes Mercado Libertad. Fare US$0.40, one-peso coins needed to buy tokens. **Car rental**: Quick, T 614-2247, VW Sedan

US$40/day, inc tax, insurance, 400 km/day; **Budget**, T 613-0027, Nissan Tsuru, a/c, US$70/day, unlimited mileage; **National**, T 614-7175, VW Sedan, US$50/day, inc 300 km/day; **Avis**, T 91 (800) 70777, VW Sedan US$40, plus US$18 insurance and 15% tax, unlimited mileage; **Hertz**, T 614-6162, VW Sedan US$15/day, inc 300 km/day. Others scattered throughout city. **Taxis**: no meters used. A typical ride in town costs US$1.50-2.50. From the centre to the new bus station is about US$4 and to the airport US$8-10.

Air Miguel Hidalgo (GDL), 20 km from town; fixed rate for 3 city zones and 3 classes of taxi: *especial, semi especial* and *colectivo*, no tip necessary. Bus No 176 'San José del 15', leaves from intersection of Corona and Calz Independencia every 20 mins, 2 pesos, grey bus. Autotransportes Guadalajara-Chapala runs 2nd class buses from old bus terminal every 15 mins, 0655-2125, 3 pesos, stop at airport on way to/from Chapala. Many flights daily to and from Mexico City, 65 mins. Connections by air with nearly all domestic airports. US cities served inc Boston, Chicago, Dallas, Houston, Los Angeles, Nashville, New York, Oakland, Portland, St Louis, San Antonio, San Diego, San Francisco, San José (California).

Trains Ferrocarriles Nacionales de México, tickets at the station, T 650-0826; Ferrocarril del Pacífico, T 650-0570 at the station, or ticket office, Av Libertad 1875, T 626-5665, 626-3102. The station has bathrooms, coin and card operated Ladatel phones and food stores. **Mexico City**-Guadalajara: Tapatío leaves the capital 2030, arr 0815, returns 2100, arrives 0830. Fares to Mexico City US$14.30 *primera preferente*, US$30 sleeper (Fri, Sat, Sun) (single) to US$60 for double cabin. 2nd class fare from Mexico City is US$8. Train to **Mexicali** and **Nogales** via Benjamín Hill (*Estrella*), by *primera preferente* train, 0930, 30 hrs, but can be as much as 57 hrs, no sleeping cars, no food and drinks, fare to Mazatlán US$14 (great scenery, tunnels, bridges), to Sufragio US$24. At Benjamín Hill the train splits: to Nogales (US$41, an extra 2 hrs 10 mins) and Mexicali (US$50, 7 hrs 10 mins). There is a 2nd class train Guadalajara-**Colima-Manzanillo** at 2000 (scheduled to arrive at 0600 but very slow, as much as 12 hrs, US$4 to Colima, US$5 to Manzanillo, 2nd class); scenery between Ciudad Guzmán and Colima is spectacular but as the train only goes at night it is best to take the bus. Daily train for **Los Reyes** involves change at Yurécuaro on the line to Mexico City.

WARNING Do not accept cups of coffee at the station however friendly or insistent the offer is, they may be drugged. If possible avoid arriving at night.

Buses New bus station nr the El Alamo cloverleaf, 10 km from centre; buses 102 and 275 go to the centre, US$0.25, frequent service (see **Local Transport** above), journey takes at least 30 mins. There is a new luxury bus service (Linea Azul) running from Zapopán, along Avila Camacho, past Plaza Patria shopping centre to the glorieta La Normal, S down Av Alcalde, through Tlaquepaque, to the new bus station and ending in Tonalá, seats guaranteed, 3.50 pesos. Another luxury bus service to the centre is Línea Cardenal. No buses after 2230. Official taxi fares from the bus station to various zones of the city are posted on the booths for buying taxi tickets located in each of the 7 modules of the terminal, to the centre US$3 day time, US$4 night time. Bus tickets are sold at 2 offices on Calzada Independencia underneath the big fountain on Plaza Tapatía, open 0900-1400, 1600-1900. Because of the distance from the centre of town, it is worth getting your departure information before you go into town. Shop around. It helps to know which company you wish to travel with as their offices are spread over a large area, in 7 modules. All modules have phones, but only Nos 1 and 2 long distance, all have left luggage, toilets, taxi booths, tourist information booths (not always manned), restaurants and shops; outside No 5 is a map of urban bus routes. A number of bus companies change dollars at rates marginally worse than *cambios*.

Module 1: Bus company: **Cienaga**, T 600-0363, to Ocotlán every 30 mins 0615-2115, US$2.50, 1 hr, to La Barca every 30 mins 0630-2100, US$3.50, to Zamora, US$5.50, 2nd class, they serve sodas on board; **La Alteña**, T 600-0770, 2nd class to Tepatitlán, US$2.50, Arandas US$4, Mexico City US$20, León US$8.50, Lagos de Moreno US$6.25, Querétaro US$12.50, Atotonilco US$3.50, Dolores Hidalgo US$12.25, Guanajuato US$10; **Costalegre**, T 600-0270, 2nd class to Barra de Navidad, US$10; **Primera Plus** (a 'plus' level service), T 600-0398/0014/0654/0142, same numbers for **Flecha Amarilla** (2nd class service), and **Servicios Coordinados** (1st class service), all part of the same group, Primera Plus to Colima US$9, Manzanillo US$12, León US$10.50, Guanajuato US$12.50, Aguascalientes US$6.50, San Miguel de Allende US$16.50, Querétaro US$13.50, Morelia US$12.25, Mexico City US$24.25 (7 hrs), also a bus that leaves at 0020

that takes the new toll road for the same price and takes 6 hrs; **Servicios Coordinados** (buses have toilets) to Morelia US$10.50, León US$9.50, Lagos de Moreno US$7.25, Colima US$8, Manzanillo US$10.50, Querétaro US$12.50. **ETN** has a ticket booth in module 1 (no credit cards) but their main ticket booth is in module 2 and all their buses leave from there. Module 1 has remodelled bathrooms, 2 pesos, and smaller free bathrooms, a magazine/snack shop (also beer), torta stand, cafetería, fruit juice stand, and phone office for long-distance and fax. There are also LADA (long-distance) phones outside the terminal entrance that take debit cards available at the snack shop inside, and other LADA phones next to them that take coins.

Module 2: Bus company: **ETN**, T 600-0477/0858/0605 (luxury service), American Express cards, round-trip tickets sold at a slight discount, own waiting room with bathrooms, snack bar, and gift shop, to Aguascalientes US$12.50, Colima US$12, Manzanillo US$15.50, Guanajuato US$15.50 (3 a day), León US$13.25 (8 a day), Morelia US$16.25 by non-toll roads (2 a day) and US$17.50 by the new toll road (7 a day), Querétaro US$17.50, Puerta Vallarta US$21.25 (8 a day, takes toll road to Tepíc part of the way), Toluca via toll road US$27.50 (3 a day), Uruapan US$12.50 (some take toll road, others don't, same price), Zamora US$8, Mexico City northern bus terminal US$31.25 (7 hrs, mostly uses old toll road via Querétaro, not the new one), Mexico City Observatorio bus terminal US$31.25 (some take the new freeway, 6 hrs), San Luis Potosí US$17; La Linea (1st class and 'plus' service), T 600-1221, to Manzanillo US$8 (plus) and US$10.50 (1st class), Colima US$9 (plus) and US$8 (1st class), Cd Guzmán US$5.50 (1st class), Morelia US$12 (plus) and US$10.50 (1st class), some take new toll road, Uruapan US$10 (plus) and US$8.75 (1st class), some take new toll road, Pátzcuaro US$9.50 (1st class), Mexico City US$22.50 at 2300 by new toll road with one stop in Toluca; **Omnibus de México**, T 600-0814, 1st class, with toilets, video, a/c, main ticket counter is in module 6, buses leave from module 6 and stop by module 2 to pick up passengers before going on to their destination; **Autobuses de Occidente**, T 600-0055, "plus", 1st and 2nd class service, to La Barca US$3 (2nd class), Zamora US$5 (2nd class), US$5.50 (1st class), US$6 (plus), Morelia US$9 (2nd class), US$10.50 (1st class), US$12.25 (plus), Toluca US$16 (2nd class), US$17.50 (1st class), Mexico City US$19.75 (2nd class),

US$22.50 (1st class), Uruapan US$8 (2nd class), US$9 (1st class), US$10 (plus), Colima US$8 (1st class), US$9 (plus), Manzanillo US$10.50 (1st class), US$12 (plus), Lázaro Cárdenas US$18.25 (1st class), US$21 (plus); **Autotransportes del Sur**, T 600-0346, 2nd class with assigned seats if you get on at the beginning of the trip in Guadalajara, to Cd Guzmán US$5, Colima US$7, Cuyatlán US$8.75, Manzanillo US$9.50, Sayula US$3.25, Lázaro Cárdenas US$16.25; **Autotransportes Mazamitla**, T 600-0733, 2nd class, 0600-1830 hourly to Mazamitla, 3 hrs. Module 2 has video games, coin operated LADA phones by entrance to bathrooms, a dulcería, juice bar, torta stand, self-service restaurant, and a computel outlet for making long-distance and fax calls that takes Visa, Mastercard, and American Express.

Module 3: Bus company: **Elite** (1st class but more like plus service, rec), T 600-0285, to Tijuana US$71, Mexicali US$67, Nogales US$62.50, Los Mochis US$36.50, Mazatlán US$19.25, Tepíc US$10; **Norte de Sonora** (1st class), T 600-0285, ticket counter here but buses leave from module 4; **Transportes del Pacífico**, T 600 0339, buses that leave after 2100 leave from module 4. Greyhound passes for US$85 good for 3 consecutive days of travel anywhere in the USA, to Tepíc US$10 (1st class) and US$9 (2nd class), Mazatlán US$19.25 (1st class) and US$16.75 (2nd class), Nogales US$62.50 (1st class) and US$54.25 (2nd class), Tijuana US$71 (1st class) and US$67 (2nd class), Puerta Vallarta US$16.25 (1st class); **Futura** (plus service), T 679-0404, all buses except those to Mexico City, US$22.50, and Tepic leave from module 7; **Autocamiones Cihuatlán** (plus service), T 600-0598, to Melaque US$12.60, to Barra de Navidad US$12.75, to Manzanillo US$15.40; **Autotransportes Guadalajara, Talpa, Mascota (ATM)**, T 600-0098, Talpa US$5 (2nd class), Ameca US$2.50 (2nd class), 1st class service weekends US$6.25 to Talpa via Ameca. Module 3 has a self-service restaurant, magazine/snack shop, shoe shine and 2 coin operated LADA phones by the entrance to the bathrooms.

Module 4: Bus company: **Transportes del Pacífico**, T 600-0339, buses that leave after 2100 leave from here (see above, module 3); **Norte de Sonora** (1st class with bathrooms, video, a/c), T 600-0285, to Tijuana US$61.50, Nogales US$54.25, Mazatlán US$16.75, Tepíc US$9.40, San Blas US$10.25; **Elite** (have ticket counter here but buses leave from module 3, see above); **ATM** (see module 3), buses leave

from both modules 3 and 4 for the same destinations; **Autocamiones Cihuatlán** (2nd class service, 'plus' service from module 3, serves same destinations,see module 3). Module 4 has shoe shine, snack/magazine shop, self-service restaurant, 2 LADA coin phones by bathrooms.

Module 5: Bus company: **Rojo de los Altos** (2nd class), T 679-0454/0455/0434, to Arandas US$4, Torreón US$22.40, Durango US$19.75, Zacatecas US$11; **Omnibus de Oriente/Linea Azul**, T 600-0231, to Mexico City US$22.50 (1st class) and US$19.75 (2nd class), Lagos de Moreno US$7.25 (1st class) and US$6 (2nd class), Querétaro US$12 (2nd class), Matamoros US$35.40 (1st class) and US$30.25 (2nd class), San Luis Potosí US$12.40 (1st class) and US$10.75 (2nd class), Reynosa US$33.50 (1st class) and US$29.75 (2nd class), Cd Victoria US$23.60 (1st class) and US$20.20 (2nd class); Tepatitlán (2nd class), T 600-0665, to Tepatitlán every 30 mins 0600-2030, US$2.75, to Zapotlanejo every 20 mins 0600-2100, also goes to the *penal* at Puente Grande for 3 pesos, if you're in the mood to visit the prison where some of the worst criminals are kept. Module 5 has a gift/snack shop, torta stand, self-service restaurant, and 24-hr phone/fax booth.

Module 6: Bus company: **Ómnibus de México** (1st class to plus service, all with bathrooms, video, a/c), T 600-0814, they have the entire module except for a small ETN ticket counter (FTN buses leave from module 2), to Mexico City US$22.50, Monterrey US$27.20, Durango US$23, Torreón US$26, Tampico US$25.50, San Luis Potosí US$12.40, Cd Juárez US$54, Reynosa US$33.50, Matamoros US$35.40, Nuevo Laredo US$36.20, Zacatecas US$12.50. Module 6 has a self-service restaurant, gift/snack shop, shoe shine, 2 LADA coin operated phones by bathrooms.

Module 7: **Futura** (plus service), T 679-0404, buses to Mexico City and Tepíc leave from here and stop at module 3 to pick up more passengers, for all other destinations the buses leave from module 7 only, to Cd Juárez US$54 (dep 1800), Chihuahua US$41.25 (dep 1800), Nuevo Laredo US$36.20 (dep 1930), Torreón US$26 (dep 2200); **Turistar Ejecutivo** (luxury service, like ETN), to Cd Juárez US$70.25 (dep 1600), Chihuahua US$54 (dep 1600), Nuevo Laredo US$47 (dep 1730 and 2100), Monterrey US$36.50 (4 buses 1730-2130), Mexico City US$30.25 (dep 2300), Saltillo US$30.25 (dep 1900 and 2230), Aguascalientes US$12.50 (dep 1600); **Transportes del Norte** and **Transportes Chihuahuenses** are affiliated with the above two companies, their ticket booths mainly sell tickets for the other two. Module 7 has a gift/snack shop, remodelled bathrooms for 2 pesos (also free bathrooms), shoe shine, a Burger Bus and Viva Pollo, an office for making long distance calls, and 2 LADA coin operated phones by bathrooms.

The old central bus station, Los Angeles y 28 Enero serves towns within 100 km. You have to pay 20 centavos to enter the terminal (open 0545-2215). It has 2 *salas* (wings): A and B, and is shaped like a U. The flat bottom of the U fronts Dr R Michel, where the main entrances are. There is a side entrance to Sala A from C Los Angeles and to both A and B from C 15 de Febrero via a tunnel. Taxi stands on both sides of the terminal of C Los Angeles and 15 de Febrero. By the entrances to the salas is a Computel outlet with long-distance and fax service. A fax to the USA costs US$2/min, to Europe US$2.50. There are lots of Ladatel phones for long distance and local calls outside the main entrance, some take coins and others debit cards. There is also a magazine stand selling maps of the city and a shoe shine service in front of the terminal. The shuttle buses to the new bus station leave from here, 2 pesos. In Sala A there are 2nd class buses to Tepatitlán and Zapotlanejo and *la penal* (the prison), with Oriente. 1st class buses to the same destinations leave from the new bus terminal. Buses to Chapala (every 30 mins, 0600-2140, US$1.60) and Ajijic (every 30 mins, 0700-2100, US$1.80) leave from here with Autotransportes Guadalajara-Chapala. Round trip package to the balneario at San Juan Cosalá, US$5.25 inc admission to the baths. In Sala B, Omnibus de Rivera sells tickets to the same balneario for US$1.50 and at La Alteña booth for the balnearios Agua Caliente and Chimulco. A Primera Plus/Servicios Coordinados booth sells tickets to places served by the new bus terminal. There is a Computel outlet with phone service, no fax, a luggage store and a magazine stand. Both salas have several food stands serving tortas, etc, and there are bathrooms.

ROUTES   "From Guadalajara to Irapuato: via **Tepatitlán** (79 km, on the León road), a small market town with a *charro* centre, in an impressive setting with steep hills all around; **Arandas** has a curious neo-gothic church and a pleasant square with a white wrought-iron bandstand; the road then winds tightly up over a range of hills and then down into a long and heavily cultivated valley. 5-hr journey," writes Tim Connell.

San Miguel El Alto (*pop* 50,000), NE of Tapatitlán, off Route 80, is an old town, typical of the Jalisco area, where the tradition of the *serenata* is still practiced. On Sun at 2000, men with confetti and roses line the square while the women promenade. The men signal their interest by throwing confetti on a girl's head; next time around he will offer her a rose. If she is interested she will walk with him round the plaza. At 2200 the police send everyone home and fortunate suitors may be allowed to walk their girlfriends home.

CHAPALA

Chapala town (*phone code* 376), 64 km to the SE on the northern shore of **Laguna de Chapala** (113 km long, 24 to 32 wide), has thermal springs, several good and pricey hotels, 3 golf courses, and is a popular resort particularly with retired North Americans and Mexican day-trippers. Watch women and children play a picture-card game called *Anachuac*.

The divided highway from Guadalajara becomes Av Francisco Madero in town, with a grassy middle and large trees, Laurel de la India, giving shade. The avenue ends at the lakefront. The street that runs along the lakefront is Paseo Ramón Corona and is closed to traffic W of Av Madero. The other main street in town is Av Hidalgo, one block in from the lake, parallel to Ramón Corona. Av Hidalgo going W becomes the road to Ajijic and beyond. Uphill from the *Villa Montecarlo* hotel on C Lourdes (cobblestone) is La Iglesia de Lourdes, a small pastel pink church with a bell tower, facing down the street to the lake. Open during masses on Thur and noon on Sunday.

The lake is set in beautiful scenery. There are boats of all kinds for hire, some go to the Isla de Alacranes (restaurant), water-fowl shooting in autumn and winter. Most fish in the lake have been killed by pollution, but the 5-cm 'XYZ' fish, called *charales*, are a delicacy. Lake water must be boiled. The water level is low

The Plumed Serpent

In May-July 1923, D H Lawrence lived in Chapala, renting a house called Los Cuentales. The house still stands at Zaragoza 307, although a second floor and some modernization have been added. The church that figures in the last pages of *The Plumed Serpent* is on the waterfront, its humble façade and interior now covered by a handsome veneer of carved stone. Lawrence's novel published in 1926 explored Mexican society in the light of the revolution and there are descriptions of the countryside around Lake Sayula (in reality Lake Chapala) and its 'sperm' coloured, shallow water: "It was a place with a strange atmosphere: stony, hard, broken with round, cruel hills and the many and fluted bunches of the organ-cactus behind the old house, and an ancient road trailing past, deep in ancient dust."

because of irrigation demand and it is getting smelly and overgrown at the edges. Beside the lake, 4 blocks E of Av Madero along Paseo Ramón Corona, Parque de la Cristiania is worth a visit, popular with families at weekends, swimming pool. Horses for hire on the beach by the Parque, bargain. There is a market on the E side of the Zócalo with stalls selling handicrafts, places to eat, dirty public restrooms, 1 peso, entrance on street behind the market. Pemex sells magna sin.

Local festivals

On the Fiesta de Francisco de Asís (2 3 Oct) fireworks are displayed and excellent food served in the streets.

Local information

● Accommodation

B-C *Villa Montecarlo*, W edge of town on Av Hidalgo at C Lourdes, family rooms or suites available, beautiful grounds with palms and mangoes, all rooms have phone, bath tub, balcony overlooking lake, pool, tennis, good restaurant, tables outside under massive laurel de la India tree.

D *Chapala Haciendas*, Km 40, Chapala-Guadalajara highway, T 52720, live music Wed and Sat, unheated pool, **D** *Nido*, Av Madero 202, close to lake, T 52116, brick building, old photos in reception hall, clean, cheaper without TV, accept Visa and MC, clean, good restaurant, swimming pool, parking for motorcycles beside pool.

E *Casa de Huéspedes Palmitas*, C Juárez 531, behind market, TV, hot water, bath, but run down, noisy, cockroaches.

furnished apartments for rent at Hidalgo 269, information at 274-A, also at Paseo Ramón Corona and C Juárez on the lake, 1 block E of Av Madero. Next door at Paseo Ramón Corona 16 is a pretty house with large lawn and gardens where rooms are rented by the week or month inc morning coffee. Lots of real estate offices on Hidalgo, W of Madero, with house or apartment rentals. Chapala Realty, Hidalgo 223, helpful, T 53676, F 53528.

Trailer Park: 1 km from the lake between Chapala and Ajijic. PAL, Apdo Postal 1 1170, Guadalajara, T 53764 or Chapala 60040, US$13 daily, 1st class, pool, good.

● Places to eat

La Leña, Madero 236, open air, serves *antojitos* and steaks, bamboo roof; next door is *Che Mary*, also attractive, outdoor seating; *Café Paris*, Madero 421, sidewalk tables, popular, *comida corrida* US$3, also breakfast, sandwiches, also on Madero are *El Patio*, good, cheap, and next door at 405A, *Los Equipales*. Where Madero reaches the lake is a restaurant/bar, *Beer Garden*, live amplified Mexican music, dancing, tables on the beach; *Bing's* ice cream parlour next door; *Cazadores*, on lake, old red brick house, mariachis sometimes, credit cards accepted; *La Langosta Loca*, Ramón Corona, seafood; 1 block further is the bar *Centro Botanero Los Caballos Locos*, and 2 doors down is the *Scotland Café*, in part of a colonial house with tables on the front porch and on the back lawn, as well as inside at the bar, open until 0200-0300. Several seafood places close by: *El Guayabo*, *El Guayabo Green*, *Cozumel*, *Huichos*, *Acapulquito*, *La Terraza Lupita*. Grocery store on SE corner of Hidalgo and Madero and another one at Madero 423 next to the plaza.

● **Banks & money changers**
Casa de cambio on Av Madero nr Beer Garden, open 0830-1700, Mon-Sat. **Banco Bital**, Madero 208, next to Hotel Nido, 24-hr ATM taking Visa, MC, and cards of Cirrus and Plus networks. Nearby is a Banamex with 24-hr ATMs. Casa de cambio at Hidalgo 204 esq Madero, has phone on street for international calls that takes Visa, MC and Amex. **Bancomer** at Hidalgo 212 nr Madero, 24-hr ATM taking Visa; across the street is a **Banco Serfín**, 24-hr ATM accepting Visa, MC, Diner's Club, Cirrus and Plus networks. **Lloyds**, Madero 232, is a real estate office, casa de cambio, travel agency and sociedad de inversión, many Americans keep their money here.

● **Hospitals & medical services**
Clinic: IMSS clinic on Niños Heroes between Zaragoza and Cinco de Mayo. Centro de salud at Flavio Romero de V and Guerrero.

Red Cross: in Parque de la Cristina.

● **Laundry**
Zaragoza y Morelos. Dry cleaners at Hidalgo 235A, also repair shoes and other leather items.

● **Post & telecommunications**
Postal services: Mail Box, etc, C Chapala-Jocotepec 155, opp PAL Trailer Park, T 60747, F 60775. Shipping office at Hidalgo 236 uses Federal Express and DHL. Just W of it is the Post Office. At Hidalgo 223 is a UPS office.

Telephones: Computel on the plaza, long distance and fax, accept Amex, MC, AT&T. Also pay phones for long distance calls on Zócalo and outside bus station.

● **Tourist offices**
Regional office at Aquiles Serdán 26, T 53141.

● **Transport**
Local Bus: bus station on Av Madero at corner of Miguel Martínez. Buses from Guadalajara every 30 mins, 0515-2030, 1 hr. 2 blocks S of bus station, minibuses leave every 20 mins for Ajijic, 2 pesos, and San Juan Cosalá, 3 pesos. **Taxi**: stand on Zócalo and at bus station.

AJIJIC

7 km to the W, a smaller, once Indian village, has an arty-crafty American colony with many retired North Americans. The village is pleasant, with cobbled streets, a pretty little plaza and many single storey villas. One block E of the plaza at the end of C Parroquia is the very pretty church of San Andrés, started in 1749. There is also a pretty stone church on the NW corner of the plaza. On Colón in the 2 blocks N of the plaza are several restaurants, boutiques and galleries. Going S from the plaza, Colón becomes Morelos, crossing C Constitución and continues some 5 blocks to the lake with lots of restaurants, galleries and shops. The lake shore has receded about 200m from the original shore line and it is a bit smelly. The Way of the Cross and a Passion Play are given at Easter in a chapel high above the town. House and garden tours, Thur 1030, 2½ hrs, US$10, in aid of Lakeside School for the Deaf, T 61881. Bus from Chapala or taxi US$3.20.

● **Accommodation** B Hotel Danza del Sol, T (376) 60220/61080, or Guadalajara 621-8878, Av Lázaro Cárdenas 3260, Planta Baja, large complex, nice units and gardens, pool; under same management as **A1** Real de Chapala, Paseo del Prado 20, T 60007, F 60025, delightful, pleasant gardens; **A3** La Nueva Posada, Donato Guerra 9, Apdo 30, T 61444, F 61344, breakfast inc, vast rooms, Canadian management, horseriding, golf, tennis, theatre, gardens, swimming pool, restaurant (large, clean, pretentious, attractive outdoor seating in garden overlooking lake), colonial décor, delightful; **B** Los Artistas Bed & Breakfast, Constitución 105, T 61027, F 60066, e-mail: artistas@acnet.net, 6 rooms, fireplaces, pool, living room, no credit cards, English and Spanish spoken; **B** La Floresta, E of Ajijic, lake views, motel style, kitchen, living room, bathroom, pool; good; **C** Laguna Bed 'n' Brunch, Zaragoza 29, T 61174, F 61188, good value, clean, comfortable, with bath, parking; **D** Mariana, Guadalupe Victoria 10, T 62221, 54813, breakfast available, weekly and monthly rates, all rooms have cable TV; **D** Las Casitas, motel-type with kitchen units, pool (just outside Ajijic, at Carretera Puente 20); similar is las Calandrias next door, furnished apartments, swimming pool, T 52819. Mama Chuy Club, and Villa Chello, on hillside, T (376) 30013 for both, good, pools, spacious, monthly rentals, good value.

● **Places to eat** Los Telares on main street, nice, courtyard garden; clean lonchería on plaza, good simple meals, cheap, grilled chicken, used by locals and Americans; Ajijic, pavement café on corner of plaza, cheap drinks, Mexican snacks, hearty *parrillada* Sat, Sun; **Los Girasoles**, 16 de Septiembre 18, moderately priced, Mexican food in walled courtyard; **Posada Ajijic**, Morelos, opp pier, T 60744, bar and restaurant, accept credit cards; pier here with fish restaurant at the end, indoor and outdoor seating and bar, used to be over water but stilts are now over dry land; **Bruno's**, on main street, excellent steaks. Fresh fish shop on plaza and other small food shops.

● **Hospitals & medical services Clinics**: *Clínica Ajijic*, Carretera Ote 33, T 60662/60500, with 24-hr ambulance service, Dr Alfredo Rodríguez Quintana (home T 61199). Two dentists' offices on Colón, just S of plaza.

● **Useful services Post Office**: 1 block S of plaza, corner of Colón and Constitución; artisan clothes shops; newspaper shop nr plaza sells *Mexico City Times*; small art gallery but few cultural events advertised. On the NW corner of the plaza is a Computel booth for long distance phone and fax, open daily, 0800-2100. About ¹/₂ block N at Colón 24A is a *lavandería*, US$2 to wash and dry a load. Taxi stand on W side of plaza, next to it is a large map of Ajijic on one side and Chapala on the other, showing businesses and tourist sites. Opp taxi stand at Colón 29 is a *casa de cambio*. On SW corner of plaza is Banco Promex with 2 ATMs open 24 hrs, accept Cirrus, Plus, Visa, MC, Diner's Club. Ajijic Real Estate at Morelos 4, T 62077, is an authorized UPS outlet. *El Ojo del Lago* is a free English newspaper, available at hotels and chapala@infosel.net.mx.

Beyond Ajijic on the lake is the Indian town of **Jocotepec**, a sizeable agricultural centre (*Pop* 18,000, recently invaded by more cosmopolitan types, little budget accommodation: **D** *Posada del Pescador*, *cabañas* on outskirts with bedroom, living room, kitchen and bathroom, set in a lovely garden; one other small hotel in town, **E**, bath, not clean); there is a local *fiesta* on 11-18 January. Jocotepec can be reached from Ajijic or from the Mexico-Guadalajara highway. Bus Chapala-Jocotepec US$2, every hour in each direction. The Indians make famous black-and-white *sarapes*. Tony Burton (PO Box 79, Jocotepec, T/F 376-30492), runs ecology and other tours in Western Mexico

through Odisea México and publishes *Western Mexico, A Traveller's Treasury* (US$15, US$2.95 p and p), Editorial Agata, Guadalajara, ISBN 9687310448.

Between Ajijic and Jocotepec lies the small town of **San Juan Cosalá**, less prosperous than Ajijic but pleasant, with cobblestone streets and fewer gringos. There are thermal springs (varied temperatures, crowded and noisy at weekends, 5 pools of different sizes) at *Hotel Balneario San Juan Cosalá* (Apdo Postal 181, Chapala, T (376) 10302, F 10222), which has private rooms for bathing with large tiled baths. Sunbathing in private rooms also possible. Bed and breakfast in clinical modern quarters with bar/restaurant. Rooms to let at **D** *Balneario Paraíso*. Bus service from Chapala. Fish restaurants are squeezed between the carretera and the lake at **Barrenada**, 1 km E of town.

NB Route 80 from Laguna de Chapala to the Pacific Coast at Barra de Navidad is in very poor condition. Route 15 on the southern shore of Laguna de Chapala, which leads to Pátzcuaro (6 hrs) is in good condition, if slow and winding through the hills.

40 km due S of Lake Chapala is the colonial town of **Mazamitla** (2,200m), a pleasant place on the side of a range of mountains, cold at night. It has a charming zócalo. Hotels, **D** *Posada Alpina*, on square; **E** *Fiesta de Mazamitla*, with bath, clean, rec; *La Llorona County Club*, in Sierra del Tigre Woods, T 6821186, has cabins, spa-club house and driving range. About 4 km out of town is Zona Monteverde with pine forests, small *casitas* for rent, two good restaurants at entrance, T 161826; steep hills, access only by car or taxi.

TAPALPA

About 130 km S of Guadalajara off the road (Jal 54) to Sayula and Ciudad Guzmán is **Tapalpa**, very pretty indeed. 3½ hrs' drive from Guadalajara. The bus has several detours into the hills to stop at small places such as Zacoalco (Sun market) and Amacueca. The road up to Tapalpa is winding and climbs sharply; the air becomes noticeably cooler and the place is becoming increasingly popular as a place for weekend homes. The town itself, with only 11,000 inhabitants, shows ample signs of this influx of prosperity. There are two churches (one with a curious atrium) and an imposing flight of stone steps between them, laid out with fountains and ornamental lamps. Tapalpa is in cattle country; the rodeo is a popular sport at weekends.

The main street is lined with stalls, selling *sarapes* and other tourist goods on Sun and fresh food the other days of the week. The only local speciality is *ponche*, an improbable blend of tamarind and mescal which is sold in gallon jars and recommended only for the curious or foolhardy. If you are planning a day trip get your return ticket as soon as you arrive as the last bus back to Guadalajara (1800 on Sun) is likely to be full.

● **Accommodation & places to eat** The more expensive restaurants have tables on balconies overlooking the square – the *Restaurante Posada Hacienda* (which has a US$1 cover charge) is well placed. Others are the *Buena Vista* (which also has rooms) and *La Cabaña*, and all are visited by the mariachis. Less grand is the **D** *Hotel Tapalpa*, with huge holes in the floor, but clean and fairly cheap. Some rooms are for hire (*Bungalows Rosita*, *Posada Hacienda* has nice bungalows with fireplace and small kitchen).

CIUDAD GUZMAN

Jalisco Route 54 continues through **Ciudad Guzmán** (formerly Zapotlán) to join Route 110, which heads SW from Zamora to Colima. Ciudad Guzmán is a clean, modern town with wide streets and a relaxed atmosphere. It is a good base for climbing the volcanoes, see below, **Colima**.

Local festivals There is a fair for 2 weeks in October. On one Sun in Oct the festival of San José is celebrated. Farmers march to the church to give presents to San José, who they believe will bring rain to help their crops grow. In 1996, a bull ran

through the streets on the first Sat in Oct, it is expected to become an annual event. Famous Mexican singers perform at the local theatre throughout the month.

● **Accommodation   A2** *Hacienda Nuera*, Hidalgo 177; **A2** *Real*, Colón; **B** *Posada San José*, M Chávez Madrueño 135; **C** *Reforma*, Javier Mina 33; **C-E** *Zaplotán*, on main plaza, reasonable, stores luggage; **D** *Hotel Flamingo*, nr main square, excellent value, very modern, very clean, and quiet, rec; **E** *Morelos*, Refugio B de Toscana 12.

● **Places to eat   *Juanito*, on main square, steak dishes, good service; *Bon Appetit*, upstairs on main square, views of town, excellent chef called Blas Flores, large servings, Japanese, Greek and Continental food, rec; *La Flor de Loto*, vegetarian on José Rodón 37C, cheap soya burgers; *Pilón Burgers* next to *Hotel Flamingo*, tiny, traditional. On C Priciliano Sánchez there are stalls selling juices, yoghurts and cereals. Good cheap meals in the market (upstairs).

● **Laundry   José Rodón, opp *La Flor de Loto*, cheap.

● **Transport   Trains   Go to Guadalajara at 1658, 1st class and 1120, regular, and Manzanillo via Colima, 1205 and 1345 respectively. Trains stop under highway bridge, taxi to get there is US$2.50. **Buses   To Colima 2 hrs, US$3 (Flecha Amarilla); to Uruapan and Morelia involves changes in Tamazula and Zamora.

COLIMA

(*Pop* 150,000; *State pop 1995* 487,324; *Alt* 494m; *Phone code* 331) The capital of Colima state is a most charming and hospitable town with a 19th century Moorish style **arcade** on the main square and a strange rebuilt gothic ruin on the road beyond the **Cathedral** (late 19th century). Also on the E side of the main square is the **Palacio de Gobierno** (with interesting murals of the history of Mexico). Both are attractive buildings. Behind them is the Jardín Torres Quintero, another pretty but smaller plaza. Andador Constitución is a pedestrian street, with people selling paintings on the street, several small, attractive restaurants and a state run artisan's shop at the N end on the corner of

Zaragoza. Crossing Zaragoza, Constitución is open to traffic, and one block N on the corner with Vicente Guerrero is the church of **San Felipe de Jesús** (early 18th century plateresque façade) where Miguel Hidalgo was at one time parish priest. Public swimming pool in Parque Regional Metropolitano on C Degollado about 5-6 blocks from SW corner of the main plaza. **Teatro Hidalgo** on the corner of Degollado and Morelos, has a pink colonial façade and large carved wooden doors (only open during functions). Parque Núñez, 5 blocks E of the plaza is also pretty and twice the size of the plaza. South of Parque Núñez, about 7 blocks, is Parque Hidalgo, a very large park with tall coconut palms. Young men can be seen climbing the palms to collect coconuts.

Museums

Museo de las Culturas de Occidente María Ahumada, Calzada Pedro Galván, in Casa de Cultura complex, Tues-Sun 0900-1300, 1600-1800 (closed for repairs 1996); **Museo de la Máscara, la Danza y el Arte Popular del Occidente**, C 27 de Septiembre y Manuel Gallardo, folklore and handicrafts (items for sale – in the University Institute of Fine Arts); **Museo de la Historia de Colima**, on the Zócalo.

Excursions

El Chanal An archaeological site, about 15 km to the N of Colima, with a small pyramid with 36 sculptured figures, discovered in 1944.

El Hervidero, 22 km SE of Colima, is a spa in a natural lake of hot springs which reach 25°C.

Colima volcano (3,842m), one of the most exciting climbs in Mexico, which erupted with great loss of life in 1941, and **El Nevado** (4,339m) are in the vicinity. They can be climbed by going to Ciudad Guzmán, and taking a bus to the village of Fresnito, from where it is 20 km to the hut at 3,500m (take water). Register with the police in Fresnito before climbing. At weekends it may be possible to hitch. From the hut it is a strenuous 3-4 hr hike

to the top. Sr Agustín Ibarra (T 33628, ext 103) organizes day trips to within a 2-hr climb of the summit (recommended), US$50 for 10 people to the hut, or 3½-hr horse ride to the refuge with a 3-hr climb, US$10 pp. Sr Ibarra's dog Laika is also a great companion! It may be possible to hitch a lift down next day with the TV maintenance crew who work at the top. The weather in this region is very unpredictable, beware of sudden heavy rains. Sr Ibarra provides homely accommodation in the village; otherwise ask where to camp. There are a couple of shops where you can buy basic foodstuffs. Hotels in Ciudad Guzmán, see above.

Comalá A pretty colonial town with whitewashed adobe buildings near Colima, worth a few hours' visit, bus US$0.25, 20 mins every 30 mins. The climate is somewhat cooler and more comfortable than Colima. The surrounding vegetation is lush with coffee plantations. In the town are two popular restaurants with *mariachis* and local specialities, *Los Portales* and *Comalá* on Plaza Mayor; they are open until 1800. Outside the town on the Colima road is the *Botanero Bucaramanga*, a bar with *botanas* (snacks) and *mariachis*. 8 km NE is the Escuela de Artesanía where handmade furniture, painted with fabulous bird designs, and other crafts are manufactured to order. **Suchitlán** (Sun market) has *Los Portales de Suchitlán*, a good restaurant selling local specialities at Galeanas 10, T 339-54452. The people here are very small (*chaparrito*) and it is reflected in the size of the doorways. Further down the road at Km 18, Comala-San Antonio, is a beautiful, large, open-air restaurant, *Jacal de San Antonio*, on top of a hill overlooking a lush valley with the Volcán de Colima in the distance. About 18 km beyond Comalá (look out for signposts), is the magnificent 18th century *estancia* of **San Antonio**; set in a green valley with an impressive roman-style aqueduct leading water down from a mountain spring. The road continues up and over a mountain stream; about a km further on are **Las Marías**, a private mountain lake used as a picnic site, admission US$0.65.

Local festivals

Feria The annual fair of the region (agriculture, cattle and industry, with much additional festivity) runs from the last Sat of Oct until the first Sun of November. Traditional local potions (all the year round) include *Jacalote* (from black maize and pumpkin seeds), *bate* (*chía* and honey), *tuba* (palm tree sap) and *tecuino* (ground, germinated maize).

Local information
● **Accommodation**

B-C *Hotel América*, Morelos 162, T 20366, a/c, cable TV, phone, largest rooms in new section, pretty interior gardens, travel agency, steam baths, good restaurant, central, friendly.

C *Posada San José*, M Chávez Madrueño 135, T 20756, phone, TV; **C-D** *Ceballos*, Torres Quintero 16, T 21354, main square, fine building with attractive *portales*, some huge rooms with a/c, clean, good food in restaurant (pricey), secure indoor parking, very good value, highly rec.

D *Tlayolan*, J Mina 33, T 23317, clean, quiet; **D-E** *Flamingos*, ex-*Gran Hotel*, pleasant small rooms with fan, Av Rey Colimán 18, T 22526, nr Jardín Núñez, with bath, simple, clean, breakfast expensive, disco below goes on till 0300 on Sat and Sun; **D-E** *La Merced*, Hidalgo 188, T 26969, pretty colonial house with rooms around patio filled with plants, passageway to newer section, entrance at Juárez 82 with reception, all rooms same price, 2 beds cost more than one, TV, bath, highly rec for budget travellers.

E *Galeana*, Medellín 142, nr bus terminal, basic; **E** *Núñez*, Juárez 80 at Jardín Núñez, basic, dark, with bath; **E** *San Cristóbal*, Reforma 98, T 20515, nr centre, run down. Many *casas de huéspedes* nr Jardín Núñez; **D** *Rey de Colimán*, on continuation of Medellín on outskirts, large rooms; **Motel Costeño** on outskirts going to Manzanillo, T 21925, is rec. Three motels coming in from Guadalajara: María Isabel, T 26262; Los Candiles, T 23212; *Villa del Rey*, T 22917.

● **Places to eat**

Several restaurants on the Zócalo serve inexpensive meals. *El Trébol* probably the best, on SW corner; opp on Degollado 67, is nice open-air

restaurant on 2nd floor on S side of plaza, overlooking it; *Café de la Plaza*, Portal Medellín 20, beside *Hotel Ceballos*, *comida corrida* about US$4; *Los Naranjos*, Gabino Barreda 34, ½ block N of Jardín Torres Quintero, going since 1955, nice, well-known; *Samadhi*, Filomeno Medina 125, vegetarian, good, T 32498, meal about US$3, opp *La Sangre de Cristo*, church, good yoghurt and fruit drinks, attractive, large garden with iguanas; *Café Dali* is in the Casa de Cultura complex; *Café Colima* in Parque Corregidora; *Giovannis*, Constitución 58 El Nte, good pizzas and take away. Good yoghurt and wholemeal bread at *Centro de Nutrición Lakshmi*, Av Madero 265, run by Hari Krishnas. *La Troje*, T 22680, on SE of town heading to Manzanillo, good, mariachis, very Mexican. Try the local sweet *cocada y miel* (coconut and honey in blocks), sold in *dulcerías*.

● **Airline offices**

Aero California, T 44850; AeroMéxico, T 31340; Aeromar, T 35588.

● **Banks & money changers**

Banco Inverlat at Juárez 32 on W side of Jardín Núñez, ATM takes Amex, Visa, Diner's Club. *Casa de cambio* at Morelos and Juárez on SW corner of same park. **Bancomer** at Madero and Ocampo 3 blocks E of plaza, ATM takes Visa and Plus. *Casa de cambio* across the street. **Banamex** a block S down Ocampo at Hidalgo has an ATM.

● **Hospitals & medical services**

Hospital: *Hospital Civil*, T 20227.

Pharmacy: *Farmacia Guadalupana* on NE corner of Jardín Torres Quintero behind cathedral. Another pharmacy on NE corner of Zócalo.

Red Cross: T 21451.

● **Laundry**

Lavandería Shell, 27 de Septiembre 134, open 0900-2000, inexpensive, quick.

● **Post & telecommunications**

Post Office: Av Fco I Madero y Gral Núñez, NE corner of Jardín Núñez.

Telecommunication: Computel at Morelos 234 on S side for long distance phone and fax, and at bus station, open 0700-2200, accepts Visa, MC, Amex and AT&T cards. Fax not always in use.

● **Tourist offices**

On the W side of the Zócalo, opp the Cathedral, good, but no information on climbing local volcanoes.

● **Transport**

Air Airport (CLQ) 19 km from centre, T 44160, 49817. Flights to Mexico City, San Luis Potosí and Tijuana available.

Trains 2nd class trains pass through at night.

Buses Bus station on the outskirts; buses and combis run to centre, US$0.50, or taxi about US$1. Bus companies: ETN, T 25899, La Línea, T 20508, 48179; Primera Plus T 48067; Omnibus de México, T 47190; Sur de Jalisco, T 20316; Elite, T 28499. If going to **Uruapan** it is best to go to **Zamora** (7-8 hrs, although officially 4) and change there. ETN bus to Guadalajara US$12, 2½-3 hrs by autopista; plus service US$9, regular 1st class US$8, 2nd class US$7, all take autopista, non-stop; Colima-Manzanillo US$7. ETN to **Mexico City** US$51.65.

MANZANILLO

A beautiful, 3-hr hilly route runs from Colima to **Manzanillo** (*Pop* 150,000), which has become an important port on the Pacific, since a spectacular 257-km railway has been driven down the sharp slopes of the Sierra Madre through Colima. A new toll road has been opened between Guadalajara and Manzanillo, good, double-laned in some sections, driving time about 4 hrs, but total cost US$17 in tolls. The tolls from Mexico City to Manzanillo total US$55. Occupations for tourists at Manzanillo, which is not a touristy town, include deep-sea fishing (US$250 to hire a boat for a day, including beer, *refrescos* and *ceviche*), bathing, and walking in the hills. There is a good snorkelling trip starting at the beach of *Club Las Hadas* (see below), US$40 includes soft drinks and equipment. The water is clear and warm, with lots to see. Trips 2-3 times daily, last one at 1230. There is a bullring on the outskirts on the road to Colima. The best beach is the lovely crescent of Santiago, 8 km N, but there are three others, all of which are clean, with good swimming.

Local information
● **Accommodation**

L1 *Club Las Hadas*, Península de Santiago, T 30000, a Moorish fantasy ("architecture crowned by perhaps the most flamboyantly and unabashedly phallic tower ever erected, and the palpable smell of money; should on no account be missed").

A1 *La Posada*, Calz L Cárdenas 201, nr the end of Las Brisas peninsula, T 31899, US manager, beautifully designed rooms carved into the living rock of an outcrop; *Club Maeva*, Km 12.5 Carretera Santiago-Miramar, T 30595, picturesque, opp beach, clean rooms with bath and kitchen, meals inc in price, several good restaurants; **A1** *Roca del Mar*, Playa Azul, T 21990, vacation centre; **B** *Las Brisas Vacation Club*, Av L Cárdenas 207, T 31747/32075, some a/c, good restaurant.

At **Santiago beach**: **A1** *Playa de Santiago*, T 30055, good but food expensive; **C** *Anita*, T 30161, built in 1940, has a certain funky charm and it is clean and on the beach; **C** *Parador Marbella*, Blvd M de la Madrid Km 10, T 31105, meals extra; *Marlyn*, T 30107 third floor rooms with balcony overlooking the beach, a bargain, rec.

At the **port**: **C** *Colonial*, good restaurant, México 100, T 21080, friendly, avoid rooms above the record shop (very loud music); **D** *Casa de Huéspedes Posada Jardín*, Cuauhtémoc, reasonable; **D** *Emperador*, Davalos 69, T 22374, good value, good, cheap restaurant; **D** *Flamingos*, 10 de Mayo y Madero, T 21037, with bath, quite good; **E** *Casa de Huéspedes Central*, behind bus station, with bath, fan, OK. Visitors can also rent apartments in private condominiums, eg *Villas del Palmar* at Las Hadas, or *Club Santiago* (contact Hector Sandoval at Hectours for information).

Camping: at Miramar and Santiago beaches. 4.5 km N of Manzanillo is *Trailer Park El Palmar*, T 23290, with a large swimming pool, run down, very friendly, coconut palms, US$13 for 2 in camper-van. *La Marmota* trailer park, at junction of Highways 200 and 98, cold showers, bathrooms, pool, laundry facilities, US$8/car and 2 people.

● **Places to eat**

Willy's Seafood Restaurant, Playa Azul, on the beach, French owner, primarily seafood, some meat, very good, 3-courses with wine US$15 pp; *Portofino's*, Blvd M de la Madrid, Km 13, Italian, very good pizza; next door is *Plaza de la Perlita*, good food, live music; also Italian, *Bugatti's*, Crucero Las Brisas; *Carlos and Charlie's*, Blvd M de la Madrid Km 6.9, on the beach, seafood and ribs, great atmosphere. Good but not cheap food at the two *Huerta* restaurants,

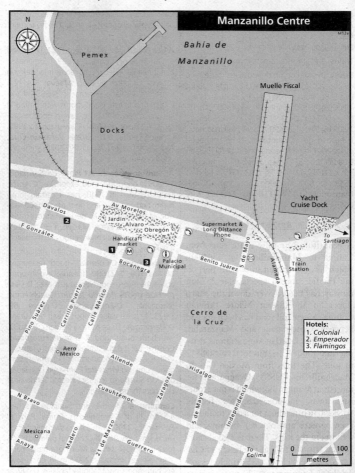

Manzanillo Centre

the original nr the centre, and *Huerta II* nr the
Las Hadas junction. *Johanna*, opp bus station
entrance, good food, cheap.

● **Tourist offices**
At Santiago beach, helpful.

● **Transport**
Air Frequent flights from airport (ZLO) 19 km
from town, to Mexico City and Guadalajara.
Other domestic destinations: Monterrey, Tepic
and Tijuana. US destinations: Los Angeles, Phoenix and San Antonio.

Trains To Guadalajara 2nd class, up to 12
hrs, US$2.50. For minibus to the **airport**
T 32470, US$5 from the beach. **Buses** To
Miramar, US$0.50, leaves from J J Alcaraz,
'El Tajo'. Several to **Guadalajara**, US$11, or
US$23 ENT, 6 hrs. To **Mexico City** with ETN,
luxury, US$62, with Autobus de Occidente, 19
hrs, 1st class, US$25. **Barra de Navidad**,
US$2.50, 1½ hrs; to **Colima**, US$4, US$7
ENT; to **Tijuana**, bus US$80, 1st class, 36 hrs.
Down the coast to **Lázaro Cárdenas** and
crossroads for Playa Azul (see page 227) by

Autobus de Occidente or Galeana, 7 hrs. To **Acapulco**, US$8.50. To **Puerto Vallarta**, 1st class with Trans Cihuatlán at 0800 and 1200, 4½ hrs, rec. Bus terminal in Av Hidalgo outside centre, local buses go there. Taxi to centre US$1.50.

Southeast of Manzanillo is **Tecomán** (*Pop* 68,000) with delightful atmosphere. **B-C** *Gran Fénix*, larger rooms have a/c, smaller rooms are noisier but hotel is recommended; unnamed *pensión* on the corner of the Zócalo, if you face the

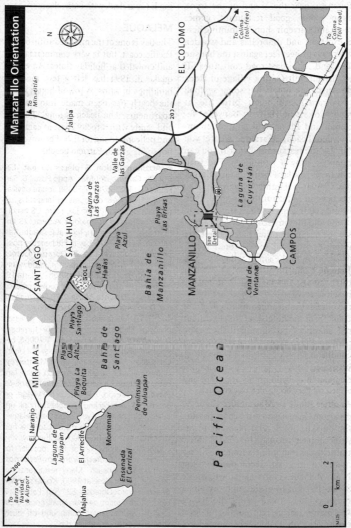

Manzanillo Orientation

To Minatitlán

EL COLOMO

To Colima (toll-free)

To Colima (toll road)

N

Jalipa

201

200

Valle de las Garzas

Laguna de Las Garzas

SALAHUA

SANTIAGO

Laguna de Cuyutlán

Playa Las Brisas

MANZANILLO

see Detail

Las Hadas

Playa Azul

Bahía de Manzanillo

Canal de Ventanas

CAMPOS

SOL

Playa Santiago

MIRAMAR

Playa Ola Alta

Bahía de Santiago

Playa La Boquita

El Naranjo

Península de Juluapan

To Barra de Navidad & Airport

Laguna de Juluapan

El Arrecife

Montemar

Ensenada El Carrizal

Majahua

Pacific Ocean

km

0   2

church it is on your left, E. Try the local deep-fried *tortillas* filled with cheese. To the W of Tecomán is the small coastal resort of **Cuyutlán**, on the fast highway between Colima and Manzanillo. It has a pleasant, black-sand beach and **D** *Hotel Bucanero*, near the N end of the front, clean rooms, good restaurant, games room and souvenir shop. Swimming here is excellent and umbrellas and wooden walkways protect feet against the hot sun and sand. The coast road continues SE to the unspoilt fishing village of **Boca de Apiza** (no hotels but some seafood restaurants). Abundant bird life at mouth of river. Halfway between Tecomán and Playa Azul is another uncrowded beach, **Maruata**, where you can ask the restaurant owner if you can camp or sling a hammock. The road continues to Playa Azul, Lázaro Cárdenas, Zihuatanejo and Acapulco: for 80 km beyond Manzanillo it is good, then Route 200 in some parts is in poor condition and for long stretches you cannot see the ocean. In other places there are interesting coastal spots. About 1 hr S of Tecomán is the small village of **San Juan de Lima**, on a small beach; two or three hotels, the farthest S along the beach is very basic, D. There are a couple of restaurants, one unnamed, about 200m from the hotels, serving excellent red snapper and shrimp dishes. The road to Playa Azul is paved, in good condition.

WARNING Local police warn against camping in the wild in this area; rape and armed robbery occur on a weekly basis.

Another Route to Manzanillo Route 80 goes from Guadalajara to the coast, passing the outskirts of several pleasant towns with cobbled streets. The road is fairly trafficked as it plummets from the Sierra Madre to the coast. **Tecolotlán**, 200 km N of Melaque, is a small town whose zócalo is 1 km from the highway along rough cobbles. It has a few hotels, eg **D** *Albatros*, 1 block E of Zócalo, modern, clean, with bath, TV, highly recommended.

Autlán de Navarro, 115 km from Melaque, is a clean, modern, mid-sized town, with public phones in the zócalo and several hotels (eg **D** *Palermo*, pleasant, clean, with bath). 74 km from Melaque is **Casimiro Castillo**, a small town with 3 hotels, including **E** *Costa Azul*, with bath, clean.

MELAQUE

The bay is one of the most beautiful on the Pacific coast, but is very commercialized and crowded at holiday times. An earthquake in 1994 has left a few, modern, buildings in ruins. A row of hotels along the beach has been made into holiday apartments. The beach is long, shelving and sandy with a rocky coast at each end and pelicans diving for fish. The waves are not so big at San Patricio beach.

● **Accommodation & places to eat L3-B** *Villas Camino del Mar*, Apdo Postal 6, San Patricio, T (335) 55207, F 55498, rooms or villas on beach, 2 pools, discounts for long stays, up to 50% for a month, inc tax, many US visitors stay all winter; **B** *Bungalows Azteca*, 23 km from Manzanillo airport, for 4 at C Avante, San Patricio, T (333) 70150, with kitchenette, pool, parking. *Club Náutico El Dorado*, Gómez Farías 1A, T 70230, very pleasant, good value, small swimming pool; **C** *Flamingo*, Vallarta 19, clean with fan, balconies, water coolers on each floor; opp is **D** *Santa María*, T 70338, friendly, rec; **D** *Posada Pablo de Tarso*, Gómez Farías 408, T 70117, facing beach, pretty, galleried building, tiled stairs, antique-style furniture; **D** *San Nicolás*, Gómez Farías 54, T 70066, beside Estrella Blanca bus station, noisy but clean. Off season, very pleasant, eg **D** *Monterrey*, Gómez Farías 27, T 70004, on beach, clean, fan, bath, parking, superb view. *Trailer Park La Playa*, San Patricio, T 70065, in the village, on beach, US$13 for car and 2 people, full hook-up, toilets, cold showers. If you follow the 'Melaque' signs, at the end of the main road is a free camping place on the beach at the bay, very good, easily accessible for RVs, popular for vehicles and tents. *Restaurant Los Pelícanos*, overpriced, on beach. Many restaurants on beach but most close at 1900. *Koala's at the Beach*, Alvaro Obregón 52, San Patricio, 2 blocks from *Camino del Mar*, small, good, great food in walled garden compound off dusty street, Canadian/Australian run.

BARRA DE NAVIDAD

The village of **Barra de Navidad** is commercial but still pleasant, where there is a monument to the Spanish ships which set out in 1548 to conquer the Philippines. Barra is 1½ hrs from Manzanillo; the beach is beautiful, very good for swimming, but at holiday times it is very crowded and a lot less pleasant. Pemex station at Route 200/Route 80 junction, has unleaded fuel. To change money, go to Cihuatlán from Barra, buses every 30 mins; no tourist office. Bus to Manzanillo, US$2.50, 1½ hrs.

● **Accommodation & places to eat** D *Tropical*, López de Legaspi 96, T 70020, on beach, seedy but pleasant; C *Delfín*, Morelos 23, T 333-70068, very clean, pool, hot water, highly rec; opp is C *Sand's*, Morelos 24, T 162859 (Guadalajara) or 70018 (Barra), bar, clean, some kitchen units, good value, pool; C *Hotel Barra de Navidad*, López de Legaspi 250, T 70122, with balcony on beach, or bungalows where you can cook, pool, very good value; D *Hotel Jalisco*, Av Jalisco 91, hot water, safe but not very clean and noisy, nightclub next door with music till 0300; D *Marquez*, T 55304, rec; *San Lorenzo*, Av Sinaloa 87, T 70139, is same price and much better, clean, hot water, good restaurant opp; E *Posada Pacífico*, Mazatlán 136, one street behind bus terminal, clean, fan, friendly, good restaurant opp. Ask about **camping** on beach. Fish restaurants eg *Antonio* on beach, many good restaurants on the Pacific side, a couple of good restaurants on the lagoon side, *Velero's*, delicious snapper and good views; *Amber*, Veracruz 101, half of menu vegetarian, real coffee, good breakfast and crêpes, highly rec, closed lunchtime; *Pacífico*, very good barbecued shrimp, and good breakfasts.

Pretty seaside villages near Barra de Navidad include **La Manzanilla**, 14 km N of Routes 200/80 junction (D *Posada de Manzanilla*, nice, recommended; *Posada del Cazador*, T 70330); camping possible. South of village at end of Los Cocos beach is the **B** hotel and RV trailer park, *Paraíso Miramar*, T 321-60434, pool, gardens, palm huts, restaurant, bar. 3 km N of beach is Boca de Iguanas with 2 trailer parks: *Boca de Iguanas*, US$7 pp, vehicle free, hook-ups, cold showers, toilets,

laundry facilities, clean, pleasant location, and *Tenacatita* (US$9d with hook-ups, US$7 without, cold showers, toilet, laundry facilities, restaurant). For both places take the unpaved road from Highway 200 to the abandoned *Hotel Bahía de Tenacatita*; at the T junction, turn right, pass the hotel, and the campsites are about 500m further on the left. This place is nothing to do with the village of **Tenacatita**. This has a perfect beach complete with palm huts, tropical fish among rocks (2 sections of beach, the bay and oceanside). D *Hotel* (no name) in village near beach, or you can sleep on the beach under a palm shelter, but beware mosquitoes. Several kilometres N of Tenacatita is **A2** pp all inclusive *Blue Bay*, ex-*Fiesta Americana* resort, Km 20 Carretera Federal 200, T 335-15020/15100, F 15050, tennis, watersports, horseriding, disco, pool, gym, credit cards.

MICHOACAN

The State of Michoacán, where the Tarascan Indians live, is a country of deep woods, fine rivers and great lakes. Fruit, game, and fish are abundant. It has some of the most attractive towns and villages in the country. Visitors are attracted by the Tarascan customs, folklore, ways of life, craft skills (pottery, lacquer), music and dance. The dance is of first importance to them; it is usually performed to the music of wooden drum, flute and occasionally, a fiddle. Masks are often worn and the dance is part of a traditional ritual. The dances which most impress outsiders are the dance of Los Viejitos (Old Men; at Janitzio, 1 Jan); Los Sembradores (The Sowers; 2 Feb); Los Moros (The Moors; Lake Pátzcuaro region, *fiestas* and carnival); Los Negritos (Black Men; *fiestas* at Tzintzuntzán); Los Apaches (4 Feb, at the churches); Las Canacuas (the crown dance; Uruapan, on Corpus Christi). At the weddings of fisherfolk the couple dance inside a fish net. In the local *fandango* the woman has fruits in her hand, the man has a glass of *aguardiente* balanced on his head, and a sword.

South of Laguna de Chapala, you come to **Jiquilpan** (on Route 110 to Colima). There are frescoes by Orozco in the library, which was formerly a church. At least 5 hotels; **D** *Posada Palmira*, on main street, pleasant, clean, good restaurant; **E** *Imperial*, on main street, good value; **E** *Colonial Mendoza*, Route 15 in the centre, with bath, clean, good value, but noisy. Good, cheap, street foodstalls in the town.

ZAMORA

Zamora (58 km E of Jiquilpan), with 135,000 people, is an agricultural centre founded in 1540. There is an interesting ruined gothic-style church in the centre, several other, fine churches, and a market on C Corregidora. Nearby is tiny Laguna de Camecuaro, with boats for hire, restaurants and wandering musicians; popular at holiday times.

● **Accommodation** C *Fénix*, Madero Sur 401, T 20266, clean, swimming pool, poor ventilation, pleasant balconies; **D** *Amalia*, Hidalgo 194, T 21327, pleasant, some rooms noisy, restaurant OK; next door to *Fénix* is **D/E** *Posada Fénix*, rooms of varying quality, nice owner, good laundry service; **E** *Posada Marena*, simple, clean; other cheap *hospedajes* nr market, none very clean. **E** *Jasmin*, 2 km on road to Morelia, opp Pemex, with bath, clean, noisy. **Motel**: **A3** *Jérico*, Km 3 on La Barca road just N of town, T 25252, swimming pool, restaurant.

● **Places to eat** *El Campanario*, Nervo 22, off main square, rec.

● **Transport** Bus station at N edge of town, local bus to centre US$0.25, taxi US$3.50. Bus to Mexico City, 1st *plus*, US$16.50, 1st US$14.20, ETN luxury US$30 (ETN to Guadalajara US$11, and US$10 to Morelia). To Pátzcuaro, 2½ hrs, with Via 2000.

On 40 km is **Carapán** (**E** *Motel La Hacienda*, friendly, clean, cold water, good restaurant), a crossroads at which a road goes N to **La Piedad de Cabadas**, a pleasant stopping place on the toll road between Guadalajara and Mexico City (**D** *Hotel*

Mansión Imperial, parking; **E** *San Sebastián*, central, hot water, old but nice, parking across the street; **E** *Gran Hotel*, on main street, OK; *Restaurant El Patio*, near church, very good, dish of the day good value). At Carapán a branch road runs 32 km S through pine woods to **Paracho**, a quaint, very traditional Indian village of small wooden houses; in every other one craftsmen make guitars and *mandolines* worth from US$10 to US$1,000 according to the wood used. A recommended workshop is that of Ramiro Castillo B, Av Independencia 259, Galeana 38, good value, friendly. Bargaining possible in all workshops. On the main plaza is the *Casa para el arte y la cultura Purhepecha* with information, library, shops etc. **E** Hotel on main road S of town, hot water arm only. *Café D'Gribet*, on main street, cheap and good snacks. Try local pancakes. Buses to/from Uruapan. Also to Morelia via Pátzcuaro.

URUAPAN

(*Pop* 250,000; *Alt* 1,610m) This road continues S to **Uruapan** ('Place where flowers are plentiful'), a town set among streams, orchards and waterfalls in the **Parque Nacional Eduardo Ruiz**, cool at night, well worth a visit (entry US$0.30). Local foods are sold in the Parque and there is a government-operated trout breeding facility. The most attractive of its three plazas is the **Jardín de los Mártires**, with the 16th century church facing it. In the *portales* or at the market can be bought the local lacquered bowls and trays, or the delicate woodwork of the Paracho craftsmen, Patamban green pottery and Capácuaro embroideries. Restored hospital, built by Fray Juan de San Miguel in the 16th century; now a ceramics museum. Adjoining it is a 16th century chapel now converted into a craft shop. In the same square, part of the former Collegiate church of San Francisco (17th century with later additions such as an interesting 1960s modern art interior) houses the attractive **Casa de**

la Cultura (small museum upstairs, free, with excellent display of the history of Uruapan). 1 km from the centre is the entrance to the Parque, on the corner of Independencia and Colver City, with a good handicraft shop selling wooden boxes and bracelets (entry US$0.35). Several stalls sell food and drink. Walk there or catch a bus 1 block S of the Zócalo marked 'El Parque'. The town suffers badly from traffic fumes.

Excursions

Through coffee groves and orchards along the Cupatitzio (meaning Singing River) to the **Tzararacua Falls** (10 km, entry US$0.15); restaurants at bus stop where you can hire a horse to the falls (US$8 pp). It is not advisable to walk to the falls alone. To extend the trip beyond the falls, cross the stone bridge to the other side of the stream. Take a path to the right which then switches back and heads up the other side of the gorge. After a while you will reach a plateau at the top of the mountain, with good views all around. A well-worn path/stream leads down the other side of the mountain to a more secluded waterfall, from the top of which are many paths down to the river and lake into which the stream flows (a great spot for a swim). Good camping some 300m below the village under the shelter on the top of a rim, with a view down into the valley to the waterfall (1 km away) and a small lake. A bus (marked Tzararacua, or Zupomita, but ask if it goes all the way) will take you from the Zócalo at Uruapan to Tzararacua, US$1 (15-25 mins), weekends and public holidays only. Alternatively, try to buy a ticket to Tzararacua on the bus to Apatzinguán (which passes the falls) and ask the driver to let you off. If on a tight schedule, take a taxi.

Parque Cholinde, 1.5 km out of town (all uphill – take a bus), swimming pool, US$1.30; Colibrí Nurseries nearby. Balneario Caracha (frequent buses), alight at cross roads by sign, then walk 1 km on road to pools, a delightful place, open daily (US$2) with restaurant, hotel, several pools and beautiful gardens. **Tingambato** ruins are half way along road to Pátzcuaro, about 2 km downhill from Tingambato town (pyramid and ball court).

Local festivals

In the first week of April the Zócalo is filled with pottery and Indians from all the surrounding villages. Around 16 Sept, in nearby village of San Juan, to celebrate the saving of an image of Christ from the San Juan church at the time of the Paricutín eruption. The 2 weeks either side of 15 Sept are *feria* in Uruapan, too.

Local information

● **Accommodation**

A3 *Victoria*, Cupatitzio 13, T 36700, good, quiet, restaurant and garage.

B *Concordia* on main square has nice restaurant, T 30500; **B** *El Tarasco*, Independencia 2, T 41500, pool, lovely, good restaurant, moderate prices; **B** *Plaza Uruapan*, Ocampo 64, T 30333, good, clean, large rooms.

C *Villa de Flores*, Emilio Carranza 15, T 21050, quiet, pleasantly furnished, lovely flowers, rec.

D *Atzimba*, in street where the mariachis are waiting, modern, rec, on main square, **D** *Nueva Hotel Alameda*, Av 5 de Febrero, with bath, clean, TV, good value; **D** *del Parque*, Av Independencia 124, with bath, very nice, by entrance to national park, clean, quiet, enclosed parking, rec.

E *Acosta*, opp bus station; nearby is *Sandy*, cheaper; **E** *Capri*, Portal Santos Degollado, by market, friendly; **E** *Mi Solar*, Juan Delgado 10, T 20912, good value, hot water, clean, rec; **E** *Santa Fe*, Constitución 20, without bath, adequate, beside open-air food stalls.

F *Moderno*, main square, lovely building, with bath, water spasmodic, friendly, very basic; **F** *Oseguera*, main square, dirty but good hot shower.

Motels: A1 *Mansión del Cupatitzio*, on the road to Guadalajara, T 32100, pool, patio, restaurant, good souvenir shop, outstanding; **B** *Paricutín*, Juárez 295, T 20303, well-maintained; **B** *Pie de la Sierra*, Km 4 Carretera a Carapán, on N outskirts, T 42510, good moderately-priced restaurant; **C** *Las Cabañas*, Km 1 Carretera a México, nr the bus terminal, T 34777, clean, local bus until 2200. One trailer park which takes small units only.

● **Places to eat**
La Pergola, on plaza, good breakfasts and coffee, rec; *Café Tradicional de Uruapan*, just off Plaza, on same side as *Hotel Villa de Flores*, freshly-ground coffee, home-made chocolates, light meals, rec. *Calypso*, Alvaro Obregón 2A, excellent cakes and hamburgers, ask for local speciality: *rumpope agua fresca*. Locals eat at open-air food stalls under one roof at back of church, very picturesque. *Monarca*, Cupatitzio opp Banco Mexicano, cheap food and yoghurt; good icecream at *Bing*, Obregón on plaza. *La Puesta del Sol*, supermarket, Juan Ayala, has good meals. Local speciality, dried meat, *cecina*. Cheap meals from comedors in the *Mercado de Antojitos*.

● **Laundry**
Emilio Carranza 51.

● **Post & telecommunications**
Post Office: Reforma 13.

● **Tourist offices**
Ocampo 64, below *Hotel Plaza Uruapan* on E side of Zócalo, T 36172.

● **Transport**
Air Three daily flights from Mexico City via Morelia.

Trains Purépecha train from **Mexico City** at 2100, returning 1910 (arr 0730), and another at 0630, US$13.70 *primera preferente*, US$11.20 1st, 2nd class to Mexico City US$7.65. Freight train to **Pátzcuaro**, daily, takes passengers, US$1.50, can take 5 hrs for the 62 km. Food vendors board at every stop, 1 train a day to Lázaro Cárdenas and Apatzingán.

Buses Bus station on the NE edge of town, necessary to get a city bus (US$0.25) into town, finishing at about 2100, or a taxi to the Plaza, US$3. To **Mexico City**, 9¼ hrs, Flecha Amarilla via Toluca leaves 0845 and then every hour, US$16.25, many stops; others less frequent but quicker, US$18.75. ETN has a deluxe service, US$23, 5½ hrs, several a day, hot and cold drinks, clean, good drivers. Omnibús de México has night buses and Tres Estrellas morning departures. To **Morelia**, 2nd class (Flecha Amarilla) US$4.60 (2½ hrs), nice ride. Parhikuni, T 38754, 1st class and plus with computerized reservations to Morelia, Apatzingan and Lázaro Cárdenas US$10.60. To **Colima** with Flecha Amarilla US$13.50, 6 hrs, and to **Los Reyes**, US$2.20, 1¼ hrs with same company. To **Zihuatanejo** (Galeana not rec, or Occidente) 1st or 2nd class, several a day, 6½ hrs, US$9 (2nd)

along winding, intermittently wooded road via Nueva Italia and Arteaga, which turns off just before Playa Azul at La Mira and on to Lázaro Cárdenas on the Río Balsas. From there, frequent buses to Zihuatanejo (see page 352). Bus to **Guadalajara**, several companies, US$9, 5 hrs, ETN US$17.75. Bus to **Pátzcuaro**, frequent, US$2, 1 hr.

PARICUTIN

The volcano of **Paricutín** can be visited from Uruapan; it started erupting in the field of a startled peasant on 20 February 1943, became fiery and violent and rose to a height of 1,300m above the 2,200m-high region, and then died down after several years into a quiet grey mountain (460m) surrounded by a sea of cold lava. The church spires of San Juan, a buried Indian village, thrusting up through cold lava is a fantastic sight. If not taking an organized tour (with horses and guides), Paricutín is best reached by taking a 'Los Reyes' bus on a paved road to Angahuán, 34 km, US$0.80, 1 hr, 9 a day each way (hourly from 0500 to 1900) with Galeana, then hire a horse or mule or walk (1 hr). Sres Juan Rivera, Francisco Lázaro (tour is a bit hurried, he lives in the second house on the right, coming from the *albergue*, see below), Atanacio Lázaro and his horse 'Conejo', and Lino Gómez are recommended, but there are a host of other guides (it is definitely worthwhile to have a guide – essential for the volcano – even though they are very persistent, best if you can speak Spanish, but it is expensive if you are on your own as you have to pay for the guide's mule too). A full day's excursion with mules to the area costs about US$10-15 per mule, with US$4-5 tip for the guide (6-7 hrs); shorter journeys cost less. To go on foot with a guide costs US$8. Distance Angahuán-San Juan ruins, 3 km, an easy walk: go from the bus stop on the main road to the new hostel, from where you can see the buried church. To the peak of the volcano is 10 km, a long, tough walk (also a long day on horseback for the unaccustomed, especially if you get a wooden saddle). Walk westwards round the lava field, through an avocado plantation. Wear good walking shoes with thick soles as the lava is very rough and as sharp as glass (some cannot make the last stretch over the cricket-ball size rocks); bear in mind the altitude too, as the return is uphill. One can continue on to the volcano itself; it takes 7-9 hrs there and back. The cone itself is rather small and to reach it, there is a stiff 30-min climb from the base. A path goes around the tip of the crater, where activity has ceased. Take something to drink because it is pretty hot and dusty out on the plains. If going in 1 day, leave Uruapan by 0800 so that you don't have to rush. Go even earlier in the rainy season as clouds usually build up by midday. Take sweater for the evening and for the summit where it can be windy and cold after a hot climb. Last bus back to Uruapan at 1900 (but don't rely on it). Much better, though, is to stay the night in **Angahuán**, where there is an *albergue*, **E** pp in *cabañas* with a log fire, or **F** pp in dormitory with bunk beds (dormitories closed in low season, both have hot showers), meals US$5, no dinner available in low season, basic facilities, but clean and peaceful, warm and highly recommended. The *albergue* is a 30-min walk from the bus stop on the main road: walk into the village, take the 3rd turning on the left and then right at the plaza. Go straight on until the road forks at an expensive-looking wooden house with a satellite TV aerial. Take the left fork. From here, the *albergue* is about 10-15 mins' walk at the end of the road. It is possible to drive to the *albergue* where they try to charge US$1.60 for the free car park. There is a panoramic view from the *albergue* of the volcano, San Juan ruins and surrounding pine forest. Camping possible near the hostel. Some families rent out rooms, eg that of Francisco Lázaro, near Zócalo, whose son, José, will guide you up the volcano. In the village are shops selling food and drink and a good local restaurant in the street behind the church. There is a water tap near the church; follow the

signs. Just outside the village, on the dirt road to the main road, is the cemetery, which is interesting. The local Tarascan Indians still preserve their dialects.

Past Angahuán and Peribán, after the volcano, over a paved road is the little town of **Los Reyes**; good swim above the electricity generating plant in clear streams (take care not to get sucked down the feed pipe!).

● **Accommodation C** *Arias* behind Cathedral, T 20792, best, clean, friendly; **D** *Fénix*, clean, between bus station and plaza, T 20807; **D** *Oasis*, Av Morelos 229, C for a suite, with bath, hot water, clean, pleasant; **D** *Plaza*, not as good as *Arias* but nice, clean, on street facing Cathedral, T 20666; **E** *Casa de Huéspedes*, clean, basic, lovely courtyard, a little further along the same road is **E** *Villa Rica*, often no water.

● **Places to eat** *La Fogata*, in main square.

● **Transport Buses** From Uruapan to **Los Reyes** go via Angahuán (so same frequency as above), depart from Uruapan bus station, not from the plaza as the tourist office says. Bus from Los Reyes on Av 5 de Mayo to Angahuán, US$2.50, 1½-2 hrs. Bus to Los Reyes from Guadalajara with Ciénaga de Chapala 4 a day, 4 hrs, US$8.25 1st class. **Trains** Guadalajara-Mexico City connects at Yurécuaro for Los Reyes, almost no wait, beautiful ride up fertile valley.

THE PACIFIC COAST OF MICHOACAN

The Pacific coast of Michoacán is only just coming under development. From Uruapan Route 37 goes to **Playa Azul**, 350 km NW of Acapulco (bus US$9, 10½ hrs minimum) and 122 km from Zihuatanejo (see page 352), a coconut-and-hammock resort frequented much more by Mexicans than foreigners, with a few large hotels. The city of La Mira, on the main road, is larger than Playa Azul. 40 km of excellent deserted beaches N of Playa Azul. At night there is much beautiful phosphorescence at the water's edge. **NB** Beware of the large waves at Playa Azul and of dangerous currents; always check with locals if particular beaches are safe.

- **Accommodation D** *El Delfín*, Venustiano Carranza s/n, T 60007, no a/c, clean, pleasant, swimming pool; **D** *Hotel del Pacífico*, opp beach, with bath, fan, clean, hammocks on roof, friendly, a bit run-down but rec. **E** *Costa de Oro*, Francisco I Madero s/n, T 60982, clean, with fan, rec, safe parking; *Hotel Playa Azul*, Venustiano Carranza s/n, T 60024/88, F 60090, has a trailer park with 20 spaces, full hook-up, bathrooms, cold shower, 2 pools, bar and restaurant, US$13 for car and 2 people. Many small fish restaurants along beach, but most close early; *Martita*, highly rec. Tap and shower water seems to smell of petrol.

- **Transport** Buses ply up and down the coast road, stopping at the road junction 4 km from Plaza Azul. Colectivos take you between town and junction. If driving N it is 5 hrs to Tecomán (where the road from Colima comes down to the coast); there is nothing along this road.

Lázaro Cárdenas is the connecting point for buses from Uruapan, Manzanillo and Zihuatanejo. There is a Tourist Office at Nicolás Bravo 475, T 21547, in the *Hotel Casablanca* building.

- **Accommodation C** *Hotel de la Curva*, Vicente Guerrero esq Nicolás Bravo, T 73656-9, F 23237; **D** *Sol del Pacífico*, Fco Javier Mina 178, T 20660, F 70490; **E** *Viña del Mar*, Javier Mina 352, T/F 20415. Avoid **E** *Hotel Sam Sam*, nr terminal; go to *Capri*, Juan Alvarez 237, T 20551, or *Costa Azul*, 5 de Mayo 276, T 20780, both **E** with bath, or **E** *Verónica*, Javier Mina 47, T 20254, 2 blocks on left as you leave bus station, friendly, pleasant, noisy, restaurant in front part of hotel has nice atmosphere but indifferent food; several eating places in streets nr bus terminal.

- **Transport Buses** Galeana to Manzanillo 7¾ hrs, US$10; to Uruapan, US$10.75, 6½ hrs; to Guadalajara, US$21.50 with La Línea; to Mexico City from 2nd US$17, 1st US$36.65 to 43.35, luxury; Flecha Roja to Zihuatanejo, 2 hrs, US$3.65. If possible, book tickets in advance at the bus terminal for all journeys. **Trains** Mexico City-Lázaro Cardenas, via Morelia, Pátzcuaro, Uruapan, dep 2100, arr 1600, returns to capital midday, arr 0730, *primera preferente* US$21.50, 2nd class US$10, crowded.

Buses continue along the coast road to La Mira, then another a short distance to **Caleta de Campos**, 76 km NW up the coast from Playa Azul. In this poor village there is little food other than seafood, but there are phone services; *Hotel Yuritzi*, **E** pp, **D** in room for 4, with bath, clean, no hot water, good views from front, nice; *cabañas* with hammock space at US$1 pp, NW of village, where Río Nexpa reaches the coast. *Fiesta*: 10-13 Dec; at 0200 on the 13th El Torito, a bull mask and sculpture loaded with fireworks appears. There are other elaborate, if dangerous fireworks. Beaches are 5 mins away, clean, with seafood restaurants. 86 km further up the coast, to the NW, is **Maruata**, unspoilt and beautiful. This is a turtle conservation area. There are floods in the rainy season. For southbound traffic seeking Maruata, road signs are inadequate.

QUIROGA

Back on the road **from Guadalajara to Morelia** via Zamora, at **Zacapu** (Km 400), see the Franciscan church (1548). At **Quiroga** (Km 357), a road turns off right for Pátzcuaro, heart of the Tarascan Indian country. The town is named after Bishop Vasco de Quiroga, who was responsible for most of the Spanish building in the area and for teaching the Indians the various crafts they still practise: work in wool, leather, copper, ceramics and canework; many Indians, few tourists. Fair and craft exhibitions in December. Good place to buy cheap leather jackets – most shops in town sell them. The night-time entertainment seems to be driving through town in a pick-up with blaring speakers in the back.

- **Accommodation C** *Misión don Vasco*, Av L Cárdenas y Gpe Victoria. Three hotels on main street (Vasco de Quiroga): **E** *Tarasco*, colonial style, courtyard, clean, hot water, pleasant but front rooms noisy; **D** pp *Quiroga* and **D** *Tarisco* (was *San Diego*), cheapest in town, last two both modern with parking. *Cabañas Tzintzuntzan*, Km 6 Quiroga-Pátzcuaro road (Ojo de Agua), swimming pool, own pier, fully-furnished (contact *Hotel Casino*, Morelia, T 31003). Trailer park 3 km N of town. Old summer residence of a former Mexican president, apparently, wonderful view over Lake Pátzcuaro.

● **Transport** Bus from Pátzcuaro bus station every 15 mins. Bus Quiroga-Mexico City, US$11, 1st *plus*.

We pass through **Tzintzuntzan**, the pre-conquest Tarascan capital; the ruins are just behind the village, a good walk from the monastery, open daily 0900-1730, US$1, Sun free. The fascinating ruins of **Yácatas**, a Purépecha ceremonial centre, with five pyramids, are across the road and up the hill (10 mins' walk) from the monastery. Wood carving and rustic furniture also here. In C Magdalena is a monastery built in 1533 but closed over 250 years ago, which has been restored, but its frescoes have deteriorated badly. The bells of its church date from the 16th century; a guard will show you round the monastery. In the grounds are some very old olive trees which are still bearing fruit, said to have been planted by Vasco de Quiroga. Fortuitously they were missed in a Spanish edict to destroy all Mexican olive trees when it was thought that Mexican olive oil would compete with Spain's. A most interesting Passion play is given at Tzintzuntzan and *fiestas* are very colourful. Beautiful and extensive display of hand-painted pottery, very cheap but also brittle. (It is available in other markets in Mexico.) Other handicrafts on sale include woodcarving, leather and basketwoven Christmas tree ornaments. Good bargaining opportunities. Bus from Pátzcuaro bus station every 15 mins, US$0.50, same bus as for Quiroga, which is 8 km further on. **NB** If taking the route Uruapan-Pátzcuaro-Morelia, Tzintzuntzan and Quiroga come after Pátzcuaro.

PATZCUARO

(*Pop* 65,000; *Alt* 2,110m; *Phone code* 434) 23 km from Quiroga (cold in the evenings), **Pátzcuaro** is one of the most picturesque towns in Mexico, with narrow cobbled streets and deep overhanging eaves. The houses are painted white and brown. It is built on Lago de Pátzcuaro, about 50 km in circumference, with Tarascan Indian villages on its shores and many islands. The Indians used to come by huge dugout canoes (but now seem to prefer the ferry) for the market, held in the main plaza, shaded by great trees.

Places of interest

There are several interesting buildings: the unfinished **La Colegiata** (1603), known locally as La Basílica, with its much venerated Virgin fashioned by an Indian from a paste made with cornstalk pith and said to have been found floating in a canoe. Behind the Basílica there are remains of the precolumbian town and of a pyramid in the precincts of the Museo de Artes Populares; the restored Jesuit church of **La Compañía** (and, almost opposite, the early 17th century church of the **Sagrario**) at the top of C Portugal. Behind this street are two more ecclesiastical buildings: the **Colegio Teresiano** and the restored **Templo del Santuario**; on C Lerín is the old monastery, with a series of small patios. (Murals by Juan O'Gorman in the Library, formerly San Agustín.) On C Allende is the residence of the first Governor. On C Terán is the church of **San Francisco**; nearby is **San Juan de Dios**, on the corner of C Romero. Visit also the **Plaza Vasco de Quiroga**. 15 mins' walk outside the town is the chapel of **El Calvario**, on the summit of Cerro del Calvario, a hill giving wide views; views also from the old chapel of the **Humilladero**, above the cemetery on the old road to Morelia. This chapel is said to have been built on the spot where the last Tarascan emperor knelt in submission to the Spanish Conquistador, Cristóbal de Olid. Do not hike there alone, it is rather isolated.

The very well arranged **Museo de Artes Populares** is in the former Colegio de San Nicolás (1540) entrance US$2, excellent for seeing regional ceramics, weaving, woodcarving and basketware, open 0900-1900 Mon-Sat, 0900-1430 Sun (free), English speaking, friendly guide. Ask there for the Casa de los Once Patios,

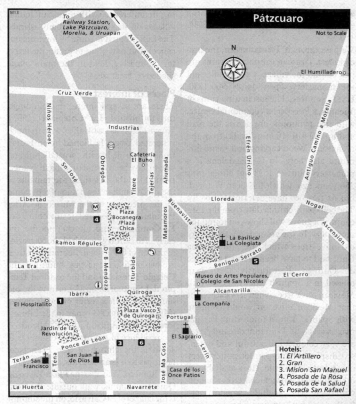

To
Railway Station,
Lake Pátzcuaro,
Morelia, & Uruapan

Pátzcuaro

Not to Scale

M13

N

El Humilladero

Cruz Verde

Industrias

Niños Héroes

San José

Obregón

Titere

Telerías

Ahumada

Cafetería
El Buho

Av las Américas

Efren Uricho

Antiguo Camino a Morelia

Libertad

Lloreda

Nogal

Plaza
Bocanegra
/Plaza
Chica

4

M

Matamoros

Buenavista

Ascensión

Ramos Régules

2

Dr B Mendoza

Iturbide

La Basílica/
La Colegiata

La Era

El Cerro

Benigno Serrato

Museo de Artes Populares,
Colegio de San Nicolás

Ibarra

Quiroga

Alcantarilla

El Hospitalito

1

Plaza Vasco
de Quiroga

La Compañía

Portugal

Jardín de la
Revolución

Ponce de León

3   6

El Sagrario

Lerín

Terán
San
Francisco

F Tena

San Juan
de Dios

José Ma Coss

Casa de los
Once Patios

La Huerta

Navarrete

Hotels:
1. *El Artillero*
2. *Gran*
3. *Misión San Manuel*
4. *Posada de la Rosa*
5. *Posada de la Salud*
6. *Posada San Rafael*

which contains boutiques selling handicrafts; you can see weavers and painters of lacquerwork in action. An 'International Hippy Crafts Market' is held every Sat and Sun in the courtyard in front of the Casa de Once Patios. See also the attractive Jardín de la Revolución (F Tena y Ponce de León) and, nearby, the old church of the Hospitalito. Excellent Fri and also Sat markets, often much cheaper than shops; good copperware on sale. Woodcarving is another local speciality. Good crafts by intersection of Benigno Serrato and Lerín near the Basílica. Some stalls open daily on the main square, selling handicrafts, and there is a friendly handicraft shop on the road

down to the lake, Vicky's, with interesting toys. There is a free medical clinic, English-speaking, on the outskirts of Pátzcuaro.

Excursions

The best-known island is **Janitzio**, which despite the souvenir shops, children asking for pesos and the tourists (visit during the week if possible) has considerable charm. It is 45 mins by motorboat, leaves when full from 0800 onwards, US$1.50 return from Muelle General (cheaper from Muelle San Pedrito, 500m further on), tickets from office at dock, last boat back (return by any boat) at 1800. There is an unfortunate monument to Morelos, with mural inside, crowning a hill, US$0.30, which nevertheless affords magnificent views, and a circular path around the island. Winter is the best time for fishing in the somewhat fish-depleted lake, where Indians throw nets shaped like dragonflies. The Government is planning to improve the lake's water quality, but there are still plenty of places selling white fish on the island, at about a quarter of the price in Pátzcuaro. Another island to visit is **Yunen**, boat from Muelle General. The island is clean and quiet. There is a cabaña (**R**) on the hill with a good restaurant. During the week there are few *lanchas*, so be sure to arrange return trip unless you want to spend the night. Bring provisions. On a lakeside estate (formerly the country house of Gen Lázaro Cárdenas) is the Educational Centre for Community Development in Latin America, better known as Crefal (free films every Wed at 1930). For a truly spectacular view of the lake, the islands and the surrounding countryside, walk to Cerro del Estribo; an ideal site for a quiet picnic. It is 1½-h walk to the top from the centre of Pátzcuaro. Follow the cobbled road beyond El Calvario, don't take the dirt tracks off to the left. Cars go up in the afternoon, the best time for walking. No buses, 417 steps to the peak. The areas round Pátzcuaro are recommended for bird watching. If intending to drive around the lake, a high-clearance vehicle is necessary.

From Pátzcuaro one can also visit Tzintzuntzan and Quiroga by regular bus service. 30 mins by local bus from Plaza Chica are **Ihuátzio** (US$0.25), on a peninsula 12 km N of Pátzcuaro, 8 km from Tzintzuntzan. This was the second most important Tarascan city; two pyramids are well-preserved and afford good views of the lake. Admission US$1.70, leaflets in Spanish or English, US$0.40. The road to the pyramids is very bad, 1 km from village, signposted. To get to Tzintzuntzan from Ihuátzio, take bus or hitch back to main road and wait for Pátzcuaro-Quiroga bus.

An excursion can be made into the hills to **Santa Clara del Cobre**, a sleepy village with red tiles and overhanging eaves, an attractive square with copper pots filled with flowers along each arcade, and a fine old church. Hand-wrought copper vessels are made here and there is a Museo del Cobre (closed Mon, free) with some excellent examples; it's half a block from the main square. There is a Banco Serfín which changes dollars cash and cheques between 1000 and 1200. (*Fiesta*: 12-15 August.) Take a bus to Pátzcuaro bus station, then another to Ario de Rosales (every 15 mins), which passes Santa Clara, fare US$0.50 each way. Nearby is the pretty **Lago Zirahuen**, where you can take boat trips, eat at lakeside restaurants and visit the huge adobe church. **C** *Motel Zirahuen*, T 23600, attractive, clean, garden restaurant, horse riding. Flecha Amarilla buses leave Pátzcuaro between 0930-1400, 30 mins direct, last bus back at 1800. Past Santa Clara, on the La Huacana road, after Ario de Rosales, one descends into the tropics; fine views all along this road, which ends at Churumuco. Pátzcuaro-Ario de Rosales-Nueva Italia-Uruapan-Pátzcuaro takes about 6 hrs, beautiful tropical countryside.

● **Accommodation At Santa Clara:**
C *Camino Real*, Av Morelos Pte 213, T 30281;
D *Real del Cobre*, Portal Hidalgo 19, T 30205;
D *Oasis*, Portal Allende 144, T 30040, both on main square.

Local festivals

1-2 Nov: Día de los Muertos (All Souls' Day), ceremony at midnight, 1 Nov, at almost every village around the lake; if you are in the region at this time it is well worth experiencing. The ceremony is most touristy on Janitzio island and at Tzintzuntzan, but at villages such as Ihuátzio, Jarácuaro and Uranden it is more intimate. The tourist office has leaflets listing all the festivities. 6-9 Dec, Virgen de la Salud, when authentic Tarascan dances are performed in front of the *basílica*. There is an interesting *fiesta* on 12 Dec for the Virgin of Guadalupe; on 12 Oct, when Columbus reached America, there is also a procession with the Virgin and lots of fireworks. Carnival in Feb when the Dance of the Moors is done. On the 8th day of every month there is a religious celebration and most accommodation is full.

Local information
● Accommodation

Rooms in some hotels are reserved 4 weeks prior to Día de los Muertos, other hotels do not take reservations, so it is pot luck at this time.

A1 *Posada de don Vasco*, attractive, colonial-style hotel on Av de las Américas (halfway between lake and town, T 20262), breakfast good, other meals poor, presents the Dance of the Old Men on Wed and Sat at 2100, no charge, non-residents welcome but drinks very expensive to compensate, also mariachi band.

B *Las Redes*, Av de las Américas 6, T 21275, nr lake, popular restaurant; **B** *Mesón del Cortijo*, Obregón, just off Américas, T 21295, rec, but often fully booked at weekends.

C *Apo-Pau*, between lake and town (closest to town of the non-central hotels), pleasant, friendly.

In the centre: **A3** *Mesón del Gallo*, Dr Coss 20, T 21474, F 21511, good value, flower garden, tasteful furnishings; **B** *Posada La Basílica*, Arciga 6, T 21108, nice restaurant with good views, central; **B** *Posada San Rafael*, Plaza Vasco de Quiroga, T 20770, safe, poor restaurant, parking in courtyard.

C *Los Escudos*, Portal Hidalgo 74, T 21290, colonial style ('Baile de los Viejitos' every Sat at 2000), rec, ask for room with fireplace, good food; **C** *Mansión Iturbe*, Portal Morelos 59, restored mansion on main plaza, breakfast inc, excellent value, very expensive restaurant; **C** *Misión San Manuel*, Portal Aldama 12 on main plaza, T 21313, restaurant, highly rec.

D *Casa de Huéspedes Pátzcuaro*, Ramos 9, without bath; **D** *Concordia*, next to *Posada de la Rosa*, with bath and hot water, cheaper without (which means use of toilet, but no bath whatsoever), in poor shape, rooms on plaza, noisy; **D** *El Artillero*, Ibarra 22, T 21331, hot water, with bath, gloomy, noisy, not too clean or secure, no drinking water, nr Zócalo (discounts for long stays paid in advance); **D** *Gran Hotel*, Portal Regules 6, on Plaza Bocanegra, T 20443, small rooms, clean, friendly, pleasant,

good food; **D** *Imperial*, Obregón 21, large clean rooms; these are all central.

E *Hostal de la Salud*, Benigno Serrato 9, T 20058, clean, quiet, pleasant, excellent value, some rooms with individual fireplaces, rec; **E** *Laguna*, Titere, with bath, cheaper rooms also with bath but no water-buckets outside!; **E** *Posada de la Rosa*, Portal Juárez 29 (Plaza Chica), with bath, F without, parking, colonial style, clean; **E** *Posada La Terraza*, Benito Juárez 46, T 21027, central, gardens, hot water, kind señora. Also on Plaza Chica is **E** *Posada San Agustín*, very good value, clean, hot water. **E** *Valmen*, Lloreda 34, T 45412-21161, with bath, hot showers, charming colonial building but noisy, closes 2200, very popular.

There are many *hospedajes* and hotels nr the bus station. Public baths next to *Hotel Valmen*, US$0.50.

Motels: **B** *Chalamu*, Pátzcuaro road Km 20, T 20948; **B** *Hostería de San Felipe*, Cárdenas 321, T 21298, friendly, clean, fireplaces in rooms, good restaurant (closes 2030), highly rec; **B** *San Carlos*, Muelle Col Morelos, T 21359; *Villa Pátzcuaro*, Av de las Américas 506, T 20767 (Apdo Postal 206), 1 km from centre, very quiet, hot water, gardens, lots of birds, tennis, pleasant, also camping and caravan site. *Trailer Park El Pozo*, on lakeside, opp *Chalamu*, T 20937, hot showers am, large, delightful, well-equipped, US$10, owner speaks English, also camping (take water for drinking from the entrance rather than taps on the trailer pads).

Camping: see **Motels** above.

● Places to eat

Local speciality is *pescado blanco* (white fish), but it is disappearing from menus as a result of overfishing and pollution. Several lakeside restaurants serve fish dishes, but it is advisable to avoid locally caught fish. Many places close before 2000. Make sure you don't get overcharged in restaurants, some display menus outside which bear no resemblance to the prices inside. *Los Escudos* restaurant, Plaza Quiroga, open till 2200, popular with tourists, try *sopa tarasca* (a flavoursome soup made with toasted tortillas, cream and cheese), good value and coffee; *San Agustín*, Plaza Bocanegra, friendly, good doughnuts on sale outside in pm. *Taquería Los Equipales*, Portal Allende 57, Plaza Vasco de Quiroga (under *Hotel Mansión Iturbe*), very good *tacos*, open from mid-afternoon into the night. *Mery Lerín*, Benigno Serrato (opp Museo de Artes Populares) cheap local dishes; *Gran Hotel*, filling *comida corrida*, excellent *café con leche*; good chicken with vegetables and *enchiladas* over the market (budget restaurants here, usually open in evening). *Cafetería Dany's*, Zaragoza between the 2 plazas, touristy, good snacks; *Cafetería El Buho*, Tejerías 8, meals, drinks, slow but very good food, good value, stylish, friendly, rec; *Cafetería Fumeiro*, below *Hotel Misión San Manuel*, good coffee house. *Camino Real*, next to Pemex, 100m from *El Pozo Trailer Park*, very good *comida corrida*, quick service; *Tortisam*, Benito Mendoza 12, *good tortas*. Excellent *paletería and ice cream* parlour at Codallos 24, also sells frozen yoghurt; fruit and yoghurt for breakfast at *El Patio, Plaza Chica* (not cheap, slow service). Breakfast available from small stands in the market, usually 0600-0700 (*licuados, arroz con leche*, etc). At the Plaza in Erongaricuaro, 17 km clockwise around the lake, is a Hindu vegetarian restaurant at the weekends; also a local crafts fair (take ADO bus from bus or rail station, US$0.65).

● **Hospitals & medical services**
Dentist: Dra María de Lourdes Cázarez Cárdenas, Av Alvaro Obregón 52-A, T 20663.

● **Laundry**
Lavandería de Pátzcuaro, on C Ponce de León.

● **Sports**
Massage: Shiatsu Massage, Stephen Ritter del Castillo, in Tocuaro, 15 mins by bus or taxi clockwise around the lake about halfway to Erongaricuaro, T 43180309, Mon-Fri 0900-1700, excellent, English/Spanish bilingual.

● **Tourist offices**
Ibarra 2, Interior 3, Plaza Vasco de Quiroga, T 21214 (poorly signed); diagonally opp NW corner of plaza, next to Veterinario. The office is 3 doors along, on the right, in the courtyard.

● **Transport**
Trains Very enjoyable and cheaper, though slower, train ride around lake and plateau to Mexico City. Train leaves daily at 2100, from Mexico City to Pátzcuaro, arrives at 0645, beautiful views between Uruapan and Acámbaro (*fiesta*, 4 July), fare from capital US$11.70 *primera preferente*. Train to Mexico City at 2115, 10 hrs. Take pullover. Train to Uruapan and Lázaro Cárdenas: 0645, *primera preferente*. No trains to Guadalajara.

Buses New bus station out of town, with left luggage office, colectivo from centre US$0.30. You can pick up buses from large roundabout 1 km N of centre. To Mexico City, Tres Estrellas

de Oro, Herradura de Plata (via Morelia – rec) and Autobuses de Occidente 1st (US$13.60) and 2nd class buses (US$12.20), 6 hrs. Regular bus service to Morelia, 1 hr, US$1.80 with ADO, Herradura de Plata, Galeana and Flecha Amarilla (departs every 30 mins). Buses to Guadalajara go through Zamora, US$10 (Flecha Amarilla), 6 hrs; to Lázaro Cárdenas, for connections to Zihuatanejo, Acapulco, etc, hourly from 0600, US$12.50, 8 hrs, long but spectacular ride through mountains and lakes (police checks likely); to Uruapan, 30 mins, US$2 (1 hr); to Toluca, 1st class US$17.50, from 0915, 5 hrs. It is cheaper to get to Toluca by taking a bus to Morelia and then changing onto a PD bus for US$9. Local buses from corner of market in town to lakeside (colectivo to lakeside US$0.25).

MORELIA

(**Km 314**; *Pop* 759,000; *State pop 1995* 3,869,133; *Alt* 1,882m; *Phone code* 43) **Morelia**, capital of Michoacán state, is a rose-tinted city with attractive colonial buildings (their courtyards are their main feature), rather quiet, founded in 1541. The narrow streets suffer from vehicle pollution. Thur and Sun are market days: specialities are pottery, lacquer, woodcarving, jewellery, blankets, leather sandals; in this connection see the **Casa de Artesanías de Michoacán**, in the ex-Convento de San Francisco, next to the church of the same name; it is full of fine regional products for sale, not cheap. Shops close early. Free weekly concerts are held in the municipal theatre. At the E edge of the downtown area, on the road to Mexico City, are the 224 arches of a ruined **aqueduct**, built in 1788 (walk 11 blocks E from Cathedral along Av Madero). Both Banamex and Bancomer have their offices in magnificent old houses; the patio of the former is especially fine. Many good language schools.

Places of interest

The **Cathedral** (1640), is set between the two main plazas, with graceful towers and a fine façade, in what is called 'sober baroque'; there are paintings by Juárez in the sacristy. The **Virgen de Guadalupe** (also known as San Diego), E of the aqueduct, has an ornate interior of terracotta garlands and buds, painted in pastels, like being inside a giant wedding cake. There are four huge oil paintings of the missionaries Christianizing the Indians. Other important churches are the modernized **Iglesia de la Cruz**, and the 18th century **Iglesia de las Rosas** in the delightful plaza of the same name (its ex-Convento now houses the Conservatorio de Música). The oldest of Morelia's churches is the **San Francisco** of the Spanish Renaissance period, but lacking many of the decorative features of that style.

Even more interesting than the colonial churches are the many fine colonial secular buildings still standing. The revolutionary José María Morelos, Melchor Ocampo, and the two unfortunate Emperors of Mexico (Agustín de Iturbide and the Archduke Maximilian of Austria) are commemorated by plaques on their

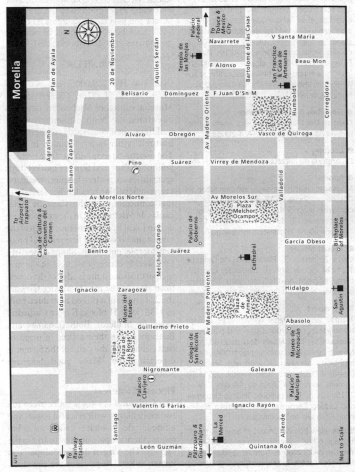

houses. Morelos' birthplace, at Corregidora 113, is open to visitors, admission free. The **Colegio de San Nicolás** (1540) is the oldest surviving institution of higher education in Latin America. (It has a summer school for foreign students.) Opposite is the Centro Cultural Universitario, with many free events. The fine former Jesuit college, now called the **Palacio Clavijero**, contains government offices, with a helpful tourist office on the ground floor (corner of Madero Pte y Nigromante). Nearby on Av Madero is a library with carved wooden balconies and many historical volumes. Also notable are the **Law School**, in the former monastery of **San Diego**, next to the Guadalupe church; the **Palacio de Gobierno** (1732-70), facing the Cathedral; the **Palacio Municipal**; and the **Palacio Federal**. Visit also the churches of **La Merced**, with its lovely tower and strange, bulging *estípites* (inverted pyramidal supports), **Capuchinas** (Ortega y Montaño), which has some Churrigueresque *retablos*, and **Santa María**, on a hilltop S of the city.

Next to the Plaza de Morelos is the Alameda de Calzones, a shady pedestrianized walkway with restored mansions leading 3 blocks to the fountain of the Tarascans (three bare-chested women holding up a giant basket of fruit)

Museums

Museo de Michoacán (archaeological remains), C Allende (open 0900-1900 daily, closed Mon, 0900-1400 Sun, US$4.35). The **Casa de la Cultura**, Av Morelos Norte, housed in the ex-Convento del Carmen, which has a good collection of masks from various regions, crucifixes (open daily, free); also workshops (nominal fee of US$1.55 for 12 weeks). The **Museo de Estado**, in the house of Iturbide's wife (Casa de la Emperatriz), SE corner of Jardín de las Rosas, is well worth a visit (open daily). Most of the ground floor is dedicated to Tarascan history and culture, lots of information about Michoacán, and, at the front, an old pharmacy with all its bottles, cabinets,

scales, etc, intact. The **Museo de Morelos**, on Morelos Sur, about 3 blocks S of the Cathedral, is a history museum, admission US$4.35 (described by one correspondent as 'intensely nationalistic').

Parks and zoos

Fairly good zoo in Parque Juárez, S of the centre (25 mins' walk S along Galeana). Planetarium.

Local information
● **Accommodation**

Some of the cheaper hotels may have water only in the morning; check. **A1** *Calinda Quality Inn*, Av Acueducto, T 145969, colonial-style, modern; **A2** *Alameda*, Av Madero Pte 313 y C de Jazmines, T 122023, F 138727, 'flashy'; **A3** *Virrey de Mendoza*, Portal Matamoros, T 120633, superb old-style building, poor restaurant, service could be better, could be cleaner, poor ventilation, ask for room at front with balcony.

B *Casino*, Portal Hidalgo 229, main square, T 131003, clean, hot water, private bath, good restaurant. Off the Plaza de Armas and much quieter is the **B** *Posada de la Soledad*, Zaragoza 90 and Ocampo, T 121888, F 122111, fine courtyards, converted chapel as dining room, TV and fireplaces in rooms, parking opp (free between 2000 and 0900, otherwise US$1/hr), good value, María Luisa speaks English; **B** *Plaza Morelos*, Glorieta Morelos 31, T 124499, large, cool, pleasant.

C *Catedral*, Zaragoza 37, T 130783, F 130467, close to Plaza, spacious, nice bar, restaurant closes quite early, rec; **C** *Florida*, Morelos Sur 165, T 121819, clean, good value.

D *del Matador*, E Ruiz 531, T 124649; another **D** hotel at E Ruiz 673, good value, but small rooms, overlooks the Casa de la Cultura, hot water; **D** *Don Vasco*, Vasco de Quiroga 232, T 121484, with shower and hot water, clean, safe, some rooms dingy, rec; **D** *Valladolid*, Portal Hidalgo 241, on main square, T 120027, with bath, good value for its location but a bit drab.

E *Carmen*, E Ruiz 63, T 121725; **E** *Mintzicini*, Vasco de Quiroga (opp *Don Vasco*), clean, small rooms, hot shower, TV, parking, helpful tourist office.

Cheap hotels on Morelos Norte: **D** *Concordia*, Gómez Farías 328, T 123052, round corner from bus station; **E** *Colonial*, corner with 20 de Noviembre 15, T 121897, pleasant, lots of hot water, good value. On Madero Poniente: **D** *San Jorge*, No 719, T 124610, with hot shower, clean; at No 670 is **E** *Vallarta*, T 124095, fair; at No 537 is **E** *Fénix*, with bath, front rooms noisy, back rooms dingy, clean, cheap; **E** *Posada Lourdes*, No 340, basic, clean, quiet, hot water. **E-F** *Señorial*, Santiago Tapiá 543, 1 block S from bus terminal, basic, with bath. Cheap *posadas* and *casas de huéspedes* tend to be uninviting, although the half-dozen around the bus station are reported clean and cheap.

On Santa María hill, S of the city, with glorious views, are hotels *Villa Montaña*, T 140231, F 151423, each room a house on its own, run by French aristocrats, very expensive but value for money, superb restaurant, *Vista Bella* (T 120248) and **C** *Villa San José* next door and much cheaper, reached only by car.

Motels: **B** *Villa Centurión*, Morelos road, T 132272, good antiques, pool, TV; **C** *El Parador*, Highway 45, with trailer park. **C** *Las Palmas*, Guadalajara road, also trailer park. Two good trailer parks on Route 126 between Morelia and the capital: *Balneario Las Ajuntas*, after Queréndaro, and *Balneario Atzimba*, hot springs at Zinapécuaro.

Youth hostel: at corner of Oaxaca and Chiapas No 180, T 133177, 1 km SW of bus station (walk W to C Cuautla, then S along Cuautla to Oaxaca) F, pp. Camping possible in a forest about 4 km S of centre on unnumbered Pátzcuaro-signposted road.

● **Places to eat**
Govinda, vegetarian, Av Morelos Sur 39, opp cathedral, delicious lunch for US$1.20, go early as food runs out, elegant setting, good breakfasts too; *Quinta Sol*, Aquiles Serdán 729, 5 blocks E of Morelos, also vegetarian, good *comida corrida*, US$4, served from 1400; both close daily at 1700 and both closed Sun. *Comidas corridas* at *El Viejo Paral*, Madero Ote and Quiroga, and in an unnamed restaurant on Gómez Farias, on right hand side heading away from bus station, US$1.50; *La Flor de las Mercedes*, Leon Guzmán, colonial-style house, beautiful decor, moderate prices; *Las Palmas*, Melchor Ocampo 215, friendly and tasty. Try stewed kid, best in cheaper restaurants. *Pizza Tony's*, Madero Ote 698; *Pollo-Coa*, Madero Ote 890, nr aqueduct, good food; *Viandas de San José*, Alvarado Obregón 263 (y E Zapata), good cheap *comida corrida*, excellent service, rec; *Los Pioneros*, Aquiles Serdán y Av Morelos Nte, cheap, good local food; *Café Pindaro*, Morelos Nte 150, good breakfasts. On Gómez

Farías, *Boca de Río*, at No 185, good fish. *Café del Olmo*, Benito Juárez 95, in a nice colonial building. There is a good café in *Casa de la Cultura*, with delicious home-made cakes. *Café Colón*, Ardiles Serdán 265, good coffee. The Mercado de Dulces, on Gómez Farías at W end of the Palacio Clavijero, is famous for fruit jams (*ates*), candies and *rompope* (a milk and egg nog).

● **Hospitals & medical services**
Dentist: Dr Leopoldo Arroyo Contreras, Abraham Gonzáles 35, T 120751, nr Cathedral, rec.

● **Language schools**
Centro Mexicano de Idiomas, Calz Fray Antonio de San Miguel 173, intensive weekly classes (US$280 for first week, other courses available inc handicrafts, accommodation with families). Baden-Powell Institute, Antonio Alzate 565, T 124070, from US$6.50/hr to US$8.50/hr, depending on length of course, lodging US$12/day, inc 3 meals, courses for all levels, plus cultural, social science and extracurricular courses, highly rec. (See National Registration Center for Study Abroad and *AmeriSpan* under **Learning Spanish** in Information for travellers.)

● **Laundry**
Lavandería Chapultepec, C J Ceballos 881. *Lavandería* on Santiago Tapiá towards bus station.

● **Post & telecommunications**
Post Office: in Palacio Federal, is said to charge different rates from the rest of Mexico.

● **Tourist offices**
Inside Palacio Clavijero (S end), has local hotel information list and map, English spoken, open 0900-2000 (closed Sun). Also kiosk at bus terminal, but not always open. Good city map available from *Casa de Cambio Troca Mex*, Melchor Ocampo y I Zaragoza.

● **Transport**
Air Many flights daily to and from Mexico City, 50 mins, also to other Mexican destinations: Guadalajara, León, Querétaro, Tijuana, Uruapán and Zacatecas. To USA: Mexicana and Taesa (T 134050) to Chicago; Mexicana to Los Angeles, San Francisco and San José (California); Taesa to Oakland. No public transport to airport, 26 km from city. Dollar and Budget car rental offices. Taxi to centre US$18.

Trains Morelia-Mexico City at 1030 and 2250, train starts at Lázaro Cárdenas, US$6 *primera preferente*; 2nd class US$3, 12 hrs. Take food and water with you. For enquiries T 163965.

Buses The terminal is on Eduardo Ruiz between León Guzmán and Gómez Farias, an easy walk to the town centre. Tourist Kiosk, though not always open, restaurants and left luggage. Many buses to **Guanajuato**, 4½ hrs, US$4.50. Guadalajara, US$10.35, also luxury service by ETN, US$20, T 37440. To Nuevo Laredo, 17 hrs, US$43. **Uruapan**, US$4.60 2nd class, Irapuato, US$4.55 2nd class, rough ride. Several direct daily to **Querétaro**, 3½ hrs. **Mexico City**, 2nd class 6½ hrs, 4½ by 1st *plus*, US$10.50, every 90 mins from 0600 to 2000, ETN luxury service US$15 to W terminal (see also diversion, below). Bus to **Acapulco** US$36.50, 15 hrs. To **Zitácuaro**, US$4.60, 2½ hrs. Bus to **Pátzcuaro** every 30 mins with ADO, Flecha Amarilla, Herradura de Plata and Parikhuni, 1 hr, US$1.80. Also about 15 a day to Zihuatanejo on the coast, US$14. For **Toluca** buses, many a day with ETN, 3 hrs, US$14.80.

NORTH OF MORELIA

Just after Morelia there is a good road N to two lakeside villages. At **Cuitzeo**, the first one (hotel, *Restaurant Esteban*, by post office), there is a fine Augustinian church and convent (begun in 1550), a cloister, a huge open chapel, and good choir stalls in the sacristy. The church houses a good collection of Mexican graphic art, spanning 4 centuries, in a gallery in the basement. **Laguna de Cuitzeo**, on which it stands, is the second largest lake in Mexico; the road crosses it on a causeway. Ecological damage in the past has caused the lake to dry up on occasion. From here one can go to **Valle de Santiago** (**D** *Hotel Posada de la Parroquia*), attractive mountain scenery. The second village, 33 km to the N, **Yuriria**, has a large-scale Indian version of the splendid church and convent at Actopán (see page 90). It is on Laguna de Yuriria, which looks like a grassy swamp. (Before Yuriria is Moreleón, the clothing distribution centre of Mexico – buses empty here.) The road continues to **Salamanca** (hotel, appalling traffic), where one turns left for Irapuato or right for Celaya and Querétaro. Mexico City-Morelia buses from the Central del Norte take the freeway to Celaya and then head S through Yuriria and Cuitzeo.

The road soon climbs through 50 km of splendid mountain scenery: forests, waterfalls, and gorges, to the highest point at (Km 253), Puerto Gartan, and **Mil Cumbres** (2,886m), with a magnificent view over mountain and valley, and then descends into a tropical valley. A new, 4-lane highway avoids the Mil Cumbres pass.

Another alternative to the Mil Cumbres pass is to take Route 126 from Morelia to **Queréndaro** (**E** *Hotel Imperial*, near church, pleasant rooms and courtyard, hot water, good value. Good *tacos* on main square), where the pavements are covered in *chiles* drying in the blazing sun, and all the shops are filled with large bags of *chiles* in the season, then at a junction 10 km short of Zinapécuaro, turn right to join Route 15 (to Toluca and Mexico City) at Huajumbaro. If, instead of turning right you carry straight on, the road climbs and descends to **Maravatío** (hotel) and then climbs steeply, towards **Tlalpujahua**, an old mining town with a museum, several churches, and cobblestoned streets, very picturesque among forests and hills (*Casa de Huéspedes*). From Maravatío Route 122 goes S to join Route 15 just E of Ciudad Hidalgo. Also from Maravatío, Route 126 to Toluca has been upgraded to a toll road, renamed 15D and is 1 hr quicker than the route over the mountains of Route 15.

Northwest of Maravatío, on the Río Lerma (18th century bridge), lies the town of **Acámbaro**, founded 1526. It has a Franciscan church of the same date and monastery (finished 1532), with the Capilla de Santa Gracia (mid-16th century) and its ornate fountain. It was the point from which the irrigation system for the whole area was laid out when the town was founded. Acámbaro continues to thrive as an agricultural centre and an important railway junction. It is also on the main highway from Celaya to Toluca.

EAST OF MORELIA

Worth a glance are the façade of the 16th century church at **Ciudad Hidalgo**

(Km 212; *Pop* 100,000). **D** *Hotel Fuente*, Morelos 37, T 40518, some rooms have no keys, clean, showers, no water in the afternoon; **E** *Florida*, damp rooms, garage US$0.50 a night; *Restaurant Manolo*, inexpensive, good; *Restaurant Lupita's*, excellent, family run. Also see the old colonial bridge and church at **Tuxpan (Michoacán)** Km 193; **F** *Mara*, on main square, dirty, hot water, wood stove; *Tuxpan*, Miguel Cabrera, T 50058, noisy. At Km 183 a side road runs, right, to the spa of **San José Purúa** at 1,800m, in a wild setting of mountain and gorge and woods. The radioactive thermal waters are strong. First-class hotel, beautiful spot, good restaurant, reservations in Mexico City, T 510 1538/4949, helpful stall. Trailers can park outside the guarded gate (24 hrs, tip the guard for security), small charge for entry to grounds. Alternatively, drive down the steep hill to the river, just over the bridge on right is Agua Amarilla, a spa where you can camp for a small fee, friendly. Smaller, cheaper hotels lie on the road past the spa and in the town of Jungapeo. If driving with a trailer, do not take the downward hill to the village, your brakes may not hold.

ZITACUARO

Then comes **Zitácuaro**, with a pleasant plaza and a good covered market.

● **Accommodation** **B** *Rancho San Cayetano*, 3 km out on Huetamo road, T 31926, chalets, friendly, clean, highly rec; **B** *Rosales del Valle*, Revolución Sur 56, T 31293, fair, some rooms hired for very short stays; **B** *Salvador*, Hidalgo Pte 7, T 31107, clean and pleasant; **C** *Lorenz*, Av Hidalgo Ote 14, T 30991, quiet, clean, TV, friendly, 9 blocks from bus station; **D** *México*, Revolución Sur 22, T 32811, clean, large rooms with cable TV, parking, restaurant, rec; **D** *Florida*, with bath, clean, garage US$0.50 a night; **D** *Hotel Colón*, reasonable, fan, not very quiet, friendly management, can store luggage; **E** *América*, Av Revolución Sur, 1st block, TV, pleasant, clean, rec; **E** *Mary*, on main street, hot shower, TV,

clean; one block from *Mary* on same street is unnamed hotel, **F**, clean, TV, basic. **E** *Posada Michoacán*, main square, TV, clean, friendly, luggage store.

● **Transport** Bus to Mexico City, 3 hrs, US$6; to Morelia, US$4.60, 2½ hrs; to Guadalajara, 11 hrs, US$14.80, 409 km (bus station at end of Av Cuauhtémoc, next to market, taxi to centre, US$1).

EL CAMPANARIO ECOLOGICAL RESERVE

A turning off the main road at Angangueo brings you to a unique site, the wintering grounds of the Monarch butterfly in **El Campanario Ecological Reserve**, above the village of El Rosario. There are several trails to see the millions of large orange butterflies, which migrate every year to SE Canada and NE USA. They leave in Mar, after which there is nothing to see until the following Nov/December. Chris Sharp writes: "Huge clusters of the butterflies hang from branches and on warm days they take to the air in swirling masses of red clouds. The most impressive component of this is the sound of their wings, like a strong breeze blowing through the trees." Entry to the reserve, 0900-1700, is US$2, plus a tip for your guide (only Spanish spoken), try to form a small group to go round the reserve. There is a small visitors' centre and food kiosks near the entrance. **NB** The reserve is at a high altitude and you need to walk a few kilometres (30 mins) to see the butterflies. Bring warm clothes. Best to go in the morning.

● **Accommodation** The best base for visiting the reserve is the village of **Angangueo**. In Dec-Mar much of the village caters for the influx of butterfly watchers. It is very cold at night. **C** *Albergue Don Bruno*, Morelia 92, T 60026, good but a little overpriced, nice setting, restaurant; **D** *Parakata 2*, Matamoros 7, T 80191; **D** *La Margarita*, Morelia, very clean, highly rec; **E** *Juárez*, Nacional s/n, T 80023, friendly, some rooms damp; **E** *Paso de la Monarca*, Nacional 20, T 80187, large comfortable rooms, hot water, friendly, meals, highly rec.

● **Places to eat** There are several cafés and restaurants nr the plaza, wholesome food, but not gourmet.

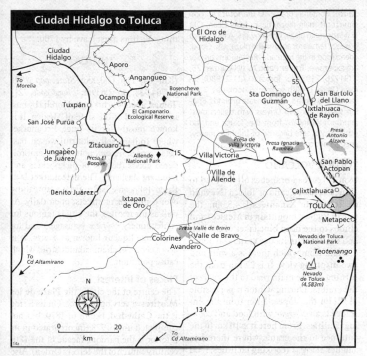

Ciudad Hidalgo to Toluca

El Oro de Hidalgo

Ciudad Hidalgo

Aporo

To Morelia

Angangueo

Bosencheve National Park

Sta Domingo de Guzmán

San Bartolo del Llano

Tuxpán

Ocampo

Ixtlahuaca de Rayón

San José Purúa

El Campanario Ecological Reserve

Zitácuaro

55

Presa de Villa Victoria

Presa Ignacio Ramírez

Presa Antonio Alzare

Jungapéo de Juárez

Presa El Bosque

Allende National Park

15

Villa Victoria

San Pablo Actopan

Denito Juárez

Villa de Allende

Calixtlahuaca

Ixtapan de Oro

TOLUCA

Metapec

Presa Valle de Bravo

Valle de Bravo

Colorines

Avandero

Nevado de Toluca National Park

Teotenango

To Cd Altamirano

N

Nevado de Toluca (4.583m)

0 20 km

134

To Cd Altamirano

● **Transport Buses** Half-hourly local bus (marked Angangueo) from Zitácuaro (Av Santos Degollado Ote, or from bus station on outskirts of town) to Ocampo, 1 hr, US$0.75, and from Ocampo another local bus (2 a day from corner 2 blocks E of plaza, 1000 and 1200, last one back at 1600, 1¼ hrs, US$0.85, 12 km on a mountainous dirt road) to El Rosario, from where it is a 10-min walk to the Reserve. A truck from Ocampo to the butterfly refuge costs US$17, this can be shared, especially at weekends. All hotels will arrange transport to the Reserve, about US$20 per vehicle, 1 hr. Alternatively, walk, about 2½ hrs (first hr steeply uphill), pleasant countryside. Aguila Tours, Amsterdam 291-C, Col Hipódromo Condesa, run tours from Mexico City from early Dec. Day trips cost around US$100-120. 4 direct buses to Mexico City, US$6. To Guadalajara, 3 a day, US$13, 8 hrs.

Ixtapan del Oro is a pleasant town in a valley, 70 km SE of Zitácuaro (*Pop* 20,000). It has a few hotels (eg **E** *Posada*

Familiar Portal Moreno, with bath, clean). A road, mostly dirt, runs between Ixtapan del Oro and Valle de Bravo SE of Zitácuaro.

VALLE DE BRAVO

(Km 86) A branch road, right, goes to the mountain resort of **Valle de Bravo**, a charming old town on the edge of an attractive artificial lake, with another Monarch butterfly wintering area nearby. This area gets the weekend crowd from Mexico City. (1 direct bus a day Zitácuaro-Valle de Bravo, US$3.30; 1st class bus to Toluca, US$3.50.)

● **Accommodation** *Loto Azul Resort*, Av Toluca, T 20157, F 22747, 4-star; *Centro Vacacional ISSEMYM*, central, pool, restaurant, satisfactory, Independencia 404; **B** *Los Arcos*, good, is several kilometres beyond, in pine woods, excellent restaurant; **C** *Refugio del*

Salto, Fontana Brava; **D** *Blanquita's*, opp church off main plaza, basic, fairly clean, OK; **D** *Mary*, main plaza, hot showers. A few cheap *posadas familiares* around the plaza, ask. Good, cheap food in the mercado. Restaurants on pier are expensive. **Trailer Park**: Av del Carmen 26, T (91726) 21972 (or Toluca 91721-21580), familia Otero, English spoken, 5 hook-ups, 7 dry camping, 3 rentals, small private grounds, English spoken, rec. **NB** Drivers with trailers must approach Avándaro from the Toluca end, no other way is safe because of the hills, narrow streets and town centre.

TOLUCA VOLCANO

(Km 75) A road branches off the road to Toluca to the volcano of Toluca (**Nevado de Toluca**, or Xinantécatl; 4,558m, the fourth highest mountain in Mexico) and climbs to the deep blue lakes of the Sun and the Moon in its two craters, at about 4,270m, from which there is a wide and awe-inspiring view. It is 27 km from the turning off the main road to the heart of the craters. During winter it is possible to ski on the slopes; 2 km from the entrance is an *albergue* with food and cooking facilities. From here it is 10 km to the entrance to the crater, where there is a smaller *albergue* (cooking facilities, food sold at weekends only, no bathroom or water, dirty), and then a further 6 km to the lakes. A short cut from the small *albergue* takes 20 mins to the crater (not possible to drive). At the third refuge (21 km from the turn-off) is an attendant. Trips to the volcano are very popular at weekends. You can stay overnight at any of the refuges (F), although they are sometimes closed during the week, and there is a restaurant, but the trip can be done in 1 day from Toluca. If walking remember the entrance to the crater is on the far left side of the volcano.

To reach the Toluca volcano take the first bus to Sultepec from Toluca at about 0700, every 2 hrs thereafter. Leave the bus where the road to the radio station branches off, just after Raices village (US$1), from there it is about 20 km to the crater, hitching fairly easy, especially at weekends. Aim to get to the crater by midday, otherwise clouds will cover everything. Visitors must leave by 1700.

TOLUCA

(Km 64; *Pop* 600,000; *State pop 1995* 11,704,934; *Alt* 2,639m; *Phone code* 721) **Toluca**, about 4¾ hrs from Morelia by bus, is the capital of the state of México. It is known mostly for its huge Fri market where Indians sell colourful woven baskets, *sarapes*, *rebozos*, pottery and embroidered goods (beware of pickpockets and handbag slashers). The new market is at Paseo Tollocan e Isidro Fabela, spreading over a number of streets, open daily. As well as for textiles, the city is famous for confectionery, *chorizos* (sausages) and for an orange liqueur known as *moscos*. It is also a centre of chemical industries which cause pollution.

Places of interest

The centre of the city is the **Plaza de los Mártires**, a very open space. On its S side is the **Cathedral**, begun in 1870, but not completed until 1978 (incorporated in its interior is the baroque façade of the 18th century church of the Tercera Orden). Also on the S side is the **Church of Veracruz**, which houses a black Christ; its interior is very attractive. On three sides of the block which contains these two churches are **Los Portales** (C Bravo, C Hidalgo and C Constitución), arcaded shops and restaurants. Northeast of Plaza de los Mártires is a park, Plaza Angel María Garibay, with trees and fountains, on which is the **Museo de Bellas Artes**, formerly the Convento del Carmen, with seven halls of paintings (from Colonial Baroque – 18th century – to 20th century) and temporary exhibitions. A tunnel is said to run from the ex-Convento to all the central churches. (Museum open Tues-Sun 1000-1800, students half price, booklet US$1.35.) Next door is the **Templo del Carmen**, a neoclassical church with a gold and white interior. Next to the Carmen is Plaza España. At the eastern end of Plaza

Garibay is the **Cosmovitral** and **Jardín Botánico** (open Tues-Sun 0900-1700, US$1.60). From 1933-1975 the building was the 16 de Septiembre market; in 1980 it was opened in its new form, a formal garden in honour of the Japanese Eizi

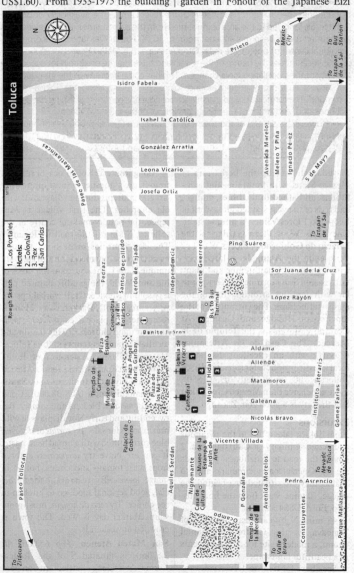

Valle de Toluca, ancient and modern

The southern section of the Valle de Toluca used to contain within its boundaries the lake and headwaters of the River Lerma. The availability of water, and fertile land, led to the area being settled from the earliest times: there is evidence of human presence in this area dating from 10,000 BC. It was later to become the regional centre of one of the main Otomi groups, the Matlazincas.

In recent times the nature of the terrain and therefore the predominant economic activity of the population have changed. This has come about with the introduction of large-scale industry in and around Toluca, particularly along the Toluca-Lerma 'corridor'. The former lake and marshlands are now dry; commercial fishing has all but disappeared, and much of the agriculture is now of the intensive variety.

However, in several of the towns in this area, traditional products continue to flourish, aided in some cases by modern technology, eg leather goods in San Mateo Atenco, pottery in Metepec, textiles in Santiago Tianguistenco.

Matuda, who set up the herbarium of Mexico State, with fountains and exhibitions, all bathed in the blues, oranges and reds of the vast stained glass work of Leopoldo Flores Valdez, a unique sight. One block W of Plaza Garibay is the **Palacio de Gobierno**. 4 blocks W of Los Portales is the **Alameda**, a large park with a statue of Cuauhtémoc and many tall trees; on Sun morning it is very popular with families strolling among the many stallholders. The entrance is at the junction of Hidalgo and Ocampo. At Ocampo y Morelos is the **Templo de la Merced**. The **Casa de las Artesanías** (Casart), with an excellent display of local artistic products for sale, is at Paseo Tollocan 700 (open daily 0930-1850), more expensive than Mexico City. 10 km S of the city is a good zoo, Zacango.

Excursions

From Toluca take a bus to the pyramids and Aztec seminary of **Calixtlahuaca**, 2 km off the road to Ixtlahuaca; pyramids are to Quetzalcoatl (circular) and to Tlaloc; they are situated just behind the village, 10 mins' walk from the final bus-stop. Entry US$4.35.

45 mins N by car, near the town of Temoaya, is the Centro Ceremonial Otomí, a modern site for cultural events in a beautiful landscape.

See above for trips to Toluca volcano.

Along Route 55 S of Toluca, or reached from it, are a number of most interesting 'art and craft' producing villages, all with old churches. The first village is **Metepec**, the pottery-making centre of the valley, 1½ km off the road to Tenango. The clay figurines made here, painted bright fuchsia, purple, green and gold, are unique. This is the source of the 'trees of life and death', the gaudily-painted pottery sold in Mexico. Craft workshops are very spread out. Market is on Mon. A recommended place to eat is *Las Cazuelitas*, near main church. Try the handmade tortillas. Interesting convent (bus Toluca-Metepec US$0.65). A detour E off Route 55 (or S from Route 15, the Toluca-Mexico City highway) goes to the town of **Santiago Tianguistenco** (*Pop* 38,000). Good *cazuelas*, *metates*, baskets and *sarapes*. Between July and early Nov displays of wild mushrooms for sale. Try *gordas* or *tlacoyos*, blue corn stuffed with a broad bean paste. If you are brave try *atepocates*; embryo frogs with tomato and chiles, boiled in maize leaves. Try restaurant *Mesón del Cid*, good regional food, go to kitchen to see choice. Try *sopa de hongos*, mushroom soup. Market day is Wed. The town is crowded at weekends.

San Mateo Atenco (*Pop* 65,000; *Alt* 2,570m), is situated S of the Toluca-Lerma 'corridor'. Settled in ancient times, it has featured in several important historical moments by virtue of occupying a bridge-head between lagoons: Axayácatl, Hernán Cortés and Hidalgo all passed this way. There is a Franciscan church and monastery, the earliest parts of which date from 1550. The town is famous for its shoes, and leather goods of all descriptions. Excellent bargains to be had. Market Fri and Sat. On 25 Oct St Crispin, patron saint of shoemakers, is honoured in the open chapel of the church in the presence of the local bishop.

Local information
● Accommodation
Holiday Inn, Carretera a México Km 57.5, T 164666, F 164099, restaurant, bar, parking; **C** *San Carlos*, Madero 210, T 49422; **D** *Colonial*, Hidalgo Ote 103, T 47066, with bath, clean, TV, cheap food (good restaurant, closed Sun), rec (bus from Terminal de Autobuses to Centro passes in front); **D** *Rex*, Matamoros Sur 101, T 50300, with bath, hot water, no restaurant. On Hidalgo Poniente: **C** *La Mansión*, No 408, T 565/8, with hot water, clean, garage, TV, no restaurant; **D** *Alameda*, No 508, with bath, hot water, TV, nice rooms, *El Patio* restaurant; **E** *Maya*, No 413, shared bath, hot water, clean, charming, towels extra. All the above are in the centre, not many cheap hotels. **D** *Terminal*, adjoining bus terminal, T 57960 (prices vary according to floor), restaurant next door.

Motels: A1 *Del Rey Inn*, T 122122, F 122567, Km 63, Mexico City road entrance (5-star), resort facilities; on same exit road, *Paseo*, T 65730 (4-star) and *Castel Plaza Las Fuentes*, Km 57.5, T 164666, F 164798 (5-star).

● Places to eat
Ostionería Escamilla, Rayón Nte 404, good fish; *San Francisco*, Villada 108; *Café L'Ambient*, Hidalgo 231 Pte, snacks, meals, quite simple, next door is *Son Jei*, oriental; opp, in Los Portales, is *Impala* for *comida corrida*, coffee; *Woolworth* restaurant, Hidalgo Pte casi Matamoros, is open Sun from 0930 for good set breakfasts; *Fonda Rosita* in Los Portales central avenue going through to Plaza de los Mártires, is also open Sun am, pleasant, Mexican; *Las Ramblas*, on Constitución side of Los Portales, Mexican food, average.

● Tourist offices
Lerdo de Tejada Pte 101, Edif Plaza Toluca, 1° p, T 50131, has a free *Atlas Turístico* of the state of México, inc street maps of all towns of interest; Federal office at Villada 123, T 48961.

● Transport
Bus station is some distance from the centre; inside, information is difficult to gather and all is confusion outside – look for a bus marked 'Centro', US$0.15; from centre to terminal buses go from, among other places Ignacio Rayón Nte e Hidalgo Ote, look for 'Terminal' on window (yellow or orange bus). To Mexico City, US$2.85, 1 hr. Bus to **Pátzcuaro**, 6 hrs, US$17.50, several daily; to **Taxco**, 4 buses a day, book in advance, 3 hrs, US$6 with Frontera, a spectacular journey. To **Morelia**, several buses daily with Herradura de Plata, 4 hrs, US$8.25, ETN US$14.80. Many buses to **Tenango de Arista** (US$0.65, 30 mins), **Tenancingo** (US$2.25); also regular buses to **Calixtlahuaca** US$2.50 (1 hr) from platform 7.

From Toluca to the coast at Ixtapa (Route 134, see page 355), via Tejupilco (**C** *Hotel Juárez*), Ciudad Altamirano and La Salitrera. the road is paved (deteriorating in parts), traffic is sparse and the landscape hilly and pleasant.

SOUTH TO TENANCINGO

Route 55 descends gradually to **Tenango de Arista**, 2 hotels with car park alongside main road (Toluca-Tenango bus, US$0.65), where one can walk (20 mins) to the ruins of **Teotenango** (Matlazinca culture, reminiscent of La Ciudadela at Teotihuacán, with five plazas, 10 structures, and one ball court). There is an interesting museum by the ruins of Teotenango; entry to museum and ruins US$4.35; to enter go to the end of town on the right hand side. If you ask the guard, you can pitch a tent at the museum inside the gate. 48 km from Toluca the road descends abruptly through gorges to **Tenancingo**, still at 1,830m, but with a soft, warm all-the-year-round climate. Half an hour by bus to the S (road unpaved) is the magnificent 18th century Carmelite convent of El Santo Desierto, where they make beautiful *rebozos*. The

Toluca to Taxco

townspeople themselves weave fine *rebozos* and the fruit wines are delicious and cheap. Overlooking this busy commercial town is a statue of Christ on a hill. The daily market area is 2 blocks from the bus terminal (continue 1 block, turn left for 2 further blocks to the main square); market day is on Sun (excellent local cheese).

● **Accommodation** Recommended hotels at Tenancingo are **D** *Lazo*, Guadalupe Victoria 100, T 20083 (1½ blocks straight on from market, away from bus terminal), with clean rooms in annex with shower, leafy courtyard, *El Arbol de la Vida* restaurant; **D** *María Isabel*, clean, well-lit; **E** *Hotel Jardín*, on main plaza, T 20108, with bath, big, airy rooms, restaurant, good value. Good bakery in private house at Guillermo Prieto 302.

● **Transport** Frequent buses to Toluca, US$2.25 with Tres Estrellas del Centro, 1 hr; also to Ixtapan de la Sal, Taxco, Malinalco, US$1.50, and Chalma.

IXTAPAN DE LA SAL

On 32 km from Tenancingo, on Route 55, is **Ixtapan de la Sal**, a pleasant forest-surrounded leisure resort with medicinal hot springs. In the centre of this quiet whitewashed town is the municipal spa, adult admission US$1.60. The municipal spa's hours are 0700-1800, it is not always open. At the edge of town is Parque Los Trece Lagos. Private baths charge US$6 for admission only, everything else is extra. For the hedonist there are private 'Roman' baths, for the stiff-limbed a medicinal hotwater pool, mud baths for the vain, an Olympic pool for swimmers, rowing boats and a water slide for the adventurous. The latter is 150m long (prohibited to those over 40; US$1.55 entry, US$0.90 for 2 slides, US$2.20 for slides all day, free midweek 1200-1400). 'The Thirteen Lake Park' is privately run and has a train running around; there are numerous picnic spots. Market day: Sun. Fiesta: second Fri in Lent.

Ixtapan de la Sal can be reached in 2 hrs or so by car from Mexico City: turn off Route 15, the Toluca highway, at La Marquesa (see below), go through Santiago Tianguistenco and join Route 55 at Tenango. The road goes on to the Grutas de Cacahuamilpa (see page 339) from where you can continue either to Cuernavaca or Taxco. Bus to/from Mexico City 3 hrs, US$5.35, every 30 mins from Terminal Oriente; to Toluca every 30 mins, US$4.20, 2 hrs. Also to Taxco, Coatepec, Cuernavaca.

● **Accommodation A1** *Ixtapan*, Nuevo Ixtapan, T 30304, inc food and entertainment; **A1** *Vista Hermosa*, T 30092, next door, full board only, good, friendly; **A3** *Kiss* (*Villa Vergel*), Blvd San Román y Av Juárez, T 30349, F 30842; **B** *Casablanca*, Juárez 615, T 30241, F 30842; **C** *María Isabel*, T 30122, good; **D** *Guadalajara*, with bath; **D** *Casa de Huéspedes Margarita*, Juárez, clean, rec; **E** *Casa Guille*, C José María Morelos, with bath, clean; **E** *Casa Yuyi*, with bath, clean, good; many others.

● **Places to eat** Plenty of reasonable restaurants on Av Benito Juárez, most close by 1900. Good value is *Fonda Jardín* on Zócalo.

MALINALCO

About 11 km E of Tenancingo is **Malinalco**, from which a path winds up 1 km, 20 mins, to Malinalco ruins (1188, Matlazinca culture, with Aztec additions), certainly one of the most remarkable pre-Hispanic ruins in Mexico, now partly excavated. Here is a fantastic rock-cut temple in the side of a mountain which conceals in its interior sculptures of eagle and jaguar effigies. Apparently you can feel movement in the rock if you lie on it or lean against it. The staircase leading to the temple has over 430 steps. The site is very small, but in a commanding position over the valley, and now overlooking the town and the wooded hills all around (open Tues-Sun 1000-1630, US$4.35, Sun free). The site is visible from the town as a ledge on the hillside; the walk up passes a tiny, blue colonial chapel. For an even better view of the ruins carry straight on where the path leading to the ruins branches off to the right. This old road is cobbled in places and rises up the mountainside pretty steeply, arriving (after about 1½ hrs walk) at a small shrine with two crosses. It is possible to camp here but there is no water. Breathtaking views can be seen from here off both sides of the ridge. The trail then carries on gently down the other side, past avocado trees, for 20 mins, to the paved road to Tenancingo, almost opposite a new brick house with arches. It is possible to catch a bus back over the mountains to Malinalco. It would also be much quicker and easier (downhill walk mostly) to do this whole hike in reverse; catch the bus out (ask for the old road) and walk back.

You should not fail to visit also the Augustinian **Templo y Exconvento del Divino Salvador** (1552), in the centre of town, the nave of which has a patterned ceiling, while the 2-storey cloisters are painted with elaborate, early frescoes. Just below the main square in front of the convent is the market (market day Wed).

You can also get to Malinalco from Toluca, or Mexico City, by taking a 2nd class bus to **Chalma**. This is a popular pilgrimage spot, and when you get off the bus you will be offered (for sale) a corona of flowers. From the bus lot, walk up hill, past the market stalls, to the crossroads where blue colectivos leave for Malinalco until 2000 (10 km, 20 mins, US$1).

Local festivals

There is a *fiesta* in Malinalco on 6 January.

Local information

● Accommodation

E *Hotel Santa Mónica*, Hidalgo 109, with bath, pretty courtyard, good value; **E** *Posada Familiar*, cabins for families at N edge of town; camping and trailer park *El Paraíso* opp the small blue chapel (not well named: "no more than a parking lot with one dirty toilet").

● Places to eat

La Playa on road to ruins, just off square, with garden, nice place; opp is *La Salamandra*, good value; trout farm and fishery has a restaurant, superb, bring own supplies of beverages, bread, salad (trout costs US$5-6); also *El Rincón del Convento*, behind the convent on road to square.

● Transport

A direct road runs from Tenancingo to Malinalco, paved to the summit of a range of hills, poor at the summit, then graded to the junction with the Malinalco-San Pedro Zictepec road; pick-up truck or buses run on this direct road

hourly, 40 mins, US$2.25 (in Malinalco bus leaves from corner of Av Progreso and the square). From Toluca you can go to Malinalco by leaving the Toluca-Tenancingo road after San Pedro Zictepec, some 12 km N of Tenancingo, which is paved and 28 km long. Terminal in Mexico City, Central del Pte, opp Observatorio, at least two companies go there. Buses to Chalma from Mexico City leave frequently from Central del Pte, 2 hrs, US$3.60 direct. This is also where you make connections if coming from Cuernavaca (take a Cuernavaca-Toluca bus to Santa Marta, then wait for a Mexico City or Toluca-Chalma bus).

TOLUCA TO MEXICO CITY

The basin of Toluca, the highest in the central region, is the first of a series of basins drained by the Río Lerma into the Pacific. To reach Mexico City from Toluca, 64 km by dual carriageway, it is necessary to climb over the intervening mountain range. The centre of the basin is swampy. (Km 50) Lerma is on the edge of the swamp, the source of the Lerma River. The road climbs, with backward views of the snow-capped Toluca volcano, to the summit at Las Cruces (Km 32; 3,035m). At this point is the **Parque Nacional Miguel Hidalgo**, or **La Marquesa**, which has many facilities for weekend recreation (lakes with watersports, hiking, running, picnics etc). Here also is the turn-off for Chalma and Santiago Tianguistenco from Route 15. There are occasional great panoramic views of the City and the Valley of México during the descent (smog-permitting).

Mexico City

MEXICO CITY, the capital (*Alt* 2,240m), founded by the Spaniards in 1521, was built upon the remains of Tenochtitlan, the Aztec capital, covering some 200 sq km. The Valley of México, the intermont basin in which it lies, is about 110 km long by 30 km wide. Rimming this valley is a sentinel-like chain of peaks of the Sierra Nevada mountains. Towards the SE tower two tall volcanoes, named for the warrior Popocatépetl and his beloved Ixtaccíhuatl (see page 296). Both are permanently snow-capped, but they are often not visible because of the smog. To the S the crest of the Cordillera is capped by the wooded volcano of Ajusco.

About 20 million people (one in four of the total population) live in this city, which has over half the country's manufacturing employment, and much of the nation's industrial smog (the worst months being Dec to Feb). Measures such as closing the huge Pemex refinery have reduced lead and sulphur dioxide emissions to acceptable levels, but the ozone level is occasionally dangerous. Common ailments are a burning sensation in the eyes (contact-lens wearers take note) and nose and a sore throat. Citizens are advised by the local authorities not to smoke and not to take outdoor exercise. The English-language daily, *The News*, gives analysis of the air quality, with warnings and advice.

The city suffers from a fever of demolition and rebuilding, especially since the heavy damage caused by the Sept 1985 earthquake. This was concentrated along the Paseo de la Reforma, Av Juárez, the Alameda, and various suburbs and residential districts. About 20,000 people are believed to have lost their lives, largely in multi-storey housing and government-controlled buildings, including Juárez hospital in which there were about 3,000 fatalities.

Mexico City has long burst its ancient boundaries and spread; some of the new residential suburbs are most imaginatively planned, though there are many appalling shanty-towns. Like all big centres it is faced with a fearsome traffic problem, despite the building of inner and outer ring roads (the Circuito Interior and the Periférico). Nine metro lines now operate, plus the *tren ligero* in the S and the *tren férreo* in the E. There is a large traffic-free area E of the Zócalo.

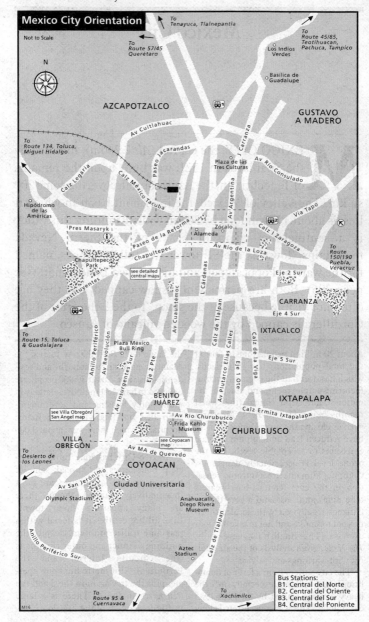

Mexico City Orientation

Not to Scale

N

To Tenayuca, Tlalnepantla

To Route 57/45 Querétaro

Los Indios Verdes

To Route 45/85, Teotihuacan, Pachuca, Tampico

Basílica de Guadalupe

AZCAPOTZALCO

GUSTAVO A MADERO

Av Cuitlahuac

Paseo Jacarandas

Carranza

Calz Legaria

To Route 134, Toluca, Miguel Hidalgo

Calz México Tacuba

Plaza de las Tres Culturas

Av Río Consulado

Av Argentina

Hipódromo de las Américas

Vía Tapo

Pres Masaryk

Paseo de la Reforma

Zócalo

Alameda

Calz I Zaragoza

Chapultepec

Av Río de la Loza

To Route 150/190 Puebla, Veracruz

Chapultepec Park

see detailed central maps

Eje 2 Sur

Av Constituyentes

L Cárdenas

CARRANZA

Eje 4 Sur

Av Cuauhtémoc

Calz de Tlalpan

IXTACALCO

Anillo Periférico

Av Revolución

Plaza México Bull Ring

Av Plutarco Elías Calles

Eje 1 Ote

Calz de la Viga

Eje 5 Sur

To Route 15, Toluca & Guadalajara

Eje 2 Pte

Av Insurgentes Sur

IXTAPALAPA

BENITO JUÁREZ

Calz Ermita Ixtapalapa

see Villa Obregón/ San Angel map

Av Río Churubusco

Frida Kahlo Museum

CHURUBUSCO

VILLA OBREGÓN

see Coyoacan map

Av MA de Quevedo

To Desierto de los Leones

COYOACAN

Av San Jerónimo

Ciudad Universitaria

Olympic Stadium

Anahuacalli, Diego Rivera Museum

Anillo Periférico Sur

Calz de Tlalpan

Aztec Stadium

To Route 95 & Cuernavaca

To Xochimilco

M16

Bus Stations:
B1. Central del Norte
B2. Central del Oriente
B3. Central del Sur
B4. Central del Poniente

Climate

Because of the altitude the climate is mild and exhilarating save for a few days in mid-winter. The normal annual rainfall is 660 mm, and most of it falls – usually in the late afternoon – between May and October. Even in summer the temperature at night is rarely above 13°C, and in winter there can be sharp frosts. Despite this, central heating is not common.

PLACES OF INTEREST

Sightseeing in and around the city can easily take up 10 days. The main places of interest are listed below.

You will find, as you explore the city, that you use two thoroughfares more than any others. The most famous is Paseo de la Reforma, with a tree-shaded, wide centre section and two side lanes; it runs somewhat diagonally NE from the Bosque de Chapultepec. At the Plaza de la Reforma it bends eastwards and becomes Av Juárez, still fairly wide but without side lanes. Beyond the Palacio de Bellas Artes this becomes Av Madero, quite narrow, with one-way traffic. The other and longer thoroughfare is Av Insurgentes, a diagonal NS artery about 25 km long. Reforma and Insurgentes bisect at a *plazuela* with a statue of Cuauhtémoc, the last of the Aztec emperors. Much of the **Centro Histórico** has been refurbished; this is roughly a rectangle from Alhóndiga/Santísma, E of the Zócalo, to Guerrero, W of the Alameda; República de Honduras N of the Alameda to Arcos de Belén/Izazaga S of the Alameda and Zócala. Calle Tacuba is especially fine; street vendors have been banished from it. The *Guía Peatonal* of Sacbe (US$1.15) is recommended, giving eight suggested walking routes, all starting from metro stations. Two ways of familiarizing oneself quickly with the Centro Histórico are to take a trip (US$5 for 45 mins) on a 1910-type street car (every 30 mins from the Museo de la Ciudad de México, Pino Suárez, or from in front of the Palacio de

Bellas Artes), or to ride on a form of rickshaw (bici-taxi) from the Zocalo, US$1.65 for 30 mins.

Mexico's 'West End', the **Zona Rosa** (Pink Zone), used to be where most of the fashionable shops were found; it is bounded by the Paseo de la Reforma, Av Chapultepec, C Florencia and Av Insurgentes Sur. It has been replaced by **Polanco**, N of Chapultepec, a luxury residential area with many interesting art galleries and shops. It does not suffer from the tourists that crowd the Zona Rosa and other chic areas. Many old houses have carved stone façades, tiled roofs, gardens, especially on C Horacio, a pretty street lined with trees and parks. The Secretaría de Turismo Offices are on Av Presidente Masaryk at the corner of Hegel.

HISTORICAL CENTRE

The Zócalo

The great main square, or Plaza Mayor, centre of the oldest part, restricted wheeled traffic 1000-1700 Mon-Fri, is always alive with people, and often vivid with official ceremonies and celebrations. The flag in the centre of the square is raised at 0600 (0500 in winter) and taken down, with ceremony, at 1800 each day (1700 in winter). On the N side, on the site of the Great Teocalli or temple of the Aztecs, is the cathedral.

The Cathedral

The largest and oldest cathedral in Latin America, designed by Herrera, the architect of the Escorial in Spain, along with that in Puebla; first built 1525; rebuilding began 1573; consecrated 1667; finished 1813. Singularly harmonious, considering the many architects employed and time taken to build it. Restoration work on the exterior has been completed; work continues inside. The Cathedral has been subject to subsidence over many years and a lengthy programme of work is under way to build new foundations. Meanwhile, the weight of much of the building is being supported by massive scaffolding inside

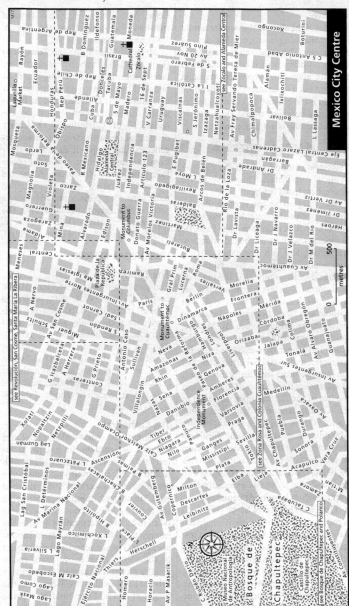

Mexico City Centre

the Cathedral. A plumb line hanging from the cupola and a notice board by the W entrance give some idea of the extent of the problem. There is an underground crypt reached by stairs in the W wing of the main part of the building (closed for restoration since 1993). Next to the Cathedral is the **Sagrario Metropolitano**, 1769, with fine churrigueresque façade. To the side of the Cathedral are the Aztec ruins of the **Templo Mayor** or *Teocalli*, which were found in 1978 when public works were being carried out. They make a very worthwhile visit, especially since the Aztecs built a new temple every 52 years, and seven have been identified on top of each other. A **Museum** (**Museo Arqueológico del Sitio**) was opened in 1987 behind the temple, to house various sculptures found in the main pyramid of Tenochtitlán and six others, including the huge, circular monolith representing the dismembered body of Coyolxauhqui, who was killed by her brother Huitzilopochtli, the Aztec tutelary god, and many other objects. The Templo Mayor and museum are at Seminario 4 y Guatemala, entrance in the corner of the Zócalo, open 0900-1730 daily except Mon, last tickets at 1700, there is a café, bookshop and left luggage office; entry to museum and temple US$5, free Sun, US$1.75 to take photos, US$3.45 to use video camera; guided tours in Spanish Tues-Fri 0930-1800, Sat 0930-1300, in English Tues-Sat 1000 and 1200, US$0.85 pp (sometimes cancelled at short notice). There are TV displays in the halls, with English subtitles.

On C Maestro Justo Sierra, N of Cathedral (between C Guatemala and C San Ildefonso – see map) is the **Mexican Geographical Society** (No 19), in whose courtyard is a bust of Humboldt and a statue of Benito Juárez, plus a display of documents and maps (ask at the door to be shown in); opposite are the **Anfiteatro Simón Bolívar**, with murals of his life in the lobby and an attractive theatre, and the **Colegio San Ildefonso**, open Mon-Sun 1100-1800, except Wed 1100-2100.

On the W side of the Zócalo are the Portales de los Mercaderes (Arcades of the Merchants), very busy since 1524. North of them, opposite the Cathedral, is: the **Monte de Piedad** (National Pawnshop) established in the 18th century and housed in a 16th century building. Prices are government controlled and bargains are often found. Auctions are held each Fri at 1000 (1st, 2nd and 3rd Fri for jewellery and watches, 4th for everything else), US dollars accepted.

The Palacio Nacional

The National Palace takes up the whole eastern side of the Zócalo. Built on the site of the Palace of Moctezuma and rebuilt in 1692 in colonial baroque, with its exterior faced in the red volcanic stone called *tezontle*; the top floor was added by President Calles in the 1920s. It houses various government departments and the Juárez museum (open Mon-Fri, 1000-1800, ID needed), free. Over the central door hangs the Liberty Bell, rung at 2300 on 15 Sept by the President, who gives the multitude the *Grito* – '¡Viva México!' The thronged frescoes around the staircase are by Diego Rivera (including *The History of Mexico*). Open daily; guides: ask them for the US$2 booklet on the frescoes. In the C Moneda and adjoining the back of the Palace is the **Museo de las Culturas**, with interesting international archaeological and historical exhibits. Open 0930-1800; closed Sun, you have to show your passport at the entrance. Also in Moneda are the site of the first university in the New World (building now dilapidated), the Palacio del Arzobispado, and the site of the New World's first printing press.

Ex-Palacio Arzobispal, on the corner of Moneda and Licenciado Verdad. The Archbishop's palace until 1861 (foundations laid 1521, subject to flood and earthquake damage, major reconstruction in late 18th century), now owned by the Finance Ministry, it was restored and opened to the public in 1994. Open 1000-1700 (closed Mon), US$1.15 (Sun free).

Zona Rosa & Colonia Cuauhtemoc

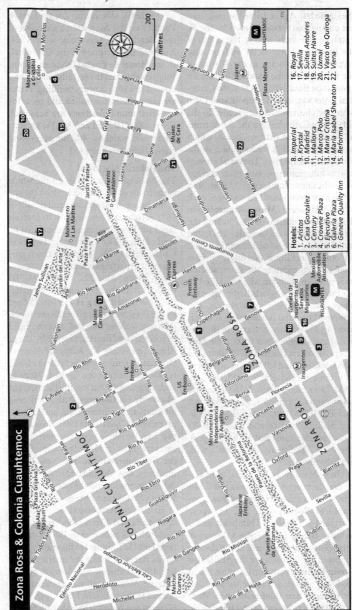

N

metres

0   200

Hotels:
1. Aristos
2. Casa González
3. Casa Gonzáles
4. Crowne Plaza
5. Ejecutivo
6. Galería Plaza
7. Geneve Quality Inn

8. Imperial
9. Krystal
10. Madrid
11. Mallorca
12. Marco Polo
13. María Cristina
14. María Isabel Sheraton
15. Reforma

16. Royal
17. Sevilla
18. Suites Amberes
19. Suites Havre
20. Uxmal
21. Vasco de Quiroga
22. Viena

Museo de Artes e Industrias Populares de México, Av Juárez 44, was closed in 1996. The building was originally the church of the Corpus Christi convent, built between 1720-24. Since 1867, the church has been used variously as a warehouse, a Protestant church, a museum of hygiene and, from 1951, by the Instituto Nacional Indigenista (INI). The area in which it stands was badly affected by the 1985 earthquake and is scheduled for redevelopment.

Suprema Corte de Justicia de la Nación, opposite Palacio Nacional, on SE corner of the Zócalo, see frescoes by Orozco. Closes at 1400.

Palacio de Bellas Artes

The Palacio was refurbished, inside and out, in 1994 to celebrate its diamond jubilee; the garden in front of the marble apron has been laid out as originally designed. A large, showy building, interesting for Art Deco lovers (see the fabulous stained glass skylight in the roof), houses a museum and a theatre, and a *cafetería* at mezzanine level (light, average continental food at moderate prices), and an excellent bookshop on the arts. Its domes are lavishly decorated with coloured stone. The museum has old and contemporary paintings, prints, sculptures, and handicraft articles. The fresco by Rivera is a copy of the one rubbed out in disapproval at Radio City, New York, and there are spirited Riveras in the room of oils and water-colours. Other frescoes are by Orozco, Tamayo and Siqueiros.

Daily, 1000-1730; Sun, 1000-1330, US$1.25. The most remarkable thing about the theatre is its glass curtain designed by Tiffany. It is solemnly raised and lowered before each performance of the Ballet Folclórico de México. The Palacio is listing badly, for it has sunk 4m since it was built. Operas are performed; there are orchestral concerts and performances by the Ballet Folclórico de México on Sun, 0930 and 2100, Wed at 2100 (check press for details), you must book in advance. Tickets US$12 on the balcony, US$20 and US$25 (cheap balcony seats are not recommended because you see only a third of the stage set, although you can see the performers). Tickets on sale from 1100; hotels, agencies etc only sell the most expensive, cheaper tickets only at the theatre. Cheap concerts at 1200 on Sun, and also at Teatro Hidalgo, behind Bellas Artes on Hidalgo, at the same time, book in advance. Student reductions are given for some shows.

The Alameda

Across the road is **Torre Latinoamericana**; on the 44th floor is a viewing platform with telescopes, open 0900-2300, US$3 to go up. (The cafetería is poor, but try the Coca Cola with lemon ice-cream.) This great glass tower dominates the gardens of the **Alameda Central**, once the Aztec market and later the place of execution for the Spanish Inquisition. Beneath the broken shade of eucalyptus, cypress and ragged palms, wide paths link fountains and heroic statues. The park is

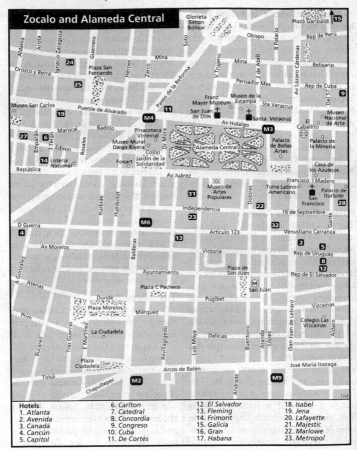

Zocalo and Alameda Central

Hotels:

1. *Atlanta*	6. *Carlton*	12. *El Salvador*	18. *Isabel*
2. *Avenida*	7. *Catedral*	13. *Fleming*	19. *Jena*
3. *Canadá*	8. *Concordia*	14. *Frimont*	20. *Lafayette*
4. *Cancún*	9. *Congreso*	15. *Galicia*	21. *Majestic*
5. *Capitol*	10. *Cuba*	16. *Gran*	22. *Marlowe*
	11. *De Cortés*	17. *Habana*	23. *Metropol*

illuminated at night. (Much rebuilding going on in this area.)

On the northern side of the Alameda, on Av Hidalgo, is the Jardín Morelos, flanked by two old churches: Santa Veracruz (1730) to the right and **San Juan de Dios** to the left. The latter has a richly carved baroque exterior; its image of San Antonio de Padua is visited by those who are broken-hearted for love. The **Franz Mayer** museum is located next to this church, in the former Hospital de San Juan de Dios, which was built in the 17th century. Recently rebuilt and exquisitely restored, it houses an important decorative arts collection (ceramics, glass, silver, time-pieces, furniture and textiles, as well as Mexican and European paintings from the 16th-20th centuries) and a library. Its cloister, with a pleasant cafeteria, is an oasis of peace in the heart of the city. Open 1000-1700 except Mon; admission US$1.15 (US$0.30 if only visiting the cloister).

On the same side of Hidalgo, next to the Franz Mayer, is the **Museo de la Estampa**

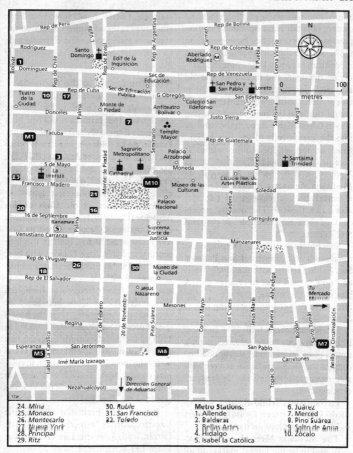

Escuela Nacional Preparatoria, N of Zócalo at Justo Sierra 27 (the street parallel to, and between, Guatemala and San Ildefonso), built 1749 as the Jesuit School of San Ildefonso in splendid baroque. There are some frescoes by Orozco and, in the Anfiteatro Bolívar, frescoes by Diego Rivera and Fernando Leal, all of which are in excellent condition. There are other Leal murals in the stairwell separating the two floors of Orozco works. The whole interior has been magnificently restored. Occasional grand exhibitions.

Secretaría de Educación Pública, on Argentina 28, three blocks from Zócalo, built 1922, contains frescoes by a number of painters. Here are Diego Rivera's masterpieces, painted between 1923 and 1930, illustrating the lives and sufferings of the common people, open daily, 1000-1800, free entry.

Plaza Santo Domingo, two blocks N of the Cathedral, an intimate little plaza surrounded by fine colonial buildings: (a) the Antigua Aduana (former customs house); (b) on the W side, the Portales de

Santo Domingo, where public scribes and owners of small hand-operated printing presses still carry on their business; (c) on the N side, the church of Santo Domingo, in Mexican baroque, 1737 – note the carving on the doors and façade; (d) the old Edif de la Inquisición, where the tribunals of the Inqusition were held (by standing on tiptoe in the men's room one can see – if tall enough – through the window into the prison cells of the Inquisition, which are not yet open to the public). It became the Escuela Nacional de la Medicina and is now the **Museo de la Medicina Mexicana**(Brasil 33). There is a remarkable staircase in the patio; it also has a theatre. The nearby streets contain some fine examples of colonial architecture.

Two blocks E of Santo Domingo are the church and convent of **San Pedro y San Pablo** (1603), both massively built and now turned over to secular use. A block N is the public market of Abelardo L Rodríguez, with striking mural decorations.

Church of Loreto, built 1816 and now tilting badly, but being restored, is on a square of the same name, surrounded by colonial buildings. Its façade is a remarkable example of 'primitive' or 'radical' neoclassicism.

La Santísima Trinidad (1677, remodelled 1755), to be seen for its fine towers and the rich carvings on its façade.

The Mercado Merced (metro Merced), said to be the largest market in all the Americas, dating back over 400 years. Its activities spread over several blocks and is well worth a visit. In the northern quarter of this market are the ruins of La Merced monastery; the fine 18th century patio is almost all that survives; the courtyard, on Av Uruguay, between C Talavera and C Jesús María, opposite No 171, is nearly restored.

The oldest hospital in continental America, **Jesús Nazareno**, 20 de Noviembre 82, founded 1526 by Cortés, was remodelled in 1928, save for the patio and staircase. Cortés' bones have been kept since 1794 in the adjoining church, on the corner of Pino Suárez and República de El Salvador, diagonally opposite the Museo de la Ciudad.

From the Zócalo to the Alameda

Avenida Madero leads from the Zócalo W to the Alameda. On it is **La Profesa** church, late 16th century, with a fine high altar and a leaning tower. The 18th century **Palacio de Iturbide**, Av Madero 17, once the home of Emperor Agustín (1821-23), has been restored and has a clear plastic roof. Wander around, it is now a bank head office. To the tourist the great sight of Av Madero, however, is the **Casa de los Azulejos** (House of Tiles) at the Alameda end of the street. Now occupied by *Sanborn's Restaurant*, it was built in the 16th century, and is brilliantly faced with blue and white Puebla tiles. The staircase walls are covered with Orozco frescoes. (There are more Orozco frescoes at Biblioteca Iberoamericana on Cuba between 5 de Febrero and Argentina.) Over the way is the **Church of San Francisco**, founded in 1525 by the 'Apostles of Mexico', the first 12 Franciscans to reach the country. It was by far the most important church in colonial days. Cortés' body rested here for some time, as did Iturbide's; the Viceroys attended the church.

Beyond San Francisco church, Eje Lázaro Cárdenas, formerly C San Juan de Letrán, leads S towards **Las Vizcaínas**, at Plaza Las Vizcaínas, 1 block E, built in 1734 as a school for girls; some of it is still so used, but some of it has become slum tenements. In spite of neglect, it is still the best example of colonial secular baroque in the city. Not open to the public; permission to visit sometimes given.

Museo San Carlos, Puente de Alvarado 50 (metro Revolución), a 19th century palace (open to visitors 1000 to 1700, closed Mon), has fine Mexican colonial painting and a first-class collection of European paintings. It is the former home of Señora Calderón de la Barca who wrote *Life in Mexico* while living there. The **Escuela Nacional de Artes Plásticas** at the corner of Academía and C Moneda, houses about 50 modern Mexican paintings. There is another picture gallery housing a collection of colonial paintings (16th-18th century), the **Pinacoteca Virreinal**, in the former church of San Diego in C Dr Mora, at the W end of the Alameda, opens at 0900, interesting. (Cheap concerts on Thur at 2000.)

Moving eastwards along Av Hidalgo, before the Palace of Fine Arts, on the right is the **Post Office**, built 1904. The postal museum (open Mon-Fri 0900-1800, Sat 1000-1400, free) on the first floor is well worth a visit: exhibits from mid-18th century.

Plaza Santiago de Tlatelolco

North from the W side of the Post Office leads to the C Santa María la Redonda, at the end of which is **Plaza Santiago de Tlaltelolco**, next oldest Plaza to the Zócalo, heavily damaged in the 1985 earthquake. Here was the main market of the Aztecs, and on it, in 1524, the Franciscans built a huge church and convent. This is now the **Plaza de las Tres Culturas** (Aztec, colonial and modern): (a) the Aztec ruins have been restored; (b) the magnificent baroque church of Santiago Tlaltelolco is now the focus of (c) the massive, multi-storey Nonoalco-Tlatelolco housing scheme, a garden city within a city, with pedestrian and wheeled traffic entirely separate. In Oct 1968, the Plaza de las Tres Culturas was the scene of serious distubances between the authorities and students, in which a large number of students were killed (see *The Other Mexico* by Octavio Paz, or *La Noche de Tlatelolco* by Elena Poniatowska, Biblioteca Era, 1971, and the very readable, and startling, *68* by Paco Ignacio Taibo II, 1991, in Spanish).

Plaza Garibaldi

About 4 blocks N of the Post Office off Eje Lázaro Cárdenas is **Plaza Garibaldi**, a must, especially on Fri and Sat night, when up to 200 *mariachis* in their traditional costume of huge sombrero, tight silver-embroidered trousers, pistol and *sarape*, will play your favourite Mexican serenade for US$5 (for a bad one) to 10 (for a good one). If you arrive by taxi you will be besieged. The whole square throbs with life and the packed bars are cheerful, though there is some danger from thieves and pickpockets, particularly after dark. The Lagunilla market is held about 4 blocks NE of the plaza, a hive of activity all week. On one side of Plaza Garibaldi is a gigantic eating hall, different stalls sell different courses, very entertaining.

Palacio de Minería, C Tacuba 9 (1797), is a fine old building, now restored, and once more level on its foundations. From 1910 to 1954 it was the Escuela Nacional de Ingeniería; here is a permanent exhibition of meteorites found all over Mexico (up to 14 tonnes). Free. (Cheap concerts on Sun at 1700, upstairs.) Moved from the Plaza de la Reforma to Plaza Manuel Tolsá opposite the Palacio is the great equestrian statue, 'El Caballito', of King Charles IV cast in 1802; it weighs 26 tons and is the second-largest bronze casting in the world.

Museo Nacional de Arte, Tacuba 8, opposite Palacio de Minería, near main Post Office. Open Tues-Sun, 1000-1730. Built in 1904, designed by the Italian architect, Silvio Contri, as the Palacio de Comunicaciones. The building has magnificent staircases made by the Florentine firm Pignone. It houses a large collection of Mexican paintings, drawings, sculptures and ceramics dating from the 16th century to 1950. It has the largest number of paintings (more than 100) by José María Velasco in Mexico City, as well as works by Miguel Cabrera, Gerardo Murillo, Rivera, Orozco, Siqueiros, Tamayo and Anguiano. Bookshop; entry US$3.35.

Along the S side of the Alameda, running E, is Av Juárez, a fine street with a mixture of old and new buildings. Diego Rivera's huge (15m by 4.80m) and fascinating mural, the 'Sueño de una tarde dominical en la Alameda Central', was

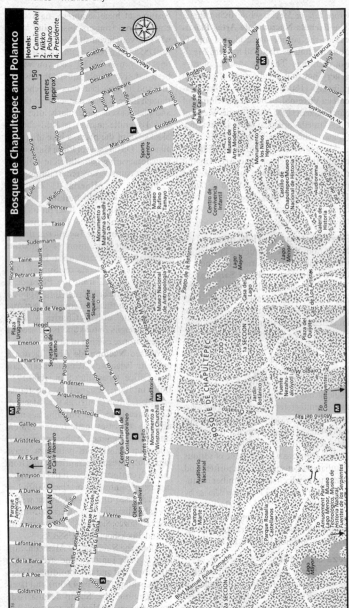

Bosque de Chapultepec and Polanco

Hotels:
1. Camino Real
2. Nikko
3. Polanco
4. Presidente

N

0   150
metres
(approx)

Darwin
Goethe
Milton
Descartes
Curie
Camila Shakespeare
Poe
Kant
Leibnitz
Victor Hugo
Dante
Escobedo
Mariano

Río Elba
Rodano
Fuente de las
Diana Cazadora

Secretaría
de Salud

Chapultepec
Liefa
Puebla

Av Melchor Ocampo

Av Veracruz
Av M Ángel
Zamora

Sports
Centre

Museo de
Arte Moderno
Monumento
a los Niños
Héroes

Av Vasconcelos

Gutenburg
Euler
Walton
Spencer
Tasso
Sudermann
Taine
Petrarca
Schiller
Horacio
Copérnico

Monumento a
Mahatma Gandhi

Museo
Rufino
Tamayo

Centro de
Convivencia
Infantil

Castillo de
Chapultepec/Museo
Nacional de Historia
Audiorama

Galería de
Historia

Av Presidente Masarik
Rubén Darío
Museo Nacional
de Antropología

Paseo de la Reforma

Lago
Mayor
Lago
Menor

Sala de Arte
Siqueiros
Lope de Vega
Hegel
Emerson
Lamartine

Calzada M Gandhi

Casa del
Lago

1a SECCIÓN

Plaza del
Quiote

Plaza de los Artistas

Plaza
Uruguay

Secretaría de
Turismo
Eliseos
Polanco
Andersen
Arquimedes

Auditorio

ZOO

Fuente
Nezahu-
alcoyotl

Código Mijilla

Tres Picos
Goldsmith

Temistocles

Centro Cultural de
Arte Contemporáneo

Andrés Bello

Monumento
Winston Churchill

Jardín
Botánico

Cruz G Nuevo

To Constitución

Molino del Rey

Polanco
Galileo
Aristóteles
Av E Sue
Tennyson
A Dumas
Musset
A France
Lafontaine
C de la Barca
E A Poe
Goldsmith

Newton

1 block North
to Calle Homero

O POLANCO

W Wylde
Virgilio

Obelisco a
Simón Bolívar

J Verne

Emilio Castelar

Parque Lincoln
Luis G Urbina

Dickens

BOSQUE DE CHAPULTEPEC

Parque
América

Parque Rosalia
Castellanos

Parque
Castellanos

Auditorio
Nacional

Campo
Marte

Blvd Manuel Ávila Camacho

2a SECCIÓN

Lago Mayor

To
Amusement Park
Lago Menor, Museo de
Tecnología, Museo de
Historia Natural,
Fuentes de los Serpientes

removed from the earthquake-damaged Hotel del Prado and now occupies its own purpose-built museum, the highly recommended **Museo Mural Diego Rivera**, on the N side of the Parque de la Solidaridad at Colón y Balderas; open Tues-Sun 1000-1800, US$1, free for students with ISIC card. A stroll down C Dolores, a busy and fascinating street, leads to the market of San Juan. The colonial church of Corpus Christi, on Av Juárez, is now used to display and sell folk arts and crafts. The avenue ends at the small Plaza de la Reforma. At the corner of Juárez and Reforma is the Lotería Nacional building. Drawings are held three times a week, at 2000: an interesting scene, open to the public. Beyond Plaza de la Reforma is the **Monumento a la Revolución**: a great copper dome, soaring above supporting columns set on the largest triumphal arches in the world. Beneath the monument is the **Museo Nacional de la Revolución**, dealing with the period 1867-1917, very interesting, lots of exhibits, videos (open Tues-Sun, 1000-1700, US$0.60).

South of this area, on Plaza Ciudadela, is a large colonial building, **La Ciudadela**, dating from 1700. It has been used for all kinds of purposes but is now a library.

The wide and handsome Paseo de la Reforma, 3 km long, continues to the Bosque de Chapultepec: shops, offices, hotels, restaurants all the way. Along it are monuments to Columbus; to Cuauhtémoc and a 45m marble column to Independence, topped by the golden-winged figure of a woman, 'El Angelito' to the Mexicans. Just before entering the park is the Salubridad (Health) Building. Rivera's frescoes in this building cannot be seen by the public, who can view only the stained-glass windows on the staircases.

Bosque de Chapultepec

The Park at the end of Paseo de la Reforma, with its thousands of ahuehuete trees, is beautiful and is now being kept litter-free and well policed (park closes at 1700). The best day to visit is Sun when it is all much more colourful. It is divided into three sections: the first, the easternmost, was a wood inhabited by the Toltecs and Aztecs; the second section, W of Blvd Manuel Avila Camacho, was added in 1964, and the third in 1974. The first section contains a maze of pathways, a large and a small lake, a Plaza del Quijote and Monumento a los Niños Héroes, shaded lawns and a zoo with giant pandas and other animals from around the world, cages spacious, animals seem content, 300 well laid out (free, closed Mon and Tues). At the top of a hill in the park is the Castillo de Chapultepec, with a view over Mexico Valley from its beautiful balconies, US$2 to enter the building (large bags have to be left at Museo Nacional de Historia, so go there first). It has now become the **Museo Nacional de Historia**, open 0900-1700 (long queues on Sun, closed Mon). Its rooms were used by the Emperor Maximilian and the Empress Carlota during their brief reign. There is an unfinished mural by Siqueiros (in Sala XIII, near the entrance) and a notable mural by O'Gorman on the theme of independence. Classical music concerts, free, are given on Sun at 1200 by the Bellas Artes Chamber Orchestra; arrive early for a seat. Entrance US$4.35, free on Sun. Halfway down the hill is the new **Galería de Historia**, which has dioramas, with tape-recorded explanations of Mexican history, and photographs of the 1910 Revolution. Just below the castle are the remains of the famous Arbol de Moctezuma, known locally as 'El Sargento'. This immense tree, which has a circumference of 14m and was about 60m high, has been cut off at a height of about 10m.

Museo Nacional de Antropología

The crowning wonder of the park was built by architect Pedro Ramírez Vásquez to house a vast collection illustrating pre-conquest Mexican culture. It has a 350m façade and an immense patio shaded by a gigantic concrete mushroom, 4,200 sq metres – the world's largest concrete expanse supported by a single pillar. The largest exhibit ($8\frac{1}{2}$m high, weighing 167 tons) is the image of Tláloc the rain god, removed (accompanied by protesting cloud bursts) from near the town of Texcoco to the museum. Open Tues-Sat, 0900-1900 and Sun, 1000-1800. Only Mexican student cards accepted. Entrance is US$5 except Sun (free, and very crowded). No written explanations in English. Guided tours in English or Spanish free with a minimum of 5 people. Ask for the parts you want to see as each tour only visits two of 23 halls. Excellent audio-visual introduction free (lasts 1 hr, includes 3D models). If you want to see everything, you need 2 days. Permission to photograph (no tripod or flash allowed) US$1.50, US$5 for video camera. Upstairs is a display of folk costumes, which may be closed Sun. Attractions include *voladores* and Maya musicians. There is an excellent collection of English, French, German and Spanish books, especially guides to Mexican ruins, including maps. Guide books of the museum itself cost US$13.50 and US$18.50. Cafeteria on site is good, recommended, particularly for the soup, but pricey with long queues at times. The nearest metro is Auditorio.

Also in the first section of the Bosque de Chapultepec is the **Museo de Arte Moderno** (US$2.30, free with ISIC card), which shows Mexican art only in two buildings, pleasantly set among trees with some sculptures in the grounds. The smaller building shows temporary exhibitions. The delightfully light architecture of the larger building is spoilt by a heavy, vulgar marble staircase, with a curious acoustic effect on the central landing under a translucent dome, which must have been unplanned; open 1100-1800 daily except Mon. The **Museo Rufino Tamayo** (on the other side of Reforma, cross near the Museo de Arte Moderno, on the way to the Anthropological Museum) has a fine collection of works by Rufino Tamayo and shows

contemporary Mexican and other painters. The interior space of the museum is unusual in that it is difficult to know which floor one is on. Open 1000-1700 (closed Mon), US$1.50, free to students with international card.

The second section has a large amusement park, open Wed, Fri and weekends, 1030-2000, entry US$1 (there is a wonderful section for children and another for adults) and huge roller-coasters including the *Montana Rusa*, one of the world's largest, on Sat and Sun only, US$0.40, bridle paths and polo grounds. Diego Rivera's famous fountain, the Fuente de Tláloc, is near the children's amusement park. Close by are the Fuentes de los Serpientes (Snake Fountains). There are two museums in this section: the **Museo de Tecnología** is free; it is operated by the Federal Electricity Commission, has touchable exhibits which demonstrate electrical and energy principles. It is located beside the roller-coasters. The **Museo de Historia Natural** is beside the Lago Menor of the second section; open 1000-1700, Tue to Sun. Both the Lago Menor and Lago Mayor are popular for boating; on the shore of each is a restaurant.

Centro Cultural de Arte Contemporáneo, Campos Eliseos y Jorge Eliot, Polanco (near *Hotel Presidente*, metro Polanco), has permanent and temporary exhibitions of painting, photography, installations (mostly Mexican), small entrance fee, highly recommended.

Modern buildings

On Av Insurgentes Sur (at the corner of Mercaderes) is a remarkable building by Alejandro Prieto: the Teatro de Los Insurgentes, a theatre and opera house seating 1,300 people. The main frontage on the Av consists of a high curved wall without windows. This wall is entirely covered with mosaic decoration, the work of Diego Rivera: appropriate figures, scenes, and portraits composed round the central motif of a gigantic pair of hands holding a mask, worth going a distance to see.

The most successful religious architecture in Mexico today is to be found in the churches put up by Enrique de la Mora and Félix Candela; a good example is the chapel they built in 1957 for the Missionaries of the Holy Spirit, in a garden behind high walls at Av Universidad 1700. (An excellent Candela church, and easy to see, is the Church of La Medalla Milagrosa, just to the E of Av Universidad at the junction of Av División Norte, metro station División del Norte.) 'All the churches and chapels built by this team have such lightness and balance that they seem scarcely to rest on their foundations.' One of the seminal works of one of Mexico's greatest modern architects, Luís Barragán, is at Los Clubes, Las Arboledas bus from Chapultepec bus station. See also the *objet trouvé* mural at the Diana cinema in the centre of the city, and Orozco's great thundercloud of composition, the 'Apocalypse', at the Church of Jesús Nazareno. Both the *Camino Real Hotel* and the IBM technical centre were designed by Ricardo Legorreto; very well worth seeing. Consult Max Cetto's book on modern Mexican architecture. In this connection, University City (see page 285) is also well worth a look.

An example of modern hospital architecture is the huge Centro Médico Benito Juárez on Av Cuauhtémoc (corner with Morones Prieto), built after the 1985 earthquake. It contains a small shopping centre, theatre and art exhibition complex (Siglo XXI); entrance from metro station Centro Médico.

MUSEUMS AND CHURCHES

Museo de la Ciudad, on Av Pino Suárez and República de El Salvador, shows the geology of the city and has life size figures in period costumes showing the history of different peoples before Cortés. It also has a photographic exhibition of the construction of the metro system. In the attic above the museum is the studio of Joaquín Clausell, with walls covered with impressionist miniatures. Free admittance, Tues to Thur (temporarily closed for renovation 1997). Two blocks S of this museum at Mesones 139 is the **Anglican (Episcopal) Cathedral**, called the Cathedral of San José de Gracia. Built in 1642 as a Roman Catholic church, it was given by the Benito Juárez government to the Episcopal Mission in Mexico. Juárez himself often attended services in it.

Museo José-Luis Cuevas, Academia 13, in a large colonial building. It houses a permanent collection of paintings, drawings and sculptures (one is 2-storeys high) by the controversial, contemporary Cuevas (**NB** the Sala Erótica), and temporary exhibitions (Tues-Fri 1000-1830, Sat-Sun 1000-1730, US$1).

Museo Legislativo, inside Palacio Legislativo, Av Congreso de la Unión 66, entrance in Sidar y Rivorosa, metro Candelaria. Entrance free, open 1000-1800, closed Mon. Shows development of the legislative processes in Mexico from pre-Hispanic times to the 20th century.

Museo Nacional de las Culturas, Moneda 13, free, open 0930-1800, closed Sun. Exhibits of countries from all over the world and some historical information.

The **Casa del Presidente Venustiano Carranza**, Lerma y Amazonas, is a museum.

Museo de Arte Carrillo Gil, Av Revolución esq Los Leones, near San Angel; another museum of striking modern features, inside and out; paintings by Orozco, Rivera (**NB** some of his Cubist works), Siqueiros and others (US$3.35 entry); good bookshop and cafeteria.

Museo de Cera de la Ciudad de México (Wax Museum) in a remarkable house at Londres 6, 1100-1900 daily.

Museo de la Caricatura, C de Doncellas 97, free.

Instituto Nacional Indigenista, Av Revolución 1297.

Museo Universitario del Chopo, E G Martínez 10, between metro San Cosme and Insurgentes, near Insurgentes Norte. Contemporary international exhibitions

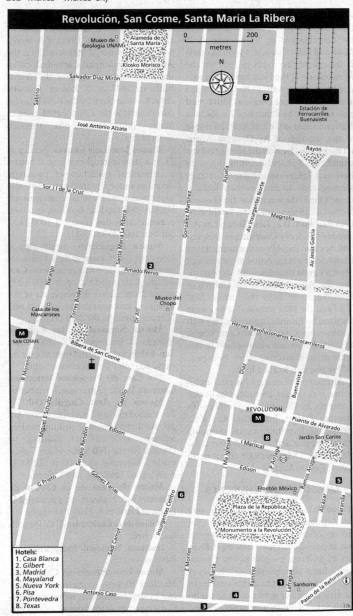

Revolución, San Cosme, Santa María La Ribera

Museo de Geología UNAM
Alameda de Santa María
Kiosko Morisco

Salvador Díaz Mirón

Estación de Ferrocarriles Buenavista

Sabino

José Antonio Alzate

Rayón

Sor J I de la Cruz

Azuela

Av Insurgentes Norte

González Martínez

Magnolia

Santa María La Ribera

Av Jesús García

Naranjo

2 Amado Nervo

Torres Bodet

Dr Atl

Museo del Chopo

Casa de los Mascarones

Héroes Revolucionarios Ferrocarrileros

M SAN COSME

Ribera de San Cosme

R Moreno

Díaz

Buenavista

Castillo

Miguel E Schultz

Serapio Rendón

Edison

REVOLUCION **M**

Puente de Alvarado

Jardín San Carlos

8

I Mariscal

Ma Iglesias

P Arriaga

Edison

Ramos Arizpe

5

G Prieto

Gómez Farías

Frontón México

Alcázar

Baranda

6

Insurgentes Centro

Plaza de la República

Sadí Carnot

Monumento a la Revolución

E Montes

1 Sanborns

Lafragua

Paseo de la Reforma

(i)

Antonio Caso

Vallarta

Ramírez

4

3

Hotels:
1. *Casa Blanca*
2. *Gilbert*
3. *Madrid*
4. *Mayaland*
5. *Nueva York*
6. *Pisa*
7. *Pontevedra*
8. *Texas*

0 — 200 metres

N

(photography, art) in a church-like building designed by Eiffel (Wed-Sun 1000-1400, 1600-1900).

Casasola Archive, Praga 16, in Zona Rosa, T 564-9214, amazing photos of the revolutionary period, reproduction for sale.

The **Siqueiros Polyforum**, on Insurgentes Sur, includes a handicraft shop and a museum of art, with huge frescoes by Siqueiros, one of the largest in the world, inside the ovoid dome. Entrance to the frescoes US$0.40; open 1000-1900, closed for lunch. Next door is the former *Hotel de México* skyscraper, which is to become Mexico's World Trade Centre.

Museo del Convento de Carmen, Av Revolución 4, San Angel, open 1000-1700 (has mummified nuns in upright cases in the cellar). **Museo Nacional de Culturas Populares**, Hidalgo 289 (see under Coyoacán, **Suburbs**).

Museo Dolores Olmedo Patiño, Av México 5843, Xochimilco (see under Xochimilco, **Suburbs**).

Museo Nacional de las Intervenciones, Gen Anaya y 20 de Agosto, see under Churubusco, **Suburbs**.

NB For details of other museums, far from the centre, see under Suburbs, page 282, and Teotihuacan, page 290.

Bull Ring

Said to be the largest in the world, it holds 60,000 spectators. Bull fights are held every Sun at 1600 from Oct through Mar (seats from US$5 at the very top, to US$20, to US$65 in the front row – even the cheaper seats afford impressive views. Admission starts at 1600; buy ticket in morning to avoid queues. The Bull Ring is in the Ciudad de los Deportes (City of Sports), Plaza México, reached by Av de los Insurgentes; metro station San Antonio, Línea 7, is a couple of blocks away. (A little to the W of where Los Insurgentes crosses Chapultepec, and on Av Chapultepec itself between C Praga and C Varsovia, are the remains of the old aqueduct built in 1779.) Besides the Bull Ring, the Sports City contains a football stadium holding 50,000 people, a boxing ring, a cinema, a *frontón* court for *jai-alai*, a swimming pool, restaurants, hotels, etc.

SANTA MARIA LA RIBERA AND SAN COSME

(North of metro San Cosme) these are two colonias which became fashionable residential areas in the late 19th century, and many elegant, if neglected façades are to be seen. On the corner of Ribera de San Cosme and Naranjo (next to San Cosme metro) note the **Casa de los Mascarones**. Built in 1766, this was the Casa de Campo of the Conde del Valle de Orizaba, later the Escuela Nacional de Música. Recently restored, it now houses a UNAM computer centre. In the pleasant Alameda de Santa María, between Pino and Torres Bodet, stands an extraordinary Moorish pavilion designed by Mexicans for the Paris Exhibition in 1889. On its return to Mexico, the *kiosko* was placed in the Alameda Central, before being transferred to its present site in 1910. On the W side of this square, on Torres Bodet, is the **Museo del Instituto Geológico** of UNAM; apart from its collection of fossils and minerals (and magnificent early 20th century showcases), the building itself (1904) is worth a visit: swirling wrought-iron staircases and unusual stained-glass windows of mining scenes by Zettler (Munich and Mexico); Tues-Sun 1000-1700, free.

Sullivan Park (popularly known as Colonia Park or Jardín del Arte) is reached by going up Paseo de la Reforma to the intersection with Los Insurgentes, and then W two blocks between C Sullivan and C Villalongín. Here, each Sun afternoon, there is a display of paintings, engravings and sculptures near the monument to La Madre, packed with sightseers and buyers; everything is for sale (beware of thieves).

Reino Aventura, S of the city near the Mall del Sur, amusement park for children along Disneyland lines, clean, orderly, popular with families.

Basilica of Guadalupe

The **Basilica of Guadalupe**, in the Gustavo A Madero district, often called La Villa de Guadalupe, in the outer suburbs to the NE, is the most venerated shrine in Mexico, for it was here, in Dec 1531, that the Virgin appeared three times, in the guise of an Indian princess, to the Indian Juan Diego and imprinted her portrait on his cloak. The cloak is preserved, set in gold, but was moved into the new basilica next door in 1992, as a massive crack has appeared down the side of the old building. Visitors stand on a moving platform behind the altar to view the cloak. The huge, modern basilica is impressive and holds over 20,000 people (very crowded on Sun). The original basilica has been converted into a museum, admission US$3. It still houses the original magnificent altar, but otherwise mostly representations of the image on the cloak, plus interesting painted tin plates offering thanks for cures, etc, from about 1860s. A chapel stands over the well which gushed at the spot where the Virgin appeared. The great day here is 12 Dec, the great night the night before: Indian dance groups provide entertainment in front of the Basilica. There are, in fact, about seven churches in the immediate neighbourhood, including one on the hill above (Iglesia del Cerrito – excellent view of the city, especially at night, free access); most of them are at crazy angles to each other and to the ground, because of subsidence; the subsoil is very soft. The **Templo de los Capuchinos** has been the subject of a remarkable feat of engineering in which one end has been raised 3,375m so that the building is now horizontal. There is a little platform from which to view this work. Buses marked La Villa go close to the site, or you can go by metro to La Villa (Line 6). The Virgin even has her own home page on the Internet, visit her on line at Interlupe. http://spin.com.mx/~msalazar.

LOCAL FESTIVALS

The largest is the Independence celebration on 15 Sept, when the President gives the *grito*: 'Viva México' from the Palacio Nacional on the Zócalo at 2300, and rings the Liberty Bell (now, sadly, electronic!). This is followed by fireworks, and on 16 Sept (0900-1400) there are military and traditional regional parades in the Zócalo and surrounding streets – great atmosphere.

Safety Take care in the centre at quiet times (eg Sun pm) and in Chapultepec (where Sun is the safest day).

LOCAL INFORMATION

● **Accommodation**

Hotel prices

L1	over US$200	L2	US$151-200
L3	US$101-150	A1	US$81-100
A2	US$61-80	A3	US$46-60
B	US$31-45	C	US$21-30
D	US$12-20	E	US$7-11
F	US$4-6	G	up to US$3

Prices of the more expensive hotels do not normally inc 15% tax; service is sometimes inc. Always check in advance. Reductions are often available; breakfast is rarely inc in the room price. There are fair hotel reservation services at the railway station and at the airport; also services for more expensive hotels at bus stations.

L1 *Camino Real*, Mariano Escobedo 700, T 203-2121, F 250-6897; **L1** *Clarion Reforma Suites*, Paseo de la Reforma 373, T 207-8944, F 208-2719, new; **L1** *Four Seasons Mexico*, Paseo de la Reforma 500, T 230-1818, F 230-1817, new (1994), beautiful, excellent restaurant; **L1** *María Isabel Sheraton*, Paseo de la Reforma 325, T 207-3933, F 207-0684, Hotel, Towers (opp Angel of Independence), 'old-fashioned', all facilities, but restaurant overpriced; **L1** *Nikko*, Campos Eliseos 204, T 280-1111, F 280-9191; **L1** *Presidente*, Campos Eliseos 218, T 327-7700, F 327-7737, good location, exercise room; **L2** *Century*, Liverpool 152, T 726-9911, F 525-7475 (Golden Tulip hotel); **L2** *Fiesta Americana*, Paseo de la Reforma 80, T 705-1515, F 705-1313, with restaurants, bars, nightclubs, superior business facilities; **L2** *Imperial*, Reforma 64, T 566-4879, very good, restaurant, café, bar, 24-hr service, business facilities, etc; **L2** *Krystal*, Liverpool

155, T 228-9928, F 511-3490. A rec hotel is the **L2** *Marco Polo*, Amberes 27, T 207-0299, F 533-3727, in the Zona Rosa, small, select hotel, price reductions at weekends, Mexican, Italian and international cuisine; **L2** *Marquis*, Paseo de la Reforma 465, Col Cuauhtémoc, T 211-3600, F 211-5561, new, all facilities, rec as very fine; **L2** *Westin Galería Plaza*, Hamburgo 195, T 211-0014, F 207-5867; **L3** *Flamingos Plaza*, Av Revolución 333, T 627-0220, F 515-4850; **L3** *Royal Zona Rosa*, Amberes 78, T 228-9918, F 514-3330, good. A *Crowne Plaza* has opened at Paseo de la Reforma 1, T 128-5000, F 128-5050.

A1 *Aristos*, Paseo de la Reforma 276, I 211-0112, F 525-6783; **A1** *Calinda Genève*, Londres 130, T 211-0071, F 208-7422, pleasant dining area; **A1** *Casa Blanca*, Lafragua 7 (1 block from Reforma and Revolución monument), T 705-1300, F 705-4197, modern; **A1** *Plaza Madrid*, Madrid 15, T 705-0836, F 705-0961; **A1-A2** *Majestic* (Best Western), Madero 73 on Zócalo, T 521-8609, F 512-6262, interesting rooms, lots of tiles, carved wooden beams, large beds, quiet rooms overlook courtyard, magnificent breakfast in 7th floor restaurant with excellent views of centre, food otherwise expensive and disappointing (1995); **A1-A2** *Ritz* (Best Western), Madero 30, T 518-1340, F 518-3466; the **A2** *Howard Johnson Gran Hotel de México* 16 de Septiembre 82 (Zócalo), T 510-4040, F 512-2085, has an incredible foyer, 30's style, 4th floor restaurant and balcony good for Zócalo-watching, especially on Sun am (breakfast buffet US$10); **A2** *María Cristina*, Lerma 31, T 703-1787/566-9688, F 566-9194, attractive colonial style, comfortable, helpful, safe parking, rec (book well in advance); **A2-A3** *Cortés* (Best Western), Av Hidalgo 85, T 518-2184, F 512-1863, is the only baroque-style hotel in Mexico City, a former pilgrims' guest house, with a pleasant patio, TV, good bathroom, no a/c or pool, quiet, good yet touristy floor show, good food; **A3** *Ejecutivo*, Viena 8, T 566-6422, staff helpful, rec; **A3** *Metropol*, Luis Moya 39, T 510-8660-1, F 512-1273, good, clean, safe, touristy, average restaurant, good value, rec; **A3** *Regente*, París 9, T 566-8933, clean, friendly, noisy at front, restaurant; **A3** *Royal Plaza*, Parroquia 1056, corner with Cuauhtémoc, T 605-8943 (B at weekends); **A3** *Viena*, Marsella 28 (close to Juárez market and Cuauhtémoc metro), T 566-0700, quiet, Swiss decor, garage, dining room, rec;

Hotels at or near the airport: L2 *Continental Plaza Aeropuerto*, Fundidora Monterrey 89, T 230-0505, entrance between sections B and C in airport, all facilities; **L2-L3** *Ramada Ciudad de México*, Blvd Puerto Aéreo 502, T 785-8522, F 762-9934, free transport to/from airport. A short walk from the airport: **A1** *JR Plaza*, Blvd Puerto Aéreo 390, T 785-5200, F 784-3221, free transport to/from airport, expensive restaurant, quiet, good rooms with solid furniture, close to metro; next door is **A3** *Aeropuerto*, T 785-5318, noisy but OK, functional, expensive restaurant.

B *Brasilia*, excellent modern hotel, nr Central del Nte bus station, on Av Cien Metros 48-25, T 587-8577, F 368-2714, king size bed, TV, 24-hr traffic jam in front; **B** *Cancún*, Donato Guerra 24, T 566-6083, F 566-6488, restaurant, safe, noisy, rec; **B** *Catedral*, Donceles 95, T 518-2532, F 512-4344, behind Cathedral, clean, spacious, good service, rec; **B** *Fleming*, Revillagigedo 35, T 510-4530, good value, central; **B** *Jena*, Jesús Terán 12, new, central, rec (but not the travel agency on the premises); **B** *Lepanto*, Guerrero 90, TV, phone, modern, attractive, good restaurant; **B** *Mallorca*, Serapio Rendón 119, T 566-4833, clean, reasonable; **B** *Mayaland*, Maestro Antonio Caso 23, T 566-6066, with bath, good value, rec, good restaurant; **B** *Palace*, Ignacio Ramírez 7, T 566-2400, very friendly, good restaurant; **B** *Polanco*, Edgar Poe 8, T 280-8082, nr Chapultepec, dark, quiet, good restaurant; **B** *Premier*, Atenas 72, T 566-2701, good location, clean, front rooms noisy, will store bags; **B** *Prim*, Versalles 46, T 592 4600, F 592-4835, clean, good in all respects; **B** *San Francisco*, Luis Moya 11, T 521-8960, F 510-8831, just off Alameda, great views, friendly, excellent value, takes credit cards, good set meals; **B** *Sevilla*, Serapio Rendón 126 and Sullivan, T 591-0522, restaurant, garage, reasonable (not to be confused with **A1** *Sevilla Palace*, Reforma 105, T 566-8877, which is smart); **B** *Vasco de Quiroga*, Londres 15 y Berlín, 3 mins' walk from Zona Rosa, T 546-2614, F 535-2257, clean, friendly, very good (ask for room away from the generator), restaurant downstairs.

C *Astor*, Antonio Caso 83, nr Sullivan Park, new, clean, restaurant, rec; **C** *Canadá*, Av 5 de Mayo 47, T 518-2106, F 521-1233, closest metro station Allende, with bath, hot water, TV, collect calls can be made for US$1, good value, friendly, helpful, no restaurant; **C** *Capitol*, Uruguay 12, T 518-1750, F 521-1149, attractive lobby, recently remodelled, TV, bath, clean, friendly, don't miss the restaurant in the same building: *El Malecón*; **C** *Casa González*, Lerma y Sena 69 (nr British Embassy), T 514-3302, full board available, shower, English spoken by Sr González, clean, quiet and friendly, no credit cards, rec; **C** *Congreso*, with bath, hot water, good, central, clean, quiet, TV, garage, at Allende 18, T 510-9888; **C** *Galicia*, Honduras 11, T 529-7791, good; **C** *Gilbert*, Amado Nervo 37, Col Buenavista, Mex 4DF, T 547-9260, good location but a bit spooky at night; **C** *Gillow*, 5 de Mayo e Isabel la Católica 11, T 518-1440, central, large, clean, many services, attractive, hospitable, good value, poor restaurant; **C** *La Villa de los Quijotes*, Moctezuma 20, nr Basílica Guadalupe (metro La Villa), T 577-1088, modern, quiet, clean, expensive restaurant; **C** *Marlowe*, Independencia 17, T 521-9540, clean, but poor restaurant (tourist office at airport refers many travellers here – if this one is too expensive, the cheaper *Concordia*, see below, is round the corner); **C** *New York*, Edison 45, large, clean rooms, expensive restaurants; **C** *Parador Washington*, Dinamarca 42 y Londres, with bath, clean, safe area, café next door; **C** *Pisa*, Insurgentes Nte 58, rec; **C** *Uxmal*, Madrid 13, quite close to Zona Rosa, clean rooms, same owner as more expensive *Madrid*, next door, No 15, T 705-0836, F 705-0961, with access to their better facilities, rec.

The best of the cheaper hotels are in the old part of town between the Zócalo and the Alameda, and there are more N of the Plaza República. **C** *Oxford*, Mcal 67, T 566-0500, very clean, radio and satellite TV, helpful, but short stay; **C** *Texas*, Ignacio Mcal 129, T 564-4626, with bath, clean, hot water, small rooms, good breakfasts.

D *América*, Buena Vista 4 (nr Revolución metro), with bath, hot water, TV, good service, rec; **D** *Antillas*, B Domínguez 34, T 526-5674, with bath and TV, friendly, stores luggage; **D** *Atlanta*, corner of B Domínguez and Allende, T 518-1201, good, clean, quiet if you ask for a room away from street, friendly, luggage store; **D** *Avenidas*, Lázaro Cárdenas 38 (Bellas Artes metro), T 518-1007, with bath, central, friendly, will store luggage, good value, cheapest hotel that can be booked at airport; **D** *Concordia*, Uruguay 13, nr Niño Perdido, clean, hot water, friendly, some rooms airless, lift, phone, noisy; **D** *Cuba*, on Cuba 69, T 518-1380, with bath, TV, good beds but sheets too small, noisy; **D** *Danky*, Donato Guerra 10, with bath, central, hot water, phone, clean, easy

parking (T 546-9960/61), rec; **D** *El Roble*, Uruguay y Pino Suárez, bath, TV, restaurant closes early, rec; **D** *El Salvador*, Rep del Salvador 16, T 521-1247, nr Zócalo, modern, clean, laundry, safe, parking, good value; **D** *Encino*, Av Insurgentes, 1 block from the railway station, clean, private bath; **D** *Florida*, Belisario Domínguez 57, TV, shower, clean, rec; **D** *Frimont*, Jesús Terán 35, T 705-4169, clean, central; **D** *Lafayette*, Motolinia 40 and 16 de Septiembre, with bath, and TV, good, clean, quiet (pedestrian precinct), but check rooms, there's a variety of sizes; **D** *Managua*, on Plaza de la Iglesia de San Fernando, nr Hidalgo metro, with bath, phone, TV, good location, car park, very friendly, run down; **D** *Mina*, Jose T Salgado 16, esq Mina, T 7031682, modern, clean, TV, large beds; **D** *Monaco* opp, Guerrero 12, T 566-8333, comfortable, TV, modern, good service; **D** *Monte Carlo*, Uruguay 69, T 518-1418/521-2559/521-9363 (D H Lawrence's hotel), elegant, clean, friendly owner (also suites), with bath, hot water, good about storing luggage, safe car park inside the hotel premises, US$3.45, rooms in front noisy, very popular, can make collect calls abroad from room, repeatedly rec; **D** *Principal*, C Bolívar 29, with bath, central, OK, friendly owner; **D** *Pontevedra*, Insurgentes Nte opp railway station, bath, hot water, TV, clean, helpful, will store luggage; **D** *San Antonio*, Callejón 5 de Mayo 29, T 512-9906, clean, pleasant, popular, friendly, TV in room, rec; **D** *Santander*, Arista 22, not far from railway station, with bath, good value and service, clean; **D** *Royalty*, Jesús Terán 21, opp *Hotel Jena*, with bath, TV, clean, very quiet, nr Hidalgo metro; **D** *Toledo*, López 22 (Bellas Artes Metro), T 521-3249, with bath, TV, warmly rec; **D-E** *Habana*, República de Cuba 77, spacious rooms, huge beds, renovated, very clean, phone, TV, friendly and helpful staff, rec; **D-E** *Isabel la Católica* (street of the same name, No 63, T 518-1213, F 521-1233) is pleasant, popular, clean, helpful, safe (taxi drivers must register at desk before taking passengers), roof terrace, large shabby rooms with bath and hot water (some without windows), central, a bit noisy, fax service, quite good restaurant, luggage held, rooms on top floor with shared bathroom are cheaper, rec.

E *Ambar*, San Jerónimo 105 y Pino Suárez, shower, fan, TV, phones in rooms, a little noisy, safe deposit, very clean, good service, highly rec; **E** *Carlton*, Ignacio Mcal 32-bis, T 566-2911, getting rough around the edges, small rooms but some with fine views, rooms at front noisy, rec, good restaurant; **E** *Fornes*, Revillagigedo 92, nr Balderas metro, 10 mins' walk to Alameda, extremely clean, bathroom, TV, radio, smarter bigger rooms for **D**, restaurant, large, indoor car park, friendly staff, Dutch-speaking, Spanish owner, very good value, highly rec; **E** *Tuxpán*, on Colombia, nr Brasil, modern, clean, TV, hot shower; **F** *Rio de Janeiro*, on Brasil, nr Colombia, dirty, noisy; **F** *Princess*, next door at No 55, with bath, good value, TV, fairly secure, front rooms noisy; **F** *San Pedro*, Mesones 126 and Pino Suárez, with bath, TV, tiny rooms, clean (but the occasional cockroach) and friendly, good value.

Near Allende metro are **D-E** *Rioja*, Av 5 de Mayo 45, T 521-8333, shared or private baths, reliable hot water, clean, popular, luggage store, well placed, rec, next door to *Canadá*, see above; opp are **E** *Juárez*, in small alley on 5 de Mayo 17, 1 min walk from Zócalo, T 512-6929, ask for room with window, safe, clean, with bath, phone, radio, TV, rec, and **F** *Zamora*, No 50, clean, cheap, hot water, some find it OK, others say it is falling apart, good *Café El Popular* next door; **D-E** *Washington*, Av 5 de Mayo 54, clean, small rooms, cable TV; **D** *Buenos Aires*, Av 5 de Mayo, safe, friendly, TV, stores luggage, hot water; **E** *Casa Blanca*, Manuel Gutiérrez Najera 34-A, T 578-3379; **D** *Detroit*, Zaragoza 55, T 591-1088, hot shower, central, clean, has parking; **D** *Nueva Estación*, Zaragoza opp Bellavista station, with bath, clean, quiet, friendly, colour TV; **D** *Savoy*, Zaragoza 10, T 566-4611 nr Hidalgo metro, convenient for Zócalo, with bath and hot water, clean, phone, TV, modernized, good value; **D** *Yale*, Mosqueta 200, 5 mins' walk from Buenavista station, showers, toilet, large room with TV and phone, very good value, rec; **E** *Pennsylvania*, Ignacio Mariscal 15, T 535-0070, with bath, clean, TV; **E** *La Marina*, Allende 30 y B Domínguez, clean, comfortable, safe, friendly, TV, hot water, will store luggage, rec; **E** *Azores*, Brasil 25, T 521-5220; **E** *Atoyac*, Eje de Guerrero 161, Col Guerrero, 200m from metro, clean, friendly, safe; **E** *El Paraíso*, Mariscal 99, T 566-8077, hot water, clean, private bath, TV, phone, recently renovated, friendly.

E-F *Casa de los Amigos*, Mcal 132 (T 705-0521/0646), nr train and bus station (metro Revolución), in dormitory, **D-E** in double room, pay 2 nights in advance, use of kitchen, rec, max 15-day stay, separation of sexes, run by Quakers for Quakers, or development-work related travellers, other travellers taken only if space is available, good information on volunteer work,

travel and language schools, breakfast US$2.50 (weekdays only) and laundry facilities on roof, safe-keeping for luggage, English library, references or advance booking rec.

For longer stays, **B** *Suites Quinta Palo Verde*, Cerro del Otate 20, Col Romero de Terreros (Mexico 21 DF) T 554-3575, pleasant, diplomatic residence turned guest house, nr the University; run by a veterinary surgeon, Miguel Angel, very friendly, speaks English and German, but the dogs are sometimes noisy. *Suites Amberes*, Amberes 64, Zona Rosa, T 533-1306, F 207-1509, kitchenette, good value, rec; *Suites Havre*, Havre 74, T 533-5670, nr Zona Rosa, rec for longer stays, 56 suites with kitchen, phone and service. *Club Med* head office for Club Med and *Villas Arqueológicas* reservations, C Masaryk 183, Col Polanco, México 11570, T 203-3086/3833, Telex 1763346.

Campsites: Campo Escuela Nacional de Tantoco, Km 29.5 on road Mexico-City to Toluca, T 512-2279, cabins and campsite. The Dirección de Villas Deportivas Juveniles, address below (Condep), has details of campsites throughout the country; site in the capital, T 665-5027. They have either camping, or camping and dormitory accommodation on sites with additional facilities, inc luggage lockers; ask in advance what documentation is required. The nearest trailer park is *Pepe's* in Tepotzotlán (see **Excursions** below), 43 km N of the capital (address: Eva Sámano de López Mateos 62, T 876-0515/0616, in Mexico City, *Mallorca Travel Service* Paseo de la Reforma 105, T 705-2424, F 705-2673); it costs about US$12 a night, 55 pads with full hook-ups, very friendly, clean, hot showers, Canadian run, rec (owner has a hotel in Mexico City if you want to leave your trailer here and stay in the capital). If you want to bring your car into the city, find a cheap hotel where you can park and leave it, while you explore the city by bus, metro or on foot. Or try camping in the parking lot of the Museum of Anthropology.

Youth hostels: Asociación Mexicana de Albergues de la Juventud, Madero 6, Of 314, México 1, D F. Write for information. There is a similar organization, Comisión Nacional del Deporte (Condep), which runs the Villas Deportivas Juveniles (see above); information office at Glorieta del Metro Insurgentes, local C-11, T 525-2916/533-1291. Condep will make reservations for groups of 10 or more; to qualify you must be between 8 and 65 and have a 'tarjeta plan verde' membership card, US$6, valid 2 years, obtainable within 24 hrs from office at Tlalpan 583, esq Soria, metro Xola, or a IYHF card. See also Setej, below, for information on hotels and other establishments offering lodging for students.

● **Places to eat**
All the best hotels have good restaurants. The number and variety of restaurants throughout the city is vast; the following is a small selection.

Mexican food: note the *Hotel Majestic's* Mexican breakfast, Sat and Sun till 1200, excellent, go to terrace on 7th floor, otherwise food mediocre. *San Angel Inn*, Las Palmas 50, in San Angel, is excellent and very popular, so book well in advance (San Angel can be reached by metro to Barranca del Muerto and bus 5 along Revolución); *Hostelería Santo Domingo*, Belisario Domínguez, 2 blocks W of Plaza Santo Domingo, good food and service, excellent music, the oldest restaurant in the city; *La Plancha Azteca*, Río Lerma 54, good tacos and tortas, moderate prices; *La Puerta del Angel*, Varsovia y Londres, local food and specializing in American cuts, very good; *Fonda del Recuerdo* for excellent *mole poblano*, Bahía de las Palmas 39A, 17DF, with music; *Club de Periodistas de México*, F Mata 8, nr C 5 de Mayo, open to public, OK; *Opera Bar*, 5 de Mayo nr Bellas Artes, good atmosphere, expensive, see Pancho Villa's bullet-hole in ceiling (cocktails made with foreign spirits are 3 times as expensive as tequila); *Cardenal*, C Palma 23, food, service and music (from 1530) is outstanding, 1930s ambience; *Casa Zavala*, Bolívar y Uruguay, cheap, large selection of dishes; *El Huequito*, Bolívar 58, casual, friendly, cheap meals for US$2; *Focolare*, Hamburgo 87 (swank and high priced); *Taquería Lobo Bobo*, Insurgentes Sur 2117, excellent food, quite cheap, very friendly; *Nadja*, Mesones 65, nr Pino Suárez, typical food, set menu for US$1.30, large portions, friendly, rec; *Vitamar*, Ayuntamiento 8, good food, pricey, good beer from the tap, normally open till 2400. A very old restaurant with stunning tile décor and not touristy is the *Café Tacuba*, Tacuba 28, it specializes in Mexican food, very good enchiladas, tamales and fruit desserts, good service, live music, rec. *México Viejo*, Tacuba 86 (nr Zócalo), excellent breakfast, not touristy, pricey; *El Refugio*, Liverpool 166, tourist-oriented, good desserts, check bill carefully; *Doneraky*, Nuevo León y Laredo (Col Condesa), good tacos, rec; *Don Albis*, Tomás Edison 100, delicious large cheap meals, popular with office workers; *La Luna*, Oslo y Copenhague, Zona Rosa, mostly Mexican, good

breakfasts; *Casa Neri*, Bélgica 211, Col Portales, excellent authentic cooking, Oaxacan specialities, huge *comida corrida* for US$4; *La Lupe*, C Industria, metro: Coyoacán, leafy patio, good and cheap, open till 1800. Almost everywhere are American-style restaurant chains, eg *Vips*, *Toks*, *El Portón*, *Lyni's* and *Sanborns*, offering Mexican and international food, clean and reliable, but by no means cheap by local standards (breakfast US$3.50, lunch US$7).

International: *Delmonico's*, Londres 87 and 16 de Septiembre 82, elegant; *Jena*, Morelos 110 (deservedly famous, à la carte, expensive); *La Cava*, Insurgentes Sur 2465 (excellent food and steaks, lavishly decorated as an old French tavern, moderate); *Andreson's*, Reforma 400, very good atmosphere, excellent local menu, not cheap; *Keops*, Hamburgo 146, nr Amberes in Zona Rosa, T 525 6706, reasonable food, good live music; also in Zona Rosa are *La Calesa de Londres*, Londres 102, good meat; and *Carousel Internacional*, Hamburgo and Niza, very popular drinking-hole for smartly-dressed Mexicans, resident Mariachi, food not gourmet but fun atmosphere, about US$15 pp. *Trevi*, Dr Mora y Colón (W end of Alameda), Italian/US/Mexican, reasonable prices. *Milomita*, Mesones 87, Centro, 0800-2000, specializes in American cuts of meat (see also Polanco restaurants below).

US and other Latin American: *Shirley's*, Reforma 108 and Londres 102-B, real American food, moderate prices, especially the buffet after midday; *Sanborn's*, 36 locations (known as the foreigners' home-from-home) soda fountain, drugstore, restaurant, English, German and Spanish language magazines, handicrafts, chocolates, etc, try their restaurant in the famous 16th century *Casa de los Azulejos*, the 'house of tiles' at Av Madero 17, many delicious local dishes in beautiful high-ceilinged room, about US$15-20 pp without wine (also has handicraft shops in basement and first floor). *New York Deli and Bagel*, Av Revolución 1321, just S of metro Barranca del Muerto, 0800-0100, good coffee and full meals available. Many US chain fast-food restaurants (eg *Burger Boy* for good value breakfasts, McDonalds and Dunkin Donuts on Madero). *Rincón Gaucho*, Insurgentes Sur 1162, Argentine food.

Spanish: *del Cid*, Humboldt 61, Castilian with medieval menu; *Mesón del Castellano*, Bolívar y Uruguay, T 518 6080, good atmosphere, plentiful and not too dear, excellent steaks, highly rec; **Centro Catalán**, Bolívar 31, open 1100-1700 only, excellent paella and other Spanish cuisine (2nd floor); **Centro Castellano**, on Uruguay, excellent, cheap, try the steaks; **Vasco**, Madero 6, 1st floor; **Mesón del Perro Andaluz**, Copenhague 26, and Luis P Ogazón 89, very pleasant.

Other European: French cuisine at **Le Gourmet**, Dakota 155, said to be most expensive restaurant in Mexico, and also said to be worth it! **Ambassadeurs**, Paseo de la Reforma 12 (swank and highly priced); **Les Moustaches**, Río Sena 88 (second most expensive in town, probably); **Bellinghausen**, Londres y Niza, excellent food (another branch **Casa Bell**, Praga 14, T 511-5733, smaller, identical menu, old house, elegant, rec); **Chalet Suizo**, Niza 37 (very popular with tourists, specializes in Swiss and German food, moderate); **Grotto Ticino**, Florencion 33, Swiss food, rec; **Rivoli**, Hamburgo 123 (a gourmet's delight, high priced); **Café Konditori**, Génova 61, Danish open sandwiches; **La Gondola**, Genova, great pasta; **La Casserole**, Insurgentes Sur 1880, nr Núcleo Radio Mil building, French. The **Piccadilly Pub**, Copenhague 23 and Génova, serves British food at its best, especially steak and kidney pie, expensive, smart dress preferred, very popular with Mexicans and expatriates alike. Similar (and dearer), is **Sir Winston Churchill**, Avila Camacho 67.

Oriental: **Mr Lee**, Independencia 19-B, Chinese, seafood, good food, value and service; **Chen Wan**, Bolívar 104, large portions, set meal US$2-3.

Seafood: **La Costa Azul**, López 127, y Delicias, Centro, good, cold lighting, reasonable prices; **Marisquito**, nr Congress on Doncelo 12, very good.

Vegetarian: **Restaurante Vegetariano**, Filomeno Mata 13, open until 2000, Sun 0900-1900, good menú del día US$3; **Chalet Vegetariano**, nr Dr Río de la Loza 11; **El Bosque**, Hamburgo 15 between Berlín and Dinamarca, rec. Vegetarian restaurant at Mololinia 31, nr Madero, is open Mon-Sat 1300-1800, reasonably priced. **Karl**, on Amberes nr junction Londres, excellent buffet lunch and dinner; **Saks**, Insurgentes Sur 1641, close to Teatro Insurgentes, very good; **Yug**, Varsovia 3, cheap vegetarian, 4-course set lunch US$3.50 (not very special). **Super Soya**, Tacuba, metro Allende, good juices and fruit salads, health food shop. Wholewheat bread at **Pastelería Ideal** on 16 de Septiembre 14 (nr Casa de Los Azulejos). The best place to buy natural products is in the San Juan market (see **Markets** below), inc tofu (**Queso de Soja**). Health food shop, **Alimentos Naturales**, close to metro Revolución, on P Arriagal; health food shops in other metro stations.

A selection of restaurants in Polanco (in the lower price ranges): **La Parrilla Suiza**, Arquimedes y Pres Masaryk, for grilled meats, alambres, sopa de tortilla and other meat-and-cheese dishes, very popular, especially 1400-1600, service fair, moderately priced; **The City Bistro**, Lope de Vega 341, N of Horacio, serves finest English and international cuisine, also stunningly inventive dishes, moderately priced; **Zeco**, Sudermann 336, T 531-5211, Mexican-Italian, very good, middle price range, wines expensive; **Addetto**, Av Revolución 1382, Col Guadalupe Inn, T 562-5434, same ownership; **El Buen Comer Marcelín**, Edgar Allan Poe 50, T 203-5337, mainly French, very good; **Cambalache**, Arquimedes N of Pres Masaryk, Argentine steak house, good steaks, wide selection of wines, cosy atmosphere, not as expensive as **El Rincón Argentino**, Pres Masaryk 181, which is very expensive; **Milomita**, steak house and piano bar, Pres Masaryk 52 y Torquato Tasso. For tacos and other tortilla-based dishes: **Los Tacos**, Newton just S of Horacio, inexpensive; **Chilango's**, Molière between Ejército Nacional and Homero, good value and service, MTV videos, rec; **El Tizoncito**, S of Ejército Nacional just W of Pabellón Polanco mall, very popular at lunchtime. **El Jarrocho**, Homero between Emerson and Hegel, informal, eat-at-counter place, inexpensive; **Embers**, Seneca y Ejército Nacional, 13 types of excellent hamburger, good French fries, rec.

Cafés etc: many economical restaurants on 5 de Mayo, eg **Café La Blanca** at No 40, popular and busy atmosphere, good expresso coffee, rec, open for Sun breakfast and early on weekdays; **París**, No 10, good breakfast and dinner; **Popular**, No 52 between Alameda and Zócalo, on corner of alley to Hotel Juárez, cheap, rushed, 24 hrs, meeting place; **Gili's Pollo**, opp Hotel Rioja, excellent chicken, eat in or take away; **El 20 de Bolívar**, Bolívar 20, excellent service and highly rec for breakfasts; **TFI Friday**, Copenhagen esq Reforma, excellent value; **Comida Económica Verónica**, República de Cuba, 2 doors from Hotel Habana (No 77), rec for tasty breakfasts and set comida corrida, very hot chilaquiles, good value and delightful staff; **La Rosita**, 2a C de Allende 14-C, cheap and good; **El Reloj**, 5 de Febrero 50, good comida and à la carte; *Rex*, 5 de Febrero 40, nr Zócalo, good café con leche and cheap *comidas*; *Shakey's*, Monte de Piedad (at the Zócalo), self-service, large helpings of pizza and chicken; *Pastelería Madrid*, 5 de Febrero 25, 1 block from *Hotel Isabel La Católica*, good pastries and breakfasts. *Bamerette*, Av Juárez 52 (*Hotel Bamer*), excellent breakfast. Good small restaurants in Uruguay, nr *Monte Carlo Hotel*; the *Maple*, next to *Hotel Roble* at No 109, has been rec for its *comida*, and *Pancho* (No 84), for its breakfasts, cheap meals and service. *Zavala*, W side of Calzada Tlalpán, between metros Nativitas and Portales, small, family-run, serves magnificent 5-course lunch for US$1.75; *Tic Tac*, Av Balderas, very good *comida corrida*. *La Habana*, Bucareli y Morelos, not cheap but good food and excellent coffee. Another centre for small restaurants is Pasaje Jacarandas, off Génova 44: *Llave de Oro* and many others; *La Casa del Pavo*, Motolinia nr 16 de Septiembre, clean, courteous, excellent *comida corrida*; also C Motilinia between 5 de Mayo y Tacuba. Cheap cafeterias in C Belisario Domínguez. *Gaby's*, Liverpool y Napolés, excellent italian-style coffee, décor of old coffee machines etc; *Duca d'Este*, Av Florencia y Hamburgo, good coffee and pastries; *Il Mangiare*, opp Siqueiros Polyforum (see above), very good sandwiches; *El Núcleo*, Lerma y Marne, excellent fruit salads, breakfasts and lunches, closes 1800 and all day Sun; *Zenón*, corner of Madero 65 and Palma, trendy decor, average Mexican food, *comida corrida* US$1.50-3.50; *Enanos de Tapanco y Café*, Orizaba 161, between Querétaro and San Luis Potosí, great coffee, warm friendly atmosphere. Good breakfasts can be had at *Woolworth*, 16 de Septiembre. *Dulcería de Celaya*, 5 de Mayo 39, good candy store and lovely old premises. Good bakeries on 16 de Noviembre, nr Zócalo; also *Panadería La Vasconia*, Tacuba 73, good, also sells cheap chicken and fries; *Jugos California* on Guerrero by Hidalgo metro, good juices; *Roxy*, Montes de Ocay Mazatlán (Col Condesa), good ice cream. Good juices and sandwiches at the *Juguería* on 5 de Mayo, next to *Hotel Rioja*.

● **Bars**

Bar Jardín, in the *Hotel Reforma*; *El Morroco*, Conjunto Marrakesh, C Florencia 36. *Casino*, Isabel La Católica, nr *Sanborn's*, superb painted glass doors and lavish interior, also has Spanish restaurant. *Abundio*, Zaragoza y Mosqueta, very friendly, free food. *Yuppies Sports Bar*, Genova, expensive but good atmosphere. Many safe gay bars in the Zona Rosa in the area between Niza and Florencia, N of Londres.

● **Airline offices**

The majority are on Paseo de la Reforma: No 325, **Avensa** (T 208-4998/3018); **Air France**, No 287, T 546-9140, 566-0066, airport 571-6150; **Delta**, No 381, T 525-4840, 202-1608, airport T 762-3588; **American Airlines**, No 314, T 208-6396/399-9222/571-3219 (airport); **Avianca**, No 195, T 566-8588/546-3059; **Iberia**, No 24, T 566-4011/592-2988/762-5844 (airport); **Aero California**, No 332, T 207-1392; **Alitalia**, No 390-1003, T 533-5590/1240/1243; **Japan Airlines**, No 295, T 533-6883/5515, 571-8742 (airport); **Canadian Airlines**, No 390, T 207-6611/3318. On C Hamburgo: **Swissair**, No 66, T 533-6363; **SAS**, No 61, T 533-0098/0177, 511-9872 (airport); **Air Canada**, No 108, 5th floor, T 511-2004, 514-2516; **Alaska Airlines**, No 213-1004, T 533-1747/6; **Ecuatoriana de Aviación**, No 213, T 533-4569, 514-1274, 762-5199 (airport). **Mexicana**, Xola 535, Col del Valle, T 660-4433/4444, 762-4011 (airport); **KLM**, Paseo de las Palmas 735, T 202-4444; **Lufthansa**, Paseo de las Palmas 239, T 202-8866; **Cubana**, Temístocles 246, Polanco, T 255-0646/0835; **Continental**, Andrés Bello 45, T 546-9503, 535-7603, 571-3661 (airport); **Aeromar**, Sevilla 4, T 207-6666, 574-9211; **Aeroflot**, Insurgentes Sur 569, T 523-7139; **United Airlines**, Leibnitz 100, loc 23-24, T 250-1657, 545-5147; **AeroMéxico**, Insurgentes Sur 724, T 207-6311/8233; **British Airways**, Mariano Escobedo 572, T 533-6375, 525-9233; **El Al Israel Airlines**, Paseo de las Palmas, T 735-1105, 202-2243; **Icelandic Airlines**, Durango 103, T 514-0159, 511-6155/8461; **Lacsa**, Río Nazas 135, T 511-0640, 525-0025; **Northwest Airlines**, Reforma y Ambares 312, T 511-3579, Reforma 300, T 525-7090; **Pan American Airways**, Plaza Comermex 1-702, T 395-0022/0077; **Taca**, Morelos 108, Col Juárez, T 546-8807/8835.

● **Banks & money changers**

Banks 0900-1330 Mon-Fri, although some branches open earlier and close later. Always see if there is a special counter where currency transactions can be effected, to avoid standing in queues which can be long, particularly on Fri. Branches of all major Mexican banks proliferate in most parts of the city. Cash advances on credit cards is easy, and good rates. TCs in most major currencies can be cashed at any branch of Bancomer or Banco Serfín without undue delay.

Banks do not charge commission for changing TCs. The exchange of foreign currency notes, other than dollars, can be difficult apart from at the airport and main bank branches in the city centre. There are two *casas de cambio* at the airport which specialize in obscure currencies. Before buying or selling currency, check the day's exchange rate from a newspaper and then shop around. There is often a great disparity between different banks and *casas de cambio* particularly in times of volatile currency markets. In general, banks are better for buying pesos and *casas de cambio* for buying 'hard' currency. Hotels usually offer very poor rates. **Banco de Comercio** (Bancomer, Visa agent), head office at Av Universidad 1200, also Venustiano Carranza y Bolívar, **Banco Nacional de México (Banamex)**, C Palmas (Banamex's offices nearby, at Av Isabel la Católica 44, are in a converted baroque palace, ask the porter for a quick look into the magnificent patio; another worthwhile building is the bank's branch in the Casa Iturbide, where Agustín de Iturbide lived as emperor, at Madero 17 with Gante); **Banco Internacional** rec, they deal with Mastercard (Carnet) and Visa (usually quicker than Bancomer or Banamex for cash advances against credit card), also **Banco Serfín**, corner of 16 de Septiembre y Bolívar, or Madero 32, nr Bolívar; **Citibank**, Paseo de la Reforma 390, for Citicorp TCs, they also give cash advances against credit cards with no commission. *American Express* office at Reforma 234 esq Havre, T 533 0380 will change cheques on Sats, 0930-1330, also open Mon-Fri until 1800 (there are 5 other AmEx offices in Mexico City, inc **Campos Eliseos 204**, local 5, Polanco, **Centro Comercial Perisur**). For more details on Visa and Master Card, see **Information for travellers** under **Credit cards**, page 522. There are many *casas de cambio*, especially on Reforma and in the centre. Their hours may be more convenient, but their rates can be poor. The Central de Cambios (Suiza), Madero 58, W of Zócalo, has been rec for rates. The Perisur shopping centre, Insurgentes and Periférico Sur, has a *casa de cambio* (T 606-3698) which is usually open until 1900, with a better exchange rate in the morning. See also under **International Airport** below.

● Cultural centres

American Community School of Mexico, complete US curriculum to age of 12, Observatorio and C Sur 136, T 516-67-20; **American Chamber of Commerce**, Lucerna 78; **Benjamin Franklin Library**, Londres 116 (has *New York Times* 2 days after publication); **Anglo-Mexican Cultural Institute** (with British Council Library), Maestro Antonio Caso 127, T 566-61-44, keeps British newspapers; **Instituto Italiano**, Francisco Sosa 77, Coyoacán, T 554-0044/53, has 3-week intensive and painless courses in Spanish, 3 hrs a day. **Goethe-Institut**, Tonalá 43 (metro Insurgentes), 0900-1300, 1600-1930; **Colegio Alemán**, Alexander V Humboldt, Col Huichapan, Del Xochimilco (CP 16030, México DF); **Instituto Francés de la América Latina**, Nazas 43, free films every Thur at 2030.

● Embassies & consulates

Check location of embassies and consulates; they tend to move frequently. Most take 24 hrs for visas; check to make sure you have a visa and not just a receipt stamp.

Guatemalan Embassy, Explanada 1025, Lomas de Chapultepec, 11000 México DF, T 540-7520/520-9249, F 202-1142, am only (take No 47 bus from Observatorio to Virreyes, then walk up hill, or No 76 'Km 15.5 por Reforma', or 'por Palmas', or taxi); to visit Guatemala some nationalities need a compulsory visa costing US$10 in US$ cash only (eg Australians and New Zealanders), others need either a free visa (take a passport photo) or a tourist card (issued at the border), the current regulations are given in Guatemala: **Information for travellers**, open 0900-1300 for visas; **Belizean Embassy**, Av Thiers 152-B, Anzures 2P, 11590 México DF, T 520-1346, F 531-8115, open 0900-1300 Mon-Fri, visa US$10, takes a day; **Honduran Consulate**, Alfonso Reyes 220, T 515-6689/211-5425 (metro Chilpancingo), visas issued on the spot (no waiting) valid up to 1 year from date of issue, cost varies per nationality, up to US$20 for Australians; **Salvadorean Embassy**, Monte Altai 320, T 202-8250, 520-0856, metro Auditorio; **Nicaraguan Consulate**, Payo de Rivera 120, Col Virreyes, Lomas de Chapultepec, T 520-4421 (bus 13 along Reforma, get out at Monte Altai and walk S on Monte Athos), visas for 30 days from date of issue, 1 photograph, US$25, plus US$5 if you want it 'on the spot'; **Costa Rican Embassy**, Río Póo 113, Col Cuauhtémoc, T 525-7764 (metro Insurgentes); **Panamanian Embassy**, Campos Eliseos 111-1, T 250-4259/4229, nr Auditorio metro (visa US$20 for Australians); **Colombian Consulate**, Reforma 195, 3rd floor, will request visa from Bogotá by telegram (which you must pay for) and permission can take up to a month to come through.

USA Embassy, Reforma 305, Col Cuauhtémoc, T 211-0042, F 511-9980, open Mon-Fri 0830-1730, if requiring a visa for the States, it is best to get it in your home country; Canadian Embassy, Schiller 529 (corner Tres Picos), nr Anthropological Museum, T 724-7900. Australian Embassy, Plaza Polanco Torre B, Jaime Balmes 11, 10th floor, Colonia Los Morales, T 395-9988; New Zealand Embassy, JL Lagrange 103, 10th floor, Polanco, T 281-5486, F 281-5212.

British Embassy, C Río Lerma 71, T 207-2593/2449 (Apdo 96 bis, Mexico 5), open Mon and Thur 0900-1400 and 1500-1800, Tues, Wed, Fri, 0900-1500; Consular Section at C Usumacinta 30, immediately behind main Embassy Building; reading room in main building; poste restante for 1 month, please address to Consular section, this is not an official service, just a valuable courtesy; British Chamber of Commerce, Río de la Plata 30, Col Cuauhtémoc, T 256-0901; German Embassy, Byron 737, Colonia Rincón del Bosque, T 280-5534, 545-6655, open 0900-1200; French Embassy, Havre 15, nr the Cuauhtémoc Monument, T 533-1360; Netherlands Embassy, Monte Urales 635-203 (nr Fuente de Petróleos), T 202-8267, F 202-6148; Swedish Embassy, Paseo de las Palmas 1375; Danish Embassy, Tres Picos 43, Colonia Polanco, Apdo Postal 105-105, 11580 México DF, T (5) 255-3405/4145/3339, open Mon-Fri 0900-1300 (nearest metro Auditorio); Finnish Embassy, Monte Pelvoux 111, 4th floor, 11000, Mexico, DF, T 540-6036; Swiss Embassy, Edificio Torre Optima, Paseo de las Palmas 405, 11th floor, Col Lomas de Chapultepec, T 520-8535, open 0900-1200 Mon-Fri; Italian Embassy, Paseo de las Palmas 1994, Col Lomas de Chapultepec, T 596-3655; Polish Embassy, Cracovia 40, CP 01000, T 550-4700; Greek Consulate, Paseo de las Palmas 2060, Col Lomas Reforma, T 596-6333/6936; Israeli Embassy, PO Box 25389, T 540-6340, F 284-4825; Sierra Madre 215 (nearest metro Auditorio), open Mon-Fri 0900-1200. Japanese Embassy, Apdo Postal 5101, Paseo de la Reforma 395, Colonia Cuauhtémoc, T 211-0028.

● Entertainment
For all cultural events, consult Tiempo Libre, every Thur from news stands, US$1, or monthly programme pamphlets from Bellas Artes bookshop.

Theatres: Palacio de Bellas Artes (for ballet, songs, dances, also concerts 2-3 times a week, see page 253), Fábregas, Lírico, Iris, Sullivan,

Alarcón, Hidalgo, Urueta, San Rafael and Insurgentes in town and a cluster of theatres around the Auditorio Nacional in Chapultepec Park (check at Tourist Office for details of cheap programmes). Spectaculars (eg presidential inauguration) are often staged in the Auditorio Nacional itself. Also in Chapultepec Park is the Audiorama (behind the Castle on the Constituyentes side) where one may listen to recorded classical music in a small open ampitheatre in a charming wooded glade. A request book is provided, for the following day. There may be a free performance of a play in one of the parks by the Teatro Trashumante (Nomadic Theatre). Variety show nightly with singers, dancers, comedians, magicians and ventriloquists, very popular with locals, at Teatro la Blanquita, on Av Lazaro Cárdenas Sur nr Plaza Garibaldi. The Teatro de la Ciudad, Donceles 36 (T 510-2197 and 510-2942) has the Ballet Folklórico Nacional Aztlán, US$3-15 for tickets, very good shows Sun am and Wed. On Sun there is afternoon bull-fighting in a vast ring (see page 263). The balloon sellers are everywhere.

Cabarets and nightclubs: every large hotel has one. El Patio, Atenas 9; Passepartout, C Hamburgo; La Madelon, Florencia 36; Brasileirinho, León 160; Guadalupana, nr Plaza Hidalgo, Coyoacán. There are many discotheques in the better hotels and scattered throughout town.

Cinemas: a number show non-Hollywood films in original language (Spanish sub-titles); check Tiempo Libre magazine, or Mexico City News for details. Some rec cinemas are: Cineteca Nacional, metro Coyoacán (excellent bookshop on the cinema and related topics, library); Cinematógrafo del Chopo, C Dr Atl, non-commercial films daily 1700 and 1930, US$1; good cinema in Ciudad Universitaria; Cine Latino, Av Reforma between the statue of Cuauhtémoc and El Angel; Cine Versalles, Versalles (side street off Av Reforma, nr statue of Cuauhtémoc); Cine Electra, Río Guadalquivir (nr El Angel); Cine Diana, Av Reforma, at the end where Parque Chapultepec starts; Cine Palacio Chino, in the Chinese barrio S of Av Juárez (also interesting for restaurants). The sound is often very low on sub-titled films, only option is to sit nr speakers at front. All cinemas, except Cineteca Nacional, charge half-price on Wed.

Folk music: a fine place for light refreshments and music is the Hostería del Bohemio, formerly the San Hipólito monastery, nr Reforma on Av Hidalgo 107, metro Hidalgo: poetry and music every night from 1700 to 2200, light snacks and refreshments US$4 minimum, expensive but no cover charge.

● **Hospitals & medical services**

Hospital: *American British Cowdray Hospital*, or the ABC, to give it its popular name, on Observatorio past C Sur 136. T 277-5000 (emergency: 515-8359); very helpful.

Medical services: *Dr César Calva Pellicer* (who speaks English, French and German), Copenhague 24, 3° p, T 514-2529. *Dr Smythe*, Campos Elíseos 81, T 545-7861, rec by US and Canadian Embassies. For any medical services you can also go to the *Clínica Prensa*, US$1.20 for consultation, subsidized medicines. *Hospital de Jesús Nazareno*, 20 de Noviembre 82, Spanish-speaking, friendly, drugs prescribed cheaply. It is a historical monument (see page 256). Most embassies have a list of rec doctors and dentists who speak languages other than Spanish.

Pharmacies: *Farmacia Homeopática*, C Mesones 111-B. *Farmacia Nosarco*, corner of 5 de Febrero and República del Salvador, stocks wide range of drugs for stomach bugs and tropical diseases, may give 21% discount. *Sanborn's* chain and *El Fénix* discount pharmacies are the largest chains with the most complete selection (the *Sanborn's* behind the Post Office stocks gamma globulin). Many supermarkets have good pharmacies.

Vaccination centre: Benjamín Hill 14, nr metro Juanacatlán (Line 1). Open Mon-Fri 0830-1430, 1530-2030, avoid last ½-hr, also open on Sat from 0830-1430; typhoid free (this is free all over Mexico), cholera and yellow fever (Tues and Fri only) US$2; will give a prescription for gamma globulin. For hepatitis shots you have to buy gamma globulin in a pharmacy (make sure it's been refrigerated) and then an injection there (cheap but not always clean), or at a doctor's surgery or the ABC Hospital (see above). Gamma globulin is hard to find (see **pharmacies** below); try Hospital Santa Elena, Querétaro 58, Col Roma, T 574-7711, about US$50 for a vaccination. Malaria prophylaxis and advice free from San Luis Potosí 199, 6th floor, Colonia Roma Nte, 0900-1400, or from the Centro de Salud nr metro Chabacano, opp Supermercado Comercial Mexicano – no typhoid vaccinations here (ask at Centro de Salud Benjamín Hill, which does not supply malaria pills). It seems that paludrine is not available in Mexico, only chloroquine.

● **Language schools**

The UNAM has excellent classes of Spanish tuition and Mexican culture: Centro de Enseñanza para Extranjeros, US$200 for 6 weeks, five different levels, free additional courses in culture, free use of medical service, swimming pool, library, a student card from here allows free entry to all national monuments and museums and half price on many bus lines (eg ADO during summer vacations). See also National Registration Center for Study Abroad and AmeriSpan under **Learning Spanish** in **Information for travellers** page 534. See also **Cultural centres** above.

● **Laundry**

Laundry on Río Danubio, between Lerma and Panuco and at Chapultepec and Toledo, nr Sevilla metro, expensive. *Lavandería* at Chapultepec y Toledo; *Lavandería Automática* at Edison 91 has automatic machines, US$3/kg. Also at Parque España 14 and Antonio Caso 82, nr British Council. Dry cleaning shops (*tintorerías* or *lavado en seco*) are plentiful. Typical charges: jacket or skirt US$1.10, suit US$2.20, can take up to 48 hrs.

● **Places of worship**

English-speaking: Roman Catholic, St Patricks, C Bondojito, Evangelical Union, Reforma 1870; Baptist, Capital City Baptist Church, C Sur 136; Lutheran, Church of the Good Shepherd, Palmas 1910; Anglican, Mexican Anglican Cathedral, Mesones 139 (see page 261) has services in Spanish, for services in English, Christ Church, Monte Escandinavos 405, Lomas de Chapultepec (services at 0800 and 1000, sung Eucharist, take bus Reforma Km 15 or Km 16 to Monte Alti, then down hill off opp side of the road); First Church of Christ Scientist, 21 Dante, Col Anzures. Jewish, Beth Israel, Virreyes 1140., Nidche Israel (Orthodox), Acapulco 70, nr Chapultepec metro.

● **Post & telecommunications**

Chief Telegraph Office: for internal telegrams, Palace of Communications and Transport, Av Lazardo Gardena/Calzada Tacuba.

Post Office: Tacuba y Lázaro Cárdenas, opp Palacio de Bellas Artes, open for letters 0800-2400 Mon-Fri, 0800-2000 Sat, and 0900-1600 Sun. For parcels open 0900-1500 Mon-Fri only; parcels up to 2 kg (5 kg for books) may be sent. It is an interesting historic building with a stunning interior, worth a visit. Philatelic sales at windows 9 to 12. Mail kept for only 10 days at poste restante window 3, rec, but closed Sat and Sun (see page 535). If they can't find your mail under the initial of your surname, ask under the initials of any other names you may happen to have. EMS Mexpost, accelerated national and international postage is available at the central post office, the airport, Zona Rosa, Coyoacán and 13 other post offices in the city; payable by weight. Other post offices (open 0800-1900 Mon-Fri, 0800-1300 Sat) which travellers may find useful: Centre, Nezahualcóyotl 184 and Academia 4; P Arriaga y Ignacio Mcal, 2 blocks N of Monumento a la Revolución; Zona Rosa, Londres 208; Tlatelolco, Flores Magón 90; San Rafael, Schultz 102; Polanco, Polanco 79A; Lomas de Chapultepec, Prado Nte 525; Buenavista, Aldama 216; San Angel, Dr Gálvez 16; Coyoacán, Higuera 23; Iztapalapa, Calzada Ermita Iztapalapa 1033; Xochimilco, Prolongación Pino 10; also at the airport and bus terminals. In all there are 155 branches in the federal capital, so there is no need to go to the Palacio de Correos.

Telephones: see **Information for travellers** for details of the LADA phone system. Finding a phone box that works can be a problem. Most public phones take phone cards (Ladatel), costing 20-50 pesos, from shops and news kiosks everywhere. Calls abroad can be made from phone booths with credit cards (via LADA system). International calls can easily be made from the phone office in the Central del Oriente bus terminal. There are several places, inc some shops, all officially listed, with long-distance phones. For information dial 07.

● **Shopping**

Mexican jewellery and hand-made silver can be bought everywhere. Among the good silver shops are *Sanborn's, Calpini, Prieto,* and *Vendome. Joyería Sobre Diseño* (local 159) at the Ciudadela Market is helpful and will produce personalized jewellery cheaply. There are also good buys in perfumes, quality leather, and suede articles. *Woolworths* on 16 de Septiembre, and on Periférico Sur, T 806-8427, for cheap food, drinks, clothes, domestic goods, etc. With the extension of the ring roads around the city, hypermarkets are being set up: there are two, *Perisur* in the S of the city (with Liverpool, Sears, Sanborn's and Palacio de Hierro), open Tues-Fri 1100-2000, Sat 1100-2100; and *Plaza Satélite* in the N (with Sumesa, Sears and Liverpool), open on Sun. There is an ISSSTE supermarket in Tres Guerras, 2 blocks from metro Balderas and 1 block from Bucaveli. Art supplies can be found on C San Salvador.

Luggage repairs (moderate prices) at Rinconada de Jesús 15-G, opp Museo de la Ciudad de México on Pino Suárez, but opening times can be unreliable; better try the shop in Callejón del Parque del Conde off Pino Suárez opp Hospital de Jesús church. At Pino Suárez metro station are several shops selling *charro* clothing and equipment (leggings, boots, spurs, bags, saddler, etc), eg *Casa Iturriaga,* rec. Many small tailors are found in and around República de Brasil; suits made to measure in a week or less at a fraction of European prices (eg *Sastrería Guadarrama,* Brasil 54).

Guatemalan Refugee shop, Yosemite 45, Col Nápoles, off Insurgentes Sur, T 523-2114.

Bookshops: many good ones, eg in the Palacio de Bellas Artes, at the airport (Area D), *El Parnaso,* Jardín Centenario Coyoacán (see **Suburbs**), one of the best in the city, has a fashionable *cafetería; Librería Británica,* Serapio Rendón 125 (stocks this *Handbook*) has a second-hand section where you can trade in old books (as long as they're neither even slightly damaged nor 'highbrow') and buy new ones, excellent selection; *Librería Británica,* has four other branches: Antonio Caso 127 (Instituto Anglo Mexicano), Av Universidad y Av Coyoacán (Casa del Libro, metro Coyoacán), Av Madero 30-A, and E Sada Muguerza 38; *American Book Store,* Madero 25, excellent selection of Penguins and Pelicans, low mark-up, stocks this *Handbook* (also has a large branch on Revolución, 3-5 mins' by bus S of metro Barranca del Muerto); *Librería Madero,* Madero 12, good, also stocks antiquarian books; *Libros, Libros, Libros,* Monte Ararat 220, Lomas Barrilaco, T 540-4778, hundreds of hardback and paperback English titles; the shop at the entrance to the Templo Mayor has a good selection of travel books and guides in many languages; *Nueva Librería Francesa,* Hamburgo 172, T 525-1173/1213; *Librería Italiana,* Pza Río de Janeiro 53, Col Roma, T 511-6180. The *Sanborn* chain has the largest selection of English-language paperbacks, art books and magazines in the country. *Casa Libros,* Monte Athos 355 (Lomas), large stock of second-hand English books, the shop is staffed by volunteers, gifts of books welcome, all proceeds to the American Benevolent Society. *Librería Gandhi,* C Miguel Angel de Quevedo (metro Quevedo), art books, discs, tapes (try coffee in restaurant upstairs). *Libros y Discos,* Madero 1. Plenty of Spanish bookshops on C Argentina. Second-hand book market on Independencia just past junction with Eje Lázaro Cárdenas has some English books;

also Puente de Alvarado, 100m from Hidalgo metro, and Dr Bernard 42, metro Niños Héroes. Secondhand Spanish and antiquarian booksellers on Donceles between Palma and República de Brasil, about 1½ blocks from Zócalo. *La Torre de Papel*, Filomeno Mata 6-A, in Club de Periodistas, sells newspapers from all over Mexico and USA.

Cycle shops: *Tecno-Bici*, Av Manuel Acuna 27 (Camarones metro station, line 7), stocks almost all cycle spares, parts, highly rec; *Benolto*, nr Polanco metro, stocks almost all cycle spares; another good shop is between San Antonio and Mixcoac metro stations. The Escuela Médico Militar, nr Pino Suárez metro station, has a very good shop, stocking all the best known international makes for spare parts.

Handicrafts: *Fonart*, Fondo Nacional para el Fomento de las Artesanías, a state organization founded in 1974 in order to rescue, promote and diffuse the traditional crafts of Mexico. Main showroom at Av Patriotismo 691 (metro Mixcoac), T 598-1666, branches at Av Juárez 89 (metro Hidalgo), Londres 136 (Zona Rosa) and Coyoacán (Presidente Carranza 115). Competitive prices, quality superb. *The Mercado de Artesanías Finas Indios Verdes* is at Galeria Reforma Nte SA, FG Bocanegro 44 (corner of Reforma Nte, nr Statue of Cuitlahuac, Tlatelolco); good prices and quality but no bargaining. For onyx, *Müllers*, Londrés y Florencia, nr Insurgentes metro, good chess sets. There is an annual national craft fair in Mexico City, first week in December.

Markets: San Juan market, C Ayuntamiento and Arandas, nr Salto del Agua metro, good prices for handicrafts, especially leather goods and silver (also cheap fruit and health food); open Mon-Sat 0900-1900, Sun 0900-1600 (but don't go before 1000). The **Plaza Ciudadela** market (Mercado Central de Artesanías, open 1100-1800 weekdays, Sun 1100-1400), Balderas y Morelos (3 blocks S of metro Juárez), government-sponsored, fixed prices, good selection, reasonable and uncrowded, is cheaper than San Juan, but not for leather; craftsmen from all Mexico have set up workshops here (best for papier maché, lacquer, pottery and Guatemalan goods) but prices are still cheaper in places of origin. **Mercado Lagunilla** nr Glorieta Cuitláhuac (take *pesero* bus from metro Hidalgo) is a flea market where antique and collectable bargains are sometimes to be found, also a lot of rubbish (open daily but Sun best day). The market, which covers several blocks,

now has all sorts of merchandise, inc a wider range of non-silver jewellery; good atmosphere. Market (Insurgentes) in C Londres (Zona Rosa) good for silver, but other things expensive, stallholders pester visitors, only place where they do so. There is a market in every district selling pottery, glassware, textiles, *sarapes* and jewellery. Try also **San Angel** market, although with little choice and expensive, many items are exclusive to it; good leather belts, crafts and silver; open Sat only from about 1100. Mexican tinware and lacquer are found everywhere. Vast fruit and veg market, **Mercado Merced** (see page 256), metro Merced. A few blocks away on Fray Servando Teresa de Mier (nearest metro Fray Servando) lies the fascinating **Mercado Sonora**: secret potions and remedies, animals and birds as well as *artesanías*. **Buena Vista craft market**, Aldama 187 y Degollado (nearest metro Guerrero), excellent quality (open 0900-1800, Sun 0900-1400). Also on Aldama, No 211, between Sol and Luna, the **Tianguis del Chopo** is held on Sat, 1000-1600, selling clothes, records, etc, frequented by hippies, punks, rockers, and police. You can bargain in the markets and smaller shops. **Jamaica** market, Jamaica metro, line 4, huge variety of fruits and vegetables, also flowers, pottery, and canaries, parrots, geese, and ducks, indoor and outdoor halls.

Photography Kodak film (Ektachrome, not Kodachrome) is produced in Mexico and is not expensive. Imported film is also available (eg Agta slide film US$6). Cheapest film reported to be on Av Madero, eg 36 Slide Kodak Ektachrome costs US$4.50, but shop around. The price for slide film does not inc processing. Small shops around República de Chile and Tacuba are cheaper than larger ones S of Av 5 de Mayo, but it may be worth paying more for good quality prints. Special offers abound, quality is good, prints normally ready in 45 mins (no express charge), slides up to 48 hrs.

● **Sports**

Charreadas: (Cowboy displays), Rancho Grande de La Villa, at very top of Insurgentes Nte (nearest metro Indios Verdes, then walk N beyond bus station and keep asking), Sun 1100-1500, US$1.30.

Football: Sun midday, Aztec and Olympic stadia (former has a great atmosphere at football matches, latter has a Rivera mural of the history of Mexican sport); also Thur (2100) and Sat (1700). Tickets from US$3.35 at Olympic Stadium. To Aztec Stadium take metro to Taxqueña terminus, then tram en route to Xochimilco to Estadio station; about 75 mins from Zócalo. To Olympic Stadium take metro to Universidad terminus, then local bus (US$0.35) or taxi (US$1), leave Zócalo at 1045 for 1200 kick-off.

Golf: at Chapultepec Golf Club and Churubusco Country Club. These are private clubs, open to visitors only if accompanied by a member. Green fees are high (US$20 upwards).

Horse races: Hipódromo de las Américas, W of Blvd Manuel Avila Camacho, off Av Conscriptos. Beautiful track with infield lagoons and flamingoes, and plenty of atmosphere. In liquidation in 1997 and closed but a buyer has been found. Best to check with Tourist Office, T 250-0123.

Hiking: every weekend with the Alpino and Everest clubs. Club de Exploraciones de México, Juan A Mateos 146, Col Obrero (metro Chabacano), DF 06800, T 578-5730, 1930-2400 Wed or Fri organizes several walks in and around the city on Sats and Suns, cheap equipment hire, slideshow Wed. Club Alpino Mexicano, Córdoba 234, Col Roma (metro Hospital General), T 574-9683, open Mon-Fri 1030-2030, Sat 1030-1530, small shop.

Ice-skating: Pista de Hielo San Jerónimo, Av Contreras 300, Col San Jerónimo, metro B Muerto then bus to arena, T 683-1625, full-sized rink, crowded, closed Mon, US$3.50. Pista de Hielo de Galerías Reforma, Carr Mexico-Toluca 1725, Lomas Palo Alto, T 259-3543, US$3.50, small rink, not crowded.

Jai-Alai: events with the foremost players in the world every day except Fri at the Frontón México across from Monumento a la Revolución, from 2000 (1900 Sun) till 2400 (closed Mon), entry US$7, drinks expensive. It seats 4,000. Jackets and ties are needed for admission. Restaurant El Rincón Pampero. The people in the red caps are the *corredores*, who place the bets. Pari-mutuel betting. Also Frontón Metropolitano, on Bahía de Todos los Santos, nr junction of Gutemberg and Calz Melchor Ocampo.

Swimming: Agua Caliente, Las Termas, Elba, Centro Deportivo Chapultepec and others.

● **Tour companies & travel agents**

Shop around. Many agencies charge high prices and don't reflect the peso devaluation. *Thomas Cook*, Campos Eliseos 345, Col Polanco, TCs agency only; *Wagons-Lits*, Av Juárez 88, T 518-1180, also Av De Las Palmas 731, T 540-0579, very helpful and knowledgeable; *Uniclam* agent in Mexico City is Srta Rosa O'Hara, Río Pánuco 146, Apto 702, Col Cuauhtémoc, T 525-5393. *Grey Line Tours*, Londres 166, T 208-1163, reasonably priced tours, car hire, produces *This is Mexico* book (free). *American Express*, Reforma 234 y Havre, T 533-0380, open Mon-Fri 0900-1800, Sat 0900-1300, charges US$3-4 for poste restante if you do not have their TCs and US$1 if no card or cheques are held for other services, service slow but helpful. *Mundo Joven Travel Shop*, Insurgentes Sur 1510 (on the corner of Río Churubusco), T 661 3233, F 663 1556. *Corresponsales de Hoteles*, Blvd Centro 224-4, T 360-3356, for hotel reservations (upmarket); *Hadad Viajes*, Torres Adalid 205, of 602, Col de Valle, T 687-0488. *Viajes Tirol*, José Ma Rico 212, Depto 503, T 534-5582/3323/1765, English and German spoken, rec; *Turisjoven*, Tuxpan 54-903 (metro Chilpancingo). For cheap tickets to Cuba, ask round agencies around Hamburgo; *W Tours and Travel*, T 682 1718/1607, are also rec.

Finding a cheap flight to Europe is difficult. Try *Vacation Planning*, Copenhague 21-203, Zona Rosa, T 511-1604; *Cultours*, Guanajuato 72 (Col Roma), T 264-0854/574/6265, highly rec, good for flights to central and S America

and for changing flight dates; *Anfitriones, Turismo y Convenciones*, Río Niágara 42, nr Reforma, T 208-2553/3752 (ask for Marco Polo, good English), rec; *Beltravel*, Londres 51, Zona Rosa; *Viajes de Alba*, Villalongín 20-2, Col Cuauhtémoc, T 705-4180.

● **Tourist offices**
The **Mexican Secretariat of Tourism** (Secretaría de Turismo) is at C Masaryk 172, 5th floor, between Hegel and Emerson, Colonia Polanco (reached by bus No 32), T 250-8555, ext 116, F 254-2636, emergency hot line 250-0123/0151. Lots of printed information but little knowledge about places off the tourist trail. Booking of hotels in other parts of the country possible here. The tourist office produces a telephone directory in English and French. There is an office for Mexico City and the state of México at the corner of Londres and Amberes, Zona Rosa, helpful. You may refer complaints here, or to the tourist police, in blue uniforms, who are reported to be very friendly. Articles from the various craft displays can be bought. Free maps not always available, but try Cámara de Comercio de la Ciudad de México, Información Turística, open Mon-Fri 0900-1400, 1500-1800, at Reforma 42, which provides maps and brochures of the city (apparently for government employees only); may otherwise be got from Department of Public Works; or buy in bookshops. Bus and metro maps available. Information bureau outside Insurgentes metro station and on Juárez, just E of Paseo de la Reforma (closed Sun). Tourist information can be dialled between 0800 and 2000 (bilingual operator) on 525-9380. For problems, eg theft, fraud, abuse of power by officials, T 516-0490, *Protectur*, Also try the *Agencia Especializada en asuntos de Turista*, C Horencia 20, Col Judice, English spoken, very helpful. Incidentally, museums are closed Mon, except Chapultepec Castle, which is open daily. A weekly magazine, *The Gazer/El Mirón* gives basic information and tips for Mexico City and elsewhere in Mexico. Also *Mexico City Daily Bulletin*, free from most hotels, good listings, exchange rate information unreliable. The magazine *Donde* (US$2) gives general information, details on hotels, restaurants, crafts and entertainment. *Concierge* is a monthly tourist guide in English and Spanish with information on Mexico City.

● **Useful addresses**
Customs: Dirección General de Aduanas, 20 de Noviembre 195, T 709-2900.

Delegation building: Av Central, the Ministry of Public Works is the place to report a theft; take a long book.

Immigration: Instituto Nacional de Migración, Av Chapultepec 284, T 795-6685. Go to Metro Insurgentes where a Mexican flag marks Servicios Migratorios, 0900-1100, long queues, no English spoken. Here you can extend tourist cards for stays over 90 days or replace lost cards. New card will be given in 10 days; you may be given 10 days to leave the country.

Maps: **Instituto Nacional de Estadística Geografía e Informática (INEGI)** sells maps and has information, branches in each state capital and in the Distrito Federal in the arcade below the traffic roundabout at Insurgentes (where the metro station is), open 0800-1600, all maps available, but only one index for consultation. The Automobile Club's (AMA) street map is good, but hard to find. Good maps of the city from HFET (see **Maps** in **Information for travellers**), *Guía Roji* (an excellent A to Z, US$14), and *Trillas Tourist Guide* (US$6.50, rec). Street vendors on Zócalo and in kiosks sell a large city map for US$3. Good large postcard/map of Coyoacán available at many bookshops.

Setej (Mexican Students' Union): Hamburgo 301, Zona Rosa, metro Sevilla, only office to issue student card, which is required to buy a hostel card, T 211-0743 or 211-6636, deals with ISIS insurance. To obtain national student card you need 3 photos, passport, confirmation of student status and US$7. Open Mon-Fri 0900-1800, Sat 0900-1400.

● **Transport**
Local Car hire agencies: Budget Rent Auto, Reforma 60; **Hertz**, Revillagigedo 2; **Avis**, Medellín 14; **VW**, Av Chapultepec 284-G; **National Car Rental**, Insurgentes Sur 1883; **Auto Rent**, Reforma Nte 604; quick service at Av Chapultepec 168, T 533-5335 (762-9892 airport); **Pamara**, Hamburgo 135, T 525-5572, **NB** 200 km free mileage; **Odin**, Balderas 24-A; and many local firms, which tend to be cheaper. It is generally cheaper to hire in the US or Europe. **NB** When driving in the capital you must check which 'día sin auto' 'hoy no circula' applies to your vehicle's number plate; if your car is on the street when its number is prohibited, you could be fined US$80. This should not apply to foreign-licensed cars. The regulation covers the state of México besides the Distrito Federal. The ban applies to the last digit of your number plate: Mon 5,6; Tues 7,8; Wed 3,4; Thur 1,2; Fri 9,0; Sat, all even numbers and 0; Sun, all odd numbers (emergency only at weekends). You

can drive freely in 'greater' Mexico City on Sat, Sun and between 2200 and 0500.

City buses: buses have been coordinated into one system: odd numbers run NS, evens EW. Fares on large buses, which display routes on the windscreen are US$0.10, exact fare only. There are 60 direct routes and 48 feeder (SARO) routes. We are informed that thieves and pickpockets haunt the buses plying along Reforma and Juárez. Be careful of your valuables! A most useful route for tourists (and well-known to thieves, so don't take anything you don't require immediately) is No 76 which runs from C Uruguay (about the level of the Juárez Monument at Parque Alameda) along Paseo de la Reforma, beside Chapultepec Park. A *Peribus* service goes round the entire Anillo Periférico (see Traffic System.) Trolley buses also charge US$0.10. *Peseros* run on fixed routes, often between metro stations and other known landmarks; destination and route displayed on the windscreen. Avoid the smaller, white VW Kombis which do not have catalytic converters and which can be unpleasant. *Peseros* can be hailed almost anywhere and stop anywhere (press the button or say 'bajan'); this can make long journeys slow. If a Ruta 100 bus runs on the same route, it is preferable as it has fixed stops. Fares are N$1 up to 5 km, N$1.50 up to 10 km and N$2 over 10 km. No tip necessary; 20% price increase between 2200 and 0600.

Metro: free maps of the network are usually available from ticket offices at big stations and tourist offices and are displayed at most stations. There is a metro information service at Insurgentes station on Pink Line which dispenses maps and most interchange stations have information kiosks. The *Atlas de Carreras*, US$1.65 has a map of Mexico City, its centre and the metro lines marked. *Pronto's* map of the metropolitan area displays the metro clearly. Good metro and bus maps at the Anthropology Museum, US$1.25. *Guía práctica del Metro*, US$9, explains all the station symbols; also *Guía cultural del Metro*, US$3, both for sale at Zócalo station. All the stations have a symbol, eg the grasshopper signifying Chapultepec. There are nine lines in service. **1** from Observatorio (by Chapultepec Park) to Pantitlán in the eastern suburbs. It goes under Av Chapultepec and not far from the lower half of Paseo de la Reforma, the Mercado Merced, and 3 km from the airport. **2**, from Cuatro Caminos in the NW to the Zócalo and then S above ground to Taxqueña; **3**, from Indios Verdes S to the University City (free bus service to Insurgentes); **4**, from Santa Anita on the SE

side to Martín Carrera in the NE; **5**, from Pantitlán, via Terminal Aérea (which is within walking distance of gate A of the airport, but some distance from the international gates – opens 0600), crossing Line 3 at La Raza, up to Politécnico (if using La Raza to connect with Line 5, note that there is a long walk between Lines 5 and 3, through the Tunnel of Knowledge); **6**, from El Rosario in the NW to Martín Carrera in the NE; **7**, from El Rosario in the NW to Barranca del Muerto in the SW; **9** parallels 1 to the S, running from Tacubaya (where there are interesting paintings in the station) in the W to Pantitlán in the E. Line **8**, the newest, runs from Garibaldi (N of Bellas Artes, Line 2), through Chabacano (Line 9), Santa Anita (Line 4), to Constitución de 1917 in the SE. In addition to the numbered lines: running SE from Pantitlán, Line A, the *metro férreo* goes as far as La Paz, 10 stations in all. From Taxqueña the *tren ligero* goes as far as Xochimilco, a very convenient way to this popular destination. Line B is to be built from Buenavista to Ciudad Azteca in Ecatepec, N of the city. Music is played quietly at the stations. Tickets 1 peso, buy several to avoid queuing, check train direction before entering turn-stile or you may have to pay again. If you want to use the metro often, you can buy an *abono*, available on 1st or 16th of month from stations, Conasupo stores, special booths in the city, and some lottery sellers), which allows you to use the whole system and the 100 buses, trolleybuses, the *metro férreo* and the *tren ligero* for 15 days: remember in this case to use the blue entrances to the metro stations, or your *abono* will be lost. An efficient, modern system (virtually impossible to get lost), and the best method of getting around the city, especially when the pollution is bad. Trains are fast, frequent, clean and quiet although overcrowded at certain times (eg early morning, 1400-1500 and 1830-2000). When carriages are crowded, be alert for pickpockets (if possible don't stand nr the sliding doors). Several reports of theft. Pino Suárez, Hidalgo and Terminal Central del Nte are particularly 'infamous' for thieves. Between 1800 and 2100 men are separated from women and children at Pino Suárez and certain other stations. Two pieces of medium-sized luggage are permitted. At the Zócalo metro station there is a permanent exhibit about the city, interesting. At Pino Suárez, station has been built around a small restored Aztec temple. Art in the metro: Line 1, Pino Suárez and Tacubaya; Line 2, Bellas Artes and Panteones; Line 3, La Raza, scientific display in the Tunnel of Knowledge, and S of Coyoacán; Line 4, Santa Anita; Line 5, Terminal Aérea; Line 6, all stations, Line 7, Barranca del Muerto; Line 9, Mixuca. **NB** Lines 1, 2, 3 and A open 0500-0030 Mon-Fri, 0600-0130 Sat and 0700-0030 Sun and holidays; the other lines open 1 hr later

on weekdays (same hours on weekends and holidays). Do not take photos or make sound-recordings in the metro without obtaining a permit and a uniformed escort from metro police, or you could be arrested. For lost property enquire at Oficina de Objetos Extraviados at

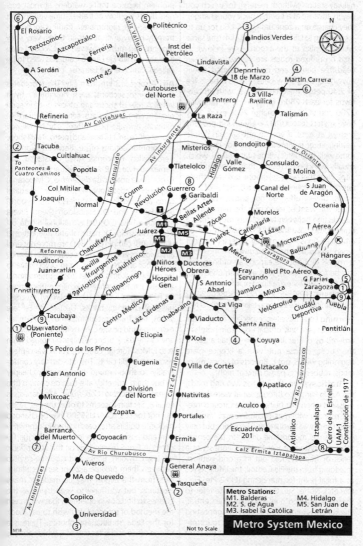

Metro Stations:
M1. Balderas
M2. S. de Agua
M3. Isabel la Católica
M4. Hidalgo
M5. San Juan de Letrán

Metro System Mexico

Not to Scale

Chabacano (intersection of lines 2,8 and 9), open Mon-Fri only.

Taxi: there are three types: 1) 'turismo' taxis which operate from first class hotels, the Museo Nacional de Antropología, etc – the most expensive. 2) Taxis from bus terminals and the railway station (without meters), for which you pay in advance at a booth (check your change); they charge on a zone basis, US$4.60 for up to 4 km, rising to US$22 for up to 22 km (the same system applies at the airport – see below). 3) Taxis on unfixed routes are yellow, and green (lead-free petrol) and can be flagged down anywhere; the yellow ones charge a basic fee of 2.40 pesos, the green ones 3, with 35 centavos for each 250m or 45 seconds; between 2200 and 0600 they charge 20% extra. They have meters (check they are working properly and set at zero); if you do not bargain before getting in, or if the driver does not know the route well, the meter will be switched on, which usually works out *cheaper* than negotiating a price. Note that radio-telephone taxis, and those with catalitic converters have a basic fee of 2.50 pesos. Drivers often do not know where the street you want is; try to give the name of the intersection between two streets rather than a number, because the city's numbering can be erratic. A tip is not normally expected, except when special help has been given. At most bus terminals (but not the airport) an ordinary taxi can be found nearby. Also avoiding unscrupulous demands for extra tips. For information, or complaints, T 605-5520/6727/ 5388/ 6894; if complaining make sure you take the taxi's ID No.

Warning Lone travellers, especially female, are advised to take only official taxis from hotels or ordered by phone. If you have to hail a taxi in the street, choose one with a licence plate beginning with S, not L. Reports of rapes, muggings, robbery etc, particularly at night.

Traffic system: the city has two ring roads, the Anillo Periférico through what were the city outskirts when first built, and the Circuito Interior running within its circumference. You can cross the city via Viaducto and Periférico but only with a *small* motorhome or car. In the centre, there is a system of Ejes Viales. It consists of a series of freeways laid out in a grid pattern, spreading from the Eje Central; the latter serves as a focal point for numbering (Eje 2 Pte, Eje I Ote etc). Norte, Sur, Oriente, Poniente refer to the roads' position in relation to the Eje Central. The system is remarkably clear in its signposting with special symbols for telephones, information points, tram stops, etc. Beware of the tram lines – trams, buses, emergency services and folk in a hurry come down at high speed; and as often as not this lane goes against the normal flow of traffic! Bicycles are permitted to go the wrong way on all roads, which also 'adds to the spice of life'. Driving is not too much of a problem because traffic wardens at most corners direct the flow of traffic (some visitors find city driving a nightmare). Traffic can be extremely heavy and, at certain times, very slow moving. You must, however, have a good map (see above). **NB** Eje Lázaro Cárdenas used to be called C San Juan de Letrán.

Air Airport, 13 km from city. The terminal is divided into sections, each designated by a letter. A row of shops and offices outside each section contains various services. Section **A**: national arrivals; post office, city of Mexico tourist office, exit to taxis and metro, INAH shop, telecommunications office. Between **A** and **B**: AeroMéxico; Bancomer ATM. Outside **B**: Banamex. Between **B** and **C**: entrance to *Continental Plaza* hotel, *casa de cambio*. **C** Mexicana; map shop. Ladatel phones just after C (Ladatel cards are sold at many outlets in the airport). Between **C** and **D**: Exposición Diego Rivera exhibition hall. **C-D**: Other national airline offices; bookshop. **D**: national and international departures; *cambio* opp. By D are more national airline desks and long distance phones. Also by D is a bar and restaurant. From D you have to leave the building to get to **E**: international arrivals; car hire offices, exchange (Banamex), 24-hr luggage lockers (US$2.50/day). **F**: international check-in; banks. Upstairs at E-F are shops, fast food restaurants (mostly US-style), exchange and phones. Pesos may be bought at any of the bank branches liberally spread from A to F. Most foreign currencies or TCs accepted, also most credit cards. The rate can vary considerably, so shop around. It is generally cheaper to buy 'hard' currency at a *casa de cambio* (the *centro de Cambio Coberturas Mexicanas*, in Local 8, Section E, seems to offer the best rates, but not for TCs). Only US$500 may be changed back into dollars after passing through immigration and customs when leaving. Exchange facilities in E or F (particularly on the upper floor) are less crowded. Banks and *casas de cambio* between them provide a 24-hr service. Phone calls from the airport may be made at many locations, but you have to keep trying all the phones to find one in operation that will accept the method of payment you wish to use. Look for the Lada 'multitarjeta' phones. There is a phone office at the far end of F, which accepts

Amex and, in theory, Visa, Mastercard and other cards. It is very expensive though. Fixed-price taxis by zone, buy tickets from booths at exits by A, E and F; rates range from US$5 upwards, according to distance (per vehicle, not per person), drivers may not know, or may be unwilling to go to, cheaper hotels. For losses or complaints about airport taxis, T 571-3600 Ext 2299; for reservations 571-9344/784-8642, 0800-0200. The fixed price taxi system is efficient and safe. A cheaper alternative (about 50%) if one doesn't have too much luggage is to cross the Blvd Puerto Aéreo by the metro Terminal Aérea and flag down an ordinary taxi outside the *Ramada* hotel. Journey about 20 mins from town centre if there are no traffic jams. There are regular buses to the airport (eg No 20, along N side of Alameda) but the drawback is that you have to take one to Calzada Ignacio Zaragoza and transfer to trolley bus at the Blvd Puerto Aéreo (ie at metro station Aeropuerto). Buses to airport may be caught every 45 mins until 0100 from outside *De Carlo Hotel*, Plaza República 35. It takes an hour from downtown and in the rush hour, most of the day, it is jam-packed. But you can take baggage if you can squeeze it in. To get to the airport cheaply, take metro to Terminal Aérea and walk, or take metro to Blvd Pto Aéreo and then a *pesero* marked 'Oceanía', which will leave you at the Terminal metro station. Avoid rush hours especially if you have luggage. There are airport information kiosks at A, D, E and F. There is an hotel desk **before** passing through customs. The tourist office at A has phones for calling hotels, no charge, helpful, but Spanish only. The travel agency at E exit will book hotels or reconfirm flights, charges 5 pesos. For air freight contact the Agencia Aduanales, Plazuela Hermanos, Colima 114, Mon-Fri 0900-1700, US$5.75/kilo.

Trains The Buenavista central station (a spacious building) is on Insurgentes Nte, junction Alzate with Mosqueta, nearest metro Revolución or Guerrero. Left luggage for US$1.25/piece/day, open 0630-2130. *Cafeteria* reasonable. At the station there are long distance phone and fax services and an information desk. For details of train services, see destinations in text. A monthly timetable, *Rutas Ferroviarias*, is available from the station (Departamento de Tráfico de Pasajeros) and from ticket offices. Reservations T 597-6177, 5 lines; information T 547-1084/1097. If planning a train journey, find out in advance whether the service is actually running, the departure time, which floor the ticket will be sold on and when, and arrive 1 hr

in advance. In general, 1st class tickets can be bought in advance, 2nd class are only available on the day. **NB** Lost or stolen tickets will not be replaced.

Buses Long-distance buses: for details of bus services, see destinations in text. At all bus stations there are many counters for the bus companies, not all are manned and it is essential to ask which is selling tickets for the destination you want (don't take notice boards at face value). On the whole, the bus stations are clean and well organized. Book ahead where possible. Buses to destinations in N Mexico, inc US borders, leave from **Central del Norte**, Av Cien Metros 4907, which has a *casa de cambio*, 24-hr cafés, left luggage, pharmacy, bakery and phone offices for long distance calls (often closed and poorly informed, very high charges). The bus station is on metro line 5 at Autobuses del Norte. City buses marked Cien Metros or Central del Norte go directly there. **Central del Sur**, at corner of Tlalpan 2205 across from metro Taxqueña (line 2), serves Cuernavaca, Acapulco, Zihuatanejo areas. Direct buses to centre (Donceles) from Central del Sur, and an express bus connects the Sur and Norte terminals. It is difficult to get tickets to the S, book as soon as possible; the terminal for the S is chaotic. The **Central del Poniente** is situated opp the Observatorio station of line 1 of the metro, to serve the W of Mexico. You can go to the centre by bus from the 'urbano' terminal outside the Poniente terminal (US$0.10). The **Central del Oriente**, known as TAPO, Calzada Ignacio Zaragoza (metro San Lazaro, Line 1), for buses to Veracruz, Yucatán and SE, inc Oaxaca (it has a tourist information office open from 0900, luggage lockers, US$2.65/day, key is left with guard; post office, *farmacia* changes TCs). To Guatemala, from TAPO, take a bus to Tapachula, Comitán or Ciudad Cuauhtémoc, pesos only accepted. There are also buses departing from Mexico City airport (outside Sala D), to Puebla, Toluca, Cuernavaca and Querétaro, very convenient. Buy ticket from driver.

All bus terminals operate taxis with voucher system and there are long queues (check change carefully at the taxi office). It is much easier to pay the driver, although beware of extra charges. Easier still is to flag down a yellow VW taxi on the street outside the terminal. In the confusion at the terminals some drivers move each other's cabs to get out of the line faster and may take your voucher and disappear. Fares are given under **Taxis** above. The terminals are connected by metro, but this is not a good option at rush hours, or if carrying too much luggage. Advance booking is rec for all trips, and very early reservation if going to *fiestas* during Holy Week, etc. At Christmas, many Central American students return home via Tapachula and buses from Mexico City are booked solid for 2 weeks before, except for those lines which do not make reservations. You must go and queue at the bus stations; this can involve some long waits, sometimes 2-2½ hrs. Even if you are travelling, you may sometimes be required to buy a *boleto de andén* (platform ticket) at many bus stations. Note that many bus companies require luggage to be checked in 30 mins in advance of departure.

Bus companies: (tickets and bookings) Going N: Transportes del Nte, at Av Insurgentes Centro 137, nr Reforma (T 587-5511/5400); dep from Central Nte. Omnibús de México, Insurgentes Nte 42, at Héroes Ferrocarrileros (T 567-6756 and 567-5858). Greyhound bus, Reforma 27, T 535-2618/4200, F 535-3544, closed 1400-1500 and all day Sun; information at Central Nte from Transportes del Nte (Chihuahuenses) or Tres Estrellas bus counters, prices only, no schedules. Going to Central States: Autobuses Anáhuac, Bernal Díaz 6 (T 591-0533); Central Nte departures. Going NW: ETN, Central México Nte, T 567-3773, or Central del Pte T 273-0251; Tres Estrellas de Oro, Calzada Vallejo 1268 Nte (Col Santa Rosa), T 391-1139/3021, Central Nte. Going NE: ADO, Av Cien Metros 4907 (T 567-8455/5322). Beware of ADO selling tickets for buses and then not running the service. Although the ticket will be valid for a later bus, there are then problems with overbooking (your seat number won't be valid). Going S (inc Guatemala): Cristóbal Colón, Blvd Gral Ignacio Zaragoza 200, T 542-7263 to 66; from Central del Ote; also ADO, Buenavista 9 (T 592-3600 or 542-7192 at terminal). Going SW: Estrella de Oro, Calzada de Tlalpan 2205 (T 549-8520 to 29). **Warning** Beware of con men at bus terminals or airport. Reports of one, Bernardo Kan, who claims to have been robbed and unable to get his flight. He pledges to return your borrowed money in Palenque where his mother lives, but this is fictitious.

SUBURBS OF MEXICO CITY

CHURUBUSCO

Churubusco, 10 km SE, reached from the Zócalo by Coyoacán or Tlalpan bus, or from General Anaya metro station, to see the picturesque and partly ruined convent (1762) at Gen Anaya y 20 de Agosto, now become the **Museo Nacional de las Intervenciones** (open 0900-1800, closed Mon, US$3.35, free Sun and holidays). 17 rooms filled with mementoes, documents, proclamations and pictures recounting foreign invasions, incursions and occupations since independence (also has temporary exhibitions). The site of the museum was chosen because it was the scene of a battle when the US Army marched into Mexico City in 1847. Adjoining the ex-convento is the church of San Diego (16th century, with 17th and 18th century additions). Near the church, on the other side of Calzada Gen Anaya is the delightful Parque de Churubusco. One block from Tlalpan along Héroes del 47, to the left, is the 18th century church of San Mateo. There is a golf course at the Churubusco Country Club. Churubusco has the principal Mexican film studios. The new Olympic swimming pool is here. Near enough to Coyoacán (see page 287) to walk there.

TLALPAN

Tlalpan, 6½ km further out, or direct from Villa Obregón (see page 285) a suburb with colonial houses, gardens, and near the main square, Plaza de la Constitución, an early 16th century church (San Agustín) with a fine altar and paintings by Cabrera. Reached by bus or trolley bus from the Taxqueña metro station. 2½ km W is the suburb of Peña Pobre, near which, to the NE, is the Pyramid of **Cuicuilco**, believed to be the oldest in Mexico (archaeological museum on site, Insurgentes Sur Km 16, intersection with Periférico, open 0800-1800, closed Mon). The pyramid dates from the 5th or 6th century BC; it is over 100m in diameter but only 25m high.

AJUSCO

Another excursion can be made to **Ajusco**, about 20 km SW of Mexico City. Catch a bus from Estadio Azteca on Calzada Tlalpan direct to Ajusco. From the summit of the extinct **Volcán Ajusco** (3,929m), there are excellent views on a clear day. The way up is 10 km W of the village, 400m W of where the road branches to Xalatlaco (there is a hut S of the road where the path goes to the mountain). Foothills are also pleasant.

XOCHIMILCO

Some 20 km to the SE of the city centre, **Xochimilco** has many attractions, not least the fact that it lies in an unpolluted area.

Easiest access is by bus, pesero or metro to Metro Tasqueña, then (about 20 mins) *tren ligero*. Get off at terminal (misleadingly named 'Embarcadero', as there are several embarcaderos, see map and below).

Meaning 'The place where flowers are grown', it was an advanced settlement long before the arrival of the Spaniards. Built on a lake, it developed a form of agriculture using 'chinampas', or 'floating gardens'; the area is still a major

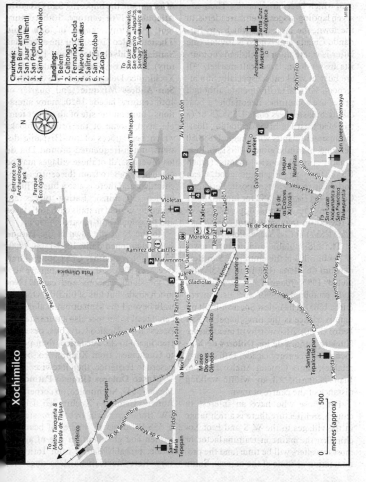

supplier of fruit and vegetables to Mexico City. The Spaniards recognized the importance of the region and the need to convert the indigenous population: evidence of this is the considerable number of 16th and 17th century religious buildings in Xochimilco itself and in the other 13 pueblos which make up the present-day Delegación, or municipality.

Xochimilco is famous for its canals and colourful punt-like boats, or *trajineras*, which bear girls' names. There are seven landing-stages, or embarcaderos, in the town, the largest of which are Fernando Celada and Nuevo Nativitas (the latter is where most coach-loads of tourists are set down, large craft-market). All are busy at weekends, especially Sun afternoon. Official tariffs operate, although prices are sometimes negotiable: a boat taking 6 passengers costs US$5.75/hr (a trip of at least 1½ hrs is desirable); floating mariachi bands will charge US$3.50 per song, marimba groups US$1.50. Reasonably priced tourist menus (lunch US$2) from passing boats; good, clean and cheap restaurants opposite Fernando Celada (eg *Beto's*, US$2 for lunch); more expensive restaurants opposite Nuevo Nativitas; in town, excellent *comida corrida* (US$2) at *Con Sazón*, Pino 70.

The indisputable architectural jewel of Xochimilco is the church of **San Bernardino de Siena** (begun in 1535, completed 1595; magnificent Renaissance style retable, 1580-90) and its convent (circa 1585). The oldest Spanish-built religious edifice is the tiny chapel of **San Pedro** (1530). Also worthy of mention are **Nuestra Señora de los Dolores de Xaltocán** (17th century façade, 18th century retable), Santa Crucita Analco and San Juan Tlatentli. All are within walking distance of the centre of town.

For those who have an interest in church architecture there is a rich range in the villages to the W, S and E of Xochimilco; the main constraining factor for most travellers will be time (and the pronunciation of some of the names). **Santa María Tepepan** (1612-21), unique decorated earthenware font dated 1599; *tren ligero* Tepepan, walk up 5 de Mayo; **Santiago Tepatcatlalpan** (1770); **San Lucas Xochimanca** (16th century); **San Francisco Tlanepantla** (small 17th century chapel), village right in the country, superb views; **San Lorenzo Atemoaya** (16th century). After **Santa Cruz Acalpixca** (16th century with 17th century façade), near a mediocre Archaeological Museum, are the imposing **San Gregorio Atlapulco** (17th century; 16th century font), the tiny chapel of **San Luis Tlaxiatemalco** (1633) and the enormous **Santiago Tulyehualco** (late 18th century). Finally, beyond the boundary of the Xochimilco Delegación, is the church of **San Andrés Míxquic** (2nd quarter of 16th century; façade 1620; many alterations), built on the site of an earlier temple, using some of the original blocks which bear traces of pre-Hispanic designs; much-frequented around Día de los Muertos. All of these villages may be reached by pesero from the centre of Xochimilco, and there is also a bus to Tulyehualco (30 mins). Eating places are generally limited to stalls with rolls, tacos and occasional spit-roasted chicken.

To the N of the town is the **Parque Ecológico** (open daily, 1000-1800, 1000-1700 winter months, US$1.50, children free, over-60s US$0.75), an extensive area of grassland, lagoons and canals. Not much shade, but lots of birdlife. One can walk beyond the asphalt paths along the canal banks. There is also a punt-station. Access from Mexico City: bus, pesero or tren ligero to the Periférico, then pesero to Cuemanco; from Xochimilco, bus or pesero to Periférico, then likewise.

Museo Dolores Olmedo Patiño (Av México 5843, Xochimilco, on corner with Antiguo Camino a Xochimilco, 1 block SW from La Noria *tren ligero* station, T 555-1016), set in 8 acres of beautiful garden and grassland on site of an old estate, probably dating from 16th century. Rare Mexican hairless dogs and peacocks parade. Houses 137 works by Diego Rivera, 25 by Frida Kahlo, and an important collection of drawings by Angelina Beloff. There are also pre-Hispanic artefacts, 19th century antiques and Mexican folk art. Highly recommended (open 1000-1800, Tues-Sun, US$1.50, students US$0.75). (Very pleasant open and covered cafés; **D** *Hotel Plaza El Mesón*, Av México 64, T 676-4163, restaurant.) Tourist office at Pino 36, open 0800-2100.

IXTAPALAPA

At the foot of the Cerro de Estrella, whose top is reached by a paved road or a path for some ruins, it has a small museum, a good view of volcanoes and two good churches: the Santuario del Calvario (1856), and San Lucas (1664), original roof timbers restored in 19th century, main door embodies Aztec motifs, fine interior. One of the most spectacular of Mexican passion-plays begins at Ixtapalapa on Holy Thursday.

CIUDAD UNIVERSITARIA

(University City), world-famous, founded in 1551, is 18 km via Insurgentes Sur on the Cuernavaca highway. Perhaps the most notable building is the 10-storey library tower, by Juan O'Gorman, its outside walls iridescent with mosaics telling the story of scientific knowledge, from Aztec astronomy to molecular theory.

The **Rectoría** has a vast, mosaic-covered and semi-sculptured mural by Siqueiros. Across the highway is the **Olympic Stadium**, with seats for 80,000, in shape, colour, and situation a world's wonder, but now closed, and run down. Diego Rivera has a sculpture-painting telling the story of Mexican sport. A new complex has been completed beyond the Ciudad Universitaria, including the newspaper library (the **Hemeroteca Nacional**), **Teatro Juan Ruiz de Alarcón**, **Sala Nezahuacoyotl** (concerts etc), bookshop and post office; also the **Museo Universitario Contemporáneo de Arte** and the **Espacio Escultórico** (sculptures – a large circular area of volcanic rock within a circle of cement – monoliths; on the opposite side of the road is another large area with many huge sculptures; stick to the path as it is possible to get lost in the vegetation). In the University museum there is an exhibition of traditional masks from all over Mexico. Beyond the Olympic Stadium is also the **Jardín Botánico Exterior** which shows all the cactus species in Mexico (ask directions, it's a 30-min walk, open 0700-1630).

The University offers 6-week courses (US$200, plus US$35 if you enroll late, good, student card useful).

● **Transport** Bus (marked CU, one passes along Eje Lázaro Cárdenas; also bus 17, marked Tlalpan, which runs the length of Insurgentes) gets you there, about 1 hr journey. Another way to the university is on metro line 3 to Copilco station (20 mins' walk to University) or to Universidad station (30 mins' walk). At the University City there is a free bus going round the campus.

Further E is **Anahuacalli** (usually called the **Diego Rivera Museum**, open Tues-Sun 1000-1400, 1500-1800, closed Holy Week, US$1.70, free Sun). Here is a very fine collection of precolumbian sculpture and pottery, effectively displayed in a pseudo-Mayan tomb built for it by Diego Rivera. Reached by Kombi 29 bus from the Taxqueña metro station to Estadio Azteca, or take the bus marked División del Norte from outside Salto del Agua metro. Calle Museo branches off División del Norte. There is a big display here for the Day of the Dead at the beginning of November.

VILLA OBREGON

(Popularly known as **San Angel**) 13 km SW, has narrow, cobble-stone streets, many old homes, huge trees, and the charm of an era now largely past. Most of the distinguished architecture is of the 19th century. See the triple domes of its church, covered with coloured tiles, of the former Convento del Carmen, now the **Museo Colonial del Carmen**, which

Villa Obregón/San Angel

houses 17th and 18th century furniture and paintings (open 1000-1700). See also the beautifully furnished and preserved old house, **Casa del Risco** (photographic ID required for entry, open Tues-Sun 1000-1700, free), near the Bazar del Sábado, on Callejón de la Amargura; also the church of San Jacinto, once belonging to a Dominican convent (1566). The **Museo de Arte Carrillo Gil**, Av Revolución 1608, has excellent changing exhibits and the **Museo Estudio Diego Rivera** (Av Altavista y C Diego Rivera, opposite Antigua Hacienda de Goicochea – now *San Angel Inn*); the museum shows many of Rivera's personal belongings, the building was built by Juan O'Gorman. The Bazar del Sábado is a splendid Sat folk art and curiosity market. Reach San Angel by bus from Chapultepec Park or by metro line 3 to MA Quevedo. There is a YWCA (ACF) at San Angel, but it is expensive (E) with hot water for 2 hrs in the morning only,

and use of kitchen 1800-2200. Excellent restaurants: the *San Angel Inn* is first class; good *panadería* by post office (which is no good for letters abroad). Between Villa Obregón and Coyoacán is the monument to Obregón on the spot where he was assassinated in 1928 (by the junction of Av Insurgentes Sur and Arenal); the monument is open 0900-1400. Desierto de los Leones (see below) is reached from Villa Obregón by a scenic road. The **Centro Cultural San Angel** (on Revolución opposite Museo del Carmen) stages exhibitions, concerts, lectures etc; **La Carpa Geodésica**, Insurgentes Sur 2135 has theatre of all types from works for children to very avant-garde; the **Centro Cultural Helénico** (Insurgentes 1500, metro Barranca del Muerto) always has a lively and diversified programme of drama, music and dance.

Magdalena Contreras has many characteristics of the old Spanish village. Up in the hills in the SW of the city, it can be reached by *pesero* or bus from San Angel (or by bus direct from Taxqueña), about 30-45 mins. There is an attractive main square and an 18th century church on the site of an earlier structure. *Artesanías* and multiple *taquerías*, etc; good *comida corrida* at *Restaurante del Camino* and *Local 29* in the main square. From the village take another bus (bus station behind church), or *pesero*, up to **Los Dinamos** ($3\frac{1}{2}$ km), site of former pumping stations, now a National Park with picnic areas, waterfalls, horseriding, breathtaking scenery and, above all, clean air. There are *pulquerías* invitingly placed at intervals. If walking, bear in mind that you are quite a lot higher than in the city.

COYOACAN

The oldest part of Mexico City, Coyoacán is the place from which Cortés launched his attack on Tenochtitlán. It is also one of the most beautiful and best-preserved parts of the city, with hundreds of fine buildings from the 16th-19th centuries, elegant tree-lined avenues and carefully tended parks and, in the Jardín Centenario and the Plaza Hidalgo, two very attractive squares. There are no supermarkets, no high-rise buildings, no hotels, no metro stations (see below). It is an area that is best explored on foot. (An excellent postcard-cum-pedestrian map of the Centro Histórico of Coyoacán to be found in local book and gift shops.)

It is culturally one of the most lively parts of Mexico City, and with its attractive cafés and good shops it is much frequented by the inhabitants of the capital, particularly at weekends. From Villa Obregón, one can reach Coyoacán via a delightful walk through Chimalistac, across Universidad and down Av Francisco Sosa; or one can take a bus or *pesero* marked 'Tasqueña' as far as Caballocalco.

Places of interest

From the city centre, it is easiest to take the metro to Viveros, or General Anaya.

Alternatively, metro to Coyoacán then *pesero* for Villa Coapa, which drops you in the historic centre. If coming from metro Viveros (a large park in which trees are grown for other city parks), it is worth making a slight detour in order to walk the length of **Francisco Sosa**, said to be the first urban street laid down in Spanish America. At the beginning of this elegant avenue is the church of **San Antonio Panzacola** (18th century), by the side of Río Churubusco; nearby, on Universidad, is the remarkable, beautiful (and modern) chapel of **Nuestra Señora de la Soledad**, built in the grounds of the 19th century ex-hacienda El Altillo. A little way down, in Salvador Novo, is the **Museo de la Acuarela** (free admission; open Tues-Sun). The terra-cotta fronted residence at No 383 is said to have been built by Alvarado (courtyard and garden may be visited 0900-1600 Mon-Fri, no charge, enquire at entrance). Many fine houses follow, mostly built in the 19th century. **Santa Catarina**, in the square of the same name, is a fine 18th century church; on Sun, at about one o'clock, people assemble under the trees to tell stories (all are welcome to attend or participate). In the same square, the **Casa de la Cultura Jesús Reyes Heroles** should not be missed, with its delightful leafy gardens. Just before arriving at the **Jardín Centenario**, with its 16th century arches, is the **Casa de Diego Ordaz**. From metro General Anaya, there is a pleasant walk along Héroes del 47 (1 block along on the left, 16th century church of **San Lucas**), across División del Norte and down Hidalgo (1 block along on the left, and 2 blocks down San Lucas is the 18th century church of **San Mateo**). The **Museo Nacional de Culturas Populares** is at Hidalgo 289, and should be seen: open Tues-Sun 1000-1600, free, permanent and temporary exhibitions, cinema-cum-auditorio; good bookshop on Mexican culture and folklore. Another good bookshop next door, entrance on to street.

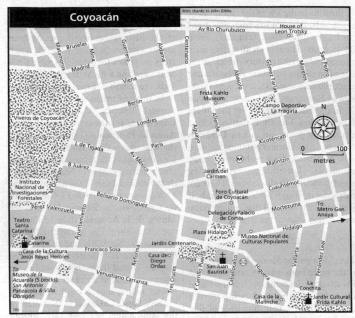

The centre of Coyoacán is dominated by the church of **San Juan Bautista** (16th century with later additions; magnificent interior); also 16th century Franciscan monastery. Centenario is 16th century. The building which now houses the **Delegación** (Plaza Hidalgo) was built 244 years after the Conquest, on the site of the Palacio de Cortés. The beautiful 18th century church of **La Conchita** (in square of the same name) is reached by taking Higuera from Plaza Hidalgo; the interior, especially the altarpiece, is magnificent, but the church is normally open only on Fri evenings and Sun mornings. On the corner of Higuera and Vallarta is what is reputed to be the house of La Malinche, Cortés' mistress. Admirers of Frida Kahlo will be pleased to know that the **Museo Frida Kahlo** (Allende and Londres 247) is now open again; two rooms are preserved as lived in by Frida Kahlo and Diego Rivera, and the rest contain drawings and paintings

by both; open Tues-Sun 1000-1700, admission US$1.50. (In the Parque de la Juventud Frida Kahlo, near Plaza de La Conchita, there is a striking bronze statue of Frida.) **Trotsky's house** is at Río Churubusco 410 (between Gómez Farías and Morelos); open Tues-Sun 1000-1700 (entry US$2, half-price with ISIC card). **NB** Also the **Museo del Retrato Hablado** (Universidad 1330-C), the **Museo Geles Cabrera** (sculpture; Xicoténcatl 181; prior appointment, T 688-3016) and the **Museo del Automóvil** (División del Norte 3752).

Coyoacán has several theatres, medium and small, and similar establishments, eg: the *Coyoacán* and *Usigli* theatres (Eleuterio Méndez, 5 blocks from metro Anaya), the *Foro Cultural de Coyoacán* (Allende; most events free of charge), the Museo de Culturas Populares (Hidalgo), the *Foro Cultural Ana-María Hernández* (Pacífico 181), the *Teatro Santa Catarina* (Plaza Sta Catarina), the

Rafael Solana theatre on Miguel Angel de Quevedo (nearly opposite Caballocalco), the *Casa del Teatro*, Vallarta 31 and *Foro de la Conchita*, Vallarta 33. Also note *El Hábito* (Madrid) and *El hijo del cuervo* (Jardín Centenario) for avant-garde drama and cabaret, *Los talleres de Coyoacán* (Francisco Sosa) for dance and ballet, *Cadac* (Centenario) for traditional and experimental drama. On the edge of the Coyoacán Delegación (SE corner of Churubusco and Tlalpan, Metro General Anaya) is the *Central Nacional de las Artes*, a huge complex of futuristic buildings dedicated to the training and display of the performing and visual arts. Good bookshop, library and cafeterías. Details to be found in *Tiempo Libre* and local broadsheets. At weekends there are many open-air events especially in Plaza Hidalgo. Also at weekends, the Artesanía market, in a site off Plaza Hidalgo, is well worth a visit; reasonable prices, and lots of potential for bargaining; as at most places where bargaining is possible, the best deals are to be had either early or late in the day.

Local information
● **Places to eat**

There are several pleasant *cafeterías* in the Jardín Centenario, some of which serve light snacks and *antojitos*; the best known is *El Parnaso*, adjacent to the bookshop of the same name. Two of the best-known *cantinas* in Mexico are *La Guadalupana* (Higuera) and the *Puerta del Sol* on Plaza Hidalgo. No shortage of restaurants with *comida corrida*, though prices tend to be higher than in other parts of the city (US$1.75-2.50). Very good value are: *Rams*, Hidalgo, almost opp Museo de Culturas Populares, excellent fish, US$1.75; *Fabio's*, overlooking Plaza Hidalgo and the Delegación, credit cards accepted; *Rincón Oaxaqueño*, Carrillo Puerto 12, US$1.75. Good value, too in the *Mercado*, between Malintzin and Xichoténcatl, US$1.15, possibly the most exquisite *quesadillas* in the whole of Coyoacán are found at local 31 (outside, opp Jardín del Carmen) stall holders are very friendly and fruit and veg sellers are ready to explain the names and uses of their goods; frequent musical entertainment particularly lunchtime and weekends. The *Restaurante*

Vegetariano, Carranza y Caballocalco, offers an excellent US$5 buffet lunch; *El Morral*, Allende No 2, set lunch US$3, double at weekends, no credit cards, highly rec, quieter upstairs, palatial lavatories. The *Caballocalco*, on Plaza Hidalgo, is expensive, although the seats are comfortable. There is a *Sanborn's* on Jardín Centenario, nr to *El hijo del cuervo*. *Hacienda de Cortés*, Fernández Leal 74, behind Plaza de la Conchita, exceptionally pleasant surroundings, large, shaded, outdoor dining area, excellent breakfast, good value, *comida corrida* US$5, try the *sábana de res con chilaquiles verdes*.

● **Shopping**

Many gift shops in the area, good taste and prices at *Etra*, on corner of Francisco Sosa opp Jardín Centenario; *Mayolih*, Aldama with Berlín, 2 blocks from Museo Frida Kahlo; *La Casita* on Higuera. Also on Higuera are *La Rosa de los Vientos* (maps of all parts of the country) and the Post Office with Mexpost service. *Foto Coyoacán*, Fco Sosa 1, opp the Arches, excellent, rapid developing, printing, English, French, German spoken. *Sakurafoto*, Plaza Hidalgo, excellent service, English, German spoken.

● **Transport**

The *pesero* from metro Anaya to the centre of Coyoacán is marked 'Santo Domingo', alight at Abasolo or at the Jardín Centenario; it also goes past the Mercado (Malintzin). Alternatively, get off the metro at Ermita and get the *pesero* (Santo Domingo) from C Pirineos, on the W side of Tlalpan just N of the metro station. The *pesero* passes in front of the Frida Kahlo museum.

The **Huayamilpas Ecological Park** can be reached by *pesero* from the centre of Coyoacán. The lake and surrounding area are protected by local inhabitants.

TENAYUCA

The pyramid of **Tenayuca**, 10 km to the NW, is about 15m high and the best-preserved in Mexico. The Aztecs rebuilt this temple every 52 years; this one was last reconstructed about 1507; well worth seeing, for it is surrounded with serpents in masonry. The easiest way to get there by car from Mexico City centre is to go to Vallejo, 11 km N of the intersection of Insurgentes Norte and Río Consulado. Admission US$4.35. By metro, take the

290 Mexico – Mexico City

line to the Central de Autobuses del Norte (see page 281), La Raza, and catch the bus there. By bus from Tlatelolco; ask driver and passengers to advise you on arrival as site is not easily visible. An excursion to Tula may go via Tenayuca. It is not far from the old town of **Tlalnepantla**: see the ancient convent (ask for the *catedral*) on the Plaza Gustavo Paz and the church (1583), which contains the first image, a Christ of Mercy, brought to the New World. 2½ km to the N is the smaller pyramid of **Santa Cecilia**, interesting for its restored sanctuary.

Los Remedios, a small town 13 km NW of Mexico City, has in its famous church an image, a foot high, adorned with jewels. See the old aqueduct, with a winding stair leading to the top of two towers. It can be reached by car or by taking the Los Remedios bus at Tacuba metro. Fiesta: 1 Sept to the climax 8 September.

At **Naucalpan**, NW of the city (just outside the city boundary on Blvd Toluca), pre-classic Olmec-influenced figurines can be seen in the **Museo de la Cultura de Tlatilco** (closed Mon), opposite the *Hotel Naucalpan* on Vía Gustavo Baz. This is said to be the oldest settlement in the Cuenca de México.

EXCURSIONS FROM MEXICO CITY

DESIERTO DE LOS LEONES

This a beautiful forest of pines and broad-leaved trees, made into a national park, can be reached from Mexico City (24 km) by a fine scenic road through Villa Obregón. In the woods is an old Carmelite monastery (begun 1602, finished 1611, abandoned because of cold and damp in 1780); around are numerous hermitages, inside are several subterranean passages and a secret hall with curious acoustic properties. Take a torch.

Take an hour's bus ride from Observatorio metro to La Venta and ask bus-driver where to get off for the path to the monastery (about 4 km walk). One can either

get there via the paved road or via the beautiful conifer-forest path, but the latter splits frequently so stick to what looks like the main path; or take the fire-break road below the row of shops and cheap restaurants near the main road. Food stalls abound, particularly at weekends when it is crowded. Do not leave valuables in your car. Many birds may be seen in the valley reached from the picnic area 6 km S of La Venta on Route 15.

Acolman has the formidable fortress-like convent and church of San Agustín, dating from 1539-60, with much delicate detail on the façade and some interesting murals inside. Note the fine portal and the carved stone cross at the entrance to the atrium. Reached by bus from Indios Verdes metro station, or from the Zócalo. It is 35 km NE of the city and can be visited on the way to/from Teotihuacan.

TEOTIHUACAN

49 km from Mexico City, with some of the most remarkable relics of an ancient civilization in the world. Thought to date from around 300 BC, the builders of this site remain a mystery. Where they came from and why the civilization disppeared is pure conjecture. It seems that the city may have housed 250,000 who were peace-loving but whose influence spread as far as Guatemala. So completely was it abandoned that it was left to the Aztecs to give names to its most important features.

Places of interest

There are three main areas: the **Ciudadela**, the **Pyramid of the Sun** and the **Pyramid of the Moon**. The whole is connected by the almost 4 km-long Street of the Dead which runs almost due N. To the W lie the sites of Tetitla, Atetelco, Zacuala and Yayahuala (see below). To the NE lies Tepantitla, with fine frescoes on a palace. The old city is traceable over an area of 3½ by 6½ km. Reckon on about 5-8 hrs to see the site properly, arrive early before the vast numbers of the *ambulantes* (wandering sales people with obsidian, flutes, silver bangles and, in Plaza of the Sun, straw hats) and the big tourist groups at 1100. There is a perimeter road with a number of car parking places – go anti-clockwise. The small pebbles embedded in mortar indicate reconstruction (most of the site apparently!).

Capable of holding 60,000 people, the citadel's main feature is the **Temple of Quetzalcoatl** (the Plumed Serpent, Lord of Air and Wind). Go to E side of the 1 km square. Behind the largest of the temples (take the right hand path), lies an earlier pyramid which has been partially restored. Lining the staircase are huge carved heads of the feathered serpents.

Follow the Street of the Dead to the **Plaza of the Sun**. You will pass small grassy mounds which are unexcavated temples. The Plaza contains many buildings, probably for the priests, but is dominated by the massive **Pyramid of the Sun** (64m high, 213m square at the base) and covering almost the same space as the Great Pyramid of Cheops in Egypt. The sides are terraced, and wide stairs lead to the summit. The original 4m covering of stone and stucco was removed by mistake in 1910. The view from the top gives a good impression of the whole site. But beware, it is a steep climb particularly between the third and fourth terrace. The car park to the N leads to Tepantitla. The murals here depict the rain god Tláloc. The museum (admission included in price of ticket) now lies S of Pyramid of the Sun. It is beautifully laid out and contains a large model of Teotihuacan in its heyday as well as many beautiful artefacts, recommended. There is an expensive restaurant at the museum, indifferent service, not always open.

The **Pyramid of the Moon** is about 1 km further N and on your right a tin roof covers a wall mural of a large, brightly coloured jaguar (the **Jaguar Temple**). The plaza contains the 'A' altars – 11 in a peculiar geometric pattern. The Pyramid is only half the size of the Pyramid of the Sun. There are excellent views looking S down the Street of the Dead.

To the W of the Plaza of the Moon lies the **Palace of Quetzalpapalotl** (quetzal-mariposa, or quetzalbutterfly), where the priests serving the sanctuaries of the Moon lived, it has been restored together with its patio. Note the obsidian inlet into the highly decorated carved pillars. There is a sign here forbidding high heels. Follow the path left under the Palace through the Jaguars' Palace with catlike murals protected from the sun by green canvas curtains to the **Temple of the Feathered Shells**. The base of the simple altar is decorated with shells, flowers and eagles.

You will pass several more temples on the W side of the Street of the Dead. If you want to visit Atetelco, go through the car park opposite the Pyramid of the Sun, turn right past *Restaurant Pirámides Charlies* (reputed to be the best on the site) and turn right along a small track. Alternatively to get to them from the museum, exit W and walk right up to main road, turning left after crossing the stream. They are well worth a visit; **Tetitla** a walled complex with beautiful frescoes and paintings, **Atetelco** with its three tiny temples and excellent murals and the abandoned sites of **Zacuala** and **Yayahuala**.

At the spring equinox, 21 Mar, the sun is perfectly aligned with the W face of the Pyramid of the Sun; many ad hoc sun worshippers hold unofficial ceremonies to mark the occasion (this is also Benito Juárez's birthday so entry is free).

NB If short of time, try to get lift from a tourist bus to the Pyramid of the Moon car park. This is the most interesting area. Also take food and water – most of the shops are on the W side and you may be some distance from them. There is a handicraft centre with weavings, obsidian carvings and explanations (and tastings) of the production of tequila and mescal.

Site open daily 0800-1700. (If the entrance near the bus stop is not open when it says it is, at 0800, try entrance near the Pyramid of the Moon.) Entrance, US$2.10, cars free, free on Sun (extra charge for videos, tripods not permitted).

The outside sites may be closed on Mon. *Son et lumière* display, costs US$4 per person (good *lumière*, not so good *son*); lasts 45 mins, 1900 in Spanish, 2015 in English (Oct-June only); take blanket or rent one. Official guidebook on sale, US$1, gives a useful route to follow. The Bloomgarden guide contains a useful map, good description and is recommended. At weekends, students give free guided tours, ask at the entrance. One recommended guide is Ricardo Cervantes C, T 61415-60540.

Local information
● Accommodation

A2 *Villas Arqueológicas*, pool (Apdo Postal 44 55800, San Juan Teotihuacan, Edo de México, T 60909/60244, F 60928; in Mexico City, reservations at Club Med office).

● Transport

Buses From Terminal del Nte, Gate 8, platform 6 (Autobuses del Nte metro), Mexico City, which takes at least 45 mins, US$1 one way (Pirámides buses are white with a yellow stripe). Bus returns from Door 1 at Teotihuacan site, supposedly every 30 mins. Some return buses to the capital terminate in the outskirts in rush hour without warning. You can also get a bus from Indios Verdes metro station. If driving, the toll on the Autopista Ecatepec-Pirámides is US$3. You can ride back to town with one of the tourist buses for about US$3. Note that the site is more generally known as 'Pirámides' than as 'Teotihuacan'. Train to Teotihuacan, 2 hrs, US$2.65, frequently delayed. You can also take the metro to Indios Verdes (last stop on line 3), then a public bus (US$1) to the pyramids. Tours to Teotihuacan, picking you up at your hotel and usually inc the Basílica de Guadalupe, normally cost US$30-35, with little time at the site.

The village of **San Juan Teotihuacan** is well worth a visit, if time permits (*pesero* from the road running round the site of the pyramids, US$0.20). It has a magnificent 16th century church (a few blocks down Cuauhtémoc from the square). Good, clean restaurant, *Los Pinos*, in Guadalupe Victoria, 1 block from the square, *comida corrida* US$1.65. Bus back to Mexico City (Terminal del Norte, or Metro Indios Verdes, US$1.25).

TEPOTZOTLAN

About 43 km NW of Mexico City just off the route to Querétaro, with a splendid Jesuit church of San Francisco Javier in churrigueresque style. There are fine colonial paintings in the convent corridors. The old Jesuit monastery has been converted into the Museo Nacional del Virreinato, a comprehensive and well-displayed collection covering all aspects of life under Spanish rule. Open 1000-1700, closed Mon, entry US$4.35, Sun free. It is also a tourist centre with restaurants. There is a big market on Wed and Sun when the town gets very congested; good selection of handicrafts and jewellery, as well as meat, cheese, and other foods. 28 km NW is the 18th century Acueducto del Sitio, 61m at its highest, 438m long.

● Accommodation **A2** *Hotel Tepotzotlán*,
C Industrias, about 3 blocks from centre, TV, restaurant, swimming pool, good views, secure parking, highly rec; *Hotel San José*, Zócalo, nice rooms, poor service and value.

● Places to eat The *Hostería del Monasterio* has very good Mexican food and a band on Sun; try their coffee with cinnamon. *Restaurant Artesanías*, opp church, rec, cheap. Also good food at *Brookwell's Posada*.

● Transport Bus from nr El Rosario metro station, US$1.50, 1 hr ride. Many Querétaro or Guanajuato buses from Terminal del Nte pass the turn-off at 'Caseta Tepotzotlán' from where one can take a local bus or walk (30 mins) to the town. (Do not confuse Tepotzotlán with Tepoztlán, which is S of Mexico City, nr Cuernavaca).

In the third week of Dec, *pastorelas*, morality plays based on the temptation and salvation of Mexican pilgrims voyaging to Bethlehem, are held. Tickets are about US$10 and include a warming punch, the play, a procession and litanies, finishing with a meal, fireworks and music. Tickets from Viajes Roca, Neva 30, Col Cuauhtémoc, Mexico City.

TULA

Another 1/2-day excursion is to **Tula**, some 65 km, thought to be the most important Toltec site in Mexico; two ball courts, pyramids, a frieze in colour, and remarkable sculptures over 6m high have been uncovered. There are four huge warriors in black basalt on a pyramid, the great Atlantes anthropomorphic pillars. The museum is well worth visiting and there is a massive fortress-style church, dating from 1553, near the market. Admission to site and museum, US$2 weekdays, free Sun and holidays. The small restaurant is not always open. Multilingual guidebooks at entrance, fizzy drinks on sale. Site is open Tues-Sun 0930-1630 (museum open Wed-Sun till 1630). The town itself is dusty, however, with poor roads. If driving from Mexico City, take the turn for Actopán before entering Tula, then look for the Parque Nacional sign (and the great statues) on your left.

● **Accommodation & places to eat C** *Hotel Catedral*, clean, pleasant, TV; *Restaurant la Cabaña*, on main square, local dishes, also *Nevería*, with good soup.

● **Transport** 1½ hrs by train from Buenavista station; at 0700 and 0900, returns at 1744 and 1955, US$1.20 (excellent breakfast for US$0.65), but can be several hours late; it follows the line of the channel cut by Alvarado to drain the lakes of Mexico Valley, visible as a deep canyon (from station walk along track 30 mins to site). One can take bus back, which leaves earlier. It can also be reached by 1st class bus, 'Valle de Mesquital', from Terminal del Nte, Av de los Cien Metros, goes to Tula bus terminal in 2-2½ hrs; US$2.50 each way, hourly service; Tula bus terminal is 3 km from the site, take a 'Chapantago' bus (every 20 mins) to the entrance, 5 mins (badly signposted), or a taxi, US$1, an alternative route is 200m to the Zócalo, to C Quetzalcoatl, to small bridge, sandy road to the right, and opening in the fence. Also bus or car from Actopán, on the Pan-American Highway (see page 90). Tula-Pachuca US$3.30; safe to leave belongings at bus station. Grey Line excursions from Mexico City have been rec.

Mexico City-Veracruz-Mexico City

A ROUND TOUR by way of Tlaxcala, Cholula, Puebla, Tehuacán, Orizaba, Córdoba, Veracruz, and Xalapa. The route encompasses volcanoes, remains of the Tlaxcalan, Olmec and Totonac cultures, many fine colonial buildings in cities and villages and leads to the distinct Caribbean culture of Veracruz. A major detour goes to the Papaloapan region, in the S of Veracruz state, often neglected by visitors.

By road, the principal route is paved all the way (no Pemex service station on road between Puebla and Orizaba, a distance of about 150 km); total distance: 924 km, or 577 miles. A new toll *autopista* (motorway) now runs all the way from Mexico City to Veracruz (4 tolls which range from US$4.35 to US$9). If wishing to avoid the toll route, note that the Vía Libre is very congested initially, and, at Ixtapulaca, just out of Mexico City, there is a series of *topes* (speed bumps) so high that they are a danger to ordinary saloon cars.

Our description is a trip along the old road, which goes E along the Puebla road, past the airport and swimming pools, and some spectacular shanty-towns. At (Km 19) Los Reyes, a road runs left into a valley containing the now almost completely drained Lake Texcoco, a valley early settled by the *conquistadores*. Along it we come to **Chapingo**, where there is a famous agricultural college with particularly fine frescoes by Rivera in the chapel. Next comes **Texcoco**, a good centre for visiting villages in the area. Bus from

Mexico City, from Emiliano Zapata 92, near Candelaria metro station. Near Chapingo a road runs right to the village of **Huexotla** (see the Aztec wall, with ruined fortifications and pyramid, and the 16th century Franciscan convent of San Luis Obispo). Another road from Texcoco runs through the public park of Molino de las Flores. From the old *hacienda* buildings, now in ruins, a road (right) runs up the hill of Tetzcotzingo, near the top of which are the Baños de Netzahualcoyotl, the poet-prince. (San Miguel de) **Chiconcuac** (road to San Andrés and left at its church), 4 km away, is where Texcoco *sarapes* are woven. Tues is market day and there is a rousing *fiesta* in honour of their patron saint on 29 September.

POPOCATEPETL AND IXTACCIHUATL

At Km 29 is **Ixtapaluca** where a road on the right (S) leads to the small town of Amecameca, the starting point for Popocatépetl and Ixtaccíhuatl. where there is a

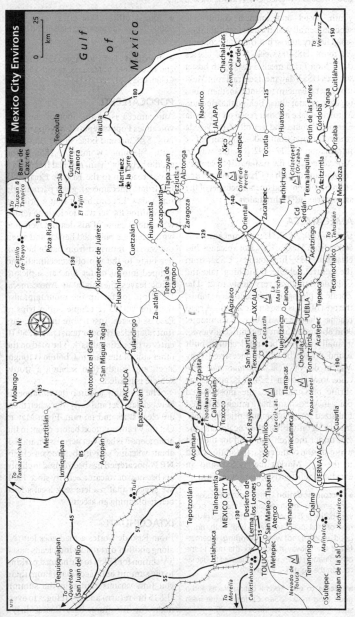

Mexico City Environs

0 — 25 km

youth hostel and Spanish countryside school: open all year, it caters for all abilities, small library, tourist information, economical tours. US$100/week, 5 hrs of classes daily, Mon-Fri, 3 meals a day. Youth hostel services US$3/day, meals extra. From Mexico City, take metro to Pantitlán, then a bus or *pesero* to Ixtapaluca. Behind the Mercado Municipal take another *pesero* on the 'Avila Camacho' route and get off at La Vereda (transportation from 0600-2100 daily). For information F 512-5992. On the way to Amecameca, see the restored 16th century convent and church at **Chalco**, and the fine church, convent and open-air chapel of the same period at **Tlalmanalco**.

AMECAMECA

(*Pop* 57,000; *Alt* 2,315m) **Amecameca** is 60 km from Mexico City, Los Volcanos 2nd class bus 1-1½ hrs' journey, US$2, from the Central del Ote; if hitching, take the Calzada Zaragoza, very dusty road. The Zócalo is pleasant, with good taco stands; the post office is also on the Zócalo. A road reaches the sanctuary of El Sacromonte, 90m above the town (magnificent views), a small and very beautiful church built round a cave in which once lived Fray Martín de Valencia, a *conquistador* who came to Mexico in 1524. It is, next to the shrine of Guadalupe, the most sacred place in Mexico and has a much venerated full-sized image of Santo Entierro weighing 1½ kg only. From the Zócalo, take the exit under the arch and head for the first white station of the cross; the stations lead to the top. Market day is Sat, and an excellent non-touristy market on Sun.

- **Accommodation** Three hotels, E, close to Amecameca's main square (*Ameque*, clean, with bath), and rooms at the *San Carlos* restaurant on the main square, **F** with bath, noisy, good, modern, hot water. **Camping**: is permitted at the railway station, ask the man in the office (leaving town, it's after the road to Tlamacas, on the right, 1-2 km away).

- **Places to eat** Several eating-places and a good food market. *San Carlos*, on the main square, good food, set lunch US$1.75.

- **Tourist office** Near plaza. Open 0900-1500. They can provide information and guides for Ixtaccíhuatl.

- **Transport** Trains to Mexico City US$1.50, 2nd class. Buses to Mexico City with Cristóbal Colón, US$1.20.

POPOCATEPETL

Amecameca is at the foot of the twin volcanoes **Popocatépetl** ('smoking mountain', 5,452m) and Ixtaccíhuatl (Eestaseewatl, 'sleeping woman', 5,286m); the saddle between them, reached by car via a paved road up to the Paso de Cortés (25 km from Amecameca), gives particularly fine views. Legend has it that a princess was waiting for her warrior lover to return when news came of his death. Overcome with grief, she poisoned herself and when the warrior returned from battle he took her body to the top of Ixtaccíhuatl and jumped into its crater. On Sats a pickup truck leaves the plaza at Amecameca, US$2 pp, for far up the mountain; also taxis for US$15 (2 people), offer trips to Paso de Cortés. Just before the pass, cars (but not pedestrians or taxis) pay US$0.10 entry to the national park. The road on the other side of the pass to Cholula is rough, steep and sandy (but scenic), a sturdy vehicle is needed.

The best time to climb the volcanoes is between late Oct and early Mar when there are clear skies and no rain. From May to Oct the weather is good before noon; in the afternoons it is bad. Get permission and ask about volcanic activity before you climb. **NB** Popocatépetl has been closed to climbers because of volcanic activity since 1994. We suggest that readers seek local advice before planning an ascent.

IXTACCIHUATL

From Paso de Cortés a road goes left (N) along another dirt road which leads past a TV station for 12 km to the nearest parking to the summit of Ixtaccíhuatl. From there you find various routes to the summit (12-15 hrs return) and 3-4 refuges to overnight (no furniture, bare floors, dirty).

Ixtaccíhuatl has been described as "an exhilarating rollercoaster of successive summits." To climb **Ixtaccíhuatl** take a taxi to La Joya, from there follow the tracks up the grassy hill on the right, 3-6 hrs to first huts. The first two huts are at 4,750m (places for 30 people), the third at 4,850m (10-15 people), and the last hut is at 5,010m (in poor condition, 10-12 people); the Luís Menéndez hut is the most salubrious. From the last hut it is 2½ hrs to the top, over two glaciers, some rock climbing required, crampons and ice-picks are necessary, can be hired in Amecameca. Guides are available in Amecameca (Rigoberto Mendoza has been recommended). Cost is about US$110 and worth it, as walking on glaciers without knowing the conditions is hazardous.

Beyond Ixtapaluca the road climbs through pine forests to reach 3,196m about 63 km from Mexico City, and then descends in a series of sharp bends to the town of San Martín **Texmelucan**, Km 91. The old Franciscan convent here has a beautifully decorated interior, and a former *hacienda* displays weaving and old machinery. The Zócalo is beautiful, with benches covered in ceramic tiles and a central gazebo. Market day is Tues (**D-E** *Hotel San José*, with bath, variety of rooms, parking inside, rec, at Pte 115; opp is **E** *La Granja*, with bath, parking, rec).

TLAXCALA

(*Pop* 36,000; *State pop 1995* 883,630; *Alt* 2,240m) From Texmelucan a side-road leads NE for 24 km to the once quaint old Indian town of **Tlaxcala**, with its pleasant centre of simple buildings washed in ochre, pink and yellow, and its vast suburbs. It is the capital of small Tlaxcala state whose wealthy ranchers breed fighting bulls, but whose landless peasantry is still poor.

Places of interest

Church of **San Francisco**, the oldest in Mexico (1521), from whose pulpit the first Christian sermon was preached in New Spain (Mexico). Its severe façade conceals a most sumptuous interior (note the cedar and gold, star-spangled ceiling, and the 'No Photos' sign at the door); almost next door is the **Museo del Estado de Tlaxcala** (free), open 0900-1700, 2 floors of historical and artistic exhibits, interesting; also the extremely colourful murals (1966, still incomplete) depicting the indigenous story of Tlaxcala, the history of Mexico and of mankind in the **Palacio de Gobierno**. Huge market every Sat. **Casa de las Artesanías de Tlaxcala**, a 'living museum' where Otomi indians demonstrate traditional arts and customs including the sweatbath, cooking, embroidery, weaving and pulque-making, highly recommended. *La Fonda del Museo* is attached restaurant (see below).

Excursions

A remarkable series of precolumbian frescoes are to be seen at the ruins of **Cacaxtla** near San Miguel del Milagro, between Texmelucan and Tlaxcala. The colours are still sharp and some of the figures are larger than life size. One wall, in turquoise, depicts a battle between an army dressed as jaguars and another dressed as eagles. Also depicted are two princes, the jaguar (the native prince), and the eagle, representing the invading Huaxtecas. The jaguar also represents Venus, the night, the rainy season, N, death, while the eagle is the sun, day, the dry season, S and life (Helmut Zettl, Ebergassing, who quotes the theories of Prof Michel Graulich of the Free University of Brussels). To protect the paintings from the sun and rain, a huge roof has been constructed. (The paintings were featured in the Sept 1992 issue of *National Graphic*.) The site is open all day and an easily accessible visitors' centre has been opened (closed Mon). There is disappointingly little published information on the site, however. In theory there is a 'per picture' charge for photography, but this is not assiduously collected. From Puebla take a Flecha Azul bus marked 'Natividad' from C 10 Pte y C 11 Nte to just beyond that town where a sign on the right points to San Miguel del Milagro and Cacaxtla (US$1). Walk up the hill to a large sign with its back to you, turn left here for the ruins.

The ruins of the pyramid of **Xicohténcatl** at San Esteban de **Tizatlán**, 5 km outside the town, has two sacrificial altars with original colour frescoes preserved under glass. The pictures tell the story of the wars with Aztecs and Chichimecs. Amid the archaeological digs at Tizatlán are a splendid 19th century church and a 16th century chapel of San Esteban. Colectivo to Tizatlán from 1 de Mayo y 20 de Noviembre, Tlaxcala, at main square, you get out when you see a yellow church dome on the left.

The **Sanctuary of Ocotlán** (1541), on a hill in the outskirts of Tlaxcala (a stiff 20-min climb from Juárez via Guribi and Alcocer, but worth it) commands a view of valley and volcano. It was described by Sacheverell Sitwell as 'the most delicious building in the world', but others have been less impressed. Nevertheless, its façade of lozenge-shaped vermilion bricks framing the white stucco portal and surmounted by two white towers 'with fretted cornices and salomonic pillars' is beautiful. The golden interior was worked on for 25 years by the Indian Francisco Miguel.

La Malinche Volcano, 4,461m, can be reached from Tlaxcala or Puebla (buses from the market beside the old railway station, 1½ hrs, US$1, one at 0800 and others, return 1800). You go to La Malintzi Centro de Vacaciones at the base of the volcano, now closed to the public. The hike to the summit takes 4 hrs, the descent 1½ (take an ice-axe, altitude is a problem). Alternatively, stay at nearby town of Apizaco. Reasonable hotel and restaurant next to the roundabout with a locomotive in the centre, safe parking. It is a good day trip from Puebla. Another route is via Canoa (bus from Puebla, US$0.50). Long hike to top, 10 hrs return at a good pace, take warm clothes.

Local festivals
The annual fair is held 29 Oct-15 Nov each year.

Local information
● **Accommodation**
C *Alifer*, Morelos 11, uphill from plaza, T 25678, safe parking.

Several in **D** category nr centre.

E *Hotel-Mansion Xichoténcatl*, on Juárez, back rooms quieter.

● **Places to eat**
Los Portales, main square; *Restaurante del Quijote*, Plaza Felipe Xochiténcatl; *La Fonda del Museo* (see above), serves excellent 4-course traditional meals in a lovely setting, set lunch US$8; *Oscar's*, Av Juárez, nr corner of Zitlalpopocatl, excellent sandwiches and juices; *La Arboleda*, Lira y Ortega, nr square, good.

● **Entertainment**
The Cine American, on Blvd G Valle (continuation of Av Juárez) has two for the price of one on Wed.

● **Laundry**
Servi-Klim, Av Juárez, 1½ blocks from plaza, good.

● **Tourist offices**
Tourist office at Juárez y Landizábal, many maps and leaflets, very helpful, no English spoken.

● **Transport**
Frequent Flecha Azul buses from Puebla, central bus station (platform 81/82) between 0600 and 2130, 45 mins, US$1.20. Tlaxcala's bus station is about a 10-min walk to the centre.

(Km 106) **Huejotzingo** has the second-oldest church and monastery in Mexico, built 1529; now a museum. Market: Sat, Tues. Dramatic carnival on Shrove Tues, portraying the story of Agustín Lorenzo, a famous local bandit. **D** *Hotel Colonial*, secure but poor value.

CHOLULA

(Km 122) is a small somnolent town (20,000 people, with the Universidad de las Américas), but one of the strangest-looking in all Mexico. When Cortés arrived, this was a holy centre with 100,000 inhabitants and 400 shrines, or *teocallis*, grouped round the great pyramid of

Quetzalcoatl. In its day it was as influential as Teotihuacan. There used to be a series of pyramids built one atop another. When razing them, Cortés vowed to build a chapel for each of the *teocallis* destroyed, but in fact there are no more than about 70.

Places of interest

The excavated pyramid, open 1000-1700, admission US$2 on weekdays, free on Sun and holidays, has 8 km of tunnels and some recently discovered frescoes inside, but only 1 km of tunnel is open to the public, which gives an idea of superimposition (the frescoes are not open to the public). Museum near tunnel entrance has a copy of the frescos. Guides charge US$6.50, recommended as there are no signs inside (some guides claim to speak English, but their command of the language is poor). The entrance is on the main road into Cholula. The 16th century chapel of **Los Remedios** on top of it gives a fine view. The Franciscan fortress church of **San Gabriel** (1552) is in the plaza (open 0600-1200, 1600-1900, Suns 0600-1900); and next to it, the **Capilla Real**, which has 49 domes (open 1000-1200, 1530-1800, Suns 0900-1800).

Excursions

See the Indian statuary and stucco work of the 16th century church of Santa María de **Tonantzintla**, outside the town; the church is one of the most beautiful in Mexico (open 1000-1800 daily), and may also be reached by paved road from San Francisco **Acatepec**, which also has a beautiful, less ornate 16th century church (recently damaged by fire, although the façade of tiles is still intact, supposedly open 0900-1800 daily, but not always so – key is held by José Ascac, ask for his shop). They are off Highway 190 from Puebla to Izúcar de Matamoros. Both these places are easily reached from Cholula or Puebla. Best light for photography after 1500. Photography *inside* both churches is frowned upon. John Hemming says these two churches "should on no account be missed; they are resplendent with Poblano tiles and their interiors are a riot of Indian stucco-work and carving." Both churches, though exquisite, are tiny. Some visitors note that regular visiting hours are not strictly observed at Cholula, Acatepec, Tonantzintla and Huejotzingo.

One can visit Tonantzintla and Acatepec from Cholula main square with a 'peso-taxi'. Or one can take a kombi from Cholula to Acatepec or to Tonantzintla (marked Chilipo or Chipanco, ask which kombi goes to the church you want) for US$0.55 from junction of Av 5 and Av Miguel Alemán. This is 2 blocks from Zócalo, which is 3 blocks from tourist office. You can walk the 1 km to the other church, and then take a bus or kombi back to Cholula or Puebla. Acatepec from CAPU in Puebla, US$0.45, 30 mins, bus stops outside the church.

Local information
● Accommodation

B *Villas Arqueológicas*, 2 Pte 501, T 471966, F 471508, behind pyramid, affiliated to *Club Med*, heated pool, tennis, French restaurant, rooms have heating, TV, phone.

C *Cali Quetzalcoatl*, on Zócalo, Portal Guerrero 11, T 474199, clean, good restaurant; **C** *Posada Real*, 5 de Mayo 1400, at end of highway from Puebla, 3 blocks from pyramid, T 4/6677; **C-D** *Campestre Los Sauces*, Km 122, Carretera Federal Puebla-Cholula, T 471011, pool, tennis, restaurant/bar, gardens, TV and phone in rooms.

D *Super Motel* on the road from Puebla as you enter town, each room with private garage, very secure; **D** *Reforma*, nr main square.

E *Hotel de las Américas*, 14 Ote 6, T 470991, nr pyramid, actually a motel, modern with rooms off galleries round paved courtyard (car park), small restaurant, clean, good value; **E** *Trailer Park Las Américas*, 30 Ote 602, hot showers, secure, as are the furnished apartments.

Motel de la Herradura, Carr Federal, T 470100, will not quote rates by phone, close to *Los Sauces*, satellite TV, phones, hot water.

● Places to eat
Restaurant Choloyan, also handicrafts, Av Morelos, good, clean, friendly. Try *licuados* at

market stalls, fruit and milk and 1 or 2 eggs as you wish; *mixiote* is a local dish of lamb or goat barbecued in a bag. Pure drinking water sold behind the public baths, cheaper to fill own receptacle, funnel needed.

● **Tourist offices**
There is a very helpful tourist office opp the main pyramid: Cholula map and guide book for US$1.

● **Useful services**
There is a *casa de cambio* on the corner of the main plaza, and a **travel agency** in the Los Portales complex on the plaza.

● **Transport**
Trains The Mexico City to Puebla train (dep 0705) also stops right by the ruins.

Buses Frequent 2nd-class Estrella Roja buses from **Puebla** to Cholula US$0.35 from 6 Pte y 13 Nte, 9 km on a new road, 20 mins, also 1st and 2nd class Estrella Roja buses from CAPU bus terminal hourly (be ready to get out, only a quick stop in Cholula); from Cholula take a 'Pueblo Centro' bus to the city centre, or a 'Puebla-CAPU' bus for the terminal; colectivos to Cholula, US$0.40. From **Mexico City**, leave for Cholula from Terminal del Ote with Estrella Roja, every 30 mins, US$3, 2½-3 hrs, 2nd class every 20 mins, a very scenic route through steep wooded hills. Good views of volcanoes.

Just before Puebla one comes to the superb church of **Tlaxcalantzingo**, with an extravagantly tiled façade, domes and tower. It is worth climbing up on the roof for photographs.

PUEBLA

(Km 134; *Pop* 1,222,177; *State pop 1995* 4,624,239; *Alt* 2,060m; *Phone code* 22) (de los Angeles), 'The City of the Angels', one of Mexico's oldest and most famous cities and the capital of Puebla state. Puebla was founded in 1531 by Fray Julián Garcés who saw angels in a dream indicating where the city should be built, hence its name. This also explains why Puebla wasn't built over Indian ruins like many other colonial cities. Talavera tiles are an outstanding feature of Puebla's architecture and their extensive use on colonial buildings distinguishes it from other colonial cities. Puebla is a charming city, pleasant and friendly and always popular with

travellers. The centre, though still beautifully colonial, is cursed with traffic jams and pollution, except in those shopping streets reserved for pedestrians.

Places of interest

The **Congreso del Estado** in C 5 Pte 128, formerly the Consejo de Justicia, near the post office, is a converted 19th century Moorish style town house. The tiled entrance and courtyard are very attractive, it had a theatre inside (shown to visitors on request), and is now the seat of the state government. The **Patio de los Azulejos** should also be visited; it has fabulous tiled façades on the former almshouses for old retired priests of the order of San Felipe Neri; the colours and designs are beautiful; it is at 11 Pte 110, with a tiny entrance on 16 de Septiembre, which is hard to find. Ring the bell on the top right and you may get a guided tour. Worth visiting is also the library of Bishop Palafox, in the Casa de la Cultura, 5 Ote No 5, opposite the Cathedral; it has 46,000 antique volumes, open at 1000. Known as the **Biblioteca Palafoxiana**, it is in a colonial building with a large courtyard which also houses paintings and art exhibitions. Next door at 5 Ote 9 is another attractive building, the Tribunal Superior de Justicia, built in 1762; you may go in the courtyard.

The Plaza y Mercado Parián is between Avs 2 y 4 Ote and C 6 y 8 Nte. On C 8 Nte between Av 6 Ote and Av 4 Ote there are many small shops selling paintings. The area is also notable for onyx souvenir shops. Onyx figures and chess sets are attractive and cheaper than elsewhere, but the *poblanos* are hard bargainers; another attractive buy are the very tiny glass animal figures. In the adjoining Barrio del Artista the artists' studios are near to *Hotel Latino*. Live music and refreshments at small *Café del Artista*, C 8 Nte y Av 6 Ote. Just S at C 8 Nte 408 is the *Café Galería Amparo*, which serves light food. The University Arts Centre offers folk dances at various times, look for posters or enquire direct, free admission.

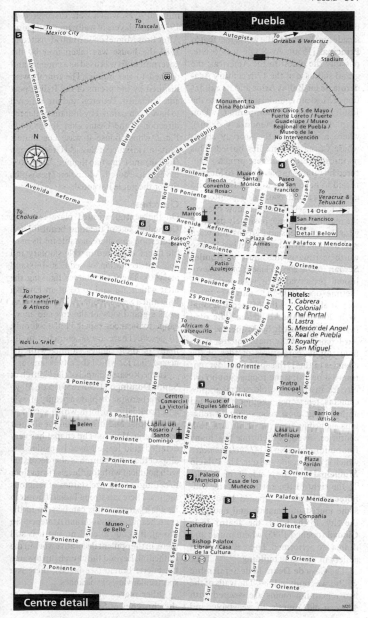

Puebla

To Tlaxcala

To Mexico City

Autopista

To Orizaba & Veracruz

Stadium

Blvd Hermanos Serdán

N

Blvd Atlixco Norte

Monument to China Poblana

Centro Cívico 5 de Mayo / Fuerte Loreto / Fuerte Guadelupe / Museo Regional de Puebla / Museo de la No Intervención

Avenida Reforma

Defensores de la República

18 Poniente

17 Norte

Tienda Convento Sta Rosa

Museo de Santa Mónica

Calz las Fuertes

To Cholula

10 Poniente

19 Norte

San Marcos

Paseo de San Francisco

To Veracruz & Tehuacán

Avenida Reforma

2 Norte

10 Ote

14 Ote

6

8

Av Juárez

Paseo Bravo

5 de Mayo

San Francisco

See Detail Below

7 Poniente

Plaza de Armas

Av Palafox y Mendoza

25 Sur

19 Sur

13 Sur

11 Sur

Patio Azulejos

7 Oriente

Av Revolución

19 Poniente

2 Sur

19

31 Poniente

25 Poniente

16 de septiembre

25 Ote

Del 5 de Mayo

Hotels:
1. *Cabrera*
2. *Colonial*
3. *Del Portal*
4. *Lastra*
5. *Mesón del Angel*
6. *Real de Puebla*
7. *Royalty*
8. *San Miguel*

To Acatepec, & Atlixco

To Africam & Valsequillo

43 Pte

Blvd Héroes

Not to Scale

Centre detail

10 Oriente

8 Poniente

7 Norte

5 Norte

3 Norte

1

0 Oriente

Teatro Principal

6 Norte

Centro Comercial La Victoria

House of Aquiles Serdaño

6 Oriente

9 Norte

7 Norte

Belen

6 Poniente

Capilla del Rosario / Santo Domingo

5 de Mayo

Casa del Alfeñique

Barrio de Artista

4 Poniente

2 Norte

4 Norte

4 Oriente

Plaza Parián

2 Poniente

Av Reforma

7

Palacio Municipal

Casa de los Muñecos

2 Oriente

Av Palafox y Mendoza

7 Sur

3 Poniente

3

La Compañia

5 Sur

3 Sur

2

3 Oriente

Museo de Bello

Cathedral

Bishop Palafox Library / Casa de la Cultura

4 Sur

5 Poniente

16 de Septiembre

5 Oriente

7 Poniente

2 Sur

7 Oriente

Also worth seeing are the church and monastery of **El Carmen**, with its strange façade and beautiful tile work; the **Teatro Principal** (1550), Av 8 Ote y C 6 Nte, possibly the oldest in the Americas; the grand staircase of the 17th century **Academia de las Bellas Artes** and its exhibition of Mexican colonial painting; and the Jesuit church of **La Compañía** (Av Don Juan de Palafox y Mendoza y 4 Sur), where a plaque in the sacristy shows where China Poblana lies buried. This mythical figure, a Chinese princess captured by pirates and abducted to Mexico, is said to have taken to Christianity and good works and evolved a penitential dress for herself which has now become the regional costume; positively dazzling with flowered reds and greens and worn with a strong sparkle of bright beads. Also worth visiting is the house of **Aquiles Serdán** (6 Ote 206), a leader of the Revolution, preserved as it was during his lifetime (open 1000-1630, entrance 10 pesos). It also houses the **Museo Regional de la Revolución Mexicana**. The tiled façade of the **Casa de los Muñecos**, 2 Nte No 1 (corner of the main square) is famous for its caricatures in tiles of the enemies of the 17th century builder (entrance 8 pesos); some rooms contain old physics instruments, old seismographs, cameras, telescopes, another has stuffed animals, but most rooms contain religious paintings from the 17th and 18th centuries. Avenida Reforma has many fine buildings, eg No 141 (*Hotel Alameda*), which is tiled inside and out. The **Palacio Municipal** is on the N side of the Zócalo. To the right of the entrance is the **Biblioteca del Palacio** (opened 1996) with some tourist information and books on the city. To the left is the **Teatro de la Ciudad** (opened 1995) where music and drama are performed. There is also an art gallery in the same building.

The **Casa de Dean**, 16 de Septiembre y 7 Pte, was built in 1580. The walls of the two remaining rooms are covered with 400-year-old murals in vegetable and mineral dyes, which were discovered in 1953 under layers of wallpaper and paint. After Pres Miguel de la Madrid visited in 1984 the house was taken over by the government (it was used as a cinema) and opened to the public. The murals were inspired by the poems of the Italian poet and humanist, Petrarca, and are believed to have been painted by Indians under the direction of the Dean, Don Tomás de la Plaza, whose house it was. The murals contain a mixture of classical Greek, pagan (Indian) and Christian themes. About 40% have been restored. Admission 7 pesos plus tip for the guide if wanted.

Churches

On the central arcaded plaza is a fine **Cathedral**, one of the most beautiful and interesting anywhere, notable for its marble floors, onyx and marble statuary and gold leaf decoration (closed 1230-1600 and at 2000). There are statues flanking the altar which are said to be of an English king and a Scottish queen. The bell tower gives a grand view of the city and snow-capped volcanoes (open 1130-1200 only, 10 pesos). There are 60 churches in all, many of their domes shining with the glazed tiles for which the city is famous.

In the Rosario chapel of the Church of **Santo Domingo** (1596-1659), 5 de Mayo 407, the baroque displays a beauty of style and prodigality of form which served as an exemplar and inspiration for all later baroque in Mexico. The chapel has very detailed gold leaf all over it inside. The altar of the main church is also decorated with gold leaf with four levels (from floor to ceiling) of life size statues of religious figures. There is a strong Indian flavour in Puebla's baroque; this can be seen in the churches of Tonantzintla and Acatepec (see above); it is not so evident, but it is still there, in the opulent decorative work in the Cathedral. Beyond the church, up towards the Fuerte Loreto (see below), there is a spectacular view of volcanoes.

Other places well worth visiting are the churches of **San Cristóbal** (1687),

4 Nte y 6 Ote, with modern churriguer-esquetowersandTonantzintla-likeplasterwork inside; **San José** (18th century), 2 Nte y 18 Ote, with attractive tiled façade and decorated walls around the main doors, as well as beautiful altar pieces inside. One of the most famous and oldest local churches is **San Francisco** (14 Ote 1009), with a glorious tiled façade and a mummified saint in its side chapel; see also the pearl divers' chapel, given by the poor divers of Veracruz, the church thought it too great a sacrifice but the divers insisted. Since then they believe diving has not claimed a life. The **Capilla de Dolores**, the other side of Blvd 5 de Mayo from San Francisco, is small but elaborately decorated. **Santa Catalina**, 3 Nte with 2 Pte, has beautiful altarpieces; **Nuestra Señora de la Luz**, 14 Nte and 2 Ote, has a good tiled façade and so has **San Marcos** at Av Reforma and 9 Nte. The Maronite church of **Belén** on 7 Nte and 4 Pte has a lovely old tiled façade and a beautifully tiled interior.

The church **La Puerta del Cielo** at the top of the Cerro de San Juan in Col La Paz, is modern but in classical style. There are over 80 figures of angels inside and from outside there are good views of the city and the volcano, El Popo.

Museums

The **Museo de Artesanías del Estado** in ex-Convento de Santa Rosa (3 Nte 1203) has a priceless collection of 16th century Talavera tiles on its walls and ceilings, well worth a visit, open 1000-1630.

The fragile-looking and extravagantly ornamented **Casa del Alfeñique** (Sugar Candy House), Av 4 Ote 418, a few blocks from the Cathedral is worth seeing, now the **Museo Regional del Estado** (entry US$0.40).

The **Cinco de Mayo** civic centre, with a stark statue of Benito Juárez, is, among other things, a regional centre of arts, crafts and folklore and has a very worth-while **Museo Regional de Puebla**, open 1000-1700, **Museo de Historia Natural**, auditorium, planetarium, fairgrounds and an open air theatre all nearby. In the same area, the forts of **Guadalupe** and **Loreto** were the scene of the Battle of Puebla, in which 2,000 Mexican troops defeated Maximilian's 6,000 European troops on 5 May 1862 (although the French returned victorious 10 days later). Inside the **Fuerte Loreto** (views of the city - and of its pollution) is a small museum (**Museo de la No Intervención**) depicting the battle of 1862 (open 1000-1700, closed Mon, entry US$1.30). 5 May is a holiday in Mexico.

Museo de Bello, the house of the collector and connoisseur Bello who died in 1938, has good displays of Chinese porcelain and Talavera pottery, Av 3 Pte 302; the building is beautifully furnished (entry 10 pesos, free Tues and Sun, guided tours, closed Mon). **Museo de Santa Mónica** (convent) at 18 Pte 103, open 1000-1800, closed Mon; generations of nuns hid there after the reform laws of 1857 made the convent illegal. **Museo Amparo**, 2 Sur 708, esq 9 Ote, has a good anthropological exhibition, modern, audiovisual explanations in Spanish, English, French and Japanese (take your own headphones, or hire them), open 1000-1800, closed Tues, free guided tour 1200 Sun, admission 16 pesos, students half-price, recommended.

For railway enthusiasts there is an outdoor museum displaying old engines and wagons at 11 Nte, between 10 y 14 Pte, **El Museo Nacional de los Ferrocarriles Mexicanos**, in the old Puebla railway station known as El Mexicano.

Excursions

On the Prolongación Av 11 Sur is **Balneario Agua Azul**, in the suburbs, a complex with sulphur springs, playing fields, amusement park etc, popular with families (entry US$3.25, children US$2.25, open daily 0600-1800, T 431330, bus from centre, route 1 on 11 Sur). 15 km S of

Puebla lies **Lago Valsequillo**, with *Africam*, a zoo of free-roaming African animals whose enclosures are nevertheless a bit cramped and uncomfortable. Entry US$4.50, children US$4, open daily 1000-1700, T 358932. Several daily Estrella Roja buses from bus station, US$2.40, round trip. Information from 11 Ote, T 460888. A good, 1 day excursion is a round trip Puebla-Cacaxtla-Tlaxcala-Tizatlán-Puebla: details are given on page 297. There is a Volkswagen factory a few kilometres from town (buses leave from terminal marked VW). Open from 1100, book ahead for guided tours.

Local festivals

Feria in mid-April for 2 weeks. The Fiesta Palafoxiano starts on the last Fri in Sept until mid-Nov for 9 weekends of dancing, music, theatre, exhibitions etc, some free performances.

Local information

● **Accommodation**

L3 *Camino Real*, 7 Pte 105, T 290909, 91 (800) 90123, F 328993, in ex-Convento de la Concepción, built 1593, bar, restaurant, room service, boutiques, dry cleaning.

A1-A2 *Del Alba*, Blvd Hermanos Serdán 141, T 486055, pool, gardens, Spanish restaurant; **A2** *Mesón del Molino*, Calz del Bosque 10, Col San José del Puente, T 305331, 91 (800) 22612, F 305519, rooms with 2 double beds, some have bath tubs, cable TV, restaurant/bar, small covered pool, chapel with mass 1300 Sun; **A2** *Real de Puebla* (Best Western), 5 Pte 2522, T 489600, F 489850, helpful staff, restaurant open until 2300; **A2-A3** *Condado Plaza*, Privada 6B Sur 3106, esq 31 Ote, Zona Dorada, T 372733, 91 (800) 22456, F 379305, cable TV, rooms have modems for computer hookup, conference halls for 40-300 people; **A3** *Del Portal*, Portal Morelos 205, T 460211, F 323194, very good, but ask for room away from Zócalo side (noisy), restored colonial, plain rooms, TV, phone, parking across the street; **A3** *Lastra*, Calz de Los Fuertes 2633, T 359755, restaurant, pool, games room; **A3** *Palacio San Leonardo*, 2 Ote No 211, T 460555, F 421176, modern rooms but wonderful colonial entrance hall with adjoining bar/restaurant; **A3-C** *Aristos*, Av Reforma 533, esq 7 Sur, T 320565, 320529, good facilities in rooms and bathrooms, gym with sauna, pool, attractive public areas, restaurant, piano bar, cheaper rates at weekends.

B *Posada San Pedro*, 2 Pte 202, T 465077, 91 (800) 22808, F 465376, attractive restaurant, parking; **B-C** *Royalty*, Portal Hidalgo 8, T 424740, F 424740 ext 113, pleasant, central, quiet, restaurant good but expensive and service slow, tables outside under the portales where a marimba band sometimes plays.

C *Cabrera*, 10 Ote 6, T 425099, 328525, with shower and phone, clean, quiet in interior rooms, don't be put off by outward appearance of hardware store, no restaurant; **C** *Colonial*, 4 Sur 105, T 464199, across pedestrian street from La Compañía church, old-fashioned and charming, very friendly, colonial style, restaurant, accepts American Express cards, ask for back room, with bath, TV and phone; **C** *Gilfer*, 2 Ote No 11, T 460611, F 423485, attractive, modern building, large rooms, reasonable restaurant, excellent service; next door is **B-C** *Palace*, 2 Ote No 13, T 322430, F 425599, price depends on number and size of beds, attractive, modern lobby, cafetería, satellite TV, phones, 60 rooms; **C** *Granada*, Blvd de la Pedrera 2303, T 320966, F 320424, very close to bus terminal, bus to centre leaves from front door, quiet, comfortable, restaurant, room service, TV in rooms; **C** *Imperial*, 4 Ote 212, T 463825, good sized plain rooms with TV and phones, shower, clean, some rooms noisy, laundry, restaurant, gym, parking, 30% discount offered to *Handbook* owners.

D *Alameda*, Reforma 141, close to the Zócalo, T 420882, old rooms at front, newer rooms at back are plainer, nice patio, very pretty tiles inside and out, iron grill work, TV, phone, bath, very clean, friendly, good value; **D** *Ritz*, 2 Nte 207 y 4 Ote, T 324457, 2 blocks from Zócalo, reasonable, drab front rooms with balcony quieter, hot water; **D** *San Miguel*, 3 Pte 721, T 424860, carpeted rooms, TV, phone; **D** *Virrey de Mendoza*, Reforma 538, T 423903, old colonial house, plain, fairly basic rooms, high ceilings, TV, bath, beautiful wooden staircase; **D-E** *Santander*, 5 Pte 111, T 463175, F 425792, nr Cathedral, colonial façade, recently renovated, hot showers, clean, simple, big bright rooms towards street, enclosed parking, rec; **D-E** *Teresita*, 3 Pte 309, T 327072, small modern rooms, with bath ('comedy showers'), hot water, friendly.

E *Casa de Huéspedes Los Angeles*, C 4 Nte 9, basic, communal bathrooms, irregular hot water, *comedor*, central; **E** *Embajadores*, 5 de Mayo 603, T 322637, 2 blocks from Zócalo, without bath but limited water and insalubrious;

other cheap places on pedestrian mall on this street; **E** *Latino*, C 6 Nte 8, T 322325, next to Barrio del Artista, basic; **E** *Victoria*, nr Zócalo, 3 Pte 306, T 328992, clean, quiet, hot showers, rec; **E-F** *Avenida*, 5 Pte 336 between 7 and 3 Sur, 2 blocks from Zócalo, price depends on number of beds and shared or private bathroom, airy rooms, quiet, friendly, clean, hot water, drinking water, rec.

Several basic *casas de huéspedes*, nr markets. Very cheap hotel (F), 2 blocks S of train station, *20 de Noviembre*, big rooms, no water 2000 to 0700, clean, bus to town.

Camping: possible on the extensive university grounds about 8 km S of centre.

Motels: L3-A1 *Mesón del Ángel* (Swiss run), Hermanos Serdán 807, T 243000, F 242227, nr first Puebla interchange on Mexico-Puebla motorway, possibly best in town, but far from the centre, 192 rooms, a/c, cable TV, conference and banqueting facilities, 2 restaurants, bar, 2 pools, tennis: **B-D** *Panamerican*, Reforma 2114, T 485466, restaurant, no bar, parking, rec.

● **Places to eat**

Local specialities. *Mole poblano* (meat or chicken with sauce of chiles, chocolate and coconut); best at *La Poblanita* D, 10 Nte 1404-B, and *Fonda Santa Clara*, 3 Pte 307, good for local specialities. *Mixiote* is *borrego* (lamb) with chile wrapped in paper with hot sauce. *Chiles en Nogada* are *chiles poblanos* stuffed with fruit and topped with a sweet cream sauce made with ground nuts, then topped with pomegranate seeds, best in July Sept, delicious. *Camotes* (candied sweet potatoes) and *dulces* (sweets). Also *nieves*: drinks of alcohol, fruit and milk, worth trying, and excellent *empanadas*. Also noted are *quesadillas*: fried tortillas with cheese and herbs inside.

El Vasco, Portal Benito Juárez 105, on Zócalo, slow, most dishes US$3, US$6 for *plato mexicano*; several others to choose from on Zócalo, eg *La Princesa*, Portal Juárez 101, good variety and good prices, breakfast US$2-3, *comida corrida* US$3, *Mac's*, US-style diner, good variety. Cheap *comidas* at *Hermilo Nevados*, 2 Ote 408, good value, rec; also *Munich*, 3 Pte y 5 Sur. Many cheap places nr main square with menus prominently displayed. *Cafetería La Vaca Negra*, Reforma 106, just off Zócalo, modern, attractive, part of a chain, meals US$2-7; *Hotel Royalty*, Portal Hidalgo 8, nice restaurant with meals around US$6-7, *platillos poblanos*, tables under the portales, marimba

band plays sometimes; *Woolworth's*, corner of 2 Pte and 5 de Playo, 1½ blocks from NW corner of Plaza Mayor, 0800-2200, good range of cheap, reasonable meals and some dearer dishes; *El Vegetariano*, 3 Pte 525, good (nr *Hotel San Agustín*), serves breakfast, rec; *Pizza Hadis*, 3 Nte between 3 Pte y Reforma, cheap, good, friendly; *Super-Soya*, 5 de Mayo, good for fruit salads and juices; several other good places for *comidas corridas* on 5 de Mayo; *Librería Cafetería Teorema*, Reforma 540, esq 7 Nte, café, books and art, live music at night, good coffee and snacks, pastries, *platillos mexicanos*, rec; *Cafetería Tres Gallos*, 4 Pte 110, good coffee and pastries. *Jugos y Licuados*, 3 Nte No 412, rec, *Tony's Tacos*, 3 Nte and Reforma, quick and very cheap; *La Super Torta de Puebla*, on 3 Pte, good sandwich bar; *Tepoznieves*, 3 Pte 150 esq 3 Sur, rustic Mexican décor, serves all varieties of tropical fruit ice cream and sherbet.

● **Airline offices**

Aero California, Blvd Atlixco 2703, locales B y C, Col Nueva Antequera, T 304855; **AeroMéxico**, T 91-800-90999, 320013/4, Av Juárez 1514, Col La Paz, flight connections at Monterrey; **Aeromar**, at airport, T 320633, 329644, 91 (800) 70429; **Mexicana**, Av Juárez 2312, entre C 23 Sur y 25 Sur, T 91 (800) 50220, 485600; **Lufthansa** and **LanChile**, at Av Juárez 2916, Col La Paz, T 484400, 301109.

● **Banks & money changers**

Bancomer, 3 Pte 116, changes TCs 0930-1300, good rates. On the Zócalo are **Banco Santander Mexicano**; **Banco Inverlat** at Portal Benito Juárez 109, changes money 0900-1400; and a *casa de cambio* at Portal Hidalgo 6 next to *Hotel Royalty*. On Av Reforma are: **Banamex**, No 135, ATMs accept Cirrus network cards; **Bancomer**, No 113, ATMs accept Visa and Plus network cards; **Banco Bital**, across the street, ATMs accept Plus and Cirrus network cards. All available 24 hrs.

● **Hospitals & medical services**

Dentist: *Dr A Bustos*, Clínica de Especialidades Dentales, 2 Pte 105-8, T 324412, excellent service, rec.

Doctors: *Dr Miguel Benítez Cortázar*, 11 Pte 1314, T 420556, US$15 per consultation. *Dr Cuauhtémoc Romero López*, same address and phone.

Hospitals: *Beneficiencia Española*, 19 Nte 1001, T 320500; *Betania*, 11 Ote 1826, T 358655; *UPAEP*, 5 Pte 715, T 466099, F 325921, outpatients T 328913, 323641; the cheapest is *Universitario de Puebla*, 25 Pte y 13 Sur, T 431377, where an outpatient consultation is US$5.

● **Laundry**
In large commercial centre on Av 21 Pte y C 5 Sur, US$4 wash and dry, 3 hrs. Another on 9 Nte, entre 2 y 4 Pte, US$2.80 for good service wash.

● **Post & telecommunications**
Post Office: 5 Ote between 16 de Septiembre and 2 Sur. Open Mon-Fri, 0800-2000. Colonial building with red/orange bricks and blue and white tiles.

● **Shopping**
5 de Mayo is a pedestrian street closed to traffic from the Zócalo to Av 10. The entire block containing the Capilla del Rosario/Templo de Santo Domingo in the SE corner has been made into a shopping mall (opened 1994), called the Centro Comercial La Victoria after the old La Victoria market. The old market building still exists. Built in 1913, it is a long, narrow building on the 3 Nte side of the mall and on its second floor are many places to eat. The mall is a metal structure, painted green with glass panes. It houses department stores, boutiques and restaurants. Craft shop sponsored by the authorities: *Tienda Convento Santa Rosa*, C 3 Nte 1203, T 28904. The famous Puebla tiles may be purchased from factories outside Puebla, or from *Fábrica de Azulejos la Guadalupana*, Av 4 Pte 911; *D Aguilar*, 40 Pte 106, opp Convent of Santa Mónica, and *Casa Rugerio*, 18 Pte 111; *Margarita Guevara*, 20 Pte 30. Mercado Venustiano Carranza, on 11 Nte y 5 Nte, good for *mole*. **Bookshop**: *Librería Británica*, C 25 Pte 1705-B, T 408549, 374705.

Bicycle shops: there are several shops in 7 Nte, N of 4 Pte, international spare parts.

● **Sports**
Las Termas, C 5 de Mayo 2810, T 329562, gay bath house, entry US$2.50, steambaths, sauna, gym; *Lidromasaje*, beer and soft drinks.

● **Tour companies & travel agents**
American Express, Centro Comercial Plaza Dorada 2, Héroes 5 de Mayo, locales 21 y 22, T 375558, F 374221, open Mon-Fri 0900-1800, Sat 0900-1300.

● **Tourist offices**
5 Ote 3, Av Juárez behind the Cathedral, next to the Post Office, T 460928, closed Sat and Sun. Also 3 Sur 1501, 8th floor and at the bus station. Administrator of Museums, T 327699.

● **Transport**
Local Taxi: radio taxi service, *Radio Omega*, T 406299, 406369, 406371, new Chevrolet cars, 24-hr service, will deliver packages or pick up food or medicine and deliver it to your hotel.

Air Hermanos Serdán airport (PBC) has flights to Guadalajara, Mexico City, Monterrey, Querétaro and Tijuana with Aero California or Aeromar.

Trains T 201664 for information. Station is a long way from centre, very run down, in questionable neighbourhood, no left luggage (if taking a night train, try to leave luggage at your hotel for the day), no services except for very dirty bathrooms. Micro bus No 1 on Sur 9 goes to station, US$0.35. Trains from **Mexico City**, 2nd class to Puebla via Cuautla at 0705, very slow (10-11 hrs, stops at the ruins of Cholula, see page 298); train to **Oaxaca** (2nd class), leaves Puebla 0720, 12 hrs, no advance booking, US$4, superb scenery, highly rec. The line weaves through cactus laden gorges recalling the Wild West. On clear days one gets a good view of Popocatépetl. There are many food sellers on train. The Oaxaqueño train from Mexico City leaves at 1900 and stops at 2350 at Puebla on its way to Oaxaca at 0010 (tickets sold 1200-1400 for reserved seats, breakfast included, supposed to arrive in Oaxaca 0925, often delayed). Fares from Mexico City: US$5.60 *primera preferente*; Puebla-Oaxaca US$13.50 1st class, US$15 *primera preferente*. 2nd class train to **Oriental** at 0830, US$1.25, for connection to **Veracruz**, US$2.50.

Buses Terminal: new, huge CAPU bus terminal for all buses N of city. From the centre to the terminal, take any form of transport marked 'CAPU', many colectivos on Av 9 Nte, fare US$1.50 pp flat rate. To the centre from the terminal take Kombi No 14, US$0.30, which stops at 11 Nte and Reforma at Paseo de Bravo (make sure it's a No 14 'directo', there is a No 14 which goes to the suburbs). The departure terminal has a *casa de cambio* (open 0900-1830), a Banco Serfín (Mon-Fri) with a 24-hr ATM compatible with Cirrus and Plus networks, *dulcería*, gift and craft shop, newsagent, 24-hr pharmacy, *pastelería*, cafetería, *caseta* for long distance phone calls, tourist information booth, booth selling taxi tickets (US$1.75 to the centre), next to it is a chart showing local bus routes, bathrooms (2 pesos), luggage store (1 peso/hr/bag), open 0700-2230. The arrivals terminal has some shops inc small grocery, free bathrooms, long distance pay phones and taxi ticket booth (but you have to take ramp to the departure terminal to get the taxi). **Companies**: **Autobuses de Oriente (ADO)**, T 497144, Mercedes Benz buses, 1st class and 'GL' plus service; **Oro**, T 497775, 497177, *gran turismo* or 1st class service; **UNO**, T 304014, luxury service, accept American Express; **Estrella Roja**, T 497099, 2nd class, 1st class and plus service; **Cristóbal Colón**, T 497144 ext 2860, plus service; **Estrella Blanca**, T 497561, 497433, 1st class, plus service and Elite; **Autobuses Unidos (AU)**, T 497366, 497405, 497967, all 2nd class without toilets.

To **Mexico City**, ADO to TAPO (eastern) terminal at 0445, 0530, then every 20 mins from 0600 to 2145, US$5; to Central del Sur terminal every hour from 0635 to 2135, US$5; to Central del Nte terminal every 20-40 mins from 0520-2150, US$5, Estrella Roja to Mexico City airport every hour from 0300 to 2000, US$7; to Mexico City 2nd class every 10 mins, US$4, 3 stops, 1st class, several a day US$5, plus service US$5.50; AU, every 12 mins from 0510 to 2300. To **Tehuacán** direct ADO every 30-45 mins from 0600-2100, US$4. To **Oaxaca**, all take new autopista, 4 hrs; ADO 'GL' plus service, 2 daily, US$28.25, 1st class, 5 daily, US$12; UNO at 1800, US$18; AU, 2nd class. To **Jalapa**, ADO 'GL' plus service at 0805 and 1700, US$7, 1st class, 8 a day, US$6, 4 hrs; AU, 2nd class. To **Villahermosa**, ADO 'GL' plus service via autopista, 2200, US$30, 1st class, 1900, 2145, US$25.50; UNO at 2100, US$41.25, 8 hrs. To **Reynosa**, ADO at 1155, US$31.60. To **Chetumal**, ADO, 1145, US$42. To **Mérida**, ADO, 2105, US$44. To **Tuxtla Gutiérrez**, ADO, 2010, US$30; UNO, 2215, US$46, 14 hrs. To **Tapachula**, UNO, 1830, US$53, 16 hrs; Cristóbal Colón, plus service, 2115, US$37.50. To **San Cristóbal de las Casas**, Cristóbal Colón, plus service, 1715, 1845, 2215, US$36. To **Cuernavaca**, Oro, *gran turismo* service, 0700, 1100, 1500, 1900, US$5, 1st class hourly 0600-2000, US$4, 2 stops. To **Nuevo Laredo**, Estrella Blanca, 1st class, 1000, US$43. To **Monterrey**, Estrella Blanca, 1st class, 1030, US$34.50. To **Matamoros**, Estrella Blanca, 1st class, 1330, US$31.50. To **Ciudad Victoria**, Estrella Blanca, 1st class, 1030, US$25. To **Acapulco**, Estrella Blanca, plus service, 2200, US$23.25, 1st class, 1030, 1230, 2130, 2230, 2300, US$20.75. To **Tijuana**, Estrella Blanca Elite service, 1400, bypassing Mexico City, goes via Guadalajara (US$31), Tepic, Mazatlán, Nogales (US$85.75) and Tijuana (US$87.25).

CUETZALAN

An interesting day-trip from Puebla is to **Cuetzalán** market (via Tetela-Huahuaztla) which is held on Sun in the Zócalo (3 hrs' walk up). In first week of Oct each year dancers from local villages gather and *voladores* 'fly' from the top of their pole. Nahua Indians sell cradles (*huacal*) for children; machetes and embroidered garments. The Día de los Muertos (2 Nov) is interesting here. Big clay dogs are made locally, unique stoves which hold big flat clay plates on which *tortillas* are baked and stews are cooked in big pots. Also available in nearby Huitzitlán. Women decorate their hair with skeins of wool. You can also go via Zaragoza, Zacapoaxtla and Apulco, where you can walk along a path, left of the road, to the fine 35m waterfall of La Gloria. It can be very foggy at Cuetzalán, even when it is fine in Puebla. Tourist information, C Hidalgo y Bravo, helpful, good map.

From Cuetzalán it is a 1½-hr walk to the well-preserved, niched pyramids of **Yohualichan** (Totonac culture); there are five excavated pyramids, two of them equivalent to that at El Tajín, and three still uncovered. There has been earthquake damage, though. Take a bus from C Miguel Alvarado Avila y C Abosolo, more frequent in morning and market days to San Antonio and get off at the sign Pirámides Yohualichan (30 mins, bad road), then walk 2 km to the site, closed Mon and Tues, entry US$2. In the Cuetzalán area are 32 km of caverns with lakes, rivers and wonderful waterfalls. These include **Tzicuilan** (follow C Emiliano Zapata, E of town) and **Atepolihuit** (follow Carretera Antigua up to the Campo Deportivo, W of town). Children offer to guide visitors to the ruins and the caves. (Claudio Rivero, Buenos Aires.)

● **Accommodation & places to eat** Several cheap, quite clean hotels, eg **E** *Hotel Rivello*, G Victoria 3, T (91) 2331-0139, 1 block from Zócalo, with bath, F without, basic, friendly, clean; **E** *Posada Jackelin*, upper end of plaza, nr market, behind church, pleasant; **E** *Posada*

Vicky, on G Victoria; *Posada Quetzal*, C Zaragoza. Good, cheap restaurant: *Yokoxochitl*, 2 de Abril, good for breakfasts, huge juices; *Casa Elvira Mora*, Hidalgo 54, rec; *Villacaiba* for seafood, Francisco Madero 6; *Café-Bazar Galería* in centre, good sandwiches and tea, nice garden, English magazines, rec.

● **Transport**   Direct buses from Puebla (Tezuitecos line only) 5 a day from 0500 to 1530, US$6.50; quite a few return buses, but if none direct go to Zaragoza and change buses there. There are many buses to Zacapoaxtla with frequent connections for Cuetzalán.

(Km 151) **Amozoc**, where tooled leather goods and silver decorations on steel are made, both mostly as outfits for the *charros*, or Mexican cattlemen. Beyond Amozoc lies **Tepeaca** with its late 16th century monastery, well worth a visit; its weekly market is very extensive. On the main square is Casa de Cortés, where Hernán Cortés signed the second of five *cartas de Relación* in 1520 (open 1000-1700). An old Spanish tower or *rollo* (1580) stands between Tepeaca's main square and the Parroquia. Beyond Tepeaca, 57½ km from Puebla, lies **Tecamachalco**: vast 16th century Franciscan monastery church with beautiful murals on the choir vault, in late medieval Flemish style, by a local Indian. **Language school**: Escuela de Español en Tecamachalco, run by Patricia O Martínez, C 29 Sur 303, Barrio de San Sebastián, Tecamachalco, CP 75480, Apdo Postal 13, T 91-242-21121, very good; US$70 for 1 week, 4 hrs a day, possible to live with families. There is a good seafood restaurant; enquire at José Colorado's *tienda* near the school.

TEHUACAN

(*Pop* 113,000;*Alt* 1,676m) Beyond, the road leads to **Tehuacán**, a charming town with a pleasant, sometimes cool, climate. It has some old churches. Water from the mineral springs is bottled and sent all over the country by Garci Crespo, San Lorenzo and Peñafiel. From the small dam at Malpaso on the Río Grande an annual race is held for craft without motors as far as the village of Quiotepec. The central plaza is pleasant and shaded; the nights are cool. From Tehuacán there are two paved roads to Oaxaca: one, very scenic, through Teotitlán del Camino (US$1.65 by 2nd class bus), and the other, longer but easier to drive, through Huajuapan (see page 365). Railway junction for Oaxaca and Veracruz; no passenger trains on line to Esperanza. Wild maize was first identified by an archaeologist at Coxcatlán Cave nearby. There is an airport.

Places of interest

The Ayuntamiento on the Zócalo is decorated inside and out with murals and tiles. **Museo de Mineralogía Romero**, 7 Nte 356, open 0900-1200, 1600-1800, am only on Sat, free, 1 room with good collection of minerals from all over the world. A short bus ride beyond Peñafiel Spa is the spa of **San Lorenzo** with spring-fed pools surrounded by trees, US$2 entry.

Local information
● **Accommodation**

México, Reforma Nte and Independencia Pte, 1 block from Zócalo, T 20019, garage, TV, restaurant, renovated colonial building, pool, quiet; **B-C** *Bogh Suites*, 1 Nte 102, NW side of Zócalo, T 23006, new, businessman's hotel, safe parking.

C *Iberia*, Independencia 217, T 21122, with bath, clean, airy, rec, pleasant restaurant, public parking nearby at reduced fee with voucher from hotel.

D *Inter*, above restaurant of same name, close to bus station (ask there), hot shower, clean, modern; **D** *Madrid*, 3 Sur 105, T 20272, opp Municipal Library, comfortable, cheaper without bath, rec. Several *casas de huéspedes* along C 3 (Nte and Sur) but low standards.

● **Places to eat**

Many eating places on Zócalo with reasonable prices (eg on same corner as Cathedral, good breakfast). The main meal is served at midday in Tehuacán. Try *Restaurant Santander*, good but pricey. *Cafetería California*, Independencia Ote 108, excellent juices and *licuados*; *Pizzería Richards*, Reforma Nte 250, quite good pizzas, good fresh salads; excellent taco stands.

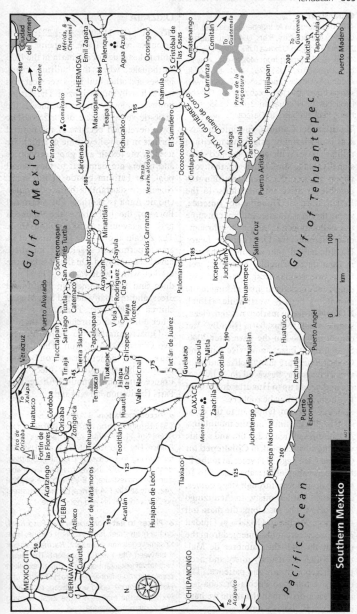

Southern Mexico

● **Transport**

ADO bus station on Av Independencia (Pte). Bus direct to **Mexico City**, 5 hrs, US$10; to **Puebla**, 2½ hrs, US$4; to **Oaxaca** (US$10.75, 5½ hrs, AU at 1430, coming from Mexico City, may be full), **Veracruz**, US$7.75, and the Gulf: Autobuses Unidos, 2nd class on C 2 Ote with several buses daily to Mexico City and Oaxaca. Local bus to **Huajuapan** 3 hrs, US$5; from there, frequent buses to Oaxaca.

Teotitlán del Camino, en route to Oaxaca, is a glaringly bright town with a military base. Vehicles are stopped occasionally; make sure, if driving, that your papers are in order. From Teotitlán it is possible to drive into the hills, to the Indian town of **Huautla de Jiménez**, where the local Mazatec Indians consume the hallucinogenic 'magic' mushrooms made famous by Dr Timothy Leary. Huautla has 'all four seasons of the year in each day; springlike mornings; wet, foggy afternoons; fresh, autumn evenings; and freezing nights.' Hiking in the mountains here is worthwhile. (Hotel: **E** *Olímpico*, above market, no sign, clean, simple, small rooms, bath, friendly.) You cannot buy food in the town after 2000. Several daily buses to Mexico City and Oaxaca. There are many police and military. Drivers may be waved down by people in the road up to Huautla; do not stop for them, they may be robbers.

The road from Tehuacán to the coast soon begins to climb into the mountains. At Cumbres we reach 2,300m and a wide view: the silvered peak of **Citlaltépetl** (or Orizaba – see page 311) volcano to the E, the green valley of Orizaba below. In 10 km we drop down, through steep curves, sometimes rather misty, to Acultzingo 830m below. The road joins the main toll road from Puebla to Orizaba at Ciudad Mendoza, where it has emerged from the descent through the Cumbres de Maltrata, which are usually misty and need to be driven with care and patience. (The expensive toll road Puebla-Orizaba is a much safer drive than the route we have described; it, too, is scenic.)

ORIZABA

(Km 317; *Pop* 115,000; *Alt* 1,283m) The favourite resort of the Emperor Maximilian, lost much of its charm in the 1973 earthquake, when the bullring, many houses and other buildings were lost, and is now heavily industrialized. The setting, however, is lovely. In the distance is the majestic volcanic cone of Orizaba. The town developed because of the natural springs in the valley, some of which are used by the textile and paper industries and others are dammed to form small pools for bathing beside picnic areas; Nogales (restaurant) is the most popular, Ojo de Agua is another. The Cerro del Borrego, the hill above the Alameda park, is a favourite early-morning climb. The Zócalo at one time lost much of its area to permanent snack bars, but these have been removed. On the N side is the market, with a wide variety of local produce and local women in traditional dress, and the many-domed San Miguel church (1690-1729). There are several other quite good churches, and there is an Orozco mural in the Centro Educativo Obrero on Av Colón. The Palacio Municipal is the actual cast-iron Belgian pavilion brought piece by piece from France after the famous 19th century Paris Exhibition, an odd sight.

● **Accommodation** **B** *Aries*, Ote 6 No 265, T 51116 (nightclub on top floor); **B** *Trueba*, Ote 6 and Sur 11, T 42744, resort facilities; **D** *De France*, Ote 6 No 186, T 52311, and US$0.25 for parking in courtyard, charming building, clean, comfortable, shower, friendly, reasonable if uninspiring restaurant; **E** *Vallejo*, Madero Nte 242, dirty, smelly; **F** *América*, on the main street no 269, very friendly and good value.

● **Places to eat** *Romanchu* and *Paso Real*, on the main street, have excellent cuisine. Hare Krishna vegetarian restaurant, *Radha's*, on Sur 4 between Ote 1 and 3, excellent. The Indian vegetarian restaurant on Sur 5, has an excellent *comida corrida*, highly rec. *Crazy Foods*, opp *Hotel De France*, good and cheap, nice sandwiches. In the market, try the local morning snack, *memelita picadita*.

Pico de Orizaba

🦶 Also known as Citlaltépetl, the highest mountain in Mexico (5,760m), it is not too difficult to climb, although acclimatization to altitude is advised and there are some crevasses to be negotiated. About 4 people a year ski on the glacier, but the surface is unpredictable. From Acatzingo one can go via a paved road to Tlachichuca (35 km, or you can take a bus from Puebla to Tlachichuca). Either contact Sr Reyes (F 24515019) who arranges trips in a 4WD up an appalling road to two huts on the mountain. He charges about US$50, including one night at his house, a former soap factory – very clean (**D** full board). His truck leaves at 1200, 3-hr journey, and he picks you up at about 1600, by prior arrangement. Sr Reyes is well-equipped and keen to give ground support to climbers. Alternatively, stay at **E** *Hotel Margarita*, no sign, then, early in the morning hitch hike to the last village, Villa Hidalgo (about 15 km). From there it's about 10 km to the huts. Take the trail which goes straight through the forest, eventually to meet the dusty road. The huts, one small, one larger and colder, are at 4,200m (small charge at each). There is no hut custodian; it's usually fairly empty, except on Sat night. No food or light, or wood; provide your own. Take a good sleeping bag and warm clothes. Water close at hand, but no cooking facilities. Start from the hut at about 0500, first to reach the glacier at 4,700m, and then a little left to the rim. It's about 7-8 hrs to the top; the ice is not too steep (about 35-40°), take crampons, if not for the ascent then for the descent which takes only 2½ hrs. At the weekend you're more likely to get a lift back to Tlachichuca. 1:50000 maps are available from INEGI information and sales office, eg in Puebla (Av 15 de Mayo 2829), Veracruz or Mexico City.

Volker Huss of Karlsruhe (Germany) informs us of an alternative route up the volcano; this is easier, because there is no glacier and therefore no crevasses, but is best done in the rainy season (April to Oct), when there is enough snow to cover the loose stone on the final stage. Crampons and ice-axe are necessary. The route is on the S face of the volcano. Stay in Orizaba and take a very early bus to Ciudad Serdán (depart 0530), or stay in Ciudad Serdán. At Serdán bus station take a bus, US$1.50, to San Antonio Atzitzintla, and then taxi US$4 to Texmalaquila; the driver will know the way. 5 hrs from Texmalaquila is the Fausto González hut at 4,760m (take own food and water). Miguel Quintero in Texmalaquila has mules for luggage transport to the shelter (US$5/bag). Spend the night there and climb the final 1,000m early in the morning, about 5 hrs. From the top are fine views, with luck even to Veracruz and Mexico City. In the rainy season the summit is usually free of cloud until midday. The entire descent takes 6 hrs and can be done the same day. A rec guide is Raimund Alvaro Torres, in Orizaba, C Sur 10 574, T 272-61940. An adventure travel shop on Pte 3 entre Sur 2 y 4, hires equipment and guides but their equipment is old and the guides not very knowledgeable.

● **Tourist office** Pte 2, across river from Zócalo. Open mornings only.

● **Transport** Bus to **Merida**, one a day (ADO), US$35, 1st class. To **Veracruz**, many buses, US$3.50, 1st class.

A road leaves Orizaba southwards, up into the mountains of **Zongolica**, a dry, poor and isolated region, cold and inhospitable, inhabited by various groups of Indians who speak Nahuatl, the language of the Aztecs. Zongolica village is a good place to buy *sarapes*; take early bus from Orizaba (ask for direct one) to get clear views of the mountains.

Beyond Orizaba the scenery is magnificent. The road descends to coffee and sugar-cane country and a tropical riot of flowers. It is very pleasant except when a northerly blows, or in the intolerable heat and mugginess of the wet season (one cyclist, en route to Córdoba, warned that "this is where the real sweating starts").

FORTIN DE LAS FLORES

(Km 331) A small town devoted to growing flowers and exporting them. Sometimes Indian women sell choice blossoms in small baskets made of banana-tree bark. Near Fortín there is a viewpoint looking out over a dramatic gorge (entry free). The *autopista* from Orizaba to Córdoba passes over this deep valley on a concrete bridge.

● **Accommodation** B *Posada la Loma*, Km 333 Carretera Nte 150, T 30658, very attractive, tropical garden with butterflies, distant view of snow-capped volcano in early morning, moderately expensive. There are others, slightly cheaper, which also offer tropical gardens for relaxation. Note that Veracruz-Mexico City night trains sound their horns when passing Fortín which can be disturbing.

CORDOBA

(*Pop* 126,000; *Alt* 923m) 8 km on in the rich valley of the Río Seco, an old colonial city, is also crazy with flowers. Its Zócalo is spacious, leafy and elegant; three sides are arcaded; two of them are lined with tables. On the fourth is an imposing church with a chiming clock. There are several hotels in the Zócalo, which is alive and relaxed at night. In one of them, the *Hotel Zevallos*, Gen Iturbide signed the Treaty of Córdoba in 1821, which was instrumental in freeing Mexico from Spanish colonial rule. There is a local museum at C 3, No 303, open 1000-1300 and 1600-2000. Córdoba has the highest rainfall in Mexico, but at predictable times. The area grows coffee.

● **Accommodation** B *Mansur*, Av 1 y C 3, T 26600, on square, smart; C *Hostal de Borreña*, C 11 308, T 20777, modern, clean, really hot water, some traffic noise but good value. Near the ADO terminal is C *Palacio*, Av 3 y C 2, T 22186; C *Marina* (T 22600), D *Iberia* (T 21301), D *Trescado* (T 22366) and *Casa de Huéspedes Regis* are all on Av 2; E *Las*

Carretas, Av 4 No 512, with bath, clean, noisy, short stay, not rec, can wash clothes; *Casa de Huéspedes La Sin Rival* and E *La Nueva Querétana* are at 511 and 508 of Av 4, respectively (latter is basic but cheap); F *Los Reyes*, C 3, rec, shower, hot water, street rooms double-glazed, street parking OK.

● **Places to eat** *Cantábrico*, C 3 No 9, T 27646, 1 block from Zócalo, excellent meat and fish dishes, fine wines and good service, 'worth a trip from Mexico City!', highly rec; *Brujes*, Av 2 No 306, good *comida corriente*.

● **Banks & money changers** *Casa de Cambio* on Av 3 opp **Bancomer**, rec.

● **Transport** **Trains** From Mexico City at 0745, 2nd class, arrive 1610, US$4, continuing also to Veracruz. At 0630, a 2nd class train departs for Tierra Blanca (US$1), Medias Aguas (US$3), Coatzacoalcos (US$4), Teapa (US$6.50), Palenque (US$8), Campeche (US$12) and Mérida (US$14), arrive 0935 next day. **Buses** Bus station is at the end of Av 6. Direct services to **Veracruz**, 2 hrs, US$4; **Puebla**, 3 hrs, US$7.70; **Mexico City**, hourly, 5 hrs, US$10; to **Coatzacoalcos**, US$13; **Oaxaca** and many others. **Car service** Nissan, Chevrolet and Dodge dealers, mechanics all on C 11.

The direct road from Córdoba to Veracruz is lined, in season, by stalls selling fruit and local honey between **Yanga** and Cuitláhuac. Yanga is a small village named after the leader of a group of escaped black slaves in colonial times. A slightly longer but far more attractive road goes from Fortín de las Flores northwards through Huatusco and Totutla, then swings E to Veracruz. For cyclists, the 125 km from Córdoba to Veracruz has no accommodation en route, but is mostly flat, so could be done in 1 day.

VERACRUZ

(Km 476; *Pop* 1,000,000; *Phone code* 29) The principal port of entry for Mexico lies on a low alluvial plain bordering the Gulf coast. Cortés landed near here, on Isla de Sacrificios, on 17 April 1519. The first settlement was called Villa Rica de la Vera Cruz; its location was changed various times, including to La Antigua, now a pleasant little colonial town with the ruins of Cortés' house (it is 1.5 km off the road to Cardel, some 30 km N of Veracruz). The present site was established in 1599.

NB If planning to visit Veracruz or the hills inland (eg Xalapa) between July and Sept, check the weather forecast because many tropical storms blow themselves out in this region, bringing heavy rain. From Oct to Jan the weather tends to be changeable, with cold, damp winds from the N. At this time the beaches and Malecón are empty and many resorts close, except over Christmas and New Year when the tourists flood in and all road transport is booked up 5 days in advance. Otherwise it is generally hot.

Veracruz is a mixture of the very old and the new; there are still many picturesque white-walled buildings and winding side-streets. It has become a great holiday resort, and can be touristy and noisy. The heart of the city is **Plaza Constitución** (Zócalo). The square is white-paved, with attractive cast iron lampstands and benches, and surrounded by the cathedral, with an unusual cross, depicted with hands, the governor's palace and colonial-style hotels. The plaza comes alive in the evening at weekends: an impressive combination of the crush of people, colour and marimba music in the flood-lit setting. From 15 July to the end of Aug there is jazz in the Zócalo from 1900.

Culturally, Veracruz is a Caribbean city, home to the *jarocho* costume (predominantly white), dance and music which features harps and guitars. The most famous dances, accompanied by the Conjunto Jarocho, are the *bamba* and *zapateado*, with much stamping and lashing of feet related to flamenco of Andalucía. Mexico's version of the Cuban *danzón* music and the indigenous *música tropical* add to the cultural richness. Many cultural events can be seen at the Instituto Veracruzano de Cultura, a few blocks from the Zócalo with a good, new café and library; a nice place to relax and mingle with students. At night the Malecón is very lively, noisy and sometimes fire-eaters and other performers entertain the public.

The food is good, the fishing not bad, and the people lively, noisy and welcoming. The local craft is tortoise shell jewellery adorned with silver, but remember that the import of tortoise shell into the USA and many other countries is prohibited.

Places of interest

There are two buildings of great interest: the very fine 17th century **Palacio Municipal** (1627), on Plaza Constitución, with a splendid façade and courtyard, and the castle of **San Juan de Ulúa** (1565), on Gallega Island, now joined by road to the mainland; take bus marked Ulúa from Malecón Av República (it is not advisable to walk there, entry to the castle US$4.35, open 0900-1700 Tues-Sun). It failed to deter the buccaneers and later became a political prison. Mexico's 'Robin Hood', Chucho el Roto, was imprisoned there, and escaped three times. In 1915 Venustiano Carranza converted it into a presidential palace. The **Baluarte de Santiago**, a small fort which once formed part of the city walls, is at Francisco Canal y Gómez Farias, open 1000-1630, Tues-Sun, (entry US$4.35). The **aquarium** has moved from the harbour breakwater to a new building at Villa del Mar; large underwater viewing tank, watch sharks and other exotic species, admission US$4.35, open 1000-1900 Mon-Fri, 0900-1900 Sat and Sun. **Plazuela de la Campana**, by Serdán and Zaragoza, is an attractive small square.

There is a **city historical museum** with a good collection of photographs, well displayed; it traces history from the Conquest to 1910; it is at Zaragoza 397 (entry US$0.35, open 0900-1500 Mon-Sat, English booklet available). The **Carranza museum** on the Malecón, Tues-Sun 0900-1700, has photos of the revolution, the life of Carranza and his battles against the Huerta Regime (the last room shows a picture of Carranza's skeleton and the trajectory of the bullet that killed him), entry free.

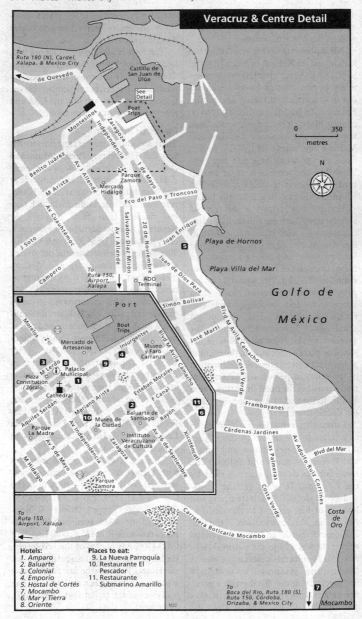

Veracruz & Centre Detail

To Ruta 180 (N), Cardel, Xalapa, & Mexico City

de Quevedo

Castillo de San Juan de Ulúa

See Detail

Boat Trips

0   350
metres

N

Montesinos

Zaragoza

Independencia

Benito Juárez

M Arista

Av I Allende

Av Cuauhtémoc

J Soto

Campero

1 de Mayo

Parque Zamora

Mercado Hidalgo

Fco del Paso y Troncoso

Salvador Díaz Mirón

20 de Noviembre

Av I Allende

Juan Enrique

Playa de Hornos

5

Playa Villa del Mar

Juan de Dios Peza

To Ruta 150, Airport, Xalapa

ADO Terminal

Simón Bolívar

Golfo de México

T

Port

Morelos

Boat Trips

Mercado de Artesanías

Insurgentes

Blvd M Ávila Camacho

Museo y Faro Carranza

José Marti

3

M Lerdo

8

Palacio Municipal

9

4

Esteban Morales

Costa Verde

Plaza Constitución Zócalo

1

Cathedral

Mariano Arista

F Canal

11

Framboyanes

Aquiles Serdán

2

Baluarte de Santiago

Rayón

6

10

Museo de la Ciudad

Cárdenas Jardines

Parque La Madre

Av Independencia

Zaragoza

Instituto Veracruzano de Cultura

Av 16 de Septiembre

Xicoténcatl

Las Palmeras

Av Adolfo Ruiz Cortines

Blvd del Mar

Av S de Mayo

M Hidalgo

Parque Zamora

Costa Verde

Costa de Oro

To Ruta 150, Airport, Xalapa

Carretera Boticaria Mocambo

To Boca del Río, Ruta 180 (S), Ruta 150, Córdoba, Orizaba, & Mexico City

7

Mocambo

M22

Beaches

The beach along the waterfront, and the sea, are filthy. There is much pollution from the heavy shipping. Amber from Simojordis is sold on the town beach. A short bus ride from the fish market takes you to **Mocambo** beach, which has a superb, 50m swimming bath (with restaurant and bar, admission US$3.30), beach restaurants, Caribbean-style beach huts and dirty sand; the water is quite a bit cleaner though still rather uninviting in colour. There are crabs and mosquitoes and much pestering by sellers. The Gulf is even warmer than the Caribbean. The beach is crowded. At holiday time cars race up and down, there are loud radios, etc. To Mocambo take a bus marked 'Boca del Río' on Av Zaragoza. There is little shade near the beach. There is a fine beach at Chachalacas, 50 km N, not crowded (see page 326).

Excursions

Harbour trips from the Malecón US$3.30 pp for 35 mins if 15 people turn up. Isla de Sacrificios (see above) is no longer included as damage from tourism has caused it to be closed to visitors. To **Zempoala** (see page 326), buses from ADO terminal 30 mins each way, via Cardel, or less frequent direct 2nd class buses; a local bus from Cardel goes to La Antigua, US$0.50. On Sun, to Mandinga for cheap fresh sea food (big prawns), and local entertainment.

Local festivals

The Shrovetide carnival 7 weeks before Easter is said to be Mexico's finest, rivalling those of New Orleans, Brazil and Trinidad. The carnival starts a week before Shrove Tuesday and ends on Ash Wednesday; Sat-Tues are the main days with parades. At this time it is very difficult to find higher-priced accommodation (especially on the Sat), or tickets for transportation.

Local information
● **Accommodation**

NB Because of the liveliness of the Zócalo at night, hotels on the square can be noisy.

A1 *Calinda* (formerly *Veracruz*, Av Independencia esq Lerdo, nr Zócalo, probably the best in the centre; **A2** *Emporio*, Paseo del Malecón, Insurgentes Veracruzanos y Xicoténcatl, T 320020, F 312261, very good, with bath, swimming pool, inexpensive *comida corrida*, rather old-fashioned; a block before the *Emporio* when approaching from the Zócalo is **A2** *Mocambo*, Boca del Río, T 371661, 8 km out on Mocambo beach, 1930s palace, good service and food, highly rec; **A2** *Puerto Bello* (aka *Howard Johnson's*), Avila Camacho 1263, T 310011, F 310867, good, clean, friendly, most rooms have sea-view, rec.

B *Baluarte*, opp the small fort of Baluarte, Canal 265, T 360844, good, clean, rec, **B** *Colonial*, on Zócalo, T 320193, swimming pool, indoor parking, rec; **B** *Hostal de Cortés*, 3-star, Avila Camacho y de las Casas, T 320065, F 315744, convenient for clean beaches, helpful, rec; **B** *Oriente*, M Lerdo 105, T 312440, secure parking, clean, friendly, balconies (noisy from street), good fans, some a/c, rec.

C *Central*, Mirón 1612, T 372222, next to ADO bus terminal, clean, fair, noisy, erratic hot water, friendly, get room at back, especially on 5th floor, laundry facilities; **C** *Cristóbal Colón*, Avila Camacho 681, T 823844, small, quiet, some rooms with sea-view balconies, clean; **C** *Ruiz Milán*, Malecón y Gómez Farias, T 361877, F 361339, good.

D *Casa de Huéspedes*, on Morelia, nr Zócalo, with bath, hot water, quiet, clean, use of mosquito net needed, economical restaurant next door; **D** *Concha Dorada*, on Zócalo, very pleasant; **D** *Impala*, Orizaba 650, T 370169, with bath, cold water, mosquitoes but clean, nr bus station; **D** *Mar y Tierra*, Figueroa y Malecón, T 313866, good value, some rooms with balconies overlooking the harbour; **D** *Príncipe*, Collado 195, some distance from centre, very clean with hot shower and toilet; **D** *Royalty*, Abasolo 34, T 361041, average, nr beach, 20 mins' walk from Zócalo, rec, but noisy as it caters mainly to student groups; **D** *Santander*, Landero y Coss 123, T 324529, with bath and TV, very clean.

E *Amparo*, Serdán 482, T 322738, with fan, insect screens, clean, hot water, good value, rec; opp is **D** *Santo Domingo*, with bath, fan, OK, bakery attached; nearby on Serdán is **C** *Mallorca*, with bath and fan, radio, newly furnished, very clean, highly rec; **E** *Casa de Huéspedes La Tabasqueña*, Av Morelos 325, fan, new bathrooms, upper rooms less good, front rooms noisy, many others without windows, cheap, clean, safe, helpful; **E** *Marsol de Veracruz*, Av Díaz Mirón 1242, T 325399, right from ADO bus station 4 blocks, quiet, with bath, highly rec, clean and helpful; **E** *Hatzin*, Reforma 6 and Avista, friendly, rec; **E** *Paloma*, E Morales y Reforma, clean, basic, fan, friendly, good value; **E** *Sevilla*, Av Morelos 359, with fan and TV, negotiate.

F *Las Nievas*, C Tenoya, off Plaza Zamora, with bath, fan, dark rooms. Many others in port area, reached by bus from the bus terminal.

Trailer Park: the only trailer park is behind *Hotel Mocambo* (see above), dry camping, showers and bathrooms dirty, swimming pools empty, US$6.50 for vehicle and two people.

Youth hostel: Paso Doña Juana, Municipio de Ursulo Galván, T 320878, 2 hrs by bus from town, US$2.30 a night; for information on Villas Deportivas Juveniles, see under Mexico City **Campsites**.

● **Places to eat**
Torros are the local drinks made of eggs, milk, fruit and alcohol, delicious and potent. *La Nueva Parroquía* on Melecón, 2 coffee houses in same block, very popular, excellent coffee and capuccino. In the main market, H Cortés y Madero, there are inexpensive restaurants in the mezzanine, overlooking the interior (watch out for extras that you did not order). In the fish market for excellent fish and shrimp cocktails, and opp are *La Garlopa* and *Doña Paz/Normita*, good seafood. There is a good local fish restaurant, *Olympica*, Zaragoza 250, nr the fish market, 2 blocks from the Zócalo. *El Pescador*, for fish, Zaragoza 335 y Morales (not evenings) good cheap *comida corrida*; and the steakhouse *Submarino Amarillo*, Malecón 472. *Karen*, Arista 574 between Landero y Coss and Zaragoza, good fish restaurant. *Café de la Catedral*, Ocampo y Parque Zamora, large, local, few tourists, good value, try fish stuffed with shrimps; *El Azteca de Cayetano*, Mario Molina 94, where *mondongos de fruta* (a selection of all the fruits in season, plus fruit-flavoured ice) are prepared on one plate; also *Mondongo de Fruta*, M Molina 88, not cheap but delicious for fruits, juices and ices. An interesting place is *Tiburón*, Av Landero y Coss 167, esquina A Serdán, 2 blocks from Zócalo, run by 'Tiburón' González, the 'Rey de la Alegría', or 'Rey Feo' of carnival; the walls are covered in pictures of him and his *comparsas*, dating back to at least 1945, has inexpensive, good food too. *La Paella*, Plaza Constitución, No 138, has its name written into the concrete of the entrance floor

as well as a sign, good *comida corrida*. *Pizza Palace*, Zamora, buffet 1200-1700, US$5; *Emir Cafetería*, Independencia 1520, nr F Canal, good breakfast. *La Quinta del Son*, on paved side street off Serdán, bar and restaurant, food nothing special but excellent Cuban-style *trova* band in pm. *Gran Café del Portal*, opp Cathedral, traditional (marimba all day) but not cheap; *La Puerta del Sol*, on Molina, 1 block S of the Zócalo, friendly pub, cheap beer. Good shellfish at Boca del Río. *Le Blé*, coffee house, on road parallel to Blvd M Avila Camacho, between F Canal and Rayón, good decor, fine variety of coffees; *Nevería y Refresquería Aparito*, A Serdán y Landero y Coss, nr fish market, good for fruit and juices, try *mondongo de frutas*.

● **Airline offices**
AeroMéxico, García Auly 231, T 350142; **Mexicana**, Av 5 de Mayo y A Serdán, T 322242.

● **Banks & money changers**
Bancomer, Independencia y Juárez (changes TCs 1000-1215), Banco Serfín, Díaz Mirón, 2 blocks from bus station, changes US$ cash and TCs; and Banamex (not Amex) changes money. American Express agency is *Viajes Olymar*, Blvd M Avila Camacho 2221, T 313406. 2 *casas de cambio*: *La Amistad*, Juárez 112 (behind the hotels on the Zócalo), rates not as good as the banks but much quicker; *Hotel Veracruz* changes money at similar rates.

● **Embassies & consulates**
US Consular Agency: C Víctimas del 25 de Junio 388, in centre.

● **Post & telecommunications**
Post Offices: main post office by bridge to San Juan de Ulúa fortress, a fine building inaugurated in 1902 by Porfirio Díaz, open 0900-1200 Mon-Fri, also Telegraph office, open 0900-1700 Mon-Fri; also at Palacio Federal, 5 de Mayo y Rayón, 0800-1900.

● **Tourist offices**
Palacio Municipal on the Zócalo, T 329942, helpful but no hotel price list; Federal office, T 321613.

● **Transport**
Air At Las Bajadas (VER), 12 km from the centre, to the capital several flights daily with Mexicana and AeroMéxico. Serolitoral, T 315232, for flights up and down the coast: Monterrey, Tampico, Torreón, Villahermosa. Aero Caribe to Ciudad del Carmen, Mérida, Cancún and Minatitlán.

Trains Rail to **Mexico City**: 2nd class train leaves Mexico City 0745 via Fortín and Córdoba, arr Veracruz, 1850 (US$5), returns 0800 arr 1855. Another train from Mexico City via Xalapa leaves at 0720. There is also a train Veracruz to Tapachula via Tierra Blanca, Medias Aguas and Ixtepec at 2100, arr 1925 next day, 2nd class, US$10.

Buses The majority of buses are booked solid for 3 days in advance throughout summer; at all times queues of up to 2 hrs possible at Mexico City booking offices of bus companies (best company: ADO). Book outward journeys on arrival in Veracruz, as the bus station is some way out of town and there are often long queues. ADO terminal, Díaz Mirón y Jalapa, T 376790; Autobuses Unidos, Lafragua y Jalapa (2 blocks from ADO), T 372376. For local buses, get accurate information from the tourist office. Buses to the main bus station along Av 5 de Mayo; marked ADO; and from the station to the centre, blue and white or red and white buses marked Díaz Mirón; pass 1 block from the Zócalo, US$0.35, or colectivos, also US$0.35. Taxi to ADO terminal from centre US$2.50. Bus to **Mexico City**, ADO, US$13.50, US$20.35 *primera plus* (4 hrs), via Xalapa, non-stop, or stops only at Perote, misses out Orizaba, Fortín and Córdoba; to **Villahermosa** US$36 *primera plus* (7½ hrs); to **Puebla**, US$9; to **Oaxaca**, ADO, 11 hrs, US$21.50 *plus* service; to **Mérida** US$43 (16 hrs).

Connections with Guatemala: there are no through buses to Guatemala, but there are connecting services. The 'directo' train leaves Veracruz 2100 daily for Ixtepec and Tapachula (US$13.25 *primera preferente*); scheduled to take almost 24 hrs, more like 38, not recommended, foul toilets, no lighting so high likelihood of robbery. Take your own toiletries and food, although there is a restaurant car, food is available at every stop. No sleeping accommodation. Local bus services run Tapachula-border and border Guatemala City; quicker than the much more mountainous route further N. Bus Veracruz-Tapachula 14 hrs, 1½-hr meal stop (at 0230), four 10-min station stops, US$30.75, *plus* service US$50, 1900 every night, 13 hrs, video, reclining seats. Alternatively, take ADO bus to Oaxaca, then carry on to Tapachula (12 hrs) by bus. This allows you to stop at intermediate points of your choice, has few 'comfort' stops. Buy bus tickets out of Veracruz in advance.

ROUTES The road is very winding from Orizaba so take travel sickness tablets if necessary. Philippe Martin, of the Touring Club Suisse, writes: 'The road from Veracruz to Oaxaca is spectacular but tiresome to drive and will take about a day. The road from Veracruz to La Tinaja and Tierra Blanca is good and fast although there are many lorries. From there to Miguel Alemán the road is bad, speed reasonable, still many lorries. The Tuxtepec area has lovely lowland, jungle areas, charming villages, and the traffic is sparser between Tuxtepec and Oaxaca, while there are no more gasoline stations. The road is very bad and winding and the fog only lifts after you leave the pinou at 2,650m above sea level. After a descent and another pass at 2,600m you enter the bare mountainous zone of Oaxaca. Very few eating places between Tuxtepec and Oaxaca.'

THE PAPALOAPAN REGION

At **Puerto Alvarado**, a modern, fishing port (1½ hrs S from Veracruz by bus, none too pleasant for women on their own, many bars and drunks; **D** *Hotel Lety*, reasonable but for grim plumbing system; **D** *Hotel del Pastor*, avoid next-door restaurant; **D** *María Isela*, quiet, clean with fan, rec; beware of small boys with pea-shooters in the plaza; exchange services 1000-1200; fair/carnival 31 Mar-5 April), cross the Río Papaloapan (Butterfly River) by a toll bridge (US$1.70), go along Route 180 into the sugar-cane area around Lerdo de Tejada and Angel R Cavada. At El Trópico shop a dirt road turns left to some quiet beaches such as Salinas and Roca Partida. Only at Easter are the beaches crowded: they are normally the preserve of fishermen using hand nets from small boats. In the dry season (Dec-May) the road is passable around the coast to Huatusco.

At **Tula**, a little further along the main road, is a spectacular waterfall, El Salto de Tula; a restaurant is set beside the falls. The road then climbs up into the mountainous volcanic area of Los Tuxtlas, known as the Switzerland of Mexico for its mountains and perennial greenness.

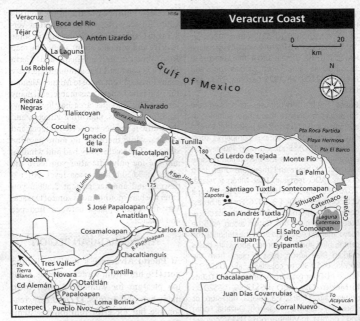

SANTIAGO TUXTLA

A pleasant town of colonial origin, set on a river. In the main square is the largest known Olmec head, carved in solid stone, and also a museum (open 0900-1500, Sat-Sun 0900-1200 and 1500-1800), containing examples of local tools, photos, items used in witchcraft (*brujería*), and the first sugar-cane press used in Mexico and another Olmec head. There is dancing to *jarana* bands in the Christmas fortnight.

The archaeological site of **Tres Zapotes** lies to the W; it is reached by leaving the paved road S towards Villa Isla and taking either the dirt road at Tres Caminos (signposted) in the dry season (a quagmire from May-Dec), or in the wet season access can be slowly achieved by turning right at about Km 40, called Tibenal, and following the dirt road N to the site of the Museum which is open 0900-1700, entrance US$1.65. (If it is closed, the lady in the nearby shop has a key.) A bus from Santiago Tuxtla goes at 1200 to the village of Tres Zapotes, the site is 1 km walk (the bus cannot reach Tres Zapotes if rain has swollen the river that the road has to cross). Travellers with little time to spare may find the trip to Tres Zapotes not worth the effort. There is an Olmec head, also the largest carved stela ever found and stela fragments bearing the New World's oldest Long Count Date, equal to 31 BC. Not far from Tres Zapotes are three other Olmec sites: Cerro de las Mesas, Laguna de los Cerros, and San Lorenzo Tenochtitlán.

• **Accommodation** C *Hotel Castellanos*, on Plaza, hot shower, clean, swimming pool (US$1 for non-residents), rec; D *Morelos*, family run, quiet, nicely furnished.

• **Places to eat** Overlooking Santiago Tuxtla is the hillside restaurant *El Balcón*, which serves excellent fish and seafood and *horchata de coco*, a drink made from the flesh and milk of coconut.

• **Banks & money changers** Exchange at Banco Comermex on Plaza, TCs 0900-1330.

• **Transport** AU bus from Veracruz, 2nd class, 3 hrs, US$2.

SAN ANDRES TUXTLA

15 km beyond lies **San Andrés Tuxtla** (112,000), the largest town of the area, with narrow winding streets, by-passed by a ring road. This town is also colonial in style and has a well-stocked market with Oaxacan foods such as *totopos, carne enchilada*, and *tamales de elote* (hard tortillas, spicy meat, and cakes of maize-flour steamed on leaves). It is the centre of the cigar trade. One factory beside the main road permits visitors to watch the process and will produce special orders of cigars (*puros*) marked with an individual's name in 30 mins.

• **Accommodation** **D** *Hotel Pasada San José*, Belisario Domínguez 10, T 22020, close to plaza, run by nice family and staff, restaurant, pick-up truck for excursions, second hotel at Monte Pío; **D** *Catedral*, nr Cathedral, very nice, **D** *Colonial*, Pino Suárez opp *Figueroa*, with bath, hot water, clean; **D** *Figueroa*, Pino Suárez 10; **D** *del Parque*, Madero 5, a/c, very clean, good restaurant; **D** *Zamfer*, ½ block from Zócalo; **E** *Casa de Huéspedes la Urizabana*, in the centre of town, without bath, clean, hot water, friendly; **E** *Juárez*, 400m down street from ADO terminal, clean, friendly, **E** *Ponce de León*, primitive, pleasant patio

• **Places to eat** Near the the town centre is the restaurant *La Flor de Guadalajara*; it appears small from the outside but is large and pleasant inside, well rec; sells *tepachue*, a drink made from pineapple, similar in flavour to cider, and *agua de Jamaica*.

• **Transport** Bus San Andrés Tuxtla-Villahermosa US$11, 6 hrs; to Mexico City, 1st class, 9 hrs, US$22.

CATEMACO

(*Pop* 31,000) A pleasant town with large colonial church and picturesque situation on lake, 13 km from San Andrés Tuxtla (bus service irregular, taxi US$5). There are stalls selling handicrafts from Oaxaca,

and boat trips out on the lakes to see the shrine where the Virgin appeared, the spa at Coyame and the Isla de Changos, and to make a necklace of lilies, are always available (boat owners charge US$30-35 per boat). The town is noted for its *brujos* (sorcerers), although this is becoming more of a tourist attraction than a reality, and the Monte del Cerro Blanco to the N is the site of their annual reunion.

Excursions

At Sihuapan, 5 km from Catemaco, is a turning S on to a paved road which leads to the impressive waterfall of Salto de **Eyipantla** (well worth a visit); there are lots of butterflies. There is a stairway down to the base and a path winding through a small village to the top. Small boys at the restaurant near the falls offer their services as guides. Take 2nd class AU bus Catemaco-Sihuapan; from 1030 buses leave every 30 mins from Sihuapan to Eyipantla, otherwise it's a 20-min walk to Comoapan, then take a taxi for US$2. There are also buses from the plaza in San Andrés Tuxtla.

Local information
● **Accommodation**
A number of hotels are situated at the lakeside.

A3 *la Finca*, just outside town, T 30430, pool, attractive grounds, beautiful setting beside lake, full at weekends, a/c, comfortable rooms, but poor food and service.

B *Motel Playa Azul*, 2 km on road to Sontecomapan, T 30042, modern, a/c; in a nice setting, comfortable and shady, with water-skiing on lake, will allow trailers and use of showers.

C *Posada Komiapan* (swimming-pool and restaurant), very comfortable, T 30063; **C** *Catemaco*, T 30203, excellent food and swimming pool, and *Berthangel*, T 30411, a/c, satellite TV, similar prices; both on main square.

D *Del Cid*, 1 block from ADO bus terminal, with fan and bath, OK; **D** *Los Arcos*, T 30003, clean, fan, good value; **D** *del Brujo*, Ocampo y Malecón, fan, a/c, shower, nice clean rooms, balcony overlooking the lake, rec.

E *Posada Viki*, on Zaragoza, next to *Gallardo*; **E** *San Francisco*, Matamoros 26, with bath, basic, but good and clean.

Trailer park: at Solotepec, on the lakeside on the road to Playa Azul, US$6.50/vehicle, very clean, hook-ups, bathrooms, rec; also *La Ceiba*, restaurant and trailer park, Av Malecón, 6 blocks W of Zócalo, by lakeshore, camping and hook-ups, bathrooms with hot water, restaurant and lakeside patio.

● **Places to eat**
On the promenade are a number of good restaurants: *María José*, best; *7 Brujas*, wooden restaurant open till 2400, good, try *mojarra* (local fish); *La Julita*, also lets rooms, E, with bath, pleasant, rec; *La Pescada*, opp cathedral, good fish, US$5; *La Ola*, built almost entirely by the owner in the local natural materials, and *La Luna*, among others. At the rear of the market, diagonally from the back of *La Luna*, are some inexpensive, good restaurants serving *comida corrida* for US$2-2.50, *La Campesina* is rec. Restaurant on 1st floor opp Cathedral, nice atmosphere. Best value are those not directly on the lake, eg *Los Sauces*, which serves *mojarra*. *Bar El Moreno*, 2 de Abril, at the beach, 'not too fancy' but good cuba libres and live synthesizer music.

● **Transport**
Catemaco can be reached by direct AU 2nd class bus from Veracruz, every 10 mins, many stops, 4 hrs, US$5, also ADO 1st class; buses also from Santiago Tuxtla, 2nd class. It is about 120 km NW of Minatitlán (see page 407); buses also from/to Villahermoso, 6 hrs, US$10 (ADO). To Tuxtepec, change in San Andrés Tuxtla.

SONTECOMAPAN AND GULF COAST

The Gulf Coast may be reached from Catemaco along a dirt road (which can be washed out in winter). It is about 18 km to Sontecomapan, crossing over the pass at Buena Vista and looking down to the Laguna where, it is said, Francis Drake sought refuge. The village of **Sontecomapan** (*Pop* 1,465), (*Hotel Sontecomapan*) lies on an entry to the Laguna and boats may be hired for the 20 mins' ride out to the bar where the Laguna meets the sea (US$10 return). A large part of the Laguna is surrounded by mangrove swamp, and the sandy beaches, edged by cliffs, are almost deserted except for local fishermen and groups of pelicans. Two good restaurants in Sontecomapan. Beaches are accessible to those who enjoy isolation, such as **Jicacal** and **Playa Hermosa**. Jicacal can be reached by going straight on from the Catemaco-Sontecomapan road for 9 km on a good dirt road to La Palma where there is a small bridge which is avoided by heavy vehicles; immediately after this take left fork (poor dirt road, there is a bus) for **Monte Pío**, a pretty location at the mouth of the river (**D** *Hotel Posada San José Montepío*, Playas Montepío, T 21010, rec, family-run, also basic rooms to let, **E**, and a restaurant), and watch out for a very small sign marked Playa Hermosa; road impassable when wet, about 2 km, and then continuing for about 4 km from there. Playa Jicacal is long and open, the first you see as you near the water. The track reaches a T-junction, on the right Jicacal, to the left to Playa Hermosa, *Hotel*, **E** and restaurant. It is not recommended to sleep on the beaches (assaults and robberies) although at Easter time many people from the nearby towns camp on the beaches. The place is busy at weekends.

CROSSING THE ISTHMUS

At **Acayucán**, a pleasant town with several cinemas (**D** *Hotel Joalica*, Zaragoza 4; **D** *Hotel Ritz*, Av Hidalgo 7, T 50024, shower, fan, noisy, parking; **D** *Los Angeles*, cheaper without TV, clean, fans, friendly, pool, owners speak some English, space for car inside; **E** *San Miguel*, with bath, hot water and fan, not very attractive, but OK; **E** *Iglesias*), 267 km from Veracruz on toll road (1st class buses 'de paso', very hard to get on, 4 hrs to Veracruz, 2nd class 5½ hrs), turn right for Route 185 if you want to go across the Isthmus to Tehuantepec, Tuxtla Gutiérrez and Central America, but continue on Route 180 for Minatitlán, Coatzacoalcos and Villahermosa (Tabasco). The road across the Isthmus is straight but is not always fast to drive because of high winds (changing air systems from Pacific to Atlantic). Gasoline and food on sale at the half-way point,

Palomares, where there is a paved road to Tuxtepec (see page 323), 2½ hrs' drive. A few kilometres S of Palomares a gravelled road enters on the eastern side; this passes under an imposing gateway 'La Puerta de Uxpanapa' where some 24,500 families are being settled on land reclaimed from the jungle. There is a good hotel at **Matías Romero**, *Real del Istmo*, a/c, by the road, safe parking, good restaurant. The road crosses the watershed and passes across the flat coastal plain to Juchitán (see page 381).

ALVARADO TO PAPALOAPAN

About 15 km from Alvarado a new bridge replaces the old ferry-crossing at Buenavista over the Papaloapan Río and the 175 road heads southwards to the fishing village of **Tlacotalpan** where the Papaloapan and San Juan rivers meet. This town, regarded as the centre of Jarocho culture (an amalgam of Spanish, mainly from Seville, African and Indian cultures), has many picturesque streets with 1-storey houses all fronted by stuccoed columns and arches painted in various bright pastel colours. Two churches in the Zócalo, and a Casa de las Artesanías on Chazaro, 1½ blocks from the Zócalo. The **Museo Funster** contains interesting local paintings and artefacts. There is a famous *fiesta* there on 31 Jan which is very much for locals rather than tourists (accommodation is impossible to find during *fiesta*).

● **Accommodation & places to eat** The **D** *Viajero* and *Reforma* hotels are good; so is the **B** *Posada Doña Lala*, Carranza II, T 42580, F 42111, with a/c and TV, restaurant good but expensive; **E** *Jarocho*, seedy. Excellent *sopa de mariscos* and *jaiba a la tlacotalpina* (crab) at the *Restaurant La Flecha*.

● **Transport** Buses go to Veracruz via Alvarado (US$2, 45 mins), to San Andrés, Tuxtla Gutiérrez, Santiago Tuxtla (US$2.50, 1½ hrs) and Villahermosa.

Cosamaloapan, some 40 km beyond Tlacotalpan (*Pop* 103,000) on Route 175, is the local market centre with a number of hotels, and the staging point for most bus lines from Veracruz, Orizaba and Oaxaca.

One of the largest sugar mills in Mexico is situated just outside the town – Ingenio San Cristóbal – and there is a local airstrip. From Cosamaloapan to Papaloapan the banks on either side of the river are lined with fruit trees. Chacaltianguis, on the E bank of the river, reached by car ferry, has houses fronted by columns.

40 km beyond Cosamaloapan is a ferry to **Otatitlán**, also on the E bank of the river (it leaves whenever there are sufficient passengers, US$0.25 the ride). The town, also known as El Sanctuario, dates back to early colonial times, its houses with tiled roofs supported by columns, but most interesting is the church. The padre maintains that the gold-patterned dome is the largest unsupported structure of its kind in Mexico, measuring 20m wide and 40 high. El Sanctuario has one of the three black wooden statues of Christ brought over from Spain for the son of Hernán Cortés. During the anti-clerical violence of the 1930s attempts to burn it failed, although the original head was cut off and now stands in a glass case. The first weekend in May is the saint's day and fair, for which pilgrims flock in from the *sierra* and from the Tuxtlas, many in local dress. (*Restaurant-Bar Pepe* serves delicious but unusual local food; *Restaurant-Bar Ipiranga III* also offers excellent cooking; both by embarkation point.)

At **Papaloapan** on the eastern bank of the river, the main road from Orizaba to Rodríguez Clara (145) crosses the main road from Alvarado to Oaxaca (175); the railway station has services to Yucatán and Chiapas, and to Orizaba or Veracruz. On the W bank is the bus terminal of Santa Cruz (almost under the railway bridge) where all second class buses stop. A passenger ferry may be taken from here to Papaloapan (US$0.50). Although Papaloapan is the route centre for the area the most convenient centre is Tuxtepec, 9 km further S (see below).

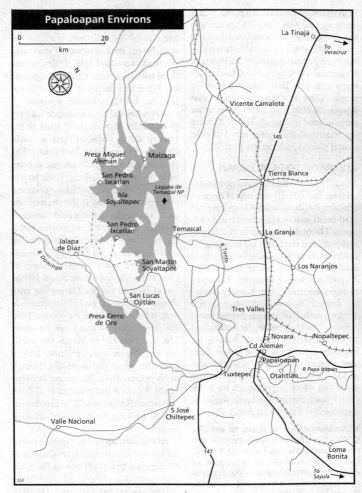

Papaloapan Environs

La Tinaja
To Veracruz
Vicente Camalote
145
Tierra Blanca
Presa Miguel Alemán
Maizaga
San Pedro Ixcatlan
Laguna de Temascal NP
Isla Soyaltepec
San Pedro Ixcatlan
Temascal
La Granja
Jalapa de Díaz
R Domingo
San Martin Soyaltapee
R Tonto
Los Naranjos
San Lucas Ojitlán
Presa Cerro de Oro
Tres Valles
Novara
Nopaltepec
Cd Alemán
Papaloapan
R Papa Itapan
Tuxtepec
Otatitlán
S José Chiltepec
Valle Nacional
147
Loma Bonita
To Sayula

0 — 20 km

PRESA MIGUEL ALEMAN

The river basin drained by the Papaloapan and its tributaries covers some 47,000 sq km, about twice the size of the Netherlands, and is subject to a programme of regional development by the Comisión del Papaloapan, which includes the construction of two large dams to control the sometimes severe flooding of the lower basin. The lake formed behind Presidente Alemán dam at Temascal is scenically very attractive and boats may be hired to go to Mazatec Indian settlements on the islands or on the other side. There is also a daily ferry passing round the lake. **Soyaltepec** is the closest settlement, situated high above the water on an island, the peak crowned by a church. **Ixcatlan** lies on a peninsula jutting into the lake on the S side;

it has one hotel and one restaurant, as well as a large beer repository. Ixcatlan may also be reached by dirt road from Tuxtepec, but it is less nerve-racking to take a ferry.

Temascal (Sun is the most active day) may be reached by taking Route 145 from Papaloapan through Gabino Barreda, Ciudad Alemán (no facilities, centre of the Papaloapan Commission), Novara (petrol and 3 restaurants of varying prices, 1 air-conditioned), as far as La Granja where the turn to Temascal is clearly marked. (In Temascal there is a woman who offers very basic accommodation.)

PAPALOAPAN TO LA TINAJA

Route 145 continues paved and straight past Tres Valles (cheap, good regional food; annual fair mid-Nov), and on to **Tierra Blanca**, a railway junction on the Tapachula-Veracruz and Mérida-Córdoba-Mexico City lines (Hotels **D** *Principal*, own shower and fan, clean, just above bus station, noisy; **E** *Balun Canán*, cheap, hot; *Bimbis* restaurant by ADO bus station, good; shopping centre, market, car repairs, eg Volkswagen agent). Route 145 passes under a sign saying 'La Puerta del Papaloapan', to join the main Orizaba-Veracruz road (Route 150) at **La Tinaja**, a second class bus junction, also gasoline, and restaurants (1 air-conditioned at service station). Papaloapan to La Tinaja takes about 1 hr, the road often has a lot of lorries and in the cane-cutting season great care should be taken at night for carts travelling on the road without lights. There are three railway crossings on the road, also poorly marked, two near La Granja and one near Tierra Blanca. The tarmac is often damaged in the wet season (June-Dec).

PAPALOAPAN TO SAYULA

From Papaloapan a paved road runs eastwards to Rodríguez Clara and on to Sayula de Alemán on the Trans-Isthmian road. This road passes through the main pineapple-producing region of Mexico, which has encouraged the development of towns such as **Loma Bonita** (local airstrip, hotels, restaurants and gasoline) and **Villa Isla**

(Hotels: *La Choca* restaurant good, railway station, ADO bus terminal, and centre for the rich cattle-producing area that surrounds it).

From Villa Isla a good dirt road runs S to **Playa Vicente** (*Pop* 6,974), another ranching town, located beside a wide river (**F** *Hotel Ros Bal*, clean, safe, fan, good); excellent crayfish may be eaten at the *Restaurant La Candileja*, while the café on the central plaza serves tender steaks. Another dirt road leaves the Villa Isla-Playa Vicente road for **Abasolo del Valle** (*Pop* 2,000), but only reaches to within 7 km. The last few kilometres can be impassable by vehicle in the wet season. The town is set beside a lagoon and the houses are surrounded by fruit trees (no hotels or restaurants). Gasoline can be bought – ask at a shop who has some to sell.

At the cross-roads of the Papaloapan-Sayula road about 80 km from Papaloapan, where the S turn is to Villa Isla, the N turn is a paved road which in about 30 mins will take you past two turnings to Tres Zapotes and up to Santiago Tuxtla.

The road from Papaloapan continues E to a point just N of **Rodríguez Clara**, which is reached by branching off S down a dirt road. This is a compact, thriving town. There are 2 hotels, the better is in the centre of the town, **D** *Hotel Roa*; *Restaurant Mexicana* rec.

TUXTEPEC

Tuxtepec is the natural centre for a stay in the Papaloapan area. It is a large city in the state of Oaxaca, some 9 km S of Papaloapan (toll for Caracol bridge, US$0.40). There is a fascinating mixture of the music and exuberance of Veracruz with the food and handicrafts of Oaxaca. The town is built on a meander of the Río Santo Domingo and a good view can be had from the rear balcony of the market on Av Independencia; there are other viewpoints beyond the main shops. A hand-pulled ferry crosses the river from below the viewpoint next to *Hotel Mirador*.

NB Near the river watch out for gnats (*rodadores*), which bite sensitive skins leaving itchy welts.

NB Also many street names and numbers are not marked.

Excursions

To Temascal to see the dam (see above); also a visit to the Indian villages of **Ojitlán** and **Jalapa de Díaz** (bus Tuxtepec-Jalapa de Díaz, 1½ hrs from the end of C 20 de Noviembre, US$5; hotel, E and food stores, good and cheaper *huipiles* from private houses) is well worth the ride; easily reached by car along semi-paved road. The Chinantec Indians' handicrafts may be bought on enquiry; hotels non-existent and eating facilities limited but some superb scenery, luxuriant vegetation and little-visited area. Ojitlán is best visited on Sun, market day, when the Chinanteca *huipiles* worn by the women are most likely to be seen (bus Jalapa de Díaz-Ojitlán, 1½ hrs). Part of the area will be flooded when the Cerro de Oro dam is finished and the lake will join that of Temascal. Heavily armed checkpoint on the road from Tuxtepec to Tierra Blanca (bus 1½ hrs, US$1.50), non-uniformed men, very officious, do not get caught with any suspicious goods.

Local information
● Accommodation

El Rancho, Avila Camacho 850, T 50641, restaurant, bar, evening entertainment, most expensive, accepts TCs as payment, rec.

C *María de Lourdes*, Av 5 de Mayo 1380, T (91-287)50410, hot water, clean, excellent car park, rec; *Tuxtepec*, Matamoros 2, T 50944, good value.

D *Catedral*, C Guerrero, nr Zócalo, very friendly, fan and shower; D *Robles*, Av 5 de Mayo, clean, basic, enclosed parking; D *Mirador*, Av Independencia, hot showers, fairly safe car park, with view of filthy river, good; nearby on same Av, E *Posada Guadelupana*, and E *Posada Real*; E *Sacre*, C Libertad, good, quiet; nearby is E *Casa de Huéspedes Ocampo*, with bath, clean, friendly, room 10 is the best. Very good value is the E *Avenida* in Independencia round the corner from ADO bus station, with bath and

fan, basic, clean but restaurant below not very good value; E *Posada del Sol*, basic and noisy, opp Fletes y Pasajes bus station.

● Places to eat

El Estero, in a side street opp market on Av Independencia (fish dishes and local cuisine excellent), *El Mino* (nr Fletes y Pasajes bus terminal), *Mandinga*, Av 20 de Noviembre, for fish dishes, *Avenida*, next to hotel of same name; *Pata Pata*, around corner, on side street, half way down the block. *Ronda*, C Independencia, cheap and good; *La Mascota de Oro*, 20 de Noviembre 891, very friendly, cheap. *Las Palmas*, Riva Palacios, palm-thatched, excellent local food, friendly, heartily rec. Beer from the barrel can be bought from the bar next to the Palacio Municipal, and the best ices are found in *La Morida*.

● Transport

There are 4 bus terminals in town, clear street signs for each one. ADO bus services to **Mexico City** (Thur, US$16.50), **Veracruz** and regular daily minibus (taking 5-6 hrs) to **Oaxaca** leaving at 2230. AU (Autobuses Unidos, on Matamoros, ½ block from Libertad) daily to wide variety of destinations. AU to Oaxaca, US$10 2nd class, 8 hrs, slow, Buses Cuenca del Papaloapan, direct route, every 2 hrs in am and pm, US$8.25, ADO at 2230, 10 hrs, US$16.50. Also Transportes Chinantecos. Bus to **Acayucán**, ADO, 4 hrs, US$3.30.

ROUTES The Tuxtepec-Palomares road provides a short cut to the Transístmica; it passes through many newly cleared jungle areas. Armed robberies are said to be a danger on this road; the route via Sayula is 20 km longer, but safer as well as quicker. The route from Tuxtepec to Minatitlán is being made into a toll road; the 56 km from Tuxtepec to Isla is under construction, while Isla to Minatitlán has been finished. The 'vía libre' remains in good condition, through Sayula and Acayucan.

The road to Tuxtepec N from Oaxaca (Route 175) is in bad repair but is a spectacular, steep and winding route, cars need good brakes and it is reported to be difficult for caravans (also very tough for cyclists, with few services and no accommodation en route – advised to take a bus!). "The road is good from Oaxaca as far as the national shrine at Juárez's birthplace at Ixtlán. North from there to the crestline of the mountain range is pretty dreadful – potholed and rutted with a scrubby pine forest cutting off any views for almost the whole route. It gets much better coming down the other side, however. The surface is smooth, the curves are well-engineered and the descent from alpine evergreen down into tropical rainforest is fascinating and exhilarating. Valle Nacional, at the bottom of the descent, is notable for what are surely the highest and most diabolically-shaped *topes* in the Mexican republic: at any speed, at any angle of approach, it was almost impossible to keep a VW from bottoming out on them." (Eric Mankin, California, USA.)

It takes about 5 hrs to drive this journey in reverse, up **Valle Nacional**. This valley, despite its horrific reputation as the 'Valle de los Miserables' in the era of Porfirio Díaz, for political imprisonment and virtual slavery from which there was no escape, is astoundingly beautiful. The road follows the valley floor, on which are cattle pastures, fruit trees and a chain of small villages such as Chiltepec (very good bathing in the river), Jacatepec (reached by ferry over the river, produces rich honey and abounds in all varieties of fruit), Monte Flor (where swimming and picnicking are possible beside natural springs, but *very* cold water, and an archaeological site) and finally Valle Nacional. (Bus to Valle Nacional from Tuxtepec, 1½ hrs, basic hotel, restaurants, stores, and gasoline available; river swimming.) The road climbs up into the Sierra, getting cooler, and slopes more heavily covered with tropical forest, and there are panoramic views.

San Pedro Yolox lies some 20 mins' drive W of this route down a dirt road; it is a peaceful Chinantec village clustered on the side of the mountain, while Llano de Flores is a huge grassy clearing in the pine forest with grazing animals and cool, scented air. Wood from these forests is cut for the paper factory in Tuxtepec. Ixtlán de Juárez has gasoline. While houses in the lowlands are made of wood with palm roofs, here the houses are of adobe or brick. From Guelatao (see page 379) it is about 1½ hrs' drive, mainly downhill, to Oaxaca (see page 365), with the land becoming drier and the air warmer. About 30 km before Oaxaca is *Restaurant del Monte*, by the roadside, ranch-style, good views, tasty soup, meat indifferent.

VERACRUZ TO MEXICO CITY

By the road followed to Veracruz, the driving time from Mexico City is about 9 hrs. One can return to the capital by a shorter route through Xalapa which takes 6 hrs; this was the old colonial route to the port, and is the route followed by the railway.

XALAPA

(*Pop* 213,000; *State pop 1995* 6,734,545; *Alt* 1,425m) (Also spelt Jalapa) Capital of Veracruz state, 132 km from the port, Xalapa is in the *tierra templada*. The weather is variable, hot with thunder storms, the clouds roll down off the mountains in the evening. There was a passion for renovation in the flamboyant gothic style during the first part of the 19th century. It is yet another 'City of Flowers', with walled gardens, stone built houses, wide avenues in the newer town and steep cobbled crooked streets in the old.

Places of interest

The 18th century cathedral, with its sloping floor, has been recently restored. Just outside, on the road to Mexico City, is an excellent, modern museum (opened 1986) showing archaeological treasures of the Olmec, Totonac and Huastec coastal cultures. The colossal heads displayed in the grounds of the museum, are Olmec; the museum has the best collection of Olmec monumental stone sculptures in Mexico (open 1000-1700, take the Foviste de Tejada bus). Xalapa has a University; you can take a pleasant stroll round the grounds, known as El Dique. Pico de Orizaba is visible from hotel roofs or Parque Juárez very early in the morning, before the haze develops. 2.5 km along the Coatepec road are lush botanical gardens with a small museum.

Excursions

Hacienda Casa de Santa Ana, 20 mins' drive, was taken over in the revolution and is now a museum with the original furniture, entrance free, no bags allowed in. **Palo Gacho** falls are worth a visit. Take the route 40 from Xalapa, towards Cardel, to Palo Gacho. The waterfalls can be reached on a dirt road next to the church, 4 km steep descent. Avoid weekends. To ruins of **Zempoala**, 40 km N of Veracruz (hotel, *Chachalaca*, near sea, spotless, rec), the coastal city which was conquered by Cortés and whose inhabitants became his allies. The ruins are interesting because of the round stones uniquely used in construction. (Entry US$3.45, small museum on site.) Take 2nd class bus to Zempoala via Cardel, which will let you off at the ruins, or take a taxi from the Plaza of Zempoala, US$3 return. You can also get there from Veracruz. **Chachalacas** is a beach with a swimming pool and changing facilities in an expensive hotel of the same name, US$1 adults. Thatched huts; local delicacies sold on beach, including *robalito* fish. It is worth asking the restaurants on the beach to let you hang up your hammock, most have showers and toilets. They charge US$2 if you agree to eat at their restaurant.

To **Texolo** waterfalls, some 15 km SW of Xalapa near the village of Jico (or Xico), just beyond the neighbouring town of **Coatepec** (famous for its ice-cream); there is a deep ravine and an old bridge, as well as a good, cheap restaurant at the falls. It's a 5 km walk through Jico to the falls. The village itself is pretty, US$0.60 by bus from Xalapa every 30 mins. (The film *Romancing the Stone* used Texolo as one of its locations.)

Naolinco is 30 mins' ride, 40 km NE of Xalapa up a winding hilly road, *Restaurant La Fuente* serves local food and has nice garden. Las Cascadas, with a *mirador* to admire them from, are on the way into the town: two waterfalls, with various pools, tumble several thousand feet over steep wooded slopes. Flocks of *zopilotes* (buzzards) collect late in the afternoon, soaring high up into the thermals.

2 hrs from Xalapa between Tlapacoyan and Martínez de la Torre is the archaeological site of **Filobobos**. It includes El Cuajilote, a 400m wide ceremonial centre and Vega de la Peña, an area of basalt rocks decorated with bas-reliefs, a ball court and several pyramids by the river banks. Abundant wildlife here including toucans, parrots and otters. At the end of the Veracruz mountain range is the spectacular Encanto waterfall.

Local festivals

Feria de Primavera, mid-April.

Local information

● **Accommodation**

Cheaper hotels are up the hill from the market, which itself is uphill from Parque Juárez (there is no Zócalo).

L2 *Xalapa*, Victoria y Bustamante, T 82222, good restaurant, excellent bookshop, changes TCs.

A2 *María Victoria*, Zaragoza 6, T 80268, good; **A2** *Posada Coatepec*, Hidalgo 9, Centro, T 160544, F 160040 (in Mexico City T 514-2728/207-5666), tastefully modernized colonial house, highly rec, reserve in advance, restaurant with Mexican and international cuisine; *Hostal del Tejar*, 20 de Noviembre Ote 552 esq Av del Tejar, T 72459, F 83691, 3-star, a/c, pool, parking.

B-C *Hotel/Restaurant Mesón del Alférez*, Zaragoza y Sebastián Camacho, T/F 186351, charming, small rooms, free parking opp, good food, highly rec.

C *Hotel Suites Araucarias*, Avila Camacho 160, T 73433, with large window, balcony and view (D without), TV, fridge, good cheap restaurant; **C** *México*, Lucio 4, T 75030, clean, with shower, will change dollars; **C** *Salmones*, Zaragoza 24, T 75435, restaurant, excellent view of Orizaba from the roof, good restaurant, rec.

D *Principal*, Zaragoza 28, good if a bit shabby, safe parking nearby.

E *Amoro*, nr market, no shower but public baths opp, very clean; **E** *Continental*, on Enríquez, owner speaks some English, good lunches, friendly; **E** *Plaza*, Enríquez, clean, safe, friendly, will store luggage, good view of Orizaba from the roof, rec.

F *El Greco*, Av Revolución (opp church), with bath, hot water, clean.

● **Places to eat**
La Casona del Beaterio, Zaragoza 20, good atmosphere; *Quinto Reyno*, Juárez 67 close to Zócalo, lunches only, excellent vegetarian with health-food shop, very good service. *Terraza*, opp Parque Juárez, the cheapest breakfast in the centre; *Estancia*, opp Barranquilla, good food; *Aladino*, Juárez, up from ADO, excellent Mexican food; *Pizzaría*, Ursulo Galván; *La Sopa*, on Diamante, an alleyway just off Enríquez, great tapas, cheap; *Fruitlandia* on Abasolo (uphill from Cathedral), wonderful fresh juices; *La Tasca*, a club, good music, rec; another club is *La Cumbre* (rock). Health food shops, Ursulo Galván, nr Juárez, good bread and yoghurt, another opp the post office on Zamora. The famous Xalapeño chilli comes from this region.

● **Banks & money changers**
Banco Serfín will change TCs, **Bancomer** will not. *Casa de Cambio*, on right side of Zamora going down hill, English spoken. Banks are slow, money transferred from abroad comes via Mexico City. **American Express** at Viajes Xalapa, Carrillo Puerto 24, T 76535, in centre, sells cheques against Amex card. The liquor shop in Plaza Cristal will change dollars.

● **Entertainment**
Centro de Recreación Xalapeño has exhibitions; live music and exhibitions in Ayora, underneath Parque Juárez; 10 pin bowling, Plaza Cristal, next to cinema.

Cinemas: there are 2 cinemas next to *Hotel Xalapa*, off Camacho; 3-screen cinema in Plaza Cristal; cinemas in the centre tend to show soft porn and gore.

Theatre: *Teatro del Estado*, Av Avila Camacho; good Ballet Folklórico Veracruzano and fair symphony orchestra.

● **Hospitals & medical services**
Dentists: there are 2 dentists on Ursulo Galván.

Hospitals: *Nicolás Bravo*, entrance in street on right. *Dr Blásquez*, Hidalgo, speaks English.

● **Laundry**
2 on Ursulo Galván, same day service.

● **Post & telecommunications**
Post Office: letters can be sent to the Lista de Correos in C Diego Leño, friendly post office,

and another at the bottom of Zamora. There is a telegraph office next door where telegrams marked Lista de Correos are kept.

Telephone: radio-telephone available opp *Hotel María Victoria*; long distance phone in shop on Zaragoza, with a sign outside, others behind the government palace also in Zaragoza.

● **Shopping**
Artesanía shop on Alfaro, more on Barcenas, turn off Enríquez into Madero, right again at the top, the owner of *El Tazín* on the corner speaks English.

Books: *Instituto de Antropología*, Benito Juárez, has books in English and Spanish, student ID helps.

● **Tour companies & travel agents**
Travel agents: there are four on Camacho, the one nearest Parque Juárez is very helpful.

● **Tourist offices**
Av Camacho, a long walk or short taxi ride. Look out for *Toma Nota*, free sheet advertising what is on, available from shop in front of *Hotel Salmones*.

● **Transport**
Local Car hire: Automoviles Sanchez, Av Ignacio de la Llave 14, T 79011, rec. **Moped hire**: in Camacho US$4-6/hr, Visa accepted.

Air Airport 13 km SE, on Veracruz road

Trains Railway station on outskirts, buses from nr market to get there. Train to **Mexico City** at 1140 (unreliable, dirty, crowded), to **Veracruz** at 1530 (4 hrs).

Buses A new 1st and 2nd class bus station has been built; taxi from centre US$1.75. 5 hrs from Mexico City by AU or ADO, from the Central de Ote (TAPO). Frequent ADO service Xalapa-Veracruz, US$5. To **Puebla**, ADO, 'GL' Plus service, US$7, 1st class US$6, 4 hrs, scenic route; also AU 2nd class. To **Villahermosa**, ADO, 3 a day, 10 hrs. To **Poza Rica**, the coast road is faster, while the impressive route via Teziutlán requires a strong stomach for mountain curves.

The 140 road towards the capital continues to climb to **Perote**, 53 km from Xalapa. The San Carlos fort here, now a military prison, was built in 1770-77; there is a good view of Cofre de Perote volcano. A road branches N to **Teziutlán** (**D** *Hotel Valdez*, hot water, car park), with a Fri market, where good *sarapes* are sold, a local fair, *La Entrega de Inanacatl*, is held in the 3rd week in June. The old convent at **Acatzingo**, 93 km beyond Perote on route 140, is worth seeing. Another 10 km and we join the road to Puebla and Mexico City.

NORTH FROM VERACRUZ

The 180 coast road from Veracruz heads to **Nautla** (one hotel, E, rec; on main street; pleasant town, but nothing to see or do) 3 km after which Route 131 branches inland to Teziutlán (see above). 42 km up the coast from Nautla is **Tecolutla**, a very popular resort on the river of that name, toll bridge US$2.50. A fiesta takes place 2 days before the carnival in Veracruz, recommended.

• **Accommodation** B Hotels *Villas de Palmar*; D *Playa*, good; D *Tecolutla*, best, and *Marsol* (run down) are on the beach; E *Posada Guadalupe* and E *Casa de Huéspedes Malena* (pleasant rooms, clean) are on Av Carlos Prieto, nr river landing stage. Other hotels, D, on road to Nautla. *Torre Molina* trailer park, 16 km before Nautla on coastal Route 180 (coming from Veracruz), electricity, water and sewage disposal, hot showers, bathrooms, swimming pool, on beach, US$10/vehicle with 2 people, rec. *Restaurant Paquita*, next to *Hotel Playa*, rec.

EL PITAL

El Pital (15 km in from the Gulf along the Nautla River, 80 km SE of Papantla and named after a nearby village), was identified early in 1994 as the site of an important, sprawling precolumbian seaport (approximately AD 100-600), which lay hidden for centuries under thick rainforest. Now planted over with bananas and oranges, the hundred or more pyramid mounds (some reaching 40m in height) were assumed by plantation workers to be natural hills. Little excavation or clearing has yet been done, but both Teotihuacan-style and local-style ceramics and figurines have been found, and archaeologists believe El Pital may mark the principal end point of an ancient cultural corridor that linked the N-central Gulf Coast with the powerful urban centres of Central Mexico. As at nearby El Tajín, ball courts have been discovered, along with stone fragments depicting what may be sacrificed ball players.

PAPANTLA

(*Pop* 280,000) Some 40 km inland from Tecolutla is **Papantla**, built on the top of a hill overlooking the lush plains of northern Veracruz. It was the stronghold of a Totonac rebellion in 1836. Traditional Totonac dress is still seen: the men in baggy white trousers and sailor shirts and the women in lacy white skirts and shawls over embroidered blouses. Papantla is also the centre of one of the world's largest vanilla-producing zones, and the distinctive odour sometimes lingers over the town. Small animal figures, baskets and other fragrant items woven from vanilla bean pods are sold at booths along Highway 180, as well as the essence; packaged in tin boxes, these sachets are widely used to freshen cupboards and drawers. The vanilla is processed in **Gutiérrez Zamora**, a small town about 30 km E (close to Tecolutla), and a 'cream of vanilla' liqueur is also produced.

Places of interest

The Zócalo, formally known as **Plaza Téllez**, is bordered by Enríquez on its downhill N edge; on the S uphill side is the Cathedral of **Señora de la Asunción** with a remarkable 50m-long mural in its northern wall called *Homenaje a la Cultura Totonaca*, with the plumed serpent Quetzalcoatl along its entire length. *Voladores* perform each Sun at 1100 in the church courtyard and as many as three times daily during the colourful 10 days of Corpus Christi (late May or early June), along with games, fireworks, artistic exhibitions, dances and cockfights. For a sweeping view of the area walk up Reforma to the top of the hill where the giant **Monumento al Volador** was erected in 1988. Murals and mosaic benches in the Zócalo also commemorate Totonac history and their conception of creation. Beside the main plaza is the **Mercado Juárez** (poultry and vegetables); more interesting is **Mercado Hidalgo**,

20 de Noviembre off the NW corner of the Zócalo (open daily 0600-2000), where traditional handmade clothing is sold amid fresh produce and livestock.

Excursions

About 12 km away, in the forest, is **El Tajín**, the ruins of the capital of the Totonac culture (6th to 10th century AD, the name means 'hurricane') entry, US$4.35, free on Sun. Guidebook US$1.25, available in Museo de Antropología, Mexico City. At the centre of this vast complex is the Pyramid of El Tajín, whose 365 squared openings make it look like a vast beehive. There is a fine, modern museum, a cafetería and souvenir shops. Traditionally, on Corpus Christi, Totonac rain dancers erect a 30m mast with a rotating structure at the top. Four *voladores* (flyers) and a musician climb to the surmounting platform. There the musician dances to his own pipe and drum music, whilst the roped *voladores* throw themselves into space to make a dizzy spiral descent, sometimes head up, sometimes head down, to the ground. *Voladores* are now in attendance every day, most of the day, and fly if they think there are enough tourists, donations expected. In the wet season beware of a large, poisonous creature like a centipede.

Local festivals

The *Fiesta de la Vainilla* is held throughout the area in early June.

Local information

● **Accommodation**

C *Tajín*, C Dr Núñez 104, T 20121, F 21062, restaurant with good value breakfast and bar, fairly clean, parking, reasonable.

E *Pulido*, Enríquez 205, modern, T 20036, but noisy, with bath, parking; **E** *Trujillo*, C 5 de Mayo 401, rooms with basin, friendly. (It is better to stay in Papantla than in Poza Rica if you want to visit El Tajín.)

● **Places to eat**

(Most open 0700-2400) *Las Brisas del Golfo*, C Dr Núñez, reasonable and very good. *Enríquez*, Enríquez 103, attached to *Hotel Premier*, modern, expensive seafood, popular, pleasant; *Sorrente*, Zócalo, covered in decorative tiles,

good, cheap, rec; *Rodeo*, on Zócalo, cheap, popular; *Catedral*, Núñez y Curado, behind Cathedral, plain, clean, cheap breakfasts and good 'fast' meals, 0630-2100.

● **Banks & money changers**

Bancomer and Banamex, on Zócalo, 0900-1300, change cash and TCs till 1200; Serfín, between the two, does not change TCs.

● **Hospitals & medical services**

Farmacia Aparicio, Enríquez 103, daily 0700-2200.

● **Post & telecommunications**

Post Office: Azueta 198, 2nd floor, Mon-Fri 0900-1300, 1500 1800, Sat 0900-1200.

● **Tourist offices**

On 1st floor of Palacio Municipal, on the Zócalo, T 20177, helpful, good local information and maps, bus schedules, English spoken, Mon-Fri 0900-1400 and 1800-2100.

● **Transport**

Buses ADO terminal, Juárez 207, 5 blocks uphill from centre. To **Mexico City**, 4 a day, 5 hrs via Poza Rica, US$7; **Poza Rica**, 8 daily, 35 mins, US$0.50; to **Xalapa**, 8 daily, 6 hrs, US$6.25; 4 hrs to **Veracruz**, US$14. 2nd class terminal (Transportes Papantla), 20 de Noviembre 200, many services to local destinations, inc El Tajín, buses leave when full. Occasional minibus to El Tajín from SW corner of Zócalo, US$2, unreliable schedule about every 1-1½ hrs.

POZA RICA

(*Pop* 210,000) 21 km NW of Papantla is **Poza Rica**, an oil city, with an old cramped wooden market, but little else to recommend it. The streets are busy, there are several comfortable hotels and bus connections are very good. Flaring gas burn offs light up the night sky.

● **Accommodation** **B** *Poza Rica Inn*, carretera a Papantla, Km 4, 'Holiday Inn look-a-like', poor restaurant; **B** *Robert Prince*, Av 6 Nte, 10 Ote, T 25455, Col Obrera; **C** *Nuevo León*, Av Colegio Militar, T 20528, opp market, rooms quite spacious, fairly clean and quiet, rec; **C** *Poza Rica*, 2 Nte, T 20134, fairly comfortable, good *comida corrida* in restaurant; **C** *Salinas*, Blvd Ruiz Cortines, 1000, T 20706, good central hotel, a/c, TV, restaurant, pool, secure parking; **E** *Aurora*, Bolívar 4, basic but quiet and fairly clean; **E** *Fénix*, basic, opp ADO bus station; **E** *Juárez*, Cortines y Bermúdez, average; **E** *San*

Román, 8 Nte 5; **F** *Cárdenas*, Bermúdez y Zaragoza, T 26610, basic, not central.

● **Transport** **Air** Airport 8 km S; 3 flights a week to both Ciudad Victoria and Mexico City, AeroMéxico (Edif Geminis, Parque Juárez, T 26142/28877). **Buses** All buses leave from new terminal about 1½ km from centre, take white bus from centre. Terminal is divided into ADO and all others, good facilities, tourist office. ADO 1st class to **Mexico City** and **Tampico**, 21 daily each, 5 hrs, US$11. Estrella Blanca 2nd class to Mexico City, 23 daily, US$7.25. To **Monterrey**, 4 a day, US$11. To **Veracruz**, 4 hrs, US$13.75. To **Pachuca**, Estrella Blanca, 4½ hrs, US$6, change in Tulancingo. To **Tecolutla** (see below), US$2.20, 1¼ hrs. 2nd class with Transportes Papantla to **El Tajín**, 10/day (with different destinations), US$0.40.

From Poza Rica you can head N to visit the **Castillo de Teayo**, a pyramid with the original sanctuary and interesting carvings on top, buses every 30 mins, change halfway. 25 km along Route 8 is Barra de Cazones with a little developed, good beach.

TUXPAN

On the coast, 55 km from Poza Rica, 189 km S of Tampico is **Tuxpan** (**Veracruz**), tropical and humid, 12 km from the sea on the Río Tuxpan. Essentially a fishing town (shrimps a speciality), it is now decaying from what must have been a beautiful heyday. Interesting covered market, but beware of the bitter, over-ripe avocados; fruit sold on the quay. Beach about 2 km E of town, reached by taxi or bus (marked 'Playa'), at least 10 km long. White sands, few people, no hasslers, some sandflies; hire deckchairs under banana-leaf shelters for the day (US$2). Many restaurants line the beach, with showers for the use of bathers (US$0.35), it is worth asking to hang up a hammock for US$2 per night.

● **Accommodation** **B** *Hotel Florida*, Av Juárez 23, clean, hot water; **C** *Plaza Palmas*, on edge of town along bypass route, a/c, tennis, pool, secure parking, clean, boat launch to river, TV, good restaurant, fenced all round compound, rec; **C-D** *Riviera*, Blvd Jesús Reyes Heroles 17a, on waterfront, parking, rooms vary in size so check first; **D** *California*, clean, hot water, good breakfast; **D** *Parroquia*, Berriozabal 4, beside Cathedral, T 41630, clean, friendly, hot water, fan, noisy; **E** *Tuxpan*, OK; **F** *Santa Ana*, one of cheapest, 'friendliness makes up for dirtiness'; and others.

● **Places to eat** *El Arca*, restaurant serves good fish and shrimp and the owners are very friendly and helpful; also *Bremen*, a/c, food good and cheap.

● **Entertainment** *Hotel Teján*, over the river, S side, then about 1 km towards the sea, very plush, good singers but US$6.50 cover charge; *Aeropolis* disco, dull, no beer.

● **Transport** Buses to Mexico City (Terminal del Nte), US$14.80, 6½ hrs via Poza Rica.

Mexico City-Cuernavaca-Taxco-Acapulco

FROM THE CAPITAL to the Pacific, with long-established resorts such as Acapulco, newer developments (Puerto Escondido, Huatulco) and the only-recently discovered (Zipolite). The route passes through Cuernavaca, the country seat of Aztecs and Spaniards, now a major tourist town, and the silver city of Taxco.

A 106 km 4 lane toll motorway connects Mexico City with Acapulco. (Total toll for the route at 8 booths is US$89.) Driving time is about 3½ hrs. The highest point, La Cima, 3,016m, is reached at Km 42. The road then spirals down through precipitous forests to Cuernavaca (Km 75).

CUERNAVACA

(*Pop* 1,000,000; *State pop 1995* 1,442,587; *Alt* 1,542m; *Phone code* 73) Capital of Morelos state (originally Tlahuica Indian territory) 724m lower than Mexico City. The temperature never exceeds 27°C nor falls below 10°C, and there is almost daily sunshine even during the rainy season. The city has always attracted visitors from the more rigorous highlands and can be overcrowded. The Spaniards captured it in 1521 and Cortés himself, following the custom of the Aztec nobility, lived there. The outskirts are dotted with ultra-modern walled homes and most of its charm has been swamped by the city's rapid growth and a new industrial area to the S.

The centre of the city has two adjacent squares, the larger Zócalo and the smaller Zócalo. At the western end of the Zócalo is the Palacio de Gobierno; N of the Zócalo, E of the Alameda is the Centro Las Plazas shopping mall. Heading N from the Alameda, C Vicente Guerrero is lined with shops in arcades. Calle Degollado leads down to the main market in a labyrinth of shops and alleys.

Places of interest
The palace Cortés built in 1531 for his second wife stands at the eastern end of the tree-shaded Alameda; on the rear balcony is a Diego Rivera mural depicting the conquest of Mexico. It was the seat of the State Legislature until 1967, when the new legislative building opposite was completed; it has now become the **Museo Regional de Historia Cuauhnáhuac**, showing everything from mammoth remains to contemporary Indian culture, explanations are none-too-logical and most are in Spanish (US$1.80, open 1000-1700, closed Mon). West of the centre, C Hidalgo leads to one of the main areas of historical interest in the city.

The **Cathedral** (entrance on Hidalgo, near Morelos), finished in 1552, known as Iglesia de la Asunción, stands at one end of an enclosed garden. 17th century murals were discovered during restoration; they depict the martyrdom of the Mexican saint San Felipe de Jesús on his journey to Japan. The scenes show monks in open boats, and mass crucifixions. The interior is bathed in different colours from the modern stained-glass windows. At the W end is a stone font full of water; the E end painted gold, contains the modern altar. In the entrance to the chapel of

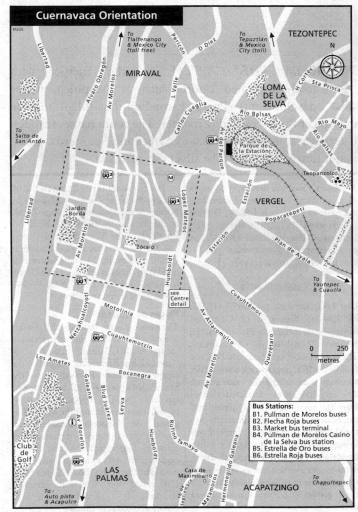

Cuernavaca Orientation

Bus Stations:
B1. Pullman de Morelos buses
B2. Flecha Roja buses
B3. Market bus terminal
B4. Pullman de Morelos Casino de la Selva bus station
B5. Estrella de Oro buses
B6. Estrella Roja buses

0   250
metres

Cuernavaca Centre

Bus Stations:
B1 Pullman de Morelos
B2 Flecha Roja Buses
B3 Market bus terminal

the Reserva de la Eucariota is a black and white fresco of the crucifixion. There are also 2-storey cloisters with painted friezes and a fragment of massed ranks of monks and nuns. The Sun morning masses at 1100 are accompanied by a special *mariachi* band. *Mariachis* also perform on Sun and Wed evenings in the Cathedral. By the entrance to it stands the charming small church of the **Tercera Orden** (1529), whose quaint façade carved by Indian craftsmen contains a small figure suspected to be one of the only two known statues of Cortés in Mexico. (The other is a mounted statue near the entrance of the *Casino de la Selva* hotel.) Beside the cathedral, in the Casa de la Torre, is the **Museo Robert Brady**, housing a collection of paintings by, among others, Diego Rivera, Frida Kahlo, Paul Klee and Francisco Toledo. It also has colonial furniture, textiles, prehispanic objects and African art and ceramics. It is open 1000

to 1800, closed Mon, US$1.30, café and shop. The 18th century **Jardín Borda**, on C Morelos, was a favourite resort of Maximilian and Carlota; it has been restored and is in fine condition; it is open 1000-1730, closed Mon, US$0.80 (open-air concerts, exhibition rooms, café, good bookshop, museum); boats can be rented on the small lake, US$1-3 depending on duration. Next to the Jardín Borda is the church of Nuestra Señora de Guadalupe (neoclassical). 2 km on the right up Morelos (pesero), side by side are the churches of San José Tlaltenango (1521-23) and Nuestra Señora de la Natividad (early 19th century); bazaar on Sun, second hand English books.

The weekend retreat of the ill-fated imperial couple, in the Acapantzingo district, is now the **Herbolario y Jardín Botánico**, with a museum, Matamoros 200, Col Acapatzingo (open daily 0900-1700), peaceful, interesting, free. To get there take a bus from the centre to Acapantzingo and ask the driver for the Museo del Herbolario, or, more easily, take a taxi US$1.75. Acapantzingo is a pleasant district. The house of David Alfaro Siqueiros, the painter, is now a museum (**Taller Siqueiros**) at C Venus 7 (a long way E of the centre) and contains lithographs and personal photographs. The very unusual **Teopanzolco** pyramid is to be found just E of the railway station (open 1000-1630, entry US$1.50). At the pyramid's summit, remains of the temple can be seen. Also in the complex are various structures including a circular building, probably dedicated to Quetzalcoatl.

Excursions

To the Chapultepec Park, SE of the city centre, with boating facilities, small zoo, water gardens, small admission charge. Also E of the centre is a zoo and recreation centre at Jungla Mágica, built around a series of natural springs. To the potters' village of **San Antón**, perched above a waterfall, a little W of the town, where divers perform Sun for small donations. In the vicinity of Cuernavaca are many spas, such as Xochitepec, Atotonilco, Oaxtepec, Temixco, Las Huertas and Los Manantiales at Xicatlocatla.

Local information
● Accommodation

Good value, cheap hotels are hard to find.

L3 *Hostería Las Quintas*, Av Díaz Ordáz No 9 Col Cantarranas, T 183949, F 183895, built in traditional Mexican style, owner has splendid collection of bonsai trees, restaurant, 2 pools, spa, outdoor jacuzzi, magnificent setting, fine reputation; **L3** *Las Mañanitas*, Linares 107, T 124646 (one of the best in Mexico), Mexican colonial style, many birds in lovely gardens, excellent food, reservation necessary.

A1 *Hacienda de Cortés*, Plaza Kennedy 90, T 160867/158844, 16th century sugar *hacienda*, magnificent genuine colonial architecture, garden, suites, pool, excellent restaurant, access by car; **A1** *Posada Jacarandas*, Cuauhtémoc 805, T 157798, garden, restaurant, parking; **A1** *Posada San Angelo*, Privada la Selva 100, T 141499, restaurant, gardens, pool; **A1** *Posada Maria Cristina*, Francisco Leyva 200, T 185767, nr Zócalo, restaurant, pool, garden; **A2** *Suites Paraíso*, Av Domingo Díaz 1100, T 133365, family accommodation; on same avenue, *Villa Bejar*, No 2350, T 175000, F 174953, Gran Turismo class, all facilities; **A3** *Posada Quinta Las Flores*, Tlaquepaque 210, Colonia Las Palmas, T 141244/125769, 2 mins' walk from Estrella de Oro bus station, 30 mins from centre on foot, inc breakfast, no TV, helpful, pool, gardens, restaurant (set evening meal), small parking space, very pleasant, highly rec.

B *Papagayo*, Motolinia 13, T 141711, 5 blocks from Zócalo, 1 block from Estrella Roja bus station, on Fri-Sat rooms are available only if one takes 2 meals a day, on other days price is **C**, room only, pool, gardens, convenient, good value, suitable for families, parking.

C *Bajo el Volcán*, Humboldt 117, T 124873, 187537, pool, restaurant, fair; **C** *Las Hortensias*, Hidalgo 22, T 185265, takes Visa, pretty courtyard, central, long-distance phone service; **C** *Papagayo*, Motolinia 13, T 141715, inc breakfast, 1 block from Pullman de Morelos bus

station, 5 blocks from Zócalo, excellent value, clean, cool, large pool, garden, billiard table, parking, suitable for families.

D *Roma*, Matamoros 405, T 120787, with hot water 0700-0800 and shower, noisy.

Several cheaper hotels in C Aragón y León between Morelos and Matamoros: eq **E** *América*, No 111, safe, good value but noisy, clean, basic; some rent rooms by the hour.

Motels: **A3** *Posada Cuernavaca*, Paseo del Conquistador, T 130800, view, restaurant, grounds; **B** *El Verano*, Zapata 602, T 17-0652; **E** *Royal*, Matamoros 19, hot water 0700-2300, central, clean, rec; *Suites OK Motel* with *Restaurant Las Margaritas*, Zapata 71, T 131270, special student and long-term rates, apartments, trailer park; swimming pool and squash courts.

● **Places to eat**

Hacienda de Cortés, (see above); *Las Mañanitas*, Ricardo Linares 107, beautiful but expensive, Amex accepted; also beautiful is *La India Borita*, Morrow 20, excellent Mexican food but expensive. On the Zócalo and Alameda: *Villa Roma*, *Café/Pastelería Viena* (expensive), *La Parroquia*, *La Universal* (on corner of Zócalo and Alameda). Next to *La Universal* on the Alameda is *McDonalds*. Also for fast food, *Subway* (on Alameda) and others in Centro Las Plazas. *Carlos 'N' Charlie's (Harry's Grill)*, with bar, grill and *Clothesline*; *Parrots*, next to the Museo Regional, opp which, at Hidalgo y Juárez, are *La Adelita* and *Flash Taco*. *Marco Polo*, opp Cathedral, good, Italian, good pizzas, popular meeting place; there are other *cafés* opp the cathedral. Near the Glorieta Niña in Col Las Palmas, *Los Vikingos*, restaurant and *pastelería*, good. There is also a large *panadería pastelería* on this roundabout. Generally, it is not

easy to find good, authentic Mexican cooking at reasonable prices. A major exception is *La Pasadita*, Morelos esq Abasolo, where there is usually an amazingly wide choice at very good prices, quieter upstairs.

Pollo y Más, Juárez, decent, cheap *comida corrida*. *Malvias*, Matamoros, next to *Motel Royal*, friendly, good value *comida corrida*. *Jugos Hawai* in Centro Las Plazas. Fruit juices are sold from stalls beneath the bandstand on the Zócalo.

● **Banks & money changers**

Cambio Gesta, Dwight D Morrow 9, T 183750, open 0900-1800; **Divisas de Cuernavaca**, Morrow 12; many banks in the vicinity of the Zócalo.

● **Language schools**

There are about 12 Spanish courses on offer. These start from US$100/week, plus US$60 registration at the *Centro de Lengua, Arte e Historia para Extranjeros* at the Universidad Autónoma del Estado de Morelos, Río Panuco 20, Col Lomas del Mirador, T 161626 (accommodation with families can be arranged). Private schools charge US$100-150 a week, 5-6 hrs a day and some schools also have a US$75-125 registration fee. The peak time for tuition is summer: at other times it may be possible to arrive and negotiate a reduction of up to 25%. There is a co-operative language centre, *Cuauhnahuac*, Morelos Sur 123, T 123673/189275, F 182693, e-mail: cuauhna@mail.giga.com, intensive Spanish 6 hrs a day and flexible private classes, registration US$70, US$200/week or US$630/month high season, US$160/week, US$530/month low season, family stays US$18/day shared room with meals or US$25 single room with meals, efficient, helpful. *Center for Bilingual Multicultural Studies*, Apdo

Postal 1520, T 171087/172488, F 170533 or Los Angeles, LA, 213-851-3403; *Spanish Language Institute*, Pradera 208, Col Pradera, T 175294/157953; *Instituto Fénix*, Salto Chico 3, Col Tlaltenango, T 131743, which also has excursions and minor courses in politics, art and music; *Cetlalic*, Apdo Postal 1-201, 62001 Cuernavaca, T 126718, F 180720, a non-profit organization teaching the Spanish language, themed courses, plus Mexican and Central American history and culture, rec; *Cemanahuac*, C San Juan 4, Las Palmas, T 186407, F 125418, e-mail: 74052.2570@compuserve .com, claims high academic standards, field study, also weaving and pottery classes; *Experiencia*, which encompasses all these features, free 'intercambios' (Spanish-English practice sessions) Tues and Wed pm, C Leyva, Colonia Las Palmas; *Centro de Artes y Lenguas*, Nueva Tabachín 22-A, T 173126/130603, F 137352, 5 hrs a day, registration US$125, 1 week minimum, classes US$160, US$150-200 a week accommodation with families inc meals. *Encuentros*, Morelos 36, Col Acapantzingo, CP 62440, T/F 125088, e-mail: encuent@infosel.net.mx; *Universal*, JH Preciado 332, Col San Anton, T 124902 (Apdo Postal 1-1826), 3 levels of language course, tutorials and mini courses on culture; and *Idel*, Apdo 1271-1, Calz de los Actores 112, Col Atzingo, T/F 130157, 5 levels of course. Staying with a local family will be arranged by a school and costs US$12-20 a day inc meals; check with individual schools, as this difference in price may apply even if you stay with the same family. See also *National Registration Center for Study Abroad*, which represents three schools in Cuernavaca, and *AmeriSpan* under **Learning Spanish** in Information for travellers.

● **Laundry**
In Las Palmas: *Oaxaca* behind Confía buildings, almost opp *Restaurante Vikingos*, good; *Euro Klin*, Morelos Sur 700 block, a short way from Glorieta Niña towards centre. There is a good laundry behind the Cathedral.

● **Post & telecommunications**
Post Office: on Hidalgo, just off the Alameda.

Telephone: Telmex on Hidalgo, just off the Alameda, LADA phones are outside, almost opp junction of Netzahualcoyotl. There is a telephone office at *Parrots* restaurant and bar on the Alameda, next to the Museo Regional.

● **Shopping**
Bookshop: secondhand English books at Guild House, C Tuxtla Gutiérrez, Col Chipitlán, T 125197.

Handicrafts market: behind Cortés' palace, moderately priced and interesting silver, textiles and souvenirs. When the tour buses arrive there are lots of handicraft sellers outside the cathedral gates.

● **Tour companies & travel agents**
Marín, Centro Las Plazas, local 13, Amex agent, changes Amex TCs but poorer rate than *casas de cambio*, charges US$1 to reconfirm flights. Also in Centro Las Plazas, *Pegaso*, French, Italian, German, English spoken (the sign says), charges US$2 to reconfirm. *Viajes Adelina*, Pasaje Bella Vista, on Zócalo.

● **Tourist offices**
Tourist kiosk on Vicente Guerrero outside *Posada San Angelo*. For cultural activities, go for information to the university building behind the Cathedral on Morelos Sur.

● **Transport**
Air Daily flight from Tijuana via Hermosillo and Guadalajara with Aerolíneas Internacionales.

Trains Station on C Amacuzac; only passenger service is daily train to Iguala and Apipilulco.

Buses Each bus company has its own terminal;

Estrella de Oro (B5), Morelos Sur 900, Col Las Palmas, T 123055, 1st class buses to Mexico City, Taxco (0915, 2100), Ixtapa (2145), Lázaro Cárdenas (2015), Chilpancingo (0900, 1100, 1345, 1630), Aguascalientes (2200), Acapulco (7 daily 0715-2230) and Zihuatanejo (2015); this bus station is a US$3.25 taxi ride, or 25 mins' walk from the centre. Local buses from the bus station up Morelos, marked Centro, or Buena Vista, all go to the Cathedral. From the centre take bus on Galeana marked Palmas. **Pullman de Morelos** has 2 termini: (B1) at Abasolo 106 y Netzahualcoyotl in the centre, T 180907, for Mexico City (*ejecutivo dorado*) every 30 mins from 0530, and some local departures to Alpuyeca, Tehuixtla, Zacatepec, Jojutla, Grutas de Cacahuamilpa, and (B4) at 'Casino de la Selva', Plan de Ayala 102, opp Parque de la Estación, T 189205, for *ejecutivo dorado* to Mexico City and 10 daily buses to Mexico airport (book 24 hrs in advance at either terminal, US$6). **Flecha Roja** (B1) on Morelos Nte 503 y Arista, T 125797, 2nd class to Mexico City (0530-2100), Taxco (0805-2005), Iguala, Tijuana (via Guadalajara, Mazatlán, Hermosillo, 1815, 2200), Querétaro (1400), San Luis Potosí (1701), Nuevo Laredo (via Saltillo, Monterrey, 1615), Acapulco (several daily) and Grutas de Cacahuamilpa (left luggage open 0700 to 2100 daily, US$0.25/hr/item). **Estrella Roja** (B6), Galeana y Cuauhtemotzín, S of the centre, for Cuautla (every 15 mins) via Yautepec, Matamoros and Puebla (via Izúcar de Matamoros, hourly 0500-1900). Many minibuses and 2nd class buses leave from a terminal by the market (B3).

To **Mexico City** 1½ hrs, fares US$3.65 ordinary to US$4.25 *ejecutivo dorado*. Pullman de Morelos is said to be the most comfortable and fastest, from Southern Bus Terminus, Mexico City every 30 mins.

To **Acapulco**, 4 hrs, Estrella de Oro, US$14.75 (US$19.50 *plus*). For advance tickets for Acapulco or other points on the Pacific Coast, be at Estrella de Oro office between 1645 and 1700, 2-3 days before you want to travel, this is when seats are released in Mexico City and full fare from Mexico City to the coast must be paid. To **Zihuatanejo**, Estrella de Oro, 1 a day, US$23. To **Taxco**, Flecha Roja, 2nd-class buses, hourly on the ½-hr, or Estrella de Oro, 1st class, US$4.25; to **Puebla**, Estrella de Oro, *gran turismo* service, US$5, 1st class hourly, US$4, 2 stops; **Cuautla** (page 363) either Estrella Roja every 20 mins, US$1.85, or 2nd class or minibus from market terminal, via Yautepec every hour, 1 hr, interesting trip; go there for

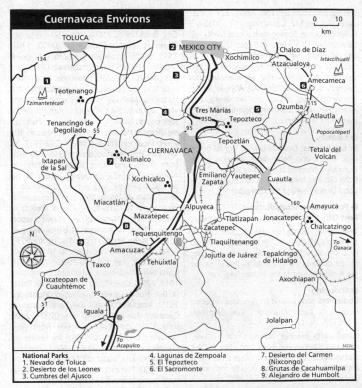

Cuernavaca Environs

0 — 10
km

TOLUCA

2 MEXICO CITY

Chalco de Díaz

134

Xochimilco

Atzacualoya

Ixtaccíhuatl

1

Teotenango

3

6

Amecameca

Tzimantetécatl

Tres Marías

5

Ozumba

115

95D

Tepozteco

Atlautla

Tenancingo de Degollado 55

95

Tepoztlán

Popocatépetl

Tetala del Volcán

CUERNAVACA

Ixtapan de la Sal

7

Malinalco

Xochicalco

Emiliano Zapata

Yautepec

Cuautla

Miacatlán

Alpuyeca

160

Amayuca

Mazatepec

Tlatizapán

Jonacatepec

Chalcatzingo

8

Tequesquitengo

Zacatepec

N

9

Amacuzac

Tlaquiltenango

Jojutla de Juárez

Tepalcingo de Hidalgo

To Oaxaca

Taxco

Tehuixtla

Axochiapan

Ixcateopan de Cuauhtémoc

95

51

Iguala

Jolalpan

To Acapulco

M22c

National Parks
1. Nevado de Toluca
2. Desierto de los Leones
3. Cumbres del Ajusco

4. Lagunas de Zempoala
5. El Tepozteco
6. El Sacromonte

7. Desierto del Carmen (Nixcongo)
8. Grutas de Cacahuamilpa
9. Alejandro de Humbolt

long-distance buses going S (Puebla buses do not stop at Cuautla).

Warning Theft of luggage from waiting buses in Cuernavaca is rife; don't ever leave belongings unattended. Robberies have been reported on the non-toll mountain road to Taxco and on the road to Mexico City.

NB to Drivers Cuernavaca to points W of Mexico City: on the toll road, N from Cuernavaca is a sign at Las Tres Marías to Toluca. Do not be tempted to take this route; it is well-surfaced but narrow over the pass before leading to the lakes at Zempoala, but thereafter it is almost impossible to navigate the backroads and villages to Toluca. Among the problems are livestock on the road, unsigned intersections, signposts to villages not marked on the Pemex atlas, heavy truck traffic, potholes, *topes* and congested village plazas. (Eric Mankin, Venice, CA.)

TEPOZTLAN

Tepoztlán is 24 km NE of Cuernavaca at the foot of the spectacular **El Tepozteco national park**, with the small Tepozteco pyramid high up in the mountains (US$3, free with student card, open anytime between 0900 and 1030, officially 1000-1630). The only way into the park is on foot. It takes 40 mins-1 hr to climb from the car park at the end of Av de Tepozteco to the pyramid. It is 2 km uphill, strenuous, climb up before the sun is too high, although most of the climb is through trees. The trip is well worth it. The altitude at the top of the pyramid is 2,100m; the view from the top is expansive. Signs remind you on the way that you must pay at the top; 5 mins before the entrance a steel ladder has to be scaled. Cold drinks are sold at the entrance for US$1.

Places of interest

The town (*Pop* 4,000) has picturesque steep cobbled streets, an outdoor market and a remarkable 16th century church and convent (María de la Natividad): the Virgin and Child upon a crescent moon above the elaborate plateresque portal, no tripod or flash allowed. The mural by Juan Ortega (1887) covering the eastern end of the church is being restored (1994). There is a small archaeological museum with objects from all over Mexico behind the church (Tues-Sun 1000-1800, US$0.75). There is a Sat/Sun arts and crafts market on the plaza with a good selection of handicrafts from Mexico, Guatemala and East Asia, expensive. Every Nov, first week, there is an arts festival with films and concerts (open air and in the main church's cloister). This was the village studied by Robert Redfield and later by Oscar Lewis. In 1997 the main road to the town was blocked by a wall of stones as a protest against a planned golf links by a foreign investment group. There have been demonstrations by villagers.

Local information
● Accommodation

A3 *Posada del Tepozteco*, a very good inn, quiet, old fashioned, with swimming pool, excellent atmosphere and view; **A3** *Hotel Tepoztlán*, largest hotel, towering over the village, grand pool, popular, crowded at weekends, as they all are; *Hotel Restaurant Anatlán de Quetzalcoatl*, T 91739/51880, F 51952, pool, children's park, gardens; **A3** *Posada Ali*, Netzahualcóyotl 2 'C', off Av del Tepozteco, T 51971, 4 rooms, 2 family suites (A1) breakfast, pool, fine view; **A3** *Casa Iccemanyan*, Familia Berlanga, C del Olvido 26, 62520, Tepoztlán, T (91-739) 50096/99 with 3 meals, **B** without meals, monthly rates available, 4 cabañas, swimming pool, clothes washing facilities, use of kitchen, laundry, restaurant, English, French and German spoken, beautiful garden.

D *Mesón del Indio*, Av Revolución 44, no sign, Sr Lara, basic.

● Places to eat

Los Colorines, Av de Tepozteco 13-B, good, Mexican vegetarian; next door is *El Chinelo*, Mexican. *El Jardín del Tepozteco*, Italian, Wed-Sun 1300-2200; *Axitla*, at beginning off path up to Tepozteco, open Fri, Sat, Sun and holidays; *La Costa de San Juan*, by plaza on opp side of street, meat and seafood; *Tapatía*, Av Revolución 1910 (just across street from church wall), good food and pleasant view from 1st floor, takes credit cards.

● Transport

Local bus (Autobus Verde) from Cuernavaca market terminal, takes 1 hr, US$1 (bus returns to Cuernavaca from the top of the Zócalo); bus to Mexico City, US$3.35 1st class, US$3.65 *primera plus*, hourly. There are buses from Tepoztlán to Yautepec.

SOUTH OF CUERNAVACA

(Km 100) **Alpuyeca**, whose church has good Indian murals. A road to the left runs to **Lago Tequesquitengo** (*Paraíso Ski Club*) and the lagoon and sulphur baths of **Tehuixtla**. Near the lake a popular resort, with swimming, boating, water skiing and fishing, is **A2** *Hacienda Vista Hermosa*, Hernán Cortés' original *ingenio* (sugar mill), and several lakeside hotels. East of the lake is **Jojutla** (**D** *Hotel del Sur*, central, clean, simple; and others). Near Jojutla is the old Franciscan convent of **Tlaquiltenango** (1540), frequent bus service from Cuernavaca, US$1.75, Pullman de Morelos. The route through Jojutla can be used if coming from the coast heading for Cuautla and wishing to avoid Cuernavaca. Enquire locally of road conditions off the major highways.

From Alpuyeca also a road runs W for 50 km to the **Cacahuamilpa** caverns (known locally as 'Las Grutas'); some of the largest caves in North America, well worth a visit, open 1000 to 1700 (take a torch); strange stalactite and stalagmite formations; steps lead down from near the entrance to the caverns to the double opening in the mountainside far below, from which an underground river emerges (entry, US$1, US$2.50 including 1¼ hrs guided tour, every hour on the hour up to 1600 – crowded after 1100 and at weekends). Guided tours take you 2 km inside; some excursions have gone 6 km; the estimated maximum depth is 16 km. It is worth going with a guided tour as the caves are then lit properly (Spanish only). Don't miss the descent to the river exits at the base of the cliff, called Dos Bocas, tranquil and less-frequently visited.

WARNING The disease *histoblastose* is present in the bat droppings in the cave (if you breathe in the tiny fungus it can cause a tumour on the lungs); to avoid it you can buy a dentist's face mask (*cobre boca/protección de dentista*) at a pharmacy.

● **Transport** There are direct Pullman de Morelos buses from Cuernavaca at 1030 and 1200, returning 1700 and 1830, 1 hr, US$2; also Flecha Roja; they are usually overcrowded at weekends; enquire about schedules for local buses or buses from Taxco to Toluca, which stop there (from Taxco, 30 km, 40 mins).

XOCHICALCO

At 15 km on the westerly road from Alpuyeca is the right-hand turn to the **Xochicalco** ruins (36 km SW of Cuernavaca), topped by a pyramid on the peak of a rocky hill, dedicated to the Plumed Serpent whose coils enfold the whole building and enclose fine carvings which represent priests. The site is large: needs 2-3 hrs to see it properly (open 1000-1700). There is a new museum which is well laid out and well explained.

Xochicalco was at its height between 650 and 900 AD. It is one of the oldest known fortresses in Middle America and a religious centre as well as an important trading point. The name means 'place of flowers' although now the hilltops are barren. It was also the meeting place of northern and southern cultures and, it is believed, both calendar systems were correlated here. The sides of the Pyramid of the Plumed Serpent are faced with andesite slabs, fitted invisibly without mortar. After the building was finished, reliefs 3-4 ins deep were carried into the stone as a frieze. There are interesting underground tunnels (open 1100-1400); one has a shaft to the sky and the centre of the cave. There are also ball courts, an avenue 18.5m wide and 46m long, remains of 20 large circular altars and of a palace and dwellings. Xochicalco is well worth the 4 km walk from the bus stop; take a torch for the underground part, entry US$2. Tickets must be bought at the museum about 500m from ruins. This new and striking edifice incorporates many ecological principles and houses some magnificent items from the ruins.

● **Transport** To get to Xochicalco, take a Pullman de Morelos bus from Cuernavaca en route to El Rodeo (every 30 mins), Coatlán or Las Grutas; alight from any of these buses at the turn-off, 4 km from the site, then take a colectivo taxi, US$0.35-US$1.20 pp, or walk up the hill. From Taxco, take bus to Alpuyeca and pick up bus from Cuernavaca there.

TAXCO

From the toll road at Amacuzac (Km 121) an old road (39 km) runs to **Taxco** (*Pop* 120,000), a colonial gem, with steep, twisting, cobbled streets and many picturesque buildings, now wholly dedicated to tourism. The first silver shipped to Spain came from the mines of Taxco. José de la Borda made and spent three fortunes here in the 18th century; he founded the present town and built the magnificent twin-towered, rose-coloured parish church of **Santa Prisca** which soars above everything but the mountains. Large paintings about Mexican history at the Post Office. The roof of every building is of red tile, every nook or corner in the place is a picture, and even the cobblestone road surfaces have patterns woven in them. It is now a national monument and all modern building is forbidden. Gas stations are outside the city limits. The plaza is 1,700m above sea-level. A good view is had from the **Iglesia de Guadalupe**. There are superb views also from the *Teleférico* to Monte Taxco, US$3 one way, you can return by bus. The *Teleférico* is reached by microbus along the main street from Santa Prisca.

Shopping for silver

📍 Silverwork is a speciality and there are important lead and zinc mines. Vendors will bargain and cheap silver items can often be found. Beware of mistaking the cheapish pretty jewellery, *alpaca*, an alloy of copper, zinc and nickel, for the real stuff. By law, real silver, defined as 0.925 pure, must be stamped somewhere on the item with the number 925. The downtown shops in general give better value than those on the highway, but the best value is among the booth-holders in the Pasaje de Santa Prisca (from the Zócalo). Prices usually drop in the low season. On the 2nd Sun in Dec there is a national silversmiths' competition. The colourful labyrinthine produce and general market beneath the Zócalo is spectacular among Mexican markets; reasonable meals in the many *fondas*.

NB All silver jewellers must be government-registered. Remember to look for the 925 stamp and, if the piece is large enough, it will also be stamped with the crest of an eagle, and initials of the jeweller. Where the small size of the item does not permit this, a certificate will be provided instead.

The climate is ideal, never any high winds (for it is protected by huge mountains immediately to the N); never cold and never hot, but sometimes foggy. The processions during Holy Week are spectacular. The main central area is full of shops and shopping tourists; the district between the 4-storey Mercado and the Carretera Nacional is quieter and free of tourists. Also quieter are those parts up from the main street where the taxis can't go. Wear flat rubber-soled shoes to avoid slithering over the cobbles.

Places of interest

One of the most interesting of Mexican stone-age cultures, the Mezcala or Chontal, is based on the State of Guerrero in which Taxco lies. Its remarkable artefacts, of which there are many imitations, are almost surrealist. The culture remained virtually intact into historic times. **Museum of the Viceroyalty** (formerly Casa Humboldt), where Baron von Humboldt once stayed, recently renovated with beautiful religious art exhibits, many from Santa Prisca, admission US$3.30, students US$1.65, (open Tues-Sat 1000-1700, Sun 0900-1500). The **Casa Figueroa**, the 'House of Tears', so called because the colonial judge who owned it forced Indian labourers to work on it to pay their fines, is now a private house. **Museo Guillermo**

Spratling, behind Santa Prisca, is a museum of prehispanic artefacts bought by William Spratling, a North American architect who came to Taxco in the 1920s. His designs in silver helped bring the city to world recognition and revived a dwindling industry. On his death bed Spratling donated his collection to the state, entry US$3.30, open Tues-Sun 1000-1700. The **Museo de la Platería** is a new museum devoted to modern silverworking, on Plaza Borda 1; at the **Platería La Mina** on John F Kennedy you can see mining techniques.

Excursions

Visit *Posada Don Carlos*, Bermeja 6, also Ventana de Taxco in *Hacienda del Solar* for view. 'Combi' to Panorámica every 30 mins from Plaza San Juan, US$0.20, or you can walk up the steep hill from Plaza San Juan for views of the hills and volcanoes. About 20 km out of Taxco a rodeo is held on some Suns at El Cedrito, costs about US$4-5, tickets in advance from Veterinario Figueroa on C Nueva near Flecha Roja terminal. 21 km from Taxco to Acuitlapán waterfalls, with colectivo or Flecha Roja bus (US$1.20); 4 km narrow path from nearest village (snakes) to large clear pools for swimming. Taxis about US$7.50/hr. To **Cacahuamilpa** for caverns, 40 mins, see page 339. Buses from 0820 but service erratic, US$1.65, or take a long white taxi marked 'Grutas' from opposite the bus station, US$3.50. Take an Ixtapan bus from opposite the Flecha Roja bus terminal, US$1.50, 1 hr, which passes the turn off to the site, 1 km downhill; Ixtapan-Taxco buses go to the site car park. Alternatively, to return, take bus coming from Toluca at junction, 500m from the caves.

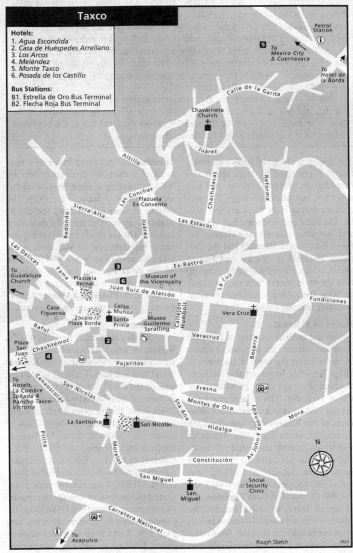

Taxco

Hotels:
1. Agua Escondida
2. Casa de Huéspedes Arrellano
3. Los Arcos
4. Meléndez
5. Monte Taxco
6. Posada de los Castillo

Bus Stations:
B1. Estrella de Oro Bus Terminal
B2. Flecha Roja Bus Terminal

Rough Sketch

M23

Visit the villages where *amate* pictures are painted (on display at Museum of the Viceroyalty/Casa Humboldt and in the market). Xalitla is the most convenient as it is on the road to Acapulco, take 2nd class bus there. Other villages: Maxela, Ahuelicán, Ahuehuepán and San Juan, past Iguala and before the Río Balsa. 33 km from Taxco, at Km 55 on the road to Cuernavaca, is Zoofari, a private safari park with many animals roaming free (entrance US$5), well worth a visit, T/F Cuernavaca 209794.

Ixcateopán de Cuauhtémoc (Cuauhtémoc's birthplace), is a beautiful and peaceful village, where most of the buildings, and even the cobblestones, are made of marble. A statue honouring Cuauhtémoc stands at the entrance to the village. To get there, take a *pesera* from the road out of Taxco towards Acapulco. 22-23 Feb is the anniversary of Cuauhtémoc's death, called Día de la Mexicanidad. Runners come from Mexico City to Ixcateopán via Taxco, carrying a torch representing the identity of the Mexican people. Aztec dancers (in traditional dress and colourful plumed head-dresses) come from all over Mexico to dance all night and most of the following day.

Local festivals

There is much festivity in Semana Santa (Holy Week); at this time the price of accommodation rises steeply. At any time it is best to book a room in advance because hoteliers tend to quote inflated prices to those without reservations.

Local information

● Accommodation

A1 *De la Borda*, on left as you enter Taxco, largest, all facilities, great views, T 20225, dearest and best; **A1** *La Cumbre Soñada*, 1.5 km or so towards Acapulco on a mountain top, colonial, exquisite; **A1** *La Hacienda del Solar*, Acapulco exit of town, T 20323, best restaurant in Taxco (*La Ventana*); **A1** *Rancho Taxco-Victoria*, Soto la Marina 15, walk to centre, fantastic view, good restaurant, rec; **A2** *Monte Taxco*, on right entering Taxco, T 21300, F 21428, special prices sometimes available

from Mexico City offices, T 525-9193, F 533-0314, spectacular hilltop setting, pool, riding, golf course, beware mosquitoes; **A3** *Posada de la Misión* Cerro de la Misión 32 (Mexico City – Cuernavaca buses stop outside), T 20063, F 22198, Juan O'Gorman mural, restaurant, good, pool, no a/c, quiet, rec.

B *Posada Don Carlos*, Cerro de Bermeja 6, converted old mansion, restaurant, good view; **B-C** *Agua Escondida*, nr Zócalo at C Guillermo Spratling 4, T 20726, with bath, nice view, rooftop bar, parking, pool.

C *Posada San Javier*, down a small street opp Municipalidad, clean, lovely garden, pool (sometimes dirty), excellent value, no restaurant; **C** *Meléndez*, 1 20006, somewhat noisy as it is nr market, good breakfast, excellent good value lunch; **C-D** *Los Arcos*, Juan Ruiz de Alarcón 2, T 21836, magnificently reconstructed 17th century ex convent, delightful rooftop garden, charming, friendly, breakfast available, best rooms for views are 18 and 19, rooms overlooking street are noisy, otherwise rec; **C-D** *Posada de los Castillos*, Alarcón 7, T 23471, off main square, Mexican style, friendly, excellent value.

D *Casa de Huéspedes Arellano*, Pajaritos 23, by Santa Prisca and Plaza Borda, with bath (E without), basic, no single rooms, old beds, hot water, overpriced.

E *Casa Grande*, Plazuela San Juan 7, T 21108, pleasant, well furnished, rooms at the top are better, takes credit cards, good value; **E** *El Jumil*, Reforma 6, nr Tourist Office North, without bath, hot water, basic, friendly, but noisy; **E** *Posada Santa Anita*, John F Kennedy 106, T 20752, close to Flecha Roja buses, with hot shower and toilet, cheaper without, very clean, basic, overpriced, noisy at night, friendly, secure parking; the cheapest hotels are in this area.

F *Central*, round the left hand corner of *Casa de Huéspedes Arellano*, shared bath, quite clean, some rooms without windows.

● Places to eat

Restaurants tend to be pricey. There are many places on the Zócalo: *Alarcón*, overlooking Zócalo, very good; *Sr Costilla*, next to church on main square, good drinks and grilled ribs; *Papa's Bar*, on Zócalo, a discotheque and a small pizza place in an arcade; *Bora-Bora*, overlooks Zócalo, Guadalupe y Plaza Borda, good pizzas; *Pizzería Mario*, Plaza Borda, beautiful view over city, excellent pizzas, the first pizzeria in town, opened 30 years ago, highly rec; *La Parroquia*, Plaza Borda 5, terrace with excellent views, good food and service, cheap; *La Hacienda*, Plaza Borda 4 (entrance is off the square), excellent, fair prices, exquisite *quesadillas* in the *neveria* on top of the silver shop Perlita looking on to the Plaza Borda; *Mi Taverna* next to the Post Office, excellent Italian food, friendly; *Concha Nuestra*, Plazuela San Juan (beneath *Hotel Casa Grande*), food and live Latin American music excellent, cheap for breakfasts, other meals pricey; *La Hamburguesa*, off Plaza San Juan, excellent *comida corrida*, US$1.80, home-cooked food, despite name; *De Cruz*, C Veracruz, good Mexican food at low prices; *Armando*, Av Plateros 205, opp Flecha Roja bus station, excellent tacos; *Pozolería Betty*, Mora 20 (below bus station), good food inc the local beetle (jumil) sauce. Many small restaurants just nr *Hotel Meléndez*. Excellent *comida corrida* (US$6) at *Santa Fe*, opp *Hotel Santa Prisca* but disappointing *enchiladas*. Cheap *comida corrida* in market and good cheap restaurants on San Nicolás.

● **Banks & money changers**
Good rates at *Cambio de Divisar Argentu* on Plazuela San Juan 5; **Bancomer**, between Plazuela San Juan and Plaza Principal is OK.

● **Laundry**
Lavandería La Cascada, Delicias 4.

● **Post & telecommunications**
Post Office: on Carretera Nacional about 100m E of Estrella de Oro bus terminal.

● **Tourist offices**
Tourist Office at Av de los Plateros 1, T 22274, open 0900-1400 and 1600-2000 every day. City tours from Tourist Office North, US$35 for up to 5 people.

● **Transport**
Book onward bus tickets to Mexico City on arrival. (Taxis meet all buses and take you to any hotel, approximately US$2.) Taxco is reached from **Mexico City** from the Central del Sur, Estrella de Oro, luxury US$10.65, *plus* US$8.65, non-stop, with video, 3 a day, 1st class US$7.65, only one stop in Cuernavaca, quick, no over-crowding, 3 a day (3 hrs); last bus back to Mexico City at 1800, but computerized booking allows seat selection in the capital; also Flecha Roja, excellent buses, 5 a day for US$7.50, up to 5 hrs. Buses to **Cuernavaca**; 1st class buses at 0900, 1600, 1800 and 2000 (Estrella de Oro), 2nd class about 5 a day, 2½ hrs (Flecha Roja), US$3 but can be erratic and crowded (watch out for pickpockets); buses en route to Mexico

City drop passengers on the main highway, away from centre of Cuernavaca. Little 24-seaters, 'Los Burritos' (now called 'Combis'), take you up the hill from the bus terminal on main road, US$0.35, same fare anywhere in town. Spectacular journey to **Toluca**, missing out Mexico City, 2nd class buses only, from Flecha Roja Terminal, US$6, 3 hrs, change at Toluca for Morelia. To **Acapulco**, Estrella de Oro, or Flecha Roja, US$11, 5 hrs.

36 km S of Taxco join the road at **Iguala**, (**E** *Hotel Central*, basic; **E** *Pasajero*; **E** *Mary*, OK, enclosed parking; bus to Taxco US$1, to Cuernavaca US$4.25, to Mexico City from US$9.35 to US$15.35).

CHILPANCINGO

(*Pop* 120,000; *State pop 1995* 2,915,497; *Alt* 1,250m) Beyond the Mexcala river, the road passes for some 30 km through the dramatic canyon of Zopilote to reach **Chilpancingo**, capital of Guerrero state at Km 302. The colourful reed bags from the village of Chilapa (see below) are sold in the market. The Casa de las Artesanías for Guerrero is on the right-hand side of the old main highway Mexico City – Acapulco. It has a particularly wide selection of lacquerware from Olinalá. It has a University.

Excursions

Not far from Chilpancingo are Oxtotitlán and Juxtlahuaca, where Olmec cave paintings can be seen.

To reach the **Grutas de Juxtlahuaca** caves, drive to Petaquillas on the non-toll road then take a side road (paved, but poor in parts) through several villages to Colotlipa (colectivo from Chilpancingo – see below – US$1.50, 1½ hrs). Ask at the restaurant on the corner of the Zócalo for a guide to the caves. They can only be visited with a guide (3 hrs' tour US$25, popular at weekends for groups; if on your own, try for a discount). The limestone cavern is in pristine condition; it has an intricate network of large halls and tunnels, stalagmites and stalactites, a huge underground lake, cave drawings from about 500 AD, a skeleton and artefacts.

Take a torch, food and drink and a sweater if going a long way in.

Chilapa, E of Chilpancingo, is accessible by several local buses and is worth a visit (about 1 hr journey). On Sun there is an excellent craft market selling especially good quality and well-priced Olinalá lacquer boxes as well as wood carvings, textiles, leather goods, etc. The Grutas de Oxtotitlán are about 18 km N of Chilapa.

Local festivals

Its *fiesta* starts on Dec 16 and lasts a fortnight.

Local information

● **Accommodation**

La Posada Meléndez, large rooms, helpful, swimming pool, cheap *comida corrida* in restaurant, rec; **D** *María Isabel* and *Cardeña*, both on same street; **F** *Chilpancingo*, 50m from Zócalo, clean, shower.

● **Transport**

Buses Cuernavaca-Chilpancingo, Estrella de Oro US$8.30, or *plus* US$11 (9 a day). Buses Mexico City-Chilpancingo from US$11 to US$23.35 super luxury.

OLINALA

(*Alt* 1,350m) This small town is known to most Mexicans for the beautiful lacquered wooden objects made here (boxes, chests, screens, trays etc), but is visited by few. Situated in the E of the State of Guerrero, it lies in an area of mountains, rivers and ravines, which make access difficult. Most of the population is involved in the production and selling of the lacquer work, which is available from the artesans direct as well as from the more expensive shops on the square. The wood chiefly used is *lináloe*, which gives the objects a gentle fragrance. The lacquering techniques include both the scraping away of layers and applying new ones. Other villages in the area similarly devote themselves almost exclusively to their own *artesanías*. The church on the square is decorated inside with lacquer work. A chapel dedicated to Nuestra Señora de Guadalupe crowns a

hill just outside the town, offering striking views. The hill is pyramid-shaped and there are said to be tunnels, but to date no archaeological investigations have been carried out.

● **Accommodation** **F** Three hotels around the square.

● **Places to eat** Restaurant (no name displayed), above furniture shop on main square, exquisite Mexican cooking.

● **Transport** **Buses** Direct from Mexico City via Chilpancingo (Terminal Sur); also via Izúcar de Matamoros to Tlapa, then local bus. Local bus also from Chilapa. **By car**, there is one paved road (1 hr) from the Chilpancingo-Tlapa road to the S, the turning to Olinalá is between the villages of Tlatlauquitepec and Chiepetepec, about 40 km W of Tlapa. There is an unpaved road (4 hrs) from Chiautla to the N, but you have to cross rivers whose bridges are often washed away in the rainy season. A better unpaved road (2½ hrs) from Santa Cruz to the E, nr Huamuxtitlán on the route 92, fords the river Tlapaneco, which is feasible for most vehicles except in the rainy season. The scenery is spectacular, with huge bluffs and river valleys, but filling stations are infrequent. If *Pemex* in Olinalá has no fuel, local shops may sell it. Fill up when you can.

The new section of 4-lane toll freeway runs from Iguala W of the old highway as far as Tierra Colorada, where it joins the existing 4-lane section to Acapulco. Chilpancingo is bypassed, but there is an exit. This is the third improvement: the first motor road was pushed over the ancient mule trail in 1927, giving Acapulco its first new lease of life in 100 years; when the road was paved and widened in 1954, Acapulco began to boom.

About 20 km from the coast, a branch road goes to the NW of Acapulco; this is a preferable route for car drivers because it avoids the city chaos. It goes to a point between Pie de la Cuesta and Coyuca, is signed, and has a drugs control point at the junction.

WARNING Do not travel by car at night in Guerrero, even on the Mexico City-Acapulco highway and coastal highway. Always set out early to ensure that you reach your destination in daylight. Many military checkpoints on highway. *Guerrilleros* have been active in recent years, and there are also problems with highway robbers and stray animals.

ACAPULCO

(*Pop* 1 million; *Phone code* 74) Acapulco is the most popular resort in Mexico, particularly in winter and spring. During Holy Week there is a flight from the capital every 3 mins. It does not fit everyone's idea of a tropical beach resort. The town stretches for 16 km in a series of bays and cliff coves and is invading the hills. The hotels, of which there are 250, are mostly perched high to catch the breeze, for between 1130 and 1630 the heat is sizzling; they are filled to overflowing in Jan and February. It has all the paraphernalia of a booming resort: smart shops, nightclubs, red light district, golf club, touts and street vendors and now also air pollution. The famous beaches and expensive hotels are a different world from the streets, hotels and crowded shops and buses of the city centre, which is only 2 mins' walk away. The Zócalo is lively in the evenings, but the surrounding streets are grimy.

Acapulco in colonial times was the terminal for the Manila convoy. Its main defence, **Fuerte de San Diego**, where the last battle for Mexican independence was fought, is in the middle of the city and is worth a visit. (Open 1000-1800, Tues and Sun only, free admission.)

Beaches

A campaign to tidy up the whole city and its beaches is in process. There are some 20 beaches, all with fine, golden sand; deckchairs on all beaches, US$0.50; parachute skiing in front of the larger hotels at US$12 for 5 mins. Every evening, except Mon, there is a water skiing display opposite Fuerte de San Diego. The two most popular beaches are the sickle-curved and shielded **Caleta**, with its smooth but dirty water yet clean sands, and the surf-pounded straight beach of **Los Hornos**. Swimmers should look out for motor boats

close in shore. At **Revolcadero** beach, development is continuing, with new luxury hotels, new roads and landscaping; it is being called Acapulco Diamante. Take local bus to **Pie de la Cuesta**, 12 km, now preferred by many budget travellers to Acapulco itself, but also commercialized. There are several bungalow-hotels and trailer parks (see below), lagoon (6 hrs' boat trip US$10), now used for laundry, and long, clean, sandy beaches (**Warning** The surf is dangerous on the beach W of the road and the beaches are unsafe at night). At Pie de la Cuesta you drink *coco loco*, fortified coconut milk, and watch the sunset from a hammock. One can swim, and fish, the year round. Best free map of Acapulco can be obtained from the desk clerk at *Tortuga Hotel*.

Excursions

Daily, amazing 40m dives into shallow (polluted) water by boys can be watched from the **Quebrada** (US$1.20, at 1915, 2015, 2115 and 2215).

The **lagoons** can be explored by motor boats; one, **Coyuca Lagoon** (also known as **La Barra**), is over 10 km long (38 km NW of Acapulco); strange birds, water hyacinths, tropical flowers.

At **Playa Icacos** there is a marineland amusement park *Ci-Ci*, with a waterslide, pool with wave-machine and arena with performing dolphins and sea-lions, US$5.70 for whole day, open 1000-1800 (nothing special). Pleasant boat trip across beach to **Puerto Marqués**, US$2 return (or 30 mins by bus); one can hire small sailing boats there, US$12 an hr. Bay cruises, 2½ hrs, from Muelle Yates, US$9, including free bar, at 1100, 1630 and 2230. *Yate Bonanza* has been recommended, stops 30 mins for swim in bay. Visit the island of **La Roqueta**, in a glass-bottomed boat; tours leave at 1100 and 1300 from Fuerte San Diego and return at 1500 and 1700, US$4; once on the island follow the path which goes over the hill towards the other side of the island (towards the right) where there is a small,

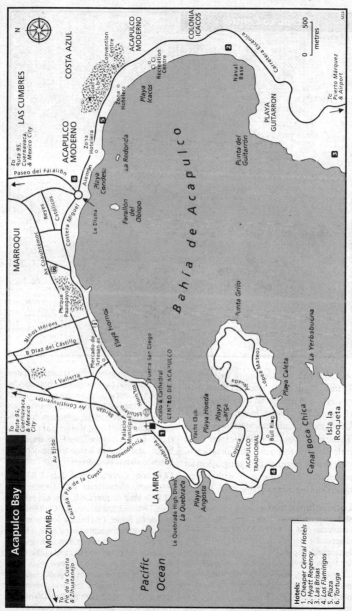

Acapulco Bay

Hotels:
1. Cheaper Central Hotels
2. Hyatt Regency
3. Las Brisas
4. Los Flamingos
5. Plaza
6. Tortuga

Acapulco Centre

Not to Scale

Hotels:
1. Añorve
2. California
3. Chamizel
4. Colimense
5. Isabel
6. Mama Helène
7. Misión
8. Sacramento
9. Santa Lucía

secluded and usually empty bay (about 15 mins' walk). Take food and drink with you as it is expensive on the island. Parachute sailing (towed by motor boats), US$12 for a few minutes, several operators. There is an Aqua Marine museum on a little island (Yerbabuena) off Caleta beach, with sharks, piranhas, eels, stingrays in an aquarium, swimming pool with waterchute, and breezy bar above, entry US$7.

Local information
● Accommodation
Hotels can cost up to US$200 a night double; cheaper for longer stays, but this also means less expensive hotels insist on a double rate even for 1 person and for a minimum period. In the off-season (May-Nov) you can negotiate lower prices even for a single for 1 night. For hotels in our C range and above in Acapulco you can make reservations at the bus terminal in Mexico City, helpful; similarly, at the 1st class bus station in Acapulco you can arrange hotel packages, eg 3 nights in 4-star accommodation for US$60. Hotel recommendations, and reservations, made at the bus terminal, often turn out to be dingy downtown hotels. If seeking a hotel in the D or C range, go to the *Doral Playa*, on Hornos beach, and use it as a base for exploring the hotels in surrounding streets.

L2 *Elcano*, Costera nr golf club, T 841950, renovated, many rooms with terrace, pool; **L2** *Villa Vera Raquet Club*, luxurious celebrity spot, T 840333. The fabulous **L1** *Club Residencial de las Brisas*, T 841733, a hotel where the services match the astronomical price, it begins at sea-level and reaches up the mountain slope in a series of detached villas and public rooms to a point 300m above sea-level, each room has own or shared swimming pool, guests use pink jeeps to travel to the dining-room and recreation areas; **L1** *Camino Real Diamante*, T 812010, on edge of Diamante development at Revolcadero beach, luxury resort; **L1-A1** *Acapulco Plaza*, Costera 123, T 859050, 3 towers, 2 pools, 5 bars, 4 restaurants, a city in itself; *Hyatt Regency*, next to naval base, Av Costera M Alemán 1, T 842888, F 843087; **L3** *Acapulco Tortuga*, T 848889, good discounts in low season; and **L3** *Caleta*, Playa Caleta, T 39940, remodelled; **L3** *Romano Days*, T 845332, both on Costera, many groups.

A1 *Fiesta Americana Condesa del Mar*, Costera at Condesa beach, T 842828, all facilities; **A1** *Maris*, Alemán y Magallanes, T 858440, very good; **A2** *Acapulco Imperial*, Costera 251, T 851918; **A3** *Los Flamingos*, López Mateos, T 820690/2, F 839806, one of the finest locations in Acapulco, glorious cliff-top views, in the 1950s it was a retreat for John Wayne, Johnny Weissmuller et al, and the present owner preserves the atmosphere of those days, gardens, pool, restaurant, highly rec, breakfast inc. The *Acapulco Princess Country Club*, part of the *Acapulco Princess*, T 843100, 20 km away on Revolcadero beach, is highly fashionable, delightful resort, all facilities, taxi to town US$10. **A3** *Maralisa*, C Alemania s/n, T 856677, smallish and elegant, Arab style, private beach, rec.

B *Casa Blanca Tropical*, Cerro de la Pinzona, T 821212, with swimming pool, is rec; **B** *do Brasil*, Costera Miguel Alemán on Hornos beach, T 854364, shower, TV, all rooms with sea view balcony, pool, restaurant, bar, travel agency, friendly, rec; **B** *Club Majestic* nr Yacht Club and above city (a little hard to find), T 834710, quiet, reasonable, good views; **B** *Playa Suites*, Costera Miguel Alemán, on beach, suites sleeping up to 6, good value; **B** *Real del Monte*, clean, friendly, on the beach, pool, good food, Playa del Coco opp new convention centre, T 841010; *Boca Chica*, Playa Caletillo, T 836741, on promontory opp island, pool, clean, direct access to bathing, free drinking water on each floor.

C *Doral Playa*, Hornos beach, T 850103, a/c, pool, ask for front upper floors with balcony, good value; **C** pp *El Cid*, Hornos beach, T 851312, clean, pool, rec; **C** *Embassy*, Costera Miguel Alemán, T 840273, clean, a/c, pool; opp *Costa Linda* is **D** *Casa de Huéspedes Johnny*, hammocks on porch, etc, OK; **D** *Los Pericos*, Costera Miguel Alemán nr Playa Honda, T 824078, fan, clean, friendly, pool, rec; **D** *Olivieda*, Costera Miguel Alemán, 1 block from cathedral, clean, fan, hot water, great views from top floor rooms; **D** *El Tropicano*,

Costera Miguel Alemán 150, on Playa Icacos, a/c, clean, big garden, 2 pools, bars, restaurant, very friendly and helpful, rec; **D** *San Francisco*, Costera 219, T 820045, old part of town, friendly, good value, noisy in front.

Most cheaper hotels are grouped around the Zócalo, especially **C** *La Paz* and **C** *Juárez*. **C** *Acuario*, Azueta 11, T 821784, popular; **C** *Añorve*, Juárez 17, T 822093, 2 blocks off Zócalo, clean, with bath, front rooms better than back (but can be noisy from street in mornings); opp *Añorve* is **E** *Mama Helène*, who owns 2 hotels in same price range, and offers laundry service, homemade lemonade, rec; **C** *Fiesta*, clean and nice, with bath, fan, 2 blocks NW from Zócalo, Azueta 16, T 820019; **C** *Misión*, Felipe Valle 12, T 823643, very clean, colonial, close to Zócalo, rec; **D** *California*, La Paz 12, T 822893, 1½ blocks W of Zócalo, good value, fan, hot water, pleasant rooms and patio; **D** *Colimense*, JM Iglesias II, off Zócalo, T 822890, pleasant, limited parking; **D** *Isabel*, La Paz y Valle, T 822191, with fan, rec, nr Zócalo; **D** *Sacramento*, E Carranza y Valle, with bath and fan, no towel, soap or loo paper, friendly, noisy, OK, purified water, T 820821; **D** *Santa Cecilia*, Francisco Madero 7, off Zócalo, with bath and fan, noisy, but otherwise fine; **D** *Santa Lucía*, López Mateos 33, T 820441, family-owned, will negotiate if not full, good value; **E** *Aca-Plus*, Azueta 11, T 831405, with bath and fan, clean, safe; **E** *La Posada*, Azueta 8, nr Zócalo, with bath, more expensive in high season; **E-F** *Chamizal*, López Mateos 32, close to Zócalo, shower, OK.

Many cheap hotels on La Quebrada, basic but clean with fan and bathroom, inc **D** *El Faro* (No 63, T 821365, clean); **D** *Casa de Huéspedes Aries*, No 30 (with bath, nice); **D** *Asturia* (No 45), with bath, no single rooms, clean, friendly, pool, a few cockroaches on lower floor, otherwise rec; **D** *Coral* (No 56, T 820756, good value, friendly, reasonably quiet, small pool); **E** *Sagamar* (No 51), with bath, basic, friendly, some English spoken, safe, clean, use mosquito coil; **E** *Beatriz*, 3 blocks from Flecha Roja terminal, 2 from beach, for more than one night, central, fan, shower, pool; **D** *Betty*, Belisario Domínguez 4, T 835092, 5 mins from bus station, with bath, fan, short stay, dirty, not rec; just around corner on same street is **E** *Alberto*, much better. Turn left at *Betty* for several cheap *casas de huéspedes*.

Several nice places at Pie de la Cuesta, **D**, in clean rooms with shower: **C** *Villa Nirvana*, Pie de la

Cuesta, Canadian/Mexican owners (depending on season) with kitchen, clean, pool, good value, rec; **D** *Casa Blanca*, rooms for 3, management nice, food good; *Puesta del Sol*, expensive places for hammocks; **D** *Quinta Dora Trailer Park*, for hammock, managed by American, helpful.

The student organization Setej offers dormitory accommodation, D, if one has a valid international student card, at Centro Vacacional, Pie de la Cuesta, 0700-2400. For longer (1 month plus) stays, try *Amueblados Etel*, Av la Pinzona 92 (nr Quebrada) for self-catering apartments, cheap off-season (before Nov), short stays possible in rooms (**C**), a/c, fan, hot shower, sundeck, large pool, rec; **C** *Apartamentos Maraback*, Costera M Alemán; **D** *Amueblos Caletilla Diamante*, López Mateos 28, Las Playas, T 827975, apartments with kitchen, pool, close to beach and market, safe parking. The Tourist Bureau is helpful in finding a hotel in any price range.

Camping: *Trailer Park El Coloso*, in La Sabana, small swimming pool, and *Trailer Park La Roca* on road from Puerto Márquez to La Sabana, both secure; *Estacionamiento Juanita* and *Quinta Dora* at Pie de la Cuesta (latter is 13 km up the coast on Highway 200, palapas, bathrooms, cold showers, hook-ups, US$12 for 2 plus car, US$4 just to sling hammock); *Quinta Carla*, *Casa Blanca*, *J Kae Kim*, all US$50 a week upwards, but negotiable; *Acapulco West KDA*, on Barra de Coyuca, opened 1996, beachfront, security patrol, pool, restaurant, hot showers, laundry, store, volleyball, basketball, Spanish classes, telephones.

Motels: **B** *Impala*, T 840337, *Bali-Hai*, T 857045, *Mónaco*, T 856415, all along the Costera; **B** *Victoria*, Cristóbal Colón, 1 block behind Costera.

● **Places to eat**
There are a number of variously-priced restaurants along and opp Condesa beach, inc *Embarcadero* on the Costera, Thai/Mexican/US food, extraordinary decor with waterfalls, bridges, bamboo huts and 'a hall of mirrors on the way to the loo', expensive but worth it for the atmosphere; many cheap restaurants in the blocks surrounding the Zócalo, especially along Juárez: for example, *El Amigo Miguel*, *Ricardo* (popular), Juárez 9 (nr Zócalo), fixed menu lunch, good; *Nachos*, on Azueta, at corner of Juárez, popular, excellent prawns; *El Pulpo*, Miguel Alemán 183, 1½ blocks from Zócalo, good filling breakfasts, friendly. By La Diana roundabout is *Pizza Hut*, reliable, with 'blissful a/c';

Italianissimo, nearby, decent pizza and garlic bread, average price for area; *Parroquia*, on Zócalo, excellent; *El Zorrito*, opp *Ritz Hotel*, excellent food with live music, average prices, reputedly popular with Julio Iglesias when he is in town. The *cafetería* at the SE corner of the Zócalo serves good coffee. Another group of restaurants along the Caleta beach walkway; better value on Caleta beach itself is *La Cabaña*, good food, delightful setting. Yet another group with mixed prices on the Costera opp the *Acapulco Plaza Hotel*. 250 or so to select from.

● **Airline offices**
AeroMéxico, T 847009; American, T 669248; Delta, T 840716; Mexicana, T 841215; Taesa, T 864576.

● **Embassies & consulates**
British Consul (Honorary) Mr DB Gore, MBE, *Hotel Las Brisas*, T 846605; Canadian, *Hotel Club del Sol*, Costera Miguel Alemán, T 856621; Dutch, *El Presidente Hotel*, T 837148; Finnish, Costera Miguel Alemán 500, T 847641; French, Av Costa Grande 235, T 823394; German, Antón de Alaminos 46, T 847437; Norwegian, *Maralisa Hotel*, T 843525; Spanish, Av Cuauhtémoc y Universidad 2, T 857205; Swedish, Av Insurgentes 2, T 852935; US, *Club del Sol Hotel*, T 856600.

● **Entertainment**
Nightclubs: there are dozens of discos inc *Discoteca Safari*, Av Costera, free entry, 1 drink obligatory, good ambience; *Disco Beach*, Costera Miguel Alemán, between the *Diana* and *Hotel Fiesta Americana Condesa*, by beach, informal dress, open till 0500, good; every major hotel has at least one disco plus bars. Superb varied night-life always.

● **Laundry**
Tintorería Bik, 5 de Mayo; *Lavadín*, José María Iglesias 11a, T 822890, next to *Hotel Colimense*, rec.

● **Post & telecommunications**
Post Office: Costera, 2 blocks S of Zócalo.

Telephones: public offices will not take collect calls; try from a big hotel (ask around, there will be a surcharge).

● **Tourist offices**
Costera Miguel Alemán at Hornos beach, T 840599/7621, helpful, but double-check details; useful free magazines, *Aca-Sun* and *Acapulco guide*. Also at 'Flechas' bus station, very helpful, will make hotel bookings, but not in cheapest range.

● **Useful addresses**

Immigration: Juan Sebastian el Cuno 1, Costa Azul el Lado, T 849021, open 0800-1400, take a Hornos Base bus from Miguel Alemán, US$0.20, 30 mins, visa extensions possible.

● **Transport**

Local Taxis US$9 an hour; sample fare: Zócalo to Condesa Beach US$3.65. Taxis more expensive from bus terminal, walk half a block round corner and catch one on the street. Several bus routes, with one running the full length of Costera Miguel Alemán linking the older part of town to the latest hotels, marked 'Caleta-Zócalo-Base', US$0.50, another operating to Caleta beach. Buses to Pie de la Cuesta, 12 km, 1.50 pesos. Bus stops on the main thoroughfare are numbered, so find out which one you need. Many buses along the beach front may turn off at right angles; read the destination boards carefully.

Air Airport Alvarez Intl (ACA) 23 km from Acapulco. Direct connections with New York, Miami, Chicago, Dallas, Houston, Los Angeles, Memphis, Minneapolis, Montréal, Orlando, Phoenix, San Antonio and San Diego by Mexican and US carriers. ITU has a weekly scheduled flight from Dusseldorf. Also many charter flights from Europe and North America. Mexico City, 50 mins, with AeroMéxico, Mexicana and Taesa. Also domestic services to Cuernavaca, Guadalajara, Oaxaca, Puerto Vallarta and Tijuana AeroMéxico and Mexicana offices in Torre Acapulco, Miguel Alemán 1252, Mexicana T 841428/1215, AeroMéxico T 847009/1625. Flights to Mexico City are worth booking at least a week in advance, especially in high season. Transportaciónes de Pasajeros Aeropuerto taxi service charge return trip (*viaje redondo*) when you buy a ticket, so keep it and call 24 hrs in advance for a taxi, US$11. Airport bus takes 1 hr, US$3.35 and *does* exist (ticket office outside terminal)!

Buses Bus terminal is on Av Ejido. There is a left luggage office. Estrella de Oro buses leave from the bus station on Av Cuauhtémoc. **Mexico City**, 406 km, 5½ (1st class or above) – 8 hrs; de luxe air-conditioned express buses (*futura*, highly rec), US$28.35 and super luxury US$36.65; ordinary bus, US$21.65 1st and US$25.65 *plus*, all-day services from Estación Central de Autobuses del Sur by the Taxqueña metro station, Mexico City, with Estrella de Oro (10 a day, one stop) or Flecha Roja (part of Líneas Unidas del Sur, hourly). Taxi to Zócalo, US$5.50; bus, US$0.50. To **Manzanillo**, direct bus

US$8.50. To **Cuernavaca**, with Estrella de Oro, 6 hrs, US$14.75-19.50. To **Oaxaca**, 402 km: 6 hrs on main road, 264 km, 6 hrs on good road through mountains by bus, change at Pochutla (8 hrs, bad road) for night bus (only one at 2200), 11 hrs, waiting room and luggage deposit at Pochutla; also via Pinotepa Nacional (one bus at 2100) but worse road. Several 1st class buses, Estrella de Oro, 5 hrs, and Flecha Rosa buses a day to **Taxco** US$11. Bus to **Puerto Escondido** every hour on the ½-hr from 0430-1630, plus 2300, 2400, 0200, US$9, and *directo* at 1330 and 2300, US$20, seats bookable, advisable to do so the day before, 7½ hrs, many checkpoints, bad road; Flecha Roja, Transportes Gacela (US$15.65). To **Tapachula**: take Impala 1st class bus to Huatulco, arriving 1930; from there Cristóbal Colón at 2030 to Salina Cruz, arriving about midnight, then take 1st or 2nd class bus.

COAST NW OF ACAPULCO

Between Acapulco and Zihuatanejo is **Coyuca de Benítez**, 38 km from Acapulco, close to the Laguna Coyuca (see above, **Acapulco excursions**), a lagoon with little islands: Coyuca is a market town selling exotic fruit, cheap hats and shoes. There is no bank but shops will change US dollars. Pelicans fly by the lagoons, there are passing dolphins and plentiful sardines, and young boys seek turtle eggs.

● **Accommodation** D *Parador de los Reyes*, clean, pool; **E** *Imperial*, off the main square. There is a *jai-alai* palace.

1½ km beyond Coyuca is a turn-off to **El Carrizal** (7½ km), a village of some 2,000 people, a little paradise with a beautiful beach (many pelicans) with a steep drop-off (unsafe for children), dangerous waves and sharks behind them; good for spotting dolphins and, if you are lucky, whales.

● **Accommodation & places to eat** Good restaurant (opp *Hotel-Bungalows El Carrizal*) which has 6 rooms with bath and toilet, E, closes early (1800 for food), poor food, not very clean; more basic; **E** *Aída*, friendly, rec, but little privacy, more expensive rooms more secure and mosquito-proof, all rooms with bath and fan, Mexican food (good fish).

• **Transport** Frequent VW minibuses from Acapulco or Pie de la Cuesta, US$0.55.

ROUTES If driving, take Route 200, direction Zihuatanejo. If heading towards Mexico City, it is better to go via Acapulco, from where there is a new, fast toll-road to Chilpancingo, than via Ciudad Altamirano, see page 356. Highway 200, between Tecomán and Acapulco, has many badly potholed stretches.

A couple of km SE of El Carrizal is **El Morro** on an unpaved road between the ocean and the lagoon: the waves on the ocean side are very strong, while swimming in the lagoon is excellent. El Morro is a small fishing village (carp) reminiscent of African townships as it is constructed entirely of *palapa* (palm-leaf and wood). Every other house is a 'fish-restaurant'; ask for bungalow rental (F), no running water but there is a toilet, mosquito nets on requests. One shop sells basic provisions; fruit and vegetables from Coyuca may be available. At El Morro you can rent a canoe for US$2/hr and sail down river, past El Carrizal; you can also go up river to the lagoon, an all day trip, very beautiful with plenty of birdlife. Minibuses run Coyuca-El Carrizal-El Morro.

San Jerónimo, 83 km from Acapulco, has an 18th century parish church, you can make canoe trips up river to restaurants; **Técpan de Galeana**, 108 km from Acapulco, is a fishing village. 10 km N of Técpan is a turn-off to another El Carrizal, which is 7 km from the Pacific Highway. There is some public transport from Técpan, but plenty of cars go there (the road is rough). Very little accommodation, but plenty of hammock space; there is a beautiful beach and lagoon and the place is very friendly. There is a beach further on at **Cavaquito** where a series of small rivers join the ocean and there is a large variety of birds and dense vegetation; three restaurants offer fish dishes, there is a reasonable modern hotel, *Club Papánoa*, with lovely views and a camping site; a cheaper, nameless hotel with restaurant on the beach, **E**; and one can also visit the lovely bay of Papanóa.

ZIHUATANEJO

(*Pop* 22,000) A beautiful fishing port and expensive, commercialized tourist resort 237 km NW of Acapulco by the paved Route 200, which continues via Barra de Navidad along the Pacific coast to Puerto Vallarta (see page 185). This road goes through coconut plantations where you can buy *tuba*, a drink made from coconut milk fermented on the tree, only slightly alcoholic.

Places of interest

Despite being spruced up, 'Zihua', as it is called locally, still retains much of its Mexican village charm. There is an Indian handicraft market by the church, some beachside cafés and a small **Museo Arqueológico**, in the old Customs and Immigration building on Av 5 de Mayo (entry US$0.70). At sunset thousands of swallows meet in the air above the local cinema in the centre of town and settle for the night within 1 min on the telephone poles. The *plaza de toros* is at the town entrance with seasonal *corridas*.

Beaches There are 5 beaches in the bay, including Playa de la Madera, near town and a bit dirty; better is Playa de la Ropa, 20 mins' walk from centre, with the *Sotavento* and other hotels, and some beach restaurants. Also good is Las Gatas beach, secluded, a haven for aquatic sports which can be reached by boat from the centre (US$2 return) or a 20 mins' walk from La Ropa beach over fishermen-frequented rocks (the boat is much safer, muggings on the path have occurred). Watch out for coconuts falling off the trees! Off the coast there are rock formations, to which divers go, and Isla Ixtapa, a nature reserve with numerous restaurants. Playa Linda is a beautiful beach (no hotels) easily reached by collectivo (30 mins). The yacht, *Fandango Zihua*, takes bay cruises from the municipal pier.

Local information
● Accommodation

Difficult to find accommodation in Mar, and around Christmas/New Year.

L1 *Villa del Sol*, Playa La Ropa, T 42239, F 4758, Apdo 84, no children under 12 in high season, very expensive but highly regarded;

Fiesta Mexicana, Playa La Ropa, T 43776, F 43738, a/c, satellite TV, fine views, pool, restaurant, bar.

A1 *Catalina* and *Sotavento*, Playa de la Ropa, T 42032, F 42975, 105 steps to hotel, same facilities; **A1** *Irma*, Playa la Madera, T 42025, F 43738, good hotel but not best location.

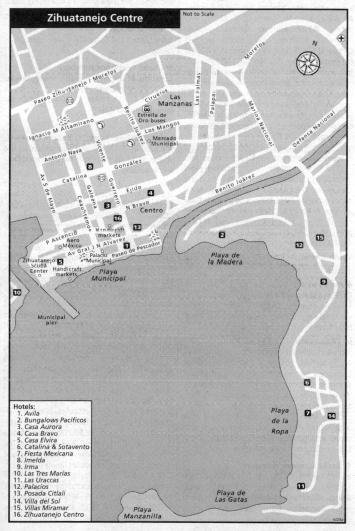

Zihuatanejo Centre

Not to Scale

N

Paseo Zihuatanejo / Morelos

Ignacio M Altamirano

Antonio Nava

Catalina

Av 5 de Mayo

Galeana

Cuauhtémoc

Vicente

Guerrero

Gonzáles

Ejido

N Bravo

Centro

Benito Juárez

Ciruelos

Las Manzanas

Estrella de Oro buses

Los Mangos

Mercado Municipal

Las Palmas

Palapa

Morelos

Marina Nacional

Defensa Nacional

Benito Juárez

8

3

16

13

4

2

12

15

9

Handicraft markets

P Ascencio Aero México

Av Gral J N Alvarez

Palacio Municipal

Paseo de Pescador

Zihuatanejo Scuba Center

Handicraft markets

5

1

Playa Municipal

10

Municipal pier

Playa de la Madera

Playa de la Ropa

6

7

14

11

Playa de Las Gatas

Playa Manzanilla

Hotels:
1. *Avila*
2. *Bungalows Pacíficos*
3. *Casa Aurora*
4. *Casa Bravo*
5. *Casa Elvira*
6. *Catalina & Sotavento*
7. *Fiesta Mexicana*
8. *Imelda*
9. *Irma*
10. *Las Tres Marías*
11. *Las Uraccas*
12. *Palacios*
13. *Posada Citlali*
14. *Villa del Sol*
15. *Villas Miramar*
16. *Zihuatanejo Centro*

M24a

B *Bungalows Pacíficos*, T 42112, highly rec, advance reservation necessary; **B** *Las Uraccas*, Playa La Ropa, T 42049, cooking facilities, good value; **B** *Palacios*, T 42055, good, on Playa de la Madera.

Several other hotels along Playa de la Madera, try **A2** *Villas Miramar*, T 42106, F 42149, suites, pool, lovely gardens, rec. Central hotels: **A3** *Avila*, Juan N Alvarez 8, T 42010, a/c, phone; **A3** *Zihuatanejo Centro*, Agustín Ramírez 2, T 42669, bright rooms, a/c, rec; **C** *Posada Citlali*, Vicente Guerrero 3, T 42043; **D** *Las Tres Marías*, C La Noria 4, T 42191, cross the wooden footbridge, very pleasant with large communal balconies overlooking town and harbour, clean but sparely decorated, tiny baths, nice plants, hotel has an annex on C Juan Alvarez 52, part of restaurant, similar rooms and tariffs, best on 2nd floor, note that price doubles during Christmas holidays; **E** *Casa Elvira* hotel-restaurant, on Juan N Alvarez, T 42061, in older part of town on waterfront, very basic but clean, fan, with bath, the restaurant is on the beach front (*the* place to watch the world go by), good and reasonable; **D-E** *Casa La Playa*, on Juan N Alvarez, similar to *Elvira*, but not as good; **D** *Casa Aurora*, N Bravo 27, clean with bath and fan, not all rooms have hot water, and **D** *Casa Bravo*, T 42528; **C** *Imelda*, Catalina González 11, T 43199, clean, rec, no restaurant.

Youth hostel: Av Paseo de las Salinas s/n, CP 40880, T 44662.

● **Places to eat**

On Playa la Ropa: *La Perla* (very popular, good food, slow service), *Elvira* (by *Hotel Sotavento*, small, attentive service, good value) and *Rossy* (good, live music at weekends).

In Zihuatanejo: many inc *El Patio*, excellent food and atmosphere, beautiful patio/garden, live music occasionally; *Il Piccolo*, restaurant and video bar, excellent value, good pizzas; *Gitano's*, *Coconuts* (good atmosphere, pricey, dinner only, rec), *La Marina* (popular, rec). *Puntarenas*, close to *Hotel Las Tres Marías*, excellent cooking, friendly, not expensive, popular, slow service. *Stall 27* at marketplace is very popular, cheap and good. Try local lobster for about US$10; most meals cost US$6 or over.

● **Banks & money changers**

Banca Serfín will change TCs at lower commission than in banks in hotel district; **Banco Mexícana**, on same street, has good rates; **Banamex**; **Bancomer**. Several *casas de cambio*.

● **Sports**

Scuba diving: hire of all equipment and guide from Zihuatanejo Scuba Center, T 42147, English spoken. Off Playa de las Gatas is an underwater wall built, according to legend, by the Tarascan king Calzonzin, to keep the sharks away while he bathed; the wall is fairly massive and can be seen clearly while scuba diving. Many fish too. US$3 a day for mask, snorkel and fins.

● **Tourist offices**

Tourist Office and Complaints, see under Ixtapa, below.

● **Useful telephone numbers**

Customs at airport: T 43262; **Immigration**: T 42795; **Ministerio Público**: (to report a crime), T 42900; **Police**: T 42040; **Red Cross**: (ambulances), T 42009.

● **Transport**

Local Car hire: Hertz, N Bravo and airport, T 43050 or F 42255; also with offices at the airport and in Ixtapa hotels: **Avis**, **Budget**, **Dollar**, **Economy**.

Air Ixtapa/Zihuatanejo international airport (ZIH), 20 km from town, T 42070/42100. Many flights from Mexico City and others from Chihuahua, Ciudad Juárez, Durango, Guadalajara, Monterrey and Torreón, and, in the USA, Atlanta, Detroit, Greenville/Spartanburg, Houston, Los Angeles, Minneapolis, St Louis and San Francisco. Other destinations via Mexico City. AeroMéxico, T 42018/32208/09; Delta (airport), T 43386/686; Mexicana, *Hotel Dorado Pacífico*, Ixtapa, T 32208-10.

Buses Estrella de Oro operates its own terminal on Paseo Palmar, serving, Acapulco and **Mexico City**; to the capital 0830, 1130, 1930 (with stops), US$24.20, direct (no stops) at 2000; 'Diamante' (wider seats, movie, stewardesses serving free drinks) non-stop 2100, arriving 0600, US$50; *plus* (wider seats, non-stop) 2200 arriving 0700, US$33. To **Lázaro Cárdenas** at 0600, 1500 and 1900, US$3.65, 2 hrs. Direct to **Acapulco** 0600, US$8, *plus* at 1630.

The Central de Autobuses is on the Zihuatanejo-Acapulco highway opp Pemex station (bus from centre US$0.20); 3 lines operate from here, all using good, 32-seater buses. The terminal is clean, with several snackbars. Estrella Blanca: to Mexico City almost hourly from 0600-2130, US$24.20; to Lázaro Cárdenas daily, for connections further N and to the interior, US$4; to **Manzanillo**, US$15, 9 hrs; to **Acapulco**, US$9; to **Laredo** at 1730, 30 hrs, US$65. Blancas Fronterea to Mexico City 2100 or 2200,

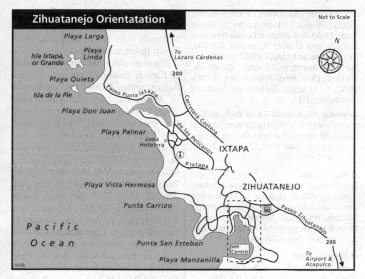

Zihuatanejo Orientatation

Not to Scale

Playa Larga

Isla Ixtapa, or Grande

Playa Linda

To Lázaro Cárdenas

Playa Quieta

Isla de la Pie

Playa Don Juan

Playa Palmar

Zona Hotelera

IXTAPA

P Ixtapa

Playa Vista Hermosa

ZIHUATANEJO

Punta Carrizo

Paseo Zihuatanejo

Pacific Ocean

Punta San Esteban

see Centre

200

Playa Manzanilla

To Airport & Acapulco

US$33 (direct) to Acapulco 0100, 0900 and 1700, US$10.65; to Lázaro Cárdenas 4 a day, US$4.75, to Puerto Escondido and Huatulco 2130, US$34. Cuauhtémoc serves all towns between Zihuatanejo and Acapulco almost half hourly from 0400 to 2000. To Acapulco, Líneas Unidas del Sur, US$8, leave hourly, rec. The old Central de Autobuses is half a block from the new; old buses use it, with erratic service to Mexico City via the less-used dangerous road through Altamirano (to be avoided it possible, robberies).

By **car** from Mexico City via the Toluca-Zihuatanejo highway (430 km) or via the Acapulco-Zihuatanejo highway (405 km). To Acapulco can be done in 3½ hrs, but sometimes takes 6 hrs. To Lázaro Cárdenas, 103 km, takes 3½ hrs, the road is very bad.

IXTAPA

From Zihuatanejo one can drive 7 km or take a bus (US$0.30) or taxi (US$5, colectivo, US$1) to **Ixtapa**, 'where there are salt lakes' (*Pop* 32,000). The resort, developed on a large scale, boasts 14 beaches: La Hermosa, Del Palmar, Don Juan de Dios, Don Juan, Don Rodrigo, Cuata, Quieta, Oliveiro, Linda, Larga, Carey, Pequeña, Cuachalate and Varadero. There are turtles, many

species of shellfish and fish, and pelicans at El Morro de los Pericos, which can be seen by launch. There is an island a few metres off Quietas beach; boats go over at a cost of US$5. Ixtapa has 10 large luxury hotels and a *Club Méditerranée* (all obtain food-supplies from Mexico City making food more expensive, as local supplies aren't guaranteed); a shopping complex, golf course, water-ski/parachute skiing and tennis courts. There is a yacht marina and an 18-hole golf club, Palma Real. Isla Grande has been developed as a nature park and leisure resort. **NB** The beach can be dangerous with a strong undertow; small children should not be allowed in the sea unaccompanied. Also, there are crocodiles in the beautiful lagoons at the end of the beach.

Local information

● Accommodation

All in L2-A3 range: *Westin Resort Ixtapa*, T 32121, F 31091, spectacular, in a small jungle; *Krystal*, highly rec, book in advance, T 30333, F 30216; *Dorado Pacífico*, T 32025, F 30126, *Sheraton*, Blvd Ixtapa, T 31858, F 32438, with panoramic lift, reductions for AAA members, rec; *Stouffer Presidente*, T (753) 30018, F 32312; *Aristos*, T 31505, the first to open in Ixtapa; **L3-A1** *Best Western Posada Real*, next to *Carlos and Charlie's Restaurant*, T 31745, F 31805; *Fontan Ixtapa*, T 30003; *Holiday Inn SunSpree Resort*, Blvd Ixtapa, T 800-09346, F 31991. *Club Med*, Playa Quieta, T 743-30742, F 743-30393. Taxi between centre and main hotels, US$3.

Camping: *Playa Linda Trailer Park*, on Carretera Playa Linda at *Playa Linda Hotel*, just N of Ixtapa, 50 spaces, full hook-ups, restaurant, recreation hall, baby sitters, on beach, US$14 for 2, comfortable.

● **Places to eat**
Besides those in every hotel, there are many others, inc *Villa de la Selva*, rec for food and views, book in advance, T 30362; *El Sombrero*, Mexican, very good; *Montmartre* (French), *Onyx*, *Bogart's* (opp *Hotel Krystal*), *Gran Tapa*, all more costly than in Zihuatanejo.

● **Entertainment**
Nightclubs: every hotel without exception has at least one nightclub/disco and two bars.

● **Tourist offices**
In Ixtapa Shopping Plaza, T 31967/68.

● **Transport**
NB for motorists: although paved Highway 134 leads directly from Mexico City and Toluca to Ixtapa, there is no fuel or other supplies after **Ciudad Altamirano** (188 km, pleasant motel on SW edge of city, C with a/c). This road also runs through remote country, prone to landslides, and there is occasional bandit activity, with unpredictable army check-points (looking for guns and drugs). It is not recommended for non-Spanish speaking, or lone motorists.

The coastal route continues NW to Lázaro Cárdenas and Playa Azul in Michoacán (see page 227).

COAST EAST OF ACAPULCO

Highway 200, E from Acapulco along the coast, is paved all the way to Puerto Escondido; this stretch is known as the Costa Chica. There is a bridge missing about 55 km from Acapulco, near Playa Barra Vieja on the road past the airport along the coast. It is better to take the parallel inland road to San Marcos (**D** *Hotel San Marcos*, clean, restaurant, pool). This road, which is windy, hilly and with few services and little traffic, has been reported dangerous due to bandit hold ups of lone cars, check locally before driving this route.

Further along the coast is Copala (**F** *Casa de Huéspedes*, not rec), 123 km from Acapulco. Another 19 km brings you to **Marquelia**, with excellent beaches about 3 km from town (transport well nigh impossible, taxi US$6); there are no hotels, but you can spend the night in a hammock in one of the little restaurants on the beach (US$3 per night). The restaurant owners will look after luggage, but keep an eye on it anyway. Very good seafood, about US$5 per meal. Bus to Puerto Escondido US$7.35, 5-6 hrs, very full coming from Acapulco. Another 65 km brings you to **Cuajinicuilapa** (**F** *Hotel Marín*, clean, restaurant, rec), from where it is an hour's *colectivo* ride to **Faro**, US$1.50. Last one leaves at about 1800. Faro (on Punta Maldonado) is a beautiful beach, unspoilt and clean. Simple hotel (**F**) right on beach, authentic fishing village, several huts serving food (check prices before ordering). From Cuajinicuilapa it is 51 km to **Santiago Pinotepa Nacional**.

"From Pinotepa Nacional you can visit the Mixtec Indian village of **Pinotepa de Don Luis** by *camioneta*. These leave from the side street next to the church in Pinotepa Nacional, taking a dirt road to Don Luis (last one back to Pinotepa Nacional at 1300, or wait till next morning, nowhere to stay). The women there weave beautiful and increasingly rare sarong-like skirts (*chay-ay*), some of which are dyed from the purple of sea snails. Also, half-gourds incised with various designs and used both as caps and cups can be found. The *ferias* of Don Luis (20 Jan) and nearby San Juan Colorado (29-30 Nov) are worth attending for the dancing and availability of handicrafts." (Dale Bricker, Seattle.)

● **Accommodation D** *Hotel Carmona*, restaurant, good value but poor laundry service, parking; **D** *Massiel*; **E** *Tropical*, fan, clean, large rooms, quiet, parking.

PUERTO ESCONDIDO

(*Pop* 25,000; *Phone code* 958) **Puerto Escondido**, 144 km SE of Pinotepa Nacional, is on a beautiful bay almost due S of Oaxaca, very touristy for much of the year, good surfing. Palm trees line the beach, which is not too clean. The expansion of the SE end of town, 'to make it the next Acapulco' (in the words of one developer) is well-advanced. Many visitors are disappointed by the high costs and the commercialization in the main part of the town. There are, however, a number of beaches to visit and villages close by. 15 mins by taxi or bus to the W is Manialtepec, with a lagoon, wild birds (Canadian ornithologist Michael Malone recommended for guided tours, US$35 approx), and watersports such as water skiing; the village has rivers and hot springs. Villages inland include San Pedro and San Gabriel Mixtepec on the direct road to Oaxaca and, just-off this road, Santa Catarina Juquila, with a sanctuary. A trip to **Lagunas de Chacahua** is recommended. The excursion goes through mangroves and there are many birds to watch. Available through travel agencies in town. Recommended guide is Ana Márquez, located in Cooperative boating office, Av Marinero Principal, tours from US$15 a day.

Beaches

Next to the Bahía Principal is Playa Marinero, with small bars, restaurants and handicrafts market. Further SE is Zicatela, good for surfing. 2 km W of the centre is Puerto Angelito, recommended by locals as a safe and clean beach. Launches take passengers from the bay in Puerto Escondido, US$3.50 pp for max 10, or taxi US$2. At Manzanillo, with a small creek, is a coral reef and tropical fish; access to the beach on foot only.

NB There can be dangerous waves, and the cross-currents are always dangerous; non-swimmers should not bathe except in the bay on which the town stands. Also, a breeze off the sea makes the sun seem less strong than it is, be careful. Do not stray too far along the beach; armed robbery by groups of 3-5 (or rape) is becoming more and more frequent, even in daylight, take as little cash and valuables as possible, US$ sought after. Also at La Barra beach 10 km away. Be alert for dogs.

Local information
● Accommodation
Very crowded during Holy Week; prices rise on 1 Nov because of the local Fiesta de Noviembre. Most hotels are on the beach, little air-conditioning. Many cheaper hotels have no hot water and cheap *cabañas* are often full of mosquitoes.

L3-A1 *Best Western Posada Real* (ex-*Bugambilias*), Blvd Benito Juárez II, T 20133, F 20192, about 2½ km from town, off road to Acapulco, very pleasant, lovely gardens, pool, path to beach, attentive, a/c, good service, food inc (à la carte, also lobster).

A3 *Paraíso Escondido*, Unión 1, T 20444, noisy a/c, not on beach (up the hill almost all the way to the Crucero) but with own swimming pool, rec, clean, colonial style, in summer when not full bar and restaurant open according to demand.

B *Bungalows Barlovento*, very comfortable, highly rec, but a little way out of town and not advisable to walk there at night; **B** *Cabañas Zikatela*, on Zicatela beach, large clean rooms with fan and mini-fridge, swimming pool, bar service, small restaurant serving breakfast and cheese burgers; **B** *El Rincón del Pacífico*, Pérez Gasca 900, T 20056, very popular, always full, on beach, with restaurant, hot water; **B** *Loren*, Pérez Gasca 507, T 20448, clean, friendly, safe, rec; **B** *Hotel Santa Fe*, Carretera Costera, on beach at N end of bay, noisy a/c, restaurant expensive but very good food.

C *Casa Blanca*, Pérez Gasca, middle of beach, with fan and hot water, clean and well-furnished, balconies, pool; **C** *Margot's*, 30m S of the pedestrian zone in the centre, nice big rooms, good, cheap food; **C** *Nayar*, Pérez Gasca 407, T 20113, big rooms, views, pool, TV, some with bath and fan, more expensive with a/c, hot water, restaurant, safe parking; **C** *Rocamar*, Pérez Gasca 601, T 20339, by beach, upper rooms a/c and balconies, fans, hot water, restaurant, rec.

D *Alderete*, opp bus station, with private bath; **D** *Art and Harry's*, on oceanfront, free board use, great barbecues, good food; **D** *Bungalows*

Villa Marinero, on Marinero beach, can also be reached from the main road to Zicatela, own cooking possible, friendly, kitchen/eating area, pool; **D** *Cabañas San Diego*, down a sand road just before bridge on road to Puerto Angel, safe, nice grounds but few facilities; **D** *Central*, 2 mins uphill from bus terminal, clean, friendly; **D** *La Posada Económica*, one big dormitory, attached to restaurant, but also runs hotel across the road, ask for a room opp the flat, good *huachinango*; **D** *Ribera del Mar*, behind Iglesia de la Soledad, uphill, fan, quiet, no hot water, laundry facilities, cheaper for longer stays, rec; **D** *San Juan*, downhill from bus station, some rooms with seaview, English spoken, fair, small, enclosed car park, 2-3 cars; **D-E** *Castillo del Rey*, Av Pérez Gasca, T 20442, nr beach, clean, nice rooms, hot water, quiet, good beds, friendly, good value, highly rec.

E *Alojamiento Las Cabañas* has dormitories with bunks, on main road (S side), friendly, very nice, food is good, you will be charged for all beds regardless of whether they are occupied, unless you share the cabin; *Cabañas Cocoa Beach*, in the town nr the church, US$4.50/cabin (6 or 7 available), mosquito nets, cold shower, family-run; **E** *Cabañas Cortés*, for small, basic huts or large, basic huts, in all cases, take mosquito nets; **E** *Casa de Huéspedes Las Dos Costas*, fairly clean, acceptable for budget travellers. Lots of bungalows and *cabañas* at S end of the beach; **E** *Real del Mar*, nr bus station (cheaper for longer stays), bath, no hot water, clean, nice view.

F *Acuario*, on Zicatela beach, shared bath, some with bath more expensive, pool, gym, scuba diving centre, rec; **F** *Mayflower*, just off Pérez Gasca (pedestrian street) on Andador Libertad, T 20367, T 20422, shared rooms with fans, communal bathrooms, some more expensive rooms, **D**.

Apartments: *La Maison*, Andador Puerto Juárez C, Lomas de Puerto, Box 243, Puerto Escondido, Oax 71980, F 958-20612 'para entregar a Pierre', 1 room (shared kitchen and patio), 3 apartments for 2, 3 and 5 people, with kitchen, all with bath, hot water, rates from US$180 for 2 to US$480 for 5/week, high season (Christmas/New Year, Easter and 15 July to 31 Aug), low season US$130-370, reductions for long stays.

Camping: if camping, beware of clothes being stolen. *Carrizalillo Trailer Park*, nr old airport on W side of town (follow signs from Tourist Office), on cliff top with path leading down to secluded beach, bathroom, cold showers, laundry facilities, swimming pool and bar, very pleasant, prices from US$8 to US$20 for 2 plus car depending on location and whether you have hook-up. *Neptuno* campsite for vehicles, tents and hammocks on water front in centre of town, vehicles and tents accepted, swimming pool, electricity, cold showers, US$10/car with 2 people, rather rundown and noisy; next door is *Las Palmas* (better), about US$10 for 2 plus car, US$5 for tent, clean bathrooms, shade, rec. *Hotel Playa Azul* has a constricted trailer park (not very convenient for large vehicles), access from a side road, has a good swimming pool.

● **Places to eat**
Many restaurants on main street, Pérez Gasca, eg: *Lolys*, cheap and good, try *pescado a la parrilla*, with sweet onion sauce, and lemon pie after; *San Angel* for fish; *La Galería*, Italian, good pizzas but pricey; *Extacea*, good cheap meals and live music; *7 Regiones*, good for very late night tacos and frijoles; *La Estancia*, good, warm service, but expensive; *La Sardino de Plata*, popular; *Hermann's*, main street, good, cheap; S end of main street is *Mario's Pizzaland*, excellent pizzas at reasonable prices, friendly; *Lisa's Restaurant*, nice location on beach (just off Carretera Costera) good food, also has rooms to let, D off season, with fan, very clean, safe deposit, highly rec; *Los Crotos*, also on the beach, good and varied food at reasonable prices, good service, rec; *El Tiburón*, on beach, corner of Felipe Merbelín, lots of good food for US$2-3; *Cappuccino*, Pérez Gasca, good coffee, fruit salads, some dishes pricey. Good *licuados* at *Bambú Loco*, also fish. *Las Palapas*, good, it is just over the stream (sewer) on the right. *Carmen's*, on a path from beach to main road to Zicatela, great pastries baked on the premises, also second-hand books and magazines; *Pepe's*, great sandwiches. *Alícia*, in town, best value but be careful with seafood. Food is good quality, but very expensive nr the beach. *El Cafecito*, next door to *Acuario* *cabañas* on Zicatela beach, excellent breakfasts *pain au chocolat* made with Swiss chocolate, highly rec, and next along is *Bruno's*, with "starving surfer" meals of rice, frijoles, and tortillas for US$2, popular place for watching sunsets.

● **Banks & money changers**
Bancomer, Pérez Gasca, open 0900-1200 slow service, no commission; Banamex, open 0900-1330. *Casa de cambio*, on Pérez Gasca open till 2000, poor rates.

● Entertainment

Discos: *Tubo*, on the beach; *El Son y La Rumba*, opp, live salsa daily; *Tequila Bum-Bum* (pronounced Boom-Boom), downtown, international crowd, varied music, open air; *Bacocho*, popular with locals, Mexican pop, indoors.

Video bar: *Bartly*, regular screenings of films and videos, upstairs area with hammocks, candle-lit, gives out wax crayons to encourage budding artists to doodle on the paper table cloths.

● Hospitals & medical services

Dr Francisco Serrano Severiano, opp Banpeco, speaks English, 0900-1300, 1700-2000. *Farmacia La Moderna*, Av Pérez Gasca 203, T 20214, open 24 hrs.

● Shopping

Small selection of foreign language books at *Papi's*, souvenir shop 3 doors from Mercado de Artesanías, buy or swap. Local crafts best not bought from vendors on the beach, but in the non-gringo part of town up the hill nr where the buses stop.

● Transport

Air Airport (PXM) 10 mins' drive from town, orange juice and coffee sold. Puerto Escondido-Mexico City, with Mexicana (T 20098) 5 days a week, non-stop. Puerto Escondido-Oaxaca, see under Oaxaca **Air**. Taxis to centre in VW combis, US$2.25 pp, Colectivos Combi, T 20030.

Road The best route between Puerto Escondido and Oaxaca is via San Pedro Pochutla, using the coast road 200 and Route 175 inland. Bus drivers on the paved route have a radio for checking road conditions. The direct highway to Oaxaca is being upgraded. Don't take a stopping bus to Oaxaca on the direct road as robberies have been reported.

Buses To Oaxaca, 3 a day (inc overnight), US$11.50 1st class, US$18.75 *plus* with Trans Oaxaca-Pacífico (direct), advertised as 7 hrs' trip, but can take up to 17 hrs; also Estrella del Valle (1st class, from 2nd class terminal); Auto Transportes Oaxaca-Pacífico, via Pochutla, 10-18 hrs (depending on roadworks), leaves at 0700, 2nd class, 2300 1st class; all have bookable seats. Puerto Escondido-**Pochutla**, for Puerto Angel, several hourly from 0500 to 2000, about 1 hr, US$2, and on to **Salina Cruz**, Oaxaca-Pacífico company rec. The road to Salina Cruz is now paved (bus US$9.75, about 7 a day, 10 hrs). Bus to **Acapulco**, US$15.65, Flecha Roja (nr La Solteca terminal), at least 7½ hrs, not exciting. The 1030 bus stops for 2 hrs' lunch at Pinotepa, book tickets at least 1 day in advance. First bus

to Acapulco at 0400, hourly up to 2100 thereafter. Transportes Gacela has 3 direct buses a day to Acapulco at 1030, 1330 and 2300, only 2 short stops. The road is in bad condition. To/from **Mexico City** US$38.35 1st class, US$40.35 *plus*. To **Tehuantepec**, go to Salina Cruz and change there; 2 direct buses a day to **San Cristóbal de las Casas**, US$21.

POCHUTLA

San Pedro Pochutla is the crossroads of Route 175 from Oaxaca, Route 200 from Acapulco to Salina Cruz and a 10-km road to Puerto Angel and the beaches. It is therefore important for bus connections. At Pochutla there is a prison; you can buy black coral necklaces made by prisoners very cheaply (but remember that black coral is an endangered species); they make and sell other handicrafts. Take vitamins or other useful small items to trade or give away. Leave documents and valuables outside (an 'interesting, eye-opening, if noisy, shopping trip').

● **Accommodation** A3 *Costa del Sol*, on main street nr the market, with a/c, C with ceiling fan, credit cards, bar, restaurant; D *Hotel Izala*, on main street (Lázaro Cárdenas) nr plaza, shower, fan, clean comfortable; D *San Juan*, with bath, good view, pleasant; E *Puchutla*, on Plaza, entrance on side street; E *Posada Sta Cruz*, opp bus stop to Oaxaca, OK for 1 night; F/a *Tropical*, on La Constitución, by prison, basic. Excellent ice-cream factory.

● **Banks & money changers** Bancomer, only 0930-1100, exchanges AmEx and Visa TCs but only US$100 pp a day; Banamex handles AmEx and Mastercard. Banks here sometimes run out of money, so best not to rely on them.

● **Hospitals & medical services** There is a hospital outside Pochutla, US$2 for a consultation, medicines free. There is also a private doctor in Puerto Angel, but he charges US$17 minimum for a consultation, and it is hard to find him home.

● **Useful services** A **post office**. Snorkel equipment can be bought in Pochutla.

● **Transport** Hourly bus to **Salina Cruz** (US$5, 4 hrs), to which a new road is finished (occasionally closed by landslides). Pochutla-**Puerto Angel**, same regular service as for **Zipolite**, below; alternatively take a colectivo, or taxi, US$2.50, 30 mins. Pochutla-**Oaxaca**, either direct, on a paved, winding road (a safer route than Puerto Escondido-Oaxaca) from 0500-2300, 5-9 hrs, US$8 (Estrella del Valle, 1st class), 1st class not always available, 2nd class US$6, 5 hrs (Oaxaca-Pacífico). San José del Pacífico is a pleasant stop on the way, with good restaurant; or via Salina Cruz, US$13.25, 8 hrs (2nd class US$6). The bus service between Pochutla and **Puerto Escondido** (US$1, several every hour from 0500 to 2000, 1¼ hrs) links with the bus to Puerto Angel. Bus Pochutla-**San Cristóbal de las Casas** at 1000 and 2200, 12-15 hrs, 1st class (Cristóbal Colón, US$23, bus starts at Puerto Escondido so very few seats available in Pochutla, book in advance if possible), goes via **Huatulco, Salina Cruz, Tehuantepec** and **Tuxtla Gutiérrez**; to **Acapulco** at 2200 direct, 1st class, 12 hrs, US$20. Estrella Blanca run an hourly bus to **Acapulco**, US$17, 8 hrs.

PUERTO ANGEL

Puerto Angel is a coffee port on the Pacific with a good, popular beach, 69 km from Puerto Escondido, 240 km from Oaxaca, with road connection but no direct buses; all services involve change at Pochutla. It is 6-7 hrs by bus from Oaxaca, see under Oaxaca **Buses**. Just before Puerto Angel, a dirt road leads left to some small bays which have no people, are good for snorkelling, but can have dangerous waves. Playa del Panteón has been recommended as a relaxing place to stay with good restaurants.

In Puerto Angel take care of your belongings, but, more important, take extra care in the sea, the currents are very dangerous. The sea water is said to be polluted from animals on the beach, 'immediate stomach problems' reported. Lots of dogs everywhere. Scuba diving is possible with *Hotel La Cabaña* on Playa del Panteón. Experienced instructors, up-to-date equipment, English spoken, PADI services available, T (958) 43116.

Local festivals 1 October.

● **Accommodation** On a hill away from the beach, **B** *Angel del Mar*, fan, dirty, run down, good view; **C** *Buena Vista*, nice rooms up hill, clean, relaxing but not very friendly; **D** *El Rincón Sabroso*, beautiful views, clean, quiet, friendly,

no hot water; **D** *La Cabaña*, nr the *Cañón de Vata*, fan, free coffee in morning, clean, friendly owner, no restaurant, rec; **D-E** *Hotel Soraya*, fan, bath, very clean (changes dollars and TCs), unfriendly; **E** *Capis*, clean rooms, cold water, fan, excellent food, rec; **E** *Anahi*, on road to *Angel del Mar*, with fan, Indonesian-style wash basins; **E** *Casa de Huéspedes Gladys*, just above *Soraya*, balcony, fine views, clean, rec, owner can prepare food, no hot water; **F** *Casa de Huéspedes Leal*, shared bath, washing facilities, friendly, rec; **F** *Familiar*, clean, friendly, fan; **E** *Casa de Huéspedes Gundi y Tomás* (Gundi and Tomás López), without bath, clean, or hammocks (**G**), popular with travellers, will store luggage, good value, snacks and breakfast (US1.50-3), sells food and beverages, often rec; Gundi also runs *Pensión El Almendro*, with café (good ice-cream) and library; similar is the **D** *Pensión Puesta del Sol*, run by Harald and Maria Faerber (suite more expensive), very friendly, English and German spoken, excellent restaurant, on road to Playa Panteón, clean, rec; 50m along is **E** *Casa de Huéspedes Copy*, great rooms; **D** *Posada Cañón de Vata*, on Playa Panteón, Apdo Postal 74, Pochutla 70900, clean but dark, lovely setting, booked continuously, popular with Americans, quite good restaurant, mainly vegetarian. Possible to sleep on beach away from the naval base and soldiers who will move you on. **Estacahuite**, a beautiful, clean beach, 1 km from town, 20 mins' walk, has cabins (beware of jelly fish on the beach). There is a hut at the beach selling beer and fries, and it lends snorkelling gear. **Camping**: there is a campsite half way between Puerto Angel and Pochutla, very friendly, driveway is too steep for large vehicles, US$8.50 for two in camper van, rec.

● **Places to eat** An excellent restaurant at *Villa Valencia* hotel, charming place, good food if a bit pricey. Good restaurant *Capís* (has 10 rooms above). *Beto's* restaurant, just up hill on road to Zipolite, 5 mins' walk from centre, good fish (fresh tuna) and cheap beer; *Mar y Sol*, cheap, good seafood; *Sirenita*, popular for breakfasts, and bar, friendly; *Cangrejito*, by Naval base gate, popular bar, also good breakfasts and excellent tacos. Many fish restaurants along the main street. Two restaurants by fishing harbour used by locals, cheap.

● **Post & telecommunication Post Office**: for post office, go to Customs office; for other services go to Pochutla (eg exchange). **Telephone**: long distance phone next to *Soraya* at Telmex, open 0800-2200.

ZIPOLITE

4 km W (30 mins' walk) is the lovely but dangerous **Zipolite** beach (name means 'the killing beach', according to legend; several drownings a month). It is dangerous for bathing if you swim behind the waves or when the tide changes. It may be the last nude beach in Mexico (only at the far end), but do not walk to the beach at night, packs of dogs have attacked people. As far as personal safety goes, the eastern end is safer than the western end, it is also quieter. It has much less of a Mexican atmosphere than Puerto Angel, but is very popular with travellers.

● **Accommodation & places to eat** Places to stay are usually either basic or overpriced. Hammock spot and vegetarian restaurant *Shambhala* run by Gloria, an American woman (30 mins' walk to far W end coming from Puerto Angel), F pp with hammock or US$10, wonderful views, basic, rustic, but no longer receiving the good reports it used to get; *Lo Cósmico*, just before *Shambhala*, cabañas and very good crêpes, open all year: hammocks for rent from Philippe at 'Gloria end' of the beach, US$1; also at 'Gloria end', *Cristóbal Cabañas*, family run, clean, good meals, E for room, E basic *cabaña*, US$1.65 for hammock, shared bathrooms; **E** *Roca Blanca*, friendly, helpful, hammock space US$1.40, good and cheap food, good service, also at W end; **E** *Cabañas El Tao*, 'rooms with a view', clean, friendly, shared bath, expensive breakfast; **G** pp *Lyoban's*, basic rooms, hammock space on 1st floor terrace, filling dishes served by family, table tennis; *Cabañas Montebello*, next to *La Puesta* bar, with hammocks, quiet and very clean, run by Luis and María; *Hamacas La Choza*, on way to *Shambhala*, with cheap restaurant but poor service, family atmosphere, hammocks to rent for under US$2/night, luggage store. *Cabañas Palapa del Pescador*, US$1.50 for hammock, US$7 for a *palapa*, fresh fish available, English and French spoken, use of kitchen, safe luggage store, next door is *Restaurant Genesis*, 3rd on beach, ask for rooms, E, clean, charming, helpful, good meals (ask for house on the hill). There is a campsite suitable for tents only, water and bathroom: follow paved road, then unpaved road for 1 km, then small road to the left. RVs can stay overnight in the parking lot,

but no facilities. Every hut on the beach is a fish restaurant with cold drinks and hammock space, US$2 pp but lots of mosquitoes. There are a couple of informal discos. At the E end of the beach is *Lola's*, great views along beach, excellent food, also rooms (E) without bath, fan, basic, clean; good pizzas at *Gemini Pizzas*; there is a good *Panadería* on the road behind the beach, through the green gate.

● **Transport** Bus service from Pochutla to Zipolite every 20 mins from 0600 to 1830, last bus back from Zipolite to Pochutla at 1900, US$0.70; fare to Puerto Angel US$0.35. Buses stop on the paved road behind the beach just after the 'Zipolite/Playa de los Muertos' sign. Taxi Puerto Angel-Zipolite, US$3.50 pp for any amount of passengers; to Pochutla US$5 (add US$3.50 to be taken to your *cabaña* door).

Several kilometres further up the coast is San Agustín beach, accessible by a path behind Shambhala (ask directions), beautiful, safe for swimming, with an extraordinary cave in the cliffs. Accommodation is now available (**F** for a room with shared toilet and shower, basic, dirty, but friendly; restaurant next to bus stop; hammock rental US$5). Beyond is Mazunte beach, with accommodation, **E-F**, and restaurant. There is also the Museo de la Tortuga (US$1.25, closed Mon). From here you can walk along the shore to more empty beaches. About 15 km from Zipolite on a dirt road is a sign to Ventanilla beach; follow the rough track until you find a thatched ranch and ask for Hilario Reyes. The beach is long and empty and there are 2 lagoons with fresh water. There are no cabins: you need your own tent (or hammock/ mosquito net). Ventanilla beach is also dangerous for bathing. Playa de Mina is 20 mins' walk from Zipolite towards Pochutla, turn right at the soccer pitch to the coast; it is 'a serene beach, paradise'.

HUATULCO

East of Puerto Angel (50 km, 1 hr) and 112 km W of Salina Cruz, on the coast road, is the new resort of **Huatulco** being built on about 34,000 ha around nine bays. Some estimate that it will surpass Cancún by the

Huatulco's legendary cross

The name Huatulco means 'place of the wood', which refers to a cross planted on the beach, legend tells, by Quetzalcoatl. After resisting efforts to pull it down, it was found to be only a few feet deep when dug up; small crosses were made from it. A more likely history of the cross is told by Michael Turner in his research into Francis Drake's voyages. Until the establishment of Acapulco as the departure point for the Spanish Pacific fleet, Huatulco (Guatulco) was the main port on the Pacific, its heyday being from about 1537 to 1574. Drake sacked the port on his voyage around the world (1577-80) and Thomas Cavendish raided it in 1587. Cavendish burnt the church to the ground, but the crucifix (La Santa Cruz) survived, thereafter being incorporated into the village's name. The Spanish viceroy ordered Huatulco's abandonment in 1616.

year 2000. Population in 1992 was 15,000 and growing as more hotels and businesses spring up. Santa María Huatulco, near the airport, is now the town for the construction workers, while Santa Cruz Huatulco, the original village, is destined to become an 'authentic Mexican village' for the tourists. There are 3 separate areas of development: Zona Hotelera on Tangolunda Bay, with 4 luxury hotels, Santa Cruz Bay with a hotel, 3 banks, a tourist market and boats for hire, and Crucecita, downtown, with 5 hotels, all C, all within 1 block W of Plaza Principal. There are also a number of shopping centres around Plaza La Crucecita, with *artesanías* and boutiques. *Colectivos*, US$0.20, and taxis connect the three areas. Great care is to be taken to blend the resort into the landscape: about 80% of the total area is to be set aside as a nature reserve.

Beaches

The nearest beach to Crucecita is Chahue Bay, about 3 km, dangerous undertow, better to go to the Zona Hotelera, about 6 km, which has a good beach. Other beaches are accessible by car or boat. *Lanchas* can be hired from Cooperativa Tangolunda for exploring the coves, US$10/day. Guided tours of the Bahías de Huatulco from the major hotels or from Agencia de Viajes García Rendón, Av

Alfonso Pérez Gasca, Puerto Escondido, T 20114.

Local information
● **Accommodation & places to eat**
Sheraton, T 958-10055, F 10335; *Royal Maeva*; *Holiday Inn Crowne Plaza*, Blvd Benito Juárez 8, T 928-10044, F 958-10221; and the *Club Méditerranée* (5-star, T 958-10033, F 958-10101; reservations are cheaper when made at head office in C Masaryk, Mexico City. *Suites Bugambilias*, T 70018, rec, clean); **D** *Grifer*, good accommodation, friendly. There are 18 restaurants, some overpriced, and many *comedores*. *Palma Real*, opp Cristóbal Colón bus terminal, rec.

Camping: there is a trailer park at Chahue (bathrooms, snackbar, but sites are quite stark).

● **Tourist offices**
On Av Guamuchl.

● **Transport**
Air The airport, Bahías de Huatulco (HUX), is 17 km from town, off the road to Pochutla, with daily, non-stop flights from Mexico City with Mexicana (T 70243, airport 42805) and other airlines. Also flights from Los Angeles (Mexicana), Monterrey (Mexicana), Oaxaca (Aerocaribe) and Salina Cruz.

Buses 3 bus companies; Gacela has direct buses to Acapulco at 0815 and 1315, and to Puerto Escondido at 1015. Several buses to Salina Cruz.

Mexico City to Guatemala

O UT OF A NUMBER of routes, we describe that through Oaxaca, a popular tourist town with many fine colonial buildings, markets, Indian traditions and, close by, several magnificent archaeological sites (Monte Albán, Mitla, and others). From Oaxaca, there is a coastal route to Guatemala and the more interesting Chiapas highland route. The main town of interest on the latter is San Cristóbal de Las Casas, which gives access to Maya villages, archaeological sites and lakes.

The National Railway runs daily from Mexico City to Tapachula, the border town. Taxi to Talismán, on the Guatemalan border, for bus to Guatemala City (also accessible from Puebla). There is a new bridge which links Ciudad Hidalgo with Tecún-Umán (formerly Ayutla) in Guatemala. Cristóbal Colón bus Mexico City-Guatemala City takes 23 hrs, with a change at the border to Rutas Lima. Mexico City-Tapachula, 20 hrs.

NB Motorists who know the area well advise that anyone driving from Mexico City to Tehuantepec should go via Orizaba-La Tinaja-Papaloapan-Tuxtepec-Palomares. This route is better than Veracruz-Acayucán and, if drivers are in a hurry, far preferable to the route which follows, via Izúcar de Matamoros and Oaxaca. Between Oaxaca and Tehuantepec the road, although paved throughout and in good condition, serpentines unendingly over the Sierras and is quite beautiful. But as the Oaxaca route is far more interesting and spectacular we describe it below. For the alternative journey through the Papaloapan region, see page 317.

Tolls Total road toll Mexico City – Oaxaca, US$8.35.

This road through southern Mexico is 1,355 km long. It can be done in 3 or 4 days' driving time. There are bus services from Mexico City along the route through Oaxaca to Tehuantepec and on to the Guatemalan frontier through San Cristóbal de Las Casas to Ciudad Cuauhtémoc or through Arriaga to Tapachula. A road now runs (still rough in places) from Paso Hondo near Ciudad Cuauhtémoc via Comalapa and Porvenir to Huixtla on the S road, and from Porvenir to Revolución Mexicana.

CUERNAVACA TO OAXACA

CUAUTLA

(*Pop* 94,000) Take Route 160 via Yautepec to the semi-tropical town of **Cuautla**, with a popular sulphur spring (known as *aguas hediondas* or stinking waters) and bath, a crowded weekend resort for the capital.

Tourist Cuautla is divided from locals' Cuautla by a wide river, and the locals have the best bargain: it is worth crossing the stream. The plaza is pleasant, traffic-free and well maintained. There is a market in the narrow streets and alleyways around 5 de Mayo. The tourist office is opposite *Hotel Cuautla*, on Av Obregón, satisfactory. The **Casa de la Cultura**, 3 blocks N of Zócalo offers useful information and maps. There is a museum/ex-convent next door.

● **Accommodation** C *Jardín de Cuautla*, Dos de Mayo 94, opp Colón bus station, modern, clean, but bad traffic noise, pool; 1 block from *Jardín de Cuautla* is C *Colonial*, modern, pool; **D** *Hotel Colón* in Cuautla is on the main square, good, clean; *Hotel-restaurante Valencia*, 4 blocks N of Cristóbal Colón terminal; **E** *Hotel España*, Dos de Mayo 22, 3 blocks from bus station, very good, clean, rec; **D** *Hotel Madrid*, Los Bravos 27. 11 km from Cuautla, on road to Cuernavaca the **A1** *Hacienda de Cocoyoc*, an old converted *hacienda* with a swimming pool backed by the mill aqueduct. Glorious gardens, 18-hole golf-course, tennis and riding, but isolated, Amex not accepted, reservations at Centro Comercial El Relox, Local 44, Insurgentes Sur 2374, México 01000 DF, T 550-7331. **Youth Hostel**: Unidad Deportiva, T 20218, CP 60040.

● **Places to eat** Try the delicious *lacroyas* and *gorditas*, tortillas filled with beans and cheese. 4 good restaurants in main square, all serving cheap *comidas*, try the one in the *Hotel Colón*; good restaurant at *Hotel Granada*, Defensa de Aguas 34.

● **Transport** Buses from Mexico City to Cuautla from Central del Ote (Volcanes terminal), 2nd class US$1. Buses from Cuautla at Cristóbal Colón terminal, 5 de Mayo and Zavala, to **Mexico City** hourly US$3.65 1st class, US$4.65 *plus*; Estrella Roja 1st class, 2nd class buses or minibuses to **Cuernavaca** at least hourly, 1 hr, US$1.85; to **Oaxaca**, US$14.80, 2 Cristóbal Colón buses/day (2nd class 1430 and 1st class 2330), 7-8 hrs, also ADO, most overnight and en route from Mexico City so book ahead, also try Fletes y Pasajes 2nd class buses, or change twice, at Izúcar de Matamoros and Huajuapan. Cristóbal Colón terminal will store luggage until they close at 2200. The 115 road leads to Amecameca (page 296).

Chalcatzingo From Cuautla, this interesting Olmec sanctuary can be reached. It has an altar, a pyramid and rock carvings, one of which depicts a procession of warriors led by a prisoner with a beard and horned helmet (a Viking, some say), others depict battles between jaguars and men. To get there take Route 160 SE, direction Izúcar de Matamoros; at Amayuca turn right towards Tepalcingo. 2 km down this road turn left towards Jonacatepec and it's 5 km to the village of Chalcatzingo (take a guide). There are buses from Puebla to Amayuca. A taxi from Amayuca costs US$5. Near Jonacatepec are the ruins of Las Pilas. Some 7 km further down the road to Tepalcingo is Atotonilco where there is a *balneario* for swimming (bus from Cuautla). (We are grateful to Helmut Zettl of Ebergassing for much of this information.)

After Cuautla take Route 160 with long descent and then ascent to **Izúcar de Matamoros** (*Pop* 58,000), famous for its clay handicrafts, 16th century convent of Santo Domingo, and two nearby spas, Los Amatitlanes (about 6 km away) and Ojo de Carbón.

● **Accommodation** C *Premier*, on Zócalo; **D** *Hotel Ocampo*, next to bus station; **E** *Las Fuentes*, bath and hot water, clean, quiet, TV, courtyard, rec; **F** *La Paz*, off Zócalo, friendly, clean basic rooms, hot water.

A road leads SW from Izúcar to **Axochiapan** (Morelos state; **E** *Hotel Primavera*, bath, hot water, clean, tiny room), leading to a paved road to the village of **Jolalpan** with the baroque church of Santa María (1553). Very few restaurants in Jolalpan; ask where meals are to be had. Bus from Axochiapan stops in front of the church in Jolalpan. The road (and bus) continues to Atenango del Río in Guerrero state, the last 20-30 km unpaved.

Route 190 heads N from Izúcar to Puebla (side road to Huaquechula: 16th century renaissance-cum-plateresque chapel) via **Atlixco** ('the place lying on the water'), with interesting baroque examples in the Capilla de la Tercera Orden de San Agustín and San Juan de Dios. There is an annual festival, the Atlixcayotl, on San Miguel hill (**B** *Molina de Herrera*, Km 40 of carretera Puebla-Izúcar de Matamoros, 15 mins from Atlixco, T 448171, 50 a/c rooms with satellite TV, pool, restaurant, bar, convention hall for 300 people; **E** *Hotel Colonial* behind parish church, shared bath; *Restaurant La Taquería*, Av Libertad, 1 block from Plaza, highly rec). Nearby, 20 mins, are the curative springs of Axocopán. Thence to Acatepec (page 299) and, 30 km, Puebla.

From Izúcar de Matamoros, route 190 S switchbacks to Tehuitzingo. Then fairly flat landscape to **Acatlán** (Hotels **E** *Plaza*, clean, hot showers, TV, new, good restaurant, rec; **E** *México*, 'grungy', cockroaches, try elsewhere; *Lux*; *Romano*, both E) a friendly village where black and red clay figures, and palm and flower hats are made. Carry on to Petlalcingo (restaurant), then ascend to **Huajuapan de León**, with *Hotel García Peral*, on the Zócalo, good restaurant; *Hotel Casablanca*, Amatista 1, Col Vista Hermosa, also good restaurant (just outside Huajuapan on the road to Oaxaca); **C-D** *Plaza de Angel*, Central, nice, clean; **D** *Playa*, El Centro, hot water, clean, big windows, good value; and **D** *Hotel Bella Vista*; and **D** *Colón*, very good. 2nd class bus from Oaxaca to Huajuapan, 4 a day, US$3.50. The next town on Route 190 is **Tamazulapan** (Hotels **D** *Gilda*, 1 block S of Highway 190, central, new, large clean rooms, safe parking; **D** *México*, on highway, modern, clean, has lush courtyard, balconies, good restaurant with *comida corrida*; **D** *Santiago*, without sign on Zócalo; **E** *Hidalgo*, behind church; restaurant *Coquiz*, on Highway 190, good). 72 km NW of Oaxaca on Route 190 is **Yanhuitlán**, with a beautiful 400-year-old church, part of a monastery (Santo Domingo). Yanhuitlán is in the Sierra Mixteca, where Dominican friars began evangelizing in 1526. Two other important centres were San Juan Bautista at Coixtlahuaca and the

open chapel at Teposcolula. The scenery and the altars, the huge convents in such a remote area, are a worthwhile day trip from Oaxaca. The new highway from **Nochixtlán** (**D** *Mixli*, outskirts at intersection with new highway, large beds, TV, parking, rec but 20 mins' walk from town; **E** *Hotel Sarita*, around corner is **E** *Elazcan*, clean, OK) to Oaxaca (103 km) has been recommended for cyclists: wide hard shoulders and easy gradients.

The major route from Mexico City first runs generally eastwards to Puebla, where it turns S to wind through wooded mountains at altitudes of between 1,500 and 1,800m, emerging at last into the warm, red earth Oaxaca valley.

OAXACA

(*Pop* 300,000; *State pop 1995* 3,224,270; *Alt* 1,546m; *Phone code* 951) **Oaxaca**, 413 km from Puebla, 531 km from Mexico City, is a charming Indian town, of airy patios with graceful arcades, famous for its colourful market, its *sarapes*, crafts, dances and feast days.

The Zócalo with its arcades is the heart of the town; its bandstand has a few food stalls underneath. Since the streets surrounding the sides of the Zócalo and the adjacent Alameda de León have been closed to traffic it has become very pleasant to sit there or stroll. It is always active. Free music and dance events are often held in the evenings. In the daytime vendors sell food, in the evening their tourist wares and gardenias in the square. It is especially colourful on Sat and Sun nights when Indian women weave and sell their wares. Their weavings can also be seen during the week, on the Plazuela del Carmen, up Alcalá, 1 block beyond Santo Domingo.

Places of interest
Worth visiting is the state-government, Palacio de Gobierno, on the S side of the Zócalo; it has beautiful murals and entry is free. There are often political meetings or protests outside. Visit also the **Arcos**

Xochimilco on García Vigil, starting at Cosipoji, some 10 blocks N of the Zócalo. This picturesque area is the remains of an aqueduct, with narrow, cobbled passageways under the arches, flowers and shops. There is a grand view from the amphitheatre on the Cerro de Fortín. The monument to Juárez is in the valley below. The house of the Maza family, for whom Bénito Juárez worked and whose daughter he married, still stands at Independencia 1306 (a plaque marks it). Similarly, a plaque marks the birthplace of Porfirio Díaz at the other end of Independencia, in a building which is now a kindergarten, near La Soledad. DH Lawrence wrote parts of 'Mornings in Mexico' here, and revised 'The Plumed Serpent'; the house he rented is on Pino Suárez. There is an observatory and planetarium on the hill NW of the town, shows on Wed, Fri, Sat and Sun at 1900, US$2, best to take a taxi (about US$3.50) the walk is dark and deserted.

Churches

On the Zócalo is the 17th century **cathedral** with a fine baroque façade (watch the raising and lowering of the Mexican flag daily at 0800 and 1800 beside the cathedral), but the best sight, about 4 blocks from the square up the pedestrianized C Macedonio Alcalá, is the church of **Santo Domingo** (reckoned by all to be beautiful, closed 1300-1700) with its adjoining monastery, now the Regional Museum (see below). The church's gold leaf has to be seen to be believed. The ceilings and walls, sculptured and painted white and gold, are beautiful. There is an extraordinary vaulted decoration under the raised choir, right on the reverse of the façade wall: a number of crowned heads appear on the branches of the genealogical tree of the family of Santo Domingo de Guzmán (died 1221), whose lineage was indirectly related to the royal houses of Castilla and Portugal. The entire ceiling of the central nave is painted. By making a donation (say US$1) to the church you can get the lady at the bookstall to light up the various features after 1800. The Capilla del Rosario in the church is fully restored; no flash pictures are allowed.

The massive 17th century church of **La Soledad** (between Morelos and Independencia, W of Unión) has fine colonial ironwork and sculpture (including an exquisite Virgen de la Soledad). Its interior is predominantly fawn and gold; the plaques on the walls are painted like cross-sections of polished stone. The chandeliers at the sides are supported by angels. The fine façade is made up of stone of different colours, pinks and greens. The church was built on the site of the hermitage to San Sebastian; begun in 1582, it was recommended in 1682 because of earthquakes. It was consecrated in 1690 and the convent was finished in 1697. The **Museo Religiosa de la Soledad** on Independencia 107 (open 0900-1400 Mon-Sun, US$0.30 donation requested) has a display of religious artefacts; it is at the back of the church. In the small plaza outside the encircling wall, refreshments and offerings are sold. There are elaborate altars at the church of **San Felipe Neri** (Av Independencia y García). There is an Indian version in paint of the Conquistadores arrival in Oaxaca and of an anti-Catholic uprising in 1700 at **San Juan de Dios** (20 de Noviembre y Aldama). On the ceiling are paintings of the life of Christ. This was the first church in Oaxaca, originally dedicated to Santa Catalina Mártir. The church of **San Agustín** (Armenta y López at Guerrero) has a fine façade, with bas-relief of St Augustine holding the City of God above adoring monks (apparently modelled on that of San Agustín in Mexico City, now the National Library).

Museums

The **Museo Regional de Antropología e Historia** on M Alcalá, next to Santo Domingo (entry US$2, free on Sun, open Tues-Fri 1000-1800, Sat, Sun and holidays 1000-1700, being renovated in 1997, not all rooms open during the work) has fine displays of pottery, glass, alabaster, jewellery and other treasures from Monte Albán, whose jewellery is copied with great skill in several workshops near Oaxaca.

The **Instituto de Artes Gráficos de Oaxaca** (IAGO) is almost opposite the Museo Regional at Alcalá 507 (open Mon-Sun 0900-2000, closed Tues); it has interesting

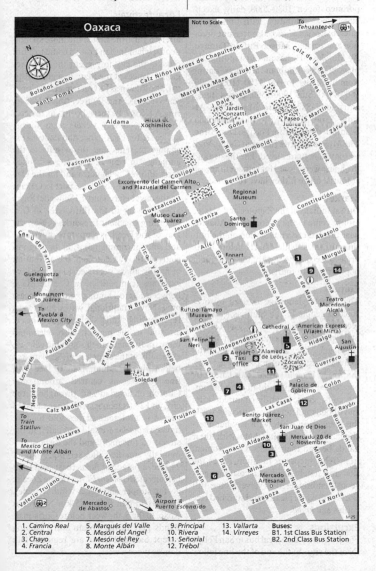

1. Camino Real	5. Marqués del Valle	9. Principal	13. Vallarta
2. Central	6. Mesón del Angel	10. Rivera	14. Virreyes
3. Chayo	7. Mesón del Rey	11. Señorial	**Buses:**
4. Francia	8. Monte Albán	12. Trébol	B1. 1st Class Bus Station
			B2. 2nd Class Bus Station

exhibition rooms, a good reference library and beautifully kept courtyards filled with flowers (free, but donation appreciated). At Alcalá 202 is **Museo de Arte Contemporáneo** (open 1030-2000 daily, except Tues), good exhibition with library and café, *Amigos del Museo*, also free but donation appreciated. **Museo Rufino Tamayo**, Av Morelos 503, has an outstanding display of precolumbian artefacts dating from 1250 BC to AD 1100 (1000-1400, 1600-1900, Sun 1000-1500, closed Tues); entry for US$2. **Teatro Macedonio Alcalá**, 5 de Mayo with Independencia, beautiful theatre from Porfirio Díaz' time. The **Museo Casa de Juárez** at García Vigil 609, is where Juárez lived. The theatre and the house were closed for remodelling, ask at tourist office if they have reopened.

Market

On Sat Indians of the Zapotec and Mixtec groups come to the **Mercado de Abastos** near the 2nd class bus station on the outskirts of town, which starts before 0800; prices are rising because of the city's great popularity with tourists.

Culture

The Zapotec language is used by over 300,000 people in the State as a first or second language (about 20% of Oaxaca State population speaks only an Indian language). The Zapotec Indians, who weave fantastic toys of grass, have a dance, the *Jarabe Tlacolula Zandunga* danced by barefooted girls splendid in most becoming coifs, short, brightly coloured skirts and ribbons and long lace petticoats, while the men, all in white with gay handkerchiefs, dance opposite them with their hands behind their backs. Only women, from Tehuantepec or Juchitán, dance the slow and stately *Zandunga*, costumes gorgeously embroidered on velvet blouse, full skirts with white pleated and starched lace ruffles and *huipil*.

Excursions

For good hikes, take local bus to San Felipe (N of the city); at the end of the line follow the dirt road to the left along the valley, cross the bridge and turn right (uphill) after the bridge, trails go into the mountains and to a waterfall (ask for La Cascada).

Local festivals

Los Lunes del Cerro, on the first two Mon after 16 July (the first is the more spontaneous, when Indian groups come to a hill outside the city to present the seven regional dances of the State in a great festival, also known as La Guelaguetza). Upper seats (rings C and D) free, ring B US$46, ring A US$62, be there 1½ hrs in advance to get a good seat, tickets from Tourist Office. After each dance the dancers exchange presents and throw gifts to the audience in ring A. Hotels get booked early for the Guelaguetza and for the Day of the Dead, as does transport to Oaxaca on the days beforehand. El Señor del Rayo, a 9-day event in the third week of Oct, including excellent fireworks. 2 Nov, the Day of the Dead, is a mixture of festivity and solemn commemoration, best appreciated at the Panteón Gen; the decoration of family altars is carried to competitive extremes (competition in C 5 de Mayo between Santo Domingo and the Zócalo on 1 Nov); traditional wares and foods, representing skulls, skeletons, coffins etc are sold in the market. Also celebrated more traditionally, in the outlying villages, especially in the cemetery of Acotlán. Ask before photographing. 8 to 18 Dec with fine processions centred around the Church of Soledad and throughout the city, and 23 (Rábanos) with huge radishes carved in grotesque shapes sold for fake money; *buñuelos* are sold and eaten in the streets on this night, and the dishes ceremonially smashed after serving. Night of 24 Dec, a parade of floats (best seen from balcony of *Merendero El Tule* on the Zócalo; go for supper and get a window table). Posadas in San Felipe (5 km N) and at Xoxo, to the S, the week before Christmas. Bands play in the Zócalo every evening except Sat, and there are regional folk dances twice a week.

Local information

● Accommodation

L3 *Camino Real*, 5 de Mayo 300, T 60611, beautifully converted convent, very elegant, good pool; **L3** *Victoria*, colonial house turned into hotel, bedrooms with showers built round the garden, good value, swimming pool, TV (with 2 US satellite channels), discount for elderly couples who book directly, up to 30%, many tour groups, but out of town (around 15 mins' walk) at Km 545 on Pan-American Highway (noisy), T 52633, F 52411.

A1 *Hacienda La Noria*, Periférico con La Costa, T 67555, F 65347, motel-type, pool, good and convenient; Best Western also has **A1** *Hostal de la Noria*, Hidalgo 918, T 147844, F 163992, 2 blocks from Zócalo, new colonial style; **A2** *Misión de Los Angeles*, Calzada Porfirio Díaz 102, T 51500, F 51680, motel-style, 2 km from centre, quiet and most attractive, with swimming pool; **A2** *Misión Oaxaca*, San Felipe del Agua, some way out, attractive; **A3** *Calesa Real*, García Vigil 306, T 65544, F 67232, modern colonial but many small dark rooms, good but expensive, *Los Arcos* restaurant, parking, central, slow service; **A3** *Gala*, Guerrero y Bustamante 103, SE corner of Zócalo, also suites, cable TV, with a/c, very nice (no elevator).

B *Mesón del Rey*, Trujano 212, T 60033, 1 block from Zócalo, clean, modern, fun, quiet except for street-facing rooms, good value, restaurant and travel agency, no credit cards; **B** *Posada San Pablo*, M Fiallo 102, T 64914, with bath, hot water, kitchen, large rooms in old convent, quiet, safe, clean, must stay more than 2 nights, highly rec; **B** *Santa Rosa*, Trujano y 20 de Noviembre, T 46714, TV, phone, restaurant/bar, hot water, laundry, central; **B-C** *Marqués del Valle*, Portal de Clavería, on Zócalo, attached to cathedral, T 63677, F 69961, modern colonial style, clean, friendly, many rooms with balconies, good restaurant, rec; **B-C** *Mesón del Angel*, Mina, nr Díaz Ordaz, clean, large rooms, good services, with pool, tours to ruins (see below), bus to Pochutla passes hotel at 0800 and 2200, rec; **B-C** *Villa de Canpo*, Macedonia Alcalá 910, T 59652, rooms and 4 suites, new, clean, quiet, tiled floors, safe, friendly, parking, pool, restaurant.

C *Antonio's*, Independencia 601, T 67227, F 63672, 1 block from Zócalo, colonial patio, with bath, hot water, spotless, good restaurant, closed in evening; **C** *Anturius*, Privada Emilio Carranza, new, clean, friendly, cafetería, rec; **C** *California*, Chapultepec 822, T 53628, nr 1st

class bus station, with bath, friendly, pleasant, restaurant; **C** *Del Arbol*, Calzada Madero 131, T 64887, modern, comfortable, bath; **C** *Del Bosque*, exit road to Mitla, T 52122, modern, restaurant; **C** *La Casa de la Tía*, 5 de Mayo 108, T 68201, reductions for longer stays, has triples and a suite, restaurant and bar; **C** *Las Golondrinas*, Tinoco y Palacios 411, T 68726, F 42126, uphill from centre, 3 courtyards, cash only, pleasant; **C** *Monte Albán*, Alameda de León 1, T 62777 friendly, colonial style, opp Cathedral; regular folk dance performances are given here at 2030, US$3.50, photography permitted; **C** *Plazuela*, La Bastida 115, pleasant, friendly; **C** *Posada de Chencho*, 4a Privada de la Noria 115, T 40043, with shower, hot water, quiet, breakfast inc, hospitable, enclosed parking, warmly rec; **C** *Primavera*, Madero 438, T 64508, opp railway station, with bath, warm water, clean, friendly, good value, front rooms noisy, 2 blocks from the Zócalo at 5 de Mayo 208 is **C** *Principal*, T 62535, colonial house, very clean, private shower with hot and cold water, rooms overlooking street are a bit noisy, English spoken, heavily booked; **C** *Rivera*, 20 de Noviembre 502, esq Aldama, T 63804, and in 600 block); **C** *Santa Clara*, Morelos 1004, T 67144, clean, hot showers, friendly, quiet, no English spoken, very nice, rec (same owner as *Reforma*, below); **C** *Señorial*, Portal de Flores 6 (on Zócalo), T 63933, will store luggage, suites or rooms, with bath, swimming pool, on main square, good restaurant, no personal cheques or credit cards, cockroaches, rec; **C-D** *Trébol*, Av Las Casas y Cabrera, T 61256, F 40342, pleasant, clean, with bath, breakfast available, friendly, good value, transport to Monte Albán, Mitla, Puerto Escondido; **C-D** *Veracruz*, Chapultepec 1020, T 50511, next to ADO bus station, spotless, welcoming, comfortable, good if you arrive late at night by bus, expensive restaurant.

D *Aurora*, Bustamante 212, T 64145, no private bath, 2 blocks from Zócalo; **D** *Chayo*, 20 de Noviembre 508, T 64112, bath but no fan, water not always hot, clean, large courtyard used as car park (several others in same block); **D** *Francia*, 20 de Noviembre 212, T 64811, around enclosed courtyard, popular, some rooms scruffy without windows, friendly and helpful, rec but noisy; **D** *La Cabaña*, Mina 203, M Cabrera, with bath, cheaper without, safe, clean, hot water 0700-1000, 1700-2100; **D** *Las Rosas*, Trujano 112, old charm, nice patio, clean, excellent, quiet, friendly, good view from roof; **D** *Vallarta*, Díaz Ordaz 309, T 64967, clean, good value, enclosed parking, street rooms noisy, good set lunch; **D** *Villa Alta*, Cabrera 303, T 62444, 4 blocks from Zócalo, friendly service, clean, stores luggage, rec; many cheap hotels in the block Mina, Zaragoza, Díaz Ordaz y García (not a safe area at night); **D** *del Valle*, Díaz Ordaz 105, with bath, run down, friendly, a bit noisy, poor breakfast, next door to tourist bus to Monte Albán; **D-E** *Central*, 20 de Noviembre 104, T 65971, private bathroom, hot water, good value but very noisy, fills up early; **D-E** *Chayo*, C 20 de Noviembre 508, clean, friendly, synthetic bed sheets; **D-E** *Virreyes*, Morelos 1001 y Reforma, problems with water, quiet, a bit tatty, rooms on street a bit noisy and unfriendly front desk, otherwise rec.

E *Arnel*, Aldama 404, T 52856, homely, pleasant patio, good for meeting people, parking, not central, organize good tours, reservations not always honoured, not even after confirmation and arrival; **E** *Pasaje*, Mina 302, nr market, with bathrooms, parakeets in patio, hot water but you have to ask, clean; **E** *Posada Margarita*, La Bastida 115, with shower, clean, quiet, basic, nr Santo Domingo; **E** *Reforma*, Av Reforma 102 between Independencia and Morelos, T 60939, back rooms quieter, upper floors have good views, terrace on roof, friendly, rec; **E** *Yagul*, Mina 103 nr market and Zócalo, family atmosphere, no hot water, use of kitchen on request. At Díaz Ordaz 316 is **E-F** *Díaz Ordaz*, clean and friendly, water problems; and 2 doors along is **F** *Lupita*, large, pleasant rooms, upstairs rooms are bright and have mountain views, rec; **E** *Posada El Palmar*, C JP García 504 and Aldama (2 blocks from the market), cheaper rooms without bathroom, convenient, friendly, family-run, hot water am, only one shower upstairs, electricity late pm only, safe motorcycle parking; **E** *Pombo*, Morelos 601 y 20 de Noviembre, nr Zócalo, rooms vary so check first, hot shower, clothes washing not allowed, good value, friendly and clean; **E** *Regional de Antequera*, Las Casas 901, 5 mins' walk from 2nd class bus station, pleasant, clean, good value; **E** *San José*, Trujano 412, basic, dirty, cheap, lively, friendly. Many other cheap hotels in 400 block of Trujano.

There is also accommodation in private houses which rent rooms (*casas de huéspedes*); **E** *Bengalí*, C de Las Casas 508, more expensive with bath, basic, friendly, quiet, clean; **E** pp Mariana Arroyo runs a B&B from her home, Reforma 402, restaurant *La Olla*, also offers traditional Aztec massage from her cottage in San Felipe de Agua, N of town.

Villa María, Arteaga 410A, T 65056, F 42562, 5 blocks from the Zócalo, pleasant modern well furnished apts from US$180/month with 24-hr security, maid service if required, rec. On the road to Tehuantepec (Km 9.8): **C** *Hotel Posada Los Arcos*, Spanish-style motel at San Sebastián Totla; *Tourist Yu'u*, several tourist houses (**F** pp) in Oaxaca environs. Each house has room with 4 beds, kitchen, bathroom. For details: T 60123, F 60984.

Camping: Oaxaca Trailer Park S of town off the road to Mitla at a sign marked 'Infonavit' (corner of C Pinos and C Violetas), US$4.50 for a tent, US$6 for a camper van, secure, clothes washing facilities not always available, try the delicious tamales across the road in the green restaurant; bus 'Carmen-Infonavit' from downtown.

Youth hostel: *El Pasador*, Fiallo 305, T 61287, F pp in dormitories, full of tourists, friendly, kitchen and laundry facilities, water supply problems, seldom any hot water, stores luggage, purified water, good place to meet travellers. Villa Deportiva Juvenil, office at Belisario Domínguez 920, Col Reforma, bus from Las Casas y JP García in centre, 5 mins, US$0.15, cold water, dormitories, clean, friendly, G with YHA card, F without, sheets and blankets provided.

● **Places to eat**
Most restaurants on the main square cater for tourists, and are therefore pricey (efficiency and standards depend a bit on how busy they are, but generally they are good): on the W side are *El Jardín*, a nice place to sit and watch all the activity (music, parades, aerobics, etc) in the Zócalo; upstairs is *Asador Vasco*, live Mexican music, good food and service; *La Primavera*, good value meals, good expresso coffee, slow; *La Casa de la Abuela*, upstairs on corner of Zócalo and Alameda de León. On the N side are *El Marqués*, very slow service, and *Pizza, Pasta y Más*, popular. On the E side, *Café El Portal*, Portal Benito Juárez, good food, quick service; *de Antequera*; *Café Amarantos*; and *Mario's Terranova Restaurant*, excellent food, friendly and efficient service, pricey. *Flor de Oaxaca*, Armenta y López 311, pricey but excellent meals and delicious hot chocolate; *Los Arcos*, García Vigil 306 under *Calesa Real* hotel, good food in pretty setting and friendly service; *La Fuente de la Catedral*, corner of Gral García Vigil and Morelos, 1 block from cathedral, good for international and local specialities, steaks, good *tamales*, classical music, excellent buffet for US$7; *La Casita*, nr main Post Office, Av Hidalgo 612, 1st floor, good food, reasonable prices, live music; *La Gran Torta*, on Independencia opp

Post Office, small, simple, family-run, cheap, good *pozole* and *tortas*; *Alameda*, JP García between Trujano and Hidalgo, excellent regional food, crowded Sun, closes 1800; *Flami*, on Trujano nr Zócalo, good food; *Hostería Alcalá*, C Macedonio Alcalá 307, 5 mins from Zócalo, not cheap but excellent food and quiet atmosphere, good service (at No 303 is *Plaza Garibaldi*); *La Quebrada*, Armenta y López, excellent fish, open only to 1800; *Guitarra, Pan Y Vino*, Morelos 511, regional food, music *soirées*; *Quince Letras*, Abasolo opp *Hotel Santo Tomás*, excellent food, friendly service; *Santa Fe*, 5 de Mayo 103, open till 2400, good, not cheap.

Vegetarian *Café Fuente y Señor de Salud*, Juárez just N of Morelos, pleasant, reasonable food; *Arco*, dearer, opp ADO bus station, Niños Héroes de Chapultepec, loud music; *Manantial Vegetariano*, Tinoco y Palacios 303, excellent cheap meals, buffet US$3, pleasant patio, rec; *Girasoles*, 20 de Noviembre 102, small but good food, rec; *Flor de Loto*, Morelos 509, good value, clean, vegetarian and Mexican.

Alfredo's Pizzería, Alcalá, about 4 blocks N of the Zócalo, expensive wine by the glass, *Pizza Rústica Angelo y Domenico*, Allende y Alcalá, opp Santo Domingo, very good, reasonable prices, rec; *El Sol y la Luna*, on N Bravo, good although not cheap, live music some nights, open evenings only. *Las Chalotes*, Fiallo 116, French food, friendly service, expensive. The best Oaxacan food is found in the *comedores familiares* such as *Clemente, Los Almendros, La Juchita*, but they are way out of town and could be difficult to get to, or in *comedores populares* in the market; *El Bicho Pobre II*, Calzada de la República, highly rec, lunch only, very popular; *La Verde Antequera*, Matamoros 3 blocks N of Zócalo, good daily lunch specials, best *comida corrida* in town for US$1; *Los Olmos*, Morelos 403, regional specialities, popular, friendly; *El Mesón*, buffets 0800-1930 good at US$2.50, breakfast, *comida corrida* 1200-1630 poor value at US$2, good tacos, clean, quick service, on Hidalgo at NE corner of Zócalo; almost opp is *La Piñata*, good chicken in *mole* lunches; *El Laurel*, N Bravo 210, tasty home-style cooking, try the *mole*, open to 1800 Tues-Thur, and to 2200 on Fri and Sat; also close to Zócalo, *Bamby*, García Vigil 205, cheaper beer than elsewhere, good breakfast; *Pan Bamby*, García Vigil y Morelos, excellent bakery, rec; *El Paisaje*, 20 de Noviembre, good, cheap chicken dishes; *Arte y Tradición*, García Vigil 406, craft centre with courtyard café, excellent

service and food, open Mon-Sat 1100-2200; *Los Canarios*, 20 de Noviembre, nr *Hotel Chayo*, good *comida corrida*; *María Cristina's* in Mercado 20 de Noviembre, excellent *caldos* and *comidas*; the bar *El Favorito*, on 20 de Noviembre, a couple of blocks S of the Zócalo, is supposedly the original that inspired Malcolm Laury's bar in *Under the Volcano*; *Café Pitapé*, García Vigil 403 y N Bravo, friendly, good value; *Fiesta*, Las Casas 303, good for breakfast or *comida corrida*; *El Shaddai*, Av Hidalgo 121 y Galeano, family-run, good and cheap; *Gala*, Bustamante, just off Zócalo, opens 0730 for good coffee and breakfast; *Trece Cielos*, Matamoros 101, good, cheap daily *menú*; *French Pastry Shop*, Trujano, 1 block W of Zócalo, good coffee, pastries, desserts; *Cafetería Alex*, Díaz Ordaz y Trujano, good *comida corrida*, coffee and breakfasts, delicious pancakes with fruit, good value; *Café y Arte Geono*, Alcalá 412, nice garden, good coffee and cakes; *TLC*, corner of Aldama y García, excellent tacos, tortas and juices in a calm patio setting; *Tartamiel*, Valerio Trujano, ½ block E of Zócalo, good bakery and cake shop; as is *La Luna*, Independencia 1105, 5 blocks E of cathedral. Several good places for cheap *menú del día* on Porfirio Díaz, such as *Guidos*, popular, with cheap pasta and coffee. Good restaurant opp 1st class bus station, good value, one of the only sit-down places among taco stands. Good *dulcería* (sweet shop) in the 2nd class bus station. On C Mina y 20 de Noviembre, opp the market are several mills where they grind cacao beans, almond, sugar and cinnamon into a paste for making delicious hot chocolate, eg *Mayordomo*, 20 de Noviembre y Mina, and *Guelaguetza*, next to Hotel *Galaxia*. Also at Mina y 20 de Noviembre is *La Casa de Dulce* sweet shop. In the Mercado 20 de Noviembre there are *comedores* and lots of stalls selling breads and chocolate. A local bread called *pan de yema*, is made, with egg-yolk, at the Mercado de Abastos (the Hermanas Jiménez bakery is most rec). In the Oaxaca area you can find *chapulinas*, grasshoppers roasted with garlic, lemon and lots of salt, often sold on trains.

● **Airline offices**

Líneas Aéreas Oaxaqueñas office at Av Hidalgo 503, T 65362, airport 61280. There is a **Mexicana** office at Fiallo 102 y Av Independencia, T 68414 (airport T 62337); **AeroMéxico**, Av Hidalgo 513 Centro, T 67101 (airport T 64055); **Aviacsa**, agency on Zócalo, T 31809/51500 (airport T 62332); **Aero Caribe**, at *Hotel Misión de los Angeles*, T 56373 (airport T 62247).

● Banks & money changers

Get to banks before they open, long queues form. **Bancomer**, 1 block from Zócalo, exchanges TCs, 0900-1330, on García Vigil, and has cash dispenser for Visa card. **Banpais** at corner of Zócalo has a better service. For Thomas Cook cheques, **Banco Internacional**. Amex office *Viajes Micsa*, at Valdivieso 2, T 62700, just off Zócalo, very helpful, but lots of paperwork (no travel reservations). *Interdisa*, Valdivieso nr Zócalo, Mon-Sat 0800-2000, Sun 0900-1700, cash, TCs, sells quetzales and exchanges many Western currencies, also changes TCs into dollars cash. *Comermer*, on Periférico nr Abastos Market, best rates. *Casa de Cambio* 105, 0800-2000 changes TCs. *Casa de Cambio* at Armenta y López, nr corner with Hidalgo, 0800-2000 Mon-Sat, shorter hours on Sun; another *cambio* at García Vigil 215. No problem to change TCs at weekends, many *casas de cambio* around the Zócalo. **Western Union** at Elektra store, Colón 210, money from abroad can be sent here in 24 hrs.

● Embassies & consulates

US Consular Agency, Alcalá 201, suite 204, T 43054; **Canadian Honorary Consul**, Dr Liceaga 119-8, T 33777; combined **Honorary British** and **German** consul, address available at Federal Tourist Office.

● Entertainment

Folk dancing at the *Hotel Señorial* most nights of the week, advance booking rec. *Eclipse* nightclub on P Diaz, free on Thur; *Snob*, Niños Héroes Chapultepec, free Wed; live salsa at *Rojo Caliente* on P Diaz.

Cinemas: *Ariel 2000*, Juárez y Berriozabal, subtitled films for US$2, half price Mon; *Cine Versalles*, Av Melchor Ocampo, N of Hidalgo (3 blocks E, ½ block N of Zócalo); *Cine Oaxaca*, Morelos nr Alcalá; another cinema on Trujano, 1 block W of Zócalo.

● Hospitals & medical services

Chemist/pharmacy: 20 de Noviembre y Ignacio Aldama, open till 2300.

Dentist: *Dra Marta Fernández del Campo*, Armenta y López 215, English-speaking, very friendly, rec.

Doctor: *Dr Victor Tenorio*, Clínica de Carmen, Abasolo 215, T 62612, close to centre (very good English); *Dr Marco Antonio Callejo* (English-speaking), Belisario Domínguez 115, T 53492, surgery 0900-1300, 1700-2000.

● Language schools

There are many in the city; the following have been recently rec: *Instituto Johann Goethe*, JP García 502, T/F 43516, wide variety of courses, eg 4 weeks, 2 hrs a day US$160; *Instituto de Comunicación y Cultura*, M Alcalá 307-12, 2nd floor, T 63443, US$75/week; accommodation can be arranged (part of the National Registration Center for Study Abroad consortium; see **Learning Spanish** in Information for travellers). *Centro de Idiomas*, Universidad Autónoma Benito Juárez, C de Burgoa, 4 blocks S of Zócalo, weekly or monthly classes (US$200/month), or private tuition, very professional and good value for money, rec. *Becari*, M Bravo 210, Plaza San Cristóbal, T/F 46076, e-mail: becari@antequera.antequera.com; or web: www.mexonline.com/becari.htm. 4 blocks N of Zocalo, US$60/15-hr week, fully-qualified teachers, courses inc culture, history, literature and politics, with workshops on dancing, cooking or art, flexible programmes, rec. *Instituto de Lengua y Cultura Natipaa*, 4½ blocks N of Zócalo, García Vigil 509-4 2nd floor, T 30728, also cultural activities, arranges stay with host family. See also **Learning Spanish** in Information for travellers.

In addition to Spanish classes, local crafts (inc cooking, weaving and pottery) are also taught at the *Instituto Cultural Oaxaca*, Av Juárez 909, T 53404/51323, F 53728, US$105/week, more time spent on cultural classes than learning Spanish.

● **Laundry**

ELA, Super Lavandería Automática, Antonio Roldán 114, Col Olímpica, washes and irons; *Lavandería Azteca*, on Hidalgo between Díaz Ordaz y J P García, 0800-2000, 1000-1400 on Sun, quick service, delivers to nearby hotels, 1½ kg US$5.50. There is another laundry at Hidalgo y J P García, 3½ kg, US$3.

● **Libraries**

English lending library with very good English books, a few French and Spanish, also English newspapers (*The News* from Mexico City), used books and magazines for sale, at Macedonio Alcalá 305, looks like an apartment block on the pedestrian street, a few blocks N of Zócalo (open Mon-Fri, 1000-1300, 1600-1900, Sat 1000-1300), US$13/year plus US$13 returnable deposit. *The News* is also sold round the Zócalo by newsboys, from mid morning, or from street vendor at Las Casas y 20 de Noviembre. The local library at Alcalá 200 (no sign) has a lovely courtyard and a reading room with Mexican newspapers and magazines. Next door is the library of the Museo de Arte Contemporáneo.

● **Post & telecommunications**

Post Office: on Alameda de León, Independencia y 20 de Noviembre.

Telephone: shop around. Self-service, long-distance phone at pharmacies at 20 de Noviembre y Hidalgo, Porfirio Díaz y Av Morelos, and at C Rayón 504. Caseta Larga Distancia Mesón del Rey, Trujano 212, open till 2200, F 61434, night rate 2000-2200 and Sun till 1700; Computel which is almost next door, for long distance calls and fax, evening discounts, Trujano, 2 blocks W of Zócalo. Phone service to USA, collect or with credit card, in lobby of *Hotel Marqués del Valle*.

E-mail: Makedonia, Trujano 22, US$1.50 to send and US$1 to receive.

● **Shopping**

There are endless shopping temptations such as green and black pottery, baskets and bags made from cane and rushes, embroidered shirts, skirts, and blankets; Sat is the best day for buying woollen *sarapes* cheaply. Unfortunately some of the woven products are of a different quality from the traditional product – more garish dyes and synthetic yarns are replacing some of the originals; but you can still find these if you shop around. *Aripo*, on García Vigil 809, T 69211, Government run, cheaper and better than most, service good, with very good small market nearby on junction of García Vigil and Jesus Carranza, for beautiful coloured belts and clothes. Superior craft shops at *Arte y Tradición*, García Vigil 406, good prices. *Sedetur* (see under **Tourist offices**), now run a shop selling crafts and all profits go to the artisans, good prices, rec. *Casa Breno*, nr Santo Domingo church, has unusual textiles and spindles for sale, happy to show visitors around the looms. *Fonart*, N Bravo 116, wide range of Mexican crafts, excellent quality, but pricey. *Lo Mexicano*, García Vigil, at end furthest from centre, excellent selection of high quality crafts at reasonable prices, run by young Frenchman. *Pepe*, Av Hidalgo, for jewellery; cheap local crafts. Good for silver, *Plata Mexicana*, 20 de Noviembre 209-C. *Yalalag*, Alcalá 104, has good selection of jewellery, rugs and pottery, somewhat overpriced; *El Palacio de Gemas*, next door, is rec for gemstones, good selection at reasonable prices; cheapest and largest selection of pottery plus a variety of fabrics and sandals at *Productos Típicos de Oaxaca*, Av Dr B Domínguez 602; city bus nr ADO depot goes there. *Casa Aragón*, JP García 503, famous for knives and *machetes*; a large **Mercado Artesanal** also at JP García y Zaragoza. Fine cream and purple-black pottery (Zapotec and Mixtec designs) available at *Alfarería Jiménez*, Zaragoza 402. Other potteries at Las Casas 614, makers of the Oaxacan daisy design, and Trujano 508, bold flower designs. The nearby village of Atzompa (NW of the city, buses from 2nd class terminal) is worth a visit for its interesting ceramics; local potters are very friendly. There are several Mezcal factories on the Mitla road which show the process of making Mezcal and sell it in black pottery bottles.

Bookshop: *Librería Universitario*, Guerrero 104, buys and sells books inc English and a few German books.

Hairdressers: *Salón de Belleza Londres*, Morelos y Reforma, shampoo and set US$9.25, rec.

Markets: the Mercado Juárez, just SW of the Zócalo in the block bounded by 20 de Noviembre, Las Casas, Cabrera and Aldama, sells fruit, vegetables, meat, cheeses, household goods, flowers, hats and some handicrafts (good leather bags are sold in and around this market). Immediately S of Mercado Juárez is **Mercado**

20 de Noviembre, for baked goods, with lots of good *comedores*. Look for the sautéd chilli insects sold on the streets. The **Mercado de Abastos** (referred to also as the Tianguis), open daily, which sells just about everything inc baskets and pottery, is close to the 2nd class bus station. There is a large and interesting straw section here. Gilberto Segura T, 2 Galería de Artesanías, puesto 140, Mercado de Abastos, makes hammocks to your own design and specification, price depends on size, about US$20 for a single. Sr Leonardo Ruiz of Teotitlán del Valle, has an excellent carpet stall here. Market stall-holders drive very hard bargains and often claim 'no change'; it may be possible to barter rather than bargain. Those disappointed with it should go to the Sun market at **Tlacolula**.

Specialities: black earthenware, tooled leather, blankets, ponchos, shawls, embroidered blouses, the drink *mescal*. The best *mescal* in the region is El Minero. *Mescal* sours are good at the bar of *Misión Los Angeles*. The poor man's drink is *pulque*. Local *sarapes* are more varied and cheaper than in Mexico City.

● **Sports**
Public baths: Baños Reforma, C Reforma 407, open 0700-1800, US$4 for steam-bath for 2, sauna for one, US$3. Baños San Rafael, Tinoco y Palacios 514, Mon-Sat 0600-1800, Sun 0600-1530, hot water.

● **Tour companies & travel agents**
There are many in town. Most run the same tours, eg daily to Monte Albán; El Tule, Mitla and, sometimes, another village on this route; city tour; Fri to Coyotepec, Jalietza and Octotlan; Thur to Cuilapan and Zaachila; Sun to Tlacolula, Mitla and El Tule. Basically, the tours tie in with local markets. Judith Reyes at *Arte y Tradición*, García Vigil 406, runs good tours to outlying villages in her VW van, US$8/hr.

● **Tourist offices**
5 de Mayo y Av Morelos, open 0900-2000 every day, excellent free map of city and surroundings. Sedetur tourist office at Independencia y García Vigil (Mon-Fri 0830-2000, Sat-Sun 0900-1500), has maps, posters, postcards, information; ask here about the *Tourist Yu'u* programme (T 60123, F 60984) in local communities. Tourist Police on Zócalo nr cathedral, friendly and helpful. Instituto Nacional de Estadística, Geografía e Informática, Calz Porfirio Díaz 241A, for maps. There is a monthly tourist newspaper called *Oaxaca*, in Spanish, English and French.

● **Useful addresses**
Immigration: Periférico 2724 at Rayón, open Mon-Fri 0900-1400, 2nd floor.

Luggage storage: Servicio Turístico de Guarda Equipaje y Paquetería, Av Tinoco y Palacios 312, Centro, T 60432, open 24 hrs.

● **Transport**
Local Bus: local town minibuses, mostly US$0.30. To the bus station, buses marked 'VW' go from Av Juárez. To airport US$1.45. **Car hire**: phone ahead to book, a week before if possible. **Car park**: safe parking at *Estacionamiento La Brisa*, Av Zaragoza y Cabrera, US$3.50/night, closed Sun.

Air The Xoxocotlan (OAX) airport is about 9 km S, direction Ocotepec. The airport taxis (*colectivos*) cost US$3 pp. Book at Transportaciones Aeropuerto Oaxaca on Alameda de León No 1-6, opp the Cathedral in the Zócalo (T 64350) for collection at your hotel to be taken to airport, office open Mon-Sat 0900-1400, 1700-2000. From Mexico City several daily in less than an hour by AeroMéxico, Mexicana, Aero Caribe and Aviacsa. Aero Caribe fly daily to Havana, Acapulco, Huatulco, Palenque, Tuxtla Gutiérrez (also Aviacsa, US$56), Villahermosa, Mérida and Cancún. Flights to other Mexican, and to any US destination, except Los Angeles with Mexicana and AeroMéxico daily, involve a connection in Mexico City. Daily flights to Puerto Escondido, 40 mins, eg Aero Caribe; Aerovías Oaxaqueñas at 1100, returns at 0730 or 1200; Líneas Aéreas Oaxaqueñas fly at 1030 Mon-Sat and 0830 Sun; Aeromorelos at 0730, returns at 0830, US$64 one way (new 40-seater Fokker). Most flights are in small, modern planes, 35 mins' journey, spectacular, eg Aero Veca. Be very careful when booking flights to Puerto Escondido on a small airline, they tend to be very erratic.

Trains Station on Calzada Madero at junction with Periférico, 15 mins' walk from Zócalo. From Mexico City, 563 km, 14-17 hrs, magnificent scenery after dawn in either direction, El Oaxaqueño, with *primera preferente*, 1st and 2nd class, no sleepers; take food for 2nd and 1st class (although there are colourful foodsellers on the train), at 1900 daily. To **Mexico City** daily also at 1900. Tickets must be bought the same day; the office is open 0600-1100 and 1500-1900, long queues. Numbered seats in 2nd class, US$5.50, 1st class, US$11; *primera preferente* US$15.60. Route is via Tehuacán and Puebla to the capital.

Buses 1st class terminal is NE of Zócalo on Calzada de Niños Héroes (no luggage office, taxi from centre US$1.40). Note that many 2nd class buses leave from here too, especially towards the Guatemalan border; 2nd class, Autobuses Unidos (AU), is W of Zócalo on Calz Trujano (referred to as 'Central'), has left-luggage office, open until 2100. 1st class terminal is the only one for Villahermosa and the Yucatán. ADO and Cristóbal Colón have a ticket sales office in the centre at 20 de Noviembre 204-A, open Mon-Sat 0900-1400, 1800-1900. Beware of double-booking and short-changing, especially when obtaining tickets from drivers if you have not booked in advance, beware also of thieves at both bus terminals, but especially on arrival of *plus* services. Cristóbal Colón to **Mexico City**, 6 hrs, about 8 a day, mostly evenings; 2nd class by Fletes y Pasajes, comfortable, frequent departures with UNO, about 10 a day with ADO, 6 hrs, robberies have been reported on these buses. Fares to the capital: 2nd class US$10.50, 1st class US$12.50, US$20 *plus*. Buses now travel via the new highway, through spectacular scenery. If buses to the capital are fully booked travel via Puebla. It is difficult to get tickets for buses from the capital to Oaxaca on Fri pm without booking in advance (you can book in advance and pay on day of travel); bus companies require 2 hrs checking-in time in Mexico City on this route. 1st class to **Cuautla**, US$14.80 with ADO, 7 hrs (change there for Cuernavaca and Taxco); **Puebla** (1st class, 4 hrs, US$12, several companies, 2nd class, daytime bus 0730, local people, few tourists, cheap, superb scenery); to **Tuxtepec**, 1st class, 6 hrs, US$16.50 with ADO, from same terminal, Cuenca goes by a more direct, but still beautiful route 1st class US$8.25 (police have reported robberies on this route). To **Veracruz**, ADO, 2 a day from 1st class bus station, via Huajuapan, Tehuacán and Orizaba, 11 hrs, US$21.50 *plus*, book early, or change as above, allow 16 hrs. Cristóbal Colón to **Villahermosa**, US$27.50, book well ahead, 12 hrs, daily at 1700 and 2100. **San Cristóbal de Las Casas** (US$17, at 1930, 2000 and 2015, 12 hrs, the first 2 hrs are on very windy roads, don't eat just before travelling) book 1-2 days in advance with C Colón, there are daytime buses if you go 2nd class; and **Tapachula**, 10 hrs, US$19, 1st class (Cristóbal Colón, also Fipsa, from 1st and 2nd class terminals). Book well in advance as buses often come almost full from Mexico City. To **Tuxtla Gutiérrez**, C Colón or ADO, 4 a day, 10 hrs, *especial* at 2230, US$16, 2nd class US$10, daytime buses if you go 2nd class. To **Tehuantepec**, scenic, 5 a day, 2nd class US$6.50, Cristóbal Colón US$8, 7½ hrs. To **Ciudad Cuauhtémoc**, US$33, 12 hrs. To **Arriaga** US$7, 6 hrs, 5 a day. To **Puerto Escondido**, 0900, 2130 1st class, US$20.25, gruelling 13 hrs journey (can be longer) 3 a day, partly along dirt roads, interesting scenery. Night bus 5 hrs faster. Probably better to go Oaxaca-**Pochutla** on new road with spectacular scenery, especially the cloud forest and 2 hrs descent into Pochutla, 6½-10 hrs, US$6 2nd class, US$8 1st-class, Estrella del Valle buses at 0800 and 2200, then change for Puerto Angel/Puerto Escondido; 1st class Cristóbal Colón bus 0930, 1030, US$13, 9 hrs to Pochutla via Salina Cruz and Huatulco, much further but nice scenery. Oaxaca-Pacífico has good 2nd class buses (5 a day to Pochutla, 1 a day to Puerto Angel, US$5, at 1730 arrives in middle of the night). 1st class buses from 2nd class terminal to Pochutla via Salina Cruz and Huatulco, 7 hrs, several daily. Buses to most local villages go from this terminal, too.

ARCHAEOLOGICAL EXCURSIONS FROM OAXACA

MONTE ALBAN

Monte Albán about 10 km (20 mins) uphill from Oaxaca, to see the pyramids, walls, terraces, tombs, staircases and sculptures of the ancient capital of the Zapotec culture. The place is radiantly colourful during some sunsets, but permission is needed to stay that late (take a torch/flashlight).

To the right, before getting to the ruins, is Tomb 7, where a fabulous treasure trove was found in 1932 (take a torch); most items are in the Museo Regional in the convent of Santo Domingo and the entrance is closed off by a locked gate. Tomb 172 has been left exactly as it was found, with skeleton and urns still in place. Tomb 104 (closes at lunchtime) contains an interesting statue of the rain god, Tlaloc. The remarkable rectangular plaza, 300 by 200m, is rimmed by big ceremonial platforms: the Ball Court, and possibly a palace to the E, stairs rising to an unexcavated platform to the S, several platforms and temples to the W and one, known as Templo de los

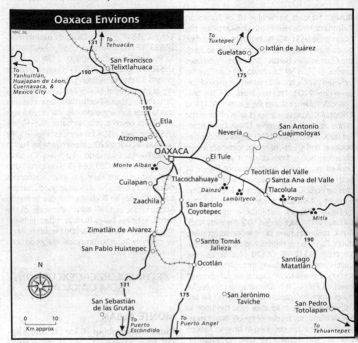

Oaxaca Environs

MAC 26

To Tehuacán — 131

San Francisco Telixtlahuaca — 190

To Yanhuitlán, Huajapan de Léon, Cuernavaca, & Mexico City

190

To Tuxtepec

Guelatao ○ Ixtlán de Juárez

175

Etla ○

Atzompa ○

Nevería ○   San Antonio Cuajimoloyas

OAXACA

Monte Albán ●●   El Tule ○

Cuilapan ○   Tlacochahuaya ○   Teotitlán del Valle ○
   Santa Ana del Valle ○
Dainzu   Tlacolula

Zaachila ○   San Bartolo Coyotepec   Lambityeco   ● Yagul

Zimatlán de Alvarez ○   Mitla

San Pablo Huixtepec ○   Santo Tomás Jaliezta ○   190

N   Ocotlán ○   Santiago Matatlán ○

131   San Jerónimo Taviche ○

San Sebastián de las Grutas ○   San Pedro Totolapan ○

0   10
Km approx

To Puerto Escondido   To Puerto Angel   To Tehuantepec

Danzantes but in reality, probably a hospital, with bas-reliefs, glyphs and calendar signs (probably 5th century BC). A wide stairway leads to a platform on the N side. Most of the ruins visible are early 10th century, when the city was abandoned and became a burial place. Informative literature is available at the site. Explanations are in English and Spanish. (Recommended literature is the Bloomgarden *Easy Guide* to Monte Albán or *Easy Guide* to Oaxaca covering the city and all the ruins in the valley, with maps. In major hotels or the bookshop at Guerrero 108, and all the ruins.)

● **Admission** The ruins are open 0830-1700. Entrance to ruins US$2, free on Sun and public holidays (and for Mexican students). A charge of US$4 is made to use video cameras; guides charge US$15. Most people go in the morning, so it may be easier to catch the afternoon bus. There is a museum at the entrance. There is a drinks and snack bar and a handicrafts shop.

● **Transport** To Monte Albán: Autobuse Turísticos depart from behind *Hotel Mesón de Angel*, Mina nr Díaz Ordaz (bus tickets availabl from hotel lobby) hourly on the 1/2-hr from 083(to 1530 fare US$1.50 return, last bus back a 1730; 2 hrs at the site, allowing not enoug time to visit ruins before returning (you ar permitted to come back on another tour on on ticket for an extra US$1 but you will not, o course, have a reserved seat for your return) There is a bus from *Hotel Trébol*, 1 block S c Zócalo, US$2.50, at 1030, returning 1330. Loca buses also run from outside *Hotel Mesón de Angel*, which leaves you to walk or hitch th remaining 3 km (uphill) to the site. Taxis charg about US$5/hr to go to any site. To give yourse enough time (3 hrs is adequate at the site), yo can walk 4 km downhill from the ruins t Colonia Monte Albán and get a city bus bac from there. Some prefer to walk up and tak the bus back.

ROUTE TO MITLA

To Mitla, paved road (Route 190), but wit

many potholes and occasional flooding, 42 km from Oaxaca past (1) **El Tule** (12 km from Oaxaca) which has what is reputed the world's largest tree, a savino (*Taxodium mucronatum*), estimated at 2,000 years old, 40m high, 42m round at base, weighing an estimated 550 tons, fed water by an elaborate pipe system, in churchyard, US$0.50 entry (bus from Oaxaca, 2nd class bus station, every 30 mins, US$0.15, buy ticket on bus, sit on the left to see the Tule tree; bus El Tule-Mitla US$0.40); El Tule has a good market with good food on sale and *La Sonora* restaurant on eastern edge of town has quite tasty food. (2) **Tlacochahuaya**, 16th century church, vivid Indian murals, carpets and blouses sold in market nearby, admission US$0.45 to church, visit cloisters at back. Bus from Oaxaca 2nd class terminal, US$0.30. (3) A paved road leads off Route 190 to **Teotitlán del Valle**, where Oaxaca *sarapes* and *tapetes* (rugs) are woven, which is now becoming rather touristy. If you knock at any door down the street, you will get them only a little cheaper than at the market, but there is greater variety. The best prices are to be had at the stores along the road as you come into town, but may be even cheaper in Oaxaca where competition is stronger (Make sure whether you are getting all-wool or mixture and check the quality. A well-made rug will not ripple when unfolded on the floor.) Buses leave every 1-1½ hrs from 0800 from 2nd class bus terminal (US$0.60); the 3rd class bus may provide all the contacts you need to buy all the weavings you want! *Juvenal Mendoza*, Buenavista 9, will make any design any size into a rug to order (daily at 1100). Recommended for rugs is Pedro Guitiérrez, Cuauhtémoc 29. Just before the turning for Teotitlán, turn right at Km 23.5 for **Dainzu**, 1 km off the road, another important ruin recently excavated (open daily 1000-1700, US$2.15, Sun free). At the base of the most prominent structure (called Cluster A) are bas reliefs of ball players and priests, similar to the Monte Albán dancers. The nearby site of **Lambityeco** is

also well worth visiting, to see several fine and well-preserved stucco heads.

TLACOLULA

Tlacolula (**D** *Hotel Guish-Bac*, Zaragoza 3, T 20080, clean), has a most interesting Sun market (beware pickpockets) and the renowned Capilla del Santo Cristo in the church. The chapel is similar in style to Santo Domingo in Oaxaca, with intricate white and gold stucco, lots of mirrors, silver altar rails and sculptures of martyrs in gruesome detail. Two beheaded saints guard the door to the main nave (fiesta 9 Oct). There is a pleasant walled garden in front of the church. A band plays every evening in the plaza, take a sweater, cold wind most evenings, starts at 1930. The square is colonnaded. On the main street is a *casa de cambio* Tlacolula can be reached by bus from Oaxaca, from the 2nd class bus station every 30 mins, but every 15 mins on Sun, US$0.60. Taxis and *peseros* stop by the church, except on Sun when they gather on a street behind the church; ask directions. Tlacolula's bus station is just off the main highway, several blocks from the centre.

Quality weavings can be found at **Santa Ana del Valle** (3 km from Tlacolula). Sr Alberto Sánchez García, Sor Juana I de la Cruz No 1 sells excellent wool with natural dyes. Turn right just after the school and left at the T-junction at the top of hill. Sr Sánchez's home is several compounds along on the right with a faded blue metallic gate door. Good prices. The village is peaceful and friendly with a small museum. Ask any villager for the keyholder. Cheap guesthouse. There are two *fiestas*, each lasting 3 days. One takes place the 2nd week of Aug, the other at the end of January. Buses leave from Tlacolula every 30 mins.

YAGUL

The ruins of **Yagul** (on the way to Mitla), are an outstandingly picturesque site where the ball courts and quarters of the priests are set in a landscape punctuated by candelabra cactus and agave. Yagul was a large Zapotec and Mixtec religious centre; the ball courts are perhaps the most perfect discovered to date; also fine tombs (take the path from behind the ruins, the last part is steep) and temples. There is a superb view from the hill behind the ruins.

● **Admission** Entrance to ruins daily 0800-1700, US$1. Guided tours in English on Tues, US$10, from Oaxaca travel agencies. Fletes y Pasajes buses and taxis from Oaxaca. Ask to be put down at paved turn off to Yagul. You will have to walk 2 km from the bus stop to the site, and you can return the same way or walk 3 km to Tlacolula to catch a bus (signposted). Car park US$0.20.

MITLA

From the main road a turn left leads 4 km to **Mitla** (whose name means 'place of the dead') where there are ruins of four great palaces among minor ones. Some of the archaeology, outside the fenced-in site, can be seen within the present-day town.

Magnificent bas-reliefs, the sculptured designs in the Hall of Mosaics, the Hall of the Columns, and in the depths of a palace, La Columna de la Muerte (Column of Death), which people embrace and measure what they can't reach with their fingers to know how many years they have left to live (rather hard on long-armed people). The museum just W of the Zócalo in the village is interesting (US$2). There is a soberly decorated colonial church with three cupolas (no access from church to ruins, or vice versa). Beautiful traditional Indian clothes and other goods may be bought at the new permanent market behind the church, bargaining possible. On the cobbled road from the town to the church and ruins are many *artesanía* shops and others selling good *mescal*. Sellers of carved wooden animals and figures congregate near the site entrance. A car and bus park is located behind the church also.

● **Admission** Entry US$1.30 (Sun free, students with ID free, use of video US$4.50), open 0800-1700 daily, literature available on site.

● **Accommodation** C *Hotel y Restaurante Mitla*, on town square, clean, local food; C *Hotel y Restaurante La Zapoteca*, before bridge on road to ruins, newer and better than *Mitla*, cheaper food, good. The University of the Americas has a small guest-house, and runs the small Frissell museum in the Zócalo at Mitla, with very good and clean restaurant, *La Sorpresa*, good, cheap food, in a patio; restaurant opp site, *Santa María*; *María Elena* restaurant 100m from site towards village, good *comida corriente*. The local technical college provides accommodation, showers and a bathroom; it is also possible to arrange rooms with families.

● **Transport** Taxi costs US$10 each to Mitla for 4 sharing, with time to take photographs at Tule and Mitla and to buy souvenirs at ruins. Tours (1000 till 1300, rather rushed) to Tule, Mitla and Tlacolula from Oaxaca agencies, cost US$7.50, not inc entry fees. Fletes y Pasajes bus from Oaxaca, 2nd class bus station, every 20 mins to Mitla, 1 hr, US$0.75; the ruins are 10 mins' walk across the village (from the bus stop on the main road, 2 blocks from the square). Minibuses from Oaxaca leave a shorter walk to the ruins than regular buses.

From Mitla take a bus to San Lorenzo (1 hr, US$1). 3 km from there is the village of **Hierve El Agua**. There are also two 2nd class buses a day to Hieve El Agua at 0700 and 1400, returning 0900 and 1600. A cliff over which water from pools flows has created a stalactite, which looks like a petrified waterfall. You can swim in the mineral pools. There is no water in the dry season. There is a village-run hotel. **E** *Tourist-Yu'u*, T (951) 60123, rooms for 6 people with kitchen, hot water, discounts for students, good restaurant, rec. Also several excellent foodstalls (quesadillas etc) above the car park.

From Mitla the road is paved as far as Ayutla, but an unpaved single track runs from then on to Playa Vicente (4WD rec) Beautiful mountain scenery and cloud forest. No accommodation between Ayutla and Playa Vicente.

EXCURSIONS SOUTH OF OAXACA

Sat trips from Oaxaca to market at **San Antonio Ocotlán** on the road to Puerto

Angel, with good prices for locally woven rugs and baskets, also excellent fruit and veg (stallholders prefer not to be photographed); buses leave every 30 mins for Ocotlán (not to be confused with another village called San Antonio) from the microbus station SE of the Mercado Artesanal on Armenta y López (30 mins' journey, US$0.35). Outside the Mercado de Abastos a steady stream of colectivos leave for US$0.70. Stop in **San Bártolo Coyotepec** to see black pottery (Doña Rosa's, she's been dead for years but her name survives, is a target for tours, but other families are just as good) and don't try to bargain (also red and green ceramics in the village), and in **Santo Tomás Jalieza**, where cotton textiles are made.

CUILAPAN

17 km SW of Oaxaca is **Cuilapan**, where there is a vast unfinished 16th century convent, now in ruins, with a famous nave and columns, and an 'open chapel', whose roof collapsed in an earthquake. "At the back of the unfinished chapel is a board on which the Zapotec and Mixtec calendars had been correlated. On the left side is the date 1555 in Arabic numerals; the two calendars differed by 13 years, Zapotec 1555, Mixtec 1568. The last Zapotec princess, Donaji, daughter of the last ruler Cosijoeza, married a Mixtec prince at Tilantongo and was buried at Cuilapan. On the grave is an inscription with their Christian names, Mariana Cortez and Diego Aguilar." (Helmut Zettl, Ebergassing.) Reached by bus from Oaxaca from 2nd class bus station, on C Bustamante, near de Arista (US$0.50), take bus to Zaachila (US$0.60) which leaves every 30 mins, then walk to unexcavated ruins in valley. **Zaachila** is a poor town, but there are ruins, with two Mixtec tombs, with owls in stucco work in the outer chamber and carved human figures with skulls for heads inside, admission US$4.35. No restrictions on flash photography. There is an Indian market on Thur. 80 km S on Route 131 is **San Sebastián** (about 10 km

off the road) where there are caves. Ask for a guide at the Agencia Municipal next to the church; guide obligatory, US$1.50. Take bus 175 from Oaxaca.

EXCURSIONS NORTHEAST OF OAXACA

To San Pablo de **Guelatao** (65 km from Oaxaca), the birthplace of Benito Juárez. The town is located in the mountains and can be reached by bus (US$1.50, 3 hrs) along a paved but tortuously winding road. There are a memorial and a museum to Juárez on the hillside within the village (entry, US$0.20), and a pleasant lake with a symbolic statue of a shepherd and his lambs. The area is beautiful although the town is rather neglected.

ISTHMUS OF TEHUANTEPEC

We are approaching a more traditional part of Mexico; Tehuantepec isthmus and the mountains of Chiapas beyond, a land inhabited by Indians less influenced than elsewhere by the Spanish conquest. Only about 210 km separate the Atlantic and the Pacific at the hot, heavily-jungled Isthmus of Tehuantepec, where the land does not rise more than 250m. There are a railway (to be renewed) and a Trans-Isthmian Highway between Coatzacoalcos and Salina Cruz, the terminal cities on the two oceans. Winds are very strong on and near the isthmus, because of the intermingling of Pacific and Caribbean weather systems. Drivers of high-sided vehicles must take great care.

NB In southern Mexico the word 'Zócalo' is not often used for the main square of a town: 'Plaza (Mayor)' is much more common.

Route 190 heads SE from Oaxaca towards the Golfo de Tehuantepec and the Pacific. At Km 116, in **San José de Gracia**, is the hotel and restaurant *El Mirador*, **D**, clean, very friendly, noisy from passing trucks, overlooking a beautiful valley, parking in front. At Km 134 in the village of **El Camarón** is **E** *Hotel Santa Elena*, new, clean, friendly, fan and TV. There are some basic restaurants in the village.

TEHUANTEPEC

(Km 804; *Pop* 45,000; *Alt* 150m) **Santo Domingo Tehuantepec** is 257 km from Oaxaca. A colourful place, it is on the bend of a river around which most of its activities take place and which makes it very humid. Tehuantepec is probably a better place to break the journey to Tapachula than Salina Cruz, but some find it a smelly, rundown city, others find it friendly nonetheless. The plaza has arcades down one side, a market on the other, and many stands selling *agua fresca*, an iced fruit drink. At dusk the trees of the square are filled with black birds roosting and making an incredible noise. There is more noise from the music played through loud speakers at high volume. Houses are low, in white and pastel shades. The Indians are mostly Zapotecs whose social organization was once matriarchal: the women are high-pressure saleswomen, with some Spanish blood; their hair is sometimes still braided and brightly ribboned and at times they wear embroidered costumes. The men for the most part work in the fields, or as potters or weavers, or at the nearby oil refinery. Hammocks made in this area are of the best quality.

Excursions

To neighbouring villages for *fiestas*. Near the town are the ruins of **Guingola**, 'the Mexican Machu Picchu', so called because of its lonely location on a mountain. It has walls up to 3m high, running, it is said, for 40 km; there are the remains of two pyramids and a ball court. This last fortress of the Zapotecs was never conquered; Alvarado and his forces marched past it in 1522. Take the 0500 bus Tehuantepec towards Oaxaca and alight at Km 141, at the bridge (8 km from Tehuantepec). Take the turn at the signpost 'Ruinas Guingola 7 km'. Walk 5 km then turn left, uphill, to the car park. From here it is 1½ hrs to the ruins.

Try to return before 0900 because it gets very hot; take plenty of water. Alternatively, take a taxi to the car park and ask the driver to return for you 3 hrs later, or drive there. (With thanks to Helmut Zettl of Ebergassing for these details.)

Local festivals

The town is divided into 15 wards, and each holds a *fiesta*, the main one at the end of Holy Week, when the women wear their finest costumes and jewellery. A large fair takes place the week leading up to Easter. There is another splendid *fiesta* in honour of St John the Baptist on 22-25 June. Jan and Feb are good months for the ward *fiestas*.

Local information
● **Accommodation**

Mostly overpriced and basic. **D** *Donají*, Juárez 10, a/c, nr market, clean, friendly, rec; **D** *Oasis*, on Av Juana C Romero, 1 block from plaza, good atmosphere, with bath and a/c, simple, safe parking, owner Julín Contreras is head of local Casa de Cultura and is looking for volunteers to help restore convent, good information on local history and traditions; **E** *Casa de Huéspedes Istmo*, Hidalgo 31, 1½ blocks before the main plaza, quiet, basic, with lovely patio.

Camping: *Santa Teresa* Trailer Park, E side of town, 8 km off Route 190 (take side road at *Hotel Calli* and follow signs), US$6.50 for car and 2 people, cold showers, restrooms, drinking water, restaurant, lovely mango grove, very friendly owner.

● **Places to eat**

Cheap food on top floor of market. *Colonial*, good *comida corrida*. *Mariscos Silvia*, ½ block off route 190 on main road into town, excellent shrimp, moderate; *Restaurant Colonial*, around corner from *Hotel Donají*, good food, clean, friendly; *Restaurant Scaru*, on Leona Vicario, good food, reasonable, nice courtyard; *Jugos Hawaii*, Av Juárez, on plaza, freshly squeezed juices, snacks, ice-cream, friendly. The local *quesadillas* made of maize and cheese are delicious; sold at bus stops. Tehuantepec is noted for its mangoes.

● **Transport**

Road The highway between Tehuantepec and Tapachula is being made into a dual carriageway; the construction work may cause delays to road transport.

Buses 3-wheeled rickshaws take locals around town, you have to stand and hold on to the railing. There are several bus companies at N end of town, taxi to Zócalo US$1, or 15 mins' walk. One bus a day to **San Cristóbal** at 1230, it may be full, standing is not allowed but the driver may accept a present and let you on (7½ hrs, US$14.80). To **Coatzacoalcos** at 0730, 9-10 hrs, US$8 2nd class. Bus to **Arriaga** at 0600, 0800, 1800 to connect to Tonalá. To **Tuxtla Gutiérrez**, 2130, 2200, 0030, 0400, 4½ hrs, 2nd class at 0130, and Tapachula, US$14.80 (Cristóbal Colón). Bus to **Tonalá** (Cristóbal Colón) at 0030 and 0130. To **Oaxaca**, US$6.50, 5 hrs, with Istmo, US$8 Cristóbal Colón, US$7 2nd class; to **Salina Cruz**, US$0.25 with Istmeños; to **Pochutla**, and **Puerto Escondido**, with Istmo at 1300; to **Villahermosa**, Cristóbal Colón 1st class, US$14, 8 hrs, 2nd class US$10.50. (**NB** Some buses from Salina Cruz do not stop at Tehuantepec.)

SALINA CRUZ

(*Pop* 43,000) 21 km from Tehuantepec, a booming and evil-smelling port with a naval base, extensive oil-storage installations and an oil refinery. Bathing is dangerous because of the heavy swell from Pacific breakers and also sharks. Beware of overcharging in the marketplace. Car drivers should not park close to the beach in windy weather unless they want their vehicle sandblasted.

- **Accommodation C** *Costa Real*, Progreso, nr Manuel A Camacho, with parking; *Fuente*, bath, basic. *Río*, reasonable, nr Cristóbal Colón bus station. **E** *Magda*, on 5 de Mayo, ½ block from Zócalo. *Parador*, on road to Juchitán, a/c, pool, rec.

- **Places to eat** *Costa del Pacífico*, hires shower cabin, stores luggage. *El Lugar*, corner of Acapulco y 5 de Mayo on 1st floor.

- **Transport Buses** Two daily buses from Salina Cruz to **San Cristóbal** come from Oaxaca and are very often full (2nd class, US$14); take instead a 2nd class bus to **Juchitán**, then to Arriaga and from there to Tuxtla and San Cristóbal; a long route. To **Coatzacoalcos**, US$12.15, 6 hrs. Salina Cruz-**Pochutla**, US$5, 4 hrs; 2nd class to **Puerto Escondido**, 6 hrs, slow, US$9.75. Frequent buses to **Tehuantepec**, 30 mins, US$0.75. To **Tapachula** by Cristóbal Colón 2nd class, along the coast,

9-10 hrs, 0740 and 2030, US$14.50, 1st class bus at 2000. No luggage storage at bus station. Cristóbal Colón terminal is on Av 5 de Mayo, ½ block from Zócalo. Istmeños are on Av Tampico at Progreso, new comfortable buses, rec.

10 km to the SE is a picturesque fishing village with **La Ventosa** beach which, as the name says, is windy. Buses go to the beach every 30 mins from a corner of the main square. Accommodation: **D** *La Posada de Rustrian*, overlooking the sea, with bath in new block, half in old block, poor value; unnamed *pensión*, **E**, on right of road before asphalt ends. Friendly family at the top of the dirt road coming from Salina Cruz (on the right) and 200m after the first path that leads down to the beach, rents hammocks, US$1 a night, fried fish US$1. *Champas*, or hammocks under thatch shelters by the beach, US$1 a night. The owners serve drinks and food (fish, shrimps, crabs just caught) from early morning on. Prices often high. At the end of the road which crosses the village is a good restaurant under a high palm roof, excellent fish.

WARNING It is not safe to wander too far off along the beach alone, nor to sleep on the beach or in your car.

JUCHITÁN

27 km beyond Tehuantepec on the road to Tuxtla Gutiérrez is **Juchitán de Zaragoza** The town is very old, Indian, with an extensive market, many *fiestas* and a special one on 19 June. The women wear Zapotec dress as everyday costume.

- **Accommodation & places to eat E** *Hotel Don Alex*, clean, cheapest; *El Palacio de Gemas*, next door, is rec for gemstones, good selection at reasonable prices; **D** *Hotel Casa Río*, has an Indian name, *Coty*, not posted, next to Casa Río shop, nr market, clean, (be prepared to bargain in cheap hotels); the Casa de Cultura can help if you want to stay with local people and learn about their culture, eg with Florinda Luis Orozco, Callejón de los Leones 18, entre Hidalgo y Aldana; good restaurant in the Casa Grande, a beautifully restored colonial house on the main square. *Café Colón*, close to the bus station, good.

• **Transport** 2nd class bus Oaxaca-Juchitán, at least twice a day, US$8.25, 6 hrs, frequent Juchitán-Tuxtla, 1st class, 4 hrs, US$7.15. Connect here with train from Veracruz to Tapachula, 18 hrs, US$6, but Juchitán station is very dangerous (at night you are strongly advised to wait for the train in Ixtepec).

A road runs 6 km NW to **Ixtepec** (airport), railway junction on the lines Veracruz- Tapachula and Salina Cruz-Medias Aguas (**Accommodation E** *Casa de Huéspedes San Gerónimo*, close to train station and market, clean, good; **E** *Panamericano*, noisy from railway station; **E** *San Juan*, bath, acceptable). Natural and man-made pools are fed by springs rising in Santiago Laollaga, free bathing, popular with Mexicans.

JUCHITAN TO TAPACHULA

Routes from W to E. merge to cross the isthmus from W to E. Accommodation is available at **Zanatepec** (Motel: **C-D** *Posada San Rafael*, very comfortable, safe parking); and at **Tapanatepec** (**D** *Motel La Misión* on Highway 190 on northern outskirts, T (91971) 70140, fan, hot water, clean, TV, hammock outside each room, affiliated restaurant, very good), where Highway 190 heads NE to Tuxtla Gutiérrez and Highway 200 continues SE to the Guatemalan border. **Arriaga** (*Pop* 12,000) is a good stopping place; many banks around Zócalo for exchange. The road from Arriaga to Tapachula is a 4-lane divided freeway.

• **Accommodation & places to eat C** *Ik-Lu-maal*, nr Zócalo, a/c, clean, quiet, good restaurant; *El Parador*, Km 47 on road to Tonalá, T 20199, clean with swimming pool; **D** *Colonial*, Callejón Ferrocarril, next to bus station, clean, friendly, quiet, limited free parking; **E** *Arbolitos*, fan, basic, clean, off main road; *Restaurant Xochimilco*, nr bus stations.

• **Buses** To many destinations, mostly 1st class, to Mexico City, US$26.50, 12-13 hrs, at 1645. To Tuxtla with Fletes y Pasajes at 1400 and 1600, 4 hrs, US$7. To Oaxaca, 6 hrs, US$7.

TONALA

The 200 road then goes to **Tonalá**, formerly a very quiet town but now noisy and dirty, with a small museum; good market (bus Tonalá-Tapachula, 3 hrs, US$6.75; also buses to Tuxtla). Beyond Tonalá the road is mostly straight and in perfect condition. This is by far the most direct road for travellers seeking the quickest way from Mexico City to Guatemala.

• **Accommodation B** *Galilea*, Av Hidalgo y Callejón Ote, T 30239, with bath, air-conditioned, good, basic cheap rooms on 1st floor, balconies, on main square, with good restaurants; **D** *Tonalá*, Hidalgo 172, T 30480, opp museum; **E** *Casa de Huéspedes El Viajero*, Av Matamoros, nr market, with bath, rough but OK; **E** *Faro*, 16 de Septiembre 24, nr Plaza.

• **Places to eat** *Santa Elena Restaurant*, at the S end of town, nr Cristóbal Colón bus station on outskirts, good. On the Plaza, *Restaurant Nora*. Numerous Chinese-named restaurants; good breakfast at restaurants on Zócalo.

Excursions from Tonalá

Along the coast from Tonalá to Tapachula there are several fine-looking and undeveloped beaches (although waves and/or currents are dangerous). **Puerto Arista** (17 km S of Tonalá) is now being built up, but it is still a relatively peaceful area with 30 km of beach to relax on; bus from Tonalá every hour, 45 mins, US$0.50, taxi US$2; plenty of buses to Arriaga, US$0.75.

• **Accommodation & places to eat** Many hotels, motels and restaurants on the beach; hot, muggy, lots of mosquitoes and, in the wet season, sandflies. Take your own water. **B** *Arista Bougainvilla*, with private beach, a/c, pools, restaurant; **E** *Casa Diana*, N end of beach road, run by 2 Canadians, with breakfast, nice, friendly. Some restaurants (closed by 2000) have rooms to rent, eg *Restaurant Turquesa*; small hotel/restaurant 3 blocks down on the right from where the road reaches the beach coming from Tonalá and turns right, next to bakery, no fan, basic, **F**. **Camping**: at E edge of town, Canadian run, well organized, clean, US$1.50 pp.

Buses also from Tonalá to Boca del Cielo further down the coast, which is good for bathing and has *cabañas* with hammocks, and similarly Cabeza del Toro. **Paredón**, on the huge lagoon Mar Muerto, 14 km W of Tonalá, has excellent seafood and one very basic guest house. One can take a local fishing boat out into the lagoon to swim; the shore stinks because fishermen clean fish on the beach among dogs and pigs. Served by frequent buses.

En route for Tapachula one passes through **Pijijiapan** where there is the *Hotel Pijijilton* (!) next to the Cristóbal Colón bus station; also **C** *Hotel El Estraneo*, very nice, parking in courtyard and **E** *Sabrina*, nice, clean and quiet, safe parking; many on Ruta México 200, cg *El Navegante Los Reyes*, E per bed, doubles only. Also **Huixtla**, which has a good market, no tourists (**E** *Casa de Huespedes Regis*, Independencia Nte 23).

TAPACHULA

(*Pop* 144,000; *Phone code* 962) **Tapachula** is a pleasant, neat, but expensive, hot commercial town (airport; cinemas in centre). Avenidas runs N-S, Calles E-W (Oriente-Poniente). Odd-numbered Calles are N of Calle Central, odd Avenidas are E of Av Central. It is the road and rail junction for Guatemala (road crossings at the Talismán bridge, or at Ciudad Hidalgo).

Local information
● Accommodation

AJ *Motel Loma Real*, Carretera Costera No 200, Km 244, T 61440, 1 km N of city, operates as a 1st class hotel, use of swimming pool, cold showers.

C *Don Miguel*, 1 C Pte No 18, T 61143; **C** *San Francisco*, Av Central Sur 94, T 61454, F 52114, 15 mins from centre, good, a/c, large rooms, hot water, TV, restaurant, safe parking; **C** *Posada Michel*, 5 C Pte No 23, T 52640, a/c; **C** *Santa Julia*, next to Cristóbal Colón terminal, bath, phone, TV, a/c, clean, good. In centre within 1 block of Plaza Central.

D *Fénix*, 4 Av Nte 19, T 50755; **D** *Tabasco*, with shower, close to first-class bus station, poor value but friendly.

E *Cinco de Mayo*, 5 C Pte y 12 Av Nte, with bath (cheaper without), not very clean, convenient for Talismán colectivos which leave ½ block away; **E** *Colonial*, 4 Av Nte 31, attractive courtyard, about 1 block from central square, good value, clean, safe; **E** *El Retorno*, opp, on 5 C Pte, is unhelpful and noisy; **E** *Plaza Guizar*, 2 Av Nte, old, pleasant, clean, hot water, rooms differ so ask to see more than one; **E** *Rex*, 8 Av Nte 43, T 50376, similar *Hospedaje Carballo*, 6 Av Nte 18, T 64370; **E** *San Román*, 9 C Pte entre 10 y 12 Av Nte, shower, fan, safe motorcycle parking, clean, quiet, friendly, drinks for sale.

On 11 C Poniente: **D** *Alfa*, No 53, T 65442, clean, fan, cold shower, similar *Posada de Calu*, No 34, T 65659; **E** *Hospedaje Santa Cruz*, No 36, clean, fan, bath, no windows in some rooms; all a long way from Cristóbal Colón 2nd class terminal (15-20 blocks). Many hotels along Avenidas 4, 6, 8 (nr Plaza); **E** *Pensión Mary*, Av 4 Nte No 28, T 63400, has cheap *comidas*; **E** *Atlántida*, 6 Av N, C 11/13 Pte, T 62136, helpful, clean, cheaper without window, fans, noisy, safe parking for 2; **E** *Hospedaje Madrid*, 8 Av Nte, No 43, T 63018, shared bath.

● Places to eat
Good restaurant next to Cristóbal Colón terminal and on main square. *Snoopy*, 4 Av 19, friendly, excellent tortas, breakfasts; *Viva Pizza*, Av Central, good pizza, reasonable price. Good, cheap chicken on Central Nte; *Heladas Irma*, C 13 Pte between Av 4 y 6, good ice-cream.

● Banks & money changers
Avoid the crowds of streetwise little boys at the border; exchange is rather better in the town, bus station gives a good rate (cash only). **Banamex**, Blvd Díaz Ordaz, open 0830-1230, 1400-1600, disagreement over whether TCs are charged. *Casa de cambio Tapachula*, 4 Av Nte y 3 C Pte, changes dollars, TCs, pesos, quetzales, lempiras and colones (open late Mon-Sat), but not rec, poor rates, very difficult to change money on Sun. Try the supermarket.

● Embassies & consulates
Guatemalan Consulate, 2 C Ote 33 and 7 Av S, T 61252, taxi from Colón terminal, US$1. (Open Mon-Fri 0800-1600; visa US$10, friendly and quick, take photocopy of passport, photocopier 2 blocks away, the consul may give a visa on Sat if you are willing to pay extra.)

● Laundry
There is a laundry, at Av Central Nte 99 between 13 y 15 C Ote, US$3 wash and dry, 1 hr service, about 2 blocks from Cristóbal Colón bus station, open Sun. Also on Central Nte between Central Ote y 1 C, opens 0800, closed Sun.

● Post & telecommunications
Telephone: several long-distance phone offices, eg *Esther*, 5 Av Nte 46; *La Central*, Av Central Sur No 95; *Monaco*, 1 C Pte 18.

Tapachula

M26a

N

To Tonalá & Tuxtla Gutiérrez

Migración

17 C Pte

Av 14 Norte

12 Av Norte

8 Av Norte

6 Av Norte

4 Av Norte

2 Av Norte

9 C Pte

Colectivos to Talismán

5 C Pte

Iglesia San Agustín

Parque Hidalgo

Av Central Norte

Av 1 Norte

Av 3 Norte

Av 5 Norte

Av 7 Norte

Av 9 Norte

17 C Ote

Cristóbal Colón buses

To Talismán

15 C Ote

13 C Ote

11 C Ote

9 C Ote

C Central Pte

2 C Pte

4 C Pte

Templo de Buena Esperanza

C Central Oriente

5 C Ote

3 C Ote

1 C Ote

8 C Pte

C 6 Ote

Guatemalan Consul

C 8 Ote

Av 4 Sur

Av 2 Sur

Av Central Sur

Av 3 Sur

Av 5 Sur

Av 7 Sur

Av 9 Sur

To Airport & Puerto Madero

Hotels:
1. *Colonial*
2. *Fénix*
3. *Mary*

● **Shopping**

Rialfer, supermarket, Blvd Díaz, 2 doors from Banamex.

● **Tour companies & travel agents**

Viajes Tacaná, operated by Sr Adolfo Guerrero Chávez, 4 Av Nte 6, T 63502/63501/63245; trips to Izapa ruins, to mountains, beaches and can gain entry to museum when closed.

● **Tourist offices**

4 Nte 35, Edif del Gobierno del Estado, 3rd floor,

between 3 and 5 Pte, T 65470, F 65522, Mon-Fri, 0900-1500, 1800-2000, helpful.

● **Useful addresses**

Migración/Gobernación: 14 Av Nte 57, T 61263.

● **Transport**

Air Aviacsa, C Central Nte 52-B, T 63147, T/F 63159, flies daily Tapachula-Tuxtla Gutiérrez-Mexico City; AeroMéxico, 2 Av Nte 6, T 63921, flies daily to Mexico City, as does Taesa,

T 63732. Kombis to airport from 2 C Sur 40, T 51287. From airport to border, minibuses charge US$26 for whole vehicle, so share with others, otherwise take colectivo to 2nd class bus terminal and then a bus to Ciudad Hidalgo.

Trains To Veracruz at 0730, US$10, 2nd class, via Ixtepec, Medias Aguas and Tierra Blanca, arr 0600 next day. To get a seat, board the train hours in advance. Train also to Cd Hidalgo at 1315, arr 1435, US$0.50.

Buses Buses (Cristóbal Colón 1st class, Av 3 Nte y 17 Ote, T 62880; 2nd class Prolongación 9 Pte s/n, T 61161) to/from Tapachula to **Mexico City**, US$40, 5 a day, all pm, 18 hrs in theory (frequent stops for toilets and food, also frequent police checks, no toilet or a/c on bus), much better to take 'plus' service, 1915, US$58. Buses from Mexico City all leave pm also; the 1545 and 1945 go on to Talismán. Bus to **Oaxaca**, Cristóbal Colón and Fipsa (9 C Ote, T 67603) has luggage store, US$19, 14 hrs, many passport checks (Fipsa has 4 a day, continuing to Puebla and Córdoba, take 1830 to see sunrise over the Sierra Madre; also has 2 a day to Mexico City). Cristóbal Colón, plus service to **Puebla**, US$37.50; UNO, US$53, 16 hrs. To Tehuantepec and Salina Cruz 0915, 8 hrs, US$14.80; to San Cristóbal de las Casas and Tuxtla Gutiérrez at 1100. The second class bus station is at 3 Av Nte, 9 C Ote. To **Oaxaca**, 10 hrs, US$14.

FRONTIER WITH GUATEMALA-TALISMAN

It is 8 km from Tapachula to the frontier at the Talismán bridge (open 24 hrs a day).

● **Immigration**

The Mexican customs post is 200m from the Guatemalan one. Exit tax US$0.45. Lots of pushy children offer to help you through border formalities; pay US$2-3 for one, which keeps the others away.

NB The toilet at immigration at the crossing is dangerous, hold-ups have been reported day or night.

● **Guatemalan consulate**

In Tapachula, above.

● **Crossing by private vehicle**

Crossing into Guatemala by car can take several hours. If you don't want your car sprayed inside it may cost you a couple of dollars. Do not park in the car park at the control post, it is very expensive.

Motoring into Mexico See **Information for travellers**, **Automobiles**, on the temporary importation of vehicles, page 528. Car papers are issued at the Garita de Aduana on Ruta 200 out of Tapachula. There is no other road, you can't miss it. Photocopies of documents must be made in town; no facilities at the Garita.

● **Accommodation**

There is a *hospedaje* at the border.

● **Exchange**

Exchange in town rather than with men standing around customs on the Guatemalan side (check rates before dealing with them, and haggle; there is no bank on the Guatemalan side).

● **Transport**

Kombi vans run from near the Unión y Progreso bus station, about US$1; *colectivo* from outside *Posada de Calu* to Talismán, US$0.60, also from C 5 Pte between Avs 12 y 14 Nte. Taxi Tapachula-Talismán, negotiate fare to about US$2. There are few buses between the Talismán bridge and Oaxaca or Mexico City (though they do exist); advisable therefore to travel to Tapachula for connection, delays can occur there at peak times. A taxi from Guatemala to Mexican immigration will cost US$2, but it may be worth it if you are in a hurry to catch an onward bus. Hitchhikers should note that there is little through international traffic at Talismán bridge.

FRONTIER WITH GUATEMALA-CIUDAD HIDALGO

There is another crossing S of Tapachula, at **Ciudad Hidalgo**, opposite Tecún Umán (you cannot change TCs here); there are road connections to Coatepeque, Mazatenango and Retalhuleu.

● **Immigration**

A few blocks from the town plaza is Mexican immigration, at the foot of the kilometre-long bridge across the Río Suchiate; cycle taxis cross the bridge for about US$1, pedestrians pay US$0.15.

● **Transport**

From C 7 Pte between Av 2 Nte and Av Central Nte, Tapachula, buses go to 'Hidalgo', US$1.25.

Excursions from Tapachula

The coastal town of **Puerto Madero**, 18 km from Tapachula (bus US$1.80), is worse than Puerto Arista, because it is more built up and the beaches stink from rubbish being burned. Intense heat in summer. (**E** *Hotel Pegado*, run down, not rec, better is unnamed *hospedaje*, also E; **F** *Hotel Puerto Madero*, accommodation in what are really remains of cement block room.) Water defences are being built, but the graveyard is under threat of being washed into the sea (watch out for skulls, etc). Many fish restaurants on beach.

Visit the ruins of **Izapa** (proto-classic stelae, small museum) just off the road to Talismán; the part of the site on the N is easily visible but a larger portion is on the S side of the highway, about 1 km away, ask caretaker for guidance. These buildings influenced Kaminal Juyú near Guatemala City and are considered archaeologically important as a Proto-Mayan site. Some findings from the ruins are displayed in the **Museo Regional del Soconusco** on the W side of the Zócalo in Tapachula. To reach Izapa take kombi from Unión Progreso bus station. 45 km NE of Tapachula, beyond the turning to Talismán is **Unión Juárez** (**E** *Hotel Alijoat*, hot shower, reasonable restaurant; **E** *Hotel Colonial*; *Restaurant Carmelita* on the square is modest with fair prices). In Unión Juárez one can have one's papers stamped and proceed on foot via Talquián to the Guatemalan border at Sibinal. Take a guide.

A worthwhile hike can be made up the **Tacaná volcano** (4,150m), which takes 2-3 days from Unión Juárez. Ask for the road to Chiquihuete, no cars. The Tapachula tourist office can help; in Unión Juárez ask for Sr Umberto Ríos at *Restaurante Montaña*, he will put you in touch with guide Moises Hernández, who charges US$15 a day. It is possible to stay overnight in Don Emilio Velásquez' barn half way up, US$2; he offers coffee and tortillas. At the top are some *cabañas* in which you sleep for free, sleeping bag essential.

CHIAPAS HEARTLAND

Beyond Las Cruces (near the Oaxaca-Chiapas border) we enter the mountainous Chiapas state, mostly peopled by Maya Indians whose extreme isolation has now been ended by air services and the two main highways. Chiapas ranks first in cacao production, second in coffee, bananas and mangoes, and cattle-grazing is important. Hardwoods are floated out down the rivers which flow into the Gulf.

NB Following the EZLN uprising in early 1994, check on political conditions in Chiapas state before travelling in the area. At the time of going to press, there was no fighting between the EZLN and the Mexican army.

From Las Cruces to Tuxtla Gutiérrez, Route 190 carries on to **Cintalapa** (**D** *Hotel Leos*, rec and restaurant; **E** hotel on main street, clean, with bath and fan) whence there is a steep climb up an escarpment. Mike Shawcross writes: Anyone with a vehicle who has time to visit or is looking for a place to spend the night would find it well worth while to make a 4-km detour. 30 km beyond Cintalapa a gravel road leads N (last section very rough, only accessible with 4WD with high clearance) to the beautiful waterfall in **El Aguacero National Park** (small sign), which falls several hundred feet down the side of the Río La Venta canyon. There is a small carpark at the lip of the canyon. 798 steps lead down to the river and the base of the waterfall. Good camping but no facilities.

Carry on to **Ozocoautla** (airport for Tuxtla; **D** *Posada San Pedro*, noisy, not rec), make a long ascent followed by descent to (Km 1,085) **Tuxtla Gutiérrez**.

TUXTLA GUTIERREZ

Capital of Chiapas (*Pop* 240,000; *State pop 1995* 3,606,828; *Alt* 522m; *Phone code* 961), 301 km from Tehuantepec. It is a hot, modern city with greatest interest to the tourist during the fair of Guadalupe.

Tuxtla Gutiérrez Centre & Orientation

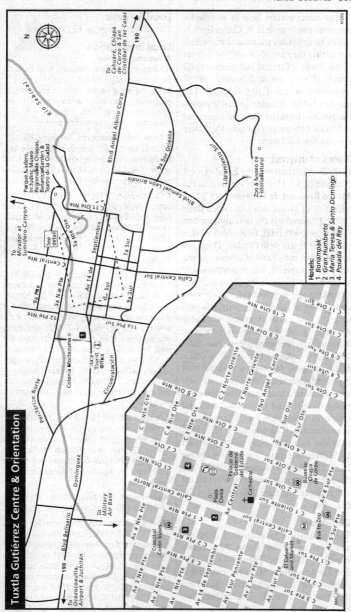

Hotels:
1 Bonampak
2 Gran Humberto
3 María Teresa & Santo Domingo
4 Posada del Rey

The street system here is as follows: Avenidas run from E to W, Calles from N to S. The Avenidas are named according to whether they are N (Norte) or S (Sur) of the Avenida Central and change their names if they are E (Oriente) or W (Poniente) of the Calle Central. The number before Avenida or Calle means the distance from the 'Central' measured in blocks. Drivers should note that there are very few road signs.

Places of interest

In the Parque Madero at the E end of town (Calzada de los Hombres Ilustres) is the **Museo Regional de Chiapas** with a fine collection of Mayan artefacts, open daily (US$1.25); nearby is the botanical garden (Tues-Sun, 0900-1600, free). Also in this park is the Teatro de la Ciudad. There is a superb **zoo** some 3 km S of town up a long hill (too far to walk), which contains only animals and birds from Chiapas, wild ("monkeys and hundreds of agoutis wandering around") and in captivity. It is said to be the best zoo in Mexico, if not Latin America, good for birdwatchers too, *quetzales* may be seen (open Tues-Sun, 0830-1730, aviary, nocturnal wildlife house, reptiles, insects, everything well explained, in Spanish only, free, but voluntary donation to ecological work recommended, shirts and posters for sale); the colectivos 'Zoológico' and 'Cerro Hueco' from Mercado, C 1a Ote Sur y 7 Sur Ote, pass the entrance every 20 mins; taxi US$2.50 from centre. Town buses charge US$0.15. When returning catch the bus from the same side you were dropped off as it continues up the hill to the end of the line where it fills up.

Excursions

Two vast artificial lakes made by dams are worth visiting: the **Presa Netzahualcoyotl**, or Mal Paso, 77 km NW of Tuxtla, and **La Angostura**, SE of the city. Information from the tourist office. Mal Paso can also be visited from Cárdenas (see page 408).

Local festivals

Fair of Guadalupe on 12 December.

Local information

● Accommodation

A2 *Bonampak* (Best Western), Blvd Belisario Domínguez 180, T 32050, F 22737, W end of town, the social centre, clean, noisy at night, expensive restaurant; *Flamboyant*, Blvd Belisario Domínguez 1081, T 50888, F 91961, comfortable, good swimming pool.

B *Gran Hotel Humberto*, Av Central Pte 180, T 22080, central, a/c, noisy disco; **B** *Palace Inn*, Blvd Belisario Domínguez Km 1081, 4 km from centre, T 50574, F 51042, generally rec, lovely garden, pool, noisy videobar.

C *La Mansión*, 1 Pte Nte 221, T 22151, a/c, bath, safe, clean, but street-facing rooms are noisy and affected by traffic fumes; all centrally located; **C** *Posada del Rey*, 2 Av Nte Ote 310, T 22911, a/c, but damp; **C** *Regional San Marcos*, 1 Sur y 2 Ote No 176, T 31940, cheaper without TV, close to Zócalo, bath, fan or a/c, clean.

D *Mar-Inn*, pleasant, clean, 2 Av Nte Ote 347, T 22715. Opposite Cristóbal Colón bus station are **D** *María Teresa* (2 Nte Pte 259-B, T 30102), and **E** *Santo Domingo*, with shower, good if you arrive late, but noisy and very basic; **E** *Estrella*, 2 Ote Nte 322, T 23827, with bath, friendly, clean, quiet, comfy, a bit run-down but safe, free drinking water, rec; **E** *La Posada*, 1 Av Sur Ote y 5 C Ote Sur, with or without bath, laundry facilities, friendly; **E** *Plaza Chiapas*, 2 Av Nte Ote y 2 C Nte Ote, T 38365, clean, with fan and hot shower, good value, enclosed car park, rec.

F *Posada del Sol*, 3 Nte Pte, 1 block from Cristóbal Colón buses, with hot shower and fan, good service, good value; **F** *Posada Maya*, 4 Pte Sur 322, fan, clean; *Posada Muñiz*, 2 Sur Ote 245, nr 2nd class bus station, not rec, but useful for early departures; **F** *Santa Elena*, Ote Sur 346, basic.

Youth hostel: Calz Angel Albino Corzo 1800, CP 29070, T 33405, run down, meals available.

Motels: **C** *Costa Azul*, Libramiento Sur Ote No 3722, T 13364/13452, comfy, clean, but everything designed for short-stay couples; **C** *El Sumidero*, Panamericana Km 1093, on left as you enter town from E, a/c, comfortable, but much passing trade; **C** *La Hacienda*, trailer-park-hotel, Belisario Domínguez 1197 (W end of town on Route 190), T 50849, camping US$7-8/tent, 4 spaces with hook-up, hot showers, restaurant, minipool, US$13.50 for car and 2 people, a bit noisy and not easily accessible for RVs over 6m, owner speaks English.

● **Places to eat**
Parrilla La Cabaña, 2 Ote Nte 250, excellent *tacos*, very clean; *Los Arcos*, Central Pte 806, good international food; *Las Pichanchas*, pretty courtyard, typical food, dancing from Chiapas with *marimba* music between 1400-1700 and 2000-2300, on Av Central Ote 857, worth trying; good pizza restaurant by cinema on Plaza, reasonable; *Mina*, Av Central Ote 525, nr bus station, good cheap *comida*; *Café Mesón Manolo*, Av Central Pte 238, good value, reasonably priced; *La Parcela*, 2C Ote, nr *Hotel Plaza Chiapas*, good, cheap, good breakfasts, rec; *Los Gallos*, 2 Av Nte Pte, 20m from Cristóbal Colón terminal, open 0700-2400, good and cheap; *Las Delicias*, 2 Pte between Central and 1 Nte, close to Cristóbal Colón terminal, good breakfasts and snacks; *Super Cocina Uno*, on 1 Nte Ote between 2 and 3 Nte Ote, good cheap *comida corrida*; *Pizzería San Marco*, behind Cathedral, good; *Bing*, 1 Sur Pte 1480, excellent ice-cream; many others. Coffee shop below *Hotel Avenida*, Av Central Pte 224, serves excellent coffee.

● **Banks & money changers**
Bancomer, 1 Sur Pte 1600, nr *Hotel Bonampak* for Visa, open 0900-1330; Banco Bital, opens 0800, good rates and service. For cheques and cash at 1 Sur Pte 350, nr Zócalo.

● **Post & telecommunications**
Post Office: on main square.

Telephone: international phone calls can be made from 1 Nte, 2 Ote, directly behind post office, 0800-1500, 1700-2100 (1700-2000 Sun).

● **Tour companies & travel agents**
Carolina Tours, Sr José Narváez Valencia (manager), Av Central Pte 1138, T 24281; reliable, rec; also coffee shop at Av Central Pte 230.

● **Tourist offices**
For Chiapas Av Central Pte 1500 block (on left-hand side going up), next to Bancomer building, in a complex with *artesanía* shop and cheap, a/c café, open 0900-1900 every day Col Moctezuma, has information on all Chiapas, inc very useful state and other maps, English spoken, free; also in Zoo, am only.

● **Transport**
Buses Cristóbal Colón 1st class bus terminal is at 2 Av Nte Pte 268; has buses daily to **Villahermosa** at 0620, 1300 and 1730, 8½ hrs,

US$14.80; to **Oaxaca** 4 a day, 10 hrs, US$16.50 1st class, US$10 2nd class; ADO to **Puebla**, US$30, departs 1845, UNO US$46, 14 hrs; ADO to **Veracruz**, US$25, at 2100; 8 a day to **Mexico City**, US$39, plus frequent buses 0430 to 2115 to **San Cristóbal de Las Casas**, 2 hrs, US$2.50, superb mountain journey; colectivos do the journey for the same price. To **Comitán** 0530 then each hour to 1800, Cristóbal Colón, US$5.80; to Ciudad Cuauhtémoc, same company, US$8, 0730 and 1245. Tuxtla-**Tapachula**, US$11, 4 a day; there are more 1st class than 2nd class to the Talismán bridge (1st class is less crowded). Oaxaca Pacífico buses to Salina Cruz, from 1st class bus terminal. Take travel sickness tablets for Tuxtla-Oaxaca road if you suffer from queasiness. To **Pochutla** with Cristóbal Colón at 0900 and 2000, 10 hrs, US$18. To **Palenque**, 2nd class, US$8, 7 hrs. To **Mérida** change at Villahermosa if no direct service at 1330, US$35. The scenery between Tuxtla and Mérida is very fine, and the road provides the best route between Chiapas and Yucatán.

Air The new airport (Llano San Juan, TGZ) for Tuxtla is way out at the next town of Ocozocoautla, a long drive to a mountain top. It is often shrouded in cloud and has crosswinds: there are times when aircraft do not leave for days! There are VW taxis at the bus station and opposite *Hotel Humberto*, but they will not drive to the airport unless they have a full passenger load and may tout hotels before going there. Journey takes 45-50 mins. Good facilities, inc restaurant. There is also Terán airport, souvenir shop, cafeteria, 10 mins by taxi from the centre, US$3.50. Direct taxi to San Cristóbal from Terán airport for US$35. Tuxtla Gutiérrez to Tapachula, daily with Aviacsa (Av Central Pte 1144, T 26880/28081, F 27086), new jets, 40 mins; to Villahermosa daily, 30 mins, Aerocaribe. Frequent to Mexico City, direct 1 hr 20 mins, Aerocaribe and Aviacsa, US$60. Aerocaribe also flies to Oaxaca, Palenque, Villahermosa, Mérida, Cancún and Havana. There are also charter flights from many destinations.

SUMIDERO CANYON

By excellent paved road through spectacular scenery, to the rim of the tremendous Canyon, over 1,000m deep. Indian warriors unable to endure the Spanish conquest hurled themselves into the canyon rather than submit. The canyon is in a national park, open 0600-1800, camping permitted outside the gate (bus US$3; taxi fare US$25 return; try to get a group together and negotiate with a *kombi* driver to visit the viewpoints on the road into the canyon, US$15 per vehicle, leave from 1 Nte Ote). To get to the first viewpoint only, take colectivo marked 'Km 4', get out at the end and walk about 3 km up the road. With your own car, you can drive up to the last mirador (restaurant), especially recommended at sunset (2-3 hrs' trip, 20 km W of the city). At Cahuaré, 10 km in the direction of Chiapa de Corzo, it is possible to park by the river. If going by bus, US$1.50 each way, get out just past the large bridge on the Chiapa de Corzo road. Boat trip into the Sumidero Canyon costs US$6.50 pp for the boat for 1½-2 hrs; boats often set out with 6 passengers but can take 10 (take a sweater, the boats go very fast). Tour from San Cristóbal including boat trip costs around US$18 with numerous travel agencies. It is easier to find people to make up numbers in Chiapa de Corzo than in Cahuaré, as the former is a livelier place with more restaurants, launches and other facilities. Good birdlife but sadly hundreds of plastic water bottles pollute the river. It is not recommended for swimming, besides, there are crocodiles.

CHIAPA DE CORZO

(*Pop* 35,000) 15 km on, a colonial town on a bluff overlooking the Grijalva River, is more interesting than Tuxtla: see a fine 16th century crown-shaped fountain, the 16th century church of Santo Domingo whose engraved altar is of solid silver, and famous craftsmen in gold and jewellery and lacquer work who travel the fairs. Painted and lacquered vessels made of pumpkins are a local speciality. There is a small lacquer museum. Chiapa de Corzo was a preclassic and proto-classic Maya site and shares features with early Maya sites in Guatemala; the ruins are behind the Nestlé plant, and some restored mounds are on private property in a field near modern houses. There are 1½ and 2-hr boat trips along the river to spot crocodiles, turtles, monkeys and hummingbirds, cost US$50 or US$60 for 12 passengers, wait by water's edge, boats soon fill up, rec.

Local festivals The *fiestas* here are outstanding: they reach their climax on 20-23 Jan (in honour of San Sebastián) with a pageant on the river, but there are daylight *fiestas*, Los Parachicos, on 15, 17 and 20 Jan, and the Chunta *fiestas*, at night, from 9-23 January. The musical parade is on 19 January. There is another *fiesta* in early Feb and San Marcos festival on 25 April, with various *espectáculos*.

- **Accommodation D** *Hotel Los Angeles*, on Plaza, often full, warm shower, fan, beautiful rooms; **C** *La Ceiba*, T 60773, with fan, a/c extra, bath, restaurant, pool, rec.

- **Places to eat** *Jardín Turístico* on main plaza, good restaurant, open until 2000 (*plato jardín* is a selection of different regional dishes); good seafood restaurants by the riverside. Along the pier there are many restaurants, inc the *Veronica*, good food, cheap, slow service.

- **Entertainment Bars**: plaza filled with bars playing jukeboxes.

- **Transport** Buses from Tuxtla Gutiérrez, 380 C 3C Ote Sur, US$0.50, frequent; several buses a day (1 hr) to San Cristóbal de Las Casas, 2nd class, US$3.50. Cristóbal Colón from Mexico City, 1815, US$36.50.

Mike Shawcross tells us: The waterfall at the **Cueva de El Chorreadero** is well worth a detour of 1 km (one restaurant here, rec). The road to the cave is 10 km past Chiapa de Corzo, a few kilometres after you start the climb up into the mountains to get to San Cristóbal. Camping possible but no facilities; take a torch to the cave.

ROUTES 35 km E of Tuxtla, just past Chiapa de Corzo, a road runs N, 294 km, to Villahermosa via Pichucalco (see page 411), paved all the way. If driving to Villahermosa, allow at least 5 hrs for the endless curves and hairpins down from the mountains, a very scenic route, nevertheless.

SAN CRISTOBAL DE LAS CASAS

(Km 1,170; *Pop* 90,000; *Alt* 2,110m) **San Cristóbal de Las Casas**, 85 km beyond Tuxtla Gutiérrez, founded in 1528 by Diego de Mazariegos and the colonial capital of the region stands in a high mountain valley. It was named after Bishop Las Casas, protector of the Indians. There is a plaque to him in the plaza. San Cristóbal was at the centre of the Zapatista uprising in 1994, see **History** for details.

Places of interest

There are many old churches; two of them cap the two hills which overlook the town. **Santo Domingo**, built in 1547, has a baroque façade, a gilt rococo interior and a famous carved wooden pulpit (see below). Museum in the **Convent of Santo Domingo** (entry US$2, closed Mon), gives a very good history of San Cristóbal, and has a display of local costumes upstairs, with English explanations. At the back of the building is a small library with books on Chiapas. Other churches include **San Nicolás**, with an interesting façade, **El Carmen**, **La Merced**, and **La Caridad** (1715). From the **Temple of Guadalupe** there is a good view of the city and surrounding wooded hills (from the N side of the Zócalo, go E along C Real de Guadalupe). At the opposite side of the city, behind the **Iglesia de San Cristóbal** at the top of Cerrito San Cristóbal is a crucifix made of licence plates (reached via Hermanos Domínguez at Ignacio Allende); parking area with stone benches, popular with picnickers, also good view over city. Churches are closed Sun pm. 25 July is *fiesta* day, when vehicles are taken uphill to be blessed by the Bishop. Two other museums: **Museo del Ambar**, Av Gen Utrilla, and **Museo Etnográfico**, Casa de la Artesanía, Av Hidalgo/Niños Héroes.

Various kinds of craftwork are sold in the new market, open daily, and in the Sun markets of the local Indian villages. Most Indian tribes here are members of the Tzotzil and Tzeltal groups. The Tenejapans wear black knee-length tunics; the Chamulans white wool tunics; and the Zinacantecos multicoloured outfits, with the ribbons on their hats signifying how many children they have. The Chamula and Tenejapa women's costumes are more colourful, and more often seen in town, than the men's.

NB Check on the situation before you visit the surrounding villages. Travellers are strongly warned not to wander around on their own, especially in the hills surrounding the town where churches are situated, as they could risk assault. Warnings can be seen in some places frequented by tourists. Heed the warning on photographing, casual clothing and courtesy (see page 399). It is cold at night, in winter extremely so (eg Sept), bring warm clothing and night clothes.

Excursions

Caves (**Las Grutas de San Cristóbal**) 10 km SE of the town (entrance US$0.30) contain huge stalagmites and are 2,445m long but only lit for 750m. Refreshments available. Horses can be hired at Las Grutas for US$13 for a 5-hr ride, guide extra, for rides on beautiful trails in the surrounding forest. Some of these are best followed on foot. Yellow diamonds on trees and stones mark the way to beautiful meadows. Stay on the trail to minimise erosion. **NB** Parts of the forest are a military zone. The land next to the caves is taken up by an army football pitch, but once past this, it is possible to walk most of the way back to San Cristóbal through woods and fields. Las Grutas are reached by Autotransportes de Pasaje/31 de Marzo colectivos every 15 mins (0600-1900) from Av Benito Juárez 37B, across the Pan-American Highway just S of Cristóbal Colón bus terminal. Colectivos are marked 'San Cristóbal, Teopisca, Ciudad Militar, Villa Las Rosas', or ask for minibus to 'Rancho Nuevo'. To the bus stop take 'San Diego' colectivo 1 block E of Zócalo

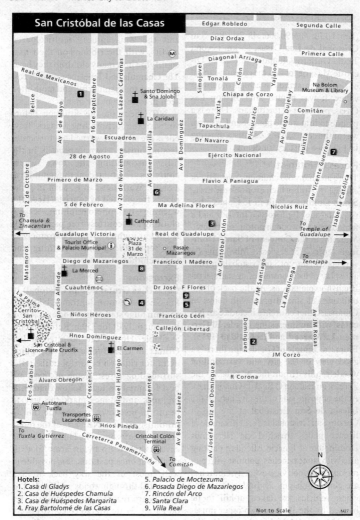

San Cristóbal de las Casas

Hotels:
1. Casa di Gladys
2. Casa de Huéspedes Chamula
3. Casa de Huéspedes Margarita
4. Fray Bartolomé de las Casas
5. Palacio de Moctezuma
6. Posada Diego de Mazariegos
7. Rincón del Arco
8. Santa Clara
9. Villa Real

Not to Scale   M27

to end of Benito Juárez. When you get to Las Grutas, ask the driver to let you out at Km 94, caves are poorly signed.

Local festivals

There is also a popular spring festival on Easter Sun and the week after.

Local information
● Accommodation

A3 *Arrecife de Coral*, Crescencio Rosas 29, T 82125/82098, modern, clean, TV, hot water, garden, off-street parking, friendly owners; **A3** *Posada Diego de Mazariegos*, María A Flores 2, T 81825, F 80827, 1 block N of Plaza, rec, comfortable, quiet,

San Cristóbal de Las Casas **393**

reception at 5 de Febrero, restaurant, live music regularly in the evening in bar *El Jaguar*.

B *Bonampak* (Best Western), Calzado México 5, T 81621, F 81622, pool, restaurant, bar and excellent travel agency run by Pilar; **B** *Casa Mexicana*, 28 de Agosto 1, T 80698, F 82627, cable TV, telephone, indoor patio with fountain, very plush and comfy, same owner as *La Galeria* restaurant, highly rec; **B** *Español*, 1 de Marzo 16, T 80045, hot water morning and evening, clean, beautiful courtyard, restaurant, some rooms noisy, **B** *Molino de La Alborada*, Periférico Sur Km 4, S of airstrip, T 80935, modern ranch-house and bungalows; *Parador Ciudad Real*, Diagonal Centenario 32, T 81886, F 82853, W edge of city; **B** *Rincón del Arco*, 8 blocks from centre, friendly, Ejército Nacional 66, T 81313, F 81568, warmly rec, bar, restaurant, discotheque; **B-C** 2 *Hoteles Mónica*, larger at Insurgentes 33, T 80732, F 82940, nice patio, restaurant, bar, rec, and smaller at 5 de Febrero 18, T 81367 (also have furnished bungalows to rent on road to San Juan Chamula); **B** *Ciudad Real*, Plaza 31 de Marzo 10, T 80187, F 80469, clean, good value, TV in rooms, good restaurant, attractive rooms, but noisy parrot talks a lot.

C *Capri*, Insurgentes 54, nr Cristóbal Colón bus terminal, T 80015, clean, helpful, rec; **C** *Casa Vieja*, María A Flores 27, T 80385, elegant converted colonial house, relaxing, TV, good restaurant, parking, laundry service; **C** *Mansión del Valle*, C Diego de Mazariegos 39, T 82582/3, F 82581, chic, classic colonial building, safe parking; **C** *Maya Quetzal*, on Pan-American Highway, Km 1171, T 81181, F 80984, adjoining restaurant; **C** *Parador Mexicano*, Av 5 de Mayo 38, T 81515, tennis court, quiet and pleasant; **C** *Posada de los Angeles*, Madero 17, T 81173, F 82581, very good value, hot water, with bath and TV; **C** *Santa Clara*, Insurgentes 1, on Plaza, T 81140, F 81041, colonial style, clean, some rooms noisy, good restaurant, pool bar, pool, highly rec.

D *Fray Bartolomé de Las Casas*, Insurgentes and Niños Héroes, T 80932, with bath, nice rooms (some dark) and patio with *Café Kate*, can be noisy, extra blankets available, safe parking; **D** *Palacio de Moctezuma*, Juárez 16, T 80352, F 81533, colonial style, good Mexican food, highly rec; **D** *Pensión Ramos*, Cuauhtémoc 12, with bath and hot water, small, rec; **D** *Posada El Paraíso*, Av 5 de Febrero 19, T/F 80085, Mexican-Swiss owned, impeccable

rooms varying in size, many open onto pretty patio, excellent restaurant, nearby parking beneath cathedral, highly rec; **D** *Posada Los Morales*, Ignacio Allende 17, cottages with open fires (wood US$0.80), kitchen and hot showers, beautiful gardens overlook city, parking possible (some cottages are very basic, with no water), beautiful bar/restaurant with live music; **D** *Real del Valle*, Av Real de Guadalupe 14, T 80680, F 83015, next to Plaza, with breakfast, very clean, friendly, avoid noisy room next to kitchen, new wing added, very nice, hot water, but no heating, good café, English spoken, laundry, credit cards accepted, parking; **D** *San Cristóbal*, Insurgentes 2 nr Plaza, with bath, colonial style, renovated, pleasant, **D** *Villa Real*, Av Benito Juárez 8, T 82930, clean, hot water, luggage deposit, safe, rec.

E *Posada Lucella*, Av Insurgentes 55, T 80956, opp Iglesia Santa Lucía (noisy bells!), some rooms with bath, hot water, others shared, good value, clean, safe, quiet rooms around patio, large beds, rec; **E-F** *Jovel*, C Flavio Paniagua 28, T 81734, villa style, roof terrace, clean, quiet, good, hot water, extra blankets available, friendly, will store luggage, restaurant, good breakfast available, horses (OK) for hire, laundry facilities, highly rec; **E** *San Martín*, Real de Guadalupe 16, T 80533, nr Plaza, clean, highly rec, hot water, left-luggage; **E** *Posada Margarita*, Real de Guadalupe 34, T 80957, in private room without bath, spotless communal sleeping F, washing and toilets, clean, friendly, hot water, laundry, rec, popular with backpackers, often full, attractive restaurant serves good breakfast and dinner (not cheap), wholefood, live music in evenings. Next door is **D** *Posada Santiago*, No 32, T 80024, with private bath, clean, hot water, good cafeteria, rec.

E *Casa di Gladys* (Privates Gästelhäus Casa Degli Ospiti), Real de Mexicanos 16, Caja Postal 29240, 2 blocks from Santo Domingo, or F pp in dormitory, patio, hot showers, clean bathrooms, comfortable, breakfast available, Gladys meets Cristóbal Colón buses, highly rec, laundry facilities, horseriding arranged, luggage store; **E** *Posada del Barón*, Belisario Domínguez 2, clean and comfortable, good value; **E** *Casa de Huéspedes Chamula*, C Julio M Corzo, clean, hot showers, washing facilities, friendly, parking, noisy, with shared bath, some rooms without windows, rec; **E** *Paris-México*, on Dr José Flores 34, clean, pretty patio, rec, ask at nearby restaurant of same name (see below); **E** *Posada Casa Blanca*, Insurgentes 6-B, 50m S of Zócalo, with shower, clean, hot water, friendly owner; **E** *Posada El Cerillo*, Av B Domínguez 27, hot showers, laundry facilities, no electricity 1300-1700, reports vary; **E** *Posada Insurgente*, Av Insurgentes 73, clean, refurbished, good bathrooms with hot water, cold rooms, 1 block from Cristóbal Colón station; **E** *Posada Isabel*, Francisco León 54, nr Av JM Santiago, with shower, clean, quiet, good value, parking; **E** *Posada Lupita I*, Benito Juárez 12, T 81421, beds like hammocks, small, enclosed car park, strict controls of hot water and *No II* at Insurgentes 46, T 81019; **E** *Posada Poganda*, Insurgentes, nr Cristóbal Colón terminal, good laundry, hot showers, comfortable; **E** *Posada Tepeyac*, Real de Guadalupe 40, 1 block from *Margarita*, with bath, friendly, clean, hot shower, avoid ground floor rooms, dark and gloomy, otherwise rec; **E** *Posada Virginia*, C Cristóbal Colón and Guadalupe, for 4 in room with bath, hot water, clean, rec; **E** *Posadita*, Flavio Paniagua 30, with bath, clean, friendly, laundry facilities, rec; **E** *Santo Domingo*, 28 de Agosto 4, 3 blocks from Zócalo, with bath, F without, clean, hot showers, very friendly; **E** *Villa Betania*, Madero 87, T 84467, not central, airy rooms with bath and fireplace (US$3 extra if you want to light a fire), hot water in morning, clean, rec.

F *Baños Mercederos*, C 1 de Marzo 55, shared quarters, good cheap meals, steam baths (highly rec, $2 extra); **F** *Casa de Huéspedes Santa Lucía*, Clemente Robles 21, T 80315, shared bath, ask for hot water, refurbished, one of the cheapest, rec; **F** *Posada del Candil*, Mexicanos, hot shower, but erratic, clean, laundry facilities, good value; **F** *Posada Chilan Balam*, Niños Héroes 9, family-run, hot water, very pleasant; **F** *Posada Maya*, Av Crescencio Rosas II, hot water in shared showers, cheap café next door, rec. Look on the bulletin board outside the tourist office for guesthouses advertising rooms at US$3.50 pp, bed and breakfast (ie *Madero 83 Hospedaje Bed and Breakfast*, clean, small breakfast, popular with backpackers), US$5 with lunch or dinner; **F** *Casa 7*, Benito Juárez 48, shared bath, hot water, friendly.

Camping: *Rancho San Nicolás*, at end of C Francisco León, 1½ km E of centre, beautiful, quiet location, is a trailer park, but do take warm blankets or clothing as the temperature drops greatly at night, hot showers, US$7 for room in cabaña, US$5 to camp, US$12 for camper van with 2 people (electricity hook-up), children free, laundry facilities, rec. Trailer Park *Bonampak* on

Route 190 at W end of town, 22 spaces with full hook-up, hot shower, heated pool in season, restaurant, US$10/vehicle and 2 people. 'White gas' available at small store on corner across from NE corner of main market (Chiwit).

● **Places to eat**

La Parrilla, Av Belisario Domínguez 32, closed Sat, not cheap but excellent grilled meats and cheese, open fire, cowboy decor with saddles as bar stools, rec; *La Pergola*, Plaza de la C Real, Real de Guadalupe 5, pasta and coffee, good but not cheap; *La Margarita*, Real de Guadalupe 32, concerts, good tacos; *La Selva*, Real de Guadalupe, good pizza, concerts almost nightly, rec; *Copal*, Real de Guadalupe 43, Italian, imported ingredients and wine, good atmosphere and food, US$5 a meal, rec; *El Mural*, 20 de Noviembre 8, good, excellent coffee and cakes; *La Galería*, Hidalgo 3, a few doors from Zócalo, popular with tourists, best coffee, good breakfast, good pasta, international (many German) newspapers, art gallery, videos at night, pool table, live music at weekends; *El Unicornio*, Av Insurgentes 33a, good; *Capri*, Insurgentes 16, good food, set meals at reasonable prices; *El Circo*, Av Crescencio Rosas 7, opp Correo, Italian, good, reasonably priced, rec; *Tikal*, Insurgentes 77A, nr bus station, open 0600 to midnight, excellent and not expensive, good breakfasts, bright and pleasant, sells toys made by SODAM (see below); *Cafetería Palenque*, Insurgentes 40, nr C Colón terminal, cheap, good and friendly, open 0800-1900, closed Sun; *Tuluc*, Insurgentes 5, open 0630-2200, good value especially breakfasts, nr Plaza, popular, classical music, art for sale and toys on display (sold at SODAM, see below), rec; *Merendero*, JM Corzo y Insurgentes, OK, cheap; *El Teatro*, 1 de Marzo 8, café, bar, restaurant; *Oasis*, also 1 de Marzo, excellent milk shakes; *París-México*, Madero 20, smart, French cuisine, excellent cheap breakfasts, reasonably-priced *comida corrida*, good value for all dishes, classical music, rec, now own hostel of same name (see above); *Faisán*, Madero, nr Plaza, good breakfasts, excellent food and service; *Los Arcos*, Madero 6, varied menu, family run, inexpensive, good *comida corrida*, excellent service, closes 2100; several other cheap, local placed on F Madero E of Plaza 31 de Marzo; *Fulano*, on Madero 12, nr Plaza, excellent set meal at reasonable price; *La Langosta* opp, Madero 9, good *comida corrida*; *Flamingo*, Madero 14, nice décor, reasonable food (good paella); next door is *El Mirador II*, good local and international food, excellent *comida corrida* US$3, rec; *Los Payasos*, Madero 19, cheap and good, huge breakfasts, Dutch owner, very friendly, rec.

The town is a 'health food and vegetarian paradise'; shop around. *Madre Tierra*, Insurgentes 19 (opp Franciscan church), Anglo-Mexican owned, European dishes, vegetarian specialities, good breakfasts, wholemeal breads from bakery (also take-away), pies, brownies, chocolate cheese cake, classical music, popular with travellers, not cheap, good nightlife; *Noria*, 20 de Noviembre 21, good and cheap Mexican food; *Las Estrellas*, Dr Navarro entre 20 de Noviembre y Gen Utrilla, good cheap food, inc vegetarian, good brown bread, try the *caldo Tlapeño*, live music from 2030, nice atmosphere, Mexican/Dutch owned, rec; *Tienda Vegetariana* at 28 de Agosto 2, sells a variety of health foods; *Café San Cristóbal* on Cuauhtémoc, good coffee sold in bulk too; *Café Altura*, at 1 de Marzo No 6-D, vegetarian, organic coffee, also has information on ecotours to the Finca Irlanda and to the Huitepec nature reserve, ask for Roland Lehmann; *Café Centro*, on D Domínguez and Real de Guadalupe, popular for breakfast, good *comida*; *La Casa del Pan*, on B Domínguez and Dr Navarro, excellent wholemeal bread, breakfasts, live music, closed Mons, highly rec; *Tortas Tortugas*, Guadalupe Victoria, nr corner of Av 20 de Noviembre, excellent sandwiches. Many others. San Cristóbal is not lively in the evenings. main meeting place is around *ponche* stall on Plaza.

● **Banks & money changers**

Casa Margarita will change dollars and TCs. Banks are usually open for exchange between 0900 and 1100 only, check times; this leads to queues. **Bancomer** charges commission, cash advance on Visa, American Express or Citicorp TCs, good rates and service; **Banco Internacional**, Diego de Mazariegos, good rates for cash and TCs (US$ only), fast efficient, cash advance on Mastercard; **Banamex** changes cheques without commission, 0900-1100; **Banco Serfin** on the Zócalo, changes Euro, Amex, Mastercard TCs. *Casa de Cambio Lacantún*, Real Guadalupe 12, open daily 0900-1400, 1600-1900, Sat/Sun 0900-1300 (supposedly, may close early), no commission, at least US$50 must be changed. Quetzales can be obtained for pesos or dollars in the *cambio* but better rates are paid at the border.

● **Culture centres**

The *Casa de Cultura*, opp El Carmen church on junction of Hnos Domínguez and Hidalgo, has a busy range of activities on offer: concerts, films, lectures, art exhibitions and conferences.

Na Bolom, Vicente Guerrero 33, the house of the archaeologists Frans (died 1963) and Trudi Blom (died Dec 1993, aged 92), and a beautiful but shabby 15-room guest house (**B** double room with bath and fireplace, 3 meals available, lunch and dinner for US$5, require 3 hrs' notice, excellent Sun buffet), with good library (open Mon-Fri 0800-1500). At 1100 (Spanish) and 1630 sharp, guides (English) take you round display, rooms of beautiful old house, and garden (1½ hrs, US$2.20 inc video, a US PBS TV programme, at 1800, rec, 50% discount with ISIC card). You cannot see the museum on your own. It is well worth visiting: beautifully displayed artefacts, pictures of Lacandón Indians, with information about their history and present way of life (in English). Also only easily-obtainable map of Lacandón jungle. There is a wonderful photographic book by Ms Blom for sale called *Bearing Witness*. Na Bolom is closed Mon for tours. They also organize tours to villages, leaving at 1000, returning at 1430, US$8.50 pp, and special request tours for study programmes for groups. *Pepe*, a Tzeltal Indian, guides tours to Chamula and Zinacantán, rec. For further information contact Yosefa T (967) 81418, F 85586. Na Bolom is non-profit making, all money goes towards helping the Lacandón Indians. The volunteer programme has been tentatively reinstated, contact Suzanna Paisley. *Centro Cultural El Puente*, Real de Guadalupe 55, has excellent cafe, bookshop, information centre, travel agency and gallery (see also under **Language schools**). *Casa/Museo de Sergio Castro*, Guadalupe Victoria 47 (6 blocks from plaza), T 84289, excellent collection of indigenous garments, talks (in English, French or Spanish) and slide shows about customs and problems of the indigenous population, open from 1900, entry free but donations welcome.

● **Entertainment**

Free videos offered on several screens, eg *Centro Bilingue*, on C Real de Guadalupe 55 and *La Galería*, Av Miguel Hidalgo 3. Film schedules are posted around town.

● **Hospitals & medical services**

Dra Carmen Ramos, Av Insurgentes 28, T 81680, or make an appointment through Tourist Office.

● **Language schools**

Roberto Rivas Bastidas, Centro Bilingüe, Insurgentes 57-D, Santa Lucía, Caja Postal 29250, T 84157, F 83723 (English programme) at Centro Cultural *El Puente*, Real De Guadalupe 55, Caja Postal 29230, T/F 83723 (Spanish programme), rates range from US$4.50/hr to US$7.50/hr depending on number in class and length of course, home stay programmes available, registration fee US$100; Universidad Autónoma de Chiapas, Av Hidalgo 1, Dpto de Lenguas, offers classes in English, French and Tzotzil. Instituto Jovel, María Adelina Flores 21, Apdo Postal 62, T/F 84069, runs language classes and handicraft workshops, tours offered, accommodation with families, US$285 for 2 weeks, US$130 each subsequent week, homestay US$80-95/week, deposit US$80, rec for good tuition and accommodation.

● **Laundry**

Superklin, C Crescencio Rosas 48, T 83275, US$3 for washing and drying for up to 3 kg, for collection after 5 hrs. Lavorama at Guadalupe Victoria 20A; another opp *Posada del Candil*, 6 hrs, US$1/kg. Clothes washed and mended by Isaiah and friendly staff, on Av B Domínguez, nr corner of Real de Guadalupe.

● **Post & telecommunications**

Post Office: Cuauhtémoc 13, between Rosas and Hidalgo, Mon-Fri 0800-1900, Sat 0900-1300.

Telephone: long distance phone calls can be made from the *Boutique Santo Domingo* on Utrilla, esquina Paniagua, takes credit cards, collect possible; and at shops at Av 16 de Septiembre 22, Madero 75 and Av Insurgentes 60. Phone and fax services available at the Tourist Office in the Plaza. Reliable fax, phone and computer services at *Calidad Total*, next to Post Office on Cuauhtémoc. Cheap international calls from 2nd class bus station, no waiting. No operator-assisted phone calls are possible on Sun after 2000 in Chiapas.

Public Internet and **e-mail**: on Real de Guadalupe.

● **Shopping**

Part of the ex-convent of Santo Domingo has been converted into a cooperative, *Sna Jolobil*, selling handicrafts from many Indian villages (best quality and expensive; also concerts by local groups). *SODAM* (Mutual Aid Society) with their shop at Casa Utrilla, Av Gral Utrilla 33, is a cooperative of Indian craftsmen selling beautiful wooden dolls and toys. Sales go towards a training fund for Chamula Indians, with

a workshop based at Yaalboc, a community nr San Cristóbal. For local goods try *Miscelánea Betty*, Gen Utrilla 45, good value. Souvenir markets on Gral Utrilla between Real de Guadalupe and Dr A Navarro. Amber museum in Plaza Sivan shop, Gen Utrilla 10, T 83507. Many shops on Av Real de Guadalupe. For good leather cowboy boots: *Santiag*, C Real de Guadalupe 5; very good prices. *Postelería*, Real de Guadalupe 24, open late for maps, postcards, water and cakes. *Tzantehuitz*, Real de Guadalupe 74, sells textiles with original designs hand made on the premises. Main market is worth seeing as well. Pasaje Mazariegos (in the block bounded by Real de Guadalupe, Av B Domínguez, Madero and Plaza 31 de Marzo) has luxury clothes and bookshops, restaurants and travel agents.

Bookshops: *Soluna*, has a few English guidebooks, a wide range of Spanish titles and postcards. *Librería Chilam Balam*, Casa Utrilla, Av Gral Utrilla 33, good range of books, mostly in Spanish, also cassettes of regional music. *Librería El Rincón*, Diego de Mazariegos, some 2nd hand books, exchange only, 2 for 1. *La Pared*, C Hidalgo next to La Galería, bookshop which also hires books by the day, deposit required, excellent quality books, also fax service. On same street, *Terra Amata*, rec.

● **Sports**

Horse hire: Carlos, T 81873/81339; Olivier at *Bar-Restaurante La Galería*, Hidalgo 3, T 81547, reserve 1600-2230, US$10, groups of 4-6, not for the inexperienced. Horses can be hired from *Casa de Huéspedes Margarita*, prices US$16-20 for horse and guide, reserve the day before; or from Sr José Hernández, C Elias C 10 (1 block from Av Huixtla and C Chiapa de Corzo, not far from Na Bolom), T 81065, US$10 for half a day, plus guide US$11.50; the tourist office also has a list of other stables which hire out horses. Check the saddles; those made of wood are uncomfortable for long rides if you are not used to them.

● **Tour companies & travel agents**

Mercedes Hernández Gómez, leads 5-6 hrs tours of local villages, inc Chamula and Zinacantán, starting at 0900 from Kiosk on the Plaza 31 de Mayo, returns about 1500, about US$8 pp, repeatedly rec. Mercedes is very informative and can be recognized by her long skirts and flowery umbrella. Many others take tours for same price, eg Raul and Alejandro (T 83741) who leave from in front of the cathedral at 0930, returning at 1400, in blue VW minibus, US$7, good. *Chincultic*, at *Posada Margarita* (address above),

T/F 80957, runs tours to local sites and organizes horse riding tours to San Juan Chamula. Longer tours such as to Bonampak and Yaxchilan can be booked by tour operators in San Cristóbal de las Casas.

● **Tourist offices**
Helpful, at the Palacio Municipal, W side of main Plaza, some English spoken. Ask here for accommodation in private house. Good free map of town and surroundings. Another office at Hidalgo 2, a few paces from Zócalo. Maps of San Cristóbal US$0.35, also on sale at *Kramsky*, Diego de Mazariegos y 16 de Septiembre, behind Palacio Municipal (one way traffic shown for Av 16 de Septiembre and Av Ignacio Allende actually goes in the opp direction).

● **Useful addresses**
Immigration: on Carretera Pan Americana and Diagonal Centenario, opp *Hotel Bonampak*. From Zócalo take Diego de Mazariegos towards W, after crossing bridge take Diagonal on the left towards Highway, 30-min walk. Only 15 day extensions given.

● **Transport**
Local Bike hire: *Los Pingüinos* on Av 5 de Mayo 10B, T 80202, rents mountain bikes for US$1/hr or US$7.50/day. Guided biking tours half or full days, prices from US$7 to US$12.50, beautiful countryside and knowledgeable guides, highly rec. Also tours to Agua Azul and Palenque, US$30/day. *Bicirent*, Belisario Domínguez 5B (on corner with Real de Guadalupe), good new equipment, US$1.30/hr. **Bike shops**: *Bicipartes*, on Alvaro Obregón and 2 shops on Utrilla between Navarro and Primero de Marzo have a good selection of bike parts. **Car hire**: Budget, Mazariegos 36.

Air San Cristóbal no longer has an airport; it has been consumed by urban growth. The nearest airport is at Ocosingo (see page 400) about 50 km along the Palenque road. To Tuxtla Gutiérrez Tues, Thur, Sat at 1345, 84 km (Tuxtla is the major local airport but see page 389). Regular daily flights, except Sun, to Palenque, 0715 (some crashes); booking only at airport. Charter flights to see Lacanjá, Bonampak and Yaxchilán on the Usumacinta River, 7 hrs in all (US$100 pp if plane is full, more if not). All with Aerochiapas at airport. Aviacsa, Pasaje Mazariegos, local 16, T 84441, F 84384, for flights from Tuxtla Gutiérrez.

Buses Beware of highly proficient pickpockets at bus stations. Some restaurants on Insurgentes nr bus stations display signs saying they store luggage. From Mexico City direct, Cristóbal

Colón at 1415, 1815, 2300, US$30. Cristóbal Colón 1st class bus to **Oaxaca**, about 12 hrs, at 1700, US$17, 1900, US$21, daily, book well in advance, monotonous trip, 622 km, robberies have been reported on these buses. Buses are regularly stopped and passengers questioned along this route. To do the trip in daytime, you need to change at Tuxtla Gutiérrez (0745 Cristóbal Colón to Tuxtla, then 1100 on to Oaxaca), C Colón has hourly buses to Tuxtla between 0130 and 2030, US$2.50; to **Tehuantepec**, US$10; to **Mexico City**, via Tuxtepec, about 18 hrs, 1,169 km, many buses daily, US$30; to **Tapachula**, 9 hrs, at 0600, US$14.80, 483 km; to **Puebla** at 1530 and 1730, US$30, 1,034 km. Bus to **Huatulco**, 0730. Book tickets as far in advance as possible, during Christmas and Holy Week buses are sometimes fully booked for 10 days or more. Cristóbal Colón has its own bus station on Insurgentes, 1st class; to **Villahermosa**, 6 hrs, US$9 (direct at 1415); to **Arriaga**, at 1200 via Tuxtla Gutiérrez, 235 km, US$6; to **Coatzacoalcos** at 0630, 10 hrs, US$14.80; to **Orizaba** 845 km; to **Chiapa de Corzo**, 64 km, several daily at 0800, 0830, 1100, 1400, 2 hrs, US$3.35; *servicio plus* to Campeche 2100; direct to **Mérida** at 1730, US$21, to **Chetumal** at 1535, US$19. (There is a direct bus to Tulum at 0030 with Autotransportes del Sur.) To **Puerto Escondido** with Cristóbal Colón, 1st class, 0700 and 1800, US$24 (US$23 to **Pochutla**). There is a new 210 km paved road with fine views to **Palenque**; Lacandonia 2nd class bus to Palenque from 2nd class bus station on C Allende (where the 1st class bus station is also) 7 a day between 0100 and 2015, 4 hrs, US$4 (via Agua Azul, US$4); Cristóbal Colón, 1st class service, up to 4 times daily (inc at least one *servicio plus*) US$4.50, bookings 5 days in advance; Maya de Oro, from Cristóbal Colón terminal, 3 times daily, a/c, videos, non-stop; Rodolfo Figueroa, 5 times a day, US$4.50, a/c. Other buses leave one at **Ocosingo**; Lacandonia 2nd class to Ocosingo, 3 hrs, US$2.75. Refunds of fares to Palenque when reaching Ocosingo are not rare, and you then have to make your own way. Autotransportes Na-Bolom to **Tuxtla Gutiérrez**, Comitán and Palenque from just E of 1st class bus terminal (across the bridge): to Tuxtla 13 departures (1600 *servicio plus*), US$3, 2 hrs, to Palenque 0700 and 1300, US$6.50, to **Comitán** 1100 and 1500, US$3.75, 2 hrs. Autotrans Tuxtla, F Sarabia entre Carretera Panamericana y Alvaro Obregón 2nd class to Palenque, reserved seats, US$5. Minibuses to

Tuxtla Gutiérrez leave from in front of 1st class bus station, when full, US$1.65.

Buses to Guatemala: Cristóbal Colón, S end of Av Insurgentes (left luggage facilities open 0600-2000 exc Sun and holidays), clean station, direct 1st class buses to the Guatemalan border at Ciudad Cuauhtémoc, 170 km, several daily from 0700, 3 hrs, US$3.50 (leave bus at border, not its final destination). Cristóbal Colón to Comitán (if you can't get a bus to the border, take one to Comitán and get a pick-up there, US$0.50), hourly from 0700, US$3.50, 87 km (a beautiful, steep route). Colectivos also leave for Comitán from outside the Cristóbal Colón bus station. 2nd class to border with Autotrans Tuxtla, US$2.75 (do not take 1430 ACL 2nd class, next to Trans Lacandonia, on Carretera Panamericana, it arrives too late for onward transport). For details on crossing the border at La Mesilla see page 402.

VILLAGES NEAR SAN CRISTOBAL

You are recommended to call at Na Bolom before visiting the villages, to get information on their cultures and seek advice on the reception you are likely to get. Photography is resisted by some Indians (see below) because they believe the camera steals their souls, and photographing their church is stealing the soul of God. Many Indians do not speak Spanish. On Sun you can visit the villages of San Juan Chamula, Zinacantán and Tenejapa. While this is a popular excursion, especially when led by a guide (see above), several visitors have felt ashamed at going to look at the villagers as if they were in a zoo; there were many children begging and offering to look after private vehicles in return for not damaging them.

Zinacantán is reached by VW bus from market, US$0.75, 30 mins' journey, sometimes frequent stops while conductor lights rockets at roadside shrines. The men wear pink/red jackets with embroidery and tassels, the women a vivid pale blue shawl and navy skirts. Annual festival days here are 6 and 19-22 Jan, 8-10 Aug, visitors welcome. At midday every day the women prepare a communal meal which the men eat in shifts. Main gathering place around church; the roof was

destroyed by fire (US$1 charged for entering church, official ticket from tourist office next door; photography inside is strictly prohibited). There is a new museum called **Ik'al Ojov**, off C 5 de Febrero, 5 blocks down Av Cristóbal Colón from San Lorenzo church, and 1 block to the left. The museum includes two buildings which are traditional *palapas* or huts that people used to live in. Small collection of regional costumes. It occasionally holds shows and annual festival on 17 February. Tiny gift shop. Donation requested. Another new museum opened in 1996: the **Museo Comunitario Autzetik ta jteklum**, run by women from Zinacantán, 1 block from San Lorenzo church. Also exhibits local culture and plans to extend with hothouses of local flowers.

Chamula You can catch a VW bus ride from the market every 20 mins, last at 1700, last one back at 1900, US$0.70 pp (or taxi, US$10) and visit the local church; another popular excursion. A permit (US$1) is needed from the village tourist office and photographing inside the church is absolutely forbidden. There are no pews but family groups sit or kneel on the floor, chanting, with rows of candles lit in front of them, each representing a member of the family and certain significance attached to the colours of the candles. The religion is centred on the 'talking stones', and three idols and certain Christian saints. Pagan rituals held in small huts at the end of August. Pre-Lent festival ends with celebrants running through blazing harvest chaff. Just after Easter prayers are held, before the sowing season starts. Festivals in Chamula should *not* be photographed, if you wish to take other shots ask permission, people are not unpleasant, even if they refuse (although children may pester you to take their picture for US$0.15). The men wear grey, black or light pink tunics, the women bright blue blouses with colourful braid and navy or bright blue shawls. There are many handicraft stalls on the way up the small hill SW of the village. This has a good viewpoint of the village and valley: take the road from SW corner of square, turn left towards ruined church then up flight of steps on left.

Interesting walk from San Cristóbal to Chamula along the main road to a point one km past the crossroads with the Periférico ring road (about 2½ km from town centre); turn on to an old dirt road to the right, not sign-posted but first fork you come to between some farmhouses. Then back via the road through the village of Milpoleta, some 8 km downhill, 5 hrs for the journey round trip (allow 1 hr for Chamula). Best not done in hot weather. Also, you can hike from Chamula to Zinacantán in 1½ hrs: when leaving Chamula, take track straight ahead instead of turning left onto San Cristóbal road; turn left on small hill where school is (after 30 mins) and follow a smaller trail through light forest. After an hour you reach the main road 200m before Zinacantán.

NB Signs in Chamula warn that it is dangerous to walk in the area, robberies have occurred between Chamula and both San Cristóbal and Zinacantán (these warnings persisted in 1996; the police in San Cristóbal are reported to charge for statements of robberies). Also seek full advice on any travel outside San Cristóbal de las Casas in the wake of events in early 1994 (see above).

3½ km from San Cristóbal, on the road to Chamula, is the **Huitepec** nature reserve; entrance US$0.80, 2½ km trail with Spanish and English information, administered by Pronatura-Chiapas. The 135-ha reserve contains grassland, oak-wood forest, rising to cloud forest at 2,400m. As well as a wide diversity of plants, there are many birds, including some 50 migratory species. Colectivos go there, US$0.50. Tours can be organized 2-3 days in advance at Pronatura. Roland in the *Café Altura* takes guided tours to the reserve, about 5 hrs hiking, few explanations, US$10 pp, bargaining possible.

Tenejapa The Sun market is traditionally fruit and vegetables, but there are a growing number of music cassette and shooting gallery stalls. Excellent woven items can be purchased from the weavers' cooperative near the church. They also have a fine collection of old textiles in their regional ethnographic museum adjoining the handicraft shop. The cooperative can also arrange weaving classes. The village is very friendly and many men wear local costume. Few tourists (**F** *Hotel Molina*, simple but clean; several *comedores* around the market). Buses leave from San Cristóbal market at 0700 and 1100 (1½ hrs' journey), and colectivos every hour, US$1. The paved road is very bumpy and landslides are common, not recommended for an ordinary car in the wet. Ask permission to take pictures and expect to pay. Market thins out by noon.

Two other excursions can be made, by car or local bus, from San Cristóbal S on the Pan-American Highway (30 mins by car) to **Amatenango del Valle**, a Tzeltal village where the women make and fire pottery in their yards, and then SE (15 mins by car) to **Aguacatenango**, picturesque village at the foot of a mountain. Continue 1 hr along road past Villa las Rosas (hotel) to **Venustiano Carranza**, women with fine costumes, extremely good view of the entire valley. There is a good road from Las Rosas to Comitán as an alternative to the Pan-American highway. Frequent buses.

NB Remember that locals are particularly sensitive to proper dress (ie neither men nor women should wear shorts, or revealing clothes) and manners; persistent begging should be countered with courteous, firm replies. It is best not to take cameras to villages: there are good postcards and photographs on sale. Drunkenness is quite open and at times forms part of the rituals. Best not to take umbrage if accosted.

● **Transport** Get to outlying villages by bus or communal VW bus (both very packed); buses leave very early, and often don't return until next day, so you have to stay overnight; lorries are more frequent. To Zinacantán catch also VW bus from market. Buses from the market area to San Andrés Larrainzar (bus at 1000, 1100, 1400, with return same day, US$0.80 one way) and Tenejapa. Transportes Fray Bartolomé de Las Casas has buses to Chanal, Chenalhó (US$15 with taxi, return, 1 hr stay), Pantelhó, Yajalón and villages en route to Ocosingo. Transportes Lacandonia on Av Crescencio Rosas also go to the villages of Huistán, Oxchuc, Yajalón, on the way to Palenque, Pujiltic, La Mesilla and Venustiano Carranza. If you are in San Cristóbal for a limited period of time it is best to rent a car to see the villages.

ROAD TO PALENQUE

Palenque (see page 411) can be reached by paved road from San Cristóbal de Las Casas, a beautiful ride via **Ocosingo**, a not particularly attractive place (70,000 people) which has a local airport and several hotels (**D** *Central* on Plaza, shower, clean, verandah; **E** *Bodas de Plata*, 1 Av Sur, clean, hot water; **E** *San Jacinto*, just off lower side of plaza, with bath, hot water, clean, friendly; *Aqua Azul*, simple rooms around courtyard, parking; *Posada Morales*) and clean restaurants, including *La Montura*, on the plaza, good. It was one of the centres of fighting in the Ejército Zapatista de Liberación Nacional uprising in Jan 1994. Many buses and colectivos to Palenque, 2½ hrs, US$3.30 and San Cristóbal de Las Casas.

Toniná Road to ruins, 12 km away, is unpaved but marked with signs once you leave Ocosingo (possible in ordinary car, taxi US$25); a tour from San Cristóbal costs US$15. To walk from Ocosingo, start in front of the church on the plaza and follow the signs, or take the 0900 bus from the market to the jungle and get off where the road forks (ask). There is a short cut through the fields: after walking for 2 hrs you come to an official sign with a pyramid on it: don't follow the arrow but take the left fork for about 15 mins and go through a wooden gate on your right; follow the path for 2-3 km (across a little stream and two more gates, ask farmers

when in doubt). You end up in the middle of the site, with the palace high on a hill to your left. It is well worth visiting the ruins, which were excavated by a French government team (open 0900-1600). Temples are in the Palenque style with internal sanctuaries in the back room, but influences from many different Maya styles of various periods have been found. The huge pyramid complex, seven stone platforms making a man-made hill, is 10m higher than the Temple of the Sun at Teotihuacan. Stelae are in very diverse forms, as are wall panels, and some are in styles and in subject unknown at any other Maya site. A beautiful stucco mural was discovered in Dec 1990. Ask the guardian to show you the second unrestored ballcourt and the sculpture kept at his house. He will show you round the whole site; there is also a small museum. Entry US$4.35. (Drinks available at the site; also toilets and parking.) Beside the Ocosingo-Toniná road is a marsh, frequented by thousands of swallows in January.

Some 15 km from Ocosingo on the road to San Cristóbal de las Casas is a beautiful cave with stalagmites and stalactites and bats. It is visible from the road on the left (coming from Ocosingo), close to the road, but look carefully for it. Take a torch/flashlight and walk 15m to a 10m diameter chamber at the end of the cave (don't touch the geological formations as many stalactites have already been damaged).

ROUTE TO GUATEMALA

COMITAN

For Guatemala, follow the 170-km paved road via **Teopisca** (*pensión*, E, comfortable; *La Amistad* trailer park, run down, one dirty shower and bathroom, no electricity, not rec) past **Comitán de Domínguez** (85 km), a lively, attractive town of 87,000 people at 1,580m above sea level with a large, shady plaza.

● **Accommodation** Accommodation inferior in quality and almost twice the price of San Cristóbal; **B** *Internacional*, Av Domínguez 22, T 20112, nr Plaza, good, decent restaurant; **B** *Los Lagos de Montebello*, T 21092, on Pan-American Highway, Km 1,257, noisy but good; **B** *Real Balún Canán*, 1 Av Pte Sur 5, T 21094, restaurant; **E** *Delfín*, Av Domínguez 19-A, T 20013, on Plaza, small rooms but hot water, helpful and clean; **F** *Hospedaje Primavera*, C Central B Juárez 42, ½ block off Plaza, room without bath; **E** *Posada Panamericana*, 1 Av Pte Nte 2, T 20763, dirty; 1 block away is **E** *Hospedaje Montebello*, clean, sunny courtyard, laundry, fax service, friendly, rec.

● **Places to eat** *Helen's Enrique*, on Plaza opp church, good food in pleasant surroundings; *Nevelandia*, Central Nte 1, clean, rec, and *Café Casa de La Cultura*, on the Plaza. Live music daily at 2030 at *Buffalo Café*, nr Plaza, Av Central y C Nte. Several small *comedores* on the Plaza.

● **Airline offices** Aviacsa, 3 C Sur Pte, 12a, T 23519, F 20824, helpful, rec.

● **Banks & money changers** Bancomer, on plaza will exchange Amex TCs; 2 others on plaza, none changes dollars after 1200; also a *casa de cambio*.

● **Embassies & consulates** Guatemalan Consulate, open Mon-Fri 0800-1200, 1400-1700, Sat 0800-1400 at la C Sur Pte 26 y 2 Av Pte Sur, T 2-26-69; visa (if required) US$10 (even for those for whom it should be free), valid 1 year, multiple entry; tourist cards available at border.

● **Tourist offices** On main square, in Palacio Municipal, ground floor, open till 2000.

● **Transport** Buses from San Cristóbal de las Casas with Cristóbal Colón, frequent between 0730 and 2030, US$2.75, 2 hrs, last bus back at 1930. One Cristóbal Colón bus goes on to Tuxtla (via San Cristóbal), US$3.50, 4 hrs. Minibuses from Comitán to Tuxtla leave from by the Cristóbal Colón bus station. Buses, kombis and pick-up trucks from Comitán run to the border at Ciudad Cuauhtémoc. Unleaded petrol is available in Comitán, in centre of town on E side of Pan-American Highway, and another 2 km S of town, open 24 hrs.

LAGUNAS DE MONTEBELLO AND CHINKULTIC

A road branches off the Pan-American Highway 16 km after Comitán to a very beautiful region of vari-coloured lakes, the **Lagunas de Montebello** (a national park). Off the road to Montebello, 30 km from the Pan-American Highway, lie the ruins of **Chinkultic**, with temples, ball-court, carved stone stelae and *cenote* (deep round lake, good swimming) in beautiful surroundings; from the signpost they are about 3 km along a dirt road and they close at 1600 (entry US$3). Watch and ask for the very small sign and gate where road to ruins starts (about 1 km back along the main road, towards Comitán, from Doña María's, see below, don't attempt any short cuts), worth visiting when passing. Colectivo from Comitán US$1.

Kombi vans or buses marked Tziscao or Lagos to the Lagunas de Montebello (60 km from Comitán, US$1.30 about 1 hr), via the Lagunas de Siete Colores (so-called because the oxides in the water give varieties of colours) leave frequently from 2 Av Pte Sur y 3 C Sur Pte, 4 blocks from Plaza in Comitán; buses go as far as Laguna Bosque Azul, 1 hr journey. For those with their own transport there are several dirt roads from Comitán to the Lagunas, a recommended route is the one via La Independencia, Buena Vista, La Patria and El Triunfo (beautiful views) eventually joining the road W of Chinkultic ruins. **Tziscao** is 9 km along the road leading right from the park entrance, which is 3 km before Bosque Azul; five buses a day Comitán-Tziscao; the last bus and colectivo back is at 1600 and connects with the 1900 bus to San Cristóbal. A trip to the Lagunas de Siete Colores from Comitán can be done in a day (note that the less accessible lakes are hard to get to even if staying in the vicinity). It is also possible to hire a Kombi, which takes 12 people, to go to the Lakes and Chinkultic for US$15/hr. A day trip to Chinkultic and the lakes from San

Cristóbal de Las Casas is also possible, if exhausting (take passport and tourist card with you). The Bosque Azul area is now a reserve. The area is noted for its orchids and birdlife, including the famous *quetzal*; very crowded at weekends and holidays. Horse hire US$5/hr.

● **Accommodation** There are, as well as picnic areas, an *Albergue Turístico* on the shores of Lake Tziscao (10 km, **F** pp, rooms for 4-6, toilet, blankets available, no hot water, reasonable kitchen facilities and bathrooms, excellent, reasonably-priced meals, dinner US$2, camping US$1.60 per site including use of hotel facilities; boats for hire, highly rec, friendly owners, one of whom, Leo, speaks good English and has an intimate knowledge of the region), a small, family-run restaurant at Laguna Bosque Azul with a wooden hut for sleeping, G, bring sleeping bag, two very basic food shops in the village (best to bring your own food from Comitán market), and there are small caves. Young boys are good guides, take powerful torch. *Posada Las Orquídeas* (better known as 'Doña María', Km 31, on the road to Montebello near Hidalgo and the ruins of Chinkultic, dormitory or cabin, **G** pp, family-run, very basic (no washing facilities, often no water, 2 toilets, urn in a shack) but friendly, small restaurant serving plentiful Mexican food. **Youth Hostel**: Las Margaritas. *Hotel Bosque Bello*, 34 km, reservations in Tuxtla, T 10966, or Comitán T 21702. On the Montebello lake, a friendly family offers accommodation.

NB Mexican maps show a road running along the Guatemalan border from Montebello to Bonampak and on to Palenque; this road is not complete and no public transport or other traffic makes the trip.

From Hidalgo you can get to Comitán by pick-up or paying hitchhike for US$1 (not recommended for women); to the Guatemalan border go from Hidalgo to La Trinitaria and catch a bus or pick-up there.

FRONTIER WITH GUATEMALA – CIUDAD CUAUHTEMOC

From Comitán the road winds down to the Guatemalan border at **Ciudad Cuauhtémoc** via La Trinitaria (near the turn-off to Lagunas de Montebello, restaurant but no hotel). In Ciudad Cuauhtémoc, not a town, despite its name; just a few buildings; the Cristóbal Colón bus station is opposite Immigration, with an overpriced restaurant and an excellent **E/F** *Hotel Camino Real*, extremely clean and quiet, changes dollars to pesos, highly recommended. Be sure to surrender your tourist card and get your exit stamp at Mexican immigration in Ciudad Cuauhtémoc before boarding a pick-up for Guatemalan immigration; you will only have to go back if you don't. A pick-up to the Guatemalan border, 4 km, costs US$0.65 pp. Walk 100m to immigration and customs, open until 2100. Beyond the Guatemalan post at La Mesilla, El Tapón section, a beautiful stretch, leads to Huehuetenango, 85 km. This route is far more interesting than the one through Tapachula; the border crossing at Ciudad Cuauhtémoc is also reported as easier than that at Talismán. Remember that Mexico is 1 hr ahead of Guatemala.

● **Entering Mexico from Guatemala**
1) Entry charge 20 pesos. Tourist cards and visas are available at the border, recent reports say only 15 days is being given, but extensions are possible in Mexico City; 2) it is forbidden to bring in fruit and vegetables; rigorous checking at two checkpoints to avoid the spread of Mediterranean mosquito.

● **Crossing by private vehicle**
Drivers entering Mexico: at the border crossing your vehicle is fumigated, US$7.25, get receipt (if re-entering Mexico, with documents from a previous entry, papers are checked here). Proceed 4 km to Migración to obtain tourist card or visa, or have existing visa checked. Then go to Banjército to obtain the necessary papers and windscreen sticker or, if re-entering Mexico, to have existing papers checked (open Mon-Fri 0800-1600, Sat-Sun 0900-1400).

● **Exchange**
Don't change money with the Guatemalan customs officials: the rates they offer are worse than those given by bus drivers or in banks (and these are below the rates inside the country). There is nowhere to change TCs at the border and bus companies will not accept cheques in payment for fares. The briefcase and dark glasses brigade changes cash on the Guatemalan side only, but you must know in advance what quetzal rates are.

● **Transport**

Buses are 'de paso' from San Cristóbal so no advance booking is possible. The Cristóbal Colón bus leaves Comitán 0800, 1100 (coming from San Cristóbal) and in pm for the border at Ciudad Cuauhtémoc, fare US$2.75. Autotransportes Tuxtla leave from Comitán (on the main highway at approximately 2 Av Sur) at regular intervals for the border, 1½ hrs. There are at least 8 buses to Comitán 0800-1930 from Ciudad Cuauhtémoc, with 2nd class buses during the evening. Pick-ups charge US$1.55 pp Comitán-border; beware short-changing. From here take a taxi, US$1.65, or colectivo, to the Guatemalan side (4 km uphill, minimum 3 people) and get your passport stamped. Cristóbal

Colón (terminal nr the Pan-American Highway, Comitán) has 1st class buses to **Mexico City** at 0900, 1100 and 1600 (which leave the border 2½ hrs earlier), fare US$40.75 (from Mexico City to Comitán at 1415 and 2040, fully booked 2 hrs in advance); to **Oaxaca** at 0700 and 1900, US$33; to **Tuxtla Gutiérrez** at 0600 and 1600, US$8, and to **Tapachula** (via Arriaga) at 1200 and 2000, US$20. Entering Mexico from Guatemala, to San Cristóbal, direct buses US$3.50, or take a minibus to Comitán, US$1.55; these connect with Kombis at the Autotransportes Tuxtla terminal for San Cristóbal de Las Casas.

Yucatán Peninsula

T HE STATES OF Yucatán, Campeche and Quintana Roo, sold to tourists as the land of Maya archaeology and beach and island resorts (Cancún, Cozumel, etc). It pays to explore beyond the main itineraries, for lesser-known Maya sites, caves, lagoons, flamingo feeding grounds and villages with old churches. There are two road and river routes into Guatemala, and the main road access to Belize.

The peninsula of Yucatán is a flat land of tangled scrub in the drier NW, merging into exuberant jungle and tall trees in the wetter SE. There are no surface streams. The underlying geological foundation is a horizontal bed of limestone in which rainwater has dissolved enormous caverns. Here and there their roofs have collapsed, disclosing deep holes or *cenotes* in the ground, filled with water. Today this water is raised to surface-level by wind-pumps: a typical feature of the landscape. It is hot during the day but cool after sunset. Humidity is often high. All round the peninsula are splendid beaches fringed with palm groves and forests of coconut palms. The best time for a visit is from Oct to March.

In Yucatán and Quintana Roo, the economy has long been dependent on the export of *henequén* (sisal), and chicle, but both are facing heavy competition from substitutes and tourism is becoming ever more important.

HISTORY

The early history and accomplishments of the Maya when they lived in Guatemala and Honduras before their mysterious trek northwards is given in the introduction to the book. They arrived in Yucatán about AD 600 and later rebuilt their cities, but along different lines, probably because of the arrival of Toltecs in the 9th and 10th centuries. Each city was autonomous, and in rivalry with other cities. Before the Spaniards arrived the Maya had developed a writing in which the hieroglyphic was somewhere between the pictograph and the letter. Fray Diego de Landa collected their books, wrote a very poor summary, the *Relación de las Cosas de Yucatán*, and with Christian but unscholarlike zeal burnt all his priceless sources.

In 1511 some Spanish adventurers were shipwrecked on the coast. Two survived. One of them, Juan de Aguilar, taught a nahuatl-speaking girl Spanish. She became interpreter for Cortés after he had landed in 1519. The Spaniards found little to please them: no gold, no concentration of natives, but Mérida was founded in 1542 and the few natives handed over to the conquerors in *encomiendas*. The Spaniards found them

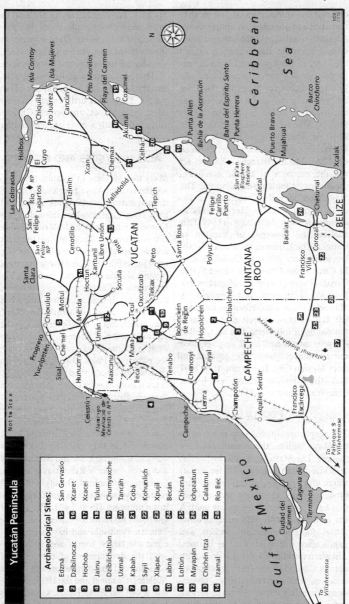

Yucatán Peninsula

Archaeological Sites:

1. Edzná
2. Dzibilnocac
3. Hochob
4. Jaina
5. Dzibilchaltún
6. Uxmal
7. Kabah
8. Sayil
9. Xlapac
10. Labná
11. Loltún
12. Mayapán
13. Chichén Itzá
14. Izamal
15. San Gervasio
16. Xcaret
17. Xcacel
18. Tulum
19. Chumyaxche
20. Tancáh
21. Cobá
22. Kohunlich
23. Xpujil
24. Becán
25. Chicaná
26. Ichpaatun
27. Calakmul
28. Rio Bec

Not to Scale

difficult to exploit: even as late as 1847 there was a major revolt, arising from the inhuman conditions in the *henequén* plantations, from the discrimination against the Maya in the towns and from the expropriation of their communal lands. In July 1847 a conspiracy against the Blancos, or ruling classes from Mexico, was uncovered in Valladolid and one of its leaders, Manuel Antonio Ay, was shot. This precipitated a bloody war, the Guerra de Castas (Caste War) between the Maya and the Blancos. The first act was the massacre of all the non-Maya inhabitants of Tepich, S of Valladolid. The Maya took control of much of the Yucatán, laying siege to Mérida, only to abandon it to sow their crops in 1849. This allowed the governor of Yucatán to counter-attack, driving the Maya by ruthless means into southern Quintana Roo. In Chan Santa Cruz, now called Felipe Carrillo Puerto, one of the Maya leaders, José María Barrera, accompanied by Manuel Nahuat, a ventriloquist, invented the 'talking cross', a cult that attracted thousands of followers. The sect, called Cruzob, established itself and renewed the resistance against the government from Mexico City. It was not until 1901 that the Mexican army retook the Cruzob's domain.

PEOPLE

The people are divided into two groups: the Maya Indians, the minority, and the *mestizos*. The Maya women wear *huipiles*, or white cotton tunics (silk for *fiestas*) which may reach the ankles and are embroidered round the square neck and bottom hem. Ornaments are mostly gold. A few of the men still wear straight white cotton (occasionally silk) jackets and pants, often with gold or silver buttons, and when working protect this dress with aprons. Carnival is the year's most joyous occasion, with concerts, dances, processions. Yucatán's folk dance is the Jarana, the man dancing with his hands behind

his back, the woman raising her skirts a little, and with interludes when they pretend to be bullfighting. During pauses in the music the man, in a high falsetto voice, sings *bambas* (compliments) to the woman.

The Maya are a courteous, gentle, strictly honest and scrupulously clean people. They drink little, except on feast days, speak Mayan, and profess Christianity laced with a more ancient nature worship.

ACCESS TO SITES AND RESORTS

Many tourists come to Yucatán, mostly to see the ancient Maya sites and to stay at the new coastal resorts. A good paved road runs from Coatzacoalcos through Villahermosa, Campeche and Mérida (Route 180 – one ferry crossing). Most of the great archaeological sites except Palenque are on or just off this road and its continuation beyond Mérida. An inland road from Villahermosa to Campeche gives easy access to Palenque. If time is limited, take a bus from Villahermosa to Chetumal via Escárcega, which can be done overnight as the journey is not very interesting (unless you want to see the Mayan ruins off this road, see page 482). From Chetumal travel up the coast to Cancún, then across to Mérida. A train from Mexico City to Mérida goes through Palenque; Pullman passengers can make the whole trip without leaving the car in 2 nights. Route 307 from Puerto Juárez and Cancún to Chetumal is all paved and in very good condition. Air services from the USA and Mexico City are given under Villahermosa, Mérida, Cancún and Cozumel. Details of the road route between Guatemala and Yucatán are given on pages 416 and 439. The state of Quintana Roo is on the eastern side of the Yucatán Peninsula and has recently become the largest tourist area in Mexico with the development of the resort of Cancún, and the parallel growth of Isla Mujeres, Cozumel and the 100-km corridor S of Cancún to Tulum. Growth has been such, in both Yucatán and Quintana

Roo, that there are insufficient buses at peak times, old 2nd class buses may be provided for 1st class tickets and 2nd class buses take far too many standing passengers. There is a lack of information services. Where beaches are unspoilt they often lack all amenities. Many cheaper hotels are spartan. **Warning** So many of the tourists coming to the coastal resorts know no Spanish that price hikes and short-changing have become very common there, making those places very expensive if one is not careful. In the peak, winter season, prices are increased any way, by about 50%.

NB The use of tripods for photography at sites is subject to an extra fee of US$3.50, but for using video cameras the fee is US$7.50. Since the major archaeological sites get very crowded, it is best to visit them just before closing time. Note also that in spring and summer temperatures can be very high; take plenty of drinking water and adequate protection against the sun if walking for any length of time (eg around a large Maya site). See page 536 for recommended reading.

COATZACOALCOS

(*Pop* 186,000) The Gulf Coast gateway for Yucatán, 1½ km from the mouth of its wide river. It is hot, frantic and lacking in culture, and there is not much to do save watch the river traffic (river too polluted for fishing and swimming, less than salubrious discos on the beach by the pier at the river-mouth; beach is dangerous at nights, do not sleep there or loiter). Ocean-going vessels go upriver for 39 km to **Minatitlán**, the oil and petrochemical centre (*Pop* 145,000; airport), whose huge oil refinery sends its products by pipeline to Salina Cruz on the Pacific. Pollution can be bad at times. The road between the two towns carries very heavy industrial traffic. The offshore oil rigs are serviced from Coatzacoalcos. Sulphur is exported from the mines, 69 km away.

● **Accommodation In Coatzacoalcos**: very difficult as all hotels are used by oil workers. Don't spend the night on the street if you can't find lodging. Prices double those of hotels elsewhere. **A3** *Enríquez*, Ignacio de La Llave, good; **C** *Alex*, JJ Spark 223, T 24137, with bath, fan, clean, safe parking; **D** *Oliden*, Hidalgo 100, with fan, clean, noisy (other similar hotels in this area); **E** *San Antonio*, Malpica 205, nr market, with shower. *Motel Colima* at Km 5, Carretera Ayucan-Coatzacoalcos, may have rooms if none in Coatzacoalcos; it is clean, in a quiet position, but does have a lot of red-light activity. **In Minatitlán**: **B** *César*; **B** *Palacio* on main street; **B** *Plaza*; **C** *Tropical*, with bath, no hot water. **D** *Hotel Nacional*, opp *Palacio*, with bath, fan, hot water, clean, rec.

● **Places to eat In Coatzacoalcos**: *Los Lopitos*, Hidalgo 615, good *tamales* and *tostadas*; *Mr Kabubu's* bar and restaurant, nr *Hotel Alex*, good food and drinks. Cheap restaurants on the top floor of the indoor market nr the bus terminal. *Cafetería Sanborn*, Carranza 406 on Plaza Independencia, good breakfast. There is a 24-hr restaurant in one of the streets just off the main Plaza, good empanadas with cream.

● **Post & telecommunications Post Office**: Carranza y Lerdo, Coatzacoalcos.

● **Transport Air** Minatitlán airport, 30 mins. **Trains** Railway station is 5 km from town at Cuatro (for Mexico City and Mérida) at end of Puerto Libre bus route and on Playa Palma Sola route, smelly and dingy, the through train is swept out here; irregular bus services. Better walk about 500m to the main road and get a bus there, US$0.25. Train to **Mérida**, via Palenque and Campeche at 1540. Another station, in the city centre, serves Tehuantepec and Salina Cruz, via Medias Aguas. The train to **Salina Cruz** leaves daily at 0605, 9½ hrs journey 2nd class. **Buses** To Mexico City, US$26.50; to Mérida US$31; to Córdoba, US$13; to Veracruz (312 km), US$9, 7¼ hrs; to Ciudad del Carmen, US$16.50; to Salina Cruz, US$12.15; to Minatitlán, to which taxis also ply. To Villahermosa, US$7. Buses from Minatitlán, ADO to many destinations: Mexico City, Puebla, Villahermosa, Veracruz, Mérida, Palenque, Chetumal, but not Cancún.

39 km E of Coatzacoalcos, on a side road off Route 180 is **Agua Dulce**, where there is a campground, *Rancho Hermanos Graham*, nice location, full hook-up, cold

showers, only one bathroom for whole site, US$6.50 for car and 2 people.

On the Gulf Coast, further E (turn off Route 180 at Las Piedras, 70 km from Coatzacoalcos, signposted), is **Sánchez Magallanes**, a pleasant, friendly town. You can camp safely on the beach.

CARDENAS TO VILLAHERMOSA

Cárdenas, 116 km from Coatzacoalcos and 48 km from Villahermosa by dual carriageway, is the headquarters of the Comisión del Grijalva, which is encouraging regional development. Between Cárdenas and Villahermosa are many stalls selling all varieties of bananas, a speciality of the area, and the road passes through the Samaria oilfield. (From Chontalpa there is irregular transport to Raudales on the lake formed by the Netzahualcoyotl dam.) It is very hard to find accommodation in Cárdenas, **D** *Hotel Yaxol*, cheapest, with bath, a/c, parking, clean, on main plaza. **D** *Turista*, on main plaza, hot water, clean, parking, restaurant.

VILLAHERMOSA

(*Pop 275,000; State pop 1995 1,748,664; Phone code* 931) Capital of Tabasco state, **Villahermosa** is on the Río Grijalva, navigable to the sea. It used to be a dirty town, but is now improving, though it is very hot and rainy.

Places of interest

The **cathedral**, ruined in 1973, has been rebuilt, its twin steeples beautifully lit at night; it is not in the centre. There is a warren of modern colonial-style pedestrian malls throughout the central area. The **Centro de Investigaciones de las Culturas Olmecas** (CICOM) is set in a new modern complex with a large public library, expensive restaurant, airline offices and souvenir shops, a few minutes' walk S out of town along the river bank. The **Museo Regional de Antropología Carlos Pellicer Cámara** on three floors, has well laid out displays of Maya and Olmec artefacts, with an excellent

bookshop. Entry US$1, open 0900-2000, closed Mon.

Museo de Cultura Popular, Zaragoza 810, open daily 0900-2000; **Museo de Historia de Tabasco**, Av 27 de Febrero esq Juárez, same hours.

At the NW side of town (W of the downtown area) is Tabasco 2000, a futuristic mall/hotel/office area with an original statue of fishermen.

In 1925 an expedition discovered huge sculptured human and animal figures, urns and altars in almost impenetrable forest at La Venta, 120 km from Villahermosa. Nothing to see there now: about 1950 the monuments were threatened with destruction by the discovery of oil nearby. The poet Carlos Pellicer got them hauled all the way to a woodland area near Villahermosa, now the **Parque Nacional de La Venta**, Blvd Adolfo Ruíz Cortines, with scattered lakes, next to a children's playground and almost opposite the old airport entrance (W of downtown). There they are dispersed in various small clearings. The huge heads, one of them weighs 20 tons, are Olmec, a culture which flourished about 1150-150 BC; this is an experience which should not be missed. Be sure to take insect-repellent for the visit. It takes up to 2 hrs to do it justice, excellent guides, speak Spanish and English (US$6.65 for 1 hr 10 mins). There is also an excellent zoo with creatures from the Tabasco jungle: monkeys, alligators, deer, wild pigs and birds. Open 0900-2000, closed Mon, entrance US$1, rec. Take a bus marked 'Gracitol' from ADO bus terminal US$0.30 (don't take a bus going to 'La Venta', if in doubt, ask). Bus Circuito No 1 from outside 2nd class bus terminal goes past Parque La Venta (taxi to La Venta park US$2). From Parque Juárez in the city, take a 'Fracc Carrizal' bus and ask to be let off at Parque Tomás Garrido, of which La Venta is a part.

Villahermosa is heaving under pressure from the oil boom, which is why it is now such an expensive place. Buses to Mexico City are often booked up well in advance, as are hotel rooms, especially during the holiday season (May onwards). Overnight free parking (no facilities) in the Campo de Deportes. It is hard to find swimming facilities in Villahermosa: Ciudad Deportiva pool for cardholders only. There is a bull ring.

Excursions

Northwest of Villahermosa are the Maya ruins of **Comalcalco**, reached by bus (2 a day by ADO, 1230 and 1800, US$2.50, or local Souvellera bus, US$2, 1½ hrs over paved roads, Souvellera bus leaves from near the bridge where Av Universidad crosses Ruiz Cortines, 4-5 blocks N of Central Camionera in Villahermosa), then taxi to the ruins US$4.50 or to the entrance, US$0.35, and walk 1 km, or walk the full 3 km. The ruins are unique in Mexico because the palaces and pyramids are built of bricks, long and narrow like ancient Roman bricks, and not of stone (entry US$4.35, open daily 0800-1700). From Comalcalco go to **Paraíso** near the coast, frequent buses from town to the beach 8 km away. Interesting covered market, good cocoa. **D** *Centro Turístico* beach hotel, clean, no hot water, food and drink expensive. Also **E** *Hotel Hidalgo*, in centre, clean.

Local festivals

Ash Wednesday is celebrated from 1500 to dusk by the throwing of water in balloon bombs and buckets at anyone who happens to be on the street.

Local information
● **Accommodation**

The price difference between a reasonable and a basic hotel can be negligible, so one might as well go for the former.

Best is **L2** *Exalaris Hyatt*, Juárez 106, T 34444, F 55808, all services.

A1 *Holiday Inn Villahermosa Plaza*, Paseo Tabasco 1407, T 64400, F 64569, 4 km from centre, restaurant, bar, entertainment; **A3** *Maya-Tabasco* (Best Western), Blvd Ruiz Cortines 907, T 21111, F 21133, all services, ask for special offers, sometimes as cheap as **D**.

B *Don Carlos*, Madero 418, T 22493, F 24622, central, clean, helpful, good restaurant (accepts American Express card), nearby parking; **B** *Plaza Independencia*, Independencia 123, T 21299, F 44724.

C *Chocos*, Merino 100, T 129444, F 129649, friendly, clean, a/c, nr ADO terminal; **C** *María Dolores*, Aldama 104, a/c, hot showers, excellent restaurant (closed Sun); **C** *Palma de Mallorca*, Madero 516, T 20144, **C** *Ritz*, Madero 1009, T 121611, safe parking; many other hotels along Madero (eg **D** *La Paz*, central).

D *Oviedo*, Lerdo 303, good; **D** *Sofia*, Zaragoza 408, T 26055, central, tolerable but overpriced, a/c.

E *Madero*, Madero 301, T 20516, damp, good value, some rooms for 4 are cheaper; **F** *Oriente*, Madero 441, clean, hot shower, fan, rec, good restaurant; **E** *San Miguel*, Lerdo 315, T 21500, good value, quiet, clean, shower, fan, very friendly, run down; **E** *Tabasco*, Lerdo 317, T 20077, not too clean, cold water, mosquitoes; several others on Lerdo. Cheap hotels, from E pp, on C Constitución (come out of main entrance of bus terminal, turn right then 1st left and continue for 5 blocks, but it's the red-light district).

Youth hostel: there is a youth hostel at the back of the Ciudad Deportiva, but it doesn't accept travellers arriving in the evening (4 km SW of the bus station), CP 80180, T 50241.

NB Tourists are often wiser to go directly to Palenque for accommodation; cheaper and no competition from business travellers. Villahermosa can be difficult for lone women: local men's aggressive behaviour said to be due to the effect of eating iguanas.

● **Places to eat**

A good restaurant at *Hotel Madan*, Madero 408, good breakfast, inexpensive fish dishes, a/c, newspapers, a good and quiet place to escape from the heat; *VIPs*, next door, reliable and moderately priced a/c alternative; *Cafetería La Terraza*, Reforma 304, in *Hotel Miraflores*, good breakfast; *Café Casino*, Suárez 530, good coffee, *Bruno's*, Lerdo y 5 de Mayo, cheap, good, noisy, good atmosphere; *Café La Barra*, Lerdo, nr *Bruno's*, good coffee, quiet, pleasant; *El Torito Valenzuela*, next to *Hotel Madero*, Mexican specialities, excellent and inexpensive, highly rec; *El Fogón*, Av Carlos Pellicer 304-A, good value; *Blanca Mariposa*, nr entrance to Parque La Venta, rec; *Aquarius*, Fco Javier Mina 309, nr Av Méndez, vegetarian food, juice bar and health food store. Avoid the bad and expensive tourist eating places on and nr the river front.

● **Airline offices**
AeroMéxico office, Periférico Carlos Pellicer 511, T 26991 (airport 41675); **Mexicana**, Av Madero 109, or Desarollo Urbano Tabasco 2000, T 163785 (airport 21164); **Aerocaribe**, Fco Javier Mina 301-A, T 43202 (airport 44695); **Aviacsa**, T 45770.

● **Banks & money changers**
Banco Internacional, Suárez y Lerdo, changes TCs at good rates; **Banamex**, Madero y Reforma; **American Express**, Turismo Nieves, Sarlat 202, T 41818.

● **Post & telecommunications**
Postal services: DHL, parcel courier service, Paseo Tabasco.

● **Tour companies & travel agents**
Viajes Villahermosa, 27 de Febrero 207.

● **Tourist offices**
In the 1st class bus station (English spoken) and another not far from La Venta park, in Edif Administrativo Tabasco 2000, at Paseo Grijalva and Paseo Tabasco (T 163633, F 163632), both good, closed 1300-1600. Many *papelerías* sell a city map for US$0.10.

● **Transport**
Local Taxis run mainly on a fixed-route collective system (US$1/stop), which can be a problem if you want to go somewhere else. You may have to wait a long time before a driver without fares agrees to take you. **Car hire**: Hertz car rental is available from the airport.

Air Daily services to Mexico City, Mérida, 1 hr, Oaxaca, Monterrey, Tampico, Tuxtla Gutiérrez, Veracruz and Cancún, 3 a week to Palenque, 6 a week to Chetumal, Torreón and Durango, 1 a week to Minatitlán, 6 a week to Havana, Cuba, 6 a week to Houston, from airport 15 km SE, out along the Palenque road, VW bus to town US$3 pp, taxi US$9.50 for 2. Airlines inc AeroMéxico, Mexicana, Serolitoral, Aviacsa and Aerocaribe.

Buses 1st class, ADO bus terminal is on Javier Mina between Méndez and Lino Merino, 12 blocks N of centre, computerized booking system, staff unhelpful. A taxi to the ADO terminal costs US$6, expensive but hard to avoid. Left luggage at ADO terminal, 0700-2300, US$0.30/piece/hr, alternatively, go to Sra Ana in minute restaurant/shop at Pedro Fuentes 817, 100m from ADO, reliable, open till 2000, small charge made. Other private luggage depositories by the bus station also make a small charge. The Central Camionera 2nd class bus station is

on Av Ruiz Cortines, nr roundabout with fisherman statue, 1 block E of Javier Mina, opp Castillo, 4 blocks N of ADO (ie 16 from centre); usually in disarray and it is difficult to get a ticket. Mind your belongings. Several buses (1st class) to **Mexico City**, US$30, 12 hrs, direct bus leaves 1815 (Cristóbal Colón) or 1650 (ADO) then frequent through the night, expect to wait a few hours for Mexico City buses and at least 30 mins in the ticket queue. To **Jalapa** with ADO, 3 a day, 10 hrs; to **Campeche**, US$16.50 (6 hrs), reservation required; to **Coatzacoalcos**, US$7; to **Tapachula**, US$20, 14 hrs. Many buses a day to **Mérida** 8-10 hrs, with ADO, US$19.50, 11 a day, or Cristóbal Colón at 1030 and 2230, US$22; or go 2nd class from Palenque; if coming from Oaxaca to make a connection for Mérida, be prepared for long queues as most buses pass through en route from México City. To **San Andrés Tuxtla**, 6 hrs, US$12.50. To **San Cristóbal**, US$9, 6 hrs; also 2nd class bus with one change at Tuxtla, leaves 0800, arrives 2100, fine scenery but treacherous road. To **Puebla**, ADO 'GL' plus service via autopista, US$30, 1st class US$25.50; UNO, 8 hrs, US$41.25. Cristóbal Colón from ADO terminal to **Oaxaca** via Coatzacoalcos and Tehuantepec at 1930 and 2130, 1st class, stops at about seven places, US$27.50. Bus to **Veracruz**, many a day with ADO, 7 hrs, US$36 *primera plus*; to **Chetumal**, US$16, 10 hrs, but the road is now in a very bad state and it can take much longer, 4 buses, erratic service. To **Catazajá**, US$4, 1½ hrs. To **Palenque**, from ADO terminal, US$4, 1st class, US$2.50, 2nd class, 2½ hrs, 8 a day in all from 0430 (difficult to get on a bus on Sun). Circuito Maya, US$5.60, ADO; 1st class 1000 (buy ticket day before) and 1700, 1½ hrs. To **Emiliano Zapata** and **Tenosique** (for Río San Pedro crossing into Guatemala, see page 416), buses 0700, 0800, 1330, 3-4 hrs.

SOUTH OF VILLAHERMOSA

Teapa is a nice, clean little town with several hotels and beautiful surroundings. The square is pleasant, and you can swim in the river or in the sulphur pool, El Azufre and cavern of Cocona. From Teapa, Tapijulapa on the Chiapas border can be visited, beautiful views.

● **Accommodation & places to eat** C *Quintero*, Eduardo R Bastar 108, T 20045, behind Zócalo, a/c, fan, clean, friendly, enthusiastic restaurant; **D** Simple hotel in grounds of El Azufre, entry to pool inc, no restaurant; **E** *Casa de Huéspedes Miye*, in the main street; good restaurant on main square, *El Mirador*.

● **Transport Trains** If the Villahermosa-Mexico City bus is booked up, try taking the train from Teapa. Check in rainy season whether bridges are OK. Vendors ply the train with local foods and drinks. Journey to the capital 14 hrs US$9.25. **Buses** Buses run hourly between Teapa and Villahermosa on a paved road, 50 km 1 hr, US$1.65. Bus to Chiapa de Corzo at 0730, 7 hrs, US$10, lovely, mountainous landscape (see page 390).

80 km SW of Villahermosa on Route 195 is **Pichucalco**, an affluent town with no beggars and a lively and safe atmosphere. The Zócalo is thronged in the evening with people on after-dinner *paseo*.

● **Accommodation & places to eat** There are many good restaurants and bars. **D** *Hotel La Loma*, Francisco Contreras 51, T 30052, bath, a/c, or fan, ample parking, clean (opp is a cheaper *posada* with resident monkey); **E** *Hotel México*, on left turn from bus station, with bath, fan, clean but musty, *Vila*, on Plaza, **D** *Jardín*, noisy; **D** *La Selva*.

● **Transport** Buses almost every hour to Villahermosa, US$4.

South of Pichucalco on Highway 195 on the way to Tuxtla Gutiérrez, is **Bochil**, an idyllic stopover (**D** *Hotel/Restaurant María Isabel*, 1st Av Sur Pte 44, basic but nice, delicious simple food).

VILLAHERMOSA TO GUATEMALA

By car: 1) via Palenque to San Cristóbal de Las Casas (see below); 2) by Route 195 and 190 to Ciudad Cuauhtémoc via San Cristóbal de Las Casas (Highway 195 is fully paved, but narrow and winding with landslides and washouts in the rainy season, high altitudes, beautiful scenery). If this route is impassable, travel back by Route 180 to Acayucan, to 190, via 185 and go to Ciudad Cuauhtémoc or by Route 200 to Tapachula.

VILLAHERMOSA TO PALENQUE

Palenque is reached by turning off the inland Highway, 186, at **Playas de Catazajá**, 117 km from Villahermosa (no petrol stations until Catazajá; unleaded Magna-sin is available in Catazajá; if you look like running out, turn left for **Macuspana**, where there is one; hotel in Macuspana; **D** *America*, basic, clean, comfortable, safe parking). (Macuspana municipal *fiesta* 15-16 August.) Palenque is 26 km away on a good paved but winding road (minibus US$1.15, 30 mins, taxi US$10). Coming from Campeche it is 5 hrs' drive on a good road, apart from one rough stretch about 1 hr from Palenque; toll bridge US$0.60.

PALENQUE

The town of Palenque is an ugly place but visitors come for the archaeological site 8 km from the town (143 km from Villahermosa), a splendid experience, with its series of Maya hilltop temples in remarkably good condition. It is best to visit the ruins just before they close to avoid the crowds, but to avoid the heat arrive early. On the road to the ruins there are several waterfalls, one is just 250m from the entrance on the right (2 mins' walk from road).

Places of interest

The site is in a hot jungle clearing on a steep green hill overlooking the plain and crossed by a clear cascading brook. Interesting wildlife, mainly birds, also includes howler monkeys and mosquitoes. The ruins are impressive indeed, particularly the Templo de las Inscripciones, easy to climb from the back, in the heart of which was discovered an intact funerary crypt with the Sarcophagus of Lord Pacal, Palenque's greatest ruler, buried in AD 683 (you walk from the top of the pyramid into a staircase, descending to ground level, very humid; usually illuminated when the site is open, but check). The temples around, with fantastic comb-like decorations on their intact roofs, and the sculptured wall panels, are undoubtedly the most exquisite achievement of the Maya. Groups of buildings and several tombs have been discovered in the last few years.

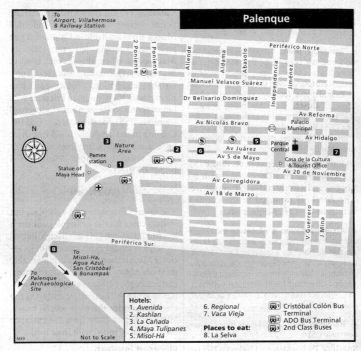

Palenque

To Airport, Villahermosa & Railway Station

Periférico Norte

Manuel Velasco Suárez

Dr Belisario Domínguez

Av Reforma

Av Nicolás Bravo

Palacio Municipal

Av Hidalgo

Parque Central

Casa de la Cultura & Tourist Office

Av 20 de Noviembre

Nature Area

Av Juárez

Av 5 de Mayo

Pemex station

Statue of Maya Head

Av Corregidora

Av 18 de Marzo

Periférico Sur

To Misol-Ha, Agua Azul, San Cristóbal & Bonampak

To Palenque Archaeological Site

Not to Scale

Hotels:
1. *Avenida*
2. *Kashlan*
3. *La Cañada*
4. *Maya Tulipanes*
5. *Misol-Há*
6. *Regional*
7. *Vaca Vieja*

Places to eat:
8. La Selva

Cristóbal Colón Bus Terminal
ADO Bus Terminal
2nd Class Buses

Explanations in three languages on each temple are now legible (pamphlet with brief explanations in English available at the ticket office, US$1.30). You can also wander around in the jungle, many unexcavated ruins, take a torch and look out for spiders and snakes.

There is a 5-hr hike starting to the left side of the Templo de las Inscripciones, follow the path uphill for 1½ hrs until you reach a fence. Walk along several fields until you reach the village at the bottom of the valley (1 hr). Coconut milk is available here. Turn right and follow the track uphill to a pass with fine views. Walking on through farmland you arrive back on the road by the museum at the ruins. Start early.

An excellent **museum**, with restaurant and gift shop, about 1 km outside the ruins has some fine Maya carvings – stuccos,

jade pieces, funerary urns, pottery and other artefacts excavated at the site (open 1000, more like 1100, to 1700, closed Mon). Entry to ruins, US$2.50 (Sun free), charge for car parking. The site opens at 0800 and closes at 1700 (guide, up to 10 people). Beware of thieves at all times. A restaurant by the cascades serves a limited range of food, basic but friendly (stores luggage for US$0.25); shops quick to overcharge and souvenirs are dearer than elsewhere. A path runs from the museum to the main road via waterfalls with good swimming. Hail a colectivo on the road, US$0.80 to town. The climate is hot and dry Mar-April, the coolest months are Oct to February. **Warning** The area can have many mosquitoes; make sure you're up-to-date with your tablets (Dec-April usually few mosquitoes).

Local festivals

Santo Domingo, first week in August.

NB Visitors should respect the local customs and dress so as not to offend – footwear and shirts should always be worn.

Local information

● **Accommodation**

It is convenient to stay at hotels nr the Pemex service station, as they are also nearer the ruins and the bus stations. (Prices treble around *fiesta* time.)

A1 *Misión Palenque*, far end of town in countryside, T 50241, F 50499, complete resort, noisy a/c, although poor service in restaurant reported, has a minibus service from Villahermosa airport for about US$20 return (2 hrs' journey, avoids backtracking from airport into Villahermosa for transport to Palenque), has courtesy bus to ruins and to airfield for trips to Bonampak and Yaxchilán; **A1-C** *Plaza Palenque* (Best Western), Km 27, Carretera Catazajá-Palenque, T 50555, F 50395, free transport Mon-Sat 0800-1700, a/c, pool, relaxing, disco, 1.5 km from centre, 8 km from ruins; **A2** *Maya Toucan*, on road into town, T 50290, pool, a/c, bar, restaurant, lovely views from rooms; **A2** *Hotel Maya Tulipanes*, C Cañada 6, T 50201, F 50230, a/c, cable TV, rooms vary in size, price and quality, garage, pool, bar/restaurant next door; **A3** *Motel Chan-Kah Inn*, at Km 03 Carretera Ruinas, T 51134, F 50820, closest to ruins, cool bungalows, swimming pool fed from river, beautiful gardens, perfectly clean, rec, poor restaurant, with marimba music Fri-Sun, and affiliated to **B** *Chan Kah Centro*, corner of Juárez and Independencia, T 50318, F 50489, a/c, restaurant, terrace bar with happy hour.

B-C *Motel Los Leones*, Km 2.5, about 5 km before ruins on main road, T 50201, F 50033, hot water, a/c, TV, quiet, large restaurant, gringo food.

C *Hotel La Cañada*, T 50102, F 50446, very rustic but very clean, with fan, good value, lovely garden, expensive restaurant, the owner, Sr Morales, is an expert on the ruins; **C** *Casa de Pakal*, Juárez 8, T 50042, 1 block from Plaza, a/c, good but poor plumbing and not very friendly; next door is **E** *Misol-Há*, at Juárez 12, T 50092, fan, with bath, hot water, clean, owner Susana Cuevas speaks English; **C** *Palenque*, 5 de Mayo 15, off Plaza, T 50188, F 50030, with bath, a/c restaurant, vast, rambling menage, 'going downhill fast', pool.

D *Kashlan*, 5 de Mayo 105, T 50297, F 50309, with bath, fan, **C** with a/c, hot water, quiet, clean, will store luggage, video each pm, mosquito nets, helpful owner Ada Luz Navarro, laundry opp, restaurant with vegetarian food in same building, bus and boat tours to Flores offered, rec; **D** *Lacroix*, Hidalgo 30, T 50014, next to church, with bath, fan, no hot water, some cheaper rooms, pleasant place; **D** *Posada Mallorca*, on highway, T 50838, small rooms, comfortable; **D** *Regional*, Av Juárez 79, T 50183, 3 blocks from Plaza, 100m from bus station, hot showers (US$1.50 extra), lights located behind fans ensure constant flickering lights, noisy; **D** *Xibalba*, Merle Green 9, T 50411, F 50392, spacious rooms, clean, hot water, a/c, fan, rec.

E *Avenida*, Juárez 216, T 50116, opp 2nd-class bus station (can be very noisy), with restaurant, clean, large rooms with fan, parking, but does not display price in rooms so ask for government list to check, no hot showers, some rooms with balcony; **E** *Casa de Huéspedes León*, Hidalgo (s/n) nr junction with Abasolo, T 50038, with bath, only cold water, some mosquitoes; **E** *La Posada*, at La Cañada, 200m from Cristóbal Colon buses, T 50437, hot water, fans, basic, a little run down but OK, 'designed for young travellers, international ambience', peaceful; **E** *La Selva*, Av Reforma 69, clean, hot water extra; **E** *Naj K'in*, Hidalgo 72, with bath and fan, hot water 24 hrs, purified water in room and cooler in hallway, safe parking, excellent value; **E** *Posada Alicia*, Av Manuel Velasco Suárez 59, T 50322, between new market and C Novelos, with fan (ask for one), cold water, no towels, cheap, grubby, rooms on left as you enter are cooler, ask for rooms with communal bathroom; **E** *Posada San Francisco*, Hidalgo 113 and Allende, with bath, clean, quiet, no curtains, basic; **E** *Posada Shalom*, Av Juárez 156, T 50944, new, friendly, clean, stores luggage, rec; **E** *Santa Elena*, C Jorge de la Vega, by *Restaurant Oaxaqueña*, with bath, good value, 2 blocks from ADO terminal, clean, simple and quiet, fan, safe parking; **E** *TRF*, above 2nd class bus terminal, with bath, not noisy, rec; **E** *Vaca Vieja*, 5 de Mayo 42, T 50388, 3 blocks from Plaza, with bath, popular with gringos, good restaurant; **E-F** *Posada San Juan*, T 50616 (from ADO go up the hill and first right, it's on the 4th block on the left), with bath, cheaper without, cold water, and fan, clean, quiet, firm beds, secure locks, nice courtyard, very good for budget accommodation, safe parking available (also nr ADO, *Santo Domingo*, 20 de Noviembre 19, T 50146, stores luggage).

F *Joanna*, 20 de Noviembre y Allende, large, clean, airless rooms with fan and bath; **F** pp *Posada Charito*, Av 20 de Noviembre 15-B, T 50121, clean, friendly, family run, very good value, basic, some rooms very airless, ground floor best, laundry service; opp is **E** *Posada Canek*, 20 de Noviembre, dearer rooms have bath, all with fan and toilet, very clean, ground floor rooms nr reception noisy, helpful staff, prices are pp and sharing is often required (regardless of sex), fills up early, arrive before 1000 check-out time.

Camping: *Trailer Park Mayabel*, on road to ruins 2 km before entrance (bus from town US$0.30), for caravans and tents, US$8/vehicle with 2 people. US$2.35 for tent or to sling hammock (an *ambulante* sells hammocks once a day, or you can hire them for an additional US$2.50), palmleaf huts, bathrooms, cold showers, good restaurant but not cheap, nice setting, popular so can be noisy, the place is not to everyone's taste; many mosquitoes and many ticks in long grass (we're told they avoid people who eat lots of garlic!). Watch your belongings; management sometimes stores luggage during the day (reluctant to store valuables). At night, around 0100, you can often hear the howler monkeys screaming in the jungle; quite eerie. The path between the campground and the ruins is not open; do not attempt to use this path. *Panchan Camping*, on road to ruins, cabins (**E**), rent a hammock for US$3 or camp for US$2, hot showers, clean, small pool, vegetarian meals, library, owner is archaeologist and is friendly and informative. *Trailer Park María del Mar*, 5 km from Palenque, along road to ruins, T 50533, US$12 for 2 in camper van with hook-up, camping US$5, restaurant and swimming pool, cold showers, clean, pretty setting (check that water is turned on). Good swimming at *Calinda Nututún* (entry US$1), 3.5 km along Palenque-Ocosingo road, T 50100, US$3.30 pp, vehicle free, US$2/camping site/night, rather run down, no tent rentals, rooms (**B**) are neglected, toilets and bath; and beautiful lake and waterfall open to the public for a small fee. Misol-Ha, 2 km off same road at Km 19, see below.

● **Places to eat**

Some restaurants accept dollars, but at less than the current rate. *Montes Azules*, Av Juárez, very tasty food in generous portions and at low prices, friendly and helpful owner, live marimba music Fri, Sat, Sun nights; *La Quebrada*, Av Juárez 120, opp ADO terminal, breakfast and reasonably-priced meals, fast service, rec; *El Patio*, Av Juárez, opp *Girasoles*, cheap set menu, excellent service, good Mexican food, friendly; *Merolec*, down street from *La Posada*, new, good atmosphere and service, reasonable prices; *Lakan-Ha*, Juárez 20, fast, cheap, efficient; also on Av Juárez, *La Jícara Pícara*, Allende junction, very good value and very friendly, specializes in *pozole*, a maize stew; *El Rodeo*, Juárez 10, nr Plaza, does inexpensive breakfasts and meat dishes, rec, popular with travellers, good source of information; *La Ceiba* (Hnos Cabrera) on Juárez, good café for breakfast; *Girasoles*, Juárez 189, roof terrace, very good food and value, popular with backpackers, good breakfasts, slow service; *Francesa*, Juárez, 2 doors down from ADO bus office, nothing French but reasonable steak and chips; *Pizzería Palenque*, Juárez, T 50332, good pizzas and prices; *Mara*, on 5 de Mayo by the Zócalo, excellent food, very welcoming; *Mariscos and Pescados*, off Juárez, opp large *artesanía* market; *Las Tinajas*, 20 de Noviembre 41 y Abasolo, good, family run, excellent food, huge portions food but not cheap; *Los Portales*, Av 20 de Noviembre e Independencia, cheap, good, rec; *Artemio*, Av Hidalgo, nr Plaza, reasonably-priced food, rec; *Chan Kah*, on Plaza, good value, accepts credit cards. At Km 0.5 on Hidalgo (road to ruins) is *La Selva*, expensive, but excellent, smart dress preferred, live music at weekends. *Yunuen*, at *Hotel Vaca Vieja*, generous portions at reasonable prices, good steaks, popular with local ranchers; *Oaxaqueña*, at entrance to town, nr Mayan head statue, memorable food; *La Palapa de Apo-Hel*, Av 5 de Mayo, s/n, between Independencia and Abasolo, a delightful little bamboo shack specializing in sea food, rec; *California*, Av 5 de Mayo, opp *Avenida*, nr 2nd class buses, good value, Mexican specialities; opp *Hotel Kashlan*, **Café de los Altos**, good coffee; *El Rinconcito*, Allende, across from *Kashlan*, good, economical; *El Fogón de Pakal*, C Merle Green, La Cañada, delightful, good and varied menu. Good *pollo rostizado* in restaurant inside ADO office. Good *tacos* at food stalls E of Parque Central. Try the ice-cream at *Holanda* on Av Juárez, s/n, 4 doors W of Banamex, in the centre.

● **Banks & money changers**

Exchange rate only comes through at 1000, then banks open until 1200. Bancomer, changes TCs, good rates. **Yax-Ha Cambio** on

Juárez, next to Banamex, open 0700-2000 daily, changes US$ cash and TCs. *Restaurante El Rodeo* also changes TCs at bank rate. At weekends TCs can be changed at many travel agencies and other shops on Av Juárez; also, the owner at Farmacia Central will change US$ at a reasonable rate.

● Laundry

Opposite *Hotel Kashlan*, 3 kg for US$2, mixed reports. At the end of Juárez is a laundry, US$3 for 3 kg.

● Post & telecommunications

Post Office: Independencia, next to Palacio Municipal, helpful.

Telephone: long-distance telephones at ADO bus terminal, cheaper than many other telephone offices; at *Mercería* bookshop in Aldama nr Juárez, and a shop by *Hotel Palenque* in Zócalo.

● Shopping

Cotton, nylon and sisal hammocks can be bought along Av Juárez. Bargain.

● Sports

Horse riding: tours can be booked at the Clínica Dental Zepeda, Av Juárez s/n. The dentist is the owner of the horses.

● Tour companies & travel agents

Tonina, Juárez 105, T 50384, or small office on Juárez ½ block from plaza, mixed reports, tours to Bonampak and Yaxchilán, 2 days, US$55 pp. *STS*, nr Post Office, good prices for group tours; *Yax-Ha*, Av Juárez 123, T 50/98, F 50787, English spoken, rec; *Shivalva* (Marco A Morales), Merle Green 1, La Cañada, T 50411, F 50392, tours of Palenque, Yaxchilán, Bonampak, Tikal, Guatemala City, Belize, Copán (also offers hotel booking for San Cristóbal de las Casas, but it's best to make your own choice). One way trips to Tikal can be arranged for about US$30 pp.

● Tourist offices

In the Casa de la Cultura on plaza entrance at side of building, corner of Jiménez and 5 de Mayo, open 0900-1300 and 1700-2000, useful map with hotel and restaurant listings, helpful and informative staff.

● Transport

Air Aerocaribe flies 4 times a week to Palenque from Cancún via Chetumal and Flores, Guatemala. There are also flights from Mérida, Villahermosa, and Oaxaca via Tuxtla Gutiérrez. For flights to Bonampak and Yaxchilán, see below.

Trains Railway station for Palenque is 10 km outside town (bus goes from in front of *Posada Alicia* at 2000; from station to town, irregular service, be patient). Much better is a taxi colectivo to/from railway station and Pemex service station US$1.50 for 2. Latest timetables show trains to Palenque and Mérida starting at Córdoba at 0630, arr Palenque 2250, US$8 2nd class, and continuing to **Campeche** (7 hrs) and **Mérida** (10½ hrs); keep your luggage with you, (only one car, no sleeper) no light, take a torch and insect repellent. Tickets on sale 1 hr before train arrives. The train may be crowded so it may be necessary to stand all the way. The trains are unreliable with delays of up to 11 hrs. The station is not a pleasant place to wait in the dark. Do not rely on timetables, check all times in person before travel. **NB** If returning from Palenque to Mérida by train, bear in mind that in Dec and Jan it is nearly impossible to make reservations.

Buses Micro buses run back and forth along the main street, passing the bus station area, to and from the ruins, every 10 mins, US$0.50 (taxi US$5). All bus companies have terminals at W end of Av Juárez. The Cristóbal Colón terminal is on the road to the ruins. Buy ticket to leave on arrival, ADO 1st class on sale the day before, buses are often full; very heavy ticket sales on 1 and 15 of each month when salaries are paid. 1st class bus to/from **Mexico City**, ADO, at 1800, 15 hrs, 1,006 km, US$43. First-class bus to **Villahermosa** with ADO, 6 a day between 0700 and 1900, 2½ hrs, US$4. 2nd class bus to Villahermosa at 0800 and 1200, US$2.50. To Veracruz, only via Villahermosa, from there 7½ hrs with ADO, many a day, US$14.80. ADO buses, 7 a day, to **Ciudad del Carmen**, US$13.25. Direct bus to **Campeche** from Palenque at 1700, 2nd class (Transportes del Sur), 5 hrs, US$10.65, or 2 with ADO, 0800 and 2100, US$10, 5 hrs, change here for Mérida (a further 2½ hrs). Daily ADO 1st class bus direct to **Mérida** at 0800, US$23, book in advance, 8 hrs, luxury service at 0100 daily, Cristóbal Cólon (US$25). 2nd class to Mérida US$17, dep 1700 and 2300. Another possibility is to go for connections to Campeche or Mérida at Emiliano Zapata, bus from Palenque at 0700, 0900, 1400, and 2000 (from ADO terminal) bus to Palenque at 0600 and 1230 (taxi Emiliano Zapata-Palenque US$28). See page 419. Another possiblity is to take a bus to Catazajá (see page 410), where the 1500 Cristóbal Colón bus Villahermosa-Campeche bus stops. To **Chetumal** with ADO, daily at 2030, with a/c, toilets, stops at Escárcega for a meal, 8-10 hrs; Maya de Oro 1st class, US$23; Cristóbal Colón at 2100, 7-8 hrs; also 2nd class with Lacandonia at 0100 from their office next to *Restaurante Oaxaqueña*, US$14.80. Note that ADO and Cristóbal Colón buses arrive between 0400 and 0500, a bad time to look for a hotel or find a bus to Belize. To **San Cristóbal de Las Casas**, good road throughout, 4 hrs' journey, Rodolfo Figueroa, a/c, TV, toilet, 3-4 a day, US$4.50 (beware travel sickness, many bends); luxury service with Cristóbal Colón, a/c, video, 0230 and 2300 daily, also goes on to Tuxtla Gutiérrez. ADO leaves at 0930, US$5. Autotransportes Tuxtla 5 expresses a day, US$7, also 1st class US$5.25 and 2nd class US$4.30. **Tuxtla Gutiérrez**, 5 a day, 377 km, US$11, 3¹/₂ hrs, 2nd class, via San Cristóbal de Las Casas. **NB** There are military checks between Palenque and San Cristóbal de las Casas; buses and cars are stopped. If stopped at night in a private car, switch off engine and lights, and switch on the inside light. Always have your passport handy.

ROAD AND RIVER TRAVEL TO GUATEMALA

1) The Río San Pedro route starts at **Tenosique**, a friendly place (money exchange at clothing shop Ortiz y Alvarez at C 28, No 404, good rates for dollars to quetzales, poor for dollars to pesos) on the Palenque-Mérida railway line. From here you go by road to La Palma, boat to El Naranjo, Guatemala, and road to Flores.

● **Accommodation D** *Rome*, C 28, No 400, T 20151, clean, will change dollars for residents, bath, not bad; **E** *Azulejos*, C 26 No 416, with bath, fan, clean, hot water, friendly, helpful owner speaks some English, opp church; **E** *Casa de Huéspedes La Valle*, C 19, with bath, clean, good, and others. Excellent and cheap *Taquería Pipirrín*, C 26, 512, nr *Hotel Azulejos*.

● **Tour companies & travel agents** For planes to Bonampak contact Sr Quintero, T 20099. *Hotel Kashlan* offers 2 and 3 day trips to Flores via Yaxchilan and Bonampak, reliable and rec. *Kim Tours*, Av Juárez 27, T 51499, do similar trips "strenuous but great", US$100 pp, rec.

● **Transport** You can get to Tenosique from Villahermosa by ADO bus (0430, 0700, 0800, 1330), 4 hrs, from Emiliano Zapata by frequent 1st or 2nd class bus, US$2, or on the México-Mérida railway line, 1 hr **E** by train from Palenque,

US$0.75. From Palenque by road minibuses Libertad leave from 20 de Noviembre y Allende from 0700 to Emiliano Zapata, 1 hr, US$2.50 (take 0700 to be sure of making the boat at La Palma); and from there to Tenosique at 0800 or 0900, 90 mins, US$2. ADO have a direct bus to Tenosique from Palenque at 0430, 2 hrs, US$3.25. Many travel agents in Palenque organize colectivos direct to La Palma at 1000, US$14 pp to connect with the boat to El Naranjo (4 passengers minimum). Alternatively, take a colectivo before 0645 to Playas de Catazajá from the stop just up from ADO (US$1, 30 mins); alight at the El Crucero de la Playa crossroads on the Villahermosa – Tenosique road and wait for the bus to pass at 0730 (2 hrs to Tenosique, US$2). Similarly, from Tenosique to Palenque, take the Villahermosa bus (every hour or so during the day) as far as El Crucero de La Playa, and then take one of the regular minibuses running to Palenque. Bus also from Mexico City, ADO, 16¹/₂ hrs, arrives 0700, US$45.50.

From Tenosique to **La Palma** on the Río San Pedro, orange *colectivos*, starting at 0600 from in front of the market, 1 hr, US$1, 2 hrs by bus (from Tenosique bus station, which is outside town, take taxi, US$1.70 or colectivo to 'Centro', or walk 20 mins). Taxi to La Palma US$7, shared by all passengers. From La Palma boats leave to El Naranjo (Guatemala) at 0800 (or when they have enough passengers) but timings are very irregular (they wait for a minimum of 5 passengers before leaving), at least 4¹/₂ hrs, US$22 (to check boat times, T 30811 Rural at the Río San Pedro). Be at boat 1 hr early, it sometimes leaves ahead of schedule; if this happens ask around for someone to chase it, US$3-4 pp for 3 people. If there are fewer than 5 passengers, the boat may be cancelled, in which case you must either wait for the next one, or hire a *rápido* (US$125, max 4 people). It is a beautiful boat trip, through mangroves with flocks of white herons and the occasional alligator, dropping people off at homesteads. There is a stop at the border post 2 hrs into the journey to sign out of Mexico, a lovely spot with a lake and lilies. In the rain, luggage will get wet; take a raincoat and a torch. There is a pier at El Naranjo. In La Palma, two restaurants are poor value; one restaurant will change money at weekends at a reasonable rate. There are no officials on arrival at the jetty in El Naranjo; immigration is a short way uphill on the right (entry will cost US$5 in quetzales or dollars, beware extra unofficial charges at customs); bus tickets to Flores sold here.

At **El Naranjo** there are hotels (basic), a video cinema (US$0.50) and restaurants (you can wait in a restaurant till the 0100 bus departs, but electricity is turned off at 2300). The grocery store opposite immigration will change dollars into quetzales at a poor rate, accommodation also available here, US$1.50 per room. From El Naranjo there is a dirt road through the jungle to Flores; buses leave at 0100, 0400 and 1200 for Flores (minimum 4½-5 rough, crowded hours, US$3) or hitchhiking apparently possible.

● **Tour companies & travel agents** Travel agencies in Palenque do the trip to Flores via La Palma and El Naranjo, US$55 pp, 3 passengers minimum (agencies will make up the number), dep 0500, arrive Flores 1900; via Corozal/Bethel, US$35 pp, via Yaxchilán and Bonampak, see below, minimum 5 people. It may take several days before you can join an organized trip in low season.

2) The Río Usumacinta route by road to Benemérito, boat to Sayaxché, Guatemala and road to Flores: Autotransportes Comitán Lagos de Montebello buses (Av Manuel Velasco Suárez, Palenque, 3 blocks from food market) run daily at 0330, 0530, 0800 to Benemérito, on the Mexican side of the Usumacinta, 7-12 hrs, basic buses, dreadful road, crowded (it's about half the time in a *camioneta* if you can hitch a ride in one). You must visit immigration, about 3 km from Benemérito, to sign out of Mexico (the bus will wait). Once in Benemérito, hope for a boat to Guatemala; this may take a couple of days (accommodation is possible). The boat goes to Sayaxché and should stop at Pipiles for immigration formalities. A trading boat takes 2 days, US$4-5; a motorized canoe 8 hrs, US$5-10. From Sayaxché, buses run to Flores.

Alternatively, one bus a day runs Palenque-Frontera Echeverría, 0930 (same company), 6-8 hrs, US$5; or a minibus at 0730 from 5 de Mayo by *Restaurante El Caimito*, US$4 (many travel agencies in Palenque run minibuses on this route, leaving at 0600, to connect with the boat to Bethel, 35 mins, and on to Flores as below). Echeverría is also called Corozal. From Echeverría/Corozal there is a 5-min launchride to La Técnica, then 20 mins by bus to Bethel in Guatemala, from where a regular bus service goes to Flores at 1400, 1-2 hrs (see Guatemala chapter, **El Petén**, page 659). At Echeverría/Corozal there is an immigration office which has a basic room where people can stay for US$3.50 (the only place to stay here) and a cheap *comedor*. Coming from Guatemala you may well get stuck at the border as the 0500 Santa Elena-Bethel bus does not connect with buses to Palenque (you may be able to get a lift with one of the tour buses which start arriving around 1200, bargain hard). Passengers have to wait until 0400 next day. Bus from Frontera Echeverría to Palenque, 0500, US$3 and at 1230, US$4. Many military checkpoints.

PALENQUE TO BONAMPAK AND YAXCHILAN

Flights from Palenque to **Bonampak** and **Yaxchilán**, in light plane for 5, about US$600 per plane, to both places, whole trip 6 hrs. Prices set, list available; Viajes Misol-Ha run charter flights to Bonampak and Yaxchilán for US$150 pp return, minimum 4 passengers. ATC Travel Agency, agents for Aviacsa, at Av Benito Juárez and Allende, open 0800-1800 daily except Sun, to Bonampak; book at airport, may be cheaper from Tenosique, best to visit in May – the driest month. Do not visit ruins at night, it is forbidden.

From Palenque, a 2-day road and river trip to Bonampak and Yaxchilán is sold by travel agencies, US$100 pp, all transport and food included; or 1 day trip to Yaxchilán, US$65; entrance to sites included in cost. Strenuous, but good value: the usual schedule is 4-hrs bus ride to Echeverría/Corozal (mostly tarmac), 1 hr boat to Yaxchilán, next day boat to Echeverría, 1 hr bus to Bonampak turn-off, walk to Bonampak and back (see below), 6 hrs bus to Palenque (arriving 2200). Colectivos Chambala at Hidalgo y Allende, Palenque, also run 2-day trips, slightly cheaper, again all inclusive, minimum 6 passengers. However you go, take suitable footwear and rain protection for jungle walking, drinking water, insect repellent and passport (there are many military checkpoints). Bonampak is over 30 km from Frontera Echeverría/Corozal (see above for how to get there: food, petrol and accommodation; you must register at the Migración office) and can be reached only on foot from the crossroads to Lacanjá (see below) on the road to Echeverría. Autotransportes Comitán Lagos de Montebello buses at 0300, 0430, 0630, 0900 and 2000 all pass the turn off to Bonampak, US$5.50, check details in advance. It is a 12 km walk from the crossroads to the ruins, 2-4 hrs depending on mud and fitness. Walk 4 km along the road until the blue house, then follow the track straight ahead into the jungle. It's an 8 km walk direct to the ruins. Local people take passengers in 3-wheelers to the ruins. Beware of sandflies, black flies which cause river blindness, and mosquitoes; there is basic accommodation at the site, take hammock and mosquito net. The workers are not to be trusted. At **Lacanjá** (9 km from Bonampak) there is a community of Lacandonian Indians. They have curly hair, rare in Mexico, and wear white gowns. For more details ask Lewis at Na-Bolom in San Cristóbal de las Casas. There are three campsites here where you can sling a hammock, *Kin Bor*, *Carmelo* and *Manuel Chan Bor*. Local guides can be hired for hikes in the jungle and to the ruins of Bonampak. A new road is in the process of being built to Bonampak: 2 lanes, paved. Buses from Palenque leave from Chancala bus terminal every

3 hrs or so, from 0730 to San Javier US$3.50, 3 hrs. From San Javier a jungle trail leads to Bonampak, easy to follow but several hours walk with nowhere to stay en route. Take your own tent, hammock, sleeping bag as it gets cold at night, food and drink.

Yaxchilán is reached by 1-hr boat journey from Echeverría, you must register at the immigration office here (US$50 to hire a motorboat for the round trip, no problem finding a boat, cost includes boatman staying overnight); a beautiful ride, and beautiful ruins, open 0800-1600. The custodian of the ruins is very helpful; outside the excavation season (Mar-June) you can sling a hammock anywhere. There are more howler monkeys than people in Yaxchilán.

At **Bonampak** there is a series of remarkable murals depicting many aspects of Maya life: ceremonies, battles and festivals. An article in *National Geographic*, Feb 1995, reproduces some of the murals with computer enhancement to show their original colours and most of the details.

AGUA AZUL AND MISOL-HA

A series of beautiful waterfalls aptly named for the blue water swirling over natural tufa dams on 7 km of fast-flowing river, is a popular camping spot reached by a 4-km paved road (in fair condition) from the junction with the paved road to San Cristóbal, 65 km from Palenque. Best visited in dry season as in the rainy season it is hard to swim because of the current (don't visit if it was raining the day before). **Warning** One of the falls is called 'The Liquidiser', an area of white water in which bathing is extremely dangerous. On no account should you enter this stretch of water; many drownings have occurred. Obey the notice posted in an adjacent tree. If you walk some way up the lefthand side of the river you come to uncrowded areas where the river is wider and safer for swimming. 3 km upstream is the Balcón Ahuau waterfall, good beach for sunbathing. It is extremely popular at holiday time (visit in the morning, less crowded). Entrance fee to this *ejidal* park US$0.65 on foot, US$1.75 for cars.

Horses can be rented for riding downstream where there are also uncrowded pools for swimming. It is possible to walk upriver to the rainforest; follow the river till you come to a rickety bridge across a stream, cross this and continue through a meadow until you rejoin the river; carry on to a lovely beach with trees and the river thundering through a gorge. Further progress is difficult. Beware of ticks when camping in long grass, use kerosene to remove them (or eat raw garlic to repel them!). Flies abound during the rainy season (June-Nov). The river near the campsite is often badly polluted with soap and detergents.

Between Palenque and Agua Azul are the **Misol-Ha** waterfalls (entry US$0.65, US$1.65 for a car). There is an interesting cave to the right of the big falls, about 25m deep, with a pool inside and another waterfall; take a torch and beware of bats! It is also worth going behind the waterfall.

● **Accommodation & places to eat** There are a few restaurants and many food stalls (if on a tight budget, bring your own). There are 2 places with *cabañas* for hammocks (hammock rental US$1.50 and up, US$3.45 pp in beds in dormitory); if staying, be very careful of your belongings; thefts have been reported. *Camping Agua Azul* is popular and reliable, opposite the parking lot; camping costs US$1.75, US$3.30 for 2 in camper van, and US$0.15 for use of toilets (100m further on are free public toilets), no other facilities. RVs can stay overnight at Agua Azul, using the facilities, without paying extra (as long as you do not leave the park). Plenty of food stalls, 2 restaurants. Follow the path up the falls to a second site, cheaper, less crowded. There are also more *cabañas* and nice places to sling a hammock further upstream, all cheaper and less touristy than lower down. *Hamacas Casa Blanca* next to *Comedor El Bosque*, 2 km upstream, big room with mosquito-netted windows, accommodates 10, shared toilet, US$2 pp (US$1.70 with own hammock), free locked luggage store. 750m upstream from *Casa Blanca* is the last house on this

path. Here you can sling a hammock for US$1 (US$0.50 with own hammock), friendly family atmosphere, good views, store luggage, basic but good dinner, rec. *Restaurant Económico* will rent out a small hut with hammocks, friendly, helpful, excellent food, safe luggage store.

● **Transport** Coop Chambalum, C Allende, and Viajes Aventura Maya, Av Juárez 123, Palenque run tours to Agua Azul and Misol-Ha for US$8, leaving 1000 returning 1630, and 1200 returning 1900 (30 mins at Misol-Ha, 4 hrs at Agua Azul, take swimsuit). Other minibuses from minibus terminal (nr 4 Esquinas): they leave 0930-1000 from Palenque, 2 hrs at Agua Azul, arriving back in Palenque at 1500, stopping for 15 mins at Misol-Ha, US$6.65-8 (½ price one way). Colectivos from Hidalgo y Allende, Palenque, for Agua Azul and Misol-Ha, 1000-1500, US$5; colectivos can also be organized between Misol-Ha and Agua Azul, in either direction. Several buses from Palenque daily (direction San Cristóbal de las Casas or Ocosingo), to crossroads leading to the waterfall, US$3.35, 2nd class, 1½ hrs. From the crossroads walk the 4 km downhill to the falls (or hitch a ride on a minibus for US$0.20). Back from the junction 1400-1600 with transportes Maya buses. There are buses between San Cristóbal de Las Casas and Palenque (to 2nd class bus station, Transportes Maya) which will stop there, but on a number of others you must change at Temo, over 20 km away, N of Ocosingo, which may require a fair wait.

VILLAHERMOSA TO CAMPECHE

There are two highways: inland Highway 186, via Escárcega, with two toll bridges (cost US$4.25), and the slightly longer coastal route through Ciudad del Carmen, Highway 180, on which all but one of the former ferries have been replaced by bridges; both converge at Champotón, 66 km S of Campeche. Highway 186 passes Villahermosa's modern international airport and runs fast and smooth in a sweeping curve 115 km E to the Palenque turnoff at Playas del Catazajá; beyond, off the highway, is **Emiliano Zapata** (*Pop* 13,000; *Fiesta* 26 Oct), a busy cattle centre, with Pemex station. There is a mediocre hotel here, painted blue, on a quiet plaza by the river, 200m from main road. On the main road is restaurant *La Selva*, good food.

● **Transport** From Emiliano Zapata, all ADO: to **Tenosique**, frequent, first at 0700, 0830, 0900, last at 2000, 2100, US$2, 90 mins (plus 2 2nd class companies); to **Villahermosa**, 17 departures between 0600 and 2000, US$6; to **Mérida**, 5 a day between 0800 and 2100, US$21; to **Escárcega**, 5 between 0630 and 2100, US$5.50; to **Chetumal**, 2130, US$14.

The river town of **Balancán** is a further 60 km NE and has a small archæological museum in its Casa de Cultura (**E** *Hotel Delicias*); *fiesta* 14 December. In 10 km the main highway has crossed the narrow waist of Tabasco state and entered Campeche, a popular destination for hunters and fishermen.

● **Accommodation C** *Maya Uscumacinta*, **D** *Ramos*, opp bus station, with a/c, E with fan, reasonable restaurant, friendly; *Bernat Colonial*, all basic.

ESCARCEGA

Route 186 is paved for the 140 km run to **Escárcega** (officially Francisco Escárcega). The condition of this route is good up to Escárcega, but poor around the town itself, good around Champotón (see below), and paved right up to Campeche. Escárcega is a hot, straggling town of 20,300 which relies heavily on the many buses passing through. Service stations (fill up here if going E to Chetumal), a few overpriced hotels and cafés and the ADO 1st class bus station cluster near the junction of Highways 186 and 261. The rest of town spreads 2 km E along the Chetumal highway (186) and C Justo Sierra (which parallels it a block S) to the 2nd class Autobuses del Sur terminal just E of the railway crossing. The oil boom has expanded the town's services considerably in recent years.

● **Accommodation C** *Motel Akim Pech*, on Villahermosa highway, a/c or fans and bath, reasonable rooms, restaurant in motel, another across the street, also Pemex station opp (sells unleaded *magna sin*); **D** *Berta Leticia*, C 29 No 28, with bath, fairly clean; **D** *Casa de Huéspedes Lolita* on Chetumal highway at E end of town, pleasant; **D** *María Isabel*, Justo Sierra 127, T 40045, a/c, restaurant, comfortable, back rooms noisy from highway;

D-E *Escárcega*, Justo Sierra 86, T 40186, bath, TV, parking, hot water, noisy, good restaurant, small garden, about 500m E of ADO, on the road Chetumal-Villahermosa; **E** *El Yucateco*, C 50 No 42-A, T 40065, D with a/c, central, tidy, fair value; **E** *Las Gemelas*, behind Pemex on Highway 186 W of intersection and ADO, noisy, decrepit, overpriced; **E** *San Luís*, C 28 facing the Zócalo, simple and lazily-maintained.

● **Places to eat** *La Choza*, on Chetumal highway by railway line, local atmosphere, good, inexpensive; budget prices and *típico* fare also at *Juanita*, same building as *Akim-Pech*; nearby is *Mi Ranchito*, grilled meal or chicken, popular; plenty of food in the town market (begins at C 31 on the corner of the plaza).

● **Banks & money changers** Bancomer, C 31 No 26 with limited currency exchange facilities.

● **Post & telecommunications Post Office**: on C 28a.

● **Transport** Escárcega is an important transport hub and buses run regularly from the 2nd class bus station to Palenque beginning at 0430 (US$6.60, 3 hrs); for other connections to Palenque, go to Emiliano Zapata, not all Villahermosa buses stop there, though. 1st class services on to Campeche (US$2), Mérida and Villahermosa depart from the ADO terminal; buses plying beautifully-surfaced Highway 186 E to Chetumal are ADO, 4 a day, and Autobuses del Sur, 3 at night, US$5 and US$4.60 respectively, 4 hrs. Buses to Xpujil leave from central terminal, 3 hrs, US$4.

Off this road are many interesting ruins (see page 482), such as **Balamku** (105 km, discovered only in 1990), **Chicanná** (145 km), **Becán** (watch for very small sign) and **Xpujil** (153 km); little excavation has yet been undertaken in this region, but these ruins do give a good idea of how such sites look when stumbled upon by archæologists.

CHAMPOTON

Highway 261 runs 86 km due N from Escárcega through dense forest to the Gulf of Mexico, where it joins the coastal route at **Champotón** (*Pop* 18,000), a relaxed but run down fishing and shrimping port spread along the banks of the Río Champotón. In prehispanic times it was an important trading link between Guatemala and Central Mexico; Toltec and Maya mingled here, followed by the Spaniards (where blood was shed when Francisco Hernández de Córboba was fatally wounded in a skirmish with the inhabitants in 1517). On the S side of town can be seen the remnants of a 1719 fort built as a defence against the pirates who frequently raided this coast. The Feast of the Immaculate Conception (8 Dec) is celebrated with a joyous festival lasting several days.

● **Accommodation & services** C *Snook Inn,* C 30 No 1, T 80088, a/c, fan, pool, owner speaks English, favourite with fishing enthusiasts and bird hunters; for larger game (plentiful in the surrounding jungle) there are three primitive but comfortable jungle camps to the S; rec guide is José Sansores (*Hotel Castelmar*, Campeche); *Gemenis*, C 30 No 10; *D'Venicia*, C 38; *Imperial*, C 28 No 38, all **E**, simple, with fans, river views, regular food. A few unpretentious restaurants, usually seafood menus but venison (*venedo*) and *pato* plentiful in season: *La Palapa*,on the seafront, covered terrace, speciality fish stuffed with shrimp, "very fresh and tasty, splendid place". Gasoline available.

● **Banks & money changers** Try the Banco del Atlántico for currency transactions, open Mon-Fri 0900-1230.

VILLAHERMOSA TO CAMPECHE VIA THE COAST

Although Highway 180 is narrow, crumbling into the sea in places and usually ignored by tourists intent on visiting Palenque, this journey is a beautiful one and more interesting than the fast toll road inland to Campeche. The road threads its way from Villahermosa 78 km N through marshland and rich cacao, banana and coconut plantations, passing turnoffs to several tiny coastal villages with palm-lined but otherwise mediocre beaches, to the river port of **Frontera** (*Pop* 28,650), from where Graham Greene began the research journey in 1938 for his novel *The Power and the Glory*. The Fería Guadalupana is held from 3-13 Dec, agricultural show, bullfights, *charreadas*, regional dances.

● **Accommodation & places to eat** D *Chichén Itzá*, on Plaza, not very clean, fan, shower, hot water; **E** *San Agustín*, very basic, fan, no mosquito net; *Restaurant Conquistador*, beside church, very good.

The road briefly touches the coast at the Tabasco/Campeche state border before running E beside a series of lakes (superb bird watching) to the fishing village of **Zacatal** (93 km), at the entrance to the tarpon-filled **Laguna de Términos** (named for the first Spanish expedition which thought it had reached the end of the 'island' of Yucatán). Just before Zacatal is the lighthouse of **Xicalango**, an important precolumbian trading centre near where Cortés landed in 1519 on his way to Veracruz and was given 20 female slaves, including 'La Malinche', the Indian princess baptized as Doña Marina who, as the Spaniards' interpreter, was to play an important rôle in the Conquest. A bridge crosses the lake's mouth to Ciudad del Carmen.

CIUDAD DEL CARMEN

(*Pop* 151,400; *Phone code* 938) is the hot, bursting-at-the-seams principal oil port of the region and is being developed into one of the biggest and most modern on the Gulf. Its important shrimping and prawning fleets are also expanding (good photo possibilities along the trawler-filled docks E of the ferry landing) and much ship building is undertaken. The site was originally established in 1588 by a pirate named McGregor as a lair from which to raid Spanish shipping; it was infamous until the pirates were wiped out by Alfonso Felipe de Andrade in 1717, who then named the town after its patroness, the Virgen del Carmen.

Places of interest

Her attractive, cream-coloured **Cathedral** (notable for its stained glass), along with the Palacio Municipal and Library, stands on the **Plaza Principal**, or Plaza Zaragoza, a lush square conveniently sited on the waterfront at the ferry terminal, with wooden gazebo (free band concerts Thur and Sun evenings), Spanish lanterns, brick walkways and elegant wrought-iron fencing. There is a modest **Archæological Museum** in the Liceo Carmelita showing locally-excavated items (US$0.25 admission). Carmen is inescapably associated with the ugliness accompanying an oil boom and is little-frequented by tourists; nevertheless, it is a good place for those curious to see the development of the Mexican oil and fishing industries: there is a wide range of facilities available and it is a convenient place to break the journey to Campeche. Delays and long queues at the ferry (which in extreme weather can be seriously disrupted) may sometimes force a stopover. Calle 20 is the seaside *malecón*, even-numbered streets run parallel to the E, with 20a, b, c, etc, being separate streets.

Local festivals

The town's patroness is honoured with a cheerful fiesta each 15-30 June, bullfights, cultural events, fireworks, etc.

Local information
● **Accommodation**

A2 *EuroHotel*, C 22a No 208, T 31030, large and modern, 2 restaurants, pool, a/c, disco, built to accommodate the flow of Pemex traffic.

B *Hotel del Parque*, C 33 No 1; **B** *Isla del Carmen*, C 20 No 9, T 22350, a/c, restaurant, bar, parking; **B** *Lli-Re*, C 32a y 29a, T 20588, commercial hotel with large sparsely-furnished a/c rooms, TV, servibars, oddly old-fashioned but comfortable, restaurant with good but not cheap fish dishes.

C *Aquario*, C 51 No 60, T 22547, a/c, comfortable; **C** *Lino's*, C 31 No 132, T 20738, a/c, pool, restaurant, also has 10 RV spaces with electricity hook-ups.

D *Zacarías*, C 24a No 58, T 20121, modern, some cheaper rooms with fans, brighter a/c rooms are better value, rec.

E *Internacional*, C 20a No 21, T 21344, uninspiring outside but clean and friendly, 1 block from Plaza, some a/c; **E** *Roma*, on C 22, fan, cold showers, good value; other budget class places nearby are *Casa de Huéspedes Carmen*, C 20 No 142, *Villa del Mar*, C 20 y 33.

● **Places to eat**

The better hotels have good restaurants (the shrimp and prawns are especially tasty); others rec are *Pepe's*, C 27a No 15, a/c, attractive seafood dishes; *Vía Veneto*, in the *EuroHotel*, reasonable prices, good breakfasts; *El Kiosco*, in *Hotel del Parque* with view of Zócalo, modest prices, eggs, chicken, seafood and Mexican dishes, but not clean, poor service; *La Mesita*, outdoor stand across from ferry landing, well-prepared shrimp, seafood cocktails, extremely popular all day; *La Fuente*, C 20a, 24-hr snack bar with view of the Laguna; for 'best coffee in town' try *Café Vadillo* or other tiny cafés along pedestrian walkway (C 33a) nr the Zócalo; inexpensive snacks also in the thriving Central Market (C 20a y 37a, not far NW of Zócalo), many bakeries and supermarkets throughout the city, eg *Conasuper*, C 20a y 37a.

● **Banks & money changers**
Banco del Atlántico or Banamex, both at C 24a y 31a.

● **Post & telecommunications**
Post Office: at C 29 y 20b, 1 block from the Plaza.

● **Tourist offices**
On C 20c nr C 23 has little to promote in this non-tourist town, emphasis is on fishing excursions, basic street map available. **Fishing excursions** can be arranged through the *Club de Pesca Nelo Manjárrez* (T 20073) at C 40a and C 61a, coastal lagoons are rich in tarpon *(sábalo)* and bonefish.

● **Transport**
Local Car rentals (not cheap): Auto-Rentas del Carmen, C 33 No 121 (T 22376); Fast (T 22306), and Auto Panamericana, C 22 (T 22326).

Air Carmen's efficient airport (Av Aviación, only 5 km E of the Plaza) has also benefited from the oil traffic, with Mexicana (C 22 y 37, T 21171) flights daily to Mexico City and Aero Caribe 4 days a week to Villahermosa, Veracruz and Mérida (more frequent at certain times of year); Aero-Campeche and Aviatur service many regional towns and oilfields.

Buses New ADO bus terminal some distance from centre. Take bus or colectivo marked 'Renovación' or 'ADO', they leave from around the Zócalo. At least 8 ADO services daily to Campeche (3 hrs) and Mérida (9 hrs, US$14.80), inc three departures between 2100 and 2200 (worth considering if stuck for accommodation); hourly bus to Villahermosa via the coast, 3 hrs. A connection can be made to **Palenque** at 2330 or 0400, a slow but worthwhile trip. Buses also travel via **Escárcega**, where connections can be made for Chetumal and Belize.

11 km beyond Carmen is the *Rancho El Fénix*, with an interesting iguana (*lagarto*) hatchery. Highway 180 runs NE along the 38-km length of the Isla del Carmen and is now linked to the 'mainland' at Puerto Real by the 3.25 km long Puente de la Unidad (US$1.85 toll), built in 1982 and claimed to be the longest bridge in Mexico. Isla del Carmen is little more than a narrow sandspit, heavily forested (coconuts) and with Playa Nte occupying most of the Gulf side; Playa Bahamita extends it to the bridge at Puerto Real. Both have gritty sand mixed with shells and generally good swimming (although oil processing in the region can periodically affect the water), few facilities but a great place for beachcombing; camping is poor because of the shells and biting chiggers. The bridge crosses to the **Isla Aguada** (**C** *Hotel Tarpon Tropical*, **D** *Motel La Cabaña* and Trailer Park at former boat-landing just after the toll bridge, full hook-up, hot showers, laundry facilities, quiet, US$12 for vehicle and 2 people), actually a narrow peninsula with more deserted shell littered beaches on the Gulf shore, and undulates its way NE through tiny fishing villages towards Campeche; there are many offshore oil rigs to be seen. At Sabancuy (85 km from Carmen) a paved road (57 km) crosses to the Villahermosa-Escárcega highway. 63 bumpy km later, Highway 180 reaches Champotón (see above).

Continuing N, Highways 180 and 261 are combined for 17 km until the latter darts off E on its way to Edzná and Hopelchen (bypassing Campeche, should this be desired). A 66-km toll *autopista*, paralleling Highway 180, just inland from the southern outskirts of Champotón to Campeche, is much quicker than the old highway. Champotón and Seybaplaya are bypassed. We describe the places reached from Highway 180, narrow and slow (beware many speed bumps), which runs on a little further to the resort of **Sihoplaya**. Here is the widely-known **C** *Hotel Siho Playa* (T 62989), a former sugar hacienda with a beautiful setting and beach facilities, pool, disco/bar, breezy rooms, etc, but, despite remodelling in the past, it has seen better days; camping possible, US$5; restaurant is overpriced and poor but nowhere else to eat nearby; very popular, nonetheless, with *campechano* families and good views from the iguana-covered jetty of pelicano diving for their supper. Regular buses from Campeche US$1. A short distance further N is the larger resort of **Seybaplaya**, an attractive place where fishermen mend nets and pelicans dry their wings on posts along the beach. On the Highway is the open-air *Restaurant Veracruz*, serving delicious red snapper (fresh fish at the seafront Public Market is also good value), but in general there is little to explore; only the *Balneario Payucán* at the N end of the bay makes a special trip worthwhile; this is probably the closest decent beach to Campeche (33 km) although a little isolated, since the water and sand get filthier as one nears the state capital.

CAMPECHE

(*Pop* 230,000; *State pop 1995* 642,082; *Phone code* 981) Highway 180 enters the city as the divided Av Resurgimiento, which passes either side of the huge **Monumento al Resurgimiento**, a stone torso holding aloft the torch of Democracy. The city, capital of Campeche state, is beautifully set on a small bay on the western coast of Yucatán, 252 km from Mérida and 444 km from Villahermosa. Originally the trading village of Ah Kim Pech, it was here that the Spaniards, under Francisco Hernández de Córdoba, first landed on Mexican soil (20 March 1517) and thus made the first contact between Maya and European. The city was founded by Francisco de Montejo in 1540; export of local dyewoods, chiclé, timber and other valuable cargoes soon attracted the attention of most of the famous buccaneers, who constantly raided the port from their bases on Isla del Carmen, then known as the Isla de Tris. Combining their fleets for one momentous swoop, they fell upon Campeche on 9 February 1663, wiped out the city and slaughtered its inhabitants. 5 years later the Crown began fortifying the site, the first Spanish colonial settlement to be completely walled. Formidable bulwarks, 3m thick and 'a ship's height', and eight fortress/bastions (*baluartes*) were built in the next 36 years. All these precautions soon defeated pirate attacks and Campeche prospered until Mexican independence (only Campeche and Veracruz had the privilege of conducting international trade), after which it declined into an obscure fishing and logging town. Only with the arrival of a road from the 'mainland' in the 1950s and the oil boom of the 1970s has Campeche begun to see visitors in any numbers, attracted by its historical monuments and relaxed atmosphere (*campechano* has come to mean an easy-going, pleasant person).

Like many of the Yucatán's towns, Campeche's streets in the Old Town are numbered rather than named. Even-numbers run N/S beginning at Calle 8 (no-one knows why) near the Malecón, E to Calle 18 inside the walls; odd-numbers run E (inland) from Calle 51 in the N to Calle 65 in the S. Most of the points of interest are within this compact area. The full circuit of the walls is a long walk; buses marked 'Circuito Baluartes' provide a regular service around the perimeter. Running in from the NE is Av Gobernadores, on which are situated the bus and railway stations.

Places of interest

Of the original walls, only seven of the *baluartes* and an ancient fort (now rather dwarfed by two big white hotels on the seafront) near the cathedral remain. Some house museums: **Baluarte La Soledad** (just W of the Central Plaza), the largest

of the seaward defences, there are three rooms of Maya stelae and sculpture, first class (open Tues-Sat, 0900-1400, 1600-2000; Sun 0900-1300, 5 pesos); **Baluarte San Carlos** (near the Palacio de Gobierno) houses the city's museum, there are also interesting scale models of the 18th century defences and a collection of colonial arms and seafaring equipment, small library, a fine view from the cannon-studded roof, dungeons and a government-sponsored handicrafts market; for a few pesos, guides will conduct you through underground passageways which once provided escape routes from many of the town's houses (most have now been bricked up), open 0900-2000, free; **Baluarte San Pedro** (C 18 y 51, 5 blocks S of the Plaza) has a permanent *artesanía* exhibition open Mon-Fri, 0900-1300, 1700-2000, free; **Baluarte Santiago**, 1 block N of the Plaza, with the Xmuch Haltun Botanical Gardens: 250 species of Yucatecan plants exhibited in a courtyard of fountains, a delightful spot to relax (free, open Tues-Sat, 0900-2000; Sun 0900-1300).

The heart of Campeche is its **Plaza Principal** or Zócalo, bounded by C 8, C 10, C 55 y 57 and filled with a strange mixture of colonial past and ultramodern; an atmosphere of small-town Spain gives it a delightful ambience during the evening *paseo*. The old houses within the walls are warmly coloured but often in a bad state of repair; efforts are now being made to spruce the place up. The best way to see the Old City is to walk its narrow streets; the shady **Alameda** (bottom of C 57 opposite the Baluarte San Francisco) offers respite from the sun and contains the unusual **Puente de los Perros** (Bridge of the Dogs), a colonial bridge guarded by carved stone dogs honouring the Dominican missionaries called the 'Hounds of God' for their zealous pursuit of converts.

Representative of the city's increasing modernity are big white luxury hotels on the sea-front, and the square glass **Palacio de Gobierno** (colourful murals) and adjoining concrete **Congreso**;

although both were designed to blend in with the native architecture, conservative Campechanos dismiss them as 'The Jukebox' and 'The Flying Saucer' respectively. The futuristic Ciudad Universitaria almost rivals that of Mexico City. Other interesting sights include: the **Fuerte José El Alto**, some distance NE on C 7 beyond the railway ('San José El Alto' bus from the market), with excellent views, and adjacent refurbished church and Jesuit college (1756), now a museum and cultural centre with frequently changing exhibits, gift shop; incorporated into the church is Yucatán's first lighthouse (1864). Remnants of the **Convento de San Francisco** (1546) lie 20 mins' walk NE along the seafront, where the first Mexican Mass was celebrated and Cortés' grandson, Jerónimo, was baptized (1563) in the font, which is still in use; close by is **Pozo de la Conquista**, the spring from which Hernández de Córdoba's men filled their casks in 1517.

Churches

The somewhat dull and crumbling Franciscan **Cathedral** (1540-1705), facing the Plaza, the oldest church in the Yucatán, has an elaborately carved façade and the Santo Entierro (Holy Burial), a sculpture of Christ in a mahogany sarcophagus with silver trim. There are, however, several better 16th and 17th century churches. The most interesting are **San Francisquito** (16th century with wooden altars painted in vermilion and white), Jesús, San Juan de Dios, Guadalupe and Cristo Negro de San Román.

Museums

The **Fuerte de San Miguel**, on the Malecón 4 km SW, is the most atmospheric of the forts (complete with drawbridge and a moat said to have once contained either crocodiles or skin-burning lime ... take your pick!); it houses the **Museo Arqueológico**, with a well-documented display of precolumbian exhibits including a display of jade masks and black funeral pottery from Calakmul

and recent finds from Jaina (open Tues-Sat, 0900-2000, Sun 0900-1300, admission US$2.20, recommended).

Excursions

Lerma is virtually a small industrial suburb of Campeche, with large shipyards and fish processing plants; the afternoon return of the shrimping fleet is a colourful sight; *Fiesta de Polk Kekén* held on 6 Jan, traditional dances. Close by is **Playa Bonita**, touted as a wonderful place to go (and hordes of Yucatecanos do during the *temporada* season); the beach has lockers, showers, palapas and dressing sheds but the water is now polluted and the sand hopelessly littered. Oil storage tanks nearby do little to improve the view, but the *malecón* is useful for car parking. Rickety buses marked 'Lerma' or 'Playa Bonita' run from Campeche, crowded, US$1, 8 km. A short distance to the S is the slightly better but less accessible San Lorenzo beach, rocky and peaceful but littered with cans and bottletops nonetheless.

Local festivals

Fería de San Román, second 2 weeks of Sept; *Fiesta de San Francisco*, 4-13 Oct; good Carnival in Feb/Mar; 7 Aug is a state holiday.

Local information
● Accommodation
In general, prices are high. Beware of overcharging and, if driving, find a secure car park.

A1 *Ramada Inn*, Av Ruiz Cortines 51, T 62233, F 11618 (5-stars), on the waterfront; **A2** *Alhambra*, Av Resurgimiento 85, T 66822, F 66132, 4-star, S end of town, a/c, disco, pool, satellite TV, quiet but popular with Mexican families in summer.

B *Baluartes*, Av Ruiz Cortines, T 63911, nice, parking for campers, who can use the hotel washrooms, very good restaurant, pool.

Several on C 10 inc **C** *América-Plaza*, No 252, T 64588, hot water, friendly, no safe deposit, clean, fans but hot, safe parking, night watchman, at the back of the *Ramada Inn*; **E** *Posada Del Angel*, C 10 No 307, T 67718 (opp cathedral), a/c, attractive, some rooms without windows, clean, rec; **E** *Roma*, C 10 No 254, T 63897, run down, dirty, dark, difficult parking, not safe (often full).

D *Autel El Viajero*, López Mateos 177, over-charges, but often only one left with space in the afternoon, T 65133; **D** *Central*, on Gobernadores opp ADO bus station, misleadingly named, a/c, hot water, clean, friendly, noisy; **D** *Colonial*, C 14 No 122, T 62222, clean, good, several blocks from Zócalo; **D** *López*, C 12 No 189, T 63344, interesting art deco design, clean if a bit musty, with bath, uncomfortable beds, a/c.

E *Campeche*, C 57 No 1, across from the park at the end of C 57, T 65183, fan, cold water, washing facilities, dirty, noisy, not rec; **E** *Reforma*, C 8 No 257, T 64464, upper floor rooms best, basic, clean bathrooms, reasonable value.

F *Hospedaje Teresita*, C 53 No 31, 3 blocks NE of Plaza, quiet, welcoming, very basic rooms with fans, no hot water.

Camping: *Trailer Park Campeche*, on Agustín Melgar and C 19, 5 km S of centre, close to the Bay in uninviting suburb of Samulá (signposted), 25 spaces and tent area, full hook-ups, good amenities, cold showers, pleasant site, owners speak some English, US$3.25 pp, US$6.50 for car with 2 people, 'Samulá' bus from market (US$0.15) or a 'Lerma' bus down coast road, alight at Melgar and walk. Tourist Office often gives permission to pitch tents in their grounds, as will the Youth Hostel. There is a trailer park near the tourist office, open evenings only, until 2000, no tent or hammock facilities.

Youth hostel: Av Agustín Melgar s/n, Col Buenavista, CP 24020, T 61802/67718, in the S suburbs, nr University, Fuerte San Miguel and Trailer Park, take Samulá or ISSSTE bus from market US$0.15 (ISSSTE bus also from bus station), segregated dormitories with 4 bunk beds in each room (US$1.50 pp), lovely grounds, pool, cafeteria (breakfast 0730-0930, lunch 1400-1600, dinner 1930-2130, about US$1.50), clean and friendly, towels provided.

● **Places to eat**
La Perla, C 10 No 345, good fish, busy and popular, venison, squid, locals' haunt, sometimes erratic service, off Plaza; *Lonchería Puga*, corner of C 8 and C 53, open 0700, rec; *Café Artista*, on Zócalo, good breakfasts, good fish from 1200-1400, also popular in evening, cheap; *Del Parque*, on Zócalo, good, US$5 meal and drink; *Marganza*, C 8, upmarket, good breakfast and meals, excellent service; *Heladería Bing*, corner of C 12 y 59, good ice-cream. *Ave Fénix*, on Juárez where the street bends towards the terminal, generous breakfasts. Good food in the market, but don't drink the tap water. It is hard to find reasonably-priced food before 1800; try the restaurant at the ADO terminal, or *La Parroquia*, C 55 No 9, open 24 hrs, good local atmosphere, friendly and clean, rec. Opposite is *Los Portales*, authentic local atmosphere, try the sopa de lima. *Disco Bar Bali Hai*, on Malecón S of town, good drinks and *tapas*, moderately priced.

Campeche is widely-known for its seafood, especially large shrimps (*camarones*), black snapper (*esmedregal*) and *pan de cazón*: baby hammerhead shark sandwiched between corn tortillas with black beans. Food stands in the Market serve *típico tortas, tortillas, panuchos* and *tamales* but hygiene standards vary widely; barbecued venison is also a marketplace speciality. Fruit is cheap and in great variety; perhaps best to resist the bags of sliced mangoes and peel all fruit yourself. (The word 'cocktail' is said to have originated in Campeche, where 17th century English pirates enjoyed drinks adorned with palm fronds resembling cock's tails.)

● **Banks & money changers**
Banamex, C 10 No 15; **Bancomer**, opp the Baluarte de la Soledad; **Banco del Atlántico**, C 50 No 406; open 0900-1300 Mon-Fri; all change TCs and give good service. **American Express** (T 11010), C 59 in Edif Belmar, oficina 5, helpful for lost cheques, etc. It is difficult to withdraw cash on credit cards here.

● **Cultural centres**
Centro Manik, C 59 No 22 entre 12 y 14, T/F 62448, opened 1997 in restored house in centre, vegetarian restaurant, bookshop, handicrafts, art gallery, music lessons, conferences, concentrates on ecology, environmentalism and health, also developing ecotourism in southern Campeche.

● **Laundry**
C 55 entre 12 y 14, 5 pesos/kg.

● **Post & telecommunications**
Post Office: Av 16 de Septiembre (Malecón) y C 53 in the Edif Federal (go to the right upon entry for telegraph service); open Mon-Fri 0800-2000, Sat 0900-1300 for *Lista de Correos*, registered mail, money orders and stamps.

● **Shopping**
Excellent cheap Panama hats (*jipis*), finely and tightly woven so that they retain their shape even when crushed into your luggage; cheaper at the source in Becal (see under **From Campeche to Mérida**). Handicrafts are generally cheaper than in Mérida. The attractive new

market, from which most local buses depart, is beside Alameda Park at the S end of C 57 and is worth a visit. Plenty of bargains here, especially Mexican and Maya clothes, hats and shoes, fruit and vegetables; try ice-cream, though preferably from a shop rather than a barrow. *Super 10* supermarket behind the post office has some English magazines, excellent cheap bakery inside. There are souvenir shops along C 8a, such as *Artesanía Típica Naval* (No 259) with exotic bottled fruit like *nance* and *maranón*, or *El Coral* (No 255) with a large variety of Maya figurines; many high-quality craft items are available from the *Exposición* in the Baluarte San Pedro; *Artesanías Campechanos*, C 55 No 25, rec. Camping and general supplies, and laundrette, at *Superdíaz* supermarket in Akim-Pech shopping area at Av Miguel Alemán y Av Madero, some distance N of the Zócalo (open 0800-2100).

● **Tourist offices**
C 12, 153, T 66068/66767. Tourist information is also available at Baluarte Santa Rosa, C 14, T 67364, open 0900-1600, 1800-2000, library.

● **Useful addresses**
The **Oficina de Migración** at the Palacio Federal will extend Mexican visas. Take copies of your passport.

● **Transport**
Local Car hire: next to *Hotel Ramada Inn*, Av Ruiz Cortines 51, T 62233 **Hertz** and **Autorent** car rentals at airport (good for neighbourhood excursions).

Air Modern and efficient airport (CPE) on Porfilio, 10 km NE. AeroMéxico direct daily to Mexico City (T 65678). If on a budget, walk 100m down service road (Av Aviación) to Av Nacozari, turn right (W) and wait for 'China-Campeche' bus to Zócalo.

Trains Railway station is at Gobernadores y Av Héroes de Nacozari (3 km), plenty of 'Centro' buses; some banditry in this region, trains from Campeche not really rec. Train to Mexico City, 34 hrs. Mexico City-Campeche train leaves at 2115 daily, change trains at Córdoba, very crowded in holiday times. Train Campeche-**Palenque**, 2nd class only, at 2140, US$3.50, 7 hrs (coming from Mérida, and continuing to Córdoba for Mexico City). To Mérida at 0545 (3½ hrs).

Buses ADO bus terminal at Gobernadores 289, esq Chile, on way to train station ('Gobernadores' or 'Centro' buses to the Plaza Principal, taxis about US$2, or 30 mins' walk). First class buses almost hourly to Mérida, 3 hrs, US$4.50.

First class buses go by the Via Corta, which does *not* pass through Uxmal, Kabah, etc. Check bus times. Campeche-Uxmal, US$4.50, 2nd class, 3 hrs, 0600 and 1200. To **Escárcega**, hourly from 0600 to 1700, 2 hrs, US$2. Buses along inland road to **Villahermosa**; take posted times with a pinch of salt, 2nd class, 5 a day, US$14.25, 1st class US$16.50, 6½ hrs, 2300 bus comes from Mérida but empties during the night. Bus via Emiliano Zapata (US$7.75, 2 hrs before Villahermosa) to **Palenque**, change at Emiliano Zapata, or direct, 1 daily, 2nd class (Transportes del Sur), US$10.65, 2 with ADO, US$10, 5 hrs, see page 415. ADO bus to **Mexico City**, US$56.

MAYA SITES IN CAMPECHE STATE

A number of city remains (mostly in the unfussy Chenes architectural style) are scattered throughout the rainforest and scrub to the E of Campeche; little excavation work has been done and most receive few visitors. Getting to them by the occasional bus service is possible in many cases, but return trips can be tricky. The alternatives are one of the tours run by some luxury hotels and travel agencies in Campeche (see below) or renting a vehicle (preferably with high clearance) in Campeche or Mérida. Whichever way one travels, carrying a canteen of drinking water is strongly advised.

EDZNA

The closest site to the state capital is **Edzná** ('House of Grimaces'), reached by the highway E to Cayal, then right turn onto Highway 261 (the road to Uxmal, see page 429), a total distance of 61 km. A paved short cut SE through China and Poxyaxum (good road) cuts off 11 km; follow Av Nacozari out along the railway track. Gracefully situated in a lovely, tranquil valley with thick vegetation on either side, Edzná was a huge ceremonial centre, occupied from about 600 BC to AD 200, built in the simple Chenes style mixed with Puuc, Classical and other influences. Centrepiece is the magnificent, 30m-tall, 60 sq metres **Temple of the Five Storeys**, a stepped pyramid consisting of four levels of living quarters for the priests and a shrine and altar at the top; 65 steep stairs ascend it from the Central Plaza. Opposite is the recently-restored **Paal U'na**, Temple of the Moon. Excavations are being carried out on the scores of lesser temples by Guatemalan refugees under the direction of Mexican archaeologists, but most of Edzná's original sprawl remains hidden away under thick vegetation; imagination is still needed to picture the extensive network of irrigation canals and holding basins built by the Maya along the below-sea-level valley. Some of the site's stelae remain in position (two large stone faces with grotesquely squinting eyes are covered by a thatched shelter); others can be seen in various Campeche museums. There is also a good example of a *sacbe* (white road). Edzná is well worth a visit especially in July (date varies) when a Maya ceremony to Chac is held, either to encourage or to celebrate the arrival of the rains.

• **Admission** Edzná is open Tues-Sun 0800-1700, US$2; small *comedor* at the entrance. Local guides available. There is a tourist bus which leaves from the town wall at 0900, US$10 pp. At weekends take a bus towards Pich from Campeche market place at 0700, 1000 and 1030 (1 hr trip) but may leave hours late, return buses pass the site (5 mins' walk from the Highway) at 0930, 1230 and 1300. In the week, the Pich bus leaves Campeche at 1400, which is only of any use if you are prepared to sleep rough as there is nowhere to stay in the vicinity; hitching back is difficult, but you may get a ride to El Cayal on the road to Uxmal. *Viajes Programados*, C 59, Edif Belmar, in Campeche offers daily 2-hr tours at 1000 (US$15 pp); tours from the *Baluartes Hotel* cost US$10 pp; *Picazh Servicios Turísticos*, C 16 No 348 entre 357 y 359, T 64426, run transport to ruins, US$8 return, or US$14 tour with guide; the Tourist Office can also recommend reliable guides for regional tours, eg Sr Antonio Romero. Maestro Zavala (from Puerto de Tierra) offers personal and friendly service for US$12.25.

HOCHOB

Of the remoter and even less-visited sites beyond Edzná, Hochob and Dzibilnocac are the best choices for the non-specialist. **Hochob** is reached by turning right at

Hopelchén on Highway 261, 85 km E of Campeche. This quiet town has an impressive fortified 16th century church but only one hotel, **D** *Los Arcos*; a traditional honey and corn festival is held on 13-17 April, another *fiesta* takes place each 3 May on the Día de la Santa Cruz. From here a narrow paved road leads 41 km S to the village of **Dzibalchén**; no hotels but hammock hooks and toilet facilities upon request at the Palacio Municipal, there are some small eating places around the Zócalo. Don Willem Chan will guide tourists to Hochob (he also rents bikes for US$3.50 per day), helpful, speaks English. Directions can be obtained from the church here (run by Americans); essentially you need to travel 18 km SW on a good dirt road (no public transport, hopeless quagmire in the rainy season) to the village of Chenko, where locals will show the way (4 km through the jungle). Remember to bear left when the road forks; it ends at a small *palapa*, from which the ruins are a kilometre's walk up a hill with magnificent view over the surrounding forest. Hochob covered a large area but, as at Edzná, only the hilltop ceremonial centre (the usual Plaza surrounded by elaborately decorated temple buildings) has been properly excavated; although many of these are mounds of rubble, the site is perfect for contemplating deserted yet accessible Maya ruins in solitude and silence. The one-room temple to the right (N) of the plaza is the most famous structure: deep-relief patterns of stylized snakes moulded in stucco across its façade were designed to resemble a mask of the ferocious rain god Chac, a door serving as the mouth (some concentration is need to see this due to erosion of the carvings; a fine reconstruction of the building is on display at the Museo de Antropología in Mexico City).

• **Admission** Open daily 0800-1700, US$4.35. Early-morning 2nd class buses serve Dzibalchén but, as always, returning to Campeche later in the day is often a matter of luck.

DZIBILNOCAC

20 km NE of Dzibalchén at Iturbide, this site is one of the largest in Chenes territory. Only three temples have been excavated here (many pyramidal mounds in the forest and roadside *milpas*); the first two are in a bad state of preservation, but the third is worth the visit: a unique narrow edifice with rounded corners and remains of a stucco façade, primitive reliefs and another grim mask of Chac on the top level. Much of the stonework from the extensive site is used by local farmers for huts and fences, keep an eye out in the vegetation for thorns and snakes. Other sites in the region would require 4WD transport and be likely to appeal only to professional archaeologists.

● **Admission** Open daily 0800-1700, US$4.35. A bus leaves Campeche at 0800, 3 hrs, return 1245, 1345 and 1600, US$3.35. If driving your own vehicle, well-marked 'km' signs parallel the rocky road to Iturbide (no accommodation); bear right around the tiny Zócalo and its attendant yellow church and continue on (better to walk in the wet season) for 50m, where the right branch of a fork leads to the ruins.

JAINA AND PIEDRA

Two small limestone islands lie just off the coast 40 km and 55 km N of Campeche. Discovered by Morley in 1943, excavations here have revealed the most extensive Maya burial grounds ever found, over 1000 interments dating back to AD 652. The bodies of religious and political leaders were carried long distances from all over the Yucatán and Guatemala to be buried beneath the extremely steep **Pyramids of Zacpol** and **Sayasol** on Jaina. The corpses were interred in jars in crouching positions, clutching statues in their folded arms, some with jade stones in their mouths; food, weapons, tools and jewellery accompanied the owner into the after-life. Terracotta burial offerings (including figurines with movable arms and legs) have provided a revealing picture of Maya customs, dress and living habits; many of

these are now on display in Campeche or in the museum at Hecelchakán (see below). Although a vehicular track from Hecelchakán on Highway 180 leads W to the beach opposite Jaina, the islands are Federal property and are guarded; consequently, written official permission is needed to visit. Some tour operators in Campeche are allowed to run boat tours if there are enough people (about US$10 pp, but bargain), 3 hrs each way. This is practically the only way for a non-professional foreigner to make the excursion. The Tourist Office can provide details.

CAMPECHE TO MERIDA

There are two **routes**: the so-called 'Camino Real', Vía Corta or Short Route (173 km via the shortcut along the railway line to Tenabó), using Highway 180 through Calkiní, Becal and Umán (taken by all first class and *directo* buses), and the 'Ruta Maya' or Long Route (254 km), Highway 261 through Hopelchén and Muná, which gives access to many of the Peninsula's best-known archaeological sites, especially Uxmal.

On the direct route, State Highway 24 provides a convenient link from Campeche to Highway 180 at **Tenabó** (36 km against 58 km), from where the well-paved road runs on through rising ground and sleepy villages, each with its traditional *Zócalo*, solid church and stone houses often made from the materials of nearby Maya ruins, to **Hecelchakán** (18 km, large service station on the bypass), with a 1620 Franciscan church and the rustic Museo Arqueológico del Camino Real on the Zócalo. Although dusty, the museum's 5 rooms give an informative overview of Mayan cultural development with the help of maps, stelae, a diorama and many Jaina burial artefacts (open Tues-Sat 0900-1400, US$1.85).

The highway bypasses **Calkiní** (**E** *Posada del Viajero*, not rec, in a state of decay; service station) and after 33 km arrives at **Becal** (*Pop* 4,000), the centre for weaving Panama hats, here called *jipis* (pronounced 'hippies') and ubiquitous throughout the Yucatán. Many of the town's families have workshops in cool, moist backyard underground caves, necessary for keeping moist and pliable the shredded leaves of the *jipijapa* palm of which the hats are made; most vendors are happy to give the visitor a tour of their workshop, but are quite zealous in their sales pitches. Prices are only marginally higher for *jipis* and other locally-woven items (cigarette cases, shoes, belts, etc) in the *Centro Artesanal, Artesanías de Becaleña* (C 30a No 210a), or the shops near the Plaza, where the hat is honoured by a hefty sculpture of three concrete sombreros! More celebrations of homage take place each 20 May during the *Feria del Jipi*.

Just beyond Becal, the Highway passes under a 19th century stone arch which is supposed to mark the Campeche/Yucatán border (although nobody seems totally sure of where the line is) and runs 26 km to **Maxcanu**. Here the road to Muná and Ticul branches right (see page 441); a short way down it (right) is the recently-restored Maya site of **Oxkintoc**. The Pyramid of the Labyrinth can be entered (take a torch) and there are other ruins, some with figures; entrance US$3, ask for a guide at Calcehtoc which is 4 km from the ruins and from the Grutas de Oxkintoc (no bus service). These, however, cannot compare with the caves at Loltún or Balancanché. Highway 180 continues N towards Mérida through a region of numerous *cenotes*, soon passing a turnoff to the turn-of-the-century Moorish-style *henequén* (sisal) hacienda at **San Bernardo**, one of a number in the state which can be visited (another to the E at Yaxcopoil on Highway 261); an interesting colonial museum chronicling the old Yucatán Peninsula tramway system is located in its lush and spacious grounds. Running beside the railway, the highway continues 47 km to its junction with the inland route at **Umán**, an *henequén* processing town of 7000 with another large 17th century

church and convent dedicated to St Francis of Assisi; there are many *cenotes* in the flat surrounding limestone plain. Highway 180/261 is a divided 4-lane motorway for the final 18 km stretch into Mérida. A new ring road around the city is now open.

MERIDA

(*Pop* 525,000; *State pop 1995* 1,555,733; *Phone code* 99) Capital of Yucatán state, **Mérida** was founded in 1542 on the site of the Mayan city of Tihoo.

In Paseo de Montejo, together with many shops and restaurants, there are a few grand late 19th century houses. Calle 65 is the main shopping street and the Plaza Mayor is between C 61/63 y 60/62. Odd-number streets run E and W, even numbers N and S. In colonial times, painted or sculpted men or animals placed at intersections were used as symbols for the street: some still exist in the small towns of Yucatán. All streets are one-way. The houses are mostly of Spanish-Moorish type, painted in soft pastel tones, thick walls, flat roofs, massive doors, grilled windows, flowery patios. The water supply, once notorious, is improved. Redevelopment is rapid; many of the old houses are being pulled down. The city suffers from pollution caused by heavy traffic, narrow streets and climatic conditions favouring smog-formation. Mérida is a safe city in general (though be careful on C 58 and near the market), but the large influx of visitors in recent years is creating 'mostly quiet hostility' towards them. Begging and much molestation from car-washers, shoe-shiners, souvenir-peddlers and others wishing to 'help you find the right hammock, just to practise English'.

Addresses Check that the address you need is in the centre; there are many *fraccionamientos* (estates) around the town.

Places of interest

Its centre is the Plaza Mayor, green and shady; its arcades have more than a touch of the Moorish style. It is surrounded by the severe twin-towered 16th century **Cathedral**, the Palacio Municipal, the Palacio de Gobierno, and the **Casa Montejo**, originally built in 1549 by the *conquistador* of the region, Francisco de Montejo, rebuilt around 1850 and now a branch of the Banco Nacional de México (Banamex). The **Casa de los Gobernadores**, or Palacio Cantón, on Paseo de Montejo at C 41, is

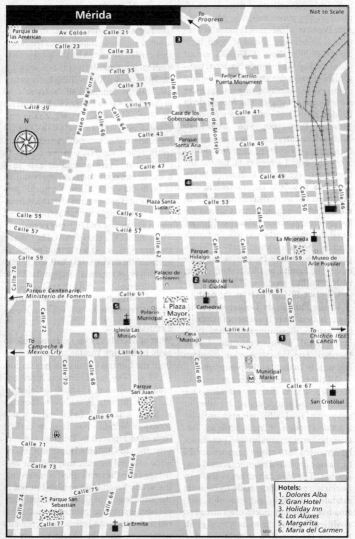

Hotels:
1. *Dolores Alba*
2. *Gran Hotel*
3. *Holiday Inn*
4. *Los Aluxes*
5. *Margarita*
6. *María del Carmen*

an impressive building in the turn-of-the-century French style of the Porfirio Díaz era. It now houses the **Museo de Antropología e Historia** (very good on Maya history), closed on Mon (open 0800-1400 Sun, 0800-2000 all other days, US$4.35, photography permitted). The **Museo de Arte Popular** (Museum of Peninsular Culture, C 59, between 50 and 48, open Tues-Sat 0800-2000, Sun 0900-1400, closed Mon), run by the Instituto Nacional Indigenista (INI), a contemporary crafts museum, is well worth visiting (inexpensive gift shop, small stock). The **Museo de la Ciudad** is on C 61 entre C 58 y 60, open Tues-Sat 0800-2000, Sun 0800-1400, closed Mon, entry free. There are several 16th and 17th century churches dotted about the city: La Mejorada, behind the Museum of Peninsular Culture (C 59 between 48 and 50), Tercera Orden, San Francisco and San Cristóbal (beautiful, in the centre). Along the narrow streets ply horse-drawn cabs of a curious local design. In all the city's parks you will find *confidenciales*, S-shaped stone seats in which people can sit side by side facing each other. The **Ermita**, an 18th century chapel with beautiful grounds, is a lonely, deserted place 10-15 mins from the centre.

In the **Palacio de Gobierno**, on the Plaza Mayor, there is a series of symbolic and historical paintings, finished 1978, by a local artist, Fernando Castro Pacheco. The Palacio is open evenings and well lit to display the paintings.

All the markets, and there are several, are interesting in the early morning. One can buy traditional crafts: a basket or *sombrero* of sisal, a filigree necklace, also a good selection of Maya replicas. Tortoiseshell articles are also sold, but cannot be imported into most countries, as sea turtles are protected by international convention. The Mérida market is also particularly good for made-to-measure sandals of deerskin and tyre-soles, panama hats, and hammocks of all sizes and qualities. Some of the most typical products are the *guayabera*, a pleated and/or embroidered shirt worn universally, its equivalent for women, the *guayablusa*, and beautiful Mayan blouses and *huipiles*. In **Parque El Centenario** is a zoo; a popular place for family outings on Sun. In the Parque de las Américas is an open-air theatre giving plays and concerts, and bands play in various plazas in the evenings. Enquire at hotels about the house and garden tours run by the local society women for tourists to raise money for charity. Every Thur evening there is free local music, dancing and poetry at 2100 in the **Plaza Santa Lucía**, two blocks from the Plaza Mayor (C 55 y 60), chairs provided. Every Sun (from 0900 to 2100) all the roads in the centre are closed to motor traffic: everyone takes to the streets to stroll, chat, cycle around or ride in a horse-drawn open carriage ('the best time to be in the city'). There is a weekly programme of events organized by the Municipality (every night except Sat), including regional dancing and folk guitar concerts. The Tourist Office has details. The Casa de Cultura (C 63 y 64) has several rooms; an open-air theatre, concert hall, art gallery and display of regional handicrafts. There are monuments to Felipe Carrillo Puerto, an agrarian labour leader prominent in the 1910 revolution.

Excursions

West of Mérida (29 km) is **Hunucmá**, an oasis in the dry Yucatán, about 30 mins from the Central Camionera bus station, US$0.50. The road divides here, one branch continuing 63 km W to Celestún, the other running 24 km NW to the coast at **Sisal**, a languid, faded resort which served as Mérida's port from its earliest days until replaced by Progreso last century; the old Customs House still retains some colonial flavour, snapper and bass fishing from the small wharf is rewarding; the windy beach is acceptable but not in the same league as Celestún's. Sisal's impressive lighthouse, painted in traditional red-and-white, is a private residence and permission must be sought to visit the tower, the expansive view is worth the corkscrew climb. Frequent buses (0500-1700) from Mérida, C 50 between C 65 y 67, 2 hrs, US$1.50.

● **Accommodation & places to eat** *Sisal del Mar Hotel Resort*, luxury accommodation, T in USA 800-451-0891 or 305-341-9173. More modest are **E** *Club Felicidades*, a 5-min walk E of the pier, bathrooms not too clean; **E** *Club de Patos*, similar but a slight improvement; **E** *Club Balnearios*, with shower (cold water) and fan, prickly mattresses; **E** *Yahaira* (**F** low season), large clean rooms. *Restaurant Juanita*, reasonable.

Local festivals

Carnival during the week before Ash Wednesday (best on Sat). Floats, dancers in regional costume, music and dancing around the Plaza and children dressed in animal suits. On 6 Jan Mérida celebrates its birthday. **NB** Banks closed Mon following carnival.

Local information
● **Accommodation**
Cheaper hotels tend to be S of the main Plaza (odd streets numbered 69 and higher), nr the market and especially the bus station (C 69 y 68). More expensive hotels are on the N side of the city and nr the Paseo Montejo. Sometimes there are special deals at the more expensive hotels, offers available through counter at ADO terminal. The narrow streets in the city centre tend to amplify noise making it difficult to sleep in hotels in this part of town.

L3 *Hyatt Regency*, C 60 No 344 x Colón, T 256722, F 257003, luxury hotel with boutiques, car hire, money exchange, tennis, gym, *Peregrina* restaurant; opp and open late 1994 is a *Fiesta Americana*; **L3-A1** *Holiday Inn*, Av Colón No 489 x Montejo, T 256877, F 247755 (connected with LADA International direct dialling), all facilities, elegant but a long way from the centre.

A1 *Calinda Panamericana*, C 59, No 455 x 52, T 239111, F 248090, good, expensive, with elaborate courtyard in the Porfirian style, very spacious and airy, ordinary rooms in new building behind, good buffet breakfast, with swimming pool, 5 blocks from centre; **A1** *Casa del Balam*, C 60, No 488 x 57, T 248844, F 245011 (Mayaland Resort, in USA T 305-344-6547/800-451-8891), a/c, close to centre, noisy at front, restaurant, bar, pool, neocolonial style, facilities

rather below 5-star; **A1-A2** *Best Western María del Carmen*, C 63, No 550 x 68, T 239133, F 239290, pool, a/c, good value; **A2** *Castellano*, C 57, No 513 x 62, T 230100, modern, clean but a bit run-down, friendly, pool; **A2** *El Conquistador*, Paseo del Montejo 458 x 35, T 262155, modern, specializing in package tours, unhelpful, poor value for independent travellers, good buffet breakfast; **A2** *Los Aluxes*, C 60 No 444, T 242199 x 49, delightful, pool, restaurants, very convenient, first class, two large new wings away from traffic noise; **A3-C** *Del Gobernador*, C 59, No 533 x 66, T 237133, a/c, bar, restaurant, good pool, excellent value, highly rec; and others in our A range and above.

B *Gran Hotel*, Parque Hidalgo, C 60 No 496, T 247730, F 247622, does not accept Amex card, with a/c, TV, hot water, phone, clean, helpful, owner speaks English, turn-of-the-century atmosphere (inaugurated 1901, renovated 1993 not to everyone's taste), Fidel Castro has stayed here frequently, as have other politicians, film and stage stars, good restaurant attached, free parking nearby on C 61 between 56 and 54 (opp Banco BCI I, ask front desk to stamp the parking receipt); **B** *Maya Yucatán*, C 58 No 483 x 57, between C 55 y 57, T 235395, F 234642, with bath, a/c, clean, swimming pool, TV, good restaurant; **B** *Reforma*, C 59, No 508 x 62, T 247922, swimming pool, refurbished, nice.

C *Caribe*, Parque Hidalgo, C 59 No 500, T 249022, F 248733, tiny pool, a/c, cheaper with fan, modern, elegant, tasteful patio; **C** *Colón*, C 62, No 483, T 234355, rooms old and shabby, pool, dirty, not rec; **C** *Del Parque*, C 60 No 495 x 59, T 17840, with bath and a/c, clean, friendly, rec; **C** *México*, C 60, No 525 x 67, T 219255, good restaurant attractive; **C** *Peninsular*, C 58, No 519 x 65 y 67, T 236996, 1 block from post office and market, small pool, a/c, clean, comfortable, convenient, friendly; **C** *Posada Toledo*, C 58, No 487 x 57, T 231690, good value, central, a/c extra, in charming old house, lots of plants, has paperback exchange; **C** *Sevilla*, C 62, No 511 x 65, T 215258, nr Zócalo, private bath, clean, quiet, fan, but rooms without proper windows.

D *América*, simple, private shower and toilet, noisy, will look after luggage, C 67, No 500, x 58 y 60, T 215133, about 10 mins from bus station and nr centre, good value, rec; **D** *Dolores Alba*, C 63 No 464 x 54, T (99) 285650, F (99) 283163, does not take credit cards, rooms with bath and fan, some with a/c (have to pay extra), quiet, friendly, safe parking in courtyard, pool, cool on 1st floor, have to pay for children under 10, good value, good breakfast for US$2.40 0700-1000, will make reservations for sister establishment at Chichén Itzá; **D** *Flamingo*, C 58 y 59, T 217740, nr Plaza, with private shower, swimming pool, noisy, so get room at the back, clean, helpful, laundry; **D** *María Teresa*, C 64 No 529 x 65 y 67, T 211039, friendly, safe, central, with bath and fan, a bit noisy, some rooms E, rec; **D** *Montejo*, C 57 No 507 x 62 y 64, T 280277, noisy a/c, fan, clean, comfortable, convenient, safe, rec; **D** *Mucuy*, C 57, No 481 x 56 y 58, T 211037, good, but 1st floor rooms very hot, with shower, use of fridge, washing facilities, efficient, nice gardens, highly rec (although owner can be irritable, his wife is nice), but long way from bus station; **D** *Posada del Angel*, C 67, No 535, x 66 y 68, T 232754, clean, with shower and fan; **D** *Príncipe Maya Airport Inn*, T 214050, some rooms noisy from nightclub, convenient for airport; **D** *San Jorge*, across from ADO bus terminal, T 219054, with fan and bath, stores luggage, clean, but take interior room as the street is noisy; **D** *Hospedaje San Juan*, 1 block N of arch by Iglesia San Juan, clean rooms with fan and bath; **D** *Santa Lucía*, C 55 No 508, almost opp Plaza Santa Lucía, T 282662, parking, small pool, TV, a/c, very clean, very good value, rec; **D-E** *Pantera Negra*, C 67 No 547B x 68 y 70, T 240251, inc lavish breakfast, beautiful old Mexican house, with cool quiet patio, well-stocked bookshelves, clean, very friendly English owner, rec; **D-E** *Trinidad Galería*, C 60, esq 51, T 232463, F 232419, excellent value, pool, hot water, fan, nice atmosphere and arty décor, a bit run down, laundry service, mixed reports; same ownership.

E *Alamo*, T 218058, double rooms much better than singles, with bath, clean, next to bus station (noisy), on C 68, rec, storage; **E** *Casa Becil*, C 67 No 550-C, x 66 y 68, convenient for bus station, fan, bath, hot water, clean, safe, popular, owner speaks English, quiet, friendly, make you feel at home, rec; **E** *Casa Bowen*, restored colonial house (inside better than out), corner of C 66, No 521-B, x 65, nr ADO bus station, often full at weekends, rooms on the main street noisy, bath, hot water but irregular supply, exchanges dollars, cheap laundry service, stores luggage, clean, mosquitoes, some rooms with kitchen (but no utensils), good; **E** *Casa de Huéspedes*, C 62, No 507 x 63 y 65, shared Victorian showers and toilets, very poor water

supply but drinking water available, run down, will keep luggage for small fee, mosquitoes, so take coils or net, pleasant and quiet except at front, laundry expensive; **E** *Centenario*, with bath, friendly, clean, safe on C 84 x 59 y 59A, T 232532; **E** *Del Mayab*, C 50, No 536A x 65 y 67, T 285174, with bath, clean, friendly, tiny swimming pool and car park; **E** pp *Latino*, C 66, No 505 x 63, T 213841, with fan and shower (water supply problems), friendly and clean, parking outside; **E** pp *Lol-be* C 69 x 66 y 68, with bath, fan, friendly, excellent value; **E** *Margarita*, C 66, No 506 x 63, T 213213, with shower, clean, good, rooms a bit dark, friendly; **E** *Oviedo*, C 62, next to *Sevilla*, nr main Plaza, with bath, friendly, clean, luggage deposit, quieter rooms at the back; **E** *Rodríguez*, C 69, C 54 y 56, T 236299, huge rooms, with bath, central, clean, safe; **E** *San Luis*, C 61, No 534 x 68, T 217580, with fan and shower (and US$2.25 for noisy a/c), basic, friendly, patio pool, restaurant; **E** *Trinidad*, C 62, No 464 x 55, T 213029, old house, cheaper rooms with shared bath, hot water, clean bathrooms, tranquil, courtyard, sun roof, lovely garden, can use pool at the other hotel, lots of rules and regulations, rec.

F *Centenario II*, C 69, No 563 x 68 y 70, opp ADO bus station, fan, hot water, quite clean, friendly; **F** *San José*, W of Plaza on C 63, No 503, bath, hot water, basic, clean, friendly, one of the cheapest, popular with locals, will store luggage, good cheap meals available.

Camping: *Trailer Park Rainbow*, Km 8, on the road to Progreso, is preferable, US$5 for 1 or 2, hot showers. *Oasis Campground*, 3 km from Mérida on Highway 180 to Cancún, F 432160, with hook-ups, hot showers, laundry, rundown, US manager, US$7 for car and 2 people.

● **Places to eat**

On main plaza: *Louvre* (NW corner), good, cheap, quick friendly service; *Lido* (C 62 y 61), good value meals and breakfast; *Pizza Bella*, good meeting spot, pizzas US$4-7, excellent cappuchino; *La Choza*, Av Reforma y C 23 (nr Plaza de Toros), bands play there daily except Mon, from 1300-2100. *Los Almendros*, C 50A, No 493 x 59, in high-vaulted, whitewashed thatched barn, for Yucatán specialities, first rate, expensive, mind the peppers, especially the green sauce and avoid both the leathery poc chuc and the watery ice-cream, sometimes live music played, popular! *Pórtico del Peregrino*, C 57, x 60 y 62, dining indoors or in an attractive leafy courtyard, excellent food but not cheap;

next door is *Pop*, a/c, excellent snacks, popular with foreigners, very charming; *Patio de las Fajitas*, C 60 No 482 x 53, 7 blocks from Zócalo, not cheap but pleasant open air setting; meat served on a hot griddle at the table; also in the same building is *La Casona*, Italian dishes, quite smart. The *Patio Español*, inside the *Gran Hotel*, well cooked and abundant food, local and Spanish specialities, breakfasts, moderate prices; *La Bella Epoca* in *Hotel Parque*, pricey but excellent with vegetarian selections and nice atmosphere on 1st floor; another good hotel restaurant for value and cooking is *El Rincón* in *Hotel Caribe*. *La Prosperidad*, C 53 y 56, good Yucateca food, live entertainment at lunchtime; *El Escorpión*, just off plaza on C 61, good cheap local food. *Tianos*, C 59 No 498, corner of C 60 (outdoor seating), friendly, touristy, good food, pricey, sometimes live music; next door, on Parque Hidalgo, is *El Mesón*, pleasant with tables on the square. *El Faisán y El Venado*, C 59 No 617 x 80 y 82, expensive, regional food, Mayan dance show, nr zoo. *Pizzería Vita Corleone*, C 59 No 508, nr Plaza, good; the café at the *Gran Chopur* dept store serves good food, large portions, a/c; *Amano*, C 59 No 507, x 60 y 62 with open courtyard and covered patio, good food, try *chaya* drink from the leaf of the *chaya* tree, their curry, avocado pizza and home-made bread, are also very good, open 1200-2200, closed on Sun; *Mily's*, C 59 x 64 y 66, *comida corrida* for under US$3; *La Pérgola*, warmly rec (both drive-in and tables), at corner C 56A and C 43, good veal dishes, also in Colonia Alemán at C 24 No 289A. *Los Cardenales*, C 69 No 550-A x 68, close to bus station, good food at reasonable prices, good value, open for breakfast, lunch and dinner; *El Ardillo* and *El Viajero*, both nr bus station, offer good cheap, local meals. Cold sliced cooked venison (venado) is to be had in the Municipal Market.

Café Restaurante Express, on C 60, at Parque Hidalgo, breakfast, traditional coffeehouse where locals meet; *Mil Tortas*, good cheap sandwiches, not very cheap, C 62 y 65 x 67; *El Trapiche*, C 62 No 491, excellent fruit salads and licuados, highly rec; *Tortacos*, C 62 y 65, good, cheap Mexican food; many other *torta* places on C 62, but check them carefully for best value and quality. *Govinda*, C 55 No 496, x 60 y 58, open until 1600, a good range of vegetarian dishes, fruit juices, at reasonable prices, pleasant atmosphere, also makes whole-meal bread and pastries to take away; *Kuki's*, C 61 x 62, opp taxi stand, very good coffee, snacks, expresso, cookies by the kilo, highly rec;

Naturalmente, C 20 No 104, corner of C 23, Colonia Chuburrá, not in centre, vegetarian, rec; banana bread and wholemeal rolls at *Pronat* health shop on C 59, No 506, corner of C 62 (but don't have breakfast there); *Jugos California*, good, expensive fruit juices, C 60, in C 65, at the main bus station and many other branches all over city. *Bing*, Paseo Montejo (56A) y C 37, 13 blocks from centre, about 30 different flavours of good ice-cream. Good *panadería* at C 65 y 60, banana bread, orange cake. Another good bakery at C 62 y 61. Try Xtabentun, the liqueur made from sweet anise and honey since ancient Mayan times.

● **Airline offices**
Mexicana office at C 58 No 500 x 61 y 246633, and Paseo Montejo 493, T 247421 (airport T 461332); **AeroMéxico**, Paseo Montejo 460, T 279000, airport T 461400; **Taesa**, T 202077; **Aviacsa**, T 269193/263253; **AeroCaribe**, Paseo Montejo 500B, T 286790, airport T 461361; **Aviateca**, T 243605.

● **Banks & money changers**
Banamex (passport necessary), at C 56 y 59 (Mon-Fri 0900-1300, 1600-1700), ATM cash machine, quick service, good rates. **Banco Atlántico**, C 61 y 62, quick, good rates. Many banks on C 65, off the Plaza. Most have ATM cash machines, open 24 hrs, giving cash on Visa or Mastercard with PIN-code. Cash advance on credit cards possible only between 1000 and 1300. *Centro Cambiario*, C 61 x C 54 y 52; *Casa de Cambio*, C 56 No 491 x 57 y 59, open 0900-1700 Mon-Sun.

● **Cultural centres**
Alliance Française, C 56 No 476, x C 55 y 57, has a busy programme of events, films (Thur 1900), a library and a cafeteria open all day.

● **Embassies & consulates**
British Vice Consul, also Belize, Major A Dutton (retd), MBE, C 58-53 No 450, T 286152, 0900-1600. Postal address Apdo 89; USA, Paseo Montejo 453 y Av Colón (T 255011); Canada, Av Colón, No 309-D-19 x 62, T 256419; Cuba, C 1-C No 277A, x 38 y 40, T 444215.

● **Entertainment**
Nightlife: most bars open 1000-2300, but a few expensive discos remain open until 0300. Two recommended spots: *El Tuche*, C 60 No 482 x 55 y 57, just N of Plaza, cabaret with live music and dance, salsa, local bands, good food at reasonable prices, very popular with locals; *Trovador Bohemia*, Parque Santa Lucía, guitar

trios (*trova*) nightly at 2100, entrance US$3. Seven good cinemas regularly show films in English, US$2, try the *Cine Plaza Internacional*, C 58, x 62 y 64 and the cinema at Parque Hidalgo, C 60.

Theatre: *Teatro Peón Contreras*, C 60 with 57. Shows start at 2100, US$4, ballet etc.

● **Hospitals & medical services**
Doctor: Dr A H Puga Navarrete (speaks English and French), C 13 No 210, x C 26 y 28, Colonia García Gineres, T 250709, open 1600-2000.

Hospital: *IDEM*, C 66, x 67 y 65, open 24 hrs, specializes in dermatology.

● **Language schools**
See under **Learning Spanish** in **Information for travellers** for AmeriSpan which has an affiliated school in Mérida.

● **Laundry**
C 59, x C 72 y 74, at least 24 hrs. *Lavandería* on C 69, No 541, 2 blocks from bus station, about US$3 a load, 3-hr service. *La Fe*, C 61 No 518, x C 62 y 64, US$3.30 for 3 kg, highly rec (shoe repair next door). Self-service hard to find.

● **Post & telecommunications**
Post Office: C 65 y 56, will accept parcels for surface mail to USA only, but don't seal parcels destined overseas: they have to be inspected. For surface mail to Europe try Belize, or mail package to USA, *poste restante*, for collection later if you are heading that way. An air mail parcel to Europe costs US$15 for 5 kg. Also

branches at airport (for quick delivery) or on C 58. DHL on Av Colón offers good service, prices comparable to Post Office prices for air mail packages over 1 kg.

Telephone: international telephones possible from central bus station, airport, the shop on the corner of C 59 y 64, or public telephones, but not from the main telephone exchange. Many phone card and credit card phone booths on squares along C 60, but many are out of order. Collect calls can be made on Sat or Sun from the *caseta* opp central bus station, but beware overcharging (max US$2). Telegrams and faxes from C 56, x 65 y 65A (same building as Post Office, entrance at the back), open 0700-1900, Sat 0900-1300. *Tel World* offer long distance fax service from offices on C 60 No 486a, x 55 y 57.

● **Shopping**
The Mercado de Artesanías has many nice things, but prices are high and the salespeople pushy. Good postcards for sale, though. There are several frequently recommended shops for hammocks (there is little agreement about their respective merits, best to compare them all and let them know you are comparing, shops employing touts do not give very good service or prices): *El Hamaquero*, C 58 No 572, x 69 y 71, popular, but beware the very hard sell; *El Campesino*, the market, Eustaquio Canul Cahum and family, will let you watch the weaving; *El Mayab*, C 58, No 553 y 71, friendly, limited choice but good deals available; and *La*

Know your hammock

Different materials are available for hammocks. Some you might find are: *sisal*, very strong, light, hard-wearing but rather scratchy and uncomfortable, identified by its distinctive smell; *cotton*, soft, flexible, comfortable, not as hard-wearing but good for 4-5 years of everyday use with care. It is not possible to weave cotton and sisal together although you may be told otherwise, so mixtures are unavailable. Cotton/silk mixtures are offered, but will probably be an artificial silk. *Nylon*, very strong, light but hot in hot weather and cold in cold weather. Never buy your first hammock from a street vendor and never bargain then accept a packaged hammock without checking the size and quality. The surest way to judge a good hammock is by weight: 1,500 grams (3.3 lbs) is a fine item, under 1 kg (2.2 lbs) is junk (advises Alan Handleman, a US expert). Also, the finer and thinner the strands of material, the more strands there will be, and the more comfortable the hammock. The best hammocks are the so-called 3-ply, but they are difficult to find. There are three sizes: single (sometimes called *doble*), matrimonial and family (buy a matrimonial at least for comfort). If judging by end-strings, 50 would be sufficient for a child, 150 would suit a medium-sized adult, 250 a couple. Prices vary considerably so shop around and bargain hard.

Poblana, C 65, x 58 y 60, will bargain, especially for sales of more than one, huge stock; also *Jorge Razu*, C 56 No 516B, x 63A y 63, very convincing salesman, changes TCs at good rates; *El Aguacate*, C 58 No 604, corner of C 73, good hammocks; *Rada*, C 60 No 527, x 65 y 67, T 241208, F 234718, good; *Santiago*, C 70 No 505, x 61 y 63, very good value. To mail a hammock abroad can be arranged through some shops, try *La Poblana*, or *El Aguacate* for help with the forms and method of parcelling and addressing. In the market prices are cheaper but quality is lower and sizes smaller. There are licensed vendors on the streets and in the main plaza; they will bargain and may show you how hammocks are made; some are very persistent. Good silver shops and several antique shops on C 60, x 51 y 53; *Bacho Arte Mexicano*, C 60 No 466, x C 53 y 55, also sells other jewellery and ornaments; *La Canasta*, No 500, good range of handicrafts, reasonable prices. Good panama hats at *El Becaliño*, C 65 No 483, esq 56A, diagonally opp Post Office. *Paty*, C 64 No 549, x C 67 y 69, stocks reputable 'Kary' brand guayaberas, also sells hammocks. C 62, between C 57 y 61, is lined with *guayabera* shops, all of a similar price and quality. Embroidered *huipil* blouses cost about US$25. Clothes shopping is good along C 65 and in the García Rejón Bazaar, C 65 y 60. Good leather sandals with soles made from old car tyres, robust and comfortable, from the market, US$10. Excellent cowboy boots for men and women, maximum size 10, can be bought around the market for US$46. *Casa de las Artesanías*, C 63, x 64 y 66, good. There is a big supermarket, *San Francisco de Assisi*, on C 67 y 52, well stocked; also *San Francisco de Assisi* at C 65, x Av5 50 y 52.

Bookshop: *Librerías Dante*, C 59, No 498 x 58 y 60.

Cameras and film: repairs on C 53/62. Mericolor, C 67 y 58, rec for service and printing; also Kodak on Parque Hidalgo. Many processors around crossing of C 59 y 60. Prices are high by international standards.

● **Tour companies & travel agents**
Travel agents: *Wagon-Lits (Cooks)*, helpful, Av Colón 501 (Plaza Colón), T 55411; *American Express*, Paseo Montejo 494, x 43 y 45, Col Centro, T 284222, F 244257; *Yucatán Trails*, C 62, No 482, is very helpful, run by Canadian, Denis Lafoy; *Viajes Colonial*, in lobby of *Hotel Colonial*, C 62 No 476, T 236444, F 283961, trips to Cuba, very helpful, rec; *Viajes T'Ho*, lobby of *Hotel Reforma*, C 59, No 508 y 62,

T 236612/247922, for tours in private cars, also for flights to Havana and to Palenque; *Ecoturismo Yucatán*, C 3 No 235, x 32-A y 34, Col Pensiones, T 252187, F 259047, Alfonso Escobedo. *Bon Voyage*, C 59, x 60 y 62, T 232258, very helpful, speak English; *Ceiba Tours*, C 60 No 459, T 244477, efficient and friendly staff.

● **Tourist offices**
C 59 between 62 and 64, also has exchange facilities. Also tourist office at the airport, which has maps, and at the bus station. Instituto Nacional de Estadística, Geografía e Informática (INEGI), C 40 x 39 y 41, for maps and information.

● **Useful addresses**
Immigration Office: C 60, No 448, entre 51 y 49, Dpto 234, 1st floor, T 214824/211714, Pasaje Camino Real, extension of stay easy and quick, open 0830-1300, Mon-Fri. Also helpful in the case of lost tourist cards.

● **Transport**
Local Car hire: car reservations should be booked well in advance wherever possible; there is a tendency to hand out cars which are in poor condition once the main stock has gone, so check locks, etc, on cheaper models before you leave town. **Avis**, C 57 No 507A x 62, T 236191; **Hertz**, C 55, No 479, x 54, T 242834; **Budget**, Prol Paseo Montejo 49, T 272708; **Panam**, *Hotel Montejo Palace*, T 234097, or C 56A No 483 x 43, T 231392; **Ximbal**, C 44, No 500, Col Jesús Carranza (owner Roger de Jesús García Pech), English spoken, VW Beetles in good condition, accepts Amex; **Easy Way** (*turismo Planeta*), C 59, No 501 x 60, T 281560, competitive prices, new cars. Most car hire agencies have an office at the airport and, as all share the same counter, negotiating usually takes place. Many agencies also on C 60 (eg **Executive**, down from *Gran Hotel*, good value, **Mexico-Rent-a-Car**, cheap, and **Veloz Rent a Car**, No 488, in lobby of *Hotel Casa del Balam*, good). VW Beetles from **Agencia de Viajes America** have been rec, US$19 a day, friendly. All agencies allow vehicles to be returned to Cancún at an extra charge. Be careful where you park in Mérida, yellow lines mean no parking. **Car service**: *Servicillos de Mérida Goodyear*, very helpful and competent, owner speaks English, serves good coffee while you wait for your vehicle. Honest car servicing or quick oil change on C 59, nr corner of Av 68. **Taxi**: we are warned that taxi drivers are particularly prone to overcharge by taking a long route, so always establish the journey and fare

in advance. There are a dozen taxi stands in the city, eg beside the Cathedral (T 212136), at C 57A y 60 (T 212133), at C 59 y 60 (T 212500), and at the airport (T 230391). Stands display fixed charges. Taxi from centre to bus terminal, US$4.50, to airport US$15. Taxis are hard to find on Sun pm. **Toll road**: there is a toll road from Kantunil, 68 km E of Mérida, to Xcan, whereafter it is a divided free way to Cancún; the toll is about US$15, which has to be paid in full however little of the road you use. The only exits from the toll road are at Chichén-Itzá and Valladolid. The toll road, Route 180D, is free of traffic, has a speed limit of 110 kph and takes under 3 hrs, boring but fast. The old road, Route 180, is free and goes through lots of villages with speed bumps (*topes*), about 5 hrs.

Air From C 67, 69 and 60 bus 79 goes to the airport, marked Aviación, US$0.20, roughly every 20 mins. Taxi US$8, voucher available from airport, you don't pay driver direct; colectivo US$2.50. There is a tourist office with a hotel list. No left luggage facilities. Mexicana and AeroMéxico both have about 10 flights between them to Mexico City daily, 1¾ hrs, both also fly Miami-Mérida daily (about 2 hrs), while Aviateca flies 3 times a week to Houston and Guatemala City. Other internal flights to Oaxaca (4 hrs 20 mins); to Cancún, 45 mins; Tuxtla Gutiérrez, 2 hrs; Villahermosa, 80 mins; Ciudad del Carmen, 65 mins; Minatitlán and Veracruz. Package tours Mérida-Havana-Mérida are available. See **Cuba** in **Information for travellers** (page 590) for details. A description of Cuba will be found elsewhere in this volume. For return to Mexico ask for details at Secretaría de Migración, C 60, No 285. Food and drinks at the airport are very expensive.

Trains Fees for red-capped porters posted at the station (C 48 y 55). The through train to Mexico City no longer runs (1996). It is possible to go via Córdoba, but there is no convenient connection, you have to stay overnight. To Córdoba at 1815 arr next day 2105, US$14. From Córdoba 0630, arr next day 0935, via Tierra Blanca, Medias Aguas, Coatzacoalcos, Teapa, Palenque, Campeche. 2nd class, one carriage, no lights, crowded after Campeche (US$19.50 to Córdoba). No clean running water, lavatory dirty. No food except for vendors at stations, stock up. There are still services to Valladolid and Tizimín, 2nd class only. Check locally for other trains. Fruit nr station, bread and cheese a couple of streets away from station, better bought before leaving centre. To Tizimín at 0600, about

6 hrs, arrives back in Mérida at 1750, US$2 one way. There are two picturesque railway lines SE of Mérida – one to **Sotuta** and the other to **Peto** (dep 1425) via Ticul and Oxcutzcab.

Buses Almost all buses except those to Progreso, or Tizimín etc (see below) leave from the 1st class terminal on C 70, No 555, between C 69 y 71 (it is called CAME). The station has lockers; it is open 24 hrs a day. About 20 mins' walk to centre, taxis are expensive (US$4.50). Most companies have computer booking. Schedules change frequently. ADO terminal has nowhere to store luggage. To **Mexico City**, US$42, 24-28 hrs, about 6 rest stops (eg ADO, 5 a day); direct Pullman bus Mexico City 2200. 14 hrs to **Coatzacoalcos**, US$31. Bus to **Veracruz**, ADO 1430 and 2100, US$43, 16 hrs; to **Chetumal**, see **Road to Belize** below. To **Ciudad del Carmen** 8 a day, 1st class, ADO, US$14.80, 9 hrs. Buses to **Tulum**, via Chichén Itzá, Valladolid, Cancún and Playa del Carmen, several daily, from main terminal, 6 hrs, US$7, 2nd class, drops you off about 1 km from the ruins. For buses to Uxmal and Chichén Itzá see under those places. Regular 2nd class buses to **Campeche** (US$3.50, 4½ hrs) also pass Uxmal, 6 a day between 0630 and 1900; 1st class fare (not via Uxmal) US$4.50. Buses to **Puerto Juárez** and **Cancún** (Autobuses de Oriente), every hour 0600 to 2400, US$8 2nd class, US$14 1st class, US$20 *plus*, 4½ hrs. Buses to and from Cancún stop at C 50, x C 65 y 67. If going to Isla Mujeres, make sure the driver knows you want Puerto Juárez, the bus does not always go there, especially at night. Buses to **Progreso** (US$1.65) with Auto Progreso, leave from the bus station on C 62, x C 65 y 67 every 15 mins from 0500-2100. To **Valladolid**, US$4.50 2nd class, US$6, 1st express (10 a day). Many buses daily to **Villahermosa**, US$22, 1st class (several from 1030 to 2330) better than 2nd class, 11 hrs, US$19.50; one direct bus daily at 1330 via Villahermosa and Campeche to **Tuxtla Gutiérrez**, arrives 0630 next day, US$35 with Autotransportes del Surente de Yucatán. Buses to **Palenque** 0800, 2200 (US$23) and 2330 (US$17) from ADO terminal, 8-9 hrs, Cristóbal Colón luxury service US$25; alternatively take Villahermosa bus to Playas de Catazajá (see page 411), US$16.50, 8½ hrs, then minibus to Palenque, or go to Emiliano Zapata, 5 buses a day US$21, and local bus (see page 415). To **Tenosique** at 2115, US$23.35. To **San Cristóbal de las Casas**, at 1800, US$21 (arr 0800-0900), and one other at 0700

(Autotransportes del Sureste de Yucatán). Buses to Celestún and Sisal from terminal on C 71, x C 64 y 66. To Celestún, 2½ hrs, US$2, from bus station on C 71, entre 64 y 66, frequent departures. To Tizimín, **Cenotillo** and **Izamal** buses leave from C 50 x C 65 y 67. Route 261, Mérida-Escárcega, paved and in very good condition.

To Guatemala by public transport from Yucatán, take a bus from Mérida to San Cristóbal and change there for Comitán, or to Tenosique for the routes to Flores. A more expensive alternative would be to take the bus from Mérida direct to Tuxtla Gutiérrez (times given above), then direct either Tuxtla-Ciudad Cuauhtémoc or to Tapachula.

    Road to Belize: paved all the way to Chetumal. Bus Mérida Chetumal US$18.50 luxury, US$16.50, 1st class, takes 7 hrs (Autotransportes del Caribe, Autotransporte Peninsular), US$13 2nd class.

CELESTUN

A small, dusty fishing resort much frequented in summer by Mexicans, standing on the spit of land separating the Río Esperanza estuary from the ocean. The long beach is relatively clean except near the town proper (litter, the morning's fishing rejects, insects, weeds that stick to feet, etc), with clear water ideal for swimming, although rising afternoon winds usually churn up silt; along the beach are many fishing boats bristling with *jimbas* (cane poles), used for catching local octopus. A plain Zócalo watched over by a simple stucco church is the centre for what little happens in town. Cafés (some with hammock space for rent) spill onto the sand, from which parents watch offspring splash in the surf. Even the unmarked post office operating Mon-Fri, 0900-1300, is a private residence the rest of the week.

    The immediate region is a National Park, created to protect the thousands of migratory waterfowl (especially flamingoes and pelicans) who inhabit the lagoons; fish, crabs and shrimp also spawn here, and manatees, toucans and crocodiles may sometimes be glimpsed in the quieter waterways. Boat trips to view the wildlife can be arranged with owners at the river bridge 1 km back along the Mérida road (US$30 for one large enough for 6-8, 1½ hrs, bargaining possible). Trips also arranged at *Restaurant Avila*, US$25 per boat, 2-3 hrs. Ensure that the boatman will cut his motor frequently so as not to scare the birds; morning is the best viewing time, important to wear a hat and use sun-screen. Hourly buses to Mérida 0530-2030, 1 hr, US$3.

● **Accommodation D** *Gutiérrez*, C 12 (the *malecón*) No 22, large beds, fans, views, clean; **D** *María del Carmen*, new, spacious and clean, rec; **E** *San Julio*, C 12 No 92, also large bright rooms and clean bathrooms.

● **Places to eat** Many beachside restaurants along C 12, but be careful of food in the cheaper ones; rec is *La Playita*, for fried fish, seafood cocktails; bigger menu and more expensive is *Restaurant Chemas*, for shrimp, oysters and octopus; *Restaurant Avila* also safe for fried fish; food stalls along C 11 beside the bus station should be approached with caution.

DZIBILCHALTUN

Halfway to Progreso turn right for the Maya ruins of **Dzibilchaltún**. This unique city, according to carbon dating, was founded as early as 1000 BC. The most important building is the Templo de las Siete Muñecas (Seven Dolls, partly restored and on display in the museum). The Cenote Xlaca contains very clear water and is 44m deep (you can swim in it, take mask and snorkel as full of interesting fish); ruined church nearby; very interesting nature trail starting half way between temple and cenote, rejoins the sacbé ('white road') half way along.

● **Admission** Open 0800-1700, US$3. Museum at entrance by ticket office where you can buy drinks. VW combis leave from Parque San Juan, corner of C 62 y 67A, every 1 or 2 hrs between 0500 and 1900, stopping at the ruins en route to Chablekal, a small village further along the same road. There are also five direct buses a day on weekdays, from Parque San Juan, marked 'Tour/Ruta Polígono'; bus returns from site entrance on the hour, passing the junction 15 mins later, taking 45 mins from junction to Mérida (US$0.60).

PROGRESO

(*Pop* 14,000) A port 39 km away from Mérida, reached by road (45 mins) or railway (no passenger services); temperatures range from 27° to 35°C. Main export: *henequén*. It claims to have the longest stone-bridge pier in the world (it is being extended to 6 km, unfortunately not open to the general public). The beach has no shade but there is always a breeze and plenty of new hotels and houses have been built. The shallow waters are good for swimming. Most of the palm trees along the front are dying from a virus (*amarrillamiento letal*). It is very popular with Mexican tourists at weekends and holiday times (July-Aug), but is quiet otherwise.

● **Accommodation On beach**: C *Progreso*, clean, friendly, traffic noise; **C** *Tropical Suites* (more with kitchen), clean, rec; **E** *San Miguel*, C 78 No 148, hot shower, fan, clean; **E** *Playa Linda*, by beach, with shower, kitchen and fan, cockroaches, quiet; **E** *Hostal*, clean, big rooms. Police permit free beach camping; huts for hammocks. Many homes, owned by Mexico City residents, available for rent, services included.

● **Places to eat** Good restaurants are *Capitán Marisco*, and *Charlie's* expensive but good; *Soberanis*, for seafood tacos; *El Cordobés*, rec, good service; *La Terraza*, variable results, expensive; *Pelícanos*, corner of C 21 y 20 on sea front, good and friendly, rec; *La Conkaleña* is a good deli (Dutch owner). Many good restaurants along the beach. Good local market with lowest food prices in Yucatán, especially seafood. You can buy fresh shrimps cheaply in the mornings on the beach. The beach front by the pier is devoted to cafés with seafood cocktails as their speciality. They also have little groups performing every weekend afternoon in summer; and the noise can be both spirited and deafening.

● **Entertainment** Two cinemas.

● **Transport Buses** Progreso-Mérida US$1.15 every 15 mins. The bus and train stations are close together, 3 blocks inland, 5 mins' walk E of the pier. **Boats** Can be hired to visit the reef of Los Alacranes where many ancient wrecks are visible in clear water.

A short bus journey (4 km) W from Progreso are **Puerto Yucalpetén** and **Chelem**, a dusty resort. Balneario Yucalpetén has a beach with lovely shells, but also a large naval base with further construction in progress. **A2** *Fiesta Inn* on the beach and *Mayaland Club* (Mayaland Resorts, T in USA 800-4510-8891/ 305-341-9173), villa complex. Yacht marina, changing cabins, beach with gardens and swimming pool. Between the Balneario and Chelem there is a nice hotel with some small bungalows, *Hotel Villanueva* (2 km from village, hot rooms), and also *Costa Maya*, on C 29 y Carretera Costera, with restaurant. In Chelem itself is a new hotel, **B** *Las Garzas*, C 17 No 742, T 244735, a/c, cable TV, bar, good restaurant, private beach club, pool, pleasant. Fish restaurants in Chelem, *Las Palmas* and *El Cocalito*, reasonable, also other small restaurants. 5 km E of Progreso is another resort, **Chicxulub**; it has a narrow beach, quiet and peaceful, on which are many boats and much seaweed. Small restaurants sell fried fish by the *ración*, or kilo, served with tortillas, mild chilli and *cebolla curtida* (pickled onion). Chicxulub is reputed to be the site of the crater made by a meteorite crash 65 million years ago which caused the extinction of the dinosaurs. Studies were in progress in 1996. The beaches on this coast are often deserted and, between Dec and Feb, 'El Norte' wind blows in every 10 days or so, making the water turbid and bringing in cold, rainy weather.

UXMAL

(Pronounced Ooshmál) is 74 km from Mérida, 177 km from Campeche, by a good paved road. If going by car, there is a new circular road round Mérida: follow the signs to Campeche, then Campeche via *ruinas*, then to Muná via Yaxcopoil (long stretch of road with no signposting). Muná-Yaxcopoil about 34 km. The Uxmal ruins are quite unlike those of Chichén Itzá (see below), and cover comparatively little ground. Uxmal, the home of the Xiu tribe, was built during the Classic Period (AD600-900). Its finest buildings seem to have been built much later. See El Adivino (the Sorcerer, a 30m high pyramid, topped by two temples with a splendid view); the Casa de las Monjas (House of Nuns), a quadrangle with 88 rooms much adorned on their façades; the Casa del Gobernador (House of the Governor), on three terraces, with well preserved fine sculptures; the Casa de las Tortugas (Turtle House) with 7 rooms; the Casa de las Palomas (House of Doves), probably the oldest; and the so called 'Cemetery Group'.

There are caves which go in for about 100m near the main entrance (rather dull). Many iguanas (harmless) wandering about, watch out for occasional scorpions and snakes, and beware of biting insects in the long grass.

● **Admission** Ruins open at 0800, close at 1700, entrance US$4 weekdays, free on Sun (students with Mexican ID, US$1.75). A new visitors' centre at the entrance to the ruins houses a museum, souvenir shops and a restaurant (no refreshments sold in the ruins), also a good selection of guide books here. A free film is shown in English at 1000 and 1200. Guided tours cost US$20. Luggage can be left at the visitors' centre There is a car park, US$1.50. There is a son et lumière display at the ruins nightly, English version (US$5) at 2100, Spanish version US$3.20) 2000 (check for times), rec (special bus for Spanish version only leaves at 1730 from terminal at C 69, between 60 and 70, returning 2100, US$4.10 return). 2nd class bus from Mérida to Campeche ('Via Ruinas') passes Uxmal, can buy tickets on bus, 2 hrs' journey, 4 hrs just enough to see ruins. From Mérida at least six 2nd-class buses a day from 0600, 1½ hrs, US$1.50, 1st class bus (Autotransportes del Sur) at 0800, returns 1430 (can be overcrowded). Advance seat booking is strongly recommended. ATS buses stop outside main entrance to site to drop off and pick up passengers, including those going on to Campeche. After the Spanish show it may be possible for those without tour bus tickets to get a ride to Muná from where the last bus to Mérida leaves at 2200. (There may be spare seats in VW colectivos for those without return tickets, US$2.50.) There is, however, a bus to Campeche

at 2315 (can be crowded). Good service with Yucatán Trails, informative but hurried (see page 437). For best photographs early morning or late afternoon arrival is essential.

Local information
● **Accommodation & places to eat**
A1 *Misión Park Uxmal*, T/F 247308, Km 78, 1-2 km from ruins on Mérida road, rooms a bit dark; **A3** *Hacienda Uxmal*, T 247142, 300-400m from ruins, is good, efficient and relaxing, (3 restaurants open 0800-2200), a/c, gardens, swimming pool (the pottery that decorates the rooms is made by Miguel Zurri, C 32, Ticul).

B *Club Méditerranée Villa Arqueológica*, T 47030, beautiful, close to ruins, good and expensive restaurant, excellent service, swimming pool, rec. For cheap accommodation, go to Ticul, 28 km away (see below). Restaurant at ruins, good but expensive; restaurant of **D** *Hacienda Uxmal*, about 4 km N of ruins, reasonable food but not cheap. **NB** There is no village at Uxmal, just the hotels.

Camping: no camping allowed, but there is a campsite, *Sacbe*, at Santa Elena, about 15 km S, between Uxmal and Kabah, on Route 261, Km 127 at S exit of village. Postal address: Portillo, Ap 5, CP 97860, Ticul, Yuc. (2nd class buses Mérida-Campeche pass by, ask to be let out at the Campo de Baseball.) 9 electric hook-ups (US$7-10 for motor home according to size), big area for tents (US$2.75 pp with tent), palapas for hammocks (US$2.65 pp), cars pay US$1, showers, toilets, clothes washing facilities also 3 bungalows with ceiling fan (**E**), breakfast, vegetarian lunch and dinner available (US$2.65 each), French and Mexican owners, a beautifully landscaped park, fastidiously clean, and impeccably managed, highly rec. *Restaurante Rancho Uxmal*, 3 km N of Uxmal, T 20277, has comfortable rooms (**D**) with hot and cold water, fan, also camping for US$5 and a pool, also good local food.

On the road from Uxmal to Mérida is **Muná** (15 km from Uxmal, 62 from Mérida); delightful square and old church, no hotel, but ask in *Restaurant Katty*, just on plaza, whose owner has two rooms with two double beds at his home, E, clean, friendly, hot showers, recommended (restaurant has good, cheap *enchiladas en mole*). Also ask in shops by bus stop in town centre for accommodation in private homes. There is a new direct road (Highway 293) from Muná to Baca-lar, Quintana Roo, just N of Chetumal.

KABAH

On either side of the main road, 37 km S of Uxmal and often included in tours of the latter, are the ruins of **Kabah**; on one side there is a fascinating Palace of Masks (or Codz-Poop), whose façade bears the image of Chac, mesmerically repeated over and over again about 250 times, each mask made up of thirty units of mosaic stone: even the central chamber is entered via a huge Chac mask whose curling snout forms the doorstep. On the other side of this wall, beneath the figure of the ruler, Kabal, are impressive carvings on the door arches which depict a man about to be killed, pleading for mercy, and of two men duelling. This side of the road is mostly reconstructed; across the road the out-standing feature is a reconstructed arch marking the start of the sacbe (sacred road), which leads all the way to Uxmal, and several stabilized, but unclimbable mounds of collapsed buildings. The style is classic Puuc. Watch out for snakes and spiders. Admission, US$1.50, free on Sun.

SAYIL, XLAPAK AND LABNA

Further S of Uxmal, about half-way be-tween Mérida and Campeche, a paved road branches off to the left to the **Sayil** ruins (5 km), **Xlapak** (about 11 km) and **Labná** (about 14 km). Both Sayil and Labná are in low, shrubby bush country. Sayil has several fine structures scattered over a wide area, including the massive Gran Palacio with a colonnaded façade; walks of several 100m are involved, but do not stray from the marked paths as many mapping trails merely lead off into the forest (admission, US$1.50). Xlapak has one, well-reconstructed palace and two partially reconstructed buildings (entry US$1.65). Labná has an astonishing arch, two palace structures and a pyramid all within a 200m radius, quiet, lovely setting among trees (admission US$1.50). These sites can each be explored in 1-2 hrs (all

are free on Sun). Refreshments and water are available, at the sites. From Labná, continue to immense galleries and caves of **Bolonchen** which are now illuminated (bus from Mérida).

Autotransportes del Sur run a 'Ruta Puuc' bus at 0800 from the main bus terminal in Mérida, which passes Uxmal at 0930 before leaving passengers for 30 mins each at Labná, Sayil, Kabah and Xlapak, returning to Uxmal at 1330 for 1½ hrs; back to Mérida at 1530; cost is US$4 (entry to ruins extra). The only disadvantage is that you get to Uxmal in the midday heat when the crowds are there. If visiting Sayil, Xlapak and Labná only, you can take a taxi from the village of Santa Elena at the turn-off (see camping *Sacbe*, above), costing US$22 for 1-3 persons. By hire-car one can continue to Oxcutzcab (see below).

TICUL

The road from Mérida (and also from Uxmal) to Chetumal is through Muná, **Ticul** (where pottery, hats and shoes are made; quite a good base for visiting Uxmal and Loltún), and Felipe Carrillo Puerto.

- **Accommodation & services** C *Motel Bougambileas*, C 23, clean but overpriced; D-E *Sierra Sosa*, shower, fan, cheapest rooms dungeon-like but clean, helpful, friendly; E *Cerro Motor Inn*, run down; E *San Miguel*, C 28 nr Plaza, fan, quiet, good value, parking, rec; next door is a good little *pizzería*; next door again is *Los Almendros* restaurant, opp Cinema Ideal.

OXCUTZCAB

16 km after Ticul is **Oxcutzcab**, a good centre for catching buses to Chetumal, Muná, Mayapán and Mérida (US$2.20). It is a friendly place with a large market on the side of the Plaza and a church with a '2-dimensional' façade on the other side of the square.

- **Accommodation** D *Tucanes*, with a/c, E with fan, not very clean, by Pemex station; E *Casa de Huéspedes*, nr bus terminal, large rooms with bath, TV, fan, friendly, rec; *Bermejo*, C 51, No 143; E *Trujeque*, just S of main plaza, a/c, TV, clean, good value, discount for stays over a week. Hammocks provided in some private houses, usually full, fluent Spanish needed to find them. (No money exchange facilities; go to Banco Atlántico in Tekax, 25 mins away by bus.)

LOLTUN

Nearby, to the S, are the caverns and precolumbian vestiges at **Loltún** (supposedly extending for 8 km). Caves are open Tues-Sun, admission at 0930, 1100, 1230 and 1400 (US$3 with obligatory guide, 1 hr 20 mins), recommended. Caretaker may admit tours on Mon, but no lighting. Take pickup (US$0.30) or truck from the market going to Cooperativa (an agricultural town). For return, flag down a passing truck. Alternatively, take a taxi, US$10 (can be visited from Labná on a tour from Mérida). The area around Ticul and Oxcutzcab is intensively farmed with citrus fruits, papayas and mangos. After Oxcutzcab on Route 184 is **Tekax** with restaurant *La Ermita* serving excellent Yucateca dishes at reasonable prices. From Tekax a paved road leads to the ruins of **Chacmultun**. From the top you have a beautiful view. There is a caretaker. All the towns between Muná and Peto, 14 km NE of Tzucacab off the Route 184, have large old churches. Beyond the Peto turn-off the scenery is scrub and swamp as far as the Belizean frontier.

MAYAPAN

Route 18 leads SE from Mérida to join Route 184 at Ticul. It passes first through **Kanasin**, to which there are frequent buses. The restaurant, *La Susana*, is known especially for local delicacies like *sopa de lima*, *salbutes* and *panuchos*. Clean, excellent service and abundant helpings at reasonable prices. There are two large pyramids in village of **Acanceh** en route. Between Acanceh and Mayapán is Tecóh, with the caverns of **Dzab-Náh**; you must take a guide as there are treacherous drops into *cenotes*. Mayapán is a large, peaceful late Maya site easily visited by bus from Mérida (every 30 mins from terminal at

C 50 y 67 behind the municipal market, 1 hr, US$1 to Telchquillo). It can also be reached from Oxcutzcab. Beware of snakes at site (entrance US$4.35).

CHICHEN ITZA

120 km by a paved road (Route 180) running SE from Mérida. The scrub forest has been cleared from over 5 sq km of ruins. The city was built by the Maya in late Classic times (AD 600-900). By the end of the 10th century, the city was more-or-less abandoned. It was reestablished in the 11th-12th centuries, but much debate surrounds by whom. Whoever the people were, they were heavily influenced by the Toltecs of Central Mexico.

The major buildings in the N half display a Toltec influence. Dominating them is El Castillo, its top decorated by the symbol of Quetzalcoatl, and the balustrade of the 91 stairs up each of the four sides is decorated at its base by the head of a plumed, open-mouthed serpent. There is also an interior ascent of 61 steep and narrow steps to a chamber lit by electricity where the red-painted jaguar which probably served as the throne of the high priest burns bright, its eyes of jade, its fangs of flint (see below for entry times). There is a ball court with grandstand and towering walls each set with a projecting ring of stone high up, at eye-level is a relief showing the decapitation of the winning captain (sacrifice was an honour, some theories, however, maintain that the losing captain was killed). El Castillo stands at the centre of the northern half of the site, and almost at right-angles to its northern face runs the sacred way to the Cenote Sagrado, the Well of Sacrifice. Into the Cenote Sagrado were thrown valuable propitiatory objects of all kinds, animals and human sacrifices. The well was first dredged by Edward H Thompson, the US Consul in Mérida, between 1904 and 1907; he accumulated a vast quantity of objects in pottery, jade, copper and gold. In 1962 the well was explored again by an expedition sponsored by the National Geographic Society and some 4,000 further artefacts were recovered, including beads, polished jade, lumps of copal resin, small bells, a statuette of rubber latex, another of wood, and a quantity of animal and human bones. Another *cenote*, the Xtoloc Well, was probably used as a water supply.

Old Chichén, where the Maya buildings of the earlier city are found, lies about 500m by path from the main clearing. The famous El Caracol, or observatory is included in this group as is the Casa de las Monjas, or Nunnery. A footpath to the right of Las Monjas takes one to the Templo de los Tres Dinteles (the Three Lintels) after 30 mins' walking. The Temple of the Warriors was closed in late 1996 because of tourists littering the place. It requires at least 1 day to see the many pyramids, temples, ballcourts and palaces, all of them adorned with astonishing sculptures, and excavation and renovation is still going on. Interesting birdlife and iguanas can be seen around the ruins.

● **Admission** Entry to Chichén Itzá, 0800-1700, US$4 (free Sun and holidays, when it is incredibly crowded, students with Mexican ID US$1.75); you may leave and re-enter as often as you like on day of issue. Check at entrance for opening times of the various buildings. Best to arrive before 1030 when the mass of tourists arrives. *Son et lumière* (US$1.85 in English, US$1.35 in Spanish) at Chichén every evening, in Spanish at 1900, and then English at 2100; nothing like as good as at Uxmal. A tourist centre has been built at the entrance to the ruins with a restaurant, free cinema (short film in English at 1200 and 1600), a small museum, books and souvenir shops (if buying slides, check the quality), with exchange facilities at the latter; luggage deposit free, open 0800-1700. Car park US$1.50. Entry to see the jaguar in the substructure of El Castillo along an inside staircase at 1100-1500, 1600-1700, closed Sun (but entry time does vary). Try to be among the first in as it is stuffy inside and queues form at busy times. Drinks and snacks available at entrance (expensive), also guidebooks, clean toilets. Also toilets on the way to old Chichén, and a drinks terrace

with film supplies. The site is hot, take a hat, sun cream, sun glasses, shoes with good grip and drinking water. The *Easy Guide* by Richard Bloomgarden is interesting though brief, available in several languages. *Panorama* is the best. José Díaz Bolio's book, although in black and white (and therefore cheaper) is good for background information, but not as a guide to take you round the ruins. Guides charge US$4-6 pp for a 1½-hr tour (they are persistent and go too fast).

There are tours daily to the **Balankanché** caves, 3 km E, just off the highway (caretaker turns lights on and off, answers questions in Spanish, every hour on the hour, 0900-1600, US$5.30, US$2 on Sun); minimum 6, maximum 20 persons. Worth the trip: there are archaeological objects, including offerings of pots and *metates* in a unique setting, except for the unavoidable, 'awful' *son et lumière* show (5 a day in Spanish; 1100, 1300 and 1500 in English; 1000 in French; it is very damp and hot, so dress accordingly). Open 0900-1700, US$3.45, free Sun (allow about 45 mins for the 300m descent), closed Sat and Sun afternoons. Bus Chichén Itzá or Pisté – Balankanché hourly at a quarter past, US$0.50, taxi US$15.

An interesting detour off the Chichén – Mérida highway is to turn in the direction of Yaxcaba at Libre Unión, after 3 km turn on to a dirt road, singposted to cenote **Xtojil**, a beautiful cenote with a Maya platform, which has well-preserved carvings and paintings.

Local information
● **Accommodation**
All are expensive for what they offer. The three hotels closest to the ruins are **A1** *Hacienda Chichén*, once owned by Edward Thompson with charming bungalows; **A1** *Mayaland Hotel*, inc breakfast and dinner, pool, but sometimes no water in it, no a/c, just noisy ceiling fans, but good service and friendly (in USA T 800-451-8891/305-341-9173); **A1** *Villas Arqueológicas*, T (985) 62830, Apdo Postal 495, Mérida, pool, tennis, restaurant (expensive and poor). Both are on the other side of the fenced-off ruins from the bus stop; rather than walk through ruins take taxi (US$1-1.50).

Further away: A3 *Lapalapa Chichén*, with breakfast and dinner, a few kilometres from the ruins, excellent restaurant, modern, park with animals; **B** *Sunset Club*, 10 mins' walk from Pisté village, 30 mins from Chichén Itzá, takes credit cards, room with bath, hot water, fan, TV, swimming pool, rec; nearby is **C** *Pirámide Inn*, 1½ km from ruins, at the Chichén end of Pisté, clean, with good food, swimming pool, friendly English-speaking owner, Trailer Park and camping US$6.50 for 2 plus car in front of hotel, US$4.50 in campground (owned by *Stardust*, see below, but still check in at hotel reception, cold showers); **D** *Dolores Alba*, small hotel (same family as in Mérida, where you can make advance reservations, advisable in view of long walk from ruins), 2½ km on the road to Puerto Juárez (bus passes it), in need of renovation, with shower and fan, clean, has swimming pool and serves good, expensive meals, English spoken, RVs can park in front for US$5, with use of restroom, shower and pool, free transport to the ruins (be careful if walking along the road from the ruins after dark, there are many trucks speeding by, carry a flashlight/torch).

Other hotels at **Pisté** about 2 km before the ruins if coming from Mérida (taxi to ruins US$2.50): no accommodation under US$10 **B-C** *Stardust Posada Annex*, good value, especially if you don't want TV or a/c (fans available), swimming pool, popular with German tour groups, average restaurant; **D** *Maya Inn*, on main road to Chichén Itzá, with bath, E without, also hammock space, clean; **D** *Posada Chac Mool*, fan, shower, clean, laundry service, safe parking, a bit noisy but rec; **D** *Posada Olalde*, quiet, 100m from main road at end of C 6; **E** *Posada Novelo*, nr *Pirámide Inn*, run by José Novelo who speaks English, good cheap restaurant. **D** *Posada el Paso*, on main road into village from Chichén, with shower, good value, very friendly, safe parking, nice restaurant. **D** *Posada el Paso*, on main road into village from Chichén, with shower, good value, very friendly, safe parking, nice restaurant. A lot of traffic passes through at night, try to get a room at the back.

There is a small pyramid in the village opp the **A3** *Hotel Misión Chichén Itzá*, a/c, pool (disappointing, gloomy, poor restaurant), not easily seen from the road; it has staircases with plumed serpents and a big statue facing N on top; close by is a huge plumed serpent, part coloured, almost forming a circle at least 20m long. Unfortunately the serpent has been largely destroyed to make way for the *Posada Chac Mool*. There is no sign or public path, climb over gate into scrubland, the serpent will be to right, pyramid to left. The whole construction is an unabashedly modern folly made 25 yrs ago by a local stone-mason who used to work on the archaeological expeditions. Bank in Pisté, Banamex, open 0900-1300.

● **Places to eat**

Mostly poor and overpriced in Chichén itself (cafés inside the ruins are cheaper than the restaurant at the entrance to the ruins, but they are still expensive). *Hotel Restaurant Carrousel* (rooms D); *Las Redes*; *Nicte-Ha* opp is cheaper and has chocolate milk shakes; *Fiesta* in Pisté, C Principal, Yucatecan specialities, touristy but good. Next door is a place serving good *comida corrida* for US$5.35; *Poxil*, Mérida end of town, for breakfast; *El Paso* in Pisté, good meals but doesn't open for breakfast as early as it claims. *Sayil* in Pisté has good *pollo pibil* for US$2.60. Restaurants in Pisté close 2100-2200.

● **Post & telecommunications**

Telephone: international calls may be placed from Teléfonos de México, opp *Hotel Xaybe*.

● **Shopping**

Hammocks are sold by *Mario Díaz* (a most interesting character), excellent quality, huge, at his house 500m up the road forking to the left at the centre of the village. 35 km from Chichén is Ebtún, on the road to Valladolid. A sign says 'Hammock sales and repairs': it is actually a small prison which turns out 1st class cotton or nylon hammocks; haggle with wardens and prisoners; there are no real bargains, but good quality.

● **Transport**

Road If driving from Mérida, follow C 63 (off the Plaza) out as far as the dirt section, where you turn left, then right and right again at the main road, follow until hypermarket on left and make a left turn at the sign for Chichén Itzá. Hitchhiking to Mérida is usually no problem.

Buses Chichén Itzá is easily reached (but less easily during holiday periods) from Mérida by (ADO) 2nd class, 2½ hrs, US$2.50 from 0500, bus station on C 50 between 65 and 67. Buses drop off and pick up passengers until 1700 (thereafter take a taxi to Pisté or colectivo to Valladolid for buses). Mon am 2nd class buses may be full with workers from Mérida returning to Cancún. Many buses a day between 0430 and 2300 go to **Cancún** and **Puerto Juárez**, US$6.20. The first bus from Pisté to Puerto Juárez is at 0730, 3 hrs. ADO bus office in Pisté is between *Stardust* and *Pirámide Inn*. Budget travellers going on from Mérida to Isla Mujeres or Cozumel should visit Chichén from Valladolid (see below). Buses from **Valladolid** go every hour to the site, the 0715 bus reaches the ruins at 0800 when they open, and you can return by standing on the main road 1 km from the entrance to the ruins and flagging down any bus going straight through. Colectivo entrance-Valladolid, US$1.65. Bus Pisté-Valladolid US$1.50; Pisté-**Tulum**, one bus only at 1300, US$4. Chichén Itzá-Tulum, bus at 1330, 4 hrs, very crowded.

IZAMAL

On the way back, turn to the right at Kantunil (68 km from Mérida) for a short excursion to the charming, friendly little city of **Izamal** (*Pop* 15,385). (It can be reached by direct bus either from Mérida or Valladolid, a good day excursion.) Once a major Classic Maya religious site (founded by the priest Itzamná), Izamal became one of the centres of the Spanish attempt to Christianize the Maya. Fray Diego de Landa, the historian of the Spanish conquest of Mérida (to whom there is a statue in the town), founded the huge convent and church which now face the main Plaza de la Constitución. This building, constructed on top of a Maya pyramid, was begun in 1549 and has the second largest atrium in the world. The image of the Inmaculada Virgen de la Concepción in the magnificent church was made the Reina de Yucatán in 1949 and the patron saint of the state in 1970. Just 2½ blocks away, visible from the convent across a second square, are the ruins of a great mausoleum known as Kinich-Kakmo pyramid. The entrance is on C 27, next to the tortilla factory (open 0800-1700, free). You climb the first set of stairs to a broad, tree-covered platform, at the end of which is a further pyramid (still under reconstruction). From the top there is an excellent view of the town and surrounding *henequén* and citrus plantations. Kinich-Kakmo is 195m long, 173 wide and 36 high, the fifth highest in Mexico. In all, 20 Maya structures have been identified in Izamal. Another startling feature about the town is

that the entire colonial centre, including the convent, the arcaded government offices on Plaza de la Constitución and the arcaded second square, is painted a rich yellow ochre, giving it the nickname of the 'golden city'.

Four blocks up C 27, at the junction with C 34 is a small church on a square. The front door may be locked, but a little door outside leads to a spiral staircase to the interior gallery (note the wooden poles in the ceilings) and to the roof. The treads on the stairs are very narrow.

● **Accommodation & places to eat** On Plaza de la Constitución, **D** *Kabul*, poor value, cell-like rooms; **E** *Canto*, basic, room 1 is best, friendly. Several **restaurants** on Plaza de la Constitución; *Gaby* just off the square on C 31; *El Norteño* at bus station, good, cheap; *Wayane*, nr statue of Diego de Landa, friendly, clean.

● **Banks & money changers** Bank on square with statue to Fray Diego de Landa, S side of convent.

● **Entertainment** Activity in town in the evening gets going after 2030.

● **Post & telecommunications** Post Office: on opp side of square to convent.

● **Shopping** Market: C 31, on Plaza de la Constitución, opp convent, closes soon after lunch.

● **Transport Trains** Mérida-Izamal leaves at 0600, returns 1520. **Buses** Bus station is on C 32 behind government offices, can leave bags; 2nd class to **Mérida**, every 45 mins, 1½ hrs, US$1.50, lovely countryside; bus station in Mérida, C 50 entre C 65 y 67. 6 a day to/from **Valladolid** (96 km), about 2 hrs, US$2.30-3.

From Izamal one can go by bus to **Cenotillo**, where there are several fine *cenotes* within easy walking distance from the town (avoid the one *in* town), especially Ucil, excellent for swimming, and La Unión. From Mérida, take 0600 train to Tunkas, and then bus to Cenotillo (direct bus from Mérida, same service as to Izamal), the train continues from Tunkas to Tizimín, arr 1140. Lovely train ride, 2½ hrs, US$1.50. Past Cenotillo is Espita and then a road forks left to Tizimín (see below).

The cemetery of **Hoctun**, on the Mérida-Chichén road, is also worth visiting, impossible to miss, there is an 'Empire State Building' on the site. Take a bus from Mérida (last bus back 1700) to see extensive ruins at **Aké**, a unique structure. Public transport in Mérida is difficult: from an unsigned stop on the corner of C 53 y 50, some buses to Tixcocob and Ekmul continue to Aké; ask the driver.

VALLADOLID

(*Pop* 19,300) Beyond Chichén Itzá, and easily reached from Mérida is **Valladolid**, a pleasant Yucatecan town bypassed by the paved road between Mérida and Puerto Juárez/Cancún. Here also is a large Franciscan church, situated on the pleasant plaza, in the middle of which is a fountain with a statue of a woman wearing a *huipil*, pouring water from a jar. Good nightlife in the plaza where at dusk there is a cacophony of birdsong. In the western outskirts, in the Barrio del Convento de Sisal, is the former convent of San Bernardino de Siena; built in 1552, it is one of the oldest church in the Yucatán, worth a visit, guide US$1 (closed Mon). See **History** for a description of the Caste War, which took place around Valladolid. Indigenous people were prohibited to enter the plaza or walk in the adjoining streets.

A lovely *cenote*, Zací, with a thatched-roof restaurant and lighted promenades, is on C 36 between C 37 y 39, but you cannot swim in it because of the algae, admission US$1 (children half-price), open 0800-1800. Road turns left from Cancún road a couple of blocks from main plaza.

Excursions

One can swim in the very clean electrically-lit *cenote* of Xkeken at **Dzit-Nup**, a huge cave with blue water: wonderful swimming with stalactites and flying bats

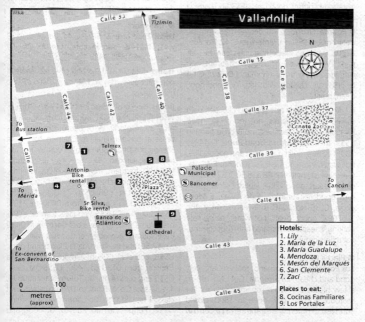

Valladolid

Hotels:
1. *Lily*
2. *María de la Luz*
3. *María Guadalupe*
4. *Mendoza*
5. *Mesón del Marqués*
6. *San Clemente*
7. *Zací*

Places to eat:
8. *Cocinas Familiares*
9. *Los Portales*

overhead. Go early to avoid tour groups and take a torch for exploring (entry US$0.70, open until 1700, taxi US$2 one way from Valladolid 7 km away). Colectivos leave several times a day in front of *Hotel María Guadalupe*, or take Valladolid-Mérida bus and alight at Dzit-Nup junction, US$0.80, then hitch or walk the last couple of km, or it's 30 mins by bicycle (take C 39 towards Mérida; leaving town you reach a fork in the road, go left, unsigned for Mérida and after 10 mins or so in a car you'll see the sign for Dzit-Nup; turn left and the cenote is on the left).

Local information
● Accommodation

B *Mesón del Marqués*, N side of Plaza Principal, T 62073, F 622680, takes Amex, a/c, with bath, on square, with good but pricey restaurant and shop (helpful for information), cable TV, swimming pool, excellent value, rec.

C *María de la Luz*, C 42 No 193-C, Plaza Principal, T 62071, takes Visa, good, a/c, swimming pool (non-residents, US$0.50), excellent restaurant, buffet breakfast US$3.50, *comida corrida* US$5, closes at 2230.

D *Posada Osorio*, C 40 between 35 and 33, clean, quiet; **D** *San Clemente*, C 42 No 206, 62208, with a/c, spacious, quiet, clean, has car park, TV, small swimming pool, restaurant, opp cathedral, in centre of town, rec; **D** *Zací*, C 44 No 191, a/c, cheaper with fan, TV, good pool, clean, quiet.

E *Lily*, C 44, with hot shower, cheaper with shared bath, fan, basic, not too clean, good location, laundry facilities, motorcycle parking US$3, friendly; **E** *María Guadalupe*, C 44 No 188, T 62068, quiet, fan, clean and good value, hot water, washing facilities, parking; **E** *Maya*, C 41 No 231, between 48 and 50, T 62069, fan or a/c, clean, good value, laundry service, also runs good restaurant 2 doors away; **E** *Mendoza*, C 39 No 204C (between C 44 y 46), T 62002, good, clean, hot water, noisy, safe parking, cheaper with shared bath (but communal toilets dirty).

● Places to eat

Los Portales on SE corner of main square, very good and cheap; *La Sirenita*, C 41 No 168-A, a few blocks E of main square, highly rec for seafood, popular, only open to 1800, closed Sun. Next to *Hotel Lily* are *Panadería La Central*

and *Taquería La Principal*. Good, cheap food at the *cocinas familiares*, Yucatecan food, pizzas, burgers, etc, NE corner of Plaza Principal, next to *Mesón del Marqués*, try the *Janet*, half way back. Cheap meals in the market, C 37, 2 blocks E of the cenote Zací. There is a well-stocked supermarket on the road between the centre and bus station.

● Banks & money changers

Bancomer on E side of square, changes TCs between 0900 and 1330; **Banco del Atlántico**, corner of C 41 y 42, quick service for TCs, from 1000.

● Laundry

Teresita, C 33 between 40 and 42, US$6 for 5½ kgs.

● Post & telecommunications

Post Office: on E side of Plaza, 0800-1500 (does not accept parcels for abroad); Telecom telegraph office on same side of Plaza, next to Palacio Municipal.

Telephones: Telmex phone office on C 42, just N of square; expensive Computel offices at bus station and next to *Hotel San Clemente*; Ladatel phonecards can be bought from *farmacias* for use in phone booths.

● Transport

Local Bike hire: Sr Silva, C 44, between C 39 y 41, US$1/hr. Antonio, in front of *Hotel María Guadalupe*, US$0.50/hr.

Trains Station at the S end of C 42. There is one train every day to Mérida at 0400, 7 hrs, great views.

Buses New bus station is at C 54 y 37, 6 blocks W of plaza, taxi US$0.80 (old terminal is at C 46 y 39, 4 blocks W of plaza). Check all bus times at bus terminal. To **Chichén Itzá**, take Mérida bus (make sure it takes you to the stop opp the Unidad de Servicios), 2nd class, US$1.50, frequent, from 0600-2400, 1 hr ride, also to Balankanché caves; many buses go to **Mérida**, first at 0600, US$6, 2nd class US$4.50 (3 hrs); and to **Cancún** from 0400 to 2100, US$5.20, 2 hrs, US$5 2nd class (can take 3½ hrs), from 0700. To **Playa del Carmen** at 0430 (reservations available) and 1300 via Cobá (US$2.50) and the crossroads 1 km from Tulum, US$8, 2nd class (3½ hrs), more frequently via Cancún from 0130 to 1400, US$8 1st class, US$6 2nd class (4 hrs); to **Tulum**, daily at 0830, 1st class via Cobá, 3 hrs; to **Tizimín**, hourly 2nd class, 1 hr, US$1; to **Rio Lagartos** (via Tizimín), US$2; **Felipe Carrillo Puerto**, at 0600 and

0930 and others for **Chetumal** (most 'de paso', buy tickets on the bus, only two direct, at 0630 and 1330), 2nd class, US$8, 5 hrs.

TIZIMIN

(*Pop* 30,000) A paved road heads N from Valladolid to **Tizimín**, a pleasant, busy town with an austere 16th century church and a convent (both may be closed), open squares and streets with low houses. It has a famous New Year *fiesta*. There is also a local *cenote*, Kikib, and the Maya ruins of **Kulubá** are 1 hr, 50 km away (taxi US$18,50). 15 km N of Temozón, on the road from Valladolid to Tizimín, are the interesting Maya ruins of Ek Balam (US$1.50). A colectivo leaves from La Candelaria park, Wed-Sun only.

● **Accommodation** There are several hotels, eg **D** *San Jorge*, on main plaza, a/c, good value; **D** *San Carlos*, 2 blocks from main square, with bath, fan, clean, good; **D** *Tizimín*, on main square; **D** *posada* next to church.

● **Places to eat** There is a good but expensive restaurant, *Tres Reyes*, also *Los Portales* on main square, and others, the many serving cheap *menú del día* around the plaza.

● **Entertainment** On the edge of town is a vast pink disco, popular with Meridanos.

● **Post & telecommunications Telephone**: long-distance phone at C 50 No 410, just off plaza.

● **Transport Trains** To Mérida 1240, 5 hrs, US$2. **Buses** From Mérida from C 50 entre C 65 y 67, 1st class, 3 hrs, US$6. In Tizimín there are two bus terminals side-by-side: Expreso del Oriente for Valladolid, Mérida, Cancún (3 hrs, US$6), and Playa del Carmen, and Pullman Ejecutivo Noreste for Mérida (3 *ejecutivo* and at least 7 1st class), Río Lagartos (3 1st class and 11 2nd class between 0515 and 1900, US$1), San Felipe (2 1st, 5 2nd class), Chiquilá, Valladolid (5 a day, US$1), and Felipe Carrillo Puerto, Bacalar and Chetumal (0530 and 1430).

RIO LAGARTOS

The road continues N over the flat landscape to **Río Lagartos**, itself on a lagoon, where the Maya extracted salt. Río Lagartos has been declared a nature reserve to protect waterfowl habitat (local and migratory) and turtle nesting beaches. The town however, is filthy. *Fiesta*, 12 Dec, La Virgen de Guadalupe. Swimming from the island opposite Río Lagartos, where boats are moored; access to beach by boat only.

Bus from Río Lagartos to **San Felipe** (13 km), where you can bathe in the sea, access to beach here, too, only by boat; basic accommodation in the old cinema, F, ask in the shop *Floresita*; also houses for rent; Miguel arranges boat trips to the beach (US$3); he lives next door to the old cinema; good cheap seafood at *El Payaso* restaurant; on the waterfront is *La Playa* restaurant, recommended; on a small island with ruins of a Maya pyramid, beware of rattlesnakes. One can also go from Río Lagartos to **Los Colorados** (15 km) to swim and see the salt deposits with red, lilac and pink water (no shade, beware of sunburn). Early morning boat trips can be arranged in Río Lagartos to see the flamingoes (US$40, in 8-9 seater, 2½-3 hrs, cheaper in 5-seater, but no shade, fix the price before embarking; in mid-week few people go so there is no chance of negotiating, but boat owners are more flexible on where they go, at weekends it is very busy, so it may be easier to get a party together and reduce costs). There are often only a few pairs of birds (but thousands in July-Aug) feeding in the lagoons E of Los Colorados; ask for Adriano who is a good guide and bird expert, or for Manuel at the Río Lagartos bus stop. Make sure you are taken to the furthest breeding grounds, to see most flamingoes, and pelicans. There is also a road around the main congregating area. (Check before going whether the flamingoes are there. Salt mining is disturbing their habitat.) Not a lot else here, certainly no accommodation, but if you are stuck for food, eat inexpensively at the *Casino* (ask locals).

● **Accommodation & places to eat E** *Hotel Nefertiti*, run down, fish restaurant; *Cueva Macumba* restaurant nr harbour, good Mexican food, friendly, will arrange breakfast if requested in advance; restaurant at seashore, good, well decorated, evening only; *lonchería*, opp hotel, open for lunch. There are a number of small eating-places.

● **Transport** There are frequent buses from Tizimín (see above), and it is possible to get to Río Lagartos and back in a day from Valladolid, if you leave on the 0630 or 0730 bus (taxi Tizimín-Río Lagartos US$25, driver may negotiate) and last bus back from Río Lagartos at 1730.

EL CUYO

The road goes E along the coast on to **El Cuyo**, rough and sandy, but passable. El Cuyo has a shark-fishing harbour. Fishermen cannot sell (co-op) but can barter fish. Fry your shark steak with garlic, onions and lime juice. El Cuyo is a very quiet, friendly place with a beach where swimming is safe (there is less seaweed in the water the further from town you go towards the Caribbean). *La Conchita* restaurant (good value meals) has *cabañas* with bath, double bed and hammock (D). Opposite *La Conchita* bread is sold after 1700. From Tizimín there are kombis (US$2.70, 1½ hrs) and buses (slower, 4 times a day) to El Cuyo, or take a kombi to Colonia and hitch from there (Sheila Wilson, Stoke Poges, UK).

HOLBOX ISLAND

Also N of Valladolid, turning off the road to Puerto Juárez after Nuevo Xcan, is **Holbox Island**. Buses to **Chiquilá** for boats, 3 times a day, also direct from Tizimín at 1130, connecting with the ferry, US$2.20. The ferry leaves for Holbox 0600 and 1430, 1 hr, US$1, returning to Chiquilá at 0500 and 1300. A bus to Mérida connects with the 0500 ferry. If you miss the ferry a fisherman will probably take you (for about US$14). You can leave your car in the care of the harbour master for a small charge; his house is E of the dock. Take water with you if possible. The beach is at the opposite end of the island to the ferry, 10 mins' walk. Hurricane Hugo uprooted or broke all the palm trees. During 'El Norte' season, the water is turbid and the beach is littered with seaweed.

● **Accommodation E** *Hotel Holbox* at dock, clean, quiet, cold water, friendly; house with 3 doors, ½ block from plaza, rooms, some beds, mostly for hammocks, very basic, very cheap, outdoor toilet, no shower, noisy, meals available which are rec; rooms at pink house off plaza, **D**, clean, with bath; *cabañas*, **D**, usually occupied; take blankets and hammock (ask at fishermen's houses where you can put up), and lots of mosquito repellent. **Camping**: best camping on beach E of village (N side of island).

● **Places to eat** *Lonchería* on plaza. Restaurant on main road open for dinner. All bars close 1900. Bakery with fresh bread daily, good. Fish is generally expensive.

● **Entertainment Disco**: opens 2230, admission US$2.75.

There are five more uninhabited islands beyond Holbox. Beware of sharks and barracuda, though few nasty occurrences have been reported. Off the rough and mostly unpopulated bulge of the Yucatán coastline are several islands, once notorious for contraband. Beware of mosquitoes in the area.

At the border between Yucatán and Quintana Roo states, Nuevo Xcan (see page 475), police searches are made for those leaving Quintana Roo for items which may transmit plant and other diseases.

THE CARIBBEAN COAST

Further to the information given in the introduction of this section (see page 404), Quintana Roo (and especially Cozumel) is the main area for Diving and Watersports in the Yucatán Peninsula. More dive sites are found off the Belize Cayes. The text below gives information on some of the options available, with addresses of dive shops, etc. It should be noted that watersports in Quintana Roo are expensive and touristy, but operators are generally helpful; snorkelling is often organized for large groups. On the more accessible reefs the coral is dying and there are no small coral fishes as a necessary part of the coral life cycle. Further from the shore, though, there is still much reef life to enjoy.

CANCUN

(*Pop* 30,000; *Phone code* 98) This famous resort near the northeastern tip of the Yucatán peninsula, is a thriving holiday resort and town. The town is on the mainland; the resort, usually known simply as the Zona Hotelera (Hotel Zone), is on an island shaped like the number 7, encompassing the Laguna Nichupté. The population is almost all dedicated to servicing the tourist industry. A bridge at each end of the island links the hotel zone with the mainland in a seamless ribbon, not yet developed along its entire length, but not

far off. Beaches stretch all along the seaward side of the Zona Hotelera; both sand and sea are clean and beautiful. Watersports take place on the Caribbean and on the Laguna, but when bathing, watch out for the warning flags at intervals along the shore.

Zona Hotelera

Its scale is huge, with skyscraper hotels and sprawling resorts between the beach and Bulevar Kukulkán, which runs the length of the island. At the northern end are shopping malls and an archaeological museum with local finds, next to the old

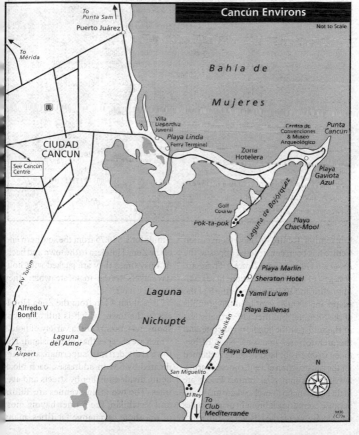

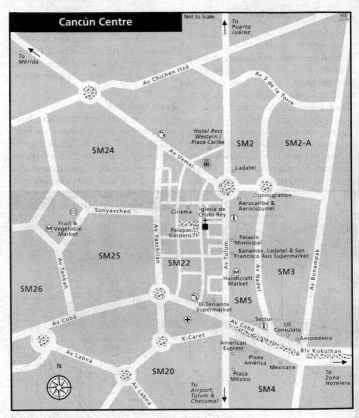

Cancún Centre

Not to Scale

To Puerto Juárez

To Mérida

Av Chichén Itzá

Av S de la Torre

SM24

Hotel Best Western / Plaza Caribe

Av Uxmal

SM2

SM2-A

Ladatel

Immigration
Aerocaribe & Aerocozumel

Sunyaxchen

Cinema

Iglesia de Cristo Rey

Fruit & Vegetable Market

Palapas Gardens

Palacio Municipal

Banamex, Ladatel & San Francisco Asis Supermarket

SM25

Av Yaxchilán

SM22

Av Tulum

Av Nader

SM3

Av Bonampak

SM26

Av Tankah

Handicraft Market

SM5

El Teniente Supermarket

Sectur

Av Cobá

US Consulate

Aeroméxico

Av Cobá

X-Caret

American Express

Blv Kukulhán

Av Labná

Plaza América

Mexicana

SM20

Plaza México

To Zona Hotelera

Av Labná

SM4

To Airport, Tulum & Chetumal

N

Convention Centre (a new Convention Centre has been constructed opposite the *Fiesta Americana Coral Beach*.) There are vestiges of Maya occupation here, San Miguelito and El Rey towards the S of the island and a small temple in the grounds of the *Sheraton*, but they are virtually lost in the midst of the modern concrete and the architectural fantasies. Near El Rey (open 0800-1630), land is being reclaimed for the construction of a golf course, marina, hotel and commercial centre. Prices are higher on Cancún than elsewhere in Mexico because everything is brought in from miles outside. Buses, marked 'Hoteles', run every 5 mins for US$0.75 from the southern end of the Zona Hotelera to the town and back. At busy times they are packed with holidaymakers trying to locate where they should get off.

It is about 4 km from the Zona Hotelera to the town, which is full of tourist shops, restaurants and a variety of hotels which are cheaper than on the island. The town is divided into 'supermanzanas', indicated by SM in addresses, each block being divided further by streets and avenues. The two main avenues are Tulum and Yaxchilán, the former having most of the shops, exchange facilities, many restaurants and hotels. Its busiest sector runs from the roundabout at the junction with Bulevar Kukulkán to the roundabout by the bus station.

Local information
● Accommodation
Hotels fall roughly into two categories: those in the Zona Hotelera, which are expensive and tend to cater for package tours, but which have all the facilities associated with a beach holiday; those in the town are less pricey and more functional. The list below gives more detail on the latter.

In the Zona Hotelera: *Camino Real*, T 830100, F 831730; *Sheraton Cancún Resort and Towers*, in the **L2** range (PO Box 834, Cancún, T 831988, F 85-02-02); **L3** *Hyatt Cancún Caribe*, T 830044, F 83-15-14, and *Hyatt Regency*, T 830966, F 831349; *Stouffer Presidente*, T 830200, F 832515, *Miramar Misión Park Plaza*, T 831755, F 831136.

In our **L2-L3** range: *Playa Blanca*, Av Kukulkán Km 3.5, T 830071, F 830904, resort facilities; and *Krystal*, T 831133, F 831790. *Oasis Cancún*, T 850867, F 850131, huge hotel but well separated to give intimate feel, nice pool, helpful staff, about 15 km from centre. Slightly less expensive: *Aristos*, T 830011, F 830078, *Calinda Quality Cancún Beach*, T 830800, F 831857, and *Calinda Viva*, same phone, F 832087; *Club Lagoon Marina*, T 831101, F 831326. Also represented are hotels in the *Fiesta Americana* chain (three in all), *Days Inn*, *Holiday Inn* (two, one in the Zona Hotelera, one in the centre), *Marriott*, *Meliá* (two), *Radisson* (also two), and many more hotels, suites and villas. At the southern end of the island is the *Club Méditerranée* with its customary facilities (T 98842409, F 98842090), **B** *Laguna Verde Suites Hotel*, on Pok-ta-pok island, nicely furnished suites sleeping up to 4, kitchens, pool, shuttle to beach, good value.

Hotels in Cancún town: most are to be found on Av Tulum and Av Yaxchilán and the streets off them. In Cancún town you will be lucky to find a double under US$20; many do not serve meals. **A2** *Best Western Plaza Caribe*, Av Tulum y Uxmal, T 841377, F 846352, opp bus terminal; **A2** *Plaza del Sol*, Yaxchilán y Gladiolas, T 843888, F 844393, modern, comfortable; **A3** *Caribe Internacional*, at the junction of Yaxchilán and Sunyaxchén, T 843499, F 841993.

In our **B** range: *Antillano*, Av Tulum y Claveles, T 841532, F 841132, a/c, TV, phone, pool; *Cancún Rosa*, Margaritas 2, local 10, T 842873, F 840623, close to bus terminal, a/c, TV, phone, comfortable rooms; *El Alux*, Av Uxmal 21, T 840662, turn left and first right from bus station, a/c with bath, clean, TV, some rooms cheaper, good value, rec; *Hacienda*, Sunyaxchén 38-40, a/c, TV; *Margarita*, Yaxchilán y Jazmines, T 849333, F 849209; *María de Lourdes*, Av Yaxchilán SM 22, T 844744, F 841242; *Batab*, Av Chichen 52 SM23, Apdo Postal 555, T 843821, 843720, e-mail: hotel-batab@mail.interacces.com.mx, a/c, TV, clean, hot water, phone, OK.

In our **C** range: *Coral*, Sunyaxchén 30 (towards post office), T 842901; *Cotty*, Av Uxmal 44, T 840550, nr bus station, a/c, TV, clean; *El Rey del Caribe*, Av Uxmal y Náder, T 842028, F 849857, a/c, kitchenettes, pool, garden with hammocks, parking, older style, friendly, rec; *Lucy*, Gladiolas 25, between Tulum and Yaxchilán, T 844165, a/c, kitchenettes, takes credit cards; *Novotel*, Av Tulum y Azucenas, T 842999, F 843162, close to bus station, rooms start at under US$30 with fan, but rise to **B** range with a/c, popular, noisy on Av Tulum side; *Parador*, Av Tulum 26, T 841310, F 849712, close to bus terminal, some rooms noisy, inefficient, a/c, TV, phone, pool, restaurant attached, clean; *Rivemar*, Av Tulum 49-51 y Crisantemas, T 841708, a/c, phone, TV; *Villa Maya Cancún*, Uxmal 20 y Rubia, T 842829, F 841762, a/c, pool, *La Francesa* bakery next door; *Villa Rossana*, Yaxchilán, opp *Plaza del Sol*.

D *Azteca*, Av López Portillo, hot water, good, cheap restaurant next door; **D** *Colonial*, Tulipanes 22 y Av Tulum, T 841535, a/c with bath, cheaper with fan, quiet, TV, phone, poor service, not too clean; **D** *Jardín*, SM64, Mza 14, Lote 20, No 37, T 848704, clean, friendly, a bit noisy; *Posada Mariano*, Av Uxmal SM 62, nr Av Chichén Itzá, T 842266, shower, fan, clean; **D** *María Isabel*, Palmera 59, T 849015, nr bus station and Av Tulum, fan and a/c, hot water, TV, small and clean, friendly, helpful, avoid rooms backing onto noisy air shaft.

E *San Carlos*, Cedro 14, T 840786, W side of Av Tulum, 300m N of bus station, with shower, fan, quiet, rec; **E** *Tropical Caribe*, Cedro 10 SM 23, T 411442, bath and fan, quiet, secure, run down, not too clean (walk N up Av Tulum from junction with Uxmal for about 5 blocks, turn left at *Suites Dokamar* and hotel is on the right).

Camping: is not permitted in Cancún town except at the Villa Deportiva youth hostel. There is a trailer park, *Rainbow*, just S of the airport. *El Meco Loco*, campground, 2 km N of passenger ferry to Isla Mujeres, full hook ups for RVs, good showers, small store, access to small beach, buses into town.

Youth hostel: F *Villa Deportiva Juvenil*, is at Km 3.2 Blvd Kukulkán, T 831337, on the beach, 5 mins' walk from the bridge towards Cancún town, next to *Club Verano Beat*, dormitory style, price pp, US$10 deposit, 10% discount with membership card, 8 people/room, friendly, basic, dirty, plumbing unreliable, sketchy locker facilities, camping US$5.

● **Places to eat**

There is a huge variety of restaurants, ranging from hamburger stands to 5-star, gourmet places. Just about every type of cuisine can be found. The best buys are on the side streets of Cancún town, while the largest selection can be found on Avs Tulum and Yaxchilán. The ones on the island are of slightly higher price and quality and are scattered along Av Kukulkán, with a high concentration in the shopping centres (of which there are about 10). If you are in no hurry to eat, look at what the restaurants are offering in the way of dishes, prices and drinks specials, then decide, if you can resist the pressurized selling.

The best is said to be *100% Natural*, opp *Hotel Caribe Internacional* on Yaxchilán y Sunyaxchén freshly-prepared food, friendly staff, 'invigorating eating'; *La Doña*, on Av Yaxchilán between Av Uxmal and Av Sunyaxchén, good cheap breakfast, and lunch, clean, a/c, friendly; *Rincón Yucateca*, Av Uxmal 24, opp *Hotel Cotty*, good Mexican breakfasts, popular; *Pericos*, Av Yaxchilán 71, Mexican seafood and steaks, live Mexican music, not cheap; *Los Huaraches*, on Uxmal opp Yaxchilán, fast food, cheap *empanada* specials after 1300; many others on Av Uxmal, not too expensive. *Los Almendros*, Av Bonanpak y Sayil, Lote 60, 61 and 62, in front of bull ring, good local food; *El Pescador*, Tulipanes 28, good seafood but expensive; *Pop*, next to *Hotel Parador*, for quicker-type food, good value; *Bing*, Av Tulum y Uxmal, close to Banpais bank, best ice-cream. *Jaguari*, Zona Hotelera, opens 1700, set price, has been rec. *Piemonte Pizzería*, Av Yaxchilán 52, good food and value, appetizing aperitifs on the house, rec; *Las Tejas*, Av Uxmal, just before C Laurel, good food at reasonable prices. On Av Tulum, *Olé Olé*, good meat, friendly. *Tacolote*, Av Cobá 19, good food and excellent value, cheerful, popular; taco stands can be found each evening on and around the squares between Avs Tulum and Yaxchilán, good family atmosphere. *Comida Casera*, Av Uxmal opp bus terminal, good coffee. The native Mexican restaurants in the workers' colonies are cheapest. Best bet is to buy food and beer in a store such as *chedravi* on Av Tulum y Cobá.

● **Airline offices**

AeroMéxico, Av Cobá 80, T 84-11-86; **Mexicana**, Av Cobá 13, T 844444; **Aerocaribe** and **Aerocozumel**, Av Tulum 29, T 842000; **American Airlines**, Aeropuerto, T 860055; **Continental**, Aeropuerto, T 860040; **NW**, Aeropuerto, T 860044; **Aviacsa**, Av Cobá 55, T 874214; **Aviateca**, Av Tulum 200, T 843938; **Lacsa**, Av Bonampak y Cobá, T 860008; **Cubana**, T 860192, outside the departure terminal at the airport, or down town, Yaxchilán 23, T/F 877373.

● **Banks & money changers**

Many Mexican banks, best rates. Many small *casas de cambio*, which change cash and TCs (latter at poorer rates) until 2100 and give cash against credit cards (Visa, Mastercard and some others); rec is *Cunex*, Av Tulum 13, half way round the roundabout, close to Av Cobá. **American Express**, Av Tulum, for money transfers in cash or TCs, plus flight service. Rates are better in town than at the airport. It is possible to change dollar TCs into dollars cash, but not one-for-one.

● **Embassies & consulates**

Consulates: downtown, unless stated otherwise, most open am only: **Costa Rica**, C Mandinga, manzana 11, SM 30, T 84-48-69; **Canada**, Plaza México 312, 2nd floor, T 84-37-16, 1100-1300; **France**, Instituto Internacional de Idiomas, Av Xel-Há 113, SM 25, T 84-60-78, 0800-1100, 1700-1900; **Germany**, Punta Conoco 36, SM 24, T 84-18-98; **Italy**, La Mansión Costa Blanca Shopping Center, Zona Hotelera, T 83-21-84; **Spain**, Cielo 17, Depto 14, SM 4, T 84-18-95; **Sweden**, Av Náder 34, SM 2-A, T 84-72-71, 0800-1300, 1700-2000; **USA**, Av Náder 40, T 84-24-11, 0900-1400, 1500-1800.

● **Entertainment**

Ballet Folclórico de México, nightly dinner shows at 1900 at *Continental Villas Plaza Hotel*, Zona Hotelera, T 85-14-44, ext 5706. *La Boom* disco, almost opp Playa Linda dock, nr the youth hostel, US$7 for all you can drink. Salsa club *Batachá* in *Miramar Misión* hotel, US$5 entry charge, popular with locals, good music. Crococun crocodile ranch, 30 km on road to Playa del Carmen. Good cinema at Kulkulcan Plaza showing English language films.

● **Post & telecommunications**
Post Office: at end of Av Sunyaxchen, a short distance from Av Yaxchilán.

Telephones: Telmex *caseta* just off Av Cobá on Alcatraces; another *caseta* on Av Uxmal next to *Los Huaraches* restaurant. Ladatel phones in Plaza América, at San Francisco de Asís shopping centre and opp the bus station on the end wall of a supermarket at Tulum y Uxmal. Computel phone and fax, more expensive, at Yaxchilán 49 and other locations. Fax público at Post Office, Mon-Sat, and at San Francisco de Asís shopping, Mon-Sat until 2200.

● **Shopping**
The market, at Av Tulum 23, is basically a handicrafts market, with jewellery, clothing, hats, etc. Downtown there are several supermarkets, big and small, for food and drink, eg *Comercial Mexicana*, nr Ladatel; *San Francisco de Asís*. Next to *Hotel Caribe Internacional*, on Yaxchilán, are two 24-hr *farmacias*.

Bookshop: *Fama*, Av Tulum 105, international books and magazines, English, French, German.

● **Sports**
Bungee jumping: from a crane hoist.

Parasailing: from beaches on Zona Hotelera.

Sailing: and many other watersports. *Nautibus*, a vessel with seats below the waterline, makes trips to the reefs, 1½ hrs, a good way to see fish, Playa Linda dock, T 83 35 52. There are a number of other cruises on offer. Atlantis submarines offer trips in a 48-passenger vessel to explore natural and man-made reefs off Cancún. For more information contact Robert Theofel in Cancún on T 834963.

● **Tour companies & travel agents**
American Express, Av Tulum 208, esq Agua, Super Manzana 4, T 845441, F 846942.

● **Tourist offices**
State Tourist Office, Av Tulum, between Comermex and city hall; **Sectur Federal Tourist Office**, corner of Av Cobá and Av Náder, closed weekends, but kiosk on Av Tulum at Tulipanes is open sometimes at weekends. There are kiosks in the Zona Hotelera, too, eg at Mayfair Plaza. Downtown and in the Zona Hotelera closest to downtown most street corners have a map. See free publication, *Cancún Tips*, issued twice a year, and *Cancún Tips Magazine*, quarterly, from Av Tulum 29, Cancún, QR 77500, Mexico.

● **Transport**
Local Car hire: Budget Rent-a-Car in Cancún has been rec for good service. A 4-door Nissan Sentra, a/c, can be hired for US$24/day from Budget at the airport, insurance US$15. **Avis**, Plaza Caracol, cheapest but still expensive. There are many car hire agencies, with offices on Av Tulum, in the Zona Hotelera and at the airport; look out for special deals, but check vehicles carefully. Beware of overcharging and read any documents you sign carefully. Rates vary enormously, from US$40 to US$80 a day for a VW Golf (VW Beetles are cheaper), larger cars and jeeps available. **Car parking**: do not leave cars parked in side streets; there is a high risk of theft. Use the parking lot on Av Uxmal.

Air Cancún airport is 16 km S of the town (very expensive shops and restaurant, exchange facilities, double check your money, especially at busy times, poor rates too, 2 hotel reservation agencies, no rooms under US$45). From Cancún by AeroMéxico to Miami (and other airlines), Mérida, Mexico City, and other Mexican destinations. Aviacsa daily to Mexico City. Continental flies to Atlanta, Buffalo, Houston, New York. To Los Angeles daily with Mexicana or AeroMéxico (less frequent out of high season). Other flights to the USA: Dallas (American, 4 a day); Detroit (Northwest, American); Indianapolis (American Trans Air); Memphis (Northwest); New Orleans (Lacsa, AeroMéxico); New York (AeroMéxico, Mexicana, Lacsa); Philadelphia (American); San Francisco (Mexicana); Tampa (Northwest); Washington (Midway, American); Baltimore and Charlotte (US Air); Columbus (Northwest). Cheap flights to USA and Canada can be found. Flights to Mexico City are heavily booked; try stand-by at the airport, or go instead to Mérida. Aviateca to Guatemala City, Flores and San Salvador. Aerocaribe to Flores (Tikal ruins) on Mon, Wed, Fri 0700, returning at 1730. Lacsa flies Cancún-San Pedro Sula, Tegucigalpa and San José. There are weekly flights to Bogotá (Ladeco), Caracas (Viasa), Lima and Buenos Aires (Aero Perú), Santiago (Ladeco) and Rio and São Paulo (Varig). Cubana and Aero Caribe fly daily to Havana; Cubana charges US$225 return (1997), special deals available for US$170, Aerocaribe fare US$286 return, flights heavily booked, visa US$15 and airport tax extra. Condor flies once a week to Cologne and Frankfurt, while LTU flies to Dusseldorf. AeroMéxico flies twice a week to Paris and Iberia flies 4 times a week from Madrid and Barcelona via Miami. Nouvelles Frontières fly charter Zurich-Cancún, 66 Blvd St Michel, 75006 Paris, France. Many charters from North America. Reconfirm flights at a travel agent, they charge, but it is easier than phoning.

On arrival at Cancún, make sure you fill in documents correctly, or else you will be sent back to the end of the long, slow queue. At customs, press a button for random bag search. Colectivo taxi buses run from the airport to Av Tulum via the Zona Hotelera, US$8; taxis on the same route charge US$25.35. Only taxis go to the airport, US$8 minimum, usually US$11.50 (beware of overcharging; even if you take a 'Hotelera' bus to the last hotel, the taxi fare remains the same). Irregular bus from Cancún to the airport 4 times a day, US$3, allow 1 hr. At Cancún airport, official ticket for taxi to Playa del Carmen costs US$50, paid in advance. If you leave the airport area on foot, walk along main road to Cancún, about 500m outside the area is a control booth; behind it taxis are allowed to pick you up for Playa del Carmen for about US$20 after bargaining. From the airport to the main road is 4 km; you can hitch on the main road.

Buses Local bus ('Hoteles' Route), US$0.75 (taxis cost about US$15); to Puerto Juárez from Av Tulum, marked 'Puerto Juárez or 'Colonia Lombardo', US$0.70. Cancún bus terminal, at the junction of Avs Tulum and Uxmal, is the hub for routes W to Mérida and S to Tulum and Chetumal. The station is neither large nor very well organized. It is open 24 hrs. Many services to **Mérida**, 4 hrs, ranging from *plus* with TV, a/c, etc, US$20, to 1st class US$14, to 2nd class US$8; all services call at **Valladolid**, US$5.50 1st class, US$5 2nd class; to **Chichén Itzá**, many buses, starting at 0630, 4 hrs, Expreso de Oriente 1st class en route to Mérida, US$6.20. Expreso de Oriente also has services to **Tizimín** (3 hrs, US$6), Izamal, Cenotillo and Chiquilá. Caribe Express (T 74173/4) has a 1330 service to **Campeche** via Mérida, US$38. Caribe Inter 3 times a day to Mérida via Francisco Carrillo Puerto, US$17.50, calling at Polyuc, Peto, Tekax, Oxkutzcab, Tikul, Muná and Uman. To **San Cristóbal** at 1900. To **Villahermosa**, US$60. Autotransportes del Oriente to **Playa del Carmen** have been rec, 2nd class, US$2.25. Inter Playa Express every 30 mins to **Puerto Morelos**, US$1, **Playa del Carmen**, US$2.25 and **Xcaret**, US$2.25; 3 times daily to **Puerto Aventuras**, US$2.50, **Akumal**, US$3, **Xel-Há**, US$3.30 and **Tulum**, US$4.25. Other services to Playa del

Carmen and Tulum are more expensive, eg 1st class Caribe Inter to Playa del Carmen US$3, 2nd class US$2.35 to Playa del Carmen and US$4.75 to Tulum. Last bus to Playa del Carmen 2000. These services are en route to **Chetumal** (US$17 luxury, US$13.50 1st class, US$10 2nd, 5 hrs). Several other services to Chetumal, inc Caribe Express, deluxe service with a/c.

Boat The Playa Linda boat dock is at the mainland side of the bridge across Canal Nichupté, about 4 km from centre, opp the *Calinda Quality Cancún Beach*. It has shops, agencies for boat trips, a snack bar and Computel. Trips to Isla Mujeres, with snorkelling, bar, shopping, start at US$27.50, or US$35 with meal; ferry to Isla Mujeres 0900, 1100, 1330, returning 1600 and 2000, about 45 mins, US$6.25 one way. Cheaper ferries go from Puerto Juárez, see below. *M/V Aqua II* has all inclusive day cruises to Isla Mujeres starting from US$44 (30% for user of the *Handbook*), T 871909.

PUERTO JUAREZ

About 3 km N of Cancún. It is the dock for the cheaper ferry services to Isla Mujeres; there is also a bus terminal, but services are more frequent from Cancún. There are many buses between Cancún and Puerto Juárez, eg No 8 opposite bus terminal (US$0.70), but when the ferries arrive from Isla Mujeres there are many more taxis than buses (taxi fare should be no more than US$2, beware overcharging).

● **Accommodation & services A3** *Hotel Caribel*, resort complex, with bath and fan; in the same price range is *San Marcos*; other hotels inc **D** *Kan Che*, first hotel on right coming from Cancún, fan, clean, swimming pool on beach, good value; *Posada Hermanos Sánchez*, 100m from bus terminal, on road to Cancún; **D** *Fuente Azul* opp the dock. *Restaurants Natz Ti Ha* and *Mandinga* by the ferry dock, serve breakfast. **E** *Pina Hermanos*, SM 68, Manzana 6, Lote 14, Col Puerto Juárez, T 842150, 10 mins from Cancún by depot, excellent value, friendly, clean, secure. *Cabañas Punta Sam*, clean, comfortable, on the beach, **D** with bath (**C** in high season). Possible to camp, with permission, on the beach nr the restaurant next door. A big trailer park has been built opp *Punta Sam*, 150 spaces, camping **F** pp, shop selling basic commodities. Irregular bus service there, or hitchhike from Puerto Juárez. Check to see if restaurant is open evenings. Take mosquito repellent.

● **Transport Buses** On the whole it is better to catch outgoing buses in Cancún rather than in Puerto Juárez: there are more of them. **Ferry** Passenger ferry to Isla Mujeres leaves from the jetty opp the bus terminal at Puerto Juárez 16 times a day between 0600 and 2100, returning 0500-1930; sometimes leaves early, last boats back may not sail at all (US$1.50, 1 hr, 5 vessels; *Caribbean Queen* is faster, US$3; *Caribbean Express* is faster still). There are also small water taxis, but these are much more expensive (US$6 at least to the town or El Garrafón). At the jetty is a luggage store (0800-1800) and a tourist information desk. Car ferry from Punta Sam to Isla Mujeres (about 75 cars carried), 5 km by bus from Cancún via Puerto Juárez (facilities to store luggage), US$1.50 pp and US$6-7/car; 6 times a day between 0830 and 2200, returning between 0715 and 2200 (45-mins' journey).

ISLA MUJERES

The island (which got its name from the large number of female idols first found by the Spaniards) has long silver beaches (beware sandflies), palm trees and clean blue water at the N end (although the large *Del Prado* hotel dominates the view there). There is pollution near the town, and a naval airstrip to the SW of it. There are limestone (coral) cliffs and a rocky coast at the S end. A lagoon on the W side is now fouled up. The island has suffered from competition from Cancún and although it is touristy, it is worth a visit. A disease destroyed practically all the palms which used to shade the houses and beach, but now, disease resistant varieties have been planted and are growing to maturity. There was considerable damage from hurricane Gilbert. The main activity in the evening takes place in the square near the church, where there are also a supermarket and a cinema. The Civil Guard patrol the beaches at night.

Local festivals

Between 1-12 Dec there is a fiesta for the Virgin of Guadalupe, fireworks, dances until 0400 in the Plaza. In Oct there is a festival of music, with groups from Mexico and the USA performing in the main square.

EL GARRAFON

At **El Garrafón**, 7 km (entry US$3.05, and the same for a locker with an extra US$3.35 key deposit), there is a tropical fish reserve (fishing forbidden) on a small coral reef. With a snorkel you can swim among a variety of multicoloured tropical fish. They aren't at all shy, but the coral is dead and not colourful (rental US$4 a day for mask and snorkel, same again for fins, US$5 for underwater camera, plus deposit of US$30, passport, driver's licence, credit card or hotel key, from shops in the park). Reef trips by boat cost US$11.65 without equipment hire, US$15 with hire. El Garrafón is a very popular excursion on the island and from Cancún; the water is usually full of snorkellers between 1100 and 1400. It is open 0800-1630; there are showers, toilets, expensive restaurants and bars, reasonable snack bar, shops and a small museum-cum-aquarium.

Taxi from the town to El Garrafón costs US$7, fixed rate. There is a bus which goes half-way to El Garrafón, the end of the line being at the bend in the road by the entrances to Casa Mundaca and Playa Paraíso (bus fare US$0.85). You can walk from El Garrafón to Playa Paraíso in 30 mins. Near Playa Paraíso is a turtle farm for presentation of the species (signposted), well worth a visit. This beach, and its neighbour, Lancheros, is quite clean, with palms, restaurants and toilets. The area of sand is quite small. Sadly, there are pens at the shore containing nurse sharks, which swim up and down their cages like big cats in a zoo. If so moved, you can join them in the water. Playa Indios, S of Lancheros, towards El Garrafón, has similar facilities and 'entertainment'.

The curious remains of a pirate's domain, called **Casa de Mundaca**, is in the centre of the island; a big, new arch gate marks its entrance. Paths have been laid out among the large trees, but all that remains of the estate (called Vista Alegre) are one small building and a circular garden with raised beds, a well and a

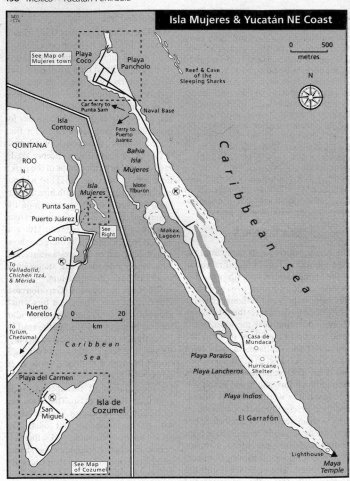

Isla Mujeres & Yucatán NE Coast

gateway. Fermín Mundaca, more of a slave-trader than a buccaneer, built Vista Alegre for the teenage girl he loved. She rejected him and he died, broken-hearted, in Mérida. His epitaph there reads 'Como eres, yo fui; como soy, tu serás' (what you are I was; what I am you shall be). See the poignant little carving on the garden side of the gate, 'La entrada de La Trigueña' (the girl's nickname).

At the southern tip is a small, ruined Mayan lighthouse or shrine of Ixtel, just beyond a modern lighthouse. The lighthouse keeper sells coca-cola for US$1, hammocks and conch shells. The view from the Maya shrine is beautiful, with a pale turquoise channel running away from the island to the mainland, deep blue water surrounding it, and the high-rise hotels of Cancún in the distance. Looking N from the temple you see both coasts of the island stretching away from you.

The town is at the NW end of the island; at the end of the N-S streets is the northern beach (Playa Coco), the widest area of dazzling white sand on the island (watersports equipment is rented at very high prices, also umbrellas and chairs). The island is best visited April to Nov, off-season (although one can holiday here the year round). **NB** Bathing on the Caribbean side of the island can be unsafe because of strong undertows and cross-currents.

Trips to **Isla Contoy** (bird and wildlife sanctuary), while suspended from Cancún, are still possible from Isla Mujeres, US$40, 9 hrs, with excellent lunch, 2 hrs of fishing, snorkelling (equipment hire extra, US$2.50) and relaxing. Boats from the cooperative at the town pier may not leave until full, their trips are warmly recommended and include an excellent fish lunch and 2 hrs snorkelling. From the same point boat trips go to the lighthouse at the entrance to the harbour, Isla Tiburón, El Garrafón and Playa Lancheros for lunch, 3-4 hrs, US$16.65 pp. You will be approached by boatmen on the boat from Puerto Juárez, and on arrival.

There is public transport on Isla Mujeres, ie taxis at fixed prices, and the bus service mentioned above. You can walk from one end of the island to the other in 2½ hrs. At the top of the rise before El Garrafón, by the speed humps and the houses for rent, is a point where you can see both sides of the island. A track leads from the road to the Caribbean coast, a couple of minutes stroll. You can then walk down the E coast to the southern tip.

Local information
● **Accommodation**

At Christmas hotel prices are increased steeply and the island can heave with tourists, especially in January. The island has several costly hotels and others, mainly in the **D** category, and food, especially fresh fruit, is generally expensive.

Reasonable hotels to stay at on Isla Mujeres are **A2** *Posada del Mar*, Alte Rueda 15, T 20212, (inc meals) has pleasant drinks terrace but expensive drinks, restaurant for residents only; **A3** *Belmar*, Av Hidalgo 110 x Madero y Abasolo, T 70430, F 70429, a/c, TV, restaurant *Pizza Rolandi* downstairs; **A3** *El Mesón del Bucanero*, Hidalgo 11, T 20210, F 20126, all rooms with fan; **A3** *Las Perlas del Caribe*, Caribbean side of town, clean, a/c, pool, rec.

B *Cabinas María del Mar*, overlooks Coco beach, a/c, lovely beach bar with hammocks and rocking chairs for two.

C *Berny*, Juárez y Abasolo, T 20025, with bath and fan, basic, problems with water supply, swimming pool, long-distance calls possible, residents only, but does not even honour confirmed reservations if a deposit for one night's stay has not been made; **C** *Caracol*, Matamaros 5, T 70150, F 70547, cheaper with fan, hot water, terrace balcony, stoves for guests' use, bar, coffee shop, laundry, central, clean, good value; **C** *El Paso*, Morelos 13, with bath, clean, facing the pier, 2nd floor; **C** *Isla Mujeres*, next to church, with bath, renovated, run by pleasant Englishman; **D** *María José*, Madero 25, T 20130, clean, fans, friendly; **C** *Rocas del Caribe*, Madero 2, 100m from ocean, cool rooms, big balcony, clean, good service; **C** *Vistalmar*, on promenade about 300m left from ferry dock (D for longer stays),

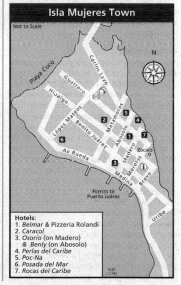

Isla Mujeres Town

Hotels:
1. Belmar & Pizzeria Rolandi
2. Caracol
3. Osorio (on Madero)
   & Benly (on Abosolo)
4. Perlas del Caribe
5. Poc-Na
6. Posada del Mar
7. Rocas del Caribe

ask for rooms on top floor, bath, balcony, fan, insect screens, good value.

D *Caribe Maya*, Madero 9, central, modern, a/c, cheaper with fan, very clean and comfy; **D** *Carmelina*, Guerrero 4, T 70006, central with bath and a/c, clean, safe, but no toilet paper, soap, blankets or hot water, unfriendly family, rents bikes and snorkelling gear, advance payment for room required daily; **D** *Isleñas* Madero and Guerrero, with bath, cheaper without, very clean, helpful; **D** *Las Palmas*, central, Guerrero 20, 2 blocks from N beach, good, clean; **D** *Xul-Ha*, on Hidalgo towards N beach, with fan.

E *Osorio*, Madero, 1 block from waterfront, clean, fan, with bath and hot water, rec, friendly, reception closes at 2100, *La Reina* bakery nearby.

F-G *Poc-Na Hostal*, T 70090, price pp, is cheapest, dormitories or 3 rooms, try for central section where there are fans, clean, everything works, no bedding, but linen is included in price, gringo hang-out, good and cheap café, book exchange, video, take insect repellent, book in advance, but get receipt if paying in advance (San Jorge laundry is just 1 block away, US$2/kg).

Camping: there is a trailer park on the island, with a restaurant. At Playa Indios is *Camping Los Indios* where you can put up your hammock. **NB** If you arrive late, book into any hotel the first night and set out to find what you want by 0700-0800, when the first ferries leave the next morning.

● **Places to eat**
Many beach restaurants close just before sunset. *El Limbo* at *Roca Mar Hotel* (Nicolás Bravo y Guerrero), excellent seafood, good view, reasonable prices; *Miriti*, opp ferry, quite good value; *Miramar*, on Rueda Medina, next to ferry, fine seafood; *Pizza Rolandi*, see above, good breakfast, popular. *Gomar*, Madero and Hidalgo, expensive, possible to eat outside on verandah or in the colonial-style interior, popular; *Chen Huayo*, Hidalgo, nr basketball courts, excellent Mexican food, cheap; *Arriba*, Hidalgo, popular, lively, delicious food, good value; *Las Gemelas*, also on Hidalgo, US-owned, vegetarian options, good value; *Mano de Dios*, nr the beach, cheap, quite good. *Eric's*, very good inexpensive Mexican snacks; *Tropicana*, 1 block from pier, simple, popular, cheap; *Cielito Lindo*, waterfront, open air, good service; good fish restaurant 50m to left of jetty; *La Peña*, overlooks beach, good pizzas, happy hour, nice atmosphere; *La Langosta*, good Mexican dishes,

lovely view; *Bucanero*, downtown, steak, seafood, prime rib, classy for Islas Mujeres; *Red Eye Café*, breakfast and lunch only, closed Mon, excellent buffet, good coffee, friendly; *Robert's* on square, cheap and good; *Giltri*, in town, good value; *Café Cito* on B Juárez, 1 Block W of *Tequila*, best breakfast, small portions, good health food, rec; *Lomita*, Benito Juárez Sur, blue house, excellent Mexican food, cheap, friendly; *Ciro's* lobster house, not too good but *Napolito's*, opp, is excellent. Small restaurants round market are good value. Daily fish barbecue at El Paraíso beach. At Garrafón Beach: *El Garrafón*, *El Garrafón de Castilla*, catering for tour boats from Cancún; between Playa Indios and El Garrafón, *María's Kankin Hotel and Restaurant*, French cuisine.

● **Banks & money changers**
Banco del Atlántico, Av Juárez 5, 1% commission, but better on mainland.

● **Entertainment**
Disco-bars: *Tequila*, on Hidalgo, video bar and restaurant. *Bad Bones* has live rock-and-roll.

● **Laundry**
Tim Pho, on corner of Juárez and Abasolo, fast and cheap, US$2 for big load.

● **Post & telecommunications**
Telephone: Ladatel cards are sold at *Artesanía Yamily*, Hidalgo, just N of the square.

● **Shopping**
Opposite the restaurant *Gomar* are several souvenir shops, selling good stone Maya carvings (copies), macramé hangings and colourful wax crayon 'Maya' prints. *El Paso Boutique*, opp ferry, trades a small selection of English novels.

● **Sports**
Watersports: you can rent skin and scuba diving equipment, together with guide, on the waterfront N of the public pier, a boat and equipment costs about US$50 pp for ½ day, check how many tanks of air are inc and shop around. They can set up group excursions to the Cave of the Sleeping Sharks; English spoken. It is no cheaper to hire snorkel gear in town than on the beach. Deep sea fishing for 10 in a boat from *Aguamundo*. Diving is not in the class of Cozumel.

● **Tourist offices**
Tourist office on square, opp the basketball pitch.

● **Transport**
Bike hire: worth hiring a bicycle, US$5 a day (about US$7 deposit eg *Sport Bike*, Av Juárez y

Morelos), or a moped (US$5/hr, US$15-20 all day, shop around, credit card, passport or money deposit, helmet not required), to explore the island in about 2 hrs. Do check if there is any damage to the bicycle *before* you hire. Bicycles for hire from several hotels. Try Ciro's Motorrentor by *Hotel Caribe* for good motorbikes.

Puerto Morelos, not far S of Cancún (bus US$1), has three hotels, two expensive, one basic, **D** *Amor*, nr bus stop, quiet, clean, safe motorcycle parking, good restaurant; also free camping. Hotels close in the low season, but one of the restaurants in town has good value rooms. Popular with scuba divers and snorkellers, but beware of sharks.

PLAYA DEL CARMEN

A fast growing beach centre, with many new hotels and restaurants. In Maya times it was a departure point for boats to Cozumel; modern services have resumed with the development of Playa del Carmen as a resort. This has only happened more-or-less concurrently with the expansion of Cancún. 'Playa', as it is usually known, has several kilometres of white sand beaches, which are relatively clean; those to the N of town are the most pleasant. There are sandflies though, and, from time to time, certain plankton in the water cause an itchy rash that the locals call *Agua Mala*. Pharmacists stock cream and pills to treat it. Avenida Juárez runs from Highway 307 to the park which fronts the sea. 1 block S of the park is the ferry terminal. All along Av 5, the street which parallels the beach, are restaurants and shops, with hotels on the streets running back from the beach. Playa is conveniently placed between Cancún and Tulum, giving easy access to these and other tourist sites on the coast and inland.

Local information
● **Accommodation**
Hotels fill up early; cheaper rooms are hard to find in January.

Outside town are: at Km 297/8, N of Playa del Carmen, **A1** *Cabañas Capitán Lafitte*, very good, pool, excellent cheap restaurant on barren beach; under same ownership is

A1 *Shangri-Lá Caribe*, T 22888, 7 km S, closer to town (at N end of the bay N of Playa), cabins, equally good, excellent beach with diving (Cyan-Ha, PADI) and snorkelling, sailing, easy birdwatching beside hotel; beside *Shangri-Lá* is **L3** *Las Palapas*, breakfast and dinner included, cabins with hammocks outside, good, T 22977, F 41668 (F Mexico City 379-8641); at Km 296, **A1** *El Marlín Azul*, swimming pool, good food.

Most luxurious is **L1** *Continental Plaza Playacar*, T 30100, F 30105, a huge new development just S of the ferry terminal, excellent in every respect, non-residents can use swimming pool, no charge; in the same development as this 5-star hotel is the 5-star *Diamond Resort*, Apdo Postal 149, T 30340, F 30348 and the 4-star *Caribbean Villages*, T 30434, F 30437, both all-inclusive club operations, the latter in the middle of the golf course; there are also villas for rent from US$65 to US$280, PO Box 139, Playa del Carmen, T/F 30148.

At the N end of town, on a popular stretch of beach between C 12 y 14, is **A1-B** *Blue Parrot*, T 30083, F 44564 (reservations in USA 904- 775 6660, toll free 800-634 3547), price depends on type of room and facilities, has bungalows, no a/c, with excellent bar (Happy Hour 2200) and café, volley ball court, deep sea fishing expeditions, highly rec; **A1** *Molcas*, T 30070, nr ferry pier, pool, a bit shabby, friendly staff, interesting architecture, its open-air restaurant across street is good and reasonable; **A1** *Cabañas Tucán*, Av 5 beyond C 14, clean, good, mosquito net, highly rec; **A3** *Hotel Maranatha*, Av Juárez between Avs 30 and 35, T 30143, F 30038 (US Res T 1-800-3298388), luxury with all facilities.

B *Azul Profundo*, next to *Blue Parrot*, with bath and balcony; **B** *Costa del Mar*, T 30058, on little road between C 10 y 12, clean, restaurant (disappointing) and bar, pool; **B** *Rosa Mirador*, behind the *Blue Parrot*, **A2** in high season, hot showers, fan, best views from 3rd floor, owner Alberto speaks English, rec; **B-F** *Cabañas Alejari*, C 6 going down to beach, T 30374, very nice, shop has long distance phones; next to *Alejari* on the beach is **A2** *Pelícano*, inc good breakfast, impersonal, and **A3** *Albatros Royale*, T 30001, clean, very good, no pool.

B *Mom's*, Av 30 y C 4, T 30315, about 5 blocks from bus station or beach, clean, comfortable, small pool, good restaurant with US home cooking and plenty of vegetables, *Yax-Ha* cabins, on the beach, via Av 5 by C 10 (price depending on size and season), excellent; **B-C** *Cabañas Banana*, Av 5 entre C 6 y 8, T 30036, cabins and rooms, kitchenettes; **B-C** *Casa de Gopala*,

C 2 Nte and Av 10 Nte (PO Box 154), T/F 30054, with bath and fan, 150m from beach, quiet and central, pool, American/Mexican owned, large rooms, quiet and comfortable, rec.

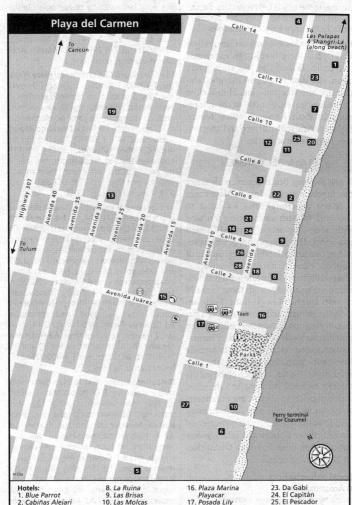

Playa del Carmen

Hotels:
1. Blue Parrot
2. Cabiñas Alejari & Phones
3. Cabañas Banana
4. Cabañas Tucán
5. Cabañas Tuxatah
6. Continental Plaza Playacar
7. Costa del Mar
8. La Ruina
9. Las Brisas
10. Las Molcas
11. Maya Bric & Tank-Ha Diving
12. Mi Casa
13. Mom's Hotel & Restaurant
14. Nuevo Amanecer
15. Playa del Carmen
16. Plaza Marina Playacar
17. Posada Lily
18. Sian Ka'an
19. Villa Deportiva Juvenil
20. Yax-Ha

Places to eat:
21. Bip Bip & La Opción
22. Chicago
23. Da Gabi
24. El Capitán
25. El Pescador
26. Karen's
27. Máscaras
28. Pez Vela

🚌1 Playa Express
🚌2 Caribe
🚌3 Expreso Oriente

C *Cabañas Tuxatah*, 2 mins from sea, 2 blocks S from Av Juárez (Apdo 45, T 30025), German owner, Maria Weltin speaks English and French, with bath, clean, comfortable, hot water, laundry service, beautiful gardens, rec, breakfast US$4; **C** *Delfín*, Av 5 y C 6, T 30176, with bath; **C** *Maya Bric*, Av 5, between C 8 and 10, T 30011, hot water, clean, friendly, pool, Tank-Ha dive shop (see below); **C** *Nuevo Amanecer*, C 4 W of Av 5, very attractive, fans, hot water, hammocks, mosquito nets, clean, laundry area, pool room, helpful, rec; **C** *Sian Ka'an*, Av 5 y C 2, T 30203, 100m from bus station, modern rooms with balcony, clean, rec.

Others in the **C** range inc *El Elefante*, Av 10 y C 10, T 30037, with bath, modern but basic, and *Playa del Carmen*, Av Juárez, between Avs 10 y 15, T 30293, opp bank; **C** *Posada Freud*, Av 5 entre C 8 y 10 Nte, T/F 30601, with bath, fan, some with kitchenette, Palapa-style, quiet, clean, Austrian owner, simpler rooms without bath available priced at **D-E**, rec.

D *Casa Tucan*, C 4 N, between 10 y 15 Av Nte, T/F 30283, nice patio, small but clean rooms; **D** *Posada Lily*, with shower, fan, safe, clean, but noisy in am and cell-like rooms, Av Juárez at Caribe bus stop; under same ownership *Dos Hermanos*, 3 blocks W and 2 blocks N of *Posada Lily*, clean, hot showers, fan, quiet. **D-E** *Posada Papagayo*, Av 15 between C 4 y 6, with fan and bath, mosquito net, very nicely furnished rooms, friendly, highly rec.

E *Posada Fernandez*, Av 5 opp C 1, with bath, hot water and fan, friendly, rec; **E-F** *Cabañas La Ruina*, at the beach end of C 2, popular, crowded, noisy, clean, lots of options and prices, from 2- to 3-bedded cabins, hammock space under *palapa*, with or without security locker, hammock in open air, camping US$2.50, space for vehicles and camper vans, linen rental, bath extra, cooking facilities; **E-F** *Mi Casa* (painted red), Av 5 opp *Maya Bric*, also apartments (E) with kitchenette, mosquito net, fan, clean, well-furnished, bath, cold water, owner speaks German, English, and Spanish, nice garden, rec. Lots of new places going up, none under US$10 a night. Small apartments on Av 5, esq C 6, approx US$200/month, with kitchen; also rooms nr basketball court, US$100/month.

Youth Hostel: *Villa Deportiva Juvenil*, from US$2 camping, US$5 in dormitory ("hot with only two fans and a lot of beds"), to US$20 for up to 4 in cabin with fan and private shower, comfortable, with basketball court, clean, rec, but difficult to find, especially after dark, but it is signposted: it's 5 blocks up from Av 5, on C 8 Nte (T 525-2548).

Camping: see above under *La Ruina*; also *Camping Las Brisas* at the beach end of C 4. *Punta Bete*, 10 km N, the right-hand one of three at the end of a 5 km road, on beach but no sand in 1997 because of hurricane damage, US$3 for tent, also 2 restaurants and cabañas. *Outback*, small trailer park on beach at end of C 6, US$10 for car and 2 people.

● **Places to eat**

Máscaras, on square, highly rec; also on the square, *El Tacolote*, tacos, etc, and *Las Piñatas*. *Da Gabi*, just up C 12 from *Blue Parrot*, good pastas, Mexican dishes, "best pizzas in town", breakfast buffet, also has rooms in C range. Next to *Cabañas Yax-Ha* is *El Pescador*, fish, has a variety of beers. On or nr Av 5: *Pez Vela*, Av 5 y C 2, good atmosphere, food, drinks and music (closed 1500-1700); *Pollo Caribe*, nr bus station between C 2 and Juárez, set chicken menu for US$2, good, closes early when chicken runs out; *Nuestra Señora del Carmen*, Av 5 y C 2, family-run, cheap, generous portions, rec; *Playa Caribe*, 1 block up Av 5 from plaza, fish and seafood specialities, good breakfast, nice atmosphere, cheap, and popular with budget minded travellers, drinks for US$1 but small; *Karen's Pizza*, Av 5 entre C 2 y 4, pizzas, Mexican dishes, cable TV, popular; *El Capitán*, C 4 just off Av 5, good meals and music, popular; next door is *Sabor* for sandwiches, juices, breakfast, English-spoken, rec. *Los Almendros*, C 8, excellent Mexican food, cheap, friendly; *Lonchería Maquech*, C 1 entre Av 5 y 10, vegetarian lunch daily, cheap, friendly, rec; *Limones*, Av 5 y C 6, good food, popular, reasonable prices; across C 6, still on Av 5 is *Flippers*, good atmosphere, good food especially fish, moderately priced. *Bip Bip*, Av 5 between C 4 and 6, best pizza in town; *La Hueva del Coronado*, same block, seafood and local dishes, reasonable; *Calypso House* also in same block. *La Lunada*, Av 5 entre C 6 y 8. *El Correo*, just beyond *Posada Fernández*, Mexican, cheap, excellent *menú del día* and *pollo pibil*, rec; *Marinelly*, Av 10 No 110, clean, good food and prices, not touristy; *La Choza*, 5 Av entre Juárez y C 2, great food, cheap set menus; *Sophie's*, C 2 (opp *Cabañas La Ruina*), good food, videos shown; *Media Luna*, Av 5 y C 15, good atmosphere, delicious poached eggs for breakfast, and Italian food; *El Chino*, C 4 Nte entre C 10 y 15, popular with Mexicans, seafood, Yucatán specialities, good breakfast, inexpensive, friendly; *Panadería del Caribe*, Av 5 entre C 4 y 2, for breads and cakes; *Panificadora del Carmen*, Av 30, just before

Youth Hostel, excellent, open until 2300, has a café/restaurant at the side called *La Concha*; *Zermat Bakery* at extreme end of pedestrian C Nte, 5 blocks from bus station, rec for pastries. Various places serve breakfast close to Post Office. Many places have 'happy hour', times vary, shop around.

● **Banks & money changers**
Banks open 0900-1300, get there early to avoid crowds. **Banco del Atlántico** on Av Juárez y Av 10, 2 blocks up from plaza; **Bancomer**, Av Juárez, 5 blocks W of Av 5, only bank giving cash advances on credit cards, prefer visa; *casa de cambio* on Av 5 opp tourist information booth, reasonable rates for US$ cash, no commission.

● **Entertainment**
La Opción, Av 5 beside *Bip Bip*, upstairs, shows video films, usually 2 a night. *Ziggy's Bar and Disco* on the square, very busy Fri/Sat night, expensive drinks; live music in a number of places at night, look for notices. *Pez Vela* has live music at about 2000 followed by Happy Hour. *Blue Parrot*, C 12, live music and shows most evenings, happy hour 1700-2000, and 2300-0200, very popular. *Señor Frags* (Carlos 'n Charlie's chain), by the pier, "a sure sign that this small town is developing fast".

● **Hospitals & medical services**
Dentist: *Perla de Rocha Torres*, Av 20 Nte s/n entre 4 y 6, T 30021, speaks English, rec.

● **Laundry**
Av Juárez, 2 blocks from bus station; another on Av 5.

● **Post & telecommunications**
Post Office: Av Juárez y Av 15, open 0800-1700 Mon-Fri, 0900-1300 Sat.

Telephones: Computel next to bus station on Av Juárez. Long distance phones at shop at *Cabañas Alejari*. International fax service at Turquoise Reef Realty, in same block as *Hotel Playa del Carmen*, cost of phone call plus US$3.65 for first sheet, US$1.65 for second.

● **Sports**
Diving: Tank-Ha Dive Center, at *Maya Bric Hotel*, resort course US$60 (diving lesson in the hotel pool before first dive), 1-tank dive US$35, 2-tank US$50, packages from US$90-395, PDIC certification course US$350. Dive shop at *Yax-Ha Cabañas*. Also El Oasis Dive Shop, C 4 between Avs 5 and 10; Albatros Water Sports; Costa del Mar Dive Shop, beside *Blue Parrot*; and others. Cavern diving with Yucatech Expeditions has been rec; 2 tank day trip costs

US$100 all inclusive. Check Dive shops carefully, there have been reports of drunken dive masters.

● **Tour companies & travel agents**
Tierra Maya Tours, T 47918, F 30537, Box 24, professional and nice.

● **Tourist offices**
Tourist kiosk on square, with information and leaflets, books, guided tours to Tulum and Cobá, US$30 inc transport, entry to site, and English-speaking guide, Mon and Fri, 0930. *Destination Playa del Carmen* bulletin gives details of many of the services in town, plus map.

● **Transport**
Local Car hire: Continental Car Rental, Av Juárez; **Playa**, at Plaza Marina Playacar; **National** at *Hotel Molcas*.

Air Aerocaribe has flights to Chichen Itzá and Cozumel twice a week.

Buses To/from **Cancún**, 1 hr 15 mins, Playa Express (Av Juárez, between Avs 5 y 10) goes every 30 mins, US$2.25; also Caribe (Av Juárez, by *Posada Lily*) to Cancún luxury bus at 1215, 1st class 3 times a day. To Cancún international airport, take a 2nd class bus to the crossroads (US$2.50) and walk, or take a taxi (US$1.65) the 4 km to the terminal (a *camioneta* will pick you up at your hotel, minimum 3 people, US$1.50, reserve seat in restaurant at *Hotel Maya Bric* 24 hrs in advance). Caribe luxury buses to **Mérida**, US$25.30, **Campeche** US$42, and **Chetumal** US$13.50, also 1st (US$11.50) and 2nd class (US$10) to Chetumal, Felipe Carrillo Puerto; 2nd class calls at **Tulum**, US$1.40. Expreso Oriente (Av Juárez y Av 5) has luxury, 1st and 2nd class buses to Mérida via Cancún, many a day, US$17.50, US$14.30 and US$12 respectively; also to **Valladolid** 1st class US$8.50, US$6 2nd, 4 hrs; **Tizimín**, US$9, and 2nd class Tulum (US$1.20), **Cobá** (US$3.30), Valladolid (US$8.50) at 0500, 1000 and 1700. In all, several buses a day to Tulum between 0530 and 1845, 1 hr. To **Puebla**, ADO at 1800, 20 hrs, US$40; to **Mexico City**, ADO at 0700, 1200, 1800, 24 hrs, US$35; to **San Cristóbal de las Casas**, different classes, US$22-30, 3 a day, can book only 1 day in advance, Maya de Oro 1st class at 1845.

Taxis: to Cancún airport cost US$25. Beware of those who charge only US$5 as they are likely to charge an extra US$20 for luggage. Tours to Tulum and Xel-Há from kiosk by boat dock US$30; taxi tours to Tulum, Xel-Há and Xcaret, 5-6 hrs, US$60; taxi to Xcaret US$6.65. Taxis congregate on the Av Juárez side of the square (Sindicato Lázaro Cárdenas del Río, T 30032/30414).

Ferry For **Cozumel**, 3 companies, *Mexico I* and *Mexico II* waterjets, US$4 one way, minimum 30 mins' journey, and Naviera Turística, US$4, 6 times a day. Naviera Turística Waterjets have 8-9 a day from 0530-2045, returning 0400-2000 (schedules change frequently). **Cozumeleño** have slower boats (1¼ hrs), US$3 one way. **NB** Waterjets are like floating buses and you have to sit inside.

COZUMEL

The island is not only a marvellous place for snorkelling and scuba diving, but is described as a "jewel of nature, possessing much endemic wildlife including pygmy species of coati and raccoon; the bird life has a distinctly Caribbean aspect and many endemic forms also" – Jeffrey L White, Tucson, Arizona. A brief visit does not afford much opportunity to see the flora and fauna on land; the forested centre of the island is not easy to visit, except at the Maya ruins of San Gervasio (see below), and there are few vantage points. On the other hand, the island has a great deal to offer the tourist. The name derives from the Maya 'Cuzamil', land of swallows.

Maya pilgrims hoped to visit once in their lifetime the shrine to Ix-Chel (goddess of the moon, pregnancy, childbirth, all things feminine, but also floods, tides and destructive waters), which was located on the island. By the 14th century AD, Cozumel had also become an important trading centre. The Spaniards first set foot on the island on 1 May 1518 when Juan de Grijalva arrived with a fleet from Cuba. Spanish dominance came in 1520. By the 18th century, the island was deserted.

Places of interest

In all, there are some 32 archaeological sites on Cozumel, those on the E coast mostly single buildings (lookouts, navigational aids?). The easiest to see are the restored ruins of the Maya-Toltec period at **San Gervasio** in the N (7 km from Cozumel town, then 6 km to the left up a paved road, toll US$1). Entry to the site is US$4.35, open 0800-1600; guides are on hand, or you can buy a self-guiding booklet at the *librería* on the square in San Miguel, or at the *Flea Market*, for US$1. It is an interesting site, quite spread out, with *sacbes* (Maya roads) between the groups of buildings. There are no large structures, but a nice plaza, an arch, and pigment can be seen in places. It is also a pleasant place to listen to birdsong, see butterflies, animals (if lucky), lizards and landcrabs (and insects). **Castillo Real** is one of many sites on the northeastern coast, but the road to this part of the island is in very bad condition and the ruins themselves are very small. **El Cedral** in the SW (3 km from the main island road) is a 2-room temple, overgrown with trees, in the centre of the village of the same name. Behind it is a ruin, and next to it a modern church with a green and white façade (an incongruous pairing). In the village are large, permanent shelters for agricultural shows, rug sellers, and locals who pose with *iguanas doradas*. El Caracol, where the sun, in the form of a shell, was worshiped is 1 km from the southernmost Punta Celarain. At Punta Celarain is an old lighthouse.

SAN MIGUEL DE COZUMEL

This is the main town on the sheltered W coast. Here the ferries from the mainland and the cruise ships dock. The town is particularly touristy and expensive during Christmas and Easter. The waterfront, Av Rafael Melgar, and a couple of streets behind it are dedicated to the shoppers and restaurant-goers, but away from this area the atmosphere is quite Mexican. Fishermen sell their catch by the passenger ferry pier, which is in the centre of town. It is a friendly town, with a good range of hotels (both in town and in zones to the N and S) and eating places.

Museums On waterfront between C 4 y 6, history of the island, well laid-out (entry US$3). Bookshop, art gallery, rooftop restaurant has excellent food and views of sunset, good for breakfast, too from 0700 ('The Quick' is excellent value). Recommended.

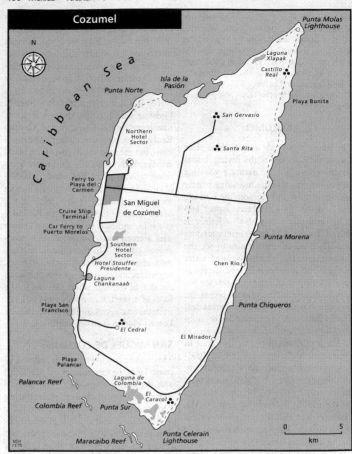

Cozumel

Punta Molas Lighthouse

Laguna Xlapak

Castillo Real

Playa Bonita

San Gervasio

Santa Rita

Caribbean Sea

Punta Norte

Isla de la Pasión

Northern Hotel Sector

Ferry to Playa del Carmen

San Miguel de Cozúmel

Cruise Ship Terminal

Car Ferry to Puerto Morelos

Punta Morena

Southern Hotel Sector

Hotel Stouffer Presidente

Chen Rio

Laguna Chankanaab

Playa San Francisco

Punta Chiqueros

El Cedral

El Mirador

Playa Palancar

Palancar Reef

Laguna de Colombia

El Caracol

Colombia Reef

Punta Sur

Maracaibo Reef

Punta Celerain Lighthouse

0   5
km

Beaches The best public beaches are some way from San Miguel town: in the N of the island they are sandy and wide, although those at the Zona Hotel Norte were damaged in 1989 and are smaller than they used to be. (At the end of the paved road, walk up the unmade road until it becomes 'dual carriageway'; turn left for the narrow beach, which is a bit dirty. Cleaner beaches are accessible only through the hotels.) S of San Miguel, San Francisco is good if narrow (clean, very popular, lockers at *Pancho's*, expensive restaurants), but others are generally narrower still and rockier. All the main hotels are on the sheltered W coast. The E, Caribbean coast is rockier, but very picturesque; swimming and diving on the unprotected side is very dangerous owing to ocean underflows. The only safe place is at a sheltered bay at Chen Río. Three good (and free) places for snorkelling are the beach in front of *Hotel Las Glorias*, 15 mins' walk S from ferry, you can walk through the hotel's reception; **Playa Corona**, further S, too far to walk, so hitch or take a taxi, small restaurant and pier; **Xul-Ha**, further S, with a bar and comfortable beach chairs.

Excursions A circuit of the island on paved roads can easily be done in a day (see **Local Transport** below). Head due E out of San Miguel (take the continuation of Av Benito Juárez). Make the detour to San Gervasio before continuing to the Caribbean coast at *Mescalito's* restaurant. Here, turn left for the northern tip (road unsuitable for ordinary vehicles), or right for the S, passing Punta Moreno, Chen Río, Punta Chiqueros (restaurant, bathing), El Mirador (a low viewpoint with sea-worn rocks, look out for holes) and Paradise Cove. At this point, the paved road heads W while an unpaved road continues S to Punta Celarain. On the road W, opposite the turnoff to El Cedral, is a sign to *Restaurante Mac y Cía*, an excellent fish restaurant on a lovely beach, popular with dive groups for lunch. Next is Playa San Francisco (see above). A few more km lead to the former *Holiday Inn*, the last big hotel S of San Miguel. Just after this is Parque Chankanab, which used to be an idyllic lagoon behind the beach (9 km from San Miguel). After it became totally spoilt, it was restored as a National Park, with the lagoon, crystal clear again, a botanical garden with local and imported plants, a 'Maya Area' (rather artificial), swimming (ideal for families with young children), snorkelling, dive shops, souvenirs, expensive but good restaurants and lockers (US$2). Entry costs US$4, snorkelling mask and fins US$5, use of underwater camera US$25, open 0800-1600. Soon the road enters the southern hotel zone at the *Stouffer Presidente*, coming to the cruise ship dock and car ferry port on the outskirts of town.

Diving

The island is famous for the beauty of its underwater environment. The best reef for scuba diving is Palancar, reached only by boat. Also highly recommended are Santa Rosa and Colombia. There are at least 20 major dive sites. Almost all Cozumel diving is drift diving, so if you are not used to a current choose an operator you feel comfortable with. There are over 20 dive operators. PADI, NAUI or SSI certification are all available; most trips are 2-tank dives, US$40-50, but one-tank and night-time dives are easily arranged. The better establishments have more dive masters accompanying reef trips. There are two hyperbaric chambers on the island, which treat about one tourist a week. Don't let the next one be you and follow safe diving practices with a concerned dive master. A resort course costs on average US$60, a certification course US$350, including equipment. Lots of packages are available. The following operators have been recommended: *Chino's Scuba Shop*, T/F 24487, ask for Ruben Maldonado; *Caribbean Diver's*, T 21080, F 21426, 2-tank dive US$45, good boat, friendly; *Ecotour Caraibe*, C 1 Sur between Av 5 y 10, small groups, safe, friendly, inexpensive; *Studio Blue*, C Dr Salas, safe diving, there are many others, shop around. It is also possible to go cavern diving in Cenotes.

Local information
● **Accommodation**
Prices rise 50% around Christmas.

L2 *Meliá Mayan Cozumel*, in northern hotel zone, 5 km from airport, T 20072, F 21599; *El Cozumeleño*, also in N zone, T 20149, F 20381, good, but like all hotels in this area, a bit inconvenient. South of San Miguel are *Stouffer Presidente*, T 20322, F 21360, first class, but some distance from town; *Fiesta Inn*, T 22900, F 21301, linked to beach by tunnel, and 5 km S, new *Fiesta Cozumel*, 4-star; *La Ceiba*, T 20844, F 20065, and others (all in the **L2-A1** range); **A3** *Tontan*, 3 km N of town (taxi US$1) on waterfront, pool, clean, safe, snorkelling, cheap restaurant, rec.

Hotels in San Miguel town: in **A2-3** range *Bahía*, Av Rafael Melgar y C 3 Sur (above *Kentucky Fried Chicken*), a/c, phone, cable TV, fridge, even-numbered rooms have balcony, T 20209,

F 21387, rec; *Barracuda*, Av Rafael Melgar 628, T 20002, F 20884, popular with divers; *Mesón San Miguel*, on the plaza, T 20233, F 21820; *Plaza Cozumel*, C 2 Nte 3, T 22711, F 20066, a/c, TV, phone, pool, restaurant, car hire, laundry.

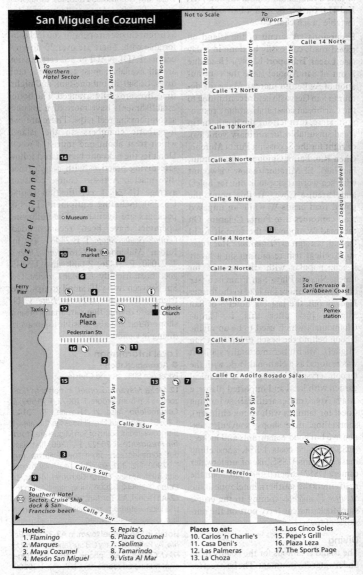

San Miguel de Cozumel

Not to Scale — To Airport

To Northern Hotel Sector

Cozumel Channel

Calle 14 Norte
Calle 12 Norte
Calle 10 Norte
Calle 8 Norte
Calle 6 Norte
Calle 4 Norte
Calle 2 Norte

Av 5 Norte
Av 10 Norte
Av 15 Norte
Av 20 Norte
Av 25 Norte
Av Lic Pedro Joaquin Coldwell

Museum
Flea market

Ferry Pier
Taxis

Main Plaza
Pedestrian Sts

Catholic Church

Av Benito Juárez

To San Gervasio & Caribbean Coast

Pemex station

Calle 1 Sur
Calle Dr Adolfo Rosado Salas
Calle 3 Sur
Calle Morelos
Calle 5 Sur
Calle 7 Sur

Av 5 Sur
Av 10 Sur
Av 15 Sur
Av 20 Sur
Av 25 Sur

To Southern Hotel Sector, Cruise Ship dock & San Francisco beach

Hotels:
1. Flamingo
2. Marques
3. Maya Cozumel
4. Mesón San Miguel
5. Pepita's
6. Plaza Cozumel
7. Saolima
8. Tamarindo
9. Vista Al Mar

Places to eat:
10. Carlos 'n Charlie's
11. Casa Deni's
12. Las Palmeras
13. La Choza
14. Los Cinco Soles
15. Pepe's Grill
16. Plaza Leza
17. The Sports Page

B range hotels inc: *Maya Cozumel*, C 5 Sur 4, T 20011, F 20781, a/c, pool, good value; *Safari*, T 20101, F 20661, a/c; *Soberanis*, Av Rafael Melgar 471, T 20246, a/c, restaurant terrace bar; *Tamarindo*, C 4 Nte 421, entre 20 y 25, T/F 23614, bed and breakfast, 3 rooms, shared kitchen, hammocks, dive gear storage and rinse tank, purified drinking water, laundry, safe deposit box, TV, run by Eliane and Jorge, Spanish, English and French spoken, child care on request; and *Vista del Mar*, Av R Melgar 45, T 20545, nr ferry deck, pool, a/c, restaurant, parking, good value.

C *Al Marestal*, C 10 y 25 Av Nte, T 20822, spacious, clean rooms, fan or a/c, cool showers, swimming pool, very good; **C** *Elizabeth*, Adolfo Rosado Salas 44, T 20330, a/c, suites with fridge and stove, also has villas at C 3 Sur con Av 25 Sur; 2 doors away is **C** *Flores*, a/c, D with fan; **C** *López*, on plaza, C Sur 7 A, T 20108, hot showers, clean, main square, no meals; **C** *Marqués*, 5 Av Sur between 1 Sur and A R Salas, T 20677, a/c, cheaper with fan, rec; close by are *Mary Carmen* and *El Pirata*, both C but cheaper with fan; *Posada Cozumel*, C 4 Nte 3, T 20314, pool, showers, a/c, cheaper with fan, clean.

D *Blanquita*, 10 Nte, T 21190, comfortable, clean, friendly, owner speaks English, rents snorkelling gear and motor-scooters, rec; *José de León*, Av Pedro J Coldwell y 17 C Sur, fairly clean, showers; *Posada del Charro*, 1 block E of *José de León*, same owner, same facilities; **D** *Flamingo*, C 6 Nte 81, T 21264, showers, fan, clean, family-run, good value, rec; **D** *Kary*, 25 Av Sur y A R Salas, T 22011, a/c, showers, pool, clean; *Paraíso Caribe*, 15 Av Nte y C 10, fan, showers, clean; **D** *Pepita's*, 15 Av Sur 120, T 20098, a/c, fan, fridge, owner, Eduardo Ruiz, speaks English, Spanish, French, Italian, German and Mayan, clean, rec.

E *Posada Letty*, C 1 Sur y Av 15 Sur, clean, hot water, good value, rec; **E** *Saolima*, A R Salas 260, T 20886, clean, fan, showers, hot water, rec.

Camping: is not permitted although there are two suitable sites on the S shore. Try asking for permission at the army base.

Places to eat

In general, it is much cheaper to eat in town than at the resort hotels to the N or S. Very few hotels in town have restaurants since there are so many other places to eat. *Las Palmeras*, at the pier (people-watching spot), rec, very popular for breakfast, opens 0700, always busy;

Morgans, main square, elegant, expensive, good; *Plaza Leza*, main square, excellent and reasonable; *La Choza*, A R Salas 198, expensive, Mexico City food, rec; *Miss Dollar*, AR Salas y Av 20, good Mexican food, US$2 *comidas*, very friendly; *Karen's Pizza and Grill*, Av 5 Nte between Av B Juárez and C 2 Nte, pizza cheap, good; *Western Grill*, Av 5, nr Zócalo, excellent breakfasts; *Gatto Pardo*, 10 Av Sur 121, good pizzas and try their 'tequila slammers'; *Café del Puerto*, 2nd floor by pier, South Seas style; *El Moro*, 75 Bis Nte 124, between 4 y 2, good, closed Thur; *Santiago's Grill*, 15 Av Sur y A R Salas, excellent, medium price-range, popular with divers; also popular with divers is *Las Tortugas*, 10 Av Nte, just N of square, good in the evening; *El Capi Navegante*, 2 locations: by market for lunch, and C 3 y 10 Av Sur, more up market, seafood at each; *Alfalfa*, C 5 Sur, between RE Melgar and 5 Av, mostly vegetarian meals but owner Dawne Detraz expanding with more fish and chicken and health food shop, daily hot special US$3 with salad and drink, excellent coffee, friendly, highly rec; *La Yucatequita*, 9 C Sur y 10 Av Sur, genuine Mayan food, closes at 2130, best to go day before and discuss menu; *La Misión*, Av Benito Juárez y 10 Av Nte, good food, friendly atmosphere; *Pepe's Grill*, waterfront, 2 blocks S of pier, expensive and excellent; *Acuario*, on beach 6 blocks S of pier, famous for seafood, aquarium in restaurant (ask to see the tanks at the back); *Carlos and Charlie's* restaurant/bar, popular, 2nd floor on waterfront 2 blocks N of pier; *Pancho's Backyard*, Rafael Melgar 27, in *Los Cinco Soles* shopping complex. Mexican food and wine elegantly served, good food; *Mi Chabalita*, 10 Av Sur between C 1 Sur and C Salas, friendly, cheap and good Mexican food; *Pepe Pelícano*, 2 houses left of *Saolima Hotel*, cheap and clean; *Casa Deni's*, C 1 Sur 164, close to Plaza, open air restaurant, very good, moderate prices; *The Sports Page*, C 2 Nte y Av 5, US-style, breakfasts, burgers, steaks, lobster, satellite TV, money exchange, phones for USA; US-style breakfasts also at *Los Cocos*, next to ProDive on A R Salas; *Diamond Bakery*, 15 Av y 1 Av Sur, inconspicuous sign, good bread and pastries, also have a café on the waterfront; *Zermatt*, Av 5 y C 4 Nte, good bakery.

Naked Turtle, on E side (has basic rooms to let); *Mescalito's*, see above, another place, like *The Sports Page*, to write a message on your T-shirt and leave it on the ceiling; several other bar restaurants on the E side.

● **Banks & money changers**
4 banks on the main square, all exchange money in am only, but not at same hours; **Bancomer** has ATM machines. *Casas de cambio* on Av 5 Nte (eg next to Banco Atlántida) and around square, 3.5% commission, open longer hours.

● **Entertainment**
Nightclubs: *Joman's* (very seedy), *Scara-mouche* (the best, Av R Melgar y C A R Salas), *Neptuno* (Av R Melgar y C 11, S of centre, these two are state-of-the-art discos), as well as hotel nightclubs.

● **Laundry**
On A R Salas between Avs 5 and 10, coin op or service wash. Cheap laundry opp *Posada Letty*.

● **Post & telecommunications**
Post Office: Av Rafael Melgar y C 7 Sur.

Telephone: credit card LADA phones on main square at corner of Av Juárez y Av 5, or on A R Salas, just up from Av 5 Sur, opp *Roberto's Black Coral Studio* (if working). For calls to the USA go to *The Sports Page*. Telmex phone offices on the main square next to *Restaurant Plaza Leza*, open 0800-2300, and on A R Salas between Avs 10 and 15. There are also expensive Computel offices in town, eg at the cruise ship dock.

● **Shopping**
Film: two shops develop film, both quite expensive (about US$20 for 36 prints). Best to wait till you get home.

● **Tour companies & travel agents**
Aviomar, Av 5 No 8a, and 2 y 4 Nte, T 24622, F 21728.

● **Tourist offices**
Sectur tourist office in Plaza Cozumel on Av Juárez, between 5 Av and 10 Av, 1st floor, English-speaking service in am, opens 1800 in pm. On arrival, cross the road from the pier to the square where lots of information kiosks give maps, tour information, etc. A good map (*The Brown Map*), inc reef locations, is available from stores and shops. *The Blue Guide*, free, has maps and practical details, available everywhere. Booklets on archaeological sites and the region, and Mexico City newspapers are available at the *papelería* on the E side of the square.

● **Transport**
Local Bus: the main road around Cozumel is paved, but public buses serve only the expensive hotels N of town. **Bike hire**: it is best to hire a bicycle (quiet) when touring around the island so one can see wildlife: iguanas, turtles, birds.

Rental charges are US$5 for 12 hrs, US$8 for 24 hrs, eg from *Splash*, on C 6 Nte, T 20502, 0800-2000. **Taxi**: all carry an official price list. Downtown fare US$1.15; to N or S hotel zones US$2.35; San Francisco beach US$10; Maya ruins US$30; island tour inc San Gervasio US$50. **Vehicle rental**: many agencies for cars, jeeps and mopeds. Eg Avis, Budget, Hertz, National, and local companies. Car hire ranges from about US$55 a day for a VW Beetle to US$70 minimum for a jeep. Discounted vehicle hire plus free breakfast at a 5-star hotel in return for listening for 1 hr about an offer to buy holiday units, no commitments, "a great deal for the budget traveller". Ask at information desks around town. Scooter rental is US$27 a day high season, US$22 low. One Pemex filling station, at Av Juárez y Av 30; beware overcharging. If taking a moped be aware of traffic laws, helmets must be worn, illegal parking is subject to fines, etc (single women should not ride alone on the eastern side of the island).

Air Cozumel-Mexico City direct with Mexicana, US$122, via Mérida (40 mins); Mexicana also flies daily to Miami; Continental to Houston and Northwest to Detroit and Minneapolis; Aero Caribe to Cancún, Chichén Itzá and Playa del Carmen.

Ferry See under Playa del Carmen for passenger ferries. Car ferry goes from Puerto Morelos twice a day (inc 1200): US$27 for a car, US$3/passenger; the entrance to the car ferry on Cozumel is just past the cruise ship dock. Because of the treatment cars receive on the ferry, it may be better to leave your car on the mainland and do without it on the island.

XCARET

There are some Maya ruins on the mainland at **Xcaret**, a turnoff left on Route 307 to Tulum, after Playa del Carmen. This was once an undeveloped spot, with the unrestored ruins near three linked *cenotes* and sea water lagoons. The Maya site, an ancient port called Pole, was the departure point for voyages to Cozumel. It has now been redesigned as a daytrip from Cancún. The ruins and lagoons form part of a clean well-kept park, catering exclusively for day-trippers, which costs US$18.50 (children under 5 years free) to enter. This entitles you to visit the small ruins, the aviary, the beach, lagoon and inlet, to take an underground river trip (life vest included) and to use all chairs, hammocks and *palapas*. Everything else is extra: food and drink (none may be brought in), snorkel rental (US$7), snorkel lessons, reef trips (US$10), diving, horse riding (US$30) and lockers (for which you have to pay US$1 each time you lock the door). There are also dolphins in pens with which you may swim for US$50. No sun tan lotion may be worn in the sea, but there is a film of oils in the sea nonetheless. Buses from Playa del Carmen leave you at the turnoff (US$0.65), by a roadside restaurant which is very clean (accepts Visa). This is a 1 km walk from the entrance to Xcaret. The alternative is to take a taxi, or a tour from Playa del Carmen or Cancún (in a multicoloured bus). You can also walk along the beach from Playa del Carmen, 3 hrs.

Paamul, about 92 km S of Cancún, is a fine beach on a bay, planned for development, with chalets (C with bath, fan, terrace for hammocks, comfortable, pretty, clean, rec) and campsites (recommended). Snorkelling and diving. 2nd-class buses from Cancún and Playa del Carmen pass.

AKUMAL

A luxury resort, 20 km N of Tulum, is reached easily by bus from there or from Playa del Carmen (30 mins). Cove owned by Mexican Skin Divers Society, 102 km S Cancún. **L2** *Hotel Club Akumal Caribe*, restaurant (there is a small supermarket nearby at Villas Mayas), poor service, overpriced, no entertainment, excellent beach, linked to two buildings separated by *Villas Mayas*, with coral reef only 100m offshore. Eat at restaurant marked *Comidas Económicas* outside the gate. **L2** *Club Aventuras Akumal*, T (987) 22887, all inclusive resort owned by Oasis group, small pool, on pleasant beach. In addition at *Villas Mayas*, bungalows A1, with bath, comfortable, some with kitchens, on beach, snorkelling equipment for hire, US$6 per day, restaurant with poor service. Recom-

mended as base for excursions to Xelhá, Tulum and Cobá. There is a small lagoon 3 km N of Akumal, good snorkelling. **Playa Aventuras** is a huge beach resort S of Akumal. **L2** *Club Puerto Aventuras*, another Oasis hotel, sandwiched between the sea and marina, all inclusive with 309 rooms. Two ferries run daily to Cozumel. Also just S of Akumal are **Chemuyil** (*palapas*, thatched shelters for hammocks, US$4, free shower, expensive restaurant, laundry facilities) and **Xcacel** (campground has water, bathrooms, cold showers and restaurant, very clean, US$2 pp, vehicles free, snorkel hire US$5 a day, beautiful swimming in the bay). Xcacel has a cenote, with excellent clear water and underwater rock formations (Ron's dive shop with gear for hire). Ask guards if you can go on turtle protection patrol at night (May-July). The large underwater caves of Cenote Dos Ojos are being explored; dive shop at Dos Ojos, or ask for the instructor, Ron, at Xcacel.

LAGUNA XELHA

13 km N of Tulum, 122 km from Cancún (bus from Playa del Carmen, 45 mins), this beautiful clear lagoon, is full of fish, but no fishing allowed as it is a national park (open 0800-1630), entry US$10. Snorkelling gear can be rented at US$7 for a day, but it is often in poor repair; better to rent from your hotel. Lockers cost US$1. Arrive as early as possible to see fish as the lagoon is full of tourists throughout most of the day. Snorkelling areas are limited by fencing (you need to dive down about a metre because above that level the water is cold and fresh with few fish; below it is the warm, fish-filled salt water). Bungalows, first-class hotels, fast food restaurants being built. Very expensive food and drink. There is a marvellous jungle path to one of the lagoon bays. Xelhá ruins (known also as Los Basadres) are located across the road from the beach of the same name. Entry US$3.35, few tourists but not much to see. You may have to jump the fence to visit; there is a beautiful cenote at the end

of the ruins where you can have a lovely swim. Small ruins of **Ak** are near Xelhá. Closer to Tulum, at **Tancáh**, are newly-discovered bright post-classical Maya murals but they are sometimes closed to the public.

TULUM

The Tulum ruins, Maya-Toltec, are 131 km S of Cancún, 1 km off the main road. They are 12th century, with city walls of white stone atop coastal cliffs. The temples were dedicated to the worship of the Falling God, or the Setting Sun, represented as a falling character over nearly all the W-facing doors (Cozumel was the home of the Rising Sun). The same idea is reflected in the buildings, which are wider at the top than at the bottom.

The main structure is the Castillo, which commands a view of both the sea and the forested Quintana Roo lowlands stretching westwards. All the Castillo's openings face W, as do most, but not all, of the doorways at Tulum. Look for the alignment of the Falling God on the temple of that name (to the left of the Castillo) with the pillar and the back door in the House of the Chultún (the nearest building in the centre group to the entrance). The majority of the main structures are roped off so that you cannot climb the Castillo, nor get close to the surviving frescoes, especially on the Temple of the Frescoes. In 1993 the government began a major improvement and conservation programme to improve facilities at the site.

Tulum is these days crowded with tourists (best time to visit is between 0800 and 0900). Take towel and swimsuit if you wish to scramble down from the ruins to one of the two beaches for a swim (the larger of the two is less easy to get to). The reef is from 600 to 1,000m from the shore, so if you wish to snorkel you must either be a strong swimmer, or take a boat trip.

● **Admission** The site is open 0800-1700, about 2 hrs needed to view at leisure (entry US$2, students with Mexican ID free, Sun free). There is a tourist complex at the entrance to the ruins. Guide books can be bought in the shops; Panorama guide book is interesting, others available. Local guides can also be hired. The parking area is near Highway 307, and a handicraft market. A small train takes you from the parking area to the ruins for US$1, or it is an easy 500m walk. The paved road continues down the coast to Bocapaila and beyond, access by car to this road from the car park is now forbidden. To reach the road S of the ruins, access is possible 1 km from Tulum village.

Public buses drop passengers at El Crucero, a crossroads 500m N of the car park for Tulum Ruinas (an easy walk); at the crossroads are some hotels, a shop (will exchange TCs), on the opposite side of the road a naval base and airstrip, and a little way down Highway 307 a Pemex station. The village of **Tulum** is 4 km S of El Crucero. A taxi from the village to the ruins costs US$1.50. It is not very large and has a post office but no bank; TCs can be changed at the offices of the GOPI Construction Company, though not at a very good rate; there are shops and a hotel.

Local information
● **Accommodation**

When arriving by bus, alight at El Crucero for the ruins and nearby accommodation. Note that since the damage caused by Hurricane Roxane in Oct 95, electricity supply may still be intermittent along this stretch of coast.

At El Crucero: **C** *El Faisán y El Venado*, TV, a/c, OK, restaurant serving pizzas, Mexican dishes and very expensive drinks; across the road is **E** *Hotel El Crucero de Tulum*, much more basic, damp, dirty, but a/c, hot water, staff unhelpful, good restaurant with shop attached. Almost opp bus stop is a new hotel, **C**, large, clean, a/c, parking, with restaurant (24 hrs), good food and service; and *Chilam-Balam*, across the road, also serves good food.

At Tulum village: **D-E** *Hotel Maya*, good, a/c or fan, shower, clean, rec, restaurant with slow service, nr bus stop, small shop, parking in front. Near *Hotel Maya* is *La Isla*, Italian-owned, very friendly, great coffee and Italian/Mexican food, moderate prices. Several chicken restaurants and *Leonor's* for fish and Mexican food, good but pricey.

A new hotel is under construction at the site.

To reach the following accommodation it is better to get off the bus in town and take a taxi (US$3.25). Accommodation is generally expensive for the facilities offered, and in high season cabañas are difficult to get. Establishments are listed according to proximity to the ruins (in all these places, beware theft); E *Cabañas El Mirador*, small, quiet, cabins (won't rent to singles), hammocks available F, camping G, 2 showers, use of restaurant toilets (clean), expensive bar and restaurant, slow service, 10 mins' walk from ruins; next is E *Santa Fe*, about 1½ km from the ruins (a path leads along the beach and then through forest to the ruins, 20 mins), basic cabañas, new toilets and showers, US$1 extra for mosquito net, hammocks or tents, G (free camping possible further up the beach), has a restaurant, good breakfasts and fish dinners, reggae music, English, French and Italian spoken, basic toilets, not very safe; next, with good restaurant, are *Cabañas Don Armando*, T 43856/ 44539/44437, cabañas from E to C for up to 4, no singles, prices variable, the best, very popular, most (but not all) staff are friendly and helpful, mixed reports on atmosphere, you can have problems if you don't speak good Spanish, good restaurant, bar with noisy disco till 0200. Next along is the Fishing Association, rent out cabañas, G, friendly. C-E *Los Gatos*, cabins on beach, clean, nice atmosphere, price depends on whether in room or hammock, torch/flashlight necessary, food poor value; E *Cabañas Mar Caraibe*, 15 mins from ruins, C *Bungalows Paraíso*, 3 km from ruins, nice cabins with fan, hot shower, clean, electricity 1800-2200; A3 *Sian Ka'an/Osho Oasis* (owned by Sanyasins), for reservations phone US office T/F (707) 778 1320, 5 km S from ruins by beautiful secluded beach, wooden huts, well-equipped, electricity, mosquito net, good showers, washing facilities, clean, full board option for US$18, excellent vegetarian food, meditation and yoga groups, relaxed, highly rec, credit cards not accepted; on same road, 500m N is *Zamas Cabañas*, simple restaurant on beach, highly rec; *La Perla*, 5 km S of Tulum, cabañas, F pp, camping and restaurant, comfortable, good food, family atmosphere, nr beach, rec (Monica Koestinger, Lista de Correos, Tulum, Quintana Roo); next to *La Perla* is D *Nosho Tunich*, 1 hr walk from ruins, clean cabañas, good food; C *Hotel Posada Tulum*, 8 km S of the ruins on the beach, has an expensive restaurant. *Anna y José* restaurant, 6 km S of ruins, rec, which also has cabañas

(A3) and rooms (B), some are right on the beach, very clean, comfortable, very hospitable, taxi to Tulum, US$2.50. For places to stay in Sian Ka'an Biosphere Reserve, see below.

● **Banks & money changers**
Travellers' cheques can be changed at a cambio in the corner of the shops nr the ruins.

● **Post & telecommunications**
Telephone: long-distance phones in ADO terminal in town.

● **Sports**
Diving: Buzos Maya, nr *Don Armando*, run by American, John, good value, rec for scuba, snorkelling and fishing. Many untrained snorkelling and diving outfits, take care.

● **Transport**
Buses 2nd class buses on the Cancún-Playa del Carmen-Felipe Carrillo Puerto-Chetumal route stop at Tulum; also 3 Inter Playa buses a day from Cancún, US$4.25. To Felipe Carrillo Puerto, several between 0600-1200 and 1600-2200, 1 hr, US$2, continuing to **Chetumal**, 2nd class, US$7, 1st class US$8.50, 4 hrs. To Cobá: the Playa del Carmen-Tulum-Cobá-Valladolid bus passes El Crucero at 0600, 1100 and 1800 (in the other direction buses pass Tulum at 0715 and 1545, all times approximate, may leave 15 mins early). Fare Tulum-Cobá US$1.35, 45 mins. To Mérida, several daily, US$7, 2nd class, 6 hrs. To Tizimín daily at 1400, via Cancún and Valladolid. Autobuses del Caribe offices are next door to *Hotel Maya*. Buy tickets here rather than wait for buses at the crossroads, but this still does not ensure getting a seat. It may be better to go to Playa del Carmen (US$1.40) for more connections to nearby destinations. If travelling far, take a bus to Felipe Carrillo Puerto and transfer to ADO there. **Taxis**: Tulum town to ruins US$2, to the cabañas US$3.25; to Cobá about US$25. **Bicycles**: can be hired in the village at US$1/hr, a good way to visit local centres (Cristal and Escondido are rec as much cheaper, US$2, and less commercialized than Xcaret).

SIAN KA'AN BIOSPHERE RESERVE

The **Reserve** covers 1.3 million acres of the Quintana Roo coast. About one third is covered in tropical forest, one third in savannas and mangrove and one third coastal and marine habitats, including 110 km of barrier reef. Mammals include jaguar, puma, ocelot and other cats, monkeys, tapir, peccaries, manatee and deer; turtles

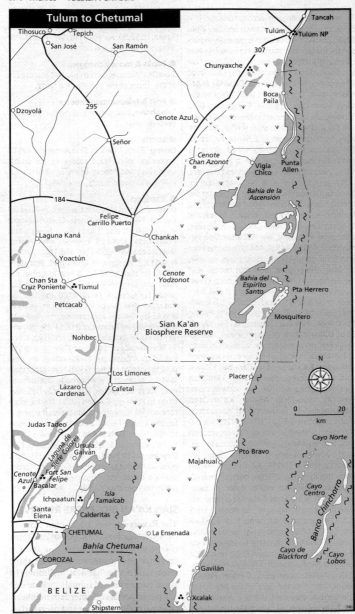

Tulum to Chetumal

Tancah
Tulúm
Tulúm NP
307
Chunyaxche
Boca Paila
Tihosuco
Tepich
San José
San Ramón
Cenote Azul
Dzoyolá
295
Señor
Cenote Chan Azonot
Vigía Chico
Punta Allen
Bahía de la Ascensión
184
Felipe Carrillo Puerto
Chankah
Laguna Kaná
Yoactún
Cenote Yodzonot
Bahía del Espíritu Santo
Pta Herrero
Chan Sta Cruz Poniente
Tixmul
Petcacab
Mosquitero
Nohbec
Sian Ka'an Biosphere Reserve
N
Los Limones
Placer
Lázaro Cardenas
Cafetal
0 20
km
Judas Tadeo
Cayo Norte
Laguna de Siete Colores
Ursula Galván
Pto Bravo
Cenote Azul
Fort San Felipe
Bacalar
Majahual
Cayo Centro
Banco Chinchorro
Ichpaatun
Isla Tamalcab
Santa Elena
Calderitas
CHETUMAL
La Ensenada
Cayo de Blackford
Cayo Lobos
COROZAL
Bahía Chetumal
Gavilán
BELIZE
Xcalak
Shipstern

nest on the beaches; there are crocodiles and a wide variety of land and aquatic birds. For all information, go to the office of Los Amigos de Sian Ka'an, Plaza América, Av Cobá 5, 3rd floor, suites 48-50, Cancún (Apdo Postal 770, 77500 Cancún, T 849583), open 0900-1500, 1800-2000, very helpful. Do not try to get there independently without a car. Los Amigos run tours to the Reserve, US$115 for a full day, starting at 0700, everything included: in winter the tour goes through a canal, in summer it goes bird watching, in both cases a visit to a Maya ruin, a cenote, snorkelling, all equipment, breakfast and evening meal are included. 2-day camping trips can be arranged. 2-hr boat trips through the Biosphere can be taken for US$50. Trips can also be arranged through *Cabanas Ana y José*, near Tulum, US$50, daily except Sun. It is possible to drive into the Reserve from Tulum village as far as Punta Allen (beyond that you need a launch). From the S it is possible to drive to Punta Herrero (unmade road, see **Majahual**, below). No explanations are available for those going independently.

● **Accommodation** At **Punta Allen** is a small fishing village with houses for rent (cooking facilities), and a good, non-touristy restaurant, *La Cantina* (US$3-4 for fish). There are also 2 comfortable *cabañas* at a place called **A3** *Rancho Sol Caribe*, with bath, restaurant, rec. Reservations to: Diane and Michael Sovereign, Apdo Postal 67, Tulum, CP 77780, T 12091/F 12092. **Punta Herrero** is 6 hrs from Chetumal, 10 from Cancún; *rancheros* are very hospitable, camping is possible but take all food and plenty of insect repellent. In the Reserve, 8 km S of Tulum, are the quiet, pleasant **A2** *Cabañas Los Arrecifes*, with smart chalets on the beach and others behind, cheaper, with good fish restaurant shaped like a ship (no electricity), limited menu. 100m away are **D** *Cabañas de Tulum*, also with good restaurant, clean cabins with shower, electricity 1730-2100; interesting fish in the cenote opp, take taxi there (US$5-6 from ruins car park), empty white beaches; *Pez Maya* and *Boca Paila* are expensive fishing lodges; *Casa Blanca* is an exclusive hotel reached only by small plane; *Rancho Retiro*, camping US$2, food and beer served, very relaxed atmosphere.

The ruins of **Chumyaxche**, three pyramids (partly overgrown), are on the left-hand side of the road to Felipe Carrillo Puerto, 18 km S of Tulum (they are mosquito-infested). Entry US$4. Beyond the last pyramid is Laguna Azul, which is good for swimming and snorkelling in blue, clean water (you do not have to pay to visit the pool if you do not visit the pyramids).

The road linking Tulum with the large but little-excavated city of Cobá (see below) turns off the main Highway 307 just before Tulum Pueblo. This road joins the *vía libre* Valladolid-Cancún road at **Nuevo Xcan**, thus greatly shortening the distance between Chichén Itzá and Tulum (do not take the *cuota* road which no longer exits at Nuevo Xcan). The Cobá-Valladolid bus passes Nuevo Xcan (no hotel but the owner of the shop where the road branches off to Cobá may offer you a room). There is an *aduana* post in Nuevo Xcan. If going from Valladolid or Cancún to Cobá, look for the *Villas Arqueológicas* sign at Nuevo Xcan. Note, many maps show a road from Cobá to Chemax, W of Xcan. This road does not exist; the only road from the N to Cobá is from Nuevo Xcan. For drivers, there is no Pemex station between Cancún and Valladolid, or Cancún-Cobá-Tulúm, or Valladolid-Cobá-Tulúm, all are journeys of 150 km without a fill-up.

Between Nuevo Xcan and Cobá is the tiny village of **Punta Laguna**, which has a lake and forest, preserved through the efforts of ecotourists. Ask for Scrapio to show you round; he does not speak English, and depends mainly on tourists for his income.

COBA

An important Maya city in the 8th and 9th centuries AD, whose population is estimated to have been between 40,000 and 50,000, but which was abandoned for unknown reasons, is 47 km inland from Tulum. The present day village of Cobá lies on either side of Lago Cobá, surrounded by dense jungle. It is a quiet friendly village, with few tourists staying overnight.

The entrance to the ruins is at the end of the lake between the two parts of the village. A second lake, Lago Macanxoc, is within the site. There are turtles and many fish in the lakes. It is a good bird-watching area. Both lakes and their surrounding forest can be seen from the summit of the Iglesia, the tallest structure in the Cobá group. There are three other groups of buildings to visit: the Macanxoc group, mainly stelae, about 1.5 km from the Cobá group; Las Pinturas, 1 km NE of Macanxoc, a temple and the remains of other buildings which had columns in their construction; the Nohoch Mul group, at least another km from Las Pinturas. Nohoch Mul has the tallest pyramid in the northern Yucatán, a magnificent structure, from which the views of the jungle on all sides are superb. You will not find at Cobá the great array of buildings which can be seen at Chichén Itzá or Uxmal, nor the compactness of Tulum. Instead, the delight of the place is the architecture in the jungle, with birds, butterflies, spiders and lizards, and the many uncovered structures which hint at the vastness of the city in its heyday (the urban extension of Cobá is put at some 70 sq km). An unusual feature is the network of ancient roads, known as *sacbes* (white roads), which connect the groups in the site and are known to have extended across the entire Maya Yucatán. Over 40 *sacbes* pass through Cobá, some local, some of great length, such as the 100 km road to Yaxuná in Yucatán state.

At the lake tucans may be seen very early; also look out for greenish-blue and brown mot-mots in the early morning. The guards at the site are very strict about opening and closing time so it is difficult to gain entry to see the dawn or sunset from a temple.

The paved road into Cobá ends at Lago Cobá; to the left are the ruins, to the right *Villas Arqueológicas*.

● **Admission** Cobá is becoming more popular as a destination for tourist buses, which come in at 1030; arrive before that to avoid the crowds and the heat (ie on the 0430 bus from Valladolid, if not staying in Cobá). Take insect repellent. The site is open 0800-1700, entry US$2.50, free on Sun. Guide books: Bloomgarten's *Tulum and Cobá*, and *Descriptive Guide book to Cobá* by Prof Gualberto Zapata Alonzo, which is a little unclear about dates and details, but is still useful and has maps. Free map from *Hotel Restaurant Bocadito*.

Local information
● **Accommodation**

B *Villas Arqueológicas* (Club Méditerranée), about 2 km from site on lake shore, open to non members, excellent, clean and quiet, a/c, swimming pool, good restaurant with moderate prices, but expensive beer. Do not arrive without a reservation, especially at weekends; on the other hand, making a reservation by phone seems to be practically impossible.

In the village, on the street leading to the main road, is **E** *Hotel Restaurant Bocadito*, run down, spartan rooms with fan, intermittent water supply, poor security, good but expensive restaurant (which is popular with tour groups), books and handicrafts for sale, rec.

● **Places to eat**

There are plenty of restaurants in the village, on the road to *Villas Arqueológicas* and on the road to the ruins, they are all quite pricey, also a grocery store by *El Bocadito* and souvenir shops. *Nicte-Ha*, good and friendly; *Pirámides*, on corner of track leading to *Villas Arqueológicas*, highly rec.

● **Banks & money changers**

Sterling Store, opp entrance to ruins.

● **Transport**

Local Buses into the village turn round at the road end. Buses are 3 a day to Valladolid, coming from Playa del Carmen and Tulum, passing through at 0630, 1130 and 1830, 2 hrs to Valladolid, US$2.50; 2 buses a day to Tulum and Playa at 0630 and 1500, US$1 to Tulum. A taxi to Tulum costs around US$25. If you miss the bus there is a taxi to be found at *El Bocadito*.

FELIPE CARRILLO PUERTO

The cult of the 'talking cross' was founded here (see page 406). The Santuario de la Cruz Parlante is 5 blocks W of the Pemex station on Highway 307. The beautiful main square is dominated by the Catholic church, built by the Cruzob in the 19th century. Legend has it that the unfinished bell tower will only be completed when the descendants of those who heard the talking cross reassert control of the region. In the plaza is lots of playground equipment for children. (With thanks to Suzanne Elise Tourville, St Louis, Missouri.)

● **Accommodation & places to eat** *Hotel Carrillo Puerto* has been rec; **C** *El Faisán y El Venado*, 2 blocks NE of main square, mixed reports on cleanliness, but hot water and good value restaurant, popular with locals; **D** *Tulum*, with better restaurant; **E** *Chan Santa Cruz*, just off the plaza, good, basic, clean and friendly (*Restaurante 24 Horas* is open 24 hrs, OK); **E** *Hotel Esquivel*, just off Plaza, fair, noisy; **D** *San Ignacio*, nr Pemex, good value, a/c, bath, towels, TV, secure car park; next door is restaurant *Danburger Maya*, good food, reasonable prices, helpful; **F** *María Isabel*, on same road, clean, friendly, laundry service, quiet, safe parking; *Restaurant Addy*, on main road, S of town, good, simple. There are a few food shops in the village selling sweet breads, and mineral water.

● **Transport** Bus station opp Pemex. Autotransportes del Caribe (Playa Express) to Cancún daily from 0600, 1st and 2nd class to Tulum, US$2, and Playa del Carmen en route. Bus Felipe Carrillo Puerto-Mérida, via Muná, US$10, 4½ hrs; to Valladolid, 2nd class, 2 hrs, US$3.75; to Chetumal, 1st class, 2 hrs, US$3.35.

CHETUMAL

(*Pop* 120,000; *State pop* 1995 703,442; *Phone code* 99) Capital of the state of Quintana Roo, Chetumal is now being developed for tourism (albeit slowly). It is a free port with clean wide streets, and a pleasant waterfront with walks, parks and trees from where you can see Belize. It is 240 km S of Tulum. The Chetumal Bay has been designated a Natural Protected Area for manatees, which includes a manatee sanctuary.

Places of interest

The 'paseo' near the waterfront on Sun night is worth seeing. The State Congress building has a mural showing the history of Quintana Roo. Avenida Héroes is the main shopping street. Good for foreign foodstuffs – cheaper at the covered market in the outskirts than in the centre. A new commercial centre is being built at the site of the old bus station. **Museo de la Cultura Maya** is on Av Héroes de Chapultepec by the market, good models of sites and touchscreen computers explaining Mayan calendar and glyphs, some explanations in English, guided tours available, good bookshop with English magazines, open Tues-Thur, 0900-1900, Fri and Sat 0900-2000, Sun 0900-1400, US$1.75, cold a/c, highly rec.

Local information
● **Accommodation**
Accommodation may be a problem during the holiday season.

A1 *Los Cocos*, Héroes de Chapultepec 138, T 20544, reductions for AAA members, a/c, pool, restaurant, breakfast rec; **A3** *Continental Caribe/Holiday Inn*, Av Héroes 171, T 21100, F 21676; **A3** *El Marqués*, Av Lázaro Cárdenas 121, T 22998, 5 blocks from centre, fan, a/c, hot water, restaurant, rec; *Marlon*, Av Benito Juárez, new, no details as yet.

C *Real Azteca*, Belice 186, T 20720, cheerful, friendly, but no hot shower (2nd floor rooms best, but still not too good).

D *Caribe Princess*, Av A Obregón 168, T 20520, a/c, TV, good, very clean, no restaurant, rec; **D-F** *Jacaranda*, Av Obregón 201, T 21455, clean; **D-E** *Luz María*, Carmen de Merino 204, T 20202, friendly but not very clean, owner speaks English.

E *Big Ben*, Héroes 48-A, T 20965, clean, shabby, safe, cheaper rooms for 4, with bath; **E** *Brasilia*, Aguilar 186, T 20964, clean, quiet, some rooms small and dark, nowhere to leave luggage; **E** *Motel Casablanca*, Alvaro Obregón 312, clean, quiet, very good value, rec; **E** *Crystal*, Colón y Av Belize, fan, bath, parking; **E** *El Dorado*, Av 5 de Mayo 21, T 20316, hot water, a/c, very friendly, quiet, rec; **E** *María Dolores*, Alvaro Obregón 206, T 20508, bath, hot water, fan, clean, windows don't open, noisy, restaurant *Solsimar* downstairs good and popular; **E** *Tulum*, Héroes 2, T 20518, above market, noise starts 0530, but clean, with bath and fan, friendly, large rooms; **E** *Ucum*, Gandhi 4, T 20711 (no singles) with fan and bath, clean, pleasant, quiet, enclosed car park, good value;

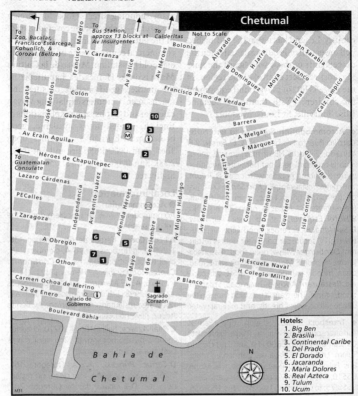

Chetumal

Hotels:
1. Big Ben
2. Brasilia
3. Continental Caribe
4. Del Prado
5. El Dorado
6. Jacaranda
7. María Dolores
8. Real Azteca
9. Tulum
10. Ucum

E-F *Boston*, Belice 290, between bus station and centre, a/c, not very good; **E-F** *Cuartos Margot*, 5 de Mayo 30, some with bath, clean, charming.

F *Ejidal*, Av Independencia entre Obregón y P Blanco, bath, clean, rec. Plenty more.

Camping: *Sunrise of the Caribbean*, Trailer Park on the road to Calderitas, US$15 for car and 2 people, cold showers, electricity, laundry facilities, *palapas*, boat ramp.

Youth hostel: **G** pp, Calzada Veracruz y Alvaro Obregón, referred to as CREA, T 23465, CP 77050, hot water, clean, comfortable, friendly, good breakfast, rec, camping US$2.

● **Places to eat**
Next door to *Hotel Ucum*, reasonable, good value, rec. Cheap snacks at *Lonchería Ivette* on Mahatma Gandhi 154. *Pandoja*, Gandhi y

16 de Septiembre, good food; *La Charca de las Ranas Verdes*, Blvd Bahía, opp bandstand, cheap and good; *Pérez Quintas*, next door, good; *Chicho's Lobster House*, Blvd Bahía esq Vicente Guerrero, T 27249, expensive but good seafood, friendly; *Bambino Pizzas*, P Blanco 215, good; *Maria's*, 5 de Mayo y Obregón, delicious local food, good and inexpensive fish; *Sergio Pizza*, Obregón 182, pizzas, fish, and expensive steak meals, a/c, good drinks, excellent service; *La Cabaña Azul*, 5 de Mayo 23 nr waterfront, good and cheap; *Mar Caribe*, 22 de Enero entre F Madero y Independencia, snacks only. Good breakfasts at the *Hotel Los Cocos*, US$5 but well worth it. Several 1 block W of intersection of Héroes y Obregón, eg *Bienvenidos*, good. *Solsimar*, Obregón 206 (closed Sun), popular, reasonable prices; *El Vaticano*, popular with locals, good atmosphere,

cheap; *Arcada*, Héroes y Zaragoza, open 24 hrs, with mini-market at the back. Another area with many restaurants is about 4 blocks N of market, then 3 blocks W, eg *Barracuda*, good seafood. *Pacho Tec*, small lunch room next to electricity plant, try the chicken broth. Delicious yoghurt ice in shop opp market. Try *Safari* roadhouse in Calderitas suburb for enterprising nightlife. Good juices at *Jugos Xamach*, corner of Salvador y Quintana Roo, friendly local spot.

● **Banks & money changers**
For exchange, **Banamex**, Obregón y Juárez, changes TCs; **Banco Mexicano**, Juárez and Cárdenas, TCs or US$ cash, quick and courteous service. Banks do not change quetzales into pesos. Good rates at *Bodegas Blanco* supermarket beside bus terminal; will change US dollars and Belize dollars (only if you spend at least 15% of the total on their groceries!). Batty Bus ticket counter will change pesos into Belizean dollars. Try also *Casa Medina*, L Cárdenas. Pemex stations will accept US and Belizean dollars, but at poor rates for the latter. *San Francisco de Assisi* supermarket changes TCs, next to bus station.

● **Embassies & consulates**
Guatemala Av Héroes de Chapultepec 354, T 26565, open for visas, Mon-Fri 0900-1700. There is a Guatemalan consul in Belize, where **visas to Guatemala** may be obtained, see Guatemala **Information for travellers** for requirements and fees, usually takes 15 mins, 30 days only available, passport photo and photocopy of passport required. **Belize** Hon Consul, Lic Francisco Lechón Rosas, Av Alvaro Obregón 232-1, T 20100; visas usually given in 10 mins (US$25). **NB** A list of nationalities who do *NOT* need a visa for Belize is given in the Belize **Information for travellers** section. All others **must** have a visa in advance. The surest place to get one is in Mexico City at the Belize Embassy, or in Mérida.

● **Hospitals & medical services**
Malaria prophylaxis available from Centro de Salud, opp hospital (request tablets for 'paludismo').

● **Laundry**
Lavandería Automática 'Lava facil', corner of Héroes and Confederación Nacional Campesina.

● **Shopping**
Shops are open from 0800-1300 and 1800-2000. **Super San Francisco** supermarket, nr bus station, is better than the one behind *Arcada* restaurant.

● **Tour companies & travel agents**
Turismo Maya at *Hotel Continental Caribe* will arrange flights to and within Belize, T 20555. For a trip to Belize, the Cayes, or Guatemala, contact Moisés Vega Beall at the 24-hr restaurant *Arcada*, speaks good English, helpful in finding something to suit your budget and in dealing with paper work, eg immigration.

● **Tourist offices**
Secretaría Estatal de Turismo, Av Miguel Hidalgo 22, 1st floor, corner with Carmen Ochoa de Merino. Office on Blvd Bahía and 5 de Mayo, useful city booklet and map of Quintana Roo; also a kiosk in the small plaza on Héroes and Aguilar (closed Sun).

● **Transport**
Local Taxis: no city buses; taxis operate on fixed price routes, US$0.50 on average. Cars with light-green licence plates are a form of taxi. **Fuel**: *Magna Sin* (unleaded fuel) is sold at the petrol station just outside Chetumal on the road N at the beginning of the road to Escárcega, also at Xpujil (see page 482). **Garage**: Talleres Barrera, helpful, on Primo de Verdad; turn E off Héroes, then past the electrical plant.

Air With flights to Cancún and Flores (Aero Caribe), Mexico City and Villahermosa (Aviacsa, T 27765).

Buses The main bus station is 2-3 km out of town at the intersection of Insurgentes y Belice, clean facilities, reasonable café; left luggage in the shop, US$0.75/day; all passengers have to go through the customs *semáforo* (red/green light) on entry. Taxi from town US$2. Colectivo taxi from town US$0.80, bus to town from Av Belice. Many buses going to the border, US$0.30; taxi from Chetumal to border, 20 mins, US$6 for two. Buses are often all booked a day ahead especially long distance journeys, so avoid unbooked connections. Expect passport checks on buses leaving for Mexican destinations. Autobuses del Caribe to **Mexico City**, 22 hrs, US$40, once a day via **Villahermosa** at 0800 (US$16, 8 hrs, the road is bad and it can take longer); also 2 ADO buses to Mexico City, and 3 ADO to Villahermosa; to **Puebla**, US$40; bus to **Escárcega**, four between 1300 and 2100, 3½ hrs, US$7.25, 2nd class; from Chetumal to **Palenque**, ADO 1st class at 2215, Maya de Oro 1st class at 2200, US$23, 9 hrs (2 stops), 2nd class at 2130, US$14.80, otherwise a change is necessary at Emiliano Zapata (bus to there at 0900, 1300, US$11.50), then change again at Catazajá, or Catazajá itself (then take a colectivo), or Escárcega. Lacandonia has 2nd class bus to **San Cristóbal** via Palenque at 2130, US$19. Bus to **Mérida**, luxury US$18.30, US$16.50 1st class (Caribe Express and Autobuses del Caribe), about 7 hrs, 2nd class US$13. To **Felipe Carrillo Puerto**, US$3.35, 1½ hrs, many, on excellent road. To **Cancún**, 6 hrs, boring road, several daily, between 0700 and 2400 (luxury US$17, 1st class US$13.50, 2nd class US$10). To **Tulum**, several 2nd class from 0630, US$7, 1st class from 0700, 4 hrs, US$8.50. To **Minatitlán**, 12 hrs, US$22.50. There are also buses to Veracruz, Campeche, Villahermosa, Córdoba, Xpujil and Puerto Juárez. Green *colectivos* at Francisco Primo de Verdad y Av Hidalgo go along the coast to Cancún.

To Belize Batty Bus from the new market to **Belize City**, three afternoon departures, schedules change frequently, taking 4-5 hrs on paved road, US$5 in pesos, US dollars or Belize dollars. Venus Bus to Belize City leaves from the square by Mercado Nuevo on Calzada Veracruz y 2° Circuito Periférico, 3 blocks from main terminal (US$1 taxi ride), morning departures, again frequent schedule changes, first bus leaves at 0600. Be there in good time; they sometimes leave early if full. If intending to stay in Belize City, do not take a bus which arrives at night as it is not recommended to look for a hotel in the dark. Bus Chetumal-**Orange Walk**, 2½ hrs, US$2.50. **San Juan Travel** at the main bus station has a direct daily service to Flores (US$30) and Tikal (US$33) in **Guatemala**, at 1430 from ADO terminal, 8 hrs to Flores, 6 hrs to Tikal.

FRONTIER WITH BELIZE

● Mexican customs
Mexican customs procedure can be slow; bus passengers en route to Belize walk across the bridge, with personal luggage, for Belizean passport control, where the buses wait. Visitors who have been to Ecuador, or any of its neighbouring countries recently, require a health certificate, available from the Centro de Salud at the border. Note that fresh fruit cannot be imported into Belize.

● Entering Mexico
Tourist cards are available at the border. It is reported that in 1996 only 15 days were being given but you can get an additional 30 days at the Servicios Migratorios in Chetumal.

● Crossing by private vehicle
Leaving Mexico by car: go to the Mexican immigration office to register your exit and surrender your vehicle permit and tourist card; very straightforward, no charges. Go to the office to obtain compulsory Belizean insurance (also money changing facilities here). Entering Belize, your car will be registered in your passport.

● Exchange
Money checked on entering Belize. Excess Mexican pesos are easily changed into Belizean dollars with men waiting just beyond customs on the Belize side, but they are not there to meet the early bus. You can change US for Belizean dollar bills in the shops at the border, this is not necessary as US$ are accepted in Belize.

● Transport
It is difficult to hitch to the Belizean border. To hitch once inside Belize, it is best to take the *colectivo* from in front of the hospital (1 block from the bus station, ask) marked 'Chetumal-Santa Elena', US$1. For buses to Belize, see above.

NORTH OF CHETUMAL

6 km N are the stony beaches of **Calderitas**, bus every 30 mins from Colón, between Belice and Héroes, US$1.80 or taxi, US$5, many fish restaurants. Camping at Calderitas, signposted, OK, US$2.75. 16 km N **Laguna de los Milagros**, a beautiful lagoon for swimming, and 34 km N of Chetumal, on the road to Tulum (page 472), is **Cenote Azul**, over 70m deep, with a waterside restaurant serving inexpensive and good seafood and regional food (but awful coffee) until 1800 and a trailer park (Apdo 88, Chetumal, relaxing place to camp; other *cenotes* in area). Both are deserted in the week. About 3 km N of Cenote Azul is the village of **Bacalar** (nice, but not special) on the Laguna de Siete Colores; swimming and skin-diving; colectivos from terminal (Suchaa) in Chetumal, corner of Miguel Hidalgo y Primo de Verdad, from 0700-1900 every 30 mins, US$1.60, also buses from Chetumal bus station every 2 hrs or so, US$1.60. There is a Spanish fort there overlooking a beautiful shallow, clear, fresh water lagoon; abundant birdlife on the lakeshore. This is the fort of San Felipe, said to have been built around 1729 by the Spanish to defend the area from the English pirates and smugglers of logwood (there is a plaque praying for protection from the

British). The British ships roamed the islands and reefs, looting Spanish galleons laden with gold, on their way from Peru to Cuba. There are many old shipwrecks on the reef and around the Chinchorro Banks, 50 km out in the Caribbean (information kindly provided by Coral Pitkin of the Rancho Encantado, see below).

● **Accommodation & places to eat** Hotel and good restaurants on the Laguna. At Bacalar is **D** *Hotel Refugio* (closed Sept 1996), 10 mins' walk from main plaza, N, lovely gardens and thatched bar overlooking lagoon; *Restaurant La Esperanza*, 1 block from plaza on same road, thatched barn, good seafood, not expensive and one cheap place on the plaza, *Punta y Coma*. *Orizaba*, 3 blocks from Zócalo, cheap, large menu, rec. Several lakeside bars also serve meals, mostly fish: *Ojitos, Los 6 Hermanos, Sian Kaan, El Pez de Oro, El Fuerte*, but no details on any of these. Camping possible at the end of the road 100m from the lagoon, toilets and shower, US$0.10, but lagoon perfect for washing and swimming; Balneario Ejidal, with changing facilities and restaurant (good fried fish), rec; gasoline is sold in a side-street. About 2 km S of Bacalar (on left-hand side of the road going towards the village) is **D** *Hotel Las Lagunas*, very good, wonderful views, helpful, clean, comfortable, hot water, swimming pool and opp a sweet-water lake; restaurant is poor and overpriced. 3 km N of Bacalar is the resort hotel **A1** *Rancho Encantado*, on the W shore of the lagoon, half-board also available, Aptdo 233, Chetumal, T/F 983-80427 (USA res: 800 748 1756 or F 505-751-0972, PO Box 1644, Taos, New Mexico) with private dock, tour boat, canoes and windsurf boards for rent, private cabins with fridge and hammock, very good. North of Bacalar a direct road (Route 293) runs to Muná, on the road between Mérida and Uxmal.

North of Chetumal are also the unexcavated archaeological sites of **Ichpaatun** (13 km), Oxtancah (14) and Nohochmul (20).

Just after the turn off to Muná, at Cafetal, is an unpaved road E to **Majahual** on the coast (56 km from Cafetal), a peaceful, unspoilt place with clear water and beautiful beaches. Kombi from the bus terminal next to *Hotel Ucum* in Chetumal at 0600, returns 1300. Accommodation at *Restaurant Los Piratas del Caribe*, owned by a French family, simple rooms without bath, excellent restaurant, inexpensive. Excursion possible to Banco Chinchorro offshore, where there is a coral bank and a white sandy beach.

About 2 km before Majahual a paved road to the left goes to Puerto Bravo and on to Placer and Punta Herrero (in the Sian Ka'an Biosphere Reserve, see above). 3.5 km along this road a right turn goes to the *Sol y Mar* restaurant, with rooms to rent, bathrooms and spaces for RVs, also coconut palms and beach. 10.5 km along the Punta Herrero road, again on the right, is *Camidas Trailer Park*, with palm trees, *palapas*, restaurant and restrooms, space for 4 RVs, US$5 pp, car free.

EAST OF CHETUMAL

Across the bay from Chetumal, at the very tip of Quintana Roo is **Xcalak**, which may be reached from Chetumal by private launch (2 hrs), or by the unpaved road from Cafetal to Majahual, then turning S for 55 km (186 km from Chetumal, suitable for passenger cars but needs skilled driver). Daily colectivos from 0700-1900, from 16 de Septiembre 183 y Mahatma Ghandi (T 27701), check return times. Bus runs Fri 1600 and Sun 0600, returning Sat am and Sun pm (details from Chetumal tourist office). Xcalak is a fishing village (*Pop 230*) with a few shops with beer and basic supplies and one small restaurant serving Mexican food. A few kilometres N of Xcalak are two hotels, *Costa de Cocos* and *Villa Caracol*, both American run, latter is good, comfortable *cabañas*, expensive. From here trips can be arranged to the Banco Chinchorro or to San Pedro, Belize. *Villa Caracol* has sport fishing and diving facilities. In the village you may be able to rent a boat to explore Chetumal Bay and the unspoiled islands of Banco Chinchorro. Do *not* try to walk from Xcalak along the coast to San Pedro, Belize; the route is virtually impassable.

WEST OF CHETUMAL

From Chetumal you can visit the fascinating Mayan ruins that lie on the way (route 186) to Escárcega. There are few tourists in this area and few facilities. Take plenty of drinking water. About 25 km from Chetumal at Ucum (fuel), you can turn off 5 km S to visit **Palmara**, located along the Río Hondo, which borders Belize, swimming holes and restaurant. Just before Francisco Villa (61 km from Chetumal) lie the ruins of **Kohunlich** 8.4 km S of the main road, 1½ hrs' walk, take plenty of water (hitching difficult), where there are fabulous masks (early classic, AD 250-500) set on the side of the main pyramid, still bearing red colouring; they are unique of their kind (allow an hour for the site). 200m W of the turning is a *migración* office and a stall selling beer; wait here for buses, which have to stop, but 1st class will not pick up passengers. Colectivos 'Nicolás Bravo' from Chetumal, or bus marked Zoh Laguna from bus station pass the turning.

Xpujil (119 km from Chetumal, leaded and unleaded fuel is available), has one large pyramid, 8th century AD, recently restored and worth a visit, about 1 km W of bus terminal/junction, open daily 0800-1700 entry US$2, Sun free. If stuck overnight there is accommodation in Xpujil in *cabañas* (**D**) at Hotel El Mirador Maya, which also has a good restaurant. *Restaurant Calakmul* has *cabañas* (**E**), with mosquito nets and fan, some with bath, basic, restaurant good, rec.

7 km beyond Xpujil lies the large Maya site of **Becán** (open 0800-1700 every day) shielded by the forest with wild animals still wandering among the ruins, surrounded by a water-less moat and a low wall, now collapsed, with vast temples and plazas and a decayed ball court (site is visible from the road, entry US$2, Sun free, lots of mosquitoes, RVs may be parked at the ruins, no facilities).

2 km further on and 10 mins down a paved road lies **Chicanná**, with a superb late classic Maya temple with an ornate central door which has been formed in the shape of the open-fanged jaws of the plumed serpent. A 10-min path leads from the first site to a second, which has a pyramid with lovely Chac masks (about 1 hr is enough to see both sites). At Chicanná there is **A1** *Ramada Chicanná Eco Village*, opened 1995, in Mexico City T 705-3996, F 535-2966, in Campeche T (981) 62233, 100 rooms in thatched cabins, restaurant, bar, pool, jacuzzi, solar heating, rainwater showers etc, most waste recycled. No camping permitted at either site.

Two sites, a bit further away, accessible from Xpujil village are **Hormiguero** (Hill of the Ants), and **Río Bec**. Helmut Zettl (Ebergassing) writes: "The latter was discovered in 1912 by an American, but was later lost for almost 60 years. It was rediscovered in 1973 by an American couple who were researching a documentary on the Maya and were shown the overgrown temple by a *chiclero*. Try to find a driver and guide in Xpujil to make the 6-7 hrs' expedition, well worth it, but only possible in the dry season (Dec-Mar)." Rec is Serge 'Checo' Rion, who lives in the *Hotel Mirador Maya* (see below), US$200 for 5-6 people in 4WD, full day's trip. On either side of the Chetumal-Francisco Escárcega road at this point stretches the **Calakmul Biosphere Reserve** (S it reaches to the Guatemala border). 180 species of birds have been registered here, including the endangered king vulture, 2 species of eagle, and others. At Km 98 on the Escárcega road is a paved turn off (65 km, 1¼ hrs) to the ruins of **Calakmul**, which are undergoing restoration. The government is now suggesting that Calakmul was the largest of all Mayan sites with about 1,500 structures. There are some 116 carved monuments studied so far but most of the inscriptions have been eroded. One theory is that Calakmul, or Oxte'tun, which was its old name, was an important centre, maybe the capital of the Serpent's Head Kingdom. There is evidence that the kingdom attacked Palenque in 599 and 611 AD and Tikal, another superpower, in 657. In 695 the king, Pata de Jaguar, attacked Tikal again but was defeated, and from this time the influence of Calakmul declined, with a loss of power and prestige. Entrance US$3 per car, US$1.50 pp.

● **Transport** Buses leave from Chetumal bus terminal along the road to Francisco Villa and Xpujil, passing the entrance to Becán. Many taxis and colectivos in Xpujil for the ruins (US$8 for taxi inc waiting time). 2nd class buses from Chetumal to Xpujil at 0630, 1200, 1400, 1930 (confirm all prices with bus station) and others later, stopping service, 4 hrs; 1st class (direct),
US$3.30, 0900,1130, 1230, 1300 and others; 2nd class fare Chetumal-Francisco Villa US$1.65, 1 hr 10 mins, Francisco Villa-Xpujil US$2.20, 2 hrs 20 mins. Last bus from Xpujil to Chetumal at 1700 (1st class ADO); similarly, last bus back from Becán is just before 1700. Taxi from Xpujil to Chicanná costs US$5, 30 mins. Bus from Cancún (goes on to Villahermosa), leaves at 1700, US$13.50, 6½ hrs, returns Cancún 0700 (ADO). Colectivos, a bit more expensive, leave from E of the electricity plant in Chetumal. Xpujil, Becán and Chicanná are in Campeche state and, at the state border, passports and tourist cards must be shown.

Maps of roads in Quintana Roo are obtainable in Chetumal at Junta Local de Caminos, Secretaría de Obras Públicas.

Baja California

A LAND OF HOT, parched deserts, but deserts of infinite variety and everchanging landscapes, clothed in a fascinating array of hardy vegetation. Most visitors find Baja a magical place of blue skies, fresh air, solitude and refuge from the rat race N of the border.

THE LAND

Baja California (Lower California) is that long narrow arm which dangles southwards from the US border between the Pacific and the Gulf of California for 1,300 km. It is divided administratively into the states of Baja California and Baja California Sur, with a 1 hr time change at the state line. The average width is only 80 km. Rugged and almost uninhabited mountains split its tapering length. Only the southern tip gets enough rain: the northern half gets its small quota during the winter, the southern half during the summer. Not only the northern regions near the US, but also the southern Cape zone is attracting increasing numbers of tourists. The US dollar is preferred in most places N of La Paz.

Stretching 1,704 km from Tijuana to Cabo San Lucas, Highway 1 is generally in good repair, although slightly narrow and lacking hard shoulders. Roads in the N are more potholed than those in Baja California Sur. Service stations are placed at adequate intervals along it, but motorists should fill their tanks at every opportunity and carry spare fuel, particularly if venturing off the main roads. Stations in small towns may not have fuel, or may sell from barrels at inflated prices. The same conditions apply for Highways 5 (Mexicali-San Felipe), 3 (Tecate-Ensenada-San Felipe road) and 2 (Tijuana 196 Mexicali-San Luis-Sonoita). Hitchhiking is difficult, and there is very little public transport off the main highway.

The costs of food and accommodation are more expensive than the rest of Mexico, but less than in the USA. Tijuana, Ensenada and La Paz all have a good range of duty-free shopping. Stove fuel is impossible to find in Baja California Sur. Beware of overcharging on buses and make a note of departure times of buses in Tijuana or Ensenada when travelling S: between Ensenada and Santa Rosalía it is very difficult to obtain bus timetable information, even at bus stations. Don't ask for English menus if you can help it, prices often differ from the Spanish version. Always check change, overcharging is rife. Note also that hotels have widely divergent winter and summer rates; between June and Nov tariffs are normally lower than those given in the text below (especially in expensive places).

Border crossing There is no immigration check on the Mexican side of the

Northern Baja California

USA

0   50
km

Tijuana
Rosarito
Tecate
La Rumorosa
Calexico
MEXICALI
Laguna
Salada
Ensenada
PN
Constitución
de 1857
San Luis
Río Colorado
To
Sonoita
Maneadero
Santo Tomás
Golfo de
Santa
Clara
San Vicente
Crucero la
Trinidad
Colonet
PN
Sierra San
Pedro Mártir
Picacho
del Diablo
San Felipe
Pacific
Ocean
San Quintín
El Rosario
Puertecitos
Punta
Baja
Cataviña
Bahía
San Luis
Gonzaga

available locally. Motorcycle insurance costs about US$3 a day. If you require x-ray facilities after an accident it appears that the only place between Tijuana and Los Cabos with X-ray equipment and an on-call technician is Ciudad Constitución.

Maps There are only two really comprehensive maps: the road map published by the ACSC, which gives highly detailed road distances (but in miles) and conditions, and which is available only to AAA members (the AAA also publishes a *Guide to Baja California* for members only); and International Travel Map (ITM) Production's *Baja California 1:1,000,000* (2nd edition 1992-93), which includes extra geographical and recreational detail on a topographic base. Many specialist maps and guides are available in book stores in Southern California. Both guidebooks and maps are sadly rare in Baja itself.

HISTORY

border. The buffer zone for about 120 km S of the frontier allows US citizens to travel without a tourist card. Some have reported travelling in Baja California Sur without a tourist card. If you are bringing in a vehicle you should try to get a tourist card/vehicle permit in Tijuana (see page 492); if you are travelling beyond Baja California, with or without a vehicle, getting a tourist card in Tijuana will save a lot of trouble later. Immigration authorities are also encountered at Mexicali, at Ensenada, at Quitovac, 28 km S of Sonoita (Sonora) on Highway 2, and when boarding the ferries to cross the Gulf. Ferries ply from Pichilingüe (N of La Paz) and Santa Rosalía to various places on the mainland (see text). As a car needs an import permit, make sure you get to the ferry with lots of time and preferably with a reservation if going on the Pichilingüe-Mazatlán ferry. (See under La Paz below.)

Insurance and Medical Services Insurance covering bodily injury is not

Cortés attempted to settle at La Paz in 1534 after one of his expeditions had become the first Europeans to set foot in Baja, but the land's sterile beauty disguised a chronic lack of food and water; this and sporadic Indian hostility forced the abandonment of most early attempts at settlement. Jesuit missionary fathers arrived at Loreto in 1697 and founded the first of their 20 missions. The Franciscans and then Dominicans took over when the Jesuits were expelled in 1767. The fathers were devoted and untiring in their efforts to convert the peninsula's three ethnic groups, but diseases introduced unknowingly by them and by ships calling along the coasts soon tragically decimated Indian numbers; some Indians remain today, but without tribal organization. Scattered about the Sierras are the remains of 30 of these well-meaning but lethal missions, some beautifully restored, others only eroded adobe foundations. Most are within easy reach from Highway 1, although 4WD is necessary for remoter sites such as San Pedro Mártir and Dolores del Sur.

Today's population of about 2.8 million has increased by two-thirds in the past decade through migration from Mexico's interior and Central Pacific coast.

ECONOMY

The development of agriculture, tourism, industry, migrant labour from California, and the opening of the Transpeninsular Highway has caused an upsurge of economic growth and consequently of prices, especially in areas favoured by tourists.

The Morelos dam on the upper reaches of the Colorado River has turned the Mexicali valley into a major agricultural area: 400,000 acres under irrigation to grow cotton and olives. The San Quintín Valley and the Magdalena Plain are other successful areas where crops have been wrenched from the desert. Industries are encouraged in all border regions by investment incentives; called *maquiladoras*, they are foreign-owned enterprises which import raw materials without duty, manufacture in Mexico and ship the products back to the United States.

MEXICALI

(*Pop 850,000; State pop 1995 2,108,118; Phone code* 65) Capital of Baja California, Mexicali is not as geared to tourism as Tijuana and thus retains its busy, business-like border town flavour. It is a good place to stock up on supplies, cheap clothing and footware, and souvenirs.

The new **Centro Cívico-Comercial**, Calzada López Mateos, is an ambitious urban development comprising government offices, medical school, hospitals, bullring, bus station, cinemas, etc.

Places of interest
The **City Park**, in the SW sector, contains a zoo, picnic area and **natural history museum** (open Tues-Fri 0900-1700; weekend 0900-1800). University of Baja California's **Regional Museum**, Av Reforma y Calle L; interesting exhibits illustrating Baja's archaeology, ethnography and

missions (Tues-Fri 0900-1800; weekend 1000-1500, admission free). **Galería de la Ciudad**, Av Obregón 1209, between C D y E, former state governor's residence, features work of Mexican painters, sculptors and photographers (Mon-Fri 0900-2000). There are *charreadas* (rodeos), held on Sun during the April-Oct season, at two separate *charro* grounds on eastern and western outskirts of Mexicali. Mexicali has numerous Chinese restaurants, the legacy of immigration which began in Sonora in the late 19th century.

Calexico, the much smaller city on the California side of the border, is so thoroughly Mexicanized that it can be difficult to find a newspaper from San Diego or Los Angeles. Mexican shoppers flock here for clothing bargains.

Local information
● **Accommodation**
A1 *Crowne Plaza*, Blvd López Mateos y Av de los Héroes 201, T 573600, F 570555; **A1** *Holiday Inn*, Blvd Benito Juárez 2220, T (656) 61300, F 664901, a/c, best in town; also **A3** *Castel Calafía*, Calzada Justo Sierra 1495, T 682841, a/c, plain but comfortable, dining room; **A3** *Lucerna*, Blvd Juárez 2151, T 541000, a/c, meeting rooms, bar, nightclub.

B *Del Norte*, C Melgar y Av Francisco Madero, T 540575, some a/c and TV, across from border crossing, pleasant but a little noisy, has free parking for guests and offers discount coupons for breakfast and dinner in its own restaurant.

C *La Siesta*, Justo Sierra 899, T 541100, reasonable, coffee shop.

D *Rivera*, nr the railway station, a/c, best of the cheaper hotels; *Fortín de las Flores*, Av Cristóbal Colón 612, T 524522, and **D** *Las Fuentes*, Blvd López Mateos 1655, T 571525, both with a/c and TV but noisy, tolerable if on a tight budget.

Motels: **B-C** *Azteca de Oro*, C Industria 600, T 571433, opp the train station and only a few blocks from the bus terminal, a/c, TV, a bit scruffy but convenient. Others around town and in Calexico just across the border around E 4th St. **B-C** *Hotel De Anza*, on the Calexico side, excellent value for money.

Youth hostel: Av Salina Cruz y Coahuila 2050, CP 21050, T 551230.

● **Airline offices**
Mexicana, T 535402; **Taesa**, T 663921; AeroMéxico, T 91-800-90999.

● **Banks & money changers**
All major banks: currency exchange is only from 0900-1330. *Casas de cambio* in Calexico give a slightly better rate. Several *cambios* on López Mateos.

● **Entertainment**
Many good nightclubs on Av Justo Sierra, and on your left as you cross border, several blocks away.

● **Tourist offices**
State Tourism Office, C Comercio, between Reforma and Obregón ('Centro Cívico' bus); better is **Tourist and Convention Bureau**, Calzada López Mateos y C Camelias, helpful, English spoken, open Mon-Fri 0800-1900, Sat 0900-1300. The Procuraduría de Protección al Turista, which provides legal assistance for visitors, is in the same building as the State Tourism office.

● **Transport**
Air 25 km E, Blvd Aviación; daily flights to Mexico City, Chihuahua, Guadalajara and Hermosillo, Matamoros, Ciudad Obregón, Culiacán, Monterrey, Torreón and Phoenix, Arizona, with Mexicana, AeroMéxico, Aviación del Noroeste and Serolitoral. Charter services.

Trains The railway station on the S is about 3½ km from the tourist area on the border and C 3 bus connects it with the nearby bus terminal. There is a passport desk at the station. The ticket information office closes at 1230 but there are timetables on the wall. Phone 572386 (1000-1200) or 572101 to verify departure times and make reservations. The ticket office is open 0900-1100 for 1st class tickets for following day. For the slow train the office is open from 1630 to 2040. A special 1st class train, El Tren del Pacífico, leaves at 1000 daily for the **capital**, via Benjamín Hill and Guadalajara, a/c, book in advance. Passengers have to change carriages at Benjamín Hill. Slow train (leaves 2050, 2nd class cars) to Benjamín Hill, **Guadalajara** and **Mexico City** takes up to 57 hrs. Be sure to take your own food. There is no pullman service or dining car between Mexicali and Mazatlán. 1st class consists of one a/c car with reclining seats and a non a/c car where drinks and snacks are available. Food and drink sold on station platforms. Guards are not always reliable, thieves especially active if lights are turned off. Thorough police luggage searches for drugs and guns possible. Toilets in each class are inefficient and therefore unpleasant. Very hot and dusty in desert part of trip, though train is cleaned twice, cold at night between Los Mochis and Mexico City, take a blanket. *Primera preferente* fare Mexicali-Guadalajara US$74; 2nd class US$22; Mexicali-Benjamín Hill US$14.50 and US$8 respectively. If you come from the N on the slow train and want to go to Chihuahua you'll arrive at 2015 at the junction, **Sufragio** (the Tren del Pacífico arrives at 0215, easy to miss in the dark, but can be too late for the Chihuahua connection). For a hotel, go to San Blas, where the train also stops, 5 mins away by local bus (every 15 mins from 0500 in either direction), where there are 3 hotels. *Santa Lucía*, *San Marco*, both often full; *Pérez* dirty, cold water, but adequate, E. If the next morning you are refused a ticket because the train is full, try getting in and getting a ticket on the train.

Buses Tijuana, 3 hrs, US$16.50 luxury liner, US$6.50 1st class, US$5 2nd class, sit on right for views at the Cantú Grade; **San Felipe**, 3 hrs, 4 a day, US$8, **Guadalajara**, US$77. **Mazatlán**, US$50. **Hermosillo**, 10 hrs, US$22. **Mexico City**, US$96. **Ensenada**, US$9. **Santa Rosalía**, US$33. **La Paz**, daily 1630, 24 hrs, US$60.50. All trips leave from the new central bus station (Camionera Central) on Av Independencia, four major bus companies have their offices here under one roof. Autotransportes Tres Estrellas de Oro serves both Baja and the mainland. Golden State buses from Mexicali to Los Angeles (US$40) tickets available at trailer/kiosk across from *Hotel del Norte*. Greyhound from Los Angeles to Calexico (901 Imperial Av), US$33, 6 hrs. San Diego to Calexico via El Centro, US$20, 3 to 4 hrs. The 1200 bus from San Diego connects with the Pullman bus to Mazatlán, US$40, 21 hrs. Local buses are cheap, about US$0.55. 'Central Camionera' bus to Civic Centre and bus station.

Crossing the border The border is open 24 hrs a day for all formalities. Day visitors may prefer to park on the California side, since the extremely congested Av Cristóbal Colón, which parallels the frontier fence, is the only access to the US port of entry; entering Mexico, follow the diagonal Calzada López Mateos, which leads to the tourist office and train and bus stations. Mexican automobile insurance is readily available on both sides of the border.

Pedestrians travelling from Mexicali to Calexico should take the underpass beneath Calzada López Mateos, which passes through the utterly indifferent Mexican immigration office before continuing to the US side.

Highway 2 runs E from Mexicali through San Luis Río Colorado, Sonoita and Caborca to join the Pacific Highway at Santa Ana; see page 166.

SAN FELIPE

Paved Highway 5 heads S from Mexicali 196 km to San Felipe, passing at about Km 34 the Cerro Prieto geothermal field. After passing the Río Hardy (one of the peninsula's few permanent rivers) and the **Laguna Salada** (Km 72), a vast dry alkali flat unless turned into a muddy morass by rare falls of rain, the road continues straight across sandy desert until entering San Felipe around a tall, white, double-arched monument. Floods (as in Jan 1993) can cut the road across the Laguna Salada; when it is closed, motorists have to use Highway 3 from Ensenada to get to San Felipe.

San Felipe is a pleasant, tranquil fishing and shrimping port on the Gulf of California with a population of about 13,000, with about 3,000 North American RV temporary residents and a further 3,000 on winter weekends. Long a destination for devoted sportfishermen and a weekend retreat for North Americans, San Felipe is now experiencing a second discovery, with new trailer parks and the paving of many of the town's sandy streets. A public library is planned, recycling plant, artificial breakwater reef and two golf courses are under construction. Even the *Las Macetas* hotel (the 'grey ghost') may see completion in the near future. There is an airport 8 km S. San Felipe is protected from desert winds by the coastal mountains and is unbearably hot during the summer; in winter the climate is unsurpassed; and on weekends it can become overcrowded and noisy. A good view of the wide sandy beach can be had from the Virgin of Guadalupe shrine near the lighthouse.

Local festivals

Navy Day is celebrated on 1 June with a carnival, street dancing and boat races.

Local information
● **Accommodation**

A2 *Aquamarina Condohotel and Villas*, 4 km S on Punta Estrella road, B Sun-Thur, on beach, pool, attractive rooms, a/c; **A2** *Castel*, Av Misión de Loreto 148, T 71282, a/c, 2 pools, tennis etc, best in town.

B *La Trucha Vagabunda*, Mar Báltico, nr *El Cortés Motel*, T 71333, also a few RV spaces and *Restaurant Alfredo* (Italian), seafood, international cuisine; **B** *Vagabond Inn*, on same street, 3 km S of town, a/c, pool and beach; **B** *Villa del Mar*, pool, volley ball court, restaurant.

C *Fiesta San Felipe*, 9 km S on the airport road, isolated, every room has Gulf view, tennis, pool, restaurant, VAT (IVA) not inc in bill. **C** *Riviera*, 1 km S on coastal bluff, T 71185, a/c, pool, spa, restaurant.

Motels: B *Chapala*, some a/c, free coffee, clean but pricey, on beachfront, T 71240; **B** *El Capitán*, Mar de Cortés 298, T 71303, a/c, some balconies, pool, lovely rancho-style building, hard beds but otherwise OK; **B** *El Cortés*, on Av Mar de Cortés, T 71055, beachside esplanade, a/c, pool, palapas on beach, launching ramp, disco, restaurant; **C** *El Pescador*, T 71044, Mar de Cortés and Calzada Chetumal, a/c, modest but comfortable.

Camping: many trailer parks and campgrounds in town and on coast to N and S, inc **D** *El Faro Beach and Trailer Park*, on the bay 18 km S; *Ruben's, Playa Bonita, La Jolla, Playa de Laura, Mar del Sol*, and the more primitive *Campo Peewee* and *Pete's Camp*, both about 10 km N. All from US$8/night for two.

● **Places to eat**

Green House, Av Mar de Cortés 132 y Calzada Chetumal, good food (beef or chicken *fajitas* a speciality) and friendly service, cheap breakfasts, 'fish filet for a fiver'! 0730-0300 daily. *Clam Man's Restaurant*, Calzada Chetumal, 2 blocks W of Pemex station, used to belong to the late, famous Pasqual 'The Clam Man', oddly decorated, but excellent clams, steamed, fried, barbecued, at budget prices. *Los Misiones* in *Mar del Sol* RV park, small menu, moderately-priced, seafood crêpes a speciality, popular with families, good service. *Las Redes*, Mar de Cortés Sur; *Ruben's Place*, Junípero Serra, both favourites for seafood; *El Toro II*, Chetumal, Mexican and American food, popular for breakfasts; other pleasant places on Av Mar de Cortés: No 300 *Corona*, No 348; *El Nido*, grilled fish and steaks (closed Wed), No 358; *Puerto Padre* (Cuban); *George's*, No 336, steaks, seafood, live music, pleasant, friendly, popular with US residents, rec.

● **Tourist offices**
Mar de Cortés y Manzanillo, opp *El Capitán Motel*, helpful, little handout material, open Tues-Sun 0900-1400 and 1600-1800.

● **Transport**
Transportes ABC and TNS buses to **Ensenada**, direct, over the mountains, at 0800 and 1800, 3½ hrs, US$9. Bus to **Mexicali** US$8, 4 a day from 0730, 2 hrs. Hitching to Mexicali is not difficult (much traffic), but beware the desert sun. Bus station is on Mar Báltico near corner of Calzada Chetumal, in town centre.

COASTAL ROUTE SOUTH OF SAN FELIPE

The road S has been paved as far as **Puertecitos**, a straggling settlement mainly of North American holiday homes. There is an airstrip, a simple grocery store, a Pemex station and the 8-room *Puertecitos Motel*. Fishing is good outside the shallow bay and there are several tidal hot springs at the SE point. The road continues S along the coast (well graded with improvements continuing, acceptable for standard vehicles), leading to the tranquil **Bahía San Luís Gonzaga**, on which are the basic resorts of Papa Fernández and Alfonsinas; the beach here is pure sand, empty and silent. From here, the 'new' road heads W over hills to meet Highway 1 near Laguna Chapala, 53 km S of Cataviña, opening up a circular route through northern Baja California.

COASTAL ROUTE WEST OF MEXICALI

The road from Mexicali W to Tijuana is fast and well surfaced, it runs across barren desert flats, below sea level and with organ-pipe cacti in abundance, until

reaching the eastern escarpment of the peninsula's spine; it winds its way up the Cantú Grade to **La Rumorosa**, giving expansive, dramatic vistas of desert and mountain. The numerous wrecked trucks and cars which litter the canyons along the Cantú Grade, together with countless crosses, emphasize the need for careful driving and better than adequate brakes. If pulling off the highway for the view, do so only on wide shoulders with good visibility in both directions. La Rumorosa, sited high enough on a boulder-strewn plateau to receive a sprinkling of snow in winter, has a service station. There are three more Pemex stations along the highway before it reaches Tecate after 144 km.

TECATE

Visitors will find that placid **Tecate** (*Pop* 40,000) more resembles a Mexican city of the interior rather than a gaudy border town, perhaps because there is no population centre on the US side. It is a pleasant place to break the journey, especially around the shady Parque Hidalgo, where families promenade on weekends. The Baja California Secretary of Tourism, opposite the park at Libertad 1305, provides a useful map of the town and other information. English spoken.

Brewing is the most important local industry; the landmark Tecate Brewery, which produces Tecate and Carta Blanca beers, offers tours on the first three Sat of the month between 0800 and 1200. There are many *maquiladora* industries.

● **Accommodation** A3 *Motel El Dorado*, Juárez 1100, T 41102, a/c, central, comfortable; **C** *Hotel Hacienda*, Juárez 861, T 41250, a/c, clean; **C** *Hotel Paraíso*, Aldrete 83, T 41716. 10 km S of Tecate, on the road to Ensenada, is **A3** *Rancho Tecate*, T 40011. Budget-minded travellers may try **E** *Hotel México*, Juárez 230, gloomy rooms with or without bath, rumoured to be a staging post for unauthorized border crossings; **D** *Hotel Frontera*, Callejón Madero 131, T 41342, basic but clean and friendly, is probably a step up in quality (Antonio Moller Ponce, who resides here, is knowledgeable on the area's history and ethnohistory).

• **Places to eat** Excellent Mexican and Italian specialities at *El Passetto*, Libertad 200 nr Parque Hidalgo. Many other good ones.

Border crossing The border crossing is open from 0700-2400. To get to border immigration facilities, go N 3 blocks, uphill, from the W side of the Parque. You will pass the theatre. Mexican offices are on the left, US on the right. The orderly and friendly Mexican immigration and customs officers will only process vehicle papers between 0800 and 1600; at other hours, continue to Mexicali or Sonoita. All documents obtainable at the border. Tourist cards may also be obtained at the bus terminal; services to the interior resemble those from Tijuana (Tres Estrellas de Oro to Mexico City, US$93.50).

The highway continues W past the Rancho La Puerta, a spa and physical fitness resort, strictly for the rich, vegetarian meals, petrol station. Leaving the Rodríguez Reservoir behind, Highway 2 enters the industrial suburb of La Mesa and continues into Tijuana as a 4-lane boulevard, eventually to become Av Revolución, one of the city's main shopping streets.

A new alternative to Route 2 is the only completed segment of the 4-lane Tijuana-Mexicali motorway, between Tecate and Otay Mesa, Tijuana. It is very fast, but carries almost no traffic because of the US$4 toll.

TIJUANA

(*Pop* 1,500,000; *Phone code* 66) On the Pacific, where 35 million people annually cross the border, fuelling the city's claim to be 'the world's most visited city'. It came to prominence with Prohibition in the United States in the 1920s when Hollywood stars and thirsty Americans flocked to the sleazy bars and enterprising nightlife of Tijuana and Mexicali. Today, tourism is the major industry; although countless bars and nightclubs still vie for the visitor's dollar, it is duty-free bargains, horse racing and inexpensive English-speaking dentists which attract many

visitors. This area is much more expensive than further S, especially at weekends. Modern Tijuana is Mexico's fourth-largest city and one of the most prosperous.

Places of interest

Centro Cultural, Paseo de los Héroes y Av Independencia (museum, excellent book *Las Californias*, handicraft shops, restaurant, concert hall, and the ultra-modern spherical Omnimax cinema, where three films are shown on a 180° screen, best to sit at the back/top so you don't have to lean too far back: English performance at 1400 daily, US$4.50, Spanish version at 1900 costs US$3.75); **Casa de la Cultura**, a multi-arts cultural centre with a 600-seat theatre; the Cathedral of **Nuestra Señora de Guadalupe**, C 2. The **Jai-Alai Palace** (Palacio Frontón) is at Av Revolución y C 7 (games begin at 2000 nightly except Wed; spectators may bet on each game). Tijuana has two bullrings, the **Plaza de Toros Monumental** at Playas de Tijuana (the only one in the world built on the sea shore). A few metres away is an obelisk built into the border chain-link fence commemorating the Treaty of Guadalupe Hidalgo, 1848, which fixed the frontier between Mexico and the USA. **El Toreo** bullring is 3 km E of downtown on Búlevard **Agua Caliente**; *corridas* alternate between the two venues between May and Sept; Sun at 1600 sharp. Tickets from US$4.50 (*sol*) to US$16 (sombra). Horse and dog racing is held at the Agua Caliente track, near the Tijuana Country Club; horse racing Sat and Sun from 1200; greyhound meetings Wed-Mon at 1945, Mon, Wed, Fri at 1430. Admission US$0.50, reserved seats US$1. *Charreadas* take place each Sun from May to Sept at one of four grounds, free. Tourism office will give up-to-date information. A walk along the barrio beside the border (don't go alone) to see the breached fence will demonstrate the difference between the first and third worlds.

Immigration There is no passport check at the border, although US freeways funnelling 12 lanes of traffic into three on the

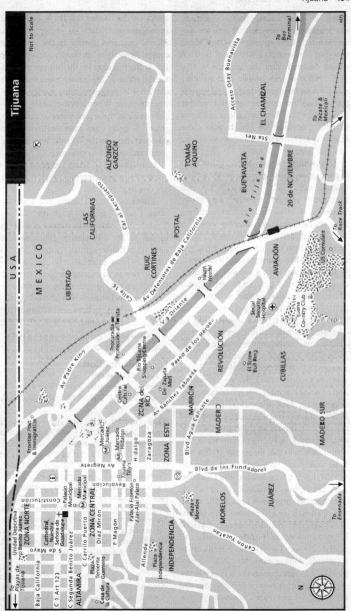

Mexican side means great congestion, particularly at weekends. A quieter recommended alternative is the **Otay Mesa** crossing (open 0600-2200) 8 km E of Tijuana, reached from the US side by SR-117. Traffic is less frantic and parking much easier but car insurance and vehicle permit facilities are no longer available here. From the Mexican side it is harder to find: continue on the bypass from Highway 1-D to near the airport to 'Garita de Otay' sign.

If travelling on into Mexico, don't follow the crowds who cross without visiting immigration: try to deal with US exit formalities and get an entry stamp at the border as it will avoid serious problems later on. Be sure to get an entry stamp on your tourist card as well as your passport. The Migración office is difficult to find: try the right hand lane marked 'Customs'. When entering with a vehicle or motorcycle you should be able to obtain your tourist card/vehicle permit at this office, then you are supposed to get a stamp from a vehicle registry office about 100m S. The officials will ask for copies of your documents, including the vehicle permit. As they have no photocopier you can look for the copy shop opposite, above a liquor store, or return to the USA, go 2 blocks N and look for the mail box rental company opposite the *Jack-in-the-Box*. There is an immigration office for tourist cards and vehicle documents on the righthand side of Highway 1 as it enters Ensenada. Alternatively, you can forget the stamp and hope you won't be asked for it later (do not do this if going beyond Baja California). If entering by bicycle, go to 'secondary', the immigration area to the right, where an official will process your tourist card to travel beyond Ensenada. Cyclists are not allowed on highway 1-D (the toll road), so head for Highway 1 (libre) to Ensenada. Going into the USA, be prepared for tough immigration procedures.

If entering without a vehicle, you can get a tourist card from Tijuana airport or at the bus terminal; there is no passport check at the border but there is a small immigration office for entry stamps. Money changers operate in the shopping centre 200m from the border and opposite this is the bus stop for the bus terminal. A tourist office at the border gives out maps of the border area explaining money changing, buses, etc. When leaving the USA without a vehicle, there is nowhere to surrender your US entry card because there is no passport check on the US side. You can send your card to a US Consulate.

Immigration officials are reluctant to grant visa extensions; you need to get one at your next port of call.

Those visiting Tijuana for the day often find it easier to park on the San Ysidro side and walk across the footbridge to the city centre. (Parking fees near the border range from US$5 to US$7/24 hrs.) Alternatively, the 'San Diego Trolley' is an entertaining way to reach the border, taking visitors from downtown San Diego to 'la línea' from US$1-3; departures every 15 mins between 0500 and 0100 (tickets sold from machines at stops). There is a visitor information kiosk at the Trolley's southern terminus.

Local information
● Accommodation

L2 *Fiesta Americana Tijuana*, Blvd Agua Caliente 4500, T 817000, heated pool, suites, etc, first rate.

A2-3: *Country Club*, Blvd Agua Caliente y Tapachula 1, T 817733, F 817066, *Hacienda de Río*, Blvd Sánchez Taboada 10606, T 848644, F 848620, and *La Mesa Inn*, Blvd Díaz Ordaz 50 y Gardenia, T 816522, F 812871; *Centenario Plaza*, Blvd Agua Caliente 22400, T 818183; *Lucerna*, Héroes y Av Rodríguez in new Río Tijuana development, T 841000, a/c, pool, piano bar, popular with business travellers; *Paraíso-Radisson*, Blvd Agua Caliente 1 at the Country Club, T 817200, pool, sauna, bar, a/c, etc; **A3-B** *El Conquistador*, Blvd Agua Caliente 700, T 817955, colonial style, a/c, pool, sauna, disco.

B *Calinda Tijuana*, nr the Paraíso-Radisson, a/c, pool, disco, convention centre; **B** *Palacio Azteca*, Highway 1 S, T 865301, a/c, modern, cocktail bar, extensively remodelled, in older, congested part of city; **B-C** *Hotel Caesar*, C 5 y Av Revolución, T 851606, a/c, restaurant, decorated with bullfight posters, unique character, good.

C *La Villa de Zaragoza*, behind the Jai-Alai *frontón*, a/c, comfortable; **C** *Nelson*, Av Revolución 502, T 854302, central, simple clean rooms, coffee shop.

D *Adelita*, hot showers, cockroaches, basic, C 4 2017; **D** *Hotel del Pardo*, C 5 y Niños Héroes, acceptable, noisy in parts; **D** *París*, C 5a 1939, adequate, value-for-money budget hotel; **D** *Rey*, C 4 2021, central, old but comfortable; **D** *St Francis*, Benito Juárez 2A, more with bath, rec, central.

E *Hotel del Mar*, C 1 1448, opp *Nelson*, central but in a poor section, communal bathroom, good budget hotel. Recommended along C Baja California are **E** *Hotel Virrey* and **F** *Pensión Noche Buena*; nearby and as good are **D** *Rivas*, on Constitución, friendly, clean, a little noisy; **E** *Fénix*, Miguel Martínez 355; **E** *Machado*, restaurant, basic, reasonable, C 1 No 1724; **E** *San Jorge*, Av Constitución 506, old but clean, basic.

If entering from the USA, it is easier to sightsee in Tijuana without luggage, so stay in San Diego and make a day excursion before travelling on. Two rec places: **C** *Park Regency Hotel*, nr Balboa Park, 3-room apartment, good value; **E** *Imperial Beach Youth Hostel*, the grade for members, take bus 933 from trolley station Palm City to 3rd St.

Motels: B-C *León*, C 7 1939, T 856320; **C-D** *La Misión*, in Playas de Tijuana nr the bullring, T 806612, modern, a/c, restaurant, pool, popular with businessmen; **D** *Golf*, T 862021, opp each other on Blvd Agua Caliente, next to Tijuana Country Club, both OK, and **D** *Padre Kino*, T 864208, *Golf*, an older-type motel.

Youth hostel: T 832680/822760, far from centre, Vía Ote y Puente Cuauhtémoc, Zona del Río, dirty, not rec, inexpensive cafeteria on premises, open 0700-2300.

● **Places to eat**

Tijuana Tilly's, excellent meal, reasonably priced. *La Leña*, downtown on Av Revolución between C 4 y 5, excellent food and service, beef and Mexican specialities; countless others, inc new complex nr border crossing. *Casa del Taco*, Revolución y Hidalgo, has taco buffet.

● **Airline offices**

Aero California, T 842100; **AeroMéxico**, T 854401; **Mexicana**, T 832851; **Taesa**, T 848484.

● **Banks & money changers**

Many banks, all dealing in foreign exchange. For Visa TCs, go to **Bancomer**. Better rate than *cambios* but less convenient. Countless *casas de cambio* throughout Tijuana open day and night. Some *cambios* collect a commission (up to 5%), even for cash dollars; ask before changing.

● **Embassies & consulates**

Canadian Consul, C Germán Gedovius 5-201, T 84-0461; **Mexican Consulate-General**, in San Diego, CA, 549 India St, Mon-Fri 0900-1400, for visas and tourist information; **US Consulate**, C Tapachula 96, between Agua Caliente racetrack and the Country Club, Mon-Fri 0800-1630, T 681-7400.

● **Entertainment**

Nightclubs: recommended: *Flamingos*, S on old Ensenada road; *Chantecler*.

● **Post & telecommunications**

Telephones: Computel, C 7 y Av Negrete, metered phones, fax, computer facilities.

● **Shopping**

The Plaza Río Tijuana Shopping Centre, Paseo de Los Héroes, is a new retail development; opp are the Plaza Fiesta and Plaza del Zapato malls, the latter specializing in footware. Nearby is the colourful public market. Downtown shopping area is Avs Revolución and Constitución. Bargaining is expected at smaller shops, and everyone except bus drivers is happy to accept US currency.

● **Tourist offices**

State Tourism Secretariat, main office on Plaza Patria, Blvd Agua Caliente, Mon-Fri 1000-1900. Branch offices at airport, first tollgate on Highway 1-D to Ensenada, and at the Chamber of Commerce, C 1 and Av Revolución, English-speaking staff, helpful, Mon-Fri 0900-1400, 1600-1900; Sat 0900-1300. Brochures and schematic maps available; no hotel lists. Chamber of Commerce also offers rest rooms and first aid facilities to visitors. **Procuraduría de Protección al Turista** is in the Government Centre in the Río Tijuana development; 0800-1900.

● **Useful telephone numbers**

Emergency: **Fire**: 135; **Police**: 134; **Red Cross**: 132; valid for Tijuana, Rosarito, Ensenada, Tecate, Mexicali and San Luis Río Colorado.

● **Transport**

Air 20 mins from San Diego, CA; cheaper flights than from the US. Prices vary considerably so shop around. Lots of flights to Mexico City, also to Los Mochis, La Paz, Aguascalientes, Colima,

Guadalajara, Durango, Culiacán, Mazatlán, Puebla, Tepic, Torreón, Zacatecas, Ciudad Juárez, Cuernavaca, Puerto Vallarta, León, Morelia, Monterrey, Acapulco, Chihuahua, Ciudad Obregón, Hermosillo, Manzanillo, Oaxaca and San Luís Potosí. Taxi between airport and centre is quoted at US$15 (bargaining may be possible from centre to airport); colectivo from airport to border, 'La Línea', US$3.20. Mexicoach run from San Diego to Tijuana airport for US$15, combination bus to Plaza La Jolla and taxi to airport.

Buses Local buses about US$0.30, taxis ask US$10 (but shouldn't be that much), 'Central Camionera' or 'Buena Vista' buses to bus station, downtown buses to border depart from C 2a nr Av Revolución. Local buses also go to the border from the bus station, every 30 mins up to 2300, marked 'La Línea/Centro', US$0.50. New bus station is 5 km SE of centre on the airport road at the end of Vía Ote (at La Mesa). It is very crowded and inefficient; take advantage of toilet facilities as long distance buses are usually so full of luggage and goods that getting to the toilet at the back is impossible. There is a bank which changes TCs. Parking at bus terminal US$1/hr. To **Mexico City** (every couple of hours) 1st class (Tres Estrellas de Oro, T 869515/869060), normal about 38-45 hrs, US$100, express US$110, poor, expensive food at stops, *plus* service US$115, or special (with video and more comfort), US$132, 38 hrs. (Transportes del Pacífico, similar fares, express only). 2nd class (Transportes del Norte de Sonora), US$86. Other 1st class routes: **Guadalajara**, 36 hrs, US$82.50; **Hermosillo**, 12 hrs, US$35; **Los Mochis**, 22 hrs, US$53, Tres Estrellas de Oro; **Mazatlán**, 29 hrs, US$62.75; Sonoita US$16.50, Culiacán US$54; Querétaro US$99. By ABC line: **Ensenada**, about hourly 0500-2400, 1½ hrs, US$2.90, bus leaves from behind Centro Comercial at border; **Mexicali**, hourly from 0500-2200, US$6.50 first class; **San Quintín**, 7 a day, US$7.15; **Santa Rosalía**, 1600, direct, US$37; La Paz, 0800, US$60.50, packed full; Tres Estrellas to La Paz, cheaper, 4 a day, 24 hrs. There are also many services E and S from the old bus station at Av Madero and C 1a (Comercio). From Tijuana bus terminal Greyhound has buses every 2 hrs to San Diego via the Otay Mesa crossing, except after 2200, when it uses the Tijuana crossing; coming from San Diego stay on the bus to the main Tijuana terminal, entry stamp given at border (ask driver to get it for you), or at bus station. Long queues for immigration at lunchtime. Fare San Diego-Tijuana US$12.50, 2 hrs. Walk across 'La Línea' border and catch a Golden State bus to downtown Los Angeles, US$13 (buy ticket inside *McDonalds* restaurant), 12 a day, or take trolley to downtown San Diego and there get Greyhound, US$20, or Amtrak train, US$25, to Los Angeles. Golden State is the cheapest and fastest; its terminal is about 1 km from Greyhound terminal in downtown LA, but stops first at Santa Ana and elsewhere if requested. If travelling beyond Los Angeles, ask about layovers in LA before buying a through ticket. Tijuana is a major transportation centre and schedules are complex and extensive.

SOUTH OF TIJUANA

A dramatic 106-km toll road (Highway 1-D) leads along cliffs overhanging the Pacific to Ensenada; the toll is in three sections of US$2 each. There are emergency phones approximately every 2 km on the toll road. This is the safest route between the two cities and 16 exit points allow access to a number of seaside developments and villages along the coast.

ROSARITO

Largest is **Rosarito** (*Pop* 50,000), variously described as a drab resort strung out along the old highway, or 'a breath of fresh air after Tijuana', with numerous seafood restaurants, curio shops, etc. There is a fine swimming beach; horseriding on N and S Rosarito beaches US$4/hr. In Mar and April accommodation is hard to find as college students in great numbers take their holiday here.

● **Accommodation** Many hotels and motels, inc: **A3-B** *Festival Plaza*, Blvd Benito Juárez, T 20842, F 20224, deluxe, pool, shopping, 1 block from beach; **A3-B** *Quinta del Mar Resort Hotel*, pool, sauna, tennis, also condos and townhouses with kitchens (T 21145), *Beachcomber Bar*, good food, relatively cheap, good for watching the sunset; *Motel Quinta Chico*; **B-C** *Motel Colonial* (T 21575); **D** *Rene's Motel* (T 21020), plain but comfortable; **D** *Motel La Prieta*. Best is the **A3-B** *Rosarito Beach Hotel*, T 21106 (US toll free 1-800-343-8582), Benito Juárez 31, which was one of the casinos which opened during Prohibition; its architecture and decoration are worth a look.

● **Tourist offices** Quinta Plaza Mall, Benito Juárez 96, 0900-1600 daily.

The coast as far as Puerto Nuevo and nearby **Cantamar** (Km 26 and 28) is lightly built-up (toll between Cantamar and Highway 1 US$2.30, none heading towards Cantamar); there are several trailer parks and an amazing number of restaurants specializing in lobster and seafood (impressive is *Jatay*, built on 4 levels, Puerto Nuevo). There is fine surfing to the N and 'hassle-free' hang-gliding areas S of Cantamar. 11 km S is an archaeological garden (Plaza del Mar) with an exhibition of precolumbian stone art, open to visitors. At **Punta Salsipuedes**, 51 km S of Tijuana by the tollway, a *mirador* affords sweeping views of the rugged Pacific coast and the offshore Todos Santos Islands. The section of Highway 1-D for several km beyond this point is subject to landslides.

ENSENADA

(*Pop* 255,700) Baja's third city and leading seaport. It is a delightful city on the northern shore of the Bahía de Todos Santos, whose blue waters sport many dolphins and underline the austere character of a landscape reduced to water, sky and scorched brown earth. Sport and commercial fishing, canning, wineries, olive groves and agriculture are the chief activities. The port is rather unattractive and the beach is dirty.

Places of interest

Tourist activity concentrates along Av López Mateos, where most of the hotels, restaurants and shops are located. The twin white towers of **Nuestra Señora de Guadalupe**, C 6a, are a prominent landmark; on the seafront boulevard is the new **Plaza Cívica**, a landscaped court containing large busts of Juárez, Hidalgo and Carranza. A splendid view over city and bay can be had from the road circling the Chapultepec Hills on the western edge of the business district. Steep but paved access is via the W extension of C 2a, 2 blocks

from the bus station. The **Bodegas de Santo Tomás** is Mexico's premier winery, Av Miramar 666, between C 6 y 7, T 82509; daily tours at 1100, 1300, 1500, US$2. *Charreadas* are held on summer weekends at the *charro* ground at Blancarte y C 2a. A weekend street market is held from 0700-1700 at Av Riversoll y C 7a; the fish market at the bottom of Av Macheros specializes in 'fish tacos' (a fish finger wrapped in a taco!). *Ensenada Clipper Fleet* runs daily fishing trips (0700-1500) from the sportfishing terminal. Also seasonal whale-watching trips and bay and coastal excursions.

Local information
● **Accommodation**

L2 *Las Rosas Hotel and Spa*, on Highway 1, 7 km W of town, suites, spectacular ocean views, pool, sauna, restaurant; **L2** *Punta Morro Hotel Suites*, on coast 3 km W of town, rooms have kitchens and fridges, 2 and 3-bedroom apartments available, pool; **L2** *San Nicolás Resort Hotel*, López Mateos y Av Guadalupe, T 61901, a/c, suites, dining room, disco.

In the ranges **A1-A3**: *Villa Marina*, Av López Mateos y Blancarte, T 83321, heated pool, coffee shop; *La Pinta*, Av Floresta y Blvd Bucaneros (on Fri-Sat, B Sun-Thur), TV, pool, restaurant; *Punta Morro*, 3 km N on Highway 1, rooms and suites, a/c, pool, kitchens, etc; *Quintas Papagayo*, 1½ km N on Highway 1, T 44575, landscaped beach resort complex with all facilities, Hussong's *Pelican* restaurant attached, seafood and local specialities, 0800-2300, best value for an Ensenada 'splurge'.

B *Bahía*, López Mateos, T 82101, balconies, suites, fridges, quiet, clean, parking, a/c, good value, popular; **B** *Misión Santa Isabel*, López Mateos and Castillo, T 83616, pool, suites, Spanish Mission-style, attractive.

D *América*, López Mateos opp State Tourist Office, T 61333, basic, hard beds, kitchenettes, good; **D** *Plaza*, López Mateos 540, central, plain but clean, rooms facing street noisy; **D** *Ritz*, Av Ruiz y C 4, No 381, T 40573, central, a/c, TV, phone, coffee shop, parking; **D** *Royal*, Av Castelum, bath, parking.

Several cheaper hotels around Miramar and C 3, eg **C-D** *Perla del Pacífico*, Av Miramar 229, quite clean, hot water; **E** *Río*, Av Miramar and C 2, basic, noisy until 0300 when local bars shut. Note that some of the larger hotels have different rates for summer and winter; cheaper tariffs are given above, check first! All hotels are filled in Ensenada on weekends, get in early.

Motels: in our **A1-A3** ranges: *Ensenada Travelodge*, Av Blancarte 130, T 81601, a/c, heated pool, whirlpool, family rates available, restaurant; *Cortés*, López Mateos 1089 y Castillo, T 82307, F 83904; *Casa del Sol* (Best Western), López Mateos 101, T 81570, F 82025, a/c, TV, pool, comfortable; *El Cid*, on Fri-Sat, B on Sun-Thur, Av López Mateos 993, T 82401, Spanish-style building, a/c, fridges, suites available, dining room, lounge, disco. **C** *Balboa*, Guerrero 172 y Cortés, T 61077, modern, comfortable, some way E of downtown; **C** *Villa Fontana*, López Mateos y **C** Blancarte, T 83434, good location, old but large clean rooms, cheerful, English spoken; **D** *Costa Mar*, Av Veracruz 319 at Playa Hermosa (1 km S), ½ block from beach, T 66425, TV, phones, etc, agreeable; **E** *Pancho*, Av Alvarado 211, shabby but clean rooms, opp the *charro* ground, cheapest habitable motel in town. A great many good trailer parks.

● **Places to eat**
El Rey Sol, López Mateos 1000 y Blancarte, French/Mexican, elegant, reasonable prices; *La Góndola*, López Mateos between Miramar and Macheros, clean, Mexican dishes and pizzas, inc lobster pizza!; *Mesón de Don Fernando*, López Mateos, good breakfasts, tacos and seafood, good value; *Taco Factory*, López Mateos y Av Gastelum, good tacos, many varieties. *Cantina Hussong's*, Av Ruíz 113, an institution in both the Californias, 1000-1400. *Cha-Cha Burgers*, Blvd Costero 609, 'American' style burgers', fish, chicken, fast food 1000-2200; *Pancho's Place* (don't confuse with *Motel Pancho*), Ejército Nacional (Highway 1) y San Marcos, well-run, wide menu, pleasant; *Restaurant Muylam*, Ejército Nacional y Diamante, seafood and Chinese cuisine, 1200-2400; *China Land*, Riveroll 1149 between C 11 y 12, Sichuan, Mandarin and Cantonese cuisine, authentic, not cheap, 1200-2300; *El Pollo*, Macheros y C 2, grilled chicken 'Sinaloa style', fast food 1000-2200 every day of year; *Las Brasas*, López Mateos 486, between Ruíz and Gastelum barbecue chicken and fish, Mexican specialities, attractive patio dining, 1100-2200, closed Tues; *Mandarin*, López Mateos 2127, between Soto and Balboa (Chinese), elegant surroundings, good food, expensive, considered to be the best *chifa* in Ensenada. *Domico's*, Av Ruiz 283, also Chinese restaurants in same avenue; *Lonchería*

la Terminal, opp bus station, cheap and filling *comida*, good but basic.

● **Tourist offices**
Av López Mateos y Espinoza, part of the Fonartartesan centre, Mon-Sat 0900-1900, accommodation literature; the Procuraduría is next door, same hours plus Sun 0900-1600. **Tourist and Convention Bureau**, Lázaro Cárdenas y Miramar, Mon-Sat 0900-1900, Sun 0900-1400, helpful; free copies of *Ensenada News and Views*, monthly English-language paper with information and adverts on northern Baja, Tijuana and Ensenada.

● **Useful addresses**
Immigration: Oficina de Migratorios, beside the shipyard, for tourist entry permits.

● **Transport**
Air Airport 8 km S. No scheduled services.

Buses To Tijuana, US$2.90, 1½ hrs.

SOUTHEAST TO SAN FELIPE

Highway 3 E to San Felipe leaves Ensenada at the Benito Juárez *glorieta* monument as the Calzada Cortés. 26 km out of Ensenada, an 8-km dirt road branches S for a steep descent to the basic resort of **Agua Caliente** (**C** *Hotel Agua Caliente*, restaurant, bar, closed in winter; adjoining is a campground and large concrete pool heated to 38° by nearby hot springs; access road should not be attempted in wet weather). Free camping at the end of the road 3 km beyond Agua Caliente, no facilities but good hiking in the area.

At Km 39, a paved road leads off 3 km to Ojos Negros, continuing E (graded, dry weather) into scrub-covered foothills. It soon climbs into the ponderosa pine forests of the Sierra de Juárez. 37 km from Ojos Negros, the road enters the **Parque Nacional Constitución de 1857**. The jewel of the park is the small Laguna Hanson, a sparkling shallow lake surrounded by Jeffery pines; camping here is delightful, but note that the lake is reduced to a boggy marsh in dry seasons and that the area receives snow in mid-winter. A high-clearance vehicle is necessary for the continuation N out of the park to Highway 2 at El Cóndor 15 km E of La Rumorosa.

At Km 92½, Ejido Héroes de la Independencia, a graded dirt road runs 8 km E to the ruins of Mission Santa Catarina, founded in 1797 and abandoned after a raid by the Yuman Indians in 1840; the Paipái women in the village often have attractive pottery for sale.

Highway 3 descends along the edge of a green valley to the rapidly developing town of Valle de Trinidad. A reasonable dirt road runs S into the **Parque Nacional Sierra San Pedro Mártir** and Mike's Sky Rancho (35 km), a working ranch which offers motel-style accommodation, a pool, camping and guided trips into the surrounding mountains; rooms **E**, good meals.

After leaving the valley, the highway follows a canyon covered in dense stands of barrel cacti to the San Matías Pass between the Sierras Juárez and San Pedro Mártir which leads onto the desolate Valle de San Felipe. The highway turns E and emerges onto open desert hemmed in by arid mountains. 198½ km from Ensenada it joins Highway 5 at the La Trinidad T-junction, 148 km from Mexicali and 50 km from San Felipe.

SOUTH FROM ENSENADA

Highway 1 S from Ensenada passes turn-offs to several beach resorts. Just before the agricultural town of **Maneadero**, a paved highway runs 23 km W onto the Punta Banda pensinsula, where you can see **La Bufadora** blowhole, one of the most powerful on the Pacific. Air sucked from a sea-level cave is expelled as high as 16m through a cleft in the cliffs. Concrete steps and viewing platform give easy access. Tourist stalls line the approach road and boys try to charge US$1 for parking (restaurants *Los Panchos* and *La Bufadora*, Mesquite-grilled seafood, *palapa* dining, both 0900 to around sunset). This is one of the easiest side trips off the length of Highway 1.

NB Tourist cards and vehicle documents of those travelling S of Maneadero are supposed to be validated at the immigration checkpoint on the southern outskirts of the town; the roadside office, however, is not always in operation. If you are not stopped, just keep going.

SANTO TOMAS

Chaparal-clad slopes begin to close in on the highway as it winds it way S, passing through the small towns of **Santo Tomás** (**D** *El Palomar Motel*, adequate but overpriced rooms, restaurant, bar, general store and gas station, RV park with full hook-ups, campsite with swimming pool, clean, refurbished, US$10, nearby ruins of the Dominican Mission of 1791, local Santo Tomás wine, cheaper out of town) and **San Vicente** (**E** *Motel El Cammo*, Highway 1, S of town, without bath, friendly, OK restaurant; two Pemex stations, cafés, tyre repairs, several stores), before reaching **Colonet**. This is a supply centre for surrounding ranches; several services. A dry weather dirt road runs 12 km W to **San Antonio del Mar**, many camping spots amid high dunes fronting a beautiful beach renowned for surf fishing and clam-digging.

14 km S of Colonet a reasonable graded road branches to San Telmo and climbs into the mountains. At 50 km it reaches the *Meling Ranch* (also called San José), which offers resort accommodation for about 12 guests. 15 km beyond San José the road enters the **Parque Nacional Sierra San Pedro Mártir** and climbs through forests (4WD recommended) to three astronomical observatories perched on the dramatic eastern escarpment of the central range. The view from here is one of the most extensive in North America: E to the Gulf, W to the Pacific, and SE to the overwhelming granite mass of the **Picacho del Diablo** (3,096m), Baja's highest peak. The higher reaches of the park receive snow in winter. The observatories are not open to visitors.

SAN QUINTIN

(Pop 15,000) 179 km from Ensenada, **San Quintín** is a thriving market city almost joined to Lázaro Cárdenas 5 km S. There are service stations in both centres (check pump readings carefully) and San Quintín provides all services. Rising out of the peninsula W of San Quintín bay is a line of volcanic cinder cones, visible for many kilometres along the highway; the beaches to the S near Santa María are hugely popular with fishermen, campers and beachcombers.

Local festivals

20 Nov: *Day of the Revolution*, street parades with school children, bands and the military.

Local information
● **Accommodation**

A2 *La Pinta*, isolated beachfront location 18 km S of San Quintín then 5 km W on paved road, a/c, TV, balconies, tennis, nearby airstrip, reasonably priced breakfasts, even for non-residents.

E *Hada's Rooms*, just N of Benito Juárez army camp in Lázaro Cárdenas, cheapest in town, shabby, basic, sometimes closed when water and electricity are cut off.

Motels: A3-C *Molino Viejo/The Old Mill*, on site of old English mill, part of an early agricultural scheme, upgraded by new American owners, new wing, new bar and dining room with good food and drink, on bay 6 km of W of highway and S of Lázaro Cárdenas, rough access road, some kitchenettes, also one 6-bed dormitory, 15 RV spaces with full hook-up (US$15), camping (US$10), electricity 0800-0900, 1800-2200, various sizes of boat for rent, rec as 'delightfully well-run and cosy' (in USA, representative is The Baja Outfitter, 223 Via de San Ysidro, Ste 76, San Ysidro, CA 92173, T 619-428-2779, F 619-428-6269, or T 800-479-7962); **C** *Cielito Lindo*, 2 km beyond the *La Pinta Hotel* on S shore of bay, restaurant, cafeteria, lounge (dancing Sat nights), electricity Mon-Sat 0700-1100, 1500-2400, Sun 0700-2400, modest but pleasant, US$5 for vehicles to camp overnight (use of showers), last km of access road unpaved, messy after rain; **C** *San Carlos*, at Old Pier restaurant, large rooms, friendly, good value; **D** *Ernesto's*, next door, rustic, overpriced, popular with fishermen,

electricity 0700-2100; **D** *Muelle Viejo*, between *Ernesto's* and the old English cemetery, restaurant, bad access road, hot showers, bay views; **E** *Chávez*, on highway N of Lázaro Cárdenas, family-style, clean rooms, TV, plain but good value; **E** *Romo*, about 200m from post office, clean, OK, convenient if arriving late; **E** *Sánchez*, a few kilometres before town in Col Guerrero, large rooms, clean; **E** *Uruapan*, very clean and friendly.

Camping: *Pabellón RV Campground*, 15 km S and 2 km W on coast, 200 spaces, no electricity, disposal station, toilets, showers, beach access, US$5/vehicle, great area for clam-digging. *Posada Don Diego*, off Highway in Colonia Guerrero (S of town, Km 174), wide range of facilities, laundry, restaurant, etc, 100 spaces, US$7; at S end of Colonia Guerrero is *Mesón de Don Pepe RV Park*, smaller and more modest, full hook-ups, restaurant with view of campground so you can watch your tent, US$5. *Campo Lorenzo* is just N of Molino Viejo, 20 spaces, full hook-ups but mostly permanent residents. Trailer park attached to Cielito Lindo Motel, comfortable.

● **Places to eat**

El Alteño, on highway next to the cinema, bare but clean roadhouse, fresh seafood and Mexican dishes, Mariachi music, moderate prices, closed July-Sept; *Tres Estrellas de Oro*, where the bus company stops for lunch, reasonably priced and sized meals. *Muelle Viejo*, next to motel, overlooks old pier, reasonably-priced seafood, modest decor. *Mi Lien* on Highway 1, N end of town, very good Chinese food.

● **Banks & money changers**
Banco International, off highway behind the Pemex station and small plaza.

● **Post & telecommunications**
Post Office: on highway opp the *El Alteño*.

EL ROSARIO

After leaving the San Quintín valley, bypassing Santa María (fuel), the Transpeninsular Highway (officially the Carretera Transpeninsular Benito Juárez) runs near the Pacific before darting inland at El Consuelo Ranch. It climbs over a barren spur from which there are fine views, then drops in a succession of tight curves into **El Rosario**, 58 km from San Quintín. This small, agricultural community has a Pemex station, small supermarket, a basic museum, and meals, including Espinosa's famous lobster *burritos* (expensive and not particularly good) and omelettes, also a good *taco* stand outside the grocery store at night. 3 km S is a ruined Dominican Mission, founded 1774 upstream, then moved to its present site in 1882; take the graded dirt road to Punta Baja, a bold headland on the coast, where there is a solar-powered lighthouse and fishing village.

● **Accommodation D** *Motel Rosario*, small, basic; new motel at S end of town; **D** *Sinai*, comfortable, very clean, small RV park, friendly owner makes good meals, but beware of overcharging.

CENTRAL DESERT OF BAJA CALIFORNIA

Highway 1 makes a sharp 90° turn at El Rosario and begins to climb continuously into the central plateau; gusty winds increase and astonishingly beautiful desertscapes gradually become populated with many varieties of cacti. Prominent are the stately *cardones*: most intriguing are the strange, twisted *cirios* growing to heights of 6 to 10m. They are unique to this portion of Baja California as far S as the Vizcaíno Desert, and to a small area of Sonora state on the mainland. At Km 62 a 5 km track branches S to the adobe remains of **Misión San Fernando Velicatá**, the only Franciscan mission in Baja, founded by Padre Serra in 1769. 5 km further on, Rancho El Progreso offers expensive meals and refreshments (possible to camp behind Rancho, and RV park, fill up with water if possible). The highway is now in the **Desierto Central de Baja California Natural Park** (as yet not officially recognized). About 26 km N of Cataviña a strange region of huge boulders begins, some as big as houses; interspersed by cacti and crouching elephant trees, this area is one of the most picturesque on the peninsula.

Cataviña is only a dozen buildings, with a small grocery store/*Café La Enramada*, the only Pemex station on the 227-km stretch from El Rosario to the Bahía de Los Angeles junction (there are in fact 2 fuel stations, but do not rely on either having supplies), and the attractive **A3** *La Pinta Hotel*, a/c, pool, bar, electricity 1800-2400, good restaurant, tennis, rooms, rec. Attached to the *La Pinta* is the *Parque Natural Desierto Central de Baja California Trailer Park*, flush toilets, showers, restaurant, bar, US$3 per site. 2 km S of Cataviña is Rancho Santa Inés, which has dormitory-style accommodation (E), meals and a paved airstrip.

Highway 1 continues SE through an arid world of boulder strewn mountains and dry salt lakes. At 53 km the new graded road to the Bahía San Luís Gonzaga (see under San Felipe) branches off to the E. After skirting the dry bed of Laguna Chapala (natural landing strip at southern end when lake is totally dry), the Transpeninsular Highway arrives at the junction with the paved road E to Bahía de Los Angeles; **C** *Parador Punta Prieta*, fair, 20 RV spaces with full hook-ups, few facilities; gas station at junction, fuel supply sometimes unreliable, small store at the junkyard opposite the gas station.

BAHIA DE LOS ANGELES

The side road runs 68 km through *cirios* and *datilillo* cactus-scapes and crosses the Sierra de la Asamblea to **Bahía de Los Angeles** (no public transport but hitch-hiking possible), a popular fishing town which, despite a lack of vegetation, is one of Baja's best-known beauty spots. The bay, sheltered by the forbidding slopes of Isla Angel de la Guarda (Baja's largest island), is a haven for boating (winds can be tricky for kayaks and small craft). The series of tiny beaches at the foot of the Díaz *cabañas* are good for swimming, but watch out for stingrays when wading. There is good clamming and oysters. Facilities in town include: gas station, bakery, grocery stores, two trailer parks and four restaurants, paved airstrip; water supply is inadequate, a water truck visits weekly, electricity is cut off about 2200 nightly.

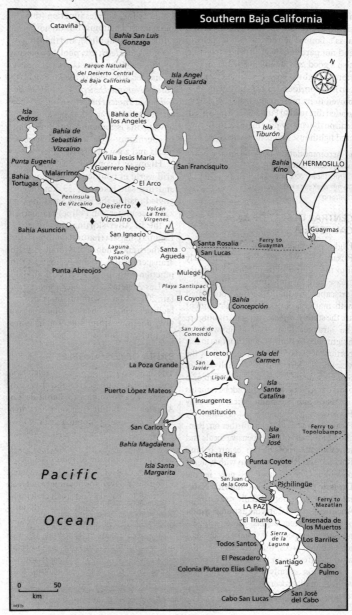

Southern Baja California

Cataviña

Bahía San Luis Gonzaga

Parque Natural del Desierto Central de Baja California

Isla Angel de la Guarda

Isla Cedros

Bahía de Sebastián Vizcaíno

Bahía de los Angeles

Punta Eugenia

Malarrimo

Villa Jesús María

Guerrero Negro

San Francisquito

Isla Tiburón

Bahía Kino

HERMOSILLO

Bahía Tortugas

El Arco

Península de Vizcaíno

Desierto Vizcaíno

Volcán La Tres Vírgenes

Bahía Asunción

San Ignacio

Laguna San Ignacio

Santa Agueda

Santa Rosalía

San Lucas

Ferry to Guaymas

Guaymas

Punta Abreojos

Mulegé

Playa Santispac

El Coyote

Bahía Concepción

San José de Comondú

Loreto

Isla del Carmen

La Poza Grande

San Javier

Ligüí

Isla Santa Catalina

Puerto López Mateos

Insurgentes

Constitución

Isla San José

San Carlos

Ferry to Topolobampo

Bahía Magdalena

Santa Rita

Punta Coyote

Isla Santa Margarita

San Juan de la Costa

Pichilingüe

Ferry to Mazatlán

Pacific

LA PAZ

El Triunfo

Ensenada de los Muertos

Ocean

Sierra de la Laguna

Los Barriles

Todos Santos

El Pescadero

Colonia Plutarco Elías Calles

Santiago

Cabo Pulmo

0   50
km

Cabo San Lucas

San José del Cabo

There is also a modest but interesting museum in town, good for information on the many mines and mining techniques used in the region around the turn of the century, such as the San Juan Mine high in the mountains 24 km SSW which had its own 2-ft guage railway and wire rope tramway down to a smelter at Las Flores as early as 1895; the relic steam locomotive and mine car on display beside the airstrip are from this remarkable mine (which returned US$2mn in gold and silver before closing down in 1910).

Lynn and Walt Sutherland from Vancouver write: "Bahía de los Angeles (*Pop* 1,245) is worth a visit for its sea life. There are thousands of dolphins in the bay June-December. Some stay all year. In July and Aug you can hear the whales breathe as you stand on shore. There are large colonies of seals and many exotic seabirds. Fishing is excellent. A boat and guide can be rented for US$40 a day; try Raúl, a local fisherman, who speaks English." Camping free and safe on beach.

La Gringa is a beautiful beach 13 km N of town, many camping sites, pit toilets, rubbish bins, small fee.

● **Accommodation & places to eat** C *Villa Vita Motel*, modern, a/c, pool, jacuzzi, boat launch, trailer park, electricity 0700-1400, 1700-2000, bar, dining room; D *Casa de Díaz*, 15 rooms, restaurant, grocery store, campground, boat rentals, clean but cockroaches, well-run, popular; *Guillermo's Trailer Park*, flush toilets, showers, restaurant, gift shop, boat ramp and rentals; *Guillermo's* also has a restaurant in a white building on main street, above the gift shop, well-prepared Mexican food, attractive, reservations advised at weekends; *La Playa RV Park*, on beach, similar facilities and tariff (US$4/site); *Sal y Mauro* campsite, first gravel road on left before entering town, friendly, rec. *Restaurant Las Hamacas*, on N edge of town, budget café with bay view, slow service, popular for breakfast.

The highway now runs due S. 3 km from the highway is **San Ignacio** (D-E *Hotel La Posada*; grocery stores). There is a small and interesting museum on the edge of the square about nearby cave paintings. Trips to the caves are available. Before you enter Baja California Sur you pass Punta Prieta (3 stores) and Rosarito (1 store and 1 restaurant) and go through **Villa Jesús María** (gas station, store, cafés) to the 28th parallel, the state border between Baja California and Baja California Sur

Whale watching

Whale watching is the main attraction on nearby **Laguna Ojo de Liebre**, usually known as **Scammon's Lagoon** after the whaling captain who entered in 1857. California Grey Whales mate and give birth between end Dec and Feb, in several warm-water lagoons on central Baja's Pacific coast, most leave by the beginning of April, but some not departing until as late as May or June. They can be seen cavorting and sounding from the old salt wharf 10 km NW of Guerrero Negro on the Estero San José, or from a designated 'whale watching area' with observation tower on the shore of Scammon's Lagoon 37 km S of town. The access road branches off Highway 1, 8 km E of the junction (if going by public transport, leave bus at the turn off and hitch). US$3 is charged to enter the park. Local personnel may collect a small fee for camping at the watching area, this pays to keep it clean. The shores of Scammon's are part of the **Parque Natural de Ballena Gris**. Watch between 0700 and 0900 and again at 1700. The authorities in Guerrero Negro say that boats are not allowed on to the lagoon to watch whales, but *pangas* are available for hire (US$10 pp). There are also daily tours including 1½ hrs boat trip, sandwiches and transport to the lagoon, US$30 pp.

The road to the park was repaired in 1991 and now has little whale signs at regular intervals. It is still sandy in places, so drive with care.

(soaring stylized eagle monument and **A3** *Hotel La Pinta*, a/c, pool, dining room, bar, trailer park attached, 60 spaces, full hook-ups, US$5, laundry and gasoline at hotel).

NB Advance clocks 1 hr to Mountain time when entering Baja California Sur, but note that Northern Baja observes Pacific Daylight Saving Time from first Sun in April to last Sun in Oct; time in both states and California is thus identical during the summer.

GUERRERO NEGRO

(Pop 9,000) 3 km beyond the state line and 4 km W of the highway; 714 km S of Tijuana, 414 from San Quintín, Guerrero Negro is the halfway point between the US border and La Paz. There are 2 gas stations, bank, hospital, cafés, stores, an airport with scheduled services (just N of the Eagle monument), and the headquarters of Exportadora de Sal, the world's largest salt-producing firm. Seawater is evaporated by the sun from thousands of salt ponds S of town; the salt is loaded at the works 11 km SW of town and barged to a deepwater port on Cedros Island. From there ore carriers take it to the USA, Canada and Japan.

● **Accommodation** *San Ignacio*, on road into town from highway, new, clean, good but exact prices unknown; **D** *San José*, opp bus terminal, clean, will help to organize whale-watching tours; **E** *Cuartos de Sánchez-Smith*, C Barrera, W end of town, basic rooms, some with showers, cheapest in town. **Camping**: *Malarrimo Trailer Park*, on highway at E end of town, flush toilets, showers, bar, US$10/vehicle, whale watching tours arranged. **Motels**: **C** *Cabañas Don Miguel* (same owner and location as *Malarrimo Restaurant*), E end of town, very clean, TV, fan, quiet, rec; **D** *El Morro*, on road into town from highway, modest, clean; **E** *Las Dunas*, few doors from *El Morro*, modest, clean; **E** *Gámez*, very basic, nr city hall.

● **Places to eat** Good restaurant at bus station. *Malarrimo Restaurant-Bar*, fishing decor, good fish and steak menu, moderate prices, music, open for breakfast, runs whale-watching tours, US$30 pp, inc transport to boats and lunch; *Mario's Restaurant-Bar*, next to *El Morro*, modest surroundings and fare, disco. Excellent taco stall a few blocks towards town from *El Morro*. Good bakery on main street.

● **Transport Air** Seroliteral flies from Tucson, Arizona and Hermosillo 5-6 days a week. Flights go to Cedros Island and Bahía Tortugas; information from airfield downtown.

After Guerrero Negro the highway enters the grim Vizcaíno Desert. A paved but badly potholed road leads due E (42 km) to El Arco, other abandoned mining areas and crossing to **San Francisquito** on its beautiful bay on the Gulf (77 km), and to Santa Gertrudis Mission (1752), some of whose stone ruins have been restored; the chapel is still in use. It should be stressed that these minor Bajan roads require high-clearance, preferably 4x4, vehicles carrying adequate equipment and supplies, water and fuel. A new gravel road from Bahía de Los Angeles (135 km) gives easier road access than from El Arco and opens up untouched stretches of the Gulf coast.

Vizcaíno Peninsula which thrusts into the Pacific S of Guerrero Negro is one of the remotest parts of Baja. Although part of the Vizcaíno Desert, the scenery of the peninsula is varied and interesting; isolated fishcamps dot the silent coast of beautiful coves and untrodden beaches. Until recently only the most hardy ventured into the region; now an improved dry-weather road cuts W through the peninsula to Bahía Tortugas and the rugged headland of Punta Eugenia. It leaves Highway 1 at Vizcaíno Junction (also called Fundolegal, Pemex station, café, market, pharmacy and auto parts store; *Motel Olivia* at Vizcaíno, reasonably priced, hot water), 70 km beyond Guerrero Negro is paved for 8 km to Ejido Díaz Ordaz. The new road passes Rancho San José (116 km) and the easily-missed turn-off to Malarrimo Beach (where beach-combing is unparalleled). After another bumpy 50 km is **Bahía Tortugas**, a surprisingly large place *(Pop 3,200)* considering its remoteness. Many facilities

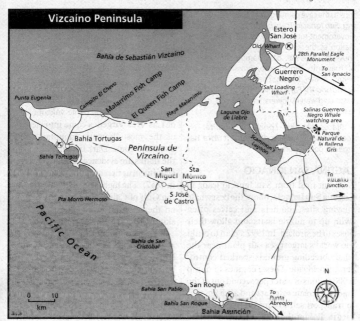

Vizcaíno Peninsula

Estero
San José
Old Wharf
28th Parallel Eagle
Monument
To
San Ignacio
Guerrero
Negro
Salt Loading
Wharf
Bahía de Sebastián Vizcaíno
Campito El Chevo
Malarrimo Fish Camp
El Queen Fish Camp
Playa Malarrimo
Laguna Ojo
de Liebre
Salinas Guerrero
Negro Whale
watching area
Parque
Natural de
la Ballena
Gris
Punta Eugenia
Scammen's Lagoon
Bahía Tortugas
Península de
Vizcaíno
Bahía Tortugas
San
Miguel
Sta
Mónica
To
Vizcaíno
junction
Pta Morro Hermoso
S José
de Castro
Pacific Ocean
Bahía de San
Cristóbal
Bahía San Pablo
San Roque
Bahía San Roque
To
Punta
Abreojos
Bahía Asunción
N
0   10
km

including eating places, health clinic, gas station, airport with services to Cedros Island and Ensenada, and the small **D-E** *Vera Cruz Motel*, restaurant, bar, very modest but the only accommodation on the peninsula apart from a trailer park at Campo René, 15 km from Punta Abreojos. Two roads leave the Vizcaíno-Bahía Tortuga road for Bahía Asunción (*Pop* 1,600), which has the peninsula's only other gas station, then following the coast to Punta Prieta, La Bocana and Punta Abreojos (93 km). A lonely road runs for 85 km back to Highway 1, skirting the Sierra Santa Clara before crossing the salt marshes N of Laguna San Ignacio and reaching the main road 26 km before San Ignacio.

SAN IGNACIO

The Highway continues SE on a new alignment still not shown on most maps and, 20 km from Vizcaíno Junction, reaches the first of 23 microwave relay towers which follow Highway 1 almost to the Cape. They are closed to the public but make excellent landmarks and, in some cases, offer excellent views 143 km from Guerrero Negro is the turnoff for **San Ignacio** (*Pop* 2,200). Here the Jesuits built a mission in 1728 and planted the ancestors of the town's date palm groves. On the square is the beautifully-preserved mission church, completed by the Dominicans in 1786. Near the mission is a good museum. The town is very attractive, with thatched-roof dwellings and pastel-coloured commercial buildings; there is limited shopping but several restaurants, service station, mechanical assistance and bank.

● **Accommodation A3** *La Pinta*, on road leading into town, a/c, pool, all facilities, built in mission style, attractive but overpriced; **E** *Cuartos Glenda*, with shower, basic but cheapest in town, on highway E. **Motel: D** *La Posada*, on rise 2 blocks from zócalo (difficult to find), well-maintained, fans, shower, best value in town, worth bargaining (owner can arrange trips to the cave paintings for US$25 pp). **Camping**: *San Ignacio Transpeninsula Trailer Park*, Government-run, on Highway 1 behind Pemex station at the junction, full hook-ups, toilets, showers, US$4/site; basic campground on left of road into San Ignacio, grass, run down, helpful owner, Martín, cheap dates in season; *El Padrino RV Park*, on same road on the right, basic, cold water showers, sites on sand, decent restaurant.

● **Places to eat** *Loncheria Chalita*, on Zócalo, excellent value; *Restaurant Tota* has received poor reports.

LAGUNA SAN IGNACIO

A 70-km road from San Ignacio leads to **Laguna San Ignacio**, one of the best whale viewing sites; mothers and calves often swim up to nuzzle boats and allow their noses to be stroked. In 1997 a plan to build the world's largest sea salt plant near the whale breeding grounds sparked controversy worldwide. Diesel engines to pump 6,000 gallons of water per second out of the lagoon to create salt flats and a 1.5 km pier to transport salt to cargo ships were forecast to disrupt the whales' migration and reproduction. The company, Essa, 51% owned by the Mexican government and 49% owned by Mitsubishi, already operates in the Laguna Ojo de Lievre. The Cooperativa Laguna de San Ignacio, C Juárez 23, off the Zócalo in San Ignacio, takes fishermen to the lagoon every day and can sometimes accommodate visitors. The road is rough and requires a high clearance vehicle.

There are many cave painting sites around San Ignacio; colourful human and animal designs left by Baja's original inhabitants still defy reliable dating, or full understanding. To reach most requires a trek by mule over tortuous trails; Oscar Fischer, owner of the *La Posada Motel*, arranges excursions into the sierras (about US$10 per person to Santa Teresa cave). The cave at the **Cuesta del Palmarito**, 5 km E of Rancho Santa Marta (50 NW of San Ignacio), is filled with designs of humans with uplifted arms, in brown and black; a jeep and guide (if one

can be found) are required. A better road leads E from the first microwave station past Vizcaíno Junction up to **San Francisco de la Sierra**, where there are other paintings and petroglyphs in the vicinity (US$120 pp for trip with own car).

Highway 1 leaves the green *arroyo* of San Ignacio and re-emerges into the arid central desert. To the N, the triple volcanic cones of **Las Tres Vírgenes** come into view, one of the most dramatic mountain scenes along this route. Dark brown lava flows on the flanks are evidence of relatively recent activity (eruption in 1746, smoke emission in 1857). The highest peak is 2,149m above the Gulf of California; the sole vegetation on the lunar-like landscape is the thick-skinned elephant trees.

2½ million ha of the Vizcaíno Desert are now protected by the **Reserva de la Biósfera El Vizcaíno**, supposedly the largest in Latin America. It was decreed in Nov 1988 and has absorbed the Parque Nacional Ballena Gris. It runs S from the state border to the road from San Ignacio to Laguna San Ignacio and Highway 1 near Santa Rosalía; it stretches from the Pacific to the Gulf. Encompassed by the reserve are the desert, the Vizcaína Peninsula, Scammon's Lagoon, Las Tres Vírgenes volcano, the Laguna San Ignacio and several offshore islands.

SANTA ROSALIA

72 km from San Ignacio is **Santa Rosalía**, a bustling city of 14,500. It was built by the French El Boleo Copper Company in the 1880s, laid out in neat rows of wood frame houses, many with broad verandahs, which today give Santa Rosalía its distinctly un-Mexican appearance. Most of the mining ceased in 1953; the smelter, several smokestacks above the town and much of the original mining operation can be seen on the N of town.

Places of interest

There is a small museum off C Francisco next to the Impecsa warehouse, historic exhibits of mining and smelting. The port was one of the last used in the age of sail. The church of Santa Bárbara (Av Revolución y Calle C, a block N of the main plaza), built of prefabricated galvanized iron for the 1889 Paris Worlds' Fair from a design by Eiffel, was shipped around the Horn to Baja. A car ferry leaves for Guaymas, from the small harbour, 7 hrs (T 20014, fares are the same as for the La Paz-Topolobampo ferry, see schedule, page 532; tickets sold on day of departure).

Drivers should note that Santa Rosalía's streets are narrow and congested; larger vehicles should park along the highway or in the ferry dock parking lot. The Pemex station is conveniently located on the highway, unlike at Mulegé (see below), so larger RVs and rigs should fill up here.

Local information
● **Accommodation**

D *El Morro*, on Highway 2 km S of town, T 20414, on bluff with Gulf views, modern, Spanish-style, a/c, bar, restaurant (good food, generous portions, reasonable prices); **D** *Francés*, Av 11 de Julio on the N Mesa, T 20829, a/c, restaurant, bar, pool not always filled, historic 2-storey wooden French colonial building overlooking smelter and Gulf, photos of sailing vessels on walls, charming, lukewarm water; **D** *Olvera*, on main plaza, 2nd floor, a/c, showers, clean, good value; **D** *Playa*, Av la Playa between C B y Plaza, central, fans, bathrooms, good budget hotel; **D** *Real*, Av Manuel Montoya nr C A, similar to *Olvera*, rec.

E *Blanca y Negra*, basic but clean, Av Libertad at end of C 3.

Camping: possible on the beach under *palapas*, access via an unmarked road 500m S of *El Morro*, free, no facilities, a beautiful spot. Also trailer park *El Palmar*, 3 km S of town, US$5 for 2, showers, laundry, good value.

● **Places to eat**

Balneario Selene, T 20685, on Highway opp Pemex; *Palapa Mauna Loa*, T 21187, on Highway below copper smelter, good spaghetti and pizzas, popular; *Panadería El Boleo*, widely noted for its delicious French breads.

● **Post & telecommunications**

Post Office: only from here and La Paz can parcels be sent abroad; customs check necessary first, at boat dock.

● **Transport**

Tres Estrellas de Oro bus station (T 220150) nr tourist office and Pemex station 2 km S of ferry terminal; stop for most Tijuana-La Paz buses, several per day. To **La Paz**, 1100, US$24. Autobus Aguila, C 3a y Constitución, T 20374.

Painted cave sites can be visited from the farming town of **Santa Agueda**, turnoff 8 km S of Santa Rosalía then rough dirt road for 12 km. (4WD necessary, guide can be arranged at the Delegado Municipal, C Madero, Mulegé.) The caves are in the San Borjita and La Trinidad deserts; the drawings depict animals, children and, some claim, female sexual organs. The fishing village of **San Lucas**, on a palm-fringed cove, is 14 km S of Santa Rosalía; camping is good and popular on the beaches to N and S. *San Lucas RV Park*, on beach, no hook-ups, flush toilets, boat ramp, ice, restaurant, US$5 per vehicle, 35 spaces, rec. Offshore lies Isla San Marcos, with a gypsum mine at the S end.

Just beyond **San Bruno** is a reasonable dirt road to **San José de Magdalena** (15 km), a picturesque farming village dating back to colonial days; ruined Dominican chapel, attractive thatched palm houses, flower gardens. An awful road leads on for 17 km to Rancho San Isidro, from where the ruined Guadalupe Mission can be reached on horseback. At San Bruno, *Costa Serena* beach camping, no hook-ups, one shower, clean beach with good fishing and shrimping. Similar is *Camp Punta Chivato*, just before Mulegé, no hook-ups but clean toilets and shower, beautiful location.

MULEGE

61 km S of Santa Rosalía, is another oasis community (*Pop* 5,000) whose river enters the gulf as a lushly-vegetated tidal lake. There are lovely beaches, good diving, snorkelling and boating in the Bahía Concepción. The old Federal territorial prison (La Cananea) is being converted into a museum. There is a good cheap fish restaurant 40 mins' walk along the river; the lighthouse, 10 mins further on provides

tremendous views and the sunsets are unforgetable. South of the bridge which carries the highway over the river is the restored Mission of Santa Rosalía de Mulegé, founded by the Jesuits in 1705; good lookout point above the mission over the town and its sea of palm trees. Locals swim at an excellent spot about 500m inland from the bridge and to the right of the track to the Mission. The bank will only change a minimum of US$100. **NB** One Pemex station is in the centre; not convenient for large vehicles, and a one-way system to contend with, but there is another Pemex station 4½ km S of the bridge, on the road out of town towards Loreto, with restaurant and mini-market.

Local information
● Accommodation

B *Baja Hacienda*, C Madero 3, lovely courtyard, pool, rooms refurbished, bar, trips to cave paintings and kayaking offered (US$25 pp), rec; **B** *Serenidad*, 4 km S of town nr the river mouth on beachside road, closed 1997 because of long-running dispute with members of a local *ejido* who claim the land and have occupied the resort developed and run for many years by the Johnsons, T 20111; **B** *Vista Hermosa*, opp the *Serenidad*, a/c, pool, excellent restaurant, bar with satellite US TV.

C *Las Casitas*, Callejón de los Estudiantes y Av Madero, central, a/c, showers, restaurant next door, shady garden patio, fishing trips arranged, pleasant older hotel, well-run.

D *Suites Rosita*, Av Madero nr main plaza, a/c, kitchenettes, clean and pleasant, hot water, a bit run down but good value; **D** *Terraza Motel*, C Zaragoza y Moctezuma, in business district, 35 rooms, rooftop bar, TV, parking, clean.

E *Casa de Huéspedes Manuelita*, sloppily run but reasonably clean.

F *Casa Nachita*, next door, with fan, basic and pleasant, fairly clean, hot water in am.

Camping: *The Orchard (Huerta Saucedo) RV Park*, on river S of town, partly shaded, off Highway 1, pool, boat ramp, fishing, up to US$10.50 for 2, rec; *Villa María Isabel RV Park*, on river and Highway E of *Orchid*, pool, recreation area, disposal station, American-style bakery; *Jorge's del Río Trailer Park*, grassy, on river at E end of Highway bridge by unpaved road, hot water, clean, plenty of shade but

watch belongings at night; *Pancho's RV Park*, next to *María Isabel*, off Highway 1, little shade; *Oasis Río Baja RV Park*, on same stretch as those above, reasonable. All the foregoing have full hook-ups, flush toilets, showers, etc. From here on down the Bahía Concepción coast and beyond are many *playas públicas* (*PP*); some have basic facilities, most are simple, natural camping spots on beautiful beaches where someone may or may not collect a fee. At Mulegé is the Playa Sombrerito at the hat-shaped hill (site of Mexican victory over US forces in 1847), restaurant and store nearby. White gas is sold at the *ferretería* 'on the far side of town from the main entrance' in large cans only.

● Places to eat

Patio El Candil, C Zaragoza, simple outdoor dining; *Azteca* and *Vista Hermosa* at *Hotel Terraza*, good food, budget prices; *Paco y Rosy's*, signed turnoff from Highway 2 km S, rustic, friendly, Chinese, open from 1800; *Tandil* and *Las Casitas*, romantic and quiet atmosphere, good; *Equipales*, C Zaragoza, 2nd floor, rec for good local cooking and for breakfasts; *Baja Burger*, between *Las Casitas* and *Hotel Baja Hacienda*, traditional burgers and *quesadillas*, ice-cream; *Doney's Tacos*, Fco Madero, end farthest from centre, good food and clean. Good pizza place under the bridge, on the river between *Jorge's Trailer Park* and town, reasonable prices, English book exchange. Good fish restaurant on the beach nr the lighthouse. In the plaza next to the *Hacienda* is a good *taco* stand in am and vendors selling chips and *churros* in pm. Next to *Doney's* on Madero is a Corona beer store, selling ice-cold beer with plastic bags of ice supplied.

● Laundry

Lavimática, C Doblado, opp Tres Estrellas bus station.

● Post & telecommunications

Telephone and fax abroad at mini-supermarket *Padilla*, 1 block from Pemex station.

● Sports

Dive shop: C Madero 45, rents equipment and runs trips around Bahía Concepción.

● Transport

Buses to the S do not leave at scheduled times. Allow plenty of time to complete your journey.

SOUTH OF MULEGE

Beyond Mulegé the Highway climbs over a saddle and then runs along the shores of the bay for 50 km. This stretch is the most heavily-used camping and boating area on the Peninsula; the water is beautiful, swimming safe, camping excellent, varied marine life. Bahía Concepción and Playa Santispac, 23 km S of Mulegé, are recommended, many small restaurants (eg *Ana's*, which sells water, none other available, food good value) and *palapas* (shelters) for hire (day or overnight, US$2.50). You can get to Santispac from Mulegé on the La Paz bus. Beyond Santispac is Playa Burro and, beyond that, an unnamed beach. Further S from El Coyote is Playa Buenaventura, which has *palapas* and 3 *cabañas* for rent (US$20), and an expensive restaurant serving wine, burgers and spaghetti. From the entrance to the beach at Requesón, veer to the left for Playa La Perla, which is small and secluded. In summer this area is extremely hot and humid, the sea is too salty to be refreshing and there can be midges.

A new graded dirt road branches off Highway 1 to climb over the towering **Sierra Giganta**, whose desert vistas of flat-topped mesas and *cardón* cacti are straight out of the Wild West; it begins to deteriorate after the junction (20 km) to San José de Comondú and limps another 37 km into San Isidro after a spectacular drop into the La Purísima Valley. San Isidro has a population of 1,000 but little for the visitor; 5 km down the valley is the more attractive oasis village of La Purísima (*Pop* 800). The road leads on southwards to Pozo Grande (52 km) and Ciudad Insurgentes (85 km), it is now beautifully paved and is probably the fastest stretch of road in Baja. Two side roads off the San Isidro road lead down to the twin towns of San Miguel de Comondú and San José de Comondú (high-clearance vehicles are necessary); both oasis villages of 500 people each. One stone building remains of the mission moved to San José in 1737; the original bells are still at the church. A new graded road leads on to Pozo Grande and Ciudad Insurgentes.

LORETO

(*Pop* 7,500; *Phone code* 113) 1,125 km from Tijuana, Loreto is one of the most historic places in Baja. Here settlement of the Peninsula began with Father Juan María Salvatierra's founding of the Mission of Nuestra Señora de Loreto on 25 October 1697. Nestled between the slopes of the Sierra Giganta and the offshore Isla del Carmen, Loreto has experienced a tourist revival; fishing in the Gulf here is some of the best in Baja California.

Places of interest

The Mission is on the Zócalo, the largest structure in town and perhaps the best-restored of all the Baja California mission buildings. It has a gilded altar. The museum beside the church is worth a visit: there are educational displays about the missions, Bajan history and historic horse and ranching equipment, book shop, open Tues-Sat 0900-1700. Inscription over the main door of the mission announces: 'Mother of all the Missions of Lower and Upper California'.

Local information
● **Accommodation**

L2 *Diamond Eden*, all-inclusive, luxury, beachfront, 10 mins from airport, 224 rooms, a/c, 2 pools, fitness centre, 2 restaurants, 6 bars, golf, John McEnroe Tennis Centre, mostly package holiday business.

A3 *Oasis*, C de la Playa y Baja California, T 30112, on bay at S end of Loreto in palm grove, large rooms, pool, tennis, restaurant, bar, skiffs (pangas) for hire, fishing cruises arranged, pleasant and quiet, a/c; **A3-B** *La Pinta*, on Sea of Cortés 2 km N of Zócalo, a/c, showers, pool, tennis, restaurant, bar, considered by many the best of the original 'Presidente' paradores, 30 rooms, fishing boat hire, rec.

C *La Siesta Bungalows*, small, manager owns the dive shop and can offer combined accommodation and diving trips; **C** *Misión de Loreto*, C de la Playa y Juárez, T 30048, colonial-style with patio garden, a/c, pool, dining rooms, bar, fishing trips arranged, very comfortable, but poor service, check for discounts.

D *Villa del Mar*, Colina Zaragoza, nr sports centre, OK, restaurant, bar, pool, bargain rates, on beach. **Motel**: **E** *Salvatierra*, C Salvatierra, on S approach to town, a/c, hot showers, clean, good value; **E** *Casa de huéspedes San Martín*, Benito Juárez, 200m from beach, with shower, good.

Camping: *Ejido Loreto RV Park*, on beach 1 km S of town, full hook-ups, toilets, showers, laundry, fishing and boat trips arranged, US$7.50/site. *PPs* in the area average US$2-3 pp. Butter clams are plentiful in the sand.

● **Places to eat**
On C de la Playa, *Embarcadero*, owner offers fishing trips, average prices for food; *El Nido* and *El Buey*, both good (latter barbecues); several *taco* stands on C Salvatierra. *Playa Blanca*, Hidalgo y Madero, rustic, American meals, reasonable prices; *César's*, Emiliano Zapata y Benito Juárez, good food and service, candelit, moderate prices; *Café Olé*, Madero 14, Mexican and fast food, palapa-style, open-air breakfasts, budget rates.

● **Sports**
Diving: scuba and snorkelling information and equipment booth on municipal beach nr the fishing pier; the beach itself stretches for 8 km, but is dusty and rocky. Beware of stingrays on the beach.

● **Transport**
Air International, 4 km S; Aero California (T 50500) to Los Angeles; Aerolitoral to Ciudad Obregón and La Paz, all daily flights. Charter flights to Canada.

Buses Bus station at C Salvatierra opp intersection of Zapata; to **La Paz** 6 a day, from 0700, US$10.75; to **Tijuana** 1500, 1800, 2100, 2300, US$30, 17 hrs.

ROUTE SOUTH OF LORETO

Just S of Loreto a rough road runs 37 km through impressive canyon scenery to the village of **San Javier**, tucked in the bottom of a steep-walled valley; the settlement has only one store but the Mission of San Javier is one of the best-preserved in North America; it was founded by the Jesuits in 1699 and took 59 years to complete. The thick volcanic walls, Moorish ornamentation and bell tower are most impressive in so rugged and remote a location. Near San Javier is Piedras Pintas, 16 km from the main road, close to Rancho Las Parras; there are eight prehistoric figures painted

here in red, yellow and black. The road to San Javier Mission is in poor shape, sturdy vehicle required. In San Javier, you can stay in hostal and restaurant *Palapa*, close to the church, or in a **E** 2-bed house with kitchen rented by Ramón Bastida in a beautiful, quiet garden, 5 mins' walk along the path behind the church.

The highway S of Loreto passes a picturesque stretch of coast. Fonatur, the government tourist development agency, is building a resort complex at **Nopoló** (8 km), which it was hoped would one day rival its other resort developments at Cancún, Ixtapa and Huatulco. An international airport, streets and electricity were laid out, then things slowed down; today there is the 15-storey **L2** *El Presidente Hotel*, T 30700; international class, self-contained, on its own imported-sand beach; nearby lighted Loreto Tennis Center, half-finished foundations, weeds and an absence of people. 16 km further on is Puerto Escondido, with a new yacht harbour and marina; although the boat landing and anchoring facilities are operating, the complex is still far from complete, slowed by the same diversion of funds to other projects as Nopoló. There is, however, the *Tripui Trailer Park*, claimed to be the best in Mexico (PO Box 100, Loreto), landscaped grounds, paved roads, coin laundry, groceries, restaurant and pool, lighted tennis court, playground; 116 spaces (most rented by the year), US$17 for 2, extra person US$5 (T 706-833-0413). There are three lovely *PPs* between Loreto and Puerto Escondido (none has drinking water); Notrí, Juncalito and Ligüí: palm-lined coves, which are a far cry from the bustle of the new resort developments nearby. Beyond Ligüí (36 km S of Loreto) Highway 1 ascends the eastern escarpment of the Sierra Giganta (one of the most fascinating legs of Highway 1) before leaving the Gulf to strike out SW across the Peninsula again to Ciudad Constitución.

CIUDAD CONSTITUCION

The highway passes by **Ciudad Insurgentes**, a busy agricultural town of 13,000 with two service stations, banks, auto repairs, shops and cafés (no hotels/motels), then runs dead straight for 26 km to **Ciudad Constitución**, which is the marketing centre for the Magdalena Plain agricultural development and has the largest population between Ensenada and La Paz (50,000). Although not a tourist town, it has extensive services of use to the visitor: department stores, restaurants, banks, public market, service stations, laundries, car repairs, hospital (see introduction to this section, **Insurance and Medical Services**) and airport (near Ciudad Insurgentes). Many businesses line Highway 1, which is divided and doubles as the palm-lined main street, with the first traffic lights since Ensenada, 1,158 km away.

● **Accommodation** **D** *Casino*, a block E of the *Maribel* on same street, T 20754, quieter, 37 clean rooms, restaurant, bar; **D** *Maribel*, Guadelupe Victoria y Highway 1, T 20155, 2 blocks S of San Carlos road junction, a/c, TV, restaurant, bar, suites available, clean, fine for overnight stop; **E** *El Arbolito*, basic, clean, central. **Camping**: *Campestre La Pila*, 2½ km S on unpaved road off Highway 1, farmland setting, full hook-ups, toilets, showers, pool, laundry, groceries, tennis courts, ice, restaurant, bar, no hot water, US$10-13 for 4. *RV Park Man fred*, on left of main road going N into town, very clean, friendly and helpful, Austrian owner (serves Austrian food).

● **Places to eat** *Panadería Superpan*, N of market hall, excellent pastries.

Excursions

Deep artesian wells have made the desert of the Llano de Magdalena bloom with citrus groves and a chequerboard of neat farms growing cotton, wheat and vegetables; this produce is shipped out through the port of **San Carlos**, 58 km to the W on **Bahía Magdalena**, 40 mins by bus from Ciudad Constitución. Known to boaters as 'Mag Bay', it is considered the finest natural harbour between San Francisco and Acapulco. Protected by mountains

and sand spits, it provides the best boating on Baja's Pacific coast. Small craft can explore kilometres of mangrove-fringed inlets and view the grey whales who come here in the winter season. The best time to whale-watch is Jan-Mar, US$25 per hour for a boat for up to 6 persons.

● **Accommodation** **C** *Hotel Alcatraz*; **E** *Las Palmas*, on same street as bus station, clean, fan, hot water; **E** *Motel Las Brisas*, 1 block behind bus station, clean, friendly, quiet.

On the narrow S end of Magdalena Island is Puerto Magdalena, a lobstering village of 400. 7 km away is a deepwater port at Punta Belcher. Whales can be seen at Puerto López Mateos further N (access from Cd Insurgentes or Cd Constitución); no hotel, but take a tent and camp at the small harbour near the fish plant, or stay in Ciudad Constitución, several daily buses. On **Santa Margarita Island** are Puertos Alcatraz (a fish-canning community of 300) and Cortés (important naval base); neither is shown on the ACSC map.

Highway 1 continues its arrow-straight course S of Ciudad Constitución across the flat plain to the village of Santa Rita. 28 km beyond Santa Rita, it makes a 45° turn E, where a road of dubious quality runs to the remote missions of San Luis Gonzaga (64 km) and La Pasión (49 km); it is planned to extend it to the ruins of Dolores del Sur (85 km) on the Gulf of California, one of Baja's most inaccessible mission sites. There is a service station at the village of El Cien; meals and refreshments are available at the Rancho San Agustín, 24 km beyond.

LA PAZ

(*Pop* 168,000, 1991; *State pop* 1995 375,450; *Phone code* 112) Capital of Baja California Sur, La Paz is a fast-changing, but relaxed modern city, nestled at the southern end of La Paz Bay (where Europeans first set foot in Baja in 1533). Sunsets can be spectacular. Prices have risen as more tourists arrive to enjoy its winter climate, but free port status ensures that there are plenty of bargains (although some goods, like certain makes of camera, are cheaper to buy in the USA). Oyster beds attracted many settlers in the 17th century, but few survived long. The Jesuit mission, founded here in 1720, was abandoned 29 years later. La Paz became the territorial capital in 1830 after Loreto was wiped out by a hurricane. Although bursting with new construction, there are still many touches of colonial grace, arched doorways and flower-filled patios. The early afternoon *siesta* is still observed by many businesses, especially during summer.

Places of interest

Heart of La Paz is the **Plaza Constitución**, facing which are the Government Buildings and the graceful **Cathedral of Nuestra Señora de la Paz**, built in 1861-65 on or near the site of the original mission. The Post Office is a block NE at Revolución de 1910 y Constitución. The street grid is rectangular; westerly streets run into the Paseo Alvaro Obregón, the waterfront **Malecón**, where the commercial and tourist wharves back onto a tangle of streets just W of the main plaza; here are the banks, City Hall, Chinatown and many of the cheaper *pensiones*. The more expensive hotels are further SW. A must is the **Museo Antropológico de Baja California Sur**, Ignacio Altamirano y 5 de Mayo (4 blocks E of the Plaza), with an admirable display of peninsula anthropology, history and prehistory, folklore and geology. (The bookshop has a wide selection on Mexico and Baja. Open Tues-Sat 0900-1800; entry free.) A carved mural depicting the history of Mexico can be seen at the **Palacio de Gobierno** on Isabel La Católica, corner of Bravo.

Excursions

There are boat tours from the Tourist Wharf on the Malecón around the bay and to nearby islands like Espíritu Santo. Travel agencies offer a daily boat tour to **Los Lobos Islands** ranging from US$40 (basic) to US$80; the tour should include lunch and snorkelling, 6 hrs, you can see

pelicans, sealions and dolphins, with luck whales, too. 17 km W of La Paz a paved road branches NW off Highway 1 around the bay leading to the mining village of **San Juan de la Costa**, allowing a closer look at the rugged coastal section of the Sierra de la Giganta. Pavement ends after 25 km, the road becomes wide, rolling, regularly graded; OK for large RVs to San Juan, which is a company town of neat-rowed houses; phosphorus is mined and loaded by conveyor and deep-water dock, to be shipped to processing plants for fertilizer production. After San Juan (45 km), the road is passable for medium-size vehicles to Punta Coyote (90 km), closely following the narrow space between mountains and coast; wonderful untouched camping spots. From Coyote to **San Evaristo** (27 km) the track is poor, rugged vehicle recommended, travel time from Highway 1 about 4½ hrs; San Evaristo is a sleepy fishing village on a delightful cove sheltered on the E by the Isla San José. Ideal boating area but as yet undiscovered. Visit the salt-drying operations near San Evaristo or on San José. This is a rewarding excursion for those with smaller, high-clearance vehicles (vans and pick-ups with shells) for the steep final 20 mile stretch.

State Highway 286 leads SE out of La Paz 45 km to **San Juan de Los Planes** (*Pop* 1,350), a friendly town in a rich farming region. A fair road continues another 15 km to the beautiful **Ensenada del los Muertos**, good fishing, swimming and 'wild' camping. A further 11 km is the headland of **Punta Arena de la Ventana**, with a magnificent view of the sterile slopes of Isla Cerralvo. (**L2** *Hotel Las Arenas*, resort overlooking Ventana Bay). 6 km before Los Planes, a graded road leads to the Bahía de la Ventana and the small fishing villages of La Ventana and El Sgto; lovely beaches facing Cerralvo Island.

Local festivals

Pre-Lenten Mardi Gras (carnival) in Feb or Mar, inaugurated in 1989, is becoming

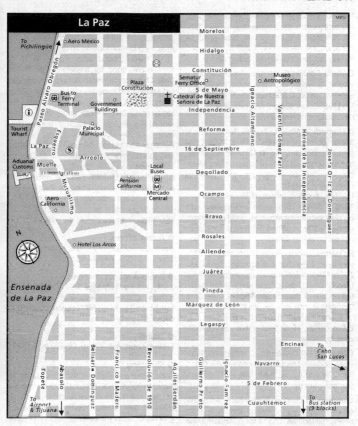

La Paz

Morelos

Hidalgo

Constitución

○ Aero México

To Pichilingüe

Sematur Ferry Office

Plaza Constitución

Bus to Ferry Terminal

Government Buildings

Palacio Municipal

La Paz

Aduana/Customs

Muelle

Inmigración

Pensión California

Mercado Central

Local Buses

5 de Mayo

Catedral de Nuestra Señora de La Paz

Museo Antropológico

Independencia

Reforma

16 de Septiembre

Degollado

Ocampo

Bravo

Rosales

Allende

Juárez

Pineda

Márquez de León

Legaspy

Encinas

Navarro

5 de Febrero

Cuauhtémoc

Hotel Los Arcos

Ensenada de La Paz

Paseo Alvaro Obregón

Esquerro

Mutualismo

Aero California

Arreola

Tourist Wharf

Ignacio Altamirano

Valentín Gómez Farías

Héroes de la Independencia

José Ortiz de Domínguez

Topete

Abasolo

Belisario Domínguez

Francisco I Madero

Revolución de 1910

Aquiles Serdán

Guillermo Prieto

Ignacio Ramírez

To Cabo San Lucas

To Bus station (9 blocks)

To Airport & Tijuana

one of Mexico's finest. The Malecón is converted into a swirling mass of dancing, games, restaurants and stalls, and the street parade is happy and colourful. Well worth a visit, but book accommodation far in advance.

Local information
● Accommodation

A1 *Los Arcos*, Paseo Alvaro Obregón 498 at Allende, T 22744, a/c, pool, restaurant, coffee shop, across the Malecón from the beach, walking distance of centre, fishing trips arranged, excellent value; **A1** *Cabañas de los Arcos*, opp with shared facilities, a/c, pool, slightly cheaper, T 22297; **A1** *Gran Hotel Baja*,

'the only high-rise structure S of Ensenada', so easy to find, T 23844, restaurant, bar, pool, disco, etc, on beach, trailer park adjacent; **A1** *La Posada*, on bay 3½ km SW of centre, 5 blocks off Highway 1 on Colima, T 20653, a/c, pool, tennis, bar, restaurant, quiet and relaxing, rec but away from the centre; **A2** *El Morro*, 3½ km NE on Palmira Beach, Moorish-style, a/c, TV, fridges, apartments with kitchenettes, pool, restaurant, bar; **A2** *El Presidente Sur*, 6½ km NE at Caimancito Beach, T 26544, good location but furthest from town, a/c, pool, restaurant, bar, next door to Governor's mansion; **A2** *Misiones de La Paz*, on El Mogote sandspit, isolated, accessible by launch from *Hotel La Posada*, T 24021, a/c, showers, pool, restaurant, cocktail bar, quiet; **A2** *Palmira*,

T 24000, 3¹/₂ km NE of Pichilingüe road, a/c, pool, tennis, restaurant, disco, convention facilities, fishing trips arranged, popular with families; **A3** *La Perla*, on the water front, T 20777, clean, a/c, friendly, restaurant expensive, locked garage.

C *María Dolores Gardenias*, Aquíles Serdán y Vicente Guerrero, a/c, pool, restaurant (good), excellent, value; **C** *Mediterraneo*, Allende 36, T 51195 (D low season) a/c, beautiful setting, has outstanding restaurant.

D *Hospedaje Marelí*, Aquíles Serdán 283 y Bravo, a/c, clean, 10 mins' walk to Plaza Constitución, pleasant, rec; **D** *Lorimar* on Bravo, hot showers, clean, very helpful, run by a Mexican/American couple, popular, good place to meet fellow travellers, good value restaurant, free ferry booking service; **D** *Veneka*, Madero 1520, T 54688, nice, clean and friendly, safe parking, excellent *margaritas*, good restaurant, specials are rec, chained monkey in courtyard, not rec for animal lovers.

E *Cuartos Jalisco*, Belisario Domínguez 251, very basic; **E** *Pensión California*, C Degollado 209 nr Madero, fan, shower, garden patio, noisy, friendly, weekly deals, basic and not too clean, but popular; **E** *Posada San Miguel*, C Belisario Domínguez Nte 45, nr plaza, colonial-style, bathroom, clean, friendly, hot water, quiet, rec; **E** *San Carlos*, 16 de Septiembre y Revolución, clean but noisy.

F *Hostería del Convento*, C Madero 85, fans, clean, shower, tepid water between 0700 and 0900, beautiful patio; **F** *Miriam*, Av 16 de Septiembre, price pp.

Camping: *El Cardón Trailer Park*, 4 km SW on Highway 1, partly-shaded area away from beach, full facilities, US$11 for 2; *Aquamarina RV Park*, 3¹/₂ km SW, 400m off Highway 1 at C Nayarit, on bay, nicely landscaped, all facilities, marina, boat ramp, fishing, scuba trips arranged, US$17 for 2; *La Paz Trailer Park*, 1¹/₂ km S of town off Highway 1, access via C Colima, deluxe, nearest RV Park to La Paz, very comfortable, US$12 for 2. The *ferretería* across from the main city bus terminal sells white gas stove fuel (*gasolina blanca*). *La Perla de la Paz* department store, C Arreola y 21 de Agosto, sells general camping supplies. CCC Supermarket, opp Palacio de Gobierno, is good for supplies.

Youth hostel: on Carretera al Sur (Highway 1), Blvd Forjadores de Sudcalifornia Km 3, CP 23040, T 24615, dormitory bunk **G**, open 0600-2300, good value, '8 de Octubre' bus from market.

● **Places to eat**
Palapa Adriana, on beachfront, open air, excellent service but beware overcharging; *Antojitos*, next to *Pirámide* on 16 de Septiembre de 1810, friendly, good value. *Rossy*, Av 16 de Septiembre, good for breakfast, fish, cheap; *Café Chanate*, behind tourist office, open evening only, good atmosphere, jazz music, sometimes live. *La Caleta* on the waterfront nr La Paz Lapa, rec; *La Tavola Pizza*, good value. Restaurant of *Aquarius Hotel*, rec, fish burgers, free coffee; *La Revolución*, Revolución, between Reforma and Independencia, cheap breakfast and lunch. Vegetarian restaurant *El Quinto*, Independencia y B Domínguez, expensive (whole wheat bread is half the price at the *panadería* in the market place). Excellent and cheap tacos at a restaurant with no name on Av 16 de Septiembre, nr the bus station. Good *lonchería* and juice bars in the market.

● **Airline offices**
Aero California, city office at Malecón y C Bravo, T 51023; **AeroMéxico**, T 20091.

● **Banks & money changers**
Banks will not exchange TCs after 1100. **Banamex**, C Arreola y Esquerro. Two *casas de cambio* on 5 de Mayo off Obregón, 0800-2000, better rates than banks.

● **Laundry**
Laundromat Yoli, C 5 de Mayo y Rubio.

● **Shopping**
A duty-free port (but see above). *Casa de las Artesanías de BCS*, Paseo Alvaro Obregón at Mijares, just N of *Hotel Los Arcos*, for souvenirs from all over Mexico; *Centro de Arte Regional*, Chiapas y Encinas (5 blocks E of Isabel La Católica), pottery workshop, reasonable prices; *Fortunato Silva*, Highway 1 (Abasolo) y Jalisco at S end of town, good quality woollen and hand-woven cotton garments and articles. *Bazar del Sol*, Obregón 1665, for quality ceramics and good Aztec art reproductions; *Solco's*, Obregón y 16 de Septiembre, large selection of Taxco silver, leather, onyx chess sets. The Mercado Central, Revolución y Degollado, and another at Bravo y Prieto, have a wide range of goods (clothes, sandals, guitars, etc), plus fruit and vegetables. Tourist shops are concentrated along the Malecón between the Tourist and Commercial Wharves.

● **Sports**
Diving: *Baja Diving and Service*, Obregón 1680, hires equipment and takes diving trips

(US$320 for 4-day PADI course); snorkelling day trip about US$35, very good.

● **Tour companies & travel agents**
Sea kayaking and whale watching tours starting in La Paz, are offered by OARS, PO Box 67, Angels Camp CA 95222, T (209) 736 4677, European office: 67 Verney Ave, High Wycombe, Bucks HP12 3ND, England, T (01494) 448901.

● **Tourist offices**
On Tourist Wharf at bottom of 16 de Septiembre, helpful, English spoken, open Mon-Fri 0800-1500, Sat 0900-1300, 1400-1500, open till 1900 high season, will make hotel reservations, some literature and town maps. Fax facilities here (send and receive worldwide), also noticeboard for rides offered, crew wanted etc.

● **Useful addresses**
Immigration: second floor of large building on Paseo Alvaro Obregón, opp the pier, reported to be very helpful, possible to extend visa here.

● **Transport**
Local Rentals. *Viajes Palmira* rents cycles and mopeds, Av Obregón, opp *Hotel los Arcos*, T 24030. **Budget, Avis, Hertz, Auto Renta Sol** and **Auto Servitur** booths at airport.

Air. Gen Manuel Márquez de León International Airport (LAP), 11 km SW on paved road off Highway 1. Taxi fare US$6, supposedly fixed, but bargain. AeroMéxico and Aero California: to Tijuana non-stop, Mexico City, Guadalajara and Culiacán. AeroMéxico to Guaymas and Tucson, Arizona. Aero California: to Los Mochis, Los Angeles (California), Hermosillo, and Mazatlán. Serolitoral to Chihuahua, Culiacán, Ciudad Obregón, Mazatlán, El Paso (Texas), Los Mochis, Hermosillo, Los Cabos, Phoenix (Arizona), San Antonio (Texas), León, Loreto and Monterrey.

Buses. Local buses about US$0.50, depot at Revolución de 1910 y Degollado by the Public Market. Central Bus Station (Central Camionera): Jalisco y Héroes de la Independencia, about 16 blocks from centre, terminal for Tres Estrellas de Oro and Autotransportes Aguila (a/c buses, video, toilet); Autotransportes de La Paz leave from Public Market. **Ciudad Constitución**, 13 departures a day, US$7.70; **Loreto**, 3/day, US$11.50; **Guerrero Negro**, 6/day, US$24; **Ensenada**, US$43; **Tijuana**, US$60.50, **Mexicali**, US$55. To the Cape: **San Antonio**, US$1.75, **Miraflores** US$5, **San José del Cabo**, US$6.60, **Cabo San Lucas**, US$8 (all 10 departures/day), **Todos Santos**, 6/day, US$4.40; Cabo San Lucas via W loop US$7.70.

Ferry. For schedule to Mazatlán and Topolobampo, see page 532. Modern ferry terminal at Pichilingüe, 21 km N on paved highway. Tickets for the same day are sold at the terminal itself. In advance, tickets may be bought at Sematur, 5 de Mayo y Guillermo Prieto, between Reforma and Independencia, T 53833/54666, open 0700-1200.) Travel agents sell ferry tickets, eg *Turismo Express*, Esplanada Alvaro Obregón y 16 de Septiembre, 23000 La Paz, T 56310-3, F 56310. Tourist cards must be valid, allow 2 hrs as there are long queues, trucks have loading priority. It should be noted that many motorists have had difficulty getting reservations or having them honoured. Try to book at least 2 weeks ahead (6 weeks at Christmas, Easter, July and Aug). If you have left it to the last minute, get to the ticket office at 0400 and you may be able to get a cancellation. **NB** Vehicles must have car permits, obtainable at ferry terminal and at Sematur, or at Registro Federal de Vehículos in Tijuana; automobile clubs will provide information. Conditions on the ferry are reported to have improved from the former 'cockroach haven'. The deck gets wet during the night, but the top deck is very refreshing in summer (OK to sleep on deck); toilets quickly get blocked and are then locked up, so make an early call and bring your own toilet paper. Restaurants on board are reasonably priced and food OK. To get a tourist cabin, insist that you will share with strangers, a friendly chat may help. At busy periods, the queue for seats starts at 0630. Book cars 4 weeks in advance. On arrival, buses to Mazatlán may be full, ask about rides on the ferry. Bus to ferry terminal from Medira Travel Agency, Paseo Alvaro Obregón y C 5 de Mayo, frequent departures; from terminal, C Ejido (first on the left after leaving the ferry). Reasonable facilities at terminal but crowded; large parking lots, officials may permit RVs to stay overnight while awaiting ferry departures. **NB** On all ferry crossings, delays can occur from Sept if there is bad weather, which could hold you up for 3 days; fog at the entrance to Topolobampo harbour is often a problem; mechanical breakdowns are not unknown! Keep a flexible schedule if travelling to the mainland.

Beaches Many, most popular on the Pichilingüe Peninsula, most have restaurants (good seafood restaurant under *palapa* at Pichilingüe). Going N from La Paz to ferry terminal on Highway 11; Palmira, Coromuel (popular with paceños), El Caimancito (admission fee), Tesoro. Wind surfing and catamaran trips can be arranged. Pichilingüe (bus from 1000-1400 and 1600-1800, US$1.30 from station at Paseo Alvaro Obregón y Independencia), 100m N of ferry terminal is a *playa pública*. Balandra (rubbish bins, *palapas*, US$2) and Tecolote (same but camping free under *palapas*) are reached by the road beyond the ferry terminal (paved for some distance beyond this point), which ends at a gravel pit at Playa Cachimba (good surf fishing), 13 km NE of Pichilingüe; beaches facing N are attractive but can be windy, some sandflies. El Coyote (no water or facilities) is on the E coast and reached by a road/track from La Paz running inland along the middle of the peninsula. El Comitán and El Mogote, are to the SW of La Paz on the bay, tranquil, no surf. In Oct (at least) and after rain, beware of stinging jelly fish in the water.

LA PAZ TO SANTIAGO

South of La Paz and its plain, the central mountain spine rises again into the wooded heights of the Sierra de la Laguna and bulges out into the 'Cape Region', Baja's most touristically-developed area. The highway winds up to **El Triunfo**, a picturesque village (almost a ghost town); silver was discovered at El Triunfo in 1862. The town exploded with a population of 10,000 and was for a while the largest town in Baja. The mines closed in 1926 but small-scale mining has resumed in places. **Warning** Present-day miners are using arsenic in the old mine tailings; these areas are fenced and signed. There is a craft shop at the village entrance where young people make palm-leaf objects.

8 km further on is the lovely mountain town and farming centre of **San Antonio** (gasoline, groceries, meals), which was founded in 1756 and served briefly as Baja's capital (1828-30) when Loreto was destroyed. 8 km S of San Antonio was the site of Santa Ana, where silver was first discovered in 1748. It was from this vanished village that the Viceroy and Padre Junípero Serra planned the expedition to establish the chain of Franciscan missions in Alta California.

Highway 1 climbs sharply from the canyon and winds past a number of ancient mines, through the peaceful orchard-farming town of San Bartolo (groceries and meals) and down to the coastal flats around **Los Barriles**, a small town with fuel, meals and limited supplies. A number of resort hotels are situated near here along the beautiful Bahía de Palmas and at nearby Buena Vista; none is in the 'budget' class but all are popular (**A1** *Hotel Palmas de Cortez*, nice beach location; *Victor's* campground is clean, well-organized with all facilities; nearby is *Tío Pancho's* restaurant, mediocre food but good atmosphere).

The Highway turns inland after Los Barriles (106 km from La Paz). An 'East Cape Loop' turns E off the Highway through La Rivera (**E** *La Rivera RV Park* in palm grove next to beach, excellent swimming, hot showers, laundry, friendly, rec), where a new spur leads towards **Cabo Pulmo**; it is being paved at a rapid rate and will eventually take a slightly inland route paralleling the coast to San José del Cabo. Off Cabo Pulmo, a beautiful headland, is the Northern Pacific's only living coral reef; fishing, diving and snorkelling are excellent (56 km from Los Barriles). There are many camping spots along the beautiful beaches of this coast.

SANTIAGO

Santiago (*Pop* 2,000) is a pleasant, historic little town 3 km off Highway 1. On the tree-lined main street are a Pemex station, café and stores grouped around the town plaza. A kilometre further W is the Parque Zoológico, the Cape's only zoo, modest but informative, free admission. The Jesuits built their 10th mission in Santiago in 1723 after transferring it from Los Barriles. The town was one of the sites of the Pericué Indian uprising of 1734.

● **Accommodation D** *Palomar*, a/c, hot showers, restaurant, bar, on main street, modest, good meals).

3½ km S of the Santiago turnoff Highway 1 crosses the Tropic of Cancer, marked by a large concrete sphere, and runs S down the fertile valley between the lofty Sierra de la Laguna (W) and the Sierra Santa Clara (E), to the Cabos International Airport. There are direct jet services to Los Angeles, San Francisco, San Diego in California, Phoenix, Arizona and Seattle, USA, and Mexican destinations; modern terminal, expensive shops, parking and good transportation to San José del Cabo, 10 km S and Cabo San Lucas, bus 1 hr, US$9.

SAN JOSE DEL CABO

The largest town S of La Paz has a population of 10,000. Although founded in 1730, it is now essentially a modern town divided into two districts: the resort sectors and new Fonatur development on the beach, and the downtown zone to the N, with the government offices and many businesses grouped near the tranquil Parque Mijares, and numerous shops and restaurants along C Zaragoza and Doblado. The N end of Blvd Antonio Mijares has been turned into a "mini-gringoland ... which could have been transplanted from the Main St of Disneyland" (Scott Wayne). San José also has two service stations, hospital, auto parts and mechanical repairs. The attractive church on the Plaza Mijares was built in 1940 on the final site of the mission of 1730; a tile mosaic over the entrance depicts the murder of Padre Tamaral by rebellious Indians in 1734. Most of the top hotels are located W of San José along the beaches or nearby estero; the Fonatur development blocks access to much of the beach near town; best are Playas Nuevo Sol and California, about 3 km from downtown. Unofficial camping is possible on those few not fronted by resort hotels.

● **Accommodation L2** *Palmilla*, one of the top resorts in Baja, 8 km W at Punta Palmilla (outstanding surfing nearby), some a/c, showers, pool, beach, tennis, narrow access road, restaurant, bar, skin diving, fishing cruisers and skiffs for hire (daily happy hour allows mere mortals to partake of margarita and appetizers for US$3 and see how royalty and film stars live!); **L2** *Stouffer Presidente Los Cabos*, Blvd Mijares s/n, T 20038, F 20232, on lagoon S of town, a/c, all facilities, boat rentals, centrepiece of the Fonatur development at San José del Cabo; **L3-A1** *Posada Real Cabo* (Best Western), next door, T 20155, F 20460, a/c, colour TV, showers, pool, tennis, restaurant, bar, gift shop, fishing charters; **A2** *Calinda Aquamarina-Comfort Inn*, next to *Posada Real Cabo*, T 20077, US Comfort Inn chain, a/c, beach, pool, restaurant, bar, fishing, clean and comfortable; *Aston Cabo Regis Resort and Beach Club*, in hotel zone on Blvd Finisterra, a/c, colour TV, showers, kitchenettes, private balconies, pool, tennis, golf course, restaurant; **A2** *Castel Cabo*, on beach off Paseo San José S of town, T 20155, a/c, another Fonatur hotel; **C** *Nuevo Sol*, on beach S of intersection of Paseo San José and Highway 1, pool, restaurant, sports facilities, nicely-landscaped, acceptable and good beachside value; **C** *San José Inn*, on last paved street N of beach, clean, quiet, cool, comfortable, ceiling fans, good value; **D** *Collí*, in town on Hidalgo above Budget Rent-a-Car, T 20052, fans, hot showers, 12 clean and adequate rooms; **D** *Pagamar*, Obregón between Degollado y Guerrero 3½ blocks from plaza, fans, café, hot showers, clean, good value; **E** *Ceci*, Zaragoza 22, 1 block W of plaza, T 20051, fans, hot showers (usually), basic but clean, excellent value, central. **Youth hostel**: Domicilio Conocido Anikan s/n. **Motel**: **D** *Brisa del Mar*, on Highway 1, 3 km SW of town nr Hotel Nuevo Sol, 10 rooms, restaurant, bar, pool, modest but comfortable, at rear of trailer park on outstanding beach. **Camping**: *Brisa Del Mar Trailer Park*, 100 RV sites in fenced area by great beach, full hook-ups, flush toilets, showers, pool, laundry, restaurant, bar, fishing trips arranged, popular, rec, good location ('unofficial' free camping possible under *palapas* on beach)

● **Laundry** Self-service at Playa de California.

● **Transport** Bus station on C Manuel Doblado opp hospital, about 7 blocks W of plaza. To **Cabo San Lucas** (Tres Estrellas) daily from 0700, US$1.25, 30 mins; to **La Paz** daily from 0630, US$6.60, 2 hrs.

All the beaches and coastal areas between San José del Cabo and Cabo San Lucas have become public after protests by local inhabitants against private developments. These include: *Hotel Cabo San Lucas*, *Twin Dolphin* (T 30140), and *Calinda Cabo Baja-Quality Inn* (T 30045), part of Cabo Bello residential development (all **L1-2**). At Km 25, just after the *Twin Dolphin*, a dirt road leads off to Shipwreck Beach, where a large ship rots on the shore. 5 km before Cabo a small concrete marker beside the highway heralds an excellent view of the famous Cape. The Highway enters Cabo San Lucas past a Pemex station and continues as Blvd Lázaro Cárdenas to the Zócalo (Guerrero y Madero) and the Kilómetro 0 marker.

CABO SAN LUCAS

Grown rapidly in recent years from a sleepy fishing village (*Pop* 1,500 in 1970) to a bustling, expensive international resort with a permanent population of 8,500. There are trailer parks, many cafés and restaurants, condominiums, gift shops, discos and a marina to cater for the increasing flood of North Americans who come for the world-famous sportfishing or to find a retirement paradise. Everything is quoted in US dollars and food is more American than Mexican. The town fronts a small harbour facing the rocky peninsula that forms the 'Land's End' of Baja California. Francisco de Ulloa first rounded and named the Cape in 1539. The sheltered bay became a watering point for the treasure ships from the Orient; pirates sheltered here too. Now it is on the cruise ship itinerary. A popular attraction is the government-sponsored regional arts centre, located at the cruise liner dock.

● **Accommodation** In our **L2-3** range: *Finisterra*, perched on promontory nr Land's End, T 30000, a/c, TV, shower, pool, steps to beach, poolside bar with unsurpassed view, restaurant, entertainment, sportfishing cruisers; *Giggling Marlin Inn*, central on Blvd Marina y Matamoros, a/c, TV, showers, kitchenettes, jacuzzi, restaurant, bar, fishing trips arranged, lively drinking in attached cocktail bar; *Hacienda Beach Resort*, at N entrance to harbour, some a/c, showers, pool, tennis, yacht anchorage, various watersports, hunting, horseriding, restaurant, etc, claims the only area beach safe from strong Pacific swells; *Marina Sol Condominiums*, high season 16 Oct-30 June, on 16 de Septiembre, between Highway 1 and Bay, full hotel service in 3- and 7-storey buildings; *Solmar*, T 30022, the southernmost development in Baja California, a/c, showers, ocean view, pool, tennis, diving, restaurant, poolside bar, fishing cruisers, beach with heavy ocean surf. **B** *Mar de Cortez*, on Highway 1 at Guerrero in town centre, T 30032, a/c, showers, helpful, pool, outdoor bar/restaurant, good value; **C** *Casablanca*, C Revolución between Morelos y Leona Vicario, central, ceiling fan (**D** in rooms with floor fan), hot shower, clean, but basic in cheaper rooms, quiet and friendly; **C** *Marina*, Blvd Marina y Guerrero, T 30030, central, a/c, restaurant, bar, can be noisy, pricey. **D** *Dos Mares*, Hidalgo, a/c, TV, clean, small pool, parking space, rec. Nothing cheaper than US$12d. **D** **Youth Hostal** Av de la Juventud s/n, T 30148, private bath, F pp in dormitory, not very central, but quite smart and clean. **Motel**: **C** *Los Cabos Inn*, Abasolo y 16 de Septiembre, central, 1 block from bus station, fans, showers, central, modest, good value; **D** *El Dorado*, Morelos (4 blocks from bus terminal), clean, fan, hot water, private bath. **Camping**: *El Arco Trailer Park*, 4 km E on Highway 1, restaurant; *El Faro Viejo Trailer Park*, 1½ km NW at Matamoros y Morales, shade, laundry, ice, restaurant, bar, clean, out-of-town but good; *Vagabundos del Mar*, 3½ km E on Highway 1, pool, snack bar, laundry, good, US$15 for 2; *Cabo Cielo RV Park*, 3 km E on Highway 1; *San Vicente Trailer Park*, 3 km E on Highway 1, same as Cabo Cielo plus pool, both reasonably basic, rates unknown. All have full hook-ups, toilets and showers.

● **Places to eat** As alternatives to expensive restaurants, try the two pizza places just beyond *Mar de Cortez*, one next to the telephone office, the other in the block where the street ends; also *Flor Guadalajara*, C Lázaro Cárdenas, on the way out of town a few blocks beyond 'Skid Row', good local dishes. Half a block uphill from *Hotel Dos Mares*, is **San Lucas**, Hidalgo s/n, good food at very reasonable prices, highly rec. *Edith's*, 1 block from Medeno beach, evenings only, great views. *Mi Casa*, behind Plaza. **The Office Restaurant**, on Medeno beach, good food, moderate prices, live dance show every Thur, rec. There is a good bakery in front of the large modern supermarket in the centre of town. The supermarket is stocked with a full range of US foodstuffs.

- **Post & telecommunications** Post Office: is at Morelos y Niños Héroes.

- **Tourist offices** Next to ferry landing, town maps, Fonatur office.

- **Transport Air** To Los Cabos International Airport (SJD), 14 km, take a local bus, US$3, which drops you at the entrance road to the airport, leaving a 2-km walk, otherwise take a taxi. Flights to the USA: Milwaukee (America West), Anchorage (Alaska Airlines), Denver (Mexicana), San Antonio via Houston (Continental), Las Vegas (America West), Los Angeles (Alaska Airlines, Aero California, Mexicana), Phoenix (Alaska Airlines, America West), Portland (Alaska Airlines), Dallas (American Airlines), Minneapolis (Northwest), San Diego (AeroMéxico, Alaska Airlines), San Francisco (Alaska Airlines), San José (Alaska Airlines), Seattle (Alaska Airlines, America West), Spokane (Alaska Airlines) and Wichita (America West). Domestic flights: Guadalajara (Mexicana, Aero California), Mazatlán (Mexicana), Mexico City (Mexicana, AeroMéxico), Puerto Vallarta (Mexicana), Chihuahua (Serolitoral), Culiacán (Serolitoral), La Paz (Serolitoral), Los Mochis (Serolitoral). **NB** There are no ferries from Cabo San Lucas to Puerto Vallarta. **Buses** Bus station at 16 de Septiembre y Zaragoza, central, few facilities. To **San José del Cabo**, 8 departures a day, US$1.25. To **La Paz** 6 a day from 0630, US$8; **Tijuana** US$44, 1600 and 1800 daily via La Paz.

Ringed by pounding surf, columns of fluted rock enclose Lover's Beach (be careful if walking along the beach, huge waves sweep away several visitors each year), a romantic sandy cove with views out to the seal colonies on offshore islets. At the very tip of the Cabo is the distinctive natural arch ('el arco'); boats can be hired to see it close-up, but care is required because of the strong rips. At the harbour entrance is a pinnacle of rock, Pelican Rock, which is home to vast shoals of tropical fish; it is an ideal place for snorkelling and scuba diving or glass-bottomed boats may be rented at the harbourside. (45 mins harbour cruise in glass-bottomed boat to 'el arco', Lover's Beach, etc US$5 pp; most hotels can arrange hire of skiffs to enable visits to the Arch and Land's End, about US$5-10/hr.)

Many firms rent aquatic equipment and arrange boating excursions, etc; the beaches E of Cabo San Lucas offer endless opportunities for swimming, scuba diving and snorkelling: Cabo Real, 5 km, has showers and restrooms, modest fee; Barco Barrado (Shipwreck Beach), 10 km, is a lovely beach.

WEST COAST BEACHES

Highway 19, the western loop of the Cape Region, was not paved until 1985 and the superb beaches of the W coast have yet to suffer the development and crowding of the E. The highway branches off Highway 1 just after San Pedro, 32 km S of La Paz, and runs due S through a cactus-covered plain to **Todos Santos**, a quiet farming town of 4,000 just N of the Tropic of Cancer. There has been a recent influx of expats from the USA and there is a community of artists and craftspeople. There is a Pemex station, cinema, stores, cafés, a bank, clinic and market, a museum: the Casa de la Cultura (C Topete y Pilar). Todos Santos was founded as a Jesuit mission in 1734; a church replacing the abandoned structure, built in 1840, stands opposite the Civic Plaza on C Juárez. The ruins of several old sugar mills can be seen around the town in the fertile valley. Fishing is also important. *El Tecolote*, on Juárez, has a selection of books in English, some on the region, and the US owner is helpful with local information such as access to the Sierra de la Laguna.

- **Accommodation B** *Hotel California*, formerly the *Misión de Todos Santos Inn*, historic brick building nr town centre, C Juárez, a block N of Highway 19, fans, showers, pool, a/c, dining room; opp is **D** *Motel Guluarte*, fan, fridge, shower, pool, good value; **E** *Miramar*, S end of village, new, with bath, hot water, fan, pool, clean, safe, parking, rec. **Camping**: *El Molino Trailer Park*, off Highway at S end of town, 30 mins from beach, full hook-ups, flush toilets, showers, laundry, American owner, very helpful, US$8 for 4, better value than the hotels! No camping here but apparently OK to use the beach (clean – but look out for dogs – see below). Several kilometres S is *Trailer Park San*

Pedrito (see below), on the beach, closed to camping in 1996, new hotel being built, full hook-ups, flush toilets, showers, pool, laundry, restaurant, bar, US$12 for RVs.

● **Places to eat** On main plaza is *Café Santa Fe*, gourmet Italian food, pricey but very highly rated restaurant.

2 km away is the Pacific coast with some of the most beautiful beaches of the entire Peninsula. Nearest is **Playa Punta Lobos**, a popular picnic spot, but too much rubbish and unfriendly dogs for wild camping; better is the sandy cove at **Playa San Pedro** (4 km SE). Backed by groves of Washingtonia fan palms and coconut palms, this is one of the loveliest wild camping spots anywhere. Opposite the access road junction is the Campo Experimental Forestal, a Botanical Garden with a well-labelled array of desert plants from all regions of Baja; staff are very informative. Here too is the *San Pedro RV Park* (see above), an open area on the beach, one of the most beautifully-sited RV parks in Baja. 11 km S of Todos Santos is **El Pescadero**, a fast-growing farming town with few facilities for visitors.

Excursions

In the rugged interior E of Todos Santos is the **Parque Nacional Sierra de la Laguna** (under threat and not officially recognized). Its crowning peak is the Picacho La Laguna (2,163m), beginning to attract a trickle of hikers to its 'lost world' of pine and oak trees, doves and woodpeckers, grassy meadows and luxuriant flowers; there is nothing else like it in Baja. The trail is steep but straight forward; the panoramic view takes in La Paz and both the Gulf and Pacific. Cold at night. It can be reached from Todos Santos by making local enquiries; 3-day guided pack trips are also offered by the *Todos Santos Inn*, US$325 per person. Alternatively, take a taxi from Todos Santos to La Burrera, from where it is 8 hrs walk along the littered path to the Laguna.

7 km S of El Pescadero is *Los Cerritos RV Park* on a wide sandy beach, 50 RV or tent sites but no hook-ups, flush toilets, US$3 per vehicle. Playa Los Cerritos is a *playa pública*; there are several camping areas but no facilities, US$2 per vehicle. The succession of rocky coves and empty beaches continues to Colonia Plutarco Elías Calles, a tiny farming village in the midst of a patchwork of orchards. The highway parallels the coast to Rancho El Migriño, then continues S along the coastal plain; there are no more camping spots as far as Cabo San Lucas. Many now prefer the W Loop to the main highway; it is 140 km from the junction at San Pedro, thus cutting off about 50 km and up to an hour's driving time from the Transpeninsular Highway route.

Information for travellers

BEFORE TRAVELLING

ENTRY REQUIREMENTS

● Documents

A passport is necessary, but US and Canadian citizens need only show birth certificate (or for US, a naturalization certificate). Tourists need the free tourist card, which can be obtained from any Mexican Consulate or Tourist Commission office, at the Mexican airport on entry, from the offices or on the aircraft of airlines operating into Mexico, and at land borders, ask for at least 30 days (maximum 180 days); if you say you are in transit you may be charged US$8, with resulting paper work. **NB** Not all Mexican consuls in USA are aware of exact entry requirements; it is best to confirm details with airlines which fly to Mexico. Tourist cards are available for citizens of W European countries (except France, Andorra, Cyprus and Malta), the USA, Canada, Australia, New Zealand, Japan, Singapore, South Korea, Argentina, Bermuda, Chile, Costa Rica, Uruguay, Venezuela and Israel. The tourist card is also available at border offices of the American Automobile Association (AAA), which offers this service to members and non-members. There is a multiple entry card valid for all visits within 6 months for US nationals. The normal validity for other nationals is 90 days, but sometimes only 15-30 days are granted at border crossings; insist you want more if wishing to stay longer. Although technically you are only supposed to stay 180 days a year on a tourist card (also known as an FM-T), one correspondent has

been living in Mexico for 5 years on a tourist card, making short visits to the USA 3-4 times a year, with no problems. Tourist cards are not required for cities close to the US border, such as Tijuana, Mexicali, etc.

If you are travelling with a person under 18 years of age, you must go to a Mexican Consulate to have 2 photographs stamped by the Consulate on the back of the person's tourist card. If a person under 18 is travelling alone or with one parent, both parents' consent is required, certified by a notary public or authorized by a Consulate. A divorced parent must be able to show custody of a child. Exact details are available from any Mexican Consulate.

Renewal of entry cards or visas must be done at Servicios Migratorios, Av Chapultepec 284, Glorieta de Insurgentes, Mexico City, only 60 days given, expect to wait up to 10 days for a replacement tourist card, open 0900-1400, T 626-7200 (Metro Insurgentes), or in Guadalajara, or at international airports (there is a helpful office at Room 78 in the International Airport). There are also immigration offices in cities such as Oaxaca or Acapulco who can renew tourist cards. To renew a tourist card by leaving the country, you must stay outside Mexico for at least 72 hrs. Take TCs or credit card as proof of finance. The Oaxaca immigration office will renew your tourist card for only 15 days unless you have US$1,000 in cash for 1 month's stay, credit cards not accepted.

Travellers not carrying tourist cards need visas (French, South Africans and those nationalities not listed above need a visa), multiple entry not allowed, visa must be renewed before re-entry.

Business visitors and technical personnel who want to study the Mexican market, appoint an agent, or enter the country for technical purposes should apply for the requisite visa and permit. (Since 1 April 1994, business visas for US and Canadian citizens are free.) For a *Visitante Rentista* visa, or FM-3 (non-immigrant pensioner) for stays over 6 months (up to 2 years) the following are required: passport, proof of income from abroad of US$750/month (or 400 days of the minimum wage), which is reduced by half if you own a house in Mexico, and your tourist card.

We would warn travellers that there have been several cases of tourist cards not being honoured, or a charge being imposed, or the validity being changed arbitrarily to 60 days or less. In this case, complaint should be made to the authorities in Mexico City. If, on leaving Mexico, your tourist card is not taken from you, post it to the Mexico City address above. Above all, do not lose your tourist card, you cannot leave the country without it (except at some of the US border crossings which are very lax) and it can take up to a week to replace. If you want to return to Mexico after leaving there to visit Belize or Guatemala, remember that you will need a new visa/tourist card if yours is not marked for multiple entry.

At the land frontiers with Belize and Guatemala, you may be refused entry into Mexico if you have less than US$200 (or US$350 for each month of intended stay, up to a maximum of 180 days). This restriction does not officially apply to North American and European travellers. If you are carrying more than US$10,000 in cash or TCs, you must declare it. In most cases entering Mexico from Belize and Guatemala only 30 days entry is given, possibly renewable for up to 60 days.

● **Tourist information**
All Mexican Government tourist agencies are grouped in the Department of Tourism building at Av Masaryk 172, nr corner of Reforma. See under Mexico City for full details. A few cities run municipal tourist offices to help travellers. The Mexican Automobile Association (AMA) is at Orizaba 7, 06700 México DF, T 208-8329, F 511-6285; they sell an indispensable road guide, with good maps and very useful lists of hotels, with current prices. The ANA (Asociación Nacional – Automobilística) sells similar but not such good material; offices in Insurgentes (Metro Glorieta) and Av Jalisco 27, México 18 DF. For road conditions consult the AMA, which

is quite reliable. A calendar of *fiestas* is published by *Mexico This Month. Travellers Guide to Mexico*, published annually by the Secretaría de Turismo, lists resorts, attractions, hotels, sports, businesses, etc, US$17.

In a similar vein to the Ruta Maya (see the Introduction to this book), but purely Mexican, is the Colonial Cities Schedule, which links 51 cities in 8 circuits. Full details are available from the Secretaría de Turismo, T/F 250-7414.

If you have any complaints about faulty goods or services, go to the Procuraduría Federal de Protección del Consumidor of which there is a branch in every city (head office in Mexico City, José Vasconcelos 208, CP 06720, México DF, T 761-3801/11). Major cities, like Acapulco, also have a Procurador del Turista. The Tourist Office may also help with these, or criminal matters, while the Agente del Ministro Público (Federal or State District Attorney) will also deal with criminal complaints.

● **Maps**
The Mexican Government Tourist Highway map is available free of charge at tourist offices (when in stock). If driving from the USA you get a free map if you buy your insurance at Sanborn's in the border cities. The official map printers, Detenal, produce the only good large-scale maps of the country.

The Dirección Gen de Oceanografía in C Medellín 10, near Insurgentes underground station, sells excellent maps of the entire coastline of Mexico. Good detailed maps of states of Mexico and the country itself from Dirección Gen de Geografía y Meteorología, Av Observatorio 192, México 18, DF, T 515-1527 (go to Observatorio underground station and up C Sur 114, then turn right a short distance down Av Observatorio). Best road maps of Mexican states, free, on polite written request, from Director Gen de Programación, Xola 1755, p 8°, México 12 DF. Building is on the corner of Xola with Av Universidad. Mapas Turísticos de México has Mexican (stocks Detenal maps) and world-maps, permanent exhibition at Río Rhin 29, Col Cuauhtémoc, Mexico 5, T 566-2177. Maps also available from Instituto Nacional de Estadística, Geografía e Informática (INEGI), which has branches in Mexico City (see page 277) and in state capitals. Pemex road atlas, *Atlas de Carreteras y Ciudades Turísticas*, US$5 in bookshops (eg Sanborns), has 20 pages of city maps, almost every road one may need, contour lines, points of interest, service stations, etc (it is rarely on sale in Pemex stations), rec. Similar, and good, is *The Green Guide*. As well as its maps of *Mexico City* and *Baja California*, ITM of Vancouver (PO Box 2290, Vancouver, BC, V6B 3W5, Canada) publish a map of *Mexico* (1:3,300,000, 1993-94), *Mexico: South* (1:1,000,000, 1992-93) and *Yucatán* (1:1,000,000, 3rd edition, 1993-95). The AAA road map is fine for major roads, less good off the beaten track. Also rec, maps published by HFET SA, Fresas 27, Col de Valles, Mexico DF, T 559-2310/559-2320, Mexico City, Estado de México and Mapectual Road Atlas of whole country, US$6 (from Sanborns). The best road map obtainable outside the country is Berndtson & Berndtson *Yucatán* 1:1,000,000, plastic coated, but soon to be outdated (as they all are) by ambitious road building programme undertaken by Pemex (rural roads) and the Federal government.

● **Tourist offices overseas**
Canada, 2 Bloor St West, Suite 1801, Toronto, Ontario, M4W 3EZ, T 416 925-0704; **France**, 4 Rue Notre Dame des Victories, 75002 Paris, T 331 4020-0734; **Germany**, Welsenhutten-platz 26, D600 Frankfurt am Main 1, T 4969 25-3413; **Italy**, Via Barberini 3, 00187 Rome, T 396 474-2986; **UK**, 60-61 Trafalgar Square, 3rd Floor, London, WC2N 5DS, T 0171 839-3177; **USA**, 405 Park Ave, Suite 1401, New York, NY 10022, T 212 755-7261.

There are telephone numbers that tourists can call to clarify problems. In USA, phone Mexican Tourism, Miami, 1 000 446 8277. In North America T 1-800-44-MEXICO, for English information for US and Canadian citizens (separate offices in USA and Canada), 24 hrs a day, 7 days a week. There is a Houston number which anyone can call, 1-713-880-8772 for information on surface tourism. In Mexico, tourists can call 91-800-00148 and in Mexico City 604-1240. The Secretaría de Turismo has an emergency hot line, open 24 hrs a day: (05) 250-0123/0151.

WHEN TO GO

● **Best time to visit**
The best season for a business visit is from late Jan to May, but for pleasure between Oct and early April, when it hardly ever rains in most of the country. Aug is not a good time because it is a holiday month throughout Central America and most internal flights and other transport are heavily booked (also see above under **Travel in Mexico**).

HEALTH
The Social Security hospitals are restricted to members, but will take visitors in emergencies; they are more up to date than the Centros de Salud and Hospitales Civiles found in most centres, which are very cheap and open to everyone. There are many homeopathic physicians in all parts of Mexico. You are recommended to use bottled or mineral water for drinking, except in hotels which normally provide purified drinking water free. Ice is usually made from *agua purificada*. Coffee water is not necessarily boiled. Bottled water is available everywhere. Mineral water is sold all over Mexico; both plain and flavoured are first class. Water-sterilizing tablets and water purification solution, Microdyn, can be bought at pharmacies. Raw salads and vegetables, and food sold on the streets and in cheap cafés, especially in Mexico City, may be dangerous. Women who are breast-feeding should avoid eating chile. Advisable to vaccinate against hepatitis, typhoid, paratyphoid and poliomyelitis if visiting the low-lying tropical zones, where there is also some risk of malaria; advice and malaria pills from 6th Floor, San Luis Potosi 199, Colonia Roma Nte, Mexico City, 0900-1400 (chloroquine is available in most large chemists/pharmacies under the brand name Aralen; mefloquire-Lárium, is not available). Dengue fever is spreading in Mexico so seek advice on where the Aedes mosquito is present and protect yourself against being bitten. Note also that cholera is on the rise. Hepatitis is a problem in Mexico and, if you have not been vaccinated, gamma globulin is available at better pharamacies/chemists. Heavy eating and drinking of alcohol is unwise in the capital because of its altitude; so is overdoing it physically in the first few days. Some people experience nose-bleeds in Guadalajara and Mexico City because of pollution; they cease with fresh air. Locals recommend Imecol for 'Montezuma's Revenge' (the very common diarrhoea).

MONEY
● **Currency**
Until 1 Jan 1993, the monetary unit was the Mexican peso (represented by an 'S' crossed with one vertical line, unlike two vertical lines on the US dollar sign), divided into 100 centavos. On that date three zeros were eliminated from the peso, so that 1,000 peso now equals 1 new peso. The word 'new' has now been dropped and the currency is again referred to as the peso. There are notes for 10, 20, 50, 100, 200 and

500 pesos; coins for 5, 10, 20 and 50 centavos and for 1, 2, 5, 10, 20 and 50 pesos. The 1 and 2-peso coins and the 10 and 20 are similar in size, check the number on the coin. Older coins up to a previous value of 1,000 (old) pesos are no longer legal tender, nor are 2/2,000 old and 5/5,000-peso notes.

Local cheques are easier to cash in the issuing branch. There is a charge for cashing a cheque in a different city; if you can take someone along as a guarantor who has an account in the branch it helps.

● **Exchange**

In the border states such as Baja California Norte, the most-used currency is the US dollar, and the Mexican peso is often accepted by stores on the US side of the border. Travellers' cheques from any well-known bank can be cashed in most towns if drawn in US dollars; TCs in terms of European currencies are harder to cash, and certainly not worth trying to change outside the largest of cities. The free rate of exchange changes daily and varies from bank to bank and even from branch to branch (Banamex usually has the best rates). Until the new day's rate is posted, at any time between 1000 and 1100, yesterday's rate prevails. Many banks, including in Mexico City, only change foreign currency during a limited period (often between 1000 and 1200, but sometimes also 1600-1800 in Banamex), which should be remembered, especially on Fri. Many people pay in their wages on Fri, so longer queues can be expected. *Casas de cambio* are generally quicker than banks for exchange transactions, and stay open later, but their rates are not as good. Telegraphic transfer of funds *within* Mexico is not reliable. Beware of short-changing at all times. For information on Western Union services (for USA only), T 1-800-325-4045.

● **Credit cards**

American Express, Mastercard and Visa are generally accepted in Mexico and cash is obtainable with these credit cards at certain banks. Automatic Teller Machines (ATM, *cajero automático*) of Banamex accept Visa, Mastercard and ATM cards of the US Plus and Cirrus ATM networks for withdrawals up to 1,500 pesos. ATM withdrawals on Visa can also be made at branches of Bancomer and Cajeros RED throughout the country. ATMs are now found even in small towns allowing you to travel without carrying large amounts of cash or TCs. Many banks are affiliated to Mastercard but locations of ATMs should be checked with Mastercard in advance.

Visa is more commonly found. There have been repeated instances of Banamex ATMs stating that cash cannot be given, 'try again later', only for the card holder to find that his/her account has been debited anyway. If you get a receipt saying no cash dispensed, keep it. **NB** An American Express card issued in Mexico states 'valid only in Mexico', and is used only for peso transactions. All other American Express cards are transacted in US dollars even for employees living in Mexico. Amex TCs are readily accepted and can easily be purchased with an Amex credit card. If you are enrolled in the Amex Express Cash programme you can withdraw cash with your Amex card from Banco Inverlat ATMs. There is a 6% tax on the use of credit cards. Before you travel, check that your credit cards have not been accidentally demagnetized.

● **Cost of living**

Budget travellers should note that there is a definite tourist economy, with high prices and, on occasion, unhelpful service. This can be avoided by seeking out those places used by locals; an understanding of Spanish is useful. The prices of accommodation and transport in this chapter can only be taken as representative. You are advised to check all local prices before booking. VAT (IVA) is charged on all but some basic goods; it is generally 15% on almost all consumer goods, including hotel and restaurant bills, but 25% is charged on some luxury items. VAT is already included in the final price of the good or service.

Doctors and dentists provide good quality care at high prices (taking appropriate insurance is highly rec). Film is reasonably cheap, but developing is expensive and of poor quality.

GETTING THERE

AIR

● **From Europe**

Several airlines have regular direct flights from Europe to Mexico City. Air France from Paris 5 a week, also AeroMéxico, 4 a week of which one is via Cancún; Iberia and AeroMéxico from Madrid; KLM from Amsterdam; British Airways from London (Heathrow); Lufthansa from Frankfurt, 5 times a week (LTU and Condor charter flights from Germany to Mexico City or Cancún). Aeroflot fly to Mexico City from Moscow via Shannon on Wed. Most connecting flights in Europe are through Madrid or Heathrow.

● From North America

Mexico City from New York (Newark, JFK and La Guardia), under 4 hrs (Delta, AeroMéxico, Continental, Mexicana, United); from Chicago, 3 hrs (Mexicana, Taesa, United and American Airlines); from Los Angeles, 4½ hrs with Mexicana, AeroMéxico, Lacsa, Delta, Continental, United; from Houston, 1 hr (AeroMéxico, Continental); from Washington DC, with United Airlines. Other flights from the USA inc: Atlanta (Delta, AeroMéxico), Baltimore (Northwest Airlines), Detroit (Northwest Airlines), Laredo (Taesa), Las Vegas (America West Airlines), Little Rock (American Airlines), McAllen (Continental), New Orleans (AeroMéxico), Oakland (Taesa), Orlando (Delta), Phoenix (America West Airlines, AeroMéxico), Philadelphia (American, Northwest Airlines), San Diego (AeroMéxico), San José, California (Mexicana), Seattle (United). San Antonio (Mexicana, Aeromar), Denver (Mexicana, United, America West Airlines), Dallas (American Airlines, AeroMéxico), Miami (United, American, AeroMéxico, Mexicana), San Francisco (Mexicana, United, America West Airlines), Tucson (AeroMéxico). Other flights from the USA to Mexican cities are given in the text. From Canada, Japan Airlines fly from Vancouver, Canadian Airlines and Mexicana fly from Toronto and Montreal.

● From the Far East

Japan Airlines twice weekly flight from Tokyo stops at Vancouver.

● From Latin America

Flights from South and Central America: Lan Chile, Mexicana and Lacsa from Santiago, Chile (Lacsa via San José); Mexicana and Lan Chile from Buenos Aires; Lacsa, AeroMéxico, Mexicana and AeroPerú from Lima, some flights via Panama City; Lloyd Aéreo Boliviano from Santa Cruz, Bolivia via Panama City; Servivensa from Caracas; Avianca and Mexicana from Bogotá, also Variq en route from Rio and São Paulo; AeroPerú and AeroMéxico also fly from São Paulo; Aviateca, KLM and Mexicana from Guatemala City; Copa from Managua, Panama City, San Pedro Sula; also Lacsa from Panama; Lacsa, United and Mexicana from San José, Costa Rica; Taca from Tegucigalpa, who fly via San Salvador.

● From the Caribbean

Mexicana and Cubana fly from Havana; Air Jamaica and American Airlines have connecting flights from Kingston and Montego Bay via Miami.

CUSTOMS

The luggage of tourist-card holders is often passed unexamined. If flying into Mexico from South America, expect to be thoroughly searched (body and luggage) at the airport. US citizens can take in their own clothing and equipment without paying duty, but all valuable and non-US-made objects (diamonds, cameras, binoculars, typewriters, computers, etc), should be registered at the US Customs office or the port of exit so that duty will not be charged on returning. Radios and television sets must be registered and taken out when leaving. Anyone entering Mexico is allowed to bring in: clothing, footwear and personal cleaning items suitable for the length of stay; camera, or video recorder, and 12 rolls of film, or videocassettes; books and magazines; one used article of sporting equipment; 20 packs of cigarettes, or 50 cigars, or 250 grams of tobacco; medicines for personal use. Foreigners who reside legally outside Mexico are also allowed: a portable TV, stereo, 20 records or audio cassettes, a musical instrument, 5 used toys, fishing tackle, tennis racket, a pair of skis, a boat up to 5m without an engine, camping equipment, a tent. Those entering by trailer, private plane or yacht may also bring a videocassette recorder, bicycle, motorbike and kitchen utensils. Anything additional to this list with a value of over US$300, if entering by land, air or sea, is taxable and must be declared as such (for Mexicans returning by land the value is US$50). This stipulation is rarely invoked for those entering by motor home. There are no restrictions on the import or export of money apart from gold but foreign gold coins are allowed into the US only if they are clearly made into jewellery (perforated or otherwise worked on). On return to the US a person may take from Mexico, free of duty, up to US$100 worth of merchandise for personal use or for personal gifts, every 31 days, if acquired merely as an incident of the trip. 1 litre of alcoholic drinks may be taken across the border from Mexico (beer is counted as an alcoholic drink); Texas will allow you to pay the small state tax, Arizona will not. All foreign citizens are subject to this law. Archaeological relics may not be taken out of Mexico. US tourists should remember that the US Endangered Species Act, 1973, prohibits importation into the States of products from endangered species, eg tortoise shell. The Department of the Interior issues a leaflet about this. Llama, alpaca, etc, items may be confiscated at the airport for fumigation and it will be necessary to return to the customs area on the Mexico City airport perimeter 2-3 days later to collect and pay for fumigation. Production of passport will be required and proof that goods are to be re-exported otherwise they may also be subject to import duties.

ON ARRIVAL

● Airport information
When arriving in Mexico by air, make sure you fill in the immigration document before joining the queue to have your passport checked. If you are not given one on the plane, find one in the arrivals hall. Also at Mexico City airport you may be subject to a brief interview by the Federal District Health Service; this is in relation to the control of cholera, yellow fever and other diseases.

● Books
If looking for something to read in English, German or French, ask at the front desk of a first class hotel. Previous visitors may have left books behind which the receptionist may give you, often without charge.

● Clothing
People are usually smartly dressed in Mexico City. There is little central heating, so warm clothing is needed in winter. Four musts are good walking shoes, sun hats, dark glasses, and flip-flops for the hot sandy beaches. Topless bathing is now accepted in parts of Baja California, but ask first, or do as others do. Men may need a jacket and tie in some restaurants. It is difficult to obtain shoes over US size $9\frac{1}{2}$, but it is possible to have them made.

● Friends
To meet interesting people, it is probably a good idea to visit the Casa de Cultura in any sizeable town.

● Hours of business
The hours of business in Mexico City are extremely variable. All banks are open from 0900 to 1330 from Mon to Fri, some stay open later, and (head offices only) 0900 to 1230 on Sat. Business offices usually open at 0900 or 1000 and close at 1300 or 1400. They reopen at 1400 or 1500, but senior executives may not return until much later, although they may then stay until after 1900. Other businesses, especially those on the outskirts of the city, and many Government offices, work from 0800 to 1400 or 1500 and then close for the rest of the day. Business hours in other parts of the country vary considerably according to the climate and local custom.

● Official time
US Central Standard Time 6 hrs behind GMT; Daylight Saving Time, from 1st Sun in April to last Sun in Oct, 5 hrs behind GMT. In Sonora, Sinaloa, Nayarit and Baja California Sur, 7 hrs behind GMT; and in Baja California Norte (above 28th Parallel) 8 hrs behind GMT (but 7 hrs behind GMT between 1 April and end Oct).

● Photography
There is a charge of US$4 for the use of video cameras at historical sites. If you want to use professional equipment including use of a tripod, the fee is US$150 per day.

● Safety
Mexico is generally a safe country to visit, although crime is on the increase and the usual precautions over personal safety should be taken, especially in Mexico City. Never carry valuables visibly or in easily picked pockets. Leave passports, tickets and important documents in an hotel safety deposit, not in your room. Underground pedestrian crossings are hiding places for thieves, take extra care at night. Cars are a prime target for theft. There has also been a rapid rise in robbery by taxi drivers in Mexico City. The drivers most often pick up their victims on Av Cuauhtémoc, Alvaro Obregón or Insurgentes after 2200, stop in poorly lit streets where accomplices get in the cab and assault the passenger. As with driving at night in the States of Guerrero and Oaxaca, avoid travelling by bus at night in these districts; if at all possible make journeys in day light. Also (and it is very sad having to write this), beware of getting too friendly with young gringos who seem to be living in Mexico permanently, unless, of course, they have jobs. Many of them stay in Mexico for the cheap drugs, and are not above robbery and assault to finance their habit. Couples, and even more, women on their own, should avoid lonely beaches. Those on the W coast are gaining a reputation as drug landing points. Some women experience problems, whether accompanied or not; others encounter no difficulties at all. (In discos women are supposed to wait until asked to dance by a man.) The police service has an equivalent to the Green Angels (see above), the Silver Angels, who help victims of crime to file a report. US citizens should present this report to the nearest embassy or consulate.

Speaking Spanish is a great asset in avoiding rip-offs for gringos, especially short changing and overcharging (both rife), and to make the most of cheap *comedores* and market shopping.

Gay travellers should be aware of 'public decency' laws which allow the police much latitude: for as little as holding hands on the beach you can be arrested, even in Acapulco which has many attractions for gay visitors.

Drugs Note that anyone found in possession of narcotics, in however small a quantity, is liable to a minimum prison sentence of 10 years, with a possible 1-year wait for a verdict. Narcotics include 'magic mushrooms'.

Smoking Smoking is not allowed on most forms of public transport, including intercity buses, the metro and *peseros*; there are generally non-smoking areas in the better restaurants. However, the attitude towards smoking is more relaxed than in the USA and some other countries. The price of a pack of cigarettes ranges from US$0.30-US$1.20, most pharmacies stock cigarettes. Mexican brands are available in airport duty free shops but only for US dollars and at a much higher equivalent price. Ordinary airport shops charge up to 30% more than standard shops.

● **Student cards**

Only national, Mexican student cards permit free entry to archaeological sites, museums, etc, see **Setej** page 277. The surest way to get in free is to go on Sun, when all such places have no entry charge, but are crowded in consequence.

● **Tipping**

Tipping is more or less on a level of 10-15%; the equivalent of US$0.25/bag for porters, the equivalent of US$0.20 for bell boys, theatre usherettes, and nothing for a taxi driver unless he gives some extra service. It is not necessary to tip the drivers of hired cars.

● **Weights and measures**

The metric system is compulsory.

ON DEPARTURE

● **Airport departure tax**

US$13.60 on international flights (dollars or pesos accepted); US$10.50 on internal flights, may be included in ticket price.

NB VAT is payable on domestic plane tickets bought in Mexico. Domestic tax on Mexican flights is 10%, on international flights 3.75%.

WHERE TO STAY

● **Accommodation**

Hotel rates were freed from government control in early 1993; some establishments may raise

prices above the rate of inflation, so some shopping around may be required to find the best value. Complaints about standards, etc, may be reported to the Department of Tourism, Presidente Masaryk 172, Colonia Polanco, Mexico City, T 250-1964 and 250-8555. English is spoken at the best hotels.

In 1996, the introduction of a hotel tax was raised. No formal announcement had been made at the time of writing, but indications are that it will be applied on a state-by-state basis, and only on those bills accompanied by a formal invoice.

Casas de huéspedes are usually the cheapest places to stay, although they are often dirty with poor plumbing. Usually a flat rate for a room is charged, so sharing works out cheaper. Sleeping out is possible anywhere, but is not advisable in urban areas. Choose a secluded, relatively invisible spot. Mosquito netting (*pabellón*) is available by the metre in textile shops and, sewn into a sheet sleeping bag, is ample protection against insects.

Beware of 'helpfuls' who try to find you a hotel, as prices quoted at the hotel desk rise to give them a commission. If backpacking, it is best for one of you to watch over luggage while the other goes to book a room and pay for it; some hotels are put off by backpacks. During peak season (Nov-April), it may be hard to find a room and clerks do not always check to see whether a room is vacant. Insist, or if desperate, provide a suitable tip. The week after Semana Santa is normally a holiday, so prices remain high, but resorts are not as crowded as the previous week. When using a lift, remember PB (*Planta Baja*) stands for ground floor. Discounts on hotel prices can often be arranged in the low season (May-Oct), but this is more difficult in Yucatán and Baja California. There is not a great price difference between single and double rooms. Rooms with double beds are usually cheaper than those with 2 singles. Check out time from hotels is commonly 1400. When checking into a hotel, always ask if the doors are locked at night, preventing guests from entering if no nightguard is posted. Always check the room before paying in advance. Also ask if there is 24-hr running water.

Motels and Auto-hotels, especially in central and South Mexico, are not usually places where guests stay the whole night (you can recognize them by curtains over the garage and red and green lights above the door to show if the room is free). If driving, and wishing to avoid a night on the road, they can be quite acceptable (clean, some have hot water, in the Yucatán they have a/c), and they tend to be cheaper than respectable establishments.

NB In the highlands, where it can be cold at night, especially in winter, many hotels do not have heating; be prepared. The cheaper hotels often provide only one blanket so you may need a sleeping bag. This applies in popular tourist centres such as San Cristóbal de las Casas, Oaxaca, Pátzcuaro.

Experiment in International Living Ltd, 'Ostesaga', West Malvern Rd, Malvern, Worcestershire, WR14 4EN, T 01684-562577, F 562212, or Ubierstrasse 30, 5300 Bonn 2, T 0228-95-7220, F 0228-35-8282, with offices in 38 countries, can arrange stays with families in Mexico from 1 to 4 weeks. This has been recommended as an excellent way to meet people and learn the language.

● **Youth Hostels**
21 *albergues* exist in Mexico, mostly in small towns; they are usually good value and clean. The hostels take YHA members and non-members, who have to pay more. You have to pay a deposit for sheets, pillow and towel; make sure that this is written in the ledger or else you may not get your deposit back. Hostels have lockers for valuables; take good care of your other possessions.

● **Camping**
Most sites are called Trailer Parks, but tents are usually allowed. For camping and youth-hostel accommodation, see under **Campsites**, Mexico City (page 267) for *Villas Deportivas Juveniles*. Beware of people stealing clothes, especially when you hang them up after washing. *Playas Públicas*, with a blue and white sign of a palm tree, are beaches where camping is allowed. They are usually cheap, sometimes free and some have shelters and basic amenities. You can often camp in or near National Parks, although you must speak first with the guards, and usually pay a small fee. Paraffin oil (kerosene) for stoves is called *petróleo para lámparas* in Mexico; it is not a very good quality (dirty) and costs about US$0.05/litre. It is available from an *expendio*, or *despacho de petróleo*, or from a *tlapalería*, but not from gas stations. Methylated spirits is called *alcohol desnaturalizado* and is available from chemists. Calor gas is widely available, as it is throughout Central America. Gasolina Blanca may be bought in *ferreterías*, ironmongers or paint shops, prices vary widely, also ask for Coleman fuel. Alcohol for heating the

burner can be obtained from supermarkets. Repairs to stoves at Servis-Coleman at Plaza de San Juan 5, Mexico City. Katadyn water-purifying filters can be bought in Mexico City at: Katadyn/Dispel, Distribuidores de Purificadores y Electrodomésticos, Fco Javier Olivárez Muñoz, Sinaloa 19 PB, Colonia Roma, CP 06700, Mexico DF, T 533-0600, F 207-7174, spare parts also available.

FOOD AND DRINK

● **Food**
Usual meals are a light breakfast (although this can consist of several courses), and a heavy lunch between 1400 and 1500. Dinner, between 1800 and 2000, is light. Many restaurants give foreigners the menu without the *comida corrida* (set meals), and so forcing them to order à *la carte* at double the price; watch this! Try to avoid eating in restaurants which don't post a menu. Meals in modest establishments cost about US$1.50-2 for breakfast, US$2-3 for lunch (*comida corrida*, US$3-5.50 for a special *comida corrida*) and US$5-8 for dinner (generally no set menu). A la Carte meals at modest establishments cost about US$7; a very good meal can be had for US$11 at a middle level establishment. Much higher prices are charged by the classiest restaurants (eg, in Mexico City, US$15-22 medium class, US$30 1st class, US$40 luxury). The best value is undoubtedly in small, family-run places. For those who are self-catering the cost of food in markets and supermarkets is not high. In resort areas the posh hotels include breakfast and dinner in many cases. Check bills and change, even if service is included waiters may deduct a further tip from the change, they will hand it back if challenged. In some restaurants, beer will not be served unless a meal is ordered.

Among the least appetizing places to eat in Mexico are fast food chain restaurants named after their American counterparts.

What to eat *Tamales*, or meat wrapped in maize and then banana leaves and boiled. Turkey, chicken and pork with exotic sauces: *mole de guajolote* and *mole poblano* (chile and chocolate sauce with grated coconut) are famous. *Tacos* (without *chiles*) and *enchiladas* (with all too many of them) are meat or chicken and beans rolled in *tortillas* (maize pancakes) and fried in oil; they are delicious. Try also spring onions with salt and lime juice in *taquerías*. *Nopales* are opuntia leaves cooked with onions and spices, wrapped in tortilla, slimy but delicious. Indian food is found everywhere: for instance, *tostadas* (toasted fried tortillas with chicken, beans and lettuce), or *gorditas*, fried, extra-thick tortillas with sauce and cheese. Black kidney beans (*frijoles*) appear in various dishes. Try *crepas de cuitlacoche*, best during rainy season, this consists of a pancake stuffed with maize fungus, which has a delicate mushroomy taste, very moreish. In the Pátzcuaro area ask for *budín de cuitlacoche*, with tomato, cream and *chiles*. Red snapper (*huachinango*), Veracruz style, is a famous fish dish, sautéd with *pimientos* and spices. Another excellent fish is the sea bass (*róbalo*). Fruits include a vast assortment of tropical types: avocados, bananas, pineapples, *zapotes*, pomegranates, guavas, limes and *mangos de Manila*, which are delicious. Don't eat fruit unless you peel it yourself, and avoid raw vegetables. Try *higos rebanados* (delicious fresh sliced figs), *guacamole* (a mashed avocado seasoned with tomatoes, onions, coriander and *chiles*) and of course, *papaya*, or pawpaw. Mexico has various elaborate regional cuisines. Some Maya dishes are *sopa de lima* (chicken, rice, *tostada* and lime), *pok chuk* (pork in achiote sauce), *pibil* (a mild sauce on meat or chicken, cooked in banana leaves), *longanizo* sausage from Valladolid. Chinese restaurants, present in most towns, generally give clean and efficient service.

European continental breakfast is very hard to find. For those who like a light, sweet breakfast, try *avena*, a fairly liquid porridge prepared with milk or water, with liberal amounts of cinnamon. Mexican chocolate made with milk is quite filling. In markets, *arroz con leche* is rice boiled in milk until it starts to dissolve, flavoured with cinnamon and sugar. Milk is only safe when in sealed containers marked *pasteurizado*. Fried eggs are known as *huevos estrellados*. On 6 Jan, Epiphany, the traditional *rosca*, a ring-shaped sweet bread with dried fruit and little plastic baby Jesuses inside, is eaten. The person who finds a baby Jesus in his piece must make a crib and clothes for Him, and invite everyone present to a *fiesta* on 2 Feb, Candelaria.

● **Drink**

The beer is good: brands include Dos Equis-XX, Montejo, Bohemia, Sol and Superior. Negra Modelo is a dark beer, it has the same alcohol content as the other beers. Beer *suero* is with lime juice and a salt-rimmed glass, or *michelada* with chile sauce (both available in Oaxaca). Local wine is cheap and improving in quality; try Domecq, Casa Madero, Santo Tomás, etc; the white sold in oyster restaurants *ostionerías* is usually good. Cetto Reisling Fumé has been rec. The native drinks are *pulque*, the fermented juice of the agave plant (those unaccustomed to it should not over indulge), *tequila*, made mostly in Jalisco, and *mescal* from Oaxaca; also distilled from agave plants. Mescal usually has a 'gusano de maguey' (worm) in the bottle, considered by Mexicans to be a particular speciality. Tequila and mescal rarely have an alcoholic content above 40-43%; tequila Heredura, Sauza and Cuervo have been recommended. Also available is the Spanish aniseed spirit, *anís*, which is made locally. Imported whiskies and brandies are expensive. Rum is cheap and good. *Puro de caña* (called *chinguere* in Chinanteca and posh in Chamula) is distilled from sugar cane, stronger than mescal but with less taste; it is found in Oaxaca and Chiapas. There are always plenty of non-alcoholic soft drinks (*refrescos*), try the *paletas*, safe and refreshing (those of Michoacán are everywhere) and mineral water (bottled water is available throughout the country). Fresh juices (as long as not mixed with unpurified water) and milk shakes (*licuados*) are good and usually safe. If you don't like to drink out of a glass ask for a straw, *popote*. Herbal teas, eg camomile, are available. There are few outdoor drinking places in Mexico except in tourist spots.

GETTING AROUND

AIR

Note that the majority of internal routes involve a change in Mexico City, eg there is no direct flight Acapulco-Cancún. Promotional packages for local tourism exist, with 30-40% discount, operated by hoteliers, restauranteurs, hauliers and AeroMéxico and Mexicana. These may be the best value if going from and returning to the same city. Their tickets are not interchangeable. Mexicana and AeroMéxico in combination offer MexiPlan 97 tickets, which are for a minimum of 2 coupons covering five zones of the country; the pass is eligible only to those arriving on transatlantic flights, valid 3-90 days. Fares range from US$50-145/coupon; extra coupons may be bought and reservations may be changed. There are several other airlines flying internal routes (a few with international flights as well), eg Aero California, Aeromar, Serolitoral, Taesa, Saro, Aviacsa and Aero Caribe (details are given in the text above).

OTHER LAND TRANSPORT
● **Motoring**

Vehicles may be brought into Mexico on a Tourist Permit for 180 days each year. The necessary documents are: passport, birth certificate or naturalization papers; tourist card; vehicle registration (if you do not own the car, a notarized letter from the vehicle's owner, be it the bank, company, whoever, is necessary); a valid driver's licence. National or international driving licences are accepted. The original and 2 photocopies are required for each. It takes 10 days to extend a permit, so ask for more time than you expect to need. Don't overstay, driving without an extension gets a US$50 fine for the first 5 days and then rises abruptly to *half the value of the car!* US$12 is charged for the permit, payable only by credit card (Visa, Mastercard, American Express or Diners Club), not a debit card, in the name of the car owner, as recorded on the vehicle registration. The American Automobile Association (AAA) is permitted to issue Tourist Permits for 'credit card' entry, free to members, US$20 to non-members, but this service in California is available only to members. If you do not have a credit card, you have to buy a refundable bond in cash to the value of the vehicle according to its age (a set scale exists), which is repaid on leaving Mexico. The bond is divided into 2 parts, the bond itself and administration; the latter, accounting for about 43% of the total cost, is retained by the authorities; the bond is refunded. The bond is issued by Afianzadora Mexicana at US/Mexican border crossings, or by Sanborn's (see below). It may be waived if you are only going to the State of Sonora, under the Sonora Department of Tourism's 'Only Sonora' programme.

English versions of leaflets giving the rules on temporary importation of vehicles state that you must leave at the same crossing by which you entered. The Spanish versions do not say this and in practice it is not so. The temporary importation permit is multiple entry for 180 days; within that period you can enter and leave by whatever crossing, and as often as you like. Remember, though, that you must have a new tourist card or visa for each new entry.

On entry, go to Migración for your tourist card, on which you must state your means of transport. This is the only record of how you entered the country. At the Banjército desk sign an 'Importación Temporal de Vehículos' 'Promesa de retornar vehículo', which bears all vehicle and credit card details so that, if you sell your car illegally, your credit card account can be debited for the import duty. Next you purchase the 'Solicitud de importación temporal', which costs US$12; it bears a hologram which matches the dated sticker which must be displayed on the windscreen, or, on a motorcycle, on some safe surface. Then go to 'Copias' to photocopy all necessary documents and papers issued. The sticker and other entry documents must be surrendered on departure. They can only be surrendered at a Mexican border crossing, with date stickers cancelled by Banjército at Immigration. If you neglect to do this, and re-enter Mexico with an expired uncancelled sticker on you car, you will be fined heavily for each 15-day period that has elapsed since the date of expiry. If you intend to return to Mexico within the 180-day period, having surrendered your sticker and documents, keep safe the 'Importación Temporal de Vehículos' form, stamped 'Cancelado', as a receipt. If entry papers are lost there can be much delay and expense (including enforcement of the bond) in order to leave the country. Banjércitco (Banco del Ejército) offices at borders are open daily, for 24 hrs, except at Naco (daily 0800-2400), Tecate (daily 0800-1600), Tijuana (Mon-Fri 0800-2200, Sat 0800-1800, Sun 1200-1600), Columbia, Texas (Mon-Fri 1000-1800), Ojinaga (Mon-Fri 0730-2100, Sat 0730-1600, Sun 0800-1600). Each vehicle must have a different licensed driver (ie, you cannot tow another vehicle into Mexico unless it has a separate driver).

On arrival, you have to find the place where car permits are issued; this may not be at the border. If driving into Mexico from California, Nogales is probably the easiest crossing, which means going first into Arizona. The main car documentation point here is Km 21, S of Nogales. Entering at Tijuana, it seems that car entry permits are given at Mexicali (which means taking the very busy Route 2 through Tecate), or, if you drive through Baja California, at the ferry offices in Santa Rosalía or La Paz. This does not apply if you are not going beyond Baja. In Nuevo Laredo permits are issued at a new complex in town, opposite the train station. If crossing from Brownsville to Matamoros and require longer than 10 days, send a fax with car details to immigration at the border 3 days before leaving the country. Before crossing the border, pick up the fax and show it at the US side of the border. Most visitors to Mexico at this border are just crossing for shopping and only need a 10 day visa.

According to latest official documents, insurance for foreign cars entering Mexico is not mandatory, but it is highly recommended to be insured. Arranging insurance when crossing from the USA is very easy as there are many offices at US border crossings. Policy prices vary enormously between companies, according to age and type of vehicle, etc. **NB** In Mexico foreign insurance will not be honoured; you must ensure that the company you insure with will settle accident claims outside Mexico.

Sanborn's Mexican Insurance Service, for example, with offices in every US border town, and many more, will provide insurance services (many comprehensive plans available, including full-year cover) within Mexico and other parts of Latin America, and provides free 'Travelogs' for Mexico and Central America with useful tips. A selection of offices: Brownsville, Johnny Ginn Travel Center, 1845 Expway US, 77-83 exit, T 512-542-5457; El Paso, Associated Insurance Agency, 440 Raynolds off IH-10, T 915-779-3588; Nogales, PO Box 1584, 3420 Tucson Hwy (US-89), T 602-281-1873; San Antonio, Broadway Insurance Agency, 8107 Broadway, S off loop 410-E, T 512-828-3587. Also, *Tepeyac,* with offices at most Mexican cities, towns and border crosings (including Lapachula), and in USA (eg in San Diego, Mexican American Insurance Agency, corner of 6th and A sts, downtown, T 233-7767); *Aseguradora Mexicana SA* (Asemex), with offices in Tijuana, T 85-03-01/04, 24 hrs, Ensenada, Mexicali, La Paz, and adjusters throughout Baja California and that border zone; *International Gateway Insurance Brokers* (also offers insurance for Mexican residents visiting USA), PO Box 609, Bonita, CA 92002-0609, T (619) 422-3022, F (619) 422-2671; also 2981 N Grande Ave, Nogales, T 281-9141, F 281-0430; 1155 Larry Mahan, Suite H, El Paso, T 595-6544, F 592-1293; Hidalgo 79F, Riberas del Pilar, Centro Comercial Máscaras, Chapala, T 52559, F 543-16; Escuela Militar de Aviación 60, Chapultepec, Guadalajara, T 152992, F 341448; Misión de San Diego, No 1517 Despacho 1C, Tijuana, T 341446, F 341448; Revolución Morelos s/n, Cabo San Lucas, T 31174, F 30793; Blvd Costera Miguel de la Madrid, Km 10, Plaza Galerías local 3, Manzanillo. *Mex-Insur* in San Diego CA, T 425-2390, will issue a policy and refund each full 24 hrs not used as long as you return over the Mexican/US border. *Points South Caravan Tours*, 11313 Edmonson Ave, Moreno Valley, CA 92560-5232, T (909) 247-1222 or toll free USA and Canada 1-800-421-1394, offers Mexican insurance.

Entering Mexico from Guatemala presents few local insurance problems now that *Tepeyac* (see above), has an office in Tapachula, and *Seguros La Provincial*, of Av Gen Utrillo 10A, upstairs, San Cristóbal de las Casas, have an office in Cuauhtémoc, Av Cuauhtémoc 1217 PB, Sr García Figueroa, T (5) 6-04-0500. Otherwise, try in Tuxtla Gutiérrez (Segumex). In Mexico City, try *Grupo Nacional Provincial,* Río de la Plata 48, T 286-7732, who have offices in many towns.

British AA and Dutch ANWB members are reminded that there are ties with the AAA, which extends cover to the US and entitles AA members to free travel information including a very useful book and map on Mexico (note that some AAA offices are not open at weekends or on US holidays). Luggage is no longer inspected at the checkpoints along the road where tourist cards and/or car permits are examined.

Spare parts: the only Japanese makes for which spare parts are sold in Mexico are Datsun and Nissan. Most other cars are US makes.

Gasoline is either unleaded, 90 octane, called *magna sin*, which costs about 3 pesos/litre and *nova,* leaded, 80 octane, 3 pesos/litre. *Magna sin* is sold from green pumps from green and white Pemex stations; *nova* from blue pumps and diesel from purple pumps. They are in the process of introducing diesel sin and withdrawing regular diesel. Unleaded petrol is now available in almost all stations, very few have only nova. Always fill up when you can and carry spare fuel. If your own vehicle is fitted with a catalytic converter you can remove it to use either leaded or unleaded fuel. (Mexican petrol is not very clean, so check spark plugs frequently; most mechanics will let you use their wire brushes free of charge.) There are dozens of minor swindles, including overcharging, practised at filling stations. Make sure you are given full value when you tank up, that the pump is set to zero before your tank is filled, that both they and you know what money you've proffered, that your change is correct, that the pump is correctly calibrated, and that your filler cap is put back on. There is no legal surcharge for service at night, nor additional taxes: two more games frequently tried.

The Free Assistance Service of the Mexican Tourist Department's green jeeps (*ángeles verdes*) patrol most of Mexico's main roads. Every state has an Angeles Verdes Hotline and it is advisable to find out the relevant number when entering each state. The drivers speak English, are trained to give first aid and to make minor auto repairs and deal with flat tyres. They carry gasoline and have radio connection. If you want your vehicle to be escorted through Mexico City, offer to pay about US$15, and the police will do it for you. All help is completely free. Gasoline at cost price. Parking: Multi-storey car parks are becoming more common but parking is often to be found right in city centres under the main square.

A useful source of information and advice (whose help we acknowledge here) is the Recreation Vehicle Owner's Association of British Columbia, Box 2977, Vancouver, BC, V6B 3X4 (members receive *RV Times* publication; Mexican insurance arranged for members). RV tours including Mexico are available from RV Adventuretours, 305 W Nolana Loop #2, McAllen, TX 78505, USA. Another recommended source of information in Canada is *Mexi-Can Holidays Ltd*, 150-332 Water St, Vancouver, BC V6B 1B6, T (604) 685-3375, F (604) 685-3321. Motorists are referred to: *Clubmex*, PO Box 1646, Bonita, California 91908, USA, T (619) 585 3033, F (619) 420 8133, publishes a regular newsletter for its members (annual subscription US$35). The newsletter gives useful information and advice for drivers, specialist trips for sport fishing enthusiasts, and some interesting travel articles. *Clubmex* also arranges insurance for members. *Mexico Travel Monthly Report*, Carolyn Files, Box 1498, Imperial Beach, CA 91933-1498, T/F 619-429-6566, has also been recommended. *Winter in Mexico Caravans Inc* (a member of *The Escapees Club*, which issues a bi-monthly newsletter), 101 Rainbow Drive, Livingston, Texas 77351, T (303) 761-9829, offers advice on caravan trips to Mexico, runs tours for caravanners, including a birdwatching tour, and issues its own bulletin. *R Ving in Mexico, Central America and Panamá*, by John and Liz Plaxton (Travel 'N Write, Canada, 1996) has been rec as full of useful information. Also *Aim*, on retirement and travel in Mexico, Apdo postal 31-70, Guadalajara 45050, Jalisco.

In Case of Accident Do not abandon your vehicle. Call your insurance company immediately to inform it of the accident. Do not leave Mexico without first filing a claim in Mexico. Do not sign any contract or agreement without a representative of the insurance company being present. Always carry with you, in the insured vehicle, your policy identification card and the names of the company's adjusters (these are the recommendations of Asemex). If, in an accident, bodily injury has occurred or the drivers involved cannot agree who is at fault, the vehicles may be impounded. Drivers will be required to stay in the vicinity in cases of serious accidents, the insured being confined to a hotel (or hospital) until the claim is settled (according to Sanborn's). Should parties to an accident be incarcerated, a bail bond will secure release. A helpline for road accidents is available by phoning 02 and asking the operator to connect you to Mexico City T 6849715/6849761.

Warnings On all roads, when two vehicles converge from opposite directions, or when a vehicle is behind a slow cart, bicycle, etc, the driver who first flashes his lights has the right of way. This also applies when a bus or truck wishes to turn left across the opposing traffic: if the driver flashes his lights he is claiming right of way and the oncoming traffic must give way. At 'Alto' (Halt) signs, all traffic must come to a complete stop. At a crossroad, however, the first person to come to a complete halt then has precedence to cross. This requires a lot of attention to remember your place in the sequence (this is the same system as in the USA). Do not drive at night. If it is unavoidable don't drive fast; farm and wild animals roam freely. Night-time robberies on vehicles are on the increase especially in Guerrero and Oaxaca States. 'Sleeping policemen' or road bumps can be hazardous in towns and villages as often there are no warning signs; they are sometimes marked '*zona de topes*', or incorrectly marked as *vibradores*. In most instances, their distinguishing paint has worn away.

Roadworks are usually well-marked. If your vehicle breaks down on the highway and you do not have a warning triangle or a piece of red cloth to act as a warning, cut branches from the roadside and lay them in the road in front of and behind your vehicle.

Searches of foreigners for drugs on the W coast were reinstated in 1993. The following precautions should help towards an incident-free passage of a drug search. Carry copies of all prescriptions for medicines (typed). Keep medicines in the original container. Carry a notice of all medical conditions that need a hypodermic syringe or emergency treatment. Never take packages for another person. Never take hitchers across a border. Always cross a border in your own vehicle. Check your vehicle carefully for suspicious packages secreted by someone other than yourself. If you have bodywork done in Mexico, supervise it yourself and keep records, even photos, of the workshop that did it. If you did have work done on your vehicle, call for a sniffer dog to cover yourself. Prior to inspections, open all doors, hatches, etc. Put away all money and valuables. Offer no drinks, cigarettes or gifts to the inspectors; accept none. When searched, cooperate with narcotics officers (who wear black and yellow, and have an identity number on a large fob attached to the belt); do not intrude, but watch the proceedings closely.

If you are stopped by police in town for an offence you have not committed and you know you are in the right, do not pay the 'fine' on the spot. Take the policeman's identity number, show him that you have his number and tell him that you will see his chief (jefe) at the tourist police headquarters instead. It is also advisable to go to the precinct station anyway whenever a fine is involved, to make sure it is genuine. In 1994-96, we received reports of drivers being subject to demands for bribes frequently, especially on the Mexico City-Guadalajara route. If stopped in a remote area, it is not advisable to get into a dispute with a policeman; drugs may be planted in your vehicle or other problems may occur.

Note that cars must by law display a number/license plate front and back, as this is not the case in some US States, you may have to improvise.

Tourists' cars cannot, by law, be sold in Mexico. This is very strictly applied. You may not leave the country without the car you entered in, except with written government permission with the car (and trailer if you have one) in bond.

If your car breaks down and cannot be repaired, you must donate it to the Mexican people. This is done through the Secretaría de Hacienda. If you have to leave Mexico in a hurry and cannot take the car with you, you have to get permission from the Secretaría de Hacienda which will guard your car until you return.

Road Tolls (See also page 162.) A toll is called a 'cuota', as opposed to a non-toll road, which is a 'vía libre'. There are many toll charges, mostly of US$1 to 2, on roads and bridges. Some new freeways bypassing city centres charge US$7 or more for 50 km. Because of the high cost of toll roads, they are often quite empty, which means that good progress can be made on them. With the privatization of many freeways, hefty tolls are charged to roadusers (double the car fee for trailers and trucks). Some can be avoided if you seek local, or motoring club (see above) advice on detours around toll gates (follow trucks). This may involve unpaved roads which should not be attempted in the wet. Two advantages of toll

roads are that they are patrolled and safe, even at night, and drivers are insured against accident or breakdown.

● **Bus**
Bus services have been upgraded in recent years and are generally organized, clean and prompt. However, the ordinary traveller should not be beguiled into thinking that it is necessary to purchase an expensive ticket in order to travel comfortably. On many routes, the 2nd, or 'normal', class has disappeared. 1st class is perfectly satisfactory, but there now exist three superior classes, usually called 'Primera Plus', 'Futura' and 'Ejecutiva', which offer various degrees of comfort and extra services. Companies offering these services include UNO (rec) and ETN, as well as the major bus companies. The extras are reclining seats, toilets, drinks, videos, etc. ETN has exceptional buses with 3 seats in a row but prices about 35-40% (in some cases double) above regular 1st class. The superior classes are probably best for journeys over 6 hrs, but take a warm garment at night because a/c can be very cold. On day time journeys consider whether you want to see the scenery or a video. If going on an overnight bus, book seats at the front as toilets get very smelly by morning. No standing (in theory), and you may have to wait for the next one (next day, perhaps) if all seats are taken. You *must* book in advance for buses travelling in the Yucatán Peninsula, especially around Christmas, but it is also advisable to book if going elsewhere. Some companies, eg ADO, are computerized in main cities, so advance reservations can be made. Bus seats are particularly hard to get during school holidays, Aug and the 15 days up to New Year when many public servants take holidays in all resorts; transport from Mexico City is booked up a long time in advance and hotels are filled, too. In the N especially, try to travel from the starting-point of a route; buses are often full at the mid-point of their routes. Beware of 'scalpers' who try to sell you a seat at a higher price, which you can usually get on a stand-by basis, when somebody doesn't turn up, at the regular price. Sometimes it helps to talk to the driver, who has two places to use at his discretion behind his seat (don't sit in these until invited). Lock your luggage to the rack with a cycle lock and chain. If protecting luggage with chicken wire it will set off metal detectors used by Cristóbal Colón bus line in southern Mexico. Stowing your luggage on the roof is not advisable on night buses since theft can occur. Luggage racks on both classes of

Sematur Ferry Schedule

Route	La Paz - Mazatlán	Mazatlán - La Paz	La Paz - Topolobampo	Topolobampo - La Paz	Sta Rosalia - Guaymas	Guaymas - Sta Rosalia
Frequency and Class	Thur - Tues	Fri - Wed	Wed, Thur	Wed, Thur	Sun, Wed	Tues, Fri
	Salón US$20 Turista US$40 Cabina US$60 Especial US$80	Salón US$20 Turista US$40 Cabina US$60 Especial US$80	Salón US$13 Turista US$27 Cabina US$40 Especial US$53	Salón US$13 Turista US$27 Cabina US$40 Especial US$53	Salón US$13 Turista US$27	Salón US$13 Turista US$27
	Wed Load Ferry	Thur Load Ferry	Mon, Tues, Fri, Sat	Mon, Tues, Fri, Sat		
	Salón US$20	Salón US$20	Salón US$13	Salón US$13		
Departure	1500	1500	1100	2200	0800	1100
Arrival	0900	0900	1900	0700	1500	1800

Fare pp sharing accommodation
children under 12, ½ price
children under 2 free
no pregnant women allowed on board

SALON - General seating
TURISTA - Cabin with bunkbeds, washbasin
CABINA - Cabin with bunkbeds, bathroom
ESPECIAL - Cabin with living room, bedroom, bathroom & closet

Routes on request for cars, motor homes, trailers, motorcycles etc

SEMATUR OFFICES:

Central reservation T 91(800) 69696
Guillermo Prieto y 5 de Mayo, La Paz T (112) 53833/54666
Terminal Pichilingüe, La Paz T (112) 29435, F 56588
Terminal de Transbordadores, Mazatlán T (69) 817020/21, F 817023
Muelle Fiscal, Topolobampo T (686) 20141, F 20035
Muelle Fiscal, Sta Rosalia T (115) 20014/13
Muelle Fiscal, Guaymas T (622) 23390, F 23393
Festival Tours, Texas 36, Col Napoles, Mexico DF, CP 03810 T 682-7043, 682-6213, F 682-7378

long-distance bus are spacious and will take a rucksack with a little persuasion (either of the rucksack itself, or the bus driver). However well-organized a company (eg ADO), always check that your luggage is on your bus if you are putting it in the hold.

Second-class buses usually operate from a different terminal from 1st class buses and are often antiques (interesting, but frustrating when they break down) or may be brand new. They call at towns and villages and go up side roads the first-class buses never touch. They stop quite as often for meals and toilets as their superiors do and, unlike the first-class buses, people get on and off so often that you may be able to obtain a seat after all. Autobuses Unidos (AU) are usually a little cheaper than other services, but they stop more often, including at the roadside when flagged down. They will not stop on curves, walk until you find a straight stretch. It is not unusual to have to stand on these buses. Some second class seats are bookable (eg in Baja California), others are not, it depends on the company. In general, it is a good idea to take food and drink with you on a long bus ride, as stops may depend on the driver. When a bus stops for refreshment, remember who your driver is and follow him; also memorize your bus' number so you do not miss it when it leaves. First class fares are usually 10% dearer than 2nd class ones. Some companies give holders of an international student card a 50% discount on bus tickets, especially during summer holiday period; persistence may be required. Look out for special offers, eg ADO tickets in 1996/97 gave you a 20% reduction at Best Western hotels throughout Mexico. If making a day trip by bus, do not lose your ticket; you will have to show the driver and operator proof that you have paid for the return. There seem always to be many buses leaving in the early morning. All classes of bus invariably leave on time. Buses are sometimes called camiones, hence central camionero for bus station. A monthly bus guide is available for US$1 (year's subscription) from Guía de Autotransportes de México, Apdo 8929, México 1, DF.

● Car hire

Car rental is very expensive in Mexico and 15% VAT is added to rental costs. Rates will vary from city to city. It can be cheaper to arrange hire in the US or Europe, but rentals booked abroad cannot be guaranteed (though usually they are). Proceed with caution. At some tourist resorts, however, such as Cancún, you can pick up a VW beetle convertible for US$25/day, which you will not be told about abroad. Renting a vehicle is nearly impossible without a credit card. It is twice as expensive to leave a car at a different point from the starting point than a round trip. Check the spare tyre, that the fuel gauge works and that you have been given a full tank, that the insurance is valid on unmade roads and that you know how the alarm (if fitted) turns off, the car will not go if the alarm is set off. A short length of strong chain and a padlock for securing the trunk are worthwhile, for VW beetles (Mexican models are the cheapest cars available for hire but do not come with any frills, a/c, radio, etc).

● Cycling

Peter Cossins (of Bath) writes: 'Considering that it is a large country with many sparsely populated areas, Mexico offers plenty of enjoyable places for riding. The main problems facing cyclists are the heavy traffic which will be encountered on many main roads, the poor condition of the same main roads and the lack of specialized spare parts particularly for mountain bikes. It is possible to find most bike spares in the big cities, but outside these places it is only possible to find the basics: spokes, tyres, tubes etc. Traffic is particularly bad around Mexico City and on the road between Mazatlán and Guadalajara. The easiest region for cycling is the Gulf of Mexico coast, however the roads are dead flat, straight and generally boring. The mountains may appear intimidating, but gradients are not difficult as clapped-out buses and trucks have to be able to climb them. Consequently, much of the best riding is in the sierra. If cycling in Baja, avoid riding in mid-Summer, even during Oct temperatures can reach 45°C+ and water is very scarce all the time. Also beware of Mexican bike mechanics who will attempt to repair your bike rather than admit that they don't know what they are doing, particularly when it comes to mountain bikes.' Wolfgang Schroppel from Urbach and Friedemann Bar from Plüderhausen in Germany also advise that 'for cyclists the toll roads are generally preferable to the ordinary highways. There is less traffic, more lanes and a wide paved shoulder. Some toll roads have 'no cyclists' signs but even the police pay no attention. If you walk your bicycle on the sidewalk through the toll station you don't have to pay (if using the toll roads, take lots of water, there are few facilities). Overland buses, especially on the Pacific Coast highway from Tijuana to Guadalajara, forced us off the road several times as there is no shoulder. They believe more in God than in their brakes. This is very dangerous for cyclists. It is useful to fit a rear mirror, so you can jump off the road before you get hit'. It is reported to be allowed to take bicycles on any bus in Mexico, free of charge, if you feel like a break. Some drivers, however, will expect a tip when loading the luggage. If leaving Mexico City towards Veracruz, consider taking a bus as far as Texmelucan avoiding Chalco – not so much because of the traffic but from risk of robberies. There are about 20 bicycle shops in Mexico City, one next to the other, on the street that leads from the Mercado Merced towards the Zócalo Merced metro station. Make sure you insist on quality, known brand parts, as some of the Mexican brands are made out of inferior/soft material. Most Mexican bicycles have 28 ins wheels, so this size tyres are easy to find; good 26 ins tyres for road use can be found, but rare.

● **Hitchhiking**

Hitchhiking is usually possible for single hikers, but apparently less easy for couples. It is generally quick, but not universally safe (seek local advice). Do not, for example, try to hitch in those parts of Guerrero and Oaxaca States where even driving alone is not recommended. In more out of the way parts, short rides from village to village are usually the rule, so progress can be slow. Getting out of big cities is best done by taking a local bus out of town in the direction of the road you intend to take. Ask for the bus to the 'Salida' (exit) to the next city on that road. From Mexico City to the US border, the route via Tula, Ciudad Valles and Ciudad Victoria, the Sierra Madre Oriental, is scenic but slow through the mountains. The quicker route is via Querétaro, San Luis Potosí and Matehuala. Elsewhere, the most difficult stretches are reported to be Acapulco-Puerto Escondido, Santa Cruz-Salina Cruz and Tulum-Chetumal. It is very easy to hitch short distances, such as the last few kilometres to an archaeological site off the main road; offer to pay something, like US$0.50.

● **Motorbikes**

Grant and Susan Johnson, of Horizons Unlimited, Vancouver, tell us that motor-cycling is good in Mexico as most main roads are in fairly good condition and hotels are usually willing to allow the bike to be parked in a courtyard or patio. This advice is confirmed by Francesca Pagnacco of Exeter, UK.

In the major tourist centres, such as Acapulco, Puerto Vallarta or Cancún, motorbike parts can be found as there are Honda dealers

for bike and jet ski rentals. All Japanese parts are sold only by one shop in Mexico City at extortionate prices (but parts and accessories are easily available in Guatemala at reasonable prices for those travelling there). For BMW repairs and some parts, Ashley Rawlings recommends BMW Mexico City, Grupo Baviera SA de CV, Calzada de Tlalpan 4585, Apdo postal 22-217-CP 14330, T 573-4900.

● **Taxis**

To avoid overcharging, the Government has taken control of taxi services from airports to cities and only those with government licences are allowed to carry passengers from the airport. Sometimes one does not pay the driver but purchases a ticket from a booth on leaving the airport. No further tipping is then required, except when the driver handles heavy luggage for you. The same system has been applied at bus stations but it is possible to pay the driver direct.

● **Trains**

Much of the passenger equipment in use dates from the forties or fifties, including a number of *autovías*. There are modern trains between Mexicali and Guadalajara in 36 hrs, and overnight good Pullman trains between Mexico City and Monterrey, Guadalajara and Veracruz. In 1996 the train from Mexico City to Mérida was not running. A difficult, 2nd class connection was possible via Córdoba but not recommended. The *primera preferente* services (see text for routes) provide reclining seats and heating in carpeted carriages. The railways claim that you can see more from a train than from any other form of transport; this may well be true, but trains are slower than the buses (they can, however, be very crowded); they sometimes have comfortable sleeper cars with *alcobas* (better berths) and *camarines* (small sleepers). Tickets are best booked at the stations: agencies tend to add a large commission and the tickets they issue sometimes turn out not to be valid. A condensed railway timetable is published monthly, see under Mexico City, **Trains**.

● **Walking**

Do not walk at night on dark, deserted roads or streets.

COMMUNICATIONS

● **Learning Spanish**

The National Registration Center for Study Abroad, 823 N 2nd St, PO Box 1393, Milwaukee, WI 53201, USA, T (414) 278-0631, F (414) 271-8884, Telex 8100071205, will advise on tuition within a worldwide consortium of language schools. It will also make all arrangements for study in Mexico. The catalogue costs US$3; phone for information and newsletter. Affiliated schools in Mexico are in San Miguel de Allende, Cuernavaca, Mazatlán, Mérida, Morelia, Guadalajara, Puebla, Acapulco, Mexico City, Aguascalientes, Toluca, Saltillo, Oaxaca. *AmeriSpan Unlimited*, PO Box 40513, Philadelphia, PA 19106-0513, T (USA and Canada) 800-879-6640, 215-829-0996 (worldwide), F 215-829-0418, e-mail: info@amerispan.com, has affiliated schools in eight Mexican cities and also provides many services and advice for travellers (see also under Antigua, Guatemala).

● **Newspapers**

The more important journals are in Mexico City. The most influential dailies are: *Excelsior*, *Novedades*, *El Día* (throughout Mexico), *Uno más Uno*; *The News* (in English, now available in all main cities (Grupo Novedades, which comprises *Novedades* and *The News* has a web site at http://www.novedades.com); *The Mexico City Times* (in English, less US-oriented than *The News*); *El Universal* (*El Universal Gráfico*); *La Jornada* (more to the left), *La Prensa*, a popular tabloid, has the largest circulation. *El Nacional* is the mouthpiece of the Government, *El Heraldo*; *Uno más Uno* publishes a supplement, *Tiempo Libre*, on Thur, listing the week's cultural activities. In Guadalajara, *El Occidental*, *El Informador* and *Siglo 21*. The *Guadalajara Reporter*, the weekly English-language newspaper, has a monthly on-line edition at http://www.guadalajara-reporter.com/. *Siglo 21* is on-line at http://mexplaza.udg.mx/Siglo 21, and *El Informador* at http://www.infored.com.mx. There are influential weekly magazines *Proceso*, and *Siempre*; *Epoca*, and *Quehacer Político* weekly also. The political satirical weekly is *Los Agachados*.

● **Postal services**

Rates are raised periodically in line with the peso's devaluation against the dollar but are reported to vary between towns. They are posted next to the windows where stamps are sold. Rates are: within Mexico, letters up to 20g $1.90, postcards $1.30; to North and Central America and the Caribbean: letters $2.80 (20g), postcards $2.10; South America and Europe $3.50, postcards $2.50; Asia and Australia $3.90, postcards $2.90. International service has improved and bright red mail-boxes, found in many parts of the city, are reliable. Weight limit from the UK to Mexico: 22 lb, and 2 kg (5 kg for books) in the reverse direction. About

3 months to Europe. Small parcel rate cheaper. Parcel counters often close earlier than other sections of the post office in Mexico. See below for the accelerated service, Mexpost. As for most of Latin America, send printed matter such as magazines registered. Many travellers have recommended that one should not use the post to send film or cherished objects as losses are frequent. A permit is needed from the Bellas Artes office to send paintings or drawings out of Mexico. Not all these services are obtainable outside Mexico City; delivery times in/from the interior may well be longer than those given above. Poste restante ('general delivery' in the US, *lista de correos* in Mexico) functions quite reliably, but you may have to ask under each of your names; mail is sent back after 10 days (for an extension write to the Jefe de la Administración of the post office holding your mail, any other post office will help with this). Address '*favor de retener hasta llegada*' on envelope.

Within Mexico many businesses use 1st and 2nd class passenger buses to deliver letters and parcels. Each piece is signed for and must be collected at the destination. The service is considered quick and reliable. Should it be necessary to send anything swiftly and safely (in Mexico and other countries), there are many courier firms; the post office's own EMS/Mexpost accelerated service, paid for by weight, is quick and reliable, otherwise the best known is DHL (Mexico City T 227-0299), but it is about twice the cost of Estrella Blanca (T 368-6577) or Federal Express (T 228-9904).

● **Telephone services**

Most public phones take phone cards only (Ladatel) costing 20-50 pesos from shops and news kiosks everywhere. AT&T's USA Direct service is available, for information in Mexico dial 412-553-7458, ext 359. From LADA phones (see below), dial **01, similar for AT&T credit cards. To use calling cards to Canada T 95-800-010-1990. Commercially-run *casetas*, or booths (eg Computel), where you pay after phoning, are up to twice as expensive as private phones, and charges vary from place to place. Computel's main office is on the 27th floor of Torre Latinoamericana in Mexico City. They have offices countrywide with long opening hours (if using commercial booths to make credit-card calls, check in advance what charges are imposed). It is better to call collect from private phones, but better still to use the LADA system. Collect calls on LADA can be made from any blue public phone, silver phones for local and direct long distance calls, some take coins. Others take foreign credit cards (Visa, Mastercard, not Amex, 'a slot machine scenario', not all phones that say they take cards accept them, others that say they don't do). **NB** You cannot make transatlantic calls on a 20 peso LADA phone card. LADA numbers are: 91 long distance within Mexico, add city code and number (half-price Sun); 92 long distance in Mexico, person to person; 95 long distance to USA and Canada, add area code and number; 96 to USA and Canada person to person for collect calls; 98 to rest of the world, add country code, city code and number; 99 to rest of the world, person to person; it is not possible to call collect to Germany, but it is possible to Israel. Cheap rates vary according to the country called. For information dial 07 or 611-1100. Foreign calls (through the operator, at least) cannot be made from 1230 on 24 Dec until the end of Christmas Day. The *Directorio Telefónico Nacional Turístico* is full of useful information, including LADA details, federal tourist offices, time zones, yellow pages for each state, places of interest and maps.

NB With the imminent ending of Telmex' monopoly, there may be significant changes in Mexico's phone numbering system by 1997.

Telecommunications Telégrafos Nacionales maintains the national and international telegraph systems, separate from the Post Office. There is a special office at Balderas 14-18, just near corner of Colón, in Mexico City to deal with international traffic (open 0800-2300, Metro Hidalgo, exit C Basilio Badillo). There are three types of telegraph service: *extra urgente*, *urgente* and *ordinario*; they can only be prepaid, not sent collect. There is a telegraph and telex service available at Mexico City airport. Fax is common in main post offices.

HOLIDAYS AND FESTIVALS

Sun is a statutory holiday. Sat is also observed as a holiday, except by the shops. There is no early-closing day. National holidays are as follows:

New Year (1 Jan), Constitution Day (5 Feb), Birthday of Benito Juárez (21 Mar), Maundy Thursday, Good Friday and Easter Saturday, Labour Day (1 May), Battle of Puebla (5 May), President's Annual Message (1 Sept), Independence Day (16 Sept), Discovery of America (*Dia de la raza*) (12 Oct), Day of the Revolution (20 Nov), Christmas Day (25 Dec).

Santos Reyes 6 Jan, Mother's Day 10 May, All Souls' Day 1-2 Nov and Our Lady of Guadalupe 12 Dec, are not national holidays, but are widely celebrated.

FURTHER READING

Travellers wanting more information than we have space to provide, on archaeological sites for instance, would do well to use the widely available *Panorama* guides and the *Easy Guides* written by Richard Bloomgarden, with plans and good illustrations. Also available are Miniguides to archaeological and historical sites, published in various languages by INAH, US$0.75 each. You will appreciate archaeological sites much more if you do some research before visiting them. Do not expect to find leaflets or books at the sites, stock up before you visit. For ornithologists: *A Field Guide to Mexican Birds*, Peterson and Chalif, Houghton Mifflin, 1973, has been recommended; *Finding Birds in Mexico*, by Ernest P Edwards, Box AQ, Sweet Briar, Virginia 24595, USA, recommended as detailed and thorough. 2 books by Rudi Robins: *One-day Car Trips from Mexico City*, and *Weekend trips to Cities near Mexico City*. Highly recommended, practical and entertaining is *The People's Guide to Mexico* by Carl Franz (John Muir Publications, Santa Fe, NM), now in its 8th edition, 1990; there is also a *People's Guide Travel Letter*. *Back Country Mexico, A Traveller's Guide and Phrase Book*, by Bob Burlison and David H Riskind (University of Texas Press, Box 7819, Austin, Texas, 78713-7819) has been recommended. *Mexico From The Driver's Seat*, by Mike Nelson, is published by Sanborn's (see **Automobiles**, above). Also *Hidden Mexico* by Rebecca Brüns.

Recommended reading for the Maya archaeological area: *The Maya*, by MD Coe (Pelican Books, or large format edition, Thames and Hudson); C Bruce Hunter, *A Guide to Ancient Mayan Ruins* (University of Oklahoma Press, 1986); Joyce Kelly, *An Archaeological Guide to Mexico's Yucatán Peninsula* (the states of Yucatán, Quintana Roo and Campeche) (University of Oklahoma Press, Norman and London, 1993, with maps, photos, 364 pp, accessible, informative and very good). *More Maya Missions. Exploring Colonial Chiapas*, written and illustrated by Richard D Perry (Espadaña Press, PO Box 31067, Santa Barbara, CA 93130, USA) is the latest in a series; also published, *Maya Missions* (in Yucatán) and *Mexico's Fortress Monasteries* (Central Mexico and Oaxaca). For the Puuc region, *Guide to Puuc Region*, Prof Gualberto

Zapata Alonzo (US$7.30), has been recommended. For a contemporary account of travel in the Maya region, see *Time among the Maya*, by Ronald Wright. Perhaps the most descriptive of travel in the region is John L Stephens, *Incidents of Travel in Central America, Chiapas and Yucatán*, with illustrations by Frederick Catherwood (several editions exist). *Western Mexico: A Traveller's Treasury*, by Tony Burton (Editorial Agata, Guadalajara), has also been suggested for further reading.

For a short guide to the people, politics, geography, history, economy and culture, *In Focus, Mexico* by John Ross is recommended as part of the In Focus series published by Latin America Bureau in 1996, ISBN 1 899365 05 2.

ACKNOWLEDGEMENTS

The editors would like to thank John Gibbs (Mexico City) for much invaluable updating material and answering queries. The sections on Guadalajara, Puebla and Colima have been substantially rewritten by the tireless Jim Hardy (Guadalajara), to whom we are most grateful. The chapter has been updated with the most welcome help of Caitlin Hennessy and Huw Clough (London, UK). In addition to the names listed at the end of the book, we should like to thank Tim Burford for writing on national parks, Anne McLauchlan for information on Celaya and maps, and Richard Robinson for updating Puerto Vallarta and other areas.

Cuba

T HE ISLAND OF CUBA, 1,250 km long, 191 km at its widest point, is the largest of the Caribbean islands and only 145 km S of Florida. The name is believed to derive from the Arawak word 'cubanacan', meaning centre, or central. Gifted with a moderate climate, afflicted only occasionally by hurricanes, not cursed by frosts, blessed by an ample and well distributed rainfall and excellent soils for tropical crops, it has traditionally been one of the largest exporters of cane sugar in the world.

HORIZONS

THE LAND

About a quarter of Cuba is fairly mountainous. To the W of Havana is the narrow Sierra de los Organos, rising to 750m and containing, in the extreme W, the strange scenery of the Guaniguánicos hill country. South of these Sierras, in a strip 145 km long and 16 km wide along the piedmont, is the Vuelta Abajo area which grows the finest of all Cuban tobaccos. Towards the centre of the island are the Escambray mountains, rising to 1,100m, and in the E, encircling the port of Santiago, are the most rugged mountains of all, the Sierra Maestra, in which Pico Turquino reaches 1,980m. In the rough and stony headland E of Guantánamo Bay are copper, manganese, chromium and iron mines. About a quarter of the land surface is covered with mountain forests of pine and mahogany. The coastline, with a remarkable number of fine ports and anchorages, is about 3,540 km long.

PEOPLE

Some 66% of Cubans register themselves as whites: they are mostly the descendants of Spanish colonial settlers and immigrants; 12% are black, now living mostly along the coasts and in certain provinces, Oriente in particular; 21% are mixed and about 1% are Chinese; the indigenous Indians disappeared long ago although there is evidence of Amerindian ancestry in some Cubans. Some 73% live in the towns,

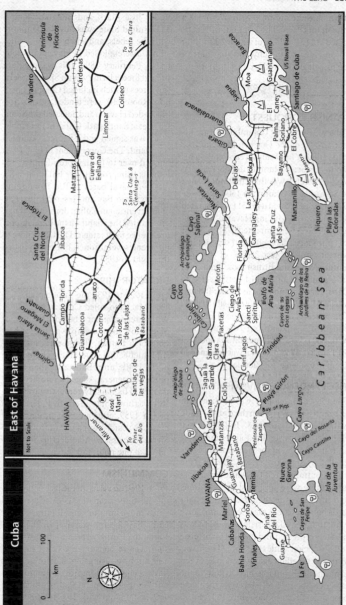

Cuba

East of Havana

Not to Scale

0 ____ 100
km

N

Caribbean Sea

of which there are nine with over 50,000 inhabitants each. The population is estimated at 11.0 million, of which 2.1 million live in Havana (the city and that part of the province within the city's limits).

HISTORY

SPANISH CONQUEST

Cuba was visited by Columbus during his first voyage on 27 October 1492, and he made another brief stop 2 years later on his way to Jamaica. Columbus did not realize it was an island; it was first circumnavigated by Sebastián de Ocampo in 1508. Diego de Velázquez conquered it in 1511 and founded several towns, including Havana. The first African slaves were imported in 1526. Sugar was introduced soon after but was not important until the last decade of the 16th century. When the British took Jamaica in 1655 a number of Spanish settlers fled to Cuba, already famous for its cigars. Tobacco was made a strict monopoly of Spain in 1717. The coffee plant was introduced in 1748. The British, under Lord Albemarle and Admiral Pocock, captured Havana and held the island in 1762-63, but it was returned to Spain in exchange for Florida.

INDEPENDENCE MOVEMENT

The tobacco monopoly was abolished in 1816 and Cuba was given the right to trade with the world in 1818. Independence elsewhere, however, bred ambitions, and a strong movement for independence was quelled by Spain in 1823. By this time the blacks outnumbered the whites in the island; there were several slave rebellions and little by little the Créoles (or Spaniards born in Cuba) made common cause with them. A slave rising in 1837 was savagely repressed and the poet Gabriel de la Concepción Valdés was shot. There was a 10-year rebellion against Spain between 1868 and 1878, but it gained little save the effective abolition of slavery, which had been officially forbidden since 1847. From 1895 to 1898 rebellion flared up again

under José Martí and Máximo Gómez. The United States was now in sympathy with the rebels, and when the US battleship *Maine* exploded in Havana harbour on 15 February 1898, this was made a pretext for declaring war on Spain. American forces (which included Colonel Theodore Roosevelt) were landed, a squadron blockaded Havana and defeated the Spanish fleet at Santiago de Cuba. In December peace was signed and US forces occupied the island. The Government of Cuba was handed over to its first president, Tomás Estrada Palma, on 20 May 1902. The USA retained naval bases at Río Hondo and Guantánamo Bay and reserved the right of intervention in Cuban domestic affairs, but granted the island a handsome import preference for its sugar. The USA chose to intervene several times, but relinquished this right in 1934.

DICTATORSHIP

From 1925 to 1933 the 'strong man' Gerardo Machado ruled Cuba as a dictator. Widespread popular rebellion throughout Machado's dictatorship was utilized by Fulgencio Batista, then a sergeant. Corrupt, ineffectual governments held office in the 1940s, until Batista, by then a self-promoted general, staged a military coup in 1952. His harshly repressive dictatorship was brought to an end by Fidel Castro in Jan 1959, after an extraordinary and heroic 3 years' campaign, mostly in the Sierra Maestra, with a guerrilla force reduced at one point to 12 men.

COMMUNISM

From 1960 onwards, in the face of increasing hostility from the USA, Castro led Cuba into communism. All farms of over 67 ha have been taken over by the state. Rationing is still fierce, and there are still shortages of consumer goods. However, education, housing and health services have been greatly improved. Infant mortality fell to 9.4 per 1,000 live births in 1994, compared with 19.6 in 1980. It is claimed that illiteracy has been wiped out.

Considerable emphasis is placed on combining productive agricultural work with study: there are over 400 schools and colleges in rural areas where the students divide their time between the fields and the classroom. Education is compulsory up to the age of 17 and free.

US RELATIONS

Before the Revolution of 1959 the United States had investments in Cuba worth about US$1,000mn, covering nearly every activity from agriculture and mining to oil installations; it took 66% of Cuba's exports and supplied 70% of the imports in 1958. Today all American businesses, including banks, have been nationalized; the USA has cut off all imports from Cuba, placed an embargo on exports to Cuba, and broken off diplomatic relations. Promising moves to improve relations with the USA were given impetus in 1988 by the termination of Cuban military activities in Angola under agreement with the USA and South Africa. However, developments in Eastern Europe and the former USSR in 1989-90 provoked Castro to defend the Cuban system of government; the lack of political change delayed any further rapprochement with the USA. Prior to the 1992 US presidential elections, President Bush approved the Cuban Democracy Act (Torricelli Bill) which strengthened the trade embargo by forbidding US subsidiaries from trading with Cuba. Many countries, including EC members and Canada, said they would not allow the US bill to affect their trade with Cuba and the UN General Assembly voted in November in favour of a resolution calling for an end to the embargo. The defeat of George Bush by Bill Clinton did not, however, signal a change in US attitudes, in large part because of the support given to the Democrat's campaign by Cuban exiles in Miami.

1990'S CRISIS AND CHANGE

In an effort to broaden the people's power system of government introduced in 1976, the central committee of the Cuban Communist Party adopted resolutions in 1990 designed to strengthen the municipal and provincial assemblies and transform the National Assembly into a genuine parliament. In Feb 1993, the first direct, secret elections for the National Assembly and for provincial assemblies were held. Despite calls from opponents abroad for voters to register a protest by spoiling their ballot or not voting, the official results showed that 99.6% of the electorate voted, with 92.6% of votes cast valid. All 589 official candidates were elected.

Economic difficulties in the 1990s brought on by the loss of markets in the former USSR and Eastern Europe, together with higher oil prices because of the Gulf crisis, forced the Government to impose emergency measures and declare a special period in peace time. Rationing was increased, petrol became scarce, the bureaucracy was slashed and several hundred arrests were made in a drive against corruption. As economic hardship continued into 1993, Cuba was hit on 13 March by a winter storm which caused an estimated US$1bn in damage. Agricultural production, for both export and domestic consumption, was severely affected. In mid-1994, economic frustration and discontent boiled up and Cubans began to flee their country. Thousands left in a mass exodus to Florida on any homemade craft they could invent. It was estimated that between mid-Aug and mid-Sept 30,000 Cubans had left the country, compared with 3,656 in the whole of 1993. In contrast, the number of US visas issued in Jan-Aug was 2,059 out of an agreed maximum annual quota of 20,000. Eventually the crisis forced President Clinton into an agreement whereby the USA was committed to accepting at least 20,000 Cubans a year, plus the next of kin of US citizens, while Cuba agreed to prevent further departures.

As the economic crisis persisted, the government adopted measures (some of which are outlined below) which opened up many sectors to private enterprise and

Hurricane Lili

After several days of hesitation, during which Cubans frantically speculated and evacuated, Hurricane Lili finally moved towards the Cuban coast on 17 October 1996. It was at first thought that she would pass over the island to the W of Havana through Pinar del Río; the next forecast was that the route would be to the E and hit Matanzas. Once she got started and headed due N over Isla de la Juventud, it was assumed she would strike Havana, wreaking untold damage to the fragile colonial city. However, she changed course at the last minute, and, having reached the coast veered SE again towards Trinidad and sharply NE across Villa Clara province to the Atlantic Ocean and on to the Bahamas. There was extensive damage to crops and housing, but no one was killed because of highly efficient civil defence procedures involving evacuation of the most vulnerable areas. Heaps of rubble for renovation were cleared from the streets of Havana to prevent storm drains being blocked, leaving them cleaner than ever before. Half the buildings in the colonial city were judged to be at risk and 200,000 people were moved from their homes. Tourists were evacuated from Cayo Largo to Varadero and some Havana hotels were emptied, although a few Italian and Spanish visitors professed to be looking forward to the 'adventure' and refused to move. Crop damage was compounded by heavy rain later in October which flooded eastern Cuba and further storms in mid-November affecting the whole country. Several buildings collapsed in Havana while thousands of tonnes of bananas, citrus, rice, sugar and root vegetables were destroyed.

recognized the dependence of much of the economy on dollars. The partial reforms did not eradicate the imbalances between the peso and the dollar economies, and shortages remained for those without access to hard currency.

Cuba then intensified its economic liberalization programme, speeding up the opening of farmers' markets throughout the country and allowing farmers to sell at uncontrolled prices once their commitments to the state procurement system were fulfilled. Importantly, the reforms also allowed middlemen to operate. It had been the emergence of this profitable occupation which had provoked the Government to close down the previous farmers' market system in 1986. Markets in manufactured goods and handicrafts also opened and efforts were made to increase the number of self-employed.

US PRESSURE IN THE 1990s

Cuba's foreign policy initiatives in 1994-95 succeeded in bringing international pressure to bear on the USA over its trade embargo. In its third and worst defeat in 1994, the USA lost a resolution in the UN General Assembly which called for an end to the embargo by 101 votes to 2. In 1995 it lost again by 117 votes to 3. The European Parliament meanwhile adopted a resolution which described the 1992 Torricelli Act as contrary to international law and called for its repeal. The Russian parliament passed a similar motion. However, right wingers in the USA continued to push for further economic pressure on Cuba.

In 1996, another US election year, Cuba faced another crackdown by the US administration. In Feb, Cuba shot down 2 light aircraft piloted by Miami exiles allegedly over Cuban air space and implicitly confirmed by the findings of the International Civil Aviation Organization (ICAO) report in June. The attack provoked President Clinton into reversing his previous opposition to key elements of the Helms-Burton bill to tighten and internationalize the US embargo on Cuba and on 12 March he signed into law the Cuban Freedom and Democratic

Solidarity Act. The new legislation allows legal action against any company or individual benefiting from properties expropriated by the Cuban government after the Revolution. Claims on property nationalized by the Cuban state extended to persons who did not hold US citizenship at the time of the expropriation, thus including Batista supporters who fled at the start of the Revolution. It brought universal condemnation: Canada and Mexico (Nafta partners), the EU, Russia, China, the Caribbean Community and the Rio Group of Latin American countries all protested that it was unacceptable to extend sanctions outside the USA to foreign companies and their employees who do business with Cuba. In 1997 the EU brought a formal complaint against the USA at the World Trade Organization (WTO), but suspended it when an EU/US agreement was reached under which Pres Bill Clinton was expected to ask the US Congress to amend Title IV of the law (concerning the denial of US entry visas to employees and shareholders of 'trafficking companies'). Clinton was also expected to carry on waiving Title III (authorizing court cases against 'trafficking' of expropriated assets).

The Cuban Communist Party is to hold its 5th Congress in October 1997, the first since 1991. It is expected to highlight issues such as social indiscipline, corruption and other illegal activities, while promoting nationalism in the months leading up to the centenary of the US occupation of Cuba in 1898.

GOVERNMENT

In 1976 a new constitution was approved by 97.7% of the voters, setting up municipal and provincial assemblies and a National Assembly of People's Power. The membership of the Assembly was increased to 589 in 1993, candidates being nominated by the 169 municipal councils, and elected by direct secret ballot. Similarly elected are numbers of the 14 provincial assemblies.

The number of Cuba's provinces was increased from six to 14 as a result of the decisions of the First Congress of the Communist Party of Cuba in Dec 1975. Dr Fidel Castro was elected President of the Council of State by the National Assembly and his brother, Major Raúl Castro, was elected First Vice-President.

THE ECONOMY

Following the 1959 revolution, Cuba adopted a Marxist-Leninist system. Almost all sectors of the economy were state controlled and centrally planned, the only significant exception being agriculture, where some 12% of arable land was still privately owned. The country became heavily dependent on trade and aid from other Communist countries, principally the USSR (through its participation in the Council of Mutual Economic Aid), encouraged by the US trade embargo. It relied on sugar, and to a lesser extent nickel, for nearly all its exports. While times were good, Cuba used the Soviet protection to build up an impressive, but costly, social welfare system, with better housing, education and health care than anywhere else in Latin America and the Caribbean. The collapse of the Eastern European bloc, however, revealed the vulnerability of the island's economy and the desperate need for reform. A sharp fall in gdp of 35% in 1990-93, accompanied by a decline in exports from US$8.1bn (1989) to US$1.7bn (1993), forced the Government to take remedial action and the decision was made to start the complex process of transition to a mixed economy.

Transformation of the unwieldy and heavily centralized state apparatus has progressed in fits and starts. The Government is keen to encourage self-employment to enable it to reduce the public sector workforce, but Cuban workers are cautious about relinquishing their job security. Some small businesses have sprung up, particularly in the tourism

Self-employment – Cuban style

When the Cuban government realized it would have to lay off thousands of workers in state enterprises in order to achieve some sort of efficiency, while thousands of others were already idle because of the lack of fuel and spare parts which paralysed industry, it hit upon self-employment as a convenient way to mop up surplus labour. It was hoped that it would boost the income of non-working women and people on pensions, and provide some services the state was unable to offer. Initially cautious, Cubans accepted the scheme as the only way to increase their income from the average state employee's monthly salary of 200 pesos. The positive response led to the categories of work being extended. Craft markets and street vendors appeared on street corners and many families opened their doors to feed tourists and Cubans with small restaurants, known as *paladares*, a term coined from a Brazilian soap opera. The boom was short-lived, however. As soon as the new entrepreneurs started to make money, the authorities saw the need to tax and control them to reduce distinctions in income. Restaurant owners have to buy a licence to operate, they are limited to 12 chairs in their *paladar* and are not permitted to employ anyone other than relatives, who also have to buy a licence. In Feb 1996, tax payments were increased sharply from 500 to 1,000 pesos for restauranteurs, 100 to 400 pesos for taxi drivers and 45 to 500 pesos for car mechanics. No wonder that the number of registered self-employed fell in one month from 208,000 to 205,694. The Government, however, maintains that self-employment is here to stay and is aiming to triple the number to 600,000. Tax revenues from the self-employed sector now account for 10% of the national budget income.

sector (see box). Free farm produce markets were permitted in 1994 and these were followed by similar markets at de-regulated prices for manufacturers, including goods produced by state enterprises and handicrafts. Cubans are now allowed to hold US dollars and in 1995 a convertible peso at par with the US dollar was introduced, which is fully exchangeable for hard currencies.

Although commercial relations with market economies were poor in the late 1980s, because of lack of progress in debt rescheduling negotiations, Cuba has made great efforts in the 1990s to improve its foreign relations. The US trade embargo and the associated inability to secure finance from multilateral sources has led the Government to encourage foreign investment, principally in joint ventures. All sectors of the economy, including sugar and real estate, are now open to foreign investment and in some areas majority foreign shareholdings are allowed. About US$1,500mn was registered between 1990-94, in areas such as tourism, oil and mining. Some 400 foreign companies are now established in Cuba, with capital from 38 countries in 26 economic sectors. In 1996 Cuba attracted US$2bn in foreign investment and the number of joint ventures rose to 260. The leading investors are from Spain, Canada, France, Italy and Mexico, in that order. Bilateral investment promotion and protection agreements have been signed with 12 nations including Italy, Spain, Germany and the UK. Under new legislation passed in 1996, free-trade zones are being established, the first one at Havana with others to follow at Cienfuegos, Mariel and Wajay, outside Havana. 75% of production must be exported but the rest can be sold in Cuba on the dollar market. Employees will be paid in pesos. By mid-1997, 35 foreign companies had applied for licences to operate.

Structure of production

Sugar is the major crop, providing about 70% of export earnings. However, the industry has consistently failed to reach the targets set. Cuba's dream of a 10 million tonne raw sugar harvest has never been reached. Poor weather and shortages of fertilizers, oil and spare parts cut output to 3.3 million tonnes in 1994-95, but it recovered to 4.4 million in 1995-96. Sugar mills have been converted to use bagasse as fuel, but the canefields use large quantities of oil for machinery to cut and transport the cane. Earnings from sugar exports are devoted to purchasing oil. Trade agreements with the ex-USSR, involving oil and sugar, survived US pressure on Russia to end oil shipments in order to receive US aid.

Citrus is now the second most important agricultural export contributing about 4% of revenues. Cuba became a member of the International Coffee Agreement in 1985 and produces about 22,000 tonnes of **coffee** a year but exports are minimal. **Tobacco** is a traditional crop with Cuban cigars world famous, but this too has suffered from lack of fuel, fertilizers and other inputs. Production fell to about 13,800 tonnes, a third of previous levels, but is recovering with the help of Spanish credits and importers from France and Britain. The 1996 crop was expected to increase to some 34,500 tonnes, from which about 65 million cigars will be produced for export, earning over US$100mn.

Diversification away from sugar is a major goal, with the emphasis on production of **food** for domestic use because of the shortage of foreign exchange for imports. The beef herd declined from an average 5.2 million head in 1979-81 to 4 million in the first half of the 1990s because of the inability to pay for imports of grains, fertilizers and chemicals. Production is now less intensive, with smaller herds on pastures, and numbers are beginning to rise again. Similarly, milk production is also increasing. The opening of farmers markets in 1994 has

Cuba: fact file

Geographic

Land area	110,861 sq km
forested	23.7%
pastures	27.0%
cultivated	30.7%

Demographic

Population (1996)	11,117,000
annual growth rate (1990-95)	0.8%
urban	72.8%
rural	27.2%
density	100.3 per sq km
Religious affiliation	
Roman Catholic	39.6%
Non religious	48.7%
Birth rate per 1,000 (1993)	14.0
	(world av 25.0)

Education and Health

Life expectancy at birth,	
male	73.9 years
female	77.6 years
Infant mortality rate	
per 1,000 live births (1994)	9.4
Physicians (1992)	1 per 231 persons
Hospital beds	1 per 134 persons
Calorie intake as %	
of FAO requirement	135%
Population age 25 and over	
with no formal schooling	39.6%
Literacy (over 15)	95.7%

Economic

GNP (1991 market prices)	
	US$17,000mn
GNP per capita	US$1,580
Public external debt (1993)	
	US$10,800mn
Tourism receipts (1994)	US$850mn
Inflation	na
Radio	1 per 3.1 persons
Television	1 per 4.4 persons
Telephone	1 per 31 persons

Employment

Population economically active	
(1988)	4,570,236
Unemployment rate	6.0%
% of labour force in	
agriculture	20.4
mining and manufacturing	21.8
construction	9.8
Military forces (1996)	100,000

Source *Encyclopaedia Britannica*

helped to stimulate diversification of crops and greater availability of foodstuffs, although shortages still remain.

The sudden withdrawal of **oil** supplies when trade agreements with Russia had to be renegotiated and denominated in convertible currencies, was a crucial factor in the collapse of the Cuban economy. Although trade agreements involving oil and sugar remain, Cuba has had to purchase oil from other suppliers, such as Iran and Colombia, with extremely limited foreign exchange. As a result, Cuba has stepped up its own production to 1,287,000 tons in 1994, providing 27% of electricity generation. Foreign companies have been encouraged to explore for oil on and off-shore and investment has borne fruit. Two Canadian companies have found oil in Cárdenas Bay, E of Havana, in a well capable of producing 3,750 barrels a day. Nevertheless, shortages of fuel remain, which, combined with a lack of spare parts for ex-Soviet and Czechoslovakian generating plants, does result in power cuts and unreliable public transport.

Mining is a sector attracting foreign interest and at the end of 1994 a new mining law was passed. A Mining Authority was created and a tax system set up. 40,000 sq km have been allocated for mining ventures and all were expected to have been allocated by the end of 1995. Major foreign investors included Australian (nickel), Canadian (gold, silver and base metals) and South African (gold, copper, nickel) companies. Nickel and cobalt production declined by 11.3% to 26,362 tonnes in 1994, but with greater investment output rose to 43,900 tonnes in 1995 and a record 55,800 tonnes in 1996, nearly half of which came from the Moa Bay plant run as a joint venture between Canadian interests and the Cuban state. Cuba has one small gold mine at Castellanos in Pinar del Río province which produced 200 kg in 1995 and was expected to increase that to 300 kg in 1996. New, Canadian-backed projects in Pinar del Río at the Hierro Mantua site will produce gold and copper, and on Isla de Juventud, gold and silver.

Tourism is now a major foreign exchange earner and has received massive investment from abroad with many joint ventures. New hotel projects are coming on stream and many more are planned. An estimated 5,000 new or renovated rooms came into use in 1996, bringing the total available to foreign visitors to 33,600. Most of the development has been along the Varadero coast, where large resort hotels attract package tourism. By the year 2000, Cuba aims to have 50,000 hotel rooms, of which 33,000 will be in beach resorts and 10,000 in cities. Despite political crises, numbers of visitors have risen steadily from 546,000 in 1993 to 630,000 in 1994, 741,700 in 1995 and 1,001,739 in 1996. The target is for 2,550,000 tourists a year bringing earnings of about US$3.1bn.

Recent trends

There has been considerable success in reducing the fiscal deficit, which was bloated by subsidies and inefficiencies. A deficit of 5,000mn pesos in 1993 was cut to 775mn in 1995 and 570mn in 1996, only 2.4% of gdp, reflecting subsidy reductions. More reforms are planned, which may include the removal of subsidies from almost all state enterprises, new legislation on property ownership and commercial practice, development of the tax system and restructuring of the banking system. Financial services will have to be overhauled to cater for the accumulation of capital by owners of small businesses, who currently have to operate in cash. In 1997 legislation was approved to transform the Banco Nacional into a central bank.

There are signs that the Cuban economy has turned the corner, although these have yet to be felt by the population in general. In 1994 gdp showed a small growth rate of 0.7%, exports rose by about 3.5% and the black market exchange rate for the US dollar strengthened from

130 to 40 pesos. In 1995 gdp grew stronger by 2.5% and the exchange rate strengthened further to 20 pesos = US$1. 1996 was even better, with growth of 7.8% due to increases in output of nickel, oil, fertilizers, tobacco, sugar, steel and cement as well as greater tourism earnings. The external accounts remain weak, however. Foreign debt hovers around US$11bn, or 4.6% of gdp, and Cuba's dependence on high-interest, short-term trade finance is a burden. Cuba is ineligible for long-term development finance from multilateral lending agencies because of the US veto.

CULTURE

The Cuban Revolution has had a profound effect on culture both on the island itself and in a wider context. Domestically, its chief achievement has been to integrate popular expression into daily life, compared with the pre-revolutionary climate in which art was either the preserve of an elite or, in its popular forms, had to fight for acceptance. The encouragement of painting in people's studios and through a national art school, and the support given by the state to musicians and film-makers has done much to foster a national cultural identity. This is not to say that the system has neither refrained from controlling what the people should be exposed to (eg much Western pop music was banned in the 1960s), nor that it has been without its domestic critics (either those who lived through the Revolution and took issue with it, or younger artists who now feel stifled by a cultural bureaucracy). Furthermore, while great steps have been made towards the goal of a fully-integrated society, there remain areas in which the unrestricted participation of blacks and women has yet to be achieved. Blacks predominate in sport and music (as in Brazil), but find it harder to gain recognition in the public media; women artists, novelists and composers have had to struggle for acceptance. Nevertheless, measures are being taken in the cultural, social and political spheres to rectify this.

The major characteristic of Cuban culture is its combination of the African and European. Because slavery was not abolished until 1886 in Cuba, black African traditions were kept intact much later than elsewhere in the Caribbean. They persist now, inevitably mingled with Hispanic influence, in religion: for instance *santeria*, a cult which blends popular Catholicism with the Yoruba belief in the spirits which inhabit all plant life. This now has a greater hold than orthodox Catholicism, which lost much support in its initial opposition to the Revolution. In 1994 Cardinal Jaime Ortega was appointed by the Vatican to fill the position left vacant in Cuba since the last cardinal died in 1963. Pope John Paul II is to visit Cuba in Jan 1998.

Death of a film maker

1996 marked the end of the notable and prolific career of Tomás Gutiérrez Alea, who died on 16 April at the age of 67. He was an internationally admired and respected film maker and a moving force in the founding of the Cuban Film Institute (ICAIC) in 1959. In the 1960s he directed *Historias de la Revolución* (1961), *Las Doce Sillas* (1962), *Cumbite* (1964), *Muerte de un Burocrata* (1966) and the award-winning *Memorias del Subdesarrollo* (1968), which made the *New York Times* list of the year's top 10 films. He continued to live in Cuba, making films which generated debate about the Cuban revolution, the bourgeoisie and the bureaucracy, with a satirical sense of humour. In 1993 he dealt with another taboo when he made *Fresa y Chocolate* about a gay man struggling for acceptance in a macho society. The film won a Silver Bear at the Berlin Film Festival and was submitted to the US Oscar awards foreign film category.

MUSIC

Music is incredibly vibrant on the island. It is, again, a marriage of African rhythms, expressed in percussion instruments (batá drums, congas, claves, maracas, etc), and the Spanish guitar. Accompanying the music is an equally strong tradition of dance. A history of Cuban music is beyond the scope of this book, however there are certain styles which deserve mention. There are four basic elements out of which all others grow. The *rumba* (drumming, singing about social preoccupations and dancing) is one of the original black dance forms. By the turn of the century, it had been transferred from the plantations to the slums; now it is a collective expression, with Sat evening competitions in which anyone can partake. Originating in eastern Cuba, *son* is the music out of which *salsa* was born. *Son* itself takes many different forms and it gained worldwide popularity after the 1920s when the National Septet of Ignacio Piñeiro made it fashionable. The more sophisticated *danzón*, ballroom dance music which was not accepted by the upper classes until the end of the last century, has also been very influential. It was the root for the *cha-cha-cha* (invented in 1948 by Enrique Jorrin). The fourth tradition is *trova*, the itinerant troubadour singing ballads, which has been transformed, post-Revolution, into the *nueva trova*, made famous by singers such as Pablo Milanés and Silvio Rodríguez. The new tradition adds politics and everyday concerns to the romantic themes.

There are many other styles, such as the *guajira*, the most famous example of which is the song 'Guantanamera'; *tumba francesa* drumming and dancing; and Afro-Cuban jazz, performed by internationally renowned artists like Irakere and Arturo Sandoval. Apart from sampling the recordings of groups, put out by the state company Egrem, the National Folklore Company (Conjunto Folklórico Nacional) gives performances of the traditional music which it was set up to study and keep alive.

LITERATURE

The Cuban Revolution had perhaps its widest cultural influence in the field of **literature**. Many now famous Latin American novelists (like Gabriel García Márquez, Mario Vargas Llosa and Julio Cortázar) visited Havana and worked with the Prensa Latina news agency or on the *Casa de las Américas* review. As Gordon Brotherston has said, "an undeniable factor in the rise of the novel in Latin America has been a reciprocal self-awareness among novelists in different countries and in which Cuba has been instrumental." (*The Emergence of the Latin American Novel*, Cambridge University Press, 1977, page 3.) Not all have maintained their allegiance, just as some Cuban writers have deserted the Revolution. One such Cuban is Guillermo Cabrera Infante, whose most celebrated novel is *Tres tristes tigres* (1967). Other established writers remained in Cuba after the Revolution: Alejo Carpentier, who invented the phrase 'marvellous reality' (*lo real maravilloso*) to describe the different order of reality which he perceived in Latin America and the Caribbean and which now, often wrongly, is attributed to many other writers from the region (his novels include *El reino de este mundo, El siglo de las luces, Los pasos perdidos*, and many more); Jorge Lezama Lima (*Paradiso*, 1966); and Edmundo Desnoes (*Memorias del subdesarrollo*). Of post-revolutionary writers, the poet and novelist Miguel Barnet is worth reading, especially for the use of black oral history and traditions in his work. After 1959, Nicolás Guillén, a black, was adopted as the national poet; his poems of the 1930s (*Motivos de son, Sóngoro cosongo, West Indies Ltd*) are steeped in popular speech and musical rhythms. In tone they are close to the work of the *négritude* writers (see under Martinique), but they look more towards Latin America than Africa. The other poet-hero of the Revolution is the 19th-century writer and fighter for freedom from Spain, José Martí. Even though a US radio and TV station beaming propaganda, pop music and North American culture usurped his name, Martí's importance to Cuba remains undimmed. 19 May 1995 was the centenary of his death in action against Spanish forces which was commemorated around the world by Cuban *aficionados*.

FLORA AND FAUNA

The National Committee for the Protection and Conservation of National Treasures and the Environment was set up in 1978. There are six national parks, including three in Pinar del Río alone (in the Sierra de los Organos and on the Península de Guanahacabibes), the swamps of the Zapata Peninsula and the Gran Piedra near Santiago. The Soledad Botanical Gardens near Cienfuegos house many of Cuba's plants. The Royal Palm is the national tree. Over 200 species of palms abound, as well as flowering trees, pines, oaks, cedars, etc. Original forest, however, is confined to some of the highest points in the SE mountains and the mangroves of the Zapata Peninsula.

There are, of course, a multitude of flowers and in the country even the smallest of houses has a flower garden in front. The orchidarium at Soroa has over 700 examples. To complement the wide variety of butterflies that can be found in Cuba, the buddleia, or butterfly bush, has been named the national flower. In fact, about 10,000 species of insect have been identified on the island.

Reptiles range from crocodiles (of which there is a farm on the Zapata Peninsula) to iguanas to tiny salamanders. Cuba claims the smallest of a number of animals, for instance the Cuban pygmy frog (one of some 30 small frogs), the almiquí (a shrew-like insectivore, the world's smallest mammal), the butterfly or moth bat and the bee hummingbird (called locally the *zunzuncito*). The latter is an endangered species, like the *carpintero real* woodpecker, the cariara (a hawk-like bird of the savannah), the pygmy owl, the Cuban green parrot and the *ferminia*. The best place for birdwatching on the island is the Zapata Peninsula, where 170 species of Cuban birds have been recorded, including the majority of endemic species. In winter the number increases as migratory waterbirds, swallows and others visit the marshes. The national bird is the forest-dwelling Cuban trogon (the *tocororo*).

Also protected is the manatee (sea cow) which has been hunted almost to extinction. It lives in the marshes of the Zapata Peninsula. Also living in the mangrove forests is the large Cuban land crab. Many species of turtle can be found around the offshore cays.

DIVING AND MARINE LIFE

Cuba's marine environment is pristine compared with most Caribbean islands, where there has often been overharvesting and overdevelopment of the dive industry. The majority of coral reefs are alive and healthy and teeming with assorted marine life. The Government has established a marine park around the Isla de la Juventud and much marine life is protected around the entire island, such as the hawksbill turtle, the manatee and coral.

The main dive areas are Isla de la Juventud, Havana, Varadero, Faro Luna, Santa Lucía and Santiago de Cuba. New areas are being developed as hotels are built around the island. Most areas offer a variety of diving, including reefs and walls and an assortment of wrecks, from remains of ancient Spanish ships to many modern wrecks sunk as dive sites. Cuban diving is a new frontier in the Caribbean and has much to offer the adventurous diver.

Varadero sites include the *Neptune*, a 60m steel ship lying in only 10m. This is home to a number of fish including 4 massive green moray eels and 4 very large, friendly French angel fish. The wreck is broken up, but there are places where the superstructure is interesting to explore and there are good photo sites. Among the many reef dive sites in the area are Clara Boyas (Sun Roof), a massive 60 sq metres coral head in 20 metres of water with tunnels large enough for 3-4 divers to swim through. These connect with upward passages where the sunlight can be seen streaming through. Playa Coral is a barrier reef W of Varadero with a large variety of fish and coral.

Faro Luna, S of Havana, has over 18 reef sites and a variety of modern wrecks, including 7 sunk as diving sites just outside the harbour. One of the best is *Camaronero II*, only 5 mins from the dive shop. Others are the cargo ships, *Panta I* and *II*, sunk in 1988, the *Barco R Club* in 8m, the *Barco Arimao* in 18m and the steel fishing boat *Itabo* in 12m.

Santiago de Cuba offers a great deal of diving with 4 dive shops: Bucanero, Daiquiri Dive Centre, Siqua Dive Centre and Sierra Mar. Popular wreck sites near the Siqua Dive Centre include the 30-m passenger ship, *Guarico*, lying in 15m. She lies on her port side with the mast covered in soft sponges. A ferry/tug wreck lies upside down in 35m of water and the two vessels together span around 150m. The metal structure is covered with large yellow and purple tube sponges. The 35-m *Spring Coral* lies in 24m. Most of the structure is still intact with a great deal of marine growth offering many photo opportunities. An unusual site dived by Bucanero and the Daiquiri Dive Centre is the Bridge. In 1895 a large bridge broke and fell into the sea in 12m, along with a train. Later a ship sunk and was blown into the bridge underwater, adding to the mass of structures. The Sierra Mar Dive Shop offers a special wreck dive on the *Cristóbal Colón*, a Spanish ship lying on a slope in 9-27m. She was sunk, along with 4 others around 1895 by the US Navy during the Spanish American War. The other 4 are in shallow water and are ideal for a snorkel.

Santa Lucía on the Atlantic side of the island has 2 dive shops and offers one of the most interesting wrecks dived. The 66-m *Mortera* sank in 1905 on a slope of 7-27m and is home for a host of marine life, including 8 massive bull sharks, who have been hand fed by the dive masters from Sharks Friend Dive Shop since the early 1980s (very exciting to watch). Other wrecks include the *Sanbinal*, in 17m and the British steel ship, *Nuestra Senora de Alta Gracia*, sunk around 1973 and completely intact, allowing divers to penetrate the entire ship, entering the engine room where all the machinery is still in place. An exciting historical site is Las Anforas, under an old fort dating from 1456. The fort was attacked several times by pirates and artifacts from Spanish ships are scattered across the sea bed. Four anchors were seen on one dive, with the largest being at least 2m.

All dive shops are government owned in Cuba, but run as joint ventures with foreign investors. There are 3 main companies, the largest (14 dive shops) is Cubanacan (Marlin). The others are Puerto Sol and Gaviota. Most staff speak Spanish, English and often other languages. Diving is usually done as part of all-inclusive packages, although dives can be booked direct with dive shops for around US$35, including all equipment. Most companies use European dive gear. In Europe for details on dive packages contact Cubanacan UK Ltd, Skylines, Unit 49, Limeharbour, Docklands, London E14 9TS, T 0171 537 7909, F 537 7747.

You should be prepared with all spares needed for diving and photography (batteries, film etc) as these are either not available or excessively expensive. In the summer months, on the S of the island, tiny jelly fish may abound and can cause nasty stings on areas not covered by a wet suit. A tropical hood is a good idea to protect the neck and face in jelly fish season. A well-stocked first aid kit is recommended, for although the medical profession is well-trained, supplies are limited. Havana has a Hyperbaric Medicine Centre and Varadero has a chamber at the main hospital at Cárdenas, both staffed by doctors trained in hyperbaric medicine.

Dives can sometimes be delayed for a variety of reasons, including limited available fuel, Coast Guard clearance to depart port, etc, so patience is needed.

FESTIVALS

Festivals of dance (including ballet), theatre, jazz, cinema and other art forms are held frequently. Annual festivals in Havana which receive international recognition include ballet (April), traditional Cuban music (May), cinema (Dec) and the international jazz festival (Dec). Tickets (in dollars) are usually available from the box office at the place of performance and although little information about the events is published it is worth checking with the tourism desk in major hotels. Last minute changes and cancellations are common.

Carnival was moved by the revolutionary government from Feb to July to coincide with the end of the sugar harvest. From 1990 there was no carnival because of economic hardships, but in Feb 1996 it took place again and will be an annual event. Festivities are mostly along the Malecón, which is closed to traffic, Prado and terminating outside El Capitolio. Dancing to rap, techno, salsa, rock, reggae etc, very lively if something of a drunken brawl. Celebrations take place Fri-Sun nights during February. A lack of resources means there are no elaborate costumes as in other countries' carnivals.

HAVANA

Havana, the capital, is situated at the mouth of a deep bay; in the colonial period, this natural harbour was the assembly point for ships of the annual silver convoy to Spain. Its stategic and commercial importance is reflected in the extensive fortifications, particularly on the E side of the entrance to the bay (see below). Notably the shield of Havana depicts 3 towers and

a key, illustrating the importance of the city's defences. Before the Revolution, Havana was the largest, the most beautiful and the most sumptuous city in the Caribbean. Today it is rather run-down, but thanks to the Government's policy of developing the countryside, it is not ringed with shantytowns like so many other Latin American capitals, although some have reappeared in the 1990s. With its suburbs it has 2.1 million people, half of whom live in housing officially regarded as substandard. Many buildings are shored up by wooden planks. Some of it is very old, the city was founded in 1515, but the ancient palaces, plazas, colonnades, churches and monasteries merge agreeably with the new. The old city is being substantially refurbished with Unesco's help, as part of the drive to attract tourists, and has been declared a World Heritage Site by the United Nations. There are good views over the city from the top floor restaurant and bar of *Hotel Habana Libre* and of the *Hotel Sevilla* and from the lookout at the top of the José Martí monument in Plaza de la Revolución (see **Museums**).

The centre is divided into five sections, three of which are of most interest to visitors, Habana Vieja (Old Havana), Central Havana and Vedado. The oldest part of the city, around the Plaza de Armas, is quite near the docks where you can see cargo ships from all over the world being unloaded. Here are the former palace of the Captains-General, the temple of El Templete, and La Fuerza, the oldest of all the forts. From Plaza de Armas run two narrow and picturesque streets, Calles Obispo and O'Reilly (several old-fashioned pharmacies on Obispo, traditional glass and ceramic medicine jars and decorative perfume bottles on display in shops gleaming with polished wood and mirrors). These two streets go W to the heart of the city: Parque Central, with its laurels, poincianas, almonds, palms, shrubs and gorgeous flowers. To the SW rises the golden dome of the Capitol. From the NW corner of Parque

Central a wide, tree-shaded avenue, the Paseo del Prado, runs to the fortress of La Punta; at its N sea-side end is the Malecón, a splendid highway along the coast to the W residential district of Vedado. The sea crashing along the seawall here is a spectacular sight when the wind blows from the N. On calmer days, fishermen lean over the parapet, lovers sit in the shade of the small pillars, and joggers sweat along the pavement. On the other side of the six-lane road, buildings which look stout and grand, with arcaded pavements, balconies, mouldings and large entrances, are salt-eroded, faded and sadly decrepit inside. Restoration is progressing slowly, but the sea is destroying old and new alike and creating a mammoth renovation task.

Further W, Calle San Lázaro leads directly from the monument to General Antonio Maceo on the Malecón to the magnificent central stairway of Havana University. A monument to Julio Antonio Mella, founder of the Cuban Communist Party, stands across from the stairway. Further out, past El Príncipe castle, is Plaza de la Revolución, with the impressive monument to José Martí at its centre. The large buildings surrounding the square were mostly built in the 1950s and house the principal government ministries. The long grey building behind the monument is the former Justice Ministry (1958), now the HQ of the Central Committee of the Communist Party, where Fidel Castro has his office. The Plaza is the scene of massive parades and speeches marking important events. The May Day parade is also held here.

From near the fortress of La Punta a tunnel runs E under the mouth of the harbour; it emerges in the rocky ground between the Castillo del Morro and the fort of La Cabaña, some 550m away, and a 5-km highway connects with the Havana-Matanzas road.

The street map of Old Havana is marked with numerals showing the places of most interest to visitors.

1. **Castillo del Morro** was built between 1589 and 1630, with a 20-m moat, but has been much altered. It stands on a bold headland, with the best view of Havana; it was one of the major fortifications built to protect the natural harbour and the assembly of Spain's silver fleets from pirate attack. The flash of its lighthouse, built in 1844, is visible 30 km out to sea. The castle is open to the public, Wed-Sun, 1000-1800, as a museum with a good exhibition of Cuban history since Columbus. On the harbour side, down by the water, is the Battery of the 12 Apostles, each gun named after an Apostle. It can be reached by bus through the tunnel to the former toll gates.

2. **Fortaleza de la Cabaña**, built 1763-1774. Fronting the harbour is a high wall; the ditch on the landward side, 12m deep, has a drawbridge at the main entrance. Inside are Los Fosos de los Laureles where political prisoners were shot during the Cuban fight for independence. Every night at 2100, the cannons are fired in an historical ceremony recalling the closing of the city walls in the 17th century. Open to visitors at the same hours as El Morro.

The National Observatory and the railway station for trains to Matanzas are on the same side of the Channel as these two forts, at Casablanca, a charming town, also the site of a statue to a very human Jesus Christ. Access by ferry, alternating with crossing to Regla from opposite Calle Santa Clara, 20 centavos.

3. **Castillo de la Punta**, built at the end of the 16th century, a squat building with 2½-m thick walls, is open to the public, daily. Entrance (free) through gap in makeshift fencing, custodian with dogs shows you around. Opposite the fortress, across the Malecón, is the monument to Máximo Gómez, the independence leader.

4. **Castillo de la Real Fuerza**, Cuba's oldest building and the second oldest fort in the New World, was built 1558-1577

after the city had been sacked by buccaneers. It is a low, long building with a
picturesque tower from which there is a
grand view. Inside the castle is a museum
with armour and ceramics, open daily,
0830-1830, US$1. The downstairs part is
used for art exhibitions. Upstairs there is
a small shop and cafetería. The Castillo
reopened (1994) after renovation. **NB**
There are two other old forts in Havana:

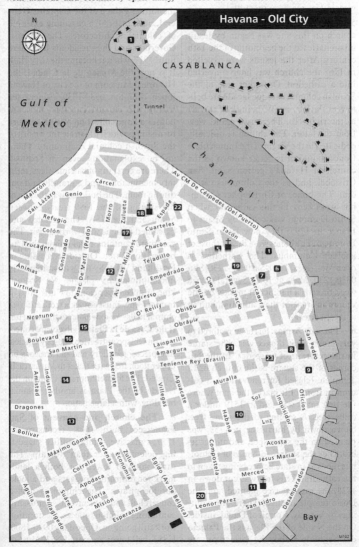

Havana - Old City

Atarés, finished in 1763, on a hill overlooking the SW end of the harbour; and **El Príncipe**, on a hill at the far end of Av Independencia (Av Rancho Boyeros), built 1774-1794, now the city gaol. Finest view in Havana from this hill.

5. **The Cathedral**. Construction of a church on this site was begun by Jesuit missionaries at the beginning of the 18th century. After the Jesuits were expelled in 1767 the church was later converted into a cathedral. On either side of the Spanish colonial baroque façade are belltowers, the left one (W) being half as wide as the right (E). There is a grand view from the latter. The church is officially dedicated to the Virgin of the Immaculate Conception, but is better known as the church of Havana's patron saint, San Cristóbal, and as the Columbus cathedral. The bones of Christopher Columbus were sent to this cathedral when Santo Domingo was ceded by Spain to France in 1795; they now lie in Santo Domingo. The bones were in fact those of another Columbus. The Cathedral is open Mon-Tues, Thur-Sat 0930-1230, Sun 0830-1230, Mass at 1030. Several days a week there is a handicraft market on the square in front of the Cathedral, and in adjacent streets.

6. **Plaza de Armas**, has been restored to very much what it once was. The statue in the centre is of Céspedes. In the NE corner of the square is the church of El Templete (closed for renovation); a column in front of it marks the spot where the first mass was said in 1519 under a ceiba tree. A sapling of the same tree, blown down by hurricane in 1753, was planted on the same spot, and under its branches the supposed bones of Columbus reposed in state before being taken to the cathedral. This tree was cut down in 1828, the present tree planted, and the Doric temple opened. There are paintings by Vermay, a pupil of David, inside. On the N side of the Plaza is the **Palacio del Segundo Cabo**, the former private residence of the Captains General, now housing the Feria Cubana del Libro. Its patio is worth a look. Outside there is a small book market daily except Mon.

7. On the W side of Plaza de Armas is the former **Palace of the Captains General**, built in 1780, a charming example of colonial architecture. The Spanish Governors and the Presidents lived here until 1917, when it became the City Hall. It is now the **Museo de la Ciudad**, the Historical Museum of the city of Havana (open Mon-Sat 0930-1830, camera fee US$3) and rec to visit. The museum houses a large collection of 19th-century furnishings which illustrate the wealth of the Spanish colonial community. There are no explanations, even in Spanish. There are portraits of patriots, flags, military memorabilia and a grandly laid out dining room. The building was the site of the signing of the 1899 treaty between Spain and the USA. The arcaded and balconied patio is well worth a visit. The courtyard contains royal palms, the Cuban national tree. Outside is a statue of Ferdinand VII of Spain, with a singularly uncomplimentary plaque. No Spanish king or queen ever came to Cuba. Also in front of the museum is a collection of church bells. An extension to the museum is the **Casa de la Plata**, a silverware collection on Obispo entre Mercaderes y Oficios, fine pieces, jewellery and old frescoes on upper floor, free with ticket to Museo de la Ciudad. The former Supreme Court on the N side of the Plaza is another colonial building, with a large patio.

8. **The church and convent of San Francisco**, built 1608, reconstructed 1737; a massive, sombre edifice suggesting defence rather than worship. The three-storeyed tower was both a landmark for returning voyagers and a lookout for pirates. The church is now a concert hall and the convent is a museum containing religious pieces. Restoration work still going on. Open daily 0930-1800, US$2, bell tower an extra US$1. Most of

the treasures were removed by the government and some are in museums.

9. The Corinthian white marble building on Calle Oficios S of the Post Office was once the legislative building, where the House of Representatives met before the Capitol was built.

10. **The Santa Clara convent** was founded in 1644 for the Clarisan nuns. Guided tours of main convent. The quaint old patio alongside has been carefully preserved; in it are the city's first slaughter house, first public fountain and public baths, and a house built by a sailor

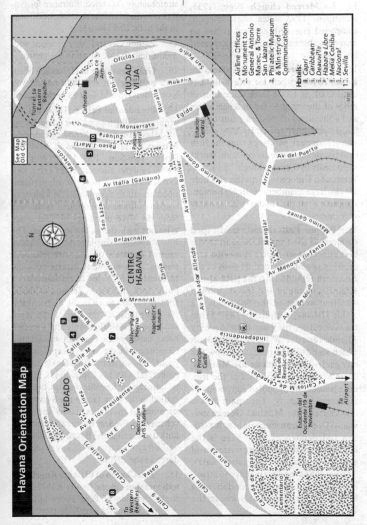

Havana Orientation Map

for his love-lorn daughter. It is now a *Residencia Académica* for student groups (and independent travellers if room). You can still see the nuns' cemetery and their cells. Open Mon-Fri 0900-1500, US$2 for guided tour in Spanish or French, entrance on Cuba.

11. La Merced church, begun 1755, incomplete 1792, when work stopped, completed late 19th century. It has an unremarkable exterior and a redecorated lavish interior.

12. The Museo Nacional Palacio de Bellas Artes, closed for refurbishment until 2001, it has a large collection of relics of the struggle for independence, and a fine array of modern paintings by Cuban and other artists. Its huge collection of European paintings, from the 16th century to the present, contains works supposedly by Gainsborough, Van Dyck, Velázquez, Tintoretto, Degas, et al. There are also large chambers of Greek, Roman, Egyptian sculpture and artefacts, many very impressive.

13. Parque Fraternidad, landscaped to show off the Capitol, N of it, to the best effect. At its centre is a ceiba tree growing in soil provided by each of the American republics. In the park also is a famous statue of the Indian woman who first welcomed the Spaniards: La Noble Habana, sculpted in 1837. From the SW corner the handsome Avenida Allende runs due W to the high hill on which stands Príncipe Castle (now the city gaol). The **Quinta de los Molinos**, on this avenue, at the foot of the hill, once housed the School of Agronomy of Havana University. The main house now contains the **Máximo Gómez museum** (Dominican-born fighter for Cuban Independence). Also here is the headquarters of the young writers and artists (Asociación Hermanos Saiz). The gardens are a lovely place to stroll. North, along Calle Universidad, on a hill which gives a good view, is the University.

14. The Capitol, opened May 1929, has a large dome over a rotunda; it is a copy, on a smaller scale, of the US Capitol in Washington. At the centre of its floor is a 24-carat diamond, zero for all distance measurements in Cuba. The interior has large halls and stately staircases, all most sumptuously decorated. Entrance for visitors is to the left of the stairway, US$1 to go in the halls, US$3 for a tour.

15. Parque Central Very pleasant with monument to José Martí in the centre.

16. Gran Teatro de la Habana, a beautiful building but they will not let you look around inside. Go to a performance.

17. Presidential Palace (1922), a huge, ornate building topped by a dome, facing Av de las Misiones Park; now contains the **Museo de la Revolución** (T 62-4091). Open Tues-Sun 1000-1700, entrance US$3, cameras allowed, US$3 extra. (Allow several hours to see it all, explanations are all in Spanish.) The history of Cuban political development is charted, from the slave uprisings to joint space missions with the ex-Soviet Union. The liveliest section displays the final battles against Batista's troops, with excellent photographs and some bizarre personal momentos, such as a revolutionary's knife, fork and spoon set and a plastic shower curtain worn in the Sierra Maestra campaign. At the top of the main staircase are a stuffed mule and a stuffed horse used by Che Guevara and Camilo Cienfuegos in the same campaign. The yacht *Granma*, from which Dr Castro disembarked with his companions in 1956 to launch the Revolution, has been installed in the park facing the S entrance, surrounded by planes, tanks and other vehicles involved, as well as a Soviet-built tank used against the Bay of Pigs invasion and a fragment from a US spy plane shot down in the 1970s.

18. The Church of El Santo Angel Custodio was built by the Jesuits in 1672 on the slight elevation of Peña Pobre hill. The original church was largely destroyed by a hurricane in 1844 and rebuilt in its present neo-Gothic style in 1866-71. It has white, laced Gothic towers and 10 tiny chapels, the best of which is behind the high altar.

19. **Museo de Arte Colonial**, Plaza de la Catedral (in the former Palacio de los Condes de Casa Bayona), open Mon-Sat 1000-1800, Sun 0900-1300, US$2, contains colonial furniture and other items, plus a section on stained glass, exquisite (T 61-1367).

20. **Museo Casa Natal de José Martí**, Leonor Pérez 314 entre Picota y Egido, opposite central railway station (Tues-Sat 0900-1700, Sun 0900-1300, entrance US$1, T 61-3778).

21. **Museo Histórico de Ciencias Carlos J Finlay**, Calle Cuba 460 entre Amargura y Brasil (Mon-Fri 0800-1700, Sat 0900-1500, entrance US$2, T 63-4824).

22. **Palacio Pedroso**, now the **Palacio de la Artesanía**, a beautiful Arab building housing shops and restaurant/bar. Open 0900-0200 Fri-Sun with traditional dance at 2200; see **Shopping** below.

23. **La Plaza Vieja**, an 18th century plaza, undergoing restoration since Feb 1996 as part of a joint project by UNESCO and Habaguanex, a state company responsible for the restoration and revival of old Havana. The former house of the Spanish Captain General, Conde de Ricla, who retook Havana from the English and restored power to Spain in 1763 can be seen on the corner of San Ignacio and Muralla. As restoration continues, 18th century murals are being uncovered on the external walls of the buildings, many of which boast elegant balconies overlooking the plaza. Art exhibitions in the colonial house on the corner of San Ignacio and Brasil. The newly-restored Cuban Stock Exchange building, **La Lonja**, Oficios and Plaza San Francisco, is worth a look, as is the new cruise ship terminal opposite.

Other museums

For US$9 you can buy a 1-day ticket allowing you entrance to about 9 museums. **Museo Napoleónico**, San Miguel No 1159 esq Ronda (Mon-Sat 1100-1830, entrance US$2, T 79-1460), houses paintings and other works of art, a specialized library and a collection of weaponry (T 79-1412); **Museo de Artes Decorativas**, Calles 17 y Este Vedado (Wed-Sun 0930-1630, entrance US$2, T 32-0924); **Museo José Martí**, Plaza de la Revolución, in base of memorial, beautifully restored and most impressive museum, with lookout accessed by mirrored lift (Mon-Sat 0900-1600, US$3, lookout US$5 extra); **Postal Museum**, Ministry of Communications, Plaza de la Revolución (Mon-Fri 0900-1700, entrance US$1, T 81-5551), also **Numismatic Museum** (Calle Oficios 8 between Obispo and Obrapía, T 63-2521, Tues-Sat 1000-1700, Sun 1000-1300). **Museo de Finanzas**, Obispo y Cuba, in the old Ministry of Finance building, has a beautiful stained-class ceiling in the foyer, Mon-Fri 0830-1700, Sat till 1230 only. **Vintage Car Museum**, Oficios y Jústiz (just off Plaza de Armas, open daily 0900-1900, US$1). There are a great many museum pieces, pre-revolutionary US models, still on the road especially outside Havana, in among the Ladas, VWs and Nissans. **Casa de los Arabes** (with restaurant) opposite, on Oficios between Obispo and Obrapía, a lovely building with vines trained over the courtyard for shade, open daily 0930-1830, US$1; **Casa de Africa**, on Obrapía 157 between San Ignacio and Mercaderes (Mon-Sat 1030-1730, Sun 0930-1230, US$2); small gallery of carved wooden artefacts and handmade costumes. **Museo Nacional de la Música**, Cárcel 1, entre Habana y Aguilar, Habana Vieja; small and beautifully furnished old house; interesting collection of African drums and other instruments from all around the world, showing development of Cuban *son* and *danzón* music (Mon-Sat 0900-1645, US$2, T 61-9846). **Museo Nacional de Historia Natural** is at Obispo

61, Plaza de Armas, open Tues-Sat 1000-1730, Sun 0900-1230.

Suburbs

The western sections of the old city merge imperceptibly into Vedado. West of it, and reached by a tunnel under the Almendares river, lies **Miramar**, some 16 km W of the capital, and easily reached by bus. Miramar was where the wealthy lived before the Revolution; today there are several embassies and government buildings, and also many old, abandoned villas. The **Maqueta de la Ciudad** (scale model of Havana) is on Calle 28 113 entre 1 y 3, open Tues-Sat 1000-1800, US$3.

The **Cuban pavilion**, a large building on Calle 23, Vedado, is a combination of a tropical glade and a museum of social history. It tells the nation's story by a brilliant combination of objects, photography and the architectural manipulation of space. **Casa de la Amistad**, 646 Paseo, entre 17 y 19, Vedado, a former mansion, a beautiful building with gardens, now operated by ICAP (Cuban Institute for Friendship among the Peoples) and housing the *Amistur* travel agency (see **Travel agents** below). It has a reasonably priced bar, cafetería and tourist shop (0930-1800). The bar and cafetería are open Mon-Fri 1100-2300 (with sextet), Sat 1100-0200 (with Cuban bands).

Museo Nacional de la Alfabetización, Av 29E esq 86, Marinao, vivid history of the 1960 literacy campaign (Mon-Fri 0830-1200, 1300-1600, T 20 8054).

The **Escuela Superior de Arte**, located in the grounds of the former Havana Country Club in Cubanacan, SW of Miramar, houses schools for different arts and was designed by Ricardo Porro. Architects will be interested in this 'new spatial sensation'.

The **Cementerio Colón** should be visited to see the wealth of funerary sculpture, including Carrara Marbles; Cubans visit the sculpture of Amelia de Milagrosa and pray for miracles; entry US$1.

Expocuba completed in Jan 1989, a sprawling new facility SW of Havana, past Lenin Park, near the botanical gardens, features a score of pavilions showing Cuba's achievements in industry, science, agriculture and the arts and entertainment. Open weekdays Wed-Fri 1400-1600 and Sat-Sun 1000-1800 (times subject to change), T 44-7324. Special trains leave from main terminal in Old Havana. Information on times (and special buses) from hotels.

South of the centre, in Cerro district, is the **Estadio Latinoamericano**, the best place to see baseball (the major league level), entrance 1 peso.

● **Jardín Botánico Nacional de Cuba**
Km 3½, Carretera Rocío, S of the city, beyond Parque Lenin. Open Mon-Fri 0800-1700, US$3, T 44-5525. The garden is well-maintained with excellent collections; it has a Japanese garden with tropical adaptations. Rosa Alvarez, one of the guides, is knowledgeable and speaks some English. There are few signs, so despite the extensive plant collection it is not informative as it might be. There is a good eco-vegetarian restaurant which uses solar energy for cooking, book at the gate and it costs 14 pesos, just turn up at the restaurant and you'll be charged US$14. Private taxi from Old Havana US$8.

● **Zoo**
Parque Zoológico Nacional, Km 3, Carretera de Capdevila, Wed-Sun, 0900-1515, T 44-7613. Parque Zoológico de la Habana, Av 26, Nuevo Vedado (open daily 0930-1700, US$2).

● **Cigar factory**
Partagas on Calle Industria behind the Capitolio, gives tours twice daily, in theory, at 1000 and 1330, US$5. The tour lasts for about an hour and is very interesting. You are taken through the factory and shown the whole production process from storage and sorting of leaves, to packaging and labelling (explanation in Spanish only). Four different brand names are made here; Partagas, Cubana, Ramón Allones and Bolívar (special commission of 170,000 cigars made for the Seville Expo, Spain, 1992). These and other famous cigars can be bought at their shop here, open 0900-1700, and rum, at good prices (credit cards accepted). Cigars are also made at many tourist locations (eg Palacio de la Artesanía, the airport, some hotels).

● **El Bosque De La Habana**
Worth visiting. From the entrance to the City Zoo, cross Calle 26 and walk a few blocks until you reach a bridge across the Almendares. Cross this, turn right at the end and keep going N, directly to the Bosque which is a jungle-like wood.

● **Aquaria**
National Aquarium, Calle 60 and Av 1, Miramar, specializes in salt-water fish and dolphins, entrance US$2, while the Parque Lenín aquarium has fresh-water fish on show.

Beaches and watersports

The beaches in Havana, at Miramar and Playa de Marianao are rocky and generally very crowded in summer (transport may also be difficult and time consuming). The beach clubs belong to trade unions and may not let non-members in. Those to the E, El Mégano, Santa María del Mar and Bacuranao, for example, are much better (see also **East from Havana**). To the W of Havana are Arena Blanca and Bahía Honda, which are good for diving and fishing but difficult to get to unless you have a car.

The Marina Hemingway, 20 mins by taxi from Havana (see **West from Havana**), at Santa Fe, hosts annual fishing tournaments. Fishing and scuba diving trips can be arranged here as well as other watersports and land-based sports. The Offshore Class 1 World Championship and the Great Island speedboat Grand Prix races have become an annual event in Havana, usually held during the last week in April, attracting power boat enthusiasts from all over the world.

Local information
● **Accommodation**

Hotel prices

L1	over US$200	L2	US$151-200
L3	US$101-150	A1	US$81-100
A2	US$61-80	A3	US$46-60
B	US$31-45	C	US$21-30
D	US$12-20	E	US$7-11
F	US$4-6	G	up to US$3

(Payment for hotels used by tourists is in US$). Foreign tourists should obtain a reservation through an accredited government agent (see

Travel agents at the end of this chapter). Always tell the hotel each morning if you intend to stay on another day. Do not lose your 'guest card' which shows your name and room number. Tourist hotels are a/c, with 'tourist' TV (US films, tourism promotion), restaurants with reasonable food, but standards are not comparable with Europe and plumbing is often faulty or affected by water shortages.

The Vedado hotels (the best) are away from the old centre; the others reasonably close to it. Several important hotel renovation projects are in progress in Old Havana. A huge colonial building on the Plaza de Armas was due to open end-1996 as the luxury *Hotel Santa Isabel*, which will be the best situated hotel in the old city. *Hotel Ambos Mundos*, Calle Obispo on the corner of San Ignacio (also due to open end-1996) is well-located: Hemingway lived here for 10 yrs before moving to La Vigía in 1939. The *Parque Central* on park of same name was also due to open end-1996.

L1-L2 *Nacional de Cuba* (Gran Caribe), Calle O esq 21, Vedado, T 33-3564-7, F 33-5054/5, 467 rooms, some package tours use it at bargain rates, generally friendly and efficient service, faded grandeur, dates from 1930, superb reception hall, note the vintage Otis high speed lifts, steam room, 2 pools, restaurants, bars, shops, gardens with old cannons on hilltop overlooking the Malecón and harbour entrance, great place the watch people and vehicles, the hotel's tourist bureau is also efficient and friendly; **L2** *Meliá Cohiba* (Sol Meliá), Paseo entre 1 y 3, Vedado, T 33-3636, F 33-4555, international grand luxury, high rise and dominating the neighbourhood, 462 rooms, 120 suites, shops, gym, healthclub, pool, gourmet restaurant, disco, piano bar; **L2** *Santa Isabel*, Baratillo y Obispo, Plaza de Armas, T 33-8201, F 33-8391; **L3** *Victoria* (Gran Caribe), 19 y M, Vedado, T 33-3510, F 33-3109, 31 rooms, small, quiet and pleasant, tasteful if conservative, rec.

A1 *Habana Libre* (Tryp), L y 23, Vedado, T 33-4011, F 33-3141, 606 rooms, prices depend on the floor number, ugly exterior but most facilities are here, eg hotel reservations, excursions, Polynesian restaurant, buffet, 24-hr coffee shop, *Cabaret Turquino* 2200-0400, US$20, shopping mall under construction; **A1** *Habana Riviera* (Gran Caribe), Paseo y Malecón, Vedado, T 33-3733, F 33-3738, 330 rooms, 1950s block, Mafia style, appearance suffers from being so close to the glitzy *Meliá Cohiba*, comfortable, does a good breakfast; **A2** *Inglaterra* (Gran Caribe),

Prado 416 esq San Rafael y San Miguel, T 33-8254, 86 rooms, next to Teatro Nacional, old style, regal atmosphere, beautifully restored, balconies overlook Parque Central, highly rec, helpful staff, several of whom speak English, good breakfast, lovely old tiled dining room, also *Ristorante La Stella* (Italian), open to non-guests, snacks available in pleasant inner courtyard, piano music at meal times in *Restaurante Colonial*, the bar often has music or shows at 2200, US$5 cover; **A2** *Presidente* (Gran Caribe), Calzada y G, Vedado, T 33-4075, F 33-3753, 142 rooms, oldest hotel in Havana, 1940s furniture, pool, TV, restaurant OK, cafetería, piano bar, nightclub; **A2** *Plaza* (Gran Caribe), Ignacio Agramonte No 267, T 62-2006, F 33-8591, 186 rooms, comfortable, street front rooms very noisy, ask for one in the inner courtyard, good breakfast, poor dinner, service generally poor; **A2** *Ambos Mundos* (Habaguanex), Obispo, on corner of Mercedes, Old Havana, T 66-9530, F 66-9532, beautifully restored, re-opened 1997, Hemingway lived here for 10 years before moving to La Vigia in 1939; **A2** *Sevilla* (Gran Caribe), Trocadero 55 y Prado, T 33-8560, 33-8580, F 33-8582, recently restored, 188 rooms on edge of Old Havana, pool, shops, sauna and massage, tourism bureau, buffet restaurant on ground floor, elegant restaurant on top floor with great night time views over Vedado and the Malecón; **A2** *Capri* (Horizontes), 21 y N, Vedado, T 33-3571/3747, F 33-3750, 215 rooms, showing their age, public areas also with signs of wear and tear, a/c, pool, cabaret, shops, currency exchange, parking, car rental; **A3** *Hostal Valencia* (Horizontes), Oficios 53 esq Obrapía, T 62-3801, Old Havana, joint Spanish/Cuban venture modelled on the Spanish *paradores*, 12 rooms, each named after a Valencian town, tastefully restored building, nicely furnished, good restaurant (see below); **A3** *Vedado* (Horizontes), Calle O, No 244, T 32-6501, 33-4072, F 33-4186, 192 rooms, a/c, pool, restaurants, nightclub; **A3** *Deauville*, Galiano y Malecón, T 62-8051, 33-8213, F 33-8148, 144 rooms, noise from Malecón, very tatty, weather damage, poor food.

B *St John's* (Horizontes), O, entre 23 y 25, Vedado, T 32-9531, 33-3740/4187, F 33-3561, 93 rooms, sparse, a/c, pool, avoid rooms close to noisy nightclub, closed for repairs 1997; **B** *Colina* (Horizontes), L y 27, Vedado, T 32-3535, 33-4071, F 33-4104, 79 rooms, hot water, street noise, small rooms, excellent buffet breakfast, open to non-residents US$3, popular with airport Cubatur desk; **B** *Lincoln* (Islazul),

Galiano 164 esq Virtudes, T 62-8061, 135 rooms, friendly, TV, hot water, a/c, radio, clean, good value, guests are mostly Cuban honeymooners; **B** *Morro* (Horizontes), Calle 3 entre C y D, Vedado, T 33-3907, 32-7584, 30-9943, 20 rooms, restaurant and bar; **B-C** *Lido* (Horizontes), Consulado entre Animas y Trocadero, T 33-8814, F 62-7000/0653, 65 rooms, a/c, not bad for the price, laundry expensive, central, slightly dodgy area at night with prostitutes heckling, but 1 block from Prado, very friendly reception and cafetería, food bland and overpriced, bar on roof terrace, live music, rec.

The cheaper hotels are usually hard to get into; often full. **C** *Caribbean* (Horizontes), Paseo Martí 164 esq Colón (bus 82 from Vedado), T 62-2071, lobby full of smoke and prostitutes, 36 rooms, only 2 have windows, hot water (sporadic supply), fan and TV, popular with travellers, clean, old city, rec, but avoid noisy rooms at front and lower floors at back over deafening water pump, and beware of theft from rooms, small café serves mostly sandwiches and eggs at a low price; **C-D** *Residencia Santa Clara*, in convent buildings, see 10 above, lovely, peaceful, nice café, T 61-2877, 66-9327, F 33-5696; **D** *Isla de Cuba* (Islazul), 169 Máximo Gómez, T 62-1031, refurbished, great character, central, no hot water, noisy disco, friendly, helpful; nearby is **C-D** *New York* (Islazul) at 156 Dragones, T 62-7001, OK; **D** *Bruzón* (Islazul), on Calle Bruzón No 217, with P Dulces y Independencia, near the Plaza de la Revolución and the bus station, T 70-3531, fan, bath, TV in some rooms, no hot water, drinking water on each floor, back rooms noisy from bus station, staff from sleepy to helpful, club at side, free to guests.

Tourists have to pay for accommodation in US dollars in Havana. Cubans use the national Islazul chain. However Cubans may offer you their house, apartment or a room for about US$20-25/day and cook for you for US$5/day. A taxation system for this form of 'self-employment' was introduced in 1997 so that it is now legal. See **Information for travellers**. Private homes are often dirty with cockroaches, things don't work, there is cold water only, once a day, and the lights often go off. A torch is useful. The families will usually offer you cheap transport too.

If you have a car, the eastern beaches are good places to stay for visiting Havana. The hotels are usually booked up by package tours but you can rent an apartment on the beach away from the main tourist area for US$30. The office is at the end of the main road running along the beach nearest to Havana and furthest from the main hotel area.

● **Places to eat**

Restaurants are not cheap. The choice of food is limited to 'dollar' restaurants, recognizable by the credit card stickers on the door, where meals are about US$20-25, paid only in US dollars. Check the bill carefully as overcharging is common in some Havana 'dollar' restaurants, also the bill may not record what you actually ate. As a rule, in Havana, outside the hotels, the 'dollar' places have been the only option, but since 1995 it has been legal for private houses to operate as restaurants, charging for meals in dollars or pesos. Known as *paladares*, they are licensed and taxed and limited to 12 chairs as well as having employment restrictions (see box, above). Some very good family-run businesses have been set up, offering a 3-course meal for US$6-8 pp, excellent value. They are not allowed to have lobster or shrimp on the menu as these are reserved for the dollar hotels and the export market. However, if you ask, there are often items available which are not on the menu.

Paladares: *Doña Eutimia*, Callejón del Chorro, just off Plaza Catedral in Old Havana, highly rec, open daily 1200-2400; *Bellamar*, Virtudes entre Amistad e Industria, good, US$3 for fish, salad, rice, service slow; *Sevilla's*, Obispo 465, altos, entre Villegas y Aguacate, open from 1130, good seafood but expensive; *La Julia*, O'Reilly 506A, T 62-7438, meals US$6-8, beer US$1, large portions, good creole food, can help with finding accommodation; *Doña Blanquita*, Prado 153 entre Colón y Refugio, near Hotel Caribbean, run by English-speaking lawyer; another *paladar* on Malecón 27 entre Prado y Cárcel, 1st floor, you are served on balcony, lovely view of city, bay and prostitutes plying their trade; *Chez Aimée*, upstairs at San Ignacio 68, near Plaza Catedral, T 61-2545, great lobster, shrimp or fish, US$12 for full meal and coffee, friendly, highly rec; in central Havana, *La Guarida*, Concordia 418 entre Gervasio y Escobar, T 62-4940, film location for *Fresa y Chocolate*; in Vedado try *Doña Nieves*, Calle 19, entre 2 y 4, T 30-6282, open Tues-Sun, 1200-2400, rec. Also in Vedado, *El Helecho*, Calle 6 entre Línea y 11; *El Moro*, Calle 25 1003, entre Paseo y 2; *Los Amigos*, M y 19, opp *Victoria*, cheap and tasty. Near the university are *La Reina*, San Lázaro 1214, apto 1, entre M y N, open 1230-0100, T 78-1260; opp is *Casa Karlita*, San Lázaro 1207, T 78-3182, both have small signs on street.

Restaurants: *La Bodeguita del Medio*, Empedrado 207, near the Cathedral, was made famous by Hemingway and should be visited if only for a drink (*mojito* – rum, crushed ice, mint, lemon juice and carbonated water – is a must, US$4), food poor, expensive at US$35-40 for 2 but very popular, open 1030-0100, T 33-8857. *Floridita*, on the corner of Obispo and Monserrate, next to the Parque Central, T 33-8856, open 1200-0100, was another favourite haunt of Hemingway. It has had a recent face-lift and is now a very elegant bar and restaurant reflected in the prices (US$6 for a daiquiri), but well worth a visit if only to see the sumptuous decor and 'Bogart atmosphere'. *La Zaragozana*, almost next door, Monserrate entre Obispo y Obrapía, oldest restaurant in Havana, international cuisine, good seafood, rec; *El Patio*, San Ignacio 54 esq Empedrado, Plaza Catedral, nearby, is rec for national dishes, open 24 hrs, T 61-8504 and *La Mina*, on Obispo esq Oficios, Plaza de Armas, open 1200-2400, T 62-0216, traditional Cuban food but both have uneven service, waits can be long and cooking gas shortages are common; nearby, *Oasis*, Paseo Martí 256-58, in Arab Cultural Institute, cold a/c, very good hummus and lamb dishes, T 61-4098, open 1000-2400; and *D'Giovanni*, Italian, Tacón between Empedrado and O'Reilly, lovely old building with patio and terrace, interesting tree growing through the wall, but food very bland. Handicrafts shop in doorway specializes in miniature ornaments. *Al Medina*, Oficios, entre Obrapía y Obispo, Arab food in lovely colonial mansion, show at 2130 Fri, Sat, also Mosque and Arab cultural centre off beautiful courtyard, open 1200-2300, T 63-0862; *Torre de Marfil*, Mercaderes, entre Obispo y Obrapía, good, inexpensive Cantonese menu, open 1200-2200, T 62-3466. *Hostal Valencia* restaurant *La Paella* features the best paella in Havana, good food, charming, open 1200-2300; *El Tocororo* (national bird of Cuba), excellent food at US$40-50 a head, Calle 18 y Av 3a, Miramar, T 24-2209, open Mon-Sat 1230-2400, old colonial mansion with nice terrace, rec as probably the best restaurant in town; *La Cecilia*, Calle 5a No 11010e/110 y 112, Miramar, good international food, mostly in open air setting, rec, open 1200-2400, T 24-1562. *La Divina Pastora*, fish restaurant, Fortaleza de la Cabaña, open 1230-2300, T 33-8341, expensive, food praised; *Los XII Apóstoles*, nearby on Vía Monumental, fish and good criollo food, good views of the Malecón. *Las Ruinas*, Calle 100 esq Cortina

Presa in Parque Lenín, Cuba's most exclusive restaurant, and aptly named for its prices, is most easily reached by taxi; try to persuade the driver to come back and fetch you, as otherwise it is difficult to get back, open 1200-2400, T 44-3336. *El Conejito*, Calle M esq 17, Vedado, T 32-4671, open 1800-2200, specializes in rabbit, and *La Torre* (17 y M, at top of Edificio Fosca, T 32-5650, open midday-midnight, poor food but good view), are quite expensive. *Restaurante 1830*, Vedado, at far W end of Malecón, overlooks bay, excellent seafood, relatively inexpensive, open air show in gardens at 2200, rec; *El Ranchón*, Av 19 y 140, Playa, T 23-5838, good barbecued chicken, meats, typical *criolla* cuisine; *La Ferminia*, Av 5, entre 182 y 184, Playa, T 33-6555, international, elegant, lovely gardens, expensive. In the *Habana Libre Hotel*, try *El Barracón*, traditional Cuban with good fish and seafood at lobby level, open 1200-midnight, T 30-5011, and *Sierra Maestra* restaurant and *Bar Turquino* on the 25th floor (spectacular views of Havana which makes the food acceptable, service bad). Along and near La Rampa there are some cheaper pizzerías and self-service restaurants. *Hanoi*, on Av Brazil, Cuban food, and *La Azucena China* on Calle Cienfuegos, Chinese food, both charge US$1-2 for a main course. *Café París*, Obispo y San Ignacio, serves good and reasonably priced chicken, snacks and pizza around the clock, as does *Casa de la Amistad*, Paseo entre 17 y 19, 1100-2300. At Marianao beach there are also some cheaper bars and restaurants. Inside the hard currency shopping centre, Av 5 and Calle 42 in Miramar, is an outdoor fast-foodery and an indoor restaurant, the latter with moderate dollar prices.

A visit to the *Coppelia* open-air ice-cream parlour, 23 y L, Vedado, is rec, open 1000-midnight, payment in pesos, you might have to queue for an hour or so, not unpleasant in the shade, or pay in dollars to avoid the queue, US$2 for small portion. The parlour found movie fame in *Strawberry and Chocolate*. Alternatively, sample the Coppelia ice-cream in the tourist hotels and restaurants and some dollar food stores.

● **Bars**

Visitors find that ordinary bars *not* on the tourist circuit will charge them in dollars, if they let foreigners in at all. If it is a local bar and the Cubans are all paying in pesos, you will have to pay in US dollars. Even so, the prices in most places are not high by Caribbean standards.

The best bar in Old Havana is *La Bodeguita* (see above, also for *La Floridita*). *Lluvia de Oro*, Calle Obispo esq a Habana, good place to drink rum and listen to rock music, also food, open 24 hrs. Try a *mojito* in any bar. Tour groups are often taken to *O'Reilly*, on the street of the same name, for a *mojito*, pleasant upstairs, with balcony and musicians.

● **Banks**

Banco Nacional and its branches. For dollar services, credit card withdrawals, TCs and exchange, *Banco Financiero Internacional*, Línea esq O, open Mon-Fri 0800-1500, last day of the month until 1200, branch in *Habana Libre* complex, open daily 0900-1900. Exchange bureau in *Hotel Nacional*, open 0800-1200, 1230-1930. *Banco Internacional de Comercio*, Ayestarán esq Paseo, Plaza de la Revolución, open 0830-1400. (See also under **Currency** below.)

● **Entertainment**

Casa De La Trova: San Lázaro, entre Belascoán y Gervasio, closed for repairs 1997. There are Casas de la Trova around the country, they are houses where traditional Cuban music can be heard for free, thoroughly recommended. For bolero admirers, try *Dos Gardenias*, with restaurant and bar, Av 7, esq 26, Miramar, Playa, T 24-2353, open 2100-0500. UNEAC, Av 17 entre G y H, rumba Sat and other Cuban band performances. Events listed at entrance. Radio Taino FM 93.3, English and Spanish language tourist station gives regular details of wide range of Cuban bands playing and venues, particularly in the programme at 1700-1900.

Cinemas: best are *Yara* (opp *Habana Libre* hotel, T 32-9430); *Payret*, Prado 503, esq San José, T 63-3163, and *La Rampa*, Rampa esq O, evenings only. Many others.

Jazz: *Maxim Club*, Calle 10, closed 1997 for repairs; *Coparrun*, *Hotel Riviera* (big names play there), jazz in the bar rec; Fri nights at *Meliá Cohiba* from 2100.

Nightclubs: the *Tropicana* (closed Mon, Calle 72 No 4504, Marianao, T 33-7507, F 33-0109, 2000-0200) is a must; book with *Havanatur*, *Amistur*, Rumbos Tour, etc, US$30-55, depending on seat, drinks extra. Despite being toned down to cater for more sober post-revolutionary tastes, it is still a lively place with plenty of atmosphere, open-air (entry refunded if it rains). Drinks are expensive: a bottle of rum is US$60; payment in dollars. Bringing your own bottle seems acceptable. Foreigners may be admitted without booking if there is room. All the main hotels have their own cabarets, eg *Parisien* at *Hotel Nacional*, make a reservation. *Capri* is rec, at US$15 and longer show than *Tropicana* but the drinks are expensive at US$40 for a bottle of best rum. *Aché* in the *Meliá Cohiba* and next door *Palacio de Salsa* in the *Riviera*, which is full of life and atmosphere. Also the *Commodore* disco (US$10), crowded, Western-style, free to *Hotel Neptune* guests; *Café Cantante*, Teatro Nacional, Paseo y Calle 39, Plaza de la Revolución, open nightly from 2200, 3 bands, US$10; *La Finca* at Playas del Este. The *Cabaret Nacional*, San Rafael y Prado, is a nightclub for Cubans, you must be invited by a Cuban friend.

Theatres: *Teatro Mella*, Línea entre A y B, Vedado, T 3-8696, specialiaze in modern dance; more traditional programmes at *Gran Teatro de la Habana* on Parque Central next to *Hotel Inglaterra*, T 61-3076-9. The Conjunto Folklórico Nacional and Danza Contemporánea dance companies sometimes perform here, highly rec, US$0.60. Havana has some very lively theatre companies. *Amistur* travel agency can help with theatre and nightclub bookings.

● **Post & telecommunications**

Post Office: there is a post office at Oficios 102, opp the Lonja, and postal facilities in the *Hotel Nacional* and in the *Hotel Habana Libre* building. Also on Calle Ejido next to central railway station and under the Gran Teatro de La Habana. For stamp collectors the Círculo Filatélico is on Calle San José 1172 between Infanta and Basarrata, open Mon-Fri, 1700-2000, and there is a shop on Obispo 518 with an excellent selection (Cuban stamps are very colourful and high quality).

Telephones & cable offices: Ministerio de Comunicaciones, Plaza de la Revolución, T 81-0875, for national and international telegraphs (Cuban pesos). The *Habana Libre* and *Nacional* have international telephone, telex and fax facilities.

● **Shopping**

Local cigars and rum are excellent. Original lithographs and other works of art can be purchased directly from the artists at the *Galería del Grabado*, Plaza de la Catedral (Mon-Fri 1400-2100, Sat 1400-1900). On Sat afternoons there are handicraft stalls in the Plaza. Reproductions of works of art are sold at *La Exposición*, San Rafael 12, Manzana de Gómez, in front of Parque Central. Handicraft and tourist souvenir markets have sprung up, especially around the Cathedral, on D and Av 1, Vedado, and on the Rampa, open Tues-Sun 0900-1600;

Che Guevara and religious *Santería* items lead the sales charts. There is a special boutique, the *Palacio de la Artesanía*, in the Palacio Pedroso (built 1780) at Calle Cuba 64 (opp Parque Anfiteatro) where the largest selection of Cuban handicrafts is available; the artisans have their workshops in the back of the same building (open Mon-Sat 0900-2000) it has things not available elsewhere: jewellery, Cuban coffee, local and imported liqueurs, soft drinks, T-shirts, postcards and best retail selection of cigars (2 cigar-makers in attendance, lower prices than at factory); Visa and Mastercard accepted, passport required. *Artex* shop on Av 23 esq L has excellent music section and tasteful T-shirts and postcards. The *Caracol* chain, formerly 'Inturshops' in tourist hotels (eg *Habana Libre*) and elsewhere, which sell tourists' requisites and other luxury items such as chocolates, biscuits, wine, clothes, require payment in US$ (or credit cards: Mastercard, Visa). *La Maison* is a luxurious mansion on Calle 16, 701 esq 7 in Miramar, with dollar shops selling cigars, alcohol, handicrafts, jewellery and perfume. There is sometimes live music in the evening in lovely open-air patio, and fashion shows displaying imported clothes sold in their own boutique, free entry. The large department stores are along Galiano (Av Italia) near San Rafael and Neptuno. Calle Monte is being redeveloped, with a variety of shops operating in dollars or Cuban pesos, starting from the Capitolio end with a food supermarket. At the other end is Cuatro Caminos market (see **Markets** below). In Miramar there is a dollar shopping complex on Av 5 y 42 and a large diplomatic store, *Diplomercado* (Av 5 esq 24 y 26), with a bakery next door. Bread is also available at the new French bakery on Av 42 y 19 and in the Focsa shopping complex on Av 17 entre M y N. For food shopping, there is the *Focsa Supermarket*, or the *Panamericana*, on San Lázaro just below Infanta. There are tourist mini-stores in most hotels, but they do not sell fresh food. The International Press Centre (open to the public) on La Rampa sells items like chocolate for dollars in a shop to the right of the entrance.

Markets Farmers are allowed to sell their produce (root and green vegetables, fruit, grains and meat) in free-priced city *agromercados*. You should pay for food in pesos. There are markets in Vedado at Calle 19 y B; in Nuevo Vedado, Tulipán opp Hidalgo; in the Cerro district at the Monte and Belascoaín crossroads; and in Central Havana, the Chinese market at the junction of Zanja and Av Italia. Cadeca exchange bureaux at the first 5 listed.

Bookshops International bookstore at end of El Prado, near Parque Fraternidad and Capitol, English, French, German books but selection poor and payment has to be in dollars. Other good bookshops near Parque Central and *La Internacional* on Calle Obispo esq Bernaza (books are very good value). *Librería La Bella Habana*, in the Palacio del Segundo Cabo, O'Reilly 4 y Tacón, open Mon-Sat 1000-1800, has both Cuban and international publications. *El Siglo de las Luces* (Neptuno), near Capitolio, good place to buy *son*, *trova* and jazz (rock) records.

● **Photography**
Films developed at *Publifoto*, Edificio Focsa, Calle M entre 17 y 19, and *Photoservice*, Calle 23 esq P, Vedado, 0800-2200, camera repairs 0800-1700, T 33-5031 (another branch in Varadero, *Hotel Cuatro Palmas*, Av 1 entre 61 y 62, open 0900-1900.

● **Travel agents**
There is a large number of state owned travel agencies, which cooperate fully with each other and have bureaux in all the major hotels (see **Information for travellers**). *Amistur*, Paseo 646, entre 19 y 17, T 33-3544/1220, F 33-3515, is more geared towards independent travellers and can book you into good hotels in all the major cities at reduced rates. They are helpful with transport and tours and can also book excursions, restaurants, theatre and nightclubs, or help you find a guide. They arrange sociocultural tours with specific interest groups if contacted in advance.

Guides Many Cubans in Havana tout their services in their desperate quest for dollars and it can be easier to accept one of them to prevent being pestered all the time. Both male and female single travellers have recommended using a guide as long as you are careful who you choose; avoid young Cubans hanging around main tourist areas, especially if they approach you in pairs. Lots of Cubans speak English and are keen to practise it. If you feel you trust someone as a guide, make sure you state exactly what you want, eg private car, *paladar*, accommodation, and fix a price in advance to avoid shocks when it is too late. You may find, however, that the police will assume your guide is a prostitute and prohibit him or her from accompanying you into a hotel.

● **Transport**
The economic crisis and shortage of fuel has led to severe transport problems and public transport is only slowly recovering. There is now very little local traffic, there are long queues at petrol stations and public transport have dwindled. Tourists are expected to use dollar transport, such as taxis or hired cars, or not travel at all. Organized tours out of town are rarely more than day trips. Always check when booking that departure is definite, agencies will cancel through lack of passengers or fuel. You must have 4-6 people to get a tour started but arranged tours can be better than tackling the problems of public transport.

Taxis A fleet of white 'Turistaxis' with meters has been introduced for tourists' use; payment in US$: sample fare, Ciudad Vieja to Vedado US$3.50. A cheaper way of getting around is via **Panataxi**, a company set up for the 1992 Pan American Games. Basically a call-out service, T 81-3311, Panataxis also wait just outside the Plaza de la Catedral, the *Meliá Cohiba*, on 17 entre L y M, and at the airport, or ask your hotel to call one. In the older taxis there are no meters and there is normally a fixed charge between points in or near the city. The fare should be fixed before setting out on a journey. Cuban peso taxis are mostly reserved for hospital runs, etc. Several private car owners operate as taxi drivers, some legitimately, others without a licence, always for dollars. Beware of overcharging until you know the regular rates. In Habana Vieja and Vedado tricycle taxis are cheap and readily available, a pleasant way to travel.

Buses Town buses used to be frequent and cheap but the crisis since 1993 means that they are scarce and crowded. The out-of-town bus services leave from the Terminal de Omnibus Interprovinciales, Av Rancho Boyeros (Independencia). See **Information for travellers** for advance booking addresses.

Trains Trains leave from the Estación Central in Av Egido (de Bélgica), Havana, to the larger cities. The Estación Central has what is claimed to be the oldest engine in Latin America, *La Junta*, built in Baltimore in 1842. *Ferrotur*, Calles Arsenal y Egido, use side entrance, official government outlet for dollar tickets, is very helpful. Tickets easily purchased from LADIS ticket office at opp end of platform from main building, pay in US$, carriage, a/c, spacious, food and drink on board. The 'special' leaves Estación Central daily at 1620, arrives Matanzas 1800, US$4, arrive Santa Clara 2033, US$12, arrive Ciego de Avila 2313, US$18, arrive Camagüey 0054, US$22, arrive Las Tunas 0258, US$27, arrive Holguín 0505, US$31, arrive Santiago de Cuba 0645, US$35, arrive Guantánamo

0835, US$38. A long distance dollar taxi may well do the same journey in a fraction of the time for the same cost as the train, eg Havana-Pinar del Río, US$15 one way, 2 hrs or less by taxi, 7-8 hrs by train.

Bicycle hire *Hotel Neptune*, charges US$3 for the first hour then US$1 for each subsequent hour. Also *Hotel Riviera*. Check the bicycle carefully (take your own lock, pump, even a bicycle spanner and puncture repair kit; petrol stations have often been converted into bicycle stations, providing air and tyre repairs). Cycling is a good way to see Havana, especially the suburbs; some roads in the Embassy area are closed to cyclists. The tunnel underneath the harbour mouth has a bus designed specifically to carry bicycles and their riders. Take care at night as there are few street lights and bikes are not fitted with lamps.

● **Airport**
José Martí, 18 km from Havana. A new terminal is to be built by 1998 to allow 3 million passengers a year. Turistaxi to airport, US$16-18 depending on time of day or night and destination. Panataxi are US$9-12. The Cubatur desk will book a taxi for you from the airport. The return journey in a private taxi could cost as little as US$5. The duty free shop at the airport is good value. City buses run from Terminal 4 (Air Cubana terminal) to town, ask around. To catch a bus to the airport from town, the M2 buses leave from Parque Fraternidad, but are always full, long queues, difficult with luggage.

EAST FROM HAVANA

BEACH RESORTS

An easy excursion, 15 mins by taxi, is to **Cojímar**, the seaside village featured in Hemingway's *The Old Man and the Sea*. He celebrated his Nobel prize here in 1954 and his bust is here. The coastline (no beach) is covered in sharp rocks and is dirty because of effluent from tankers, but it is a quiet, pretty place to relax. *La Terraza* is a restaurant with a pleasant view, reasonably priced seafood meals; photographs of Hemingway cover the walls. Further E is the pleasant little beach of **Bacuranao**, 15 km from Havana. At the far end of the beach is a villa complex with restaurant and bar. Another 5 km E is **Santa María del Mar**, with a long, open beach which continues eastwards to **Guanabo** (4 train departures daily), a pleasant, non-touristy beach but packed at weekends. Cars roll in from Havana early on Sat mornings, line up and deposit their cargo of sun worshippers at the sea's edge. The quietest spot is **Brisas del Mar**, at the E end. Tourism bureaux offer day excursions (min 6 people) for about US$15 pp to the Playas del Este, but its worth hiring a private car for the day for US$20-25.

● **Accommodation A2** *Tropicoco Beach Club*, Av Sur y Las Terrazas, Santa María del Mar, T 687 2530, price inc beer rum 3 meals wonderful view of beach but food boring after 2 days, nothing to do but drink and bathe, 188 rooms; **A3** *Itabo*, Laguna Itabo entre Santa María del Mar y Boca Ciega, T 687-2550/58/80, F 33-5156, 198 rooms, good accommodation, poor food, dirty pool; **A3-B** *Panamericano* (Horizontes), Calle A y Av Central, Cojímar, T 33-8810, 68-4101, F 33-8001, 81-room hotel and 421 2/3-room apartments, restaurants, bars, pool; **B** *Hotel Atlántico* (Gran Caribe), Av Las Terrazas, entre 11 y 12 Santa María del Mar, T 687-2560/69, 92 rooms, also has an *Aparthotel* (opposite the hotel is the self-catering complex's shop selling fresh food, inc eggs, bread, cheese and meat). It may be possible to find privately rented apartments in Guanabo for US$15 a night with kitchen, ask around; **C** *Villa Playa Hermosa*, 5 Av y Calle D, T 2774, Guanabo, 33 rooms or chalets, good value, often used by party faithful and honeymooners, pizzería, good quality, US$1-2, rich French pastries US$1, well worth the culinary experience, rents bikes (in poor condition).

● **Places to eat** There are many *paladares* in Guanabo and elsewhere along the coast, reasonable prices. If you are self-catering, there is a farmers' market in Guanabo selling fresh fruit and vegetables 6 days a week.

Guanabacoa

Guanabacoa is 5 km to the E of Havana and is reached by a road turning off the Central Highway, or by launch from Muelle Luz (not far from No 9 on the map) to the suburb of Regla, then by bus (if running) direct to Guanabacoa. It is a well preserved small colonial town; sights include the old parish church which has a splendid altar: the monastery of San Francisco; the Carral theatre;

and some attractive mansions. The **Museo Histórico de Guanabacoa**, a former estate mansion, with former slave quarters at the back of the building, Calle Martí 108, between San Antonio and Versalles, T 90-9117. Closed for repairs 1997, the African religion section has been transferred to Casa de Africa.

Santa María del Rosario

A delightful colonial town, founded in 1732, 16 km E of Havana. It is reached from Cotorro, on the Central Highway, and was carefully restored and preserved before the Revolution. The village church is particularly good. See the paintings, one by Veronese. There are curative springs nearby.

San Francisco de Paula

Hemingway fans may wish to visit his house, 11 km from the centre of Havana, where he lived from 1939 to 1960 (called the **Museo Ernest Hemingway**, T 91-0809, US$3, open 0930-1600, closed Tues). The signpost is opposite the Post Office, leading up a short driveway. Visitors are not allowed inside the plain whitewashed house which has been lovingly preserved with all Hemingway's furniture and books, just as he left it. But you can walk all around the outside and look in through the windows and open doors, although vigilant staff prohibit any photographs unless you pay US$5 for each one. There is a small annex building with one room used for temporary exhibitions, and from the upper floors there are fine views over Havana. The garden is beautiful and tropical, with many shady palms. Next to the swimming pool (empty) are the gravestones of Hemingway's pet dogs, shaded by a flowering shrub. Hemingway tours are offered by hotel tour desks for US$35.

Some 60 km E of Havana is **Jibacoa** beach, which is excellent for snorkelling as the reefs are close to the beach. (D *Camping de Jibacoa*, cabins for 4 or 2. *El Abra* campsite has 2-4-bed cabins, organized activities, pizza house, bar, restaurant and pool, transport and booking provided by Cubamar.)

MATANZAS

The old provincial town of **Matanzas** lies 104 km E of Havana along the Vía Blanca, which links the capital with Varadero beach, 34 km further E. The drive is unattractive along the coast and smelly because of the many small oilwells producing low-grade crude en route, but once you get into the hills there are good views. It is a sleepy town with old colonial buildings and a busy, ugly industrial zone. Walk along the riverside at dusk to watch the fishermen and take in the tranquility and murmur of fellow observers.

The old town is on the W bank of the estuary, the new town on the E, although this also has colonial buildings; both the rivers Yumurí and San Juan flow through the city. In Matanzas one should visit the **Museo Farmacéutico** (Milanés, 4951 entre Santa Teresa y Ayuntamiento, T 3179, Mon-Sat 1000-1800, Sun 0900-1300), the **Museo Provincial** (Milanés entre Magdalena y Ayllón, T 3195, Tues-Sun 1500-1800, 1900-2200), and the cathedral, all near Parque La Libertad. The **Palacio de Justicia** has been restored and nicely painted, serving to highlight the crumbling buildings which surround it. There is a wonderful view of the surrounding countryside from the church of Montserrat. The road out to Varadero goes past the university and the Escuela Militar. Bellamar Cave is only 5 km from Matanzas.

• **Accommodation** B *Hotel Canimao*, Km 3½ Carretera Matanzas a Varadero, T 6-1014, good restaurant; **B-C** *Hotel Louvre*, variety of rooms and prices, opt for the a/c room with bathroom and balcony overlooking the square, beautiful mahogany furniture, rather than the small, dark, cupboard room in the bowels of the hotel.

• **Transport** There used to be frequent buses but the journey via the Hershey Railway is more memorable (4 trains daily, 3 hrs, from the Casablanca station, which is reached by public launch from near La Fuerza Castle). Those who wish to make it a day trip from Havana can do so, long queues for return tickets, best to get one as soon as you arrive.

VARADERO

From Matanzas one can continue on a good dual carriageway to **Varadero**, 144 km from Havana, Cuba's chief beach resort with all facilities. The toll at the entrance to the resort can be paid in pesos or foreign currency, choose your channel. It is built on a 20-km sandspit, the length of which run two roads lined with dozens of large hotels, some smaller ones, and many chalets and villas. Many of the villas date from before 1959. Development of the peninsula began in 1923 but the village area was not built until the 1950s. The Du Pont family bought land, sold it for profit, then bought more and built a large house, now *Las Americas* restaurant on a cliff near the new hotel of the same name, and constructed roads. Varadero is undergoing large scale development of new hotels and cabins and joint ventures with foreign investors are being encouraged with the aim of expanding to 30,000 rooms by the turn of the century. The southern end is more downmarket, with hustlers on the beaches by day and prostitutes in the bars at night. The northern end is where the Sol/Meliá and other international hotels are; you can pay to use their facilities even if you are not staying there. Check out the price of sun loungers for an indication of hotel prices, eg US$1/day at the *Internacional*, US$2/day at Sol/Meliá resort. In Varadero all hotels, restaurants and excursions must be paid in US dollars. Don't bother to buy any pesos for your stay here. Book excursions at any hotel with a Tour Agency office. Despite the building in progress it is not over exploited and is a good place for a family beach holiday. The beaches are quite empty, if a bit exposed, and you can walk for miles along the sand, but you are totally isolated from the rest of Cuba. Beach vendors will try to sell you T-shirts, crochet work and wooden trinkets, don't buy the black coral, it is protected internationally and you may not be allowed to take it in to your country. Distances are large. Avenida 1, which runs NE-SW the length of the spit, has a bus service; calle numbers begin with lowest numbers at the SW end and work upwards to the NE peninsula. There is a **Municipal Museum** at Calle 57 y Av de la Playa. The **Centro Recreativo Josone**, Av 1 y Calle 59, is a large park with pool, bowling, other activities and a café. There are three marinas: Acua, Chapelín and Gaviota, all full service with sailing tours, restaurants, fishing and diving.

Festival

Some years in Nov a festival is held in Varadero, lasting a week, which attracts some of the best artists in South America. Entrance US$2-10 per day. Carnival is held in Jan with lots of tourist participation, encouraged by the hotel entertainment teams.

Excursions

From Varadero it is possible to explore the interesting town of **Cárdenas**, where the present Cuban flag was raised for the first time in 1850. The sea here is polluted with oil and the air smells of phosphorous which sometimes drifts as far as Varadero. Many of the Cubans who work in the hotels live in Cárdenas and old Canadian buses, mostly blue, go from the town all the way to the last hotel, US$1. Another excursion is to **Neptune's Cave** (thought a more appealing name than the old one, Cepero), which is S of the town of **Carboneras**, half-way between Matanzas and Varadero. It has an underground lagoon, stalagmites and stalactites, evidence of Indian occupation and was used as a clandestine hospital during the war of independence.

There are many sailing tours to the offshore cays. The *Jolly Roger* is rec, not a pirate ship as in other parts of the Caribbean, but a catamaran, US$70 inc lunch and open bar, good food, several stops for snorkelling or beaches, ask for a detour to the dolphinarium on Cayo Macho if not already included, isolated, large pens for dolphins, US$5 for show, US$5 to swim with them. *Varasub*, a Japanese semi-submersible carrying 48 passengers, has

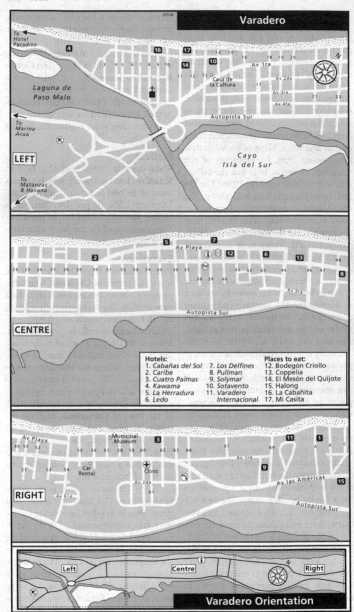

Varadero

M104

To Hotel Paradiso

4   16   17   14 15   16   18 19 20   Av 1ra
3 4 5 6 7 8 9 10   14   10   Av 2da
11 12 13   Casa de la Cultura   17   Av 3ra
Laguna de Paso Malo   Av 4ta
21   23

To Marina Acua   Autopista Sur

LEFT   Cayo Isla del Sur

To Matanzas & Havana

5   7   Av Playa
2   12   6   13
24 25 26 27 28 29 30 31 32 33 34 35 36 37   41 42 43   44   46 47   48
Pol   8
38 39 40   Av 3ra

Autopista Sur

CENTRE

Hotels:
1. Cabañas del Sol   7. Los Delfines
2. Caribe   8. Pullman
3. Cuatro Palmas   9. Solymar
4. Kawama   10. Sotavento
5. La Herradura   11. Varadero
6. Ledo   Internacional

Places to eat:
12. Bodegón Criollo
13. Coppelia
14. El Mesón del Quijote
15. Halong
16. La Cabañita
17. Mi Casita

Av Playa   Municipal Museum   3   11   1
49 50 52   55 56 57 58 59 60   62 63 64   67   69   A B C
51   53 54   Car Rental   Clinic   Av 1ra
Av 2da   9
Av 61a   61   Av las Américas   15
Autopista Sur

RIGHT

Left   Centre   Right

Varadero Orientation

6 daily departures from the *Hotel Paradiso*, adults US$25, children US$20. Reservations can be made with Havanatur representatives or the Varasub offices: Av Playa 3606, entre 36 y 37, T 66-7279; Calle 31, entre Av 1 y Playa, T 66-7154; Av Kawama y Calle O, T 66-7165; Av de las Américas y Calle 64, T 66-7203, and others. For an all-round view of the península, Matanzas and the Yumurí valley, you can ride in a noisy 32-seater Russian helicopter, landing in the valley for lunch, a visit to a local farm, horse riding or boating on a lake, Wed, Fri, Sun, 0930-1530, US$75. Many more excursions are available from hotel tour operators, including to the Bay of Pigs, US$47, or to Trinidad, US$99 by plane.

Local information
● **Accommodation**

(All prices high season, double. Hotels can be booked in the tourist office. Many hotels now offer all-inclusive rates, but these can be disappointing with lack of variety in food and drinks.)

A Cuban-Spanish joint venture has opened three resort hotels managed by Sol/Meliá Hotels of Spain: **L2** *Meliá Las Américas*, T 66-7600, F 66-7625, 5 stars, 250 rooms, suites, 125 luxury bungalows, comfortable, glitzy public areas, restaurants, breakfast rec, nice pool but cold, good beach, golf, tennis, watersports, disco, Plaza América shopping centre alongside, new shops still opening up; **L2** *Sol Palmeras*, T 66-7013, F 66-7162, 375 rooms, 32 suites, 200 bungalows, well-landscaped, quiet, shady, attractive, cool lobby bar, 4 stars, same facilities, Chinese restaurant rec, buffet breakfast poor, and the star-shaped **L2** *Meliá Varadero*, T 66-7013, F 66-7162, 490 rooms, 5 stars, on rocky promontory, tennis, watersports, disco, nightclub, spa, sauna, jacuzzi. There is a shuttle service through the Sol/Meliá complex 0730-2300. **L3** *Cuatro Palmas Resort* (Gran Caribe), Av 1 entre 60 y 62, T 66-7640, F 66-7583, 343 a/c rooms, also in bungalows and villas, on beach, opp Centro Comercial Caiman, very pleasant, pool, tennis, bicycle and moped hire, tourism bureau, Post Office, lots of services; **L3-A3** *Varadero Internacional* (Gran Caribe), Av Las Américas, T 66-7038/9, F 66-7246, formerly the *Hilton*, now dated compared with Sol/Meliá resorts but has charm, 371 rooms, also new villas, Porto Carrero original painting on tiles in lobby, ghastly pink paint outside, friendly

bar staff, best bit of beach on whole peninsula, nice rooms, solid wooden furniture, dodgy wiring, cheap packages available, dancing classes on beach, good value lunches, rec cabaret. Jamaican investors have built the 160-room, all-inclusive *Superclubs Club Varadero*, T 66-7030, F 66-7005, for singles and couples, no children under 16, lots of activities and sports, plenty of equipment, popular, crowded even in low season.

A1-A3 *Kawama* (Gran Caribe), Carretera de Kawama y Calle O, T 66-7155/6, F 66-7334, 202 rooms, refurbished older hotel, at the S end **A1-A3** *Paradiso*, attached to *Puntarena* (Tryp), T 66-7120, F 66-7074, with all resort facilities, 3 pools, watersports, all shared by both hotels, smart, modern, 518 rooms in total, 5 stars, good restaurants, fresh seafood, rec; **A2** *Acuazul*, Av 1 entre Calles 13 y 14, 156 rooms, with pool, older style, not on beach, blue and white, lots of concrete; **A2** *Villa Punta Blanca*, T 66-7090/7083, F 66-7004, 320 rooms, made up of a number of former private residences with some new complexes; **A3-C** *Villa La Herradura*, Av Playa entre 35 y 36, T 6-3703, well-equipped suites, balcony, restaurant bar, *Caracol* shop, etc.

B *Brisas del Caribe*, Av de la Playa y Calle 30, T 66-8030, F 66-8005, 124 rooms; **B** *Los Delfines*, Av Playa y Calle 39, T 6-3630, F 66-7496; **B** *Pullman*, Av 1 entre 49 y 50, T 6-2575, F 66-7495, best value for the Independent traveller, only 15 rooms, very popular; **B** *Varazul*, Av 1 entre Calles 14 y 15, T 66-7132/4, F 66-7229, aparthotel, 69 rooms, quiet; **B** *Villa Sotavento*, dependency of *Acuazul*, Calle 13 between Av 1 and Av Playa, T 66-2953, 130 rooms, next to beach, clean, with bath, breakfast, US$5, buffet, very good.

● **Places to eat**

Recommended restaurants, all between US$9-15, are *Mi Casita* (book in advance), Camino del Mar entre 11 y 12, T 63787, meat and seafood, open 1800-2300; *La Cabañita*, Camino del Mar esq Calle 9, T 62215, meat and seafood, open 1900-0100; *Oshin*, Chinese, in grounds of *Sol Palmeras*, open 1200-1500, 1800-2300, good, popular, reservations essential; *Halong*, Camino del Mar esq Calle 12, T 63787, Chinese, open 1900-2300; *El Mesón del Quijote* (Spanish) at *Villa Cuba*, Cra Américas, T 63522, open 1500-2300; *Albacora*, at *Hotel Copey*, Calle C entre Av 62 y 63, T 6-3650, open 1200-1245, disappointing, all dishes except *pescado*, US$12-18, but if you want fish you may be told '*no hay*'; *Lai-Lai* bar/restaurant, Oriental, Av 1 y Calle 18, T 66-7793, 1900-0045; *Castelnuovo*, Av 1 y Calle 11, T 66-7794, 1200-2345, Italian; *Las Américas*, Av Las Américas, T 6-3856, open 1200-2215, international food, beautiful setting, food good one night, inedible the next; *El Mirador*, at *LTI Bella Costa Resort*, on cliff overlooking the sea, lovely fish restaurant, lobster US$18.50, shrimp US$14, open 1200-2300; *Bodegón Criollo*, Av Playa esq Calle 40, T 66-7795, open 1200-0100, pleasant atmosphere, popular, music, no vegetarian food; *La Casa del Chef*, Av 1 entre 12 y 13, T 6-3606, 1200-2245, set menu US$9 inc salad, black bean soup, rice, meat and chips, flan, coffee not rec, chicken dry, fish tasteless; *La Sangría*, snack bar on sea front, Av 1 entre Calle 8 y 9, T 6-2025, open 24 hrs; *Coppelia*, Av 1 entre Calle 44 y 46, T 62866, open 1000-2245, in town centre, ice cream US$0.90. It is now easier to buy food in Varadero because the new Aparthotels (*Varazul, La Herradura*) have a small food store.

● **Entertainment**

Discos: in most large hotels. *Kastillito*, Av de la Playa y Calle 49, T 63888, open 2300-0600; *La Patana*, Canal de Kawama, T 66-7791, open 2100-0300; *La Bamba*, hottest in town; *Tuxpán*, biggest, most popular; *Havana Club* in old *centro comercial*, matinées Sun pm, frequented by locals.

Nightclubs: *Cabaret Continental* at *Hotel Internacional*, US$40 with dinner, 2000, show and disco US$25 at 2200, rec by Canadians; *Cabaret Cueva del Pirata*, Autopista Sur Km 11, T 66-7751, 2100-dawn, closed Sun.

● **Services**

Bank: Banco Financiero Internacional, Av Playa y C 32, cash advance service with credit cards, open 0900-1900 daily.

Clinic: 1 Av y C 61, T 66-7226, international clinic, doctor on duty 24 hrs, a medical consultation in your hotel will cost US$15.

Phones, telex and telegrams: C 64 y 1 Av.

Police: C 39 y 1 Av, T 116.

● **Tour companies & travel agents**

Most hotels have a tour agency on site offering local and national excursions, boat trips, etc. A rec travel agency is *Fantástico*, Calle 24 y Playa, T 66-7061, F 66-7062, helpful multilingual guides, transfers, booking and confirmation of air tickets, air charters, car rentals, reception and representation service, linked to Cubanacan hotels.

● **Transport**

Car hire: Havanautos, T 33-7341 at airport, or through many hotels. Hot tip: hire a car rather than jeep to avoid having your spare wheel stolen, insurance covers 4 wheels, not the spare. **Moped rental**: US$9 per hour, US$15 3 hrs, extra hours US$5, a good way to see the city. **Bicycle hire**: from hotels, US$1/hour. **Horse drawn vehicles** sometimes act as taxis. **Taxis** (cars) charge US$0.50/km; from *Hotel Internacional* to the bank is US$3, to Plaza América US$5.

A cheap method of getting to Varadero from Havana is to take the **train** to Matanzas (see above), then a taxi to Matanzas bus terminal from where you catch a bus, about 1 hr (state destination, take ticket, wait for bus and then your number to be called, and run for the bus). About 5½ hrs in all, if buses are running. Bus station in Varadero is at Calle 36. There is an **airport**; bus to hotels US$10 pp.

SANTA CLARA

300 km from Havana and 196 km from Varadero, **Santa Clara** is a pleasant university city in the centre of the island. It was the site of the last battle of the Cuban revolution before Castro entered Havana, and the Batista troop train captured by Che Guevara can be seen. A monument and museum to Che, built 1994, is just off Calle Marta Abréu, entrance on Calle Rafael Trista, good displays and personal effects, rec, open Tues-Sun 0900-1200, 1400-1700, US$2.

● **Accommodation** There are two hotels, **B** *Los Caneyes* (Horizontes), Av de los Eucaliptos y Circunvalación, T 422-4512, F 33-5009 (outside the city), chalet-style cabins, hot showers, good buffet, supper US$12, breakfast US$4, excellent value; and **C** *Santa Clara Libre*, central, ugly concrete building on Parque Vidal, T 27548/27550, clean, water shortages, reasonable lunch, noisy disco on 11th floor.

● **Places to eat** *Sol de Cuba* on Candelaria (Machado) entre Alemán y Central, up spiral staircase, limited menu, US$6-8 for main dish, make sure rice and salad are included, not charged extra, slightly overpriced; *El Rápido* café, Calle Marta Abréu, opp interprovincial bus station, if you have a wait; dollar shop next door sells food and bread as well as clothes, shoes, etc; *Coppelia* ice cream, Calle Colón just off Parque Vidal, corner of Calle Mugica, 1000-2330; *Rincón Criollo*, Cuba 410, entre Serafín Sánchez y Estrada Palma, T 7-1309, chicken and pork dishes US$2-3, others can be ordered, lunch 1200-1500 by reservation, dinner 1800-2400, food OK, nice surroundings, clean; *Mandarín*, Chinese, Calle Marta Abréu beyond bus stations, reservations needed with Islazul on Calle Lorda, open 1830-2230; *La Casona*, Carretera Central 6 entre Padre Chao y Marta Abréu, T 5027, meals US$1-2, side dishes US$0.25, very tasty, nice old house, friendly hosts, open 1200-2400; *La Marquesina*, 24-hr café next to theatre, pleasant place for a drink, Rumbos Cuba desk for tours and information.

● **Entertainment** *Club Mejunje* (mishmash), 2½ blocks N from Parque Vidal, Calle Marta Abréu 107 entre Lubián y Juan Bruno Zayas, cultural centre and Casa de la Trova in a backyard full of artefacts and graffiti-covered walls, opens 1700, Wed-Sun, free, pay for rum in pesos, composers, singers, musicians and friends sing, play and drink together, friendly, enjoyable. Larger events and shows staged in courtyard, US$1 for foreigners.

● **Transport Bus** From Havana, US$16, 4 hrs. The provincial bus station is on Calle Marta Abréu, 1 km from centre, on corner with Calle Pichardo, white building. The interprovincial bus station is on the same road, 1 km further out, in blue building. Horse-drawn *coches*, or taxi-buses go all over town and down Calle Marta Abréu to the bus stations, 1 peso. There are also some buses, 40 centavos.

CIENFUEGOS

Cienfuegos, on the S coast, is an attractive seaport and industrial city 80 km from Trinidad and 70 km from Santa Clara. Interesting colonial buildings around the central Parque Martí, notably the Cathedral, built in 1868, and the Teatro Thomas Terry, built 1889 with ornate gilt and paintings. The Palacio de Ferrer, now the Casa de Cultura, has a tower with great views, on the corner. On the S side the Museo Provincial is open 0800-1630 daily, US$0.50, but suffered hurricane damage in 1996 and upstairs is closed.

The Meliá Don Juan cruise starts from here, taking in Cayo Largo, Grand Cayman, Cienfuegos, Montego Bay, Santiago de Cuba, Cayman Brac, Santiago de Cuba, 7 days US$630, 3 days US$270, 4 days US$360.

● **Accommodation** There is one hotel, 45 mins' walk from station, **B** *Jagua* (Gran Caribe), Punta Gorda, Calle 37 No 1, T 3021-4, F 66-7454, 145 a/c rooms with view over bay, comfortable, palatial restaurant next door, gorgeous decor, live piano music, simple but good food in snack bar (expensive restaurant next door). Many of the hotels are out of town or booked solid by Cubans. **B** *Hotel Pasacaballo*, Carretera a Rancho Luna, Km 22, T 9-6280/90, and **B** *Rancho Luna*, Km 16, T 4-8120/3, F 33-5057, 225 rooms with balcony, salt water pool, scuba diving, are seaside complexes with cafeteria etc. People offering private accommodation meet buses and trains but charge you for gasoline to their houses, **D** *Dr R Figueroa*, Calle 35 4210, entre 42 y 44, T 9108; also his brother, *Dr A Figueroa*, Av 56 3927, entre 39 y 41, T 6107, hot shower, nice family, excursions offered.

● **Transport Bus** Terminal at Calle 49 esq Av 56. To Havana, daily, 0600, 1000, 1230, 1500, 2350, 5 hrs, US$14. From Havana, 0630, 1220, 1630, 1945, 2130. To Santiago de Cuba, every other day, 1700, US$31. To Camagüey, every other day, 0800, 1400. To Trinidad, 0630, arrive 1200, US$3. To Santa Clara, 0500, 0910, 1550, 11½-2 hrs, US$2.50. **Train** Terminal at Calle 49 esq Av 58. To Havana, direct or via Santa Clara, on alternating days, 1030, 9 hrs, US$9.50, or 1430, arrive Santa Clara 1700, Havana 2300, US$12.10.

PLAYA GIRON

From Cienfuegos take a taxi to **Playa Girón** and the **Bay of Pigs** (1½ hrs). Ask the driver to wait while you visit the beach and tourist complex, and the site of national pilgrimage where, in 1961, the disastrous US-backed invasion of Cuba was attempted.

● **Accommodation** **C** *Villa Horizontes Playa Girón*, T 59-4118, 292 rooms, a/c with bath, good self-service meals, bar pool, disco, tourist information desk, shop.

ZAPATA PENINSULA

Further W from Girón is the **Zapata Peninsula**, an area of swamps, mangroves, beaches and much bird and animal life. It is the largest ecosystem in the island and contains the Laguna del Tesoro, a 92 sq km lagoon over 10m deep. It is an important winter home for flocks of migrating birds. There are 16 species of reptiles, including crocodiles. Mammals include the jutia and the manatee, while there are over 1,000 species of invertebrate of which more than 100 are spiders. Access from Playa Larga or Guamá, inland. There is a crocodile farm at the Zapata Tourist Institute in **Guamá**, which can be visited. Varadero, Havana and other hotels and tourist agencies organize day excursions inc lunch, multilingual guide and a boat ride on the lagoon through the swamps to a replica Siboney Indian village. If you go on your own, entrance to the crocodile farm is US$3 and the boat trip to Guamá island US$10. Tours are interesting and good value but involve a lot of travelling. Birdwatchers are advised to go there from Ancón and spend a few nights, or go on a tour one day and return with the next tour the following day.

● **Accommodation** **B** *Horizontes Villa Guamá*, Laguna del Tesoro, T 59-2979, 59 a/c rooms with bath, phone, TV, restaurant, bar, *cafetería*, nightclub, shop, tourist information desk; **C** *Villa Horizontes Playa Larga*, at Playa Larga, T 59-7219, 59 a/c rooms with bath, radio, TV, restaurant, bar, nightclub, shop, birdwatching and watersports.

TRINIDAD

Trinidad, 133 km S of Santa Clara is a perfect relic of the early days of the Spanish colony: beautifully preserved streets and buildings with hardly a trace of the 20th century anywhere. It was founded in 1514 as a base for expeditions into the 'New World'; Cortés set out from here for Mexico in 1518. The five main squares and four churches date from the 18th and 19th centuries; the whole city, with its fine palaces, cobbled streets and tiled roofs, is a national monument and since 1988 a UNESCO World Heritage Site. The **Museo Romántico**, Calle Hernández 52, next to the church of Santísima Trinidad on the main square, is excellent. It has a collection of romantic-style porcelain, glass, paintings and ornate furniture dating from 1830-1860 displayed in a colonial

mansion, with beautiful views from the upper floor balconies. No cameras allowed, open Tues, Thur 0800-2200, Sat-Mon, Wed, Fri 0800-1800, US$2, T 4363. **Museo Municipal de Historia** is on Calle Simón Bolívar 423, an attractive building but rather dull displays, walk up the tower for a good view of Trinidad, open Sun, Mon, Tues, Thur 0900-1800, Wed, Fri 0900-2200, US$1.50, T 4460. Other museums worth visiting include the **Museo de Arqueología Guamuhaya**, Simón Bolívar 457, esq Villena, Plaza Mayor, T 3420, open Mon, Wed 0900-2200, Sun, Tues, Thur, Fri 0900-1700, US$1; **Museo de Arquitectura Colonial**, Desengaño 83, T 3208, exhibits specifically on the architecture of Trinidad, open Mon, Thur 0900-2200, Sat, Sun, Tues, Wed 0900-1700, US$1; **Museo Nacional de Lucha Contra Bandidos**, Calle Hernández esq Piro Guinart, housed in old San Francisco convent, exhibits about campaign in Escambray mountains, open Tues, Fri 0900-2200, Wed, Thur, Sat, Sun, 0900-1700, US$1, T 4121.

Excursions

Nearby are the excellent beaches of **La Boca** (8 km), a small fishing village, restaurant on beach, some buses or taxi, or rent a bicycle from local people for about US$1. Private accommodation with Iliana Serrano, Villa La Piedra, Calle Real 47. Inland from Trinidad are the beautiful, wooded Escambray mountains. There is no public transport but day trips are organized to **Topes de Collantes National Park** by Rumbos. A Jeep Safari for 6 hrs costs US$25, min 3 passengers, lunch not included. A Truck Safari, min 10 passengers, including lunch, costs US$37, both take in swimming in a waterfall. You can see hummingbirds and the tocororo, the national bird of Cuba. A great day out. Hiring a private car with driver to Topes de Collantes and the Caburni falls will cost you about US$15-20. Private tours do not go to the same places as organized tours. There is also a huge hospital in the mountains, *Kurhotel Escambray*, which offers special therapeutic treatments for patients from all over the world, and a hotel C *Los Helechos*, T 40117.

Local information
● Accommodation

In the town centre only private accommodation is available.

B *Motel Las Cuevas* (Horizontes), Finca Santa Ana, T 419-4013/9, on a hill 10 mins' walk from town (good road), chalets with balconies, 84 very comfortable rooms with a/c, phone, radio, hot water, and very clean, 2 swimming pools, bar, beer US$1.50, discotheque (most rooms are far enough away not to be disturbed by noise), dollar shop, restaurant with buffet meals, breakfast US$4, evening meal US$12, not bad.

D *Bárbara Vásquez* hostal, Simón Bolívar 312 entre José Martí y Maceo, T 4107, clean room, fan, hot water, not far from historic centre; **D** *Casa de Huésped Mercedes Albalat Milord*, José Martí 330 entre Rosario y Desengaño, T 3350, large house full of antiques, quiet, good food on request, lobster rec, will guide if you want

E *Maritza Hernández*, Francisco Cadahía (Calle Gracia) 227 entre Colón y Lino Pérez T 3160, warmly rec, she speaks only Spanish but is fluent in sign language, 2-3 rooms, family atmosphere, pleasant courtyard, wonderful rocking chairs, excellent meals, US$7 for dinner, king prawns, fish, etc, more than you can eat, generous breakfast US$2.50; **E** *Aleida Calzada*, Juan Manuel Márquez 20 entre José Mendoza y Jesús Menéndez.

Camping: campsites at Ancón beach (see below) and La Boca (5-bed apartments). Camping at Base Manacal in the mountains, tent or small hut for US$5 per day; take No 10 bus from Cienfuegos.

● Places to eat

El Jigüe, Calle Real esq a Boca, T 4315, open 1100-1700 only unless a group comes in and then they open at night, live music, good food and atmosphere. A Rumbos restaurant is *El Mesón del Regidor*, Simón Bolívar 424, opp Calle Toro, T 3756, open 0900-1800 daily, US$7-8. The price of beer in some restaurants drops from US$2 to US$0.60 after 1700 when the tourist tours leave but all the state-run places shut then too. Family-run restaurants, *paladares*, have opened. Some which have been rec inc *Paladar Inés*, José Martí 160, entre Lino Pérez y Camilo Cienfuegos, T 3241, open 1200-2300, US$5-7 inc rice, salad, etc, nice place;

Daniel's, Camilo Cienfuegos 20, T 4395, open 1100 until everyone leaves, some courtyard tables, US$5-6 inc side dishes, also rooms US$15, a/c, but may be noisy from restaurant music downstairs; *Cocodrilo*, next door at Camilo Cienfuegos 28, entre Cárdenas y Zerquera, T 2108, open 0900-2400, nice old house, meals US$8, house pork special called Cocodrilaso US$7, also rooms for US$10; *Colonial*, Maceo 402, esq Colón, open daily 0900-2200, US$5-6, nice place, locally popular; *Sol y Son*, Simón Bolívar 283, entre Frank País y José Martí, run by English-speaking ex-architect Lázaro, open 1200-2400, in 19th century house, nice décor, courtyard, vegetarian special US$4.50, tasty stuffed fish US$7, all meals cost US$3 extra if you go with a guide, highly rec. On the road to Cienfuegos, *Hacienda María Dolores*, serving creole food, 0900-1600, has a collection of tropical birds, cockfighting and a fiesta on Thur, 1800-2300.

● Entertainment

One block from the church is the *Casa de la Trova*, open weekend lunchtimes and evenings, entry free. Excellent live Cuban music with a warm, lively atmosphere. There are mostly Cubans here, of all age groups, and it's a great place to watch, and join in with, the locals having a good time. All drinks paid for in dollars. Another venue for live music is *La Canchanchara*, Calle Real 70, T 4345. Open 0900-1900, cocktails, no food. More touristy than *Casa de La Trova* (cigar and souvenir shop), but good traditional music at lunchtimes.

● Transport

Bus Terminal on Piro Guinart entre Izquiedo y Maceo. Bus for Havana leaves 1330 every other day, arrives 1930, US$21 a/c, US$17 without a/c; also every other day a/c minibuses carrying 8 foreigners at 1500, US$25, comfortable. To Sancti Spíritus, daily, 0400, 0700, 0930, 1200, 1500, 2000, all take 2 hrs except 0400, 1200, which take 2 hrs 40 mins, 2.10 pesos. To Cienfuegos, daily, 0900, 1415, US$3. *Camión* (truck) leaves every other day, 0700, 1300, 2 hrs, 2.30 pesos. To Santa Clara, daily, 1715, arrive 2030, US$6. Ticket office open daily, 0800-1130, 1330-1700. Transport to the E of Cuba is difficult from Trinidad as it is not on the Carretera Central. Best to go to Sancti Spíritus through beautiful hilly scenery (see below) and bus from there. As elsewhere, severe shortages and huge queues, trucks and tractors with trailers may be laid on as a back-up.

Taxi Cienfuegos-Trinidad US$75; tour US$30 pp inc lunch. A taxi *particular* from Sancti Spíritus costs US$12, 1 hr, 70 km.

PLAYA ANCON

13 km from Trinidad is **Playa Ancón** not a town as such, just two resort hotels. The beach is lovely, pure white sand and clean turquoise water, highly recommended. A metered taxi from Trinidad costs US$5.20. The rainforest tour offered by both hotels for US$30 pp is superb (min 3 people, but can negotiate higher price for 2), knowledgeable and adaptable guides, good hiking, swimming through a river inside a cave coming out behind a waterfall, through which you have to dive.

● **Accommodation** **A2** *Ancón* (Gran Caribe), F 66-7424, though they encourage you to go all-inclusive, inc three meals, drinks and such extras as snorkels, bicycles and horse riding, good restaurant, snack bar and many facilities, inc scuba diving and watersports, best beach here, popular for families; **A2-A3** *Costa Sur* (Horizontes), 11 km from Trinidad, T 419-6100/2524, 131 rooms and chalets, new block best, occasional hot water, a/c, bath, phone, restaurant, good value breakfast buffet, bar, nightclub, pool, shop, good value, car rental and taxis.

SANCTI SPIRITUS

Sancti Spíritus, about 80 km E of Trinidad and 90 km SE of Santa Clara, can be reached by road from Cienfuegos, Santa Clara or Trinidad (2 hrs over a mountain road through the Escambray). In the San Luis valley, between Trinidad and Sancti Spíritus are many 19th century sugarmills. Among them is the 45-m Manacas-Iznagas tower (entry US$1), with a café nearby. It is one of Cuba's seven original Spanish towns and has a wealth of buildings from the colonial period. Refreshments in town available at the *Casa de las Infusiones*.

● **Accommodation** The nearest tourist hotel is the **B** *Zaza* (Horizontes), T 412-6012/5334, 10 km outside the town on the Zaza artificial lake, 128 a/c rooms with bath, phone, restaurant, bar, nightclub, pool, shop, car rental, rather run down but service and food praised by Cubans. For private accommodation, **E** *Sergio*

Orihuela Ruíz, room in apartment, Agramonte 61, Apto 5 Altos entre Jesús Menéndez y Llano, CP 60 100, T 2-3828, 5 mins walk from station opp Iglesia Parroquial Mayor del Espíritu Santo, English spoken, meets most trains.

● **Transport Train** Station at end of Av Jesús Menéndez. Daily trains to Santa Clara (2 hrs), Cienfuegos (4 hrs) and Havana (9 hrs). Sancti Spíritus can also be reached by getting the 'special' from Havana to Santiago and changing at Guayos, 15 km N.

Ciego de Avila

The next province E is **Ciego de Avila**, largely flat, with mangrove swamps on the coasts and cayes to the N. 2 km outside the province's capital is B *Hotel Ciego de Avila*, T 2-8013, with good food. At Morón on Av Tarafa, N of Ciego de Avila, is B *Morón*, T 3901/3904, very smart, renovated 1994, 144 rooms with balcony, pool, games room, good a/c and food.

CAYO COCO

Cayo Coco has become a focal point in the Government's ecotourism interests. It is a large island of mostly mangrove and bush which shelter many migratory birds as well as permanent residents. The Atlantic side of the island has excellent beaches, particularly Playa Flamenco (15 mins' drive from hotels), with some 5 km of white sand and shallow, crystalline water. Beach bar and horses for hire. Anyone looking for solitude can explore Playa Prohibida, appropriately named as the Government has banned construction here in the interests of ecology. Day trips and 2-night packages from Havana.

● **Accommodation** *Hotel Tryp Cayo Coco*, Spanish and Cuban, 458 rooms, 5 restaurants, 2 bars, piano bar, 2 snack bars, 2 pools, shops, disco, watersports, volleyball, floodlit tennis, beach a bit disappointing but facilities well planned; second hotel alongside under construction 1996. A joint French-Cuban venture is to construct 1,300 rooms on the cay by 2001. There is also a hotel on **Cayo Guillermo**, W of Cayo Coco, *Cayo Guillermo*, in the Gran Caribe chain, T 30-1012/1160, F 33-5221, 80 rooms, a/c, bath, restaurant, watersports, scuba diving, etc. The 13 sq km cay with 5 km of beach is protected by a long coral reef which is good for diving with plentiful fish and crustaceans, while on land there are lots of birds.

CAMAGUEY

The **Museo Casa Natal Ignacio Agramonte** in the large city of **Camagüey**, halfway between Santa Clara and Santiago, is one of the biggest and most impressive museums in the country (Av Ignacio Agramonte 59, T 9-7116, open Mon, Wed, Sat 1300-1600, Sun 0800-1200).

● **Accommodation A3** *Maraguán* (Cubanacán), Circumvalación Este, on outskirts, T 7-2017, 7-2170, 35 rooms and suites, 3 bars, restaurant, cafetería, car rental, pool, horseriding; **B** *Hotel Camagüey* (Horizontes), Av Ignacio Agramonte, T 7-2015, good condition, modern, pool, disco show, bar, cafetería, good buffet restaurant; **B** *Puerto Príncipe*, Av de los Mártires 60 y Andrés Sánchez, La Vigía (in town), T 8-2469, a/c, bar, restaurant, nightclub on roof; **B** *Gran Hotel*, Maceo 67, T 92093/4, under renovation, swimming pool added, restaurant on top floor, good view, also cafetería and snack bar; **C-D** *Plaza* (Islazul), Calle Van Horne 1, entre República y Avellaneda, T 8-2413, 8-2457, 67 rooms with TV, fridge, colonial building, restaurant, bar; **D** *Isla de Cuba*, República y San Estéban, T 9-1515, in the heart of the city.

Nuevitas, on the coast N of Camagüey, was the original site of the city, founded in 1514 by Diego de Velázquez as Santa María del Puerto del Príncipe. Constant pirate attacks forced the town to be moved inland. Several resort hotels have been built at **Santa Lucía**, near Nuevitas on the coast, about 2 hrs by bus from Camagüey. The beach is over 20 km long, with no rocks or cliffs but protected by a large coral reef not far offshore. There are great diving opportunities here (see **Diving and marine life**), with abundant fish and more than 50 species of corals. The water is clean with good visibility and an average temperature of 24°C. Now and then you can see dolphins near the shore and flamingos inland. 8 km from Santa Lucía is Playa Los Cocos, which is even better than Santa Lucía, with white sand and translucent water. There are some bars and the *Lazo Lobster House*.

● **Accommodation At Santa Lucía**: most of the hotels offer full board and all facilities, but room only is available if you want more flexibility and variety. Tour desks offer trips to Camagüey, Havana, diving etc. **A2** *Villa Coral*, choice of independent bungalows, snack bar, disco, pool; **A3** *Cuatro Vientos*, the newest on the beach, all facilities inc pool, disco show; **A3** *Villa Caracol*, T 30402/3, 4-star, *cabañas*, pool, disco, restaurant, snack bar, 24-hr entertainment, Cuban dance lessons; **B** *Mayanabo*, T 33-5533, 33-1131/2, 3-star, pool, a/c, hot water; *Villa Tararaco*, T 3-6222/3, 6310, under renovation 1997.

● **Places to eat** *Las Brisas*, creole food; *Bonzai*, Chinese; *La Casa del Pescador*, seafood; *paladares* are opening up.

HOLGUIN

(*Pop* 250,000, *Province* 1,011,977) **Holguín** is a provincial capital in the E, with easy access to some of the best beaches in the country. The local economy is traditionally based on sugar and there is a sugar mill at Rafael Freyre. Further to the E of the province is the hugely important nickel plant with shipping facilities at Moa. The countryside is attractive, hilly and covered with luxuriant vegetation. There are picture book views of hillsides dotted with royal palms, towering over thatched cottages, called *bohíos*, while the flatter land is green with swathes of sugar cane.

Holguín was founded in 1545 and named after García Holguín, a captain in the Spanish colonization force. It officially received the title of Ciudad de San Isidro de Holguín on 18 January 1752, when the population numbered 1,426. It is known as the 'city of the parks', four of which, Parque Infantil, Parque Carlos Manuel de Céspedes, the Plaza Central and Parque José Martí, lie between the two main streets: Antonio Maceo and Libertad (Manduley). There is a statue of Carlos Manuel de Céspedes in the parque named after him, he is remembered for having freed the slaves on 10 October 1868 and starting the war of independence. The Plaza Central is named after General Calixto García Iñiguez (statue in the centre), who was born in Holguín in 1837 and took part in both wars of independence. His statue is in the centre and his birthplace on Calle Miró, one block from the plaza, is now a museum. Around the plaza are the Commander Eddy Suñol Theatre (he fought against Batista), the Library, **Museo Provincial** (open Mon-Fri 0900-1700, Sat 0900-1300, US$1, US$3 with camera), **Galería Bayado** (ceramics, carvings, furniture, all for sale, courtyard at back with small bar, singing, music at night), **Casa de Cultura** (handicrafts, dancing), cafetería and both peso and dollar stores. Off the square, the **Museo de Ciencias Naturales** is good and popular. The city has a university, a paediatric hospital, coffee roasting plant, brewery and baseball stadium and is busy, although all traffic moves at the pace of the thousands of bicycles which throng the streets. There are many statues and monuments to national heroes, several of which are around the Plaza de la Revolución on the edge of the city, the location of the City Hall and the Provincial Communist Party building.

Above the city is **La Loma de la Cruz**, a strategic hill with a cross on top. On 3 May 1790, a Franciscan priest, Antonio de Alegría, came with a group of religious people and put up the cross, 275m above sea level, 127m above the town. All the streets of the town were laid out from that strategic point, which has a look out tower, built by the Spanish during the 10 Years War. In 1929 stone steps were begun up the hill, which were finished 3 May 1950. Every 3 May locals celebrate the Romerías de la Cruz de Mayo. There is a road, but if you wish to walk up, there are lots of benches for resting on. The way is lit up at night with street lights. Candles are lit and offerings of coins are made at the cross, but you are more likely to meet gangs of boys waiting for tourists than religious devotees. A policeman is usually on patrol in the morning.

Excursions

The **Mirador de Mayabe** is a popular excursion for Cubans and tour parties. A restaurant and hotel have been built on a hillside a few km out of town with a splendid view over the valley and the whole city. Water towers stand out like mushrooms in the distance. C *El Mirador de Mayabe*, T 422160, T/F 425347, has 24 rooms in cabins under the trees, tiled floors, a/c, TV, wooden furniture, fridge, hot water, adequate bathroom, quiet, also a suite and A3 4 rooms in a house at the top of the hill with a fantastic view. The restaurant has good Cuban food, open air but under cover and the usual strolling musicians. There is a swimming pool perched on the edge of the hill and beside it a bar, where Pancho, the beer-drinking donkey entertains guests. *La Finca Mayabe* has a second restaurant, normally open only for tour parties, with a *bohío*, and a collection of chickens, turkeys, ducks etc which you might find around a typical farmer's house.

Local information
● **Accommodation**

B *Pernik*, T 48-1011/1140, near Plaza de la Revolución on Av Jorge Dimitrov y Av XX Aniversario, 202 rooms, mostly overnighters passing through, shops, bar, restaurant, empty swimming pool, TV, a/c, nice view from top floor rooms, blue furniture, small bathrooms, adequate; C *Villa El Bosque*, T 48-1012, just off Av Jorge Dimitrov, 69 rooms in spread out villas, patio garden, fridge, basic shower room, TV, a/c, also 2 suites, **A3**, good security, car rental, large pool, *El Pétalo* disco, popular; in the centre are D *Turquino*, T 46-2124 on Martí, 40 rooms with bath, TV, basic; and 3 peso hotels, *Santiago, Praga* and *Majestic*, which only occasionally take foreigners and have little to recommend them. Famous guests at the *Majestic* in the 1950s included Fidel Castro in room 13 and the Mexican singer Jorge Negrete, but now it is more of a short-stay hotel, painted red.

● **Places to eat**

There are several *paladares. Aurora*, on Martí, has a good reputation and is popular; *Jelly Boom*, also on Martí, near the cemetery, is supposed to be the best in town; ask around for others as they change quickly; *Pizzería Roma* on Maceo with Agramonte at the corner of

Parque Céspedes, is state-run; *La Begonia*, is a *cafetería* on the Plaza Central, outdoors under a flowering creeper, very pretty.

● **Post & telecommunications**

The Post Office is on Maceo, opp Parque Céspedes. DHL is on Libertad, opp Plaza Central, open Mon-Fri 1000-1200, 1300-1600, alternate Sats 0800-1500. Telecorreos on Plaza Central charges US$5.85/min to Europe, US$3/min to North America, minimum 4 mins, for phone calls. For a fax you have to go to *Hotel Pernik*, where they charge a commission of US$1.

● **Transport**

There is very little motorized public transport. The city is choked with *bicitaxis*, bicycles with an extra wheel and seat on the side, or cart behind, or horse drawn buses and taxis, charging 50-80 centavos. Out of town people wait at junctions for the *Amarillos* (traffic wardens dressed in yellow) to stop any truck or large vehicle and bundle on as many passengers as possible. The interurban bus terminal, notable for the number of horses, rather than vehicles, is on Av de los Libertadores after the coffee roasting plant and opp the turning to Estadio Calixto García. The interprovincial bus terminal is W of the centre on Carretera Central.

Air Frank País international airport (HOG), 8 km from the centre, receives direct scheduled flights from Amsterdam (Martinair), Dusseldorf (LTU), Buenos Aires and Montevideo (Cubana), while others connect through Havana. There are also charter flights from other cities which vary according to the season. There are domestic flights from Havana and Varadero.

Train Holguín is on the Havana-Santiago line (see Havana, **Transport**).

GUARDALAVACA

Guardalavaca has been developed as a tourist resort along a beautiful stretch of coastline, indented with horseshoe bays and sandy beaches. The resort is in two sections: the older part is rather like a village, apartments for workers are here and there are a few shops, discos, bank, restaurant and bus stop, while two newer hotels further W on the beach Estero Ciego (also referred to as Playa Esmeralda), are very isolated and there is nothing to do outside the hotels. Nevertheless, Estero Ciego beach is idyllic, a very pretty

horseshoe shape with a river coming down to the sea in the middle and rocks at either end providing good snorkelling opportunities. There is a reef offshore for diving, which is very unspoilt and has a lot to offer. The hills surrounding the beach are green and wooded, helping to make the two Sol hotels here unobtrusive. Further W, Playa Pesquero is visited by tour parties on a boat excursion and is mostly empty, although it fills up with Cubans on holiday in July/August. It is a lovely sandy beach, the E end is better for children as there are strong currents and deceptive sand bars to the W. There is a lifeguard on duty even out of season. There are plans to build a hotel here with Italian investment. The tour desks in the hotels have lots of excursions on offer along the coast or inland, even to Santiago de Cuba. Alternatively you can hire a car, scooter or bike, or contract a local private driver to take you wherever you want, eg to Gibara for US$25 return with the option of having a meal with a Cuban family. Private operators can not pick you up from your hotel, so you have to meet in the Centro Comercial or on the main road.

A few km from Guardalavaca on a hill with a wonderful view, is the **Museo Aborigen Chorro de Maita**, a small but well-presented museum displaying a collection of 56 skeletons dating from 1490-1540, exactly as they were found. One is of a young Spaniard, but the rest are Amerindians, buried in the Central American style, lying flat with their arms folded across their stomachs. Open Tues-Sat 0900-1700, Sun 0900-1300, US$1 per photo, plus US$5 per film, small shop with souvenirs.

Local information
● **Accommodation**

Delta Las Brisas opened 1994 and became all-inclusive 1996, sea view or inland rooms all same price, 3 restaurants, non-motorized watersports inc, small man-made beach, nice pool, organized entertainment, good sized rooms and bathrooms, TV, phone, a/c, safety box, family rooms with garden; **A1-A2** *Atlántico*, T 30180/30280, F 30200, on beach, 233 rather small rooms with shower, adequate but nothing special for the price, parts under renovation 1997, shops, pool, tennis, long dark corridors; **A1** *Villa Turey*, opp bus stop, not on beach, spread out villas and apartments around pool, 136 rooms, 3 suites (with 2 bedrooms, 2 bathrooms upstairs, sitting room, kitchenette and toilet downstairs), large rooms, cupboards, TV, safe box, balconies, 2 restaurants, shop, short walk to beach through other hotels; **A2-A3** *Guardalavaca*, T 30121, F 24-30145 (in Holguín), 234 smallish rooms, TV, basic bathroom, shower, outside a/c, restoration 1996/97; along the coast at Estero Ciego are the best hotels in the area, *Sol Río de Luna* (all-inclusive) and sister hotel next door, **L3-A3** *Sol Río de Mares*, upmarket, half board only, most people on discounted packages, comfortable, open, well-designed for ventilation, not so good when it rains, pool, restaurants, bars, organized entertainment, some of it excruciatingly embarrassing, lovely beach, diving and other watersports, shade, sunbeds US$2.

● **Places to eat**
El Cayuelo, short walk along coast from *Las Brisas*, good for lobster. Most hotel restaurants in the hotels offer buffet meals which get very dull after a few days. There are restaurants in the Centro Comercial but no *paladares* in the area.

● **Watersports**
There are dive shops on the beach near the *Atlántico* and the *Sol Río de Mares*, offering courses and fun dives. The *Sea Lovers Diving Centre* at the latter hotel has dives at 0900 and 1400 (US$30, US$140/5 dives, equipment US$10 or US$35/5 dives), and snorkelling trips at 1100 (US$8, plus US$5 for equipment), several good dive sites on the reef offshore, can be rough at certain times of the year, no dock so you have to swim and carry tank and gear out to boat. Good, well-maintained equipment and safety record. Safety not so good with other watersports, where life-jackets are not always offered or worn. The lifeguard on duty is not always in his chair. Hobie cats US$10/hr, windsurfers and kayaks US$5/hr, pedalo bikes US$2/hr. The lagoon in the Bahía de Naranjo is being developed as a small marina, sailing trips and fishing expeditions can be arranged. Near the mouth of the lagoon is an aquarium, 10 mins by boat from the dock, with dolphins and a sea lion, and a restaurant. An evening excursion, US$45, inc dolphin show, extra US$8 to swim with the dolphins, lobster supper and an Afro-Cuban show.

On the road from Holguín to Baracoa is the small town of **Mayarí** on the river of the same name. Inland and up in the hills the soil turns to a deep red; known as *mocarrero*, it is 85% iron. Visit the scientific station at the **Jardín de Pinare National Park**. There are trails in the park through 12 different eco-systems. The **Salto de Guayabo** is 85m high, one of the highest waterfalls in Cuba, and there is a tremendous view across the fall, down the valley to the Bahía de Nipe. In Feb 1997 a forest fire destroyed more than 100 ha of pine forest in the Mayarí Arriba area. Seek local information on where to walk.

● **Accommodation** *Pinares de Mayarí*, rustic timber and stone, isolated, pool, nature trails, pine trees, lake, 25 rooms, restaurant, bar, billiards, horse riding.

SANTIAGO DE CUBA

Santiago de Cuba, near the E end of the island, 970 km from Havana and 670 km from Santa Clara, is Cuba's second city and 'capital moral de la Revolución Cubana'. It is a pleasant colonial Caribbean city, with many balconies and *rejas* (grills), for instance on Calles Aguilera and Félix Pena. The **Cathedral**, dating from 1522, is on the S side of Parque Céspedes, entrance on Félix Pena, open 0800-1200 daily, services Mon, Wed 1830, Sat 1700, Sun 0900, 1830. The national hero, José Martí, is buried in Santa Ifigenia cemetery, just W of the city.

Museums
Of the several museums, the best is the **Museo de Ambiente Histórico Cubano** located in Diego de Velázquez' house (the oldest in Cuba, started by Cortés in 1516, completed 1530), at the NW corner of Parque Céspedes. It has been restored after its use as offices after the Revolution and is in two parts, one 16th century, one 18th century. Each room shows a particular period; there is also a 19th-century extension. Open Mon-Sat 0900-1700, Sun 0900-1300, US$1, with guided tour in English or German. Two blocks E of the

Parque, opposite the Palacio Provincial is the **Museo Emilio Bacardí** (exhibits from prehistory to the Revolution downstairs, paintings upstairs), open Tues-Sat 0900-2000, Sun 0900-1300, US$2, T 2-8240. Visit the **Museo Histórico 26 de Julio**, Av Moncada esq General Portuondo, open Mon-Sat 0800-1800, Sun 0800-1200, US$1. Formerly the Moncada Garrison, it was attacked (unsuccessfully) by Castro and his revolutionaries on 26 July 1953. When the revolution triumphed in 1959, the building was turned into a school. To mark the 10th anniversary of the attack, one of the buildings was converted to a museum, featuring photos, plans and drawings of the battle. Bullet holes, filled in by Batista, have been reconstructed on the outer walls. The **Museo Casa Natal de Frank País** (General Banderas 226), is in the birthplace of the leader of the armed uprising in Santiago on 30 November 1956, who was shot in July 1957. The **Museo de la Lucha Clandestina** has an exhibition of the citizens' underground struggle against the dictatorship. It was originally the residence of the Intendente, then was a police HQ. It is at the top of picturesque Calle Padre Pico (steps), corner of Santa Rita, and affords good views of the city (T 2-4689). Open 0900-1700 Tues-Sun, US$1. Another historical site is the huge ceiba tree in the grounds of the *Motel San Juan* (formerly *Leningrado* hotel), beneath which Spain and the USA signed the surrender of Santiago on 16 July 1898; at the Loma de San Juan nearby are more monuments of the Hispano-Cuban-American war (only worth visiting if staying at the *San Juan*, or going to the zoo and amusement park behind the hotel).

Excursions

The Ruta Turística runs along the shore of the Bahía de Santiago to the Castillo del Morro, a clifftop fort with the **Museo de la Piratería**, a museum of the sea, piracy and local history (open Tues-Sun 0900-1800, T 9-1569). Recommended, even if only for the view. Turistaxi to El Morro,

US$10 round trip with wait. Transport along the road passes the ferry at Ciudadmar to the resorts of **Cayo Granma** and La Socapa in the estuary (hourly, 5 cents each way). Cayo Granma was originally Cayo Smith, named after its wealthy owner; it became a resort for the rich. Now most of its 600 inhabitants travel to Santiago to work. There are no vehicles; there is a fish restaurant and bar (try the house speciality in the restaurant) in an idyllic setting looking across the bay towards Santiago.

Excellent excursions can be made to the **Gran Piedra** (32 km E) a viewpoint from which it is said you can see Haiti and Jamaica on a clear day, more likely their lights on a clear night. It is a giant rock weighing 75,000 tonnes, 1,234m high, reached by climbing 454 steps from the road ('only for the fit'). Santiago-La Gran Piedra buses are no use because daily buses leave La Gran Piedra early morning and return in the evening (the *Turismo Buró* in any hotel will arrange a tour, good value). 2 km before La Gran Piedra are the **Jardines de la Siberia**, on the site of a former coffee plantation, an extensive botanical garden; turn right and follow the track for about 1 km to reach the gardens. The **Museo Isabelica** is 2 km past La Gran Piedra (Carretera de la Gran Piedra Km 14), a ruined coffee plantation, the buildings of which are now turned into a museum (open daily 0800-1600, US$1) housing the former kitchen and other facilities on the ground floor. Upstairs is the owners' house in authentic 19th-century style. On view in the ground floor are instruments of slave torture. After the slave revolt in Haiti, large numbers of former slave owners were encouraged to settle in the Sierra de la Gran Piedra. This influx led to the impact of Haitian/French culture on Santiago, especially in music. Here they built 51 *cafetales*, using slave labour. During the Ten Years War (1868-78) the revolutionaries called for the destruction of all the *cafetales*. The owner, Victor Constantin Cuzeau, named the plantation after his

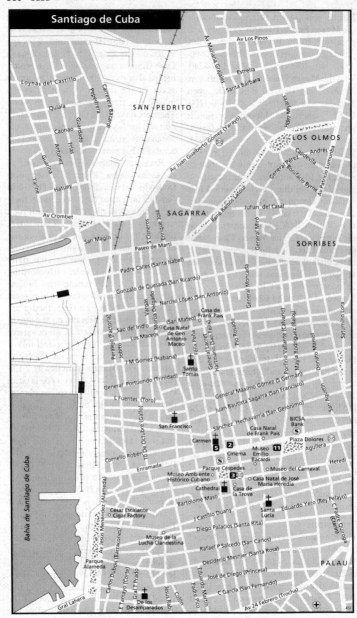

Santiago de Cuba

Av Los Pinos

Loynas del Castillo

Quiala

Caonao

Guardado

Antúnez

Frías

Guarina

Yarine

Hatuey

Estrella

Santa Bárbara

SAN-PEDRITO

Carretera Central (Av Libertadores)

Pepedrera

Av Juan Gualberto Gómez (Yarayó)

Hdez Mayarte

Candelva

Andrés

LOS OLMOS

General Pérez

Bonifacio Byrne

Av Patricio Lumumba

General Miró

Julián del Casal

René Ramón Latour

SORRIBES

SAGARRA

Av Crombet

San Maún

Paseo de Marti

San Cisneros

Enrique José

General Moncada

Padre Calles (Santa Isabel)

Gonzalo de Quesada (San Ricardo)

Narciso Lópes (San Antonio)

Casa de Frank País

Vargas

Morúa Delgado

(San Mateo)

Casa Natal de Gen Antonio Maceo

Sao del Indio

Los Maceos

Perralejo (Factoría)

Jobito

Félix Peña

General Lacret

Hartmann (San Félix)

Pío Rosado

Porfirio Vallante (Calvario)

Mayía Rodríguez (Reloj)

Donato Mármol

Saturnino Lora

J M Gómez (Habana)

Santo Tomás

General Portuondo (Trinidad)

General Máximo Gómez (S Germán)

San Agustín

L Fuentes (Toro)

Juan Bautista Sagarra (San Francisco)

10 De Octubre (Gallo)

San Francisco

Sánchez Hechavarría (San Gerónimo)

Casa Natal de Frank País

BICSA Bank

Plaza Dolores

Carmen

5

2

Cinema

Aguilera

Heredi

Cornelio Robén

Museo Emilio Bacardí

11

Enramada

Parque Céspedes

Museo del Carnaval

Museo Ambiente Histórico Cubano

3

Casa Natal de José María Heredia

Cathedral

Casa de la Trova

Bartolomé Masó

Santa Lucía

Eduardo Yero (Rey Pelayo)

C Padre Quiroga (Sta Ana)

Av Jesús Menéndez (Alameda)

Bahía de Santiago de Cuba

César Escalante Cigar Factory

J Castillo Duany

Diego Palacios (Santa Rita)

Rafael P Salcedo (San Carlos)

Museo de la Lucha Clandestina

Desiderio Mesnier (Santa Rosa)

José de Diego (Princesa)

PALAU

Parque Alameda

Carlos Dubois (Corte)

E Tamayo (Corte)

Gral T Prado

Jesús Rabí

Colón

Padre Pico

Eduardo Martín

C García (San Fernando)

De los Desamparados

Gral Lahera

Av 24 Febrero (Trocha)

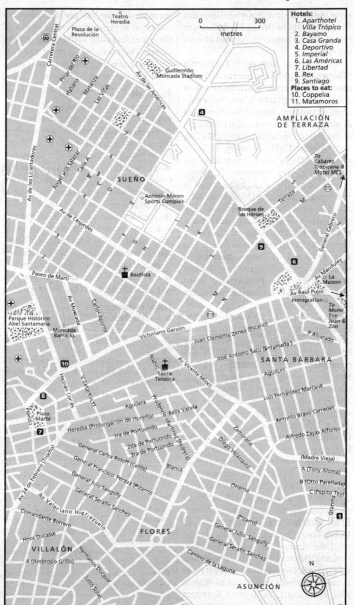

Teatro Heredia

Plaza de la Revolución

Carretera Central

Av de las Américas

Guillermón Moncada Stadium

0   300

metres

Hotels:
1. *Aparthotel Villa Trópico*
2. *Bayamo*
3. *Casa Granda*
4. *Deportivo*
5. *Imperial*
6. *Las Américas*
7. *Libertad*
8. *Rex*
9. *Santiago*

Places to eat:
10. *Coppelia*
11. *Matamoros*

Pinar del Río

Habana

Matanza

Las Villas

Av de los Libertadores

Ángel de Salazar

Calle K

J

SUEÑO

Antonio Maceo Sports Complex

Av de Céspedes

H

G

Paseo de Martí

Bautista

AMPLIACIÓN DE TERRAZA

To Cabaret Tropicana & Motel MES

Terraza

Bosque de los Héroes

General Cebreco

M

S

9

6

Av Manduley

La Maison

Av Raúl Pujol

Immigration

To Motel Faro Juan & Zoo

Parque Histórico Abel Santamaría

Moncada Barracks

Carlos Aponte

Av Moncada

Victoriano Garzón

Juan Clemente Zenea (Escario)

P Alvarado

José Antonio Saco (Enramada)

SANTA BÁRBARA

Aguilera

10

Hernán Cortés

Villalón

Plaza Marté

Av 24 de Febrero (Trocha)

8

7

Nibane

Santa Teresita

Av Vicente Miret

Patricio Lumumba (Trinidad)

Heredia (Prolongación de Heredia)

1ra de Portuondo

2da de Portuondo

3ra de Portuondo (Padre)

Félix Varela

Aguilera

Zamorana

Luis Fernández Marcané

Antonio Bravo Carreasa

Alfredo Zayas Alfonso

(Madre Vieja)

A (Tony Aloma)

B (Otto Parellada)

C (Pepito Tey)

General Carlos Roloff (Celda)

General Francisco Peraza (Pizarro)

General Julio Sanguily

General Serafín Sánchez

Av Valeriano Hierrezuelo

Comandante Borrero

Hnos Ducasse

Blanca

Diego Velázquez

Oriente

(Pizarro)

General Julio Sanguily

General Serafín Sánchez

Granma

1

FLORES

VILLALÓN

A (Ambrosio Grillo)

Hermanos Ducasse

Justo Solar

Camino de la Laguna

ASUNCIÓN

N

45r

lover and house slave, but when Céspedes freed the slaves he fled and Isabelica was thrown by the former slaves into a burning oven.

13½ km E of Santiago is **La Granja Siboney**, the farmhouse used as the headquarters for the revolutionaries' attack on the Moncada barracks. It now has a museum of uniforms, weapons and artefacts as well as extensive newspaper accounts of the attack (open Tues-Sun 0900-1700, T 9836, entry US$1). **Siboney**, 16 km E of the city is the nearest beach to Santiago, pleasant and unpretentious (D cabins, private rooms to rent and *paladares*, all in US$), mostly frequented by Cubans. Take bus 214 from near bus terminal. Very crowded at weekends. Even nicer is **Juraguá** beach, bus 207, along the same road; further development is projected in this area. Further E is **Parque Bacanao**, a wonderful amusement park in which you can visit **El Valle Prehistórico** (with lifesize replicas of dinosaurs), an old car and trailer museum (free, recommended). There are no buses to Parque Bacanao; a private car hired for a whole day will cost about US$50. Beyond the Parque, on the coast, is an aquarium/dolphinarium, US$3, rec. **Daiquirí** beach at Km 25 is beautiful and quiet and the resort there was due to re-open Summer 1997, entrance US$2 if not staying the night. A3 *Daiquirí* (Cubanacán), T 24849/24724, 150 rooms, 3-star, takes Visa; also C cabins, bookable in any hotel or agency in Santiago.

10 mins from the centre of Santiago there is a rum factory, open to visitors, but you can only go in the bar, the factory is closed to visitors since tourists 'stole' the technology by taking too many photos. From Santiago, it is possible to visit **El Cobre** where the shrine of Cuba's patron saint, the Virgen de la Caridad del Cobre, is located (there is a very cheap *hospedería* for pilgrims, but tourists can stay if there is room, payment in pesos, and reasonable restaurant). Built over a copper mine, there is a moving shrine set up by

the relatives of the 'raft' people. Interesting collection of personal offerings at foot of the statue, including a gold model of Fidel Castro. There is no bus, so either hire a car and driver, about US$10, or get on a truck at the bus station for a few pesos.

Festivals

The *Festival de Caribe* begins in the first week in July with theatre, dancing and conferences, and continues later in July to coincide with the Moncada celebrations on 26 July. The Carnival, already in full swing by then (as it was in 1953, the date carefully chosen to catch Batista's militia drunk and off-guard and use the noise of the carnival to drown the sound of gunfire), traditionally stops for a day of more serious celebration, then continues on 27 July. Carnival is 18-29 July, taking in Santiago's patron saints day, 25 July. This carnival is regaining its former glory and is well worth seeing. Visit the **Carnival Museum** on Calle Heredia to get the feel of it.

Local information
● **Accommodation**

L3 *Hotel Santiago*, Av Las Américas y M, T 4-2612/2654, F 4-1756, 5-star, clean, good service, excellent breakfast buffet US$7, good *La Cubana* restaurant, highly rec, open 1200-2100, swimming pool, tennis, sauna, discotheque, has post office and will change almost any currency into dollars.

A1 *Casa Granda* on Parque Céspedes, T 86600, F 86035, fax service, laundry, car hire, satellite TV, nanny service, post office, disabled access, Havanatur office, excellent central location with terrace bar overlooking park, has a café, open 2000-0300, good.

B *Balcón del Caribe*, next to Castillo del Morro, T 9-1011, overlooking the sea, quiet, pool, basic food, cold water in bungalows, pleasant but inconvenient for the town; **B** *Las Américas* (Horizontes), T 4-2011, F 86075, Av de las Américas y Gen Cebreco, easy bus/truck access to centre, private cars around bus stop in plaza opp hotel, lively, restaurant, discotheque, non-residents may use swimming pool, bicycle hire; **B** *Motel San Juan*, Km 1 Carretera a Siboney, T 4-2434, too far out of town, turistaxi US$3.95, private car US$2, a complex with cabins, very nice rooms, large and clean, no hot water, pool, bar and several restaurants, high quality by Cuban standards, accepts pesos, queues at weekends and during festivals; **B** *Villa* (Gaviota), Av Manduley 502, entre 19 y 21, Reparto Vista Alegre, T 41368, 3-star, car hire, tourist office, nearby pool for guests, quiet.

C *MES*, Calle L esq 7, Reparto Terrazas (about 5 blocks N of *Las Américas*), T 4-2398, TV and fan, 2 rooms share bath and fridge.

E *Imperial*, Saco 251, T 48917, basic, central; **E** *Libertad* on Plaza Marte, T 23080, good central location, good value if slightly downmarket, very noisy fans.

Private accommodation available for about US$10-15; touts around Parque Céspedes, also near all hotels.

● **Places to eat**
The hotels have restaurants and mostly serve buffet meals. 3 restaurants (*Matamoros* is the collective name) on Plaza Dolores (known as Búlevar locally), Italian, Chinese and creole food. Lots of good *paladares* around Calles Heredia and Aguilera, and in Reparto Vista Alegre, near the hotels *Santiago*, *Las Américas* and *San Juan*. *Mujeres de Arena*, Félix Pena 554 entre Aguilera y Enramada, main dish US$3-7, side dishes extra, simple décor but food delicious and nicely presented, open all the time; *Paladar Mireya*, Padre Pico 368-A, Frente a la Escalinata, US$5-6 inc rice and salad, open 1200-2400, in smokey back room; *El Balcón*, Independencia 253, Reparto Sueño, T 2-7407, good food, US$3, open 24 hrs, popular with locals; *Terrazas*, Calle 5 50 entre M y Terraza, Ampliación de Terraza, T 4-1491, 1000-2400, tasty food, rec.

● **Banks & money changers**
Possible to get US dollar cash advance on Visa at **Banco Financiero Internacional**, corner of Parque Céspedes and Aguilera. **BICSA**, is on Enramada opp Plaza Dolores.

● **Entertainment**
Club Tropicana Santiago, local version of Havana show, on Autopista Nacional Km 1.5, T 43036/43610, open until 0300, book in any hotel. *Casa de la Trova*, Calle Heredia 206 around the corner from *Casa Granda*, 2 daily shows of traditional music, morning and evening, open until 2400, US$1, nice venue. Lively nightly disco in *Santiago* and *Las Américas* hotels.

● **Shopping**
Casa de la Artesanía, under the cathedral in Parque Céspedes, open 0800-1730. Handicraft shop also on Lacret 724.

● **Post & telecommunications**
Post office: main Post Office is on Aguilera y Clarín, near Plaza Marte.

Telephones: for calls outside Santiago, Centro de Comunicaciones Nacional e Internacional, Heredia y Félix Pena, underneath the cathedral.

● **Transport**
Train Book tickets in advance in LADIS office on Aguilera near Plaza Marte. Terminal at N end of Malecón, new terminal being built further N, supposed to be finished by end-1997. Train travel is not as reliable or comfortable as bus travel. Take sweater for Havana journey, freezing a/c. Daily to Manzanillo 0545, US$8; Camagüey 0855, US$13; Havana 1635, US$35.

Bus Terminal near Plaza de la Revolución at the top of Av Libertadores. Arrive 1 hr before departure, jump queue paying in dollars, buy ticket in office before boarding. To **Moa**, 0700, US$9; **Manzanillo/Niquero/Bayamo**, 0720, US$7.50; **Baracoa**, 0640, US$9; **Guantánamo** (Baracoa bus), US$3. Also trucks available at terminal to most destinations, drivers shout destination prior to departure, pay in pesos. Urban buses run until about 0100, 20 centavos, truck 1 peso.

Taxis *Cubataxi*, T 51038, are the cheapest (name on windscreen). Motorbike transport can be arranged at Plaza Marte for about US$1.

GUANTANAMO

80 km from Santiago on the Baracoa road, Guantánamo is close to the US base of the same name (which cannot be easily visited from Cuba). Peter Hope, Public Relations Officer, can arrange tours to Mt Malones, where you can view the US base through Soviet binoculars. He also arranges a tour of the city and environs, including a traditional Haitian dance show (*La Tumba Francesa*) and lunch on a farm with *Son* music show; tour to Baracoa also available. He speaks English, German and French and is based in room 117, *Hotel Guantánamo*, Mon-Sat.

● **Accommodation C** *Guantánamo*, Plaza Mariana Grajales, T 3-6015, pool, 2 bars, food average, clean, a/c, bar and restaurant, telephone service to Havana and beyond.

● **Transport** Private cars run from the train and bus station to *Hotel Guantánamo*/town centre, US$1.

BARACOA

150 km E of Santiago, close to the most easterly point of the island, is an attractive place surrounded by rich, tropical vegetation. It is the wettest region in Cuba with annual rainfall of 2m in the coastal zone to 3.6m in the middle and upper Toa Valley. White water rafting is possible down the Río Toa, with different levels of difficulty. It is well worth the trip from Santiago (4 hrs drive) for the scenery of the last section of road, called La Farola, which winds through lush tropical mountains and then descends steeply to the coast. In the church you can see a cross said to have been planted there by Columbus in 1492.

Excursions Rent a private car (US$10) or take a colectivo taxi E to the Río Yumurí where the road ends. A canoe will ferry you across or take you upriver for US$1. You can continue walking upriver and swim, very quiet and peaceful. 25 km N of Baracoa is Maguana, where there is a beach and a hotel, 1 hr on unpaved road in private car, US$10.

● **Accommodation** B *El Castillo*, Calixto García, Loma del Paraíso, T 214-2103/2115, 35 a/c rooms with bath, phone, TV in lobby lounge, rec, friendly staff, food OK, excellent views, highly rec breakfast; **A1-B** *Porto Santo*, T 214-3578/3590, 36 rooms, 24 cabañas or suites, a/c, bath, restaurant, bar, shop, beautiful swimming pool, car hire, next to airport, beach, peaceful atmosphere, friendly, highly rec, speak to Wilder Laffita, Public Relations Officer, to organize day trips, many available inc beautiful local rivers, mountains and beaches; **C-D** *La Rusa* (Islazul), on the Malecón, Máximo Gómez 13, T 4-3011, e-mail islazul@gtmo.cu, basic, food OK, nice location, good *paladar* opp. Private accommodation easily arranged, ask in Parque Central in front of church.

● **Places to eat** Lots of *paladares*. One of the best is *Walter's*, on Rubén López 47, T 4-3380.

● **Entertainment Casa de la Trova**, Tues-Sun from 2100, US$1, the place where all the young of Baracoa go, near church, ask in square, good *son* and friendly atmosphere.

● **Transport Air** Airport next to *Hotel Porto Santo*. Cubana flight to Havana Tues, Fri, to

Santiago Sun, 1200. Cubana office on Martí 181, T 4-2171. **Bus** Main bus terminal at the end of Martí near Av de los Mártires, T 4-2239, 4-3670, for buses to Havana, Santiago, Camagüey. Trucks to other destinations from 2nd bus terminal on Coroneles Galana.

Guardalavaca (see page 577) on the N coast is a lovely drive through the mountains from Santiago. Take a day driving to Frente II (eat at *Rancho México*), down to Sagua and across to Guardalavaca. You can stay at Don Lino beach, which is small but pleasant, where there are comfortable huts (US$14) with refrigerator for cooling beer. Restaurant food is basic.

West from Santiago runs a wonderful coastal road along the **Sierra Maestra** with beautiful bays and beaches, completely deserted, some with black sand. It is only possible to visit by car. At **La Plata**, about 150 km from Santiago in the mountains, is a little museum about the Cuban guerrillas' first successful battle. There is no curator so ask the local people to open it. En route you pass **Las Coloradas**, the beach where *Granma* landed. You can make a circular route back to Santiago via **Manzanillo** (C *Hotel Guacanayabo* (Islazul), on Circunvalación Camilo Cienfuegos, T 54812, a/c, pool, noisy poolside disco, mostly Cuban guests), **Bayamo** (both in Granma province; in Bayamo B *Hotel Sierra Maestra*, Av Gen Manuel Cedeño, Km 7½, on Santiago road, T 48-1013, a/c, bath, restaurant, pool and other usual facilities, guided tour of the revolutionaries' bases and routes, inc Comandancia de la Plata, in the mountains) and **Palma Soriano**.

WEST FROM HAVANA

The western end of the island is dominated by the Cordillera de Guaniguanico. The eastern end of the range, known as the Sierra del Rosario, contains the Pan de Guajaibón, at 699m its highest point. UNESCO has classified 20,000 ha as a Biosphere Reserve covering an area of mesophytic tropical forest with over

50 bird species and several reptiles, including a water lizard found only in the Sierra del Rosario.

West from Havana a dual carriage highway has been completed almost to **Pinar del Río**, the major city W of Havana. The province of Pinar del Río produces Cuba's best cigars.

SOROA

If travelling by car on this route, you can make a detour to **Soroa** in the Sierra del Rosario, 81 km SW of the capital. It is a spa and resort in luxuriant hills. As you drive into the area, a sign on the right indicates the **Mirador de Venus** and **Baños Romanos**. Past the baths is the *Bar Edén* (open till 1800), where you can park before walking up to the Mirador (25 mins). From the top you get fine views of the southern plains, the palm-covered Sierra and the tourist complex itself; lots of birds, butterflies, dragonflies and lizards around the path; many flowers in season.

The road continues into the complex where there is an orchidarium with over 700 species (check if they are in bloom before visiting, guided tours between 0830-1140, 1340-1555 daily, US$2) and the *Castillo de las Nubes* restaurant (1200-1900, entrées US$5-6), a mock castle. Across the road from the orchidarium is a waterfall (250m, paved path, entry US$1), worth a visit if you are in the area.

- **Accommodation** At the resort, **B** *Horizontes Villa Soroa*, T 82-2122, 49 cabins and 10 houses, a/c, phone, radio, TV, VCR, some have private pool, restaurant *El Centro* (quite good), disco, bar, Olympic swimming pool, bike rental, riding nearby and handicrafts and dollar shops. Despite the ugly, gloomy cabins, it's a peaceful place and would be more so without the loud juke box.

Nearer Pinar del Río another detour N off the main road is to the spa of **San Diego de los Baños**, also in fine scenery in the Sierra de los Organos.

PINAR DEL RIO

The city has many neoclassical villas with columns, but is not especially interesting for tourists.

- **Accommodation** At the E entrance to the city is the **C** *Hotel Pinar del Río*, Calle Martí final, T 5070-7, slow reception, swimming pool, nightclub etc; **D** *Cabañas Aguas Claras*, T 2722, 6 km N on road to Viñales, chalets in landscaped garden around (unchlorinated?) pool, hot showers, chicken US$5 but tastier than most, excellent value, rec.

- **Places to eat** The state-run *Rumayor*, 1 km on Viñales road, specializes in *pollo ahumado* (smoked chicken), overpriced at US$6.50, grim toilets, open 1200-2200, closed Thur, cabaret at night, US$5.

- **Transport** For travel to Pinar del Río, train from Havana's Estación 19 de Noviembre/del Occidente, rather than bus, is recommended (leaves Havana 0500, book 1300 day before, leaves Pinar del Río 1702, 8 hrs); slow but comfortable. Shared taxi from Havana US$4 pp.

VIÑALES

North of Pinar del Río, on a road which leads to the N coast and eventually back to Havana is **Viñales**, a delightful small town in a dramatic valley. Stands of palm and tobacco fields with their drying barns (*vegas*, steep, thatch-roofed buildings which you can enter and photograph with ease) lie amid sheer and rounded mountains (*mogotes*) reminiscent of a Chinese landscape, especially at dawn and dusk. These massifs were part of a cave system which collapsed millions of years ago and, on some, remnants of stalactites can still be seen.

Viñales itself is a pleasant town, with trees and wooden colonnades along the main street, red tiled roofs and a main square with a little-used cathedral and a Casa de Cultura with art gallery.

Excursions 2 km N is the **Mural de la Prehistoria**, painted by Lovigildo González, a disciple of the Mexican Diego Rivera, between 1959 and 1976; tourist restaurant nearby. 6 km beyond Viñales is the **Cueva del Indio** which can be approached from two ends, neither far apart. Inside, though, you can travel the cave's length on foot and by boat (US$3 for foreigners), very beautiful. There is a restaurant at the cave (also at a smaller cave nearer Viñales) where tour parties are given a huge lunch of suckling pig (*lechón*).

● **Accommodation** **A3-B** *Los Jazmines* (Horizontes), Carretera de Vinales Km 25, 3 km before the town, in a superb location with travel brochure view of the valley, T 89-3205/6, 62 nice rooms and 16 *cabañas*, nightclub, unexciting restaurant, bar with snacks available, shops, (unchlorinated?) swimming pool, riding, easy transport, highly rec; **B-C** *Horizontes La Ermita*, Carretera de la Ermita Km 2, 3 km from town with magnificent view, T 89-3204, 62 rooms, a/c, phone, radio, shop, tennis court, wheelchair access, pool (not always usable), food not bad, rec as beautiful, the farmers in the valley below are friendly and hospitable, they may invite you for a meal of their own fruit and vegetables or offer a home grown cigar; **B** *Horizontes Rancho San Vicente*, Valle de San Vicente, near Cueva del Indio, T 89-3200, 34 rooms in a/c cabañas, bar, restaurant, nightclub, shop, tourist information desk, nice pool, pleasant. Book your hotel before you arrive as everywhere is often full.

● **Places to eat** *Paladar Restaurant*, or *Valle Bar*, T 93183, on the main street, small, friendly, rec, music, can find you local accommodation with private families.

● **Transport** Turistaxi from Havana to *Motel Los Jazmines* takes $2\frac{1}{2}$ hrs, there may be a bus back to the capital, $3\frac{1}{2}$ hrs. Tour buses from Havana will drop you off if you want to stay more than a day and collect you about 1600 on the day you want to return.

Offshore, N of Viñales is **Cayo Levisa**, part of the Archipiélago de los Colorados, with a long, sandy beach and reef offshore with good snorkelling and scuba diving (lots of fish). One small hotel, *Cayo Levisa* (Gran Caribe) with 20 cabins, a/c, restaurant, bar, shop, waterskiing, windsurfing and sailing.

VINALES TO HAVANA

From Viñales to Havana along the coast road takes about 4 hrs by car. It is an attractive drive through sugar and tobacco plantations, pines, the mountains inland, the coast occasionally visible. All the small houses have flower gardens in front. You pass through **La Palma**, **Las Pozas** (which has a ruined church with a boring new one beside it), **Bahía Honda** and **Cabañas**; many agricultural collectives along the way. After Cabañas the road deteriorates; either rejoin the motorway back to the capital, or take the old coast road through the port of **Mariel** to enter Havana on Av 5.

Near Mariel is **El Salado** beach, small, secluded, with calm, clear water, although some parts are rocky. Taxi from Havana US$25. There is a reasonably-priced restaurant, part of a small hotel used by German holidaymakers; the hotel has good value tours. Taxis back to Havana can be ordered at the hotel, but you may have to wait.

Marina Hemingway

Off Avenida 5 is the Marina Hemingway tourist complex, in the fishing village of **Santa Fe**. In May and June the marina hosts the annual Ernest Hemingway International Marlin Fishing Tournament and in Aug and Sept the Blue Marlin tournament. The resort includes the hotel *El Viejo y El Mar*, a Canadian-Cuban joint venture, restaurants, bungalows and villas for rent, shopping, watersports, facilities for yachts, sports and a tourist bureau. Building continues for more villas and apartments. Excursions include a day trip to the Castillo del Morro in Old Havana with swimming and lunch (US$30); a snorkelling excursion along the reef W of Havana with equipment and lunch (US$35); by yacht to the beaches E of Havana with swimming and lunch (US$45). Shorter trips available as well as scuba diving and fishing trips, T 33-1909. VHF radio channels 16, 72, or 55B 2790.

● **Accommodation** *El Viejo y El Mar*, Calle 248 y Av 5, Santa Fe, T 33-1150/57, F 33-1149, pleasant enough hotel on seafront but out of the way and nothing to do unless you are busy at the marina, package tourists come here before going off on excursions, small pool, restaurant with buffet meals, lobby bar, clean, bath tub, tricky shower; heading E from the Marina towards Havana there are lots of new hotels going up, with villas, apartments, many in pastel colours with tiled roofs: *Triton, Neptune, Chateau Miramar* (Cubanacán), *Copacabana*, etc, all aimed at package tourism.

● **Places to eat** Several restaurants and a grocery store at the Marina: *La Tasca*; *Pepe's* at the end of the 'dock'; *Fiesta*, Spanish, OK.

THE ISLANDS

In the Gulf of Batabanó is the **Isla de la Juventud** (Isle of Youth), 97 km from the main island, reached by daily Cubana flights or hydrofoil, the *Kometa*. At about 3,050 sq km, it is not much smaller than Trinidad, but its population is only 60,000. It gets its present name from the educational courses run there, particularly for overseas students. Columbus, who landed there in 1494 called the island Evangelista and, until recently, it was called the Isla de Pinos. It was a pirate's haunt and *Treasure Island* by R L Stevenson is believed to have been inspired by its legends. From the 19th century until the Revolution its main function was as a prison and both José Martí and Fidel Castro served time there. It was here that Castro wrote his famous speech ending with the words, "History will absolve me". The prison building is a Panopticon, devised in 1791 by Jeremy Bentham, to give total surveillance and control of its inmates and built by Gerardo Machado in 1932 (closed by Castro in 1967). The building is now decaying but you can wander around the rotundas and guard towers, see the numbered cells and imagine the horrors of incarceration there.

Today the main activities are citrus-growing, fishing and tourism. Cuba's largest known gold deposit is on the island; the Delita property is a gold-silver project expected to start operations in 1998 with Canadian investment. There are several beaches and ample opportunities for water sports. The capital is **Nueva Gerona**. There is a museum in the old Model Prison (El Presidio) and four others. Main tourist hotel is **A2** *El Colony*, 83 rooms, T 98181.

CAYO LARGO

Cayo Largo, E of Isla de la Juventud, is a westernized island resort reached by air from Havana (US$94 day trip) and Varadero, or by light plane or boat from Juventud, or by charter plane from Grand Cayman. Snorkelling and scuba diving can be done at Playa Sirena, 10 mins' boat ride from the hotels. Very tame iguanas can be spotted at another nearby cay, **Cayo Rico** (day-trips available for US$37 from Cayo Largo). Hotel expansion is planned to cater for watersport tourism. **Cayos Rosario** and **Avalos**, between Juventud and Largo, have not yet been developed.

Island information
● **Accommodation**
There are several hotels here at present, all in the Gran Caribe chain, T 79-4215, F 52108, with all facilities shared and included in the package cost (prices quoted are high season per person and include 3 meals and free use of all water sports and other activities). **L3** *Villa Capricho*, 60 rooms in cabañas, **L3** *Isla del Sur*, 62 rooms, **L3** *Pueblito (Villa Coral)*, 72 rooms and suites, **L3** *Hotel y Villa Pelícano*, 144 rooms, and **A2** *Club (Villa Iguana)*, 114 rooms. The hotels and the thatched cabañas are low-lying and pleasantly spread out in gardens by the beach.

● **Places to eat**
There are several restaurants attached to the hotels, including a highly recommended Italian place and a good pizzería. As with many Cuban resort hotels restaurants are run on a self-service buffet basis and food is reported to be plentiful and fresh.

Information for travellers

BEFORE TRAVELLING

● **Documents**

Visitors from the majority of countries need only a tourist card to enter Cuba, as long as they are going solely for tourist purposes. A tourist card may be obtained from Cuban embassies, consulates, airlines, or approved travel agents (price in the UK £10 from the consulate, £12-15 from travel agents, some other countries US$15). From some countries (eg Canada) tourist cards are handed out by the tour operator or on the plane and checked by visa control at the airport; the first one is free but replacements cost US$10. Immigration in Havana airport give you only 30 days on your tourist card. You can get it extended a further 30 days at Immigration in Miramar (see below). Nationals of other countries without visa-free agreement with Cuba, journalists and those visiting on other business must check what visa requirements pertain (in the UK a business visa costs £25, plus US$13 for any telex that has to be sent in connection with the application). The US government does not normally permit its citizens to visit Cuba. US citizens should have a US licence to engage in any transactions related to travel to Cuba, but tourist or business travel are not licensable, even through a third country such as Mexico or Canada. They should contact Marazul Tours, 250 West 57th St, Suite 1311, New York City, 10107 New York, T 212-582 9570, or Miami T 305-232 8157 (information also from *Havanatur*, Calle 2 No 17 Miramar, Havana, T 33-2121/2318). Many travellers do conceal their tracks by going via Mexico,

the Bahamas, or Canada, when only the tourist card is stamped, not the passport. The Cuban Consulate in Mexico City refuses to issue visas unless you have pre-arranged accommodation and book through a travel agent; even then, only tourist visas are available, US$20. In Mérida, a travel agent will arrange your documents so you do not need to go to a Consulate for a visa. In the USA, the Cuban interests section is at 2630 16th St NW, Washington DC 20009, T 202-797 8518, and will process applications for visas. Visas can take several weeks to be granted, and are apparently difficult to obtain for people other than businessmen, guests of the Cuban Government or Embassy officials. However, a British citizen was able to obtain a Tourist Card there in half an hour (US$26, photographs essential). When the applicant is too far from a Cuban consulate to be able to apply conveniently for a visa, he may apply direct to the Cuban Foreign Ministry for a visa waiver.

Visitors travelling on a visa must go in person to the Immigration Office for registration the day after arrival. The office is on the corner of Calle 22 and Av 3, Miramar. When you register you will be given an exit permit.

Travellers coming from or going through infected areas must have certificates of vaccination against cholera and yellow fever.

The Cuban authorities do not insist on stamping your passport in and out but they often do so. They will stamp your tourist card instead if you ask.

US citizens on business with Cuba should contact Foreign Assets Control, Federal Reserve Bank of New York, 33 Liberty St, NY 10045.

● **Airport**

On arrival immigration can be painfully slow if you come off a busy Iberia DC10 flight but speedy off smaller Cubana aircraft. At Havana airport there are taxi dispatchers who can get you in a taxi or minibus for US$12, cheaper than Turistaxi which charges US$15 to the centre on a meter.

● **Customs**

Personal baggage and articles for personal use are allowed in free of duty; so are 200 cigarettes, or 25 cigars, or 1 lb of tobacco, and 2 bottles of alcoholic drinks. Visitors importing new goods worth between US$100 and US$1,000 will be charged 100% duty, subject to a limit of 2 items a year. No duty is payable on goods valued at under US$100. Many things are scarce or unobtainable in Cuba: take in everything you are likely to need other than food (say razor blades, medicines and pills, heavy duty insect repellent, strong sun protection and after-sun preparations, toilet paper, tampons, reading and writing materials, photographic supplies, torch and batteries).

● **Climate**

Northeast trade winds temper the heat. Average summer shade temperatures rise to 33°C (91.4°F) in Havana, and higher elsewhere. In winter, day temperatures drop to 20°C (68°F). Average rainfall is from 860 mm in Oriente to 1,730 mm in Havana; it falls mostly in the summer and autumn, but there can be torrential rains at any time. Hurricanes come in August-November. The best time for a visit is during the cooler dry season (Nov to April). In Havana, there are a few cold days, 8°-10°C (45° 50°F), with a N wind. Walking is uncomfortable in summer but most offices, hotels, leading restaurants and cinemas are air-conditioned. Humidity varies between 75 and 95%.

● **Health**

Sanitary reforms have transformed Cuba into a healthy country, and tap water is generally safe to drink (check if renting privately); bottled and mineral water are recommended. Doctors abroad will advise you to get Hepatitis A and typhoid innoculations.

Medical service is no longer free for foreign visitors in Havana, Santiago de Cuba, and Varadero, where there are international clinics that charge in dollars (credit cards accepted). Visitors requiring medical attention will be sent to them. Emergencies are handled on an ad hoc basis. Check with your national health service or health insurance on coverage in Cuba and take a copy of your insurance policy with you. Remember you can not dial any toll-free numbers abroad so make sure you have a contact number. Charges are generally lower than those charged in Western countries. According to latest reports, visitors are still treated free of charge in other parts of the country, with the exception of tourist enclaves with on-site medical services.

The Cira García Clinic in Havana (Calle 20 No 4101 esq 43, Playa, T 33-2811/14, F 33-1633, payment in dollars) sells prescription and patent drugs and medical supplies that are often unavailable in chemists, as does the Camilo Cien fueqos Pharmacy, L and 13, Vedado, T 33-3599, open daily 0800-2000. Bring all medicines you might need as they can be difficult to find. You might not be offered even a painkiller if you have an accident, as they are in very short supply.

Between May and Oct, the risk of sunburn is high, sun blocks are rec when walking around the city as well as on the beach. In the cooler months, limit beach sessions to 2 hrs.

Always carry toilet paper with you, it is not available in public toilets and even some hotels do not have it.

● **Working in Cuba**

Those interested in joining International Work Brigades should contact Cuba Solidarity Campaign, c/o The Red Rose, 129 Seven Sisters Rd, London N7 7QG, or 119 Burton Rd, London SW9 6TG.

MONEY

● **Currency**

The monetary unit is the peso Cubano. The official exchange rate is US$1=1 peso. Watch out for pre-1962 peso notes, no longer valid. There are notes for 3, 5, 10, and 20 pesos, and coins for 5, 20, and 40 centavos and 1 peso. You must have a supply of 5 centavo coins if you want to use the local town buses (20 centavos, 40 centavos in *ruteros*) or pay phones (very few work). The 20 centavo coin is called a *peseta*. In 1995 the Government introduced a new freely 'convertible peso' at par with the US dollar with a new set of notes and coins. It is fully exchangeable with authorized hard currencies circulating in the economy.

● **Exchange**

As a result of currency reforms the black/street exchange rate has fallen from 130 pesos Cubanos = US$1 in May 1994 to 20 pesos = US$1 in May 1997. Official Casas de Cambio (CADECA) rates fluctuate between 19-22 pesos to the dollar. The 'peso convertible' is equal to the dollar and can be used freely in the country. Cubans are allowed to hold US$ and to have a bank account. There is very little opportunity for foreigners to spend pesos Cubanos unless you are self-catering or travelling off the beaten track and you are advised to change only the absolute minimum, if at all. Food in the markets (*agromercados*), at street stalls, on trains, postcards, stamps and books, popular cigarettes, but not in every shop, can be bought in pesos. Away from tourist hotels, in smaller towns, there are very few dollar facilities and you will need pesos for everything. Visitors on pre-paid package tours are best advised not to acquire any pesos at all. Bring US$ in small denominations for spending money, dollars are now universally preferred. US dollars are the only currency accepted in all tourist establishments.

Travellers' cheques expressed in US or Canadian dollars or sterling are valid in Cuba. TCs issued on US bank paper are not accepted so it is best to take Thomas Cook or Visa. Amex TCs are accepted if issued in Europe. Commission ranges from 2-4%. Don't enter the place or date when signing cheques, or they may be refused.

There are branches of the **Banco Financiero Internacional** and CADECAS (exchange houses) for changing money legally. Non-dollar currencies can be changed into dollars. Visitors have difficulties using torn or tatty US dollar notes.

● **Credit cards**
Credit cards acceptable in most places are Visa, Master, Access, Diners, Banamex (Mexican) and Carnet. No US credit cards accepted so a Visa card issued in the USA will not be accepted. American Express, no matter where issued, is unacceptable. Many restaurants which claim to accept credit cards make such a performance that it is not worthwhile. A master list of stolen and rogue cards is kept at the *Habana Libre* and any transaction over US$50 must be checked there; this can take up to 3 hrs. You can obtain cash with a credit card at branches of the Banco Financiero Internacional, but best to bring plenty of cash as there will often be no other way of paying for what you need.

GETTING THERE

AIR
● **To Havana**
From Europe: Cubana flies from London Gatwick, Berlin, Frankfurt, Brussels, Rome, Lisbon and Paris (also AOM French Airlines), Iberia and Cubana from Barcelona and Madrid (Cubana also from Vitoria and Gran Canaria, Spanair also from Madrid). LTU from Dusseldorf. Cubana and Aeroflot from Moscow. Aeroflot flights continue on to Lima. It is essential to check Aeroflot's flights to make sure there really is a plane going. Since Havana no longer enjoys the close relationship with Moscow that it used to have, these flights are now reported to be increasingly unreliable.

From North America: Cubana from Montréal and Toronto, Cubana and Mexicana de Aviación from Mexico City with Mexicana also from Veracruz via Mérida, AeroCaribe also flies from Oaxaca via Tuxtla Gutierrez, Villahermosa, Mérida and Cancún, Cubana and Mexicana also from Cancún.

From Central and South America: Cubana from Caracas, Cubana and Lacsa from San José, Costa Rica, Mexicana de Aviación and Aviateca from Guatemala City, Cubana from Buenos Aires via Montevideo, São Paulo via Rio de Janeiro, Lima, Mendoza via Santiago de Chile, Cubana, Copa and Tame from Panama; Avianca and Cubana from Bogotá; Cubana from Quito and Guayaquil, Tame from Quito.

From the Caribbean: Cubana flies from Kingston, Jamaica and Fort-de-France and Pointe-à-Pitre in the French Antilles. Air France from Cayenne via Martinique and Guadeloupe. Air Jamaica and Avianca from Montego Bay.

● **To Varadero**
From Europe: Martinair from Amsterdam, Condor from Cologne/Bonn, LTU from Dusseldorf, Condor from Frankfurt, Cubana from London, Air Europe and Spanair from Madrid, AOM from Paris, Cubana from Rome.

From North America: Cubana from Montréal and Toronto. There are charters direct from Vancouver with Air Transat.

From South America: National Airlines Chile from Santiago de Chile via Guayaquil and Cancún, Mexico.

From the Caribbean: Tropical from Montego Bay.

● **To Holguín**
From Europe: Martinair from Amsterdam, LTU from Dusseldorf.

From South America: Cubana from Bogotá and Buenos Aires.

● **To Santiago de Cuba**
From Europe: Cubana from Berlin, Frankfurt, Lisbon, Madrid, Paris, Rome and Vitoria.

From North America: Cubana from Mexico City.

From the Caribbean: Tropical from Montego Bay.

The frequency of these flights depends on the season, with twice weekly flights in the winter being reduced to once a week in the summer. Some of the longer haul flights, such as to Buenos Aires, are cut from once every 2 weeks in winter to once a month in summer. There are charters to Cancún, Mexico, and between Santiago de Cuba and Montego Bay, Jamaica. Regular charters between Cayo Largo and Grand Cayman. Occasional charters between Providenciales, Turks and Caicos Islands and Santiago de Cuba. The Cuban air charter line AeroCaribbean has an arrangement with Bahamasair for a daily service Miami-Nassau-Havana, changing planes in Nassau; the Cuban tourist agency *Amistur* organizes the service. Havanatur has 8 weekly charter flights, 5 to Cancún and 3 to Nassau, in 1997 it inaugurated a flight between Holguín and Nassau. At certain times of year there are special offers available from Europe; enquire at specialist agents. There are also many combinations of flights involving Cuba and Mexico, Venezuela, Colombia and the Dominican Republic; again ask a specialist agent.

Mexicana de Aviación organizes package tours. Several Canadian tour operators have departures from Toronto and Montréal and run package tours to Cuba for all nationalities. Package tours also available from Venezuela, the Bahamas and Jamaica (see **Travel agencies** below).

SEA

See **Shipping** in Introduction and hints for Sprante Shiffahrts regular service from Amsterdam to Cuba. No other passenger ships call regularly.

● **Ports of entry**
Havana, Cienfuegos and Santiago receive tourist cruise vessels. There are several marinas, including the Hemingway, Tarará and Veneciana (in Havana), Acua, Chapelín, Gaviota (in Varadero), and Cayo Largo. Arriving by yacht, announce your arrival on VHF channel 16, 72 or 55B.

ON ARRIVAL

● **Airlines**
All are situated in Havana, at the seaward end of Calle 23 (La Rampa), Vedado: eg Cubana, Calle 23, esq Infanta, T 33-4949/50, F 3-6190; Aeroflot, Calle 23, No 64, T 33-3200/3759, F 33-3288. Iberia, Calle 23, No 74, T 33-5041/2, F 33-5041/2; Mexicana, T 33-3531/2, F 33-3729. Lacsa has an office in the *Habana Libre* which sells tickets for cash only, T 33-3114/3187, F 33-3728. If staying at Old Havana, allow sufficient time if you need to visit an airline office before going to the airport.

● **Clothing**
Generally informal. Summer calls for the very lightest clothing. Sunglasses, sun factor and some kind of head cover rec for those with fair complexions. A jersey and light raincoat or umbrella are needed in the cooler months.

● **Embassies and consulates**
All in Miramar, unless stated otherwise: **Argentina**, Calle 36 No 511 between 5 and 7, T 24-2972/2549, F 24-2140; **Austria**, Calle 4 No 101, on the corner with 1st, T 24 2852, F 24-1235; **Belgium**, Av 5 No 7408 on the corner with 76, T 24-2410, F 24-1318; **Brazil**, Calle 16 No 503 between 5 and 7, T 24-2026/2141, F 24-2328; **Canada**, Calle 30 No 518, on the corner with 7, T 24-2516/2527, F 24-2044; **UK**, Calle 34, No 708, T 24-1771, F 24-8104 or 24-9214 Commercial Section, open Mon-Fri 0800-1530; **France**, Calle 14 No 312 between 3 and 5, T 24-2132/2080, F 24-1439; **Mexico**, Calle 12 No 518 between 5 and 7, T 24-2294, F 24-2719, open 0900-1200, Mon-Fri; **Netherlands**, Calle 8 No 307 between 3 and 5, T 24-2511/2, F 24-2059; **Peru**, Calle 36 No 109 between 1 and 3, T 24-2477, F 24-2636; **Sweden**, Av 31A, No 1411, T 24-2563, F 24-1194; **Switzerland**, Av 5, No 2005, T 24-2611, F 24-1148; **Venezuela**, Calle 36A No 704 corner of 42, T 24-2662, F 24-2773, **Greece**, Av 5, No 7802, Esq 78, T 24 2854, F 24-1784. In Vedado, **The US Interests Section** of the Swiss Embassy, Calzada between L and M, T 33-3550/9; **Germany**, Calle B, esq 13, T 33-2460; **Italy**, Paseo No 606 between 25 and 27, T 33-3378, F 33-3416; **Japan**, Calle N No 62, on the corner with 15, T 33-3454/3508. In the old city, **Spain**, Cárcel No 51 on the corner of Zulueta, T 33-8025-6, F 33-8006; **Denmark** and **Norway** are at the Prado No 20, Apartment 4C, T 33-8128, F 33-8127.

● **Gifts**
If you are planning to stay with Cubans, whether with friends or in private rented accommodation, there are some items in short supply in Cuba which they may appreciate: T-shirts (preferably with something written on them), household medicines such as Paracetamol, cosmetics, soap, refillable cigarette lighters, and for children, pens and pencils.

● **Hours of business**
Government offices: 0830-1230 and 1330-1730 Mon to Fri. Some offices open on Sat morning. Banks: 0830-1200, 1330-1500 Mon to Fri. Shops: 0830-1800 Mon to Sat, 0900-1400 Sun. Hotel tourist (hard currency) shops generally open 1000-2100.

● **Official time**
Eastern Standard Time, 5 hrs behind GMT; Daylight Saving Time, 4 hrs behind GMT.

● **Photography**
It is forbidden to photograph military or police installations or personnel, port, rail or airport facilities.

● **Public Holidays**
Liberation Day (1 Jan), Victory of Armed Forces (2 Jan), Labour Day (1 May), Revolution Day (26 July and the day either side), Beginning of War of Independence (10 Oct).

● **Security**
In general the Cuban people are very hospitable. The island is generally safer than many of its Caribbean and Latin neighbours, but certain precautions should be taken. Visitors should never lose sight of their luggage or leave valuables in hotel rooms (most hotels have safes). Do not leave your things on the beach when going swimming. Guard your camera closely. Pickpocketing and purse-snatching on buses is quite common in Havana (especially the old city) and Santiago. Also beware of bagsnatching by passing cyclists. Walking in Havana involves a constant escort of small children, or even teenagers, asking for chewing gum and small change. This is an issue of social concern because of what it could lead to as much as because of the general harassment. You need to be equipped with pockets full of little gifts or a very hard heart. In the capital, street lighting is poor so care is needed when walking or cycling the city at night. The police are very helpful and thorough when investigating theft, ask for a stamped statement for insurance purposes. In the event of a crime, make a note of where it happened. Visitors should remember that the government permitting Cubans to hold dollars legally has not altered the fact that some of the local population will often do anything to get hard currency, from simply asking for money or dollar-bought goods, to mugging. Latest reports suggest that foreigners will be offered almost anything on the street 'from cigars to cocaine to chicas'. Buying cigars on the street is not rec, they are often not genuine and may be confiscated at customs if you cannot produce an official receipt of purchase. Prostitution is common, beware of sexually transmitted diseases. Cubans who offer their services (whether sexual or otherwise) in return for dollars are known as *jineteros*, or *jineteras* ('jockeys' because they 'ride on the back' of the tourists). Take extra passport photos and keep them separate from your passport. You will waste a lot of time getting new photos if your passport is stolen.

● **Shopping**
Essentials, rent and most food, are fairly cheap; non-essentials are very expensive. Everything is very scarce, although imported toiletries and camera film (Kodak print only, from Mexico), are reasonably priced. Take your own toilet paper. A sandwich in a restaurant or bar costs about US$4, a coffee costs US$1. The street price of a bottle of rum ranges from US$2-4 for poor quality to US$4-8 for a 5-year-old rum, beware of some diabolical doctoring processes. A beer costs US$0.75-1.50 in both restaurants and shops. Compared with much of Latin America, Cuba is expensive for the tourist, but compared with many Caribbean islands it is not dear.

● **Tipping**
Tipping customs have changed after a period when visitors were not allowed to tip in hotels and restaurants. It is now definitely recommended. Tip a small amount (not a percentage) in the same currency as you pay for the bill (typically US$1-2 on a US$25 meal). At times taxi drivers will expect (or demand) a tip. Turistaxis are not tipped, but the drivers still appreciate a tip. Musicians in bars and restaurants depend on your tips, give generously, they are worth it. If you want to express gratitude, offer a packet of American cigarettes. Leaving basic items in your room, like toothpaste, deodorant, paper, pens, is recommended.

● **Voltage**
110-230 Volts. 3 phase 60 cycles, AC. Plugs are usually of the American type, an adaptor for European appliances can be bought at the Intur shop at the *Habana Libre*. In some tourist hotel developments, however, European plugs are used, check in advance if it is important to you.

● **Weights and measures**
The metric system is compulsory, but exists side by side with American and old Spanish systems.

ON DEPARTURE

It is advisable to book your flight out of Cuba before actually going there as arranging it there can be time-consuming. Furthermore, it is essential to reconfirm onward flights as soon as you arrive in Cuba and certainly 48 hrs prior to departure, otherwise you will lose your reservation. Independent travellers should have tickets stamped in person, not by an agent and, for Mexico, should make sure they have a Mexican tourist card and that Cuban departure tax is collected. The airport departure tax is US$15. The international terminal is Terminal 1. On departure, check in, pay tax at separate booth, go upstairs for immigration control and X-ray. Seating in the departure lounge is uncomfortable. Restaurant OK for sandwiches or full meals, welcome during 3-hr check-in. Last chance to hear live Cuban band while eating. Limited shops, lots of rum, coffee, a few books and magazines.

ACCOMMODATION

● **Hotels**

Accommodation for your first day should be booked in advance of travelling. You have to fill in an address on your tourist card and if you leave it blank you will be directed to the reservations desk at the airport, which is time consuming. A voucher from your travel agent to confirm arrangements is usual and the hotels expect it as confirmation of your reservation. This can be done abroad through travel agencies, accredited government agencies, or through Turismo Buró desks in main hotels. It's a good idea to book hotel rooms generally before noon. In the peak season, Dec to Feb, it is essential to book in advance. At other times it is possible to book at hotel reception. Prices given in the text are high season (15 Dec-15 Mar); low season prices are about 20% lower. Shop around for prices, eg one reader was quoted US$48 in the Hotel Presidente by Cubatur, US$42 when contacting the hotel direct, and US$28 through the agency Mexihabana, who have an office in the hotel. After 31 Aug many hotels go into hibernation and offer limited facilities, eg no restaurant, no swimming pool. All hotels are owned by the government, solely or in joint ventures with foreign partners. All Cubanacán hotels are 4-5 star and were finished after 1991, they are the most expensive and are usually joint ventures. Gaviota hotels also date from after 1990 and some of them are joint ventures, eg Gaviota Club Med and Sol Club Sirenas, both all-inclusives in Varadero. Gran Caribe also has 4-5 star hotels while Horizontes hotels are 3-star and Islazul has the cheaper end of the market, mostly for national tourism but foreigners are welcome. A 3-star hotel in Varadero costs US$30-50d bed and breakfast in high season, US$20-25 in low season, while a 4-star hotel will charge US$ 80-90 and US$60-70 respectively. Most 3-star hotels were built in the 1940s and 1950s and are showing their age, but some have been refurbished and are now considered 4-star.

● **Camping**

Official campsites are opening up all over the island; they are usually in nice surroundings and are good value. One such is El Abra International Campsite halfway between Havana and Varadero, which has extensive facilities (car hire, bicycles, mopeds, horses, watersports, tennis etc) and organizes excursions. Camping out on the beach or in a field is forbidden. Cubamar, Calle 15 No 752 esq Paseo, Vedado, T 30-5536/9, F 33-3111, will arrange bookings and transport to villa or cabin-style accommodation in most provinces, open Mon-Fri 0830-1700, Sat-Sun 0830-1200.

● **Private accommodation**

Cuba is geared more to package tourism than to independent visitors but self-employment is opening up opportunities which can prove rewarding for the visitor. Lodging with a family is possible (at US$10-25 per day) following new legislation in 1997 introducing taxation on a practice which had been going on for some time. Cubans are now allowed to rent out their houses, apartments or rooms, subject to health and hygiene regulations and incorporation into the tax system. Hustlers on the street will offer accommodation, but it is safer to arrange rooms through contacts if you can. A guide or hustler taking you to a private home will expect US$5 commission, which goes on your room rate. **Note** Be prepared for long waits for everything: buses, cinemas, restaurants, shops etc. Service has improved somewhat in Havana tourist facilities with foreign investment and the passage of new legislation allowing employees to be sacked if they are not up to the job. Officials in the tourist industry, tour guides, agencies and hotel staff are generally efficient and helpful 'beyond the call of duty'. Take care with unofficial guides or 'friends' you make; if they take you to a bar or nightclub or restaurant you will be expected to pay for them and pay in dollars.

FOOD AND DRINK

Visitors should remember that eating is often a problem and plan ahead. If you are going to a concert or the theatre (performances start at 2030 or 2100 in Havana). You will only be able to get a meal beforehand if you go to a *paladar*.

Breakfast can be particularly slow although this is overcome in the larger hotels who generally have buffets (breakfast US$3, lunch and dinner US$10-20). If not eating at a buffet, service, no matter what standard of restaurant or hotel, can be very slow (even if you are the only customers). Look out for the *oferta especial* in small hotels which gives guests a 25% discount on buffet meals in larger hotels. Also, the 'all-you-can-eat' vouchers for buffets in tourist hotels do not have to be used in the hotel where bought. Breakfast and one other meal may be sufficient if you fill in with street or 'dollar shop' snacks. All towns and cities have street stalls for sandwiches and snacks; change about US$10 for a 2-wee!: stay if planning to avoid restaurants.

In Havana the peso food situation is improving. Outside Havana, including Havana province, shortages are not so bad. Self-catering has become easier with the farmers' markets and the new fish shops. The dollar shops sell mostly imported supplies. Tourists do not have access to local stores, or *bodegas*, as these are based on the national ration card system. Cubans are rationed to one small round bread a day and local products such as rice, beans, sugar and coffee, although available to dollar holders are severely rationed to Cuban families. Milk is allowed only for children up to the age of 7; chicken and beef are rare.

For vegetarians the choice is very limited, normally only cheese, sandwiches, spaghetti, pizzas, salads and omelettes. Generally, although restaurants have improved in the last few years, the food in Cuba is not very exciting or enjoyable. There is little variety in the menu and menu items are frequently unavailable. Always check restaurant prices in advance and then your bill. Private restaurants are better; these are now licensed, subjected to health inspections and regulations, and taxed, which may limit their scope in the short term. The national dish is *congris* (rice mixed with black beans), roast pork and yuca (cassava) or fried plantain. Salads in restaurants are mixed vegetables which are slightly pickled and not to everyone's taste. Hatuey is the best of Cuba's many beers, named after an Indian chief ruling when the Spanish arrived.

GETTING AROUND

AIR TRANSPORT

Cubana de Aviación services between most of the main towns. From Havana to Camagüey (US$58 one way), Holguín (US$70), Baracoa (US$80), Guantánamo (US$80), Manzanillo (US$66), Moa (US$80), Nueva Gerona/Isla de Juventud (US$20), Bayamo (US$66), Ciego de Avila (US$48), Las Tunas (US$64), Santiago (US$76), Cayo Largo and Cayo Coco (US$48), Varadero (US$22), all have airports. Return fare is twice the single fare. Tourists must pay airfares in US$; it is advisable to prebook flights at home as demand is very heavy. It is difficult to book flights from one city to another when you are not at the point of departure, except from Havana, the computer is not able to cope. Airports are usually a long way from the towns, so extra transport costs will be necessary. Delays are common.

Although theoretically possible to get a scheduled flight as listed above, it is often only possible for tourists to travel on excursions: day trips or packages with flights, accommodation, meals and sightseeing.

LAND TRANSPORT

● Motoring

Petrol for foreigners is available in Cupet stations, costs US$0.75 per litre and must be paid for in US$. If possible, get the rental company to fill the car with fuel, otherwise your first day will be spent looking for petrol. Hiring a car is recommended, in view of difficulties of getting seats on buses and trains and you can save a considerable amount of time but it is the most expensive form of travel. Breakdowns are not unknown, in which case you may be stuck with your rented car many kilometres from the nearest place that will accept dollars to help you. Be careful about picking up hitchhikers, although it can be an interesting and pleasant way of meeting Cubans.

● Car hire

Through state rental companies at the International Airport and most large hotels. Nacional Rent A Car is at Av 47, 4701 y 40, Rpto Kohly, Playa, Havana, T 81-0357, 23-7000, 20-6897, F 33-0742; in Matanzas (Varadero), T 056-2968/2620; Sancti Spíritus (Trinidad), T 042-40117/40330; Holguín, T 024-30102/30115; Santiago de Cuba, T 0226-41368; Isla de la Juventud, T 2-3290, 24486. Minimum US$40 a day (or US$50 for a/c) with limited mileage, and US$8-20 a day optional insurance, or US$50-84/day unlimited mileage; cheaper rates over 7 days. Visa, Mastercard, Eurocard, Banamex, JCB and Carnet accepted for the rental, or cash or TCs paid in advance, guarantee of US$200-250 required; you must also present your passport and home driving licence. Fly and drive packages can be booked from abroad, eg in the UK, Journey Latin America, T 0181-747-8315, can organize rentals of Suzuki Samurai jeeps (or equivalent). Most vehicles are Japanese makes, Suzuki jeeps can be hired for 6-12 hrs in beach areas, US$11-22, plus US$8 insurance, extra hrs US$5. Moped rental at resorts is around US$5-9/hr, cheaper for longer, US$25-30/day, US$80/week.

● Bus

The local word for bus is *guagua*. The urban bus fare throughout Cuba is 20 centavos and it helps to have the exact fare. In the rush hours they are filled to more than capacity, making it hard to get off if you have managed to get on. Buses are running but fuel shortages limit services. Urban tickets can only be bought in pesos Cubanos. For bus transport to other provinces from Havana there is a dollar ticket office in the Terminal de Omnibus Nacional, Boyeros y 19 de Mayo (3rd left via 19 de Mayo entrance), T 70-3397, open daily 0700-2100, very helpful staff. You don't have to book in advance but it might be wiser to do so. There may be cancellations. If you want the hassle of paying in pesos cubanos tickets between towns must be purchased in advance from: Oficina Reservaciones Pasajes, Calle 21, esq 4, Vedado (main booking office for buses and trains from Havana to anywhere in the country, one-way only, open Mon to Fri 0900-1745, organized chaos); Plazoleta de la Virgen del Camino, San Miguel del Padrón; Calzada 10 de Octubre y Carmen, Centro; Terminal de Omnibus Nacional, Boyeros y 19 de Mayo (all in Havana). Look for notices in the window for latest availabilities, find out who is last in the queues (separate queues for buses and trains, sometimes waiting numbers issued), and ask around for what is the best bet. Maximum 3 tickets sold per person. Seat reservations are only possible on a few long distance routes (eg Havana-Trinidad Express) but you still need pesos Cubanos, or a Cuban entrepreneur to obtain one. Cubans queue professionally and make a profit out of selling places near the top of the queue. You may end up paying the same as if you'd gone to the dollar ticket office.

● Hitchhiking

With the shortage of fuel and decline in public transport since 1991, Cubans have taken to organized hitchhiking to get about. At every major junction outside towns throughout Cuba you will find the *Amarillos*, traffic wardens dressed in yellow, who organize a queue, stop traffic to find out where the trucks or vans are going, and load them with passengers. You pay a nominal amount in pesos, eg 6 pesos for a 4-hr ride Cienfuegos-Havana in an open truck.

● Taxis

The best you can do is avoid the most expensive tourist taxis. See **Transport** under Havana. **Dollar tourist taxis** can be hired for driving around; you pay for the distance, not for waiting time. On short routes, fares start at US$1. Airport to Havana (depending on destination), US$9-12 with Panataxi, to Playas del Este US$25, to Varadero US$71; Havana to Varadero US$65; Varadero airport to Varadero hotels US$13; Santiago de Cuba airport to *Hotel Las Américas* US$8, to *Balcón del Caribe* US$5. Taxis can work out cheaper than going on organized tours, eg US$60 pp to tour the Viñales area but US$25 (206 km) Havana-Viñales by taxi, US$15 (183 km) Havana-Pinar del Río. Shorter journeys are comparatively more expensive: Pinar del Río-Viñales US$10 (23 km). Cubans are not allowed to carry foreigners in their vehicles, but they do; private taxis are considerably cheaper, eg airport to Havana centre US$8-12, from Havana to Santa María del Mar beach US$8-10, from Santiago to the airport US$5.

● Train

Recommended whenever possible, although delays and breakdowns must be expected. Be at station at least 30 mins before scheduled departure time, you have to queue to reconfirm your seat and have your ticket stamped. Fares are reasonable, eg US$13 to Sancti Spíritus (for Trinidad), 9 hrs. There is a dollar ticket office in the Estación Central, Calles Arsenal y Egido (on Arsenal), open daily 0630-1600, T 61-4259. Alternatively, the Tourist Desk in the *Habana Libre*, *Inglaterra* and *Plaza* hotels sell train tickets to foreigners, in dollars. Tourists will find it is only possible to pay for rail tickets in dollars. Bicycles can be carried as an express item only.

NB In major bus and train terminals, ask if there are special arrangements for tourists to buy tickets without queuing; payment would then be in dollars. You can waste hours queuing and waiting for public transport. Travel between provinces is usually booked solid several days or weeks in advance. If you are on a short trip you may do better to go on a package tour with excursions. Trains and some buses are air-conditioned, you may need a warm jersey. All train carriages are smokers; there is no food service.

COMMUNICATIONS

● Language
Spanish, with local variants in pronunciation and vocabulary. English is becoming more commonly used; it is a university entrance requirement and encouraged by the influx of Canadian tourists. German, Italian and French are now spoken by people working in the tourist industry and tour guides are usually multilingual.

● Language study
Any Cuban embassy will give details, or, in Santiago, contact Cecilia Suárez, c/o Departamiento de Idiomas, Universidad de Oriente, Av Patricio Lumumba, Código Postal 90500, Santiago de Cuba. Spanish courses at the University of Havana cost US$300-350 depending on the level and begin the first Mon of every month. For language combined with social study, contact Projecto Cultural EL1, PO Box 12227, 6000 Luzern, Switzerland, T/F 4141360 8764, 3-week courses all year at the University of Havana.

● Postal services
When possible correspondence to Cuba should be addressed to post office boxes (Apartados), where delivery is more certain. Stamps can only be bought at Post Offices, or at certain hotels. All postal services, national and international, have been described as appalling. Letters to Europe, for instance, take at least 4-5 weeks, up to 3 months. Cubans will stop you in the street and ask you to bring letters out of Cuba for them. Telegraphic services are adequate. You can send telegrams from all post offices in Havana. Telegrams to Britain cost 49 centavos a word. The night letter rate is 3.85 pesos for 22 words.

● Telecommunications
Local telephone calls can be made from public telephones for 5 centavos. A telephone call to Europe costs US$6/minute. The cost of phoning the USA is US$4.50/minute from Havana, US$3 from Varadero and Guadalavaca hotels. Many hard currency hotels and airports (including Havana departure lounge and Santiago) have telephone offices where international calls can be made at high prices. No 'collect' calls allowed and only cash accepted. Collect calls to some

places, including London, are possible from private Cuban telephones. At least one Havana hotel, the *Nacional*, can arrange for you to direct dial foreign countries from your room. Phonecards are in use at Etecsa call boxes, in different denominations from US$10-50, much cheaper for phoning abroad than in a hotel. Telephone sockets (for computer users) are standard US type. The cost of these calls is high, connections are hard to make and you will be cut off frequently. In 1994 the US Federal Communications Commission approved applications from 5 US companies to provide direct telephone services to Cuba and for AT&T to expand its existing service. Mobile phones are commonly used in Cuba.

MEDIA

● Newspapers
Granma, mornings except Sun and Mon; *Trabajadores*, Trade Union weekly; *Tribuna* and *Juventud Rebelde*, also only weekly. *Opciones* is a weekly national and international trade paper. *Granma* has a weekly edition, *Granma International*, published in Spanish, English, French and Portuguese, and a monthly selected German edition, all have versions on the Internet, Website: http://www.granma.cu; main offices: Avenida General Suárez y Territorial, Plaza de la Revolución, La Habana 6, T 81-6265, F 33-5176, Telex: 0511 355; in UK 928 Bourges Boulevard, Peterborough PE1 2AN. *El País* is the Mexican edition of the Spanish newspaper, available daily, 2 days late. Foreign (not US) newspapers are sometimes on sale at the telex centre in *Habana Libre* and in the *Riviera* (also telex centre, open 0800-2000). The previous day's paper is available during the week. Weekend editions on sale Tues.

TOURIST INFORMATION

● Local tourist office
The Government has a decentralized system for receptive tourism and there is a large number of state-owned travel agencies/tour companies, which cooperate fully with each other and with the tourism bureaux in the major hotels. Their main function is to sell excursions and package tours. Individual tourism is relatively new but growing, with agencies like *Amistur*, overseas agent Cubanacán.

● Tourist offices overseas
The Cuba Tourist Office also has offices in: **Canada**, 440 Blvd René Levesque, Suite 1402,

Montréal, Quebec H2Z 1V7, T (514) 875-8004/5, F 875-8006; 55 Queen St E, Suite 705, Toronto, M5C 1R5, T (416) 362-0700/2, F 362-6799.

Belgium, Robert Jones Straat 77, Brussels 18, T 02-343-0022; **France**, 280 Bd Raspail, 75014 Paris, T 14-538-90-10, F 14-538-99-30; **Italy**, Via General Fara 30, Terzo Plano, 20124 Milan, T 66981463, F 6690042; **Spain**, Paseo de la Habana No 28 iro derecha, 28036 Madrid, T 411-3097, F 564-5804; **Switzerland**, Gesellschaststrasse 8, 3012 Berne, Case Postale 52725, T/F 31 3022111; **UK**, 167 High Holborn, London WC1V 6PA, T 01891-880-820, 0171-379-1706, F 0171-379-5455.

Russia, Room 627, Hotel Belgrado Kutuzovskii 14KB7, Moscow, T 2-48-2454/3262, F 2-43-1125.

Argentina, Paraguay 631, 2° piso A, Buenos Aires, F 311-4198, T 311-5820; **Mexico**, Insurgentes Sur 421 y Aguascalientes, Complejo Aristos, Edificio B, Local 310, México DF 06100, T 574-9651, F 574-9454.

● **Travel agents abroad**

In the **UK**, agents who sell holidays in Cuba include Regent Holidays, 15 John St, Bristol BS1 2HR, T (0117) 9211711, F (0117) 9254866, ABTA members, holding ATOL and IATA Licences; South American Experience Ltd, 47 Causton St, Pimlico, London SW1P 4AT, T 0171-976 5511, F 0171-976 6908, ATOL, IATA; Progressive Tours, 12 Porchester Place, Marble Arch, London W2 2BS, T 0171-262 1676, F 0171-724 6941, ABTA, ATOL, IATA. Cubanacan UK Ltd, Skylines, Unit 49, Limeharbour Docklands, London E14 9TS, T 0171-537 7909, F 0171-537-7747. Check with these agents for special deals combined with jazz or film festivals. Cubanacan SA, Calle 148/11 y 13, Playa, Aptdo Postal 16046, Zona 16, Havana, T 7-219-457/200-569/336-006, operates all diving packages (**see p 549**), as well as Veracuba excursions by bus or fly/drive packages; Club Amigo all-inclusives; Servimed health organization for special treatments; Cubacar car hire; Tropicana Club; ExpoCuba at Havana International Conference Centre. A recommended agent in **Eire** for assistance with Aeroflot flights is Concorde Travel, T Dublin 763232; Cubatur agent is Cubatravel, T Dublin 713385. See above under **Documents** for Marazul Tours in the USA. If travelling from **Mexico**, many agencies in the Yucatan peninsula offer packages, very good value and popular with travellers wanting to avoid Mexico City. From Cancún Cubana flights cost US$225 return, although you can get special deals for

US$170; Aerocaribe charges US$286. Flights are heavily booked.

From **Canada**, Air Canada Vacations has year-round packages or air tickets only to Varadero, from economy to first class hotels; Canadian Holidays (division of Canadian Airlines) to Varadero and other destinations inc ecological tour of Sierra Maestra; Alba Tours, year-round packages up to 4 weeks to all parts of the island, or flights only; Magna Holidays books individual travel and custom tours out of Toronto; several more inc Fiesta Sun, Hola Holidays (Cuban) offer individual travel arrangements from Canada. The Canadian-Cuban Friendship Association, Box 57063-2458 E Hastings Street, Vancouver, BC, V5K 5G6, coordinates specialist group tours, eg medical, children's study, cycling tours, also lots of information on who is doing what in Canadian-Cuban aid and cultural exchange, membership Can$10/year, newsletter. From **Venezuela**, Ideal Tours, Centro Capriles, Plaza Venezuela, T (010 582) 793-0037/1822, have 4-day or 8-day package tours depending on the season, flight only available. From **Jamaica**, UTAS Tours offer weekends in Cuba for US$199 inc flight, hotel etc, PO Box 429, Montego Bay, T (809) 979-0684, F 979-3465. In the **Bahamas**, Havana Tours in Nassau, T 394-7195, sells package tours to Cuba.

● **Local travel agents**

Several state-owned tour companies offer day trips or excursion packages inc accommodation to many parts of the island as well as tours of colonial and modern Havana. Examples (one day, except where indicated): Viñales, inc tobacco and rum factories, US$39; Guamá, US$39; Cayo Coco (by air), US$89; Soroa, US$29; Varadero, US$27; Cayo Largo (by air), US$94; Trinidad (by air), daytrip US$79 or US$139 inc overnight stay; Santiago de Cuba (by air) and Baracoa, US$159 inc 1 night's accommodation, rec, you see a lot and cover a lot of ground in 2 days. Tours can also be taken from any beach resort. Guides speak Spanish, English, French, Italian or German; the tours are generally rec as well-organized and good value. A common complaint from individual tourists is that, when they sign up for day trips and other excursions (eg Cayo Largo), they are not told that actual departure depends on a minimum number of passengers (usually 6). The situation is made worse by the fact that most tourists are on pre-arranged package tours. They are often subject to long waits on buses and at points of departure and are not informed of delays in departure times. Always ask the organizers when they will know if the trip is on or what the real departure time will be.

● **Travel assistance**

Asistur, Paseo del Prado 254, entre Animas y Trocadero, Habana Vieja, for 24-hr service T 33-8527, 62-5519, F 33-8088, cellular Asis 2747, linked to overseas insurance companies, can help with emergency hospital treatment, robbery, direct transfer of funds to Cuba, etc. Also office in *Hotel Casa Granda,* Santiago.

● **Maps**

Mapa Turístico de la Habana, Mapa de la Habana Vieja, and similar maps of Santiago de Cuba, Trinidad, Camagüey and Varadero are helpful, but not always available. The best shop for maps of all kinds inc nautical maps is *El Navegante,* Mercáderes entre Obispo y Obrapía in Old Havana.

ACKNOWLEDGEMENTS

The editor is most grateful to Angie Todd in Havana for her extensive work in updating the chapter and to Gavin Clark for research based in Santiago de Cuba and the east. The editor would also like to thank Rigoberto Herrera Romero in Varadero and Orestes Cordoví Quintana in Guardalavaca for help during her visit to Cuba.

Central America

C ENTRAL AMERICA comprises the seven small countries of Guatemala, Belize (formerly British Honduras), El Salvador, Honduras, Nicaragua, Costa Rica and Panama. Together they occupy 544,700 square km, which is less than the size of Texas. The total population of Central America in 1993 was about 31.0 million and it is increasing by 2.7% each year.

The degree of development in these countries differs sharply. Costa Rica and Panama have the highest standard of living, with two of the highest rates of literacy in all Latin America. At the other end of the scale, Honduras and Nicaragua have the lowest standards of living.

Geographically, these countries have much in common, but there are sharp differences in the racial composition and traditions of their peoples. Costa Ricans are mostly white, Guatemalans are largely Amerindian or *mestizo*; Hondurans, Nicaraguans and Salvadoreans are almost entirely *mestizo*. Panama has perhaps the most racially varied population, with a large white group. Most of these countries also have a black element, the largest being found in Panama, Nicaragua and Belize.

HISTORY

EARLY, POST-CONQUEST HISTORY

At the time of the coming of the Spaniards there were several isolated groups of Indians dotted over the Central American area: they were mostly shifting cultivators or nomadic hunters and fishermen. A few places only were occupied by sedentary agriculturists: what remained of the Maya (see **Precolumbian Civilizations**) in the highlands of Guatemala; a group on the south-western shores of Lakes Managua and Nicaragua; and another in the highlands of

Costa Rica. The Spanish conquerors were attracted by precious metals, or native sedentary farmers who could be christianized and exploited. There were few of either, and comparatively few Spaniards settled in Central America.

It was only during his fourth voyage, in 1502, that Columbus reached the mainland of Central America; he landed in Panama, which he called Veragua, and founded the town of Santa María de Belén. In 1508 Alonso de Ojeda received a grant of land on the Pearl Coast E of Panama, and in 1509 he founded the town of San Sebastián, later moved to a new site called Santa María la Antigua del Darién (now in Colombia). In 1513 the governor of the colony at Darién was Vasco Núñez de Balboa. Taking 190 men he crossed the isthmus in 18 days and caught the first glimpse of the Pacific; he claimed it and all neighbouring lands in the name of the King of Spain. But from the following year, when Pedrarias de Avila replaced him as Governor, Balboa fell on evil days, and he was executed by Pedrarias in 1519. That same year Pedrarias crossed the isthmus and founded the town of Panamá on the Pacific side. It was in April 1519, too, that Cortés began his conquest of Mexico.

Central America was explored from these two nodal points of Panama and Mexico. Cortés' lieutenant, Pedro de Alvarado, had conquered as far S as San Salvador by 1525. Meanwhile Pedrarias was sending forces into Panama and Costa Rica: the latter was abandoned, for the natives were hostile, but was finally colonized from Mexico City when the rest of Central America had been taken. In 1522-24 Andrés Niño and Gil Gonzales Dávila invaded Nicaragua and Honduras. Many towns were founded by these forces from Panama: León, Granada, Trujillo and others. Spanish forces from the N and S sometimes met and fought bitterly. The gentle Bartolomé de Las Casas, the 'apostle of the Indies', was active as a Dominican missionary in Central America in the 1530s.

SETTLEMENT

The groups of Spanish settlers were few and widely scattered, and this is the fundamental reason for the political fragmentation of Central America today. Panama was ruled from Bogotá, but the rest of Central America was subordinate to the Viceroyalty at Mexico City, with Antigua Guatemala as an Audiencia for the area until 1773, thereafter Guatemala City. Panama was of paramount importance for colonial Spanish America for its strategic position, and for the trade passing across the isthmus to and from the southern colonies. The other provinces were of comparatively little value.

The small number of Spaniards intermarried freely with the local Indians, accounting for the predominance of *mestizos* in present-day Central America. In Guatemala, where there were the most Indians, intermarriage affected fewer of the natives, and over half the population today is pure Indian. On the Meseta Central of Costa Rica, the Indians were all but wiped out by disease; as a consequence of this great disaster, there is a buoyant community of over 2 million whites, with little Indian admixture, in the highlands. Blacks predominate all along the Caribbean coasts of Central America; they were not brought in by the colonists as slaves, but by the railway builders and banana planters of the 19th century and the canal cutters of the 20th, as cheap labour.

INDEPENDENCE AND FEDERATION

On 5 November 1811, José Matías Delgado, a priest and jurist born in San Salvador, organized a revolt in conjunction with another priest, Manuel José Arce. They proclaimed the independence of El Salvador, but the Audiencia at Guatemala City quickly suppressed the revolt and took Delgado prisoner.

It was the revolution of 1820 in Spain itself that precipitated the independence of Central America. When on 24 February 1821, the Mexican general Agustín de

Iturbide announced his Plan of Iguala for an independent Mexico, the Central American *criollos* decided to follow his example, and a declaration of independence, drafted by José Cecilio del Valle, was announced in Guatemala City on 15 September 1821. Iturbide invited the provinces of Central America to join with him, and on 5 January 1822, Central America was declared annexed to Mexico. Delgado refused to accept this decree, and Iturbide, who had now assumed the title of Emperor Agustín the First, sent an army 3 under Vicente Filísola to enforce it in the regions under Delgado's influence. Filísola had completed his task when he heard of Iturbide's abdication, and at once convened a general congress of the Central American provinces. It met on 24 June 1823, and established the Provincias Unidas del Centro de América. The Mexican republic acknowledged their independence on 1 August 1824, and Filísola's soldiers were withdrawn.

The congress, presided over by Delgado, appointed a provisional governing *junta* which promulgated a constitution modelled on that of the United States on 22 November 1824. The Province of Chiapas was not included in the Federation, for it had already adhered to Mexico in 1821. No federal capital was chosen, but Guatemala City, by force of tradition, soon became the seat of government.

BREAKDOWN OF FEDERATION

The first President under the new constitution was Manuel José Arce, a liberal. One of his first acts was to abolish slavery. El Salvador, protesting that he had exceeded his powers, rose in Dec 1826. Honduras, Nicaragua, and Costa Rica joined the revolt, and in 1828 Gen Francisco Morazán, in charge of the army of Honduras, defeated the federal forces, entered San Salvador and marched against Guatemala City. He captured the city on 13 April 1829, and established that contradiction in terms: a liberal dictatorship. Many conservative leaders

were expelled and church and monastic properties confiscated. Morazán himself became president of the Federation in 1830. He was a man of considerable ability; he ruled with a strong hand, encouraged education, fostered trade and industry, opened the country to immigrants, and reorganized the administration. In 1835 the capital was moved to San Salvador.

These reforms antagonized the conservatives and there were several risings. The most serious revolt was among the Indians of Guatemala, led by Rafael Carrera, an illiterate *mestizo* conservative and a born leader. Years of continuous warfare followed, during the course of which the Federation withered away. As a result, the federal congress passed an act which allowed each province to assume what government it chose, but the idea of a federation was not quite dead. As a result, Morazán became President of El Salvador. Carrera, who was by then in control of Guatemala, defeated Morazán in battle and forced him to leave the country. But in 1842, Morazán overthrew Braulio Carrillo, then dictator of Costa Rica, and became president himself. At once he set about rebuilding the Federation, but was defeated by the united forces of the other states, and shot on 15 September 1842. With him perished any practical hope of Central American political union.

THE SEPARATE STATES

Costa Rica, with its mainly white population, is a country apart, and Panama was Colombian territory until 1903. The history of the four remaining republics since the breakdown of federation has been tempestuous in the extreme. In each the ruling class was divided into pro-clerical conservatives and anti-clerical liberals, with constant changes of power. Each was weak, and tried repeatedly to buttress its weakness by alliances with others, which invariably broke up because one of the allies sought a position of mastery. The wars were rarely over boundaries; they were mainly ideological wars between conservatives and liberals, or wars motivated by inflamed nationalism. Nicaragua, for instance, was riven internally for most of the period by the mutual hatreds of the Conservatives of Granada and the Liberals of León, and there were repeated conflicts between the Caribbean and interior parts of Honduras.

Of the four republics, Guatemala was certainly the strongest and in some ways the most stable. While the other states were skittling their presidents like so many ninepins, Guatemala was ruled by a succession of strong dictators: Rafael Carrera (1844-1865), Justo Rufino Barrios (1873-1885), Manuel Cabrera (1898-1920), and Jorge Ubico (1931-44). These were separated by intervals of constitutional government, anarchy, or attempts at dictatorship which failed. Few presidents handed over power voluntarily to their successors; most of them were forcibly removed or assassinated.

Despite the permutations and combinations of external and civil war there has been a recurrent desire to reestablish some form of *la gran patria centroamericana*. Throughout the 19th century, and far into the 20th, there have been ambitious projects for political federation, usually involving El Salvador, Honduras and Nicaragua; none of them lasted more than a few years. There have also been unsuccessful attempts to reestablish union by force, such as those of Barrios of Guatemala in 1885 and Zelaya of Nicaragua in 1907.

During colonial times the area suffered from great poverty; trade with the mother country was confined to small amounts of silver and gold, cacao and sugar, cochineal and indigo. During the present century the great banana plantations of the Caribbean, the coffee and cotton trade and industrialization have brought some prosperity, but its benefits have, except in Costa Rica and Panama, been garnered mostly by a relatively small landowning class and the middle classes

of the cities. Nicaragua is now a case apart; extensive and radical reforms were carried out by a left-leaning revolutionary government, but protracted warfare and mistakes in economic management have left the country still extremely poor.

REGIONAL INTEGRATION

Poverty, the fate of the great majority, has brought about closer economic cooperation between the five republics, and in 1960 they established the Central American Common Market (CACM). Surprisingly, the Common Market appeared to be a great success until 1968, when integration fostered national antagonisms, and there was a growing conviction in Honduras and Nicaragua, which were doing least well out of integration, that they were being exploited by the others. In 1969 the 'Football War' broke out between El Salvador and Honduras, basically because of a dispute about illicit emigration by Salvadoreans into Honduras, and relations between the two were not normalized until 1980. Despite the handicaps to economic and political integration imposed by nationalist feeling and ideological differences, hopes for improvement were revived in 1987 when the Central American Peace Plan, drawn up by President Oscar Arias Sánchez of Costa Rica, was signed by the Presidents of Guatemala, El Salvador, Honduras, Nicaragua and Costa Rica. The plan proposed formulae to end the civil strife in individual countries, achieving this aim first in Nicaragua (1989), then in El Salvador (1991). In Guatemala, a ceasefire after 35 years of war led to hopes of a peace accord before the end of 1996. In Oct 1993, the presidents of Guatemala, El Salvador, Honduras, Nicaragua and Costa Rica signed a new Central American Integration Treaty Protocol, to replace that of 1960 and set up new mechanisms for regional integration. The Treaty was the culmination of a series of annual presidential summits since 1986 which, besides aiming for peace and economic integration, has established a Central American Parliament and a Central American Court of Justice.

In 1994, problems emerged which cast doubt on the intention of the Central American republics forming a strong regional bloc. Although intraregional trade grew to US$1.3bn in 1994 (compared with US$450mn in 1986), economic circumstances were forcing each government to pursue independent policies. For example, Costa Rica signed a bilateral agreement with Mexico, undermining the region's aim of negotiation as a group with the North American Free Trade Agreement. Guatemala adopted a 10% tariff on most imports, only to revert to the previous rates following private sector protests. El Salvador announced plans to reduce import tariffs and to fix its exchange rate, in contravention of regional accords. In addition, Nicaragua and Costa Rica were in dispute over the illegal immigration of Nicaraguan workers into Costa Rican agricultural jobs.

NB In the chapters below, information is given on border crossings and entry and exit taxes. Travellers should note that official policy may be disregarded by officials who prefer to set their own, more arbitrary regulations. This may be for a variety of reasons (including the wish to supplement low pay). If you want to debate the issue at the border, find out from a consulate what the regulations are in advance.

Guatemala

GUATEMALA is the most populous of the Central American republics and the only one which is largely Indian in language and culture. It still has large areas of unoccupied land, especially in the north; only about two-thirds is populated. Two-thirds of it is mountainous and about the same proportion forested. It has coastlines on the Pacific (240 km), and on the Caribbean (110 km).

HORIZONS

THE LAND

A lowland ribbon, nowhere more than 50 km wide, runs the whole length of the Pacific shore. Cotton, sugar, bananas and maize are the chief crops of this lowland, particularly in the Department of Escuintla. There is some stock raising as well. Summer rain is heavy and the lowland carries scrub forest.

From this plain the highlands rise sharply to heights of between 2,500 and 3,000m and stretch some 240 km to the N before sinking into the northern lowlands. A string of volcanoes juts boldly above the southern highlands along the Pacific. There are intermont basins at from 1,500 to 2,500m in this volcanic area. Most of the people of Guatemala live in

these basins, drained by short rivers into the Pacific and by longer ones into the Atlantic. One basin W of the capital has no apparent outlet and here, ringed by volcanoes, is the splendid Lake Atitlán. The southern highlands are covered with lush vegetation over a volcanic subsoil. This clears away in the central highlands, exposing the crystalline rock of the E-W running ranges. This area is lower but more rugged, with sharp-faced ridges and deep ravines modifying into gentle slopes and occasional valley lowlands as it loses height and approaches the Caribbean coastal levels and the flatlands of El Petén.

The lower slopes of these highlands, from about 600 to 1,500m, are planted with coffee. Coffee plantations make almost a complete belt around them. Above 1,500m is given over to wheat and the main subsistence crops of maize and

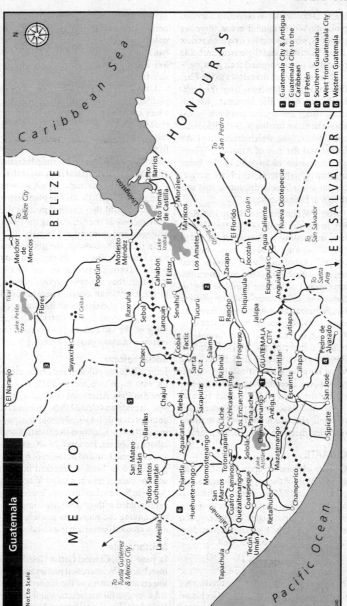

Guatemala

Not to Scale

N

Caribbean Sea

BELIZE

HONDURAS

MEXICO

EL SALVADOR

Pacific Ocean

1 Guatemala City & Antigua
2 Guatemala City to the Caribbean
3 El Petén
4 Southern Guatemala
5 West from Guatemala City
6 Western Guatemala

To Belize City

To Tuxtla Gutiérrez & Mexico City

To Barrios

To San Pedro

To San Salvador

To Santa Ana

GUATEMALA CITY

beans. Deforestation is becoming a serious problem. Where rainfall is low there are savannas, where water for irrigation is now drawn from wells and these areas are being reclaimed for pasture and fruit growing.

Two large rivers flow down to the Caribbean Gulf of Honduras from the highlands: one is the Río Motagua, 400 km long, rising among the southern volcanoes; the other, further N, is the Río Polochic, 298 km long, which drains into Lake Izabal and the Bay of Amatique. There are large areas of lowland in the lower reaches of both rivers, which are navigable for considerable distances; this was the great banana zone.

To the NW, bordering on Belize and Mexico, in the peninsula of Yucatán, lies the low, undulating tableland of El Petén (36,300 sq km). In some parts there is natural grassland, with woods and streams, suitable for cattle, but large areas are covered with dense hardwood forest. Since the 1970s large-scale tree-felling has reduced this tropical rain forest by some 40%, especially in the S and E. However, in the N, which now forms Guatemala's share of the Maya Biosphere Reserve (with Mexico and Belize), the forest is protected, but illegal logging still takes place. Deep in the tangled rain forest lie the ruins of Maya cities such as Tikal and Uaxactún. In the Department of Petén, almost one-third of the national territory, there are only 250,000 people.

CLIMATE

Climate, dependent upon altitude, varies greatly. Most of the population lives at between 900 and 2,500m, where the climate is healthy and of an even springlike warmth – warm days and cool nights. The pronounced rainy season in the highlands is from May to Oct; the dry from Nov to April.

HISTORY

For early history see the introductory chapter to Central America. Cochineal and indigo were the great exports until 1857, when both were wiped out by competition from synthetic dyes. The vacuum was filled by cacao, followed by coffee and bananas, and essential oils. The upland soil and climate are particularly favourable to coffee.

Only coffee of the Bourbon variety is planted below 600m, and until 1906, when bananas were first planted there, the low-lying *tierra caliente* had been used mostly for cane and cattle raising. The first plantations of the United Fruit Company were at the mouth of the Motagua, near Puerto Barrios, then little more than a village. Blacks from Jamaica were brought in to work them. The plantations expanded until they covered most of the *tierra caliente* in the NE – along the lower Motagua and around Lake Izabal.

In the 1930s, however, the plantations were struck by disease and the Company began planting bananas in the Pacific lowlands; they are railed across country to the Caribbean ports. There are still substantial plantations at Bananera, 58 km inland from Puerto Barrios, though some of the old banana land is used for cotton and *abacá* (manila hemp).

Social reform

Jorge Ubico, an efficient but brutal dictator who came to power in 1931, was deposed in 1944. After some confusion, Juan José Arévalo was elected President and set out to accomplish a social revolution, paying particular attention to education and labour problems. He survived several conspiracies and finished his term of 6 years. Jacobo Arbenz became President in 1950, and the pace of reform was quickened. His Agrarian Reform Law, dividing large estates expropriated without adequate compensation among the numerous landless peasantry, aroused opposition from landowners.

Military rule

In June 1954, Colonel Carlos Castillo Armas, backed by interested parties and with the encouragement of the United States, led a successful insurrection and became President. For the following 29 years the army and its right-wing supporters suppressed left-wing efforts, both constitutional and violent, to restore the gains made under Arévalo and Arbenz; many thousands of people, mostly leftists but also many Indians, were killed during this period.

Return of democracy
In Aug 1983 Gen Oscar Mejía Victores took power. He permitted a Constituent Assembly to be elected in 1984, which drew up a new constitution and worked out a timetable for a return to democracy. Presidential elections, held in Dec 1985, were won by Vinicio Cerezo Arévalo of the Christian Democrat party (DC), who took office in Jan 1986. In the 1990 elections the Christian Democrats fared badly, their candidate failing to qualify for run-off elections between Jorge Serrano Elías, the eventual winner, of the Solidarity Action Movement (MAS) and Jorge Carpio of the National Centrist Union (UCN).

Civil unrest
By 1993 when President Serrano's government reached mid-term, the country was in disarray. Political, social and economic policies pursued by the government had alienated nearly everybody and violence erupted on the streets led by a wave of student riots. The Christian Democrats and the UCN centrists withdrew their support in Congress, leaving the government without a majority. Amid growing civil unrest, President Serrano suspended the constitution, dissolved Congress and the Supreme Court and imposed press censorship, with what appeared to be military support for his auto-coup. International and domestic condemnation for his action was immediate and most foreign aid was frozen. After only a few days, Serrano was ousted by a combination of military, business and opposition leaders and a return to constitutional rule was promised. Congress approved a successor to Serrano immediately, electing as president Ramiro de León Carpio, who had previously been the human rights ombudsman. This spectacular choice led to

much optimism, which proved short-lived. Although progress was made in talks between the government and URNG, assassinations, kidnapping and human rights violations continued. Some communities, displaying no faith in the security and justice systems, took the law into their hands to deal with criminals. Land invasions also continued and strikes in the public and private sectors continued in 1994 and early 1995. In this climate, the public's distaste at corrupt congressional deputies and ineffectual government was not diminished. The president seemed powerless to restore any confidence because Congress deliberately failed to approve bills on constitutional, police, or tax reform, and other laws. The reform of election procedures and political parties had been called for by a referendum in 1994, which obliged Congressional elections to be called. The result gave a majority of seats to the Guatemalan Republican Front (FRG), led by ex-president Efraín Ríos Montt. Voter turnout was under 20% of the electorate. Despite an alliance of four parties against the FRG's control of Congress, Ríos Montt was elected to the presidency of Congress for 1994-96.

Ríos Montt's candidate in the 1995 presidential election, Alfonso Portillo, lost by a slim margin to Alvaro Arzú of the National Advancement Party (PAN). Although backed by the business élite, the army and the urban middle class, Arzú proposed to increase social spending, curtail tax evasion, combat crime and bring a speedy conclusion to peace negotiations with the URNG guerrillas.

Towards peace
One of the earliest moves made by President Serrano was to speed up a process of talks between the government and the Guatemalan National Revolutionary Unity (URNG), which began in Oslo in Mar 1990. The sides, including the military, met in Mexico City in April 1991 to discuss such topics as democratization and human rights, a reduced role for the

military, the rights of indigenous people, the resettlement of refugees and agrarian reform. Progress was slow and several rounds of talks were held with little achieved. The URNG remained active, but in late 1993 negotiations recommenced, leading to a Global Human Rights accord signed between the government and rebels on 29 March 1994. Further talks and the setting up of a Civil Society Assembly (to deliberate on the displaced and victims of war, a truth commission and other issues) raised hopes, but by Mar 1995 no solution to the civil war had been found. The main stumbling block was the issue of the identity and rights of indigenous people; while the government and URNG could not reach agreement, indigenous groups were excluded from the talks. A related problem, land ownership, also had to be addressed by the Peace Commission. After UN Secretary Gen Boutros Boutros Ghali expressed the frustration of many in late-1994, talks were given new impetus and a timetable for decisions, leading to an acccord by Aug 1995, was drawn up with the aid of the UN's Guatemala mission (MINUGUA) and the Norwegian government. The timetable proved overambitious, but, on taking office, President Arzú committed himself to signing a peace accord. In Feb 1996 he met the URNG leadership, who called a ceasefire in March. Arzú immediately ordered the military to suspend anti-guerrilla operations. In May a vital social and agrarian reform agreement was signed, raising hopes for a formal end to the civil war. Areas still requiring agreement were: constitutional reform, the reintegration of guerrillas into civilian and political life, the future role of the military and the question of an amnesty for those on each side accused of human rights violations. In Oct the Government suspended peace talks because of a guerrilla leader's involvement in a kidnapping, but pressure from mediators brought them back to the negotiating table with a compromise and

the URNG agreed to sign a bilateral ceasefire. On 29 December 1996 a peace treaty was signed, ending 36 years of armed conflict during which an estimated 100,000 people were killed and 40,000 disappeared. An amnesty was agreed which would limit the scope of the Commission to Clarify the Past and prevent it naming names in its investigations of human rights abuses. The 3,000 URNG guerrilla troops congregated in 6 special camps, ready for demobilization in Mar 1997 when a 60-day disarmament process began, supervised by the UN. Although the demobilization was completed successfully, difficulties remained over human rights in the peace process. One of the guerrillas involved in the earlier kidnapping was allegedly beaten to death under interrogation. His disappearance was covered up by the peace negotiators who gave priority to securing a peace treaty. The case had adverse repercussions on the UN envoy to Guatemala, and head of Minugua, Jean Arnault, who was accused of involvement in the scandal.

PEOPLE

About half the total population are classed as Amerindian. (Estimates of the Amerindian population vary, from 40% to 65%.) Over 40% are *ladino*, while 5% are white, 2% black and 3.9% other mixed race or Chinese. UN statistics show that 87% of the population live in poverty and 72% can not afford a minimum diet. Some 65% of the people live at elevations above 1,000m in 30% of the total territory; only 35% live at lower elevations in 70% of the total territory.

CULTURE

The indigenous people of Guatemala are mainly of Maya descent. There are 22 recognized language groups of the Guatemalan Maya, with 100 or more dialects. Among the groups are the Mam, Cakchiquel, Kekchi, Quiché, Chuj, Maya-Mopan and Ixil. A brief description of their culture follows.

When the Spaniards arrived from Mexico City in 1523 they found little precious metal: only some silver at Huehuetenango. Those who stayed settled in the intermont basins of the southern highlands around Antigua and Guatemala City and intermarried with the groups of native subsistence farmers living there. This was the basis of the present *mestizo* population living in the cities and towns as well as in all parts of the southern highlands and in the flatlands along the Pacific coast; the indigenous population is still at its most dense in the western highlands and Alta Verapaz. They form two distinct cultures: the almost self-supporting indigenous system in the highlands, and the *ladino* commercial economy in the lowlands. At first sight the two seem to have much in common, for the Indian regional economy is also monetary, but a gulf opens between the two systems when it is realized that to an Indian trade is seen as a social act, not done out of need, and certainly not from any impulse to grow rich.

The scenery of the Indian regions W of the capital is superb and full of colour. In the towns and villages are colonial churches, some half ruined by earthquakes but often with splendid interiors. The coming of the Spaniards transformed outer lives: they sing old Spanish songs, and their religion is a compound of image-worshipping paganism and the outward forms of Catholicism, but their inner natures remain largely untouched.

Their markets and *fiestas* are of outstanding interest. The often crowded markets are quiet and restrained: no voice raised, no gesture made, no anxiety to buy or sell; but the *fiestas* are a riot of noise, a confusion of processions, usually carrying saints, and the whole punctuated by grand firework displays and masked dancers. The chief *fiesta* is always for a town's particular patron saint, but all the main Catholic festivals and Christmas are celebrated to some extent everywhere.

COSTUME AND DRESS

Indian dress is unique and attractive, little changed from the time the Spaniards arrived: the colourful head-dresses, *huipiles* (tunics) and skirts of the women, the often richly patterned sashes and kerchiefs, the hatbands and tassels of the men. It varies greatly, often from village to village. Unfortunately a new outfit is costly, the Indians are poor, and denims are cheap. While men are adopting western dress in many villages, women are slower to change. As a result of the increase in employment opportunities and the problems of land distribution (see below), many Indians are now moving from the highlands to the *ladino* lowland areas; other Indians come to the southern plains as seasonal labourers whilst retaining their costumes, languages and customs and returning to the highlands each year to tend their own crops.

NB The word *ladino*, used all over Central America but most commonly in Guatemala, applies to any person with a 'Latin' culture, speaking Spanish and wearing normal Western clothes, though he may be pure Amerindian by descent. The opposite of *ladino* is *indígena*; the definition is cultural, not racial.

RELIGION

There is no official religion but about 70% consider themselves Roman Catholic. The other 30% are Protestant, mostly affiliated to evangelical churches, which have been very active in the country in the past 25 years.

EDUCATION

50% of the population aged 25 and over have had no formal schooling and a further 22% failed to complete primary education.

CONSTITUTION

Guatemala is a Republic with a single legislative house with 80 seats. The Head of State and of government is the President. The country is administratively divided into 22 Departments. The Governor of each is appointed by the President, whose term is for 5 years. The latest constitution was dated May 1985.

THE ECONOMY

STRUCTURE OF PRODUCTION

The equitable distribution of occupied land is a pressing problem. US Aid statistics show that 68% of the cultivable land is in the hands of 2% of the landowners, 20% in the hands of 22%, and 10% in the hands of 78%, these figures corresponding to the large, medium and small landowners. A quarter of the land held by the small owners was sub-let to peasants who owned none at all. There were 531,636 farms according to the 1979 census, of which 288,083 (54%) were of less than 1.4 ha, 180,385 (34%) were of under 7 ha, while 482 (less than 1%) were of more than 900 ha. Between 1955 and 1982, 665,000 ha were redistributed (compared with 884,000 between 1952 and 1954), but it was estimated that in 1982 there were 420,000 landless agricultural workers. A peaceful movement of *campesinos* (farm labourers) was formed in 1986 to speed land distribution.

In international trade the accent is still heavily on agriculture, which accounts for two thirds of total exports. Coffee is the largest export item, followed by sugar, but bananas, vegetables, sesame and cardamom are also important crops. There has been an attempt to diversify agricultural exports with tobacco, fruit and ornamental plants, and beef exports are increasing.

The industrial sector has been growing steadily; the main activities, apart from food and drink production, include rubber, textiles, paper and pharmaceuticals. Chemicals, furniture, petroleum products, electrical components and building materials are also produced. The encouragement of *maquila* industries in the mid-1980s attracted foreign investment, much of it from the Far East, and created low-paid jobs for about 80,000 Guatemalans,

Guatemala: fact file

Geographic

Land area	108,889 sq km
forested	53.6%
pastures	24.0%
cultivated	17.6%

Demographic

Population (1996)	10,928,000
annual growth rate (1985-94)	2.9%
urban	35.0%
rural	65.0%
density	97.5 per sq km
Religious affiliation	
Roman Catholic	75%
Protestant	25%
Birth rate per 1,000 (1994)	35.4
	(world av 25.0)

Education and Health

Life expectancy at birth,	
male	61.9 years
female	67.1 years
Infant mortality rate	
per 1,000 live births (1994)	53.9
Physicians (1987)	1 per 2,356 persons
Hospital beds	1 per 602 persons
Calorie intake as %	
of FAO requirement	103%
Population age 25 and over	
with no formal schooling	45.2%
Literate males (over 15)	71.7%
Literate females (over 15)	57.3%

Economic

GNP (1993 market prices)	US$12,237mn
GNP per capita	US$1,190
Public external debt (1994)	
	US$2,368mn
Tourism receipts (1994)	US$258mn
Inflation	
(annual av 1991-95)	14.5%
Radio	1 per 19 persons
Television	1 per 22 persons
Telephone	1 per 43 persons

Employment

Population economically active (1995)	
	3,095,058
Unemployment rate	na
% of labour force in	
agriculture	58.1
mining	0.1
manufacturing	13.6
construction	4.1
Military forces	44,200

Source *Encyclopaedia Britannica*

mostly in garment manufacturing. In 1994, *maquila* exports were the third largest item in Guatemala's foreign sales (US$147mn to USA alone). At the same time, though, 60 factories moved to Mexico to be within the NAFTA bloc, with a loss of 20,000 Guatemalan jobs. The decline was forecast to continue.

Petroleum has been discovered at Las Tortugas and Rubelsanto in the Department of Alta Verapaz and in the northern Petén in a basin known as Paso Caballos. The Rubelsanto find is estimated to have proven and probable reserves of 27.3 million barrels. Production in 1996 was running at around 20,000 b/d. A pipeline transports oil from Rubelsanto to the port of Santo Tomás de Castilla. Several new wells are under development in El Petén and Guatemala is nearly self-sufficient. Several foreign oil companies are interested in exploration in Guatemala. Offshore exploration has so far been unsuccessful. There are three oil refineries. In order to lessen imports of petroleum, five hydroelectricity projects have been developed including Aguacapa (90 Mw) and Chixoy (300 Mw). A 120 Mw coal power plant is under construction on the Pacific coast. The first coal facility in Central America, it should be completed by 1999 at a cost of US$170mn.

RECENT TRENDS

Guatemala's poor growth record in the first half of the 1980s was attributable to the world recession bringing low agricultural commodity prices, particularly for coffee, and political instability both at home and in neighbouring Central American countries. The return to democracy and economic restructuring brought confidence and higher rates of growth as inflows of foreign funds were renewed. Other factors improving the balance of payments included moderate imports, rising exports, a rebound in tourism and selective debt rescheduling arrangements. An attempt at economic liberalization in 1989, involving the floating of the exchange rate,

was reined in in 1990. The Government reintroduced control over the rate after it fell sharply, causing a surge in inflation. Measures were announced to reduce liquidity and curb the fiscal deficit by raising tax income, although two previous efforts to increase taxes were followed by military coup attempts and had to be diluted.

The Government which took office in Jan 1991 sought an agreement with the IMF to reduce the fiscal deficit and inflation and stabilize the exchange rate. Efforts were also made to refinance the external debt owed to official international financial institutions. Inflation was cut from 41.1% in 1990 to 10.1% in 1992 and has remained at around that level ever since.

Gdp rose by 3.2% in 1991 and 4.8% in 1992. Growth slowed to 4% in 1993 and 1994 as investment was restricted after the insecurity of the Serrano *auto-coup*. Growth did not translate into higher investment in agriculture or industry. Nor did it produce improvements in under- or unemployment, land use or raise standards of living. High interest rates attracted capital inflows and international reserves increased from US$19mn in 1990 to US$786mn by end-1994. A 15-month standby arrangement was signed with the IMF in Dec 1992 but had to be renegotiated by the de León Carpio government. A new agreement was signed in late 1993 and much of the administration's economic planning was tied to IMF structural adjustment.

The credit and investment picture improved in 1995, led by multilateral lending to the private sector in areas such as tourism, agroindustry and energy. In 1996, confidence improved as talks progressed with the URNG for peace and social and agrarian reform but there was a slowdown in investment reflected in slower import demand and gdp grew by only 3.1%.

The Government estimates it needs US$2.3bn to fulfill its commitments agreed in the peace accords. While about

US$1.9bn is to be provided by international lending institutions and donors, the balance has to come from taxes. The Government has pledged to combat poverty and inequality by increasing social spending, with a doubling of health and education expenditure over 4 years. Funds are also needed to reform the judiciary, the police and the army and provide aid for returning refugees. Privatization is now a priority with 95% of the state telecommunications company Guatel, to be sold in 1997. Others under consideration are the National Electricity Institute (INDE), the Guatemala Electricity Company (EEGSA) and the rail network (FEGUA).

COMMUNICATIONS

There are 18,000 km of roads, 16% of which are paved. A railway links the Caribbean seaboard with the Pacific, running from Puerto Barrios up the Motagua valley to Guatemala City and on to the port of San José. From Santa María a branch line runs W through Mazatenango to the port of Champerico and the Mexican frontier. With the closure in 1995 to passengers of the line Guatemala City – Puerto Barrios, there are only freight services on Guatemala's railways. There are 867 km of public service railways and 290 km of plantation lines.

CONSERVATION

The quetzal, a rare bird of the Trogon family, is the national emblem. A stuffed specimen is perched on the national coat of arms in the Presidential Palace's ceremonial hall and others are at the Natural History Museums in Guatemala City, Quezaltenango, the Camino Real Hotel in Guatemala City and in the Historical Exhibit below the National Library. (Live ones may be seen, if you are very lucky, in the Biotopo on the Guatemala City-Cobán road, or in heavily forested highlands.)

CONSERVATION AND NATIONAL PARKS

Cecon (Centro de Estudios Conservacionistas) and Inguat (addresses under **Tourist Information**, Guatemala City) are setting up Conservation Areas (Biotopos) for the protection of Guatemalan wildlife (the quetzal, the manatee, the jaguar, etc). Several other national parks (some including Maya archaeological sites) and forest reserves have been set up or are planned. The main ones are given in the text. Those interested should see Thor Janson's books *Animales de Centroamérica en Peligro*, *Maya Nature* and *The Quetzal* (in English) available at Editorial Piedra Santa bookstores in Guatemala City and Antigua.

Guatemala City and Antigua

THE PRESENT CAPITAL, commercial and administrative centre of the country, smog-bound and crowded, and the former capital, now one of Latin America's most popular places for learning Spanish. Antigua has many major ruins, evidence of the earthquakes that have bedevilled its history. Both cities are overlooked by volcanoes active and dormant.

GUATEMALA CITY

Guatemala City was founded by decree of Charles III of Spain in 1776 to serve as capital after earthquake damage to the earlier capital, Antigua, in 1773. The city lies on a plateau in the Sierra Madre. The lofty ranges of these green mountains almost overhang the capital. To the S looms a group of volcanoes.

The city was almost completely destroyed by earthquakes in 1917-18 and rebuilt in modern fashion or in copied colonial; it was further damaged by earthquake in 1976, but most of the affected buildings have been restored.

BASICS *Pop* 1,150,452; *alt* 1,500m. The *climate* is temperate, with little variation around the year. The average annual temperature is about 18°C, with a monthly average high of 20° in May and a low of 16° in Dec-January. Daily temperatures range from a low of 7°C at night to a high of about 29° at midday. The rainy seasons are from late April to June (light), Sept to Oct, with an Indian summer (*canicula*) in July and Aug; the rain is heaviest in early Sept. It averages about 1,270 mm a year, and sunshine is plentiful. The city has a serious smog problem. Guatemala City is large. Any address not in Zona 1 – and it is absolutely essential to quote Zone numbers in addresses – is probably some way from the centre. Addresses themselves, being purely numerical, are easy to find. 19 C, 4-83 is on 19 C between 4 Av and 5 Av.

PLACES OF INTEREST

At the city's heart lies the **Parque Central**: it is intersected by the N-S running 6 Av, the main shopping street. The eastern half has a floodlit fountain; on the W side is **Parque Centenario**, with an acoustic shell in cement used for open-air concerts and public meetings. The Parque Central is popular on Sun with many *indígenas* selling textiles. To the E of the plaza is the Cathedral; to the W are the Biblioteca Nacional and the Banco del Ejército; to the N the large Palacio Nacional. Behind the **Palacio Nacional**, built of light green stone, is the Presidential Mansion.

Many of the hotels and boarding houses are in the main shopping quarter between 2 Av and 11 Av and between 6 C and 18 C, Zona 1. The railway station is

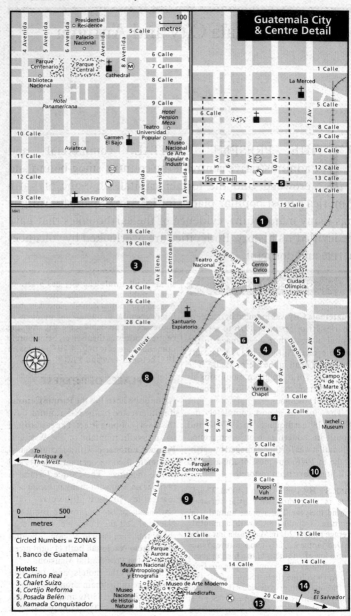

Guatemala City & Centre Detail

0   100
metres

Circled Numbers = ZONAS

1. Banco de Guatemala

Hotels:
2. *Camino Real*
3. *Chalet Suizo*
4. *Cortijo Reforma*
5. *Posada Belén*
6. *Ramada Conquistador*

in the southern part of Zona 1, at 10 Av, 18C, facing the Plaza named for Justo Rufino Barrios, to whom there is a fine bronze statue on Av las Américas, Zona 13, in the southern part of the city. To see the finest residential district go S down 7 Av to Ruta 6, which runs diagonally in front of Edif El Triángulo, past the Yurrita chapel (Zona 4), into the wide tree-lined **Av La Reforma**. At the beginning of the avenue are the Botanical Gardens; at its southern end is **Parque El Obelisco** (also known as Próceses or Independencia) with the obelisk to Guatemalan independence. La Aurora international airport, the Zoo, the Observatory, the Archaeological and the Modern Art Museums and racetrack are in **Parque Aurora**, Zona 13, in the southern part of the city.

There is a magnificent view all the way to Lake Amatitlán from **Parque de Berlín** at the S end of Av las Américas, the continuation of Av La Reforma, though some recent poor quality building has spoilt the foreground.

In the northern part (Zona 2) is the fine **Parque Minerva**, where there is a huge relief map of the country made in 1905 to a horizontal scale of 1 in 10,000 and a vertical scale of 1 in 2,000 (open 0800-1700, entrance US$0.25). Buses 1 (from Av 5, Zona 1) and 18 run to the park, where there are basketball and baseball courts, swimming pool, bar and restaurant and a children's playground (it is unsafe at night).

The most notable public buildings built 1920-44 after the 1917 earthquake are the **Palacio Nacional** (the guards have keys and may show you round the rooms of state), the Police Headquarters, the Chamber of Deputies and the Post Office. The modern Centro Cívico includes the Municipalidad, the Palacio de Justicia, the Ministerio de Finanzas Públicas, the Banco de Guatemala, the mortgage bank, the social-security commission and the tourist board.

The **Teatro Nacional** dominates the hilltop of the W side of the Civic Centre. There is an excellent view of the city and surrounding mountains from the roof. An old Spanish fortress provides a backdrop to the Open Air Theatre adjoining the blue and white mosaic-covered Teatro Nacional; open Mon-Fri (unaccompanied tours not permitted in the grounds).

On the W outskirts in Zona 7 are the Mayan ruins of **Kaminal Juyú** (Valley of Death). About 200 mounds have been examined by the Archaeological Museum and the Carnegie Institute. The area is mainly unexcavated, but there are three excavated areas open to the public, and a sculpture shed. Open 0900-1600, free. Approach from C de San Juan Sacatepéquez, then turn right along Av 30; park is at the far end.

CHURCHES

Cathedral Begun 1782, finished 1815. Paintings and statues from ruined Antigua. Solid silver and sacramental reliquary in the E side chapel of Sagrario. Next to the Cathedral is the colonial mansion of the Archbishop.

Cerro del Carmen A copy of a hermitage destroyed in 1917-18, containing a famous image of the Virgen del Carmen, situated on a hill with views of the city, was severely damaged in 1976 and remains in poor shape.

La Merced (11 Av y 5 C, Zona 1), dedicated in 1813, which has beautiful altars, organ and pulpit from Antigua as well as jewellery, art treasures and fine statues.

Santo Domingo (12 Av y 10 C, Zona 1), 1782-1807, is a striking yellow colour, reconstructed after 1917, image of Nuestra Señora del Rosario and sculptures.

Santuario Expiatorio (26 C y 2 Av, Zona 1) holds 3,000 people; colourful, exciting modern architecture by a young Salvadorean architect who had not qualified when he built it. Part of the complex (church, school and auditorium) is in the shape of a fish.

Las Capuchinas (10 Av y 10 C, Zona 1) has a very fine St Anthony altarpiece, and other pieces from Antigua.

Santa Rosa (10 Av y 8 C, Zona 1) was used for 26 years as the cathedral until the present building was ready. Altarpieces again from Antigua (except above the main altar).

San Francisco (6 Av y 13 C, Zona 1) has a sculpture of the Sacred Head, originally from Extremadura. Interesting museum with paintings at the back, though in poor condition.

Capilla de Yurrita (Ruta 6 y Vía 8, Zona 4), built in 1928 on the lines of a Russian Orthodox church as a private chapel. It has been described as an example of 'opulent 19th century bizarreness and over-ripe extravagance.' There are many wood carvings.

Carmen El Bajo (8 Av y 10 C, Zona 1) built in the late 18th century; the façade was severely damaged in 1976.

MUSEUMS

Museo Nacional de Antropología y Etnología, Salón 5, Parque Aurora, Zona 13, T 472-0489, contains stelae from Piedras Negras and typical Guatemalan costumes, and good models of Tikal, Quiriguá and Zaculeu, and other Maya items. Open 0900-1600, Tues-Fri; admission US$0.40. Contains sculpture, murals, ceramics, textiles, and a collection of masks. Its excellent jade collection is closed at weekends.

Museo de Arte Moderno, Salón 6, Parque Aurora, Zona 13, T 472-0467, 'modest, enjoyable collection'. Open Tues-Fri, 0900-1600, US$0.12.

Museo Nacional de Historia Natural, collection of national fauna: stuffed birds, animals, butterflies, geological specimens etc, in Parque Aurora, 7 Av, 6-81, Zona 13, T 472-0468; open Tues-Fri, 0900-1600, Sat-Sun, 0900-1200, 1400-1600, US$0.20.

Museum of Natural History of the University of San Carlos, C Mcal Cruz 1-56, Zona 10, T 334-6065, free, open Mon-Fri, 0900-1200, 1400-1800, closed 1 Dec-15 Jan, Holy Week and holidays, botanical garden and stuffed animals.

Museo Nacional de Arte Popular e Industrias, 10 Av, 10-72, Zona 1, T 238-0334, small exhibition of popular ceramics, textiles, silversmiths' work etc. Hours Tues-Fri 0900-1600, Sat and Sun 0900-1200, 1400-1600 (US$0.12).

Museo Ixchel del Traje Indígena, Complejo Cultural del Campus de la Universidad Francisco Marroquín, 6 C Final, Zona 10, has a collection of Indian costumes. Open Mon-Fri, 0800-1630, Sat 0900-1300, entrance US$2. Costumes are not yet all on display in the new premises, but photos from early 20th century, paintings and video. Has a shop selling textiles not usually available on the tourist market, prices are fixed.

Museo Popol Vuh de Arqueología, also at 6 C Final, Zona 10. Extensive collection of precolumbian and colonial artefacts. Has a replica of the Dresden Codex, one of the only Maya parchment manuscripts in existence. Open Mon-Fri, 0900-1700, Sat, 0900-1600. Admission US$1.20 (students US$0.60, children US$0.10-20). US$5 charge to take photographs.

Museo Nacional de Historia, 9 C, 9-70, Zona 1, T 253-6149 (Mon-Fri 0830-1600), historical documents, and objects from independence onward; and colonial furniture and arms.

Museo Fray Francisco Vásquez, 13 C, 6-34, Zona 1, 18th century paintings, Mon-Fri 0900-1200.

Museo Puiz de Arte Contemporaneo, Av 7, 8-35, Zona 9, Tues-Sat 0900-1700, Sun 0900-1400.

NB Each museum has a sign in four languages to the effect that 'The Constitution and Laws of Guatemala prohibit the exportation from the country of any antique object, either pre-columbian or colonial'. The USA in fact prohibits the import of such items and penalties are severe.

GARDENS AND ZOOS

Botanical Gardens, 1 C in Zona 10, off Av
La Reforma, open Mon-Fri, 0800-1200,
1400-1800, Sat 0830-1230, opened in 1922
and there are over 700 species of plants;
most of them labelled. Admission free.

The **Parque Zoológico La Aurora** is
in La Aurora park; entry US$1, newer
areas show greater concern for the animals' well-being.

LOCAL FESTIVALS

7 Dec, Devil's Day, hundreds of street fires
are lit, any old rubbish burnt so the smell
is awful, but it's spectacular.

LOCAL INFORMATION

● Warning

Thieves and handbag snatchers operate openly
throughout the centre of Zona 1, especially
between 4 Av and 8 Av from the Cathedral to
18 C. Some operate in pairs on motorbikes. Take
extra care walking at night. Do not park on the
street, either day or night, or your car may well
be broken into. There are plenty of lock-up
garages and parking lots (*estacionamientos*). If
you are robbed, report the incident to the Policia
Nacional, 6 Av, 13-71, Zona 1. Obtaining the
Police report may take a couple of days.

● Accommodation

Hotel prices

L1	over US$200	L2	US$151-200
L3	US$101-150	A1	US$81-100
A2	US$61-80	A3	US$46-60
B	US$31-45	C	US$21-30
D	US$12-20	E	US$7-11
F	US$4-6	G	up to US$3

(Av=Avenida; C=Calle). **NB** Hotel prices are subject to 10% VAT and 10% service. Thefts from
hotel rooms and baggage stores have been
reported; do not leave valuables unsecured.
Better prices in the more expensive hotels may
be obtained by booking corporate rates through
a reputable travel agent.

NB also The water supply in hotels tends to be
spasmodic, and water for showering is often
unobtainable between 1000-1800. Hotels are
often full at holiday times, eg Easter, Christmas,
when visitors from other countries and the
interior come to shop. At the cheaper hotels it

is not always possible to get single rooms. There
are many cheap *pensiones* nr bus and railway
stations and market; those between C 14 and
C 18 are not very salubrious.

The following list gives hotels by Zone; hotels
are listed according to category. Zona 1 is where
the majority of medium and lower-priced establishments are to be found. The higher numbered
Zones tend to be more expensive, but cheaper
alternatives can be found, eg in the Zona 9.

Zona 1: **A1** *Ritz Continental*, 6 Av 'A', 10-13,
T 238-1671, F 232-4659, clean, TV, a/c, pool,
restaurant, rec, recently refurbished; **A2** *Pan
American*, 9 C, 5-63, T 251-8709, F 251-8749,
central and rec as quiet and comfortable, TV and
baths with plugs, try to avoid rooms on the main
road side, restaurant with good and reasonably-
priced food (lunch rec, served by staff in typical
costumes), parking; **A3** *Del Centro*, 13 C, 4-55,
T 238-1281, F 230-0208, large comfortable
rooms, cable TV, good restaurant (but expensive
wines), live entertainment in bar, excellent service, rec; **A3** *Maya Excelsior*, 7 Av, 12-46, T 238-
2761, crowded, noisy and commercial but
comfortable rooms, good service and rec restaurant; **B-C** *Posada Belén*, 13 C, 'A' 10-30, T/F
251-3478, with bath in a colonial-style house,
quiet, good laundry service, friendly Francesca
and René Sanchinelli speak English, highly rec,
often full, will store luggage safely, good dining
room, avoid room next to front door, rather
noisy; **C** *Centenario*, 6 C, 5-33, T 238-0381,
clean, clothes washing facilities on top floor;
C *Chalet Suizo*, 14 C, 6-82, T 251-3786, with
or without shower (triples available) popular,
often crowded, locked luggage store
US$0.50/day but theft reported from locked
store, noisy rooms on street (avoid rooms 9 to
12, noisy pump will disturb sleep and 19-21 very
thin walls), nice new extension, big rooms,
constant hot water, Café Suizo, next door,
breakfast (with muesli) and snacks, nothing
special; **C** *Colonial*, 7 Av, 14-19, T 232-6722, F
232-8671, reasonable restaurant for breakfast,
quiet and rec, although ground floor rooms are
small and poorly ventilated, ask for 2nd floor;
C *Lito*, 10 C, 1-35, T 232-5565, popular with
Swiss travellers, with bath, quiet, clean;
C *Spring*, 8 Av 12-65, T 230-2858, F 232-0107,
with shower and hot water, cheaper without,
quaint, good breakfasts, guarded parking lot
nearby, popular, highly rec; **C-D** *Monteleone*,
18 C, 4-63, T 238-2600, F 253-9205, in front
of Antigua terminal, good clean rooms, secure,
friendly; **D** *Alameda*, C 12, Av 10, with bath,

E without, hot water, no water after 1900, cable TV, radio cassette, fan, insufficient sheets, towels etc, secure; **D** *Capri*, 9 Av 15-63, T 232-8191, F 230-0496, with shower, **F** without, some rooms noisy, clean, helpful, good restaurant, hot water, cable TV; **E** *Ajau*, 8 Av, 15-62, T 232-0488, clean, good, close to El Petén buses; **E** *Lessing House*, 12 C, 4-35, T 251-3891, small, clean, friendly; **E** *Hernani*, 15 C, 6-56, no restaurant, clean, friendly, safe to leave luggage while travelling, Spanish owner; **E** *Costa del Sol*, 17 C, 8-35, bath, hot water, noisy, adjoining *cafetería* poor value; **E** *La Fuente*, 16 C, 3-46, T 253-9924, quiet, will store luggage; **E** *San Diego*, 15 C, 7-37, unfriendly, run down, uncomfortable beds, no bag storage facilities, annex opp, **F**, good value, full by 1000; **E** *CentroAmérica*, 9 Av 16-38, with 3 meals, US$1 extra with bath, staff very helpful, bright, hot water, iced drinking water, peaceful; next door is **E** *Albergue*, courtyard, friendly, very basic but pleasant; **E** *Sevilla*, 9 Av 12-29, T 238-2226, F 232-8431, with bath, cheaper without, restaurant, bar, hot water, cable TV, Turkish bath, laundry, accepts major credit cards, very good value; **F** *Bilbao*, 8 Av y 15 C, some English spoken, shared showers but some rooms with private bath, good toilets; also **E** *Bilbao II*, fairly clean, functional, safe; **F** *Bristol*, 15 C, 7-36, shared bath, pleasant, back rooms are brighter, but noisy and not too clean; **F** *Diligencia*, 14 C, 7-36, reasonable but unfriendly; **F** *Fénix*, 7 Av, 16-81, nice old building, some rooms with bath, hot water, clean, safe, very helpful, corner rooms noisy, good meals, breakfast available; **F** *San Martín*, 16 C, 7-59, round the corner from the *Fénix*, same management, with or without bath, modern, clean, helpful, a bit noisy; **F** *San Angel*, 14 C between 10 and 11 Av, with or without bath, large rooms, good beds, intermittent hot water, bad electric wiring in some rooms and rats, kitchen; **F** *Pensión Meza*, 10 C, 10-17, beds in dormitories **F**, other rooms **E**, popular, helpful staff, English spoken, hot electric showers, noisy, dirty, damp, inhabited mainly by young travellers, motorcycle parking, good place to arrange travel with others, basic, beware of petty theft; **F** *El Virrey*, 7 Av, 15-46, OK, Estrellita del Sur, C 16, 7-37, good; **F** *Flores*, 12 C between Av 11-12, basic, shared bath, parking. If the popular tourist hotels are full try one of 3 *Hoteles Metropolitanos* at: 17 C, 1-69 (**E**); 19 C, 1-53 (**E**); and 8 C, 0-40 (**F**).

Zona 4: **L3** *Ramada Conquistador*, Vía 5, 4-68, T 331-2222, F 334-7245, luxurious; **A2** *Plaza*, Vía 7, 6-16, T 331-6173, outdoor pool, squash court, satisfactory; **E** *Venecia*, 4 Av 'A', 6-90, T 331-6991, with bath, comfortable, meals poor but cheap.

Zona 9: **L3** *El Dorado Marriott*, 7 Av, 15-45, T 331-7777, F 334-5132, being refurbished 1996-7 (ask for modernized room), expects to rival *Camino Real* as best hotel; **L3** *Princess Reforma*, 13 C 7-65, T 334-4545, F 334-4546, expanded in 1995, attractive, a/c, excellent service, cable TV, phone, pool, Hertz, travel agency; **A1** *Cortijo Reforma*, Av La Reforma 2-18, T 332-0712, F 331-8876, attractive rooms, suites, good restaurant, rec; **A2** *Apartotel Alamo*, 10 C, 5-60, T 332-4942, large rooms, bare walls and under airport flight path; **A2** *Villa Española*, 2 C, 7-51, T 332-2515, motel style, reasonably clean and modern, restaurant, bar, reasonable prices, parking, colonial atmosphere, good security, rec; **B** *Carillon*, 5 Av, 11-25, T 332-4036, noisy, uncomfortable beds, only breakfast in restaurant; **D** *Aguilar*, 4 Av, 1-51, T 334-7164, modern, good cheap food, a bit noisy, handy if you are going on to El Salvador by bus; **D** *Istmo*, 3 Av, 1-38, good restaurant, good value.

Zona 10: **L2** *Camino Real*, Av La Reforma 14-01, T 333-4633, F 337-4313, first class hotel, no airport transfers, good restaurant; **L3** *Radisson Suites Villa Magna*, 1 Av, 12-46, T 332-9797, F 332-9772, large, luxurious suites with kitchenette, a/c, laundry, garage, credit cards accepted, no restaurant but many nearby, good for long rental; **L3** *Guatemala Fiesta*, 1 Av, 13-22, T 332-2555, F 368-2366, overpriced; **A2** *Posada de Los Próceres*, 16 C, 2-40, T 368-1405, new 1995, friendly staff, free transport from airport, secure; **A2** *Residencial Reforma* (*Casa Grande*: colonial style), Av La Reforma 7-67, T 332-0914, F 360-1388, nr US Embassy, rec; **B** *Glovve Joffmar*, 12 C, 6-16, T 331-0411, with bath, free laundry included, meals, clean, safe, run by Doña Gloria Esperanza Robles; **C** *Mr Toni*, 4 C, 4-27, T/F 334-8416, hot showers, big rooms, TV, clean, parking, credit cards accepted, quiet, English spoken; **D** *Alameda Guest House*, 13 Av, 17-14, T 368-2281, English and German spoken.

Zona 13: **L3** *Crowne Plaza Las Américas*, Av Las Américas, 9-08, T 361-2535, F 339-0690, good, new, suites available; *Apartotel Casa Blanca*, Av Las Américas 5-30, US$920 a month, pleasant, a bit noisy from highway and airport; *Aeropuerto Guest House*, 15 C 'A', 7-32, see under **Airport** below; **B** *Hincapié Guest House*, Av Hincapié 18-77, T 332-7771, on far side of airport runway, nr old terminal building.

Camping: for campsites within easy access of Guatemala City, see page 681 under Amatitlán. Parking is available free at the Airport from 1900-0700. Camping-gas cartridges not hard to find (they are stocked at Almacén Orval, 11 C, y 8 Av, Zona 1 and *Supermercado Norte*, 6 Av, 2-47, Zona 1). For equipment, try *El Globo*, 7 Av, 9-61, Zona 1.

● **Places to eat**

(Restaurants at hotels. Food prices vary less than quality.) In the capital, the visitor can easily find everything from the simple national cuisine (black beans, rice, meat, chicken, soup, avocado, cooked bananas – *plátanos* – and tortillas with everything) to French, Chinese, Italian and German food (and pastries). A meal in a smart restaurant will cost US$25-30. Fashionable places, such as *Hola* (French and Italian), Av Las Américas, Zona 14, *Romanello* (Italian), 1 Av, 13-38, Zona 10, *El Parador*, 4 Av y C Montúfar, Zona 9, excellent *platos típicos*; *Hacienda de los Sánchez*, 12 C, 2-25, Zona 10, good steaks, good Guatemalan dishes; *Hacienda Real*, 13 C, 1-10, Zona 10, excellent steaks, good wine list; *El Rodeo*, 7 Av, 14-84, Zona 9, excellent steaks, rec; *Estilo Campo*, 14 C y 5 Av, Zona 10, good steak house; *Estro Armonico* (French), Vía 4, 4-30, also at 15 C, 1-11, Zona 10, Zona 4, *Puerto Barrios* (seafood), 7 Av, 10-65, Zona 9, *Marios*, 13 C, 0-43, Zona 10, superb Spanish, US$12-13, or *Grischun* (Swiss), 14 Av, 15-36, Zona 10, charge on average US$10 for a 3-course meal, without wine. Other rec restaurants: *Lai-Lai*, 7 Av, 14 C, Zona 9, Chinese, popular; *Canton*, 6 Av, 14-20, Zona 1, good Chinese, good value; *Teppanyaki*, 7 Av y 10 C, Zona 10, good Japanese; *Young Bin Guan*, 6 C, 1-57, Zona 9, T 334-3290, good Korean and Japanese; *Mesón de Don Quijote*, 11 C, 5-27, Zona 1, good budget lunch, US$2, good service, lively at night, and *Altuna*, 5 Av, 12-31 Zona 1, run by Basque family, about US$6 main course, excellent service, both good Spanish; *Arrin Cuan*, 5 Av, 3-27 Zona 1, serving food from Cobán, with marimba music and other entertainments, good food, lively atmosphere; *Bologna*, Plaza Rosa, 13 C, 1-62, Zona 10, Italian, friendly, cheap, also branch in Zona 1, at 10 C, 6-20; *Mediterráneo*, 7 Av, 3-31, Zona 9, Italian/Spanish with nice garden, good food. For local food served in 14 different 'menus', try *Los Antojitos*, Av La Reforma, 15-02, Zona 9, with music, though a bit pricey; other locations inc 7 Av y 12 C Zona 9. *La Escudilla del Tecolote*, 14 C, 4-73, Zona 10, good local dishes from

around the country, live music at weekends. Fast food is available in all parts of the city, and is relatively safe, eg *Piccadilly*, 6 Av y C11, good, modern, bright, busy, Italian food; *Los Cebollines*, 6 Av, 9-75, also in Zonas 7, 9 and 12, Mexican, good but expensive, accepts Visa cards. *El Gran Pavo*, 13 C, 4-41, Zona 1, regional Mexican, well patronized, comfortable place to talk. *Lido*, on 11 C between 7 Av y 8 Av, Zona 1, good, inexpensive set lunch. A rec pizza chain is *Giorgios*, formerly *A Guy from Italy*, Centro Comercial Pradera, Zona 10, and elsewhere, good daily lunch menu; another is *La Spaghettería*, eg Av La Reforma y 11 C, Zona 10. A simple, but nourishing, 3-course meal can be had for US$2 at any *comedor*.

Rec vegetarian restaurants: *Señor Sol*, 5 C, 11-32, Zona 1; *100% Natural*, Plaza de Villa Centre, 18 C, 10-55, Zona 10, extensive variety of dishes; *Vegetariano Devanand* chain, several branches (eg corner of 8 Av and 11 C, Zona 1), also take-away; *El Vegetariano*, 14 C, 6-74, Zona 1, next to *Chalet Suizo*, small, cheap, friendly, good international food; *Vegetariano Rey Sol*, 7 Av, 8-56, also good breads and pastries, *Antros Café*, 4 Av, 15 53, Zona 10; *Café de la Libra*, 7 Av, 12 01, Zona 9; *Señor Tenedor*, 15 C, 3-52, Zona 10 in Plaza Santander.

The best cafeterías for pies, pastries and chocolates (German, Austrian and Swiss styles) are *Los Alpes*, 10 C, 1-09, Zona 10, good cakes; *Café Wien*, annex to *Hotel Camino Real*, probably the best for coffee and cakes; *Jensen*, 14 C, 0-53, Zona 1; *Pasteleria Lins 2 C, 9-32, Zona 1, and other branches, rec; *American Doughnuts*, 5 Av, 11 47, Zona 1, and several other branches in the capital; *Pumpernik's*, 13 C, 1½ blocks from Av Reforma, Zona 10, bagels and cream cheese and other Stateside deli items, well patronized by US nationals; *Pastelería Las Américas*, 6 Av 8-44, Zona 1, delicious cakes and pastries, also at 5 Av/9 C; *Bäckerei-Konditorei Viena*, 7 Av 8-56, Zona 1, good breads and pastries. For German food eg sausages and other European specialities, try *Gourmet Center*, 18 C between 8-9 Av, Zona 10.

● **Airline offices**

Local airlines: **Aviateca**, 10 C, 6-30, Zona 1, T 238-1415, poor service, and at airport, T 334-7722; **Aerovías** T 332-7470/361-5703, for Flores and Belize City, **Tapsa**, T 331-4860, F 334-5572, for Flores: these 3 have offices at Av Hincapié and 18 C, Zona 13 at the national part of the airport. **Copa**, 1 Av 10-17, Zona 10, T 361-1567, airport, T 331-8790; **Avianca** and

SAM, Av La Reforma 13-89, Zona 10, T 334-6801, T/F 334-6797; **Lacsa**, 7 Av, 14-39, Zona 9, Ed Galería, T 332-2360/334-7722; **Iberia**, Edif Galerías Reforma 204, Av La Reforma 8-60, Zona 9, T 334-3816, F 334-3817; **Aero México**, 13 C, 8-44, Zona 10, T 333-6001; **Mexicana**,13 C 8-44, Zona 10, T 333-6048; **KLM** 6 Av 20-25, Zona 10, open 0900-1700, T 337-0222); **Aerolíneas Argentinas**, 10 C 3-17, Zona 10, T 331-1567, **United**, Edif El Reformador, Av La Reforma 1-50, Zona 9, T 332-2995, F 332-3903; **Lufthansa**, Diagonal 6 10-01, Zona 10, T 336-5526, F 339-2995; **British Airways**, 1 Av, 10-81, Zona 10, T 332-7402, F 332-7401; **JAL and American**, 7 Av 15-45, Zona 9, T (JAL) 331-8531, T (American) 334-7379. **Jungle Flying**, Av Hincapié, 18 C, Zona 13, T 360-4917, 360-4920.

● **Banks & money changers**

Banks change US dollars into quetzales at the free rate. **Banco de Guatemala**, 7 Av and 22 C, Zona 1, open Mon-Thur 0830-1400, Fri 0830-1430. There is a **Banco del Quetzal** office open 7 days a week at the airport, weekdays 0800-2100, Sat, Sun and holidays 0800-1100, 1500-1800, sometimes open earlier or may stay open for late flights (only place to change foreign banknotes). When shut, try airport police or porters who may be able/willing to change US$ cash for quetzales. There are several banks on 7 Av, open from 0830. Try the **Banco Industrial** (with Visa ATM), Av 7, nr Central Post Office, will only change TCs with proof of purchase, **Banco Internacional**, or **Bandesa**, 9 C between 9 and 10 Avs, Zona 1. **Lloyds Bank plc**, 6 Av, 9-51, Edif Gran Vía, Zona 9, T 332-7580, F 332-7641; agencies at El Reformador, Av Roosevelt, Zona 1, Zona 10, La Parroquía and Petapa. Open weekdays, 0900-1500. **Citibank**, Av Reforma 15-45, Zona 10, T 333-6574, open Mon-Fri 0900-1500. **American Express**, Edif Plaza Panamericana, Av La Reforma, 9-00 (Bancafé building) planta baja, Zona 9, T 334-0040/334-7463, F 331-1418 (bus 101 from Av 10), open Mon-Fri 0900-1630, will hold mail, Apartado Postal 720-A, for all services, agencies throughout the country. Quetzales may be bought with Visa or Mastercard at **Credomatic**, minimum withdrawal US$100, in the basement of **Banco del Quetzal** 7 Av, 6-22, Zona 9 (open until 2000, Mon-Fri, 0800-1300 Sat), T 331-8333, also 7 Av 6-26, Zona 9, T 331-7436, and at 11 C, 5-6 Av, Zona 1 (next to *Bar Europa*). You can also draw quetzales on Diners Club card, not less than US$125 or more than US$1,000 equivalent, once every 2 weeks maximum, 12 C, 4-74, Zona 9, Edif Quinta Montufar, 4th floor, T 331-6075/332-9615. Other places to use Mastercard are: **Shell/Circle K**, Av Las Américas, 18C, Zona 14 and **Banco Agrícola Mercantil**, 7 Av, 7 C Zona 9; Visa: **Construbanco**, also 7 Av, 7C Zona 9, *Hotel Radisson* and *Hotel Camino Real* both in Zona 10. Thomas Cook TCs are not easy to cash, but try Banamex on Av La Reforma, Zona 10.

The **legal street exchange** for cash and cheques may be found on 7 Av, 12-14 C, nr the Post Office (Zona 1). Be careful when changing money on the street; never go alone.

● **Cultural centres**

Goethe Institut, 11 C between 3 and 4 Av, German newspapers. **Alianza Francesa**, 4 Av, 12-39, Zona 1, free film shows on Mon, Wed and Sat evenings; other activities on other evenings, rec. **Sociedad Dante Alighieri** (Italian cultural centre), 4 Av, 12-47. **American Society**, Diagonal 6 at 13 C, Zona 10, 4th floor, Edif Rodríguez, T/F 337-1416, Mon-Fri 1300-1800. **Instituto Guatemalteco Americano** (IGA), 4 Av, 12-47, Zona 4, offers 6-week Spanish courses, 2 hrs a day, for US$60, also houses US Embassy commercial library. Several other schools in the city.

● **Embassies & consulates**

Addresses change frequently. **USA**, Av La Reforma 7-01, Zona 10 (T 331-1541/55, 336-6205/9), Mon-Fri 0800-1200, 1300-1700. **Canada**, 13 C 8-44, Zona 10, T 333-6104, Mon-Fri 0830-1100. **Mexico**, Consulate, 13 C, 7-30, Zona 9, T 331-8165, open 0815-1530 for tourist card applications and issues cards at 1500 that afternoon, those with straightforward applications, eg US, can get them at the border and avoid queues. **El Salvador**, 18 C, 14-30, Zona 13, T 334-3942, Mon-Fri, 0800-1400. **Honduras**, 13 C, 12-33, Zona 10, T 337-4344 (visas take 24 hrs, quicker in Esquipulas). **Belize**, Casa El Reformador, Av La Reforma 1-50, Zona 9, p 8, open 0800-1130, T 334-5531. **Nicaragua**, 10 Av, 14-72, Zona 10 (open Mon-Fri 0900-1300, English spoken T 368-0785). **Costa Rica**, Edificio Galerías Reforma Oficina 320, Av La Reforma, 8-60, Zona 9, T 332-0531. **Panama**, 5 Av, 15-45, Centro Empresarial, Zona 10, T 333-7182, 0830-1300 Mon-Fri, visa given on the spot, US$10, valid for 3 months for a 30-day stay, English spoken.

Argentina, 2 Av, 11-04, Zona 10, T 331-4969. **Bolivia**, 7 Av, 15-13, Zona 1, T 232-6153. **Brazil**, 18 C, 2-22, Zona 14, T 337-0949.

Colombia, Edificio Géminis 10, 12 C 1-25, Zona 10, T 335-3604. Chile, 14 C, 15-21, Zona 13, T 332-1149. Ecuador, 4 Av 15-67,Zona 14, T 337-2902. Paraguay, 7 Av, 7-78 (p 8), Zona 4. Peru, 2 Av, 9-67, Zona 9, T 331-8558. Uruguay, 6 Av 20-25, Zona 10, T 337-0228. Venezuela, 8 C, 0-56, Zona 9 T 331-6505.

Israel, 13 Av 14-07, Zona 10, T 333-6951. Japan, Ruta 6, 8-19, Zona 4, T 331-9666. South Africa, 10 Av, 30-57, Zona 5, T 332-6890.

Austria, 6 Av, 20-25, Zona 10, T 368-2324 Mon to Fri 1100 to 1300. Belgium, 15 C A 14-44, Zona 10, T 368-1150. Denmark, 7 Av 20-36 (Apartment 1, p 2), Zona 1, T 238-1091. Finland, 2 C, 18-37, Zona 15, T 365-9270. France, 16 C, 4-53, Zona 10, T 337-3639/337-2207. Germany, 6 Av, 20-25, Edif Plaza Marítima, p 2, Zona 10, T 337-0028/337-0031, open 0900-1200 (bus 14 goes there). Netherlands, Consulate General, 12 C, 7-56, Edif La Curaçao, Zona 9, p 4, T 331-3505 (open 0900-1200). Norway, 6 Av, 11-77, Zona 10, p 5, T 332-9296, F 332-9301; Italy, 5 Av, 8-59, Zona 14, T 337-4558, Mon, Wed, Fri 0800-1430, Tues, Thur 0800-1330, 1500-1800; Portugal, 5 Av, 12-60, Zona 9, T 334-1054; Spain, 6 C, G 48, Zona 9, T 331-2757. Sweden, 8 Av, 15-07, Zona 10, T 333-6536. Switzerland, Edif Seguros Universáles, 4 C, 7-73, Zona 9, T 334-0743, Mon-Fri 0900-1130; British Embassy, Ed Centro Financiero, Torre 2, p 7, 7 Av 5-10, Zona 4 (T 332-1601/02/04/06), Mon-Thur 0900 1200, 1400-1600, Fri 0800-1100, passports replaced in 4 days inc weekend, helpful, compiling new database for security rating in 1997 so report all attacks/thefts (Australian/New Zealand citizens should report loss or theft of passports here).

● Entertainment

Cinemas: are numerous and often show films in English with Spanish subtitles. Prices are US$1.50-$2.

Concerts: of the Philharmonic Orchestra take place in the Teatro Nacional, Civic Centre, 24 C, Zona 1. During the rainy season at the Conservatorio Nacional, 5 C, y 3 Av, Zona 1, and occasionally in the Banco de Guatemala.

Discothèques: After Eight, Ed Galerías España, Zona 9; Kahlúa, 1 Av, 13-21, Zona 10; Manhattan, 7 Av opp Hotel El Dorado, Zona 9; El Optimista, Av La Reforma 12-01, Zona 10; La Petite Discothèque, La Manzana, Ruta 4, 4-76, Zona 4; La Bodeguita, 12 C, 3 Av, Zona 1, rec dance club; El Establo, Av La Reforma 11-83, Zona 10, is a bar with excellent music, 1900-0100 (1200-1900 it is a bookshop and

restaurant); Pandora's Box, Ruta 3-38, Zona 4, popular. Another popular bar with live music is Concierto de los 60, 7 Av y 8 C, Zona 1, no entrance charge and normal prices for drinks. Also in Zona 1 are Madrid, 8 Av y 12 C, opp Guatel, good, and Cavi, 17 C between 7 and 8 Av, both Spanish style bars. Shakespeare's Pub is an English-style bar, at 13 C, 1-51, Zona 10, good atmosphere, live music at weekends. Bar Europa, 11 C, 5-16, Zona 1, popular peace corps/travellers' hangout, Don Mauricio will change dollars and TCs, good rates, honest. Lots of bars, discos and restaurants in Zona 10 open till 0300 at weekends.

Music: Guatemala (with southern Mexico) is the home of marimba music (see page 17). The marimba is a type of xylophone played with drum sticks by from one to nine players. Up country the sounding boxes are differently sized gourds, the marimbas de tecomates. The city ones are marvels of fine cabinet work.

Nightclubs: La Quebrada, 6 Av, 4-60, Zona 4; Plaza Inn, Motel Plaza, Vía 7, 6-16, Zona 4; Brasilia in Hotel Ritz Continental.

Theatres: Teatro Nacional. Teatro Gadem, 8 Av, 12-15, Zona 1; Antiguo Paraninfo de la Universidad, 2 Av, 12-30, Zona 1; Teatro Universidad Popular, 10 C, 10-32, Zona 1; Teatro Artistas Unidos, 3 Av, 18-57, Zona 1; La Cúpula, 7 Av/13 C, contemporary plays, concerts and classic cinema, details in press. Occasional plays in English, and many other cultural events, at Instituto Guatemaltoco Americano (IGA), Ruta 1 and Vía 4, Zona 4. List of current offerings outside Teatro del Puente, 7 Av, 0-40, Zona 4, and in local English-language publications and city newspapers.

● Hospitals & medical services

Dentists: Dr Freddy Lewin, Centro Médico, 6 Av 3-69, Zona 10, T 332-5153 (German, English); Dr Bernal Herrera, 6 C, 1-50, Zona 1, T 251-8249 (English, Japanese); Amicelco, 5 Av, 4 12, Zona 1, sells drugs to pharmacies but will also supply gamma globulin etc to the public at reasonable prices.

Doctors: Dr Mariano A Guerrero, 5 Av, 3-09, Zona 1, German-speaking, understands English (US$10 for treatment); Dr Manuel Cáceres, 6 Av, 8-92, Zona 9, 1600-1800, speaks English and German; Dr Boris Castillo Camino, 6 Av, 7-55, Zona 10, office 17, T 334-5932, rec; also Dr Román Ferrate Felice at 5 Av, 2-63, Zona 1, rec for consultation (US$6) by tourist who had amoebic dysentery.

Emergency: T 334-5955/332-3555 for hospitals, T 128 for ambulance, T 125 for Red Cross (Cruz Roja).

Hospitals: *Centro Médico Hospital*, 6 Av, 3-47, Zona 10, private, but reasonably priced, all senior doctors speak English, very helpful.

● **Laundry**
Lava-Centro Servimatic, Ruta 6, 7-53, Zona 4 (opp Edif El Triángulo) sometimes has hot water; *Lavomatic*, 8 Av, 17/18 C, Zona 1; *Lavandería Super Wash*, Av 12, 12-28, Zona 1, T 232-9362, US$1.50/load, US$1.80/dryer; *Express* (dry cleaners), 7 Av, 3-49, Zona 4; *El Siglo* (dry cleaners), 7 Av, 3-50, Zona 4, 11 Av, 16-35, Zona 1, and 12 C, 1-55, Zona 9, 4 Av, just up from 13 C, Zona 1. Dry cleaner also at Vía 2, 4-04, Zona 4, open Mon-Fri, 0730-1830.

● **Places of worship**
Non-Catholic Churches: *Episcopalian Church of St James*, Av Castellana 40-08, Zona 8, and the *Union Church of Guatemala* (Plazuela España, Zona 9). Sun morning service in English at the first: 0930; at the second: 1100.

Synagogue: 7 Av, 13-51, Zona 9. Service at 0930 Sat.

● **Post & telecommunications**
Central Post Office: 7 Av, 12 C, Zona 1, T 232-6101/6107, open Mon-Fri 0800-1600. Ground floor for overseas parcel service (airmail only, very expensive), at the back (allow plenty of time). Watch your belongings when standing in queues here. This is the only post office in the country from which parcels over 2 kg can be sent abroad. You have to show your goods, which will be weighed, make a customs list before packing (cardboard box or flour sack, staff will lend a needle and give instructions), all in an office at the back of the building. Airmail to US; 1-3 kg US$22, 3-5 kg US$33, 5-10 kg US$59; to Europe, 1-3 kg US$33, 3-5 kg US$48, 5-10 kg US$80. Poste restante keeps mail for 2 months (US$0.03/letter). Amex will hold mail for cardholders, office below Bancafé, Av Reforma y 9 C, Zona 9. If you are awaiting an incoming parcel, the Post Office will inform you at a private address that the item has arrived. You must then clear customs, Aduana de Fardos Postales, 10 C, 13-92, Zona 1, and pay the charges, which may be high. At customs, there are lists of parcels received, which you can ask to see. There may also be information in rooms 110 and 233 in the main post office.

Telecommunications: **NB** See **Telephone services** in **Information for travellers**, page 733. Empresa Guatemalteca de Telecomunicaciones (Guatel), 7 Av, 12-39, Zona 1 or 4 Av, 6-54 for international calls; open 0700-2400, 7 days a week, national and international telephone service. Local telegrams from central post office. Calls within Guatemala are surprisingly cheap on Sun, Q1 will get you a brief call anywhere in the country.

● **Shopping**
The **Central Market** operates behind the Cathedral, from 7 to 9 Av, 8 C, Zona 1; one floor is dedicated to native textiles and crafts, and there is a large, cheap basketware section on the lower floor. Apart from the **Mercado Terminal** in Zona 4 (large, watch your belongings), there is the **Mercado del Sur**, 6 Av, 19-21, Zona 1, primarily a food market though it has a section for popular handicrafts. There is also an *artesanía* market in Parque Aurora, nr the airport, where marimba music is played, and which is strictly for tourists. Silverware is cheaper at the market than anywhere else in Guatemala City. The market is, however, rec for all local products. Bargaining is necessary at all markets in Guatemala. Also, *4 Ahau*, 11 C, 4-53, Zona 1, very good for *huipiles*, other textiles, and crafts and antiques, run by *Dr Italo Morales* who has a great knowledge of local cultures; hand-woven textiles from *Miranda* factory, 8 Av, 30-90, Zona 8; *El Patio*, 12 C, 3-57, Zona 1; *Rodas Antiques*, 5 Av, 8-42, Zona 1 and *Barrientos Antigüedades*, 10 C, 4-64, Zona 1, have high priced silver and antiques. *Mayatex*, 12 C, 4-46, good choice, wholesale prices. *Maya Exports*, 7 Av, 10-55, Zona 1, credit cards accepted. Opp is *Sombol*, Av Reforma 14-14 and C 7-80, good for handicrafts, dresses and blouses. *La Momosteca* has a stall in Plaza Barrios and a shop at 7 Av, 14-48, Zona 1, and sells both textiles and silver. *Pasaje Rubio*, 9 C nr 6 Av, Zona 1, is good for antique silver charms and coins. Shop hours 0900-1300, 1500-1900 weekdays; may open all day on Sat.

Bookshops: *Géminis*, 6 Av, 7-24, Zona 9, T 331-0064 (good selection), has English books; *La Plazuela*, 12 C, 6-14, Zona 9, US magazines, English and Spanish books, large selection of 2nd hand books; *Vista Hermosa* 2 C, 18-50, Zona 15, T/F 369-1003 (English, German, Spanish); *Don Quijote*, Av Reforma y 14 C, Zona 10 (in Galería), good selection in Spanish. *Museo Popol Vuh* bookshop has a good selection of books on pre-columbian art, crafts and natural history; also bookshop of *Camino Real* hotel which has US newspapers. *Arnel*, Edif El Centro 108, 9 C, 7 Av, Zona 1, excellent range of English and French books, usually stocks *Handbooks*, friendly owner, speaks English. Bookshops also at *Conquistador-Ramada*, Museo Ixchel, and the airport. *Librería del Pensativo*, La Cupola, Av 7, 13-01, Zona 9; *Librería Artemis*, 5 Av, 12-11, Zona 1, T 253-3532, good selection. *Instituto Guatemalteco Americano* (IGA), Ruta 1 and Vía 4, Zona 4 (also library). *Luna y Sol*, 12 C, 3-55, Zona 1, good selection of books, cassettes etc; *Eximia*, 12 C, 0-85, Zona 9, Local 5, Plaza Lorenzo, T 331-7073, a good place to browse, stocks English and Spanish books on ecology, mysticism, psychology, also posters, cards, crystal, quartz and gemstones; *Piedra Santa*, 11 C, 6-50, Zona 1, 5a C, 8-61 Zona 1, 6a C, 9-68, Zona 1, 12 C, 1-25, Zona 10 (Edif Géminis 10, L 202 y 203) and Calz Roosevelt 22-50 Zona 7 (Edif Econocentro, L20).

Camera repairs: *Fototécnica*, Av Centro América 15-62, efficient, good stock. Batteries for cameras hard to come by but try *Celcomer* in Centro Comercial Montufar on 12 C in Zona 9. Kodak's main local distributor is nr the zoo for a wide supply of camera products. Film is easy to find; slide film, Ektachrome 36 exp 100 ASA costs around US$10, shop at 9C, 0-88.

Maps: can be bought from the *Instituto Geográfico Militar*, Av Las Américas 5-76, Zona 13, T 332-2611, open 0800-1600 Mon to Fri, closed Sat and Sun; the more detailed maps can be bought over the counter, just explain why they are needed and wait until the paperwork is done, US$3 5 each. Those that cannot be bought may be copied by hand from the book containing all the 1:50,000 and 1:250,000 maps of the country. Also good map of city on back of map of country, from Hertz at airport when in stock. (See also Casa Andinista in Antigua under **Bookshops**.)

● **Sports**

Bowling: ten-pin variety and billiards at Bolerama, Ruta 3, 0-61, Zona 4, 2 blocks from *Ramada-Conquistador* hotel.

Golf: there is an 18-hole golf course at the *Guatemala Country Club*, 8 km from the city, and a 9-hole course at the *Mayan Club*. You must be invited by a member (enquire at *Shakespeare Pub*).

Hang gliding: *Asociación de Vuelo Libre*, 12 C, 1-25, Zona 10, Oficina 1601, Edif Géminis 10, T 335-3215, flying over Lakes Atitlán and Amatitlán, best time Nov to May.

Swimming pools: apart from those at the Parque Minerva (page 615) there are pools at *Ciudad Olímpica*, 7 C y 12 Av, Zona 5 (monthly membership only, US$2.50 a month – photograph required; you may be allowed in for a single swim); *Piscina Ciudad Vieja*, Zona 15; Baños del Sur, 13 C 'A' 7-34, Zona 1, has hot baths for US$0.50, saunas for US$1.50. Try also the hotels and the campsites nr Amatitlán. The *Camino Real* sells tickets for its pool to non-guests.

Tennis: *Guatemala Lawn Tennis Club* and the *Mayan Club* are the chief centres for tennis.

● **Tour companies & travel agents**
Archaeological tours: *Turismo Kim'Arrin*, Edif Maya, Oficina No 103, Vía 5, 1 50, Zona 4, and *Panamundo Guatemala Travel Service* also arrange tours to Maya sites.

Travel agents: *Clark Tours*, 7 Av 6-53, in Edif El Triángulo, Zona 4, T 331-0213, F 331-5919 long established, very helpful, tours to Copán, Quiriguá, etc. For address of **American Express**, see under **Banks & money changers** above; *Setsa Travel*, 8 Av, 14-11, very helpful, tours arranged to Tikal, Copán, car hire; *Aire, Mar y Tierra*, Plaza Marítima, 20 C, y 6 Av, Zona 10, and Edif Herrera, 5 Av y 12 C, Zona 1; *Tourama*, Av La Reforma 15-25, Zona 10, both rec, German and English spoken. *Izabal Tours*, Alfredo Toriello, 7a Av 14-44, Zona 9, Local 14, T 334-0323, F 334-3701, highly rec for special interest and educational tours, very knowledgeable. *Servicios Turísticos del Petén*, 2 Av, 7-78, Zona 10, trips to Flores and Tikal (owns *Hotel Maya Internacional*, Flores) *Maya Expeditions*, 15 C, 1-91, Zona 10, T 363-4955, F 337-4666, very experienced, varied selection of short and longer river/hiking tours, white-water rafting, bungee jumping, cultural tours, official guides to Piedras Negras archaeological excavations. *Interconti Travel*, Av Reforma 6-46, Zona 9, T 339-0990, F 339-1001, English and German. *Nancy's*, 11 C, 5-16, Zona 1, T 251-6995, very helpful. *Aventuras Vacacionales*, 4 C, 6-63, Zona 13, T/F 473-6253, for sailing trips from Río Dulce to local destinations and the Belize Cayes (see page 656). For the cheapest flights out of Guatemala, speak to Josefina at 6 Av, 9-28, Zone 1, T 253-6346, in English, German or French. *Viajes de Guatemala*, 15 C, 7-75, Zona 10, T/F 368-2252, arranges helicopter flights from Flores to Uaxactún, Río Azul and Mirador, and helicopter rental. *Jungle Flying*, Av Hincapié and 18 C, Zona 13, T 360-4917/4920 at airport, tours to Copán, Honduras, US$180 inc flight, entry to site, guide and lunch; *Mersans*, 43 Av, 0-44,

Zona 11, T/F 591-0789, good for bus excursions, German spoken. *Mayapan*, 6 Av 7-10, Zona 2, T 251-8840, F 232-1866. *Viajes Internacionales*, 6 Av 9-62, Zona 1, T 238-3191, helpful, English spoken. *Destinos Turísticos*, SA, 12 C 1-25, Zona 10, Edif Géminis 10, Torre Norte, Oficina 1102, T/F 335-2819/2821, e-mail: destinos@guate.net, UK Agent: Penelope Kellie, Winchester 01962 779317, F 01962 779458.

● **Tourist offices**

Inguat, 7 Av, 1-17, Zona 4 (Centro Cívico), T 331-1333/47, F 331-2127/331-4416, very friendly, English and some German spoken, provides hotel list from the inexpensive to the most expensive, has general information on buses, market days, museums, etc, open Mon-Fri 0815-1600, accurate map of city, other maps, information, major tourist attractions. The Citur office on the 2nd floor of the Inguat building can arrange air fare discounts for International Student Identity card holders. A letter from a Guatemalan language school may work. Sra Betty López, in the department of residences, 10th floor, is the person to see regarding any queries about residency; she speaks English, for information, T 124. Information on nature from **Inafor**, 7 Av y 13 C, Zona 9, T 332-5064. For information on the Biotopos (Nature reserves) contact CECON, Av La Reforma 0-63 Zona 10, T 331-0904, who can also advise on voluntary work opportunities.

● **Useful addresses**

Fire service: T 122.

Immigration office: Dirección General de Migración 41 C, 17-36, Zona 8, T 471-4670/475-1390, F 471-4678 (for extensions of visas, take photo to 'Inspectoría'). If you need new entry stamps in a replacement passport (ie if one was stolen), go to room 201, police report required, plus a photocopy and a photocopy of your passport. They need to know date and port of entry to check their records. Whole process takes only about 30 mins. Take bus 71 'Terminal' from 10 Av. See **Documents** under **Information for travellers**, page 726.

Police: T 120 or 137 or 138.

Voluntary work: Casa Guatemala, 14 C, 10-63, Zona 1, T 232-5517, can arrange voluntary work in an orphanage in Río Dulce (Fronteras) nr the road bridge.

● **Transport**

Local Bus: in town, US$0.12/journey on regular buses, US$0.16 on express buses. Not many before 0600 or after 2000. In 1995 trailer buses were introduced, charging US$0.10, and fixed route taxis, charging US$0.36 for the first 700m, or 2 mins, then US$0.10 for each additional 200m/40 secs. **Taxis**: from US$1 for a short run to US$5-9 for longer runs inside the city (eg US$6 Zona 9 to centre). Hourly rates are from US$5. Prices double at night. Taxis of the Amarillo Express, Azules, Concordia and Palace companies rec. Taxis Circulante Rojo, T 289-4415 also rec, otherwise service is generally bad. No meters, so agree fares in advance and make arrangements to share before you approach the taxi or you will pay double. Taxis always available in Parque Central and Parque Concordia (6 Av and 15 C, Zona 1) and at the Trébol (the main crossroads outside city if coming from Pacific or Highlands by bus, convenient for airport).

Car Insurance: Granai y Townson, 7 Av, 1-82, Zona 4.

Car rental: **Hertz**, 7 Av, 14-76, Zona 9, T 331-5374, F 331-7924; **Avis**, 12 C, 2-73, Zona 9, T 331-2750, F 332-1263; **Budget**, Av La Reforma y 15 C, Zona 9, T 331-6546; **National**, 14 C, 1-42, Zona 10, T 368-0175, F 337-0221; **Dollar**, 6 Av 'A', 10-13, Zona 1, T 232-3446 (at *Hotel Ritz*); **Tikal**, 2 C, 6-56, Zona 10, T 332-4721; **Quetzal**, 19 Av 0-56, Zona 11, T 473-5197; **Tabarini**, 2 C, 'A', 7-30, Zona 10, T 331-6108, airport T 331-4755 (have Toyota Land Cruisers); **Rental**, 12 C, 2-62, Zona 10, T 361-0672, good rates, also motorbikes. **Tally**, 7 Av, 14-60, Zona 1, T 232-0421 (have Nissan and Mitsubishi pick-ups), very competitive, rec; **Uno**, 10 Av, 19-50, Zona 10, T/F 337-2347 (Sr Manuel Pacas), or T 203-6987 La Aurora Airport. **Ahorrent**, at airport, good service, hotel delivery.

Check carefully the state of the car when you hire. You may be charged for damage already there. Average rates are US$50-60 all inc (US$60-80 Hertz, or Avis)/day. Local cars are usually cheaper than those at international companies; if you book ahead from abroad with the latter, take care that they do not offer you a vehicle which is not available. If you wish to drive to Copán, you must check that this is permissible; Tabarini and Hertz do allow their cars to cross the border. Insurance rate (extra) varies from US$4-6 a day, check carefully what excess will be charged (could be as high as US$500 but travel insurance should cover this in the event of an accident).

Car repairs: Christian Kindel, 47 C, 16-02, Zona 12. Chevrolet *Automecánica Cidea*, 10 Av, 30-57, Zona 5, T 334-1531-5 (good supply of parts); Honda, Frank Autos, 7 Av, 10-01, Zona

Win two Iberia flights to Latin America

We want to hear your ideas for further improvements as well as a few details about yourself so that we can better serve your needs as a traveller.

We are offering you the chance to win two Iberia flights to Latin America, currently flying to 25 destinations. Every reader who sends in the completed questionnaire will be entered in the Footprint Prize Draw. 10 runners up will each receive a Handbook of their choice.

Fill in this form using a ball-point pen and return to us as soon as possible.

Mr ☐ Mrs ☐ Miss ☐ Ms ☐   Age

First name

Surname

Permanent Address

Postcode/Zip

Country

Email

Occupation

Title of Handbook

Which region do you intend visiting next?

North America ☐	India/S.Asia ☐	Africa ☐
Latin America ☐	S.E. Asia ☐	Europe ☐
Australia ☐		

How did you hear about us?

Recommended ☐	Bookshop ☐
Used before ☐	Media/press article ☐
Library ☐	Internet ☐

There is a complete list of Footprint Handbooks at the back of this book. Which other countries would you like to see us cover?

Offer ends 30 November 1998. Prize winners will be notified by 30 January 1999 and flights are subject to availability.

If you do not wish to receive information from other reputable businesses, please tick box ☐

Win two Iberia flights to Latin America

IBERIA

Affix
Stamp
Here

Footprint Handbooks

6 Riverside Court
Lower Bristol Road
Bath
BA2 3DZ
England

Thailand Handbook

Andalucia Handbook

Zimbabwe & Moçambique Handbook with Malawi

Caribbean Islands Handbook with the Bahamas

Goa Handbook

Indonesia Handbook

Chile Handbook

Cambodia Handbook

India Handbook

Bolivia Handbook

Israel Handbook with the Palestinian Authority Areas

Vietnam Handbook

East Africa Handbook with Kenya, Tanzania, Uganda and Ethiopia

Tibet Handbook with Bhutan

Peru Handbook

South Africa Handbook

Morocco Handbook with Mauritania

Malaysia & Singapore Handbook

Namibia Handbook

Myanmar (Burma) Handbook

Egypt Handbook

Nepal Handbook

Ecuador & Galápagos Handbook

Mexico & Central America Handbook

Laos Handbook

South American Handbook

Tunisia Handbook with Libya

9, T 331-9287. For muffler service (or to remove a catalytic converter if you are heading into countries without lead-free petrol), Leonardo's, Av Castellana 40-76, Zona 8. General Motors (Cofiño Stahl)T 368-0446; Isuzu (Canella S.A) T 334-8051. Honda **motorcycle** parts from FA Honda, Av Bolívar 31-00, Zona 3, T 471-5232, general manager and chief mechanic are German, former speaks English. Car and motorcycle parts from FPK, 7 Av, 8-08, Zona 4; T 331-9777.

Motorbike rental: *Moto-Rent*, 11 C, between 2 and 3 Av, Zona 9. Good Hondas for rent at reasonable prices, about US$15/day for a Honda XL 185. Bikes can also be rented at the airport, a Jawa 180 cc for US$15, primitive but it works. Rec to take jacket and gloves, particularly when touring the countryside. Avoid riding a bike in Guatemala City, it is very polluted.

Motorcycle repairs: Mike and Andy Young, 27 C, 13-73, Zona 5, T 331-9263, open 0700-1530, excellent mechanics for all vehicles, extremely helpful.

Traffic: some traffic lights operate at rush hours; at dangerous junctions they operate 24 hrs. Avenidas have priority over Calles (except in Zona 10, where this rule varies). City traffic is very heavy during weekdays.

Air The airport is in the S part of the City at La Aurora, 4 km from the Plaza Central; restaurant with cheap 'meal of the day'; all prices marked up in the shops. Tourist information desk close to immigration office, open 0600-2100, T 331-4256, has maps and general information. No left luggage facilities. Banco del Quetzal, see above under **Banks and money changers**. Taxi to town, US$4.50-6, bargaining difficult. The Inguat kiosk for the purchase of taxi vouchers is just outside the arrivals terminal on right. Beware of rogue taxis (*taxis fantasmas*) that operate as part of a robbery network. Buses nos 5 (in black not red), 6, 20 and 83 from 8 Av, Zona 1, and the Zona 4, 4 Av, 1 C, bus terminal, run the 30-min journey between airport and centre (US$0.20). (Bus 20 runs from Centro Cívico to Aeropuerto Local.) There is also a bus to 7 Av, 18 C (price increases at night). From airport, buses leave just outside the upper level every 5-10 mins, until 1930. For transport to Antigua, ask at the *Ramada* desk when their shuttle is leaving, US$7-9 pp (last shuttle around 1600-1730). Some domestic flights (check!) to Flores (see page 662) leave from a separate terminal at La Aurora. This is located on the opp side of the runway and reached via Av Hincapié, in Zona 13. There are no scheduled flights to other

domestic airfields in Guatemala, any chartered flights will leave from this terminal. It is 150m to Av Américas and buses to town. **NB** The airport is officially closed from 2100-0400, so you cannot stay the night there, but there is **C** *Aeropuerto Guest House*, 5 mins' walk from the airport at 15 C A, 7-32, Zona 13, T 332-3086, with free transport to and from the airport, shared baths, clean, safe, will order take-away food from nearby.

Trains Passenger trains to Puerto Barrios and Tecún Umán have been suspended.

Buses NB Information on interior bus services is available at Inguat, see Tourist Information above. The Zona 4 bus terminal (2nd class service only, not rec for tourists, poor and unsafe) between 1-4 Av and 7-9 C serves the Occidente (West), the Costa Sur (Pacific coastal plain) and El Salvador. The area of 19 C, 8-9 Av, Zona 1, next to the Plaza Barrios market, contains many bus offices and is the departure point for the Oriente (East), the Caribbean zone, Pacific coast area toward the Mexican border and the N, to Flores and Tikal. 1st class buses often depart from company offices in the south-central section of Zona 1. The following companies operate from Guatemala City: Transportes Unidos, 15 C, 3-4 Av, Zona 1, T 232-4949, 253-6929 (Antigua); Delta y Tropical, 1C y 2 Av, Zona 4; Escobar y Monja Blanca, 8 Av, 15-16, Zona 1, T 251-1878, 238-1409 (Biotopo del Quetzal and Cobán); Veloz Quichelense (Chichicastenango), Chatia Gomerana (La Democracia), Transportes Cubanita (Reserva Natural de Monterrico) all at Zona 4 terminal; Galgos, 7 Av, 19-44, Zona 1, T 232-3661, 253-4868 (Quezaltenango, Mexican border – rec); Rutas Orientales, 19C, 8-18, Zona 1, T 253-7282/251-2160 (Honduran border); Buses Vilma, Parque de Chiquimula (Florido); Los Halcones, 7 Av, 15-27, Zona 1, T 238-1929 (Huehuetenango); Transportes Velásquez, 20C, 2 Av, Zona 1 (Mexican border); Transportes Rebuli, 21C, 1-34, Zona 1, T 230-2748/474-1539 (Panajachel); Transportes Litegua, 15C, 10-42, Zona 1, T 253-8169 (Puerto Barrios); Transportes Esmeralda, 8 Av 38-41, Zona 3, T 471-0327 (Pacific coast); Fuente del Norte, 17C, 8-46, Zona 1, T 251-3817 (Río Dulce); Línea Máxima del Petén, 9 Av, 17-28, Zona 1; Melva Internacional, 3 Av, 1-38, Zona 9, T 331-0874 (El Salvador border); Transportes Poaquileña, 20C, Av Bolívar, Zona 1 (Tecpán); Transportes Fortaleza, 19C, 8-70, Zona 1, T 232-3643,(Tecún Umán – not rec). See under destinations for schedules and fares.

International buses: to San Salvador: Quality, Círculo Maya, 6 Av, 9-85, Zona 9, T 334-7954, leaves from *Hotel Villa Española* (0615 and 1515) and *Hotel Guatemala Fiesta* (0630 and 1530) daily for San Salvador, about 5 hrs, bus takes care of border formalities, a/c,video, snacks, US$18 one way, US$35 return (valid 90 days). Confort Lines leaves *Hotel El Dorado*, 7 Av, 16 C, Zona 9, 0800 and 1400, same price and service. Tickets from all travel agencies in Guatemala City and Antigua. Ticabus (11 C 2-72, Zona 9, T 331-4279) at 1230 daily, to San Salvador (US$16) with connections to Tegucigalpa, Managua, US$43, San José, and Panama, US$78.10. All other San Salvador buses leave from 3 Av, between 1 C and 2 C, Zona 9, all companies are part of a cooperative and buses leave between 0400 and 1630, US$7.50. Companies are: Transportes Centroamérica, 7 Av, 15-59, Zona 1, T 238-4985 (minibus service to hotel on request), can book in advance, US$6 to San Salvador, 4 hrs, comfortable minibus, leaves Zona 1 at 0530 and Zona 9 at 0700-0715; Melva and Pezzarossi.

Reserve the day before if you can (all except Pezzarossi go also to Santa Ana). Taking a bus from Guatemala City as far as, say, San José is tiring and tiresome (the bus company's bureaucracy and the hassle from border officials all take their toll).

To **Honduras** avoiding El Salvador, take bus to Esquipulas, then minibus to border.

To **Mexico**: Fortaleza has buses to Tecún Umán, US$4; Galgos have several buses daily to Talismán, US$6.50, connections with Cristóbal Colón bus line – rebookings at the border may be necessary, they also have a luxury service at 0630 to Tapachula, US$16. Velásquez have 0830 bus daily to La Mesilla, connections with Cristóbal Colón.

GUATEMALA CITY TO ANTIGUA

The shortest route to **Antigua** is 45 km via San Lucas Sacatepéquez (see page 639) by paved double-lane highway (Calzada Roosevelt/Calzada Internacional) passing (25 km out) El Mirador (1,830m), with fine view of the capital. Road then rises to 2,130m and gradually drops to 1,520m at Antigua. The main road between Guatemala City and Antigua suffers from heavy traffic at weekends.

ANTIGUA

Antigua (*Pop* 43,000; *Alt* 1,520m) was the capital city until it was heavily damaged by earthquake in 1773. Founded in 1543, after destruction of a still earlier capital, Ciudad Vieja, it grew to be the finest city in Central America, with a population of 80,000, numerous great churches, a University (1676), a printing press (founded 1660), and famous sculptors, painters, writers and craftsmen.

Agua volcano is due S of the city and the market is to the W. Avenidas are numbered upwards running from E (Oriente) to W (Poniente), and Calles upwards from Norte to Sur. Avenidas are Norte or Sur and Calles Oriente or Poniente in relation to the central Plaza; however, unlike Guatemala City, house numbers do not give one any clue towards how far from the central Plaza a place is.

Places of interest

Entry fees in 1997 were Q10 for most ruins for foreigners, Q2 for Guatemalans. **Colonial architecture** Centre of the city is the **Parque Central**, the old Plaza Real, where bullfights and markets were held. The **Cathedral** (current structure 1680 – first cathedral was demolished 1669) is to the E (entry to ruins US$0.35), the **Palace of the Captains-General** to the S (1764 – the original building, begun 1543, was demolished), the **Municipal Palace** (Cabildo – see **Museums** below) to the N (all have been repaired since the 1976 earthquake) and an arcade of shops to the W. Alvarado was buried in the Cathedral, but whereabouts is not known. All the ruined buildings, though built over a period of 3 centuries, are difficult to date by eye, partly because of the massive, almost romanesque architecture against earthquakes. For example, the cloisters of the convent of **Capuchinas** (1736), look 12th century, with immensely thick round pillars. The most interesting ruins (apart from those mentioned) are of the monastery of **San Francisco**, the convent of

Santa Clara (1700, 6 C Oriente y 2 Av Sur),
El Carmen, San Agustín (the last two may
only be viewed from outside), La Compañía de Jesús (being restored by the
Spanish government), Santa Cruz, Escuela de Cristo church, La Recolección
(1700), C de la Recolección, off the road,
set among coffee groves (particularly
worth a visit), Colegio y Ermita de San
Jerónimo (Real Aduana), C de la Recolección, open daily, 0800-1700, La Merced
(said to have largest fountain in the Americas), the Hospital (operated by Las Obras
Sociales del Hermano Pedro; restoration

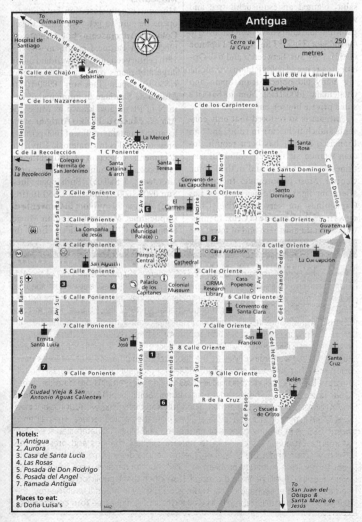

Hotels:
1. Antigua
2. Aurora
3. Casa de Santa Lucía
4. Las Rosas
5. Posada de Don Rodrigo
6. Posada del Angel
7. Ramada Antigua

Places to eat:
8. Doña Luisa's

after 1976 earthquake almost complete; donations welcome), and the **Museum**. Other ruins, such as **Santa Isabel**, **San Cristóbal**, **El Calvario** and **San Gaspar Vivar**, all S of the town, are well worth visiting. El Calvario, 1618, was where Pedro de Betancourt, Guatemala's unique saint, planted an esquisuchil tree and worked as a gardener. Many sculptures, paintings and altars have been removed to Guatemala City. **The Casa Popenoe** (1632), 1 Av Sur, between 5 and 6 C Oriente, is a restored colonial house containing many old objects from Spain and Guatemala; 1400-1600, Mon to Sat (it's still a private house), entry US$1.

Antigua is so restored that only convents and churches are in ruins, and San Francisco church has been rebuilt. Indian women sit in their colourful costumes amid the ruins and in the Parque Central. Most picturesque. In the late afternoon light, buildings such as Las Capuchinas are very attractive. Good views from the **Cerro de la Cruz**, 15 mins' walk from the northern end of town.

This is certainly the cultural centre of Guatemala as shown by the sections on museums and shopping below. Indigenous music can be heard everywhere, and the Marimba Antigua plays Bach and Mozart.

Museums

Museums usually close Mon, but ruins are open. Be sure to get your entry ticket. **Colonial Art museum**, C 5 Oriente, ½ block from Parque Central, mostly 17-18th century religious art, well-laid out in large airy rooms round a colonial patio, US$0.10 (open Tues-Sun 0900-1600). **Museo de Santiago** in municipal offices to N of Plaza (also known as Museo de Armas); **Museo del Libro Antiguo** (same location), contains replica of 1660 printing press (original is in Guatemala City), old documents, collection of 16th-18th-century books (1500 volumes in library, open afternoons, US$0.05). Both open Tues-Sun 0900-1600. Admission US$0.10 (free Sun). Also small museum in **Convento de Capuchinas**. **Museum of Indian Music**, K'ojam, 5 C Poniente a la final (by

From archaeological site to cultural centre

The *Hotel Casa Santo Domingo* (3 C Oriente 28) purchased most of the old Dominican church and monastery property to create a Cultural Centre with a theatre for performing arts, contemporary art gallery, colonial art museum for the hotel's fine collection and an open air theatre-chapel. In 1997 the Cultural Centre was opened and activities included historical national cinema, music, dance, theatre and more. In progress is a projection room for school children's cultural heritage programmes, coordinated by Elizabeth Bell. Recent archaeological excavations have turned up some startling finds at the site. Prehispanic burials and ceramics have confirmed that there was never a formal Maya settlement under the colonial capital. Isolated Maya burials date from 1300 AD while other remains pre-date this time. Quite unexpectedly, when cleaning out a burial vault in Sept 1996, the greatest find in Antigua's history was unearthed. The vault had been filled with rubble but care was taken in placing stones a few feet away from the painted surface. The painting, from 1683, is in pristine colours of natural red and blue. A Guatemalan specialist, Margarita Estrada, was called in to prevent climatic changes and preserve the 'Calvary' scene under the chapel of Nuestra Señora del Socorro. While opening a vent to resolve a humidity problem in 1997, human remains were found. These were 'feeding' the lichens on the mural. Now open to the public on a limited basis, you can see other archaeological findings on display in a burial vault nearby; the site is also included in Elizabeth Bell's walking tour of Antigua (see **Tour companies**).

Alameda Santa Lucía), good collection of traditional musical instruments, slide shows on music and culture with free coffee, open 0930-1600 Mon-Sat, US$0.85.

Local festivals

Holy Week. The most important and colourful processions are those leaving La Merced on Palm Sunday and Good Friday, and Escuela de Cristo and the Church of San Felipe de Jesús (in the suburbs) on Good Friday. Bright carpets, made of dyed sawdust and flowers, are laid on the route. The litter bearers wear purple until 1500 on Good Friday afternoon, and black afterwards. Only the litter bearing Christ and His Cross passes over the carpets, which are thereby destroyed. Reserve accommodation at least 6 months in advance during Holy Week or stay in Guatemala City. Also 21-26 July and 31 Oct-2 Nov (All Saints and All Souls, in and around Antigua). On 7 Dec, the citizens celebrate the Burning of the Devils by lighting fires in front of their houses thereby starting the Christmas festivities.

Local information
● Warning

Despite its air of tranquility, Antigua is not without incidents of robbery and violent crime. Take care and take advice (eg from Casa Andinista or the Tourist Office) on where not to go. Cerro de la Cruz is a notorious area for muggings and worse. Similarly, seek advice before visiting ruins S of the centre. Report incidents to police, tourist office and Casa Andinista. Firemen (*bomberos*) can also be helpful.

● Accommodation

In the better hotels, advance reservations are advised for weekends and Dec-April. During Holy Week hotel prices are generally double.

L1 *Casa Santo Domingo*, 3 C Oriente No 28, T 832-0140, F 832-0102, inc breakfast, beautifully designed in ruins of 17th century convent with prehispanic archaeological finds, good service, beautiful gardens, good restaurant, worth seeing even if you don't stay there (see box); **L3** *Antigua* (best), 5 Av Sur and 8 C (4 blocks S of Parque), T 832-0331, F 832-0807, beautiful gardens, pool (see **Swimming** below); **L3** *Ramada Antigua*, 9 C Poniente and Carretera Ciudad Vieja, T 832-3002, F 832-0237 (tax inc), 2 pools (see below), horse hire and riding, tennis courts, discotheque, gymnasium, sauna.

A1 *Posada del Angel*, 4 Av Sur 24 A, T/F 832-0260, 1-800-934-0065, e-mail: Elangel@IBM.net, **A2** in May, Sept and Oct, **L3** in Christmas week, price inc taxes and breakfast, colonial style, wood fires, beautifully furnished, attention to detail, USA T/F 617-934-0065 (A-006, P O Box 669004, Miami Springs, FL 33266); **A2** *Posada de Don Rodrigo*, 5 Av Norte 17, T 832-0291, very agreeable if a little worn, good food, buffet breakfast rec, in colonial house (Casa de los Leones), marimba music pm; **A2** *Quinta de las Flores*, C del Hermano Pedro 6, T 832-3721, F 832-3725, well-equipped apartments, pool, beautiful garden, good value, rec; **A2** *Panchoy*, 1 Av Norte 5A, T 832-4029, F 832-3919, large new hotel at town exit; **A3** *Aurora*, 4 C Oriente 16, T/F 832-0217, breakfast available, the oldest hotel in the city, old plumbing but it works, clean, English spoken, quieter rooms face the patio, beautiful gardens, parking, good value.

B *Convento Santa Catalina*, 5 Av Norte 28, T 832-3000, F 832-3079, under the arch, friendly, nice atmosphere but some rooms dark and small; **B** *Del Centro*, 4 C Poniente, 22, T/F 832-0657, bijou colonial around a tiny courtyard; **B** *Posada del Farol*, C Los Nazarenos No 17, T/F 832-3735, 7 rooms with bathroom, hot water, fridge, cable TV, laundry, convenient, friendly, clean, rec; **B** *Unicornio*, 4 C Poniente 22A, T/F 832-3229, very nice; **B** *Posada Santiago de los Caballeros*, 7 Av Norte No 67, T 832-0465, nr Parque San Sebastián.

C *Posada San Sebastián*, 3 Av Norte No 4, T 832-2621, breakfast, laundry, English-speaking owner, use of kitchen, good; **C** *Posada de Doña Marta*, 7 Av Norte 100, T 832-0948, clean, attractive, good value; **C** *El Descanso*, 5 Av Norte 9, T 832-0442, 4 rooms on 2nd floor, with private bath, clean, pleasant, family atmosphere; **C** *Posada Asjemenou*, 5 Av Norte 31, nr La Merced, T 832-2670, nice gardens, friendly, laundry, popular with tour groups and with Dutch tourists but some adverse comments; **C-D** *Santa Clara*, 2 Av Sur 20, T 832-0342, 8 rooms, 4 with private bath, hot water, dark rooms, safe parking, breakfast and bar service, Doña María Panedes, the owner, very helpful.

D *Bougambilia*, C Ancha de Los Herreros 27, T 832-2732, with bath, parking, cable TV, kitchen, very good; **D** *Don Valentino*, 5 C Poniente 28, T 832-0384, clean, with bath; **D** *El*

Confort, 1 Av Norte 2, T 832-0566, beautiful gardens; **D** *El Rosario Lodge*, 5 Av Sur 36, T 832-0336, very quiet, with garden, some bungalow rooms with fireplace, good parking; **D** *La Tatuana*, 7 Av Sur 3, T 832-0537, rooms rather small, colourful, friendly, clean, safe; **D** *Plaza Real*, 5 Av S 8, T 832-0581, basic, friendly, hot water, cheap restaurant downstairs; **D** *Posada de San Luquitas*, C de San Luquitas 30, nr *Ramada*, good for longer stays, nice rooms and patio, cable TV; **D** *Cristal*, C del Desengaño 25, 7 blocks from Parque Central, T 832-4177, noisy day and night, clean, friendly, good, not all rooms have hot water, beautiful courtyard, will store luggage, cooking facilities, rec; **D** *San Vicente*, 6 Av Sur 6, T 832-3311, central, nice view from upper rooms, clean, friendly, hot showers, safe parking, storage, cycles for hire.

E *Las Rosas*, 6 Av Sur 8, T 832-0644, clean, quiet, hot water, family atmosphere; **E** *Los Capitanes*, 5 Av Sur, between 5 and 6 C, all rooms with bath, restaurant downstairs, commercial; **E** *Posada de Doña Angelina*, 4 C Poniente 33, with hot shower, **F** without (rooms in new part more expensive, but good), noisy, nr market and bus station; **E** *Posada La Merced*, 7 Av Norte, 43A, friendly, hot shower, clean but occasional bed bugs; **E** *Posada Landivar*, 5 C Poniente 23, T 832-2962, cheaper without bath, good beds, close to bus station, safe, hot water all the time, clothes washing facilities, rec; **E** *Posada Pedro de Alvarado*, 4 C Poniente 27, above gas station, nr bus station, with bath, cheaper without, clean, laundry and cooking facilities, see also **Language schools** below; **E** *Tienda Pati*, 8 Av Norte 23, private guesthouse, very friendly, clean; **E-F** *Primavera*, 3 C Poniente nr Alameda de Santa Lucía and bus station, hot water, clean and friendly, good value; **E-F** *Villa San Francisco*, 1 Av Sur 15, T/F 832-3383, some rooms without window, clean, quiet, inexpensive T/F service, bicycle rental, rec.

F *Angélica Jiménez*, 1 C Poniente 14A, offers accommodation for more than a week only and meals, cheap, clean; **F** *Casa de Santa Lucía*, Alameda de Santa Lucía 5, nr bus terminal, very popular, rec, luggage stored, with bath, hot water all day, good value but rooms small, they have 3 houses, clean, safe, noisy, camping behind hotel, US$4-5, only place in town to camp; **F** *Hospedaje El Pasaje*, Alameda de Santa Lucía 3, T 832-3145, more expensive at Easter, clean, friendly, noisy, washing facilities, use of kitchen, will store luggage for US$0.50, doors shut at 0100, good view of volcanoes from roof, avoid damp ground floor rooms, rec; **F** *Pensión El Arco*, 5 Av N between 1 and 2 C Poniente, clean, shared bath, hot shower, good value, single rooms available; **E** *Plácido*, 3 C Poniente 33, communal bathrooms with hot electric shower, laundry facilities, use of kitchen, long stays cheaper, family atmosphere, friendly, clean, parking; **F** *Posada El Refugio*, 4 C Poniente 28, with or without showers, hot water, popular, cooking and laundry facilities, lots of comings and goings (not very secure), good for breakfast, parking Q5 in adjacent courtyard (pay at end of stay), close to bus station but don't stay here if you have to catch an early bus, the gate is locked and nobody around to open it; **F** *Posada La Quinta*, 5 C Poniente, clean, friendly, good value, hot water, laundry service, parking; **F** *Posada Ruiz*, Alameda de Santa Lucía 17, hot water, washing machine, noisy, basic, friendly, good café opp, nr bus station; **F** *Posada Ruiz No 2*, 2 C Poniente between 6 and 7 Av Norte, hot water, safe, busy, washing machine, good view from veranda.

G *San Francisco*, 3 C Oriente 19, clean.

For longer stays, ask around. Full service apartments available eg at *Suites Bouganvillas*, 9 C Poniente 48, price negotiable, T 334-6078, F 334-6075. Rooms, from about US$50/month, and houses, from about US$150/month, can be found on the noticeboard at Casa Andinista (see **Bookshops**) and sometimes advertised in the Tourist Office and in Doña Luisa's café. You do not have to be on a language course to stay with local families, it is cheap and convenient, about US$30-35 a week inc meals, and a good way of meeting local people. Look on noticeboards for rec families or ask in shops outside central area of town. Gladys Rivera, Callejón Hermano Pedro 20, very nice house with patio and roof terrace, US$40/week with board; Martha, 2 Av Sur 53, US$48 for 2, inc meals, for a week. Estela López, 1 C Poniente No 41A, US$35/week for room and 3 meals/day, clean, friendly; Doña Alicia Reyes, Colonia Candelaria 62, spotless, 4 rooms, roof patio, excellent meals, rec, US$50/week. Familia Cuellar de Toledo, 8 Av Norte, No 23, friendly, family rents rooms, clean. Good accommodation in Jocotenango, 15 mins' walk, 5 mins in kombi (on road to Chimaltenango), Doña Marina's, 13 C 1-69, Colonia los Llanos; Carmen Urrutia, 12 C 1-69, Colonia Los Llanos, Jocotenango, T 832-2216, excellent house and food.

Camping: see *Casa de Santa Lucía* above. Campervan parking, try the Texaco station by the *Ramada Inn*, otherwise camping around Antigua is not advisable.

● **Places to eat**

In several of the more expensive hotels. *El Sereno*, 4 Av Norte 16 (T 832-0501), well-prepared meals in beautifully-reconstructed colonial-style house, open 1200-1500, 1830-2200 Wed to Mon, expensive but highly rec, reservations advised, especially Sun lunch (children under 8 not served). *Welten*, 4 C Oriente 21, not cheap but very good, interesting food in a delightful garden setting, reservations T 832-0630, closed Tues, also shows films most evenings. *Asados de la Calle de Arco*, 5 Av, 4 C Poniente, charming, good food, not very expensive; *Doña Luisa*, 4 C Oriente 12, 1½ blocks E of the Plaza, a popular meeting place with an excellent bulletin board, serves pies and bread, breakfasts, ice cream, good coffee, good burgers, but meals, service and value criticized in 1996; *La Fuente*, next to Doña Luisa, good pasta and light meals, tables set around fountains, relaxing, huipil market held in courtyard Sat 0900-1400; *Café de las Américas*, 5 C y 6 Av, best chocolates in town, though somewhat expensive and others now claim *La Cenicienta* on 5 Av Norte, decidedly has the best cakes, eg cinnamon roll, New York cheesecake, etc. *Café Flor*, 4 Av Sur, good, helpful owners, Thai food, shows videos, and *La Estancia*, steakhouse, 4 C Poniente. *Peregrinos*, 4 Av Norte 1, Mexican pizzas and salads, open air eating, pleasant atmosphere, good value; *Katok*, 4 Av Norte 2, small patio, good food, *Martedino*, 6 Av Norte nr La Merced, good, not cheap; *Dianchi*, 4 C, between Av 5 and 6, consistently good food, pizzas, not cheap; *El Mesón Panza Verde*, 5 Av Sur 19, expensive but good (has 3 excellent rooms to let, B range, and 3 suites with great views of the volcanoes, A3 range); *El Oasis*, 7 Av Norte, European dishes, good brunch on Sun a favourite among locals. *Su Chow*, 5 Av Norte nr La Merced, good and inexpensive; *Fonda de la Calle Real*, 5 Av Norte No5, speciality is *queso fundido*, guitar trio on Sun evenings; good; *La Fonda a la Vuelta*, 3 C Oriente 8, same ownership, menu and music, equally good; *Quesos y Vino*, 5 Av Norte 31A, good Italian food, open late, another branch on 2 C Poniente up from Capuchinas; *El Capuchino*, 6 Av, between C 4 and 5, good Italian food, especially pizzas, and salads, try the garlic spaghetti, friendly English-speaking owner from Philadelphia, has US cable TV; *Café Opera*, 6 Av Norte y 2 C Poniente, Italian owned, good food and atmosphere; *Coco Loco*, 1 C Poniente 3, nr La Merced, Asian; *Fénix*, 6 Av Norte 33, Italian and international, vegetarian dishes, midnight and Sun specials; *Emilio*, Santa Inés 8 at entrance to town (great noodles, much better than branch at 4 C Poniente), and *Gran Muralla* opp, both sell reasonable Chinese food; *Luna Llena*, 6 Av Norte 32, nice atmosphere, candlelight; *San Carlos*, on main square, sells good set meals; *Café Jardín*, on W side of main square, good value, nice atmosphere; *Hamburguesa Gigante* on main square, cheap; *Panchoy's*, 6 Av 1-8, good beef and fondue, very good choice and quality; *Comedor Veracruz* in the market, good; *Asjemenou*, 5 C Poniente No 4, serves Italian dishes, good food, excellent expresso, very small, therefore always full, good breakfast, excellent bread, slow service, but rec; *Lina*, nr market on Alameda de Santa Lucía, serves good, cheap meals; *Santa Bárbara*, 4 C Oriente 53, 'super asados', seafood, grilled meats, etc, music, good for breakfast too, rec. *Sueños del Quetzal*, 4 C Oriente, in shopping centre beyond *Doña Luisa's*, good vegetarian, Cable TV, good breakfast, message board, soda fountain has excellent sandwiches; *Da Vinci*, 7 Av Norte 18B, Guatemalan food and pasta, good atmosphere, lunch specials; on Alameda Santa Lucía *Jugocentro*, *Peroleto*, for fruits and yoghurt; *Tostaduria Antigua*, 6 Av Sur No 12A, good coffee roasted and brewed, many say best coffee in town, pies, cheap, friendly American owner, *Rainbow Room*, 7 Av Sur, between 6-7 C Poniente (open 0700-2200), bookshop with vegetarian food, good breakfasts, but beware of 10% service charge added to bill, video bar, popular with travellers, rec for word-of-mouth information, also poetry evenings, see under **Bookshops**; *Café Condesa*, 5 Av Norte 4, W side of main plaza, favourite gringo hangout, capuccino, second cup of coffee free, breakfast, desserts, Sun buffet, friendly, moderate prices, rec; *Don Diego's*, 1 C Poniente with Alameda Santa Lucía, cheap, good Tex Mex food; *Maná*, 5 Av Norte 31, crêpes, 20 varieties of tea, light meals, good breakfasts, soft background music; *Pastelería Okrassa*, 6 Av, C, 1-2, for meat and fruit pies; *La Manzana Grande*, 2 Av Sur, between C 4/5, American style breakfasts, sandwiches and pies; *Punto Internacional*, 5 Av 35, very clean, good food; *Masala*, 6 Av Norte y 4 C Poniente, Chinese and Japanese vegetarian, nicely decorated, good; *Los Tacos*, Alameda Santa Lucía, C 3y4, best lunch special.

NB Some establishments have introduced microwave ovens; make sure your food is piping hot.

● **Bars**

Bar Picasso, 7 Av Norte, entre 2 y 3 C, popular, loud music, closed some Sun; *Latinos*, 7 Av Norte, entre 3 y 4 C, live music occasionally, good dance floor, also *Abstracto* next door, loud music; *Moscas y Miel*, 2 blocks from Parque Central, open late; *Jazz Gruta*, Calzada Santa Lucía 17,live music at weekends, cover charge US$1.25-3.50, food, happy hour Mon-Thur 1900-2200; *Bar Chimenea*, 7 Av Norte y 2 C Poniente, large dance floor, cheap drinks; *Casbah*, 5 Av Norte just past the arch, good dance floor, night club atmosphere, open after 2400, popular after all the others have closed; *Macondo*, C del Arco, 'English-style pub', good Western and local music, rec. Most bars have a happy hour betrween 1800-2100.

● **Banks & money changers**

Lloyds Bank plc, 4 C Oriente 2 on NE corner of Plaza, Mon-Fri 0900-1500, changes Amex TCs at Q10 commission, also changes TCs into US$ cash at 2% plus Q10; **G&T Bank**, 5 Av Norte about 4 doors N of junction with 5 C Poniente, also changes Amex TCs, any amount between 1000-1200 Mon-Fri, US$100 only 1200-1800 and 1000-1400 on Sat; **Banco del Agro**, N side of Plaza, open Mon-Fri until 2000; **Banco Industrial**, 5 Av Sur 4, nr Plaza, gives cash on Visa ATM (24 hr) and Visa credit card at normal rates, no commission. Branch of **Banco del Agro**, Alameda Santa Lucía y 5 C, nr Post Office, open 0900-1800, Mon-Sat, US dollars not obtainable, may exchange personal cheques for quetzales; **Banco del Occidente**, 4 C Poniente y 5 Av Norte, open to 1900, Mon-Fri, and Sat am. **Banco Continental**, 5 Av Sur 20 A, good rates, open Sat am. Cash advances on a Mastercard at Jades, SA (see **Shopping**). **NB** No banks change money in the week between Christmas and New Year. At this time, at weekends, etc, *Hotels Don Rodrigo* and *Villa San Francisco* will change money.

● **Cultural centres**

The Alianza Francesa, 3 C Oriente 19, has French music on Fri between 1600 and 2000, regular talks and slide shows, films (information from Casa Andinista or *Doña Luisa's*), also French newspapers. **Proyecto Cultural El Sitio**, 5 C Poniente 15, has concerts and other cultural activities, and a very good library inc books in English, Tues-Sun 1100-1900. Concerts also at La Fonda a la Vuelta (see above) and *Hotel Posada Don Rodrigo* (marimba 1900-2100, Grupo Folklórico Hunapú in bar 2000-2100). In 1997 a Cultural Centre opened at the **Casa Santo Domingo**, 3 C Oriente 28, with cinema, music, dance, theatre and art galleries (see tinted box).

● **Entertainment**

Cinemas: *Cinemala*, Antigua Coneplex, with increased schedules and film choice; *Rainbow Video*, 7 Av Sur 8; *Ciné Géminis*, 4 C Oriente 7; *Ciné Sin Ventura*, 7 C Poniente 7; *Bistro*, 5 Av Norte, nice atmosphere, food available; all show films or videos in English, or with subtitles, none is a large theatre.

Dance lessons: Escuela de Danza, 5 Av Norte 25. *Ritmo Latino Dance Academy*, 3 Av Sur 4, merengue, salsa, punta, US$4/hr, open 1600-1900; *Nahual*, 6 Av Norte 9 (Spanish school), similar programme and cost.

Workshops: *Art Workshops in La Antigua*, 4 C Oriente, PO Box 14, F 320602, or 4758 Lyndale Ave South, Minneapolis, MN 55409-2304, T (612) 825-0747, F 825-6637, USA, e-mail: Artguat@aol.com: a wide variety of courses offering instruction in all forms of expression (weaving, painting, photography, writing, etc), Nov-April, all-inclusive packages available, tuition costs about US$350.

● **Hospitals & medical services**

Doctor: *Dr Julio R Aceituno*, 2 C Poniente, No 7, T 320512, speaks English; *Dr José del Valle Monge*, 8 C Oriente 5, good English and German, US$4 for consultation; *Dr Joel Alvarado*, 4 C Poniente 21, keeps regular hours and a quick cure for dysentery; *Dr Sergio Castañeda*, 6 Av Norte 52, rec by Alianza Francesa. Centro de Especialidades, Alameda Santa Lucía 35, several specialists, will check for parasites as will *Hospital Privado Herman Pedro*, Av El Desengaño 12A. **Hospital emergency**: T 320301.

Dentist: *Dr Asturias*, a few doors up from *Doña Luisa's*.

Public toilets: 4 C Oriente, nr square, 35 centavos pp, dirty.

● **Language schools**

There are about 60 Spanish schools, consequently Antigua is full of foreigners learning the language. Not all schools are officially authorized by the Ministry of Education and Inguat. Rates depend on how many hours tuition you have a week and vary from school to school; as a rough guide the average fee for 4 hrs a day,

5 days a week is US$85 (US$125 for 8 hrs a day), at a reputable school, though many are cheaper. You will benefit more from the classes if you have done some study before you arrive. There are guides who take students around the schools and charge a high commission (make sure this is not added to your account). They may tackle tourists on the bus from the capital. Before making any commitment, find somewhere to stay and shop around at your leisure. Mary Cano at Alianza Lingüística 'Cano' (see address below) is rec. She is honest, helpful, speaks English and knows the budget hotels. Also check in *The Revue*. Some points to bear in mind; accommodation with families is often linked to a particular school so be sure about one before you pay a week in advance for the other. Average accommodation rates with a family with 3 meals a day are US$40-60/week. In some cases lodging is group accommodation; if you prefer single accommodation, ask for it. All schools offer one-to-one tuition; if you can meet the teachers in advance, so much the better, but don't let the director's waffle distract you from asking pertinent questions. Paying more does not mean you get better teaching and the standard of teachers varies within schools as well as between schools. Some schools are cheaper in the afternoons than in the mornings. Beware of 'hidden extras' and be clear on arrangements for study books. Some schools have an inscription fee. Several schools use a portion of their income to fund social projects. Latest indications are that learning Spanish in Quezaltenango or Huehuetenango is preferable to Antigua if you want to avoid Antigua's international atmosphere. Some, eg Francisco Marroquín, also offer Indian language tuition.

We list only those schools of which we have received favourable reports from students: **Proyecto Lingüístico Francisco Marroquín**, 7 C Poniente 31 T 832-3777; **Sevilla Academia de Español**, Apartado Postal 380, 1 Av Sur 8, T/F 832-0442; **CSA (Academia Cristiana de Español)**, 6 Av Norte No 15, Apartado Postal 320, T/F 832-0367; **Centro Lingüístico Maya**, 5 C Poniente 20, T/F 832-0656; **Nahual**, 6 Av Norte 9, T 832-2548; **Tecún Umán**, 6 C Poniente 34, T/F 832-2792; **Quiché**, 3 Av Sur No 15A, T 832-0575, F 832-2893; **Español Dinámico**, 6 Av Norte 63, T 832-2440; **Jiménez**, nr La Merced, 1 C Poniente 41; **Centro Lingüístico Antigua**, 6 Av Norte 36, director speaks good English, discounts for couples and for longer study period; **Don Pedro de Alvarado**, 1 C Poniente 24, T 832-4180 (also a hotel, see above); **Instituto Antigüeño de Español**, 1 C Poniente No 33, T 832-2682; **El Quetzal**, 7 C Poniente 7, Apartado Postal 426, T 832-3331; **Centro Lingüístico Atabal**, 1 Av Norte 6, T 832-0791. **Popol Vuh Professional Language School**, 7 Av Norte No 82, PO Box 230, Roberto King and Lesvia Arana Gallardo (directors); **La Enseñanza**, C El Portal 1, T 832-0692, run by Aura and Paty Miranda; **Hombres de Maíz**, Callejón Camposeco 5, 2 blocks from La Merced run by Rosa and Nery Méndez; **Don Quijote**, 9 C Poniente 7, T 832-0651; **Latinoamérica Spanish Academy**, José Sánchez Corado, 7 Av Poniente, F 832-2667; **Academia de Español Colonial** (ACADEC), Calzada Santa Lucía Sur, Pasaje Matheu No 7, Director Alvaro Coronado Estrada; **Alianza Lingüística 'Cano'**, 2 Av del Chajón No 8A (Mary Cano also has office at Sta Lucía Norte 3A, opp bus terminal), PO Box 366. Rec private teachers: Julia Solís, 5 C Poniente 36; María Elena Estrada, *La Cenicienta*, 5 Av Norte 7; Sandra Rosales, 7 C Oriente 21; Amalia Iarquín, *El Desengaño* No 11, T 832-2377; Julio César Pérez, 1 C Poniente 10. Also rec is **Proyecto Bibliotecas Guatemala**, 6 Av Norte 41B, T 832-3768, 25% of profits go towards founding and maintaining public libraries in rural towns. See also *AmeriSpan* in **Introduction and hints**, page 51. Also check advertisements in *Doña Luisa's* and the Tourist Office (Director helpful) for private lessons (about US$2/hr).

● **Laundry**

All charge about US$0.75/kg and close Sun and half-day Sat. *Lavandería Gilda*, 5 C Poniente entre 6 y 7 Av, very good; *Central*, 5 C Poniente 7 B. There are many others around the centre of town.

● **Libraries**

Research: The Centro de Investigaciones Regionales de Mesoamérica (Cirma), 5 C Oriente 5, offers good facilities for graduate students and professional scholars of Middle American history, anthropology and archaeology. Open Mon-Fri 0800-1800, Sat 0900-1300. **Public Library**: The Granai y Townson library, just N of the Plaza on 4 C Oriente, is open to the public, Mon-Fri 0900-1200, 1300-1700. Biblioteca Internacional de Antigua, 5 C Poniente, 15, Tues-Sat 1100-1800.

● **Post & telecommunications**

Post Office at Alameda Santa Lucía and 4 C, nr market (local cables from here), open 0800-1600 Mon-Fri; *lista de correos* keeps letters for a month. Boxes of books up to 2 kg can be sent from the post office, but other packages weighing more than 2 kg must be posted from Guatemala City (do not seal parcels before going to the capital). There are strict rules on how to wrap parcels, see instructions at counter 3.

Courier services: *Quick Shipping*, 6 C Poniente 27; *DHL*, 6 C Poniente y 6 Av Sur; *Aéreo Systems*, 6 Av Norte.

International cables in Guatel building, SW corner of main square.

Telephones: you can make collect calls from a public phone to some countries (see **Information for travellers**). Some hotels and restaurants will also let you use their fax machines to send and receive messages eg *Sueños del Quetzal* restaurant. For a small charge you can phone abroad, leave the number and be called back.

Conexión is an electronic mail service, fax, telex, e-mail, telegrams, send and receive, message service, translations, word processing, computers available for customers' use, 4 C Oriente No 14, T 832-3768, F 832-0082, e-mail: 5385706@MCImail.com or conex@ibm.net; cost: sending to arrive before 1800 US$5, after 1800 US$4, receiving US$1. *Tecnicámaras Antigua*, 3 C Poniente 21, e-mail: garlo@tikal.net.gl, US$2 to send 40 lines, US$1 to receive 1 page, also repair cameras, good service. *Intertel*, 5 Av Norte 30, T/F 832-2640, Mon-Fri 0700-2200, Sat-Sun 0800-1800, to Europe 1 min US$3.50, 1 page fax US$7.50, USA US$1.75 and US$4.50, Canada US$2.25 and US$5.50 respectively. Check bulletin board in *Doña Luisa's* for cheap ways to telephone overseas. See also *AmeriSpan* under **Tourist Offices** below.

● **Shopping**
Mercado de Artesanías At 7 Av between 4 C and 3 C (in La Compañía ruins, touristy). Main market is by the bus terminal. *Casa de Artes* for traditional textiles and handicrafts, antiques, jewellery, etc, 4 Av Sur. *Casa de los Gigantes* for textiles and handicrafts opp San Francisco Church. *Fábrica de Tejidos Maya*, 1 Av Norte, C, 1-2, makes and sells good cheap textiles, wall hangings, etc. *Armario*, 5 Av Sur y 6 C Poniente, modern design, traditional weaving, nice patio with café. The *Utatlán* cooperative on 5 Av Norte specializes in good handicrafts and antiques (expensive). There are many other stores selling textiles, handicrafts, antiques, silver and jade on 5 Av Norte and 4 C Oriente (*Ixchel* on 4 C Oriente sells blankets from Momostenango; *Kashlan P'ot*, in Galería La Fuente, 4 C Oriente

14, T 832-2369). *Galería de Arte Estipite*, 4 C Oriente 7 (also *Restaurante Patio de las Delicias*), Wed-Sun 1200-1530, 1830-2200, Central American artists, will ship works of art abroad. A number of jade-carving factories may be visited, eg *Jades, SA*, 4 C Oriente 34 (branches on same street Nos 1 and 12), open daily 0900-2100 (also coffee shop), *La Casa del Jade*, 4 C Oriente 3 (open daily 0900-1800) or *JC Hernández*, 2 Av Sur 77, *San José*, Calzada Santa Lucía N, No 23 A. Jade is sold on the Parque Central on Sat more cheaply. Painted ceramics can be obtained from private houses in 1 Av del Chajón (C San Sebastián) nr C Ancha, and glazed pottery from the *Fábrica Montiel*, N of C Ancha on the old road to San Felipe. Near San Felipe is the silver factory where many of the silver ornaments sold in Antigua and Guatemala City are made. Various local handicrafts at *Hecht House* in the same area. *Colibrí*, 4 C Oriente 3B, sells quality weavings. Ceramic birds at handicrafts shop in the *Posada de Don Rodrigo* (see under Hotels above). *Calzado Fase*, 6 Av Norte 61, makes made-to-measure leather boots. *El Unicornio*, 4 C Poniente 38A, entre 7 Av y Calzada, near market, tobacco shop, owned by JM Cunningham (British), open 0700-1800 daily; *Doña María Gordillo's* sweet (candy) shop on 4 C Oriente is famous throughout the country. *Zapote*, 6 Av Sur between 5 and 6 C Poniente, top quality fruit, vegetables, herbs, spices, imported cheese etc, Canadian run, good; *Dulces Típicos y Artesanías*, 7C Poniente 17, good value candies, candles etc; *La Bodegona* is a discount supermarket on 4 C Poniente between Alameda Sta Lucía and 7 Av Sur, dingy but well-stocked.

Bookshops: *Casa Andinista*, 4 C Oriente 5A, sells books in Spanish and English (inc the *Mexico and Central America* and the *South American Handbooks*), photographs, posters, rubbings, maps (easier than the Instituto Geográfico in Guatemala City), large selection of postcards, cards, weavings from Ixil Triangle, camping gear for rent (opp *Doña Luisa's*, which sells *Time* and *Newsweek*), has photocopying machine, good information on reputable language schools, repeatedly rec. *Un Poco de Todo*, on W side of Plaza, sells (and buys) English, French and German language books, postcards, maps. *Casa del Conde*, 5 Av Norte 4, opp *Café Condesa*, sells books in English and Spanish and guides to Guatemalan sites, good for books on Central America. *Librería Pensativo*, 5 Av Norte 29, good for books in Spanish about Central America. *Librería Marquense*,

6 C Poniente between 5 and 6 Av. *Rainbow Reading Room*, 7 Av Sur, 6-7 C Poniente, campfire in evenings with musicians, nice atmosphere, videos, secondhand books, popular with travellers.

Film developing: *Unifoto Fuji Antigua*, 4 C Oriente nr square, open Sun, 1 hr service; *Rapi Revelado*, next to *Café Condesa* on square, closed Sun, 1 hr service; *Foto Juárez Gonzáles*, 4 C Poniente 32, closed Sun, good, all day service; *Foto Solís*, 5 Av Norte 13, open Sun, 1 hr service. US$8.75 for 24 exposures, US$12.30 for 36.

Hairdressers: for men, all over town. For women, 6 C Poniente 29A, around corner from *Rainbow Café*, US$3.30 for cut and blow dry, good.

Market: there is an extensive daily market, particularly on Mon, Thur and Sat (best) next to the bus terminal at end of 4 C Poniente, W of Alameda Santa Lucía. Good handmade textiles, pottery and silver. A wider selection of *típicas* can be found at the market at the NW corner of 6 Av Norte y 4 C Poniente. Several women sell *típicas* in front of Convento Santa Clara, on 4 C Oriente between 2 Av Sur y 3 Av Sur.

● **Sports**

Karate school: Bie Sensei (Danish), 3rd degree black belt gives hour-long lessons. For more information ask at Tourist Office.

Riding: for horse riding English style, see San Juan del Obispo, below page 636.

Swimming: non-residents may use the pool at the *Hotel Antigua* for a charge of US$9, more on Sun (US$45/month), you may be obliged to have a buffet meal (eg breakfast) as well, also, at *Ramada Antigua* for US$4/day or US$35/month. Both hotels have special Sun prices for buffet lunch, swimming and marimba band (the *Ramada* also has children's shows). At the latter, weekly and monthly rates for use of sports facilities can be negotiated. *Antigua Spa Resort*, T 311456, swimming pool, steam baths, sauna, gymnasium, jacuzzi, beauty salon. Also *Casa Solmor*, Av San Sebastián, nr Parque San Sebastián. Warm mineral springs (public pool and private cubicles, less than US$1) at San Lorenzo El Tejar: Chimaltenango bus to San Luis Las Carretas (about 8 km) then 2 km walk to 'Balneario', or direct bus to San Lorenzo and a 5 mins' walk, popular with local families on Sun, good day trip by motorbike. The last part of the road was reported unsafe for pedestrians on their own in 1996. At Jocotenango, *Fraternidad Naturista Antigua*, C Real 30,

T 832-2443, with public saunas US$2, massage US$5.20, health foods, medicinal herbs, dietary advice, open Sun-Thur 0700-1800, Fri 0700-1300, closed Sat, 2 km NW of Antigua. Pool El Pilar 30 mins' walk on road to San Juan del Obispo, US$0.60 entrance.

● **Tour companies & travel agents**

Lots. *Connection Travel*, at *Ramada Antigua*, rec. *Tivoli Travel*, 4 C Oriente 10, T 832-3041, highly rec, helpful with any travel problem, speak English, French, Spanish, German, Italian, reconfirm tickets, good value tours, manager Kathy Töpke's husband, Sr Nuñez, is rec as good car mechanic (he owns taller at Km 41). *Club de Viajeros*, 1 C Poniente. *Sin Fronteras*, 3 C Poniente 12, T 832-2674, local tours, rafting, horseriding, bicycle tours, national and international air tickets inc discounts with ISIC and GO25 cards. *Adventure Travel Center-Viareal*, 4 C Oriente No 14, T/F 832-3228 (in *La Fuente*), and at 5 Av Norte 25B, T 832-0162, weekend trips to Guatemalan destinations (especially Río Dulce sailing, river and volcano trips), El Salvador, Honduras. *Space*, 1 C Poniente No 6 B, T 832-4182, F 832-0938, and *Total Petén*, 6 C Poniente No 6, T 832-0478, good service to El Petén. *Turansa*, main office on 5 Av Norte opp *Posada de Don Rodrigo*, T 832-0011/15, good for flights, eg to Tikal. Elizabeth Bell, *Antigua Tours*, Casa Santo Domingo, 3 C Oriente 28, T 832-0140 ext 341, T/F 832-0228, e-mail: elizbell@guate.net, also at *Adventure Travel*, above, author of *Antigua Guatemala: An Illustrated History of the City and its Monuments* (11th ed, 1995, also in Spanish and Italian) and *Lent and Easter Week in Antigua* (1st ed, 1995), offers walking tours of the city (US$12 pp), book in advance, daily 0930-1430 (Tues 1430 only) T 832-0228, and 45 mins' slide lecture at Christian Spanish Academy, 6 Av Norte 15, Tues 1800, US$2.55 pp (in USA 7907 NW 53rd St, Suite 409 L570, Miami, FL33166). Shop around for tours. *Area Verde Expeditions*, 4 Av Sur 8, T 832-3132, T/F in USA (719) 539-7102, rec for whitewater rafting and kayaking, US$160 for 3 day trip. Birdwatching and historical tours inc trips to Honduras and Belize. *Servicios Turísticos Atitlán*, in *Villa San Francisco*, sells return flights to Flores for day trip to Tikal, around US$80, but reports of difficulties with 0500 pick up and delays in getting to airport. *Eco-Tour Chejo's*, 3 C Poniente 24, well guarded walks up volcanoes, to Pacaya with police armed escort on the road and 6 armed security guards going up the volcano.

A bi-weekly magazine, *The Revue* (4 C Oriente No 23, T/F 832-0767, e-mail: Revue@ guate.net), has information, articles and advertisements in English, free.

● **Tourist offices**

Inguat office at 4a C Oriente No 12A. Very helpful, lots of maps and information, English and a little German spoken. Open: 0800-1700 (Tues-Sun), T 832-0763. The tourist office can arrange guides for visits to monuments for between US$3 and US$6/day.

● **Transport**

Local Bike hire: Mayan Mountain Cycle Tours offer tours around Antigua, Lake Atitlán and other areas, 6 Av Sur No 12B, T/F 832-3316, Spanish, English, German, French, Italian spoken, US$15 for half day with guide, US$30 full day, rec. **Car rental**: Avis, 5 Av Norte between the square and the arch. Also at *Turansa* (see **Travel agents** above). **Motorcycle hire**: Jopa, 6 Av Norte 3, T 832-0794, Yamaha 175, and Kawasaki 125, ask for Juan Pablo, who is very knowledgeable about what excursions to make; US$109 and US$115/week respectively, also 4-hrly, 1, 2 and 3-day rates, all with free km. Good bikes, locks, tools and helmets (in poor shape, but better than nothing) available. **Motorcycle spares**: *Moto-Repuestos CMA*, Alameda de Santa Lucía 16A, open Mon-Fri 0800-1800, Sat 0800-1200, can get spares from the capital, but doublecheck prices. Good mechanic.

Buses From Guatemala City, buses leave when full between 0500 and 1900, US$0.50, 45 mins, from several locations: Av Bolívar, 32 C, Zona 3, 2 Av 19-62, Zona 1, 15C between Avs 3 y 4, Zona 1 and 18C, Av 4-5 (at least 10 bus lines, ask your hotel in the capital which is nearest). Buses to Guatemala City leave from Alameda Santa Lucía nr the market, with the same frequency as buses to Antigua. To **Chimaltenango**, on the Pan-American Highway, half-hourly, US$0.25, for connections to Los Encuentros (for Lake Atitlán and Chichicastenango), Cuatro Caminos (for Quezaltenango) and Huehuetenango (for the Mexican border). It is possible to get to Chichicastenango and back by bus in a day, and tourist minibuses run for US$12, especially on Thur and Sun for the market. Direct Rebuli bus to **Panajachel** at 0700, from 4 C Poniente opp gas station, a few doors E of Alameda Santa Lucía, US$2 (pay on board, sometimes it doesn't turn up), 2½ hrs; tourist minibus costs US$20. To **Escuintla**, Grenadiña and Ruta América, at 0600, 0630 and 1300, 2 hrs, US$0.60. Buses and minibuses also to nearby villages.

Buses Inter-Hotel y Turismo run a transfer service (1 hr) from Antigua to **La Aurora airport**, at 0440, 1100 and 1500, starting at *Ramada*, calling at *Antigua Hotel, Posada Don Rodrigo, Doña Luisa's* and *Hotel Aurora*; for tickets T 832-0011/15, US$7. Tickets available at *Doña Luisa's* and *Casa Andinista*. *Servicios Turísticos* runs a shuttle service to and from airport, Chimaltenango, Río Dulce and Copán, at 6 Av Sur 7, T 832-0486, rec. Travel agencies charge US$7 for the shuttle service to the airport at 0420 and 0515 (US$9 pick-up at hotel). Shuttles arranged by travel agencies, typically: to Guatemala City US$8, to Panajachel US$11, to Chichicastenango US$11. Taxi to Guatemala City US$22.50.

EXCURSIONS FROM GUATEMALA CITY AND ANTIGUA

Whether you are staying in Guatemala City or Antigua, the places in this section can be conveniently visited on a day or overnight basis.

Ciudad Vieja

To **Ciudad Vieja**, 5½ km SW of Antigua at the foot of Agua volcano, this was the original capital, from 1527 to 1541. On 11 September 1541, after days of torrential rain, an immense mud-slide came down the mountain and overwhelmed the city. Alvarado's widow, Doña Beatriz de la Cueva, newly elected Governor after his death, was among the drowned; you can see the ruins of the first town hall. Today it is a mere village (*Hospedaje Shigualita*, cheap, at S end of village), but with a handsome church, founded 1534, one of the oldest in Central America. Larrys Macadamia factory, 2 blocks down from the market, is worth a visit. *Fiesta*: Dec 5-9. Bus US$0.10. At **San Juan del Obispo**, not far, is the restored palace of Francisco Marroquín, first bishop of Guatemala, now a convent. The parish church has some fine 16th century images. For horse riding, English style, Fred and Paula Haywood offer instruction and scenic rides from their stables at 2 Av Sur 3, 1 block from the Palacio and bus terminal.

Santa María de Jesús

Behind San Juan del Obispo, on the side of Agua volcano, is the charming village of **Santa María de Jesús**, with a beautiful view of Antigua. In the early morning, there are good views of all three volcanoes 2 km back down the road towards Antigua. Beautiful *huipiles* are worn, made and sold from a couple of stalls, or ask at the shops on the plaza. Frequent buses to and from Antigua on main market days, US$0.20 (Mon, Thur, Sat) otherwise 0700 only; last bus returns at 1700. *Fiesta* on 10 January. **Accommodation** at *Municipalidad* G; **E** *Hospedaje y Comedor El Oasis* on road to Antigua has clean, pleasant rooms. The road, very steep in places, high clearance vehicle necessary, continues on to the main road to Escuintla at Palín. Excellent views of Pacaya Volcano.

San Antonio Aguas Calientes

About 3 km NW of Ciudad Vieja, the village has many small shops selling locally made textiles; *Carolina's Textiles* is recommended for a fine selection, while just down the road *Alida* has a shop almost as large. Carmelo and Zoila Guarán give weaving lessons for US$1/hr, as do Rafaela Godínez, very experienced, and Felipa López Zamora, on the way to the church, 30m from bus station (bring your own food and she will cook it with you), US$2 daily. Sra María Natividad Hernández is also recommended. You will need some time (say several afternoons) to make some progress. *Fiestas*: 16-21 Jan; Corpus Christi, 1 November. Frequent buses from Antigua.

A good off-road route to Lake Atitlán can be made by suitable car or motorbike: just past Ciudad Vieja, take the unmade road W to the village of Acatenango, then take the unmade road N to Patzicía (see page 689). This route can be incorporated in a 1-day round trip Antigua-Atitlán-Antigua.

Volcanoes

The three nearby volcanoes provide incomparable views of the surrounding countryside and are best climbed on a clear night with a full moon or with a very

early morning start. Altitude takes its toll and plenty of time should be allowed for the ascents. Plenty of water must be carried and the summits are cold. Ankle boots, preferably full climbing boots recommended, especially on Fuego to cope with the cinders. Descents take from a third to a half of the ascent time. Tourist Office in Antigua helpful. Enquire there about conditions (both human and natural) before setting out. There is a volcano-climbing club: *Club de Andinismo*, Chigag, Volcano Tours, Daniel Ramírez Ríos (helpful), 6 Av Norte, No 34, Antigua, T/F 832-3343, the only guide certified by the Guatemalan Tourist Commission (he has a guest house, *Albergue Andinista*, with use of kitchen). Recommended for volcano tours are *ICO's Expeditions*, C del Desengaño 2, and *Gran Jaguar* at 4 C Poniente 30. Prices from US$6/8 pp. **Warning Robberies and rapes have occurred even where large parties are climbing these volcanoes. Nov 1996, Cerro de la Cruz, group of 20 students held up at gunpoint, robbed of all belongings, teacher killed. Jan 1997, Pacaya, group of 17 held up at gunpoint, security guard and robber killed in shoot out. Any attack should be reported to your embassy. The Antigua tourist office does not recommend volcano tours, but plenty of people offer them.**

Agua Volcano 3,760m, the easiest of the three (or the least difficult as one traveller described it), is climbed from Santa María de Jesús (directions to start of ascent in village). Crater with small shelter (dirty), which is/was a shrine, and about 10 antennae at top. Fine views (though not guaranteed) of Volcán de Fuego; 3 to 5 hrs' climb if you are fit, at least 2 hrs down. Make sure you get good directions; there is an old avalanche you have to cross and regain the trail, if you do not you may get lost. To get the best views before the clouds cover the summit, it is best to stay at the radio station at the top. Climbing at night is recommended by torchlight/moon with help from fireflies, Sat-Sun is rec for the ascent, often 100 or more locals will spend the night on the top. A bus from Antigua to Santa María de Jesús around 0600 (irregular) allows you to climb the volcano and return to Antigua in 1 day. Guided tours US$30; information from *El Oasis* restaurant.

Agua can also be climbed from **Alotenango**, a village between Agua and Fuego volcanoes (*fiesta* 18-20 Jan), S of Ciudad Vieja, 9 km from Antigua. Looking at the market building, take the left route up; turn left at the T junction, then first right and up. Only two decision points: take the right fork, then the left. It is not advisable to descend Agua towards Palín (SE – see page 681) as there is precipitous forest, steep bluffs, dry watercourses which tend to drop away vertically and a route is hard to plot.

Acatenango Volcano 3,976m. The best trail (W of the one shown on the 1:50,000 topographic map) heads S at La Soledad, 2,300m (15 km W of Ciudad Vieja on Route 10) 300m before the road (Route 5) turns right to Acatenango (good *pensión*, **G**, with good cheap meals). A small plateau, La Meseta on maps, known locally as El Conejón, provides a good camping site two-thirds of the way up (3-4 hrs). From here it is a further 3-4 hrs harder going to the top. There is a shelter, holding up to 15 people, on the lower of the two summits. Though dirty and in poor condition, this is the best place to sleep. The climb to the higher peak takes about 45 mins. Excellent views of the nearby (lower) active crater of Fuego and you can watch the activity of Pacaya at night. To reach La Soledad, take a bus heading for Yepocapa or Acatenango (village) and get off at La Soledad, or from Antigua to San Miguel Dueñas, and then hitch to La Soledad. Alternatively, take an early bus to Ciudad Vieja from where you can hitch to Finca Concepción Calderas (bus Ciudad Vieja-Calderas 0645 Sat only), then 1 hr walk to La Soledad. Be sure to take the correct track going down (no water on the way). Guided tours US$14, rec is Martin Sis who lives by the main junction at Soledad.

Fuego Volcano 3,763m, for experienced hikers only. Can be climbed either via Volcán de Acatenango (sleeping on the col between the two volcanoes where there is a primitive shelter), up to 12 hrs hiking, or from Alotenango. For the first hour or so, until the trees, take a guide, or follow these instructions (given by Will Paine, Maidstone): down from Alotenango market place, over river, and at the concrete gateway turn right, up the main track. Ignoring the initial left fork, plantation/orchard entrances and all 90° turnoffs, take the next three left forks and then the next two right forks. Do not underestimate water needed for the climb. It is 7 hrs ascent with an elevation gain of 2,400m. A very hard walk, both up and down, and easy to lose the trail. Steep, loose cinder slopes, very tedious in many places. It is possible to camp about three quarters of the way up in a clearing. Fuego has had frequent dangerous eruptions in recent years though generally not without warning. Check in Antigua before attempting to climb.

Another popular excursion is to the still active **Pacaya** volcano (last major eruption Jan 1987, but still steaming early 1997). Tours are available for US$7 pp upwards, depending on the number in the party, with Eco-Tour Chejo's, Ceprotur, Tivoli and other Antigua tour agencies. Tours on large buses do not always provide enough guides/torches and people get lost on the descent. The popular time for organized trips is to leave Antigua at 1400 and return 2200. Security officers and often police escorts go with the trips (do not go on a tour without), but take torch, refreshments and water with you. Tour agencies will arrange camping with guide and guard, US$20 if you need a tent, US$17 if you have your own. The volcano can be reached by private vehicle, the road from Antigua is unpaved. Alternatively take a bus from the central bus station in Zona 4 to **San Vicente de Pacaya**, 0700 and 1530 (US$0.35); then walk to **San Francisco** (1½ hrs); or Guatemala City-Palín bus to turn-off to San Vicente, wait for bus to San Vicente and San Francisco, last at 1800 (buses from San Francisco to junction on Guatemala City-Escuintla road 0500, 0900, 1200 and 1500). There are guides available in both San Vicente and San Francisco US$2 to 2.50. The road to San Francisco is not easy to drive, even in 4WD. Part of the crater has collapsed and the route has had to be changed. The last part up the cone is steep and takes about 30 mins. Check the situation in advance in San Francisco for both climbing and camping (if safe, take torch, warm clothing and a handkerchief to filter dust and fumes). It is recommended to go up overnight with a good camera, tent and sleeping bag, camp at a respectful distance from the cone or at a local home, all arranged by a guide from ICO's Expeditions (see above). To get good night-time photographs, a tripod or similar required for exposure 8 secs at f2.8 on 100 ASA film. Beware cold and cloud; however, you can warm your hands on the lava blocks, or keep warm overnight if you camp near the hot ash. Sunrise comes with awesome views over the desolate black lava field to the distant Pacific (airborne dust permitting) and the peaks of Fuego, Acatenango and Agua. People do scramble up from the 40m view-point to watch the venting in the crater below ("scary but unmissable"). Be warned, though, that this can be very dangerous. Enquire if the volcano is active before going – much more exciting trip if it is.

If you miss the last bus back to Palín or San Vicente, you can stay overnight with Luis the Mexican in San Francisco (a good guide), or you can sleep in the porch at the school in El Cedro, the village below San Francisco, or in a house at the entrance to San Vicente (US$1), or with other locals. Another recommended guide is Salvador, whose house is near the bus stop for Guatemala.

At the village of **San Felipe** (US$0.05 by bus, or 15 mins' walk from Antigua) is a figure of Christ which people from all over Latin America come to see. *Restaurant El Prado* is rec. There is a small silver workshop which is worth visiting.

NORTH OF GUATEMALA CITY

Two Indian villages N of Guatemala City are easily reached by bus. At **Chinautla** (9½ km), the village women turn out handmade pottery. 8 km beyond is another small village, **San Antonio las Flores**: good walking to a small lake (70 mins) for bathing.

At **San Lucas Sacatepéquez**, the Fábrica de Alfombras Típicas Kakchikel at Km 29½, Carretera Roosevelt (usually known as the Pan-American Highway), will make rugs for you. Restaurants: *La Parrilla, La Cabaña, Nim-Guaa, La Diligencia*, and *El Ganadero*, all good for steaks; *Delicias del Mar* for seafood. 5 km beyond San Lucas is **Santiago Sacatepéquez**, whose *fiesta* on 1 Nov is characterized by colourful kite-flying; also 25 July. Market Wed and Fri.

A most interesting short trip by car or bus from the capital is to **San Pedro Sacatepéquez**, 22½ km NW. Good view over Guatemala valley and mountains to the N. Its inhabitants, having rebuilt their village after the 1976 earthquake, are returning to the weaving for which the village was renowned before the disaster. Bus from Guatemala City, Zona 4 bus terminal, US$0.20, 1 hr. *Fiestas*: Carnival before Lent; 28-30 June (rather rough, much drinking) and great ceremony on 15 Mar when passing the Image of Christ from one officeholder to the next, and in honour of the same image in May. About 10 km W of San Pedro is **Santo Domingo Xenacoj**, reached by bus from the Zona 4 terminal, Guatemala City. It has a fine old church and produces good *huipiles*.

6½ km N of San Pedro, through a flower-growing area, is **San Juan Sacatepéquez**, where textiles are also made.

28 km N of San Juan Sacatepéquez is **Mixco Viejo**, the excavated site of a post-classic Mayan fortress, which spans 14 hilltops, including 12 groups of pyramids. Despite earthquake damage it is worth a visit, recommended. It was the 16th century capital of the Pokomam Maya; there are a few buses a day from the Zona 4 bus terminal in Guatemala City, departures at 1000 and 1700. The bus goes to Pachalum; ask to be dropped at the entrance. A new bridge now enables you to drive to the site where you can buy refreshments.

RABINAL

In Baja Verapaz, N of the capital, the village of **Rabinal** was founded in 1537 by Las Casas as the first of his 'peaceful conquest' demonstrations to Emperor Charles V. It has a handsome 16th century church (under reconstruction), Sun market interesting; brightly lacquered gourds, beautiful *huipiles* and embroidered napkins, all very cheap. The local pottery is exceptional. Local festival on 17-25 Jan with mask dancers.

● **Accommodation** F *Hospedaje Caballero*, 1 C, 4-02, without bath; F *Pensión Motagua*, friendly, has bar attached, not rec for women travelling alone; F *Posada San Pedro*, clean, friendly, will do laundry, hard beds, no hot water.

● **Places to eat** *Restaurant El Cevichazo* has good food; *Los Gauchos*, simple meal with beer US$3.

● **Buses** From Guatemala City 5½ hrs, a beautiful, occasionally heart-stopping ride. Buses go N through Rabinal to Cobán (see page 643).

SALAMA

This is the capital of Baja Verapaz and is normally reached from the capital through El Rancho on the Atlantic Highway, paved all the way. Alternatively, it can be reached from San Juan Sacatepéquez and Rabinal through San Miguel Chicaj along another road which offers stunning views (bus Rabinal-Salamá US$0.50, takes 1-1½ hrs; Salamá-Guatemala, US$1.60). Its church contains carved gilt altarpieces. Market day is Mon; worth a visit. Exchange at Banco de Guatemala, 5 Av, 6-21.

● **Accommodation** D *Tezulutlán*, Ruta 4, 4-99, Zona 1, just off plaza, best, with bath, cheaper without, some rooms have hot water, clean, quiet; F pp *Pensión Verapaz*, 3 C, 8-26 and F pp *Hospedaje Juárez*, 10 Av, 8-98, both with bath, cheaper without; F *San Ignacio*, 4 C 'A' 7-09 with bath, cheaper without, clean, friendly.

● **Places to eat** *Restaurante Las Tejas*, opp Shell station as you enter town from the E, good, specialty is *caldo de chunto* (turkey soup); *El Ganadero*, good steaks; *Deli-Donus*, good coffee and fresh orange juice.

Guatemala City to the Caribbean

THE ATLANTIC HIGHWAY is the main road to Guatemala's Caribbean coast with its two main ports. From Puerto Barrios there is access by the Jungle Trail to Honduras and to Lake Izabal. Biotopo, of the national quetzal bird, is found just off an alternative route to Lake Izabal, through Alta Verapaz (via Cobán: nearby are natural rock formations at Lanquín and Semuc Champey). Easier routes to Honduras go through Chiquimula, either to Esquipulas, or to the Maya site at Copán across the border.

The Atlantic Highway from Guatemala City to the Caribbean port of Puerto Barrios (Route CA9) is fully paved and gives access to the Honduran border, Cobán and the Peten. **NB** The distances between filling stations are greater than in other parts of the country. At Km 19 the San Juan bridge, which was destroyed by URGN guerrillas in Mar 1994, has been rebuilt. Along the way is **Sanarate** (**F** *Hotel Las Vegas*, 1 Av 1-21, T 925-2197), **El Progreso** (also known as Guastatoya – **E** *Casa Guastatoya*, T 945-1589, bath, swimming pool, good restaurant, relaxed, friendly, do not confuse with *Central Guastatoya*, which should be avoided), **Teculután** (**G** *Paty*, friendly, clean; and 1 other basic hotel), and Santa Cruz (for some reason a whole clutch of hotels). Shortly after Santa Cruz is Río Hondo (see page 647) and the turn off for the new road to Esquipulas and the Honduran border.

ROUTE TO ALTA VERAPAZ

The branch road to Cobán is at **El Rancho**, Km 85, between El Progreso and Teculután, this is better than the route through Rabinal and Salamá (see page 640). North of El Rancho is San Agustín, an entrance for the **Sierra de las Minas** National Park. Get a *permiso* in Salamá at the Oficina Defensores Naturales.

BIOTOPO DEL QUETZAL

Between Cobán and Guatemala City at Km 160.5, 4 km S of Purulhá and 53 km from Cobán, is the **Biotopo del Quetzal**, a reserve established by Mario Dary Rivera, a biologist of San Carlos university, for the preservation of the quetzal bird and its cloud-forest habitat; trails in the jungle.

A series of trails, taking up to 3 hrs to cover on foot, lead more than 300m up the mountainside. The reserve is in two parts. The lower part has two trails (1 hr and 2½ hrs), the other is inaccessible except

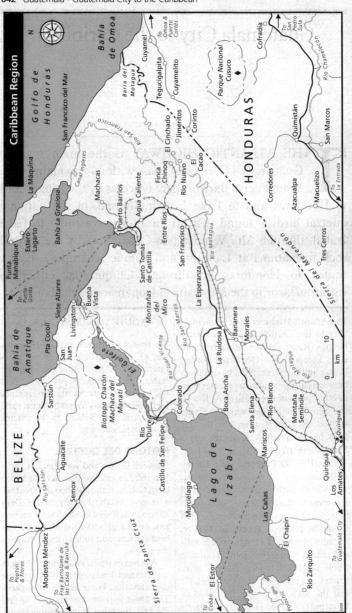

Caribbean Region

with permission. Most animals have naturally retreated from tourists. Nevertheless, there are now reported to be increasing numbers of quetzales in the Biotopo, but still very elusive (some are tagged electronically and the wardens can tell if they are in the vicinity). They feed on the fruit of the aguacatillo and guaramo trees early in the morning or early evening. Ask for advice from the rangers. There are two cold water swimming pools. Camping possible, toilets and showers. Open 0600 to 1600 every day, nominally free but you are asked for a donation of US$1 pp. Parking overnight and camping permitted for a small donation to the park. It was reported in mid 1996 that the Biotopo was closed. No reason was given. Check before planning to visit.

● **Accommodation** At Km 156 is the hotel and restaurant **B** *Posada Montaña del Quetzal*, bungalows or room, café, bar, swimming pool, gardens (T 335-1805 in Guatemala City for reservations although they may get lost by inefficient front desk staff, book in advance, especially at weekends). 100m N of the entrance to the Biotopo is the **E** *Hospedaje Los Ranchitos*, in 3-room, 10-bed cabins, fairly basic, also two stone houses each with 4 double rooms with bathrooms, spacious, clean, hot water, limited restaurant. The *Hospedaje* is a good place to see the bird (not frequent, but more likely in the early morning July to Nov).The *farmacia* at **Purulhá** has rooms to let, **F**. *Comedor San Antonio* in Purulhá, simple meals. Electricity is a problem, a torch is handy in this area.

● **Buses** Cobán-Purulhá, US$0.50; from Guatemala City, take a Cobán bus and ask to be let out at the Biotopo; more difficult to get a bus back to the capital, last one at 1600; bus El Rancho-Biotopo, US$1.25, 1½ hrs; Biotopo-Cobán, US$0.75.

TACTIC

Tactic, on the main Guatemala City-Cobán road, is famous for beautiful *huipiles* and for its 'living well', in which the water becomes agitated as one approaches. (Ask for the Pozo Vivo; it is along a path which starts opp the Esso station on the main road – now reported dirty and

disappointing.) Colonial church with Byzantine-influenced paintings, well worth a visit. Market Sun and Thur. Balneario Cham Che, entrance free, cold water from natural springs, take picnic, barbecues possible. *Fiesta* 3rd week in Aug and a colourful parade on Good Friday.

● **Accommodation E** *Villa Linda*, nr the plaza with bath; **G** *Hotel Sulmy*, nice, clean, meals, US$0.75; **G** *Pensión Central*, clean, cheap meals.

● **Shopping** Doña Rogelia sells *huipiles* made in the surrounding area, and the silversmith nr her shop will make silver buttons etc to order. The Cooperativa Origen Maya Pocom 'Ixoq Aj Kemool', is an association of 60 weavers, open Tues, Thur, Sun, 0900-1700 for sales, orders and to watch the women weaving (contact Rosalía Asig locally for more information).

SANTA CRUZ VERAPAZ

Santa Cruz Verapaz is 15 km NW of Tactic at the junction with the road to Uspantán (see page 704) which has a fine 16th century church and a festival 1-4 May. **C** *Hotel Park*, on main road near the junction, Km 196.5, T 950-4539, 48 rooms, some bungalows, restaurant, bar, excellent gardens small zoo, Italian owner, rec. 6 km W towards Uspantán is **San Cristóbal Verapaz**, which has a large colonial church with interesting altar silver and statue of San Joaquín (**G** *Hospedaje Oly*, quiet, friendly, nice patio/garden, good value; restaurant: *Viajeros*, OK). The lake is popular for fishing and swimming. Market: Sun; festival 21-26 July.

COBAN

Cobán (*pop* 59,310; *alt* 1,320m; *climate* semi-tropical), capital of Alta Verapaz Department, is the centre of a rich district producing coffee and cardamom, of which Guatemala is the world's largest exporter. The plant is tall, reed-like, with coarse leaves and white spiky flowers. It is 130 km by road S to El Rancho on the Guatemalan Railway and the highway to Guatemala City. Founded by Apostle of the Indies, Las Casas, in 1544. See the church of El Calvario (1559), now completely renovated, original façade still intact. Daily market. Cobán is a good place for finding textiles. There are two cinemas near the main plaza.

Excursions

Near Cobán is the old colonial church of **San Juan Chamelco**, well worth a visit. 1 hr walk from San Juan Chamelco is Aldea Chajaneb, where there is C *Don Jerónimo's Bungalows* to rent, including vegetarian meals. From Chamelco take road to Barrio San Luis, continue straight for 5 km, take first path on left after the last electricity post and continue 500m till you reach the bridge, or take the bus from Chamelco towards Chamil and ask to be put down at *Don Jerónimo's*. **San Pedro Carchá** (5 km E of Cobán, bus US$0.10, 15 mins, frequent; buses from the capital as for Cobán; F *Hotel La Reforma*, 4 C, 8-45 'A', T 952-1448, basic, motorcycle parking). Local speciality *kackic*, a turkey broth. Used to be famous for its pottery, textiles and wooden masks, and silver, but only the pottery and silver are available. Small local museum displays examples of local crafts. Balneario Las Islas is on a small river popular with the locals for bathing, BBQ facilities. Truck to Sebol (see page 677), 7 hrs, US$1.20. Also visit Vivero Verapaz, the orchid farm of Otto Mittelstaedt (2.5 km SW, entry US$1), more than 23,000 specimens, which mostly flower from Oct-Feb, the best time to go.

Local festivals

Holy Week (which is said to be fascinating), Rabín Ahau, in July, meeting of cultural groups from the whole country and election of a 'reina indigenista', and 3 Aug (procession of saints with brass bands, pagan deer dancers and people enjoying themselves), followed by a folklore festival, 22-28 August.

Local information
● **Accommodation**

C *La Posada*, 1 C, 4-12, T 952-1495, attractive hotel with well-kept gardens, full board available, reasonable, no credit cards, see **Places to eat**; **C** *Hostal Doña Victoria*, 3 C, 2-38, Zona 3, T 952-2213, F 952-2214, opened 1996 in 400-year-old convent, colonnaded gallery, attractive gardens, good restaurant, excursions arranged rec.

D *El Recreo*, 10 Av, 5-01, Zona 3, T 952-2160, F 952-2333, clean, good breakfast; **D** *Oxib Pec*, 1 C, 12-11, T 952-1039, with bath; **D** *Posada de Don Antonio*, 1 C, 5 Av, Zona 4, T 952-2287, with bath, comfortable rooms, TV, garden, car park.

E *Central*, 1 C, 1-74, T 952-1442, check you are not overcharged, very clean, with hot shower, good restaurant entered through *Café San Jorge*; **E** pp *Hostal Casa de Acuña*, 4 C, 3-11, Zona 2, T 952-1547, F 952-1268, excellent meals, owner's wife is from USA, clean, family runs Tourist Office (see below), pleasant courtyard, hot water, good restaurant, laundry, cheap fax and phone arranged; rec; **E** *La Colonia*, 2 C, 10-88, Zona 4, T 952-2029, clean, hot water sometimes, restaurant, family-owned, friendly, car parking; **E** *Perta Maria*, 4 Av, 1 C, Zona 4, T 952-1988, hot water, with bath, TV, car park; **E** *Posada de Carlos*, 1 Av, 3-44, Zona 4, T 952-3501, restaurant, car park. On the edge of town, 2 km towards Chisec, **E** *Posada la Hermita*, same owner as *El Recreo*, who can arrange transport, very clean, superb view.

F *El Chino*, 14 C at the end of 4 Av, good; **F** *Hospedaje Maya*, opp Ciné Norte, cold showers, friendly, rec; **F** *La Paz*, 6 Av, 2-19, T 952-1358, with extension which is rec, hot water, safe parking, pleasant, comfortable beds, laundry facilities, garden; **F** *Monterrey*, 6 Av, 1-12, T 952-1131, clean, big rooms, good value, rec; **F** *Pensión Familiar*, Diagonal 4, 3-36, Zona 2, 1 block N of Parque Central, hot water in am, clean, basic, 3 pet toucans, airless rooms in basement; **F** *Santo Domingo*, Col Chichochoc, Zona 5, T 952-1569, on road to Caribbean Highway, cheaper without bath, clean, OK, restaurant; **F** *Villa Imelda*, 2 C, 2 Av, Zona 3, nr Monja Blanca bus station, OK; **F** *María Elena Wohlers de la Cruz*, 3 Av, 2-12, Zona 2, nr the bus terminal, has rooms to let, hot water, clean, friendly, will provide meals or you can cook your own. Accommodation is hard to find in Aug and even at other times of the year in the town centre. At no time be tempted to spend the night in the covered market, very dangerous.

● **Places to eat**

La Posada (address above), good soups, good lunch menu US$6; rec; *El Bistro*, in Hostal Casa Acuña, excellent menu, often crowded; rec;

Kam Mun, 1 C, Zona 2, 100m from main plaza, inexpensive Chinese and local food, good; *Café Norte* (good fast food), *El Refugio* 2 Av, 2 C, Zona 3, good steaks; *Café Santa Rita*, on main plaza, good *típico* menu, open 0700-2100, good breakfasts, friendly, popular, good value; *Café El Tirol*, on main plaza, good meals, 33 different coffees, also homemade wholemeal bread, good cakes, nice garden, slow service; *El Chino*, 4 C, 3 Av, small, good typical dishes; *Cantonés*, Diag 4-24, just off main plaza, good menu, quality food, good value, friendly, rec; *Renée Yoghourt y Helados*, 1 C, behind church, delicious fresh fruit yogurt, good ice creams, rec; *Convite Café*, 1 C, 3-28. K'ekchi specialities, good, cheap.

● **Banks & money changers**
Most banks around the main plaza will change money. Mastercard accepted at **G & T Bank** (also has ATM). Visa ATM at **Banco Industrial**.

● **Hospitals & medical services**
Doctor: Dr Juan José Guerrero P, 6 Av, 4-49, Zona 3, T 952-1186, rec.

● **Post & telecommunications**
Telephones: you can make international calls from Guatel. Cheaper from *Hostal Acuña* or *Hostal Doña Victoria*.

● **Tour companies & travel agents**
Epiphyte Adventures, Apartado Postal 94 A, 2 Av, 2 C, T/F 512169, for off the beaten track tours.

● **Tourist offices**
Tourist office on main plaza, run by knowledgeable Acuña family from *Hostal Acuña*, who also run day trips to the caves of Lanquín and Semuc Champey, from US$30, highly rec, stop several times on the way to look at plants and taste fruits, T 952-1547, English spoken.

● **Transport**
Local Car rental: *Ochoch Pec*, at entrance to town, T 951-3474, about US$60/day inc insurance.

Buses From Guatemala City: US$4.50. Transportes Escobar-Monja Blanca (hourly from 0400 till 1700, 4 hrs, arrive early in the morning and book a seat on the first available bus, or book in advance). Also Transportes Expreso Verapaz, 16 C, 8 Av, deluxe service daily at 1315, US$3.50. To **El Estor**, 0500, 0800, 1000, 1100 and 1400, 8 hrs, US$2.50. Similar return service. The trip from the capital via Rabinal, along an old dirt road, takes about 12 hrs (change buses in Salamá). To **Uspantán**, 1015, 5 hrs, scenic,

US$1.40. To **Sacapulas**, daily, 1000. Cobán can also be reached from **Quiché** (page 702) and from **Huehuetenango** (page 709). There are also buses from **Flores** via Sayaxché and Sebol.

ROUTES To the W of Cobán is Nebaj which can be reached by taking a truck from Cobán to Sacapulas and travelling on from there, or by bus from Huehuetenango. See page 704 and 712 for places en route to Sacapulas, Nebaj and Huehuetenango.

There are 2 roads from Cobán to the Petén. One goes 66 km due N from Cobán through Chisec and is described on page 678. The better road N goes through San Pedro Carcha (see above) and continues unpaved 40 km to Pajal, thence to Sebol on the road between Raxruhá and Modesto Méndez.

About 20 km along the road to Chisec, near Finca Sonté, there is an even more dreadful road NW to **Playa Grande**, from where there is a track to the **Laguna Lachua National Park**. The lake, at 170m, is surrounded by dense jungle and is virtually unspoilt. You can camp, or sling a hammock and there is water laid on (though it needs to be purified before drinking). There is a friendly caretaker who will rent canoes and may allow you to stay the night in his cabin. Bring your own food. There are buses and pick-ups from Cobán which take 12-15 hrs, presumably only in the dry season. This area of Alta Verapaz is quite close to the Mexican border (Chiapas). Enquire carefully about the safety of the zone before visiting.

LANQUIN AND SEMUC CHAMPEY

At Pajal there is a turning right and a bad 10 km to **Lanquín** cave, in which the Lanquín River rises. The road is very rough, and particularly bad for the last 12 km (it can take 2½ hrs). The views are superb, though. You can camp at the cave. Caves are normally open 0800-1200, 1330-1700, US$2. The sight of the bats flying out at dusk is impressive. The cave is very slippery and the ladders and handrails are poor, so wear appropriate shoes. The caretaker will leave the lights on for 1 hr only so take a torch for additional lighting or in case of a power failure. It may take you up to 1¹/₂ hrs to go to the end of the caves and back. Outside the cave you can swim in the deep, wide river, and camp (free) or sling a hammock under a large shelter.

In Lanquín church, there are fine images and some lovely silver. Lanquín *fiesta* 22-28 August.

From Lanquín one can visit the natural bridge of **Semuc Champey** stretching 60m across the Cahabón gorge, 10 km walk, or 2 to 3 hrs along a new road which runs to the footbridge over the river, 20 mins from Semuc Champey. At the end of the road, which is very steep in places, is a car park (occasional cars for a hitch, and pickups from Lanquín will take you for US$0.50). A steep track heads down to the new bridge half-way along the road (the route is not signposted so ask frequently for the shortest route). US$1 charge to cross the new bridge. The natural bridge has water on top of it as well as below, and the point where the river Cahabón goes underground is spectacular, though very dangerous, about 10 mins unsigned walk upstream. One can swim in the pools on top of the bridge. At Semuc Champey are places where you can camp. Insect repellent and a mosquito net are essential. If planning to return to Lanquín the same day, start early to avoid the midday heat. There are a couple of places en route where you can get a drink. Camping is possible at Semuc Champey, US$1.45, resin cedar wood from local market useful for starting fires.

You can hike from Cobán or San Pedro Carchá to Lanquín via Semuc Champey in 5 or 6 days camping beside rivers, visiting caves and canyons in this limestone region. There are coffee, cardamom and banana plantations on the way. Unless you speak K'ekchí, conversation is difficult with the people in the countryside, few of whom speak Spanish. For information and guide possibilities enquire at *Hostal Acuña* in Cobán.

24 km E of Lanquín is **Cahabón** village, from where it is possible to cross the mountains to Senahú (see below). The hike takes a full day (if setting out from Sehahú, it may be possible to hitch a lift to Finca Volcán, then it's only 6 hrs; either way it is quicker than by road).

Local information
● Accommodation
C *El Recreo*, T 952-2160 (through hotel of same name in Cobán) at entrance to Lanquín village, clean, good meals, friendly, rec.

G *El Hogar del Turista*, new 1995, clean, helpful, very friendly, sling a hammock for Q3, good pancakes in *comedor* downstairs, limited water and electricity, basic; **G** *Hospedaje La Divina Providencia*, hot water and a good (for Lanquín), cheap restaurant, friendly; **G** *Hospedaje El Centro* (no sign), close to church, friendly, good simple dinner, basic. There is another *comedor* in town, which is good. There is accommodation, **G**, in **Cahabón**.

● Transport
Buses From Cobán 0600, 1230, 1300, 1400, 1500, 3 hrs, continue to Cahabón. Return from Cahabón, similar service (you can try hitching from San Pedro Carchá, from the fumigation post, where all trucks stop, to the turn-off to Lanquín, then 12 km walk – very little traffic). From Lanquín to Flores: take the 0730 or 0800 Cobán bus to Pajal, 1 hr, US$0.30, the 0930 Pajal to Sebol, 5¹/₂ hrs, US$1 (page 675), pick-up, hitch or bus to Flores. The road is beautiful and quiet and probably in better condition than the normal route to Flores. However, not rec for women alone. Pajal is just a shop. Pick-up Lanquín-Sebol, US$1. Petrol/gas station in Lanquín by the church.

COBAN AND TACTIC TO EL ESTOR

From Tactic, a reasonable and very beautiful unpaved road runs down the Polochic valley to El Estor (see page 657). This road is served by the Cobán-El Estor buses and is quite easy to hitch. **Tamahú** (12 km) and **Tucurú** (28 km, 2 hotels) produce pretty *huipiles*; main market days are Sun and Thur and there are interesting images in the Tucurú church. *Fiesta* in Tamahú 23-25 January.

47 km beyond Tucurú is a turnoff to **Senahú**, where there is magnificent walking in the area. Climb to the cemetery for good views. *Fiesta* in Senahú 9-13 June.

● **Accommodation** **Pensiones at Senahú**: *Senahú*, same group as *El Recreo* in Cobán; **G** *González*, good meals for US$0.60, at entrance to village, no sign, old finca, romantic exterior; **G** *Edilson*, good for information on hikes: *Pensión Oly*, in centre, not rec; **G** *Gladys*, nr main square, meals for US$0.55.

● **Buses** From Cobán, 8 hrs, Autotransportes Valenciano and Brenda, departures from Cobán 2 direct a day, but check, US$1.25, particularly crowded on Sun.

Beyond the turn-off to Senahú, the road continues to **Telemán** (bus from Senahú at 0300 and 1030), **Panzós** (pick-up from Telemán; guest house; bus to El Estor pm) and Cahaboncito (6 km from Panzós). Here you can either carry on to El Estor, or take the road to Cahabón and Lanquín. Coming from El Estor, alight at the Senahú turn off, hitch or wait for bus from Cobán which should pass on its way to Senahú around 1200 and 1600. Trucks take this road, passing the turning at about 0800, on Fri and Sun, and possibly Thur, otherwise no traffic (the alternative is to go back to Cobán and go from there to Lanquín).

CONTINUING ON THE ATLANTIC HIGHWAY

At Km 126 on the Atlantic Highway is the **B** *Motel Longarone*, T 934-7269, with bungalows and a/c, good service, good food, pool, in a delightful setting, good place for trips to Quiriguá and Copán. Nearby is **B** *Hotel Atlántico*, T 934-7160, also good, with good value restaurant. **F** *Hotel Santa Cruz*, bath, fan, no a/c, clean, good value. The Pasabien waterfall and swimming hole is a few km N at the bottom of the Sierra de las Minas at the end of a dirt road, pleasant. Geologists will be interested in the Motagua fault nr Santa Cruz. At **Río Hondo**, 138 km from Guatemala City there is **F** *Hotel Hawaii*, helpful, rather individual idea of door locks, clean except for resident cockroaches. Also *Posada del Río*, Km 137.

ROUTES TO HONDURAS

ZACAPA

Before the entry to Río Hondo, a paved road, poorly signed, runs S to **Zacapa** (*pop* 15,000; *alt* 187m; climate hot and dry). Sulphur springs for rheumatic sufferers at Baños de Agua Caliente, well worth a visit (closed on Mon: two baths, one private, US$3, good value, the other state-owned, semi-abandoned and usually closed; camping possible nearby. No bus). It is an attractive town with a colourful market, 148 km from Guatemala City. Just outside the town is Estanzuela (minibus, US$0.30), a village whose museum houses a complete skeleton of a pre-historic monster.

Local festivals 4-9 Dec, 30 April-1 May, small local ceremony.

● **Accommodation** Next to station is **D** *Ferrocarril*; other *pensiones* (basic) opp; **E** *Wong*, 6 C, 12-53, cold showers, friendly, secure, will store luggage, noisy; **F** *De León*, **G** without bath, clean, good value but make sure your room is securely locked; **F** *Posada Doña María*, E of Zacapa at Km 181 on road to Puerto Barrios, with bath, rec; **G** *Central*, opp market, clean, friendly, noisy parrots, very good, delightful setting, rec.

● **Places to eat** *Chow Mein*, Chinese food, varying reports. *Comedor Lee*, 50m from *Pensión Central*, good rice, friendly Chinese owners.

● **Banks & money changers** Several banks in the centre will change TCs.

● **Buses** From Guatemala City to Zacapa, US$1.25 with Rutas Orientales, every 30 mins, 3½ hrs. To Esquipulas 0700 daily, Rutas Orientales, US$0.80, 1½ hrs.

CHIQUIMULA

From Zacapa the paved road runs S to Chiquimula and Esquipulas. **Chiquimula** (21 km; *pop* 42,000), capital of its Department, has a number of interesting churches including the Templo Santuario facing the plaza, with a colonnaded vault, dome and fine stained glass windows. On the outskirts is the Iglesia Vieja, a church ruined by 1765 earthquake. Daily market.

The town has an attractive central plaza surrounded by a circle of ceiba trees. A road, 203 km, runs W through splendid scenery to the capital (see page 650) There is a lively daily market, biggest on Sun mornings.

Local festivals 11-18 Aug, Virgen del Tránsito.

● **Accommodation E** *Chiquimulja*, 3 C, 6-51, T 942-0387, on the central plaza, with bath, good quality, clean, but poor staff and beware of biting ants; **E** *Posada Perla del Oriente*, 2 C y 11 Av, T 942-0014, restaurant, quiet, rec; **E** *Victoria*, 2 C, 9-99, T 942-2238, next to bus station so ask for rooms away from street, all rooms with bath, cold water, fan, TV, towels, soap, shampoo, drinking water all provided, good restaurant, good value, will store luggage, rec; **E** *Hernández*, good, cheap, swimming pool, friendly; **F** *Cabrera*, green building to right of bus terminal, market outside, shower, fan, clean, friendly; **F** *Dario*, 8 Av, 4-40, 1½ blocks from main plaza, with or without bath, rec; **F** *Hospedaje Martínez*, round the corner from the bus station, clean, safe cod showers but noisy am with buses; **G** *Hospedaje Río Jordan*, 3 C, 8-81, between main plaza and bus station, shared bath, very basic, only for the desperate; **G** *Los Arcos*, by the market and bus station, shared bath, cold water, plant-filled courtyard, poor reports. The town's water supply is often cut off.

● **Places to eat** *Las Vegas*, 7 Av, 4-40, S side of Plaza, extensive menu, good typical dishes, also pizza, good selection of wines and beers, main dishes US$4-7, rec; *El Tesoro*, also on Plaza, good Chinese; *El Chino*, 8 Av, 2-3 C, 1½ blocks from plaza, also Chinese, very large helpings; *Deli Pizza*, 8 Av, 3 C, above Esso, good pizza selection; *Cafetería Rancho Típico*, 3 C, 9 Av, good typical lunch; *Holanda Helados*, next to Rest. *El Chino*, ice creams and milk shakes; *Cherry Helados*, 8 Av, 3 C, opp Shell, cheese, yogurt, ice cream, fruit juices; *Guayacán*, 3 C, 7 Av, buffet style lunch 1100-1500; *La Bandeja*, 7 Av, 5 C, open wood fired parrillada, open air seating; *Ranchen Chileno*, 8 Av, 5 C, churrascos, seafood, grills, not cheap; *Pastelería Las Violetas*, 2 C, 8, 9 Av, nr *Hotel Victoria* is a good bakery as is *Superpanadería Las Violetas*, 7 Av, 4, 5 C. Many small *comedores* between 3 C and 4 C with good *liquados* and *batidos* eg *Via Lactea*, *Albrita*, *Jumena María*, all good.

● **Banks & money changers** Banco de Comercio, 3 C, 5-91, Zona 1, corner of main plaza, Mon-Fri 0830-1400; **Banco del Agro** will change Amex cheques, helpful; **Bancafé** is agent for Amex; **Banco Granai y Townson**. All have extended opening hours mostly to 2000. Also Almacén Nuevo Cantón, on the Plaza, will change quetzales into dollars.

● **Buses** From **Guatemala City**, Transportes Guerra and Rutas Orientales, on the hour every hour, US$3, 3½ hrs; from **Zacapa** US$0.12, from **Quiriguá**, US$1, from **Puerto Barrios** US$3, 4 hrs, several companies, and from **Cobán** via El Rancho (where a change must be made) US$1.65. Buses to El Florido (Honduras border), see below.

SW of Chiquimula, an interesting excursion can be made to the (1650m). Take an early bus to Ipala (basic pension) and look for transport to Amatillo, 12km, from where you can ascend the volcano to the W and the crater lake surrounded by forest. Take plenty of water, 2 hrs up and 1 hr down. Before making the ascent, check on returning transport.

ROUTE TO COPAN – HONDURAS

At **Vado Hondo** (10 km from Chiquimula) on the road to Esquipulas, a smooth dirt road branches E to the Honduran border (48 km) and on (11 km) to the great Mayan ruins of Copán (see Honduras section, **Copán and Western Honduras**, page 938). It goes through the small town of **Jocotán** (**G** *Pensión Ramírez*, showers, pleasant, very friendly, good local food from *comedor*; **G** *Pensión Sagastume*, very friendly, garden, safe parking for motorcycles, bus will stop outside, good meals on request. Meals also at the bakery; exchange at *farmacia*, with 10% commission). Good place to buy cheap hammocks in the market. *Fiesta* 25 July. Hot springs 4 km from town. The road goes on to the border at **El Florido** and to Copán (paved on the steep parts, dirt on the flat road). If driving, note that in wet weather there may be several fords to cross on the Guatemalan side.

FRONTIER WITH HONDURAS – EL FLORIDO

The border is 1 km past the village

● **Guatemalan immigration**
Border open 0700-1800. If you need a visa for Guatemala, you must have one in advance. Tourist cards are available at the border. If going to Copán for a short visit, the Guatemalan official will give you a 72-hr pass, stapled into the passport. You must return through this frontier within the period, but you will not require a new visa.

● **Crossing by private vehicle**
Crossing by car normally takes ½-1 hr, you need 11 stamps, 5 in Guatemala and 6 in Honduras and you will have to pay for almost every one. Ask for receipts and try bargaining. The vehicle will be sprayed: make sure none of the disinfectant gets inside.

● **Honduran consulate**
See Esquipulas.

● **Transport**
There are through buses from Chiquimula to the border at El Florido at 0600, 0900, 1030-1530 hourly. Transportes Vilma, US$2.50, 3½ hrs, booking the day before can help, it is often chaotic in the morning. Hang on to your bags at all times. At 1400 and 1730 there are buses as far as Jocotán, bus Jocotán to the border US$0.50, taxi US$5. Taxi Chiquimula – border US$10 (there may be colectivos for US$3). Chiquimula-Copán and back same day US$25. Bus (Vilma) from Zacapa-El Florido at 0530 that will allow you 2-3 hrs in Copán and return same day. It is impossible to visit Copán from Guatemala City by bus and return the same day. However travel agents do a 1-day trip for about US$35 pp.

If you have any undue difficulties at this border, ask to see the *delegado*. You can leave your car at the border and go on to Copán by public transport thus saving the costs of crossing with a vehicle.

For a better road to Honduras from Chiquimula, see below – Agua Caliente.

To visit the Mayan ruins of El Petén, take a bus from Chiquimula to Río Hondo (US$0.35, 1 hr) to connect with the 0730 bus from Guatemala City to Flores which leaves Río Hondo at 1030, cost US$3, or a bus to Bananera (Morales) and change there.

ESQUIPULAS

The main road continues S from Vado Hondo to San Jacinto and **Quezaltepeque** (no hotel, but a *comedor* 1 km towards Esquipulas has rooms). Thence to Padre Miguel where you turn E to **Esquipulas** (*pop* 7,500; *alt* 940m), a typical market town in semi-highland and pleasantly cool. At the end of its 1½-km main avenue is a magnificent white basilica, one of the finest colonial churches in the Americas. In it is a black Christ carved by Quirio Cataño in 1594 which draws pilgrims from all Central America, especially on 1-15 Jan, during Lent and Holy Week and 21-27 July. It attracted 1.2 million visitors in 1995, and a visit from Pope John Paul II in Feb 1996. The image was first placed in a local church in 1595, but was moved to the basilica, built to house it, in 1758. The old quarter near the Municipal Building is worth a visit.

The Benedictine monks who look after the shrine are from Louisiana and therefore speak English. They show visitors over their lovely garden and their extensive library. If you wish to see this, go midweek; on Sun in particular the town is very busy with pilgrims.

Esquipulas was host to the Peace Congress in 1986 that helped to settle the civil wars in Nicaragua and El Salvador.

Local information
● **Accommodation**
Plenty of hotels, *pensiones* and *comedores* all over town.

A2 *Gran Chortí*, at Km 222 on the highway to Chiquimula, T 943-1148, all you would expect from a luxury hotel; 2 km S on road to Honduras at Km 224 is **D** *Posada del Cristo Negro*, T 943-1482, motel style, swimming pool, restaurant, good; **D** *Internacional*, 2 blocks from basilica, clean, hot showers, noisy, TV.

Near the basilica are **B** *Payaquí*, D in annex, T 943-1371, hot water and drinking water, swimming pool, protected car parking; **C** *Los Angeles*, T 943-1254, with bath, **D** without, rec; **E** *El Angel*, with bath, cold water; **F** *Pensión Casa Norman*, nice rooms with bath, hot water; **F** *Pensión Santa Elena*, behind market;

nr the Rutas Orientales bus stop, **E** *Santa Rosa*
(1 block opp), hot water; **G** *París*, 2 Av, 10-48.
Several good restaurants on main road.

● **Banks & money changers**
Bancafé and Banco Granai y Townson, latter
changes TCs. No bank will exchange anything
for lempiras. Plenty of money changers in the
centre. Better rates than at the borders.

● **Embassies & consulates**
Honduran consulate: in the lobby of the *Hotel
Payaquí*, very helpful. Quicker to get your Honduran visa here than in the capital. Cost is US$5,
though latest reports indicate that there may be
no one there empowered to issue visas.

● **Transport**
Buses from the capital every 30 mins 0400-
1800, US$4 (4-5 hrs), Rutas Orientales and Rutas
Guatesqui (unreliable).

FRONTIER WITH HONDURAS – AGUA CALIENTE

The Honduran frontier is 10 km beyond
Esquipulas.

● **Guatemalan immigration**
Open 0700-1200, 1400-1800.

● **Honduran consulate**
See Esquipulas, above.

● **Crossing by private vehicle**
Paperwork is reported as a tedious experience
here, insisting on receipts will keep costs down.

● **Transport**
Minibuses run from Esquipulas to the border
US$0.60 and then continue to Nueva Ocotepeque.
They like to overcharge in order to 'help you
to use up left over quetzales'.
We have received complaints about this border crossing reflecting badly on both sides, but
differences seem to depend on the individual
officials. Standard tariffs should apply.

Part of the Department of Chiquimula falls
within the International Biosphere **Montecristo-Trifinio**, a reserve of cloud forest
and its surroundings in the Montecristo
range. The reserve is administered jointly
by Guatemala, Honduras and El Salvador.
35 km S of Chiquimula at the Padre
Miguel junction, turn R on highway
CA12 for El Salvador, or from Esquipulas,
take the road to Concepción Las Minas
and then join the same road to **Anguiatú**.

FRONTIER WITH EL SALVADOR – ANGUIATU

19 km from Padre Miguel.

● **Guatemalan immigration**
Open 0700-1800.

● **Transport**
Colectivos to/from Padre Miguel junction connecting with buses to Chiquimula and Esquipulas.

ALTERNATIVE ROUTE TO CHIQUIMULA AND ESQUIPULAS

From the SE corner of Guatemala City
(Zona 10) the Pan-American Highway
leads out toward the Salvadorean border.
After a few kilometres a turning to **San
José Pinula** (**G** *Hotel San Francisco*, large
rooms, no running water, but they will
fill a tub for you; most people don't stay
the whole night; one other hotel, poorer;
fiesta 16-20 Mar) leads to an unpaved
winding branch road, 203 km long
through fine scenery to **Mataquescuintla** (**G** *Pensión Olimpia*, small rooms,
clean, cold showers, good value), Jalapa,
San Pedro Pinula, San Luis Jilotepeque,
and Ipala to Chiquimula (see page 647).
This road is impassable in the wet; buses
San José Pinula to Mataquescuintla at
1130, and Mataquescuintla-Jalapa, several. It was the route to the great shrine at
Esquipulas, but visitors now use the Atlantic Highway to Río Hondo and the new
road to Honduras past Zacapa (see page
647) and Chiquimula.

JALAPA

(*Pop* 42,000) Capital of Jalapa Department, 114 km from Guatemala City, Jalapa
is set in an attractive valley at 1,380m.
Fiesta 2-5 May.

● **Accommodation F** *Méndez*, 1 C 'A', 1-27,
Zona 2, T 922-4835, 1 block from market, hot
water, towels, rec; *Pensión Casa del Viajero*,
1 Av 0-70, T 922-4086, clean, bath, warm
water. At least 2 other *hospedajes*.

● **Places to eat** *Casa Real*, one block from
market, reasonable prices, pleasant.

● **Buses** To Esquipulas 0900, 7½ hrs,
US$1.60; to Chiquimula, 8 hrs.

ATLANTIC HIGHWAY TO PUERTO BARRIOS

Back on the Atlantic Highway the highway improves after Rancho Grande, being very good to Puerto Barrios.

QUIRIGUA

Quiriguá is about half way between Zacapa and Puerto Barrios on the Atlantic Highway and about 4 km from some remarkable Maya late classic period remains: temple, carved stelae, etc. It is believed that Quiriguá was an important trading post between Tikal and Copán, rose to prominence in its own right in the middle of the 8th century but was abandoned at the end of the 9th at about the same time as Tikal. The Kings of Quiriguá were involved in the rivalries and wars and shifting alliances between Tikal, Copán and Calakmul. One of the stelae tells of the decapitation of the Copan king here in the plaza as a sacrifice after a battle in 738 AD. In 1975 a stone sun-god statue was uncarthed here. The tallest stone is over 8m high with another 3m or so buried. Some stelae have been carved in the shapes of animals, some mythical, all of symbolic importance to the Maya. Many of the stelae are now in a beautiful park (but all have shelters which makes photography difficult). Take insect-repellent. The best reference book is S G Morley's *Guide Book to Ruins of Quiriguá*, which should be obtained before going to the ruins.

● **Admission** Open 0800-1800, entry US$0.25.

● **Accommodation E** *Eden*, safe, helpful, nice rooms, shared bath, clean; **F** *Hotel Royal*, with bath, clean, mosquito netting on all windows, unfriendly, poor value, but social centre for locals who come for a drink with their horses and good restaurant; **G** *Pension San Martín*, nr train station. **Camping** in car park of the ruins, US$0.50.

● **Transport** From the main highway to the ruins, there is an occasional bus; alternatively ride on the back of a motorbike, US$0.50, walk or take a taxi. From *Hotel Royal* walk past church towards train station, follow tracks branching

off to right through banana plantation for about 45 mins to the ruins. Reached by road from Guatemala City to Los Amates, then a 3½-km dirt road (ask to be put down at the 'ruinas de Quiriguá', 4 km after Los Amates), Velázquez bus at 0700, US$1.25, 3½ hrs. If driving the road branches off the Atlantic Highway at Km 205 which is where the bus stops (free overnight vehicle parking at ruins, check with warden).

PUERTO BARRIOS

Puerto Barrios (*pop* 37,800), on the Caribbean, 297 km from the capital by the Atlantic Highway (police check), has now been largely superseded as a port by Santo Tomás. It is the capital of the Department of Izabal. The beach of Escobar on the northern peninsula is recommended, access by car or taxi, toll, US$0.25. The launch to Lívingston leaves from here, and one can take a boat to Puerto Modesto Méndez, on the Sarstún River.

Local festivals
12-22 July.

Local information
● **Accommodation**
C *El Reformador*, 16 C y 7 Av, T 948-0533, rooms on 2 levels around a green courtyard, restaurant, clean, quiet, rec. **C** *Del Norte*, 7 C, and 1 Av, T 940-0087, 'rickety old wooden structure' on sea front most rooms with bath, cheaper without, a timeless classic, but with a concrete newer part, pool, will change US$ cash at good rate, expensive restaurant but worth it for atmosphere.

D *Caribe*, 7 C 6 y 7 Av, T 948-1221, a/c, TV, parking, cold shower, clean, boat trips; **D** *Europa*, 8 Av, 8 and 9 C, clean, with bath, but water problems, good restaurant, car parking outside hotel.

E *Español*, 13 C between 5 and 6 Av, T 948-0738, with bath, clean, friendly.

F *Caribeña*, 4 Av, between 10 and 11 C, T 948-0860, rec, close to boat and bus terminals, has popular restaurant; **F** *El Dorado*, 13 C between 6 and 7 Av, with bath, noisy, friendly.

G *Pensión Xelajú*, 8 Av, between 9 and 10 C, quiet, clean. There are other cheap hotels on 7 and 8 Calles between 6 Av and 8 Av (eg **F** *Canadá*, 6 C, between 6 and 7 Av), cockroaches, unfriendly, otherwise reasonable, and on and nr 9 C towards the sea.

● **Places to eat**
Most hotels. *Cafesama*, 7 C, and 6 Av, open 24 hrs, reasonable. *Ranchón La Bahía*, 7 C and 6 Av, good seafood, snacks and sandwiches, reasonable prices but watch the bill; *Al Mar Caribe*, on the waterfront, has open air section where you can sit and watch the cargo boats loading; *Pizzería Pastelería Salinas*, 7 C and 7 Av, clean, pleasant, cheap; *Copos* and *Frosty* ice-cream parlours, 8 C between 6 and 7 Av, both good and clean; *Frutiland*, good juices, sandwiches. Numerous others, undistinguished, in centre and several good places on streets facing the market. Avoid *Quick Burger*. Nightlife is aimed at visiting seamen, with lots of nightclubs and prostitutes.

● **Banks & money changers**
Lloyds Bank, 7 C and 2 Av, open 0900-1500, Mon-Fri, also handles Mastercard; Banco de Guatemala on seafront (9 C Final), opens and closes 30 mins earlier; Bancafé, 13 C and 7 Av, open Mon to Fri until 2000 and on Sat 1000-1400; Banco Granai y Townson, 7 C and 6 Av, also opens late; Construbanco, 7 C y 7 Av, does visa advances, and changes TCs, open till 1900. The only other bank to change TCs is Banco del Comercio. *Quinto* store in the market place changes money.

● **Entertainment**
Cinemas: *Palacio Del Cine*, 7 Av y 7 C, historic building. Also cinema next to the Banco Granai y Townson. Both show US movies.

● **Post & telecommunications**
Post Office: 3 Av and 7 C, behind Bandegua building.
Cables/Telephones: Guatel, 10 C and 8 Av.

● **Shopping**
Market: in block bounded by 8 and 9 C and 6 and 7 Av. Footwear is cheap.

● **Transport**
Air Charter flights only to Guatemala City with Aerovías.
Buses To Guatemala City, Litegua, regular bus 8 a day from 0700, US$5, special with a/c US$6.20, 4 daily, first at 0630, 6 hrs, address in Puerto Barrios 6 Av entre 9 y 10 C. Fuentes del Norte runs a regular service; Unión Pacífica y Las Patojas (9 Av, 18-38, Zona 1, Guatemala City), has 4 2nd-class buses and one semi-pullman to capital a day, with luggage on top (US$5). Bus to El Rancho (turn-off) for Biotopo del Quetzal and Cobán, US$2.40, 4 hrs. To Chiquimula, first at 0500 operated by Carmencita, 4 hrs, US$3. Bus station is in the centre, by the railway.

FRONTIER WITH BELIZE – PUERTO BARRIOS and LIVINGSTON/PUNTA GORDA

For foot passengers, bicycles and motorcycles only.

● **Guatemalan immigration**
There are immigration offices in Puerto Barrios (Calle 7, 100m from the sea front) and Livingston (C 9, nr landing). Best to get your exit and entry stamps in Puerto Barrios. At Puerto Barrios, the boat is met by immigration officials who collect passenger's tickets and passports. Passports with entry stamp are returned in the immigration building.

● **Transport**
Ferry to Belize: passenger boat to Punta Gorda, Belize, Tues and Fri 0700, from Puerto Barrios, 3 1/2 hrs, US$8; return same days at 1200 sharp. Get your tickets in good time from Agencia Líneas Marítimas (ALM) offices at 1 Av, between 11 C and 12 C; trips are often sell-outs. There is also a daily fast skiff which takes 1 hr, US$10. You must have your exit stamp before you can buy a ticket. Be warned also that your luggage will get wet and the boats do not handle well in rough weather (see also the corresponding comments under Belize). While waiting for the ferry in Puerto Barrios, you can buy a good quality hammock from the prison (penitenciaria).

Transporting a motorcycle: for US$52.50, payable in quetzales only at the Guatemalan side whichever direction you are going, the 'loading boat' takes motorbikes. The small tourist boat does not. The bike will get covered in spray and salt so grease it down or wash it thoroughly on arrival. Vehicle permits in Guatemala are given in the Puerto Barrios Aduana, opp Immigration, 1 1/2 hrs for 2 permits: Q30 plus receipt for document and sticker to go on bike, Q30 and no receipt for the other. Make sure all details are filled in accurately. Aduana is supposed to open at 0700.

FRONTIER WITH HONDURAS

● **Guatemalan immigration**
Best to get your exit stamp in Puerto Barrios before leaving There is an immigration office in Entre Ríos and at the El Cinchado river crossing but they are not always attended. Coming into Guatemala, see if you can use these facilities.

● **Honduran consulate**
If you need a visa, you must obtain it in Guatemala City.

Jungle trail to Honduras

🦶 Over the past few years a route between Guatemala and Honduras has been pioneered, mainly by back-packers, through the plantations and jungles of the lower Río Motagua. It follows routes taken by local people but remains only a semi-official crossing. A road between the two countries is reportedly being built now with international funding.

There are two recognized overland routes from Puerto Barrios to Puerto Cortés. For both, take an early bus from the market in Puerto Barrios through Entre Ríos to the banana plantations. There are buses from 0500, approximately hourly.

The first crossing starts near Finca Chinoq (to which there is a plantation railway from Entre Ríos on which you may be able to hitch a ride),where you ask for the river crossing at El Cinchado. A few families live here and can change your quetzales, sell you warm sodas and very local food. Ask for the path to Corinto, which is about 3 hrs' walk and can be very hot and/or very wet. Look for tree trunks that act as bridges over the canals and ask frequently for the trail. You should pass Jumeritos in about 1 hr where drinks and fruit are available. You will pass through jungle, farms and plantations and see the mountains of Honduras to the E and S, Corinto is at their base. Look out for snakes and be prepared for swarms of mosquitoes. You can pay someone to guide you through this section. From Corinto, you can get a bus to Puerto Cortés.

For the second route, now well frequented, take a canoe downstream from El Cinchado or stay on the bus to Punto Cuatro or La Inca (US$1) where you can find a boat to take you to the border (min 5 people, US$2, about 30 mins). From there, find another canoe to take you up the narrow waterways into Honduras (US$2, 45 mins) and leave you with a walk or possibly a pickup truck to Cuyamelito, which is on the road from Corinto to Puerto Cortés. The pickup passes the immigration office for entry stamps. Other boats make the longer trip towards Tegucigalpito closer still to Puerto Cortés, but this can depend on the water level and is not recommended. This trip can leave you with a 2-hr walk to the road. Make sure you know where you are when you leave the boat. From Tegucigalpita there are buses to Omoa and Puerto Cortés.

Check carefully on conditions before you leave dry land. You will be crossing the Río Motagua flood plain and rain here or upstream can cause difficulties. We have received several accounts from travellers who have been caught by rising water levels. Heavy rain may also close the road from Corinto to Omoa in Honduras. Take food and water with you and make sure you are at least on the road by dark. It is useful to have both quetzales and lempiras with you. An average time from Entre Ríos to the road in Honduras is 7 hrs, but much depends on how long you have to wait for transport.

Boats can be hired in either Lívingston or Puerto Barrios to take you directly to Puerto Cortés or Omoa, which may be worth it if there is a group of you. The fare is about US$200 for 4 people, about 3 hrs, weather permitting.

SANTO TOMAS DE CASTILLA

A few km S of Puerto Barrios on Santo Tomás bay, this is now the country's largest and most efficient port on the Caribbean. It was formerly known as Matías de Galvez and now handles 77% of the country's exports and half the imports as well as 20% of El Salvador's imports and 10% of its exports. Cruise ships put into Santo Tomás. Apart from *Hotel Puerto Libre* (see below), no good hotel or eating place as yet, and no shops, and nothing to do save sea bathing; the sea and beach are none too clean. There is fresh water bathing past the port and the garrison.

- **Accommodation** D *Puerto Libre*, 25 rooms, at highway fork for Santo Tomás and Puerto Barrios, a/c and bath, TV, phone for international calls, restaurant and bar, swimming pool.

- **Banks & money changers** Bancafé, Banoro, Banco del Quetzal.

- **Transport Buses** To Guatemala City one has either to take a local bus to Puerto Barrios or the highway fork by the *Hotel Puerto Libre* to catch the Pullman bus. **Sea Shipping**: it is possible to ship a car to New Orleans: the cost depends on size of car.

Above Santo Tomás, to the SW, is the Cerro San Gil which rises to 1,300m and is classified as "super humid rainforest". This is being conserved as a wildlife refuge. A good place from which to visit the area is **Las Pavas**, 8 km NW of Santo Tomás; **B** *Cayos del Diablo*, T 948-2361, F 948-2364, US management, rustic bungalows, a/c, restaurant.

LIVINGSTON

Lívingston (*pop* 5,000, mostly Garifuna blacks, a few English-speaking) is very quiet, now there is little trade save some export of famous Verapaz coffee from Cobán, and bananas. It is the centre of fishing and shrimping in the Bay of Amatique. Many young travellers congregate here for the Caribbean atmosphere. Beach discotheques at the weekend are popular. The beach is rather dirty and dangerous. No phone service between 1900 and 0700.

Excursions

Northwest along the coast towards the Río Sarstún, which is the border with Belize, is Río Blanco beach followed by **Playa Quehueche** (also spelt Keueche), where there is *Hotel El Chiringuito*, thatched roof, good music, relaxing atmosphere and good food, with 6 bungalows available – a good place to stop for a few days. Guided jungle trips arranged. 5 mins before *El Chiringuito* is **E** *Hotel Seaguilan*, bungalows with bath, comfortable, clean, shop nearby, good and cheap breakfast and dinner, rec. 10 mins' walk beyond Quehueche,

about 6 km (2 hrs) from Lívingston, is **Los Siete Altares**, beautiful waterfalls and pools, at their best during the rainy season (well recommended). Early Tarzan movies were filmed here. Beware of theft when leaving belongings to climb the falls. **Warning** People are frequently robbed on their way to the Falls, single women should not go. Also paddle up the Río Dulce gorge. *Cayucos* can be hired nr Texaco station, US$5/day. Tours by boat from Lívingston US$7, 4 hrs. You need a boat to visit these beaches from Lívingston, the river is too deep to wade.

Boats can be hired in Lívingston to cross Amatique Bay to the N to the tip of the long finger of land beyond Puerto Barrios. At **Estero Lagarto**, nr Punta Manabique, there was a laid-back resort called *Pirate's Point*, now closed, but you can still visit the miles of white sand, good snorkelling, fishing and birdwatching. A boat for the day costs about US$25-30 shared between several passengers, 45-60 mins crossing. Transport may also be arranged through the Empresa Portuaria in Puerto Barrios or with one of the fishermen whose boats leave from the house of Doña Licha, nr *African Place*. At the 'neck' of the peninsula there is a channel (Canal Ingleses) which connects the bay with the Caribbean. You can take a boat through the channel.

Local festivals 24-31 Dec, Garifuna fiesta, 26 November.

- **Accommodation A1** *Tucán Dugú* (Fri-Sun, less in week – all rooms with bath), sea view, swimming pool, restaurant, bars, laundry service, mini zoo, overpriced, to book T 948-1572/588, or Guatemala City 332-1259; **C** *Hospedaje Doña Alida*, 200m beyond Tucán Dugú, on right, T 948-1567, clean, tepid water, in bungalows or rooms, with or without bath, pleasant, quiet charming owner; **C** *Pensión Adila*, opp *Hotel Berisford*, family run, welcoming, clean; **D** *Flamingo*, turn right nr *African Place* then left along the beach, with garden, own water supply and generator, German owner, run down; **D** *Henry Berrisford*, T 948-1030, nr *Casa Rosada*, 28 rooms, restaurant, run down; **E** *African Place*, looks like a cross between a mosque and a castle, main street

800m from dock, with bath, **F** without, clean, huge rooms, pleasant, good restaurant, good breakfasts, left on paved road at top of hill; **E** *Casa Rosada*, 800m first left from dock, 5 thatched cabins for 2-3 persons each, new owner (Cathy), attractively decorated, hand-painted furniture, good meals set for the day, swimming and trips can be arranged, peaceful, rec, often full, call Guatel in Livingston for reservations, hotel will call back; **E** *Garifuna*, T 481091, first paved road to the right on the way to the *African Place*, halfway to the beach, 10 rooms some with private bath, comfortable, laundry, rec; **F** *Caribe*, T 948-0494, 100m first left from dock, same road as *Casa Rosada* and *Henry Berrisford*, with bath, cheaper rooms without, noisy but good; **F** *El Viajero*, from port turn left, clean, friendly, rec; **F** *Minerva*, left off road to *African Place*, nr *Restaurant Margoth*, basic but clean; **G** *Río Dulce*, 300m from dock on the main street, basic, clean, but beware of the odd rat. Beach bungalows can be rented just outside Livingston on the way to Siete Altares, **E** *Livingston Seagull Bungalows*, owned by Manuel García de la Peña, T 331-3908/331-8449, F 331-0784. Camping is said to be good around Livingston, but check on security and use hammock to avoid rats. Beware of theft from hotel rooms and rats in cheaper hotels.

● **Places to eat** *El Tiburón*, restaurant of the *Iucan Dugu*, very good but expensive; *El Malecón*, 50m from dock, on left, reasonable; *Margoth*, don't be put off by the building, the food is good and reasonably priced; *La Cabaña Garifuna*, down from *African Place*, relaxed, good but a little pricey, rec; *Dante's*, on the street going to the *Garifuna* and *African Place* hotels, grilled fish and seafood, fresh fruit and vegetables, try jumbo shrimp wrapped in bacon and marinated in tequila, large portions, competitive prices, clean kitchen, nicely decorated, book exchange, friendly, helpful, good information, highly rec, live music most nights, bar; *El Jaguar*, main street, Caribbean style, Garifuna background music, fish and seafood, good; *La Cueva*, opp Catholic church, nice decoration, music, extensive menu; *Cafetería Coni*, clean, good, cheap; *Café McTropic*, opp *Hotel Río Dulce*, great breakfasts, 2 menus lunch and dinner; *Café Lily*, cheap, friendly, food OK; *Happy Fish*, good; *Bahía Azul*, excellent breakfasts with huge pancakes, good fruit and home-made yoghurt, will arrange trips to beaches and Río Dulce and to both Omoa and Puerto Cortés in Honduras, quicker than going by road, US$30

pp, 2 hrs, 0800; *Bala Bala*, nr the ferry dock, international food, good. Fresh fish is available everywhere. Women sell *pan de coco* on the streets. You can buy cold, whole coconuts, US$0.20, from the orange crush stand on the main street, which they split for you with a machete.

● **Banks & money changers** Banco de Comercio will change TCs. Some hotels will change TCs, as will the Chinese shop, *Café McTropic* and *El Malecón*.

● **Post & telecommunications** Guatel next to the *Tucán Dugú*, open 0700-2100. Opposite is a store/gift shop whose French owner will allow you to use his satellite telephone at good rates.

● **Security** Don't stroll on the beach after dark, or in daylight at the Siete Altares end as there is a serious risk of robbery. Never drink from unsealed liquor bottles, they may be drugged as a prelude to robbery. Also there are many stray dogs that get aggressive at night.

● **Transport Ferries** A ferry from Puerto Barrios to Livingston (22½ km), at the mouth of the Río Dulce, leaves daily, 0500, 1030 and 1700 (schedules change frequently) taking 1½ hrs; arrive at least 1 hr in advance to ensure a seat, cost US$1.20. Tickets on the boat, or from the ALM shipping office, 1 Av, between 11 C and 12 C, who will advise if there are other sailings and details of excursions. Launch returns to Puerto Barrios 0500 and 1400 daily, buy ticket previous afternoon, office in front of *Tucán Dugú*. The ferry has been referred to as the 'barfy barque', there is much pitching and heaving. Private launches taking 10-12 people also ply this route, 30-40 mins, US$3, much better, leave when full, about once an hour. From Puerto Barrios-Livingston to Río Dulce, with stops at Aguas Calientes and Biotopo, cost US$9 one way, easy to arrange, enquire at the ALM office in Puerto Barrios. One can get the mail boat from Livingston up to the new bridge at Río Dulce (from where you can catch the bus to Tikal) at 0600, Tues and Fri (1300 in the other direction), but schedules subject to change. Other boats will also do the trip to Río Dulce, cost about US$8 one-way, US$12.50 return. Take food and drink with you, though there are some places for refreshments on the way. *Cayucos* are cheaper than *lanchas*, and if you want to share, get a group together; fare about US$10 pp for a group of 6. Taking a boat is the best way to reach Livingston, travelling through beautiful scenery. Try asking for Carlos at the *Cafetería Coni* who can arrange trips and act as guide (Spanish). Rec boats: Nery's boat *Yertzy*; Mariel or Cambell with *Lidia II* (speaks good English). **To Omoa or Puerto Cortés in Honduras**, boats go Wed, Sat, return Tues, Fri, 1000, US$25, also see *Bahía Azul* restaurant, above. **To Punta Gorda in Belize**, there is a more or less regular ferry service from Lívingston, Sat at 0700, US$50; exit fee Q10, though you may be able to arrange a private boat, and most days fast motor boats make the trip, enquire at the jetty. Anyone who says they will take you must have a manifest with all passengers names stamped and signed at Immigration Office. Boats can be hired to go to southern Belize cayes, US$14/day, max 6 passengers, rec.

LAGO DE IZABAL

Fronteras, commonly known as **Río Dulce**, is 23 km upstream at the entrance to **Lago de Izabal** (site of new bridge, toll US$1).

RIO DULCE

There are yachting facilities at Río Dulce. *Once Around Suzanna Laguna Marina* is reached by 2 mins shuttle boat from NE corner of the bridge across the Río Dulce; good, inexpensive food and drinks at the Marina. In the Río Dulce there are hot springs at Aguas Calientes; there is no beach so you have to swim to them from a boat. However, swimming in Lago de Izabal near the hotels is not advisable.

● **Accommodation & places to eat** **A2** *Turicentro Marimonte*, 500m to right at Shell station, bungalows (T 947-8585 for reservations, F 334-4964), restaurant, pool, no real camp site but you can park a camper van overnight, US$2/car, US$6 pp, use of showers and pool; the US-owned **A3** *Catamaran* (taxes extra), T 947-8361, F 336-4450, bungalows, pool, friendly and helpful, expensive restaurant but good food, is reached by outboard canoe (US$1.50 from Río Dulce, 2 km or 10 mins downstream; T 336-4450, Guatemala City for reservations); **A3** *Del Río*, a few km downstream, inc 3 meals, **F** without meals, has seen better days (Guatemala City T 331-0016 for reservations); **C** *Viñas del Lago*, on the lake, pool, clean, attractive, friendly service, restaurant slow and overpriced; **D** *Río Dulce*, beside bridge, fan, clean but damp and basic; **E** *Café Sol*, 500m N of bridge, friendly, clean, own boat dock; **F** *Hospedaje* at Río Dulce bus stop, clean,

shower, reports vary; **F** *Hospedaje Riverside*, cold water, shared bath, fan, friendly, good (no water in late pm), about 200m on left from bridge (the first hotel on the right after the bridge going NE is not rec, overcharges, unfriendly); **F** *Marilú*, El Relleno on N side, with bath, but rooms are sheds full of holes, uncertain water supply, no electricity late pm, beware of overcharging; *Comedor El Quetzal*, nr the bridge at Río Dulce, has excellent sea food; at Punta Bacadilla, 30 mins downstream, there is a bar, restaurant and a place to sling your hammock for US$1/night, tent sites and hammock rentals available, mosquitoes abound however, and not all reports are favourable; *Hacienda Tijax* nr the bridge at Río Dulce, has 4 jungle lodges, **A3-E**, depending on season, beautiful jungle trail on property; *Restaurant Hollymar*, US-run, on waterfront nr Hacienda Tijax, good food, delicious cinnamon buns and good Bloody Marys, owner Holly is a good source of information (and, if encouraged, will entertain with rhythm and blues).

● **Sports Sailing**: Captain John Clark offers sailing trips from Brunos – under the N end of the bridge on his 46-foot Polynesian catamaran, *Las Sirenas*, highly rec. One 3-day sail is to Río Dulce canyon, Lívingston, Lago Izabal, hot waterfalls, Castillo de San Felipe, US$150 pp double occupancy. The other 6 day sail is to Río Dulce, Lívingston and the Belize Cayes, US$338 pp double occupancy, inc food, taxes, snorkelling and fishing gear, windsurf boards. Trips leave on Fri, credit cards accepted. Also offered are swimming, kayaks, canoes, sailing, windsurfing and accommodation (**E** in rooms, **F-G** in tents, **G** in hammocks or **F** in a Chinese junk); restaurant and bar. For information contact *Aventuras Vacacionales SA*, 1 Av Sur, 11 B, Antigua, T/F 832-3352 or Tivoli Travel, Antigua T/F 832-3352. Alternatively, Captain Tom Patten and Gisela run the *Osprey*, and offer 6 day sailing trips at around US$150, good food, enquire at Fronteras pier; also shorter trips. A boat from the bridge to Lívingston costs US$60 for 2 people, a day trip with a stopover at the Biotopo, Aguas Calientes, hot springs where you can bathe, and some lagoons, highly rec. It is probably cheaper to hire a boat here than in Lívingston for this trip. All prices, tours and numbers of passengers negotiable.

● **Buses** To Guatemala City and Flores: through buses stop at Río Dulce. Both destinations 6-7 hrs, about US$6.

CASTILLO DE SAN FELIPE

At the entrance to Lake Izabal, 2 km upstream, is the old Spanish fort of **Castillo de San Felipe** (open 0800-1700, US$2) with a pleasant park, restaurant and swimming pool. The fortification was first built about 1600, was rebuilt and expanded in 1688 and restored as a national monument in 1955-56.

● **Accommodation** E *Hotel Don Humberto*, at San Felipe, good value; also basic *pensión*, G, which is not rec.

● **Transport** US$0.40 boat from El Relleno, Río Dulce, below the new bridge, US$2.50 return for one, US$0.50 pp in groups; it is a 5 km walk (practically impossible after rain) or take a camioneta from 2 blocks up the road to Tikal US$ 0.15.

EL ESTOR

On the NW shore of Lago Izabal the name, El Estor, dates back to the days when the British living in the Atlantic area got their provisions from a store situated at this spot. Nickel-mining began here in 1978 but was suspended after the oil crisis of 1982 because the process depended on cheap sources of energy. The mine is still closed, but oil prospecting has started. It is a good place to relax, quiet, cheap and in a beautiful setting. You can hire a boat from Río Dulce to El Estor for about US$60, passing near the hot waterfall at Finca El Paraíso, which can be reached by a good trail in about 40 mins from the shore. El Estor can also be reached by

going to Mariscos on the S side of Lago Izabal, then crossing on the boat. Coming by road from Guatemala City or Puerto Barrios, get off at La Trinchera and continue by pick-up to Mariscos. For the routes from El Estor to Cobán via either Panzós and Tactic, or Cahabón and Lanquín, see page 647.

● **Accommodation & places to eat D** *Hotel Vista al Lago*, 6 Av, 1-13, owned by Oscar Paz who will take you fishing, clean, friendly; **E** *Hotel Los Almendros*, T 948-7182, away from the lake, pleasant, clean, safe, rec; **F** *Santa Clara*, friendly, basic, clean, others at similar prices; **F** *Villela*, big rooms with bath, nice, clean, friendly, patio, rec. Also restaurants: *Hugo's*, good; *Rancho Mari*, fish and beer only, big helpings, delicious; *Marisabella*, good spaghetti; *Dorita*, at ferry point for Mariscos friendly, very good meals, good value; a *comedor* 1 block from *Hotel Vista al Lago* on waterfront is good and cheap, eggs, beans and coffee for US$0.50.

● **Banks & money changers** Corpobanco accepts TCs and Mastercard.

● **Transport Ferry** From Mariscos on the S side of the lake, 0800 and 1200, 1½ hrs, return 0500 and 1030, US$2. **NB** If taking the 1200 boat from Mariscos to El Estor, there is no bus connection on to Lanquín or Cobán. All buses leave El Estor in the morning.

On the shore of Lago Izabel is *Casa Guatemala*, a children's orphanage, run by a lady called Angie, where you can work in exchange for basic accommodation and food. There are about 200 children. Ask for information in Fronteras.

Biotopo Chacon-Machaca del Manatí

The Lake Izabal area is a habitat for the manatee (sea cow). A reserve has been set up halfway between San Felipe and Livingston on the northern shore of El Golfete, where the Río Dulce broadens into a lake 5 km across. The reserve has been set up to protect the mangrove swamps and the local wildlife including jaguars and tapirs as well as the endangered manatee. It covers 135 sq km, with both a land and an aquatic trail. The Park, like the Biotopo del Quetzal, is run by Centro de Estudios Conservacionistas (Cecon) and Inguat; entry US$5. Ask for booklet at entrance. There is a good campsite in the Biotopo, 400m from the entrance US$1/night, toilets but no food. The likeliest way to see manatees is to hire a rowing boat and allow plenty of time; the animals are allergic to the noise of motor boats. Better, stay overnight.

MARISCOS TO BANANERA

From Mariscos there are buses to the twin town of **Bananera/Morales**, US$0.60 and Puerto Barrios, US$1; from Bananera there are buses to the Río Dulce crossing (road paved, 30 km, US$0.80 in minibus), Puerto Barrios and the Petén (US$4, 10 hrs to Flores); return buses from Río Dulce to Bananera start at 0600. Morales is a short distance off the main road, check carefully where the bus you want will stop. *Fiesta*: 15-21 March.

● **Accommodation   At   Bananera**: **G** *Hospedaje Liberia*, basic, but OK; *Simon's*, basic, dirty, not rec; **G** *Pensión Montalvo*, next to station, basic but clean, friendly, quiet. Best place to eat cheaply, *Carnita Kelly*, good meat, homemade tortillas. One decent restaurant in Morales, *Nineth*. **At Mariscos**: **F** *Hospedaje Karilinda*, good food, right on the lake, rec; **G** *Marinia*, next door, restaurant; **G** *Cafetería/Hospedaje Los Almendros*, good. Many Guatemalans have holiday homes on Lago Izabal, particularly around Mariscos. *Cauca* (dory) trips can be arranged to Livingston, via San Felipe, from Mariscos, 5 hrs, US$18 for 3 people.

El Petén: the Maya Centres and the Jungle

MOSTLY DEEP IN the jungle and reached only in the dry season, or, as with the majestic Tikal, full-blown tourist sites, ancient Maya cities are the main attraction of El Petén. Flores on Lake Petén Itzá is the chief starting point; another, but less developed and less-easily accessible is Sayaxché. From both there are tough road and river routes into Mexico; from Flores is the principal road route to Belize.

El Petén Department in the far N, which was so impenetrable that its inhabitants, the Itzáes, were not conquered by the Spaniards until 1697, is now reached by road either from Km 245, opposite Morales, on the Atlantic Highway, or from Cobán, through Sebol and Sayaxché, or by air. The local products are chicle and timber (the tropical forest S of Flores is being rapidly destroyed) and mosquitoes in the rainy season; take plenty of repellent, and reapply frequently.

In 1990 16,000 sq km of the N of Petén was declared as the Maya Biosphere Reserve, the largest protected tropical forest area in Central America. Within the Reserve are several of the most important Mayan sites including Tikal (in its own National Park), Uaxactún, El Mirador, El Zotz and Río Azul. It is a sparsely inhabited area and, apart from Tikal, contains none of the standard tourist attractions though the route from Flores to Mexico via El Naranjo more or less follows the Reserve's southern border.

From either Guatemala City or Puerto Barrios, the road from the Atlantic Highway is paved to **Modesto Méndez** (no accommodation, but you can borrow a hammock). A new bridge has been built over the Río Sarstún, then 215 km on a road which is narrow and winding in stretches, otherwise broad, dusty and potholed. Despite the first paved 45 km to San Luis, it takes 7 hrs to drive in a private car. There are plans to pave the road to Flores, but in the meantime this bad road is getting progressively worse.

Those who wish to break the journey could get off the bus and spend a night in Morales, **San Luis** (G *Pensión San Antonio*, nice; *Comedor Oriente*, cheap, good), Río Dulce or Poptún.

Poptún is 100 km before Flores. At certain times of the year delicious mangoes are on sale in this area. Good view of the town from Cerro de la Cruz, a 15 mins' walk from the market. *Fiesta* 26-30 April.

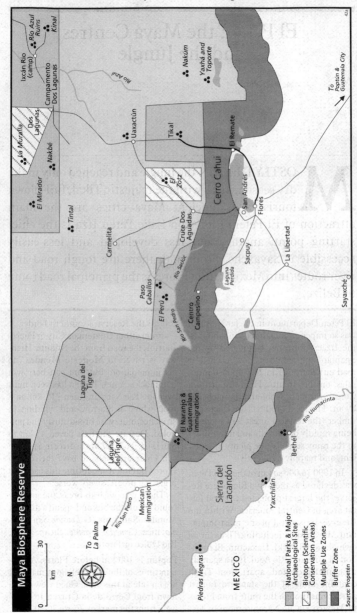

Maya Biosphere Reserve

N

km
0   30

Source: Propetén

National Parks & Major
Archaeological Sites

Biotopes (Scientific
Conservation Areas)

Multiple Use Zones

Buffer Zone

Maya Biosphere Reserve

👣 Created by congressional decree in 1990, the 16,000 sq km **Maya Biosphere Reserve** is (at least in theory) by far the largest protected area in Guatemala, covering the northern third of El Petén. Following UNESCO's model, biosphere reserves aim to link conservation of biodiversity with sustainable human development by having several zones of protection and use. In the Maya Biosphere Reserve, strictly protected **core areas**, the National Parks and *biotopos* (areas set aside for scientific study by the University of San Carlos) are bordered by a **multiple use zone**, where some non-destructive extractive use is permitted. To the S of these protected zones a 15 km-wide **buffer zone** is designed to inhibit further encroachment into the reserve proper.

A number of major international conservation organizations work with Guatemalan government agencies in developing sustainable economic alternatives for villagers in the reserve. These include extraction of traditional forest products, primarily *pimienta* (allspice), *chicle* (tree sap used in chewing gum), *xate* (pronounced shatay, small palm fronds used in flower arrangements) and lesser quantities of ornamental and medicinal plants. The main threats to the integrity of the reserve are illegal logging and waves of settlers from Guatemala's impoverished southeastern departments. The rate of forest clearance has begun to slow down over the last year as the reserve management programmes take effect, but real protection is marginal and fragile. While the extractive use is sustainable, the income generated is insufficient to halt the threat to the forest. Much of the hope for the future of the forest is pinned on sustainable tourism. With a wealth of neotropical wildlife and hundreds of remote Maya sites, there is much to see. On a low-key, small-scale expedition with a good guide, you could expect to encounter some of the following: jaguars, pumas, monkeys, tapirs, peccaries, crocodiles, turtles and some of the 500 bird species in the reserve.

Peter Eltringham

● **Accommodation F** *Pensión Isabelita*, clean, rec, but no electricity at night; **G** *Pensión Gabriel*.

● **Buses** Five minibuses a day from Flores, US$3 or take Fuentes del Norte bus, US$1.15, 4 hrs; bus Poptún-Guatemala City at 0900 and 2400 (en route from Flores), 11 hrs; US$6, long and bumpy; take this bus also for Cobán, alight at the turn-off to Sebol, 5 km before Modesto Méndez, hitch to Fray Bartolomé de las Casas (see page 677), then take 0500 bus to Cobán. Alternatively, take bus (4 daily, 2½ hrs, US$1) to Sayaxché and to Cobán via Chisec with pick up truck or hitch, a long ride, need a day to recover from bruises (see page 678). La Pinita has a service from Flores to Poptún and Sayaxché, see below. Bus Poptún-Río Dulce US$5.

3 km S of Poptún is *Finca Ixobel*, T/F 050-7363, a working farm owned by Carole DeVine, widowed after the assassination of her husband in 1990. At this highly acclaimed 'paradise', one may camp for US$2 pp. There are shelters, tree houses, hot showers, free firewood, one unforgettable parrot, swimming, riding, rafting, many short and longer treks in the jungle, farm produce for sale; excellent family-style meals available, and there is a small guest house, **E**, **F** in dormitory, TCs exchanged. Beware of the thief (Toni, the spider monkey and his friend). This is a popular stop for backpackers. They have a restaurant-bar (also called *Ixobel*, excellent too, and *hospedaje* next door) in the centre of Poptún where the buses stop. Ask there for transport to the *Finca*. Expeditions are organized; the 1-day River Cave Trip is rec, US$3.50. 3 day jungle expeditions are also organized. Héctor Gómez also offers jungle treks of 4 days

visiting caves and forest on his own property with groups of 4-12 people, rec (organized through the Finca).

35 km E of Poptún are the caves of Najtunich, discovered in 1980, with Mayan cave paintings dating from around 750 AD with hieroglyphs referring to Popul-Vuh. The Mayans believed that caves were the entrance to the underworld.

7 km N of Poptún is Machaquilá, **B** *Hotel Ecológico Villa de Los Castellanos*, T 927-7222, F 927-7365, mailing address 13C 'B' 32-69, Zona 7, Tikal III, Guatemala City, 01007 Guatemala: an ecotourist project and hotel on the Río Machaquilá, international, local and vegetarian food, hot water, laundry, T/F, money exchange, excursions to archaeological sites, caves, jungle trails, rec. Also on the Río Machaquilá, *Cocay Camping*, hammocks available, good food, trips arranged, also rooms nearby.

24 km N of Poptún, 8 km NE of Dolores, is the small Maya site of **Ixcún**, unexcavated, with a number of monuments (some carved), and a natural hill topped by the remains of ancient structures. The access road is impassable in the rainy season.

Never drive at night, nor alone, robberies reported by motorcyclists. Some drivers suggest driving in front of a truck and, if you break down, do so across the road, then you will be assured of assistance. Alternatively after rain, it is advisable to follow a truck, and do not hurry.

FLORES/SANTA ELENA

NB Since Tikal is a 'must' on the visitor's itinerary, there are many tourists at Flores and the ruins. Demand has outstripped supply, prices are therefore high and quality of service often poor. If you have several days available, consider staying in Flores/Santa Elena and making the easy trip to the ruins each day, though this will involve paying daily to enter the Park. Sadly theft is common, and watch out for rip-offs. Tikal, however, will not disappoint you.

The Department's capital, **Flores** (*pop* 5,000), lies in the heart of the Petén, and is built on an island in the middle of Lake Petén Itzá. There is a small cathedral on the highest point of the island overlooking the central plaza. It is linked by a causeway with **Santa Elena** (airport) and **San Benito**, to the W. There have been heavier than average rains in the past few years and the level of the lake, which has no surface outlet, has been rising, giving problems to some lakeside properties and making the causeway difficult. From Flores the ruins of Tikal and other Maya cities can be reached. Many hotels have inclusive daily trips to Tikal. (For description of Maya culture, see the section on **Precolumbian civilizations** at the beginning to this book).

Lake excursions

Dugouts or fibreglass one or 2-seaters can be hired to paddle yourself around the lake (US$2/hr). Check dugouts for lake-worthiness. 'Radio Petén' island, the small island which used to have a radio mast on it, is US$0.12 by boat. Petencito (La Guitarra) island in the lake is being developed for tourism (known as 'Paraíso Escondido'); there is a small zoo of local animals (including spider monkeys, collared peccaries, pumas and jaguars), birds (parrots, toucans, and macaws etc), and reptiles. However, the zoo conditions are not good. There are two water toboggan slides, and plant-lined walks, good but popular at weekends, entry US$2. Dugout to island, US$3 pp. Boat tours of the whole lake cost about US$10/boat, calling at these islands, a lookout on a Maya ruin and *Gringo Perdido* (see page 666); whatever you may request, the zoo will almost certainly be included in the itinerary. **San Benito**, a US$0.05 (US$0.10 after 1800) ride across the lake (or walk from Santa Elena), has some small restaurants (eg *Santa Teresita*), which are cheaper but less inviting than those in Flores. A dirty village, but good football matches at weekends. *Fiesta* 1-9 May. Regular launch service from San Benito across the lake to

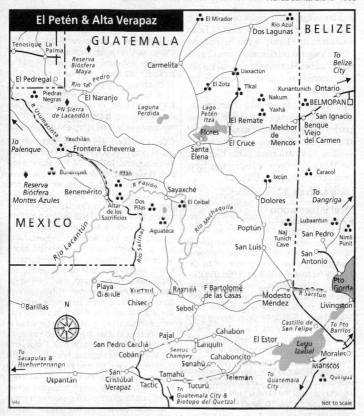

El Petén & Alta Verapaz

GUATEMALA

El Mirador
Río Azul
Dos Lagunas
BELIZE

Tenosique La Palma

Reserva
Biósfera
Maya

Carmelita

To
Belize
City

El Pedregal

R San Pedro

Piedras
Negras
PN Sierra
de Lacandón

El Naranjo

Uaxactún

El Zotz Tikal

Xunantunich Ontario

Nakum

BELMOPAN

Laguna
Perdida

Lago
Petén
Itzá

Yaxhá

San Ignacio

El Remate

To
Palenque

R Usumacinta

Yaxchilán

Frontera Echeverría

Flores

Santa
Elena

El Cruce

Melchor
de
Mencos

Benque
Viejo
del Carmen

Bonampak

Itzán

Sayaxché

Ixcún

Caracol

Reserva
Biósfera
Montes Azules

Benemérito

R Pasión

El Ceibal

Dolores

To
Dangriga

MEXICO

Altar
de los
Sacrificios

Dos
Pilas

Aguateca

Río Machaquila

Poptún

Lubaantun

Naj
Tunich
Cave

San Pedro

Nimli
Punit

San
Antonio

Río Lacantún

R Salinas

San Luis

Playa
Grande

Yurtzul

Raxrujá

F Bartolomé
de las Casas

Modesto
Méndez

Pto
Gorda

Barillas

Chisec

Sebol

R Sarstún

Livingston

N

Pajal

Cahabón

El Estor

Castillo de
San Felipe

To Pto
Barrios

San Pedro Carchá

Semuc
Champey

Lanquín

Cahaboncito

Lago
Izabal

Morales

To
Sacapulas &
Huehuetenango

Cobán

Sanahú

To
Guatemala
City

Mariscos

Quiriguá

Uspantán

San
Cristóbal
Verapaz

Tactic

Tamahú

Tucurú

Telemán

To
Guatemala City &
Biotopo del Quetzal

Not to Scale

San Andrés (US$0.12) and San José (US$0.15) on NW shore.

San Andrés, about 16 km by road from Santa Elena is a quiet, pleasant village on a hillside with a Spanish language school, Eco-Escuela, T/F 926-8106, office in Flores, founded by Eco-Escuela, 1015 18th St NW, Suite 1000, Washington DC 20036, USA, T 202-973-2264, F 202-887-5188, e-mail: m.sister@conservation.org, with normally about 15 pupils in residence with local families. Courses cost about US$120/week for 25 hrs' study and accommodation and meals with a family. This is a good starting point for visiting El Mirador as the bus from Santa Elena

stops outside *Comedor Angelita* at the junction of the road to Carmelita. Local accommodation inc: **G** *Hospedaje El Reposo Maya*, clean, good. 2 km from the village on the Santa Elena road is **A2** *Hotel Nitún*, T/F 926-0494 in Flores, luxury cabañas on wooded hillside above lake, run by friendly couple Bernie and Lauren, who cook fantastic meals and organize expeditions to remote sites. Bus to Santa Elena at 1330 daily, but most people go by boat, every hour from 0500 to 1100 and on demand (20 people) until late.

2 km further NE on the lake is **San José**, a traditional Maya Itzá village, where efforts are being made to preserve the

Itzá language. Most buses come this far (lakeside bungalows, **E**, check at *El Tucán* restaurant in Flores). 4 km beyond the village a signed track leads to the Classic period site of **Motúl**, with several plazas, tall pyramids and some stelae depicting Maya kings.

NB Swimming in the lake is not recommended anywhere. There are various nasties in the water including fungi and bacteria. Ear infections are common.

3 km S by road from Santa Elena are the Aktun Kan caves, a fascinating labyrinth of tunnels, entry US$1.20.

Local festivals 12-15 January.

Local information
● **Accommodation**

In Flores: B *Sabana*, T/F 926-1248, inc breakfast and evening meal, huge rather spartan rooms, good service, clean, pleasant, good view, caters for European package tours; **C** *La Casona de las Islas*, T 926-0523, F 926-0593, on the lake, elegant rooms, fans, clean, friendly, good restaurant, bar, garden, takes major credit cards, also caters for tour groups; **C** *La Mesa de los Mayas*, T 926-1240, clean, friendly, good bathrooms, rec; **C** *Petén*, T 926-0692, F 926-0662, with hot water, lake view, clean, pool, take care with the electrics, breakfast a little extra, helpful travel agency (will change TCs), rec minibus service to Tikal, may give free ride to airport, very obliging, will store luggage, ask for the new rooms at the front; **C** *Yum Kax*, T 926-0686, with bath and a/c; **D** *Santa Rita*, with bath, clean, excellent service, rec; **D** *Villa del Lago* next door, T 926-0629, smart, very clean, hot water, cheaper with shared bath, balcony over lake, breakfast on terrace overlooking the lake, cool drinks, friendly, rec; **E** *El Itzá*, T 926-0686, basic, no hot water, dangerous fixtures, but friendly; **E** *El Itzá II*, nice rooms, shower, but watch your belongings; **E** *El Tucán*, T 926-0677, on the lakeside, 4 rooms only, fan, comfortable, good restaurant in garden with collection of birds, friendly, nice view over lake; **E** *La Canoa*, nr the causeway to Flores, with bath, small restaurant, OK; **E** *La Jungla*, bath, fan, hot water, clean, rec, travel agent, restaurant behind, see below; **E** *Tayazal*, T 926-0568, rooms with 2 double beds, can sleep 4, clean sheets, fan, hot showers downstairs, roof terrace, drinking water available, very accommodating, can arrange Tikal trip; **F** *El Tucán II*, near *El Tucán*, fan, clean,

unreliable water, nice common room on second floor, basic; **G** *Continental*, clean, hot water.

In Santa Elena: A2 *Del Patio Tikal*, T 926-0104, clean, hot water, a/c, modern, colour TV, expensive restaurant, best booked as part of package; **A2** *Maya Internacional*, T 926-1276, tax extra, beautifully situated on the lake front, subject to flooding, restaurant not rec; **A3** *Tziqui Na Ha*, nr airport, T 926-0175, a/c pool, overpriced; **B** *Del Trópico*, T 926-0728, new commercial hotel at top end of main road.

C *Costa del Sol*, T 926-1336, 1 block from bus station, pool, friendly; **D** *Posada Santander*, opp Banco Industrial, T 926-0574, free airport transport; **D** *Sac Nicte*, by lake below road to Flores, rooms with balcony upstairs, electric shower, fan, some trouble with water and electricity, not very clean, friendly, minibus to Tikal; **D** *San Juan I*, close to the Catholic Church, T 926-0562, F 926-0041, bus stop outside, travel agency inside acts as Aviateca office, tours arranged, pleasant, full of budget travellers, luxurious remodelled rooms (**C** with a/c, TV, hot water) and older (seedy) rooms, **F** with shared bath, credit cards accepted, also cash advances on credit cards and TC exchange, clean, safe, public phone, parking, take care with the electric heaters, not to be confused with *San Juan II*; **E** *Alonzo*, 6 Av, 4-99, T 926-0105, with bath, **F** without, fan, quiet, popular, minibus to Tikal, laundry facilities, but reported run down 1996; **E** *Coral Pek*, clean, friendly; **F** *Jade*, very simple, intermittent electricity, helpful, just by the causeway to Flores, will store luggage, share with ants and cockroaches, try to choose your room; **F** *Leo Fu Lo*, on lake, quiet, hot water (sometimes), possible toilet problems, will store luggage; **F** *San Juan II*, close to the lake, cheaper without bath, front rooms noisy, staff helpful and friendly, luggage store, money exchange.

In San Benito: F *Hotel Miraflores*, good, private showers; **G** *Calle Real*, clean, comfortable, friendly; **G** *Hotel Rey*, friendly, untidy, noisy; **G** *San Juan*, clean.

Between Santa Elena and Tikal: L3 *Camino Real*, T 926-0204, F 926-0222 30 km from Santa Elena, at El Remate, 1 km beyond *El Gringo Perdido*, see page 666, on shore of lake, all rooms have views, free minibus from airport, good restaurant, a/c, free use of boats on the lake, cable TV rec; **A1** *Villa Maya*, T 926-0086, on Lake Peténchel, 8 km from Santa Elena airport on road to Tikal, bungalows, nice setting beside lake, helpful, pool, rec, only drawback is set menu, if you do not like it you are a long way from an alternative restaurant.

● Places to eat

In Flores: *El Jacal*, on road to left of causeway, good regional dishes, good fish, animal skins on walls; *Gran Jaguar*, pleasant, very good, rec, relocated to other side of lake because of flooding; *La Jungla*, pleasant, reasonably priced, good portions, avoid spaghetti bolognese; *El Faisán*, reasonable prices, good food; *El Tucán*, see **Hotels**, the best place at sunset but slow service; *La Mesa de los Mayas*, cheap set lunch, clean, toucan in cage, mixed reports; *Pizzería Picasso*, good Italian food, normal prices, try their spaghetti con pesto, also Mexican dishes; *La Canoa*, very friendly, good breakfasts (try the pancakes), dinners start at US$1.50; *El Koben*, open patio, friendly, expensive but good value.

In Santa Elena: *El Rodeo*, 2 C y 5 Av, excellent, reasonable prices but slow service, classical music; opp is *Doña Amintas*, good value café/restaurant, fresh homemade pasta, friendly; *Jennifers*, on road to causeway, good sandwiches, cheap, popular; *El Lago Azul*, good value; *La Parranda* on the lake; *Petenchel*, next to *El Rodeo*, vegetarian and other food, music, reasonable prices.

Santa Elena market, well-stocked, 2 blocks from *Hotel San Juan*, just off Guatel road. Several ice cream shops (*Gémini* 'artificial').

NB In restaurants, do not order *tepescuintle*, a rabbit-sized jungle rodent that is endangered. Imported goods, especially soft drinks, are expensive in Flores.

● Banks & money changers

Flores: Banco de Guatemala, C 30 de Junio between 1 and 2 Av, open Mon-Thur, 0830-1400, Fri 0830-1430, changes Amex TCs; Banco Hipotecario also for Amex TCs. **Santa Elena:** Banco del Café, best rates for Amex TCs; Banco Granai y Townson. Banco Industrial, Visa ATM. Also Banco del Quetzal (see airport). The major hotels and travel agents change cash and TCs. Others nr bus terminal. For cash advances, see *Hotel San Juan I*.

● Hospitals & medical services

Centro Médico Maya, Santa Elena, Dra Sonia de Baldizón, speaks some English, rec.

● Laundry

Lavandería Fénix with dryer, US$2 wash and dry (in Flores).

● Post & telecommunications

Post Office: Flores: nr the church. Santa Elena: close to *Hotel San Juan I*, on opp side of street.

Fax: *Cahui-Intertel*, T/F 926-0494, Flores, nr where the boats leave for San Benito.

Telephone: Guatel in Santa Elena.

● Tour companies & travel agents

Flores: *Petén Travel Agency*, can arrange trips in Tikal, Sayaxché and region and to other Maya sites. *Total Petén*, T 926-0662/0692, F 926-0662/1258. **Santa Elena:** *San Juan Travel Agency*, T/F 926-0041/2, reliable transport to Tikal 0400 (in time to see sun rise), 0600, 0800, 1000, returns, 1400, 1600, 1700, US$6 return, US$30 inc tour, also excursions to Ceibal US$30, and Uaxactun US$20, with non-bilingual guide. Excellent service to Belize, US$20 (except driver sometimes stops for breakfast after only 30 mins) 0500, arrives 1100, wake up call if you stay at *San Juan* hotel, otherwise collect from your hotel, bus links with Chocolate's boat to Caye Caulker, ticket US$8 from *San Juan* but US$6 in Belize; also to Chetumal at 0500, US$30, arrives 1300. *Transportes Inter-Petén*, 10 C, 10-32, Zona 1, San Benito, T 926-0574, for transport to archaeological sites, Belize, etc.

● Tourist offices

Propetén, on Flores main plaza, T/F 926-0495, associated with Conservation International, 1015 18th St NW, Suite 1000, Washington, DC 20036, T (202) 973-2264, F 887-5188, has an Eco-Escuela in San Andrés for learning Spanish and about conservation; a project on the Chicleros, part of Cincap (ecological, cultural and craft information centre for El Petén); also has free maps of Tikal and other local information inc details of the Scarlet Macaw Trail, a 5-day hike through the Maya Biosphere Reserve. Open 0800-1700. Always check with Propetén before setting out to any sites, to see whether they have vehicles going, eg to El Mirador.

● Volunteer work

Check with Arcas office in Flores for local work with wild animal rehabilitation, min 2 weeks, food and accommodation cost about US$17/week (see page 730).

● Transport

Local Car hire: at airport, mostly Suzuki jeeps, cost about US$65-80/day; Jade agency is rec; also ask at *Hotel San Juan I*. Petrol is sold in Santa Elena.

Air Three companies fly from Guatemala City to Flores: Aviateca, Tapsa (rec) and Tikal Jet – check carefully which terminal. Aviateca charges more than the others, but enquire about special offers: eg Aviateca may offer reduction if you buy an international ticket from them. Aviateca and Aero Caribe fly to and from Cancún (Mexico) 4-5 days a week each. AeroCaribe's flights go via Chetumal, 4 days a week they also fly to Palenque. Tropic Air fly to Belize City. Be early for flights, overbooking is common and reconfirming is no help. The schedules appear to change frequently, but all fly daily at 0700 or 0800; flights leave between 1600 and 1700, but check. Banco del Quetzal, 0800-1200, 1400-1700, and a cambio booth. See **Information for travellers** for flights to other countries. You must have passport (or identity documents) to pass through Santa Elena airport. *Inguat Tourist Office* at Santa Elena airport, T 926-0533, open 0800-1700.

Buses The Flores bus terminal is in Santa Elena, a 10-min walk from Flores (urban bus US$0.10, taxi whatever you can bargain). Services from **Guatemala City** are run by La Petenera, T 926-0070 (early morning and late afternoon each way) US$10, 15 hrs; Fuentes del Norte, throughout the day inc express buses, US$12-15 depending on time of day, and ordinary buses, US$9, 12-15 hrs with refreshment stops, take food anyway and your passport in case of army checks, very crowded (try riding on roof for breathing space); and Guatemala City-Santa Elena, Línea Máxima del Petén overnight, US$13; all these buses leave Guatemala City from 9 Av, 17-28, Zona 1. There is another service, Línea Dorada from 16 C/10 Av, leaving at 2000, US$18 inc sandwich, pillow and blanket. If you are going only to Poptún or Fronteras/Río Dulce make sure you do not pay the full fare to Guatemala City. Route is via Morales and Modesto Méndez; from Flores 'the first 6 hrs are terrifying, a virtual rollercoaster: book early if you want a front seat!'. Also minibus, more expensive, faster but beware owner saying nothing else is available. Bus Flores to **Río Dulce**, US$4, Fuentes del Norte, 8 hrs. Bus between Flores and **Quiriguá** (see page 651), US$5, 11 hrs. In the rainy season the trip can take as much as 28 hrs, and in all weathers it is very uncomfortable and crowded (flights warmly rec). To **Sayaxché** from behind the market, 0600, 1300. Buses run around the lake to San Andrés, with one at 1200 continuing to Cruce dos Aguadas and Carmelita for access to El Mirador. There is a minibus to **Belize City** at 0500, US$20, 5 hrs, 3 hrs to border, see below.

To travel overland to **Copán**, take a bus from Flores to Morales, then from Morales to Chiquimula, then from Chiquimula to El Florido (see page 648) and finally from there to Copán. Santa María buses to Chiquimula at 0600, US$10, 12 hrs, half dirt half paved road.

CERRO CAHUI

In 1982, the **Cerro Cahui Conservation Park** was opened on the northern shore of Lake Petén Itzá near its eastern end; this is a lowland jungle area where one can see three species of monkeys, deer, jaguar, peccary, ocellated wild turkey and some 450 species of birds; run by Cecon and Inguat. There are several trails through hilly country with good views of the lake. Interesting though some say that you will see more in the jungle around Tikal.

Local information
● **Accommodation**

800m from the entrance to the Cerro Cahui Conservation Park is **C** *El Gringo Perdido Parador Ecológico* (T Guatemala City 232-5811, F 253-8761, Viajes Mundial, 5 Av, 12-44, Zona 1), with a restaurant, cabin (**D** without food), camping (US$3 a night) and good swimming in the lake though some parts muddy, good meals, owner keen on triathlon. Good walking. It is about 4 km from El Cruce on the Tikal road, turning off to the left along the N shore of the lake. To get there walk 3 km from El Remate, or ask for a boat in *El Gringo Perdido* store, El Remate. The road from El Remate to *El Gringo Perdido* is sometimes flooded.

There is also accommodation up the hill overlooking **El Remate: E** *La Casa de Don David*, clean, friendly owner, good meals, good value; *Eco-Camping*, El Mirador del Duende, El Remate, Km 30 on road to Tikal, Community phone 926-0269, F Guatel 926-0397, run by Manuel Soto Villafuente and his family, overlooks lake Petén Itzá, **F** pp for bed or hammock, camping US$2.50, vegetarian food, jungle trips highly rec, US$25/day. Canoes (US$4/day), boat trips, mountain bikes, horses and guides are available. No electricity, take flashlight.

● **Shopping**

In El Remate is a handicraft shop selling carvings in tropical hardwood made by a group of local farmers; items cost from US$6 to US$60, rec. Tourist and minibuses stop here. 20 mins walk NE of El Cruce.

EL PERU

A visit to **El Perú** is included in the *Scarlet Macaw Trail*, a 5-day trip into the Laguna del Tigre National Park (see page 673), through the main breeding area of the scarlet macaw. The trip begins by road to Centro Campesino, served by daily bus from Santa Elena (in wet conditions the road is only passable as far as Sacpuy), then on horseback to the Río Sacluc, where you pick up the boat to El Perú. The site is large though little excavated, but contains some carved stelae; the attraction is the wild setting. Upstream the route continues to the campsite at the 150m Buena Vista cliffs and on to the road at Cruce dos Aguadas, between San Andrés and Carmelita. The tour is run by *Epiphite Adventures* (contact at Propetén, Flores), the cost depends on the level of support required. Doing it on your own is possible, though you may have to wait for connections and you will need a guide, about US$20/day. El Perú can be reached by hiring a boat to go upstream on the Río San Pedro from El Naranjo.

TIKAL

The road from Flores/Santa Elena to Tikal is the only paved road in El Petén, although it can still be closed in wet weather. The great Maya ruins of vast temples and public buildings are reached by bus from Santa Elena (see below).

The ruins

The site of Tikal was first occupied around 300 BC and became an important Mayan centre from AD 300 onwards. The oldest stela found has been dated as AD 292. The main structures which cover 2.5 sq km were constructed from AD 600 to AD 800 and at its height, the total 'urban' area was over 100 sq km. From this time, Tikal declined and the last stela recorded date is AD 889. The site was finally abandoned in the 10th century.

An overall impression of the ruins (a national park) may be gained in 4-5 hrs, but you need at least 2 days to see everything. A nature trail, with signs in Spanish labelling trees and plants, leads eventually to the ruins (turn left at the first and second roads you meet). All the

pyramids can be climbed except Temple I; Temple IV, the highest, especially recommended. A network of tunnels linking some of the temples has recently been discovered near El Mundo Perdido, but these are now closed owing to vandalism. **NB** Take care on the pyramids, every year there are fatal accidents often involving children. Take water and snacks with you, it is likely to be hot, and you will walk several kilometres. There is officially nowhere to store luggage at Tikal while you are visiting the ruins but you may be able to persuade the Inspectoría to help.

● **Admission** Ruins (open 0600-1730 daily) charge US$5/day. If you enter after 1500, your ticket is valid the following day. Extended passes to see the ruins at sunrise/sunset (until 2100) are easy to obtain from the Inspectoría office on the slope by the path to the ruins (especially good for seeing animals, eg around Temple III between sunrise and 0800). It is best to visit the ruins after 1400, or before 0900 (fewer tourists). A photocopied plan of the site is available at the entrance gate for US$1. It rains here most days for a while between April and December. It is busiest Nov to Jan and during the Easter and Northern Hemisphere summer holidays.

The museum

The new Museum (on same side of the road as *Jungle Lodge*) is worth a visit; a good collection of Maya ceramics and a reproduction of the tomb of the ruler Chac. Entrance US$2, open Mon-Fri 0900-1700, Sat and Sun 0900-1600; restaurant and gift shop in same building. There is also a stelae museum, entrance free.

Wildlife

It is a marvellous place for seeing animal and bird life of the jungle. Take binoculars. There is a secluded part, called 'El Mundo Perdido', in which wildlife can be seen. *Birds of Tikal*, by Frank B Smithe, is available at the museum, but for the serious bird watcher, Peterson's *Field Guide to Mexican Birds* is recommended (covers most Central American birds also) and a quality guide to North American birds is helpful if visiting Tikal in the early months of the year. Ask for Normandy Bonilla González

Decline and fall of the Tikal Empire

🐾 Dr Patrick Culbert, University of Arizona, found two different kinds of skeletons in Tikal: those who died well fed and others who suffered from malnutrition and lack of iron. He concluded that the normal dead must have been priests, who fed on the sacrifices of food and drinks given by the peasants to the gods to ward off a poor harvest. The farmers must have died from starvation when the harvest failed. This theory has been confirmed by findings in Belize of Dr David Pendergast, University of Toronto, where peasants looted the tombs of dead priests, but dared not threaten the living. The Tikal astronomer priests who prophesied good harvests erred in 790, after which there was drought, failed harvests and soil erosion, accompanied by malnourishment, starvation and death among the peasants. There was rebellion among the peasants, while frustration and disillusionment followed within the priesthood. Their subsequent lack of interest in astronomy is reflected in the decline in the number of calendar stela: 20 were dated 790 AD, 12 of them 810, only 3 dated 830 and the last one 889 AD. Competition between the Maya cities and the decline of the peasantry, leaving them outnumbered by the priesthood, led to the abandonment of Tikal around this time. Further research by scholars from the University of Florida who conducted chemical analyses of lime and burned grass and roots of the Lake Chichancanab in the Yucatán has shown that the lake was at its driest between 800-900 AD. Similar effects on other lakes in Costa Rica, Mexico and wood fires in Costa Rica, point to a massive drought in the area at that time, leading to the collapse of the Maya Empire.

Helmut Zettl

if you would like a local expert. Wildlife includes spider monkeys, howler monkeys (re-established after being hit by disease), three species of toucan (most prominent being the 'Banana Bill'), deer, foxes and many other birds and insects. Pumas have been seen on quieter paths and coatimundis (*pizotes*) in large family groups, sometimes rummaging through the bins. Mosquitoes can be a real problem even during the day if straying away from open spaces.

Local information
● **Guides**

The guide book (Spanish or English), *Tikal*, by W R Coe, has an essential map (updated 1988) price US$13 at Tikal, slightly more in Antigua; some visitors find the text difficult to connect with what is seen. Without a guide book, a guide US$10-20, is essential as outlying structures can otherwise easily be missed – and there are many km of trails (Maximiliano has been rec, he will meet you at 0500, US$20, speaks Spanish; another is Yolanda Quintana, T Flores 926-0265; guides who speak English charge US$40). Guides are available by the

hotels, at the Rangers' Office (Inspectoría), or where the buses park.

● **Access**

To visit Tikal you can take package tours from Guatemala City, but due to tourist demand these are now expensive, at least US$250 for 3 days/2 nights with not necessarily much time to see the ruins. A 1-day inclusive air trip can cost US$250, which includes the bus to Tikal, lunch while there and a guide. If you are in a party of say 6 to 10 it may be worth investigating a private plane, cost similar to the US$250 pp quoted, and more time flexibility at Tikal. Servicios Turísticos del Petén, 2 Av 7-78, Zona 10, Guatemala, T 334-1813/334-6236, highly rec. Check in Belize for air tour packages, with eg Tropic Air, 3 days for around US$400, day return US$120. Buses from Guatemala City are all on 17 C between 8-10 Avs, and cost under US$10: La Petenera, dep 1600, 1800, 2000; Fuentes del Norte, 0100, 0200, 0300, 0700, 2100; Maya Express, 1600, 2000. If you wish to drive, you will need a sturdy vehicle though not 4WD.

From Santa Elena, it is possible to visit Tikal in a day. San Juan Travel Agency minibuses leave 0400, 0600, 0800, 1000, return 1200, 1400, 1600, 1700, 1 hr, US$6 return. Several other companies and hotels also run minibuses at the same price although out of season you can bargain. If you have not bought a return ticket you can often get a discounted seat on a returning bus if it is not full. The 0400 bus should get you to Tikal in time to see the sunrise, but do not rely on it. Minibuses meet Guatemala City-Flores flights to take visitors to Tikal, but check arrangements with your airline or hotel. They tend to leave when full, so you might miss your return flight. Taxi to Tikal costs US$20/vehicle, or US$35 waiting for return. Mario Grijalba, T 926-0624, has been rec.

● **Accommodation**

NB It is advisable to book hotel rooms or camping space as soon as you arrive, in high seasons, book in advance. The telephone numbers given are in Flores, Tikal has no phones.

A3 *Jungle Lodge*, reservations direct T 926-1519, or may be made at 29 C, 18-01, Zona 12, Guatemala City, T 476-8775, although this is not rec as you have to pay for one night in advance and reservations may get lost somewhere down the line, new, spacious bungalows, with bath, hot water and fan (electricity 1800-2230 max), **C** without bath, it is cheaper to pay in quetzales than dollars at the lodge, they will cash TCs (poor rate), full board available (food fair, but service slow and portions small), *Jungle Lodge's* Tikal tours (US$5) have been rec, runs bus to meet incoming flights, US$3.50 one way, **A3** *Tikal Inn*, T 926-0065, in room (1 to 4 people) and **D** for up to four in a lodge, cheap accommodation without electricity also available, quests only restaurant, breakfast and dinner inc in room price, mediocre food, pool (dirty), they have a pet ocelot who is very cute but its teeth are sharp.

C *Jaguar Inn*, full board, triple rooms **C** (without board: **D**), will provide picnic lunch at US$1.30, its electricity supply is the most reliable (1800-2200), will store luggage, you may share your room with bugs and lizards. Tents can be hired at about US$10, to use in their campground, inc mattress and sheets, sleep 2-3, if you have your own tent, you pay about US$3 pp, wife of proprietor, Patricia (English) is very knowledgeable on local wildlife.

Camping: there is one campsite (US$6 for tent or hammock space), by the old airstrip (which is closed except for emergencies for ecological reasons), rents tents US$10 pp, a few small hammocks with mosquito netting for US$3 best to bring your own, very popular. Take your own water as the supply is very variable, sometimes

rationed, sometimes unlimited, depending on season. Bathing is possible in a pond at the far end of the airstrip (check first). Beware of chiggers in the grass. Same charge for vehicle overnight parking.

Wear light cotton clothes, a broad-brimmed hat and take plenty of insect repellent. The nights can be cold, however; at least one warm garment is advisable.

● **Places to eat**

Comedor Tikal, good food and reasonably priced, will store luggage for small fee; *Imperio Maya* (opens 0530), good food and lots of it at reasonable prices, friendly; *Restaurant del Parque*, annex to the stelae museum, consistently poor reports. Sometimes the restaurants only have chicken on the menu.

Economical travellers are best advised to bring their own food (you can pay US$2 for a candy bar), and especially drink. Soft drinks are available near every major temple or pyramid (at least US$0.75) but you will need plenty of water so bring some with you. No banking services available, and exchange rates locally in hotels, etc are poor. Bring enough quetzales with you. If staying the night, take a torch: electricity at Tikal is only available 1800-2200 and then is intermittent.

● **Warning**

There are increasing numbers of bats in Tikal, and anyone bitten must seek medical aid right away. This means an immediate return to Guatemala City and a visit to the Centro de Salud, 9 C between Av 2 and 3 for treatment, including tetanus shots if necessary. The treatment is free.

NB For all expeditions in the Petén involving overnight stops, make sure you take enough water purification tablets with you from Flores. If not provided by your guide, take tents, torches, mosquito nets and hammocks. Cooking gear is not essential as the guide will make a fire. Ticks can be a menace as well as mosquitoes, and in some areas there are scorpions to watch for, or nocturnal snakes. A working knowledge of Spanish is recommended as not all the guides speak anything else. You need to be fit as the hiking is strenuous. It is always best to pick up information beforehand, from Propetén, Calle Central, Flores, T 926-0370, e-mail: ciguatemala@conservation.org, or CINCAP, on the plaza.

UAXACTUN

25 km N of Tikal is **Uaxactún** (pronounced Wash-ak-tún), which has a stuccoed temple with serpent head decoration.
Uaxactún is one of the longest-occupied
Maya sites and contains the oldest complete Mayan astronomical complex. It was
researched by the Carnegie Institution between 1926 and 1937. The ruins lie either
side of the village, the main group to the
N and a smaller group with observatory to
the S. Beneath lies the oldest building yet
found in Petén. At the moment there is no
charge and you can wander freely through
the tranquil site, usually accompanied by
a group of children selling handmade corn
husk dolls. The road from Tikal is in good
condition and takes less than 1 hr in any
vehicle. The village is little more than a
row of houses either side of a disused
airstrip. At the *Hotel El Chiclero* there is a
museum of the life and work of the *chicleros*, which also includes objects, especially vases, discovered in the excavations
here and nearby. These mainly date from
the late pre-classical period 250 BC-300
AD. Entry free. At the W end of the airstrip
a dirt road, passable by vehicles, leads 30
km SW to **El Zotz**. The road is hardly ever
used by trucks except to go specifically to
El Zotz, but it is easy to walk, camping
halfway at an *aguada* for water. The site is
in a *biotopo* and, as always, there is some
basic infrastructure for the guards, and
you can camp. The temples are 2 km from
the camp and completely unrestored but
tragically slashed by looters. The tallest
group, El Diablo, is a little further on and
you are advised to take a guide from the
biotopo. Each evening the sky is darkened
by the fantastic spectacle of tens of thousands of bats flying out of a cave next to
the camp. 'Zotz' means 'bat' in Mayan. You
can continue on the dirt road for 4-5 hrs
to reach Cruce dos Aguadas, where you
can pick up a bus or truck, or, if time and
supplies permit, head N to Carmelita and
El Mirador.

Local information
● Accommodation
E *Hotel El Chiclero*, is the best accommodation
in the village, neat and clean, hammocks and
rooms in a garden, also best food and the
owners, Antonio and Neria Baldizón, have the
best information on organizing an expedition.

F pp *El Tecomate*, cabins and hammocks at the
village entrance, run by Manuel Soto.

G *Ecocampamento*, a campsite 150m from
the ruins with toilets, showers and guard service,
but reported not well run. There is a village
laundry service and *comedores*.

● Tour companies & travel agents
Contact the *Association of Eco-Cultural
Guides of Uaxactún* for tours and expeditions
to Xultún, Río Azul, El Zotz, Nakbé and El
Mirador. A guided tour of the ruins is US$15 for
2 people, US$20 for 3 or more. Jungle treks inc
food, mules, guides etc are US$30 pp/day for
8-10 days. Antonio and Neria Baldizón have
high clearance pick-ups, used to supply the
chicle and *xate* camps, and have plenty of
experience in organizing both vehicle and mule
trips to any site. Manuel Soto or the village
guides can take you on foot, with more chance
of seeing wildlife.

● Transport
A daily Pinita bus leaves Santa Elena at 1300 via
Tikal, 1530, arriving with luck at about 1630,
returning next day at 0500, US$2.

From Uaxactún a dirt road leads N to the
campamento of **Dos Lagunas**, where the
guards of the *biotopo* live by the side of a
small, tranquil lake. It is a lovely place to
camp, with few mosquitoes, but swimming will certainly attract crocodiles. The
guards' camp at **Ixcán Río**, on the far
bank of the Río Azul can be reached in 1
long day's walk, crossing by canoe if the
water is high. If low enough to cross by
vehicle you can drive to the **Río Azul**
archaeological site, a further 6 km on a
wide, shady, track. It is also possible to
continue into Mexico if your paperwork
is OK. A barely passable side track to the
E from the camp leads to the ruins of
Kinal. The big attraction at Río Azul are
the famous painted tombs, technically off
limits to visitors without special permission, though the guards may show you one

or two for a tip. The early classic standing architecture includes a 47m pyramid, under investigation each dry season. It is a difficult climb up it, but the view from the top reveals the forest canopy (you will almost certainly see monkeys) over to the Calakmul Biosphere Reserve to the W and the Río Bravo Conservation Area to the E.

Tours The cost can be surprisingly reasonable if you get a small group together with your own food and camping equipment. Hire a truck and driver, about US$120/day, from Uaxactún. A guide can be hired in either Uaxactún or Dos Lagunas, and he will be essential to help clear the road. The best place to pick up information beforehand is to visit David Kuhn at the *Casa de Don David* in El Remate. He can contact Antonio at *El Chiclero* and arrange a guide from the nearby *Biotopo Cerro Cahui*.

EL MIRADOR

The largest Maya site in the country is at **El Mirador**, just short of the northern border with Mexico, 36 km direct from **Carmelita**, which is itself 64 km N of Flores. So far there has been only minimal clearing and excavation. No permission is needed to visit the site because there are permanent guards there to check you are not removing any souvenirs. If you are uncertain, check with the Archaeology Dept behind the Gobernación in Flores. There are paintings and treasures; guards will show you around if no one else is on hand. The larger of the two huge pyramids, called La Danta, is 70m high. The other is called El Tigre and is a wonderful place to be on top of at night, with a view of endless jungle and other sites, including Calakmul, in Mexico.

El Tintal, a day's hike from El Mirador, is said to be the second largest site in Petén, connected by a causeway to El Mirador, with great views from the top of the pyramids. **Nakbé**, about 10 km SE of El Mirador, is the earliest known lowland Maya site

(1000 BC-400 BC), with the earliest examples of carved monuments. It is currently being excavated by Richard Hansen, who leads trips to the site, recommended, organized by *Far Horizons*, PO Box 91900, Albuquerque, New Mexico, T 505-343-9400, e-mail: journey@farhorizon.com.

Local information
● Accommodation
In Carmelita ask around for space to sling your hammock or camp. Simple accommodation and meals at **F** *Campamento Nakbé*. Brigido, who has worked with archaeologists at El Mirador and Nakbé may offer you hospitality for the night, **G**. There is a basic *comedor*. Local *tiendas* are notoriously understocked, bring sufficient food and water purification tablets for onward journeys from Flores.

● Tours
Ask in Carmelita for guides with mules to go to El Mirador and/or other sites. Carlos Catalán is highly rec, you can contact him through the Propetén office, T 926-0495. Sebastián Hernández and Rudy are also rec, but Chepe, who lives next door to the doctor, is not, he doesn't have mules and may not be able to obtain them. A guide with a mule costs about US$25-30/day but a full 5-day trip for 4 people with guide, mules, horses for riding, hammocks and nets will cost around US$300. Take water, food, tents and torches. Allow 2 days each way, unless you want a forced march. It is about 25 km to El Tintal, a camp where you can sling a hammock, or another 10 km to El Arroyo, where there is a little river for a swim near a *chiclero* camp and fewer mosquitoes than at El Tintal. It takes another day to El Mirador or longer if you detour via Nakbé. You will pass *chiclero* camps on the way, who are very hospitable, but very poor. Gifts in return for staying with them are much appreciated: food, batteries for torches (used to guard against nocturnal snakes). At El Mirador you can camp near the guards' camp; they may let you use their kitchen if you are polite (they also appreciate gifts, eg a giant can of peaches). Watch out for scorpions.

● Transport
Drive or hitchhike to Carmelita beyond San Andrés on Lake Petén Itzá, 1 bus daily. Also usually 1 truck a day, San Andrés to Carmelita. Ask at Propetén in Flores to see whether they have any vehicles going. You are unlikely to get to El Mirador in the rainy season, Sept-January.

YAXHA

The road from Flores to the Belize border passes through **Puente Ixlú**, where the road to Tikal heads N. There is a *campamento*, information and the ruins of **Ixlú**. About 65 km from Flores, on the same road, is a turning left, a dry weather road which brings you in 8 km to Lake Yaxhá. On the northern shore is the site of **Yaxhá**, the third-largest known classic Maya site in the country, accessible by causeway (recent work has restored some of the main temples). In the lake is the site of **Topoxte**. (The island is accessible by boat.) The site is unique since it flourished between the 12th and 14th centuries, long after the abandonment of all other classic centres.

Local information
● **Accommodation**

On the S shore, **C** *El Sombrero*, T 926-5299, offers comfortable cabins and rooms in a beautiful setting. The owners, Juan and Gabriela de la Hoz, organize riding trips to Yaxhá and Nakúm, and have a boat to take you to the island site of Topoxte. Inguat have constructed a campsite with thatched shelters (free at the moment) on the N shore, just below the ruins, a wonderful place to stay.

20 km further N lies **Nakum**, with standing Maya buildings. The road is bad and subject to flooding, but work is taking place here as well so more facilities may be available soon. A number of other sites are being opened up to promote tourism. At the moment the only one easily visited is **El Pilar**, the largest site in the Belize River valley and straddling the border, set in an international archaeological park. Best reached from San Ignacio, Belize. Plenty of mosquitoes.

MELCHOR DE MENCOS

Since the establishment of formal diplomatic relations between Guatemala and Belize in Sept 1991, travel between the two countries has improved and been simplified. **Melchor de Mencos** has thus become a busy border town for travellers and trade between Guatemala and Mexico as well as Belize.

Local festivals 15-22 May.

● **Accommodation & services E** *Mayab*, clean, comfortable, fan, **F** with shared showers and toilets, cold water, no nets on windows, take own mosquito net, safe parking; **F** *Zacaleu*, T 926-5163, clean, good value, shared toilets/showers; *La Chinita*, 1 block from *Mayab*, good dinner under US$2; *El Hilton*, good meals, reasonable prices; *Ribera*, at the border, good, pleasant view. Also at the border the new **D** *Hotel Palace Frontera*, with restaurant, car rental services, on the banks of the Río Mopan, T 926-5196. Tienda Unica will change TCs, but at a poor rate.

FRONTIER WITH BELIZE – MELCHOR DE MENCOS/BENQUE VIEJO
● **Belizean and Mexican consulates**

If you need a visa for either of these countries, obtain them in Guatemala City. However, 72-hr transit visas are available at the border which will cover you to the Mexican border at Chetumal but not into Mexico. If you intend to stay in Belize, you may be able to extra get a visa at the border but there could be extra charges when you leave the country.

● **Crossing by private vehicle**

There is unleaded fuel at the Melchor de Mencos petrol station but none in Belize.

● **Exchange**

There are good rates for quetzales, Belize dollars and Mexican pesos both on the street but better at the Banco de Guatemala office at the border, open 0800-1400, Mon-Thur, to 1430 Fri. Street changers accept TCs when the bank is closed.

● **Transport**

There are several buses from Santa Elena to Melchor de Mencos, starting at 0500, about 3½ hrs inc breakfast stop, US$2.65. Bus from Melchor de Mencos to Flores include Autobuses de Rosita, on main street near *Hotel Mayab* or better at the market. These buses call at El Cruce/Puente Ixlú (the turn off for Tikal). Bus El Cruce to Tikal US$1.80, El Cruce to Melchor de Mencos, US$2. Connecting buses for San Ignacio, Belmopan and Belize City wait at Melchor de Mencos (if you catch the 0500 bus from Santa Elena you can be in Belize City by noon). In addition, there is a non-stop minibus service at 0500 to Belize City, reserve previous day with travel agents, cost US$20. This service terminates at the Shell Station in Belize from where boats to the Cayes leave.

TO MEXICO THROUGH BELIZE

From Flores or Tikal to Chetumal in a day is possible if the 0500 bus from Flores to Melchor de Mencos, or 0630 from Tikal (change at El Cruce) connects with a bus at 0920 from the border to Belize City, from where you can take an afternoon bus to Chetumal. Total cost about US$12, 12 hrs. You may be able to lower the price by taking slower, cheaper transport at the risk of not getting to Mexico the same day. There are also daily minibuses Santa Elena to Chetumal, US$30, 0500, with San Juan Travel Agency, about 7 hrs, but check in advance if it is running.

MEXICO THROUGH EL PETEN

A rough, unpaved road runs 160 km W from Flores to **El Naranjo** on the Río San Pedro, a centre for oil exploration, unfriendly, near the Mexican border. There is a big army base there. At **G** *Posada San Pedro*, basic (under same ownership as *Maya Internacional* in Santa Elena) there is information, group travel, guides, and arrangements for travel as far as Palenque; reservations can be made through travel agencies in Guatemala City; there is one other basic hotel and accommodation by the landing stage. The restaurant by the dugouts is expensive, others in town better value. Electricity is turned off at 2200. An orphanage, run by an American and his Guatemalan wife, advertises for volunteers in *Doña Luisa's*, Antigua (they have a clinic, school, garden, etc).

FRONTIER WITH MEXICO – EL NARANJO/LA PALMA

● **Guatemalan immigration**

Immigration office near the landing stage in the same building as the hotel.

● **Accommodation**

F *Quetzal*, by the dock, basic, poor service, overpriced restaurant, bathe in river. Several even more basic *hospedajes* in town, but across the river, upstream from the ferry, **D** *Posada San Pedro* has neat, simple *cabañas* with mosquito nets, T 926-1276 in Flores, T 334-1823 in Guatemala City.

● **Exchange**

You can change money at the grocery store opp immigration, which will give you a better US$/Q rate than the Mexican side of the border. Even so, rates here are poor. Better to buy pesos in Flores.

● **Transport**

Pinita buses leave Santa Elena from *Hotel San Juan* for El Naranjo, daily at 0500, 1000, 1200, 1400, 4 hrs, US$3. To be sure of a seat you are better off heading to the marketplace where you can pick up Del Rosío buses until 1600. The bus drops you at the side of the ruins (adorned with machine gun posts) by the dock. Several travellers have said that there is no point in getting the 0500 bus if going to Mexico because the boat almost always waits for the arrival of the next bus. Boat is supposed to leave for Mexico at around 1300, but often goes about 1400. Probably what happens is that the boat leaves when full, so if there are many travellers leaving Santa Elena, better get the earlier bus. There are buses back to Santa Elena at 0100, 0400, 1230 and 1400.

From El Naranjo, daily boats leave at 0600 and sometime around 1300, for La Palma in Mexico, US$22, cheaper to pay in quetzales, 4-5 hrs inc Mexican border crossing, from where buses go to Tenosique and on to Palenque. **NB** The 1300 boat will often get you to La Palma just in time to miss the last bus to Tenosique, be prepared to stay the night. If there are fewer than 5 passengers for the boat, it may be cancelled and your alternatives are to wait for the next boat, or take a *rápido*, max 4 persons US$125. Return from La Palma to El Naranjo at 1400. Bus La Palma-Tenosique at 1700, and one other; it is not possible to go Palenque the same day unless you hire a taxi in La Palma. Mexican tourist cards can be obtained at the border. Beautiful trip, but take waterproofs, a torch and some food with you. Beware mosquitoes. Expect thorough searches on both sides of the border. Depending on the level of the water, this can be an exciting trip through the narrower, rocky stretches. Look for the border marked by a straight line cleared up to a distant white obelisk.

LAGUNA DEL TIGRE

The **Laguna del Tigre National Park and Biotopo** is a vast area of jungle and wetlands N of El Naranjo. The best place to stay is the CECON camp, the headquarters of the *biotopo*, across the river below the ferry; a boy will paddle you over in a canoe. This is where the guards live and they will let you stay in the bunk house and use their kitchen. Getting into the reserve is not easy and you will need to be equipped for a week or more, but a few people (occasionally scientists) go up the Río Escondido. The lagoons abound in wildlife, including enormous crocodiles and spectacular birdlife. There is a cluster of ruins near the border, extremely difficult to reach.

FRONTIER WITH MEXICO – RIO USUMACINTA

Further S, another route leads into the Mexican state of Chiapas. There are two points on the Río Usumacinta which you can reach by launch and continue by bus into Mexico. They are Benemérito de las Américas (frontier post upstream at Pipiles) and Frontera Echeverría (immigration office near the wharf). You are advised, however, to get your exit stamp in Flores and your visa or free Mexican tourist card in advance.

For the first option, take a bus from Santa Elena via La Libertad to **Bethel** (regular Pinita bus service, 0500, 1100, 5 hrs, US$4); ask the driver to drop you at immigration while he drives around the village, then collect you for the 20-min ride to La Técnica village (an extra US$1.10). From here it is a 5-min ferry ride to **Frontera Echeverría/Corozal** on the Río Usumacinta. Immigration at Bethel charges US$3/Q15 exit tax. In Bethel there is lodging at the **E** *Posada Maya*, just over 1 km outside the village run by the village co-op as part of an eco-tourism project, the only place to stay but a bit inconvenient, superb setting, open-sided thatched shelters with tents or hammocks and mosquito nets, all with clean sheets, built in plaza of a Maya site overlooking the river, *cabañas* ready 1997, mainly used by passing tour groups. If you need to stay in the village you can borrow a hammock from a *comedor* or camp by the riverbank. There are guides with horses to take you to nearby attractions, including a lovely *cenote*; further afield are more ruins in the jungle. Bethel itself has sizeable ruins. Bus leaves Bethel for Flores at 1200. You get your Mexican immigration stamp at Corozal. No hotel. A dirt road leads up 18 km to the equally unpaved Frontier Highway (35 km to the San Javier junction for Lacanjá and Bonampak). From Frontera Echeverría it is 6-8 hrs by bus to Palenque, US$5. **NB** The 0500 bus from Santa Elena does not get you to Bethel for an onward connection to Palenque. You have to wait until the 0400 direct bus from Frontera Echeverría next morning. However, there are often pickups and the main road has buses day and night.

Alternatively, go from Santa Elena to Sayaxché, 61 km (see below), then take a boat down the Río de la Pasión to the military post at **Pipiles** (exit stamps must be given here) and on to the town of **Benemérito** on the Río Usumacinta (trading boat twice a week US$4-5, 2 days; motorized cargo canoe US$5-10, 8 hrs; private launch US$100, 4 hrs). The trading boats (maize) give a good insight into riverside life, stopping frequently at hamlets to drop and pick up passengers. Grapefruit are in such plentiful supply that no one bothers to sell them (still, it is polite to ask before picking them up off the ground). If stuck at Pipiles, a farmer who lives 800m upstream may take you to Benemérito in his launch. If there is more than one maize boat at Pipiles move up to the first one because they often wait up to 3 days to get a better price. At Benemérito, a shop near the river lets out rooms at the back, no electricity, water from well. From Benemérito, buses go at 0600, 0700, 0800 and 1300 to immigration just past the Río Lacantún (or hitch in a truck); buses wait here before continuing to Palenque. Unpaved road, 7-12 hrs by bus Benemérito-Palenque (more in the wet). There are also boats from Sayaxché to Frontera Echeverría/Corozal, but they charge from US$275 for a 20-seater. Get Mexican tourist card in advance to avoid offering bribes at border, and get your exit visa in Flores. Take also hammock, mosquito net, food and insect repellent; the only accommodation between Sayaxché and Palenque is a basic room in Benemérito, and dollars cannot be exchanged. Yaxchilán and Bonampak in Mexico can be visited from the road Benemérito-Palenque.

SAYAXCHÉ

Sayaxché is a good centre for visiting the Petén, whether your interest is in the wildlife or the Maya ruins. To cross the ferry near the village costs US$2 for a car (free for motorcycles). Up to recently, foot passengers were free, but we have heard of a charge of US$0.10 in 1996.

Local festivals

5-13 June.

Local information
● **Accommodation & places to eat**

All places are pretty grim.

E *Guayacán*, known locally as *Hotel de Godoy* after the owner Julio Godoy, is a good source of information on the area, on S bank of river, close to ferry, 2 rooms with bathrooms, new rooms built, but pretty basic.

F *Mayapán*, friendly, clean, basic, rents bicycles to visit El Ceibal US$5/day.

G *Casa de Huéspedes Carmen Kilkan*, nr the football field, very friendly, no running water or electricity, rats, otherwise OK!, camping permitted, US$0.75 pp, ask there for Juanita (American), knowledgeable, will arrange trips and accompany you; or **G** *Hotel Sayaxché*, basic, dirty, food not bad. *Yaxkin*, good food, friendly, cheap, owner speaks English, very informative; *Restaurant Montaña*, Julián Mariona Morán, T/F 926-6114, will give you information, he also owns **A3** *Posada Caribe* at Laguna Petexbatún, T 926-0436 (see below), and at *Los Charros*, Maguin is helpful, good food, nice. If travelling S, stock up with fruit in the market and, if driving, fuel at the service station.

● **Banks & money changers**

You can change US$ bills at various places in town and TCs at the bank. Pesos can be bought in the store *La Moderna* or *Hotel Guayacán*.

● **Transport**

Buses There are buses to and from Guatemala City via Sebol from 0700 when conditions allow. You can also catch pickup trucks to Sebol from 0630 or earlier, 7^1/$_2$ hrs, terrible road, police checks, reported great fun (especially on an off-road bike)! Also buses to and from Santa Elena, Flores, 0600, 1300 (US$0.80, 3 hrs); La Pinita has a bus to Flores, US$2 (intermittent transport S in the rainy season), but note that Pinita has a policy of charging foreign tourists double the normal fare. If hitching to Flores, try for a ride on an oil truck at the river crossing in Sayaxché to La Libertad (oil refinery), then truck or bus to Flores.

River *Viajes Don Pedro* runs launches to El Ceibal, Petexbatún and Aguateca, 4 hrs, and 2-day trips to Yaxchilán (in Mexico). Although Don Pedro organizes interesting jungle tours, his son, the guide, tends to change the plans and alter the length of the trip once you have started. *Viajes Turísticos La Montaña* (Julián Mariona Morán, see above); good guide Antonio Chiquín Cocul, at *Hotel Guayacán*, good tours to Maya sites, US$7 pp.

Driving Flores-Cobán: take the road from Santa Elena to Sayaxché, unpaved, lots of potholes, dusty (don't follow a truck), many oil transporters, especially nr the La Libertad intersection to Bethel. In Sayaxché the road to Cobán is signed (200 km): go left for Cobán. After a few km is an intersection to El Ceibal. The road improves up to the first mountain ridge. Keep asking for the road to Sebol, which is better than the direct route to Cobán via Chisec. At all times, ask directions. Do not drive at night, there is a real danger of getting lost and of hitting cattle. Petrol/gasoline is available in La Libertad and Sayaxché.

EL CEIBAL

Up the Río de la Pasión from Sayaxché is **El Ceibal** (also known as Seibal in the archaeological literature), where the ruins were excavated by Peabody Museum and Harvard. The ceremonial site is about 1 km from the left bank of Río de la Pasión and extends for 1.5 sq km. One of the main structures to be seen is the 30m temple, partially restored, with 4 staircases, linked by a sacbé (causeway) to an unusual circular pyramid, believed to be unique in the Petén. Some of the best preserved *stelae* in Guatemala are found in a jungle park setting. There is now a difficult road linking Sayaxché with El Ceibal – impassable in the wet (leave bus at El Paraíso on the main road – local pick-up from Sayaxché US$0.20 – then walk to the ruins, a further 7 km, 1½ hrs) so the trip can be made either by road or by river (launch hire US$35 round trip 4 passengers, 2 hrs each way – *pensión* **G**). You can sling a hammock at El Ceibal and use the guard's fire for making coffee if you ask politely – a mosquito net is advisable, and take repellent for walking in the jungle surroundings. If you leave belongings at El Ceibal, make sure they are in reliable care, theft is not uncommon. Tours can be arranged in Flores for a day visit to Sayaxché and El Ceibal but there is limited time to see the site.

From Sayaxché the ruins of the **Altar de Sacrificios** at the confluence of the Ríos de la Pasión and Usumacinta can also be reached. Also within reach of Sayaxché is **Itzán**, discovered in 1968. Further down the Usumacinta Río is Yaxchilán, just over the border in Mexico (temples still standing, with sculptures and carved lintels – see Mexico, page 417, **Yucatán Peninsula**). You can sometimes talk your way onto one of the boats leaving Corozal (see above) with a tour group aboard to visit Yaxchilán. Best to have good Spanish, but you will pay less than the tour party.

PIEDRAS NEGRAS

Still further down the Río Usumacinta in the W of Petén is **Piedras Negras**. A huge Classic period site, Piedras Negras has been saved from the major looting which afflicted most other sites in Petén by its role as a base for guerrillas during Guatemala's protracted insurgency. With the signing of the peace treaty, a 5-year research project, undertaken by Prof Stephen Houston of Brigham Young University and Dr Héctor Escobedo of San Carlos University, has recently begun. In the 1930s Tatiana Proskouriakoff first recognized that the periods of time inscribed on stelae here coincided with human life spans or reigns, and so began the task of deciphering the meaning of Maya glyphs. Until 1997 no research had taken place at Piedras Negras since 1939. The site on a cliff high above the river is today one of the best places to observe how modern archaeological techniques interpret the Maya world. If plans to construct hydroelectric dams on the Usumacinta go ahead, this and many other sites will be inundated.

Advance arrangements are necessary with a rafting company to reach Piedras Negras. Maya Expeditions in Guatemala City, 15 C, 1-91, Zona 10, Oficina 104, T 363-4955, F 594-7748, e-mail: mayaexp@guate.net, is the official tour operator for the project; they run 2-week expeditions, taking in a number of sites, including Piedras Negras, where they provide logistic support for the current archaeological research. Each participant contributes US$200 towards the project's expenses, an amount matched by Maya Expeditions. The archaeologists give special tours and presentations and visitors are given full details of the latest research. This trip is a real adventure. The riverbanks are covered in the best remaining tropical forest in Guatemala, inhabited by elusive wildlife and hiding more ruins. Once you've rafted down to Piedras Negras, you have to raft out. Though most of the river is fairly placid, there are the 30m Busilhá Falls, where a crystal clear tributary cascades over limestone terraces and two deep canyons, with impressive rapids to negotiate, before reaching the take-out 2 days later.

LAGUNA PETEXBATUN

The Río de la Pasión is a good route to visit other, more recently discovered Maya ruins. From **Laguna Petexbatún** (16 km), a fisherman's paradise, which can be reached by outboard canoe from Sayaxché (US$10 or more for 6 people and luggage) excursions can be made to unexcavated ruins: these include **Arroyo de la Piedra** (a small site with a number of mounds and stelae, between Sayaxché and Dos Pilas), **Dos Pilas** itself (many well-preserved stelae, important tomb find of a King here in 1991), **Aguateca**, where the ruins are so far little excavated, giving a feeling of authenticity, and where an excursion can be made over the only known Maya bridge and down into a huge chasm. Lagoon fishing includes 150-lb tarpon, snoek and local varieties. Many interesting birds, including toucan and *guacamayo*.

● **Accommodation** Highly rec is **A3** *Posada Caribe*, run by Julián Mariona Morán, T/F 926-6114/ 0436, inc 3 meals, comfortable *cabañas* with bathroom and shower, excursion to Aguateca by launch and a guide for jungle excursions where you can see lots of animals and birds. The only other hotel, **A1** *Posada Mateos*, with bath, hot water, electricity, in bungalows, T 926-0505, or can be booked in advance by tour agencies. Jungle guides can be hired for US$1.50-2.50/day. Camping is possible at Escobado, on the lakeside, occasional public launches from Sayaxché. Take water and food.

SEBOL

100 km NE of Cobán, 50 km N of Lanquín is **Sebol** from where roads go N into the Petén and E to Izabal. There is nowhere to stay in Sebol but, if you get stuck there, ask at the control station (the big house) if you might sleep on the floor. There is (hopefully) a bus Raxrujá 0400, Sebol 0500, to Cobán 1330, which is 120 km in 9½ hrs! The Río Sebol (part of the Río de la Pasión system) offers good bathing a short distance to the N (follow the signs to La Playa). 2 hrs N at Balneario Las Islas there is also good swimming and walks, well signposted, crowded at weekends, good camping, good *comedor* (US$3 by boat, 1½-2 hrs). On 24 Aug, all-night mass is celebrated in Sebol (free food at 0100) with games played on the church lawn in the daylight hours.

10 km from Sebol is **Fray Bartolomé de Las Casas** (**F** *Hospedaje Ralíos*, shared bath, OK; **F** *Damelito*, on main sqare, own generator, clean friendly, good breakfast; **F** *Evelyne*, main street, no meals; restaurants), a pleasant village which has a *fiesta*

from 30 April-4 May with a parade and rodeo on 1 May. No bus service to Fray Bartolomé from 16 Jan to end of wet season, bargain with pick-up drivers to/from Sebol. There is an airstrip nearby, charters possible. A rough dirt road links Sebol with Sayaxché via **Raxrujá**, 'a hole', with strong military presence. Most of this 120-km road is in poor condition, particularly the section from Raxrujá to (Cruce) El Pato. Thereafter going N, the road improves though it can be very difficult in the wet season (coming S it is often not possible to travel Sayaxche-Sebol in 1 day and you get stuck overnight in Raxrujá, from where transport only leaves in the morning). Hitching with oil tankers is possible. Near to Raxrujá is an extensive river cave. In the wet season there is occasional boat transport Sebol-El Pato-Sayaxché.

● **Accommodation in Raxrujá**: **G** *Pensión Aguas Verdes*, basic, pleasant; **G** *Pensión La Reina*, rough, no water, dirty, bad; good *pensión* nr bridge, **G** pp, no bath (except the river!) *comedor* opp; many *comedores*, eg **El Piloto**, good, meal US$1, *El Ganadero*, quite good. In **El Pato**: 2 *hospedajes*, first at the port, dirty, monkey in garden; second at **G** *Farmacia Margarita/Hospedaje El Amigo*, better, basic, mosquito net necessary, owner's son has pick-up transport; good *comedor*, *Tonito*, behind soccer field.

● **Transport** Local transport connects most of these towns, but do not travel at night: from Sayaxché there are buses at 0600, 0730 and 1430 to within 20 km of Raxrujá, at which point you have to change to a pick-up because buses cannot cope with the road; there are also pick-ups all the way, check times, several a day, 6 hrs, US$2.60; after about 2½ hrs is a road junction with a comedor, at least 2 buses a day from here to Sayaxché (one at midday), 3½ hrs. There are many more roads in this area than maps show, there are also plenty of military camps, so expect checks by the army and other types of (non-military) hold-up. El Pato-Raxrujá (minibus 0500 daily); Raxrujá-Sebol, occasional bus, US$0.40, pick-up from 0700 more common, US$0.75 (very bad road, 2 hrs for 25 km) or El Pato-Sebol; Fray B de Las Casas-Cobán, 0500, 9 hrs, US$1.50 (Cobán-Sebol at 0530). You can also go from Lanquín to Sayaxché via Pajal, Las Casas, Sebol and Raxrujá (see page 646), not rec as a 1-day journey, better to rest in Raxrujá. The road from Raxrujá via Chisec to Cobán is very steep and rocky. Part, over the Sierra de Chamá, is known as the staircase! It is passable in the dry season with high clearance vehicle (not advisable for a standard car). In the wet even 4WD cannot manage this road. Recommended for spectacular scenery but you need lots of time. Several army checkpoints on the Chisec route; friendly, will give advice on directions. Even well after the wet season, ie mid-Jan, a bus may not be able to get all the way from Sayaxché to Cobán, even though tickets may be sold. Pick-ups will do the trip via Chisec, 11-12 hrs, US$4, a terrible squash, but ask as many people as possible before embarking if a bus is running via Sebol. **Chisec** to Cobán takes 5 hrs driving in normal conditions.There is a petrol station in

Chisec (on the right heading for Cobán). The owner of *Pinchazo* workshop also owns *Costa Sur* hotel and restaurant, good entering from Sayaxché; meals US$1, car park outside, friendly, good advice on road conditions. From Sebol, there is an 0300 bus to Poptún (see page 659), via Fray Bartolomé de Las Casas and San Luis (on the Morales-Río Dulce-Poptún-Flores road). This route is impassable in the rainy season. From San Luis there is an 0630 bus to Flores, stopping at Poptún (4½ hrs). It is easy to get a ride on one of the many trucks which run on all these routes. You can also go from Sebol to Modesto Méndez on the Morales-Flores road but it is extremely slow going because of potholes, winding narrow roads and big rocks (very difficult in the wet).

Southern Guatemala

FROM GUATEMALA CITY to San Salvador, and to the Pacific ports of San José and Puerto Quetzal: some of the busiest roads in the country passing through major agricultural areas. Several beach resorts, and bird and turtle reserves near Monterrico.

ROUTES TO EL SALVADOR

There are three routes through Southern Guatemala to El Salvador. The first is the paved Pan-American Highway through Barberena and Cuilapa which keeps to the crest of the ridges most of the way to the border, 166 km.

CUILAPA

At **Cuilapa**, capital of Santa Rosa Department, **F** *Hospedaje Posada K-Luy*, 4 C, 1 166, T 886-5372, clean, comfortable, parking, friendly owner, cable TV. Beyond Cuilapa the Highway crosses the Río de los Esclavos by a bridge first built in the 16th century. At **Los Esclavos** is **C** *Turicentro Los Esclavos*, T 886-5139, F 886-5158, pool, hot water, restaurant, a/c. 50 km on is **Jutiapa** (*pop* 9,200), a pleasant, lively town with a big food market in Zona 3; at least 6 hotels/*hospedajes* nearby, eg **B** *Linda Vista*, 4 Av, 3-55, Zona 3, T 844-1115, a/c, parking; **E** *Ordóñez*, 4C, 8-33, Zona 3, T 844-1273, a/c, restaurant, parking; **D** *Posada del Peregrino*, C 15 de Septiembre 0-30, Zona 3, T 844-1770; **E** *Posada Belén*, T 844-1767. Beyond, it goes through the villages of El Progreso and Asunción Mita, where another road

runs left to Lago de Güija. Between Jutiapa and El Progreso is the *Centro Turístico Guantepec*, swimming pool and restaurant, camping permitted (free). Before reaching the border at San Cristóbal it dips and skirts the shores (right) of **Lago Atescatempa**, an irregular sheet of water with several islands and set in heavy forest. From the border to San Salvador is 100 km.

FRONTIER WITH EL SALVADOR – SAN CRISTOBAL

As the Pan-American Highway, this the principal crossing between the two countries. Heavy transport and international buses favour this route.

● **Tourist offices**
There is a tourist office (Inguat) by the border, who will advise you on accommodation and travel.

● **Guatemalan immigration**
Open 0600-2000 but it is usually possible to cross outside these hours with additional charges.

● **Transport**
Local services on the Guatemalan side are poor but hitchhikers should have no problem.

A right turn after Cuilapa (just before Los Esclavos) towards Chiquimulilla (road No 16, with old trees on either side, some with orchids in them) leads after 20 km to a sign to Ixpaco. A 2-3 km steep, narrow, dirt road goes to the **Laguna de Ixpaco**, an impressive, greenish-yellow lake, boiling in some places, emitting sulphurous fumes, set in dense forest. There is a bus service.

JALPATAGUA

The second, quicker way of getting to San Salvador is to take a paved highway which cuts off right from the first route at Molino, about 7 km beyond the Esclavos bridge. This cut-off goes through El Oratorio and **Jalpatagua** (F *Hotel El Centenario*, clean, a/c, pool) to the border, continuing then to Ahuachapán and San Salvador.

FRONTIER WITH EL SALVADOR – VALLE NUEVO/CHINAMAS

Since the construction of the Santa Ana bypass, this has become a popular route for lighter traffic between the two countries.

● **Guatemalan immigration**
We have heard that bargaining with officials can reduce the costs of transit.

● **Accommodation**
F *Motel Martha*, 15 km into Guatemala, pool, excellent breakfast.

● **Tourist offices**
There is a helpful tourist office on the Salvadorean side.

PEDRO DE ALVARADO

The third route goes SW from Guatemala City past Amatitlán to Escuintla where it joins the Pacific Highway. East from Escuintla the road is paved through Guazacapán to the border bridge over the Río Paz at La Hachadura (El Salvador), then through the coastal plain to Sonsonate and on to San Salvador, 290 km in all; this road gives excellent views of the volcanoes. It takes 2 hrs from Escuintla to the border. At **Pedro de Alvarado** (formerly Pijije) on the border there are several *hospedajes* (all **G**, basic).

FRONTIER WITH EL SALVADOR – PEDRO DE ALVARADO/LA HACHADURA

This is a comparatively lightly used frontier partly because the road on the Salvadorean side was so poor. However this has now been much improved and traffic may well increase. Transit is normally straightforward. There is basic accommodation on both sides and food at the service station restaurant. However, it is not recommended that you plan to stay here. The last bus for Sonsonate in El Salvador leaves at 1800.

See **Getting around** in **Information for travellers** for entry and exit procedures with a vehicle. It is possible to leave Guatemala without the aid of the 'helpers' who hang around this border.

GUATEMALA CITY TO THE PACIFIC COAST

The first part of this route to Escuintla is one of the busiest roads in the country, paved throughout, much of it a divided highway. It connects the capital with all the Pacific ports and with the most important agricultural area of the country. In 1997 this highway was particularly dangerous because although some repair work had recently been done, some sections were still in a poor state of repair.

A good section of dual highway bypasses Villa Nueva (minor but scenic roads to Antigua and to the N side of Lake Amatitlán), goes past the entrance to the UN park (see below) then drops steeply down to:

AMATITLAN

Amatitlán (*pop* 12,225; *alt* 1,240m) is 27 km by road SW of the capital, on Lake Amatitlán, 12 by 4 km (but diminishing in size as a result of sedimentation in the Río Villalobos which drains into it – caused by deforestation). Fishing and boating; bathing is not advisable, as the water has become seriously contaminated. Sun boat trips cost US$1, or less, for 30 mins; beware of people offering boat trips which last no more than 10 mins. Very popular and colourful at weekends. The thermal springs on the lake side, with groves of trees and coffee plantations, feed pools which *are* safe to bathe in. The lake is surrounded by picturesque chalets with lawns to the water's edge. Grand view from the United Nations Park, 2½ km N, above Amatitlán. A road goes round the lake; a branch runs to the slopes of Pacaya volcano, US$0.15 by bus (see page 639). The town has two famous ceiba trees; one is in Parque Morazán. Bank changes dollars cash but not TCs. Buses from Guatemala City (every ½-hr, US$0.20) go right to the lakeside.

Local festivals Santa Cruz, 1-7 May.

● **Accommodation** D *Blanquita*, on the road to Guatemala City, with bath; E *Amatitlán*, 3 blocks from *Karla*, parking inside, dirty bathrooms, overpriced, friendly but noisy; E *Los Arcos y Anexo Rocareña*, on lakeside, T 633-0337, with bath, pool, a/c, parking, restaurant; E *Motel Seul*, Km 27.5; F *Hospedaje Don Leonel*, 8 C, 3-25, shared bath, clean, secure; F *Hospedaje y Comedor Kati*, clean, pleasant dining room; F *Pensión Karla*, clean, friendly, family-run. **Camping**: the by-road to the UN Park (turning at 19½ km from Guatemala City) ends at camping sites and shelters; it is rather steep and narrow for caravan trailers. View of Lake Amatitlán and Pacaya Volcano, US$0.12 entrance fee. On the main highway S of Amatitlán, accessible by any bus going to Palín, Escuintla or beyond, is *Automariscos* (Km 33.5, T 633-0479), English-speaking owner, electric and water hook-ups, large warm swimming pool (thermal), hot jacuzzi, baby pool, good toilets, restaurant, noisy at weekends. Next door in the direction of Escuintla, is *La Red*, which has swimming pools fed by volcanic springs; quieter, restaurant/bar and good toilet facilities (camping **G**). Bus, Guatemala City to any of these 3, US$0.25.

● **Places to eat** Many restaurants are nr the lake, beware of local fish because of water pollution.

PALIN

Palín, 14½ km from Amatitlán, has a Sun Indian market in a square under an enormous ceiba tree. Grand views to E, of Pacaya, to NW, of Agua volcano, to W, of Pacific lowland. Power plant at Michatoya falls below town. An unpaved road runs NW to Antigua through Santa María de Jesús (see page 637). See old Franciscan church (1560). *Fiestas*: 25-30 July, and movable feasts of Holy Trinity and Sacred Heart. Textiles here are exceptional, but are becoming hard to find.

● **Accommodation G** *Pensión Señorial*, basic; **G** *Napolitana*, also basic; **G** *Miramonte*, C Central, friendly.

ESCUINTLA

Escuintla (*pop* 62,500; *alt* 335m), 18 km from Palín on the road to San José, is a large, rather ugly provincial centre in a rich tropical valley. There is a large market on Sun, and a daily market over 2 blocks. Near the market is the police HQ, fortress-like, painted sky blue. Marimbas frequently play in the central plaza. The local banana bread is worth trying and *basitas*, real fruit ice-lollies. The town is crowded with lots of streetlife, eating places, bars (many with prostitutes from San Salvador) and, at weekends, much drunkenness. Agua volcano looms to the N. Road N to Antigua. There is a meat packing and several industrial plants.

The Department of Escuintla, between the Pacific and the chain of volcanoes, is the richest in the country, producing 80% of the sugar, 20% of the coffee, 85% of the cotton, and 70% of the cattle of the whole country.

Local festivals

6 (holiday) to 15 December.

Local information
● **Accommodation**

A3 *Hotel Sarita*, Av Centroamérica 15-32, Zona 3, T 888-0482, F 888-1959, pool, a/c, good restaurant.

D *Costa Sur*, 12 C, 4-13, Zona 1, T 888-1819, a/c, TV, clean, friendly owner, speaks English, good value.

E *Istcuintlan*, 4 Av, 6-30, next to Bancafé, with bath, fan, clean, sparcely furnished, courteous owner speaks English; E *Rosario*, 4 Av, 11-46;

E *Las Rosas*, 4 Av, 11-21, about 400m from bus terminal heading into town, for a clean, basic room, better rooms also.

● **Places to eat**
Pizzería Al Macarone, 4 Av, 6-103, modern, smart, excellent pizzas and pastas, Italian ice cream, set lunch US$2, good value; *Los Camarones*, 4 Av, 10-90, seafood at reasonable prices,spacious dining area, off street parking; *Cevichería El Delfín*, 1 C, 3-87, clean, good *caldo de mariscos*, rec; *Chungking*, 4 Av 4-41, Chinese, good, inexpensive, also operates adjoining well stocked supermarket; *El Fuente*, 4 Av, 3-10, also Chinese, pleasant modern setting; *Pastelería Diveli*, 3 Av, just off central plaza; *Martita*, Av Centroamericana, 6-01, Zona 3, good café open for breakfast. Earliest for breakfast is *Campero*, 4 Av, 5-21, open at 0700. Several other sandwich places with good milk shakes.

● **Banks & money changers**
Lloyds Bank (agency) 7 C 3-09, Zona 1, T 888-0226, open 0830-1200, 1400-1600; Banco G&T, 4 Av, 2 C. Others on 4 Av; Banco Industrial, Banco del Agro, Banco Occidente, Banco Continental. Most change TCs and service Visa/Mastercard.

● **Embassies & consulates**
Consulate: El Salvador, 16 C, 3-20, nr the Esso Station, will issue visas. Honduras, 6 Av, 8-24.

● **Transport**
Many buses to the capital (US$0.50) also direct to Antigua at 0700, US$0.60 (poor road).

The Pacific Highway goes W to the Mexican border at Tecún Umán (200 km). As a route to Mexico, it is shorter, faster and easier to drive, but hotter and much less picturesque, than the El Tapón route to the N. The road is paved all the way but has a lot of heavy traffic; be wary of the large, decrepit tractor-trailers carrying sugar cane to the several large mills in the season.

PUERTO SAN JOSE TO MONTERRICO

South of Esquintla, the railway follows the road for 11 km to **Santa María**, near Masagua where the line to Mexico branches W. The railway (now closed), the road and a new motorway completed 1991

continue S to **San José** (*pop* 8,000), 52 km beyond Escuintla, 109 km by road from the capital.

SAN JOSE

San José used to be the country's second largest port. The climate is hot, the streets and beaches filthy and at weekends the town fills up with people from the capital. Fishing, swimming, though beware the strong undercurrent. San José has the big disadvantage of requiring most ships to anchor offshore and discharge by lighter. A new harbour, **Puerto Quetzal**, to take all shipping alongside, has been completed, 3 km to the E, although the oil terminal remains at San José. Restaurants at the entrance to Puerto Quetzal: *Cafetería Sol y Mar*, seafood specialities; *Taberna Tarro Dorado*, Km 115, open air deck, seafood etc.

Local festivals 16-22 Mar, when town is crowded and hotel accommodation difficult to get.

● **Accommodation** A2 *Turicentro Agua Azul*, Km 106, T/F 881-1667, 4 different swimming pools, food reasonable, 24 rooms; A3 *Posada Quetzal*, Av 30 de Junio, 1 Av, T 881-1892, F 881-1601 and A3 *Posada Quetzal II*, Barrio Miramar No 26, same T and F as above, 500m from the mole, rec; A3 *Eden Pacific*, Barrio El Laberinto, T 881-1133, pools, beach cabins, guarded parking; A3 *Turicentro Martita*, 5 C, Av del Comercio, Lote No 26, T/F 881-1504; B *Real Toledo*, Barrio Peñate, Lote No 1, T 881-1405; B *Perla del Mar*, Av del Comercio 8-38, T 881-1011, 100m from beach, a/c, garage; D *Casa San José*, Av del Comercio, 9 C, T 776-5587, with bath, fan, cable TV, restaurant, bar, parking; D *Papillon*, Barrio Miramar, T 881-1064, on the beach, with bath, fan, bar, restaurant; E *Viñas del Mar*, on the beach, with bath, run down, friendly; G *Veracruz*, on the main street, very basic, dark but friendly. No accommodation at present in Puerto Quetzal.

● **Places to eat** Best food is in the hotels eg *Papillon*, on the beach, serves *cacerolas* (fish and shrimp soup).Plenty of other places on the beach.

● **Buses** San José-Guatemala City (Transportes Unidas), half hourly from 0530, US$1.50,

2 hrs 30 mins; from Iztapa to San José US$0.12. To Escuintla, US$0.50.

5 km to the W of San José is **Chulamar**, a popular beach at weekends, good bathing; **B** *Santa María del Mar*, T 881-1283, a/c, pools, restaurant, private beach with changing facilities. Some chalets can be hired. Many new houses are being built. It is lifeless during the week with nowhere but expensive resorts to stay. To the E of San José is the smart resort of **Likin**, which fronts on both the Chiquimulilla canal and the Pacific. The construction of Puerto Quetzal has altered the configuration of the coast and the outer beach, with bungalows and restaurant, is being severely eroded by tides and sand. For the time being, the only remaining place to stay is **A3** *Hotel Likín*, on road to Iztapa, T 756-1061, directly on beach, a/c, restaurant, pool.

IZTAPA

Interesting trip can be taken through Chiquimulilla canal by launch from the old Spanish port of **Iztapa**, now a bathing resort a short distance to the E. At Iztapa you can camp on the beach (take great care if bathing, waves are particularly dangerous along this coast) and rent launches. Buy food before crossing. By road you need to cross the canal by ferry which takes cars.

● **Accommodation L3** *Fins 'n' Feathers Inn*, Aldea Buena Vista, T/F 201-3790, pool, restaurant, parking etc; **E** *Playa del Sol*, with swimming pool, non-residents US$2, friendly staff, rooms OK, good food; **F** *Pollo Andra*, owned by Tex Mex (from Tennessee), nice beds, overhead fans, attached restaurant good fish good value; **F** *Brasilia*, 1C, 4-27, Zona 1, basic; some local people may put you up. Cabins along the beach for hire but few have water and they are very rustic.

● **Places to eat** *Marina del Capitán*, good *ceviches*, packed lunches for fishing trips; *Playa Grande*, similar.

MONTERRICO

Further E is the less expensive resort of **Monterrico**, best approached from Taxisco on the main lowland route to El Salvador.

It is a small black sand resort (beach shoes advisable), a few shops and *comedores*. Its popularity is growing fast but mainly as a weekend and holiday resort. Bird and turtle reserves in the mangrove swamps nearby combine estuarine and coastal ecosystems with a great variety of waterbirds and aquatic plants. Turtles normally visit Oct-December. The reserve is operated by the Conservation Department of the Public University (USAC) and Inguat. Free, but donations welcome. Take insect repellent, guides available. Well worth taking a boat trip at sunrise or sunset, negotiate the price. This reserve is also on the migratory routes of North and South American birds.

● **Accommodation B** *San Gregorio*, E of *Baule Beach*, nice modern rooms with bath, pool, tienda, friendly, quiet, good value; **D** *Johnny's Place*, cabins for 4, well-furnished, refrigerator, stove for rent, fan, nets on windows; **D** *Baule Beach Hotel*, with bath, mosquito nets, run by ex Peace Corps volunteer, Nancy, expensive, seafood restaurant, mixed reports, good surfing but busy at weekends. **E** *Kaiman*, next to *Baule Beach*, Italian run, with bath, fan, mosquito nets, pool, good value restaurant. **Camping** possible at E end of beach, US$3, take drinking water with you.

● **Places to eat** *El Divino Maestro*, good shrimps and shark, but order am for evening; *Pig Pen*, on beach, run by two Australians, also bar and surfboard rental. Look for a good plate of shrimps at *comedores* on the main street. *Comedor Susy* is good.

● **Buses** To San José nominally at 0500 and 1100, but check. Best to take a boat from Monterrico 'inland' through the canals to **La Avellana** (US$0.50) and then by bus to Taxisco. Buses run by Cubanita from Guatemala City, Terminal Zone 4, to La Avellana via Taxisco at 1030, 1230 and 1430, 5 hrs.

SOUTH AND WEST OF ESCUINTLA

Between Escuintla and **Santa Lucía Cotzumalguapa** at Siquinalá (**F** *El Recreo*, in the centre, good) is a turn off S to **La Democracia** (7 km), where sculptures found on the Monte Alto and Costa Brava estates (*fincas*) are displayed in the main plaza. These remarkable stones are believed to date from 400 BC or earlier. Visit the Museo del Pueblo on the main plaza (closed Mon). This road continues 40 km to **Sipacate** on the coast (see below) with a half hourly bus service through La Democracia to Guatemala City.

At Santa Lucía, a friendly town, is the 9th century site of **Bilbao** (or **Cotzumalguapa**), which shows Teotihuacan and Veracruz influences. Three large statues in sugar cane fields can be reached on foot from the tracks leading from Av 4. Ask locals for guidance. **El Baúl**, a pre-classic monument (stelae) which dates back to the Izapan civilization (see the Horizons to this book), is 6 km N of Santa Lucía: go along 3 Av past El Calvario church, taking the left fork about half way, signposted 'Los Tarros', to the timberyard where numerous interesting stelae are displayed. From this early art, the classic Maya art developed. El Castillo, between Bilbao and El Baúl, has some small sculptures dating back to Maya times. On the Las Ilusiones and Finca Pantaleón estates are ruined temples, pyramids and sculptures, and there are other stelae to be found in the area, though most items have now been transferred to museums in Guatemala City.

● **Accommodation** At Santa Lucía: **B** *Santiaguito*, swimming pool, good restaurant, T 882-5435, rec; **D** *El Camino*, T 882-5316, bath, hot water, fan, clean, TV, both at Km 90.5. **At La Democracia**: **G** *Pensión San Marcos*, 2 blocks from central plaza, very basic. Good restaurant on main road nr Shell station, *La Casa de los Olmecas*, palm thatched building, simple menu.

● **Buses** From the Zona 4 terminal in the capital run to both places.

SIPACATE

The Chiquimulilla Canal runs along much of this coast separating the mainland from the narrow black sand beach. To get to the beach here, take a canoe across the canal where there is the pleasant *Rancho Carrillo* (see below). Good swimming in the ocean provided there are calm conditions (The dangers of bathing along this coast must be understood). There is good beach E towards San José as far as Buena Vista in the Sipacate-Naranjo National Park, mainly a bird and turtle sanctuary. There are also mangrove wetlands in this area. At Buena Vista the Río Acamé reaches the sea. You can reach the Park (no facilities) by pick-up from Sipicate along the mainland side of the lagoon, or by motorized canoe.

● **Accommodation** **E** *La Costa*, pleasant rooms round a fine grass lawn, peaceful, owner speaks English, good value, warmly rec; **E** *Hospedaje La Bendición*, noisy, overpriced. Across the canal: **E** *Rancho Carrillo*, take the canoe from their private wharf, rustic wooden cabins, running water, electricity, bar, excellent seafood in the restaurant, private launch for fishing or sightseeing, packed lunches arranged.

COCALES

23 km beyond Santa Lucía is **Cocales**. A few km before Cocales a bridge was destroyed by guerrillas as a 'Christmas present' in 1989. Two other bridges between here and Mazatenango suffered the same fate. The bridge near Cocales was reopened in 1994. Road works continue at several places along this road (1997).

At Cocales a road N leads to Patulul and in 30 km to Lake Atitlán at San Lucas Tolimán. This is a good surfaced road which climbs up from the Pacific plains to the coffee region dominated by volcanoes, Agua and Fuego to the right and Atitlán in front. Excellent cheese, ice cream and other dairy products at Lacteos Parma, 16 km short of San Lucas. This area suffered an earthquake in 1991 with the epicentre near Pochuta, 20 km N of Cocales. There were many landslides including one affecting a steep half km just short of San Lucas which still needs high clearance to drive. Bus from Panajachel to Cocales, 2½ hrs, US$1.05, 5 a day between 0600 and 1400.

TECOJATE

60 km S of Cocales on a good paved road is the coastal resort of **Tecojate**, popular

with Guatemalans specially at holiday times. The road stops at the *estero* (tidal lagoon) and motor launches cross to the excellent black sand beach, 5 mins, US$0.25 pp, or you can paddle across at low tide. Private, rustic beach houses, but no formal public accommodation. Beachside places to eat. Buses from Guatemala City and other closer centres mostly passing though Cocales. Parking for the day US$1, more at holiday times. Do not bathe in the *estero*.

The Pacific Highway continues through San Antonio Suchitepéquez to Mazatenango, see in the **Western Guatemala** section.

West from Guatemala City

T HERE is some beautiful scenery west of the capital, with interesting markets and colourful Indian costumes in the towns and villages. Lake Atitlán, in the shadow of three volcanoes, is a jewel of the region, the villages around it having acquired varying degrees of tourist consciousness. In the highlands is the famous market of Chichicastenango; north of here are the Quiché and Ixil regions, very traditional and yet suffering heavily in Guatemala's bloody recent past.

GUATEMALA CITY TO LAKE ATITLAN

The Pacific Highway goes W from Guatemala City to Tapachula in Mexico. The Pan-American Highway (fully paved) cuts off NW at San Cristóbal Totonicapán and goes into Chiapas by El Tapón, or Selegua, canyon. This is a far more interesting route, with fine scenery. A railway also runs through southwestern Guatemala from Guatemala City to the Mexican frontier.

About 12 km W of the capital a road (right) leads to San Pedro Sacatepéquez (see page 639) and Cobán (see page 643). Our road twists upwards steeply, giving grand views, with a branch to **Mixco** (16½ km from Guatemala City). Here, local priests will provide tourists lodging at E *Casa Sacerdotal*, 12 C Final, Colonia El Rosario, Zona 3, behind the seminary. Call Gladys Montes de Rubio, T 595-4684, for reservations. At Km 18.5, *Restaurante Los Tilos*, open 1000-1900, good lunches, pies a specialty, rec. About 14 km beyond, at San Lucas Sacatepéquez, the road to Antigua turns sharp left. **Sumpango**, which is a little over 19 km beyond this turn-off, has a daily market, best on Sun, and *huipiles* can be bought from private houses; they are of all colours but preponderantly red, as it is believed to ward off the evil eye. Good font in church. *Fiesta* 27-29 August.

CHIMALTENANGO

At **Chimaltenango**, another road runs left, 20 km, to Antigua; this road is served by a shuttle-bus (US$0.25 or US$0.40 in minibus), so Antigua can be included in the Guatemala-Chichicastenango circuit. Chimaltenango is the capital of its Department. Excellent views at 1,790m, from which water flows one side to the Atlantic, the other side to the Pacific. Thermal swimming pool at San Lorenzo El Tejar, which can be reached by bus from Chimaltenango. Market: Wed. *Fiesta*: 22-27 July.

At Km 56 is a gallery, Comalapa, open 0800-1800 daily, prices lower than Antigua and Guatemala City, worth a trip. Bus to Panajachel, US$1.70.

● **Accommodation** 4-5 km W of Chimaltenango is **A3** *Hotel y Restaurant La Villa*, T 839-1130; **E** *San Angel*, 1 C, 4-37, T 839-1423, restaurant, pleasant; **G** *Pensión Los Alamos*, pleasant rooms, shared toilets/showers, cold water, clean, helpful, rebuilt since the earthquake; **G** *Pensión Río*, OK. Good restaurant nearby: *La Marylena*.

● **Banks & money changers** Banco Continental, BAM and Bancor.

Buses to Antigua pass the famous park of **Los Aposentos**, 3 km (lake and swimming pool). At **San Andrés Itzapa** (4 km off Antigua road, 6 km from Chimaltenango) there is a very interesting chapel to Maximón (San Simón) which is well worth a visit. Open till 1800 daily. Shops by the chapel sell prayer pamphlets and pre-packaged offerings. **NB** The turning is signposted from the Chimaltenango direction, but not from the Antigua direction.

A side-road runs 21 km N to San Martín **Jilotepeque** over deep *barrancas*; markets on Sun, Thur. Bus from Chimaltenango, US$0.50. *Fiesta*: 7-12 Nov (main day 11). Fine weaving. Striking *huipiles* worn by the women. 10 km beyond Chimaltenango is Zaragoza, a former Spanish penal settlement, and beyond that (right) a road (13 km) leads N to the interesting village of **Comalapa**: markets 1000-1430, Mon-Tues, bright with Indian costumes. Fine old church of San Juan Bautista (1564). *Fiestas*: 22-26 June.

There are several local artists working in Comalapa; no studios, so best to ask where you can see their work. There is a *pensión* here, **G**.

6 km beyond Zaragoza the road divides. The southern branch, the old Pan-American Highway, goes through Patzicía and Patzún to Lake Atitlán (see below), then N to Los Encuentros. The northern branch, the new Pan-American Highway, much faster, goes past Tecpán and over the Chichoy pass, also to Los Encuentros. From Los Encuentros there is only the one road W to San Cristóbal Totonicapán, where the new road swings NW through El Tapón and La Mesilla to Ciudad Cuauhtémoc, the Mexican border settlement; and the old route goes W through Quezaltenango and San Marcos to Tapachula, in Mexico.

TECPAN

The northern road to Los Encuentros: from the fork the Pan-American Highway runs 19 km to near **Tecpán**, which is slightly off the road at 2,287m. It has a particularly fine church: silver altars, carved wooden pillars, odd images, a wonderful ceiling which was severely damaged by the 1976 earthquake. The church is being slowly restored: the ceiling is missing and much of its adornment is either not in evidence, or moved to a church next door. The women wear most striking costumes. Market: Thur and Sun.

Near Tecpán are the very important Mayan ruins of **Iximché**, once capital and court of the Cakchiqueles, 5 km of paved road from Tecpán (nice walk), open 0800-1700 (admission US$0.10). Iximché was the first capital of Guatemala after its conquest by the Spaniards; followed in turn by Ciudad Vieja, Antigua and Guatemala City. The ruins are well-presented with three plazas, a palace, and two ball-courts on a promontory surrounded on three sides by steep slopes. There is a museum at the site.

Local festivals 25 Sept-5 October.

● **Accommodation & places to eat C** *Hotel Iximché*, T 839-1656; **F** *El Sucro*, basic, water only at night; **G** *Posada de Doña Ester*, clean, hot water; *Casa de Don Pedro*, good churrasco; *Restaurant de la Montaña*, 1 km after the road to Tecpán; the owner of *Zapatería La Mejor* has a guest house. G Also *Restaurante Katok*, on the highway, good hams, pork, *chorizos*, cheeses and hot chocolate, but expensive, and opp *El Encinal del Río*, wider menu, expensive. Better value at *El Pedregal*, just off the main road at Km 90, toward Xetzac, 2 km after junction to Tecpán, run by a German family, open 0730-1030 and 1200-1500, excellent breakfasts for US$2.30 and lunches US$3.50, fresh homemade dishes.

● **Buses** From Guatemala City (Zona 4 terminal), 2¼ hrs, every hour; easy day trip from Panajachel.

Beyond Tecpán the road swings up a spectacular 400m to the summit of the Chichoy pass. The pass is often covered in fog or rain but on clear days there are striking views. 58 km from the fork is Los Encuentros (and the road to Chichicastenango) and 3 km further on the new northern road joins the old southern one from Sololá. 12 km before Los Encuentros is Las Trampas intersection with the new paved road to Godínez and Lake Atitlán. This is a good road apart from one section of earthquake damage; buses now run along it, and it's worth taking if in a car. The road from Los Encuentros to Sololá and down to the lake is paved.

SOLOLA

Sololá (*pop* 40,785; *alt* 2,113m), 11 km from the junction, has superb views across Lake Atitlán. Fine Tues and even better Fri markets, to which many of the Indians go (mornings only, go early, Fri market gets underway on Thur). Good selection of used *huipiles*. Note costumes of men. Great *fiesta* 11-17 August. Hot shower 500m from market on Panajachel road, behind Texaco station, US$0.18. If driving in Sololá, follow only the yellow arrows on the road.

Tightly woven woollen bags are sold here: far superior to the usual type of tourist bags. Prices are high because of nearness of tourist centres of Panajachel and Chichicastenango.

● **Accommodation E** *Del Viajero*, 7 Av, 10-45, T 762-3683, on Parque Central, no windows or bath but spacious, clean and friendly, good food; **F** *El Paisaje*, 9 C, 5-6 Av 2 blocks from Parque Central, pleasant colonial courtyard, shared baths and toilets, clean, cold water, restaurant, good breakfast, family run, laundry facilities; **F** *Santa Ana*, 6 Av, 8 C, basic, clean, friendly, rooms around a lawn, shared facilities,

good value; **F** *Tzoloj-yá*, 11 C, 7-70, T 762-1266, nr Parque Central, tepid shower, mixed reports.

● **Places to eat** *El Cafetín*, Parque Central, delicious lake fish, *mojarra*; *Cafetería Karol* and *Café Favy*, open all day for cheap meals and snacks, but coffee expensive; *Helados Topsy* for ice cream, all within a block of Parque Central.

● **Banks & money changers** Banco G y T, 7 Av y 9C, Zona 2.

● **Buses** To Chichicastenango US$0.35, 2 hrs. Bus to Panajachel, US$0.25, or 1½-2 hrs walk; to Chimaltenango, US$1; to Quezaltenango at 1200, US$1.50. Colectivo to Los Encuentros, US$0.15; to Guatemala City (Rebuli) direct US$1.50, 3 hrs.

From Sololá the old Pan-American Highway (all newly paved) drops 550m in 8 km to Panajachel: grand views on the way. Take the bus up (US$0.25, they stop early in the evening). It is quite easy to walk down direct by the road (the views are superb, particularly early in the morning), you also miss the unnerving bus ride down! You can return to Panajachel either by taking the southern road from the plaza, which rejoins the main road, off which another road S strikes through a very steep, wooded hill down to the tower block flats. Alternatively, take the western road out of Sololá's plaza direct to the lake shore. Once you get to the tower blocks, it is impossible to carry on along the shore because of fenced-off private land; you must return to the main road. It is a 2-hr walk. A longer, but rewarding walk is along the road W from Sololá to San José Chacayá, then down to the lake through the Finca María Linda. About 4-5 hrs to Santa Cruz La Laguna on the lake and another 3 hrs along, below San Jorge to Panajachel.

The southern road from Zaragoza to Lake Atitlán is much more difficult than the northern, with several steep hills and many hairpin bends. This was the original Pan American highway but several sections were severely damaged by the 1976 earthquake and some sections were

Lake Atitlán

Lake Atitlán is 147 km from the capital via the northern road and Los Encuentros, 116 km via the southern road and Patzún, and 148 km via Escuintla and Cocales to San Lucas Tolimán (see **Section 4**). It is a further 31 km from San Lucas to Panajachel. The lake, 1,562m above sea-level, about 7-10 km across and 18 km long, is one of the most beautiful and colourful lakes in the world. It changes colour constantly – lapis lazuli, emerald, azure – and is shut in by purple mountains and olive green hills. Over a dozen villages on its shores, some named after the Apostles, house three tribes with distinct languages, costumes and cultures. The lake was the only place in the world where the *poc*, a large flightless water grebe, could be seen. The *poc* is now extinct because of loss of habitat, increased human population, pollution and the introduction of non-native fish. The British Royal Society for the Protection of Birds also cites replacement by, or hybridization with, the pied-billed grebe, which it closely resembled. There is no surface outlet now, though at some time in the past it presumably drained through the gap S of San Lucas, at present 30m above the water surface. The water level varies, but has been falling slowly for several years.

not repaired and the route diverts on to other roads. Parts were repaved in 1995 but others are in a poor state. Nevertheless, if you have the time and a sturdy vehicle, it is a rewarding trip. The route goes through **Patzicía**, a small Indian village founded 1545 (no accommodation). Market on Wed and Sat. *Fiesta* for the patron, Santiago, on 22-27 July. The famous church, which had a fine altar and beautiful silver, was destroyed by the 1976 earthquake; some of the silver is now in the temporary church. 14 km beyond (road in good condition, with one steep hill) is the small town of **Patzún**; its famous church, dating from 1570, was severely damaged; it is still standing, but is not open to the public. Sun market, which is famous for the silk (and wool) embroidered napkins worn by the women to church, and for woven *fajas* and striped red cotton cloth; other markets Tues and Fri. *Fiesta*: 17-21 May (San Bernardino). Lodgings at the tobacco shop, G, or nr market in unnamed *pensión*.

The road descends in two stages, then climbs steeply to meet the paved road to Las Trampas (see above) just short of **Godínez**, 19 km W of Patzún. Here there is a good place for meals and 5 buses a day

to Panajachel, US$0.35. There is no bus Patzún-Godínez, and very little motor traffic of any sort. From Godínez, a good paved road turns off S to the village of San Lucas Tolimán and continues unpaved to Santiago Atitlán; the latter can be reached by a lake boat from Panajachel. The main road continues straight on for Panajachel; it is poor between Godínez and San Andrés Semetabaj, dirt and worse thereafter. The high plateau, with vast wheat and maize fields, now breaks off suddenly as though pared by a knife. From a viewpoint here, there is an incomparable view of Lake Atitlán, 600m below; beyond it rise three 3,000m-high volcano cones, Tolimán, Atitlán and San Pedro, to the W. The very picturesque village of San Antonio Palopó is right underneath you, on slopes leading to the water. It is about 12 km from the viewpoint to Panajachel. For the first 6 km you are close to the rim of the old crater and at the point where the road plunges down to the lakeside is **San Andrés Semetabaj** with a beautiful ruined early 17th century church. Market on Tues. Bus to Panajachel, US$0.20.

NB The Patzicía and Patzún route to Panajachel is reported unsafe at night.

PANAJACHEL

Visitors to Lake Atitlán tend to stay at or near **Panajachel**, which extends 1 km up from the lake. Six hotels are actually on the lakeshore: *Atitlán, Visión Azul, Monterrey, Del Lago, Playa Linda* and *Tzanjuyu*. The main attraction is the scenery. The town itself, now suffering severely from the tourist invasion, is inhabited by many *gringos* ('Gringotenango'). (Visitors planning to travel round the lake should note that banks are here and one in Santiago Atitlán in the market place.) The main tourist season is the second half of Nov to February. There is water-skiing (at weekends), private boating (kayaks for hire) and swimming, but be warned, there are parasites in the water as in many lakes.

Places of interest
The town has a newly laid out promenade. Good market in the upper part of town on Sun mornings, especially for embroidery; you are expected to bargain (despite the amount of tourism and some hassling, prices are reasonable). Visit La Galería (near *Rancho Grande Hotel*), where Nan Cuz, an Indian painter, sells her pictures which evoke the spirit of village life. The village church, originally built in 1567, was restored, only to be badly damaged by the 1976 earthquake.

Local festivals
1-7 October.

Local information
● **Accommodation**

A1 *Atitlán* (check price beforehand), T 762-1441/2060 (T 476-1582 Guatemala City for reservations), 3 meals US$10 (breakfast is very good, less choice at other 2 meals – restaurant caters for travel groups), 1 km W of centre on lake, excellent rooms and service; **A1** *Del Lago*, T 762-2047/1555, on lakeshore, pool (non-residents US$2), rec, although the restaurant is not as good for other meals as it is for breakfast; **A3** *Tzanjuyu*, T 762-1317/18, 3 meals US$10, on the lake, balconies and private beach, excellent service; **A3** *Cacique Inn* (full board available), T 762-1205, large comfortable rooms, no credit cards, swimming pool, magnificent house

and garden, English spoken, good food, rec; **A3** *Monterrey*, T 762-1126, without breakfast, discounts for longer stays, clean, friendly, good food, restaurant open 1100-1400, 1900-2100; **A3** *Playa Linda*, T 762-1159, above public beach, rooms sleep up to 6, fireplace, beautiful view, slow service in restaurant; **A3** *Visión Azul*, T 762-1426, nr *Hotel Atitlán*, friendly staff, good meals but grubby pool, hot water in evenings.

B *Dos Mundos*, Av Santander 4-72, T/F 762-2078, pool, cable TV, fireplaces, good mid-level place to stay; **B** *El Aguacatal*, T 762-1482, also nr *Hotel del Lago*, has bungalows, for 4-6, good value; **B** *Rancho Grande*, T 762-1554, cottages in charming setting, 4 blocks from beach, popular for long stay, good, simple food, inc breakfast, rec; **B** *Regis*, T 762-1149, Av Santander, well-kept house, rooms or apartments, garden, friendly, good service but breakfast expensive; **B** *Turicentro Los Geranios*, T 762-1433, nr *Hotel del Lago*, has fully-equipped new bungalows which sleep 6, this price on Sat and Sun, **C**, on other days, outdoor pool.

C *Bungalows Guayacán*, T 762-1479, beautifully located among coffee bushes 700m from centre on road to Santa Catarina Palopó; **C** *Fonda del Sol*, C Real, T 762-1162, with bath, occasional hot water, or **E** without, comfortable, good restaurant; **C** *Mini Motel Riva Bella*, C Real, T 762-1353, bungalows, with bath, good, clean, rec; **C** *Paradise Inn*, C del Río, on the lake, clean, friendly, showers in rooms.

D *El Centro*, next to Texaco station, T 762-2167, nice rooms, hot water, parking, washing facilities; **D** *Galindo*, C Real, T 762-1168, with bath, hot water, thin walls, nice garden and good set meal, US$3.50, but smelly and noisy; **D** *Hospedaje Santa Isabel*, T 762-1462, nr the jetty, new rooms built in an orchard, private bath, safe; **D** *Mayan Palace*, C Real, with shower, hot water, clean, friendly, but a bit small and noisy; **D** *Posada de los Volcanes*, Av Santander 5-51, T 762-2367, with bath, hot water, clean, comfortable, quiet, friendly owners, Julio and Janet Parajón; **D** *Primavera*, Av Santander, T 762-1427, clean, expensive restaurant serves German food, washing machine, friendly, rec. **D** *Bungalows El Rosario*, T 762-1491, about half block S of *Hotel del Lago*, safe, clean, run by Indian family, hot water.

E *Casa Linda*, on C Santander between *Mayan Palace* and tourist office, hot shower, nice garden, friendly, central, quiet; **E** *Del Camino*, next

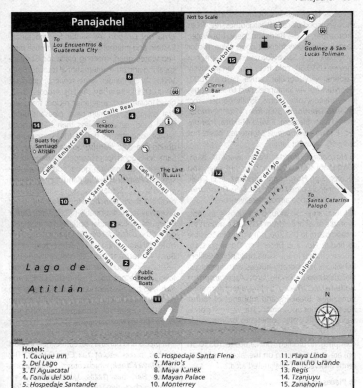

Hotels:

1. Cacique Inn	6. Hospedaje Santa Elena	11. Playa Linda
2. Del Lago	7. Mario's	12. Rancho Grande
3. El Aguacatal	8. Maya Kanek	13. Regis
4. Fonda del Sol	9. Mayan Palace	14. Tzanjuyu
5. Hospedaje Santander	10. Monterrey	15. Zanahoria

to Texaco, with bath (private bathrooms separate from bedrooms), clean, comfortable; **E** *Hospedaje Mi Chosita*, just beyond *Last Resort*, clean, friendly, family atmosphere, warm water, but very small cabins; **E** *Hospedaje Ramos*, close to lake shore, run by an Indian family, friendly, safe, loud music from nearby cafés; **E** *Mario's Rooms*, Av Santander, T 762-1313, with garden, clean, hard beds (try to pick your room), laundry, hot showers US$0.20 (sheets US$0.35, good breakfast; **E** *Maya Kanek*, T 762-1104, good, clean, friendly, good value; **E** *Posada La Casita*, with bath, hot shower, basic, friendly, next to police station and market, buses stop outside but quiet at night; **E** *La Zanahoria Chic*, above restaurant *La Zanahoria*, friendly, good value; **E** *Montufar*, next door to *Casa Linda*, family owned, friendly, hot shower, safe.

F *Cabaña Country Club*, C del Balneario, cheaper rooms, hot showers, clean, sheets 100% nylon, parking for 2 cars; **F** pp *Hospedaje García*, C El Chali, shared shower, hot water extra, mixed reports; **F** *Hospedaje Eddy*, C Chinimaya, basic, friendly, quiet; **F** *Hospedaje Pana*, on side street opp *Restaurant Zanahoria*, clean, friendly, hot water, coffee, fruit juice and beer available, luggage store, gymnasium; **F** *Hospedaje Sanches*, Av Santander y C El Chali, clean, quiet, comfortable, rec; **F** *Hospedaje Santa Ana*, off Av Los Arboles, without bath, simple, adequate; **F** *Hospedaje Santa Elena* C Real, Av Santander, with bedding, cheaper without, all facilities charged extra, friendly, safe parking for motorcycles; has annex (C Monterrey, off Santander), also **F**, hot showers US$0.40, clean, family atmosphere; **F** *Hospedaje Zulema*, C del Balneario y 5 C, nr

Hotel del Lago, upstairs rooms best, clean, hot showers, good place to wash clothes, rec; **F** *Las Jacarandas*, C del Balneario, new, hot water, garden, quiet, very friendly, good value, motor cycle parking; **F** *Salvavidas*, without bath, hot shower US$0.50, cold free, nice family, lovely gardens, very popular, arrive before 1000; **F** *Santander*, Av Santander, next to the *Grape-vine*, friendly, nice rooms, lovely garden, rec; **F** *Santo Domingo*, 30m from *Vista Hermosa*, shared bath, pleasant; **F** *Villa Martita*, friendly, rec; **F** *Vista Hermosa*, C Monterrey, basic, hot showers, pleasant family.

G *Hospedaje Buena Vista*, without bath, **F** with, hot showers extra, basic but clean and secure; **G** pp *Hospedaje Sánchez*, C El Chali, clean, friendly, family-run, quiet, safe; **G** *Londres*, C Santander, good atmosphere, very basic.

For long stay, ask around for houses to rent; available at all prices from US$125 a month for a basic place, to US$200, but almost impossible to find in Nov and December. Domingo Can, whose office is in the same building as Gallery Bookstore, rents pretty houses with fireplaces, electric showers, private yards. *Apartamentos Boheme* at Callejón Chinimaya rent furnished bungalows. Break-ins and robberies of tourist houses are not uncommon. The water supply is variable, with water sometimes only available 0630-1100.

Camping: no problem, but campsites (US$0.50 pp) are dirty. Camping on the lakeshore is currently allowed in a designated area.

● **Places to eat**

Many of the higher priced hotels have restaurants open to the public, as does *Fonda del Sol* (large varied menu, reasonable prices, rec). *Casa Blanca*, C Real, very expensive, but good, German owned. Opposite is *La Laguna*, excellent cooking, nice garden, log fire indoors. *The Last Resort*, C El Chali, 'gringo bar', all-you-can-eat breakfast, reasonable prices, bar, table tennis, good information. *El Patio*, Av Santander, good food, very good breakfast, quiet atmosphere. *El Cisne*, opp *Hotel del Lago*, attractive, clean, good cheap set meals. *Brisas del Lago*, good meals at reasonable prices, on lake shore; a number of others on beach front, eg *El Pes-cador* for fish (good bass), about US$4. Next door *Los Pumpos*, good fish dishes, but over-priced. There are a number of vegetarian restaurants: *Comedor Hsieh*, Av Los Arboles, vegetarian, friendly, good quality, fair prices, rec; *Casa de Pays*, Av Los Arboles (pie shop, also known as *La Zanahoria*, or *The Carrot*), good

food, good value, clean, also has rooms (shows English language videos in evening US$1); *Tav-erna del Dragón*, Av Santander, vegetarian, Eastern and international dishes, only use puri-fied water, good, meeting place for German-speaking and other international tourists; *Bella Vista*, Av Santander, large servings, good set menu US$3; *Bombay*, Av Los Arboles, 0-42, good Indian food, vegetarian recipes from sev-eral countries, German beer, pleasant patio, good food, set lunch less than US$2, good service, operates as the *East/West* restaurant during the day; *Hamburguesa Gigante*, Av Santander, good honest burgers; *Papagayo*, Av Santander, German run, good food, a bit expen-sive; *Las Palmeras*, Av Santander, cheap; *Gua-jimbo's*, Av Santander, good atmosphere, excellent food; *Rancho Mercado Deli*, good takeaway food, reasonably priced wine; *Deli 2* at end of Av Santander both rec for all meals, go for the *pastel de día*; *Tocoyal*, on beach nr *Hotel del Lago*, good for breakfast, good value; *Bar y Restaurant Las Gaviotas*, 2 Av del Bal-neario, very good, national and international food, service not up to same standard; *Pana Pan* also has excellent wholemeal breads and pastries, banana bread comes out of the oven at 0930, wonderful, cinnamon rolls also rec; *Pizza Hot* at Flyin' Mayan Yacht Club, on corner of C Real 00-54 and Los Arboles, US run, excel-lent pizzas and banana pie, coffee, newspapers to read; pizzas also at *Yax Che*, C Real 1-04; opp *Maya Kanek*, which caters for vegetarians. *Circus Bar*, has pizzas, good coffee, German/French owners, popular. *Ranchón Típico*, Av Santander. *Chisme*, Av Los Arboles, good food, try eggs McChisme for breakfast, good fresh pasta, excellent banana cake, good atmos-phere, popular, a bit pricey, open 0700-2200 daily except Wed, English and German maga-zines. The yoghurt dishes at *Mario's* restaurant are good, his crêpes filled with yoghurt and fruit are rec. *Connections*, Av Santander, good value. *Don Cokey* is a new restaurant on Av Los Arboles nr *Circus Bar*, open 1200-0100, typical cuisine, popular; *El Bistro*, at end of Santander, dinner only, homemade dishes, great salads, pasta and chocolate mousse, expensive but rec; *Cafetería Panajachel*, C Real, good breakfasts, comidas US$3, cable TV; *Amigos*, Av Los Ar-boles, attractive, popular, good, rec; *La Típica*, C Real 50m from church, good *comida corri-ente*, good value. It is reported that the best hot dog in the universe is to be found in the evening on a stall on the C Real, confirmation welcomed.

● **Banks & money changers**
Banco Inmobilario on Av Los Arboles, open Mon-Thur 0900-1500, Fri to 1530, Sat 0900-1300 will change TCs. Also **Banco Industrial**, Av Santander (TCs and Visa ATM), and **Banco Agrícola Mercantil**, C Real, also changes TCs. There is a *cambio* on the street nr *Mayan Palace* for US dollars cash and TCs, good rate. The barber's shop nr the bank will change TCs. The Kodak Camera Club nr the Tourist Office, slightly better rates.

● **Entertainment**
Chapiteau, discotheque, open 2000 to early morning Tues to Sat, US$1-1.50 cover charge. Opp *Hotel del Lago*, **Circus Bar**, good live music at weekends, open 1700-0100 daily. *Grapevine Video Bar*, Av Santander, 2 screens, about 10 films a day, US$1.15, good coffee and brownies, also snacks and sandwiches, open 1500-0100. *Nuan's Bar*, in small shopping arcade just down road from Circus Bar, happy hour 2200-2300, small dance floor. A number of other video bars.

● **Hospitals & medical services**
Health: Centro de Salud on C Real, just downhill from the road to San Antonio Palopó. *Dr Hernández Soto*, office nr Texaco station, US$5 for a short consultation. There are good clinics at Santiago Atitlán and San Lucas Tolimán, which specialize in treating dysentery. Outbreaks of cholera have been reported in the lake area since 1991; enquire locally about the safety of water, lake fish, etc. Amoebic dysentery and hepatitis are less common than in the past. Treatment free, so a donation is appropriate. Fleas endemic. Take care to treat bites in case of infection. 1 litre plastic bags and larger plastic containers of water are sold in Panajachel.

● **Language schools**
0 **Pana Atitlán Language School**, C de la Navidad 0-40, rec. See *AmeriSpan* under Antigua, **Tourist offices**.

● **Post & telecommunications**
Post Office: nr the church. It is difficult but not impossible to send parcels of up to 1 kg abroad as long as packing requirements are met. *Get Guated Out*, Centro Comercial, Av Los Arboles, T/F 762-2015, good and inexpensive service to send larger parcels, they use the postal system but pack and deal with formalities for you. Next to *Restaurant Chisme*, a parcel service in the handicrafts shop claims economy rates to USA cheaper than post office (more expensive to Europe); can send over 2 kg. Central America Link sends parcels to USA, US$18.50 plus US$4.10/kg, and to Europe US$24.50 plus about US$10/kg, 6 days to Miami. If you can collect your parcel in Miami and mail it from there to Europe it is cheaper (7790 NW 64th St, Miami, FL 33166, T (305) 592 5219).

Telephones: good service from Panajachel, internal and external. *Maya Communications* office is in new shopping centre on Av Santander, next to Inguat, T/F 502-9-622194, interlinked with Antigua and Quezaltenango, also e-mail.

● **Shopping**
Many small stores selling local handicrafts. *The Chocolate Factory* (*Casa de Pájaros*) sells books as well as chocolate. Another chocolate shop is on the other side of the main street, nr the bank, good, but expensive. Also on road to San Andrés Semetabaj is the *Idol's House*, an antique shop where you must bargain. Indians sell their wares cheaply on the lakeside; varied selection, bargaining easy/expected. You can buy daily Guatemalan and international newspapers at *Almacén Rosales*, C Real 0-32. *Chalo's Tienda*, on C Real, is the town's 'mini-supermarket'. *Tienda Las Golondrinas*, C Real, good value store; *Tienda Típica Luxitó*, C El Chali, typical products at sensible prices.

● **Tour companies & travel agents**
Turísticos San Nicolás, C Santander, T 762-2078, ask for Gregorio, one of the few agencies prepared to negotiate private taxi services to towns and villages in the area. Other agencies operate fixed schedules at expensive rates.

● **Tourist office**
Inguat is in Centro Comercial Pana, on Av Santander nr C Real, T 762-1392. Open Mon-Sat, 0900-1700; has maps. Bus and boat timetables posted on door when closed. Hector is very helpful and speaks excellent English. They can also help booking internal flights, sometimes with discounts. Check with Inguat whether it is safe to climb the volcanoes.

● **Transport**
Local Bicycle hire: US$1/hr or US$5 for 8 hrs. Mayan Mountain Cycle Tours offers mountain bike tours around Antigua, Lake Atitlán and other places (see under Antigua). **Car rental**: 2 doors down from post office, cheapest US$40 a day with unlimited mileage. **Horse hire**: at riding club close to *Hotel Atitlán*, US$8/hr. **Kayak hire**: US$1.70/hr, good Kayaks. **Motorcycle rental**: about US$6/hr, plus fuel and US$100 deposit. Shop nr the Church, another at the junction of C Real and Av Santander, and

two places nr *Circus Bar*. Bikes generally poor, no locks or helmets provided. Motorcycle parts from *David's Store*, opp *Hotel Maya Kanek*, good prices, also does repairs and rents bikes.
Ultralight flights: US$26 for 15 mins, thrilling and nerve-racking first time up, but a good way to see the lake.

Buses Rebuli to **Guatemala City**, 3 hrs, US$1.75, crowded; 9 a day between 0500 and 1430. Direct bus to **Quezaltenango** 8 a day between 0530 and 1415, US$1.25, 2 hrs (from there to Mexico, bus to Tecún Umán via Coatepeque). The fastest way to Mexico is probably by bus S to Cocales, 2½ hrs, 5 buses between 0600 and 1400, then many buses along the Pacific highway to Tapachula on the border. There are direct buses to **Los Encuentros** on the Pan-American Highway (US$0.50, the junction for routes to the capital, Quezaltenango and Chichicastenango and the cheapest way to travel). To **Chichicastenango** direct, 11 a day between 0645 and 1700, US$1, although a minibus tour can cost US$6.50 (no buses from Los Encuentros to Panajachel after 1830). There are direct buses to **Cuatro Caminos**, US$0.50 (see page 708) from 0530, for connections to Totonicapán, Quezaltenango, Huehuetenango, etc. Bus to **Chimaltenango** (for Antigua), US$1.40, change there for **Antigua**. There is also a direct bus (Rebuli) 1030, US$2, which leaves from opp the bank and a tourist minibus, US$20 Guatemala City and Antigua. Bus to **Sololá**, US$0.25, every 30 mins. Best to wait for buses by the market, not by the Guatel road to the lake. If there are no buses for your destination, take one to Sololá where there are better services.

AROUND THE LAKE

There are regular boat trips across the lake, mainly to Santiago Atitlán and San Pedro La Laguna, but there are a number of stopping services to places along the W shore, so you can take a boat to eg Santa Cruz, walk on to San Marcos and catch a boat back from there. (Note that for return to Panajachel boats may not stop at Santa Cruz and San Pablo unless someone is going to get off.) If you buy a return ticket (US$2.75) you must travel back with the same owner. Buy ticket on boat or from *Hotel Maya Kanek*, but do not buy tickets from touts on the shore. Typical fares: Panajachel-Santiago US$1.50, Panajachel-San Pedro

US$1.50, Santiago-San Pedro US$1.50 (1996). You can also hire boats for trips (a 6-hr tour costs about US$5, dep 0930). The Tourist Office has the latest information on boats pinned on its door, schedules change too frequently for us to publish.

The lake is some 50 km in circumference and you can walk on or near the shore for most of it. Here and there the cliffs are too steep to allow for easy walking and private properties elsewhere force you to move up 'inland'.

Santa Catarina Palopó is within walking distance of Panajachel, about 4 km, the road hugs the side of the hill with a continous view of the lake. The town has an attractive adobe church. Reed mats are made here, and you can buy *huipiles* (beautiful, green, blue and yellow) and men's shirts. Must bargain for articles. **Local festivals** 25 November.

● **Accommodation** **A2** *Villa Catarina*, T 762-1291, nice setting, modern, traditional style; also **A3** *Bella Vista*, T 762-1566, on road to San Antonio Palopó, overlooking lake, quiet. Look for the art gallery 'El Dzunum'. Houses can be rented here. From Santa Catarina you can walk to the Mirador of Godínez for views, but the path is very steeply uphill for quite a while.

● **Transport** Truck from Panajachel US$0.12, bus at 0915 US$0.20, also minibuses and 2 boats a day, US$1.

San Antonio Palopó (6 km beyond Santa Catarina), has another splendid church; it lies in an amphitheatre formed by the mountains behind. The village is noted for the costumes and headdresses of the men, and *huipiles* and shirts are cheaper than in Santa Catarina. Unfortunately there is a lot of pressure selling now and women and children have learned some European languages to encourage you to buy. A good hike is to take the bus from Panajachel to Godínez, take the path toward the lake 500m S along the road to Cocales, walk on down from there to San Antonio Palopó (1 hr) and then along the new road back to Panajachel via Santa Catarina Palopó (3 hrs). You can walk on round the lake from San Antonio, but you

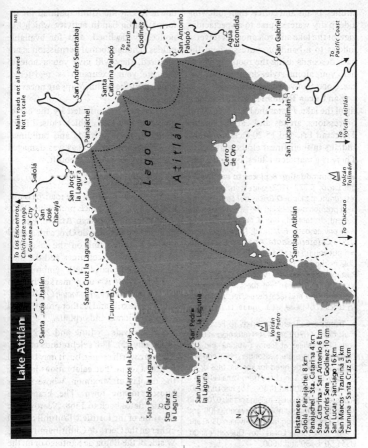

Lake Atitlán

Main roads not all are paved
Not to scale

To Patzún
To Pacific Coast
Godínez
San Antonio
Palopó
Agua
Escondida
San Gabriel
Santa Catarina Palopó
San Andrés Semetabaj
To Chichicastenango
& Guatemala City
To Los Encuentros,
Panajachel
Sololá
San José
Chacayá
San Jorge
la Laguna
Cerro
de Oro
San Lucas Tolimán
To Volcán Atitlán
L a g o d e A t i t l á n
Volcán
Tolimán
To Chicacao
Santa Cruz la Laguna
Santiago Atitlán
Santa
Lucía Atitlán
Tzununá
San Marcos la Laguna
San Pablo la Laguna
Volcán
San Pedro
Sta. Clara
la Laguna
San Pedro
la Laguna
San Juan
la Laguna
N

Distances:
Sololá - Panajache: 8 km
Panajachel - Sta. Catarina 4 km
Sta. Catarina - San Antonio 6 km
San Andrés Sem - Godínez 10 km
San Lucas - Santiago 16 km
San Marcos - Tzununá 3 km
Tzununá - Santa Cruz 5 km

must eventually climb steeply up to the road at Agua Escondida. **Local festival** 12-14 June.

● **Accommodation C** *Hotel Terrazas del Lago*, T 232-6741 (Guatemala City), on the lake with view, bath, clean, restaurant, Polish born owner speaks German and English; you can stay in private houses (eg Don Tiedera nr the Post Office) or rent rooms (take sleeping bag).

● **Transport** The only bus from Panajachel to San Antonio is at 0915, US$0.35, but there are pick-ups, US$0.55, and 2 boats a day, 40 min, US$1.60.

1½ km S along the road is **Panaranjo** from where a track leads towards the lake and down to Finca Tzanpetey, 30-40 mins. From there it is possible to walk to San Lucas Tolimán but the path is narrow and delicate in places where it climbs up 50-100m to negotiate the steepest drops to the lake. After 1 km you reach the N end of the San Lucas lake shore and it is an easy walk. Less strenuous is to walk on from Panaranjo to San Gabriel, ask for the 'extravio para San Lucas' for a delightful route through fields of corn, tomato, potatoes, chillies, beans and coffee, then following a deep dry water course to a spectacular view of the lake and volcanoes. A traverse follows to a band of cypress where the path descends using the roots of trees to help you, alpine-style, down to San Lucas. Good footwear essential.

San Lucas Tolimán is on the southern tip of the lake. *Fiestas* inc Holy Week with processions, arches and carpets on the Thur and Fri, and 15-20 October. Many Indians in their finest clothes take part. There is a market on Tues, Fri and Sun.

● **Accommodation & places to eat D** *Villa del Lago*, T 722-0102, with bath, hot water, restaurant, parking; **D** *Brisas del Lago*, prominent position overlooking the lake, 10 rooms at present, restaurant, bar; **E** *Pensión Central*, with private bath, **F** without, hot water, meals US$1. *Cafetería Santa Ana*, shop and café, will put you up for US$2, clean. Camping possible nr the lake but ask, and check for safety. Restaurants: *Comedor Victoria*, Guatemalan food; *Café Tolimán*, on the lakeside, home made yoghurt and local dishes, rec; *La Fonda*, 1/2 block N of plaza, clean, good local food.

● **Transport** There are boats to Panajachel most days at 0700 and 1300 returning at 0930 and 1400 calling at Santa Catarina and San Antonio if there are passengers, but enquire. Boats can also be hired for specific trips or for the day. Bus to San Lucas from Panajachel 5 a day between 0600 and 1400, 1 1/2 hrs, US$0.60. A bus leaves San Lucas to Panajachel, 0700 and 1800; to Santiago, hourly between 0900 and 1800, 1 hr, returning hourly between 0300 and 1300. Bus San Lucas to Quezaltenango, US$1.50, 0430 and 0600.

From San Lucas the cones of **Atitlán**, 3,535m, and **Tolimán**, 3,158m, can be climbed. The route leaves from the S end of the town and makes for the saddle (known as Los Planes, or Chanán) between the two volcanoes. From there it is S to Atitlán and N to the double cone and crater of Tolimán. Though straightforward, the climb of both is complicated by many working paths and thick cover above 2600m. Cloud on the tops is common, least likely Nov-March. If you are fit, either can be climbed in 8 hrs, 5 hrs

down. Ask at the Municipalidad for information on bandit activity, which has noticeably declined, and for available guides. Though formal permission is not required, they will give you a note to indicate your excursion is registered, which could be useful. Maps are not available locally.

This area was affected by the earthquake of Nov 1991, which caused landslides, damage to roads and buildings. The church in San Lucas was damaged and the façade is being rebuilt.

SANTIAGO ATITLÁN

From San Lucas, a poor dirt road, passable only with high clearance, preferably 4WD, goes 16 km to **Santiago Atitlán**. On the right is the hill, **Cerro de Oro**, with a small village of that name on the lake. The women wear fine costumes and the men wear striped, half-length embroidered trousers. There is a daily market, best on Fri. A coooperative, *Asociación Q'Na Wnaq* sells local textile and leather products and supports widows and orphans.

Local festivals 5 June and 23-27 July (main day 25). The celebrations of Holy Week are worth seeing, but it may be hard to find a room. The celebrations include the display of Maximón, whose idol is housed in the town. The Franciscan church dates back to 1568. Nearby were the ruins of the fortified Tzutuhil capital either on the Cerro de Chuitinamit on the W side of the Bahía de Santiago or on the E side just N of the village. There is nothing now to see at either location.

● **Accommodation B** *Posada de Santiago*, to leave message, T 721-7158/7168, cabins, inc breakfast, American owners, 2 km on the road to San Pedro, good restaurant, boat trips on lake for US$5/hr. **E** *Tzutuhil Atitlán*, with bath, clean, comfortable, great views, good; **E** *Hospedaje Chi-Nim-Ya*, good (good café opp, also 50m away, huge Pepsi advert on wall, cheap, large helpings); **F** *Pensión Rosita*, nr the church, clean, friendly, safe, basic, restaurant. Houses can be rented, but be extremely careful to check for, and protect against, scorpions and poisonous spiders in the wooden frames. *Santa Rita* restaurant good and cheap. The *Galería Nim Pot* is worth a visit, nr the school, the family Chávez exhibit their own paintings and carvings and sell hand woven cloth, etc.

● **Transport   Buses**   To Guatemala City, US$1.50 (5 a day, first at 0300). Buses to Panajachel at 0600, 2 hrs, or take any bus and change on the main road just S of San Lucas. **Boats** Seven a day to and from Panajachel, 1 hr, US$1,50.

From Santiago Atitlán, a rough road goes S towards the coast, passing through a town called Chicacao (where the road becomes paved). The road passes through little villages and coffee plantations.

Parque Nacional Atitlán 5 km N of Santiago Atitlán had a small reserve for the *poc*, the Atitlán grebe, now extinct, see box, page 689. Also in the reserve is the *pavo del cacho* (a big black bird with a red horn on its head), though there is some doubt if any are now left there. To get there, go by canoe from Santiago (US$0.65), with the reserve workers, or on foot, about 30 mins on the San Lucas Tolimán road, but ask directions. Safe camping, take food and water; the guards may put you up in one of their cabins.

7 km S of Santiago Atitlán is a mirador and *refugio* called **Quetzal Reserve** where a path winds up and down through rain forest. Follow the path past the *Posada de Santiago*, then go left at the fork and stay on the road until you come to the reserve and viewpoint, both on the left.

SAN PEDRO LA LAGUNA

San Pedro has taken over as the young people's laid back haven that was Panajachel 10 years ago. It is a small, poor village but living costs are low and it is known as a good place to hang out for a short or longer period. Some of these semi-permanent inhabitants now run bars and cafés or sell home made jewellery. Correspondents refer to San Pedro as a 'wired' town, and 'freaky'.

San Pedro is at the foot of the **San Pedro volcano**, which can be climbed in 4-5 hrs, 3 hrs down, not difficult except for route finding through the coffee plantations and heavy cover. A guide is therefore advisable unless you walk part of the way the day before to make sure you know where you are going. The route starts 1½ km along the road to Santiago, and where the road takes a sharp turn to the right, go left through coffee plantations to the W flank of the volcano; after 1 hr there is only one path and you cannot get lost. A rec guide is Ventura Matzar González, C Principal, Cantón Chuacante, San Pedro, T 762-1140, US$2.50 pp. Go early (0530) for the view, because after 1000 the top is usually smothered in cloud; also you will be in the shade all the way up and part of the way down. The abysmal road around the volcano to Santiago Atitlán can be cycled (boats charge half fare for a bike from Panajachel – beware overcharging); it is a tough 3-4 hrs' ride requiring some experience and good brakes. If hiring a bike in Panajachel, check the machine carefully. Set out early and allow enough time to catch the last boat back. Motorcyclists also find this stretch very demanding.

Canoes are made here (hire, US$0.50 a day) and a visit to the rug-making co-operative on the beach is of interest. Backstrap weaving is taught at some places, about US$0.50/day. Try Rosa Cruz, past the 'Colonel's Place', turn right up the hill. Local people in San Pedro speak Tzutuhil. Market days Thur and Sun (better). Horse hire in San Pedro from two houses next to each other on path closest to beach, US$6.50 for 3 hrs with guide to neighbouring villages (rather primitive saddles leave you bow-legged). You can also walk from San Pedro to San Juan along the lake and up to **Santa María Visitación**, an attractive village with spectacular views.

Fiesta 27-30 June with traditional dances.

● **Accommodation** There are many **G** *pensiones*, inc two on the public beach. All beach *pensiones* have a water supply problem so bathrooms are often smelly. **F** *Pensión Chuazanahi* (known as the Colonel's Place), charges for bedding, boating and swimming, reasonable meals, friendly staff, nice rooms; next door is F *San Francisco*, 4 good rooms with lake view, garden, cooking facilities, cold water, helpful owner, washing facilities, good value; F *Hospedaje Chuacanté*, in front of church, clean, family run, hot water; F *San Pedro*, bargain for a decent price, cold showers, cold drinks available, laundry if you stay more than one night, noisy with a lot of people coming and going, not rec for single women, very basic; rooms also at G *Blue House* down road beside *Chuazanahi*; G *Tikaaj*, good, wooden cabins a few yards from second dock, popular with backpackers, lovely garden, but very basic, restaurant opp, good and cheap; G *Domingo's*, chalets, communal toilets and cold showers; all are basic; houses can be rented from US$5 a week to US$50 a month; G *Familia Penelón*, 200m along path opp the green *farmacia*, friendly, clean, meals available, basic; G *Hospedaje Selena*, on the lake, nr *Johanna's Bar*, clean; G *Pensión Balneario*, not rec, 100m to the right is G *Villa Sol*, better, nothing fancy, no bath, excellent banana pancakes, helpful owner; G *Hospedaje Xocomil*, clean, basic, cold water, washing facilities, helpful; G *Casa Rosario*, nice garden.

● **Places to eat** Good food is available at *Chez Michel*, friendly (some French spoken), cheap but slow, interesting dishes at weekends, turn right from landing stage along beach road, past *Pensión Chuazanahi*; *Sascha*, run by Dutch woman, on right side of first pier you come to by boat, good lasagne, cakes, popular; *Restaurant Francés*, good for pancakes (chocolate and banana), cheap, steaks US$1.50, go through coffee plantation from first pier to the next one; good food but slow service at *Comedor Ranchón*, opp *Chuazanahi*, good fish, possibly the best food in town; *Pachanay*, 150m from *Villa Sol*, lunch and dinner, good, cheap, good rice dishes, reggae music, 'hippy'-type atmosphere; *Otty's* also has good, cheap food. Buy banana bread from the *Panadería El Buen Gusto*, nr centre of town; *Comedor la Ultima Cena*, opp the Municipalidad, good pizzas, pancakes, very popular, service for food can be very slow but beer comes quickly; *El Mesón*, clean, good food, nr landing stage; *Restaurant Rosalinda*, very good especially for local fish and for the banana and chocolate cakes; *El Tambor*, good bakery also serves pizzas; *Jocabed*, tofu burgers and other soya dishes; *Comedor*

Amigos Viajeros, good cooks, nice view; *Aladan*, pizzas, run by a French couple; *Johanna*, best place in the evening, music, dancing; *Thermal Bath*, good vegetarian food, good coffee, expensive; *Tulipán* has wide variety and vegetarian dishes; *Viajero*, good food, loud music, good value; *Maharishi*, run by Antonio from USA, somewhat eccentric but good vegetarian and other dishes, everything fresh. Village café, meals US$0.30. Be careful of drinking water in San Pedro, both cholera and dysentry exist here. Centro Médico opp Educación Básica school, good doctor who does not speak English.

● **Transport** Up to 10 *lanchas* a day leave from Panajachel for **San Pedro**, 20 km by dreadful road beyond Santiago (not rec for motorcycles unless you are an expert off-roader). The boat fare is about US$2 (US$5 to take motorcycle in boat). There is a launch from Santiago to San Pedro which leaves when full (45 mins, US$1.50). **NB** There are two landing stages in San Pedro, the 'pier' and the 'beach'. There is an unreliable, uncomfortable bus to San Pedro, not rec, better take the boat. There is also one daily bus San Pedro-Quezaltenango, 0430, 3½ hrs, cold, US$2.

From San Pedro, you can walk to Panajachel (about 7 hrs) through San Juan (look for Los Artesanos de San Juan, T 762-1150, and another image of Maximón displayed in the house opposite the Municipalidad), San Pablo, San Marcos and finally Santa Cruz (a difficult track – it has been done on motorbike). You can get beautiful views of the lake and volcanoes in the early morning light. Sisal bags and hammocks are made at **San Pablo La Laguna**. Further on round the lake is **San Marcos**. Boat to Panajachel about 1300.

● **Accommodation San Pablo**: D *Posada Schuman*, modern, nice bungalows close to the shore, clean, friendly; G *Hospedaje Bisente*, nice patio, the family makes meals. **San Marcos**: D *Casa La Paz*, 3 bungalows, vegetarian restaurant; E *Paco Real*, friendly; G *Hospedaje Hernández*, in the village, clean, friendly, cold water only, and an interesting 16th century church with many curious wooden statues. *Flor del Lago* restaurant serves good chicken, the owner speaks only Calchiquel, but her daughter speaks Spanish.

From San Marcos, there is a path of sorts through Tzununá and around the lake to **Santa Cruz** and Panajachel. It is possible to go 'inland' at Tzununá, climb up to the rim, and follow it to San José and Sololá with great views of the lake most of the way. A good day's walk, take plenty of water.

● **Accommodation Santa Cruz**: E *Arco de Noé*, bungalow accommodation, restaurant; E *Abaj Rosa García*, 100m along the lake, bungalows and rooms, home made meals, beautiful garden, German spoken; E *La Iguana Perdida*, F 762-1196, also **G** dormitory, 3 meals a day, 3-course dinner at 1930 round large table, vegetarian options, home-baked bread, no electricity, dive school.

● **Watersports** There is a **diving** operation at *La Iguana Perdida*, offering spectacular diving in the lake, which is quite different from diving in the sea. There are spectacular walls that drop off, rock formations you can swim through, trees underwater, and because of its volcanic nature, hot spots. Prices: US$25 single tank, US$45 2-tank dives, US$150 PADI Open Water Course, US$150 PADI Advanced Course, PADI Rescue and Dive Master also available.

Half way between Santa Cruz and Panajachel is the intermittant river bed of the Río Quiscab, shortly after which is the **Finca San Buenaventura**, which has been transformed into an interesting **Nature Reserve**. This was one of the largest coffee plantations in the area and includes some 100 ha of forest. There is now a Visitor Centre, a Butterfly Reserve, a Bird Refuge, an Orchid Garden and several nature trails. It is associated with the *Hotel Atitlán* (see under Panajachel). The Reserve is open 0800-1700, US$4, students US$2. For further information T 762-2059, Felipe Marín.

WARNING   The lake is not a safe area for women to go walking alone, on the E and S shores, even in Panajachel. Beware of theft, including clothes hanging out to dry. Equally, there are stories of money stolen from tourists being recovered and returned to owners by local people. Also beware of overcharging on private boats crossing the lake: practices include doubling the price half-way across and if you don't agree, out you get.

LOS ENCUENTROS

The old and new Pan-American Highways rejoin 11 km from Sololá. 3 km E is Los Encuentros, the junction of the Pan-American Highway and the paved road 18 km NE to Chichicastenango. Altitude 2,579m. (Very poor accommodation available, G, if you miss a bus connection, easy to do as they are often full.) Buses for Panajachel stop outside the green police office, about 250m from where the bus stops en route between the border and capital.

CHICHICASTENANGO

(Often called "Chichi" and also known as Santo Tomás) Chichicastenango (*alt* 2,071m) is the hub of the Maya-Quiché highlands, and is very popular with tourists. Nights are cold. About 1,000 *ladinos* in the town, but 20,000 Indians live in the hills nearby and flood the town, almost empty on other days, for the Thur and Sun markets.

Derivation of town's name: *chichicaste*, a prickly purple plant like a nettle, which grows profusely, and *tenango*, place of. The town itself is charming: winding streets of white houses roofed with bright red tiles wandering over a little knoll in the centre of a cup shaped valley surrounded by high mountains. Fine views from every street corner. The costumes are particularly splendid: the men's is a short-waisted embroidered jacket and knee breeches of black cloth, a gay woven sash and an embroidered kerchief round the head. The cost of this outfit, over US$200, means that fewer and fewer men are in fact wearing it. Women wear *huipiles* with red embroidery against black or brown and skirts with dark blue stripes. The Sun market is much the same as the one on Thur: but it certainly becomes very touristy after the buses arrive from Guatemala City (bargains may be had after 1530 when the tourist buses depart). Articles from all over the Guatemalan highlands may be bought including rugs, carpets and bedspreads. In fact the markets begin on the previous afternoon. You

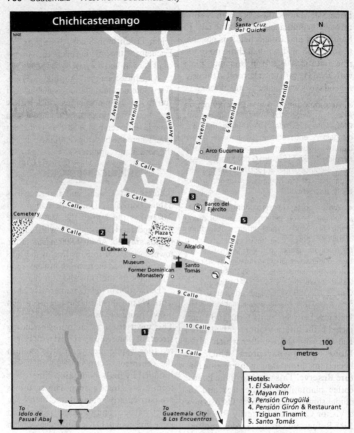

Chichicastenango

To Santa Cruz del Quiché

N

2 Avenida
3 Avenida
4 Avenida
5 Avenida
6 Avenida
8 Avenida

○ Arco Gucumatz

5 Calle

4 Calle

6 Calle

7 Calle

4   **3**   Ⓢ Banco del Ejército

Cemetery

8 Calle   **2**   ✝   Plaza   ○ Alcaldía   7 Avenida   **5**

El Calvario   Ⓜ

Museum   ✝   Santo Tomás   ○

Former Dominican Monastery ○

9 Calle

1   10 Calle

11 Calle

0   100
metres

To Idolo de Pasual Abaj

To Guatemala City & Los Encuentros

Hotels:
1. El Salvador
2. Mayan Inn
3. Pensión Chugüilá
4. Pensión Girón & Restaurant Tziguan Tinamit
5. Santo Tomás

must bargain hard, although reductions may be limited owing to the non-bargaining of package tourists. Good value handicrafts at the shop next door to Cooperativo Santo Tomás, opp *Mayan Inn* on market place; also from *Popol Vuh*, opp *Pensión Girón*, which has a good range of clothing in modern designs, good value. However, prices are generally cheaper in Panajachel.

Places of interest

The town is built around a large square plaza, with two churches facing one another: **Santo Tomás** parish church and **Calvario**. Santo Tomás is now open again

to visitors, although restoration work is still going on; photography is not allowed, and visitors are asked to be discreet and enter by a side door. Groups burn incense and light candles on steps and platform before entering. Inside, from door to high altar, stretch rows of glimmering candles, Indians kneeling beside them. Later they offer copal candles and flower-petals to the 'Idolo', a black image of Pascual Abaj, a Maya god, on a hilltop 1½ km SW of the plaza (beware of armed robbery on the way), boys act as guides for US$1; be very respectful at the ceremony and do not take photographs. Next to Santo Tomás are the cloisters of the Dominican monastery (1542) where the famous Popol Vuh manuscript of Maya mythology was found and translated into Spanish in 1690. Father Rossbach's jade collection can be seen in the **municipal museum** on the main plaza (open 0800-1200, 1400-1600, closed Tues), and so is the house of a mask-maker on the way up to the 'Idolo', who rents masks and costumes to the dancers and will show visitors the path to the idol (boys often don masks and do a dance for the tourists, for a small fee). This is a little difficult to find even then, and clear instructions should be obtained before setting out. You can also visit the 'mask factory' 1 block from the plaza, and buy them from Manuel Mejía Guarcas, 6 Av 9-36.

Local festivals

Santo Tomás, 18-21 Dec: processions, dances, marimba music (well worth a visit – very crowded); New Year's Eve; Holy Week; 1 Nov; 20 Jan; 19 Mar; 24 June (shepherds). There is also a *fiesta* at the end of May.

Local information

● **Accommodation**

You won't find accommodation easily on Sat evening and the prices rise to E and over.

A1 *Mayan Inn*, T 756-1176, F 756-1212, colonial style courtyard hotel, huge rooms, simple, antique furniture, fireplaces, friendly staff, bar, marimba music, laundry service, restaurant overpriced; **A2** *Santo Tomás*, 7 Av, 5-32, T 756-1316, F 756-1306, very attractive building with beautiful colonial furnishings (a museum in itself), often full at weekends, very good, friendly service, helpful owner (Sr Magermans), pool, good restaurant (set meals US$6) and bar, marimba music pm, same day laundry, nice patio; **A2** *Villa Grande*, just S of town, T 756-1053, new, single storey units set along a hillside, charmless conference venue, poorly kept, huge sunken bathtubs.

C *Chalet House*, 3 C, 7-44, T 756-1360, F 756-1347, with bath, clean, small, family atmosphere, good; **C** *Maya Lodge*, 6 C, 4-08, T 756-1177, with bath, with breakfast, mixed reports; **C** *Pensión Chugüilá*, 5 Av, 5-24, T 756-1134, clean, good, **D** without bath, meals (good) another US$3.85 (some rooms

have fireplaces, wood costs US$0.90 a day extra), marimba on Sat, front rooms noisy otherwise rec.

D *Pascual Abaj*, 5 Av Arco Gucumatz 3-38, on the road to Quiché, T 756-1055, rooms around a central courtyard, hot showers, good value; **D-E** *Pensión Girón* (cheaper without bath), on 6 C, 4-52, Edif Girón, T 756-1156, good, hot water, helpful, clean, ample parking; **D-E** *Posada El Arco*, 4 C, 4-36, helpful, clean, very pretty, small, friendly, garden, washing facilities, negotiate lower rates for stays longer than 1 night, large rooms, all-you-can-eat breakfasts, English spoken, cold water, garage.

E *El Salvador*, 10 C, 4-47, 2 blocks from main plaza, in large rooms with bath and fireplace (wood available in market), good views, **F** in small rooms without bath, mixed reports; **E** *Posada Belén*, 12 C, 5-55, T 756-1244, more expensive with bath, hot water, check electrics, balcony, clean, friendly, will do laundry, fine views.

F *El Torito*, nr where the buses stop, clean, comfortable; **F** *Posada Santa Marta*, 5 Av, 3-27, with cold water, bath and sheets (**G** without either). Local boys will show you other cheap lodgings, **G**. Try the fire station (Los Bomberos) at weekends.

Camping: free overnight vehicle parking at Shell station next to the *Hotel Santo Tomás*.

● **Places to eat**

Tapena, 5 Av, 5-21, clean, very good; *El Torito*, on the 2nd floor of Edif Girón, steaks, fish, good breakfasts, 3-course meal and drink US$5-6; *La Parilla*, next to *El Salvador*, good food, best choice, reasonable prices; *Eben Ezer*, good breakfasts; *Tziguan Tinamit*, 5 Av y 6 C, some local dishes, steaks, breakfasts, good; *Kato Cok*, opp *Hotel Chugüilá*, good budget food but check the bill; *Tita*, average quality, expensive; *La Fonda de Tzijolaj*, 2nd floor of Centro Comercial Municipal Santo Tomás, N side of main plaza, good meals, good service, reasonable prices (ask the waitress for the booklet written by the owner, a useful English-Spanish-Quiché phrase book). Also above the market at local 17 is *Buenaventura*, reasonable, friendly owner, Manuel Ventura; *Antojitos Tzocomá*, 5 Av, beyond *Hotel Pascual Abaj*, good food, cheap and friendly, a locals' place; *K'umarkaaj*, next to food market, good *comida* US$2, good breakfasts and cheap coffee, very friendly; *Comedor Isabel*, 5 C 4-16, good; *La Villa de los Cofrades*, good food; *Cafetería Tuttos*, nr *Posada Belén*, pizzas, good breakfasts, reasonable prices.No meals anywhere under US$2.50 (except in the market).

● **Banks & money changers**
Banco del Ejército, open Tues-Sun, very slow, but nowhere else changes TCs, beware queues on market days; **Bancafé** open every day. *Mayan Inn* will exchange cash, *Santo Tomás* cheques and cash at holiday times.

● **Post & telecommunications**
Courier service: opp Post Office in main square, open Mon-Sat; DHL, 5 Av, 1 block N of Plaza.

● **Transport**
Veloz Quiché bus direct from/to **Guatemala City**, US$1.60 (Zona 4 Terminal), half hourly service, 0500-1800, 3½ hrs. The slower Reina de Utatlán bus from the capital, 4-5 hrs (Zona 4 Terminal) costs only US$1.50, several daily. 4 a day to **Sololá** and several to **Panajachel**, direct (US$0.65, 1 hr 15 mins) or via Los Encuentros, prices and schedules vary according to type of service. For **Antigua**, change at Chimaltenango until 1730, after that at San Lucas Sacatepéquez until 2000 (or taxi from Chimaltenango, US$8-9). To **Huehuetenango**, via Los Encuentros, US$1.75. 2 weekly buses Chichicastenango-**Nebaj**, US$1, may have to change at Sacapulas, otherwise take a bus to **Santa Cruz del Quiché** (half-hourly, 30-min journey, paved road, also lots of trucks on market day, US$0.40) and change there. Beware of overcharging on buses in the Panajachel/Chichicastenango area.

QUICHE AND THE IXIL TRIANGLE

SANTA CRUZ DEL QUICHE

(Pop 7,750; *Alt* 2,000m) 19 km N by paved road from Chichicastenango is **Santa Cruz del Quiché**, commonly known simply as Quiché, a quaint, friendly town, colourful daily market. There are few tourists here and prices are consequently reasonable. Good selection of local cloth. Quiché's speciality is palm hats, which are made and worn in the area. Remains 3 km away of palace and temples of former Quiché capital, **Gumarcaj**, sometimes spelt **K'umarkaaj** and now generally called **Utatlán**. This was largely destroyed by the Spaniards, but the stonework of the original buildings can be seen in the ruins, in a very attractive setting. They can be reached on foot (from the bus station, walk W along 10 C to a lane on the R which winds upward marked to K'umarkaaj. Open 0700-1800, entry US$0.60. There are two subterranean burial chambers (take a torch, there are unexpected drops) still used by the Indians for worship; small but interesting museum at the entrance which should be visited before the site. Ask at the site for a good guide, Leopoldo.

On the road NW to San Antonio Ilotenango are the thermal baths of Balneario Pachitac, in a delightful location about 4 km from Quiché. There is a fine tiled swimming pool, and a smaller one for children, fed from a warm underground spring, clean and refreshing. Free entry, changing rooms and picnic area. Bring your own food but cold drinks available. It is a pleasant walk from Quiché along the road bordered by massive clumps of sunflowers, go W along 2 C from the centre and straight on for 4 kms. Hitching possible, probably an occasional bus to and from San Antonio.

Local festivals
About 14-20 Aug (but varies around Assumption).

Local information
● **Accommodation**
D *Rey K'iché*, 8 C, 0-9, 2 blocks from bus terminal, opened 1996, comfortable, hot water, parking.

F *Posada Monte Bello*, 4 Av, 9-20, clean, peaceful, nice garden, off street parking; **F** *Posada Calle Real*, 2 Av, 7-36, 25 very small rooms, parking, hot shower, clean, friendly, good value; **F** *Hospedaje Hermano Pedro*, 9 C, 0-2, friendly, clean, private shower, close to bus terminal so arrive early; **F** *Hospedaje San Francisco*, past church uphill, clean, good value; **F** *La Cascada*, 10 Av, 10 C, friendly, clean; **F** *San Pascual*, 7 C, 0-43, T 555-1107, occasional hot showers, clean, quiet, locked parking, rec; **F** *Tropical*, 1 Av, 9 C. Basic accommodation nr bus terminal.

● **Places to eat**
El Torito Steak House, 4 C, ½ block W of parque central, good meat and chicken dishes; *Pic Nic*, 2 Av, 0-45, reasonable prices; *Video 2000*, 3 C, 1 Av, inexpensive menu, *churrascos*,

pizzas, hamburgers etc; *La Casona*, 2 C, 4-05, old colonial house, good selection, also vegetarian, good quality, rec; *Las Rosas*, 1 Av 28, opens for good breakfasts at 0700, good *almuerzos*; *Café Kail* on main plaza, good ice cream, cakes, also main dishes, popular with foreign visitors; *Musicafé*, 1 Av 16, good food, reasonable; *La Cabañita Café*, 1 Av 13, charming small café with pinewood furniture, home made pies and cakes, great vanilla shakes, excellent breakfasts (waffles, cereals, etc) great snacks eg *sincronizadas* (hot tortillas baked with cubed ham, spiced chicken and cheese) rec; *Celajes*, on main square, good food; good *comedor* 2 blocks N of NE corner of main plaza, clean, cheap, friendly, pretty wooden tables; *Comedor Los Viajeros*, 1 Av, 8 C, nr bus terminal, clean, good, simple meals; *La Esquina*, in the bus terminal, good for snacks while waiting for bus

● **Banks & money changers**
Banco Industrial, 3 C y 2 Av; Banco G y T, 6 C y 2 Av, open 0900-1900 Mon-Fri, 1000-1400 Sat, Visa and Mastercard, does not cash TCs.

● **Post & telecommunications**
Post Office: on 3 C, Zona 5. **Guatel**, on 1 Av, Zona 5.

● **Transport**
Bus terminal at 10 C y 1 Av, Reina de Utatlán from **Guatemala City**, Zona 4 bus terminal, 0600-1600, 4-5 hrs (US$1.60), via Los Encuentros and Chichicastenango (US$0.30, from Pensión Chuguilá). To **Nebaj** and **Cotzal**, 5 a day, US$1.20, 4-5 hrs; a rough but breathtaking trip, arrive in good time to get a window seat (may leave early if full). To **Uspantán**, via **Sacapulas**, 3 a day, 5 hrs, US$1.80, ride on top for good view (for continuation to **Cobán** and **San Pedro Carchá**, see below). To **Joyabaj**, several daily, via Chiché and Zacualpa, US$0.50, 1½ hrs.

It is possible to get to **Huehuetenango** in a day via Sacapulas (0930 bus), then truck from bridge to Aguacatán, bus from there 1430 to Huehuetenango. There are also daily buses to **Quezaltenango** and **San Marcos**, and to **Panajachel**.

There is a paved road E from Quiché to (8 km) **Santo Tomás Chiché**, normally known simply as **Chiché**, a picturesque village with a fine rarely-visited Indian Sat market (*fiesta*, 25-28 Dec). Buses and vans (US$0.25) run from Quiché. (There is also a road to this village from Chichicastenango. Although

it is a short-cut, it is rough and now virtually impassable in any vehicle. It makes a good 3 to 4 hrs' walk however.)

45 km further E from Chiché is **Zacualpa**, where beautiful woollen bags are woven. There is an unnamed *pensión* near the plaza; on the plaza itself is a private house which has cheap rooms and meals. (Mosquito coils are a must.) Market: Sun, Thur. Church with remarkably fine façade. Two shops opposite each other on the road into town sell weavings, good prices.

JOYABAJ

On another 11 km is **Joyabaj**, where women weave fascinating *huipiles*, with a colourful Sun market, followed by a procession at about noon from the church led by the elders with drums and pipes. This was a stopping place on the old route from Mexico to Antigua. There is good walking in the wooded hills around, eg N to Chorraxaj (2 hrs) or across the river Cocol S to Piedras Blancas to see blankets being woven (ask for Santos López). Ask at the Conalfa office in Joyabaj for information or a guide. The Centro Xoy, C de la Hospital, arranges tours (for the benefit of community development) and offers Spanish and Quiché lessons. During *fiesta* week (9-15 Aug) Joyabaj has a *palo volador*, two men dangle from a 20m pole while the ropes they are attached to unravel to the ground. The villages of San Pedro and San Juan Sacatepéquez (see page 639) can be reached from Joyabaj by a dry-season road suitable only for strong vehicles and thence to Guatemala City. The scenery en route is spectacular.

● **Accommodation** F *Pensión Mejía*, nr the church, basic but clean. If staying for several days, ask at Centro Xoy for families to stay with. There is a restaurant next to the Esso station on the Santa Cruz end of the plaza with a bank (will change US$ cash) opp.

● **Buses** Joyita bus, Guatemala City 3-4 Av, 7-9 C, Zona 4, to Joyabaj, 10 a day between 0200 and 1600, 5 hrs, US$1.50.

SACAPULAS

A poor road goes N from Quiché, 48 km, to **Sacapulas** (*alt* 1,220m), a quiet, friendly town at the foot of the Cuchumatanes mountains. Here there are the remains of a bridge over Río Negro, built by Las Casas. Primitive salt extraction. Market under two large ceiba trees on Thur and Sun (larger, selling local wares, baskets, some traditional clothing). The colonial church has surprising treasures inside, built 1554. There are hot springs along the S bank of the river a few hundred metres E of the bridge, which are rec for a hot bath. They are shallow, dug out depressions along the bank and a small bucket (a *guacal* or a *palangana*) is rec to assist in bathing.

● **Accommodation & places to eat G** *Restaurante Río Negro (Gloris)*, 20 rooms, basic, friendly, cold communal showers, but hot springs opp, clean, good meals well-prepared, excellent milkshakes; *Elvi's*, on edge of town towards Chichi, good breakfast and evening meals; *Panadería Karla*, nr square, good *chocobananos* with nuts; *Comedor Central* nr the market; small *tiendas* nr the square and women nr the bridge sell *enchiladas*, *tamales*, etc.

● **Buses** The ride from Quiché to Sacapulas is rec, fabulous views on switchback road. All buses from Quiché to Uspantán and Aguatán go through Sacapulas, US$1, 3 hrs. Try to persuade them to let you ride on the roof, you will see much more! Return buses, Sacapulas-Quiché appear all to be in the early hours. Bus to Huehuetenango via Aguacatán (see below), at 0300 and 0530, basically for those taking local produce to market, 4½ hrs; this road is beautiful, but can be closed in rainy season (it's a tough road to drive at any time).

THE ROAD EAST TO COBAN

The road E from Sacapulas is one of the most beautiful, and roughest, mountain roads in all Guatemala, with magnificent scenery in the narrow valleys. Truck to Cobán, several daily am, US$1.25, 7 hrs, if lucky, usually much longer. There is no direct bus to Cobán; instead, take one of the three Quiché-Uspantán buses (passing Sacapulas at about 1230, 1400, 1600), or a truck, to **Uspantán**, *fiesta* 6-10 May.

Stay the night at the **G** *Hospedaje El Viajero*, 2 blocks E of Plaza, then 2 blocks S, basic, clean, pleasant, informative about the area, or **G** *Galindo*, 4 blocks E of parque central, clean, friendly, rec. There are several places to eat, *Comedor Kevin* is good, serves vegetables, or *Cafetería Los Pericos*, on the road to Quiché, good food, good value. Then take the early morning bus at 0300-0400 to Cobán; you may be able to spend the night on the bus before it leaves. Hitchhiking to Cobán is also possible. (Truck Uspantán-San Cristóbal Verapaz, US$1.25.) Buses to Quiché at 0300, 2200.

Between Sacapulas and Uspantán is **Cunén** (*fiesta* several days around the beginning of Feb, with parades of Eskimos, parrots, bears, Arabs etc, who gather at the Church and make their way round the town, especially interesting at night; one pension, **F** across the road from the yellow *tienda* with the satellite dish, friendly, clean, cold shower. *Tienda y Comedor Rech Kanah María*, next to church, good; no food after 2000 anywhere). The road is not suitable for road motorcycles; off-road bikes and high-clearance vehicles OK. Fuel is sold at Uspantán, Chicamán (10 km beyond) and San Cristóbal Verapaz, but supply is unreliable.

It is a 5-hr walk from Uspantán S to **Chimul**, the birthplace of Rigoberta Menchú, the Nobel Peace Prize winner in 1992. The village was virtually erased during the 1980s, but settlement is coming to life again. You can get a lift on market day in the afternoon, but not all the way.

THE IXIL TRIANGLE

13 km N of Sacapulas, 5 km before Cunén, is a spectacular road to the village of Nebaj (see below). It is easy enough to get by truck to Nebaj (US$0.50) and there are buses from Quiché. It is not so easy to get to the other two villages of the Ixil Triangle, **Chajul** and **San Juan Cotzal** (a new road has been built between the two), but the 0500 bus from Quiché and Sacapulas to

Nebaj on Sun seems to continue to both. Chajul has a *pensión*, basic, G; also a small *comedor*. Chajul's main festival is the 2nd Fri in Lent. Cotzal also has a *pensión*. The village's fiesta is 21-24 June, culminating in the day of St John the Baptist on 24 June. There is a conquistador dance and it is very colourful. The local women's headwear has huge pom poms. Nebaj to Cotzal is a pleasant 4-hr walk. There are no formal lodging or restaurant facilities in other small villages and it is very difficult to specify what transport facilities are available in this area as trucks and the occasional pick-up or commercial van (probably the best bet – ask, especially in *Las Tres Hermanas*, Nebaj) are affected by road and weather conditions. For this reason, be prepared to have to spend the night in villages. Chajul has a pilgrimage to Christ of Golgotha on the second Fri in Lent, beginning the Wed before (the image is escorted by 'Romans' in blue police uniforms!) Chajul has market Tues and Fri. In Cotzal the market is on Sat. Look out for the attractive local *huipiles*.

NEBAJ

On the main plaza of **Nebaj** are two weaving cooperatives selling *cortes*, *huipiles* and handicrafts from the town and the surrounding area, bargaining possible. *Huipiles* may be bought from María Santiago Chel (central market) or Juana Marcos Solís who can be found in the parque central on market days or at home (see under **Places to eat**) who gives weaving lessons from 1 day to 6 months. The local costume is colourful and very beautiful; the *corte* (skirt) is bright red and the *huipil* is of a geometric design in red, purple, green and yellow. The women also wear a headdress with pompoms on it. Visitors are asked by young women to visit their homes to see (and buy) 'típicas', weavings (prices are usually better than in the market, but the sellers are very persistent and there is much rivalry between them); boys meet all incoming buses and will guide

you to a *hospedaje*. This village has very good Sun and Thur markets. Nebaj has a *fiesta* on 12-15 August. There are magnificent walks from Nebaj along the river or in the surrounding hills. The views of the Cuchumatanes mountains are spectacular.

Excursions
To a waterfall take the road to Chajul and after 20 mins take the left fork to follow the river; another 40 mins brings you to a pretty waterfall; lovely scenery. A guide is Jacinto (has a notebook of testimonials); he charges US$2 for a morning's walking.

There is good walking W of Nebaj, and the roads are better in this direction than to Chajul and Cotzal since there are a number of 'model villages' resettled by the government. These include **Acul**, follow 5 C out of town, downhill, over the bridge then, 50m further, the main path veers left, but go straight on; from here the route is self-evident, any forks come back together. By road leave town on Av 4, the Shell station road, at the first main fork after the 'turret', follow the main road left and at the next fork take the small, unsigned track to the left). There is a good cheese farm 1 km W of the village, whose late Italian owner was making Swiss cheese for 50 years (the cheese is for sale, US$3.50 for about 500g). **Tzalbal**, 2½ hrs walking; **Salquil Grande**, 26 km NW of Nebaj (several hours walk); **La Pista**, where the airstrip is. None has accommodation or restaurants. Apart from the rare bus, there is no public transport, only pick-ups; ask for advice at *Las Tres Hermanas*. **Las Violetas**, 15 mins' walk from the centre of Nebaj, is a squatters' village where people who have come down from the mountains live when they arrive in Nebaj.

Local information
● Accommodation
F *Ilebal Tenau*, Av Salida Chajul, no sign, hot water, shared bath, very clean, friendly, parking inside; **F** *Ixil Hotel*, 5 Av, 10 C, in a colonial house, pretty central patio with fountain, clean, pleasant and comfortable, big rooms, rec.

G *Hospedaje Esperanza*, 6 Av, 2-36, very friendly, clean, hot shower extra, owner's daughter gives weaving lessons, US$7/day; **G** *Las Clavellinas*, nice, basic, without bath, rec; **G** *Las Tres Hermanas*, 5 Av y 4 C, no sign, 2 blocks from square, friendly, full of character, popular with foreigners, wood-fired hot water, not too clean, basic, some beds very hard, good food available for about US$1.

● **Places to eat**
Comedor Irene, 5 C close to square, painted blue-green, good food, plenty of vegetables, full of character, rec; *Comedor Las Delicias*, good *comida corriente*; *Los Boxboles* a *comedor* at the home of the weaver Juana Marcos Solís (see above) in Cantón Simacol, head towards Chajul from the plaza on Av 15 de Septiembre, turn right up 0 Av at the pila on Salida Chajul, take first left and her house is last on the left, excellent *tamalitos*, *boxboles* (squash leaves with *masa* and chopped meat or chicken spread on them, rolled tightly, boiled and served with *salsa* and fresh orange juice) and other local dishes, but food only prepared with several hours notice, rec. Juana also has a sauna, US$1.75 for 2 or more, US$2.65 for 1, 2 hrs' notice required.

● **Banks & money changers**
Bancafé changes Amex TCs.

● **Transport**
Buses to **Quiché** (US$1.60) and **Guatemala City** all leave early am or late at night. From Nebaj, bus to **Sacapulas** and Quiché 0100, 0400, 0500 (coming from Cotzal), and on Sun 0800, 2½ hrs to Sacapulas (US$0.60), a further 1½ to Quiché (service times unreliable). Direct buses daily to **Huehuetenango**, Rutas Garcías, 5-6 hrs, at 0100 and 2330. You can travel to Cobán in a day by getting a truck or pick-up from outside the village or earliest bus to Sacapulas, get off at junction to Cunén and hitch or catch a bus from there. There is a Shell station, but supply is unreliable and prices are high.

Western Guatemala

YET MORE MARKET towns and villages, with characteristic weaving or other crafts, can be found on the routes through western Guatemala. The volcanic chain is also still in evidence. In the cool highlands, Quezaltenango is a good centre for reaching Indian villages, or for heading to Mexico, including a descent to the Pacific lowlands. Another good centre is Huehuetenango, on the highland route to Mexico. Also from Huehuetenango you can go to the Indian village and weaving centre of Todos Santos Cuchumatán, or head east to Aguacatán and the scenic road to Quiché.

TOTONICAPAN TO LA MESILLA

The stretch of Pan-American Highway between Los Encuentros and San Cristóbal Totonicapán runs past **Nahualá** (*Pop* 1,370; *Alt* 2,470m), an Indian village where *metates*, or stones on which maize is ground to make *tortillas*, are made. The inhabitants wear distinctive costumes, and are considered by other Indians to be somewhat hostile. Good church. Market on Thur and Sun (this is the time to visit), at which finely embroidered cuffs and collars are sold, also very popular *huipiles*, but check the colours, many run. No accommodation except perhaps with Indian families at a small cost. *Fiesta* (Santa Catalina) on 23-26 Nov (main day 25). Remember the Indians do not like to be photographed.

There is another all-weather road a little to the N and 16 km longer, from Los Encuentros to San Cristóbal Totonicapán.

In 40 km it reaches Totonicapán. The route Chichicastenango-Quiché-Xecajá-Totoni capán takes a day by car or motorcycle, but is well worth taking and recommended by cyclists in 1996. No buses.

TOTONICAPAN

(*Pop* 52,000, almost all Indian; *Alt* 2,500m) 14½ km E of Cuatro Caminos (see below), is the capital of its Department. There are sulphur baths, but they are dirty and crowded. Market (mind out for pickpockets) considered by Guatemalans to be one of the cheapest, and certainly very colourful, on Tues (small), and Sat (the main market noted for ceramics and cloth); annual fair 24-30 Sept with main *fiesta* on 29 Sept. *Casa de Cultura*, 3 C, displays collection of fiesta masks and stuffed animals. *Chuimekená* cooperative is at 9 Av between C 1 and 2, Zona Palín, fine variety of handicrafts and woven cloth.

- **Accommodation** F pp *Hospedaje San Miguel*, 3 C, 7-49, Zona 1, T 766-1452, clean, comfortable, hot water, prices treble on market day; F *Pensión Blanquita*, 13 Av, 4 C, hot showers, good; G *El Centro*, 7 C, 7-33, Zona 4.

- **Places to eat** *Centro Siam*, 2 blocks from church, Thai and Chinese dishes; *Comedor Lety*, opp *Hospedaje San Miguel*, excellent; *Comedor Brenda*, 8 Av, 6 y 7 C, also good.

- **Banks & money changers** Banco G&T, 2 C, 1-95, Zona 1.

- **Buses** Frequent buses to Quezaltenango along a paved road (fine scenery), US$0.35. Bus to Los Encuentros, US$1.50.

SAN CRISTOBAL TOTONICAPAN

San Cristóbal Totonicapán (*pop* 3,168; *alt* 2,340m), 1 km from the **Cuatro Caminos** road junction (Pan-American Highway, with the roads to Quezaltenango, Totonicapán, Los Encuentros and Huehuetenango), San Cristóbal has a huge church, built by Franciscan friars, of which the roof has recently been renovated. The silver-plated altars and screens, all hand-hammered, are well worth seeing. Noted for textiles (and *huipiles* in particular) sold all over Guatemala. Also well known for ceramics. Market, Sun, on the other side of the river from the church (only 2 blocks away), spreading along many streets. Bus service to Quezaltenango.

Local festivals 22-27 July.

- **Accommodation** D *Nuevo Hotel Reforma*, T 766-1051, with bath, hot water, a/c, parking; E *Pensión Reforma*, T 766-1438, a/c, parking, restaurant, in Barrio La Reforma, T/F 766-1438; F *Hospedaje Amigo*.

SAN FRANCISCO EL ALTO

2 km W of the Cuatro Caminos junction a road runs N to San Francisco El Alto (3 km) and Momostenango (19 km). **San Francisco** (*alt* 2,640m), also reached by a new paved road 5 km W of Cuatro Caminos, at Km 191, stands in the mountain cold, above the great valley in which lie Totonicapán, San Cristóbal and Quezaltenango. Church of metropolitan magnificence, notice the double-headed,

Hapsburg eagle. Visit the roof on market days for a fine view of activities and surroundings (US$0.20). Crammed market on Fri, said to be the largest in the country; Indians buying woollen blankets for resale throughout country, and fascinating cattle market at the entrance to town. An excellent place for buying woven and embroidered textiles of good quality, but beware of pickpockets. Go early, the market begins to close about 1030. Colourful New Year's Day celebrations. It is a pleasant walk from San Francisco down to the valley floor, then along the river to San Cristóbal. Frequent buses to Quezaltenango and Totonicapán, about 1 hr to either. Close by in the mountains to the W is San Andrés Xecul, see under Quezaltenango **Excursions**.

- **Accommodation** F *Vista Hermosa*, 3 Av, 2-22, T 766-1030, no showers, fleas. F *Galaxia*, 2 Av, 2-63, with bath, spacious rooms, check for water problems; G *Hospedaje Central San Francisco de Asís* on main street nr market. Good restaurant, *Dixie*.

MOMOSTENANGO

At 2,220m this is the chief blanket-weaving centre. Indians can be seen beating the blankets on stones to shrink them. The Feast of the Uajxaquip Vats (pronounced 'washakip') is celebrated by 30,000 Indians every 260 days by the ancient Mayan calendar. Frequent masked dances also. Momostenango means 'place of the altars', and there are many on the outskirts but they are not worth looking for; there is, however, a hilltop image of a Mayan god, similar to the one outside Chichicastenango. There are said to be 300 medicine-men practising in the town; their insignia of office is a little bag containing beans and quartz crystals. Outside town are three sets of *riscos*: eroded columns of sandstone with embedded quartz particles, which are worth visiting. The most striking are the least accessible, in the hills to the N of the town. The town is quiet except on Wed and Sun, the market days (the latter being larger, and interesting for weaving; also try Tienda Manuel del Jesús Agancel, 1 Av, 1-50, Zona 4 for good bargains, especially blankets and carpets; on non-market days, ask for weavers' houses). It has a spring-fed swimming pool; also a sulphur bath (5 in all) at Pala Grande, 4 km NW of Momostenango (take the road first towards Santa Ana); the water is black, but worth experiencing, take soap. Bus service from Cuatro Caminos (US$0.35) and Quezaltenango, US$0.45.

● **Accommodation** G *Hospedaje Paclom*, on main street, clean, pretty inner courtyard, water mornings only, no showers, friendly but watch out for overcharging, cheap meals (reported deteriorating 1996); G *Galaxia*, ½ block S of market, clean cold water, shower; G *Hospedaje Roxane*, bad, avoid. *Comedor Tonia*, friendly, cheap. *Flipper*, 1 C y 2 Av 'A', good *liquados*. Bottled water can be bought in *Tienda Xela*.

At San Cristóbal the old and the new routes of the Pan-American Highway, which joined at Los Encuentros, part again. The new route to the Mexican border at Ciudad Cuauhtémoc goes NW. It climbs for several km before dropping down past the *ladino* town of Malacatancito (48 km) and swinging NW, bypassing Huehuetenango before entering the **Selegua (El Tapón) gap** to Mexico. The road is in good condition.

HUEHUETENANGO

A 6½ km spur from this road leads to **Huehuetenango** (*pop* 39,000; *alt* 1,905m), a mining centre in farming country, with Indians from remote mountain fastnesses coming in for the daily market, and particularly Wed. Huehuetenango is the last town before the La Mesilla border post, on the Pan-American Highway into Mexico. It is also an appropriate town for the serious Spanish language student: there is very little English spoken here, and the language schools are good.

Excursions

Ruins of **Zaculeu**, old capital of the Mam tribe, pyramids, a ball court and a few other structures, completely reconstructed, concrete stepped forms, devoid of any ornamentation (museum), disappointing, 5 km NW on top of a rise ringed by river and *barrancas* (admission US$0.30, open 0800-1800). Yellow Alex bus runs at 1030, 1330 and 1530 as long as at least 5 people are going (fare US$0.20). It is possible to walk to the ruins in about 1 hr.

Chiantla, 5 km N of Huehuetenango, has a great pilgrimage to the silver Virgin of La Candelaria on 28 Jan to 2 February. The statue is set behind glass, upstairs; ask the priest's permission to take photos. Another *fiesta* on 8 Sept and interesting processions in Holy Week. The church is well worth a visit. Good walking in the neighbourhood. Daily market, largest on Sun. G *Hospedaje Cuchumatanes*, 7 C, 1 block from plaza, friendly, clean, big rooms, communal shower. Buses leave regularly from 1 Av and 1 C. Some 13 km N of Chiantla is a viewpoint with 9 obelisks, which has magnificent views over mountain and valley.

It is also possible to walk NW from Chiantla to Todos Santos Cuchumatanes, 13 hrs, or better, 2 days, staying overnight at El Potrillo in the barn owned by Rigoberto Alva. This route crosses one of the highest parts of the Cordillera at over 3500m. Alternatively, cycle the 40 km gravel road, steep in places but rewarding. If you camp, secure your belongings.

Local festivals

Fiesta 12-17 July and festivities 7 December for the *quemando del Diablo* (burning the Devil) with fireworks etc.

Local information
● **Accommodation**
Out of town: **A3** *Los Cuchumatanes*, about 3 km out of town, Zona 7, T 764-1951, F 764-2816, good restaurant, clean swimming pool (known as Brasilia), good value; **C** *Centro Turístico Pino Montano*, at Km 259 on the Pan-American Highway, 2 km past the fork to Huehuetenango on the way to La Mesilla, a bit run down, pool, a/c, restaurant, parking, T 764-1637; **C** *El Prado*, Cantón San José, Zona 5, T/F 764-2150/51, just beyond the new bus

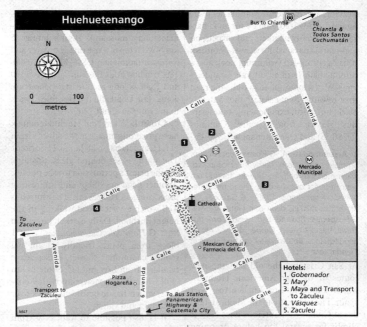

Huehuetenango

N

0   100
metres

To
Chiantla &
Todos Santos
Cuchumatán

Bus to Chiantla

1 Calle

1 Avenida

2 Avenida

3 Avenida

2

1

5

Plaza

2 Calle

3 Calle

4

Cathedral

4 Avenida

5 Avenida

3

Mercado
Municipal

M

To
Zaculeu

7 Avenida

4 Calle

Mexican Consul /
Farmacia del Cid

5 Calle

To
Zaculeu

Transport to
Zaculeu

Pizza
Hogareña

6 Avenida

To Bus Station,
Panamerican
Highway &
Guatemala City

6 Calle

M47

Hotels:
1. *Gobernador*
2. *Mary*
3. *Maya* and Transport
   to *Zaculeu*
4. *Vásquez*
5. *Zaculeu*

terminal, clean; **C** *Cascata*, Lote 4, 4-42, Colonia Alvarado, Zona 5, T 764-1188, new, rooms on top floor best, clean, hot showers, restaurant disappointing.

In town: **C** *Zaculeu*, 5 Av, 1-14, Zona 1, T 764-1086, attractive hotel, with charming lounge, cable TV, restaurant (varying reports but good breakfasts); **E** *Gran Hotel Shinula*, 4 C, 2-3 Av, T 764-1225, clean, bath, restaurant; **E** *Mary*, 2 C, 3-52, Zona 1, T/F 764-1228/1618, with bath, cheaper without, good beds, hot water, parking, clean, safe, good value; **E** *Gobernador*, 4 Av, 1-45, T 764-1197, clean, shower, cafetería serves breakfast; **E** *Río Lindo*, 3 Av, 0-20, Zona 1, T 764-2641, 3 blocks from Plaza, shower, hot water (but beware poor electrical installation), small rooms, clean, nice; **E** *Todos Santos Inn*, 2 C, 6-74, Zona 1, T 764-1241, shared bath, hot water, helpful, clean, luggage stored, rec; **F** *Vásquez*, 2 C, 6-67, T 764-1338, 2 blocks W of Plaza, with bath, clean, good value; **F** *Hospedaje Huehueteco*, 2 C between 2-1 Av, close to market, basic but clean, small single rooms, larger doubles with bath, no electricity 0700-1800; **F** *Jenni*, 6 Av between 4 C and 5 C, with bath, cheaper without, run down;

F *Maya*, 3 Av, 3-55, with bath, tepid water, safe, basic; **F** *Central*, 5 Av, 1-33, communal baths, hot water, basic, laundry facilities, cheap, nice roof to sit on, parking, good breakfast, lunch and dinner; **G** *Centroamericana*, 1 Av, 4-85. There are a number of cheap *pensiones* on 1 Av, by the market, inc **G** *Pensión San Ramón*, nr 1 Av, basic, dirty toilets, friendly, convenient for bus stations; **G** *San Antonio*, very cheap, unpleasant toilets, good hot showers for US$0.50, also charge for cold showers; **G** *Tikal* (reasonably clean); **G** *Tikal 2*, next door to *San Antonio*, friendly, bed bugs, hot shower extra. **NB** The cheap *hospedajes* (F and under) are not rec for single women.

Camping: camping at Zaculeu ruins, or further on the same road at the riverside, unofficial, no facilities.

● **Places to eat**

All hotel restaurants are open to the public. *Las Bouganvillas*, on the Plaza, large, popular; *Las Brasas*, 4 Av, corner of 2 C, steak house and Chinese dishes, rec; *La Fonda de Don Juan*, 2 C, 5-35, Italian, excellent sandwiches, big choice of desserts, *licuados*, good pizzas, reasonable prices; *Los Pollos*, 3 C, 5 y 6 Av, full chicken meal US$3, also takeaway, open 24 hrs; *Los Amigos*, behind the cathedral, good, low prices; *Bon Apetit*, 5 Av, reasonable prices. There are numerous cheap *comedores* nr the market, but check for hygiene. *El Edén*, 2 km down road to Chiantla, good food; *El Jardín*, 6 Av y 4 C, Zona 1, meat dishes, good pancakes and milkshakes; rec; *Pizza Hogareña*, 6 Av between 4 C and 5 C, rec, popular, always full; *Rico Mac Pollo*, 3 Av, for chicken; *Le Kaf*, 6 C, 6-40, Western-style, varied menu, live music every evening, good travel information, rec; *Doña Estercita's*, 2 C entre 6 y 7 Av, coffee, licuados and pastries, rec; *Ebony*, 2 C nr market, cheap but poor service, particularly if your Spanish is not perfect; *Pan Deli's*, 2 C entre 3 y 4 Av, next to Hotel Mary, good breakfasts. Also on 2 C, *Cafetería y Panadería La Regis* and *Restaurante Los Alpes* (at 5 Av); *Rinconcito Huehueteco*, nr bus station in Zona 4, good. Good *taco* stand on corner opp bus station.

● **Banks & money changers**
Several local banks, some open Sat am; good rates at Banco G&T, 2 C y 5 Av, changes TCs. Some others change TCs, but no bank changes pesos. Visa advances from Construbanco. Try the *Farmacia del Cid* for good rates for pesos.

● **Embassies & consulates**
The Honorary Mexican Consul at the *Farmacia del Cid* (5 Av and 4 C) will provide you with a Mexican visa or tourist card for US$1; open Mon-Fri 0800-1200, 1500-1700, T 764 1366, F 764-1353, helpful, has latest information

● **Language schools**
Spanish: most operate in the summer months only (see notes on schools in Antigua and Quezaltenango). **Casa Xelajú**, Apdo Postal 302, 6 C, 7-42, Zona 1. **Fundación XXIII**, 6 Av, 6-126, Zona 1, T 764-1478. **Instituto El Portal**, 1 C, 1-64, Zona 3; **Rodrigo Morales** (at Sastrería La Elegancia), 9 Av, 6-55, Zona 1, private classes, rec. **Instituto Zaculeu de Español**, 4 C, 9 25, Zona 1, **Spanish Academy Xinabajul**, 6 Av, 0-69, Zona 1, T 764-1518. Private teacher, Abesaida Guevara de López, 10 C A, 10-20, Zona 1, T 764-2917, US$100/week inc room and board, rec. Information on schools is posted in several restaurants: *Pizza Hogareña*, *El Jardín*, *La Fonda* and at the Post Office.

● **Post & telecommunications**
Guatel: 4 Av, between C 5-6.

Post Office: on 2 C across the street from *Hotel Mary*.

● **Shopping**
Artesanías y Antigüedades Ixquil, 5 Av, 1-56, good selection of *huipiles* from local villages, reasonable prices, rec.

● **Useful addresses**
Car insurance: for Mexico and Guatemala can be arranged at Banco Granaí & Townson, next door to Mexican Consulate (see above).

● **Transport**
There is a new **bus** terminal on SW outskirts of town about 2 km from the centre. Yellow urban buses shuttle between 'Terminal' and 'Centro', ruta 11, US$0.08. To **Guatemala City** (about 5 hrs): US$3.75, Los Halcones, 7 Av, 3 62, Zona 1, 0700, 1400 in each direction, reliable; Rápidos Zaculeu, 3 Av, 5-25, 0600 and 1500, good service; Transportes Velásquez, 10 a day, rec; El Cóndor, 5 a day. To **Zaculeu**, Los Flamingos, S side of market, 0445. To **La Mesilla**: frequent buses, US$2, 2½ hrs; Los Verdes, 1 Av, 1-34, 0500 and 1330; Osiris, 1 Av y 3 C, 0430, 1030, 1230; López, 4 C, 2-39, 0630. El Cóndor, office at the top of 7 Av, 0600, 1000, 1300, 1500. To **Quezaltenango**, US$1, 2½ hrs. To **Cuatro Caminos**, US$1, 2 hrs; to **Los Encuentros**, for Lake Atitlán and Chichicastenango, US$2.50; also, direct to **Chichicastenango**, Rutas García, 0300 and 1100, US$3.20, via Sacapulas and Santa Cruz del Quiché, others inc Rutas Zaculeu to **Sacapulas**, US$0.75; to **Nebaj** 1130 daily, 5-6 hrs, direct, Rutas Garcías, US$2, 3-4 hrs (bus stops in Aguacatán); to **Cobán**, take 1100 bus to Sacapulas and continue by truck; to **Nentón**, **Cuilco** and other outlying villages, enquire at the new bus station. Several bus companies go to **Todos Santos Cuchumatán** between 1100 1300, 3-4 hrs, US$1, note that the first to leave is not necessarily the first to arrive. Travellers arriving from the Mexican border should check the posted timetables for onward buses. Also, buy your tickets to where the bus takes you, eg Cuatro Caminos, Los Encuentros, not to your final destination if a change of buses is involved.

AGUACATÁN

The views are fine on the road which runs between Huehuetenango and Sacapulas. **Aguacatán** (*alt* 1,670m) is 26 km E of Huehuetenango, 36 km from Sacapulas (**G** *Nuevo Amanecer*, clean, quiet, friendly, meals; **G** *Pensión La Paz*; **G** *Hospedaje Aguacatán*, 2 blocks E of market and 1 N, noisy, above arcade). Aguacatán has an interesting market on Sun (beginning Sat night) and Thur (excellent peanuts). The women wear beautiful costumes and head-dresses. *Fiesta* 40 days after Holy Week, Virgen de la Encarnación.

The source of the Río San Juan is about 2 km down the C Principal N of the centre of Aguacatán, then 3 km down a signposted turnoff. There is a 2 km walking route, turn left up a dirt road by the evangelist Templo Buenas Nuevas, and straight to the 'fuente'. There is a US$0.20 admission charge to the park, which is a delightful place for a freezing cold swim. It is surrounded by onion and garlic fields. Take a picnic, only soft drinks available nearby. Camping is permitted.

● **Buses** Los Verdes, 1 Av, 2-34, Huehuetenango, has buses to Aguacatán at 1300 (last return bus at 1500), US$0.50, and buses for Sacapulas, Quiché, Nebaj and Cobán pass through the village. There are jeeps, Huehuetenango-Aguacatán. Taxi Huehuetenango-Aguacatán US$15 for a 3-hr trip inc source of Río San Juan. Zaculeu, 1 Av, 2-53, to Sacapulas, 1400, 2 hrs, US$1 (truck at 1630, arrives 2000, US$1), and from the same place Alegres Mañanitas has a bus to Quiché at 0415. Bus to Chichicastenango from Aguacatán 0400, very crowded, or take a truck. The Campo Alegre company has buses to Nebaj from the *Hospedaje San José*, 1 Av and 4 C 'A', and buses for Cobán leave from the same area.

SAN MATEO IXTATAN

The road runs N 117 km to **San Mateo Ixtatán**, at 2,530m, in the Cuchumatanes mountains. The *huipiles* made there are unique and are much cheaper than in Huehuetenango. Market, Sun and Thur. The road passes through San Juan Ixcoy, **Soloma** (watch out for young pickpockets in plaza and market; *Mansión Kathy*, run down; **F** *Hospedaje San Ignacio* basic, fleas, noisy; **G** *Hospedaje San Juan*, charge for hot shower, secure parking), and **Santa Eulalia** (**G** *Hospedaje El Cisne*). San Mateo itself (**G** *Pensión El Aguilar*, very basic, no showers, bring own sheets or sleeping bag) is a colourful town, with an interesting old church and black salt mines nearby. There are some impressive ruins on the outskirts

of the town. The European Community has an office here.

After San Mateo the road runs 27 km E to **Barillas** (several cheap *pensiones* including **G** *Terraza*, friendly, clean; **G** Montecristo, on main road, basic, irregular water, clean, good breakfast), a fine scenic route.

● **Transport** Buses from Huehuetenango to San Juan Ixcoy, Soloma, Santa Eulalia, San Mateo Ixtatán (US$2) and Barillas leave at 0930, 1000, 2330 and midnight, very crowded, be early and get your name high up on the list as passengers are called in order. The bus returns to Huehuetenango from San Mateo (at least 5 hrs) at 0200, 0300, 0700, 1100 and 1330, but it is advised to take 2 days over the trip. Solomarita buses (1 Av and 2 C) run as far as Soloma, at 0500 and 1300. 5 km beyond the turn off to Todos Santos Cuchumatán (see below) the road becomes rough, narrow and steep.

TODOS SANTOS CUCHUMATAN

The village of **Todos Santos** is very interesting. Beware of sunburn on days when it is not cloudy; it can be cold at night (*alt* 2,481m). Some of Guatemala's best weaving is done there, and fine *huipiles* may be bought in the cooperative on the main street (cash and TCs exchanged) and direct from the makers. There are also embroidered cuffs and collars for men's shirts, and colourful crocheted bags made by the men. A fair selection of old woven items can be bought from a small house behind the church and from a few other shops on, or just off, the main road. The Sat-Sun market is fascinating (best Sat); also Wed. A museum (US$1 entrance) in the main plaza has a collection of antiques, farm tools and (poorly) stuffed animals. The attendant is pleased to explain everything. Proceeds go to the city park fund. A Spanish Language School, Proyecto Lingüístico de Español, is one block from the Parque Central (June-Aug, US$125, Sept-May, US$100), food rather basic; you can also learn Mam, the local dialect; one of the teachers, Benito, offers dinner and sauna for US$5 for 2 at his home, he also plays chess. The school is part of La Hermandad Educativa non-profit language study organization with a school in Quezaltenango and offices in the USA (PO Box 205-337, Sunset Park, NY 11220-0006, T (718) 965 8522, F (718) 965 4643) and Europe (c/o R Bjordal, Johs Bjordalsv 8, 6400 Molde, Norway, T (072) 51376, F (072) 54050).

Excursions

From Todos Santos, one can walk to **San Juan Atitán**, 5 hrs (more interesting costumes; market Thur) and from there the highway, 1 day's walk. **G** *Hospedaje San Diego*, basic, friendly, clean, food US$1.15. Also, walk to San Martín (3 hrs), or **Santiago Chimaltenango** (7 hrs, stay in school, ask at Municipalidad), then to San Pedro Necta, and on to the Pan-American Highway for bus back to Huehuetenango.

The highest point of the Cuchumatanes, 3,837m is to the NE of Todos Santos and can be reached from the village of Tnichem on the road to Concepción Huista. The hike takes about 5 hrs and is best done in the late afternoon, spending the night near the top on a plateau at about 3,700m, convenient for camping (wood but no water). A compass is essential in case of mist. A 1.50000 map is available at the Casa Andinista in Antigua.

Local festivals

1 Nov, characterized by a horse race in which riders race between two points, having a drink at each turn until they fall off. The festival begins on 21 October.

Local information

● **Accommodation & places to eat**

F *Hospedaje Casa Familiar*, close to central park, clean though now fleas reported, friendly family of Santiago Mendoza Pablo, hot shower and sauna extra (about US$1), breakfast, dinner US$2.50, delicious banana bread, spectacular view, popular and rec. Santiaga's sister-in-law, Nicolasa Jerónimo Ramírez, owns the *Tienda Maribe* further up the hill and rents rooms, **G**, friendly. Both women make and sell *típicas* and give weaving lessons, US$1/hr: other families offer basic accommodation; **F** *Hospedaje La Paz*, friendly but fleas and cold, enclosed parking, shared showers; **F** *Pension Katy*, nice people, good food, will prepare vegetarian meals on request, good value; **F** *Mam*, just below *Casa Familiar*, friendly, clean, hot water, great view of valley, good value; **G** *Hospedaje Tres Olguitas*, very basic, dark, hot showers US$0.40, cheap meals, require a couple of hours notice; *comedor* also in market.

● **Transport**

Bus to **Huehuetenango**, 3-4 hrs, US$1.25, crowded on Mon and Fri, at 0430, 0500, 1130 and 1300, arrive early for a seat, best views from roof. The drive is spectacular, ascending to 3,290m (approximately), but much of the land has been overgrazed and there is much soil erosion. If you have not much luggage you can walk 4 hrs to Tres Caminos, the junction, where you can pick up the buses. For petrol, ask at *El Molino*, US$2/gallon.

The road from Todos Santos continues NW through Concepción Huista (where the women wear towels as shawls) to **Jacaltenango** (bus from Todos Santos at 1600, bus to Huehuetenango at 0230 and 0300, may be others, also pick-ups). In this area Jacalteco is spoken; the *feria titular* is 29 Jan to 3 Feb, with a firework jamboree (mostly at ground and eye level) and a community dance. Much pride is taken in marimba playing, eg at football matches. The hat maker in Canton Pilar supplies the hats for Todos Santos, he welcomes viewers and will make a hat to your specifications (but if you want a typical Todos Santos leather *cincho*, you must get it there).

Beyond Jacaltenango, the road goes N to Nentón (two *hospedajes*, very basic) and then on to Gracias a Dios and the Mexican border near Tziscao, from where there is a road and buses to Hidalgo and Comitán. So far as we are aware this is not an official crossing point. Apparently a bus goes from Todos Santos to **Buenavista** (NW) near the Mexican border, 4 hrs there, 4 hrs back, passing through highlands and tropical lowlands; it leaves 0700, but it's not known if this is only on market days. **NB** Check on safety in this region before visiting especially in the light of the recent problems in the border area with Chiapas.

The Pan-American Highway runs W from Huehuetenanango, swinging gently from one side of a gorge to the other, reaching the Guatemalan border post at **La Mesilla**.

FRONTIER WITH MEXICO – LA MESILLA/CIUDAD CUAUHTEMOC

This is the Pan-American Highway route to Mexico, the most scenic (certainly in Guatemala), faster and cooler than the coastal roads which are preferred by heavy transport.

● Guatemalan immigration

Open 0800-1200, 1400-1800. You may be able to pass through out of hours for a US$0.50 surcharge.

There is a tourist office (**Inguat**) in the Guatemalan immigration building.

The Mexican border post is in Ciudad Cuauhtémoc (just a few buildings, not a town) which is about 4 km from the Guatemalan frontier at La Mesilla. There are pick-ups during the day US$1.65 pp.

● Entering Guatemala

A tourist card for Guatemala can be obtained at the border, normally available for 30 days (though some readers asked for and were given 90 days, late 1996, early 1997) renewable in Guatemala City. See under **Guatemala – Information for travellers** for those who need visas. Visas are not available at the border for all nationalities who need them (eg Australians) and buses do not wait for those who alight to obtain them. It is advisable to obtain a visa in advance, ie from Comitán. You pay US$1, or US$5 quetzales to enter Guatemala, and the border is open until 1800 (beware of extra charges and bribery. There is sometimes a US$1 charge at customs for **not** searching your luggage. If unsure, request a receipt, and if asked if you are doubting his word, confess you are a writer and interested in official documents).

● Crossing by private vehicle

Some charges are posted, or printed on the documentation. Read the small print, ask for receipts and watch out for overcharging. Full details under **Getting around – car** in Information for travellers.

● Mexican consulates

Mexican visas are available at the border, but better at *Farmacia El Cid* in Huehuetenango for US$1, which saves time at the border. See also under Quezaltenango, **Embassies & consulates**.

● Accommodation & places to eat

At the first gas station, 7 km from La Mesilla, is **E** *Hotel Reposo La Gasolinera*, with hot shower, cheaper without, clean, good breakfast in restaurant (other meals, US$1.75, poor), rec, ample parking; **F** *Hotel Mirasol*, insanitary, no running water, front rooms reasonable; **F** *Mily's*, hot water, with bath, good views. *Restaurant Yamy*, opens 0700, good breakfast, popular; in La Democracia, 14 km from La Mesilla, is an unsigned *mesón*, 1 block N of the market, basic, clean, **G**.

● Exchange

Rates are not usually favourable at the border in either currency. You can try Banco Quetzal in La Mesilla or haggle in the street, but it is probably better to change a minimum amount and go for more favourable rates in Huehuetenango, Quezaltenango or Guatemala City. Bus drivers may give you a better deal than money changers, no harm in trying!

● Transport

Buses from La Mesilla to Huehuetenango US$1.50-1.85 (1st class – foreigners tend to be overcharged – 2nd class US$1). Express buses run by El Cóndor and Velásquez, who have the better service, go to Guatemala City (US$5, 6 hrs, allow 10). Do not buy a ticket at the border until a bus leaves as some wait while others come and go. If you miss the last bus to Huehuetenango, you may be able to negotiate a ride out of La Mesilla, If not, there are rooms at the border and a few kilometres beyond; the border officials are helpful with accommodation. From Guatemala City, 19 C, 2-01, Zona 1, at 0400, 0900, 1000 and 1100. Change at Los Encuentros for Lake Atitlán and Chichicastenango, and at Chimaltenango or San Lucas for Antigua. When changing buses at the border, note that Mexican buses are more spacious for luggage; the Guatemalan ones often put large bags on the roof, so keep valuables, breakables, etc in your hand luggage. Also be prepared to push for a seat.

TOTONICAPAN TO TALISMAN AND TECUN UMAN

SALCAJA

The old route of the Pan-American Highway runs W from San Cristóbal Totonicapán through Quezaltenango to Tapachula, in Mexico. 5 km from San Cristóbal it reaches the small *ladino* town of **Salcajá**, where jaspé skirt material has been woven since 1861, well worth a visit. Yarn is tied and dyed, then untied and warps stretched around telephone poles along the road or along the riverside. Many small home weavers will sell the lengths – five or eight *varas* – depending on whether the skirt is to be wrapped or pleated. The finest, of imported English yarn, cost US$40. Market, Tues, mostly fruit and vegetables; it is early, as in all country towns. The church of San Jacinto behind the market is 16th century and also worth a visit. The taxi rate is US$2.50-3/hr. Several minibuses a day from new commercial centre, 10 Av and 8 C.

● **Accommodation & places to eat** There are 2 hotels in town: **E** *La Mansión de Don Hilario*, 3 Av, 3-21, Zona 2, T 768-9569, next door to *Cafesama* restaurant, which is good; **F** *Salcajá*, 3 Av final, Zona 1, T 768-9594, restaurant. Excellent unnamed bakery on third street up the hill parallel to main street where buses pass in town centre. Try *caldo de frutas*, a highly alcoholic, but clandestine drink, 'when it's well made it's sweet and doesn't hit you until you try to stand up' It is not openly sold. There is also *rompopo*, made with eggs.

QUEZALTENANGO

Quezaltenango (commonly known as Xela (*pop* over 125,000; *alt* 2,335m), 14½ km SW of Cuatro Caminos, is the most important city in western Guatemala. The climate is decidedly cool and damp, particularly Nov to April, and there is no heating anywhere. Set among a group of high mountains and volcanoes, one of which, Santiaguito, the lower cone of Santa María (which can be easily climbed), destroyed the city in 1902 and is still active. A modern city, but with narrow colonial-looking streets and a magnificent plaza (between 11 and 12 Av and 4 and 7 C).

Places of interest

Especially interesting is the stately but quaint **Teatro Municipal** (14 Av and 1 C). There is a modern gothic-style church, the

Sagrado Corazón, on the Parque Juárez nr the market; other churches inc **San Juan de Dios** on 14 Av and **La Transfiguración**, from which there is a good view. The **cathedral** is modern with a 17th-century façade. The **Museo de Historia Natural** on the S side of the Parque Central, open Mon-Fri, 0900-1800, Sat 0800-1600 (closed in Dec) has a delightful collection of historical documents, precolumbian pottery, stuffed birds, and many other items. There is also the **Museo de Arte**, 12 Av y 7 C, in the Casa de la Cultura, interesting collection of contemporary Guatemalan art with special exhibitions and a strange collection of stuffed animals.

Excursions

Many places of interest around on roads N to Huehuetenango, W to San Marcos and Mexico, S to Ocós and Champerico. According to folklore, on the Llanos de Urbina near **Olintepeque**, an Indian town 6 km N from Quezaltenango (on a road parallel to the main road), the greatest battle of the conquest was fought, and Alvarado slew King Tecún Umán in single combat. When Tecún Umán was struck, a quetzal is said to have flown out of his chest. The river is still known as Xequizel, the river of blood. Market, Tues, with an unusual emphasis on animals; *fiestas*, June 20-25. The local idol, San Pascual Baillón, has its own little church. Frequent buses from Quezaltenango, US$0.12. A further 8 km to the NE is **San Andrés Xecul**, a small village in beautiful surroundings and a very colourful church with extraordinary figurines (some claim that the church is the oldest in Central America). There is also an attractive chapel, up the cobbled street, similarly painted. Rituals can be observed at the Altar 'Maya'. Small but attractive market, Thur. Direct buses to Quezaltenango, US$0.25. The direct road climbs 18 km to San Carlos Sija, at 2,642m, with wide views. The Spanish strain is still noticeable amongst the inhabitants, most of whom are tall and fair. A climb through conifers for another

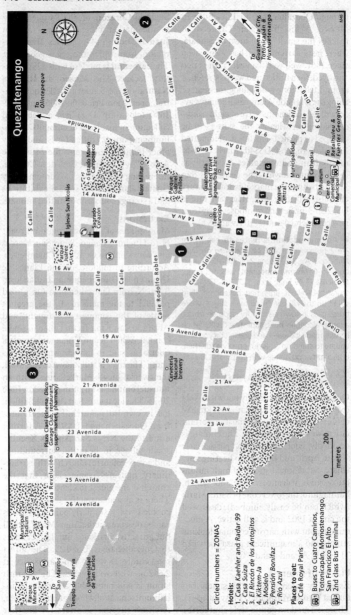

Quezaltenango

Circled numbers = ZONAS

Hotels:
1. Casa Kaehler and Radar 99
2. Casa Suiza
3. El Rincón de los Antojitos
4. Kiktem-Ja
5. Modelo
6. Pensión Bonifaz
7. Río Azul

Places to eat:
8. Café Royal Paris

Buses to Cuatro Caminos, Totonicapán, Momostenango, San Francisco El Alto
2nd class Bus Terminal

Volcanoes and views

To reach the **Santa María volcano** (3,772m) take the bus to Llano del Piñal from the Central bus station (every 30 mins or when full from the Shell station on Av 9; last bus back from Llano del Piñal leaves at 1830; taxi about US$5). Get off at the crossroads and follow the dirt road towards the right side of the volcano until it sweeps up to the right (about 40 mins), where you should take the footpath on the left (marked for some distance); bear right at the saddle where another path comes in from the left – look carefully, it is easily missed. A rough 5½-hr climb (1,500m – take plenty of water) but worth it for the superb views of the Pacific and to watch the still active crater, **Santiaguito** (2,488m), on the Pacific side. Do not attempt to climb this cone, several people were killed in 1990 when overtaken by an eruption. There are frequent clouds of poisonous gas. The volcano can also be reached from Retalhuleu (see page 727) by bus to Palajunoz, from where it is also a 4½-hr climb. It is possible to camp at the summit, or on the saddle W of the summit, but cold and windy. Early morning is the best time for views, and the dawn can be 'magic'. Santa María is popular with picknickers on Sun. You can arrange a guide in Llano del Piñal for about US$6 (eg Alfonso, who lives in the last house on the right before the road turns upward on to the foot of Santa María). There is a good view from the **Siete Orejas volcano** (inactive, 3,370m) 10 km NW of Santa María.

10 km to **Cumbre del Aire**, with grand views behind of volcanoes, and ahead of Cuchumatanes mountains. Another 25 km to the junction with the Pan-American Highway. There are hot steam baths at Los Vahos, reached by a dirt road to the right (3 km) on the outskirts of town on the road to Almolonga; a taxi will take you there and back with a 1 hr wait for US$1.50. 6 km SE is **Almolonga**, which is noted for its fine 16th century church (may be locked) and beautiful costumes, especially skirts, which are hard to buy. There is also a very interesting vegetable market, market days Wed and Sat. *Fiesta* 28-30 June. Good swimming pool (entrance, US$0.25). About 1 km further on are the thermal baths of Cirilo Flores (US$0.50 for large pool, US$1 to soak for an hour, hot, soothing water but heavily used – frequently cleaned) and El Recreo (entrance, US$0.30); bus from Quezaltenango, US$0.15. It is a good 3-4 hrs' walk back over El Baúl; ask in the village. El Baúl itself is a hill to the E of the city, reached by winding road, or direct trail to the top where there is a cross (visible from the city), monument to Tecún Umán.

Local festivals

9-17 Sept and Holy Week (very interesting).

Local information

NB All addresses are Zona 1 unless stated.

● **Accommodation**

At Easter, 12-18 Sept and Christmas, rooms need to be booked well in advance.

A3 *Pensión Bonifaz*, 4 C, 10-50, T 761-4241, F 761-2850, good restaurant (really not a *pensión* but an excellent hotel), clean, comfortable, US cable TV in all rooms, central heating but lower rooms are warmer than upper rooms, quiet, lounge with fireplace (good for taking afternoon coffee and cakes); **A3** *Villa Real Plaza*, 4 C, 12-22, T/F 761-6780, dignified colonial building nicely converted, restaurant has good vegetarian food.

B *Del Campo*, a Best Western lookalike, Km 224 Carretera a Cantel, T 761-1165, F 761-0074, at city limits (4 km) at turn-off to Retalhuleu, good meals (*El Trigal*, European and Chinese), rec; **B** *Modelo*, 14 Av 'A', 2-31, T 761-2529, friendly staff, hot showers, good restaurant (4 course meal US$3) and early breakfast.

C *Casa del Viajero*, 8 Av, 9-17, T 761-0743, with bath, hot water, limited but good restaurant, English-speaking manager, parking (US$0.30 extra), has fax but charges US$10 for one page to USA.

D *Casa Suiza*, 14 Av A, 2-36, T 763-0242, with bath, breakfast US$1.50, pleasant; **D** *Anexo Hotel Modelo*, 14 Av 'A', 3-22, T 761-2606, good value; **D** *Centroamericana Inn*, Blvd Minerva 14-09, Zona 3, T 763-0261; **D** *Gran Hotel Americano*, 14 Av, 3-47, T 761-2118, good, friendly, restaurant, breakfast rec, TV; **D** *Kiktem-Ja*, 13 Av, 7-18, T 761-4304, good location, colonial-style rooms, all with bath, hot water, open fires, car parking inside gates, rec; **D-E** *Río Azul*, 2 C, 12-15, T 763-0654, all rooms with bath, clean, comfortable, friendly, good location, secure, rec; *Arturos*, 14 Av y 3 C, nice atmosphere, friendly, food good.

E *Casa Kaehler*, 13 Av, 3-33, T 761-2091, very nice, clean, hot water all day, some rooms very cold, seen better days but OK; **E** *Los Alpes*, Diagonal 3, 31-04, Zona 3, T 763-5721, Swiss-owned, private bath, rec; **E** *Pensión Altense*, 9 C, 8-48, T 761-2811, with bath (cheaper without), new part rec, hot water extra, restaurant, parking, secure; **E** *Pensión Andina*, 8 Av, 6-07, T 761-4012, hot water am only, friendly, clean, restaurant, good value.

F *El Aguila*, 12 Av y 3 C, no sign, friendly, hot water extra; **F** *El Rincón de los Antojitos*, 15 Av, 4-59, nr the Post Office, see Restaurants below, apartments, minimum 4 days (though may allow one night stops **E**), use of kitchen, English, French and Spanish spoken; **F** *Oriental*, 14 Av nr C 4, shared bath, cable TV, door closes 2100, hot water, safe, friendly; **F** *Pensión El Quijote*, 8 Av A, 7-25, hot water, clean, helpful, good views; **F** *Pensión Horiana*, 14 C, 0-07, clean and friendly; **F** *Radar 99*, 13 Av nr C 4, with bath and hot water (advise the previous night for the morning), cheaper without bath, friendly, not too clean, use of kitchen, padlock useful, will arrange parking in guarded car park opp (Q3); **F** *Casa Argentina*, Diagonal 12, 8-37, hot water, cooking facilities, clean, friendly.

G *Pensión Emperador*, 15 C y 1 Av, clean, no hot water; **G** *Pensión San Nicolás*, Av 12, 3-16, very basic, dirty, friendly, sunny patio, parking; **G** *Regia*, 9 Av y 10 C, narrow rooms, basic; **G** *Quetzalteca*, 12 Av y 3C, basic, clean, cold at night, icy water if there is any.

● **Places to eat**
Kopetin, 14 Av, 3-31, friendly, good, meat and seafood dishes, about US$5.50/meal; *El Maruc*, 23 Av A, 1-16, good, medium-priced, barbecued meat, dancing, rec; *Royal París*, 14 Av A, 3-06, T 761-1943, French owners Bruno and Suzanne moved here 1997, small but reasonably

priced, good food, excellent choice, inc vegetarian, cheap snacks and soups, main course US$5-8, table d'hôte US$2,50, chocolate crêpes, nice atmosphere, live music at weekends, rec; *El Rincón de los Antojitos*, 15 Av y 5 C, French café (French/Guatemalan owned, Thierry y María Antonieta Roquet), French, vegetarian and local cuisine, good food, US$3-4 main course, see also **Travel Agents** below; *Shanghai*, 4 C, 12-22, Chinese, reasonable prices; *Pizza Ricca*, 14 Av, 2-42, good, value, friendly staff, mixed reports; *Pizza Bambino*, 14 Av y 4 C, Zona 3, good prices, popular with gringos, excellent vegetarian pizza; *Giuseppe's Gourmet Pizzas*, Edif Santa Rita, 15 Av, 3-68, excellent pizzas, friendly service; *Pizza Cardinali*, 14 Av, 3-41, good food, owned by Benny, a NY Italian, large pizzas, rec; *Arturo's*, 14 Av 'A', 03-9, good for meat; *Casa Grande*, 4 C, 16-29, Zona 3, good but expensive. **Steakhouses**: *La Rueda*, 4 C, 28-40, Zona 3, 100m from Templo Minerva, Zona 3, expensive; *Pocholo's*, 7 Av, 10-17, Zona 5, international and Spanish; *Panchoy*, 0 C 8-81, Zona 9, expensive. *Albamar*, 4 C 13-84, Zona 3, 12 Av 7-18, Zona 1 and other locations, good meals, nice atmosphere, good service; *El Deli Crepe*, 14 Av, 3-15, good tacos, *almuerzo* US$1.50, great milkshakes, reasonable prices, rec; *Ut'z Hua*, Av 12 y C 3, typical food, very good, filling, inexpensive; *El Chaparral*, 1 C y 14 Av, Zona 3, for good grills, good atmosphere; *Café Baviera* (often called Bavaria), 5 C, 12-50, nice atmosphere, good cheap meals and praised for excellent pies and coffee, good for breakfasts; *Café Berna*, 16 Av, 3-35, Zona 3, good breakfasts, excellent sandwiches, cheesecake, open until 2000, expensive; *La Vienesa*, 9 Av entre 4 y 5 C, bakery/coffee shop, popular with locals, nice place to study local scene; *La Esperanza*, Diagonal 11, good food in evenings, with or without meat, good local information; *Los Balcones*, 7 C, 10-67, next to the cathedral, small, good, classical music; *Café y Chocolate La Luna*, 8 Av, 4-11, good cheap snacks, also very good chocolates, pleasant atmosphere in a colonial house, classical music (more or less), good meeting place, open till 2100; *Café Armadillo Pie*, 4 C, 22-15, Zona 3, new 1997, imported Zurich chocolates and marzipan for sale, good pies and coffee, play dominoes, nice place; *Blue Angel Video Café*, 7 C, 15-22, Zona 1, great salads, light meals, good selection of movies; *Taverna Alemana*, C Rodolfo Robles, 24 Av, away from the centre but worth it, typical German food, run by Guatemalans, variety of imported beers, great giant subs for US$5; *Van Gogh*, 12 Av, 17 C, decorated in Van Gogh style, good; *La Taberna de Don Rodrigo*, 14 Av entre 1-2 C, warm and cosy bar, reasonable food, draught beer in pint glasses; *Aladino's Bar and Restaurant*, 20 Av, 0-66 Zona 3, T 763-1608, Mexican bar, good selection of drinks, excellent food, good music, not expensive; *Salón Tecún*, Edif Pasaje Enríquez, 12 Av, on plaza, bar, local food, video. *Los Antojitos*, 9C, 11-05, good food, draught beer, inexpensive; *Xelapán*, several locations, good cakes and bread, inc wholemeal; *Helados La Americana*, 14 Av, 4-41, Zona 1, best ice cream; *Pan y Pasteles*, 4 C, 26-19, Zona 3, excellent bakery, only open Tues and Fri, 0900-1430, rec. The *comedor* opp Galgos office is rec for good, filling breakfast before a journey.

● **Banks & money changers**
Many banks on the central plaza. **Banco Occidente**, 12 Av, 5-12, on W side, Mon-Fri 0900-1900, Sat 0930-1400. **Banco Inmobiliario**, NW corner; **Banco Industrial**, Visa ATM. Many other banks do Visa but for Mastercharge, go to 2nd floor of the Montblanc commercial building, 4 C, 19 Av, Zona 3 (also Visa); many banks are open 0900-1800 and on Sat am.

● **Cultural centres**
Alianza Francesa de Quezaltenango, 14 Av 'A', A-80, T 761-4076, runs French courses inc one on one tuition, many cultural events (exhibitions, films on Thur evening, lectures, etc).

● **Embassies & consulates**
Consulate: Mexican, 9 Av, 6-19, T 761-1312 to 1316, Mon-Fri 0900-1230, 1400-1600, take photocopies of passport and some nationalities have to show copy of international credit card.

● **Entertainment**
Cinemas: *Cadore*, 13 Av and 7 C, *Roma*, 14 Av 'A' and C 'A'; from US$0.85. *Alpino*, Plaza Ciani, 24 Av y 4 C, Zona 3. See also *Blue Angel Video Café*.
Theatre: *Green House Café-Teatro*, or *Casa Verde*, 12 Av, 1-40, T 763-0271, daily programme of live music, poetry, dance, theatre etc, board games, cheap international calls and fax, useful bulletin board, café/restaurant, bar, best meeting place in town.

● **Hospitals & medical services**
Dr Oscar Armando de León A at the hospital is an English speaking doctor, 9 C, 10-41, T 761-2956. *Dr Luis Méndez*, 1 C 23, Zona 3, also speaks English.

● **Language schools**
There are many schools, most of which offer individual tuition, accommodation with families, extra-curricular activities and excursions. Mayan languages are also offered by some. Several schools fund community development projects and students are invited to participate with voluntary work. Extra-curricular activities are generally better organized at the larger schools (despite the factory atmosphere). Prices start from US$100/week inc accommodation but rise in June-Aug to US$120-150. The following have been rec by students: **English Club and International Language School**, 3 C, 15-16, Apdo Postal 145, T 763-2198. Harry Danvers is an expert on indigenous culture, worth a visit. **Projecto Lingüístico Quezalteco de Español**, 5 C, 2-40, T/F 763-1061, see also under Todos Santos Cuchumatán for US and European offices. For information also write to National Registration Center for Study Abroad, 823 N 2nd St, PO Box 1393, Milwaukee, WI 53201, USA; **Casa de Español Xelahú**, 9 C, 11-29, T/F 761-2628, USA contact: 2206, Falcon Hill Drive, Austin TX 78745, T 512-416-6991, F 512-414-8965; **Spanish School Juan Sisay**, 15 Av, 8-38, Apartado Postal 392, T/F 763-1684; **Instituto Central América (ICA)**, 1 C, 16-93, T/F 763-1871, in USA: RR Box 101, Stanton, Nebraska, 68779 T 402-439-2943, Internet access for students' use (for a fee); **Centro de Estudios de Español Pop Wuj**, 1 C, 17-72, 5 C, 2-40, T/F 761-8286; **Desarrollo del Pueblo**, 19 Av 0-34, Zona 3, T/F 761-6754, Apartado Postal 41, in UK, Hannah Roberts, 48 Thorncliffe Rd, Oxford OX2 7BB, T (01865) 552653; **Ulew Tinimit**, 8 Av 3-30, PO Box 346, T/F 763-1713; **Academia Latinoamericana Mayense (ALM)**, 15 Av, 6-75, PO Box 375 and 376, T 761-2707; **Projecto Lingüístico de Santa María**, 14 Av 'A', 1-26, Apartado Postal 230, T 761-2570, F 761-8281; **Utatlán**, 12 Av, 4-32, PO Box 239, T 763-0446, possibility of voluntary work with under-privileged children; **Centro del Lenguaje América Latina**, 19 Av, 3-63, Zona 3, T 761 6416; **Minerva Spanish School**, 24 Av, 4-39; **Guatemalensis**, 19 Av, 2-41; **Kie-Balam**, Diagonal 12 4-46, T 761-1636; also rec is **Q'anil**, Encuentro de Expresión Cultural, 15 Av, 6-24, Zona 3, small, non-profit collective, also teaches traditional music; **La Paz**, 2 C, 19-30, T 761-4253; **INEPAS**, 15 Av, 5 C, information at *Rincón de los Antojitos*. See also *AmeriSpan* under Antigua, **Tourist offices**.

● **Libraries**
Bellas Letras, C 3, between Avs 12 and 13, Zona 1, good, Spanish, English, German books, lots about Guatemala, language books.

● **Laundry**
Minimax, 14 Av C-47, T 761-2952, 0730-1930, US$2.15, wash and dry; *Lavandería Pronto*, 7 C, 13-25, Zona 1, good cheap service; *Lavandería El Centro*, 15 Av, 3-51, Zona 1, US$2 wash and dry, very good service.

● **Post & telecommunications**
Post and Telegraph Office: 15 Av and 4 C, Telephone (Guatel) 13 Av between 6 and 7 C, Zona 1, and 15 Av and 3 C, Zona 3, nr Mercado La Democracia. The Tourist Service Centre (CEDEM) on C Rodolfo Robles 17-23 will send a fax cheaper than Guatel, eg US$10/min to UK compared with US$22/sheet at Guatel, you can also receive phone calls here. Other places to try are *Maya Communications*, Edif Salón Tecún, Pasaje Enríquez, also e-mail, which is interlinked with offices in Antigua and Panajachel, T/F 761-2832; *Green House Café*, see under **Theatre**; *Speed Calls*, behind the Post Office. Check around for the best rates.

● **Shopping**
For local items try the markets of which there are 4: main market at **Templo de Minerva** at Western edge of town (take local bus, US$0.04), has craft section; at the SE corner of **Parque Centro América** (central park) is a shopping centre with craft stalls on the upper levels, food, clothes, etc below; another market at 2 C y 16 Av, Zona 3, S of Parque Benito Juárez. *Típica Chivita*, Centro Comercial Municipal, 2nd level, makes up locally produced woollen blankets into jackets. *Xekijel*, 7 C, 10/11 Av, T 761-4734, just off plaza, same side of road as tourist office, very good for textile lengths and *artesanía*. *Talabartería Quetgo*, C Rodolfo Robles, 15-53, excellent selection, good starting prices. Every first Sun of the month, there is an *artesanía* market in central park, with a marimba band playing in the morning. Of the markets around Quetzaltenango, the more interesting are in Zunil, San Andrés Xecul and San Francisco el Alto. For food shopping, in the *Mont Blanc* commercial centre, *El País*, 4 C y 19 Av, Zona 3. Good shops, boutiques and food in El Portal commercial centre, 13 Av, 5-38. *Mérida* supermarket in the *mercado*, Av 15, C 1, Zona 3.

Bookshops: *Bellas Letras*, 3 C, 12-31, T 763-4680, new and second hand books in several languages, maps etc; *Vrisa*, 15 Av, 0-67, has a good range of English language 2nd hand paperbacks, rec.

Photography: good quality development at Konica, 15 Av opp Post Office.

● **Sports**
Climbing: for rock climbing on neighbouring volcanoes, contact Miguel Morales, 4 C, Diag 3-67, T 756-2105 (home), 761-4673 (office). For general mountain climbing: *Asociación Quezalteca de Andinismo*, trekking and volcano climbing, meetings at 5 C, 8-43 on Tues 2030, good Spanish and some experience very useful.

Tennis: *Club Tenís Quezalteco*, 4 C, 18-50, Zona 3, T 761-2356, for information and temporary membership

● **Tour companies & travel agents**
SAB Agencia de Viajes, 1 C, 12-35, T 761-6402. Thierry Roquet at *El Rincón de los Antojitos* restaurant arranges trips to volcanoes, hot springs, markets, etc. A guide, José, advertises in Post Office, cafés, friendly Spanish teacher, speaks English, can take you to Santa María Volcano, US$8 pp, Laguna Chicabal, US$7 pp, or hot springs, usually at weekends.

● **Tourist office**
Oficina Regional de Turismo, 7 C, 11-35, SW corner of the Plaza, Mon-Fri, 0900-1200, 1430-1700, T 761-4931, helpful, free maps of city.

● **Useful addresses**
Hairdresser: Sala de Belleza Anny, good haircut US$6, 13 Av, 4-60, Zona 3, Plaza Monterrey, ask for Anny.

Insurance: Granai and Townson motoring insurance from Seguros Occidental behind Banco del Café, which is on main plaza.

Mechanic: Taller Enderezad, corner of 8 Av and 3 C, Zona 1, rec for car repairs. Also Don Abdullio at 6 C, 5-48, Zona 2.

Volunteer work: SCDRYS, Sociedad Civil para Desarrollo Replicable y Sostenible, Diagonal 11, 7-17 (1 block from *Blue Angel Video Café*) for social work opportunities in the area and Quiché (ask for Guillermo Díaz).

● **Transport**
Local Bicycle hire: *Xela Sin Límites* travel agency, 12 Av, 1 C, T/F 761-6043, US$6/day, US$30/week, deposit required.

Buses Rutas Lima, 11 Av, 3-68, Zona 1 and 2 C, 6-32, Zona 2, T 761-4134 and 761-2033 (best), 4 a day to **Guatemala City** (US$2.50, 4 hrs). The 0800 bus has connections to Chichicastenango, Panajachel (US$1.25, 3 hrs) and

Sololá (US$1.25, 2½ hrs). Galgos, C Rodolfo Robles 17-43, T 761-2248, Zona 3, 1st class buses to Guatemala City, 7 a day from 0330-1645 (US$4.15, 4 hrs, will carry bicycles); Marquensita twice a day, US$2.50 (office in the capital 21 C, 1-56, Zona 1). Líneas América to Guatemala City, 2 a day from 7 Av, 3-33 Zona 2, T 761-4587. For **Antigua**, change at Chimaltenango (Galgos, US$3 to Chimaltenango 0800, 1000, Rutas Lima 0715, 1415). To **Huehuetenango** 0500 and 1530, US$1. From Quezaltenango you can get to three border crossings: La Mesilla via Huehuetenango (if you cannot get a regular bus catch a chicken bus from behind the market, no 13 on map, plenty of them and not too crowded early in the morning); Talismán bridge and Tecún Umán (frequent buses from there to Tapachula), buses run all day from Minerva terminal, but you will probably have to change buses in Malacatán. To **San Pedro** (see page 723) at 1200. Regular buses to **Cuatro Caminos** US$0.40 (where buses for Guatemala City and Huehuetenango stop on the highway), bus Guatemala City-Cuatro Caminos, US$1.65), **Totonicapán**, 1 hr (US$0.35), **San Francisco El Alto** (US$0.35) and **Momostenango** (0600, US$0.55). Also many second class buses to many parts of the country from Zona 3 market by Parque Minerva (13 Av y 4 C'A'), eg Transportes Velásquez to **Huehuetenango**, US$1, 2 hrs; to **Malacatán**, 5 hrs, US$2; to **Los Encuentros**, US$2; to **Chichicastenango**, Transportes Veloz, US$1, 2½ hrs; to **Panajachel**, Transportes Morales, US$2, 2½ hrs; to **Zunil**, US$0.30, 40 mins; also to **La Mesilla** at 0800. Bus to town from 2nd class terminal, No 3 from just below Templo de Minerva through the market.

QUEZALTENANGO TO CHAMPERICO

Via Retalhuleu the 53-km link between the old Pan-American Highway and Pacific Highway, is paved all the way. A toll (Quezaltenango-Retalhuleu, US$0.25) is collected. The first town (11 km) is **Cantel**, which has the largest textile factory in the country. Market, Sun; *fiestas*, 12-18 Aug (main day 15) and a passion play at Easter.

ZUNIL

9 km from Quezaltenango is **Zunil**, picturesquely located in the canyon of Río Samalá. Market, Mon, Fri, small and colourful but drowned if two busloads of tourists come in (beware pickpockets); *fiesta*, 22-26 Nov (main day 25), and a very colourful Holy Week. On the Sat there is a very slow procession through the village, followed by a performance of Christ's life in the plaza outside the church (fascinating to watch the crowd's enjoyment), lots of comedy. No market that Mon when the inhabitants go to the cemetery and pray for their dead. Striking church, inside and out. The local sacred idol is San Simón, a life size dummy, dressed differently at different times, eg in ski wear: hat, scarf, gloves and sunglasses, or in a black suit and wide-brimmed hat, complete with cigar; the statue is moved from time to time to different houses. Enquire locally for the present location. A small charge is usually made or a donation expected. Behind the church is a cooperative (*Santa Ana*) which sells beautiful *huipiles*, and shirt and skirt materials.

Zunil mountain, rises to 3,542m to the SE of the town. On its slopes are the thermal baths of **Fuentes Georginas**, entrance US$1, closed Mon for cleaning; **E** *Turicentro Fuentes Georginas*, bungalows (a bit run down) with 2 double beds, cold shower, fireplace with wood, no electricity after 2100, candles provided, fair restaurant, beware overcharging, barbecue grills for guests' use near baths, in attractive surroundings. Reasonably priced food and drinks available. The Fuentes' temperature and water level have been reduced as a result of a geothermal energy project nearby and are now only lukewarm. There are steam vents in the slopes above the Fuentes, worth a 45 mins' hike up the hill. The path is in good condition, but keep left to avoid a cul-de-sac. Fuentes Georginas can be reached either by walking the 8 km, uphill (300m ascent; take right fork after 4 km, robbery is common here, latest report end 1994) to S of Zunil, by pickup truck (US$5.50), or hitch a ride. Alternatively, take the bus from Quezaltenango to Mazatenango, but get out at the sign to Fuentes Georginas, or ask for advice in Zunil. Taxi from Quezaltenango is about US$11. The springs are 13 km from Almolonga (see page 717). The thermal baths of Aguas Amargas are also on Zunil mountain, below Fuentes Georginas; they are reached by a road E before Santa María de Jesús is reached.

The road descends through Santa María de Jesús (large hydro-electric station) to **San Felipe**, at 760m, 35 km from Zunil. Tropical jungle fruits. Beyond, 3 km, is San Martín, with a branch road to Mazatenango. **NB** The main road bypasses San Felipe, which has a one-way road system (delays of up to 1½ hrs if you go through the town).

MAZATENANGO

18 km from San Martín, **Mazatenango** (*pop* 37,850; *alt* 380m) is the chief town of the Costa Grande zone. It is not especially attractive though the Parque Central is very pleasant with many fine shade trees. Chitalón airfield is 3 km away. The Pacific Highway passes through. The road is paved to Quezaltenango. There is a huge festival in the last week of Feb, when hotels are very full and double their prices. At that time, beware of children carrying (and throwing) bags of flour. There is a cinema.

● **Accommodation D** *Hotel Alba*, 1 C, 0-26, Zona 2, T 872-0264, OK; **E** *Roma*, 6 Av, 3-30, T 872-2129, quiet street in pleasant area, very nice; **E** *La Gran Tasca*, 7 Av, 4-53, T 872-0316, with bath, fan, cable TV, friendly owners, good value, rec; **E** *Recreo*, Av La Libertad 8-27, T 872-0435, friendly family, close to main plaza but noisy; **F** *Sarah*, by railway station, with bath; **F** *Santa Bárbara*, bottom of 6 Av facing railway station, clean, nice; **G** *Chinchilla*, 4 C, 5-17, beside church on Parque Central, clean, friendly, cafetería attached; **G** *Gloria*, 5 C, 1-13, ½ block from Texaco station, quiet side street, clean, decent; **G** *Costa Rica*, 1 Av, 7 C.

● **Places to eat** *Maxim's*, 6 Av, 9-23, extensive *churrasco* and Chinese menus, reasonable prices, spotless, interesting range of Chinese porcelain for sale, highly rec; *Pagoda Dorada*, 9 C, 6-17, average Chinese, locally popular,

inexpensive; *Pizza Cardinale*, 1 Av, 10 C, good pizzas, take away service; *Yogen Früz*, 6 Av, 9-33, fresh fruit yogurts a speciality; *Holanda Helados*, Parque Central, huge choice of ice creams; *Croissants Pastelería*, Parque Central, excellent pastries, juice etc.

● **Banks & money changers** Banco de Los Trabajadores, 7 C, 3-18, Zona 1; Banco Occidente, 6 Av, 8 C (Visa); Banco Industrial, 7 C, 2-52 (TCs); Bancor, 1 C, 1 Av (Visa and Mastercard); Bancafé, 1 C, 1 Av, Zona 2 (TCs).

● **Buses** They leave frequently from Esso station to Guatemala City, US$1.50; to the border at Tecún Umán US$1.50.

7 km W of Mazetenamgo is **Cuyotenango** (**C** *Posada del Sol*, T 872-0166, bungalows, a/c, hot water, pool, parking, restaurant, quiet, clean, friendly), where a dirt road goes 65 km down to the coast, at **El Tulate**. There is a white sand bar with a lagoon behind.

RETALHULEU

NB Retalhuleu is normally referred to as 'Reu', both in conversation and on bus signs.

Southwest 11 km from San Martín is **Retalhuleu** (*pop* 42,000; *alt* 240m), capital of the Department of the same name with a fine *Palacio del Gobierno*. It serves a large number of coffee and sugar estates. **Museo de Archaeología y Etnología**, next to the *Palacio*, small but interesting collection and a permanent exhibition of photos of old Retalhuleu, entry US$1. *Fiesta*, 6-12 December.

● **Accommodation B** *Posada de Don José*, 5 C, 3-67, T 771-0180, good food, closed for renovations, reopening late 1997; **C** *Siboney*, 5 km NW of Reu in San Sebastián, Km 179, T 771-0149, F 771-0711, with bath, bungalow style round large pool, excellent restaurant, try *caldo de mariscos* US$6, *paella* for two US$11; **D** *Astor*, 5 C, 4-50, Zona 1, T 771-0475; **E** *Modelo*, 5 C, 4-53, T 771-0256, front rooms noisy; **G** *Pacífico*, 7 Av, 9-29, opp Mercado San Nicolás, dismal, last resort only; **G** *Santa Bárbara*, opp station, fan, bath, clean, secure, parking. **Motel: B** *La Colonia* (swimming pool), 1½ km to the N at Km 178, T 771-0054, is good, good food, rec.

● **Places to eat** *La Luna*, 5 C, 4-97, on Parque Central good *típico* meals: breakfast US$2.15, lunch and dinner US$2.65, also Chinese menu, OK; *El Volován*, on Parque Central, delicious cakes, pies and ice creams; *Stivi's Café*, 5 Av, 2 C, good snacks, salads, milk shakes, better than average coffee, modern, comfortable, pleasant atmosphere; *Pollo Llanero*, 7 Av, 8-39, clean, good, inexpensive.

● **Banks & money changers** Banco del Agro, TCs; Banco Industrial, TCs, Visa; Banco Occidente, Mastercard; Banco Inmobiliario, Mastercard.

CHAMPERICO

43 km SW of Retalhuleu by a paved road, Champerico was once the third most important port in the country, is little used now (*pop* 4,500). Good black sand beach but there is a strong undercurrent; good fishing. There is a municipal fresh water swimming pool US$0.50. Mosquitoes, day and night.

● **Accommodation D** *Posada del Mar*, on outskirts of town, Km 222, T 773-7104; **E** *El Submarino*, at beach end of 3 Av, T 773-7237, cheerful rooms with comfortable beds and modern plumbing, TV, good restaurant overlooking beach; **F** *Miramar*, 2 C, Av Coatepeque, T 773-7231, nice restaurant with dark wood bar, Spanish owners, good; **F** *Martita*, opp *Miramar*, with bath cheaper without, fan, restaurant; **G** *Hospedaje Buenos Aires*, 3 Av, 4 C, clean, neat rooms in nice clapboard house with balcony, bit noisy from traffic; **G** *Hospedaje Recinos*, 7 C, Av Coatepeque, clean but small dark rooms, basic.

● **Places to eat** *Alcatraz*, next to *El Submarino*, good; *Frutilandia*, 3 Av opp market, juices, *liquados*, ice cream. Other good restaurants on the beach.

● **Post & telecommunications Post Office** 1 C, just off 3 Av. **Guatel**: 2 C, 3 Av, beside Palacio Municipal.

● **Buses** To Quezaltenango direct 0400, 0600 and 0800. Later, change at Reu. Every 30 mins to **Retalhuleu**. Direct bus to **Guatemala City**, 0245, 0545, 1030, 4-5 hrs.

QUEZALTENANGO WEST TO MEXICO

15 km to **San Juan Ostuncalco** (*alt* 2,530m), a pleasant, prosperous town, noted for good weekly market on Sun and beautiful sashes worn by men. *Fiesta*, Virgen de la Candelaria, 29 Jan-2 February. See below for road S to Pacific town of Ocós. The road, which is paved, then switchbacks 37 km down valleys and over pine-clad mountains to a plateau looking over the valley in which are San Pedro and San Marcos, also known as La Unión. **San Marcos** (*alt* 2,350m), is 1 km or so beyond San Pedro. **San Pedro** (full name San Pedro Sacatepéquez, same name as the town near Guatemala City) has a huge market Thur. Its Sun market is less interesting. There is an interesting Palacio Municipal (known as the Palacio Maya) built in 1926, with a wooden clocktower. The Indian women wear golden-purple skirts.

Tajumulco volcano, 4,220m (the highest in Central America), can be reached by taking the road from San Marcos to San Sebastián; after the latter, several km on is the summit of a pass at which a junction to the right goes to Tacana, and to the left is the start of the ascent of Tajumulco, about 5 hrs' climb. Once you have reached the ridge on Tajumulco, turn right along the top of it; there are two peaks, the higher is on the right. The one on the left is used for shamanistic rituals; people are not very friendly, so do not climb alone. The last bus back from Tajumulco village leaves about 1500 so you need to start out from San Marcos very early, 0200 bus rec, very slow road, 20 km takes 2 hrs, no accommodation available on the way. Ask in the village of Tuchán for Juan Pérez y Pérez, a guide who lives at the start of the climb, US$5 pp. Take a bus early in the morning from San Pedro to Tuchán. **Tacana** volcano may be climbed from Sibinal village.

About 15 km W of San Marcos the road begins its descent from 2,500m to the lowlands. In 53 km to **Malacatán** it drops

to 366m. This was one of the toughest
stretches in Central America, but now
the surface is paved. It is a tiring ride
with continuous bends, but the scenery
is attractive.

● **Accommodation & places to eat** At **San
Juan Ostuncalco**: F *Ciprés Inn*, 6 Av, 1-29,
T 761-6174, clean, hot water, good atmosphere,
TV, good restaurant, traditional blue wooden
building, converted private house (1992), modern
bathrooms, highly rec; F *El Embajador*, 7 C, 1 Av,
good views; *Ricafé* for burgers and sandwiches,
aquarium. At **San Marcos**: **E-F** *Maya*, negotiate
price, shower, hot water; **E** *Pérez*, 9 C, 2-25,
T 760-1007, with good dining room, meals US$2.
At **San Pedro**: **G** *Bagod*, fallen on hard times,
noisy; **G** *Bethalonia*, 3 blocks N of main plaza;
G *El Valle*, simple but clean; *Pensión Victoria*,
4C and 9 Av, basic but clean, rooms around a
central courtyard, pleasant owner. **Restaurants**:
La Cueva de Los Faraones, 5 C, 1-11, a real Italian
menu, chef Sr Franco Manzini, moderate prices,
rec; *Brasilia*, 7 Av, 4-19, excellent typical breakfast
for US$0.85. At **Malacatán**: **E** *La Estancia*, 3 C,
3-43, T 776-9382; F *América*, lunch, US$1,
good; F *Pensión Santa Lucía*, 5 C, 5-25, Zona 1,
T 776-9415. Several *hospedajes*, **G**.

The international bridge over the
Suchiate River at **Talismán** into Mexico
is 18 km W of Malacatán. Beyond the
bridge the road goes on to Tapachula.

FRONTIER WITH MEXICO – TALISMAN/TAPACHULA

● **Guatemalan immigration**
Normally open 24 hrs. It is a 200m walk between
the two border posts.

NB We have received reports of armed robberies
at the border day and night eg in the toilets.

● **Mexican consulate**
There is a service at the border and at Malacatán
(closed at 1300).

● **Crossing by private vehicle**
If entering by car, especially a rented car, be
prepared for red tape, miscellaneous charges,
vehicle fumigation and frustration. See **Information for travellers**. There are lots of pushy
children around, employing one of them for
US$2-3 could smooth progress.

● **Accommodation**
There is a *hospedaje* at the border but better
accomodation nearby (see above) or in Mexico.

● **Exchange**
Money changers offer the same (reasonable)
rates on both sides of the border. There is no
bank on the Guatemalan side.

● **Transport**
From the border to Quezaltenango, it is best to
go via Retalhuleu (take Galgos bus from the
border), but you can go by bus to Malacatán,
then bus (or taxi US$5) to San Marcos, 1½ hrs,
lovely scenery, walk up hill to Parque Central,
ask for Galgos bus stop or catch a van, US$0.70
pp plus US$0.70 for bags on top, to Quezal-
tenango). Beware of overcharging on buses
from the border to Quezaltenango. Bus Talis-
mán-Guatemala City, US$4, Galgos 6 a day, 5
hrs because of checkpoints, or you can go to
Malacatán for direct buses to Guatemala City.
Guatemala City-Mexico City in 1 day is possible
if you start early enough and allow plenty of
time for the border crossing.
  This border is not used much by heavy transport. Hitchhikers will find Tecún Umán better.

Travelling by bus to Mexico is quicker from
Quezaltenango than from San Marcos. Most
traffic seems to go via Coatepeque and not via
San Marcos; the former road is longer but is
reported very good. From Quezaltenango, there
are frequent buses to Talismán via San Marcos
or Coatepeque, and probably more via
Coatepeque to Ciudad Tecún Umán; buses from
Xela marked 'Talismán' usually involve a change
in Malacatán, 40 mins from border (US$0.30 by
bus from shelter at back of Malacatán bus
station). From San Pedro, frequent local buses
from 0430 to 1630 to Malacatán, from where
colectivos, often crowded, will get you to the
border. Or take bus from Quezaltenango to
Retalhuleu, 1½ hrs, US$0.55, then another to
the border, 2 hrs, US$1.85.

After San Juan Ostuncalco (see above), go S
for 1½ km to **Concepción Chiquirichapa**,
one of the wealthiest villages in the country.
It has a small market early every Thur morning. *Fiesta* 5-9 December.

SAN MARTIN SACATEPEQUEZ

5½ km beyond is **San Martín** (sometimes
known as Chile Verde, famous for its hot
chillies; this village appears in Miguel Angel Asturias' *Mulata de Tal*), in a windy,
cold gash in the mountains. *Huipiles* and
shirts from the cottage up behind the
church. Accommodation next door to the

Centro de Salud (ask at the Centro), US$0.50. Food in *comedor* opp church, US$0.20. Indians speak a dialect of Mam not understood by other Maya tribes, having been separated from them during the Quiché invasion of the Guatemalan highlands. The men wear very striking costumes. Market, Sun. *Fiesta* 7-12 Nov (main day 11). Ceremonies of initiation held on 2 May at nearby **Laguna Chicabal**, in the crater of a volcano. The walk to the lake from San Martín takes about 2 hrs, ask any campesino for the path to Laguna Chicabal. It is possible to camp at the lake. The last bus to Quezaltenango leaves at 1900.

COATEPEQUE

The road descends to lowlands. From Colomba a road branches S (28 km) to Retalhuleu: the road to Ocós runs 21 km W from Colomba to **Coatepeque** (*pop* 13,657; *alt* 700m); one of the richest coffee zones in the country; also maize, sugarcane and bananas, and cattle. *Fiesta*, 11-19 March.

● **Accommodation A3** *Virginia*, at Km 220, T/F 775-1801; **D** *Villa Real*, 6 C, 6-57, T 775-1939; **E** *Baechli*, 6 C, 5-35, T 775-1483; **E** *Europa*, 6 C, 4-01, T 775-1860; **F** *Posada Santander*, 6 C, 6-43; **F** *Residencial*, 0 Av, 11-49, Zona 2, T 775-2018.

● **Banks & money changers** Banco Continental, BAM, Bancafé and several others.

● **Buses** Bus from Quezaltenango, US$0.40 (buses to/from the capital as for Talismán).

Both railway and paved Pacific Highway go to **Tecún Umán**, 34 km W, on the Mexican frontier, separated by the Río Suchiate from the Mexican town of Ciudad Hidalgo.

FRONTIER WITH MEXICO – TECUN UMAN/CIUDAD HIDALGO

● **Guatemalan immigration**
The 1 km bridge over the river separates the two border posts. Pedestrians pay US$0.15, cycle taxis cost US$1, toll for cars. For a fee, boys will help you with your luggage. Open normally 24 hrs

● **Mexican consulates**
See Malacatán and Quezaltenango.

● **Accommodation**
E *Maxcel*, 3 Av, 1 C, Zona 2; **F** *Lourdes*, 1 Av A, Zona 1.

● **Exchange**
Banco de Guatemala, 1 Av entre 4 y 5 C, Zona 2, and other banks will not cash pesos. Money changers on the street, will. Reasonable rates reported.

● **Transport**
Buses run from the Mexican side of the border to Tapachula, 30 mins, cheap (beware of overcharging). The bus to Guatemala City costs US$4, run by Fortaleza, 4 direct buses daily, 5 hrs, frequent slower buses via Retalhuleu and Mazatenango. Colectivo from Coatepeque, US$0.50. Trains to Guatemala City have been suspended. See also under the Talismán crossing.

Ocós, a small port now closed to shipping, is served by a 22-km road S from Tecún Umán. Across the river from Ocós is **Tilapa**, a small resort; buses from Coatepeque and ferries from Ocós (**G** *Pensión Teddy*, friendly). The swimming is good, but both here and at Ocós there are sharks, so stay close to the shore.

Information for travellers

BEFORE TRAVELLING

ENTRY REQUIREMENTS

● Documents

Only a valid passport is required for citizens of: all Western European countries; USA, Canada, Mexico and all Central American countries; Panama, Brazil, Chile, Paraguay, Uruguay and Venezuela; Australia, Israel, Japan and New Zealand. Visas (US$10) or Tourist Cards (US$5) are required by citizens of Bahrain, Kuwait, Saudi Arabia, Czech Republic, Slovakia, Poland, Philippines, Iceland and South Africa. All others must have a visa, which may require prior reference to immigration authorities in Guatemala which takes 3-4 weeks. Visas, tourist cards and passport stamps are normally valid for 30 days (but may be granted for longer if you ask). Tourist cards may be given to you at land frontiers and should be free if not otherwise required. However, regulations change frequently, best to check in advance with consulates in your home country before leaving. Children under 13 do not require a tourist card provided their name is included on their parents' document.

Tourist cards must be renewed in Guatemala City after 30 days (visas also after 30 days or on expiry) at the immigration office: *Dirección General de Migración*, 41 C, 17-36, Zona 8, T 475-1390, open weekdays 0800-1600. This office extends visas and renews tourist cards on application (before noon) for 30 days at a time (up to 90 days maximum), this takes at least 1 day, usually two (but you will have to insist in

any event), costs US$10, fingerprints and photograph required, and you may not be given the full 90 days. To stay more than 6 months, seek permission at the Immigration Department in Guatemala City. You may need stamped paper (*papel sellado*). Avoid Fri, get there early. Diplomatic passport holders go to the Ministerio de Relaciones Exteriores in the National Palace, Zona 1. Multiple entry visas for tourist purposes only are free for US citizens and are valid for 3 or 5 years (very useful if travelling back and forth between neighbouring countries). Business visas cost US$10. Two photographs and a letter from the company (in duplicate) required. If experiencing obstruction in renewing a visa, it is easier to leave the country for 3 days and then come back.

Although not officially required, some airlines may not allow you to board a flight to Guatemala without an outward ticket (eg SAM in Colombia).

Apart from the visa or tourist card charge, there should be no other entry fees if you are travelling by public transport; see note on **Taxes** below. For cars, see under **Road Travel**. If entering overland it is most advisable to have obtained a visa in advance (fewer hassles).

Identification must always be carried while you are in Guatemala for police and military checks.

● Representation overseas

Argentina, Avenida Santa Fe No 830, 5th floor, CP 1059, Buenos Aires, T (1) 3139180, F 3139181 (also covers **Paraguay**); **Austria**, Salesianergasse 25/5, A-1030, Vienna, T (1)

7143570, F 7143569 (also covers **Hungary** and **Romania**); **Barbados**, 2nd floor, Trident House, Broad Street, Bridgetown, T 4352542, F 4352638; **Belgium**, Avenue Winston Churchill, 185, 1180, Brussels, T (2) 3456992, F 3446499 (also covers **Holland** and **Luxembourg**); **Belize**, 1 St John St, Belize City, T (2) 33314, F 35140; **Brazil**, Shis QL. 08, Conjunto 05, Casa 11, Brasilia, CEP 70460, T (61) 2483164, F 2484383; **Canada**, 130 Albert St, Suite 1010, Ottawa, Ontario, KIP 5G4, T (613) 2337237, F 2330135; **Chile**, Casilla No 36, Correo 10 Los Condes, Santiago, T (2) 3414012, F 2253630; **China (Taiwan)**, 12, Lane 88 Chien Kuo, North Road, Section 1, Taipei, T (2) 5077043, F 5060577; **Colombia**, Transversal 29 A, No 139A-41, Bogotá, T (1) 2580746, F 2745365; **Costa Rica**, De la *Pizza Hut* en Plaza del Sol, Curridabat, 50m E, 100m N, 50m E, Casa No 3, San José, T 2245721, F 2832556.

Dominican Republic, Pedro Enriquez Ureña, No 136-A, Ensanche La Esperilla, Santo Domingo, T 5670110, F 5670115 (also covers **Haiti**); **Ecuador**, Avenida Republica No 192, y Diego de Almagro, Edif Casa Blanca, 4th floor B, Quito, T (2) 545714, F 501927; **Egypt**, Mohamed Fahmi El Mohdar St, No 8, Madinet Nasr, Cairo, T (2) 2611114, F 2611814 (also covers **Turkey**); **El Salvador**, 15 Avenida Norte, No 135, San Salvador, T 2712225, F 2213019; **France**, 73 Rue de Courcelles, 75008 Paris, T (1) 42277863, F 47540206 (also covers **Portugal** and **Switzerland**); **Germany**, Zietenstrasse 16, 53173, Bonn, T (228) 351579, F 354940; **Honduras**, Calle Principal, Colonia Loma Linda Norte, Tegucigalpa, T 325018, F 315655; **Israel**, 74 Hey De'lyar St, Apt 6, Kikar Hamedina, 62198, Tel Aviv, T (3) 5467372, F 5467317 (also covers **Greece**); **Italy**, Via Dei Colli della Farnesina 128, 00194, Rome, T (6) 36303750, F 3291639; **Japan**, Nr 38 Kowa Bldg, Room 905, Nishi-Azabu, Minato-Ku, Tokoyo 106, T (3) 38001830, F 34001820 (also covers **Australia**, **Bangladesh**, **India**, **Iraq**, **Philippines** and **Thailand**); **Korea (South)**, 602 Garden Tower Building, 98-78 Wooni-Dong, Chongro-Ku, Seoul, 110-350, T (2) 7653265, F 7636010.

Mexico, Avenida Explanada No 1025, Lomas de Chapultepec, 11000 Mexico, DF, T (5) 5407520, F 2021142; **Nicaragua**, Km 11½ de la carretera a Masaya, Managua, T (2) 799609, F 799610; **Norway**, Oscars Gate 59, 0258, Oslo, T (22) 556004, F 556047 (also covers **Denmark**); **Panama**, Calle Abel Bravo y Calle 57, Bella Vista, Edif Torre Cancún, Apt 14-A, Panama City, T 269-3475, F 223-1922;

Peru, Inca Ricap No 309, Lima 11, T/F (14) 635885 (also covers **Bolivia**); **Poland**, Ul Genewska 37, 03-940 Warsaw, T (22) 6178342 (also covers **Ukraine**); **Russia**, Karoby Val No 7, Apt 92, 117049, Moscow, T (095) 2382214, F 9566270; **Spain**, Calle Rafael Salgado No 3, 4th Izquierda, 28036, Madrid, T (1) 3441417, F 4587894 (also covers **Morocco**); **Sweden**, Wittstockgaten 30, S 115, 27 Stockholm, T (8) 6805229, F 6604229 (also covers **Finland**); **Uruguay**, Rambla República del Perú 757, Apt 602, Montevideo, T (2) 719497, F 701366; **USA**, 2220 R St NW, Washington DC, 20008, T (202) 7454952, F 7451908; **Venezuela**, Avenida Francisco Miranda Torre Deaza, Primer Nivel, Urb El Rosal, Caracas, T (2) 9521166, F 9521992.

● **Tourist information**

Instituto Guatemalteco de Turismo (Inguat), 7 Av 1-17, Zona 4, Centro Cívico, Apartado Postal 1020-A, Guatemala City, T 331-1333, 331-1347, F 331-8893, 331-4416, e-mail: inguat@geo2.poptel.org:uk, INGUAT@Guate.net, www.travel-guatemala.org.gt. Inguat provides bus timetables, hotel and camping lists and road maps. Tourist information is provided at the Mexican border for those entering Guatemala. Maps inc Belize as Guatemalan territory. Roads marked in the Petén are inaccurate.

Amerindia, based in Quito, is a new regional ground operator, who operates in Guatemala, Costa Rica and Belize (as well as in Peru, Bolivia and Ecuador). It has been created to rediscover the wonders of Latin America. Tours of the highest quality with experienced guides are offered. Accommodation is in superb lodges. Among the tours available will be yacht charters along coasts, luxury safari-style tents and Land Rover circuits. Further information from Amerindia's head office T (543) 2 439 736/469 455, F (543) 2 439 735, e-mail: amerindi@pi.pro.ec; in UK from Penelope Kellie T (44) 1962 779317, F (44) 1962 779458, e-mail: pkellie@yachtors.u-net.com; in USA T (1) 305 599 9008, F (1) 305 592 7060.

● **Tourist offices overseas**

Inguat: **USA**, 299 Alhambra Circle, Suite 510, Coral Gables, Florida 33134, T 305-442-0651/442-0412, F 442-1013, 1-800-742-4529; **Mexico**, Río Nilo 55, Mezzanine 1, Col Cuauhtémoc, CP 06500, DF, T/F 525-208-1991; **Dominican Republic**, Pedro Enríquez Ureña, 136-A, Apdo 235, Santo Domingo, T 809-563-1792, F 809-567-0115; **Italy**, Viale Prassilla 152, 00124, Rome, T 396-50-91-2740,

F 505-3406; **Spain**, Calle Rafael Salgado 3, 4th Izquierda, 28036 Madrid, T/F 341-344-1559; **Canada**, 72 McGill St, Toronto, Ontario, M4B 1H2, T/F 416-348-8597.

In the UK, information on Guatemala and the Maya of Guatemala, Mexico, Belize and Honduras can be found at The Guatemalan Indian Centre, 94A Wandsworth Bridge Rd, London SW6 27F, T 0171-371 5291, library, video archive, textile collection and travel advice. Open Wed, Thur, Sat 1000-1800; closed Jan and August.

● **Maps**
The **Instituto Geográfico Militar** produces detailed maps which can be bought in Guatemala City at Av Las Américas, 5-76, Zona 13, T 332-2611. Some are not for sale but can be copied by hand from the book containing all the 1:50,000 and 1:250,000 maps of the country.

HEALTH

Guatemala is healthy enough if precautions are taken about drinking-water, milk, uncooked vegetables and peeled fruits; carelessness on this point is likely to lead to amoebic dysentery, which is endemic. In Guatemala City the Bella Aurora and Centro Médico hospitals are good. Herrera Llerandi is a good private hospital. Most small towns have clinics. At the public hospitals you may have an examination for a nominal fee, but drugs are expensive. There is an immunization centre at Centro de Salud No 1, 9 C, 2-64, Zona 1, Guatemala City (no yellow fever vaccinations). In the high places avoid excessive exertion. If going to the Maya sites and the jungle areas, prophylaxis against malaria is strongly advised; there may also be a yellow fever risk. Cholera has been reported since 1991 and you should be particularly careful buying uncooked food in market *comedores* where good hygiene may be doubtful. You may pick up parasites if you swim in lakes.

MONEY

● **Currency**
The unit is the *quetzal*, divided into 100 centavos. There are coins of 25, 10, 5 and 1 centavos. The paper currency is for 50 centavos and 1, 5, 10, 20, 50 and 100 quetzales. If you have money sent to Guatemala, you can opt to take in US$ or quetzales. Miami airport is sometimes a good place to buy quetzales at favourable rates.

Warning Torn notes are not always accepted, so avoid accepting them yourself if possible. There is often a shortage of small change, but

when you arrive in Guatemala and change money, especially at weekends, insist on being given some small notes to pay hotel bills, transport, etc.

● **Exchange**
When changing TCs, ensure that your two signatures are a perfect match. Banks usually charge about 2% per transaction to advance quetzales on Visa card or other, and you will probably get a less favourable rate of exchange. Visa is the most widely recognized card. ATMs for the withdrawal of cash are available for Visa at Banco Industrial, and Mastercard/Cirrus sometimes at Banco Granai y Townson (G y T). Visa ATMs are much more common than Mastercard. Visa assistance, T 099-0115. Amex cards are not widely accepted. For Western Union, T 331-2841.

● **Credit cards**
All credit card transactions are subject to a 7% government tax.

GETTING THERE

BY AIR
● **From Canada**
Connections are made through Mexico City, Los Angeles or Miami.

● **From the Caribbean**
Copa from Santo Domingo and San Juan; American Airlines also from San Juan; Copa from Kingston and Montego Bay, Jamaica, and Port au Prince via Panama. Mexicana de Aviación from Havana.

● **From Central America**
From San Salvador: Taca, Aviateca, Lacsa, Copa. From Tegucigalpa: Taca. From San Pedro Sula: Taca (via San Salvador). From Mexico City: Aviateca, Mexicana, KLM. From Cancún: Aviateca, Mexicana. From Mérida: Aviateca. From Belize: Taca. From Managua: Copa, Aviateca. From San José: Aviateca, Lacsa, United Airlines, Copa, Mexicana. From Panama: Copa, Aviateca, Taca (via San Salvador), Lacsa (via San José). See **Introduction and Hints**, page 27, for regional airpasses.

● **From Europe**
KLM flies from Amsterdam via Mexico City, Iberia flies from Barcelona and Madrid via Miami, with connecting flights from other European cities. Alternatively, fly British Airways, Lufthansa, Air France, Alitalia, Aeroflot, Virgin

Atlantic, Continental or Delta to Miami and connect with daily flights to Guatemala City with Aviateca and American.

● **From South America**
SAM from Bogotá and San Andrés; flight connections through Panama. **NB** You will have to have an outward ticket from Colombia to be allowed a visa (though worth checking with Colombian embassy first); round trip tickets Guatemala-Colombia are stamped 'Refundable only in Guatemala', but it is possible either to sell the return part on San Andrés island – at a discount – or to change it to an alternative destination. There are no direct flights to Peru; connections with Lacsa via San José.

● **From the USA**
American (Philadelphia; Miami), Continental (Houston), Aviateca (Houston; Miami), United (Los Angeles; San Francisco), Lacsa (San Francisco), Taca (Los Angeles; New Orleans; New York; Washington DC).
Round-trips Miami-Guatemala are good value, and useful if one does not want to visit other Central American countries. MCOs are not sold in Guatemala.

● There are flights to **Flores** from Belize City with TropicAir; from Cancún with Aviateca and Aero Caribe (also from Chetumal and Palenque); from Guatemala City with Aviateca; connecting with flights from Managua, Mexico City, Miami and San Salvador.

CUSTOMS

You are allowed to take in, free of duty, personal effects and articles for your own use, 2 bottles of spirit and 80 cigarettes or 100 grams of tobacco. Once every 6 months you can take in, free, dutiable items worth US$100. Temporary visitors can take in any amount in quetzales or foreign currencies; they may not, however, take out more than they brought in. The local equivalent of US$100 pp may be reconverted into US dollars on departure at the airport, provided a ticket for immediate departure is shown.

ON ARRIVAL

● **Clothing**
Remember that most of the tourist areas you are likely to visit in Guatemala are over 1,500m and it will be cold in the evening and at night. Bad weather may bring noticeable drops in temperature. In many tropical areas where mosquitoes and other biting insects are common,

take long trousers and long-sleeved shirts for after dusk.

● **Entry tax**
There is no entry tax, officially, except for those nationalities which need a tourist card. See **Documents**, above; see also **Airline ticket and departure taxes**, below.

● **Hours of business**
Business and commercial offices are open from 0800-1200, and 1400-1800 except Sat. Shops: 0900-1300, 1500-1900, but many am only on Sat. Banks in Guatemala City: 0900-1500. In the interior banks tend to open earlier in the morning and close for lunch, and be open later. In the main tourist towns, some banks are open 7 days a week. Government offices open 0700-1530.

● **Official time**
Guatemalan time is 6 hrs behind GMT; 5 hrs during Summer Time, which was first introduced in 1976 after the earthquake and has been used intermittently since. Check carefully when you arrive.

● **Safety**
Following the 1996 ceasefire between government and URNG forces, travellers should not encounter difficulties, but if going to very isolated areas it may be wise to check conditions prior to travelling. In some parts of the country you may be subject to military or police checks. Local people are reluctant to discuss politics with strangers; it is best not to raise the subject. Do not necessarily be alarmed by 'gunfire' which is much more likely to be fireworks etc, a national pastime, especially early in the morning.
Robberies and assaults on tourists are becoming more common. Single women should be especially careful, but tourist groups are not immune and some excursion companies take necessary precautions. Specific warnings are given in the text, but visitors are advised to seek up-to-date local advice on places to avoid at the earliest opportunity.

● **Shopping**
Woven goods are normally cheapest bought in the town of origin, or possibly even cheaper at big markets held nearby. Try to avoid middlemen and buy direct from the weaver. You won't do better anywhere else in Central America. Guatemalan coffee is highly rec, although the best is exported; that sold locally is not vacuum-packed.
Kerosene is called 'Gas corriente', and is good quality, US$0.80/US gallon; sold only in gas stations.

Film for transparencies is hard to find (it is available at 9 C, 6-88, Zona 1, Guatemala City, also in large cities like Antigua, Xela and Cobán.

● **Tipping**
Hotel staff: bell boys, US$0.25 for light luggage, US$0.50 for heavy. Chamber maids at discretion. Restaurants: 10%, minimum US$0.25. Taxi drivers: none. Airport porters: US$0.25/piece of luggage. Cloakroom attendants and cinema usherettes are not tipped.

Guatemalan children are becoming persistent in asking for money in some tourist areas. It may be better to pass on items like soap, shampoo, sewing kits picked up from hotels.

● **Voltage**
Generally 110 volts AC, 60 cycles, but for variations see under individual towns. Electricity is generally reliable in the towns but can be a problem in the remoter areas eg Petén. Take a torch to be on the safe side.

● **Volunteer work**
If you would like to volunteer to help in local children's homes, write to: Casa Guatemala, 14 C, 10-63, Zona 1, Guatemala City, or Casa Alianza, Apartado Postal 400, Antigua, Guatemala. Also contact Ac'tenamit, AP 2675, 09001 Guatemala City, T 251-1136; they are based at Clínica Lámpara, near Livingston, supported by the British Commonwealth Association. The Permanent Commission on Refugees is at 6 Av, 3-23, Zona 1, Oficina 301, Guatemala City (T/F 251-7549). They sometimes require assistants to help with returning refugees from Mexico; you pay your own way. Several language schools in Quezaltenango and Huehuetenango fund community development projects and seek volunteers from among their students. Also, Asociación de Rescate y Conservación de Vida Silvestre (ARCAS), which returns wild animals to their natural habitat, takes volunteer workers (1997 report that there are plenty of paid staff, you may feel unnecessary); contact ARCAS, Flores, Petén, Guatemala, T/F 926-0566 or their Guatemala City office, 11 C 6-66, Zona 1, T/F 253-5329. Their centre is 15 km from Flores towards Tikal. An orphanage in El Naranjo takes volunteers, see page 673.

● **Weights and measures**
The metric system is obligatory on all Customs documents: specific duties are levied on the basis of weight, usually gross kilograms. United States measures are widely used in commerce; most foodstuffs are sold by the pound. The metric tonne of 1,000 kg is generally used; so is the US gallon. Old Spanish measures are often used; eg *vara* (32.9 inches), *caballería* (111.51 acres), *manzana* (1.727 acres), *arroba* (25 lbs), and *quintal* (101.43 lbs). Altitudes of towns are often measured in feet.

ON DEPARTURE

● **Airline ticket and departure taxes**
There is a 17% ticket tax, single or return, on all international tickets sold in Guatemala. A stamp tax of 2% is payable on single, return, baggage tickets and exchange vouchers issued in Guatemala and paid for in or out of the country. Hence it is usually cheaper to buy air tickets outside the country. A US$5 tourism tax is levied on all tickets sold in Guatemala to Guatemalan residents for travel abroad. There is also a Q50/US$10 airport and departure tax, and a Q5/US$1 (officially) tourist tax at all borders, charged on leaving overland (borders may not be open 24 hrs). These taxes vary from one border crossing to another, and from one official to another, and may be charged on entry as well as departure. Bribery is rife at border crossings, whether you are entering with a car or on foot. Always ask for a receipt and, if you have time and the language ability, do not give in to corrupt officials. Report any complaint to ISTU office or Inguat representative.

WHERE TO STAY

● **Hotels**
The tourist institute Inguat publishes a list of maximum prices for single, double and triple occupancy of almost 300 hotels throughout the country in all price ranges, though the list is thin on the budget hotels. They will deal with complaints about overcharging if you can produce bills etc. Room rates should be posted in all registered hotels. Hotel rooms are subject to 10% sales tax and 10% tourism tax. Most budget hotels do not supply toilet paper, soap or towels. Busiest seasons, when hotels in main tourist centres are heavily booked, are Easter, Dec and the European summer holiday (July-Aug).

FOOD AND DRINK

● **Food**
Traditional Central American/Mexican food such as tortillas, tamales, tostadas, etc are found everywhere. Tacos are less spicy than in Mexico. *Chiles rellenos* are a speciality in Guatemala, chiles stuffed with meat and vegetables which may be *picante* (spicy) or *no picante*. *Churrasco*,

charcoal-grilled steak, is often accompanied by *chirmol*, a sauce of tomato, onion and mint. *Guacamole* (avocado mashed with onion and spices) is also excellent. Local dishes inc *pepián* (thick meat stew with vegetables) in Antigua, *patín* (tomato-based sauce served with *pescaditos*, ie small fish from Lake Atitlán, wrapped in leaves), *sesina* (beef marinated in lemon and bitter orange) from the same region. On All Saints Day (1 Nov) *fiambre* is widely prepared for families and friends who gather on this holiday. It consists of all kinds of meat, fish, chicken, vegetables, eggs, cheese served as a salad with rice, beans etc.

Desserts inc *mole* (plantain and chocolate) *torrejas* (sweet bread soaked in egg and panela or honey) and *buñuelos* (similar to profiteroles) served with hot cinnamon syrup.

For breakfast try *mosh* (oats cooked with milk and cinnamon), fried plantain with cream, black beans in various forms. *Pan dulce* (sweet bread), in fact bread in general, and local cheese are rec. Try *borracho* (cake soaked in rum).

● **Drink**

Local beers are good (Monte Carlo and Cabra, which are better than Gallo, and Moza, a dark beer); bottled, carbonated soft drinks (*gaseosas*) are safest, milk should be pasteurized. Cold, freshly made *refrescos* and ice creams are delicious made of many varieties of local fruits, *licuados* are fruit juices with milk or water, but the standard of hygiene varies, take care. Water should be filtered or bottled 'Salvavidas' (although bottled water may not always be available). If you are planning to spend some time travelling in Guatemala, take an orange squeezer with you. Oranges are plentiful and cheap but a glass in a café or hotel will cost up to US$1.

GETTING AROUND

LAND TRANSPORT

● **Train**

There are railways from Atlantic to Pacific and to the Mexican border. Passenger services were terminated in 1995 pending privatization of the network.

● **Bus**

Most buses are in a poor state of repair and breakdowns can be expected; they are always overloaded. Although recent government legislation has reduced problems of overcrowding, it is still difficult to get on buses in mid route.

The correct fare should be posted up; if not, ask your neighbours. Many long distance buses leave very early in the morning. Try to arrange your passage the previous day and arrive in good time to get a seat. Make sure you can get out of your hotel/*pensión*. For long trips, take snacks and water. For international bus journeys make sure you have small denomination local currency or US dollar bills for border taxes. In the smaller towns, you will probably be woken up by the horns of arriving and departing buses. At Easter there are few buses on Good Friday or the Sat but they run again on Easter Sunday.

On several popular tourist routes, eg airport-Antigua, Antigua Panajachel, there are mini buses, comfortable, overpriced, not as much fun as regular buses but convenient. They can be booked through hotels and travel agencies and will usually pick you up from your hotel. We receive complaints that bus drivers charge tourists more than locals. This is becoming more widespread. One way to keep your bus fares down, ask the locals, then tender the exact fare on the bus. Also check carefully that the bus is going all the way to your destination. In the country, travellers frequently say it is great to travel on the roof of the bus. However, you should know that it is illegal and, of course, can be dangerous.

NB Many long names on bus destination boards are abbreviated: Guate = Guatemala City, Chichi = Chichicastenango, Xela = Xelajú = Quezaltenango, Toto = Totonicapán, etc. Buses in the W and N are called *camionetas*. Regarding pronunciation, 'X' is pronounced 'sh' in Guatemala, as in Yucatán.

● **Car**

Bringing a vehicle into Guatemala requires the following procedure: visit immigration and pay Q5 for an entry stamp; visit cuarantena agropecuario (Ministry of Agriculture quarantine); at Aduana (Customs), pay US$20 for all forms and permits and a sticker for your vehicle; go to Guardia de Hacienda for a final stamp. All stamps are put on a strip of paper. When entering the country, ask the officials to add any important accessories you have to the paper eg spare wheels, radio, a/c unit etc. If border officials try to charge you more than the above, demand a written receipt or resist if one is not given. Always double check 'Ingreso' papers before leaving the border. A private vehicle may not re-enter Guatemala within a month of leaving the country, except on a transit permit. A normal, renewable permit is orange; a transit permit is green and is valid for anything up to 30 days. It is not renewable. The orange entry permit is renewable at the Aduana, 10 C, 13-92, Zona 1, after completion of forms at 12th floor of Edif Financiero, 8 Av y 21 C, Zona 1, Centro Cívico. The process costs around US$7 and can take several days. Your passport must contain a visa for the period requested. On leaving by car, four stamps on a strip of paper are required: exit stamp from Migración (Q5, or Q10 at weekends, or for any other excuse); surrender of vehicle permit at Aduana; cuarantena agropecuaria (quarantine); vehicle inspection (not always carried out). You are then supposed to surrender your stamped strip of paper. Motorcycle entry permit costs the same as a car, better to pay in quetzales if you can. The description of your vehicle on the registration document must match your vehicle's appearance exactly. Spare tyres for cars and motorcycles must be listed in the vehicle entry permit, otherwise they are liable to confiscation. It is better not to import and sell foreign cars in Guatemala as import taxes are very high. We understand you can air freight a motorcycle and maybe a car to Colombia from Guatemala without too much hassle. Check with SAM office in Guatemala City.

The paved roads are generally quite good, but can be poor in places; the dirt roads are often very bad. There has, however, been a general deterioration in the state of the busiest roads since 1993-4 owing to strikes and a lack of funds for maintenance. High clearance is essential on many roads and 4WD useful. Identification should be carried at all times. There are frequent transit police stops, especially near borders. Stopping is compulsory: if driving your own vehicle, watch out for the 'ALTO' sign. When driving, keep at least 200m in front of, or behind, army vehicles; their drivers are concerned about attacks on military personnel. For a minor traffic offence, you should only be given a citation by the police, but they may impound your licence if you are stopped for an infraction, which can take some time to redeem. To avoid this if your papers are in order, a tip of say US$3.50-9, depending on circumstances, will help. If your papers are not in order, a larger tip may be necessary. Another suggestion is to take one or more International Driving Licences as well as your national licence. Tourists involved in traffic accidents will have to pay whether the guilty party or not. If someone is injured or killed, the foreigner will have to pay all damages. Car insurance can be arranged at **Seguros G & T**, 7 Av, 1-82, Zona 4, Guatemala City, T 334-1361

and at their offices in Coatepeque, Mazatenango, Zacapa, Jalapa and Huehuetenango, depending on length of stay, also La Ceiba SA, 13 C 3-40, Zona 10, Edif. Atlantis Of. 1001, T 366-1606/1616, F 366-1658/9. Sanborns in the USA (see **Automobiles**, Mexico **Information for travellers**), provides insurance for Guatemala only if you buy Mexico cover through them.

Gasoline costs US$1.55 'normal', US$1.62 'premium' for the US gallon. Unleaded is available in major cities, at Melchor de Mencos (Belize border) and along the Pan-American Highway but not in the countryside. Diesel costs US$1.10 a gallon. If coming in from Mexico fill up before you enter. Just about all motorbike parts and accessories are available at decent prices in Guatemala City at **Canella**, 7 Av, 8-65, Zona 4, T 334-8051/55, open Mon-Fri 0830-1730, closed for lunch, Sat 0830-1230; opp is **FPK**, 7 Av, 8-08, Zona 4, T 331-9777/81, F 331-6012; better availability than anywhere else in Central America. Excellent BMW bike mechanic, Johann Ferber, Autofix, Av Petapa 11-00, Zona 12, Guatemala City, T 714189.

Border crossings from Mexico to Western Guatemala: **Tecún Umán/Ciudad Hidalgo** is the main truckers' crossing. It is very busy and should be avoided at all costs by car (hitch hikers, on the other hand, are sure to find a long-distance lift here). **Talismán** is more geared to private cars; there are the usual hordes of helpers to guide you through the procedures, for a fee. **La Mesilla** is the simplest for private cars and you can do your own paperwork with ease. All necessary documents can be obtained here. Any of the three crossings is straightforward going from Guatemala to Mexico (with thanks to Francesca Pagnacco, Exeter).

● **Car hire**
Hired cars may not always be taken into neighbouring countries (none is allowed into Mexico); rental companies that do allow their vehicles to cross borders charge US$7-10 for the permits and paperwork. Credit cards or cash are accepted for car rental.

● **Cycling**
Shirley Hudson (Mosier, Oregon) writes: The scenery is gorgeous, the people friendly and colourful. The hills are steep, steep and sometimes long. The Pan-American Highway is OK from Guatemala City W; it has a shoulder and traffic is not very heavy. South from Guatemala City has no shoulder and heavier traffic. Cycling is hard, but enjoyable. Buses are frequent and easy to

load a bicycle on the roof; many buses do so, charging about two thirds of the passenger fare. On the road, buses are a hazard for cyclists, Guatemala City is particularly dangerous.

● **Hitchhiking**

Hitchhiking is comparatively easy, but increasingly risky, especially for single women, also beware of theft of luggage, especially in trucks. The best place to try for a lift is at a bridge or on a road out of town; be there no later than 0600, but 0500 is better as it is when truck drivers start their journey. Trucks usually charge US$1-1.50 upwards for a lift/day. It may be worth asking around the trucks the night before if anyone is going your way. Recently, travellers suggest it can be cheaper by bus. The only way to retrieve 'lost' luggage is by telling the police the vehicle registration number.

COMMUNICATIONS

● **Newspapers**

The main newspapers are *Prensa Libre* and *El Gráfico* in the morning; *La Hora* in the afternoon (best). *Siglo Veintuno* is a good new newspaper, started in 1989, *El Regional*, excellent weekly paper (Antigua). *Tinamit* is a left-wing weekly, on Thur. Weekly magazine *La Crónica* is worth reading, rec. There are several free booklets and newsletters aimed at the tourist: *The Revue*, produced in Antigua bi-weekly, carries advertisements, lodgings, tours and excursions, covering Antigua, Panajachel, Xela, Río Dulce and Guatemala City; *Guía Turística* covers Antigua, Atitlán, Tikal and Copán. *Guatemala News* and *Guatemala Weekly* are English language newspapers, free and widely available in Guatemala City, Antigua and Panajachel.

● **Postal services**

Airmail to Europe takes 10-14 days (letters cost Q0.60 for first 10 grammes, Q0.40 for each additional 10 grammes, max weight, 2 kg). Airmail letters to US cost Q0.25. Airmail rates sometimes vary between Post Offices. Airmail parcel service to the US is reliable (4-14 days). Parcels sent abroad must be checked before being wrapped for sending; take unsealed package, tape and string to office 119 at the Central Post Office between 0800 and 1530. Note, though that parcels over 2 kg may only be sent abroad from Guatemala City (except 2 kg of books from Antigua); in all other cities, packets under 2 kg must be sent registered abroad. (See in the text for alternative services to the Post Office for sending packets abroad.) **NB** The Lista

de Correos charges US$0.03/letter received. Correos y Telégrafos, 7 Av y 12 C, Zona 1; Guatel next door. Also, no letters may be in parcels: they will be removed. All Post Offices are closed Sat and Sun. Urgent telegrams are charged double the ordinary rate but are generally cheap and reliable within the country.

● **Telephone services**

NB All telephone numbers in the country were changed on the 15 August 1996 from 5 and 6 figure numbers to a new 7 figure basis. No prefixes (eg 0 for numbers outside Guatemala City) are now necessary. All numbers in this edition have been revised but we ask that you advise us of any errors discovered. For directory enquiries, dial 124.

Telephone calls to other countries can be made at any time; to Europe, these are slightly cheaper between 1900 and 0700. The cost of overseas calls will fluctuate according to the current exchange rate: USA/Canada direct dialled US$1/min; Europe US$3.50, less to Spain; Australia/New Zealand US$5. Operator calls are more expensive, usually minimum 3 mins. For Sprint, dial 195; for MCI dial 189. Collect calls may be made from public phones in Guatemala City, Antigua, Quezaltenango (possibly elsewhere) only to Central America, Mexico, USA (inc Alaska) dial 196 for the operator. For direct calls, dial USA (190), Spain (191). For other countries, enquire Canada (198), Italy (193), Spain (191). Collect calls cannot be made to the UK; from a private phone you can call for 1 min and ask the person at the other end to phone back (at Guatel you have to pay for a minimum of 3 mins). All telephone services and the international cable service are in the hands of Guatel (due to be privatized in 1997), but local telegrams are dealt with at the post office. Remember there are very few public telephones outside the main towns.

Fax: US$3.50 (US$2/additional minute) to the US; US$5 (US$4/additional minute) to Europe; and US$5.50 (US$4.50/additional minute) to other countries. However, check around, there are wide variations in fax charges made, some by the page, some by time. Rates available in Antigua and Quezaltenango are cheaper than elsewhere, Guatemala City prices are high.

HOLIDAYS AND FESTIVALS

1 Jan; Holy Week (4 days); 1 May: Labour Day; 30 June; 15 Aug (Guatemala City only); 15 Sept: Independence Day; 12 Oct: Discovery of

America; 20 Oct: Revolution Day; 1 Nov: All Saints; 24 Dec: Christmas Eve: from noon; 25 Dec: Christmas Day; 31 Dec (from noon).

12 Oct and Christmas Eve are not business holidays. During Holy Week, bus fares may be doubled.

Although specific dates are given for *fiestas* there is often about a week of jollification beforehand.

FURTHER READING

Guatemala for You by Barbara Balchin de Koose (Piedra Santa, Guatemala City). *I, Rigoberta Menchú*, by Rigoberta Menchú; *Sweet Waist of America: Journeys around Guatemala*, by Anthony Daniels (London: Hutchinson, 1990). The novels of Miguel Angel Asturias, notably *Hombres de Maíz, Mulata de tal* and *El señor presidente*. Mario Payeras' *Los días de la selva* is a first-hand account of the guerrilla movement in the 1970s.

ACKNOWLEDGEMENTS

Our warmest thanks go to Peter Pollard for updating this chapter. We should also like to thank Peter Eltringham for his work on the Petén, and Elizabeth Bell of Antigua.

Belize

BELIZE, FORMERLY KNOWN as British Honduras, borders on Mexico and Guatemala, and has a land area of about 8,867 sq miles, including numerous small islands. Its greatest length (N-S) is 174 miles and its greatest width (E-W) is 68 miles.

HORIZONS

THE LAND

The coastlands are low and swampy with much mangrove, many salt and fresh water lagoons and some sandy beaches. In the N the land is low and flat, but in the SW there is a heavily forested mountain massif with a general elevation of between 2,000 and 3,000 ft. In the eastern part are the Maya Mountains, not yet wholly explored, and the Cockscomb Range which rises to a height of 3,675 ft at Victoria Peak. To the W are some 250 sq miles of the Mountain Pine Ridge, with large open spaces and some of the best scenery in the country.

From 10 to 40 miles off the coast an almost continuous, 150-mile line of reefs and cayes (meaning islands, pronounced 'keys') provides shelter from the Caribbean and forms the longest coral reef in the Western Hemisphere (the fifth-longest barrier reef in the world). Most of the cayes are quite tiny, but some have been developed as tourist resorts. Many have beautiful sandy beaches with clear, clean water, where swimming and diving are excellent. (However, on the windward side of inhabited islands, domestic sewage is washed back on to the beaches, and some beaches are affected by tar.)

The most fertile areas of the country are in the northern foothills of the Maya Mountains: citrus fruit is grown in the Stann Creek valley, while in the valley of the Mopan, or upper Belize River, cattle raising and mixed farming are successful. The northern area of the country has long proved suitable for sugar cane production. In the S bananas and mangoes are cultivated. The lower valley of the Belize River is a rice-growing area as well as being used for mixed farming and citrus cultivation.

CLIMATE

Shade temperature is not often over 90°F (32°C) on the coast, even in the hotter months of Feb to May (the 'dry season',

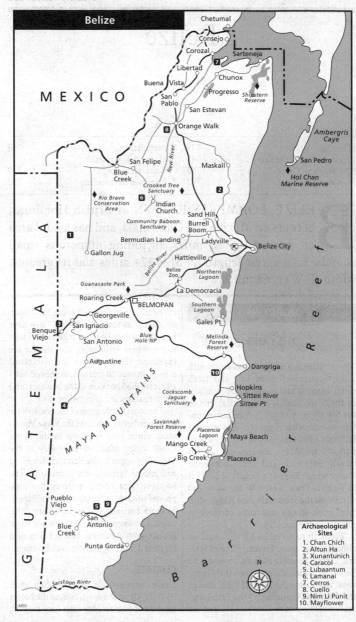

Belize

MEXICO

Chetumal
Consejo
Corozal
Sarteneja
Libertad
Buena Vista
San Pablo
Chunox
Progresso
Shipstern Reserve
San Estevan
Orange Walk
Maskall
San Felipe
Blue Creek
New River
Crooked Tree Sanctuary
Indian Church
Rio Bravo Conservation Area
Community Baboon Sanctuary
Sand Hill
Burrell Boom
Bermudian Landing
Ladyville
Belize River
Hattieville
Belize City
Gallon Jug
Belize Zoo
Northern Lagoon
Guanacaste Park
La Democracia
Roaring Creek
BELMOPAN
Southern Lagoon
Georgeville
Gales Pt
San Ignacio
Benque Viejo
Blue Hole NP
San Antonio
Augustine
Melinda Forest Reserve
MAYA MOUNTAINS
Dangriga
Cockscomb Jaguar Sanctuary
Hopkins
Sittee River
Sittee Pt
Savannah Forest Reserve
Placencia Lagoon
Mango Creek
Maya Beach
Big Creek
Placencia
Pueblo Viejo
San Antonio
Blue Creek
Punta Gorda
Sarstoon River

Ambergris Caye
San Pedro
Hol Chan Marine Reserve

GUATEMALA

Reef

Barrier Reef

N

Archaeological Sites
1. Chan Chich
2. Altun Ha
3. Xunantunich
4. Caracol
5. Lubaantum
6. Lamanai
7. Cerros
8. Cuello
9. Nim Li Punit
10. Mayflower

M50

but see below). Inland, in the W, day temperatures can exceed 100°F (38°C), but the nights are cooler. Between Nov and Feb there are cold spells during which the temperature at Belize City may fall to 55°F (13°C). Humidity is normally high, making it 'sticky' most of the time in the lowlands.

There are sharp annual variations of rainfall – there is even an occasional drought – but the average at Belize City is 65 ins, with about 50 ins in the N and a great increase to 170 ins in the S. Generally, the driest months are April and May; in June and July there are heavy showers followed by blue skies; Sept and Oct tend to be overcast and there are lots of insects. Hurricanes can threaten the country from June to Nov, but there have been only four in the past 30 years. An efficient warning system has been established and there are hurricane shelters in most towns and large villages. Hurricane Preparedness instructions are issued annually.

HISTORY

Throughout the country, especially in the forests of the centre and S, are many ruins of the Classic Maya Period, which flourished here and in neighbouring Guatemala from the 4th to the 9th century and then somewhat mysteriously (most probably because of drought) emigrated to Yucatán. It has been estimated that the population then was 10 times what it is now.

The first settlers were English with their black slaves from Jamaica who came about 1640 to cut logwood, then the source of textile dyes. The British Government made no claim to the territory but tried to secure the protection of the wood-cutters by treaties with Spain. Even after 1798, when a strong Spanish force was decisively beaten off at St George's Caye, the British Government still failed to claim the territory, though the settlers maintained that it had now become British by conquest.

When they achieved independence from Spain in 1821, both Guatemala and Mexico laid claim to sovereignty over Belize as successors to Spain, but these claims were rejected by Britain. Long before 1821, in defiance of Spain, the British settlers had established themselves as far S as the river Sarstoon, the present southern boundary. Independent Guatemala claimed that these settlers were trespassing and that Belize was a province of the new republic. By the middle of the 19th century Guatemalan fears of an attack by the United States led to a *rapprochement* with Britain. In 1859, a Convention was signed by which Guatemala recognized the boundaries of Belize while, by Article 7, the United Kingdom undertook to contribute to the cost of a road from Guatemala City to the sea 'near the settlement of Belize'; an undertaking which was never carried out.

Heartened by what it considered a final solution of the dispute, Great Britain declared Belize, still officially a settlement, a Colony in 1862, and a Crown Colony 9 years later. Mexico, by treaty, renounced any claims it had on Belize in 1893, but Guatemala, which never ratified the 1859 agreement, renewed its claims periodically.

Independence

Belize became independent on 21 September 1981, following a United Nations declaration to that effect. Guatemala refused to recognize the independent state, but in 1986, President Cerezo of Guatemala announced an intention to drop his country's claim to Belize. A British military force was maintained in Belize from independence until 1993, when the British government announced that the defence of Belize would be handed over to the government on 1 January 1994 and that it would reduce the 1,200-strong garrison to about 100 soldiers who would organize jungle warfare training facilities. The last British troops were withdrawn in 1994 and finance was sought for the expansion of the Belize Defence Force. Belize was admitted into the OAS in 1991 following negotiations between Belize, Guatemala and Britain. As part of Guatemala's recognition of Belize as an independent nation (ratified by Congress in 1992) Britain will recompense Guatemala by providing financial and technical assistance to construct road, pipeline and port facilities that will guarantee Guatemala access to the Atlantic. In Belize there will be a referendum to decide whether to accept the proposed Maritime Areas Bill which will delimit Belize's southern maritime borders in such a manner as to allow Guatemala uncontested and secure access to the high seas.

Elections

Mr George Price, of the People's United Party, who had been re-elected continuously as Prime Minister since internal self-government was instituted in 1964, was defeated by Mr Manuel Esquivel, of the United Democratic Party (UDP), in general elections held in Dec 1984 (the first since independence), but was returned as Prime Minister in 1989. The National Alliance for Belizean Rights (NABR) was created in 1992 by a defector from the UDP. General elections were held early, in 1993, and contrary to forecasts, the PUP was defeated. The UDP, in alliance with the NABR, won 16 of the 29 seats, many by a very narrow margin, and Mr Esquivel took office as Prime Minister with the additional portfolios of Finance and Defence. In the months following the elections, a corruption scandal rocked Belizean politics. Several PUP members, including the former Foreign Minister were arrested on charges of offering bribes to two UDP members of the House of Representatives to persuade them to cross the floor. They were later acquitted.

Mr Price retired from the PUP party leadership in 1996, aged 77, after 40 years in the post. He was succeeded by Mr Said Musa, a lawyer. In 1977 the PUP had a spectacular success in the municipal elections, winning all 7 Town Boards for the first time ever, reversing the position since 1994 when the UDP won them all. General elections are due by mid-1998.

CONSTITUTION

Belize is a constitutional monarchy; the British monarch is the chief of state, represented by a Governor-General, who is a Belizean. The head of government is the Prime Minister. There is a National Assembly, with a House of Representatives of 29 members (not including the Speaker) elected by universal adult suffrage, and a Senate of eight: five appointed by the advice of the Prime Minister, two on the advice of the Leader of the Opposition, one by the Governor-General after consultation. General elections are held at intervals of not more than 5 years.

CULTURE

PEOPLE

About 40% of the population are of mixed ancestry, the so-called Creoles, a term widely used in the Caribbean. They predominate in Belize City and along the coast, and on the navigable rivers. 43% of the population are mestizo; 11% are Indians, mostly Mayas, who predominate in the N between the Hondo and New rivers and in the extreme S and W. About 7% of the population are Garifuna (Black Caribs), descendants of the Black Caribs deported from St Vincent in 1797; they have a distinct language, and can be found in the villages and towns along the southern coast. They are good linguists, many speaking Mayan languages as well as Spanish and 'Creole' English. They also brought their culture and customs from the West Indies, including religious practices and ceremonies, for example Yankanu (John Canoe) dancing at Christmas time. The remainder are of unmixed European ancestry (the majority Mennonites, who speak a German dialect, and are friendly and helpful) and a rapidly growing group of North Americans. The Mennonites fall into two groups, generally speaking: the most rigorous, in the Shipyard area on The New River, and the more 'integrated' in the W, Cayo district, who produce much of Belize's poultry, dairy goods and corn. The newest Mennonite settlements are E of Progresso Lagoon in the NE. There are also East Indian and Chinese immigrants.

LANGUAGE

English is the official language, although about 75% speak mostly 'Creole' English. Spanish is the mother tongue for about 15%. About 30% are bilingual, and 10% trilingual (see above). Spanish is widely spoken in the northern and western areas. Free elementary education is available to all, and all the towns have secondary schools.

THE ECONOMY

Structure of production

Belize's central problem is how to become self-sufficient in food: imports of food are still some 20% of the total imports. Necessity is forcing the people to grow food for themselves and this is gathering pace. One difficulty is that the territory is seriously under-populated and much skilled labour emigrates. Three immigrant Mennonite communities have already increased farm production, and new legislation provides for the development of lands not utilized by private landowners.

This is still the most important sector of the Belizean economy, directly or indirectly employing more than half the population, and bringing in 65% of the country's total foreign exchange earnings. The main export crops, in order of importance, are sugar, citrus and bananas. Maize, beans, cocoa and rice are grown, and attempts are also being made to increase the cattle herd. Poultry, eggs and honey production grew significantly during the 1980s.

Belize: fact file		
Geographic		
Land area		22,965 sq km
forested		92.1%
pastures		2.1%
cultivated		2.5%
Demographic		
Population (1996)		219,000
annual growth rate (1985-94)		2.6%
urban		47.5%
rural		52.5%
density		9.5 per sq km
Religious affiliation		
Roman Catholic		57.7%
Protestant		34.3%
Birth rate per 1,000 (1995)		33.7
		(world av 25.0)
Education and Health		
Life expectancy at birth (1995),		
male		66.4 years
female		70.4 years
Infant mortality rate		
per 1,000 live births (1995)		34.7
Physicians (1993)	1 per 1,708 persons	
Hospital beds	1 per 350 persons	
Calorie intake as %		
of FAO requirement		118%
Population age 25 and over		
with no formal schooling		13.0%
Literacy (over 15)		93%
Economic		
GNP (1994 market prices)		US$535mn
GNP per capita		US$2,550
Public external debt (1994)		
		US$159.6mn
Tourism receipts (1994)		US$71.4mn
Inflation		
(annual av 1990-95)		2.3%
Radio		1 per 7.2 persons
Television		1 per 9.1 persons
Telephone		1 per 7.2 persons
Employment		
Population economically active		
(1994)		69,670
Unemployment rate (1994)		11.6%
% of labour force in		
agriculture		19.9
mining		0.5
manufacturing		8.6
construction		5.8
Military forces		1,065
Source Encyclopaedia Britannica.		

Timber is extracted during the first 6 months of the year. Forest products were for a long time the country's most important export, but their relative importance has fallen. The government has encouraged the establishment of a veneer plant to increase the domestic value added in wood product exports. There were local protests in 1995-96 against the granting of logging licences; 17 concessions totalling 555,000 acres were granted in the Toledo district, some of which overlapped with Maya reserves. The largest, of 159,000 acres, belonging to a Malaysian company, was accused of violating the conditions of the licence. Marine products (eg shrimp and conch) are around 9% of exports, though some of the traditional grounds have been overfished and restrictions necessary for conservation are enforced.

There is also some light industry and manufacturing (dominated by sugar refining and citrus processing) now contributes about 14% of gdp. The value of clothing exports has risen to 11% of domestic exports (excluding re-exports), making garments the fourth most important export item in 1996. Oil was discovered, near the Mexican border, in 1981; the search for oil is being intensified on and off shore.

With the emergence of ecotourism and natural history-based travel as a major expansion market within the travel industry, the Belize government is encouraging the development of tourism facilities and services. Tourism in Belize is the second largest foreign revenue earner, behind agriculture. Tourist arrival numbers have grown steadily from 77,542 in 1991 to 121,270 in 1995 of whom 60% came from the USA and 24% from Europe. A further 7,953 cruise ship passengers visited in 1995.

The 1995 Banks and Financial Institutions Act brought the regulation and supervision of the financial sector in line with Caricom requirements. New or amended legislation is pending on offshore banking and ship registration following a 1994 report by a British Government adviser, which recommended 'more regulation and supervision and rather less free enterprise'. Some 1,000 International Business Companies (IBCs) have been registered in Belize under 1990 legislation, while the open marine register numbers about 300 ships.

Recent trends

The slowing down of economic growth at the beginning of the 1980s was attributable to decline in the sugar industry and pressures on Belize's international accounts. Prudent financial policies in the mid-1980s led to the elimination of external debt arrears and the increase of foreign exchange reserves. In 1985-94 gdp grew at an average of 7.9% a year, and by end-1996 official reserves stood at US$56.1mn, the highest level for 6 years.

The departure of the British army garrison meant the loss of US$30mn to the Belize economy and the rise in gdp slowed from 6% in financial year 1992/93 to 3.8% in 1993/94. The decline in fiscal receipts led the Government to raise taxes and curb public sector pay rises (which led to strikes and demonstrations). A 1995 IMF mission highlighted the sluggish economy, the scarcity of domestic savings and high unemployment, with the large government deficit worsening the balance of payments.

COMMUNICATIONS

Formerly the only means of inland communication were the rivers, with sea links between the coastal towns and settlements. The Belize River can be navigated by light motor boats, with enclosed propellers, to near the Guatemalan border in most seasons of the year, but this route is no longer used commercially because of the many rapids. The Hondo River and the New River are both navigable for small boats for 100 miles or so. Although boats continue to serve the sugar industry in the N, the use of waterborne transport is much diminished.

Some 1,684 miles of roads, of which 18% are paved, connect the eight towns and many villages in the country. Many of the dirt roads are of high quality, smooth and well-maintained, but in outlying areas others are impassable in the wet season. There arc road links with Chetumal, the Mexican border town, and the Guatemalan border town of Melchor de Mencos. The main roads are the Northern Highway (from the Mexican border at Santa Elena to Belize City via Orange Walk), the Western Highway (from Belize City to the Guatemalan border at Benque Viejo del Carmen via San Ignacio), the Hummingbird Highway (from the Western Highway at Belmopan to Dangriga on the coast), the new Coastal Highway (from La Democracia on the Western Highway also to Dangriga) and the Southern Highway (from the Hummingbird Highway 6 miles W of Dangriga to Punta Gorda further down the coast). The road system has been upgraded in the interests of tourism and further improvements are planned. There are no railways in Belize.

NATURE CONSERVATION

Convention is now a high priority, with nature reserves sponsored by the Belize Audubon Society, the Government and various international agencies. 'Nature tourism' is Belize's fastest growing industry. By 1992 18 national parks and reserves had been established, including: Half Moon Caye, Cockscomb Basin Wildlife Sanctuary (the world's only jaguar reserve), Crooked Tree Wildlife Sanctuary (swamp forests and lagoons with wildfowl), Community Baboon Sanctuary, Blue Hole National Park, Guanacaste Park, Society Hall Nature Reserve (a research area with Maya presence), Bladen Nature Reserve (watershed and primary forest), Hol Chan Marine Reserve (reef eco-system), Rio Bravo Conservation Area (managed by the Programme for Belize, 1 King St, Belize City, T 02-75616/7, or John

Burton, Old Mission Hall, Sibton Green, Saxmundham, Suffolk, IP17 2JY), the Shipstern Nature Reserve (butterfly breeding, forest, lagoons, mammals and birds: contact PO Box 1694, Belize City, T 08-22149 via BCL Radio phone, or International Tropical Conservation Foundation, Box 31, CH-2074 Marin-Ne, Switzerland). Five Blue Lakes National Park, based on an unusually deep karst lagoon in Cayo District off the Hummingbird Highway was designated in April 1991. On 8 December 1991 the government created three new forest reserves and national parks: the Vaca Forest Reserve (52,000 acres), Chiquibul National Park (containing the Maya ruins of Caracol, 265,894 acres), both in Cayo District, and Laughing Bird Caye National Park (off Placencia). The first eight listed are managed by the Belize Audubon Society, 12 Fort St, Belize City (PO Box 1001), T 02-34988, F 02-34985. Glovers Reef was declared a marine reserve in 1993.

Belize Enterprise for Sustained Technology (BEST) is a non-profit organization committed to the sustainable development of Belize's disadvantaged communities and community-based ecotourism, eg Gales Point and Hopkins Village; PO Box 35, Forest Drive, Belmopan, T 08-23043, F 08-22563.

A wildlife protection Act was introduced in 1982, which forbids the sale, exchange or dealings in wildlife, or parts thereof, for profit; the import, export, hunting or collection of wildlife is not allowed without a permit; only those doing scientific research or for educational purposes are eligible for exporting or collecting permits. Also prohibited are removing or exporting black coral, picking orchids, exporting turtle or turtle products, and spear fishing in certain areas or while wearing scuba gear.

On 1 June 1996 a National Protected Areas Trust Fund (PACT) was established to provide finance for the "protection, conservation and enhancement of the natural and cultural treasures of Belize".

Funds for PACT will come from a BZ$7.50 Conservation Fee paid by all foreign visitors on departure by air, land and sea, and from 20% of revenues derived from protected areas entrance fees, cruise ship passenger fees, etc. **NB** Visitors pay only one PACT tax every 30 days, so if you go to Tikal, for example, then leave from Belize airport, show your receipt in order not to pay twice.

Bird watchers are recommended to take Petersen's *Field Guide to Mexican Birds*.

Fishing The rivers abound with tarpon and snook. The sea provides game fish such as sailfish, marlin, wahoo, barracuda and tuna. On the flats, the most exciting fish for light tackle – the bonefish – are found in great abundance. Seasons are given below. In addition to the restrictions on turtle and coral extraction noted above under **Nature Conservation**, the following regulations apply: no person may take, buy or sell crawfish (lobster) between 15 Feb and 14 July, shrimp from 15 April to 14 Aug, or conch between 1 July and 30 Sept.

Fishing seasons: Billfish: blue marlin, all year (best Nov-Mar); white marlin, Nov-May; sailfish, Mar-May. Oceanic: yellowfin tuna, all year; blackfin tuna, all year; bonito, all year; wahoo, Nov-Feb; sharks, all year. Reef: kingfish, Mar-June; barracuda, all year; jackfish, all year; mackerel, all year; grouper, all year; snapper, all year; permit, all year; bonefish, Nov-April; tarpon, June-Aug. River: tarpon, Feb-Aug; snook, Feb-Aug; snapper, year round.

Operators In Belize City: *Blackline Marine*, PO Box 332, Mile 2, Western Highway, T 44155, F 31975; *Sea Masters Company Ltd*, PO Box 59, T 33185, F 026-2028; *Caribbean Charter Services*, PO Box 752, Mile 5, Northern Highway, T 45814 (have guarded car and boat park), fishing, diving and sightseeing trips to the Cayes.

Belize River Lodge, PO Box 459, T 025-2002, F 025-2298, excellent reputation.

Diving The shores are protected by the longest barrier reef in the Western Hemisphere. Lighthouse Reef, the outermost of the three N-S reef systems, offers pristine dive sites in addition to the incredible Blue Hole, a sinkhole exceeding 400 feet. Massive stalagmites and stalactites are found along overhangs down the sheer vertical walls of the Blue Hole. This outer reef lies beyond the access of most land-based diving resorts and even beyond most fishermen, so the marine life is undisturbed. An ideal way to visit this reef is on a liveaboard dive boat. An exciting marine phenomenon takes place during the full moon each Jan in the waters around Belize when thousands of the Nassau groupers gather to spawn at Glory Caye on Turneffe Reef.

Old wrecks and other underwater treasures are protected by law and cannot be removed. Spear fishing, as a sport, is discouraged in the interests of conservation. The beautiful coral formation is a great attraction for scuba diving, with canyons, coves, overhangs, ledges and walls. There are endless possibilities for underwater photography: schools of fishes amid the hard and soft coral, sponges and fans. Boats can only be hired for diving, fishing or sightseeing if they are licensed for the specific purpose by the government. This is intended to ensure that tourists travel on safe, reliable vessels and also to prevent the proliferation of self-appointed guides. Try to see that the boat which is taking you to see the reef does not damage this attraction by dropping its anchor on, or in any other way destroying, the coral. The coral reefs around the northerly, most touristy cayes are dying. There are decreasing numbers of small fishes as a necessary part of the coral lifecycle in more easily accessible reefs, including the underwater parks.

Belmopan and Belize City

BELMOPAN, THE CAPITAL, suffers from being created for political rather than economic reasons, and apart from some interesting buildings, it has little to offer the visitor. The real centre of the country remains Belize City which, while typical of the main cities of Central America – considerable historical interest, all the main services, good communications to everywhere else, and a certain amount of street crime, is quite Caribbean in appearance.

BELMOPAN

Belmopan (*pop* 3,927; *phone code* 08) is the capital; the seat of government was moved there from Belize City in Aug 1970. It is 50 miles inland to the W, near the junction of the Western Highway and the Hummingbird Highway to Dangriga (Stann Creek Town) – very scenic. It has a National Assembly building (which is open to the public), 2 blocks of government offices (which are copies of Mayan architecture), police headquarters, a public works department, a hospital, over 700 houses for civil servants, a non-governmental residential district to encourage expansion, and a market. It was projected to have a population of 40,000, so far there are only a fraction of that. Many government workers still commute from Belize City. The Department of Archaeology in the government plaza has a vault containing specimens of the country's artefacts, as there is no museum to house them. Guided tours are offered on Mon, Wed and Fri 1330-1430 only (a 2-day

prior appointment is necessary, T 08-22106). Visits are free, but donations are encouraged to help preserve the country's treasures. The city can be seen in less than an hour (break Belize City-San Ignacio bus journey, storing luggage safely at Batty Bus or Novelo terminal – but see below). A recent addition is the civic centre. The Western Highway from Belize City is now good (1-hr drive), continuing to San Ignacio, and there is an airfield (for charter services only).

Excursions
Nearby are Belize Zoo and Guanacaste Park both well worth a visit (as Belmopan's accommodation is so expensive it may be better to take an early bus to either from Belize City rather than go from the capital). See under **Western Belize**, below.

Local information
NB Belmopan has been described as 'a disaster for the budget traveller'; also, taxi drivers tend to overcharge.

● **Accommodation**
L3-A2 *Belmopan Convention*, 2 Bliss Parade,

T 22130, F 23066 (opp bus stop and market), a/c, hot water, swimming pool, restaurant, bars. **A3** *Bull Frog*, 23/25 Half Moon Ave, T 22111, a/c, good, reasonably priced, laundry (these 2 are a 15-min walk E of the market through the Parliament complex).

C *El Rey Inn*, 23 Moho St, T 23438, big room with fan, hot and cold water, basic, clean, friendly, restaurant, laundry on request, central.

● **Places to eat**
There are 3 restaurants (*Caladium*, next to market, limited fare, moderately priced, small portions, and *El Rey*, see above); there is a *comedor* at the back of the market, which is very clean; also a couple of bakeries nearby. Local food is sold by vendors, 2 stands in front sell ice cream (closed Sat and Sun), fruit and vegetable market open daily, limited produce available Sun. Shops close 1200-1400. No cafés open Sun.

● **Banks & money changers**
Barclays Bank International (0800-1300, Mon-Fri; and 1500-1800 Fri). Visa transactions, no commission (but see under Belize City, below).

● **Embassies & consulates**
British High Commission, North Ring Rd, next to the Governor's residence (PO Box 91, T 22146/7, F 22761). Officially 'visits' Belize City, 11 Marks St, T 45108, Mon, 0900-1100. The Commission has a list of rec doctors and dentists. **El Salvador**, 2 Ave Rio Grande, visa on the spot valid 1 month for 90-day stay, 1 photo, US$38 cash, better to get it in Guatemala, maps available, (PO Box 215, T/F 23404); **Costa Rica**, 2 Sapodilla St, T 22725, F 22731; **Panama**, 79 Unity Blvd, T 22714 (Embassy, for Consulate see under Belize City); Venezuelan Consul General, 18/20 Unity Blvd, T 22384.

● **Buses**
To **San Ignacio**, 1 hr, US$1, frequent service by Batty and Novelo from 0730-1700. To **Belize City**, 60 mins, US$1.50 frequent service by Batty, Z line and others. To **Dangriga**, **Mango Creek** and **Punta Gorda**, see under those towns. To **Orange Walk** and **Corozal** take an early bus to Belize City and change. Novelo's bus terminus will store luggage, but note that on Sun it closes at 1500.

BELIZE CITY

Belize City (*pop* 48,655; *phone code* 02, unless otherwise indicated) is the old capital and chief town. Most of the houses are built of wood, often of charming design, with galvanized iron roofs; they stand for the most part on piles about 7 ft above the ground, which is often swampy and flooded. There are vast water butts outside many houses, with pipes leading to the domestic supply. Ground-floor rooms are used as kitchens, or for storage. A sewerage system has been installed, and the water is reported safe to drink, though bottled water may be a wise precaution. Belize City hotels and tourist board are keen to develop the city. It has been improved over recent years with the canal being cleaned. There are plans to develop the sea front from the centre towards the *Ramada Royal Reef Hotel*. The introduction of tourist police has had a marked effect on crime levels. Just under a quarter of the total population live here, with the African strain predominating. Humidity is high, but the summer heat is tempered by the NE trades.

Hurricane Hattie swept a 10-ft tidal wave into the town on 31 October 1961, and caused much damage and loss of life. In 1978, Hurricane Greta caused extensive damage.

PLACES OF INTEREST

Haulover Creek divides the city; the swing bridge across the river is opened at 0530 and 1730 daily to let boats pass. Among the commonest craft are sandlighters, whose lateen sails can be seen off Belize City. Three canals further divide the city. The main commercial area is either side of the swing bridge, although most of the shops are on the S side, many being located on Regent and Albert streets. The area around **Battlefield** (formerly Central) **Park** is always busy, but it is no distance to Southern Foreshore with its views of the rivermouth, harbour and out to sea. At the southern end of Regent St, the **Anglican Cathedral** (St John's) and **Government House** nearby are interesting; both were built in the early 19th century. In the days before the foundation of

1. A & R Station, Boats to Caye Caulker & other Cayes
2. Baron Bliss Institute
3. Baron Bliss Memorial & Ft George Lighthouse
4. Battlefield Park
5. Brodie's Department Store
6. Catholic Church
7. Court House
8. Courthouse Wharf for Boats to San Pedro & Caye Caulker
9. Government House
10. Honduran Consulate
11. James Bus
12. Marine Terminal & Museum
13. MCC Grounds
14. Memorial Park
15. Mexican Embassy
16. National Stadium
17. Novello's Bus
18. Swing Bridge
19. Venus Bus & Z-Line
20. W Collut Canal, Cemetery Road Taxi Stand

Hotels:
21. *Bellevue*
22. *Fort George*
23. *Ramada Royal Reef*
24. Area of cheaper Hotels

To Municipal Airport

Guatemalan Consulate

Princess Margaret Drive

19th St
18th St
17th St
H St
G St
E St
D St
A St

12th St
11th St
8th St
K St
I St
14th St

St Thomas St
3rd St
bth St
7th St

Princess Margaret Dr

Nulin St
Hopkin St
Landivar St
St Peter's St

Newtown Barracks Rd
Baymen Av
Barracks Rd

St Joseph St

Freetown Rd

To International Airport & Northern Highway to Mexico

Simon Lamb St
Nurse Seay St

Calle Al Mar

Mom's Restaurant
Slaughterhouse Rd
Cran St
Mapp St

Cinderella Plaza Taxi Stand

Wilson St
Kelly St

Haulover

D Jones St
Cleghorn St
North Front St

New Rd
Castle St
York St

Eve St
Craig St

Mopan St
Eittee St
Sasstoon St
Magazine Rd

Belchina Bridge

Ebony St

Creek

Victoria St

Pickwrock St

Hyde's Lane
Caly Rd
Green St

Gaol La
Gabourel La

US Embassy

Logwood St
Banak St

Vernon St
Johnson St

Regent St W

Water Lane

Hutson St

Angel La
Handy de

Eyre St

Marine Parade

To Belmopan & Dangriga

Cemetery Rd

Orange St

Church St

Bishop St
King St

Fort St

N Park St
S Park St

Cork St

Curasson St
Gibnut St
Iguana St

W Collett Canal St
E Collett Canal St
Amara Av
Euphrates Av
West St
George St
W Canal St

Prince

Dean St
South

Dredge St

Raccoon St
Dolphin St

Allenby St

Berkley St
Albert St
Regent St

Southern Foreshore

To Belmopan & Guatemala

Mex Av

Anglican Cathedral

Caribbean

Sea

Neal's Pen Rd

Yarborough Rd
Queen Charlotte St

Rivero St
Waight St

Birds Isle

Not to Scale

Belize City

the Crown Colony the kings of the Mosquito Coast were crowned in the Cathedral, built with bricks brought from England as ships' ballast. In the Cathedral (not always open), note the 19th century memorial plaques which give a harrowing account of early death from 'country fever' (yellow fever) and other tropical diseases. The museum in Government House is open Mon-Fri, 0830-1200, 1300-1630, entry US$5. It contains some interesting pictures of colonial times, displays of furniture and silver and glassware, as well as a display showing fishing techniques and model boats.

On the N side of the swing bridge, turn left up North Front St for some of the cheaper hotels and the A and R Station, from which most boats leave for the Cayes. Turn right for the Post Office, Tourist Office and roads which lead to **Marine Parade** (also with sea views). Opposite the Post Office is the new **Marine Terminal** and **Museum** housed in a colonial building. It features a mangrove exhibition, reef exhibition and aquarium, entry US$3. At the junction of Cork St at Marine Parade is the *Fort George Hotel* whose Club Wing, a copper-coloured glass tower, is a considerable landmark. **Memorial Park** on Marine Parade has a small obelisk, two cannon, concrete benches, and is peppered with the holes of landcrabs. The small park by the **Fort George Lighthouse** has a children's play area and is a popular meeting place.

Coming in by sea, after passing the barrier reef, Belize City is approached by a narrow, tortuous channel. This and the chain of mangrove cayes give shelter to what would otherwise be an open roadstead.

Belize is the nearest adequate port to the State of Quintana Roo (Mexico), and re-exports mahogany from that area. It also handles substantial container traffic for Yucatán.

LOCAL INFORMATION

● **Security**

Tourist police patrol the city centre to prevent attacks on tourists, give safety advice, etc. They wear greenish uniforms and have, since their introduction in Aug 1995, greatly reduced crime in the city by nearly 40%. It is planned to station the police elsewhere in the country.

Watch out for conmen, some in uniform, who would like to disappear with your money. Do not trust the many self-appointed 'guides' who also sell hotel rooms, boat trips to the Cayes, drugs, etc. Local advice is not even to say "no"; just shake your head and wag your finger if approached by a stranger. Street money changers are not to be trusted either. It is wise to avoid small, narrow side streets and stick to major thoroughfares, although even on main streets you can be victim to unprovoked threats and racial abuse. Hostility and racial abuse towards whites is common. A common sense attitude is needed and a careful watch on your possessions is recommended. No jewellery or watches should be worn. Travel by taxi (cheap) is advisable particularly at night and in the rain. Areas which are best avoided at night (because they are frequented by crack users) are near Pinks and Bride's Alleys opp Tourist Office, on the Southern Foreshore and the area bounded by the Southside Canal, Haulover Creek and Collet Canal (where the bus stations are).

Cars should only be left in guarded carparks. For a tip, the security officer at the *Ramada* will look after your car for a few days while you go to the Cayes.

The whole city closes down on Sun except for a few shops open on Sun morning, eg Brodies in the centre of town. Banks and many shops are closed on Wed afternoons.

● **Accommodation**

Hotel prices

L1	over US$200	**L2**	US$151-200
L3	US$101-150	**A1**	US$81-100
A2	US$61-80	**A3**	US$46-60
B	US$31-45	**C**	US$21-30
D	US$12-20	**E**	US$7-11
F	US$4-6	**G**	up to US$3

All hotels are subject to 7% government tax (on room rate only).

L1-L3 *Ramada Royal Reef and Marina*, Newtown Barracks (PO Box 1758), T 32670, F 34322, on sea front (but not central), marina facilities, a/c, good food and service in restaurant

Local information 747

and bar (a/c with sea views, expensive), good business facilities, informal snack bar near the dock is lively at night, nice pool and children's play area; **L2-A1** *Belize Biltmore Plaza*, Mile 3 Northern Highway, T 32302, F 32301, Best Western since 1995, comfortable rooms, a/c, restaurant (nice atmosphere, a/c, good selection), excellent English pub-style bar (but karaoke in bar most evenings), pool, conference facilities, a long way from town (US$3.50 or more by taxi); **L2-A3** *Bellevue*, 5 Southern Foreshore (T 77051, F 73253), a/c, private bath, good laundry service, restaurant (nice atmosphere, good lunches with live music, steaks), leafy courtyard pool, nice bar with live music Fri and Sat nights, good entertainment, rec; **L3** *Radisson Fort George*, 2 Marine Parade (PO Box 321, T 33333, F 73820), in 3 wings (Club Wing, Colonial Section and former *Holiday Inn Villa*), each with excellent rooms, refurbished 1995, a/c, helpful staff, reservations should be made, safe parking, good restaurant, good pool (non-residents may use pool for US$10), rec; **L3-A3** *Belize International*, at Ladyville, 9 miles on Northern Highway, T 52150 or 44001, 1½ miles from airport, tennis court, restaurant and bar; **L3-A3** *Chateau Caribbean*, 6 Marine Parade, by Fort George (T 30800, F 30900), a/c, with good bar, restaurant (excellent Chinese and seafood, sea view, good service) and discotheque, parking, but a decaying seafront mansion.

A3 *Alicia's Guest House*, corner Dean St and Chapel Lane, T 75082, with a/c, some with fan, fruit and tea/coffee inc, owner Anselmo Ortiz (Alicia, his daughter) friendly and helpful; **A3** *Bakadeer Inn*, 74 Cleghorn St, T 31286, F 31963, private bath, breakfast US$4, a/c, TV, fridge, friendly, rec; **A3** *Colton House*, 9 Cork St, T 44666, F 30451, named after owners, delightful 1928 colonial style home, private bath, some a/c, overhead fans, large rooms, friendly, helpful, quiet; **A3** *Four Fort Street* (address as name), T 30116, F 78808, full breakfast inc, 6 rooms, all with 4-poster beds and shared bath, charming, excellent restaurant, rec.

B *El Centro*, 4 Bishop St, T 72413, a/c, restaurant, good value; **B** *Glenthorne Manor*, 27 Barrack Rd. (T 44212), with or without bath, colonial-style, safe, getting run down, meals available, overpriced; **B** *Mopan*, 55 Regent St, T 77351, with bath, breakfast, a/c, in historic house, has restaurant and bar (owners Tom and Jean Shaw), nice but pricey, helpful with information, transport arrangements; **B** *Royal Orchid*, 153 New Rd and Douglas Jones St,

T 32783, F 32789, a/c, with bar, restaurant, laundry service, Chinese, not central.

C *Freddie's*, 86 Eve St, T 44396, with shower and toilet, fan, hot water, clean, very nice, secure, very small; **C** *Isabel Guest House*, 3 Albert St, above Matus Store, PO Box 362, T 73139, 3 double rooms, 1 huge triple room, quiet, private shower, clean, friendly, safe, Spanish spoken, highly rec; **C** *Orchidia*, Regent St, clean, safe; **C** *Sea Side Guest House*, 3 Prince St, T 78339, E pp in bunk room, popular, very clean, pleasant verandah, owned by Quaker Group.

D *Annis Louise*, 3 Freetown Rd, T 44670, shared bath, fan; **D** *Belize River Lodge*, Ladyville, PO Box 459 Belize City, T 52002, F 52298, 10 mins from airport on Belize River, excellent accommodation, food and fishing (from lodge or cruises), also scuba facilities, numerous packages; **D** *Bon Aventure*, 122 North Front St, T 44248, **E** in dormitory, purified water available, a bit run down, not very clean, but one of the best cheap options in Belize City, Hong Kong Chinese owners helpful and friendly, secure, Spanish spoken, laundry service, good meals at reasonable prices, a few rooms rented by 'working girls'; opp are **D** *Mira Rio*, 59 North Front St, shared hot shower, fan, toilet, clean, covered verandah overlooking Haulover Creek, Spanish spoken, good food, noisy bar opp; **D** *Downtown Guest House*, 5 Eve St, T 30951, small rooms, hot shower, secure, friendly, clean, breakfast available, noisy but rec; **D** *North Front Street Guest House*, T 77595, 1 block N of Post Office, 15-min walk from Batty bus station, 124 North Front St, no hot water, fan, book exchange, TV, friendly, laundry, good information, keep windows closed at night and be sure to lock your door; **D** *Venus*, Magazine Rd, T 77390, at Venus Bus Station; **C** with a/c, rooms without a/c have ceiling fans, and are quieter and lighter, private bath, clean, safe.

E *Marin Travel Lodge*, 6 Craig St, T 45166, good, fans, shared hot showers, clean, safe, regretfully keep unhappy coati on short chain; **E** *Riverview*, 25 Regent St West, T 73392, basic.

Camping: no tent sites. Camping on the beaches, in forest reserves, or in any other public place is not allowed. **NB** Butane gas in trailer/coleman stove size storage bottles is available in Belize.

● **Places to eat**

It can be difficult to find places to eat between 1500 and 1800. See also Hotels above. *Four Fort Street* (at that address), nr Memorial Park, nice atmosphere, sit out on the verandah, desserts a speciality, rec (see **Accommodation** above); *Macy's*, 18 Bishop St (T 73419), rec for well-prepared local game, Creole cooking, different fixed menu daily, charming host; *Grill*, 164 Newtown Barracks (a short taxi ride from major hotels), English owner Richard Price, considered by many as best restaurant in the city, varied menu, T 45020; *DIT's*, 50 King St, good, cheap; *GG's Café and Patio*, 2-3 King St, popular for lunches, about US$5 for a main dish, good quality, good service, George Godfrey well informed host, ask for his extra hot home made sauce, rec; *King's*, St Thomas St, good value; *Big Daddy's*, Church St opp BTL office, good cheap food; *Mom's*, 7145 Slaughterhouse Rd, nr Freetown Rd, good breakfasts, Mexican dishes, salad bar; *Marlin*, 11 Regent St West, overlooking Belize River, T 73913, varied menu, good seafood.

New Chon Saan, 55 Euphrates Av, T 72709, best Chinese in town, pleasant atmosphere (taxi ride), take away; *Hong Kong*, 50 Queen St, Chinese, reasonably priced, good lobster salad; *Canton*, New Rd, large portions, good, cheap; *China Garden*, 46 Regent St, lunch specials; *Shek Kei*, 80 Freetown Rd, Chinese, good; *Ding Ho*, North Front St, good Chinese, try their 'special' dishes; other Chinese (fair): *Yin Kee*, 64 Freetown Rd, *Taiwan*, 93 Cemetery Rd. *Sea Rock*, Queen and Handyside Sts, good Indian food. *Pop 'n' Taco*, Regent St, good sweet and sour chicken, cheap, friendly service; *Edward Quan Fried Chicken*, New Rd, take away, good. *H & L Burgers*, 4 locations; *Playboy*, 11 King St, good sandwiches; *Blue Bird*, Albert St, cheap fruit juices; specialities, modest, clean, reasonable; *Babb's*, Queen and Eve Sts, good pastries, meat pies, juices, friendly; *De-Lites*, opp Brodies Department Store, quick, tasty snacks; *Flores Fruit*, N end of Barrack Rd, tamale lunch US$1, good juices.

● **Bars**

Best and safest bars are found at major hotels, Fort George, Biltmore Plaza, Bellevue and Four Fort Street. If you want a little local charm *Lindbergh's Landing*, 164A Newtown Rd (next to *Grill*) is fun, open air with sea view. Lots of bars some with juke boxes and poolrooms. *Privateer*, Mile 4½ on Northern Highway, on seafront, expensive drinks but you can sit outside. Try the local drink, anise and peppermint, known as 'A and P'; also the powerful 'Old Belizeno' rum. The local beer, Belikin, is good, as is the 'stout', strong and free of gas. Guinness is also served, but is expensive.

● **Airline offices**

Local: Tropic Air, Belize City T 02-45671, San Pedro 026-2012/2117/2029, F 062-2338; **Island Air**, Belize City T 02-31140, International airport 025-2219, San Pedro 026-2435/2484, F 026-2192; **Maya Air**, 6 Fort St, PO Box 458, Belize City T 02-35794/5, municipal airport 02-44234/44032, International 025-2336, San Pedro 026-2611, F 02-30585/30031.

International: Taca (Belize Global Travel), 41 Albert St (T 02-77363/77185, F 75213), International T 025-2163, F 025-2453, also **British Airways**, T 77363, International T 025-2060/2458. **American**, Valencia Building, T 02-32522/3/4 and **Continental Airlines**, 32 Albert St, T 02-78309/78463/78223, International 025-2263/2488. **Aerovías**, in *Mopan Hotel*, 55 Regent St, T 02-75383/ 75445/6, F 75383, for Flores/Guatemala.

● **Banks & money changers**

All banks have facilities to arrange cash advance on Visa card. The **Belize Bank** is particularly efficient and modern, US$0.50 commission on Amex cheques but a big charge for cash against Visa and Mastercharge; also **Barclays Bank International**, with some country branches, slightly better rates, 2% commission, no charge for Visa/Mastercharge. **Atlantic Bank**, 6 Albert St, or 16 New Rd (the latter in a safe area), quick efficient service, small charge for Visa/Mastercharge, smaller queues than Belize Bank or Barclays. **Bank of Nova Scotia**. Banking hours: Mon-Thur 0800-1300, Fri 0800-1200 and 1300-1630. It is easy to have money telexed to Belize City. Guatemalan quetzales are very easy to obtain at the borders, less easy in Belize City. American Express at **Global Travel**, 41 Albert St (T 77185/77363/4). Good exchange rates at **Belize Global Travel Services**, 41 Albert St. Money changers at Batty Bus terminal just before departure of bus to Chetumal (the only place to change Mexican pesos except at the border). Some shops change without commission.

● **Cultural centres**

Baron Bliss Institute, public library, temporary exhibitions; has 1 Stela and 2 large discs from Caracol on display. Audubon Society: see under Nature Conservation in the Introduction.

● **Embassies & consulates**

See also under Belmopan. **Mexican Embassy**, 20 Park St, T 30193/4 (open 0900-1230, Mon-Fri, documents returned 1530-1630; if going to Mexico and requiring a visa, get it here, not at the border, tourist card given on the spot, note that long queues are normal, arrive early, get visa the afternoon before departure; **Honduras**, 91 North Front St, T 45889; **El Salvador**, 120 New Rd, T 44318; **Costa Rica**, 8-18th St, T 44796; **Panama Consulate**, 5481 Princess Margaret Drive, T 34282; **Guatemala Embassy**, 1 St John St, Belize City, T 33314, F 35140; **Guatemala Consulate**, 6A Saint Matthew St, nr municipal airstrip, T 33150, open 0900-1300, will not issue visas or tourist cards here and tell you to leave it till you reach San José Succotz (see page 778); **Jamaica**, 26 Corner Hyde's Lane and New Rd, T 45926, F 23312.

USA Embassy, 29 Gabourel Lane, T 77161/2, consulate is on Hutson St, round corner from embassy's entrance on Gabourel Lane, consulate open 0800-1000 for visitor visas, library 0830-1200, 1330-1630 Mon-Fri, but am only on Wed; **Canada**, 83 N Front St, T 31060; **Belgium**, Marcelo Ltd, Queen St, T 45769; **The Netherlands**, 14 Central American Blvd, T 73612; **France**, 9 Barrack Rd, T 32708; **German Honorary Consul**, 123 Albert St, T 73343; **Denmark**, 13 Southern Foreshore, T 72172; **Norway**, 1 King St, T 77031, F 77062; **Sweden**, 13 Queen St, T 77234; **Italy**, 18 Albert St, T 78449; **Israel**, 4 Albert and Bishop St, T 73991/73150, F 30750.

● **Entertainment**

Clubs and discos: *The Big Apple*, North Front St, live music at weekends, good, *The Louisville Democratic Bar*, psychedelic decor, lively and amusing, good loud music, best Fri-Sun, rec.

● **Laundry**

Central American Coin-Op Laundry, junction Barrack Rd and Freetown Rd, wash US$3.50, dryer US$1.50, powder US$0.50, self-service.

● **Places of worship**

There are an Anglican Cathedral, a Catholic Cathedral, a Methodist and a Presbyterian church. The Baptist Church is on Queen St.

● **Post & telecommunication**

Post Office: letters, Queen St and N Front St, 0800-1700 (1630 Fri); parcels, beside main Post Office, these must be wrapped in brown paper, sold by the yard in large stationery shop around the corner in Queen St. Letters held for 1 month. Beautiful stamps too.

International telecommunications: telegraph, telephone, telex services, Belizean Telecommunications Ltd, No 1 Church St just off Central Park, 0800-1800, 0800-1200 on Sun. Also public fax service and booths for credit card and charge calls to USA, UK.

● **Shopping**

Handicrafts, woodcarvings, straw items, are all good buys. The Belize Chamber of Commerce has opened a Belize crafts sales room on Fort St, opp *Four Fort Street* restaurant, to be a showcase and promote the efforts of crafts people from all over Belize, come here first. *Nile*, 49 Eve St, Middle East. *Go Tees*, 23 Regent St, T 74082, excellent selection of T-shirts (printed on premises), arts and crafts from Belize, Guatemala and Mexico: jewellery, silver, wood carvings, clothes, paintings, etc; also has a branch at Belize Zoo, good zoo T-shirts and cuddly animals. Zericote (or Xericote) wood carvings can be bought in Belize City, for example at *Brodies Department Store* (Central Park end of Regent St), which also sells postcards, the *Fort George Hotel*, the small gift shop at *Four Fort Street*, or from Egbert Peyrefitte, 11a Cemetery Rd. Such wood carvings are the best buy, but to find a carver rather than buy the tourist fare in shops, ask a taxi driver. (At the Art Centre, nr Government House, the wood sculpture of Charles Gabb, who introduced carving into Belize, can be seen.) Wood carvers sell their work in front of the *Fort George* and *Holiday Inn Villa* hotels. A new craft centre at the southern end of the swing bridge, on the site of the old market, should be open by 1993. The market is by the junction of North Front St and Fort St. *Ro-Macs*, 27 Albert St, excellent supermarket inc wide selection of imported foods and wines. *Thrift Center*, 2 Church St, good food store.

Bookshops: *Book Centre*, 2 Church St, above Thrift Center, very good, has secondhand books and back issues of US magazines. *Belize Bookshop*, Regent St (opp *Mopan Hotel*), ask at counter for 'racy' British greetings cards. *Angelus Press*, 10 Queen St, excellent selection of stationery supplies, books, cards, etc. *The Book Shop*, 126 Freetown Rd, new and secondhand books, also exchange books. *Book Centre*, Church St, good selection.

● **Tour companies & travel agents**

Tours: *S and L Guided Tours*, 91 North Front St, T 77593, F 77594, rec group travel (minimum 4 persons for most tours, 2 persons to Tikal); *Native Guide Systems*, 2 Water Lane, T 75819, F 74007, PO Box 1045, individual and group tours. A great many others both inside and outside Belize. Tourist Bureau has a full list. If booking tours in Belize from abroad it is advisable to check prices and services offered with a reputable tour operator in Belize first.

● Tourist offices

Belize Tourist Bureau, 83 North Front St, Belize, PO Box 325, T 77213/73255, F 77490 (open 0800-1200, 1300-1700 Mon-Thur, and till 1630 Fri), provides complete bus schedule (care, may be out of date) with a map of Belize City, as well as list of hotels and their prices. Also has *Mexico and Central American Handbook* for sale and a list of rec taxi guides and tour operators, and free publications on the country and its Maya ruins, practical and informative. Excellent maps of the country for US$3 (postage extra). **Belize Tourism Industry Association** (private sector body for hotels, tour companies, etc), 99 Albert St, T 75717, F 78710, brochures and information on all members throughout Belize. Enquire for all details of all Belize tour operators. Suggested reading is *Hey Dad, this is Belize*, by Emory King, a collection of anecdotes, or more seriously, *Warlords and Maize Men, a guide to the Mayan Sites of Belize*, Association for Belize Archaeology, available in bookshops. Maps (US$3), books on Belizean fauna etc available at Angelus Press, Queen St. Above the Post office is the Survey Office selling maps, 2-sheet, 1:250,000 US$10, dated, or more basic map US$2 (open Mon-Thur 0830-1200, 1300-1600, but 1530 on Fri).

Caribbean Charter Services, Mile 5 North Highway, PO Box 752. Belize City, T 30404, F 33711, is a tourist information centre and agency for airline flight tickets, boat charters, inland resorts and other facilities, Bulletin Board Service, owned by Ms Ruha'mah Stadtlander.

● Transport

Local Car hire: only 1 car rental company will release registration papers to enable cars to enter Guatemala or Mexico (Crystal–see below). Without obtaining them at the time of hire it is impossible to take hire cars across national frontiers. It is best to take a scheduled tour to Tikal or Flores in Guatemala, if intending to return to Belize, because the road is in a poor state and because entry through military checkpoints is quicker. Car hire cost is high in Belize owing to heavy wear and tear on the vehicles. You can expect to pay between US$65 for a Suzuki Samuri to US$125 for an Isuzu Trooper/day. Cautious driving is advised in Belize as road conditions, while improving steadily, are generally poor except for the Northern and Western Highways and there is no street lighting in rural areas. When driving in the Mountain Pine Ridge area it is prudent to check carefully on road conditions at the entry gate; good maps are essential. Emory King's *Drivers Guide to Belize* is helpful when driving to the more remote areas. **Budget** PO Box 863, 771 Bella Vista (nr International Airport, can pick up and drop off car at airport, office almost opp *Biltmore Plaza Hotel*), T 32435, good service, well-maintained vehicles, good deals (Suzukis and Isuzu Troopers); **Crystal**, Mile 1.5 Northern Highway, T 31600, Jay Crofton, helpful, cheapest deals in town, but not always most reliable, wide selection of vehicles inc 30-seater bus, will release insurance papers for car entry to Guatemala and Mexico (speak to Jay about his scheme to drive imported vehicles from Houston to Belize), he also buys second hand cars but at a poor price; **Pancho's**, 5747 Lizarraga Av, T 45554; **National**, International Airport, T 31586 (Cherokee Chiefs); **Avis**, at *Fort George Hotel*, T 78637, airport T 52385, largest fleet, well-maintained, Daihatsus and Isuzu Troopers. **Smith & Sons**, 125 Cemetery Rd, T 73779 (less reliable than in the past); **Gilly's**, 31 Regent St, T 77613; **Lewis**, 23 Cemetery Rd, T 74461. CDW ranges from US$10 to US$20/day. **Safari**, 11a Cork St, beside *Radisson Fort George Hotel*, T 30268, F 35395, Isuzu Troopers.

Taxis: have green licence plates (drivers must also have identification card); within Belize, US$2.50 for 1 person; for 2 or more passengers, US$1.75 pp. International Airport to Belize centre, US$15; municipal airport to centre, US$7.50. (**NB** If you check several hotels, you may be charged for each ride.) There is a taxi stand on Central Park, opp Barclays, another on the corner of Collet Canal St and Cemetery Rd. Outside Belize City, US$1.75/mile, regardless of number of passengers. Belize City to the resorts in Cayo District approx US$100-125, 1-4 people (ask for Edgar August or Martin at *Radisson Fort George* desk, they are reliable and can do guided tours around Belize). Best to ask price of the ride before setting off. No meters, so beware of overcharging and make sure fare is quoted in BZ$. No tips necessary. If you have a complaint, take the licence plate and report to the Taxi Union.

Air There is a 10-mile tarmac road to the Phillip SW Goldson International Airport; modern check-in facilities, toilets, restaurant, bank (open 0830-1100 and 1330-1630, not Sun), viewing deck and duty-free shop, a/c. No facilities on Arrivals side. Taxi fare US$15; make sure your taxi is legitimate. Any bus going up the Northern Highway passes the airport junction (US$0.75), then 1½ mile walk.

There is a municipal airstrip for local flights, 15 mins out of town, taxi, US$7.50, no bus service. Services to San Pedro, Caye Chapel, Caye Caulker with Tropic Air, Island Air and Maya Airways, flights every 30 mins, 0700 to 1630, US$39 municipal to San Pedro return, US$34 municipal to Caye Chapel return and US$35 to Caye Caulker return (US$19 one way). Flights to and from the islands can be taken from the International Airport and companies link their flights to meet or leave international departures; add approx US$12 each way to the price to/from municipal airport.

Services also to Corozal (Tropic Air), 30 mins, US$44. To Big Creek US$47; San Ignacio, Placencia, Dangriga, US$29; Punta Gorda, US$70 (from international) or US$58 (from municipal) with Maya Air and Tropic Air, 5 flights daily from 0700, last return flight 1705 (one way fares).

Buses Within the city the fare is US$0.50. There are bus services to the main towns. To **Chetumal** (see Mexico, **Yucatán Peninsula**, Section 10), several daily each way (there are several express Batty Buses from 0600 stopping at Orange Walk and Corozal only), US$5, up to 4 inc crossing, with 2 companies: Batty Bus, 54 East Collet Canal St, T 74924, F 78991, and Venus, Magazine Rd, T 73354. If taking a bus from Chetumal which will arrive in Belize City after dark, decide on a hotel and go there by taxi. Batty Bus to **Belmopan** and **San Ignacio**, 4 hrs, US$4.50, Mon-Sat frequent 0600 to 1900, Sun 0630 to 1700. Novelo's run until 2000. The 0600, 0630 and 1015 buses connect at the border with services to Flores, Guatemala. To San Ignacio, Benque Viejo and the Guatemalan border via Belmopan, Novelo's, West Collet Canal, T 73372 (can store luggage US$0.50), US$1.25 to Belmopan, US$3 to Benque, US$2.50 to San Ignacio, hourly Mon-Sat, 1100 to 1900. The last possible bus connection to Flores leaves the

border at 1600, but it is better to get an earlier bus to arrive in daylight. Several Batty buses leave for **Melchor de Mencos**, from 0600 to 1030. To **Flores, Guatemala**, minibuses leave the A & R Station on Front St at 0500, make reservation the previous day. To **Dangriga**, via Belmopan and the Hummingbird Highway 7-line (T 73937), from Venus bus station, daily, 0800, 1000, 1100, 1500, 1600, plus Mon 0600, US$5; James Bus Line, Pound Yard Bridge (Collet Canal), unreliable, slow, 9-12 hrs, to **Punta Gorda** via Dangriga, Cockscomb Basin Wildlife Sanctuary and Mango Creek, daily 0800 and 1500, US$11. **NB** The bus stations are in an unsafe area of town. If taking a bus early in the morning, try to stay nr the bus station as you will find it difficult to find a taxi before about 0530, and walking through this part of town in darkness with luggage is dangerous. If arriving at in the late evening, you should be able to find a taxi, eg Batty Bus Station to centre, US$2.50. During the day, since it is not far from the bus terminals to the centre, or to the boat dock for the Cayes, don't be given the run-around by taxi drivers.

Shipping The only boat to Guatemala goes from Punta Gorda; for Puerto Cortés, Honduras, boats leave from Dangriga, Mango Creek and Placencia. Obtain all necessary exit stamps and visas before sailing. See under each town for details. For boats to the Cayes and other places in Belize, see under destinations.

At Ladyville, on the other side of the Northern Highway from the turning to the airport, the Secretariat for Mundo Maya is being built at Bella Vista. This will be the headquarters for all the countries involved in this regional tourism promotion.

The Northern Cayes

THE CAYES OFF the coast are most attractive, relaxing, slow and very 'Caribbean'. An excellent place for all forms of diving and sea fishing.

The Cayes are popular destinations, especially from Feb to May and in Aug. Ask around (for example, the skippers of the boats to Caye Caulker or Chapel) for information on staying with families on the smaller, lesser populated cayes.

There are 212 sq miles of cayes. **St George's Caye**, 9 miles NE of Belize, was once the capital and was the scene of the battle in 1798 which established British possession. The larger ones are Turneffe Island and Ambergris and Caulker Cayes. Fishermen live on some cayes, coconuts are grown on others, but many are uninhabited swamps. The smaller cayes do not have much shade, so be careful if you go bathing on them. Sandflies infest some cayes (eg Caulker), the sandfly season is Dec to beginning of Feb; mosquito season June, July, sometimes Oct.

Travel by boat to and between the islands is becoming increasingly regulated and the new licensing requirements will probably drive the cheaper boats out of business. In general, it is easier to arrange travel between the islands once there, than from Belize City. All authorized boats leave from Jan's Station (A and R) on North Front St, or, especially for San Pedro, from the boat dock on Southern Foreshore outside *Bellevue Hotel*. There is a new Marine Terminal opposite the Post Office for fares to Caye Caulker,

US$7.50. Cargo boats are no longer allowed to carry passengers, too many have capsized with tourists on board, causing loss of life.

On **St George's Caye**: *A1-A2 Cottage Colony*, PO Box 428, Belize City, T 02-77051, F 02-73253, colonial-style cabañas with dive facilities, price varies according to season, easy access from Belize City. *St George's Island Cottages*, PO Box 625, Belize City, 6 rooms. Boat fare is US$15, day trips are possible.

Caye Chapel is free of sandflies and mosquitoes and there are several beaches, cleaned daily. 40 mins by boat from Belize City, US$7.50. The *Pyramid Island Resort* owns the island (A3 price range, credit cards not accepted); it has an excellent beach and dive courses (PADI). Be careful if you hire a boat for a day to visit Caye Chapel: the boatmen enjoy the bar on the island and your return journey can be unreasonably exciting. Also, there are very few fish now round this caye. There is a landing strip used by local airlines, which stop flights between Belize and San Pedro on request.

On **Long Caye** the guesthouse is now closed to the public. The Caye is being taken over by a private corporation.

Small caye resorts within easy reach of Belize City: *Moonlight Shadows Lodge*, **Middle Long Caye**, T 08-22587, still in

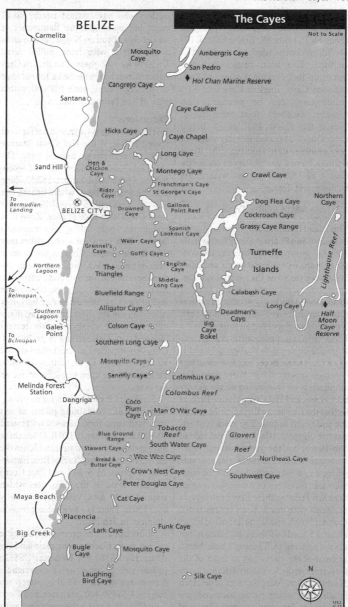

BELIZE

The Cayes

Not to Scale

Carmelita

Mosquito Caye

Ambergris Caye

San Pedro

Hol Chan Marine Reserve

Cangrejo Caye

Santana

Caye Caulker

Hicks Caye

Caye Chapel

Sand Hill

Long Caye

Hen & Chicken Caye

Montego Caye

Crawl Caye

Frenchman's Caye

Rider Caye

St George's Caye

Dog Flea Caye

Northern Caye

To Bermudian Landing

BELIZE CITY

Drowned Caye

Gallows Point Reef

Cockroach Caye

Grassy Caye Range

Spanish Lookout Caye

Lighthouse Reef

Grennel's Caye

Water Caye

Turneffe

Goff's Caye

English Caye

Islands

Northern Lagoon

The Triangles

Middle Long Caye

To Belmopan

Bluefield Range

Calabash Caye

Southern Lagoon

Alligator Caye

Long Caye

Gales Point

Colson Caye

Deadman's Caye

Half Moon Caye Reserve

To Belmopan

Big Caye Bokel

Southern Long Caye

Mosquito Caye

Sandfly Caye

Columbus Caye

Melinda Forest Station

Columbus Reef

Dangriga

Coco Plum Caye

Man O'War Caye

Tobacco Reef

Glovers Reef

Blue Ground Range

Stewart Caye

South Water Caye

Bread & Butter Caye

Wee Wee Caye

Northeast Caye

Crow's Nest Caye

Southwest Caye

Peter Douglas Caye

Maya Beach

Cat Caye

Placencia

Funk Caye

Big Creek

Lark Caye

Bugle Caye

Mosquito Caye

Laughing Bird Caye

Silk Caye

N

early stages of development. *Ricardo's Beach Huts*, Blue Field Range (59 North Front St, PO Box 55, Belize City, T 02-44970), recommended, charming and knowledgeable host, rustic, authentic fish camp feel, overnight camps to Rendez-vous Caye, English Caye and Sargeants Caye can be arranged with Ricardo, excellent food, snorkelling. *Spanish Bay Resort*, PO Box 35, Belize City, T 02-77288, also in early stages of development, dive facilities. *The Wave*, Gallows Point Caye (9 Regent St, Belize City, T 02-73054), 6 rooms, watersports facilities and diving.

AMBERGRIS CAYE

This island (pronounced Amb*er*gris), with its town of **San Pedro** (*pop* 1,527; *phone code* 026), has grown rapidly over the last couple of years, with over 50 hotels and guest houses restricted on the island. Buildings are still restricted to no more than 3 storeys in height and the many wooden structures retain an authentic village atmosphere. New hotels are opening all the time and a US$250mn resort and casino is proposed. It should be noted that, although sand is in abundance, there are few excellent beach areas around San Pedro town. The emphasis is on snorkelling on the nearby barrier reef and Hol Chan Marine Park, as well as the fine scuba diving, sailing, fishing and board sailing. The main boat jetties are on the E (Caribbean sea) side of San Pedro, but the yacht harbour is increasingly moving to the W (lagoon) side where a new marina will shortly be completed. In fact it can be dangerous to swim near San Pedro as there have been serious accidents with boats. Boats are restricted to about 5 mph within the line of red buoys about 25 yards offshore but this is not always adhered to. There is a 'safe' beach in front of the park, just to the S of the Government dock. A short distance to the N and S of San Pedro lie miles of deserted beach front, where picnic barbecues are popular for day-tripping snorkellers and birders who have visited nearby small cayes hoping to glimpse flamingoes or scarlet ibis. If you go N you have to cross a small inlet with hand pulled ferry, US$0.50 for foreigners. The British Ordnance Survey has published a Tourist Map of Ambergris Caye, scale 1:50,000, with a plan of **San Pedro**, 1:5,000.

Excursions

Just S of Ambergris Caye, and not far from Caye Caulker, is the **Hol Chan Marine Park**, an underwater natural park. Divided into 3 zones, zone A is the reef, where fishing is prohibited. Entry US$2.50. Zone B is the seagrass beds, where fishing can only be done with a special licence; the Boca Ciega blue hole is here. Zone C is mangroves where fishing also requires a licence. Only certified scuba divers may dive in the reserve. Contact the Reserve Manager in San Pedro for further information. Several boatmen in San Pedro offer snorkelling trips to the park, US$15 (not including entry fee), 2 hrs. At Shark-Ray Alley, you can see shark, manta ray, many other fish and coral; a highly recommended trip. Fish feeding is prohibited. Only very experienced snorkellers should attempt to swim in the cutting between the reef and the open sea; seek advice on the tides.

San Pedro is well known for its diving. Long canyons containing plenty of soft and hard coral formations start around 50-60 ft and go down to 120 ft. Often these have grown into hollow tubes which make for interesting diving. Tackle Box, Esmeralda, Cypress, M & MS and Tres Cocos are only some of the dive sites which abound in the area. Visability is usually over 150 ft. There is now a recompression chamber in San Pedro.

Tours can also be arranged from here to visit many places on the mainland (eg Altun Ha US$60 pp; Lamanai US$125 pp) as well as other water experiences (catamaran sailing US$40 pp, deep sea fishing US$150-400, manatee and Coco Solo US$75). Among the many operators

Hustler Tours, T 26-2538 (Billy and his brothers are experienced and very helpful) are recommended. Day cruises to Caye Caulker and barrier reef on the island trader MV Winnie Estelle is good value at US$45 pp to include snacks and soft drinks. Other day snorkelling trips from US$25 to Caye Caulker with stops at Sting Ray Alley and coral gardens. Snorkel rental US$5, discount through tour group.

Local information
● Accommodation

In San Pedro: L1-L2 Belize Yacht Club, PO Box 1, T 2777, F 2768, all rooms are suites with fully-furnished kitchens, bar and restaurant, pool, docking facilities; L2-L3 Paradise Villas, condominiums alongside Paradise Resort, owners let villas when not occupied, T 3077, F 3831, a/c, the collection of 20 villas around a small (and not always very clean pool) are well equipped and convenient; L2-A1 Ramon's Village Resort, T 2071/2213, F 2214, or USA 601-649 1990, F 601-425-2411 (PO Drawer 4407, Laurel, MS 39441), agree on which currency you are paying in, 61 rooms, a diving and beach resort, all meals and all diving, highly rec even for non-divers (fishing, swimming, boating, snorkelling), very efficient, comfortable rooms, pool with beach club atmosphere; L3 Mayan Princess, T 2778, F 2784, centre of village on seafront, clean, comfortable; L3 A2 Paradise Resort Hotel, T 2083, F 2232, wide selection of rooms and villas, good location, villas better value, cheaper summer rates, all watersports; A1 Rock's Inn Apartments, T 2326, F 2358, good value and service; A1 San Pedro Holiday Hotel, PO Box 1140, Belize City, T 2014/2103, F 2295, 16 rooms in good central location, fun atmosphere with good facilities, reasonable value; A1 Sun Breeze, T 2347/2191/2345, F 2346, nr airport, Mexican style building, a/c, comfortable, all facilities, good dive shop, rec; A1-B Coral Beach, T 2013, F 2001, central location, slightly run down but good local feel and excellent watersports facilities inc dive boat charter, tours for fishing and scuba available; A2 Changes in Latitudes, T/F 2986, next to Yacht Club, new, breakfast inc, Canadian owners; A2-A3 Spindrift, T 2018, F 2251, 24 rooms, 4 apartments, unattractive block but central location, good bar and restaurant, popular meeting place, trips up the Belize River, a/c, comfortable; A2-B Barrier Reef, T 2075, F 2719, handsome wooden house in centre, a/c, pool.

Just outside San Pedro: L1-L2 Caribbean Villas, T 2715, F 2885, 10 units, homely, attractive development, bird-watching tower; L1-L2 Journey's End, PO Box 13, San Pedro, T 2173, F 2028, 4.5 miles N, excellent resort facilities inc diving, resort club theme, but overpriced; L2-L3 Captain Morgan's Retreat, 3 miles N of town, T 2567, F 2616, access by boat, thatched roofed cabañas with private facilities, pool, dock, secluded, rec; L2-L3 El Pescador, on Punta Arena beach 3 miles N, PO Box 793, Belize City, T/F 2398, access by boat, specialist fishing lodge with good reputation, a/c, good food and service; L2-A1 Victoria House, PO Box 22, San Pedro, T 2067/2240, F 2429, inc meals, 1 mile from town, 3 different types of room, excellent facilities, good dive shop and watersports, windsurfing US$15/hr, highly rec; L3 Royal Palm, PO Box 18, San Pedro, T 2148/2244, F 2329, good location nr Victoria House, 12 new villas with pool and full facilities just completed, further expansion planned; L3-A1 Playador, nr Belize Yacht Club, T 2870, F 2871, 20 rooms, cabañas on the beach.

For those staying in villas, contact Denny "The Bun Man", for fresh coffee, orange juice, and excellent cinnamon buns. He will deliver in time for breakfast, T 263490.

Other, cheaper hotels: A3 Lily's, rooms with sea view, some with a/c, others with fan, clean, T 2059; B Casa Blanca, San Pedro town, T 2630; B Conch Shell Inn, facing sea, some rooms with kitchenette, T 2062; B Hide Away Lodge, PO Box 484, Belize City, T 2141/2269, good value but a bit run down; B Martha's (D in low season), PO Box 27, San Pedro, T 2054, F 2589, good value, rec; La Joya del Caribe, San Pedro, T 2050/2385, F 2316, nice location just out of town, rec; B Pirate's Lantern, in town, T 2146; B Ruby's, San Pedro Town on the beach, fan, private bath, good views, beach cabaña, central, rec as best value in town, T 2063/2434; B San Pedrano, San Pedro, T 2054/2093, clean and good value; B San Pedro Guesthouse, T 3243, breakfast inc, cheaper dormitory (D); B Seychelles Guesthouse, opp Jade Garden restaurant, T 263817, 3 rooms, full breakfast, quiet neighbourhood, run by Harte Lemmle and popular with divers; C Thomas, airy rooms, fan, bath (tub, not shower), drinking water, clean, friendly; D Milo's, T 2033, private or shared bath, mosquito nets advised, comfortable, clean, no hot water; Seven Seas, T 2382/2137. At Coral Beach, the Forman, Gómez, González and Paz families provide room and meals for US$9 each. At Sea Breeze, the Paz and Núñez families offer the same accommodation at the same price.

● **Places to eat**

The *San Pedro Grill* is a good place to meet other travellers and swap information on boats, etc.

Other eating places are: *Elvi's Kitchen*, popular, newly upmarket, live music and roof built around flamboyant tree, can be very busy, won international award 1996; 1 block N is *Ambergris Delight*, pleasant, inexpensive, clean; 1 block S of *Elvi's* is *Marinos*, excellent food, good prices, popular with locals, erratic service; *Lily's Restaurant*, best seafood in town, friendly, good breakfast, excellent value but quite basic; *Alijua*, in San Pedro, Croatian owned, good food, also rents suites with kitchen, US$100 for 4 persons; *Jade Garden Restaurant*, Chinese, sweet and sour everything, drinks expensive; *The Hut*, Mexican, friendly; *Estel's* on the beach, good food and '40s-'50s music; *Celi's*, behind *Holiday Hotel*, good seafood, rec; *La Parilla*, opp *Holiday Hotel*, small, Tex-Mex, quite good; *Little Italy*, at *Spindrift Hotel*, popular but expensive; *Pier*, in *Spindrift* complex, very Mexican, dinners from US$10.

● **Bars**

Big Daddy's Disco, open evenings but gets cranked up at midnight; *Tarzan Disco*, nearby on Front St, good atmosphere; *Fido's Yard*, towards N end of Front St, lively bar-restaurant. For entertainment, try 'Chicken Drop' at *Sea Breeze Hotel*, you bet US$1 on which square the chicken may leave its droppings on, also at *Spindrift Hotel*.

● **Banks & money changers**

Atlantic Bank and *Bank of Belize*, open Mon-Thur 0800-1300, Fri 0800-1630. Small denominations of US currency in regular use.

● **Shopping**

Rocks Supermarket has good range of supplies. There are many gift shops in the centre of town. Try *Fidos* which has *Sunsation Gift Shop*, *Belizean Arts* (paintings and prints by local artists), *Amber Jewellry* and *Realty Café*. Wave runners (US$50/hr), hobie cats (US$25/hr) and parasailing (US$40) can be hired here.

● **Sports**

Diving: instruction to PADI open water widely available, from US$350-400 at Amigos del Mar, opp *Lily's*; freelance instructor Lynne Stevens can be contacted through *Marinos* restaurant. Larry Parker at Reef Divers, *Royal Palm Villas*, T 262943, is the most experienced operation on the island, highly rec; Blue Hole (Colin and Fiona, in centre of town, T 26735) and Amigos del Mar (opp *Lily's*) have been repeatedly rec. Harte Lemmle, a Canadian, who sometimes works for Reef Divers, can be contacted at *Seychelle Guesthouse*, T 263817 and is also recommended. Check diving shop's recent safety record before diving.

Vehicle rental: golf carts US$10/hr, make sure battery is fully charged before hiring; gives quick access to southern, quieter end. Bicycles US$5/hr, try negotiating for long-term rates, good way to get around.

● **Transport**

Air Several flights daily to and from Belize City municipal airport with Tropic, Island and Maya Airways, prices under Belize City. *Universal Travel* at San Pedro airfield and *Travel and Tour Belize* in town helpful. They can arrange charter flights to Corozal, with a request stop at Sarteneja (for the Shipstern Butterfly Farm see page 766).

Sea More interesting than going by air are the boats, most of which leave from the Courthouse Wharf on Southern Foreshore: boats leave for San Pedro, Mon-Fri 1600, return 0700, Sat 1300, return 0800, none on Sun, US$10, 1½ hrs. A new service, the yellow 'Banana' boat, leaves Mon-Fri 1500, returning 0800 from Spindrift pier, San Pedro, US$10 one way. *Triple J* boat leaves from Courthouse Wharf, daily round trip to **Ambergris Caye** (1¾ hrs in covered boat, US$12.50, video), **Caye Caulker** and **San Pedro** leaving Belize City 0900, return 1500, to San Pedro US$10 one way, US$17.50 return, fast, dependable, rec. Boats, irregular, between **Ambergris** and **Caye Caulker**, no set fare, but around US$6. Remember, pay on arrival.

NB One cannot in practice walk N along the beach from San Pedro to Xcalak, Mexico.

CAYE CAULKER

A lobster-fishing island (closed season 15 Feb-14 July), used to be relatively unspoilt, but the number of tourists is now increasing. The houses are of wood, the majority built on stilts. It has been allowed to run down and the main landing jetty has been closed. Some services are reported to have deteriorated, and theft and unpleasantness from some mainlanders who go to the caye with tourists; on the other hand the islanders are friendly. The atmosphere seems to be much more re-laxed out of the high tourist season; nevertheless, women should take care if alone at night. There are no beaches as the coast is largely mangrove forest, but you can swim at the channel ('cut' or 'split', formed by a recent hurricane) or off one of the many piers. **NB** If swimming in the 'cut', beware of fishing and powerboats using it as a route from the ocean to the west side; several serious accidents have occurred. A reef museum has opened with enlarged photos of reef fish, free for school parties, tourists are asked for a US$2 donation to help expansion. There are only 10 vehicles on the island, one of which is used solely to transport Belikin beer. Sandflies are ferocious in season (Dec-Feb), take trousers and a good repellent. Make sure you fix prices before going on trips or hiring equipment, and clarify whether you are talking US$ or BZ$. Do not pay the night before. One trickster is known as 'Jimmy the Worm'.

A walk S along the shore takes you to the new airstrip, a gash across the island, and to mangroves where the rare Black Catbird (*Melanoptila glabirostris*) can be seen and its sweet song heard. In this area there are lots of mosquitoes. A campaign to make the Black Catbird's habitat and the associated reef a Nature Reserve (called Siwa-Ban, after the catbird's Maya name) can be contacted at *Galería Hicaco* (Ellen McCrea, near *Tropical Paradise*), or 143 Anderson, San Francisco, California.

Excursions

Reef trips (see also under **Accommodation**) Prices are regulated: Manatees US$27.50; San Pedro, Hol Chan and Shark Alley US$17.50. Both are all day trips. They seem to be cheaper from Caye Caulker than Ambergris Caye. It is almost impossible to arrange boat trips the evening before; just wander down the main street at 1000, ask around for names of boat men, and you can not fail. Hol Chan gets very crowded and the earlier you get there the better. Try to ascertain that the boat

operator is reliable. As from Sept 1996 anyone taking trips must be approved by the Tour Guide Association and should have a licence to prove it. So far few guides have obtained the permission. Try to go with a group of 5 to 7 people, larger numbers are less enjoyable. We have received reports of theft of valuables left on board while snorkelling and even of swimmers being left in the water while the boat man went off to pick up another group. Protect against sunburn on reef trips, even while snorkelling.

● **Reef trip operators** Neno Rosado has been approved by the association and is reliable and knowledgeable. Contact him at *The Big Fish Little Fish Snorkelling Shop*, T 022-2250. Mervin, a local man, is reliable for snorkelling trips, he will also take you to Belize City. Another is Ignacio. Also Gamoosa, who may spend all day with you on the reef and then sometimes invites you to his house to eat the fish and lobster you have caught; also offers a healthy breakfast of banana, yoghurt, granola and honey for US$2.50. Also recommended are Ras Creek, "a big man with a big heart", in his boat *Reggae Muffin*, US$12.50 inc lunch; Alfonso Rosardo, a Mexican, reef trips for up to 6 people, 5-6 hrs, sometimes offers meals at his house afterwards. Also recommended are Lawrence (next to *Castaways*), Obdulio Lulu (a man) at *Tom's Hotel* goes to Hol Chan and San Pedro for a full day (if he catches a barracuda on the return, he will barbecue it at the hotel for US$0.75); Raoul and Charles, also from *Tom's Hotel*, US$12.50; also Harrison (ask around for him, he goes to see manatees, then to a small island to see the coral reef, US$25, recommended). Lobster fishing and diving for conch is also possible. 'Island Sun', near the 'cutting', local husband and American wife, very conscientious; day tours to reef, plus snorkel hire (1000-1400), day tour to San Pedro and Hol Chan, plus snorkel hire, plus entry fee for reserve, recommended. Snorkel Equipment Rental and Pastries Shop, do tour, rental gear, on same route 1015-1630, boat has sunshade. Capt Jim Novelo, of *Sunrise* boat, does daily trips to Hol Chan and San Pedro, 1000-1600, and snorkelling excursions to the Turneffe Islands, Half Moon Caye, Bird Sanctuary and Blue Hole, 0630-1700, every Tues, Dec-April, July-Aug, or on request, US$67.50 inc lunch and drinks, T 022-2195, F 022-2239. A sailing boat also goes to Hol Chan, but the trip takes a long time, leaving only a short while for snorkelling, departs 1000, US$12 for a day. Mask, snorkel and fins for US$2.50, cheapest (for instance at the post office, or *Sammie's Pastry Shop*). Benji, owner of a small sailboat and Joe Joe, his Rasta captain, will take you to Placencia or the Cayes, fun.

Watersports

Windsurfing equipment hire from Orlando, US$10/hr, poor quality, bring your own or go to San Pedro. **Canoes** for hire from Salvador, at painted house behind *Marin's* restaurant, US$10 a day; sea kayaks from Ellen at *Galería* Hicaco. Go **fishing** with Rolly Rosardo, 4 hrs, US$45, up to 5 people, equipment, fresh bait and instruction provided. **Diving** Frank and Janie Bounting of Belize Diving Service (PO Box 667, T 44307, ext 143 mainland side, past the football pitch) charge US$55 for 2 scuba dives, day and night, good equipment, good value; they also offer a 4-day PADI certificate course for US$300, recommended, also 2 and 3-day trips to Lighthouse Reef on the *Reef Roamer*, highly recommended; the 3-day trip comprises 7 dives, including the Blue Hole, a visit to a bird reserve, good food and crew, US$290. Frenchie's Diving Service, T 022-2234, charges US$330 for a 4-day PADI course, friendly and effective, 2-tank dive US$60, also advanced PADI instruction. Day excursion diving Blue Hole, etc, US$65, snorkellers welcome. Many **sailing** trips available for US$18 pp (stops for snorkelling too). For sailing charters, Jim and Dorothy Beveridge, 'Seaing is Belizing', who also run scuba trips to Goff's Caye Park and the Turneffe Islands (5-10 days). They arrange slide shows of the reefs and the Jaguar Reserve (Cockscomb) at 2000, from time to time, US$2, excellent photography, personally narrated (they, too, have a book exchange; they have an office next to *Dolphin Bay Travel*, which itself is good for information, booking flights and trips); PO Box 374, Belize City, T 022-2189. Ask Chocolate for all-day trips to the manatee reserve in the S of Belize. There is a sailing school, charging US$30 for a 5-hr, solo beginner's

course. It may be possible to hire a boat for 6-8 people to Chetumal. There are also boats leaving for Placencia and Honduras from Caye Caulker, but be sure to get exit stamps and other documentation in Belize City first if going to Honduras.

Local information
● Accommodation
The cheapest end of town is the S, but it is a long way from the 'cutting' for swimming or snorkelling. A map which can be bought on arrival lists virtually everything on the island. Camping on the beach is forbidden.

B *CB's*, further S than *Tropical Paradise*, T 022-2176, with bath, clean 12 beds, no advance bookings, good, small beds, restaurant; **B** *Out Island Beach Club*, by the Split, 9 bungalows on the beach, hot showers, a/c; **B** *Rainbow*, on the beach, T 022-2123, 10 small bungalows, with shower, rooms also, **C**, hot water, good. Beach houses can also be rented for US$50-150 a month; **B** *Tropical Paradise*, T 022-2124, F 022-2225 (PO Box 1206 Belize City), cabins, rooms from **D**, hot showers, clean, not very comfortable, restaurant (see below), good excursions.

C *Edith's*, rooms with bath or private chalet, rec, hot water, fan; **C** *Jiminez's Cabins*, delightful self-contained huts, some cheaper rooms, friendly staff; **C** *Martínez*, T 022-2196, small rooms, smelly recycled shower water, basic, but reasonable for the caye; **C** *Shirley's Guest House*, T 022-2145, S end of village, very relaxing, rec; **C** *Tree Tops*, T 022-2008, F 022-2115, clean, comfortable beds, beach views, German spoken, powerful fan, cable TV, friendly, good value, rec; **C** *Vega's Far Inn* rents 7 rooms, all doubles, T 022-2142, with ceiling fan and fresh linen, flush toilets and showers (limited hot water) shared with camping ground, which is guarded, has drinking water, hot water, clean toilets, barbecue, can rent out camping gear (camping costs US$6 pp, overpriced).

D *Anchorage*, nr *Ignacio's*, basic, large cabañas with cold showers, fan OK, discounts for stays of over 4 days, pleasant atmosphere, friendly family, breakfast and drinks served under shade on the beach; **D** *Deisy's*, T 022-2150, with shower, toilet and fan, reductions for longer stays, clean, friendly, safe, cheaper rooms downstairs, cash TCs, rooms with communal bathroom not good value, hot water; **D** *Ignacio Beach Cabins*, T 022-2212, (PO Box 1169, Belize City), small huts or hammocks just outside town, for double room, **C** for a hut for 3-4, quiet, clean, rec, toilet and shower facilities in private cabins only, cheap lobster tails and free coconuts (Ignacio runs reef trips and he has equipment, he is principally a lobster fisherman); **D** *Marin*, T 022-44307 (also private hut) with bath, clean, helpful, rec (the proprietor, John Marin, will take you out for a snorkelling trip on the reef); **D-E** *Mira Mar*, T 022-44307, 2nd floor rooms best, clean showers, rec, bargain if staying longer, helpful owner Melvin Badillo, he owns liquor store, his family runs a pastry shop and grocery store.

E *Castaways*, T 022 2294, inc morning coffee, run by Bob and Angela Wiles, good food (see below), hospitable; **E** *Sandy Lane*, T 022-2217, 1 block back from main street, bungalow-type accommodation, clean, shared toilet and hot showers, run by Rico and Elma Novelo, rec; **E-D** *Tom's*, T 022-2102, with shared bath and fan, up to C in cabin with 3 beds, basic, clean, cold water, long walk from beach, laundry service US$5, safe deposit, barbecue. Tom's boat trips go to various destinations, inc Hol Chan and coral gardens, and to Belize City. In all accommodation take precautions against theft.

● **Places to eat**

Rodriguez for dinner at 1800 onwards for US$3.50, US$5 for lobster, very good (limited accommodation available). *Melvin's*, excellent lobster meals (opp *Riva's*); *Tropical Paradise* for excellent seafood, varied menu, slightly more expensive than others (also the only place selling ice cream); *The Sandbox*, run by American couple, one of the Caye's social centres, good chocolate cake, rec. Cakes and pastries can be bought at houses displaying the sign, rec are *Daisy's*, *Jessie's* (open 0830-1300, 1500-1700, behind *Riva's*), and a very good one nr the telephone exchange office; *Glenda's*, nr *Hotel Marin*, try the delicious lobster, or chicken 'Burritos', chicken, vegetables, chile and sauce wrapped in a tortilla for US$0.50, also good breakfast with cinnamon rolls, closed evenings, also good for 'Burritos', *Rainbow*, on waterfront near channel, good value, beautiful view; *Castaways*, good shrimp and lobster, rec; *Popeye's*, on shore, excellent pizzas; *Claudette*, next to Fishermen's Wharf, US$1.25, delicious. *Marin's*, good seafood in evening, expensive but worth it; *Ocean Side* home cooking, big portions, rec; *Martinez*, good seafood, good prices; *Paradise Burgers*, nr the Split, also fish sandwiches; *Cindy's*, on main street, good coffee, fresh yoghurt; *I & I Bar*, mellow, laid back, good view from upper deck, pricey; *Reef Bar*, good atmosphere, reggae music. Many private houses serve food. Buy lobster or fish from the cooperative and cook up at the barbecue on the beach; beer is sold by the crate at the wholesaler on the dock by the generator; ice for sale at *Tropical Paradise*.

● **Banks & money changers**
Rates for changing cash and TCs are reasonable; **Atlantic Bank** (Visa advances available) and many places for exchange. Gift shops will charge a commission.

● **Post & telecommunications**
International telephone and fax connections available on Caye Caulker (telephone exchange is open 0900-1230, 1400-1630; cardphone outside office can be used for international calls. Collect calls possible at least to North America at no charge. Fax number at telephone exchange is 501-22-2239). The island also boasts 2 book swaps, inc *Seaing is Belizing* (see also under **Sailing** above) and Belize Diving Service. Bookstore on opp side of island to ferries has many magazines, inc *Time* and *Newsweek*. Dolphin Bay is a helpful travel agency on the island.

● **Shopping**
There are at least four small 'markets' on the island where a variety of food can be bought; prices are 20-50% higher than the mainland.

● **Transport**
On the Island You can rent golf carts, US$5/hr, popular, the locals rent them to take the family for a drive.

Air The airstrip has been newly constructed; all 3 airlines fly every 30 mins most of the day to and from San Pedro and/or Belize City), flight details under Belize City. Flying is rec if you have a connection to make. There are also direct flights to Chetumal (Mexico) with Aerobelize.

Sea Boats leave from behind A & R Station on North Front St (see above), for Caye Caulker, at 0645, 0800, 1000 and 1500, daily (US$7.50 pp, US$5 on 'sunrise boat', buy tickets at the departure depot opp Post Office, 45 mins one way (boats depend on weather and number of passengers – can be 'exciting' if it's rough), return boats from 0645 till pm (if booked in advance at some places, inc *Edith's Hotel*, US$6). You can sometimes catch a boat as late as 1600, but do not rely on it. The Caye Caulker Water Taxi Association regulates schedules and fares; the office on Caye Caulker is opp BTL. Rec boats: Emilio Novelo's *Ocean Star* (good, cheaper than others); Chocolate's *Soledad* ('Chocolate' is white, over 70 yrs old and has a white moustache). *Rainbow Runner*, 0830 from Belize City via Caye Chapel, boat in good condition, 2 motors, and *C Train*. Boat to San Pedro departs at 1000, US$6. Boats from San Pedro en route to Belize City 0700-0800, US$7.50. *Triple J* (see above, San Pedro) boat, rec, daily service, from Ambergris Caye 0700, 45 mins, US$7.50. To get to Flores on the San Juan Travel minibus, buy a ticket at Chocolate's gift shop the day before and take the boat at 0800.

English Caye 12 miles off Belize City, English Caye is beautiful, with no facilities; take a day trip only. It is part of the reef so you can snorkel right off the beach. Sunrise Travel, Belize City, T 72051/ 32670, can help arrange a trip, book in advance, US$15.

TURNEFFE ISLANDS

The islands are one of Belize's 3 atolls. On **Big Caye Bokel** is *Turneffe Islands Lodge*, PO Box 480, Belize City, which can accommodate 16 guests for week-long fishing and scuba packages. *Turneffe Flats*, 56 Eve St, Belize City, T 02-45634, in a lovely location, also offers week-long packages, for fishing and scuba; it can take 12 guests, but is to be expanded. *Blackbird Caye Resort*, c/o Blackbird Caye Co, 11a Cork St, Belize, T 02-32772, F 02-34449, Manager, Kent Leslie, weekly packages arranged, is an ecologically-oriented resort on this 4,000 acre island used by the Oceanic Society and is a potential site for a Biosphere Reserve two underwater project. Reservations in the USA, T (713) 658-1142, F (713) 658-0379. Diving or fishing packages available, no bar, take your own alcohol. On Calabash Caye, *Coral Cay Conservation* in conjunction with University College of Belize has a marine studies programme. For information contact CCC in the UK, T 0171-498 6248, F 0181-773 9656.

LIGHTHOUSE REEF

Lighthouse Reef is the outermost of the 3 N-S reef systems off Belize, some 45 miles to the E of Belize City. There are two cayes of interest, Half Moon Caye (on which the lighthouse stands) and 12 miles to the N, the caye in which Blue Hole is found. **Half Moon Caye** is the site of the **Red-Footed Booby Sanctuary**, a national reserve. Besides the booby, which is unusual in that almost all the individuals have the white colour phase (normally they are dull brown), magnificent frigate birds nest on the island. The seabirds nest on the western side, which has dense vegetation (the eastern side is covered mainly in coconut palms). Of the 98 other bird species recorded on Half Moon Caye, 77 are migrants. Iguana, the wish willy (smaller than the iguana) and the *anolis allisoni* lizard inhabit the caye, and hawksbill and loggerhead turtles lay their eggs on the beaches. The Belize Audubon Society, 12 Fort St, maintains the sanctuary; there is a lookout tower and trail. The lighthouse on the caye gives fine views of the reef. It was first built in 1820: the present steel tower was added to the brick base in 1931 and now the light is solar powered. Around sunset you can watch the boobies from the lookout as they return from fishing. They land beside their waiting mates at the rate of about 50 a minute. They seem totally unbothered by humans.

There are no facilities; take all food, drink and fuel. On arrival you must register with the warden near the lighthouse (the warden will provide maps and tell you where you can camp).

It is possible to stay on one of the private islands in the reef, 12 km from the Blue Hole, all inclusive 1 week stays, contact PO Box 1435, Dundee, Fla, USA, T 1-800-423-3114, F 1-813-439-2118 (USA).

In Lighthouse Reef is the **Blue Hole**, recently declared a National Monument, an almost circular sinkhole, 1,000 ft across and with depths exceeding 400 ft. The crater was most likely formed by a meteor, thousands of years ago. It was studied by Jacques Cousteau in 1984. Stalagmites and stalactites can be found in the underwater cave. Entry to the Blue Hole is US$4. Scuba diving is outstanding at Lighthouse Reef, including two walls which descend almost vertically from 30-40 ft to several thousand.

Excursions Frenchie, of *Frenchie's Diving*, runs regular trips from Caye Caulker to **Half Moon Caye** and the **Blue Hole**, US$65 for snorkellers, more for divers. To charter a motor boat in Belize City costs about US$50 pp if 10 people are going (6 hrs' journey). Bill Hinkis, in San Pedro Town, Ambergris Caye, offers 3-day sailing cruises to Lighthouse Reef for US$150 (you provide food, ice and fuel). Bill and his boat *Yanira* can be found beside the lagoon off Back St, just N of the football field. Out Island Divers, San Pedro, do various 2-3 day trips. Other sailing vessels charge US$150-250/day. Speed boats charge US$190 pp for a day-trip including lunch and 3 dives, recommended. The main dive in the Blue Hole is very deep, at least 130 ft (almost 50m); the hole itself is 480 ft deep. Check your own qualifications as the dive operator probably will not. It is well worth doing it you are qualified. Keep an eye on your computer or dive charts if doing subsequent dives.

For southern cayes, see under **Southern Belize**.

Northern Belize

NORTH BELIZE is notable for its agricultural productivity, sugar, fruit, market gardening, providing much of Belize's food. There are some notable wildlife sanctuaries and nature reserves, and a fair share of the country's countless Maya sites, many recently found and yet to be fully explored.

BELIZE CITY TO MEXICAN BORDER

Two main roads penetrate the country from Belize City: one to the N and other to the W. The Northern Highway is very patched up as it leaves Belize City until it divides into the New Alignment, which is well paved to the Mexican border, and the Old Northern Highway (narrow, paved, in reasonable condition).

BERMUDIAN LANDING/ COMMUNITY BABOON SANCTUARY

15 miles out of Belize City there is a turning left to **Bermudian Landing** (12 miles on a rough road from the turn off). The village was once a transfer point for timber floated down the Belize River and now a small Creole village. Here there is a local wildlife museum (sponsored by the World Wildlife Fund) and the **Community Baboon Sanctuary** nearby, with black howler monkeys, locally called baboons. Trails have been made in and around the reserve, which encompasses eight villages, all of whose inhabitants collaborate to protect the howlers' habitat. Check with the Sanctuary warden if you wish to visit. Boats can be hired from the warden for river trips to see monkeys and birds. Booklet (US$3, excellent) from the Audubon Society, 12 Fort St, Belize City. A guided walk costs US$6 pp. The warden will also arrange accommodation locally and may allow overnight parking at the site for a small donation, T 44405. Many freelance guides seek business from arriving vehicles, but it is better to get a licensed guide from the visitor's centre.

• **Accommodation** At Burrell Boom Cutoff, just before the Belize River bridge on the road to Bermudian Landing, is ***Little Eden*** (Fred and Sally Cuckow, T/F 028-2052, PO Box 1317, Belize City), 2 bedrooms, B, bed and breakfast, weekly rates available, camping possible, ceramics made and sold; at Bermudian Landing, **A3-C** ***Jungle Drift Lodge***, 400 yds from museum, cabañas have been built by John and Madeline Estephan of the tour company, Jungle Drift (PO Box 1442, Belize City, T 014-9578, F 02-78160), screened windows, fans, cheaper with shared bath, discounts for students, meals available in village, camping US$5 pp, bring tent, river tours US$20 pp recommended, transport from Belize City in pick up, US$40, 1-4 people, on request; meals with local families, breakfast, lunch and dinner, US$2.50-7.50; canoe rentals in Burrell Boom for trips on Belize River to see birds, howler monkeys, manatee, hicatee.

• **Transport** Bus from Belize City about midday (ask at Batty Bus terminal for directions, near Cemetery Rd), return 1700, 1 hr, US$1 one way. Also Russell's bus to Bermudian landing from corner Orange St and Euphrates Av at 1215 and 1615 Mon-Fri and 1200 and 1300 Sat, US$2. A day trip is very difficult by public transport so it is best to stay the night.

CROOKED TREE

The Northern Highway continues to **Sand Hill** where a dusty or muddy 3 mile road turns off to the NW to the **Crooked Tree Lagoons and Wildlife Sanctuary**, set up in 1984, an exceptionally rich area for birds. The network of lagoons and swamps attracts many migrating birds and the dry season, Oct-May, is a good time to visit. You may see the endangered jabiru stork, the largest flying bird in the Western Hemisphere, 5 ft tall with a wingspan of 11-12 ft, which nests here, as well as herons, gnabes, pelicans, ducks, vultures, kites, ospreys, hawks, sand pipers, kingfishers, gulls, terns, egrets and swallows. In the forest you can also see and hear howler monkeys. Other animals include coatimundi, crocodiles, iguanas and turtles. Glenn Crawford is a very good guide as is Sam Tillet (see **Accommodation** below). The turn off to the Sanctuary can be hard to find as the sign is difficult to spot, especially if coming from the south. The intersection is 22 miles from Orange Walk and 32 miles from Belize City. There is another sign further S indicating the Sanctuary but this does not lead to the Wildlife Sanctuary – just the park boundary. The mango and cashew trees in the village of Crooked Tree are said to be 100 years old. Birdwatching is best in the early morning, but, as buses do not leave Belize City early, for a day trip take an early Corozal bus, get off at the main road (about 1¼ hrs from Belize City) and hitch to the Sanctuary. The village is tiny and quaint, occupied mostly by black Garifunas. Boats and guides can be hired for approx US$70 per boat (max 4 people). It may be worth bargaining as competition is high. Trips include a visit to an unexcavated Mayan site. Lots of birds can be seen, especially near the lagoon. It is easy to get a lift, and someone is usually willing to take visitors back to the main road for a small charge. Entry is US$4 (Belizeans US$1); you must register at the visitor's centre, drinks are on sale, but take food. There is a helpful, friendly warden, Steve, who will let you sleep on the porch of the visitors' centre.

• **Accommodation A3** *Bird's Eye View Lodge*, T 02-32040, F 02-24869 (owned by the Gillett family; in USA T/F New York 718 845 0749, e-mail: BirdsEye@aol.com), single and double rooms, shower, fan, also bunk accommodation, US$10, camping US$5, meals available, boat trips, horseriding, canoe rental, nature tours with licensed guide, ask for information at the Audubon Society (address above); **A3** *Paradise Inn*, run by the Crawfords, cabins with hot showers, restaurant, is well maintained and friendly, T 02 44333, boat trips, fishing, horse riding and tours available; **B-C** *Sam Tillet's Hotel*, T 021-12026, in centre of village, wood and thatch cabin, tiny restaurant, great trips. Cabins may be rented at US$33 for a night, up to 4 people. Camping and cheap rooms (house of Rev Rhayburn, E, recommended, meals available) can also be arranged if you ask.

• **Transport** Buses from Belize City with JEX and Batty, former 1035 and others, latter 1600; return from Crooked Tree at 0600-0700, sometimes later.

ALTUN HA

North of Sand Hill the road forks, the quicker route heading direct to Orange Walk, the older road looping N then NW.

The Maya remains of **Altun Ha**, 31 miles N of Belize City and 2 miles off the old Northern Highway, are worth a visit, entrance US$1.50 (insect repellent necessary); they are open 0900-1700. Since there is so little transport on this road, hitching is not recommended, best to go in a private vehicle or a tour group. Vehicles leave Belize City for **Maskall** village, 8 miles N of Altun Ha, several days a week, but same-day return is not possible. With warden's permission, vehicle overnight parking is permitted free, but there is no accommodation in nearby villages. Tourist Board booklets on the ruins are out of print now. Altun Ha was a major ceremonial centre in the Classic Period (250-900 AD) and a trading station linking the Caribbean coast with Maya centres in the interior. The site consists of two central plazas surrounded by thirteen partially excavated pyramids and temples. What the visitor sees now is composite, not how the site would have been at any one time in the past. Nearby is a large reservoir, now called Rockstone Road ('Altun Ha' is a rough translation of the modern name). The largest piece of worked Maya jade ever found, a head of the Sun God Kinich Ahau weighing 9½ pounds, was found here, in the main temple (B-4) in 1968. It is now in a bank vault in Belize City.

● **Accommodation** Just N of Maskall is **L2** *Maruba Resort*, T 03-22199 also USA 713-719-2031, a hotel, restaurant and spa, all rooms different, some a/c, German spoken, good bird-watching, inc storks in the nearby swamp; has caged animals and birds. Also **L3** *Pretty See Ranch*, lovely cabins, sign by the roadside.

ORANGE WALK

The New Alignment runs to (66 miles) Orange Walk, centre of a district where about 17,000 Creoles, Mennonites and Maya Indians get their living from timber, sugar planting and general agriculture.

Orange Walk (*pop* 12,155; *phone code* 03) is an agricultural centre and the country's second city. A toll bridge (BZ$0.25 for motorbikes, BZ$0.80 for cars) now spans the New River a few miles S of the town at Tower Hill. Spanish is the predominant language. It is a centre for refugees from other parts of Central America, although Mennonites from the surrounding colonies also use it as their marketing and supply town. There are some pleasant wooden buildings on the streets leading off Queen Victoria Ave, which is the main road through town. The clock tower, town hall and Park, on this street at the heart of the city, is where the

Belize City-Mexico border buses stop. Also on this street, which is dusty in dry weather, are some concrete buildings such as 'Big Pink', otherwise known as *Mi Amor Hotel*, Chinese restaurants, shoe shops, electrical goods sellers and purveyors of reggae music. The other public buildings are beside the football pitch, while the Catholic cathedral and school are towards the river from the Park (take Church St out of the Park). The only battle fought on Belizean soil took place here, during the Yucatecan Race Wars (1840-1860s); the Maya leader, Marcus Canul was shot in the fighting (1872).

Local information
● **Accommodation**
C *Chula Vista*, Trial Farm, T 22227, at gas station (closed) just N of town, safe, clean, helpful owner, but overpriced; **C** *d'Victoria*, 40 Belize Rd (Main St), T 22518, a/c, shower, hot water, parking, quite comfortable, pool.

D *Camie's Hotel and Restaurant*, on Park at Queen Victoria Ave, T 22661, with bath and fan, hot rooms, spartan but OK, offstreet parking; **D** *Mi Amor*, 19 Belize-Corozal Rd, T 22031, with shared bath, **C** with bath and fan, **B** with a/c, nice, clean, restaurant; **D** *Tai San*, beside Batty Bus stop, small rooms, fan.

E *Jane's*, 2 Baker's St, T 22473 (extension on Market Lane), large house in pleasant location but smelly; **E** *La Nueva Ola*, 73 Otro Benque Rd, T 22104, large car park, run down, probably the cheapest. Parking for vehicles is very limited at hotels.

● **Places to eat**
The majority of restaurants in town are Chinese, eg *Hong Kong II*, next to *Mi Amor*; *Golden Gate*, Baker's St, Chinese specialities, cheap; *King Fu*, Baker's St, excellent Chinese, filling, US$5. *Julie's*, nr police station, good, inexpensive creole cooking; similarly at *Juanita's*, 8 Santa Ana St (take road beside Shell station), open 0600 for breakfast and all meals. Most restaurants and bars are open on Sun. Many good bars eg *San Martín*. On Clarke St behind hospital is *The Diner*, good meals for US$3, very friendly, taxi US$4 or walk.

● **Banks & money changers**
Scotia Bank on Park, BZ$1 commission/transaction; Bank of Belize on Main St (down Park St from Park, turn left); same hours as Belize City (see page 748). Shell Station will change TCs.

● **Buses**

Bus Station is near the fire station. All Chetumal buses pass Orange Walk Town (hourly); Belize-Orange Walk, US$1.75.

A road heads W from Orange Walk, then turns S, parallel first to the Mexican border, then the Guatemalan (where it becomes unmade). Along this road are several archaeological sites: **Cuello** is 4 miles W on San Antonio road, behind Cuello Distillery (ask there for permission to visit); taxi about US$3.50. Site dates back to 1000 BC; although it has yielded important discoveries in the study of Maya and pre-Maya cultures, there is little for the layman to appreciate and no facilities for visitors. At **Yo Creek**, the road divides, N to San Antonio, and S, through miles of cane fields and tiny farming settlements parallel to the Mexican border as far as **San Felipe** (20 miles – via San Lazaro, Trinidad and August Pine Ridge). At August Pine Ridge there is a daily bus to Orange Walk at 1000. You can camp at the house of Narciso Novelo, T (03) 33019, relaxing place to stay. At San Felipe, a branch leads SE to Indian Church (35 miles from Orange Walk, 1 hr driving on improved, white marl road, passable all year, 4WD needed when wet). Another road heads W to Blue Creek Village (see below).

LAMANAI

Near **Indian Church**, one of Belize's largest archaeological sites, **Lamanai** stretches along the W side of New River Lagoon 22 miles by river S of Orange Walk. While the earliest buildings were erected about 700 BC, culminating in the completion of the 112 ft-high major temple, N10-43, about 100 BC (the tallest known preclassic Maya structure), there is evidence the site was occupied from 1500 BC. With the Spanish and British sites mentioned below, and the present day refugee village nearby, Lamanai has a very long history. The Maya site has been partially cleared, but covers a large area so a guide is recommended. The views from temple

N10-43, dedicated to Chac, are superb; look for the Yin-Yang-like symbol below the throne on one of the other main temples, which also has a 4m tall mask overlooking its plaza. Visitors can wander freely along narrow trails and climb the stairways.

At nearby Indian Church a Spanish mission was built over one of the Maya temples in 1580; the British established a sugar mill here last century; remains of both buildings can still be seen. Note the huge flywheel engulfed by a strangler fig. The archaeological reserve is jungle again and howler monkeys can be seen (with luck) in the trees. There are many birds, and mosquitoes (wear trousers, take repellent) in the wet season, but the best way to see birds is to reach Lamanai by boat. The earlier you go the better.

The community phone for information on Indian Church, including buses, is 03-23369.

Local Information

● **Accommodation**

At Indian Church: A1 *Lamanai Outpost Lodge*, Colin and Ellen Howells, T/F 23-3578, a short walk from Lamanai ruins, overlooking New River Lagoon, package deals available, day tours, 28ft pontoon boat, canoes, thatched wooden cabins with bath and fan, hot water, electricity, restaurant, still expanding. Nazario Ku, the site caretaker, permits camping or hammocks at his house, opp path to Lamanai ruins, good value for backpackers.

● **Transport**

Boats can be hired in Orange Walk, Shipyard or Guinea Grass (US$100 for 6). Herminio and Antonio Novelo run boat trips from Orange Walk (T 03-22293, F 03-22201, PO Box 95, 20 Lovers Lane), 5 passengers/boat, US$30 pp inc lunch, 1½-2 hrs to Lamanai. If staying in Orange Walk, leave after a 0600 breakfast; if coming from Belize City, take the 0600 Batty Express to be in Orange Walk by 0700, you return from Lamanai in time to take a pm bus back to Belize City.

Bus A cheaper way of getting to Lamanai is to take the daily bus, Orange Walk-San Felipe, 1000, continues to Indian Church on Tues and Thur at 1530. Bus from Indian Church to Orange Walk on Tues and Thur at 0500, 3 hrs; good road.

West of San Felipe is **Blue Creek** (10 miles), largest of the trim Mennonite settlements. Many of the inhabitants of these close-knit villages arrived in 1959, members of a Canadian colony which had migrated to Chihuahua to escape encroaching modernity; they preserve their Low German dialect, are exempt from military service, and their industry now supplies the country with most of its poultry, eggs and vegetables. Some settlements, such as Neustadt in the W, have been abandoned because of threats by drug smugglers in the early 1990s. A large area to the S along the **Rio Bravo** has been set aside as a conservation area (see **Nature Conservation** in the Introduction). Within this Conservation Area, there is a study and accommodation centre near the Mayan site of Las Milpas, **A2** *Rio Bravo Field Station*, 3 cabañas, spacious, comfortable, with a thatched roof overhanging a large wooden deck. For more information call T 03-30011, or contact the Project for Belize in Belize City. To reach the site, go 6 miles W from Blue Creek to Tres Leguas, then follow the signs S towards the Rio Bravo Escarpment. The site of Las Milpas is at present being excavated by a team from the University of Texas and Boston University, USA. A good road can be followed 35 miles S to Gallon Jug, where **Chan Chich**, **L1** with meals, **L2** without, a jungle tourism lodge has been built around a small Maya ruin, recommended, PO Box 37, Belize City, T 02-75634, F 02-76961 (flights to Chan Chich from Belize City, 0900 Mon, Wed and Fri, US$98 return, and can be chartered from elsewhere). Another road has recently been cut S through Tambos to the main road between Belmopan and San Ignacio; travel in this region is strictly a dry weather affair. Phone before setting out for *Chan Chich* for reservations and information on the roads.

NORTHEAST OF ORANGE WALK

From Orange Walk a road crosses New River and runs 6 miles NE to **San Estevan**. San Estevan can also be reached either by a poor road going N from Carmelita (the junction of the Old and New Alignments of the Northern Highway, 7 miles S of Orange Walk), or by a road heading SE from the Northern Highway between San José and San Pablo. These two towns, some 10 miles N of Orange Walk, merge into one another; the turning, unsigned on the right is before San Pablo proper. Drive 4 miles on a rough road through sugar cane field to a T-junction; turn right and after 3 miles you come to a hand-cranked ferry across the New River (fare anything from nothing to US$1.50, operates 0600-2200). If going to Progresso and Sarteneja, after the ferry turn left up the hill to the police station, where the road bears right. Follow this road straight through San Estevan. The Maya ruins near San Estevan have reportedly been 'flattened' to a large extent and are not very impressive. 10 miles from San Estevan is a road junction: straight on is **Progresso**, a village picturesquely located on the lagoon of the same name. The right turn, signposted, runs off to the Mennonite village of Little Belize and continues (in poor condition) to **Chunox**, a village with many Maya houses of pole construction. In the dry season it is possible to drive from Chunox to the Maya site of Cerros (see below).

SARTENEJA

The main road continues E, in improved state, over swampy land to **Sarteneja** (40 miles from Orange Walk; 1-hr drive, only impassable in the very wet), a small fishing and boat-building settlement founded by Yucatán refugees in 19th century. There are many remains of an extensive Maya city scattered throughout the village. You can stay at *Diani's*, on the seashore, D, restaurant. Houses can be rented for longer stays. The main catch is lobster and conch. On Easter Sun there is a regatta, with all types of boat racing, dancing and music; very popular. There is also windsurfing.

• **Transport** Sarteneja can be reached by **boat** from Corozal in ½ hr, but only private charters, so very expensive (compared with 3 hrs by road). **Bus** from Belize City daily, around noon, through Orange Walk; return bus 0330.

SHIPSTERN NATURE RESERVE

3 miles before Sarteneja is the visitors' centre for the **Reserve**, which covers 9,000 ha of this NE tip of Belize. Hardwood forests, saline lagoon systems and wide belts of savannah shelter a wide range of mammals (all the fauna found elsewhere in Belize, except monkeys), reptiles and 200 species of birds. Of the mammals you are most likely to see coatis and foxes. Also, there are mounds of Maya houses and fields everywhere. The remotest forest, S of the lagoon, is not accessible to short-term visitors. There is a botanical trail leading into the forest with trees labelled with Latin and local Yucatec Maya names; a booklet is available. At the visitor's centre is the Butterfly Breeding Centre, where pupae are bred for sale to European butterfly houses; 200 species can be seen in the reserve. Entry US$5 inc excellent guided tour, open daily 0900-1200, 1300-1600 except Christmas and Easter. (Choose a sunny day for a visit if possible, on dull days the butterflies hide themselves in the foliage.) In the wet season mosquito repellent is essential. There is dormitory accommodation at the visitors' centre, US$10 pp. A day trip by private car is possible from Sarteneja or Orange Walk.

NORTH OF ORANGE WALK

1 mile from the Northern Highway, in San José and San Pablo, is the archaeological site of **Nohmul**, a ceremonial centre whose main acropolis dominates the surrounding cane fields (the name means 'Great Mound'). Permission to visit the site must be obtained from Sr Estevan Itzab, whose house is opposite the water tower.

COROZAL

The Northern Highway continues to **Corozal** (96 miles from Belize City, *pop* 7,794), formerly the centre of the sugar industry. It is a mixture of modern concrete commercial buildings and Caribbean clapboard seafront houses on stilts. Much of the old town was destroyed by Hurricane Janet in 1955. Like Orange Walk Town it is economically depressed; there is a greater dependence on marijuana as a result. Corozal is much the safer place. It is open to the sea with a pleasant waterfront where the market is held. There is no beach but you can swim in the sea and lie on the grass. Fishermen return to Sartaneja from Corozal pm, you can bargain for a ride.

Excursion A road leads 7 miles NE to **Consejo**, a seaside fishing village on Chetumal Bay; taxi about US$10.

• **Accommodation** Two motels: **A3-B** *Tony's*, South End, T 04-22055, F 04-22829, C with a/c, clean, comfortable units in landscaped grounds, rec, but restaurant overpriced; **D** *Caribbean Village Resort*, South End (PO Box 55, T 04-22045, F 23414), hot water, US$5 camping, US$12 trailer park, rec, restaurant, **D** *Nestor's*, 123, 5th Av South (T 04-22354), with bath and fan, OK, refrescos available, good food; next door **E** *Papa's Guest House*, good value; **E** *Capri*, 14 Fourth Ave, on the seafront, T 04-22042, somewhat run down; **E** *Maya*, South End, T 04-22082, hot water, quieter than *Nestor's* but food not as good, plain meal US$5. Pleasant, clean guest house, **E**, to the N of town, on E side of main street, no name but look for sign which reads: *rooms/comfortable and clean*, next to used car dealer, very friendly, fan, good value. **Camping**: *Caribbean Motel and Trailer Park*, see above, camping possible but not very safe (US$4 pp), shaded sites, restaurant.

• **Places to eat** *Club Campesino*, decent bar, good fried chicken after 1800; *Skytop*, 5th Av South, friendly, good food, excellent breakfast, rec, good view from roof; *Border*, 6th Av South, friendly Chinese, good food, cheap; *Rexo*, North 5th St, Chinese; also Chinese: *Bumpers* (rec); *King of Kings*; *Hong Kong*.

• **Banks & money changers** Bank of Nova Scotia, Atlantic Bank and Belize Bank (does not accept Mexican pesos), open same hours as Belize City. For exchange also ask at the bus station (see page 748).

• **Transport Air** Maya Airways, 2 flights daily to San Pedro (Ambergris Caye), and on to Belize City, 0800 and 1530 (not Sun). Airstrip 3m S, taxi US$1.50. **Buses** There are 15 buses a day from Belize to **Corozal** by Venus Bus, Magazine Rd, and Batty Bus, 54 East Collet Canal, 3½-5 hrs, US$3.75. Both continue to Chetumal where there is a new bus terminal on the outskirts of town; because of the frequency, there is no need to take a colectivo to the Mexican border unless travelling at unusual hours (US$2.50). The increased frequency of buses to Chetumal and the number of money changers cater for Belizeans shopping cheaply in Mexico – very popular, book early. For those coming from Mexico who are more interested in Tikal than Belize, it is possible to make the journey border to border in a day, with a change of bus, to Novelo's, in Belize City. Timetables change frequently, so check at the time of travel. There are also tourist minibuses which avoid Belize City.

6 miles NE of Corozal, to the right of the road to Chetumal, is **4 Miles Lagoon**, about ¼ mile off the road (buses will drop you there). Clean swimming, better than Corozal bay, some food and drinks available; it is often crowded at weekends.

CERROS AND SANTA RITA

Across the bay to the S of Corozal stand the mounds of **Cerros**, once an active Maya trading port whose central area was reached by canal. Some of the site is flooded but one pyramid, 21m high with stucco masks on its walls, has been partially excavated. Boat from Corozal, walk around bay (boat needed to cross mouth of the New River) or dry-season vehicular trail from Progresso and Chunox (see above). More easily accessible are the ruins of **Santa Rita**, only a mile out on the Northern Highway, opposite the Coca Cola plant; once a powerful and cosmopolitan city, and still occupied when the Spaniards arrived in Belize, the site's postclassic murals and buildings have long been destroyed; only 50 ft tall Structure 7 remains standing, entry US$1.

FRONTIER WITH MEXICO

8 miles N beyond Corozal is the Mexican frontier at **Santa Elena**, where a bridge across the Río Hondo connects with Chetumal, 7 miles into Mexico. Contact Henry Menzies in Corozal, T 04-23415, who runs taxis into Chetumal for about US$25, quick and efficient way to get through to the border. If coming from Mexico, he will collect you in Chetumal.

• **Belizean immigration**
Border crossing formalities are relatively relaxed. The border is open 24 hrs a day. Exit tax by PACT, see page 741.

• **Crossing by private vehicle**
If driving to Belize, third party insurance is obligatory. It can be purchased from the building opp the immigration post.

• **Mexican Embassy**
In Belize City. Mexican tourist cards for 30 days are available at the border most of the time but it is safer to get one in Belize City. To extend the tourist card beyond 30 days, go to immigration in Cancún.

• **Exchange**
You can buy pesos at good rates at the border with US and Belizean currency. Rates for Belizean dollars in Mexico will be lower. Coming from Mexico, it is best to get rid of pesos at the border. Compare rates at the small bank nr the frontier with the street changers. The shops by the border will also change money.

• **Transport**
The Northern Highway is in good condition. Driving time to the capital 3 hrs. There are frequent buses from Corozal to Belize City, see under Corozal. All northbound buses from Belize City go to Chetumal: Batty in am, Venus in pm up to 1900.

If entering for a few days only, you can ask the Mexican officials to save your tourist card for you (but this may not work).

Western Belize

WEST BELIZE, from Belmopan to the Guatemalan border, has some spectacular natural sights, exciting rivers and, in the Mountain Pine Ridge area, some of the best limestone scenery in Central America, notably waterfalls and caves. There are many Maya sites.

BELIZE CITY TO SAN IGNACIO

The Western Highway leaves Belize City past the cemetery, where burial vaults stand elevated above the boggy ground, and runs through palmetto scrub and savannah landscapes created by 19th century timber cutting. At Mile 16 is Hattieville was originally a temporary settlement for the homeless after hurricane Hattie in 1961. It has become a permanent town of some 2,500 people and is also home to the new Belize prison with its many juvenile offenders. From here, an all-weather road runs N to **Burrell Boom** (Texaco station) and the Northern Highway, a convenient bypass for motorists wishing to avoid Belize City. The Highway roughly parallels the Sibun River, once a major trading artery where mahogany logs were floated down to the coast in the rainy season; the placename 'Boom' recalls spots where chains were stretched across rivers to catch the logs.

BELIZE ZOO

The small but excellent **Belize Zoo**, moved in 1992 to a new location close to its old site at Mile 28.5, see yellow sign; it is open daily 0900-1600, US$7.50, T 08-13004.

Wonderful collection of local species (originally gathered for a wildlife film), lovingly cared for and displayed in wire-mesh enclosures amid native trees and shady vegetation, including jaguar and smaller cats, pacas (called 'gibnuts' in Belize), snakes, monkeys, parrots, crocodile, tapir ('mountain cow'), peccary ('wari') and much more. Recommended, even for those who hate zoos. Get there early to avoid coach parties' arrival. There is an 0900 bus from Belize City, 1 hr. Tours by enthusiastic guides; T-shirts and postcards sold for fundraising. Nearest restaurant 45 mins' walk away at La Democracia, only cold drinks and snacks sold at the zoo.

The highway gently climbs toward the foothills of the Maya Mountains through stands of Caribbean pine. Look out for the foothill known as the 'Sleeping Giant', seen in profile S of the highway when heading W. Between the Zoo and *JB's* (see below) the coastal road to Dangriga heads S.

● **Accommodation L3** *Jaguar Paw Jungle Lodge*, on curve of Caves Branch River on road S at Mile 31, enquiries T 02-35395, with 3 meals, opened 1996. Possible basic lodging at the Education Centre at Belize Zoo, ask at the reception, take a torch.

MONKEY BAY WILDLIFE SANCTUARY

At Mile 31.5 the **Wildlife Sanctuary** is sponsored by the Belize Center for Environmental Studies (PO Box 666, Belize City, T 02-45545) and Rainforest Action Information Network (RAIN, PO Box 4418, Seattle, Washington 98104, T 206-324-7163). It contains 1,070 acres of tropical forest and savannah between the Highway and the Sibun River ('no monkeys and no bay, but lots of natural beauty, hospitality and peace' – Darrell Hutchinson, Olds, Canada). Birds are abundant and there is a good chance of seeing mammals. Pedro, the caretaker, can be hired for guided tours of the trails. Dormitory accommodation US$7.50 pp, or you can camp on wooden platform with thatched roof for US$5, swim in a river, showers available, take meals with family for US$4 (it is planned to provide cooking facilites in the future). Nearby at mile 33 is *JB's*, a bar and restaurant 'in the middle of nowhere', a popular stopping place decorated with the insignia of the British soldiers who have passed through, good food, reasonably priced.

47 miles from Belize City, a minor road runs 2 miles N to *Banana Bank Ranch*, resort accommodation, B with meals, horseriding, birding, river trips, etc, American-owned, Carolyn and John Carr (T/F 08-12020, PO Box 48, Belmopan). A mile further on is the highway junction for Belmopan and Dangriga. At the confluence of the Belize River and Roaring Creek here is the 50-acre **Guanacaste Park**, a national park protecting a parcel of rainforest and a huge 100-year-old guanacaste (tubroos) tree, which shelters a wide collection of epiphytes including orchids. Many mammals (jaguarundi, kinkajou, agouti, etc) and up to 100 species of birds may be seen from the 3 miles of nature trails cut along the river. This is a particularly attractive swimming and picnicking spot at which to break the journey to Guatemala. It has a visitors'

centre, where luggage can be left. Entrance US$2.50. Take an early morning bus from Belize City, see the park in a couple of hours, then pick up a bus going to San Ignacio or Dangriga.

Soon after the junction is **Roaring Creek** (*pop*, 1,000), once a thriving town but now rather overshadowed by the nearby capital. 500 yds from the Texaco station on the main road, follow the oasis sign for free overnight parking. 6 miles beyond the turning to the capital is **A2** *Warrie Head Lodge*, Ontario, T 08-23826 or for reservations T 02-77257, F 02-75213 (PO Box 244, Belize City), a working farm offering accommodation. They cater mainly for groups but it is well kept, homely and a lovely spot for river swimming. Just before the *Warrie Head*, at Teakettle, there is a turning S along a dirt road for 5 miles to Pook's Hill Reserve and **A2** *Pook's Hill Lodge* (T 081-2017), on Roaring Creek, run by Ray and Vicki Snaddon, 6 cabañas, horses, rafting, birdwatching etc.

The Highway now becomes narrower and curves through increasingly lush countryside. At Mile 60 is **A3** *Caesar's Place*, 4 rooms with bath, clean riverside campground with security, 4 full hookups for RVs, with showers and bathroom facilities, restaurant and bar, good general store, swimming, musicians welcome to play with 'in-house' group, highly rec, T 092-2341 (PO Box 48, San Ignacio, under same ownership as *Black Rock* – see below). The important but unimpressive **Baking Pot** archaeological site is just beyond the bridge over Barton Creek (Mile 64); 2 more miles brings us to **Georgeville** (another Mennonite community; try the ice cream and cheese), from where a gravel road runs S into the Mountain Pine Ridge Forest Reserve (see below). The highway passes the turnoff at Norland for **Spanish Lookout**, a Mennonite settlement area 6 miles N (*B & F Restaurant*, Centre Rd, by Farmers Trading Centre, clean, excellent value); ask in San Ignacio if you are interested in visiting this area.

Climbing up a forested valley the road reaches Santa Elena, linked by the substantial Hawkesworth suspension bridge to its twin town of San Ignacio. (At the bridge is Belize's first set of traffic lights; the bridge is only one vehicle's width.)

SAN IGNACIO

(*Pop* 9,891 including Santa Elena; *phone code* 092) 72 miles from Belize City and 10 miles from the border, **San Ignacio** (locally called Cayo) is the capital of Cayo District and western Belize's largest town, an agricultural centre serving the citrus, cattle and peanut farms of the area, and a good base for excursions into the Mountain Pine Ridge and western Belize. It stands amid attractive wooded hills at 200-500 ft, with a good climate, and is a nice town to rest in after Guatemala. The town is on the eastern branch of the Old, or Belize River, known as the Macal. The river journey of 121 miles from Belize, broken by many rapids, needs considerable ingenuity to negotiate the numerous 'runs' More Spanish is spoken than English in San Ignacio.

Tours

Local taxis which offer tours of Mountain Pine Ridge (described below) in the wet season probably won't get very far; also, taking a tour to Xunantunich (also described below) is not really necessary. Canoe trips up the Macal River are well worthwhile. They take about 3 hrs upstream, half that on return, guides point out iguanas in the trees and bats asleep on the rock walls. Ask at *Eva's Bar* (T 2267) for information on canoe trips with Toni, bird and wildlife watching, visiting medicinal plant research farm (US$5 extra), small rapids, etc, 0830-1600, good value; or with Bob, who does jungle river trips, US$30 for 2 people in a canoe, all-day tour, highly recommended. Bob is very helpful and will organize tours for you but you may end up with an indifferent guide, make sure you tell him exactly what you want. Tours to Tikal can also be arranged.

Westland Tours charge US$40 pp for tour to Caracol including Río Frío Cave, Río On pools and García sisters gift shop, 12 hrs; cheaper to hire a car if with a group, difficult to get lost. Another trip is to Barton Creek Cave, 1½-hr drive followed by a 3½-hr canoe trip in the cave; cost is US$20 pp min 3 people. Hiring a canoe to go upstream without a guide is not recommended unless you are highly proficient as there are class 2 rapids 1 hr from San Ignacio. A rec guide is Ramon Silva from *International Archaeological Tours*, 23 Burns Av, T 3991.

Excursions

A short walk from San Ignacio (800m from *Hotel San Ignacio*) is **Cahal Pech**, a Maya site and nature reserve on a wooded hill overlooking the town. A Visitor's Centre was opened in 1997. A museum is being built on site. Admission US$2.50, open daily. The man who sells tickets will lend you a guidebook written by some of the archaeologists who worked on the site; it is now out of print so must be returned.

4 miles W of San Ignacio on a good road is Bullet Tree Falls on the western branch of the Belize River, here in its upper course known as the Mopan River; a pleasant cascade amid relaxing surroundings.

12 miles N of San Ignacio, near Bullet Tree Falls, is **El Pilar** Archaeological Reserve for Maya Flora and Fauna, an archaeological site which straddles the border with Guatemala. Although it is a large site (about 38 ha), much of it has been left intentionally uncleared so that selected architectural features are exposed within the rainforest. The preserved rainforest here is home to hundreds of species of birds and animals. There are five trails, three archaeological, two nature, the longest of which is a mile and a half long. There are more than a dozen pyramids and 25 identified plazas. Unusually for Maya cities in this region, there is an abundance of water (streams and falls). Take the Bullet Tree Road N of San Ignacio, cross the Mopan River Bridge and follow the signs to El Pilar.

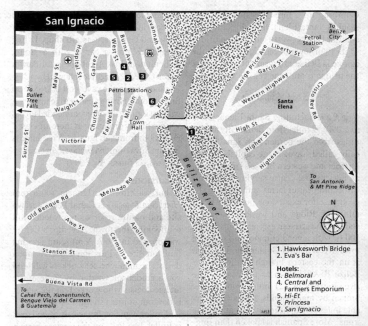

San Ignacio

1. Hawkesworth Bridge
2. Eva's Bar

Hotels:
3. *Belmoral*
4. *Central* and
   Farmers Emporium
5. *Hi-Et*
6. *Princesa*
7. *San Ignacio*

The Reserve is 7 miles from Bullet Tree on an all-weather limestone road. It can be reached by vehicle, horse or mountain bike (hiking is only recommended for the experienced; carry lots of water). The caretakers, who live at the S end of the site in a modern green-roofed house, are happy to show visitors around. The Cayo Tour Guides Association works in association with the Belize River Archaeological Settlement Survey (BRASS) and can take visitors. See also *Trails of El Pilar: A Guide to the El Pilar Archaeological Reserve from Maya Flora and Fauna* (published 1996).

About 10 miles S of San Ignacio, above the river and adjacent to the Chaa Creek Cottages at Ix Chel Farm (see below), is the unusual **Panti Rainforest Trail**, established as a place for study and preservation of native medicinal plants by Dr Rosita Arvigo, an American disciple of Mayan healer Eligio Panti of San Antonio in the Mountain Pine Ridge (he died Mar 1996, aged 104). From the turn off on the Benque road it is a pleasant 4-mile walk to Ix Chel; lifts are often possible. The plants are labelled in four languages. Visits can be arranged by calling 08-23180; self-guided tour with field guide, US$5 pp, guided tours with local guide, US$7.50 pp, group tours with the director by arrangement (Belizeans free). Dr Arvigo sells selections of herbs (the jungle salve, US$5, has been found effective against mosquito bites) and a book on medicinal plants used by the Maya (US$8, US$2 postage and packing, from General Delivery, San Ignacio, Cayo District).

At nearby Tipu are the remains of one of the few old Spanish mission churches established in Belize.

Local information
● Accommodation
In centre of town: up the hill, as you turn left on the San Ignacio side of the suspension bridge, is **A2-B** *San Ignacio*, 18 Buena Vista St,

T 2034/2125, F 2134, on road to Benque Viejo, with bath, a/c or fan, hot water, clean, helpful staff, swimming pool, excellent restaurant, visited by the Queen in 1994, highly rec; **B** *Plaza*, 4a Burns Av, T 3332, a/c, cheaper without, with bath, parking; **C** *Venus*, 29 Burns Av, with bath, D without, fan, clean, hot water, free coffee and fruit, thin walls, noisy, Sat market and bus station behind hotel, rec; **C-D** *Piache*, 18 Buena Vista Rd, around the bend in the road from *San Ignacio* (PO Box 54, T 2032/2109) with or without bath, cold water, basic, overpriced, bar in pm, also tour agent; **D** *Martha's Guest House*, 10 West St, T 2276, good restaurant, friendly, clean, kitchen facilities, the family also runs August Laundromat, **D** *New Belmoral*, 1/ Burns Av, T 092-2024, with shower, cable TV, hot water, fan or a/c, a bit noisy (clean and friendly); **D** *Tropicool*, Burns Av, shared bath, fan, clean; **D** *Princesa*, Burns Av and King St, with bath, clean, helpful, secure, manager Mathew Galvez; **E** *Central*, 24 Burns Av, T 2253, clean, secure, fans, shared hot showers, book exchange, friendly, verandah with hammocks, uncomfortable beds but rec, no restaurant but eat at *Eva's Bar* next door; **E** *Hi-Et*, 12 West St, T 2828, noisy, fans, low partition walls, family run, clothes washing permitted, no meals; **E** *Imperial*, 22 Burns Av, basic, noisy, shared bath, dirty, but popular; **F** *Mrs Espat's*, up the hill from *Hi-Et*, rooms next door to small shop and house. **NB** San Ignacio has a lively disco on Fri and Sat, some hotels may be noisy.

In Santa Elena: **D** *Snooty Fox*, 64 George Price Av, overlooking Macal River, rooms and apartments, some with bath, others shared bath, good value canoe rental.

Camping. *Mida's*, 1 km from town, nr river, go down Burns Av, turn right down unpaved road after wooden church, after 200 yds turn left, campground is 300 yds on right, US$15/car and 2 people inc electricity, cabins available at US$20, hot showers, electricity, water, restaurant, owner Maria, very helpful, good value, also organize trips to Tikal. 1 km further is *Cosmos* camping, US$2.50 pp for tents, washing and cooking facilities, cabins **E**, run by friendly Belizean family, canoe and bikes for hire, good.

Other places to stay nearby South of San Ignacio: **L3** *Chaa Creek Cottages*, on the Macal River, 5 miles upstream from San Ignacio, inc breakfast, lunch US$9, dinner US$16.50, discounts June-Oct, set on a working farm in pleasant countryside, highly rec. Electricity in

restaurant/bar area only; cabins have oil lamps. You can swim or canoe in the river. Trips on the river, to Xunantunich, to Tikal, to Mountain Pine Ridge, to Caracol, nature walks, horse riding and jungle safaris organized by Chaa Creek Inland Expeditions; also joint vacations arranged with *Rum Point Inn*, Placencia. Latest project is blue morpho butterfly breeding centre. If coming by road, turn off the Benque road at Chial, 6 miles from San Ignacio; hotel will collect you by boat from San Ignacio (US$25 for 4), or from international airport (US$125); reservations PO Box 53, San Ignacio, T 092-2037, F 092-2501, or hotel office at 56 Burns Av, San Ignacio.

Nabitunich Cottages (Rudi and Margaret Juan), turn off the Benque road 1½ miles beyond Chial, offers spectacular views of Xunantunich and another, unexcavated Maya ruin, jungle trails, excellent birdwatching, with fields going down to beautiful Macal river on working farm, own transport recommended, excursions not arranged, very homely if slightly basic, T 093-2309, F 093-2096 or c/o Benque Viejo Post Office, Cayo. Room rates from **A3** without meals to **A1** full board. You may camp here, US$0.25.

L3 *duPlooys'*, turn left on the road to Benque on same road for Chaa Creek, then follow signs (inc one steep hill), on the Macal River, T 092-3101, F 092-3301, inc all meals in jungle lodge, bar with deck overlooking trees and river, a small jungle area on the 20-acre property, trips arranged to many local activities and sites. Run by Ken and Judy du Plooy formerly of Charleston, S Carolina. Good food, rec.

A3 *Ek Tun*, 10-min walk before *Black Rock* but across the river, owned by the Darts, a Colorado couple, 2 4-person cabins, good food, T cellular 091-2002, in USA (303) 442-6150, or check for space through *Eva's Bar*.

A2-B *Black Rock Lodge*, on the Macal River, road sometimes requires 4WD depending on weather, 6 stone and thatch cabañas, solar-powered electricity and hot water, hiking, riding, canoeing, birdwatching, excursions, breakfast US$7, lunch US$8, dinner US$15; Caesar Sherrard, PO Box 48, San Ignacio, Cayo, T 092-2341/3296, F 092-3449, e-mail: blackrock@btl.net, web site: http://www.belizenet.com/black-rock.html (see also *Caesar's Place*, above); **A2** *Windy Hill Cottages*, on Graceland Ranch 2 miles W off highway, T 092-2017, F 092-3080, 14 cottage units, all with bath, dining room, small pool, nature trails, horse riding and river trips can be arranged, expensive.

C *Parrot Nest*, run by Fred, nr village of Bullet Tree Falls, 3 miles from San Ignacio (taxi US$5), small but comfortable tree houses in beautiful grounds by the river, breakfast and dinner inc, Fred is a good cook, canoeing, bird-watching, horse riding available. Also nr Bullet Tree Falls is a restaurant, *Terry's*, limited menu but good food.

East of San Ignacio: A2-B *Maya Mountain Lodge* (Bart and Suzi Mickler), ¾ mile from San Ignacio at 9 Cristo Rey Rd in Santa Elena (taxi from town US$2.50, bus US$0.25), welcoming, special weekly and monthly rates and for families, restaurant, excursions are more expensive than arranging one in town, 10% service charge added to total bill, T 092-2164, F 092-2029, PO Box 46, San Ignacio, laundry, postal service, self-guided nature trail. Swimming, hiking, riding, canoeing, fishing can be arranged. Explore Belize Tours in the region and beyond; also 'Parrot's Perch' social and educational area with resident naturalist and ornithologist. Edgar is a good taxi driver/guide.

Mountain Equestrian Trails, Mile 8, Mountain Pine Ridge Rd (from Georgeville), Central Farm PO, Cayo District, T 092-3310, F 092-3361, T 082-3180 for reservations, 082-2149 for office, reservations in US T 941-488 0522, F 941-488 3953 or 1-800-838-3913, offers ½-day, full-day and 4-day adventure tours on horseback in western Belize, 'Turf' and 'Turf and Surf' packages, and other expeditions, excellent guides and staff; birdwatching tours in and around the reserve; accommodation in 4 *cabañas* doubles with bath, no electricity, hot water, mosquito nets, good food in *cantina*, *Chiclero Cultural Trails*, tents under rainforest canopy are a new development, US$499 for 4 nights, incl meals, trip to Caracol, birdwatching, caving etc; highly rec (owners Jim and Marguerite Bevis, in conjunction with neighbouring landowners, have set up a biosphere reserve, incorporating nearby Salvadorean refugees).

L1-A1 *Blancaneaux Lodge*, Mountain Pine Ridge Rd, Central Farm, PO Box B, Cayo District, T/F 092-3878, once the mountain retreat of Francis Ford Coppola and his family, now villas and cabañas, full amenities, overlooking river, private air strip; *A1* *Five Sisters Lodge*, 2½ miles beyond *Blancaneaux Lodge*, T/F 092-2985, new 1995, rustic cottages lit by oil lamps, great views, rec, good value restaurant; *A2* *Pine Ridge Lodge*, on road to Augustine, just past turning to Hidden Valley Falls, T 092-3310, F 092-2267, cabañas in the pinewoods, inc breakfast.

● **Places to eat**

Doña Elvira Espat serves good meals at her house (inc breakfast), advance notice required, good, friendly with good local information (no sign, corner of Galvez St and Bullet Tree Rd). Her daughter (Elvira Quiróz) is also an excellent cook, meals served in her home: 6 Far West St, T 092-2556, advance notice required, vegetarian available, reasonable prices. *Maxim's*, Bullet Tree Rd and Far West St, Chinese, good service, cheap, very good food, popular with locals, noisy TV at the bar; *Serendib*, 27 Burns Av, good food and good value, Sri Lankan owners, good, tasty Indian-style food, open 1030-1500, 1830-1100, closed Sun; *Eva's Bar*, 22 Burns Av, T 092-2267, good, helpful, local dishes, excellent breakfasts, bike rental, tours (see above); *The Sand Castle*, take a right turn off King St to river, the open air restaurant is at the back of the building, music, good food and prices; *Belbrit*, 30 Burns Av, good breakfast and service, clean; *Bushwacker's Grill*, Burns Av, good steak sandwiches and Buffalo wings (named after Buffalo, New York, not bison); *Roots*, vegetarian, nr square, good; *Nablo's Bakery*, breads, meat pies, biscuits, cakes etc, good, rec; *Belize Chinese*, below *Jaguar Hotel*, good Chinese and Italian, good breakfasts, cheap; *Café Maya*, Burns Av, owned by Mel and Eric Barber, very good; *HL Burgers*, Burns Av, good food; *Martha's Kitchen*, below *Martha's Guest House*, very good breakfasts and Belizean dishes. Fruit and vegetable market every Sat am.

On a hill, with TV station, beside the road to Benque Viejo before the edge of town is *Cahal Pech* tavern, serving cheap drinks and meals, with music and dancing at weekends, the place to be, live bands are broadcast on TV and radio all over Belize, good views. On a hill across the track from the tavern is Cahal Pech archaeological site (see above). The *Blue Angel* on Burns Av is popular with the younger crowd, very dark, fun, live bands, dancing, small admission charge.

● **Banks & money changers**

Belize Bank offers full service, TCs, Visa and Mastercard cash advances; Atlantic Bank, Burns Av also does cash advances. Both change US$5 commission for cash advances. *Eva's Bar* changes TCs at a very good rates. Changers in the town square give better rates of exchange for dollars cash and TCs than you can get at the border with Guatemala. The best place to change dollars into quetzales is in Guatemala.

● **Post & telecommunications**

Post Office: above the police station, reliable parcel service. **NB** All shops and businesses close 1700-1900.

Telecommunications: *BTL* office at further end of Burns Av, opp *Venus Hotel*, long distance calls and fax service.

● **Shopping**

Black Rock Gift Shop, near *Eva's*, linked to *Black Rock Lodge*, luggage can be left here if canoeing from Black Rock to San Ignacio, large selection of arts and crafts, workshop.

● **Sports**

Riding: *Easy Rider*, Bullet Tree Rd, T 3310, full day tours for US$40 inc lunch.

● **Buses**

To **Belize City**: Batty Bus departs 1300, 1400, 1500 and 1600; early morning buses from the border stop at the bridge in front of the police station and from the bus terminal at 0500, 0600 and 0700. Later morning trips go from Benque Viejo at parking area behind Burns Ave, US$2.50, 3½ hrs. A 1000 or 1100 bus will connect with the 1500 bus to Chetumal. Novelo, starts at 0400 and runs on the hour until about 1200. To **Belmopan**, 1 hr, US$1. **Taxi**: to Guatemalan border, about US$5 (colectivo US$1.50, bus US$0.70), to Xunantunich US$20, to Belize City US$75, to Tikal US$100. **Mini-buses**: also run to Tikal, US$20 pp return, making a day trip possible. Ask taxi drivers for information. Organized tours cost about US$60.

XUNANTUNICH

At **Xunantunich** ('Maiden of the Rock'), now freed from heavy bush, there are Classic Maya remains in beautiful surroundings; the heart of the city was three plazas aligned on a N-S axis, lined with many temples, the remains of a ball court, and surmounted by the 'Castillo'; at 130 ft this was thought to be the highest man made structure in Belize until recent measurement of the Sky Palace at Caracol; the impressive view takes in jungle, the lowlands of the Petén and the blue flanks of the Maya Mountains. Maya graffiti can still be seen on the wall of Structure A-16; friezes on the Castillo, some restored in modern plaster, represent astronomical symbols. Extensive excavations took place in 1959-60 but only limited restoration

work has been undertaken. A leaflet on the area is available from the Archaeological Dept for US$0.15. About 1½ miles further N are the ruins of Actuncan, probably a satellite of Xunantunich; both sites show evidence of earthquake damage.

Xunantunich is open 0800-1700, entry US$2.50 and, apart from a small refreshment stand, no facilities for visitors, but a new museum is now being built, helpful guides at the site, bring own refreshments; beware of robbery on the road up to the ruins, government employees accompany visitors up the hill (try hitching back to the ferry with tourists travelling by car). It is in any case an extremely hot walk up the hill on the white, limestone road with little or no shade. Start early! You can swim in the river after visiting the ruins. Just E of the ferry, Magaña's Art Centre and the Xunantunich Women's Group sell locally made crafts and clothing in a shop on a street off the highway.

● **Access** To reach Xunantunich hitch, or take a 0800-0830, or 0900-0930 bus from San Ignacio towards the border to the village of San José Succotz (7 miles, US$0.75), where a hand-operated ferry takes visitors and their cars across the Mopan River (0800-1700, free weekdays, US$0.50 at weekends); there is then a 20-min walk uphill on dirt road (even motorcyclists may find the track impossible after rain). Return buses to San Ignacio pass at about lunchtime.

● **Accommodation** Opposite the ferry, a 1½ mile walk brings you to *Rancho de los Amigos*, a farm run by Americans Edward and Virginia Jenkins, T 093-2483 where you can stay in rural surroundings, **C** pp including two home-cooked meals, vegetarian available, open air dining room built on the side of a Mayan temple, cabins, bucket showers, quiet, peaceful, also herbal healing and acupuncture, will pick you up at Xunantunich bus stop on highway. **D** *Clarissa Falls*, along river, book through *Eva's Bar*, comfortable cabins in beautiful setting, quiet, clean, good meals for about US$5, take a green taxi there for US$0.50.

San José Succotz is a large Yucatec Maya village below Xunantunich where Spanish is the first language and a few inhabitants preserve the old Maya customs of their ancestral village (San José in the Petén); the colourful fiestas of St Joseph and the Holy Cross are celebrated on 19 Mar and on a variable date in early May respectively each year. There is a Guatemalan Consulate on the Western Highway, opposite the Xununtunich ferry (see **Frontier with Guatemala**, below).

MOUNTAIN PINE RIDGE

Mountain Pine Ridge is a Forest Reserve (59,000 ha) covering the NW portion of the Maya Mountains. The undulating country is well-watered and covered in largely undisturbed temperate pine and gallery forest; in the valleys are lush hardwood forests filled with orchids, bromeliads and butterflies. The enjoyable river scenery, high waterfalls, numerous limestone caves and shady picnic sites attract about 50 visitors/day during the dry season – a popular excursion despite the rough roads. Hitching is difficult but not impossible. Try contacting the Forestry Conservation Officer, T 092-3280, who maybe able to help. Two reasonable roads lead into the reserve: from Georgeville to the N and up from Santa Elena via Cristo Rey; these meet at **San Antonio**, a Mopan Maya village with many thatched-roof houses and the nearby Pacbitun archaeological site (where stelae and musical instruments have been unearthed). At San Antonio, the García Sisters have their workshop, museum, shop where they sell carvings in local slate and guest house (**D**). You can sample Maya food and learn about use of medicinal plants; this is a regular stop on tours to the Mountain Pine Ridge. A donation of US$0.50 is requested; US$12.50 is charged to take photos of the sisters at work. Two buses a day from San Ignacio, 1000 and 1430, from market area.

The main forest road meanders along rocky spurs, from which unexpected and often breathtaking views emerge of jungle far below and streams plunging hundreds of feet over red-rock canyons; a lookout point has been provided to view the impressive **Hidden Valley Falls**, said to be over 1,000 ft high (often shrouded in fog Oct-Jan); on a clear day it is said you can see Belmopan from the viewpoint. There is a picnic area and small shops here. It is quite a long way from the main road and is probably not worth the detour if time is short particularly in the dry season when the flow is restricted. On many heights stand forestry observation towers: bushfires are a constant threat in the dry season. 18 miles into the reserve the road crosses the **Río On**. Here, where the river tumbles in inviting pools over huge granite boulders, is one of Belize's most beautiful picnic and swimming spots. The rocks from little water slides are good for children. The rocks can be slippery and, in the wet season, bathing is not possible.

5 miles further is **Augustine** (also called Douglas D'Silva, or **Douglas Forest Station**), the main forest station (pop 170) where there is a shop, accommodation in two houses (bookable through the Forestry Dept in Belmopan, the area Forestry Office is in San Antonio) and a camping ground, US$1, no mattresses (see rangers for all information on the area). Keep your receipt, a guard checks it on the way out of Mountain Pine Ridge. A mile beyond Augustine is a cluster of caves in rich rainforest; the entrance to the **Rio Frio Cave** (in fact a tunnel) is over 65 ft high; many spectacular rock formations and sandy beaches where the river flows out. Trees in the parking area and along the Cuevas Gemelas nature trail, which starts 1 hr from the Rio Frio cave, are labelled. A beautiful excursion; highly recommended. In the Mountain Pine Ridge note the frequent changes of colour of the soil and look out for the fascinating insect life. If lucky you may see deer.

Forestry roads continue S further into the mountains, reaching San Luis (6 miles), the only other inhabited camp in the area (pop 100, post office, sawmill and forest station), and continuing on over the granite uplands of the Vaca Plateau into the Chiquibul Forest Reserve (186,000 ha).

The four forest reserves which cover the Maya Mountains are the responsibility of the Forestry Department, who have only about 20 rangers to patrol 400,000 ha of heavily-forested land. A hunting ban prohibits the carrying of firearms. Legislation, however, allows for controlled logging; all attempts to have some areas declared National Parks or biosphere reserves have so far been unsuccessful.

NB At the driest time of year, normally Feb to May, is when the Mountain Pine Ridge is reasonably accessible, there is an ever-present danger of fire. Open fires are strictly prohibited and you are asked to be as careful as possible.

CARACOL

About 24 miles SSW of Augustine **Caracol** (about 1 hr by 4WD), is a rediscovered Maya city; the area is now a National Monument Reservation. Caracol was established about 300 BC and continued well into the Late Classic period; glyphs record a victorious war against Tikal. Why Caracol was built in such a poorly-watered region is not known, but Maya engineers showed great ingenuity in constructing reservoirs and terracing the fields. The Sky Palace ('Caana') pyramid climbs 138 ft above the site, which is being excavated by members of the University of Central Florida. Excavations take place Feb-May but there are year-round caretakers who will show you around. Admission US$15. Currently very knowledgeable guides escort groups around the site twice daily and there is a new information centre being built. As the site is largely unprotected you are free to walk and examine parts of the buildings which would be closed to visitors or well protected. For this reason unescorted visitors are not welcome. Best to obtain an officially authorized permit to visit the site from the Forestry Office in San Antonio. Throughout this largely unknown region are vast cave systems stretching W into Guatemala, but there are absolutely no facilities and none of the caves is open to the casual traveller. The only months in which a trip by road to Caracol can be guaranteed are April and May, but the road has been improved and with 4WD is passable for much of the year. The road is interesting as you pass many chiclero trees in the rainforest, crosses over a river and then immediately climbs the Mountain Pine Ridge – the difference is very pronounced. A number of places in San Ignacio, and Mountain Equestrian Trails (see above), offer horseback tours to Caracol, US$185.

• **Transport** Mountain Pine Ridge has no public transport. Apart from tours, hiring a mountain bike (from *Eva's Bar*), a vehicle or a taxi are the only alternatives. Everything is well signposted. The private pick-ups which go into San Ignacio from Augustine are usually packed, so hitching is impossible. Taxis charge US$88 for 5 people. Roads are passable but rough between Jan and May, but after June they are marginal and are impossible in the wet (Sept-Nov); essential to seek local advice at this time.

BENQUE VIEJO

9 miles up-river from San Ignacio on a good road is the tranquil town of **Benque Viejo del Carmen**, near the Guatemalan frontier. Population, 3,312, many of whom are Maya Mopan Indians. There are police and military barracks near the border.

There are caves nearby, open 0800-1600, ask locals to show you the road, near the hydroplant.

Local information
● **Accommodation**
E *Maya*, 11 George St, T 093-2116, and **E** *Okis*, George St, T 093-2006, opp the bus station, are the least bad. There is a green hotel, **F**, good on left side of main road to Guatemala. The hotels on the Guatemalan side are much cheaper than Belize so if on a tight budget try to cross the border even late in the afternoon. From Benque to the border is a 20-min walk, 1.6 km.

● **Places to eat**
Meals at *Riverside Restaurant*, on main square; *Restaurant Los Angeles*, Church St; *Hawaii*, on main street, rec; or at one of picturesque huts.

● **Transport**

Road Novelo's run many daily buses from Belize City to **Benque Viejo**, US$3, 0330-1100; frequent buses from San Ignacio to Benque Viejo, taxi US$10, or colectivo from central square, US$2 (or US$2 to Melchor de Mencos in Guatemala, 30 mins).

FRONTIER WITH GUATEMALA

● **Belizean immigration**

Border hours are 0800-1200 and 1400-1700. Everyone leaving Belize has to pay the PACT exit tax (see page 741).

● **Guatemalan consulate**

Opposite the ferry in San José Succotz, open Mon-Fri 0900-1300; visas for those who need them easily arranged. Most nationalities can obtain a tourist card (sometimes a visa) at the border.

● **Exchange**

You will get better rates purchasing quetzals at the border than anywhere before Puerto Barrios or Guatemala City. Compare rates at the **Banco de Guatemala** with the money changers. Check what you receive and do not accept damaged notes.

● **Transport**

From Benque Viejo to Melchor de Mencos, by taxi US$1.50, by colectivo US$0.50. For bus services, see under Benque Viejo.

On the Guatemalan side someone will carry the luggage to **Melchor de Mencos** (see Guatemala, Section 3, **El Petén**), where there is a landing strip (flights to Flores). There is also a road (very rough) on to Santa Elena, for Flores (a bus leaves the border for Flores at 1330, US$2.65, or several daily buses from Melchor de Mencos, 3½ hrs, US$2.65, leave Belize City at 0600, 0630 or 1015 to make a connection to Flores); unless you take a tourist minibus, US$10, it is only possible to get to Tikal by bus by asking the driver of the border-Flores bus to let you off at the road junction (El Cruce), where you can get a connecting bus to Tikal (see same section of Guatemala chapter). See that section also, under **Flores Travel Agents** for direct minibus services between Flores/Santa Elena and Belize City.

Southern Belize and the Southern Cayes

S OUTHERN BELIZE is the remotest part of the country, sparsely populated but with many Indian settlements akin to those across the border in Guatemala. Maya ruins abound and nature reserves are increasing in numbers. Roads are poor, not helped by the wetter climate. However, access to the attractive coast is improving.

BELIZE CITY TO PUNTA GORDA

GALES POINT

About 2 miles beyond the Belize Zoo on the Western Highway a good dirt road runs SE to **Gales Point**, a charming fishing village of 300 on a peninsula at the S end of Manatee Lagoon, 15 miles N of Dangriga. The villagers are keen to preserve their natural resources and there are a lot of the endangered manatee and hawksbill turtles. Boat tours of the lagoon are recommended. Turn off the highway at **La Democracia** (signed Manatee Rd) and head E, then SE, around Cumberland Hill, to join the Gales Point-Melinda road about 3 miles S of Gales Point (La Democracia to the junction 23.2 miles). At **Melinda Forest Station** turnoff it is signed Belize New Rd. The government has upgraded the road as a short cut to Dangriga, bypassing Belmopan and it is now the quickest route, called the Coastal Highway. Day and overnight excursions of a wide variety, from US$30/boat holding 6-8 people, contact Kevin Andrewin of Manatee Tour

Guides Association on arrival. Community phone, T 05-22087, ask for Alice or Josephine. Gales Point can be reached by inland waterways from Belize City, but boat services have largely been superceded by buses. At least 2 daily Z-line buses between Belize City and Dangriga use the coastal road.

- **Accommodation L2** *Manatee Lodge*, resort fishing camp; about US$1,000 for 7-day all-inclusive package, T 77593, US res: T 800-782-7238. The Gales Point Bed and Breakfast Association arranges basic accommodation, E, no indoor plumbing, meals available, contact Hortence Welch on arrival.

ALONG THE HUMMINGBIRD HIGHWAY

The narrow Hummingbird Highway branches off the Western Highway 48 miles W of Belize City, passes Belmopan and branches 52 miles SE to Dangriga. Its surface is partly dirt and partly newly paved. It climbs through rich tropical hardwood forest until reaching Mile 13, where a track leads off to **St Herman's Cave**; the path passes through shady ferns until descending in steps to the cave entrance. You can walk for more than a mile underground: torch and spare batteries essential.

2 miles further on is the **Blue Hole National Park**, an azure blue swimming hole fringed with vines and ferns, fed by a stream which comes from St Herman's Cave and re-enters another 100 ft away (entry US$4). This is typical karst limestone country with sinkholes, caves and underground streams. The water appearing here is deliciously cool after a long journey underground to disappear into the top of a large underwater cavern. Eventually this joins the Sibun River which enters the sea just S of Belize City. There is a rough 2½ mile trail, through low secondary forest, between St Herman's Cave and the Blue Hole, good walking shoes required. A sign on the roadway warns visitors against thieves; lock your car and leave someone on guard if possible when swimming. An armed guard and more wardens have been hired to prevent further theft and assaults.

There is a rest area and snack bar at Mile 21 and several *tiendas* thereafter for snacks and drinks, but otherwise few other stopping places. The peaks of the mountains continue to dominate the S side of the highway until about Mile 39, when the valley of the Stann Creek begins to widen out into Belize's most productive agricultural area. Large citrus groves stretch along the highway: grapefruit, bananas and Valencia oranges, which are processed into canned juices and concentrates at centres like Pomona (Mile 40). The drive to Dangriga from Belmopan can take from 2-2½ hrs, depending on road conditions.

Canoeing or tubing trips can be organized from Over-the-Top Camp on the Hummingbird Highway (try Kingfisher in Placencia) down the Indian Creek, visiting Caves 5, 4, 3 and then Daylight Cave and Darknight Cave. Vehicle support is brought round to meet you on the Coastal Highway near Democracia.

Turn E at Mile 32 for 4 miles along a gravel road to **Tamandua**, a wildlife sanctuary in **Five Blue Lakes National Park**. For further information on Five Blue Lakes National Park contact Friends of 5 Blues, PO Box 111, Belmopan, T 08-12005, or the warden, Lee Wengrzyn, a local dairy farmer, or Augustus Palacio (see above).

● **Accommodation On the Hummingbird Highway**: at Mile 31, **E** *Palacios Mountain Retreat*, Augustus Palacio, St Martha, Hummingbird Highway, Cayo District, good for relaxing, *cabañas*, friendly, helpful, family atmosphere, safe, good local food; swimming in river, tours to waterfall in forest, caves and lagoon, Five Blue Lakes National Park; beware sandflies.

There is an organic fruit farm run by Janet and Bernard Dempsey, with 7 cabins, eat with the family, local day trips arranged to see birds and wildlife. Contact the Dempseys at Tamandua, PO Box 306, Belmopan.

At Mile 41½, **B** *Caves Branch Jungle Camp*, PO Box 356, Belmopan, T/F 08-2280, camp phone 08-23180, cabins **D** pp in bunks, camping US$5, family-style meals extra, highly rec, also runs a variety of river cave, dry land, crystal cave and jungle adventure trips.

DANGRIGA

The chief town of the Stann Creek District, has a population of 10,000, largely Black Caribs (Garifunas – always ask before taking photographs – *phone code* 05). It is on the seashore, with the usual Belizean aspect of wooden houses elevated on piles, and is a cheerful and busily commercial place. The two rivers which meet the sea here – North Stann Creek and Havana Creek – are alive with flotillas of boats and fishermen. There are several gas stations, a good hospital and an airfield with regular flights. The beach has been considerably cleaned up and extended, being particularly nice at the *Pelican Beach Hotel*, where it is raked and cleaned daily. Palm trees are being planted by *Pal's Guest House* where the beach is being enlarged. Dangriga (until recently called Stann Creek) means 'standing waters' in Garifuna.

Local festivals/holiday

18-19 Nov, Garifuna, or Settlement Day, re-enacting the landing of the Black Caribs in 1823, fleeing a failed rebellion in Honduras. Dancing all night and next day; very popular. All transport to Dangriga is booked up a week in advance and hotel rooms impossible to find. Private homes rent rooms, though. At this time, boats from Puerto Barrios to Punta Gorda (see below) tend to be full, but launches take passengers for US$10 pp.

Local information

● **Accommodation**

L3-A1 *Pelican Beach*, outside town (PO Box 14), on the beach N of town, T 22044, F 22570, with private bath, hot water and a/c, verandah, pier with hammocks, 20 rooms, excellent restaurant, bar, games lounge, gift shop, tours arranged, helpful (taxi from town US$2.50, or 15-min walk from North Stann Creek).

A2 *Bonefish*, Mahogany St, T 22165, on seafront on outskirts of town, a/c, colour TV with US cable, hot water, takes Visa, good, refurbished 1993, good restaurant.

B *Pal's Guest House*, 10 new units on beach, 808A Magoon St, Dangriga, T 22095, all units with balconies, sea views, bath, fan, cable TV, cheaper rooms in main building, Dangriga Dive Centre, T 23262, runs from next door, Derek Jones arranges fabulous trips to the cayes (see also Hangman's Cay below).

D *Riverside*, 5 Commerce St, T 22168, F 22296, clean, shared bathroom, nice common area; **D** *Rio Mar*, 977 Southern Foreshore, friendly, good, music piped into all rooms, you will hear your neighbour's even if yours is turned off; **D** *Sofie's Hotel & Restaurant*, Chatuye St, unimpressive but pleasant.

E *Bluefield Lodge*, 6 Bluefield Rd, T 22742, bright new hotel, owner Louise Belisle very nice, spotless, comfortable beds, very helpful, secure, highly rec; **E** *Catalina*, 37 Cedar St, T 22390, very small, dirty but friendly, store luggage. Also you can stay in private homes (basic), eg Miss Caroline's. There is a cooperative which runs a place to pitch a tent or sling a hammock. Unfurnished houses are rented out for US$20-30 a month. **E** *New Central*, 119 Commerce St, T 22008, shared cold shower, fans, thin walls, cramped but reasonably safe and friendly; **E** *Cameleon*, fan and shared bath, clean, nice balconies.

● **Places to eat**

Sea Flame, 42 Commerce St, excellent fish and chicken; *Riviera Bar/Restaurant*, good meals, clean; *Starlight* nr *Cameleon*, towards bridge, Chinese, cheapish, good; *Ritchie's Dinette*, on main street N of Police Station, creole and Spanish food, cheap, simple, large portions, popular for breakfast, bakeries; *Sunrise*, similar; *Pola's Kitchen*, 25a Tubroose St, nr *Pal's Guest House*, excellent breakfasts, cheap, clean, good atmosphere; *Ricky's*, good reasonable local food; *Burger King* (not the international chain) do good breakfasts, lunches and take-aways; *River Café*, S bank of river, just E of main road, nicer inside than it looks, good breakfast, good for information.

● **Banks & money changers**

Bank of Nova Scotia; Barclays Bank International (Mastercard and Visa); Belize Bank (Visa cash advances). Same hours as Belize City. (See page 748.) Change TCs at Z-line bus station, good rates.

● **Entertainment**

Listen for local music 'Punta Rock', a unique Garifuna/African based Carib sound, now popular throughout Belize. *Local Motion Disco*, next to *Cameleon*, open weekends, Punta rock, reggae, live music. A local band, the Turtles, maintain a Punta museum in town. Studios can be visited. Homemade instruments are a Garifuna speciality, especially drums.

● **Tour companies & travel agents**

Treasured Travels, 64 Commerce St, T 22578, is very helpful, run by Diane; *Pelican Beach Hotel* runs tours to Cockscomb Basin, Gales Point and citrus factories; *Rosado's Tours*, T 22110/22020, 35 Lemon St; *Rodney* at the airstrip also runs tours, T 22294.

● **Transport**

Air Maya Airways flies from Belize City 5 daily (continuing to Independence and Punta Gorda). Tickets from Rodney at the airstrip (T 22294), or at *Pelican Beach Hotel*.

Buses From **Belize City**, Z Line, Magazine St, several daily from 0800, plus 0600 Mon, returning daily from 0500, Sun at 0900, 1000, 1500, US$5, 4½ hrs (buy ticket in advance to reserve numbered seat – the bus stops at the Blue Hole National Park); truck, US$1.25. 5 buses daily to **Punta Gorda**, 1000, 1100, 1200, 1600, 1900, 4-5 hrs, US$6.50 (very crowded), stops at Independence, nr Mango Creek. Bus to **Placencia** daily at 1200 direct, 1300 via Hopkins and Sittee River, US$4 (schedules change often, as do bus companies); to **Belmopan**, 2½ hrs, US$3. The Z-line bus terminal is at the road junction at the S end of town.

Sea A fast skiff leaves 0900 (be there at 0800) on Sat for Puerto Cortés, Honduras, US$40; departs from N bank of river by bridge, T 23227, ask for Carlos. Crossing takes 3 hrs and can be dangerous in rough weather. Check in advance procedures for exit formalities, if PACT exit tax has to be paid and you will have to pay to enter Honduras. You can hire a boat for around US$25 pp in a party to Belize City, enquire locally.

CAYES NEAR DANGRIGA

Tobacco Caye 1 hr by speedboat from Dangriga (US$15), this tiny island, quite heavily populated, has lots of local flavour and fishing camp charm. It is becoming a little commercialized, but still has an authentic feel. It sits right on the reef; you can snorkel from the beach although there are no large schools of fish. No sandflies on the beach; snorkelling equipment for rent. Boats go daily, enquire at *River Café*, run by English couple, Katherine and Jim, *The Hub* or *Rio Mar* restaurants, Dangriga, Captain Buck or Anthony charge US$12-15 pp.

• **Accommodation** *Reefs End Lodge*, PO Box 10, Dangriga, basic, small rooms, excellent host and food, boat transfer on request from Dangriga; **C** *Island Camps*, PO Box 174 (51 Regent St, Belize City, T 02-72109), owner Mark Bradley will pick up guests in Dangriga, A-frame huts and campground US$5 pp a night, meals on request, reef excursions, friendly, good value, rec. Several families on the island take guests; accommodation very basic and grubby, 3 meals are usually provided. **A1** *Ocean's Edge*, full board, 6 cabins on stilts joined by elevated walkways, excellent food, diving and fishing can be arranged, T USA 713-894-0548. There is no electricity on the island.

Hangman's Caye There is a new dive resort on this tiny, private island; 6 attractive cabañas with balcony over the sea, private bath, restaurant and bar.

South Water Caye is a lovely palm-fringed tropical island, with beautiful beaches, particularly at the S end.

• **Accommodation** Part of the caye is taken up by *Blue Marlin Lodge*, PO Box 21, Dangriga, T 05-22243, F 05-22296, an excellent dive lodge offering various packages; small sandy island with snorkelling off the beach; good accommodation and food; runs tours. *Frangipani House* and *Osprey's Nest* are two comfortable cottages owned by the *Pelican Beach Hotel*, available for rent; the *Hotel* also has *Pelican University*, which is ideal for groups as it houses 10-22 at US$55 pp/day inc 3 meals (details from *Pelican Beach Hotel* as above). *Leslie Cottages*, 5 units, T 05-22004, US contact T 800-548-5843 or 508-655-1461.

DANGRIGA TO PLACENCIA

The Southern Highway connects Dangriga with Punta Gorda in the S. It is a wide, flat, dirt road: dusty in the dry season, muddy in the wet but being paved with international funding. Public transport is limited and may be suspended after heavy rain. Hitching possible, but little traffic. 6 miles inland from Dangriga the road branches from the Hummingbird Highway and heads S through mixed tropical forests and palmettos and pines along the fringes of the Maya Mountains. West of the road, about 5 miles from the junction with the Hummingbird Highway, a track leads to **Mayflower**, a Mayan ruin. Work has begun on opening it up and they say it will be the biggest archaeological site in southern Belize.

HOPKINS

15 miles from Dangriga a minor road forks off 4 miles E to the Garifuna fishing village of **Hopkins**. Watch out for sandflies when the weather is calm. The villagers throw household slops into the sea and garbage on the beach.

• **Accommodation D-E** *Caribbean View*, at N end of village, basic rooms, shared bath; **D-E** *Sandy Beach Lodge*, T 05-22023, a women's cooperative, run by 10 women who work in shifts, arrive before 1900 or they will have gone home, 9 beachside rooms and large restaurant, 20-min walk S of village, quiet, safe, friendly, clean; **E** *Swinging Armadillos*, on the pier, 2 rooms, outdoor shower, seafood restaurant, bar. For longer stays, ask for *Seaside Garden*, owner Barry Swan. South of Hopkins, just N of Sittee River, is **L3-A2** *Jaguar Reef Lodge*, T/F 212041, postal address Hopkins

General Delivery, Stann Creek District, 14 thatched cabañas and central lodge on sandy beach, diving, snorkelling, kayaking, C-Breathe Center, non-divers can go down to 25 ft with special breathing equipment, mountain bikes, birdwatching and wildlife excursions.

● **Places to eat** *Over The Waves* has good food.

● **Buses** From Dangriga at 1215 daily; Z-line, maybe others.

COCKSCOMB BASIN WILDLIFE SANCTUARY

4 miles further on, the Southern Highway crosses the Sittee River at the small village of **Kendal** (ruins nearby); 1 mile beyond (20 miles from Dangriga) is the new village of **Maya Centre** (cabins and campground at *Nuck Cheil*, community phone 05-22666, ask for Aurora Saqui; small restaurant), from where a bad 7-mile track winds W through Cabbage Haul Gap to the **Cockscomb Basin Wildlife Sanctuary** (41,457 ha), the world's first jaguar sanctuary (entry US$5; Belizeans US$1.25). This was created out of the Cockscomb Basin Forest Reserve in 1986 to protect the country's highest recorded density of jaguars (*Panthera onca*) and their smaller cousins, the puma ('red tiger'), the endangered ocelot, the diurnal jaguarundi, and the exquisite margay. Many other mammals share the heavily-forested reserve, including coatis, collared peccaries, agoutis, anteaters, Baird's tapirs, and tayras (a small weasel-like animal). There are Red-eyed Tree Frogs, boas, iguanas and fer-de-lances, and over 290 species of birds, including King Vultures and Great Curassows. Park HQ is at the former settlement of Quam Bank (whose milpa-farming inhabitants founded Maya Centre outside the reserve); here there is an informative visitors' centre, picnic area and camping area (US$1.50); there are several 6-person basic cabins for rent (US$8 pp) with cooking facilities. Potable water is available, also earth toilets, but you must bring your own food, other drinks, matches, torch, sheet sleeping bag,

eating utensils and mosquito repellent; nearest shop is at Maya Centre. 3 miles of jungle trails spread out from the visitors' centre, but walkers are unlikely to see any of the big cats. Note that the guards leave for the day at 1600. You will see birds, frogs, lizards and snakes. Longer hikes can be planned with the staff; it is an arduous 4-5 day return climb to Victoria Peak (3,675 ft) and should not be undertaken casually. There is virtually no path, a guide is essential; Feb-May best for the climb. The Sanctuary is a good place for relaxing, listening to birds (scarlet macaws can be seen), showering under waterfalls, etc. This unique reserve is sponsored by the government, the Audubon Society, the World Wildlife Fund and private firms like the Jaguar car company; donations are very welcome. Before a visit travellers should contact the Belize Audubon Society, 12 Fort St, Belize City, T 02-34985, Dangriga T 05-22044 (*Pelican Beach Hotel*), or write to Ernesto Saqui, PO Box 90, Dangriga. Transport can be booked at the time of reservation, or locals will drive you from Maya Centre for US$15 (shared by passengers), otherwise it is a 6-mile, uphill walk from Maya Centre to the reserve. All buses going S from Dangriga go through Maya Centre, 40 mins, US$2.50-3; and N from Placencia, return bus at 0700, 0900, etc to Dangriga (allow 2 hrs for the walk down to Maya Centre). If walking, leave all unneeded gear in Dangriga in view of the uphill stretch from Maya Centre, or you can leave luggage at the little store in Maya Centre for US$0.50/day; note also that radio communication is not always perfect and may lead to problems of accommodation. A taxi from Dangriga will cost about US$50, it is not difficult to hitch back. The rainy season here extends from June to January.

GLOVER'S REEF

Turning E towards the Caribbean just before Kendal a road leads down the Sittee River to **Sittee River Village** and **Possum Point** Biological Station.

• **Accommodation** The Biological Station has a 16-room hotel, restaurant, **D**, specialise in student package tours from the USA and discourage casual guests; **F** pp *Glover's Atoll Guest House*, T 08-22505, 5 rooms, on river bank, restaurant, camping, jungle river trips, run by Lomont-Cabral family and starting point for boat to their *North East Caye* (see below); **B-E** *Toucan Sittee*, 400 yds down river from *Glovers*, run by Neville Collins, lovely setting, rooms with screens and fans, hot water, or fully-equipped riverside apartments, great meals around US$6, grow most of their fruit and veg, also over 50 medicinal plants; **F** *Isolene's*, family house, Isolene cooks good meals in restaurant opp; **B** *Bocatura Bank*, T 05-22006, cottages, restaurant.

Glover's Reef, about 45 miles offshore, is an atoll with beautiful diving and a Marine Reserve since 1993. *Manta Reef Resort*, Glover's Reef Atoll, PO Box 215, 3 Eyre St, Belize City, T 02-31895/32767, F 02-32764; 9 individual cabins with full facilities, in perfect desert island setting, 1 week packages available only, reservations essential; excellent diving and fishing, good food, highly recommended (E6 photo lab available). On 9-acre **North East Caye** is *Glover's Atoll Resort* (Gilbert and Marsha-Jo Lomont and Becky and Breeze Cabral, PO Box 563, Belize City, T 0148351/523048, F 08-23505/23235, no reservations needed). There are 8 cabins with wood burning stoves, US$95-145 pp/week + 7% room tax. Camping US$80 pp a week (inc trip out and back). Restaurant. No beach but the resort also comprises Lomont Caye and Cabral Caye which do have beaches, both of 1 acre and within swimming distance. Boats for hire, with or without guide, also canoes, rowboats, windsurfer; full PADI/NAUI dive centre, snorkel and scuba rental, tank of air US$12; no diving alone, certified divers must do tune-up dive, US$20, 4-day NAUI certification course US$295. Fly fishing with Breeze as guide, US$75/½ day. The reef here is pristine, and the caye is unspoilt. Families welcome. Contact the Lomonts in advance to obtain a full breakdown of all services and costs. Best

to bring everything you will need inc torch, soap, candles, sun screen, toilet paper, allowing for possible supply shortages or bad weather when boats stop running. Facilities are simple, don't expect luxury and guests are invited to help out occasionally. To get there take the 1230 daily Z-Line bus on Sat from Dangriga to Sittee River and go to the *Glover's Atoll Guest House* at Sittee River Village (see above). Alternatively, take any bus going S to the Sittee junction and take a ride to the guest house. If you get lost, phone ahead for help. At 0800 Sun a sailing boat leaves for the Reef 5 hrs, US$20 pp one way (price inc in accommodation package), returns Sat. At other times, charter a boat (skiff or sailing boat, US$200 one way, up to 8 people, diesel sloop US$350, up to 30 people).

MAYA BEACH

Further down the Southern Highway watch for signs to hotels (nothing official, look carefully). 9 miles leads to Riverside, then down a spit of land to **Maya Beach**.

• **Accommodation A1** *Green Parrot Beach Houses*, T/F 06-22488, beach houses on stilts, all with sea view, sleep up to 5, kitchen, open air restaurant and bar, highly rec; **A1** *Singing Sands Inn*, T/F 06-22243, run by Bruce Larkin and Sally Steeds, 6 thatched cabins with bathrooms, hot water, fans, ocean view, snorkelling in front of the resort at False Cay, diving instruction with Sally, windsurfing, canoe and mountain bike hire, fishing, tours arranged, restaurant and bar on the beach; **A2** *Tropical Lodge*, T 06-22077, full board, camping **G**, hot showers, own dock and diving facilities, run by Ted and Peggy Williams, remote, good place to relax, or enjoy the Caribbean, US reservations T 813-639-5717.

The road continues S to **Seine Bight**, becoming rougher, with sand mixed into mud, 4WD advisable, huge holes appear and fill up with water in wet season. **L1-L2** *Rum Point Inn*, T 06-23239, F 06-23240 (in USA T 504-465 0769, F 464 0325), full board, delightful cabins, owned by an American entomologist, good food, dive shop; **B** *Hotel Seine Bight*,

T 06-22491, small, very good restaurant, run by English couple Pamela and Mike. Visit the *Kulcha Shack* restaurant, gift shop, bar with dancing, run by Dewey, promoting Garifuna culture and traditions. 5 miles further is Placencia.

PLACENCIA

Placencia (also spelt Placentia – *phone code* 06), is a little resort 30 miles S of Dangriga, at the end of a long spit of land reached by bus. There are no streets, just a network of concrete footpaths and wooden houses under the palms. No riding of bicycles or motorbikes on footpaths or you face a fine of BZ$25. Electricity and lighting on the main path have been installed. Although the village is rather dirty, the atmosphere has been described as good, laid back, with lots of Jamaican music. **Big Creek**, on the mainland opposite Placencia, is 3 miles from Mango Creek (see below). Fresh water is now piped from Mango Creek and is of good quality.

Excursions

Trips can be made to the coral reef, 16 km off-shore. Day trips including snorkelling, lunch, from US$25 pp; scuba diving also available, ask for Bryan Young. Prices are from about US$65 for two dives (gear extra). Ellis, of Kingfisher/Belize Adventures, has been recommended as knowledgeable and pleasant local guide, T 06-23104/23204, good for land-based tours, while Jimmy Westby (lives behind *Flamboyant Bar*) is good for water excursions, snorkelling day trip including lunch to Laughing Bird Cay, 6-12 people, US$20 pp, kayaking tours, 2-7 days, US$100 for 2 including camping gear and food. There are day tours by kayak or boat to Monkey River and **Monkey River Town**, S along the coast, you can see howler monkeys, toucans, manatees, iguanas, cost US$115 including guiding for 5-6 people. The town can be reached by a rough road, but not recommended in wet weather. The road ends on N side of river and the town is on the S side, so call over for transport.

There is accommodation. Trips up river can also be arranged here with locals but kayaking is best organized in Placencia. Dave Dial, *Monkey River Magic*, T 06-23204, runs good tours, usually leaves 0700 daily, US$40. José Oh can be contacted at *Turtle Inn* for tours inc hiking, birdwatching, etc, rec.

Local information
● **Accommodation**
(**NB** That rooms may be hard to find in pm, eg after arrival of the bus from Dangriga.)

A1 *Serenity Resort*, at entrance to town, T 23232, F 23231, alcohol free, good beach, well run; **A1** *Turtle Inn*, on beach close to airstrip, T 23244, F 23245, inc delicious breakfast, thatched cabañas, dive shop, a little basic for price but friendly, restful; **A2** *Cove Resort*, PO Box 007, Placencia, T 22024; **A2** *Ranguana Lodge*, T 23112, wooden cabins on the ocean, very clean; **A3** *Trade Winds Cottages*, South Point, Mrs Janice Leslie.

B *Barracuda and Jaguar Inn*, T/F 23250, comfortable cabins with deck, inc good breakfast, good restaurant, English/Canadian run.

C *Paradise Vacation Resort*, full board or single meals available, clean, creole cooking, run by Dalton Eiley and Jim Lee, they offer reef fishing, snorkelling, excursions to the jungle, Pine Ridge, Mayan ruins and into the mountains. If arriving by air at Big Creek, first contact Hubert Filey, T 23118 who will arrange for a boat to take you to Placencia; **C** *Sonny's Resort*, T 23103, cabins on the ocean, good restaurant (see below).

D *Conrad and Lydia's Rooms*, T/F 23117, 5 double room with shared toilet and shower, situated on a quiet part of the beach, with excellent breakfast, good other meals, excellent coconut bread, rec, Conrad is a boat owner, ask for his prices; *Kitty's Place*, T 23227, F 23226, beach apartment **B**, weekly rates cheaper, rooms **D** with hot showers, restaurant with buffet Fri and Sat evenings; **D** *Lucille's Rooms*, run by Lucille and her family, private bath, clean rooms, good beds, fans, good value, meals by arrangement.

E *Julia's Budget Hotel*, T 23185 no private bath, stuffy and hot, central, friendly, reliable wakeup call for bus. Mr Clive rents 2 houses, **F** pp/day, also camping; George Cabral has a 2-bed apartment to rent in town, T 23130. Camping on the beach or under the coconut palms. Ask at *Jennie's Restaurant*, or T 23148 for lodgings at **B** *Seaspray* with bath, **D** without, cheaper in low season, very nice, good value, bar. The bus stop outside Kingfisher office is the best place to start looking for rooms, lots of budget accommodation nearby.

● **Places to eat**

The Galley, good fish and shellfish (depending on the day's catch), try the seaweed punch, information on fishing and snorkelling, slow service, rec; *Flamboyant Restaurant and Bar*, a bit of cool luxury and excellent food, popular and good place for meeting local guides, catch them early before they get drunk; *Sunrise*, good, reasonably-priced food; *Tentacles*, thatch roof, nice balcony, good music; *De Fatch*, opp *Seaspray Hotel*, good food, excellent atmosphere, sea views; *Brenda's*, on S shore, good filling local food, full dinner US$7.50; *Ed's*, 20m behind *Lydia's* on sandy road out of town, pleasant, good value, great specials, bacon for breakfast; *King Fisher's*, on beach, thatched roof, seafood, tour arrangements; *Sonny's Resort Restaurant*, excellent fish and seafood; *Daisy's*, has good, homemade ice cream; *Dockside Bar*, good music, dancing at weekends; *Chili's*, good hamburgers and American-style breakfasts with potatoes; *Omar's Fast Food*, fish, meat, burgers, *burritos*, good cheap breakfasts. At least 5 shops (fresh fruit and vegetables supplied to *The Market*, opens 0800-1200, 1500-1800, Sun 0800-1200, closed Thur, changes TCs and cash, a video-cassette movie theatre, 4 bars (*Cosy's* is rec, disco every night, good hamburgers), the fishing cooperative, open Mon-Sat, am, sells fish cheaply, also ice, and supplies the town's electricity. Most places close Thur.

● **Banks & money changers**

Nearest bank in Mango Creek (**Barclays**) open Fri only 0900-1200, but shops and market change TCs.

● **Post & telecommunications**

There is a *BTL* office next to the petrol station where you can make international calls and receive and send fax messages.

Post Office: open Mon-Fri 0800-1200, 1330-1600.

● **Useful services**

There is a police station. Visa extensions obtainable in Mango Creek.

● **Transport**

Air Placencia has its own airstrip. Maya Airways fly 5 times a day Belize City (international and municipal)- Dangriga-Placencia/Big Creek-Punta Gorda (flight tickets are sold at Placencia's post office), about US$45 one way. Flights to Punta Gorda US$30, several daily.

Buses From Dangriga at 1200 direct, or 1215 via Hopkins and Sittee River; times and operators change constantly, US$3.50, 3½ hrs. Return at 0530 and 0600, connecting with 0900 bus to Belize City.

Boats Regular service Mango-Creek-Placencia, *Hokey Pokey*, 0830 and 1430; return 1000 and 1600, US$10 return; meets Dangriga and Punta Gorda buses. Kingfisher (see **Excursions**) sails to Puerto Cortés, Honduras, Sat 0900, US$50.

RANGUANA CAY

Ranguana Cay is private, leased from the Government, and reached from Placencia. Reservations through the Resort's Office in Placencia near *Sea Spray Hotel*, T/F 06-23112, open Mon-Sat, 0800-1830, accepts major credit cards or ask at BTL for Jean on the Cay. Getting there costs US$75 for up to 4 people. A room sleeps 3, **B**, with bathroom and fan. Camping possible, **F** pp, bathrooms and barbecue pits provided but bring food. Kayaks US$30/day. Divers must bring their own scuba equipment.

SAPODILLA CAYS

At the southernmost end of the Belize Barrier Reef are the Sapodilla Cays. Tours are arranged from Guatemala (eg see under Río Dulce-El Tortugal Resort) or can be made from Placencia. There are settlements on a few of the Cays including Hunting Cay.

MANGO CREEK

Mango Creek is a banana exporting port, 30 miles (40 by road) S of Dangriga.

● **Accommodation & places to eat** **C** *Hello I Hotel* (at Independence) run by Antonio Zabaneh at the shop where the Z-Line bus stops, clean, comfortable, helpful; **D** *Ursella's Guest House*, 6 rooms. Hotel above **F** *People's Restaurant*, clean, basic, ask to borrow a fan and lamp, at night you can listen to 'the sounds of the whole Belizean Zoo on the wooden floor, walls and ceiling', shower is a bucket of water in a cabin, 'don't use too much soap or you'll have to go back to the house for a refill; restaurant basic also' (Harry Balthussen); food better at the white house with green shutters behind it (book 2 hrs in advance if possible). *Goyo's Inn/Restaurant Independence* (no accommodation), family-owned, good food.

● **Transport Buses** Belize City-Mango Creek, Z-Line, or the less regular James Bus Service, from Pound Yard Bridge, US$8.50; bus Mango Creek-Belmopan, US$6.50. There is an **airport** at **Independence**, nearby. **Sea** Motorized canoe from Mango Creek to **Puerto Cortés**, Honduras, irregular; ask Antonio Zabaneh at his store, T 06-22011, who knows when boats will arrive, US$50 one way, 7-9 hrs (rubber protective sheeting is provided – hang on to it, usually not enough to go round, nor lifejackets – but you will still get wet unless wearing waterproofs, or just a swimming costume on hot days; it can be dangerous in rough weather). Remember to get an exit stamp, preferably in Belize City, but normally obtainable at the police station in Mango Creek, not Placencia (the US$10 departure tax demanded here is not official). See under Placencia **Transport** for Mango Creek-Placencia boats.

The turnoff from the Southern Highway for Mango Creek, Independence and Big Creek comes 15 miles after the Riversdale turnoff, running 4 miles E through the **Savannah Forest Reserve** to the swampy coast opp Placencia. The Highway itself continues through forest and limestone outcrops, as the foothills of the mountains press in on the W. The road surface deteriorates as you get further S, some sections are very stoney. About 35 miles beyond the junction, 10½ miles N of the T-junction for Punta Gorda, ½ mile W of the road, is the **Nim Li Punit** archaeological site; unrestored, partially cleared, Nim Li Punit ('Big Hat') was only discovered in 1974; a score of stelae, 15-20 ft tall, were unearthed, dated 700-800 AD. A ball court, several groups of buildings and plazas, only southernmost group open to visitors. Worth visiting. Signed trail from the highway.

A short distance beyond, the highway passes **Big Falls**, where there are hot springs; here you can swim, camp or sling a hammock, but first seek permission of the landowner, Mr Peter Alaman, who runs the general store on the highway and

has a guest house, **D. E** pp *Xaiha*, cooperatively owned cabins on the bank of the Rio Grand, bunks and private rooms. This is a popular weekend picnicking spot and a pleasant place to break the dusty (or muddy) journey S. 4 miles from Big Falls, the Highway reaches a T-junction (Shell station), the road to San Antonio branches right (W), the main road turns sharp left and runs down through another forest reserve for 13 miles to Punta Gorda. This part is in better condition. There are plans to pave the whole of the Southern Highway.

PUNTA GORDA

The capital of Toledo District (*pop* 4,000; *phone code* 07), is the last town of any size in Belize, a marketing centre and fishing port with a varied ethnic makeup: Creoles, Kekchi, Mopan, Chinese, East Indians, etc, descendants of the many races brought here over the years as labourers in ill-fated settlement attempts. At **Toledo**, 3 miles N, can be seen the remains of the sugar cane settlement founded by Confederacy refugees after the Civil War. Rainfall in this region is exceptionally heavy, over 170 ins annually, and the vegetation suitably luxuriant. The coast, about 100 ft above sea level, is fringed with coconut palms. Punta Gorda is a pleasant, breezy, quiet place; the seafront is clean (once you get away from Front St, where it is smelly with fish and rotting vegetables) and enjoyable, but swimming is not recommended. The Voice of America has a tall antenna complex on the edge of town. On Main St is a pretty park with a new clock tower, and the bus terminus, while on the parallel Front St are the civic centre and post office/government office. Most of the (little) activity takes place around the pier. Market days Wed and Sat.

Local information
● **Accommodation**
A2 *Traveller's Inn*, nr Z-line bus terminal, inc breakfast, bath, a/c, restaurant, bar, clinical atmosphere, information on tours and services;

A3-C *Mira Mar*, 35 Front St, T 2033 (PO Box 2), overpriced, fishing on local rivers arranged, pool room, restaurant not rec.

C *Punta Caliente*, 108 José María Nuñez St, T 22561, double or king size, excellent value, very good restaurant; **C** *Tate's Guest House*, 34 José María Nuñez St, T 22196, a/c, cheaper without, clean, hot water, bathroom, TV, parking, frienldy, Mr Tate is the Postmaster, Mrs Tate is a teacher so breakfast has to be before 0730, laundry service.

D *Circle C*, 1 block from bus terminal, OK; **D** *Goyo's*, facing clocktower, new, bath, clean, cable TV; **D** *Nature's Way Guest House*, 65 Front St, T 2119 (PO Box 75), clean, good breakfast, will arrange accommodation in Maya villages (Guesthouse Program), ecologically-aware tours, fishing, sailing, has van, camping gear and trimaran for rent, rec; **D** *Pallavi*, 19 Main St, T 22414, recently enlarged, tidy, balcony, clean, friendly; **D** *St Charles Inn*, 23 King St, T 22149, with or without bath, spacious rooms, fan, cable TV, good.

E *Mahung's Hotel*, corner North and Main St, T 2044, cockroaches, reasonable, also rents mountain bikes, US$10/day; **E** *Wahima*, on waterfront, clean and safe, owner Max is local school teacher, friendly and informative.

F pp *Airport Hotel*, quiet, OK, communal bathrooms, clean, spartan. You can flag down the 0500 bus to Belize in front of *Wahima* or *Pallavi* – buy ticket the night before. Sony's Laundry Service nr airstrip.

● **Places to eat**
Kowloon, 35 Main Middle St, good food; *Lucille's Kitchen*, Main St next to Texaco, friendly, good, cheap meals, open until about 2200, but if she's not there, 'just holler'; *Marmars*, good breakfasts, dinner 'US$5, popular. *Bavarian Restaurant*, waterfront nr Texaco, owner Otto, excellent, expensive, new 1995; *Fishermans Inn*, Front St, opened 1995 by Americans Darcy and Billy, good food and conversation, excellent breakfasts with free coffee refills. Bakery selling excellent 'sticky buns' nr *Wahima*. *Honeycomb* bar on Front St, especially around Garifuna Day when spontaneous music, singing and dancing bursts forth.

● **Banks & money changers**
Belize Bank, at one end of the park (a/c, a cool haven), will change excess BZ$ for US$ on production of passport and ticket out of the country. They do not change Quetzales and charge US$7.50 for advancing cash against Visa card. You can change BZ$ for Quetzales at the Customs in Punta Gorda and Puerto Barrios, but don't expect a good rate.

● **Tourist offices**
Toledo Visitors Information Center, also called 'Dem Dats Doin', in booth by pier, PO Box 73, T 22470, Alfredo and Yvonne Villoria, information on travel, tours, guiding, accommodation with Indian families (Homestay Program), message service, book exchange, for the whole of Toledo district, free. **Toledo Explorers Club**, 46 José María Nuñez St, T 22986, offer local trips. **Tourist Information Centre**, Front St, T 22834, F 22835, open Mon-Fri, 0830-1200, 1300-1800, Sat 0800-1200, flight reservations worldwide, hotels, tours, boat trips to Honduras.

● **Transport**
Air Daily flights to Big Creek, Dangriga, Placencia, Belize City and to International airport. Tickets at Alistair Kings (at Texaco station) and Bob Pennell's hardware store on Main St. Advance reservations essential. Maya Airways plans a flight to Puerto Barrios (about US$20).

Buses From Belize, 9 hrs (longer in heavy rain), US$11, Z-Line, Mon to Sat 0800, 1200 and 1500, Sun 1000 and 1500, ticket can be bought day before, beautiful but rough ride; Z-line bus to Belize City 0500, 0900, 1200 stopping at Mango Creek, Dangriga and Belmopan (schedules change on holidays). Z-Line terminal is at very S end of José María Núñez St; lobby of *Traveller's Inn* serves as ticket office. James Bus line to Belize City from Tues, Fri, 1100, after ferry from Puerto Barrios arrives, also 0600 Sun; departs from government buildings near ferry dock. To San Antonio from square, see below for schedules; buses to San Pedro Columbia and San José Wed and Sat 1200, return Wed and Sat am. Buses are usually delayed in the wet season.

FERRY TO GUATEMALA

● **Belizean immigration**
Exit stamps for people and vehicles can be obtained at the Customs House next to the pier on Front St.

Be there at least 1 hr before departure, or 2 hrs if loading a motorcycle.

PACT exit tax payable, see page 741.

● **Guatemalan consulate**
If you need a visa it must be obtained in Belize City. Tourist cards are available in Puerto Barrios.

● **Exchange**

There are money changers at both ends of the crossing, but it is better to wait until in Guatemala before buying quetzals. Neither side changes TCs.

● **Transport**

For buses into Belize, see above.

Ferry to Guatemala The ferry to **Puerto Barrios** leaves Tues and Fri at 1200, 3 hrs BZ$15 (US$7.50), ticket must be purchased from the office of the Agencia de Líneas Marítimas Tomás de Castillo, which opens at 1400 the day before departure (ie Mon and Thur), may be possible on day of departure. The office is half a block N of the clocktower on Middle Main St in the same building as the Tienda Indita-Maya. Tickets can be reserved by phone (T 07-22065, Carlos Godoy), even from overseas. If taking a bike check with Carlos Godoy (T 07-22065) that the incoming boat is the 'loading boat' (not the small tourist boat) which can take about 4 motorbikes, cost US$52.50 payable in quetzales cash at Puerto Barrios. Grease your bike, they are put at the front and get covered in seaspray. If the ferry is not running the day you wish to travel, or is full, small boats are available. There are also boats to Puerto Barrios (US$12.50) usually leaving around 0900, enquire an hour or 2 earlier. Regular safe boat to Puerto Barrios Tues and Fri 0830, 0900 on other days, 1 hr, US$10, T 07-22070, Requena's Charter Service, 12 Front St, to charter a boat to Guatemala costs US$100 (good for a group). There are sometimes boats to Livingston but in 1996 they were suspended because the boat owners were protesting about slow immigration procedures there. **NB** Officials in Livingston do not have the authority to issue vehicle permits to anything other than water craft. Beware however of unsafe, unseaworthy craft. The weather can be treacherous, and you and your luggage will certainly get wet.

SAN PEDRO COLUMBIA

Inland from Punta Gorda there are several interesting villages in the foothills of the Maya Mountains. Take the main road as far as the Dump (to be paved 1996), the road junction (so named because they dumped soil there when clearing land for rice paddies) with the Southern Highway. Take the road to San Antonio. After nearly 2 miles is a branch to **San Pedro Columbia**, a Kekchi village. (Kekchi is a sub-tribe of Maya speaking a distinct language.) The Maya and Kekchi women wear picturesque costumes, including Guatemalan huipiles. There are many religious celebrations, at their most intense (mixed with general gaiety) on San Luis Rey day (5 Aug).

● **Accommodation C-D**, with Alfredo and Yvonne Villaria, *Dem Dats Doin'*; **E** *Guest House*, dormitory. You can buy drinks and get breakfast at the large, yellow stone house.

4 km beyond the village, up some very steep, rocky hills, is Fallen Stones Butterfly Ranch, owned by an English man, leave messages at Texaco gas station, T 07-22126, not only butterfly farm exporting pupae but also hotel, **L3** inc tax, service and breakfast, jungle tours, laundry, airport transfers.

LUBAANTUN

Beyond San Pedro, continuing left around the church, then right and downhill to the new concrete bridge, then left for a mile, is the trail to the Maya remains of **Lubaantun** ('Fallen Stones'), the major ceremonial site of southern Belize. It was last excavated by a Cambridge University team in 1970 and found to date from the 8th-9th centuries, late in the Maya culture and therefore unique. A series of terraced plazas surrounded by temples and palaces ascend along a ridge from S to N; the buildings were constructed with unusual precision and some of the original limemortar facings can still be discerned. Excavation revealed some interesting material: whistle figurines, iron pyrite mirrors, obsidian knives, conch shells from Wild Cane Caye, etc. The site is little visited and, according to latest reports, could be better maintained. Opening hours are 0800-1600 daily; a caretaker will point out things of interest. Refreshments should be taken; dubious local food at a hut nearby. Toilets provided. This whole region is a network of hilltop sites, mostly unexcavated and unrecognizable to the layman.

Blue Creek is another attractive Indian village with a marked trail to Blue Creek caves (caretaker is guide, US$12.50 pp, Maya drawings in middle of cave) through forest and along rock strewn creeks. Good swimming nearby but choose a spot away from the strong current. Turn off 3 miles before San Antonio at *Roy's Cool Spot* (good restaurant; daily truck and all buses pass here). Halfway to Blue Creek is **E** pp *Roots and Herbs*, a couple of simple cabins with mosquito nets, Pablo is an excellent guide, good food. Turn left at *Jim's Pool Room* in Manfredi Village, then continue about 5 miles. Blue Creek is 35 mins by bicycle from San Antonio. Very basic accommodation at the house at the beginning of the trail to the caves.

Close to the Guatemalan border is one of the most interesting Maya cities, **Pusilhá**, which is only accessible by boat. Many stelae were found here dating from 573 to 731 AD; carvings are similar to those at Quiriguá, Guatemala. Rare features are a walled-in ball court and the abutments remaining from a bridge which once spanned the Moho River. Swimming in the rivers is safe and refreshing. There are plenty of logging trails and hunters' tracks penetrating the southern faces of the Maya Mountains, but if hiking in the forest do not go alone.

SAN ANTONIO

San Antonio (21 miles) was founded by refugees from San Luis in Guatemala in the late 19th century. Nearby there are Maya ruins of mainly scientific interest. Community phone for checking buses and other information, T 07-22144.

● **Accommodation & places to eat D** *Bol's Hilltop Hotel*, showers, toilets, meals extra, clean; meals also from *Theodora*, next to hotel, and *Clara*, next to hotel and Theodora, both with advance notice: local specialities are *jippy jappa/kula*, from a local plant, and chicken *caldo*.

● **Shopping** 8 stores: *Lucio Cho* sells cold beer and soda and has the local post office;

Matildo Salam is building a hotel above his shop; medical centre in the village. Crafts such as basketry made from *jippy jappa* and embroidery can be found in this area.

● **Transport** Bus from Punta Gorda, US$1.50, 1-1½ hrs, Mon, Wed, Fri, Sat 1230, from W side of Central Park, also 1200 on Wed and Sat, continuing to Santa Cruz, Santa Elena and Pueblo Viejo (1 hr from San Antonio). Alternatively, hire a pick-up van in Dangriga, or get a ride in a truck from the market or rice co-operative's mill in Punta Gorda (one leaves early pm); or go to the road junction at Dump, where the northern branch goes to Independence/Mango Creek, the other to San Antonio, 6 miles, either hitch or walk. Bus from San Antonio to **Punta Gorda** Mon, Wed, Fri, Sat 0530 also 0500 Wed and Sat (having left Pueblo Viejo at 0400); if going to **Dangriga**, take the 0500, get out at Dump to catch 0530 Z-line bus going N. This area is full of places to explore and it is well worth hiring a vehicle.

Into Guatemala: transport can sometimes be arranged from Pueblo Viejo along a rough road to Jalacté (also reached by trail from Blue Creek and Aguacate), from where it is a 30-min hike to Santa Cruz del Petén (often muddy trail). From here trucks can be caught to San Luis on the highway nr Poptún. There is no Guatemalan government presence at this border; entry stamps cannot be obtained. Although locals cross to shop in Guatemala, it is officially illegal to cross this border. Guatemalan maps are purposely inaccurate.

Neil McAllister writes: An interesting alternative from Punta Gorda is to stay in Indian villages. Two schemes exist; one is run by villagers as a non-competitive co-operative. **San Miguel**, **San José (Hawaii)**, **Laguna**, and **Santa Cruz** are isolated villages beyond Dump towards San Ignacio. **Barranco** is a Garifuna village S of Punta Gorda, accessible by boat or poor road. These have joined together and have developed a visitor scheme which benefits the villages. Each village has built a well appointed guest house, simple, but clean, with sheets, towels, mosquito nets, oil lamps, ablutions block, and total of eight bunks in 2 4-bunk rooms. Visitors stay here, but eat in the villagers' houses on strict rotation, so each household gains equal income and only has to put up with intruding foreigners for short periods. They have their privacy, and so do you.

Village children and many men speak English. Many expressed fears for what the arrival of power (and television) will do to their culture, and are keen to protect their heritage. Dancing and music were previously banned by the Church, but the Indians have relearned old dances from elderly villagers and are buying and learning instruments to put on evening entertainments. Home-made excursions are arranged, these vary from 4-hrs' trek through local forest, looking at medicinal plants, and explaining agriculture (very interesting) as well as seeing very out-of-the-way sights like caves and creeks (take boots, even in dry season). The village tour could be skipped, as it is easy to walk around and chat to people, although by doing this freelance, you deprive the 'guide' of income.

This experience does not come cheap: 1 night for 2 people, with a forest tour and 2 meals came to almost US$50 but all profits go direct to the villages, with no outsiders as middlemen. Dormitory accommodation costs US$9 pp. All villagers share equally in the venture, so there is no resentment, or pressure from competing households, and gross profits from the Guest House are ploughed back into the villages infrastructure, schools etc. The

scheme is co-ordinated by Chet Smith at *Nature's Way Guest House*, Punta Gorda, who donates assistance and booking facilities for the scheme. You may have to arrange your own transport (see below for public transport), or a vehicle can be hired. Hitching not recommended, as some villages are remote, and may have one car a day visiting. Enquire also at the Toledo Information Centre in Punta Gorda. Local attractions include San Antonio waterfall, 30-min walk from San Antonio towards Santa Cruz; caves at San José (Hawaii); Uxbenka ruins and caves 2½-hr walk from San Antonio (turn off right just before Santa Cruz), commanding view from ruins; Santa Cruz waterfalls, 10 mins beyond the village, deep and cold. For Uxbenka and Santa Cruz, take Chun's bus on Wed and Sat at 1300 from San Antonio and arrange return time. Do not take Cho's bus, it does not return.

Agricultural 'roads' push down to the southern border with Guatemala along the Sarstoon (Sarstún) River but there is little permanent settlement. At **Barranco**, the only coastal hamlet S of Punta Gorda, there is a village guest house. A bad track leads to Barranco through Laguna and Santa Theresa (turn off left before Dump), or through Blue Creek and San Lucas, or go by boat. Information can be had at *Nature's Way*, Punta Gorda.

Information for travellers

BEFORE TRAVELLING

ENTRY REQUIREMENTS

● Documents

All nationalities need passports, as well as sufficient funds and, officially, an onward ticket, although this is rarely requested for stays of 30 days. Visas are usually not required from nationals of all the countries of EC, some Commonwealth countries, eg Australia, New Zealand, most Caribbean states, USA, Canada, Leichtenstein, Mexico, Norway, Finland, Panama, Sweden, Turkey, Uruguay, Venezuela. Citizens of India, Austria and Switzerland do need a visa. There is a Belizean Consulate in Chetumal, Mexico, at Av Alvaro Obregón 226A, T 24908, US$25. Visas may not be purchased at the border. Free transit visas are available at borders (for 24 hrs). It is possible that a visa may not be required if you have an onward ticket, but check all details at a Consulate before arriving at the border. Those going to other countries after leaving Belize should get any necessary visas in their home country. Visitors are initially granted 30 days' stay in Belize; this may be extended every 30 days for US$12.50 up to 6 months at the Immigration Office, Government Complex, Mahogany St, Belize City, T 02-24620 (to the W of the city, nr Central American Blvd). At the end of 6 months, visitors must leave the country for at least 24 hrs. Visitors must not engage in any type of employment, paid or unpaid, without first securing a work permit from the Department of Labour; if caught, the penalty for both the employer and

the employee is severe. Travellers should note that the border guards seem to have complete power to refuse entry to people whose looks they do not like. There have also been reports that tourists carrying less than US$30 for each day of intended stay have been refused entry. Cyclists should get a passport stamp to indicate an 'imported' bicycle.

● Representation overseas

Canada, 1080 Cote Beaver Hill, Suite 1720, Montréal, Québec, H2Z 1S8, T (514) 871-4741 (according to High Commission in London, this is the only consul in Canada); **UK**, High Commission, 22 Harcourt House, 19 Cavendish Sq, London W1M 9AD, T 0171 499-9728; F 0171 491-4139; **USA**, 415 Seventh Ave, New York, NY 10001, T 800 624-0686, F 212 695-3018.

● Tourist information

The Belize Tourist Board, as well as its office in Belize City (83 North Front St, PO Box 325, T 02-77213/73255, F 02-77490, e-mail: bttbb@btl.net, website: http://www.belizenet. com), also has offices in the **USA**, 15 Penn Plaza, 415 Seventh Ave, 18th Floor, New York, NY 10001, T 800-624-0686, 212-268-8798, F 212-695-3018; **Canada**, Belize High Commission, 273 Patricia Ave, Ottawa, K1Y V6C, T 613-722-7187; **Germany**, Belize Tourist Board/WICRG, Lomenstr-28, 2000 Hamburg 70, T 49-40-695-8846, F 49-40-380-0051; **UK**, c/o Belize High Commission (see **Representation Overseas** above).

Amerindia, based in Quito, is a new regional ground operator, who operates in Belize, Costa Rica and Guatemala (as well as in Peru, Bolivia and Ecuador). It has been created to rediscover the wonders of Latin America. Tours of the highest quality with experienced guides are offered. Accommodation is in superb lodges. Among the tours available will be yacht charters along coasts, luxury safari-style tents and Land Rover circuits. Further information from Amerindia's head office T (543) 2 439 736/469 455, F (543) 2 439 735, e-mail: amerindi@pi.pro.ec; in UK from Penelope Kellie T (44) 1962 779317, F (44) 1962 779458, e-mail: pkellie@ yachtors.u-net.com; in USA T (1) 305 599 9008, F (1) 305 592 7060.

HEALTH

Those taking common precautions find the climate pleasant and healthy. Malaria was reportedly under control, but once again precautions against the disease are essential. Also use mosquito repellent. Dengue fever exists in Belize. Inoculation against yellow fever and tetanus is advisable but not obligatory. No case of either has been reported in years.

MONEY

● **Currency**

The monetary unit is the Belizean dollar, stabilized at BZ$2=US$1. Currency notes (Monetary Authority of Belize) are issued in the denominations of 100, 50, 20, 10, 5, 2 and 1 dollars, and coinage of 1 dollar, 50, 25, 10, 5 and 1 cent is in use. Notes marked Government of Belize, or Government of British Honduras, are only redeemable at a bank; all notes should be marked **Central Bank** of Belize. The American expressions Quarter (25c), Dime (10c) and Nickel (5c) are common, although 25c is sometimes referred to as a shilling. US dollars are accepted in many places.

● **Exchange**

See under **Banks & money changers**, Belize City, above. For Western Union, T 275924. Good rates for Mexican pesos in Belize. Best rates of exchange at the borders.

● **Cost of living**

The cost of living is high because of the heavy reliance on imports and extra duties. This applies especially to food, car hire, driving. In addition, licences are required to provide many services, which involve payment. Budget travellers also find exploring the interior difficult because public transport is limited and car hire is beyond the means of many. VAT of 15% is charged on all services, but should **not** be charged in addition to the 10% hotel tax.

GETTING THERE

BY AIR

From Miami, American Airlines and Taca have daily flights; flights from Europe (eg British Airways from London) or Canada connect with Taca. From Houston, Continental and Taca daily, allowing similar connections with European flights. American flies from Baltimore daily, and Dallas daily via Houston. Taca flies from Los Angeles daily and New Orleans 4 times a week. Also daily flights to Guatemala City, San Pedro Sula, San Salvador, San José, and Panama (all Taca). Flights to Flores (Guatemala), with TropicAir. Caribbean Air flies from Roatán, Honduras, on Sat.

BY SEA

For ferry services to Honduras and Guatemala, see under Dangriga, Placencia, Mango Creek and Punta Gorda. American Canadian Caribbean Line has a Ship *MV Caribbean Prince* which visits cayes and mainland Belize, 75 passengers, well organized, excellent food.

CUSTOMS

Clothing and articles for personal use are allowed in without payment of duty, but a deposit may be required to cover the duty payable on typewriters, dictaphones, cameras and radios. The duty, if claimed, is refunded when the visitor leaves the country. Import allowances are: 200 cigarettes or ½ lb of tobacco, 20 fluid ozs of alcohol; 1 bottle of perfume. Visitors can take in an unspecified amount of other currencies (charges were brought in 1993 against 2 people who brought in an excessive amount of US dollars, later dropped, maximum amount may now be set). No fruit or vegetables may be brought into Belize; searches are very thorough. Firearms may be imported only with prior arrangements. Pets must have proof of rabies inoculations and a vet's certificate of good health. CB radios are held by customs until a licence is obtained from Belize Communications Ltd.

ON ARRIVAL

● **Clothing**

The business dress for men is a short-sleeved cotton or poplin shirt or *guayabera* (ties not often worn) and trousers of some tropical weight material. Formal wear may inc ties and jackets, but long-sleeved embroidered *guayaberas* are commoner. Women should not wear shorts in the cities and towns; acceptable only on the cayes and at resorts.

● **Hours of business**
Retail shops are open 0800-1200, 1300-1600 and Fri 1900-2100, with a ½-day from 1200 on Wed. Small shops open additionally most late afternoons and evenings, and some on Sun 0800-1000. Government and commercial office hrs are 0800-1200 and 1300-1600 Mon to Fri.

● **Medical facilities**
Out-patients' medical attention is free of charge. Myo' On Clinic Ltd, 40 Eve St, Belize City, T 02-45616, has been rec, it charges reasonably for its services. Nearby is the Pathology Lab, 17 Eve St, rec. Also rec are Belize Medical Associates, next to the new city hospital, and Dr Lizama, Handyside St, consultation US$17.50. The British High Commission in Belmopan, T 22146/7 has a list of rec doctors and dentists.

● **Official time**
Official time is 6 hrs behind GMT.

● **Safety**
Apart from taking certain precautions in Belize City, the visitor should feel at no personal risk anywhere in Belize. The authorities are keen to prevent the illegal use of drugs. The penalties for possession of marijuana are 6 months in prison or a US$3,000 fine, minimum.

● **Selling cars**
Sellers of cars must pay duty (if the buyer pays it, he may be able to bargain with the customs official). The easiest type of vehicle to sell is either a pick-up or a 4-door sedan. Smaller more economical cars are becoming more popular. Prices are quite good particularly in Orange Walk (ask taxi drivers in Belize City). Also, O Perez & Sons, at their grocery store, 59 West Canal St, Belize City, T 73439, may be able to help or refer you on to Norm, who sells cars for people at 10% commission (rec for fast sale). The Belikin bridge over Haulover Creek on W side of town is a prime site for buying and selling cars. At parking lot here you pay a small fee only if you sell your car. *Freetown Auto World and Club*, 150 Freetown Rd, T 02-30405, also buys and sells. If all else fails try selling car for spare parts, Santos Díaz and Sons, CA Boulevard, T 02-24545/6.

● **Tipping**
In restaurants, 10% of the bill; porters in hotels US$2; chambermaids US$0.50/day. Taxi drivers are not tipped.

● **Voltage**
110/220 volts single phase, 60 cycles for domestic supply. Some hotels use 12 volt generators.

● **Weights and measures**
Imperial and US standard weights and measures. The US gallon is used for gasoline and motor oil.

ON DEPARTURE

● **Airport tax**
Departure tax of US$15 on leaving from the international airport, but not for transit passengers who have spent less than 24 hrs in the country. There is also a security screening charge of US$1.25.

All visitors must pay the BZ$7.50 PACT tax on departure; see page 741.

FOOD AND DRINK

● **Food**
Seafood is abundant, fresh and reasonably cheap; beef is plentiful. Presentation varies: vegetables are not always served with a meat course. For the cheapest meals, order rice. It will come with beans and (as often as not) banana or plantain, or chicken, vegetables or even a blending of beef with coconut milk. Better restaurants have a selection of Mexican dishes; there are also many Chinese restaurants, not always good and sometimes overpriced.

● **Drink**
Belikin beer is the local brew, average cost US$1.75 a bottle; many brands of local rum available. The local liqueur is called *nanche*, made from crabou fruit; it is very sweet. All imported food and drink is expensive. Rainwater is commonly served as drinking water. See **Fishing**, page 742, with regard to the closed season for certain seafoods: do not order these items during these periods unless you are certain they have been legally caught.

GETTING AROUND

AIR TRANSPORT

Maya Airways (see **Airline offices**, Belize City) flies daily to each of the main towns and offers charter rates to all local airstrips of which there are 25; only twin-engined planes are used and their safety record is good. Tropic Air flies to San Pedro, Caye Chapel also Caye Caulker, Placencia, Punta Gorda and Corozal.

Five other companies have charters from Belize City to outlying districts. (Belize Aero Company, T 02-44021; Cari Bee Air Service, flies mainly to the Cayes, also scheduled service to San Pedro, T 02-44253; Javier Flying Services, T 02-45332; National Charters, T 02-45332; Island Air Service flies mainly to the Cayes, also to Corozal and scheduled service to San Pedro and Caye Caulker, indifferent service but no major problems, T 02-31140/ 026-2435).

LAND TRANSPORT

● Bus
Public transport between most towns is by bus, trucks carry passengers to many isolated destinations, although they are no longer allowed to carry passengers to places served by buses. Enquire at market place in Belize City. By law, buses are not allowed to carry standing passengers; some companies are stricter than others. Most buses are ex-US school buses, small seats, limited legroom. There are a few ex-Greyhounds. All bus companies sell seats in advance. Most buses have no luggage compartments so bags which do not fit on the luggage rack are stacked at the back of the bus. Get a seat at the back to keep an eye on your gear; rough handling is more of a threat than theft.

● Car hire
For details of car hire, see under Belize City.

● Hitchhiking
Hitchhiking can be difficult as there is little traffic.

● Motoring
Motorists should carry their own driving licence and certificate of vehicle ownership. Third party insurance is mandatory, and can be purchased at any border (BZ$25 a week, BZ$50 a month, cars and motorbikes are the same, cover up to BZ$20,000 from the Insurance Corporation of Belize). Border offices are open Mon-Fri 0500-1700, Sat 0600-1600, closed Sun. Also offices in every district. Valid International Driving Licences are accepted in place of Belize driving permits. Fuel costs BZ$4.82 (regular) or BZ$4.98 (super) for a US gallon but can be more in remote areas. Unleaded gasoline is now available in Belize.

Traffic drives on the right. When making a left turn, it is the driver's responsibility to ensure clearance of both oncoming traffic and vehicles behind; generally, drivers pull over to the far right, allow traffic from behind to pass, then make the left turn. Many accidents are caused by failure to observe this procedure. All major

roads have been, or are being, improved, but they are still poor in many areas, particularly when it rains. One reader claims there are more visible jaguars than road signs in Belize and finding your way can be problematic.

COMMUNICATIONS

● Language
English is the official language, but Spanish is widely spoken. Belize Broadcasting Network (BBN) devotes about 40% of its air-time to the Spanish language. A Low German dialect is spoken by the Mennonite settlers, and Mayan languages and Garifuna are spoken by ethnic groups.

● Newspapers
Belize: *Belize Times* (PUP supported), in total opposition to *People's Pulse* (UDP supported), *Reporter* (weekly); *Amandala*; monthlies *Belize Today*, and *Belize Review*; bi-monthly *Belize Currents*.

Belize First, published 5 times a year in the USA, has articles on travel, life, news and history in the country: Equator Travel Publications Inc, 280 Beaverdam Rd, Candler, NC 28715, USA, F (704) 667-1717 (US$27 a year in Belize, USA, Canada, Mexico, US$37 elsewhere); *Belize On line* http://www.belize.wm.

● Postal services
Airmail postage to UK 4-5 days. US$0.38 for a letter, US$0.20 for a postcard; US$0.50 for letter to European continent; US$0.30 for a letter to USA, US$0.15 for a post card; US$0.30 postcard, US$0.50 letter to Australia, takes 4-6 weeks. Parcels: US$3.50/½-kilo to Europe, US$0.38/½-kilo to USA. The service to Europe and USA has been praised, but sea mail is not reliable. Belize postage stamps are very attractive. Mail may be sent to any local post office, c/o General Delivery.

● Telephone services
All towns have a telephone office and in most villages visitors can use the community phone. Payphones are being improved and cardphones are fairly commonplace in Belize City. There is a direct-dialling system between the major towns and to Mexico and USA. Local calls cost US$0.25 for 3 mins, US$0.12 for each extra minute within the city, US$0.15-0.55 depending on zone. Belize Telecommunications Ltd (known as BTL), Church St, Belize City, open 0800-1800 Mon-Sat, 0800-1200 Sun and holidays, has an international telephone, telegraph and telex service. To make an international call from Belize costs

far less than from neighbouring countries. US$3/min to UK and Europe (a deposit of US$15 required on all international calls); US$1.60 to North, Central and South America and the Caribbean; US$4 to all other countries. Collect calls to USA, Canada, Australia and UK only. For the international operator, dial 115. International telex US$1.60/min to USA, US$3 to Europe, US$4 elsewhere; telegram US$0.16/word to USA, US$0.30 to Europe, US$0.40 elsewhere. AT&T's USA Direct, UK Direct, Hong Kong Direct must have AT&T card and ID. BT Chargecard service to the UK is available. Fax US$4.80 to North, Central and South America and the Caribbean, US$9 to Europe, US$12 elsewhere, plus US$2.50 service charge.

Many establishments have direct dial numbers using radio or cellular phones. Belize Communications, Belmopan (Rick and Sue Simpson), is a telephone and fax service used by many establishments not yet reached by direct phone line: T 08-23180, F 08-23235. Those on the service, who will be contacted by Belize Communications by radio, inc the US Embassy, CARE, Maya Airlines, Guanacaste Park, The Blue Hole, Cockscomb, Shipstern Nature Reserve, Chaa Creek, Ix Chel Farm, Mountain Equestrian Trails, Maya Mountain Lodge, duPlooy's, Banana Bank Ranch, Warrie Head, Belize Audubon Society.

HOLIDAYS AND FESTIVALS

1 Jan: New Year's Day; Feb: San Pedro Carnival, Ambergris Caye; 9 Mar: Baron Bliss Day; 14-18 Mar: San José Succotz Fiesta; Good Friday and Saturday; Easter Monday; 21 April: Queen's birthday; 1 May: Labour Day; 3-4 May: Cashew Festival (Crooked Tree); 17 May: Coconut Festival (Caye Caulker); 24 May: Commonwealth Day; 29 June: San Pedro Day; 18-19 July: Benque Viejo Fiesta; 10 Sept: St George's Caye Day; 21 Sept: Belize Independence Day; 12 Oct: Pan American Day (Corozal and Orange Walk); 19 Nov: Garifuna Settlement Day; 25 Dec: Christmas Day; 26 Dec: Boxing Day.

NB Most services throughout the country close down Good Friday to Easter Monday: banks close at 1130 on the Thur, buses run limited services Holy Saturday to Easter Monday, and boats to the Cayes are available. St George's Caye Day celebrations in Sept start 2 or 3 days in advance and require a lot of energy.

ACKNOWLEDGEMENTS

We are grateful to Caitlin Hennessy for updating this chapter.

El Salvador

EL SALVADOR IS the smallest, most densely populated and most integrated of the Central America republics. Its intermont basins are a good deal lower than those of Guatemala, rising to little more than 600m at the capital, San Salvador. Across this upland and surmounting it run two more or less parallel rows of volcanoes, 14 of which are over 900m. The highest are Santa Ana (2,365m), San Vicente (2,182m), San Miguel (2,130m), and San Salvador (1,893m). One important result of this volcanic activity is that the highlands are covered with a deep layer of ash and lava which forms a porous soil ideal for coffee planting.

HORIZONS

THE LAND

The total area of El Salvador is 21,041 sq km. Guatemala is to the W, Honduras to the N and E, and the Pacific coastline to the S is approximately 321 km long.

Lowlands lie to the N and S of the high backbone. In the S, on the Pacific coast, the lowlands of Guatemala are confined to just E of Acajutla; beyond are lava promontories till we reach another 30-km belt of lowlands where the 325 km long Río Lempa flows into the sea. The northern lowlands are in the wide depression along the course of the Río Lempa,

buttressed S by the highlands of El Salvador and N by the basalt cliffs edging the highlands of Honduras. The highest point in El Salvador, Cerro El Pital (2,730m) is part of the mountain range bordering on Honduras. After 160 km the Lempa cuts through the southern uplands to reach the Pacific; the depression is prolonged SE till it reaches the Gulf of Fonseca.

El Salvador is located on the SW coast of the Central American Isthmus on the Pacific Ocean. As the only country in the region lacking access to the Caribbean Sea it does not posses the flora associated with that particular coastal zone. El Salvador nevertheless has a wide variety of colourful, tropical vegetation; for example over

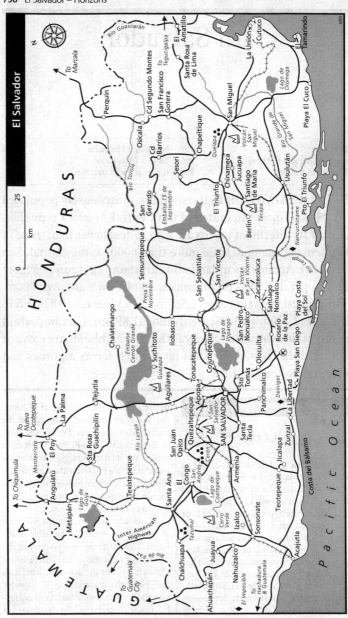

El Salvador

200 species of orchid grow all over the country. As a result of excessive forest cutting and therefore the destruction of their habitats, many of the animals (such as jaguars and crested eagles) once found in the highlands of the country have diminished at an alarming rate. In response to this problem several nature reserves have been set up in areas where flora and fauna can be found in their most unspoilt states. Among these nature reserves are the Cerro Verde, Deininger Park, El Imposible Woods, El Jocatal Lagoon and the Montecristo Cloud Forest.

CLIMATE

El Salvador is fortunate in that its temperatures are not excessively high. Along the coast and in the lowlands it is certainly hot and humid, but the average for San Salvador is 28°C with a range of only about 3°. Mar, April and May are the hottest months; Dec, Jan and Feb the coolest. There is one rainy season, from May to Oct, with April and Nov being transitional periods; there are only light rains for the rest of the year: the average is about 1,830 mm. Occasionally, in Sept or Oct, there is a spell of continuously rainy weather, the *temporal*, which may last from 2 or 3 days to as many weeks. The pleasantest months are from Nov to Jan. From time to time the water shortage can become acute.

HISTORY

When Spanish expeditions arrived in El Salvador from Guatemala and Nicaragua, they found it relatively densely populated by several Indian groups, of whom the most populous were the Pipiles. By 1550, the Spaniards had occupied the country, many living in existing Indian villages and towns. The settlers cultivated cocoa in the volcanic highlands and balsam along the coast, and introduced cattle to roam the grasslands freely. Towards the end of the 16th century, indigo became the big export crop: production was controlled by the Spaniards, and Indians provided the workforce, many suffering illness as a result. A period of regional turmoil accompanied El Salvador's declaration of independence from the newly-autonomous political body of Central America in 1839: Indian attempts to regain their traditional land rights were put down by force.

Coffee emerged as an important cash crop in the second half of the 19th century, bringing with it improvements in transport facilities and the final abolition of Indian communal lands.

The land question was a fundamental cause of the peasant uprising of 1932, which was brutally crushed by the dictator Gen Maximiliano Hernández Martínez. Following his overthrow in 1944, the military did not relinquish power: a series of military coups kept them in control, and they protected the interests of the landowning oligarchy.

THE 1980s CIVIL WAR

The most recent military coup, in Oct 1979, led to the formation of a civilian-military junta which promised far-reaching reforms. When the reforms were not carried out, the opposition unified forming a broad coalition, the Frente Democrático Revolucionario, which adopted a military wing, the Farabundo Martí National Liberation Front (FMLN) in 1980. Later the same year, the Christian Democrat, Ing José Napoleón Duarte was named as President of the Junta. At about the same time, political tension reached the proportions of civil war.

Duarte was elected to the post of President in 1984, following a short administration headed by Dr Alvaro Magaña. Duarte's periods of power were characterized by a partly-successful attempt at land reform, the nationalization of foreign trade and the banking system, and violence. In addition to deaths in combat, 40,000 civilians were killed between 1979 and 1984, mostly by right-wing death squads. Among the casualties was Archbishop Oscar Romero, who was shot while saying mass in Mar 1980. Nothing came of meetings between Duarte's government and the FMLN, aimed at seeking a peace agreement.

The war continued in stalemate until 1989, by which time an estimated 70,000 had been killed. The Christian Democrats' inability to end the war, reverse the economic decline or rebuild after the 1986 earthquake, combined with their reputation for corruption, caused a resurgence of support for the right-wing National Republican Alliance (ARENA). An FMLN offer to participate in presidential elections, dependent on certain conditions, was not accepted, and the ARENA candidate, Lic Alfredo Cristiani, won the presidency comfortably in Mar 1989, taking office in June.

Peace talks again failed to produce results, and in Nov 1989, the FMLN guerrillas staged their most ambitious offensive ever, which paralysed the capital and caused a violent backlash from government forces. FMLN-government negotiations resumed with UN mediation following the offensive, but the two sides could not reach agreement about the purging of the Armed Forces, which had become the most wealthy institution in the country after 10 years of US support.

PEACE NEGOTIATIONS

Although El Salvador's most left-wing political party, the Unión Democrática Nacionalista, agreed to participate in municipal elections in 1991, the FMLN remained outside the electoral process, and the civil war continued unresolved. Talks were held in Venezuela and Mexico after initial agreement was reached in April on reforms to the electoral and judicial systems, but further progress was stalled over the restructuring of the armed forces and disarming the guerrillas. There were hopes that human rights would improve after the establishment in June 1991 of a UN Security Council human rights observer commission (ONUSAL), charged with verifying compliance with the human rights agreement signed by the Government and the FMLN in Geneva in April 1990. Offices were opened in San Salvador and the departments of San Miguel, San Vicente, Morazán and Chalatenango. Finally, after considerable UN assistance, the FMLN and the Government signed a peace accord in New York in Jan 1992 and a formal ceasefire began in February. A detailed schedule throughout 1992 was established to demobilize the FMLN, dismantle five armed forces elite battalions and initiate land requests by ex-combatants from both sides. The demobilization process was reported as completed in Dec 1992, formally concluding the civil war. The US agreed at this point to 'forgive' a substantial portion of the US$2bn international debt of El Salvador. In Mar 1993, the United Nations Truth Commission published its investigation of human rights abuses during the civil war. 5 days later, the legislature approved a general amnesty for all those involved in criminal activities in the war. This included those named in the Truth Commission report. The Cristiani government was slow to implement not only the constitutional reforms proposed by the Truth Commission, but also the process of land reform and the establishment of the National Civilian Police (PNC). By 1995, when Cristiani's successor had taken office, the old national police force was demobilized, but the PNC was already facing criticism for abuses of human rights and other excesses. Part of the problem was that the PNC suffered from a lack of resources for its proper establishment. In fact, the budget for the implementation of the final peace accords was deficient and El Salvador had to ask the UN for financial assistance.

1994 ELECTIONS AND AFTER

Presidential and congressional elections on 20 March 1994 failed to give an outright majority to any presidential candidate. The two main contenders, Armando Calderón Sol of Arena and Rubén Zamora, of a coalition of the FMLN, Democratic Convergence and the National Revolutionary Movement, faced a run-off election on 24 April. Calderón Sol won 70% of the vote and took office on 1 June 1994. Besides his government's difficulties with the final stages of the peace accord, his first months in office were marked by rises in the cost of living, increases in crime, strikes and protests, and occupations of the Legislature by ex-combatants. The government's failure to solve these problems continued into 1996, with the United Nations adding its weight to criticisms, especially of the lack of progress on implementing the social projects designed to reintegrate civil war combatants into civilian life. This contributed to the electorate's sense of disillusion, exacerbated by considerable realignment of the country's political parties. The congressional and mayoral elections of Mar 1997 highlighted these issues further. Only 41% of the electorate bothered to vote. In the National Assembly, Arena won 29 seats, FMLN increased its tally to 28 seats, the National Conciliation Party (PCN) won 11, the Christian Democrats (PDC) 9 and minority parties 7 seats. Arena, PCN and PDC were expected to form a coalition to keep FMLN from power. Nevertheless, FMLN's role will remain in the spotlight as its candidate, Héctor Silva, was elected mayor of San Salvador. His success, or otherwise, in the post, now that the marxist rhetoric has been abandoned in favour of social democracy, will be a major indicator for the 1999 presidential elections.

CULTURE

PEOPLE

The population is far more homogeneous than that of Guatemala. The reason for this is that El Salvador lay comparatively isolated from the main stream of conquest, and had no precious metals to act as magnets for the Spaniards. The small number of Spanish settlers intermarried with those Indians who survived the plagues brought from Europe, to form a group of mestizos. There were only about half a million people as late as 1879. With the introduction of coffee, the population grew quickly and the new prosperity fertilized the whole economy, but internal pressure of population has led to the occupation of all the available land. Several hundred thousand Salvadoreans have emigrated to neighbouring republics because of the shortage of land and the concentration of land ownership, and more lately because of the civil war.

Of the total population, some 20% are regarded as ethnic Indians, although the traditional Indian culture has almost completely vanished. Other estimates put the percentage of pure Indians as low as 5%. The Lenca and the Pipil, the two surviving indigenous groups, are predominantly peasant farmers. Less than 5% are of unmixed white ancestry, the rest are mestizos.

With a population of 280 to the sq km, El Salvador is the most densely populated country on the American mainland. Health and sanitation outside the capital and some of the main towns leave much to be desired, and progress was very limited in the 1980s and early 1990s because of the violence.

EDUCATION AND RELIGION

Education is free if given by the government, and nominally obligatory. There are 43 universities, three national and the others private or church-affiliated. There is also a National School of Agriculture. The most famous are the government-financed Universidad Nacional and the Jesuit-run Universidad Centroamericana (UCA). Roman Catholicism is the prevailing religion.

CONSTITUTION

Legislative power is vested in a unicameral Legislative Assembly, which has 84 seats and is elected for a 3-year term. The head of state and government is the president, who holds office for 5 years. The country is divided into 14 departments.

THE ECONOMY

Structure of production

Agriculture is the dominant sector of the

Handicrafts of El Salvador

The artists' village of La Palma, in a pine-covered valley under Miramundo mountain, is 84 km N of the capital, 10 km S of the Honduran frontier. Here, in 1971, the artist Fernando Llort "planted a seed", known as the *copinol* (a species of the locust tree) from which sprang the first artists' cooperative, now called *La Semilla de Dios* (Seed of God). The *copinol* seed is firm and round; on it the artisans base a spiritual motif that emanates from their land and soul. The town and its craftspeople are now famous for their work in wood, including exotically carved *cofres* (adorned wooden chests), and traditional Christmas *muñecas de barro* (clay dolls) and ornamental angels. Wood carvings, other crafts and the designs of the original paintings by Llort are produced and exported from La Palma to the rest of El Salvador and thence worldwide. In 1971 the area was almost exclusively agricultural; today 75% of the population of La Palma and neighbouring San Ignacio are engaged directly or indirectly in producing handicrafts. The painter Alfredo Linares (born 1957 in Santa Ana, arrived in La Palma 1981 after studying in Guatemala and Florence) has a gallery in La Palma, employing and assisting local artists. His paintings and miniatures are marketed abroad, yet you will often find him working in the family pharmacy next to the gallery. Many of La Palma's images are displayed on the famous Hilasal towels. If you cannot get to La Palma, visit the shop/gallery/workshop of Fernando Llort in San Salvador, *Arbol de Dios*.

20 km from the capital is the indigenous town of Panchimalco, where weaving on the loom and other traditional crafts are being revived. Many *nahaut* traditions, customs, dances and the language survived here as the original Indians hid from the Spanish conquistadores in the valley beneath the Puerta del Diablo (now in Parque Balboa). In 1996 the painter Eddie Alberto Orantes, and his family opened the *Centro de Arte y Cultura Tunatiuh*, named after a *nahuat* deity who is depicted as a human face rising as a sun over a pyramid. The project employs local youths (from broken homes, or former addicts) in the production of weavings, paintings and ceramics.

In the mountains of western El Salvador, villages in the coffee zone, such as Nahuizalco, specialize in weaving henequen, bamboo and reed into table mats and in wicker furniture. There are also local artists like Maya sculptor Ahtzic Selis, who works with clay and jade. East of the capital, at Ilobasco (60 km), many ceramic workshops produce items including the famous *sorpresas*, miniature figures enclosed in an egg shell. In the capital, there are crafts markets in which to bargain for pieces, while throughout the country outlets range from the elegant to the rustic. Everywhere artists and artisans welcome visitors into their workshops.

economy, accounting for three quarters of export earnings. Coffee, sugar and cotton are the most important crops, but attempts have been made at diversification and now soya, sesame, vegetables, tropical flowers and ornamental plants are being promoted as foreign exchange earners. The sector was badly affected by drought in 1994-95; worst affected were production of basic grains, cotton and hemp, and pasture for cattle (average weight and milk yields were greatly reduced). Shrimp farming investment has risen and shrimp is now an important export item.

Land ownership has been unevenly distributed with a few wealthy families owning most of the land, while the majority of agricultural workers merely lived at subsistence level; this led to serious political and social instability despite attempts at agrarian reform by successive governments, including a determined one involving cooperatives in 1980. The Arena Government put an end to the formation

El Salvador: fact file

Geographic

Land area	21,041 sq km
forested	5.0%
pastures	29.5%
cultivated	35.2%

Demographic

Population (1996)	5,897,000
annual growth rate (1991-96)	2.2%
urban	50.4%
rural	49.6%
density	280.3 per sq km
Religious affiliation	
Roman Catholic	75.0%
Birth rate per 1,000 (1995)	28.6
	(world av 25.0)

Education and Health

Life expectancy at birth,	
male	65 years
female	72 years
Infant mortality rate	
per 1,000 live births (1995)	33.0
Physicians (1993)	1 per 1,219 persons
Hospital beds	1 per 588 persons
Calorie intake as %	
of FAO requirement	116%
Population age 25 and over	
with no formal schooling	34.7%
Literate males (over 15)	77.4%
Literate females (over 15)	71.3%

Economic

GNP (1994 market prices)	US$8,365mn
GNP per capita	US$1,480
Public external debt	
(1994)	US$1,994mn
Tourism receipts (1994)	US$86mn
Inflation	
(annual av 1990-95)	12.9%
Radio	1 per 2.8 persons
Television	1 per 12 persons
Telephone	1 per 32 persons

Employment

Population economically	
active (1992)	1,762,002
Unemployment rate	
(urban, 1993)	8.1%
% of labour force in	
agriculture	34.0
mining	0.1
manufacturing	13.9
construction	4.7
Military forces	30,500

Source *Encyclopaedia Britannica*

of cooperatives and encouraged existing cooperatives to divide into individual farms. In 1992 the Government and the FMLN agreed a Land Transfer Programme (PTT) designed to distribute 166,000 ha of land to about 48,000 Salvadoreans at a cost of US$143mn. The plan was beset by problems with implementation and acquisition of land which caused serious delays in the distribution of land to potential beneficiaries.

The most important industries are food processing and petroleum products: others include textiles, pharmaceuticals, shoes, furniture, chemicals and fertilizers, cosmetics, construction materials, cement (and asbestos cement), drink processing, rubber goods. Maquila factories have grown rapidly in recent years, particularly garment assemblers, providing an estimated 20,000 jobs. Exports of manufactured goods, mostly to other Central American countries, account for some 24% of foreign exchange earnings.

There are small deposits of various minerals: gold, silver, copper, iron ore, sulphur, mercury, lead, zinc, salt and lime, but only limited amounts of gold, silver and limestone are produced. There is a gold and silver mine at San Cristóbal in the Department of Morazán. In 1975 a geothermal power plant came into operation at Ahuachapán, with capacity of 30 mw. The plant was expanded by 60 mw in 1978. Hydraulic resources are also being exploited as a means of generating power and saving oil import costs, but the intention of closing thermal plants has been thwarted by the poor condition of the infrastructure and disruption during the civil war. Electricity has been in short supply since 1991, first as a result of extensive sabotage, then as a result of a lack of rain to fill the hydroelectricity lakes. With electricity demand growing at 6% a year, new investment for the sector from Japan and the Inter American Development Bank announced in 1996 was much needed.

Recent trends

The country's agricultural and industrial production, and consequently its exporting capability, were severely curtailed by political unrest. In 1986 further economic and social damage was caused by an earthquake; damage to housing and government property alone was estimated at US$311mn, while the total, including destruction and disruption of businesses was put at US$2bn. El Salvador was heavily dependent upon aid from the USA to finance its budget. Total US assistance was estimated at over US$4bn in the 1980s. In 1989 the new government outlined a national rescue plan to provide jobs, food and low cost housing to those most in need but it was not fully implemented. Efforts were also made to put order into public finances, reduce inflation and encourage exports, but the initial effect was to increase inflation, unemployment and poverty. However, the lack of foreign exchange reserves remained a serious constraint and El Salvador was declared ineligible for World Bank lending after arrears exceeded limits.

By 1990 progress was becoming evident as inflation eased, gdp grew slightly and the fiscal deficit was reduced. The privatization of banks and other state-run enterprises got under way, the trade deficit was lowered by an 18% increase in exports, private savings rose and so did foreign exchange reserves. International creditors praised the Government's economic stabilization efforts, with the IMF, the World Bank and the InterAmerican Development Bank all committing finance during the year. Improvement in economic indicators continued in 1991 and a second stage of the World Bank structural adjustment loan was initiated. Nevertheless, it was expected that real progress would take some time and alleviation of poverty (some two-thirds of the population are classified as living in extreme poverty) and unemployment would be slow (official estimates put the unemployment rate at 10%, under-employment 29%; unofficial estimates are much higher,

unemployment rose as ex-combatants sought jobs).

The Consultative Group for El Salvador (22 donor countries and 15 international and regional organizations) agreed in 1992 to provide about US$800mn to support the National Reconstruction Plan (PNR), a 5-year, US$1.4bn project to alleviate poverty and consolidate peace. Foreign aid and loans in 1993 helped to boost private investment and stabilize the colón against the US dollar. Other positive factors were growth in construction and services as rebuilding and rehabilitation of infrastructure after the civil war progressed, overall gdp growth and a fall in inflation. Cristiani's administration also reduced the foreign debt and cut the fiscal deficit.

President Calderón Sol vowed to continue his predecessor's economic policies, aiming for growth and low inflation. He also proposed to attract foreign investment, increase competitiveness of exports, privatize state industries, fix the exchange rate, reduce import tariffs and increase VAT from 10% to 13%. The government's policies succeeded in slowing inflation from 11.4% in 1995 to about 9% in 1996, but tight monetary control also limited demand. Consequently gdp growth fell from around 6% in both 1994 and 1995 to 4% in 1996. Imports also declined, which helped to improve the trade balance, but exports also fell, especially coffee, contributing to the general slowdown in the economy. In mid-1996, the president announced measures to stimulate investment in production, promote jobs and increase social spending, since no progress had been made in alleviating poverty or raising living standards.

COMMUNICATIONS

There are 562 km of railway but no long-distance passenger services. In 1993 the road length was 15,562 km, of which 13% was paved.

San Salvador and Environs

A CITY WHICH has suffered from natural and man-made disasters from which it has not had the ability to recover. Probably not a place to stay for long, but the best point to start from to see the many attractions of El Salvador.

SAN SALVADOR

San Salvador, the capital, is in an intermont basin on the Río Acelhuate, with a ring of mountains round it. The valley is known as 'Valle de las Hamacas' because of its frequent seismic activity. It was founded in 1525, but not where it now stands. The city was destroyed by an earthquake in 1854, so the present capital is a modern city, most of its architecture conditioned by its liability to seismic shocks. However, in the earthquake of 10 October 1986, many buildings collapsed; over 1,000 people died. The city centre is still in bad condition, and many people have not returned to proper housing.

BASICS The *pop* of the central city is 478,000, but when outlying suburbs are included, estimates rise to 1.5 million. *Alt* 680m. The *climate* is semi-tropical and healthy, the water-supply relatively pure. Days are often hot, especially in the dry season, but the temperature drops in the late afternoon and nights are usually pleasantly mild. Since it is in a hollow, the city has a very bad smog problem, caused mainly by traffic pollution.

Four broad streets meet at the centre: Av Cuscatlán and its continuation Av España run S to N, C Delgado and its continuation C Arce from E to W. This principle is retained throughout: all the *avenidas* run N to S and the *calles* E to W. The even-numbered *avenidas* are E of the central *avenidas*, odd numbers W; N of the central *calles*, they are dubbed Norte, S of the central *calles* Sur. The even-numbered *calles* are S of the two central *calles*, the odd numbers N. East of the central *avenidas* they are dubbed Oriente, W of the central *avenidas* Poniente. Although it sounds complicated, this system is really very straightforward, and can be grasped quickly.

PLACES OF INTEREST

A number of important buildings are near the main intersection. On the E side of Av Cuscatlán is the **Plaza Barrios**, the heart of the city. A fine equestrian statue looks W towards the renaissance-style **Palacio Nacional** (1904-11). To the N is the new **cathedral**, which was left unfinished for several years after Archbishop Romero suspended its construction (to use the money to alleviate poverty): work was resumed in 1990. To the E of the Plaza Barrios, on C Delgado, is the **Teatro Nacional** (the interior has been magnificently restored). If we walk along 2 C Oriente we come on the

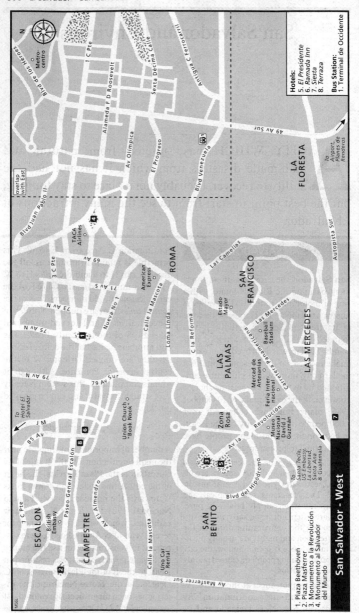

N

Metro-
centro

1 C Pte

Sexta Decima Calle

Antigua C Ferrocarril

Overlap
with East

Alameda F D Roosevelt

Av Olímpica

El Progreso

Blvd Juan Pablo II

49 Av Sur

Blvd Venezuela

To
Airport,
Planos de
Renderos

**LA
FLORESTA**

Autopista Sur

4
TACA
Airlines

Av 69

3 C Pte

71 Av S

73 Av N

75 Av N

Nueva No 1

American
Express

Calle la Mascota

Loma Linda

C la Reforma

ROMA

Las Camelias

**SAN
FRANCISCO**

Estado
Mayor

Las Mercedes

Baseball
Stadium

**LAS
PALMAS**

Mercado
de
Artesanías

Feria Inter-
nacional

Carretera Panamericana

LAS MERCEDES

1

79 Av N

79 Av Sur

To
Hotel El
Salvador

J M

85 Av

8 **6**

Paseo General Escalón

Union Church
"Book Nook"

Zona
Rosa

Revolución

Museo
Nacional
David J
Guzmán

Av 1a

3
5

To
Santa Tecla,
US Embassy,
La Libertad,
Santa Ana
& Guatemala

7

ESCALON

7 C Pte

British
Embassy

CAMPESTRE

Av El Almendro

Blvd del Hipódromo

**SAN
BENITO**

Calle la Mascota

Uno Car
Rental

Av Masferrer Sur

M661

San Salvador - West

1. Plaza Beethoven
2. Plaza Masferrer
3. Monumento a la Revolución
4. Monumento al Salvador
   del Mundo

Hotels:
5. El Presidente
6. Ramada Inn
7. Siesta
8. Terraza

Bus Station:
1. Terminal de Occidente

right to the **Parque Libertad**: in its centre is a flamboyant monument to Liberty looking E towards the rebuilt church of El Rosario where José Matías Delgado, father of the independence movement, lies buried. The **Palacio Arquiepiscopal** is next door. Not far away to the SE (on 10 Av Sur) is another rebuilt church, **La Merced**, from whose bell-tower went out Father Delgado's tocsin call to independence in 1811.

Across C Delgado, opposite the theatre, is **Plaza Morazán**, with a monument to Gen Morazán. Calle Arce runs W to the **Hospital Rosales**, in its own gardens. On the way to the Hospital is the great church of **El Sagrado Corazón de Jesus**, which is well worth a visit – don't miss the stained glass windows. Turn left (S) here and you come after 1 block to the **Parque Bolívar**, with the national printing office to the S and the Department of Health to the N. Four streets N of C Arce is the Alameda Juan Pablo II, on which stands **Parque Infantil**, in which is the Palacio de los Deportes. One block W is the **Centro de Gobierno**, with many official buildings. New offices are under construction further W between 17 and 19 Avs Norte.

The N side of Parque Bolívar is C Rubén Darío (2 C Poniente), which becomes Alameda Roosevelt, then Paseo Gen Escalón as it runs through the commercial and residential districts W of the centre. Heading W this boulevard first passes **Parque Cuscutlán**. A major junction is with 49 Av: to the S this avenue soon passes the national stadium, **Estadio Olímpico Flor Blanca**, before becoming the main highway to the international airport. To the N, 49 Av crosses Alameda Juan Pablo II. Beyond this junction it changes name to **Boulevard de los Héroes**, on which are the fashionable shopping centres, Metrocentro and the newer Metrosur, the *Camino Real* hotel, some of the city's better restaurants and a glut of fast food places, a busy area at all times, especially at night. At the Shell

station by Metrocentro, mariachis and other musicians gather each evening, waiting to be hired; others wander around the restaurants, playing to the diners.

Continuing W along Alameda Roosevelt, the next landmark is the **Monumento Al Salvador del Mundo**, a statue of Jesus standing on the Earth atop a column, in the middle of the Plaza Las Américas. From this junction the Carretera Panamericana heads SW to Santa Tecla. Straight ahead is **Paseo Gen Escalón**, Parque Beethoven and an area with many restaurants, shops and the Colonia Escalón residential district. Another important residential and entertainment region is the **Zona Rosa** and **Colonia San Benito**, reached either from the Carretera Panamericana, or from Escalón. In this leafy suburb, some of the most elegant restaurants and the *Hotel Presidente* are found.

MUSEUMS

Museo Nacional David J Guzmán, opposite Feria Internacional on Av de la Revolución, was under reconstruction in 1997; the only operating archaeological museums until the new museum has been built are at Joya de Cerén and Tazumal. **Museo de Historia Nacional**, end of C Los Víveros, Col Nicaragua, Wed-Sun 0900-1600, entry US$0.65, parking in the grounds US$0.65, microbus No 12 from city centre.

LOCAL FESTIVALS

During Holy Week, and the fortnight preceding 6 Aug, is held the *Fiesta of the Saviour* ('El Salvador'). As a climax colourful floats wind up the Campo de Marte (the park encompasssing the Parque Infantil and Palacio de Deportes; 9 C Poniente and Av España). The celebrations of El Salvador del Mundo last from 3-6 Aug: on 5th, an ancient image of the Saviour is borne before a large procession: there are church services on the 6th, Feast of the Transfiguration. On 12 Dec, Day of

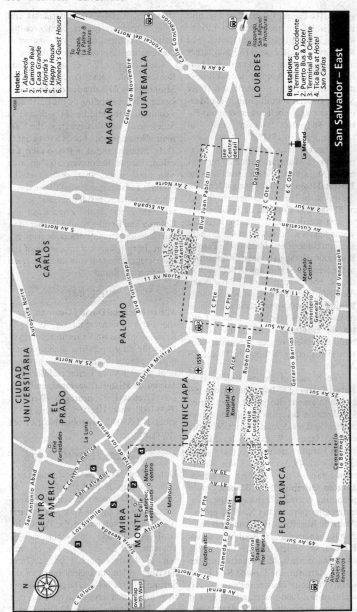

San Salvador – East

Hotels:
1. Alameda
2. Camino Real
3. Casa Grande
4. Florida's
5. Happy House
6. Ximena's Guest House

Bus stations:
1. Terminal de Occidente
2. Puerto Bus & Hotel
3. Terminal de Oriente
4. Tica Bus at Hotel
   San Carlos

To
Apopa,
La Palma &
Honduras

To
Ilopango,
San Miguel
& Honduras

Troncal del Norte

Calle Concepción

Calle 5 de Noviembre

GUATEMALA

MAGAÑA

24 Av N

LOURDES

La Merced

see Centre
detail

Delgado

2 C Ote

6 C Ote

2 Av Sur

Av Cuscatlán

Blvd Juan Pablo III

2 Av Norte

Av España

5 Av Norte

13 Av N

Parque
Infantil

11 Av Norte

SAN
CARLOS

PALOMO

25 Av Norte

Autopista Norte

Gabriela Mistral

SSS

3 C Pte

1 C Pte

Arce

Rubén Darío

Gerardo Barrios

Mercado
Central

Cementerio
General

Blvd Venezuela

17 Av Sur

11 Av Sur

25 Av Sur

CIUDAD
UNIVERSITARIA

EL
PRADO

Blvd Tutunichapa

TUTUNICHAPA

Hospital
Rosales

Parque
Cuscatlán

6 C Pte

Cementerio
La Bermeja

CENTRO
AMÉRICA

San Antonio Abad

cine
Variedades

La Luna

C Centro América

San Salvador

Los Sisimiles

MONTE
MIRA

Sierra Nevada

Atitlán

La calle,
restaurants

Metro-
centro

Metrosur

39 Av

41 Av

1 C Pte

Credomatic

National
Stadium
Flor Blanca

Alameda F D Roosevelt

FLOR
BLANCA

49 Av Sur

57 Av Norte

Av Bernal

C Toluca

C Bernal

To
Airport &
Planes de
Renderos

overlap
with West

N

MS9R

the Indian, there are processions honouring the Virgin of Guadalupe in El Salvador (take bus 101 to the Basílica de Guadalupe, on the edge of the city on the Carretera a Santa Tecla, to see colourful processions.)

TOURS

A good **sightseeing tour** of from 2 to 3 hrs by car starts along Av Cuscatlán: it includes the Zoo (which though small, is quiet and attractive, US$0.60 – open Tues-Sun 0900-1600, T 270 0728, buses 2 – zoo, and 12 from centre) and, 550m from the zoo, **Saburo Hirao Park and Museum of Natural History** (Col Nicaragua, bus 2 – zoo, or 12), US$0.60, beautiful Japanese gardens and small, interesting museum. You pass the Casa Presidencial and go on up to the new residential district in the mountain range of **Planes de Renderos**. This place is crowned by the beautiful Parque Balboa (good view of city from El Mirador at foot of Park). Parque Balboa is a Turicentro, with cycle paths, playground, gardens, etc, open daily 0800-1800. From the park a scenic road runs to the summit of **Cerro Chulo**, from which the view, seen through the Puerta del Diablo (Devil's Door), is even better. The Puerta consists of two enormous nearly vertical rocks which frame a magnificent view of the San Vicente volcano. The rocks are very steep but the sides can be climbed for an even better view. A little beyond the car park and drinks stands at the Puerta is a path climbing up a further summit, from which there are 360° views: to the coast, Lago Ilopango, the capital and volcanoes, including San Salvador, Izalco and Cerro Verde and San Vicente.

There are local buses to Parque Balboa (12, US$0.20 from eastern side of Mercado Central, and 17, from same location to the Mirador), and to Puerta del Diablo (No 12-MC marked 'Mil Cumbres') about every hour. There are reports that mugging is increasingly common at Cerro Chulo; it is unsafe to make the trip alone, and do not be there after dark. At the foot of Cerro Chulo is Panchimalco (see below); the road to Panchimalco and the coast branches off the road to Parque Balboa at the village of Los Planes, some km before the park.

The Teleférico on Cerro San Jacinto overlooking the city and Lago de Ilopango has good views, cafeterias and a children's funfair. Reached by bus 9 from centre, US$3 return, new cars, highly rec. Open daily, but best on weekdays, T 293-0546/5711, F 293-0478.

LOCAL INFORMATION

NB In 1997 many phone numbers in San Salvador were being changed. Prefixes 223, 224, 225, 226, some 298 and 279 will be replaced by 260, 261, 262 and 263, but not according to a logical system. A full list was not available at the time of going to press. You are advised to seek information from Antel, T 114.

● **Security**

NB The city centre is dangerous after dark, but Boulevard de los Héroes, the Zona Rosa and Escalón are relatively safe. In general robberies, particularly on crowded city buses, have increased of late: pickpocketing and bag-slashing are common. In the downtown markets, don't carry cameras, don't wear watches or jewellery and don't flash dollars around. In fact, women are advised not to wear expensive jewellery anywhere; they are also advised to carry a whistle at night, to attract attention in case of assault. Drivers, especially women, should take care at night at traffic junctions where windows should be kept closed (if the glass is tinted, so much the better).

● **Accommodation**

Hotel prices

L1	over US$200	L2	US$151-200
L3	US$101-150	A1	US$81-100
A2	US$61-80	A3	US$46-60
B	US$31-45	C	US$21-30
D	US$12-20	E	US$7-11
F	US$4-6	G	up to US$3

Prices are without meals unless otherwise stated. In the downtown area, some hotels lock doors very early. Value added tax (IVA) added to bills at major hotels. This tax (1996 – 13%) is not inc in our classifications.

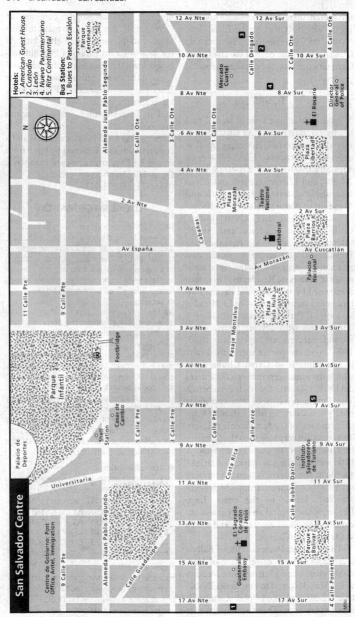

San Salvador Centre

Hotels:
1. American Guest House
2. Custodio
3. León
4. Nuevo Panamericano
5. Ritz Continental

Bus Station:
1. Buses to Paseo Escalón

Parque Centenario

12 Av Nte   12 Av Sur

Calle Delgado

4 Calle Ote

2 Calle Ote

10 Av Nte   10 Av Sur

Mercado Cuartel

8 Av Nte   8 Av Sur

El Rosario

Director General of Police

Alameda Juan Pablo Segundo

5 Calle Ote

3 Calle Ote

1 Calle Ote

6 Av Nte   6 Av Sur

Plaza Libertad

4 Av Nte   4 Av Sur

2 Av Nte

Plaza Morazán

Teatro Nacional

2 Av Sur

Cabañas

Plaza Barrios

Av España

Cathedral

Av Cuscatlán

Av Morazán

Palacio Nacional

11 Calle Pte   9 Calle Pte

1 Av Nte

1 Av Sur

Plaza Hula Hula

3 Av Nte   3 Av Sur

Pasaje Montalvo

Parque Infantil

Palacio de Deportes

Footbridge

5 Av Nte   5 Av Sur

Casas de Cambio

Shell Station

7 Av Nte   7 Av Sur

5 Calle Pte

3 Calle Pte

1 Calle Pte

Calle Arce

Universitaria

9 Av Nte   9 Av Sur

9 Calle Nte

Costa Rica

Instituto Salvadoreño de Turismo

Centro de Gobierno: Post Office, Antel, Immigration

11 Av Nte   11 Av Sur

Calle Rubén Darío

9 Calle Pte

Alameda Juan Pablo Segundo

Calle Guadalupe

13 Av Nte

El Sagrado Corazón de Jesús

13 Av Sur

Parque Bolívar

15 Av Nte   15 Av Sur

Guatemalan Embassy

4 Calle Poniente

17 Av Nte   17 Av Sur

L3 *Camino Real*, Blvd de los Héroes, T 279-3888, F 223-5660 (a Westin hotel), completely renovated, smart, formal atmosphere (popular with business visitors), Avis car hire, Taca desk, shop selling souvenirs, postcards, US papers and magazines, etc; **L3** *Hotel El Salvador* (formerly *Sheraton*), T 263-2643/0777, F 263-2583, 11 C Poniente y 89 Av Norte on the slopes of the volcano in Colonia Escalón, outdoor pool, renovated, very pleasant, friendly, security guard on every floor; **L3** *Presidente*, T 298-2044, F 223-2044, Av La Revolución, San Benito, pool, garden, very pleasant, good buffets some nights, excellent service but expensive. The *Princess Reforma* chain is building a new hotel in Col San Benito, due open Nov 1997.

A1 *Siesta (El Presidente)*, T 279-0377, F 224-6575, on Autopista Sur, off Pan-American Highway, W of the city, very friendly, good service and restaurant; **A1** *Terraza*, T 279-0083, F 223-3223, 85 Av Sur and C Padre Aguilar, 4-star, cable TV, hot water, English spoken, pool, weekly rates available; **A2** *Alameda*, T 279-0299, F 279 3011, 43 Av Sur and Alameda Roosevelt, good service, tour information, parking, TV; **A2** *Jesusalén*, C del Mirador 5005, Col Escalón, T 279-1491, F 279-1488, pool, restaurant, cable TV, private parking; **A2** *Mediterráneo Plaza*, 15 C Poniente 4319, Escalón, T 279-0977, F 279-1508, a/c, cable TV, pool, garden, good; **A2** *Novo Apart Hotel*, T 279-0099, F 279-2688, 61 Av N 4617 (in cul-de-sac), rooms with bath and kitchen, mini swimming pool, garden, pleasant, US$900/month; **A2** *Ramada Inn*, T 279-1820, F 279-1889, 85 Av Sur and J J Cañas, just off Paseo Escalón, TV, pool, bar, restaurant; **A2** *Suky Aparto-Hotel*, Paseo Escalón, Edif Alpine 5262, T 279-4009, F 279-4208; **A3** *Austria*, T 224-0791, F 278-3105, 1 C Poniente 3843 (between 73 and 75 Av), small, quiet, family atmosphere, English and German-speaking owner, price inc coffee and toast, convenient; also **A3** *Casa Austria*, C Jucuaran, pl G No 1, Santa Elena, 400m from US Embassy, hard to find (turn left Blvd Knights of Malta), buses 34, 44, renovated, clean, popular with business travellers, inc breakfast, good service, parking, T 278-3401, F 278-3105; **A3** *Casa Blanca*, 89 Av Norte 719, T 224-1830, F 278-4466, with continental breakfast, new, cable TV, with bath, clean, good; **A3** *Escalón Plaza*, 89 Av Norte 1416, Col Escalón, T 223-2141, F 298-6254, elegant, a/c, cable TV, good value, limited parking; **A3** *Hacienda Santa Fe*, C La Ceiba 254, Col Escalón, T/F 298-4069, a/c,

cable TV, bath, phone, inc breakfast, takes credit cards; **A3** *Posada Los Abetos*, C Los Abetos 15, Col San Francisco T/F 224-3260, nr the Zona Rosa and the Carretera Panamericana, inc breakfast, quiet, TV, cafeteria, discount with this *Handbook*, English, French and German spoken by owner Jill Lacaya.

B *Casa Grande*, C Los Sisimiles y Av Bernal, Col Miramonte, T 274-7450, F 274-7471, discount for longer stay, pleasant; **B** *Internacional Puerto Bus*, Alameda Juan Pablo II y 19 Av Norte, at Puerto Bus terminal, T 221-1000, F 222-2138, a/c, TV, wake-up service, etc; **B** *Townhouse* Bed and Breakfast, 3 C Poniente 4400, Col Escalón, between Avs 85-87 Norte, T 223-0247, discount for groups and long stay, very nice, parking, English-speaking owner; **B** *Villa Antigua*, C Mirador 4420, 1 block from *Hotel El Salvador*, T/F 245-2763, small, colonial-style, inc continental breakfast, reservations required, limited parking.

Non-luxury hotels not in the centre: **B** *Good Luck*, Av Los Sisimiles 2943, Col Miramonte (turn left at *Camino Real* and go uphill 200m), T 226-8287, F 226-0476, TV, shower, **C** without a/c, hot water, bright but simple, restaurant, secure parking; **C** *Florida's*, T 226-1858, F 226-0301, Pasaje Los Almendros 115, off Blvd de los Héroes, all rooms with bath, recently renovated, fan, laundry service, secure, proprietor speaks English, good value, tours arranged, rec (nr *Camino Real*: popular with journalists); **C** *Happy House*, Av Sisimiles 2951, Col Miramonte, T 226-6892, F 226-6866, good, friendly, often full, parking, restaurant, good breakfast; **C** *International Guest House*, 35 Av Norte 9 Bis, T 226 7343, towards University, nr Cine Variedades, friendly, with bath, good; **D** *Casa Clementina*, Av Morazán y Av Washington 34, Col Libertad, T 225-5962, very friendly, clean, pleasant, garden; **D** *Occidental*, 49 Av Norte 171, T 223-7715, renovated building, parking, popular with local business visitors, good; **D** *Ximena's Guest House*, T 260-2481, F 260-2427, C San Salvador 202-A, Colonia Centroamérica (René and Lisa Carmona), **C** with cable TV, a variety of rooms, **E** pp in 4-bed dormitory, discounts for long stay, clean, pleasant, cable TV in lobby, kitchen, breakfast US$1.75, other meals if ordered in advance, conveniently located, but not easy to find (it's roughly behind the Esso station on Blvd Los Héroes, take the little pathway up from abandoned restaurant at Av Sisimiles y Blvd Los Héroes).

Downtown hotels: **NB** If staying in the older downtown area, note that there are few places open to eat after 1830. Restaurants are open late in the W sections of the city. **B** *Ritz Continental*, T 222-0033, F 222-9842, 7 Av Sur 219, pool, a/c, big rooms, friendly, quiet, good restaurant, charm of a somewhat run down luxury hotel; **C** *American Guest House*, T 271-0224, F 271-3667, 17 Av Norte No 119 entre C Arce y 1 C Poniente, 3 blocks from Puerto Bus, with bath (cheaper without), hot water, fan, helpful, will store luggage, accepts credit cards, discounts for groups, weekly rates, *Cafetería La Amistad*, parking nearby, good; **C** *Family Guest Home*, T 222-1902, F 221-2349, 1 C Poniente Bis 925, safe inside (don't walk alone outside late at night), clean, friendly, helpful, expensive meals available, convenient for Puerto Bus (but advise owner if you have an early start), but overpriced and they may overcharge you if you arrive late; **D** *Centro*, 9 Av Sur 410, T 271-5045, a bit boxy, checkout 0900, TV, phone, friendly, washing facilities, clean, safe, rec.

E *Custodio*, T 222-5503, 10 Av Sur 109, basic, clean, safe, and friendly; **E** *Hospedaje Izalco*, T 222-2613, C Concepción 666, parking, most rooms with bath, TV lobby, dangerous area after dark; **E** *Imperial*, T 222-5159, C Concepción 659, serves reasonable meals and has car park, more expensive with toilet and shower, rec; **E** *Panamericano*, 8 Av Sur 113, T/F 222-2959, with cold shower, safe, closes early (but knock on the door), meals from US$2 and parking space, rec; **E** *Pensión Rex*, 10 Av N 213, quiet, safe, run by Sra Rosalinda, rec; **E** *Roma*, Blvd Venezuela nr Terminal de Occidente, good but front rooms noisy; **E** *San Carlos*, T 222-8975, C Concepción 121, with bath, early morning call (extra charge), doors locked 2400, cold drinks available, good, resident cockroaches but otherwise clean, Tica bus leaves from outside (ticket reservations in lobby office hours), owner arranges evening tours of the city US$6 pp (don't go into town any other way at night); **E** *Yucatán*, C Concepción, shared bath, safe, with parking; **E-F** *León*, T 222-0951, C Delgado 621, friendly, poor water supply, safe, parking.

F *Hospedaje El Turista*, 1C y 12 Av N 210, fan, clean, quiet, dingy, little privacy, does laundry; **F** *Hospedaje Espana*, 12 Av N, No 123, fan, clean, bright, good value. Many cheap *hospedajes* nr Terminal de Oriente, dubious safety, not rec for single women, avoid *La Avenida*; 3 doors along Concepción is **F-G** *Emperador*, with bath, friendly, good value, clean, laundry facilities on roof, rec.

Apartments: **B** Two fully-furnished apartments at home/office of dentist Luis Hurtado (see below for address), hot water, bath, stove or microwave, fridge, TV, phone, 30% discount weekly, 50% discount monthly (agent Donald Lee, see also below).

● **Places to eat**
On the Paseo General Escalón: *Diligencia* (at 83 Av Sur, for good steaks) and *El Bodegón* (at 77 Av Norte, Spanish style – proprietor Spanish), both excellent; *La Mar* (at 75 Av Sur, seafoods), and *Siete Mares*, T 224-3031, good seafood; *Betos* (Italian), next door at No 4352, *Asia* moderately-priced Chinese. *La Fonda del Sol*, No 4920, opp Villas Españolas shopping centre, Italian, popular with business set, good value, highly rec; *La Pampa Argentina*, highly rec for steaks, popular; *Quecos*, opp Plaza Alegre, Mexican, good variety; *Las Carnitas*, Parque Beethoven, good beef, reasonable prices, less pretentious and costly than similar places; *Rancho Alegre*, Parque Beethoven, good choice of food, relatively cheap, travellers' meeting place – also at Metrosur, S of Metrocentro, a whole group of different restaurants sharing the same space; *Dino's*, Leonel Fuentes, 83 Av Norte y 9 C Poniente, Escalón, pizzas and Italian, English, German and Italian spoken (Klaus Heistermann, Vincent Geoffredo, T 263-3188). *Pizzería Capri*, 85 Sur y J J Cañas, 1 block S of Paseo Escalón; *Pastelería Suiza/Salón de Té Lucerna*, 85 Sur y Paseo Escalón 4363; *Le Bavarois* for cakes, in same block as *Mister Donut* and *Biggest*, between 85 and 87. *Sports Bar and Grill*, lower level Villavicencio Plaza, Paseo Escalón y 99 Av Norte, 1 block below Redondel Masferrer, 1100-2400 Mon-Thur, 1100-0200 Fri-Sat, 1100-2200 Sun, good varied menu, popular, English-speaking owner, friendly staff, trendy, TV screens, American-football theme. *Tacos* and *pupusas* at Redondel Masferrer (good view over the city, lively atmosphere, mariachis). In Colonia Escalón, *Rosal*, 93 Av Norte y C El Mirador, nr *Hotel El Salvador*, Italian, good; *Kamakura*, 93 Av Norte 617, T 223-1274, Japanese, expensive, good.

In the Metrocentro area on Blvd Los Héroes there are many restaurants, inc US and US-style fast food places. *Neskazarra*, C Sierra Verde 3008, Col Miramonte, T 226-8936, Basque, moderately priced, good; *Pueblo Viejo*, in Metrosur, T 298-5318, open 1100-2000, popular for lunch, local and steak dishes, inc *parrillada*, and seafood; *La Casa del Gran Buffet*, between *Camino Real* and Esso, T 225-8401, all you can eat, lunch and dinner US$9; *Felipe's*, 27 C Poniente off

Blvd de Los Héroes, popular Mexican, good value. Behind *Camino Real* is a row of restaurants on C Lamatepec: *Hola Beto's*, No 22, T 226-8621, seafood; *Caminito Real*, No 19, local food, popular, good value, tasty; *Comida Lo Nuestro/Taco Taco*, local food, simple; *Hang Ly*, good Chinese, cheap; *Asia*, also Chinese, good portions, reasonable prices. Restaurant at *Hotel Good Luck* (see above) does good lunch specials, Chinese; *Tabasco*, Gabriela Mistral y Centroamérica, just up from Esso station on Blvd Los Héroes, Mexican, open 1200-2200; *Que Taco*, Av Pasco, Col Miramonte, good Mexican, *La Taberna del Viejo*, C Gabriela Mistral/Av 4 de Mayo 104, pupusas a speciality, good service; *Ipanema Grill*, Antigua C San Antonio Abad 1, T 274-4887, Brazilian chef, good; *La Ventana-El Café*, C San Antonio Abad 2335, T 225-6893, opp Centro Comercial San Luis, about 500m up from Cine Variedades, European-style, international food, popular with foreigners, open 0800-2400, 0900-2300 Sun, US and European newspapers.

Restaurants in the Zona Rosa, Blvd Hipódromo, San Benito, are generally very good, but expensive. These inc: *La Ola*, very good meals and moderately priced; *L'Opera*, C La Reforma 222, T/F 223-7284, French, good lunch specials, expensive; *Osteria dei Cualtro Galti*, C La Reforma 232, T 223-1625, Italian, good but expensive; *München*, Germany; *Paradise*, corner of Reforma, T 224-4201 for steak and lobster, excellent food and service (*Pizza Hut* next door), another branch on Blvd de los Héroes (all popular); *Basilea/Schaffer's*, nice garden atmosphere and small shopping centre, restaurant and excellent cakes (from *Shaw's Bakery* next door; see also *Coffee shops* below). *Dynasty*, No 738-B, known for best Chinese food in city, but not cheap. Next door is *Madeira*, No 738, T 298-3451, pleasant atmosphere, international, expensive. Also in San Benito, *Dallas*, T 279-3551, 79 Av Sur 48, for steaks and seafood, very good, exaggerated service, prices from moderate to expensive, another branch on Autopista Sur (bus 44). Nearby, in Col La Mascota, *El Cortijo Español*, 79 Av Sur y Pasaje A, Spanish; *Texas Meats*, C La Mascota, good for steaks.

Others inc *China Palace*, Alameda Roosevelt 2731, excellent value (oldest Chinese restaurant in San Salvador); *Pupusería Margot*, opp Estado Mayor on the road to Santa Tecla, good.

Vegetarian restaurants: *La Zanahoria*, C Arce 1144, T 222-2952; *Govinda's*, 51 Av Norte 147, Col Flor Blanca, T 23-2468, take bus 44 (a bit hard to find, but worth it); *Kalpataru*, Av Masferrer 127, 100m N of Redondel Masferrer, T 279-2306, open 2230, full restaurant service and lunch buffet, nice atmosphere; *El Tao*, 21 Av Norte, C 27 y C 29 Poniente, and Centro de Gobierno, 19 C Poniente, and 19 Av Norte, Col Layco; *Todo Natural*, 39 Av Norte 934, T 225-9918, nr Cine Variedades, good, meals US$2-4, also has rooms **D** pp; *Koradi*, 9 Av Sur y 4 C Poniente; *Arbol de Vida*, 21 Av Norte y Arce.

Branches of fast-food restaurants may be found in many parts of town: *Pizza Hut*, *Sir Pizza*, good pizzas and pasta, *Toto's Pizza*, *MacDonalds* and *Biggest* (hamburgers), *Wendy*, Blvd Los Héroes and Paseo Escalón; *Pollo Campero* (fried chicken); *Mr Donut* (US-style breakfasts, pastries, sandwiches, soups, salad, fresh juice, newspapers) at Metrocentro, Paseo Escalón, and elsewhere, open 0700-2000 daily. *Pops* and *Holanda* (ice cream parlours), several outlets throughout town, rec.

Cafés: there are numerous *cafeterías* serving cheap traditional meals such as *tamales, pupusas, frijoles*, rice with vegetables, etc. Often these places can be found around the major hotels, catering for guests who find the hotel meals overpriced. *Café Don Alberto*, C Arce and 15 Av Sur, good and cheap; *Actoteatro*, 1 C Poniente (between 15 and 13 Av N, nr *American Guest House*), good atmosphere, patio, music, clown shows and theatre at weekends 1900, good buffet lunch, cheap, central, rec; *Café de Don Pedro*, Roosevelt y Alameda, next to Esso filling station, good range of food, mariachi groups, open all night; *Bandidos*, Blvd Hipódromo 131, snacks, drinks, live music Thur-Sat, cover US$3, opens 1900; *Café Teatro*, attached to the Teatro Nacional, serves very good lunches, good value (see also *La Ventana* above and **Nightclubs** below).

Comedores: good, cheap *comedores* in Occidente bus terminal. Food markets in various parts of the city have stalls selling cheap food; Gourmet and delicatessen fare at *Señor Tenedor*, Plaza Jardín, Av Olímpica 3544, opp Ciné Deluxe, 0900-2200, nearest thing to an American deli, good value, breakfast buffet, good choice of salads and sandwiches; *Pronto Gourmet*, lunch counter service, good value; *Kreef Deli*, in Metrosur nr Pueblo Viejo, German style, and in Paseo Escalón 77 Av Sur 3945, T 223-8063; *Comida a la Vista*, buffet comedores around centre, clean, cheap.

Coffee shops: *Shaw's* (good coffee and chocolates), Paseo Escalón 1 block W of Plaza
Beethoven, Zona Rosa (see above) and at Metrocentro, also sell US magazines and greetings
cards; *Victoria*, bakery, good for pastries.

● **Bars**
Las Antorchitas, Blvd de los Héroes, good local
orchestra with a dance floor, French and English
spoken, cover charge US$1.20; *La Luna*, C
Berlín 228, off Blvd de los Héroes, Urb Buenos
Aires 3, T 225-4987/5054, good mixture of
music, different themes each night, shows start
2100-2130, matched well by mixed arty clientèle, very popular, reasonably-priced drinks and
snacks, cover charge US$2.30, closed Sun and
Mon, but open for lunch Mon-Fri, 1200-1500,
set menu about US$2.50, no cover except Fri
Salsa nights, US$6, take taxi late at night; *Club
'M'*, C José Martí 7, San Benito, T 223-9321,
trendy; *Sinatra's Bar*, Centro Comercial Loma
Linda, T 224-5736, piano-bar, expensive; *Villa
Fiesta*, Blvd de los Heroes opp Hospital Bloom,
live music, popular, US$6 cover, good. See also
British Club, and **Nightclubs**, below.

● **Airline offices**
Taca, **Aviateca**, **Lacsa**, **Copa** and **Nica**, main
office Edif Caribe, p 1, Plaza Las Américas,
0800-1730 Mon-Fri, reservations T 298-5066,
tickets T 298-5077, luggage claims T airport
339-9060, airport office T 339-9155, 24-hr
switchboard T 298-5055 (Taca)/5088 (Aviateca)/1322 (Lacsa)/9129 (Copa), F 223-3757
(all airlines). **Mexicana**, *Hotel Presidente*, T 279-
3744; **American**, Edif La Centroamericana,
Alameda Roosevelt 3107, p 1, T 298-0777,
F 298-0762, open 0800-1730, 0800-1130 on
Sat (also at Redondel Masferrer, 800m W of
British Club, end Paseo Escalón, bus 52 Paseo,
0800-1800 Mon-Sat); **United**, Galerías Escalón,
planta baja, 71 Av Norte y Paseo Gen Escalón,
Col Escalón, reservations T 279-3900, sales
T 279-4469, F 298-5536; **Continental**, Edif
Torre Roble, p 9, Blvd Los Héroes, T 260-
2180/3265, F 260-3331; **Iberia**, Centro
Comercial Plaza Jardín, local C, Carretera a
Santa Tecla, T 223-2600, F 223-8463; **Air
France**, Blvd El Hipódromo, T 279-0891;
Lufthansa, 87 Av Norte, Fountain Blue Plaza,
Col Escalón, T 298-2654, F 223-9194; **KLM**,
Centro Comercial La Mascota, local 10, Car-
retera a Santa Tecla y C La Mascota, T 223-0757,
F 223-0248; **British Airways**, 43 Av Norte 216,
T 298-1322, F 298-3064; **Aerolíneas Argenti-
nas**, T 223-7320, F 224-3936.

● **Banks & money changers**
Since the colón now floats, exchange has been
liberalized. Banks generally accept dollars cash;
TCs may be changed at *casas de cambio* (several
opp Parque Infantil on Alameda Juan Pablo
Segundo) with passport and one other form of
photograpic ID. Street changers (see below) will
change TCs with passport at a pinch. It is difficult
to cash TCs in a bank unless accompanied by
an account holder. **Banco Agrícola Comercial
de El Salvador**, Paseo Escalón 3635, T 279-
1033, F 224-3948, good for remittances from
abroad, English spoken. **Banco Salvadoreño**,
C Rubén Darío 1236, good rates for TCs and
Visa card advances. Changing dollars cash is not
a problem. International department of **Banco
Cuscatlán** has moved to Santa Tecla (bus 101D)
international currencies may be cashed here,
0900-1300, 1345-1600 Mon-Fri, 0900-1200
Sat, except branch at *Hotel El Salvador*, 0900-
2000 Mon-Fri, 0900-1200 Sat.

There are *casas de cambio* throughout the
city, offering prices that differ by no more than
a few centavos. The black market still exists
along Alameda Juan Pablo Segundo between 9
and 11 Av Norte, and concentrated around the
Central Post Office in Centro de Gobierno (assaults are not infrequent, changers carry calcu-
lators, but they do not pressure tourists; do not
use them at night or at weekends, never go
alone or on foot to change money with them).
Quetzales, Mexican pesos and lempiras may be
changed at **Casa de cambio El Quetzal**,
Alameda Juan Pablo Segundo y 19 Av Norte
(Puerto Bus terminal), 0800-1700 Mon-Fri,
0800-1200 Sat. Dollars may be bought freely at
casas de cambio and on the black market, with
little variation in price.

Accounts in dollars may be opened at **Citibank**, Edif SISA, 2nd floor nr El Salvador del
Mundo. **Credomatic**, for obtaining funds with
either Visa or Mastercard, Edif Cidema, Alameda
Roosevelt and C 51, offers a poor rate and
charges commission. **Aval-Visa**, Av Olímpica y
55 Av Norte (in Centro Comercial, behind Credomatic), does cash advances on Visa, T 279-
3077. In emergency, for Visa International or
Mastercard, T 224-5100; Visa TCs can only be
changed by Visa cardholders. **Western Union**
for money transfers, c/o Banco Salvadoreño
branches, T 225-2503 (48 other branches
throughout the country, look out for the black
and yellow sign), head office Almeda Roosevelt
y 43 Av Sur 2273-B, T 279-1611, Mon-Fri 0800-
1700, Sat 0800-1200, take passport and photographic ID to claim funds in colones (30 mins

from USA/Canada, 2-3 hrs from Europe). **American Express** is at *El Salvador Travel Service*, Carretera Panamericana y C Mascota (by Shell Station, bus 42 and 101), T 279-3844, F 223-0035; to change TCs, get them stamped at the Amex desk then go upstairs round the back to Banco del Comercio, open 0900-1700, to get the cash; must take passport. Amex loss or theft, T 223-0177. When making purchases with credit cards, identity may be asked for, as well as an address in El Salvador. Most banks (except Cuscatlán – see above) open 0900-1700 Mon-Fri, 0900-1200 Sat, *casas de cambio* keep the same hours but most close 1300-1400 for lunch.

● **Cultural centres**
British Club, Paseo Escalón 4714, 2nd floor, Aptdo postal (06) 3078, opp Farmacia Paseo, T 223-6004, F 224-0420, open Mon-Sat 1700-2400, Sun 1200-2100, has bar (with imported British beer, US$2.50-US$3.50), restaurant open to non-resident visitors (great fish and chips, US$4.50), British newspapers, an English language library, darts (open night on Wed), live music Fri (cover US$3.50 for non-members), snooker and a small swimming pool (temporary visitor's cards if introduced by a member, monthly membership US$20, but free for non-resident visitors up to 2 months with use of pool and tennis courts). *American Society*, T 224-1330, Chester Stemp, 0800-1600 Mon-Fri, at International School, or Pastor Don Dawson, T 223-5505 (Union Church), or Donald Lee, cultural activities, open only to US citizens and their spouses and children, emergency assistance for US citizens. Family membership US$20 pa, single US$14. *El Centro Español*, off the Paseo Escalón, is open to non-members, has 2 pools (one for children), tennis courts, weight training room and aerobics salon. *Club Arabe*, C Mirador, 3 blocks above *Hotel El Salvador*, open to members' guests, swimming pool, sauna, tennis, bar. *La Centro Cultural*, Pasaje Senda Florida Sur, behind Edif Sisa, Carretera Santa Tecla, nr Salvador del Mundo, T 279-1868, Mon-Fri 0800-1800, Sat 0800-1200, art exhibitions, monthly shows.

● **Embassies & consulates**
Embassies: Guatemalan, 15 Av Norte 135 y C Arce (0900-1200), T 222-2903/271-2225, F 221-3019, visas issued within 24 hrs; **Honduran**, 37 Av Sur 530, Col Flor Blanca, T 271-2139, F 221-2248, Mon-Fri 0900-1200, 1300-1500; **Nicaraguan**, 71 Av Norte y 1 C Poniente 164, Col Escalón, T 223-7729, F 223-7201, Mon-Fri 0800-1300, 1500-1700; **Belizean**, Condominio Médico, local 5, 2nd floor, Blvd Tutunichapa, Urb la Esperanza, T 226-3588, F 226-3682; **Mexican**, Pasaje 12 y C Circunvalación, San Benito, behind *Hotel Presidente*, T 298-1079, Mon-Fri 0800-1100; **Panamanian**, Alameda Roosevelt y 55 Av Norte 2838, T 298-0884, F 298-0773; **Costa Rican**, Edif La Centroamericana, 3rd floor, Alameda Roosevelt 3107, T 279-0303.

US, Boulevard Santa Elena, Antiguo Cuscatlán, Unit 3116, T 278-4444, F 278-6011, outside the city, reached by bus 101A, open Mon Fri 0800 1600; **Canadian Honorary Consulate**, Av Las Palmas III, Col San Benito, T 224-1648; **British**, Edif Inter Inversiones, Paseo Gen Escalón 4828, PO Box 1591, T 298-1763, F 298-3328, has British newspapers (British citizens are requested to register here), open Mon-Fri 0800-1300; **German**, 77 Av Norte y 7 C Poniente 3972, T 223-6140, F 298-3368; **French**, 1 C Poniente 3718, Col Escalón, T 279-4018; **Swiss**, *Pastelería Lucerna*, 85 Av Sur y Paseo Escalón 4363, T 279-3047; **Norwegian Consulate**, 73 Av Norte, Escalón, 100m N of Paseo Escalón, nr Galerías; **Finnish**, C Circunvalación y Av de la Revolución, Ap 3B, Col San Benito, T 279-1912; **Italian**, Av La Reforma 154, Col San Benito, T 223-7325; **Israeli**, 85 Av Norte 614, Col Escalón, T 223-9221/8770.

● **Entertainment**
Many cinemas, inc: *Presidente*, nr *Hotel Presidente* in Col San Benito; *Colonial*, Col La Sultana, nr entrance to the UCA; *Variedades*, C San Antonio Abad; *Beethoven*, Plaza Beethoven, Paseo Escalón. Best quality cinemas cost US$2, films in English with Spanish subtitles. The new *Masferrer* 5-screen complex, Redondel Masferrer at end of Paseo Escalón, charges US$3.50, screenings 1500-2100, take bus 52 or taxi late at night. Similarly *Paseo-Uraya* twin-screen complex, Paseo Escalón y 75 Av Norte, next to El Sol Supermarket. "Art" films are shown at *La Luna* (see *Bars*) on Tues 1800, free, *Cine Presidente* and *Cine Caribe*, Plaza Las Américas, see press for details. Alliance Française arranges film seasons, T 223-8084. Ballet and plays at the **Teatro Nacional de Bellas Artes**, and music or plays at the Teatro Cámera. Folk music in *Café Teatro*, in the Teatro Nacional.

Clubs: *Club Salvadoreño* admits foreigners, owns a fine Country Club on Lago Ilopango called Corinto (with a golf course, green fee US$23), cabins for rent US$30/day (not holidays), and has a seaside branch at Km 43 on the coast road, nr La Libertad, much frequented during the dry season, Nov to April;

T/F 225-1634, Lic Oscar Paloma, Mon-Fri 0800-1200, 1330-1600. The *Automobile Club of El Salvador* has a chalet for bathing at La Libertad. See also *Atami Beach Club* under La Libertad, page 825. The *Country Club Campestre* (Paseo Escalón), admits foreigners with cards only. *Club Náutico*, at the Estero de Jaltepeque, famous for its boat races across the mud flats at low tide.

Conventions: facilities, inc organized tours for delegates, may be arranged by the Bureau of Conventions and Visitors, *Hotel El Salvador*, T 279-0777, F 245-1063, or Asiprotur (Salvadoran Association of Investors and Promoters), T/F 224-1606.

International Industrial Fair, held in Nov, every year in the International Fair buildings, C a Santa Tecla, turnoff for Colonia San Benito (nr *Hotel Presidente*). For fairground take buses 101A, B, C, 42B, 79, 34, 306. Admission to Fair US$1.25. Site is also used for other functions such as the Aug fair.

Nightclubs: all leading hotels have their own night club. Zona Rosa, Colonia San Benito, has many bars/discos/open-air cafés in a 5-block area, well-lit, crowded Fri-Sat night (discos' cover charge is US$7), take bus 306 from nr Esso/Texaco/Mundo Feliz on Blvd Los Héroes before 2000, taxi thereafter. *Mario's* on Blvd Hipódromo, Zona Rosa, with good live music; also in Zona Rosa *Le Club* and *Calipso*, both lively; *Papasitos*, Blvd Los Próceres (Autopista Sur); nr *Dallas* restaurant and Cuscatlán tower, popular up-market nightspot, T 273-5770; *Habana Club*, final 61 Av Norte, Col Escalón, shows, restaurant, bar, cover US$6.50, Tues-Sat 1900-0100; *Memories*, Paseo Gen Escalón; *My Place*, Paseo Gen Escalón and 83 Av Norte; *Lapsus*, Paseo Escalón, lively; *Santa Fe*, Av Masferrer Sur 26, T 298-6217, also lively. *Café Teatro*, by National Theatre, Tues-Sat, jazz on Tues, various music other nights; *La Luna*, C Berlín 228, Urb Buenos Aires 3, 2 blocks from Blvd de Los Héroes, see under **Bars**, above; *Villa Fiesta*, Blvd de Los Héroes Norte, T 226-2143 for reservation Fri-Sat, restaurant/bar, Mon-Wed Latin music (Grupo Fiesta), Thur Rumba Seis, Fri-Sat Latin music with guest bands (cover US$11); *Liverpool*, Blvd Constitución, Col Escalón, good live rock, Tues-Sat (see also *British Club*, above, Fri pm rock). Check *La Prensa Gráfica* and *El Diario de Hoy*.

● **Hospitals & medical services**
Chemist/Pharmacy: *Americana*, Alameda Roosevelt entre 59 y 61 Av Norte, good service and selection, 0800-1800 Mon-Sat, next to *Mr Donut*.

Dentist: *Servidenpro*, Luis Hurtado, in Merliot district, T 228-0444, PO Box 143, Santa Tecla, La Libertad, take bus 101D, stops in front of house, his son speaks English, US-trained.

Doctors: *Medicentro*, 27 Av Norte is a good place to find doctors in most specialist fields in the afternoon mostly after 1500.

Hospitals: *Hospital de la Mujer*, entre 81 y 83 Av Sur y C Juan José Cañas, Col Escalón (S of Paseo), bus 52 Paseo, T 223-8955, F 279-1441; *Hospital Pro-Familia*, 25 Av Norte 483, 11 blocks E of Metrocentro, T 225-6100/4771, clinics and 24-hr emergency, reasonable prices; *Hospital Baldwin*, 37 Av Norte 297 y Prolongación C Arce, nr Metro Sur, T 298-5131, emergency, excellent; if short of cash or in emergency, public *Hospital Rosales*, 25 Av Norte y 3 C Poniente, long waits.

● **Libraries**
The library of the UCA, Universidad Centro Americana José S Cañas, Autopista Sur, the road to the airport, is said to be the most complete collection in the capital. **Centro Cultural Salvadoreño**, Av Los Sisimiles, Metrocentro Norte, T 226-9103, 0800-1100, 1400-1700, English library, excellent. **Intercambios Culturales de El Salvador**, 67 Av Sur 228, Col Roma, T 245-1488, F 224-3084, extensive Spanish and English reference library, local artistic exhibitions, computer school. US information library at **American Chamber of Commerce**, 87 Av Norte 720, apto A, Col Escalón, Aptdo Postal (05) 9, Sr Carlos Chacón, speaks English, helpful.

● **Language schools**
Spanish: *Escuela de Idiomas Salvador Miranda*, PO Box 3274, Correo Centro de Gobierno, T 222-1352, F 222-2849, US$125-150/ week inc board. *Cihuatan Spanish Language Institute* (Ximena's), C San Salvador 202-B, San Salvador, Col Centro América (nr *Hotel Camino Real*), T (503) 260-2481, René or Lisa Carmona, F 260-2427, or Lisa Carmona F 224 1330 daytime; rates are US$125/week inc board at *Ximena's Guesthouse* in the city or nearby farm, *Lisa's Inn*, 17 km from the capital between Apopa and Guazapa (buses San Salvador-Aguilares stop at the farm).

● **Places of worship**
Anglican Centre (St John's Episcopal Church), 63 Av Sur and Av Olímpica, services on Sun, 0900 in English, 1000 in Spanish; **American Union Church**, C 4, off C La Mascota, T 223-5505, has services in English on Sun at 0930, and also has a gift shop (local crafts

and textiles) and an English paperback library with a wide selection, free (both open Wed and Sat 0900-1200, 1400-1700); take bus 101D. **Community Bible Church** (evangelical), International School, Col San Benito, opp Spanish Embassy, T 225-3549 (Sam Hawkins, e-mail shawkins@es.com.sv), English service Sun 1000, guarded parking. **Chapel in San Benito**, Av La Capilla, English mass Sun 1600, T US embassy 278-4444 0830-1530 for information. **Lutheran**, C 5 de Noviembre y 8 Av Norte 242, T 226-6010, German and English spoken. **Synagogue** (conservative), Rabino Gustavo Kraselnik, Blvd El Hipódromo, No 626, casa 1, Col San Benito, Hebrew services Fri 1830, Sat 0745, most members speak English.

● **Post & telecommunications**
Post Office: central Post Office at the Centro de Gobierno with EMS, super-fast service: branches at Almacenes Siman (Centro), Librería Hispanoamérica, Centro Comercial Gigante (Col Escalón), Metrocentro, with EMS, Mercado Local No 3, Mercado Modelo, 1st floor above PHL stationer on Plaza Morazán, Av Olímpica y 57 Av Norte, next to *Super Selectos* (behind *Casa de Negulos*, owned by Canadian Moe Heft, who repairs watches and is helpful, T 223 5944, open 0830-1700 and Sat am). Good service to Europe. Open Mon-Fri 0730-1700, Sat 0730-1200. Lista de Correos, Mon-Fri 0800-1200, 1430-1700, good service for mail collection.

Fax service: Antel Centro, C Rubén Darío y 3 Av Norte, charge by the minute, Guatemala US$0.92, USA US$2.35. More expensive at Antel Metrocentro.

Many courier services throughout the city. *DHL*, 43 Av Norte 228, T 279-0411, F 223-2441, *Gigante Express*, C Rubén Darío 1003, T 222-4969, F 222-4809; *León Express*, Alameda Roosevelt entre 49 y 51 Av Sur, No 2613, T 224-3005, F 224-3660, has *casa de cambio*. *International Bonded Couriers*, 1 C Poniente y 63 Av Norte, Escalón, Edif Comercial A&M 15, T 279-0347, F 279-1814. *UPS*, C El Progreso 3139, Col Roma, T/F 245-3844/5.

Telephones: Antel at the Centro de Gobierno, Metrocentro (open 0700-1930, 1830 for fax), and other locations. T 114 for information on new phone numbers (see above).

● **Shopping**
Mercado Cuartel, crafts market, 8 Av Norte, 1 C Oriente, a few blocks E of the Teatro Nacional, rebuilt after a disastrous fire in 1995. Towels (Hilasal brand) may be bought here with various

Maya designs. Crafts may also be bought at the *Mercado Nacional de Artesanías*, opp the Estado Mayor on the road to Santa Tecla (buses 101A, B or C, 42B, 79, 34, 30B), at prices similar to the Mercado Cuartel, but better than Metrocentro or elsewhere is San Salvador; most stalls have similar items, open 0800-1800 daily. *Tienda Artesanías La Cosecha*, in Casa Cultural La Mazorca, C San Antonio Abad 1447, T/F 226-5219, 100m N of entrance to university, on left, good prices, large selection (bus 30B, 26, 44). *Acogipiri*, handicapped and women's project, ceramics retail and wholesale, Gabriela Mistral 4 pje 11, No 563, Col Centroamérica, T 226 5269, Eileen Girón Batres (speaks English), e-mail eilgiro@es.com.sv. Custom-made handicrafts (pottery, wood, jewellery, jade), antiques at *Pedro Portillo*, Antigua C San Antonio Abad, Urb Lisboa, Casa 3, p 2, T 284-4753 in advance.

Metrocentro, the large shopping precinct with adequate parking on the Boulevard de los Héroes, NW of the city centre, contains 2 of best known department stores, *Siman* and *Swartz*, together with boutiques, gift shops and a small supermarket. A new extension (1996) has some 35 further shops, inc *El Rosal* 8a Etapa, Local 278, wide variety of local handicrafts. It is accompanied by another shopping complex, *Metrosur*, to the S, which has fewer shops (0900-2000 Mon-Sat, 0900-1900 Sun). Another shopping centre, *Villas Españolas*, is on the Paseo Escalón, 1 block S of the Redondel Masferrer; it is rather more exclusive, with expensive boutiques, several impressive furniture stores, and a minimarket specializing in tinned food from around the world. The supermarket *La Tapachulteca* is on Redondel Masferrer itself. There is another called *Feria Rosa* opp the Foreign Ministry on the road to Santa Tecla (Pan-American Highway), which is by no means fully occupied; similarly the *Plaza Merliot* in Merliot suburb. Also *Plaza San Benito*, San Benito, with *La Despensa de Don Juan*, best supermarket in the city. Paseo Escalón has a wide variety of boutiques and gift shops in all price ranges. Prices in shopping centres are much higher than in the centre of town. There are also some exclusive shops in the Zona Rosa. *El Sol* and *Europa* are 2 major supermarkets in Plaza Beethoven, Paseo Gen Escalón and Av 75 Norte.

Towels can also be bought in the centre at *Hula Hula*, 2 blocks E of the Cathedral, where there are also street traders. For modern art and antiques try *Galería Rosenthal*, Centro Comercial El Manantial, C Reforma 232, San Benito, run by Pietro Yanelli, T 224-0158, speaks Italian, some English, helpful. *Viejos Tiempos*, 3 C Poniente entre 9 y 11 Av Norte, Centro, T 222-6203, Jorge Antonio Sibrian, antiques, frames, odd articles, rec. Visa and Mastercard are increasingly accepted in shops.

Bookshops: at the Universidad de El Salvador (UES) and the Universidad Centroamericana (UCA). *Cervantes*, 9 Av Sur 114 in the Centre and Edif El Paseo No 3, Paseo Escalón. *Bautista* (T 222-2457), 10 C Poniente 124, religious bookshop. *Cultura Católica*, opp Teatro Nacional. *El Arabe* (T 222-3922) 4 Av Norte. *Clásicos Roxsil* (T 228-1212), 6 Av Sur 1-6, Santa Tecla. *Editorial Piedra Santa*, 1 C Poniente, 21 Av Norte 1204, T 222-2147 (bus 29). *Etc Ediciones* in Basilea Shopping Centre, San Benito. *The Book Shop*, Galerías, Local 357, Paseo Gral Escalón at 71 Av Norte (5 blocks from Salvador del Mundo, buses 16, 52), books and magazines in English, good prices, owners Alejandro and Carol Morales speak English, also at Metrocentro 8a Etapa, Local 274, also branches in Guatemala City and San Pedro Sula; *Eutopia*, Av La Capilla 258, San Benito, new and used books, good prices. Regular book fairs at the Teatro Nacional. Some English books at *Librería Cultural Salvadoreña* (T 24-5443) in Metrosur. Others at *Librería Quixaje*, C Arce, and a few at *Shaw's* chocolate shops. American magazines and secondhand books at *La Revista*, Hipódroma 235, Zona Rosa, large selection. Magazines and newspapers in English can be bought at leading hotels (eg *Miami Herald* at *Hotel Presidente*, 1 day old, US$2.25, also *Camino Real*); many shops sell US magazines.

Hairdressing: *Pino di Roma*, Colonia San Benito, for ladies, high standards, latest styles, US$10 cut, shampoo and blow-dry. Many unisex parlours all over the city, US$3-US$5.

Tobacco: for those interested in cigars: *Timber Box* in *Hotel El Salvador*, T 298-5444, fine cigars and other tobaccos, accessories, open Mon-Fri 0930-1230, 1330-1900, Sat 0930-1230, Lic Edward Neuwald Meza. For information on Cigar Factory in Suchitoto, and on other outlets in Guatemala and Honduras, contact Donald Lee.

● **Sports**

Basketball, tennis, international swimming, fishing, target shooting, wrestling, boxing and boat and sailing boat races, but in private clubs only.

Baseball: on the field opp Mercado Nacional de Artesanías, Tues-Fri 1700, Cuban and US coaches, local teams, admission US$1.25.

Bowling: at Bolerama Jardín and Club Salvadoreño.

Motor racing: at new El Jabalí autodrome on lava fields nr Quetzaltepeque. For all sporting events, check *La Prensa Gráfica* and *El Diario de Hoy*.

Mountain Bikes: at *Bike Doctor Racing*, Centro Comercial Juan Pablo II 313A, Blvd San Antonio Abad, T/F 225-5657.

Rollerskating rink: Av La Reforma, 100m from international school and Spanish Embassy, open daily, large, new, ample parking, skate rental, bus 30B.

Soccer: is played on Sun and Thur according to programme at the Cuscatlán and Flor Blanca Stadiums.

Watersport equipment: *Amphibious*, Centro Comercial Plaza San Benito, C La Reforma 114, local 1-16, T/F 335-3261, owner Robert Rotherham (and 2 sons), surfboard rental US$15/day, kayak rental, windsurf lessons, excursions arranged, English spoken, equipment for sale; also has mountain bike rental.

● **Tour companies & travel agents**

Numerous Tourist agents, inc: *El Salvador Travel Service*, Centro Comercial La Mascota, see **American Express** under **Banks & money changers**. *Central American Travel Exchange*, a full service travel agency in Denver, CO, USA, with a branch office in San José, Costa Rica, T 1 (800) 711-5055 toll-free in USA, F (303) 860-0864, e-mail cate@travelexchange.com, website http://www.travelexchange.com, El Salvador representative, Donald Lee (see below), offers excursions in El Salvador, Guatemala, Honduras and Nicaragua, using local companies, guides, unique lodgings, cultural and eco tours, couples or small groups, singles accommodated; discounts for Spanish speakers, students with ID, over 60s and disabled; handicrafts export service. Contact in Antigua, Guatemala, Elizabeth Bell at *Colonial Antigua Tours*, *Agencia de Viajes Tívoli* (Kathy Topke de Núñez – see page 635 for full addresses), *Dutch Travel-SBA* (Edgar Boussen, 4 C Oriente 14, T 432-2676, F 832-0602, e-mail greenacres@conexion.com); in Honduras, Eli Gonzales, T (504) 57-8011, San Pedro Sula, e-mail ayalaser@simon.intertel.hn, speaks English. *Donald Lee* can be contacted by beeper T (503) 298-1122/1222, unit 90185, ask for operator 75 televip-English to leave message 24 hrs, or F 260-2427 (c/o *Ximena's*), toll free from USA or Canada T 1-888 667-7852, e-mail evallada@rdi.uca.edu.sv (from Mexico or Central America) or ettelber@ecst.csuchico.edu (from elsewhere, state re D T Lee info El Sal CA, allow 10 days for reply). He offers the following services: information for tourists and business travellers, help in emergencies (lost or stolen documents etc), local excursions, tours to craft centres, national parks, archaeological and historical sites, arranging guides who speak French and German, train information, corporate rates, vehicle rental, security advice (tours using local buses will not be arranged free of charge). In USA and Canada, send enquiries to Mr and Mrs J Walp, F (208) 377-0205, e-mail jayjay@ rmci.net.

U Travel, Av Revolución, Col San Benito, T 243-0566. For bus tours for groups (US$45-US$60/day pp): *Amor Tours*, 73 Av Sur, Col Escalón, local 21 Edif Olímpic Plaza, T 223-5130, F 279-0363, 20 years' experience, expensive; *Set Tours*, Av Olímpica 3597, T 279-3236, F 279-3235; *Pullmantur*, in *Hotel El Presidente*, T 279-4166, F 223-7316, besides luxury bus service to Guatemala (see below), offers excellent package tours to Antigua.

Dive Pacific, 79 Av Sur 135, Col Escalón, T 223-8304, F 223-2774, Rodolfo González, PADI instructor, excellent but expensive, English spoken, for diving off the Pacific coast at Playa Los Cóbanos, fishing tours, and dives in lakes Coatepeque and Ilopango; *El Salvador Divers*, 3 C Poniente 5020A, Col Escalón, T/F 223-0961, owner speaks English and German; *Oceánica*, diving school, Centro Comercial Campestre (frente al Club Campestre), Paseo Gral Escalón, I (cellular) 887-6488 all hours, English spoken; *Magic Tours*, Galería Rosa 5, San Benito, T 279-3536, local and Central America, contact Ana Lucía Flores; *Jaguar Tours*, Hotel Siesta, nr Col San Benito, T 278-8968, F 278-8973, for horse riding tours.

● Tourist offices

Corporación Salvadoreña de Turismo, Blvd del Hipódromo 508, Col San Benito, T 243-0427, F 278-7310 (**Corsatur**): take bus 34 from centre, or 30B from Mundo Feliz or Salvador del Mundo; walk 4 blocks uphill from roundabout. The tourist office at the international airport is open 0800-1600 Mon-Sat, T 339-9454/9464. Good information on buses, turicentros, archaeological sites, beaches, national parks, etc. Texaco and Esso also sell good **maps** at some of their respective service stations. The best maps of the city and country (US$3 and $2 respectively) are available from the **Instituto Geográfico Nacional**, Av Juan Bertis No 79, Ciudad Delgado.

See also **Tourist Information**, page 853.

● Useful addresses

Ambulance/rescue: (Comandos de Salvamento), T 222-0817/221-1310.

Immigration department: in the Ministry of Interior Building, Centro de Gobierno, T 221-2111, open Mon-Fri 0800-1600. They will consider sympathetically extending tourist visas, but be prepared with photos and plenty of patience.

Complaints: Director General of Police, 6 C Oriente, T 271-4422.

Police: emergency T 121, 123, or 228-1156, no coin needed from new coin phones. In San Salvador, metropolitan police respond to tourist complaints.

Red Cross: T 222-5155/5333.

For women visitors: Instituto de Estudios de la Mujer, Cemujer, Blvd María Cristina 144, T/F 226-5466, Spanish only (Raquel Cano, T/F 221-5486, works with Cemujer; her husband is editor of *El Salvador Maya*, good for information). American Women's Association, T Patricia Arias 273-3204 for information, cultural and social events for English-speaking women, US$4.60/year. *La Luna*, see above, is owned by women and has access to many women's organizations; ask for Beatriz, who speaks English and French; it is a safe place for women to go alone or in a group; office at C Berlin y 4 de Mayo, look for 'Ropero' sign, open daytime, T 225-5054 (tell them Pato sent you). At *Ximena's Guest House* (see **Accommodation**) ask for Norwegian Lena, resident, who speaks 7 languages. There is a small women's crisis centre 50m from *Florida's Guest House* on the Pasaje at the corner, Spanish only.

Centro Internacional de Solidaridad (CIS), Urb Padilla Cuellar, Pasaje Los Pinos 17, San Salvador, T 225-0076 (PO Box 1801, New York, NY 10159, T 212-229-1290, F 212-645-7280), for language classes, brigade work, FMLN programmes and schools. **Instituto para la Rescate Ancestral Indígena Salvadoreña (RAIS)**, Av Santiago 20, Col San Mateo, has programmes for local aid to Indian communities and the Nahual language and customs.

● Transport

Local Bus: city buses are either blue and white for normal services, or red and white for special services, *preferenciales*; most routes have both normal and special buses. Fares are ¢1.50 (US$0.18) for normal services, more expensive after 1800; ¢2 (US$0.23) for special services. Most run 0500-2000, after which use taxis.

Route 101 buses to/from Santa Tecla are blue and white for either class of service. Some useful routes: 29 from Terminal de Oriente to Metrocentro via downtown; 30 Mercado Central to Metrocentro; 30B from Mundo Feliz (100m up from Esso station on Blvd de Los Héroes) to Escalón, 79 Av Norte, Zona Rosa (San Benito), Alameda Roosevelt and back to Metrocentro along 49 Av; 34 San Benito-Mercado de Arte-sanías-Terminal de Occidente-Mercado Central-Terminal Oriente; 52 'Paseo' Parque Infantil-Metrocentro-Plaza Las Américas-Paseo Escalón-Plaza Masferrer; 52 'Hotel' Parque In-fantil-Metrocentro-*Hotel El Salvador*-Plaza Masferrer. **Car hire**: local insurance is mandatory and 13% IVA applies: rentals from Avis, 43 Av Sur 137 (T 224-2623, F 224-6272, airport 339-9268), also at leading hotels (*Camino Real* 223-9103, *El Salvador* 224-2710) can rent in advance from abroad; **Uno**, member of Affinity International, Edif Sunset Plaza, Av Masferrer Sur y C Mascota, Col Maquilishuat (bus 101D), T 279-4127, F 279-4128, 24-hrs emergency service, cellular 298-1122, unidad 11988, e-mail un-orent@gbm.net, homepage http://www.un-orentacar.com/uno, English and French spoken by owner, Xavier Deprez, best prices and service, airport office to open 1997, office in San Miguel, 24-hr emergency service, cellular phone in vehicles, free transfer from airport, excursions arranged, USA T 800-761-7787 (or e-mail Mr and Mrs Jim Walp, Boise, Idaho, jay-jay@rmci.net), UK T 01932 240000, F 01932 253067 (Affinity International, United House, 4 The Quintet, Churchfield Rd, Walton-on-Thames, Surrey KT12 2TZ), Australia T 008-801-660, Germany T 6102-254108; **Budget**, Cond Balam Quitzé, 89 Av Sur y Escalón (T 298-5187, Airport 339-9186); **Hertz**, Av Los Andes behind *Hotel Camino Real* (T 226-8099, Airport 339-9481); **Horus**, Cond Balam Quitzé 29, Escalón, T 298-5858, F 298-0500; **Tropic Car Rental**, Av Olímpica 3597, Escalón, T 223-7947, F 279-3236 (runs tours, has 4WD vehicle, good service). **Taxis**: plenty (all yellow), none has a meter, ask fare before getting in. Fares: local journeys 3-4 km US$4 by day, US$6-US$7 at night. On longer trips, negotiate, about US$12/hr or US$75 for a 6-7 hr day. Few drivers speak English. They will charge more in the rain. More expensive taxis may be hired from: Acontaxis (T 270-1176/8), Cobra (T 279-2258), Dos Pinos (T 221-1285/1286, 222-2321), Acomet (T 276-5136). Taxis Acacya specializes in services to the airport (see below). **Car repairs**: Carlos Granicio, San Jacinto, Colonia Harrison T 270 6830

for general car repairs. Julio Henríquez, *Auto-Inter*, 10 Av Sur 1-7, Santa Tecla, T 228-8433, 0800-1600 Mon-Fri, speaks English, or contact through Rene Carmona or Donald Lee at *Ximena's Guest House*. Be aware that spare parts are hard to come by in El Salvador. **Insurance**: Francisco Ernesto Paz, Asesor (for El Salvador and Central American companies), Blvd Los Héroes, Pasaje Los Angeles 151 (turn right at *Toto's Pizza*), T 225-7491. **Car papers**: Ministerio de Hacienda, 'Tres Torres', turn left on Blvd Los Héroes 300m past Texaco station.

Air The new international airport (SAL) at Comalapa is 44 km from San Salvador towards Costa del Sol beach, reached by a 4-lane highway. Acacya minibus to airport, from 3 C Poniente y 19 Av Norte (T San Salvador 271-4937/4938, Airport 339-9271/9282), 0600, 0700, 1000, 1400 (be there 15 mins before), US$3 one-way. (Leave from airport when full, on right as you go out, but unreliable.) Acacya also has a taxi service, US$16, the same as other radio taxi companies; ordinary taxis charge US$18, US$25 at night. A luxury bus service runs to 2 hotels for US$8.50, known as Aerobuses, T 223-9206, and leaving the airport 4 times a day. Taxi to La Libertad beach US$13-16; to Costa del Sol US$8-10. Airport carpark US$1.25 initial charge, plus US$1.25/hr. The prices in the gift-shops at the airport are exorbitant; there is a post office, a tourist office, two exchange desks, inc Banco Hipotecario (open daily 0700-1900) and duty-free shopping for departures and arrivals.

The old airport is at Ilopango, 13 km E of the city. It is primarily used by the air force. However, small planes fly from Ilopango to San Miguel (30 mins, good), Usulután, Santa Rosa de Lima, San Francisco Gotera and La Unión; tickets from the civilian traffic offices (TAES, Taxis Aéreos El Salvador, T 295-0363 or T/F 295-0330 – in San Miguel T Sra de Domínguez 661-3954 – or Gutiérrez Flying Service). Linea Aérea Salvadoreña – LASA (T 243-1015, F 243-2540) runs a daily service to San Miguel at 0630 and 1630, returning at 0715 and 1715 for US$35 return plus tax. This airline also connects both San Miguel and Ilopango with the international airport at Comalapa. Also charter flights are easily arranged.

Trains San Salvador-Sonsonate-Metapán, through coffee plantations (details from Donald Lee, see above).

Buses Long distance: domestic services go from Terminal de Occidente, off Blvd Venezuela,

T 223-3784 (take city buses 4, 7C, 27, 44 or 34); Terminal de Oriente, end of Av Peralta in Centro Urb Lourdes (take city buses 29 from Metrocentro, 42 from Alameda, or 4, 7 C), very crowded with buses and passengers, keep your eyes open for the bus you want; and Terminal Sur, San Marcos, Zona Franca, about 10 km from the city, take city bus 26 from Universidad Nacional area or Av España downtown, take taxi to city after 1830. Routes and fares are given under destinations.

International buses Standard service to Guatemala: a confederation of buses (Pezzarossi, Taca, Transesmer, Melva, Vencedora, Daniel Express and Centro América) operate to Guatemala City (5½ hrs) from the Puerto Bus terminal at Alameda Juan Pablo II y 19 Av Norte; T 222-3224, T/F 222-2138; you can walk there from city centre, but not advisable with luggage; take bus 101D from Metrocentro, or bus 29, 52 to 21 Av Norte, 2 blocks S of terminal (city buses don't permit heavy luggage). The terminal has a *casa de cambio*, good rates, open daily, a restaurant (overpriced) and a hotel, alternatively stay at *American Guest House*, 5 mins' walk or US$3 by taxi with luggage (see above). There are 16 departures daily 0330-1600 Mon-Sat, 12 on Sun, and the fare is US$7.

Luxury service to Guatemala: King Quality, Condominio Balam Quitzé, Paseo Escalón y 89 Av, T 243-3633, F 223-7616, runs a daily service at 0630 and 1530 from *Hotel Presidente*, to Guatemala City for US$20 (US$39 return), luxury service, with a/c, film, drinks and meals; also to Tegucigalpa 0700, US$45 return. Confort Line (T 279-3382/84), US$15 (US$25 return), departing daily from *Hotel El Salvador* at 0800 and 1400, and will arrange border crossing formalities for US$3. Pullmantur, luxury hostess coaches, a/c, snacks, from *Hotel Presidente* 0630, 1530, 4 hrs, US$25 single, US$45 return (main office, Paseo Escalón, Centro Comercial Porteño No 4, T 279-4176, F 223-3718). Tica Bus (from address below, but calls at Puerto Bus) runs to Guatemala at 0530, US$16. Reserve all Tica Bus services in advance. Also from Terminal de Occidente, El Cóndor goes to Talismán, Mexico, via Sonsonate, La Hachadura and Escuintla, US$9.75, 0330, 10 hrs, also 0700-0800 to Guatemala City, compared with Galgos on the same route from Puerto Bus, 0300, 9 hrs, better service, US$10.30.

To Tegucigalpa: through Pullman services: Cruceros del Golfo from Puerto Bus, T 222-2158, 0600 and 1600 daily, US$18, 7 hrs, arrive early; Ticabus from *Hotel San Carlos*, C Concepción 121, T 222-4808, US$15, leaves 0500, ticket office opens 0430, change buses in Honduras, direct to Managua. Alternatively, take local services from Terminal de Oriente Ruta 306 to Santa Rosa de Lima, 4 hrs, US$2.20, less time by express US$2.50, then Ruta 346 to the border at El Amatillo, 30 mins, US$0.40, last bus to border 1730; see Honduras chapter for onward transport.

To countries further South: Ticabus to Managua US$35, San José US$50, Panama City US$75.

AROUND SAN SALVADOR

Many places can be visited in a day from San Salvador by car or by frequent bus services. These include trips to Panchimalco and Lago de Ilopango; to the crater of San Salvador volcano (see Santa Tecla, below); and to the volcano of Izalco (1,910m) and the near-by park of Atecosol, and Cerro Verde (see page 827); or to Lago de Coatepeque (lunch at *Hotel del Lago* or *Torre Molinos*) and to Cerro Verde in 90 mins; to the garden park of Ichanmichen (see Zacatecoluca, page 851); Sihuatehuacán and the pyramid of Tazumal (page 833). At weekends the coast around La Libertad (see below) is very popular. Bus 495 from the Terminal del Occidente goes to the seaside resort of Costa del Sol (see page 850).

The Mountaineering Club of the University of San Salvador sponsors day hikes every Sun morning. Transportation from downtown San Salvador is provided. See local papers on Sat for details. The club is extremely friendly and the excursions are strongly recommended.

Panchimalco is 14½ km S by a paved road. Around it live the Pancho Indians, descendants of the original Pipil tribes; a few have retained more or less their old traditions and dress. Streets of large cobbles, with low adobe houses, thread their way among huge boulders at the foot of Cerro Chulo (see also page 809). A very fine baroque colonial church, Santa Cruz, has a white façade with statues of eight saints. Inside are splendid woodcarvings and wooden columns, altars, ceilings and benches. Note especially the octagonal ceiling above the main altar, painted a silvery blue. There is a bell incised with the cypher and titles of the Holy Roman Emperor Charles V, and the cemetery is said to be colourful. An ancient ceiba tree shades the market place (disappointing market). The **Centro de Arte y Cultura Tonatiuh**, gallery, museum and shop, C Principal 14 bis, T 280-8836/27, has a good atmosphere, fair prices and supports local youth projects, ask for the painter, Eddie Alberto Orantes. The *fiesta* of Santa Cruz de Roma is held on 12-14 Sept, with music and traditional dances; on 3 May (or the second Sun of the month) there is the procession of Las Palmas. Bus 17 from Mercado Central at 12 C Poniente, San Salvador, every 45 mins, US$0.30, 45 mins, or minibus from near Mercado Central, very crowded but quicker (30 mins), and cheaper (US$0.35).

Lago de Ilopango A 4-lane highway, the Boulevard del Ejército, runs E for 14½ km from San Salvador to Ilopango airport, beyond which is Lago de Ilopango, 15 km by 8, in the crater of an old volcano, well worth a visit. Pre-Conquest Indians used to propitiate the harvest gods by drowning four virgins here each year. There are a number of lakeside cafés and bathing clubs, some of which hire dug-outs by the hour. The cafés are busy in the dry season (try *Teresa's* for fish dishes), but often closed in the middle of the year. *Hotel Vista del Lago*, T 227-0208, 3 km from Apulo turn off on Highway, is on a hill top. Private chalets make access to the lake difficult, except at clubs and the Turicentro Apulo. Bus 15, marked Apulo, runs from the bus stop on Parque Hula Hula to the lake (via the airport), 70 mins, US$0.30. Entrance to the Turicentro camping site costs US$0.60; bungalow US$3.45; parking US$0.60; plenty of hammock hanging opportunities; showers and swimming facilities, all rather dirty. The water is reported to be polluted in parts near the shore and it is busy at

weekends. The eastern shore is less polluted and is reached from Cojutepeque.

Santa Tecla (*pop* 63,400), also known as Nueva San Salvador, 13 km W of the capital by the Pan-American Highway, is 240m higher and much cooler, in a coffee-growing district. It has a training school for factory technicians, set up with British funds and technical help.

• **Accommodation** D *Hotel Monte Verde*, on the main road towards Los Chorros, T 228-1263; F *Hospedaje San Antonio*, 4 Av Poniente, 2 blocks S of Plaza, and a F *Hospedaje*, no name, C Daniel Hernández y 6 Av, 3 blocks from Parque San Martín, green door, good, safe, will store luggage; F *Posada La Libertad*, La Libertad, Av Melvin Jones No 4-1, 3 blocks S of Parque, T 228-4071, with bath, will store lugggage.

• **Places to eat** *Restaurant La Tortuga Feliz*, 4 C Poniente 1-5, marimba music, garden, pleasant setting, good local food. *Comedor y Pupuseria Tikal*, 2 C, half block W of 1 Av Sur, pleasant, clean, cheap.

• **Buses** 101 and 101-A, B and D, leave 3 Av Norte, nr the junction with C Rubén Darío, San Salvador, every 10 mins for Santa Tecla (US$0.20).

San Salvador volcano consists of a large massif with an impressive crater, 1½ km wide and 543m deep known as **El Boquerón** and a significant 1,960m peak about 2 km to the E, called **El Picacho**, which dominates the capital. A rough road goes N from 1 block E of Plaza Central in Santa Tecla which climbs up and passes between the two features. Ruta 103 buses at 0800, 1100 and 1400, returning at 0930, 1230 and 1530, leave from 4 Av Norte y C Hernando for El Boquerón (US$0.30), or pick-ups from the Parque Central; from the end of the busline you must walk 45 mins to the crater, but you can drive to within 50m. A walk clockwise round the crater takes about 2 hrs; the first half is easy, the second half rough. Take care not to fall from the ridge. The views are magnificent, if somewhat spoilt by TV and radio towers and litter. The inner slopes of the crater are covered with trees, and at the bottom is a smaller cone left by the eruption of 1917. The path down into the crater starts at the westernmost of a row of antennae studding the rim, 45 mins down (don't miss the turn straight down after 10 mins at an inconspicuous junction with a big, upright slab of rock 20m below), 1 hr up. Near the summit is La Laguna botanical garden. You can follow the road N and then turn right through extensive coffee plantations and forest to reach the summit of **El Picacho**. This also makes an excellent climb from the Escalón suburb of San Salvador, in the early morning preferably, taking about 3-4 hrs return trip (take a guide).

At **Los Chorros**, in a natural gorge 6 km NW of Santa Tecla, there is a beautiful landscaping of four pools below some waterfalls. The first pool is shallow, and bathers can stand under the cascades, but there is good swimming in the other three. Entry, US$0.60. Car park fee: US$0.60. There is a trailer park at Los Chorros, with restaurant and showers and a hotel **D** *Monte Sinai*, T 226-6623. Bus 77 or 79 from 11 Av Sur y C Rubén Darío in San Salvador.

THE PACIFIC COAST SOUTH OF SAN SALVADOR

Just before Santa Tecla is reached, a branch road turns S for 24 km to **La Libertad**, 34 km from San Salvador (*pop* 22,800). It is a fishing port and, in the dry season, a popular seaside resort. The pier is worth seeing for the fish market awnings and, when the fleet is in, the boats hauled up out of the water along its length. On the seafront are several hotels, lodgings and restaurants. At a small plaza, by the *Punta Roca* restaurant, the road curves left down to the point, for views of La Libertad bay and along the coast. The cemetery by the beach has tombstones curiously painted in the national colours, blue and white. The market street is two streets inland from the seafront.

The coast E and W has good fishing and surf bathing (El Zunzal beach is the

surfers' favourite, see below). Watch out for undercurrents and sharks. The beaches are black volcanic sand (which can be very hot); they are dirty but the surf is magnificent (watch your belongings). Surf season is Nov-April. There are also swimming pools, admission US$0.15.

The Costa del Bálsamo (the Balsam Coast), between La Libertad and Acajutla (see below), is a historical name, but on the steep slopes of the departments of Sonsonate and La Libertad, scattered balsam trees are still tapped. The pain-relieving balsam, once a large export, has almost disappeared. Bus along the coast to Sonsonate at 0600 and 1300, about 4 hrs.

NB La Libertad is very crowded at weekends and holidays. Service can be offhand and assaults, especially on women, are on the increase (1997). Do not stay out alone late at night.

● **Accommodation In La Libertad**: turning right from 4 C Poniente at the *Punta Roca* restaurant, the following are on the road to the point: **A3** *La Posada de Don Lito*, T 335-3166, and beside it **B** *La Hacienda de Don Rodrigo*, older hotel with character, OK; next to *Don Lito* is **C** *Rick*, T 335-3033, with bath, clean, friendly, restaurant, good value; signed behind *Rick's* is *El Retiro Familiar*, with café; **C-D** *Puerto Bello*, 2 C Poniente, on the main avenue, with bath, run-down, small rooms. By the park at 4 C Poniente are **C** *Rancho Blanco*, cheaper without a/c, cheaper still without bath, 4 rooms, pool, garden; **D** *La Posada Familiar* on opp corner, **F** without bath, popular with surfers and backpackers, basic, meals, clean, good value, hammocks, parking; next door is *La Paz*, budget accommodation. Nearby is **E** *Pensión Amor y Paz*, very basic, small rooms, no ventilation, dirty, friendly owner, cheapest in town; **E** *Nuevo Amanecer*, 1 C Poniente No 24-1, safe, clean; *Bar Gringo* on the beach front lets rooms, so does the *Miramar* restaurant (negotiable). **At Playa Conchalío**: **D** *Conchalío*, T 335-3194, large, nice, and **C** *Los Arcos*, T 335-3490, safe, quiet, with pool, garden and restaurant.

● **Places to eat** Seafood is good in the town, especially at *Punta Roca* (American-owned, by Don Bobby Rotherham), try the shrimp soup, T/F 335-3261, open 0800-2000, or 2300 weekends, safe, English-spoken, daughter-in-law

Gringos in El Salvador and Guatemala – a short history
(A personal view by Donald T Lee)

🐾 In the late 1960s, thousands of young wanderers, I among them, went "on the road" (using the *South American Handbook*, of course), emulating the 1950s Beat Generation, inspired by writers like Jack Kerouac and William Burroughs. Both generations of travellers were in search of adventure and, in the times before faxes, call-back services and e-mail, it was a golden age. We arrived, and we kept on arriving, some for only a short visit, some still going strong today, running successful businesses and raising grandchildren. In El Salvador, scores of ex-pats stayed in guesthouses like *Casa Clarke* in the then laid-back capital. They taught English during the week (no certificates were needed in those days, as long as you were a native speaker), then headed for the pristine Pacific beaches of La Libertad less than an hour's drive away. News of the lifestyle spread on the gringo-graph up N, inspiring thousands of visitors to El Salvador between 1969 and 1979. The flow dried up during the civil war that escalated after 1980. Many El Salvadoreans, both wealthy and poor, fled N, legally or illegally, to the USA and Canada (now *El Hermano Lejano*, still numbering some 1.2 million, remits an average of US$3mn daily to families back home). The ex-pats who stayed lived a kind of barricaded life, often staying in La Libertad, looking out for one another, unable to do anything regarding the conflict. Besides, most of us were not politically motivated and never will be. The Peace Accord was signed in 1992, ushering in a new era of reconstruction. Locals began travelling again and research and development began for receptive tourism in a climate of intense competition between the Central American republics. The El Salvadorean American Society was revived in 1993 and now has more than 200 active members and the *British Club*, with many ex-pat US members, provides a social and cultural centre. There are also foreign NGOs, the US Peace Corps and other international services to increase the ex-pat numbers.

In Guatemala, a number of 'gringo-friendly', ex-pat 'ghettos' existed, in the wealthier areas of Guatemala City, in Antigua, in Panajachel on Lago Atitlán, and at Río Dulce on the Caribbean coast, where yachts docked at the marinas. Scores of ex-pats also deserted the country during the worst days of the Guatemalan conflict in the early to mid-1980s. A different type of 'grifter and grafter' began arriving in Guatemala City in the mid-1980s, bringing a shadier colour to the downtown drinking spots. With the return to democracy in the late 1980s, early 1990s, tourism picked up. Antigua became more and more crowded as its Spanish-student population grew. Panajachel became a commercial centre for exporters of traditional weavings and Chichicastenango market seemed to get busier and larger each week. Quezaltenango developed as an alternative Spanish school centre, gearing itself more to those who wanted to practice their Spanish with locals, rather than in Antigua's or Panajachel's bars and clubs. These changes encouraged many ex-pats to head for El Salvador, Honduras or elsewhere, preferring to move on, sort of fade away, or (in cases of illness or economic necessity) move back with extreme reluctance to North America or Northern Europe.

Now that Guatemala has its own peace agreement, Central Americans are entering an era of upscale tourism, trade and commerce. Means of rapid communications proliferate and emergency funds can be transferred to a traveller who has been 'caught short' in less than two hours. A far cry from when I once waited in southern Mexico in the late 1960s for a bank transfer via Laredo, Texas: 3 weeks later and some 13 pounds lighter, down to my last peso, I finally received my money.

Erika offers advice for women travellers, see *Amphibious*, under San Salvador **Watersports**; opp *La Posada de Don Lito* is *Rancho Mar El Delfín*. By 4 C Poniente: *El Nuevo Altamar* for good seafood and *El Viejo Altamar*; *La Fonda Española*, *Los Amigos* and *Sandra* are also in this area. *Sagrado Corazón de Jesus*, 1 Av Norte, good value, large helpings, try their *pupusas de queso*. *Pupusería*, specializes in snacks, rec. *Los Mariscos*, good, reasonable prices, popular, closed Mon. *The Fisherman's Club*, excellent seafood, expensive, bar, swimming pool, tennis court, private beach, entry fee US$2. Cheap restaurants nr the pier; also cheap food in the market.

● **Transport Local Bus**: No 102 from San Salvador leaves from 4 C Poniente, between 13 and 15 Av Sur, 1 hr via Santa Tecla, US$0.45. To Zacatecoluca at 0500, 1230 and 1530. La Libertad's bus terminal is on 2 C Oriente, E of the pier. **Car repairs**: good workshop on 7 Av Sur, Francisco is helpful, good quality work, you can sleep in vehicle while the job is done.

La Libertad is at Km 34 from San Salvador. Continuing W from the port, at Km 36 is Playa Conchalío, quieter than La Libertad. At Km 38 are the **D** *Cabañas Don Chepe* at the start of the **Playa El Majahual**, at the other end of which is **D** *Hospedaje El Pacífico*, a surfers' hotel. This beach does not have a safe reputation, nor is it clean. Other cheaper hotels include **G** pp *Hospedaje Surfers-Inn*, very basic but friendly, run by Marta, who serves meals. Bus 80 from La Libertad.

Zunzal, Km 42 is the best surfing beach in this area and where the Club Salvadoreño and the Automobile Club have their beach premises. *El Bosque Club*, T 335-3011, day cabins only, closes 1800: *El Pacífico* is nearby, another hotel close to the village is overpriced and dirty. Many local houses for rent. At Km 49.5 is the *Atami Beach Club*, T 223-9000, with large pool, private beach, expensive restaurant, 2 bars, gardens, a beautiful place.

In the grounds of *Atami* is a private 'rancho' (kitchen, 2 bedrooms, small pool, hammocks, 150m from private beach, cooking, safe, US$100 for max 4). Access to *Club Atami* for US and other non-Central American passport-holders US$8, inc cabaña for changing. A short distance beyond, Km 51, is El Zonte and the *Turicentro Bocana*.

At Km 64, turn inland to the large village of **Jicalapa**, on high rockland overlooking the ocean. There is a magnificent festival here on St Ursula's day (21 Oct). Jicalapa is 3 km beyond Teotepeque. The Carretera Litoral continues for a further 40 km or so to Acajutla past rocky bays and remote black sand beaches and through tunnels. Take great care with the sea if you bathe along this coast.

From La Libertad going E 2 km is **Playa Obispo**. (**A3** *El Malecón de Don Lito*, T 335-3201; **D** *Rancho Blanco*, T 335-3584; near the beach several good value seafood restaurants. Nearby is *Motel Siboney*, good.) Opposite the motel there is a trail up the Río San Antonio, 1 km to the waterfall Salto San Antonio (50m) and 2 km to the Salto y Cueva Los Mangos (60m). Bus 287 from La Libertad to the San Antonio quarry will get you there. 8 km from La Libertad, on a turn off from the Carretera Litoral, is **Playa San Diego**, nice but deserted (*Río Mar Club*, T 222-7879). Bus for San Diego beach, from C 2 Oriente in La Libertad, US$1, 30 mins. The Carretera Litoral heads E, but inland, to join the airport highway by San Luis Talpa; it then continues to Zacatecoluca. Between Playa San Diego and San Luis Talpa the Carretera is under major repair.

Western El Salvador

S OME VERY interesting natural features and beautiful countryside. The trip to Cerro Verde and Izalco is a 'must'. Santa Ana is an important coffee-growing centre and the city is worth a visit.

SAN SALVADOR TO GUATEMALAN BORDER

The route from the capital S to La Libertad and along the coast to the port of Acajutla, has already been given. A quicker route to Acajutla goes W on the Pan-American highway through Santa Tecla, past Los Chorros and then in 3½ km, bears left to Sonsonate and S to the port. There are four roads which cross into Guatemala, through La Hachadura (see under Sonsonate, below), San Cristóbal (via the Pan-American Highway), Las Chinamas (see under Santa Ana) and Anguiatú (beyond Metapán).

SAN SALVADOR-SONSONATE – ACAJUTLA-LA HACHADURA

From the junction with the Pan-American Highway, route CA 8 (heavy lorry traffic) runs W, past Armenia, to the town of **Izalco** at the foot of Izalco volcano (*pop* 43,000, 8 km from Sonsonate, bus 53C, US$0.10). The town of Izalco and Izalco volcano are not directly connected by road. A paved road branches off the highway 14 km before the turning for Izalco town (about 22 km from Sonsonate) and goes up towards Cerro Verde and Lago de Coatepeque (see below). The town has resulted from the

gradual merging of the *ladino* village of Dolores Izalco and the Indian village of Asunción Izalco (**G** *Hospedaje San Rafael*, next to the church on the Central Park, very basic, no shower, dirty, noisy, motorcycle workshop, but safe and friendly, no alternative). **Festivals**, 8 to 15 Aug and during the Feast of St John the Baptist from 17 to 24 June.

Near Izalco, at the edge of town, is the spacious swimming pool of Atecozol, in the middle of a beautiful park with a restaurant (Turicentro, admission US$0.60, parking US$0.60, bungalow US$3.45). The park is shaded by huge mahogany trees, palms, aromatic balsam trees and *amates*. There is a battlemented tower; a monument to Tlaloc, god of rain; another to Atlacatl, the Indian who, on this spot, shot the arrow which lamed the *conquistador* Pedro de Alvarado; and a statue to the toad found jumping on the spot where water was found.

Just S of Izalco, a few kilometres off the main road to San Salvador is **Caluco** which has a colonial church and a ruined Dominican church, bus 432 from Sonsonate. 2 km from Caluco are Las Victorias Falls on the Río Chiquihuat, with two caves above the falls. On the same road out of Caluco is the meeting of hot and cold streams at Los Encuentros to form the Río Shuteca/Aguas Calientes. 5 km SE of the town is La Chapina pool and springs on the farm of the same name.

SONSONATE

64 km from the capital, Sonsonate (*pop* 60,900; *alt* 225m), produces sugar, tobacco, rice, tropical fruits, hides and balsam. It is in the chief cattle-raising region. The city was founded in 1552 and is now hot, dirty and crowded. The beautiful El Pilar church (1723) is strongly reminiscent of the church of El Pilar in San Vicente. The Cathedral has many of the cupolas (the largest covered with white porcelain) which serve as a protection against earthquakes. The old church of San Antonio del Monte (completed 1861), 1 km from the city, draws pilgrims from afar (*fiesta* 22-26 Aug). There is a small railway museum, look for the locomotive at the entrance to the city on the highway from San Salvador, Km 65. An important market is held each Sun. The market outside the church is quite well-organized. In the northern outskirts of the city there is a waterfall on the Río Sensunapán. Legend has it that an Indian princess drowned there, and on the anniversary of her death a gold casket appears below the falls.

Excursions

CA 8 NW to Ahuachapán (see page 834), 40 km all paved, spectacular scenery, frequent buses from Sonsonate, No 285, US$0.50, 2 hrs: the road goes through the Indian village of **Nahuizalco**. The older women still wear the *refajo* (a doubled length of cloth of tie-dyed threads worn over a wrap-round skirt), and various crafts are still carried on, although use of the Indian language is dying out. *Fiestas* 19-25 June, religious festival, music, *Danza de los Historiantes* (see **The Music of the Region** at the beginning of the book) and art exhibitions; 24-25 Dec, music and *Danza de los Pastores*. (Bus 53 from Sonsonate, US$0.10). Beyond is **Jayúya** (just off the main road), with Los Chorros de la Calera 2 km N (bus 205 from Sonsonate),

E *Hotel El Típico*, 1 C Oriente 1-2. Take care in this town, there has been much gang (*mara*) activity (1997).

Apaneca, see under Ahuachapán, is also passed.

In the Sonsonate district are a number of waterfalls and other sites of natural beauty: to the W, near the village of **Santo Domingo de Guzmán** (bus 246 from Sonsonate) are the falls of El Escuco (2 km N), Tepechapa (1½ km further) and La Quebrada (further still up the Río Tepechapa), all within walking distance of Santo Domingo and each other. Walk through the town, then follow the river. Several spots to swim. Festival in Santo Domingo, 24-25 Dec, with music and dancing. From **San Pedro Puxtla** (bus 246; modern church built on the remains of a 18th century edifice) you can visit the Tequendama Falls on the Río Sihuapán. Bus 219 goes to **Cuisnahuat** (18th century baroque church, *fiesta*, 23-29 Nov, San Judas), from where it is 2 km S to the Río Apancoyo, or 4 km N to **Peñón El Escalón** (covered in balsam trees) and El Istucal Cave, at the foot of the Escalón hill, where Indian rites are celebrated in November.

Local information
● Accommodation

B-C *Agape*, at Km 63 on outskirts of the town in the Asociación Agape complex, converted convent, gardens, suites and rooms, a/c or fan, safe parking, good restaurant, cable TV, rec, ask Father Flavian Mucci, the director of the Association, to show you round.

E *Castro*, on main street 3 blocks from Parque, with bath, fan, good, safe, friendly, some rooms with bed and hammock; **E** *Hospedaje Veracruz*, Av Rafael Campo, T 451-0616, very noisy, unfriendly, not rec; **E** *Orbe*, 4 C Oriente y 2 Av Sur, T 451-1416, parking, good restaurant.

F *El Brasil*, 4 Av Norte, basic, clean and friendly; **F** *Hospedaje Blue River*, nr bus station, with bath, large, clean rooms; *Florida*, beside bus terminal, fan, basic, manager speaks English.

● Places to eat

My Mom's at Agape, highly rec; *Nuevo Hilary*, Av Rafael Campos No 1-3, local and Chinese food, generous servings, moderate prices; *Caften Teto*, nearby, clean, friendly, good servings.

● **Airline offices**
Taca, T 451-0694.

● **Transport**
Trains The train up to the mountains and Metapán passes here about 1030-1100; see museum above.

Buses No 248 to Santa Ana, US$1 along CA 12 N, 39 km a beautiful journey through high, cool coffee country, with volcanoes in view; to Ahuachapán, 2 hrs, slow, best to go early in the day; San Salvador to Sonsonate by No 205, US$0.80, 80 mins, very frequent. There is also a bus from San Salvador along the coast at 0600 and 1300, beautiful ride. Take care at the bus terminal and on rural routes (eg in Nahuizalco area).

ACAJUTLA

Route CA 12 goes SW from Sonsonate to **Acajutla** (*pop* 36,000), Salvador's main port serving the western and central areas, 85 km from San Salvador (the port is 8 km S of the Coastal Highway). It handles about 40% of the coffee exports and is a popular seaside resort during the summer (good surfing, though beaches are dirty, suffering from occasional oil spills). It is not an attractive town.

● **Accommodation C** *Kilo 2*, at San Julián just outside town, T 452-3192; **C** *Miramar*, with bath and fan, clean, reasonable restaurant/bar; *Lara*, by beach, with bath and fan, clean, car parking; **E** *Pensión Gato Negro*, opp Belinda store, run by Japanese couple, with good restaurant, varied food, generous portions, meals US$1 to US$1.50. There are 2 motels, **D**, on the outskirts of town.

● **Places to eat** *Pizza y Restaurante Perla del Mar* serves good shakes and food at reasonable prices.

● **Buses** 207 from Occidente terminal, San Salvador, US$2.80, or 252 from Sonsonate US$0.30. 58 km from Santa Ana.

Route CA 2 turns off CA 12 about 4 km N of Acajutla, 16 km S of Sonsonate, and runs, repaved 1995, 43 km W to the Guatemalan frontier point of **La Hachadura**.

The coastline here is mainly black sand with few public facilities. Some turtles use this area and it is worth enquiring if you can visit a conservation unit.

FRONTIER WITH GUATEMALA – LA HACHADURA-PEDRO DE ALVARADO

The border is at the bridge over the Río Paz, with a filling station and a few shops nearby.

● **Salvadorean immigration**
The immigration facilities are on either side of the bridge; a relaxed crossing.

● **Crossing by private vehicle**
The border crossing is quite straightforward but a private vehicle requires a lot of paperwork (about 2 hrs).

● **Accommodation**
In La Hachadura: **G** *El Viajero*, fans, safe, clean, good value.

● **Transport**
To **San Salvador**, Terminal de Occidente, No 498, 3 hrs; to **Ahuachapán**, by market, No 503, US$0.75, 50 mins.

The beaches NW of Acajutla at Metalío (safe for camping, but no formal place to stay) and **Barra de Santiago** are rec. At Barra de Santiago, 30 km W of Acajutla, the beach is across a beautiful lagoon. A bird sanctuary is being developed on the estuary; nearby is a turtle farm and museum. René Carmona of *Ximena's* in San Salvador rents rooms at a rancho here (US$35 pp/day, clean, safe, inc gas stove, maid service, guardian has motor launch for excursions, US$12/hr, US$75/day, closed May-June); transport can be provided from the capital with advance notice (address under San Salvador **Accommodation** reservation required). There are government plans to develop the Isla del Cajete nearby into a tourist complex, to attract Guatemalans. Also rec is Salinitas, scenic, peaceful but too many rocks for safe bathing; a modern tourist complex here contains cabins, restaurants, gardens, pool, and a zoo. **Los Cóbanos** (14 km S of Acajutla – bus from Sonsonate) has seen some improvement. 2 hotels: **D** *Sol y Mar*, T 451-0137, weekends only; **E** *Mar de Plata*, at Punta Remedios, 24 cabins, T 451-3914. *Dive Pacific* (see San Salvador, **Tour companies**) has a guesthouse for clients.

Abraham Ríos runs deep-sea fishing charters, US$180/day, 4 people, English spoken, enquire locally. Fishermen arrange boat trips, negotiate a price.

Reserva Nacional Bosque El Imposible is so called because of the difficulty of getting into it. This 'impossibility' has also helped to preserve some of the last vestiges of El Salvador's flora and fauna on the rocky slopes and forests of the coastal Cordillera de Apaneca. Among the mammals are puma, ocelot, agouti and ant bear; birds include black crested eagle, white hawk and other birds of prey, black and white owl, and woodpeckers; there is also a great variety of reptiles, amphibians and insects, the greatest diversity in the country. There are eight different strata of forest, with over 300 species of tree identified. The park, of 3,130 ha, is managed by the Centro de Recursos Naturales (CEREN) and the Servicio de Parques Nacionales y Vida Silvestre (SPNVS), under the auspices of the Ministerio de Agricultura y Ganadería. The park is maintained by Salvanatura and US Peace Corps volunteers: contact Dora Eugenia Coen/Communications, Pasaje Istmania 315 (77-79 Av Norte), Col Escalón, San Salvador, T/F 223-3620, T 298-4001, messages 223-4225. Access (suitable only for 4WD or hiking) is from the road to La Hachadura, either from the turnoff by the archaeological site of **Cara Sucia** (12 km before La Hachadura), or by two routes leading to San Francisco Menéndez. Cara Sucia is being excavated; it is an Olmec site.

SANTA TECLA TO SANTA ANA

The Pan-American Highway, good dual carriageway road, parallels the old Pan-American Highway, bypassing Santa Ana; toll: US$0.40. The road, with turnoffs for Sonsonate and Ahuachapán, carries on to San Cristóbal on the Guatemalan frontier.

15 km from Santa Tecla, 7 km from the junction with the Sonsonate road, there is a junction to the right. This road forks

immediately, right to Quezaltepeque, left (at *Joya de Cerén* café) to **San Juan Opico**. After a few km on the San Juan road, you cross the railway by the Kimberley-Clark factory; at the railway is *Restaurante Estación Sitio del Niño* (seafood, steak, local dishes, in an old station, open from 0730 Tues-Sun, horseriding tours to San Andrés – see below – contact *Jaguar Tours* in San Salvador, US$60-70/day pp inc lunch and a/c transport). After a girder bridge across a river is a grain store, beside which is **Joya de Cerén**. This is a major archaeological site, not for spectacular temples, but because this is the only known site where ordinary Mayan houses have been preserved having been buried by the ash from the nearby Laguna Caldera volcano about 600 AD. Buildings and construction methods can be clearly seen; a painted book and household objects have been found. All the structures are covered with protective roofing. The site has a small but good museum, café, toilets and car park, entrance US$3 (El Salvador and Central American nationals US$0.80), open Tues-Sun, parking charge US$0.60. Children offer replicas for sale. Bus from San Salvador No 108, Terminal de Occidente, to San Juan, US$0.45, 1 hr.

SAN ANDRES

There is an excavated archaeological site at **San Andrés**, half-way between Santa Tecla and Coatepeque on the estate of the same name. (Its full name is La Campana de San Andrés.) A group of low structures stand in the valley (Structure 5, the furthest from the entrance, is closed because of erosion). There are good views of the nearby hills. Colonial era ruins about 1 km away are being excavated. The site is open 0900-1700, Tues-Sun, US$3; it is popular for weekend picnics, otherwise it is quiet. There is a café. It is at Km 32.5 on the Pan-American Highway, just after the Hilasal towel factory (bus 201 from Terminal de Occidente, US$0.80). A walkway between San Andrés and Joya de Cerén, 5 km through a Mayan Park, is due for completion in late 1997.

LAGO DE COATEPEQUE

At El Congo, some 13 km before Santa Ana a short branch road leads (left) to **Lago de Coatepeque**, a favourite weekend resort with good sailing and fishing near the foot of Santa Ana volcano. The surroundings are exceptionally beautiful. Many weekend homes line the N and E shore, making access to the water difficult, but there are public *balnearios*: *Casa Blanca* and *Recreativa El Jordán*, US$0.05 pp, parking US$0.25. Two islands in the lake can be visited, Anteojo close to the hotels and Teopán on the far side from the hotels (private, with nature reserve, archaeological excavations and hiking trails, permission from owners for ferry across and hiking, weekdays only, T 226-0301 at least 5 days in advance and ask Donald Lee to contact owner; no access at weekends). Launches charge US$5.75-8.60 pp for lake trips, depending on the size of the group, or about US$15 for 2 hrs (negotiate with the owners). Cerro Verde is easily reached in 90 mins by good roads through impressive scenery (see below). *Fiesta*, Santo Niño de Atocha, 25-29 June.

● **Accommodation** B *Del Lago*, T 446-9511, San Salvador T 279-1143, F 224-5875, manager Lic Lucio Bastillo speaks English and German, pool, old (cheaper) and new rooms, good beds, nice setting, beautiful lakeside view, good restaurant (try the crab soup), very busy on Sun, rec (for midweek specials, contact Donald Lee in San Salvador); B *Torremolinos*, T 446-9437, F 441-1859, in Santa Ana C J Mariano Méndez Pontiente 33, T 440-4836, F 440-4130, pool, good rooms (a couple with hot showers), restaurant, bar, good service, boating excursions, pool, popular at weekends with music, lively; C *Amacuilco*, 300m from Antel, very helpful manager (Sandra), 6 rooms (but avoid those which overlook the kitchen), reductions for weekly and monthly stays, art gallery, offers marimba classes and Spanish and Nahuat lessons, all meals available, live music Fri and Sat night, pool, good view, secure, rec, boat excursions on lake, tours arranged from US$30-40/day (US$100 d/week inc breakfast and dinner); in Santa Ana, contact through *Almacén Silueta*, Av Independencia Sur 11 b, 1 block from *Pollo Campero*, T 441-0608, Amita Gutiérrez;

basic, dirty rooms next to *Torremolinos*, towards the Antel office, **F**, unfriendly; also **F**, in white house across the street from *Amacuilco*, friendly. Plenty of *comedores*.

● **Post & telecommunications** Antel, 50m from *Torremolinos*, good phone service, helpful, local and long distance, cash only, can arrange for messages to be left here (US$0.60).

● **Buses** From Santa Ana, hourly bus 220 'El Lago' to the lake, US$0.40; from San Salvador, bus 201 to El Congo (bridge at Km 50) on Pan American Highway, US$1, then pick up the 220 bus to the lake, US$0.45. Other buses to Guatemala may also stop at El Congo, check. Taxi from Santa Ana US$10.

CERRO VERDE

From El Congo another road runs S, above the E shore of Lago Coatepeque. When you reach the summit, a paved road branches right, climbing above the S end of the lake to **Cerro Verde** (2,030m) with its fine views of the **Izalco volcano** (1,910m). The road up to Cerro Verde is lined with beautiful flowers. A 30-min walk, including a nature trail, around the Cerro Verde National Park leads to a series of miradores with views of Lago Coatepeque and Santa Ana volcano, with Finca San Blas at its foot. There is an orchid garden. Cerro Verde can be very busy at weekends. For the best view of Izalco go in the morning, but in the afternoon clouds around the cone can be enchanting.

The volcano, as can be seen from the lack of vegetation, is recent. Historical records show that activity began in the 17th century as a sulphurous smoke vent, but in Feb 1770, violent eruptions formed a cone which was in more or less constant activity until 1957. It was known as the "Lighthouse of the Pacific" because of the regularity of the fiery explosions. There was a small eruption in 1966 through a blowhole on the SE slope evidenced by two 1000m lava flows. Since that time, it was been quiescent.

To climb Izalco: a path leads off the road (signposted) just below the car park on Cerro Verde. In 20-30 mins descend to the saddle between Cerro Verde and Izalco, then 1-1½ hrs up (steep, but manageable); 3 hrs from base, go in a group, thieves congregate at the base. Beware of falling rocks when climbing. A spectacular view from the top. For a quick descent, find a rivulet of soft volcanic sand and half-slide, half-walk down in 15 mins, then 45 mins to 1 hr back up the saddle. This 'cinder running' needs care, strong shoes and a thought for those below. You are probably also aiding erosion.

Try to ensure that low cloud is not expected before planning to go.

● **NB** Well-dressed, bilingual thieves operate around Cerro Verde and Izalco. Don't give personal details (eg itinerary, room number) to smart, English-speaking strangers and refuse offers of assistance, meals, etc. If driving to Cerro Verde, take care late afternoon/evening as assaults have been reported. PNC (police) can arrange escorts for small groups on Izalco; do not go alone.

● **Accommodation & services** The fine **A3-B** *Hotel Montaña* (T 271-2434, F 222-1208, or reserve through Corsatur in San Salvador) at the top of Cerro Verde was originally built so that the international set could watch Izalco in eruption; unfortunately, the eruptions stopped just as the hotel was completed. The hotel is due for renovation in 1997-98. Room prices vary according to view and which meals are taken; from Mon-Thur room price is **C** without meals (better anyway to pay for meals separately); very comfy rooms with views of Izalco volcano or forest, huge fireplaces, but no wood available for fires, and can be cold at night; relaxing. There is a restaurant and café; food is good, at fairly reasonable prices. Non-residents pay US$0.60 to enter hotel. To enter the Cerro Verde park costs US$0.60 (has to be paid before you can reach the hotel), car park (US$0.60). There are cabañas for rent, US$20 a night at weekends, US$9 in the week without water, and camping (tent or motorhome) is permitted, good (ask the warden if you need basics for preparing meals). About 3 km before the park is **E** *Miramundo*, hotel and *tienda*.

The junction 8 km from the top of Cerro Verde can be reached by the Santa Ana-Sonsonate bus, No 248 (US$1), leaving Santa Ana at 0600 and 1530 with several others in between. It can also be caught at El Congo, or, in the other direction, from the highway outside Izalco town; from the junction, hitch up to the National Park and hotel (no problem, especially at weekends). 3 buses daily go up to Cerro Verde: two buses from El Congo arrive at the park at 0630 and 1700-1730, one from Santa Ana arrives at 1230 (dep Santa Ana 1030). On Sat and Sun am there are direct buses from Santa Ana to Cerro Verde car park. Check carefully the times of the buses leaving Cerro Verde in the afternoon.

Three quarters of the way to Cerro Verde, a track branches off to the right to Finca San Blas (also can be reached on foot from Cerro Verde car park, 20 mins). From there it is 30 mins down to the saddle and a 1½ hrs walk straight up the very impressive **Santa Ana volcano**. There are four craters inside one another; the newest crater has a lake and fuming columns of sulphur clouds. You can walk around the edge and down on to the ledge formed by the third crater (beware of the fumes). Views can be hazy in the dry season. A rough map is available at reception in *Hotel Montaña*.

SANTA ANA

Santa Ana, 55 km from San Salvador and capital of its Department, is the second largest city in the country (*pop* 208,322; *alt* 776m). The intermont basin in which it lies on the NE slopes of Santa Ana volcano is exceptionally fertile. Coffee is the great crop, with sugar-cane a good second. The city is the business centre of western El Salvador. There are some fine buildings, the neo-gothic **cathedral**, and several other churches, especially El Calvario, in neo-classical style. Of special interest is the classical **Teatro Nacional** on the N side of the plaza, originally completed in 1910, now being restored and one of the finest in Central America. A guide (small charge) will show you round on weekdays. A donation from the Organization of

Hotels:
1. La Libertad
2. Livingston
3. Hospedaje San Miguel

0   150
metres

American States is being used to replace the seating. *Fiesta* 1-26 July, Fiestas Julias.

Excursions

On the W of the town is the El Trapiche swimming pool. Bus 51 or 50 goes to **Turicentro Sihuatehuacán**, on city outskirts; US$0.60 admission to pools, café, park, etc, same price for parking, but run down.

Local information
● Accommodation

B-C *Internacional*, 25 C Poniente y 10 Av Sur, T 440-0810, with bath, restaurant in same building, safe parking for motorcycles, TV, not the most conventional of hotels; **B-C** *Sahara*, 3 C Poniente y 10 Av Sur, T/F 447-8865, good service.

D *Roosevelt*, 8 Av, Sur y 5 C Poniente, T 441-1702, rooms with bath and cold water, choose between noisy monkeys at the front, cockroaches in back rooms, meals available when full, free parking.

E *Colonial*, 8 Av Norte 2, clean, helpful, good breakfasts for less than US$1, a little noisy, not rec for single women; **E** *La Libertad*, nr cathedral, 4 C Oriente 2, T 441-2358, with bath, friendly, clean, helpful, safe car park across the street US$2 for 24 hrs; **E** *Livingston*, 10 Av Sur, 29, T 441-1801, with bath, cheaper without, cheap and clean; **E** *Pensión Lux*, on Parque Colón, Av JM Delgado No 57, T 440-3383, large rooms; **E** *Monterrey*, 10 Av Sur, 9-11, T 441-2758, without bathroom; *Venecia*, 11 C Poniente between 14 and 16 Av Sur, T 441-1534; **E** *Viajero*, 6 Av, 2 blocks N of main plaza, T 441-1090, clean, friendly.

F *Hospedaje San Miguel*, Av J Matías Delgado 26, T 441-3465, cheaper without bath, basic, clean, car park; **F** 3 *hospedajes* S of Parque Colón.

G *Hospedaje Tikal*, 10 Av Sur y C 9, clean, quiet, large rooms, free chilled drinking water.

● Places to eat

Kiyomi, 4 Av Sur between 3 and 5C, good food and service, clean, reasonable prices; *Los Horcones*, on main square next to church, like a jungle lodge inside, good cheap meals; *Las*

Canoas, 2 blocks from cathedral, gourmet meals at fair prices; *Parrillada Texana*, Av Independencia Sur, good grilled chicken, garlic bread and salads, good value; *Kyjau*, C Libertad nr park, Chinese, large portions, good; *Talitunal*, 3 Av Sur, 2 blocks below Antel, vegetarian, open 0900-1900, attractive, good lunch, owner is a doctor and expert on medicinal plants; *Kikos*, Av Independencia Sur, nr 5 C, good chicken and pizza; *Veras Pizza*, Av Independencia Sur, good salad bar; *Pollo Campero*, Av Independencia Sur, accepts US dollars; *Pupusería Memita*, 25 C Poniente, rec for fresh *pupusas* made to order. It is cheaper and usually good value to eat in *comedores*, or at the market in front of the cathedral. There are also food stalls on the side of the square. Look for excellent pineapples in season. Everything closes at about 1900

● **Banks & money changers**
All banks will change dollars cash; for TCs you have to go to San Salvador. **Banco Salvadoreño**, English spoken. Black market around the banks (called Wall Street by the locals!).

● **Entertainment**
Two dance clubs on 15 C Poniente nr 4 Av Sur, good music Wed-Sat, dinner served.

El Gato, Av Independencia Sur 24, theatrical cooperative, T 447-6264 for programme, coffee house atmosphere.

● **Laundry**
Lavandería Solución, 7C Poniente 29, wash and dry US$2.50/load, ironing service, rec.

● **Post & telecommunications**
Post Office: 7 C y 2 Av Sur.

● **Useful addresses**
Police: emergency T 121.

● **Transport**
Buses No 201 from Terminal del Occidente, San Salvador, US$0.60, 1 hr, every 10-15 mins, 0400-1830. Buses (Melva, Pezzarossi and others) leave frequently from 25 C Poniente y 8 Av Sur (T 440-3606) for Guatemala City, full fare as from San Salvador, 4-4½ hrs inc border stops. Alternatively there are local buses to the border for US$0.45; they leave from the market. Frequent buses to Metapán and frontier at Anguiatú.

The border with Guatemala is 30 km from Santa Ana along the paved Pan-American Highway (rough surface, but being repaired 1997) at **San Cristóbal** (**F** *Hotel El Paso*, basic, friendly).

FRONTIER WITH GUATEMALA – SAN CRISTOBAL

This is the Carretera Panamericana crossing to Guatemala taken by the international buses and much heavy traffic. There is an Inguat office on the Guatemalan side.

● **Salvadorean immigration**
The border is open from 0600-2000. Some inconsistency has been reported about fees charged but, in general, expect standard procedures.

● **Transport**
To Santa Ana, No 236, US$0.60, 1½ hrs, 0400-1800.

TEXISTEPEQUE

Texistepeque, 17 km N of Santa Ana on the road to Metapán, has an 18th century baroque church, with *fiestas* on 23-27 Dec and 15 January. The town is on the San Salvador-Sonsonate-Metapán railway, on which there are passenger services. A railway runs eastwards along the S bank of the Río Lempa to Aguilares on Troncal del Norte (San Salvador – Cerrón Grande reservoir – El Poy, on the border with Honduras, see next section). A passenger service of sorts operates, every day except Sun. About 7 km E is the starting point for river trips on the Río Lempa (contact Carolina Nixon at Corsatur; her company, *Ríos Tropicales* has equipment rental, T/F 223-2351 San Salvador – tours service temporarily suspended).

CHALCHUAPA

16 km from Santa Ana, on the road to Ahuachapán is **Chalchuapa** (*pop* 34,865; *alt* 640m). President Barrios of Guatemala was killed in battle here in 1885, when trying to reunite Central America by force. There is some good colonial-style domestic building; the church of Santiago Apóstol is particularly striking, almost the only one in El Salvador which shows strong indigenous influences (being restored 1997-98). (*Fiestas* 18-21 July, Santiago Apóstol, and 12-16 Aug, San Roque.) See the small but picturesque lake, and the **Tazumal** ruin next to the cemetery in

Chalchuapa, built about AD 980 by the Pipil Indians but with its 14-step pyramid now, alas, restored in concrete. The site has been occupied since 5000 BC and in the simple museum are the artefacts found in the mud under the lake. There are very interesting bowls used for burning incense, intricately decorated with animal designs. Some of the exhibits of the Museo de Archeologia in San Salvador, damaged in the 1996 earthquake, are temporarily on show here. The ruin, which is open 0900-1200 and 1300-1730, closed on Mon, costs US$3 entry and is only 5 mins' walk from the main road. Near the ruins is a souvenir shop, *Tienda Tazumal* (selling good reproductions and jewellery, dollars accepted or changed) run by Elida Vides de Jaime, 11 Av Sur 31, T 444-0803, on the main road. Elida's husband can act as a guide to Tazumal and other nearby ruins, helpful, speaks some English. Bus (No 236) from Santa Ana, 30 mins, US$0.25.

● **Accommodation & places to eat**
E *Gloria*, Av 2 de Abril, T 444-0131. A new hotel is under construction. Opposite the entrance to the ruins is *Manhattan Bar and Grill*, 7 Av Sur y 5 C Oriente 32, T 444-0074, has disco 7 days a week, good service, clean, helpful. Also **5** *Calles* by entrance to ruins.

● **Embassies & consulates** Guatemalan consul in Chalchuapa, Av Club de Leones Norte, between Primero and C Ramón Flores – unmarked blue house, knock for attention.

The road continues 12 km W to Atiquizaya a small, quiet town with one Hospedaje (**F**), several good *pupuserías* (1600-2100) and *Restaurante Atiquizaya*, 1 km at intersection with main highway to Ahuachapán, good. Also at the intersection a sculptor in metal exhibits and sells his work (Km 89). A *turicentro* is being developed 5 km W at hot springs (park, camping, turn off road to Ahuachapán at Finca La Labor, Km 94, 7 km on dirt road); at Cataratas del Río Malacachupán is a 50m waterfall into a lagoon, very beautiful, 1 km hike to get there. Nearby is Volcán Chingo on the Guatemalan border. For a local guide, contact José Luis Estrada, who speaks English, T 444-1672 (not Sun, or via Donald Lee in San Salvador) and who arranges long-term accommodation (**E-F**) in the area, English teachers welcome (will trade lessons Spanish-English). Camping is possible. All Ahuachapán buses stop in the central parque.

AHUACHAPAN

(*Pop* 80,000; *alt* 785m) The capital of its Department, is 35 km from Santa Ana. It is a quiet town with low and simple houses, but an important distribution centre. Coffee is the great product. Like many places in the area, it draws the mineral water for its bath-house from some hot springs near the falls of Malacatiupán, nearby. You can bathe in the river above the falls, and camp in the vicinity. The falls are over 70m high and, especially in the early morning, steam impressively. Downstream, where the hot water merges with the cold of the Río Frio, steam rises everywhere. This can be reached by bus (hourly most of the day) or 4WD along a 5 km dirt road from Atiquizaya (see above), or the same distance N of Ahuachapán. Pick-ups can be hired with driver for US$9/day. Power is generated from the falls of Atehuezián on the Río Molino, which cascade prettily down the mountain-side. See also the *ausoles* – geysers of boiling mud with plumes of steam and strong whiffs of sulphur, which have been harnessed to produce electric power.

The *ausoles* are interesting – an area of ground which is warm to the touch. They are used for generating electricity; only the smallest remains uncovered by drums and pipes. One can take a bus from Ahuachapán to El Barro, take a taxi or walk the 5 km to the area. Permission to visit the power station can be obtained from the barracks on the hill overlooking the town as the site is guarded by the Army.

● **Accommodation B** *Casa Blanca*, 2 Av Norte y Gerardo Barrios, T/F 443-2505, 2 rooms a/c, clean, good, rec (owner's husband is a doctor, Dr Escapini); **B-C** *El Parador*, Km 103, 1½ km W of town, hotel and restaurant, a/c, good service, motel-style, relaxing, helpful owner, Sr Nasser, rec, buses to border stop outside, T/F 443-0331, T 443-1637; **E** *San José*, 6 C Poniente, opp the park, with bath, clean, friendly, parking but run down; **F** *Hospedaje Granada*, 3 blocks down from plaza by market, shared bath, clean, friendly; also **F**: *La Ahuachapaneca*; *Hospedaje San Juan* guest house; *Hospedaje Milagro*, clean, basic, nr bus station.

● **Places to eat** One can get good meals at *Restaurant El Paseo*, *Restaurant Tanya* and *El Parador*. Good and inexpensive meals at *Mixta's Restaurante*; *Pastelería María*, good cakes and biscuits. *Super Selectos* supermarket in Centro Comercial at entrance to town.

● **Buses** Ahuachapán is 100 km from the capital by bus 202 from San Salvador (US$0.90), every 20 mins 0430-1830, 0400-1600 to the capital, 2 hrs via Santa Ana. Microbuses to border in front of Almacén NW corner of parque, US$0.45, 25 mins, slower buses same price.

Tacuba is an indigenous town, 15 km NE of Ahuachapán. There are large, interesting colonial ruins at the entrance to town (open 0900-1600, look for guard, or visit Casa de la Cultura office, *Concultura*, some 3,000m on main street N, interesting photos on display same hours, closed 1230-1330). The town is near the northern entrance of El Imposible National Park; access by hiking or 4WD in the dry season, with permit only. There are no lodgings in town, but *Café Tacuba*, 500m above Casa de la Cultura, serves excellent food, fresh vegetables, inexpensive (Lydia de González, daughter Mónica and husband – US citizen – speak English), 0800-1600. The town is worth a visit, especially for the scenic ride through coffee plantations en route. Buses, US$0.60, 45 mins, rough road, leave the terminal in Ahuachapán every 30 mins, 0500-1530, return 1630-1700, via Ataco.

A road runs NW through the treeless Llano del Espino, with its small lake, and across the Río Paz into Guatemala.

FRONTIER WITH GUATEMALA – LAS CHINAMAS-VALLE NUEVO

This is a busy crossing as it is the fastest road link from San Salvador (117 km from Las Chinamas) to Guatemala City, 121 km (via the Santa Ana bypass, then to Ahuachapán and on to the border).

● **Salvadorean immigration**
A straightforward crossing: quick service if your papers are ready.

● **Crossing by private vehicle**
If driving with non-Central American licence plates, expect about 45 mins for formalities, hire a *tramite* (young boy) to hustle your papers through, US$2-3. Your vehicle will probably be searched by antinarcotics officers (DOAN); do not refuse as your papers will be checked again 300m into El Salvador. PNC (police) are courteous and efficient.

● **Exchange**
Coming from Guatemala, cash your quetzales at the border, check what you are given. Change money with the women in front of the ex-ISTU office next to Aduana, they are honest. Good quetzal-dollar rate, cash only.

● **Transport**
300m above immigration, frequent buses to Ahuachapán, No 265, US$0.45, 25 mins. Change there to No 202 to San Salvador. Between 0800 and 1400 you may try for a space on one of the international pullmans, negotiate with drivers' aide, about US$3.50 to capital

Between Ahuachapán and Sonsonate is **Apaneca**, founded by Pedro de Alvarado in 1543 (*pop* 12,000; *alt* 1,450m, the highest town in the country, *average temperature* 18°C). It is 90 km from San Salvador, 29 km from Las Chinamas, with a colonial centre, one of the oldest parochial churches in the country, a traditional parque and a municipal market selling fruit, flowers and handicrafts. Other local industries include coffee, flowers for export and typical furniture. There are two small lakes nearby to the N, Laguna Verde and Laguna Las Ninfas, whose crater-like walls are profusely covered in tropical forest. This is the Cordillera de Apaneca, part of the narrow highland belt running SE of

Ahuachapán. The lakes are popular with tourists. It is possible to swim in the former, but the latter is too shallow and reedy. There is also a beautiful natural pool called the Balneario de Azumpa. (Accommodation at Apaneca, **A3** *Cabañas de Apaneca*, T 279-0099, F 452-2536; *Apaneca Tennis Club*; also two restaurants, *La Casona* and *La Casa de Mi Abuela*.) Local buses run some distance away, leaving one with a fairly long walk. Laguna Verde can be reached by walking from Apaneca to Cantón Palo Verde and Hoyo de Cuajuste, then a further km from where the road ends. South of Apaneca is the Cascada del Río Cauta (take bus 216 from Ahuachapán towards Jujutla, alight 3 km after the turn-off to Apaneca, then walk along trail for 300m).

9 km W of Ahuachapán near the village of **Los Toles** are the Tehuasilla falls, where the Río El Molino falls 60m (take bus 293 from Ahuachapán to Los Toles, then walk 1 km, or go by car).

METAPAN

Metapán (32 km N of Santa Ana; *pop* 51,800) is about 10 km NE of Lago de Güija. Its colonial baroque cathedral of San Pedro is one of the very few to have survived in the country (it was completed by 1743). The altarpieces have some very good silver work (the silver is from local mines) and the façade is splendid. (*Fiesta patronal*, San Pedro Apóstol, 25-29 June.) Lots of easy walks with good views towards Lago de Metapán and further on Lago de Güija. There are many lime kilns and a huge cement plant.

● **Accommodation B** *San José*, Carretera Internacional Km 113, nr bus station, T 442-0556/0320, a/c, quiet, cable TV, safe parking, good, restaurant on ground floor (Sra García, the manager, will help with transport to Montecristo); **F** *Ferrocarril*, W end of town; **F** *Hospedaje Central*, 2 Av N y C 15 de Septiembre, with bath, clean friendly, popular.

● **Places to eat** *Rincón del Pelon*, best in town, helpful, friendly; *Comedor Carmencita*, 2 Av N, clean, popular, basic meals but cheap.

● **Buses** From Santa Ana No 235, US$0.80, 1 hr. If driving San Salvador-Metapán, a new bypass skirts Santa Ana.

MONTECRISTO NATIONAL NATURE RESERVE

A mountain track from Metapán gives access to El Salvador's last remaining cloud forest. There is an abundance of protected wildlife. This now forms part of El Trifinio, or the International Biosphere 'La Fraternidad', administered jointly by Guatemala, Honduras and El Salvador. Near the top of Cerro Montecristo (2,418m), which is the point where the three frontiers meet, there is an orchid garden, with over 100 species (best time to see them in flower is early Spring – escorted visits only), an orchard and a camping ground in the forest. The views are stunning as is the change of flora and fauna with the altitude. For information, contact Sr Randolfo Cabezas, Secretary international relations, area Metapán, co-ordinator on El Trifinio with EU, T 442-0278, Spanish only.

● **Access** It is 20 km from Metapán to the park. It takes 1 1/2-2 hrs to go up, less to return. The trails to the summit take 1 1/2 hrs. Park employees escort visitors, best Mon-Fri; admission is paid 5 km before the park, US$1.25 pp, plus US$3 for vehicle. 4WD is necessary in the wet season (mid-May to mid-Oct). Camping is permitted. To hire 4WD and driver costs US$45 return, 7 hrs; eg Sr Francisco Xavier Monterosa, C 15 de Septiembre Casa 40, T 442-0373, c/o Isaac Monterosa.

If planning to walk in the hills near Metapán, seek local advice and do not walk alone.

A good paved road runs from Metapán to the Guatemalan frontier at **Anguiatú**. 3 1/2 km out of Metapán on this road is a hotel, **E** *Montecristo*, with 7 rooms.

FRONTIER WITH GUATEMALA – ANGUIATU

This is normally a quiet border crossing except when there are special events at Esquipulas in Guatemala.

● **Salvadorean immigration**
The usual requirements apply; relaxed crossing.

● **Exchange**
Good rates reported.

● **Transport**
To Santa Ana, No 235A, US$0.80, 1¾ hrs. To Metapán 40 mins, US$0.25.

This is the best route from San Salvador to NW Guatemala, Tikal and Belize but there is an alternative through Honduras (see under El Poy, page 840).

LAGO DE GÜIJA

On the Guatemalan border, the lake 16 km by 8, is very beautiful and dotted with small islands, but it is not easy to reach. A new dam at the lake's outlet generates electricity for the western part of the country. It is possible to walk round parts of the lake, but there is no proper track and fences reach down to the water's edge. Ask permission to enter the hiking trails; vehicle access is difficult. Boat trip to Isla Tipa, once a sacred Maya site, may be arranged through *Amacuilco Guest House* at Lago de Coatepeque. Ask directions to the Cerro de Figuras where there are interesting rock drawings. Special excursions may be available through *Jaguar Tours* in San Salvador. The border with Guatemala passes through the lake so there is the chance that you may have to account for your presence there. Carry a copy of your passport and entry stamp in case you are questioned. Bus 235 from Santa Ana, US$0.55, 1 hr.

Northern El Salvador

T HE ROUTE FROM San Salvador to Western Honduras passes through the delightful handicraft centre of La Palma.

SAN SALVADOR TO WESTERN HONDURAS

There was much guerrilla and counter-insurgency activity in the northern areas, but there is now freedom of movement. The Troncal del Norte (Ruta CA 4) is paved throughout; the first 12 km, due N to Apopa are autopista, then it is poor in parts, some areas of gravel, lots of potholes for the last 30 km. 1 hr 45 mins by car to La Palma, thereafter 11 dusty km to the border at El Poy.

WARNING Most, if not all, the mines laid during the Civil War have been cleared. However, if you are visiting the remoter areas, especially on foot, seek local advice.

APOPA

(*Pop* 20,000) A friendly town with a good market and a new shopping centre. It is the junction with a good road to Quezaltepeque (12 km). Bus 38B from San Salvador to Apopa, US$0.15.

TONACATEPEQUE

A paved road runs E from Apopa to **Tona-catepeque**, an attractive small town on a high plateau. It has a small textile industry and is in an agricultural setting. There has been some archaeological exploration of the town's original site, 5 km away. A paved road from Tonacatepeque runs 13 km S to

the Pan-American Highway, some 5 km from the capital. In the other direction, a dry-weather road runs N to Suchitoto (see next section).

3 km beyond Apopa, on CA 4 Km 17, is a finca belonging to the owners of *Ximena's Guest House* in San Salvador. It is being developed as an ecological centre with accommodation (due open July 1997), restaurant and language school (both open). *Restaurante Coma y Punto* is already open, serving local meals (it is planned to serve mostly natural foods, vegetarian meals with own-grown produce). *Lisa's Inn* will accommodate students in the Spanish language school, and a hotel is to be built higher up the hill. Visitors will be able to relax, or help on the finca. It is planned to run tours to Suchitoto, the Cerrón Grande lake for watersports and to Guazapa volcano, which played a prominent part in the civil war. For information, contact René Carmona at *Ximena's* (address under San Salvador **Accommodation**). Any bus from Terminal de Oriente to Aguilares passes the entrance, US$0.25.

21 km from Apopa is **Aguilares**, 4 km beyond which are the ruins of **Cihuatán**. The name means 'place of women' and it was presided over by female royalty. Entry only with permission from the watchman.

CHALATENANGO

The highway passes the western extremity of the Cerrón Grande reservoir. A branch to the right skirts the northern side of the reservoir to Chalatenango, capital of the department of the same name. Rural Chalatenango is mainly agricultural with many remote villages and many non-governmental organizations working in the area. **Chalatenango** (*pop* 30,000; *alt* 450m), 55 km from San Salvador, is a delightful little town with an annual fair and *fiesta* on 24 June. (Bus 125 from Oriente terminal, San Salvador, US$1.10, 2½ hrs.) It is the centre of an important region of traditional livestock farms. Good market and several craft shops eg *Artesanías Chalateca*, for bags, hammocks etc. Two *hospedajes*: **F** *El Nuevo Amanecer*, basic, good views of the Cathedral from the 2nd floor; one unnamed, **F**.

Take special care here if you walk in the countryside: areas off the main road may be mined. Local residents usually (but not always) know which places are safe.

LA PALMA

The main road continues N through Tejutla (beautiful views at Km 72) to **La Palma** (84 km from San Salvador; *municipal pop* 14,770; *alt* 1,100m). A charming village set in pine clad mountains, and well worth a visit. It is famous for its local crafts, particularly the brightly-painted wood carvings and hand-embroidered tapestries. Also produced are handicrafts in clay, metal, cane and seeds. There are a number of workshops in La Palma where the craftsmen can be seen at work and purchases made. Information on the town and surrounding area can be obtained from the Casa de Cultura (Concultura). *Fiesta:* mid or late Feb, Dulce Nombre de María.

● **Accommodation & places to eat A2** *Entre Pinos*, 3 km N of La Palma, reservations T (San Salvador) 270-1151/7, first class resort complex, a/c, pool, cable TV, sauna; **B-C** *Hotel La Palma y Restaurante de la Montaña*, T 335-9012/9202, book ahead for weekends

and holidays, 6 large rooms, clean, with bath, friendly, restaurant limited menu but good, beautiful gardens, ceramics workshop, ample parking, rec, owner is Lic Salvador Zepeda; there is a room for let **F** behind the store where the bus heading S stops, army cots, basic bath, not cheap but you have little choice. Ask around for a room (**E-F**), but not after dark. *La Terraza Cafetería*, 2 blocks from church on road to El Poy, upstairs, open daily 0800-1900, good typical food, cheap, T 335-9015; *El Poyeton*, 1 block down hill from *La Terraza*, 50m on left, local food, also has basic rooms; *La Estancia*, next to Gallery Alfredo Linares (see below), on C Principal, open 0000-2000, good menu, bulletin board, T/F 335-9049; *Del Pueblo*, C Principal 70, owner María Adela friendly, good basic menu, also incorporates *Artesanías El Yute*.

● **Shopping Handicrafts**: *Cooperativa La Semilla de Dios*, Plaza San Antonio, T 335-9098, F 335-9010, the original cooperative founded by Fernando Llort in 1971, huge selection of crafts and paintings, helpful, if unable to go to La Palma, visit *El Arbol de Dios*, end C La Mascota at Av Masferrer Sur, Col Maquilishuat, galleries and tiendas, concerts, cultural events, restaurant, garden, T 224-6200/279-1537, F 279-1538, tours in English, German or Spanish, managers María José Llort and Karl Hoffman; *Barrotienda* in Hotel La Palma; *Palma City*, C Principal behind church, T 335-9135, Sra Alicia Mata, very helpful with finding objects, whether she stocks them or not, wood, ceramics, telas, etc; *Gallery Alfredo Linares*, T 335-9049 (Sr Linares' house), well-known artist whose paintings sell for US$18-75, open daily 0900-1700, friendly, rec (ask in pharmacy if gallery is unattended); *Taller La Campina*, Marta Morena Solís, T 335-9029, good handicrafts, good prices (phone in advance); *Cerámica San Silvestre*, T 335-9202, opp Hotel La Palma, wholesale/retail, good; *Tienda-Taller Marta Solís*, opp Antel, C Principal, good work and prices, T 335-9028; *Artesanías El Típico*, Blanca Sola de Pineda, C Principal, T 335-9210, good; *Artesanías El Tecomate*, Carlos Alfredo Mancía, T 335-9068, F 335-9208, also good work in wood. (The products are also sold in San Salvador, but are much more expensive, eg at *Artesanías La Palma*, Av Sisimiles 2911, Col Miramonte, T 226-9948.)

● **Buses** From San Salvador, Terminal de Oriente, to La Palma, No 119, US$1.25, 3 hrs, last return leaves at 1630.

6 km N of La Palma is the picturesque village of San Ignacio, which has two or three small *talleres* producing handicrafts. 20 mins by bus, US$0.10 each way. Also near La Palma there is a river reached by rough road (14 km), beautiful, and the summit of Miramundo, about 2,000m, with trails and wilderness. Be prepared to hike. Ask in *Hotel La Palma* for a guide (recommended). Most areas are accessible by 4WD.

WESTERN HONDURAN BORDER

The road continues N to the frontier at **El Poy**, for western Honduras, **D** *Hotel Cayahuanca*, Km 93.5, T 335-9464, friendly, good but expensive restaurant.

At Citalá, 1 km off the highway just before El Poy, is a small, basic hotel, *El Trifinio*. The town itself is unexciting. From Citalá an adventurous road goes to Metapán (see page 836). 3-4 buses daily take 3 hrs for the 40 km, rough but beautiful. If driving, use 4WD. There is much reforestation under way in the area.

FRONTIER WITH HONDURAS – EL POY

The crossing is straightforward in both directions but it is best to arrive early in the day. At holiday times it is busy. The border posts are 100m apart.

● **Exchange**
Bargain with money changers at the border for the best rate for lempiras. They are unwilling to offer rates better than 1 colón = 1 lempira (Mar 1997). Cash dollars and TCs can be changed in banks in Nuevo Ocotepeque.

● **Transport**
To San Salvador, Terminal de Oriente, No 119, US$1.35, 3-4 hrs, often crowded, hourly, last bus from the capital 1600. The same bus to La Palma US$0.15, 30 mins.

This route is used from El Salvador to NW Guatemala, crossing this border then into Guatemala at Agua Caliente, 45 mins by car. However, roads are better through Anguiatú with only one frontier to cross. This is a good route for Copán and San Pedro Sula (7 hrs by car San Salvador-Copán, inc 45 mins at border).

Eastern El Salvador

AN AGRICULTURAL zone, the N of which was fiercely disputed between the army and guerrillas. Among the attractions are lakes, volcanoes, beaches and the towns of the Lempa Valley.

SAN SALVADOR TO LA UNIÓN/CUTUCO

There are two roads to the port of La Unión/Cutuco on the Gulf of Fonseca: (i) the Pan-American Highway, 185 km mostly in bad condition, through Cojutepeque and San Miguel; (ii) the Coastal Highway, also paved, running through Santo Tomás, Olocuilta, Zacatecoluca, and Usulután

PAN-AMERICAN HIGHWAY

The road is dual carriageway out of the city, but becomes single carriageway for several km either side of Cojutepeque. These sections are twisty, rough and seem to induce some very bad driving. There is also a great deal of litter along the roadside; look beyond it for fine views. A short branch road (about 2 km beyond Ilopango airport) leads off right to the W shores of Lago de Ilopango. A little further on another road branches off to the lake's N shore.

At San Martín, 18 km from the capital, a paved road heads N to **Suchitoto**, 25 km away on the southern shore of the Embalse **Cerrón Grande**, also known as Lago de Suchitlán. Suchitoto was founded by either the Pipíl or Yaqui Indians and there are archaeological sites in the area. It is a pleasant, small, colonial town with attractive balconied houses and an interesting, restored church. Arts and cultural festivals take place from time to time and there is a small museum, Casa Museo de Alejandro Cotto (open 0830-1600 daily, US$3, guided tour in Spanish). The local cigar factory can be visited. Other local specialities include *salporitas* (made of corn meal) and *chachamuchas*. Try the local *tortillas* filled with meat and beans. **B-C** *La Posada de Suchitlán*, Final 4C Poniente, T/F 335-1164, Swedish-run (Arne and Elinor Dahl) reservation required (in San Salvador F 260-2427, René Carmona or Donald Lee), colonial style, excellent hotel and restaurant, nice view; **F** *Hostal El Viajero*, at entrance to town, very basic. *Café El Obraje*, clean, reasonably priced. Boat trips go to lakeside villages associated with the FMLN in the recent civil war. 12 km away, on the road to Aguilares, a Parque de la Reconciliación is being developed at the foot of Guazapa volcano (contact Cedro – NGO – in San Salvador, T 228-0812, e-mail cedro@euromaya.com).

A road runs E from Suchitoto to Ilobasco (see below), passing Cinquera, whose villagers returned home in Feb 1991 after 6 years displacement, and Tejutepeque.

COJUTEPEQUE

The capital of Cuscatlán Department, 34 km from San Salvador is the first town on the Pan-American Highway (*pop* 31,300). Lago de Ilopango is to the SW. Good weekly market. The town is famous for cigars, smoked sausages and tongues, and its annual fair on 29 Aug has fruits and sweets, saddlery, leather goods, pottery and headwear on sale from neighbouring villages, and sisal hammocks, ropes, bags and hats from the small factories of Cacaopera (Dept of Morazán). There is also a sugar cane festival on 28-31 Jan. That part of town on the Pan-American Highway is full of foodstalls and people selling goods to passengers on the many passing buses.

Excursions Cerro de las Pavas, a conical hill near Cojutepeque, dominates **Lago de Ilopango** and gives splendid views of wide valleys and tall mountains. Its shrine of Our Lady of Fátima draws many pilgrims.

- **Accommodation & places to eat E** *Motel Edén*, with shower; **E** *Hospedaje Viajero*, 1 block E of *Turista* (also hourly rentals); **E** *Turista*, 5 C Oriente 130, beware of extra charges. *Comedor Toyita*, good value; *Comedor Familiar*, good.

- **Buses** No 113 from Oriente terminal in San Salvador, US$0.55; buses leave from here on the corner of the plaza 2 blocks from the main plaza.

From **San Rafael Cedros**, 6 km E of Cojutepeque, a 16-km paved road N to Ilobasco has a branch road E to Sensuntepeque at about Km 13. **Ilobasco** has 48,100 people, many of them workers in clay; its decorated pottery is now mass-produced and has lost much of its charm, but it is worth shopping around; try *Hermanos López* at entrance to town; also José y Víctor Antino Herrera, Av Carlos Bonilla 61, T 332-2324, look for *Kiko* sign, fine miniatures for sale. Hotel in Ilobasco, **D** *La Casona*, C Bernardo Perdomo y 3 Av Sur, T 332-2388, F 332-2050, rec. The area around, devoted to cattle, coffee, sugar and indigo, is exceptionally beautiful. Annual fair: 29 Sept. An all-weather road leads from Ilobasco to the great dam and hydroelectric station of Cinco de Noviembre at the Chorrera del Guayabo, on the Río Lempa. Bus 111 from Terminal de Oriente US$0.80, 1½ hrs. Another road with fine views leads to the Cerrón Grande dam and hydroelectric plant; good excursion by bus or truck. One can climb the hill with the Antel repeater on top for a view of the whole lake created by the dam.

SENSUNTEPEQUE

Sensuntepeque (*pop* 45,000), 35 km E of Ilobasco, is a pleasant town at 900m, in the hills S of the Lempa valley. It is the capital of Cabañas Department, once a great source of indigo. There are some interesting ceremonies during its fair on 4 Dec, the day of its patroness, Santa Bárbara. It can be reached from the Pan-American Highway from near San Vicente.

- **Accommodation E** *Hospedaje Jandy*; **E** *Hospedaje Oriental*.

From Sensuntepeque, the conventional way E is to head back to the Pan-American Highway by bus and continue to San Miguel. It is possible, however, to alight at Dolores (no accommodation), take a truck at dawn to the Río Lempa, cross in a small boat to San Juan, then walk 3 hrs to **San Gerardo**, from where one bus at 1100 goes daily to Ciudad Barrios (see below). Before visiting this area check in advance on conditions, as there was much damage to infrastructure during the war. Roads are appalling and water and electricity are often cut.

4 km from the turning to Ilobasco, further S along the Pan-American Highway at **Santo Domingo** (Km 44 from San Salvador) a paved road leads in 5 km to **San Sebastián** where colourfully patterned cloth hammocks and bedspreads are made. You can watch them being woven on complex looms of wood and string, and can buy from the loom. Behind *Funeraria Durán* there is a weaving workshop. Sr Durán will take you past the

caskets to see the weavers. The Casa de Cultura, about 50m from the plaza, will direct visitors to weaving centres and give information on handicrafts. Before buying, check prices and beware overcharging. Market on Mon. The 110 bus from the Oriente terminal runs from San Salvador to San Sebastián (1½ hrs, US$0.80). There are also buses from Cojutepeque.

SAN VICENTE

61 km from the capital, San Vicente (*pop* 56,800) lies a little SE of the Highway on the Río Alcahuapa, at the foot of the double-peaked **San Vicente volcano** (or **Chinchontepec**), with very fine views of the Jiboa valley as it is approached. The city was founded in 1635. Its pride and gem is El Pilar (1762-69), the most original church in the country. It was here that the Indian chief, **Anastasio Aquino**, took the crown from the statue of San José and crowned himself King of the Nonualcos during the Indian rebellion of 1832. El Pilar stands on a small square 1½ blocks S of the Parque Central. On the latter is the cathedral, whose nave is draped with golden curtains. In the middle of the main plaza is a tall, open-work clock tower, quite a landmark when descending the hill into the city. 3 blocks E of the main plaza is the *tempisque* tree under which the city's foundation charter was drawn up. The tree was decreed a National Monument on 26 April 1984. There is an extensive market area a few blocks W of the centre and hammock sellers can be found on nearby streets. An army barracks takes up an entire block in the centre. A small war museum opened in 1996-97; ask the FMLN office here or in San Salvador. Although all street signs have names, it seems that numbers are preferred. San Vicente has a lovely setting and is a peaceful place to spend a night or two. Carnival day: 1 November.

Excursions

3 km SE of the town is the Balneario **Amapulapa**, a Turicentro. There are three pools at different levels in a wooded setting. US$0.60 entry and US$0.60 parking charges. Unfortunately the site has a bad litter problem and a reputation for petty crime. Women should not walk there alone. Reached by buses 158, 177 and 193 from San Vicente bus station, US$0.10. **Laguna de Apastepeque**, near San Vicente off the Pan-American Highway, is small but picturesque. The Turicentro at the lake costs US$0.60 to enter and to park. Take bus 156 from San Vicente, or 499 from San Salvador. Ask in San Vicente for guides for climbing the volcano.

Local information
● **Accommodation**

D *Central Park*, on Parque Central, T 333-0383, with bath, TV, a/c, phone, good, clean, cheaper with fan, cheaper still without TV, café downstairs; **D** *Villas Españolas*, ½ block from main square, smart, good value, parking.

E *Casa Romero*, after the bridge, first turning on the left, no sign, clean, good meals; **E** *Las Orquídeas*, 1 Av Norte y 3 C Poniente 11, T 333-0900, big rooms, balcony, restaurant.

F *Casa de Huéspedes Germán y Marlon*, T 333-0140 1 block from plaza, shared bath, 1 bed and 1 hammock in each room, very clean and friendly; **F** *Casa de Huéspedes El Turista*, Indalecio Miranda y Av María de los Angeles, fan, good.

● **Places to eat**

Taiwan, Parque Central; *La Casona*, on same plaza as El Pilar church; *Comedor Rivoli*, Av María de los Angeles Miranda, clean, good breakfast and lunches; *Comedor La Cabaña*, just off main plaza; *Casablanca*, good shrimp, steaks, and you can swim in their pool for US$1.15; *Chentino's Pizza*, good fruit juices; *Salón de Té María*, opp barracks, café, cakes and snacks. *Pops*, next to Banco Hipotecario on main plaza, ice cream; *La Nevería*, close to bus station, good ice cream.

● **Banks & money changers**

Banco Hipotecario on main plaza, exchange counter at side, 'leave guns and mobile phones with the guard, please'. Casa de Cambio León, C Dr Antonio J Cañas, off NE corner of main plaza.

● **Post & telecommunications**

Post Office: in Gobernación, which is 2 Av Norte y C 1 de Julio 1823.

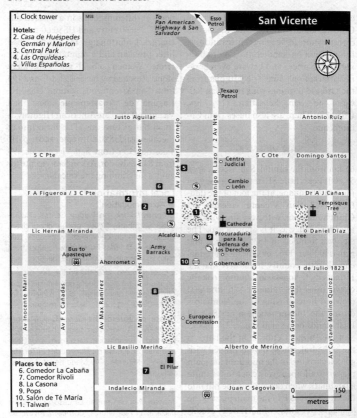

1. Clock tower

Hotels:
2. Casa de Huéspedes Germán y Marlon
3. Central Park
4. Las Orquídeas
5. Villas Españolas

San Vicente

To Pan American Highway & San Salvador

Esso Petrol

N

Texaco Petrol

Justo Aguilar

Antonio Ruiz

5 C Pte

5 C Ote / Domingo Santos

Centro Judicial

Cambio León

F A Figueroa / 3 C Pte

Dr A J Cañas

Tempisque Tree

Lic Hernán Miranda

Cathedral

Alcaldía

Procuraduría para la Defensa de los Derechos

Daniel Díaz

Zorra Tree

Army Barracks

Ahorromet

Gobernación

1 de Julio 1823

European Commission

Lic Basilio Meriño

Alberto de Merino

El Pilar

Places to eat:
6. Comedor La Cabaña
7. Comedor Rivoli
8. La Casona
9. Pops
10. Salón de Té María
11. Taiwan

Indalecio Miranda

Juan C Segovia

0   150
metres

Bus to Apasteque

1 Av Norte
Av José María Cornejo
2 Av Nte
Av Canónigo R Lazo

Av inocente Marín
Av F C Cañadas
Av Max Ramírez
Av María de los Angeles Miranda
Av Pres M A Molina y Cañasco
Av Ana Guerra de Jesús
Av Cayetano Molino Quiroz

Telephones: Antel, 2 Av Norte/Av Canónigo Raimundo Lazo, SE of plaza.

● **Transport**

Bus 116 from Oriente terminal, San Salvador, US$0.90, 1½ hrs, every 10 mins or so. Returning to the capital, catch bus at bus station (Av Victoriano Rodríguez y Juan Crisóstomo Segovia), or outside the Cathedral, or on the road out of town. To **Zacatecoluca**, No 177, US$0.40 from bus station. Buses to some local destinations leave from the street that goes W-E through the market (eg No 156 to **Apasteque**). You have to take 2 buses to get to **San Miguel** (see below), first to the Pan-American Highway (a few km), where there is a bus and food stop, then another on to San Miguel, US$1.30 total.

The Highway (in reasonable condition after San Vicente) used to cross the Río Lempa by the 411m-long Cuscatlán suspension bridge (destroyed by guerrillas in 1983). It now crosses an emergency bridge.

BERLIN

10 km S of the Pan-American Highway is **Berlín**, known for its quality coffee plantations. *Hotel Berlines* and *Villa Hermosa*, both **E**. (Take care if driving in this area, especially after 1300.)

From Berlín there is a road round the N of Volcán de Tecapa to **Santiago de María**, which itself is on a road between the Pan-American and coastal highways (**E** *Villa Hermosa*, 3 Av Norte 4, T 663-0146; bus 309 from Terminal del Oriente, 2½ hrs, US$1.15). Half way is Alegría from which you can visit the **Laguna de Alegría** in the crater of the volcano, fed by both hot and cold springs. (The volcano last erupted in 1878.) The lake level is low during the day but rises at 1600 each afternoon. Local guides charge US$12/day.

SAN MIGUEL

136 km from San Salvador, the capital of its Department, was founded in 1530 at the foot of the volcanoes of **San Miguel** (**Chaparrastique** – which erupted in 1976, and **Chinameca**). San Miguel (*pop* 250,000 approximately) has some very pleasant plazas and a bare 18th century cathedral. The city's theatre dates from 1909, but from the 1960s it was used for various purposes other than the arts. Some silver and gold are mined. It is an important distributing centre. The arid climate all year round makes the region ideal for growing maize, beans, cotton and sisal. Fiesta of the Virgen de la Paz: 3rd Sat in November. A new Metrocentro shopping centre has opened SE of the centre. The Turicentro of Altos de la Cueva is 1 km N; take town bus 60, admission, car parking US$0.60; swimming pools, gardens, restaurants, sports facilities, bungalows for rent US$3.45, busy at weekends. A popular spot is El Copulín, whose warm waters are said to be medicinal; the waters run from a cave with walls of pumice stone, which gives the place an air of mystery. There is a charming church with statues and fountains in its gardens about 16 km away at Chinameca.

Local information
● **Accommodation**
Very few in centre, most on the entrance roads: **A3** *Trópico Inn*, Av Roosevelt Sur 303, T 661-1800, F 661-1399, clean, comfortable, reasonable restaurant, swimming pool, garden.

C *Motel Milián*, Panamericana Km 136, T 661-1970, pool, good value, rec, good restaurant.

D *del Centro*, 8 C Oriente 505, T 661-5473, TV, parking, very nice, rec; **D** *China House*, Panamericana Km 137, T 669-5029, clean, friendly; **D** *Greco*, 10 C Poniente 305, T 661-1411, fan, good food and service, often full weekdays; **D** *Hispanoamericano*, 6 Av Norte y 8 C Oriente, T 661-1202, with toilet and shower, parking, unpleasant.

E *Santa Rosa*, 8 Av Norte y 6 C, good; **E-F** *Caleta*, 3 Av Sur 601, T 661-3233, basic, inexpensive, ample parking, fan, popular with local business travellers, ask directions how to find it.

F pp *Hospedaje Argueta*, 4 C Oriente y 6-8 Av; **F** *Pension Lux*, 4 C Oriente, 6 Av Oriente, reasonable.

Plenty of cheap places nr the bus station, eg **E** *San Rafael*, 6 C Oriente y 10 Av Norte, T 661-4113, with bath, clean, fan, parking; **F** *Migueleña*, 4 C Oriente No 610, very basic but good value, clean, large rooms, towels, bath, fan.

● **Places to eat**
La Puerta del Sol, 3 Av Sur 4 C Poniente, good variety; *El Gran Tejano*, 4 C Poniente, nr cathedral, great steaks; *Chetino's Pizzería*, 5 C Poniente, nr Centro Médico; *Bati Club Carlitos*, 12 Av Norte. There are branches of *Pollo Campero*, all accept dollars, and a *Burger King* and a *Wendy's* for fast food lovers, and a good *Pizza Hut* 2 blocks N of the cathedral. Try *bocadillos de totopostes*, maize balls with either chilli or cheese; also *tustacos*, which are like small tortillas with sugar or honey. Both are delicious and traditional in San Miguel. S towards El Cuco at Km 142.5 is the *La Pema* restaurant, an interesting octagonal structure with the Chaparrastique volcano framed in one of the rear sections, popular, seafood specialities, moderate prices, open 1100-1700, closed Mon, T 667-6055. All buses to El Cuco and to Usulatán will stop there if requested.

● **Airline offices**
Taca, Condominio San Benito, opp *Hotel Trópico Inn*, Av Roosevelt, T 661-1477.

● **Banks & money changers**
Local banks. Open: 0830-1200, 1430-1800. **Banco Cuscatlán** will change TCs, but you must produce receipt of purchase, otherwise, TCs are difficult to change. **Casa de Cambio Lego**, 2 C Poniente, overlooking market.

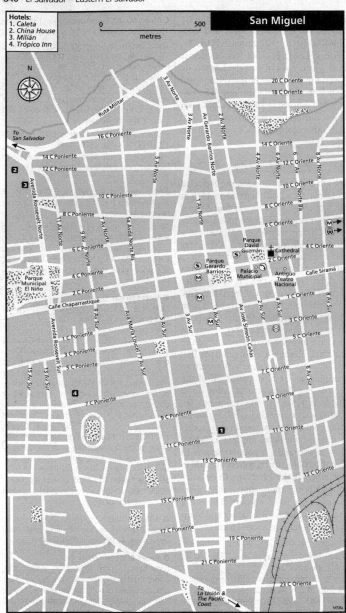

San Miguel

Hotels:
1. Caleta
2. China House
3. Milián
4. Trópico Inn

0   500
metres

N

To
San Salvador →

To
La Unión &
The Pacific
Coast →

Ruta Militar
3 Av Norte
Av Gerardo Barrios Norte
2 Av Norte
5 Av Norte
1 Av Norte
4 Av Norte
6 Av Norte
8 Av Norte
Av Norte Bis

20 C Oriente
18 C Oriente
14 C Oriente
12 C Oriente
10 C Oriente
8 C Oriente
6 C Oriente
4 C Oriente
2 C Oriente
1 C Oriente
3 C Oriente
5 C Oriente
7 C Oriente
9 C Oriente
11 C Oriente
15 C Oriente
23 C Oriente

16 C Poniente
14 C Poniente
12 C Poniente
10 C Poniente
8 C Poniente
6 C Poniente
4 C Poniente
2 C Poniente

Avenida Roosevelt Norte
7 Av Norte
9 Av Norte
5a Avda Norte Bis

Parque
Municipal
El Niño

Calle Chaparrastique

Parque
Gerardo
Barrios

Parque David
Guzmán

Cathedral

Palácio
Municipal

Antiguo
Teatro
Nacional

Calle Siramá

Avenida Roosevelt Sur
15 Av Sur
13 Av Sur
1 C Poniente
3 C Poniente
5 C Poniente
7 C Poniente
9 C Poniente
11 C Poniente
13 C Poniente
15 C Poniente
17 C Poniente
19 C Poniente
21 C Poniente

Avda María Loucel
7 Av Sur
5 Av Sur
3 Av Sur
1 Av Sur
Av José Simeón Cañas
2 Av Sur
4 Av Sur
6 Av Sur
8 Av Sur

MS8a

● **Shopping**
All San Salvador supermarkets have branches here.

● **Useful addresses**
Police: emergency T 121.

● **Transport**
Local Car rental: Uno, Av Roosevelt Sur y C Chaparrastique 701, T 661-7618, emergency 298-1122, unidad 51390.

Air Airport 5 km S of the centre, taxi US$4. Regular daily flights to the capital, see under San Salvador.

Buses No 301 from Oriente terminal, San Salvador (US$2.50, every 30 mins from 0500 to 1630, 2½ hrs). There are also 3 comfortable, express buses daily, US$5, 2 hrs. There are frequent buses to the Honduran border at El Amatillo, US$1.

From San Miguel a good paved road runs S to the Pacific Highway. Go S along it for 12 km, where a dirt road leads to Playa El Cuco (see page 851). Bus 320 from San Miguel, US$1. The climate in this area is good. A mainly paved, reasonable road goes to San Jorge and Usulután: leave the Pan-American Highway 5 km W of San Miguel. The road goes through hills and coffee plantations with superb views of San Miguel volcano. The volcano can be climbed from **Placita** on the road to San Jorge, about 4 hrs up. Ask at Placita for information, a guide costs about US$5.

To the NW are the Indian ruins of **Quelapa** (bus 99, US$0.50), but there is not much to see. From Quelapa a road continues N to **Ciudad Barrios**.

SAN FRANCISCO GOTERA

The capital of Morazán Department can be reached from the Oriente terminal in San Salvador, or from San Miguel (bus 328). Foreigners are not usually allowed beyond here on Route 7 to the Honduran border. Two places to stay: **F** *Hospedaje San Francisco*, Av Morazán 29, T 664-0066, nice garden and hammocks; *Motel Arco Iris*, next door. Beyond San Francisco, the road runs to Jocaitique (there is a bus) from where an unpaved road climbs into the mountains through pine forests to

Sabanetas, near the Honduran border. Accommodation at both Jocaitique and Sabanetas.

CORINTO

22 km NE of San Francisco is **Corinto** with two rock overhangs which show faint evidence of precolumbian wall paintings. They are 20 mins N of the village on foot, just E of the path to the Cantón Coretito. The caves are open 7 days a week; take an early bus, No 327 from San Miguel, US$1.

CIUDAD SEGUNDO MONTES

8 km N of San Francisco Gotera is **Ciudad Segundo Montes**, a group of villages housing 8,500 repatriated Salvadoran refugees (the community is named after one of the six Jesuit priests murdered in Nov 1989). If you would like to visit this welcoming, energetic place, ask for the Ciudad Segundo Montes (CSM) office in San Salvador at the UCA university, or in San Francisco Gotera (T 664-0033). When you get to CSM, ask to be let off at San Luis and go to the Oficina de Recepción. You will be put up in a communal dormitory; meals in *comedores* cost US$1; there is a bath house (spring-fed showers). Free tours of the community are given and there is beautiful hiking.

14 km N of San Francisco is **Delicias de la Concepción**, where fine decorated hammocks and ceramics are made; good prices, helpful, worth a visit. Buses every 20 mins from San Francisco.

PERQUÍN

Further along this road is **Perquín**, which was the guerrilla's 'Capital'. This was the scene of much military activity. War damage is still clearly visible around the town, but all is now peaceful. Thousands who fled the fighting in the 1980s are now returning and rebuilding. The scenery is beautiful. Nearby villages such as Arambala and El Mozote can be visited. At the latter is a memorial to a massacre in 1981. The people of Morazán are more reserved with strangers than in the rest of El Salvador; it is best not to travel alone, or else arrange an escorted tour from FMLN in San Salvador. If travelling on your own, 4WD or pickup rental is advised. There is a very interesting museum, open Tues-Sun 0830-1600, entrance US$1.20, guided tours in Spanish. *Fiesta* 1-5 Oct.

● **Accommodation** **E** pp *Casa de huéspedes Gigante*, 1 km S downhill from the centre (look for sign), T Antel Perquín 661-5077 ext 237, 4 beds per room, clean, cold showers, friendly, meals served, power turned off at 2100.

● **Transport** Bus San Miguel-Perquín, No 332B, US$1.50, 2¾ hrs bus from San Salvador takes 6 hrs. Bus or truck from Ciudad Segundo Montes. Transport back to CSM or San Miguel may be difficult in the afternoons.

FRONTIER WITH HONDURAS – PERQUIN

The Honduran border has been moved, by treaty, to within 3 km N of Perquín; this area has been the subject of disputes and definition problems for many decades. It was one of the basic causes of the 'football war' of 1959 (see reference in the introduction to the Honduras chapter) and there were military confrontations between El Salvador and Honduras in early 1997. There is a border crossing 5 km past the frontier and latest reports indicate that the route to La Esperanza, Honduras, is open. Detailed enquiries about security and conditions should be made before attempting to cross here.

It is another 42 km from San Miguel to the port of La Unión/Cutuco. Shortly before it gets there the Pan-American Highway turns N for 33 km to the Goascarán bridge at **El Amatillo** on the border with Honduras.

To save time when travelling eastwards from San Miguel, take the Ruta Militar NE through Santa Rosa de Lima to the Goascarán bridge at El Amatillo, a total of 58 km.

SANTA ROSA DE LIMA

Santa Rosa (*pop* 27,300) is a charming little place with a wonderful colonial church, set in the hills. There are gold and silver mines. Market on Wed and a curiously large number of pharmacies and shoe shops. The FMLN office here has details about the Codelum project, a refugee camp in Monte Barrios, very interesting. *Fiesta* 22-31 August.

● **Accommodation & places to eat** **F** *Florida*, Ruta Militar, helpful, fairly clean, basic, 3 parking spaces (arrive early); **F** *Hospedaje Gómez*, basic, hammocks, fan, clean; **F** *Hospedaje Mundial*, nr market, rooms OK, with fan, basic, friendly, lots of parking space; **F** *Recreo*, 2 blocks from town centre, friendly, fan, clean; *El Tejano*, behind main church, friendly. Many *comedores*, most popular is *Chayito*, 'buffet', on Ruta Militar, and *Comedor Leyla*, next to bus stop, is good. Unnamed *comedor* on the Pan-American Highway, good and cheap.

● **Banks & money changers** Banco de Comercio will change TCs, also Servicambio nr the church.

● **Buses** To the Honduran border every 15 mins, US$0.50. Direct buses also to San Salvador, No 306, US$3 from 0400 until 1400, 3½ hrs.

FRONTIER WITH HONDURAS – EL AMATILLO

The bridge over the Río Goascarán is the border, with El Amatillo on both sides.

● **Salvadorean immigration**
The border closes at 1700 and may close for 2 hrs at lunchtime. This is a very busy crossing, but is easy for those going on foot.

● **Crossing by private vehicle**
You will be hounded by *tramitadores* offering to help. Accepting one will make it easier to get through but try to choose carefully and monitor progress. Procedures are detailed in **Information for travellers**, **Motoring**. Car searches are thorough at this crossing.

● **Accommodation**
Near the border there are two *hospedajes*, both basic, **F** *Anita* with *comedor* and *Dos Hermanos*.

● **Exchange**
There are many money changers, accepting all Central American currencies and TCs, but beware of short-changing on Nicaraguan and Costa Rican currencies. Good rates for colones to lempiras.

● **Transport**
To San Miguel, No 330, US$1.50, 1 hr 40 mins.
See also Santa Rosa de Lima.

Duty free shops and prices in general are at
present cheaper here than across the border.

LA UNION/CUTUCO

The port of **La Unión/Cutuco** (*pop*
43,000), on the Gulf of Fonseca, handles
half the country's trade.

Excursions

To **Conchagua** to see one of the few old
colonial churches in the country. The
church was begun in 1693, after the original Conchagua had been moved to its
present site after repeated attacks on the
island settlements by the English. *Fiestas
patronales* 18-21 Jan and 24 July. (Good bus
service from La Unión, No 382, US$0.10.)
Conchagua volcano (1,243m) can also be
climbed and is a hard walk, particularly
near the top where stout clothing is useful
against the vegetation. About 4 hrs up and
2 hrs down. You will be rewarded by superb
views over San Miguel volcano to the W
and the Gulf of Fonseca which is bordered
by El Salvador, Honduras and Nicaragua
(where the Cosigüina volcano is prominent) to the E.

One can take an early morning boat to
the Salvadorean islands in the Gulf of Fonseca. These include Isla Zacatillo (about 1
hr), Isla Conchaguita and the largest **Isla
Meanguera** (about 4 km by 7 km) which
takes about 2½ hrs. Meanguera has attractive small secluded beaches with good
bathing, eg Marahual, fringed with palm
trees. You must obtain permission and may
have to leave your passport. The customs
will check your luggage. Take your own
provisions, although there is excellent seafood, lobster, shark steaks, etc, available
from fishermen. There are no official
hospedajes, but locals will allow you to camp
and may offer a room (better to arrange in
La Unión before you arrive). Launches
leave La Unión between 0900 and 1200,
back very early, 0200 Mon and Fri from
Marahual beach, cost US$1. For informa-

tion of excursions to the islands, contact
Carolina Nixon through Corsatur in San
Salvador, otherwise go to *Hotel El Pelícano*
and enquire. Lots of local boatmen offer
trips; negotiate a price.

You can reach El Tamarindo on the
mainland coast (see below) from La
Unión, bus 383, US$0.50. Also from La
Unión, the ruins of Los Llanitos can be
visited.

Local information
● **Accommodation**
C *Centroamérica*, 1C Oriente between 1-3 Av,
T 664-4029, with fan, more with a/c, noisy.

E *El Pelícano*, Final C Principal El Hüisquil,
T 664-4649, 20 rooms; **E** *San Carlos*, opp railway station, good meals available.

F *Hospedaje El Dorado*, 1 block from plaza,
shared bath, nice rooms with fan, some with
bath, very clean, rec; opp *Hospedaje Annex
Santa Marta*, a bit further away from plaza is
E *San Francisco*, T 664-4159, clean, friendly,
some rooms with hammocks and fan, safe
parking, noisy, but OK; **F** *Hospedaje Annex
Santa Marta*, with shower and fan, not bad; **F**
Miramar, good; *Hospedaje Santa Rosa*.

● **Places to eat**
La Patia, for fish; *Comedores Gallego* and
Rosita rec. *Comedor Tere*, Av Gen Menéndez
2.2, fairly good; *Amanacer Marino*, beautiful
view of the bay. Bottled water is impossible to
find, but 'agua helada' from clean sources is sold
(US$0.05 a bag).

● **Banks & money changers**
Exchange at *Cafetín Brisas del Mar*, 3 Av Norte
y 3 C Oriente. **Banco Agrícola Comercial** for
US$ cash and TCs. Black market sometimes in
centre.

● **Security**
Some gang (*mara*) activity has been reported
here (1997).

● **Useful addresses**
Customs: 3 Av Norte 3.9.
Immigration: at 3 C Oriente 2.8.

● **Transport**
Road Bus: Terminal is at 3 C Poniente (block
3); to San Salvador, No 304, US$2, 4 hrs, many
daily, direct or via San Miguel, one passes the
harbour at 0300. (No 320 to San Miguel
US$0.45). Bus to Honduran border at El Ama-
tillo, No 353, US$1.65.

Ferry There is no longer a ferry to Puntarenas (Costa Rica). It may be possible to take a cargo boat to Costa Rica; ask the captains in Cutuco. Outboards cross most days from La Unión to Potosí (Nicaragua), weather permitting. You must get your exit permission in La Unión. Make arrangements 1 day ahead, and check at customs office. There is reportedly a boat to Honduras, but it is easier to go by land.

COASTAL HIGHWAY

This is the second road route, running through the southern cotton lands. It begins on a 4-lane motorway to Comalapa airport. The first place of any importance after leaving the capital is (13 km) **Santo Tomás**. There are Indian ruins at **Cushu-lulitán**, a short distance N.

Beyond, a new road to the E, rising to 1,000m, runs S of Lago de Ilopango to join the Pan-American Highway beyond Cojutepeque.

10 km on from Santo Tomás is **Olo-cuilta**, an old town with a colourful market on Sun under a great tree. Good church. (Both Santo Tomás and Olocuilta can be reached by bus 133 from San Salvador.)

The highway to the airport crosses the Carretera Litoral (CA 2) near the towns of San Luis Talpa and Comalapa. The coastal highway goes E, through Rosario de la Paz, across the Río Jiboa and on to Zacatecoluca.

COSTA DEL SOL

Just after Rosario, a branch road to the S leads to La Herradura (Bus No 153 from Terminal del Sur to La Herradura, US$0.90, 1½ hrs) and the Playa **Costa del Sol** on the Pacific, being developed as a tourist resort. Before La Herradura is a small supermarket on the left. The beach is on a narrow peninsula, the length of which are private houses which prevent access to the sand until you reach the Turicentro (0800-1800). Here cabañas can be rented for US$3.45 for the day, or US$6 for 24 hrs (not suitable for sleeping), admission and car parking US$0.80 each, US$1.60 overnight. It is crowded at weekends and on holidays.

Vehicle camping possible on the beach. There are extensive sandy beaches; the sea has a mild undertow, go carefully until you are sure.

● **Accommodation**   Some luxury hotels: **L2** *Pacific Paradise*, T 334-0601, F 298-0537, rooms and bungalows, overpriced; **L3** *Tesoro Beach*, T 334-0600, F 279-1287, apartment style rooms, swimming pool, 9-hole golf course, but overpriced and poor service reported; **A3** *Izalco Cabaña Club*, T 223-6764, F 224-0363, best value in the resort, 30 rooms, pool, seafood a speciality. Take bus 495 from Terminal Sur, San Salvador; buses are very crowded at weekends, but the resort is quiet during the week. Cheaper accommodation can be found 1 km E on the next beach, Los Blancos, and also in La Herradura, eg **E** *La Sirena*, by the bus terminal, 10 rooms, fan, restaurant.

At the SE end of the Costa del Sol road, near the *Pacific Paradise* hotel, a ferry (US$1.75) leaves for **Tasajera** island in the Estero de Jaltepeque (tidal lagoon). For boat excursions, take Costa del Sol bus to the last stop and negotiate with local boat-men. To hire a boat for the day costs US$75 (per boat), inc pilot, great trip into the lagoon, the mangroves, dolphin watching and up the Río Lempa. There is interesting wildlife on the island. (**Accommodation A3** *Suites Jaltepeque*, resort with suites and rooms, new 1996, a/c, pool, private beach, special mid-week rates, T 223-1984 (880-5054 cellular), F 223-3151; **A1-B** *Oasis de Tasajera*, caters for groups, has 24-passen-ger boat, latest reports poor, run down, long walk to beach.)

Between Rosario de la Paz and Zacatecoluca, a road branches N to the small towns of **San Pedro Nonualco** and **Santa María Ostuma** (with an interesting colonial church and a famous *fiesta* on 2 Feb); both are worth visiting, but not easy to get to. Bus 135 from Terminal del Sur goes to San Pedro. If you get off this bus at the turn off to San Sebastián Arriba, you can walk to the **Peñón del Tacuazín** (or del Indio Aquino), 480m above sea level, which is 4½ km N of Santiago Nonualco. A cave at its summit was used as a refuge by Anastasio Aquino (see page 843), before his execution in April 1833.

ZACATECOLUCA

The capital of La Paz Department (*pop* 81,000; *alt* 201m) is 56 km from San Salvador by road and 19 km S of San Vicente. Good place to buy hammocks, eg nylon 'doubles', US$13. José Simeón Cañas, who abolished slavery in Central America, was born here.

● **Accommodation** D *El Litoral*, on the main road Km 56; E *Hospedaje Viroleño*; F *Hospedajes América* and *Popular* clean; F *Hospedaje Primavera*, clean, friendly, fan. *Comedor Margoth* (beware high charging).

● **Buses** Bus 133 from Sur terminal, San Salvador. Direct bus to La Libertad 1540, US$0.65, or take San Salvador bus and change at Comalapa, 2 hrs.

ICHANMICHEN

Near the town is the garden park and Turicentro of **Ichanmichen** ('the place of the little fish'). It is crossed by canals and decorated with pools: there is, in fact, an attractive swimming pool. It is very hot but there is plenty of shade. Admission and car parking each US$0.40, bungalow rental US$3; take bus 92 from Zacatecoluca.

Both the road and a railway cross the wide Río Lempa by the Puente de Oro (Golden Bridge) at **San Marcos**. (The road bridge has been destroyed; cars use the railway bridge.) Off the main road near here is **La Nueva Esperanza** where there is a community that has returned from Nicaragua, dormitories to sleep and a good place to go and help if you have a few days to spare. 20 km beyond the bridge, a branch road (right) leads to tiny **Puerto El Triunfo** on the Bahía de Jiquilisco, with a large shrimp-freezing plant (E *Hotel/Restaurant Jardín*). Boats can be hired to take you to the islands in the Bahía de Jiquilisco, which are being developed with holiday homes, but are very beautiful.

USULUTAN

About 110 km from the capital is **Usulután** (*pop* 69,000), capital of its Department (90m above sea level); large, dirty, unsafe, a useful transit point only. Bus 302 from San Salvador, US$1.40.

● **Accommodation** E *Central*; E *España*, on main square, T 662-0378, rec, nice patio, restaurant, bar and discotheque; E *Florida*; E *Motel Usulután*.

PLAYA EL ESPINO

Playa El Espino can be reached from Usulután, by slow bus from Usulután or car (4WD) or pickup; it is very remote but lovely. A luxury resort complex is under construction, but there is no other lodging.

The Coastal Highway goes direct from Usulután to La Unión/Cutuco.

LAGUNA EL JOCOTAL

Beyond Usulután, two roads go NE to San Miguel, the first from 10 km along at El Tránsito, the second a further 5 km E, which keeps to the low ground S and E of San Miguel volcano. 2 km beyond this turning on the Carretera Litoral is a short road to the right leading to **Laguna El Jocotal**, a national nature reserve supported by the World Wildlife Fund, which can be visited, enquire at the entrance. You will see more if you hire a boat. It has an abundance of birds and snakes.

PLAYA EL CUCO

12 km from junction for San Miguel there is a turn to the right leading in 7 km to **Playa El Cuco**, a popular beach with several places to stay (**F**), near the bus station (bus 320 to San Miguel, US$0.45, 1 hr last bus 1600; ISTU buses from the capital on Sun and holidays). The main beach is liable to get crowded and dirty at weekends and holidays, but is deserted midweek (single women should take care here). Locals warn against walking along beach after sunset.

● **Accommodation** D *Cucolindo*, 1 km along the coast, cabin for 4, basic, cold water, mosquitos; *Posada*, cold showers, parking US$6; E *Palmera*, with or without bath, impersonal and no direct beach access; D *Los Leones Marinos*, T 619-9015, with bath, clean and tidy.

Nearby is the **B** *Trópico Club*, T 661-1288, with several cabins, run by the *Trópico Inn* in San Miguel which can provide information. **G** pp *El Rancho*, hammocks only, in cane shacks, basic, friendly, shower from bucket drawn from well. Another popular beach, **El Tamarindo**, is reached by another right turn off the road to La Unión, *cabañas* for rent (**A2** *Playa Negra*, T 661-1726, F 661-2513; **A3** *Torola Club*, run by *Izalco Club* at Costa del Sol, T 664-4516, F 224-0363, rec; also **C** *Las Tunas*), and basic *pensión*. In Tamarindo you can stay at the

Workers' Recreational Centre, but first obtain a permit from the Ministry of Labour, 2 Av Sur 516, San Salvador. Entry is usually only granted to those related to members and smartly-dressed ones at that.

● **Hospitals & medical services Warning** Cases of malaria have been reported from El Cuco.

● **Transport** Boat from El Tamarindo across the bay leads to a short cut to La Unión; bus from La Unión 20 mins.

Information for travellers

BEFORE TRAVELLING

ENTRY REQUIREMENTS

● **Documents**

Every visitor must have a valid passport. No visas or tourist cards are required for nationals of the following countries: Austria, Belgium, Chile, Colombia, Costa Rica, Finalnd, Germany, Guatemala, Honduras, Italy, Liechtenstein, Luxembourg, Nicaragua, Norway, Panama, Spain, Sweden, Switzerland, United Kingdom. Tourist cards are required by nationals of: USA, Canada, Australia, New Zealand, Israel and Mexico. These should preferably be obtained free at a consulate before arriving in El Salvador, but can normally be obtained at the frontier for US$10. Nationals of all other countries require a visa for which an application form should be requested from your nearest Salvadorean embassy/consulate that will detail the requirements and cost (approx US$30). Evidence of your travel plans may be requested. Allow 2 weeks for processing. Immigration officials can authorize up to 90 days stay in the country, extensions may be permitted on application to Migración, Centro de Gobierno (see under San Salvador). Multiple entry visas are only permitted to US citizens.

Special arrangements can be made for business visitors, journalists, those wishing to study in El Salvador, residency/work permits etc requiring authenticated documents to support the application, eg photographs, police good conduct reports, certificates of good health, with varying charges up to US$100. Business visas can be arranged in 48 hrs.

Always check at a Salvadorean consulate for changes to these rules (April 1997).

Journalists should register on arrival with the Secretaría Nacional de Communicaciones (SENCO), T 271-0058, office near the Casa Presidencial.

● **Representation overseas**

UK, Tennyson House, 159 Great Portland St, London W1N 5FD, T 0171 436 8282, visa information line T 0891 444 580. **Belgium**, Av de Tervuren 171, 7th floor, B-1150 Brussels, T 733-0485. **Canada**, 209 Kent St, Ottawa, Ontario. T (613) 238-2939; **USA**, consulates at 1212 North Broadway Av, Suite 100, Santa Ana, CA 92701, T (714) 542-3240, and 7730 Forsyth, Suite 150, San Luis, MI 63105, T (314) 862-1354. There are also consulates in **France** (Paris), **Germany** (Bonn), **Spain** (Madrid), **Switzerland** (Geneva).

● **Tourist information**

Local information can be got from the Corporación Salvadoreña de Turismo (Corsatur), Blvd del Hipódromo 508, Col San Benito, San Salvador, T 243-0427, F 278-7310. Other sources of information: *El Salvador Maya*, tourist newspaper in Spanish, edited by Hugo Villarroel (who speaks English and Italian), T/F (503) 221-5486, Internet http://www.elsalvador.com (the home page of *El Diario de Hoy*), available in Salvadorean consulates in USA, Canada and Europe. *La Prensa Gráfica's* home page also has information: http://www.gbm.net/la_prensa_grafica/, e-mail lpg@gbm.net or lpgred@es.com.sv.

WHEN TO GO
● **Best time to visit**
Business is active all year round, except in Aug, which is the holiday season. Christmas and Easter periods should also be avoided by business visitors. Business is centralized in the capital, but it is as well to visit Santa Ana and San Miguel.

For tourists, see **Climate**, page 799. Resorts, particularly on the coast, are busy at weekends and holiday times.

HEALTH
The gastro-enteritic diseases are most common. Visitors should take care over what they eat during the first few weeks, and should drink *agua cristal* (bottled water). Specifics against malaria should be taken if a night is spent on the coast, especially in the E of the country. Cases of dengue have been reported, even in the capital city. The San Salvador milk supply is good, and piped water is relatively pure.

MONEY
● **Currency**
The unit is the colón (¢), divided into 100 centavos. Banknotes of 5, 10, 25, 50 and 100 colones are used, and there are nickel coins for 1 colón, and for fractional amounts. The colón is often called a peso. Black market trading is done in the street, but *casas de cambio* may give better rates. If arriving by air, change money at the airport for convenience. Do not find yourself in the countryside without cash: TCs and credit cards are of no use outside cities. See under San Salvador, **Banks & money changers**, regarding exchange of TCs. Most hotels and lodging places accept US$ cash and many, except the smallest, accept credit cards. Branches of *Pollo Campero* (fastfood) in San Salvador, San Miguel and Santa Ana accept US$ cash at a rate slightly worse than the bank rate, open 0700-2100 daily. Always have some cash dollars available for emergencies. Credit cards are accepted in most upscale establishments. Transactions are subject to 5% commission and are charged at the official rate. There are no international ATMs in El Salvador; for cash advances on Visa or Mastercard, go to **Credomatic** or **Aval-Visa** in San Salvador, see page 814. **NB** Change all colones before entering Guatemala or Honduras, where they may only be changed at international bus terminals at unfavourable rates.

Warning Prices in El Salvador are sometimes quoted in US dollars. Make sure which currency is being used.

GETTING THERE

BY AIR
● **From Europe**
From London: to Miami with any transatlantic carrier, thence to San Salvador with American, Aviateca, or Taca. From Frankfurt, Lufthansa to Miami, connecting with Taca. Alternatively, fly KLM or Iberia to Guatemala City and connect with Taca, Aviateca, Copa or Lacsa there.

● **From the USA**
Apart from Miami other cities with flights to San Salvador are: Houston (American, Aviateca, Continental, Taca), New Orleans (American, Aviateca, Taca), Los Angeles (Aviateca, United, Taca), San Francisco (Lacsa and Taca direct), New York (Taca via Washington and Guatemala, Continental via Houston), Washington (Taca).

● **From Central America**
Taca flies to all Central American capitals, and also to San Pedro Sula and Mexico City. Copa flies to the other Central American capitals, except Belize City and Tegucigalpa; three times a week it has connections in Panama City to Kingston, Jamaica. Lacsa flies to San José. Nica flies to Managua. Connections for South America through San José or Panama. See **Introduction and Hints** for the Visit Central America Programme air pass.

CUSTOMS
All personal luggage is allowed in free. Also allowed: 50 cigars or 200 cigarettes, and 2 litres of liquor, two used cameras or a video recorder, 1 tape machine, 1 portable computer or typewriter and new goods up to US$500 in value (best to have receipts). There are no restrictions on the import of foreign currency; up to the amount imported and declared may be exported. The import and export of local currency is limited to 200 colones, although at land borders you may bring in more. All animal products are prohibited from importation, with the exception of boned, sterilized and hermetically sealed meat products. Fruits are inspected carefully and destroyed if necessary. Hide, skins and woollen goods will be fumigated against disease. Animals must be free of parasites, fully inoculated and have a veterinary certificate and import permit. **NB** If electing to go through the 'Nothing to Declare' channel at the airport, you must not be carrying more than three bags.

ON ARRIVAL

● Border taxes
Border formalities tend to be relatively brief, although thorough searches are common. There is an entry and an exit tax of about US$0.65 (¢5). These taxes are payable only at the 'colecturía' office at borders; do not pay any other official.

● Conduct
Because tourism infrastructure is rebuilding, visitors may need some patience. They should also expect curiosity towards tourists of an unkempt appearance. Some rudeness has been reported, as has unwarranted attentions towards women, but most El Salvadoreans are friendly and eager to practice English. El Salvadoreans are hard workers and are not used to the custom of foreigners spending long hours writing and talking in a café. San Salvador has few places where foreigners gather (so far). Better for this are La Libertad, Zunzal and recognized tourist areas.

● Hours of business
0800-1200 and 1400-1730 Mon to Fri; 0800-1200 Sat. Banks in San Salvador 0900-1700 Mon to Fri, 0900-1200 Sat; different hours for other towns given in text. Government offices: 0800-1600 Mon to Fri

● Official time
Time in El Salvador is 6 hrs behind GMT.

● Safety
The legacy of many years of civil war is still visible in certain areas. In addition, poverty abounds. Peace has left many ex combatants armed but unemployed, which has resulted in cases of robbery at gunpoint, especially in the countryside and of people in cars. Since Mar 1996, the army and the civil police (PNC) have been patrolling the highways in an effort to reduce crime. Do not stop for lone gunmen dressed in military-looking uniforms. Visitors to San Salvador should seek advice on where is not safe inside and outside the city.

Foreigners are prohibited from participating in politics in Salvadorean law. Stay clear of any student rallies. It is wise not to camp out. Be prepared for police checks and possibly body searches on buses (the officers are polite, if respected.)

You are strongly advised to register with your embassy if staying for more than just a few days. Carry your Embassy's phone number with you. The British consulate, for example, advises on local legal procedures, lawyers, English-speaking doctors, help with money transfers and with contacting banks or relatives, and will make local hospital visits. The consulate cannot give free legal advice, supply money or obtain employment or accommodation. The services it does provide are only for those who have registered. Other consulates may provide the same services, but you should find out in advance what your own country's diplomatic procedures are.

● Shopping
Turtle products, live and stuffed birds, live orchids and cacti, reptile skin handicrafts are sold on the streets of the capital despite being prohibited by law. The División Medio Ambiente of PNC is helpful if you wish to complain: 5 C Poniente entre 77 y 79 Av Norte, Col Escalón, San Salvador.

● Tipping
In up-market restaurants: 10%, in others, give small change. Nothing for taxi-drivers except when hired for the day; airport porters, 'boinas rojas', US$1/bag; haircut US$0.20, not obligatory.

● Voltage
110 volts, 60 cycles, AC (plugs are American, 2 flat pin style). Supply is far from stable; mains supply alarm clocks will not work and important electrical equipment should have surge protectors.

● Weights and measures
The metric system of weights and measures is used alongside certain local units such as the *vara* (836 mm, 32.9 ins), *manzana* (7,000 sq m, or 1.67 acres), the *libra* (0.454 kg, about 1 English pound), an' the *quintal* of 100 libras. Some US weights and measures are also used. US gallons are used for gasoline and quarts for oil.

WHERE TO STAY

● Hotels
Do not check into the first hotel you come to: if you have the time, shop around. There are new places opening all the time.

FOOD AND DRINK

● Food
Try *pupusas* – stuffed *tortillas* made of corn or ricemeal, in several varieties (inc *chicharrón* – pork; *queso* – cheese; *revueltas*, typical, tasty and cheap). They are sold at many street stalls, and are better there than at restaurants, but beware stomach infection. On Sat and Sun

nights people congregate in *pupuserías*. *Pavo* (turkey) is common and good, as are the red beans *(frijoles)*. *Tortillas* in El Salvador are smaller, but thicker than in neighbouring countries. A *boca* is an appetizer, a small dish of yucca, avocado or chorizo, served with a drink before a meal. Do not eat in restaurants whose menus do not give prices; you will very likely be over-charged. Apart from San Salvador, restaurants tend to close early – around 2000.

● **Drink**

Coffee makes an excellent souvenir and is good value. Beers: *Suprema* is stronger than *Pilsener*, while *Golden Light* is a reduced alcohol beer.

ON DEPARTURE

● **Airport tax**

There is a 13% tax on international air tickets bought in El Salvador. There is also an airport tax of US$22.50 if staying more than 6 hrs. MCO tickets can be bought.

GETTING AROUND

LAND TRANSPORT

● **Train**

Passenger rail services exist in some rural areas.

● **Bus**

Bus services are good and cover most areas every 15-30 mins, although buses themselves are usually crowded and their drivers are not always very careful. The best time to travel by bus is 0900-1500; avoid Fri and Sun pm. If travelling across borders, take international pullmans for luggage safety. The buses are always brightly painted, particularly so around San Miguel. Bags on bus seats will be charged as passengers – unfortunately, roof racks are rare.

● **Hitchhiking**

Hitchhiking is comparatively easy.

● **Motoring**

At the border, after producing a driving licence and proof of ownership, you are given a *comprobante de ingreso* (which has to be stamped by immigration, customs and quarantine) costing 100 colones to stay for 30 days. You receive a receipt, vehicle permit and vehicle check document. Permission to stay can be extended for 60 days at the Dirección Gen de la Renta Aduanas in San Bartolo, to the E of San Salvador. Other fees for bringing a car in amount to 50 colones. A few km from the border the *comprobante* will be checked. Leaving the country, a *comprobante de ingreso*, must be stamped again and, if not intending to return, your permit must be sur-rendered; total cost 15 colones. Do not overstay your permitted time if you do not wish to be fined. To extend permission to stay with a vehicle contact a *tramitador* such as Arévalo Díaz y Cía, T 225-0871/242-1880, beeper 298-1122, Unidad 13634, good service, apply 2 weeks before permit expires. A good map, both of republic and of capital, can be obtained from Texaco or Esso, or from the Tourist Institute. Petrol costs/US gallon US$2.25 (sin plomo – leadfree), US$2.25 (super), US$2 (regular), US$1.30 (diesel). Roads are generally good throughout the country, but look out for crops being dried at the roadside or in central reservations. Take care of buses, which travel very fast, and other forms of bad driving.

Insurance: compulsory third party pro-gramme in El Salvador by end-1997 (can be arranged at the border – enquire first at consulates). Under the 1996 seat-belt law, you must wear one: fine for not doing so is US$34. The fine for driving intoxicated is US$55. Do not attempt to bribe officials.

Selling a vehicle is possible, older (ie cheaper)and diesel cars/vans preferred. You need a good lawyer (ask at your embassy for guidance),visits to the Ministerio de Hacienda (Finance Ministry) and Aduana (Customs) re-quired and you must find a buyer – there are dealers on the outskirts of San Salvador towards Santa Ana. A time consuming process.

COMMUNICATIONS

● **Language**

Spanish, but English is widely understood in business circles. Spanish should be used for letters, catalogues etc.

● **Postal services**

Air mail to and from Europe can take up to 1 month, but normally about 15 days, US$0.35; from the USA, 1 week. Certified packets to Europe cost US$9.40, good service; swifter, but more expensive is EMS (US$23 to Europe). Courier services are much quicker, but cost more. The correct address for any letter to the capital is 'San Salvador, El Salvador, Central America'. The main post office is at the Centro de Gobierno.

● **Telephone services**

ANTEL, the state telecommunications company, was due to be privatized in mid-1997. T 114 for information and details on new phone numbers in San Salvador. The charge for a local telephone call is 0.75 centavos for 3 mins. New coin phones are being introduced, which accept all coins. A private call, fax or telex to Europe costs US$5/minute (if made from private telephones or ANTEL). To the USA, the rate depends on which part of the country you are calling. Cheap rate for calls to Europe starts at 2400, to the USA at 2000. Calls made from hotels are more expensive. Direct dialling is available to Europe, 3 mins, minimum, USA (US$1.30/minute) and other parts of the world. For collect calls to USA, Mexico and Central America, dial 113 from any public phone, 120 from a private phone. No collect calls to Europe, except to Spain, Australia or Asia. For long-distance calls within El Salvador, T 110 for enquiries, national collect calls and to leave messages (citas) at ANTEL; international long-distance 119; for collect calls to USA, Canada, Mexico and Central America, dial 113 on coin phones, 120 on private phones; US Sprint operator 191; MCI operator 195; AT&T 800-1785 (bilingual service).

Radio Inc communicates with all parts of the world through local stations. Public fax and telex at ANTEL. British business travellers can use the telex system at the Embassy.

ENTERTAINMENT

● **Newspapers**

In San Salvador: *Diario de Hoy* (right wing) and *La Prensa Gráfica* (centre) every morning, inc Sun; both have the most complete listings of cultural events in San Salvador. *El Mundo* and *Diario Latino* (left wing) in the afternoons, except Sun. Relatively new is *La Noticia*, weekly, popular. There are provincial newspapers in Santa Ana, San Miguel (eg *Periódico de Oriente*, weekly) and elsewhere. *Tendencias* is a leftish monthly magazine. US newspapers and magazines available at leading hotels and *The Bookshop*, Galerías, Paseo Escalón, San Salvador. British newspapers can be read at the *British Club*.

● **Radio**

There are 80 radio stations: one is government owned, one belongs to the armed forces, 7 to the FMLN and several are owned by churches.

● **Television**

There are four commercial television stations, all with national coverage, and one government-run station with two channels. There are three cable channels, all with CNN news, etc. All luxury and first class hotels and some guesthouses in San Salvador have cable for guests.

HOLIDAYS AND FESTIVALS

The usual ones are 1 Jan, Holy Week (3 days, government 10 days), 1 May, 10 May, Corpus Christi (half day), first week of Aug, 15 Sept, 2 and 5 Nov (half day), 24 Dec (half day) and Christmas Day. Government offices are also closed on religious holidays. Little business in Easter Week, the first week of Aug, and the Christmas-New Year period. Banks are closed for balance 29, 30 June and 30, 31 December.

Look in the newspapers for details of regional fiestas, rodeos, etc. There are many artesan fairs, eg at San Sebastián and San Vicente, which are worth a visit but which go largely unnoticed in the capital.

FURTHER READING

For information about investment and export, see '*El Salvador is Your Best Buy*,' from FUSADES, Boulevard Santa Elena, Urbanización Santa Elena, Antiguo Cuscatlán, La Libertad, El Salvador (off the road to Santa Tecla – Pan American Highway – to SW of the capital) T 278-3386, F 278-3354 (in USA Vip Sal No 1313, PO Box 02-5364, Miami, FL 33102-5364, T 1-800-788-8144). *Rincón Mágico de El Salvador* and *El Salvador Prehistórico*, both available at Banco Agrícola Comercial, Paseo Escalón 3635, San Salvador (US$72). The El Salvador Iguana Foundation (a private project in aid of the environment) publishes an illustrated book on the country, tourism and business, US$15, in English and Spanish; Alex Salaverino, Aptdo Postal 121 C G, San Salvador, T 886-1524 (cellular), F 279-3276. *Amor de Jade*, by Walter Raudales, to be published in English too, is a novel based on the life of El Salvador's Mata Hari (now ex-comandante Joaquín Villalobos' wife). See also the novels of Manlio Argueta, *Un día en la vida* (1980) and *Cuzcatlán, donde bate la mar del sur* (1986), both about peasants during El Salvador's conflict.

ACKNOWLEDGEMENTS

We are grateful to Peter Pollard for updating the chapter, to Donald T Lee for a detailed review of the whole chapter and to Edilberto Valladares Guevara and Michelle Marie Cormier Valladares for their invaluable assistance.

Honduras

HONDURAS IS LARGER than all the other Central American republics except Nicaragua, but has a smaller population than El Salvador, less than a fifth its size. Bordered by Nicaragua, Guatemala, and El Salvador, it has a narrow Pacific coastal strip, 124 km long, on the Gulf of Fonseca, but its northern coast on the Caribbean is some 640 km long.

HORIZONS

THE LAND

Much of the country is mountainous: a rough plateau covered with volcanic ash and lava in the S, rising to peaks such as Cerro de las Minas in the Celaque range (2,849m), but with some intermont basins at between 900 and 1,800m. The volcanic detritus disappears to the N, revealing saw-toothed ranges which approach the coast at an angle; the one in the extreme NW, along the border with Guatemala, disappears under the sea and shows itself again in the Bay Islands. At most places in the N there is only a narrow shelf of lowland between the sea and the sharp upthrust of the mountains, but along two rivers: the Aguán in the NE, and the Ulúa in the NW, long fingers of marshy lowland stretch inland between the ranges. The

Ulúa lowland is particularly important; it is about 40 km wide and stretches southwards for 100 km. From its southern limit a deep gash continues across the highland to the Gulf of Fonseca, on the Pacific. The distance between the Caribbean and the Pacific along this trough is 280 km; the altitude at the divide between the Río Comayagua, running into the Ulúa and the Caribbean, and the streams flowing into the Pacific, is only 950m. In this trough lies Comayagua, the old colonial capital. The lowlands along the Gulf of Fonseca are narrower than they are along the Caribbean; there is no major thrust inland as along the Ulúa.

The prevailing winds are from the E, and the Caribbean coast has a high rainfall and is covered with deep tropical forest. The intermont basins, the valleys, and the slopes sheltered from the prevailing winds

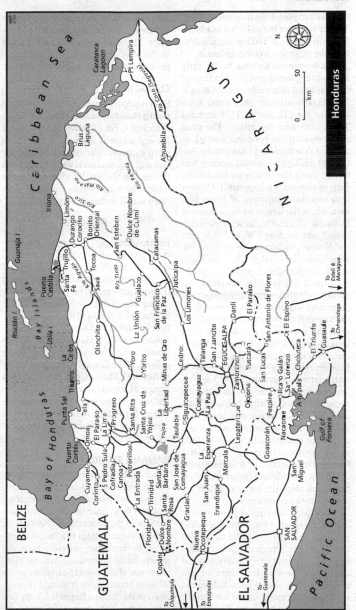

bear oak and pine down to as low as 600m. Timber is almost the only fuel available. In the drier areas, N and S of Tegucigalpa, there are extensive treeless savannas.

The Spaniards, arriving in the early 16th century, found groups of Indians of the Maya and other cultures. Pushing E from Guatemala City they came upon silver in the SE, and in 1578 founded Tegucigalpa near the mines. The yield was comparatively poor, but enough to attract a thin stream of immigrants. Settlement during the ensuing century was mostly along the trail from Guatemala City: at Gracias, La Esperanza, Comayagua and the department of Santa Bárbara, where the largest white population is found. Gradually these settlements spread over the S and W, and this, with the N coast, is where the bulk of the population lives today. The Spaniards and their descendants ignored the northern littoral and the Ulúa lowlands, but during the 19th century US companies, depending largely on black workers from the British West Indies and Belize, developed the northern lowlands as a great banana-growing area. Today the largest concentration of population per square kilometre is in the Department of Cortés, which extends northwards from Lago Yojoa towards the Caribbean; it includes the major portion of the river basins of Ulúa and Chamelecón, also known as the Sula valley: the most important agricultural area in the country, with San Pedro Sula as its commercial centre and Puerto Cortés as its seaport. The Atlantic littoral consumes two-thirds of the country's imports, and ships the bananas which are the country's major export.

Even today, land under some form of cultivation is only 18% of the total, while meadows and pastures make up 14% of total land use. Rugged terrain makes large areas unsuitable for any kind of agriculture. Nevertheless, there are undeveloped agricultural potentials in the flat and almost unpopulated lands of the coastal plain E of Tela to Trujillo and Puerto Castilla, in the Aguán valley southward and in the region NE of Juticalpa. The area further to the NE, known as the Mosquitia plain, is largely unexploited and little is known of its potential.

CLIMATE

Rain is frequent on the Caribbean littoral during the whole year; the heaviest occurs from Sept to Feb inclusive. In Tegucigalpa the dry season is normally from Nov to April inclusive. The coolest months are Dec and Jan, but this is when heavy rains fall on the N coast, which may impede travel. The driest months for this area are April and May, though very hot.

HISTORY

For Honduras' early history, see the introductory chapter to Central America. Honduras was largely neglected by Spain and its colonists, who concentrated on their trading partners further N or S. The resulting disparity in levels of development between Honduras and its regional neighbours caused problems after independence in 1821. Harsh partisan battles among provincial leaders resulted in the collapse of the Central American Federation in 1838. The national hero, Gen Francisco Morazán was a leader in unsuccessful attempts to maintain the Federation and the restoration of Central American unity was the main aim of foreign policy until 1922.

BANANA REPUBLIC

Honduras has had a succession of military and civilian rulers and there have been 300 internal rebellions, civil wars and changes of government since independence, most of them in the 20th century. Political instability in the past led to a lack of investment in economic infrastructure and sociopolitical integration, making Honduras one of the poorest countries in the Western Hemisphere. It earned its nickname of the 'Banana Republic' in the first part of the 20th century following the founding of a company in 1899 by the Vaccaro brothers of New Orleans which eventually became the Standard Fruit Company and which was to make bananas the major export crop of Honduras. The United Fruit Company of Boston was also founded in 1899 and in 1929 was merged with the Cuyamel Fruit Company of Samuel Zemurray, who controlled the largest fruit interests in Honduras. United Fruit (UFCo), known as El Pulpo (the octopus), emerged as a major political influence in the region with strong links with several dictatorships.

The 1929 Great Depression caused great hardship in the export-oriented economies of the region and in Honduras it brought the rise of another authoritarian régime. Tiburcio Carías Andino was elected in 1932 but through his ties with foreign companies and other neighbouring dictators he was able to hold on to power until renewed turbulence began in 1948 and he voluntarily withdrew from power in 1949. The two political parties, the Liberals and the Nationals, came under the control of provincial leaders and after two more authoritarian Nationalist governments and a general strike in 1954 by radical labour unions on the N coast, young military reformists staged a palace coup in 1955. They installed a provisional junta and allowed elections for a constituent assembly in 1957. The assembly was led by the Liberal Party, which appointed Dr Ramón Villeda Morales as President, and transformed itself into a national legislature for 6 years. A newly created military academy graduated its first class in 1960 and the armed forces began to professionalize its leadership in conjunction with the civilian economic establishment. Conservative officers, nervous of a Cuban-style revolution, preempted elections in 1963 in a bloody coup which deposed Dr Villeda, exiled Liberal Party members and took control of the national police, which they organized into special security forces.

FOOTBALL WAR

In 1969, Honduras and El Salvador were drawn into a bizarre episode known as the 'Football War', which took its name from its origin in a disputed decision in the third qualifying round of the World Cup. Its root cause, however, was the social tension aroused by migrating workers from overcrowded El Salvador to Honduras. In 13 days, 2,000 people were killed before a ceasefire was arranged by the Organization of American States. A peace treaty was not signed, though, until 1980, and the dispute provoked Honduras to withdraw from the Central American Common Market (CACM), which helped to hasten its demise.

TRANSITION TO DEMOCRACY

The armed forces, led chiefly by Gen López Arellano and his protegés in the National Party, dominated government until 1982. López initiated land reform, but despite liberal policies, his régime was brought down in the mid-1970s by corruption scandals involving misuse of hurricane aid funds and bribes from the United Brands Company. His successors increased the size and power of the security forces and created the largest air force in Central America, while slowly preparing for a return to civilian rule. A constituent assembly was elected in 1980 and general elections held in 1981. A constitution was promulgated in 1982 and President Roberto Suazo Córdoba, of the Liberal Party, assumed power. During this period, Honduras cooperated closely with the USA on political and military issues, particularly in moves to isolate Nicaragua's left wing government, and became host to some 12,000 right wing Nicaraguan contra rebels. It was less willing to take a similar stand against the FMLN left wing guerrillas in El Salvador for fear of renewing border tensions. In 1986 the first peaceful transfer of power between civilian presidents for 30 years took place when José Azcona del Hoyo (Liberal) won the elections. Close relations with the USA were maintained in the 1980s, Honduras had the largest Peace Corps Mission in the world, non-governmental and international voluntary agencies proliferated and the government became increasingly dependent upon US aid to finance its budget.

In 1989, general elections were won by the right wing Rafael Leonardo Callejas Romero of the National Party, which won a 14-seat majority in the National Assembly. Under the terms of the Central American Peace Plan, the contra forces were demobilized and disarmed by June 1990. The Honduran armed forces have come under greater pressure for reform as a result of US and domestic criticism of human rights abuses. An Ad

Decline of the Military

The Honduran armed forces were at their most powerful in the 1980s, when with US support in the attempt to destabilize the Sandinista régime in Nicaragua, their numbers rose to about 25,000. Since then they have seen their political and economic power eroded and their size cut to around 7,000 with the loss of compulsory military service. They have lost control of key enterprises, such as the telecommunications monopoly, the merchant marine and the state migration authority. Their allocation from the state budget has also been cut. In the 1997 budget, announced in Sept 1996, they received only US$29mn, despite having asked for US$52mn, as the money was diverted to social programmes. President Reina has also curbed military influence in government and started to bring those responsible to task for human rights abuses.

In 1994 the military-controlled security force, the DNI, was officially dismantled and a new Directorate for Criminal Investigations (DIC) began operations in 1995. The US State Department 1994 report on human rights in Honduras noted that disappearances had ceased but that arbitrary detentions by the Public Security Forces (FUSEP), impunity for the civilian and military elite, corruption and racial discrimination of indigenous peoples still continued. In 1996 an ad hoc commission was set up to oversee the creation of a new Civilian National Police (PNC) to replace the discredited, military-controlled FUSEP of 6,500 men and draw up new public security legislation. The process was expected to take up to 5 years.

The disgruntled armed forces were further dismayed with the indictment by a civilian court in 1995 of 11 military officers accused of human rights violations in the 1980s including a case when 6 students were kidnapped and tortured. The order highlighted the role of the USA and Argentina in training the Honduran military intelligence unit, the Battalion 3-16, in the 1980s. As clandestine cemeteries were discovered, the military denied there were any human rights violations. In a show of force, the Commander in Chief, Gen Luís Alonso Discua, sent armoured cars into Tegucigalpa as a warning to the Government, saying he did not trust the justice system. Gen Discua was the first commander of the B3-16 and there was an outcry from international human rights groups when he was appointed in 1996 to Honduras' delegation on the UN Security Council. The Committee of Relatives of the Detained and Disappeared (COFADEH) also took legal action against high-ranking army officers to uncover human rights abuses by the B3-16 and allegations were made against Gen Discua and the subsequent armed forces chief, Gen Mario Hung Pacheco. Several bombs exploded in key political locations which were suspected to have been planted by disaffected elements in the army and there were also suspicions that the military was a factor behind the rising crime wave of kidnappings and bank robberies.

Hoc Commission, set up by President Callejas, published a report in April 1993 recommending a series of institutional reforms in the judiciary and security services, including the resolution by the Supreme Court of all cases of jurisdictional conflict between civilian and military courts. This and other measures led to some, but not complete improvement in the respect for human rights.

THE REINA ADMINISTRATION

In the campaign leading up to the 1993 general elections, the Liberal candidate, Carlos Roberto Reina Idiáquez, promised a 'moral revolution' if he won. His targets were human rights abuse, government corruption and partisan state institutions. He also pledged to provide every citizen 'techo, trabajo, tierra y tortilla' (roof, work, land and food), arguing for a more socially-conscious face to the economic adjustment programme inaugurated by President Callejas. Reina duly won the elections with a 53.4% majority over his National Party rival, Oswaldo Ramos Soto. In the National Assembly the Liberals won 71 seats, the Nationals 55 and the Innovation and Unity Party (Pinu) 2. The Liberals also won 60% of elections for town mayors throughout the country. President Reina took office on 27 January 1994. Although many of his economic policies were unpopular and he was unable to alleviate widespread poverty in the short term, President Reina received approval for his handling of the military and investigations of human rights abuses (see box). Presidential elections are due 30 November 1997. The main candidates are Carlos Flores Facusse of the Liberal Party and Nora Gúnera de Melgar of the National Party.

CULTURE

PEOPLE

There are few pure Indians (an estimated 7% of the total population), and fewer of pure Spanish and other European ancestry. The two largest concentrations of Indians are 1) the Chortis from Santa Rosa de Copán westwards to the border with Guatemala; the Lencas in the departments of Lempira, Intibucá and, above all, in the highlands of La Paz. 2) There are about 45,000 Miskito Indians who live on the Caribbean coast, as well as several communities of Garifunas (black Caribs). The population is 90% *mestizo*. Some 53% are peasants or agricultural labourers, with a relatively low standard of living. It was estimated in 1993 that 40% of Hondurans are unemployed and that 68-80% of the population live below the poverty line.

RELIGION AND EDUCATION

Education is compulsory, but not all the rural children go to school. 33% of the population over the age of 10 have no formal schooling. The National University is based in Tegucigalpa though it also has departments in Comayagua, San Pedro Sula and La Ceiba. Also in Tegucigalpa is the Universidad José Cecilio del Valle, the Universidad Católica (with campuses in San Pedro Sula and Choluteca) and the Universidad Tecnológica Centro Americana; there is also the Universidad de San Pedro Sula. The majority of the population is Catholic, but there is complete freedom of religion.

GOVERNMENT

Honduras is a multi party republic. The Legislature consists of a single 128-seat Chamber. Deputies are elected by a proportional vote. Executive authority rests with a President, directly elected for 4 years. No President may serve two terms in succession. The National Assembly elects members of the Supreme Court, which, together with the Court of Appeal, Justices of the Peace and lesser tribunals, constitute the judiciary. The Constitution was revised by a Constituent Assembly elected in April 1980. The country is divided into 18 departments, each with an administrative centre, and further subdivided into 297 municipalities.

THE ECONOMY

Structure of production

Honduras has traditionally been the poorest economy in Central America with one of the lowest income rates per head in all Latin America although the war in Nicaragua depressed income levels there below even those of Honduras. The distribution of land continues to be a pressing problem, with an estimated 170,000 farming families lacking sufficient land for subsistence agriculture. New legislation in 1992 was designed to encourage private enterprise, making it easier to sell land and prompting large landholdings, leaving campesinos with only small parcels of land. Unemployment (and under-employment) is about 40% of the working population, owing to low investment, and poor harvests and labour disputes in the agricultural sector. After decades of low inflation when the currency was fixed, the 1990s have been a severe shock to the population and real incomes have fallen sharply as the effects of economic liberalization have been felt. It is estimated that 80% of the population live in poverty and the minimum wage has not kept pace with inflation.

Over half of the population lives by the land: coffee, bananas and shrimp are the main export crops and Honduras is the world's fourth largest exporter of bananas. Cotton, once important, is now far less so. Tobacco, maize, beans, rice and sugar are grown mostly for domestic use but small quantities are sometimes exported. Cigars have a good international reputation. Cattle raising is important and exports of both meat and livestock are growing. Timber is a major export; controversy over the development of forestry reserves in the Department of Olancho has laid the future expansion of the industry open to doubt.

Honduras has considerable reserves of silver, gold, lead, zinc, tin, iron, copper, coal and antimony, but only lead and zinc and small quantities of gold and silver are mined and exported. Japanese agencies are assisting in further exploration for lead and zinc deposits. Considerable offshore exploration for petroleum is in progress. There is an oil refinery at Puerto Cortés and exports of petroleum derivatives are becoming significant. The US$600mn hydroelectric scheme at El Cajón was constructed to reduce the country's oil bill. The Government has begun the process of privatizing the National Electric Energy Company (ENEE) as part of its policy to privatize the energy sector.

Local industries are small, turning out a wide range of consumer goods, besides being engaged in the processing of timber and agricultural products. The more important products are furniture, textiles, footwear, chemicals, cement and rubber. Maquila industries in the free trade zone grew rapidly in the 1980s but stagnated in the mid-1990s. Several companies relocated in 1995-96 to other countries and Honduras was criticized for labour abuses, low pay and poor conditions in the sector. Maquiladoras account for 20% of total exports. Most are in clothing, but there are others processing wood and a variety of goods, employing about 38,000 people.

Recent trends

Honduras' total external debt amounted to some US$4.6bn at end-1996, and spends about a third of its foreign exchange receipts on debt servicing. From 1982 the government held negotiations to reschedule its debt with commercial banks but failed to sign any agreement. Arrears mounted and in 1989 the negotiating committee disbanded to allow banks individually to recover their debts as best they could. In 1990 a new economic package was introduced with emergency spending cuts and revenue raising measures designed to reduce the fiscal deficit. The lempira was allowed to float freely against

Honduras: fact file

Geographic
Land area	112,492 sq km
forested	53.6%
pastures	13.8%
cultivated	18.1%

Demographic
Population (1996)	5,666,000
annual growth rate (1985-94)	3.0%
urban	42.9%
rural	57.1%
density	50.4 per sq km
Religious affiliation	
Roman Catholic	85.0%
Birth rate per 1,000 (1993)	35.8
	(world av 25.0)

Education and Health
Life expectancy at birth,	
male	64.8 years
female	69.2 years
Infant mortality rate	
per 1,000 live births (1993)	47.2
Physicians (1990)	1 per 1,586 persons
Hospital beds (1994)	1 per 1,126 persons
Calorie intake as %	
of FAO requirement	102%
Population age 10 and over	
with no formal schooling	33.4%
Literate males (over 15)	75.5%
Literate females (over 15)	70.6%

Economic
GNP (1994 market prices)	US$3,162mn
GNP per capita	US$580
Public external debt	
(1994)	US$3,884mn
Tourism receipts (1994)	US$33mn
Inflation (annual av 1990-95)	20.5%
Radio	1 per 2.9 persons
Television	1 per 34 persons
Telephone	1 per 48 persons

Employment
Population economically active (1994)	
	1,722,700
Unemployment rate (1990)	40%
% of labour force in	
agriculture	43.5
mining	0.2
manufacturing	11.8
construction	6.4

Source Encyclopaedia Britannica

the US dollar in a legalization of the black market rate where the currency had been trading at L4=US$1 compared with the official rate since 1926 of L2=US$1. President Callejas thereby attempted a rapprochement with the international financial community; Honduras had previously been declared ineligible to borrow from the IMF, the World Bank and the Inter-American Development Bank (IDB), while US aid had been cut by 30%. Negotiations with the multilateral agencies led to the clearing of arrears and new loans to support the economic programme. In 1991 the USA forgave US$435mn of the US$600mn debt owed by Honduras. At the same time, the private foreign debt was reduced from US$225mn to US$80mn through debt conversions and privatizations of state enterprises.

The effect of structural adjustment measures on the population, however, were not favourable: unemployment rose, inflation soared and poverty grew, causing considerable social problems. By 1992 inflation was down to 8.8% and gdp rose by 4.6% although structural adjustment remained unpopular. Inflation began to creep up in 1993 and by 1994 the new President faced a deteriorating economy. Gdp fell by 1.5% while inflation rose to 21.7%. Not only had the foreign debt risen and targets not been met in the last year of Callejas' term, but also the foreign lending institutions' loss of confidence in Honduras made it difficult for Reina to fund social programmes. Renegotiation of external debt was only possible to a limited extent as over half was owed to multilateral lending agencies, principally the IDB and the World Bank. In 1995 gdp growth improved but inflation remained high and monetary policy had to be tightened with higher lending rates.

In 1996 the Government approved a 25% increase in the minimum wage, but this was immediately wiped out by a 30% rise in the price of basic foodstuffs. Strikes in the public sector to demand further wage rises, no job cuts and price controls put pressure on the Government, which was already struggling to meet the targets of its IMF economic programme. The Government increased social spending in the 1997 budget in the face of rising crime, labour unrest and widespread poverty, despite jeopardizing its IMF programme and potential future debt forgiveness if budget deficit targets were missed. The Government aimed to cut the fiscal deficit to 2.5% of gdp in 1997, from 3.5% in 1996, as the economy was projected to grow by up to 5% compared with 4.5% in 1996 and 3.6% in 1995.

A US$18bn, 2-phase, 10-year, National Transformation Plan was announced in late 1996, involving large scale infrastructure, agriculture and industry projects. These include motorways and airports to improve regional communications; a 'dry canal' rail link between container ports on the Atlantic and Pacific coasts; a tourist, commercial and industrial zone at Trujillo and Puerto Castilla; 2 new hydroelectricity plants and new banana plantations. Tax incentives would be used to promote the massive private investment required, backed up by the InterAmerican Development Bank (IDB) and the Central Bank for Economic Integration (BCIE).

COMMUNICATIONS

The railways are in the N. In 1993 the Tela Railroad Company closed its entire operation along the Atlantic coast, while the Ferrocarril Nacional de Honduras has since downgraded its one remaining passenger service between Tela and Puerto Cortés to a twice-weekly ferrobus (Fri, Sun, return same day).

A light aeroplane is the only way of getting to La Mosquitia, but the road system in the rest of the country has improved rapidly in recent years and Honduras probably has the best roads in Central America. Total road length is now 14,602 km, of which 2,584 km are paved, 9,942 km are all-weather roads and 2,076 km are passable in the dry season. The main paved roads are the Northern Highway linking Tegucigalpa, San Pedro Sula and Puerto Cortés; the road W from Puerto Cortés along the N coast, through Omoa, to the Guatemalan frontier; the highway from Tegucigalpa to Olancho, passing through Juticalpa and Catacamas; the Pan-American Highway in the SW between El Salvador and Nicaragua, and the Southern Highway which runs to it from Tegucigalpa; the North Coast Highway joining San Pedro Sula with Progreso, Tela, La Ceiba and Trujillo; from Progreso a paved road runs S through Santa Rita to join the San Pedro Sula-Tegucigalpa highway 44 km S of San Pedro; there is also a paved road from Santa Rita to Yoro; the Western Highway links San Pedro Sula with Santa Rosa de Copán, Nueva Ocotepeque and the Guatemalan and Salvadorean frontiers, with a branch from La Entrada to Copán ruins; the road from Santa Rosa de Copán to Gracias is also paved, as are the Carretera de Santa Bárbara and on to the Western Highway (Carretera del Occidente), from Lago Yojoa to Santa Bárbara, and the stretches from La Paz to Marcala in the Department of La Paz and Siguatepeque to La Esperanza; the road linking Choluteca on the Pan-American Highway with the Nicaraguan frontier at Guasaule; the Eastern Highway linking Tegucigalpa, Danlí, El Paraíso and Las Manos (Nicaraguan frontier); the road from Tegucigalpa to Santa Lucía and Valle de Angeles; some of the road along the island of Roatán. Travel is still by foot and mule in many areas. Tegucigalpa, La Ceiba, San Pedro Sula and Roatán all have international airports. More details in the text below.

NATIONAL PARKS

The National Parks office, Conama, is next to the Instituto Nacional Agrario in Tegucigalpa, chaotic but friendly, a good source of information. Cohdefor, the national

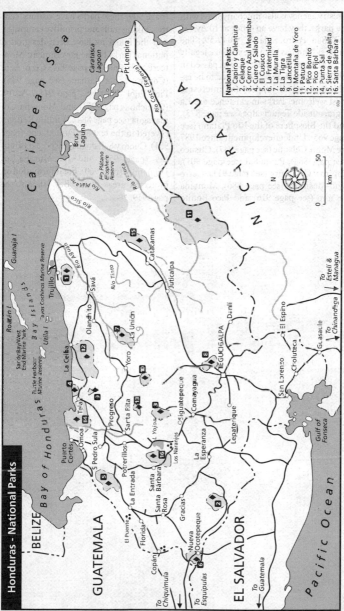

Honduras - National Parks

National Parks:
1. Capiro y Calentura
2. Celaque
3. Cerro Azul Meambar
4. Cuero y Salado
5. El Cusuco
6. La Fraternidad
7. La Muralla
8. La Tigra
9. Lancetilla
10. Montaña de Yoro
11. Patuca
12. Pico Bonito
13. Pico Pijol
14. Punta Sal
15. Sierra de Agalta
16. Santa Bárbara

forestry agency is also much involved with the parks, they have an office at 10 Av 4 C NO, San Pedro Sula, T 53-49-59. The parks system has been in existence legally since a congressional decree was passed in 1987. Natural Reserves continue to be established and all support and interest is most welcome. Parks in existence are La Tigra, outside Tegucigalpa (see page 873), and the Biosphere of the Río Plátano (see page 965). Under development since 1987 are Monte Celaque (see page 947), Cusuco (see page 888), Punta Sal (see page 901), Capiro y Calentura (see page 911), Cerro Azul-Meámbar (see page 886), Montaña de Yoro (see page 916) and Pico Bonito (page 909) these parks have visitors' centres, hiking trails and primitive camping), and the following have been designated national parks by the government: Montecristo-Trifinio (see page 951), Cerro Azul (Copán), Santa Bárbara (see page 935), Pico Pijol (Yoro, see page 915), Agalta (Olancho – page 963) and Montaña Comayagua (see page 884). Wildlife Refuges covered in the text are Punto Izopo (page 901), Cuero y Salado (page 909), Las Trancas (page 950) and La Muralla-Los Higuerales (page 960). For information on protected areas in the Bay Islands, see page 919.

Tegucigalpa

T HE CAPITAL and nearby excursions to old mining settlements in the forested mountains: a great contrast between the functional modern city and some of the oldest villages in the country.

TEGUCIGALPA

The city (*Pop* 800,000; *Alt* 1,000m) stands in an intermont basin at between 950 and 1,100m above sea level. It was founded as a mining camp in 1578: the miners found their first gold where the N end of the Soberanía bridge now is. The name means 'silver hill' in the original Indian tongue. It did not become the capital until 1880. On three sides it is surrounded by sharp, high peaks. It comprises two former towns: Comayagüela and Tegucigalpa built at the foot and up the slopes of El Picacho. A steeply banked river, the Choluteca, divides the two towns, now united administratively as the Distrito Central. Tegucigalpa has not been subjected to any disaster by fire or earthquake, being off the main earthquake fault line, so retains many traditional features. Many of the stuccoed houses, with a single heavily barred entrance leading to a central patio, are attractively coloured. However, the old low skyline of the city has now been punctuated by several modern tall buildings. Its altitude gives it a reliable climate: temperate during the rainy season from May to Nov; warm, with cool nights, in Mar and April, and cool and dry, with very cool nights, in Dec to February. The annual mean temperature is about 74°F (23°C).

The Carretera del Sur (Southern Highway), which brings in travellers from the S and from Toncontín Airport, 6½ km from Plaza Morazán, runs through Comayagüela into Tegucigalpa. It goes past the obelisk set up to commemorate a hundred years of Central American independence, and the Escuela Nacional de Bellas Artes, with a decorated Mayan corridor and temporary exhibitions of contemporary paintings and crafts.

PLACES OF INTEREST

Crossing the river from Comayagüela by the colonial Mallol bridge, on the left is the old **Casa Presidencial** (1919, now the Museo Presidencial, the new one is a modern building on Blvd de las Fuerzas Armadas). Calle Bolívar runs through the area containing the Congress building and the former site of the University, founded in 1847. The site is now the **Galería Nacional de Arte**, with a permanent art exhibition (see **Museums** below). In Colonia Palmira, Tegucigalpa, is the Blvd Morazán, with shopping and business complexes, embassies, banks, restaurants, cafeterias, bars, etc. You can get a fine view of the city from the **Monumento a La Paz** on Juana Laínez hill, near the Estadio Nacional (National Stadium), open till 1700.

The backdrop to Tegucigalpa is the summit of **El Picacho** looming up to the N (see **Excursions**, below), although it is hard to see during spring because of smog. From Plaza Morazán go up 7 Av and the Calle de la Leona to Parque La Leona, a handsome small park with a railed walk overlooking the city. Higher still is the reservoir in El Picacho, also known as the United Nations Park, which can be reached by a special bus from the number 9 bus stop, behind Los Dolores church (in front of Farmacia Santa Bárbara), Sun only, US$0.15; alternatively,

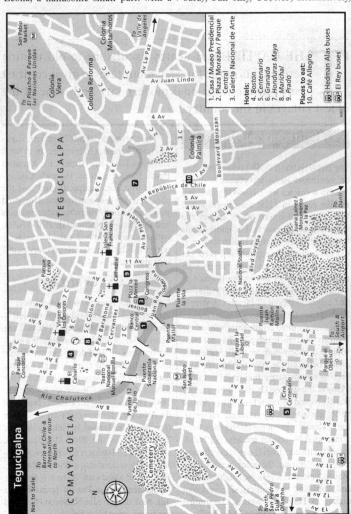

1. Casa / Museo Presidencial
2. Plaza Morazán / Parque Central
3. Galería Nacional de Arte

Hotels:
4. Boston
5. Centenario
6. Granada
7. Honduras Maya
8. Marichal
9. Prado

Places to eat:
10. Café Allegro

B1 Hedman Alas buses
B2 El Rey buses

take a bus to El Piligüin or Corralitos (daily) at 1300 from the N side of Parque Herrera in front of the Teatro Nacional. The bus to Jutiapa takes you to La Tigra, but note that the park is closed at 1400.

Calle Bolívar leads to the main square, Plaza Morazán (commonly known as Parque Central). On the eastern side of the square are the **Palacio del Distrito Central**, and the domed and double-towered **Cathedral** built in the late 18th century. See the beautiful gilt colonial altarpiece, the fine examples of Spanish colonial art, the cloisters and, in Holy Week, the ceremony of the Descent from the Cross.

Av Miguel Paz Barahona, running through the northern side of the square, is a key avenue. On it to the E is the church of **San Francisco**, with its clangorous bells, and (on 3a C, called Av Cervantes) the old **Spanish Mint** (1770), now the national printing works. If, from Plaza Morazán, we go along Av Miguel Paz Barahona westwards towards the river, by turning right along 4 Av (Calle Los Dolores) we come to the 18th century church of **Virgen de los Dolores**. Two blocks N and 3 blocks W of the church is Parque Concordia with good copies of Maya sculpture and temples.

Back on Av Miguel Paz Barahona and further W are the **Teatro Nacional Manuel Bonilla**, with a rather grand interior (1915) and, across the square, the beautiful old church of **El Calvario**. Built in elegant colonial style, El Calvario's roof is supported by 14 pillars. It contains images of the Virgen de la Soledad, San Juan and the archangels San Miguel and San Rafael. On Easter Friday processions start and end here. Crossing the bridge of 12 de Julio (quite near the theatre) one can visit Comayagüela's market of San Isidro.

MUSEUMS

On Calle Bolívar, next to Congress, in a beautifully restored building (1654) adjoining the church in Plaza La Merced, is the **Galería Nacional de Arte** (opened in Aug 1996), housing a very fine collection of Honduran modern and colonial art, also prehistoric rock carvings and pre-Colombian ceramics (some remarkable pieces). There are useful descriptions of exhibits, and explanations of the mythology embodied in the prehistoric and pre-Colombian art (in Spanish only but a brochure in English and Spanish is in preparation). Admission US$0.85, open Tues-Sat 1000-1700, Sun 1000-1400, bookshop and cafetería. **Museo Nacional Villa Roy**, in 1936 home of a former President, Julio Lozano, was restored, reconstructed and reopened in 1997 and is now called the **Museum of Republican History**. There are seven main rooms presenting Honduras' history from independence in 1821 to 1963, as well as supporting cultural presentations and temporary exhibits. It is situated on a hilltop 1 block above the beautiful Parque Concordia on Calle Morelos 3A (entry US$1.50, open 0900-1630, closed Sun). In the Edif del Banco Central, 12 C entre 5 y 6 Av, Comayagüela, is the **Pinacoteca Arturo H Medrano**, with a collection of approximately 500 works by five Honduran artists and, in the same building, the **Museo Numismático**, with a collection of coins and banknotes from Honduras and around the world (open Mon-Fri, 0900-1200, 1300-1600). **Museo de la República de Honduras** (formerly the **Museo Histórico**), in the former Presidencial Palace, better on the 19th century than the 20th, visitors can see the President's office and the Salón Azul state room, open 0830-1630, Mon-Sat, entry US$1.20, reduced for Central Americans, children and students.

NB Generally speaking, Tegucigalpa is cleaner and safer (especially at night) than Comayagüela. If you have anything stolen, report it to Dirección de Investigación Criminal (DIC), 5 Av, 7-8 C (next to Edificio Palermo), T 37-47-99.

EXCURSIONS

Southeast of Tegucigalpa is **Suyapa**, a village with a big church which attracts pilgrims to its wooden figure of the Virgin, a tiny image about 8 cm high set into the altar. 1-4 Feb is a fiesta, during which they hold a televised 'alborada' with singers, music, fireworks etc, from 2000-2400 on the second evening. Take a bus to the University or to Suyapa from 'La Isla', 1 block NW of the city stadium.

Santa Lucía

Northeast of Suyapa, on the way to Valle de Angeles take a right turn off to visit the quaint old mining village of **Santa Lucía** (*Pop* 4,230; *Alt* 1,400-1,600m), perched precariously on a steep mountainside overlooking the wide valley with Tegucigalpa below. You can also walk, it is 24 km from Tegucigalpa to the Jutiapa entrance to the park. Then hike to the visitors' centre of La Tigra (10 km). A recommended hike is the Sendero La Esperanza, which leads to the road; turn right then take the Sendero Bosque Nublado on your left. The whole circuit takes about 1 hr 20 mins. At Km 17 on Zamorano road (at the summit of the range overlooking Suyapa church) take dirt road left to TV tower. From here a delightful 2-hrs' walk over forested ridges leads to Santa Lucía. The town has a beautiful colonial church with a Christ given by King Philip II of Spain in 1592; there is a festival in the 2nd and 3rd weeks of January. There is a charming legend of the Black Christ which the authorities ordered to be taken down to Tegucigalpa when Santa Lucía lost its former importance as a mining centre. Every step it was carried away from Santa Lucía it became heavier. When impossible to carry it further, they turned round and by the time they were back to Santa Lucía, it was as light as a feather. The town is lively with parties on Sat night. There are souvenir shops in the town, including *Cerámicas Ucles* just past the lagoon, 2nd street on left, and another ceramics shop at the entrance on your right. There are good walks up the mountain on various trails; fine views of Tegucigalpa from above.

A good circuit is to descend E from the mountain towards San Juan del Rancho through lovely landscapes on a good dirt road, then connect with the paved road to El Zamorano. From there continue either to El Zamorano, or return to Tegucigalpa (see below for opposite direction).

● **Places to eat** One small *comedor* next to the plaza/terrace of the municipality, but on Sun there is more food available on the streets; also Czech restaurant *Miluška* serving Czech and Honduran food, rec.

● **Transport** Bus to Santa Lucía from Mercado San Pablo, hourly service, US$0.30, past the statue of Simón Bolívar by the Esso station, Av de los Próceres, Tegucigalpa.

Valle de Angeles

(*Pop* 6,635; *Alt* 1,310m) About a 30-min drive from Tegucigalpa, **Valle de Angeles** is on a plain below **Monte San Juan**, of which **Cerro El Picacho**, 2,270m (at the top is a zoo of mostly indigenous animals, open Thur-Sun, US$0.25), is the highest point, and **Cerro La Tigra**. It is surrounded by pine forests and the climate stays cool the year round. There are old mines, many walks possible in the forests, picnic areas, swimming pool, crowded on Sun. Hospital de los Adventistas, in the valley, a modern clinic, sells vegetables and handicrafts; there are many handicraft shops in town, good for leather goods, items in wood, hats, etc. A visit to the pavilion of arts and crafts organized by the national Asociación de Artesanías is recommended. 3 km before the town is *Cerámicas Ucles* which has a wide variety of ceramics.

● **Accommodation & services** D *Hotel y Restaurante Posada del Angel*, service indifferent, moderate prices; *Restaurante La Canterita*, good food, cosy, nice atmosphere, rec; *Restaurante Turístico de Valle de Angeles*, on top of hill overlooking town, also good; *Restaurant Papagayo* for typical dishes; *Comedor La Abejita*; several others.

Tegucigalpa environs

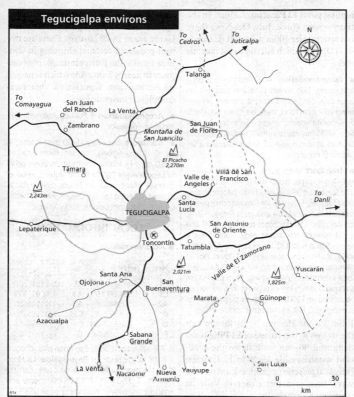

To Cedros

To Juticalpa

N

Talanga

To Comayagua

San Juan del Rancho

La Venta

Zambrano

Montaña de San Juancito

San Juan de Flores

El Picacho 2,270m

Villa de San Francisco

Támara

Valle de Angeles

To Danlí

2,243m

TEGUCIGALPA

Santa Lucía

Lepaterique

Toncontín

Tatumbla

San Antonio de Oriente

2,021m

Valle de El Zamorano

Yuscarán

Santa Ana

Ojojona

San Buenaventura

1,825m

Marata

Güinope

Azacualpa

Sabana Grande

To Nacaome

La Venta

Nueva Armenia

Yauyupe

San Lucas

0   30
km

• **Banks & money changers** Banco del Occidente.

• **Transport** Buses to Valle de Angeles hourly on the hour, US$0.40, 1 hr, leaves from San Felipe, nr the Hospital; to San Juan de Flores 1000, 1230, 1530.

Continue to San Juan de Flores (also called Cantarranas) and San Juancito, an old mining town. From here you can climb the La Tigra cloud forest and even walk along the top before descending to El Hatillo and then to Tegucigalpa.

There are bracing climbs to the heights of Picacho in the **La Tigra National Park** cloud forest. Sun morning early is a good time but weekdays are quieter. Single hikers should keep to the road, there have

been violent robberies on the short cuts, check before setting out. There are two approach routes: go to El Piligüin, from where you can start hiking, or to *Gloriales Inn*, in El Hatillo (see below, **Accommodation**). To **San Juancito** (**G** *Hotelito San Juan*, 6 rooms with shared bathroom, grocery store next door also sells fuel, drinks and can prepare *comida corriente*, same owners, T 76-22-37), above which is the National Park (well worth a visit, a stiff, 1-hr uphill walk to El Rosario visitor centre, park offices and six trails ranging from 30 mins to 8 hrs, US$10 entry, bring insect repellent); a few quetzal birds survive here; do not leave paths when walking as there are precipitous drops;

highest point **El Picacho**, 2,270m. In the rainy season (June, July, Oct-Nov) there is a spectacular 100m waterfall (Cascada de la Gloria) which falls on a vast igneous rock.

● **Accommodation** At El Rosario, it is on a first come, first served basis (no problem on weekdays, can be cold at night, showers are icy), bring your own food; there are many bunkbeds in separate rooms, water, electricity, friendly host, US$5 payable at visitors' centre. Meals can be had at the house of Señora Amalia Elvir, before El Rosario.

● **Transport** Buses leave from San Pablo market, Tegucigalpa, from 1000, 1½ hrs, on Sat and Sun bus at 0800 packed with people visiting their families, US$0.75 for San Juancito; passes turn-off to Santa Lucía and goes through Valle de Angeles. On Sat, buses return at 0600 and 1200 from church, board early. Note that the return Sun bus at 1300 is even more full, board early, leaves from near edge of town not at terminal point where it dropped you, double check local information. Alternatively, from behind Los Dolores church in Tegucigalpa you can take a bus to Jutiapa at 1300; it passes through beautiful scenery by El Hatillo and other communities.

From Parque Herrera buses throughout the day go to the village of **El Piligüin**; a delightful 40-min walk down the pine-clad mountainside leads to El Chimbo (meals at *pulpería* or shop, ask anyone the way), then take bus either to Valle de Angeles or Tegucigalpa.

At Km 24 on Zamorano road, climb the highest peak through the Uyuca rain forest, information from Escuela Agrícola Panamericana in the **Valle del Zamorano**, or from their office in the Edif Glasso, T 33-27-17, in Tegucigalpa. The school has rooms for visitors. Visits to the school are organized by some tour operators. On the NW flank of Uyuca is the picturesque village of **Tatumbla**.

Ojojona

A 1-hr drive, 24 km S of Tegucigalpa, is **Ojojona** (*Pop* 6,670; *Alt* 1,400m), another quaint old village; turn right down Southern Highway. The village's pottery is interesting (but selection reported to be poor). There is a small museum. The

Galería de Arte, open 0900-1500, is owned by the noted landscape painter Carlos Garay. *Fiesta* 18-20 January. There are two well preserved colonial churches in Ojojona (notice the fine paintings), plus two more in nearby Santa Ana which is passed on the way from Tegucigalpa. Ojojona is completely unspoiled.

● **Accommodation** F *Posada Joxone*, comfortable; *comedor*.

● **Transport** Bus every 15-30 mins from C 4, Av 6, Comayagüela, nr San Isidro market, US$0.40, 1 hr. From same location, buses go W to **Lepaterique** ('place of the jaguar'), another colonial village, over an hour's drive through rugged, forested terrain. Distant view of Pacific on fine days from heights above village.

LOCAL INFORMATION

● **Accommodation**

Hotel prices

L1	over US$200	L2	US$151-200
L3	US$101-150	A1	US$81-100
A2	US$61-80	A3	US$46-60
B	US$31-45	C	US$21-30
D	US$12-20	E	US$7-11
F	US$4-6	G	up to US$3

A 7% sales tax is added to hotel bills; check if it is inc in the price. **In Tegucigalpa**: L3 *Honduras Maya*, Av República de Chile, Colonia Palmira, T 32-31-91, F 32-76-29, rooms and apartments, casino, swimming pool US$3.50, bars (the main bar is relaxed and you get appetizers with every alcoholic drink, US TV channels), cafeterias (*Black Jack's Snack Bar*, *Cafetería 2000*), restaurant (*El Candelero*), conference hall and convention facilities for 1,000, view over the city from uppermost rooms; **L3** *Plaza San Martín*, on Plaza San Martín (nr *Honduras Maya*), Colonia Palmira, T 32-82-67, F 31-13-66, good cafeteria, nice bar, great views of the city from the top terrace; **A2** *Alameda*, Blvd Suyapa (some distance from centre), T 32-68-74, F 32-69-32, comfortable, pool, restaurant *Le Chalet* (T 32-69-20). **A2** *Suites La Aurora*, Apart-Hotel, Av Luis Bográn 1519, Colonia Tepeyac, T 32-98-91, F 32-01-88, rooms with kitchenette, cable TV, excellent restaurant, swimming pool, helpful staff; **A2** *Humuya Inn Guest House*, Colonia Humuya 1150, 5 mins from airport, T 39-22-06, F 39-50-99, e-mail rguillen@ns.hondunet.net, rooms and service apartments, US owner, rec. At El Hatillo, on the hill N of Tegucigalpa is the comfortable mountain inn *Gloriales*, beautiful setting and fine views of La Tigra forest, T 22-49-50, lovely rooms, fine cuisine, reservations essential; also the new *La Estancia Country Resort*, Corralitos, with restaurant, T 21-86-51, F 21-86-53. **Downtown: A1-B** *Excelsior*, Av Cervantes 1515, T 37-26-38, currently closed for refurbishment; **A2** *Plaza*, on Av Paz Barahona, in front of Post Office (T 37-21-11, F 37-21-19), good, *Papagayo* restaurant good for breakfast and set lunch; **A2** *La Ronda*, 6 Av, 11 C, 5 blocks from cathedral (T 37-81-51/55, F 37-14-54) a/c TV restaurant, cafeteria (*Rondalla*) and nightclub; **A3** *Prado*, Av Cervantes, 7 y 8 Av, T 37-01-21, F 37-14-54, *La Posada* restaurant.

C *Istmania*, 5 Av, 7 and 8 C (T 37-16-38/39, F 37-14-46) nr Church of Los Dolores, *Versalles* restaurant; **C** *MacArthur*, 8 C, 4 y 5 Av, T 37-98-39, F 38-02-94, a/c, TV, private bath, cheaper without a/c, rec; **C** *Nuevo Boston*, Av Jérez No 321, T 37-94-11, good beds, spotless, cable TV, hot water, central, repeatedly rec, good value, no credit cards, rooms on street side noisy, friendly, free coffee, mineral water and cookies in lounge, stores luggage, well run; **C-D** *Krystal*, 6 Av and 6 C, T 37-88-07, F 37-89-76, TV, a/c, good rooms, not very welcoming, parking, restaurant for 1,000 (special events only), rooftop bar with good view.

D-E *Imperio Maya*, 7 Av, 1225, good, reasonably-priced restaurant

E *Don Tito*, 3 Av, 7-8 C, clean, comfortable, hot water; **E** *Fortuna*, 5 Av, nr Los Dolores church, with or without bath, good, clean, friendly, basic, stores luggage; there are several other cheap hotels in this area; **E** *Granada 1*, Av Gutemberg 1401, Barrio Guanacaste (hot water on 2nd floor only), good, clean, safe, TV lounge, table tennis, T 37-23-81; **E** *Granada 2 and 3*, on the street leading uphill (to Barrio Casamate) from NE corner of Parque Finlay, T 37-40-04/22-05-97 (fax service for guests 38-44-38), better beds, hot water in all rooms, safe parking, both can be noisy from passing traffic, but rec, popular with Peace Corps; **E** *Marichal*, 5 Av, 5 C (T 37-00-69) (ask for a back room), noisy, clean, centrally located; **E** *Nan Kin*, Av Gutemberg, Barrio Guanacaste, opp San Miguel gas station, T 38-02-91, 38-02-71, F 38-02-99, clean, friendly, safe, hot water, huge cheap Chinese meals, clothes washing service, good value.

F *Iberia*, Peatonal Los Dolores, hot showers, clean, friendly, T 37-92-67, stores luggage. **F** pp, 5 rooms for 4 people each above *Café Allegro* (see **Places to eat** below), run similar to a youth hostel, shared accommodation, shared bathrooms, comfortable, very clean, cable TV room, popular with Peace Corps, safe area, very international, information on Honduras, changes money, possible work available in exchange for room and board, please contact Jorge, he can also arrange country weekends, 3 nights, all meals, hiking, horses, staying with Honduran family in their country house, relaxing, pleasant, US$150 pp.

G pp *Hospedaje Sureño*, opp *Fortuna*, friendly, safe, shared bath, room to dry laundry; **G** pp *Tegucigalpa*, Av Gutemberg 1645, basic but OK.

Comayagüela: is convenient for buses to the N and W and there are many cheap *pensiones* and rooms. It is noisier and dirtier than Tegucigalpa, and many establishments are unsuitable for travellers. If you are carrying luggage, take a taxi; **C-D** *Centenario*, 6 Av, 9-10 C, T 37-10-50, safe parking, rec; **D-E** *Real de Oro*, Av Cabanas, 11 and 12 C, clean, friendly; **D-E** *Palace*, 8-9 Av, 12 C, T 37-66-60, new; **E** *Condesa Inn*, 7 Av, 12 C, clean, hot shower, a/c, TV, cafeteria, very friendly, a bargain, rec, not far from Tica bus office; **E** *Ismary*, 4-5 Av, 5 C, T 38-13-93, with bath, new; **E** *Renieri*, 10 C, 3-4 Av, T 37-24-30; **E** *San Pedro*, 9 C, 6 Av, with bath, F without or with private cold shower, popular, restaurant; **E-F** *Hotel Richard No 1*, 4 C, 6 and 7 Av, 'laundry' on roof; **F** *California*, 6 Av, 22-23 C, private bath, friendly, changes US$3, close to MI Esperanza bus station for Nicaragua; **F** *Colonial*, 6a y 7a Av, 6 C, No 617, T 375785, price pp with bath, hot water, clean, good value, restaurant next door; **F** *Hotelito West*, 10 C, 6-7 Av, towels and soap, hot water all day, very friendly, change TCs, rec; **F** *Teleño*, 7 Av, clean, friendly; **G** *Hotelito Latino*, 6 Av, 8 C, very basic, friendly, safe, cafeteria; **G** *Lisboa*, 7 C, 4-5 Av, small rooms, OK.

● **Places to eat**

A meal in a good restaurant costs between US$6-11; for hotel restaurants, see above. Most places are closed on Sun.

Latin American: *Taco Loco*, Blvd Morazán, Mexican fast food; *José y Pepe's*, Av República de Panamá, excellent steaks, good service, good value, warmly rec.

International food: *El Arriero*, Av República de Chile, nr *Honduras Maya*, very good steaks and seafood, expensive; *Alondra*, Av Rep de Chile on E side of *Honduras Maya*, fine, expensive; *Marbella*, 6 C, 3-4 Av, central, good for breakfast. *El Trapiche*, Blvd Suyapa, opp National University, colonial ranch atmosphere, good steaks, expensive, rec.

Chinese: *China Food*, 2 blocks before the easternmost bridges on Blvd Morazán, ½ block to the right, the best Chinese in town, good value; on same road No 2001 is *China Town Palace*, T 32-82-55, delicious meals, excellent value, rec; *On-Lock*, Blvd Morazán, good; *Pekín*, 3 C, No 525, Barrio San Rafael, 1 block from *Hotel Maya*; *Mei-Mei*, Pasaje Midence Soto, central, rec; *Ley-Hsen*, Pasaje Fiallos Soto. There are several good Chinese restaurants in 4 Av in centre, enormous helpings at reasonable prices. *Hong Kong*, 6 Av, between 6 and 7 C, excellent large meals, good value.

Italian: *Café Allegro*, Av Rep de Chile 360, Col Palmira, T 32-81-22, very good coffee and pastas, magazines to read, international atmosphere, changes money, owner Jorge provides good information on diving, national parks, forests, etc, welcoming, will store luggage, warmly rec (*Mexico and Central America/South American Handbook* sold here, jazz bar, *Il Piano Roto*, TV room, souvenirs room with Honduran ceramics and handicrafts and 22 bunk beds to rent, see above). **Pizzerias**: *Tito*, Blvd Morazán, Col Palmira.

Meat: *El Patio 2*, Blvd Morazán, excellent traditional food and kebabs, good service and atmosphere, good value for the hungry, rec; *Jack's Steak House*, same street, also burgers and American style sandwiches; *Bar Mediterráneo*, city centre, delicious goat meat, and cheap set meals; *Duncan Maya*, opp central *Pizza Hut*, good and cheap.

Others: for Garifuna food, try *Yurumey*, Av JM Gálvez; 2 **Burger Huts**, one N of Parque La Merced, in the centre and one on Blvd Morazán. *Pizza Huts*: one nr Parque Central (with good salad bar) and at 7 other locations. '*Stacolosal*, 5 C, 4 Av, is a good cheap eating place, classical music and friendly owner, open 0700-1900. *Super Donuts*, Peatonal, Blvd Morazón, good for filling buffet breakfasts (not just doughnuts!), popular with locals; *Café y Librería Paradiso*, Av Paz Barahona 1351, excellent coffee and snacks, good library, paintings, prints and photos to enjoy, newspapers and magazines on sale, good meeting place; *Don Pepe's Terraza*, Av Colón, nr Bancahsa, T 22-10-84, downtown, cheap, live music, but typical Honduran atmosphere, rec. *Au Natural*, Calle Hipólito Matute y Av Miguel Cervantes, some vegetarian, some meat dishes, huge fresh fruit juices, antiques, caged birds, nice garden atmosphere but sadly deteriorating. *La Gran Muralla*, opp *Hotel Nan Kin* (see above), good cheap food, very friendly, rec; *Dunkin Donuts*, several outlets. *Basilio's*, *repostería y panadería*, Calle Peatonal off Plaza Morazán, good cakes, breads and pastries; *Sirias*, next door to *Hotel Granada 3*, best place to eat in the immediate neighbourhood; *Pastelería Francesa*, opp French embassy, rec; *Salman's* bakeries, several outlets in the centre, good bread and pastries; *Brik Brak*, Calle Peatonal just off the Parque Central, open 24 hrs, rec.

● **Airline offices**

For national flights: **Isleña airlines**, T Toncontín airport 33-11-30. **Caribbean Air** at the airport, T 33-19-06. **Taca International** and **Lacsa**, both at Edif Interamericana, Blvd Morazán, T 31-24-72 or airport 33-57-56; **Iberia**, Ed Palmira, opp *Honduras Maya*, T 31-52-23, 31-52-47, also **American** in this building, 1st floor, T 32-13-47 (airport 33-96-80), F 32-13-80; **KLM**, Ed Ciicsa, Av Rep de Chile y Av Rep de Panamá, Col Palmira, T 32-64-10; **Lufthansa**, Edif Plaza del Sol, No 2326, Av de la Paz, T 36-75-60, F 36-75-80.

● **Banks & money changers**

All banks have several branches throughout the city; we list the main offices. **Lloyds Bank**, Av Ramón E Cruz, off Blvd Morazán and Av de la Paz, take any San Felipe bus (Rivera y Cía), get out above US Embassy, walk back, turn left and bank is 300m on right. Open 0900-1500, closed Sat, Sterling and Canadian dollars changed. **Banco Atlántida**, 5 C in front of Plaza Morazán (may agree to change money on Sat up to 1200); **Banco de Honduras (Citibank)**, Blvd Suyapa; **Bancahorro**, 5 C in front of Plaza Morazán; **Banco Ficensa**, Blvd Morazán, does Visa advances. All accept TCs, and cash TCs. Visa and Mastercard cash advances (no commission) and TCs at **Credomatic de Honduras**, Blvd Morazán. Visa advances in lempiras at branches of **Futuro** and **Banco Occidente**. **Mundirama Travel Agency**, Edif Ciicsa, Av Rep de Panamá, Colonia Palmira, T 32-39-09, American Express agents, sells and cashes Amex TCs etc (to Amex cardholders only), also travel service. Banks are allowed to trade at the current market rate (see **Currency** in **Information for travellers**), but there is a street market along the Calle Peatonal off the Parque Central, opp the Post Office and elsewhere. Exchange can be difficult on Sat, try Coin, a *casa de cambio* on Av La Paz inside Supermercado Más y Menos, same rates as banks, no commission, Mon-Fri 0830-1730, Sat 0900-1200; another branch of Coin on Calle Peatonal, good rates, rec.

● **Cultural centres**
Alianza Francesa, Colonia Lomas del Guijarro, cultural events Fri pm, French films Tues 1930, T 39-15-29; **Centro Cultural Alemán**, 8 Av, Calle La Fuente, German newspapers to read, cultural events, T 37-15-55; **Instituto Hondureño de Cultura Interamericana** (IHCI), Calle Real de Comayagüela has an English library and cultural events, T 37-75-39.

● **Embassies & consulates**
El Salvador, Colonia San Carlos No 219, 1 block from Blvd Morazán, T 36-80-45, 36-73-44, F 36-93-94, friendly; **Guatemala**, Calle Principal, Colonia Loma Linda Norte, Tegucigalpa, T 32-50-18, F 31-56-55, Mon-Fri, 0900-1300, take photo, visa given on the spot, US$10; **Nicaragua**, Colonia Lomas del Tepeyac, Av Choluteca 1130, bloque M-1 (T 32-90-25, F 31-14-12), 0800-1200, US$25, visa issued same day, but can take up to 2 days, has to be used within 4 weeks of issue; for Guatemalan and Nicaraguan embassies, take Alameda bus from street behind Congress building (from Parque Merced descend towards river, but don't cross bridge, instead turn left behind Congress and ask for bus stop on right-hand side), alight before Planificación de Familia and climb street on left beside Planificación: 250m up on right is Guatemalan Embassy; can also be reached with a very steep climb from Av Juan Lindo by the *gasolinera* on corner of Av La Paz below the US Embassy. **Costa Rica**, Colonia El Triángulo, 1a C, frente a casa 104, T 32-17-68, F 32-18-76, bus to Lomas del Guijarro to last stop, then walk up on your left for 300m; **Mexico**, Av República de México, Paseo República de Brasil 2402, Col Palmira, T 32-64-71, F 31-47-19, opens 0900, visa takes 24 hrs; **Panama** (T/F 31-54-41, 2nd floor) and **Colombia**, T 32-97-09 (Embassy 32-51-31), both in Ed Palmira, opp *Honduras Maya*. **Belize Consulate**, in *Hotel Honduras Maya*, T 39-01-34.

Argentina, Col Rubén Darío 417, T 32-33-76; **Brazil**, Paseo Virgilio Zelaya Rubí 123, Colonia Castaño Sur, S of Blvd Morazán, T 32-20-21 **Chile**, Ed Interamericana, p 6, Blvd Morazán, T 31-37-03; **Ecuador**, Av Juan Lindo 122, Col Palmira, T 36-59-80; **Peru**, Calle Rubén Darío 1902, Col Alameda, T 31-52-61; **Uruguay**, Ed Palmira, p 4, T 31-53-64; **Venezuela**, Av 1 FAO, Casa 265, Col Loma Linda Norte, T 32-26-28, F 32-10-16.

USA, Av La Paz (0800-1700, Mon-Fri, take any bus from N side of Parque Central in direction 'San Felipe', T 36-93-20/29, F 36-93-20); **Canada**, Ed Comercial Los Castaños, p 6, Blvd Morazán, T 31-45-38. **Japan**, Colonia San Carlos, 4 Av, 5 C, 2 blocks off Blvd Morazán and Av de la Paz, T 36-68-29, behind Los Castaños Shopping Mall.

UK, Ed Palmira, 3rd floor, opp *Hotel Honduras Maya* (Apdo Postal 290, T 32-54-29); **Germany**, Ed Paysen, 3rd floor, Blvd Morazán, T 32-31-61. **France** Av Juan Lindo 416, Colonia Palmira, T 36-68-00. **Spain**, Col Matamoros 801, T 36-65-89, nr Av de la Paz and US Embassy; **Italy**, Av Principal 2602, Col Reforma, T 38-33-91; **Netherlands**, Edif Barahona, Av Juan Manuel Gálvez, Col Alameda, next to Festival, T 31-50-07, F 31-50-09; **Norway**, Av Juan Lindo, Col Las Minitas; **Switzerland**, consul at Oficina de Cosude (Cooperación Suiza al Desarrollo), Ed Galerías, Blvd Morazán, T 32-96-92/32-62-39; **Swedish Consulate**, Av Altiplano, Retorno Borneo 2758, Colonia Miramontes, T/F 32-49-35; **Danish Consulate**, Ed La Paz, 206 Blvd Los Próceres, T 36-64-07; **Czech Consul**, Santa Lucía nr football field.

To get to Colonia Palmira where most Embassies are, take buses marked 'San Miguel' and 'Lomas' Take 'San Felipe' bus from Rivera y Coy, 3 mins' walk from Parque Central for the following consulates: USA, Mexico, Venezuela and El Salvador.

● **Entertainment**
In front of the Universidad Nacional on Blvd Suyapa is *La Peña*, where every Fri at 2100 there is live music, singing and dancing, entrance US$1.40. On Av Rep de Chile: bars *Café Allegro*; *Backstreet Pub*, Av Rep de Uruguay in Colonia Tepeyac, bar/disco, good atmosphere, no cover except when live music. Boulevard Morazán has plenty of choice in night life inc *Taco Taco*, a nice bar, sometimes with live Mariachi music; next door *Tequila*, a popular drinking place only open at weekends; *Cocteles*, the in-place in Tegucigalpa for dancing. Blvd Juan Pablo II has discos with various types of music, eg *Rock Castle*, plays punta, dance music and after midnight rock music, relaxed atmosphere, entry US$4, women free, check your bill.

Cinemas: Plaza 1, 2 3, and 4 in Centro Comercial Plaza Miraflores; Regis, Real and Opera at Centro Comercial Centroamérica, Blvd Miraflores (all have good US films). In city centre, double cinemas Lido Palace, and Variedades. Tauro and Aries, 200m up Av Gutemberg leading from Parque Finlay to Colonia Reforma (same street as *Hotels Granada 2 and 3*), tickets US$1.65.

● **Hospitals & medical services**
Dentist: *Dra Rosa María Cardillo de Boquín*, Ed Los Jarros, Sala 206, Blvd Morazán, T 31-05-83, rec. *Dr Roberto Ayala*, DDS, Calle Alfonso XIII 3644, Col Lomas de Guijarro, T 32-24-07.

Pharmacy: *Farmacia Rosna*, in pedestrian mall off Parque Central, T 37-06-05, English spoken, rec; *Regis Palmira*, Ed Ciicsa, Av República de Panamá, Col Palmira; *El Castaño*, Blvd Morazán.

Private hospitals: Hospital y Clínica Viera, 5 C, 11 y 12 Av, Tegucigalpa, T 37-71-36; Hospital la Policlínica SA 3 Av, 7 y 8 C, Comayagüela, T 37-35-03; Centro Médico Hondureño, 3 Av, 3 C, Barrio La Granja, Comayagüela, T 33-60-28.

● **Laundry**
Lavandería Maya, 1 block off Blvd Morazán, 0700-1900, Mon-Sat; *Mi Lavandería*, opp *Reposteria Calle Real*, 3 C, 2 Av, Comayagüela, T 37-65-73, Mon-Sat 0700-1800, Sun and holidays 0800-1700, rec; *Lavandería Super Jet*, Av Guthemberg, about 300m E of *Hotel Granada*, US$0.20/kilo, rec; *La Cisne*, 1602 Calle La Fuente, US$1.80 up to 5 kg, same day service, rec; *Lavandería Italiana*, Barrio Guadalupe, 4 blocks W of *Café Allegro*.

● **Places of worship**
Churches: Episcopal Anglican (Col Florencia, take Suyapa bus) and Union Church, Colonia Lomas del Guijarro, with services in English. Catholic mass in English at the chapel of Instituto San Francisco at 1000 every Sun.

● **Post & telecommunications**
Post Office: Av Miguel de Cervantes y Calle Morelos, 4 blocks from Parque Central. *Lista de Correos* (Poste Restante) mail held for 1 month. Mail boxes in main supermarkets. Books should be packed separately from clothes etc when sending packages. The Post Office will send and receive faxes.

Telecommunications: Hondutel, 5 C and 4 Av, has several direct AT&T lines to USA, no waiting. Phone, fax and telegrams; open 24 hrs for phone services only.

● **Shopping**
Bookshops: *Metromedia*, Edif Casa Real, Av San Carlos, behind Centro Comercial Los Castaños, Blvd Morazán, English books, both new and secondhand, for sale or exchange (small fee

for exchange), wide selection of US magazines. *Shakespeare's Books*, Av Gutemberg (nr *Hotel Granada*), has a large selection of second-hand English-language books, US owner also runs *Tobacco Road Tavern* on the same premises. *Librería Paradiso* (see under café listing above). For books in Spanish on Honduras and Central America, *Editorial Guaymuras*, Av Miguel Cervantes 1055. Good book and news stand, and maps in *Hotel Honduras Maya*. Secondhand bookstalls in Mercado San Isidro (6 Av y 2 C, Comayagüela), good value.

Markets: Mercado Colón or San Isidro, 6 Av at 1 C, Comayagüela, many things for sale, fascinating but filthy, do not buy food here. Sat is busiest day. Mercado de Artesanías, 3 Av, 15 C next to Parque El Soldado, good value. Good supermarkets: Sucasa, in Blvd Morazón, Más y Menos, in Av de la Paz.

Photography: *Kodak* on Parque Central and Blvd Morazán for excellent, professional standard development of slides. *Fuji* in front of the Cathedral and on Blvd Morazán. *Ultracolor* scratched the slides, not rec.

Souvenir shops: *Candú*, opp *Hotel Maya*, and in Av Rep de Chile; *Café Allegro* (see above). Also in Valle de Angeles, see **Excursions**. *El Mundo Maya*, Calle Adolfo Zuniga 1114, T 22-29-46, art gallery, souvenir shop and tourist information, also changes US dollars, cash and TCs, run by Alejandro Villela Franco, open Mon-Fri 0900-1830, Sat 0900-1600.

● **Tour companies & travel agents**
Trek Hoñduras, Ed Midence Soto 218, T 39-07-43, F 37-57-76, downtown, tours of the city, Bay Islands, Copán, San Pedro Sula, Valle de Angeles and Santa Lucía; *Mundirama*, see **Exchange** above; *Explore Honduras Tour Service*, Ed Medcast, 2nd level, Blvd Morazán, T 39-76-94, F 36-98-00, Copán and Bay Islands; *La Moskitia Ecoaventuras*, PO Box 3577, Tegucigalpa, T/F 37-93-98, for trips to Mosquitia; *Centro Americana de Turismo*, W side of Blvd Morazán before the bridges, Tegucigalpa, specializing in Honduras; *Gloria Tours* across from N side of Parque Central in Casa Colonial, information centre and tour operator.

● **Tourist offices**
Instituto Hondureño de Turismo, Ed Europa, Av Ramón E Cruz y Calle Rep de México, 3rd floor, above Lloyds Bank, Col San Carlos, T 22-40-02, F 38-21-02, also at Toncontín airport. Open 0830-1530, provides lists of hotels and sells posters, postcards (cheaper than elsewhere) and slides.

Information on cultural events around the country from Teatro Manuel Bonilla, better than at regional tourist offices. El Mundo Maya, a private tourist information centre, behind the cathedral next to the Parque Central, T 22-29-46. For information on **National Parks**, see page 866.

● **Useful addresses**
Immigration: Dirección Gen de Migración, Av Máximo Jérez, next to *Hotel Ronda*, Tegucigalpa.

Peace Corps: opp Edif Ciicsa, on Av República de Chile, up hill past *Hotel Honduras Maya*. The volunteers are a good source of information.

● **Transport**
Local Buses: cost US$0.08-US$0.12, stops are official but unmarked. **Taxis**: about US$1.40-US$2 pp (no reduction for sharing, but bargaining possible), never pay what they say first; more after 2200, but cheaper (US$0.25) on designated routes eg Miraflores to centre.
Car rentals: Avis, T 32-00-88 or 33-95-48, *Hotel Honduras Maya* and airport; **Toyota**, Col El Prado, T 33-40-04; **Molinari**, T 37 53-35 or 33-13-07, Av Comayagüela No 1002, *Honduras Maya* and airport; **Budget**, T 32-68-32 or 33-51-70, *Honduras Maya* and airport; **National**, T 33-26-53 or 33-49-62, Col El Prado, *Honduras Maya* and airport. **Car repairs**: Metal Mecánica, 1 block S of Av de los Próceres, Colonia Lara. Volkswagen dealer nr Parque Concordia, good for repairs. **Routes**: motorists leaving Tegucigalpa for San Pedro Sula or Olancho can avoid the congestion of Comayagüela market by driving N down to Barrio Abajo, crossing the river to Barrio El Chile and taking the motorway up the mountainside, to turn right to Olancho, or left to rejoin the northern outlet to San Pedro Sula (at the second intersection, turn right for the old, winding route, go straight on for the new, fast route). A peripheral highway is being built around the city.

Air Toncontín, 6½ km from the centre, opens at 0530. The airport is in a narrow valley creating difficult landing conditions: early morning fog or bad weather can close the airport. Check-in at least 2 hrs before departure; snacks, souvenir shops, several duty free stores. Buses to airport from Comayagüela, Loarque Rutas No 1 and No 11, on 4a Av between 6 and 7 C, or opp Ciné Palace in downtown Tegucigalpa; into town US$0.06-0.19, 20 mins from left-hand side outside the airport; yellow cabs, US$4, smaller colectivo taxis, US$2 or more. Agree taxi fare at the airport.

Buses To **San Pedro Sula** on Northern Highway, 4 hrs (7 companies inc Sáenz, Centro Comercial Perisur, Blvd Unión Europea, T 33-30-10, El Rey, 6 Av, 9 C, Comayagüela, same phone number, Hedmán Alas, 13-14 C, 11 Av, Comayagüela, T 37-71-43, 7 a day, Norteños, T 37-07-06, and a new company: Viajes Nacionales (Viana) Servicio Ejecutivo Clase Oro, terminal in Comayagüela by Gasolinera Esso, El Prado, next to Toyota, T 25-42-35, 0630, 1300, 1800), all charge US$3, except Hedmán Alas (rec), US$6, first bus leaves at 0530, then 9 more at intervals to 1730. Saenz and Hedmán Alas both have a highly rec luxury service, US$8, Saenz at 0600, 1000, 1400, 1800 (book in advance), Hedmán Alas at 0545, 1130 and 1645, with a/c, film, snacks and refreshments, 3 hrs 15 mins. To **Tela** and **La Ceiba**, Traliasa, 12A 816 C, 8 Av, Comayagüela, T 37-75-38, at 0600 and 0900, US$4 50 (to Tela), US$5 to La Ceiba. Also Etrusca to Tela at 0700 and La Ceiba at 1700, US$6, 6½-7 hrs. Mi Esperanza, 6 Av, 23 or 26 C, Comayagüela, T 38-28-63, to **Choluteca**, 4 hrs, US$1.90, 0600 onwards. To **Trujillo**, Cotraibel, 8 Av 11-12 C, Comayagüela, direct 9 hrs, US$6.20, 0500 and 1200. To **Santa Rosa de Copán**, Sultana, from Comayagüela, 0600 and 1000, US$3, 7 hrs. To **La Esperanza**, Empresa Joelito, 4 C, No 834, Comayagüela, 8 hrs, US$2.60. To **Comayagua**, US$1.20, Transportes Catrachos, Col Torocagua, Blvd del Norte, Comayagüela, every 45 mins, 1½-2 hrs. To **Valle de Angeles** and **Santa Lucía**, from stop on Av La Paz (nr filling station opp hospital). To **Juticalpa** and **Catacamas**, Empresa Aurora, 8 C, 6-7 Av, Comayagüela. For **Danlí** and **El Paraíso**, for the Nicaraguan border at Los Manos, see under those towns in **East of Tegucigalpa**.

For travellers leaving Tegucigalpa, take the Tiloarque bus in Av Máximo Jérez, by Cine Palace, and alight in Comayagüela at Cine Centenario (Av 6a) for nearby Empresa Aurora buses (**for Olancho**) and El Rey buses (for San Pedro Sula or **Olancho**); 3 blocks NW is Cine Lux, nr which are Empresas Unidas and Maribel (8 Av, 11-12 C, T 37-30-32) for **Siguatepeque**, US$1.25 (to town centre, US$0.50 cheaper but 1 hr slower than San Pedro Sula buses which drop you on the main road, a US$0.50 taxi ride from Siguatepeque). Tiloarque bus continues to Mi Esperanza bus terminal (for Choluteca and Nicaraguan frontier). Take a 'Carrizal' or 'Santa Fe' bus from Tegucigalpa for the hill ascending Belén (9a C) for Hedmán Alas buses to San Pedro Sula and for Comayagua buses (to town centre, cheaper but slower than main line buses to San

Pedro Sula which drop passengers on main road, a taxi ride away from the centre). By the Mamachepa market is the Norteños bus line for San Pedro Sula; also nearby are buses for **Nacaome** and **El Amatillo** frontier with El Salvador.

International buses: Tica Bus, 16 C, between 5 and 6 Av, Comayagüela, T 20-05-79, 20-05-81, to Managua (US$20, 9 hrs), San José (US$35), San Salvador (US$15), Guatemala City (US$24) and Panama (US$60) daily, early morning departures. Make sure you reserve several days ahead, you have to go to the office to reserve. Alternatively to **Nicaragua**, take Mi Esperanza bus from 6 Av, nr *Hotel California* to San Marcos de Colón, then taxi or local bus to El Espino on border. To San Marcos, 4 a day from 0730, and direct to frontier at 0400, US$2.50, 5 hrs (0730 is the latest one that will get you into Nicaragua the same day). To **San Salvador**, Cruceros del Golfo, Barrio Guacerique, Blvd Comunidad Económica Europea, Comayagüela, T 33-74-15, US$16, at 0600 and 1300, 6 hrs travelling, 1 hr or more at border, connections to Guatemala and Mexico; direct bus to border at El Amatillo, US$2.50, 3 hrs, several daily; alternatively from San Pedro Sula via Nueva Ocotepeque and El Poy. To **Guatemala**, go to San Pedro Sula and take either Impala or Congolón to Nueva Ocotepeque and the frontier at Agua Caliente, or take the route via Copán (see page 942).

NORTH OF TEGUCIGALPA

Taking the Olancho road, you come to **Talanga** with post office and Hondutel near the market on the main road. (From the Parque Central an unpaved road S leads to the Tegucigalpa-Danlí road making a triangular route possible back to the capital.) Just beyond Talanga, an unpaved road turns N to Cedros and Minas de Oro, 66 km. After 41 km, take the small road to your left; at Km 58 is the turn off to Esquías (8 km away). The last part of the road to Minas de Oro is in poor condition, high clearance recommended.

Cedros, one of Honduras' earliest settlements, dates from Pedro de Alvarado's mining operations of 1536. It is an outstanding colonial mining town, with cobbled streets, perched high on an

North of Tegucigalpa

eminence, amid forests. The festival of El Señor del Buen Fin takes place in the first 2 weeks of January. A daily bus from Comayagüela to Minas de Oro passes Cedros.

MINAS DE ORO

(*Pop* 6,000; *Alt* 1,060m) On a forested tableland, Minas de Oro is a centre for walking in attractive hill country. It is a picturesque old mining town. There is a fine view from Cerro Grande which overlooks the town, and a more interesting hike up Cerro El Piñón about 3 km N towards Victoria. Poor road Minas de Oro to Victoria 18 km, on to Sulaco (bus service) with connections from Sulaco to Yorito, Yoro and San Pedro Sula and to Cedros. Several buses daily Sulaco-Yoro.

- **Accommodation & places to eat** Several *pensiones*, inc **G** *Hotelito Girón* and *Los Pinares* (meals US$1); *Comedor El Rodeo*, or eat at Doña Gloria's house, good, large helpings, US$0.80.

- **Transport Buses** 4-hr bus ride with Transportes Victoria, 10 Av 11 Calle Barrio Belén, Comayagüela al 1300, returning from Minas de Oro at 0400 daily (US$1.90).

To the W of Minas de Oro it is 3 km to Malcotal and a further 4 km to Minas de San Antonio both surrounded by hills, mostly stripped of trees (high clearance vehicle, 4WD in wet, recommended between Minas de Oro and San Antonio). There is a fine 2-hrs forested walk over to **Esquías** (good comedor, *Tita's*, accommodation available in private houses, ask at *Tita's*) with a fine church with one of the most fascinating colonial façades in Honduras, extravagant palm motifs, floating

angels and, at the apex, a bishop with hands outstretched in blessing. There is a monument in the plaza to a local hero, the American Harold Brosious, 1881-1950, who arrived in Malcotal in 1908 to prospect for gold. He founded a school there (closed since his death), for the children of local illiterate peasants. As Brosious' fame as a teacher spread, pupils arrived from throughout Honduras and neighbouring countries. Daily bus services Esquías-Tegucigalpa and Esquías-Comayagua.

10 km E of Minas de Oro is San José del Potrero beyond which is **Sulaco**. Above Sulaco is the Montaña de la Flor region where there are settlements of Xicaque Indians. They are also to be found in the lowlands around Victoria where they sell their handicrafts.

Tegucigalpa to San Pedro Sula

O N OR NEAR THE country's main road route are the former capital of Comayagua, Lago Yojoa and some beautiful scenery with Lenca Indian communities.

Támara The Northern Highway between Tegucigalpa and San Pedro Sula leaves the capital and enters the vast intermont basin of **Támara**. A turning at Támara village leads to San Matías waterfall, a delightful area for walking in cool forested mountains.

● **Accommodation** ½ km SW of the toll station nr the Balneario San Francisco is **F** *Hotel Posada/Posada Don Willy*, with bath (electric shower), clean, quiet, fan, excellent value.

The road climbs to the lovely forested heights to **Parque Aventuras** at Km 33, open at weekends, good food, swimming pools, horses, bikes, then to **Zambrano** at Km 34 (*Alt* 1,460m) and **Parque Aurora** at Km 36, midway between Tegucigalpa and Comayagua, about 50 km from the capital. It has a small zoo and picnic area among pine-covered hills, a lake with rowing boats (hire US$1/hr), a snack bar and lovely scenery. Good birdwatching. This spot would be perfect for camping and for caravans, which need to avoid the narrow streets and congestion of Tegucigalpa (camping US$0.50 pp, admission US$0.20, food supplies nearby).

● **Accommodation A3-B** *Casitas Primavera*, Barrio La Primavera, 1,600m W of main road, cosy, rustic houses, lovely setting, sleep 4-6, T 98-66-25 weekends, T 39-23-28 weekdays; **L3** *La Serenísima*, nr *Casitas Primavera*, same phone numbers, 6 suites, meals inc, weekend plans, new 1997. Good walking in the area with waterfalls 100m high.

● **Places to eat** *Merendero La Estancia*, on the main road, very good *comida corriente*, very good bread. Near Parque Aurora is the *Comedor Los Novillos*, good food, nice atmosphere, one of the best spots between Tegucigalpa and Comayagua.

Before descending to the Comayagua valley the Northern Highway reaches another forested mountainous escarpment. A track leads off to the right (ask for directions), with about 30 mins climb on foot to a tableland and natural fortress of **Tenampua** where Indians put up their last resistance to the *conquistadores*, even after the death of Lempira. It has an interesting wall and entrance portal.

LA PAZ

(*Pop* 19,900; *Alt* 690m) Soon after the Tenampua turning, a short road runs W, through Villa San Antonio, to **La Paz**, capital of its Department in the western part of the Comayagua valley. From the new church of the Virgen del Perpetuo Socorro, on the hill, there is a fine view of the town, the Palmerola airfield, and the Comayagua Valley. The town has all paved roads, a soccer stadium and many public services thanks to ex-president Córdoba who lives there.

Comayagua **883**

Hiking around San José

Hike 1: from San José, head NW down through Limón. Take a small path to the left towards some high ground, a large area covered with pine above some rocky escarpments, about 1hr from the centre of San José. A 30-min trail runs along the outer edge of the high ground with many vantage points overlooking the forest, canyons and mountains. There are many paths which lead down into valleys and canyons below, and a couple of small communities.

Hike 2: 5 km from San José is a turnoff called Cerro Bueno (ask locally for directions), with a few houses and a *comedor*. Explore the terrain to the S, where there are valleys, canyons and waterfalls. Ask for the path to Portillo Norte and Sapotal. Sapotal is a small community in an attractive valley from where you can continue via Aguacatal and Grandeo back to the main La Paz-Marcala road. There are many small villages in this fertile area and almost no tourists.

(Mike and Pauline Truman)

Excursions A paved road runs SW from La Paz to Marcala (see page 950, frequent minibuses 2 hrs, US$1). 2 km off this road lies **San Pedro de Tutule** (*Alt* 1,400m), the marketplace for the Indians of **Guajiquiro** (one of the few pure Indian communities in Honduras, several km S of Tutule). Market: Sun morning and Thur. (**G** *Hospedaje Valestia*, good, basic, *comedor* opp.) After San Pedro de Tutule, a turning NW goes to the village of **San José** (*Alt* 1,700m), another Lenca Indian community, 5 km downhill from turning on unpaved road. The climate here can be cool and windy even in the hottest months. The scenery is superb. Good hill walking (see box). Frequent pick-ups from Marcala, and two daily minibuses at about 0815 and 0900; from San José to Marcala minibuses depart at 0615 and 0645, 1 hr, US$1. In San José, a sleepy village, the women make rustic ceramics. There is a good *comedor* 500m before plaza on main road, clean and cheap. (**F** *Hotel Suyaguare*, run by British man, Nayo, or Nigel Potter, basic but comfortable and clean, with meals, he also takes groups to stay in Lenca villages, US$5 pp plus US$10 pp for accommodation in a village; ask for Nayo on the main square in San José, or for Profesora Vinda or Doña Gloria Morán. At least one of these three will be present to meet visitors. Nayo

knows most of the local pathways. Write to Nigel Potter at Barrio Concepción, Marcala, Depto La Paz, CP15201, Honduras.)

5 km N of La Paz, on the paved road to Comayagua, is **Ajuterique**, which has a fine colonial church, worth a visit.

● **Accommodation & places to eat** All **F**: *Pensión San Francisco* (quite nice); *Ali*, friendly, 5 rooms, bath, hot water, eat at *Ali's Restaurant*, food and lodging excellent. *Rico Lunch*, nr church, good and friendly.

● **Banks & money changers** Bancahsa, Banco Atlántida, Banadesa.

● **Transport** Buses from Comayagua, Cotrapal (opp Iglesia La Merced), every hour from 0600, US$0.30, passing Ajuterique and Lejamani; frequent minibus Comayagua-La Paz, 25 mins, US$0.50. Lila bus from the capital, from opp Hispano cinema in Comayagüela. Colectivo taxi from main N-S highway to La Paz, US$2. In La Paz all buses leave from Blvd crossroads, look for the statue of the soldier. Minibus to Marcala, 3 daily, 0530, 0630, 0800, 1½ hrs, US$1.

COMAYAGUA

(*Pop* 59,535; *Alt* 550m) Comayagua is a colonial town in the rich Comayagua plain, 1½ hrs' drive (93.5 km) N from the capital. It was founded on 7 December 1537 as Villa Santa María de Comayagua, on the site of an Indian village by Alonzo de Cáceres. On 3 September 1543, it was designated the Seat of the Audiencia de los Confines by King Felipe II of Spain. President Marco Aurelio Soto transferred the capital to Tegucigalpa in 1880.

Places of interest

There are several old colonial buildings: the former University, the first in Central America, founded in 1632, closed in 1842 (it was located in the Casa Cural, Bishop's Palace, where the bishops have lived since 1558); the churches of La Merced (1550-58) and La Caridad (1730); San Francisco (1574); San Sebastián (1575). San Juan de Dios (1590, destroyed by earthquake in 1750), the church where the Inquisition sat, is now the site of the Santa Teresa Hospital. El Carmen was built in 1785. The most interesting building is the Cathedral in the Central Park, with its square plain tower and its decorated façade with sculpted figures of the saints, which contains some of the finest examples of colonial art in Honduras (closed 1300-1500). The clock in the tower was originally made over 800 years ago in Spain; it was given to Comayagua by Felipe II in 1582. At first it was in La Merced when that was the Cathedral, but moved to the new Cathedral in 1715. There are two colonial plazas shaded by trees and shrubs. A stone portal and a portion of the façade of Casa Real (the viceroy's residence) survives. It was built 1739-41, but was damaged by an earthquake in 1750 and destroyed by tremors in 1856. The army still uses a quaint old fortress built when Comayagua was the capital. There is a lively market area.

Museums

There are two museums: the ecclesiastical museum, ½ block N of Cathedral (daily 0930-1200, 1400-1700, US$0.60) and the Museo de Arqueología (housed in the former Palacio de Gobernación, 1 block S of Cathedral at the corner of 6 C and 1 Av NO, open Wed-Fri 0800-1600, Sat, Sun 0900-1200, 1300-1600, US$1.70). The latter is small scale but fascinating, with 6 rooms each devoted to a different period. Much of the collection comes from digs in the El Cajón region, 47 km N of

Comayagua, before the area was flooded for the hydroelectricity project.

Excursions

To the coffee town of **La Libertad** (hourly bus, 2 hrs, US$0.75), several *hospedajes* and *comedores*; a friendly place. Before La Libertad is **Jamalteca** (1½ hrs by bus US$0.50), from where it is a 40-min walk to a large, deep pool into which drops a 10m waterfall surrounded by lush vegetation. Here you can swim, picnic or camp, but it is on private property and a pass must be obtained from the owner (ask at Supermercado Carol in Comayagua). Best to avoid weekends, when the owners' friends are there.

The **Parque Nacional Montaña de Comayagua** is only 13 km from Comayagua, reached from the villages of San José de la Mora (4WD necessary) or San Jerónimo and Río Negro (usually passable in 2WD). Contact Fundación Ecosimco at 0 C y 1 Av NO in Comayagua for further information. The mountain, 2,407m, has about 6,000 ha of cloud forest and is a major watershed for the area.

Local information
● **Accommodation**

D *Norymax*, Calle Central y 3 Av E, Barrio Torondón, T 72-12-10, a/c, cheaper rooms also, all with bath, hot water, car park.

E *América Inn*, 2 Av y 1 C NO, T 72-03-60, F 72-00-09, a/c, hot water, private bath, TV, cheaper with fan; **E** *Emperador*, Calle Central y 4 Av SO, Barrio Torondón, T 72-03-32, good, a/c, cable TV, cheaper with fan; **E** *Imperial*, 3 Av SO, Barrio Torondón, opp *Norymax*, T 72-02-15, with bath and fan, clean, friendly, good value, parking; **E** *Libertad*, S side of Parque Central, nice courtyard, much choice of room size, clean apart from the toilets, cold water shower outside, helpful, good restaurant 2 doors away; **E** *Motel Puma*, off the same Blvd, garage parking, hot water, with bath (catering for short-stay clientèle); **E** *Quan*, 8 C NO, 3 y 4 Av, T 72-00-70, excellent, with private bath, popular.

F *Boulevard*, small, clean, economic, dark rooms; **F** *Honduras*, 2 Av NO, 1 C, clean, friendly, some rooms with bath; **F** *Luxemburgo*, 4 Av NO y 2 C, reasonable, rooms at front are noisy.

Plenty of places at **G** pp, eg *Hospedajes Tío Luís* and *Miramar*, 1 C NO y 1 Av NO, *Hospedajes Galaxia* and *Primavera* 2 C NO y 1 Av NO by Texaco station on Panamericana by bus stop, *Hospedaje Terminal*, 2 C NO y 3 Av NO, all basic, not very clean but cheap.

Camping: possible 2 km N of town, beside the stream; beware of mosquitoes.

● **Places to eat**
Parque Central is surrounded by restaurants and fast food establishments. *Hein Wong* on Parque Central, Chinese and international food, good, a/c, reasonable prices; *Flipper*, 1 Av NO y 6 C, ice cream, tacos, etc; *Juanis Burger Shop*, 1 Av NO, 5 C, nr SW corner of Parque Central, friendly, good food, OK; *La Fonda*, 4 Av NO, just off Parque Central, Mexican food, clean, friendly, cheap; *Las Palmeras*, S side of Parque Central, good breakfasts, open 0800, good portions; *Fruty Tacos*, 4 C NO, just off SW corner of Parque Central; good snacks and licuados. In the Centro Turístico Comayagua is a restaurant, bar, disco, and swimming pool; good for cooling off and relaxing; Calle del Estadio Hispano, Barrio Arriba.

● **Banks & money changers**
Banco Atlántida, Banco de Occidente, Rancahsa (good rates), Bancahorro, Banco Sogerín, Banhcafé, Ficensa, Banadesa, Bamer and Banffaa.

● **Entertainment**
Cinema: Valladolid, at N end of 2 Av.

● **Hospitals & medical services**
Dentist: *Dr José de Jesús Berlioz*, next to Colegio León Alvarado, T 72 00 54.

● **Tour companies & travel agents**
Cramer Tours in Pasaje Arias; *Rolando Barahona*, Av Central; *Inversiones Karice's*, 4 Av NO, very friendly and helpful.

● **Useful addresses**
Immigration: Migración is at 6 C NO, 1 Av, good place to get visas renewed, friendly.

● **Transport**
Air The US military base at Palmerola, 8 km from Comayagua, was designated a commercial national and international airport in 1993, to operate initially as a cargo export/import facility and later to take passenger traffic.

Buses To Tegucigalpa, US$1, every 45 mins, 2 hrs (Hmnos Cruz, Comayagua, T 72-08-50); to Siguatepeque, US$0.40 with Transpinares. To San Pedro Sula, US$1.50, 3 hrs, either catch

a bus on the highway (very crowded) or go to Siguatepeque and change buses there. Incoming buses to Comayagua drop you on the main road outside town. From here you can walk or taxi into town. For some destinations you need to be on the Tegucigalpa-San Pedro Sula road, take a taxi (US$0.25) to **El Conejo** (a restaurant where the buses stop). **Car rental**: Amigo, on the road to Tegucigalpa and San Pedro Sula, T 72-03-71.

SIGUATEPEQUE

(Pop 39,165; *Alt* 1,150m) The Northern Highway crosses the Comayagua plain, part of the gap in the mountains which stretches from the Gulf of Fonseca to the Ulúa lowlands. 32 km NW of Comayagua is **Siguatepeque**, a town set in forested highlands with a cool climate. It is the site of the Escuela Nacional de Ciencias Forestales (which is worth a visit) and, being exactly half-way between Tegucigalpa and San Pedro Sula (128 km), a collection point for the produce of Intibucá, Comayagua and Lempira departments. The Cerro and Bosque de Calanterique, behind the Evangelical Hospital, is 45 mins' walk from town centre. The Parque Central is pleasant, shaded by tall trees with the church of San Pablo on the N side and the cinema, *Hotel Versalles* and *Boarding House Central* on the E side; Hondutel and the Post Office are on the S side.

● **Accommodation D** *Panamericano*, T 73-22-02, new, rude reception, not impressive; **D** *Zari*, T 73-20-15, hot water, cable TV, own generator, parking; **E** *Boarding House Central*, T 73-21-08, simple, but very good value, beware of the dog which bites; **E** *Internacional Gómez*, 21 de Junio, T 73-28-68, with bath, **F** without, hot water, clean, use of kitchen on request, parking; **F** *Mi Hotel*, 1 km from highway on road into town, with bath, parking, restaurant; **F** *Versalles*, on the main square, excellent, restaurant.

● **Places to eat** *China Palace*, Chinese and international; *Pizzería Venezia*, one on main street, another on highway S to Tegucigalpa, excellent pizzas, also serves good sandwiches and fruit drinks; *Pollos Kike*, next door, pleasant setting for fried chicken addicts; *Juanci's*, also on main street, American-style hamburgers, good steaks and snacks, open until 2300; *Bicos*, SW corner of Parque Central, nice snack bar/patisserie; *Supermercado Food* has a good snack bar inside; *Cafetería Colonial*, 4 Av SE (just behind the church), good pastries and coffee, outside seating. On the Northern Highway there are several restaurants: 3 km N, *Restaurante y Cafetería* (with supermarket); *Granja d'Elia*, open all day, lots of vegetables, meat too, buffet, all you can eat US$2.50, French chef, not to be missed, veg from own market garden and bakeries on sale outside; *Nuevo* and *Antiguo Bethania*, quite a long way out of town, good, abundant, inexpensive meals.

● **Banks & money changers** Bancahsa, Banco Atlántida, Banco de Occidente, Banco Sogerin.

● **Shopping** A good leatherworker is Celestino Alberto Díaz, Barrio San Antonio, Casa 53, 2A C NE, 6A Av NE. 1 block N of Celestino's is a good shoemaker, leather shoes made for US$25.

● **Transport** Bus to **San Pedro Sula**, from the W end of town every 35 mins, US$1.35; **Tegucigalpa** with Empresas Unidas or Maribel, from W plaza, S of market, US$1.50, 3 hrs. Alternatively take a taxi, US$0.30, 2 km to the highway intersection and catch a Tegucigalpa-San Pedro Sula bus which passes every 30 mins; to **Comayagua**, Transpinares, US$0.50, 45 mins; to **La Esperanza** buses leave from nr *Boarding House Central*, first departure 0530, several daily, taxi from town centre US$0.50.

From Siguatepeque, a beautiful paved road goes through lovely forested mountainous country, SW via **Jesús de Otoro** (2 basic *hospedajes* and Balneario San Juan de Quelala, US$0.30 entry, *cafetería* and picnic sites) to La Esperanza (see page 949).

From Siguatepeque the Highway goes over the enormous forested escarpment of the continental divide, before descending towards Lago Yojoa. Just S of **Taulabé** on the highway are the caves of Taulabé, with stalactites and bats (illuminated and with guides, open daily). 16 km S of the lake and just N of Taulabé is the turnoff NW of a paved road to Santa Bárbara (see page 935).

LAGO YOJOA

81 km S of San Pedro Sula, 635m high, 22½ km long and 10 km wide, the lake is splendidly set among mountains. Changes in the water level may affect the lake's appearance. To the W rise the Montañas de Santa Bárbara; to the E the **Parque Nacional Montaña Cerro Azul-Meámbar**. Pumas, jaguars and other animals can be seen in the forests and pine-clad slopes. It also has a great many waterfalls, the cloud forest forming part of the reservoir of the Lago Yojoa basin. The 50 sq km park is 30 km N of Siguatepeque and its highest point is 2,047m. To get to any of the entry points (Meámbar, Jardines, Bacadia, Monte Verde or San Isidro), 4WD is necessary. A local ecological group, Ecolago, has marked out the area and is to offer guided tours of the park. Contact Enrique Campos at *Motel Agua Azul*. Ecolago has guides who are expert in identifying regional birds; at least 373 species have been identified around the lake. For more information, contact Proyecto Humuya, Atrás Iglesia Betel, 21 de Agosto (T 73-24-26) Siguatepeque, or Proyecto de Desarrollo Río Yure, San Isidro, Cortés, Apdo 1149, Tegucigalpa. The Northern Highway follows the eastern margin to the lake's southern tip at **Pito Solo**, where sailing boats and motor boats can be hired. On the northern shore of Lago Yojoa is a complex of precolumbian, non-Maya settlements called **Los Naranjos** which are believed to have had a population of several thousand. It is considered to be the country's second most important archaeological zone. The site is being developed for tourism by the Institute of Anthropology and History. From the lake it is about 37 km down to the hot Ulúa lowlands. (Bus to Lake from San Pedro Sula, US$1, 1½ hrs; bus from Lake to Tegucigalpa with Hedmán-Alas, US$3, 3-5 hrs, 185 km.)

● **Accommodation & places to eat** **L3** *Gualiqueme*, luxurious cottage at edge of lake, originally built for executives of the Rosario mine, now a hotel, 4 bedrooms in main house, 2 in annex, daily, weekly, monthly rental, weekend packages inc ferry and fishing boat, for information contact Richard Joint at Honduyate, T 39-26-84/5, F 39-23-24; **A2-C** *Brisas del Lago*, T 52-70-30, F 53-33-41, good restaurant but overpriced, launches for hire; **C** *Finca Las Glorias*, T 56-07-36, bath, a/c, hot water, TV, bar, restaurant, pool; **C-D** *Motel Agua Azul* (at N end of lake, about 3 km W from junction at Km 166), T 53-47-50, simple, clean cabins for 2 or more persons, meals for non-residents, food average, beautiful gardens, manager speaks English, swimming pool, fishing, horseriding and boating, launches for hire, mosquito coils, rec; **D** *Los Remos*, T 57-80-54, has cabins and camping facilities at Pito Solo, at the S end of the lake, and rooms in E range, clean, beautiful setting, good food, nice for breakfasts, no beach but swimming pool, boat trips, parking US$3. *Only Bass*, 500m from *Motel Agua Azul* serves fresh fish from lake, highly rec. *Comedores* on the road beside the lake serve the fish (bass) that is caught there (*Restaurant Margoth*, 1 km N of *Los Remos*, rec) and roadside stalls nr Peña Blanca sell fruit. Buses between Tegucigalpa and San Pedro stop to let passengers off at *Los Remos*, and at Peña Blanca, 5 km from the turning for *Agua Azul*. At Peña Blanca on N side of lake are **G** *Hotel Maranata*, clean, nr bus stop, friendly, and *Comedor El Cruce*, very good home cooking; *Brisas del Canal*, local food, rec, but small portions; *Panadería Yoja*, one block from *Hotel Maranata*, good juices and pastries.

A paved road skirts the lake's northern shore for 12 km via Peña Blanca. One unpaved road heads SW to **El Mochito**, Honduras' most important mining centre. A bus from 2 Av in San Pedro Sula goes to Las Vegas-El Mochito mine where there is a cheap *pensión* (**F**) and walks along the W side of Lago Yojoa. Buses will generally stop anywhere along E side of lake. Another unpaved road heads N from the northern shore, through Río Lindo, to **Caracol** on the Northern Highway. This road gives access to the Pulhapanzak waterfall, with some unexcavated ceremonial mounds adjacent, and to Ojo de Agua, a pretty bathing spot nr Caracol.

The impressive waterfall at **Pulhapanzak** is on the Río Lindo; by car it's a 1½ hrs drive from San Pedro, longer by bus.

There is a bus from Peña Blanca every 2 hrs to the falls, or take a Mochito or Cañaveral bus from San Pedro Sula from the bus station near the railway (hourly 0500-1700) and alight at the sign to the falls, at the village of Santa Buena Ventura, US$0.95. Alternatively stay on the bus to Cañaveral (take identification because there is a power plant here), and walk back along the Río Lindo, 2 hrs past interesting rock formations and small falls. There is swimming in terrace-like pools about 20 mins' walk from Pulhapanzak (for a small tip boys will show off their diving skills). The waterfall (42m) is beautiful in, or just after the rainy season, and in sunshine there is a rainbow at the falls. There is a picnic area and a small *cafetería*, but the site does get crowded at weekends and holidays; there is a small admission charge (US$1). The caretaker allows camping for a tip, rec. Leave early for this trip. Last return bus leaves at 1630 during the week.

10 km N of the lake on the Northern Highway is the turn-off for the village of **Santa Cruz de Yojoa** (**G** *Hospedaje Paraíso*, with bath, clean, fan, friendly), and at 24 km is the **El Cajón** hydroelectric project (to visit the dam, apply at least 10 days in advance: T 22-21-77, or in writing to Oficina de Relaciones Públicas de la ENEE, 1 Av, Ed Valle-Aguiluz, Comayagüela, DC). El Cajón hydroelectric dam (226m high) has formed a 94 sq km lake, which lies between the departments of Cortés, Yoro and Comayagua. The dam is 22 km from Santa Cruz de Yojoa.

At Km 46, S of San Pedro Sula, there is a paved road leading E through banana plantations to Santa Rita, thence either E to Yoro, or N to Progreso and Tela, thus enabling travellers between Tegucigalpa and the N coast greatly to shorten their route by avoiding San Pedro Sula. Shortly before San Pedro Sula, the road divides and becomes a toll road. The toll road's surface is poor in places.

SAN PEDRO SULA

(*Pop* 500,000; *Alt* 60-150m) **San Pedro Sula**, 58 km S of Puerto Cortés by road and railway, 265 km from Tegucigalpa, the second largest city in Honduras, is a centre for the banana, coffee, sugar and timber trades, a focal distributing point for northern and western Honduras with good road links, and the most industrialized centre in the country. Its business community is mainly of Arab origin. It is considered the fastest growing city between Mexico and Colombia.

The city was founded by Pedro de Alvarado on 27 June 1536. The large neo-colonial-style cathedral, started in 1949, was completed many years later. San Pedro Sula is situated in the lush and fertile valley of the Ulúa (Sula) river, beneath the forested slopes of the Merendón mountains and, though pleasant in the cooler season from Nov to Feb, reaches very high temperatures in the rest of the year with considerable humidity levels.

The higher and cooler suburb of Bella Vista with its fine views over the city affords relief from the intense heat of the town centre. The cafeteria and foyer swimming pool of *Hotel Sula* provide a cool haven for visitors.

The city is divided into four quadrants: noreste (northeast, NE), noroeste (northwest, NO), sudeste (southeast, SE) and sudoeste (southwest, SO), where most of the hotels are located.

Museums

Museo de Antropología e Historia, 3 Av, 4 C NO, with displays of the cultures that once inhabited the Ulúa valley, up to Spanish colonization, and, on the first floor, local history since colonization; open Tues-Sun 1000-1600, US$0.35, gift shop (handicrafts, books etc). Museum café in adjacent garden with fine stela, good set lunch.

Exhibitions

Expocentro, Av Junior, off Blvd to Puerto Cortés, temporary exhibitions, conferences and fairs.

EXCURSIONS

One can take a taxi up the mountain behind the city for US$2-2.50; good view, and interesting vegetation on the way up. Lake Ticamaya, near Choloma, is worth visiting between June and December.

La Lima

The head office of the Chiquita United Brands subsidiary is at **La Lima** (45,000 inhabitants), 15 km to the E by road (bus frequent, US$0.25). It is possible to visit a Chiquita banana plantation at Finca Omanita, near El Progreso, with permission from the head office (private car needed). It is best to go in the early part of the day because the workers have a long midday break from 1100. There is a club (golf, tennis, swimming) which takes members from outside; branches of several local banks.

● **Accommodation & places to eat** D *Hotel La Lima*, central, a/c, phone, cable TV, cafeteria, restaurant; *Restaurante Los Marinos*, opp Supermercado Manuel Bonilla, live Caribbean music twice a week; *Cafetería Jacky's*, Lima Vieja, next to Hondutel, shrimp, beef, chicken, soups, etc; a cheap place to eat is *Golosinas Cristy* (from US$0.70).

A little to the E, near the Ulúa river, is Travesía (not the Travesía nr Puerto Cortés, see under **The North Coast**, Puerto Cortés), where Mayan pottery remains have been found, but no ruins as such.

Cusuco National Park

20 km W of San Pedro Sula, the cloud forest national park is managed by Fundación Ecológica Hector Rodrigo Pastor Fasquelle (HRPF), 7 Av, 1 C NO, San Pedro Sula, T 52-10-14/59-65-98, F 57-66-20. Also contact Cohdefor, 10 Av, 5 C NO, Barrio Guamilito, San Pedro Sula, T 53-49-59/29-29, or Cambio CA, who run tours. In the 1950s this area was exploited for lumber but was declared a protected area in 1959 when the Venezuelan ecologist, Geraldo Budowski reported that the pine trees here were the highest in Central America. Cutting was stopped and the lumber company abandoned the site. The

Hike from Buenos Aires to Tegucigalpita

👣 This route to the coast follows a mule trail around the NE side of the Cusuco National Park. The scenery is superb and you see a good range of wildlife.

From Buenos Aires walk E along an unpaved track to Bañaderos. A smaller track branches left just before you enter Bañaderos and immediately twists its way down, with frequent switchbacks, to a river in the valley below the road. It takes about an hour to reach the river, from where the path is fairly straightforward. Heading NE, the trail climbs steeply away from the river before dropping again to another village (2 hrs), where there is a small shop selling drinks.

From the village the path climbs to the pass (4-5 hrs). Much of the ascent is steep and water sources are scarce. There are some flat areas to camp as you approach the pass. After the pass head N to the village of Esperanza. Signs that you are nearing the village are clear as you begin to enter small coffee plantations, among the heavily forested slopes. On this side of the pass water sources are plentiful. Esperanza has two shops and it is possible to camp on the village football field.

It is about 4 hrs, almost all downhill, from Esperanza to the coast road. There are no more water sources and temperatures can be very high. Where the path meets the road there is a well-stocked shop. From there it is a 30-min walk on a tarmac road to Tegucigalpita (*hospedaje*). The bus terminal is on this road, just past the turning for the village.

(Mike and Pauline Truman)

area includes tropical rainforest and cloud forest with all the associated flora and fauna. It includes **Cerro Jilinco**, 2,242m and **Cerro San Ildefonso**, 2,228m. HRPF produces a bird checklist. Quetzals can be seen here. There are four trails, ranging from 30 mins to 2 days. They use old logging roads, traversing forested ridges with good views. Entrance to the park is US$9. Permission from HRPF is required to walk through the Park to Tegucigalpita on the coast. There is a visitors' centre with kitchen, bathroom, shower and bunk beds; take your own food. Camping is possible. Access by dirt road from Cofradía (*Cafetería Negro*, 1 block NW of plaza, good food), on the road to Santa Rosa de Copán, then to Buenos Aires: 2 hrs by car from San Pedro Sula, 4WD recommended; bus San Pedro Sula-Cofradía, 1 hr, US$0.15, from 5 Av, 11 C SO (buses drop you at the turnoff, 1 km from town); pick-up Cofradía-Buenos Aires 1½ hrs, US$1.75, best on Mon at 1400 (wait at the small shop on outskirts of town on Buenos Aires road); the park is 12 km from Buenos Aires. Ask in Buenos Aires for Carlos Al-varéngez-López who offers lodging and food half-way to the park, very friendly, camping possible US$3 pp. No hotels in the village but you can stay in the small house owned by the Park authorities (many cockroaches). Two *comedores* in town.

Local festivals

The city's main festival, Feria Juniana, is in the last days of June.

Local information

● **Accommodation**

L2 *Hotel y Club Copantl*, Col Los Arcos, Blvd del Sur, T 56-89-00/56-71-08, F 56-78-90, e-mail Copantl2@simon.intertel.hs, corporate rates available, Olympic sized pool, tennis courts, gym, sauna, disco, casino (the only one in town, foreigners only, take passport), car and travel agencies, the best; **L3-A1** *Gran Hotel Sula*, 1 C, 3 y 4 Av, on N side of Parque Central, T 52-99-91, F 57-70-00, pool, restaurant (upstairs, very good, reasonably priced) and café (for authentic North American breakfast, view of pool), also good, 24-hr service; **L3-A1** *St Anthony*, 3 Av 13 C SO, T 58-07-44/50-48-68, F 58-10-19, rooms and suites all with balcony, a/c, phone, cable TV, pool, pool bar, jacuzzi, gym, new in 1996.

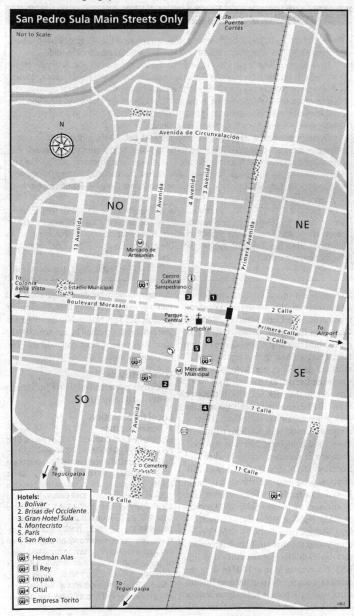

San Pedro Sula Main Streets Only

Not to Scale

To Puerto Cortés

N

Avenida de Circunvalación

NO

NE

13 Avenida

7 Avenida

4 Avenida

3 Avenida

Primera Avenida

To Colonia Bella Vista

Mercado de Artesanías

Centro Cultural Sampedrano

Estadio Municipal

Boulevard Morazán

2 Calle

Parque Central

Cathedral

Primera Calle

To Airport

2 Calle

SE

Mercado Municipal

7 Avenida

7 Calle

SO

11 Calle

Cemetery

To Tegucigalpa

16 Calle

To Tegucigalpa

Hotels:
1. *Bolívar*
2. *Brisas del Occidente*
3. *Gran Hotel Sula*
4. *Montecristo*
5. *París*
6. *San Pedro*

1 Hedmán Alas
2 El Rey
3 Impala
4 Citul
5 Empresa Torito

M62

A1 *Honduras Plaza*, 6 C 4 Av NO, T 53-24-24, F 53-21-40, a/c, restaurant/bar, cable TV, own generator, parking, in respectable area but over-priced; **A2** *Hotel-Suites Los Andes*, Av Circun-valación 84, T 53-44-25, F 57-19-45, restaurant, café, jacuzzi, 40-channel cable TV, bilingual secretarial service, garden, parking, own generator; **A2** *Plaza Cristal Suites Hotel*, 10 Av 1-2 C NO, T 52-23-02, F 52-32-27, phone, cable TV, bank, travel agency; **A3** *Aparthotel Almendral*, Av Circunvalación, Colonia Trejo, behind *Wendy's*, T 56-39-89, F 56-64-76, a/c, cable TV, kitchenette.

B *Gran Hotel Conquistador*, 2 C 7 y 8 Av SO, opp *Cine Tropicana*, T 52-76-05, F 52-92-90; **B** *Internacional Palace*, 3 C 8 Av SO, Barrio El Benque, T 52-28-38, F 57-79-22, a/c, helpful staff, restaurant OK; **B** *Javier's House*, C 9 239 D, 23 y 24 Av SO, Rio Piedras, T 57-40-56, inc breakfast and return pick-up from airport.

C *Ejecutivo*, 2 C 10 Av SO, T 52-42-39, F 52-58-68, a/c, cable TV, café/bar, phone, own generator.

D *Acrópolis*, 3 C 2 y 3 Av SE, T/F 52-75-16, a/c, cable TV, parking, café, comfortable, friendly, good value; **D** *Ambassador*, 5 Av 7 C SO, T 57-68-24/5, F 57-58-60; **D** *Bolívar*, 2 C 2 Av NO, T 53-32-74, F 53-48-73, recently redeco rated, a/c, TV, own generator, pool, restaurant; **D** *Gran Hotel San Pedro*, 3 C 2 Av SO, T 53-15-13, F 53-26-55, private bath, a/c, **E** with fan, popular, clean, good value, rooms overlooking street are noisy, stores luggage, self-service res-taurant next door, book exchange; **D** *Manhat-tan*, 7 Av 3 4 C SO, T 53-23-16, a/c, a bit run down; **D** *Palmira 1*, 6 C 6 y 7 Av SO, 157-65-22, 53 36-74, clean, convenient, large parking area; **D** *Terraza*, 6 Av 4 5 C SO, T 53-31-08, F 57-47-98, dining room dark, friendly staff, **E** without a/c; **D-E** *Colombia*, 3 C 5 y 6 Av SO, a/c or fan.

E *El Nilo*, 3 C 2 Av SO, T 53-46-89, nice rooms, friendly; **E** *La Siesta*, 7 C 2 Av SE, T 52-26-50, F 58-02-43, private bath, a/c or fan, double or twin beds, clean, safe, rec but noisy.

F *Brisas del Occidente*, 5 Av 6-7 C SO, T 52-23-09, 5-storey building, fan, ask for room with window, laundry facilities, friendly, dirty; **F** *Montecristo*, 2 Av 7 C SE, T 57-13-70, noisy, not very clean, fan, safe; **F** *París*, 3 Av 3 C SO, nr *El Nilo* and bus station for Puerto Cortés, shared bath, poor water supply, clean but noisy; **F** *San José*, 6 Av 5 y 6 C SO, T 57-12-08, cheap and cheerful; **F-G** *San Juan*, 6 C 6 Av SO, T 53-14-88, modern building, very noisy, clean, helpful, good value. **F-G** cheap hotels between

bus terminals and downtown market, often dirty and noisy.

● **Places to eat**

La Espuela, Av Circunvalación, 16 Av 7 C NO, good grilled meats, rec; *Don Udo's*, Blvd Los Próceres, restaurant and café-bar, T 53-31-06, Dutch owner, big international menu, good wine list, Sun brunch 1000-1400; *Pamplona*, on plaza, opp *Gran Hotel Sula*, pleasant décor, good food, strong coffee, excellent service; *Gamba Tropic*, 4 C 5 y 6 Av SO, delicious seafood, good wine, medium prices, a/c, rec; *Copa de Oro*, 2 Av 2 y 3 C SO, extensive Chinese and western menu, a/c, pleasant, rec; *Shang-hai*, Calle Peatonal, good Chinese; *Sim Kon*, 17 Av 6 C NO, Av Circunvalación, Chinese; *La Fortuna*, 2 C 7 Av NO, big menu of Chinese and international, Chinese food very good, not expensive, smart, good service, a/c; *Las Tejas*, 9 C 16 y 17 Av, Av Circunvalación, good sea-food, as also at nearby sister restaurant *La Tejana*, 16 Av 19 C SO, Barrio Suyapa, T 57-52-76, fine seafood and steaks; *José y Pepe's*, Plaza Ibiza, Av Circunvalación SO, end of 6 C, T 57-92-23, Mexican, smart, friendly; *Cafetería Ma-yan Way*, 6 Av 4-5 C SO, very clean, good typical breakfast and set meal, cheap, closed Sun English spoken; many branches of *Popeye's* for greasy chicken, *Pizza Hut*, *Wendy's* and *Bur-ger King*, also *Taos* for ice-cream; *Espresso Americano*, 2 branches, in Calle Peatonal off SW corner of Parque Central, and in Megaplaza shopping mall, closed Sun, great coffee, cook-ies; *Chef Mariano*, 16 Av 9-10 C SO, Barrio Suyapa, T 52-54-92, Garífuna management and specialities, especially seafood, Honduran and international cuisine, attentive service, a/c, not cheap but good value, open daily for lunch and dinner; *Friday's*, Blvd Los Próceres, 1 block from Av Circunvalación, first branch of US chain in Honduras, new, smart, a/c; *La Huerta de España*, 21 Av 2 C SO, Barrio Rio de Piedras, 4 blocks W of Av Circunvalación, supposedly best Spanish cuisine in town, open daily until 2300; *Bar El Hijo del Cuervo*, 13 C 7-8 Av NO, Barrio Los Andes, authentic Mexican cuisine, informal setting of *champas* in tropical garden with foun-tain, à la carte menu, tacos, quesadillas etc; *Café del Campo*, 5 C 10 Av NO, best coffee in town, 20 varieties, good à la carte breakfasts, big sandwiches, fish and prawn specialities US$6-8, bartender is cocktail specialist, smart, a/c, good service, very nice; *Café Skandia*, ground floor, *Gran Hotel Sula*, open 24 hrs, best place for late night dinners and early breakfasts, good club sandwiches etc, good service; *Café des Artes*, 1 C 14 y 15 Av SO, Blvd Morazán, just across from the stadium, owned and managed by Parisienne, informal, elegant, good music (rock, techno), snacks, in tropical garden setting, open Mon-Sat from 1600, happy hour 1900-2100; *Café Nani*, 6 Av 1-2 C SO, very good pastelería; *Café Venecia*, 6 Av 4-5 C, good juices, cheap.

● **Bars**
Mango's, 16 Av 8-9 C SO, Barrio Suyapa, open 1900 onwards, open terrace, pool tables, dance floor, rock music, snacks; *Frogs Sports Bar*, Blvd Los Próceres, just above *Don Udo's*, 3 different bars, a/c, pool tables, 2nd-storey open deck overlooking their own beach volleyball court, giant TV screens showing US sports, snack bar, disco at weekends (karaoki), open 1700 until late, happy hour 1800-1900.

● **Airline offices**
The following can all be booked at Centro Comercial Prisa, Blvd Morazán: **Lacsa** (T 52-68-88, 52-66-90, airport T 56-23-91), **Copa** (T 52-08-83, 52-06-28, airport T 68-25-18), **Taca** (T 53-26-46/9, airport T 68-10-91), **Aviateca** and **Nica**. **Iberia**, Edif Quiroz 2nd floor, T 53-15-30, airport T 68-10-91; **Isleña**, Edif Trejo Merlo, 1 C 7 Av SO, T 52-83-35, airport T 68-22-18; **American**, Ed Firenze, Barrio Los Andes, 16 Av, 1-2 C, T 58-05-18/23, airport T 68-21-65, 68-13-06; **Continental**, at *Gran Hotel Sula*, 1 C, 3 y 4 Av NO, T 57-41-41, airport T 59-05-77.

● **Banks & money changers**
Banco Atlántida, on Parque Central, changes TCs at good rates; **Lloyds Bank** at 4 Av SO 26, between 3 y 4 C; **Banco de Honduras** (Citibank); **Bancahorro**, has a beautiful mural in its head office, 5 Av, 4 C SO; **Bancahsa**, 5 Av, 6-7 C SO, changes TCs; **Banco Continental**, 3 Av, 3-5 C SO No 7; **Banffaa, Banco de Occidente**, 6 Av, 2-3 C SO; **Bancomer**, 4 C, 3-4 Av NO; **Banhcafé**, 1 C, 1 Av SE and all other local banks. **Amex** is at *Mundirama Travel*, Edif Martínez Valenzuela, 2 C 2-3 Av SO. Open 0830-1500, closed Sat except Bancomer and Banhcafé, open Mon-Fri 0900-1900, Sat 0900-1200. Good rates at **Lempira Cambios**, 4 C and 3 Av SO for cash and TCs; also at **Casa de Cambio DICORP**, Centro Comercial Galerías, 1 C 15 Av SO, Blvd Morazán, open Mon-Fri 0900-1600. A host of dealers buy dollars in Parque Central and the pedestrian mall.

● **Cultural centres**
Centro Cultural Sampedrano, 3 C, 4 Av NO No 20, T 53-39-11, USIS-funded library, cultural

events, occasional concerts, art exhibitions and theatrical productions. **Alianza Francesa**, on 23 Av 3-4 C SO, T 52-43-59/53-11-78, has a library, French films on Wed, and cultural events on Fri.

● **Embassies & consulates**
Belize, Km 5 Blvd del Norte, Col los Castaños, T 51-01-24, 51-07-07, F 51-17-40; **Guatemala**, T/F 53-35-60; **Nicaragua**, T 53-17-39; **Costa Rica**, *Hotel St Anthony*, T 58-07-44, F 58-10-19; **El Salvador**, Edif Bancatlán, 12th floor 1204, Parque Central, T 57-58-51, F 52-97-06; **Mexico**, 2 C 20 Av SO 201, Barrio Río de Piedras, T 53-26-04, F 52-32-93; **UK**, 2 C 2-3 Av SO, T 57-20-63, 57-40-66; **France**, Col Zerón, 9 Av 10 C 927, T 57-41-87; **Germany**, 6 Av NO, Av Circunvalación, T 53-12-44, F 53-18-68; **Spain**, 2 Av 3-4 C NO 318, Edif Agencias Panamericanas, T 58-07-08, F 57-16-80; **Italy**, Edif La Constancia, 3rd floor, 5 Av 1-2 C NO, T 52-36-72, F 52-39-32; **Netherlands**, 15 Av 7-8 C NE, Plaza Venecia, Local 10, T 57-18-15, F 52-97-24.

● **Entertainment**
Cinemas: there are 8 cinemas, a/c, look in local press for details.

Discotheques: *Henry's*, *Confetis*, both on Av Circunvalación NO; more exclusive is *El Quijote*, 11 C 3-4 Av SO, Barrio Lempira, cover charge.

Nightclubs (with shows): *Cherrie's*, 7 C 14-15 Av SO, Barrio Suyapa, and *Cocktail*, next door, open 2100-0200.

Theatre: *The Círculo Teatral Sampedrano* stages occasional amateur productions (see above, **Cultural centres**). The *Proyecto Teatral Futuro*, formed in 1995, is a semi-professional company presenting contemporary theatre of Latin American countries and translations of European playwrights (ranging from Molière to Ionesco), as well as ballet, children's theatre, and workshops. Offices and studio-theatre at 4 C 3-4 Av NO, Edif INMOSA, 3rd floor, T 52-30-74, contact the project's artistic director, Oscar Zelaya, for news of current activities.

● **Hospitals & medical services**
Dentist: *Clínicas Dentales Especializadas*, Ed María Antonia, 3a C entre 8 y 9 Av NO, apartamento L-1, Barrio Guamilito, T 58-04-64.

● **Laundry**
Lavandería Almich, 9-10 Av, 5 C SO No 29, Barrio El Benque; *Excelsior*, 14-15 Av Blvd Morazán; *Rodgers*, 4a C, 15-16 Av SO, No 114. *Lava Facil*, 7 Av, 5 C NO, US$1.50/load.

● **Places of worship**

Churches: Episcopal Church, round corner from Sports Stadium, English service, Sun, 1000. High Mass on Suns, 1030, at Orthodox church at Río Piedras is picturesque and colourful.

● **Post & telecommunications**

Post Office: 3 Av SO between 9 10 C.

Telephone: Hondutel, 4 C 4 Av SO. Collect calls can be made from lobby of *Gran Hotel Sula*.

● **Shopping**

Bookshops: *Librería Editorial Guaymuras*, 10 Av 7 C NO, wide range of Hispanic authors, inc their own publications; *La Casa del Libro*, 1 C 5-6 Av SO, comprehensive selection of Spanish and English language books, good for children's books and games, microfiche information, central, just off Parque Central; *Librería Atenea*, Edif Trejo Merlo, 1 C 7 Av SO, wide choice of Latin American, US and British fiction, philosophy, economics etc; *Librería Cultura*, 1 C 6-7 Av SO, cheap paperbacks, Latin American classics.

Food: *Gourmet Foods*, Blvd Los Próceres, between *Don Udo's* and *Frogs*, delicatessen, lots of expensive goodies eg French and Dutch cheeses, caviar, smoked salmon, Italian sausages, French champagne etc, T 53-31-06 (home delivery).

Handicrafts: large artesan market, Mercado Guamilito Artesanía, 6 C 7-8 Av NO, typical Honduran handicrafts at good prices (bargain), but mostly imported goods from Guatemala and Ecuador, also good for fruit and vegetables. *Honduras Souvenirs*, Calle Peatonal No 7, mahogany woodcraft. The *Museum Gift Shop*, has lots of cheap *artesanía* gifts, basketwork, pottery etc, open during museum visiting hours. For fine leatherwork, *Latino's Leather*, 7 C 12-13 Av SO, superb bags, belts, briefcases etc; *Danilo's Pura Piel*, factory and shop 18 Av B/9 C SO; *La Maison du Cuir*, Av Circunvalación opp *Los Andes* supermarket; *Lesanddra Leather* at Megaplaza Shopping Mall. The *IMAPRO Handicraft School* in El Progreso has a retail outlet at 1 C 4-5 Av SE, well worth visiting, fixed prices, good value, good mahogany carvings. For fine art and handicrafts, *MAHCHI Art Gallery* has no rival, exuberant paintings, ceramic vases, beautiful *artesanía*.

● **Tour companies & travel agents**

Cambio CA, Edif Copal, p 2, 1 C, 5-6 Av SO, T 52-72-74, F 52-05-23, PO Box 2666, tours to all the most interesting ecological sites in Honduras inc Mosquitia, professional guides, German and English spoken, equipment, rec; *Explore Honduras*, Edif Paseo del Sol, 1 C 2 Av NO, T 52-62-42, F 52-62-39, interesting 1-day and overnight tours with a/c bus, to Copán from US$55, Lake Yojoa and Pulhapanzak waterfall, to Lancetillo Botanical Park, Omoa, all around US$65 inc guided tour, entrance fees, lunch; *Maya Tropic Tours* in lobby of *Gran Hotel Sula*, T 52-24-05, F 57-88-30, run by helpful Jorge Molamphy and his wife; *Avia Tours*, Edif Bolívar, behind cathedral, very helpful; *Mundirama Travel Service*, Ed Martínez Valenzuela, 2 C 2-3 Av SO, T 52-34-00, American Express here; several others. **Private tour operator**: *Javier Pinel*, PO Box 2754, T/F 57-40-56, local and regional tours, also offers bed and breakfast.

● **Tourist offices**

Sectur, Edif Inmosa, 4C, NO, 3-4 Av, T 52-30-23/95, and at airport, road maps US$2.25 but no other maps.

● **Useful addresses**

Police: Dirección de Investigación Criminal, DIC, regional HQ at 9 Av 12 C NO, T 52-92-38. Report all theft, assault etc. A new, civilian, police force should be created by end-1997.

● **Transport**

Local Car rentals: American, 3 Av, 3-4 C NO (T 52-76-26), *Hotel Copantl* and airport (T 56-23-37); **Avis**, 1 C, 8 y 9 Av, T 53-09-55; **Blitz**, *Hotel Sula* and airport (T 52-24-05 or 56-24-71); **Budget**, airport T 56-24-67; **Maya Eco Tours**, 3 Av NO, 7-8 C and airport (T 57-50-56 or 68-24-63); **Molinari**, *Hotel Sula* and airport (T 53-26-39 or 56-24-63); **Toyota**, 4 Av, 2-3 C NO, T 57 26 44. Rental of a 4WD car costs US$85/day inc tax and insurance after bargaining, good discounts for long rental. **Car repairs**: Invanal, 13 C, 5 y 6 Av NE, T 52-70-83, excellent service from Sr Víctor Mora. **Bike repairs**: there are few shops for parts. One with some imported parts is *Dibisa* on 3 Av y 11 C SO. **Motoring**: if coming from the S, and wishing to avoid the city centre when heading for La Lima or El Progreso, follow signs to the airport. **Taxi**: ask the price first and bargain if necessary. Parque Central to Av Circunvalación costs about US$1.50, to *Hotel Copantl* US$4.

Air La Mesa airport (SAP), 17 km from city centre, US$6 pp by taxi, but bargain hard. No hotels nr the airport. Yellow airport taxis cost US$13. Buses and colectivos do not go to the airport terminal itself; you have to walk the final 1 km from the La Lima road (bus to this point, US$0.10). A new terminal, opened Oct 1996, has a tourist office, duty free, PO, Hondutel, café (money changers at the airport give a good rate for dollars and will exchange lempiras into dollars). Flights to Tegucigalpa (35 mins), La Ceiba, Utila and to Roatán. One passenger rec that, for local flight arrivals, it was better to collect your own bags as they come off the plane. See **Information for travellers** for international flights.

Buses Local buses cost US$0.10, smaller mini-buses cost US$0.20. To **Tegucigalpa**, 4-4½ hrs, 250 km by paved road. Main bus services with comfortable coaches and terminals in the town centre are Hedmán Alas, 7-8 Av NO, 3 C, Casa 51, T 53-13-16, 4/day 0630 to 1730 4 hrs (US$6), which is good, no meals, TV movies, and Transportes Sáenz (Av 9 y 10, C 9 SO, T 53-18-29), better buses, meals, US$8, El Rey, Av 7, C 5 y 6, T 53-42-64, Transportes Norteños (US$3), last bus at 1900, Viana, Av Circunvalación, 200m SW of *Wendy's*, T 56-92-61. The road to **Puerto Cortés** is paved; a pleasant 1-hr journey down the lush river valley. Buses to Puerto Cortés (Empresa Impala, 2 Av, 4-5 C SO No 23, T 53-31-11, several each hour, or Citul, 6 Av, 7-8 C, US$0.75), to **Omoa** (3 C E from 0600), E to **La Lima**, **El Progreso** (US$0.60), **Tela** (US$1.15) and **La Ceiba** (Tupsa and Catisa, 2 Av S, 5-6 C, hourly on the hour, US$2, 2½-3 hrs) with a change of bus in El Progreso. To **Trujillo**, 3/day, a/c, US$4.50,

departs from 2 Av, 8-9 C. Adventure Shuttle, *Suites Hotel*, Plaza Cristal, 10 Av 1-2 C NO, T 52-32-02, a/c van service between San Pedro and Copán, US$20, 0700, 2½ hrs, Thur-Sun.

Buses run S to **Lago Yojoa** and Tegucigalpa, and SW to **Santa Rosa** and then through the Department of Ocotepeque with its magnificent mountain scenery to the **Guatemalan border** (US$3.40 to the border by bus). Congolón and Torito/Copanecos serve **Nueva Ocotepeque** and **Agua Caliente** on the Guatemalan border on alternate days, Congolón dep 2400, Torito 2400 and early am and early pm; Congolón, 8 Av 10 C SO, T 52-22-68, Torito, 11 C 7 Av SO, T 57-36-91, one block apart; to **Santa Rosa de Copán**, with connections at La Entrada for **Copán**, Empresa Toritos (T 53-49-30) and Transportes Copanecos (T 53-19-54) both leaving from 6 Av, 8-9 C, every 45 mins, 0330-1700, US$1.80 to Santa Rosa. Take these buses to La Entrada, 2 hrs, US$1.30, or US$1.45 on the fast bus, for connection to **Copán**. Road paved all the way. Direct bus to Copán with Etumi, 5 hrs, from opp *Hotel Palmira* but better to take Cheny Express at 1600 or Gama Express at 1500, 3 hrs in comfortable, fast buses, see under Copán for details.

The North Coast

HONDURAS' Caribbean coast has a mixture of banana-exporting ports, historic towns (in particular Trujillo), beach resorts, and Garifuna villages. There is Pico Bonito national park, other wildlife refuges, and the overland 'Jungle Trail' to Guatemala.

PUERTO CORTÉS TO GUATEMALA

PUERTO CORTÉS

(*Pop* 65,000) **Puerto Cortés**, on a large bay backed by Laguna de Alvarado, is 58 km by road and rail from San Pedro Sula, 333 from Tegucigalpa, and only 2 days' voyage from New Orleans. Most of Honduran trade passes through it and it is now the most important port in Central America. The climate is hot, tempered by sea breezes; many beautiful palm-fringed beaches nearby; rainfall, 2,921 mm. Ferocious mosquitoes in this area, especially during the rainy season. It has a small oil refinery, and a free zone. The Central Park contains many fine trees with a huge Indian poplar in the centre providing an extensive canopy. The tree was planted as a sapling in 1941. The park was remodelled in 1996/97 with new flowerbeds, fountain and bronze statues.

Excursions

West to **Tulián**, along the bay, for picnics and very good freshwater bathing. Mini-buses departing from the Esso petrol station in the centre (US$0.35 each way) ply along the tropical shoreline past Tulián W to the 'laid-back' village of Omoa (or 3 hrs' walk, 15 km from Puerto Cortés) with its popular beach (see below).

Tours from Puerto Cortés to La Lima to visit the banana plantations, trips to Copán to visit the Maya ruins and tourist parties at the Ustaris Hacienda can be arranged with travel agents.

Beaches Buses from Puerto Cortés go E to beaches of coconut palms at **Travesía**, **Baja Mar**, etc, which are beautiful and unspoilt. Café at Travesía, and at Baja Mar. The best stretch of beach is between the two villages, but the width of sand is narrow even at low tide. The black fishing communities are very friendly. Beware of sunburn, and mosquitoes at dusk.

Local festivals

In Aug, including 'Noche Veneciana' on 3rd Sat.

Local information

● **Accommodation**

A1 *Playa*, 4 km W at Cienaguita, T 55-11-05, F 55-22-87, hotel complex, directly on beach, cable TV, good fish dishes in restaurant; **A3** *Mary Mas Club*, at Cienaguita, T 55-14-95, bath, a/c, restaurant, cable TV.

C *Costa Azul*, Playa El Faro, T 55-22-60, F 55-22-62, restaurant, disco-bar, billiards, table

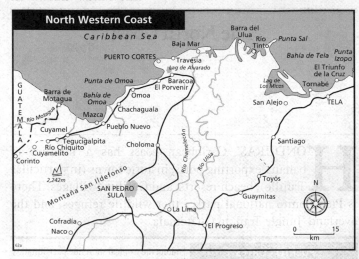

North Western Coast

Caribbean Sea

Barra del Ulua
Río Tinto
Punta Sal
Punta Izopo
Baja Mar
PUERTO CORTES
Travesía
Lag de Alvarado
Baracoa
El Porvenir
Bahía de Tela
El Triunfo de la Cruz
Tornabé
Punta de Omoa
Bahía de Omoa
Omoa
Chachaguala
Lag de Los Micas
San Alejo
TELA
Barra de Motagua
Mazca
Pueblo Nuevo
Río Motagua
Cuyamel
Tegucigalpita
Río Chiquito
Cuyamelito
Corinto
Choloma
Santiago
2,242m
Montaña San Ildefonso
SAN PEDRO SULA
Toyós
Guaymitas
La Lima
Cofradía
Naco
El Progreso
N
0   15
km
62a

tennis, pool, horse riding, volley ball, good value; **C** *International Mr Ggeerr*, 9 C, 2 Av E, T 55-04-44, F 55-07-50, no hot water, very clean, a/c, bar, video, satellite TV, rec, no restaurant; **C** *Los Arcos*, at Cienaguita, T 55-18-89.

D *El Centro*, 3 Av 3-4 C, T 55-11-60, bath, a/c, hot water, cable TV, 14 rooms by mid-1997, parking, garden, café, pleasant, well-furnished; **D** *Hotel-restaurante Costa Mar*, Playas de la Coca Cola, T 55-15-39/55-13-67, new, pleasant.

E *Frontera del Caribe*, Playas de Camaguey, Calle a Travesía, T 55-19-14, very friendly, quiet, safe, on beach, restaurant on first floor, open, airy, good food, 7 rooms on 2nd floor, private bath, cold water, linen changed daily, fan, rec.

F *Formosa*, 3 Av 2 C E, with bath, good value, friendly Chinese owner; *Las Vegas* and *Puntarenas*, short stay for visiting seamen in the docklands area. This area, 1 Av E, opp dockyards has lots of bars and prostitutes, unpleasant by day, lots of drunks, dangerous at night. Avoid.

G *Colón*, 3 Av 2 C O, opp *Puerto Limón* in clapboard building, clean, safe, basic.

● **Places to eat**
Café Viena, on Parque, good, reasonable, but check the prices when you order and pay, excellent coffee; *Chun Wa*, 2 Av, 9 C E, good, big *comidas* but noisy and uncomfortable; *Pekin*, 2 Av 6-7 C, Chinese, a/c, excellent, good service, a bit pricey but rec; supermercado *Pekin* next door best in town; on same block *Matt's*, a/c,

nice bar, good food, not expensive, and *La Cabaña* bar and restaurant; *Burger Boy's*, 2 Av 8 C, lively, popular with local teenagers; *Kasike's Restaurant-Bar-Peña*, 3 Av 4-9 C and *Carnitas Tapadera*, grills, same block; *Jugos Chapala*, 3 Av 2 C, excellent *licuados*, fresh juices; *Café Consulado*, 2 Av 8 C, very pleasant, nice snacks, fish, prawn dishes, a/c, bar, rec; next door to *Candiles*, 2 Av, 7-8 C, good grills, reasonable prices, open-air seating; *Repostería Ilusión*, 4 C E, pastries, bread (turtle, crocodile loaves), coffee, nice for breakfast; *Romanos*, nr *Hotel Mr Ggeerr*, for good large pizzas; *Príncipe Maya* on road to Omoa; *Repostería y Pastelería Plata*, corner of 3 Av and 2 C E, nr Parque Central, good bread and pastries, excellent cheap *almuerzo*, buffet-style, kids' playroom, rec, 2 older branches of *Plata* at 3 Av 3 C and 2 Av 2 C.

● **Banks & money changers**
Banco de Comercio cashes TCs; Banco de Occidente, 3 Av 4 C E, cashes Amex TCs, accepts Visa/Mastercard; Bancahsa, 2 Av, 2 C. All banks open Mon-Fri 0800-1700, Sat 0830-1130. Banks along 2 Av E, inc Sogerín, Bamer, Atlántida, Bancomer, Bancahsa.

● **Places of worship**
Protestant Church: Anglican/Episcopal.

● **Post & telecommunications**
Telephone: Hondutel, at dock entrance, Gate 6, inc fax and AT&T. Direct to USA.

Post Office: next door to Hondutel.

● **Shopping**
There is a souvenir shop in the Aduana administration building (opp Hondutel), *Marthita's*. The market in the town centre is quite interesting.

● **Tour companies & travel agents**
Bahía Travel/Maya Rent-a-Car, 3 Av, 3 C, T 65-30-64, F 55-11-23; *Ocean Travel*, Plaza Eng, 3 Av 2 C, T 55-09-13; *Irema*, 2 Av 3-4 C, T 55-15-06, F 55-09-78.

● **Useful addresses**
Immigration: the Immigration Office is on 3 Av, 5 C (it is not noted for its efficiency, exit stamps cost US$2.50-US$5, depending on the official). If entering Puerto Cortés by boat, go to Immigration immediately. Passports are sometimes collected at the dock and you must go later to Immigration to get them; US$1 entry fee, make sure that you have the stamp. This is the only official payment; if asked for more, demand a receipt.

● **Transport**
Trains The railway station is nr the harbour entrance. There are 2 trains a week (Fri and Sun) to Tela, 0700, 4 hrs, 1,067m gauge. Timetables change, check if you wish to travel.

Buses Bus service hourly to San Pedro Sula, US$0.75, 45 mins, Citul and Impala lines (T 55-06-06). Bus to Omoa, old school bus, loud music, very full, guard your belongings

Sea To Guatemala A boat leaves from Omoa for Livingston Tues and Fri, around 1200, US$25 pp, return Wed, Sat. Ask at *Fisherman's Hut*, Omoa, for Sr Juan Ramón Menjivar (phone line pending). In Puerto Cortés information from Ocean Travel at 3 Av, 2 blocks W of plaza. **To Belize** Boats to Belize leave from beside the bridge over the lagoon (Barra La Laguna), buy tickets at wooden shack facing *Kokito* bar just before bridge. A launch leaves Puerto Cortés for Mango Creek, Belize, US$30, 7 hrs, no fixed schedule; can be dangerous in rough weather. A fast skiff sails usually Wed and Sat to Dangriga and/or Placencia, US$50, about 3 hrs. Remember to get your exit stamp.

Once a week the 73 ft yacht *Osprey* sails from Puerto Cortés to Utila, German/American crew, 2 days passage, all included US$46, ask at Restaurant *El Delfin*. There are occasionally other boats **to the Bay Islands**, but none scheduled. It is possible to visit the harbour on Sun morning, ask at the gate. Most boats wait until they have sufficient cargo before they set sail. Price is around US$10.

OMOA

Omoa, 15 km from Puerto Cortés has an 18th century castle, Fortaleza de San Fernando, now renovated and worth a visit. Entrance US$0.85, tickets on sale at gate, guides available, open Tues-Sun 0800-1700. There is a Visitors' Centre (closed for renovation early 1997) and a small interesting museum. During the week Omoa is a quiet fishing village, but at weekends it is overwhelmed by Hondurans from San Pedro and the place gets littered. Roli and Berni (Swiss) run tours of Honduras and Guatemala and to the *cayos* (a handful of small islands, 1½ hrs by boat), good snorkelling. Near Omoa are waterfalls (Los Chorros) and good hiking in attractive scenery both along the coast and inland.

● **Accommodation** At Omoa you can stay at **C** *Bahía de Omoa*, on beach, with bath, a/c, English, German and Dutch spoken, use of washing machine, comfortable and clean, owner Heinz has motor launch for fishing or scuba diving and catamaran, sleeps 4, US$3,000/week; **B** *Prado Mar Lodge*, Barrio Motrique, T San Pedro Sula 53-28-80, behind beach, cabins with bath, fridge; **D** *Gemini B*, on main access road to beach, bath, fan, cafetería, parking, lawn, new, comfortable; **F** *Hospedaje Champa Julita*, on beach, friendly, fan, basic, run down; **F** *Roli and Berni's Place*, 300m from beach, clean rooms with private bath and hot water, more planned, good information here of the region; also on the road to the beach is *Hospedaje Puerto Grande*, but rooms are boxlike and sanitation unspeakable. **F** the *tienda* where the bus stops has cheap, basic rooms, shared bathroom, OK; **G** *Hospedaje El Centro* is in the centre of the village. The alternatives are going back to Puerto Cortés or going back 3 km to Chivana, where there is the **A2** *Acantilados del Caribe* **(Caribbean Cliff Marine Club)**, on the road to Omoa from Puerto Cortés, **A1** at weekends, restaurant, good food, bar, discotheque, supermarket, small nature reserve with hiking and riding trails, beach, speed boats, nice atmosphere (PO Box 23, Puerto Cortés; T 55-14-61, F 55-14-03; in USA T 1-800-327-4149, F (305) 444-8987).

● **Places to eat** Restaurants inc *El Delfín*, *Pancho*, *Champa Julita*, *Wahoo*, good seafood and *El Botín del Suizo*, run by the popular Ulrich Lang and his wife Dionicia, excellent seafood, standards fall when the boss is not around (also has beds, **G**, shower and toilets, more being built). *Virginia*, 200m on left of pier, small, friendly, good seafood; *Fisherman's Hut*, 200m to right of pier, new, clean, good food, seafood, rec.

● **Useful addresses Immigration**: Migración has an office on the main road opp Texaco.

The coastal road heads SW from Omoa towards the Guatemalan border at Corinto, where it stops. About 8 km from Omoa is a nice stretch of beach at the mouth of the Río Coto, with the very pleasant **D** *Río Coto Hotel-Restaurant*, a/c, pool, good. 15 km SW of Omoa (Km 30½, Carretera de Puerto Cortés a Cuyamel) at **Pueblo Nuevo** on the banks of the Río Coco, is **A3** *EcoRancho*, a dairy *hacienda* owned by César López. It is a beautiful ranch at the foot of the Omoa mountain range with luxury accommodation, fine family cooking, hiking, riding, bird and butterfly watching, swimming, fishing, learning to milk a cow. Also **B** cabins in two mountain sites, one at Esmeralda (500m), the other at Río Coco (1,000m), both organic coffee and cardamom plantations, camping also available, equipment provided. Tour packages arranged to include Ranguana Cay (Belize), Río Dulce (Guatemala) and other lodges. Contact the manager, Rafael Aguilera at PO Box 130, San Pedro Sula, T/F 56-61-56, T 56-87-80. Continuing along the coast road you come to a Garífuna village, **Mazca** (or Masca), where Doña Lydia has built bamboo and palm-thatched cabins on stilts beside her house behind the beach, **G**, warm family atmosphere, good Garífuna cooking. A few *champas* on the beach provide fish meals and cold drinks.

FRONTIER WITH GUATEMALA

● **Honduran immigration**
Before leaving for the frontier, obtain your exit stamp from the Oficina de Migración in Puerto Cortés (see under Puerto Cortés **Shipping**), or Omoa.

Entering Honduras You must have a Guatemalan exit stamp in your passport before crossing the frontier and obtain an entry stamp in Puerto Cortés as soon as possible. Any custom formalities will take place there.

● **Guatemalan Consulate**
See San Pedro Sula.

● **Transport**
Buses leave Puerto Cortés for Omoa and **Corinto** on the frontier every hour or so (Línea Costeños, Ruta 3 or 4).

For a crossing on foot from Guatemala to Honduras, see the description of the 'Jungle Trail' in **Guatemala**, **Section 2**. A summary of accounts we have received on the trip from Honduras to Guatemala is as follows: from Corinto (first bus from Puerto Cortés at 0600) there is a 2-3 hr walk (there may be a pick-up going) to the Guatemalan frontier post at **El Cinchado** on the Río Motagua. There are many birds through the forest, waterways to cross and to avoid. You will have to ask frequently if you are on the right trail or, better, engage a guide with a horse to carry the luggage as far as the river. Thereafter, negotiate a river crossing. Make your way along the river bank to Finca Chinoq to the light railway and hitch a lift if possible, or take a bus, for the 15 km to Entre Ríos and Puerto Barrios. Start early, this is not a route to be caught on overnight or in bad weather.

A better route recommended by many of our readers, is first to obtain your exit stamp in Omoa or Puerto Cortés, then catch the 0600 or 0715 bus from Puerto Cortés market via Tegucigalpita to **Cuyamelito**. (Or take a bus to Tegucigalpita as early as possible; a pick-up driver will turn up and take you to the place where the boat leaves (at the fence), stopping on the way at an *Oficina de Migración* where you can get an exit stamp if you do not already have one.) From Cuyamelito (**G** *Hospedaje Monte Cristo*, behind the bridge) it is a 2-km walk to the wharf from where a dug out takes you through the swamps to the border, US$1.50, first one at 0600, no controls. Another boat, US$2.50, on the Guatemalan side (Río Tinto) takes you to the Barra de Motagua and on to Finca la Inca banana plantation where you have to wait for a bus or hitch to Puerto Barrios. The whole trip takes 6-7 hrs but may take longer if it is raining hard.

A compass could be useful. Beware of snakes, wear high factor sun cream, wear strong boots if possible, especially in the rainy season, take plenty of water (buy some from the villagers if you run out) and keep your arms covered if you can stand it as the mosquitoes are plentiful.

NB Work has started on a road between Corinto and Puerto Barrios with a bridge across the Río Motagua, funded by the OAS.

TELA TO TRUJILLO

TELA

(*Pop* 67,890) **Tela**, some 50 km to the E, is reached from San Pedro Sula (bus service via El Progreso, watch out for thieves on bus, padlocks are no deterrent, stay with your bags at all times). Tela used to be an important banana port before the pier was partly destroyed by fire. It is pleasantly laid out, with a sandy beach. Tela Viejo to the E is the original city; Tela Nuevo is the residential area built for the executives of the American banana and farming company which established itself in the city. Old and new Tela are joined by two bridges. There is a pleasant walk along the beach E to Ensenada (a café and not much else) and Triunfo, or W to San Juan (see **Excursions**). Do not walk on the beach after 1730, muggings and rape reported, even in daylight.

A **Garífuna Museum** opened in 1996 at the river end of C 8 (also known as J C del Valle, its original name), PO Box 127, T 48-22-44. It is an interesting and colourful introduction to Garífuna history and culture, with special emphasis on the contribution made by Honduran and Belizean Garífunas to contemporary music in the form of the frenetic rhythms of Punta, a blend of rock and roll, Afro-Caribbean and Spanish influences, originally a ritual dance. Also here is the art gallery of the Tela Artists Association, exhibiting many local artists. The museum shop sells *artesanía*, oil paintings etc, usually open until 2100.

Excursions

Jardín Botánico at **Lancetilla** (established 1926), 5 km inland; open Mon-Fri, 0730 1530; Sat, Sun and holidays 0830-1600, admission US$3.85. The garden was founded as a plant research station by United Fruit Co, then from 1975 was run

---

Prolansate

The **Fundación Para la Protección de Lancetilla, Punta Sal y Texiguat (Prolansate)** is a non-governmental, apolitical, non-profit organization based in Tela. Originally set up by Peace Corps volunteers, it is now operated by local personnel and is involved in environmental programmes to protect and educate in conjunction with community development and ecotourism. It is currently managing four protected areas: Parque Nacional 'Jeannette Kawas' (Punta Sal), Jardín Botánico Lancetilla, Refugio de Vida Silvestre Texiguat, Refugio de Vida Silvestre Punta Izopo. There are plans to extend the area of the national park (see map), named after a former Treasurer and President of Prolansate who was assassinated in 1995, but there are complications with the location of several Garífuna villages. The Prolansate Visitors' Centre is at C 9 Av 2-3 NE, T 48-20-35. They organize trips to Punta Sal, Punta Izopo and Lancetilla, with expert guides, as well as providing information about other national parks, wildlife refuges and bird sanctuaries.

by Cohdefor, but is now managed by Prolansate. Over 1,000 varieties of plants and over 200 bird species have been identified. It has fruit trees from every continent, the most extensive collection of Asiatic fruit trees in the Western Hemisphere, orchid garden, plantations of mahogany and teak alongside a 1,200-ha virgin tropical rainforest. Guided tours rec. Ask for a good guided tour at the Cohdefor office. *Hospedaje* (**E** *Turicentro Lancetilla*, T 48-20-07, a/c) and *comedor*, full at weekends,

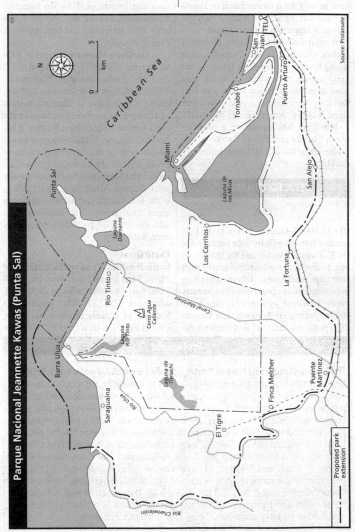

Parque Nacional Jeannette Kawas (Punta Sal)

Source: Prolansate

Proposed park extension

and camping facilities in gardens for price of admission. Either take employees' bus from town centre at 0700, or local bus to the main road turn-off, 4 km from the botanical gardens. Alternatively take a taxi from Tela, US$5, but there are few in the park for the return journey in the afternoon, so organize collection in advance. Be warned, there are many mosquitoes. Good maps available in English or Spanish US$0.30.

Local buses and trucks from the corner just E of the market go E to the Black Carib village of **Triunfo de la Cruz**, site of the first Spanish settlement on the mainland, in a beautiful bay, in which a sea battle between Cristóbal de Olid and Francisco de las Casas (2 of Cortés' lieutenants) was fought in 1524. Bus to Triunfo de la Cruz, US$0.40 (about 5 km, if no return bus, walk to main road where buses pass). **F** *Hotel El Triunfo* with bath or **D** furnished apartments. Cheap houses and *cabañas* for rent in Triunfo de la Cruz. A recommended day trip is by bus to Triunfo, lunch on seafood there, then walk back to Tela, if you have sturdy shoes on (the stretch of beach towards the headland is rugged but rewarding). Otherwise, take the easier route inland to Ensenada, then along the beach to Tela. Beyond Triunfo de la Cruz is an interesting coastal area including the cape, **Punta Izopo** (1½-hr walk along the beach, take water) and the mouth of the Río Leán. This and the immediate hinterland was declared a National Wildlife Refuge in 1992. For information contact Prolansate. To get right into the forest and enjoy wildlife, it is best to take an organized tour.

The area W of Tela is being developed for tourism, with investment in infrastructure (roads, bridges) and hotels and resorts. The Carib villages of **Tornabé** and **San Juan** (4 km W of *Villas Telamar*), are worth a visit, beautiful food (fish cooked in coconut oil). In Tornabé (taxi US$3) there are 8 bungalows for rent, some a/c, some fan, hot water, at **A3** *The Last Resort*, with breakfast, T/F 48-25-45. A great place to relax, full board available, good restaurant. Further NW, along palm-fringed beaches and blue lagoons, is **Punta Sal**, a lovely place. To get there you need a motor boat or take a bus to Tornabé and hitch a ride 12 km on to **Miami**, a small, all-thatched fishing village (2 hrs' walk along beach from Tornabé), beer on ice available, and walk the remaining 10 km along the beach. There are also pick-ups from Punta Sal to Miami, contact Prolansate for information. *Garífuna Tours*, 9 C y Parque Central, Tela, run tours for US$10, food extra. Alternatively, take a motorized *cayuco* from Tela to **Río Tinto** beyond Punta Sal, and explore from there. This area is now a 80,000 ha National Park (see map), contact Prolansate for information. It includes forest, mangroves, wetlands and lagoons. Once inhabited only by Garífuna, the area has recently suffered from immigration of cattle farmers who have cleared the forest, causing erosion, and from a palm oil extraction plant on the Río San Alejo, which has dumped waste in the river and contaminated the lagoons. Conservation and environmental protection programmes are now under way.

There is a small hotel in Río Tinto, two *comedores* and accommodation is also available in private houses. From Río Tinto it is possible to walk W along the beach to Puerto Cortés; it is about 20 km from Río Tinto to Baja Mar (4-5 hrs' walk), from where buses run to Puerto Cortés. This would be quicker than taking buses Tela-Progreso-San Pedro Sula-Puerto Cortés, but not quicker than the train. *Cayucos* arrive in Tela early am for shopping, returning to Río Tinto between 1000 and 1200, very good value.

NB As with all the beaches in or near the major towns on the N coast, it is dangerous to walk on or near them after dark. Robbery and rape are commonplace.

Local festivals

Fiesta: San Antonio in June.

Local information

● **Accommodation**

During Easter week, the town is packed; room rates double and advance booking is essential.

A3 *Sherwood*, T 48-24-16, on waterfront, a/c, TV, hot water, upper rooms have balconies and are airy, new pool, hotel under renovation 1996 with annex under construction, English speaking helpful owner, TCs or credit cards accepted, staff friendly and honest, restaurant busy at weekends; **A3** *Villas Telamar*, T 48-21-96, F 48-29-84, a complex of wooden bungalows, set on a palm-fringed beach, price for rooms, villas from **A1**, restaurant, bar, golf club, swimming pool, conference centre, redeveloped 1996.

C *Apart-Hotel Ejecutivos*, 8 C 3 Av NE, T 48-20-47, a/c, hot water, TV, 8 rooms with kitchenette; **C** *César Mariscos*, T 48-20-83, on beach, new, a/c, large rooms, restaurant; **C** *Maya Vista*, new in 1996, at top of hill, steep flight of steps starting opp *Preluna*, Canadian-owned, French and English spoken, bath, a/c, hot water, bar, restaurant, delicious French-Canadian cuisine, fantastic views; **C** *Presidente*, on central park, T 48-28-21, F 48-29-92, good restaurant and pleasant bar.

D *Bahía Azul*, 11 C, 6 Av NE, T 48-23-81 (with a/c or fan, on western end of beach), hot water, good restaurant overlooking the sea, fine location; **D** *Bertha's*, 8 C, 9 Av NE, nr bus terminal, new brick building, with bath, a/c, cheaper with fan, clean, rec; **D** *Nuevo Puerto Rico*, T 48-24-14, on the waterfront, lovely situation but exposed in June-Dec wet season, a/c or fan, small rooms, fridge, balcony, TV, poor service, large restaurant; **D** *Sinai*, 6 Av 6 C, previously Av Honduras, T 48-26-61, 3 blocks S of Parque Central, with bath and a/c, **E** without, very friendly owner, clean; **D** *Tela*, 9 C, 3-4 Av NE, T 48-21-50, clean, airy, fans, hot water, with restaurant, but meagre breakfast, otherwise very good; **D** *Tía Carmen*, 8 C 5 Av, next to Bancahorro, T 48-26-06, a/c, hot water, TV, comfortable, well-furnished rooms, friendly, efficient, excellent restaurant.

E *Caribe*, 7 Av 7 C, T 48-28-50, next to Shell, with bath, friendly, clean, a/c; **E** *Mar Azul*, 11 C, 5 Av NE, T 48-23-13, with fan and bath, charming helpful owner; **E** *Minihotel La Posada del Sol*, 8 C 3 Av NE, opp *Ejecutivos*, T 48-21-21, with bath, **F** without, clean, nice garden; **E-F** *Mi Casa es Su Casa*, 6 Av 10-11 C, bed and breakfast, private house, sign outside, friendly, family atmosphere.

F *Hotelito Porvenir*, 9 C, 2 blocks from Plaza, very small rooms, poor bathroom facilities, very cheap; **F** *Ocean View*, facing W side of Parque Central, T 48-29-46, a/c; **F** *Playa*, 11 C, 3-4 Av NE, basic, bedbugs; **F** *Preluna*, 9 C, 7-8 Av NE, delightful clapboard building, restaurant, quiet but reported deteriorating; **F** *Robert*, 9 C, 6 Av NE, basic, **G** with shared bathroom, will do laundry, noisy, close to bus station, short stay clients, mixed reports; **F** *Boarding House Sara*, 11 C, 6 Av behind the restaurant *Tiburón Playa*, basic, with bath, or without, poor sanitation, has 3 good cabins priced according to number of occupants, popular with backpackers, friendly, noisy especially at weekends from all night discos.

Out of town, 3 km on highway to La Ceiba, *El Retiro*, set back from the road by a small river, attractive setting, camping in vehicle allowed.

● **Places to eat**

The best eating in Tela is in the hotel restaurants. *Luces del Norte*, of Doña Mercedes, 11 C, 2 Av NE, towards beach from Parque Central, next to *Hotel Puerto Rico*, delicious seafood and good typical breakfasts, very popular, also good information; *César's* (also new hotel – see above), on the beach, serves good seafood, open from 0700, very good breakfast menu; next door, *Alejandro's*, good for drinks; also *Sherwood's*, see above, good food, attractive, popular, enjoy the view from the terrace, also opens 0700 and serves excellent breakfast; *Los Angeles*, 9 C, 2 Av, NE, Chinese, run by Hong Kong owners, large helpings, good; *Vista Maya*, in new hotel (see above), run by Québécois Pierre, fine cuisine; *Tuty's Café*, 9 C NE nr Parque Central, excellent fruit drinks and good cheap lunch specials, closed Sun, very slow service, take a book; *Comedor Acuario*, nr Boarding House Sara, local food, cheap, rec; *Bahía Azul* (see hotel above), excellent cheap meals; *Pizzería El Bambino*, 11 C, 50m from new bridge, good pasta, pizza, open-air eating on terrace, nice children's playground; *Garífuna*, at river end of 8 C, with *champas* at river's edge, typical garífuna fare, conch soup, *tapado* (fish stew with coconut and yuca); *Merendero Tía Carmen*, at the hotel, good food, Honduran specialities, good almuerzo; *El Magnate*, 11 C 1 Av NE, close to old bridge, à la carte menu, pork chops speciality, open until midnight, good, disco Fri, Sat, Sun; *Alexandro's*, pedestrian mall, international menu, popular, often crowded, seafood specialities; also on pedestrian mall are *La Cueva*, smart, big menu inc steak, chicken, seafood, pricey; *La Cascada*, next door, modest *comedor* in clapboard shack, cheap, home cooking, good, open early until late.

In Tela Nueva, all along the boulevard, *Los Pinchos*, shish-kebab speciality, meat and seafood, very good, nice patio, soothing music, closed Mon; *Marabú*, excellent, also rooms to rent, **C**; *Cafetería La Oso*, offshoot of *Hotel Tia Carmen's Merendero*; *Repostería y Baleadas Tía Carmen*, across the boulevard, same excellent Honduran specialities, very good; *Estancia Victoria*, new, elegant restaurant/bar, a/c, not cheap, good, international menu.

● **Banks & money changers**
Banco Atlántida, Bancahsa, 9 C 3 Av, Visa and Mastercard. Banadesa, Bancahurro, 8 C 5 Av, changes TCs. Casa de Cambio La Teleña, 4 Av, 9 C NE for US$, TCs and cash. Exchange dealers on street outside Post Office.

● **Entertainment**
Cinema: 9 C, US$0.40-0.60.

● **Hospitals & medical services**
Centro Médico CEMEC, 8 Av 7 C NE, open 24 hrs, X-rays, operating theatre, smart, well-equipped, T/F 48-24-56.

● **Laundry**
El Centro, 4 Av 9 C, US$2 wash and dry; *Lavandería San José*, 1 block NE of market; *Lavandería Banegas*, Pasaje Centenario, 3 C 1 Av.

● **Places to worship**
Protestant Church: Anglican.

● **Post & telecommunications**
Hondutel and Post Office: both on 4 Av NE. Fax service and collect calls to Europe available and easy at Hondutel

● **Tour companies & travel agents**
Garifuna Tours, SW corner of Parque Central, knowledgeable and helpful, day trips to Punta Sal (US$15) and Punta Izopo (US$11), good value, also mountain bike hire, US$4.60/day. *Galaxia Travel Agency*, 9 C 1 Av NE, nr river, T 48 21 52, F 48-20-82, for reservations and confirmations of national and international flights.

● **Useful addresses**
Immigration: Migración is at the corner of 3 Av and 8 C.

● **Transport**
Local **Bicycle**: hire from Garifuna Tours, 9 C y Parque Central (see above).

Trains The railway service to Puerto Cortés was running in 1997, 2 days a week, 4 hrs, Fri, Sun,

1300, 1st class US$1.15, 2nd class US$0.75. Check locally for exact schedule, can be daily in high season.

Buses Catisa or Tupsa lines from San Pedro Sula to **El Progreso** (US$0.45) where you must change to go on to **Tela** (3 hrs in all) and **La Ceiba** (last bus at 1900). Bus from Tela to El Progreso every 30 mins, US$0.95; to La Ceiba, 2½ hrs, US$1. Direct to Tegucigalpa, Traliasa, 1 a day from *Hotel Los Arcos*, US$4.50, same bus to La Ceiba (this service avoids San Pedro Sula).

LA CEIBA

(Pop 80,160) 100 km E of Tela, known as 'Ceibita La Bella', the capital of Atlántida Department, it stands on the narrow coastal plain between the Caribbean and the rugged Nombre de Dios mountain range, crowned by the spectacular Pico Bonito (2,435m). It was once the country's busiest port but trade has now passed to Puerto Cortés and Puerto Castilla. There is still some activity mainly to serve the Bay Islands; La Ceiba is the usual starting point for visits to the Bay Islands. The climate is hot, but tempered by sea winds. The main square is worth walking around; it has statues of various famous Hondurans including Lempira and two ponds with alligators or turtles basking in one of them; also a tourist information kiosk. There are some white sand beaches and good river bathing (eg Venado, 3 km up the Río Cangrejal) out of town, but the beaches near the dock are not rec (for details see under **Excursions** below). There is a Garifuna community by the beach at the end of C 1E.

A butterfly and insect museum has a collection of 5,000 butterflies and 1,000 other insects at Colonia El Sauce, Segunda etapa Casa G-12, open Mon Sat 0800-1200, 1400-1700, closed Wed pm, US$1.25, student reductions, T 42-28-74, e-mail: rlehman@ns.gbm.hn. You get a 25-min video in both Spanish and English and Robert and Myriam Lehman guide visitors expertly through the mysteries of lepidopterae. Interesting for all ages. Hand-painted butterfly T-shirts for sale.

Excursions

Jutiapa, a small, dusty town with a pretty little colonial church. Contact United Brands office in La Ceiba (off main square) to visit a local pineapple plantation. Two interesting Garífuna villages near La Ceiba are **Corozal** at Km 209½ (with beach Playas de Sambrano, and **C** *Hotel Villa Rhina*, T 43-12-22, F 43-35-58, with pool and restaurant near the turn off from the main road) and **Sambo Creek** (also nice beaches and simple hotel-restaurant **E** *Hermanos Avila*, clean, food OK; *La Champa* restaurant, seafood Garífuna style, bar, delightful location, rec).

Near the towns of Esparta and El Porvenir thousands of crabs come out of the sea in July and Aug and travel long distances inland. Catarata El Bejuco, 7 km along the old dirt road to Olanchito (11 km from La Ceiba): follow a path signposted to Balneario Los Lobos to the waterfall about 1 km up the river through the jungle. Good swimming from a pebbly beach where the river broadens. 20 km down the old road to Olanchito is Yaruca, reached by bus; good views of Pico Bonita. **Eco-Zona Río María**, 5 km along the Trujillo highway, signposted path up to the foothills of the Cordillera Nombre de Dios, a beautiful walk through the lush countryside of a protected area. Just beyond Río María is Balneario Los Chorros (signposted) a series of small waterfalls through giant boulders into a deep rock pool. Great for swimming. Refreshments nearby. Upstream there is some beautiful scenery and you can continue walking through the forest and in the river, where there are more pools. Another bathing place, Agua Azul with restaurant is a short distance away.

Beaches

White sand beaches in and near La Ceiba include: Playa Miramar (dirty, not rec), La Barra (better), Perú (across the Río Cangrejal at Km 205½, better still, quiet except weekends, deserted tourist complex, restaurant, access by road to Tocoa, 10 km, then signposted side road 1½ km, or along the beach 6 km from La Ceiba), La Encenada (close to Corozal). The beaches near the fishing villages of Río Esteban and Balfate are very special and are near Cayos Cochinos (Hog Islands) where the snorkelling and diving is spectacular. The Hog Islands (see page 918) can be reached by *cayuco* from **Nuevo Armenia**, a nondescript Garífuna village connected by road to Jutiapa: **E** *Chichi*, 3 small rooms, fan, mosquito net, clean, friendly, good food available. Bus from La Ceiba at 1100 US$0.75, 2½ hrs. At the bus stop is the office of the man who arranges boat trips to Hog Islands, US$10, trips start at 0700, you may see dolphins, quite an experience. Take whatever you need with you as there is almost nothing on the smaller cays. However, the Garífuna are going to and fro all the time.

Local festivals

San Isidro, La Ceiba's patron saint, is on 15 May. The celebrations continue for 2 weeks, ending 28 May, the highlight being the international carnival on the third Sat in May, when La Ceiba dons party dress and dances all night to the Afro-Caribbean rhythms of the country's Garífuna bands.

Local information
● Accommodation

B *La Quinta*, exit carretera La Ceiba-Tela, opp Club de Golf, T 43-02-23, F 43-02-26, restaurant, laundry, cable TV, swimming pool, immaculate, good value; **B** *Siesta VIP*, Blvd 15 de Septiembre, next to Banco Central, T 43-09-68, F 43-09-74, phone, TV, room service, bar, restaurant, airport pick-up; **B** *Tesla's Guest House*, T/F 43-09-33, T 43-38-93, C Montecristo 212, Col El Naranjal, opp Hospital La Fé, 5 rooms, private bathrooms, hot water, a/c, pool, phone, minibar, barbecue, laundry, friendly family owners speak English, German, French and Spanish, airport collection; **B** *Welcome Guest House*, 1162 C de el Naranjal, Barrio el Imán, Apdo Postal 1043, T/F 43-14-75, French owned, a/c, shared or private bath, next to *Expatriate's Grill*; **B-C** *Partenon Beach*, T 43-04-04, F 43-04-34, Greek-owned, family apartments, new annex with very nice rooms, cable TV, English speaking desk staff, swimming pool,

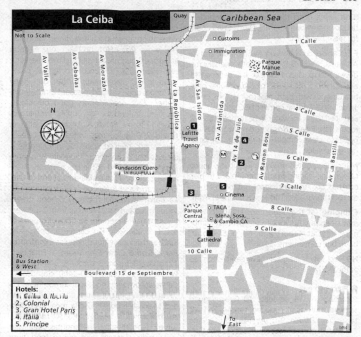

La Ceiba

Caribbean Sea

Quay

Not to Scale

Customs

Immigration

Parque Manue Bonilla

1 Calle

Av Valle

Av Cabañas

Av Morazán

Av Colón

Av La República

Av San Isidro

Av Atlántida

Av 14 de Julio

Av Ramón Rosa

Av La Bastilla

4 Calle

5 Calle

6 Calle

7 Calle

8 Calle

9 Calle

10 Calle

N

Lafitte Travel Agency

Fundación Cuero TARGETPOLL

Parque Central

Cinema

TACA

Isleña, Sosa, & Cambio CA

Cathedral

To Bus Station & West

Boulevard 15 de Septiembre

To East

Hotels:
1. Ceiba & Iberia
2. Colonial
3. Gran Hotel París
4. Italia
5. Príncipe

expensive but excellent restaurant, home made pasta, lovely salad bar, highly rec.

C *Apart-Hotel Caribbean Suites*, 14 Av San Isidro with Av La República, T 43-12-22, 43-44-05, F 43-35 58, rooms with kitchenette, sitting room, TV, phone, hot shower, room service, laundry, bar, restaurant, good value; **C** *Colonial*, Av 14 de Julio, entre 6a y 7a C, T 43-19-53/4, F 43-19-55, a/c, sauna, jacuzzi, cable TV, rooftop bar, restaurant with varied menu, nice atmosphere, tourist office, tours available; **C** *Gran Hotel París*, Parque Central, T/F 43-23-91, some rooms cheaper, a/c, own generator, faded, swimming pool (open to non-residents for US$2), parking.

D *Ceiba*, Av San Isidro, 5 C, T 43-27-37, with fan or a/c and bath, restaurant and bar, uncomfortable, but good breakfast; next door from *Ceiba* is **D** *Iberia*, T 43-04-01, a/c, window without screen, rec; **D** *Italia*, four doors from the *Colonial*, on Av 14 de Julio, T 43-01-50, clean, a/c, good restaurant with reasonable prices, parking in interior courtyard; **D** *Martín Fierro*, Av San Isidro at 13 C, T/F 42-28-12,

bath, a/c, hot water, **E** with fan, TV, bar, restaurant, new, comfortable; **D** *Paradiso*, C 4 E, Barrio La Isla, T 43-35-35, bath, a/c, hot water, TV, restaurant, 4 blocks from beach, bar, restaurant; **D** *Príncipe*, 7 C between Av 14 de Julio and Av San Isidro, T 43-05-16, cheaper with fan and shared bath, bar/restaurant, TV. **D** *San Carlos*, Av San Isidro, 5 y 6 C, rooms are clean with fan, colourful cafeteria, and its own bakery, good breakfasts, where Bay Islanders assemble Tues mornings for boat trip to Utila; **D-E** *El Conquistador*, Av La República, T 43-28-51, cheaper with fan, shared bath, safe, clean, TV; **D-E** *Gran Hotel Líbano*, at bus terminal, new, good, restaurant, a/c or fan, bath; **D-E** *Tropical*, Av Atlántida between 4 y 5 C, T 42-25-65, with bathroom, fan, basic, small rooms noisy, cold drinks and water sold in foyer.

E *Florencia*, Av 14 de Julio, clean, bath, friendly, dark rooms but rec; **E** *Granada*, Av Atlántida, 5-6 C, T 43-24-51, bath, a/c, clean, cheaper with fan; **E** *Rotterdam Beach*, 1 C, Barrio La Isla, on the beach, with bath, fan, clean, friendly, pleasant garden, good value, rec; next door is **F-G** *Amsterdam 2001*, run by Dutchman Jan

(Don Juan), good for backpackers, dormitory beds or rooms, with laundry, *Dutch Corner Café* for great breakfasts.

F *El Caribe*, 5 C between Av San Isidro and Av Atlántida, T 43-18-57, with bath, friendly, run down, cockroaches; **F** *La Isla*, 4 C between 11 and 12 Av, T 43-28-35, nice weatherboard clapboard house with bath, nice rooms, fans; on Av 14 de Julio **F** *Real* (at corner of 6 C), cold shower and need to ask for water to be turned on, small rooms, fan; **F** *Las 5 Rosas*, C 8 nr Av Le Bastilla, opp Esso, clean, simple rooms, bath, fan, laundry, good value.

Many cheap hotels on Av La República, beside railway line leading from central plaza to pier, eg *Arias*, *Los Angeles* (clean), but most of them are short stay places. This area is unsafe at night.

Camping: at the airport for US$0.20. You may sleep in your vehicle but no tent camping. Hotel at airport entrance **F** *El Cique*, basic but convenient.

NB Electricity is irregular, have candles/torches at the ready.

● **Places to eat**
Ricardo's, Av 14 de Julio, 10 C, very good seafood and steaks, garden setting and a/c tables, rec; *Palace*, 9 C, Av 14 de Julio, large Chinese menu, seafood, churrasco, rec; *La Carreta*, 4 C, 2 Av E, Barrio Potrerito (nr Parque Manuel Bonilla), good value, charcoal-broiled meat, about US$17 for 2, try *anafre*, a bean and cheese dish, rec; *Toto's*, Av San Isidro, 17 C, good pizzería; *Las Dos Fronteras*, Av San Isidro, 13 C, good Mexican and American food, open 0700-2200, another branch at Plaza del Sol Shopping Centre, good food, limited choice; *Cafetería Mi Delicia*, Av San Isidro, 11 C, good food at low prices, plentiful breakfasts, family atmosphere; *Cri Cri Burger*, Av 14 de Julio, 3 C, facing attractive Parque Bonilla good fast food, several branches in town, rec; *Masapán*, 7 C Av San Isidro-Av República, self-service, varied, well-prepared choice of dishes, fruit juices, good coffee, open 0630-2200, rec; *Café El Pastel*, Av San Isidro with 6 C, good cheap breakfasts, set lunches, snacks, open 0700-2100; *El Canadiense*, Parque Manuel Bonilla, N end of Av 14 de Julio, western food, steaks etc, busy bar, open 0800-2300, closed Sun, book exchange, operates Harry's Horseback Riding trips to Pico Bonito, 6 hrs, US$25, expat guide, food provided; *La Plancha*, C 9, Av la Bastilla, behind Esso, T 43-23-04, a/c, *churrasquería*; *Café le Jardin*, Av La Bastilla, 7-8 C,

Barrio La Isla, owners Michel (chef) and Lisette (la patronne), outstanding French cuisine, good value wine, open lunch and dinner Mon-Sat, highly rec; *Pizza Hut*, on main square, good salad bar, though pizzas criticized by some, large restaurant, US$2.25 lunchtime special, pizza, salad, drink, playground; opp *Hotel Partenon*, good seafood, pleasant atmosphere. *Cobel*, 7 C, opp *Príncipe*, good breakfasts, excellent set lunches, very popular with locals, closes 1730, rec. *Paty's*, Av 14 de Julio between 6 and 7 C, milkshakes, wheatgerm, cereals, donuts, etc, purified water, clean. Opposite is an excellent pastry shop. There are two more *Paty's* at 8 C E and at the bus terminal. There are several good fish restaurants at end of C IE, *El Pescado* and *Brisas de la Naturaleza* and *La Barra*, overlooking the river, good prawn soup, music and dancing in bar from 2100, very pleasant garden setting; *La Chavelita*, end of 4 C E, overlooking Río Cangrejal, open daily, lunch and dinner, seafood, popular. *Expatriates Bar & Grill & Cigar Emporium*, at Final de C 12, above Refricón, 3 blocks S, 3 blocks E of Parque Central, open 1600-2400, closed Wed, Canadian owned, very expat atmosphere, US TV and newspapers, sports shown, barbecue and Mexican food, US$2-5 a meal; *Deutsch-Australian Club*, beach end of Av 14 de Julio, run by German retired to Honduras after living in Australia, German food and seafood, busy bar, open 1200 until very late.

● **Banks & money changers**
Bancahsa, 9 C, Av San Isidro and *Bancomer*, Parque Central, both cash TCs. Open 0830-1130, 1330-1600; Sat 0800-1200. Cash advances on Visa and Mastercard from Credomatic on Av San Isidro. Better rates for US$ cash from *cambistas* in the lounges of the bigger hotels (and at travel agency next door to *Hotel Príncipe*). **Money Exchange**, at back of Supermercado Los Almendros, 7 C Av San Isidro with Av 14 de Julio, open daily 0800-1200, 1400-1800, T 43-27-20, good rates for US$ cash and TCs. **Honducard**, Av San Isidro for Visa, next to Farmacia Aurora.

● **Entertainment**
Cinema: 8 C y Av San Isidro in Plaza Tropical commercial centre, new, comfortable, digital Dolby stereo.

Discotheques: *Leonardo's*; *D'Lido*; *Buho's*, 1 C, Thur, Fri, Sat 2000-0400, disco free with dinner Thur; several others along 1 C; *Safari*, *Golding Rock*, *La Kosta*, *La Concha*, *Santé's*, reasonable prices.

● **Hospitals & medical services**

Doctor: *Dr Gerardo Meradiaga*, Edif Rodríguez García, Ap No 4, Blvd 15 de Septiembre, general practitioner, speaks English; *Dr Siegfried Seibt*, Centro Médico, 1 C and Av San Isidro, speaks German.

Hospital: *Vincente D'Antoni*, Av Morazán, T 43-22-64, private, competent, well equipped. Private room and doctor's fees about US$40/day for in-patients.

● **Places of worship**

Non-Catholic Churches: Anglican, Methodist, Mennonite, Evangelist and Jehovah's Witnesses, among others.

● **Post & telecommunications**

Post Office: Av Morazán, 13 C O.

Telephone: Hondutel for international telephone calls is at 2 Av, 5 y 6 C E.

● **Shopping**

El Regalito, good quality souvenirs at reasonable prices in small passage by large Carrión store; *T Boot*, store for hiking boots, C 1, E of Av San Isidro, T 43-24-99

● **Tour companies & travel agents**

EuroHonduras, Ed Hospital Centro Médico beach end of Av Atlántida, T/F 43-09-33, T 43-38-93, local tours (also Mosquitia), river trips, kayaking, good value, information, German, French, Spanish and English spoken, highly rec, also guest house, see above; *Hondutours*, 9 C, Av 14 de Julio, T 43-04-57; *Laffite*, Av San Isidro between 5 y 6 C, T 43-01-15, F 43-03-54, help ful and informative; *Trans Mundo*, at Hotel París, T 43-28-20; *Atlántida*, Blvd 15 de Septiembre y Av La República, T 43-03-37; *Pedal and Paddle*, Av 14 de Julio, T 43-27-62, rafting possible all year; *Caribbean Travel Agency*, run by Ann Crichton, Av San Isidro, Edif Hermanos Kawas, Apdo Postal 66, T 43-13-60/1, F 43-13-60, helpful, shares office with *Ríos Honduras* (affiliate of Rocky Mountain Outdoor Center, Howard, Colorado, USA), offering white-water rafting, trips on the Río Cangrejal, spectacular, reservations 1 day in advance. Oscar Pérez, T 43-27-79, PO Box 471, informative guide, 3-day rafting trip on Río Sico, also white-water rafting US$50 pp, exciting, entertaining day, other tours available, highly rec; *Omega Tours*, write to Udo Wittenam, Correos Nacional, Apdo 923, La Ceiba, runs rafting and kayaking trips and jungle hikes, and own hotel 8 hrs upstream on the River Cangrejal. Other tour companies offering whitewater rafting on

the Río Cangrejal (class II, III and IV rapids) include *Tropical River Rafting and Tropical Jungle Tours*, 1 C, facing *Hotel Rotterdam*, 4 hrs down the rapids with expert guide, US$50, T/F 43-20-55; *La Moskitia Eco Aventuras*, Av 14 de Julio at Parque Manuel Bonilla, T 42-01-04, F 21-04-08.

● **Transport**

Local Car rental: **Molinari** in *Hotel París* on Parque Central, in *Hotel Ceiba*, and **Aries Rent-a-Car** in *Hotel Iberia* (César Quesada, the owner, can assist in all types of travel arrangements, T 43-05-24). *Maya Rent-a-Car, Hotel La Quinta*, T 43-30-70, F 43-02-20; *Dino's Rent-a-Car, Hotel Partenon Beach*, T 43-04-34.

Air Golosón (LCE), 9.7 km out of town, with direct services to Belize City, San Salvador, Grand Cayman, Miami, Houston and New Orleans with Taca or Isleña, as well as internal destinations. For full details of flights to Bay Islands, see next section. Isleña (T 43-01-79, airport T 43-23-26), flies to Tegucigalpa, San Pedro Sula, Trujillo (daily except Sun), Guanaja; Caribbean Air flies to Roatán and San Pedro Sula. Rollins Air also fly to the Bay Islands. Sosa flies to Ahuas, Brus Laguna, Puerto Lempira, San Pedro Sula, Roatán and Utila. At weekends there are some charter flights which may be better than the scheduled flights. Taxi to town US$4 pp or walk 200m to the main road and share for US$1 with other passengers, also buses from bus station nr *Cric Cric Burger* at end 3 Av, US$0.15

Buses Taxi from centre to bus terminal, which is a little way W of town (follow Blvd 15 de Septiembre), costs US$0.40 pp, or there are buses from Parque Central. Most buses leave from here. Traliasa and Etrusca bus service to **Tegucigalpa** via Tela US$6, avoiding San Pedro Sula (US$1 to Tela, 2 hrs); also hourly service to **San Pedro Sula**, US$2 (3-4 hrs). To **Trujillo**, 3 hrs *directo*, 4 hrs *local*, every 1½ hrs or so, US$3; daily bus La Ceiba-Trujillo-Santa Rosa de Aguán; to **Olanchito**, US$1, 3 hrs; also regular buses to Sonaguera, Tocoa, Balfate, Isletas, San Esteban and other regional locations.

Sea *M/V Tropical* sails daily (except in bad weather) to the Bay Islands (see next section for full details) from the new dock (Muelle de Cabotaje), 6 km outside town. Take taxi, US$1.50 pp, if sharing with 4 people, bus will only take you part of the way, inconvenient 1½ hrs walk from there, some assaults reported early morning.

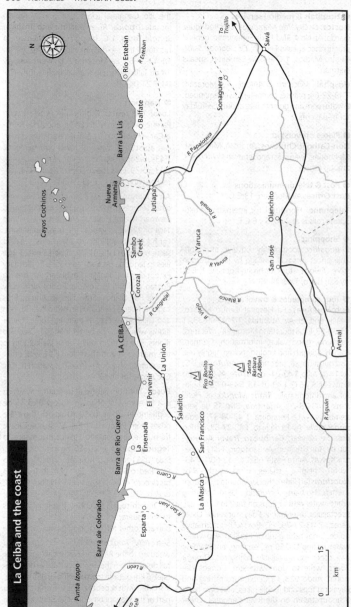

La Ceiba and the coast

NATIONAL PARKS

1. Pico Bonito

The **Pico Bonito** national park (674 sq km) is the largest of the 11 parks designated in 1987. It has deep tropical hardwood forests which shelter, among other things, jaguars and three species of monkey, deep canyons and tumbling streams and waterfalls (including Las Gemelas which fall vertically some 200m). Development of the park by CURLA (Centro Universitario Regional del Litoral Atlántico) continues under the supervision of Cohdefor, the forestry office. CURLA has a *campamento* with accommodation under construction for visiting scientists, but you can camp. The camp is 5 km (1½ hrs' walk) on a good path from **Armenia Bonito** to the W of La Ceiba, frequent buses from Parque Manuel Bonilla by the Ruta 1 de Mayo urban bus, 1 hr. Visitors can take the path to the Río Bonito with some spectacular river scenery. Swimming possible in deep rock pools. A route is being created around the foothills and there are a few interesting trails in the forest. Guide recommended: Oscar Zelaya, a forest inspector appointed by CURLA, who can be contacted in Armenia Bonito. Pico Bonito itself (2,435m) has been climbed infrequently, it takes at least 9 days. The preferred route is along the Río Bonito, starting from near the *campamento*, and from there up a ridge which climbs all the way to the summit. Expertise in rock climbing is not necessary, but several steep pitches do require a rope for safety; good physical condition is a necessity. Poisonous snakes, including the ter-de-lance (*barba amarilla*) will probably be encountered en route.

For further information on the Park contact Cohdefor at their local office 6 km out of town along the Carretera La Ceiba-Tela, T 43-10-33, where the project director is Sr Allan Herrera. Maps are being prepared by CURLA but not yet available. Take care if you enter the forest: tracks are not yet developed, a compass is advisable. Tour companies in La Ceiba arrange trips to the Park. A day trip, horse riding through the Park can be arranged through Harry's at *Bar El Canadiense*, 14 de Julio, near Parque Manuel Bonilla. Trip includes food and guide, US$25, rec.

2. Cuero y Salado

37 km W of La Ceiba between the Cuero and Salado rivers, near the coast, is the **Cuero y Salado Wildlife Reserve**, which has a great variety of flora and fauna, with a large population of local and migratory birds. It extends for 13,225 ha of swamp and forest. The reserve is managed by the Fundación Cuero y Salado – Refugio de Vida Silvestre, Fucsa, 1 block N and 3 blocks W of Parque Central (see map) to the left of the Standard Fruit Company, La Ceiba, T/F (504) 43-03-29, Apdo Postal 674, which was formed in 1987. The Foundation is open to volunteers, preferably who speak English and Spanish. Part of the programme is to teach environmental education at two rural schools. Travel agencies in La Ceiba run tours there, but Fucsa arranges visits and owns the only accommodation in the reserve. Before going to the Reserve, check with Fucsa in La Ceiba. Although the office only has basic information, they are helpful and there are displays and books about the flora and fauna to be found in the park. Worth visiting before you go to the Park. A charge of about US$10 is made to enter the reserve, plus US$5 pp for accommodation. Boatmen charge about US$20 for a 2-hr trip or US$40 for 5 hrs (6-7 persons maximum) US$6 to US$7 for the guide. To get there independently, take a bus to **La Unión** (every hour, 0600 until 1500 from La Ceiba terminus, US$0.30, 1½ hrs, ask to get off at the railway line (ferrocarril) or Km 17), an interesting journey through pineapple fields. There are several ways of getting into the park from La Unión. Walking takes 1½ hrs (avoid midday sun), take water. Groups usually take a *moto-carro*, a dilapidated train which also transportes the coconut crop – there is no fixed

timetable – but if you're lucky enough to catch it, it costs US$12, payable at the Park office, 15 mins' journey. From near Doña Tina's house (meals available), take a *burra*, a flat-bed railcar propelled by two men with poles (a great way to see the countryside) to the community on the banks of the Río Salado (9 km, 1 hr, US$8 each way). Here is Fucsa's administration centre, with photos, charts, maps, radio and a 2-room visitors house, sleeping 4 in basic bunks, electricity from 1800-2100. No mosquito nets (so avoid Sept and Oct if you can). Don't wear open footwear as snakes and yellow scorpions can be found here. The refuge is becoming increasingly popular, so book lodging in advance. There is space for tents. Meals cost extra and are served by Doña Estela Cáceres (refried beans, egg, tortillas, etc) in her main family room, with pigs, chickens and children wandering in and out. Give her prior notice. It is worth bringing your own provisions too, especially drinking water.

Nilmo, a knowledgeable biologist who acts as a guide, takes morning and evening boat trips for those staying overnight, either through the canal dug by Standard Fruit, parallel to the beach, between the palms and the mangroves, or down to the Salado lagoon. Five kayaks are available for visitors' use. The early morning is the best time for views of the Pico Bonito national park, for birdlife and for howler monkeys. Also in the reserve are spider and capuchin monkeys, iguanas, jaguar, tapirs, crocodiles, manatee, hummingbirds, toucans, ospreys, eagles, and vultures. The 5-hr trip will take you to Barra de Colorado where the manatees are. Ask to see the garden where local people are taught to grow food without burning the forest. The beach along the edge of the reserve is 28 km long, with a strip of the sea also protected by Fucsa. Fishing is possible, and camping at Salado Barra but you need a permit for both. There are extensive coconut groves along the coast owned by Standard Fruit Co. Although it is possible to go to the

Salado and hire a villager and his boat, a qualified guide will show you much more. It is essential to bring a hat and sun lotion with you.

To return to La Unión, it is another *burra* ride or a 2-hr walk along the railway, little shade; then, either wait for a La Ceiba bus, last one at 1500, or ask for the short cut through grapefruit groves, 20 mins, which leads to the main La Ceiba-Tela road on which there are many more buses back to town, 20 mins, US$0.40.

ROUTES A paved road runs from La Ceiba to Trujillo (see below) and Puerto Castilla. At Savá, the La Ceiba-Trujillo road meets the road heading SW to Olanchito and Yoro, newly paved to Olanchito and a good gravel surface thereafter, which involves a river crossing (for continuation to El Progreso, see page 915). It is possible to go La Ceiba-Jaruca-San José-Olanchito, but Yaruca-San José is no more than a mule track.

TOCOA

Between Savá and Trujillo is the rapidly-growing town of **Tocoa**, also in the Aguán valley. The Catholic church is the modern design of a Peace Corps Volunteer.

● **Accommodation** *La Esperanza*, T 44-33-71; *Victoria*, T 44-30-31; *Jamil*, T 44-35-62, all in Barrio El Centro; *La Confianza*, T 44-33-04, Barrio Abajo; **E** *San Patricio*, Barrio El Centro, T 44-34-01, with bath, a/c, cheaper without; TV; **F** *Hotelito Rosgil*, nr bus station, with bath but water problems.

● **Places to eat** *Rigo*, Barrio El Centro, good Italian food and pizzas; *Gran Vía*, on E side of park.

● **Banks & money changers** Banadesa, Banffaa, Bancahsa, Banco Atlántida, Banco Sogerín.

● **Entertainment Cinema:** Cine Maya.

TRUJILLO

(*Pop* 45,000) 90 km from Savá, was a port and former capital. The population includes a rapidly expanding North American community. This quiet town with a pleasant atmosphere was founded in 1525 (the oldest in Honduras) by Juan de Medina; Hernán Cortés arrived there after his famous march overland from Yucatán in pursuit of his usurping lieutenant, Olid. It was near here that William Walker (see under Nicaragua) was shot in 1860 (a commemorative stone marks the spot in the rear garden of the hospital, 1 block E of the Parque Central); the old cemetery where he is buried (near *Hotel Trujillo*) is interesting, giving an idea of where early residents came from. It is rather overgrown, with collapsed and open tombs. **Fortaleza Santa Bárbara**, a ruined Spanish fortress overlooking the Bay, is worth a visit, entrance US$1. Most of the relics found there have been moved to the museum of Rufino Galán (see below) but there are a few rusty muskets and cannon balls. The beach is clean and the water is calm and shallow, safe for children.

Excursions

The **Parque Nacional Capiro y Calentura** can be reached by walking (or taking a taxi) up the hill past the *Villa Brinkley Hotel*. The road to the summit is in poor condition from the entrance of the park and can be driven only with 4WD. It takes 4-6 hrs to walk it and on a clear day you can see Roatán. There used to be a secret military tracking station at the top but this is now a Hondutel relay installation and there are no longer any restrictions on access. The walk is best done very early in the morning and there are lots of forest sounds of birds and monkeys. Insect repellent needed if you pause. As with all walking in this area, it is best to go in a group to avoid attacks. The park is run by the Fundación Capiro Calentura Guaimoreto (Fucagua), which has an office on the 2nd floor of the library in the middle of the Parque Central, T/F 44-42-94, open Mon-Fri. They have information on all the reserves in the area and also on hiking and tours. They are opening up new trails, improving old ones and organizing guided tours through parts of the forest. The hike along the Sendero de la Culebrina uses the

remnants of a colonial stone road used to transport gold from the mines in the Valle de Aguán. It runs along the Río Mojagua and leads to **Cuyamel**, 37 km from Trujillo, just off the road to Sonaguera. Half way up the Cerro de las Cuevas, 7 km beyond Cuyamel, are impressive caves showing vestiges of occupation by pre-Columbian Pech Indians.

Fucagua also administers the **Refugio de Vida Silvestre, Laguna de Guaimoreto (RVSLG)**, NE of Trujillo, where there is a bird island (Isla de los Pájaros), monkeys and good fishing. To visit, either arrange a trip with Fucagua, a tour agency such as Turtle Tours, or take a bus from Trujillo towards Puerto Castilla, alight just after the bridge which crosses the lagoon, then walk away from the lagoon for about 200m to a dirt track on the left. Follow this and cross a low bridge and on the left is the house of a man who rents dugout canoes. The Isla de los Pájaros is about 3 km up the lagoon, a bit too far for a dugout. Another alternative is to go down to the wharf in Trujillo and ask for Reinardo, who runs the local fishermen's co-op. He hires out motorized canoes and launches (price depends on the number of passengers and length of trip). There are no roads, paths or facilities in the area.

20 mins' walk from Trujillo plaza (follow on road beyond *Hotel Trujillo*) is the **Museo y Piscina Rufino Galán Cáceres** which has a swimming pool filled from the Río Cristales with changing rooms and picnic facilities. Close by, the wreckage of a US C-80 aircraft which crashed in 1985 forms part of Sr Galán's museum; inside the museum is more information and memorabilia about the accident. The rest of the collection is a mass of curios, but with some very interesting objects. Entry US$1, US$0.50 for swim.

West of Trujillo, just past the football field on the Santa Fe road is the Río Grande, which has lovely pools and waterfalls for river bathing, best during rainy season. Take the path on far side of river, after about 10 mins cut down to the

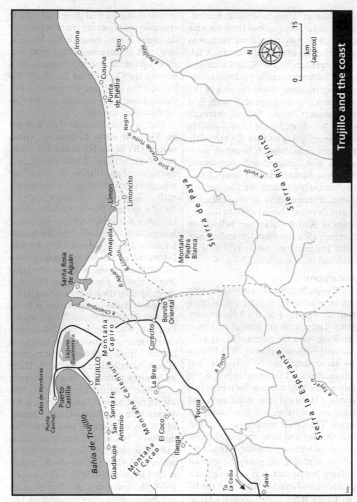

Trujillo and the coast

rocks and follow the river upstream along the boulders.

2 km along the road is **C** *Campamento*, T 44-42-44, round thatched bar, good food, and 10 rooms, lovely setting, mountain backdrop, on unspoilt beach, showers, palm trees, shade, basic but clean, ask about camping, two unfortunate chained monkeys. There are interesting villages

of Black Caribs (Garifuna) W of Trujillo. The road is rough, often impassable in wet weather, jeeps needed even in dry season. **Santa Fe**, 10 km W of Trujillo (US$0.30 by bus, leaves when full, get there by 0800 for seat), is a friendly place with several good Garífuna restaurants eg *Comedor Caballero* (also known as *Pete's Place*, good for lunch, huge portions, lobster, vegetarian food, highly rec) and *Las Brisas de Santa Fe*, on the endless white sandy beach. The bus service continues to San Antonio (good restaurant behind the beach) and Guadalupe. Walk in the morning along the beach to Santa Fe and then get a bus back to Trujillo, taking plenty of water and sun block. This stretch of beach is outstanding, but watch out for *marea roja*, a sea organism which colours the water pink and can give irritating skin rashes to bathers. Also, be warned, there have been attacks on the beach and local people consider this walk unsafe. Best to go in a large group.

Beaches

Good beaches are on the peninsula and around the Trujillo Bay. Take a bus from near the Parque Central towards Puerto Castilla and ask the driver to let you off at the path about 1 km beyond the bridge over the lagoon. The other beaches around Puerto Castilla are separated by mangroves, are littered and have sandflies. Other sandy beaches can be reached by taking any bus from the Parque Central, or walking, 1½ km, to the side road leading to the landing strip and *Bahía Bar-Restaurant*; the white sand stretches for many km northwards. The beaches around the airport area are safer than heading towards Santa Fe, but do not walk on any beach after dark.

Local festivals

San Juan Bautista in June, with participation from surrounding Garífuna (Black Carib) settlements.

Local information
● **Accommodation**
A2-A3 *Christopher Columbus Beach Resort*, T 44-43-95, 44-49-66, F 44-49-71, 51 rooms and suites (**L3-A2**), a/c, cable TV, swimming pool, restaurant, watersports, tennis, painted bright turquoise, outside town along the beach, drive across airstrip; the other side of the airstrip at road turnoff is **C** *Trujillo Bay*, T 44-37-32, F 44-47-32, 25 a/c rooms with cable TV, inc continental breakfast, tasty cooking at their in-house restaurant *Schooners*, laundry.

C *Villa Brinkley* (known locally as Miss Peggy's), T 44-44-44, F 44-40-45, on the mountain overlooking the bay, swimming pool, good view, large rooms, wooden furniture in Maya style, big bathrooms, sunken baths, fan, cheaper rooms in annex, second pool (still empty) and condos completed 1995, full of character and friendly, but reported very run down in 1996, restaurant still good though for evening meal only (in USA T 412-791-2273, Rd 3, Parker, PA16049); **C-D** *Colonial*, T 44-40-11, F 44-48-78, with bath, on plaza, restaurant (*El Bucanero*, see below), a/c, safe and clean, recently refurbished; **C-D** *O'Glynn*, T 44-45-92, new, smart, clean, good rooms and bathrooms, a/c, TV, fridge in some rooms.

E *Albert's Place*, T 44-44-31, 2 blocks S of Parque Central, red brick house, beautifully restored, nice garden, good value, English spoken; **E** *Coco Pando*, Barrio Cristales, behind beach, Garífuna-owned, clean, bright airy rooms, restaurant serving typical Garífuna dishes, runs popular weekend disco nearby; **E-F** *Catracho*, 2 blocks SW of Parque Central, T 44-44-38, basic, clean, noisy, no water at night, wooden cabins facing a garden, camping space, parking; **E-F** *Emperador*, T 44-44-46, with bath and fan, small, dark rooms, rather depressing, **E-F** *Mar de Plata*, not very clean, up street W, upstairs rooms best, with bath, fan, friendly, beautiful view from roof; **E-F** *Trujillo*, T 44-42-02, up the hill from the market, fan, clean sheets daily, rooms with shower and toilet, TV, good value, rec, but ask for a corner room, cockroaches in ground floor rooms, nice breeze.

F *Buenos Aires*, monthly rates available, pleasant, clean, peaceful, organizes tours to national park.

In the village of Silin, on main road SE of Trujillo, is **B** *Resort y Spa Agua Caliente Silin*, T 44-42-47, F 44-42-48, cabañas with cable TV, pool, thermal waters, restaurant, massage given by Pech Indian, Lastenia Hernández, very relaxing.

● **Places to eat**
El Bucanero, on main plaza, a/c, video, good *desayuno típico* for US$2; *Galaxia*, 1 block W of plaza, good seafood at reasonable prices, popular with locals; *Oasis*, new, opp Bancahsa, outdoor seating, Canadian owned, good meeting place, information board, good food, bar, English books for sale, book exchange, local tours; *Granada*, in the centre, good Garífuna dishes, seafood and standard meals, great *sopa de camarones*, rec, breakfasts and snacks, also

bar, friendly service, good value; *Nice and Ease*, sells ice cream and cakes; nearby is *Pantry*, Garifuna cooking and standard menu, cheap pizzas, a/c; *Don Perignon*, uphill from *Pantry*, some Spanish dishes, good local food, cheap.

On the beach is a row of thatched bars, *champas*, with hammocks, toilets, showers, shade, they keep the beach clean and some offer excellent food. Ask here too about bungalows to hire. Ownership tends to change frequently so ask around for latest recs. *Los Amigos*, beach front (British owners keep their patch clean), excellent fish, barracuda steaks; *Bahía Bar-Restaurant*, T 44-47-70, on the beach by the landing strip next to *Christopher Columbus*, popular with ex-pats, also Hondurans at weekends, good vegetarian food, showers, toilets.

● **Banks & money changers**
Banco Atlántida on Parque Central. Banco de Occidente, Bancahsa, both cash US$, TCs and cash, the former handles Mastercard and Visa, the latter Visa.

● **Entertainment**
Nightlife: Barrio Cristales, weekends only, Punta music, lively atmosphere, rec, hand made tambore drums and turtle shells, conch horn, dancing is a challenge. The **cinema** shows US current releases.

● **Hospitals & medical services**
Hospital on main road E off square towards La Ceiba.

● **Language schools**
Two schools: Centro Internacional de Idiomas, Belinda Linton, Apdo Postal 71, Trujillo, T/F 44-47-77 (Spanish and Garífuna courses, culture, music and dance, branch in La Ceiba), and Ixbalanque, T 44-44-61, F 57-62-15 (branch in Copán T 98-34-32, F 98-00-04), both charge about US$85/week for 4 hrs/day instruction, staying with locals is possible.

● **Libraries**
Library in middle of square.

● **Post & telecommunications**
Post Office and Hondutel: (F 44-42-00) 1 block up from church.

● **Laundry**
Next to *Disco Orfaz*, wash and dry US$2.50.

● **Shopping**
Gari-Arte Souvenir, T 44-42-07, in the centre of Barrio Cristales, is highly rec for authentic Garífuna souvenirs. Owned by Ricardo Lacayo and open 7 days a week. *Tienda Souvenir*

Artesanía next to *Hotel Emperador*, handicrafts, hand-painted toys. Three supermarkets in the centre.

● **Tour companies & travel agents**
Turtle Tours at *Hotel Villa Brinkley* (address above, run trips to Río Plátano, 6 days, 5 nights US$400, also to beaches, jungle hikes, etc. Guided tours by motorbike, 7-17 days with back-up vehicle. Bike rental US$35/day. Very helpful even if you want to travel independently to Mosquitia, German, English, Spanish spoken, T 44-44-44, F 44-42-00 at Hondutel. Several other enterprises organize tours to Capiro, Calentura, Guaimoreto and the **Hacienda Tumbador Crocodile Reserve**, privately owned, accessible only by 4WD and with guide, US$5 entry, eg *Oasis*, *Gringo's Bar*. *Gringo's* also advertises trips to Tumbador followed by visit to beach nr Puerto Castilla and lunch.

● **Useful addresses**
Immigration: Migración has an office opp *Mar de Plata*.

● **Transport**
Air Trujillo has an airstrip E of town nr the beach hotels. Isleña flies Mon-Sat 1215 to La Ceiba to connect with onward Isleña flights to San Pedro Sula and Tegucigalpa. Booking office at *Christopher Columbus Resort*, T 44-49-66.

Buses The town can be reached by bus from San Pedro Sula, Tela and La Ceiba by a paved road through Savá, Tocoa and Corocito. From La Ceiba it is 3 hrs by direct bus, 4 hrs by *local*. 3 direct buses in early am from Trujillo, buses every 1½ hrs, US$4.50. Bus from **Tegucigalpa** (Comayagüela) with Cotraipbal, 7 Av between 11 and 12 C, US$6, 9 hrs return 0300, 0500 and 0900. To **San Pedro Sula**, 5 daily 0200-0800, US$5. Public transport also to San Esteban and Juticalpa (from plaza at 0400, but check locally, arriving 1130, US$5.20 – see page 960). Bus to **Santa Fe** at 0930, US$0.40, leaves from outside *Glenny's Super Tienda*; to **Santa Rosa de Aguán** and **Limón** daily.

Sea Cargo boats leave for ports in Mosquitia (ask all captains at the dock, wait up to 3 days, see page 964), the Bay Islands (very difficult) and Honduran ports to the W. Enquire at the jetty.

PUERTO CASTILLA

There is a meat-packing station and active shrimping centre. Puerto Castilla is one of the two containerized ports of the Honduran Caribbean coast, mainly exports including bananas, grapefruit and palm oil. There is a naval base and helicopter station. Near the village, a large crucifix marks the spot where Columbus reputedly conducted the first mass on American soil in 1502. (Restaurant *Brisas de Caribe*, good.)

Santa Rosa de Aguán is an interesting coastal town of 7,000 hospitable English and Spanish-speaking inhabitants some 40 km from Trujillo, one of the largest Garífuna communities. The spreading settlement lies at the mouth of the Río Aguán, the greater part on the E of the bay. Bus from Trujillo 1015 from Parque Central Mon-Sat, returns at 1230. Also bus service from La Ceiba. If driving from Trujillo, turn left at Km 343, 20 km along the highway, where a good gravel road runs another 20 km to Santa Rosa. From where the road ends at the W bank, take a canoe ferry across to the E side. One simple hotel, **G**, clean, good beds, green house, ask for directions, not easy to find, pleasant bar/restaurant nearby. White sand beach stretches all the way to Limón (see page 967), the thundering surf is an impressive sight. Take drinking water, insect repellent, mosquito coils and high factor sun screen.

EL PROGRESO TO OLANCHITO

EL PROGRESO

(*Pop* 106,550) This important but unattractive agricultural and commercial centre (no longer just a banana town) on the Río Ulúa, is 30 mins' drive on the paved highway SE of San Pedro Sula en route to Tela.

Local festivals *Fiesta*: La Virgen de Las Mercedes, third week of September. Visit the Santa Isabel handicraft centre, where women are taught wood carving.

● **Accommodation** **D** *Gran Hotel Las Vegas*, 2 Av, 11 C N, T 66-46-67, smart, a/c, good restaurant called *La Copa Dorada*; **D** *Municipal*, 1 Av, 7-8 C N, T 66-40-61, with a/c and bath, clean; **E** *Plaza Victoria*, 2 Av, 5-6 C S, T 66-21-50, opp Migración, pool, good; **F** *Emperador*, 2 Av, 4-5 C S, 8 blocks W of bus

terminal, attractive, with bath, **G** without; **F** *Honduras*, 2 Av 3 C, T 66-42-64, in front of Banco Atlántida, price pp, with bath, run down, meals US$1.25; **F** *La Casa Blanca*, 4 C, 2 Av N, traditional white and yellow clapboard house with covered balcony, quiet but beware of giant cockroaches.

● **Places to eat** *Comida Buffet América*, 2 Av N, ½ block E of market, open 0700 to 1500, good vegetarian food; *Elite*, 1 Av, 4-5 C N, mixed reports; *Mr Kike* (pronounced Keekeh) on the ground floor of the *Hotel Municipal* building, a/c, good; *Red Dragon Pub*, 4 C, 1-2 Av N, owned by an Englishman, Steve, good source of local information, good bar and restaurant; *Los Tarros*, on San Pedro Sula road just before bridge, good but not cheap; *La Parrilla*, next to gasolinera on road to Santa Rita, good steaks and international food, a/c.

● **Banks & money changers** Bancahsa, Banco Atlántida, Banco del Comercio, Banco Continental, Banco de El Ahorro Hondureño, Banco del País, Banhcafé, Banco Sogerín, Banadesa, Banffaa, Banco de Occidente, Ficensa, Bamer.

● **Shopping** Good artesanía, *Imapro*, T 66-47-00, on the road to Tela.

● **Tour companies & travel agents** *Agencia de Viajes El Progreso*, 2 Av 3-4 C N, T 66-41-01.

5 km S of El Progreso is the Santuario Señor de Esquipulas in the village of Arena Blanca where there is a festival on 13 Jan in honour of the Black Christ of Esquipulas. The temple has baroque and modern architecture, with trees and gardens

The highway is paved 25 km S of El Progreso to Santa Rita; if you continue towards the San Pedro Sula-Tegucigalpa highway, you avoid San Pedro Sula when travelling from the N coast to the capital. 10 km S of El Progreso on the paved highway to Santa Rita, at the village of Las Minas, is El Chorro (1 km off the highway), a charming waterfall and natural swimming pool. A rugged hike can be made into the mountains and on to El Negrito from here.

Parque Nacional Pico Pijol The park is 32 km from **Morazán**, Yoro, a town 41 km from Progreso (bus from Progreso or Santa Rita). In Morazán are *Hospedaje El*

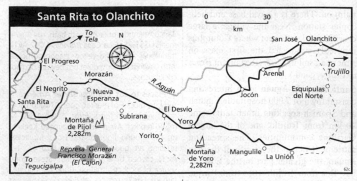

Santa Rita to Olanchito

0   30
km

To Tela
N
San José   Olanchito
El Progreso
Morazán
To Trujillo
El Negrito
Nueva
Esperanza   R Aguán   Arenal
Santa Rita   Jocón   Esquipulas
del Norte
Montaña   Subirana   El Desvío
de Pijol   Yoro
2,282m   Yorito
Represa General   Montaña   Mangulile   La Unión
Francisco Morazán   de Yoro
(El Cajón)   2,282m
To
Tegucigalpa   62c

Corazón Sagrado, several restaurants and a disco. The lower slopes of Pico Pijol have been heavily farmed, but the top is primary cloud forest, home to many quetzales. Access by vehicle is possible as far as Subirana. A guide is needed from there to Tegucigalpita (large cave nearby) and access is difficult, with no infrastructure. Another trail to the summit (2,282m) starts at **Nueva Esperanza** village (bus from Morazán, Parque Central); ask for the correct trail. The first day is tough, the second tougher: the first is all uphill with no shade, the second requires a lot of clearing with a machete. At the summit is a tree with a guest register. Take a compass and a topographical map. Also in the park is the waterfall at **Las Piratas**; take a bus from Morazán to Los Murillos and then walk to El Ocotillo. Ask for Las Piratas. Further up the river are some beautiful, deep pools.

YORO

The highway is also paved from Santa Rita to **Yoro**, a prosperous little town of ranchers and farmers, in pleasant surroundings with mountains to the N, E and S. The **Parque Nacional Montaña de Yoro** is 8 km to the SE (access from Marale), comprising 257 sq km of cloud forest, home to the Tolupanes indigenous people, also known as Xicaques. The Asociación Ecológica Amigos de la Montaña de Yoro has an office in the Parque Central in Yoro.

● **Accommodation** E *Nelson*, comfortable rooms with bath, fan, modern, good restaurant/bar and nice outdoor swimming pool on 3rd floor, bar/disco on roof with marvellous views, warmly rec; **E-F** *Palacio*, on main street, restaurant, nice, all rooms with bath and fan; **F-G** *Aníbal*, corner of Parque Central, restaurant, excellent value, private or shared bath, clean, pleasant, wide balcony.

● **Places to eat** Best restaurants in hotels, several *comedores* along main street.

● **Banks & money changers** Banco Atlántida on Parque Central.

● **Post & telecommunications** Post Office and Hondutel 1 block from Parque Central.

● **Transport** Hourly bus service to El Progreso, several daily to Sulaco.

From Yoro a dirt road continues to Olanchito via **Jocón**, through attractive country (**G** *Hospedaje*, clean, basic and other accommodation, ask around) as the road snakes along the pine-forested slopes of Montaña Piedra Blanca and Montaña de la Bellota, with fine views of the surrounding valleys and distant mountain ranges. Buses from Yoro to Olanchito go as far as Río Aguán, US$1.50, which is a bit too deep to ford. Cross the river in an ox cart or giant inner tube with waterproof floor pushed across by wading drivers, US$0.35, then get on another, waiting bus to Olanchito (see page 916), US$1. The road then runs parallel to the river through lush cattle and farming country.

OLANCHITO

(*Pop* 12,200) A prosperous but hot town (called La Ciudad Cívica) in the Aguán valley in the hills to the SE of La Ceiba. The town was founded, according to tradition, by a few stragglers who escaped from the destruction of Olancho el Viejo, between Juticalpa and Catacamas, then a wealthy town. They brought with them the crown made of hides which the image of the Virgin still wears in the church of Olanchito. There is a natural bathing spot, Balneario El Higueral.

Local festivals 2nd week of Sept, Semana Cívica.

● **Accommodation D** *Hotel Olanchito*, Barrio Arriba, Calle La Palma, T 44-63-85, a/c, under same management is **E** *Valle Aguán y Chabelito*, 1 block N of Parque Central, T 44-67-18, 44-65-46, single rooms, with a/c, double rooms with fan, all rooms with cable TV, best in town, with best restaurant; **F** *Colonial*, C del Presidio, good value, bath, fan, **G** with shared bath, restaurant, parking; opp is **E** *Olímpic*, bath, a/c, TV.

● **Places to eat** *La Ronda*, best in town, Chinese and international, main dishes US$4, rec; *Comedor Doña Luisa* in front of Radio Station and 3 blocks S of Park; *Bar/restaurant Uchapa*, *Helados Castillo*.

● **Banks & money changers** Bancahsa changes TCs; Bancahorro; Sogerín; Atlántida: Importadora Rosita has better exchange rates.

● **Entertainment Cinema**: *Cine Gardel*.

● **Transport** Buses from **La Ceiba**, 2½ hrs, US$1 via Jutiapa and Savá (Cotol 7 times a day; Cotrail); to **Trujillo**, 3 hrs, US$3.75 via Savá and Tocoa (Cotol); to **Yoro** 0430 daily, 5 hrs.

The Bay Islands

WARM CARIBBEAN waters with excellent diving, white sand beaches, tropical sunsets are some of the attractions. The culture is very un-Latin American: English is widely spoken and there are still Black Carib descendants of those deported from St Vincent in 1797.

HOG ISLANDS

The **Hog Islands** (**Cayos Cochinos**), with lovely primeval hardwood forests, are 17 km NE of La Ceiba (two small islands and thirteen palm-fringed cays). **Cochino Grande** is the larger island, rising to 143m, **Cochino Pequeño** the smaller. Both have lush tropical vegetation and fewer biting insects than the Bay Islands. There are garifuna fishing villages of palm-thatched huts at Chachauate on Lower Monitor Cay, and East End Village on Cochino Grande. Transport to the Hog Islands can be sought on the supply *cayuco* from Nuevo Armenia (see page 904), or by chartering a boat from Utila. There is a small, dirt airstrip. Dugout canoes are the local form of transport. The islands are privately owned and access to most of the cays is limited, being occupied only by caretakers. The Cayos Cochinos and surrounding waters are now a National Marine Reserve and rangers are being trained. Spear fishing, nets and traps are not allowed, although line fishing is permitted.

Local information
● Accommodation

Plantation Beach Resort on Grande, rustic cabins, on hillside, hot water, fans, diving offshore, yacht moorings, good steep walk up to lighthouse for view over cays to mainland, music festival end-July, local bands and dancers, they charge US$30 for the trip from La Ceiba, T/F 42-09-74, VHF 12, e-mail hkinett@hondutel.hn, website http://www.clearlight.com/vmoe/dive/planta.htm. At Chachauate, stay with fishing family or rent thatched hut (US$6) and a garifuna woman will cook for you. Small restaurant but bring own drinking water. A few small *tiendas* sell beer and sodas. Short wade to *Pelican Bar*, run by Al, opens on demand. This island is free of mosquitoes and sandflies. Bring snorkel equipment, kayaks can be hired. **Cayo Timón** (also known as North Sand Cay) can be visited from Utila, 1¼ hrs by boat; you can rent

Cayos Cochinos / Hog Islands

N

Cochino Grande

North East Cay

Cochino Pequeño

North West Cay

Lower Monitor

Timón

Pelon

Coral Reefs

Sandy Cays

0   2
km

the cay, **E** pp, min 6, 8 is comfortable, A-frame, Polynesian style, do overnight diving trips or combine with Eurohonduras river trips (see La Ceiba, **Travel agents**), very basic, quiet, peaceful, contact Henrik and Susan Jensen at the *Green House*, Utila, or phone Roy and Brenda at *Thompson's Bakery*, Utila, T 45-31-17, for information.

BAY ISLANDS

(*Pop* 60,000) The **Bay Islands** (Islas de la Bahía) lie in an arc which curves NE away from a point 32 km N of La Ceiba. The three main islands are **Utila, Roatán**, and **Guanaja**. At the eastern end of Roatán are three small ones: **Morat, Santa Elena**, and **Barbareta**; there are other islets and 52 cays. The traditional industry is fishing, mostly shellfish, with fleets based at French Harbour. Boat-building is a dying industry. Tourism is now a major source of income, particularly because of scuba diving attractions. There are English-speaking blacks who constitute the majority of the population, particularly on Roatán. Utila has a population which is about half black and half white, the latter of British stock descended mainly from settlers from Grand Cayman who arrived in 1830. Latin Hondurans have been moving to the islands from the mainland in recent years. Columbus anchored here in 1502, on his fourth voyage. In the 18th century the islands were bases for English, French and Dutch buccaneers. They were in British hands for over a century but were finally ceded to Honduras in 1859. The government schools teach in Spanish, and the population is bi-lingual. The islands are very beautiful, but beware of the strong sun (the locals bathe in T-shirts) and sand flies and other insects.

The underwater environment is rich and extensive; reefs surround the islands, often within swimming distance of the shore. Caves and caverns are a common feature, with a wide variety of sponges and the best collection of pillar coral in the Caribbean. Several parts have been proposed as marine reserves by the Asociación Hondureña de Ecología: the Santuario Marino de Utila, Parque Nacional Marino Barbareta and Parque Nacional Marino Guanaja. Turtle Harbour, Utila, and Sandy Bay/West End, Roatán are now Marine Parks and the latter has permanent mooring buoys at the popular dive sites. The Bay Islands have their own conservation association (see under Roatán, below). We strongly recommend snorkellers and divers not to touch or stand on the coral reefs; any contact, even the turbulence from a fin, will kill the delicate organisms. The islands are a major diving centre.

UTILA

(41 sq km; *Pop* 2,400) The island only 32 km from La Ceiba, is low lying, with only two hills, Pumpkin, and the smaller Stewarts with an aerial. The latter is nearer the town, which is known locally as **East Harbour**. The first inhabitants were Paya Indians and there is some archaeological evidence of their culture. Later the island was used by pirates; Henry Morgan is reputed to have hidden booty in the caves. The population now is descended from Black Caribs and white Cayman Islanders with a recent influx from mainland Honduras. Independence Day (15 Sept) festivities, including boxing and climbing greased poles, reported worth staying for.

Excursions

You can hike to **Pumpkin Hill** (about 4 km down the lane by Bancahsa, bikes rec) where there are some freshwater caves and a beach nearby (watch out for sharp coral). It can be very muddy after rain. It is also possible to walk on a trail from the airfield to **Big Bight** and the iron shore on the E coast, about 2 km, exploring tidal pools; nice views and beach but it is rocky so wear sandals. An interesting way of visiting the N coast is to hire a canoe (or kayak from Gunter's) and paddle from the lagoon by the *Blue Bayou* through the mangroves and the canal (about 2-3 hrs); look out for a rare sighting of a crocodile, a huge one

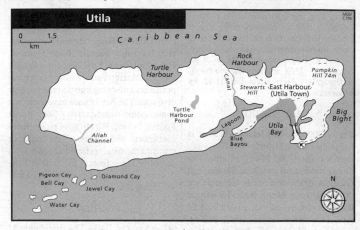

was killed in 1995; take snorkelling gear and explore the reef offshore if the sea is not too rough. Canoe hire US$10/day. Trails to the N coast are only passable in the dry months (April-Sept), through the swamp and past the dead forest, best to hire a local child to show you the way.

Utila is the cheapest and least developed of the islands to visit; there are no big resorts, although a couple of small, lodge-style, upmarket places have opened, otherwise there is rather simpler accommodation. Sunbathing and swimming are not particularly good, but there is a swimming hole near the airport. At the left-hand end of the airstrip (from the town) is one of the best places for coral and quantity of fish. Jack Neal Beach has white sand with good snorkelling and swimming; development is now starting. Snorkelling is also good off the shore by the *Blue Bayou* restaurant, a 20-min walk from town, but you will be charged US$1 for use of the facilities. There are hammocks and a jetty, which is the only place to get away from the terrible sandflies. A new resort built on the other side of the lagoon, opened 1995.

The Cays

A 20-mins motorboat ride from East Harbour are the Cays, a chain of small islands populated by fisherfolk off the SW coast of Utila known as the Cayitos de Utila. **Jewel Cay** and **Pigeon Cay** are connected by a bridge and are inhabited by a fishing community which reportedly settled there to get away from the sandflies on Utila. There is a basic hotel, *Vicky's*, a few restaurants, a Sat night disco, a dive shop run by Jan, and little else. The Cays are occasionally used by Utila dive shops as a surface interval between dives. **Diamond Cay** is privately owned, there are a few rooms in cabins for rent (**E**), and tents, a bar, restaurant, fish barbecue and snorkel gear for hire. **Water Cay** is one of the few places where you can camp, sling a hammock or, in emergency, sleep in, or under, the house of the caretaker; take food and fresh water, or rent the caretaker's canoe and get supplies from Jewel Cay. The caretaker collects a US$1.25 pp fee for landing and the same for a hammock. There are no facilities, but Jan from the Cays can bring you breakfast if you order it the day before. It is a coconut island with 'white holes' (sandy areas with wonderful hot bathing in the afternoon). The best snorkelling is off the S shore, a short walk from the beach, shallow water all around. To hire a *dory* (big motorized canoe) costs US$5 pp; many boatmen go and will collect you in the evening, rec. You may also be able to go out with a diving party and be picked up in the afternoon or persuade a boatman to take you to one of the remoter cays. *Gunter's Dive Shop* runs water taxis to the cays for US$10, also Roy at the *Green House Book Exchange*, US$6.50, plus hammock hire US$1.

Local information
● Accommodation

Utila Reef Resort, new 1996, USA T 1-800-263-9876, Utila T/F 45-32-54, on S coast, Lower Lagoon, by *Netty Bush* dive site, accommodation for 10, US$865 pp 8-day package inc 3 meals, 3 boat dives a day, unlimited shore diving, 2 double beds in each room, a/c; **L3-A1** *Laguna Beach Resort*, T/F 45-32-39, in USA, Utila Tours Inc, T 1-800-66-UTILA, (318) 893 0013, F (318) 893-5024, lodge with bungalows each with own jetty, 6-day package inc meals and diving US$750-800, non-diver US$600-650, fishing offered, can accommodate max 40, on point opp *Blue Bayou*.

A2 *Utila Lodge*, T 45-31-43, F 45-32-09, usually booked through US agent T 1-800-282-8932, an all-wooden building with decks and balconies, harbour view, a/c, 8 rooms, clean and modern, meals only when they have guests, dive shop (*Bay Islands College of Diving*) on site

C *Sharky's Reef Cabins*, the Point, T 45-32-12, a/c, cable TV, porch over lagoon, fans. Cheaper hotels are along Main St or just off it.

D *Hotel Utila*, T 45-31-40, on water next to *Lodge*, new in 1996, cheaper rooms downstairs, very clean, 24-hr water and power, fan, nice view, secure; **D** *Palm Villa*, cabins for 4, cooking facilities, good value, run by Willis Bodden; **D-E** *Bay View*, 100m from *Utila Lodge*, with or without bath, private pier, family run; **D-E** *Harbour View*, T 45-31-59, F 45-33-59, right on water, *Parrot's Dive* on site, cheaper rooms with shared bathrooms upstairs, rooms with private bath downstairs, hot water, own generator, cleaning done only on arrival, TV, fans, run by Roger and Maimee; **D-E** *Laguna del Mar*, opp and owned by *Trudy's*, T 45-31-03, terrace, very clean, fans, mosquito nets, diving offered with *Underwater Vision*.

E *Calena*, main street, new, with bath, clean, fan, Visa and Mastercard accepted, good, rec; **E** *Countryside*, 10 mins' walk out of town, new, shared bath, rooms and apartments, quiet, clean, friendly, fan, porch, ask in town for Woody and Annie; **E** *Cross Creek* (see also **Diving** below), clean basic rooms, bathrooms, for divers on courses; **E** *Margareteville*, at very end of the village, new in 1996, very clean, big rooms with 2 double beds, private bathroom, friendly, but no water or electricity at night; **E** *Sea Side*, pleasant, clean, nr *Gunter's*; **E** *Spencer*, Main St, T 45-31-62; **E** *Tropical*, Mammie Lane, 9 double rooms, kitchen, fans, mosquito nets and screens; **E** *Trudy's*, T/F 45-31-03, 5 mins from airport, with and without bath, very clean, comfortable, good breakfast, rec; *Underwater Vision* dive shop on site; **E-F** *Coopers Inn*, very clean and friendly, Danish cook, rec.

F *Blue Bayou*, 25 mins out of town, 1 hr walk from airfield, very basic, insanitary, bad sand flies, good place to hire a bike, snacks and drinks available, restaurant only in high season, hammocks on the beach US$1, free to guests, take torch for night-time; **F** *Monkey Tail Inn*, noisy, wooden building, you may share your room with bats, cooking facilities, water all the time. Cheap and very basic rooms at **F** *Blueberry Hill* and houses for rent, lots of signs along the road; **F** *Loma Vista*, beyond *Bucket of Blood Bar*, clean, fan, shared bath, very friendly, washes clothes cheaply; **F** *Delaney's*, good value, good small restaurant; **F** *Lizzie*, new in 1996, clean, fan, shared facilities, friendly, no power from 0000-0600.

● Places to eat

Menus are often limited by the supply boat, on Tues restaurants have everything, by the weekend some drinks run out. *Bahia del Mar* by airport, burgers, pizzas, etc, hammock and camping space on little pier; *Sharky's Reef*, nr airport, open Wed-Sun 1800-2100, good portions, quite expensive but good, well prepared, try steamed shark steak; *Mermaid's Corner*, breakfast from 0700, huge pizza (US$6) and pasta, about US$2.50-3 main course, good value but nothing special, no alcohol; *Sea Side* (see above under **Accommodation**) offers good fish but very slow service; *Island Café*, daily specials, good, up on covered verandah, at both these restaurants you order inside and help yourself to drinks from fridge then wait for food to be brought out to you; *Jade Seahorse*, open 0700-2300, opp *Bucket of Blood*, excellent *licuados*, good food; *Sidewalk Café*, good food and breakfasts, helpful, bicycles for hire; *Delaney's Island Kitchen*, open 1730-2200 for pizza, lasagne and veg dishes; *Las Delicias*, open 1200-2400, shark steak and local food, limited menu, music, lively bar each night; *Myrtle's*, open 1000-2330, by far the quickest lunch in town, delicious *comida corriente* served by Terricina, opp casino, locals' hangout; *News Café*, light lunch with midday matinée on huge screen, also shows latest movies at night; *Pandy's Place* for typical food and TV; *7 Seas*, open 0630-2200, breakfast, fish, burgers; *Tropical Sunset*, open 0800-2200, fish, burgers, lobster, ice cream; *Reef Bar & Grill*, open Tues-Sat 0630-1100, 1700-2300 for breakfast on the balcony, sunset drinks, also Sun barbecue 1200-1500; *Ormas*, simple but good food, excellent coconut bread, also serves beer; *Thompsons Bakery*, open 0600-1200, best place for breakfast, very informal, friendly, good cakes, lots of information. Good yogurt, cakes, bottled water at *Henderson's* store. *Green Ribbon* store has cakes and sandwiches to order; *Selly's*, very good food, closed to regular custom but Selly will cook if you get a group of 6 minimum, great kingfish, also rooms available; *Bundu Café*, in same building as *Green House Book Exchange*, excellent food, quiche, salads, sandwiches, juices and other drinks, run by friendly couple Steve and Fran, highly rec, "quite a social centre".

Bars: *Bucket of Blood*, owned by Mr Woods, a mine of information on the history of Utila and the Cays; *Reef Bar*, *Dory Bar*, *Las Delicias*, and *Casino* are lively (Sat night), as is *Captain Roy's*, next to the airport; *Bahía del Mar*, bar with pier, swimming; *Sea Breaker*, thatched bar, on waterfront behind *Orma's*, open Tues, Fri, Sat, 1730-2300, happy hour 1730-1900, jugs of cocktails, popular; *Club 07*, opens Tues and Fri, free rum 2200-2300, good dancing; *Sea Breakers*, very popular, good strong cocktails; *Barracuda*, at the end of town, good drinks.

● **Banks & money changers**

Dollars are accepted on the island. Banks open 0800-1130, 1330-1600 Mon-Fri, 0800-1130 Sat. Bancahsa changes dollars and gives cash against a Visa card, but not Mastercard. Banco Atlántida opened a branch in 1996. Henderson's Supermarket changes US$ cash at a better rate than the bank. Ronald Janssen at *Cross Creek Divers* does Mastercard advances plus 10%.

● **Places of worship**

Churches: 7th Day Adventist, Baptist, Church of God, Methodist (with a charming wooden church built in 1870).

● **Post & telecommunications**

There is a **post office** at the new pier opp *Captain Morgan's Dive Centre* (0830-1200, 1400-1700 Mon-Fri, 0830-1130 Sat) and a **Hondutel** (0700-1700 Mon-Fri, 0700-1100 Sat) office nr *Utila Lodge*. The main service is reported as unreliable. Hondutel sends (and receives) faxes, F 45-31-06, North America US$1.80, Europe US$2.25, South America and Caribbean US$2, rest of world US$3/page plus 7% tax. Ronald Janssen also runs Intertel, an international phone (no fax) service charged/minute: North America US$2.50, Europe US$5 (2 mins minimum), Mexico and Central America US$2, South America US$6, elsewhere US$7.50.

● **Shopping**

Arts and crafts: Gunter Kordovsky is a painter and sculptor with a gallery at his house, good map of Utila, paintings, cards, wood carving. Gift Shop at the *Lodge* and Annie Maud Souvenirs Gallery planned at *Tropical Sunset* for 1996 displaying local arts and crafts.

● **Sports**

Diving: there are several dive sites along the S coast, where permanent moorings have been established to minimize damage to the coral reef. Although the reef is colourful and varied, there are not a lot of fish and lobster have almost disappeared. The dive sites are close to shore at about 20m depth but they are all boat dives. Diving off the N coast is more spectacular, with drop-offs, canyons and caves. Fish are more numerous, helped by the establishment of the **Turtle Harbour Marine Reserve and Wildlife Refuge**.

Utila is essentially a dive training centre. It is very popular; you can learn to dive here cheaper than anywhere else in the Caribbean, particularly if you include low living expenses. It is best to do a course of some sort, students come first for places on boats and fun divers have to fit in. However, Utila has a reputation for poor safety and there have been too many accidents requiring emergency treatment in the recompression chamber on Roatán. Choose an instructor who may be bossy but fun, with small classes and who cares about safety, follow the rules on alcohol/drug abuse and pay particular attention to the dive tables. There is a rapid turnover of instructors; many stay only a season to earn money to continue their travels and some have a lax attitude towards diving regulations. Check that equipment looks new and well-maintained. Boats vary, you may find it difficult to climb into a dory if there are waves. Not all boats have oxygen on board. Dive insurance at US$2/day is available from the BICA office: it covers air ambulance to Roatán and the recompression chamber.

From time to time all the dive shops agree to fix prices. A PADI Open Water course in 1997 costs US$120-US$150 (inc US$14 for certificate) with 6 dives, an Advanced course costs US$110-US$150 with 5 dives. Credit cards, if accepted, are 8% extra. Competition is fierce with over 15 dive shops looking for business, so you can pick and choose. Once qualified, fun dives are US$25 for 2 tanks, US$100 for 10 tanks. Most schools offer instruction in English or German; French and Spanish are usually available somewhere, while tuition handbooks are provided in numerous languages inc Japanese. A variety of courses is available up to instructor level. If planning to do a diving course, it is helpful but not essential to take passport sized photographs with you for the PADI certificate. *Cross Creek*, run by Ronald Janssen, T 45-31-34, F 45-32-34, e-mail scooper@hondutel.hn, website http://www.ccreek.com, 2 boats, max 8 people/instructor, 2-3 instructors, new equipment, accommodation on site for students, 18 rooms. *Gunter's* dive school, T 45-31-13, F 45-31-06, is based at *Sea Side Inn*, his instructor, Pascal Floss, is experienced, has been

on the island a long time and is rec as the best person for finding fish and other aquatic life on the reef. *Utila Watersports*, run by Troy Bodden; quality of instructors varies. Troy also hires out snorkel gear, photographic and video equipment and takes boat trips, T/F 45-32-39. Chris Phillips from the *Utila Dive Centre*, T 45-33-26, F 45-33-27, very professional courses, well-maintained equipment, rec, also has photo and video equipment with an E-lab on site, sometimes takes divers to N coast in fast dory, rec but no shade, surface interval on cays. For photo courses contact Chris Watts of *Utila Aqua Videos* on the path to Cross Creek, who specializes in video and photography underwater, also camera rentals. *Captain Morgan's* has been rec for small classes, good equipment, friendly staff. *Sea Eye* has also been rec for Canadian instructor, Jackie, and for boats, but equipment needed upgrading in 1996.

● **Tour companies & travel agents**
Contact Henrik and Susan Jensen at the Green House, T 45-33-35, for tours to Timón, one of the Hog Cays; they also run boat trips to Jack Neal beach 5 km from town with white sand, blue bathing hole, excellent snorkelling, also restaurant, *Zanzibar*, for lunch and snacks, bungalows planned, 4 boats a day, US$3 return. They also run a book exchange. Shelby McNab runs *Robinson Crusoe Tours* and takes visitors on half-day tours around the island (US$10 pp) explaining his theory that Daniel Defoe based his famous book on Robinson Crusoe on Utila (not Alexander Selkirk off Chile), fascinating.

● **Useful information**
Electricity: goes off between 2400 and 0600.

Local Newspaper: *Utila Times*, in English, published monthly, excellent source of local information, 6 month subscription US$20, single copy US$1 from Utila Times, Utila, Bay Islands, Honduras, CA.

The **BICA Visitor Centre** in front of *Mermaid's Restaurant* has information on Honduran national reserves and sells Utila T-shirts. Marion Howell is the current President of BICA. Donations welcomed for conservation efforts.

Water: frequent problems.

On dry days and when there is no breeze sandflies are most active. Coconut oil, baby oil or Avon 'Skin-so-Soft' helps to ward them off. Take insect repellent. 'Off', sold at *Henderson's* supermarket is good for after dark biters.

● **Transport**

Local Bike hire is about US$2-2.50 a day, US$12.50 a week, next to Casino.

Air Sosa has scheduled flights to La Ceiba, US$16.50, 4 times a day Mon-Sat, and to San Pedro Sula once a day Mon-Sat. Caribbean Air, T/F 45-14-66, has scheduled flights to San Pedro Sula and Roatán. Always reserve flights and make onward reservations in advance. The dirt airstrip begins and ends in the sea; there is no terminal building, just a few benches under a tree; get there at 0600 for a 0615 flight. Local transport between airport and hotels, or walk.

Sea *MV Tropical* from La Ceiba to Utila scheduled service, T 45-17-96, US$6.50, buy tickets on the day, a/c, videos, comfortable, fast (1 hr), rec, Mon-Fri 1000, return 1130. Be at the landing stage 30 mins before sailing. *MV Starfish* (mainly cargo but some passengers) goes from Utila to the new harbour in **La Ceiba** Tues 0500 (be early or sleep on board Sun night) returning from La Ceiba Wed 1200, US$5 each way (information from *Green Ribbon* store). There are irregular boats to **Puerto Cortés**, times posted in main street, 7 hrs, US$7.50, ask at public dock.

Boats from Utila to Roatán can be chartered for about US$70. Occasional freight boats, eg *Utila Tom*, take passengers from Utila to Roatán. It's a 3-hrs journey between the two islands and you and your possessions are liable to get soaked.

ROATAN

(127 sq km; *Pop* 10,245) **Roatán** is the largest of the islands. It has a paved road running from West End through to French Harbour, almost to Oak Ridge, continuing unpaved to Punta Gorda and Wilkes Point; there are other, unmade roads. Renting a car or scooter gives access to many places that public transport does not reach. The capital of the department, **Coxen Hole**, or Roatán City, is on the SW shore. Besides being the seat of the local government, it has immigration, customs and the law courts. The benches in the small square by the government offices have been painted by local children. There is a Post Office, supermarket, several handicraft shops, photo shops, banks, travel agents and various stores. Buses leave from outside the supermarket. It is a scruffy little town with not much of tourist interest but some new souvenir shops are opening; there is a new bookshop: *Casi Todo II* and coffee shop, *Qué Tal* (herbal teas and good sandwiches) on the main street coming into town. *The Lucky Lemp*, just across the road provides T/F and e-mail services. You can find cheap lodgings and all public transport fans out from here. If taxis are shared, they are *colectivos* and charge the same as buses.

Sandy Bay

From Coxen Hole to **Sandy Bay**, with the **Carambola Botanical Gardens**, is a 2-hr walk, or a US$1 bus ride, hourly 0600-1700 (taxi drivers will try to charge much more. The per person fare from Coxen Hole is US$1. If you take a private taxi, *privado*, you should negotiate the price in advance. The official rate from the airport to Sandy Bay/West End is US$8 per taxi regardless of the number of passengers). For details on Carambola contact Bill or Irma Brady, T 45-11-17 (open 0700-1700 daily, entry US$3, guided tours or nature trails, well worth a visit). The gardens were begun in 1985 and contain many flowering plants, ferns and varieties of trees; a 20-min walk from the garden goes to the top of Monte Carambola past the Iguana Wall, a breeding ground for iguanas and parrots. The Roatán Museum is at *Anthony's Key Resort*, Sandy Bay. It displays the history of the islands and has a collection of artefacts, open 0900-1500, closed Wed.

West End

A further 5 mins by road beyond Sandy Bay, this is a growing community near the W tip of the island and the most popular place to stay. There are numerous good foreign and local restaurants with an abundance of pizza/pasta places, as well as hotels, cabañas and rooms to rent. It is a stiff walk from Coxen Hole over the hills (3 hrs) to West End, or take the bus on the paved road for US$0.80, 20 mins, they run until 1700. You can take a small motor boat from *Foster and Vivian's Restaurant* for a

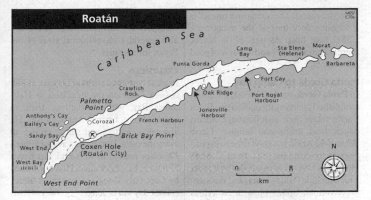

West Bay

West Bay is a beautiful, clean, beach with excellent snorkelling on the reef; there are a couple of jetties where you can escape the sandflies which lurk in the powdery white sand. Take your own food and drinks, and insect repellent. Developers have recently discovered the delights of West Bay and the atmosphere will inevitably change. Already, in 1997, a 300-room luxury resort was under construction, while in the water the 'big banana' had arrived. Beware of boats if you are snorkelling. The *Papagayo Gift Shop* beside *Café del Mar* sells insect repellent, souvenirs. Snorkel rental also available. There are a few restaurants in delightful locations serving good food, but you may want to take drinks with you to the beach. A variety of luxury cabins and homes are available for daily, weekly and monthly rental. Watch out for jellyfish in the shallow water at certain times of the year.

French Harbour

French Harbour, on the S coast, with its shrimping and lobster fleet, is the main fishing port of Roatán. There is no beach. There are two seafood packing plants: Mariscos Agua Azul and Mariscos Hybour. The road passes *Coleman's (Midway)*

Bakery, where you can buy freshly-baked products. The bay is protected by the reef and small cays which provide safe anchorage. *French Harbour Yacht Club* and Romeos Marina (at Brick Bay) offer services for visiting yachts. Several charter yachts are based here. There are a few cheap, clean places to stay, expensive hotels and dive resorts. Eldon's Supermarket is open daily and has a range of US imported food. *Gios Restaurant* and *Casa Romeos* serve top quality seafood.

Across the island

The main road goes across the mountain ridge along the island with side roads to Jonesville, Punta Gorda and Oak Ridge. You can take a bus on this route to see the island's hilly interior, with beautiful views from coast to coast. Alternatively, hire a small 4WD, which is almost as cheap if shared between 4 people, and allows you to explore the dirt roads and empty bays along the island's northern tip. **Jonesville** is known for its mangrove canal, which is best reached by hiring a taxi boat in Oak Ridge. **Oak Ridge**, situated on a cay (US$0.40 crossing in a dory from the bus stop), is built around a deep inlet on the S coast. It is a charming little fishing port, with rows of dwellings on stilts built on the water's edge (bus Coxen Hole-Oak Ridge, 1 hr depending on passengers, US$1.10). You can hire one of the many taxi boats to show you round. The 'mangrove tunnel' is a 30 mins dory tour of the mangroves, US$11/boat load. As well as its hotels, there is a grocery store and a couple of good restaurants.

Punta Gorda to Camp Bay

In **Punta Gorda** on the N coast, the oldest established community on Roatán, Black Caribs retain their own language, music, dance, food, crafts and religion. Carib Week, 8-12 April, is a good time to experience their customs. Bus from Coxen's Hole costs US$1. There are also boat tours which include Punta Gorda (and the mangrove tunnel, US$25 pp with Averyll at *Librería Casi Todo* in West End, T 45-12-55). There is a bar/restaurant serving local food. The paved road ends at the turning for Punta Gorda and from here the road is rough and sometimes too muddy for vehicles to get through. **Marble Hill Farms** is down a small track to the left on the N coast, where you can buy a variety of tropical jams, jellies and spices. The gardens have been landscaped over many years by Lisa and Brian Blancher and their produce is all home grown. Lisa also creates batik and tie dye clothing not on sale anywhere else. Open Mon-Sat, 0900-1700. Beyond here the road deteriorates but leads to Diamond Rock, Camp Bay (5 km from the paved road) and Paya Beach. **Camp Bay** has probably the best beach on the island and no sandflies. New resorts and timeshare developments are being built along this stretch of coast.

Hire a boat to **Port Royal**, famous in the annals of buccaneering but now just a community of private houses; old British gun emplacements on Fort Cay, 1 km off-shore. No bus from Port Royal to Oak Ridge, and it's a tough 3-hr walk. The **Port Royal Park and Wildlife Refuge** is the largest highland reserve on Roatán, protecting pines and endemic species of flora and fauna, threatened by hunting, the pet trade and habitat destruction. At present it lacks facilities or management and is relatively inaccessible (contact Bay Islands Conservation Association for information). There are also several archaeological sites of the Payan inhabitants.

Excursions

In glass-bottomed yacht of Dennis, at *Belvedere's Lodge* on the headland at Half-moon Bay, with snorkelling trips to secluded bays beyond Antony's Key. He also takes charters and sunset cruises all along the coast. Horseriding available from *Keifitos* or *Jimmy's* in West End. *Sea Toye*, a 57 ft yacht based in French Harbour, owned by Capt Clay Douglass, known as 'Blue', charter day sail or longer (eg 3 days Cayos Cochinos), NAUI, YMCA instructor, own tanks, compressor and weights, bring own dive equipment, 8-day charter US$895, in USA T 800-432-5828 or 708-658-5828, Jerry and Sherry Bresnakan. Gert Davidson (contact *Sunset Inn* in West End or VHF channel 10) takes charters to Cayos Cochinos, Guanaja and Utila on *Sirios*, a 37-ft ketch, 3 days US$150 pp, 7 days US$350 pp, diving available if you bring your own equipment. Far Tortugas charters, trimaran *Genesis*, does sailing trips with snorkelling and reef drag (snorkellers towed behind slow moving boat), US$45/day, US$25/half day, contact *Casi Todo*, West End, T 45-12-55. Fishing arranged through *Cindy's* next to Ocean Divers, West End, small dory, local expert, good results, or in style from French Harbour, Hot Rods sports fisher, US$500/day charter, T 45-18-62. See *Casi Todo* for the *Jimni* fishing tours, half and full day. Kayak rentals from *Ocean Divers*, with or without snorkel gear, West End, US$3/hr, US$18/day. From *Casi Todo*, Sea Blades, guided or unguided expeditions by hr, day, week. Real Sea Lion Kayaks, US$12/half day, US$20/day rental, *Genesis* used as support boat for 2-7 day trips around Roatán US$175-1,250, ask for Sally or T 43-07-80 in La Ceiba. From *Rick's American Café*, Casablanca charters on yacht *Defiance III*, sunset cruises, party trips, full day snorkelling, also can be arranged through *Casi Todo*. At West Bay beach is a glass bottomed boat, *Caribbean Reef Explorer*, US$20/1½ hrs, unfortunately fish feeding, which upsets the reef ecological balance. You can also do day trips to the mainland, white water rafting on the Río Cangrejal with Rios Honduras is US$125/day round trip with lunch, T 43-07-80, 43-13-61, or contact *Casi Todo*.

Local information
● Accommodation

At West End: A3 *Lost Paradise* T 45-13-06, F 45-13-88, rooms and cabins, most people on packages, diving, nice jetty for sunset watching, cheaper rooms, **D**, but not friendly to budget travellers; **A3-B** *Georphi's Tropical Hideaway*, T 45-12-05, individual cabins, 2 bedrooms, kitchens, coffee shop under trees with excellent cookies and pancakes, open all day; **A3-B** *Half Moon Bay*, T 45-10-80/13-82, F 45-12-13, bungalows and cabins with bath, restaurant with excellent seafood; **A3-D** *Sunset Inn*, T 45-10-05, **D** rooms above *Ocean Divers* dive shop, shared bathroom, **A3-C** in main hotel, private bath, some with kitchen and up to 5 beds, some with a/c, hot water, friendly, rec, good discounts with diving in low season, new French restaurant with homemade baguettes and croissants; **B** *Coconut Tree* (owner Vince), private cabins (3 double beds), hot water, fan, fridge, clean, friendly, discounts in low season, across the road from *Half Moon Bay*, T 45-16-48; **B** *Mermaid Beach*, T 45-13-39, new, clean, quiet, with bath, fan; **B** *Seagrape Plantation*, T 45-14-28, cabins with 2 beds, bathroom, hot water, family atmosphere, friendly, Visa accepted, nice location on rocky promontory but no beach, snorkelling; **B** *Trish's Wish*, F 45-12-05, Canadian owned, various sizes, cabin and apartments with kitchen, behind *West End Divers*, on hillside, new, clean, rec, lower rate for long term; **B** above *Cocoplum* gift shop, apartment, kitchen, nice location at entrance to village; **B-C** *Casa Calico*, F 45-19-46, F 45-11-71, new, comfortable, fan, garden, rooms and apartments, huge balconies, apartments sleep 4 or more with kitchen, hot water, noisy in morning, owned by Frances Collins, friendly, helpful; **B-C** *Foster's Cabins* and rooms, bit crowded and noisy, also house on West Bay beach with kitchen, **A2**; **B-C** *Sea Breeze*, new hotel, nice rooms, hot water, baths, a/c optional at US$5/night, suites and studios available with kitchens, windsurfers and kayaks for rent; **B-D** *Roberts-Hill*, T 45-11-76, basic rooms with bath and fan, 2-storey cabaña and new cabins on the beach next to *Keifitos*; **C** *Burke's* cottages, E end of village past Half Moon Bay, continental breakfasts available, private bath and kitchen, **D** without, cold water; **C** *Keifitos Plantation Resort*, bungalows on hillside above beach, beautiful setting, short walk from village, mosquitoes, bar, excellent restaurant serving cheap breakfasts and seafood dinners (closes at 1800), horses for rent with guide, friendly owners, very quiet, very clean, rec; **C** *Pinocchio's*, owner Patricia, 4 double rooms behind *Sea View Restaurant*, follow *Stanley's* signs, good restaurant; **C-D** *Edith's Cabins*, pink cabins on the hill beside *West End Divers*, private bath, hot water, reduced rates for longer stays; **D** *Bamboo Hut*, new cabins, shared bathroom, central, next door to *Ocean Divers*, also laundry US$4/load; **D** *Belvedere's* cabin on beach behind *Chris's Super Tienda*, private bath; **D** *Delzie* has a nice private room, ask at *Chris' Super Tienda*; **E** *Anderson's*, basic rooms, shared bath, lower rates for longer stays, behind *Chris' Super Tienda*; **F** *Dora Miller* (no sign), 2 houses behind *Jimmy's*, washing facilities, no fan, no mosquito nets, basic, noisy, friendly; **F** *Jimmy's Lodge*, hammocks or communal rooms, extremely basic, smelly, ground floor room has crabs at night, very friendly, cheap meals, snorkelling gear and horseriding available, it is very cheap to string a hammock here, but very exposed and tin roof not waterproof, you'll be bitten by sandflies, hosepipe as a shower, being reborn after a fire in late 1995; other **E-F** places to stay inc *Hotel Suárez*, *Yoly's*, *Kenny's* (also camping, **G**), all basic but friendly, water and electricity not guaranteed, take insect repellent; *Valerie's*, good clean dormitory accommodation, communal central area with cooker and fridge, private rooms **D**, hospitable, but watch your belongings, reports of theft; **F-G** *Sam's*, next to *Jimmy's*, very cheap, but hot rooms, no water, no windows, dirty, primitive, many new buildings on beach at far end of village, all **E-F**: *Helen's*, *Mermaid's*, *Zoe's*, some robberies reported here, watch security. At Gibson Bight, on the road to West End, are *Alexander's Cabins*, T 45-15-01.

At West Bay: L3-A2 *Las Roccas*, new duplex cabañas next to *Bite on the Beach*, very close together, hot water, balcony, smaller cabins sleep 3, larger ones sleep 6, contact *Foster's* restaurant;

Roatán - West End

Not to scale

Hotels:
1. Anderson's Cabins
2. Bananarama
3. Belvedere's Cabins & glass bottom boat
4. Burkes Cabins
5. Cabana Roatán
6. Casa Calico
7. Coconut Tree 2
8. Coconut Tree Cabins & Supermarket
9. Foster's Beach House
10. Foster's Cabins
11. Georphi's Tropical Hideaway
12. Half Moon Bay Cabins & Restaurant
13. Jimmy's Place
14. Keifitos Plantation Retreat
15. Las Rocas
16. Mermaid Cabins & Native sons water sports
17. Robert's Hill Cabins
18. Robert's Hill Hotel
19. Sam's Place
20. Sea Breeze
21. Seagrape Plantation Resort
22. Suárez
23. Sunset Inn (above Ocean Divers)
24. Tabayana Beach Resort
25. Trish's Wish Apartments
26. Valerie's Dormitory
27. West Bay Lodge

Places to eat:
28. Café del Mar
29. Cindy's Island Food & Fishing Trips
30. Foster's Bar & Restaurant
31. Pinnochios Restaurant & Rooms
32. Pura Vida Restaurant
33. Seaview Restaurant
34. Stanley's Island Restaurant
35. The Bite on the Beach
36. Tropico Italiano Restaurant

Caribbean Sea

Sandy Bay Marine Reserve

Halfmoon Bay

Woody's Supermarket

To Coxen Hole

Sugar Plum gift shop
Casi Todo tours & books

Chris's tienda, tel/fax service

West End

Big Blue Divers
West End Divers

Ocean Divers

Bay Island Divers

Lone's Bar

Flowers Bay/West Bay Rd (unpaved)

Coral Reef Explorer

West Bay Beach

JB's Sports Bar

N

65a

A1 *Tabayana Resort*, at far end of beach, up-market, lovely location, expensive restaurant, no alcohol permitted, outdoor freshwater showers US$1.50; **A2** *Fosters*, above *Café del Mar*, new rooms, a/c, hot water in the 'beach house', T 45-11-24; **A2-A3** *Cabana Roatana*, T 45-12-71, nice cabins on the beach, hot water; **A2-A3** *Coconut Tree 2*, T 45-16-38, luxury cabins with hot water, a/c, balcony on the beach; **B** *Bananarama*, with bath, hot water, fan, PADI dive courses available; **B** *West Bay Lodge*, behind *JB's*, follow sandy path, 2 mins' walk, cabins with hot water and fan, owners Reiner and Maran, she is a qualified masseuse, breakfast inc.

At Sandy Bay: **A1** *Anthony's Key Resort*, T 45-10-03/12-74, F 45-11-40, closes for 2 weeks in Oct, glorious situation, accommodation in small wooden cabins, launch and diving facilities (only open to resident guests), the owner, Julio Galindo, is very serious about helping the environment and local community, the resort's own cay, Bailey's, has a small wildlife reserve (parrots, cockatoo, toucan, monkeys, agoutis, turtles), it has a museum of some archaeological and colonial history, natural history laboratory, A-V lecture hall (entry for non-guests US$2); it also has a dolphin enclosure in a natural pool, guests can swim or dive with the dolphins, expensive, closed Wed (in the 1996 storms, 7 dolphins escaped but remain around the islands and occasionally approach dive boats); **A3** pp *Oceanside Inn*, T (504) 45-15-52, F 45-15-32, full board, clean, comfortable, friendly owners Joseph and Jenny, nice deck with view of bay, superb restaurant, diving packages offered, but no beach nearby, otherwise rec; **B-C** *Caribbean Seashore Bed & Breakfast*, new, on the beach at West Sandy Bay, hot water, private bath, cooking facilities, friendly management, T 45-11-23.

At French Harbour: **L3-A3** *Fantasy Island Beach Resort*, T 45-11-91/45-12-22, F 45-12-68, 80 rooms, a/c, on a 15-acre cay, man-made beach, pool, diving and many other watersports, tennis, conference facilities, mixed reports; **A2** *Coco View Resort*, T 45-10-11, in USA 1-800-282-8932, good shore diving, on lagoon; **A3-B** *French Harbour Yacht Club*, T 45-14-78, F 45-14-59, cable TV in every room, suites available, nice location, view over yacht harbour, small pool, dive packages, expensive but good food (especially lunch); **A3-C** *Buccaneer*, T 45-10-32, F 45-12-89 (Tegucigalpa T 36-90-03, F 36-98-00, San Pedro Sula T 52-62-42, F 52-62-39), dive packages, mixed reports on hotel;

B *The Faro Inn*, T 45-15-36, new hotel above *Gios* seafood restaurant, TV, phone, a/c, large rooms, inc continental breakfast; **D** *Harbour View*, a/c, private bathroom, opp *Romeo's*; **D-E** *Coral Reef*; **E** *Britos*, with fan, very good value; **E** *Dixon's Plaza*, past the *Buccaneer*, good; **E** *Hotelito*, sometimes no water, in the village; **E** *Hotelito Joe*, rooms with fan and private bath, clean restaurant downstairs serving local dishes; **E** *Isabel*, comfortable, restaurant, free transport to airport. *Romeo's Restaurant*, T 45-15-18, good for seafood.

At Brick Bay: **A2** *Caribbean Sailing Club*, modern hotel, with breakfast; **C** *Romeo's Resort Dive and Yacht Club*, T 45-11-27, F 45-15-94, dedicated dive resort, good; *Hard Rock Bodega*, at marina next to *Romeo's*, delicious homemade brown bread, salad dressings, buffalo wings and well-stocked bar.

At Mount Pleasant: **A3-B** *Executivo Inn*, on road to French Harbour opp electricity plant, new, nice rooms, a/c, hot water, TV, pool, no beach.

At Oak Ridge: **L3** *Reef House Resort*, T 45-22-97, F 45-21-42, in USA 1-800-328-8987, F (210) 341-7942, inc meals, various packages, inc diving, wooden cabins with seaview balconies, seaside bar, private natural pool, dock facilities, good snorkelling from the shore; **E** *San José Hotel*, with bath (2 rooms), cheaper without (3 rooms), clean, pleasant, good value, water shortages, good food, English-speaking owner, Louise Solórzano; *BJ's Backyard Restaurant*, at the harbour, island cooking, fish burgers, smoked foods, reasonable prices. There is a *pizzeria* and, next door, a supermarket; *Pirate's Hideaway*, at Calabash Bay, E of Oak Ridge, seafood, friendly owner.

At Port Royal: **L3** *Roatán Lodge*, accommodation in cabins, hosts Brian and Lisa Blancher provide scuba diving and snorkelling expeditions.

At Punta Gorda: **L3-A3** *Henry's Cove*, T 45-21-80, 52-71-83, secluded retreat on hill, a/c, pool, cabins sleep 6, or rooms, seafood restaurant; rooms to rent with local families. *Ben's Restaurant*, on coast road S out of village, has nice cabins to rent, **B**, dive shop (US$35/dive), limited equipment, disorganized, wooden deck over sea, local food, bar, friendly, safe parking.

At Paya Bay: **A2** *Paya Bay Beach Club and Restaurant*, cabins, private bath, hot water, wonderful ocean and beach views, owned by Mervin and Lurlene McNab, beautiful restaurant, seafood US$5-10, beach bar and showers, open breakfast, lunch, dinner, homemade soursop juice, remote, long rough drive but worth it.

At Coxen Hole: **C** *Airport View* (**D** without bath or a/c), T 45-10-74; **C** *Cay View*, Calle Principal, T 45-12-02, F 45-11-79, a/c, bath, TV, phone, laundry, restaurant, bar, overlooks water, overpriced; *Osgood Key*, cabins, max 8 people, bar, restaurant, taxi boat at end of road nr *Cay View*, T 45-15-41; **C-E** *Mom*, on main road into Coxen Hole, above pharmacy, next to hospital, private or shared bath, modern, clean, a/c, TV; **E** *El Paso*, T 45-10-59, next door to *Cay View*, shared bath, restaurant; **F** *Naomi Allen*, nr the bus depot, fan, clean, good. Many of the cheaper hotels in the **F-G** range have water shortages.

● **Places to eat**

West End: *Half Moon Bay* restaurant, nice location to sit on terrace overlooking sea, more expensive than most, dishes between US$6-US$15, but excellent food, service can be very slow; *Foster and Vivian's Restaurant* is on a jetty, good atmosphere for pre-dinner drinks, but food no longer rec, no sandflies, great sundeck, Tues is Divers' night, discounts with C Card, Thur is band/dance/party night, also rooms to rent, **B**, T 45-10-08; *Sea View Restaurant*, Italian chef/manager, extensive menu, pasta, fish, chicken, pizza, good salads; *Paris*, French restaurant in the *Sunset Inn*, seafood and vegetarian specials, excellent homemade French bread, menu changes nightly, real *coq au vin*; *Pura Vida*, Italian, pizza place next to *West End Divers*, good atmosphere; *Lighthouse*, on the point after *Belvedere's*, local dishes, good coffee and breakfasts, fried chicken and seafood; *The Cool Lizard*, Mermaid Beach, seafood and vegetarian, fresh coconut soup, limited stock so go early, closed Mon; *Rudy's*, has good pancakes and cookies for breakfast, good atmosphere, check your change, charges high prices for phone calls; *Stanley's*, up hill about 50m N of *Sunset Inn*, island cooking, menu changes daily, evening meal only, at 1900, cheap, good food, try their coconut dinner, friendly; *Pinocchio's*, along same path, excellent pasta, great stir fry and delicious salads, run by Patricia and Howard; *Belvedere's*, on water, nice setting, tasty Italian food, open 1900-2100, rec; *Cindy's*, next to *Sunset Inn*, local family lunches and breakfast in garden, fish caught same morning, also lobster and king crab, rec; *Coconut Tree*, entrance to West End, supermarket, food not special, bar shows sport, football games etc; *Woods Supermarket*,

cheap hot dogs and *baleadas* at lunch between 1100 and 1300, good; *Trópico Italiano*, now in *Bamboo Hut*, Italian cuisine, pizzas, small portions, expensive; *Punta del Ovest* music village, exotic, clay oven pizzas, 200m along path behind *Bamboo Hut*; *Rick's American Café*, Sandy Bay, tree top bar, shows all sports events, best steaks on Roatán, US$10, rec. Some children sell tasty doughnuts and cinnamon rolls. The *pastelito* boy sells vegetarian pastry puffs for L2 each and oranges for L1.

West Bay: *The Bite on the Beach*, open Wed-Sat and Sun brunch, huge deck in gorgeous position on the point over West Bay, excellent, fresh food and great fruit punch, owned by Gene and Dian, rec; *Café del Mar*, next to glass bottomed boat wharf, open daily, breakfast till late, extensive bar, good selection of dishes, try pasta with chicken and sundried tomatoes, rec; *JB's Sports Bar and Restaurant*, nice location and décor, TV sports, food diner style, hamburgers, American beer.

Coxen Hole: *Comedor Ray Monty*, very cheap, set meal US$1.50 but avoid the meat, fish good; *Gloria's*, good local food, reasonable prices, TV, popular with locals; *Qué Tal Café*, good, export quality coffee, herbal teas, sandwiches and pastries, shares space with bookstore, on road to West End; *El Punto*, bar with one basic dish, very cheap; *HB Warren*, large well-stocked supermarket (best place on island for fresh fruit) with cafeteria, mainly lunch and snacks, open 0700-1800; pizza stand opp *Warren's*, slices US$1.50; *El Paso*, next to the *Cay View*, good seafood soup; *Hibiscus Sweet Shop*, homemade fruit pies, cakes and biscuits. There is a good seafood restaurant on Osgood Cay a few minutes by free water taxi from wharf.

● **Banks & money changers**

Banco Atlántida, Bancahsa, Banco Sogerín and Banffaa in Coxen Hole, there is also a Credomatic office where you can get a cash advance on your Visa/Mastercard, upstairs, before *Cay View Hotel* on the main street; 5 banks in French Harbour; *Bancahsa* in Oak Ridge, T 45-22-10, Mastercard for cash advances. No banks in West End.

● **Entertainment**

Discotheques: informal ones which come alive about midnight, play mostly reggae, salsa, *punta* and some rock. *Harbour View*, Coxen Hole, Thur-Sun nights, late, US$0.50 entrance, very local, usually no problem with visitors but avoid local disputes, hot and atmospheric; *Al's*,

Barrio Las Fuertes, before French Harbour, closed Sat night, salsa and plenty of punta; *Bolongas*, French Harbour, weekends, late, US$1 entrance, more upmarket, modern building, sometimes live Honduran bands; *Foster's*, the late night hotspot in West End, dance music Thur night as well as band nights.

● **Hospitals & medical services**

Ambulance and Hyperbaric Chamber: Coxen Hole, next to Imapro on main road, 500m past turning to Coxen Hole towards airport, T 45-17-17, temporary location 1997 until new chamber is built in Sandy Bay.

Dentist: upstairs in the Cooper building for emergency treatment, but better to go to La Ceiba or San Pedro Sula.

Doctor: Dr Jackie Bush has a clinic in Coxen Hole, no appointment necessary, for blood or stool tests etc.

● **Post & telecommunications**

Post Office: in Coxen Hole, stamps not always available, bring them with you or try *Librería Casi Todo* in West End.

Telecommunications: very expensive, you will be charged as soon as a call connects with the satellite, whether or not the call goes through. Hondutel in Coxen Hole, fax is often broken. *The Lucky Lemp*, opp *Casi Todo II* on main road into Coxen Hole, T/F and e-mail, fax to USA US$3/page, to Europe US$6.50, phone same price per minute, e-mail US$4/3 pages. Collect calls to USA, Canada, UK, Italy, Germany. Intertel at *Supertienda Chris*, West End, T/F 45-11-71, 1 min to Europe US$5, USA, Canada and Central America US$2.50, South America and Caribbean US$5.50, Asia and Africa US$6, fax minimum 3 mins but you can send 2-3 pages; to receive, US$0.30/minute phone, US$1 for 2 pages of fax. Both *Librería Casi Todo* and *Rudy's Cabins* in West End have a fax, US$10/page to Europe, US$5 to USA. *Rudy's* charge US$2 a minute to receive phone calls. Send or receive e-mail, US$2/page, at Waterloo@globalnet.hn. Located at Waterloo Design & Publishing, Mangrove Bite, 5 mins' walk, West End. Incoming e-mail should have recipient's name in the subject line. Look for big yellow house behind the Old Pirate's Galley.

● **Shopping**

Supermarkets: best to buy food, insect repellent in Coxen Hole. *Coconut Tree* at West End expensive; *Woods* is cheaper; in French Harbour, *Eldon* is also expensive.

Local Newspaper: *Coconut Telegraph*, 6 issues/year, in English, good information on Roatán and the Bay Islands. Subscriptions: Central America and USA US$25/year, Canada US$30, elsewhere US$35 from Coconut Telegraph, Cooper Building, Suite 301, Coxen Hotel, Roatán, Honduras, CA, T 504-45-16-60, F 504-45-16-59.

● **Sports**

Diving: the establishment of the **Sandy Bay/West End Marine Park** along 4.2 km of coast from Lawson Rock around the SW tip to Key Hole has encouraged the return of large numbers of fish in that area and there are several interesting dive sites. Lobsters are still rare, but large grouper are now common and interested in divers. Mooring buoys must be used, anchoring and spear fishing are not allowed. If the sea is rough off West End try diving around French Harbour (or vice versa) where the cays provide some protection. There are more mangroves on this side, which attract fish. Flowers Bay on the S side has some spectacular wall dives, but not many fish, and it is calm during the 'Northers' which blow in Dec-February. Few people dive the E end except the liveaboards (Bay Islands Aggressor, The Aggressor Fleet, PO Drawer K, Morgan City, LA 70881-000K, T 504-385-2416, F 504-384-0817 or 800-348-2628 in USA or Canada) and people on camping trips to Pigeon Cay, so it is relatively unspoilt. Because fishing is allowed to the E, tropical fish are scarce and the reef is damaged in places. Apart from expecting some stormy days in Dec-Feb, you can also expect stinging hydroids in the top few feet of water around Mar-April which bother people who are sensitive to stings. Symptoms are itching while swimming, mostly over weed, usually on parts of the body covered by the swimsuit: vinegar is the local remedy. Divers are usually unaffected as they go below the hydroids.

As on Utila, the dive operators concentrate on instruction but prices vary (since Dec 1994 the municipal government has set minimum prices) and there is more on offer; not everyone teaches only PADI courses. Prices for courses and diving vary with the season. In low season good deals abound. Open Water US$175, Advanced US$130, fun dives US$20, snorkel rental US$5/day. Despite the huge number of dive students, Roatán has a good safety record but it still pays to shop around and find an instructor you feel confident with at a dive shop which is well organized with well-maintained equipment. As in other 'adventure' sports the cheapest is not always the best. Some operators will ask you to contribute US$2/day insurance for the hyperbaric chamber, giving you free treatment should you need it and providing funds towards treating and educating the lobster fishermen off the Mosquitia coast. The chamber will not accept insurance from people who have dived outside the sports diving safety limits (max depth 130 ft/39m).

West End: *Ocean Divers* at *Sunset Inn*, rec, T/F 45-10-05, run by Conor Megan and Phil Stevens with emphasis on safety and fun, good equipment, multilingual instructors, PADI courses, BSAC, explanation/adventure diving, 3-tank day trips to the sea mounts, also rooms and restaurant, dive/accommodation packages available; *Sueño del Mar Divers*, good, American-style operation, they tend to dive the sites closest to home; *West End Divers*, Italian owned, competant bilingual instructors, PADI Dive Centre; *Big Blue Divers*, multilingual instructors, PADI, SSI courses, good boats; *Bay Island Divers*, under *Roberts Hill Hotel*, PADI courses, new; *Native Son's Water Sports*, next to *Mermaid* cabins, run by Alvin, local instructor, PDSI courses and fun dives. **At West Bay Beach**: *Bananarama*, in centre of beach, next to *Cabana Roatana*, small, friendly, shore diving only. **Gibson Bight**: *The Last Resort*, opened 1995, mostly packages from the USA. **Sandy Bay**: *Anthony's Key Resort*, mostly hotel package diving, also swim and dive with dolphins, see above.

● **Tour companies & travel agents**
Airport travel agency at the airport, has information on hotels, will make bookings, no commission. *Bay Islands Tour and Travel Center*, in Coxen Hole (Suite 208, Cooper Building, T 45-15-85, 45-11-46) and French Harbour. *Tropical Travel*, in *Hotel Cay View*, T 45-11-46; *Columbia Tours*, Barrio El Centro, T 45-11-60, good prices for international travel, very helpful. *Casi Todo I* in West End or *Casi Todo 2* in Coxen Hole can arrange tours, locally and on the mainland, inc fishing, kayaking, island tours, trips to Barbareta and Copán. Local and international air tickets also sold here as well as new and second hand books, open Mon-Sat, 0900-1630 (see above Excursions). There is a mini tour and information desk at *Foster's* restaurant, West End, they handle boat tours. Carlos Hinds, T 45-14-46, has a van for trips, reasonable and dependable.

● **Tourist offices**
Bay Islands Conservation Association, Edif Cooper, C Principal, Coxen Hole, T 45-14-24, Charles George; Farley Smith, an American volunteer, is extremely helpful. BICA manages the Sandy Bay/West End Marine Reserve and has lots of information about the reef and its conservation. Excellent map of the island at about 1:50,000 supplied by Antonio E Rosales, T 45-15-59. Local information maps also from Librería Casi Todo, West End.

● **Transport**
Local Car rental: Sandy Bay Rent-A-Car, US$42/day all inclusive, jeep rental, T 45-17-10, F 45-17-11, agency also in West End outside *Sunset Inn*; **National**, *Hotel Fantasy Island*, T 45-11-28; **Amigo** at the airport; **Toyota**, opp airport, have pickups, US$46, 4WD, US$65, Starlets US$35/day, also 12-seater bus, US$56/day, T 45-11-66; **Avis**, T 45-15-68, Las Samurais and Coronas; **Hertz** has doorless VWs, good fun but bummer if it rains.

Air Airport is 20 mins' walk from Coxen Hole, or you can catch a taxi from *outside* the airport for US$1.50. Change in Coxen Hole for taxis to West End. US$1 pp for *colectivos*. If you take a taxi from the airport they charge US$8/taxi. Caribbean Air, Isleña, Sosa fly from **La Ceiba** several times a day, US$23 one way (fewer on Sun); flights also to and from **Tegucigalpa**, US$60, via **San Pedro Sula**, US$50, frequency varies according to season. Always buy your ticket in advance (none on sale at airport), reservations are not always honoured. From the USA, Taca flies on Fri and Sat from **Houston** on Sun from **Miami**, on Fri from **New Orleans** and 3 days a week from San Salvador; Caribbean Air fly from Belize City to Roatán Sat, daily from San Pedro Sula and at weekends from Utila. Airlines: Taca, Edif Shop and Save, Coxen Hole, T 45-12-36, at airport T 45-13-87; Isleña, airport T 45-10-88. *Casi Todo* sells all inter-Honduras and Caribbean air tickets, same price as airlines.

Sea *M/V Tropical* sails from La Ceiba to Coxen Hole, Roatán, fast (2 hrs), comfortable, a/c, videos, US$11 one way from the Nuevo Muelle de Cabotaje 6 km from town (taxi US$1.50 pp): Mon 0500, Tues-Fri depart La Ceiba again 1530; Tues-Fri Roatán-La Ceiba 0700, La Ceiba-Roatán 1530; Sat Roatán-La Ceiba 0700, La Ceiba-Roatán 1100, return 1400; Sun La Ceiba-Roatán 0700, return 1530. Times frequently change, check in good time before travelling. No sailings in bad weather. At times the crossing can be rough, sea-sick pills available at ticket counter. Irregular boats from Puerto Cortés and Utila.

BARBARETA ISLAND

East of Roatán, the island is a private nature reserve, where hiking trails have been laid out and there are beaches, good diving and sport fishing. The adjacent Pigeon Cays are ideal for snorkelling, shallow scuba, picnics. There are stone artefacts on the island, and you can hike in the hills to caves which may have been inhabited by Paya Indians. The island was once owned by the descendants of Henry Morgan. The island, plus its neighbours Santa Elena and Morat, are part of the proposed Barbareta National Marine Park.

Reservations are required for all visitors, contact the **L1** *Barbareta Beach Club*, PO Box 63, La Ceiba, F 42-26-29, no phone, VHF 88A. Accommodation inc meals in lodge or beach bungalows, restaurant, bar, tours, sports, horses included, charter flights from La Ceiba or Roatán US$72 pp, min 2 people, or charter boat from Roatán US$36 pp, min 2 people, all one way only. 1-day walking tours with guide, lunch, snorkelling, US$35. Divers should bring their own equipment, but tanks, weights, guide and boat are available, US$25 1 tank, US$40 2 tanks. Bonefishing with guide and boat, US$150 full day, deep sea fishing US$300 ½-day, US$550 full day. Also hobie cat, windsurfing, kayaks, mountain bikes for rent. In the USA: 7105 Mobile St, Suite 17, Fair Hope, Alabama 36532, T 205-990-8948, F 205-928-1659.

Averyll from *Casi Todo*, West End, Roatán, can arrange sailing tours, charter flights and accommodation, **A3-B**, T 45-12-55, 45-19-61.

GUANAJA

(56 sq km; *Pop* 5,000) Columbus called **Guanaja**, the easternmost of the group, the Island of Pines, and the tree is still abundant. The island was declared a forest reserve in 1961, and is now designated a national marine park also. Good (but sweaty) clambering on the island gives splendid views of the jungle and the sea.

Several attractive waterfalls. The first English settler was Robert Haylock, who arrived in 1856 with a land title to part of the island, two cays which now form the main settlement of Bonacca and some of the Mosquito coast. He was followed in 1866 by John Kirkconnell, who purchased Hog Cay, where the Haylocks raised pigs away from the sandflies. These two families became sailors, boat builders and landowners, and form the basis of the present population. Much of Guanaja town, locally known as **Bonacca**, covering a small cay off the coast, is built on stilts above sea water, hence its nickname: the 'Venice of Honduras'. There are three other small villages: **Mangrove Bight**, **Savannah Bight** and **North East Bight** on the main island. There are Indian graves around Savannah Bight. Bathing is made somewhat unpleasant by the many sandflies. These and mos-

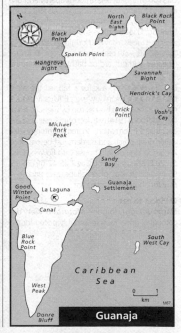

quitoes cannot be escaped on the island, all the beaches are infected (coconut oil, baby oil or any oily sun tan lotion will help to ward off sandflies). The cays are better, including Guanaja town. South West Cay is specially recommended.

Local information
● **Accommodation**

L2-A2 *Bayman Bay Club* (beautiful location, see the sunset from the tree house deck, T 45-41-79, in USA 1-800-524-1823, F 305-370-2276) and **L2-A2** *Posada del Sol* (on an outlying cay, T 45-41-86), both with launch trips, diving, fitness studio, first class, the latter has a good underwater photographic and video facility for divers.

A2 *Club Guanaja Este*, full board, many aquatic activities, and horseriding and hiking, reservations and information PO Box 40541, Cincinnati, Ohio 45240 or travel agents. *Bahía Resort*, bungalows, pool, disco, bar, Italian restaurant, T/F 45-42-12.

C *Alexander*, T 45-43-26, 20 rooms, or US$100 in 3-bed, 3-bathroom apartment, diving and fishing resort, packages: US$98 pp inc 3 dives a day, US$110 pp inc bone fishing and trawling, US$85 pp inc snorkelling and hiking, all with 3 meals a day and lodging; **C** *El Rosario*, T 45-42-40, with bath and a/c, nice; **C-D** *Miller* (cheaper without a/c or bath), TV, restaurant, T 45-43-27.

D-E *Harry Carter*, ask for a fan, all the a/c is broken down, clean however; **E** *Miss Melba*, 3 rooms in boarding house, run by friendly, talkative lady (born 1914) with lots of interesting stories and island information, shared bathroom, cold water, great porch and gardens just before *Hotel Alexander* sign on left, house with flowers; *Casa Sobre El Mar*, on Bound Cay, T 45-42-69 (31-05-95 in Tegucigalpa), offers all-inclusive packages; *Day Inn*, hotel and restaurant.

● **Places to eat**

Harbour Light, through *Mountain View* discotheque, good food reasonably priced for the island; *The Nest*, T 45-42-90, good eating in the evening; *Glenda's*, good standard meals for under US$1, small sandwiches; *Fifi Café*, named after the hurricane which wiped out most of the houses in 1974, popular local hangout.

● **Banks & money changers**

Bancahsa, Banco Atlántida.

● **Sports**

Diving and Sailing: the most famous dive site off Guanaja is the wreck of the *Jado Trader*, sunk in 1987 in about 30m on a flat bottom surrounded by some large coral pinnacles which rise to about 15m. Large black groupers and moray eels live here, as does a large shy jewfish and many other fish and crustaceans. *Jado Divers*, beside *Melba's*, US$26 for 2 dives, run by Matthew, American. Preston Borden will take snorkellers out for US$25/boat load (4-6 people), larger parties can be accommodated with larger boat, or for custom excursions, very flexible, T 45-43-26. *SV Railovy*, T (504) 45-41-35, F (504) 45-42-74, is a 40' yacht running local cruises and excursion packages; also sailing, diving and snorkelling services, and PADI courses. Ask for Hans on VHF radio channel 70.

● **Transport**

Air The airport is on Guanaja but you have to get a water taxi from there to wherever you are staying; there are no cars; Sosa and Isleña (T 45-42-08) fly daily except Sun from La Ceiba, 30 mins. Other non-scheduled flights available.

Sea The *Suyapa* sails between Guanaja, La Ceiba and Puerto Cortés. The *Miss Sheila* also does the same run and goes on to George Town (Grand Cayman). Cable Doly Zapata, Guanaja, for monthly sailing dates to Grand Cayman (US$75 one way). Irregular sailings from Guanaja to Trujillo, 5 hrs. Irregular but frequent sailings in lobster boats for next to nothing to Puerto Lempira in Caratasco Lagoon, Mosquitia, or more likely, only as far as the Río Plátano (see page 965).

Copán and Western Honduras

HONDURAS' MAJOR Maya attraction is close to the Guatemalan border; it is a lovely site, with a pleasant town nearby. This whole area has many interesting towns and villages, most in delightful hilly surroundings, often producing handicrafts. Some of these places have a colonial history, some are Lenca Indian communities.

SANTA BÁRBARA

(*Pop* 23,000; *Alt* 290m) The Western Highway runs from San Pedro Sula SW along the Río Chamelecón to Canoa (58 km, from where there is a paved road S to Santa Bárbara, a further 53 km) and Santa Rosa de Copán; it goes on to the border with Guatemala and El Salvador. **Santa Bárbara** is 32 km W of Lago Yojoa, 221 km from Tegucigalpa, in hot lowlands. Panama hats and other goods of *junco* palm are made in this, one of the nicest main towns in Honduras although it has little of architectural or historical interest compared with, for example, Gracias, Ojojona or Yuscarán. It is surrounded by high mountains (eg Cerro Guatemalilla), hills, forests and rivers. The majority of the population is fair-skinned (some red-heads) and the people are very lively. Santa Bárbara is a good base for visiting the villages in the department of the same name (see below). In the vicinity the ruined colonial city of **Tencoa** has recently been rediscovered. The paved road goes on to join the Northern Highway S of Lago Yojoa.

Excursions

Between Santa Bárbara and Lago Yojoa is the **Parque Nacional de Santa Bárbara** which contains the country's second highest peak, Montaña de Santa Bárbara, 2,744m. The rock is principally limestone with many subterranean caves (see also below). There is little touristic development as yet, only one trail has been laid out and a guide can be found in Los Andes, a village above Peña Blanca and Las Vegas. Best time to visit is the dry season, Jan-June. For more information contact Asociación Ecológica Corazón Verde, at the Palacio Municipal, Santa Bárbara. There is a Cohdefor office just below the market (look for the sign board) but they are not helpful.

The Department of Santa Bárbara is called the 'Cuna de los Artesanos', with over 10,000 manufacturers of handicrafts. The main products come from the small *junco* palm, for example fine hats, baskets, etc. The principal towns for *junco* items are **La Arada**, 25 mins from Santa Bárbara on the road to San Nicolas (see below), then branching off S, and Ceguaca, on a side road off the road to Tegucigalpa. Hats and baskets are made

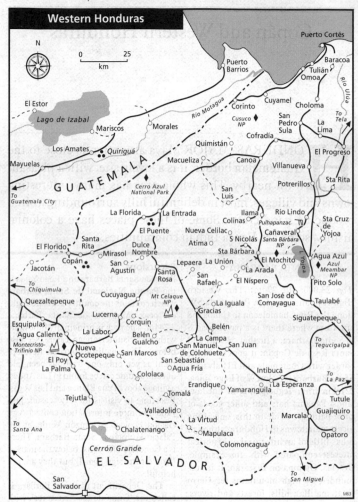

Western Honduras

in Nueva Celilac (also below). *Mezcal* is used to make carpets, rugs, hammocks, etc, it is easy to find in towns such as **Ilama** (*Pop* 7,000) on the road to San Pedro Sula, with one of the best small colonial churches in Honduras (no accommodation). *Tule* is used to make *petates* (rugs) and purses.

In the Department of Santa Bárbara is an area known as **El Resumidero**, in which are the Quezapaya mountain, and six others over 1,400m, and a number of caves (Pencaligüe, Los Platanares, El Quiscamote, and others). From Santa Bárbara, go to El Níspero and thence to El Quiscamote; or go to San Vicente

Centenario (thermal springs nearby), and on to San Nicolás, Atima, Berlín, and La Unión, all of which have thermal waters, fossils, petrified wood and evidence of volcanic activity.

San Nicolás is 20 km from Santa Bárbara on a paved road; it was founded on 20 February 1840 after the disappearance of Viejo Celilac, near Cerro Capire. In the centre of town is the big tree called 'Anacahuite' (in Lenca, place of reunion), planted in 1927. There is a nice Catholic church; other points of interest, La Peña, Las Cuevas del Masical (a local guide will take you to the caves for a fee), Quebrada Arriba and El Violín. You can drive to the ruined church of Viejo Celilac and on to Nueva Celilac, high on the mountain, a pleasant little town with a Vía Crucis procession on Good Friday.

North of Santa Bárbara is **Colinas**, reached by bus from San Pedro Sula (from near Av Los Leones). The village is picturesque, with a basic *pensión* (G), near the church; excellent set meals from *Chinita* near the gas station. Climb the mountain with El Gringo Guillermo (Bill Walton) to Laguna Colorada, US$3 (a long drive through coffee *fincas*); he plans to build tourist cabins.

Local information
● **Accommodation**
C-D *Boarding House Moderno*, Barrio Arriba, T 64-22-03, rooms with fan better value than with a/c, with hot shower, quiet, parking, rec.

E *Gran Hotel Colonial*, 1½ blocks from Parque Central, T 64-26-65, fans in all rooms, some with a/c, cold water, sparsely furnished, friendly, clean, good view from roof, rec; *Santa Marta*, on La Independencia, basic, noisy.

F *Hospedaje Rodríguez*, with bath, dark, clean, friendly, helpful, walls don't meet the ceiling, noisy; **F** *Rosileí*, clean, pleasant, *comedor* attached; **F** *Ruth*, Calle La Libertad, T 64-26-32, rooms without windows, fan.

● **Places to eat**
Pizzería Don Juan, Av Independencia, very good pizzas; *Comedor Everest*, by bus stop on Parque Central, friendly, good comida corriente; *Comedor Norma*, family food, friendly; *Las*

Tejas, nr Rodríguez, friendly, good pizzería; *Doña Ana*, 1 block above Parque Central, door and window frames painted black, no sign, restaurant in her dining room, crammed with bric-a-brac, no menu, no choice, set meal of meat, rice, beans, bananas, plentiful and good but boring; *El Brasero*, half block below Parque Central, extensive menu of meat, chicken, fish, Chinese dishes, good food, well-prepared, rec; *Repostería Charle's*, on Parque Central, excellent cakes, pastries, about the only place open for breakfast; *Helados Arco Iris*; *Cafetería Repostería Betty's*, both also on Parque Central. On main street, *McPollo*, clean, smart, good, and the delightfully named *Comedor Remembranzas del Verde*, good, cheap comida corriente.

● **Banks & money changers**
Banco Atlántida, Bancafé, Banco Sogerín, Banco de Occidente and Banadesa.

● **Entertainment**
Cinema: *Galaxia*.

● **Transport**
Buses to **Tegucigalpa**, 0700 and 1400 daily, weekends 0900, US$3, 4½ hrs with Transportes Junqueños (passing nr remote villages in beautiful mountain scenery); from **San Pedro Sula**, 2 hrs, US$1.90, 7 a day between 0500 and 1630. Bus to San Rafael at 1200, 4 hrs. Onward bus to Gracias leaves next day.

The road from San Pedro Sula towards Guatemala runs SW through Sula (*Sula Inn*, motel style 500m E of La Entrada, at La Maduna junction) to La Entrada (115 km from San Pedro), where it forks left for Santa Rosa (see below) and right for an attractive 60 km road through deep green scenery to Copán. The regular bus is rec rather than the dangerous minibus service. The road is paved throughout and in good condition.

LA ENTRADA
A hot, dusty town. Banco Sogerín will cash TCs.

● **Accommodation C-E** *San Carlos*, at junction to Copan Ruinas, T 98-52-28, a/c, modern, cable TV, bar, restaurant, excellent value; **E** *Central*, by Shell station, with 2 beds, F with 1, either with bath, fans, cold water, OK; **G** *Hospedaje Copaneco*, 1 Av No 228, T 98-51-81, Barrio El Progreso, on road to San Pedro Sula; opp is

F *Hotel Gran Bazar*, basic, E with bath; *Hospedaje Alexandra*, on the main road, T 98-50-75; *Hotel Tegucigalpa*, opp Shell station, on main road, T 98-50-46; F *Hospedaje María*, good, limited food also; G *Hospedaje Golosino Yessi*, parking, small rooms, OK. Eat in the market or at the bus station (to W, on Santa Rosa road), or at *Comedor Isis*, excellent. Plenty of other good restaurants.

El Puente, now a National Archaeological Park, is reached by taking a turn-off to the right, 1.5 km W from La Entrada on the Copán road, then turn right on a well-signposted dirt road 6 km to the Visitors' Centre. It is near the confluence of the Chamelecón and Chinamito rivers and is thought to have been a regional centre between 600 and 900 AD. There are over 200 structures, many of which have been excavated and mapped since 1984 by the Honduran Institute of Anthropology and History together with the Japanese Overseas Cooperation Volunteers. Several have been cleared and partially restored, including a 12m high pyramid; there are also stelae.

● **Admission** The visitors' centre has a *cafetería* and a souvenir shop. There is a museum of anthropology, well worth a visit and an introduction to Copán. Open 0800-1630, US$5.

A few kilometres beyond La Entrada is the small town of **La Florida** (*Pop* 24,100, primitive accommodation). The owner of the gas station here will advise archaeologists about the many Maya ruins between La Florida and Copán. There are a number of hilltop stelae between the border and Copán.

COPAN

The magnificent Maya ruins of **Copán** are 395 km by road from Tegucigalpa or 172 from San Pedro Sula, and 1 km from the pleasant village, called Copán Ruinas. There is a signposted path beside the road from the village of Copán to the ruins, passing two stelae en route (1 km, no need to take a minibus). It is advisable to get to the ruins as early as possible, or late in the day (though it takes a full day to see them

properly). There are several tame scarlet macaws (caged at night). They love shirt buttons.

● **Admission** Entry to ruins and Las Sepulturas US$10, open 0700-1700, admission valid for 1 day. There is a cafetería by the entrance to the ruins, and also a shop. Guided tours available all year (rec, US$20); recommended is Antonio Ríos, T 983414, owner of restaurant/shop opposite the ruins. Photographs of the excavation work and a maquette of the site are located in a small exhibition room at the ruins' Visitors' Centre. There is a tourist office in the Parque Arqueológico, next to the shop, with local and country maps, and a Spanish/English guide book for the ruins, which is rather generalized. Useful recent books are: *Scribes, Warriors and Kings: City of Copán*, by William and Barbara Fash (1991), and *History Carved in Stone, a guide to Copán* by William Fash and Ricardo Agarcía (1992), published locally and available at the site. (See also general account of Maya history in the Horizons to this book.) Luggage can be left for no charge (clean toilets here, too).

Museums

The **Copán Museum** on the town square has good explanations in Spanish of the Maya Empire and stelae. There is a good selection of artefacts and a burial site. It is a good idea to visit the museum before the ruins. Open Mon-Sat, 0800-1200, 1300-1600, entrance US$2.

The magnificent **Museum of Mayan Sculpture**, opened in 1996, next to the Visitor's Centre, is an impressive and huge museum and sculpture park which houses the newly excavated carvings. In the middle of the museum is a full size reproduction of the Rosalila temple, found intact buried under another structure with its original paint and carvings. The new museum houses the original stelae to prevent weather damage, while copies will be placed on site. Over 2,000 other objects found at Copán are also in the museum. It is essential to visit the museum before the ruins. The entrance is through a winding tunnel whose mouth is a serpent's head. The exit leads to the ruins via the nature trail. Admission US$5.

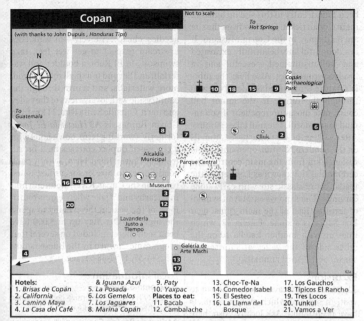

Hotels:
1. Brisas de Copán
2. California
3. Camino Maya
4. La Casa del Café

& Iguana Azul
5. La Posada
6. Los Gemelos
7. Los Jaguares
8. Marina Copán

9. Paty
10. Yaxpac
Places to eat:
11. Bacab
12. Cambalache

13. Choc-Te-Na
14. Comedor Isabel
15. El Sesteo
16. La Llama del Bosque

17. Los Gauchos
18. Típicos El Rancho
19. Tres Locos
20. Tunkul
21. Vamos a Ver

The ruins

When Stephens and Catherwood examined the ruins in 1839, they were engulfed in jungle. In the 1930s the Carnegie Institute cleared the ground and rebuilt the Great Stairway, and since then they have been maintained by the Government. Some of the most complex carvings are found on the 21 stelae, or 3m columns of stones on which the passage of time was originally believed to be recorded, and which are still in their original sites among the buildings. Under many of the stelae is a vault; some have been excavated. The stelae are deeply incised and carved with faces, figures and animals. They are royal portraits with inscriptions recording deeds and lineage of those portrayed as well as dates of birth, marriage(s) and death. (Some of the finest examples of sculpture in the round from Copán are now in the British Museum or at Boston.) Ball courts were revealed during excavation, and one of them has been fully restored. The Hieroglyphic Stairway leads up a pyramid, the upper level supported a temple. Its other sides are still under excavation. The Stairway is covered for protection, but a good view can be gained from the foot and there is access to the top via the adjacent plaza. Much fascinating excavation work is in progress, stacks of labelled carved stones under shelters, and the site looks like becoming even more interesting as new buildings are revealed. The most atmospheric buildings are those still half-buried under roots and soil.

The last stela was set up in Copán between AD 800 and 820, after less than five centuries of civilized existence. The nearby river has been diverted to prevent it encroaching on the site when in flood. 1 km beyond the main ruins, along the road to San Pedro Sula, is an area called Las Sepulturas, a residential area where ceramics dating back to 1000 BC have been found; entry to this site included in main Copán ticket. Exhibits from the site are on display in the Copán Museum. It is a delightful site, beautifully excavated and well-maintained, peaceful and in lovely surroundings. Also near the ruins is a nature trail (called Sendero Natural) through the jungle to the minor ball court; take mosquito repellent if you intend to stand still. The trail takes 30 mins. After 1600 is the best time to see animals on the Sendero Natural, open until 1700. About 4 km from the main centre is the ceremonial site known as Los Sapos (the toads), a pre-classic site with early stone carvings. The sapo was a Mayan symbol of fertility. East of the main ruins, near Los Sapos is a stone, Estella 12, which lines up with another, Estella 10 on the other side of the valley at sunrise and sunset on 12 April annually.

Excursions

There are many caves around Copán to visit, in some of which, Mayan artifacts have been found. Ask locally. Also, here and in the neighbouring part of Guatemala, are a few remaining Chorti Indian villages, interesting to visit, particularly on 1st Nov, Día de Los Muertos, when there are family and communal ceremonies for the Dead.

To **Agua Caliente**, 20 km from Copán, thermal springs, reached by a road through villages and beautiful scenery. 45 mins by vehicle, pick-ups go sometimes for about US\$17, shared between passengers. Tours are run by *Tunkul*, *Vamos a Ver* and *Tres Locos* (the last 2 in conjunction, 4-hr evening trip US\$5 pp). Cross the river and follow the trail up to the springs but only swim in the river where the very hot water has mixed with the cold. Changing facilities and toilets in the park, open 0800-1700, US\$1.10 entrance fee, take all food and water. 9 km from Copán is **Santa Rita**, a small, colonial town on the Copán river with cobblestones and red roofs (*Hospedaje Santa Rita* and unnamed restaurant rec, off main road next to Esso, speciality *tajadas*, huge portions, outdoors, floor covered in pine needles, cheap). A lovely 4-hr walk goes upstream (expect to get wet feet, take swimsuit) to El Rubí, a boulder and waterfall, and beyond to a small rock canyon, more waterfalls, and return through the countryside with lovely views of the valley and town. Outside Santa Rita, 11 km from Copán Ruinas, is **A3** *Hacienda El Jaral*, formerly a working farm, now a hotel with a cluster of duplex cottages on a broad, tropical flower lined lawn, with a pool, good horses to hire or for guided tours, tubing in the Copán River, mountain hiking nearby and a lake where egrets return most of the year in the evening to spend the night, in Oct-May up to 3,000 have been seen there; included on several tour programmes, owned by the Bueso family, T 52-44-57, F 52-48-91, rec.

Local information
● **Accommodation**

Generally hotels are expensive here compared with other places in Honduras.

A1 *Posada Real de Copán*, on hill overlooking Copán, T 98-34-80, F 98-34-99, operated by Biltmore, opened Sept 1995, in the Best Western chain, full service major hotel, restaurant, too far from town to walk; **A2-C** *Marina*, on the Plaza, T 98-30-70, F 57-30-76 (or T 39-09-56 in Tegucigalpa), swimming pool, sauna, restaurant, bar, live marimba music at weekends, large rooms with TV, very friendly, nice atmosphere, rec; **A3** *Plaza Copan*, on Parque Central, opened 1997, opened 1997, 20 a/c rooms, hot water, TV, pool, cafetería.

B *Los Jaguares* on Plaza opp *Marina*, T 98-30-75, F 39-10-80, 9 rooms, new, friendly staff, locked parking, no restaurant; **B** *Madrugada*, T 98-30-92, at end of the 1st street to the left after the bridge by the river, colonial style, nice, 15 rooms; **B-C** *Camino Maya*, corner of main square, T 98-34-46, F 39-30-56, e-mail HCMAYA@davidintertel.hn, with bath, good restaurant, extensively renovated 1996, finished rooms bright and airy, new bathrooms, cable TV, fans, rooms on courtyard quieter than street, English spoken, nice patio garden with parrot, balcony on some upstairs rooms; **B-C** *La Casa de Café*, 4½ blocks W of Plaza, T 52-72-74, F 52-05-23, new renovated colonial home, with breakfast, coffee all day, library, good information, lovely designed garden, beautiful views, friendly and interesting hosts, English spoken, tours arranged through Xupi Tours, protected parking, rec; **C** *La Posada*, N of Parque Central, remodelled 1997, private bath, hot water, fan.

D *Bella Vista*, on hill by former police barracks, T 98-35-02, clean, safe but poorly situated, good value; **D** *Hotelito Brisas de Copán*, T 98-30-18, terrace, modern rooms with bath, hot water, rooms without bath not so good, quiet, rec, limited parking; **D** *Popul Nah*, on street off SE corner of Plaza, T 98-30-95, fan, hot shower, safe parking, very clean, but cockroaches, hospitable, rec; **D-F** *Paty*, T 98-30-21, under the same ownership as one of the minibus companies, good value, rec, lots of parking.

E *California*, opp *Los Gemelos*, with *Bar Tres Locos*, run by chatty American, nice rooms with original décor, good beds, fan, nice lawn, good cooking (evening meal), good place for backpackers and women travelling alone; **E** *Hotelito Yaxpac*, opp *Tipicos El Rancho*, 1 block N of Parque Central, T 98-30-25, private bathroom, hot water, nice view of countryside from balcony; **E** *La Siesta*, 2 blocks W of main square on street that is square's northern edge, with bath, G without, clean, fan, laundry facilities on roof; **D** *Yaragua*, ½ block W of the Plaza, T 61-44-64, with bath, new in 1997, hot water, safe, clean, friendly owner Samuelito.

F *Honduras*, T 98-30-82, dark, only for the desperate; *Paty* and *Honduras* are noisy from buses after 0400; **F** *Hospedaje Los Gemelos*, T 98-30-77, without bath, clean, fans, good value, best place for backpackers, run by Doña Mafalda, friendly, use of kitchen on request, free coffee, pleasant patio, good for single women, also laundry facilties, rec; **F** *Hostel Iguana Azul*, next to *La Casa de Café* and under same ownership, dormitory style bunk beds in 2 rooms, shared bath, also 3 more private double rooms, hot water, clean, comfortable, commons area with TV, books, magazines, travel guides (inc the *Handbook*), maps, garden, fans, safe box, English spoken, new in 1997.

Camping: free camping by the Texaco station next to the ruins, no facilities. Also some houses will accommodate cheaply, enquire (eg house opp *Popul Nah*).

● **Places to eat**
Llama del Bosque, 2 blocks W of Plaza, open for breakfast, lunch and dinner, bar, pleasant, rec, large portions of reasonable food, try their carnitas típicas, touristy, long waits common because of popularity, meals about US$3, soup US$1, ugly coke sign outside; *Tunkul*, opp *Llama del Bosque*, good food inc vegetarian meals, large portions, not cheap, happy hour 2000-2100, always loud music, large outdoor patio, nice for relaxing breakfast, helpful, rec; *Comedor San Juan*, US$1 for meal, good; *Comedor Isabel*, next to *Llama del Bosque*, typical *comedor* atmosphere, green walls, slow service, relatively clean, average food, dinner US$2.50; *Café Cinema Vamos a Ver*, 1 block from Plaza, Dutch owned, Dutch cheese, lots of vegetables, complete dinner US$5, shows films at 1900, US$1, rec, pleasant, good value, open 0700-2200; *Elisa's* at *Camino Maya*, excellent food at reasonable prices, pleasant, good service, rec; *El Sesteo*, next to *Hotel Paty*, typical lunch US$3, dinner US$3-4.50, non-descript atmosphere; *Burger Zotz*, light snacks, burger US$1, sandwiches, ice creams, tacos, nr park, outdoor patio, average food; *Típicos El Rancho*, 1 block W of bridge to ruins, good and cheap, open-air restaurant, friendly, delicious tacos, turritos, licuados etc, rec; *Chuspi'p Pollo*, opp *Hotel La Siesta*, typical comedor, ugly, hangout for beer-drinking cowboys, but some of best fried chicken in Honduras, US$2.50 for chicken salad, fried bananas, sometimes open until 0130, good value, mariachis stroll in and out, be sure to request song 'Viva Copán Ruinas' for instant friendship; *Tres Locos* for New York style pizza and bar, almost opp *Los Gemelos*; *Cambalache*, Uruguayan/Honduran owned, nice outdoor patio, live music in evenings with electric organ and bongo drum, average food, lunch US$2.50-3.50, breakfast US$2, ugly coke sign outside, bar next door under same name and ownership, popular with wealthy Copanecos; *Los Gauchos*, also same owners, Uruguayan grilled specialities, excellent food, expensive but good quality meats, nice patio, renovated house, open 1000-2200, pity about the garish sign; *Carnitas Nia Lola*, 3 blocks S of Parque Central, at end of road, nice view over river and valley, popular meeting place, open 0700-2200, comida típica, inexpensive, busy bar, relaxed atmosphere; *Comedor El Jacal*, opp *El Sesteo*, typical food, rec for decent budget meal, breakfast, lunch and dinner, cable TV.

● **Banks & money changers**
Travellers' cheques may be changed at the **Banco de Occidente** on plaza (0800-1200, 1400-1600, Mon-Fri, 0800-1100 Sat, very

crowded on Sat), **Banco Atlántida**. Guatemalan currency can be changed at Copán; it is possible to change quetzales nr where buses leave for the border or Gabriela shop next to *Maya Hotel*, which also accepts Amex TCs.

● **Language schools**
Ixbalanque, T 98-34-32, F 57-62-15, one to one teaching plus board and lodging with local family, US$125 for 1 week, 4 hrs teaching a day.

● **Laundry**
Lavandería, half block E of main plaza, same day service.

● **Post & telecommunications**
Post Office: next to museum, open Mon-Fri 0800-1200, 1400-1700, Sat 0800-1200, beautiful stamps available; stamps also sold at corner shop opp.

Telephone: phone calls can be made from the office of Hondutel 0800 to 2100. **Fax**: a fax service is available Mon-Fri 0900-1600, small fee charged for incoming pages, F 98-00-04.

● **Tour companies & travel agents**
Go Native Tours, T 98-34-32, F 98-00-04, same number for *Ixbalanque* language school (see above); *MC Tours*, T 98-34-53, local and countrywide tours. Horses for hire (but around and bargain). You will probably be approached with offers of horse hire: a good way of getting to nearby attractions. Horse riding to Los Sapos and Las Sepulturas, US$10 for 3 hrs. Several birdwatching tours, contact Jorge Barraza, a local guide, or a tour operator such as *Xukoi Tours*, T 98-34-35.

● **Useful addresses**
Immigration: office in Palacio Municipal.

● **Transport**
Air 1 to 3-day trip from Guatemala City to Copán can be arranged by air (40 mins' flight to a finca airstrip, then bus, 25 mins), US$180 inc guide for 1 day, hotel accommodation extra. Try Jungle Flying (also charter flights between Tikal and Copán), Av Hincapié, 18 C, Zona 13, Guatemala City, T 60-49-20, 60-49-17, F 31-49-95, or many other agencies.

Buses Direct buses from San Pedro Sula in front of *Hotel Palmira*, to Copán Ruinas, *Hotel Paty*, 3 hrs, US$6, *Gama Express*, 1500, returns 0600, *Cheny Express*, 1600, returns 0700, both new, comfortable, reclining seats, efficient, good value, highly rec. Etumi buses also go direct but take 5 hrs. There are regular slow buses (Copanecos or Torito lines) from San Pedro Sula to

La Entrada, US$1.50 (2½ hrs), first bus leaves 0345, last bus 1700; from La Entrada to Copán, US$1.50 by bus (2 hrs), from 0500 every 45 mins (or when full) till 1630, stops at entrance to ruins. If going by bus from San Pedro Sula, and returning, it is impossible to see Copán in 1 day. 3 early am buses from Copán to Santa Rosa, 4 hrs, US$1.90. Buses from Copán to La Entrada for connecting buses going N or S, 0400-1700. An a/c van service, *Adventure Shuttle* (schedule varies according to season), dep Copán Thur-Sun 1600 from plaza nr cathedral to San Pedro Sula, US$20; also connects with service to Tela; San Pedro Sula-Copán 0700, 2½ hrs, buy tickets at *Hotel Yaragua*, Parque Central, Copán, T 98-34-64, or *Suites Hotel*, Plaza Cristal, 10 Av 1 y 2 C NO, San Pedro Sula, T 52-32-02; for special charters T/F 56-85-64.

Motoring There is a Texaco filling station by the ruins.

FRONTIER WITH GUATEMALA

● **Honduran immigration**
The Honduran immigration office is at El Florido on the border and you get stamps there. They charge US$1 entry fee, ask for a receipt for any 'extra' charges.

● **Leaving Honduras by private vehicle**
If leaving with a vehicle, you need 3 stamps on your strip from Migración US$1, Tránsito (where they take your Proviso Provisional), and Aduana (where they take your Pase Fronterizo document and cancel the stamp in your passport.

● **Guatemalan consulate**
For visas, either San Pedro Sula or Tegucigalpa. Guatemalan tourist cards are available at the border.

● **Banks & money changers**
There are many money changers but for US$ or TCs, change in Copán, better rates.

● **Transport**
Pick-up trucks run all day until 1700 every day between Copán Ruinas and the border connecting with buses to Guatemalan destinations, erratic service. The cost should be about US$2.50 but the growing number of tourists has encouraged overcharging of up to US$8; the police do nothing to stop it. Bargain for a fair price.

Just to visit Copán, those needing visas can obtain a 72-hr exit pass at the border but you must recross at the same border post before expiry.

To enter (or return to) Guatemala an alternative route is via Santa Rosa de Copán and Nueva Ocotepeque (see below and Guatemala, Section 2 for transit into Guatemala).

SANTA ROSA DE COPAN

(*Pop* 28,865; *Alt* 1,160m), 153 km by road from San Pedro Sula, Santa Rosa is the centre of a rich agricultural and cattle-raising area. The town is set in some of the best scenery in Honduras; the weather is remarkably fine. Much maize and tobacco is grown in the area. The Flor de Copán traditional hand-rolling cigar factory next to the *Hotel Elvir* is happy to give tours, ask for employee Edis Borden, very knowledgeable; large selection of cigars for sale, well worth a visit. Santa Rosa is a colonial town with cobbled streets. Originally known as Los Llanos, it was made a municipality in 1812 and became capital of the department of Copán when it was split off from Gracias (now Lempira). The central plaza and church are perched on a hilltop. It holds a festival to Santa Rosa de Lima from 21 to 31 August. The Tobacco Queen is crowned at the end of the week.

Excursions

There are buses from Santa Rosa W to the small town of **Dulce Nombre de Copán** (US$0.55). There are rooms available next to the Hondutel office. Hikers can continue W through mountains to stay at the primitive village of **San Agustín** (buses and pick-ups from Santa Rosa), take hammock or sleeping bag, continuing next day through Mirasol you reach the Ruinas road at El Jaral. Now you are 11 km E of Copán ruins (see Copán **Excursions** above).

Numerous daily buses go through **Cucuyagua**, scenic river, good swimming and camping on its banks and **San Pedro de Copán**, an attractive village and an entry point into the Parque Nacional Celaque; to **Corquín**, *alt* 850m (US$0.75, 2 hrs), 2 good *pensiones*, one with a charming garden. From here take a bus, 6 a day (also one bus a day from Santa Rosa de

Copán) or a rough, dusty, 1½-hrs ride in a pick-up truck (US$0.75) to **Belén Gualcho**, a Lenca village, 1,500m up in mountains, a good base to explore the surrounding mountains and valleys, especially N towards Monte Celaque. Belén Gualcho is perched on a mountainside, with two colonial churches, one architecturally fine with three domes and a fine colonnaded façade with twin bell towers, the other rustic. There is an interesting Sun market from 0500, over by 1000. There are numerous short walks from town in most directions, all affording postcard-type views. You can walk 2 hrs to waterfalls (90m drop). Head for El Paraíso then ask for directions. Everyone knows where they are.

- **Accommodation & places to eat In Belén Gualcho**: hotels fill up quickly on Sat as traders arrive for the Sun market. **G** *Hotelito El Carmen* (2 blocks E down from the church in the plaza), friendly, clean, good views, rec; **G** *Hotel Belén*; **G** *Hospedaje Doña Carolina*; electricity goes off at 2130 so take a torch and candle. Films are shown every evening at 1930, ask anyone, US$0.10. *Comedor Mery*, 1 block NW of plaza, good food in a welcoming family atmosphere; *Las Haciendas*, also good; 2 more *comedores* on S side of plaza and E side on corner with store.

- **Transport** To Santa Rosa daily at 0430 (Sun at 0930). To Gracias from main square at 0400, 0500, 1330.

A mule trail connects Belén Gualcho with **San Manuel de Colohuete** (*Alt* 1,500m), which has a magnificent colonial church whose façade is sculpted with figures of saints. Buses to San Manuel from Gracias at 1300, 4 hrs. There are no hotels so you must ask villagers about places to stay. There is an equally fine colonial church 30 mins by 4WD vehicle to the SW at **San Sebastián Colosuca** (*Alt* 1,550m). The village has a mild climate (2 *hospedajes*; or try Don Rubilio; food at Doña Clementina García or Doña Alicia Molina). The *feria de San Sebastián* is on 20 January. No alcohol may be sold in the village and there are no soldiers here. An hour's walk away is the Cueva del Diablo; 6 km away

Walking from San Miguel Colohuete to Belén Gualcho

There is a well-defined, well-used and therefore easy to follow mule trail linking these two villages. Maps are not essential as there are communities at many points along the way where advice can be sought. A map of the area is available from the Lenca Cultural Centre in Gracias.

The path leading away from the village leaves from opp the *pulpería* and *comedor* where the bus drops you, heading W and downhill into a valley. The path is used by 4WD vehicles and continues to San Sebastián. Just after the community of San José, after passing the last house, the path to Belén branches off. A small path leaves the 4WD track and climbs steeply up to your right and more NW.

1 hr: just after Peña Blanca, the path direction becomes unclear after it crosses an area of white chalky rocks. There are several other paths here. The main path heads N and steeply downhill at this point.

2 hrs: there is water all the year round in the Quebrada de Rogán.

3 hrs: all year round water in Río Gualmite, a short descent. After is a longish, steep ascent.

4 hrs: just after this point, the path branches on a large flat grassy area. Both paths lead to Belén Gualcho. The one to the left drops and crosses the river and then you are faced with a long, arduous and very steep ascent. We would recommend taking the path to the right, which exits to the far right of a grassy area by three small houses.

5 hrs: the path climbs as it skirts around the Cerro Capitán. Just after passing the steepest part of the Cerro Capitán, a small landslide forces the path into a descent almost to the river. From here only 20m above the river, you can walk steeply down off the path to the river bank where there is the most perfect camp site. Flat, sandy soil in some shade on the edge of a coffee plantation and 2m from the river.

6 hrs: from the camping site there is a long, continuous climb before dropping down sharply to cross the river. It is possible, but difficult to cross the river at the point the path meets it. Take a small path off to the right just before the river, which leads to a suspension bridge. From the river it is a long climb, not especially steep, but continuous, to Belén Gualcho. It is situated between two small peaks that can be seen clearly after crossing the river. There are increasing numbers of houses after crossing the river and the odd *pulpería* where you can buy *refrescos* or food.

(Mike and Pauline Truman)

is Cerro El Alta with a lagoon at the top. From San Sebastián, a mule trail goes via the heights of Agua Fría to reach the route near the frontier at Tomalá.

Alternatively, one can walk 5 hrs E from San Manuel to **La Campa** (very nice colonial church); for non-walkers there is a daily bus San Manuel-La Campa-Gracias. Irregular transport on the 18 km dirt road to Gracias. There is a *hospedaje* in La Campa, ask at Hondutel. Red pottery is made there. San Matías is the patron saint, *fiesta*: 23-24 Feb, well worth visiting, thousands celebrate the mostly indigenous traditions.

A paved road runs E from Santa Rosa to San Juan de Opoa, where it turns SE towards Gracias. From Santa Rosa there is a 2-hr, 0630 and 0730, US$1 bus ride to **Lepaera** (a few hundred inhabitants, very basic *hospedaje*, G, opp market and *comedores*, the best one adjoins the market) perched on a lovely mountainside E of San Juan de Opoa (also reached from Gracias). One can scale the peak (Cerro Puca, 2,234m, stiff climb, start early am for day trip) or descend on foot by an old mule trail heading back to Santa Rosa (4½ hrs), crossing the river on a swingbridge (*hamaca*), then hitchhiking.

Local information
● Accommodation
C *Elvir*, C Real Centenario SO, 3 Av SO, T 62-01-03, overpriced, safe, clean, quiet, all rooms have own bath, TV, hot water, drinking water, good but pricey meals in cafeteria or restaurant, rec.

D pp *Mayaland*, T 62-02-33, F 62-08-05, opp bus station, parking, restaurant, cable TV; **D-E** *Continental*, 2 C NO y 2-3 Av, T 62-08-01/2, on second floor, clean, with bath, hot water, friendly management.

E *Copán*, 1 C 3 Av, T 62-02-65, with bath, hot water, **F** without, cell-like rooms but clean, safe, hot water in morning; **E** *Hospedaje Santa Eduviga*, 2 Av NO y 1 C NO, good beds, clean, pleasant, good value but some rooms damp; **E** *Hotel Maya Central* (not to be confused with *Hospedaje Maya*), 1 C NO y 3 Av NO, T 62-00-73, hot water, private bath, very nice, **E** *Rosario*, 3 Av NE No 139, T 62-02-11, cold water, with bath, **F** without.

F *Castillo*, next door to *Maya Central*, T 62-03-68, new, clean.

G *Hospedaje Calle Real*, Real Centenario y 6 Av NE, clean, quiet, friendly, sometimes water failures; **G** *Hospedaje Maya*, 1 C NE y 3-4 Av, noisy, not clean, only for the desperate, car park.

● Places to eat
Flamingos, 1 Av SE, off main square, T 62-06-54, relatively expensive but good pasta and chop suey, popular with locals; *Las Haciendas*, 1 Av SE, varied menu, filling *comida corriente*, rec; *Rincón Colonial*, also on 1 Av SE, typical local cuisine, good, less expensive than its neighbours; *Miraflores* in Col Miraflores; *El Rodeo*, 1 Av SE, good menu, specializes in steaks, nice atmosphere (if you don't mind animal skins on the walls), pricey; *Comedor La Confianza*, 1 Av NW, friendly, helpful, good cheap food; *Pizza Pizza*, Real Centenario 5 Av NE, 4½ blocks from main square, one of the best in town, superb pizza and pasta, good wine list, pleasant surroundings in old colonial house, great coffee, cakes, best meeting place, US owned, good source of information, highly rec. There is a good *comedor* at the bus terminal, *Merendera El Campesino*. On the *carretera* *La Gran Villa*, some of the tastiest meats and meals in Santa Rosa, run by Garifuna family, rec.

● Banks & money changers
Banco de Occidente (best exchange rates) and **Atlántida**, both on main plaza; **Banadesa**, Calle Real; **Bancahsa** (fast service), Calle Centenario (Occidente and Bancahsa change TCs).

● Entertainment
Cinema: next to church on main square, dingy.

Discotheques: *Glamour*, *Tropical's* (one block from *Hotel Copán*).

● Hospitals & medical services
Dentist: *Dr Ricardo Reyes*, 3 Av 349, Barrio Santa Teresa, T 62-00-07.

● Tour companies & travel agents
Lenca Land Trails, at *Hotel Elvir*, T 62-08-05, run by Max Elvir, organizes cultural tours of the Lenca mountain villages in western Honduras, excellent source of information about the region.

● Transport
Buses from Santa Rosa to **Tegucigalpa** (lovely scenery, lush pine forests, colonial villages) (Toritos) leaves at 0400 from terminal, Mon-Sat, 0400 and 1000 Sun, US$3, 7-8 hrs. To **Gracias** Transportes Lempira, 0745, 0915, 1130, 1345, 1515, 2 hrs, US$1.50 (road paved). To **San Pedro Sula**, US$1.80, 4 hrs, every 45 mins from 0400-1730, express service at 0745, 1345, 2½ hrs, US$2 (Empresa Torito), bus to **La Entrada**, 1 hr, US$0.50. To **Copán Ruinas**, 4 hrs for 100 km on good road, US$1.90, several direct daily (eg Etumi at 1130, 1215, 1345), but you may have to change at La Entrada. South on paved road to **Nueva Ocotepeque** (0615, 0830, 1130, 1300, 1430, 1645, US$1.50, 3 hrs). There you change buses for Guatemala (1 hr to border, US$1, bus leaves hourly until 1700). Local 'El Urbano' bus to centre from bus station (on Carretera Internacional, 2 km below town, opp *Hotel Mayaland*), US$0.35; taxi US$0.50. If coming from the Guatemalan border at Nueva Ocotepeque, the bus will stop at the end of town nr Av Centenario (main street).

GRACIAS

(*Pop* 19,380; *Alt* 765m) The main road continues to **Gracias**, 50 km from Santa Rosa, the largest town on this road. It is one of the oldest and most historic settlements in the country, dominated by the highest mountains in Honduras, Montañas de Celaque, Puca and Opulaca. It is a charming, friendly town and both the town and surrounding countryside are worth a visit.

Gracias was the centre from which Francisco de Montejo, thrice Governor of Honduras, put down the great Indian revolt of 1537-38. Alonzo de Cáceres, his

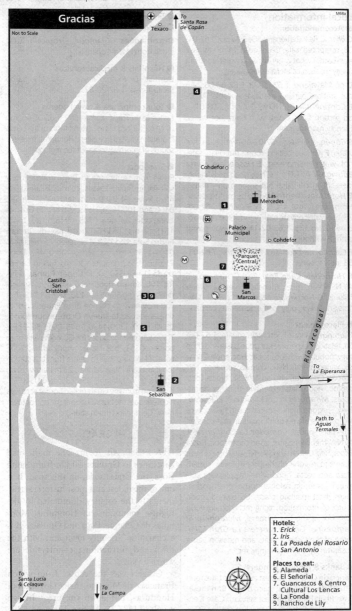

Gracias

Not to Scale

M68a

To Santa Rosa de Copán

Texaco

Cohdefor

Las Mercedes

Palacio Municipal

Cohdefor

Parque Central

Castillo San Cristóbal

San Marcos

Río Arcagual

To La Esperanza

Path to Aguas Termales

San Sebastian

To Santa Lucía & Celaque

To La Campa

N

Hotels:
1. *Erick*
2. *Iris*
3. *La Posada del Rosario*
4. *San Antonio*

Places to eat:
5. Alameda
6. El Señorial
7. Guancascos & Centro Cultural Los Lencas
8. La Fonda
9. Rancho de Lily

lieutenant, besieging Lempira the Indian leader in his impregnable mountain-top fortress at Cerquín, finally lured him out under a flag of truce, ambushed him and treacherously killed him. When the Audiencia de los Confines was formed in 1544 Gracias became for a time the administrative centre of Central America.

Places of interest

There are three colonial churches, San Sebastián, Las Mercedes, San Marcos (a fourth, Santa Lucía, is 500m SW of Gracias), and a restored fort, with two fine Spanish cannon, on a hill immediately W of centre, 5 mins' walk. The fort, **El Castillo San Cristóbal**, has been well restored, and at the foot of the northern ramparts is the tomb of Juan Lindo, President of Honduras 1847-1852, who introduced free education through a system of state schools.

Excursions

Some 6 km from Gracias along the road to Esperanza (side road signposted), swim in hot, communal thermal pools in the forest, Balneario Aguas Termales (1 hr by a path, 1 hr 20 mins by the road, the beginning of the path is a 15-min walk after the bridge on the right, next to a pebble dashed drainage channel, entry US$0.85, open daily 0600-2000, rental of towels, hammock, inner tube, restaurant/bar, rec). Good place to barbecue.

18 km away is La Campa (see page 944). From Gracias buses go through coffee plantations to San Rafael (makeshift accommodation) from where one can hitch to El Níspero (*pensión*) and catch a bus to Santa Bárbara. Also on the road to San Rafael, a short detour leads to La Iguala, a tiny village attractively set between 2 rivers, magnificent colonial church. Irregular transport from/to Gracias.

It takes at least a whole day to climb from Gracias to the summit of **Monte Celaque** (2,849m, the highest point in Honduras). Most people allow 2 days to enjoy the trip. The trail begins from behind the visitors' centre of the Celaque

National Park (1,400m) which is 8 km (2 hrs' walk) from Gracias. Entry fee US$1. The first 5½ km can be driven in a standard car, the rest only with 4WD. Transport can be arranged through the Lenca Centre at US$5 pp, minimum 3 people, worth it. Armando Mondragon, at Texaco station, T 98-40-02, does trips, including lunch. At the centre there are 7 beds, shower and cooking facilities, US$1, drinks available, well-maintained. There is another cabin nearby with 10 beds. Take a torch and sleeping bag. Behind the centre is a trail going down to the river where a crystal clear pool and waterfall make for wonderful bathing. Ask the guide the exact way or pay US$6 for the guide. There is a warden, Miguel, living nearby (he can supply food and beer), but contact Cohdefor in Gracias before leaving for full information. The Lenca Centre has maps of area and hires out camping gear. There are a number of international volunteers working on the project. Division Chief Enrique is exceedingly helpful and friendly. There is a trail all the way to the summit (trees are marked with ribbons) which takes at least 6 hrs: the first 3 hrs are easy to a campsite at 2,000m (campamento Don Tomás) where there is small hut (locked, key at the centre), the rest of the way is steep. There is another camping site, *Campamento Naranjo*, with water, at about 2,500m. Between these two sites, it is particularly steep and in cloud forest. Look out for spider monkeys. Above 2,600m quetzals have been seen. Many hikers don't bother with the summit as it is forested and enclosed. Don't forget good hiking boots, warm clothing, insect repellent, and given the dense forest and possibility of heavy cloud, a compass is recommended for safety. Also, beware of snakes. There are plans to extend the trail westward from the summit to Belén Gualcho (see above) and to create a nature trail near the visitors' centre.

Visiting the other peaks around Gracias is more complicated but interesting.

Information, maps which you can photocopy, camping gear, guided tours can be found at the Lenca Cultural Centre.

Local information
● Accommodation
E Los Lencas Cultural Centre at *Guancascos* rents 2 furnished rooms in *La Posada del Rosario*, W end of Hondutel road, old colonial house, family atmosphere, bath, hot water, also rents 2-room cabin at *Villa Verde* adjacent to Monte Celaque Visitors' Centre.

F *Iris*, 3 blocks S of Plaza, 1 block W, opp San Sebastián church, clean, cold water, closes at 2200, disco Sat; **F-G** *San Antonio*, no sign, main street, 2 blocks from Texaco station, clean, pleasant, friendly, good.

G *Erick*, same street as bus office, T 98-40-66, with bath, hot water, TV, comfortable beds, fresh, bright, clean, good value, no washing facilities, stores luggage, and shop open daily with trekker food, very convenient, same street as bus office, rec; **G** *Herrera*, shared bath, noisy, basic; **G** *Hospedaje Corazón de Jesús*, on main street by market, clean, OK; **G** *Hospedaje El Milagro*, N side of market, basic.

● Places to eat
Guancascos and popular cultural centre *Los Lencas*, on Parque Central in front of church, T 98-45-16, owned by Dutch lady, good variety of local and international food, also vegetarian, excellent breakfast, purified water used in fruit juices, rec, music, exhibition of Lenca pottery, tourist information centre, also book swap and good local maps for walking; *Alameda*, 3 blocks W of *La Fonda*, white house, no sign, open 1100-2200 for lunch and dinner, excellent cooking, meat, fish, some vegetarian dishes, salads, main courses US$3-4, *comida corriente* US$2, elegant setting, dining room faces wild garden with fruit trees, not to be missed, under same management is *La Fonda*, 2 blocks S of Parque Central, good food, good value, attractively decorated, rec; *El Señorial*, main street, simple meals and snacks, once house of Dr Juan Lindo; *Comedor Graciano* and *Pollo Gracianito* on main street; *Rancho de Lily*, 3 blocks W of Hondutel, good value, rustic cabin, bar service, good snacks. For breakfast, *comedores* nr the market, or, better, the restaurant at *Hotel Iris* (good *comida corriente* too) or *Guancascos*.

● Banks & money changers
Banco de Occidente.

● Post & telecommunications
Hondutel and Post Office: 1 block S of Parque Central, closes 1100 on Sat.

● Tour companies & travel agents
Guancascos' Tourist Centre, on Parque Central arranges tours and expeditions to Monte Celaque National Parque, local villages and other attractions.

● Transport
To **La Esperanza** a mail car goes Tues, Thur, Sat, 0400, or take bus to Erandique, 1315, get off at San Juan from where bus goes to La Esperanza the next day, or hitch, or rides can be taken on pick-up trucks for US$1.50 (dep 0700 or earlier from S end of main street on highway). The road is much improved as far as San Juan. You can easily find a pick-up this far, 1½ hrs, US$0.90. Thereafter it is all-weather and can be rough. There is a bus service from Gracias to **Santa Rosa de Copán**, US$1, from 0530, 6 times a day, 1½ hrs; beautiful journey through majestic scenery, the road is paved. Daily bus service to Lepaera 1400, 1½ hrs, US$0.85; daily bus to San Manuel de Colohuete at 1300. Cotral bus ticket office is 1 block N of Parque Central.

Southwest from Gracias, up in the Celaque mountains is Belén Gualcho. Also Corquín, San Pedro de Copán and Cucuyagua on or just off the highway between Santa Rosa and Nueva Ocotepeque (see page 943).

GRACIAS TO ERANDIQUE
After Gracias, the road runs 52 km to **San Juan del Caite** (two *hospedajes*, *Lempira* and *Sánchez*, 2 restaurants nearby, helpful people and Peace Corps workers). From here a dirt road runs 26 km S to **Erandique** (*Pop* 10,000), founded in 1560. Set high in pine-clad mountains not far from the border with El Salvador, Erandique is a friendly town, and very beautiful. Lempira was born nearby, and was killed a few kilometres away. The third weekend in Jan is the local *fiesta* of San Sebastián. Best time to visit is at the weekend. Market days are Fri and Sun. Each of the three *barrios* has a nice colonial church. There is one basic *hospedaje*, G, run by the elderly Doña Bárbara in the main street and one simple *Comedor Inestroza* which can serve you

eggs, beans and tortillas; no electricity, torch essential. For the visitor there are lakes, rivers, waterfalls, springs and bathing ponds; you need to ask around. Camping is possible outside town by the small lagoon. Nearby is **San Antonio** where fine opals (not cut gems, but stones encased in rock) are mined and may be purchased. The many hamlets in the surrounding mountains are reached by roads that have been resurfaced or recently built. The landscapes are magnificent.

● **Transport** There are minibuses to Erandique from bridge on road to La Esperanza 1100 daily, although most people go by truck from Gracias (there is sometimes a van service as far as San Juan) or La Esperanza (change trucks at San Juan intersection, very dusty). Return minibus to Gracias at 0500 daily, which connects with the bus to La Esperanza in San Juan. Trucks leave Erandique 0700 daily, but sometimes earlier, and sometimes a second one leaves around 0800 for Gracias, otherwise be prepared for a long wait for a pick-up.

There are several roads radiating from Erandique, including one to **Mapulaca** and the frontier with El Salvador (no migración or aduana or bridge here, at the Río Lempa), a road to San Andrés and another to Piraera (all passable with a car).

LA ESPERANZA

(*Alt* 1,485m) Beyond San Juan del Caite the main, but still rough and stony, road winds through beautiful mountain pine forests 43 km to **La Esperanza**. From there the road continues in good condition 98 km to Siguatepeque. Capital of Intibucá Department, La Esperanza is an old colonial town in a pleasant valley. It has an attractive church in front of the park. There is a grotto carved out of the mountainside W of the town centre, a site of religious festivals. Good views. Market: Thur and Sun, at which Lenca Indians from nearby villages sell wares and food but no handicrafts. Nearby is **Yaramanguila**, an Indian village. The area is excellent for walking in forested hills, with lakes and waterfalls. In Dec-Jan it is very

cold. You can hike to **Cerro de Ojos**, a hill to the NW and visible from La Esperanza. It is forested with a clearing on top littered with many cylindrical holes. No one knows how they were formed, a strange phenomenon. The turning to this hill is on the La Esperanza to San Juan road. Ask for directions.

Local festivals The third week in July is the *Festival de la Papa*. 8 Dec is the fiesta of the Virgen de la Concepción.

● **Accommodation** There are simple but pleasant *pensiones*, eg **E** *Hotel Solís*, T 98-20-80, 1 block E of market, bath and hot water, restaurant, rec; **F** *El Rey*, in Barrio La Morera, T 98-20-78, clean, friendly; **F** *Hotel Mina*, T 98-20-71, good beds, clean, very friendly, 1 block S of market, food available; **F** *Hotel y Comedor San Antonio*; **E** *La Esperanza*, T 98-20-68, with bath, cheaper without, hot water, clean, friendly, good meals; **F** *Rosario*, basic, on road to Siguatepeque; **F** *San Cristóbal*; **F** *San José*, 4 Av Gen Vásquez No C-0005.

● **Places to eat** *Restaurant Magus*, 1 block E of Plaza, 'good food in a formica video bar atmosphere'. Unnamed restaurant in front of Iglesia de la Esperanza, very good *comida corriente*, worth it. *Café El Ecológico*, corner of Parque Central, home-made cakes and pastries, fruit drinks, delicious home-made jams.

● **Banks & money changers** Banco de Occidente, Banco Atlántida and Banadesa.

● **Transport** Buses from La Esperanza to Tegucigalpa several daily (Cobramil, also to San Pedro Sula, and Joelito, 4 hrs, US$2.60), to Siguatepeque 0700, 0900, last at 1000, US$1.20, 2 hrs; bus, La Esperanza, Siguatepeque, Comayagua at 0600; buses also go from La Esperanza to the Salvadorean border; bus stops by market. Hourly minibuses to Yaramanguila, 30 mins. Daily bus to Marcala (time unknown). Daily minibus service to San Juan, dep between 1100-1200 from C 3 opp Quiragua's ice-cream parlour, 2½ hrs, pick-ups also do this journey, very crowded; pick-ups to Gracias, 1 hr; for Erandique, alight at Erandique turn off, 1 km before San Juan and wait for truck to pass (*comedor* plus basic *hospedaje* at intersection).

MARCALA

(*Pop* 10,770; *Alt* 1,300m) An unpaved road of 35 km, bus 2 hrs at 1230 (but check), US$0.75, runs from La Esperanza SE to **Marcala**, Department of La Paz (a paved road goes to La Paz). The Marcala region is one of the finest coffee-producing areas of Honduras. Visit 'Comarca' at the entrance to town to get a good idea of how coffee is processed. *Semana Santa* is celebrated with a large procession through main street. *Fiesta* in honour of San Miguel Arcángel, last week of September. No immigration office.

Excursions During the hotter months, Mar to May for example, a cooler climate can be found in the highlands of La Paz, pleasant temperatures during the day and cold (depending on altitude) at night. Marcala is a good base from which to visit Yarula, Santa Elena, Opatoro, San José and Guajiquiro (see page 883). In the immediate vicinity of Marcala is **Balneario El Manzanal**, 3 km on the road to La Esperanza; it has a restaurant, 2 swimming pools and a boating lake, open Sat and Sun only. For panoramic views high above Marcala, follow this hike (1 hr). Head N past *Hotel Medina*, turn right (E) after the hotel and follow the road up into hills. After 2 km the road branches. Take the left branch and immediately on the left is a football field. A small path leaves from this field on the W side taking you through a small area of pine trees then out onto a ridge for excellent views. The track continues down from the ridge back down to town, passing an unusual cemetery on a hill.

Estanzuela is an area next to a small village of the same name. It is regarded as a favourite spot to visit at weekends. It is a large grassy area next to a river, a dam has been built to provide an area for bathing, excellent camping (no food or drinks sold here). Best visited in the rainy season as the river is higher and the area greener. Take the road to La Esperanza from the Marcala to La Paz road. After 20 mins (by car) take a right hand turning to Estanzuela. It is a 1-hr walk from the turnoff passing the village of Estanzuela to the area.

There are caves nearby on Musula mountain, the Cueva de las Animas in Guamizales and Cueva de El Gigante and El León near La Estanzuela with a high waterfall close by. Other waterfalls are El Chiflador, 67m high, Las Golondrinas, La Chorrera and Santa Rosita. Transport goes to La Florida where there is good walking to the village of **Opatoro** and climbing Cerro Guajiquiro. Between Opatoro and Guajiquiro is the **Reserva Las Trancas**, a heavily-forested mountain where quetzales have been seen.

Yarula and **Santa Elena** are 2 tiny municipalities, the latter about 40 km from Marcala, with beautiful views (bus Marcala-Santa Elena 1230 returns 0500 next day, 2 hrs 45 mins, enquire at Gámez bus office opp market; truck daily 0830 returns from Santa Elena at 1300). Sometimes meals are available at *comedores* in Yarula and Santa Elena. The dirt road from Marcala gradually deteriorates, the last 20 km being terrible, high clearance essential, 4WD rec. In **La Cueva Pintada**, S of Santa Elena, there are precolumbian cave paintings ('*pinturas rupestres*') of snakes, men and dogs; ask for a guide in Santa Elena. Ask also in this village about the 'Danza de los Negritos', performed at the annual fiesta of Santiago, 24-25 Mar, in front of the church. A special performance may be organized, the dancers wearing their old, wooden masks, if suitable payment is offered.

● **Accommodation E** *Medina*, T 98-18-66, the most comfortable, clean, modern with bath, free purified water, highly rec; **F** *Margoth*, very good value; **G** *Hospedaje Edgar*, main street, beginning of town, clean, basic; **G** *Hospedaje Jairo*, with bath, 2 blocks E of main square; **G** *Hotel-Comedor Rosita* at end of main street, opp *Darwin*; **G** *Ideal*.

● **Places to eat** *El Mirador*, on entering town by petrol station, nice views from verandah, good food, rec; *Darwin*, on main street in centre, cheap breakfasts from 0700, rec; *Riviera Linda*, opp *Hotel Medina*, pleasant atmosphere, spacious, a little pricey but good food; *Jarito*, opp market entrance, good; *Café Express*, beside Esso, good breakfast and *comida corrida*, rec.

● **Banks & money changers** Banco de Occidente, Banhcafé, and Banco Sogerín.

● **Entertainment** Discotheque: *Geminis*.

● **Transport** Buses to Tegucigalpa 0500 and 1000 daily via La Paz, 4 hrs (bus from Tegucigalpa at 0800 and 1400, Empresa Lila, 4-5 Av, 7 C, No 418 Comayagüela, opp Hispano cinema); bus to La Paz only, 0700, 2 hrs, US$0.50; several minibuses a day, 1½ hrs, US$1. Bus also from Comayagua. Pick-up truck to San José at around 1000 from market, ask for drivers, Don Santos, Torencio, or Gustavo. Bus to La Esperanza at about 0830, check with driver, Don Pincho, at the supermarket next to where the bus is parked (same street as *Hotel Medina*), 1½ hrs, otherwise hitching possible, going rate US$0.80. Bus to San Miguel, El Salvador, Transportes Wendy Patricia, 0500, 1200, 7 hrs, office half block SE of market.

FRONTIER WITH EL SALVADOR

South of Marcala the road crosses into El Salvador, 3 km before Perquín (see page 797). There have been several confrontations with the Honduran military in the area but the border dispute has been settled by treaty. Ask locally for security conditions but more travellers are reporting no problems in crossing. There are buses from Perquín to the frontier early am. The rustic border crossing office is about 5 km inside Honduras. The road is not shown on some Honduran maps.

NUEVA OCOTEPEQUE

There is an old colonial church, La Vieja (or La Antigua) between Nueva Ocotepeque and the border; it is in the village of Antigua Ocotepeque, founded in the 1540s, but destroyed by a flood from Cerro El Pital in 1934.

National Parks The **Guisayote Biological Reserve** protects 35 sq km of cloud forest, about 50% virgin, reached from the Carretera Occidental. Access is from El Portillo, the name of the pass on the main road N. There are trails and good hiking. El Portillo to El Sillón, the park's southern entrance, 3-5 hrs. Twice daily *buseta* from El Sillón to Ocotepque. **El Pital**, 3 km E of Nueva Ocotepeque, but 2 km vertically above the town, 2,730m; the third highest point in Honduras with several square km of cloud forest. The park has not been developed for tourism.

The **Montecristo National Park** forms part of the Trifinio/La Fraternidad project, administered jointly by Honduras, Guatemala and El Salvador. The park is quite remote from the Honduran side, 2-3 days to the summit, but there are easy-to-follow trails. Access is best from Metapán in El Salvador. From the lookout point at the peak you can see about 90% of El Salvador and 20% of Honduras on a clear day. The natural resources office, for information, is opp Texaco, 2 blocks from *Hotel y Comedor Congolón* at S end of town. Raymond J Sabella of the US Peace Corps has written a very thorough description of the natural and historical attractions of the Department, inc hikes, waterfalls and caves.

● **Accommodation in Nueva Ocotepeque**. **C-D** *Sandoval*, opp Hondutel, T 63-30-98, F 63-34-08, reopened after fire, rooms and suites, breakfast inc, private bath, hot water, cable TV, mini-bar, phone, room service, restaurant attached, good value; **D** *Maya Chortis*, Barrio San José, 4 C 3 Av NE, T 63-33-77, new, nice rooms with bath, double beds, hot water, fan, TV, mini-bar, phone, room service, quieter rooms at back, inc breakfast, good restaurant, good value; **D** *Santander*, new, clean, good restaurant; **E-G** *San Antonio*, 1 C, 3 Av, T 63-30-72, small rooms but OK; **F** *Gran*, with bath, cold water, pleasant, clean, single beds only, about 250m from town at the junction of the roads for El Salvador and Guatemala, just N of town, at Sinuapa; **F** *Hotel y Comedor Congolón*, also bus agency, shared bath, very noisy in am; **G** *Hospedaje del Viajero*, on plaza; **G** *Hotelito San Juan*, pleasant and cheap; **G** *Hotelito Turista*, half block from San José bus terminal; **G** *Ocotepeque* (by Transportes Toritos, clean but noisy).

● **Places to eat** Best at *Sandoval* and *Don Chepe* at *Maya Chortis*, excellent food, main courses US$4-6, small wine lists, good value, rec; **Merendera Ruth**, Parque Central, and **Comedor Nora**, 2 C NE, just off Parque Central, both offer cheap *comida corriente*, preferable to *comedores* around bus terminal.

● **Transport** From Nueva Ocotepeque, buses to San Pedro Sula stop at La Entrada (US$1.70), first at 0030, for connections to Copán. There are splendid mountain views. From San Pedro Sula there are regular buses via Santa Rosa S (6 hrs, US$4.50); road is well paved.

FRONTIER WITH GUATEMALA

You can cross into Guatemala at Agua Caliente, 16 km from Nueva Ocotepeque. There is a Banco de Occidente, a tourist office on the Honduran side, the *Comedor Hermanos Ramírez* for food, and one *hospedaje* (bargain).

● **Honduran immigration**
All formalities completed at the border, open

0700-1800 though the Guatemalan offices at Atulapa are closed 1200-1400. There is an army of money changers outside the Honduran Migración building, keep L10 for exit stamp and L5 for minibus ride Agua Caliente-Atulapa.

● **Guatemalan consulate**
The nearest Guatemalan consulate is in San Pedro Sula, it is no longer possible to get a visa at the border.

● **Transport**
There are several buses a day from San Pedro Sula to Agua Caliente, first at 0300 (eg Congolón, Toritos) US$3.50, 6-7 hrs. Buses from Nueva Ocotepeque to Agua Caliente every 30 mins from 0630. Money changers get on the bus between Nueva Ocotepeque and the border, good rates for US$ cash. Minibuses go to Esquipulas, US$0.25, with connections to destinations in Guatemala.

This can be a busy crossing but in 1997 was described as quicker, cheaper (less graft) and more efficient than the crossing at El Florido.

From Tegucigalpa to the Pacific

FROM THE CAPITAL to the Gulf of Fonseca, with volcanic islands and Honduras' Pacific ports, San Lorenzo and Amapala. Also, the Pan-American Highway routes to El Salvador and Nicaragua, the latter through the hot plain of Choluteca.

TEGUCIGALPA TO GOASCARAN

A paved road runs S from the capital through fine scenery. Just off the highway is **Sabanagrande**, with an interesting colonial church (1809, Nuestra Señora del Rosario 'Apa Kun Ka', the place of water for washing); *fiesta* La Virgen de Candelaria, 1-11 February. Further S is **Pespire**, a picturesque colonial village with a beautiful church, San Francisco, with triple domes. Pespire produces small, delicious mangoes. At **Jícaro Galán** (92 km; *Pop* 3,000) the road joins the Pan-American Highway, which in one direction heads W through **Nacaome** (*Pop* 4,475), where there is a colonial church, to the border with El Salvador at **Goascarán** (*Pop* 2,190). At Jícaro Galán, international buses, eg Ticabus, from San Salvador, Tegucigalpa and Managua meet and exchange passengers.

● **Accommodation** There are hotels of a sort at Goascarán; **Nacaome**: **D** *Perpetuo Socorro*, Barrio el Centro, T 81-44-53, a/c, TV; **F** *Intercontinental* in centre, basic, tap and bucket shower, friendly; **F** *Suyapa*, basic, cheap; and **Jícaro Galán**: **C** *Oasis Colonial*, T 81-22-20, hotel, nice rooms, good restaurant and pool, luxury rest in hot sticky area, and an unnamed, basic guesthouse. Restaurants at all these places.

FRONTIER WITH EL SALVADOR

The Santa Clara bridge over the Río Goascarán is the border with El Salvador. El Amatillo appears to be on both sides of the border.

● **Honduran immigration**
The border closes at 1700. Try to avoid lunchtime when there may be a 2-hr break. This border is very relaxed.

● **Crossing by private vehicle**
Expect to be besieged by *tramitadores* touting for your business. They wear a black and white uniform of sorts with name badges and carry an identity card issued by the border station. Pick any one you like the look of, they can be as young as 12, but will take the strain out of the 3-4 hr border crossing. Expect to pay about US$25 to the various officials on both sides, not all of whom will offer to give you a receipt.

● **Salvadorean consulate**
See Choluteca.

● **Accommodation**
Two cheap *hospedajes*, *San Andrés* and *Los Arcos* on the Honduran side.

● **Exchange**
Moderate rates of exchange from money changers.

● **Transport**
Bus Tegucigalpa-El Amatillo, hourly, US$1.50, 4 hrs. El Amatillo-Choluteca, US$1, 3 hrs, every 30 mins, microbuses.

A temporary pass can be purchased on the Honduran side for US$1.50 for a visit to the Salvadorean **El Amatillo**, for an hour or so. Many Hondurans cross to purchase household goods and clothes.

SAN LORENZO

(*Pop* 21,025) In the other direction from Jícaro Galán, the Pan-American Highway goes S to the Pacific coast (46 km) at **San Lorenzo**, on the shores of the Gulf of Fonseca, a dirty town. The climate on the Pacific littoral is very hot.

● **Accommodation D** *Miramar*, Barrio Plaza Marina, T 81-20-38/39, 26 rooms, 4 a/c, good restaurant, overpriced, in rough dockside area, best not to walk there. Also **E** *Paramount*, and **E-F** *Perla del Pacífico*, fan, bath, comfortable, clean, friendly, central, charming, new block, rec.

● **Places to eat** *Restaurant-Bar Henecán*, on Parque Central, a/c, good food and service, not cheap but worth it, rec. *Restaurant and Disco Don Paco*, main street.

● **Banks & money changers** Bancahorro (changes US$ cash and TCs), **Banco de Occidente**, and **Banco Atlántida** (no exchange); Chinese grocery gives good rates for US$ cash.

● **Transport** Frequent service of small *busitos* from Tegucigalpa to San Lorenzo (US$1) and to Choluteca (US$1.50).

AMAPALA

(*Pop* 7,925) The Pacific port of **Amapala**, on Isla del Tigre, has been replaced by Puerto de Henecán in San Lorenzo, reached by a 3.5 km road which leaves the Pan-American Highway on the eastern edge of San Lorenzo. The **Isla del Tigre** is yet another place reputed to be the hiding-place of pirate treasure. In the 16th century it was visited by a number of adventurers, such as Sir Francis Drake. Amapala was capital of Honduras for a brief period in 1876, when Marco Aurelio Soto was president. Amapala has a naval base, but otherwise it is 'a charming, decaying backwater'. Fishermen will take you, but not by motor launch, to San Lorenzo for a small fee: the trip takes half a day. It is possible to charter boats to La

Unión in El Salvador. The deep-sea fishing in the gulf is good. The 750m extinct volcano, Ampala, on the island has a road to the summit, where there is a US army unit and a DEA contingent. You can walk round the island in half a day.

● **Accommodation B** *Hotel Villas Playa Negra*, Aldea Playa Negra, T 98-85-34, 98-85-80, 7 rooms with a/c, 7 with fan, pool, beach, restaurant poor value, very isolated, lovely setting; **G** *Pensión Internacional* on the harbour, very basic, otherwise only local accommodation of low standard; ask for Doña Marianita, who rents the first floor of her house, **F**; *Al Mar*, above Playa Grande, fan, scorpions, lovely view of mountains and sunset. Bancahorro on Parque Central; several clean *comedores* in the new Mercado Municipal.

● **Places to eat** *Restaurant-Bar Miramar* by the harbour, overlooking the sea, pleasant, very friendly, good meals, hamburgers and boquitas, and you can hang your hammock.

● **Banks & money changers** Banco El Ahorro Hondureño.

● **Hospitals & medical services** Dentist: Oscar Gutiérrez, T 98-81-17.

● **Sports Swimming**: at Playa Grande, black sand, 40 mins' walk from Amapala.

● **Transport** A 31 km road leaves the Pan-American Highway 2 km W of San Lorenzo, signed to Coyolito. It passes through scrub and mangrove swamps before crossing a causeway to a hilly island, around which it winds to the jetty at **Coyolito** (no *hospedajes* but a *comedor* and *refrescarías*). Motorized launches sail between Coyolito and Ampala, US$0.35 pp when launch is full (about 10 passengers), about US$4 to hire a launch (but you will have to pay for the return as well). First boat leaves Amapala at 0700 to connect with first Coyolito-San Lorenzo bus at 0800; next bus from Coyolito at 0900.

The Pan-American Highway runs SE from San Lorenzo past Choluteca and San Marcos de Colón to the Nicaraguan border at El Espino, on the Río Negro. The Pan-American Highway's total length in Honduras is 151 km: 40 km Goascarán-Jícaro Galán, 111 km Jícaro Galán-El Espino.

CHOLUTECA

(*Pop* 87,889) **Choluteca**, 34 km from San Lorenzo in the plain of Choluteca, expanding rapidly. Coffee, cotton and cattle are the local industries. The town was one of the earliest foundations in Honduras (1535) and has still a colonial centre. The church of **La Merced** (1643) is being renovated and will be reconsecrated before the end of the 1990s. The Casa de la Cultura and Biblioteca Municipal are in the colonial house of José Cecilio del Valle on the corner of the Parque Central. The social centre of San José Obrero is at 3 C SO; handicrafts can be bought there. Look out for carved wood, especially chairs. A fine steel suspension bridge crosses the broad river at the entrance into Choluteca from the N (it was built in 1937). The climate is very hot; there is much poverty here.

Excursions

40 km from Choluteca over a paved road (deteriorates after Punta Ratón turn-off) leads to **Cedeño** beach. A lovely though primitive spot, with clean sand stretching for miles and often thundering surf (**NB** the beach shelves sharply); avoid public holiday and weekend crowds. Take a good insect repellent. Spectacular views and sunsets over the Gulf of Fonseca S to Nicaragua and W to El Salvador, with the volcanic islands in the bay.

- **Accommodation & places to eat** Rough accommodation, eg **F** *Miramar*, reasonable, very noisy, loud music; *Cintia*; *Dunia*; all on beach; basic *hospedaje* on main street on road to Cedeño, restaurant *Puestas del Sol*, good, also cabins to rent. Many restaurants on beach, some open only at weekends; *El Tiburón* is popular; *El Ranchito*; and others. Fishermen sell fish straight from the beach.

- **Transport** Hourly bus from Choluteca, US$0.60 (1½ hrs).

A turn off leads from the Choluteca-Cedeño road to Ratón beach, much more pleasant than Cedeño, bus from Choluteca 1130, returns next morning.

Local festivals

The local feast day, of the Virgen de la Concepción, 8 Dec begins a week of festivities, followed by the Festival del Sur, 'Ferisur', which attracts many visitors from Tegucigalpa.

Local information

● **Accommodation**

B *Hacienda Gualiqueme*, T 82-31-29, 82-27-60, past the bridge on way to Tegucigalpa, pool, restaurant.

C *La Fuente*, Carretera Panamericana, past the bridge, T 82-02-53/63, F 82-02-73, with bath, rec, swimming pool, a/c, meals; 1 block away is **D** *Centroamérica*, T 82-35-25, F 82-29-00, a/c, good restaurant, bar, pool, good value; opp is *Restaurant Conquistador*, a bit pricey, but changes money for customers.

D *Camino Real*, road to Guasaule, T 82-06-10, F 82-28-60, swimming pool, good steaks in restaurant, rec; **D-E** *Pierre*, Av Valle y Calle Williams, T 82-06-76, with bath (ants in the taps), a/c or fan, TV, free protected parking, cafetería has good breakfasts, very central, credit cards accepted, rec.

E *Brabazola*, Barrio Cabañas, T 82-55-35, a/c, comfy beds, TV, good; **E** *Pacífico*, nr Mi Esperanza terminal, outside the city, clean, cool rooms, fan, hammocks, quiet, safe parking, fresh drinking water, breakfast US$1.50.

F *Colonial*, main street in centre, clean; **F** *Hibueras*, Av Bojórquez, Barrio El Centro, T 82-05-12, with bath and fan, clean, purified water, *comedor* attached, good value; **F** *Rosita*, with bath, G without, very basic, friendly, modest *comedor*; **F** *San Carlos*, Paz Barahona 757, Barrio El Centro, with shower, fan, very clean, pleasant; **F** *Santa Rosa*, 3 C NO, in the centre, just W of market, T 82-03-55, some with bath, pleasant patio, rec, laundry facilities, clean, friendly; *Tomalag*, moderately priced with bath and fan.

● **Places to eat**

El Conquistador, on Panamericana, opp *La Fuente*, steaks etc, outdoor seating, good, rec; *Palace Imperial*, around corner on Blvd, Chinese, a/c, inexpensive, good; *Frosty*, on main street, owned by *Hotel Pierre*, good food and juices, rec; *Alondra*, Parque Central, old colonial house, open Fri-Sun only; *Comedor Central*, opp side of Parque, *comida corriente* daily specials, *licuados*, sandwiches, good for breakfast. Local specialities are the drinks *posole* and *horchata de morro*.

● **Banks & money changers**

Banco de Honduras, Banco Atlántida, Banco El Ahorro Hondureño, Banco del Comercio,

Banco del País, Bamer, Banco Sogerín, BANFFAA, Banco de Occidente, Blvd Choluteca, open 0800-1630, and on Sat 0830-1130 or 1200. Only Banco de Comercio changes TCs. Can be difficult to exchange money in Choluteca.

● **Embassies & consulates**
The El Salvadorean Consulate is to S of town, fast and friendly, open 0800-1500 daily.

● **Post & telecommunications**
Post Office: 0800-1700, 0800-1200 on Sat, US$0.15/letter for poste restante.
Telephone: collect calls to Spain, Italy, USA only).

● **Shopping**
Mercado Municipal, 7 Av SO, 3 C SO, on outskirts.

● **Tour companies & travel agents**
Travel agency Trans Mundo. *Agencia de Viajes Tropical*, Edificio Rivera y Compañía, T 82-28-31/2.

● **Transport**
Buses to El Espino (Nicaraguan border) from Choluteca, US$1.15, 1 hr, first at 0700, last at 1400. Also frequent minibuses to El Amatillo (El Salvador border) via San Lorenzo, US$1, from bus stop at bridge. Buses to Choluteca from Tegucigalpa with Mi Esperanza, Bonanza and El Dandy; Bonanza continue to San Marcos and depart Tegucigalpa hourly from 0530, 4 hrs to Choluteca, US$1.90. The municipal bus terminal is about 10 blocks from the new municipal market, about 8 blocks from Cathedral/Parque Central; Mi Esperanza has its own terminal 1 block from municipal terminal. **Motoring**: the Texaco service station is just before the bridge.

SAN MARCOS DE COLON

(*Pop* 9,570) Beyond Choluteca is a long climb to San Marcos, 915m in the hills. This clean, tidy town is peaceful and beautifully cool.

● **Accommodation** E *Colonial*, friendly, clean, erratic water supply; F *Hotelito Mi Esperanza*, 1 block W of Banco Atlántida, nr the bus terminal, T 81-30-62, 17 rooms, nice, clean, friendly, cold showers; F *Hospedaje Flores*, friendly, clean, cell-like rooms, washing facilities, breakfast and typical dinner, good, exchange.

● **Places to eat** *Restaurante Bonanza*, nr main square, clean, good food, friendly service; *Parrillada Candilejas*, good food, children's play area; also *Taquería Bonanza*, 2 blocks

from Pan-American highway on road to centre, Mexican specialities, clean, inexpensive.

● **Transport** Bus from Choluteca throughout the day, US$0.75, 1½ hrs; buses from Tegucigalpa, Mi Esperanza, 6 Av 23 or 26 C, Comayagüela and Bonanza, 5 a day from 0530, US$2, 4 hrs.

FRONTIER WITH NICARAGUA AT EL ESPINO

10 km beyond San Marcos the road enters Nicaragua at **El Espino** (*Alt* 890m).

● **Honduran immigration**
Immigration is 100m from the border, open 0800-1600 (till 1630 on Nicaraguan side). Beware of taxis offering to take you to the border after 1600.

● **Nicaraguan consulate**
In Tegucigalpa.

● **Exchange**
Exchange is easy at this crossing for dollars, córdobas, Costa Rican colones and Salvadorean colones but the rate for buying córdobas is better on the Nicaraguan side.

● **Transport**
Taxis/minibuses run from Choluteca and San Marcos to the border. To Tegucigalpa, there is a direct bus through Choluteca with Empresa Esperanza, 4 hrs.

Border formalities can be tedious at El Espino.

FRONTIER WITH NICARAGUA AT RIO GUASAULE

There is another route for Nicaragua from Choluteca to Nicaragua through **El Triunfo** to the border at the bridge over the Río Guasaule. This route is preferred by the international buses, the road is in good condition. It may be worth choosing one of the many 'helpers' to steer you to the correct officials. Fix price beforehand.

Procedures as for El Espino except:

● **Honduran immigration**
Open 0800-1600 but the Nicaraguan side is closed 1130-1400.

● **Transport**
Bus Choluteca-Guasaule, US$1, 45 mins.
   Check conditions in the wet season. Bridge is sometimes closed because of floods.

East of Tegucigalpa

T HE ALTERNATIVE route to Nicaragua, through Danlí and Las Manos: off this road is a detour to old mining centres in the hills.

TEGUCIGALPA TO NICARAGUA

A good paved road runs E from Tegucigalpa to Danlí, 92 km away, in the Department of El Paraíso (gas at Km 28, Km 50, Danlí and El Paraíso). There are no Sigus when leaving Tegucigalpa so ask often. Some 40 km along, in the Zamorano valley (see page 874), is the Escuela Agrícola Panamericana run for all students of the Americas with US help: it has a fine collection of tropical flowers.

SAN ANTONIO DE ORIENTE

At **Zamorano** (Km 29) turn off up a narrow winding road for about 6 km to the picturesque old mining village of **San Antonio de Oriente**, much favoured by Honduran painters such as Velásquez (it has a beautiful church).

Huw Clough and Kate Hennessy describe the hike to San Antonio del Oriente: At Zamorano the bus will drop you off a few 100m before the road junction to San Antonio, from where a small path on the left goes through some trees for 10 mins before joining the main dirt road. From here on up it is a winding, rocky route through tall, thin pine woods, rising quickly for an impressive view of the broad, flat valley. After about 40 mins the main road turns sharply to the right, while a smaller track continues in roughly the same direction along the left-hand slope of a mountain. If you go to the right this leads to **San Antonio del Oriente** after a fairly long climb for an hour. If it is sunny, the path is dusty and glaring and there is little shade in the middle of the day. But reaching the village is a fine reward: red-tiled roofs and white plastered walls clinging to the hillside, with a very quaint little church overlooking the valley. There is one *pulpería*. From here, a steep, 15-mins climb over the ridge leads to San Antonio del Occidente, an even simpler, smaller village (also with one tiny *pulpería*). A much shorter (about 30 mins) walk from San Antonio del Occidente down the other side of the mountain comes back to the junction mentioned above. The hike can be done in reverse, which is probably easier. It is little problem to hitch back to Tegucigalpa.

● **Transport** Direct bus to San Antonio de Oriente from Tegucigalpa at 0630, return trip 0400, US$1.75.

From Zamorano, a road goes to **Güinope**, a pretty, white, dusty town with a church (1820) whose façade is charming. The town is famed for its oranges and jam; try the orange wine 'La Trilla', matured in oak barrels, US$2.50/bottle. Good walking in the area. *Fiesta*, Festival de la Naranja, at the end of March.

● **Accommodation G** *Merlin*, with bath, clean, good value; *Comedor Lilian*, down side street; snack bar next to bus office on Parque Central.

● **Transport** Bus from Tegucigalpa, mercado Jacaleapa, first at 0730, first from Güinope at 0515, frequent service. Some buses to Güinope continue S to San Lucas and San Antonio de Flores.

YUSCARAN

(*Pop* 9,270; *Alt* 1,070m) At Km 47½, a paved road branches S to **Yuscarán**, in rolling pine-land country.

The climate here is semi-tropical. Yuscarán was an important mining centre in colonial days and is a picturesque, typically Spanish colonial village, with cobbled streets and houses on a steep hillside. Ask to see the museum near the town plaza, you have to ask around to find the person who has the key, antiques and photographs displayed in a restored mansion which belonged to a mining family. There is a Casa de Cultura in the former Casa Fortín, open Mon-Sat. The Yuscarán distilleries, one in the centre, the other on the outskirts, are considered by many to produce the best *aguardiente* in Honduras (tours possible). Cardomom plantations are being developed here. The Montserrat mountain which looms over Yuscarán is riddled with mines. The old Guavias mine is close to Yuscarán, some 4 km along the road to Agua Fría. About 10 km further along this road, a narrow, winding road climbs steeply through pine woods to the summit of *Pico Montserrat* (1,891m), with fine views all around. The summit of Montserrat is the **Reserva Biológica de Yuscarán**.

● **Accommodation D-E** new hotel, name unknown, private or dormitory rooms, beautiful views of Nicaraguan mountains in the distance, owned by Dutchman Freek de Haan and his Honduran wife and daughter, T 81-72-13, 81-72-28; **F** *Hotel Carol*, 6 modern rooms with bath and hot water, annex to owner's fine colonial house, safe, family atmosphere, good value; *Cafeteria Colonial*, opp Banco de Occidente, which changes cash and TCs, excellent *desayuno típico* and *comida corriente*.

● **Transport** Frequent buses to Zamorano and Tegucigalpa; from the capital buses leave from Mercado Jacaleapa. For information, ask anyone in the Parque Central in Yuscarán.

DANLI

(*Pop* 30,000; *Alt* 760m) **Danlí**, 102 km from Tegucigalpa, a pleasant town, is noted for sugar and coffee production, a large meatpacking company (Orinsa), and is a centre of the tobacco industry. There are four cigar factories; visit the Honduras-América SA factory (right-hand side of Ciné Aladino) and purchase export quality cigars at good prices (open Mon-Fri, 0800-1200, 1300-1700, Sat 0800-1200), or Placencia Tabacos, on the road to Tegucigalpa to see cigar-making. Museo de Cabildo in the town hall on the Parque Central has a 'funky collection of ancient bric-à-brac, presided over by an elderly curator who is a mine of information about the town and its history' (free).

Local festivals Its *fiesta* lasts all of the 3rd week of Aug (Fiesta del Maíz, with cultural and sporting events, all-night street party on the Sat); it is very crowded with people from Tegucigalpa.

● **Accommodation** Centro Turístico Granada with **C/D** *Gran Hotel Granada*, T 93-24-99, F 93-27-74, bar, cable TV, accepts Visa, restaurant and swimming pool, locals pay half price of non-nationals, rec; **E** *La Esperanza*, Gabriela Mistral, T 93-21-06, next to Esso station, bath, hot water, fan (**D** with a/c), TV, drinking water, friendly, good car parking; **F** *Apolo*, El Canal, T 93-21-77, next to Shell station, with bath, clean, basic; **F** *Danlí*, Calle El Canal, opp *Apolo*, without bath, good; **F** *Eben Ezer*, 3½ blocks N of Shell station, T 93-26-55, basic, hot showers; **F** *Las Palmas*, next to bus terminal but not too noisy; **F** *Las Vegas*, next to bus terminal, noisy, restaurant, washing facilities, parking; **F** *Regis*, 3 blocks N of Plaza Central, with bath, car park, basic; **F** *Xilla*, Barrio Pueblo Nuevo, 4 blocks from bus terminal, with bath, cheap, basic; **G** *Hospedaje San Jorge*, 1 block from *La Esperanza*, shared bath, basic, very run down, broken fixtures, water and electricity problems, avoid.

● **Places to eat** *Pepylu's*, overpriced; *Rancho Típico* nr *Hotel Danlí*, excellent; *Pizzería Picolino*, 2 blocks SW of Parque Central, good pizzas, pleasant atmosphere; *McBeth's*, snack-bar, good ice cream; *Nan-kin 2*, Chinese; *Rodeo*, good food and service; *El Gaucho* and *España*, in the centre of town, are good; *El Paraíso de las Hamburguesas*, cheap, good, owner very friendly; *Comedor Claudio*, good *comida corriente*, good information from locals.

● **Banks & money changers** Banco Atlántida changes TCs without problems. Other banks as well.

● **Hospitals & medical services** Dentist: *Dr Juan Castillo*, Barrio El Centro, T 93-20-83.

● **Transport Local Buses** To Danlí, US$1.20, from Blvd Miraflores in Mercado Jacaleapa (from left hand side of market as you face it), Colonia Kennedy, Tegucigalpa, hourly, 2 hrs, arrive 1½ hrs before you intend to leave, long slow queues for tickets (take 'Kennedy' bus from Calle La Isla nr the football stadium in central Tegucigalpa, or taxi, US$1.20, to Mercado Jacaleapa).

One road continues E from Danlí to Santa María (several buses daily), crossing a mountain range with panoramic views. From Danlí to the N is Cerro San Cristóbal and the beautiful Lago San Julián.

EL PARAÍSO

(*Pop 27,291*) Another paved road goes S 18 km to **El Paraíso**, from which a connecting paved road, 12 km, links with the Nicaraguan road network at Las Manos/Ocotal. El Paraíso is a picturesque town in an area producing coffee, bananas and rice.

● **Accommodation E-F** *5a Av Hotel y Restaurant*, 5 Av y 10 C, T 93-42-98, with bath, hot water, parking, restaurant specializes in

Mexican-American food; **F** *Florida*; **F** *Lendy's*, Barrio Nuevo Carmelo, by bus station, T 93-44-61, clean, friendly, prepares food; **F** *Recreo*, lacking most basic facilities. There are others, but better to stay in Danlí.

● **Places to eat** *Comedor Edith*, on a small square on main road, after Parque Central towards border, US$0.85 for a meal.

● **Banks & money changers** Bancahsa, Banco Atlántida, Banadesa, Bancahorro, Banhcafé, Banco Sogerín.

● **Transport** Minibuses run from Danlí terminal to El Paraíso, frequent (0600 to 1740), US$0.40, 30 mins, don't believe taxi drivers who say there are no minibuses. Emtra Oriente, Av 6, C 6-7, runs 4 times a day from Tegucigalpa to El Paraíso, 2½ hrs, US$1.50; buses from El Paraíso to Las Manos, about every 90 mins, US$0.30, 30 mins, or taxi US$4, many people willing to share, 15 mins bumpy ride.

FRONTIER WITH NICARAGUA
● **Honduran immigration**
Border open 0800-1600. You should not be charged more than US$2 in Honduras.

● **Crossing by private vehicle**
Whether entering or leaving Honduras, you will find *tramitadores* will help you through the paperwork, and are recommended. Total costs are about US$25 and the receipts may not quite tally with what you have paid. This border can be quick: one driver was through in 15 mins (1995).

● **Exchange**
Buy and sell your córdobas in Nicaragua.
This is recommended as the best of the three routes from Tegucigalpa to Nicaragua.

Northeast of Tegucigalpa

THROUGH THE agricultural and cattle lands of Olancho a road runs to Trujillo on the Caribbean coast. Reachable only by air or sea is Honduras' Mosquitia coast with rivers and swamps, coastal lagoons, tropical forests and very few people.

TEGUCIGALPA TO LIMÓN

The Carretera de Olancho runs from the capital through Guaimaca (hotel, **F**, on plaza above restaurant *Las Cascadas*, good value, clean, friendly) and San Diego (restaurant *El Arriero*), to **Campamento**, 127 km, a small, friendly village surrounded by pine forests (*Hotelito Granada* and *Hospedaje Santos*), and on to the Río Guayape, 143 km. By the river crossing at **Los Limones** is an unpaved road N to **La Unión**, through beautiful forests and lush green countryside. **G** *Hospedaje San Carlos*, good vegetarian food; *Hotel La Muralla*, *Hotel Karol* and several *comedores* in La Unión. 14 km N is the **Refugio de Vida Silvestre La Muralla-Los Higuerales**, where quetzales and emerald toucanettes can be seen in Mar-May in the cloud forest. The Park comprises the three peaks of La Muralla, 1,981m, Las Parras, 2,064m and Los Higuerales, 1,985m. Park entrance fee US$1. Cohdefor has an office on the main square for information, closed weekends. You are now required to take a guide with you on the trail. Cost is US$4, arrange in La Unión. The four trails range from 1 km to 10 km and are recommended. Two campsites in the forest (contact Cohdefor

on T/F 22-10-27 for prior arrangements), or there is accommodation for 1-2 at the visitors' centre. When camping you may hear jaguars 'screaming' in the night. Buses from Comayagüela to La Unión, daily, take 4 hrs. (If driving from San Pedro Sula, take the road E through Yoro and Mangulile; from La Ceiba, take the Savá-Olanchito road and turn S 13 km before Olanchito.) To get to the Park, hire a truck from La Unión for about US$18. Little traffic so difficult to hitchhike.

JUTICALPA

(*Pop* 74,000; *Alt* 420m) The main road continues another 50 km from Los Limones to **Juticalpa** (capital of Olancho department), in a rich agricultural area, herding cattle and growing cereals and sugar-cane. Airfield. There is a paved road NE through the cattle land of Catacamas, continuing to just beyond Dulce Nombre de Culmi. The road from Juticalpa to Trujillo on the coast is described below.

● **Accommodation D** *Antúñez*, 1 C NO y 1 Av NO, a block W of Parque Central, T 85-22-50, with bath, E without, friendly, clean, also annex in same street; **E** *Las Vegas*, 1 Av NE, T 85-27-00, central, ½ block N of Parque, cafetería, clean, friendly; **F** *Boarding House Alemán*, rooms, breakfast, lunch and dinner; **F** *El Paso*,

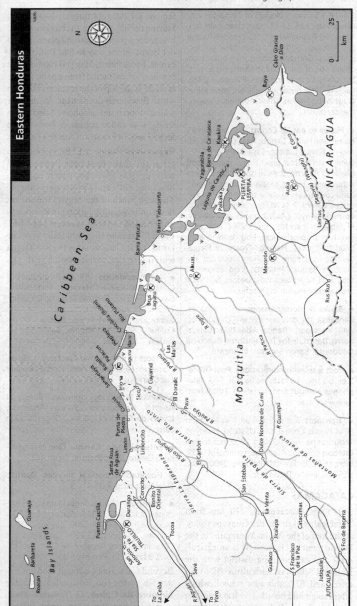

1 Av NE y 6 C No, 6 blocks S of Parque (on way to highway), T 85-23-11, quiet, clean, bath, fan, highly rec; **F** *Familiar*, 1 C NO between Parque and Antúnez, with bath, clean, basic but rec; **F** *Hotelito Granada*, 5 mins from bus station on left side of main road to town centre, basic but rooms are large and clean; **F** *Regis*, 1 C NO, balcony, 1995 building works but good value; **G** *Juticalpa*, clean, basic, shared showers, friendly owner.

● **Places to eat** *El Centro*, 2 C NO; *Dirro's Pizzería* on Parque Central; *Asia*, Chinese food, also on Parque Central; *Casa Blanca*, 1 C SE, quite smart with a good cheap menu, good paella; *El Rancho*, 2 Av NE specializes in meat dishes, wide menu, pleasant; others offering barbecued meats in same area are *El Rodeo* and *La Galera*, 2 Av NE, specializes in *pinchos*; *Comedor Any*, 1a Av NO, good value, friendly; *El Tablado*, 1 Av NE entre 3 y 4 C NO, good fish, bar; *Tropical Juices*, Blvd de los Poetas, good fruit juices; *Helados Frosty*, nr Parque Central, ice creams etc. From 0600 Sat the market in Parque Central has good selection of food, fruit, vegetables and souvenirs, said to be best outdoor market in Olancho.

● **Banks & money changers** Local banks: Bancahsa (the only one that will change TCs, with insistence), Banco Atlántida, Bancahorro, Banco de los Trabajadores, Banco de Occidente, Banco Sogerín, Banhcafé.

● **Post & telecommunications Post Office**: 2 blocks from bus station, hard to find. **Telephones**: Hondutel on main street, 1 block from Parque Central.

● **Transport** Bus station is on 1 Av NE, 1 km SE of Parque Central, taxis US$0.50. Hourly to **Tegucigalpa** from 0330 to 1800; bus to **San Esteban** from opp Aurora bus terminal at 0800, 6 hrs, US$2.25. Bus to **Trujillo** dep 0400, 9 hrs, US$5.20. Bus to **Tocoa** at 0500.

CATACAMAS

(Alt 400m) **Catacamas**, 210 km from Tegucigalpa, is in the Río Guayape valley, at the foot of the Agalta Mountains in the Department of Olancho. It is an agricultural and cattle-raising district with the National School of Agriculture (ENA) in town, and El Sembrador school, which offers room and board. The Río Guayape (named after an Indian dress, *guayapis*) is famous for the gold nuggets found in it. During the hot months, the banks near the bridge are a popular bathing place, at Paso del Burro on the way to San Pedro Catacamas. From Feb to May you can taste the *vino de coyol*, extracted from a palm (a hole is made at the top of the trunk and the sap which flows out is drunk neat). With sugar added it becomes alcoholic (*chicha*), so strong it is called *patada de burro* (mule kick). *Fiesta* St Francis of Assisi, 4 October.

Excursions Hiking to El Boquerón. Stop off at the main road near Punuare and walk up Río Olancho, which has nice limestone cliffs and a pretty river canyon. Through much of the canyon the stream flows underground. Hiking in the mountains behind Catacamas is very beautiful. From Murmullo there are trails to coffee farms. Near Catacamas is the Río Talgua with interesting caves; worth a visit.

● **Accommodation** All **F**: *Las Brisas*, Barrio El Campo, T 95-45-60; *Catacamas*, Blvd Las Acacias, T 95-40-82; *Central*, in Barrio El Centro, T 95-42-76; *Juan Carlos*, rec, good restaurant, Barrio José Trinidad Reyes, T 95-42-12; *La Colina*, T 95-44-88; *Rápalo*, Barrio San Sebastián, T 95-43-48.

● **Places to eat** *Ice and Chicken's*, Calle del Comercio; *La Cascada*, good food; *El Rodeo*; *Los Castaños*.

● **Banks & money changers** Banco El Ahorro Hondureño, Banco Atlántida, Banco de Occidente, Banco Sogerín, all in Barrio El Centro.

● **Entertainment Cinema**: *Cine Maya*, Barrio El Centro. **Discotheque**: *Tacumaca*.

● **Hospitals & medical services Dentist**: Elvia Ayala Lobo, T 95-41-29.

● **Transport** Buses **Tegucigalpa** to Juticalpa/Catacamas, Empresa Aurora, 8 C 615, Av Morazán, hourly 0400-1700, 2½ hrs US$2 to Juticalpa, 3½ hrs US$2.75 to Catacamas. Bus Catacamas-**Dulce Nombre de Culmi** (see below), 3 hrs, US$1.35, several daily.

Beyond Catacamas, a rough road continues NE up the Río Tinto valley to **Dulce Nombre de Culmí**, **G** *Hospedaje Tania*, very basic, on the main street, several *comedores* on the main square. Further on is **Paya** where the road becomes a mule track but in 3-4 days in the dry season a route can be made over the divide (Cerro de Will) and down the Paulaya Río to Mosquitia (see next section). Local police say that there is a path in the dry season from Dulce Nombre to San Esteban (about 30 km).

JUTICALPA TO TRUJILLO

There is a fine scenic road from Juticalpa to Trujillo. From Juticalpa head NE and turn left where the paved road ends, to **San Francisco de la Paz**. Beyond San Francisco is **Gualaco**, which has an interesting colonial church (cheap *hospedajes*); from here to **San Esteban** (**G** *Hotel San Esteban*, very friendly, clean; **G** *Hotel Hernández*; 3 nice *comedores* nearby) you pass Agalta mountain and some of the highest points in Honduras, and the waterfalls on the Babilonia river.

After San Esteban the road continues to **Bonito Oriental** (via El Carbón, a mahogany collection point with Paya Indian communities in the vicinity). There are four hotels here. The final 38 km from Bonito Oriental to Trujillo are paved, through Corocito. There are many dirt roads between San Francisco and Trujillo. If driving, ask directions if in any doubt. Fuel is available in each big village but there is none between San Esteban and Bonito Oriental.

Between the roads Juticalpa-Gualaco-San Esteban and Juticalpa-Catacamas-Dulce Nombre de Culmí lies the cloudforest of the **Parque Nacional Sierra de Agalta**, extending over 1,200 ha and reaching a height of 2,354m at Monte de Babilonia. Several different ecosystems have been found with a wide variety of fauna and flora: 200 species of birds have been identified so far. There are several points of entry. Contact Cohdefor in Juticalpa, Culmí, Gualaco, San Esteban or Catacamas for information on access, maps, guides, mules, lodging etc. There is no infrastructure in the park, but a base camp is being built. A good trail

leads to La Picucha mountain, the highest in E Honduras (2,354m); access strictly on foot, hiking time 2 days. From Gualaco you can hike in 4-5 days up Mt Babilonia (spectacular views over Olancho and Mosquitia); from La Venta you can visit the double waterfall of the Río Babilonia, another track from the E side skirts the flank of Montaña de Malacate.

MOSQUITIA

This is the name given to the region in the far NE of the country, which is forested, swampy and almost uninhabited, but well worth visiting. The western boundary of Mosquitia is Cabo Camarón near Plaplaya and the mouth of the Río Sico. Apart from the one road that stretches 100 km from Puerto Lempira to Leimus and a further 100 km to Ahuasbila, both on the Río Coco, there are no roads in the Honduran Mosquitia. Malaria is endemic in this area; take anti-malaria precautions.

Local information

● **Tour companies & travel agents**

La Moskitia Ecoaventuras, PO Box 3577, Tegucigalpa, T/F 37-93-98, specializes in tours and expeditions in Mosquitia. See also under San Pedro Sula, La Ceiba and Trujillo.

● **Transport**

Air From **Tegucigalpa**: Setco flies Tues and Thur to Mocorón and Puerto Lempira, US$64 one way, US$120 return. T 33-17-11/2; agent in Mocorón is Charly (who also has a restaurant), and in Puerto Lempira the wife of Federico, the local mechanic. Alas de Socorro fly on Tues to Ahuas, and other days if they happen to have a flight there; T 33-70-25. This company charters planes for US$565, but pp it is US$60 one way to Ahuas.

From **La Ceiba**: Isleña has 4 flights a week to Puerto Lempira, T 43-01-79/43-23-54. Many places can only be reached by plane, boat or on foot. SAMi flies to various villages from Puerto Lempira, for example Ahuas, Brus Laguna, Belén. There are expensive express flights to places like Auka, Raya, Kaukira. Alas de Socorro operates from Ahuas to collect sick people from villages to take them to Ahuas hospital, contact the Moravian church (in Puerto Lempira Reverend Stanley Goff, otherwise local pastors will help).

Sea Coastal vessels leave irregularly from La Ceiba to Brus Laguna and Puerto Lempira and back (2-3 day journey), carrying passengers and cargo. Information is available from the Mopawi office in La Ceiba, nr the pier at the railway track, or at the pier itself. Essential equipment: torch. From Trujillo, ask at the dock on the E part of the beach, wait 1½-3 days, take sleeping bag (not rec for women, especially single women: all-male crews). Fare Trujillo-Palacios US$4.50, Brus Laguna US$6.80; sometimes boats go to Puerto Lempira.

PUERTO LEMPIRA

Puerto Lempira is on the large Caratasca Lagoon. In Puerto Lempira is the main office of Mopawi, an organization promoting development of Mosquitia; write to Apdo 2175, Tegucigalpa, T 32-64-74. The airstrip is only 5 mins' walk from town.

Regular *tuk-tuks* (motorized canoes) cross the lagoon to Kaukira, US$1.20 (a nice place, but no hotels or anything), Yagurabila and Palkaka. The *tuk-tuks* leave Kaukira daily, except Sun, at 0500, returning during the morning. In the afternoon the lagoon is usually too rough to cross.

● **Accommodation** D *Gran Hotel Flores*, some rooms with bath, rec; *Villas Caratascas*, huts with bath, restaurant, disco; F *Pensión Moderno* (good, friendly, electricity 1800-2230), and inferior F *Pensión Santa Teresita*, Barrio El Centro, T 98-74-34.

● **Places to eat** *La Mosquitia*, Centro Comercial Segovia in main street, breakfasts and cheap fish; *Glorieta*, left of landing bridge, fish, lagoon breezes; *Delmy*, 3 blocks N of main street, chicken and other dishes, noisy; *Doña Aida*, N side of main road to landing bridge, fresh orange juice; *Quinto Patio*, good breakfasts.

● **Airline offices** SAM, T 98-74-91; Sosa, T 98-74-67.

● **Banks & money changers** Banco Nacional de Desarrollo Agrícola changes dollars at poor rates, bad reputation.

● **Entertainment** Discotheque: *Hampu*, by landing bridge.

Inland by road from Puerto Lempira are **Mocorón** (*Charly's* restaurant, see above, rooms available **F** pp) and **Rus Rus** which

may be visited with difficulty (there is no public transport but any vehicle will give a lift); a beautiful, quiet village (accommodation at Friends of America hospital's house; meals from *Capi's* next door, ask Friends about transport out). A branch off this road leads SE to **Leimus** on the Río Coco and the frontier with Nicaragua. Ask for Evaristo López (at whose house you can get breakfast) who can arrange transport to Leimus, most days, 3-4 hrs for about US$3.50. He is also knowledgeable about area safety.

FRONTIER WITH NICARAGUA

● **Honduran immigration**
If you wish to cross here, obtain your exit stamp in Puerto Lempira. The Office of *Migración* is open until 1100, Mon-Fri. This office is reported as very helpful and a good source of information.

For further details see the section on the Nicaraguan Mosquitia under **The Caribbean Coast**.

It is a 15-min scenic flight above Caratasca Lagoon and grassy, pine-covered savannas to **Ahuas**, 1 hr walk from the Patuca River (fabled for gold). There is a hospital here, as well as four missions, but poor accommodation, not much else besides. **F** *Hospedaje y Comedor Suyapa*, basic, no electricity, meals, US$1.25; mosquito repellent and coils absolutely essential here. Irregular *cayucos* sail down to **Brus Laguna** (Brewer's Lagoon) for US$2.50, at one mouth of the Patuca River, or US$12.50 (15-mins) scenic flight in the mission plane. The airstrip is 4 km from village, take a lift for US$1. There is a disco at the riverside to the left of the bridge. Plague of mosquitoes for all but 5 months of the year (winter and spring). Two tiny hilly islands near the entrance to the wide lagoon were hideouts where pirates once lurked.

● **Accommodation & places to eat** George Goff rents rooms (good but basic, limited electricity, **G**) and his wife Elga cooks tasty meals for US$1, he speaks English and will also help with mission-plane flights. Behind his house is a *hospedaje* being built by the 'Medio-Francés', Colindre (who speaks English, German, French,

'Scandinavian' and Spanish); he operates tours on the Brus Laguna and Río Plátano (can pick up people in La Ceiba if requested). Food and lodging only to those on tour with him. Write to him: Sr Colindre, Brus Laguna, Gracias a Dios, Honduras. Meals generally to be ordered in advance, try *Hospedaje Cruz* or Doña Norma, Doña Aurora or Doña Gladys.

It is better to fly direct from Ahuas via Brus and the mouth of the Río Plátano to mosquito-free **Cocobila** (Belén), picturesquely situated on a sandspit between the ocean and huge, sweetwater Ibans Lagoon. Excellent meals (US$1.25) with Miss Erlinda, but be sure to order in advance; ask at the Mopawi office about accommodation. Boats go to **Plaplaya** at the mouth of the Río Negro or Sico (bad mosquitoes and 'niguas' which burrow into the soles of your feet), or walk the distance in over 2 hrs along the beach. Room and meals with Doña Evritt de Woods at Plaplaya. After Plaplaya is the village of **Raísta**, house to rent (about US$15-US$20 for whole house, sleeps 6). The family cooks for you, rec. There is also a butterfly farm, where they breed butterflies to export. For US$3, Ed will give explanations.

● **Transport** Boats to La Ceiba, or up the Río Sico to Sico. Plátano village at the mouth of the Río Plátano can be reached by lobster boat from Guanaja or by the supply ships from La Ceiba to Brus Laguna (in all cases *cayucos* take passengers from ship to shore); Plátano-Brus Laguna, 1½ hrs, US$2.50 (plus 45 mins-1 hr on foot between the westernmost edge of the lagoon, Barra, and Plátano), Plátano-La Ceiba, US$17.50.

Río Plátano Reserve

The **Reserve** was established by the UN and the Honduran government in 1980 to protect the outstanding natural and cultural resources of the Río Plátano valley and environs. The tropical jungles that still cloak the landscape here shelter a number of endangered birds, mammals, and fish, among them scarlet macaws and harpy eagles, jaguars and tapirs, and the cuyamel, a prized food fish going extinct

throughout Honduras. In addition, there are a number of archaeological sites about which little is known, and the fabled lost White City of the Maya is said to be hidden somewhere in the thick jungles of the Plátano headwaters.

Miskito and Pech Indians living along the lower Plátano cultivate yuca, bananas, rice, corn, and beans, as well as hunting and fishing. The upper (southern) portion of the Plátano watershed was virgin jungle until quite recently, but is being quickly populated by *mestizo* immigrants from the poverty-stricken S of Honduras. These new residents are cutting down the forest to plant crops, hunting wildlife mercilessly, and using homemade dynamite in a very destructive form of fishing. The government's intention in 1995 officially to allow settlers into the Sico and Paulaya valleys, on the western edge of the reserve, was roundly criticized. It was feared that the agrarian reform programme would lead to the desertification of Río Plátano. Given the pressure the Reserve is under, it is recommended to visit it sooner rather than later.

● **Transport** To get there, you can fly or take one of the boats that periodically leave from La Ceiba and Trujillo to either Palacios, Cocobila/Belén or Barra Río Plátano, the main villages in the vicinity of the river mouth. Expect to pay perhaps US$25 for passage from Ceiba or US$5 from Trujillo. A boat from Palacios to Cocobila/Belén cost US$3 pp, US$20 for the whole boat, 45 mins. From Belén to the Biosphere headquarters in Kuri is a 45-min walk or 10-min ride (US$2). The staff and locals are friendly and the staff or the teacher (of the few who can speak Spanish) can probably put you up for the night. They can also help you contract with a *tuk-tuk* (motorized dug-out canoe) to carry you upriver as far as Las Marías, the cost is about US$80 pp return and takes 6-8 hrs (3-4 downstream). Daily boat rental costs about US$20.

Las Marías

A Miskito-Pech village that is the limit of upstream settlement. There is a hospital in Las Marías where you may be able to stay (chocolate and hand woven bags for sale to make money for the community), or ask in the village: 3-4 *pensiones* (**G**), also serving meals, US$1-2, ask for more if still hungry as only small portions served. No drinks for sale, purify your water. The journey upstream to Las Marías, although beautiful, can become very tedious and painful on the back and backside. On arrival in Las Marías, arrange return at once. Birdwatching can provide diversion; there are three species of toucan, tanagers, herons, kingfishers, vultures, hawk eagles, oropendolas. If lucky you may see crocodiles or iguanas.

An alternative route to Las Marías is by boat across Ibans Lagoon, 45 mins by *tuk-tuk*, then 6½ hrs' walk through jungle ('semi-path', hot, mosquitoes, take lots of water and insect repellent, and wear good hiking boots that don't mind getting wet). In Belén, ask for Rosendo Mejía or Segio to act as a guide. Bargain hard for a rate (about US$12.50 pp) and pay separately for the boat trip. Make sure you are paying for one way only.

Once in Las Marías, it is possible to contract villagers for trips upstream in a *pipante*. This is a shallow dugout canoe manoeuvered with poles (*palancas*) and paddles (*canaletes*): remarkably graceful. Each *pipante* can carry up to two passengers and their gear, plus three villagers who pole it upstream. The cost per day to rent *pipante* and crew is about US$12.50 pp (negotiable, you must provide all food, for crew as well). Among the sights are precolumbian rock carvings, some involve a 2-day trip. It is also possible to take an excursion into the forest for 4, or 8 hrs. The walk (or run, it's taken very briskly) is an interesting way to see neotropical jungle, but do not expect to see much wildlife. High prices are charged for everything in Las Marías, but remember that it is their only source of income. On your return, use the radio in Kuri to call Palacios for a boat to fetch you in Belén and don't forget to reserve a flight out of Palacios if you need one. On any trip take drinking water, or water purifiers, food,

insect repellent, sun protection for boat journeys, candles and camping gear.

The rainy season is from June-Dec: it is harder to advance upriver then.

Palacios

Palacios, situated in the next lagoon W of Plaplaya has few mosquitoes; cannons are relics of an old English fort.

One can also cross the lagoon by *cayuco* (US$0.50) from Palacios to the Black Carib village of **Batalla**, from which it is 112 km W along beach to Limón (see below). It is easy to get boats from Palacios to Plaplaya, Raísta (US$15) and Belén. Trips down the Río Plátano are possible, boats have to be arranged through Felix Marmol. Trips can go as far as Las Marías (see above).

● **Accommodation** Room for US$2.50 with Felix Marmol, everyone calls him Don Félix, who has information on boats to lagoons and meals for US$1. **D** *Río Tinto Lodge*, T/F 37-47-93, Don Felix has recently opened this ecotourist hotel, 10 rooms, bath, purified water, all woodwork locally made, beautiful view of Laguna Bacalar, guided tours of Río Plátano Biosphere Reserve, nearby is the World Wildlife Fund's Turtle Conservation Project, also a butterfly farm and a botanical garden. A 7-room *hospedaje* has been built by Trek de Honduras, accommodation for 14 guests, electricity, filtered water, restaurant, 5-day tours (inc fishing expeditions) arranged out of La Ceiba; T 38-19-44/5, Trek de Honduras, or USA 1-800-654-9915, Trek International. Alternatively, you can go independly, at considerably less cost, and ask around for somewhere to stay, eg the local teacher may let you sleep at the school.

● **Transport Air** There are daily flights (except Sun) to Palacios (via Trujillo) from La Ceiba with Isleña, US$25 one way. Flights from Palacios to Trujillo cost US$17 one way. A US$10 fee for entering Mosquitia was introduced at Palacios airport in 1995. **Boat** Two boats, the *Margarita* and the *Sheena Dee* sail irregularly from La Ceiba to Palacios; also fishing boats from Trujillo.

Sico

One can take a picturesque *cayuco* trip from Plaplaya and from Palacios up the Río Sico for US$50 for a hired trip or about US$6 if you can get a lift on a cargo *cayuco* to **Sico** village (contact Mr Carlos Mejía who speaks perfect English and has basic rooms to rent, G, his wife Ofelia sells meals for US$1, also possible food and meals with David Jones, who runs the store). At Sico the remains of a railway built in the late 1920s by a banana company can be seen, including the pillars of a bridge over the river. This was abandoned after disastrous floods in the 1930s. There is no public electricity or piped water in Sico but 2 schools, a health centre and alligators in the river. A strenuous 32 km walk from Sico may be made (only in dry months from Mar to May) up forested Río Paulaya Valley to stay with Mundo Jones, whose father mined gold here for 60 years and on eventually to Dulce Nombre de Culmí (see above).

The beach route out of Mosquitia from Palacios/Batalla is gruelling, past *morenales*, or Black Carib villages (honest, friendly) of Tocoamacho (meals available, boats to Palacios, Reverend Donald Grable is a godsend to benighted travellers), Sangrelaya (2 rooms available, **G**, a woman opposite cooks meals, Catholic mission, ask Max to take you to Tocoamacho by canoe, fix price first, nice trip down river but make sure you don't go out into the sea), Iriona Siraboya (dry weather walk from here across forested mountain to Sico River, and downriver to Sico village) and Cusuna. From Cusuna it is a short distance to **Punto de Piedra** (*pensión*, G) from where you can get a boat to Sangrelaya (see above). From Punto de Piedra there is a strenuous track over to the Río Sico (which at this point is quite close to the coast) at Los Fales and a road

of sorts to **Icoteya** further up river but also on the Río Sico. From Icoteya the Río Sico is navigable downstream to Sico village past the farms of Los Fales, Los Naranjos, Los Andes etc. Here and there they occasionally wash for gold. *Cayucos* can be hired, though expensive. It is also possible to go on foot/horseback along the river from Sico to Los Fales, known locally as the 'Camino Real'.

ROUTE TO LIMON

From Icoteya there are two buses daily to Tocoa through Limoncito (for Limón on the coast) and Francia. In dry weather the bus coming from Tocoa terminates at Punta de Piedra; so far the road on to Iriona is suitable for pick-ups, but no buses run on it. Some 4WD vehicles venture as far as Sangrelaya. Alternatively, you can walk along the beach from Punta de Piedra around the beautiful forested headland of Farellones to Limón, but it is about 40 'interminable' km. You are not advised to sleep on the beach (reports of robberies are increasing) but there are plenty of settlements along the coast. There are buses from La Ceiba and Trujillo to Limoncito and Limón. At **Limón** there is a fine, clean beach, with lovely swimming; accommodation is available at *Hospedaje Martínez* (also serves meals) and there is a friendly *comedor*, *Bar-Restaurant Kerolyn*. This is a Spanish-speaking Garífuna community. 2 buses a day Trujillo-Limón, first at 0830, continuing to Punto de Piedra and Cusuna; from Limón, several buses daily to Tocoa and La Ceiba. The road between Cusuna and Bonito Oriental is good, all-weather, as is the 3 km side road to Limón.

Information for travellers

BEFORE TRAVELLING

ENTRY REQUIREMENTS

● Documents

A visa is not required, nor tourist card, for nationals of all W European countries, USA, Canada, Australia, New Zealand, or Japan. Citizens of other countries need either a tourist card which can be bought from Honduran consulates for US$2-3, occasionally less, or a visa, and they should enquire at a Honduran consulate in advance to see which they need. The price of a visa seems to vary per nationality, and according to where bought. It is imperative to check entry requirements in advance at a consulate. 2-day transit visas costing US$5, for any travellers it seems, are given at the El Florido border for visiting Copán, but you must leave at the same point and your right of return to Guatemala is not guaranteed, especially if your Guatemalan visa is valid for one journey only.

Officials at land borders and airports generally allow only 30 days for visitors, regardless of arrangements made prior to arrival, although some travellers have reported 90 day permits given in airport immigrations. Make sure border officials fill in your entry papers correctly and in accordance with your wishes. Extensions of 30 days are easy to obtain (up to a maximum of 6 months' stay), cost US$5). There are immigration offices for extensions at Tela, La Ceiba, San Pedro Sula, Santa Rosa de Copán, Siguatepeque, La Paz and Comayagua, and all are more helpful than the Tegucigalpa office. A valid International Certificate of Vaccination against smallpox is required only from visitors coming from the Indian subcontinent, Indonesia and the countries of southern Africa. A ticket out of the country is necessary for air travellers (if coming from USA, you won't be allowed on the plane without one); onward tickets must be bought outside the country. (It is not impossible to cash in the return half of the ticket in Honduras, but there is no guarantee and plenty of time is needed.) Proof of adequate funds is sometimes asked for at land borders.

NB It is reported that there is now a 5-lempira tax at land borders. Nevertheless, travellers are often charged more (eg 20 lempiras on entry, 10 lempiras on exit), despite notices asking you to denounce corruption. If officials make an excess charge for entry or exit, ask for a receipt. Do not attempt to enter Honduras at an unmanned border crossing; when it is discovered that you have no entry stamp you will either be fined US$60, or escorted to the border and you have to pay the guard's food and lodging (you may be able to defray some of this cost by spending a night in jail). It is advisable always to carry means of identification, because spot-checks have increased.

● Representation overseas

Belgium, Ave des Gaulois 3, 1040 Brussels, T 322 734-0000, F 322 735-2626; **Canada**, 151 Slater St, Suite 300, Ottawa, Ontario K1P 5H3, T 613 233-8900, F 613 232-0193; **France**, 8 Rue Crevaux, 75116 Paris, T 4755-8645, F 4755-8648; **Germany**, Uberstrasse-1, 5300 Bonn 2, T 228-356394, F 228-351981; **Italy**, Via Boezio No 45, 2do Piso, 00192 Roma, T 396 687-6051, F 395 687-6051; **Japan**, 38

Kowa Bldg, 8F No 802, 12-24 Nishi Azabu 4, Chome Minato Ku, Tokyo 106, T 03 3409-1150, F 03 3409-0305; **Netherlands**, Johan Van Oldenbarneveltlaan 85, 2582 NK Den Haag, T 703-540-152, F 703-504-183; **Spain**, Calle Rosario Pino 6, Cuarto Piso Letra A, Madrid 28020, T 341 579-0251, F 341 572-1319; **Switzerland**, 6 Route de Meyrin 1202, Geneva, T 022 733-6916, F 022 734-5657; **UK**, 115 Gloucester Place, London W1H 3PJ, T 0171-486-4880; **USA**, 3007 Tilden St, Pod 4M, Washington, DC 20008, T 202 966-7702, F 202 966-9751.

● **Tourist information**

The **Instituto Hondureño de Turismo** has its main office at Edificio Europa, Av Ramón E Cruz y Calle República de México, Colonia San Carlos, Tegucigalpa, T 22-40-02, F 38-21-02. There is also an office at Toncontín airport and regional tourist offices (see also under Tegucigalpa, page 878). *HONDURAS tips*, published by *COPAN tips*, edited by John Dupuis in San Pedro Sula, Apdo Postal 2699, T/F 52-95-57, e-mail: hondurastips@globalnet.hn, is a weighty quarterly publication full of interesting and useful tourist information, in English and Spanish, free.

● **Maps**

The **Instituto Geográfico Nacional** produces two 1:1,000,000 maps (1995) of the country, one a tourist map inc city maps of Tegucigalpa, San Pedro Sula and La Ceiba, and the other with a good road network although it does not show all the roads. Both maps widely available in bookshops in major cities and some hotels. There is also a Texaco road map (1992).

HEALTH

Dysentery and stomach parasites are common and malaria is endemic in coastal regions, where a prophylactic regime should be undertaken and mosquito nets carried. Inoculate against typhoid and tetanus. There is cholera, so eating on the street or at market stalls can not be recommended. Drinking water is definitely not safe; drink bottled water which is available amost everywhere. Ice and juices are usually made with purified water. Otherwise boil or sterilize water. Salads and raw vegetables are risky. There are hospitals at Tegucigalpa and all the larger towns. Excellent ointments for curing the all-too-prevalent tropical skin complaints are Scabisan (Mexican) and Betnovate (Glaxo).

MONEY

● **Currency**

The unit is a lempira. It is divided into 100 centavos. There are nickel coins of 5, 10, 20, and 50 centavos. Bank notes are for 1, 2, 5, 10, 20, 50 and 100 lempiras. Any amount of any currency can be taken in or out.

● **Credit cards**

Mastercard and Visa are accepted in major hotels and most restaurants in cities and larger towns. Cash advances from Credomatic, Blvd Morazán, Tegucigalpa, and branches of Bancahsa, Ficensa and Futuro throughout the country. Credomatic represents American Express and issues and services Amex credit cards. Cash advances using Mastercard costs US$10 in banks. Mastercard ATMs at branches of Credomatic, Banco de Occidente or Ficensa at 11 locations, including Tegucigalpa, La Ceiba, Puerto Cortés, Roatán, San Pedro Sula and Tela. For Western Union, money transfers, T 31-10-48. That said, acceptance of credit cards in Honduras is patchy and commissions can be as high as 6%. It is advisable therefore to have available TCs and US$ in cash as well.

Money may be changed at the free rate in banks, but a street market offers rates which are usually higher than the official rate.

GETTING THERE

BY AIR

There are no direct flights to **Tegucigalpa** from Europe, but connecting flights can be made via Guatemala (with KLM or Iberia) or Miami, then American Airlines, or Taca. To Tegucigalpa from New Orleans with Lacsa; from Chicago and Dallas with American Airlines; from Houston with Continental. Taca flies daily from Guatemala City, Mexico City and San Salvador; Lacsa fly to Tegucigalpa from Cancún and San José, La Costena flies from Managua, other Central American cities have connecting flights.

Iberia flies to **San Pedro Sula** via Miami from Madrid and Barcelona twice a week. Lacsa flies to San Pedro Sula from New York, New Orleans, Cancún. American Airlines fly daily from Dallas. Taca, Iberia and American fly direct Miami-San Pedro Sula. Continental flies from Houston daily; Taca daily from Los Angeles. Lacsa flies from San José to San Pedro Sula direct; Taca flies from Belize City and San Salvador. Copa flies from Panama City and Mexico City to San Pedro Sula.

Taca flies to **La Ceiba** and on to **Roatán** from Houston, Miami, New Orleans and San Salvador. Isleña flies from Grand Cayman Island twice a week to La Ceiba.

Caribbean Air flies to Roatán from Belize City.

BY SEA

The *MV Regal Voyager* is a 112-cabin cruise line which sails from Puerto Cortés, Wed, 1800, arriving in Brownsville, Texas, Sat, 0700, returning Sun 1800, getting in to Puerto Cortés Wed, 0600, from US$80 pp, gym, restaurants, cinema, jacuzzi, sauna, casino, duty-free shop. In Tegucigalpa T 38-50-55, F 39-06-66, in San Pedro Sula T 57-58-40, F 53-35-19, in Puerto Cortés T 55-00-45, F 53-13-22.

CUSTOMS

There are no Customs duties on personal effects; 200 cigarettes or 100 cigars, or ½ kg of tobacco, and 2 quarts of spirit are allowed in free.

ON ARRIVAL

● **Border hours**
Note that the border offices close at 1700, not 1800 as in most other countries; there is an extra fee charged after that time.

● **Clothing**
Western; suits optional for most businessmen; on the N coast, which is much hotter and damper, dress is less formal. Laundering is undertaken by most hotels.

● **Hours of business**
Mon to Fri: 0900-1200; 1400-1800 Sat: 0800-1200, and some open in the afternoon. Banks in Tegucigalpa 0900-1500; 0800-1100 only along the N coast on Sat. In San Pedro Sula and along the N coast most places open and close half an hour earlier in the morning and afternoon than in Tegucigalpa. Post Offices: Mon-Fri 0700-2000, Sat 0800-1200.

● **Official time**
6 hrs behind GMT.

● **Shopping**
The best articles are those in wood: straw baskets, hats, etc, are also highly rec. Leather is cheaper than in El Salvador and Nicaragua, but not as cheap as in Colombia. The coffee is good. Note that film can be expensive, but Konica film can be bought for US$4 to US$5 for 36 exposures, eg at Laboratorio Villatoro, stores in major towns. For bulk purchases (say 50 rolls) try their head office on Calle Peatonal, Jardín de Italia, Tegucigalpa.

Sales tax is 7%, often only charged if you ask for a receipt; 10% on alcohol and tobacco.

● **Tipping**
Normally 10% of bill.

● **Voltage**
Generally 110 volts but, increasingly, 220 volts is being installed. US-type flat-pin plugs.

NB Honduras has 2 electric power producers but accidents and water shortages sometimes lead to power cuts.

● **Weights and measures**
The metric system of weights is official and should be used, but the *libra* (pound) is still often used for meat, fish etc. Land is measured in *varas* (838 mm) and *manzanas* (0.7 ha).

ON DEPARTURE

● **Airport tax**
There is a 7% tax on all tickets sold for domestic journeys, and a 10% tax on airline tickets for international journeys. There is an airport departure tax of 95 lempiras (not charged if in transit less than 9 hrs).

FOOD AND DRINK

● **Food**
Cheapest meals are the *comida corriente* or (sometimes better prepared and dearer) the *comida típica*; these usually contain some of the following: beans, rice, meat, avocado, egg, cabbage salad, cheese, *plátanos*, potatoes or yucca, and always tortillas. Pork is not rec as pigs are often raised on highly insanitary swill. *Carne asada* is charcoal roasted and served with grated cabbage between tortillas, good, though rarely sanitarily prepared. *Tajadas* are crisp, fried *plátano* chips topped with grated cabbage and sometimes meat; *nacatamales* are ground, dry maize mixed with meat and seasoning, boiled in banana leaves. *Baleadas* are soft flour tortillas filled with beans and various combinations of butter, egg, cheese and cabbage. *Pupusas* are thick corn tortillas filled with chicharrón (pork sausage), or cheese, served as snacks with beer. *Tapado* is a stew with meat or fish (especially on the N coast), plantain, yucca and coconut milk. *Pinchos* are meat, poultry, or shrimp kebabs. *Sopa de mondongo* (tripe soup) is very common.

Cheap fish is best found on the beaches at Trujillo and Cedeño and on the shores of Lago Yojoa. While on the N coast, look for *pan de* coco (coconut bread) made by *garífuna* (Black Carib) women and *sopa de camarones* prepared with coconut milk and lemon juice.

● **Drink**

Soft drinks are called *refrescos*, or *frescos* (the name also given to fresh fruit blended with water, check that bottled water is used as drinking water is unsafe); *licuados* are fruit blended with milk. Bottled drinking water is readily available in most places. Orange juice, usually sweetened, is available in paper cartons everywhere. *Horchata* is *morro* seeds, rice water and cinnamon. Coffee is thick and sweet. There are five main brands of beer, Port Royal Export, Imperial, Polar, Nacional and Salva Vida (good, more malty than the other 4). Local rum is cheap, try Flor de Caña white or amber 7 years old.

GETTING AROUND

AIR TRANSPORT

There are airstrips in the larger and smaller towns. Isleña have daily services between Tegucigalpa, San Pedro Sula, La Ceiba, and the Caribbean coastal towns and islands. Isleña, Sosa and Caribbean Air connect the mainland with the Bay Islands. Sosa (T 43-08-84 airport) has regular scheduled flights to San Pedro Sula (T 68-17-42), Tegucigalpa (T 33-73-51), Roatán (T 45-18-74 ext 244, 209), Guanaja (T 45-42-19), Utila (T 45-31-61), Puerto Lempira (T 98-74-67), Brus Laguna, Ahuas and Palacios.

LAND TRANSPORT

● **Road**

Buses tend to start early in the day; however, some night buses run between major urban centres. Try to avoid bus journeys after dark as there are many more accidents, mostly owing to the appalling road conditions, and occasional robberies. Hitchhiking is relatively easy. If hiring a car, make sure it has the correct papers, and emergency triangles which are required by law. The main arteries are in excellent condition, but off the main roads standards decline rapidly. Children fill in holes with grit in the hope of receiving a tip.

● **Motoring**

NB There are frequent police searches on entry or exit from towns and villages. Be alert if there are policemen around, they will try to spot an infraction of the laws to collect a fine, eg parking on the wrong side of the road, stopping with your wheels beyond the line at a 'Stop' sign,

seat belt violations. Your licence will be taken until the fine is paid; on-the-spot fines are not legal, but are common. Try to go to a police station. Regular gasoline/petrol costs US$1.45/US gallon on the N coast, US$1.50 in the central region and US$1.52 in remote regions such as the Mosquitia. Super costs US$1.50, US$1.52 and US$1.55 respectively. Unleaded petrol is available everywhere. Diesel costs US$1 and kerosene is US$0.90. Fuel pumps often display price per half gallon.

On entering with a car (from El Salvador at least), customs give a 30-day permit for the vehicle, but transit police only give 8 days entry. This must be renewed in Tegucigalpa (anywhere else authorization is valid for only one department). Charges for motorists appear to be: on entry, US$14 in total for a vehicle with 2 passengers, including provisional permission from the police to drive in Honduras, US$1 (official minimum) for car papers, fumigation and baggage inspection; on exit, US$2.30 in total. Motorcyclists face similar charges. These charges are changing all the time and differ significantly from one border post to another (up to US$40 sometimes). They are also substantially increased on Sat, Sun and holidays and by bribery. You will have to pass through Migración, Registro, Tránsito, Cuarentena, Administración, Secretaría and then a police vehicle check. At each stage you will be asked for money, for which you will not always get a receipt. At El Amatillo border crossing one motorbike rider had to pay US$25 to various officials. You can be fined if you do not have two reflecting triangles and a fire extinguisher in your car. Be prepared for hassle from police and military, both of whom have road check points, especially nr towns, watch out for stop signs ('Alto Repórtese'), but only stop if signalled to do so. Keep cameras and valuables hidden while driving. If unfair fines are demanded, ask to be taken to the police office. If you don't get a receipt, don't pay. No fresh food is allowed to cross the border. On arriving or leaving with a vehicle there are so many checks that it pays to hire a *tramitador* to steer you to the correct officials in the correct order (US$1-2 for the guide).

● **Bicycles**

Bicycles are regarded as vehicles but are not officially subject to entrance taxes. Bicycle repair shops are difficult to find, and parts for anything other than mountain bikes may be very hard to come by. Some buses and most local flights will take bicycles. Most main roads have smooth shoulders and most traffic respects cyclists. It is common for cars to blow their horn to signal their approach.

COMMUNICATIONS

● **Language**
Spanish, but English is spoken in the N, in the Bay Islands, by West Indian settlers on the Caribbean coast, and is understood in most of the big business houses. Trade literature and correspondence should be in Spanish.

● **Newspapers**
The principal newspapers in Tegucigalpa are *El Heraldo*, *La Tribuna* and *El Periódico*. In San Pedro Sula: *El Tiempo*, *El Nuevo Día* and *La Prensa* (circulation about 45,000). English weekly paper: *Honduras This Week*, Edif Berna Exitos 204, Col Rubén Darío, Apdo Postal 1312, Tegucigalpa, T 31-58-21, F 32-23-00, e-mail: hontweek@hondutel.hn, available at limited locations throughout the country, comes out on Sat, costs US$0.35.

● **Postal services**
Air Mail takes 4 to 7 days to Europe and the same for New York. Letters up to 20 grams cost US$0.45 to USA, US$0.62 to Europe (postcard to Europe US$0.50), US$0.70 to Asia. Small packages 500 grams-1 kg, US$3 to USA or Europe; sea mail to Europe US$3 up to 5 kg, US$4.50 up to 10 kg, takes several months. Note that this service is not available in Guatemala, so it might be convenient to send things from Tegucigalpa or San Pedro Sula main Post Offices.

● **Telephone services**
Hondutel provides international telephone, fax and telex services from stations at Tegucigalpa, San Pedro Sula, Puerto Cortés, Tela, La Ceiba, Utila, Roatán, Comayagua, Siguatepeque, Copán (Ruinas), Santa Rosa de Copán, Danlí, Choluteca, Juticalpa, La Paz, La Lima, El Progreso, Valle de Angeles, El Paraíso, Catacamas and Marcala. In 1996 Motorola won a 10-yr concession to establish a cellular phone service with networks in Tegucigalpa and San Pedro Sula.

Telephone service between Honduras and Europe costs about US$25 for a 3-mins call; calls to USA US$2.70/min. Collect calls to N America, Central America and Europe (not possible to Australia, Switzerland or Israel) can be made from Hondutel office in Tegucigalpa. Fax charges are per page, plus 7% tax, to North America US$1.80, to Europe US$2.25, to South America and the Caribbean US$2, to the rest of the world US$3. To receive a fax at Hondutel costs US$1.10/page.

● **Television**
There are six television channels and 167 broadcasting stations. Cable TV is available in every large town.

HOLIDAYS AND FESTIVALS

Most of the feast days of the Roman Catholic religion and also 1 Jan: New Year's Day; 14 April: Day of the Americas; Holy Week: Thur, Fri, and Sat, before Easter Sunday; 1 May: Labour Day; 15 Sept: Independence Day; 3 Oct: Francisco Morazán; 12 Oct: Columbus' arrival in America; 21 Oct: Army Day.

ACKNOWLEDGEMENTS

We are most grateful to Caitlin Hennessy and Huw Clough for updating this chapter on the basis of readers' letters. Our thanks also go to Simon Watson Taylor for extensive research in large parts of the country, Linda Hodson, on Roatán, for her help with the Bay Islands, and Jorge Valle-Aguiluz, in Tegucigalpa, for further revisions.

Nicaragua

NICARAGUA, the same size as England and Wales, is the largest Central American republic. It has 541 km of coast on the Caribbean and 352 km on the Pacific. Costa Rica is to the S, Honduras to the N. Only 8% of the whole country, out of a possible 28%, is in economic use.

HORIZONS

THE LAND

There are three well-marked regions. (1) A large triangular-shaped central mountain land whose apex rests almost on the southern border with Costa Rica; the prevailing moisture-laden NE winds drench its eastern slopes, which are deeply forested with oak and pine on the drier, cooler heights. (2) A wide belt of eastern lowland through which a number of rivers flow from the mountains into the Atlantic. (3) The belt of lowland which runs from the Gulf of Fonseca, on the Pacific, to the Costa Rican border S of Lake Nicaragua. Out of it, to the E, rise the lava cliffs of the mountains to a height of from 1,500 to 2,100m. Peninsulas of high land jut out here and there into the lowland, which is from 65 to 80 km wide along the Pacific.

LAKES

In the plain are two large sheets of water.

The capital, Managua, is on the shores of Lake Managua, 52 km long, 15 to 25 wide, and 39m above sea-level. The Río Tipitapa drains it into Lake Nicaragua, 148 km long, about 55 km at its widest, and 32m above the sea; Granada is on its shores. Launches ply on the Río San Juan which drains it into the Caribbean.

VOLCANOES

Through the Pacific lowland runs a row of volcanoes. The northernmost is the truncated zone of Cosegüina, overlooking the Gulf of Fonseca; then the smoking San Cristóbal, the highest of them all; a number of smaller volcanoes, of which Cerro Negro was built up during its last eruption in 1971; and the famous Momotombo, which normally smokes a little and now has a geothermal power station at its foot. Around Managua, even in the city centre, there are small craters, but none is active. Further S is the twin cone of Masaya/Santiago, which stopped smoking in late 1986, but came back to life in 1995. In Lake Nicaragua is the beautiful Concepción, the second highest, on the Isla de Ometepe, on which also stands the extinct Madera. The volcanic chain continues NW into El Salvador and to the S into Costa Rica. The volcanic ash makes rich soil for crops.

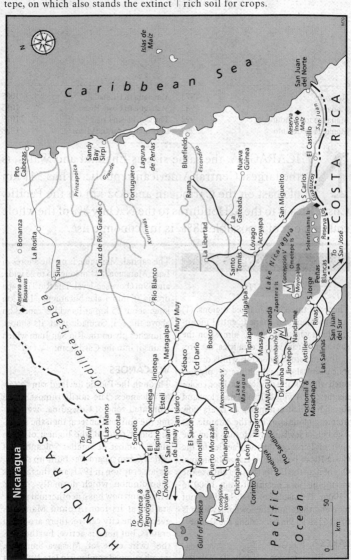

CLIMATE

The wet, warm winds off the Caribbean pour heavy rain on the Atlantic coastal zone, especially in the southern basin of the San Juan River, with more than 6m annually. While the dry season on the Atlantic coast is only short and not wholly dry, the Pacific dry season, or summer (Nov to April), becomes very dusty, especially when the winds begin to blow in February. There is a wide range of climates. According to altitude, average annual temperatures vary between 15°C and 35°C. Midday temperatures at Managua range from 30° to 36°C, but readings of 38° are not uncommon from March to May, or of 40° in Jan and Feb in the W. It can get quite cold, especially after rain, in the Caribbean lowlands. Maximum daily humidity ranges from 90% to 100%.

HISTORY

The Spanish *conquistadores* reached the lowland from Panama as early as 1519. On the south-western shores of Lake Nicaragua they found an area comparatively densely settled by peaceful Indians, who lavished gold ornaments on them. 5 years later another expedition founded colonies at Granada and León, but the flow of gold soon stopped and most of the Spaniards moved elsewhere. In 1570 both colonies were put under the jurisdiction of Guatemala. The local administrative centre was not rich Granada, with its profitable crops of sugar, cocoa, and indigo, but impoverished León, then barely able to subsist on its crops of maize, beans and rice. This reversal of the Spanish policy of choosing the most successful settlement as capital was due to the ease with which León could be reached from the Pacific. In 1858 Managua was chosen as a new capital as a compromise, following violent rivalry between Granada and León.

For more on Nicaragua's early history, see the introductory chapter to Central America. The country became an independent state in 1838. The famous (or infamous) filibustering expedition of William Walker is often referred to in the text.

WALKER'S EXPEDITION

William Walker (1824-1860) was born in Nashville, Tennessee, graduated at the University in 1838, studied medicine at Edinburgh and Heidelberg, was granted his MD in 1843, and then studied law and was called to the bar. On 5 October 1853, he sailed with a filibustering force to conquer Mexican territory, declared Lower California and Sonora an independent republic and was then driven out. In May 1855, with 56 followers armed with a new type of rifle, he sailed for Nicaragua, where Liberal Party leaders had invited him to help them in their struggle against the Conservatives. In October he seized a steamer on Lake Nicaragua belonging to the Accessory Transit Company, an American corporation controlled by Cornelius Vanderbilt. He was then able to surprise and capture Granada and make himself master of Nicaragua as Commander of the Forces. Two officials decided to use him to get control of the Transit Company; it was seized and handed over to his friends. A new Government was formed and in June 1856 Walker was elected President. On 22 Sept, to gain support from the southern states in America he suspended the Nicaraguan laws against slavery. His Government was formally recognized by the US that year. A coalition of Central American states, backed by Cornelius Vanderbilt, fought against him, but he was able to hold his own until May 1857, when he surrendered to the US Navy to avoid capture. In Nov 1857, he sailed from Mobile with another expedition, but soon after landing near Greytown, Nicaragua, he was arrested and returned to the US. In 1860 he sailed again from Mobile and landed in Honduras. There he was taken prisoner by Captain Salmon, of the British Navy, and handed over to the Honduran authorities, who tried and executed him on 12 September 1860. Walker's own book, *The War in Nicaragua*, is a fascinating document.

US INVOLVEMENT

In 1909, US Marines assisted Nicaraguan Conservative leaders in an uprising to overthrow the Liberal president, José Santos Zelaya. In 1911 the United States pledged help in securing a loan to be guaranteed through the control of Nicaraguan customs by an American board. In 1912 the United States sent marines into Nicaragua to enforce the control. Apart from short intervals, they stayed there until 1933. During the last 5 years of occupation, nationalists under Gen Augusto César Sandino waged relentless guerrilla war against the US Marines. American forces were finally withdrawn in 1933, when President Franklin Roosevelt announced the 'Good Neighbour' policy, pledging non-intervention. An American-trained force, the Nicaraguan National Guard, was left behind, commanded by Anastasio Somoza García. Somoza's men assassinated Gen Sandino in Feb 1934 and Somoza himself took over the presidency in 1936. From 1932, with brief intervals, Nicaraguan affairs were dominated by Gen Anastasio Somoza until he was assassinated in 1956. His two sons both served a presidential term and the younger, Gen Anastasio Somoza Debayle, dominated the country from 1963 until his deposition in 1979; he was later assassinated in Paraguay.

1978-79 REVOLUTION

The 1978-79 revolution against the Somoza Government by the Sandinista guerrilla organization (loosely allied to a broad opposition movement) resulted in extensive damage and many casualties (estimated at over 30,000) in certain parts of the country, especially in Managua, Estelí, León, Masaya, Chinandega and Corinto. After heavy fighting Gen Somoza resigned on 17 July 1979 and the Government was taken over by a Junta representing the Sandinista guerrillas and their civilian allies. Real power was exercised by nine Sandinista *comandantes* whose chief short-term aim was reconstruction. A 47-member Council of State formally came into being in May 1980; supporters of the Frente Sandinista de Liberación Nacional had a majority. Elections were held on 4 November 1984 for an augmented National Constituent Assembly with 96 seats; the Sandinista Liberation Front won 61 seats, and Daniel Ortega Saavedra, who had headed the Junta, was elected president. The Democratic Conservatives won 14 seats, the Independent Liberals 9 seats and the Popular Social Christians 6 (the Socialists, Communists and Marxists/Leninists won 2 seats each). The failure of the Sandinista Government to meet the demands of a right-wing grouping, the Democratic Coordinating Board (CDN), led to this coalition boycotting the elections and to the US administration condemning the poll as a 'sham'.

THE SANDINISTAS

Despite substantial official and private US support, anti-Sandinista guerrillas (the 'contras') could boast no significant success in their war against the Government. In 1988, the Sandinistas and the contras met for the first time to discuss the implementation of the Central American Peace Plan drawn up by President Oscar Arias Sánchez of Costa Rica, and signed in Aug 1987. To comply with the Plan, the Nicaraguan Government made a number of political concessions. By 1989 the contras, lacking funds and with diminished numbers, following a stream of desertions, appeared to be a spent force; some participated in general elections held on 25 February 1990. The Sandinista Government brought major improvements in health and education, but the demands of the war against the contras and a complete US trade embargo did great damage to the economy as a whole. The electorate's desire for a higher standard of living was reflected in the outcome of the elections, when the US-supported candidate of the free market National Opposition Union (UNO), Sra Violeta Chamorro, won 55.2% of the vote, compared with 40.8% for

President Ortega. The 14-party alliance, UNO, won 52 seats in the National Assembly, the FSLN 38 and the Social Christian Party one seat. Sra Chamorro, widow of the proprietor of *La Prensa*, who was murdered by Gen Somoza's forces in 1978, took office on 25 April 1990. The USA was under considerable pressure to provide substantial aid for the alliance it created and promoted, but of the US$300mn promised for 1990 by the US Congress, only half had been distributed by May 1991. President Chamorro's refusal to dismiss the Sandinista, Gen Humberto Ortega, from his post as head of the armed forces (EPS), and to drop the Nicaraguan case against the USA at the International Court of Justice, were said to be hindrances to more rapid disbursement. (The Court in The Hague found the USA guilty in 1986 of crimes against Nicaragua in mining its harbours.)

The lack of foreign financial assistance prevented any quick rebuilding of the economy. The Government's scant resources did not permit it to give the disarmed contra forces the land and services that had been promised to them. Demilitarized Sandinistas and landless peasants also pressed for land in 1991, with a consequent rise in tension. Factions of the two groups rearmed, to be known as recontras and recompas; there were many bloody conflicts. Divisions within the UNO coalition, particularly between supporters of President Chamorro and those of vice-president Virgilio Godoy, added to the country's difficulties. Austerity measures introduced in early 1991, including a devaluation of the new córdoba oro, strained the relationship between the administration, Sandinista politicians and the National Workers' Front (FNT), the so-called 'concertación', a pact which the private sector refused to sign. Pacts signed in Jan 1992 between Government, recontras and recompas failed to stop occasional heavy fighting over the next 2 years. In 1994, however, a series of bilateral meetings between previously entrenched parties and ceasefires announced by the EPS and the main recontra group, FN 3-80 (Northern Front 3-80) contributed to a disarmament accord proposed by archbishop Miguel Obando y Bravo between the Government and FN 3-80.

The achievement of a more peaceful state of affairs, if not reconciliation, did not remove other political tensions. After the UNO coalition realigned itself into new political groupings and returned to the National Assembly following a boycott in 1993, the FSLN began to fall apart in 1994. By early 1995, the Sandinistas had become irrevocably split between the orthodox wing, led by Daniel Ortega, and the Sandinista Renewal Movement (MRS), led by Sergio Ramírez. The MRS accused the orthodox wing of betraying Sandinista principles by forming pacts with the technocrats and neoliberals of the government. The MRS was itself accused of opportunism. Linked to this was considerable manoeuvring over UNO-inspired constitutional reform. The National Assembly approved 67 amendments of the constitution, among which were the strengthening of the legislative branch of government at the expense of the executive, and the prohibition of relatives of the president from seeking that office. President Chamorro denied the validity of the reforms, but the National Assembly unilaterally adopted them in Feb 1995.

In 1995 the National Assembly approved legislation governing the 20 October 1996 presidential elections. The frontrunner was Arnoldo Alemán, former mayor of Managua, of the Liberal alliance. His main opponent was Daniel Ortega of the FSLN, who regarded Alemán's policies as a return to Somoza-style government. Among other contenders were Sergio Ramírez, Antonio Lacayo (President Chamorro's son-in-law and former Minister of the Presidency), former ambassador to Italy Alvaro Robelo of Arriba Nicaragua, Virgilio Godoy and the former guerrilla leader Edén Pastora. After reviewing the vote count because of allegations of fraud, the Supreme Electoral Council (CSE) announced on 8 Nov that Arnaldo Alemán had won 51% of the vote compared with 37.7% for Daniel Ortega and the rest divided among the other 21 candidates. The FSLN appealed and called for new elections in Managua and Matagalpa but this was rejected. The OAS declared the elections fair but flawed, with administrative failings. Ortega announced he would respect the legality but not the legitimacy of the Alemán government and a period of political instability was expected. The Liberal Alliance won only 42 of the 93 seats in the National Assembly, while the Sandinistas gained 36 and 9 smaller parties won 14. 48 votes are needed to pass legislation and 56 to amend the Constitution. The outgoing administration passed a swathe of new laws in the interregnum before Alemán became president in Jan 1997 but the Supreme Court declared them null and void on procedural grounds.

SOCIAL CRISIS

As political machinations continue to create uncertainty, the country remains beset by deep economic problems. A report by the Episcopal Conference of Nicaragua (1994) criticized the weakness and corruption of government, which was largely responsible for the social crisis and widespread poverty. A separate report by the United Nations identified poverty and high levels of unemployment as major factors undermining faith in democratic institutions. This report said that 75% of Nicaraguan families lived below the poverty line. Unemployment and underemployment at over 60% was exacerbated by IMF-imposed austerity measures which included substantial lay-offs of public service employees. The inability to match progress in reducing civil conflict with economic and social advances still poses a threat to the stability of the country.

CULTURE

PEOPLE

Population density is low: 34.7 persons to the square km, compared with El Salvador's 268. An odd feature for a country so slightly industrialized is that almost two thirds of its people live in towns and urban population growth is 5.4% a year. 9 in 10 of the people of Nicaragua live and work in the lowland between the Pacific and the western shores of Lake Nicaragua, the south-western shore of Lake Managua, and the south-western sides of the row of volcanoes. It is only of late years that settlers have taken to coffee-growing and cattle-rearing in the highlands at Matagalpa and Jinotega. Elsewhere the highlands, save for an occasional mining camp, are very thinly settled.

The densely forested eastern lowlands fronting the Caribbean were neglected, because of the heavy rainfall and their consequent unhealthiness, until the British settled several colonies of Jamaicans in the 18th century at Bluefields and San Juan del Norte (Greytown). But early this century the United Fruit Company of America (now United Brands) opened banana plantations inland from Puerto Cabezas, worked by blacks from Jamaica. Other companies followed suit along the coast, but the bananas were later attacked by Panama disease and exports today are small. Along the Mosquito coast there are still English-speaking communities of African, or mixed African and indigenous, descent. Besides the *mestizo* intermixtures of Spanish and Indian (77%), there are pure blacks (9%), pure Indians (4%), and mixtures of the two (mostly along the Atlantic coast). A small proportion is of unmixed Spanish and European descent. For a brief survey of the people of eastern Nicaragua, see the introductory paragraphs of **The Caribbean Coast**.

RELIGION AND EDUCATION

Roman Catholicism is the prevailing religion, but there are Episcopal, Baptist, Methodist and other Protestant churches. Illiteracy was reduced by a determined campaign of the Sandinista government in the 1980s. Higher education at the Universidad Nacional Autónoma de Nicaragua at León, with three faculties at Managua, and the private Jesuit Universidad Centroamericana (UCA) at Managua is good. There are two separate Universidades Nacionales Autónomas de Nicaragua (UNAN).

THE ECONOMY

Structure of production

The World Bank classes Nicaragua among the world's poorest countries and its per capita income is the lowest in Latin America. The economy is based on agriculture, which contributes 30% of gdp. The principal export items are coffee, sugar, beef, seafood and bananas. The Government has encouraged a diversification of exports, and exports of tobacco and other agricultural products have gained in importance. Many coffee and cotton growers failed to sow their crops in 1992-93 because of violence and lack of credit. The agricultural sector's decline continued in 1993-94, made worse by a long drought. By 1996 debts owed by over 16,000 farmers to state development banks amounted to US$150mn. The Government announced a 5-year plan to recover the debt in an effort to balance its budget under the IMF programme, but it was deeply unpopular with farmers, who threatened to strike. Coffee prices were down by a third from 1995, while beef prices had halved and farmers called for longer repayment terms at concessionary interest rates.

Main industries are food processing (sugar, meat, shrimps), textiles, wood, chemical and mineral products. Mineral resources are scarce but there are gold deposits which yield about 10% of total exports. Copper and silver are also mined.

Nicaragua: fact file

Geographic

Land area	131,812 sq km
forested	26.3%
pastures	45.3%
cultivated	10.5%

Demographic

Population (1996)	4,272,000
annual growth rate (1991-96)	2.9%
urban	51.7%
rural	48.3%
density	35.2 per sq km
Religious affiliation	
Roman Catholic	89.3%
Birth rate per 1,000 (1995)	34.7
	(world av 25.0)

Education and Health

Life expectancy at birth,	
male	63.0 years
female	67.7 years
Infant mortality rate	
per 1,000 live births (1995)	47.6
Physicians (1994)	1 per 1,566 persons
Hospital beds	1 per 914 persons
Calorie intake as %	
of FAO requirement	102%
Population age 25 and over	
with no formal schooling	n/a
Literacy (over 15)	65.7%

Economic

GNP (1994 market prices)	US$1,395mn
GNP per capita	US$330
Public external debt	
(1994)	US$9,006mn
Tourism receipts (1994)	US$40mn
Inflation (annual av 1991-95)	15.5%
Radio	1 per 4.4 persons
Television	1 per 20 persons
Telephone	1 per 47 persons

Employment

Population economically	
active (1993)	1,489,500
Unemployment rate (1995)	over 18.0%
% of labour force in	
agriculture	30.0
mining	0.6
manufacturing	13.6
construction	2.2
Military forces	17,000

Source Encyclopaedia Britannica

Recent trends

Since the late 1970s gdp has fallen, starting with a decline of 29% in 1979. In 1981-90 it fell by an annual average of 2.4%, with only 1 year of positive growth. In the same period per capita income fell by an average of 5.6% a year. The collapse was caused by guerrilla insurgency, the US trade embargo, fluctuations in Central American Common Market trade, floods, drought and changing commodity prices. Growth has usually been led by agriculture when weather, international prices and political conditions have been favourable.

Inflation has been a problem since the 1972 earthquake; it rose to 84% in 1979 as a result of the civil war, moderating to an average of 30% in 1980-84. As an effect of insurgency requiring heavy budget spending on defence and other difficulties, the rate shot up to an estimated 750% in 1986, 1,200% in 1987 and 24,000% in 1988, while the public sector deficit rose to 27% of gnp. In 1988 a new currency was introduced as part of an anti-inflation package which realigned prices of the dollar and basic goods, but neither this nor subsequent economic packages succeeded in eliminating inflation.

Nicaragua has long been dependent upon foreign aid. It averaged US$600mn a year in 1980-89, of which the USSR is believed to have granted nearly half. The EEC and Canada were the other major donors. Nicaragua's foreign debt, including arrears, amounted to some US$12bn (1990), but reduced foreign exchange earnings since the mid-1980s (partly because of the US blockade) made it impossible for the Government to service any debt other than that owed to multilateral institutions and the Paris Club debtor countries. In Mar 1995 Nicaragua asked the Paris Club to write off US$1.2bn of debt prior to seeking major restructuring terms on commercial bank and other debts. The aim was to reduce its debts to under US$3bn and its debt service to US$120mn a year. In 1996 Russia agreed to write off 90% of Nicaragua's bilateral debt of US$3.4bn and to restructure the remainder over 15 years. Germany also agreed to forgive 80% of bilateral debt, while also granting DM250mn in aid for infrastructure and signing an investment protection agreement. By end-1996 debt forgiveness programmes had cut the total to US$3.8bn.

In 1990 the US-supported Government of Pres Violeta Chamorro took office amid great optimism that the economy could be revived on the back of renewed trade with the USA. Trade sanctions were lifted and the US Congress was asked to provide US$300mn in aid immediately, to be followed by a further US$200mn. Other countries were also asked for US$100mn. These funds were to be used to resume debt service to the IMF and multilateral development agencies, for economic restructuring, for agricultural, oil and medical supplies, to rebuild bridges, schools, roads and hospitals and repatriate and resettle the contra rebel forces and other refugees. However by mid-1991 disbursements had been insufficient to help the administration out of its extremely straightened circumstances. Emergency measures, including the introduction of another new currency, the córdoba oro, failed to stabilize the economy. With the old and new currencies in circulation side-by-side, a shortfall in foreign aid and a consequent lack of economic progress, confidence in each currency collapsed. By 1992, however, progress was apparent in some areas as slow growth resumed and inflation fell to only 3.9%. The trend was reversed in 1993 owing to deep austerity and political instability; gdp fell and inflation rose to 28.3%. In 1994, gdp growth returned, but gdp per capita continued to decline. In the 5 years to 1994 it had fallen by 48%.

Some sectors, eg energy, tourism and gold mining, benefitted from foreign investment in the mid-1990s and the seafood industry showed marked improvement. Overall, though, progress was hampered by the farm crisis, the large trade deficit, a lack of reserves and the demands on resources of what foreign debt was being repaid. Growth was also affected by uncertainties ahead of elections in Oct 1996.

President Alemán promised to continue with the structural adjustment programme of the Chamorro government and to create 100,000 jobs in his first year in office by reactivating agriculture and attracting foreign investment. A feasibility study is underway for a massive infrastructure project which could create 20,000 jobs: a 377-km rail link, or 'dry canal', to link two new deep-water Pacific and Atlantic ports and compete with the Panama Canal for container shipping.

CONSTITUTION

A new Constitution was approved by the 92-member National Constituent Assembly in 1986 and signed into effect on 9 January 1987. Legislative power is vested in a unicameral, directly elected National Assembly of 92 representatives, each with an alternate representative, with a 6-year term. In addition, unelected presidential and vice presidential candidates become representatives and alternates respectively if they receive a certain percentage of the votes. Executive power is vested in the President, assisted by a Vice President and an appointed Cabinet. The Presidential term is 5 years.

COMMUNICATIONS

The main Pacific **ports** are Corinto, San Juan del Sur and Puerto Sandino. The two main Atlantic ports are Puerto Cabezas and Bluefields. The **roads** have been greatly extended and improved. The Pan-American Highway from the Honduran border to the borders of Costa Rica (384 km), is paved the whole way and so is the shorter international road to the Honduran frontier via Chinandega; the road between Managua and Rama (for Bluefields) is paved, but is not in good condition. There are now 15,287 km of road, of which 10% are paved. Until 1 January 1994, there was one operational **railway**, the Ferrocarril del Pacífico, 349 km long, single track, with a gauge of 1.067m. On that date all railway services were suspended and the tracks were torn up although the stations were preserved. One private line remains and a railway museum is being put together. See also **Getting around** and **Further reading** in **Information for travellers**.

Managua

MANAGUA (*pop* 973,760; *phone code* 02), the nation's capital and commercial centre since 1858, is on the southern shores of Lake Managua (Lago Xolotlán), at an altitude of between 40 and 150m. It is 45 km from the Pacific, but 148 km from the main port, Corinto, though a new port, Puerto Sandino (formerly Puerto Somoza), is only 70 km away. Managua was destroyed by earthquake in March 1931, and part of it swept by fire 5 years later; it was completely rebuilt as an up-to-date capital and commercial city but the centre was again completely destroyed, apart from a few modern buildings, by another earthquake in Dec 1972. There was further severe damage during the Revolution of 1978-79.

The Sandinista Government decided that the old centre should be rebuilt, adding parks and recreational facilities, but shortage of funds prevented much progress. The UNO Government subsequently announced similar proposals, including a Parque de la Paz for central Managua; it is anticipated that this project will take years to complete. Present-day Managua has no centre as such, but rather consists of a series of commercial developments in what used to be the outskirts of the old city. No street names are in evidence, and the overall effect can be disconcerting.

The principal commercial areas of Managua are now situated on the Masaya road and the two bypass roads S of the city. These centres contain a variety of shops, cinemas and discotheques.

PLACES OF INTEREST

In the old centre of Managua, one can still see examples of colonial architecture in the **Palacio de los Héroes de la Revolución** (previously the Palacio Nacional and now to be converted to a Palacio Nacional de Cultura) and the **old Cathedral**. The Cathedral is now repaired and open as a museum. Buy the ticket at the Rubén Darío theatre. These buildings are situated on the **Parque Central** and provide a striking contrast with the modern **Teatro Rubén Darío** on the lake shore (good plays and musical events, entry US$1.50 to US$3.50 depending on show; also Sala Experimental) and the Banco de América building in the background. A **new Cathedral** has been inaugurated (1993) 500m S of the Laguna de Tiscapa. It was designed

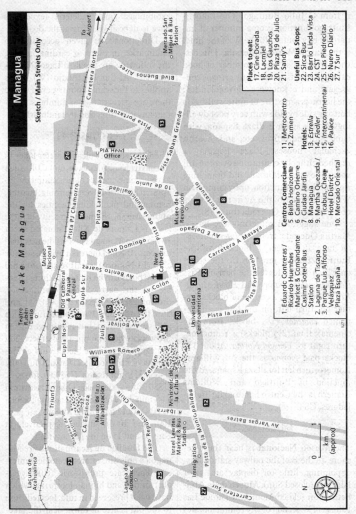

Managua

Sketch / Main Streets Only

Lake Managua

Places to eat:
17. Cine Dorada
18. Lacmiel
19. Los Gauchos
20. Plaza 19 de Julio
21. Sandy's

Useful Bus Stops:
22. Sirca Bus
23. Barrio Linda Vista
24. CST
25. Las Piedrecitas
26. Nuevo Diario
27. 7 Sur

Centros Comerciaes:
5. Bello Horizonte
6. Camino Oriente
7. Ciudac Jardin
8. Managua
9. Martha Quezada / Ticabus, Cheap Hotel District
10. Mercado Orie ıtal
11. Metrocentro
12. Zumen

Hotels:
13. Estrella
14. Fiedler
15. Intercontinental
16. Palace

1. Eduardo Contreras / Ricardo Huembes Market & Ccmandante Casimir Sotelo Bus Station
2. Laguna de Tiscapa
3. Parque Luis Alfonso Velásquez
4. Plaza España

by an Italian architect with an Arabic-style exterior, but an unimpressive interior. Access, for pedestrians only, is from the Metrocentro junction. The **Iglesia Santa María de los Angeles**, Barrio Riguero, was the initial setting for the 'misa revolucionaria' a Catholic/secular mass, interesting wall paintings. The mass is now celebrated only on special occasions and not necessarily at this church.

A significant landmark is the *Hotel Intercontinental*, designed a little like a Maya pyramid, which is about a dozen blocks S of the old Cathedral (not too far to walk). Its entrance is on Av Bolívar and in front of it an area of open land separates it from C Julio Buitrago. The Bolívar-Buitrago junction is on a number of important bus routes. To the W of the hotel is the **Barrio Martha Quezada**. This district, which also has a number of good eating places, is where many gringos congregate and is known as 'gringolandia'; the barrio is a mixture of quite well-to-do housing side by side with very poor dwellings. South again is **Plaza España**, with banks, airline offices, etc, and, nearby, exchange houses. Plaza España is reached either by continuing over the hill above the *Intercontinental* and branching right at the big junction, or by going S on Williams Romero, the Av at the W edge of Barrio Martha Quezada (bus 118).

One suggested route into the Barrio Martha Quezada: from the *Intercontinental* take the street 1 block S of the Buitrago/Bolívar junction (ie the street on which traffic leaves the barrio). Pass *Bar/Restaurant Fanny* and *Hotel Magut*. At Ciné Cabrera, a couple of blocks further on, turn left; on the left is an unnamed *comedor* (1½ blocks from the cinema), then (2½ blocks) a Y-junction; turn right for *Pensión Norma*. About 1½ blocks past *Norma* is the Av Williams Romero; turn left for Plaza España. At the junction of Buitrago and Williams Romero is the Centro Sandino de Trabajadores, CST.

MUSEUMS

The **Museo Nacional** is near the lakeshore, to the E of the railway station, disappointing, little on display and poor labelling (closed Sun). **Museo de la Alfabetización** (closed Mon) near Parque Las Palmas in W section of city commemorates the Sandinista Government's literacy programme. **Museo de Artes Contemporáneos**, opposite the Post Office, features Latin American art donated from all over the continent, open Wed-Sun, 1400-1700, free. **Centro Cultural Ruinas del Gran Hotel**, near Palacio Nacional, permanent display of 'revolutionary' art and visiting exhibitions; small cafeteria (expect to have to deposit your bag at the door).

Directions are given according to landmarks; in place of cardinal points, the following are used: Al Lago (N), Arriba (E), Al Sur (S), Abajo (W). (This applies to the whole country, even where there are street names or numbers, Nicaraguans give direction by landmarks).

EXCURSIONS

There are several volcanic-crater lakes in the environs of Managua, some of which have become centres of residential development and also have swimming, boating, fishing and picnicking facilities for the public. Among the more attractive of these lakes is **Laguna de Xiloá**, situated about 16 km from Managua just off the new road to Léon. At Xiloá there is a private aquatic club (El Náutico); small restaurants and hotels; boats can be rented; bathing possible on the narrow beach (with caves, drownings have occurred). On Sat and Sun, the only days when buses run, Xiloá gets very crowded, but it is quiet during the week, when you must walk there. You can camp there. Take bus 113 to Las Piedrecitas for bus to Xiloá, Sat and Sun only (US$0.35); admission US$1.60 for cars, US$0.30 for pedestrians. Other lakes within a 45-min drive of Managua are the Laguna de Apoyo and Laguna de Masaya (see page 1007 and 1006), situated respectively at Kms 35 and 15 on the Masaya road.

The **Huellas de Acahualinca** are Managua's only site of archaeological interest. These are prehistoric (6,000-year-old) animal and human footprints which have been preserved in tufa, located close to the old centre of town, near the lakeshore at the end of the S Highway. Bus No 102 passes the site, on which there is also a small museum which exhibits a variety of prehistoric artefacts. Entry US$1.50. (The museum was not open in 1996.)

A 10-km drive down Carretera Sur – this is the Pan-American Highway – through the residential section of Las

Piedrecitas passes the US Ambassador's residence to **Laguna de Asososca**, another small lake (the city's reservoir) in the wooded crater of an old volcano. Piedrecitas Park is to one side of the lake: there is a beautiful 3½-km ride, playgrounds for children, a café, and splendid view of Lake Managua, two smaller lakes – Asososca and Xiloá – and of Momotombo volcano. Beyond again is the little **Laguna de Nejapa** (medicinal waters). The Pan-American Highway to Costa Rica passes through **Casa Colorada** (hotel), 26 km from Managua, at 900m, with commanding views of both the Pacific and of Lake Managua, and a delightful climate (but no trees because of poisonous gases from Santiago volcano, see page 1005).

Boats can be hired on the shores of **Lake Managua** for visiting the still-smoking Momotombo and the shore villages (see also page 999). A fine drive skirts the shores of the lake. Do not swim in Lake Managua as it is polluted in places.

LOCAL FESTIVALS

Santo Domingo is the patron saint of Managua. His festival is held at El Malecón from 1 to 10 Aug: church ceremonies, horse racing, bull-fights, cock-fights, a lively carnival; proceeds to the General Hospital. 1 Aug (½ day) and 10 Aug are local holidays.

LOCAL INFORMATION

Warning Avoid arriving at night; public lighting is poor. Pickpocketing is common in the markets and on buses (don't stand near the exit; take care if you are pushed repeatedly). The bus routes to avoid are 105, 110, 112, 114, 116, 117, 118, 119; take a taxi in preference. Thieves tend to be smartly dressed, work in groups and carry knives, take care especially in and near the old cathedral. The 'Miskito Indian' mentioned under Granada, **Warning**, has appeared in Managua with the same story. When our correspondent produced his *Handbook*, he decided not to ask for money!

● Accommodation

Hotel prices

L1	over US$200	**L2**	US$151-200
L3	US$101-150	**A1**	US$81-100
A2	US$61-80	**A3**	US$46-60
B	US$31-45	**C**	US$22-30
D	US$12-20	**E**	US$7-11
F	US$4-6	**G**	up to US$3

Until recently, hotel bills had to be paid in US dollars, now invariably córdobas oro are accepted. 15% tax is added. There is regular water rationing and most hotels do not have large enough water tanks. The Government stipulates a small additional charge for rooms with a telephone (whether used or not). Several hotels have been built along the highway that bypasses the old part of the city. Try to choose a central hotel (ie nr *Intercontinental* or Plaza España) since transport to the outskirts is so difficult. There are, however, 2 good hotels close to the airport, **L2 *Camino Real*** (*Princess Reforma*), Km 9½ Carretera Norte, Apdo Postal C118, T 631381, F 631380, 2 km from terminal, shuttle bus to the airport free, superb, beautiful gardens, new conference hall, no English spoken, restaurant, live music; and **A2 *Las Mercedes***, Km 11 Carretera Norte, T 631011/28, F 631082/3, good food, but expensive, charming open-air restaurant, pleasant hotel but service generally slow, opp airport (4 mins' walk), 3 swimming pools, beware mosquitoes after dark, tennis court, barber shop, all rooms have cable TV, a/c, bath, fridge, phone, local phone calls can be made here when airport office is shut.

L3 *Intercontinental*, 101 Octava C SO, T 286991, 283530/9, F 285208/283087, PO Box 3278, service poor, sauna, use of swimming pool for non-residents on Sun, US$3, bookshop, handicraft shop, buffet, breakfast and lunch (see below), Visa cards accepted, if wishing to take photographs in vicinity, check what is permissible as there is a large military area above and behind the hotel.

A3 *Estrella*, Semáforos de Rubenia 2CN, T 897213, 897010/3, F 897104, a/c, swimming pool, with breakfast, long way from centre, book in advance as it's very popular; **B** *Bed and Breakfast El Carmen*, Costado Sureste a la Iglesia El Carmen en la C Colón, T/F 224114, inc breakfast, a/c, TV, bath, cold water, laundry, pleasant, parking; at Km 8.5 on Carretera Norte is **B** *Cesar*, T 652744, 651800, F 652888, Swiss-run, garden, safe, very good food, garage, swimming pool for children; at

Km 3.5 on Carretera Sur is **B** *D'Lido*, from match factory 2½ blocks S, T 666145, F 664560, restaurant not rec, use of swimming pool by non-residents, US$1; **B** *Las Cabañas*, nr Plaza 19 de Julio, good, helpful, with pool and decent restaurant next door; **B** *Ticomo* at Km 8½, Carretera Sur, T 651427/651273, F 651529, has parking facilities, rents apartments, a/c, with maid service and kitchenette, breakfast extra, good for longer stay; **C** *Casa de Fiedler*, 8a C Sur-Oeste 1320 (W of Barrio Martha Quezada – from CST 2 blocks S and 1½ blocks W), T 666622, with bath and a/c or fan, comfortable, soft mattresses, clean, friendly, popular, accepts TCs, cold Victoria beer sold, good breakfasts, coffee all day, has interesting collection of pre-Columbian ceramics; **C** *Casa San Juan*, C Esperanza 560, T 783220, F 670419, shared bath and private bath, clean, owner's family sleeps in, safe, excellent breakfasts for US$3; **C** *Fragata*, a few blocks from the *Intercontinental*, fan, clean, quiet, friendly; **C** *Magut*, 1 block W of *Intercontinental*, a/c, hot water; **C** *Palace*, Av Pedro A Flores, with a/c and bath (cheaper without a/c), cold shower, toilet paper on request, run down, no restaurant, helpful, TV lounge, quiet, 'free' city tour will cost you US$10-15; **D** *Colón*, nr Sirca bus terminal and road to Masaya, T 782490, with bath and fan, a bit run down, secure, clean, good restaurant.

Many hotels W of *Intercontinental Hotel* in the Barrio Martha Quezada and nr the Cine Dorado (replaced by a restaurant now called *Star Club*, but still ask for 'Cine Dorado'). To get from *Intercontinental Hotel* to the Cine Dorado, walk W for 10 mins to a main N-S road, Av Williams Romero, Cine Dorado is just S. Most hotels here have very thin walls and are therefore noisy.

C-D *Jardín de Italia*, W of *Hotel Intercontinental*, 3 blocks E and ½ block N of Cine Dorado, price depends on a/c, with bath, rec.

D *Hospedaje Carlos* 2 blocks W of Cine Dorado, cold shower, fan, a/c extra, good value, clean, good *comedor* on opp corner.

E *Hospedaje Quintana*, from Ticabus, 1 block N, then ½ a block W, rooms with fan, shared shower (cold), laundry, clean, good value, family-run, rec for longer stays; **E** *Pensión Norma*, shared rooms, basic, friendly, popular (excellent pancakes, breakfast, lunch on nearest corner to this *pensión*); **E** *Hospedaje Meza* one block away on same street (T 22046), very basic, TV; **E** *El Pueblo*, 3 blocks N, 2 blocks E from *Intercontinental*, simple, old house, big rooms,

private bath, friendly; **E** *Gabruina*, T 682169, 1 block S of Ticabus, friendly. See under **International Buses**, below, for accommodation at Ticabus. Many others in same area, eg **F** *El Portal*, shower, friendly, clean, cheap; **F** *Hospedaje Solidaridad*, 2 blocks S from Cine Dorado, with breakfast, dormitories, clean, bar, workshop for wheelchair invalids; **F** *Hospedaje Meléndez*, nr *Comedor Sara*, use of kitchen, no privacy; **F** *El Dorador*, turn left out of Ticabus station, clean, friendly.

Other accommodation in our **E** range or below: *Hospedaje Oriental*, nr Mercado Oriental, clean; *Royal*, nr railway station, shared shower and toilet, nice family, always full (though often guests not obvious); *Sultana*, by the Tica Bus Station, friendly, clean, comfortable in the circumstances, handy if you have an early bus otherwise noisy from 0500, if full, staff will arrange for you to stay at *Mi Siesta* on the other side of town (D with bath and a/c, E no a/c), good, friendly, laundry facilities; **F** *El Molinito*, one street from Tica bus station, inc evening meal, friendly, good value, basic, quiet, clean, safe luggage store, rec; **G** pp *Casa de Huéspedes Santos*, on street leading to *Intercontinental Hotel* in Barrio Martha Quezada, shared rooms, basic, sometimes dirty, spacious courtyard with hammocks, friendly, serves meals, inc breakfasts and snacks.

Camping: vehicle camping possible by the Cruz Roja (Red Cross) on the right side of the old Cathedral. However, we rec you check for security first. Also, 18½ km from the centre, W of Managua on Route 12, 2½ km after the junction with Ruta 2.

● **Places to eat**

The *Hotel Intercontinental* serves enormous breakfasts (0600-1100) for US$8 (plus 15% tax and service charge), and an excellent lunch between 1200 and 1500, US$12 for as much as you want, open to non-residents (best to dress smartly). Bill is made out in US dollars, major credit cards accepted.

In the *Intercontinental*/Plaza España /Barrio Martha Quezada area: *Antojitos*, opp *Intercontinental*, Mexican, a bit overpriced, interesting photos of Managua pre-earthquake, good food and good portions, and garden (open at 1200); a good piano bar next door; opp German Embassy, 200m N of Plaza España is *Bavaria Haus*, German and European specialities, German beer, food and service highly rec, only Spanish spoken, open Mon-Sat 1200-2300. *Taco's*, Av Williams Romero on corner

with and opp road to *Pensión Norma, tacos* and
natural *refrescos*. **Comedor Sara**, next to Ticabus, cheap, popular with gringos, serves
breakfast, has noticeboard; **Doña Pilar**, 1 block
W of Ticabus, cheap, popular; good curries,
vegetarian dishes, other cheap *comedores* in
the area. **Eskimo** ice cream, W of **Intercont**i-
nental and 2 opp Cine Dorado (you can eat at
the factory at Km 3 on Carretera Sur). Cine
Dorado is now **Star Club**. 2 blocks 'a la montaña' from *Casa de Huéspedes Santos* is an
unnamed café with white plastic tables which
serves excellent breakfasts, also lunch, closed in
evening; and a stall (ask for Doña Pilar), half a
block E from the *Santos*, and one block S,
excellent value food, filling and delicious for
about US$2. Near *Santos*, **China Bien Bien**, on
27 de Mayo, 1 block S and 1 block 'abajo' from
CST, T 669045, excellent fast food, Chinese. **La**
Bambu, 1 block E of Ticabus, excellent vegetarian breakfasts. **Las Anclas**, 1 block from Casa
Santos, good seafood. **Mirnas**, nr Pension
Norma, open 0700-1500, very good breakfasts
and comidas.

On Carretera a Masaya: *La Carreta* (Km 12),
rec; *Sacuanjoche* (Km 8), international cuisine;
Lacmiel (Km 4.5), good value, a/c, real ice
cream, *Los Gauchos*, steaks (Km 9.5), *Nerja*,
on the highway a few 100m from the bypass,
good; *La Marseillaise*, Colonia Los Robles,
French. **Sandy's** is the poor local version of
MacDonalds, one on Carretera a Masaya, Km 4,
and 2 other branches. Vegetarian: **Soya Res-**
taurant, just off the Carretera on Pista de la
Municipalidad; *Licuado Ananda*, just E of Estatua Montoya, open for breakfast and lunch.

On Carretera Sur, Km 8½, *César*, specializes in
European food and Swiss desserts; at Km 6½
is *The Lobster's Inn*, very good seafood.

Other recommendations: cheap meals at Mercado Huembes, but look to see what you're
getting first. **Bella Venezia**, Barrio San Cristobal,
1 block up, ½ S from the El Dorado traffic light,
Italian, family run, good. **Mirador Tiscapa**, overlooking Laguna Tiscapa, good food, slow service,
live music 2000-2400 (0200 Sat, closed Wed);
Naturaleza, bakery nr Tiscapa (E from **Intercon**-
tinental, turn right at drycleaners, after 2 blocks
turn left, bread sales at 1100). Opp Metrocentro
is *El Cartel*, local dishes; *Rincón Criollo* on Plaza
Julio Martínez, similar. If you can find it, try the
local fish, *guapote*, excellent eating. Another hint:
look out for private houses selling food on the
street, follow the barbecue smell. Cheap places
close by 2100.

● **Airline offices**
Around Plaza España: **Nica** (T 663136), **Aer-**
oflot, **Iberia** (T 664440), **KLM** (300m E),
Lufthansa, **Continental** (T 782834, next to
Multicambio); in Colonia Los Robles (Carretera
a Masaya), **Copa** (T 670045), **Taca** (T 662898),
Cubana (E of Plaza 19 de Julio, turn right on
road opp *Restaurant Lacmiel*, T 73976). **La**
Costeña (for the Atlantic coast), at the airport,
T 631228. **American Airlines**, T 663900; **Avi-**
ateca, T 631929; **Lacsa**, T 663136. Foreigners
may pay in dollars or córdobas for internal flight
tickets, but dollars only for international tickets.

● **Banks & money changers**
Banco Nicaragüense del Interior y Comercio
at Plaza España changes bank notes only. *Casas*
de cambio; **Buro Internacional de Cambio**,
0830-1200, 1300-1600, 250m S of traffic lights
by Plaza España, for US$ cash and TCs, 2%
commission (also Mexican and other Central
American currencies, but at very poor rates);
Multicambio SA opp Plaza España on same
road; behind Ed Oscar Pérez Cazar at Km 4.5
on road to Masaya, takes Mastercard, open
0900-1200, 1400-1600; at terminal for
Granada buses, several in Ciudad Jardín; much
quicker than banks (ask taxi drivers) It is advisable to change money in Managua as it is
difficult elsewhere, though getting easier. Present TC receipts in banks when changing them.
Córdoba cash advances on Visa, Mastercard and
Visa at **Cred o matic**, Camino Oriente on Carretera a Masaya, Mon-Fri 0800-1645, Sat 0800-
1200, commission 2½% on cash advances but
not officially detailed in the charge. **BanPro**,
Carretera a Masaya, nearer Metrocentro and
subway sandwich shop also advances cash on
Visa at 2½% commission, open Mon-Fri 0830-
1630, Sat 0830-1300. Banks on Plaza España
advertize Visa but do not have facilities to advance cash to foreigners. Many public places,
like more expensive restaurants, will change
money at the official rate (see also **Currency** in
Information for travellers). Dollars cash can be
changed on the street: first ask in a bank for the
current exchange rate, then ask the *coyotes*, the
illegal money changers on the street. Those on
Av Batahola, W of Mercado Lewites, and at
Mercado Oriental offer good rates; those nr
Hotel Intercontinental offer low rates and try to
cheat. Always take great care; always check the
rate first, ask for large denomination notes
(*coyotes* try to confuse gringos with small bills)
and leave the scene as quickly as possible.

● **Cultural centres**
Lending library, *Casa Ben Linder*, 3 blocks S
1½ blocks E of Estatua Monseñor Lezcano, also
good book exchange, T 66-4373. *Alianza
Francesa*, nr Mexican Embassy, films on Fri
evenings, friendly. A *Casa de Cultura* has
opened behind the Palacio Nacional with an art
gallery, shops and cafés.

● **Embassies & consulates**
Panamanian Consulate, Reparto Pancasán,
Hotel Colón 1 street N, 25 varas ariba, opp Super
Rápido, T/F 781619/670158, open 0830-1300,
visa on the spot, valid 3 months for a 30-day
stay, US$10, maps and information on the Ca-
nal; **Costa Rican**, Montoya 11/2 streets E, C 27
de Mayo, T 285573, F 283227. **Honduran**
Consulate, after Km 11 on Masaya road (opp
Guatemalan), open Mon-Fri, 0800-1400 (bus
118 from *Hotel Intercontinental*), Embassy,
Planes de Altamira 64, T 670184, F 670183;
Guatemalan, just after Km 11 on Masaya road,
T 799609, F 799610, visa US$10, fast service,
0900-1200 only. **Mexican**, from *Lacmiel* on
Carreta a Masaya take the 2nd street on the left
and it's at the first cross roads on your right,
T 775886, F 782886. **Venezuelan**, about 1 km
closer to city on same road (Km 10.5, T 760267,
F 678327).
  USA, Km 4½ Carretera del Sur (T 666-010,
F 663865); **Canadian Consul**, 208 C del Tri-
unfo, frente Plazoleta Telcor Central, T 24541.
  British, El Reparto, 'Los Robles', Primera
Etapa, Entrada Principal de la Carretera a
Masaya, Cuarta Casa a la mano derecha,
T 780014, F 784083, Tx 2166, Apdo Aéreo
169, it is located on a R-turn at the Telsat shop,
off Carretera a Masaya; **French**, Km 12 Carretera del Sur, T 226210, F 281057; **Dutch**, del
Canal 1 cuadra al norte, 1 cuadre al oeste, Apdo
3534, T 666175, F 660364; **Swiss**, c/o Cruz
Lovena SA, Km 6.5 Carretera Norte entrada de
la Tona, Apdo Postal 166, T 492671; **Swedish**,
from Plaza España, 1 block W (Abajo), 2 blocks
to the Lake, ½ block W (Abajo), Apdo Postal
2307, T 660085, F 666778; **Danish** Cosulate
General, Iglesia del Carmen, 2 cuadros al Oeste
No 1610, T/F 286351/668095; **Finnish**, Hospital Militar 1 street N, 1½ W, T 667947/663415;
German, 200m N of Plaza España (towards
lake), T 663917/8, open Mon-Fri 0900-1200;
Italian, Km 15 Carretera al Sur, T 666486,
F 663987.

● **Entertainment**
Ballet: Ballet Tepenahuatl, folkloric dances in
the ruins of the *Gran Hotel*.

Cinemas: most films in English with Spanish
sub-titles (US$0.50). *Cinemateca*, on Av Bolívar
(behind Cine González), Government theatre
with good programmes (only US$0.20 on Sun
am). Also good screen and sound on Carretera
Masaya.

Discotheques: *Lobo Jack*, Camino de Oriente,
T 670123, the largest disco in Central America.
La Cabaña in the *Intercontinental* and the
Piano Bar across the street, the latter is a
cultural experience. *La Cavanga*, trendy new
bar next to the Centro Cultural Managua.

● **Hospitals & medical services**
Hospitals: are generally crowded and queues
very long. Recommended is *Hospital Alemán-
Nicaragüense HNA*, from Siemens on Km 6 of
Carretera Norte, 3 blocks S, operated with German aid, mostly Nicaraguan staff, make an
appointment by phone in advance. Private clinics are an alternative, eg *Policlínica Nicaragüense*, consultation US$30. *Dr César
Zepeda Monterrey* speaks English, American-
trained. *Dr Sergio López*, Clínica SA Helena,
Monte de los Olives, Los Robles, T 787228, good
but speaks Spanish only. Medicines are in short
supply, take your own if possible though supplies to farmacias are now improving.

● **Language classes**
Spanish classes: and thorough introduction to
Nicaragua: *Casa Nicaragüense de Español*,
Km 11.5 Carretera Sur; accommodation with
families. *Universidad Centroamericana* has
Spanish courses which are cheaper, but with
larger classes.

● **Post & telecommunications**
General Post Office: 3 blocks W of Palacio
Nacional and Cathedral, 0700-1600 (closed Sat
pm). Wide selection of beautiful stamps. Poste
Restante (Lista de Correos) keeps mail for 45
days, US$0.20 per letter. There is another Post
Office in the Centro Comercial Managua.

Telecommunications: Enitel, same building as
Post Office. Mercado Roberto Huembes
(Eduardo Contreras), on bus route 109 from
Hotel Intercontinental, open 0700-2230. The
Enitel office in Barrio Altamira (take taxi) sells an
excellent phone directory for US$6 which is also
the best tourist guide. For sending faxes, use the
Enitel office in the Palace of Communications
downtown (4 pages to USA US$4).

● **Shopping**
Some handicrafts (goldwork, embroidery, etc)
are available in the Centro Comercial Managua;

good general shopping here and at Mercado Huembes (also called Eduardo Contreras), both on Pista Portazuelo (buses 110 or 119). The Mercado Huembes and the Mercado Oriental both have a wide selection of handicrafts. At the Mercado Oriental you can get just about anything, on the black market. Good shopping also at Metrocentro, Pista de la Municipalidad. Best bookshops at the Centro Sandinista de Trabajadores, Ho Chi Minh Way, and in the Centro Antonio Valdivieso, C José Martí, nr *Mirador Tiscapa* (also sells records), and at the Centro Comercial Managua; see *Amatl Libro Café* above. Many bookshops sell maps, postcards, badges, stickers and other touristy items. Postcards for sale at Tourist Office, Ministry of Culture, Mercado Huembes and *Intercontinental Hotel* (several times more expensive); also at Tarjetas Gordión. Most ordinary shops are in private houses without signs. Almacenes Internacionales (formerly Dollartienda, and Diplotienda), opp *Los Gauchos* restaurant on Carretera a Masaya, offers Western-style goods, take your passport, accepts dollars and TCs if to value of purchase. There is an a/c supermarket on Plaza España.

● **Sports**

Baseball: between Plaza de España and Plaza 19 de Julio on Sun mornings (the national game), a good seat US$0.20.

Also there are basketball, cockfighting and bullfighting (but no kill), swimming, sailing, tennis, golf.

● **Tour companies & travel agents**

Nueva Turnica, Av 11 SO, 300m, 2 mins S from Plaza España, T 661387/660303, F 668805, sells maps of Managua and of the country. It offers tours of Managua, US$20 pp, Masaya, US$20 pp, Granada and León, US$35 pp each, Matagalpa, US$38 pp, and Isla de Ometepe, US$42 pp, in all cases minimum 2 people.

● **Tourist offices**

Ministry of Tourism, 1 block W of *Hotel Intercontinental*, enter by side door, Apdo Postal 122, T 222962/223333/281337, F 281187. Airport T 331539. Information service T 112. Standard information available, inc on all types of transport in the country. Maps of Managua dated 1993, and whole country on reverse, US$2. They will help with finding accommodation with families, with full board. There is a new ecotourism pack, put together by the Nicaraguan Council of Churches, the Nature Conservancy and Ministry of Natural Resources, of special interest to those keen to visit the rainforest.

● **Useful addresses**

Customs: Km 5 Carretera del Norte, bus No 108.

Immigration: Pista de la Municipalidad, approx 1 km from Km 7 Carretera del Sur, open till 1400. Buses 118 and 110.

● **Transport**

Local Bus: service in Managua is cheap and as good as can be expected under the circumstances. US$0.13 approximately. Buses can be very full, though not always so. City buses run every 10 mins 0530-1800, every 15 mins 1800-2200, when last services begin their routes; buses are frequent but it is difficult to fathom their routes. Beware of pickpockets on the crowded urban buses particularly those on tourist routes (see **Warning** above). The principal bus routes are: 101 from Las Brisas, passing CST, *Intercontinental Hotel*, Mercado Oriental, then on to Mercados San Miguel and Mayoreo; 103 from 7 Sur to Mercado Lewites, Plaza 19 de Julio, Metrocentro, Mercado San Miguel and Villa Libertad; 109 from Teatro Darío to the Bolívar/Buitrago junction just before *Intercontinental*, turns E, then SE to Casimir Sotelo bus station/mercado Huembes, 110 runs from 7 Sur to Villa San Jacinto passing en route Mercado Lewites, Plaza 19 de Julio, Metrocentro, Mercado Huembes/Casimir Sotelo bus station and Mercado San Miguel; 113 from Ciudad Sandino, Las Piedrecitas, CST, *Intercontinental*, to Mercado Oriental; 116 runs E-W below *Intercontinental*, on Buitrago, also passing CST; 118 takes a similar route but turns S on Williams Romero to Plaza España, thence to Israel Lewites bus station; 119 runs from Plaza España to Casimir Sotelo bus station via Plaza 19 de Julio; 123 runs from Mercado Lewites via 7 Sur and Linda Vista to Telcor Sur (nr Palacio Nacional), and Nuevo Diario. A map from Mathias Hock Services (see **Further reading** in **Information for travellers**), the Tourist Office (poor), and a couple of days riding the buses will help you orient yourself. **Car hire**: Hertz, Avis and Budget. **Hertz** at the airport (T 31862/31237), *Hotel Intercontinental* (T 222320), or Edif Caribe Motors, Km 4 Carretera Sur, T 668399, F 668400. Rates are US$30/day Group A to US$65/day Group G (all a/c), unlimited mileage, US$10/day accident protection, tax not inc, discounts for 2 weeks or more. Given the poor public transport and the decentralized layout of Managua, you may find that renting a car is the best way to get around. Alternatively hire a taxi for journeys out of Managua, about US$10/hr from an office opp *Hotel Intercontinental* (opens 0930). **Renault garage**: Km 6 Carretera Norte, in front of Coca Cola; efficient spare parts service. Volvo at *Las Piedricitas*, English spoken. **Taxis**: can be flagged down along the street. They also cruise the bus stations looking for arriving passengers, but it is cheaper to get a taxi on the street nearby. There is a taxi stand just below *Hotel Magut*, W of *Intercontinental*. Taxis are the best method of transport for foreigners in Managua; bargain the fare before entering (fares range from US$0.40-US$1.50; US$10 from airport, although if you share the fare is only US$1.10 pp). You pay per zone. **NB** It may be handy to have the telephone number of your hotel with you. Street names and numbers are not universal in the city and the taxi driver may not know your destination.

Air César Augusto Sandino (MGA), 12 km E of city, nr the lake, being modernized 1997. Take any bus marked 'Tipitapa' from Mercado Huembes, Mercado San Miguel or Mercado Oriental (nr Victoria brewery), US$0.16. Alternatively take a taxi for no more than US$7. Be early for international flights since formalities are slow and thorough and can take 2 hrs. X-ray machines reported safe for film. Two duty free shops, café, toilets through immigration; some departing passengers (eg on Aviateca and Nica flights) are offered free coffee, juice and a *pastel* in the departure hall. Internal flights to eg Bluefields and the Corn Islands are given in the text below. You are not allowed to stay overnight in the airport. There is a bank at the airport which closes at 1600 and it is difficult to obtain local currency elsewhere at the airport.

Train All rail services were suspended on 31 December 1993. The ruins of the station are 5 blocks E of the old Cathedral.

Bus The Comandante Casimir Sotelo bus station by the Mercado Roberto Huembes (Mercado Eduardo Contreras), on Pista Portazuelo (see map), is for Rivas, Granada, Masaya, Estelí, Somoto, Matagalpa, etc, and all destinations in the N. Take bus 109, which starts from Parque Central and runs below the *Hotel Intercontinental*, or bus 119. For full details, see under destinations. For **León**, **Corinto** and **Pacific Coast** and **Chinandega**, the terminal is beside Mercado Israel Lewites, Pista de la Municipalidad, on SW side of city. To get from the first bus station to the second, take bus 110, or take bus 109, then change at *Intercontinental* to bus 118. It is probably simpler to take a taxi, US$3. Buses to **Boaco**, **Juigalpa** and **Rama** leave from the Terminal Atlántico at Mercado San Miguel, on Pista Sabana Grande, in the E of the city. Buses tend to be very full; children scramble on board first, grab seats and 'sell' them to passengers. Possible (and safer) to sit on your luggage than put it on the roof. You may have to pay extra for your baggage. Cotran, T 897820; Cotlántico, T 800036; AMSA, T 652138.

International buses: look in *El Nuevo Diario* Sección 2, 'Servicios', for buses running to San Salvador, Tegucigalpa, Guatemala City and Mexico. Ticabus to San José daily at 0600, 0700, US$15 single, 11 hrs; also to Panama (US$35), Tegucigalpa (0500, US$20), San Salvador (US$35) and Guatemala City (US$43), terminal is in Barrio Martha Quezada (Cine Dorado, 2 cuadras arriba, W of *Hotel Intercontinental*, T 222096/223031); passengers can stay overnight at the terminal for US$6 pp. Sirca Express leaves 0600 Mon, Wed, Fri and Sat to San José, US$30, 13 hrs (inc 1 hr minimum at border, you can stop anywhere in Costa Rica, but same price); Sirca office and terminal Puente Los Robles, Km 4.5 Carretera a Masaya, T 673833. A cheaper way of travelling to San José is to take a bus Managua-Rivas, then colectivo to border and another between the border posts, then take local bus to San José; takes 15 hrs altogether, cost about US$8. Similarly, taking local buses to Tegucigalpa will cost you about US$5. International buses are always booked-up many days in advance and tickets will not be sold until all passport/visa documentation is complete. **NB** If arriving in Managua with Ticabus beware touts who try to take you to hotels; their commission will be added to your hotel bill.

PACIFIC BEACHES

There are several beaches on the Pacific coast, about an hour's drive from Managua. The nearest are **Pochomil** and **Masachapa** (54 km from Managua, side by side, bus service from terminal in Israel Lewites market every 35 mins, US$1 to Pochomil) and **Casares** (69 km from Managua, dirty, thorns on beach; 2 restaurants. A few km from Casares is **La Boquita**, visited by turtles from Aug to Nov. Otherwise La Boquita beach is to be avoided, frequent muggings and unreliable tap water supplies. Because of their proximity to the capital, these are very popular during the season (Jan-April) and tend to be somewhat crowded. Out of season, except at weekends, Pochomil is deserted (don't sleep on the beach, mosquitoes will eat you alive); it is clean and being developed as a tourist centre with hotels and restaurants. Few hotels at present, **B** *Baja Mar*, with a/c, **C** without, basic, not worth the money; **D** *Alta Mar*, new. Masachapa is cheaper but dirtier; hotels on beach, **F** (but *Terraza* not rec); **D** *Hotel Summer* on the main street to the beach, restaurant, fair; **F** *Hotel Rex*, very very basic. Very slow bus journey from Managua. Near Pochomil and Masachapa is the *Montelimar* resort, built by the Sandinistas, now owned by Spain's Barceló group. It is expensive and becoming popular with package tours. It has a broad, unspoilt sandy beach ideal for bathing and surfing; 202 apartments in bungalows, a/c, minibar, cable TV, bathroom, 'largest swimming pool in Central America', 2 smaller ones, fine restaurant, several bars, disco, fitness centre, shops, laundry, tennis, casino. The nearest public transport is 3 km away at Masachapa, taxi from Managua US$30 (70 km), or hire a car. Reservations T Managua 284132/33/37/45, F 284146.

A visit to the broad, sandy **El Velero** beach (turn off at Km 60 on the old road to León and then follow signs) is recommended despite the US$3.50 entrance charge and poor road. All facilities controlled by the INSSBI, for the benefit of state employees, and at weekends is fully booked for weeks in advance. You may be able to rent a cabin (E for 2) in the week, pay extra for sheet and pillows. You can eat in the restaurant (*Pirata Cojo*, not cheap), at the INSSBI cafeteria (bring your own utensils, buy meal ticket in advance, or take your own food). However, the beach itself is beautiful, and the sea is ideal for both surfing and swimming. **El Tránsito** is a beautiful, undeveloped Pacific beach; bus from Managua at 1200, 1315, 1500 (from Terminal Lewites), return at 0600 or 0700, US$0.70. Good cheap meals from Sra Pérez on the beach (possible accommodation); *Restaurant Yolanda*; beach flats for 4-6 people normally available mid-week at N end (Centro Vacacional de Trabajadores, good value).

Managua to Honduras

THERE ARE THREE border crossings to Honduras, the Pan-American Highway gives access to each. After leaving Lake Managua, the road goes through hilly country, with various types of agriculture, mining and pines. A detour through Matagalpa and Jinotega enters good walking country. Estelí, a major centre, has, like many other places, evidence of Revolution damage.

The Pan-American Highway runs from Managua to Honduras (214 km) and is paved the whole way. Also paved is the branch road to Matagalpa and Jinotega. The border crossing with Honduras on the Pan-American Highway is through Somoto to El Espino (see below).

TIPITAPA

The first stretch of 21 km to Tipitapa is along the southern edge of Lake Managua. **Tipitapa**, to the SE of the lake about 2½ km away from the shore, on the other side of the Highway, was a tourist resort with hot sulphur baths and a casino. This was in ruins but the resort has been re-opened and you can swim in clean water in the baths. There is a colourful market, and a *fiesta* of El Señor de Esquipulas on 13-16 Jan. Swimming in El Trapice park, US$0.50.

● **Accommodation** There is a *Hospedaje (Lazo)* at the main road junction.

● **Places to eat** *Salón Silvia*, unpretentious. Slightly cheaper, but good, is the a/c restaurant attached to the thermal baths. *Entre Ríos*, helpful, looks like the best in town.

● **Buses** From **Managua**, Mercado Huembes, via La Fanisa, Waspan, La Subasta, Aeropuerto and Zona Franca, every 10 mins 0530-2100, 45 mins, US$0.25. Bus to **Estelí**, US$1.40, pick up on the carretera coming from Managua, every 30 mins, 0455-1755. Bus to **Masaya**, US$0.35, every 20 mins 0500-1900, 1 hr, change there for Granada.

The Pan-American Highway goes N through Tipitapa to Sébaco, 105 km. 14 km before reaching Sébaco is **Ciudad Darío** (off the main road, turning to the W), where the poet Rubén Darío was born; you can see the house, which is maintained as a museum. **F** *Hospedaje El*, 1½ blocks before the bridge on left, basic, friendly. Cheap good food from *Comedor Crismar* on Plaza Central. In **Sébaco** there is **D** *Motel El Valle*, on the highway 1 km towards Ciudad Darío, with restaurant, clean, fan, shower, quiet, patio with pool, English and Italian spoken. East of the highway is **Esquipula**, 100 km from Managua, 2½ hrs by bus, a good place for hiking, fishing, riding; **F** *Hotel Oscar Morales*, clean, shower, friendly.

MATAGALPA

From Sébaco a 24-km branch road leads (right) to **Matagalpa** (*pop* 95,270; *alt* 678m; *phone code* 061), in the best walking country in Nicaragua. Matagalpa has an old church, but it is about the only colonial style building left; the town has developed rapidly in recent years. It was badly damaged in the Revolution, but is undergoing reconstruction, regaining much of its original character. The birthplace of Carlos Fonseca is now a museum (apparently closed 1996), 1 block E of the more southerly of the 2 main squares; in the northerly square (with the Cathedral)

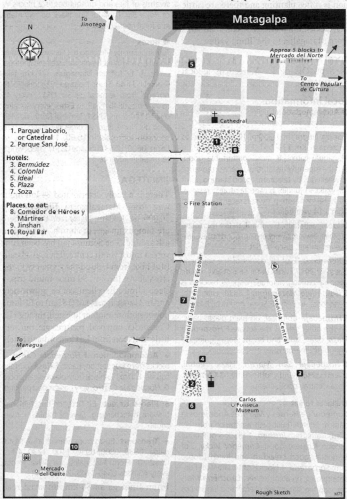

Matagalpa

To Jinotega

N

Approx 5 blocks to
Mercado del Norte

To
Centro Popular
de Cultura

5

Cathedral

1
8

9

1. Parque Laborío,
   or Catedral
2. Parque San José

Hotels:
3. *Bermúdez*
4. *Colonial*
5. *Ideal*
6. *Plaza*
7. *Soza*

Places to eat:
8. Comedor de Héroes y
   Mártires
9. Jinshan
10. Royal Bar

Fire Station

Avenida José Benito Escobar

Avenida Central

$

7

To
Managua

4

2

3

6

Carlos
Fonseca
Museum

10

Mercado
del Oeste

Rough Sketch

M75

is a Galería de los Héroes y Mártires
though little more than 30 or so photos
and used as an office. The Centro Popular
de la Cultura is 2½ blocks N, 4 blocks E
from the NE corner of the Cathedral
plaza. The town has a very erratic water
supply. There is a small zoo in the northern
suburbs along the river. The main occupation is coffee planting and there are cattle
ranges; the chief industry is the Nestlé
powdered-milk plant. A 32-km road runs
from Matagalpa to the Tuma valley.

Local festivals
24 Sept, Día de La Merced, is a local
holiday.

Local information
● **Accommodation**
Many places shut their doors by 2200-2300.

C *Selva Negra*, at 1,200m, 10 km on road to
Jinotega at Km 139½, T 23883, F 658342 (in
Managua), cabins, **B**, more comfortable, good,
as is the expensive restaurant (reserve in advance
at weekends by telegram), good starting point
for walks in jungle, private rainforest reserve,
ask hotel for free map, owners recently returned
from a 14-year exile.

D *Ideal*, with bath, **E** without, better rooms are
upstairs, beware overcharging, good but expensive restaurant, disco on Sat.

E *Bermúdez*, E of NE corner of the southerly
plaza, T 3439, with bath, reasonably clean,
good car parking, helpful, meals; ½ block W is
E *Hospedaje Matagalpa*, T 3834, with bath,
clean, light and airy; **E** *Soza*, opp river, basic.

F *Hospedaje Colonial*, on main plaza, basic;
on the other side of the square **F** *Hospedaje
Plaza*, clean, small and bright rooms, quiet, no
sign, basic, inexpensive.

G *Hospedaje San Martín*, Plaza Central,
shared bath, friendly, often dirty; **G** *Comelor*,
Plaza Central, good, cheap.

● **Places to eat**
Comedor de Héroes y Mártires Anónimos in
park nr church (built with assistance from Tilburg, Neth), rec; *Jinshan*, 1 block S of Parque
Laborio, Chinese, good; *Comedor Vicky*, S of
cathedral, good breakfast and lunch (closed
pm); *Sorbetería*, 1 block E of square with Fonseca quotes, on a corner, rec; *Lanchería Mar-
cia*, opp fire station, excellent value lunch; *Los
Pinchitos Morenos*, nr the centre, good and

cheap; *Pizzas Don Diego*, opp cinema; *Chepi*,
good and popular.

● **Banks & money changers**
Banco Nacional de Desarrollo. Money changers nr the Cathedral offer 'interesting' rates.

● **Shopping**
Mercado del Norte, close to northern highway
(filthy); Mercado del Oeste, unfriendly *comedor*,
swarms of flies and mosquitoes, is 2 blocks W
of *Royal Bar*. Look for fine black pottery made
in a local cooperative.

● **Buses**
Terminal Sur, by Mercado del Oeste for destinations N, S and W inc Managua, Estelí and Jinotega:
every ½ hr to/from **Managua**, 127 km, take
3 hrs, US$1.40. From **Tipitapa**, 2½ hrs. To Ji-
notega, from Terminal del Sur, US$1, every 45
mins, 2 hrs, 0545-1745; to Estelí, every 30 mins,
0520-1720, 2 hrs, US$1. Terminal Norte, by Mer-
cado del Norte, is for all other destinations. Taxi
between terminals US$0.50. 1 bus a day to
León, 0600, US$3 (luggage US$1); check which
terminal in advance.

JINOTEGA
There is a badly deteriorated 34-km highway from Matagalpa to **Jinotega** (*pop*
20,000; *alt* 1,004m; *phone code* 063). There
are famous images in church, if not open,
ask around. The Somoza jail has been converted into a youth centre. There is a beautiful hike from behind the cemetery to the
cross above the city, 90 mins round trip, a
steep climb. Excellent coffee grown here
and in Matagalpa. Road (18 km) to El Tuma
power station; another to Estelí, through La
Concordia, unpaved, picturesque, but very
little transport from La Concordia to Estelí.

● **Accommodation** **F** *Hospedaje Carlos*, 2
blocks from bus station, basic; **F** *Rosa*, nr main
square; **F** *Tito*, ½ block from plaza, clean, food;
G *Hospedaje Castro*, very basic, good parking.

● **Places to eat** *El Tico*, nr bus terminal,
beware overcharging. Several banks nr main
square.

● **Transport** Buses from Managua via Matagalpa, 0630, 0800, 0930, 1100, 1230, 4 hrs,
US$2.70. From Matagalpa via Selva Negra,
every 45 mins 0545-1745, 2 hrs, US$1.

From Jinotega an 80-km, unpaved road
goes to the main highway at Condega,

51 km from the Honduran border (see below). This road passes through **San Rafael del Norte** (F *Hospedaje Rocío*, shared bath, reasonable, good food; **E** *Hospedaje Aura*, basic, dirty). There are some good murals in the local church, and a chapel on the hill behind, at Tepeyak, built as a spiritual retreat; very interesting recent history, involved in Sandinista struggle. Trucks from Jinotega market to San Rafael del Norte at 0700, 0800 and 0900, thereafter regular buses; trucks to Estelí at 0700, US$1, 3 hrs. The road passes through another picturesque village, **Yalí**.

The 134-km section from Sébaco (see above) to the border at El Espino is through sharp hills with steep climbs and descents, but reasonably well banked and smooth.

A reasonable road leads off the Pan-American Highway 10 km NW of Sébaco, near **San Isidro** (F *Camposinos*), to join the Pacific Highway near León (110 km). This is an attractive alternative route to Managua through the Chinandega cotton growing area, past the spectacular chain of volcanoes running W from Lake Managua, and through León. (Bus Estelí-San Isidro, every 30 mins, 2 hrs, US$0.50, San Isidro-León, every 30 mins, 3-4 hrs, US$1.50). On this road, 12 km N of the intersection with the Chinandega-León road, is **San Jacinto**; 200m to the W of the road is a field of steaming, bubbling mud holes, worth visiting. You should approach carefully, the ground may give and scald your legs, but follow other footmarks for safety. A fast camera shutter will catch the mud in the air.

ESTELI

After San Isidro, the Pan-American Highway goes through La Trinidad (*Cafetería Los Coquitos*, good value meals) before reaching **Estelí** (*pop* 80,000 approx; *alt* 606m; *phone code* 071). This is a rapidly developing departmental capital (heavily damaged during the Revolution of 1978-79, and some of the damage still remains – perhaps intentionally). It is the site of prehistoric carved stone figures (in a park in front of the tourist information office, also has a nice playground). Worth visiting are the Casa de Cultura (fiestas, meetings, exhibitions), Galería de los Héroes y Mártires next door, opp fire station (mementoes and photographs of those killed defending the Revolution, sad but interesting, wonderful paintings on the outside walls), small café adjoining in which you are encouraged to have a drink as a way of contributing to the museum, which is poignantly run by widows and mothers of men lost in the civil war. For the Salvadorean cooperative, take Av Bolívar/C Principal from Cathedral Plaza towards bus station – some crafts, café with posters all over the walls, good. The Ministry of Health Information Centre, on Gran Vía Bolívar, 4 blocks from Plaza, is involved with projects to revive traditional medicine and healing; it offers advice on a wide range of herbal remedies. Also ask at the Reforma Agraria Office (above Banco de América) if you wish to see any local farming cooperatives. The Amnlae women's centre has social and educational projects which are interesting to visit and which may welcome volunteers. Tourist information off C Principal beyond hospital, to S of main plaza.

Local information
● Accommodation

D *Mesón*, Av Bolívar, 1 block N of Cathedral and plaza, with shower, fan, clean, restaurant, TV, changes TCs, rec; **D** *Nicarao*, 1½ blocks S of main square, Av Bolívar/C Principal, with shower (cheaper without), good restaurant, good service, leafy patio, closes at 2200, rec.

E *Barlop*, 5 blocks N of main square, 12 rooms, 6 of which good, 6 basic, former have showers, T 32486, good, friendly.

F *Bolívar*, unmarked, 2 blocks S on C Principal from *Restaurant La Plancha*; **F** *Galo*, Nicaragua y Central, clean, friendly; **F** *Hospedaje El Chepito*, 4 blocks N of bus terminal, quiet, clean, friendly; **F** *Hospedaje San Francisco*, 1 block further N; **F** *Juárez*, nr bus station, very basic, filthy, noisy, parking inside gates; **F** *La*

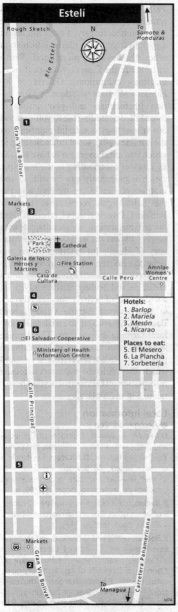

Rough Sketch

Estelí

To Somoto & Honduras

Río Estelí

Gran Vía Bolívar

1

Markets
3

Park
Cathedral

Galería de los
Héroes y
Mártires
Fire Station

Casa de
Cultura

Calle Perú

Amnlae
Women's
Centre

4

S

7 **6**

El Salvador Cooperative

Ministry of Health
Information Centre

Calle Principal

5

i

Markets

Gran Vía Bolívar

2

To Managua

Carretera Panamericana

Hotels:
1. *Barlop*
2. *Mariela*
3. *Mesón*
4. *Nicarao*

Places to eat:
5. *El Mesero*
6. *La Plancha*
7. *Sorbetería*

M74

Florida, very basic, not rec, but safe parking;
F *Mariela*, behind bus station, clean, safe,
washing facilities, very small rooms, parking
inside gates, basic.

● **Places to eat**

Opp *Sorbetería Estelí*, is *La Plancha*; *China
Garden*, on main square, good food, friendly
waiters but feel like sitting in a hanger; *El
Mesero*, off C Principal 3 blocks N of bus
station, popular and very good despite appearance. About 3 blocks N of park on Av Bolívar
Panadería España, good but pricey. *Las Brisas*, NW corner of park, good Chinese and local;
El Porchesito, on main street 5 blocks from bus
station, good, cheap, try tostones jalopeños
and jugo de guayaba; *Soda La Confianza*, 1
block S of Parque Central, cheap, good food.

Bars: *Villa Vieja*, ½ block N of Parque Central
on Av Bolívar, good atmosphere, live music at
weekends.

● **Banks & money changers**

Banco Nacional de Desarrollo. *Agencia de
Viajes Tisey* in *Hotel Mesón* changes TCs at the
official rate; many street changers, for cash only,
on Av Bolívar.

● **Language schools**

Cenac, Centro Nicaragüense de Aprendizaje y
Cultura, Apdo 40, Estelí, T 32025, two offices:
Texaco 5 cuadras al Este, ½ cuadra al Sur, and
De los Bancos 1 cuadra al Sur, ½ cuadra al Este,
frente a Farmacia San Sebastian: Spanish
classes, living with a family, full board, travelling
to countryside, meetings and seminars, opportunities to work on community projects, cost
US$100/week. Also teaches English to Nicara-
guans and others and welcomes volunteer tu-
tors. Cenac is run by women, but is separate
from the Movimiento de Mujeres, **Casa Nora
Artonga**, Apdo 72, Esteli, which also occupies
one of the Cenac buildings and offers classes.
Also **Casa de Familias**, Costado Noreste del
Hospital, 1 cuadra al Carretera, US$100/week.

● **Shopping**

2 small markets, one N, one S of Cathedral
Plaza. Big supermarket, *Supermercado economic*, on Calle Principal.

● **Tour companies & travel agents**

Travel agency *Tisey*, Apdo Postal No 63,
T 7133099, F 7134029.

● **Buses**

Leave from the market S of central plaza; walk
down Av Bolívar/C Principal, 20 mins, or take a
camioneta. To/from **Managua**, US$1.40, 3 hrs

25 mins, half-hourly service, express 2 hrs 45 mins, US$1.85. For **León**, take any bus going on the main road E towards Managua and change at San Isidro, 30 mins, US$0.50; from here buses wait by the roadside to continue S to León (see above). There is a daily minibus to **León** at 0645 (0545 Mon). For Honduras change at Somoto (for El Espino crossing), frequent service from Estelí between 0530 and 1720, US$0.90, 1 hr 40 mins, and shuttle service from there, 45 mins, US$0.50 or Ocotal (for Las Manos crossing) hourly to Ocotal, but go before 0800 to cross the border before lunch. There are two 'express' buses originating in Managua that leave Estelí for Ocotal at 0755 and 1910.

Bathing near Estelí at Puente La Sirena, 200m of the road to Condega, or Salto Estanzuela, 5 km S of Estelí, a waterfall of 25m, with a deep pool at the bottom, surrounded by trees and flowers (inc orchids – only worth it in the rainy season), at least 5 km off the Managua road, 4WD recommended. Take the dirt road, starting 500m S of Estelí on Pan-American Highway, through San Nicolás. Since there are no signs, it is worth hiring a guide.

A very poor but spectacular gravel road from Estelí runs to El Sauce, 45 km (see page 1003); after 20 km an equally rough road branches N to Achuapa. North of **Achuapa**, an unmade road continues through **San Juan de Limay** (one *hospedaje*), an *artesanía*, and marble town, and **Pueblo Nuevo** (2 basic *hospedajes*), near which is an archaeological site. From here the road goes on to join the Pan-American Highway a few km E of Somoto. The Inturismo map shows a road running from San Juan de Limay to San José de Cusmapa (5,073 inhabitants, 1,500m) and La Sabana (meals at shop on right on Parque Central when coming from Somoto), continuing to the Highway just W of Somoto. There is no road between San Juan de Limay and San José de Cusmapa.

The Highway then goes to **Condega** (5,000 people; **F** pp *Hotel Primavera*, nothing special, but plumbing works) and to **Somoto**, nice town, lovely setting (*pop* 15,000), centre of pitch-pine industry.

● **Accommodation F** *Baghal*, clean, friendly, helpful, rec; **F** *Internacional*, 1 block from central plaza, clean and basic; **F** *Panamericano*, on main square, but new section being built will be more expensive, landlord helpful, speaks English, quiet, rec; **G** *Pensión Marina*, shared shower, bargain.

● **Places to eat** *Victoria*, serves good food; *Chinatlan*, good.

Just before reaching Somoto there is a road junction at **Yalagüina** (**F** *Hospedaje*, with restaurant, at intersection). 20 km beyond Somoto is **El Espino** which is 5 km from the Honduran border at La Playa.

FRONTIER WITH HONDURAS – EL ESPINO

● **Nicaraguan Immigration**
The Nicaraguan passport control and customs are in the ruined customs house, 100m from the Honduran border. The Nicaraguan side is open 0900-1300 and 1400-1700. Immigration US$2 pp, receipt given for slightly less.

● **Crossing by private vehicle**
Motorists leaving Nicaragua should enquire in Somoto if an exit permit has to be obtained there or at El Espino. This also applies to cyclists.

● **Services**
There is a duty free shop and a food bar on the Nicaraguan side but several cafés on the Honduran side. No money changers on Nicaraguan side but locals will oblige, even with lempiras. There is nowhere to stay in El Espino.

● **Transport**
Minibuses run between Somoto and the border US$0.40 plus US$0.40/bag, and at least 2 buses daily Somoto-Estelí 0610 and 1410 which continue to Managua, US$2.15, 5 hrs; Managua-Somoto 0700 and 1400, 3¾ hrs, US$3. There are also express buses US$2.85, 4¼ hrs. On Honduran side, taxis go between border and where Mi Esperanza bus stops, when totally full, ie 9-10 people, US$1 for foreigners, less for locals. On Nicaraguan side taxis wait to take you to Somoto, they will probably try to overcharge, pay no more than US$8.

OCOTAL

A road turns off right (18 km) to **Ocotal** (*pop* 30,000; *alt* 600m), a clean, cool, white-washed town on a sandy plain (well worth a visit). It is near the Honduran border, to which a road runs N (bus marked Las Manos), wonderful scenery. Close by, at **San Albino**, there are many gold mines and gold is washed in the Río Coco (bus only from Ciudad Sandino – formerly Jícaro, 50 km from Ocotal).

Local information
● **Accommodation**
At Ocotal: **E** *Hotel Restaurant Mirador*, opp bus station, clean, friendly, with bath.

F *El Portal*, no sign, some new rooms, shared bath, clean, reasonable, rec; **F** *Pensión Centroamericana*, not as dirty as most others, but unfriendly; **F** *Pensión Wilson*, good, friendly; **F** *La Esquinita*, main street.

G *Hospedaje El Castillo*, basic, quiet, close to bus, candles provided for 2100 blackouts; *Segovia*, 1 block N of plaza on C Central, cheap, basic, OK.

There is a pleasant hotel nr the border, 8 km N of Ocotal, called *Las Colinas*, pool, safe car park, bar, information.

● **Places to eat**
Restaurant La Cabaña; *Protocoli*, main plaza; *Llamada del Bosque*, main plaza, good *comida corriente*.

● **Banks & money changers**
Banco Nicaragüense del Interior y Comercio and **Banco Banic** (nr the plaza) will change TCs. The Shell petrol station changes US$ cash.

● **Buses**
The bus station is on the highway, 1 km S of town centre, 15-20 mins walk from Parque Central. Bus (or truck) Ocotal-Somoto, US$0.40; Estelí-Ocotal, US$1.25, 2 hrs, beautiful views; Ocotal-Managua, 0850 and 1530, US$2.85; Managua-Ocotal, 0500 and 1615, 5 hrs.

FRONTIER WITH HONDURAS – LAS MANOS/OCOTAL
The Las Manos/Ocotal crossing is at 1,200m and quite cool. This is recommended as the best route from Tegucigalpa to Managua.

● **Nicaraguan immigration**
Open 0800-1200, 1300-1600. All those arriving must fill in an immigration card, then present their luggage to the customs authorities and obtain a receipt, and present these to the immigration authorities with passport and entry fees (plus up to US$35 if a visa is needed at the border). Leaving the country, fill out a card, pay the tax and get your passport stamped.

● **Crossing by private vehicle**
After completing immigration procedures, go to Tránsito to pay for the vehicle permit, obtain clearance from Revisión, and get your vehicle permit from Aduana (customs). Travellers advise that if it is busy, go first to Aduana and get your number in the queue – if necessary shout at the clerks until they give you one. On leaving the country, first complete the immigration requirements, then go to Tránsito to have the vehicle checked, and to Aduana to have the vehicle stamp in the passport cancelled. Surrender the vehicle permit at Aduana and take another form back to Tránsito; this will be stamped, signed and finally handed over at the exit gate.

● **Exchange**
Money changers operate on both sides offering córdobas at a little better than the street market rate in Nicaragua – if they have them.

● **Transport**
Bus from 4 blocks N of main plaza in Ocotal, US$0.40, otherwise take a truck or hitch. Beware of taxis: agree the fare before getting in. See above for onward buses.

Managua to Corinto

THE ROUTE FROM the capital through Pacific lowlands to the Gulf of Fonseca runs beside a chain of volcanoes, from Momotombo on Lake Managua to Cosigüina overlooking the Gulf. The city of León has been deeply involved in Nicaragua's history since colonial times. On the Pacific coast are the beaches at Poneloya and the major port of Corinto.

The first city of note along the highway is León, 88 km from Managua. The Pacific Highway between Managua and Corinto (140 km) follows the shore of Lake Managua and goes on to Chinandega; it has been continued to Corinto and to the Honduran border. The old, paved road to León crosses the Sierra de Managua, offering fine views of the lake (it is no longer than the Pacific Highway, but is in good condition).

About 60 km down the new road to León lies the village of **La Paz Centro** (road to here paved; **F** *Hospedaje El Caminante*, close to Highway, basic, friendly, cheap; **F** *Hospedaje El Buen Gusto*, friendly, fairly clean, basic. Several truck stop restaurants. Much handmade pottery here, good range and very cheap, ask to see the potters' ovens and production of bricks; try the local speciality *quesillo*, cream cheese served ready-to-eat in plastic bags, all along the highway). Frequent bus service from Managua, Terminal Lewites, every ½ hr. It is from here that one can gain access to the volcano **Momotombo**, which dominates the Managua

skyline from the W. It is also possible to camp on the lakeside here in full view of the volcano.

You have to have a permit from Empresa Nacional de Luz y Fuerza in Managua to climb Momotombo from the S, they have built a geothermal power station on the volcano's slopes; alternatively ask police in León Viejo for a permit (very difficult to get). We understand no permit is required to climb the volcano from the N.

At the volcano's foot lies **León Viejo**, which was destroyed by earthquake and volcanic eruption on 31 December 1609 and is now being excavated. It was in the Cathedral here that Pedrarias and his wife were buried (see **Early, Post-Conquest History** in Introduction to Central America). The ruins can be reached by boat from Managua or by bus from La Paz Centro. Near the large volcano is a smaller one, Momotombito.

LEON

León (*pop* 130,000; *phone code* 0311) was founded by Hernández de Córdoba in 1524 at León Viejo, 32 km from its present site. There was an Indian village called Imabite there, but an eruption of the Momotombo volcano destroyed the town. Archaeological excavations of León Viejo have revealed the Cathedral, the Convento de la Merced, the Casa del Gobernador and other foundations of buildings. The city moved to its present site in 1610. It was the capital from its foundation until Managua replaced it in 1858; it is still the 'intellectual' capital, with a university (founded 1804), religious colleges, the largest cathedral in Central America, and several colonial churches. It is said that Managua became the capital, although at the time it was only an Indian settlement, because it was half-way between violently Liberal León and equally violently Conservative Granada.

The city has a traditional air, its colonial charm unmatched elsewhere in Nicaragua, except perhaps Granada: narrow streets, roofs tiled in red, low adobe houses and time-worn buildings everywhere. The old Plaza de Armas, in front of the Cathedral, is now Parque Jérez, but is usually referred to as Parque Central; it contains a statue of Gen Jérez, a mid-19th century Liberal leader. Next to the park is an interesting mural covering the history from precolumbian times to the Sandinista revolution, completed in 1990.

Places of interest

The **Cathedral**, begun in 1746 and not completed for 100 years, is an enormous building. It has a famous shrine, 145 cm high, covered by white topazes from India given by Philip II of Spain, which is kept in a safe in the vestry, and the bishop holds the key; a very fine ivory Christ; the consecrated Altar of Sacrifices and the Choir of Córdoba; the great Christ of Esquipulas, a colonial work in bronze whose cross is of very fine silver; and statues of the 12 Apostles. At the foot of one of these statues is the tomb of Rubén Darío, the 19th-century Nicaraguan poet, and one of the greatest in Latin America, guarded by a sorrowing lion. All the entrances to the Cathedral are guarded by lions.

Churches The western end of the city is the oldest, and here is the oldest of all the churches: the parish church of **Subtiava** (1530) where Las Casas, the Apostle of the Indies, preached on several occasions. It has a fine façade, the best colonial altar in the country and an interesting representation of the sun ('El Sol') revered by the Indians. The church has been beautifully reconstructed. The roof was rebuilt, under the supervision of the 'Comisión 500 años'. Near the Subtiava church are a small town museum (entrance free) and the ruins of the parish church of Vera Cruz, now crumbling. Also in the suburb of Subtiava is the **Casa de Cultura** with interesting murals. Other churches well worth visiting include **El Calvario** (beautifully decorated ceiling), **La Recolección** (fine façade), **La Merced**, **San Felipe**, **Zaragoza**, **San Francisco** and **El Laborío**. There is a pleasant walk S across the bridge, past the church of Guadalupe, to the cemetery.

Museums The house of Rubén Darío, the famous 'Four Corners' in C Rubén Darío, is now the **Museo-Archivo Rubén Darío**, open Tues-Sat 0900-1200, 1400-1700, Sun 0900-1200, entry free but donation requested. It has an interesting collection of personal possessions, a large mural and a library with a wide range of books of poetry in Spanish, English and French. Darío died in 1916 in another house in the NW sector marked with a plaque. A plaque also marks the spot in the centre of the city where the first President Somoza was assassinated in 1956 by poet Rigoberto López Pérez.

1978-79 Revolution León was the centre of heavy fighting during the 1978-79 Revolution; much of the damage has still to be repaired, but there are also many monuments from that time in the city (descriptions of León's fight against the Somoza régime can be found in *Fire from the Mountain: The Making of a Sandinista* by Omar Cabezas). Visitors can see **El Fortín**, the ruined last stronghold of the

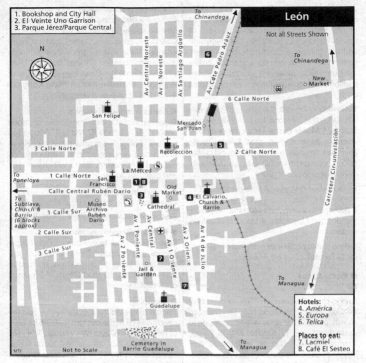

1. Bookshop and City Hall
2. El Veinte Uno Garrison
3. Parque Jérez/Parque Central

León

Not all Streets Shown

To Chinandega

To Chinandega

New Market

6 Calle Norte

Av Central Noreste
Av 1 Noreste
Av Santiago Argüello
Av Cde Pedro Aráuz

San Felipe

Mercado San Juan

La Recolección

2 Calle Norte

3 Calle Norte

La Merced

1 Calle Norte

San Francisco

To Poneloya

Calle Central Rubén Darío

To Subtiava, Church & Barrio (6 blocks approx)

Old Market

El Calvario, Church & Barrio

Cathedral

Museo Archivo Rubén Darío

1 Calle Sur

2 Calle Sur

3 Calle Sur

Carretera Circunvalación

Av 2 Poniente
Av 1 Poniente
Av Central
Av 1 Oriente
Av 2 Oriente
Av 14 de Julio

Jail & Garden

To Managua

Guadalupe

Hotels:
4. América
5. Europa
6. Telica

Places to eat:
7. Lacmiel
8. Café El Sesteo

Cemetery in Barrio Guadalupe

Not to Scale

To Managua

Somocista national guard (a commemorative march goes there each July, from the Cathedral, go W about 10 blocks, then S, best in early am, great views of town and several volcanoes); **El Veinte Uno**, the national guard's 21st garrison, also ruined, and scene of an important battle in April 1979, with the jail around the corner converted into a garden with a statue to El Combatiente Desconocido (the unknown warrior) (3 blocks S of cathedral); **statue of Luisa Amanda Espinoza**, the first woman member of the FSLN to die (in 1970), after whom the women's organization (AMNLAE) is named (7-8 blocks N of market behind Cathedral, in Barrio San Felipe); 2 blocks W of La Merced church is the **Centro Popular de la Cultura** (frequent exhibitions and events). In the blocks N of the Cathedral is a commemorative park with portraits of Sandino, Carlos Fonseca and Jérez. There is also the **Mothers Gallery of Heroes and Martyrs**, commemorating those who fell in the revolution. It has a gift shop.

Local festivals and Local holidays
The Holy Week ceremonies are outstanding, as are the festivities on 7 Dec, Día de la Concepción, much singing, dancing, fireworks, and festive crowds. 20 June (Liberation by Sandinistas), 24 Sept, 1 Nov (All Saints' Day).

Local information
● **Accommodation**
D *América*, Av Santiago Argüello, 2 blocks E of central market, with bath and fan, clean, good value, nice patio, friendly, nice garden, breakfast, slow service, cold drinks, convenient location, also secure garage nearby; **D** *Colonial*, Av

2, 2 blocks N of Parque Central, T 2279, F 3125, next to the University, pleasant, old building, fan or a/c, restaurant; **D Europa**, 2 blocks S of railway station, T 2576, F 2596, best, with bath and a/c, cheaper without bath, but with fan, comfortable patios with bar and shade, coffee available, mice, restaurant expensive, limited parking inside, guard will watch vehicles parked on street, rec.

E *Avenida*, nr Mercado San Juan, opp Esso, family run, fan, cable TV, good food, friendly, laundry facilities; **E** *Monte Cristo*, 4 blocks beyond *Hotel Avenida*, on same street, good; **E** *Restaurante Pilar*, Av Comandante, 3 blocks from old railway station, has one room with 3 beds, own bathroom, clean, owner speaks English.

F *Hospedaje Primavera*, 5 blocks N, and 1½ blocks E of railway station, not very clean, basic; **F** *Telica*, with shower, noisy, cockroaches, clean, friendly, good breakfast, 4 blocks N of railway station.

Several cheap *pensiones* nr the railway station, inc **G** *Tecotal*, good breakfast.

● **Places to eat**
NB Many restaurants are closed all day Sun.

Gringo café, *El Sesteo*, on plaza, good coffee; *La Casa Vieja*, 1 ½ blocks N of San Francisco church, pleasant bar, good quality snacks, good value, highly rec; *El Barcito*, NW of Parque Central, popular, soft drinks, milk shakes, slow service; *El Oasis*, C 5 and Av Central, good value, limited menu; *Central*, C 4 Norte, good *comida corriente*; *Marisquería Solmar*, 1 block from main square, good seafood but expensive; *La Cueva del León*, 2 blocks N of Parque Jérez, Chinese menu; *Capricornio*, nr Central University, good *comida corriente*, interesting atmosphere; good value *comida corriente* at *Comedores Emu* (nr La Recolección church, opp *Solmar*, US$2, good value) and *La Cucaracha* (moved 1996, new address not known); *Sacuanjoche*, C Darío opp Museo Archivo Darío, expensive but good steaks, good service; *Lacmiel*, 5 blocks S of Cathedral, good food, live music, open air, rec; *Los Pescaditos*, nr Subtiava church, excellent for fish at reasonable prices, rec. Excellent ice cream parlour, *Chupi's*, 1 block N of central square. *Soda Metro*, US style fast food, US$2 buys a tasty lunch; *El Rincón Azul*, C Central Rubén Darío, about 1½ blocks W of Parque Jérez, an excellent bar, very cheap, also a local art gallery, open 1500-2400, rec. *Casa Popular de Cultura*, 1 block N of plaza central, 2½ blocks abajo,

sandwiches and hamburgers, nice atmosphere, find out what's going on. *Centro Decorativo* on main square, large airy bar with roof-top roller skating rink, good views. On the Carretera Circunvalación, *Caña Brava*, good, try their 'pollo deshuesado' (boneless chicken). *Ruinas*, 1 block W of Telcor on Ruben Dario, friendly, live music at weekends. Chinese restaurant *Hong Kong*, 20 Telcor, T 6572, popular with locals.

● **Banks & money changers**
Supercambio, 1 block from cathedral, open 0800-1230, 1400-1730 Mon-Fri, 0800-1130 Sat, will change TCs at poor rates; also, *Pinolero*, a casa de cambio, ½ block E of Banco Nacional de Desarrollo. Banks will change TCs and give cash advances on Visa.

● **Entertainment**
Cinemas: two in centre.

Discos: two at weekends, one is *The Tunnel*.

● **Post & telecommunications**
Post Office and telephone: Enitel, Parque Central, opp Cathedral. Phone calls abroad possible. Small Enitel office on Darío, on road to Subtiava, about 10 blocks from main plaza, open till 2200.

● **Shopping**
The old market (dirty) is in the centre, and the new market is at the bus terminal, 5-6 blocks E of railway station. Also Mercado San Juan, not touristy, good local atmosphere. Good supermarket on C 1 Norte, by *Pollo Loco* and Banco Nacional de Desarrollo. Good bookshop next to city hall at Parque Jérez.

● **Tourist Offices**
3 C Norte and Av Central, maps and postcards. A good, multilingual guide and/or Spanish teacher, Mauricio Avellán Solórzano, works in *Hotel América*.

● **Buses**
From bus station at new market: **Managua-León**, 2 hr 15 mins, US$1.25, every 30 mins, US$1.35 express, 1½ hrs, frequent but check if it goes to the León bus terminal or the Shell station on the Managua highway. Colectivo, US$5. Bus to **Chinandega** (US$0.50) and **Corinto** (US$0.85) half-hourly between 0430 and 1800. For **Estelí**, daily express minibus at 1500, or take a bus to **San Isidro** (every 30 mins), 2½ hrs, US$1.50, then catch a bus going N from Managua or Matagalpa. To **Matagalpa** direct, 1/day at 1400, US$2.80, but cheaper to take a bus to San Isidro and catch one of the many buses there from Estelí to

Matagalpa, US$0.80. To border with Honduras take a bus from the market to Chinandega, and from there another bus to Somotillo (possible to change córdobas on the bus but better rate for US dollars at Tegucigalpa). The Tica Bus to El Salvador stops at the Shell Station on the Managua side of town sometime between 0630 and 0730 daily. Pick-up from bus terminal to centre US$0.20.

Bus to **El Sauce**, 72 km, where there is a large 19th century church, and a riotous fair in Feb (F *Hospedaje Diana*, clean, basic; *Viajero*, noisy, fan, friendly, good food; *Restaurant Mi Rancho* and others) via **Malpaisillo** (unnamed *hospedaje* at village entrance, 4 rooms, basic, F). Buses from El Sauce: to León, frequent, 2½-3 hrs, US$1.40; to Honduran border 0500 daily, 2 hrs, US$1.60. 4 daily trucks between El Sauce and Estelí, on a very rough road.

On 9 April 1992, Cerro Negro, a volcano 28 km NE of León erupted, depositing vast quantities of volcanic ash and sand on the municipality of León and surrounding areas. Many people were made homeless and there was much damage as roofs collapsed under the weight of ash. There was a further eruption in Nov 1995, but no fatalities. There is little activity now, and you can get close to the cone with a 4WD vehicle.

There is a road (20 km) to the sandy Pacific beach at **Poneloya** (main beach can have large waves, strong currents, extremely dangerous).

● **Accommodation & places to eat** D *Posada de Poneloya*, opp Lacayo, cabinas with bath, a/c or fan, car park; E *Lacayo*, great location, dusty rooms, restaurant has good repochetas, basic, meals, bats in the roof and beware of insects at night, bring coils; *Restaurante Cáceres*, good comida corriente; *La Peña del Tigre*, good but expensive fish restaurant down the road, huge portions, friendly, open air, nice views – it is nr a tall rock on the beach where bathing is dangerous and prohibited.

The place is pretty run down and all the houses of wealthy León families are locked up. It only comes alive during Semana Santa, at which time it gets crowded. Camping possible on the beach. Take bus 101 from León's Terminal Interurbana, or the central market W to the bus stop near Subtiava church on C Darío, then walk

3 mins to Terminal Poneloya, from where a small bus leaves every hour or so for Las Peñitas (US$0.45) at the S end of Poneloya beach (swimming much safer here; several small restaurants). Taxi from León costs around US$6.

CHINANDEGA

Chinandega (*pop* 101,000; *phone code* 0341), is one of the hottest and driest towns in Nicaragua, and is about 35 km beyond León. This is one of the main cotton-growing districts, and also grows bananas and sugar cane. Horse-drawn cabs for hire. Good market by the bus terminal. Local holiday: 26 July.

● **Accommodation** B *Cosigüina*, T 3636, F 3689, in city centre, just S of Banco Nacional, expensive, a/c, cable TV; D *Glomar* (shower extra), safe, may be closed Sun pm, owner (Filio) will change dollars, but mistrusts foreigners, his son is friendly, good food, cold beer; F *Hospedaje Aguirre*; F *Pensión Cortés*, S of Parque Central, basic; G *Chinandega*, basic, fan, shared bath, decent; G *Pensión Urbina*, basic.

● **Places to eat** *Corona de Oro*, Chinese, 1½ blocks E of Parque Central, T 351, expensive; *Central Palace*, same street; *Caprax Pizza*, one block E of Parque Central.

● **Banks & money changers** Banco Nacional de Desarrollo.

● **Post & telecommunications Post Office and telephones**: in Enitel building opp *Caprax Pizza*.

● **Buses** From Managua, by road, 3 hrs 15 mins, US$1.95. From León, 1 hr 15 mins, US$1.25. From Chinandega, buses leave from nr the new market at SE edge of town for **Corinto**, **León**, **Managua** and **Somotillo**. From **León**, 1 hr by bus, US$0.50. Buses to **Potosí**, **El Viejo** and **Puerto Morazán** leave from the Mercadito at NW of town. A local bus connects Terminal, Mercado and Mercadito.

Not far away, near **Chichigalpa**, is Ingenio San Antonio, the largest sugar mill in Nicaragua, with a railway between the town and the mill (6 km, 5 trains a day each way, 7 May-Nov, passengers taken, US$0.10; also bus US$0.30). While there are no official tours of the installations, you can apply at gate (portón) 14 to be shown around. On the edge of Chichigalpa itself is the Flor de Caña distillery; on leaving you will recognize the picture on all the labels, a palm-shaded railway leading towards Chichigalpa with volcanoes in the background. Enitel in Chichigalpa: from Texaco on the main road take 2nd street on left, then 1st on right, open 0800-1200, 1400-1700.

A road runs NE to Puerto Morazán. This passes through the village of El Viejo (US$0.20 by bus from Chinandega, 5 km) where there is an old church. (Restaurant: *El Retoño*, on main street, N of market; bars close to market.) **Puerto Morazán** (hotel), 26 km from Chinandega (buses, 8 a day, 1½ hrs, US$0.40), is a poor, muddy village with reed huts on a navigable river running into the Gulf of Fonseca. From Chinandega there are 4 buses a day to **Potosí**, at least 3 hrs, US$1.20. *Comedor Adela*, 24-hr service, cheap. You can sling your hammock at the *comedor* 150m past immigration for US$0.50. Ask Héctor for permission to stay in the fishing cooperative. The fishermen are very friendly. The passenger ferry from Potosí to La Unión (El Salvador) has been suspended, but there is an open boat from La Unión ad hoc. Ask around.

It is a 4-hr hike to the cone of **Cosigüina** volcano. On 23 January 1835, one of the biggest eruptions in history blew off most of the cone, reducing it from 3,000m to its present height of 870m. There are beautiful views from the cone over the islands belonging to Honduras and El Salvador. There is plenty of wildlife in the area, including poisonous snakes, so take a machete. The path is overgrown and very difficult to follow, you may need a guide. There are pleasant black sand beaches; the sea, although the colour of *café con leche*, is clean. In the centre of the village are warm thermal springs in which the population relaxes each afternoon.

From Chinandega a paved road, badly in need of repair in its middle section in 1994, goes to the Honduran border on the **Río Guasaule** near **Somotillo** (E *Las Vegas*, small rooms, fan, none too clean, restaurant) where it is continued by a better road to Choluteca, Honduras. Bus from Chinandega, 1 hr 45 mins, US$1.25.

FRONTIER WITH HONDURAS – GUASAULE

● **Nicaraguan immigration**
The border crossing is closed from 1130-1400. The distance between the border posts is 500m. There are no colectivos, so you must walk or hitch a lift.

● **Transport**
Buses run every ½ hr from the border to Chinandega, US$1.35. Express bus to Managua, Mercado Lewites terminal at 0500 and 1545, 3½ hrs, US$2.85 via Somotillo and Leon. From Managua to Río Guasaule at 1810. The international buses use this crossing.

Jiquilillo beach, 42 km from Chinandega, is reached by a mostly-paved road branching off the El Viejo-Potosí road. It lies on a long peninsula; small restaurants (eg *Fany*) and lodgings.

CORINTO

21 km from Chinandega, **Corinto** (*pop* 30,000; *phone code* 0342) is the main port of entry, and the only port at which vessels of any considerable size can berth. About 60% of the country's commerce passes through it. The town itself is on a sandy island, Punto Icaco, connected with the mainland by long railway and road bridges. There are beautiful old wooden buildings with verandahs, especially by the port. (Entry to the port is barred to all except those with a permit.) On the Corinto-Chinandega road is Paseo Cavallo beach (*Restaurante Buen Vecino*). The sea is treacherous, people drown here every year.

● **Accommodation** D *Central*, in front of Port Buildings, clean, a/c; G *Hospedaje Luvy*, fan, dirty bathrooms, 2 blocks from plaza.

● **Places to eat** *Meléndez*, on main square, good but pricey; *El Imperial*, evenings only; cheapest meals in market, but not rec.

Managua to Granada

FROM LAKE MANAGUA to Lake Nicaragua, with more volcanoes in view: Santiago is near Masaya, a centre for handicrafts in a tobacco- growing zone; Mombacho is near Granada, a richly historical city; Concepción is a perfect cone rising out of Isla Ometepe, one of a number of islands that can be visited by boat on Lake Nicaragua.

The main route is by a 61 km paved road with a fast bus service through Masaya.

SANTIAGO VOLCANO

The entrance to **Volcán Masaya National Park** is at Km 23. According to Pre-Columbian beliefs, children and young virgins had to be thrown into the volcano's crater to appease the goddess Masaya. Father Francisco de Bobadilla planted a cross on the summit of Masaya in the 16th century to exorcise the 'Boca del Infierno'; the cross visible today commemorates the event. Many Spanish chroniclers visited the crater, including Oviedo in 1529 and Blas de Castillo in 1538, who descended into it in search of gold! Volcán Nindiri last erupted in 1670, Volcán Masaya burst forth in 1772 and again in 1852, forming the Santiago crater between the two peaks; this in turn erupted in 1932, 1946, 1959 and 1965 before collapsing in 1985 and the resulting pall of sulphurous smoke made the soil in a broad belt to the Pacific uncultivable. 90 years ago German engineers Schomberg and Scharfenberg, attempting to produce sulphuric acid from the volcano's emissions, drilled into a unexpected 400m-wide lava tube, resulting in explosions and landslides; no-one has attempted anything similar since! Remains of these old installations can still be seen; consult the *guardabosques* for information.

Volcán Masaya was the first of the country's national parks (1975), 54 square km. The Visitor's Centre is 1.5 km in from the entrance (called the *Centro de Interpretación Ambiental*). Shortly after is a beautiful area with toilets, picnic facilities and barbecues (*asadores*) for the use of visitors. Camping possible here but no facilities after the Visitor's Centre closes. Next door is a good science museum, entrance free. From here a short path leads up to Cerro El Comalito, good views of Mombacho, the lakes and the extraordinary volcanic landscapes of the Park; longer trails continue to Lake Masaya and San Fernando crater. Because of the potential danger involved, visits to the fumaroles at Comalito require special authorization from rangers, who warn that they may have to place this area off-limits if visitors are injured touching or throwing the surrounding rocks. The paved road (20-25 kph speed limit) continues S across the 1670 lava flow to the

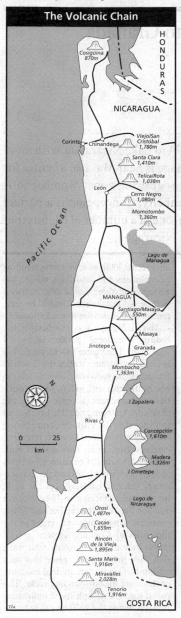

The Volcanic Chain

HONDURAS

Cosigüina
870m

NICARAGUA

Corinto Chinandega Viejo/San
Cristóbal
1,780m

Santa Clara
1,410m

Telica/Rota
1,038m

León

Cerro Negro
1,080m

Momotombo
1,360m

Pacific Ocean

Lago de
Managua

MANAGUA

Santiago/Masaya
550m

Masaya

Jinotepe Granada

Mombacho
1,363m

I Zapatera

Rivas

Concepción
1,610m

Madera
1,326m

I Ometepe

Lago de
Nicaragua

Orosi
1,487m

Cacao
1,659m

Rincón
de la Vieja
1,895m

Santa María
1,916m

Miravalles
2,028m

Tenorio
1,916m

0   25
km

N

72a

COSTA RICA

twin crests of Masaya and Nindiri, which
actually consist of 5 craters (Santiago –
still emitting sulphurous gases, San Fernando, San Juan, Nindiri and San Pedro). There is parking and a recreation
area here. Park rangers will escort groups
of no more than 5 down a path leading to
several lava caverns, visitors are not allowed to touch the fragile walls or roofs
of these caves. Park guides and
guardabosques are very knowledgeable
about the area's history and early indigenous inhabitants. The park is a wonderful excursion but take something to
drink, a hat and robust footware if planning much walking. Drivers have to pay
US$3 in córdobas (more for camper vans
etc), to get their vehicles in; pedestrians
US$2.50 (bus passengers alight at Km 23
on the Managua-Masaya route). The
Park is open 0900-1700, Tues-Fri, and
until 1900 on Sat and Sun.

MASAYA

29 km SE of Managua, **Masaya** (*pop*
101,880; *phone code* 052) is the centre of a
rich agricultural area growing many crops
including tobacco. Small **Laguna de
Masaya** (at the foot of Masaya volcano,
water too polluted for swimming), and
Santiago volcano are near the town. Interesting Indian handicrafts are sold and a
gorgeous *fiesta* is held on 30 Sept, for its
patron, San Jerónimo (Indian dances and
local costumes). The market is reportedly
commercialized now, but the selection
and quality are good. There is a new Centro de Artesanías (closed Sun), near the
former hospital and overlooking Laguna
de Masaya, but the choice is not as wide
as the market. Masaya is also the centre
for Nicaraguan rocking chairs, which can
be purchased in kit form, packed for taking by air. The Cooperativo Teófilo
Alemán has a good selection at around
US$35. The best place for Indian craft
work is **Monimbo** (visit the church of San
Sebastián here), and 15 mins from
Masaya is **Villa Nindirí**, which has a rich

museum and an old church with some even older images. There are horse-drawn carriages, some very pretty and well-kept. Statue of Sandino. The town suffered severely in the Revolution of 1978-79. Visit the Museo de Héroes y Mártires, open Mon-Fri. Another museum is that of Camilo Ortega, which has interesting exhibits on recent history; 45 mins' walk from central plaza, ask directions.

Excursions

Just outside Masaya, on the road from Managua, is an old fortress, Coyotepe, also called La Fortillera. It was once a torture centre, and is now deserted, eerie 'with a Marie Celeste feel to it' (take a torch), or offer a volunteer US$1-2 to show you around. Near the Masaya Lake, S of the town there are caves with prehistoric figures on the walls; ask around for a guide.

Niquinohomo is Sandino's birthplace, and the house where he lived from the age of 12 with his father is opposite the church in the main square. There used to be a museum here but the exhibits have now been transferred to Managua.

James N Maas writes: Take a bus from Masaya (or Granada) to **San Juan de Oriente**, a colonial village with an interesting school of pottery (products are for sale). It is a short walk to neighbouring Catarina, and a 1 km walk uphill to El Mirador, with wonderful view of **Laguna de Apoyo** (very clean, quiet during week but busy at weekends – swimming, drinking, drowning – entrance fee US$0.20; get out of bus at Km 38 on Managua-Granada road, walk 1½ hrs or hitch – easy at weekends), Granada and Volcán Mombacho in the distance. Return by bus.

Local information
● Accommodation

C *Motel Cailagua* (Km 29.5, Carretera a Granada), about 2 km from Masaya, with bath and a/c, D with bath and fan, large rooms, clean, good, very friendly, meals available (but breakfast only by arrangement), reasonably priced, parking inside gates, rec; C *Motel El Nido*, expensive, not too good.

D *Monte Carlo*, 1½ blocks from *Regis* on same side, clean, friendly, bar, no breakfast.

E *Regis*, Sergio Delgado (main street), shared bath, fan, breakfast (other meals if ordered), helpful owner, rec.

F *Rex*, dark, dirty, can be obstructive, nr the church, avoid; *pensiones* are hard to find, and dirty when you've found them.

G *Masayita*, 2 blocks W of central park, clean basic.

● Places to eat

Nuevo Bar Chegris, ½ block S around corner from *Regis*, very good food in huge portions, nice garden, rec; *Alegría*, C Real San Geronimo, ½ block N of Parque Central, good, clean, comfortable, not expensive, good pizzas; *El Arabe* at station; *Mini 16*, W end of town, nr hospital; *Jarochita*, nr park, Mexican, good; *Pochil*, nr park, good food, ask for vegetarian dishes. *Cafetín Verdi*, in central park, good atmosphere, snacks, ice cream *Panadería Corazón de Oro*, 2-3 blocks towards highway from the church, excellent cheese bread (*pan de queso*), US$0.50 a loaf. There are 2 Fuentes de Soda nr the NE corner of the Parque Central, both good, and 5 blocks N of the Parque Central is a small park with a Pepsi stand that sells excellent 'Tutti-Frutti' fresh fruit juice.

● Banks & money changers

Banco Nacional de Desarrollo, and street changer around market and plaza.

● Hospitals & medical services

Doctors: Dr Freddy Cárdenas Ortega, nr bus terminal, rec gynaecologist; Dr Gerardo Sánchez, next to town hall, speaks some English.

● Post & telecommunications

Post Office, on Parque Central.

● Tourist offices

On main highway in the block between the 2 main roads into Masaya; helpful, mostly Spanish spoken, but some English 'if you look baffled'.

● Buses

Depart from the terminal nr the market. To **Managua** every 15 mins, US$0.35; to **Granada** every 20 mins, US$0.25, to **Jinotepe** via Niquinohomo, Masatepe, San Marcos and Diriamba every 20 mins. There is also a bus service to **Tisma**.

GRANADA

Another 19 km by road is **Granada** (*pop* 89,000; *phone code* 055), on Lake Nicaragua. It is the third city of the republic and was founded by Hernández de Córdoba in 1524 at the foot of Mombacho volcano. The rich city was three times attacked by British and French pirates coming up the San Juan and Escalante rivers, and much of old Granada was burnt by filibuster William Walker in 1856, but it still has many beautiful buildings and has faithfully preserved its Castilian traditions.

Places of interest

The centre of the city, some distance from the lake, is the **Parque Central**, with many trees and food stalls in its park, civic buildings, the *Hotel Alhambra* and the Cathedral around its edge. The **Cathedral**, rebuilt in neo-classical style, is simpler in design and ornamentation than the church of **La Merced**, which was built in 1781-3, half-destroyed in the civil wars of 1854 and restored in 1862. Its interior is painted in pastel shades, predominantly green and blue. Continuing away from the centre, beyond La Merced, is the church of **Jalteva** (or Xalteva), which faces a pleasant park with formal ponds. Not far from Jalteva is **La Pólvora** church. Also nearby is **Museo de las Arenas**, in a restored fortress. If one heads towards the Managua bus terminal from Jalteva, the **Hospital** is passed. Built in 1886, it is now in very poor shape. The chapel of **María Auxiliadora**, where Las Casas, Apostle of the Indies, often preached, is hung with Indian lace and needlework (church open to public at 1600). From the Parque Central, in the opposite direction to La Merced, is the fortress-church of **San Francisco** with wonderful sculptures. Next door is the **Conjunto Histórico de San Francisco**, originally a convent (1524), then a Spanish garrison, William Walker's garrison, a university and lastly an institute. Now it is just a museum in the midst of ruined, deserted classrooms; the cloister surrounds about 3 dozen tall palms. Reconstruction has begun with financial assistance from the Swedish Government, but much work has to be done. The museum houses 28 sculptures from Isla Zapatera in the lake. They date from AD800-1200, note especially the double sculptures of standing or seated figures bearing huge animal masks, or doubles, on their heads and shoulders ('El Lagarto', 'La Tortuga', jaguars, etc). The museum is open 0800-1800; US$1.10 entrance. Horse-drawn cabs are for hire (bargain over the price – horses in very poor condition), there are many oxcarts and a fine cemetery.

A road runs from the Parque central to Plaza España by the dock on the lake; the church of **Guadalupe** is on this road. From Plaza España it is a short distance to the **Complejo Turístico** (entrance fee US$0.12), a large area with restaurants and bars (see below), paths and benches. **Casa de los tres mundos** is a beautiful renovated building, an artist's workplace and recreational centre. The lake beach is popular, but dirty; marimba bands stroll the beach and play a song for you for a small charge.

Local festivals

Holy Week: Assumption of the Virgin, 14-30 Aug; and Christmas (masked and costumed mummers).

Local information
● **Warning**

A conman operates in Granada, often near the tourist complex. He claims he is a Miskito Indian who was a political prisoner, he has just escaped and is now heading for Costa Rica. He also gives you the address of his mother, a refugee in Germany. His story is not true: do not give him money to finance his 'escape'. First reported in 1994, he or his imitators are still active 1997!

● **Accommodation**

A3-C *Alhambra*, Parque Central, T 6316/24486-9, F 2035, pleasant, comfortable rooms with bath, large restaurant serves good food, good breakfasts, often has good, live music, parked cars guarded by nightwatchman.

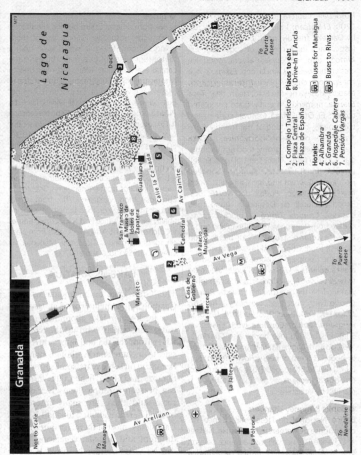

Inside the map:

Lago de Nicaragua

Dock

To Puerto Asese

To Puerto Asese

To Nandaime

To Managua

Calle la calzada

Guadalupe

Av Caimite

San Francisco & Museo de Idolos de Zapatera

Cathedral

O Palacio Municipal

Av Vega

Market

Casa de Gobierno

La Merced

La Jaltteva

Av Arellano

La Pólvora

N

Not to Scale

Granada

Places to eat:
8. Drive-In El Ancla

BR1 Buses for Managua
BR2 Buses to Rivas

1. Complejo Turístico
2. Plaza Central
3. Plaza de España

Hotels:
4. Alhambra
5. Granada
6. Hospedaje Cabrera
7. Pensión Vargas

B *Granada*, C La Calzada (opp Guadalupe church), luxury, swimming pool, a/c, restaurant for all meals, café, disco, bar, very good, T 22178, F 4128.

E *Hospedaje Cabrera*, C La Calzada, D in the one room with bath, simple wooden huts, solar heated water usually cold, clean, with fan, filtered drinking water, family run, nice garden, noisy, excellent breakfast for US$2, use of kitchen; opp *Cabrera* is **E** *Pensión Vargas*, C La Calzada, basic, very nice people, sun-heated shower, clean, nice garden; **E** *Hospedaje Esfinge*, opp market, rooms with character, patio

with washing facilities, friendly, clean, motorcycle parking in lobby, safe, laundry, rec; **E** *La Calzada*, C La Calzada nr Guadelupe church, huge rooms with bath, fan, clean, friendly, great breakfasts.

F *Central*, friendly, clean, good restaurant.

There is a shortage of hotels and restaurants in Granada (do not arrive after 2100 at the latest).

● Places to eat

Drive Inn El Ancla, opp *Hotel Granada*, clean, Western food, great Big Mac (but you can't drive in!), good; *Coffee Shop*, C La Calzada, nr

Hospedaje Cabrera, breakfasts, lunch from 1200; *El Volcán*, 1 block S of La Merced, run by Danielo, friendly, good *brochetas*, breakfasts, plans for future accommodation; *Eskimo's*, opp *Hospedaje Cabrera*, good ice cream; between *El Ancla* and *Eskimo's* is a cheap, good chicken place; *Interamericano*, road to Masaya next to Esso, clean, dear. *Tasa Blanca*, nr market, friendly, good percolated coffee; *El Otro*, Plaza Central, coffee shop with meals; cheap food at the friendly *Café Astoria*, nr plaza central; *Soyanica*, nr Plaza Central, vegetarian, grotty, food nothing special; *Las Portales*, Plaza Central, opp Enitel, simple, good; *Cafetin Amigo*, between *Hospedaje Cabrera* and the Cathedral, good food, good value; *Pollos del Norte*, opp Banco Nacional de Desarrollo, good fried chicken; *Comida Tipica*, 1 block back to square from Pension Vargas, cheap and good; *Oriente Lejano*, 1 block W of plaza, good Chinese food. Good breakfasts at the market.

In the Complejo Turístico, see above, there are restaurants and bars of all types, they tend to be expensive (lively disco Fri and Sat at night); walking from the gate they inc: *La Vista*, *Rincón Criollo* (with boat trips, see below), *Rancho Colomer*, *Omotepe*, *Restaurante Disco El Pingüino*, *Bahía*, *Carolina* (with fiestas on Sun); lots of loud juke boxes; also *Charley's*, lively, good decor, vegetarian food, share a bota (= boot – 3 litres) of beer!; *Rock Studio*, opp Banco de Desarrollo, good rock and pop music; *Cacibolca* restaurant on Isla Cacibolca is reached by launch.

● **Banks & money changers**
Banco Nacional de Desarrollo; Banco Nicaragüense de Comercio e Industria. Neither will change TCs nor will they advance cash on Visa or Amex. However, Banco de America Central and Banco Centro (1 block W of plaza) will change TCs though, for better rates change TCs and cash dollars on the street.

● **Post & telecommunications**
Telephones: Enitel in moorish building on Parque Central, left of Cathedral, open until 2200. One page fax to UK US$5, to USA US$3.40.

● **Shopping**
Market (large green building in the centre) is dark, dirty and packed; lots of stalls on the streets outside, also horse cab rank and taxis. Main shopping street runs N-S, W of plaza. *Almacén Internacional* nr Hotel Alhambra.

● **Buses**
Leave from an area 200m beyond the market behind the *Hospedaje Esfinge*, except those going to/from Managua, which leave from a 'fenced lot uptown' (see map); buses to the capital every 20 mins. Many fast minibuses to **Managua**, US$0.60, 1 hr (these do not stop in Masaya but will stop at the junction). Another bus service from the capital leaves from **La Piñata**, opp Universidad Centroamericana (UCA) every 2 hrs after 1000, US$1, no a/c but seat guaranteed. Bus to **Masaya**, US$0.30, 30 mins. Bus to **Nandaime**, every 20 mins, US$0.50. To **Rivas** 8 a day 0610-1810 (timings erratic), $1\frac{1}{2}$ hrs, US$1. It's often quicker to take a bus to Nandaime and then another on from there. Sirca Bus from Managua via Granada to **San José** Mon, Wed, Fri 0700, from corner 1 block from plaza on road to market, booking ahead essential, office is at Sr Cabezas, **Camas y Colchones Sant Ana**, $1\frac{1}{2}$ blocks from plaza on road to market. Tica from Managua via Granada to San José also at 0700.

LAKE NICARAGUA

The 'Gran Lago de Nicaragua' or Lago Cacibolca, 148 km long by 55 at its widest, is a fresh-water lake abounding in salt-water fish, which swim up the San Juan River from the sea and later return. It is said to include sharks, though none has been seen for some years; some say because Somoza had them fished out. Terrapins can be seen sunning themselves on the rocks and there are many interesting birds. There are about 310 small islands, Las Isletas (most of them inhabited), with different and unusual vegetation. They can be visited either by hired boats or motor launches, from the Complejo Turístico (see above), eg from *Rincón Criollo*, T 4317, at US$17/hr for the whole boat, or from the restaurant at the end of the road beyond the Complejo Turístico, US$50/hr for 6 in a motor launch, or US$10/hr for 2 in a rowing boat. On Sun at 1400 a boat makes a round trip to the islands, returning in the evening, US$3.30, take a picnic and drinks (those sold are expensive). Ask around for other boats. There is plenty of lakeside birdlife to see. Alternatively, take the morning bus (or taxi US$3.50) from Granada to **Puerto Asese**, 3 km further S, a tranquil town at the base of the Asese peninsula at the head of the Ensenada de Asese. (Pleasant *Restaurante Asese*, T 2269, on the lake, good value, fish specialities.) Boats can be hired for US$10-12 per hour for 2 people. Trips to various lake destinations (Zapatera, El Muerto, the Solentiname islands, Río San Juan) can be arranged in the yacht *Pacífico*, up to 15 people on day trips, 8 for overnight voyages, lunch included, rec for a group (information and reservations T Granada 4305/2269).

OMETEPE

The largest island, **Ometepe** (*pop* 20,000), has two volcanoes, one of them, **Concepción**, a perfect cone rising to 1,610m. The other is Volcán Madera, 1,394m. There are two villages on the island, on either side of Volcán Concepción: **Moyogalpa** (*pop* 4,500) and **Alta Gracia**, which are connected by bus (1 hr US$0.75). Moyogalpa is more attractive than Alta Gracia. In Moyogalpa there is a Banco Nacional del Desarrollo and a shop which changes money (sign above door, lousy rates). There is a new tourist office, up the hill from the harbour, which offers good information, tours, horseriding, bus timetables, etc. Write to: Fundación Entre Volcanes, de la Gasolinera Esso 1 C y ½ al Sur, Moyogalpa, Ometepe, Nicaragua. Local guides can be found at Ecotur Ometepe, T/F 94118. Cockfights in Moyogalpa on Sun afternoons. An unusual feature of the town are the huge trees with (modest) houses underneath.

A new museum has opened in Alta Gracia, half a block from the central park, entrance US$1. Ask for the birdwatching place about 3 km from Alta Gracia; birds fly in the late afternoon to nest on offshore islands. One can stroll to the base of Volcán Concepción for good views of the lake and the company of many birds and howler monkeys (*congos*). To climb the volcano, leave from Cuatro Cuadros, 2 km from Alta Gracia, and make for a cinder gully between forested slopes and a lava flow. There are several fincas on the lower part of the volcano. The ascent takes about 5 hrs (take water). Alpine vegetation, the crater radiating heat and the howler monkeys are attractions. Very steep near summit. You can get a guide by asking near the pier, worthwhile as visibility is often restricted by clouds, and it is easy to get lost, especially in the final stages (US$18-28). Eduardo Ortiz and his son, José, of Cuatro Cuadros, will also guide. There is an alternative route up Volcan Concepción from behind the church in Moyogalpa. South of Volcán Concepción is Charco Verde lagoon and a waterfall worth visiting.

Between Alta Gracia and Balgües is **Santo Domingo** with a wide grey sand beach.

For **Volcán Madera**, take an early bus (0430 or 0530) from Alta Gracia to Balgües, ask for *Hacienda Magdalena*, go up through banana plantations and forest to the top, beautiful lagoon in the crater, 4-5 hrs up. Hear the howler monkeys all the way up. Take water and food. On the SW flank of Volcán Madera is Salto San Ramón, a 110m waterfall. In several locations on the island are Indian petroglyphs, the best being near Hacienda Magdalena.

- **Accommodation** Alta Gracia: **D** *Cari*, half a block from pier, T 0459-4263, F 0459-4283, some a/c, restaurant; **E** *Central*, on main street to Moyogalpa, attractive courtyard and dining room, good friendly service, with bath, nice patio, cabinas in garden, rec; **F** *Castillo*, on same road, friendly, good food, slow service, owner Ramón Castillo, is 'an uncappable fount of information' and can organize trips to rock carvings on the volcano, US$4 pp or US$12 for a group guide; *Las Cabañas*, close to Playa Santa Domingo, new.

In Moyogalpa: **E** *Ometeplt*, on main street from dock, T 0459-4276, F 0459-4132, bath, fan, clean, small but comfortable rooms, service and food disappointing, car hire; **E** *Bahía*, on main street from dock; **F** *Pensión Aly*, opp Shell, clean, uncomfortable beds but best food in town, helpful, changes TCs and cash;

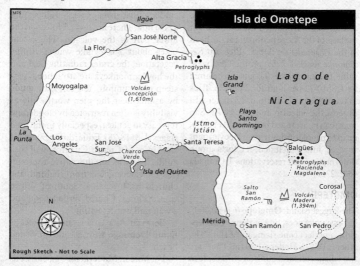

Isla de Ometepe

Ilgüe
San José Norte
La Flor
Alta Gracia
Petroglyphs
Moyogalpa
Volcán
Concepción
(1,610m)
Isla
Grand
e
Lago de
Nicaragua
Playa
Santo
Domingo
Istmo
Istián
La
Punta
Los
Angeles
San José
Sur
Charco
Verde
Santa Teresa
Balgües
Petroglyphs
Hacienda
Magdalena
Isla del Quiste
N
Salto
San
Ramón
Volcán
Madera
(1,394m)
Corosal
Mérida
San Ramón
San Pedro

Rough Sketch - Not to Scale

F pp *Asyl*, close to jetty, with restaurant; **F** *El Pirata*, on the E side of town, T 0459-4262; **G** *Pension Jade*, good atmosphere, friendly, water problems, meals available good value; *Los Ranchitos*, on same street as telephone company, excellent food, reasonable prices, highly rec.

In Santo Domingo: **E** *Villa Paraiso*, clean, lake view, friendly, peaceful, good meals, good bird-watching, rec; **F** *Pensión Santo Domingo*, comfortable.

● **Transport** Launches sail from Granada to Alta Gracia, continuing to San Carlos (see below); leave Granada Mon and Thur, 1300, ticket office open 0900, queue can be 1½ hrs. 4½ hrs to Alta Gracia, US$1.35, 10 hrs Alta Gracia-San Carlos, US$1.30 (Granada-San Carlos US$2.05). Boats arrive in San Carlos at 0500 and 0600 (passengers stay on board till daylight) and return on Tues at 1600 and 1700. Boats leave Alta Gracia for Granada on Wed at 0300 and 0400 and on Sun at 1000. Everything left on deck will get wet; as it can be very crowded, a good spot for sleeping is on the cabin roof. Snacks and soft drinks sold on board. A new direct hydrofoil service from Granada to San Carlos was started in late 1995, US$11, 3 hrs, and has become very popular. Make reservations or turn up early. It leaves Granada Wed, Fri, Sat and Sun at 0800, Thur and Mon 0900, returns Mon, Wed, Thur, Fri 1400, Sat and Sun 1330, with a stop both ways (Sat and Sun) at

Mancarrón in the Solentiname Islands. No service Tues. There is also a hydrofoil to Moyogalpa from Granada Sat and Sun 0800 returning at 1430, US$6. Ticket office in Granada is at the dock; ENAP T 2966.

SAN JORGE

Moyogalpa can be reached from **San Jorge** on the lake's SW shore; 5 boats a day Mon-Sat, 2 boats on Sun; fare US$1 on ferry, US$2.50 on yacht (2 of the weekday sailings), 1-1¼ hrs.

● **Accommodation** **F** *Nicarao*, left off the Rivas-San Jorge road, a short distance from the dock, basic meals, friendly. Meals are not easy to come by in San Jorge. On Sun in summer San Jorge is very lively with music, baseball, swimming and lots of excursion buses.

From San Jorge a road runs through Rivas (frequent bus service, US$0.30, 30 mins) to the port of San Juan del Sur.

SAN CARLOS

The Río San Juan, running through deep jungles, drains the lake from the eastern end into the Caribbean at San Juan del Norte. Launches ply down the river irregularly from the lakeside town of **San Carlos** (*pop* 15-20,000) at the SE corner of the Lake. Much of the town was destroyed by fire in 1984, but some rebuilding has been done. At San Carlos are the ruins of a fortress built for defence against pirates. A popular boat excursion is to the **Reserva Los Guatuzos**, a nature reserve along the S coast of the lake and part of the S bank of the Río San Juan.

● **Accommodation & places to eat** All hotels are basic, dirty, with bugs, rats etc. The worst is the large blue one of the corner of the plaza. One possibility is **D** *Cabanas Layca*, that has running water; another is the *Hospedaje Peña*, nr central square; **F** *Casa de Protocolo*, top of town on park opp church, clean, nets, private bath. *Restaurante Río San Juan*, good meals, room for rent, G, dirty, noisy; also *San Carlos* and 2 more basic *pensiones*; several *comedores*; *Bar-restaurant Kaoma*, Río San Carlos, T 20293, rec; *Oasis*, by the lake. If your hotel has no running water, there is a bath house by the pier.

● **Banks & money changers** Exchange (slow) at Banco Nacional de Desarrollo.

● **Transport Air** La Costeña flies from Managua Mon, Wed, Fri and on to Nueva Güinea on a circular route back to Managua, US$72 return. **Buses** There are buses to Granada and Managua at 0800, 10 hrs (not weekends), US$6 approx; on Mon there is a truck at 0600 to Santo Tomás, change in Lóvago for buses to Managua. San Carlos-Lóvago US$2, 5 hrs, a tough ride, Lóvago-Tipitapa US$2, 3 hrs. Bus Granada-San Miguelito, Mon, Tues, Wed, Thur 0830 from the pier, 8 hrs); bus San Carlos-Acoyapa, US$2.30, 'hellish' road for first 4 hrs. **Lake** See under Alta Gracia above for boat and hovercraft schedules. The slower boats stop at San Miguelito (*pop* 8,000, one primitive *pensión*). Boats can be hired to explore the shores of the lake S of the Solentiname Islands.

Some 60 km down river is **El Castillo de la Inmaculada Concepción** where there are the ruins of another 18th century Spanish fort, **Castillo Viejo** (**E** *Hospedaje Aurora*, basic, serves food; **C** *Albergue El Castillo*, new, shared bath, T 055-4635, 552-6127, in Managua 678267. Restaurant: *Naranjano*, good food). There is a daily boat from San Carlos to El Castillo at 1000 (5-6 hrs) returning at 0900, and also a hovercraft now operates downriver to El Castillo.

It is now possible to take a boat from San Carlos down to the mouth of the Río San Juan to San Juan del Norte, but there are no regular sailings (see page 1027). Descending the river, you can camp where the Río Bartola joins the Río San Juan, which is where the **Reserva Indio Maíz** has been established. There is a Ranger station here, another where the Río San Carlos comes in from Costa Rica (where boats stop for the night) and a third in the delta of the river near San Juan del Norte. The reserve can be visited by organized parties. For further information, enquire in San Juan or El Castillo.

Check in San Carlos on Lake Nicaragua with ANCUR for boats, irregular sailings. The trip takes at least 12 hrs to San Juan, up to 48 hrs upstream. You need to take food (though some is available at the Río San Carlos stopover) and a hammock is recommended. No permits to visit San Juan are now needed.

SOLENTINAME ISLANDS

Boats also run from San Carlos to the **Solentiname Islands** in the Lake, Tues, Fri, Sat, Sun, 1400. Hotels: *Hotel Isla Solentiname*, on San Fernando island, safe, acceptable but basic (you wash in the lake), cost including meals **C**; and a second hotel, **B** *Mancarrón*, overpriced but neat and comfortable rooms, on Mancarrón island, the largest, which has a library and an interesting church. Ernesto Cardenal (the poet and former Minister of Culture) lived and worked here. You can stay more cheaply with locals, ask around. The islands are home to many renowned primitive painters and are pleasant to hike around.

Warning The lake is dirty in some places, so swim in it with care.

About 14 km S of San Carlos, on the Río Frío, is Los Chiles, over the border in Costa Rica (see page 1079).

FRONTIER WITH COSTA RICA – SAN CARLOS TO LOS CHILES

Foreigners are now permitted to cross the frontier here, though some difficulties have been reported from Costa Rican officials. There is a track of sorts from the S side of the San Juan River but most travellers go by boat up the Río Frío.

● **Nicaraguan immigration**
Border is open Mon-Fri 0800-1600 only. Exit stamps must be obtained in San Carlos Mon-Fri only. Check with the police in advance for the latest position.

● **Transport**
There are 5 launches a week from San Carlos to Los Chiles, US$3.50, 1½ hrs. **NB** The entire Nicaragua-Costa Rica border along the San Juan

River is ill-defined and the subject of inter-government debate.

There is a proposal to create a national park, Sí-a-paz (Yes to Peace), which will stretch from the southern shore of Lake Nicaragua to the Caribbean coast along the Río San Juan. It will include the Solentiname islands and the Costa Rican side of the river, linking with the Caño Negro and Bara del Colorado Wildlife Refuges in Costa Rica.

Managua to Costa Rica

THE PAN-AMERICAN Highway to the Costa Rican border passes through agricultural land, with branches inland to Granada and to the Pacific coast. A useful stopping place is Rivas: from here to the border, Lake Nicaragua and Volcán Concepción are to be seen. For sunsets, go to San Juan del Sur.

The Pan-American Highway, in good condition, has bus services all the way to San José de Costa Rica (148 km). The road runs into the Sierra de Managua, reaching 900m at Casa Colorada, 26 km from Managua. Further on, at El Crucero (a cool and pleasant place), a paved branch road goes through the Sierra S to the Pacific bathing beaches of Pochomil and Masachapa (see page 990).

DIRIAMBA

The Highway continues through the beautiful scenery of the Sierras to **Diriamba** (*pop* 26,500; *alt* 760m; *phone code* 042), 42 km from Managua in a coffee-growing district. Its great *fiesta* is on 20 Jan. There is a 32-km dirt road direct to Masachapa (no buses). 5 km N of Diriamba a paved road branches off the highway to Managua and runs E through San Marcos, Masatepe and Niquinohomo to Catarina and Masaya.

● **Accommodation** E *Diriangén*, with bath, parking.

● **Places to eat** Good fish at restaurant *2 de Junio*.

JINOTEPE

5 km beyond Diriamba is **Jinotepe** (*pop* 17,600; *alt* 760m; *phone code* 041), capital of the coffee-growing district of Carazo. It has a fine neo-classical church with modern stained glass windows from Irún, in Spain. The *fiesta* in honour of St James the Greater is on 24-26 July. 5 July is celebrated here as 'liberation day'.

● **Accommodation** C *Jinotepe*, T 22978, 22947, modern, 3-storey building 1 block N and 1 block W of Parque Central, comfortable, with bath and fan, dance floor, fine restaurant, good service; F *Hospedaje San Carlos*, no sign, ask around for it.

● **Places to eat** *Pizza Danny's* is very good, 50m N of municipal building (try their *especial*, small but delicious, US$7).

● **Banks & money changers** Banco Nacional de Desarrollo for exchange; black market for dollars in Parque Central.

● **Buses** for Managua leave from the terminal in the NE corner of town, every 20 mins, US$0.55; to Nandaime every 30 mins, US$0.35; to Diriamba-Masaya every 20 mins.

From **Nandaime**, 21 km from Jinotepe, altitude 130m, a paved road runs N to Granada (bus US$0.50). Nandaime has two interesting churches, El Calvario and La Parroquia (1859-72). The annual *fiesta* is 24-27 July, with masked dancers. Unnamed *hospedaje*, E, and restaurant *La Cabaña*, good local dishes, a favourite with truck drivers.

RIVAS

About 45 km beyond Nandaime (US$0.40 by bus) is **Rivas** (*pop* 34,000; *phone code* 0461). The Costa Rican national hero, the drummer Juan Santamaría, sacrificed his life here in 1856 when setting fire to a building captured by the filibuster William Walker and his men. On the town's Parque Central is a lovely old church (in need of repair). In the dome of the Basilica, see the fresco of the sea battle against the ships of Protestantism and Communism. The parque has some old, arcaded buildings on one side, but also some new buildings. Rivas is a good stopping place (rather than Managua) if in transit by land through Nicaragua. The bus station, adjacent to the market is on the NW edge of town about 8 blocks from the main highway. The road from the lake port of San Jorge joins this road at Rivas; 11 km beyond Rivas, at La Virgen on the shore of Lake Nicaragua, it branches S to San Juan del Sur.

Local information
● Accommodation

D *Nicaragua* (or *Nicarao*), 2 blocks W of Parque Central, nr cinema (3 blocks S and 2 E from bus terminal), with a/c, cheaper with fan, comfortable, slow service, shower, cold water, best in town, clean, well-equipped, good restaurant.

E *Pensión Primavera*, small rooms but clean, shared bath, friendly, basic.

F *El Coco*, on Pan-American Highway nr where bus from frontier stops, noisy, basic, small rooms, shower, interesting bar, *comedor* with vegetarian food, nice garden; *Hospedaje El Mesón*, basic; **F** *Hospedaje Delicia*, on main Managua-border road, basic and dirty, friendly; **F** *Hospedaje Internacional*, where the SIRCS bus stops, nr the Texaco station, good breakfast; several on Highway, **E** *Hospedaje Lidia*, nr Texaco, clean, noisy, family-run. (At the Texaco station, Lenín, who speaks English, is very helpful.)

● Places to eat
Restaurant Chop Suey, in the arcade in Parque Central; *Rinconcito Salvadoreño*, in the middle of the Parque Central, open air, charming. *Comedor Lucy*, on street leaving Parque Central at corner opp Banco de Nicaragua, '*comidas corrientes y vegetarianos*'; *Restaurant El Ranchito*, nr *Hotel El Coco*, friendly, serves delicious chicken and *churrasco*.

● Banks & money changers
Banco Nacional de Desarrollo. You may have to persuade them to cash TCs. Black market nr market.

● Post & telecommunications
Enitel is 3 blocks S of Parque Central, or 7 blocks S and 3 blocks E from bus terminal.

● Buses
To the frontier Sapoá/Peñas Blancas: every hour or so: 0645, 0730 and 1100, good for connections for buses to San José (US$0.60, plus US$0.60 for each piece of luggage, 1 hr) (taxis available, about US$15 from bus terminal, add US$2 from town centre, or a place in a colectivo, US$3). Alternatively, try to get on the Sirca bus which stops at the Sirca office about 0800, Mon, Wed, Fri and Sat (NB Tica bus stops in Rivas, but only to let people off). Trucks on this section are generous with hitchhikers and are useful for continuing through the gap between customs and beyond. Bus to **Managua**, from 0400 (last one 1700), 2½ hrs, US$1.40; taxi, US$40. Several daily buses to **Granada**; it may be quicker to take the Managua bus and change at Nandaime. Frequent bus to **San Jorge** on Lake Nicaragua, US$0.25 (taxi to San Jorge, US$1.50).

A few km before Rivas, coming from Nandaime, is a road to the left to Potosí, a quiet village with *Comedor Soda Helen*, one block from the Parque Central; meals are available in the evening if you request them.

Between Nandaime and Rivas are various turnings S which lead eventually to the Pacific coast (all are rough, high clearance better than 4WD). One of these turnings, 89 km from Managua if going via Diriamba and Jinotepe (61 km from Peñas Blancas), by a metal bridge, is signposted Refugio de Vida Silvestre Chacocente. The road (45 km, dirt, rough, 4WD rec, 5 rivers to cross – no bridges) leads to Las Salinas (signed all the way Chacocente or RVS); from there go to **Astillero**, which has a fishing cooperative. (There is also a road between Rivas and Las Salinas.) Camping is safe and you can buy fish from the co-op. 5 km further by truck from Astillero (leaves very early) is **Chacocente**, at which is an Irena office, a Government-sponsored turtle sanctuary (the only signs after Astillero say 'authorized personnel only': don't be put off, they welcome visitors, but ask for directions). The Irena wardens protect newly-hatched turtles and help them make it to the sea (a magnificent sight during Nov and Dec). Unfortunately, new-laid turtle eggs are considered to have aphrodisiac properties and are used as a dietary supplement by the locals. Irena is virtually powerless to prevent egg theft, although for 2 months a year the place is protected by armed military personnel. Do not get involved since threats against the officers have been made (international smuggling rings handle the trade in stolen eggs). The Irena personnel are friendly and helpful (ask about similar projects around the country); entry US$0.70 (with thanks to Francesca Pagnacco, Exeter, for this information). Bring a tent or hammock and food if you plan to stay at Chacocente.

SAN JUAN DEL SUR

San Juan del Sur (*pop* 4,750) is 28 km from Rivas via the Pan-American Highway (regular minibus from market, crowded, 45 mins, US$0.60), 93 km from Granada. The road from the Pan-American Highway is in good condition. There is a direct dirt road from Rivas, good only when dry, going through beautiful countryside. It has a beautiful bay with a sandy beach and some rocky caves reached by walking round the point opposite the harbour. Best beaches are Playa del Coco and Playa del Tamarindo, 15 km away on the poor road to Ostional; and Marsella, 5 km N of San Juan where there is a kiosk on the beach. (Watch out for sting rays at low tide.) Sunsets here have to be seen to be believed.

Good surfing on these and nearby beaches. Check tides with officials at the Customs Office, who will give permission for camping and to park motor-caravans and trailers on the wharves if you ask them nicely.

Motor-caravans and trailers may also be parked on Marsella beach: coming S, turn right on entering San Juan, by shrimp-packing plant.

These beaches are busy at week ends and on holidays, especially at *Semana Santa*, but otherwise are quiet during the week.

Local information
● **Accommodation**

B *Barlovento*, Km 141, T (045) 82298, on hill above town with excellent views, a/c, meetings facilities.

C *Joxi*, T (045) 82348, friendly, clean, a/c, bath, Norwegian run, restaurant, bar, sailing trips on the boat 'Pelican Eyes' can be arranged here; on same street is **D** *Estrella*, on Pacific, with meals, balconies overlooking the sea, partitioned walls, take mosquito net, toilet facilities outside, rooms must be shared as they fill up, 'popular with hippies'; **D** *Lago Azul*, good, with restaurant (see below).

E *Buengusto*, opp, very basic but very friendly, helpful, good fish restaurant, on seafront; **E** *Guest House Elizabeth*, opp bus terminal, T (458) 2270, clean, tan, friendly and helpful owner; **E** *Irazú*, 1 block from beach, some rooms with bath, very run down.

F pp *Hospedaje Casa No 28*, 40m from beach, nr minibus stop for Rivas, shared showers, mosquitoes (ask owner for coils), kitchen and laundry facilities, clean, friendly owners, good; **F** *Gallo de Oro*, 500m N of town, very basic but friendly and cheapest around, nice setting at end of beach; **F** *Hospedaje La Fogata*, clean, friendly, family run, good food, rec.

● **Places to eat**

Salón Siria, good; *Soya*, vegetarian and meat dishes, fruit, *refrescos*, *chorizo de soya*, good, cheap and friendly, also has a room to rent (**F**); good *panadería* one block from beach. Good cafés along the beach for breakfast and drinks; the beach front restaurants all serve good fish (about US$4 a meal), eg *Timon Bar*, delicious *gambas*, lobster (US$9) and prawns are specialities, owner can be grumpy though. Breakfast and lunch in market; *Comedor Angelita* serves very good fish dishes. Food in the evening from a stall in street running W from the market; *Lago Azul*, good fish restaurant at N end of bay beyond the river; *Rancho Miravalle*, good for fish.

● **Banks & money changers**
Banco Nacional de Desarrollo, no TCs.

● **Laundry**
Near *Soya Restaurant* (ask there) hand wash, line dry.

● **Post & telecommunications**
Post Office: 2 blocks S along the front from *Hotel Estrella*.

● **Buses**
Minibus from **Rivas** Market, regular, crowded, 55 mins, US$0.60. Direct bus **Managua**, 3½ hrs, US$2.10.

FRONTIER WITH COSTA RICA – PEÑAS BLANCAS

This is the only road crossing between the two countries. There is a duty free shop on the Nicaraguan side.

● **Nicaraguan immigration**
Open 0900-1200 and 1300-1745. When entering the country, you show your passport at the border but the Nicaraguan Migración is at **Sapoá**, 4 km into Nicaragua, to which you can take a minibus, (they go when full), US$0.70. Allow 1½-2 hrs to complete the formalities. There is a '*municipalidad*' tax of US$10 pp.

● **Crossing by private vehicle**
Entering: after you have been through Migración, find an inspector who will fill out the preliminary form to be taken to Aduana. At the Vehículo Entrando window, the vehicle permit is typed up and the vehicle stamp is put in your passport; Next, go to Tránsito to pay for the car permit. Finally, ask the inspector again to give the final check.

Leaving: first pay your US$2 exit tax at an office at the end of the control station, receipt given. Then come back for your exit stamp, US$0.60, and complete the Tarjeta de Control Migratorio. Motorists must then go to Aduana to cancel vehicle papers: exit details are typed on to the vehicle permit and the stamp in your passport is cancelled. Find the inspector in Aduana who has to check the details and stamp your permit. If you fail to do this you will not be allowed to leave the country – you will be sent back to Sapoá by the officials at the final Nicaraguan checkpoint. Note that there is no fuel going into Nicaragua until Rivas, 37 km.

● **Exchange**
Better rates on the Costa Rican side.

● **Transport**
There is an hourly bus service from Sapoá to Rivas from 0730-1630, US$0.70, 1 hr. The last bus Rivas – Managua is at 1636, US$1.40, 2½ hrs. There can be long waits when the international buses are passing through. A good time to cross, if you are going independently, is around 0900, before the buses arrive.

The Caribbean Coast

NICARAGUA'S EASTERN tropical lowlands are very different from the rest of the country: there is heavy rainfall between May and Dec; the economy is based on timber, fishing and mining. The people are mostly Miskito Indians, but with much African influence. English is widely spoken. To reach the Caribbean port of Bluefields, from where you can go to the Corn Islands, you either have to fly or take the famous 'Bluefields Express' down river.

NB In Nicaragua, the Caribbean coast is almost always referred to as the Atlantic coast.

The area, together with about half the coastal area of Honduras, was never colonized by Spain. From 1687 to 1894 it was a British Protectorate known as the Miskito Kingdom. It was populated then, as now, by Miskito Indians, whose numbers are estimated at 75,000. There are two other Indian groups, the Sumu (5,000) and the Rama, of whom only a few hundred remain, near Bluefields. Also near Bluefields are a number of Garifuna communities. Today's strong African influence has its roots in the black labourers brought in by the British to work the plantations and in Jamaican immigration. The Afro-Nicaraguan people call themselves creoles (*criollos*). The largest number of inhabitants of this zone are Spanish-speaking *mestizos*. The Sandinista revolution, like most other political developments in the Spanish-speaking part of Nicaragua, was met with mistrust.

Although the first Sandinista junta recognized the indigenous peoples' rights to organize themselves and choose their own leaders, many of the programmes initiated in the region failed to encompass the social, agricultural and cultural traditions of eastern Nicaragua. Relations deteriorated and many Indians engaged in fighting for self-determination. About half the Miskito population fled as refugees to Honduras, but most returned after 1985 when a greater understanding grew between the Sandinista Government and the people of the E Coast. The Autonomous Atlantic Region was given the status of a self-governing region in 1987; it is divided into Región Autonomista Atlántico Norte (RAAN) and Región Autonomista Atlántico Sur (RAAS).

In late Feb 1994, elections for the Atlantic coastal autonomous regional councils were held. The party to win most votes in the North and South was the Liberals, with the Sandinistas second in each case. The poor showing of both government and FSLN was a mark of the discontent

Provisions and protection

For travel to the Atlantic Coast, a traveller should bring a mosquito net, sleeping bag, mosquito spray, flashlight, toilet paper, rain jacket, Zip-lock bags (to store toilet paper, film, cameras, etc), and sunscreen. (If not venturing beyond Bluefields or Puerto Cabezas, you may not need more than protection against the sun, rain and mosquitoes, although these are not as voracious as they are outside the large towns.) For travel inland to the rural areas, the traveller should add water, water purification tablets, more anti-mosquito protection, and carry his/her own food (such as rice, potatoes, dried soup packets, tomatoes, coffee, canned food). You should have no trouble finding someone to cook for you for a nominal fee (such as US$1 pp) or for trade (items such as sugar, inexpensive watches, tapes, etc). Ask for the village leader or pastor (either Catholic or Moravian) if you need a place to stay for the night; usually you can stay in the chapel, school, or someone's house. Do not leave your things unattended. It should be stressed that nowhere in the country are the mosquitos and other insects so voracious as in the southern Atlantic coast region; you must take particular care, and as dusk approaches, it would be wise to put on long pants and socks, and wear long sleeves. The mosquitos are particularly vicious at this time.

felt in rural areas, especially the Atlantic coast and central mountain regions.

FROM MANAGUA TO RAMA

At **San Benito**, 35 km from Managua on the Pan American Highway going N, the Atlantic Highway branches E, paved all the way to Rama on the Río Escondido, or Bluefields River. Shortly after Teustepe, a paved road goes NE to Boaco. A turn-off, unpaved, goes to **Santa Lucía**, a village inside a crater, with a women's handicraft shop. There is also a cooperative here with an organic farming programme (information from Unag in Matagalpa). *Casa de Soya*, good food, friendly owners, single room for rent, basic, F. Good views from nearby mountains. 2 trucks a day from Boaco, US$1, 1 bus a day to/from Managua. **Boaco** (*pop* 15,000), 84 km from Managua, has a nice square with good views of the surrounding countryside. **E** *Hotel Sobalvarro*, on the square, is good; **G** *Hotel Boaco*, at the entrance to the town, basic. Its specialities are white cheese and cream. From Boaco, unpaved roads go N to Muy Muy and Matagalpa, and S to Comoapa (*pop* 4,000). Bus Managua-Boaco every 40 mins from Mercado San Miguel, 2 hrs 10 mins, US$1.50.

JUIGALPA

The Atlantic Highway continues through **Juigalpa** (*pop* 30,000; 139 km from Managua, buses every ½ hr, US$1.85, 3 hrs). A pleasant town with one of the best museums in Nicaragua, with a collection of idols resembling those at San Agustín, Colombia. Small zoo in the valley below town. The bus terminal is in the town centre near the market, up the hill. Banks on main square accept US$ only, no TCs.

● **Accommodation D** *Hotel La Quinta*, T 081-2485, on main road at the east end of town, a/c or fan, bath, clean, friendly, restaurant has good food and a fine view of surrounding mountains; **E** *Hospedaje Rubio*, on main road going N, clean, friendly, with bath (**F** without), TV, laundry; **F** *Hospedaje Central*, basic and noisy; *Hospedaje Angelita* the same; the hospedaje in *Comedor San Martín* is unfriendly; better is *Presillas* (Km 269), unnamed, beside *Comedor González*; all F pp.

A gravel road goes to La Libertad, a gold-mining town at 600m (*pop* 4,000, *hospedaje*), and on to Santo Domingo. From Juigalpa a road goes direct to the shore of Lake Nicaragua at Puerto Díaz. From here pick-ups will go to the monastery of San Juan de las Aguas for about US$1.20 pp if 4 passengers (Pedro Cortéz rec, Oswaldo Melón not so). The guide will show you the path through swamps to the monastery (2-3 km) which was founded in 1689. It's a little neglected, but has several wooden statues. The monks are very friendly and will let you stay the night if you ask. Take your own food and leave a donation. Ask to see the cave/tunnel complex that was used when the monks hid from besieging Indians (Vincent van Es, Enschede, Netherlands).

25 km S of Juigalpa an unpaved road turns off to **Acoyapa** (7 km, *pop* 5,000, *hospedaje*), El Morrito, San Miguelito and San Carlos on Lake Nicaragua (see page 1012).

The main road goes E to **Santo Tomás** (*pop* 10,000, several *hospedajes*) and smaller villages (including La Gateada, turn-off to **Nuevo Güinea**, centre of cacao production, connected by air from Managua via San Carlos on Mon, Wed, Fri with La Costeña, US$64 return, T 2850160), to **Cara de Mono** (*hospedaje*), on the Río Mico, and finally to **Rama** (*pop* 35,000), 290 km from Managua. The town was badly hit by Hurricane Joan in Oct 1988 when the river rose 16m above normal height. It is now poor and dirty. *Hospedaje Ramada Inn* seems to be the best; Hotels *Amy* and *Johanna* both **E**, neither has showers, *Amy* cleaner and quieter, near main jetty. Good cheap food at *Comedor Torres*. Bus Juigalpa to Rama every 30 mins 0430 to 1430, 4½ hrs, US$2.50, terrible road even though paved. The buses connect, most of the day, with the half hourly service to Managua.

RAMA TO BLUEFIELDS

On the 'Bluefields Express', the ferry from Rama to Bluefields, some 200 people, assorted animals and goods crowd the deck. The journey passes through the sparsely populated eastern half of Nicaragua. The river is wide and fast flowing, passing land that is mostly cultivated, with the occasional poor farmer's dwelling. After the devastation of Hurricane Joan in 1988, some reconstruction has taken place

although much of the population has not returned from the capital.

● **Transport** Take a bus from Mercado San Miguel (Terminal Atlántico), Managua to Rama along the paved road (in poor condition), 7-9 hrs, leaves 2230, Mon, Wed, Fri to connect with boat to Bluefields at 1100, Tues, Thur, Sat (check days, boat US$7, combined Managua-Bluefields ticket US$12.85, buy ticket at reservation office at the terminal, preferably 1 day in advance, Cotlántico, T 280-0036, Managua). Food and soft drinks are sold on the ferry. Trip downriver takes 5-6 hrs. Return from Bluefields: boat at 0500 Tues, Thur, Sat, bus to Managua 1030 (combined tickets available, ticket office at Encab, nr dock). There is also one boat each way on Sun dep Rama 1130, dep Bluefields 0500, but no connecting bus.

An alternative service is run by Brooks-Hamilton, T Managua 496953, Bluefields 822-2496, Tues, Thur, Sat 0230 from bus station at De La Siemens 2 cuadras al lago, Km 6 Carretera Norte, Managua, boat leaves Rama 0900, return from Bluefields same day 0700, bus 1000, US$15.50 Managua-Bluefields. This is not a very interesting 6 hr river trip. Fast boats, *pangas*, can be hired for US$12-15 Rama – Bluefields, taking 1½ hrs, or hitch on a fishing boat.

BLUEFIELDS

Bluefields (*pop* 35,000; *phone code* 082), the most important of Nicaragua's 3 Caribbean ports, gets its name from the Dutch pirate Abraham Blaauwveld. It stands on a lagoon behind the bluff at the mouth of the Bluefields River (Río Escondido), which is navigable as far as Rama (96 km). In May there is a week-long local festival, Mayo-Ya!, with elements of the British Maypole tradition and local music, poetry and dancing. *Fiesta*, 30 Sept for San Jerónimo. Bananas, cabinet woods, frozen fish, shrimps and lobsters were the main exports until the hurricane in 1988 (see below).

Tragically, in Oct 1988, Hurricane Joan destroyed virtually all of Bluefields, but the rebirth is well underway. Information on the region can be found at the Cidca office. Local bands practice above the Ivan Dixon Cultural Centre, beside the library. There are several bars, a couple of reggae clubs, *comedores* and restaurants

(2 with a/c), and an Almacén Internacional. Prices are about the same as in
Managua, but the atmosphere has become tense and grasping, with many
'guides' offering their services and leading visitors to buy things at inflated
prices. Be prepared for frequent power
and water cuts.

Local information
● Accommodation & places to eat

B *South Atlantic*, nr central square, T/F 242,
next to Enitel, run by Fanny and Hubert Chambers (native language English), with bath, safe,
a/c, cable TV, fridge, clean, friendly, excellent
food, *South Atlantic II*, new annex in the main
street, T/F 640; **D** *Caribbean*, bath, a/c, nr centre of town, good cook (Angela), friendly, rec;
C pp *Costa Sur*, **E** *El Dorado*, may offer floor
space to late arrivals; **E** *Hollywood*, has its own
well and generator, friendly, restaurant, clean,
will change TCs; **E** *Marda Maus*, one of the
nicer places in its price range with bath and fan,
dark, not too clean, no restaurant, soft drinks
available, nr market; **F** *Airport*, above *Costeña*
office at airport, clean, friendly; **F** *Claudia*,
clean, comfortable, cable TV, room on street side
best; *Café Central*, good value meals, provides
accommodation, has colour TV. *Restaurant
Flottante*, built over the water at the end of
the main street, average prices, slow service,
great view. Everywhere can be full if you arrive
late, or are last off the ferry.

● Transport

Air The airport is 3 km from the city centre;
either walk 30 mins or take a taxi jeep that waits
by the runway. In 1977 only **La Costeña** had
flights to Bluefields (T 822-2750), from Managua, 0645, 0700, 1000, 1400, Mon-Sat; 0700,
1400, Sun; also 1100, Mon, Wed, Fri, via Siuna,
Bonanza, Rosita and Puerto Cabezas, US$44
one way, US$79 return (1996 prices) most flights
continue to the Corn Islands. Managua offices
of both airlines are in the domestic terminal at
the airport. Bring passport, it is sometimes asked
for in the departure lounge. There is a customs
check on return to Managua. **NB** Flights rarely
leave on time, and sometimes leave early.

Sea El Bluff is a small island with a village
harbour, some oil tanks and a small, dirty beach.
It is accessible by *panga* (speedboat) from the
wharf at the market, T 739. When the *panga* is
full, pay your fare, no more than US$1.70.
Watch out for Richard Hooker who works on

the *pangas*, he allegedly makes up stories about
needing money for medicines, and overcharges
for boat fares.

From the main wharf small boats leave irregularly for villages on the coast and Laguna
de Perlas, such as Tasbapounie (*hospedaje* run
by Mr Leonard Richard Brent); food may be
scarce in all settlements. A boat leaves most days
around 0600 to **Laguna de Perlas** (Pearl Lagoon) 80 km N of Bluefields 3-6 hrs, US$5. The
lagoon itself is some 50 km long with mostly
Creole villages round its shores, eg Pearl Lagoon,
Haulover, Brown Bank, La Fe, Orinoco, Mashall
Point and San Vicente. Raitipura and Kakabila
are Indian villages. In Raitipura there is a Danish
housing project (run by Mogens Vibe). He takes
on volunteers (min 1 week), rec. At the village
of Pearl Lagoon there is a hostel, *Miss Ingrid's*,
very friendly, stay with the entertaining family.
Larger vessels may be available for transport to
Puerto Cabezas, but there is no transport S of
Bluefields.

On outlying areas of the Región Autonomista Atlántico Sur, Cindy Gersony of
Sarasota, Florida, writes: **Río Kurinwás**
area: It might occasionally be possible to
get a boat to the town of **Tortuguero** (also
called Nuevo Amanecer) some distance
up the Kurinwás River. The Kurinwás
is a fascinating, largely uninhabited jungle area, where it is possible to see monkeys and much other wildlife. Tortuguero
(about a 6-hr speedboat ride from Bluefields, several days by regular boat) is a
mestizo town of about 1,000. It will really
give you a taste of the frontier.

Río Grande area: The Río Grande is
the next river N of the Kurinwás, connected to the Pearl Lagoon by the Top-
Lock Canal. At its mouth are five
interesting villages: the four Miskito
communities of Kara, Karawala, Sandy
Bay Sirpi, and Walpa, and the Creole
village of La Barra. **Sandy Bay Sirpi** is
situated on both the river and the Caribbean, and has a nice beach. Travelling
upriver, the Río Grande is a noticea'e
contrast to the Río Kurinwás; it is much
more settled, dotted with farms and cattle
grazing. Quite a bit upriver (also about a
6-hr speedboat ride from Bluefields, several days by regular boat), the traveller

will come to the *mestizo* town of **La Cruz de Río Grande** (*pop* about 1,700). It was founded about 1922 by Chinese traders to serve workers from a banana plantation (now defunct) further upriver. La Cruz has a very pretty church, and there are resident expatriate (US) priests of the Capuchin order in the town. The adventurous can walk between La Cruz and Tortuguero: each way takes about 10 hrs in the dry season, 12 in the rainy.

CORN ISLANDS

Corn Islands (**Islas del Maíz**), in the Caribbean opposite Bluefields, are two small beautiful islands fringed with white coral and slender coconut trees, though sadly many on the larger island were blown down by the 1988 hurricane. The smaller island escaped serious damage; it can be visited by boat from the larger island, but there are no facilities for the tourist. The larger is a popular Nicaraguan holiday resort; its surfing and bathing facilities make it ideal for tourists (best months Mar and April). Everything is naturally more expensive than on the mainland. If you climb the mountain, wear long trousers, as there are many ticks. The language of the islands is English. The islanders are very friendly but petty thievery has been reported, even clothes stolen off a washing line. The local coconut oil industry has been devastated by Hurricane Joan, but lobsters provide much prosperity.

Local information
● Accommodation

D *Hospedaje Miramar* is rec, serves meals; **D** *Hospedaje Playa Coco*, also serves meals; **E** *Brisas del Mar*, Playa Coco, basic, loud disco in same building, good breakfast, restaurant; rec is Miss Florence's house, called *Casa Blanca*, even though it is blue, **D**, at Playa Coco. She allows you to use cooking facilities. The chief problem in all the hotels is rats, which may not be dangerous, but neither are they pleasant.

● Places to eat

Comedor Blackstone; *Mini Café*; ice cream parlour; several bars and reggae clubs. *Dugout de la Tonia* has the cheapest beer and good

punta music. Ask around for where meals are available; the restaurants serve mainly chicken and chop suey, but in private houses you can find much better fare. Try banana porridge and sorrel drink (red, and ginger-flavoured). There is a severe shortage of food, water and most drinks (except rum). Main market area is nr Will Bowers Wharf and is a cheap place to eat. Dollars are widely used. Since the price of everything is generally high and there is no bank, take the cash you need with you.

● Sports

Swimming: the best beach for swimming is Long Beach on Long Bay; walk across the island from Playa Coco. For **fishing** (barracuda, etc), contact Ernie Jenkie (about US$5/hr). It is possible to **dive** off the Corn Islands although the equipment 'looks like leftovers from WW2'. The reef is good, however, and dives are very cheap.

● Transport

Air La Costeña flies twice daily from Managua and Bluefields to the Corn Islands, Mon-Sat, 0645 and 1400 from Managua, 0845 and 1520 from Bluefields; Sun, 0700 and 1400 from Managua, 0815 and 1510 from Bluefields, US$55 from Managua, US$41 from Bluefields one way, Managua return US$101, plus US$1.50 departure tax; the same advice on passport and customs applies as under Bluefields. Air services are suspended from time to time because of the poor state of the runway on Isla del Maíz. Book well in advance and book return immediately on arrival.

Sea Passenger-carrying cargo boats leave Bluefields for the Corn Islands from the docks of Copesnica, N of town, around a small bay and past the ruined church. The water around Bluefields is dirty, muddy brown, soon becoming a clear, sparkling blue. There is usually a boat from Bluefields (the *Lynx Express*), via El Bluff, on Wed at 0830, 4 hrs, but there is no guarantee. Boats back to Bluefields leave from Will Bowers Wharf on Thur; tickets available in advance from nearby office, US$5 one way. You may be able to find a lobster, or other fishing boat that will take you. Check with the Capitanía in Bluefields, or in El Bluff and with anyone else you can find who has information. Trips take 5-8 hrs.

PUERTO CABEZAS

Puerto Cabezas is the capital of the RAAN, the northern Atlantic Coast autonomous region, and it has a distinctly different atmosphere from Bluefields; it is principally a large Miskito village. Puerto Cabezas (*pop* about 30,000) can offer an excellent introduction to the Miskito part of the country. There are significant minorities of *mestizos* (referred to on the Coast as *españoles* or the Spanish) and Creoles, many of whom came to 'Port' by way of Las Minas (see below). Spanish is a second language for most residents, although most speak it well (at least those who live in Puerto itself); many speak at least some English, and for some, it is their native language. The local name for Puerto Cabezas is Bilwi, although the name is of Sumo origin. The Miskitos conquered the Sumos to obtain the town sometime in the last century. There are no restrictions on travel to Puerto Cabezas, nor to the surrounding region, although it is occasionally necessary to go through police checkpoints.

There are two main roads, the only paved streets, which run parallel to each other and to the sea. At the southern end of the town (the airport is at the northern end) is the port area; a walk along the pier at sunset is highly recommended. The main market occupies the central part of town. TCs can be changed by Augusto Chow, ask for 'El Chino'.

Beaches

There is a beach in the town limits, but it is reputed to be dirty. A clean, and lovely, beach, Poza Verde, can be found several kilometres N of town: it has white sand, calm water and sandflies. Take the road out of town for about 15 mins and turn right on the track marked *SW Tuapi* (*SW* stands for *switch*); follow it for a few kilometers to the sea. You can also walk 6 km along the beach from Puerto Cabezas, or take a taxi (US$30 for 3 hrs, with bargaining, the track is very bad).

Local information
● **Accommodation**
Hospedaje: E *Cayos Miskitos*, 2 blocks E of the plaza, good, comfortable rooms with bath, clean, friendly, breakfast by arrangement in advance only; E *El Viajante*, also clean, central,

very friendly, basic wooden rooms with fan, singles only, shared baths, *comedor* serves good breakfast to its guests; E *Ricardo Pérez*, friendly, clean, all room have windows, meals available.

● **Places to eat**
The three best restaurants are the *Atlántico*, *Jumbo*, which serves Chinese food and is close to the sea, and *Pizzería Mercedita*, nr the harbour, very good, expensive, rec, wide liquor selection, good service. *El Zaire*, popular, with TV, food and service disappointing. There are also numerous *comedores*. Prices are much higher than elsewhere in Nicaragua because almost everything has to be brought in by air.

● **Hospitals & medical services**
Hospital: a hospital was inaugurated in Feb 1993. It is located on the outskirts of Puerto, on the road leading out of town.

● **Transport**
Air The airstrip is 3 km from the town. From the airport, it is possible to get a taxi that will charge US$1 to any point in Puerto (it is also possible to walk). La Costeña (T 282-2260) flies daily from Managua in small (20 seats) planes. Price is US$52 one way or US$92 return, plus US$1.50 departure tax. On Mon, Wed, Fri, La Costeña flies from Managua via Siuna, Bonanza, Rosita and Bluefields, US$50 from Bluefields. Cancellations are not infrequent, best to make reservation and pay just before plane leaves. Bring your passport: there are 'immigration' checks by the police in Puerto, and sometimes in the waiting lounge in Managua; also, there is a customs check when returning from the Coast by air to Managua.

Road It is not possible to rent a vehicle or bicycle in Puerto, but arrangements for a car and driver can be made with a taxi driver or others (ask a taxi or at your *hospedaje*). Public bus service is available between Puerto and Waspám (see below) and from Matagalpa (14 hrs). Furthermore, Puerto is connected by road to Managua; however, this 559-km trip should only be attempted in the dry season (early Jan to mid-May) in a 4WD vehicle. With luck, it will take only 2-3 days (the road, almost all of it unpaved, is not bad from Managua to Siuna, but becomes very difficult after that); do not drive at night. **NB** If you drive back from Puerto to Managua, take the road out of town and make a left turn at the sign, *SW Wawa*.

WASPAM AND THE COCO RIVER

The road from Puerto to Waspám, on the Coco River, has been mostly rehabilitated; during the dry season, the 130-km trip takes about 3 hrs by 4WD vehicle, several hrs longer by public bus (leaves Puerto 0700, Mon-Sat, with luck returns from Waspám 1200). The bus can be boarded at several points in Puerto along the road leading out of town, cost is US$5 to go to Waspám. This trip will take you through the pine forests, red earth, and plains N of Puerto towards the Coco River (the border with Honduras), and you will pass through two Miskito villages, Sisin and Santa Marta. Hitching rides is possible, if you cannot get all the way to Waspám, make sure you are left at Sisin, Santa Marta or La Tranquera. Give rides to, or take lifts from the military. Never travel at night.

Waspám and the Coco River The Coco River (called the *Wanghi* in Miskito) is the heart of Miskito country and there are numerous Miskito villages along the river, stretching as far inland as northern Jinotega Department all the way to the Caribbean. Waspám (Spanish spelling Waspán; *pop* about 2,500) is often referred to as 'the capital of the Río Coco'. A recommended place to eat is the *Comedor La Bondad* (a delicious meal of chicken, rice, beans, tomatoes, and a soft drink costs US$4). Waspám also has *hospedajes* (one E near river, basic, straw mattresses, bath house in back yard) and other *comedores*, as well as guest houses run by international organizations and local voluntary agencies, eg Hijos de Río Coco Foundation, who provide free beds to travellers. Ask Jaime Muller for information on travelling around the area.

A project has been working to repair the roads and bridges connecting the villages of the river, and it is now possible to go by vehicle as far as Kum, in one direction, and Leimus, in the other. An irregular boat service travels upriver from Waspám to San Carlos. Flights to Managua via Puerto Cabezas with La Costeña, Tues, Thur, Sat, US$98 return.

Provisions

The same information as under *Bluefields* applies here; along the river it can sometimes get chilly at night; bring a sweater or jacket.

FRONTIER WITH HONDURAS – LEIMUS

From **Leimus**, about 30 km upstream from Waspám and the same distance by road, you can cross into Honduras.

● **Nicaraguan immigration**
If leaving for Honduras, get your exit stamp in Puerto Cabezas. If entering Nicaragua, you may find that an entry stamp in Puerto Cabezas will be charged for, up to US$50.

Make a point of checking with the military posts on both sides of the frontier. Ask for a letter which you can present to immigration in Puerto Lempira (Honduras) and Puerto Cabezas (Nicaragua).

● **Accommodation**
No formal accommodation in Leimus (either side) though you should be able to hang a hammock or find a bed locally; ask at the tienda where the river boats arrive.

● **Exchange**
Córdoba-Lempira exchange available in Leimus.

● **Transport**
Travellers advise that there is less chance of robbery if you take a truck or pick-up rather than a bus in this area. There is a regular boat from Leimus down to Waspám, daily at 1200.

This area was regarded as unsafe in 1996 because armed groups were active. Enquire before making plans.

A few words of Miskito

Tingki – Thank you; *Tingki-pali* – Thank you very much; *Nakis-ma* – How are you; *Apu* – There isn't any (*no hay*); *sirpi* – little. Most numbers are the same as English as are the words 'Christmas', 'trouser', and 'book'.

LAS MINAS

This area comprises the gold mining towns of Siuna, La Rosita, and Bonanza, and is part of the RAAN (Northern Atlantic Coast Autonomous Region), but is significantly inland from the Coast. Las Minas is a somewhat depressed region since the demise of the mines (Bonanza has the only working mine of the three towns, although Siuna's still employs some people), but the atmosphere is very much frontierish. A Canadian company has bought the mines in Siuna and Bonanza.

Siuna is the largest town, and all three are predominately *mestizo*, with a Creole minority; the surrounding rural areas have a significant Sumo population as well as some Miskitos.

● **Accommodation & places to eat**
E *Chino*, the best and most expensive; **G** *Troysa*, clean; **F** *Costeño*, 100m E of airstrip, basic; in Barrio La Luz there is a new hotel above a billiard hall; a rec place to eat is either of the 2 *comedores* called **Desnuque**, one in the market, and the other on a hill nr the baseball stadium and airstrip, the latter has good pizza as well as typical Nicaraguan food; *Comedor Siuna*, opp *Hotel Costeño*, has good *comida corriente*. In **Rosita**, a rec place to eat is *Comedor Jassy*, nr the entrance of town on the Siuna side; there is an *hospedaje*, **E**, no name, nr the market (noisy, but basically clean).

● **Transport Air** La Costeña flies from the capital to Siuna direct at 1100, Mon-Sat, also at 1100, Mon, Wed, Fri, on the flight to Bluefields via Siuna, Rosita, Bonanza and Puerto Cabezas, US$72 return from Managua, reservations in Siuna, T 2632142, 2632143.

ROUTES There are two relatively good road links from Managua, one through Matagalpa and Waslala, the other through Boaco, Muy Muy, Matiguás, and Río Blanco; the 330-km drive is very scenic (and takes about 7 hrs by 4WD vehicle in the dry season); however, check on the security situation before starting out. There is a bank in Siuna. There are also bus links. **La Rosita** is 70 km E of Siuna, and it is also possible to drive on through to Puerto Cabezas, although the road is in very poor shape. Do not drive after dark.

PARQUE NACIONAL SASLAYA

Created in 1971, Saslaya was the first national park in Nicaragua, located within the BOSAWAS Reserve which contains the largest tropical cloud forest in Central America. Development is now underway to encourage local communities to get involved in ecotourism as an incentive to preserve the area's rich natural and cultural heritage. One of these projects is the Proyecto Ecoturístico Rosa Grande, supported by Nature Conservancy and the Peace Corps. The community of **Rosa Grande**, 25 km from Siuna, is near an area of virgin forest with trails, waterfalls on the river Labú and lots of wildlife including monkeys and large cats. One path leads to a lookout with a view over the Cerro Saslaya, another, circular path to the NW goes to the Rancho Alegre falls. Guides can be hired for US$5.50 a day. Excursions for 2 or more days cost only US$13 pp for guide, food and camping equipment.

Local information
● **Accommodation & places to eat**
G *BOSAWAS field station*, on the river Labú, has hammocks, clean but simple, locally produced and cooked food about US$1.25. In Rosa Grande a meal at *Comedor Melania* costs about US$1.

● **Information**
Contact Don Trinidad at the *comedor* on arrival in Santa Rosa. In Siuna you can contact the office of the Proyecto BOSAWAS, 200m E of the airstrip, open Mon-Fri, 0800-1700. Groups of 5 or more must reserve in advance, contact the Amigos de Saslaya, c/o Proyecto BOSAWAS, Siuna, RAAN, by post or telegram. Large groups are not encouraged.

● **Transport**
Bus Daily from Siuna market at 0500 and 0730, sometimes another at 1100, US$2.25.

SAN JUAN DEL NORTE/GREYTOWN

In the S of Región Autonomista Atlántica Sur, on the Costa Rica border, San Juan del Norte was a quiet, undeveloped town until it was destroyed in the civil war. It is now being rebuilt a short distance up-river. It can be reached either down the Río San Juan or from Barra del Colorado in Costa Rica. No hotels, *pensiones* or restaurants, but the very friendly people will look after you. 150 people live here, mostly from fishing; no cars, only boats. Excellent for wildlife excursions; no nightlife. Use Costa Rican colones in town and all along the Río San Juan. The only safe bathing is in the Laguna Azul, although it is possible in the river, where there are alligators and sharks, and the sea, also sharks and can be rough.

For many years in the 19th century, the possibility was considered of constructing a transoceanic canal through Nicaragua, from San Juan up the river, across Lake Nicaragua and through a channel dug across the Rivas Isthmus. The route was used by water and land to transport prospectors in the 1848 Californian Gold Rush, known as the Vanderbilt Rd. Remains of constructions connected with these projects can still be seen in San Juan.

● **Transport** An irregular boat goes to Bluefields, possibly once a week. 3-4 boats a week upriver to San Carlos, 1 to 2 days depending on the height of the river; an interesting trip but the sun is very hot. See under **El Castillo**, page 1013.

FRONTIER WITH COSTA RICA – GREYTOWN

This area of the Caribbean coast is a narcotics zone with drugs being landed from San Andrés (Colombia). Before attempting to cross, seek information on general safety. When locals go into the jungle around Greytown, they are armed.

● **Nicaraguan immigration**
There is no official immigration in Greytown, although travellers reported in 1996 that they were able to get stamps from the authorities here that were accepted when checked elsewhere. Otherwise you must go to Bluefields or to one of the posts up the San Juan River. Equally take advice on what to do on arrival in Costa Rica.

● **Transport**
You can go by boat from Greytown to Barra del Colorado in Costa Rica, ask about fishing boats and canoes.

Information for travellers

BEFORE TRAVELLING

ENTRY REQUIREMENTS

● **Documents**

Visitors must have a passport with 6 months validity (at least), and may have to show an onward ticket and proof of at least US$200 (or equivalent in córdobas) in cash or cheques for a stay of more than a week in the country. **NB** Credit cards are becoming gradually more widely used in Nicaragua, so may be accepted instead of cash. No visa is required by nationals of most western countries except former USSR countries and some Latin American countries. Nationals of the following countries definitely need no visa: Guatemala, El Salvador, Honduras, Chile, Bolivia, Argentina, Uruguay, USA, Australia, Belgium, Denmark, Finland, Greece, Hungary, Ireland, Liechtenstein, Luxembourg, Netherlands, Norway, Poland, Spain, Sweden, Switzerland or the United Kingdom for a 90-day stay. Do not be easily persuaded that you need a visa – argue!

Visa rules are changing frequently, check before you travel. Citizens of all other countries need a visa, which can be bought before arriving at the border, is valid for arrival within 30 days, and for a stay of up to 30 days, it costs US$25; 2 passport photographs are required. A full 30-day visa can be bought at the border, but it is best to get your visa in advance. Visas take less than 2 hrs to process in the embassies in Guatemala City and Tegucigalpa, but have been known to take 48 hrs elsewhere. When consultation with Managua is required (the countries

to which this applies include India, the Arab countries, Cuba, the People's Republic of China and Hong Kong) it takes longer. Extensions can be obtained at the Dirección de Migración y Extranjería in Managua: arrive at the office before 0830. From the small office on the righthand side you must obtain the *formulario* (3 córdobas). Then queue at the *caja* in the large hall to pay US$25 or 150 córdobas for your extension. This can take hours. In the meantime you can complete forms. With the receipt of payment you queue at the window on the right. With luck you will receive the extension stamp for midday; at any event you should get it the same day. Another possibility is to leave the country for at least 72 hrs and re-enter on a new visa. Germans can obtain visas from Konsulat Nicaragua, Konstantinstr 41, 53179 Bonn. Send SAE with DM70 (cheques honoured), 2 photos and the complicated application form and allow 10 days for delivery. However, this seems to be the most expensive way to obtain a visa, see above. Commercial travellers should carry a document from their firm accrediting them as such.

An onward air ticket can be cashed if not used, especially if issued by a large company, but bus tickets are sometimes difficult to encash. It is reported, however, that the Nicaraguan Embassy in a neighbouring country is empowered to authorize entry without the outward ticket, if the traveller has enough money to buy the ticket. Also, if you have a visa to visit another Central American country, you are unlikely to be asked to show an outward ticket (this applies to all Central American countries: be 2 visas ahead!).

● **Representation overseas**
Belgium, 55 Ave de Wolvendael, 1180 Brussels,
T 02 375-6500, F 02 375-7188; **Canada**, 170
Laurier Ave West, Ottawa, Ontario KIP 5V5,
T 613 234 9361-2, F 613 238-7666; **France**, 8
Rue de Sfax, 75016, Paris, T 1 4500-4102, F 1
4500-9681; **Mexico**, Payo de Rivera 120, Lomas
de Chapultepec, CP 11000, T 540 5625-6,
F 520-6960; **Sweden**, Sandhamnsgatan 40,
6TR, 11528 Stockholm, T 8 667-1857, F 8 662-
4160; **UK**, 36 Upper Brook St, London W1Y 1PE,
I 01/1 409-2825, F 0171 409-2593; **USA**, 61
Broadway, Suite 2528-29, New York, NY 1006,
T 212 344-4491, F 212 344-4428.

● **Tourist information**
The Ministry of Tourism, PO Box 122, Managua, T (505-2) 222962/281337, F 281187, has
a wide range of brochures and information
packs. In the **USA**, PO Box 140357, Miami, FL
33114-0357, T (305) 860-0747, F 860-0746. In
Spain, Apdo Correos 10,998, 28080 Madrid.
At Managua airport, T 331539. Local information service, T 112.

● **Best time to visit**
The dry season runs from Dec to May, and the
wettest months are usually June and Oct. Best
time for a business visit: from Mar to June, but
Dec and Jan are the pleasantest months.

HEALTH
Take the usual tropical precautions about food
and drink. Tap water is not recommended for
drinking generally and avoid uncooked vegetables and peeled fruit. Intestinal parasites
abound; if requiring treatment, take a stool
sample to a Government laboratory before going to a doctor.

● **Malaria**
Malaria risk exists especially in the wet season;
take regular prophylaxis.

● **Further health information**
Medicines are in very short supply and you are
strongly advised to bring anything you may need
with you. Treatment in Centros de Salud, medical laboratories and dispensaries is free, though
we have reports that visitors may have to pay.
You may also be able to get prescribed medicines
free. Private dentists are better-equipped than
those in the national health service (but no
better trained).

MONEY
● **Currency**
The unit is the córdoba oro (C$), divided into
100 centavos. It was introduced in July 1990, at
a par with the US dollar. The córdoba oro was
devalued to 5 = US$1 in Mar 1991 and the old
córdoba was withdrawn from circulation on 30
April 1991; a further devaluation in Jan 1993
set the dollar at 6 córdobas oro, to be followed
by continuous mini-devaluations. The exchange
rate at the end of April 1997 was 9.25 córdobas
oro − US$1. Notes in circulation are for $1/2$, 1,
5, 10, 20, 50 and 100 córdobas oro. Try to avoid
obtaining the larger notes, as no-one ever has
enough change (but see **Banks & money
changers** under Managua). A decree, passed
on 22 March 1991, permitted private banks to
operate (the financial system was nationalized
in 1979). The import and export of foreign and
local currencies are unrestricted. Visa and Mastercard are accepted in nearly all restaurants and
hotels, and in many shops. This applies to a lesser
extent to Amex, Cred-o-Matic and Diners Club.
Don't rely exclusively on credit cards.
   Changing TCs is difficult outside Managua;
while the situation is improving, it is best to carry
US dollar notes and sufficient local currency
away from the bigger towns.

● **Cost of living**
In 1996 Nicaragua was a relatively expensive
country as far as hotel accommodation was
concerned, but public transport was fairly
cheap. For food, as a rough guide, a *comida
corriente* costs about US$4 (meals in restaurants
US$7-13, breakfasts US$3-4).

GETTING THERE

BY AIR
● **From Europe**
British Airways, Virgin Atlantic, American Airlines,
Continental or Delta from London to Miami and
connect to American, Nica, Lacsa, Iberia, Aviateca
via Guatemala City and San Salvador; or Taca via
San Salvador. Iberia to Managua 4 times a week
from Barcelona and Madrid via Miami (connections from other European cities).

● **From USA**
See above for Miami. Continental flies from
Houston 4 times a week. Los Angeles, Aviateca,
via Guatemala City and Salvador. Washington
DC, American Airlines daily. From other North
American cities, make connections in Miami, or
with Taca in San Salvador.

● From Latin America
Copa flies from Mexico City, Guatemala City, San José, San Salvador and Panama. Aviateca flies daily from San Salvador, Guatemala City, Panama City and San José. From Tegucigalpa, daily except Sun with La Costeña, or 4 times a week with Aviateca via San José. Lacsa also flies daily from San José. All flight tickets purchased by non-residents must be paid in US dollars.

CUSTOMS
● Duty free allowance
Duty-free import of ½ kg of tobacco products, 3 litres of alcoholic drinks and 1 large bottle (or 3 small bottles) of perfume is permitted.

ON ARRIVAL
● Entry and exit taxes
The cost of entry overland is US$7 (possibly paid in córdobas), but take care if you exchange money or expect change. Exit tax is US$2 in dollars cash, US$4 on Sat and Sun, or 15 córdobas. If in the slightest doubt about charges, insist on being given a receipt and go to the Immigration Department in Managua to verify the charge. Motorists should see under **Motoring** below.

All departing passengers must pay an airport tax of US$15, payable in US dollars. All passengers have to pay a sales tax of US$5 on all tickets issued and paid for in Nicaragua; a transport tax of 1% on all tickets issued in Nicaragua to any destination.

● Clothing
Dress is informal; business men often shed jackets and wear sports shirts, but shorts are never worn. The wearing of trousers is perfectly OK for women.

● Hours of business
0800-1200, 1430-1730 or 1800. Banks: 0830-1200, 1400-1600, but 0830-1130 on Sat. Government offices are not normally open on Sat in Managua, or in the afternoon anywhere.

● Official time
6 hrs behind GMT.

● Safety
Visitors to Nicaragua must carry their passports (or a photocopy) with them at all times. There are police checkpoints on roads and in outlying districts; the police search for firearms. They usually inspect all luggage thoroughly on entering and leaving Nicaragua. Do not photograph any military personnel or installations.

Pickpocketing and bagslashing has increased greatly in Managua, especially in crowded places, and on buses throughout the country. Apart from Managua at night, most places are generally safe. Reports of robberies and assaults in Northern Nicaragua indicate that care should be taken in this area, enquire about conditions before going, especially if proposing to leave the beaten track.

The political upheavals have produced much dislocation of all services. Be prepared for transport difficulties. Take essential personal items with you and a torch plus batteries. Keep out of politics which is still a highly-charged subject.

● Tipping
In Nicaragua: 10% of bill in restaurants (many restaurants add 10% service); US$0.50/bag for porters; no tip for taxi drivers.

● Voltage
110 volts AC, 60 cycles.

● Weights and measures
The metric system is official, but in domestic trade local terms are in use; for example, the *medio*, which equals a peck (2 dry gallons), and the *fanega*, of 24 *medios*. These are not used in foreign trade. The principal local weight is the *arroba*=25 lb and the *quintal* of 101.417 English lb. Random variety of other measures in use include US gallon for petrol, US quart and pint for liquids; *vara* (33 ins) for short distances and the lb for certain weights.

● Work opportunities
Volunteer work in Nicaragua is not as common after the 1990 elections as it was during the Sandinista years. Foreigners now work in environmental brigades supporting the FSLN, construction projects, agricultural cooperatives and environmental organizations. Certain skills are in demand, as elsewhere in the developing world; to discover the current situation, contact non-governmental organizations in your home country (eg Nicaraguan Network, 1247 E Street, SE, Washington, DC 20003, T (202) 544-9355, F 544-9360, or PO Box 4496, Fresno, CA 93744, T (209) 226-0477, in the USA), twin town/sister-city organizations and national solidarity campaigns (NSC/ENN Brigades, 129 Seven Sisters Rd, London N7 7QG, T 0171-272 9619; Dutch Nicaragua Komitee, Aptdo Postal 1922, Managua).

FOOD AND DRINK

15% tax is added to all restaurant bills. **NB** The *Colectivo de Soja* which encourages the use of soya as an alternative source of protein; vegetarian restaurants of this chain are in Masaya, Managua, Granada, San Juan del Sur and Estelí. Some Nicaraguan 'pizzas' are not much like the real thing, and the coffee can be terrible.

Try *nacatamales* – cornflower dumplings stuffed with meat and vegetables, boiled in banana leaves – an excellent value meal, or *Gallo Pinto* – tasty dish of rice and beans. Fizzy drinks are known as 'gaseosas' in Nicaragua as in neighbouring countries. Fresh drinks are 'refrescos'.

GETTING AROUND

Air

In 1997 only La Costeña was operating internal air services to San Carlos, Nueva Güinea, Siuna, Rosita, Bonanza, Puerto Cabezas, Waspám, Bluefields and Corn Islands (see text for details).

● Hitchhiking

Hitchhiking is widely accepted, but not easy because so many people do it and there is little traffic – offer to pay ('pedir un ride'). Local buses are the cheapest in Central America, but are extremely crowded owing to a lack of vehicles and fuel. Baggage that is loaded on to the roof or in the luggage compartment is charged for, usually at half the rate for passengers or a flat fee of US$0.50.

● Motoring

Motorists and motorcyclists must pay US$30 in cash on arrival at the border (bicyclists pay US$2, and up to US$9 at weekends, though this tends to vary from one customs post to the next). Several cyclists have said that you should take a 'proof of purchase' of your cycle or suggested typing out a phoney 'cycle ownership' document to help at border crossings. Motorists also pay the same entry tax as other overland arrivals (see above). Do not lose the receipts, they have to be produced when you leave; without them you will have to pay again. Vehicles not cleared by 1630 are held at customs overnight. Up to 4 hrs of formalities are possible when entering Nicaragua with a vehicle. On leaving motorists pay 5 córdobas (US$0.70), as well as the usual exit tax. For procedures at each border, see the relevant sections of text. There is nowhere to stay at either border. Make sure you get all the correct stamps on arrival, or you will encounter all sorts of problems once inside the country. Low octane gasoline costs US$2.28 a US gallon, super, US$2.65; diesel, US$1.10. Service stations close at 1700-1800. For motorcyclists, the wearing of crash helmets is compulsory. Beware when driving at night, the national shortage of spare parts means that many cars have no lights. Your car may be broken into if unattended and not in a secure place. In general, major roads are not in very good shape.

COMMUNICATIONS

● Newspapers

Managua: *La Prensa* (pro-Government), *El Nuevo Diario*, *La Tribuna*. *La Barricada*, official organ of the Sandinista Front. León: *El Centroamericano*. *La Gaceta* is the official gazette. *Ya Veremos*, monthly, covering international subjects. *Revista Conservadora* is the best monthly magazine. Other magazines: *Semana Cómica*, weekly satirical. *Envío* (monthly, English and Spanish editions, Jesuit); *Pensamiento Propio* (current affairs, monthly); *Análisis*, economic journal; *Soberanía* (Nicaraguan affairs, Spanish/English bilingual). *El Pez y la Serpiente* is a monthly magazine devoted to the arts, poetry and literature.

● Postal services

Airmail to Europe takes 2-4 weeks (letter rate US$0.70, 5 córdobas); from Europe 7-10 days; to USA 4 córdobas (3 córdobas to Miami); to Australia 6 córdobas.

● Telephone services

Telegraph and telephone lines are owned by the Empresa Nicaragüense de Telecomunicaciones (Enitel), formerly known as Telcor, which was scheduled for privatization in 1997. Automatic national and international telephone calls are possible from any private or public phone. Card phones were introduced in 1994. There are wireless transmitting stations at Managua, Bluefields and Cabo Gracias a Dios, and private stations at Puerto Cabezas, El Gallo, and Río Grande.

International or national calls can be made at any Enitel office, open 0700-2200. All phone calls can be paid for in córdobas. Rates: US$10 for 3 mins to USA, US$11.50 to Europe. You may have to wait a long time for a line, except for early in the morning on weekdays. You have to say in advance how long you want to talk for. Person to person calls are charged extra. Collect calls to the USA are easy ('a pagarse allá'), also possible to Europe. For SPRINT, dial 171; AT&T and MCI also operate. International Fax service is available in all major cities, US$4.50/page to Europe. See under Managua **Telecommunications** for Entel's excellent telephone directory.

SPORTS

Baseball is the national game, more important than soccer, and the best building in many towns is the baseball stadium. The season runs from Nov to the end of April.

HOLIDAYS AND FESTIVALS

1 Jan: New Year's Day. Mar or April: Thur of Holy Week and Good Friday. 1 May: Labour Day. 19 July: Revolution of 1979. 14 Sept: Battle of San Jacinto. 15 Sept: Independence Day. 2 Nov: All Souls' Day (Día de los Muertos). 7 and 8 Dec: Immaculate Conception (Purísima). 25 Dec: Christmas Day.

Businesses, shops and restaurants all close for most of Holy Week; many companies also close down during the Christmas-New Year period. Holidays which fall on a Sun are taken the following Mon. Local holidays are given under the towns.

FURTHER READING

Information on all Nicaragua's transport services can be found in *Nicaragua Timetable*, published twice a year in Spanish, English and German by Mathias Hock Services, Grazer Weg 38, D-60599 Frankfurt, Germany, Fax +49-69655710, US$7/issue. We acknowledge our debt here to this publication.

ACKNOWLEDGEMENTS

We are grateful to Rachel Rogers for doing the updating.

Costa Rica

COSTA RICA is the smallest but two: El Salvador and Belize, of the Central American republics and only Panama and Belize have fewer inhabitants. It is known throughout Latin America as the continent's purest democracy and in Nov 1989, celebrated its centenary of democracy. The Army was abolished in 1949, though it should be stressed that there is a very efficient-looking khaki-clad Civil Guard. Costa Rica has the highest standard of living in Central America, the second lowest birth rate (after Panama) and the greatest degree of economic and social advance.

HORIZONS

THE LAND

Costa Rica lies between Nicaragua and Panama, with coastlines on both the Caribbean (212 km) and the Pacific (1,016 km). The distance between sea and sea is from 119 to 282 km. A low, thin line of hills between Lake Nicaragua and the Pacific is prolonged into northern Costa Rica with several volcanoes (including the active volcano, Arenal), broadening and rising into high and rugged mountains and volcanoes in the centre and S. The highest peak, Chirripó Grande, SE of the capital, reaches 3,820m. Within these highlands

are certain structural depressions; one of them, the Meseta Central, is of paramount importance. To the SW this basin is rimmed by the comb of the Cordillera; at the foot of its slopes, inside the basin, are the present capital, San José, and the old capital, Cartago. Northeast of these cities about 30 km away, four volcano cones rise from a massive common pedestal. From NW to SE these are Poás (2,704m), Barva (2,906m), Irazú (3,432m), and Turrialba (3,339m). Irazú and Poás are intermittently active. Between the Cordillera and the volcanoes is the Meseta Central: an area of 5,200 sq km at an altitude of between 900 and 1,800m, where two-thirds of the population live. The northeastern

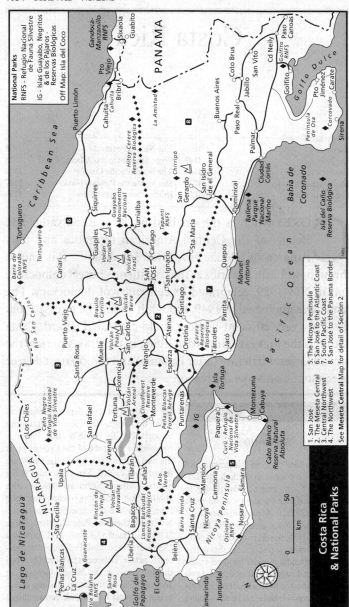

National Parks

RNFS - Refugio Nacional de Fauna Silvestre
IG - Islas Guayabo, Negritos & de los Pájaros - Reservas Biológicas
Off Map: Isla del Coco

1. San José
2. The Meseta Central
3. Central Northwest
4. The Northwest
5. The Nicoya Peninsula
6. San José to the Atlantic Coast
7. South Pacific Coast
8. San José to the Panama Border

See **Meseta Central Map** for detail of Section 2

Costa Rica & National Parks

part of the basin is drained by the Reventazón through turbulent gorges into the Caribbean; the Río Grande de Tárcoles drains the western part of it into the Pacific.

There are lowlands on both coasts. The Nicaraguan lowland along the Río San Juan is continued into Costa Rica, wide and sparsely inhabited as far as Puerto Limón. A great deal of this land, particularly near the coast, is swampy; SE of Puerto Limón the swamps continue as far as Panama in a narrow belt of lowland between sea and mountain.

The Gulf of Nicoya, on the Pacific side, thrusts some 65 km inland; its waters separate the mountains of the mainland from the 900m high mountains of the narrow Nicoya Peninsula. From a little to the S of the mouth of the Río Grande de Tárcoles, a lowland savanna stretches NW past the port of Puntarenas and along the whole northeastern shore of the Gulf towards Nicaragua.

Below the Río Grande de Tárcoles the savanna is pinched out by mountains, but there are other banana-growing lowlands to the S. Small quantities of African palm and cacao are now being grown in these lowlands. In the far S there are swampy lowlands again at the base of the Peninsula of Osa and between the Golfo Dulce and the borders of Panama. Here there are 12,000 ha planted to bananas. The Río General which flows into the Río Grande de Térraba, runs through a southern structural depression almost as large as the Meseta Central.

CLIMATE

Altitude, as elsewhere in Central America, determines the climate, but the *tierra templada* and the *tierra fría* start at about 300m lower on the Pacific than on the Atlantic side. The Pacific side is the drier, with patches of savanna among the deciduous forest; the Atlantic side has heavy rainfall, 300 days a year of it, and is covered far up the slopes with tropical forest: about 31% of Costa Rica is forested (half forested in 1950).

The climate varies from the heat and humidity of the Caribbean and Atlantic lowlands to warm temperate on the Meseta Central and chilly temperate at the greater heights. On the Cordillera Talamanca, the average temperature is below 16C. There are dry and wet seasons: on the Pacific side there is a well-defined wet season from May to Nov with a little decrease during the July-Aug *'veranillo'*. The Atlantic side has no specific dry season but there is less rainfall between Mar and September. Between May and Nov, the rainfall in the Meseta Central averages 1,950 mm and roads are often bogged down. The hottest months are Mar and April. Between Dec and Feb is the best time to visit. However, for the visitor, rain is part of the enchantment of the tropics and apart from the infrequent cyclonic storms, most of the rain is in short, sharp downpours.

HISTORY

SPANISH SETTLEMENT

During his last voyage in Sept 1502, Columbus landed on the shores of what is now Costa Rica. Rumours of vast gold treasures (which never materialized) led to the name of Costa Rica (the Rich Coast). The Spaniards settled in the Meseta Central, where there were some thousands of sedentary Indian farmers (whose numbers were soon greatly diminished by the diseases brought by the settlers). Cartago was founded in 1563 by Juan Vásquez de Coronado, but there was no expansion until 145 years later, when a small number left Cartago for the valleys of Aserrí and Escazú. They founded Heredia in 1717, and San José in 1737. Alajuela, not far from San José, was founded in 1782. The settlers were growing in numbers (many farmers emigrated from northern Spain) but were still poor and raising subsistence crops only.

INDEPENDENCE AND COFFEE

Independence from Spain was declared in 1821 whereupon Costa Rica, with the rest of Central America, immediately became part of Mexico. This led to a civil war, during which, 2 years later, the capital was moved from Cartago to San José. After independence, the government sought anxiously for some product which could be exported and taxed for revenue. It was found in coffee, introduced from Cuba in 1808, which Costa Rica was the first of the Central American countries to grow. The Government offered free land to coffee growers, thus building up a peasant landowning class. In 1825 there was a trickle of exports, carried on mule-back to the ports. By 1846 there were ox-cart roads to Puntarenas. By 1850 there was a large flow of coffee to overseas markets: it was greatly increased by the opening of a railway from San José and Cartago to Puerto Limón along the valley of the Reventazón in 1890.

From 1850, coffee prosperity began to affect the country profoundly: the birth rate grew, land for coffee was free, and the peasant settlements started spreading, first down the Río Reventazón as far as Turrialba; then up the slopes of the volcanoes, then down the new railway from San José to the old Pacific port of Puntarenas.

BANANA INDUSTRY

Bananas were first introduced in 1878; Costa Rica was the first Central American republic to grow them and is now the second largest exporter in the world. Labour was brought in from Jamaica to clear the forest and work the plantations. The industry grew and in 1913, the peak year, the Caribbean coastlands provided 11 million bunches for export, but the spread of disease lowered the exports progressively. The United Fruit Company then turned its attentions to the Pacific litoral especially in the S around the port of Golfito. However, although some of the Caribbean plantations were turned over to cacao, *abacá* (Manilla hemp) and African palm, the region has regained its ascendancy over the Pacific litoral as a banana producer (the Standard Fruit Company is an important redeveloper of the region).

DEMOCRATIC GOVERNMENT

Costa Rica's long tradition of democracy begain in 1889 and has continued to the present day with only a few lapses. In 1917 the elected president Alfredo González, was ousted by Federico Tinoco, who held power until 1919, when a counter revolution and subsequent elections brought Julio Acosta to the presidency. Democratic and orderly government followed until the campaign of 1948 when violent protests and a general strike surrounded disputed results. A month of fighting broke out after the Legislative Assembly annulled the elections, leading to the abolition of the constitution and a junta being installed, led by José Figueres Ferrer. In 1949 a constituent assembly drew up a new constitution and abolished the army. The junta stepped down and Otilio Ulate Blanco, one of the candidates of the previous year, was inaugurated. In 1952, Figueres, a socialist, founded the Partido de Liberación Nacional (PLN), and was elected President in 1953. He dominated politics for the next 2 decades, serving as President in 1953-58 and 1970-74. The PLN introduced social welfare programmes and nationalization policies, while the intervening conservative governments encouraged private enterprise. The PLN was again in power from 1974-78 (Daniel Oduber Quirós) 1982-86 (Luis Alberto Monge) and 1986-90 (Oscar Arias Sánchez).

President Arias drew up proposals for a peace pact in Central America and concentrated greatly on foreign policy initiatives. Efforts were made to expel Nicaraguan contras resident in Costa Rica and the country's official proclamation of neutrality, made in 1983, was reinforced. The Central American Peace Plan, signed by the five Central American presidents in Guatemala in 1987, earned

Arias the Nobel Peace Prize, although progress in implementing its recommendations was slow.

In the 1990 general elections, Rafael Angel Calderón Fournier, a conservative lawyer and candidate for the Social Christian Unity Party (PUSC), won a narrow victory with 51% of the vote, over the candidate of the PLN. Calderón, the son of a former president who was one of the candidates in the 1948 disputed elections, had previously stood for election in 1982 and 1986. The President's popularity slumped as the effects of his economic policies were felt on people's living standards, while his Government was brought into disrepute by allegations of corruption and links with narcotraffickers.

1994 ELECTIONS

In the Feb 1994 elections another former president's son was elected by a narrow margin. José María Figueres, 39, of the PLN, won 49.6% of the vote, 2.2 points ahead of his PUSC rival. In the Legislature, the PLN won 29 seats and the PUSC 25, while smaller parties won the remaining seats. The election was won on economic policies. Figueres argued against neo-liberal policies, claiming he would renegotiate agreements with the IMF and the World Bank, but in his first year of office, a third Structural Adjustment Programme (backed by the international agencies and drawn up by the previous administration) was approved. A subsequent National Development Plan and a Plan to Fight Poverty contained a wide range of measures designed to promote economic stability and improve the quality of life for many sectors of society. While the plans were partly responding to the protests that followed the approval of the Adjustment Programme, many of their proposals were at variance with the Programme's policies.

Labour strife increased in 1995-96 as tax increases and price rises cut into earnings. The granting of work permits to 50,000 Nicaraguan manual labourers was highly unpopular in the face of rising Costa Rican unemployment. Crime is on the increase, particularly in San José, Limón and on the Caribbean coast, but other areas are generally safe. The kidnapping of foreigners in 1996 caused alarm and helped to reduce the number of tourists that year.

Elections are due on Sunday 1 February 1998; the new president will take office on 8 May 1998.

CULTURE

PEOPLE

In all provinces save Limón over 98% are whites and *mestizos* but in Limón 33.2% are blacks and 3.1% indigenous Indians, of whom only 5,000 survive in the whole country. There are three groups, the Bribri (3,500), Boruca (1,000) and Guatuso. Although officially protected, the living conditions of the indigenous Indians are very poor. In 1992 Costa Rica became the first Central American country to ratify the International Labour Oranganization treaty on indigenous populations and tribes. However, even in Limón the percentage of blacks is falling: it was 57.1 in 1927. Many of them speak Jamaican English as their native tongue. Much of the Caribbean coastland, more especially in the N, remains unoccupied. On the Pacific coastlands a white minority owns the land on the *hacienda* system rejected in the uplands. About 46% of the people are *mestizos*. The population has risen sharply in the mountainous Peninsula of Nicoya, which is an important source of coffee, maize, rice and beans.

Contact with the rural population is easy: the people are friendly and enjoy talking. (The national adjective, *costarricense*, is rather a mouthful: the universal short form is '*tico/a*'.)

RELIGION AND EDUCATION

Roman Catholicism is the official religion and 80% of the population are Roman

Catholic, the remainder being mostly Protestant. Educational standards are high: only 12.7% of the population have no formal schooling. Consequently literacy is high at 95%.

GOVERNMENT

Costa Rica is a unitary multiparty republic with one legislative house, the Legislative Assembly of 57 deputies, elected by proportional representation for 4 years. Executive authority is in the hands of the President, elected for the same term by popular vote. Men and women over 18 have the right to vote. Voting is secret, direct and free. Judicial power is exercised by the Supreme Court of Justice.

THE ECONOMY

Structure of production

The country's economy is based on the export of coffee, bananas, meat, sugar and cocoa. The Meseta Central with its volcanic soil is the coffee-growing area: here too are grown the staple crops: beans, maize, potatoes and sugar cane, and the dairy farming is both efficient and lucrative. Diversification of exports has been successful, with non-traditional crops now accounting for about 60% of revenues. The fluctuations in coffee prices, and therefore exports, has prompted some producers to turn to other crops. Costa Rica remains the second largest banana exporter in the world, but the industry's future remains uncertain owing to difficulties caused by European import policies. The country's timber industry is very small and its resources have yet to be commercially utilized although deforestation has occurred at an alarming rate.

High growth in the industrial sector has led to considerable economic diversification, and manufacturing accounts for about 19% of gdp, compared with 16% in the case of agriculture. Industry is largely concerned with food processing but there is also some production of chemicals

Costa Rica: fact file

Geographic
Land area	51,100 sq km
forested	30.8%
pastures	45.8%
cultivated	10.4%

Demographic
Population (1996)	3,400,000
annual growth rate (1985-94)	2.5%
urban	44.0%
rural	56.0%
density	66.5 per sq km
Religious affiliation	
Roman Catholic	80.0%
Birth rate per 1,000 (1994)	25.4
	(world av 25.0)

Education and Health
Life expectancy at birth,	
male	71.9 years
female	77.5 years
Infant mortality rate	
per 1,000 live births (1994)	13.0
Physicians (1995)	1 per 870 persons
Hospital beds	1 per 564 persons
Calorie intake as %	
of FAO requirement	129%
Population age 25 and over	
with no formal schooling	12.7%
Literate males (over 15)	94.7%
Literate females (over 15)	95.0%

Economic
GNP (1994 market prices)	US$7,856mn
GNP per capita	US$2,380
Public external	
debt (1993)	US$3,139mn
Tourism receipts (1994)	US$626mn
Inflation	
(annual av 1990-95)	19.2%
Radio	1 per 4.4 persons
Television	1 per 9.8 persons
Telephone	1 per 8.8 persons

Employment
Population economically active (1994)	
	1,187,005
Unemployment rate	4.2%
% of labour force in	
agriculture	21.3
mining	0.2
manufacturing	17.9
construction	6.6
Military and Police forces	7,500

Source *Encyclopaedia Britannica*

(including fertilizers, also exported), plastics, tyres, etc. Current major industrial projects include aluminium processing, a petrochemical plant at Moín, and a tuna-fish processing plant at Golfito. The port of Caldera on the Pacific coast has been improved and manufacturing for export is being encouraged.

There are small deposits of manganese, mercury, gold and silver, but only the last two are worked. Deposits of iron ore are estimated at 400 million tons and sulphur deposits at 11 million tons. Considerable bauxite deposits have been found but have not yet been developed. In 1980, the Arenal hydroelectric plant was opened and there are projects to develop the Corobicí and other hydroelectric complexes. Oil companies are interested in offshore concessions in the Pacific. There is an oil refinery at Puerto Limón.

Tourism is now a major industry and is the main source of foreign exchange revenue generating US$660mn in 1995, from 760,000 tourists. The construction of hotels has soared and although most new businesses are small-scale eco-lodges of less than 50 rooms, the Government has allowed foreign investors to build some huge resorts for mass tourism in a controversial reversal of previous policy. This, on top of overdevelopment and overcrowding in some areas, plus a huge increase in the price of admission to national parks in Sept 1994 (reversed in April 1996), contributed to a fall in domestic tourism and no increase in international tourism. A spate of kidnappings also affected arrivals. Land prices have soared, driven up by foreign, mainly US, purchasers.

Recent trends

Despite several IMF-supported austerity programmes, the Costa Rican economy still suffers from large public sector deficits, partly because of a high level of government spending on social welfare. The country amassed a large foreign debt, which, including accumulated arrears, amounted in 1989 to US$5bn and was one of the highest per capita in the developing world. In the late 1980s, Costa Rica turned to the IMF and the World Bank for help in adjusting its economy and was one of the first countries to take advantage of a US-sponsored, debt reduction proposal. An agreement was negotiated with commercial bank creditors in 1989-90, to be supported by funds from official creditors. The economic programme was hugely unpopular as spending cuts in health, social security and education increased poverty and unemployment, leading to strikes and protests. In 1991-92 economic growth picked up, inflation declined and unemployment fell. Many new jobs were created in tourism, with 54 new hotels being built in 1992. By end-1994 total debt had fallen to just over US$3bn.

In that year a third structural adjustment loan was signed with the IMF against considerable local opposition. The new government was under pressure to reduce poverty (17.25% of the population) and, at the same time, limit the budget deficit which, was equivalent to 8% of gdp in 1994, and cut inflation, which accelerated to 20% in the same year. President Figueres intended that an increased rate of devaluation of the colón and tax reform should help reduce the balance of payments deficit, maintain gdp growth at a little below its 1994 level of 5% and prevent depletion of international reserves.

In 1995 legislation was approved to liberalize the banking system, support privatization and end state monopolies in insurance, hydrocarbons and telecommunications. Labour unions opposed many of the economic measures and the layoff of 8,000 public sector workers. There were many strikes, including an extended protest by teachers. The effort of keeping the fiscal deficit under control (3.5% of gdp in 1995) prompted congress to approve the Economic Guarantees bill in 1996 after 5 years of debate. This legislation limits the deficit to 1% of gdp, sets up a special authority to oversee state spending, grants greater autonomy to the central bank and allows Congress more control over national budgets. It will not be implemented until 1999, allowing another round of elections in the interim. The deficit was cut to 3% of gdp in 1996 (IMF target 0.5%) and was projected at 2.7% in the 1997 budget. Spending on public security was raised by 14% to tackle rising crime.

COMMUNICATIONS

Costa Rica has a total of 35,583 km of roads of which 16% are paved. The Pan-American Highway runs the length of the country, from the Nicaraguan to the Panamanian borders. A highway has been built from Orotina to Caldera, a new port on the Gulf of Nicoya which has replaced Puntarenas as the principal Pacific port, and a highway is being built from Orotina to Ciudad Colón. Another road has been completed from San José via Guápiles and Siquirres to Puerto Limón. Also a road was completed in 1993 from Orotina to Playas de Jacó to improve access to the Pacific beaches. This has still to be extended to Parrita, Quepos and Ciudad Cortés. All 4-lane roads into San José are toll roads, US$0.75; some toll roads outside San José are US$0.35.

There used to be 1,286 km of railways, all of 1.067m gauge. These are now closed. Unfortunately the spectacular line from San José to Puerto Limón suffered major damage from landslides in 1991. Some portions may be reactivated in the future, mainly for tourists.

NATIONAL PARKS

Tourists particularly enjoy the many well-kept and well-guarded national parks and nature reserves which protect some samples of the extraordinarily varied Costa Rican ecosystems. Some of the last patches of dry tropical forest, for instance, can be found in the Santa Rosa National Park, and other parks protect the unique cloud forest.

The **Servicio de Parques Nacionales** (SPN, Av 8, C 25, open Mon-Fri, 0800-1600, write in advance to Apdo 10094, or T 233-4070, 233-4246, 233-4118) in San José administers the National Park system. For information and permits to visit and/or camp in the Parks apply to **Fundación de Parques Nacionales** (FPN), 300m N y 150m E of Santa Teresita Church, Barrio Escalante, C 23, Av 15, San José, T 257-2239, open Mon-Fri 0800-1700, Sat 0800-1200. Most permits can be obtained at park entrances. To contact park personnel by radio link or make accommodation reservations,

The tourism debate

📑 A debate over development of tourism in Costa Rica raged in 1993-94 (and continues) with the Government in favour of developing mass tourism along the beaches of Nicoya and Guanacaste Provinces. Ecotourism lobbyists argued hotly that small scale tourism was more beneficial for conservation purposes, supported by many tour agents, who pointed out that at present, ecotourists spend an average of 15 days in the country, spending freely on local services, while holidaymakers to resorts average 5 days and spend almost nothing. One particular project at Tambor sparked heated criticism, when Barceló, the Spanish developers of a 400-room hotel on the beach, infringed several laws and regulations (see Tambor, page 1100). The incident dented Costa Rica's ecotourism reputation. Growth of hotels has been spectacular in the 1990s and although most have been of less than 50 rooms, there are now several large resorts along the beaches, which, like Tambor, damage habitats and the ecology.

T 233-4160, but good Spanish is a help (bilingual operators at National Parks can be reached by dialing 192). If you make reservations at their San José office, make sure they have made them direct with the park and that you have clear references on the confirmation to avoid difficulties on arrival. If you want to work as a volunteer in the parks, contact Stanley Arquedas of the SPN, mornings only. An alternative is to go to AVSO, Calle 17-19, Av 2, San José.

On 15 April 1996 a standard entrance fee of US$6 for all National Parks was introduced. Manuel Antonio, Guayabo, Cabo Blanco and Braulio Carrillo (Quebrada González ranger station) are closed Mon. Cabo Blanco is also closed Tues.

Bird watchers and butterfly lovers have long flocked to Costa Rica to see some of the 850 or so species of birds (the whole of the United States counts only about 800 species) and untold varieties of butterflies. All of these can best be seen in the parks, together with monkeys, deer, coyotes, armadillos, anteaters, turtles, coatis, raccoons, snakes, wild pigs, and, more rarely, wild cats and tapirs. Good field guides are Petersen, *Birds of Mexico and Central America* and *Birds of North America*; Stiles/Skutch, *Guide to the Birds of Costa Rica*; Ridgely, *Birds of Panama*; Golden Guide, *Birds of North America*; Daniel H Janzen, *Costa Rican Natural History*; Philip J de Vries, *Butterflies of Costa Rica*; *Birds of the Rainforest-Costa Rica*, published by FUNDECOR and USAID; *Biodiversity of Costa Rica*, published by INBio.

Nature guides can be found at The Bookshop in San José, and there is also available an illustrated book, *The National Parks of Costa Rica*, by Mario A Boza (1986), which gives a good impression of what the different parks are like.

Although the National Parks and other privately owned reserves are a main tourist attraction, many are in remote areas and not easy to get to on public transport; buses or coaches that do go

tend to stay for a short time only. There is a growing tendency for tour companies to dominate the National Park 'market' to the exclusion of other public transport. For those on tight budgets, try making up a party with others and sharing taxis or hiring a car. Descriptions of the individual parks, and how to get there, will be found in the text.

The Audubon Society holds an Eco-Tourism Seminar on Wed at 1830 at the Friends' Peace Center, C 15 y Av 8, San José. A National Park slide show with 164 slides on the National Park system, with a period for questions and answers, is held on Mon, Wed, Sat, at 1000-1130 at Cine Variedades, C 5, Av 1-Central, 50m N of Plaza de la Cultura, US$3.

WATERSPORTS

The rivers of Costa Rica have proved to be highly popular for **white water rafting**, kayaking and canoeing, both for the thrill of the rapids and the wildlife interest of the quieter sections. The seven most commonly run rivers are the Reventazón (and the Pascua section of it), Pacuare, Corobicí, Sarapiquí and El General. You can do a day-trip but to reach the big class IV rapids you usually have to take 2-3 days. The Reventazón is perhaps the most accessible but the Pacuare has been recommended as a more beautiful experience. The Corobicí is slow and popular with bird watchers. Ríos Tropicales (see San José Travel Agencies, page 1059) has been recommended for its guides and its

equipment. **NB** Heavy rain may cause cancellations, so you need flexibility in your plans. Offshore, **snorkelling** and **scuba diving** are offered by several hotels, but you have to pick your spot carefully. Anywhere near a river will suffer from poor visibility and the coral reef has died in many places because of agricultural pollutants washed downstream. Generally, on the Caribbean side you can see wrecks and coral reefs, particularly in the SE towards the Panamanian border, while on the Pacific side you see large pelagics and sportsfish. Liveaboard dive boats head for the islands of Caño and Isla del Coco. Divers are not permitted in National Parks or reserves, nor within 500m of the protected sea turtle zone N of Tortuguero National Park. **Windsurfing** is good along the Pacific coast and on Lake Arenal, particularly the W end. Lots of hotels have equipment for hire and operators in San José will know where the best conditions prevail at any time. Be careful of obstacles in the water along rocky coastlines and near river mouths. **Surfing** is also popular off the Pacific beaches, attracting professionals who follow storm surges along the coast. **Sport fishing** is done off either coast and at different times of the year. Snook and tarpon are caught in the Caribbean, the largest snook being found in Sept and Oct, mostly N of Limón (where there are several fishing lodges), but also towards Panama. In the Pacific bill fishing is well-developed.

San José

THE CAPITAL stands in a broad, fertile valley which produces coffee and sugar-cane. It was founded in 1737 but frequent earthquakes have destroyed most of the colonial buildings and the modern replacements are not very inspiring. The climate is excellent, though the evenings can be chilly. The lowest and highest temperatures run from 15 to 26°C. Slight earthquake shocks are frequent. Rainy season: May to November. Other months are dry.

SAN JOSE

(Pop 959,340, provincial pop 1,209,045; Alt 1,150m) Streets cross one another at right-angles. Avenidas run E-W; the Calles N-S. The three main streets are Av Central, Av 2 and the intersecting C Central: the business centre is here. The best shops are along Av Central. Avenidas to the N of Av Central are given odd numbers; those to the S even numbers. Calles to the W of Calle Central are even-numbered; those to the E odd-numbered. The Instituto Costarricense de Turismo has an excellent map of the city, marking all the important sights and business houses. NB Few buildings have numbers, so find out the nearest cross-street when getting directions (200m means 2 blocks, etc).

It is best not to take a car into San José between 0700 and 2000; traffic is very heavy although new traffic laws have freed up the flow. Watch out for no parking zones or you will get towed away. Many of the narrow streets are heavily polluted with exhaust fumes. Seven blocks of the Av Central, from Banco Central running E to Plaza de la Cultura, are closed to traffic. Many people prefer to stay in the suburbs or in Heredia to escape the pollution.

PLACES OF INTEREST

Many of the most interesting public buildings are near the intersection of Av Central and C Central. The **Teatro Nacional** (1897): marble staircases, statuary, frescoes and foyer decorated in gold with Venetian plate mirrors, is just off Av Central, on C 3. It has a good coffee bar. Sightseeing visits, US$3. Nearby is **Plaza de la Cultura**, Av Central, C 3/5. Along C Central is **Parque Central**, with a bandstand in the middle among trees (bands play at 1100 on second Sun of each month). To the E of the park is the **Cathedral**; to the N is the **Raventos theatre**; to the S are the **Rex Theatre** and a branch of the Banco Nacional. North of Av Central, on C 2, is the **Unión Club**, the principal social centre of the country. Opposite it is the **General**

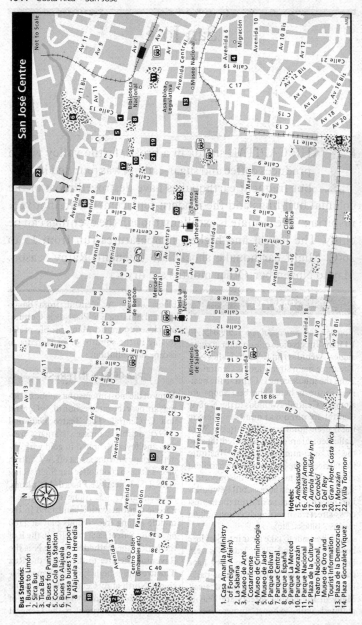

San José Centre

Not to Scale

N

Post and Telegraph Office. The **Museo Nacional**, with a good collection of precolumbian antiquities, is in the reconstructed Vista Buena barracks, E from the Plaza de la Cultura along Av Central. Facing it is the new **Plaza de la Democracia**, constructed to mark the Nov 1989 centenary of Costa Rican democracy. The **Palacio Nacional** (Av Central, C 15) is where the Legislative Assembly meets; any visitor can attend the debates, sessions start normally at 1600.

The attractive Paseo Colón continues the Av Central W to the former **La Sabana** airport (now developed as a sports centre, which is worth visiting) with a colonial-style building with frescoes of Costa Rican life in the Salón Dorado, see **Museo de Arte Costarricense** below. Further W is La Sabana, which has the **Estadio Nacional**, seating 20,000 spectators at (mainly) football matches, basketball, volleyball and tennis courts, a running track, lake and swimming pool.

MUSEUMS

NB Student cards give reductions in most museums. **Museo Nacional**, C 17, Av Central and 2, very interesting, archaeology, anthropology, national history, some gold, ex-President Arias' Nobel Peace Prize, open Tues-Sun, 0900-1500; replicas of precolumbian jewellery may be bought at reasonable prices (entrance, US$1.35, children free). **Museo de Oro** in the Plaza de la Cultura complex with art museums adjoining the Teatro Nacional, Av Central, C 3/5, excellent, entrance US$4.45, US$1.50 with student card, open Tues-Sun, 1000-1630, electronic system, Inform, costs US$2.25, mark the display numbers and the equipment tells you about the display in the language selected (Spanish or English), complete tour takes 40 mins (deposit all bags at entrance), T 223-0528/4233, ext 282; **Museo de Arte Costarricense** at the end of Paseo Colón, C 42, in La Sabana park in the old airport

building (open Tues-Sun, 1000-1700 Tues-Sat, Sun free, US$2, US$1 for students), small but interesting display of paintings and sculptures, T 222-7155/7247. In the INS building, Av 7, C 9-13, is the **Museo del Jade Fidel Tristan** on the 11th floor (Mon-Fri, 0830-1630, US$2.25), with jade carvings, pottery, sculpture etc, interesting, a 'must', and a beautiful view over the city. **Museo de Ciencias Naturales**, Colegio La Salle, Mon-Fri 0800-1600, Sat 0800-1200, Sun 0900-1600, US$1, T 232-1306 (in the grounds of the Ministry of Agriculture; take 'Estadio Sabana' bus from Av 2, C 1 to the gate). **Museo de Entomología** (entry US$1.50), in basement of School of Music building of the University of Costa Rica in San Pedro, Mon-Fri 1300-1700, to check times T 225-5555, ext 318, many beautiful insects, only museum of its kind in Central America. **Museo Histórico Imprenta Nacional**, La Uruca, open Mon-Fri 1000-1500. **Museo Nacional de la Carreta y el Campesino**, oxcart museum located in Salitral de Desamparados, display in typical old Costa Rican house of *campesino* life, temporarily closed 1997. **Railway Museum**, in the Atlántico station, Av 3 y C 21, temporarily closed 1997; **Museo de Arte Contemporáneo y Diseño**, Av 3, C 15-17, in the old liquor factory next to the Biblioteca Nacional, now the Centro Nacional de la Cultura, Tues 1300-1700, Wed 1000-1700, Thur 1000-2100, Fri-Sun 1000-1700, T 257-7202/9370. **Museo Dr Rafael Angel Calderón Guardia**, Barrio Escalante, Av 11 y C 25-27, memorial to former president and sociology museum, Mon-Sat 1000-1600, US$0.70, T 225-1218. **Museo Filatelico y Numismatico**, in General Post Office, 2nd floor, Mon-Fri 0800-1600, free. **Scientific and Cultural Centre** (**Museo del Niño** in old prison), C 4, Av 9, history and culture for children, Wed-Fri 1000-1200, 1400-1700, Sat-Sun 1000-1300, 1400-1700, US$5, children US$1.50, T 223-7003.

PARKS AND ZOOS

Two blocks N of the Museo Nacional is **Parque Nacional**, with a grandiloquent bronze monument representing the five Central American republics ousting the filibuster William Walker (see Nicaraguan chapter) and the abolition of slavery in Central America. There is also a statue donated by the Sandinista Government of Nicaragua to the people of Costa Rica. To the N of the park is the **Biblioteca Nacional**.

Still further N is **Parque Bolívar**, now turned into a recreation area, small charge for entry, with zoo (see below). Along Av 3, to the W of Parque Nacional, are the four gardens of the remodelled **Parque Morazán**, with another bandstand at the centre. A little to the NE, **Parque España**, cool, quiet, and intimate, has for neighbours the **Casa Amarilla** (Yellow House), seat of the Ministry of Foreign Affairs, and the **Edificio Metálico**, which houses several of the main schools. In the park opposite the church of La Merced is a huge carved granite ball brought from the archaeological site at Palmar Norte. There are others at the entrance to the Museo de Ciencias Naturales.

Simón Bolívar National Zoo and Botanical Gardens in Parque Simón Bolívar (Av 11, just E of C 7); entrance US$1, open Mon-Fri 0800-1530, Sat-Sun 0900-1700, also restaurant and souvenir shop. Go down C 11 about 3 blocks from Av 7. Remodelled and much improved, with all native plants numbered and listed in a brochure; animals' cages are small. Sloths can be seen in the trees. **Serpentarium**, Av 1, C 9-11, worth a visit especially if you are going to the National Parks or the jungle. Entrance adults US$3, children US$0.75, open Mon-Sun 0900-1800. Good variety of snakes and other reptiles but some not well cared for. Staff helpful if you speak Spanish. **Mundo Sumergido Aquarium**, San Francisco de Ríos (400m E, 200m N of Y-shaped roundabout to San Francisco), Mon-Sat 1000-2000.

EXCURSIONS

San José is a good centre for excursions into the beautiful Meseta Central. The excursions to the Orosí valley and volcano of Irazú are given under Cartago. Poás volcano (described on page 1072) can be visited from Alajuela. Enquire first about the likely weather when planning a visit to Poás or Irazú. To reach Barva take a bus to San José de la Montaña (see page 1109).

A road runs NE of San José to (11 km) **San Isidro de Coronado**, a popular summer resort (bus from Terminal Coronado, Av 7, C Central and 1). Those interested in medical research can visit the **Instituto Clodomiro Picado** snake farm, T 229-0335, open Mon-Fri 0800-1600 (snake feeding, Fri only 1400, Spanish only), take Dulce Nombre de Coronado bus from Av 3, C 3-5, 30 mins, or San Antonio Coronado bus to end of line and walk 200m downhill. They also sell snake-bite serum. The road goes on through fine countryside to **Las Nubes** (32 km), a country village which commands a great view of Irazú. **San Antonio de Escazú** hosts the National Oxcart Drivers' Day (Día del Boyero) festival, the second weekend in Mar, with festivities culminating on the Sun in a colourful oxcart parade from the school to the centre, accompanied by typical *payasos*. Open air dancing in the evening to a marimba.

Acua Mania water park, just off airport highway at traffic lights, 600m S of *Hotel Herradura*, San Antonio de Belén road, 0900-1900 Mon-Fri, 0900-2200 Sat-Sun. *Parque de Diversiones*, 2 km W of Hospital México, has a 'Pueblo Antiguo' theme park next to it depicting Costa Rica of 1880-1930, with areas of the city, the country and the coast, US$7. Held at the theme park is a *Vivencias Costarricenses* show, Wed-Sun, 1000-1400, US$35 inc show, lunch, transport, guide and taxes; *Noches Costarricenses* show, Sat-Sun, 1800-2100, US$35 inc show, dinner, transport, guide and taxes.

San José Main Streets & Districts

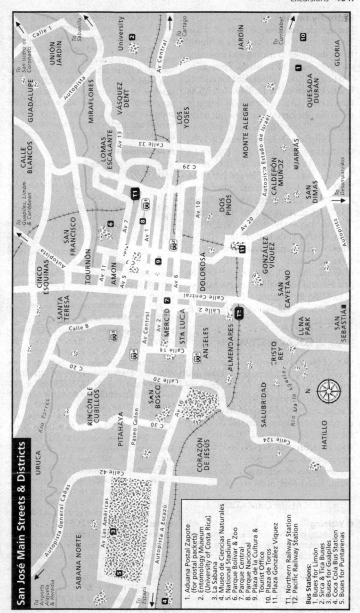

1. Aduana Postal Zapote (for postal packets)
2. Entomology Museum (University of Costa Rica)
3. La Sabana
4. Museo de Ciencias Naturales
5. National Stadium
6. Parque Bolívar & Zoo
7. Parque Central
8. Parque Nacional
9. Plaza de la Cultura & Tourist Office
10. Plaza de Toros
11. Plaza González Víquez

T1. Northern Railway Station
T2. Pacific Railway Station

Bus Stations:
1. Buses for Limón
2. Sirca & Tica Buses
3. Buses for Guápiles
4. Coca Cola Bus Station
5. Buses for Puntarenas

Butterfly farms

Just outside **Guácima**, 35 mins W of San José, 20 mins S of Alajuela, is a Butterfly Farm, dedicated to rearing and exporting over 60 species of butterfly, open daily, 0900-1500, US$12 adults, US$6 students, US$6 children under 12, T 438-0115. The farm is believed to be the second largest in the world (the largest is in Taiwan). It was created by Joris Brinckerhoff, a former Peace Corp volunteer, and his wife in 1990. Guides are most informative. Bus for La Guácima Mon-Sat from Av 1, C 20-22, 1100 and 1400, return 1500 and 1900, 1 hr, US$0.40, at last stop walk 300m from school S to butterfly sign (also minibuses, US$5). From Alajuela take bus marked 'La Guácima abajo', 0900, 1100, 1300, 40 mins, returns 1145, 1345, 1545, 1745. Another butterfly farm is **Spirogyra**, 100m E, 150m S of Centro Comercial El Pueblo (nr *Hotel Villa Tournon*), open daily, 0800-1500, printed guide in English, last guided tour 1530, US$5 for tourists, T 222-2937, take 'Calle Blancos' bus from C 3 and Av 5 to El Pueblo.

LOCAL FESTIVALS

28 to 31 December. Festivities last from 18 Dec to 5 Jan, with dances, horse shows and much confetti-throwing in the crowded streets. The annual El Tope horse parade starts at noon on 26 Dec and travels along the principal avenues of San José. A carnival starts next day at about 1700 in the same area. Fairs, firework displays and bull running (anyone can take part!) at El Zapote, frequent buses from the centre. Also parades during Easter week in the streets.

LOCAL INFORMATION

● **Warning**

Pickpockets, grab and run thieves, and muggings are on the increase in San José, especially in the centre, in the market, at the Coca Cola bus station, in the Barrios of Cuba, Cristo Rey, México, 15 de Setiembre and León XIII. Keep away from these areas at night and on Sun, when few people are around. Also be careful on buses; leave nothing unattended. Street gangs, known as *chapulines*, are mostly made up of minors. A special tourism police force is being set up which will work with the San José municipal police to help protect tourists from theft. The US embassy has produced a booklet *Helpful Hints For United States Citizens In Costa Rica*, available at the *Tico Times* office, some hotels and the US embassy. You must carry your passport (or a photocopy) with you at all times and make sure your papers are in order. A tourist helpline operated by tourist police has bilingual operators, 24 hrs (call free 800-012-3456).

● **Accommodation**

Hotel prices

L1	over US$200	L2	US$151-200
L3	US$101-150	A1	US$81-100
A2	US$61-80	A3	US$46-60
B	US$31-45	C	US$21-30
D	US$12-20	E	US$7-11
F	US$4-6	G	up to US$3

13% sales tax plus 3.39% tourism tax (total 16.39%) are added to the basic price. A deposit is rec at the more expensive hotels, especially in the high season, Dec-April, to guarantee reservations. If you arrive late at night, even a guaranteed reservation may not be honoured. Hotel stars in brackets.

In the **Barrio Amón** area are: **L1-L3** *Amstel Amon*, Av 11, C 36, in Barrio Amon, T 257-0191, F 257-0284, very helpful, clean, 75 rooms, plus suites new pink building, casino, restaurant, snack bar, underground parking; **L3-A2** *Britannia*, C 3, Av 11, T 223-6667, F 223-6411 1910 Spanish style restored mansion, high standard, antique furniture, very good service, excellent restaurant, worth the money; **A1-A2** *Casa Verde B&B*, C 7, Av 9, Barrio Amón, T 223-0969, small, renovated old house, deluxe, good breakfast, helpful; **A2** *L'Ambiance* (4), C 13, Av 9, T 222-6702, F 223-0481, US-owned, elegant 19th century restored mansion, antique furnishings, only 7 rooms, 20-seat restaurant rec, book in advance, bar, patio, very pleasant, no credit cards, front doors locked at 2300; **A2-A3** *Don Carlos*, C 9, Av 7-9, T 221-6707, F 255-0828, 36 rooms, interesting traditional building, much artwork and statuary, sundeck, free coffee, Annemarie's giftshop good selection, some noise from nearby nightclubs, credit cards accepted; **A2-A3** *Dunn Inn*, Barrio Amón, C 5, Av 11, Apdo 6241-1000, T 222-3232/3426, F 221-4596, inc breakfast and local phone calls; **A2-A3** *Hemingway*, Av 9, C 9, T/F 221-1804, central, Spanish style, inc breakfast, patio and tropical garden, 25 mins from San José; **A2-A3** *Santo Tomás*, Av 7, C 3-5, T 255-0448, F 222-3950, central, full payment requested in advance, credit cards accepted with 7% fee, several languages spoken, attractive décor, noisy; **A2-A3** *Taylor's Inn*, Av 13, C 3-3b, T 257-4333, F 221-1475, with breakfast, old house nicely restored.

C *Joluva*, C 3b, Av 9-11, T 223-7961, with breakfast, old house, friendly, safe, good laundry service, good value; **C** *Kekoldi*, Av 9, C 3b, T 223-3244, F 257-5476, old house imaginatively refurbished, colourful, 14 big rooms with bath, helpful, snacks and bar service, some traffic noise.

In **Barrio Tournón** are: **L2-L3** *Radisson Europa San José*, T 257-3257, F 221-3976, modern, well-equipped, beautiful, gym, pools, bars, restaurant, café, conference facilities, church, casino, fine views.

A2 *Villa Tournon* (3), T 233-6622, F 222-5211, attractive, excellent service, landscaped garden, pool, rooms facing the street are noisy from traffic a few minutes walk from El Pueblo (see **Shopping**).

On, or just off, **Paseo Colón** are: **L2-L3** *Quality Hotel Centro Colón*, near the Centro Colón building, off Paseo Colón, Av 3, C 38, T 257-2580, F 257-2582, luxury hotel.

A1 *Parque del Lago*, T 257-8787, F 233-1617, Av 2, C 40, E side of La Sabana, airport courtesy van, breakfast buffet inc; **L3-A2** *Rosa del Paseo*, Paseo Colón, C 28-30, T 257-3258, F 223-2776, beautifully restored mansion, breakfast inc; **A2** *Ambassador* (3), C 26, Paseo Colón, T 221-8155, F 255-3396, central, modern, casino, bar, restaurant, coffee shop, cable TV, phone in rooms, travel agency, restaurants and cinemas opp, cheaper to take your own taxi on the street, front rooms noisy from traffic, back rooms fine, nice suite; **A2** *Grano de Oro*, C 30, Av 2, T 255-3322, F 221-2782, converted 19th century mansion, 35 rooms and suites, beautiful terrace gardens, friendly, tasteful, good value.

A2-A3 *Petit Victoria*, C 26, 50m from Paseo Colón, T 233-1812, F 233-1938, bath, minibar, cable TV, kitchen, convenient, breakfast inc, but overpriced.

C *Cacts*, Av 3 bis, C 28-30, nr *Pizza Hut* Paseo Colón, T 221-2928, F 221-8616, safe, good service, breakfast inc, TV, friendly, rec.

Off **Autopista General Canas** (San José-Airport highway) are: **L2-L3** *Costa Rica Marriott*,

near Juan Santamaría airport, 700m W of Firestone, San Antonio de Belén, T 298-0000, F 298-0011, 246 rooms, 2 pools, restaurants, golf, tennis; **L2-L3** *Meliá Cariari* (4), nr airport, T 239-0022, F 239-2803, refurbished 1996, pool, tennis, 18 hole golf course, celebrity hotel; **L2-L3** *Herradura Resort and Convention Center* (4), nr the airport, Japanese-owned, *Sakura* Japanese restaurant, pool, T 239-0033, F 239-2292.

L3-A2 *San José Palacio*, nr airport, T 220-2034, F 220-2036, part of the Barceló chain, all rooms a/c, fridge, cable TV, 1 executive floor, 5 normal floors, pool, spa, squash, tennis, sauna, casino, convention centre, caters for European tours, café, piano bar, restaurant, but out of town and few shops etc nearby; **A2** *Irazú* (3), La Uruca, next to San José 2000 shopping centre, T 232-4811, F 232-4685, rooms without a/c, children under 12 free, casino, conference facilities, pool, tennis, sauna, rec, transport downtown, hotel will organize excursions and visits, good pavement café, mixed reports.

In the area of **Los Yoses, San Pedro**, University of Costa Rica (eastern suburbs) are: **A2** *Le Bergerac*, C 35 Los Yoses, T 234-7850, F 225-9103, with continental breakfast, French atmosphere, fan, TV, restaurant, bar; **A2** *Milvia*, 4 km W of downtown in San Pedro, 250m NW of De Muñoz y Nane shopping centre, T 225-4543, F 225-7801, attractive boutique hotel, converted wooden mansion once the home of a 1930s revolutionary, personal service.

B *D'Galahi* (2), behind University of Costa Rica, San Pedro, pool, nice rooms and apartments, T 234-1743; **B** *Tres Arcos*, Av 10, C 37-39, no 3773, Los Yoses, T 225-0271, Canadian-owned, close to restaurants, buses, nice area, inc breakfast.

C *Mr Tucker's Inn*, Los Yoses, T 253-7911 (in Canada 905-562-5591), inc breakfast, some rooms with bath, comfortable, rec, Mr Tucker has microbus for airport transfers, day trips, etc.

Apartotels (with kitchen, etc) can be cheaper for longer stays, weekly or monthly rates: **A** *Apartotel Los Yoses*, T 225-0033, Los Yoses, passably clean, comfortable beds, fridge and stove functional, tiny pool, attractive and secure area with supermarket, laundromat and restaurants nearby; **C** *Apartamentos Scotland*, C 27, Av 1, weekly or monthly for furnished apartments, T 223-0833; also in San Pedro, nr the University is *Casa Agua Buena*, rooms for US$150-250/month, weekly rate also, common kitchen, telephone, TV, washing machine, comfortable, quiet, call Richard (Rick)

Stern, T/F 234-2411, or write to Apdo 366-2200, Coronado, Costa Rica.

Around **La Sabana** are: **L3** *Corobicí* (3), Sabana Norte, T 232-8122, F 231-5834, Japanese-owned, same chain as *Cariari*, casino, conference facilities, pool and fitness centre, rainforest and jungle tours (by *Río Colorado Lodge* office in hotel).

L3-A2 *Torremolinos* (3), C 40, Av 5 bis, T 222-5266, F 255-3167, LanChile office, bar, restaurant, pool, sauna, 200m from Sabana, nr Yoahan commercial centre, free transport into town.

A2-A3 *Ejecutivo Napoleón*, T 223-4750, F 222-9487, Sabana Norte, C 40, 1 block from *Yoahan Supermarket* and shopping centre, 27 rooms, parking, pool; **A2-A3** *Tennis Club*, Sábana Sur, Apdo 4964, T 232-1266, F 232-3867, 2-star, 20 mins from centre, a/c, shower, TV, swimming pool, tennis courts, snack bar, restaurant, rec.

Around **Escazú** and **Santa Ana** (western suburbs) are: **L2-L3** *Camino Real* (5) Próspero Fernández Highway, Multiplaza Mall, Escazú, T 289-7000, F 289-8998, 261 rooms, golf course and luxury spa, international business hotel poor location on city margin; **L2-L3** *Tara Resort Hotel*, San Antonio de Escazú, T 228-6992, F 228-9651, beautiful mansion, inc breakfast and transport, suites, conference facilities, rec restaurant, pool, beautiful views, climb nearby Pico Blanco mountain; **L2-L3** *Sangildar*, San Rafael de Escazú, T 289-8843, F 228-6454, luxury.

A2 *Posada Canal Grande*, Santa Ana, nr airport, T 228-4101, F 282-5733, pool, peaceful area; **A2** *Posada El Quijote*, Bello Horizonte de Escazú, Apdo 1127-1250, T 289-8401, F 289-8729, renovated colonial house with modern art collection, with bath, hot water, cable TV, breakfast inc, gardens, 10 mins from centre, 15 mins from airport, airport pickup available (in USA Dept 239-SJO, PO Box 025216, Miami, FL 33102-5216, T 800-570-6750, ext 8401).

A2-A3 *Amstel Escazú*, T 228-1764, F 282-0620, 14 rooms, 2 suites, pool, parking; **A2-A3** *La Casa de las Tias*, 100m S of Centro Comercial El Cruce, San Rafael de Escazú, T 289-5517, F 289-7353, with breakfast, 5 rooms with bath, fan, airport pickup; **A2-A3** *Pine Tree Inn*, Trejos Montealegre Escazú, T 289-7405, F 228-2180, 15 rooms with bath, cable TV, pool; **A2-A3** *Tapezco Inn*, 50m S of San Miguel church, Escazú, T 228-1084, F 289-7026, with breakfast, pool, sauna, jacuzzi; **A2-A3** *Villa Escazú Bed and Breakfast*, 1 km SW of Escazú,

nr bus route, 4 rooms with private or shared bathroom, large gardens and patio, T/F 228-9566, ask for Inéz or Mary Ann.

B *Pico Blanco Inn* (1), San Antonio de Escazú, T 228-1908, F 289-5189, all rooms with balconies and views of Central Valley, several cottages, English owner, restaurant with English pub, Costa Rican flavour, pool, airport pickup can be requested, rec.

C *Bonaire*, Escazú, English-speaking bed and breakfast, nice, friendly, T 228-0866; **C** *Linda Vista Lodge Bed and Breakfast*, Escazú, cosy rooms, spectacular views.

Apartotels (with kitchen, etc) can be cheaper for longer stays, weekly or monthly rates: **L1-L2** *Apartotel Villa de Río*, San Rafael de Escazú, T 289-8833, F 289-8627, cable TV and VCR, gymnasium, pool, transportation to city centre.

Central hotels are: **L2** *Aurola Holiday Inn* (4), C 5, Av 5, pool, T 233-7233, F 222-2621, mainly business clientèle, casino, good view of city, go to 16th floor and walk up emergency stairs.

L3-A2 *Balmoral* (3), C 7, Av Central, T 222-5022, F 221-7826, unimaginative but comfortable commercial hotel, café/restaurant slow service but good food; **L3-A2** *del Rey*, Av 1, C 9, on busy corner in restored pink and white building, looks like iced cake, nice single, double, triple rooms, standard or deluxe, suites, children under 12 free, free city tour on a/c bus, walls a bit thin, restaurant, casino, Apdo 6241-1000, T 221-7272/257-3130, F 221-0096; **A2** *D' Raya Vida*, bed and breakfast villa nr by Debbi McMurray-Long, nr Hospital Calderón Guardia, inc airport transfers, 4 double rooms, children by prior arrangement, meals available, wonderful garden, T 223-4168, F 223-4157; **A2** *Europa* (3), C Central, Av 3, T 222-1222, F 221-4609, pleasant, comfortable rooms, cable TV, pool, central, good for business visitors, suites available, prior reservation rec, rooms on street side can be noisy, good restaurant; **A2** *Gran Hotel Costa Rica* (3), C 3, Av 2, T 221-4000, F 221-3501, all right for 1 night stopover, food adequate, breakfast from 0400, buffet US$7, English-speaking staff, ground floor casino, noisy.

A2-A3 *Ara Macao*, Barrio California, 50m S of Pizza Hut, 5 mins from centre, T 233-2742, inc breakfast, small, quiet; **A2-A3** *Diana's Inn*, C 5, Av 3, Parque Morazán, nr *Holiday Inn*, an old building formerly used by the president, now restored, inc breakfast and taxes, discounts available, a/c, TV, hot water, noisy, luggage storage, safety box, T 223-6542, F 233-0495;

A2-A3 *Doña Inés*, C 11, Av 2-6, PO Box 1754-1002, T 222-7443, F 222-7553, clean, quiet, safe, Italian-run; **A2-A3** *Edelweiss*, Av 9, C 13-15, 100m E of Condovac offices, T 221-9702, F 222-1241, English, German and Spanish spoken, Austrian and German cuisine, clean, comfortable, native hardwood furniture and carved doors, pleasant courtyard bar, helpful, friendly, rec; **A2-A3** *La Gran Vía* (2), C 3, Av Central, T 222-7737, F 222-7205, comfortable, helpful, good value; **A2-A3** *Costa Rica Morazán* (3), C 7, Av 1, T 222-4622, F 233-3329, book in advance, rooms vary, some **B**, rec by some, casino, parking, airport shuttle; **A2-A3** *Presidente* (3), C 7, Av Central, T 222-3022, F 221-1205, extensively refurbished 1994/5; **A2-A3** *Royal Dutch*, C 4, Av Central-2, T 222-1066, F 233-2927, 2-star, suites, restaurant, rec; **A2-A3** *Vesuvio*, Av 11, C 13-15, Barrio Otoya, T 221-7586, F 221-8325, inc breakfast, 20 rooms, private bath, secure parking, very quiet, good restaurant, show your *Handbook* for 20% discount.

B *Doral*, C 6-8, Av, T 233-5069, F 233-4827, bath, TV, central, clean, helpful staff, soft mattresses, a bit noisy, restaurant; **B** *Galilea*, Av Central, C 13, T 233-6925, friendly, hot showers, back rooms quiet, rooms on C 3 have nice view of Plaza Democracia and Museo Nacional, run by Dutch lady, English and German also spoken; **B** *Best Western San José Downtown*, Av 7, C 6-8, T 255-4766, 1-800-528-1234, F 255-4613, bath, TV, a/c, inc breakfast, rustic rooms, free coffee and bananas all day, pool, sauna, parking, rec; **B** *La Amistad*, Av 11, C 15, T 221-1597, F 221-1409, with breakfast, cosy mansion with 22 rooms all with bath, TV, fan, German owned; **B** *La Gema*, Av 12, C 9-11, T 257-2524, F 222-1074, bath, TV, pleasant, friendly; **B** *Park*, C 2, Av 4, T 221-6944, clean with bar; **B** *Plaza* (1), C 2, Av Central, T 222-5533, F 222-2614, TV, phone, bar, restaurant; **B** *Royal Garden* (3), C Central, Av 2, T 257-0023, F 257-1517, central, casino, Chinese restaurant, Dim Sum for breakfast; **B-C** *Aranjuez*, C 19, Av 11-13, T 223-3559, F 223-3528, shared or private bathroom, splendid breakfast, free coffee all day, hairdriers, friendly English speaking staff, clean, well-kept, nice gardens, bag store, rec, Apdo 457-2070.

C *Alameda* (1), C 12, Av Central, T 223-6333, F 222-9673, 5 mins from buses going to the Pacific, hot water, most rooms noisy, inside rooms quieter but no windows, staff friendly, English spoken, beds uncomfortable; **C** *Belmondo*, C 20, Av 9, T 222-9624, T 257-0816,

20 refurbished rooms, clean, inc breakfast, tiny pool; **C** *Bienvenido*, C 10, Av 1-3, very clean, hot shower, good restaurant, nr centre and airport bus, best hotel nr Coca Cola bus station; **C** *Brunelles's* bed and breakfast, T 235-1561, Bo Fletcher, Tibas, pick-up available; **C** *Capital*, Av 3-5, C 4, T 221-8497, remodelled, cable TV, bath, fan; **C** *Casa Las Mercedes*, 700m W of Colegio Sión, Los Colegios district of Moravia, T 235-9280, book in advance, breakfast US$4, quiet, clean, good food, good base for extended stays (eg language students); **C** *Centroamericano*, Av 2, C 6-8, private bath, clean small rooms, very helpful, will arrange accommodation in other towns, free shuttle (Mon-Fri) to airport, laundry facilities, rec; **C** *Fortuna*, Av 6, C 2 y 4, quiet, rec; **C** *Jardine's Inn*, 3 blocks W of *Aurola Holiday Inn*, with bath, fan, very clean, friendly; **C** *Ritz*, C Central, Av 8, T 222-4103, F 222-8849, with bath and hot water, helpful, Swiss-run, German, French and English spoken, friendly, free coffee, good breakfast, 2nd-hand book exchange, clothes washing facilities, rec, but avoid 4 rooms on ground floor by reception, small, dark and too noisy even with ear plugs; this is linked to **D-E** *Pensión Centro Continental*, same address, T 233-1731, hot water, clean, friendly, laundry, helpful, coffee available, no meals except for breakfast, rec; **C** *Talamanca* (1), C 8, Av 2, T 233-5033, F 233-5420, small rooms, good breakfast, try their rum punch.

D *Bellavista*, Av Central, C 19/21, T 223-0095, friendly and helpful, with bath, clean, opp *Dennies* restaurant; **D** *Casa Ridgeway*, Centro de Amigos para la Paz, C 15, Av 6-8, T 233-6168, F 224-8910, 1-4 beds in room, shared bath, use of kitchen, friendly, laundry possible; **D** *Berlín*, Av 8, C 2, clean, safe, quiet, fans, central; **D** *Cocorí*, C 16, Av 3, T 233-0081/233-2188, with bath, hot water, by bus to Peñas Blancas, parking; **D** *Johnson*, C 8, Av Central, T 223-7633, friendly, clean, restaurant and bar, good value, popular with Peace Corps and cockroaches, rec but can be noisy; *Pensión de la Cuesta*, Av 1, C 11-15, T 255-2896, 4 rooms with shared bath, inc breakfast; **D** *San José*, C 14 and Av 5, with shower, clean, friendly, nr bus station; **D-E** *Generaleño*, Av 2 entre C 8 y 10, with bath, cold water, good value.

E *Aurora*, Av 4, C 8, with bath, **F** without, good value, hot shower, nylon sheets and plastic mattress covers, sweaty, very noisy nightclub nearby (till 0500), rooms on 2nd floor are the least noisy, mixed reports, *Soda Aladino* next door is very good; **E** *Boston*, C Central, Av 8, T 257-4499, with or without bath, good, very friendly, but noisy, will store luggage; **E-F** *Gran Imperial*, C 8, Av 1 and Central, T 222-7899, mixed reports, small rooms, thin walls, clean, sometimes noisy, limited hot showers, new laundry downstairs, more expensive than laundromat, restaurant with good prices, best to reserve, locked luggage store, good for meeting other travellers, notice board, TV; **E** *Marlyn*, C 4, Av 7-9, T 233-3212, more with bath, hot showers, safe, will store luggage, parking for motorcycles (just); **E** *Compostela*, C 6, Av 3-5, T 221-0694, bath, friendly, small rooms, family-run, quiet, door locked at 2300, rec; **E** *Roma*, C 14, Av Central and 1, T 223-2179, uphill from Alajuela bus station, clean, safe, good value but windowless rooms, stores luggage; **E-F** *Rialto*, Av 5, C 2, 1 block from Correos, shared bath, hot water, safe, friendly but can be very noisy.

F *Nuevo Rialto*, Av 1, C 6-8, popular but leave valuables with office, noisy rooms at front, rec; **F** *Residencial Balboa*, Av 10, C 6, safe, cold shower, thin walls, basic, cheap; diagonally opp *Gran Imperial* is **F** *Valencia*, C 8 y Av 1, clean, friendly, noisy.

Pensiones are: **E** *América*, Av 7, C 4, clean, large rooms, good value; **E** *Americana*, C 2, Av 2, without bath, clean, large rooms, friendly, luggage store, laundry facilities, rec; **E** *Asia*, C 11 No 63N (between Avs Central and 1), T 223-3893, clean, friendly, but paper-thin walls, lots of noise from rapid turnover, hot showers, Chinese-run, English spoken; **E** *Astoria*, Av 7, No 749, T 221-2174, but rooms vary, cockroaches, hot showers, uncomfortable beds, thin walls, noisy; **E** *Boruca*, C 14, Av 1/3, Coca Cola market, T 223-0016, without bath, hot water, laundry service, popular with Peace Corps; **E** *Moreno*, C 12, Av 6-8, T 221-7136, with bath; **E** *Musoc*, C 16, Av 3/5, T 222-9437, F 225-0031, with or without private bath, very clean, hot water, luggage stored, friendly, nr to (and somewhat noisy because of) bus stations, but rec; **E** *Reforma Hilton*, C 11, No 105, with bath, T 221-9705, restaurant; **E** *Superfamiliar*, Av 2, C 9-11, shared bath; **F** *Araica*, Av 2 No 1125, T 222-5233, without bath, clean, dark, thin walls, friendly; **F** *Corobicí*, Av 1, between C 10 and 12, cold shared showers, run down, like a men's boarding house; **F** *Managua*, C 8, Av 1/3, small rooms, basic, hard beds, cold shared showers, clean and cheap, safe, helpful, will wash clothes, rec; **F** *Otoya*, C 1, Av 3-5, clean, friendly, luggage store, hot water, English spoken, rec.

Near **Tica Bus terminal** are: **E** *Avenida Segunda*, Av 2, C 9-11, price varies, friendly, stores luggage; **F** *Salamanca*, Av 2, C 9-11, cold water, adequate; **F** *Tica Linda*, Av 2, No 553 (tiny sign), friendly, noisy, some beds uncomfortable, redecorated, fairly clean, little privacy, cheap laundry, good information, will store luggage, good place to receive international phone calls, 'gringo' place, often full, next door is the *Esmeralda Mariachi Palace*, Av 2, C 5-7, large restaurant/bar with live bands playing requests, which operates all night except Sun. There are several hotels in **F** range nr the various markets, such as the *Comerciante* annex, C 10, Av 3/5, quite clean; *España*, Av 3/5, C 8, run by a Spanish family. Cheaper hotels usually have only wooden partitions for walls, so they are noisy. Also, they often rent only by the hour. **NB** Hotels in the red light district, C 6, Avs 1-5, nr Mercado Central, charge on average US$10 with toilet and shower for a night. **NB also** It is difficult to find cheap hotels with parking, but next to *Ribadavia*, C Central, Avs 7 y 9, is a 24-hr parking lot. There are a couple of cheap *parqueos* on C 9 between Avs 1 and 3 with cheap hotels in the vicinity.

Youth Hostel: *Toruma Youth Hostel*, the only official YHA member in Costa Rica, T 224-4085, Av Central, C 31-33, 95 beds, restaurant, clean, hot water not always available, crowded but safe, lockable compartments in each room, E pp inc breakfast, more expensive for those who do not hold International Student Identity Card or YHA membership; music, free for guests, on Fri and Sat nights; a good place for meeting other travellers to arrange group travel. You can leave bags there safely for US$0.50/day. Youth hostel information: Recaj, PO Box 10227, 1000 San José. Discounts at affiliated hotels and lodges (see text) are available if reservations are made through Recaj.

Bed and breakfast: for B-and-B accommodation in San José and Costa Rica contact *Costa Rica Bed and Breakfast Group*, c/o Debbi McMurray, Apdo 493-1000, San José, or at *D'Raya Vida*, T 223-4168, F 223-4157; also Pat Bliss, *Park Place*, Escazú, T/F 228-9200. They have 50 inns and hotels in their directory. Rec is **B** *La Casa de los Gardner*, PO Box 1028-1200, Pavas, in the suburb of Rohrmoser, convenient for airport, clean, US run; **D** *Forest Bed and Breakfast Hostel/Hotel*, Escazú, T 228-0900, youth hostel style, but also has rooms in **A2-B** range.

Trailer Park: *Belén*, in San Antonio de Belén, 2 km W of intersection at Cariari and San

Antonio, 5 km from airport, turn off Highway 1 on to Route 111, turn right at soccer field then first L for 1 km, T 239-0421, F 239-1316, US$10/day, American-owned, shade, hot showers, laundry, friendly, rec; good bus service to San José.

Camping: 16 km E of San José nr Tres Ríos, 1 km S of Pan-American Highway, turn off signed to Istaru Campo Escuela, first *finca* on the right is *Para Las Orejas*, where you can camp, bathrooms available, T/F 279-9752, back-packing Spanish goats for hikers, goats' milk

● **Places to eat**
Sales tax of 13% plus 10% service charge added to restaurant bills. Apart from the hotels, the best ones are the *Bastille*, French type (limited choice), on Paseo Colón; *Ile de France*, C 7, Av Central and 2 (T 222-4241), good French chef; next door is *La Hacienda Steak House*, expensive but good, upstairs is a good Mexican *taquería*; *La Estancia* in El Pueblo, typical Costa Rican steak house, be sure to use the garlic sauce, rec; *La Tranquera* (parking space) on the highway to Cartago at Curridabat, 6-8 km E of San José, serves good steaks and other foods (orchestra for dancing at weekends); *Los Ranchos* Steak House, Sabana Norte nr *Hotel Corobicí*, reliable, good food; *Casa de Matute Gómez*, mansion built in 1930, famous landmark in Barrio González Lehmann; on N side of old La Sabana airport on Av 3 and about C 50 are two good restaurants, *El Chicote* (country-style; good grills) and *El Molino*; *El Chalet Suizo*, Av 1, C 5-7 (T 222-3118), good food and service, international; *Il Tula*, very good, same area; *Los Anonos*, in Escazú area, grills; also *La Flecha*, Centro Colón Building, Paseo Colón, superb; *Lobster Inn*, Paseo Colón, C 24, T 223-8594, seafood, large choice, expensive; *La Cocina de Lana*, El Pueblo, seafood, excellent menu, upmarket, pricey; *Marbella*, Centro Comercial de la C Real, San Pedro de Montes de Oca, T 224-9452, fish, packed on Sun, very good; *La Casa de los Mariscos*, Los Yoses; *Italiano*, Carretera a Sabanilla, 1 block N of Av Central; *Machu Picchu*, C 32, Av 1-3, good, rec; *Peruveana*, also C 32, Av 1-3, reasonable prices; *Goya*, Av 1, C 5/7, Spanish food; *Casa de España*, in Bank of America, C 1, good lunches; *Masia de Triquell*, Edif Casa España, Sabana Norte, T 296-3528, Catalan, warmly rec, closed Sun; *Tomy's Ribs*, Av 6, C 11-13, good barbecued beef and pork; *Los Lechones*, Av 6, C 11 and 13, good food, live music Fri and Sat, reasonable prices; *Antojitos*, on Paseo

Colón, on Pavas Highway W of Sabana and in Centro Comercial Cocorí (road to suburb of San Pedro), serves excellent Mexican food at moderate prices; *La Perla*, C Central y Av 2, 24 hr, adequate, friendly staff; *El Balcón de Europa*, C 9 Av Central y 1, Italian, great atmosphere, popular, but some dishes rather small and tasteless; *Pizzería Finisterre*, next door, similar menu, good pizzas, rec, but cheaper if slightly less posh; *Pizza Metro*, Av 2, C 5 y 7, good Italian, small and cosy, not cheap, rec; *Pasta Factory*, Av 1, C 7, excellent Italian, rec; *San Remo*, Av 3-5, C 2, also Italian, local food too, *menú del día*, rec, friendly service, good value, frequently rec (closed Sun); *La Esmeralda*, Av 2, C 7, reasonably priced, clean, good local dishes, live Costa Rican music in the evenings, rec; *Morazán*, C 9, Av 3, facing Parque Morazán, not touristy, popular with locals, friendly, excellent breakfast, delicious blackberry juice.

Chinese: *Fortuna*, Av 6, C 2-4; *Kaw Wah*, Av 2, C 5-7, rec; *Kiam Kon*, C Central and Av Central-2, good, large helpings; *Kuang Chaou* on C 11 between Av Central and Av 2; *Lung Mun* on Av 1, between C 5 and 7, reasonably priced; *Tin Jo*, C 11, Av 6-8, T 217-605, good Chinese and other Asian dishes; *Wing On*, Av 7, C 13-15, good, cheap; also rec, *Fu Lu Su*, C 7, Av 2, Chinese, Korean, very good; *Tin Hao*, Av 10, C 4, T 221-1163, good; *Corona de Oro*, Av 3, round the corner from the Post Office, good and cheap; and *Kam King*, Av 10, C 19-21; *Jardín lade*, Av 4, C 4-6, good value.

Vegetarian: *Don Sol*, Av 7b No 1347, excellent 3 course lunch US$1.60, run by integral yoga society (open only for lunch); *Vishnu*, Av 1, C 1-3, good quality, cheap and good *plato del día*, try their soya cheese sandwiches and ice cream, sells good wholemeal bread, also on C 14, Av 2, open daily, 0800-2000; *El Edén*, Av 5, C Central, same food and prices as *Vishnu*; *La Mazorca*, in San Pedro, nr University of Costa Rica (Rodrigo Facio site), vegetarian and health foods; *La Nutrisoda*, Edif Las Arcadas, open 1100 to 1800, homemade natural ice cream; *Laxmi*, Av 8, C 8; *Macrobiótica*, C 11, Av 6-8, health shop selling good bread; *Naturama Uno*, Av 1, opp Omni building, cheap; *Shakti*, Av 8, C 13, excellent; *Soda Vegetariana*, next to Librería Francesa.

Churrería Manolo, Av Central, C Central and 2 (new restaurant upstairs), and another branch on Av Central, good sandwiches and hot chocolate; *Comedor* beneath 'Dorado' sign, C 8, Av 4-6, very cheap; *Pollo Obay*, Av 10, 6 C, good fried chicken; *Pollo Tico*, Av 1 C 10-12, variety of meals with good dishes around US$1, popular, open 24 hrs; *La Fánega*, in San Pedro, for excellent hamburgers, folk music some nights; *La Geishita*, C Central, Av 14, cheap *casado*; *Las Condes*, Av Central/1, C 11, inexpensive; *Lido Bar*, C 2, Av 3, for *casado*; *Orléans*, also in San Pedro, serves crêpes; *Pastel de Pollo*, C 2, Av 6-8, excellent pies; *Pizza Hut*, C 4, Av Central y 2, also several other branches, open Sun, good value pasta and salad, popular, queues to get in, rec; *Salón París*, Av 3, C 1/3, rec; *Soda Amon*, C 7, Av 7-9, good, cheap *casados*; *Soda Coliseo*, Av 3, C 10-12, next to Alajuela bus station, rec; *Soda La Casita*, Av 1, C Central, clean, breakfast US$1.25; *Soda La Luz*, Av Central, C 33, good filling meals, cheap; *Soda Magaly*, Av Central, C 23, nr Youth Hostel, good, cheap; *Soda Maly*, Av 4, C 2-4, Chinese and tico, good; *Soda Nini*, Av 3, C 2-4, cheap; *Soda Poás*, Av 7, C 3-5, good value; *Soda Puntarenas*, C 12, Av 7-9, good for light meals and breakfast, open 0500-2200; *La Vasconia*, Av 2, C 5, restaurant and soda bar, good breakfast; *The Sandwich*, good all-night soda, 1 block N of Ticabus station.

Autoservicios do not charge tax and service and represent best value; they also sell beer. Eg *Corona de Oro*, Av 3, C 2-4 (next to *Nini*) excellent, and *Kings*, Av 1, C 1-3, opp Cini Omni. Food bars in restaurants in the Mercado Central (C 6/8) are good for breakfast and lunch, but none of them is open in the evening, high standards of sanitation. Try *Soda Flor de Costa Rica*, entrada Noroeste, pabellón de las flores, very good and cheap meals, very clean, open 0700-1800, T 221-7881. At lunchtime cheaper restaurants offer a set meal called a *casado*, US$1.50-2.50, which is good value; eg in the snack bars in the *Galería* complex, Av Central-2, C 5-7. Try *Chicharronera Nacional*, Av 1, C 10/12, very popular, or *Popular*, Av 3, C 6/8, good *casado*; *El Merendero*, Av 6, C 0-2, cheap local food, popular with Ticos.

Ice cream, confectionery, etc: *Helados Rena*, C 8, Av Central, excellent; also *Helados Boni*, C Central, Av 6-8, home-made ice cream; *Pops*, nr Banco Central, and other outlets, for ice cream (excellent); *Heladería Italiano*, excellent ice cream; also for ice cream *Mönpik*, Av Central, C Central and other outlets in San José, great ice cream; *Spoon*, Av Central, C 5-7, good coffee and pastries, gives 10% ISTC discount; *Fudge*, Centro Comercial Los Lagos, Escazú, coffee and pastries; *El ABC*, Av Central between

Calles 11 and 9, self-service, good, clean, cheap; *La Selecta* bakeries rec; *Le Croissant*, Av Central, C 33, good French bakery; *Café del Teatro*, in foyer of National Theatre, reasonably priced, belle époque interior, popular meeting place for poets and writers, pleasant for a snack. At the bus station women sell *panbon* and delicious coconut pies.

● **Bars**

Good places to have a drink inc *Josephine's*, Av 9, C 2 y 4, T 256-4396, 257-2269, expensive; and *El Cuartel de la Boca del Monte*, Av 1, C 21-23, live music at weekends, popular, rec, '60s atmosphere, entrance US$5.40 but worth it; *Chelle's*, Av 0, C 9, excellent bar; *Las Abejas*, C 1, gay disco; *Las Rosas*, C 1, Av Central, bars on 3 floors, good; *Nashville South*, C 5, Av 1-3, popular; *Centro Comercial El Pueblo* has restaurants, bars and 2 discos.

● **Airline offices**

Addresses (and telephone numbers) of major airlines: **Copa**, Av 5, C 1 (222-6640, 222-6650); **SAM**, Paseo Colón, C 38-40, Edif Centro Colón 2nd floor (233-3066); **Lacsa**, Av 5, C 1 (296-0909); **Sansa**, Paseo Colón, C 24 (221-9414, see **Internal flights** below); **Taca**, Av 3, C 40 (222-1790); **Mexicana**, C 5, Av 7-9 (257-6334), Mexican Tourist Card available here; **Saeta**, C 13, Av 11, T 223-5648; **Varig**, Av 5, C 3-5 (257-0094); **Servivensa**, 2nd floor Centro Colón building, Paseo Colón, C 38-40 (257-1441); **TWA**, Paseo Colón, C 34-36 (221-4638), F 223-0226; **Continental**, Oficentro La Virgen No 2, 200m S, 300m E and 50m N of American Embassy, Pavas (296-4911); **British Airways**, C 13, Av 11, T 223-5648; **Delta**, Paseo Colón, C 40, Edif San Jorge (257-2433); **Iberia**, Paseo Colón, C 40 (257-8266); **KLM**, Sabana Sur, behind Controlaría General Building (220-4112); **Lufthansa**, Av 7-9, C 5 (221-7444); **Air France**, Condominio Vista Real, 1st floor, 50m W and 10m N of POP's, Curridabat, T 280-0069; **Swiss Air**, Av 1-3 C Central (221-6613). **Singapore Airlines**, Av 1, C 3-5 (255-3555). **Lloyd Aéreo Boliviano**, Av 2, C 2-4, upstairs (255-1530); **American**, opp *Hotel Corobicí*, Sabana Este (257-1266); **Aviateca**, Av 3, C 40 (233-8390); **Alitalia**, C 38, Av 3, Centro Comercial Los Alcazares (222-6138); **Aeroperlas**, 150m E of *Hampton Inn*, Juan Santamaría airport, T 440-0093; **Aeroperú**, Av 5, C 1-3 (223-7033); **LTU International Airways** (German charter airline), Condominio da Vinci, Oficina No 6, Barrio Dent, T 234-9292; **Condor Airlines** (German charter airline), C 5, Av 7-9,

T 221-7444; **Aero Costa Rica** (to Miami and Orlando), 200m N of Fuente de la Hispanidad, San Pedro (296-2020 for reservations); **United Airlines**, Sabana Sur, behind Controlaría General Building, T 220-4844 (at airport); **Korean Air**, Edif Alde, 2nd floor, Av Central-1, C 1 (222-1332); Travelair, T 296-1102, 296-3408, F 220-0413 (see **Internal Flights** below).

● **Banks & money changers**
Opening times: Mon-Fri, 0900-1500. **Banco Nacional** (see page 1140), head office, Av 3, C 2-4, will change TCs into dollars but you pay a commission, accepts Visa credit cards as do most of the bigger banks in San José and other major towns; **Banco de Costa Rica**, Av Central, C 4, changes TCs 1 y C 7, open 1030-1700, long queues, 3% commission; **Banco de San José**, C Central, Av 3-5, commission 2.5%. Money can be sent through Banco de San José or Banco de Costa Rica at 4% commission. Credit card holders can obtain cash advances from Banco de San José (Visa, Mastercard) and Credomatic Los Yoses in colones (Mastercard ATM) and Banco Popular y Desarrollo (Visa ATM); minimum cash advance: US$50 equivalent. ATMs which will accept international Visa/Mastercard are available at most banks, shopping malls and San José airport. **Banco Crédito Agrícola de Cartago**, 9 branches, also makes advances on Visa, no limits; **Scotiabank** (formerly Banco Metropolitano), C Central, Av 2, Visa cash advances, charges 0.49% commission on currency exchange. Banks may charge whatever commission they please on TCs (no commission on US$ cash) and other services: shop around for the best deal. The best exchange rates for Amex TCs can be found at American Express (see **Travel agents** below). **Banco Mercantil**, Av 1, C Central-2, has safe deposit lockers for US$15/month. A legal 'parallel' market has existed since Feb 1992, the centre for which is the corner of Av 2, C 2, also all around the **Banco Central** (beware fake notes, in particular US$100 notes), up to 10% better rates, will even accept TCs. Take all the usual precautions. *Hermanos Villalobos Money Exchange*, rec, better rate for cash than TCs; **Ed Schyfter**, C 2, between Av 1 and Av Central, 2nd floor, behind **Banco Central**. Most hotels will change dollars (cash or TCs) into colones, but only for guests; hotels cannot sell dollars, however.

● **Cultural centres**
Centro Cultural Costarricense Norteamericano, C 37, Av 1-5, Los Yoses, T 225-9433,

good films, plays, art exhibitions and English-language library, open to 1930, free; **Alianza Franco Costarricense**, Av 7, C 5, French newspapers, French films every Wed evening, friendly.

● **Embassies & consulates**
Nicaraguan, Av Central, Calles 25-27, opp *Pizza Hut*, T 222-2373, 233-3479, 233-8747, Mon-Fri, 0830-1200, US$25, dollars only, passport photo, 24-hr wait for visa or sometimes less; **Panamanian**, located 275m N of Centro Colón building (Paseo Colón area), T 221-4784, tough about onward ticket, open 0900-1400, you need a photograph, visa costs US$10 cash and takes 24 hrs, if they tell you to come back after 1300 to collect your visa, be there at 1245; **Honduran**, Del Itan, 300 Este y 200 Norte, T 234-9502; **Salvadorean**, Paseo Colón y Av 1, C 30, Casa 53, T 222-3648, 256-0043, receives documents 0900-1300, returns them 1430-1500; **Guatemalan**, De la *Pizza Hut* en Plaza del Sol, Curridabat, 50m E, 100m N, 50m E, Casa No 3, T 224-5721, F 283-2556, open Mon-Fri, 0900-1300, visa given on the spot, US$10 in some cases (dollars only, see Guatemala **Information for travellers**); **Mexican**, Consulate, Av 7, C 13-15, T 222-5528, 221-4448, Mon-Fri 0830-1200 to receive documents, returns them 1500-1600; **Belizean**, Rohrmoser, 25m Oriente, 75m Sur de Plaza Mayor, T 232-6637, 231-7766.

Argentine, 400m S of *MacDonalds*, Curridabat, T 234-6520, 234-6270, 0800-1530, Mon-Fri; **Bolivian**, C 19 and 21, Av 2, T 233-6244; **Brazilian**, C 20-22, Av 2, T 233-1544, T 233-1092; **Colombian**, Barrio la California, C 29, Av 1, T 221-0725 (Mon-Fri 0900-1200), issues free tourist cards for Colombia, but onward ticket must be shown and sometimes two photos provided; **Ecuadorean**, Sabana Sur, Colegio Médicos 100m E, 125m SW, T 232-1503, 231-1899, open Mon-Fri 0800-1100, 1200-1400; **Peruvian**, Los Yoses, 200m Sur, 50m Oriente del Automercado, T 225-9145; **Uruguayan**, Los Yoses, Av 14, C 35-37, T 253-2755; **Chilean**, Los Yoses, 50m Este, 225m Oriente del Automercado, T 224-4243, **Venezuelan**, Los Yoses, de la 5ta entrada, 100m S, 50m W, consulate open Mon-Fri 0900-1230, T 225-5813, 225-8810, visa issued same day, US$30, helpful.

US, Consulate and Embassy (T 220-3939, 0800-1630 Mon-Fri, T 220-3127 after hours and weekends), in the western suburb of Pavas, opp Centro Comercial, open Mon-Fri, 0800-1630 (0800-1000 only for visa applications), catch a ruta 14 bus to Pavas Zona 1 from Av 1 and C 18; **Canadian**, Building 5 (3rd floor) of Oficentro Ejecutivo La Sabana, Sabana Sur, T 296-4149, F 296-4270; **Japanese**, Rohrmoser, de la Nunciatura 400m Oriente y 100m Norte, T 232-1255; **South Korean**, Rohrmoser, 200m Oriente y 100m Sur Entrada Blvd de Rohrmoser, T 220-3141; **Israeli** C 2, Av 2-4, Edif Parque Central, 5th floor, T 221-6444, 221-6011.

British, Centro Colón, 11th floor, end of Paseo Colón with C 38 (Apdo 815-1007), T 221-5566; **German**, Rohrmoser, 200m Norte y 75m Este de la casa de Oscar Arias, T 232-5533, open Mon-Fri, 0900-1200; **Swiss**, Paseo Colón, Centro Colón, 10th floor, Calles 34/36, T 221-4829, open Mon-Fri, 0900-1200; **French**, Curridabat, 200m S, 25m W of Indoor Club, T 225-0733; **Belgian**, C 35-37, Av 3, T 225-6633; **Dutch**, Oficentro Ejecutivo La Sabana, Sabana Sur, Mon-Fri 0900-1200, T 296-1490; **Italian**, Los Yoses, C 33-35, Av 10, T 234-2326; **Spanish**, Paseo Colón, C 32, T 222-1933; **Danish**, 11th floor, Centro Colón, T 257-2695/6; **Finnish**, Centro Colón Building, 7th floor, Paseo Colón, T 257-0210; **Norwegian**, Centro Colón, 10th floor, T 257-1414; **Austrian**, C 36-38, Av 4, Edif Nagel, T 255-3007; **Swedish**, La Uruca, de la Fábrica Pozuelo, 100m al Este, T 232-8549.

● **Entertainment**

Cinemas: many excellent modern cinemas showing latest releases. *Sala Garbo*, Av 2, C 28; *Cinemateca* at the UCR's Abelardo Bonilla auditorium (university), San Pedro, shows good films at 1700 and 1900 daily. Prices, US$2.50-US$3. See *La Nación* for films and times. See also under **National parks**, page 1040.

Nightclubs: *Grill La Orquídea* at the *Hotel Balmoral*; *Les Moustaches* in Centro Colón, Paseo Colón, C 38, expensive. Many restaurants and bars with varying styles of music at El Pueblo centre on road to San Francisco (take 'Calle Blancos' bus from C 1, Av 5-7, alight 500m after river); also 3 discos here, *Cocoloco*, *Infinito* (US$2.90, not crowded) and *La Plaza* (very luxurious, US$2.90, great discothèque). Discos in the centre: *Kamakiri*, on the way to Tibas; *Top One* (US rock music); *La Rueda* (for the over 30's); *Bikini Club*, C 7, Av 0-1, topless dancing, cheap. Other nice, less expensive dance spots downtown: *El Túnel del Tiempo*, *Talamanca* and *Disco Salsa 54* (do not wear shorts, they will not let you in); *La Torre*, C 7 between Av Central and Av 1, popular gay disco. Also *Montecarlo*, corner of C 2 and Av 4

(Parque Central); *El Cuartel de la Boca del Monte*, see under **Bars**. Night spots W of C 8 are in the red light district. Some hotels have **casinos** with Black Jack and a sort of roulette shooting an arrow on a revolving wheel. No entrance fee, no formal dress required. Some night spots do not appreciate long haired men. You can buy chips with colones or dollars from the croupier and once you start to play, the drinks and cigarettes are free. The casino at the *Gran Hotel Costa Rica* has been rec.

Theatres: all are closed on Mon. *Teatro Nacional*, Av 2, C 3/5 (reopened 1993 after restoration; rec for the productions, the architecture and the bar/café), US$1.15 for guided tour, behind it is La Plaza de la Cultura, a large complex; *Teatro Carpa*, outdoor, alternative; plays, films, C 9, opp Parque Morazán; *Teatro Tiempo* (also called Sala Arlequín), C 13 between Av 2 and Central; *Compañía Nacional de Teatro*; *Teatro Melico Salazar* on Parque Central for popular, folkloric shows every Tues, T 221-4952; *Teatro del Angel*, Av Central, between C 13 and 15. Three modern dance companies. All good.

● **Hospitals & medical services**

Dentists: *Clínica Dental Dr Francisco Cordero Guilarte*, T 232-3645, Sabana Oriente, opp Colegio La Salle, take bus marked Sabana Estadio; *Dra Fresia Hidalgo*, Uned Building, San Pedro, 1400-1800, English spoken, reasonable prices, rec, T 234-2840; *Dr Otto J Ramírez González*, C 14, Av Central, Noreste Hospital San Juan de Dios, Edif Maro, T 233-4576, speaks only Spanish; *Fernando Baldioceda* and *Silvia Oreamuno*, 225m N of Paseo Colón on the street which intersects at the Toyota dealership: both speak English; *Alfonso Villalobos Aguilar*, Edif Herdocía, 2nd floor, Av 3, C 2-4, T 222-5709.

Doctor: Dr Jorge Quesada Vargas, *Clínica Internacional*, Av 14, C 3-5, speaks German.

Hospitals: Social Security Hospitals have good reputations (free to social security members, few members of staff speak English), free ambulance service run by volunteers: Dr Calderón Guardia (T 222-4133), San Juan de Dios (T 222-0166), México (T 232-6122). The *Clínica Bíblica* C 1, Av 14, 24-hr pharmacy (T 223-6422) and *Americana* (C Central-1, Av 14 (T 222-1010) have been rec; both offer 24-hr emergency service at reasonable charges and have staff who speak English; better than the large hospitals, where queues are long.

Inoculations: Bíblica will arrange TB vaccinations, prepares Spanish summaries of treatment, medication, etc, accepts credit cards, and has addresses for emergencies it cannot handle. Yellow fever inoculation, *Ministerio de Salud* (Av 4, C 16), Dpto de Enfermedades Epidémicos, Dr Rodrígo Jiménez Monge, or at his private clinic, C 5, Av 4, T 221-6658. Free malaria pills also from Ministerio de Salud, from information desk in office to left of ministry. Although the Ministerio de Salud does not have a stock of gamma globulin (Hepatitis A), they will inject it free if you buy it in a pharmacy.

Dermatologist: *Dr Elias Bonilla Dib*, C Central, Av 7-9, T 221-2025. Red Cross Ambulance, T 221-5818.

● **Language schools**
The number of schools has increased rapidly. Listed below are just a selection rec by our readers. Generally, schools offer tuition in groups of 2-5 over 2-4 weeks. Lectures, films, outings and social occasions are usually inc and accommodation with families is encouraged. Many schools are linked to the university and can offer credits towards a US course. Rates, inc lodging, are around US$1,000 a month.

Instituto Universal de Idiomas, Av 2, C 9, T 257-0441, F 223-9917, stresses conversational Spanish; *Costa Rican Language Academy*, Av Central, C 25-27, Apdo 336-2070 Sabanilla, Montes de Oca, T 233-8938, 233-8914, F 233-8670, run by Aída Chávez, offers Latin American music and dancing as well as language study and accommodation with local families; *Academia Latinoamericana de Español*, Aptdo 1280, 2050 San Pedro, Montes de Oca, T 224-9917, F 225-8125, rec; the *British Institute (Instituto Británico)* in Los Yoses, teaches English and Spanish, T 225-0256, F 253-1894, Apdo 8184, 1000 San José; *Intensa*, C 33, Av 5-7, Barrio Escalante, PO Box 8110-1000, T 224-6353, 225-6009, F 253-4337; *Instituto de Lenguaje Pura Vida*, T 237-0387, F 260-6269, Apartado 890-3000, Heredia, in USA T (714) 534-0125, F 534-1201, airport pick up, 5 days', 7 days' accommodation with local family, 2 meals a day, cultural activities, US$330 but can be less if they need to fill spaces; *Central American Institute for International Affairs*, Apdo 10302, San José, T 233-8571, F 221-5238, conversation Spanish courses; *Comunicare*, Apdo 1383-2050, San José, T/F 224-4473, offers language study (staying with families), volunteer work, and cultural activities; *Intercultura Costa Rica*, Apdo 1952-3000, Heredia, T 260-8480, F 260-9243, e-mail intercul@sol.racsa.co.cr, intensive courses with excursions to beaches, volcanoes etc, homestays available; *AmeriSpan*, PO Box 40513, Philadelphia, PA 19106-0513, T 800-879-6640 (USA and Canada), 215-985-4522 (elsewhere), F 215-985-4524, Internet info@amerispan.com, has affiliated schools in San José, Escazú, Alajuela and Heredia.

● **Laundry**
Washing and dry cleaning at Centro Comercial San José 2000, 0730-2000, US$3.75 for large load. *Sixaola*, branches throughout San José, US$3.50 a load, 2 hrs dry cleaning available, expensive; *Martinizing*, US franchise, at Curridabat, Sabana Oriente (by new ring road) and Escazú, rec; *Lavandería Costa Rica*, Av 3, C 19-21, US$3.50 for a large load; below *Hotel Gran Imperial*, US$3 to wash, US$3 to dry, quick but not rec; *Lavandería*, C 8, Av Central y 1, T 258-2303.

● **Libraries**
Biblioteca Nacional (opp Parque Nacional, has art and photography exhibitions), open Mon-Fri 0830-1630; *Universidad de Costa Rica*, in San Pedro suburb.

● **Places of worship**
Protestant, in English: The Good Shepherd, Sun 0830, Av 4, C 3-5, T 222-1560 (Anglican); Union Church, Moravia, T 235-6709, services 1000; free bus service from downtown hotels; times and locations given in Fri *Tico Times*; International Baptist Church, in San Pedro, 150m N from ex-Banco Anglo Costarricense corner, on San Pedro or Periférico bus route, T 253-7911 for information or to contact Pastor Dr Tom Hill, prayer line T 244-0569, English services at 0900 on Sun, Spanish services 1800, Sun school at 1100, nursery provided, Chinese services at 1100 on Sun. Bible study on Wed evenings, T 234-2943 for information; Escazú Christian Fellowship (Country Day School campus), Sun 1730, T 231-5444; Victory Christian Centre (from Hermanos Monge Gas Station, 200m S, 100m E, 200m S, Santa Ana, free shuttle bus, T 240-8571, Sun 1000). **Roman Catholic** services in English at *Herradura* Hotel, 1600 every Sun. **Centro de los Amigos para la Paz**, Quaker, English books, US periodicals, information, T 221-0302.

● **Post & telecommunications**
Post Office: Av 1 and 3, C 2, open for sale of stamps Mon-Fri, 0700-1700, Sat-Sun 0700-1800 (outside these hours stamps may be bought from the lottery seller who sits under the big tree opp the Post Office entrance). Stamp vending machine in main post office. Post office charges 50 colones for receiving letters (*Lista de Correos*, open 0800-1700, quick service).

Couriers: DHL, Paseo Colón, C 30 y 32, T 223-1423; Jet Ex (Federal Express agent), on Pavas Rd, T 231-6610, F 231-1488; UPS, Av 3, C 30 y 32, T 257-7447, F 257-5343.

Telephone and cable services: faxes and internal telegrams from main post office. Fax or cable abroad from Compañía Radiográfica Internacional de Costa Rica, Av 5, C 1, 0730-1000, charges per page, also receives for US$1, unlimited pages, internet access, charge by the hour (see **Information for travellers**). ICE, Instituto Costarricense de Electricidad, Av 2, C 1, has a fax service, also phone calls here, open 0700-2200, 3 mins call to UK US$10, friendly service (cheaper than Radiográfica). KitCom, 3rd level Edif Ferencz, C 3 y Av 3, T 258-0303, F 258-0606, send and receive e-mail, fax, voice mail, e-mail: kitcom@sol.racsa.co.cr. Some shops offer fax service. Collect telephone calls can be made from any public telephone. English speaking operators are available. See also under **Information for travellers**.

● **Shopping**
Market on Av Central, Calles 6/8, open 0630-1800 (Sun 0630-1200), good leather suitcases and wood. Mercado Borbón, Avs 3/5, Calles 8/10, fruit and vegetables in abundance. More and more *artesanía* shops are opening, eg *Mercanapi* (a cooperative, cheaper than most, C 11, Av 1) and *Mercado Nacional de Artesanía* (C 11, Av 4), and others on Av Central, C 1 and 3. *La Casona*, a market of small *artesanía* shops, Av Central-1, C Central, is interesting, lots of little stalls. For jade, try *Brazil Gems*, Parque Morazán. In Moravia (8 km from centre) *El Caballo Blanco*, T 235-6797, workshops alongside, and *HHH* are good for leather work. The leather rocking chairs (which dismantle for export) found in some *artesanía* shops are sometimes cheaper in Sarchí. *Amir Galería de Arte*, Av Central, C 1 y 3, Edif Galería Nacional for local paintings (will send paintings abroad promptly). Coffee is good value and has an excellent flavour (although the best quality is exported). *Automercados* are good supermarkets in several locations (eg C 3, Av 3). Generally, shopping is cheaper in the centre than in the suburbs. At the international airport on the 2nd

floor, above Continental airlines ticket counter, you can buy cut orchids which are approved by the USDA and Canadian Department of Agriculture, T 487-7086.

El Pueblo, nr the *Villa Tournon Hotel*, is an area of shops, bars, restaurants and discos, built in a traditional *'pueblo'* style. Another big new shopping centre opened in 1995 at San Pedro, on the Eastern ring road.

Bookshops: *The Bookshop*, Av 11 y C 3-5, in Casa Amón, 1/2 block W of *Hotel Amstel Amon* in Barrio Amon (T 222-7619), good selection of English language books (double US prices), buys secondhand books, but no exchange, very good range, some English, art gallery, café, open 0900-1800; *Universal*, Av Central, Calles Central and 1, T 222-4038, for Spanish books and maps; *Lehmann*, Av Central and C 3, F 233-6270, maps (large-scale topo maps not always in stock), Spanish, a few English books and magazines; *Chispas Books*, C 7, between Av Central and Av Primera, T 223-2240, F 223-4128, wide variety of new and used books in English, book exchange, open Mon-Sat 0900-1800, Sun 1000-1800; *Librería Italiana/Francesa*, C 3, Av Central/1, English, French, Italian books, German magazines; *Staufer*, nr Centro Cultural, Los Yoses, also in Centro Comercial San José 2000 and Plaza del Sol shopping mall in Curridabat, English and German books; *Book Traders*, Av 1, C 5-7, T 255-0508, open Mon-Sat, 0900-1900, buy (at 1/4 face value) and sell (at 1/2 marked price), English, French, German and Spanish used books; *Mora Books*, AV 1, C 3-5, in Omni building above *Pizza Hut*; *Librería Vlate* book exchange, Av 6, C 3-5, has large choice of Spanish books and a few in English; *Gamhit*, Av 3, C 5-7, Los Yoses, T 283-0603, used books, English, French, German; *Librería Internacional*, Barrio Dent, 400m W of Taco Bell in San Pedro, T 283-6965, English, German and Spanish titles at about 20% over US prices, special order service; *Jiménez*, C Central, Av 3-5, excellent for maps of San José and the country; *Periódicos Americanos*, in the Yaohan Shopping Centre, Sabana Norte, T 221-4664, best selection of magazines and some books; *Kiosko La Catedral*, opp Parque Central, sells American magazines, newspapers from several countries, inc *Financial Times*, books, postcards and gifts.

Photography: 1-hr colour processing available at all *IFSA* (Kodak) branches, poor reports received. Fuji processing in 1 hr at *Universal* stores. *Taller de Equipos Fotográficos*, 120m E of kiosk

Parque Morazán, Av 3, C 3-5, 2nd floor, T 223-1146 (Canon repairs – authorized workshop); *Tecfot*, Av 7, C Central, T 221-1438, repairs all types of cameras, good service, reasonable rates. Film prices are well above those of Europe. *Video Camera Rentals*, Av 7, behind *Aurola Holiday Inn*, T 257-0232, US$29/day, US$168/week for Panasonic 'Palmcorders'. **Warning** The X-ray machine at Juan Santamaría airport is not filmsafe, regardless of what the airport security guards try to make you believe.

● **Sports**

Bungee jumping: after Rafael Iglesias Bridge (Río Colorado), continue on Pan-American Highway 11 1/2 km, turn right at *Salon Los Alfaro*, down track to Puente Colorado. *Tropical Bungee* operate 0800-1400 Sat and Sun, available weekdays for groups of 5 or more, US$45 first jump, T 233-6455; full moon and water dips on request; *Geoventuras Bike Tours* run tours from San José, Tues, Thur, and Sat, 0800, return about 1700, US$85 inc lunch, T 221-2053.

Golf: several new golf courses have opened. The following hotels or clubs have golf courses: *Costa Rica Country Club* (San Rafael de Escazú), 9 holes; *Hotel Meliá Cariari Country Club* (near San José), 18 holes; *Los Reyes Country Club* (near Alajuela), 9 holes; *Hotel Tango Mar Beach Resort* (Playa Tambor), 9 holes; *Hotel Meliá Playa Conchal* (Playa Conchal), 18 holes.

Swimming pools: the best is at Ojo de Agua, 5 mins from the airport, 15 mins from San José. It is open until 1700; direct bus from Parque Carrillo, Av 2, C 20-22, US$0.25 or take bus to Alajuela via San Antonio de Belén. There is also a pool in La Sabana (at W end of Paseo Colón), entrance US$3, open 1200-1400, about 2 km from the city centre. Open air pool at Plaza González Víquez (SE section of city).

● **Tour companies & travel agents**
Swiss Travel Service, in *Hotel Corobicí*, T 231-4055, PO Box 7-1970, F 231-3030, with branches in *Hotels Sheraton, Irazú, Cariari, Amstel Amon* and *Balmoral*, large agency, good guides, much cruise business, warmly rec; *Viajes Alrededor del Mundo*, T 223-6011, at the *Holiday Inn*, Eduardo Ureña is rec for finding cheap flights to South America; *Tam Travel Corporation*, four branches, one in *San José Palacio Hotel*, open 7 days a week, PO Box 1864, 24-hr answering service T 222-2642/2732, F 221-6465; *LA Tours*, PO Box 492-1007, Centro Colón, T 221-4501, F 224-5828, Kathia

Vargas extremely helpful in rearranging flights and reservations; *Aviatica*, C 1, Av 1, T 222-7461, helpful for airline tickets; **American Express**, clients' mail, Banco de San José, Apdo 5445, 1000 San José; financial transactions, Banco de San José/Credomatic, C Central, Ave 3-5, T 223-3644/257-1792; *COOPRENA* (National Eco-Agricultural Cooperative Network of Costa Rica), is a group supporting small farmers, it offers tours of mangroves, rainforests, farms, beaches, etc, US$35 per day (accommodation and food inc), contact Leilo Solano, Apdo 6939-1000, San José, T 259-3401/8442, F 259-9430, for more details.

Aventuras Naturales, Av Central, C 33-35, T 225-3939, offers white water rafting; *Trópico Saragundi Speciality Tours*, T 255-0011, for bungee jumping (see also above, **Sports**). Those specializing in naturalist tours inc: *Costa Rica Expeditions*, Av 3, C Central/2, upmarket wildlife adventures inc white water rafting (US$89 for 1-day trip on Río Pacuare, inc lunch and transport, good, other rivers from US$69-85) etc, they own *Tortuga Lodge, Corcovado Lodge Tent Camp, Monteverde Lodge* and *Costa Rica White Water*; PO Box 6941-1000, T 257-0766/222-0333, F 257-1665, e-mail: crexped@sol.racsa.co.cr;worldwide web: WWW.crexped.co.cr; staffed 365 days a year, 0530-2100, also answering service, highly rec, good range of postcards in their souvenir shop next door; *Ríos Tropicales*, Paseo Colón, next to Mercedes Benz, PO Box 472, 1200 San José, T 233-6455, F 255-4354, specialists in white-water rafting and kayaking, good selection and careful to assess your abilities, good food, excellent guides, US$250 for 2-day trip on Río Pacuare, waterfalls, rapids, inc camping and food; *Costa Rica Sun Tours* 'Eco-Center' offers reservations and Sansa ticketing for adventure or nature lovers, regular departures for Arenal, Monteverde, Corcovado, Tortuguero and Manuel Antonio, Av 4, C 36, T 255-3418, 255-3518, F 255-4410; tours can often be arranged at very short notice, warmly rec; *Typical Tours*, 2nd and 3rd floor of Las Arcadas, next to the *Gran Hotel Costa Rica*, PO Box 623-1007, T 233-8486 24 hrs, F 233-8474, city tours, volcano tours, nature reserves, rafting, cruising; *Braun Eco Tourism*, Av 8-10, C Central (in *Hotel Ritz*), T 233-1731, F 222-8849, basic but beautiful tours to out of the way places, rec, but tour guides need to improve their biology; *Exotur*, T 227-5169, F 227-2180, Nella Fiorentini, very helpful, rec; *Green Tropical Tours*, C 1, Av 5-7, T/F 255-2859, tours to Guayabo National Monument, Los Juncos, Cloud Forest etc; *Arena Tours*, Av 7, C 13-15, tours to Tortuguero, US$74, inc boat transport, food, accommodation, 1 night; *Jungle Lodge*, T 233-0133, F 233-0778, to Tortuguero channels, 3 days, 2 nights, inc transport from San José via Siquirres to Puerto Hamburgo, very good wildlife.

Day tours to the Gulf of Nicoya with transport from San José inc: luxury yacht cruise on the *Fantasía* (T 255-0791) to Tortuga island, Wed, Sat, Sun, from San José US$65 inc lunch; Calypso Island Cruise Wed, Fri, Sun, US$69 inc lunch, T 233-3617; Bay Island Cruises to Tortuga Island (T 296-5551, F 296-5095); Blue Sea Cruises, T 233-7274, to Tortuga Island; *Cruceros del Sur*, T 220-1679, F 220-2103, PO Box 1198-1200, Pavas, San José, offers cruises to Curú Wildlife Refuge and Tortuga Island, US$79. Costa Sol Cruises, Wed, Fri, Sat, Sun, US$70 inc breakfast and lunch, visits beach nr Tambor; *Seaventures Yacht*, 2-night packages, floating hotel visits Cabo Blanco Nature Reserve in Gulf of Nicoya (T 220-0722). *Aerolineas Turisticos de America*, T 232-1125, F 232-5802, run charter flights around central Costa Rica from Tobias Bolaños airport, US$65 pp/hr, min 4 persons. **NB** It is much cheaper to take tours aimed at the local rather than the foreign tourist market.

● **Tourist offices**

Instituto Costarricense de Turismo, information office: 11th floor, ICT building, Av 4 C 5-7, T 223-1733/8423, toll free 800-012-3456, open Mon-Fri 0800-1600. Also at Juan Santamaría airport (very helpful, will check hotels for you) and at borders. Road maps of Costa Rica, San José and the metropolitan area and public transport timetables available. **Infotur** computerized hotel reservation and information system at Av 10, C 3, T 223-4481, check whether there is a commission (reports of 20%) before making a booking.

Otec, youth and student travel office and cheap lodgings, extremely helpful, C 3, Av 1-3, Edif Victoria, 2nd floor, T 222-0866, for ISTC and FIYTO members, has discount booklet for shops, hotels, restaurants, good for travel arrangements eg to Colombia by ferry or by air to South America; *Otec Tours*, Edif Ferenez, C 3 Av 1-3, T 233-8694/8678, F 233-8676, their buses tend to be rather crowded. The **Instituto Geográfico**, Av 20, C 9-11 at Ministry of Public Works and Transport, supplies very good topographical maps for walkers, 0730-1200 (which can be bought, at higher prices, at Librerías Universal and Lehmann). *American Express* office has good, free maps of San José. New up-to-date maps are available at most bookstores. Recommended city map published by Jitan, US$3.

● **Useful addresses**

Immigration: on the airport highway, opp Hospital México; you need to go here for exit visas, extensions, etc. If they are busy, you could queue all day. To get there, take bus 10 or 10A Uruca, marked 'Mexico', then cross over highway at the bridge and walk 200m along highway. Better to find a travel agent who can obtain what you need for a fee, say US$5. Make sure you get a receipt if you give up your passport.

Judiciary: thefts should be reported in San José to Recepción de Denuncias, Organismo de Investigación Judicial, C 19, Av 6-8, T 255-0122.

● **Useful phone numbers**

Emergency: **Police**: T 117; **Fire**: T 118; **Police, Fire, Red Cross** (bilingual operators): T 911.

● **Transport**

Local Buses: bus fares in **San José**: large buses: US$0.10, small: US$0.15 from the centre outwards. Hand baggage in reasonable quantities is not charged, but no trunks of any kind are taken. A cheap tour of San José can be made on the bus marked 'periférico' from Paseo Colón in front of the Cine Colón, a 45-min circle of the city. A smaller circle is made by the 'Sabana/Cementerio' bus, pick it up at the Parque Morazán or on Av 3; a 'Cementerio/Sabana' bus does the route in reverse.

Car rentals: if you can, reserve your vehicle in advance, especially if there is a particular type you want. Costa Rica's web site has been rec for advance reservations. Check your vehicle carefully as the rental company will try to claim for the smallest of 'damages'. International driver's licence and credit card generally required (see also page 1142). (Discounts available during 'green season', May-November.) Insurance costs US$10-17/day extra; deductible is between US$750 and US$1,500, depending on company, some will charge extra to waive deductible, eg Budget, US$2.50 a day; basic prices: smallest car US$38/day inc unlimited mileage or US$228/week; jeep costs US$54/day, US$324/week, inc unlimited mileage. Cash deposits or credit card charges range from US$600 to US$1,000, so check you have sufficient credit. Most local agencies are to the N of Paseo Colón. **Budget**, C 30, Paseo Colón, T 223-3284, open

Mon-Sat, 0800-1900, Sun, 0800-1800, also at international airport, T 441-4444, open Mon-Sun, 0600-2100, and at *Hotel Cariari*; **Avis**, Sabana Norte (T 232-9922); **Dollar**, C Central, Av 9 (T 233-3339); **Hertz**, C 38, Paseo Colón, T 221-1818/223-5959, F 221-1949; **Meir**, good rates for 4WD, C11, Av 14, T 257-4666; **Adobe**, T 221-5425, F 221-9286, e-mail: adobe@centralamerica.com, in North America T 1-800-826-1134, in Spain Oky de Costa Rica, 101761.2005@compuserve.com, Japanese cars and 4WD, drop-off at the beach if you fly Travelair, flexible insurance, drivers aged 18-21 accepted with US$1,500 on credit card; **National**, C 36, Av 7 (T 233-4014), easy to get on to autopista for Alajuela; and many local ones (**Elegante**, C 10 Av 13-15, T 221-0066, F 221-5761, PO Box 30-1005, San José, cars, jeeps, vans, min age 23, has branches throughout the country, rec). Various companies at airport, inc **Ada**, T 256-8383, F 233-0401, cars and jeeps, similar prices to Adobe; **Santos**, T 441-3044; **Hertz**, T 441-0097. You can often obtain lower rentals by making reservations before arrival with the major companies. If you plan to drop off a hired car, check with several firms for their charges: Elegante, Ada and National appear to have the lowest drop-off fees. Insurance will not cover broken windscreens (unless you are involved in an accident), driving on unsurfaced roads or damaged tyres. If you have an accident always call the traffic police and rental car company. Licence plates will automatically be removed. Do not move your car until the police arrive. Never bribe traffic police, ask them to issue a ticket. Some traffic police will tell you to return to San José, or another place, trying to get you to bribe them to avoid interrupting your trip. Always report any demands for money to the tourism authorities. Never leave anything in a hired car, always use car parks in San José, never leave your car on the street, even in daylight. Car parking costs US$1.25/hr, worth it when so many cars are broken into. Regular reports of robbery in the National Parks.

Car repairs: at *Repuestos Tiribí SA*, Desamparados, 50m S of Puente Tiribí, Swiss-owned, helpful, T 259-1098.

Motorcycle rental: from Heat Renta Moto, Edif Ofomeco, 7th floor, 2 Av, 11 y 13 C, T 221-6671, F 221-3786, with offices in other tourist centres, for motorcycles, scooters, mountain motorbikes, US$30-35/day, US$5-7/hr, deposit US$500; **Rent-a-Moto La Aventura**, C 8, Av 10, T 222-0055, F 223-2759, US$35/day

Honday XL250R, inc insurance, helmet and free mileage; **Moto Rental SA**, Thilo Pfleiderer, T 232-7850, Suzuki Enduro for US$200 pw unlimited mileage, deposit US$500 or credit card. An Enduro is best for seeing all the country. Keep clear of taxis and buses who will pay no attention to you. Wearing a helmet is obligatory, renters provide simple ones without front glass. You will need strong dark glasses. The paved roads offer frequent surprises, deep holes, rivers and landslides over the road, planks of bridges in a rotten state. You need good rainwear even in the dry season. However, you have increased mobility and speed on dirt roads and riding is very enjoyable outside the San José area due to low traffic (see also **Motoring**, page 1142).

Motorcycle repairs: *Taller Daytona 500*, in Pavas, 200m E of US Embassy, T/F 220-1726, run by Roberto Dachner, who speaks Spanish, English and Hebrew.

Taxis: minimum fare US$0.63 for first km, US$0.32 additional km, 20% extra 2200-0500. Waiting time US$3.15/hr. To order a taxi, T 254-5847, 235-9966. Taxis are red and should have electronic meters (called 'Marías'). Short journeys in the city are around US$2-3, bargain if you feel the price is too high. For journeys over 12 km price should be negotiated between driver and passenger. Look in the classified adverts of the *Tico Times* for car and driver hire.

Air The Juan Santamaría international airport (SJO) is at El Coco, 16 km from San José by motorway (5 km from Alajuela). Airport information, 24 hrs, T 443-2622. The Sansa terminal for domestic flights is next to the main terminal. There is another terminal about 1 km W of the main terminal used by charter flights and private planes. Bus from Av 2, C 10-12, or Av 2, C 12-14, every 10 mins from 0500-2100, US$0.50 (good service, plenty of luggage space), or by Alajuela bus via the motorway from C 14, Av 5-7. Taxi to and from airport, US$10 (can be less if ordered in advance); Sansa runs a free bus service to the airport for its passengers. Taxis run all night from the main square to the airport and for early flights, you can reserve a taxi from any San José hotel the night before. All taxi companies run a 24-hr service. During the holiday period (Dec-Jan), Juan Santamaría airport allows only ticketed passengers into the main terminal at peak times of 0600-0830, 1100-1400. Bank at the airport open 0800-1600; at other times try car rental desks, the restaurant cash desk or money changers at the entrance. ITMs at the airport accept international Visa and Mastercard. ICT has a helpful tourist office in the main terminal for maps, hotel reservations and information. There is also a booth next to the *cambio* nr the exit. X-ray machines reported unsafe for film (see **Photography** above). There is a hotel at the airport, **A2** *Hampton Inn*, T 443-0043, F 442-9523 (toll free within Costa Rica 800-HAMPTON), courtesy pick-up to both terminals (see **Alajuela accommodation**). Services at the airport are generally inadequate.

Travelair and light aircraft use the Tobias Bolaños airport (SYQ) at Pavas, about 8 km W of San José.

Internal flights: Sansa (next to the main terminal at Juan Santamaría airport) and **Travelair** (from Tobias Bolaños) operate internal flights throughout the country. Sansa check-in is at office on Paseo Colón at C 24 2 hrs before departure (free bus to and from airport). Check schedules on 221-9414 or 233-3258, F 255-2176. Sansa airport office T 441-8035/1401. For Travelair reservations, T 296-1102, 296-3408, F 220-0413. If you made reservations before arriving in Costa Rica, confirm and collect tickets as soon as possible after arrival. Book ahead, especially for the beaches. In Feb and Mar, planes can be fully booked 3 weeks ahead. On all internal scheduled and charter flights there is a baggage allowance of 12 kg/25 lb. Oversized items such as surfboards, bicycles etc are charged US$15 if there is room in the cargo hold.

Sansa and/or Travelair flights operate daily to most of the same destinations. Travelair fares are shown, Sansa flights cost up to 40% less. **Barra del Colorado** (US$74 one way), Travelair 0600, Sansa Tues, Thur and Sat; **Carrillo**, US$75 Travelair 0740; **Golfito** (US$76), Sansa 3 daily; **Quepos** (US$45) Travelair 3, Sansa 3 daily flights; **Coto 47**, daily (not Travelair); **Palmar Sur** (US$73), both daily; **Tamarindo** (US$82) Travelair 2 Sansa 1 daily; **Sámara**, Sansa daily; **Nosara** (US$82) Travelair 1045, Sansa daily; **Tambor** (US$62), both daily; **Tortuguero** (US$72), Sansa Tues, Thur, Sat, 0600 (Travelair); **Liberia** (US$82), 3 daily (Sansa), 1230 (Travelair); **Puerto Jiménez** (US$81), Sansa daily, Travelair 0815; **Punta Islita** (US$75), both daily; **Jacó** (US$34) Travelair 1115. Sansa added some new destinations at end-1996: **Limón** (Mon, Wed, Fri, Sun), **San Vito** (Mon, Wed, Fri), **Parismina** (Mon, Wed, Fri, Sun), **Los Chiles** (Tues, Thur, Sat), **Upala** (Tues, Thur, Sat). Return fares cost less than double single fare (except to Jacó). **Sansa Vacaciones**, T 221-9414, offer 1-3 night packages inc flight and accommodation at Manuel Antonio, Sámara, Nosara and Tamarindo.

Charter flights: Veasa, T 232-1010, F 232-7934, long-established, at Pavas; Alfa Romeo Aéreo Taxi, at Pavas, T 296-4344, and Puerto Jiménez, T 735-5178, Capitán Alvaro Ramírez. Helisa (Helicópteros Internacionales) operate helicopter sightseeing flights to Monteverde etc, T 222-9212, F 222-3875.

Trains During 1990-91 passenger services W to Puntarenas and E to Limón were terminated. In 1995 all remaining railway services were closed. The main station of the Ferrocarril Eléctrico al Pacífico to the Pacific ports of Puntarenas and Caldera is in the S of the city C 2, Av 20, T 226-0011 (take bus marked Paso Ancho). The journey on the Northern Railway to **Limón** used to be one of the most beautiful railway journeys anywhere but in 1990 service was suspended after a 250m section of track in the Chiz area was covered by a landslide. From the continental divide nr Cartago the line followed the narrow, wooded Reventazón valley down past Turrialba and Siquirres. The 40 km of line in the lowlands nr Limón cost 4,000 lives during building in the 1870s, mostly from yellow fever. The last 16 km into Limón ran along the seashore, amid groves of coconut palms.

Long-distance buses There are services to most towns, see text for details of times, prices etc. Check before leaving where the bus stops at your destination, some routes do not go to the centre of towns leaving passengers some distance away. Up to date timetables can be obtained from the Instituto Costarricense de Turismo (Infotur), Av 10 C 3 No 868, T 223-4481. **Cartago**, every 10 mins, 0500-1900, then every 30 mins until 2400, and every hour 2400-0500, buses depart Av 18, C 5; **Puntarenas** every 20 mins, 0600-1900, 2 hrs, good new terminal at C 16, Av 10-12; **Heredia**, every 10 mins, C 1, Av 7-9 and Av 2, C 10-12, minibuses from Av 6, C 14; **Alajuela** (inc airport and immigration office), 30 mins Av 2, C 12-14 and C 10, Av 0-1, every 10 mins, 0530-1900, every 40 mins 1900-2400; every hour 2400-0530 from C 2, Av 2; to **Sarchí**, change at Alajuela, they depart every ½ hr, express bus to Sarchí from C 16, Av 1-3; **Poás Volcano**, from C 12, Av 2/4, Sun and holidays 0830, return 1430, T 222-5325, or change at Alajuela's central park where bus leaves, Sun only; **Quepos**, from nr Coca Cola bus station, C 16, Av 1-3, 3½ hrs. Direct bus to **Manuel Antonio**, 4 hrs, from Coca Cola station, T 223-5567. Many buses for nearby towns and others to the W of San José leave from the main Coca Cola bus station or

the streets nearby (eg: *Santa Ana, Escazú, Acosta, Puriscal, Santa María Dota, San Marcos, San Ramón*). **Escazú** minibuses from Av 16, Av 0-1; buses from front of Coca Cola terminal. **San Isidro de El General**, 2 companies, Musoc and Tuasur, both on C 16, Av 1-3, frequent service, last bus 1630. **Liberia, Nicoya, Sta Cruz, Cañas** buses, Empresa Alfaro, Coca Cola bus station office at C 14-16, Av 5, also C 16, Av 1-3 to Cañas; Pulmitan de Liberia on C 14, Av 1-3, E of Coca Cola terminal, 8 a day to **Liberia** between 0700 and 2000, same company to **Coco Beach**. To the beaches on Nicoya peninsula express buses daily: **Tamarindo** from C 14, Av 3/5, Alfaro Co, T 222-2750 or from C 20, Av 3, Tralapa Co, T 221-7202; **Coco** from C 14, Av 1/3, T 222-1650; **Junquillal** from C 20, Av 3, T 221-7202; **Hermosa** from C 12, Av 5-7, Empresa Esquivel, T 666-1249; **Samara** via Nicoya from C 14, Av 3-5, T 685-5352, 222-2750. **Grecia**, bus C 6, Av 5-7. All buses to **San Carlos, Puerto Viejo de Sarapiquí, Río Frío** and **Guápiles** all now operate from Guápiles bus terminal at C 12, Av 7-9, every 30 mins 0530-1900. **Monteverde** express bus from C 14, Av 9-11 or take Puntarenas bus and change. **Tilarán**, C 14, Av 9-11. To **Fortuna** for Arenal Volcano from Coca Cola terminal, T 255-4318. **Turrialba**, hourly, 0500-2200, 1½ hrs, from C 13, Av 6. **Siquirres**, Av Ctl, C 11-13. **Limón**, hourly service, 0500-1900, 2½ hrs, good views, leaving on time, you may buy ticket the day before, C 19-21, Av 3 Transportes Unidos/Coop Limón, T 223-7811. **Paso Canoas** (Panamanian border), 5 daily, **Golfito**, 3 daily, 8 hrs, **Ciudad Neily** (Zona Sur) buses, Tracopa, C 2-4, Av 18 (T 223-7685, 221-4214). Direct to **Sixaola**, C 1-3, Av 11, tickets sold round the corner on C 1, 5 hrs. To **Cahuita**, 4 hrs, and Puerto Viejo, 4½ hrs from C Central, Av 11, Transp Mepa, T 257-8129, 4 daily. **Jacó Beach** from Coca Cola terminal, 2 express buses, 2½ hrs, and 3 indirect buses, Transp Morales, T 223-1109. **La Cruz, Peñas Blancas**, from C 14, Av 3, at *Hotel Cocorí*, on corner opp Coca Cola market, CNT (office open 0700-1600 daily), buses run from 0400, take this bus if going to Nicaragua and if international buses are fully booked, cheaper but takes longer; from same location buses to **Upala**. **San Vito de Coto Brus**, Tracopa or Alfaro from C 14-16, Av 5. *Minibuses* run on most routes to nearby towns offering better service, never crowded like the regular buses. Fares about US$0.20-0.25, always count your change. Beware of theft, which is common around buses.

International buses It is important to check how far in advance you must book tickets for international buses; in Dec-Jan, buses are often booked 2 weeks ahead, while at other times of the year outside holiday seasons, there is no need to book at all.

Sirca (C 7 between Avs 6 and 8, 2nd building from corner, on 2nd floor, open Sun-Fri, 0800-1700, Sat 0800-1200, T 222-5541, 223-1464) runs a scheduled service along the Pan-American Highway from San José to **Peñas Blancas**, on the Nicaraguan frontier, and on to **Managua** US$7.50 one-way, dep 0600 daily; (schedules appear to change frequently), about 13 hrs, reports of unreliability with this company but have more leg-room than Ticabus and can be faster (book on Fri for following week).

Ticabus terminal is at C 9-11, Av 4 (T 221-8954), office open Mon-Sun 0600-2200, book before Sat for Mon buses. It is here that all refund claims have to be made (have to be collected in person). Ticabus to **Guatemala City**, US$35, with unlimited break in **Managua**, **Teguciala** and **San Salvador**, ticket divided into 4 coupons for these 4 destinations. To Managua, US$8, 10 hrs inc 1 hr at Costa Rican side of border and another 2 hrs on Nicaraguan side while they search your bags for drugs. The Ticabus journey from San José to **Panama City** leaves at 2200 daily, US$20 one-way, 18 hrs (book at least 3 days in advance). To get a Panamanian tourist card one must buy a return ticket. **NB** The Ticabus from Panama City tends to arrive early, even at 0300, and you are left on the street. There is a 24-hr cafe nearby if you wish to avoid the expense of a hotel.

Panaline goes to Panama City daily at 1400 from C 16, Av 5, T 255-1205, US$20 one way, US$41 return, arrives 0700, TV/video, a/c, payment by Visa/Mastercard accepted.

Tracopa, moved 1996 to C 14, Av 5, sharing with another company, small signs, best to ask, goes as far as **David**, US$18 (buses daily at 0730 and 1200 sometimes, 9 hrs); book in advance. They are modern, comfortable buses, although there is not much room for long legs, but they have the advantage of covering a scenic journey in daylight. A bus to **Changuinola** via the Sixaola-Guabito border post leaves San José at 1000 daily, from a parking place a short distance from the *Hotel Cocorí*, C 14, Av 5-7, T 556-1432 Bernardo Fumero for information, best to arrive 1 hr before departure; the bus goes via Siquirres and is the quickest route to **Limón**. The journey from San José to Changuinola takes 8 hrs, US$7.

The Meseta Central

HILLY AND FERTILE, the temperate climate makes this a major coffee growing area. Fairly heavily populated, with picturesque and prosperous towns, each with a unique church, built in the shadow of volcanoes.

THE MESETA CENTRAL: EAST

CARTAGO

(*Alt* 1,439m; *Pop* 30,000) 22½ km from San José on a toll road (US$0.75), **Cartago** stands at the foot of the Irazú volcanic peak and is encircled by mountains. It was founded in 1563 and was the capital until 1823. The town is small, though the neighbourhood is densely populated. Earthquakes destroyed it in 1841 and 1910, and it has been severely shaken on other occasions. That is why there are no old buildings, though some have been rebuilt in colonial style.

Places of interest

The most interesting church is the **Basilica of Nuestra Señora de Los Angeles**, the Patroness of Costa Rica, rebuilt 1926 in Byzantine style; it houses **La Negrita**, under 15 cm high, an Indian image of the Virgin which draws pilgrims from all over Central America because of great healing powers attributed to it. In the Basilica is an extraordinary collection of very finely-made silver and gold images, no larger than 3 cm high, of various parts of the human anatomy, presumably offered in the hope of being healed. Worth seeing is the old parish church (**La Parroquia**),

ruined by the 1910 earthquake and now converted into a delightful garden retreat with flowers, fish and humming birds. There is an impressive procession on Good Friday.

Excursions

Aguas Calientes is 4 km SE of Cartago and 90m lower. Its *balneario* (warm water swimming pool) is a good place for picnics. 4 km from Cartago on the road to Paraíso is the **Jardín Lankester orchid garden** (run by the University of Costa Rica, T 551-9877), 10 mins' walk from the main road (ask bus driver to let you out at Campo Ayala, Cartago-Paraíso bus, departs every 30 mins from S side of central park in Cartago), taxi from Cartago, US$3; the best display is in April. Although off the beaten track, the gardens are definitely worth a visit; open 0900-1530 daily except Christmas, Easter and New Year, US$3.10. 1 km further on is Parque Doña Ana (La Expresión), a lake with picnic area, basketball courts, exercise track and bird watching, open 0900-1700, US$0.50. Get off bus at Cementario in Paraíso and walk 1 km S. At Paraíso, *Restaurant Continental* is rec.

Ujarrás (ruins of a colonial church and village) is 6½ km E of Cartago by a road from Paraíso and is on the shores of the artificial Lago Cachí. There is an hourly bus from Paraíso. Legend has it that in 1666, English pirates, including the youthful Henry Morgan, were seen off by the citizens of Ujarrás aided by the Virgin. The event is now celebrated each 16 April when the saint is carried in procession from Paraíso to the ruined church.

Another road runs SE from Paraíso through a beautiful valley to the small town of **Orosi**, in the enchanting Orosi valley, down which flows the tumultuous Reventazón (**C** *Hotel Río*, T 533-3128, 2 pools, dirty; **E** *Montaña Linda*, from bus stop cross the football field, turn left and after 2 blocks turn right, hotel at end of road, near hot springs, T 533-3345, cabins, double rooms and dormitory, hot showers, share kitchen, bicycle hire, camping or hammock US$2, owner Marco runs tourist information). Bus from Cartago, every 90 mins, more frequent at weekends, US$0.30. Here are magnificent views of the valley, a 17th century mission with colonial treasures (closed on Mon), and just outside the town two *balnearios* (bathing, US$1.60) and restaurants serving good meals at fair prices. The *miradores* of Ujarrás and Orosi both offer excellent views of the Reventazón valley. There are buses from Cartago to all these places.

A beautiful 1-day drive is a circular route from Cartago to Orosi, then opp Orosi, on the other side of the Reventazón, to **Palomo**, **D** *Río Palomo*, cabins, pool, laundry facilities, good restaurant. Continue round the Presa de Cachi to **Cachi** where there is a dam with artificial lake (very popular with residents of San José, Charrarra buses from 1 block N of Cartago ruins, several daily). The Charrarra tourist complex, with a good campsite, good restaurant, swimming pool, boat rides on the Orosi river and walks, can be reached by direct bus on Sun, otherwise ½-hr walk from Ujarrás. The road goes on round the N side of the lake to Ujarrás, then back to Cartago. From the dam, a dirt road continues down the valley 15 km to Tucurrique (**C** *Los Rapidos*, pleasant cabins, restaurant, good birding and horseriding, owner rents rafts with guide for US$100/day, English and German spoken). It is here where white water rafting begins. A start has been made to pave the road.

Local festivals

The feast day is 2 Aug, when the image is carried in procession to other churches in Cartago and there are celebrations throughout Costa Rica.

Local information

● **Accommodation**

E *Casa Blanca* in Barrio Asís, 2 km from centre, easy walk, not very clean, no sheets, hot water, clean towels, noisy all night.

F *El Rey*, C 5, Av 6-8, very dirty; **F** *Familiar Las Arcadas*, at railway station (rents rooms hourly late into the night); **F** *Vanecia*, cold water; **F** rooms to rent in private house, Armando Cortéz, 350 Sur de Las Ruinas, T 551-1316.

● **Places to eat**

Salón París, very good food; *City Garden*, Av 4, C 2-4; *Puerta del Sol*, in front of the Basilica; *Pizza Hut*, opp La Parroquia ruins; *Auto 88*, E of public market, meal US$2-3, cafeteria style, beer drinking room adjoining dining room. Restaurants, among other places, are closed on the Thur and Fri of Holy Week, so take your own food.

● **Banks & money changers**

Banco Fincomer changes TCs quickly with 1% commission.

● **Post & telecommunications**

Post Office: the main post office is at C 1, Av 2-4, nr the park.

● **Shopping**

Bookshop: at *Librería Cartago*, C 1, Av 2-4.

Market: there is a market facing the train station.

● **Transport**

Buses leave for **San José** as soon as they are full (every 10 mins or so throughout the day).

VOLCAN IRAZU

40 km from Cartago is the crater of **Irazú** (3,432m). Irazú crater is a half-mile cube dug out of the earth, and all around is desolate grey sand, with little wildlife other than the ubiquitous Volcano Junco,

Irazú: clouds and views

"In the afternoon the mountain top is buried in fog and mist or drizzle, but the ride up in the mist can be magical, for the mountainside is half-displaced in time. There are new jeeps and tractors, but the herds of cattle are small, the fields are quilt-work, handcarts and oxcarts are to be seen under the fretworked porches of well-kept frame houses. The land is fertile, the pace is slow, the air is clean. It is a very attractive mixture of old and new. Irazú is a strange mountain, well worth the ride up."

Mike Marlowe

"Stupendous views: you look down on mountain tops, clouds, light aircraft. Wear good shoes and a hat, the sun is strong. Those with sensitive skins should consider face cream if the sulphur fumes are heavy. By 1300 (sometimes by even 0900 or 1000) clouds have enveloped the lower peaks and are beginning to close in on Irazú."

J Douglas Porteous

a bird like a dunnock, and the few plants which survive in this desert. The phrase 'it's like the surface of the moon' describes Irazú quite well. The clouds come down early, obscuring the view, but if you can get there early (no entrance gate) it is wonderful to see the sun shining on the mountain and the clouds in the valley.

● **Admission** Entrance to Irazú, US$2, open 0800-1530 most of the year; from 1 Dec-30 April 0800-1700 on Fri, Sat, Sun, normal hours other days. There is a small museum. National Park rules forbid visitors to walk around the crater: on the N side is a 'Prohibido pasar' sign, which should not be passed. The only permitted walk is on the southerly side, which ends before the high crest.

● **Accommodation & places to eat** On the way up are the **D** *Hotel Montana* (not very helpful, no keys to rooms), **F** *Hotel Gestoria Irazú*, T 253-0827, and 10 km further on, the *Bar-Restaurant Linda Vista*, one of the highest restaurants in Central America at about 3,000m; nr Rancho Redondo, W of Volcán Irazú, is **A2-A3** *Hacienda San Miguel*, T 229-5058, F 229-1097, inc breakfast, restaurant, pool, horseriding, jacuzzi, steam bath, lake being dug 1997, magnificent views, continental divide passes through property, Pacific and Caribbean slope birds to be seen.

● **Transport** A yellow 'school' bus run by Buses Metropoli SA T 272-0651, runs from San José Sat, Sun and holidays, 0800 from *Gran Hotel Costa Rica*, stops at Cartago ruins 0830 to pick up more passengers, returns 1300 with lunch stop at Restaurant *Linda Vista* (whose

every internal surface is covered with business cards, bank notes, etc), US$5. A public bus leaves 0730 on Sat from the same place, Av 2, C 3, in front of the hotel. Taxi from Cartago is US$24 return (it is very difficult to get taxis to return for you in the morning if you have stayed at the crater overnight). A taxi tour from Orosi costs US$10 pp, min 3 people, and stops at various places on the return journey, eg Cachi dam and Ujarrás ruins. Beware of theft from hired cars. Overnight parking US$3. Since it can be difficult to find a decent hotel in Cartago, it may be easier to take one of the guided tours leaving from San José, about US$30; tours to Irazú and Orosi valley US$28-30. Horse riding tour, 5½ hrs inc lunch, transport from San José, T 255-2011, US$70. It is possible to get a bus from Cartago to Tierra Blanca (US$0.33) and hitch a ride in a pick-up truck. Alternatively you can take a bus from Cartago to Sanatorio. Ask the driver to drop you at the crossroads just outside Tierra Blanca. From there you walk to the summit, 16 km. 1½ km from the crater a road leads to Laguna Verde; the road is paved, but steep beyond the Laguna. If driving from San José, take the turn-off at the *Ferretería San Nicolás* in Taras, which goes directly to Irazú, avoiding Cartago. On Sat and Mon a bus goes from Cartago to San Juan, 12 km from the summit (0630 and 1300); **E** *Hotel Gran Irazú*, comfortable, clean.

TAPANTI NATIONAL PARK

12 km beyond Orosi is the **Refugio Nacional de Fauna Silvestre Tapantí**, run by the Forest Service, on the headwaters of the Reventazón. It is a 5,113 ha reserve of mainly cloud forest and pre-montaine

humid forest with 211 species of birds recorded, including the quetzal which nests in late spring and can be found on the western slopes near the entry point. Jaguar and ocelot are found in the reserve as well as monkeys, orchids and ferns. There are picnic areas, a nature centre with slide shows (ask to see them) and good swimming in the dry season (Nov-June), and trout fishing (1 April to 31 October).

● **Admission** Open daily 0800-1600, US$6. From June to Nov-Dec it rains every afternoon.

● **Accommodation** The **C** *Kiri Lodge* is 1½ km from the entrance (T 533-3040, good trails), or the guards may let you camp on or nr the parking lot at the entrance.

● **Transport** To get there take 0600 bus from Cartago to Orosi which goes to Puricil by 0700, then walk (5 km), or take any other Cartago-Orosi bus to Río Macho and walk 9 km to the refuge, or take a taxi from Orosi (ask for Julio who, for US$7 round trip, will take 6 passengers).

TURRIALBA

(*Alt* 625m, *pop* 40,000) **Turrialba** (57 km from San José), on the old railway between Cartago and Puerto Limón. The railway ran down to Limón on a narrow ledge poised between mountains on the left and the river on the right but no longer operates. The Centro Agronómico Tropical de Investigación y Enseñanza (CATIE) covers more than 2,000 acres of this ecologically diverse zone (with many fine coffee farms), has one of the largest tropical fruit collections in the world and houses an important library on tropical agriculture; visitors welcome. Past CATIE on the S side of the river, a large sugar mill can be seen, a conspicuous landmark. This is in Atirro which is also the centre for macadamia nuts.

Excursions The **Turrialba volcano** may be visited from Cartago by a bus from C 4 y Av 6 to the village of San Gerardo, or from Turrialba to Santa Cruz. Unpaved roads from these two villages meet at *Finca La Central*, on the saddle between Irazú and Turrialba, 2 km from **A1** *Volcán Turrialba Lodge*, where horses can be hired

(6 rooms with bath, trails and natural thermal pools, T/F 273-4335. Accessible only by 4WD but the lodge can arrange transportation. 1 hr by horseback to crater edge.

Many whitewater rafting companies are based in Turrialba, offering trips to the Reventazón and Pacuare rivers. By contacting the guides in Turrialba you can save about 30% on a trip booked in San José. Guides include Tico, at *Tico's River Adventures*; Ronald Bottger, *Serendipity Adventures*, T 556-0462, rec. New tourist information centre, Info-cen-tur, opp Parque Central above restaurant *Nuevo Hong Kong*, English spoken. The rafting is excellent; the Pascua section of the Reventazón can be class 5 at rainy times. Pacuare is more beautiful (and more expensive).

● **Accommodation** Southeast of Turrialba beyond La Suiza is **L3** *Albergue de Montaña Rancho Naturalista*, price pp inc meals, with bath, gourmet meal, horse riding, guided tours, transfers from San José and airport, 10 rooms, reservations essential, write PO Box 364-1002 San José, T 267-7138, 7-14 night programmes organized for birdwatchers and naturalists; 14 km SE of Turrialba, 2 km before La Suiza, 1 km from main road at Hacienda Atirro, **L1-L3** *Casa Turire*, 12 luxury rooms with bath, 4 suites, cable TV, phone, restaurant, pool, tennis, library, games room, in the middle of a 1,620-ha sugar/coffee/macadamia nut plantation, putting green and driving range, virgin rainforest nearby, trails, horses, bike rental, lots of excursions, T 531-1111, F 531-1075, e-mail: CasaTurire@centralamerica.com; **C** *Turrialtico*, on road to Limón, on top of hill with extensive views, clean, private bath, comfortable, friendly; **C** *Wagelia*, Av 4, Entrada de Turrialba (T 556-1596), with bath, 18 rooms, some a/c, restaurant, best, annex just outside town, beautiful gardens, pool, bar, highly rec. In a row facing the railway station are: **F** pp *Central*, with restaurant, no bath, clean and comfortable; *Clen* and *Chamango*; **F** pp *Interamericano*, with bath, clean, popular, parking, safe for motorbikes, best; **F** *Pensión Primavera*, 1 block away.

● **Places to eat** Restaurant *Nuevo Hong Kong*, good, reasonable prices; *Pizzería Julián*, on the square; *Las Palmeras*, alongside railway track, nice bar, good music; *Soda Burbuja*, local dishes very good value; *La Garza*, on main square, cheap, local good food.

● **Transport** Buses run from San José every hour 0500-2200 from C 13, Av 6-8; from Cartago, 1 hr, US$0.60, runs until about 2200.

From Turrialba you can get to the village of **Moravia del Chirripó**, E of Turrialba, where guides and horses can be hired for an excursion into the jungled, trackless area of the Talamanca Indians, where there are legends of lost goldfields (bus from Turrialba takes 4 hrs, only certain in dry season; in wet season go to Grano de Oro, from where it's 1 hr walk. No accommodation in Moravia, stay put at *pulpería* in Grano de Oro). Trips can be arranged to the **Cabeour Indian Reserve** of Alto Pacuare, also E of Turrialba; the reserve is a 2½-hr hike from Río Verch, and is good for serious naturalists and hikers; T *Jadetour* 234-9905, Flor de Lys Rojas.

GUAYABO

About 19 km N of Turrialba, near **Guayabo**, an Indian ceremonial centre has been excavated and there are clear signs of its paved streets and stone-lined water-channels. The archaeological site, 217 ha, 4 km from the town of Guayabo, is now a National Monument, and dates from the period AD 1000 to 1400. From Guayabo it is a 1½ hr walk to the site. There are excellent walks in the park, plenty of birds and wildlife to be seen.

● **Admission** Open daily except Mon, 0800-1500, US$6, local guide available, water, toilets, no food.

● **Accommodation & places to eat** *Guayabo Lodge*, 4-day packages inc meals and tours US$295 pp, located on the 200 acre Finca Blanco y Negro, home-cooked meals, riding, bird-watching and trips to Turrialba volcano arranged, T/F 556-0133; **D** *Albergue y Restaurant La Calzada*, T 556-0465, 556-6091 to leave message, best to make a reservation.

● **Transport** From Turrialba, there are buses at 1100 (returning 1250) and 1710 (returning 1750) and, on Sun, at 0900, return 1600 (check times, if you miss it is quite difficult to hitch as there is little traffic), US$0.45 to Guayabo. If you cannot get a bus all the way to Guayabo, several buses each day pass the turn-off to Guayabo, the town is a 2-hr walk uphill (taxi US$10, easy to hitch back).

Further N along this road (1½ hrs' drive) is Santa Cruz, from which the Turrialba volcano can be reached (see above). Costa Rica Expeditions and other tour operators offer day trips to Guayabo for about US$65 pp (min 4 persons).

Going NE from Turrialba, the main road follows the Río Reventazón down to Siquirres (see page 1109). On this road is Pavones with **D** *Albergue Mirador Pochotel*, T 556-0111. Following the old railway down the valley, you come in 10 km to **Peralta**, formerly a station and now more of a ghost village with a couple of sleepy bars. The old station is derelict but is the start of an interesting walk E down the track, through two tunnels full of large bats and past one of the landslides that closed the line in 1991. You can eventually reach Laguna Bonilla where there are boats for hire. The walk and return takes 4-5 hrs, requires good footwear and you may see tiny red and blue poison dart frogs. Speak to the locals en route, one used to send milk to San José by train, now makes a good cheese.

THE MESETA CENTRAL: WEST

The Pan-American Highway runs initially through the Meseta Central from San José to the Nicaraguan border, 332 km, completely paved and good. From San José it leads past the airport, bypassing Alajuela and a number of smaller towns mentioned below, to San Ramón before descending to Esparza on the coastal plain.

A paved road and a railway run from the capital to the two other main towns of the Meseta: Heredia and Alajuela.

HEREDIA

(*Alt* 1,200m; *Pop* 30,000) The capital of its province, 10 km from San José, is a great coffee and cattle centre. The town is mostly new and only the main square has a colonial atmosphere in its architecture. The main church was built in 1797. There is a statue to the poet Aquileo Echeverría

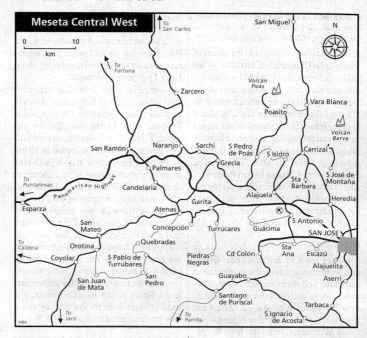

(1866-1909). The School of Marine Biology at the Universidad Nacional campus has a **Museo Zoológica Marina**, check opening times. Heredia is a convenient and pleasant place to stay, away from the pollution of San José but close to the capital and the airport, with good public transport.

Excursions

One of the largest coffee 'beneficios' is La Meseta; the bus from Heredia to Santa Bárbara will drop you at the gate and you can ask for a guided tour. There is also a coffee tour from San José to Café Britt's coffee farm near Barva de Heredia where you can see the processing factory, tasting room and multimedia presentation of the story of coffee, US$20, tours in high season 0900, 1100 and 1500, 2 hrs, in low season at 1100, T 260-2748, F 238-1848 for details. (Take 'Barva' bus from 200m N of main square to stop after 'El Castillo'.)

Above Heredia is the historic town of **Barva**, on the slope of the Barva volcano; frequent buses to/from Heredia. *Los Jardines Bed and Breakfast*, T 260-1904. At Barva the Huetar Gallery is rec for arts, crafts and delicious food. There is also a **Museo de Cultura Popular**, 500m E of the Salón Comunal de Santa Lucía de Barva. Beyond Barva is **Santa Bárbara**, good seafood at the *Banco de los Mariscos* on the N side of the central plaza.

5 km W of Heredia is **San Joaquín de Flores**, a small town in a rural setting with views of the Barva and Poás volcanoes.

Local information
● **Accommodation**

L2 *Rosa Blanca Country Inn*, de luxe suites, restaurant and bar for guests only, 1.6 km from Santa Bárbara de Heredia, Apdo Postal 41-30-09, T 269-9392, F 269-9555.

A1 *Bougainvillea de Santo Domingo*, inc breakfast, excellent service, pool, rec, T 244-1414, F 244-1313, spectacular mountain setting, free shuttle bus to San José; **A3-B** *Apartotel Vargas*, 8 large, well-furnished apartments with cooking facilities, hot water, laundry facilities, TV, enclosed patio with garage and nightwatchman, English speaking staff, Sr Vargas will collect you from airport, rec, 800m N of Colegio Santa Cecilia and San Francisco Church, Apdo 510-3000, Heredia, T 237-8526, 238-1810, F 260-4698.

B *América*, C 0, Av 2-4, just off central park, T 260-9292, F 260-9293 pick-up service from international airport; **B** *La Posada de la Montaña Bed and Breakfast* (*Heredia Mountain Inn*) at San Isidro de Heredia, T 268-8096 (USA T (417) 637-2066) inc breakfast, 2 nights min, some rooms with kitchenette, suites, airport or San José pickup; **B** *San Jerónimo Lodge*, T 292-3612, F 292-3243, 50-acre reserve, 20 mins from San José on Guápiles road, 800m E of church at San Jerónimo de Moravia, horse riding, hiking, biking; **B** *Zurquí Lodge Bed and Breakfast*, just off Limón highway at San Luís de Santo Domingo, 5 mins from entrance to Braulio Carrillo National Park, 6 rooms with private or shared bathroom, inc breakfast, T 235-2403.

E *Herediana*, C 6, friendly safe parking restaurant.

F *Colonial*, C 4-6, Av 4, clean, friendly, parking for motorcycles in restaurant, **F** *El Parqueo*, C 4, Av 6-8, T 238-2882, opp central market, friendly, and **F** *El Verano*, C 4, Av 6, T 237-1616, clean and friendly, both close to bus terminal.

● **Places to eat**
La Nueva Floresta, S side of main square, Chinese, balcony, large portions, good value, rec, pastry shop, *Pasteleria Snoopy*, ½ block W of main square, good; *Café Azzurra*, great ice cream, cakes, shakes, capuchino, on main plaza, great place to watch the world go by.

● **Language schools**
Intercultura Costa Rica, in Heredia, T/F 272-2234, mail address Apdo 487, Alajuela, small intensive classes; *Centro Panamericana de Idiomas*, in San Joaquín de Flores, PO Box 151-3007, T 265-6866, F 265-6213, accommodation with local families. See also under San José, AmeriSpan.

● **Shopping**
Bookshops: *Book Swappers*, diagonal to *MacDonalds*, run by Jill Chalfont and Frank García, new and used books, newspapers, CDs, postcards, open Mon-Sat 0930-1900.

● **Transport**
Trains Mon-Fri, 0545, 1715 from San Pedro University, returns 0630, 1800. On Sun 1000 to Heredia return 1045, in university term time only. You can take this train from the Atlantic station, San José.

Buses From the terminal at Av 4 y C Central for San José, US$0.28, frequent service. Local buses leave from Av 8, C 2-4, by market.

ALAJUELA

(*Alt* 952m; *Pop* 49,115) **Alajuela**, 13 km beyond Heredia (53 km from Juan Santamaría international airport by dual carriageway), capital of its province, is a midsummer resort for people from the capital, but easy to do as a day trip. It is famous for its flowers and its market days (Sat market is good value for food); an interesting craft cooperative produces pictures in relief metalwork. The unusual church of La Agonía in the E part of town has murals done from life. The national hero, Juan Santamaría, the drummer who fired the building at Rivas (Nicaragua) in which Walker's filibusters were entrenched in 1856, is commemorated by a monument. The **Museo Histórico Juan Santamaría** (Tues-Sun 1000-1700) tells the story of this war, confusingly. Alajuela Souvenir and Gift Center next door. 3 km outside the town is the Ojo de Agua swimming pool and sauna in beautiful surroundings: a popular bathing and boating resort. Entrance, US$1.20 pp, plus US$0.80/vehicle. The gushing spring which feeds the pool also supplies water for Puntarenas. At Río Segunda de Alajuela is *Amigo de las Aves*, an experimental bird breeding farm hoping to reintroduce native macaws back into the wild; contact owners, Richard and Margo Frisius (T 441-2658), to arrange a visit.

Local information
● **Accommodation**
A2-A3 *Hampton Inn*, airport hotel, 2 km E of Juan Santamaría, 100 rooms, double glazing, a/c, pool, bar, casino, no restaurant, fast food places nearby, discounts for children and senior citizens, T 443-0043, F 442-9532, e-mail:

Hampton@centralamerica.com; **A3** *Alajuela*, C 2, Av Central and 2 (T 441-1241), new rooms with TV and phone, C with shower, clean, friendly, free coffee, the only one appropriate for women travellers (best to book in advance); **A3** *Buena Vista*, above the city with an all-round view, T/F 443-2214, 25 rooms with bath, TV, pool, restaurant.

B *Posada Aeropuerto B&B*, T 441-7569, behind Juan Santamaría airport on road to Ojo de Agua, free transport from airport, some rooms with private bath, useful for early flights; **B** *Paraíso Tropical*, T 441-4882, cabins with tiled floors, with bath, hot water, airport shuttle, nice gardens; **B** *Islands Inn*, 500m E of central park, T 442-0573, owned by David and Erika Quesada, 8 rooms with bath, breakfast inc; **B** *Tuetal Lodge*, 3 km N of Alajuela, T 442-1804, cabins surrounded by 5 acres of gardens.

C *Pensión Alajuela*, T 441-6251, bath, hot water, fan, parking for US$5.

D pp *Villa Tourist Inn*, nr stadium, T 442-0692, parking; **D** *Charlie's Albergue*, a couple of streets from parque, need to bargain; **D** *La Posada*, T 442-9738, 100m N and 75m E of Red Cross, owner has taxi, call T 442-3333 and ask for car 990.

F *El Americano*, at Turrúcares, T 487-7192, with bath; **F** *El Real*, C 8, Av 1-Central, not rec, short stay only, opp bus terminal.

Mango Verde hostel, 50m W of Museo Juan Santamaría, T 441-6330, F 442-6257. See also hotels nr airport, given under San José.

Near Carrizal (on the road to San Miguel), which can be reached by bus from Alajuela, is *La Rana Holandesa* a Bed and Breakfast run by John and Henny Dekker, from Holland; they have 2 large, bright, clean rooms with separate entrance, **D** pp, lovely gardens, wonderful view over central valley, warmly rec, for US$60 plus fuel, John Dekker will drive you anywhere in his 4WD, free airport pickup, T/F 483-0816, 150m Noroeste Esquina Los Pérez, Carrizal de Alajuela.

● **Places to eat**

El Cencerro, on Parque Central, good meat, especially steaks, good service, nice view over park from the terrace; *Pizza Hut*, central; *La Jarra*, nr Alajuela hotel, good cheap meals in pleasant surroundings; *La Sirenita*, nothing special but OK.

● **Buses**

To San José-Alajuela US$0.33. To Sarchí US$0.50, 1½ hrs. To La Fortuna US$3.

VOLCAN POAS

From Alajuela two paved roads run to 2,708m volcano **Poás** (57 km by road from San José either through San Pedro de Poás and Fraijanes, or along the road to San Miguel, turning to Poás at the restaurant on the bend in the road just before you get to Vara Blanca. In the **National Park of Poás** (5,317 ha), the still-smoking volcano is set in beautiful tropical forest. The park has abundant birdlife and has the only true dwarf cloudforest in Costa Rica. Trails are well marked. The crater is 1½ km across (said to be the second largest in the world). In another area geysers may throw steam 600m or so. Just before the viewing point there is a path off the road leading to a still, forest-fringed lake in another crater, 30 mins return. Another path is an alternative route back to the Visitors' Centre, 30 mins' walk. Make sure you arrive at the volcano before the clouds. Clouds often hang low over the crater after 1000 permitting little to be seen.

● **Admission** Entrance to Park, US$6. The Park gates are open 0800-1600 daily (1 hr later Fri, Sat, Sun, 1 Dec-30 April), but if you wish to get in earlier you can leave your car/taxi at the gates and walk the 3 km up the hill. The main crater is 1 km along a road from the car park. There is a visitors' centre by the car park, with explanations of the recent changes in the structure, an insect museum on the 2nd floor (open 0800-1600, daily, adults US$2.50, teens US$1.50, under 10s US$0.50), and a good café next door, and toilets further along the road to the crater. The volcano is very crowded on Sun, go in the week if possible.

● **Accommodation** You cannot camp in the Park but there are several places advertising cabins on the road up to Poás; take food and water. If you get stuck in Poás ask the Peace Corps volunteer for help in finding somewhere to sleep. **A2** *Albergue Ecológico La Providencia*, nr Poás NP (2 km from green entrance gate to volcano, unpaved road), private reserve, beautiful horse-riding tour US$25-30 inc lunch, T 232-2498, F 231-2204; At San Pedro de Poás there is an interesting bar, *La Via*, with cheap food, free snacks and good music. Further on look for **A2** *Poás Volcano Lodge*, 200m from Vara Blanca junction on road to Poasito, at *El*

Cortijo farm, sign on gate, difficult to spot in cloud, rough farm track 1 km to house, T 482-2194, English-owned, inc breakfast, dinner available if only a few guests, good wholesome food, rooms in converted outbuildings with bath, or in farmhouse with shared bath, some rooms cheaper, good walking, 25 mins to volcano by car, 1½ hrs from San José, T/F 482-2194, PO Box 5723-1000, San José, or in UK T 0171-586 3538. **B** *Albergue Ecológico Los Cipreses*, Barrio San José de los Angeles de Grecia, 1 km from Poás, 11 km from Grecia, T 444-5723, F 494-4650, 2 cabins, camping available. **D** *Country Club Monte del Mago*, about 40 km away at Carrillo de Poás (T 661 2410), with bath, swimming pool, restaurant, sometimes no food or water. **Campsite**: trailer park nearby, with hookups: the *Inca*.

● **Transport** The volcano can be reached by car from San José. A taxi for 6 hrs with a side trip will cost about US$50-60. It is difficult to get to Poás by public transport midweek. On Sun and public holidays there is a regular excursion bus from the main square of Alajuela right up to the crater, leaving at 0900, connecting with 0830 bus from San José (from C 12, Av 2-4); be there early for a seat, if full before 0900 the bus will leave, although extra buses run if necessary, the area gets very crowded, US$4 return, T 237-2449 or 222-5325 for information. The bus waits at the top with ample time to see everything (clouds permitting), returning at 1400-1430. Daily bus Alajuela-Poasito 1200 (US$1). From **Poasito** hitch a lift as it is a 10 km walk. Other options include taking a 0600 or 1600 bus from Alajuela to **San Pedro de Poás**, hitch/taxi to Poasito and stay overnight there, hiking or hitching up the mountain next morning; taking a 0500 bus from Alajuela to Poasito which arrives 2 hrs before the Park gates open.

From **Vara Blanca** the road continues N round the E side of the volcano through Cinchona and Cariblanco (voluntary toll/lottery US$0.20 for road construction). The road is twisty, winding through lush forest, waterfalls down to the lowlands at **San Miguel**. Here the road splits, leading either NE to Puerto Viejo de Sarapiquí (see below) or NW to **Venecia** (3½ hrs, US$2.50 by bus from San José), interesting church; 1 hotel, **F**, clean, friendly; *Restaurant El Parque*, near church, good local food. Nearby is **Ciudad**

Cutris, precolumbian tumuli (a good road goes to within 2 km of Cutris, from there walk or take 4WD vehicle; get a permit to visit from the local *finca* owner). West of Venecia is Aguas Zarcas, another road junction. Just beyond, on the road to San Carlos, is **L2-A2** *El Tucano Country Club*, 90 rooms and suites, pleasant, hot springs of iron and sulphur, swimming pool, jacuzzi, sauna, casino, tennis, mini golf, horse riding, restaurant, T 460-3152, F 460-1692, from here it is only 8 km to San Carlos (see page 1078). About 40 km N of Aguas Zarcas is **Boca Tapada** on the Río San Carlos in the jungle and not far from its junction with the Río San Juan and the Nicaraguan border. Here there is the **A3** *La Laguna del Lagarto Lodge*, T 289-8163/5295, 12 rooms with bath, 6 with shared bath, friendly, good for watching animals, 500 ha of forest, boat trips down Río San Carlos to Río San Juan.

10 km NE of San Miguel is **La Virgen**, where *Rancho Leona* is located nr the Río Sarapiquí. Good for kayaking, T 710-6312 for 2-night packages, US$75, equipment and guides included, very basic accommodation and expensive but good home cooked dishes at the ranch and nightly frog concerts. Take the Río Frío bus from San José and ask to get off at *Rancho Leona*, the 1600 bus goes through the Braulio Carrillo National Park and ends at *Rancho Leona*, 3½ hrs. Also at La Virgen is Juan Carlos, a rec guide for rafting (class 1, 2 and 3 possible on the Río Sarapiquí) from US$25 pp, T 761-1148.

● **Accommodation A2** *La Quinta de Sarapiquí Lodge*, on Sardinal river (Bajos de Chilamate), family-run lodge, 6 rooms with bath and fan, T/F 761-1052. At Chilamate, 15 km further on, is the **B** pp *Albergue Ecológico Islas del Río*, inc meals, 5 rooms with private bathroom, 3 rooms with shared bathroom, Río Sarapiquí trips arranged, T 233-0366 in San José, 710-6898 Lodge (affiliated to the Youth Hostel network).

PUERTO VIEJO DE SARAPIQUI

Puerto Viejo de Sarapiquí is 10 km beyond Chilamate and was once an important port on the Río Sarapiquí. Launches can be taken via the Río Colorado to the Canales de Tortuguero and there is reported to be a cargo boat once a week to Barra del Colorado (no facilities, bring own food, hammock, sleeping bag) (see pages 1112-1115), and on to Moín, about 10 km by road from Puerto Limón. There is good fishing on the Río Sarapiquí.

In the neighbourhood is the **Organization for Tropical Studies** station at **La Selva Biological Station** on the Río Sarapiquí. To visit, phone in advance to book, T 710-1515. Visitors are provided with maps of the superb primary rain forest. Guided natural history walk with bilingual naturalists from 0800-1130 or 1330-1600, US$20 pp. There are different styles of accommodation, including dormitories; overnight rates reduced for a senior researcher, student researcher (letter of introduction required and prior arrangement) book well in advance. High rates for tourists help to support the scientists. Try to avoid the rainy season. To get there by car from San José, take the highway through the Braulio Carrillo National Park (Route 32) and then take Route 4, which turns off to Puerto Viejo 14 km before Guápiles, or drive via San Miguel and Le Virgen, and through Puerto Viejo: park at the suspension bridge then walk. Buses run from Puerto Viejo. The river flows into the San Juan, which forms the northern border of Costa Rica. River trips on the Sarapiquí and on the Río Sucio are beautiful (US$15 for 2 hrs); contact William Rojas in Puerto Viejo (T 766-6260) for trips on the Río Sarapiquí or to Barra del Colorado and Tortuguero, or ask for the Lao brothers who will advise you. The cost of a launch to Tortuguero is about US$150, but you may be able to find a place on a boat for US$40 or even less. **NB** The Río San Juan is wholly in Nicaragua, so you technically have to cross the border and then back into Costa Rica. This will cost US$5 and you will need passport/Visa. The whole trip takes about 5 hrs.

- **Accommodation A3** *El Bambú*, opp park, T 766-6005, F 766-6132, in centre, bath, fan, TV, inc breakfast, very nice; **D** *Mi Lindo Sarapiquí* by Park, new with 6 rooms with bath, fan, hot water, restaurant, T 766-6281; **F** *Cabinas Monteverde*, T 766-6236, with bath, but reported dirty; hotels *El Antiguo* (T 766-6205) and *Santa Marta*, both **G**; *pensiones Las Brisas* and *González*, both **F**, latter above hardware store (*ferretería*), not signed, *Pip's* restaurant, good.) There is a bus service from San José, C 1-Central, Av 11, US$2.50, via Río Frío, several daily. Buses from Puerto Viejo to Río Frío and San Carlos. Nearby is **A2** *Selva Verde Lodge*: on 600 acres of virgin rainforest reserve, 40 double rooms, 5 bungalows w/bath, caters mainly for tour groups, T 766-6266 (Lodge), T 766-6277 (reservations), extensive library, evening lectures by biologists, excellent for birdwatchers and naturalists with extensive trail system, rafting, canoeing and riding through property; tours with biologists organized. It is next to the Sarapiquí Conservation Learning Center, community library and resource centre for environmental protection. Across the river from the OTS station is the **B** *Sarapiquí Ecolodge*, 4 rooms, shared bathroom, price pp inc meals, **D** without food, riding, birdwatching, river trips, horseriding, T 235-9280 or 766-6122 (daytime only). Near La Selva Biological Station is **B** *El Gavilán Lodge*, T 234-9507, F 253-6556, inc breakfast, set in gardens by the river pier, good restaurant, good jungle paths, riding and river tours, 10 rooms private bath, 10 rooms shared bath, special group and student/reseacher rates, day trips and overnight trips from San José. **The Oro Verde Station** is located where the Río Sarapiquí flows into the Río San Juan with over 1,900 ha (almost 100% forest), 1½ hr boat ride from Puerto Viejo, US $30 pp, accommodation in **A2** range with meals, beautiful setting, quiet, excellent food, good place to unwind, T San José 233-6613, F 223-7479, Braun Eco Tourism (see above, **Tour companies & travel agents**) do 3-day all-inclusive packages, rec.

17 km S of Puerto Viejo, near **Las Horquetas de Sarapiquí** is *Rara Avis*, rustic lodges in a 1,500 acre forest reserve owned by ecologist Amos Bien. This admirable experiment in educating visitors about

rainforest conservation takes small groups on guided tours (rubber boots provided), led by biologists. You must be prepared for rough and muddy trails, lots of insects but great birdwatching. In San José T/F 256-4876, in Horquetas T 764-3131. (Affiliated to the Youth Hostel network.) The road from the Limón Highway to Puerto Viejo is now paved, the turn off is near Santa Clara, 14 km W of Guápiles, it bypasses Río Frío and goes via Las Horquetas.

● **Accommodation** Also part of *Rara Avis Lodge* are **L2** *Waterfall Lodge*, inc meals, private bath; **A3** *Albergue El Plástico*, 3 km before *Waterfall Lodge*, rustic with shared bath, min 2 nights, book well in advance.

GRECIA

The road from Alajuela to San Carlos (see page 1078) passes through several of the Meseta Central towns, with good paved roads to others. Much of this region is devoted to coffee growing and the hills are covered with green coffee bushes, interspersed with other plants for shade, often shrouded in cloud and rain. 18 km NW from Alajuela, **Grecia** is in a major pineapple-growing area and has an interesting church, made entirely of metal to replace a wooden one. The **Museo Regional de Grecia** is in the Casa de la Cultura, open Mon-Fri, 0900-1700, entrance free.

● **Accommodation D** *Cabaña Los Cipreses*; *Posada de Grecia*, bed and breakfast, T 444-5354; *Complejo Trailer y Cabinas Los Trapiches*; **G** *Pensión Quirós*, with bath.

SARCHÍ

A few kilometres further is **Sarchí**, where you can visit the factory that produces the traditional painted ox-carts, which are almost a national emblem. The three main *artesanías* are together, either side of the road and selling hand-made furniture, cowhide rocking chairs and wooden products as well as the ox-carts, which come in all sizes. Look out for the bus shelters, painted in the style of the carts. The pink church in Sarchí is especially attractive at sunset. Also **Valle de Mariposas** (next to Mercado de Artesanías), 40 species of butterflies, inc Morphos; T 454-4196 (US$6 entry, open 0900-1700 daily). Travel agents in San José charge US$20 or more, often combining Sarchí with a trip to Poás volcano.

● **Accommodation** The only place to stay in Sarchí is **B** *Villa Sarchí Lodge*, T/F 454-4006, 8 rooms, restaurant, owned by Ramon Rodrigues.

● **Transport** Express bus from San José, C 16, Av 1-3, 1215 and 1730 daily, returning 0530, 0615, 1345. Tualisa buses every 30 mins, 0500-2200 from Alajuela bus station.

The road continues on through **Naranjo** (Roberto Kopper offers balloon tours, about 30 mins, 1,000 ft, T 450-0318). On the Panamericana, 1 km W of the turnoff for Naranjo is **A3** *Rancho Mirador*, T 451-1302, F 451-1301, good value cabañas, good restaurant with local food, a spectacular view of coffee fincas and San José in the distance, owner Rick Vargas who was formerly a stunt pilot in the USA.

ZARCERO

25 km from Naranjo **Zarcero** is notable for its topiary. There are frequent bus services from San José/Alajuela through Naranjo to San Carlos (Ciudad Quesada) and buses stop in Zarcero in the main plaza, which is the highlight of the place. The bushes are clipped into the shapes of arches leading up to the white church with twin towers, animals, people dancing, a helicopter, baskets, many designs like Henry Moore sculptures, also a small grotto. The interior of the church is entirely of wood, even the pillars, painted cream and pale grey with patterns in blue, brown, green and pink; cartouches, emblems and paintings.

● **Accommodation & places to eat C** *Don Beto*, by the church, T/F 463-3137, with bath, very friendly, clean; *Soda/Restaurant El Jardín*, on first floor, overlooks the plaza with good view of topiary, local lunches and breakfasts. The town is also known for cheese and fruit preserves.

SAN RAMON

Just after Llano Bonito, before reaching Zarcero, a turning left goes to **San Ramón**, 76 km from San José. A clean town with an attractive Parque Central. Street market Sat mornings. The **Museo de San Ramón**, Frente de Parque, open Tues-Fri, 1300-1700, records the history and culture of the local community. Good walking for example to the NW, take the bus to La Paz and get off at the bridge over the Río Barranca. Also you can visit the coffee processing plant (in season) at the Cooperativa de Café in San Ramón.

● **Accommodation E** *Hotel Nuevo Jardín*, with bath, hot water; **F** *El Viajero*, basic, clean, communal bathroom, TV in lounge; **F** *Washington*, dirty, unfriendly, not rec. There are local families who offer room and board, try Sra Miriam Bamfi, T 445-6331 or Sra María del Carmen Ulate, T 445-6007, Spanish speaking only. **On the San Ramón to La Fortuna road**: heading N, is **A3** *Hotel Villa Blanca*, 800 ha of primary cloud forest, naturalist hikes, T 228-4603, F 228-4004; also **A2** *Valle Escondido Lodge*, at San Lorenzo on same road, comfortable rooms with private bath, set in 400 acres of primary forest, riding, bird watching, T 231-0906, F 232-9591.

● **Places to eat** *Restaurant Tropical*. Excellent ice cream parlour nr the NW corner of the Parque.

● **Transport** Buses run to surrounding villages and towns.

7 km SE of San Ramón is **Palmares** (one hotel), which has a pretty central park with lovely tall trees, in which are said to be five sloths. Eight paths radiate from the bandstand. On the side of the park opp the stone church is the municipal market.

ATENAS TO ALAJUELA

After Palmares you can either pick up the Pan-American Highway, or continue S to **Atenas**, which is on the road from San José to San Mateo, leading on to Esparza and the Pacific coast. This road to the coast is well-used and in good condition. The church and main plaza in Atenas lie on an earthquake fault. There is a Library on the plaza, which also serves as the office for the bus company, Cooptransatenas, T 446-5767. Many daily buses to San José, either direct or via Alajuela, US$0.60. Local speciality, *toronja rellena*, a sweet filled grapefruit. Atenas is reputed to have the best climate in the world, with stable temperatures of between 17 and 32°C the year round (plus rain of course).

● **Accommodation B** *Ana's Place*, inc breakfast, private bathroom, special weekly/monthly rates, T 446-5019; **C** *Villa Tranquilidad*, T 446-5460, 6 rooms, refurbished 1994, Canadian owned, quiet, welcoming, hard to find, phone for reservations/directions.

Driving from Atenas towards Alajuela, you pass *Fiesta de la Maíz* soda/restaurant by a green church on the side of the road, where they sell only products made of maize, you can try spoonfuls before you buy. Open weekends only, very busy, a stopping place for weekenders on their way to Jacó Beach. Nearby is the Enchanted Forest, popular with children. Also the Zooave, between Atenas and Alajuela in **La Garita de Alajuela**, Canadian owner, over 100 species of native birds and 25 exotic species, toucans, parrots, black swans, eagles, also all four monkeys as well as other mammals and reptiles. Now recognized as a Wildlife Rescue Centre, Zooave has been successful in breeding endangered birds, T 433-8989, open daily, 0900-1700, US$8.70.

● **Accommodation A2** *Chatelle Country Resort*, T 487-7081, F 487-7095, 6 rooms with bath, some rooms with kitchenette, TV, spacious, comfortable beds, beautiful gardens, good restaurant, pool, weekly/monthly rates, airport pickup available at no extra charge, opp the *Chatelle Country Resort* is an orchid nursery with a marvellous variety of blooms, run as a hobby by an enthusiastic English-speaking optometrist, who will give you a guided tour for US$3.50; **A3** *Río Real*, T/F 487-7022, inc breakfast, pool, restaurant, bar. At the Alajuela, La Garita, San Pedro de Poás fork is **B** *Las Orquídeas Inn*, T 433-9346, F 433-9740, 12 rooms with bath, 4 rooms shared bath, no children under 13 accepted, pick up from airport, pool.

● **Places to eat** *Mi Quinta*, good food, swimming pools, sports facilities also available for a small charge. The area is quiet and agricultural with fields of sugar cane and cattle pastures; pleasant walking to places of interest.

ASERRI TO SAN PABLO DE TURRUBARES

10 km S of San José is **Aserrí**, a village with a beautiful white church, where on Fri and Sat evenings, street bands play from 2000, followed by marimbas. Extremely popular among locals, the dancing is fabulous. *Chicharrones* and *tortillas* to eat, plus liquor. Further along the same road is *Mirador Ram Luna*, a restaurant with a fine panoramic view. At the end of the black-top road is **San Ignacio de Acosta**, again with a good church containing life-size Nativity figures. Buses from San José (C 8, Av 12) via Aserrí every 90 mins from 0500-2200, return 0430-1800. The unpaved road continues to **Santiago de Puriscal**, which was the epicentre for many earthquakes in 1990, the church is now closed as a result. Excellent views from the town and the road. From here it is possible to take a dirt road to the Pacific coast, joining the coastal road near Parrita (see page 1122). Alternatively, take the road to **San Pablo de Turrubares** (a soccer field, a church, a *soda* and a bar), from where you can either head W for Orotina, via an unpaved road through San Pedro and San Juan de Mata, or for Atenas via Quebradas, then E to Escobal, next stop on railway, then 4WD necessary to Atenas.

A road has been built from San José W to Ciudad Colón by-passing Escazú and Santa Ana (**A2** *Hotel Posada Canal Grande*, T 282-4089/4101/4103, F 282-5733, Apdo 84-6150), which will eventually pass San Pedro de Turrubares going to Orotina, with the aim of replacing the Pan-American Highway to the coast.

The Central Northwest

THE NORTHERN lowlands stretching to the Nicaraguan border. In the eastern foothills of the Cordillera de Tilarán is Lago Arenal, beneath the highly active Volcán Arenal. The rivers provide fine opportunities for seeing wildlife.

SAN CARLOS

Also known as **Ciudad Quesada San Carlos**, lies 48 km from the Pan-American Highway and can be reached by a road which branches off the highway near Naranjo. At the foot of the mountains it is the main town of the lowland cattle and farming region and is a hub of communications. The market (*centro comercial*) is near the Parque Central. There is a large, efficient Social Security Hospital on the N side of town on the road to Florencia, better to come here for first aid treatment rather than to local village doctors.

● **Accommodation** E *Balneario Carlos*, T 460-1822, cottages with cooking facilities, with bath, swimming pool; E *Conquistador*, with bath; E *El Retiro*, T 460-0403, with bath, clean and comfortable, but noisy; E *La Central*, T 460-0301, with bath, restaurant; several basic *pensiones*, all F; G *La Terminal*, T 460-2158, at bus station. 8 km from town is *El Tucano*, see page 1062.

● **Transport** Direct bus from Coca Cola bus station, San José, 3 hrs, hourly, from 0500 to 1900, US$2.20. From San Carlos buses go NW to Tilarán via Fortuna and Arenal (0600 and 1500), other buses go to Fortuna through El Tanque (5 daily), San Rafael de Guatuso and Upala, N to Los Chiles, NE to towns on the Río San Carlos and Río Sarapiquí, including Puerto Viejo de Sarapiquí, and E to the Río Frío district.

SAN CARLOS TO LOS CHILES

From San Carlos a paved road runs NW to **Florencia** (service station). At Platanar de San Carlos, at Hacienda Platanar is **A1** *Hotel La Garza* (8 km from Florencia, T 475-5222, F 475-5015), bungalows with bath and fan, overlooking river, guided tours, boat trips, fishing, 750 acres of forest and cattle ranch. At a junction the route to the N leads 13 km to **Muelle San Carlos**. **A1** *Country Club Tilajari Hotel Resort*, T/F 460-1083 (T 228-4603 F 228-4004, San José) 48 luxurious rooms, 4 suites, a/c, tennis, 3 pools, sauna, bar and restaurant, horses, boat trips and other excursions organized, 29 km to Arenal, rec.

A further 74 km N through flat land where orange plantations have replaced forest, leads to **Los Chiles** near the Nicaraguan border. From here you can arrange boat/fishing trips up the slow-moving Río Frío, through dense tropical vegetation into the **Caño Negro Wildlife Refuge** and Caño Negro Lake, to see alligators, turtles, monkeys, a wide variety of birdlife, fish and fauna. Ask about guides at the *Restaurant El Parque*, a 4-hr tour with Esteban, rec. Oscar and Enrique also rec. If going to Caño Negro, it is better to get a boat from Los Chiles

(Mon and Fri) rather than taking a tour or going by road. You will see much of the wildlife without going into the Parque.

● **Accommodation B** *Guajipal Lodge*, T 471-1055, with breakfast, bath, cold water, tours arranged; **F** *Cardina*, very clean, friendly; **F** *Central*, basic, mosquito nets, small rooms, camping available, and tours for US$30 for 5 people; some restaurants. **B** *Caño Negro Lagoon Lodge*, 17 km S of Los Chiles on a rough dirt road, 4WD only, rustic rooms, T 460-0124.

FRONTIER WITH NICARAGUA – LOS CHILES

This crossing point is now open to foreigners but there is no road link, and San Carlos on the Nicaraguan side is remote from the rest of that country.

● **Costa Rican Immigration**
All formalities are in Los Chiles which is a few kilometres short of the border. The office is close to the river and leaving procedures are normally straightforward. If entering Costa Rica, officials can be more difficult, mainly because they are sensitive about the many Nicaraguan immigrants wishing to enter the country.

● **Transport**
Air Sansa has flights San José-Los Chiles on Tues, Thur, Sun.

Most travellers take the (not frequent) colectivo boats that go down the Río Frío and cross the Río San Juan to San Carlos, 1-2 hrs, US$2.50. You can follow the track N to the San Juan river and then find a ferry to cross, but enquire before trying this route. Going into Costa Rica, there are 2 or 3 direct buses to San José daily 6-7 hrs, alternatively take a bus to Ciudad Quesada San Carlos from where there are good services.

See under **Nicaragua – San Carlos** and **San Juan del Norte/Greytown** for details on the Río San Juan border.

FORTUNA

(*Alt* 254m; *Pop* 4,500) The road running W from the junction in Florencia (paved, good) leads to **Fortuna**, from where you can explore the Arenal region. Banco Nacional de Costa Rica will change TCs, US$1 commission.

● **Accommodation A1** *Bosques de Chachagua*, at Chachagua on road to San

Ramón, about 12 km SE of Fortuna, individual suites, rainforest, riding, tours to Caño Negro, contact Vesa Tours, T 239-0328, F 293-4206; **A2** *Las Cabañitas*, 4 km E of La Fortuna, 30 cabins with private baths, 2 pools, observatory for viewing Arenal volcano, restaurant, highly rec, T 479-9400/9343, F 479-9408, e-mail: gasguis@sol.racsa.co.cr; **B** *Cabañas de Montaña de Fuego*, between La Fortuna and Tabacón, inc breakfast, 3 cabins with private baths, T/F 479-9106; **B** *Rancho El Corcovado*, pool, clean, overlooks river and wildlife; **B** *Villa Fortuna*, T/F 479-9139, fans or a/c, private bath, hot water, small fridge; **B-C** *San Bosco*, T 479-9050, all rooms with private bath, quiet, signs on main road, clean, friendly, nice gardens with terrace and view of the volcano, rec; **C** *Cabinas Rossi*, 1 km towards the volcano, with breakfast, friendly owner, hot water, fan, watch the volcano from the garden, horses rented, good value; **D** *Cabinas La Amistad*, clean, friendly, hot water, hard beds; *Cabinas Carmela*, 0 Av y 0 C, very central, hot showers, fairly basic, arranges tours; **D** *Las Colindas*, private bath, pleasant; **E** pp *Albergue Burío*, inc continental breakfast, private bath, T 479-9076, F 479-9010, 8 rooms with bath, try to get an inside cabin, others noisy, Arenal volcano trips, fishing arranged, motorbikes welcome, camping in garden, affiliated to the Youth Hostel network; **E** *Cabinas Jerry*, T 479-9063, new cabins with bath, hot water, mixed reports; **E** *Cabinas Sissy*, 100m S and 100m W of church, T 479-9356/9256, bath, hot water, clean; **E** *Centro Recreación Volcán Arenal*, 50m S of church, private accommodation, simple rooms, breakfast, owned by local dentist, nice garden with amusing pets; **E** *Cabinas Las Flores*, 2 km on road to Arenal, friendly, clean; **F** pp *La Central*, quiet, cold showers, friendly, restaurant good but not cheap, laundry service, squeaky beds, you may put up a tent on the lawn for US$1.50, T 479-9004 (phone this number to be put in contact with Gabino Hidalgo Solís, who runs a tourist information office on the main plaza, he also acts as a guide to the area, inc Volcán Arenal, by night, US$6.50, horse riding to the waterfalls, US$14 day trip, bring own lunch); **F** pp *Cabina Las Tejas*, private bath, bike rental, tours to Arenal and the hot springs, US$7; **F** pp *Cabinas Charlie*, run by Charlie and María Rodríguez, take good care of their guests, clean, friendly, English spoken, hot water, fan, use of kitchen, night tours to volcano US$7; **F** *Cabinas Christina*, clean, hot water; **G** *Cabinas Aduana*, hot water, tours to volcano.

- **Places to eat** *Lily and the Moon*, good vegetarian food, fresh bread for breakfast; *Choza de Laurel*, behind the church, self-service US$1.50-US$4.50, typical food, friendly; *Rancho Cascada*, on corner of Parque with high conical thatched roof, good bocas, films shown in evenings; *Soda del Rio*, good, safe, friendly, some rooms; *El Jardin*, good place to watch the world go by, *plato del dia* US$1.50, tasty; *Nene*, good food, pleasant service, not expensive; *El Jinete*, at busstop, good food, friendly, good value; *La Vaca Muca*, a bit out of the village on the way to Tabacón. Public phone with international access.

- **Tour companies & travel agents** *Aventuras Arenal*, La Fortuna, T 479-9133, Rodrigo Salazar: Caño Negro tours US$50-60; Arenal lake sunset trip US$40-50, fishing US$27/hr.

- **Buses** There are daily buses at 0615, 0840, 1130, from Coca Cola terminal, San José, C 16, Av 1-3, via San Carlos, US$2.50, return at 1330, 1430; 5 buses a day from San Carlos, 1 hr, US$1. Two buses a day to Tilarán, 0800 (connecting bus Tilarán-Puntarenas 1300) and 1600 US$2.50, 3 hrs.

About 6 km S of Fortuna are the 70m **Río Fortuna Waterfalls**, up a pleasant road through yuca and papaya plantations. Admission US$1.50. You can bathe there but it is safer 50m downstream. You can walk or drive, but 4WD is necessary, or bicycle hire US$2/hr (hard work), or you can hire a horse for the day at around US$14. White water rafting available. Take care when climbing down to falls, it is steep and slippery, take shoes with a good tread and swimming clothes. 2 hrs' climb above the falls is the crater lake of Cerro Chato. The top (1100m) is reached through mixed tropical/cloud forest, with a good view (if you are lucky) but beware of snakes on the path. A guide, if you need one, US$9.

VOLCAN ARENAL

From Fortuna the road travels N around the base of the 1,633m volcano **Arenal** to the man-made **Lago Arenal** and hydroelectric dam. The volcano has been continuously active since July 1968, when an eruption killed 78 people and more or less

destroyed three villages including Tabacón which was situated above the Balneario. It is a classic cone shape of the Stromboli type characterized by explosions sending hot grey clouds of sulphurous gases which can descend the slopes at an alarming speed. There are also lava streams, mainly on the W side. The most recent major activity was in Mar-April 1995. Although the side facing Fortuna is green, the side facing the lake is grey and barren, with lava flows clearly visible. There are three active craters and several fumaroles which spew out red hot lava and steam. The activity is particularly impressive at night, accompanied by rumbles, crashes and intermittent roars (rather like someone moving furniture upstairs) to wake you up. If you are visiting in the rainy season you will not see much as the volcano is obscured by clouds and rain. All year round, there are usually clouds and rain in the afternoons. However, if you can hire a taxi for a trip at about 0400-0500, the sky is often clearer then. On no account try to walk up the volcano beyond the level of the vegetation; some of those who have tried have not returned alive. However there is good hiking on the lower slopes from Fortuna. Rec guides are Carlos and Didier.

- **Admission** The volcano is a national park, entry US$6. There are many chalets and tourist facilities round the attractive lake, but not many people. Bathing in the warm water from quiet shady beaches is possible. Taxi from Fortuna to Tabacón US$4.50.

Thermal baths 10 km NW of Fortuna is *Balneario Tabacón*, a thermal pool with 3 bars, restaurant, rec for swimming after dark when you can see the lava coming down the volcano, a spectacular sight, not to be missed (open 1000-2200 daily). The water is hot and stimulating: there are a number of pools at descending heights and different temperatures, waterslides, a waterfall to sit under, etc. The food is good and the fruit drinks thirst quenching. The entrance fee seems to vary up to as much as US$14 but cheaper after 1800

(US$13). The resort is very popular with evening coach tours from San José and a resort hotel is planned. There are cheaper hot springs across the road. Better are the hot waters about 4 km further along the road at Quebrada Cedeña, clean and safe, no sign but look for local parked cars. Also near Fortuna are the Cavernas del Venado, limestone caves that can be visited. Tours from Fortuna with all necessary equipment, US$20. Buses from San Carlos en route to Tilarán daily, return transport to Fortuna at 2200.

● **Accommodation** 4 km after El Tabacón a left turn on to a gravel road (sign 1 km Parqueo) leads eventually to the **A1-B** *Arenal Observatory Lodge* (PO Box 1195, 1250 Escazú, Costa Rica, T 257-9489, F 257-4220 (Costa Rica Sun Tours) or T 255-2011 (Eco-Center), e-mail: Observatory@centralamerica.com, 4WD rec along this 9 km stretch (taxi-jeep from Fortuna, US$12). The Observatory was built in 1987 as a research station and now has 24 rooms in separate blocks, basic cabins with bunk beds and bath, a dining room/lodge, and newer rooms with queen size bed (some with views of volcano), double, or triple, private bathroom, hot water showers, price pp, inc taxes and meals, depending on size of group, children under 3 free, 3-10 half price; 1-day tour from San José US$60; spectacular views of volcano across valley of Río Agua Caliente and of Lake Arenal, good walking, riding and bird watching in the area, fishing with guide on the lake US$100 for 2 people. Also offers trips to Caño Negro with experienced naturalist, and hiking to Monteverde. On the N side of the lake about 2 km off the paved road from Fortuna (4WD required) is the more comfortable **L3-B** *Arenal Lodge*, meals extra, good food, 6 rooms with bath, 12 junior suites, cheaper rooms have no views, 5 chalet duplexes on ridge above lodge, great views, T 228-3189, F 228-6798, viewing deck, fishing trips arranged on the lake. **A3** *Arenal Vista Lodge*, 25 rooms with bath, arranges boat trips, riding and hiking, T 220-1712, F 232-3321. **B** *Mirador Los Lagos*, T 479-9126, 8 cabins with volcano view, 8 tents, sleep 4, **C**, camping areas, day visits US$3, excellent food and spectacular views of the volcano over the lake with a campsite. About 4 km from Fortuna on the road to Lake Arenal, turn at sign on left side of the road 'Bienvenidos a Junglas y Senderos Los Lagos'. Site is 2 km

uphill, very steep, good facilities, **G** pp, tours to hot springs at night. This is one of the best places to watch the volcanic activity at night. **C** *La Catarata Ecotourist Lodge*, 2 km W of La Fortuna on road to volcano, 6 cabins, bathroom, one of 3 lodges run by community association and supported by WWF Canada and CIDA Canada. 6 km from Arenal is **C** *Hospedaje La Ceiba*, overlooking Lake Arenal, good, helpful, great panoramic views, good breakfast. **Camping:** is possible on edge of lake, no services but good view of volcano at night, 500m past Park entrance on road to *Arenal Observatory Lodge*, take dirt road to right, 500m to lake where locals also camp.

● **Tour companies & travel agents** There are several tour agencies offering night tours to Arenal volcano and thermal baths, a typical 4-hr tour costs US$25 pp for volcano view, balneario or river hot waters, entry to park to see the lava, soft drinks and transport, hotel pickup, sometimes at 0300-0400 to be sure you see the lava. *Celin's*, in front of *Hotel Fortuna*, is rec, runs day and night tours to the volcano, inc boat on the lake and baths. The entry fee to the baths may not be inc in your tour price, check. You leave Fortuna at about 1815 and return by 2200.

The S side of the lake is very difficult to drive, with many fords; it is possible to get a boat from the dam across the lake to Río Chiquito then hike to Monteverde, or a more direct route is to hike up the Río Malanga.

FORTUNA TO MONTEVERDE

There is a road round the N of the lake, mostly paved, which leads to Tilarán. If driving yourself, you can get from Fortuna to Monteverde via Tilarán in a day, but set out in good time to avoid driving after dark. The lakeside road is frequently impassable because of fallen bridges and landslides (check before setting out), and the last 10 km just before Arenal village are rough although passable with high clearance vehicles all year (partly paved but in bad condition). An alternative route is to take the road from Fortuna to **San Rafael de Guatuso**, which runs parallel but further N. There is a 'voluntary' toll of US$1 between Jicarito and San Rafael for reconstruction work on this road. You can come back to the lake either by turning off before San Rafael through Venado (where there are caves), or from San Rafael itself, where there are a couple of basic hotels. Both roads are unpaved and very slow, 20 kph maximum speed in a car, but go through lovely countryside with beautiful views, especially when you approach the lake.

3 km from Colonia Río Celeste near San Rafael de Guatuso is the **B** *Magil Forest Lodge*, set in 800 acres on the foothills of the 1,916m volcano **Tenorio** (now a national park, 10,000 ha). The *Lodge*, inc meals, has 10 rooms with private bath. If you continue along the road from San Rafael NW towards the Nicaraguan border you come to **Upala** (airport, Sansa flights Tues, Thur, Sun) and Caño Negro. There is now a direct bus from San José to Upala (from Av 5, C 14 at 1445, 4 hrs, US$2.80), where there are the *Hotel Rigo*, *Hotel Upala*, T 470-0169, *Pensión Isabella*, **F** *Pensión Buena Vista*, basic, food available. Nearby is **A1** *Los Ceibos Lodge*, **B** without meals, T 228-0054, private reserve, riding US$6/hr, tours to Caño Negro, Río Celeste and Volcán Tenorio.

The San Rafael-Arenal road joins the lakeside road just N of Arenal town; no signs if driving from Arenal to San Rafael, it is just a track. If you turn left about 4 km out of San Rafael before the river, 4WD necessary, you come to the Guatuso Indian villages of Tonjibe, Margarita and El Sol.

ARENAL

Arenal is a pleasant little town, 20 km along the lake from the volcano, with wonderful views. 4 km E of the town is **Arenal Botanical Gardens** (T 695-5266 ext 273, F 695-5387), opened in 1993, hours 0900-1600 (closed Oct), US$3.50, with many flowers, birds, butterflies, a delightful place (still under development). Luis Diego Murillo, T 695-5008, operates sightseeing tours around the lake and the volcano.

• **Accommodation A2** *Joya Sureña*, T 694-4057, F 694-4059, 28 rooms, working cattle farm, riding, gym, sauna, pool; 10 km from Arenal towards Tilarán, **A3** *Hotel Pequeña Helvecia*, Swiss-owned, clean, pool, good food; 2 km W of the gardens is **B** *Villa Decary*, F 694-4086, 5 rooms and a bungalow for rent; **C** *Hotel-Restaurant Lajas*, breakfast inc but served too late for first bus to Fortuna at 0700, excellent restaurant, good service; **B** *Chalet Nicolás*, T 694-4041, bed and breakfast (a speciality), run by retired Americans, hot water, friendly, rec, 2 km from the centre towards Tilarán; **D-E** *Cabinas Rodríguez*, clean, friendly. There is also a campsite on Lago Coter, N of Lake Arenal. The **A2-C** *Lago Coter Eco-Lodge*, is popular with birdwatchers, 19 rooms in main building with shared bathrooms rather grim, or 16 brighter cabins with private bath and newer furniture, family-style meals, bar, pool table, games, lots of tours, watch out for snakes on roads and paths, canopy tour with platforms in the forest, T 257-5075, F 257-7065 in San José.

• **Places to eat** *Pizzería e Ristorante Tramonti*, T 695-5266, ext 282, for Italian cuisine, good.

• **Banks & money changers** Banco Nacional.

• **Sports Fishing**: several places rent fishing tackle, but if you want a boat, guide and full package try *Rainbow Bass Fishing Safaris*, run by Dave Myers, US$200 a day for 2 anglers, fishing licence US$30 for 2 months, PO Box 7758-1000, San José, T 229-2550, 222-834, F 235-7662. **Windsurfing**: the *Tilawa Windsurfing Center* is on the W side of the lake, which is the best side for windsurfing; mornings are best, particularly Dec-Jan, equipment for rent.

• **Transport** Frequent buses to Tilarán.

From Arenal, the lakeside road is good, paved, with fine views, 25 km to Tilarán.

TILARAN

Tilarán is a modern town. Tourist office ½ block from plaza, on right side of church. Cata Tours have a branch office in Tilarán, T 695-5953, offering several excursions and pickup from Cañas-Liberia area hotels.

• **Accommodation B** *Mystica Resort*, F 695-5387, hillside cabins overlooking Arenal lake, windsurfing equipment rental; **B** *Cabinas Naralit*, T 695-5393, S of church, clean, new buildings; **B** *The Spot Tourist Center*, Tilarán, 16 rooms with bath, restaurant, fishing, horses, day trips, T 695-5711, F 695-5579; **D** *Cabinas El Sueño*, T 695-5347, rooms around central patio, hot water, quiet, friendly, rec; **D** *Cabinas Mary*, T 695-5470, with bath, small pleasant rooms upstairs rec; **E** *Lago Lindo Lodge*, same street as *El Sueño*, comfortable, bright and friendly; **E** *Surf* (Youth Hostel), small, clean, very friendly; **E** *Tilarán*, with shower, cheaper without, clean, friendly, restaurant; **F** *Central*, T 695-5363, with shared bath (more with), noisy. Other hotels in the area. **B** *Rock River Lodge* on the road skirting the lake, 6 rooms with bathroom, restaurant, T 222-4547; **C** *Puerto San Luis Lake Resort*, 15 rooms with private bathroom, refrigerator, TV and fan, restaurant, boat rentals, fishing equipment, windsurf boards, trips to Arenal volcano and lake, T 695-5950. Nearby, **B** *Bahia Azul*, T 695-5950, with breakfast, fan refrigerator, TV. The office of the *Albergue La Casona del Lago* (affiliated to the Youth Hostel network), on the left hand corner (with public phone) of first main junction as you come into town from the lake, has windsurfing equipment, very helpful.

● **Buses** Direct bus from San José, 4 daily, 4 hrs, from C 14, Av 9-11, T 222-3854, and 5 daily buses from Cañas. Two daily buses to San Carlos via Fortuna. To Fortuna, 3 hrs, US$3. Daily bus to Santa Elena (for Monteverde), 1230, 3 hrs, US$1.50. Tilarán-Puntarenas 0600, 1300, 3 hrs, US$3. If you get the 1230 bus Tilarán-Liberia you can get from there to the Nicaraguan border before it closes.

To get to Monteverde (2-3 hrs, 4WD rec), go through the town until you come to a T-junction opp a green house, go left and follow paved road to Quebrada Grande. As you enter Quebrada Grande, take the unpaved road to the left before the church, it is very rough. At Dos de Tilarán is a sign: 30 km to Monteverde, follow this road to Cabeceras. There the road forks, take either the left, longer route via Nubes, or right, down dale and uphill, both poor, to Santa Elena (9 km) and thence to Monteverde.

The Northwest

THE ROUTE OF the Pan-American Highway passes near the cloud forest of Monteverde in the Cordillera de Tilarán, the marshes of the Palo Verde National Park, the active Volcán Rincón and the dry tropical forest of the Santa Rosa National Park on the Pacific coast as it crosses the great cattle haciendas of Guanacaste.

The Pan-American Highway from San José descends from the Meseta Central to **Esparza**, an attractive town with a turbulent early history as it was repeatedly sacked by pirates in the 17th century belying its peaceful aspect today. **E** *Hotel Castanuelas*, T 635-5105, a/c, quiet, cooler alternative to Puntarenas; **F** pp *Pensión Córdoba*, clean and modern.

The stretch of the Highway between San Ramón and Esparza (34 km) includes the sharp fall of 800m from the Meseta Central. (Beware of fog on this stretch if driving or cycling.) Beyond Esparza there is the *Bar/Restaurant Mirador Enis*, a popular stopping place for tour buses et al, service station opp, fruit stalls nearby, before a left turn at **Barranca** for Puntarenas, 15 km. In Barranca there is **D** *Hotel Río Mar*, with bath, restaurant, good. If going from San José to Monteverde, it is possible to change buses in Barranca, rather than going all the way to Puntarenas, if you leave the capital before 1230.

PUNTARENAS

(Pop 50,000) **Puntarenas** is on a 5 km spit of land thrusting out into Nicoya Gulf and enclosing the Estero lagoon. This is a run-down neglected town typical of small tropical ports. There are, however, plans for a face-lift. It is hot (mean temperature 27°C), the beaches are dirty, and are crowded on Sun. There is a public swimming pool on the end of the point (US$1 entrance), very hot. Good surfing off the headland. Across the gulf are the mountains of the Nicoya Peninsula. In the gulf are several islands, the Islas Negritos, to which there are passenger launches. The chief products around Puntarenas are bananas, rice, cattle, and coconuts. Puntarenas is being replaced as the country's main Pacific port by Caldera.

Places of interest
Museum of Marine History and the City of Puntarenas, in the Cultural Centre by the main church and tourist office; open 0900-1200, 1300-1700 daily, US$0.60.

Excursions
Crossing to Nicoya Peninsula see page 1098.

Isla San Lucas was a prison island, but a luxury resort has now been built. You may visit its beautiful beaches on

Sun. Launch leaves Puntarenas Sun 0900; returns 1500, US$1.50.

Isla Jesuita, in Gulf of Nicoya has an hotel: *Hotel Isla Jesuita*, lodge and cottages, hammocks reached by hotel's boat or public launch from Puntarenas. Package rates from San José, also arrangements can be made in the USA T 800-327-9408.

Isla Gitana, 13 km SW of Puntarenas has 2 rustic cabins, **A3** pp inc meals, tropical paradise island, white sand beach, lots of wildlife, swimming pool, kayaking, windsurfing. The lodge can arrange speed boat transfers from Puntarenas or meet the Puntarenas-Paquera launch. Contact Linda Ruegg, T 661-2994.

On the old San José-Puntarenas railway, near the new port of Caldera, is **Mata de Limón**, which has a beach. It is on a lagoon surrounded by mangroves, peaceful. Bus from Puntarenas market every hour (marked to Caldera). Accommodation: **E** *Casablanca*, C 2-4, Av 14, T 222-2921, full board available, or cabins; **E** *Manglares*, nr former train stop, reasonable, good restaurant; excellent bar/restaurant next to railway booking office. South of the village (care when crossing wooden bridge at night, missing planks!) there are several basic places to stay, **F**, but acceptable: *Viña del Mar*, *Villas Fanny*, *Villas América*. Good fishing nearby.

Local festivals

Fiesta de la Virgen del Mar, Sat closest to 16 July, carnival and regatta of decorated fishing boats and yachts.

Local information
● **Accommodation**

A3-B *Tioga*, Barrio El Carmen (T 661-0271), beachfront and C 17, with bath, hot water, inc continental breakfast, swimming pool, friendly, very good indeed; **C** *Colonial*, C 72-74, Av Central, a/c, swimming pool, with breakfast, T 661-1833, very friendly, comfortable, a bit run down, some distance from the centre of town; **B** *Porto Bello*, C 68 y 70, Av Central, next door, with bath, a/c, pool, quiet, clean, gardens, excellent food, helpful Italian owner, T 661-1322; *Yacht Club*, T 661-0784, at Cocal, caters for members of foreign yacht clubs. Others are **C** *Chorotega*, C 3, Av 3, T 661-0998, with bath and fan, **D** without, although price list disagrees with what they actually charge, clean, central (1 block E of river); **C** *Las Brisas*, on the waterfront, Paseo Los Turistas Al Final, with bath, good restaurant, swimming pool, T 661-2120, but reservations reported not honoured; **C** *La Punta*, Av 2, C 6-8, T 661-0696, 1 block from car ferry, with bath, friendly, clean, hot water, restaurant, secure parking, pool, American-owned, big rooms; **D** *Cabinas Los Jorón*, C 25, 7 blocks from ferry, T 661-0467, roomy, fridge, a/c, restaurant, rec; **D** *Las Hamacas* on waterfront, T 661 0308, nice rooms but noisy; **D** *Viking*, C 32, Av 2, new, on the beach; **E** *Ayo Can*, C 2, Av 1-3, a little noisy but clean; **E** *Cayuga*, C 4, Av Central, with shower, a/c, restaurant, dirty, run down; **E** *Gran Imperial*, 500m from station on road to town, friendly, hot water, private bath; **E** *Río*, Av 3, C Central/2, nr market, Chinese owners, with shower, basic and noisy, but friendly; **F** *Cabezas*, Av 1, C 2-4, with fan, cheaper without, basic, clean, very good value, rec; **F** *Miramar*, also nr market, fan, good deal; **F** *Monte Mar*, opp *El Fela Bar*, clean, small rooms, thin walls, shared bath; *Cabinas Thelma*, very good, friendly (ask at Holman Bar, C 7). Many *cabinas* on Av 2. Apartments for rent from Jacob Puister, Contigua Casino, Central, p 2, T 661-0246, US$37 for 2 weeks. Accommodation difficult to find Dec-April, especially at weekends.

At Roble, 18 km E of Puntarenas, on the coast: **L3** *Caribbean Village Fiesta*, T 663-0808, F 663-1516, all-inclusive, 174 rooms with bath, a/c, cable TV, 3 pools, boat rentals, restaurants, tennis, casino; **B** *Villa del Roble*, by the sea, T 663-0447, 5 rooms, quiet, small pool, charming; **B** *Casa San Francisco*, T 663-0148, nr regional hospital, run by 2 Canadian ladies, with breakfast, pool, friendly, clean, laundry facilities, helpful, rec.

At San Isidro de Puntarenas: **D** *Cabinas Orlando*, with bath and kitchen; *San Isidro Hotel and Club* has a Youth Hostel, **E**, T 233-2244, F 221-6822.

● **Places to eat**

Next to *Hotel Tioga* is *Aloha Restaurant* (pushy waiters). *Mariscos Kahite Blanco*, C 17, nr launch, excellent seafood; *Kahite Negro*, next door, good local food; *Casa de Mariscos*, C 7, Paseo de los Turistas, good seafood, reasonable prices. A number of Chinese restaurants on the main street (eg *Mandarín*, good value). Good food from market stalls, eg *sopa de carne*. *Fonda Brisas del Pacífico*, nr wharf, good value *casado*. *Soda Vanessa*, Av 1, clean, cheap, good breakfast for under US$1. There is a lively night life in the cheaper bars. On the beach, *Miramare*, C 17-19, good but expensive; nearby, C 19-21, is *Bierstube*, good for sandwiches, hamburgers, but beware overcharging. Rec bars: *Pier 14*, nr wharf, good pizza and hamburgers made by Captain Ed from Mobile (Alabama) and his wife; *Yate Bar*, friendly, English-speaking owner. *El Fela* bar, opp Banco Anglo Costarricense, clean, cool, a must for women just to see the toilet decor. At Roble *María Vargas*, bar and restaurant, friendly, good food, reasonable prices.

● **Banks & money changers**
Banco Nacional changes TCs, but painfully slow service.

● **Post & telecommunications**
Post Office: nr church on C 5, beach side, hard to find.

Telecommunications: ICE and Radiográfica.

● **Shopping**
Market, shops and banks on C Central, opp end to beach.

● **Tour companies & travel agents**
Turisol Travel Agency, C 1, Av 3, T 661-1212. For boat excursions (sailing or motor boats) from Puntarenas call Cath Mercer T 232-1020 at ASICS tours in San José. See under San José **Travel agents** for cruises in the Gulf of Nicoya.

Warning Thieves abound on the beach.

● **Buses**
Bus terminal for San José is at Av 4, C 2-4. Buses every 20 mins 0400-2100 to San José, 2 hrs, US$2.50. Daily bus to Santa Elena for Monteverde, see page 1087. Buses S to Quepos from around corner from San José terminal, 0500, 1100 and 1400 (high season) via Jacó, US$2.50, 3½ hrs. Several daily to Liberia from 0530, US$1.50, 3 hrs. Good café at bus terminal where you can await your bus. Tourist information office has up to date bus timetables.

MONTEVERDE

To visit the Monteverde Cloud Forest Reserve, follow the Pan-American Highway NW to km 149, turning right just before the Río Lagarto. Continue for about 40 km on mostly gravel road (allow 2½ hrs) to Santa Elena. Parts of the road are quite good, but in wet weather 4WD is recommended for the rough parts. Check that your car rental agreement allows you to visit Monteverde. A 33 km shorter route is to take the Pipasa/Sardinal turn-off from the Pan-American Highway. At the park in Sardinal turn L, then go via Guacimal to the Monteverde road. The bus from Puntarenas goes via Km 149.

SANTA ELENA

Santa Elena is a charmless place 2½ km before Monteverde village, but it is cheaper here than staying nearer to the Reserve. Next to the clinic is a Serpentarium, open daily 0700-1600, US$5. Banco Nacional, open 0900-1500, will change TCs with commission.

● **Accommodation** **B** *Finca Valverdas*, 300m E of Banco Nacional, T 645-5157, with bath, nice gardens for birdwatching, bar, restaurant; **B** *Sunset Hotel*, 1½ km on road to Tilarán, T 661-3558, on top of hill, nice location, friendly, clean, warm showers, good breakfast, German spoken; **C** *Arco Iris*, 100m N of Banco Nacional, with bath, restaurant, horses for rent, plenty of parking, T 645-5067, F 645-5022; **C** and up *Bed and Breakfast Marbella*, 10m E of National Bank, T 645-5153, owned by Carmen Acosta and Pablo Comancho, rooms without and with bath, without and with breakfast, warm, spacious, comfortable, hospitable, rec, hot water; **C** *Monte Los Olivos Ecotourist Lodge*, 6 km N of Santa Elena on road to Quebrada Grande, 4 cabins with private bathroom, 5 with shared bathroom, one of 3 lodges run by community association and supported by WWF Canada and CIDA Canada); **C** *El Gran Mirador San Gerardo*, T 645-5087, 6 km N of Santa Elena, dirt road, May-Nov you probably need a horse, cabins with bath or dormitory accommodation (E), restaurant, own private rain forest park for birdwatching nearby; **D** *Pensión Tucán*, T 645-5017, bargain for lower price in off season, with bath in nice rooms, or E in basic cabins with shower (supposedly hot), friendly management, good breakfast and restaurant rec but closed Sun lunch; **E** *Pensión Santa Elena*, T 661-1151, cheaper for YHA members, pleasant, clean, good food, vegetarians catered for, unlimited free coffee (C inc 3 meals); **F** *Canopy Tour Base Camp*, clean, friendly, electric hot shower, free transport to Monteverde for guests, riding on healthy horse, US$5/hr, food average, but good *casado*; **F** *El Colibrí*, clean, friendly, timber built with balconies; **F** *Hospedaje el Banco*, family-run, friendly, clean, good information, English spoken, good breakfast; **F** *Pensión Cabinas Marín*, 500m uphill past the Agricultural College, spacious rooms, friendly; **E** *Pensión El Sueño* (The Dream), very friendly, hot shower, small but nice rooms, clean, car park, run by Rafa Trejos who does horseback trips into the mountains to see quetzals, etc, US$35.

Chunches, good Expresso bar and snacks, used books, magazines, laundromat, opp *Pensión Santa Elena*.

● **Buses** Bus from Puntarenas, daily at 1415, 2½-4 hrs, returns 0600, US$2.20, this bus arrives in time to catch a bus to Puerto Quepos for Manuel Antonio (the company has one new bus and one old bus, take the new, safer in many respects). See Monteverde **Transport**, below, for buses from San José. For an alternative route to Santa Elena from Arenal, see pages 1080-1083. Daily bus to Tilarán 0700, 3 hrs.

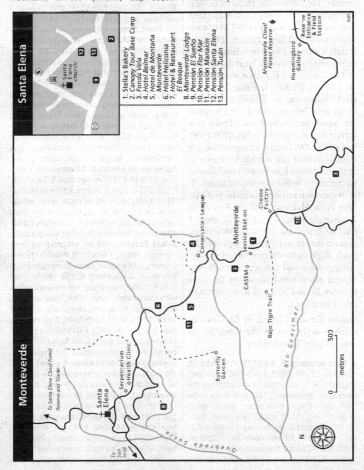

1. Stella's Bakery
2. Canopy Tour Base Camp
3. Fonda Vela
4. Hotel Belmar
5. Hotel de Montaña Monteverde
6. Hotel Heliconia
7. Hotel & Restaurant El Bosque
8. Monteverde Lodge
9. Pensión El Sueño
10. Pensión Flor Mar
11. Pensión Manakin
12. Pensión Santa Elena
13. Pensión Tucán

MONTEVERDE

The settlement at **Monteverde** was founded by American Quakers in the 1950s; it is strung out along the road without any centre. It is essentially a group of dairy farms and a cheese factory run by a cooperative, which you can tour. Excellent cheeses of various types can be bought, also fresh milk, ice cream and *cajeta* (a butterscotch spread) are sold. The Quakers have an English Library at Monteverde. The *Monteverde Butterfly Garden* is open daily, 0930-1600, US$5 inc guided tour, best time for a visit 1100-1300, beautifully presented large garden. They are mainly concerned with breeding and research and do not export. Near the Butterfly Garden is *Finca Ecológica*, entry US$5, open 0700-1700 daily, free map, bird lists, good birding and wildlife in this transitional zone between cloud- and tropical dry forest, guides available. There is a service station, open Mon-Sat, 0700-1800, Sun 0700-1200. Casem, a cooperative gift shop, is located just outside Monteverde on the road to the Reserve next to *El Bosque* restaurant. It sells embroidered shirts, T-shirts, wooden and woven articles and baskets. From Monteverde to the Reserve is a minimum 45 mins' walk uphill, about 4 km, but there are lovely views looking towards the sea and the Nicoya peninsula, particularly in the evening (when you are coming down and can appreciate them). Several places rent horses; look for signs between Santa Elena and Monteverde or ask at your hotel.

Galería Extasis, 250m S of *La Cascada*, exhibits sculptures by the Costa Rican artist, Marco Tulio Brenes.

• **Accommodation A2** *El Establo*, next to *Heliconia*, T/F 645-5033, F 645-5041, San José T 225-0569, 19 carpeted rooms with private bathroom, restaurant, 120-acre farm with 50% cloud forest, own nature guide, good birdwatching, riding stables, 35 horses, family-run, transport available, very accommodating, rec; **A2** *Monteverde Lodge*, T 800-633-4734 toll free in USA, T 645-5057 locally, F 645-5126, or book through Costa Rica Expeditions, T 222-0333, rec, restaurant, jacuzzi, daily slide shows 1815; **A2** *Sapo Dorado*, just before *Hotel de Montaña*, 10 suites with fireplace, good but expensive restaurant open 0700-2100, T 645-5010, F 645-5180; **A2-A3** *Belmar*, T 645-5201, F 645-5135, e-mail: Belmar@centralamerica.com, 300m from service station, Swiss chalet-style, beautiful views of Nicoya, restaurant, good, transport from San José available; **A3** *Cloud Forest Lodge*, 300m N of *Sapo Dorado*, T 645-5058, F 645-5168, 12 rooms with bath, restaurant, beautiful views (Canopy Tours, T 255-2463/645-5243, offer tours of 5 platforms, connected by steel cables, to explore the forest canopy, US$40 pp, at *Cloud Forest Lodge*); **A1-A2** *Fonda Vela*, T 645-5125, F 645-5119 (or San José T 223-1083, F 257-1416), e-mail: FondaVela@centralamerica.com, private bathroom, hot water, 25 rooms and suites in 7 cabins, nearest to Reserve, 25 mins' walk, on a 14-ha farm with forest and trail system, good birding, some camping, horses for hire, excellent restaurant (open to public), bar, TV room, art gallery; **A3** *Heliconia*, T 645-5109, F 645-5007, 100m before *Hotel de Montaña*, private bathroom, restaurant, very comfortable, excellent food, warmly rec; **A3** *Hotel de Montaña Monteverde*, T 645-5046, F 645-5320, in San José T 233-7078, F 222-6184, EP, just before service station on right, comfortable, rec, set meals, good, wholesome food, sauna, jacuzzi, horses for hire, good views of Nicoya, excellent birdwatching on 15-acre reserve, transport from San José available; **B-D** *El Bosque*, next to restaurant of same name, 21 rooms, T 645-5158, F 645-5129, hot showers, comfortable, clean, lovely rooms with fine views, safe parking; **C** *Villa Verde*, 2 km before reserve, rooms with hot showers, others with shared bath, cabins with kitchenette, inc good meals, restaurant, clean, nice, excellent views, T 645-5025, F 645-5115; **C** pp *Pensión Flor Mar*, T 645-5009, F 645-5088, between Monteverde and Reserve, full board, or E with breakfast in dormitory, hot shower, luggage stored, owned by Marvin Rockwell, one of the original Quaker settlers (he is a mine of information), small area for camping; **D** *Monteverde Inn*, T 645-5156, turnoff 100m before *Hotel de Montaña*, private bathroom, full board, good mattresses; **D** *Pensión Manakin*, just before *Hotel de Montaña*, turn right, drive 75m, T 645-5080, 6 cabins with bath or F with shared bath, 10% discount for students with ID, meals available (US$3-4), clean, friendly, good food.

Youth Hostel annex, E pp with breakfast, or full board, if not busy can arrange to use kitchen facilities, 800m off the main road at Cerro Plano, will collect you from bus station if you have reservation, transport to Reserve or Santa Elena, US$2 pp. Gary Diller, an American guide, highly rec, rents rooms in his house, **D**, T 645-5045, late afternoon, early evening, **F** *Hospedaje El Banco*, clean, shared bath, meals on request, non-smokers preferred; **F** pp *Pensión El Pino*, T/F 645-5005, opp *Hotel de Montaña Monteverde*, sleeps 12, hot water, English spoken by manager, Freddy Mejías, clean, secure, horse rental.

● **Places to eat** *Johnny's Pizza*, on main road between Santa Elena and Monteverde, wood oven-cooked pizzas, café, souvenir shop; *Restaurant El Bosque*, next to Casem Shop, good food, clean, open from 0630; between Gas Station and El Bosque, *La Cascada* and *Cerro Verde*; *Stella's Bakery*, opp Service Station, has good granola and cakes.

● **Language schools** A new language school, a branch of the **Centro Panamericano de Idiomas**, in Heredia, has opened, T 645-5026, accommodation with local families.

● **Transport Buses** Direct bus, Monteverde Express, runs from C 12, 125m N of Av 7, San José (4 hrs, US$5) daily at 0630 and 1430. Leaves from *Hotel Villa Verde* also at 0630, 1430. Calls at Santa Elena. Be early. Check times in advance, Sat bus does not always run in low season, T 645-5032 in Santa Elena, T 222-3854 in San José for information. Be aware that this service is not 'express', it stops to pick up passengers all along the route, and is not a comfortable ride. Alternatively, get the bus to Puntarenas and change there for Santa Elena, daily service at 1415, US$2.20. From Santa Elena to Puntarenas, 0600. Also to Tilarán, 0700, daily. **Taxis** available between Santa Elena and Monteverde, US$6.85, and between Monteverde and the Reserve, US$5.75 (hunt around for good prices). Not so easy to find a taxi for return trip, best to arrange beforehand. Road toll at Monteverde US$0.60.

MONTEVERDE CLOUD FOREST RESERVE

The 10,500 ha, private **Monteverde Reserve** (owned and managed by the non-profit research and educational association, the Tropical Science Centre) is mainly primary cloud forest. It contains over

400 species of birds (including the resplendant quetzal, best seen between Jan and May, which are the dry months, especially near the start of the Nuboso trail, 3-wattled bellbird and bare-necked umbrellabird), over 100 species of mammals (including monkeys, baird's tapir and six endangered cats: jaguar, jaguarundi, margay, ocelot, tigrillo and puma), reptiles, amphibians (including the golden toad, now thought to be extinct not having been seen since 1989). The reserve includes an estimated 2,500 species of plants and more than 6,000 species of insects. The best months are Jan to May, especially Feb, Mar and April. The entrance is at 1,500m, but the maximum altitude in the reserve is over 1,800m. Mean temperature is between 16° and 18°C and average annual rainfall is 3,000 mm. The weather changes quickly and wind and humidity often make the air feel cooler. The trails are in good condition and there are easy, short and interesting walks for those who do not want to hike all day. Trail walks take from 2 hrs to all day or more. Sendero Brillante is restricted. The Bajo Tigre trail (US$3.50) takes 1½ hrs, parking available with notice (T 645-5003) a guide can be arranged, no horses allowed on trail, open 0800-1600. There is a trail northwards to the Arenal volcano but not rec as very overgrown. Free maps of the reserve at the entrance and an excellent Nature Trail Guide. Follow the rules, sign the register, indicating where you are going in case you get lost, stay on the paths, leave nothing behind, take no fauna or flora out, no radios or tape recorders allowed.

The Reserve entrance is at the field station, 45 mins' walk from the settlement at Monteverde. The total number of visitors to the Reserve at any one time has been increased from 100 to 250, but be there before 0700 to make sure of getting in during high season (hotels will book you a place for the following day). Tour buses come in from San José every day and travellers have told us there is little chance of seeing any wildlife. Entrance fee US$8 (students with ID half-price) valid for multiple entry during the day, can not be purchased in advance; 3-day pass 20% discount. Reserve office open 0700-1630 daily; the park opens at 0600 and closes at 1700. Shelter facilities throughout the Reserve cost US$3.50 plus key deposit of US$5, bring sleeping bag and flashlight. You can make your own meals. Dormitory-style accommodation for up to 30 people at entrance, *Albergue Reserva Biológica de Monteverde*, T 661-2655, US$20 full board only. Reservations required for all Reserve accommodation (usually booked up by groups). A small shop at the office sells various checklists, postcards, slides, gifts and excellent T-shirts, the proceeds of which help towards the conservation project. Just before the Field Station is the **Hummingbird Gallery**, where masses of different hummingbirds can be seen darting around a glade, visiting feeding dispensers filled with sugared water, open 0930-1700. A small shop/photo gallery sells pictures and gifts. Slide shows daily at 1630 (3 times a week sometimes), US$3.70, T 661-1259 (photos by Michael and Patricia Fogden). There is also a slide show at *Hotel Belmar, The Hidden Rainforest*, by Bobby Maxson, 1930 daily except Fri.

Natural History walks with biologist guides, every morning and afternoon, 3-4 hrs, US$12 (children half price); reserve in advance at the office or at your hotel. If you use a private (non-Reserve) guide you must pay his entrance fee. An experienced and recommended guide is Gary Diller (Apdo 10165, 1000 San José, T 645-5045); he specializes in birds. There are six others operating, of varying specialization and experience. Tomás Guindon offers a night tour in the Reserve, 1900, T 661-1008. A guide is recommended if you want to see wildlife since the untrained eye misses a lot.

Recommended equipment includes binoculars (750s – 1040s), good camera with 400-1,000 ASA film, insect repellent, sweater and light rainwear. Rubber boots are a must for the longer walks, at all times of year but especially in the rainy season, and can be rented at the park office for US$0.80 or at hotels.

Donations to the Reserve can be made at the Reserve office or Tropical Science Centre (Apdo 8-3870, 100 San José, T 225-2649 or 253-3308, F 253-4963) at El Higuerón, 100m Sur y 125m Este, Barrio La Granja, San Pedro, or the Monteverde Conservation League (Apdo 10165, 1000 San José, T 661-2953), open 0830-1600, opp Monteverde service station. Donations are welcomed for purchasing additional land and for maintaining and improving the existing Reserve area. If you are interested in volunteer work, from non-skilled trail maintenance to skilled scientific assistance work, surveying, teaching or studying on a tropical biology programme, contact Polly Morrison at the Conservation League, or write to the address above. The Conservation League is working with schools in the area on education regarding conservation, forests, etc.

Adjoining the Monteverde Cloud Forest is the **International Children's Rainforest** (*El Bosque Eterno de los Niños*), established in 1988 after an initiative by Swedish schoolchildren to save forests. Currently at 32,000 acres, the land is bought and maintained with children's donations and the aim is to expand to include a further 14,000 acres. There are plans to bring school groups to the forest, but there are no trails open to the public so far.

Reserva Sendero Tranquilo, a private property near the Monteverde Cheese Factory arranges entrance reservations and guiding with owner David Lowther, or Julie Kraft, T 661-2754. Entry restricted to 12 people at any one time.

San Luis Biological Station and Ecolodge, T/F 645-5277, on 160 acres of farmland and cloud forest in the San Luis Valley, adjoining Monteverde Cloud Forest; **A2** pp, 5 cabins, horse riding, swimming in river and other options.

Monteverde Music Festival, classical and jazz concerts between Dec and Mar at sunset, at *Hotel Fonda Véla* (T 645-5125 for information), local and foreign musicians, entry US$9 (1996), T 661-2950; schedules and transportation from hotels.

An alternative trail network is in the **Finca Ecológica**, 2 km SW of Santa Elena, open 0700-1600. The trails are flat and there is good birdwatching and wildlife, US$3 entrance.

SANTA ELENA CLOUD FOREST RESERVE

1 km along the road from Santa Elena to Tilarán, a 5 km track is signposted to the **Reserve**, managed by the **Centro Ecológico Bosque Nuboso de Monteverde**. It is 83% primary cloudforest and the rest 17-year-old secondary forest at an elevation of 1,700m, bordered by the Monteverde Cloud Forest Reserve and the Arenal Forest Reserve. There is an 8 km path network and several lookouts where you can see and hear the Arenal volcano. The 'canopy tour' is rec, you climb inside a hollow strangler fig tree then cross between two platforms along aerial runways 30m up, good views of orchids and bromeliads, then down a 30m hanging rope at the end. There are generally fewer visitors here than at Monteverde. The Centro Ecológico Bosque Nuboso is administered by the local community and profits go to five local schools. It was set up by the Costa Rican government in 1989 with collaboration from Canada. The rangers are very friendly and enthusiastic. There is a small information centre where rubber boots can be hired. Hand-painted T-shirts for sale. Entrance US$6, students US$3, opens 0700-1600, T/F 645-5014 for information. It is a long, steep hike from the village, alternatively hire a taxi, carload US$6.50.

CONTINUING ON THE PAN-AMERICAN

43 km N of Barranca on the Pan-American Highway is the turn off for **Las Juntas**. This road is an alternative to route to Monteverde for those driving from the Tempisque ferry or Guanacaste; a third of it is paved. After Las Juntas, is the Abangares mining ecomuseum at **La Sierra de Abangares**, 0600-1800 daily, US$1.80.

47 km N of Barranca a L turn goes to the Tempisque ferry and after about 6 km a road off to the right at San Joaquín leads to the **A3** pp *Hacienda Solimar Lodge*, a 3,200-acre cattle farm with over half dry tropical virgin forest bordering Palo Verde National Park near Porozal in the lower Tempisque river basin. The freshwater Madrigal estuary on the property is one of the most important areas for waterbirds in Costa Rica, surrounded by gallery forest (only guests staying at the Hacienda can visit). Rec for serious birdwatchers. Reservations essential, T 669-0281 or contact Birdwatch, Apdo 6951, 1005 San José, T 228-4768, F 228-1573, 8 rooms with private or shared bathroom, inc meals, min 2 nights, transport available on request, local guide, horseriding.

CANAS

67 km N of Barranca is **Cañas**. Buses daily, every 2 hrs from 0830-1630 from C 16, Av 3-5, San José. Buses to Tilarán, Nuevo Arenal, past the volcano and on to San Carlos. The turn off for Tilarán is at the filling station, no signs. For a description of this route in reverse see pages 1078 1083. 5 buses a day to Tilarán, from the park, 30 mins, US$0,50, minibus US$1.

• **Accommodation & services D** *Cañas*, C 2, Av 1, with bath, clean, pleasant; **E** *El Corral*, C 4, Av Central, with bath; **E** *Gran*, with bath and fan, grubby; **F** *Guillén*, C Central, Av 2; also *Luz* and others; *Restaurant Panchitos* on main square is good and inexpensive. Good Chinese restaurants, eg *Central*, on main square, in centre of Cañas. 4 km N of Cañas is a hotel, **A1** *La Pacífica*, on Pan-American Highway, T 669-0050, F 669-0555, Swiss-run, with good restaurant, cottages, cabins, pool, and rafting down the Río Bebedero to Palo Verde. The property extends to 2,000 ha, of which half is a cattle farm and half dry, tropical forest. You can have a guided tour of the farm (US$10) and there is an extensive library on dry, tropical forests. The restaurant *Rincón Corobicí*, next to *La Pacífica*, clean and pleasant, has a small zoo and offers rafting down Río Corobicí, T 669-0544. If you turn N off the Panamerican Highway just after Corobicí, you will eventually come (58 km) to Upala (see page 1082). After 34 km you reach **Bijagua de Upala**, between the volcanoes Tenorio and Miravalles. The **C** *Bijagua Heliconias Ecotourist Lodge* is here, 6 cabins with private bathroom, one of 3 lodges run by community association and supported by WWF Canada and CIDA Canada.

● **Tour companies & travel agents**   Two local tour agencies are *Safaris Corobicí* (US$35 pp for 2 hr rafting, US$60 ½-day, T/F 669-1091, 669-0544) and *Transporte Palo Verde* (F 669-0544), run by Jay Thomas Connerly and Gregg Dean, offering bird watching, boat trips down the Corobicí, no white water but lots of wildlife, and Río Bebedero to Palo Verde, bicycling and other trips. Safaris Corobicí is 4 km past Cañas on the Pan-American Highway, 25 m before the entrance to Centro Ecológico La Pacífica; Transporte Palo Verde is in *Hotel El Corral* in Cañas on the Pan-American Highway.

PALO VERDE NATIONAL PARK

On the Nicoya Peninsula, is the **Palo Verde National Park**, over 5,700 ha of marshes with many water birds. Indeed, in the Laguna, over 50,000 birds are considered resident. Research Station, operated by OTS, T 240-5033, has accommodation facilities, ordinary visitors US$40 with meals, student researchers, US$22, senior researchers, US$32. Day visits with lunch, US$15, min 6 persons. Make advance reservations. Turn off the Pan-American Highway at **Bagaces**, half way between Cañas and Liberia, no public transport. The Palo Verde Administration offices are in Bagaces, next to service station, T 671-1062. Camping and possible lodging in park. Two ranger stations, Palo Verde and Catalina. Check roads in wet season, fantastic views from limestone cliffs.

If you turn N at Bagaces on Route 164 and drive through **Guayabo** (**E** *Las Brisas*, bath, hot water, fans), to Km 30, you get to *Parador Las Nubes del Miravalles*, T 671-1011 ext 280, home cooking for breakfast, lunch and dinner, tent and mattress rental, horse rental, good hiking to **Miravalles** volcano and waterfalls, very friendly and hospitable people on working *finca*, from here you can take a boat up the Río Pizote to Lake Nicaragua.

GUANACASTE PROVINCE

The Pan-American Highway runs for 125 km from Cañas to the Nicaraguan border. It passes through the lowhills of **Guanacaste** Province, which includes the Peninsula of Nicoya and the lowlands at the head of the gulf. The Province, with its capital at Liberia, has a distinctive people, way of life, flora and fauna. The smallholdings of the highlands give way here to large *haciendas* and great cattle estates. Maize, rice, cotton, beans and fruit are other products, and there is manganese at Playa Real. The rivers teem with fish; there are all kinds of wildlife in the uplands.

The people are open-handed, hospitable, fond of the pleasures of life: music, dancing (the Punto Guanacasteco has been officially declared the typical national dance), and merry-making (cattle and jollity often go together). There are many *fiestas* in Jan and Feb in the various towns and villages, which are well worth seeing. Rainfall is moderate: 1,000 to 2,000 mm a year, there is a long dry season which makes irrigation important, but the lowlands are deep in mud during the rainy season.

LIBERIA

(*Pop* 40,000) **Liberia** is a neat, clean, cattle town with a triangular, rather unattractive church in the most modern style and a small meticulous market (119 km from Esparza, 79 from Peñas Blancas). A well paved branch road leads SW into the Nicoya Peninsula. There is a tourist information centre, 3 blocks S of the plaza on C 1, look for signs on the main road, helpful, English spoken, leave donation as the centre is not formally funded, open 0900-1800, closed Mon (information however is not always accurate). In the same building

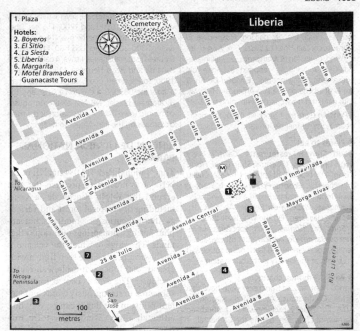

1. Plaza

Hotels:
2. *Boyeros*
3. *El Sitio*
4. *La Siesta*
5. *Liberia*
6. *Margarita*
7. *Motel Bramadero &*
   Guanacaste Tours

Liberia

is the **Museo del Sabanero** (Cowboy Museum), a poorly presented display of artefacts. Both museum and tourist centre are open 0800-1200, 1300-1600 Mon-Sat, entrance US$0.45. Social security hospital is quite good.

Local information
● Accommodation

A1-A2 *Las Espuelas*, 2 km S, good, a/c, satellite TV, swimming pool, round trip bus service from San José, day tour to San Antonio cattle ranch, US$60, American Express accepted (T 666-0144, F 233-1787; reservations, San José, T 293-4544, F 293-4839).

B *Boyeros*, on Pan-American Highway, T 666-0722, F 666-2529, pool, bath, restaurant; **B** *El Sitio*, just off highway on road to Nicoya, bath, a/c, good; **B** *La Siesta*, C 4, Av 4-6, with bath, clean, swimming pool, helpful owner who speaks English; **B-C** *Hostal Ciudad Blanca*, from Gobernación 200m S, 150m E, T 666-2715, 12 nice but dirty rooms, a/c, hot water, phone, TV, restaurant/bar, parking, rooster wake up call.

C *Bramadero Motel*, not all rooms have bath, open air restaurant and bar but somewhat noisy, swimming pool, Guanacaste Tours located here, T 666-0306; **C-D** *Casa Sinclair*, nr central park, Av Central-Av 2, with bath, fan, clean, good, early morning rooster call.

D *Guanacaste*, 4 blocks from plaza towards Pan-American Highway, 1 block S of San José bus station, 3 S of local terminal, friendly, clean, restaurant, safe parking, money exchange, camping area, English spoken, group discount, 15% student discount, rec, also has affiliated youth hostel annex, **D-E** to share 6-bedded room with own bath, T/F 666-2287; **D** *Intercontinental*, new, good; **D** *Liberia*, 50m from main square, with bath, **E** with shared bath, fans, clean, friendly, good information board and restaurant, laundry facilities, rec.

E *La Casona*, 300m S of Parque Central, T/F 666-2971, rooms for up to 5 people, shared bath, hot water, washing facilities, rooms facing street get very hot, owner José Alberto Chavarría has 2-person tent to rent, US$5/day; **E** *La Ronda* (about 2 km S on the Highway, T 666-0417), with bath, restaurant; **E** *Posada El Tupe*, C Central, 2 blocks S from square, cold shower, laundry facilities, clean, friendly, parking; *Hospedaje El Dorado*, contact *Hotel La Siesta*, C 4, Av 4-6, for booking, clean, fan; **E** *Margarita*, on La Inmaculada/Central, variously reported as "nice old house" and "filthy, not rec"; **E** *Motel Delfín*, 5 km N of Liberia on the Pan-American Highway, with bath, run down, large swimming pool.

F *Pensión Golfito*, 1 block NE of square, basic, clean, noisy, unfriendly, no fan.

● **Places to eat**
Good Chinese restaurants: *Cantón*, very good; *Chop Suey*, C Central; *Shan Ghai*; *Hong Kong*, 1½ blocks E of church, Chinese, cheap and cheerful. *Pronto Pizzeria*, C 1, Av 2-4, good food (not just pizzas) in a charming colonial house; *Pizzería da Beppe*, Av 0 y C 10, genuine clay oven. On the W side of the Plaza is *Soda Las Tinajas*, which specializes in *refrescos*; *Jardín de Azúcar*, just off plaza, self service, good variety and tasty; good coffee and fresh rolls at the bakery in the bus station.

● **Banks & money changers**
Banco Popular and **Bancrecer** both have Visa ATMs. **Credomatic**, Av Central, Mastercard ATM. For money exchange, ask around, eg *Restaurant Chun San*, behind the Cathedral.

● **Shopping**
Papers/books: *Mini Galería Fulvia*, in arcade at C Central y Av 3, sells *Tico Times*, English papers and books, English spoken, helpful.

● **Tour companies & travel agents**
Puntonorte Travel Agency, T 666-0363, Frente Banco Anglo. A rec guide for the nearby National Parks is Alejandro Vargas Rodríguez who lives in front of the Cruz Roja, T 666-1889.

● **Transport**
Air The Tomás Guardia International Airport at Liberia was reopened in 1992, revamped in 1995 and renamed Daniel Oduber Quirós Airport, after the former President who came from Guanacaste. The new runway can handle large jets and charter flights, and direct LACSA flights to Miami have been inaugurated. Local flight details under San José.

Buses The station for San José is at C 12, Av 3-5; regular Pulmitan de Liberia buses Liberia-San José, 8 a day between 0430 and 2000, 4 hrs, US$2.70, you can buy the ticket the day before from the office (blue house) diagonally opp bus terminal. Terminal for local buses C 12, Av 7-9. CNT bus Liberia-Peñas Blancas,

US$1.25, first bus at 0530, several daily, usually very crowded at 0900 and 1200, 1½ hrs. Liberia-Filadelfia-Santa Cruz-Nicoya, 14 a day between 0500-2030, 2 hrs, US$1.80, T 680-0111, Empresa Esquivel Liberia-Nicoya, 4 daily; to Playa Panamá and Playa Hermosa 1130, 1600 and 1900; to Playa de Coco 6 daily. To Puntarenas, 5 daily inc 0830. 9 a day to La Cruz and the Nicaraguan border. **NB** Not all through buses come into town but they all do stop at the main crossroads on the Pan-American highway.

RINCON DE LA VIEJA NATIONAL PARK

This National Park (14,084 ha, NE of Liberia) was created to preserve the area around the Volcán Rincón de la Vieja, including dry tropical forest and various geothermal curiosities: mudpots, hot sulphur springs, hot springs of various other kinds. The ridge of which the volcano is the highest peak can be seen from a wide area around Liberia; it is often shrouded in clouds. The area is cool at night and subjected to strong, gusty winds and violent rains; in the day it can be very hot, although always windy. These fluctuations mark all of the continental divide, of which the ridge is a part. From time to time the volcano erupts, tossing rocks and lava down its slopes. The last eruption was in November 1995. In the park are lots of birds including toucans, parrots, and also howler monkeys, armadillos and coatis. There are also lots of ticks and other biting insects. Horses can be rented from the park. The climb to the volcano requires camping near the top (need a tent), or at the warden's station, in order to ascend early in the morning before the clouds come in.

There are two ways into the park: the southern route, which has less traffic, goes from Puente La Victoria and leads to the Santa María sector, closest to the hot springs. In this part, you can stay for US$2.50 pp in an old, spacious, refurbished *hacienda* 2 km inside the park. Bring your own food and bedding, or camp. From the old *hacienda* you can hike to the boiling mudpots (Las

Santa Rosa National Park **1095**

Pailas) and come back in the same day; the sulphur springs are on a different trail and only 1 hr away. The northern route turns right off the Pan-American Highway 5 km NW of Liberia, through Curubandé. There is a morning and an afternoon bus from Liberia to Curubandé, but that leaves you with a 10 km uphill walk to the park. Beyond Curubandé, you cross the private property of Hacienda Lodge Guachipelin, US$1.80 to cross.

● **Admission** Entrance to park US$6. Camping costs US$1.70. To get there: a taxi costs US$20-30 one way from Liberia. The *Hotel Guanacaste*, will arrange transport for US$15, min 6 passengers, depart 0700, 1 hr to entrance, return 1700, take food and drink. You can also hitch, most tourist vehicles will pick you up. If you take your own transport you will need 4WD, although during the dry season a vehicle with high clearance is adequate.

● **Accommodation** B *Hacienda Lodge Guachipelin*, T 442-2848, F 442-1910, meals available, 10 rooms, naturalist guides, riding, hot springs, sulphur springs, mud pools, waterfalls (transport from Liberia arranged, US$16 pp round trip); F *Miravieja Lodge*, T 662-2004, Giovanni Murillo, rustic lodge in citrus groves, meals, transport and tours available. Also *Buena Vista Lodge*, T 695-6147, pickup arranged from Liberia. If you stay at the farm, B *Albergue Rincón de la Vieja* (affiliated to the Youth Hostel network) T/F 695-5553, inc food, pool, call the proprietor, Alvaro Wiessel, who will pick you up in Liberia. Also packages inc transport from San José. The *Albergue* is on the edge of the Park, there are horses for rent, guides, tours. From there it is 3¼ hrs to the volcano, 30 mins to Las Pailas, 45 mins to the thermal springs, Azufrales, 2¼ hrs to the Hidden Waterfalls.

20 km N of Liberia is Costa Rica's first commercial ostrich farm, blueneck and black breeds; T 228-6646/231-5068, Javnai Menahen for information on tours.

23 km N of Liberia, turn off NE to Quebrada Grande, 4 km from which is B *Santa Clara Lodge*, T 666-0473, F 666-0475, 4 rooms shared bath, 1 room with bath, cattle farm, riding, dry forest.

SANTA ROSA NATIONAL PARK

37 km N of Liberia, about half-way to the Nicaraguan border, is the **Santa Rosa National Park** (37,118 ha). Together with the Murciélago Annex, which lies N of the developed park, it preserves some of the last dry tropical forests in Costa Rica, and shelters abundant and relatively easy-to-see wildlife. They are also attempting to reforest some of the cattle ranches of the area (helped by the fact that cattle have not been profitable in recent years). During the dry season, the animals depend on the water holes, and are thus easy to find (except at the end of the season when the holes dry up). The tracks in the Park are wide with little shade; one hiker reports seeing more 4WD vehicles than animals. In the park is the Santa Rosa *hacienda* (*Casona*), at the start of the nature trail and close to the camp. The nature trail will give you a good idea of the wildlife in the Park in about 2 hrs. At the Casona, the patriots repelled the invasion of the filibuster Walker, who had entrenched himself in the main building. A **Museo Histórico de Santa Rosa** in the *Casona* is open daily 0800-1500. Look for the T shirts in the gift shop.

● **Admission** Entry US$6; camping US$2.15 pp.

● **Accommodation** There is a pleasant campground at Administration, about 7 km from the entrance with giant strangler figs that shade your tent from the stupendously hot sun, and very adequate sanitary facilities, picnic tables, and so forth. There is a small *comedor* for meals (breakfast 0600-0630, lunch 1100-1200, evening 1700-1800, good) and drinks near the camp ground but rec to bring some of your own supplies; a tent is useful: essential in the wet season. You can rent tents in Liberia for US$5/day with a US$100 deposit; ask at the tourist information centre. You may be able to sleep on the verandah of one of the scientists' houses. Bring a mosquito net and insect repellent. If the water is not running, ask at Administration. Take care, there are plenty of poisonous snakes.

● **Transport** Santa Rosa National Park is easy of access as it lies W of the Pan-American

Highway, about 1 hr N of Liberia. Any bus going to Peñas Blancas (from Liberia) on the Nicaraguan border will drop you right at the entrance at a cost of US$0.70, 30 mins. Last bus returns to Liberia at about 1800.

Michael Tesch and Leone Thiele of Cape Paterson, Australia, write "**Playa Naranjo** (12 km, 3 hrs' walk or more or use 4WD) and **Playa Nancite** (about the same distance from the entrance) are major nesting sites of Leatherback and Olive Ridley sea turtles. The main nesting season is between Aug and Oct (although stragglers are seen up to Jan regularly) when flotillas of up to 10,000 Ridley turtles arrive at night on the 7 km long Playa Nancite. Females clumsily lurch up the beach, scoop out a 2-ft hole, deposit and bury an average of 100 ping-pong-ball sized eggs before returning exhausted to the sea" (see also **Ostional**, page 1104). Playa Nancite is a restricted access beach; you need a written permit to stay there free, otherwise, US$1/day to camp, or US$1.50 in dormitories. Permits from SPN in San José, and the Park Administration building at Santa Rosa. Make sure you have permission before going, rangers may otherwise give you a hard time. Research has been done in the Playa Nancite area on howler monkeys, coatis and the complex interrelation between the fauna and the forest. No horses are available to rent. Playa Naranjo has good camping, drinking water and a barbecue. The beach is unspoilt and quiet and very good for surfing.

LA CRUZ

The last town before the border is **La Cruz**, with a bank (terribly slow service for exchange of cash or TCs) and hotels.

● **Accommodation A3** *Colias del Norte*, Ecological lodge 5 mins after La Cruz on Pan American Highway, Km 300, T 679-9132, rustic rooms with bath, transportation available; **E** *Cabinas Santa Rita*, nice, clean, secure, on main road, 200m from bus terminal; rec; **E** *Iguana*, S of Park, family run, view over the bay, good value; **F** *El Faro del Norte*, just off the Panamericana, without bath, friendly, pleasant,

clean; **F** *Pensión Tica*, without bath, dark, basic, no fan, mosquitoes. 16 km E of La Cruz is **A** pp *Hotel Hacienda Los Inocentes*, on slopes of volcano Orosí, inc meals, 11 rooms with bath, pool, horses, forest trails and guides, T 265-5484 or 679-9190. West of La Cruz, on Bahías Salinas looking over to Isla Bolaños, is *La Salinas Trailer Park y Cabinas*, drinking water, showers, toilets, tennis, barbecue, fishing boats and horses to rent, 1 km beach, T 233-6912, 228-2447, 228-0690, PO Box 449-1007, San José.

● **Places to eat** *Soda Estadio*, good, cheap; *Restaurant Mirador*, at the end of the only paved street, has superb views; *Ehecatl*, good fish and rice, also has lovely views over the bay. At nearby Ciruelas de Miramar, there is a good restaurant; *Palenque Garabito*; try their fried yucca.

Isla Bolaños is a 25-ha National Wildlife Refuge to protect the nesting sites of the brown pelican, frigatebird and American Oystercatcher. The island is covered with dry forest and you can only walk round the island at low tide. No camping allowed. The incoming tidal surge is very dangerous, be off the island before the tide comes in.

The border with Nicaragua is at **Peñas Blancas**.

FRONTIER WITH NICARAGUA – PEÑAS BLANCAS

● **Immigration**
Office hours 0800-1800 (Nicaragua 0900-1200 and 1300-1745). On leaving Costa Rica you have to go through two passport checks, trolley pullers charge US$0.50 to carry bags between these posts, a short distance. Entering Costa Rica here you must visit the Ministry of Health post and show anti-malaria tablets, you will be given a card which you must show the doctor if you become ill. Visa stamps, US$25, are given at the border, but officials may try to send you back to Rivas. Across the border, passports are inspected on the Nicaraguan side, then you must take the minibus to Sapoá, where entry formalities are carried out, 4 km away (US$0.65). Crossing to Nicaragua may be a slow process; if you arrive when a Tica or Sirca bus is passing through this is especially true (at least 3 hrs). If you have no outward ticket for Costa Rica, and are challenged, you can buy a cheap bus ticket back to Nicaragua at the border (valid for 1 year).

There is a duty free shop, a good bar and restaurant adjoining the Costa Rican immigration offices; a good free map of Costa Rica is available from the tourist office at the border (the desk opp the counter where one pays entry tax).

● **Crossing by private vehicle**
Entering Costa Rica by car, first pay your entrance stamp, then go to Aduana Permiso de Vehículo for your vehicle permit (state how long you want); at the Seguro Obligatorio window purchase insurance. Your vehicle is then briefly inspected before you can depart. Fumigation is free. Leaving by car, just hand over the printed vehicle permit you were given on arrival. For documents and other requirements, see under **Information for travellers – Documents**.

● **Exchange**
There is a bank (in *aduana*, usually changes cash, does not change TCs, open 0800-1200, 1300-1600) and a black market (good rates if you shop around; 'España' changes TCs at fair rates).

● **Transport**
There are several express or ordinary buses a day from/to San José, C 14, Av 3-5, 4 hrs or 6 hrs, US$5, only the earliest (at 0500) from San José will get you to the border before it closes). Only a few buses from La Cruz, US$0.60, taxi costs US$4-5.

The Nicoya Peninsula

FRINGED BY WHITE sand beaches, hilly and hot. Few towns and poor roads; a few large hotel resorts are increasingly taking over what were isolated coves; small reserves to protect wildlife and the geological formations of Barra Honda.

The Nicoya Peninsula can be reached by road via Liberia (bus Liberia-Nicoya, see page 1094); or one can take the Pan-American Highway to a point 62 km beyond Puntarenas, at a sign to Río Tempisque ferry. After crossing on this ferry (hourly 0630-2030, car US$2.40, bicycle or motorbike US$1, pedestrians US$0.20, queues of up to 1 hr on Sun) one can drive to Nicoya. Just across the river are **A2** *Hotel Rancho Humo* and **C** *Zapandi Lodge*, T San José 255-2463, boat trips on Ríos Tempisque and Bebedero, visits to Palo Verde and Barra Honda national parks. (At La Mansión junction there is a good restaurant, *Tony Zecca Ristorante Il Nonno*, sandwiches and steaks, reasonable prices, menu in six languages, interesting international visitor's book to sign, open Sun.) An 800m bridge is to be built across the river 5 km N of the present ferry (latest completion date 1998).

A third route is to take the Salinero car ferry from Puntarenas across the Gulf of Nicoya to Playa Naranjo, US$1.50 pp, US$3.35 for motorcycle or bicycle, US$8.50/car, 1½ hrs, crossings start at 0330 with 4 or 5 crossings a day, T 661-1069 for exact times. Snacks and drinks sold on the ferry. The ferry dock is about

1 km from Puntarenas bus station, local buses run between the two. Buses meet the ferry for Nicoya (through Carmona, 40 km unpaved, 30 km paved road, crowded, noisy, frequently break down, US$1.25, 2¼ hrs), Sámara (US$1.30), Coyote, Bejuco and Jicaral.

A fourth route is to take the launch from Puntarenas to Paquera (1½ hrs, US$2, 0615, 1100 and 1500, does not run in bad weather, has toilets, drinks and snacks). On arrival, get on the bus (which waits for the ferry) as quickly as possible (to Cóbano 2-3 hrs, US$1.25, bad road, to Montezuma US$2.60, 1½ hrs at least) pay on the bus, or get a taxi. Launch Paquera-Puntarenas (T 661-2830) at 0800, 1230 and 1700; tickets are sold only when the incoming boat has docked. In Puntarenas this boat docks in the canal N of the city centre; it is a 10-min walk due S to the bus terminal for San José.

Also, from Puntarenas to Paquera, *Hotel Playa Tambor* (see below) runs a vehicle ferry (hotel buses get priority), Naviera-Tambor SA, leaving Puntarenas 0415, 0845, 1230, 1730, leaving Paquera 0600, 1030, 1430 and 1915. All the beaches on the Nicoya Peninsula are accessible by road in the dry season. Most places can

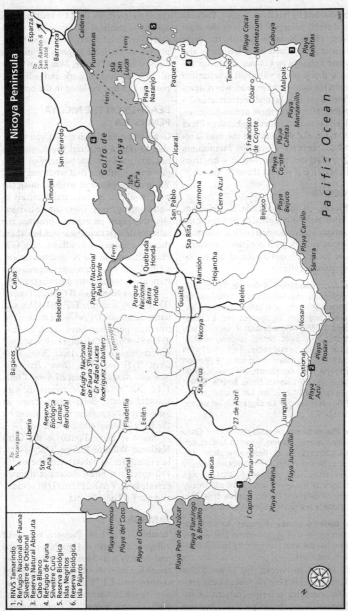

Nicoya Peninsula

1. RNVS Tamarindo
2. Refugio Nacional de Fauna Silvestre de Ostional
3. Reserva Natural Absoluta Cabo Blanco
4. Refugio de Fauna Silvestre Curú
5. Reserva Biológica Islas Negritos
6. Reserva Biológica Isla Pájaros

Pacific Ocean

Golfo de Nicoya

To Nicaragua

To San Ramón & San José

be reached by bus from Nicoya. **Paquera** is a small village 20 km along the coast from Playa Naranjo towards the main tourist areas. There are a few shops and some lodgings eg *Cabinas Rosita* on the inland side of the village. It is separated from the quay by a km or so, where apart from a good soda, one restaurnat and a public telephone, there are no facilities. There is no bus connection between Playa Naranjo and Paquera and the road is reported as barely driveable. Montezuma (popular) can be reached in 4 hrs from Puntarenas if you get the early launch.

NICOYA

Nicoya, on the Peninsula, is a pleasant little town distinguished by possessing the country's second-oldest church. The main square is leafy, with occasional concerts. Use the telephones on the square for international calls.

● **Accommodation B** *Curime*, T 685-5238, F 685-5530, with bath, TV, pool, volleyball, restaurant; **D** *Yenny*, with bath, T 685-5036, a/c, towels and soap, TV, spotless, rec; **E** *Chorotega*, T 685-5245, with bath (**F** without), very good, clean, quiet, clothes washing facilities; **E** *Las Tinajas*, nr bus station, T 685-5081 with bath, modern, clean, good value; **E** *Pensión Venecia*, opp old church, on square, good value, rec; **E/F** *Cabinas Loma Bonita*, behind hospital, T 685-5269, fans, bar, shaded parking; **F** *Ali*, dirty, avoid; **F** *La Elegancia*, on square, with bath.

● **Places to eat** A good restaurant is *Chop Suey* (Chinese); *Daniela*, breakfast, lunches, coffee, *refrescos*, good; *Restaurant Jade*, 1½ blocks behind church, Chinese, not rec; *Teyo*, nr *Hotel Yenny*, good, quick service. Opp *Chorotega* is *Soda El Triángulo*, good juices and snacks, friendly Hong Kong owners; *Café de Blita*, 2 km outside Nicoya towards Sámara, good.

● **Banks & money changers** Banks on the main square charge commission and are very slow, but the a/c is welcome; try *Soda El Triángulo*, see above.

19 km NE of Nicoya and 12 km SE of Santa Cruz, is **Guaitil**, where local artisans specialize in reproductions of indigenous Chorotegan pottery. They use the same methods used by Indians long ago, with minimal or no use of a wheel and no artificial paints. Ceramics are displayed at the local *pulpería*, or outside houses. At **San Vicente**, 2 km SE of Guaitil, local craftsmen work and sell their pottery at a new building in the centre.

BEACHES ON THE NICOYA PENINSULA

Generally, even in high season, you will be able to find a beautiful beach which is uncrowded. There are so many of them, just walk until you find what you want. You will see plenty of wildlife along the way, monkeys, iguanas and squirrels as well as many birds. There can be dangerous undertows on exposed beaches; the safest bathing is from those beaches where there is a protective headland, such as at Playa Panamá in the N. Beaches are described here working round the peninsula from where the car ferry docks in the Gulf.

At **Playa Naranjo** is **B** *Oasis del Pacífico* (**D** in rainy season), T/F 661-1555, a/c, bath, clean, quiet, pool, good restaurant, free transport from ferry, rec; **C** *El Paso*, T/F 650-0003, with bath, **D** without, cold water, clean, pool; *El Ancla*, 200m from ferry, T/F 661-4148; *Disco Bar Restaurante Maquinay*, past *El Paso*, T 661-1763, has a couple of rooms, **E** with shower, insects, Belgian-run, disco on Sun; several expensive eating places by the ferry landing, also a gas station.

North of Playa Tambor is the **Curú National Wildlife Refuge**. Only 84 ha, but five different habitats exist here with 110 species of birds. Access is through private land, T 661-2392/6392 in advance and ask for Doña Julieta.

TAMBOR

Tambor, 15km from Paquera, is a small village with a dark sand beach, some shops and restaurants. However, part of the beach has been absorbed by the large and controversial **L3** *Playa Tambor Beach Resort*, inc meals, 5-star, all amenities, tennis, pool, exercise room, TV, entertainment, bus from Montezuma stops outside gate, most people arrive by plane to the airstrip or by resort bus, T 661-1915, F 661-2069, Apdo Postal 771-1150, La Uruca, San José. Built around a cattle farm by the Barceló group, of Spain, the resort is alleged to have encroached on the public beach and drained a swamp which was a wildfowl habitat. A second stage is planned at Punta Piedra Amarilla, with 500-ship yacht marina, villas and a total of 1,100 rooms.

● **Accommodation** At Tambor, **C** *Dos Lagartos*, T/F 683-2036, cheap, clean, good value; **L3** *Tango Mar*, T 661-2798, 3 km from Tambor, all services inc golf course and its own spectacular waterfall; **L3** *Tambor Tropical*, T 381-0491, 3 km from Tambor airstrip, full services. The beach is beautiful: 14 km long, rolling surf, 1½ hrs on a boneshaking road from ferry; cruise ships from Puntarenas come here. On the beach, **D** *Cabinas Cristina*, with bath, cheaper without, good food; **D** *Cabinas del Bosque*, clean; **E** *Hotel Hermosa Playa*, basic but clean, shared bath, restaurant. Follow signs on main road as you enter town. *Bahía Ballena Yacht Club*, 15 mins' walk from Tambor, open in the high season only, friendly, free English book exchange, weekly traditional dances, good restaurant/bar, excellent place if you are looking for a crew position on a yacht June to Aug, many US craft here at that time. In the village, there is a shop with public phones, a supermarket, agency for bicycle hire, and a good American-owned restaurant on the jetty. Take a torch for returning to hotel at night.

Cóbano, near Montezuma, can be reached by bus from Paquera ferry terminal, and buses for Tambor, Cóbano and Montezuma meet the launches from Puntarenas (there is an airstrip, see **Internal Flights** San José). All roads out of Cóbano, N, W and S, require 4WD. Cóbano has a petrol/gas station.

MONTEZUMA

From Cóbano it is a ½-hr ride by taxi or hitch) to **Montezuma**, a very popular small village on the sea (hence noisy and not too clean). It has become very touristy and, in busy periods, hotels fill up every day, so check in early. Although it does get crowded, there are some wonderful beaches, many are rocky, with strong waves making it difficult to swim, but very scenic. There are beautiful walks along the beach, sometimes sandy, sometimes rocky, always lined with trees. There is a tourist information centre, Monte Aventuras, which is very helpful and often knows which hotel has space; ask here first before looking around (ask for Jaime or Rebeca). The once popular *Cabinas Karen* are now closed. Doña Karen died of cancer in October 1994. Prior to her death, she donated her land to the National Parks in memory of her late husband; it is called **Reserva Absoluta Olaf Wessberg**, not open to the public. Cabinas Karen now houses park guards.

Excursions Monte Aventuras centre hires bicycles, US$11/day and organizes tours, eg to Tortuga Island (1 hr away), white sand, palms, whole day with lunch and snorkelling, US$30; Sunset Cruise, US$17; 4-day, 3-night Ecotour to Curú, Arenal, Cano Negro and Barra Honda, US$180 pp inc transport, accommodation, breakfast, guides, minimum 6. Close to the village, 20 mins up the Montezuma river, is a beautiful, huge waterfall with a big, natural swimming pool (it's beyond a smaller waterfall). Intrepid walkers can carry on up to further waterfalls but it is very dangerous and fatal accidents have been reported. 6 km N of Montezuma is another waterfall with a pool right by the beach; the walk there passes Playa Cocal (huge, flat, sandy), and Playa Cocalito, where Sr Vásquez lives in a house with Cocalito written on the balcony and sells coconuts and mangoes in season. Horses for hire from the hotels, but carefully inspect that the horses are fit and not overworked, for the sake of the horses! Luis Angel hires horses for experienced or inexperienced riders, US$20 to waterfall, 4 hrs, along beach. Roger is good and takes care of his horses, contact him at the little white house opp the grocery store. You can change money at this store.

● **Accommodation A2** *El Jardín*, with bath, fan, ocean view, T/F 642-0025; **B-C** *Mangos*,

20 cabins, T/F 642-0259, clean, new; **B** *Los Caballos*, 3 km from Montezuma on road to Cóbano, T/F 642-0124, 8 rooms with bath, pool, outdoor restaurant, ocean views, gardens, 5 mins from beach, horses a speciality; **B** *Amor de Mar*, T 642-0262, lovely garden, breakfast and snacks available, clean, friendly, away from town, rec; **C** *Restaurant El Pargo Feliz*, has cabins with bath, and serves good food in a calm atmosphere; **C** *La Cascada*, near the river, past *Lucy's*, on the road to Cabuya, T 642-0057, with bath, fan, clothes washing facilities, restaurant; **C** *La Aurora*, run by Kenneth (German) and Angela (Costa Rican) Kock, 8 rooms with bath, fan, mosquito net, breakfast room, garden, hammocks, T/F 661 2320, also boat trips for fishing or snorkelling, overpriced; **B-D** *Alfaro*, prices vary according to demand, beware overcharging, rents tents (US$7 for 2), poor facilities but clean tents and mattresses; **D** *Cabinas Mar y Cielo*, with restaurant, good food, popular, has cabins for up to 8; **D** *Casa Blanca*, 3 rooms, fans, kitchen facilities, German-owned; **D** *Mochila Inn*, between *El Jardín* and *Cobano*, T 642-0030, cabins, clean, family-run, shared bath, hot water, use of family kitchen, keep food in your room away from marauding animals; **D** *Cabinas Las Rocas*, 20 mins S of Montezuma, good but quite expensive meals, small, seashore setting, isolated; 5 km S is **D** *Fernando Morales Cabins*; see also Cabuya below (these three places usually have space when other places are full); **D** *Montezuma Pacific*, bath, hot water, a/c, T 661-1122 ext 200; **D** *Hermanos y Hermanas de la Madre Tierra*, 2 km from village, camping F, American-run, higher up and cooler at night than on beach, vegan food, small portions, nice walks; **D** *Montezuma*, T 661-2472, next to *Mar y Cielo*, E in off season, with breakfast, balcony, private shower (cold) and fan, cheaper with shared bath, ask for sea view, large rooms (but some have cracked white asbestos wall covering), clean, restaurant (adds 23% tax and service), small book exchange; **E** *Pensión Tucán*, very clean, wood-panelled rooms, shared shower and toilet, fan, mosquito net on window, you may cook food, good value, rec; **E** *Lucy*, opp *Alfaro*, without bath, fan, mosquitoes, laundry facilities, sea views, friendly, follow road around the beach to the S, rec; **E** *Pensión Arenas*, on the beach, run by Doña Meca, basic but OK, without bath, with fan, friendly, cool, clean, also camping, but noisy cockerels at dawn; **F** *Cabinas Jenny*. A Danish family (ask for Inge and Jacob) lives a few km outside village and rents out rooms, good food, free horses.

● **Places to eat** Several restaurants, eg *Tutiles Spaghetti y Pizzas*, Italian, quite pricey, at back of village; next door to the *Cabinas Karen* (see below) there is the *Sano Banano*, a health food restaurant, good vegetarian food, large helpings, daily change of menu, milkshakes, fresh fruit and yoghurt, owned by Dutch/Americans, at night they show movies free if you spend over US$1.50 on food or US$1.25 pp (also has cabins on beach, **B**); *Burrito Bandido*, rec for good Mexican burritos, good value, big helpings; the *Soda*, by the *tienda* is good value, good breakfast, delicious shrimp and snapper; *El Jardín*, opp *Tucán*, vegetarian, good fruit juices; *Pizzería*, next to *Hotel Montezuma*, self service, good. Fruit and vegetable cars come to Montezuma.

● **Shopping** *Made in Costa Rica* souvenir shop, next to *Hotel Montezuma*, is good; a percentage of the profits goes to an ecological fund, inc clearing up the beach; also has book exchange.

● **Transport Buses** Montezuma-Paquera daily at 0530 and 1330, tickets available in advance from tourist information centre; be at bus stop in centre in good time as the bus fills up quickly, US$2.60, 1 hr 40 mins. Bus connects with boats to Puntarenas. **Taxi** Montezuma-Cóbano US$3.50; taxi Paquera-Montezuma US$12.

CABO BLANCO RESERVE

11 km from Montezuma is the **Cabo Blanco Reserve** (1,172 ha). Marine birds include frigate birds, pelicans and red-footed boobies. There are also monkeys, anteaters, kinkajou and collared peccary. Bathing in the sea or under small waterfall. Open 0800-1600 (closed Mon, Tues, entry US$6), jeep/taxi from Montezuma US$4.50-5, first at 0700, returns 1600. 6 km from the entrance is beautiful Playa Balsitas, where there are lots of pelicans and howler monkeys.

At **Cabuya**, 2 km from Cabo Blanco Reserve, the sea can be cloudy after rough weather. Cabuya Island can be visited on foot at low tide. On the road W out of Cabuya, *Cafetería El Coyote* specialises in local and Caribbean dishes, owners Wilfred and Jenny. This road goes beyond Cabuya to the attractive little village of **Mal País** on the W coast of the peninsula.

The coast here is virtually unspoilt with long white beaches, creeks and natural pools, just a few facilities, including a camping place.

● **Accommodation** 300m from the Reserve entrance is **F** *El Palenque*, camping, restaurant, American run, friendly, rec. **B** *Cabo Blanco*, Cabuya, T 284-4323, 10 rooms with bath, with breakfast, fan or a/c, pool; **C** *Cabinas y Restaurante El Ancla de Oro* (also some at E), T 642-0023, F 642-0025, some cabins with bath, others shared bathroom, seafood restaurant, lobster dinners US$10, filling breakfasts, owned by Alex Villalobos, horses US$20/day with local guide, Mountain bike rental, transport from Paquera launch available. At Mal País, **A2** *Star Mountain Eco-Resort*, T 642-0024, with breakfast, horseriding, owners Laura and Bill Clay, will meet visitors at Tambor, Cobano or Montezuma airstrips; **C** *Cabinas Mar Azul*, run by Jeannette Stewart, camping possible, T 642-0298, delicious fried fish, shrimp, lobster. Also a pleasant motel, **D** *Cabañas Bosque Mar*, T 661-3211, clean, large rooms, hot water shower, attractive grounds, good restaurant on beach nearby, 3 km to Cabo Blanco Reserve. Continuing N along the coast, the next beach is **Playa Santa Teresa** with **A3** *Tropico Latino Lodge*, T/F 642-0062, e-mail: Tropico@centralamerica.com, bamboo-decorated rooms, restaurant, pool, Italian run, good value, the manager is a keen surfer and can give you information on the best spots.

SAMARA

The beach at **Sámara**, 37 km from Nicoya on a paved road, is recommended as probably the safest major bathing beach in Costa Rica. The litter problem is being tackled with litter bins, warning signs, refuse collection and bottle banks on **Playa Carrillo** which is 5 km away at the S end of the beach. Both places have airstrips served by scheduled services from San José.

● **Accommodation & places to eat** **L3** *Guanamar Beach Resort*, on hill at end of Playa Carrillo, T/F 686-6501 (or T 293-4544, F 239-2000 San José), beautiful view from bar, pool, satellite TV, horseriding, sport fishing; **A1** *Las Brisas del Pacífico*, bungalows with a/c, hotel rooms with fan, **A3**, T 680-0876, hotel part on hill, beautiful grounds, direct access to beach, pool, expensive restaurant,

German-owned; **A2** *Isla Chora*, tourist complex with 10 bungalows and 4 fully-equipped apartments, a/c, pool, T 253-0182, F 224-4965 (San José); **A3** *Mirador de Sámara Aparthotel*, T 656-0044, F 656-0046, owned by German Max Mahlich, 6 apartments each sleep 5, information on tours and boat trips, some run by Max, restaurant; **A3** *Condominios Fénix*, on beach, fans, hot water, pool, friendly, T 656-0158, F 656-0162, or in San José on T 255-1592, F 255-0061; **B** *Marbella*, German-run, beautiful grounds, pool, good service, about 300m from beach, rec; **C** *Belvedere*, German-owned, small rooms, but very clean; **C** *Cabinas Bellavista*, horses for rent; **C** **D** *Cabinas Cecilia*, excellent food; **D** *Cabinas Arenas*, comfortable, cheaper for longer stays, good restaurant opp, pleasant bar next door; **D** *Cabinas Yoice*, with bath, kitchen, friendly; **E** *Guesthouse Pericos*, helpful, shared kitchen, luggage store; **E** *Mirador*, opp Marbella, German-owned, bargain price off-season, use of kitchen; **E** *Cabinas Atenas*, nr bus stop, rooms upstairs with fan best; **E** *Cabinas Los Almendros*, on beach, restaurant, disco Sat; **E** *Cabinas Punto*, Sámara; **E** *Doña Marta*, on beach, with bath, not too clean, camping allowed in garden US$0.75; next door is *Camping Coco*, clean, with showers, lights in trees, good for hammocks, US$2.50, rec, occasionally noisy, good restaurant behind; *Restaurant Mirador*, best seafood in town. There is another good restaurant on the beach with a fishing boat outside: *Bar El Ancla*, in front of Doña Marta, good, local food; *Bar La Góndola*, in centre of village.

● **Transport Air** Sansa operates flights Mon, Wed and Fri from San José; Travelair to Playa Carrillo, Wed, Sun.

Buses From Nicoya, US$1.15, 1½ hrs, twice daily 0700 and 1530. Express bus to San José daily at 0400; from San José, C 14, Av 3-5, at 1200, T 222-2750. It is not possible to go S from Sámara along the coast to Montezuma, except in 4WD vehicle; not enough traffic for hitching.

NOSARA

North of Sámara is **Nosara**, with 2 beaches, Guiones, which is safe for swimming, and Peladas; a colony of expatriates has formed the Nosara Civic Association, to protect its wildlife and forests, and prevent exploitation.

● **Accommodation** **A2** *Hotel Playa de Nosara* (T 680-0495), run down; excellent restaurant, *Olga's Bar*, on beach nearby; **B** *Rancho Suizo Lodge*, T/F 284-9669, Swiss-owned, bungalows, restaurant, no credit cards, whirlpool, hiking, bird-and turtle-watching; **B** *Villa Taype*, T 680-0763, 2 pools, tennis, restaurant, bar; **D** *Casa Rio Nosara*, rancho style house with cabins and nice garden, clean, friendly, camping, canoe tours and horseriding arranged, German owners; **E** *Cabinas Agnell*, with bath, good value, garage next door rents bikes; **F** *Pensión Estancia Nosara*, and a condominium. 12 km S of Nosara is **L2** *El Villaggio Beach & Casino Resort*, at Punta Guiones de Garza, an upmarket yet simply furnished beach hotel with vacation ownership plan, 30 bungalows, international restaurant, club house, bars, pool, disco, good packages arranged in San José, T 233-2476, F 222-4073.

● **Transport** Buses daily from Nicoya at 1000 and 1300, US$2, 2 hrs, 31 km and 5 flights a week from San José.

North of Nosara is **Playa Ostional** where Olive Ridley turtles lay their eggs in July-Nov and where a coastal strip is now protected by the **Refugio Nacional de Fauna Silvestre de Ostional**. The turtles arrive for nesting at high tide in the last moon of the lunar cycle. The villagers are allowed to harvest the eggs in a designated area of the beach, the rest are protected and monitored. There is very basic accommodation in cabins next to the village shop in Ostional eg *Cabinas Guacamaya*, with bath, clean, good food on request. You can camp on the beach. Outside the egg laying period it is exceptionally quiet. There is one bus a day at 0500 to Santa Cruz and Liberia. 4WD needed in rainy season if coming from Sámara.

PLAYA JUNQUILLAL

A number of beaches are reached by unpaved roads from the Nicoya-Liberia road. They can be reached by bus from the Liberia bus station. **Playa Junquillal** is one of the cleanest beaches in Costa Rica and still very empty. It is completely off the beaten track and has almost no tourist facilities.

● **Accommodation A2** *Hotel Antumalal*, with bath, pool, T 680-0506; **A2** *Villa Serena*, with meals, T 680-0737, German owners, helpful; **A3** *Iguanazú*, 3 km N of Playa Junquillal, T 680-0783 (T 232-1423 San José), 24 rooms with private bathroom, pool; **C** *Castillo Diventido*, good reports; **C-E** *El Malinche*, near *Hotel Ibiscus* on main road, Doña Haydee rents rooms and provides meals; **D** *El Manglar*, overlooking mangroves, run by Italian couple, Los Claudios, tastefully designed, shared bathroom, good showers, double mosquito netting everywhere, kitchen upstairs, Claudio has a boat for excursions, US$8/hr; **E** *Junquillal*, cabins, nice, friendly, good food.

● **Transport** Bus from Liberia to Santa Cruz (on the Nicoya road), then bus at 1000 or 1415 from Guillermo Sánchez store to Paraíso (US$0.80), from where it is a 4 km walk to Playa Junquillal, or take a car from one of the *cantinas* (road in bad shape). An express bus goes to San José daily at 0500, 5 hrs, returning 1400 from C 20, Av 3, T 221-7202.

North of Junquillal and S of Avellana is **A1-A3** *Iguanazul*, T 653-0123, 1-800-948-3770, 24 different sizes of cabins on a cliff, hot water, fan or a/c, pool, restaurant, bar, great sunsets, sport fishing on 27-ft *Marlin Genie*, close to good surfing.

PLAYA TAMARINDO

Another good beach is **Playa Tamarindo**, 70 km SE of Liberia. Road to Tamarindo is paved but for the last few km. The beach is becoming popular and it is advisable not to leave valuables unattended (even in hotels). Good surfing at N end. There is a small, expensive, mini-market. Tours to see leatherback turtles are arranged through hotels, US$12 pp with guide. Cheaper tours than through hotels from *TAM Tours*, in commercial centre opp *Tamarindo Diria Hotel*.

● **Accommodation L1-A3** *Tamarindo Vista Villas*, F 653-0115, e-mail: VistaVilla@centralamerica.com, condo-hotel, 7 luxury villas with extra sofa bed, sleep 4, a/c, verandah, safe box, kitchen, 100m from *Johan's Bakery*, internet access for guests, secure surfboard storage, owners are keen surfers; **A1** *El Jardín de Edén*, T 231-5221, F 231-6346, inc breakfast, 150m from beach on hill, 18 rooms with fan and a/c, jacuzzi, 2 pools, 2 apartments; **A1** *Tamarindo Diria*, with bath, T 289-8616,

F 289-8727, full range of services, good restaurants, house parrots, expensive tours offered with good guide; **L3-A2** *Capitán Suizo*, T 653-0075, F 653-0292, 8 villas, 22 rooms with patio or balcony, pool, restaurant, kayaking, scuba diving, surfing, sport fishing available, riding on hotel's own horses, Swiss management, a/c; **A2** *Finca Monte Fresco*, 2½ km from Tamarindo, T 653-0241, F 653-0243, very good, fully-equipped cabins, breakfast, pool, German, English, Spanish spoken, riding, sailing trips on Samonique III yacht, rec; **A3** *La Reserva*, a few kilometres before Tamarindo, T/F 654-4182, a/c, good facilities, pool, Italian run, disco; **A3** *Cabinas Pasa Tiempo*, T 653-0096, F 653-0275, 5 cabins, US$10 extra for a/c, pool, bar, restaurant, fan, friendly, negotiate for longer stays; **A3** *Pueblo Dorado*, T 222-5741, 22 rooms, a/c, pool; **C** *Pozo Azul*, cabins, a/c, cheaper in low season, cooking facilities, clean, good, swimming pool; **D** *Cabinas Marielos*, with bath, clean, use of kitchen; **D** *Cabinas Zullymar*, rec, friendly cats, good beach bar; **D** *Dolly's*, basic, some rooms with bath, bars on balcony, suspicious owner, key deposit only returned after room inspection, lots of rules and regulations (camping nearby, a cheap place to sling a hammock or rent a tent but thefts reported).

● **Places to eat** *Fiesta del Mar*, large thatched open barn, good food, good value; *Stellas*, very good, try dorado with mango cream, rec. *Johan's Bakery*, good breakfasts from 0600, exceptional breads and pizzas; *Coconut Cafe*, pizzas, pastries and best fish on beach. Check the *sodas* for good breakfasts and cheap evening meals. *Pedro's*, buy drinks from bar over road, eat the freshest fish in town.

● **Transport Air** Sansa Mon, Wed, Fri, to San José, Travelair daily. Tamarindo Investments and Developments, T 653-0031, ext 418, 2 flights on Wed, US$75. **Buses** From Santa Cruz, 0630, 1030, 1430. Tamarindo to Santa Cruz bus 0600, 1200, 1430, US$1.25. Express bus from San José daily 1600, C 20, Av 3. From San José, C 14, Av 3-5, T 222-2750, departs 0715 and 1530, 4½ hrs. Bus back to San José 0600, can be booked through *Hotel Tamarindo Diria*, US$5.

The beaches go on for many kilometres. North of Playa Tamarindo is **Playa Grande** and the **Refugio Nacional de Vida Silvestre de Tamarindo** (also known as Parque Nacional Marinas las Baulas de Guanacaste), which surrounds

A1-B *Hotel Las Tortugas*, 11 rooms with bathroom, pool, restaurant, meals inc, T 680-0496, giant leatherback turtle nesting ground Nov-March. Tours arranged, guides cost about US$6 pp, with a boat, US$12; **A2** *Villa Baula*, right behind beach, T 680-0869, bungalows with bath, fans, guided walks Sept-Feb to see leatherback turtles; **D** *Bary Restaurante Playa Grande*, 500m before beach.

Playa Flamingo has white sand but has been aggressively developed and polluted.

● **Accommodation L3** *Flamingo Marina Resort*, next to the sportfishing marina, with meals, T 290-1858; **L2** *The Presidential Suites* (T 680-0620-0444), **B** *Villas Flamingo*, T 680-0960; **A2** *Centro Vacacional Playa Bahía Flamingo*, T 680-0976; **L2** *Club Flamingo*, T 233-8056; *Flamingo Beach Condo Rentals* and **L2** *Club Playa Flamingo*, T 680-0620. Free camping on the beach. The *Flamingo Beach* operates bus service to San José Mon, Wed, Fri, Sun, and Sep San José 0800, Flamingo 1400.

At **Playa Potrero** (black sand): **D** *Hotel Potrero*, T 680-0669; good camping, US$2, signposted, bus from Santa Cruz at 0630 and 1500, returns 0900 and 1700.

Playa Conchal, a beautiful 3 km beach full of shells, now dominated by the **L1** *Meliá Playa Conchal*, T 654-4123, F 654-4181, 5-star resort, 308 suites, 18-hole golf course, largest swimming pool in Central America, tennis courts, conference centre, casino

Playa Brasilito, several unattractive hotels/cabinas along the road: **C** *Ojos Azules*, F680-0280, run by Swiss couple, 14 cabins, good breakfasts with home-baked bread, good value; **D** *Al Odisea*, cabinas, hot water, helpful owner, Marc, T 654-4125, *Bar Marisquería* attached, excellent food, reasonable prices, fresh juices rec; *Hospedaje Olga*, comfortable, horses, but parrot talks to the geese at dawn. Direct bus from San José to Flamingo, Potrero and Brasilito daily at 0800, 1100 from C 20, Av 3, 6 hrs, returning at 0900 and 1400.

Playa Pan de Azúcar: **A2** *Hotel Sugar Beach*, T 654-4242, 10 rooms, 6 with a/c,

50m from beach, fishing trips and horseriding available, 7 km N of Playa Flamingo.

Playa Ocotal: a particularly nice beach, good diving facilities, **L2-A2** *Hotel El Ocotal*, T 670-0321, F 670-0083, e-mail: Ocotal@centralamerica.com, rooms, suites and bungalows, PADI dive shop on beach, sport fishing, surfing, tennis, 3 pools, car hire, excursions; **A3** *Villa Casa Blanca*, 10 rooms, T 670-0448, with breakfast, friendly and informative, family atmosphere, small pool.

PLAYA DEL COCO

Popular is **Playa del Coco** in an attractive islet-scattered bay hemmed in by rocky headlands, the best beaches are to the S; to reach it one should leave the bus at Comunidad (road paved). There are bars, restaurants and one or two motels along the sandy beach; all activities concentrate on the beach and fishing. Snorkelling and diving are nothing special, but for a diving expedition to the Islas Murciélagos contact *Mario Vargas Expeditions*, PO Box 6398-1000, Playa del Coco, T 223-2811, F 223-1916. Be wary of excursion to secluded Playa Verde, accessible by boat only, as some boatmen collaborate with thieves and reap the rewards later.

● **Accommodation** **A3-B** *Rancho Armadillo Inn*, just S of main road to Playa del Coco, 5 rooms, a/c, T 670-0108, F 670-0441; **A3-B** *Villas Flores*, T 670-0269, 1 suite with a/c, 8 rooms with fan, spearfishing, sportfishing, and diving arranged; **B** *Flor de Itabo*, T 670-0011/0292, F 670-0003, a/c rooms, 5 bungalows, good restaurant and bar with really cold beer, pool, horse-riding, excursions, specialists in big-game fishing; **C** *Villa del Sol*, T/F (506) 670-0085, Canadian owned (Quebec), pool, clean, friendly, safe, big garden with parrots, rec; **D** *Luna Tica*, T 670-0127, also has a dormitory (friendly, clean), both usually full at weekends; **D** *Casino Playa del Coco*, with bath and cockroaches but good reasonable restaurant. Also, *Café Paris*, fresh food, French menu, good value.

● **Transport** Bus to San José 0915, return 1000, C 14, Av 1-3, T 222-1650, also 5 buses daily from Liberia 0530-1815 (Arata company).

PLAYA HERMOSA

This is one of the nicest resorts but accommodation is expensive (road paved). Walking either to the left or the right you can find isolated beaches with crystal-clear water.

● **Accommodation** **L1** *Malinche Real*, T 670-0033, F 670-0300, luxury villas with 2 guest houses, with bath, TV, pools, several restaurants, jacuzzi, sauna, conference facilities; **L3** *Costa Smeralda*, on adjacent beach (Playa Buena), T 670-0044, F 670-0379, Spanish style 68-room resort, many facilities; **A3** *El Velero*, beachfront, T 670-0330, nice rooms, fan, pool, clean, good reasonably priced restaurant; **B** *Villa del Sueño*, T 670-0027, Canadian owned, pool, good restaurant; **B** *Playa Hermosa Cabinas*, run by an American couple, T 670-0136, clean, good reasonably-priced food; also cheaper cabins (**F** pp); **D** *Ecotours and Lodge*, 50m S of Aquasport, T 670-0458; **E** *Cabinas Vallejos*; 3 small restaurants on the beach. **A1** *Condovac La Costa*, T 670-0267, luxury bungalows, a/c, more expensive are the suites with kitchenettes, TV, a/c, lots of hot water, arranges scuba-diving etc, good beach access, good restaurants and bars; **B** *Condo hotel Costa Alegre*, T 670-0218; **L3** *Complejo Turístico Los Corales*, T 670-0255; cheaper places at the other end of the beach.

● **Transport** Express bus to San José daily 0500; from San José, C 12, Av 5-7, at 1530, 5 hrs; also buses from Liberia, empresa Esquivel, 1130, 1900, return 0500, 1600, US$0.80. Bus leaves you some 500m from accommodation.

Playa de Panamá (road paved) is a peaceful place with a few basic fish restaurants and a *pulpería*.

The big Papagayo tourist complex near Playa Panama started in 1993, now appears to be in difficulties though one hotel may open soon.

● **Accommodation** **D** *Los Bananos*, cabins, restaurant and bar, with bath, friendly, English spoken, good hiking, swimming, horseriding can be arranged, rec (address is Apdo 137, Liberia, Guanacaste); **D** *Cabinas Vallejo*, with bath; camping possible on beach; *Jardín del Mar* with good facilities, restaurant, tents for hire.

SANTA CRUZ

Buy food inland in **Santa Cruz**, NW of Nicoya. Santa Cruz is known as Costa Rica's National Folklore City because of its colourful *fiestas*, dancing and regional food. Jan is the month for the *fiesta* dedicated to Santo Cristo de Esquipulas, when it can be difficult to find accommodation. There is also a rodeo fiesta in January. Much of the town was damaged by fire in Feb 1993.

● **Accommodation & places to eat** **D** *Hospedaje Avellanas*, comfortable rooms, friendly atmosphere, good value; **D** *La Pampa*, T 680 0586, close to parque, good; **D** *Palenque Diria*, bath, restaurant; **D** *Plaza* next to bus station, friendly owner, new restaurant; **E** *Pensión Isabel*, behind the church, bath, hot water; **F** *Posada Tu Casa*; *La Tortillera* is an excellent place to eat.

● **Transport** Bus to San José-Santa Cruz, 5 daily, 5 hrs, US$2.80, C 20, Av 1-3; bus Santa Cruz-Tamarindo, 2 a day, US$1, also to Playa Flamingo and nearby beaches; Santa Cruz-Liberia every 2 hrs, US$1, last bus 1930; Santa Cruz-Nicoya, US$0.35; taxi Santa Cruz-Nicoya US$10.50 for 2 people.

BARRA HONDA NATIONAL PARK

Small park in the N of the Nicoya Peninsula (2,295 ha). No permit required, entry US$6. Created to protect some caves (in particular Terciopelo) on a *mesa* and small remainders of dry tropical forest at the *mesa's* foot. First go to Nicoya, from where there are several buses a day to **Quebrada Honda** (first bus 1030, last bus returns for Nicoya 1630, giving you only 2 hrs in the park); this settlement 1 hr's walk away from the park. Alternatively, get a lift. The road to the park, after the yellow national park sign, on the main road, is 3 km paved then 6 km good gravel. The park office is at **Barra Honda**, at the foot of the *mesa*, and there are two different trails to the top; 2 hrs' hiking. Also noteworthy are the *cascadas*, bizarre limestone fountains built by sedimentation on a seasonal riverbed. You'll need a guide to get here, as the trails are hopelessly muddled by cowpaths; arrange in advance for the visit to the cave. A full visit requires harnesses, ropes and guides, US$33 for 3 guides, US$11 pp for equipment. Avoid coming in the rainy season (May to Nov), but the dry season is exceedingly hot in the open fields. Bring your own food from Nicoya. Turinsa operates a Sat tour from San José to the Barra Honda caves, T 221-9185, US$90 inc breakfast and lunch. Las Delicias Ecotourism Project, owned and operated by local community at park entrance, T 685-5580, 3 bungalows, comfortable accommodation, camping, F, Costa Rican meals at reasonable prices, guided tours available.

From San José to the Atlantic Coast

I NITIALLY DOMINATED by active volcanoes and mountainous rain forest, the land falls away to the flat Caribbean lowlands, sparsely populated, with major tropical rain forest national parks at Tortuguero and Barra del Colorado, where canals and rivers are the means of communication.

There are two routes from San José to Puerto Limón on the Atlantic coast. The main road goes over the Cordillera Central through the Braulio Carrillo National Park down to Guápiles and Siquirres. This new road is prone to fog and can be dangerous. The old road follows the route of the railway to Cartago, S of Irazú volcano to Turrialba and Siquirres.

BRAULIO CARRILLO NATIONAL PARK

This large park was created to protect the high rain forest N of San José from the impact of the new San José-Guápiles-Puerto Limón highway. It extends for 44,099 ha with five different types of forest (entry US$6). Wildlife includes many species of birds, jaguar, ocelot and Baird's tapir. Various travel agencies offer naturalist tours, approx US$65 from San José. San José to Guápiles and Puerto Limón buses go through the park. There are three main centres, two are on the highway: Zurquí (the park HQ) just after the toll station, coming from San José, before the tunnel; it has services, a visitor centre and trails.

The Carrillo centre is 2 km beyond the bridge over the Rio Sucio at the Guápiles end. There is a new administration building aimed at improving security: reports of armed robbery on tourist trails. 3 km before the bridge is the 'Sendero Botella' in the rain forest (information at the Ranger Station, closed Mon), with waterfall en route. Good birdwatching. The views down the Río Patria canyon are impressive.

An aerial tram (teleférico) takes visitors 35m up into the rainforest, interesting to see the vegetation of the canopy but best to be there early to see birds (tram hours 0600-1530, except Mon 0900-1530, tourist buses arrive 0800); 90 mins' ride costs US$47.50 (inc guided nature walk, children half price, children under 5 not allowed); T San José 257-5961, F 257-6053; office, Rainforest Aerial Tram, Av 7, C 7, behind Aurola Holiday Inn, has bus service from San José around 0800 daily, US$17.50 with pickups at most major hotels. Guarded car park for private vehicles. Restaurant for breakfast and lunch US$7.50. It can be difficult to get reservations during the high season. It is beyond the park, 5.3 km from the Río Sucio bridge, before Guápiles.

VOLCAN BARVA

The national park also includes **Barva Volcano**, 2,906m. The latter is only accessible from Heredia, there is no entrance from the new highway; take a bus to **San José de la Montaña**.

From San José de la Montaña it is 4 hrs' walk to Sacramento but some buses (about 4 a day) continue towards Sacramento halving the walk time (otherwise walk, hitchhike, or arrange a ride with the park director). Taxi Heredia-Sacramento, US$7. Ranger station and camping site nearby, from which 3 km of easy climb to the top. Good views; park entry US$6, no permit needed here. Jungle Trails (T 255-3486) offers day trips from San José to Barva Volcano. Easter Week is a good choice. The park is widely known among (illegal) birdcatchers. Be careful when leaving your car, regular reports of theft from rental cars.

● **Accommodation** In **San José de la Montaña**: all with beautiful views across the Meseta Central: **A2** *El Pórtico*, T 260-6000, F 260-6002, cosy, clean, pool, sauna, good food, rec; **A** *Hotel Chalet Tirol*, 3 km N of *Castillo Country Club*, bath, beautiful views, T 267-7070, tours to *Dundee Ranch Hotel* at Cascajal; **D** *Cabinas Las Ardillas*, T 237-6022, all with bath; **D** *Cabinas Montaña Cypresal*, T 237-4466. In **Sacramento**: **B** *Volcán Barva Lodge*, one cabin with kitchen sleeps 4, more cabins being built, T 228-3197.

Further on, at the *Soda Gallo Pinto* is the **Bosque Lluvioso** 170 ha private reserve (T 224-0819), open 0700-1700. It is at Km 56 on Guápiles highway (Rancho Redondo), 170 ha, visitors centre, restaurant, trails in primary and secondary forest, entry US$15.

See page 1074 for *Rara Avis*, NE of Braulio Carrillo.

GUAPILES

Guápiles, 1 hr from San José, is the centre of the Río Frío banana region.

● **Accommodation & places to eat A3** *Río Danta Lodge*, T 223-2421, F 255-4039, 20 acres of tropical gardens bordering the Río Danta, fresh water spring pool, restaurant; **A3** *Casa Río Blanco*, take first right before the Río Blanco bridge and follow signposts, T 710-2652, F 710-6161, with breakfatst, accommodates 12 guests, run by N Americans interested in biology and the environment; **B** *Happy Rana Lodge* (just before Guápiles), T 710-6794, cabins in rainforest, transportation from San José with 24 hrs notice, take first right before Río Blanco bridge, 3 km along gravel road; **E** *Keng Wa* and **E** *As de Oro* (with bath); all **F**: *Hugo Sánchez Cheng Cariari* and *Alfaro* (with bath, above noisy bar); *Hospedaje Guápiles*, good, T 710-6179. Restaurant *Los Guapes* good Chinese. Before reaching Guápiles, 800m off the highway at the Río Corinto is *Morpho Lodge*, good for hiking, river swimming, cooking facilities.

GUACIMO

The new highway runs alongside a railway to **Guácimo**. Costa Flores offer guided tours of the world's largest flower farm, US$15 pp, T 220-1311.

● **Accommodation B** *Las Palmas*, 1 km past Earth School, 30 rooms, private bathroom, pool, restaurant, T 760-0305, F 760-0296, the 200 ha property inc ornamental plant farm and rainforest.

SIQUIRRES

It is another 25 km from Guácimo to **Siquirres**, a clean, friendly town and junction for roads and former railways.

● **Accommodation** Hotels (all **E**) inc *Wilson*, *Cocal*, *Idamar*, *Las Brisbas* and *Vidal*. Also *Cabinas Pacaya*, on the main road.

● **Transport** Buses leave San José (C 12, Av 7-9) every 45 mins. The road Siquirres-Puerto Limón is paved.

28 km beyond Siquirres is **Matina**, a small place on the railway but off the highway. It is a short distance from the Caribbean where there is a privately owned reserve accessible by canal from Matina, the **Reserva para la Naturaleza Pacuare**, about 30 km N of Puerto Limón. Run by Englishman, John Denham, it has a 6 km stretch of leatherback turtle

nesting beach, protected and guarded by the Reserve. Volunteers patrol the beach in May and June, measuring and tagging the turtles, US$50 pp per week, inc good meals and accommodation. For volunteer working, contact Carlos Fernández, Corporación de Abogados, Av 8-10, C 19, No 837, San José, T 233-0508 or 233-0451, F 221-2820.

PUERTO LIMÓN

(*Pop* 56,525) **Puerto Limón**, on a palm-fringed shore backed by mountains, is the country's most important port. It was built on the site of an ancient Indian village, Cariari, where Columbus landed on his fourth and last voyage. It is very humid and it rains nearly every day. Much of the population is black but there is also a large Chinese contingent, involved mainly in restaurants, food stores and hotels; they even have their own part of the cemetery.

Places of interest

The seafront promenade and the **Parque Vargas** next to it are popular places for social gatherings, especially in the evening. In Parque Vargas is a botanical display, a shrine to sailors and fishermen and a bandstand. In 1994 the park was reported in bad condition and the Hoffman's 2-toed sloths which live in its trees were not easily seen. The **Museo Etnohistórico de Limón**, C 2, Av 1-2, open Mon-Thur, 1400-1700, features material relating to Columbus' arrival in Limón. The nightlife is good, particularly for Caribbean music and dancing. Some 2.8 million bunches of bananas are exported each year. New docks were recently completed.

Excursions

Moín, 6½ km N of Puerto Limón, has docks for tankers, container and ro-ro ships, and is also the departure point for barges to Barra del Colorado (8 hrs). Moín has a pleasant beach, buses run every

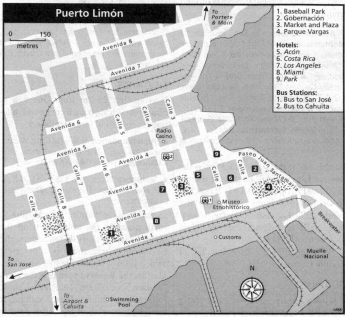

Puerto Limón

0 ——— 150
metres

1. Baseball Park
2. Gobernación
3. Market and Plaza
4. Parque Vargas

Hotels:
5. Acón
6. Costa Rica
7. Los Angeles
8. Miami
9. Park

Bus Stations:
1. Bus to San José
2. Bus to Cahuita

To Portete & Moín

Avenida 8

Avenida 7

Avenida 6

Avenida 5

Calle 3
Calle 4
Calle 5
Calle 6
Calle 7
Calle 8
Calle 9

Radio Casino

Avenida 4

Avenida 3

Avenida 2

Avenida 1

Paseo Juan Santamaría

Calle 1
Calle 2

Museo Etnohistórico

Customs

Breakwater

Muelle Nacional

To San José

To Airport & Cahuita

Swimming Pool

N

40 mins from 0600-1740, ½ hr, US$0.10. Boats run from Moín to Tortuguero (see below) and may be hired at the dockside. Go early for a good bargain. A severe earthquake struck the Caribbean coast of Costa Rica and Panama in April 1991. Many buildings were damaged or destroyed. Most bridges have been repaired, the permanent bridge across the Río Estrella has now been rebuilt, and roads to the Panamanian border are open. Because the land was raised by the earthquake, the Tortuguero canals (see below) around Matina dried up. Japdeva have started dredging work but boats for Tortuguero river now also depart from Hamburgo de Siquirres on the Río Reventazón. Boats still run from Barra del Colorado to Tortuguero.

Local festivals

Fiesta: in Oct, very crowded and expensive.

Local information

● **Warning**

Beware of theft at night, and remember it is a port as well as a tourist town; there are a lot of drunks roaming the streets.

● **Accommodation**

In Puerto Limón: A2 *Maribu Caribe*, T /58-4010, F 758-3541, on clifftop, bungalow accommodation, swimming pool, friendly, pleasant.

B *Jardín Tropical*, 5 km N of Puerto Limón, T 798-1244, F /98-1259, new holiday hotel, with breakfast, pool.

C *Acón*, C 3, Av 3, T 758-1010, with bath, a/c, clean, safe, good restaurant, a bit run down, popular discotheque *Aquarius*.

D *King*, Av 2, next to PO on main square, with bath and fan, very clean; **D** *Park*, C 1-2, Av 3, T 758-3476, sea facing rooms quiet and cool, rooms not clean but restaurant good; **D** *El Paraíso*, Av 4, C 2-3, next to Methodist church, small clean rooms, fan, basic; **D** *International*, Av 5, C 2-3, with bath, a/c, Chinese owner, reasonable.

E *Caribe*, C 1-3, Av 2, T 758-0138; **E** *Hotel Los Angeles*, Av 3, C 4-5, T 758-2068; **E** *Lincoln*, Av 5, C 2-3, with bath, fan, damp, cockroaches, rats, dirty and run down, not rec; **E** *Miami*, C 4-5, Av 2, T 758-0490, back rooms quieter, a/c, Chinese food in restaurant; **E** *Ng*, C 3, Av 5, T 758-2134, cheaper rooms without bath, fan

extra charge, basic, untidy, friendly, laundry; **E** *Palace*, nr market, small, basic, plants, chairs on balcony; **E** *Linda Vista*, Parque Vargas, basic, friendly, noisy; **E** *Linda Vista*, Parque Vargas, basic, friendly, noisy; **E** *Palmeras*, Av 2, C 3; **E** *Cariari* Av 3, C 2.

F *Hong Kong*, on main street, clean but noisy; **F** *Pensión El Sauce*, 1 block from main square, rats; **F** *Pensión Hotel Costa Rica*, 1½ blocks E of central park, small rooms, noisy; **F** *Venus*, Av 5 nr Lincoln, beach view, rats, spiders, beds 'like medical plank beds', avoid.

G *Balmoral*, nr market, basic; **G** *Pensión Los Angeles*, C 6-7, Av 7, with bath, cheap, noisy, mosquitoes, probably of ill repute; **G** *Pensión El Cano*, next to *Pensión Los Angeles*, fan, friendly, clean, share showers, OK.

At **Playa Bonita**: **A3-B** *Apartotel Cocorí*, T/F 758-2930, with bath, hot water, some with a/c, pool, restaurant popular with locals, boat trips to Tortuguero arranged; **C** *Albergue Turistico Playa Bonita*, T/F 798-3090, with bath, fan or a/c, 200m from ocean.

In nearby **Portete**: **A2** *Matama*, Playa Bonita, T 758-1123/4200, F 758-4499, recently refurbished, bath, a/c, restaurant, tennis, pool, boats for rent to Tortuguero; **C** *Cabinas Getsemaní*, cabins, bath, a/c, restaurant, pleasant (T 758-1123).

In Moín: B *Moín Caribe*, uphill from where the bus from Puerto Limón stops, friendly, nice, clean, good place to stay before Tortuguero, good value; **C** *Moín Club*, T 758-2436, F 758-1112, walking distance of Moín port, 15 rooms.

● **Places to eat**

A place to eat is harder to find than a nightclub. Several Chinese restaurants eg *Samkirson*, C 3, Av 3-4, good value; *Palacio Encantador*, 50m E of Stadium, good.

Park Hotel, C 1-2, Av 3, does good meals, US$2.25; *Restaurant La Chucheca* serves good *comidas* and breakfast; *Springfield*, serves good, Caribbean-style meals, rec, also has disco; *La Hacienda*, for steaks, cheap; *Soda/Restaurant Mares*, on market square, good food; *Soda/Restaurant Roxie*, opp hospital, some way out of town, good value *casado*. *Doña Toda*, good, nr market; *Harbour Restaurant*, good value meal of the day; *Mönpik* for good ice cream (the biggest supermarket in town); *Milk Bar La Negra Mendoza* at the central market has good milk shakes and snacks. *Casados* in market in the day, outside it at night, good, cheap food. Try *pan bon*, spicy bread from

Creole recipe, sold nr bus stop for San José. Cheap food at the corners of the Central Park and at *Familia Torres*, Av 5, ½ block from *Hotel Ng*, very good value. *Diplo's Bar*, cheap Limón food, try the soup.

● **Banks & money changers**
Banco Nacional de Costa Rica.

● **Hospitals & medical services**
Hospital: *Social Security Hospital*.

● **Places of worship**
Protestant Church: Baptist, with services in English.

● **Post & telecommunications**
Post Office: opp central market. There is a branch of ICE at Av 2 C 5-6 for international telephone calls. **Cables**: Radiográfica maintain offices in Limón.

● **Sports**
Swimming: Japdeva, the harbour authority, has a 25m pool open to the public for a small fee in the harbour area.

● **Transport**
Air Travelair and Sansa from the capital, see under San José. Keep luggage to a minimum or you will be charged for excess baggage.

Buses Town bus service is irregular and crowded. Service from **San José** with Coop Limón, T 223-7811 and Transportes Unidos del Atlántico, every 30 mins, 0530-1930, daily, return from the street between central plaza and Parque Vargas (ignore the old signs for the departure point), US$2.90, 3-4 hrs. To **Cartago**, US$2. Bus to **Cahuita** 0500, 1000, 1300, 1600, US$0.80, 1 hr, continues to Puerto Viejo and Sixaola. To **Manzanillo** at 0600, 1400, returning 0900, 1630, 2 hrs, US$1.50.

THE ATLANTIC COAST

The Río San Juan forms the border between Costa Rica and Nicaragua; the frontier is not in mid-river but on the Costa Rican bank. English is spoken widely along the coast. Between Puerto Limón and the Río San Juan is a long stretch of coastline with various settlements linked by a canal system which follows the coast.

TORTUGUERO

Tortuguero is a 18,947-ha National Park protecting the Atlantic green turtle egg-laying grounds and the Caribbean lowland rain forest inland. The turtles lay their eggs at night from June to Aug (the eggs start hatching in the second week of Sept), but before going to watch, contact the National Park administration (they have some basic but good guide books of the area for sale) for instructions, otherwise you may disturb the protected turtles (take a torch if going at night). Unfortunately people still eat turtle eggs and meat, even though they are protected. It is depressing to see the nests robbed by morning. No permission is needed to enter the park, but to visit the turtles you must pay US$6 park entrance fee and US$5 each for a guide, no matter how many you are. Guides (authorized ones only, with ID card) will let you watch one turtle laying eggs, although you may have to wait an hour; be patient. Do not swim at Tortuguero because of the sharks.

A Visitor Centre opened in Aug 1995 with information on the Park and the turtles and a gift shop. There is a 1.4 km well-marked trail with trees named, rec. Also the Caribbean Conservation Corporation has opened a natural history museum in the village of Tortuguero, open 1000-1200, 1400-1730, entrance free. Park rangers are friendly and make trips into the jungle waterways; particularly rec for viewing tropical rain forest wildlife (birds, alligators, tapirs, jaguars, ocelots, peccaries, anteaters, manatees, sloths, monkeys, gars); their trips are quite short, about US$2 pp for 3-4 hrs' trip. You can hire a canoe and guide for about US$3/hr pp, minimum 4, excellent way to see wildlife including crocodiles, ask for Damma. Johnny Velázquez (see above) does tours, US$3.55 pp/hr for tours of canals in a motor boat, US$30/hr in fishing boat on the sea, maximum 2, gear and bait inc, US$10/hr night tour. Alberto does canoe tours: US$2.25/hr pp if he goes with you, or US$1.25 if you go alone, he lives next to *Hotel Mayscar*. Rubén, who lives in the last house before you get to the National Park office, sign on pathway, is rec for

4-hrs' tour at dusk and in the dark. Chico lives behind *Sabina's Cabinas*, US$2/hr, rec as local guide and will take you anywhere in his motor boat. Ernesto was born in Tortuguero and has 15 years experience as a guide, contact him at *Tropical Lodge* or through his mother, who owns *Sabina's Cabinas*. Rafael, a biologist, is rec, speaks Spanish and English (his wife speaks French), lives ½ km behind Park Rangers' office, ask rangers for directions, he also rents canoes. There are several boats for rent from Tortuguero, ask at the *pulpería*. Take insect repellent against the ferocious mosquitoes, ticks and chiggers.

● **Accommodation** At the Southern end of the Park is Parismina, where you can stay at the **L2** *Tarpon Lodge*, T 235-7766, inc meals, boat and guide; there is also a cheap *pensión*, **F**, basic, fan, bargain. Further N is the settlement of Tortuguero itself. There are several hotels: *Río Parismina Lodge*, T 222-6633 (USA toll free 800-338-5688, F 512-829-3770), luxury, fishing packages from US$999; **L2** *Tortuga Lodge*, price pp inc meals, T 257-0766, F 257-1665, comfortable accommodation, but rooms 1-6 are dark and lack fresh air, excellent food (owner Costa Rican Expeditions, packages available from San José, better value than staying there independently though you may still be charged extra for everything, 2 mins' boat ride from village, US$8); **L3** *Ilan Ilan*, price pp inc meals, T 255-2031, clean, basic, cold showers, friendly, English-speaking owner; **L3** *Jungla Lodge*, price pp inc meals, T 233-0155, F 222-0568, 3-day, 2-night package tours with transport from San José; **L3** *Caribbean Magic Eco-Lodge*, T 296-2306, inc meals and boat trips, rustic cabins; *Pachira Lodge*, T 256-7080, F 223-1119, built 1995, 5 mins from Park, 3 day/2 night package inc transport, food, tours with bilingual guide, highly rec; **A2** *Laguna Lodge*, T 225-3740, F 283-8031, 20 rooms with bath and fan, restaurant, bar, beautiful gardens, tour packages available from San José inc unlimited boat trips; **A2** *Mawamba Lodge*, T 222-5463, 223-7490, F 255-4039, price pp inc meals, comfortable, fans, restaurant, canal and egg-laying turtles in front of property; **B** *Manatí Lodge*, 8 rooms with bath, T 221-6148; **B** *Cabinas Miss Junie*, T 710-0523, fan, bath, next to restaurant; **C** *Sabina's Cabinas*,

somewhat overpriced but clean, small, basic rooms, but next to beach, some cabinas with separate bathroom, also **F** pp for dormitory; **D** *Mayscar*, Nicaraguan-owned, fans, safe, cheap food clean, basic. North of Tortuguero is *Samay Laguna*, T 223-0867, PO Box 12767-1000, San José, tours closed, transport by seaplane possible, no travellers' reports yet.

6 km N of Tortuguero is the **Caño Palma Biological Station**, administered by the Canadian Organization for Tropical Education and Rainforest Conservation (in Canada T (905) 683-2116), basic rooms, **B** pp, inc meals, pickup from Sansa flights to Barra del Colorado can be arranged; a good place for serious naturalists or just for unwinding, accommodation for up to 16 in wooden cabin, fresh water well for drinking and washing. Don't dally on arrival if you want cheap accommodation. You can sometimes camp at the National Park office for US$2.50.

● **Places to eat** Good food is limited: *Miss Junie's* with Mona Lisa painting (order meals in advance); *El Dolar*, small menu, good casado, gift shop opp; *La Mancha*, clean, OK; *Paraíso Tropical*, drinks and light snacks, souvenir shop, public telephone.

● **Entertainment** Tío Leo's, Sat night is dancing night, happy, enjoyable, great dancing, but a notorious surplus of men. Disco nr *Sabina's Cabinas*.

● **Shopping** *The Jungle Shop* specializes in handicrafts.

● **Tour companies & travel agents** Tours from San José inc transport, meals, 2 nights lodging, guide and boat trips for US$219-252 pp (double occupancy). The main tours are *Mawamba Boats*, T 222-5463, 223-7490, F 255-4039, min 2 people, 3 days/2 nights, daily, private launch so you can stop en route, with launch tour of National Park inc, accommodation at *Mawamba Lodge*, PO Box 10050 San José, you can return to San José by charter flight (US$344 pp) or take the Río San Juan-Río Sarapiquí trip from Puerto Viejo de Sarapiquí (5 hrs, US$347 pp based on 2 people); then bus back to San José or stay at *Selva Verde Lodge*; *Miss Caribe* and *Miss America* boats, T 233-0155 operate Tues, Fri, Sun, 2-night 3-day packages using *Jungla Lodge*; *Colorado Prince* boat, 3 day/2 night package, Tues, Fri, Sun US$200, using *Ilan Ilan Lodge*, T 255-3031. *Tortuga Lodge* and *Laguna Lodge* also offer similar packages. Parismina Tarpon Rancho (PO Box 10560-1000, San José, F 222-1760) offers tours of

Tortuguero, Braulio Carrillo National Park and fishing trips. OTEC (see page 1060) runs 3-day, 2-night tours for US$180, with small student discount, a trip to see the turtles in July-Sept costs extra. Tours from Puerto Viejo de Sarapiquí, inc boat trip to Tortuguero, meals, 2 nights lodging, guide and transport to San José cost US$275-400 pp (double occupancy).

● **Transport   Boats**   A regular boat leaves Moín at 0900, US$25, 4 hrs, returning about 1400, check the times which frequently change. Tickets sold once boat is under way. You can bargain at Moín for a boat to take you to Tortuguero and bring you back 3-4 days later, at around US$50-60 provided a party of six can be arranged. *Viajes Laura*, T 758-2410, highly rec, daily service, open return US$50 if phoned direct, more through travel agencies, pick up from hotel, will store luggage, lunch provided, excellent for pointing out wildlife on the way. It is also possible to take a bus from Siquirres to Freeman (unpaved road), a Del Monte banana plantation, from where unscheduled boats go to Tortuguero; ask around at the bank of the Río Pacuare, or call the public phone office in Tortuguero (T 710-6716, open 0730-2000) and ask for Johnny Velázquez to come and pick you up, US$57, maximum 4 passengers, 4 hrs. Sometimes heavy rains block the canals, preventing passage there or back. Contact Willis Rankin (Apdo 1055, Limón, T 798-1556) an excellent captain who will negotiate rampaging rivers. All river boats for the major lodges (see below) leave from **Hamburgo** or **Freeman**. If excursion boats have a spare seat you may be allowed on. Generally it is getting more difficult to 'do it yourself', but it is still possible, ask around the boat owners in Moín. Official tours and tourist guides with accommodation inc are now normal, bargain for a good price. A 2-day, 1-night trip from Puerto Limón with basic accommodation, turtle watching trip and transport (no food) costs about US$65 pp, T 225-6220. **Road** A local municipality commenced extending a road from Guápiles to Tortuguero and cut a track of 2 km within the National Park without permits or permission. An outcry from conservation groups and other authorities has stopped the roadbuilding. The government has promised to investigate and prosecute those responsible. You can take a bus from Guápiles to **Cariari** on the Río Tortuguero and take a boat from there, 9½ hrs, US$15 return, to Tortuguero, or a boat from Puerto Viejo de Sarapiquí to Barra del Colorado and from there to Tortuguero (see

below). **Air** Flights from San José with Sansa to Tortuguero, Tues, Thur, Sun and to Parismina, Mon, Wed, Fri, Sun, see **Internal Flights**, page 1062, or charter, US$292 for up to 5 passengers.

BARRA DEL COLORADO

The canals pass many small settlements, and for many of them the barge is their only means of communication. The canals are part artificial, part natural; they were originally narrow lagoons running parallel to the sea, separated from it by ¾ km of land. Now all the lagoons are linked, and it is possible to sail as far as **Barra del Colorado**, in the extreme NE of Costa Rica, 25 km beyond Tortuguero. The town is divided by the river, the main part being on the northern bank. There is a plan to link the Parque Nacional Tortuguero with the **Refugio Nacional de Fauna Silvestre Barra del Colorado** into a continuous National Park area. The area is world famous for fishing. Boat from Barra to Tortuguero takes 1 hr and costs US$28.50. A motorized canoe can take 8 people and costs up to US$50, 2 hrs. Try and arrive in a group as boats are infrequent.

● **Accommodation   A1** *Río Colorado Lodge*, price pp inc 3 meals and fishing with guide, for serious fishermen, night-vision scopes, reservations rec, T 231-5371 or 232-6810, F 231-5987; **A2** *Hotel Pesca Casa Mar*, with bath (T 441-2820); **A2** *Silver King Lodge*, T 288-0849 (toll free in USA 1-800-847-3474), price pp, deluxe sports fishing hotel, 5-night packages inc flights, meals, rooms with bath, fan, hot water; **C** *Isla de Pesca*, with bath (T 293-4544, F 293-4839); **C** *Tarponland Lodge*, cabins, run by Guillermo Cunningham, very knowledgeable and helpful, T 710-6917; *Cabinas New Tropical Tarpon* with bath (T 227-0473). If you have a tent you may be able to camp at *Soda La Fiesta*. Lots of mosquitoes.

● **Transport   Air**   Flight San José-Barra del Colorado with Sansa and Travelair, see under **Internal Flights**, San José.

FRONTIER WITH NICARAGUA – BARRA DEL COLORADO

Once across the Río Colorado (which in fact is the S arm of the Río San Juan delta), you can walk to Nicaragua (see under Nicaragua, San Juan del Norte) along the coast, but it is a long 30 kms beach walk, take food and lots of water. Most hikers overnight en route. Seek advice before setting out.

● **Costa Rican immigration**

This is not a regular border crossing and there are no formal facilities on the Costa Rican side. Do not leave for Nicaragua by boat or on foot without checking with the Guardia Civil in Barra del Colorado or Tortuguero, who are very helpful. Similarly, check with them if arriving from Nicaragua.

● **Transport**

Transport, mostly by boat, is costly, typically US$30 for a ½-day. There are several fishermen who will take you on their way to fish in Nicaraguan waters, US$20-30. You can go by irregular boat from Barra up the Río Colorado, Río San Juan and Río Sarapiquí to Puerto Viejo, about 5-6 hrs. A small boat for 4 without roof costs US$150 (or US$50 pp), a larger boat with roof (rec) costs US$185 for 4; you see caimans, turtles and lots of birds. There are several border checkpoints. Non-Costa Rican nationals travelling along Río San Juan must pay US$5 entry and exit tax at Nicaraguan border checkpoint and receive stamp in passport.

Another alternative to going S along the coast to Puerto Limón is by bus from the river bank opposite Isla Buena Vista 25 km up the Río Colorado, daily except Sun, leaves 0600, by dirt track to Cariari and then to Guápiles. Interesting trip through rainforest and then banana plantations. Throughout this area police are on the lookout for drugs traffickers. Expect to have your luggage searched thoroughly.

SOUTH FROM PUERTO LIMON

Southward from Limón, the road is paved to **Penshurst**. Here the road (and railway) branches to Valle de Estrella, a large Standard Fruit banana plantation; camping is easy in the hills and there are plenty of rivers for swimming. (**A2** *Selva Bananita Lodge*, 20 km from Puerto Limón at Cerro Mochila near Bananito, 7 cabins on farm, solar heating, primary rainforest tours, tree climbing, horses and bikes to rent, contact Jürgen Stein, *Conselvatur SA*, Apdo 801-1007, San José, T 253-8118,

F 225-2640; **A3** *Los Aviarios del Caribe*, 30 km S of Limón, inc breakfast, Apdo 569, Limón 7300, Luis and Judy) offer canoe trips in Estrella River Delta.) Small buses leave Limón (C 4, Av 6) for Valle de Estrella/Pandora, 7 a day from 0500, at 2-hourly intervals, last at 1800, 1½ hrs (returning from Pandora at similar times). From Penshurst it is 11½ km to **Cahuita**; this stretch of the road is paved to the edge of Cahuita.

CAHUITA NATIONAL PARK

The **Cahuita National Park** has a narrow strip of beach (1,068 ha) and a coral reef offshore (600 ha), sadly badly damaged by agricultural chemicals etc from the rivers. An old Spanish wrecked ship may be seen, although the water can be very cloudy at times. Both can be reached without a boat; take snorkelling equipment. The undercurrent is strong; take care not to bump into the reef. There is a black sand beach to the N, take hammock, good swimming, beautiful. The Park extends from Cahuita town to **Puerto Vargas** further SE. Best access to the Park is from Puerto Vargas where there are the Park headquarters, a nature trail, camping facilities, toilets, take drinking water (take the bus to Km 5, then turn left at the sign; the road from the Cahuita-Bribri road to Puerto Vargas is muddy; take a torch if walking it after dark). Entry charge to the Park US$6. Latest reports indicate you may be able to enter the Park free from near Cahuita. The length of the beach can be walked in 2 hrs, passing endless coconut palms and interesting tropical forest, through which there is also a path, including fording the shallow Río Perezoso, which is brown with tannin. It is hot and humid, but a wide range of fauna can be seen, including howler monkeys, white face monkeys, coatis, snakes, butterflies and hermit crabs. Over 500 species of fish inhabit the surrounding waters. Reef tours avilable. No permission is necessary from SNP to enter the Park. Best to visit during the week when it is quieter.

- **Accommodation A2** *Magellan Inn*, inc breakfast, 2 km N of Cahuita, 6 rooms with bath and fan, pool, F 798-0652; **C** pp *Hotel Jaguar Cahuita*, 800m N of Cahuita centre, easy walk to National Park, 17-acre property with nature trails, 22 beach front rooms with private bathroom, inc breakfast and dinner, good value, T 755-0238, San José T 226-3775; **C** *Kelly Creek*, by entrance to National Park, large rooms, veranda, fan, good service; **C** *Cabinas Arrecife*, 100m E of police station, T/F 755-0081; **D** *National Park*, opp *Kelly Creek*, fan, good restaurant; **E** *Cabinas Safari*, T 755-0078, with bath, friendly owner Wayne Palmer, fan, clean, good value. There are other new developments in this area. On the street parallel to the sea, towards the Park entrance are **E** *Vaz Cabañas*, friendly, cold shower, some fans, quite clean, rec, good restaurant, safe parking, T 755-0218, and **C** *Hotel Cahuita*, renovated, pool, T 755-0238, mixed reports. **E-D** *Cabinas Surf Side*, for cabin on beach with bathroom, T 755-0203, English spoken, clean, good value, rec, get there early to get a room. A little road from the bus stop goes straight to the seafront, passing **D** *Cabinas Palmer*, T 755-0243), clean, good, friendly and helpful, but noisy; carry on to the sea, and on left is **C** *Jenny's Cabinas* T 755-0256, clothes washing area, balconies with view, Canadian owned, bath, fan, breakfast available, running water, close to the sea but surrounding area dirty; **D** *Cabinas Seaside Nan Nan*, on beach on right after *Jenny's Cabinas*, clean, English spoken, hammocks available, rec; **F** pp *Bar Hannia*, very friendly Jamaican owner, on main street, English speaking, good place for a beer, his wife also has nice cabins available. On the road from Limón to Cahuita, Km 22, is **C** *Selvamar Resort*, with bath, fans, swimming pool, T 255-6176, isolated and difficult to get to Cahuita National Park from here.

In Playa Negra: 15 mins N of the Park: **A3** *El Encanto*, on Black Beach Rd, 5 mins from town centre, F 798-0652, Spanish-style bungalows, with breakfast, restaurant; **A3** *Atlántida Lodge*, next to football ground, bungalows, nice gardens, inc tax and breakfast, free coffee and bananas, pool, rec, T 755-0213, with bath, cold water, fan, mosquito screen, pleasant, free safe parking for cars and motorcycles (also known as Canadian Jean's (French) rec); **C** *Cabinas Iguana*, Swiss-owned, cabins or houses to rent, with kitchen, fan, mosquito netting, balcony, clean, nice location, rec; **D** *Cabinas Sol y Mar*, clean, pleasant with bath and fan, quiet,

close to beach, mosquitoes; **D-E** *Cabinas Margarita*, 200m from beach, nice atmosphere, clean; **E** *Cabinas Black Beach*, clean and well situated, bar, you may camp here for US$1; **E** *Brigitte's*, friendly, quiet, Swiss run, restaurant, good for wildlife, sloth shelters from rain on verandah at night, rec; **E** *Cabinas Tito*, clean, quiet, cabins sleep 2-3, good value; **F** *Cabinas Grant* (*Cabinas Bello Horizonte*), good water service, Señorita Letty Grant (North American, also has *artesanía* shop), blue house on right of track to Black Beach, rents rooms (F) and *cabañas*, clean, nice, friendly, beautiful setting, garden and birds, good value. At the end of Black Beach, 300m on left side, **F** *Rootsman Paradise*, *cabinas*, café, juice bar, boutique, quiet, friendly, good service. There are also empty rooms to let, so take a hammock or sleeping bag, horses to rent (US$3.50/hr). On public holidays Cahuita is very crowded, expensive and difficult to get a room; the remainder of the year it is a favourite resort of backpackers (don't bathe or sun-bathe naked).

Camping: at *Vishnu's*, clean, cold showers, great breakfasts, vehicle US$6/night; at *Colibrís Paradise*, 1 km out of village, Canadian owner, US$5/tent, quiet, friendly. Also in the park (see above).

- **Places to eat** If the catch is good many restaurants have lobster at reasonable prices. *Tipico*, good; *Miss Edith's*, delicious Caribbean food, nice people, good value, no alcohol licence, take your own, many recommendations for breakfast and dinner, though don't expect quick service; *Deni*, in centre of town, original décor inc driftwood and birds' nests, reggae music, go to look but very mixed reports about food and service; *Sol y Mar*, good value, open 0730-1200, 1630-2000, need to arrive early and wait at least 45 mins for food, red snapper and volcano potato especially wicked, US$5, also good breakfasts, try cheese, egg and tomato sandwich, US$2, ask for Chepe who speaks English and is fun to talk to, also has cabins, see above; *Vista del Mar*, facing entrance to Park, good fish and Chinese dishes; *Quina*, also nr the Park, good Chinese, *casados*, best and cheapest coffee in around; *La Fiesta Italiana*, good food, nice atmosphere; *Soda Kukula*, great breakfast, fresh bread, German owner; *Soda Sedentario*, very good breakfasts, yoghurt and fruits; *Momma Mia Pizza*, good, sit outside; *Tipico*, very friendly service, good breakfasts, reggae music; *Marisquería*, at Puerto Vargas Park entrance, Italian, jovial host, also has rooms; *Cabinas Algebra* on the Black Beach has a good restaurant and the bar is away from the crowds, rec. *Salón Vaz*, lively at weekends with reggae music and Rastas, popular with travellers and locals, main gathering point, safe for lone women.

● **Banks & money changers** Money exchange is difficult except occasionally for cash dollars (Cahuita Tours changes US$ and TCs). Take plenty of colones from Limón. Several places accept credit cards.

● **Tours and rentals** Tony Mora runs glass-bottomed boats over the coral reef. Snorkelling equipment for hire. Also horses can be hired, but ensure they are in good shape. Bicycles can be hired for about US$7/day and you can cycle to Puerto Viejo and the Panamanian border through some beautiful scenery.

● **Useful information** Cahuita Tours (see above) also houses the post office and international telephone service (ICE). The National Park services have warned against muggings in the park at night, if walking the path take a torch. There have also been some rapes. Some of the jungle has been cleared for safety. Also beware of theft on the beach, and drug pushers who may be undercover police.

● **Transport Bus** service direct from San José (Av 11, C 1-Central), 0600, 1000, 1330 and 1530, T 257-8129, Transp Mepá, 4 hrs, US$4.50, and from Puerto Limón, in front of Radio Casino (0500, 1000, 1300, 1600, return 0600, 1000, 1200, 1730, US$0.80, 45 mins, T 758-1572), both continuing on paved road to Bribri, 2 basic *residencias*, and on to Sixaola on the Panamanian border (US$1, 2 hrs). The bus drops you at the crossing of the 2 main roads in Cahuita. **Taxi** Puerto Limón-Cahuita, US$20.

PUERTO VIEJO

The beaches at **Puerto Viejo (Limón)**, 19 km SE of Cahuita, are also worth a visit (be alert for thieves). They are quiet during the week, busy at weekends, good surfing. The black beach is the best for safe swimming. There is a public telephone in the Chinaman store in Puerto Viejo, the only one in the area. You need to bring towels, insect repellent and a torch. Bicycles can be rented for US$6/day but not good quality. There is a small, English book exchange, ask for directions. The

Asociación Talamanqueña de Ecoturismo y Conservación provides tourist information, sells locally made crafts and T-shirts, guide service, rainforest hikes, snorkelling and fishing trips. Tours cost US$15 (½-day), or US$22 (full day), T/F 750-0188, 750-0191. It is possible to walk along the beach from Puerto Viejo to Cahuita in 1 day (22 km, 5 hrs) but not rec. There is a channel to cross (Home Creek) and reports of tourists being robbed. **NB** Water can be scarce in Puerto Viejo.

● **Accommodation A2** *El Pizote Lodge*, cabin with bath, **B**, rooms with shared bath, T 750-0088; **B** *Black Pearl*, T 750-0111, F 750-0114, pool, restaurant; **C** *Maritza*, T 750-0199, in cabins, with bath, clean, highly rec, D, shared bathroom, clean, friendly, English spoken, a map in the bar shows all the hotels and *cabinas* in the area; **C** *Casa Máximo*, with breakfast, basic rooms; **D** *Cabinas Chimuri*, T 750-0119, N edge of town, thatched huts with balconies from which you can observe the wildlife, horseriding; **D** *Jacaranda*, T 750-0069, some rooms with bath, restaurant; **D** *Escape Caribeño Bungalows*, 500m along road to Punta Ura, German management, communal kitchen, free morning coffee, well-furnished cottages with TV, fully equipped; **D** *Pura Vida*, T 750-0002, Swiss run, friendly, very clean, hammocks, rec; **D** *Cabinas Grant*, large rooms, clean, fan, shower, parking, restaurant, nice patio; **D** *Cabinas Casa Verdes*, T 750-0047, F 750-0015, comfortable rooms, fan, shared bath. Good breakfasts at **E** *Hotel Puerto Viejo*, nice balconies, Mexican food, popular with surfers. **F** *Cabinas Manuel León*, with bath, T 758-0854; **F** *Kiskadee*, T 750-0075, small jungle lodge with 2 dormitories, kitchen available, American-run, about 200m from football field, from where it is signposted, rec, take torch and rubber boots; **F** *Cabinas Salsa Brava*, popular with surfers; *Cabinas Black Sands*, a bamboo, laurel wood and thatch cabin of Bri-Bri Indian design T 556-1132.

● **Places to eat** *Café Pizzería Coral*, good breakfasts, good main meals, not cheap, rec; *Garden Restaurant*, opens 1700, good food, highly rec; *El Parquecito*, facing sea, nice breezy atmosphere, specializes in fish and seafood (evenings only); *Green Garden*, clean, nice pastries, food from Trinidad, Californian style, very expensive; *Johnny's Place*, Chinese food, large portions, specialities of the day rec; *Soda Tamara*, open 0600-2100, local good quality homemade snacks. *Stanford's Disco*, lively nightlife; *Bambú*, nearby, good food; *Bar Sandborn*, rec for an evening beer. *Taberna Popo*, lively bar-disco, live music some nights, Carib and rock.

● **Post & telecommunications** E-mail from the Mail Office, US$2 to send, US$1 to receive, altecmail@sol.racsa.co.cr.

● **Transport** Daily bus 0600, 1000, 1330 and 1530 from San José via Cahuita, 4½ hrs, US$4.90, ½ hr from Cahuita, US$0.45.

There are a number of popular beaches SE along the road from Puerto Viejo. At about 4 km is **Playa Cocles** which has some of the best surfing on this coast.

● **Accommodation** D *Cabinas Surf Point*; F *Cabinas y Soda Garibaldi*.

2 km further on is **Playa Chiquita** with many places to stay.

● **Accommodation** A2 *Punta Cocles*, rec, 60 nice cabins, a/c, pool, forest trails, car rentals, boat trips, guides, horse riding, mountain bikes, transport from San José available, T San José 234-8055, F 234-8033. A2 *Playa Chiquita Lodge*, 11 rooms with private bathroom, French restaurant and bar, 500m from beach, naturalist guides available, T 233-6613, F 223-7479; A2 *Hotel Kasha*, 3 bungalows with bath and fan, open-air gym, jacuzzi and restaurant, T 284-6908, F 232-2056; A3 *Yare*, T 284-5921, with kitchenette, fan, hot water, restaurant; B *La Isla Inn*, 50m from beach, with bath, fan, breakfast available; D *Tío Lou Cabins*, T 227-3517; L2 *Villas del Caribe*, 2 floor apartments with kitchen, living room, bath, T 233-2200; A3 *Miraflores Lodge and Restaurant*, T 233-2822, 10 rooms, a/c, breakfast inc, with bath, fan, beautiful gardens, lots of wildlife, English and French spoken, boating tours to Monkey point.

Beyond this is **Punta Uva** with A2 *Almonds and Corals Tent Camp*, T 272-2024, tents with bath and hot water on platforms in the forest, pool, restaurant, trips arranged to Punta Mona, **Hitoy Cerere Biological Reserve**, snorkelling (equipment rental), bike hire; A3 *La Costa de Papito*, 3 bungalows managed by Eddie Ryan, fan, with bath; E *Selvin Cabins* and

restaurant, *Walaba Travellers Hostel*, with room and dormitory accommodation.

Another 5 km to **Manzanillo**, A2 *Hotel Las Palmas*, cabins, 60 ocean-view rooms, pool, snorkelling, rainforest, tours, transport from San José, Wed, Fri, Sun, US$30 return, US$20 one way, T/F 255-3939; E *Cabinas/Restaurant Maxi*, followed by white sand beaches and rocky headlands to **Punta Mona** and the **Gandoca-Manzanillo Wildlife Refuge**.

Take road from Cahuita to Hotel Creek where one road (dirt) goes to Puerto Viejo and another (paved) to **Bribri**, one of the villages at the foot of the Talamanca range, which has been declared an Indian Reserve. Halfway between Hotel Creek and Puerto Viejo is *Violeta's Pulpería*. From Limón, Aerovías Talamaqueñas Indígenas fly cheaply to **Amubri** in the Reserve (there is a *Casa de Huéspedes* run by nuns in Amubri). Villages such as Bribri, Chase, Bratsi, Shiroles and San José Cabécar can be reached by bus from Cahuita. (For a good introduction to the Talamanca mountains, read *Mamita Yunai* by Fallas, or *What Happen* by Palmer.)

FRONTIER WITH PANAMA – SIXAOLA

Continuing S from Bribri is **Sixaola**, on the border with Panama.

● **Costa Rican immigration**
The border is open 0700-1700. Remember to advance watches by 1 hr on entering Panama.

● **Accommodation**
Three hotels just before the bridge: E *Cabinas Sánchez*, with bath, F *Central*, Chinese run with good restaurant, and F *Pensión Doris*.

● **Exchange**
There are no banks in Sixaola, but it may be possible to change money in one of the shops before the bridge, eg *Soda Central*, but rates, especially to the US dollar are very poor. Shops nr the border in Panama will accept colones but shops in Changuinola and beyond do not.

● **Transport**
A narrow-gauge railway runs to Almte (Panama) from Guabito, on the Panamanian side.

If crossing to Panama take the earliest bus possible to Sixaola (see Panama, **The North-Eastern Caribbean Coast**, page 1207). Direct Sixaola-San José bus, Autotransportes Mepe, 5 hrs, US$5.45 (T 221-0524), 0500, 0800, 1430, return 0600, 1330, 1530 daily; also 3 a day to Puerto Limón via Cahuita 2½ hrs. It is cheaper to take the bus from Sixaola to Puerto Limón then another from Limón to San José rather than the through service.

In both countries, the local greeting in this area is 'OK?'. This means, 'good morning, how are you', 'I'm not going to attack you', 'can I help you?' If you don't want a chat, simply answer 'all right'.

The South Pacific Coast

A T THE FOOT of the cordillera, the narrow lowlands are cattle ranches or planted to African palm. Beaches, particularly those in the Manuel Antonio National Park, are a major attraction.

From Esparza on the Pan-American Highway a road runs 21 km SE to **San Mateo** (from where a road runs NE to Atenas – see Meseta Central section). Just before San Mateo, at Higuito de San Mateo, is *Las Candelillas*, a 26-ha farm and reforestation project with fruit trees and sugar-cane. There is a camping area with showers, pool and riding, T 428-9157, 428-8434. **A3** *El Rancho Oropéndola*, is at San Mateo, cabins with private bath or rooms with shared bath, rustic and peaceful, pool, nature trails, T/F 428-8600.

From San Mateo a road runs S to **Orotina**, which used to be an important road/rail junction on the route San José-Puntarenas. Orotina excursion: Finca Los Angeles, T 224-5828, offers 1-day nature tour on horseback US$65 through the mountains to the beach. Near Orotina, beyond the village of Coopebarre, is the Iguana Park, where you can watch, eat or buy (as pets) the reptiles. 5 km trails, gift shop (US$15 entry, US$10 for guided tour, open 0800-1600).

CARCAJAL

West of Orotina the road forks, NW to the port of Caldera, SW to the Pacific Coast at Tárcoles. Along the Caldera road is **Cascajal**.

● **Accommodation L3** *Dundee Ranch Hotel*, a working ranch, has 11 rooms with private bathroom, a/c, pool and restaurant, T 428-8776; **A3** *Hacienda Doña Marta* is a 260-ha working ranch and dairy farm with 6 cabinas, pool, bar and restaurant for guests, horseriding, next to Carara Biological Reserve, see below, reservations and information from *Finca Rosa Blanca Country Inn*, PO Box 23, Santa Bárbara de Heredia, T 269-9392, F 269-9555.

The coastal road continues through Jacó, Quepos, Playa Dominical and thence inland to San Isidro de El General. The road is paved as far as Parrita (after Jacó) and is generally good with few pot holes. Thereafter it is a good, but dusty, gravel road (difficult for motorbikes because of loose gravel), paved in villages, until Paquita, just before Quepos. Here the road deteriorates and paving is poor. After Quepos the road is still unpaved to Dominical, a hard ride, and although from Dominical the road inland through Barú to San Isidro is paved, landslides can make this section hazardous. Check the state of the roads and bridges before setting out to San Isidro if driving yourself and do not assume that if the buses are getting through, cars can too. High clearance is needed if a bridge is down. In the dry season motorists can do a round trip in a day starting from San José.

CARARA BIOLOGICAL RESERVE

Between Orotina and Jacó, just after the Río Tárcoles bridge (where crocodiles may be spotted in the river and scarlet macaws may be seen flying out of the forest into the sunset just before dusk, 1700-1730), is the **Carara Biological Reserve**, 4,700 ha with abundant wildlife. Scarlet macaws, which are using artificial nest boxes to help the birds reproduce in safety from poachers and predators, are best seen around 0630 or 1700. A good place to look for them is near the Río Tárcoles bridge, but take care: thefts and robberies reported in this area. Also to be seen in the Reserve are white-faced monkeys, coatis and crocodiles.

● **Admission** Open 0700-1600, entrance US$6. There is a 30-40 min circular path starting by the office, approximately 1,300m; trails have been improved with funds from British Embassy. San José travel agencies offer tours. If going by car, leave nothing of value in the car park.

Next to Carara is **La Catarata**, a private reserve with a 200(?)m waterfall with natural pools for bathing; take the gravel road up the hill beside *Hotel Villa Lapas*: 5 km to entrance, 2½ km hike to falls and pools. Open 0800-1500, Dec 15-April 15, entry US$7.50, information T 236-4140. There are signs on the main road.

● **Accommodation A2** *Hotel Villa Lapas*, next to the reserve (from Río Tarcolitos, turn left and go 500m), reservations T 293-2914, F 293-4104, hotel T 284-8186, with bath, pool, good restaurant, good birdwatching, easy access to mouth of Río Tárcoles, riding, guided tours to Carara, rec, animals come close to the hotel at night.

At **Playa Tárcoles**, **E** *Cabinas La Guaria*, bath (ask for Victor or Claudia of Jungle Crocodile Safari for boat trips on Río Tárcoles to see crocodiles in close-up, US$40 pp 1½ hr trip, T 661-0455); **C** *Cabinas Carara*, basic, 16 cabins with bath, small, simple restaurant, pool, superb birdwatching at mouth of Río Tárcoles about 5 km along this road, T 661-0455. 3 km from Tárcoles is *El Tico*, a good seafood restaurant. **A2-3** *Tarcol*

Lodge, basic rooms with shared bath, overpriced, on S bank of mouth of Río Tárcoles, high tide surrounds lodge on 3 sides, low tide uncovers mud flats attracting thousands of birds, packages inc transport, meals and tours, 5 bedrooms, 2 bathrooms, Apdo 364-1002, San José, T/F 284-8045, same management as *Albergue de Montaña Rancho Naturalista*, nr Turrialba.

Further S is **Punta Leona** with **B** *Punta Leona Hotel and Club*, bungalows with bath, a/c, T 231-3131, F 232-3074. **L2** *Hotel Leona Mar*, T 231-2868, 750 acres, spacious rooms with bath, a/c, cable TV, kitchen, access to Punta Leona Club pools. South of Punta Leona is **L3** *Villa Caletas*, French owned, 8 rooms, 20 bungalows, with amazing views, spectacular sunsets, lush gardens, pool, restaurant, boat and nature tours, T 257-3653, F 222-2059.

JACO

15 km from Carara is **Jacó** Beach, a large stretch of sandy beach, rather noisy and commercial, popular with surfers and weekenders from San José. Be careful of the rip tides all along this coast.

● **Accommodation & places to eat L3** *Hotel Villas Jacó Princess*, villas with kitchenette, a/c, T 643-3064, F 643-3010; **A1** *Best Western Jacó Beach Resort*, T 643-3064, F 643-3246 (or San José 220-1441, or 1-800-528-1234 in North America), a/c, IV, minibar, hot water, tennis, volley ball, restaurant and coffee shop, helpful staff, good service, recently upgraded; **A2** *Copacabana*, Apdo 15, Jacó, T/F 643-3131, Canadian-owned, on beach, attractive, clean, tours and sporting activities arranged, rooms quiet, fans, hot showers, suites for 4 with kitchenettes available, pool, bar with TV and live music, boutique, restaurant, car rentals, credit cards accepted, rec; **A2** *Jacó Fiesta*, T 643-3147, F 643-3148, bath, cable TV, phone, refrigerator, rooms hold 4/5 people, 4 pools, tennis, restaurant, highly rec, English, German, French spoken; **A2** *Paraíso del Sol*, T 643-3250, two types of room, pool and children's pool, rec; **B** *Cabinas Tanyeri*, T 442-0977, modern, attractive landscaping, pool, excellent value for groups; **A3** *Club de Mar*, T 643-3194, bath, fans, S end of beach, some rooms have separate living room and kitchenette; **B** *Zabamar*, T 643-3174, F 643-3175, large rooms, pool, American owners, helpful, small restaurant, reservations rec; **D** *Cabinas Heredia*, with bath, and **D** *Cabinas Las Brisas*, T 643-3087, attractive grounds, on beach, but run down; other hotels and many *cabinas*, inc **C** *Cabinas Las Palmas*, with bath and fan, cold water, clean; **C** *Coral*, T 643-3067, on beach S of town, 2 pools, hammocks, German owned, restaurant, warmly rec; **D** *El Jardín*, on beach, with bath, no hot water but clean, friendly, pool; **D** *Bohío*, nr beach, private bath, cold water, fan, swimming pool; **D** *Sol y Luna Cabinas*, Italian run, large rooms with bath, clean, fan, mosquito nets, restaurant; *Camping El Hicaco* and *Restaurant Los Hicacos* both down same access to the beach; *La Hacienda*, good bar and snacks; *Jacó Rock Café*, good food, good value; *Jacó Bell*, Mexican fast food.

● **Transport Air** Travelair operates daily flights to San José (Pavas). **Buses** From Coca Cola bus station, San José, 0715 and 1530 daily, returning 0500, 1500, 2½-3 hrs, US$1.60. Indirect buses also at 0730, 1030, 1530.

JACO TO PUERTO QUEPOS

From Jacó the road (with many potholes) runs along the coast giving lovely views of the ocean, several turnoffs to beaches along the way, including **Playa Hermosa** (**A1** *Hotel Terraza del Pacífico*, T 643-3939, with bath, phone, cable TV, good surfing; **A3** *David*, T 643-3737, F 643-3736, resort with fully-equipped gym); **Esterillos Este** (**A2** *Hotel El Delfín*, T 771-1640, swimming pool, all rooms with breezy balcony, secluded, clean, rec, good restaurant, considered by many one of the most delightful beach hotels in Costa Rica; other *cabinas*) and **Playa Palma**, near Parrita (**E** *Hotel Memo*, with bath, **F** *Hotel El Nopal*, and **F** *Cabinas Calevo*, with bath, clean, parking. Near Parrita, **B** *Beso del Viento* bed and breakfast, Playa Palo Seco, 5 km, T 383-7559, swimming pool, Canadian owners.) After Parrita the gravel road travels through palm plantations and the landscape is flat, becoming rather tedious after a few kilometres of palm trees. Many of the plantation villages along the

way are worth seeing for their 2-storey, balconied houses laid out around a central football pitch. On bridges along this road, the carriageway narrows to single track; take care especially at night.

PUERTO QUEPOS

Built by United Brands as a banana exporting port the town is now run down. The banana plantations were overwhelmed by Panama disease in the early 1950s and have been replaced by 8,200 ha of African Palm for oil. Mechanization was cut back when it was realized that tractors were damaging the roots of the palm trees and now oxen or mules pull carts along the rows, while tractors pulling several wagons load up at the ends of the rows. South of Quepos the coast has been developed for tourism, with numerous hotels built along the beach inevitably spoiling an attractive stretch of jungle clad coastline sweeping steeply down to the sea. Quepos is now important as a service town for local and foreign tourists. It is also cheaper to stay here than on the beach and there are many restaurants, bars and shops. The Post Office is on the walkway by the football pitch, open 0800-1700. The municipal market is at the bus station, buy fruit and bread here as the Super Mas supermarket is not well stocked. There is a good laundry near the football pitch. Immigration is on the same street as the Banco de Costa Rica, one of the three banks in town. The best place to exchange TCs or US$cash is at Distribuidora Puerto Quepos, opp Banco de Costa Rica, open 0900-1700, no paperwork, no commission, all done in 2 mins, same rate as banks. Visa card is the preferred credit card in this area, Mastercard can attract a 6% added commission. Police T 777-0196. There is a Spanish Language school, *Escuela D'Amore*, half way between Quepos and the National Park, T 777-1143, live with local families. *La Buena Nota*, souvenir shop, also sells some English language newspapers etc, a good place to seek local information, run by Anita

Myketuk and Donald Milton, who has initiated a lifesaving programme and publicity on rip tides, T 777-0345.

Local information

● Accommodation

Difficult to find accommodation on Sat, Dec-April and when local schools are on holiday.

A1 *Rancho Casa Grande*, 5 km inland close to airstrip, lovely yellow *casitas* in gardens, pool, a/c, jacuzzi, local agent for Travelair flights, nr airport, T 777-1903, F 777-1575; **A3** *Kamuk*, central, T 777-0379, shower, TV, ocean view, bar, restaurant, a/c; **D** *El Parque*, T 777-0063, on waterfront road, friendly, clean, a bit run down but good value, private bath, fan; **E-F** *Mar y Luna*, T 777-0394, with or without bath, quiet, clean, very friendly; **D** *Viña del Mar*, T 777-0070, with bath, fan, restaurant; **E** *Majestic*, noisy, shared bath, on the same street as Banco de Costa Rica; **F** *Hospedaje La Macha*, with fan, basic, noisy, little privacy, next to Post Office and soccer field behind bus station; **F** *Cabinas Cali*, 200m NE of bus station, T 777-1491, nice rooms, family run, clean, safe. On the road which leads to Manuel Antonio but still in town are **C** *Hotel Quepos*, T 777-0274, with bath, **D** without, simple, rec; **C** *Villas Mar y Sol*, T777-0307, F 777-0562, good bakery next door; **C** *Cabinas Mar-Su* in Boca Vieja district, no signs, about 300m before bridge entering town, large, clean, comfortable cabins, fan, bathroom, a/c extra, car park; **D** *Doña Alicia*, beside football pitch, big cabin with bath, friendly, quiet, parking, can wash clothes; **D** *Cabinas Mary* by football pitch behind bus station, clean, friendly, OK; **B-D** *Ceciliano* T 777-0245 with bath, family run, quiet, small rooms, hot; **D** *Mavio*, with bath, rec; **D** *Itzamaná*, cross bridge on way out of Quepos, turn half left at telephone box, continue past stop sign and along dog-leg in road, follow road to left where it peters out, hotel about 30m back on right, bath, cold water, clean, fan, friendly, good value, free bus to Manuel Antonio.

● Places to eat

In town is the *Iris* restaurant and *Arco Iris* discotheque both T 777-0449; *Isabel*, good breakfast choice, bulletin board, helpful staff, good food; *Restaurant El Turista* has good, cheap fruit juices; *El Gran Escape*, central, good food, good value, rec; *Soda La Marquesa*, very good, popular, cheap *casados*, lots of other dishes, good for breakfast; *Dos Locos*, Mexican food, good iced coffee; *Soda Nido*

and *Restaurant Ana*, cheap *casados*; *Soda Nahomi*, good sandwiches, nr park, next to laundry, *Lavanderías de Costa Rica*; *Soda El Kiosko* on seafront, nr *Hotel Kamuk*, good juices, fish dishes, international cuisine, popular; *Pan Aldas*, bakery, same road as bus station, Italian run, good; *George's American Bar and Grill*, on road to Manuel Antonio, 1 block from sea, on corner, breakfast, lunch, dinner, popular with travellers and English-speaking residents, T 777-0186; *Café Milagro*, towards Manuel Antonio, best expresso, cakes, pies, Cuban cigars, souvenirs, freshly roasted coffee for sale. The best restaurants are further along the coast towards Manuel Antonio.

● Transport

Air There are daily flights from San José, with Sansa and Travelair, see **Internal Flights** under San José. Book in advance. In Quepos the Sansa office is under *Hotel Quepos*, T 777-0161. Hustler Tours also run flights. Blue Marlin shop, run tours, information, next to *Hotel Quepos*.

Buses There are four direct buses a day from the capital, book a day in advance, 3 hrs, US$3.15; a local bus, US$3.50, takes 6$\frac{1}{2}$-7 hrs, leaving the main road at Parrita to wind its way through the mountains and rural settlements, crowded, uncomfortable, you could walk faster at times. From **Quepos** there are buses NW along the coast to **Puntarenas**, 3$\frac{1}{2}$ hrs, 0430, 1030, and 1500, US$2.10. Two daily buses via Dominical to **San Isidro de El General**, 0700 and 1330, 3$\frac{1}{2}$ hrs, connections can be made there to get to the Panamanian border. A bus from San José comes through at about 0930 on its way to Dominical and Uvita, US$1.25, 2 hrs, bad road.

Taxis: congregate at the junction of the coastal road and the park, by the road to Manuel Antonio. Minibuses meet flights at the airport.

Motorbike hire: Pico Rent-a-Bike, opp *Hotel Malinche* 200m from beach, T 777-0125, several models from US$25/day. See also information at *Restaurant Isabel*.

Taximar **boat** from Quepos to Dominical, Isla del Caño and Bahía Drake: leaves Quepos dock Tues, Thur, Sat, Sun 0700 for *Hotel Punta Dominical*, then to Isla del Caño or Bahía Drake. T 771-1903.

MANUEL ANTONIO NATIONAL PARK

7 km S of Quepos along a paved road the park is 683 ha of swamps and beaches with

a rich variety of fauna and flora. Plenty of birds, snakes, lizards, monkeys and sloths can be seen. The forest grows right down to three beautiful, but frequently crowded beaches: **Espadilla Sur**, **Manuel Antonio** and **Puerto Escondido**, and iguanas and white-faced monkeys often come down on to the sand. Hiking is good in the park. A 45-min trail, steep in places, runs round the Punta Catedral between Espadilla Sur and Manuel Antonio beaches. The walk to Puerto Escondido, where there is a blow hole, takes about 50 mins. The map sold at the entrance shows a walk up to a *mirador*, which has good views of the coastline, worth taking. The entrance to the park is reached by crossing a tidal river (plastic shoes rec, it is sometimes very high or alternatively, a boat will take you across the river for US$0.55), open 0700-1600, closed Mon, US$6. Early and late are the best times to see the wildlife. Breakfast and other meals available from stalls just before the river, where cars can be parked and minded for US$1 by the stallholders. Basic toilets and picnic tables by the beaches, cold water showers at Manuel Antonio and Espadillas Sur beaches. Keep clear of the manzanilla trees and do not eat their poisonous apples. You are not supposed to feed the monkeys but people do, which means that they can be a nuisance, congregating around picnic tables expecting to be fed and rummaging through bags if given the chance. Leave no litter and take nothing out of the park, not even sea shells. Overdevelopment outside the park and overuse within has led to problems of how to manage the park with inadequate funds. In 1992 the National Park Service (SPN) threatened to close it and a number of tour operators removed it from their itineraries. The beaches in the park are safer than those outside, but rip tides are dangerous all along the coast. Look for local safety literature. Beaches slope steeply and the force of the waves can be too strong for children. Watch out for logs and other debris in the water. Sea Kayaking, T 777-0574, Ríos Tropicales,

50m N of Manuel Antonio School, 1-day or multi-day tours, inc transport, also mountain biking, equipment and professional guides, Kelly and John have been rec.

● **Accommodation** There are hotels all along the road from Quepos to Manuel Antonio, many shut in the low season. In high season, best to book ahead. The area is full to bursting at weekends with many locals camping on the beach. Nearest the park is **D** *Hotel Manuel Antonio*, T 777-0290, restaurant, good breakfast, camping possible nearby, ask in the restaurant. On a side road just before the park is **D** *Costa Linda*, double rooms or **F** pp in 6-bedded room, with cooking facilities, fan, water shortage, T 777-0304, watch out for racoons raiding the outdoor kitchen in the night, good breakfasts, dinner rather pricey; **A3** *Hotel Villabosque*, 50m from beach, 150m from National Park, 10 rooms with a/c, private bathroom, inc breakfast, T/F 777-0401. **B** *Cabinas Espadilla*, T 777-0416, fan (not very effective), water shortages, clean, 10 mins' walk from beach; **D-B** *Vela Bar*, T 777-0413, Apt 13 Quepos, large rooms with bath, fans, safes, very good restaurant, fishing and other trips, also has a fully-equipped house to rent; further along is *Soda El Grano de Oro*, basic rooms at back, see Betty. Heading towards Quepos, on the main road, is *Bar del Mar*, T 777-0543, which rents surfboards, sells drinks and light meals and has a collection of English novels to read in the bar. Just off the road 25m further on, in a small lay-by, are the restaurants *Mar y Sombra*, T 777-0003, good *casado especial* and jumbo shrimps and *Amor y Mar*, T 777-0510, a souvenir shop, **D** *Caycosta*, and *Cabinas Ramírez*, T 777-0510 and 777-0003, with bath, food and bar, hammocks and camping free, guests can help with cooking in exchange; **C** *Cabinas Los Almendros*, cheaper for longer stays, private bath, fan, clean, quiet, reasonable restaurant, T 777-0225.

Proceeding along the main road towards Quepos, you come to *Cabinas Pisces*, T 777-0294/0046, and **A1** *Karahé*, on private road, T 777-0170, F 777-1075, inc breakfast, cabins on a steep hillside with lovely view, sleep 3/4, rec, fridge, bath, a/c or fan, good restaurant, swimming pool across the road, access to beach, can walk to park along the beach; **A2** *Costa Verde*, nr beach, apartments for 2-3 people, with kitchenette and bath, 2-bedroom villas available, T 777-0584, F 777-0560, well-appointed, rec; **A2** *Villa Nina*, unmistakable bubblegum pink, T 777-1628, F 777-1497, short walk to beach, 8 rooms, fully screened, bath, small pool, microwave ovens and fridges for hire, pleasant, friendly; **B-D** *La Arboleda*, T 777-0414, cabins on hillside leading down to beach sleep 2/3, bath, fan, good rec, Uruguayan restaurant, 8 ha wood, beware snakes, crabs and monkeys in the yard at night; **L2** *El Salto*, T 777-0130, F 441-2938, PO Box 119, Quepos, MAP in cabins with bath sleeping up to 4, inc taxes and eco-tour of own Reserve with waterfalls, 4 km of trails, horses, lovely peaceful setting on hill, open air restaurant and bar, gardens, pool; **L2-A3** *Eclipse*, Apdo 11-6350, Quepos, T/F 777-0408, F 777-1738, Costa Rican/French run, Mediterranean feel, standard rooms, junior suites or houses, 3 pools, very helpful, good service, a/c, fan, hot water, rec as 'best in the region', new restaurant opened Dec 1995, *Jardin Gourmet*, T 777-1728, delicious food, worth the price. Nearby are the cabins of John and Mavis Beisanz, T 249-1507, also expensive but very good; further on same side road, **A3** *Divisamar*, T 777-0371, low season, **A1** high season, pool, restaurant, a/c; *Barba Roja* restaurant, popular, not cheap, grilled tuna good, art gallery and gift shop, boat charter T 777-0424; **A3** *Los Mogotes*, T 777-1043 F 777-0582, inc breakfast, 8 rooms, pool and restaurant (home of singer the late Jim Croce); **L3** *Villas Nicolás*, T 777-0538, 10 rooms, 10 suites with kitchenette, pool; **A2** *Byblos*, T 777-0411, F 777-0009, low season, **L2** high season MAP, all in bungalows, sleep 1-4, French restaurant, pool, cruise in *Byblos I* boat 0800-1500, US$50 pp inc drink and sandwiches, **A2** *Villas El Parque*, 5 km from Quepos, T 777-0096, F 777-0538, large suites, attractive pool, restaurant with Mexican and S American choices; **L3** *Sí Como No*, environmental resort, T 777-1250, F 777-1093, 5 km from Quepos, 40 acre reserve, hotel, restaurant, pool, small shopping centre and 7 (**L2**) villas with 2 bedrooms will sleep 6, a/c, kitchenette; **A2** *Hotel Casablanca*, T/F 777-0253, smart, lovely view, German-owned, friendly, all facilities, pool, rec, on corner of road to **L1** *Mariposa*, T 777-0456, F 777-0050, also fine position, villas 800 ft above beach, inc breakfast, dinner, taxes and service, no credit cards, no guests under 15, bar (book meals in advance), pool (US$1 for non-residents); **L2** *El Parador*, 2 km from the road on Punta Quepos, half way between Quepos and the Park, T 777-1414, F 777-1437 (**A1** low season), 55 rooms, new all facility hotel, stunning views of the ocean, in style of Spanish parador,

helicopter landing pad; **L3** *Makanda by the Sea*, T 777-0442, F 777-1032, 1 km down from main road, 6 villas and studios; **L2** *Tule Mar*, 3 km S of Quepos, T 777-0580, F 777-1579, with breakfast, 14 octagonal 2 bedroom bungalows with domed roof lights, pool, snack bar, own beach; **A2** *Villa Oso*, T 777-0233, spectacular sea views; off the main road away from the sea, **B** *El Lirio*, T 777-0404, low season, **A1** high season inc breakfast and taxes, small, very comfortable; close to Quepos, **C** *Plinio*, T 777-0055, low season, **B** high season, on hillside, 13 rooms, restaurant, bar, pool, rec; *Cabinas Pedro Miguel*, opp, T 777-0035. Take a torch when walking on roads at night; there are snakes, some poisonous. Take all precautions against mosquitos, even in daytime.

● **Transport** There are 3-4 buses a day (depending on season) am, midday and pm, direct from **San José**, 4 hrs, US$5. At weekends buy ticket day before, bus fills to standing room only very fast. Return tickets are sold on main road between the few sodas, get them in advance, bus gets crowded in Quepos. Roads back to San José on Sun evening are packed. A regular bus service runs 6 times a day (roughly hourly in high season) from beside **Quepos** market, starting at 0545, last bus back at 1700, US$0.35. Taxi from Quepos, shared, US$0.65 pp. Minibuses meet flights from San José to the airport at Quepos (see above), US$2.25.

PUERTO QUEPOS TO DOMINICAL

30 km SE from Quepos towards Dominical along the unpaved coastal road ('carretera Costanera') is **Playa Matapalo**, a huge, beautiful sandy beach recommended for surfing and relaxing.

● **Accommodation A2** *Coicota Lodge*, nr Savegre, T 777-0161, F 777-1571, farm close to the river, rafting, walking trails; **C** *Bar y Cabinas El Coquito del Pacífico*, comfortable new cabins with bath, palm gardens, good breakfast, Swiss owned, rec (T Braun Ecoturismo in San José T 233-1731, F 222-8849); **B** *La Piedra Buena*, T/F 771 3015, cabins, good restaurant, beach access, also Swiss owned.

12 km further is **Dominical**, at the mouth of the Río Barú, where the road turns inland to San Isidro de El General. This road is very steep and has some unpaved sections, from a few metres to a few kilometres. Dominical has become very

popular with surfers, hotel prices soar in high season and most hotels are next to noisy bars, preventing sleep at night.

● **Accommodation A1** *Villas Río Mar Hotel and Resort*, T 787-0052, 500m from beach, 40 bungalows with bath, fridge and fan, pool, jacuzzi, tennis court, trails, riding, all inclusive; **A2** *Escaleras Inn*, 2 guest rooms, with breakfast, T 771-5247; **A3** *Hacienda Barú*, T 787-0003, F 787-0004, 344-ha reserve, cabins with private bath, hiking, riding; **B** *Cabinas Nayarit*, T 787-0033, beach front cabins, bath, hot water; **B** *Hotel Pacífico Edge*, 4 large cabins with views of ocean and rainforest, T 771-1903 (Selvamar reservation service); **B** *Hotel Diuwak*, T/F 223-8195, 400m from San Clemente Bar bus stop; **C** *Willis Cabañas*, restaurant opp; **C** *Cabinas Bejuco*, 300m from beach, T/F 771-1903, new cabins with bathtubs, peaceful; **D-C** *Albergue Willdale*, T 787-0023, fan and bath, bikes, boat trips, fishing and horses available; **D** *Posada del Sol*, 100m from beach, owned by Mariela Badilla, local historian, fascinating, 4 rooms, bath, fan, patio with hammocks, also 2-bedroom apartment with kitchen for US$100/week, highly rec, PO Box 126-8000, San Isidro de el General; **E-D** *Cabinas El Coco*, with or without bath, negotiate price, reported dirty, unfriendly, noisy; **E** *Cabinas Roca Verde*, T 787-0036, friendly, fan, restaurant, rec; **E** *Cabinas Costa Brava*, S of the village, restaurant, basic but friendly. 4 km S is Punta Dominical (no transport): **D** *Cabinas Punta Dominical*, T 787-0026, restaurant, fishing, riding, good value for seekers of solitude; **B-C** *Cabinas San Clemente*, T 787-0026, on beach, clean, with or without a/c, friendly, American owned, restaurant, **E** pp, rooms over bar, shared bath, fan; *Gringo Place*, bar/restaurant under same ownership, good; **B** pp *Finca Brian y Milena*, nr Dominical, 400m above ocean, T 771-1903 (for reservations), cabins with bath, inc meals, forest, waterfall, horses. 4 km S of Dominical, **B** *Bella Vista Lodge*, great view, good large meals, owned by 'Woody Dycer', local character (American), organizes trips, T 771-1903 (Selva Mar reservation service).

● **Transport** Bus Quepos-Dominical 0500, 0930, 1330; Dominical-San Isidro, 2 buses between 0700-0800, 1 hr; last bus from San Isidro to Dominical 1500; bus Dominical-Quepos 0500; to San José, 7 hrs.

18 km S of Dominical is the village of **Uvita**, where there is camping, **C** *El Chaman*, German owner, very friendly, nice beach, isolated; also *Cabinas Hegalva*, rooms with hot shower, meals, camping. In the area you can walk, swim in a waterfall in the forest or at the beach, take a boat trip, watch seabirds. The road S from Uvita was badly affected by the 1996 hurricane, but is being repaved as far as Ciudad Cortés, and access to the beaches of Playa Ballena and Playa Bahía is getting easier with consequent development of the area and the construction of *cabinas*. Bus San José to Uvita daily 1500, return 0500.

BALLENA PARQUE NACIONAL MARINO

You can hire boats to take you out to Isla Ballena, part of **Ballena Parque Nacional Marino**, wonderful views looking back to the mainland. Be careful of the surf, do not attempt to swim ashore on to the island.

● **Accommodation A3** *Cabinas Ballena* and **C** *Rocaparadiso*, both 6 km S of Uvita in front of Ballena Parque Nacional Marino, T 220-4263 for information.

Further down the road to Palmar Norte is **Las Ventanas de Osa Wildlife Refuge**, 36-ha, private reserve and lodge built by the late Fred Ross; 5-night packages inc transport, meals, guided tours, US$900 pp, T USA 1-800-561-7751, Costa Rica 236-5926/284-7780.

San José to the Panama border

THROUGH THE mountains, past El Chirripó, the highest peak, dropping down along the valley of the Río de El General to the tropical lowlands of the Pacific coast and the Panama border.

The Pan-American Highway to the Panama border runs 352 km from San José (lots of potholes, frequent rockslides during rainy season, hurricane damage in 1996 means there are roadworks and poor conditions, be careful driving, don't drive at night), first to Cartago (toll road, US$0.30), and southwards over the mountains between Cartago and San Isidro de El General (124 km). This is a spectacular journey. The climate is ideal for orchids. At Cartago begins the ascent of **Cerro Buena Vista** (3,490m), a climb of almost 2,050m to the continental divide, a little lower than the peak; the highest point of the road is 3,335m at km 89. At this height there is an interesting *páramo* ecosystem. Those unaccustomed to high altitude should beware of mountain sickness brought on by a too rapid ascent, see **Health Information**, page 59. For 16 km it follows the crest of the Talamanca ridge, with views, on clear days, of the Pacific 50 km away, and even of the Atlantic, over 80 km away.

SANTA MARIA DE DOTA

At Km 51 from San José, a side road leads off the Pan-American Highway to the peaceful and very pleasant mountain village of **Santa María de Dota** (1,460 m). Santa María is quiet, and beautifully situated; it is in a good area for walking, and 8 km away is a small lake where many waterbirds nest. From Santa María one can hike (10 hrs) to the Pacific coast of the Puerto Quepos district, or go by road (3 hrs in a 4WD vehicle). Bus from San José to Santa María and San Marcos, 5 daily from Av 16, C 19/21.

● **Accommodation** F *Hospedaje Fonda Marleuse*, T 541-1176, shared bath, clean, basic, very friendly, run by an elderly lady, Doña Elsie, rec. *Hotel and Restaurant Dota*, nr square, with bath; *Soda Gómez*, next to bus station, large portions, cheap. At **San Marcos de Tarrazú**: F *Marilú*, restaurant; E *Continental*, with bath; F *Zacateca*, with bath. *Finca El Eden*, nr Copey de Dota, on road to Providencia, no phone but T 541 1299 to leave message, 2 cabins, riding, treks into the mountains. At **San Gerardo de Dota C** pp *Cabinas Chacón*, inc meals, good cabins, simple meals, T 771-1732, good chance of seeing quetzales on the property (short trail map available), and there is trout fishing in the Río Savegre.

4½ km E of Km 58 (Cañón church) is **Genesis II**, 100-acre cloudforest reserve at 2,360m, rooms with shared bath, for birders and naturalists, advance reservation necessary, T 381-0739, transportation available from San José. There is also a student volunteer programme: write to Steve and Paula Friedman, Apdo 10303, 1000 San José (conditions are basic, the climate can be cold and damp and rooms are heated with kerosene heaters but the plant and animal life make it a worthwhile stop-over; full details of the work involved are set out in the information sent with the application form. The food is reported good, vegetarians catered for.

At Km 62 on the Pan-American Highway is the **A** *Albergue de Montaña Tapantí*, also called *Hotel Tapantí*, Spanish-owned, 6 bungalows, beautiful location, 1 hr to San José, 1-night packages inc transport and guided trips available, T 232-0436.

At Km 70: *Finca El Mirador Los Quetzales*, 43 ha forest property at 2,400m, Eddie Serrano or one of his sons will show visitors quetzales and other endemic species of the highlands, US$9 pp (Jorge, Oscar and Carlos are rec guides), 2 new cabins with wonderful view and private bath, 8 basic cabins (ask for plenty of blankets), C inc breakfast, dinner and guided hike, T 381-8456.

At Km 71 is another *Finca Quetzal*. At Km 78: *Casa Refugio de Ojo de Agua*, a historic pioneer home with picnic tables in front of the house.

The highest point is at Km 89.5 (temperatures below zero at night). At Km 95: **E** *Hotel and Restaurant Georgina*, at almost 3,300m, basic, clean, friendly, good food (used by southbound Tracopa buses), good birdwatching, ask owners for directions for a nice walk to see quetzales.

At Km 107 turn off and follow the signs to the **Reserva Privada Avalón**, where there are more than 60 species of birds recorded. Accommodation, **B**, food, guides and horses available. Contact Scott Miller, Apdo 846, San Isidro de el General, T/F 771-7226.

SAN ISIDRO DE EL GENERAL

The road then drops down into **San Isidro** (*pop* 41,513), 702m above sea-level in a fertile valley in the centre of a coffee and cattle district. The town is growing fast. The **Museo Regional de Pérez Zeledón** is in the old marketplace, now the Complejo Cultural, C 2, open Mon-Fri, 0800-1200, 1330-1630, entrance free. 7 km N of San Isidro is the **Centro Biológico Las Quebradas**, with 750 ha, trails, dormitory accommodation for researchers, open 0800-1400 Tues-Fri, 0800-1500 Sat-Sun, closed Oct, T 771-4131.

● **Accommodation A1-3** *Del Sur*, T 771-3033/3039, F 771-0527, 6 km S of town, with bath, comfortable, swimming pool, tennis, good restaurant; **B** *Talari Mountain Lodge*, 10 mins from San Isidro, 8-ha farm, T 771-0341, with bath, rustic; **E** *Amaneli*, close to San José buses, with restaurant; **E** *Hotel Chirripó*, S side of Parque Central, shared bath (**D** rooms with bath), nr bus office, clean, very good restaurant, free covered parking, good, rec; **E** *Iguazu*, modern; **E** *Manhattan*, with bath; **F** *El Jardín*, good value, and good restaurant (especially the breakfast), rec; **F** *Hotel Balboa* in the centre, bath, rec; **F** *Pensión Jerusalem*, friendly, clean. On the road towards San Gerardo de Rivas, about 4 km from San Isidro, *Centro Turístico de Praderea*, T 771-0918, wonderful views, botanical garden, hiking trails; 6 km, **B** *Talari Mountain Lodge*, T 771-0341, 8 cabins, 8-ha property, restaurant, pool, orchard, riding; 7 km, *Rancho La Botija*, T 771-1401, 382-3052, restaurant, pool, hiking, open 0900 at weekends, restaurant open daily.

● **Places to eat** *Astoria*, N side of square. *Restaurant Wu Fu* is good, *Hong Kong*, across the park from *Hotel Chirripó*, reasonable prices; *Restaurant El Tenedor*, good food, not expensive, friendly, big pizzas, rec; *Soda Mönpik*, good hamburgers, *batidos*, ice cream, N side of Parque Central; *Soda Katty*, by bus station, good reasonable food; *Panadería El Tío Marcos*, S side of Parque, very good bakery; *Café del Teatro*, small snack bar, helpful owner is planning to open a tourist office; paintings for sale and plays in Spanish every month or so. Ask in advance for early (0400) breakfast if climbing Chirripó.

● **Transport** Bus terminal at Av 6, C Central/2 at the back of the new market and adjacent streets. To and from **San José**, hourly service, US$3, 3 hrs (buses to the capital leave from the Interamericana, C 2-4). However, Tracopa buses coming from San José, going S go from C 3/Pan-American Highway, behind church, to

Palmar Norte, US$2.25; **Paso Canoas**, 0830-1545, 1930 (direct), 2100; **David** (Panama) direct, 1000 and 1500; **Golfito** direct at 1800; **Puerto Jiménez**, 0530 and 1200. Waiting room but no reservations or tickets sold.

CHIRRIPO NATIONAL PARK

From San Isidro de El General one can go to the highest mountain in Costa Rica, **Cerro Chirripó Grande** (3,820m) in the middle of the **Chirripó National Park** (50,150 ha), including a considerable portion of cloud forest (entry US$6, crowded in season, make reservations in Oficina de los Parques Nacionales in San Isidro, T 771-3155). Splendid views from the mountaintops; interesting alpine environment on the high plateau, with lakes of glacial origin and very diverse flora and fauna. The Chirripó National Park and the neighbouring **La Amistad International Park** (193,929 ha), established in 1982, extend along the Cordillera de Talamanca to the Panamanian border and comprise the largest area of virgin forest in the country with the greatest biological diversity.

● **Accommodation** At entrance to La Amistad Park there is **A2** *Monte Amou Lodge*, T 265-6149, with bath, guided walks with naturalists, electricity is generated to 2200; and a chalet lodge on a coffee plantation, **A3** pp *La Amistad*, all inclusive, good hiking, excellent guide, rec rooms and food, contact owner Roberto Montero, c/o Tropical Rainbow Tours, T 233-8228, F 255-4636, San José.

SAN GERARDO DE RIVAS

At San Isidro de El General, get food and take the Pueblo Nuevo bus from the new bus station to San Gerardo de Rivas (0500 or 1400, return at 0700 and 1600). Highly interesting trip up the Río Chirripó valley; **San Gerardo de Rivas** is situated in a cool, pleasant landscape at the confluence of two rivers. Horses can be rented. There is a hot spring 50m from the bridge in San Gerardo, free.

● **Accommodation** F *Marín*, basic but friendly and good value, good *comedor*. Sr Francisco Elizondo Badilla (the local 'champion' climber) and his family have a small cabin, **F** pp *Posada El Descanso*, with / bunks, bathroom, hearty meals available, rec, phone town administrator for information on availability,

Climbing the Chirripó peaks

🐾 If you wish to climb the mountains, you may obtain information from the SPN office in San José (see National Parks in Introduction). Start in the early morning for the 8 to 10 hrs' hike, US$6 entry for each day spent in the park, plus US$2.40 shelter fee/night, max 40 persons in park at any one time. The Park entrance is about 2½ hrs' walk from San Gerardo. Book accommodation in advance in San José, otherwise pay and obtain permit at the Park office in San Gerardo. You may be told the Refugio is fully booked, but this is not always the case when you get there. The shelter, where the horses will take you, consists of two good, but cold huts, *Refugios Base Crestones*. They are 2 hrs from the top at 3,400m where there normally is a park ranger. Hang up food or the mice will get it. Bring your own gas stove, which can be hired from *Posada El Descanso* or the shop nr *Cabinas Chirripó*. Two peaks can be reached from these huts, **Crestones**, 45 mins, and **Ventisqueres**, 1½ hrs. There is another shelter, *Refugio LlanoBonito* (2,500m), simple but clean, wooden floor, 2 levels to sleep on, no door but wind protection, drinking water, toilet, about 4 hrs' walk from San Gerardo, 3 hrs' walk on to *Refugios Base Crestones*. Plan for at least 2 nights on the mountain, and bring warm sleeping bags and waterproof clothing. It can be hot in the daytime, though. In the rainy season trails up the plateau are uncomfortably slippery and muddy, and fog obscures the views. These are stiff walks, but no technical climbing is called for. Time your descent to catch the afternoon bus back to San Isidro.

T 771-0433 ext 106, gas stove for hire, horses for rent and guide services offered, rec. Along the road beyond the Rangers office, bear right over a bridge and *El Descanso* is on the left. You can stay at the small hotel opp the football pitch called **G** *Albergue Turístico Chirripó*, hot shower, clean, basic, friendly, restaurant, or nearby at the **F** *Roca Dura*, built on a huge boulder, hot showers, good *comedor*, nice view, shop next door, ½km out of village, friendly owners. You can camp at or nr the park office, in San Gerardo nr the bus stop. Check in first and pay US$0.30.

Continuing SE along the highway, at Km 142 is **B** *Huerta de Buena Salud*, pool, good for bed and breakfast. At km 197 (from San José) is **Buenos Aires**, with **F** *Cabinas Mary*, 500m from centre, quiet clean, **F** *Cabinas La Redonda Familiares*, close to the Pan-American Highway and an un-named *cabinas* across from the bus station (with or without bath, clean, good value); next door is *Soda Refresquería El Parque*, good *casados*; *Flor de la Sabana*, good restaurant, good value. The section of the highway running alongside the Río Grande de Térraba is prone to landslides which can cut it off for days.

At **Palmar Norte** (Km 257) are **D** cabin **E** rooms *Hotel y Cabinas Casa Amarilla*, with fan, rooms at back quieter, rooms over restaurant noisy but cheaper; **G** pp *Residencia Familiar*, motorcycle parking; also *Quebrada*, noisy and basic, *El Puente Hotel y Restaurante*, and *Xinia*. From here a paved road leads to Ciudad Cortés and from there you can follow a new road along the coast NW to Dominical (see page 1125). Direct Tracopa buses from San José, 5 hrs, 6 daily from Av 18, C 2-4.

At **Palmar Sur** (gas station), 99 km from the Panamanian border, a banana plantation has stone spheres, 1½m in diameter and accurate within 5 mm, which can also be seen in other places in Costa Rica. They are of precolumbian Indian manufacture, but their use is a matter of conjecture; among recent theories are that they were made to represent the planets of the solar system, or that they were border markers. Flights with Sansa and Travelair San José-Palmar Sur, see **Internal Flights**, San José. From Palmar a bus goes to Sierpe, from where a boat sails to Bahía Drake (page 1136).

SAN VITO

Near the border is the town of **San Vito**, built by Italian immigrants among denuded hills; it is a prosperous but undistinguished town. The road from Paso Real to San Vito is now paved and has lovely views. There is a new bridge over the Río Térraba just after the Paso Real junction.

Excursions On the road from San Vito to Ciudad Neilly at **Las Cruces** there are the **Wilson Botanical Gardens**, T 773-3278, owned by the Organization for Tropical Studies, 6 km from San Vito. It consists of 145 ha of tropical plants, orchids, other epiphytes, and tropical trees, entrance US$6, good self guide booklet for the principal trail US$2.20. Many birdwatchers come here. It is possible to spend the night here if you arrange first with the Organization of Tropical Studies in San José, T 240-6696 (cost around US$64 pp double occupancy a night with food, senior researchers US$32, day visits with lunch US$18 pp). The library and other buildings were destroyed by fire in late 1994. OTS welcomes any donations; Organization for Tropical Studies, Box 90630, Durham NC 27708-0630 USA. On the same road is *Finca Cántaros*, specializing in local arts and crafts, owned by Gail Hewson Gómez. Worth a look even if you don't buy anything.

● **Accommodation & places to eat** **E** *Hotel Pitier*, ½ km out of town on road to Sabalito, new, clean, with bath; *Las Mirlas* in same location and price range but more attractive; and **D** *El Ceibo*, in new part with bath and hot water, **E** in old part, T 773-3025, good restaurant. There are also two good Italian restaurants in San Vito, *Lilianas* and *Mama Mías*, genuine Italian cuisine, reasonable prices. Hotels also in the nearby village of Cañas Gordas on the frontier with Panama (no crossing).

● **Transport** **Air** Sansa flights to/from San José, Mon, Wed, Fri. **Bus** Direct buses San José to San Vito, 4 daily, 9 hrs, C 14, Av 5; alternative route, not all paved, via Ciudad Neily (see below); from San Vito to Las Cruces at 0530 and 0700; sit on the right to admire the wonderful scenery; return buses pass Las Cruces at 1510.

The road from San Vito to Ciudad Neily is paved for the first 12 km to Agua Buena, thereafter, despite what maps say, it is unpaved to Ciudad Neily, 19 km, steep, bumpy and rocky (it would be very difficult in a passenger car). From San Vito a paved road runs to the Panama border at Sabalito/Río Sereno, but you need a visa to be allowed to cross here (if entering Costa Rica, get a tourist card in advance). Also, you may not be able to get customer clearance for a car entering Costa Rica at Río Sereno.

GOLFITO

31 km N of the border a road (26 km) branches S at Río Claro (several *pensiones* and a fuel station) to **Golfito**, the former banana port. Golfito is a 6 km long linear settlement between the gulf (Golfo Dulce) and steep forested hills. Entering the town from the S are a group of hotels leading in 2 km or so to the town centre of painted buildings with saloon bars, open fronted restaurants and cheap accommodation. Nearby is the dilapidated *'muellecito'* used by the ferries to Puerto Jiménez and water taxis. A further km N are the container port facilities and the Standard Fruit local HQ though many of the banana plantations have been turned over to oil palm and other crops. However, the port is now active with container traffic. Beyond the port is the airstrip and another set of hotels. Golfito became a free port in 1990, which has become popular with shoppers and at weekends it is difficult to get a hotel room. You must obtain a permit the previous day if you wish to shop there (passport required). There is an ICT Tourist Office, T 775-0496.

The **Refugio Nacional de Fauna Silvestre Golfito** has been created in the steep forested hills overlooking Golfito, originally to protect Golfito's watershed. It is rich in rare and medicinal plants and has abundant fauna. There are some excellent hikes in the Refuge. It is supervised by the University of Costa Rica and they have a field office in Golfito.

● **Accommodation Near airport**: A3 *Sierra*, T 775-0666, F 775-0087, 72 rooms, a/c, pool, restaurant; **B** *Golfo Azul*, with bath and a/c, T 775-0871, good restaurant. **In the 'banana town'**, **E** *Cabinas Evelyn*, with fan and bath; **E** *Cabinas Princesa del Golfo* and *Casa Blanca Lodge*, T 775-0124, 5 rooms, both in fine frame houses with beautiful gardens; **F** *Cabinas Marlin*, small neat rooms, fan, hot water, friendly; **F** *Cabinas Wilson*; **G** *Cabinas Ajilio*. **In the main town to the south**: *Del Cerro*, Edif Wachong, T 775-0006, F 775-0551, 20 rooms, private bathroom, laundry services, fishing boat rentals; **B** *Las Gaviotas*, 18 rooms, with excellent restaurant on waterfront, with bath, a/c, T 775-0062, F 775-0544; **D** *Costa Rica Surf*, also one cheap, single room, friendly; **D** *El Gran Ceibo*, next to *Gaviotas*, T 775-0403, small pool, a/c; **D** *Mar y Luna*, T 775-0192, 8 rooms, with bath, fan, restaurant on stilts above the sea; **D** *Koktsur*, T 775-0327, cabina with private bath; **D** *Golfito*, T 775 0047, with bath, run down; **E** *Delfina*, shared bath, fan, car park, friendly, owner speaks English, basic, rooms on street noisy; **E** *Cabinas Miramar*, T 775-0348, fan; **G** *El Uno*, above restaurant of same name, basic, friendly; *El Refugio*, T 775-0449. 7 km before Golfito there is good camping at *La Parruja Lodge* (US$3).

● **Places to eat** *Cubana*, nr Post Office, good food, try the *batidos*; *Luis Brenes*, opp Texaco, good simple food, good meeting place; *Soda Pavas*, in front of parque central, cheap, also have rooms in the hills, **E**. Many eating places nr centre.

● **Banks & money changers** Banco Nacional nr muelle, open Mon-Fri 0830-1535.

● **Transport Air** Daily flights San José-Golfito, with Sansa (not Suri) and Travelair, see **Internal Flights**, San José. Runway is all-weather, tight landing between trees; 2 km from town, taxi US$0.50. **Buses** From **San José** 0700, 1100, 1500 daily from C 2-4, Av 18, T 221-4214 (US$6) with Tracopa, 8 hrs; from San Isidro de El General, take 0730 bus to Río Claro and wait for bus coming from Ciudad Neily. Bus Golfito-**Paso Canoas**, US$0.80, hourly from outside *Soda Pavo*, 1¼ hrs. **Sea**

Asociación de Boteros, water taxis in and around Golfito, opp ICE building, T 775-0712, to Cacao Beach, Punta Zancudo, Punta Encanto or to order, US$20/hr up to 5 persons.

GOLFITO BEACHES

About 6 km (1½ hr walk) N round the bay from Golfito is the **Playa de Cacao**. A taxi boat from Golfito will take you there for US$2.50, or you can drive (if it hasn't rained too heavily) along an inland road, starting at the left of the police station in Golfito, and left again a few kilometres later.

● **Accommodation** B *Cabinas Palmas*, 6 cabins, American-owned, friendly, clean, shower and toilet, directly on beach, 5 mins N of Golfito by water taxi, T 775-0375 (leave message, Spanish only). Next to *Cabinas Palmas*, good, cheap restaurant, *Siete Mares*. Also at Playa de Cacao is the *Zamia Biological Station*, arrange with Sr Odette at Travelair office in Golfito, max 4 persons, student exchanges. Beyond Playa de Cacao is **Playa San Josecito** and the **A1** *Golfo Dulce Lodge*, T 775-0373, F 775-0573, cabins with bath and hot water, guided hikes and trips, Swiss owned. 30-45 mins by boat NW of Golfito, at **Playa Cativo**, is Michael Medill's **L2** *Rainbow Adventures*, cabinas, inc all meals, snacks, beer and soft drinks, transport, also double rooms, dining room, private beach with no other hotels, jungle tours, tours of the gulf, fishing, snorkelling, bordered by National Park, Apdo 63, Golfito, T/F 775-0220, in USA, 5875 NW Kaiser Rd, Portland, Oregon 97229, T 503-690-7750, F 503-690-7735 for reservations.

Also, 30 mins by water taxi from Golfito, you can visit **Casa Orquídeas**, a family owned botanical garden with a large collection of herbs, orchids and local flowers and trees, T 735-5062 for information.

At **Playa Zancudo**, about 15 km by sea S of Golfito, you can stay in cabins at **C** *Los Ultimos Paraísos*, T 776-0050, with bath, fan, mosquito nets, hammocks or **C-D** *Sol y Mar*, run by Rick and Lori, T 776-0014, F 776-0015, e-mail: solymar@zancudo.com, 4 screened cabins, hot water, fan, 3-storey rental house, US$450-550, 50m from ocean, bar/restaurant, meals 0700-2000, home baked bread, great fruit shakes, volleyball with lights

for evening play, badminton, paddleball, boogie boards, library. To get there contact staff of Yacht Club at the entrance of Golfito and ask to radiophone to Zancudo, 775-0056, well rec.

PIEDRAS BLANCAS NATIONAL PARK

To the N of Golfito is a new conservation area of tropical wet forest, **Piedras Blancas National Park**. The area was being exploited for wood products, but was purchased in 1994 with help from the Austrian government and private interests, notably Michael Schnitzler, the classical violinist. All logging has now ceased and efforts are devoted to a research centre and ecotourism. This is concentrated in an area designated **Esquinas National Park**. Near the village of **La Gamba** a tourist lodge has been built: **L2** *Esquinas Rainforest Lodge*, T/F 775-0849, or T 227-7924, full board, private baths, verandas overlooking the forest, tours, all profits to the local community. La Gamba is 6 km along a dirt road from Golfito, or 4 km from Villa Briceño on the Pan-American Highway between Piedras Blancas and Río Claro.

PUNTA BANCO

South of Golfito on the mainland, at **Punta Banco** is **A2** *Tiskita Lodge*, T 233-6890, F 255-4410, a 162-ha property including a fruit farm, with excellent birdwatching, 14 cabins overlooking ocean, owned by Peter Aspinall c/o Sun Tours, Apdo 1195-1250 Escazú. Overlooks beach, cool breezes, waterfall, jungle pools, trails through virgin forest. All-inclusive package tours from San José including roundtrip air transportation. *Tiskita* can be combined with *Corcovado Tent Lodge Camp* at Carate, Osa Peninsula. *Casa Punta Banco*, managed by Malcolm Miles, is a jungle home in 265 acres of forest, you're on your own for US$700 per week, T 775-0131. Day trips offered by boat to Sirena Ranger Station in Corcovado National Park. Near Punta Banco at Pavones is **B** *Pavones Surf Lodge*, inc meals, 2 cabins with bath, 6 rooms with shared bath, T 222-2224, F 222-2271 in San José. Also at Pavones is *Rancho La Ponderosa*, owned by two surfers, large cabins, fan, with bath, fishing diving etc, T (USA) 407-783-7184. The beach is rocky, but good surfing. A bus leaves Golfito for Pavones at 1400, and from Pavones to Golfito at 0500 3 hrs US$2.50. A spit of land continues S to Punta Burica with no roads and only one or two villages. The crest of the peninsular is the boundary with Panama.

OSA PENINSULA

Across the gulf from Golfito is the **Osa Peninsula**.

PUERTO JIMENEZ

Puerto Jiménez (*pop* 2,500), has the feel of a frontier town, perhaps because of the gold prospectors seeking riches in several mineral areas on the peninsula. In fact, most miners were cleared from the Corcovado National Park area in 1985, though there are still some licenced operations and a few pirate panners who enter the park illegally. There are gold mines near **Carate** (see below) on the Pacific coast and elsewhere on the Peninsula. Near Puerto Jiménez is **Dos Brazos**; ask for the road which goes uphill beyond town, to see the local gold mines. Several buses a day to Dos Brazos, last bus back at 1530 (often late); taxi US$7.25. The town is also popular with foreigners for its laid-back, sometimes lively atmosphere, its reasonable beaches nearby and, of course, the beautiful National Park on the other side of the peninsular. A particular charm of Puerto Jiménez is its relative freedom from road traffic. There is an ICE tourist office on the main street in town open Mon-Fri 0800-1530.

● **Accommodation & places to eat** B *Agua Luna*, facing pier, T 735-5034, new rooms with bath, good restaurant; **B** *Doña Leta's Bungalows*, close to airstrip, T/F 735-5180, cabins in gardens adjoining beach, large rooms with bath, clean, comfortable, kitchenette, fridge, fan, rec; **C** *Manglares*, with bath and fan, clean, small,

cold showers, café, bar, friendly, T 735-5002, F 735-5121, Ramón can arrange tours to Corcovado, Mangrove gardens attract many species of birds; **D** *Cabinas Puerto Jiménez*, on the gulf shore, T 735-5090, F 735-5215, big rooms, friendly, good value. **D** Sr and Sra Talí at Dos Brazos, T 775-1422, have rooms, inc breakfast, clean, shared bath, laundry facilities, jungle tours, riding, good food, rec. **E** *Cabinas Marcelina*, T 735-5007, F 735-5045, with bath, clean, friendly, nice front yard; **E** *Hotel Restaurant Choza del Maglan*, cabins in garden, **F** *Cabinas Brisas del Mar*, with bath (T 735-5012); **G** pp *Pensión Quintero*, clean, good value, ask here for Fernando Quintero, who rents horses and has a boat for up to 6 passengers, good value, he is also a guide, rec; *Restaurant El Paraíso*, typical food, cheap; *Carolina's Restaurant*, highly rec for fish; *El Rancho*, good pizzas and bar with music to 0100. 5 km from Rincón, on the road to Puerto Jiménez, at the NE side of the neck of the peninsula, is **G** pp *Profecto Boscoso*, a naturalists' camp where visitors can stay in camp beds, 3 meals US$3.65, information from Fundación Neotrópica, C 20, between Av 3 y 5, San José, T 233-0003, ask for Walter Rodríguez, who is developing ecotourism facilities. 3 km from Puerto Jiménez is **A3** *Playa Preciosa Lodge*, T 735-5005, 4 cabins, good swimming and surfing.

● **Transport Air** There are daily flights between Puerto Jiménez and Golfito, US$20 (both Sansa and Travelair planes from San José call at both airports) for information T 735-5017 or 775-0607. **Buses** From San José (C 12, Av 7-9) there are 2 buses daily to **Puerto Jiménez** at 0600 and 1200 via San Isidro, US$7, 8 hrs, return 0500 and 1100, T 771-2550. There are also buses from San Isidro, leaving from Soda Frutera del Sol at 0930 and 1500 daily, next to Castrol on Pan-American Highway, US$3, returns at 0330 and 1100, 6 hrs. To reach Puerto Jiménez from the Pan-American Highway (70 km), turn right at the restaurant about 30 km S of Palmar Sur; the road is newly paved to Rincón, thereafter best tackled with 4WD as a few rivers have to be forded (high clearance essential). They are working on bridges. Bus Puerto Jiménez-Ciudad Neily 0500 and 1400, 3½ hrs, US$2.50. There is a police checkpoint 47 km from the Pan-American Highway. Trucks, called 'taxis' run daily between Puerto Jiménez and La Palma (several, 1 hr, US$1.50); from the small settlement of La Palma an all-weather road goes to

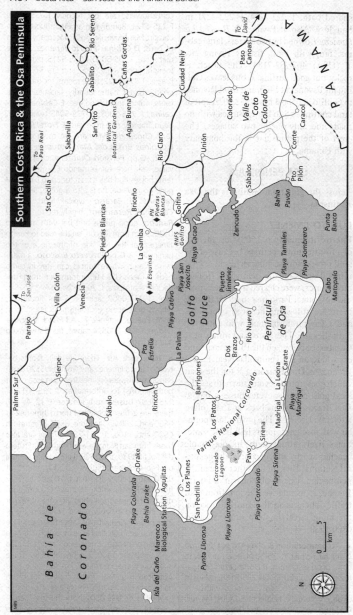

Southern Costa Rica & the Osa Peninsula

Rincón. **Sea** Two boats leave from Golfito to Puerto Jiménez at 1100, US$2.50, 1½ hrs, return 0600, or you can charter a taxi boat for about US$60, up to 8 passengers. Alternatively, if you want to visit the western side of the peninsula, take taxi or bus from Palmar Norte to Sierpe (30 mins) (see below) and for a boat going down the river. This may take some time because boats are heavily laden with the locals' shopping. It is a 2 hrs' boat trip down river and across the sea to Agujitas (see below), a small village near the **Marenco** Biological Station (information, PO Box 4025, San José, T 221-1594 or 233-9101), 3- and 4-night packages available, US$575-690 pp, with transport from San José (8 hrs by vehicle and boat, less by plane and boat).

At the tip of the Peninsula, 18 km S of Puerto Jiménez, at **Cabo Matapalo**, is **A2** pp *Bosque del Cabo Wilderness Lodge*, inc meals, T/F 735-5206 (or T 222-4547 San José), for eco-tourists, 30 mins taxi jeep ride from Puerto Jiménez; **L3** *Lapa Ríos Wilderness Resort*, T 735-5130, F 735-5179, inc meals, 14 luxury palm-thatched bungalows on private 1,000 acre reserve (80% virgin forest, owners Karen and John Lewis), camping trips, boats can be arranged from Golfito, popular with Americans but some reports suggest it goes 'over the top'. The Osa Trail, a long distance hiking trail to Sierpe, starts at Lapa Ríos. Plenty of deserted beaches (tide goes out a long way, sandflies at high tide). Inland, rubber boots are advisable as a precaution against venomous snakes (see below).

CORCOVADO NATIONAL PARK

The **Park**, including the **Isla del Caño** (200 ha), comprises over 54,000 ha. It consists largely of tropical rainforests, and includes swamps, miles of empty beaches, and some cleared areas now growing back. It is located at the western end of the Osa Peninsula, on the Pacific Ocean. If short of time and/or money, the simplest way to the park is to take the pick-up truck from outside *Carolina's Restaurant* in Puerto Jiménez to Playa Carate, most days at 0600 and 1400, 2½ hrs, US$4 one way, returning at 0800 and 1600, ask in advance about

departure (Cirilo Espinoza, T 735-5075, or Ricardo González, T 735-5068, for 4WD jeep taxi). It may be possible to book a flight with the Servicio de Parques Nacionales (SPN) in Puerto Jiménez, or take a private flight to Carate or La Sirena in the Park for US$36 pp, ask for Captain Alvaro Ramírez of Alfa Romeo Aéreo Taxi service at the airstrip, T 735-5178, F 735-5112. The SPN office in Puerto Jiménez is next to the bank, 1 block parallel to the main street, daily 0730-1200, 1300-1700, T 735-5036, ask for Carlos Quintero; they will give permits for entering the park (US$6) and will book accommodation at **La Sirena** in dormitories, maximum 20 people, **F** for bed (reservation essential), take sheets/sleeping bag, camping **F**, no reservation needed, 3 meals available. Bring mosquito netting. There is occasional trouble between gold prospectors and the park guards. If it is dangerous for visitors you will not be allowed into those parts.

At **Carate** there is a dirt airstrip and a store, run by Gilberto Morales and his wife Roxana (they rent rooms, but often full of gold miners, they also have a tent for hire, but take sleeping bag). 30 mins' walk W along the beach is *Corcovado Lodge*, **C** inc breakfast, with 20 walk-in tents with two campbeds each, in a beautiful coconut grove with hammocks overlooking the beach; to be sure of space book through Costa Rica Expeditions in San José (see under **Travel agents**). Clean showers and toilets; good food, take a flashlight. Behind the camp is a trail into the jungle with a wonderful view of the bay from a clearing; many birds to be seen, plus monkeys and frogs. The whole place is highly rec.

5 mins walk' further down the beach is **La Leona** park wardens' station and entrance to the park. To go beyond here costs US$15/day, whether you are walking to La Sirena (18 km, 6 hrs, along the beach, tough in the sun), or just visiting for the day. Lodging is available at La Leona, **F**, maximum 12 people in basic rooms or camping, meals available, book

in high season through SPN; horses for hire. Beyond here to the end of **Playa Madrigal** is another 2-2½ hrs' walk, partly sandy, partly rocky, with some rock pools and rusty shipwrecks looking like modern art sculptures. The shore rises very steeply into the jungle which grows thickly with mangroves, almonds and co-conut palms. Check with wardens about high tide so you don't get stuck. There are a couple of rivers along the beach, the first Río Madrigal, is only about 15 mins beyond La Leona (lovely and cool, clear and deep enough for swimming about 200m upstream, a good place for spotting wildlife). The best place for seeing wildlife, though, is La Sirena, where there are paths inland and the terrain is flatter and more isolated.

You can head inland from Sirena on a trail past three conveniently spaced shelters to **Los Patos** after passing several rivers full of reptiles (20 km, 5 hrs). A wooden house in dilapidated condition, but with electricity and TV, gives protection overnight. Its balcony is a great observation point for birds especially the redheaded woodpecker. From Los Patos you can carry on to the park border, then, crisscrossing the Río Rincón to **La Palma** (small hostal), a settlement near the opposite side of the Peninsula (13 km, 6 more hrs); from which there are several 'taxis' making the 1-hr trip to Puerto Jiménez (see above). An offshoot of this trail will lead you to a raffia swamp that rings the **Corcovado Lagoon**. The lagoon is only accessible by boat, but there are no regular trips. Caymans and alligators survive here, sheltered from the hunters. Horses can be rented cheaply at Sirena.

From Sirena you can walk N along the coast to the shelter at **Llorona** (adequate; plenty of water, waterfalls, in fact), from which there is a trail to the interior with another shelter at the end. From Llorona you can proceed N through a forest trail and then along the beach to the station at **San Pedrillo** on the edge of the park. You can stay here, camping or under roof, and eat with the rangers, who love company. From San Pedrillo you can take the park boat (not cheap) to Isla del Caño, a lovely park outpost with 2 men (see under Puerto Quepos for Taximar boat service from Quepos and Dominical to Isla del Caño or Bahía Drake).

AGUJITAS

Continue N to the village of **Agujitas**, outside the park. Frequent trips with the park boat from San Pedrillo to Agujitas.

● **Accommodation B** pp *Cabinas Sir Francis Drake*, with bath, meals, T 771-2436; **A3** pp *Playa Cocalito Lodge*, Punta Agujitas, 7 cabins, full board, restaurant serving organically-grown fruit and vegetables, horseriding, trips to Corcovado National Park, T/F 786-6150; **D-E** *Cecilia's Lodge*, bunk beds in dormitory with shower or rooms in the house, full board, camping possible, Cecilia rents horses, takes you riding, visit to Isla del Caño or Marenco possible, will arrange return transport to Sierpe, nice landscape, friendly family, rec; *Cabinas Jinete de Osa*, contact Isa, on beach, clean, friendly, T 273-3116.

BAHÍA DRAKE

There are new tourist facilities at **Bahía Drake**, close to Isla del Caño.

In Mar 1579, Sir Francis Drake careened his ship on Playa Colorada in Bahía Drake; a plaque commemorating the 400th anniversary of the event was erected in Agujitas.

● **Accommodation A1** pp *La Paloma Jungle Lodge*, inc meals, T 239-0954, radio phone 239-2801, 6 cabins with bath, guided tours with resident biologist; **A3** pp *Drake Bay Wilderness Camp*, with meals, cabins, tents available, pleasant family atmosphere, canoeing, ocean fishing, trips to Corcovado, Isla del Cano, horse riding facilities, large reductions for children, rec, T 771-2436, charter flights available; *Hotel El Caballito de Mar*, 7 rooms, owned by Rob Messenger, scuba diving trips to Isla de Cano sport fishing and jungle trips, T 231-5028; **L3** *Aguila de Osa Inn*, inc meals, suites L1 inc meals, fishing, hiking, canoeing and horse riding available, T 296-2190, F 232-7722.

From Agujitas you can get a boat (road under construction) to **Sierpe** on the Río

Peninsula de Osa – rain, snakes and mosquitoes

Avoid the rainy season. Bring umbrellas (not raincoats, too hot), because it will rain, unless you are hiking, in which case you may prefer to get wet. Shelters can be found here and there, so only mosquito netting is indispensable. Bring all your food if you haven't arranged otherwise; food can only be obtained at Puerto Jiménez and Agujitas in the whole peninsula, and lodging likewise. The cleared areas (mostly outside the park, or along the beach) can be devastatingly hot. Chiggers (coloradillas) and horseflies infest the horse pastures and can be a nuisance, similiarly, sandflies on the beaches; bring spray-on insect repellent. Another suggestion is vitamin B1 pills (called thiamine, or 'tiamina'). Mosquitoes detest the smell and leave you alone. Get the Instituto Geográfico maps, scale 1:50,000. Remember finally that, as in any tropical forest, you may find some unfriendly wildlife, like snakes (fer de lance and bushmaster snakes may attack without provocation), and herds of peccaries. You should find the most suitable method for keeping your feet dry and protecting your ankles; for some, rubber boots are the thing, for others light footwear which dries quickly.

Sierpe (see above; boat from Sierpe to Bahía Drake, 1½ hrs, US$60 return/boat); **L2** pp *Río Sierpe Lodge*, inc meals, 8 rooms with bath, trips to Corcovado, Isla del Cano, diving, birdwatching. Sierpe is connected by bus with the town of Palmar Sur (flights from San José, see above) on the Pan-American Highway.

ISLA DEL COCO

A thickly-wooded island and National Park of 24 sq km, 320 km off the Peninsula of Osa on the submarine Cocos Ridge which extends some 1400 km SW to the Galápagos Islands. It has a 2-man outpost. Contact Costa Rica Expeditions for reasonably priced tours; also Otec in San José, see page 1060. Arrangements for reaching it by chartered boat can be made in Puntarenas, after a permit has been got from the Government, or you can take a scuba diving cruise on the *Okeanos Agressor*, 10 days, two sailings a month, T 232-0572 ext 60 (in USA: PO Drawer K, Morgan City, LA 70381, T 504-385-2416, F 504-384-0817). It was at one time a refuge for pirates, who are supposed to have buried great treasure there, though none has been found by the 500 expeditions which have sought it. The offshore waters are a fisherman's paradise.

CIUDAD NEILY, PASO CANOAS AND PANAMA BORDER

At **Ciudad Neily**, about 18 km from the border, are the **F** *Motel Rancho*, with bath; **E** *Hotel Musuco*, with bath, **F** without, fan, good, clean, quiet; 4 sets of *cabinas* (all E with bath) and *pensiones* in F range. 10 km from the border is the **E** *Camino Real*, with restaurant, where it is possible to camp. Here and there on the road *cantinas* sell local food. Daily bus to San José, Tracopa, from main square, US$8, 7 hrs (on Sun buses from the border are full by the time they reach Ciudad Neily). The road goes (plenty of buses, 20 mins, US$0.35) to **Paso Canoas** on the Panamanian border. Colectivo to border US$1.10, very quick.

FRONTIER WITH PANAMA – PASO CANOAS
● **Immigration**
Border open 0600-1100, 1300-1700, 1800-2100 Costa Rica time. Remember Costa Rica is 1 hr behind Panama. Reports vary on border requirements, most people, but not all, have been asked for an onward ticket on entering Panama. Those without a ticket have been asked how much money they have, but have not had to prove anything. **NB** If you need a tourist card only to enter Panama, you are strongly advised to get it before the border, as Panamanian border officials often do not have them (see Panama, **Information for travellers**).

● **Customs**

No fruit or vegetables can be taken into Panama.

● **Crossing by private vehicle**

Those motoring N can get insurance cover at the border for US$17 ensuring public liability and property damage.

● **Accommodation**

E *Azteca*; **F** *Cabinas Interamericano*, with bath and fan, some rooms with a/c, very good value; **F** *Evelyn*, and **F** *El Descanso* all with bath) on the Panama border.

● **Exchange**

Banks either side of border close at 1600 local time. The bank on the Costa Rican side gives a slightly better dollar rate for colones. No difficulty in getting rid of surplus colones with money changers.

● **Transport**

Bus San José-Paso Canoas, US$9, 8 hrs, Tracopa terminal Av 18, C 2-4 at 0500, 0730, 1300, 1630, 1800, and several others, check times (T 223-7685). Care: not all buses go to the border. International buses that reach the border after closing time wait there till the following day.

At Paso Canoas shops sell luxury items brought from Panama at prices considerably lower than those of Costa Rica (eg sunglasses, stereo equipment, kitchen utensils, etc).

Information for travellers

BEFORE TRAVELLING

ENTRY REQUIREMENTS

● **Documents**

A passport is required. For visits of up to 90 days the following do not need visas: nationals of most Western European countries, the USA, Canada, Israel, Japan, Romania, Hungary, Poland, Argentina, Uruguay, Panama, Paraguay and South Korea. The following also do not need a visa, but visits are limited to 30 days: citizens of Australia, New Zealand, Iceland, Monaco, most East European countries, South Africa, Taiwan, Singapore, most Middle Eastern countries, most Caribbean countries and most Central and South America countries, including Brazil, Mexico, Ecuador, Guyana, Guatemala, El Salvador and Honduras. Notwithstanding this, some travellers report that 90 days may be allowed for nationals of some of these countries. All other nationalities need a visa, costing US$25, valid for only 30 days (this includes Italy, Greece, Eire, Nicaragua, Peru, Dominican Republic, CIS, India, Indonesia, Egypt, Turkey). Make absolutely sure that you get an entry stamp in your passport and insist even if border officials tell you otherwise. Failure to have a stamp can lead to numerous problems on departure. Some nationalities have to have a tourist card, US$2 on entry.

After requesting an extension, when departing Costa Rica you will have to pay a US$43.50 departure tax (the same as Costa Ricans or residents). If you overstay the 30 (or 90) day permitted period, you must report to Immigration before leaving the country. A fine of US$6/month will be charged, you will be given 5 days to leave the country and will have to pay the US$45 residents departure tax. For longer stays ask for a Prórroga de Turismo at Migración in San José. For this you need three passport photos, an airline or bus ticket out of the country and proof of funds (eg TCs); you can apply for an extension of 1 or 2 months, 300 colones/month. The paperwork takes 3 days. If you leave the country, you must wait 72 hrs before returning, but it may be cheaper and easier to do this and get a new 30-day entry. Travel agents can arrange all extension and exit formalities for a small fee.

An onward ticket (a bus ticket, which can be bought at the border immigration office or sometimes from the driver on Tica international buses, a transatlantic ticket or an MCO will sometimes do) is asked for, but can be refunded in San José with a loss of about US$3 on a US$20 ticket. Cashing in an air ticket is difficult because you may be asked to produce another ticket out of the country. Also, tourists may have to show at least US$300 in cash or TCs before being granted entry (especially if you have no onward ticket). Always carry a passport, or photocopy, for presentation at spot-checks. Failure to do so may mean imprisonment.

● **Tourist information**

The information offices of the **Instituto Costarricense de Turismo** are on Av 4, C 5-7, 11th floor, ICT building, San José (T 223-1733/8423, toll free 800-012-3456), open 0800-1600 Mon to Fri. All tourist information is given here. Take complaints about hotel overcharging to the Instituto. For more details, see page 1060.

There are a number of Web sites on Costa Rica; rec is Costa Rica's Travelnet at http://centralamerica.com, which contains general information, maps, descriptions of national parks, photographs, butterflies, selected hotels, car rental, airlines and schedules, tours and packages.

Amerindia, based in Quito, is a new regional ground operator, who operates in Costa Rica, Guatemala and Belize (as well as in Peru, Bolivia and Ecuador). It has been created to rediscover the wonders of Latin America. Tours of the highest quality with experienced guides are offered. Accommodation is in superb lodges. Among the tours available will be yacht charters along coasts, luxury safari-style tents and land rover circuits. Further information from Amerindia's head office T (543) 2439 736/469 455, F (543) 2439 735, e-mail amerindi@pi.pro.ec; in UK from Penelope Kellie T (44) 1962 779317, F (44) 1962 779458, e-mail pkellie@yachtors.u-net.com; in USA T (1) 305 599 9008, F (1) 305 592 7060.

HEALTH

Drinking water is safe in all major towns; elsewhere it should be boiled. Water purification tablets etc hard to find but Tratagua, SA, Apdo 141-2050, Montes de Oca will make up Superdor (a chlorine based product) for you, two drops for each litre of water, at a nominal cost. Intestinal disorders are prevalent in the lowlands although Chagas disease is now rare. Malaria is on the increase; malaria prophylaxis is advised for visitors to the lowlands, especially near the Nicaraguan border; in Costa Rica it is available only from the Ministerio de Salud in San José (free), or at the Nicaraguan border. Dengue fever broke out in several areas in 1993, with over 1,000 cases in Liberia. Puntarenas was also badly affected. Only a few cases were reported in San José. Uncooked foods should not be eaten. The standards of health and hygiene are among the best in Latin America. Ice cream, milk, etc are safe. See also notes on snakebite and mosquitoes under Corcovado National Park, page 1137.

MONEY

● **Currency**

The unit is the colón, formerly sub-divided into 100 céntimos. Old coins in use are for 1, 2, 5, 10 and 20 colones. In 1996 new, golden coloured, smaller coins were minted for 5, 10, 25,

50 and 100 colones. Public telephones use 5, 10 and 20 colón coins. Paper money in use: 50, 100, 500, 1,000 and 5,000 colones.

● **Banks & money changers**

Exchange of US dollars (etc) must be effected in a bank, and for bank drafts and transfers commission may be charged (set by the banks themselves). Most tourist and first class hotels will change dollars for guests only, the same applies in restaurants and shops if you buy something. A legal parallel (street) market has existed since Feb 1992. It is almost impossible to exchange any other major currency in Costa Rica. Every major bank issues Visa/Mastercard, inc Credomatic. Most banks (eg Banco Nacional, Banco de San José, etc) will process cash advances on Visa/Mastercard. ATMs which will accept international Visa/Mastercard are available at most banks, shopping malls and San José airport.

● **Credit cards**

Credomatic handles all credit card billings; they will not accept a credit card charge that does not have the imprint of the borrower's card plus an original signature. This is the result of fraud, but it makes it difficult to book tours or accommodation over the phone. For card loss or theft, Amex T 233-0044, Visa T 223-2211, Mastercard T 253-2155.

GETTING THERE

BY AIR

● **From Europe**

Connections can be made through US cities or direct with KLM from Amsterdam and with Iberia from Madrid and Barcelona via Miami. Condor and LTU International Airways offer scheduled and charter flights from Dusseldorf and Frankfurt, Martinair from Amsterdam and Monarch from London.

● **From Latin America and the Caribbean**

Lacsa flies from San Juan, Puerto Rico via Caracas and Barranquilla or Panama City, from Santiago, Chile, via Lima and Panama City, from Quito via Guayaquil and from Rio de Janeiro via São Paulo and Quito. Copa, Lacsa, United Airlines, Aviateca and Mexicana de Aviación all fly from Guatemala City with other flights from Belize City (Taca), Cancún (Lacsa), Managua (Copa, Lacsa, Aviateca), Mexico City (Lacsa, Mexicana, United Airlines), Panama City (Taca, Copa, Lacsa, Aviateca and KLM), San Pedro Sula (Lacsa), San Salvador (Copa, Taca, Lacsa, Aviateca),

Tegucigalpa (Lacsa). Cubana and Lacsa fly from Havana. Copa also flies from San Juan via Santo Domingo. Aeroperlas flies from David, Panama, Mon, Wed, Fri.

● **From North America**

American Airlines flies from Miami, New York, Dallas/Fort Worth, Orange County, San Juan (Puerto Rico), with connections from several other US cities via Miami. United Airlines fly from San Francisco, Los Angeles and Washington DC. Continental flies from Houston. Taca flies from Houston Lacsa flies daily from Miami direct, from Managua; from Orlando via Miami; from San Francisco via Guatemala and San Salvador; from Los Angeles via Mexico City; from New York via Cancún; from New Orleans via Cancún, Tegucigalpa. Aviateca from Miami. Aero Costa Rica has regular flights from Orlando. Canadian Airlines and Air Canada operate Charter flights.

Air Freight You can fly a motorcycle from San José to Bogotá, costs about US$1,000 for 2 bikes and 2 passengers. To Quito, 2 motorcycles costs about US$600, but it is more difficult to get them out of customs.

BY SEA

Shipping a vehicle from Puerto Limón to Guayaquil costs US$1,500 in a container (virtually impossible to travel with your car on the ship); arrange through an Agente de Vapores (look in Yellow Pages), US$200-500 for agents' fees and 'miscellaneous charges'. One agent was Rafael Angel Ulloa y Cia, C 3, Av 10-12, San José, T 223-7233, talk to Grace Barboza. High disembarcation charges in Colombia. For shipping information, see also **Introduction and Hints** at the beginning of the book.

CUSTOMS

Half a kilo of manufactured tobacco and 3 litres of liquor are allowed in duty-free. Any amount of foreign or local currency may be taken in or out.

ON ARRIVAL

● **Entering by land**

If entering from Nicaragua, you may be forced to take a blood-test for malaria at the border point, and if you are not carrying anti-malaria tablets, officials may oblige you to buy and swallow some in their presence. Some report merely being asked if they were carrying malaria tablets and no checks were made.

Warnings Those arriving by air from Colombia can expect to have their persons and baggage carefully searched because of the drug traffic in the area. In Costa Rica, particularly on the Atlantic coast, do not get involved with drugs: many dealers are undercover police agents.

There has been much illegal immigration into Costa Rica: this explains why Migración officials sometimes grill visitors in their hotels.

● **Hours of business**

0800 or 0830 to 1100 or 1130 and 1300 to 1700 or 1730 (1600, government offices), Mon to Fri, and 0800 to 1100 on Sat Shops: 0800 to 1200, 1300 to 1800 Mon to Sat.

● **Official time**

Standard time is 6 hrs behind Greenwich Mean Time.

● **Safety**

Look after your belongings in hotels (use the safe), hired cars and on beaches. Theft is on the increase and we have received reports of violent robberies in those dangerous parts of San José mentioned in the **Warning**, page 1048.

● **Shopping**

Best buys are wooden items, ceramics and leather handicrafts. **NB** Many wooden handicrafts are made of rainforest hardwoods and that deforestation is a critical problem. Coffee should have 'puro' on the packet or it may have additives.

● **Tipping**

A 10% service charge is automatically added to restaurant and hotel bills, as well as 15% sales tax. Tip porters, hairdressers and cloakroom attendants. Taxis and cinema usherettes, nil.

● **Voltage**

110, 60 cycles, AC (US flat-pin plugs).

● **Weights and measures**

For Customs the metric system of weights and measures is compulsory. Traders use a variety of weights and measures, including English ones and the old Spanish ones.

WHERE TO STAY

The Costa Rica Bed & Breakfast Group includes 50 B&B inns and small hotels around the country in its membership. They can be contacted through the president, Debbi McMurray, Apdo 493-1000, San José, T 223-4168, F 223-4157.

FOOD AND DRINK

● **Food**

Sodas (small restaurants) serve local food, which is worth trying. Very common is *casado*, a cheap lunch which includes rice, beans, stewed beef or fish, fried plantain and cabbage. *Olla de carne* is a soup of beef, plantain, corn, yuca, *ñampi* and *chayote* (local vegetables). *Sopa negra* is made with black beans, and comes with a poached egg in it; *picadillo* is another meat and vegetable stew. Snacks are popular: *gallos* (filled tortillas), *tortas* (containing meat and vegetables), *arreglados* (bread filled with the same) and *empanadas*. *Pan de yuca* is a speciality, available from stalls in San José centre. For breakfast, try *gallo pinto* (rice and beans) with *natilla* (a slightly sour cream). Best ice cream can be found in *Pops* shops. *Schmidt* bakeries are highly rec; they also serve coffee. Also *La Selecta* bakeries. In general, eating out in Costa Rica is more expensive than elsewhere in Central America.

● **Drink**

There are many types of cold drink, made either from fresh fruit, or milk drinks with fruit (*batidos*) or cereal flour whisked with ice cubes. Drinks are often sugared well beyond North American tastes. The fruits range from the familiar to the exotic; others include *cebada* (barley flour), *pinolillo* (roasted corn), *horchata* (rice flour with cinnamon), *chan*, 'perhaps the most unusual, looking like mouldy frogspawn and tasting of penicillin' (Michael J Brisco). All these drinks cost the same as, or less than, bottled fizzy products. Excellent coffee. Local beers are Bavaria, Bremen, Pilsen, Imperial and Tropical (which is low alcohol).

ON DEPARTURE

There is an airport and overland departure tax for tourists of US$17, payable in colones or dollars (TCs not accepted). There is a 5% tax on airline tickets purchased in the country.

NB Exit taxes, by air or land, and legislation regarding visa extensions, are subject to frequent change and travellers should check these details as near to the time of travelling as possible.

GETTING AROUND

AIR

● **Airports**

There are domestic airports or airstrips, with scheduled services, at Barra Colorado, Carrillo, Coto 47, Golfito, Liberia, Nosara Beach, Palmar, Puerto Jiménez, Punta Islita, Quepos, Tamarindo, Tambor, Tortuguero, with Sansa or Travelair. For details see page 1062.

LAND TRANSPORT

● **Roads and motoring**

Driving in Costa Rica allows for much flexibility of travel, with certain precautions. Main roads are not always obvious, road signs in remote areas are scarce and driving after dark is not rec. Use your mile counter to help you find the right road. Speed limits are low (80 kmph, 100 kmph on some roads) and there are rigorous radar speed traps, especially at the entry to towns and on the Pan-American Highway. If caught, you may have your number plate confiscated and have to pay a court fine (+30% tax) to get it back. Do not attempt to pay an on-the-spot fine (see below). Unpaved roads are slow going, so leave plenty of time for your trip, 20 kph may be your maximum speed. Many of the nature parks are in remote areas and 4WD may well be needed, certainly a car with high clearance is recommended; in the wet season some roads will be impassable. Check that bridges are not down. Always ask locals or bus drivers what the state of the road is before embarking on a journey, but do not assume that if the buses are running, a car can get through too. Car hire firms are not covered by tourist regulations and many complaints have been made to the authorities concerning their operations. If hiring a car, be very cautious. Most leases do not allow the use of a normal car off paved roads. Always make sure the spare tyre is in good order, as holes are frequent. You can have tyres fixed at any garage for about US$3 in $\frac{1}{2}$-hr. Tyres without rims are confiscated and burnt by the Customs. Hired cars bear special number plates and are easily identified. Be particularly careful not to leave valuables in a hired car, which is a sitting target.

Beware of policemen trying to charge on-the-spot fines. Fines in Costa Rica may only validly be paid at official stations in San José and major towns. If you pay a fine immediately, you still run the risk of getting reported and having to pay when you leave the country. It is illegal to ride in a car or taxi without wearing seatbelts. Motorcyclists must wear crash helmets.

Tourists who come by car or motorcycle pay US$10 road tax and can keep their cars for an initial period of 90 days. This can be extended for a total period of 6 months, for about US$10/extra month, at the Instituto Costarricense de Turismo, or at the Customs office, Av 3, C 14, if you take your passport, car entry permit, and a piece of stamped paper (*papel sellado*) obtainable at any bookshop. If you intend to drive in the country for more than 3 months, you are required to apply for a Costa Rican Driver's Licence at Av 18, C 5, San José (see also Car and Motorcycle Rental, page 1061). Cars are fumigated on entry: exterior US$3; interior US$1.40. It is now mandatory for foreign drivers to buy insurance stamps on entry; US$17.75 for 1 month (US$8 for motorcycles), US$27.70 for 2 months, US$37.65 for 3 months. If you have an accident, contact Policia de Tránsito, San José T 226-8436 or 277-2189.

If you want to travel on from Costa Rica without your car, you should leave it in the customs warehouse at C Blancos in San José. A customs agent is recommended unless you want to spend several weeks learning the system. Recommended, at a reasonable price, is Camilo Lacayo SA (Apdo 54-1300 San José, T 255-3174), located 100m W and 25m S of the C Blancos *Aduanas*. Boris Barrantes León is helpful and speaks English. The requisite papers are called *guías*: either for up to 2 months or up to a year (US$100 for the latter). Charges at the warehouse depend on the value of the car, eg a 1970 VW microbus valued at US$3,500 cost US$1/day. A complete inventory of the vehicle and contents is made when leaving the car. Recovering the car is a lengthy procedure of several days. You have to visit the Central Bank to certify that you have not requested dollars for the price of the car, ie, you have not sold it. The customs agency you first dealt with should guide you through this for no extra charge. The *aduanas* will either escort you to the frontier or you can buy another 3 months' insurance and have the car stamped back into your passport. This requires a visit to Central Customs (orange building, Av 1, C 14). Be sure to tell the Customs Agency that you want to reinsure the car when depositing it, doing this should save some paperwork and time. The whole operation needs time and patience.

Car parts are very expensive because of high import tax. If the parts are needed for leaving the country you can order them from abroad yourself and avoid the tax but it takes time. Ask Sr Marcheno in the Aduana de Vehículos, Av 3, C 10, Spanish required. It is best not to try and sell your car here as the import tax is 70%. Spares are available for Japanese makes in San José. San José is also the best place to get Land Rover spares. Try Oswaldo von Breymann, Av 7, Casa 27, C 5-7, T 212-274, San José, for motorcycle

spares (BMW and MZ); he is a good mechanic. Yamaha dealer, Lutz Hermanos y Cía Ltda, C 1 between Av 5 and 7, San José, T 255-3566, F 233-0658. Motorcycle spares, inc BMW, Av 7 between C 1 and 3, T 235-2173.

Main fuel stations have regular (unleaded) US$0.48 (109 colones) and diesel US$0.34 (77.30 colones)/litre; super gasoline (unleaded) is available throughout the country, US$0.51 (114.60 colones). Leaded fuel is unavailable.

Road Tolls Road tolls vary between US$0.30 and US$1. The following are 60 colones, San José-San José airport; San José-Santa Ana; San José-Cartago. 120 colones, San José airport-San Ramón. 200 colones, San José-Guápiles. San José-Cartago, San José-Santa Ana and San Ramón-airport have automatic machines accepting 5, 10, 20 colón coins.

● **Cycling**
John Gilchrist tells us that cycling is easier in Costa Rica than elsewhere in Central America; there is less heavy traffic and it is generally 'cyclist friendly'. However, paving is thin and soon deteriorates; look out for cracks and potholes, which bring traffic to a crawl. Unsurfaced roads are horrible on a bicycle. The prevailing wind is from the NE, so if making an extensive tour, travelling in the direction of Panama-Nicaragua is slightly more favourable. Be prepared for a lot of rain. It is perfectly possible to travel light, without tent, sleeping bag or cooking equipment. Particularly bad for cyclists is the Nicoya Peninsula; a mountain bike is recommended for the terrain and the poor road state.

Recommended reading for all users: *Baker's The Essential Road Guide to Costa Rica*, with detailed strip maps, km by km road logs, motoring information plus San José map and Bus Guide (130 pages: Bill Baker, Apdo 1185-1011, San José, T/F 220-1415). Cycle shop: *El Mundo de Ciclismo*, Paseo Colón, C 26, San José, good stock of newest bicycle parts; Tecnillantas, Av 10, San Martín, has cycle tyres (also motorcycle and car tyres).

● **Hitchhiking**
Hitchhiking is easy and safe by day in the week, though there is not much traffic off the main roads.

COMMUNICATIONS

● **Newspapers**
The best San José morning papers are *La Nación* and *La República*; there is also *Al Día*. La Prensa Libre is a good evening paper. *Libertad*, weekly

newspaper (socialist). *El Debate* is another good weekly. Three weekly news magazines are: *Rumbo* (political), *Triunfo* and *Perfil* (popular). *La Gazette* is the official government weekly paper. *Tico Times* (Fri, subscriptions Dept 717, PO Box 025216, Miami FL 33102) and *Costa Rica Today* (free in better hotels and restaurants, subscriptions Ediciones 2000 SA, Acc No 117, PO Box 025216, Miami FL 33102) in English (look in the classifieds for Spanish classes). The former is better for news and classifieds, the latter has weekly features of interest to travellers, eg hotels under US$10 in San José or railway news. *The Latin America*, US$1, has travel information, bed and breakfast places, local airline schedules, useful, Apdo 661, Alajuela, T 441-9263, F 441-0222. *Adventures in Costa Rica* (Starflame Productions, PO Box 508, Jackson, CA 95642) is a monthly newsletter on travel in, and the affairs of Costa Rica (US$48 for 12 issues).

● **Postal services**
Mail by sea from the UK takes from 2-3 months and 10 to 14 days by airmail. Airmail letters to Europe cost 60 colones, postcards 55 colones; to North/South America, letters 50 colones, 45 colones for postcards; to Australia, Africa and Asia, letters 70 colones, postcards 65 colones. 'Expreso' letters, 55 colones extra, several days quicker to USA and N Europe. Registered mail, 150 colones. All parcels sent out of the country by foreigners must be taken open to the post office for clearance. *Lista de Correos*, charges 50 colones/letter and will keep letters for 4 weeks. The contents of incoming parcels will be the subject of plenty of paperwork, and probably high duties. You normally have to come back the next day.

● **Telephone services**
Long-distance telephone services are run by the Instituto Costarricense de Electricidad (ICE) and by Cía Radiográfica Internacional de Costa Rica (RACSA). Local cables, though, are sent from the main post office in San José, Av 1-3, C 2. Rates at the RACSA Telecommunications Centre, Av 5, C 1, San José, to USA are US$1.45/min (reduced rate 1900-2200 and all day Sat/Sun, US$1.09/min), to Europe, Caribbean, South America, US$2.50/min (US$2), plus 13% sales tax, open 0700-2200. Internet access US$2/hr. Phone cards are available for long distance calls at US$10 and US$20. Direct dial from a private phone is cheaper than rates from a public phone or RACSA office. Calls abroad can be made from phone booths; collect calls abroad may be made

from special booths in the telephone office, Av 5, C 1, San José, or from any booth nationwide if you dial 116 for connection with the international operator. Collect calls can be made from any public phone, see page 1058 for dialling codes. Phone cards from the following countries are accepted: Brazil, Canada, France, Holland, Denmark, Hong Kong, Italy, Japan, S Korea, UK and USA. A call to USA; US$1.60/min Mon-Fri 0700-1900, US$1.20/min Mon-Fri 1900-2200, US$0.65/min Mon-Fri 2200-0700 and weekends. Call to UK, Europe, Canada; US$2.50/min Mon-Fri 0700-1900, US$2/min Mon-Fri 1900-2200, US$1.25/min Mon-Fri 2200-0700 and weekends. All rates subject to 13% sales tax. Country Direct dialling codes are (all prefix 0800): MCI -012-2222, AT&T 0114-114, Sprint -013-0123, Italy -039-1039, Germany -049-1049, Switzerland -041-1184, Belgium -032-1032, Britain -044-1044, Canada -015-1161, France -033-1033, Worldcom -014-4444, Denmark -045-1045, Spain -034-1034, Finland -358-1358, Holland -031-1111, Japan -081-1081, New Zealand -064-1064. Public telex booth at Radiográfica SA, Av 5, C 1 (telex CR 1050); the telex must show your name and Tel no or address for them to advise you; also public Fax service, to receive, 100 colones (F +506-223-1609 or +506-233-7932); to send, US$3/page to Europe, US$2.42 night rate (CRI; US$2.80 ICE), US$1.93/page to USA, US$1.45 night rate.

● **Television**
Six local TV stations, many MW/FM radio stations throughout the country (new radio station 'Welcome Radio' is in English, Spanish and German, 800 Khz AM). Local Voz de América (VOA) station. Many hotels and private homes receive one of the four TV stations offering direct, live, 24-hr TV from the USA (Canal 19, Supercanal, Cable Color and Master TV-channels 56, 58, 60. All US cable TV can be received in San José on the two cable stations).

SPORT

Association **football** (soccer) is the national sport (played every Sun at 1100, Sept to May, at the Saprissa Stadium). There are **golf** courses around the country, see under San José. There is sea-**bathing** on both Atlantic and Pacific coasts (see text). The Meseta is good country for **riding**; horses can be hired by arrangement directly with owners. Most *fiestas* end with **bullfighting** in the squares, an innocuous but amusing set-to with no horses used. Bullfights are held in San José during the Christmas period. There is no kill and spectators are permitted to enter the ring to chase, and be chased by, the bull. For **Watersports**, see page 1042.

HOLIDAYS AND FESTIVALS

1 Jan: New Year's Day; 19 Mar: St Joseph; Easter: 3 days; 11 April: Battle of Rivas; 1 May: Labour Day; June: Corpus Christi; 29 June: St Peter and St Paul; 25 July: Guanacaste Day; 2 Aug: Virgin of Los Angeles; 15 Aug: Mothers' Day; 15 Sept: Independence Day; 12 Oct: Columbus Day; 8 Dec: Conception of the Virgin; 25 Dec: Christmas Day; 28-31 Dec: San José only.

NB During Holy Week, nearly everyone is on holiday. Everywhere is shut on Thur, Fri, many shops on Sat, and Sun, and most of the previous week as well (in San José and Cartago only a small percentage of businesses and services close Mon-Wed and Sat of Holy Week; almost all transport stops on Good Friday only, with limited transport on Thur).

ACKNOWLEDGEMENTS

We are most grateful to Rachel Rogers for updating this chapter and to Simon Ellis (San José) for a complete and thorough review of the information.

Panama

THE S-SHAPED ISTHMUS of Panama, 80 km at its narrowest and no more than 193 km at its widest, is one of the great cross-roads of the world. Its destiny has been entirely shaped by that fact. To it Panama owes its national existence, the make-up of its population and their distribution: two-fifths of the people are concentrated in the two cities which control the entry and exit of the canal. The Canal Area, formerly the US Canal Zone, has been largely returned to Panamanian jurisdiction; this long process began in 1964, when Panama secured the right to fly its flag in the Zone alongside that of the USA, and is due for completion, with when Panama assumes full authority for the Canal at noon on 31 December 1999.

HORIZONS

THE LAND

Panama is most easily visualized as a horizontal S, with the 767-km Caribbean coastline on the N and the 1,234-km Pacific coast on the S. The Canal, which runs SE-NW, bisects the country from E to W; the mountains that run along the isthmus divide the country from N to S. About half the population lives in Panama City, on the E side of the Canal at its southern terminus. Most of the rural population lives in the quarter of the country S of the mountains and W of the Canal.

At the border with Costa Rica there are several volcanic cones, the boldest of which is the inactive Volcán Barú, 3,475m high and the highest point in the country. The sharp-sided Cordillera de Talamanca continues SE at a general altitude of about 900m, but subsides suddenly SW of Panama City. The next range, the San Blas, rises E of Colón (the city at the N end of the Canal) and runs into Colombia; its highest peak is Tacarcuna, at 1,875m. A third range rises from the Pacific littoral in the SE; it runs

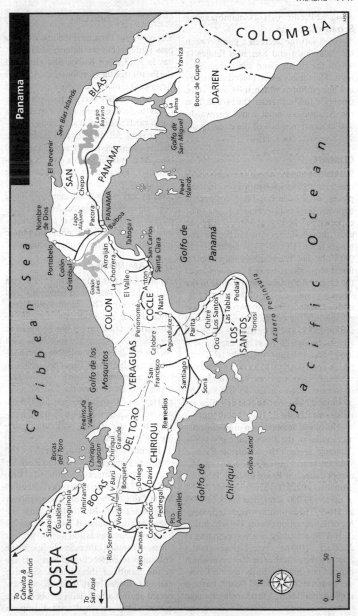

along the Pacific coast of Colombia as the Serranía de Baudó.

Good fortune decreed a gap between the Talamanca and San Blas ranges in which the divide is no more than 87m high. The ranges are so placed that there is a gap, through which the Canal runs, from NW to SE. To reach the Pacific from the Atlantic we must travel eastwards, and at dawn in much of the country the sun rises over the Pacific.

CLIMATE

Rainfall is heavy along the Caribbean coast: more than 3,800 mm a year in some places, with huge but brief downpours between April and December. Rain can be expected 365 days a year on the Caribbean coast, though. Temperature in the lowland ranges from 21°C (70°F) at night to 32°C (90°F) by day. The result is deep tropical forest along the coast and up the sides of the ranges of Panama, though little in the densely-populated SW of the country remains forested. The rain begins to shade off towards the crests of the mountains (10° to 18°C), and is much less along the Pacific, though there is no scarcity of it anywhere. At Balboa it is only 1,727 mm a year, and the tropical forest gives way to semi-deciduous trees and converted areas of savanna between the Pacific and the mountains. The wet season is called *invierno* – winter, the dry, *verano* – summer.

The rate of deforestation in Panama has accelerated in the 1980s and early 1990s. Although more of the country is forested than any other Central American republic except Belize, the loss of forest in 1990 was estimated at 220,000 acres, against felling of up to 154,000 acres/year between 1985 and 1989. The government reported a slowing of deforestation during 1993-95, but in early 1996 estimated it was continuing at 2,200 acres (100 ha) a year. Deforestation is affecting the pattern of rainfall upon which depend not only the birds (over 800 species), animals, insects and plants, but also the Panama Canal. A further threat to the Canal is silting as a result of soil erosion.

The history of Panama is the history of its pass-route; its fate was determined on that day in 1513 when Balboa first glimpsed the Pacific (see the Horizons to the Central America section). Panama City was of paramount importance for the Spaniards: it was the focus of conquering expeditions northwards and southwards along the Pacific coasts. All trade to and from these Pacific countries passed across the isthmus. As part of Colombia and its predecessors, Panama was traditionally considered part of South America until recent years, when it has more and more been classed as a Central American republic. The distinction has political significance as international economic integration increases in importance.

THE CAMINO REAL

Panama City was founded in 1519 after a trail had been discovered between it and the Caribbean. The Camino Real (the Royal Road) ran from Panama City to Nombre de Dios until it was rerouted to Portobelo. An alternative route was used later for bulkier, less valuable merchandise: a road built from Panama City to Las Cruces, now swallowed up by Gatún Lake; it ran near Gamboa on the Culebra Cut, and traces of it can still be seen. Las Cruces was on the Chagres River, which was navigable to the Caribbean, particularly during the rainy season.

Intruders were early attracted by the wealth passing over the Camino Real. Sir Francis Drake attacked Nombre de Dios, and in 1573 his men penetrated inland to Venta Cruz, further up the Chagres River on the Camino Real, plundering the town. Spain countered later attacks by building strongholds and forts to protect the route: among others San Felipe at the entrances to Portobelo and San Lorenzo at the mouth of the Chagres. Spanish galleons, loaded with treasure and escorted against attack, left Portobelo once a year. They returned with European goods which were sold at great fairs held at Portobelo, Cartagena and Veracruz. There was feverish activity for several weeks as the galleons were loaded and unloaded. It was a favourite time for attack by enemies, especially those with political as well as pecuniary motives. Perhaps the most famous was the attack by Henry Morgan in 1671. He captured the fort of San Lorenzo and pushed up the Chagres River to Las Cruces. From there he descended upon Panama City, which he looted and burnt. A month later Morgan returned to the Caribbean with 195 mules loaded with booty. Panama City was rebuilt on a new site, at the base of Ancón hill, and fortified. With Britain and Spain at war, attacks reached their climax in Admiral Vernon's capture of Portobelo in 1739 and the fort of San Lorenzo the next year. Spain abandoned the route in 1746 and began trading round Cape Horn. San Lorenzo was rebuilt: it is still there, tidied up and landscaped by the US Army.

In 1821, Gran Colombia, including Panama, won independence from Spain, celebrated in Panama annually on 28 November.

THE PANAMA RAILROAD

Some 30 years later, streams of men were once more moving up the Chagres and down to Panama City: the forty-niners on their way to the newly discovered gold fields of California. Many perished on this 'road to hell', as it was called, and the gold rush brought into being a railway across the isthmus. The Panama Railroad from Colón (then only two streets) to Panama City took 4 years to build, with great loss of life. The first train was run on 26 November 1853. The railway was an enormous financial success until the rerouting of the Pacific Steam Navigation Company's ships round Cape Horn in 1867 and the opening of the first US transcontinental railroad in 1869 reduced its traffic.

BUILDING OF THE CANAL

Ferdinand de Lesseps, builder of the Suez Canal, arrived in Panama in 1881, and decided to build a sea-level canal along the Chagres River and the Río Grande. Work started in 1882. One of the diggers in 1886 and 1887 was the painter Gauguin, aged 39. About 30 km had been dug before the Company crashed in 1893, defeated by extravagance and tropical diseases (22,000 people died). Eventually Colombia (of which Panama was then a Department) authorized the Company to sell all its rights and properties to the United States, but the Colombian Senate rejected the treaty, and the inhabitants of Panama, encouraged by the States, declared their independence on 3 November 1903. The United States intervened and, in spite of protests by Colombia, recognized the new republic. Colombia did not accept the severance until 1921.

Immediately following its independence, Panama, represented by the controversial Frenchman, Philippe Bunau-Varilla, signed a treaty granting to the USA 'in perpetuity' a 10-mile-wide corridor across the isthmus over which the USA would exercise authority 'as if it were sovereign'. The history of Panama then became that of two nations, with the Canal Zone governor, always a retired US general, responsible only to the President of the USA.

Before beginning the task of building the Canal the United States performed one of the greatest sanitary operations in history: the clearance from the area of the more malignant tropical diseases. The name of William Crawford Gorgas will always be associated with this, as will that of George Washington Goethals with the actual building of the Canal. On 15 August 1914, the first passage was made, by the ship *Ancón*.

1939 TREATY WITH USA

As a result of bitter resentment, the USA ended Panama's protectorate status in

1939 with a treaty which also limited US rights of intervention. However, the disparity in living standards continued to provoke anti-US feeling, culminating in riots in 1964 and the suspension of diplomatic relations for some months. During this period, a small, commercially-oriented oligarchy dominated Panamanian politics, although presidential successions were not always smooth and peaceful.

In 1968 Arnulfo Arias Madrid was elected president for the third time, having been ousted twice previously. After only 10 days in office he was forcibly removed by the National Guard which installed a provisional junta. Brig Gen Omar Torrijos Herrera ultimately became Commander of the National Guard and principal power in the junta, dominating Panamanian politics for the next 13 years. Constitutional government was restored in 1972 after elections for a 505-member National Assembly of Community Representatives, which revised the 1946 constitution, elected Demetrio Basilio Lakas Bahas as president, and vested temporary extraordinary executive powers in Gen Torrijos for 6 years. Torrijos' rule was characterized by his pragmatic nationalism; he carried out agrarian reform, yet satisfied business interests; he had close links with left wing movements in Cuba, El Salvador and Nicaragua, yet reached agreement with the USA to transfer sovereignty over the Canal to Panama. In 1978 elections for a new National Assembly were held and the new representatives elected Arístedes Royo Sánchez president of the country. Gen Torrijos resigned as Chief of Government but retained the powerful post of Commander of the National Guard until his death in a small-plane air crash in 1981. There followed several years of rapid governmental changes as tension rose between presidents and National Guard leaders.

GENERAL NORIEGA'S ADMINISTRATION

Following an election in May 1984, Nicolás Ardito Barletta was inaugurated in Oct for a 6-year term, though the fairness of the elections was widely questioned. He was removed from office by military pressure in Sept 1985 and was replaced by Eric Arturo Delvalle. Sr Delvalle's attempts to reduce military influence in government, by then concentrated principally in the hands of Gen Manuel Antonio Noriega Moreno, led to his own removal by Gen Noriega in Feb 1988. Manuel Solís Palma was named president in his place.

With the economy reeling and banks closed as a result of US economic sanctions, the campaign leading up to the election of May 1989 saw the growing influence of a movement called the Civic Crusade, led by upper and middle-class figures. When their coalition candidate, Guillermo Endara Gallimany, triumphed over Noriega's candidate, Carlos Duque Jaén, the election was annulled by the military.

General Noriega appointed Francisco Rodríguez as provisional President in September. However, in Dec, Gen Noriega formally assumed power as Head of State, which provoked a US military invasion (Operation Just Cause) on 20 Dec to overthrow him. He finally surrendered in mid-Jan, having taken refuge in the Papal Nunciature on Christmas Eve, and was taken to the USA for trial on charges of drugs trafficking and other corruption offences. Sr Endara was installed as President. The Panamanian Defence Forces were immediately remodelled into a new Public Force whose largest component is the civilian National Police, with a compulsory retirement after 25 years' service. More than 150 senior officers were dismissed and many were arrested.

AFTER 'JUST CAUSE'

After the overthrow of Gen Noriega's administration, the US Senate approved a

US$1bn aid package including US$480mn in direct assistance to provide liquidity and get the economy moving again. A further US$540mn aid package was requested from the USA, Japan, Taiwan and the EEC to enable Panama to help clear its US$610mn arrears with multilateral creditors and support the Panamanian banking system, but inevitably there were delays and little progress was made until 1991. The USA put Panama under considerable pressure to sign a Treaty of Mutual Legal Assistance, which would limit bank secrecy and enable investigation into suspected drug traffickers' bank accounts. Higher levels of crime and drugs trafficking led to the Government passing a law to create the Technical Judicial Police (PTJ) to pursue criminals. Charges of corruption at the highest level were made by Panamanians and US officials and President Endara was further weakened by allegations that his law firm had been involved with companies owned by drugs traffickers.

Though the economy grew under President Endara, street crime also increased. There were continuing social problems and pro-military elements failed in a coup attempt and isolated bombings.

1994 ELECTIONS AND AFTER

Fears that violence would disrupt the 1994 elections were unfounded. In the presence of 2,000 local and international observers, polling was largely incident-free and open, receiving praise worldwide. The winner of the presidency with less than a third of the popular vote was Ernesto Pérez Balladares of the Partido Revolucionario Democrático (PRD), whose campaign harked back to the record of the party's founder, Omar Torrijos, successfully avoiding any links with its more recent leader, Noriega. In second place was the widow of thrice-elected and thrice-deposed president Arnulfo Arias, Mireya Moscoso de Gruber of the Partido Arnulfista, supported by Endara, and third was the Salsa star and actor, Rubén Blades,

whose party Papa Egoró ('Mother Earth') won six seats in the legislature on its first electoral outing. Pérez Balladares, who appointed a cabinet containing members of opposition parties as well as from the PRD, gave priority in his campaign to tackling the problem of social inequality, unemployment, deteriorating education and rising crime which had characterized the end of Endara's term. In Jan 1995, it was announced by the government that a coup against Pérez Balladares had been foiled. All sides in the Assembly hastened to support the government and pledge their commitment to democracy. Suggestions that the plot was a smokescreen, designed to bolster the government's position before introducing controversial economic measures, were vigorously denied.

In the following months, many of the government's policies proved controversial. Changes in labour law (Aug 1995) led to a general strike in which several people died. New tax legislation was condemned by businesses in the Colón Free Zone. Pensioners demonstrated in support of a promised increase in the state pension, unfulfilled by mid-1996. A proposed amnesty for human rights offenders during the Noriega regime was roundly condemned at home and abroad. The president regretted the slow progress in tackling crime; he also had to admit, in mid-1996, that his election campaign had received funds from the Cali drugs cartel. His assertion that he was ignorant of this at the time was largely accepted and while the USA was satisfied that attempts were being made to control drug-trafficking in Panama, there was concern that money-laundering remained significantly important to the financial community.

CANAL AREA

The former Canal Zone was a ribbon of territory under US control extending 8 km on either side of the Canal and including the cities of Cristóbal and Balboa. The price paid by the United States Government to

Panama for construction rights was US$10mn. The French company received US$40mn for its rights and properties and US$25mn were given to Colombia in compensation. The total cost at completion was US$387mn. Panama long ago rejected the perpetuity clause of the original Canal Treaty. In April 1978 a new treaty was ratified and on 1 October 1979 the Canal Zone, now known officially as the Canal Area, including the ports of Cristóbal and Balboa, the Canal dry docks and the trans-isthmus railway, was formally restored to Panamanian sovereignty, but the US still retains much-reduced military base areas.

Though many Panamanians support retention of US bases, largely because of their employment of civilians and their expenditures in Panama (about US$350mn a year in 1995 and 1996), vocal minorities demand their departure. While some slight possibility of renegotiation remains, US phasing out of the bases is ahead of schedule. Until the final transfer of ownership in 2000 the Canal administration is in the hands of the Comisión del Canal, on which Panama now has 4 out of 9 seats. An Inter-Oceanic Regional Authority (ARI), headed by ex-president Ardito Barletta, has been created by Panama to manage the disposition of real estate handed over by the US during and after the transition. The Canal Administrator (CEO) and 95% of Canal employees are now Panamanian. According to 1996 figures, about 13,700 ships pass through the Panama Canal annually, providing US$100mn. For several years, the possibility of widening the Canal, or even building a new one, has been under study. A report in 1993 estimated that the Canal would reach maximum shipping capacity in 2025, but reevaluation led to the announcement of the widening of the Gaillard Cut, well under way by 1996.

CULTURE

PEOPLE

The population is mostly of mixed descent but there are communities of Indians, blacks and a few Asians. Most of the rural population live in the six provinces on the Pacific side, W of the Canal. There is only one rural population centre of any importance on the Caribbean: in Bocas del Toro, in the extreme NW. Of the 60 Indian tribes who inhabited the isthmus at the time of the Spanish conquest, only three have survived in any number: the Cunas of the San Blas Islands (50,000), the Guaymíes, who prefer to be called Ngöbe-Buglé, of the western provinces (80,000), and the Chocóes, now known as Emberá-Wunan, of Darién (10,000). These, and a few others, account for 6% of the total population. Indian opposition to the opening of copper mines at Cerro Colorado (see **Economy** below) and demonstrations supporting greater autonomy for Indians in the area characterized 1996, but were inconclusive. However, an administrative enclave, the Comarca, providing for some Ngöbe-Buglé home rule, has been created.

In Bocas de Toro half the population speaks Spanish, half speaks English.

Numbers of African slaves escaped from their Spanish owners during the 16th century. They set up free communities in the Darién jungles and their Spanish-speaking descendants, known as *cimarrones*, can still be seen there and in the Pearl Islands. The majority of Panama's blacks, often bilingual, are descended from English-speaking British West Indians, brought in for the building of the railway in 1850, and later of the Canal. There are also a number of East Indians and Chinese, a few of whom, especially in the older generations tend to cling to their own languages and customs.

EDUCATION

Education is compulsory from the age of 6 to 15. About 92% of children attend elementary school. English is the compulsory second language in secondary schools. There are several universities, including the mammoth **Nacional**, the important catholic **Santa María La Antigua**, and numerous small, private ones.

RELIGION

Panama's Constitution makes Roman Catholicism the official religion of the country, but guarantees freedom of practice to all others.

CONSTITUTION

Constitutional reforms were adopted by referendum in April 1983. Legislative power is vested in a unicameral, 67-member Legislative Assembly which is elected by universal adult suffrage for a term of 5 years (and whose elections are hotly contested, in part because a 5-year term yields members total compensation of US$600,000 each). Executive power is held by the President, assisted by two Vice Presidents and an appointed Cabinet. Panama is divided into nine provinces and two autonomous Indian reservations. Provincial governors are appointed by the central authorities. The magistrates of the larger districts, who combine both executive and judicial functions, are elected, others appointed. They in turn appoint subordinate authorities in the towns and villages.

THE ECONOMY

Structure of production

Panama's economy has traditionally been founded on income derived from services rendered to incoming visitors, taking advantage of its geographical position, its banking centre, and Canal employees and US military personnel spending money in the Republic. However, this contribution is lessening proportionately as the country seeks to develop new sources of income: tourism, industry, copper, etc.

Panama: fact file

Geographic
Land area	75,517 sq km
forested	43.8%
pastures	19.8%
cultivated	8.9%

Demographic
Population (1996)	2,674,000
annual growth rate (1991-96)	1.8%
urban	53.3%
rural	46.7%
density	35.4 per sq km
Religious affiliation	
Roman Catholic	80.0%
Birth rate per 1,000 (1995)	23.6
	(world av 25.0)

Education and Health
Life expectancy at birth,	
male	71.0 years
female	76.5 years
Infant mortality rate	
per 1,000 live births (1995)	30.4
Physicians (1994)	1 per 808 persons
Hospital beds	1 per 363 persons
Calorie intake as %	
of FAO requirement	97%
Population age 25 and over	
with no formal schooling	11.6%
Literate males (over 15)	88.1%
Literate females (over 15)	88.2%

Economic
GNP (1994)	US$6,904mn
GNP per capita	US$2,670
Public external	
debt (1994)	US$3,923mn
Tourism receipts (1992)	US$243mn
Inflation (annual av 1990-95)	1.1%
Radio	1 per 5.0 persons
Television	1 per 13 persons
Telephone	1 per 9.7 persons

Employment
Population economically active (1993)	940,301
Unemployment rate (1994)	13.8%
% of labour force in	
agriculture	17.7
manufacturing	10.6
construction	6.4
National Police force	11,000

Source *Encyclopaedia Britannica*

Apart from the Canal (see above), the other traditional mainstay of the Panamanian economy is agriculture, which contributes about 10% of gdp. Agrarian reform brought the post-1968 governments much support from tenant-farmers and squatters, but has been discontinued and settlements formed by the Torrijos government are in decline. 44% of the land is classified as forested, but deforestation has been occurring at an alarming rate (see above under Climate, page 1148), principally because of pressures from increasing unemployment and a rising population, as people move into isolated areas. The leading agricultural export crop is bananas, three-quarters of which are produced by the transnational Chiquita Brands, which has a monopoly on marketing. The upheavals in the world banana market, including EU constraints on imports from Central America, led to a 23% decline in exports in 1995. Shrimp is another major export, having grown to about 12% of total earnings and competing strongly with Ecuador and Honduras for the US market. Raw sugar is also an important export item, while lesser amounts of coffee and hides and skins are sold abroad. Coffee production is increasing rapidly in Chiriquí Province.

The main industry is food processing and there are textile and clothing concerns and cement, chemicals, plastics and other light industries. Petroleum products, made from imported crude, are the only industrial export. The lowering of import tariffs in 1993, as a part of trade liberalization measures, contributed to a decline in manufacturing output. At the same time, the IMF has encouraged the state to privatize many of the industries it controls. An economic programme, prepared by Planning Minister Guillermo Chapman in Oct 1994, proposed that privatization should continue.

Vast deposits of copper have been found at Cerro Colorado and if fully developed the mine could be one of the largest in the world. However, a 25-year concession granted to a Canadian company is vigorously opposed by the Ngöbe-Buglé indigenous group. There is also copper at Petaquilla, Cerro Chorca and Río Pinto; proven copper reserves are 2bn tons and export revenues are forecast at US$500mn a year by the next century. Large coal deposits have been found at Río Indio. The country also has gold and silver deposits. So far no oil has been discovered, but exploration is taking place. The country's mining code is being revised to speed up approval of mining concessions and encourage foreign investment.

One of the most dynamic sectors of the economy is banking. Since 1970 offshore banks have increased from 20 in number to 115 with the establishment of liberal conditions and the abolition of currency controls. In the mid-1980s, total assets amounted to over US$40bn, while deposits were around US$35bn. However, in 1987-88, political uncertainties severely affected the international banking centre. Loss of confidence led many banks to close their offices and move to other offshore centres such as the Bahamas or the Cayman Islands, the level of assets declined, and deposits fell to US$5bn by 1990. In 1990 the new government amended banking regulations to reduce money laundering and legislation to end banking secrecy was approved by the Legislative Assembly in July 1991. By 1993, the financial sector was flourishing again, boosted by the relaxation of restrictions on financial services throughout Latin America. Although deposits were affected by the Mexican crisis in 1995, declining by 13% to US$20bn, they have risen again since then.

RECENT TRENDS

Following a rapid accumulation of foreign debt by the public sector in the late 1970s and early 1980s, the debt service burden became intolerable. Panama received assistance after 1983 from the IMF and the

World Bank in support of its fiscal and structural adjustment programme, while commercial banks rescheduled existing loans and provided new money on easier terms. As a result of the 1988 financial crisis, Panama fell into arrears to all its creditors; consequently, capital inflows were halted; the IMF declared Panama ineligible to borrow and the World Bank cut off loan disbursements. Moreover, the US economic blockade which began in 1988 directly caused a 16% fall in gdp that year followed by a 12% fall the next. In 1990 the economy recovered slightly from its very low base, principally because of 20% increase in commercial activity in the Colón Free Zone, but delays in reaching agreements with external creditors over the repayment of US$2.7bn of arrears postponed economic recovery. In 1992 Panama succeeded in paying US$646mn in arrears to multilateral and governmental creditors, making it eligible for new credits for the first time in 4 years. Until then it had relied heavily on US aid, which amounted to US$985mn since President Endara took office in 1990, of which US$451mn were donations.

The adoption of neoliberal economic policies brought rising discontent as spending cuts caused job losses. Strikes and demonstrations became commonplace and poverty increased. The economic plan announced at the outset of Pérez Balladares' term gave priority to reducing poverty by 50%, though it remains to be seen whether it will be successful. According to official statistics in 1994, 20% of Panamanian families had insufficient income to purchase a minimum diet and a further 25% could not meet their basic needs. The plan aimed to achieve economic growth of 5% annually (between 1990 and 1993 gdp grew on average 6.9%, but it slowed to only 1.9% in 1995). Support for the government's emphasis on social development was given by the IADB, which approved a US$1.5bn loan over 5 years. The inflation rate, just over 1%, is among the lowest in the world. Contributing factors are the use of US dollar, which limits the domestic money supply, slow economic growth in recent years and high unemployment, which keeps wages low and leaves the majority of the population with little purchasing power.

In 1996 Panama signed a debt reduction and refinancing agreement with commercial banks, covering US$2bn of principal and US$1.5bn of interest arrears. It was expected that the reduction, equivalent to about 30% of Panama's total bank debt, would enable a return to the international capital markets.

COMMUNICATIONS

There are now about 9,690 km of roads, of which 3,100 km are paved. Road building is complicated by the extraordinary number of bridges and the large amount of grading required. The road running from Colón to Panama City is the only fully paved one crossing the isthmus, but another excellent and very scenic road crosses the isthmus from Gualaca in Chiriquí to the town of Chiriquí Grande in Bocas del Toro, crossing atop the spectacular, Swedish-built Fortuna hydroelectric dam (see **Buses** under **Transport**, page 1209). The Pan-American Highway connecting Panama City with Chepo to the E, and the Costa Rican border to the W, is paved throughout and is being improved. There is a modern toll road between Panama City and La Chorrera, and the highway near David is being converted into a modern, 4-lane divided highway.

NATIONAL PARKS AND RESERVES

With a relatively small population and much rugged terrain, Panama has a lot of remote, relatively unexploited areas, many of which have been declared National Parks, Wildlife Refuges and Forest Reserves. Most can be visited without hindrance or charge, that is, if you can get there. Transport can be very difficult and facilities non-existent; the largest, Darién

NP is a good example. Many of these protected places are mentioned in the text. For more information, contact Asociación de Conservación de la Naturaleza (see under Panama City – **Useful addresses**, page 1172).

WATERSPORTS

With almost exactly 2000 km of coastline split between the Pacific and the Caribbean, and situated at the northern end of one of the wettest areas of the world, there is an awful lot of water in and around Panama. The potential for water sports is great, most of which remains unexploited. There are however, some opportunities. **Diving** is the best locally developed sport and is very varied. The Caribbean coral reefs are not dissimilar to those of Belize and Honduras except that they extend SE for 100 km along from the Costa Rica border and then from Colón 300 km to the

border with Colombia. For information on these areas, see under Bocas del Toro, Portobelo and the San Blas Islands. The Pacific has quite different eco-systems owing to the much greater tidal ranges, differing water temperature and density etc. Because of easier accessibility, diving is better developed. Places to go include Taboga, the Pearl Islands, Iguana Island and Coiba National Park. A third, and perhaps unique experience, is diving in the lakes of the Panama Canal, mainly to visit wrecks and submerged villages. **Snorkelling** is popular in the less remote of the places mentioned under diving, equipment can be hired in most of the resorts. **White water rafting** and other forms of river running are limited at present to the Chiriquí river system near David and the Chagres National Park area N of Panama City.

Panama City

PANAMA CITY, capital of the Republic, was founded on its present site in 1673 after Morgan had sacked the old town, now known as Panamá Viejo, 6½ km away by road. Most of Panama City is modern; the old quarter of the city (the Casco Viejo) – the part that Spain fortified so massively just as the era of widespread piracy was coming to an end – lies at the tip of a peninsula; both it and Panamá Viejo are being extensively restored.

Population The metropolitan area has a population of over 600,000 (585,000 at 1990 census). Adjacent to the city, but constituting a separate administrative district, is the town of San Miguelito, once a squatter community, now a residential area for 300,000 people of limited means. Every available square inch of hillside is built upon here. A hospital is being built for the town. In the province of Panamá, there are 1.2 million people.

NB Some of the street names have recently been changed, which may make finding your way around a little difficult. The locals are likely still to refer to the streets by their old names, so if in doubt ask. Also, because there is no postal delivery to homes or businesses, few buildings display their numbers, so try to find out the nearest cross street.

Panama City is a curious blend of old Spain, American progress, and the bazaar atmosphere of the E. It has a polyglot population unrivalled in any other Latin American city. For the sober minded, the palm-shaded beaches, the islands of the Bay and the encircling hills constitute a large part of its charm. The cabarets and night life (very enterprising) are an attraction to those so inclined. The city has been expanding since 1979, with new developments along the southern end of the Canal and skyscrapers springing up around the Bahía de Panamá.

PLACES OF INTEREST

CASCO VIEJO

Most of the interesting sights and the budget hotels are in the Casco Viejo (the 'Old Compound', also known as the Casco Colonial or San Felipe), which occupies the narrow peninsula E of C 11. In 1992 local authorities began reviving some of the area's past glory by painting many of the post-colonial houses in soft pastels and their decorations and beautiful iron-clad balconies in relief; new shops and restaurants are being installed in restored buildings in an attempt to make the Casco Viejo

a tourist attraction. At the walled tip of the peninsula is the picturesque **Plaza Francia**, with its red poinciana trees and obelisk topped by a cockerel (symbol of the Gallic nation), which has a document with 5,000 signatures buried beneath it. Twelve large narrative plaques and many statues recall the French Canal's construction history and personalities; the work of Cuban doctor Carlos Finlay in establishing the cause of yellow fever is commemorated on one tablet. Facing the plaza is the French Embassy, housed in a pleasant early 20th century building. Built flush under the old seawalls around the plaza are *Las Bóvedas* (The Vaults), the thick-walled colonial dungeons where prisoners in tiny barred cells were immersed up to their necks during high tides. Nine 'vaults' were re-

stored by IPAT in 1982 and converted into art galleries and a handicraft centre. The French restaurant *Las Bóvedas* occupies another two 'vaults' next to the former Palacio de Justicia (partly burned during Operation Just Cause and now housing the National Institute of Culture).

Steps lead up from the Plaza Francia to the promenade (**Paseo de Las Bóvedas**) which runs along the top of the defensive walls surrounding the peninsula on three sides. This is a popular place for an evening stroll; it is ablaze with bougainvillea and affords good views of the Bahía de Panamá, the Sierra Majé on the Panamá/Darién provincial border (on a clear day), Calzada Amador (known during the Canal Zone era as the Causeway) and the islands beyond (see under Fuerte Amador, page 1176).

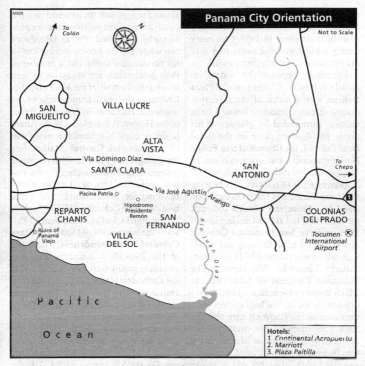

Panama City Orientation

M92R

To Colón

N

Not to Scale

SAN MIGUELITO

VILLA LUCRE

ALTA VISTA

Vía Domingo Díaz

SANTA CLARA

SAN ANTONIO

To Chepo

Piscina Patria

Vía José Agustín Arango

REPARTO CHANIS

Hipódromo Presidente Remón

SAN FERNANDO

Río Juan Díaz

COLONIAS DEL PRADO

Ruins of Panamá Viejo

VILLA DEL SOL

Tocumen International Airport

1

Pacific Ocean

Hotels:
1. Continental Aeropuerto
2. Marriott
3. Plaza Paitilla

Two blocks NW of the Plaza (Av A and C 3) are the restored ruins of the impressive **Church and Convent of Santo Domingo** (1673, but destroyed by fires in 1737 and 1756), both with paired columns and brick inlaying on their façades. The famous 15m-long flat arch (*arco chato*) which formed the base of the choir was built entirely of bricks and mortar with no internal support. When the great debate as to where the Canal should be built was going on, a Nicaraguan stamp showing a volcano, with all its implications of earthquakes, and the stability of this arch – a proof of no earthquakes – are said to have played a large part in determining the choice in Panama's favour. A chapel on the site has been converted into the interesting **Museo de Arte Colonial Religioso**, open Mon-Fri 0900-1600, T 228-2897, whose treasures include a precious golden altar, a delicate snail staircase, silver relics and wooden sculptures from as far away as Lima and México, 19th century engravings of the city, and the skeleton of a woman found by archaeologists during excavation of the Church. Behind Santo Domingo, across Av Central, the neoclassical **Teatro Nacional** (850-seat capacity) opened in 1908 with Verdi's *Aida* being performed in what was then considered the state of the art in acoustics. French-influenced sculptures and friezes enliven the façade, while Roberto Lewis' paintings depicting the birth of the nation adorn the theatre's dome. The ballerina, Dame Margot Fonteyn, who married a member of the prominent Arias family and was a long-time resident of Panama until her death in 1991, danced at the theatre's reinauguration, after many years of restoration, in 1974. Free entry during normal working hours after asking permission of the security guard.

Diagonally opposite the Teatro Nacional (Av B and C 3) is the peaceful **Plaza Bolívar**, with a statue of the Liberator, draped in robes, standing below a large vulture, surrounded by plaques of his deeds. Facing the square are the faded *Hotel Colonial*, the **Church of San Felipe Neri** (interesting but open only on 26 May), and many 19th century houses still displaying roofs of red clay tiles bearing the stamp 'Marseilles 1880'. On the E side stand **San Francisco Church** (colonial but 'modified' in 1917 and modernized in 1983) and the **San Francisco Convent** (1678), largest of all the religious buildings, which was restored by Peruvian architect Leonardo Villanueva. The Bolivarian Congress of June 1826, at which Bolívar proposed a United States of South America, was held in the Chapter Room of the Convent; here also the 1904 Constitution was drafted. This northern wing was dedicated as the **Instituto Bolívar** in 1956; its wood panelling, embossed leather benches and paintings (restored in part by the government of Ecuador) may be viewed with an authorized guide from the Bolivarian Society, T 262-2947.

Another long block W of Plaza Bolívar, on the seafront (Av Alfaro) between Calles 5 y 6, is the **Palacio Presidencial**, the most impressive building in the city, built as an opulent residence in 1673 for successive colonial auditors and governors, enlarged and restored under President Belisario Porras in 1922. Graceful patios and mother-of-pearl decorated columns give a Moorish flavour, and murals by Lewis adorn the official reception salons. The incumbent president, who commutes daily from his private house in Altos del Golf, has restricted access to the street in front of the Palacio, but visitors who ask permission at the guard office are allowed to approach the gate and view the courtyard from the outside. Exterior photography is allowed. Porras introduced two white Darién herons during one of his presidential terms and a number of their descendants are always to be seen around the fountain of the Moorish patio, leading to the popular nickname of the residence: *Palacio de las Garzas* or Palace of the Herons. A few blocks W, Av Alfaro begins to curve N around the waterfront to the colourful **Central Market** (see **Shopping**, below) and the wharves where fishermen land their catches, coastal vessels anchor (a 15m tidal range allows beaching for maintenance) and cargo boats leave for Colombia (Muelle Inglés).

Two blocks S of the Presidential Palace is the heart of the old town, the **Plaza Catedral** or **Independencia**, with busts of the Republic's founders and surrounding public buildings. On the W is the **Cathedral** (1688-1794), its twin towers, domes and classical façade encrusted with mother-of-pearl; three of the tower bells were brought from Old Panamá Cathedral. To the right of the main altar is a subterranean passage which leads to other *conventos* and the sea. On the SW corner with C 7 is the neoclassical **Palacio Municipal** (City Hall), on the 1st floor of which is the **Museo de Historia de Panamá** (see **Museums**, below). The **Post Office** next door, originally built in 1875 as the Grand Hotel ('the largest edifice of that kind between San Francisco and Cape Horn' according to a contemporary newspaper), is the city's best example of French architecture. It became de Lesseps' headquarters during Canal excavations in the 1880s and was sold back to Panamá in 1912; it has been entirely gutted in preparation for its conversion into a Museum of the Panama Canal. The E side of the Plaza is dominated by the former **Archbishop's Palace**, which was later occupied by a university and subsequently by a shelter for runaway youth (now closed), and the *Central Hotel* (1884), once

Panama City Main Streets

Not to Scale

To Miraflores Locks →

X Albrook Air Base

BALBOA

ANCÓN

Quarry Heights

Gorgas
+ Gorgas

Canal
Administration

Ancón

To Puente de las
Américas & David →

EL CHORRILLO

Av De Los Mártires

Calle D

16 Oeste

Av De Los Poetas

CURUNDÚ

Río Curundú

Juan D
Arosemena
Stadium

Gaillard

Av 2N (JF De La Ossa)

Av 2N (JF De La Ossa)

Av Simón Bolívar

AV 3N (LE Clement)

Av Perú (Sur)

Av Cuba (2 Sur)

Av Justo Arosemena

Av México

Av Balboa

Av Central

C 24 Oeste

Av 4 Sur

Av 3 Sur

CALIDONIA

Av B

Av Central

Eloy Alfaro

Av A

C 14 Oeste

Plaza de Francia

Las Bóvedas ○ ○ Palacio de Justicia

Palacio Presidencial

San José M

C. Central

Av B

Av A

PEREJIL

Martín Sosa

C 45 Este

C 42 Este

C 39 Este

Av Chile

Santo Tomás

Balboa
Monument

Instituto
Geográfico
Nacional +

Universidad
Nacional ○

Av de Fábrega

Social Security +

Via Transístmica

Av Manuel Espinoza Batista

CRESTA

BELLA VISTA

Av Federico Boyd

Aquilino De La Guardia

Main
Banking
District

CAMPO ALEGRE

Via Italia

Via Italia

EL CANGREJO

Via Argentina

Via España

Av 2 - Eusebio Morales

Av Samuel Lewis

San Gabriel

Av Nicánor de Obarrio

OBARRIO

Via España

Via Brasil

EL CARMEN

To Tocumén
& Airport →

To Panama
Viejo →

Atlapa Convention
Centre, Tourist Office,
& Hotel Marriott

Paitilla
Airport X

Bahía de Panamá

To Colón →

Bus Stations:
🚌 To the West & Chepo
🚌 To Colón
🚌 Ticabus & *Ideal*

1. Plaza 5 de Mayo, Museo Antropológico Reina Torres de Araúz.
2. Plaza Independencia/Catedral, with Cathedral, Cabildo/Post Office, Archbishop's Palace, Museo de Historia de Panamá & Hotel *Central*
3. Plaza Herrera
4. Plaza Bolívar, San Francisco &
5. Teatro Nacional
6. Santo Domingo & Museo de Arte Colonial Religioso

Hotels:
7. *Acapulco*
8. *El Panamá*
9. *Residencial Primavera*

the most luxurious in Central America (interior Palm Garden, restaurants, barber shop, 100 rooms with private baths, wooden staircase imported from New York, etc) and the centre of Panamá's social life for decades; today it is very decrepit but still retains echoes of its former elegance.

There are a number of other interesting religious structures within 2 or 3 blocks of the Cathedral but the most-visited is the church of **San José** (Av A y C 8a, 1 block W and S of the Plaza Catedral) with its famous Altar de Oro, a massive baroque altar carved from mahogany and according to common belief veneered with gold. This was one of the few treasures saved from Henry Morgan's attack on Old Panamá in 1671 and there are different versions of how it was concealed from the buccaneers (whitewashed by the priest, covered in mud by nuns, even a remark attributed to Morgan hinting that he was not deceived!). A beautiful organ, an 18th century original pulpit with a painting by an unknown artist on its tiny roof and several smaller carved wooden altars can also be seen. Two blocks further W along Av Central is the church of **La Merced**, burnt in 1963 and now completely restored. It was near here that the landward gate of the fortified city stood. A block to the S down C 9 is **Plaza Herrera**; the French influence is evident in the Mansard windows and flower-filled cast-iron balconies of the green and light pink coloured houses and *pensiones*. Behind Plaza Herrera are the ruins of the 'Tiger's Hand Bulwark', where the defensive wall ended and the landward side moat began. The strongpoint held a 50-man military post and 13 cannon, was demolished in 1856 as the town expanded westwards but restored again in 1983. Portions of the moat can still be detected.

AVENIDA CENTRAL AND CALIDONIA

From C 10 onwards the Av Central, Panama City's main commercial street, enters the 'mainland' and begins to curve NW then sweeps NE almost parallel with the shore through the whole town, changing its name to Vía España – the municipality has installed signs reading 'Av Central España' along a transitional section – on its course NE to Tocumen Airport. At its crossing with Calle B is the small Plaza Santa Ana with a colonial church (1764), a favourite place for political meetings; the plaza has many restaurants and is a good place at which to catch buses to all parts of the city. Nearby, running towards the Central Market between Av Central and Calle B is an exotic, narrow alley called **Sal Si Puedes** – 'Get out if you can' – (also known as Carrera de Chiriquí) where crowded stalls sell everything from fruit to old books to medicinal plants; 78% of the street's residents in 1892 were Chinese merchants but the city's Chinatown *(Barrio Chino)* is now largely confined to nearby C Juan Mendoza and adjacent Calle B (several good Chinese restaurants). The neighbourhood is safe enough during the day (watch for pickpockets in the throng) but don't linger late at night, best to leave before 1930.

The next section of Av Central was recently converted into a pedestrian precinct, called El Peatonal, with trees and decorations, a/c department stores, and wandering street vendors. **Plaza 5 de Mayo** (at C 22 Este) is another busy bus stop from which buses leave for the Canal and the airport. In the centre of the Plaza is an obelisk honouring firemen who died in a gunpowder magazine explosion on the site in May 1914. Housed in the old railway station (1913-46) here is the now neglected **Museo Antropológico Reina Torres de Araúz** (see **Museums**, below), formerly called the Museum of Panamanian Man, almost opposite the Plaza de Lesseps. This area is the southern fringe of the **Calidonia** district, where live the descendants of the British West Indian blacks brought in to build the railway and the Canal. Calidonia is a labyrinth of tightly-packed wooden structures, exotic and unassimilated, where outsiders should exercise extreme caution.

LA EXPOSICION

Calle 23 Este leads E from the Plaza down to the broad Av Balboa along the waterfront. The sprawling Santo Tomás Hospital is here (C 36); facing it on a semi-circular promontory jutting out from this promenade (another popular jogging stretch) is a great monument to Vasco Núñez de Balboa (1924), who stands sword and cross aloft as when he strode into the Pacific on 1 October 1513. The statue stands on a white marble globe poised on the shoulders of a supporting group representing the four races of Man. To the E a pleasant park area is being developed. A short distance up the esplanade is the US Embassy. Two more pleasant plazas, Porras and Arías, can be found behind the Santo Tomás Hospital across Av 3 Sur (Justo Arosemena). This central part of the city is known as **La Exposición** because of the international exhibition held here in 1916 to celebrate the building of the Canal. Further N, as Av Balboa begins to curve around the other end of the Bay of Panama to Punta Paitilla and the domestic airport, is **Bella Vista**, once a very pleasant residential district (many private homes now converted to business use) undergoing a renaissance and site of some of the best hotels in our **B** and **C** ranges. It includes the neighbourhood of Perejil ('Parsley'), originally called Perry Hill. Bordering this on the N, where Vía España passes the Iglesia del Carmen, is **El Cangrejo** ('the crab') apartment and restaurant district, with many upmarket stores and boutiques. The University City is on the Transisthmian Highway. Opposite the campus is the Social Security Hospital. All these areas are evidence of Panama City's sensational growth since the postwar economic boom and the spread of the centre eastwards; the attractive residential suburb of Punta Paitilla was an empty hill where hunting was practiced as recently as the 1960s.

MUSEUMS

Museo Afro-Antillano, Justo Arosemena y C 24, 1 block E of Plaza 5 de Mayo, T 262-1668, illustrated history of Panama's West Indian community and their work on the Canal, small library, Tues-Sat 0900-1600, Sun 1500-1800, US$0.50; **Museo de Arte Colonial Religioso** (Santo Domingo Convent, see above); **Museo Antropológico Reina Torres de Araúz**, Av Central at S side of Plaza 5 de Mayo, T 262-4138, five salons (partly looted during Operation Just Cause) exhibiting Panamanian history, anthropology and archaeology, rare collection of precolumbian gold objects and ceramics (Profesora Torres de Araúz was a renowned anthropologist and founder of the museum, died 1982). Opening hours change often: Tues-Sat 0830-1630, Sun 1330-1615, US$0.50. **Museo de Historia de Panamá**, in the Palacio Municipal on Plaza Catedral (see above), T 228-6231/262-8089, the nation's history since European landfall, and includes highlights of the treaty between Panama and the USA which led to the construction of the Canal. Open Mon-Fri 0800-1600, US$0.50; **Museo de Ciencias Naturales**, Av Cuba y C 30, T 225-0645, good sections on geology, palaeontology, entomology and marine biology, Tues-Sat 0900-1600, Sun 0900-1300, US$0.50; **Museo de Arte Contemporáneo**, Av de los Mártires (Ancón), entrance on Av San Blás, T 262-8012, in former Masonic Lodge (1936), permanent exhibition of national and international modern paintings and sculptures with special exhibitions from time to time; marquetry, silkscreen and engraving workshops, library of contemporary visual art open to students, entry free but donations welcomed (privately owned), open Mon-Fri 0900-1600, Sat 0900-1200; **Museo Casa del Banco Nacional**, Av Cuba y C 34, T 225-0640, large numismatic and stamp collection and history of banking from the 19th century, old postal and telephone items and historic photos, not widely-known but worth a visit, open Mon-Fri 0800-1200, 1330-1600, Sat 0830-1300; **Museum of the Independence Soldier**, Paseo de las Bóvedas near the Plaza Francia, T 228-1905, small, even less well-known museum dedicated to mementos and souvenirs of Panama's independence from Colombia in 1903, interesting for the history buff, open Mon-Fri 0800-1600, US$0.25.

PARKS

Claimed to be the only natural forest within the limits of a Latin American metropolitan capital, the 265-ha **Parque Natural Metropolitano** is located between Av Juan Pablo II and the Camino de la Amistad, W of El Cangrejo along the Río Curundú. Open Tues-Sun 0900-1500. As well as a *mirador* (150m) with a splendid view over the city and Canal, there are two interpretive walking trails from which tití monkeys, agoutis, coatis, white-tailed deer, sloths, turtles and up to 200 species of birds may be glimpsed (go early in am for best viewing); green iguanas sun themselves on every available branch. The Smithsonian Institution has installed a unique crane for studying the little-known fauna in the canopy of this remnant of tropical semi-deciduous lowland forest. The Visitor's Centre (T 232-5516) on Av Juan Pablo II runs guided 1-hr tours and holds regular slide shows. No Inrenare permit is required for this recommended, easy excursion. Bus, marked 'Tumbo Muerto', from Av Central, and ask to be dropped at the Depósito. Park is signposted from here, otherwise make for the crane.

LOCAL FESTIVALS

On Independence Day, 3 Nov, practically the whole city seems to march in a parade lasting about 3½ hrs, based in the old part of the city. Colourful, noisy, spectacular. Another parade takes place the following day. Carnival activities include a parade on Shrove Tuesday and have become more elaborate and interesting than in former years. The municipality has also instituted an annual Christmas parade, in which the growing displacement by US-style Christmas traditions of the Latin American emphasis on the Nacimiento and the Three Kings is much in evidence.

LOCAL INFORMATION

● Warning

Panamanians are generally friendly and helpful. Accustomed to foreigners, they are casual about tourists. However, as in any large city with many poor people, certain areas can be dangerous after dark and reasonable precautions should be taken at all times. Attacks have been reported in the Casco Viejo and Panamá Viejo, Marañón (around the market), San Miguelito (on the way in from Tocumen airport) and Calidonia can be dangerous; never walk there at night and take care in daylight, too. For this reason, be careful when booking into a hotel or *pensión* between Calles 9 and 30, ie W of Plaza Herrera (where most of the cheap ones are to be found). Poor districts like Curundú and Hollywood are also best avoided. Probably the safest area for visitors to stay is Bella Vista. Taxis are the safest way to travel around the city, and drivers will give you good advice on where not to go. See **Taxis** under **Transport**, below.

El Chorrillo, the area W from Plaza Santa Ana to Ancón hill, was largely destroyed in Operation Just Cause; it was a dangerous area so if you wish to visit it show a genuine interest in the district's recent history. We have received recent reports of muggings here.

Tourist Police have now appeared in the downtown areas of the city, recognisable by their broad armbands. They are proving helpful for safety and for answering questions.

● Accommodation

Hotel prices			
L1	over US$200	**L2**	US$151-200
L3	US$101-150	**A1**	US$81-100
A2	US$61-80	**A3**	US$46-60
B	US$31-45	**C**	US$21-30
D	US$12-20	**E**	US$7-11
F	US$4-6	**G**	up to US$3

Note a 10% tax on all hotel prices. Most hotels are a/c.

L2 *Miramar Inter-Continental*, Av Balboa y Av Federico Boyd, T 223-3555, F 264-5823, tallest building in the Republic, marina, pools, spa, restaurants, etc; **L3** *El Marriott Caesar Park*, Vía Israel and C 77, T 226-4077, F 226-4262, nr the sea and the Atlapa convention centre, restaurant, pool, health spa, etc; **L3** *El Panamá*, Vía España, 111 y C 55, T 269-5000, F 223-6080, former *Hilton*, tropical Art Deco style, vast rooms, good swimming pool, 'bags of charm'; **A1** *Plaza Paitilla Inn* (former *Holiday Inn*), Punta Paitilla, T 269-1122, F 223-1470, weekend cheap rates available, restaurant, café, nightclub, swimming pool; **A1** *Riande Continental*, Vía España y C Ricardo Arias, T 263-9999, F 269-4559, in the business district, pool, nightclubs, restaurants (see also **Places to eat**), but noisy till 2230 from organ music (a Wurlitzer), undergoing major expansion; **A1** *Granada*, Av Eusebio Morales, T 264-4900, F 264-0930, also with casino, pool, restaurant; **A1** *El Ejecutivo*, C Aquilino de la Guardia, T 264-3333, F 269-1944, pool, a bit shabby; **A2** *Riande Continental Aeropuerto*, nr Tocumen airport (10 mins), T 220-3333, F 220-5017, a/c (reductions for more than one night), clean, free transport to airport, good breakfasts, pool (loud music all day), tennis, casino; **A3** *Aramo*, Vía Brasil y Abel Bravo, a/c, restaurant, T 269-0174, F 269-2406.

B *Europa*, Vía España y C 42, T 263-6911, F 263-6749, opp former Teatro Della Vista, another casino hotel, restaurants and pool, rec; **B** *Gran Hotel Soloy*, Av Perú y C 30, T 227-1133, F 227-0884; **B** *Vera Cruz*, Av Perú y C 30, T 227-3022, F 227-3789, without breakfast, new, clean, good, but rooms at front noisy, **B** *Costa Inn*, Av Perú y C 39, T 227-1522, F 225-1281, a/c, hot water, TV, pool, use of fridge, safe parking, shabby, restaurant noisy and smokey, **B** *Roma*, Av Justo Arosemena y C 33, T 227-3844, F 227-3711, restaurant with Italian emphasis, rooftop pool.

C *Acapulco*, C 30 Este y Av Perú, T 225-3832, a/c, clean, comfortable, TV, private bath, excellent restaurant, safe parking, conveniently located, rec; **C** *Andino*, C 35 off Av Perú, T 225-1162 (formerly *Hotel Lux*), completely redesigned, large rooms, TV, phones, fridge, a/c, private baths, hot water, restaurant (just OK, but cheap), family-run, quiet, highly rec; **C** *California*, Vía España y C 43, T 263-7844, with bath, a/c, TV, restaurant, friendly, safe; **C** *Caribe*, Av Perú, T 225-0404, F 227-3115, a/c; **C** *Centroamericano*, Av Justo Arosemena y Av Ecuador, T 227-4555, very clean, good reading lights, TV; **C-D** *Dos Mares*, C 30 entre Perú y Cuba, T 227-6150, a/c, bath, hot water, pool on roof, TV, phone, rec; **C** *Montreal*, Vía España

nr *Restaurant Lesseps*, T 263-4422, shower, toilet, a/c, TV, phone, takes credit cards, rooms on street noisy, safe car park; **C** *Riazor*, C 16 Oriente, nr *Ideal*, T 228-0777, a/c with bath, hot water, good value, cheap restaurant downstairs next to the Ticabus office, therefore well placed as you arrive late from Costa Rica on the bus, but also much noise from buses.

D *Discovery*, Av Ecuador, T 225-1140, clean, fairly quiet, safe parking, good value; **D** *Colón*, C 12, Oriente and C 'B', T 228-8506, with shower (cheaper without), a/c, erratic water supply; **D** *Caracas*, C 12 on Plaza Santa Ana, large, clean rooms, friendly, hot showers; **D** *Central*, Plaza Catedral, T 262-8044/96), with bath, **E** shared bath, fan, very spacious foyer, faded colonial charm – ie run down, safe motorcycle parking, reasonably clean and friendly, rooms on plaza have balcony, you can bargain if staying more than a week, very good value; **D** *Ideal*, C 17 just off Av Central, T 262-2400, a/c (cold), shared hot shower, pool, cable TV, good location, between Plazas Santa Ana y 5 de Mayo, safe, westbound buses from airport pass outside, for buses to airport go to Av B, 1 block S of Av Central; **D** *Las Tablas*, Av Perú y C 29 Este, between *Hotels Soloy* and *Caribe*, with bath, **E** without, cold water, fan, clean, safe, quiet except for rooms overlooking street; **D** *Residencia Turístico Volcán*, C 29, between Avs Perú y Cuba, T 225-5263, opp Migración, next to Museo de Ciencias Naturales, fan, a/c extra, with shower, friendly, safe, clean.

Cheaper accommodation can be found in *pensiones*: **D-E** *Colonial* (also known as *Columbia*), Plaza Bolívar y C 4, Casco Viejo, T 262-3858, with bath, some balconies overlooking plaza, enjoyable; **E** *Colón*, Av Central, C 30, T 228-8510, without bath, clean, but noisy in the front room; **E** *Foyo*, Santa Bárbara 8-25, T 262-8023, similar to **E** *Herrera*, Plaza Herrera y C 9, T 228-8994, variety of prices, cheapest **F**, some dearer with a/c, TV and fridge, nice location, restaurant; **E** *Panamá*, C 6 No 8-40, T 222-6490, clean; **E** *Las Palmeras*, Av Cuba between C 38-39, T 225 0811, with shower (more with toilet as well), safe, clean, quiet; **E** *Mi Posada*, C 12 y Av Central (Plaza Santa Ana), OK; many (unlisted here) on Av México; **E** *Rivera*, Av C 11 Oriente, 8-14, off Av A, pleasant and friendly, but noisy (monthly rates available); **E** *Pensión Panamericana*, Plaza Herrera, Casco Viejo, dark rooms, balcony rooms good value; **E** *Pensión Universal*, Av Central 8-16, behind Cathedral, T 228-2796, shared bath, fan; **E** *Residencial Primavera*, Av Cuba y C 42, on edge of Bella Vista, 1 block E of Av España, T 225-1195, with bath and fan, quiet residential area, rec; **E** *Tropical*, C de San Blas No 8-18, 2½ blocks from Post Office, T 222-7034, clean; **F** *Santa Ana*, overlooking Plaza Santa Ana, helpful.

Apartments for rent at **A1** *Costa del Sol*, Vía España y Av Federico Boyd, T 223-7111, F 223-6636, central, kitchettes, rooftop restaurant, pool, tennis courts and spa, will arrange trips; **A2** *Suites Ambassador*, C D in centre of El Cangrejo district, T 263-7274, F 264-7872, well-furnished rooms, pool, gym; **A2** *Tower House Suites*, C 51 No 36, Bella Vista, T 269-2244, F 269-2869, centre of commercial district; **A3** *Apartotel Las Vegas*, C 55 y Av EA Morales, T 264-5033, F 223-0047, rec, good restaurant on the patio; **B** *Apartotel Plaza*, Av Batista opp University campus, T 264-5033, F 264-2256, and others. All have kitchenette, colour and cable TV, some with pool. Daily, weekly and monthly rates are available.

On the way to the airport are 'love motels', 'push buttons', with drive-in garages. For US$10-15 you have a nice room and shower and a few hours' relaxation, even with noble intentions. If your time is up a bell rings and you have to return to your car. You wait while they count the towels, then they open the garage.

NB Electricity and water cuts are frequent in Panama City, though usually very brief. Most better-class hotels have generators and large cisterns.

Camping: The Panamanian Embassy in London advises that it is not safe for female travellers to camp in Panama. There are no official sites but it is possible to camp on some beaches or, if in great need (they agree, but don't like it much) in the Balboa Yacht Club car park. It is also possible to camp in the Hipódromo grounds (11 km E of the city, on Vía España) but there are no facilities; this is allowed if you are waiting to ship your vehicle out of the country. Also possible, by previous arrangement, at La Patria swimming pool nearby, and at the Chorrera (La Herradura) and La Siesta beaches on the Pan-American Highway. Camping Gaz is available at *Ferretería Tam SA*, Av B, No 54; at *Super 99* grocery stores, cheap.

● **Places to eat**
There are good restaurants in most of the more expensive hotels. *Rendezvous*, at the *Riande Continental*, is very good value, open 24 hrs, superb Sun brunch from 1030-1500 US$9.50.

Good are: *Lesseps*, Vía España y C 46, La Cresta, T 223-0749, French restaurant and bar (decorated with memorabilia of the early French thwarted effort to build the canal); *Caffé Pomodoro*, Av E A Morales, N of C 55, on patio of *Apartotel Las Vegas*; *Centolla's Place*, Vía España, Río Abajo, T 221-7056, Caribbean seafood, catering to Antillean community, friendly, cheap, rec; *La Mejicanita*, Av Justo Arosemena; *Atenas*, C Ricardo Arias, excellent pizza and near-Eastern food; *Las Américas*, C San Miguel, Obarrio; *La Fregata*, Av Samuel Lewis, Obarrio, good food, medium priced; *Nápoli*, C 57, Obarrio, 1½ blocks S of Vía España, big, family-style, good Italian, pizzas with real Italian dough; *La Casa del Marisco* (sea food) on Av Balboa, is open-air; *Las Bóvedas*, in converted dungeons at seaward end of Casco Viejo, T 228-8068, good French food, expensive, art galleries adjoining. In El Cangrejo, *El Cortijo*, between Eusebio A Morales and Vía Argentina on C D; *Tinajas*, on C 51, nr *Ejecutivo Hotel*, Panamanian food and entertainment, craft shop, rec; *Le Bistrot*, Centro Comercial La Florida, C 53, expensive; *Casco Viejo*, C 50, Mansion Dante, excellent food, interesting decor, expensive but rec; *El Viejo Pipo*, C 42 No 50, Bella Vista, T 225-7924, Italian, charming, cheerful, good service, rec; *Oriental Palace*, Av Samuel Lewis No 15, just down from *Continental Hotel*, T 223-5744, Korean, Japanese and Chinese food, first class; *Taberna Bavaria*, C 50 entrance by Don Lee, T 223-1187, German cuisine, plenty of imported beers, great place; *El Hostal*, C 42 y Av Balboa, opp Banco Exterior tower, T 225-8731, good Italian dishes.

Other restaurants inc: *El Trapiche*, Vía Argentina 10, Panamanian food (*empanadas* – meat filled fritters, and *mondongo* – seasoned tripe) and entertainment, good; *Manolo*, Vía Argentina, sidewalk terrace, a favourite for politicians and young people in evenings and Sun am, beer from the tap served with *tapas*, *churros* (doughnut-like fried cakes) a speciality; *Piscolabis*, Transisthmian Highway, Vista Hermosa district, local food, reasonable; *Santana*, on pedestrian area of Av Central for Panamanian specialities; *El Jorrón*, Vía Fernández de Córdoba, Vista Hermosa district, local food, reasonable and good; *La Tablita*, Transisthmian Highway, Los Angeles district, reasonable; *Nápoli*, Av Estudiante, corner with C 16, Italian, closed Tues, good and cheap (but rough neighbourhood), and many other good Italian places. *El Rincón Suizo*, C Eusebio A Morales, charming mountain hut atmosphere, good Swiss rösti; *1985*, same street, larger than *El Rincón* but similar style; *La Cascada*, Av Balboa and C 25, beef, pork, seafood, enormous helpings, open air, 'doggy bags' given, fake waterfall, lifesize animal décor in concrete ('OTT Disneyland'), good service, credit cards not accepted, menus in charming English to take away, closed Sun, highly rec; the same management runs *Las Costillitas* on Vía Argentina, same menu (which takes 30 mins to read), same reasonable prices, open Sun; *El Dorado*, C Colombia 2, good service, excellent seafood, rec; *Los Años Locos*, opp *Caesar Park Hotel*, T 226-6966, Argentine *parrillada* steakhouse, good value. *Niko's Café*, Vía España nr El Rey supermarket, T 264-0136, and El Dorado Shopping Centre, I 260-0022, very good, cheap, self-service.

Vegetarian: *Mireya* C Ricardo Arango and C Ricardo Arias, nr *Continental Hotel*, good value, rec; *Mi Salud*, C 31 y Av México 3-30, owned by dietary specialist Carlos Raúl Moreno, open Mon-Sat 0700-1930; *Govinda's*, C 47, No 24, Marbella, many specialities.

Many good Oriental places. *Matsuei*, Av Eusebio A Morales A-12, Japanese, excellent, pricey; *Lung Fung*, Transisthmian Highway and Los Angeles, very popular with Chinese residents for Sat and Sun. Cantonese-style brunch, very good food and value; *Manhattan*, Vía España, Edif Domino, clean, reasonable, Chinese; *Kwang Chow*, in the Sal si Puedes area of Av Balboa, sells Tsingtao beer, rec; *Gran China*, Av Balboa, between Calles 26 and 27, Chinese, good value; *Modern Chang*, C 48 off Aquilino de la Guardia, elegant, good food, pricey, erratic service; *Palacio Imperial*, C 17 nr Ticabus office, Chinese, good and cheap; *Kalua*, close to the *Hotel El Panamá*, very good Chinese, reasonable prices; *Bajwa's Shamiana*, Galerías Marbella, Paitilla, T 263-8586, Indian, US$15 pp, fair; *Chipré*, Av Central y C 11 Oriente, rec.

Krispy, *McDonald's*, *Frutilandia*, *Dairy Queen*, *Hardee's*, *Burger King*, *Kentucky Fried Chicken*, *Pizza Pizza* and *Don Lee* all have their branches; *La Viña*, corner C 6 Oriente and Av A, behind Post Office, good, cheap; also *La Esquina*, Av A y C 12 Oriente; *Jimmy's*, Paseo Cincuentenario just beyond Atlapa Centre, T 226-1096, good fast food and fish, served under a thatched roof; *La Conquista*, C J, up Av Central; *La Cresta* (good food from US$1), Vía España and C 45; *A & P* on Av Central opp the National Museum, good; *Markany*, Av

Cuba y Av Ecuador, good snacks; *Café Coca Cola*, Av Central and Plaza Santa Ana, pleasant, reasonably-priced; *Café Jaime*, corner of C 12 and Av Central, for good *chichas* (natural drinks); *Cafe Central*, Av Central, between C 28 and 29, Calidonia, basic and cheap food, OK. There are good pavement cafés along Av Balboa.

● **Airline offices**

Copa, Av Justo Arosemena y C 39, T 227-5000, F 227-1952 for reservations, airport T 238-4053; **Aeroperlas**, Paitilla Airport, T 269-4555, F 223-0606; **Parsa**, Paitilla Airport, T 226-3803, F 226-3422; **Ansa**, Paitilla Airport, T 226 7891, F 226-4070; **Nica**, Vía España y C 52, Ed Oqawa, I 264-4144, F 269-4855; **Aviateca**, Suite Montecarlo p 6, T 223-2992, F 223-2993; **Lacsa**, Av Justo Arosemena 31-44, T 225-0193 for reservations, airport T 238-4116; **Taca**, C B, Suites Montecarlo, p 6, El Cangrejo, T 269-6214/6066 for reservations, airport T 238-4015; **SAM**, C MM Icaza No 12, Edif Grobman, T 269-1222 for reservations, airport T 238-4096; **Avianca**, T 223-5225; **Avensa**, C MM Icaza, T 264-9906, F 263-9022; **American**, C 50, Plaza New York, T 269 6022 for reservations, airport T 238-4140, F 269-0830; **British Airways** at Lacsa (above); **Continental**, Av Balboa y Av 4, Ed No 17, T 263-9177; **United**, I 269-8555; **Iberia**, Av Balboa y C 45, T 227-3671 reservations, airport T 238-4163, F 227-2070; **KLM**, Urb Obarrio y C 50E, T 223-3747 for reservations, airport T 238-4025, F 264-6358; **Lufthansa**, Agencias Continental, C 50, Ed Fidanque, p 1, T 269-1549, F 263-8641; **Cubana**, T 227-2122; **Aerolíneas Argentinas**, T 269-3815; **LAB**, T 263-6433; **LanChile**, T 226-0133; **Varig**, C MM Icaza, T 264-7666 for reservations, airport T 238-4501, F 263-8179; **AeroPerú**, T 269-5777.

● **Banks & money changers**

See also **Money** in **Information for travellers**. The **Chase Manhattan Bank** (US$0.65 commission on each TC), Visa advances; **Citibank** has plenty of ATMs for cash withdrawals for its own cardholders, also Visa cash advances; **Lloyds Bank**, C Aquilino de la Guardia y C 48, Bella Vista, T 263-6277, 263-8693 for foreign exchange, offers good rates for sterling (the only bank which will change sterling cash, and only if its sterling limit has not been exhausted); **Bank of America**, Av José de la Cruz Herrera, C 53 Este, no commission on own TCs, US$0.10 tax. Thomas Cook TCs exchangeable at **Banco Sudameris** and **Algemene Bank Nederland**;

Deutschmarks exchanged at **Deutsch-Süda-merikanische Bank**. Panamanian banks' hours vary, but many open 0800-1500 Mon-Fri, 0800-1200 Sat. Try to avoid 15th and last working day of the month, paydays. **Banco General** takes American Express, Bank of America and Thomas Cook TCs. Also **Banco del Istmo**, C 50, open Mon-Fri 0800-1530, Sat 0900-1200, changes TCs. You can buy Amex TCs at **Banco Mercantil del Istmo** on Vía España (they also give cash advances on Mastercard). **American Express**, Torre Exterior, Av Balboa, 9th floor, T 263-5858, Mon-Fri 0830-1600, does not exchange TCs, clients' mail only. ATMs for withdrawals from foreign bank accounts (as opposed to advances on a credit card), using bank cards with Visa symbol: **Banco General** at Av Central y 4 Sur (Balboa), and at **Banco Continental** nr hotel of same name. Visa T 264-0988; Mastercard T 263-5221; Diners T 263-8195.

Possible to change South American currencies (poor rates) at Panacambios, ground floor, Plaza Regency, behind *Adam's Store*, Vía España, nr the Banco Nacional de Panamá and opp *Hotel Riande Continental* (it also has postage stamps for collectors).

● **Cultural centres**
Alianza Francesa, C 49, Bellavista, T 264-2737, film each Wed at 2000.

● **Embassies & consulates**
Costa Rican, C Gilberto Ortega 7, Edif Miramar, T 264-2980 (open 0800-1330); **Nicaraguan**, Av Federico Boyd y C 50, T 223-0981 (0900-1300, 1500-1800); **Salvadorean**, Vía España, Edif Citibank, p 4, T 223-3020 (0900-1300); **Guatemalan**, C Abel Bravo y C 57, Bella Vista, Edif Torre Cancún, Apt 14A, T 269-3475, F 223-1922, open 0800-1300; **Honduran**, Av Justo Arosemena y C 31, Edif Tapia, p 2, T 225-8200 (0900-1400); **Mexican**, Ed Bank of America, p 5, C 50 y 53, T 263-5021 (0830-1300); **Venezuelan**, Banco Unión Building, Av Samuel Lewis, T 269-1014 (0830-1230), visa takes 24 hrs; **Colombian**, MM Icaza 12, Edif Grobman, p 6, PO Box 4407 (Zona 5), T 264-9266, open 0800-1300. The **Chilean** and **Ecuadorean** embassies are housed in the same building, T 223-5364 and 264-2654 respectively, neither is open in pm.
US, Av Balboa and 40, Edif Macondo, p 3, T 227-1777, F 227-1964, PO Box 6959 (Zona 5) (0800-1700); Consulate in new Miramar building, C 39 y Av Balboa, ground floor (hotel and restaurant in same building). **Canadian**, C MM Icaza, Ed Aeroperú, p 5, T 264-7014 (0800-1100); **British**, Torre Swiss Bank, C 53, Zona 1,

T 269-0866, F (507) 269-0866, Apdo 889 (0800-1200); **French**, Plaza Francia, T 228-7835 (0830-1200); **German**, Edif Bank of America, C 50 y 53, T 263-7733 (0900-1200); **Netherlands**, Altos de Algemene Bank, C MM Icaza, 4, T 264-7257 (0830-1300, 1400-1630); **Swedish**, Vía José Agustín Arango/Juan Díaz, T 233-5883 (0900-1200, 1400-1600); **Swiss**, Av Samuel Lewis y C Gerardo Ortega, Ed Banco Central Cancellería, p 4, T 264-9731, PO Box 499 (Zona 9A), open 0845-1145; **Italian**, C 1, Parque Lefevre 42, T 226-3111, open 0900-1200; **Danish**, C Ricardo Arias, Ed Ritz Plaza, p 2, T 263-5872, open 0800-1200, 1330-1630; **Spanish**, entre Av Cuba y Av Perú, C 33A, T 227-5122 (0900-1300); **Norwegian**, Av Justo Arosemena y C 35, T 225-8217 (0900-1300, 1400-1630); **Finnish**, Carretera Transístmica, C 85, T 236-3000; **Japanese**, C 50 y 61, Ed Don Camilo, T 263-6155 (0830-1200, 1400-1700); **Israeli Embassy**, Edif Grobman, C MM Icaza, p 5, PO Box 6357, T 264-8022/8257.

● **Entertainment**
Cabarets and discotheques: Hotel *Riande Continental*; *Josephine's*, C 50 y Av Uruguay, El Cangrejo, cover charge US$20, continuous show 2100-0400 daily except Sun; *Le Palace*, C 52, opp *Hotel Executive*, T 269-1844, no cover, shows from 2000 nightly; *Oasis*, Vía Brasil. **Recommended discos**: *Bacchus*, Vía España y Elvira Méndez, and *Magic*, C 50 diagonal a C 43 Uruguay; *Cubares*, next door; *Las Molas*, entrance to Chase Manhattan Bank, Vía España, Los Angeles district, small band, rural decor, drinks US$1.50; *Unicornio*, C 50 y R Arias 23 is nightclub with discothèque and gambling; reasonable prices, will admit foreigners for US$3 a week. *La Parrillita*, Av 11 de Octubre in Hato Pintado district, is a restaurant in a railway carriage. *El Pavo Real*, off C 50 Oriente in Campo Alegre, hard to find, pub selling British beer (at a price), darts board, popular with expats.

Casinos: more than 20, some in main hotels. State-managed and profits intended for charitable public institutions; most offer black jack, baccarat, poker, roulette and slot machines (*traganikles*). Winnings are tax-free and paid without deductions. The *National Lottery* is solemnly drawn (televised) each Wed and Sun at 1300 in Plaza de la Lotería between Avs Perú y Cuba; 4-digit tickets, called *billetes* or *pedazos*, cost US$1, 'chance' tickets, with only 2 digits cost US$0.25.

Live music clubs: *Nottingham*, Fernández de Córdoba, Vista Hermosa, T 261-0314, live salsa at weekends, no cover charge, restaurant; *Vino's Bar*, C 51 y Colombia, Bella Vista, T 264-0520, live salsa at weekends, cover charge, restaurant; *Hotels Granada* and *Soloy* (*Bar Maitai*, T 227-1133) are rec for live Latin music at weekends. *Giorgio's*, 1 block S of Vía Porras.

Theatres and cinemas: there are occasional official presentations and concerts held at the **Teatro Nacional** (folklore sessions every other Sun, check dates; monthly National Ballet performances when not on tour). The **Anayansi Theatre** in the Atlapa Convention Centre, Vía Israel, San Francisco, has a 3000-seat capacity, good acoustics, regular recitals and concerts. **Balboa Theatre** nr Steven's Circle and Post Office in Balboa, with folkloric groups and jazz concerts sponsored by National Institute of Culture. **Guild Theatre** in the Canal Area at Ancón mounts amateur productions mainly in English. *La Prensa* gives full listings of cultural events. The usual a/c cinemas (US$2.50 except Balboa cinema nr Steven's Circle, US$2); by law all foreign films must be subtitled in Spanish. Newspapers publish daily programming (*cartelera*). **Cine Universitario** in the National University, T 264-2737, US$1.50 for general public, shows international and classic movies daily (not holidays) at 1700, 1900 and 2100.

● **Hospitals & medical services**

Dentist: Dr Daniel Wong, *Clínica Dental Marbella*, Ed Alfil (ground floor), nr Centro Comercial Marbella, T 263-8998. Dr D Lindo, T 223-8383.

Hospitals: the *US Gorgas Army Community Hospital* (see map) is only for US military personnel, except in emergency though they will provide free malaria prophylaxis (the hospital is being closed and US medical facilities are moving to the Howard Air Force Base, across the Puente de Las Américas). The private clinics charge high prices; normally visitors are treated at either the *Clínica San Fernando* (T 229-2004) or the *Clínica Paitilla* (T 269-6060), both have hospital annexes. For inoculations buy vaccine at a chemist, who will rec a clinic; plenty in La Exposición around Parque Belisario Porras.

● **Laundry**

Lavamático Lavarápido, C 7 Central No 7-45, 1/2 block from Plaza Independencia, Mon-Sat 0800-2000, Sun 0900-1400, US$0.75 with hot water, US$0.60 cold, soap and drying extra. Many around Plaza Catedral; wash and dry US$2.

● **Post & telecommunications**

Post Office: there is no postal delivery in Panama. Recipients either have a post office box (*apartado*), or receive mail via General Delivery/Poste Restante (*Entrega General*). The main office is on Plaza Catedral in the Casco Viejo, open Mon-Fri 0700-1745, Sat 0700-1645; 'Poste Restante' items held for a month. Official name and zone must be inc in the address: Main Post Office = 'Zona 1, Catedral'; C 30 E nr Av Balboa = 'Zona 5, La Exposición'; El Dorado Shopping Centre = 'Zona 6A, El Dorado'; Vía España, Bella Vista (in front of Piex store) = 'Zona 7, Bella Vista'. Parcels sent 'poste restante' are delivered to Encomiendas Postales Transístmicas at the El Dorado Centro Comercial if there is duty to pay on the goods; if not they are delivered to the nearest post office. Post Office operates a courier system called EMS to most Central and South American countries, Europe, US and some Asian countries. Packages up to 20 kg: 2 to 3 days to USA (500g documents to Miami US$13); 3 to 4 days Europe US$20; Asia US$25. Also private courier services, eg *United Parcel Services*, Edif Fina, C 49, El Cangrejo, 1/2 kg to London or Paris, 3-4 days, US$30; *Jet Express* (*Federal Express*), Edif Helga, Vía España y 44 Sur/C 50, 1/2 kg to Miami, 2 days, US$10. Panamá issues highly-regarded stamps; foreigners may open a 'philatelic account' and order stamps, first-day covers, commemorative issues, etc, provided a minimum US$20 in account: Dirección de Filatelía, Dirección de Correos y Telégrafos, Apartado 3421, Panamá 1 (Vía España, Calidonia, opp Don Bosco Church).

Telecommunications: Intel offices (eg Edif Dilido, C Manuel María Icaza, nr *Hotel Continental*; Edif 843, Gavilán Rd, Balboa, and at the international airport) offer excellent but expensive international telephone, telex, fax and modem (use Bell 212A type) facilities; open every day 0730-2300. Collect calls to 21 countries, dial 106. Public payphones take 5, 10 and sometimes 25 cent coins.

● **Places of worship**

Services in English at *St John's Episcopalian*, Avs 12 de Octubre y La Paz, Betania, Sun 0700; *Baptist*, C Balboa 914, La Boca, Sun 1100 and 1900; *Methodist*, Av Central y C 16 Este, Sun 0900. *Kol Shearith Israel Synagogue*, Av Cuba y C 36, services Fri 2000, Sat 1100. *Baha'i Temple*, Mile 8 on Transístmica Highway (Ojo de Agua district), Baha'i HQ for all of Latin America, modern, white domed, worth seeing for its architecture (open daily 1000-1800, Sun service 1000), taxi round trip for US$8 with an hour to see the temple can be arranged. Church services for various denominations are also held on the US military bases.

● **Shopping**

Duty-free imported luxuries of all kinds are an attraction at the *Zona Libre* in Colón (purchases sealed and delivered to Tocumen airport), but Panama City is a booming fashion and merchandise centre where bargains are not hard to find; anything from crystal to cashmere may often be cheaper than at point of origin. (**NB** A system of US government commissaries and post exchanges serving military and Canal personnel is not available to the general public.)

The smartest shops are along C 50 and Vía España in Bella Vista and El Cangrejo, but Av Central is cheaper and the best and most popular place for clothing (not great quality), hi-fi and photographic equipment, perfumes, curios, souvenir T-shirts and Asian handicrafts. **NB** The main road artery Av 4A Sur is popularly called C 50. Colombian emeralds and pearls may also be purchased at reasonable prices from many establishments.

Traditional Panamanian *artesanía* includes *molas* (embroidered blouse fronts made by Kuna Indians, eg Emma Vence, T 261-8009); straw, leather and ceramic items; the *pollera* circular dress, the *montuno* shirts (embroidered), the *chácara* (a popular bag or purse), the *chaquira* necklace made by Guaymí Indians, and jewellery. Indigenous Darién carvings of jungle birds and animals from wood or *tagua* nut make interesting souvenirs (from US$10 up to US$250 for the best, museum-quality pieces); *Colecciones*, Vía Italia opp *Hotel Plaza Paitilla Inn*, has a wide selection. Plenty of straw articles available, inc baskets, bags, traditional masks and Panama hats (US$150 for the best quality); try *Flory Salzman* (not cheap) on Vía Venetto nr *El Panamá Hotel*, nearby *Inovación*, or *Indutípica*, Av A y C 8 Oriente (opp San José Church) for reproductions of precolumbian ceramics and jewellery, Kuna *molas* from the Darién and Guaymí dresses from Bocas del Toro. The *Gran Morrison* department store chain (best-supplied is in Paitilla, also at *Hotel Continental* and on Vía España nr C 51 Este) have good-quality handicraft sections, as well as postcards and books in English. Another good selection is at *Artesanías Nacionales* in Panamá Viejo, one of several Indian co-ops selling direct from open-air outlets, eg in the Canal Area at Balboa and along the road to Miraflores Locks at Corozal (every day if not raining). The Tourist Office has a full list of *artesanía* shops available, inc those in the main hotels. *Reprosa*, Av Samuel Lewis y C 54 (T 269-0457) features a unique collection of precolumbian gold artefacts reproduced in sterling silver vermeil; David and Norma Dickson make excellent reproductions for sale (Panamá Guacas, T 266-6176). Of the various commercial centres, with banking, entertainment and parking facilities, the largest is *El Dorado Mall and Shopping Centre*, in the Tumbo Muerto district at Av Ricardo Franco y C 71 (shops open Mon-Sat 0900-1900, Sun 1500-1900; cinema, plenty of restaurants and playgrounds). Similar are: *Plaza New York*, C 50, which has several travel agencies and a well-known disco; *Plaza California*, nr *El Dorado*; and *Bal Harbour*, Vía Italia nr Punta Paitilla (Mon-Sat 0900-1900, Sun 1100-1900); the *Balboa Mall* on Av Balboa is the newest but is closed on Sun. The *Supermercado El Rey* on Vía España just E of *Hotel Continental* and at *El Dorado*, *Super 99*, *Farmacias Arrocha*, *Casa de la Carne* (expensive) and *Machetazo* (on Av Central) are said to be the best of the city's supermarkets. Army-Navy store on Av Central nr Plaza 5 de Mayo sells camping and hiking equipment. Similarly *Army Force*, E end pedestrianized section of Av Central, W of Plaza 5 de Mayo.

The *Mercado Central*, close to the docks and Palacio Presidencial, is the place for fresh produce (pigs, ducks, poultry, geese, etc) as well as parrots and pets; bargain hard as prices are extremely competitive. Most interesting part of the Market is the chaotic shopping area along C 13 and the waterfront (Terraplen), the best place to buy secondhand jungle and military supplies (eg powerful insect repellents, machetes, webbing, cooking equipment, etc) for a trek into the forested interior. The nearby fish market is clean and prices are the best in town. Another bazaar-like shopping area lines Vía España as it passes through Calidonia beyond the Plaza 5 de Mayo; as has been said, this *barrio* is for the adventurous by day and definitely dangerous at night.

Bookshops: *Librería Argosy*, Vías Argentina y España, El Cangrejo, T 223-5344, very good selection in English, Spanish and French; rec; *Gran Morrison* department stores around the city stock books, travel guides and many magazines in English; many Spanish and English magazines also at branches of *Farmacias Arrocha*, *Super 99* and *Gago* supermarkets/drugstores. *National University Bookshop*, on campus between Av Manuel Espinosa Batista and Vía Simón Bolívar, T 223-3155, for excellent range of specialized books on Panamá, national authors, social sciences and history, open Mon-Fri 0800-1600, closed weekends, highly rec. (The campus *Simón Bolívar Library* has extensive Panamanian material, only for matriculated students but visitors engaged in special research can obtain a temporary permit from the Director, Mon-Fri 0800-2000, Sat 0900-1300.) Near the University is *La Garza* bookshop, Av José de Fábrega y C 47, good supply of Latin American literature (Spanish only). The *Smithsonian Tropical Research Institute Public Library*, Edif Topper, Av de los Mártires (opp National Assembly), has best English-language scientific library in Panamá, open Mon-Fri 0800-1600. International edition of the *Miami Herald* printed locally on *La Prensa*'s presses, widely available at news-stands and hotels, as are leading US papers and magazines.

Photographic: *Foto Enodi* and *Foto Decor*, Via Porras, Kodak slides developed in a day. Many other places for developing and equipment. In some places you will get a free film. Camera repairs at *Relojería*, watch shop, on C Medusin, off Av Central in Calidonia.

● **Sports**

Bathing: Piscina Patria (the Olympic pool), take San Pedro or Juan Díaz bus, US$0.15. Piscina Adán Gordon, between Av Cuba and Av Justo Arosemena, nr C 31, 0900-1200, 1300-1700 (except weekends to 1700 only). Admission US$0.50 (take identification), but beards and long hair frowned on (women must wear bathing caps). Many beaches within 1½ hrs' drive of the city. Fort Kobbe beach (US$7.50 admission, with vouchers given for drinks and hot dogs, bus from Canal Area bus station US$0.75, 30 mins) and Naos beach (US$1, Amador bus from same station, US$0.30, then 2 km walk along Causeway) have been rec; both have shark nets, but at low tide at the former you must go outside it to swim! Vera Cruz beach is not rec as it is both dirty and dangerous (all are dangerous at night).

Cockfights: at the *Club Gallístico*, Vía España nr junction with Vía Cincuentenario, T 221-5652, every Sun, same bus as for race track, but get out at crossing with C 150.

Golf: *Panama Golf Club*, T 266-7777, courses at Summit and Horoko; *Coronado Beach Golf Club* (open to tourists who get guest cards at Coronado office on C 50). Similarly at *Fort Amador Golf Club* tourists can play, green fees

and rented clubs US$20 for the day. A spectacular view of the canal and the city.

Horse races: (pari-mutuel betting) are held Sat, Sun and holidays at the Presidente Remón track (bus to Juan Díaz, entry from US$0.50-US$2.50).

● **Tour companies & travel agents**

Viajes Panamá SA, C 52, Av Federico Boyd, Edif Costa del Sol, T 223-0644 or 223-0630, English spoken; *Viajes Riande*, E side of *Hotel Riande Continental*, C Ricardo Arias, T 269-4569, English spoken, very helpful; *Tropic Tours*, Edif Comosa nr *El Panamá Hotel*, well organized trips, multilingual; *Eco-Tours de Panamá*, Ricardo Arias 7 (nr *Hotel Continental*), T 263-3077, F 263-3089, PO Box 465, 0800-1700 Mon-Sat, a wide variety of trips, from relaxing cultural excursions to the San Blas islands, to high altitude forest hikes, bilingual guides, highly rec; *Viajes Airemar*, C 52 y Ricardo Arias 21, T 223-5395/5336, highly rec for flights to South American destinations; *Viajes Marsal*, C 50 y Manuel M Icaza, nr Banco Iberoamericano, T 223-5321/5447/9851, helpful, efficient, English spoken; *5 Continentes*, Av Principal La Alameda, Ed Plaza San Marcos, T 260-8447/9, helpful with shipping a car, rec; *Rapid Travel*, C 53, El Cangrejo, Ed Las Margaritas, T 264-6638, F 264-6371; *Chadwick's* and *Starlite*, see page 1175; *Sun Line Tours*, C Eusebio A Morales, Edif Estela, local 2, El Cangrejo, Apdo Postal 2323, Zona 9A, Panama, T 269-6620/263-8451, F 223-7609, for Panama Canal Transits (US$99, rec) and trips to Contadora; *Viajes Arco Iris*, Av Justo Arosemena y C 45, Bella Vista, Edif Dollar, T 227-3318, F 227-3386, for full range of local tours; *Continental SA*, Av 7/Vía España, T 263-5531, in *Riande Continental* building, friendly, good. Mrs Vicky Turner (American) of *Panamá Adentro* (Inside Panama) conducts city, beach tours for 1-3 people, half-day US$50, full-day US$100, in her own car, or up to 6 people in a/c minibus, full-day US$200, T 264-8855.

● **Tourist offices**

Tourist Bureau: information office of the Instituto Panameño de Turismo (IPAT), in the Atlapa Convention Centre, Vía Israel opp *Hotel Marriott*, Apdo 4421, Panamá 5. Office open 0900 to 1600; issues good list of hotels, *pensiones*, motels and restaurants, and issues a free *Focus on Panama* guide (available at all major hotels, and airport); T 226-7000/2861, F 226-2544, ask for 'información', helpful, English spoken. *Getting to Know Panama*, by Michèle

Labrut, published by Focus Publications (Apdo 6-3287, El Dorado, Panamá, RP, F 225-0466, US$12), has been rec as very informative. Best **maps** (based on US government topographic maps) from **Instituto Geográfico Nacional Tommy Guardia (IGNTG)**, on Vía Simón Bolívar, opp the National University (footbridge nearby, fortunately), take Transístmica bus from C 12 in Santa Ana, or Tumbo Muerto bus: physical map of the country in 2 sheets, US$4 each; Panama City map in many sheets, US$4/sheet (travellers will only need 3 or so). At the back of the Panama Canal Commission telephone books are good maps of the Canal Area, Panama City and Colón.

● **Useful addresses**
Conservation: Asociación de Conservación de la Naturaleza (Ancon), on C 53, 1 block S of Argentina, N of España, Bella Vista (Apdo 1387, Panamá 1), T 264-1836, for comprehensive information on the country's natural attractions and environmental matters.

Customs: for renewal of permits and obtaining exit papers for vehicles at Paitilla airport.

Immigration: Inmigración y Naturalización, Av Cuba (2 Sur) y C 28E, T 225-8925; visa extensions and exit permits issued Mon-Fri 0800-1500.

Ministerio de Hacienda y Tesoro: Calles 35 y 36, entre Avs Perú y Cuba, T 227-4879, for tax compliance certificate (*paz y salvo*) required for exit visa (*permiso de salida*).

● **Transport**
Local Bus: the traditional small buses known as *chivas*, consisting of locally made wooden bodies grafted onto truck chassis, have all but disappeared, though occasionally may be seen on the street. Most buses in urban areas are second-hand US school buses painted in fanciful designs, but otherwise in poor condition (the small buses going into Balboa are at least 40 years old); blaring radios have recently been prohibited. Most out-bound (east) buses travel along Av Perú, through Bella Vista, before fanning out to their various destinations. In-bound (west) buses travel along Vía España and Av Central through the Calidonia shopping district. Basic fare US$0.15, usually paid to the driver upon descending; if there is a fare box, deposit upon entering. To stop at the next authorized stop, call out "*parada*" to the driver. **Car rental**: at the airport (**Hertz**, T 238-4081; **Avis**, T 238-4069; **National**, T 238-4144; also **International**, T 238-4404; **Budget** and **Dollar**). Other offices in El Cangrejo: **Avis**, C 55, T 264-0722;

International, C 55, T 264-4540; **Barriga**, Edif Wonaga 1 B, C D, T 269-0221; **Gold**, C 55, T 264-1711; **Hertz**, *Hotel Marriott*, T 226-4077 ext 6202, C 50, T 263-6966, El Cangrejo T 263-6511; **Budget** T 263-8777; **Discount**, T 223-6111; **Dollar**, T 269-7555. Rates vary from company to company and from model to model: on average they start at US$24/day for a small saloon to US$65 for 4WD jeep, free mileage, insurance US$8/day, 5% tax, US$500 deposit (can be paid by credit card), minimum age 23, home driver's licence acceptable. In general 4WDs must be booked 5 days in advance.
Motorcycle Club: Road Knights, at the Albrook Air Force base (T 286-3348) officially closed from Jan 1994. However it still has repair and maintenance workshop. Reliable information on flights and ships to Colombia. Have a look at the visitors' book for useful hints. Please leave a donation. **Cycles**: *Almacén The Bike*, C 50 opp Telemetro, good selection of cycle parts. **Taxis**: service generally good, but can be scarce during peak hours; voluntary sharing is common, but not rec after dark. Most newer taxis have a/c, look for closed windows when hailing. If taxi already has a passenger, the driver will ask your destination to see it coincides with the other passenger's. If you do not wish to share, waggle your index finger and say "No, gracias". If you are in a taxi and the driver stops for additional passengers, you may refuse politely. Zone system: US$0.75 for one passenger within one zone, US$0.25 for each additional zone. Additional passengers US$0.25 each regardless of zones. Sharing passengers each pay full fare. Panamanians rarely tip, but foreigners should add US$0.25 or US$0.50 to the fare. Hourly hire, rec for touring dubious areas, US$7/hr, US$8 with a/c. Radio taxis summoned by telephone highly rec. Listed in yellow pages under 'Taxis'. Add US$0.40 to fare for pick-up. Taxis earn enough to provide adequate vehicles; feel free to reject unsavoury-looking, battered, old cars. 'Tourist taxis' at major hotels (aged, large American cars with 'SET' number plates) have a separate fare structure, overpriced. Agree on fares in advance, or arrange through the *conserje*. **Traffic system**: several major downtown arteries become one-way during weekday rush hours, eg Av 4A Sur/C 50, one-way heading W 0600-0900, E 1600-1900. The Puente de las Américas can be used only to go into or out of town depending on time and day, mostly weekends; these directions are not always clearly signed.

Air Tocumen (PTY), 27 km. Taxi fares about US$20, but if you want to share, drivers will try to find other passengers. A full cab should be US$8 pp. (If staying for only a couple of days, it is cheaper to rent a car at the airport.) For about US$3 (should only be US$1.20) driver takes you by Panamá Viejo, just off the main airport road. Buses to airport are marked 'España-Tocumen', 1 hr, US$0.35, but if going at a busy time, eg in the morning rush hour allow 90 mins to 3 hrs. From airport to city, walk out of the terminal and across the main road to the bus shelter. There is a 24-hr left-luggage office nr the Budget car rental desk for US$1/article/day (worth it, since theft in the departure lounge is common). The tourist office at the airport remains open to meet late flight arrivals. There are duty-free shops at the airport with a wide selection and good prices.

The domestic airport is at La Paitilla (PAC), on N side of Punta Paitilla, nr Hotel Marriott and Atlapa Convention Centre (see comments on **Aeroperlas**, page 1226). No 2 bus from C 40 along Av Balboa, marked 'Boca La Caja', US$0.30. For fares, see under destinations in the text. Charter flights go to many Darién outposts. Sample hourly rates for private hire: Twin Otter 20 passenger, US$630; Rodolfo Causadias of Transpasa (T 226-0842) is an experienced pilot for photographic work. There is also an active Aero-Club.

Trains Station on Carretera Gaillard. **NB** At the time of writing in 1997, the only passenger service is on Sun as far as Summit. For information, T 252-7720.

Intercity buses NB A new central bus terminal (*piquera*) built in El Chorrillo was boycotted by operators and passengers who considered the neighbourhood dangerous. Temporary arrangements, varying for different routes, have been made pending construction of yet another new *piquera*. Ask about current arrangements.

Unlike urban versions, most long-distance buses are fairly modern and in good condition, usually a/c on long hauls. Ask if a/c on next bus out is functioning: if not, you may choose to wait for the next. Buses going W to the Interior tend to be well booked up, so make sure you reserve in advance: for the midnight express to David, early on the day of departure (only). Buses to **David** leave *piquera* at W end of Av Balboa hourly 0700-1300, then 1½ hourly till 1900, US$10.60. Express at 2400 (5½-6 hrs), 15-min rest stop at Santiago, fare US$15. Buses to **Colón** leave from Av Perú, C 30, nr Hotel

Veracruz, opp *Hotel Soloy*; express buses every 20 mins 0500-1900, less frequent at weekends, US$2.20, under 2 hrs. Orange buses to all **Canal Area** destinations (Balboa, Miraflores, Paraíso, Kobbe, etc) leave from SACA terminal nr Plaza 5 de Mayo. To **Kobbe Beach** by bus 30 mins.

International buses: buses going N to Central America tend to be well booked up, so make sure you reserve a seat in advance and never later than the night before departure. Ticabus, with office by *Hotel Ideal*, C 17 Oriente, T 262-2084/6275, run a/c buses to **San José**, daily 1000, arrives 0400, US$20 one way (but check times and prices which are for ever changing); also to **Managua** daily, US$25; this service now runs as far as Guatemala City (4 days, overnight in Managua and El Salvador), leaves 1100. A/c rarely works. (Tickets are refundable; they pay on the same day, minus 15%.) Panaline to San José from *Hotel Internacional* in the Plaza 5 de Mayo leaves daily at 1300. The buses have a/c, TV/videos and drinks and are reported more comfortable than Ticabus, also US$20. It is impossible to do Panama City-San José in 1 day on local public transport.

NEARBY EXCURSIONS

PANAMA VIEJO

A visit is recommended to the ruins of **Panamá Viejo**, 6½ km NE along the coast. This was the original site of Panama City, founded by Pedro Arias de Avila (often called 'Pedrarias') on 15 August 1519 as a storage point for Peruvian gold until it could be loaded onto mules and transported across the Isthmus, initially to Venta de Cruces and Fort San Lorenzo, later along the Camino Real to Nombre de Dios and Portobelo for shipment to Spain. The town became the centre of the New World, gold mines in Veraguas and Darién contributed 2 tons of gold a year, and many expeditions to North, Central and South America were launched from here. Panamá was recognized as a town in 1521 and granted a coat of arms. By 1570 a quarter of its 500 residents were extremely wealthy, and the town could boast a grand cathedral, a dozen religious institutions, a hospital, lavish public buildings, huge warehouses and a thriving slave market.

No enemy had ever penetrated as far as 'Golden Panama', not even Francis Drake, so the shock was all the greater when Henry Morgan and his 1,200 men, after a gruelling 9-day overland trek from San Lorenzo, fell upon the town on 28 January 1671 and captured it after a 3-hr battle. They took 600 prisoners for ransom, looted for 3 weeks and took away a fortune in gold, silver and gemstones valued at £70,000, which required 165 mules to transport it back to the Caribbean. (With this Morgan bought respectability: he was knighted and appointed Governor of Jamaica, where he died in 1688.) After the attack, the population was transferred to the present-day Casco Viejo section of Panama City, which could be enclosed by walls and defended on both landward and seaward sides.

A wander among the ruins still gives an idea of the site's former glory, although many of the structures have been worn by time, fungus and the sea. The narrow King's Bridge (1620) at the N end of the town's limits is a good starting point; it marked the beginning of the three trails across the Isthmus and took 7 years to build. Walking S brings the visitor to Convento de San José, where the Golden Altar originally stood (see above under Panama City); it was spared by the great fire that swept the town during Morgan's attack (which side started it is still debated). Several blocks further S is the main Plaza, where the square stone tower of the Cathedral (1535, 1580) is a prominent feature. In the immediate vicinity are the Cabildo, with imposing arches and columns, the remnants of Convento de Santo Domingo, the Bishop's Residence, and the Slave Market (or House of the Genovese), whose gaol-like structure was the hub of the American slave trade; there were about 4,000 African slaves in 1610, valued at about 300 pesos apiece! Beyond the plazas to the S, on a rocky eminence overlooking the bay, stand the Royal Houses, the administrative stronghold including the Quartermaster's House, the Court and Chancellery, the Real Audiencia and the Governor's Residence.

Further W along the Pacific strand are the dungeons, kitchens and meat market (now almost obliterated by the sea); a store and refreshment stands cluster here on the S side of the plaza, and handicrafts from the Darién are sold along the beach. Across C de la Carrera stands another great complex of religious convents: La Concepción (1598) and the Compañia de Jesús (1621). These too were outside the area destroyed by the 1671 fire but are today little more than rubble. Only a wall remains of the Franciscan Hospital de San Juan de Dios, once a huge structure encompassing wards, courtyards and a church. Another block W can be seen part of the Convento de San Francisco and its gardens, facing the rocky beach. 100m W is the beautiful Convento de La Merced, where Pizarro, Almagro and their men attended Mass on the morning they sailed on their final and momentous expedition to Perú; Morgan stored his plunder here until it could be counted, divided up and sent back to the Atlantic side. At the western limit of Panamá Viejo stands La Navidad Fort (1658). Its purpose was merely to defend the Matadero (Slaughterhouse) Bridge across the Río Agarroba but its 50-man garrison and half-dozen cannon were no match for the determined force of privateers; the bridge is also known as Morgan's Bridge because it was here that the attack began.

The whole area (unfenced, free entry) is attractively landscaped, with plenty of benches to rest on, and floodlit at night. Late afternoon when the sun is low is an especially nice time to visit, although at least 2 hrs should be allowed to appreciate the site fully. The main ruins are police patrolled and reasonably safe. Take care, though, between the King's Bridge and the ruins; if arriving at this N entrance by taxi, it is prudent to pause at the bridge then continue in the taxi the 1 km to San

José, where the main ruins begin. Dame Margot Fonteyn, the ballerina, is buried alongside her husband Roberto Arías Guardia in the Jardín de la Paz cemetery behind Panamá Viejo. IPAT has a handicrafts store (*Artesanía Nacional*) at the ruins, although prices are rather expensive. It also organizes free folkloric events and local dance displays on six Sat in the dry season (*verano*), which are worth seeing. The Tourist Office in Panama City (T 226-7000) has full schedules and can supply professional guides if required. Taxi from the centre, US$1.80; buses 1 or 2 from Vía España or Av Balboa, US$0.20. Panamá Viejo also makes a good excursion for passengers with time to kill at nearby Tocumen Airport; taxis are overpriced (US$3) but still reasonable, especially if this is all one will have the chance to see of Panamá.

BALBOA

Balboa docks are about 3¼ km from Panamá City, an average of 10 mins by taxi.

Balboa stands attractively between the Canal quays and Ancón hill, which lies between it and Panama City. It has been described as an efficient, planned, sterilized town, a typical American answer to the wilfulness and riot of the tropics.

The Canal administration building (with fine murals on the ground floor) and a few official residences are on Balboa Heights. At the foot of Balboa Heights is Balboa, with a small park, a reflecting pool and marble shaft commemorating Goethals, and a long parkway flanked with royal palms known as the Prado. At its eastern end is a theatre, a service centre building, post office and bank. Farther along Balboa Rd are a large YMCA (no lodging).

● **Banks & money changers** Citibank; Chase Manhattan Bank.

● **Post & telecommunications Post Office**: Av Balboa and El Prado. **Telecommunications**: INTEL; Tropical Radio & Telegraph Co Public Telex booth.

● **Tour companies & travel agents** *Chadwick's*, in YMCA building, T 272-2741/228-6329; *Starlite Travel*, in former Balboa railway station opp Canal Administration building, T 232-6401, both excellent, English spoken.

ANCON

Ancón curves round the hill of the same name N and E and merges into Panama City. It has picturesque views of the palm-fringed shore. The name has also been applied to the district, including the village of Balboa, created when the area reverted to Panama.

The following walk takes in the sights of Ancón: walk to the top of the hill in the morning for views of the city, Balboa and the Canal (conveniences and water fountain at the top – you may have to climb part of the radio tower to see anything); the entrance is on Av de los Mártires (formerly Av de Julio and briefly Av Presidente Kennedy). Return to Av de los Mártires and take a clockwise route around the hill, bearing right onto Balboa Rd (Av Estado de Jamaica), passing YMCA, Chase Manhattan and Citibank, until you reach Stevens Circle where Kuna Indians sell *molas*. Here are the Post Office and a cafetería. Then walk down the Prado lined with royal palms to the Goethals Memorial and up the steps to the Administration Building to see the recently-restored murals of the Construction of the Canal (entrance free, identity must be shown to the guards). Follow Heights Rd until it becomes Gorgas Rd. You will pass the headquarters of the Smithsonian Tropical Research Institute (where applications to visit Barro Colorado Island are made) and, among trees and flowers, the Gorgas Army Community Hospital. Gorgas Rd leads back to Av de los Mártires, but look out for the sign to the **Museo de Arte Contemporáneo** (see **Museums** below), before Av de los Mártires. Two libraries are open to the public: that of the Smithsonian Tropical Research Institute in the Canal Area, opp Plaza 5 de Mayo, and that of the Panama

Canal College, underneath the Bridge of the Americas. **NB** Take care on Ancon Hill, robberies sometimes occur.

At the foot of Ancón Hill the Instituto Nacional stands on the 4-lane Av de los Mártires (Tivoli).

FUERTE AMADOR

Before the Puente de las Américas is a long peninsula into the Pacific on which is **Fuerte Amador**, formerly the HQ of the Panamanian Defence Force, seized by US forces since in 1989 and returned to Panama in 1994. To cross the causeway costs US$0.25. There are many interesting buildings in this area bearing the marks of the conflict and some attractive lawns and parkland. Beyond Fuerte Amador are the formerly fortified islands of Naos, Perico and Flamenco, linked by the 4 km causeway (**Calzada Amador**) built during Canal construction. The Calzada is used by joggers and cyclists (bikes for hire at the causeway entrance, US$1.50-2/hr); it has fine views of the Puente de las Américas and ships lined up to enter the Canal. The charming, simple, outdoor restaurant at the far end of the Calzada is highly recommended in the evening for seeing the skyline and passing ships, as well as good food and drink (cheap). There are small charges for entry and for swimming at shark net-protected Solidaridad beach on Naos (crowded on weekends but not rec – water polluted). At Punta Culebra on Naos is the new **Marine Exhibition Center** of the Smithsonian Tropical Research Institute, interesting aquaria and exhibitions on marine fauna. Open Tues-Fri 1300-1700, Sat-Sun 1000-1700, T 227-4918/6022. There is a small restaurant on the next island, Perico, and the promise (with luck) of a cold beer. Flamenco, the last of the islands, is headquarters for the National Maritime Service and is closed to the public. The causeway and islands have been declared a 'touristic zone'.

TABOGA ISLAND

There is a launch service to **Taboga Island**, about 20 km offshore. The island is a favourite year-round resort; its pineapples and mangoes have a high reputation and its church is one of the oldest in the western hemisphere (admission to beach at *Hotel Taboga*, US$6, redeemable in 'funny money' to buy food and drink, good swimming, covered picnic huts extra). There are other good places to swim around the island.

The trip out to Taboga is very interesting, passing the naval installations at the Pacific end of the Canal, the great bridge linking the Americas, tuna boats and shrimp fishers in for supplies, visiting yachts from all over the world at the Balboa Yacht Club, and the Calzada Amador. Part of the route follows the channel of the Canal, with its busy traffic. Taboga itself, with a promontory rising to 488m, is carpeted with flowers at certain seasons. There are few cars in the meandering, helter-skelter streets, and only one footpath as a road.

The first Spanish settlement was in 1515, 2 years after Balboa's discovery of the Pacific. It was from here that Pizarro set out for Peru in 1524. For two centuries it was a stronghold of the pirates who preyed on the traffic to Panama. Because it has a deep-water, sheltered anchorage, it was during colonial times the terminal point for ships coming up the W coast of South America. El Morro, at low tide joined to Taboga, is at high tide an island; it was once owned by the Pacific Steam Navigation Company, whose ships sailed from there. For a fine view, walk through the town and up to the top of Cerro Turco, the hill with a cross at the summit (285m), to the right of the radar station (there is a shady short cut, ask locals). When surveying the view, don't miss the pelican rookery on the back side of the island; it is an easy walk down. Further S is Cerro Vigía (307m), the highest point, a 2-hr hike from the central plaza; wear ankle boots and take mosquito repellent. Another trail runs W along the N coast, about 1 hr, pleasant beaches. The southern coast of Taboga and all of neighbouring Isla Uraba are wildlife reserves; permit from Inrenare required, office near *Hotel Taboga*. All items are expensive on the island. Bring cash: there is no bank on the island.

● **Accommodation** **A3** *Taboga*, T 250-2122, F 223-0116, Apdo 55-0357, Paitilla, Panamá, 300m E of wharf, a/c, TV, restaurant, café, beach, tropical birds; **C** *Chu*, on main street, 200m left of wharf, T 250-2036, wooden colonial style, thin walls, no bath, beautiful views, own beach, terrace restaurant serving traditional fish and chicken dishes. You may be able to find locals to stay with, ask around.

● **Transport Boats** Taboga is reached in 1-1½ hrs from Pier 17-18 in Balboa (check the times in advance – T 228-4348 office, or 232-5395 pier); taxi Bella Vista-Pier 18, US$3-4 pp. There are 2 boats daily during the week (0830 and 1500 or 1700-Thur) and 3 boats on Sat, Sun and holidays (0830, 1130 and 1600). Return boats at 1000 and 1630 or 1830-Thur; 1000, 1430 and 1700 at weekends. From Nov to Jan there are 3 boats daily. Return fare US$7. You can charter a boat for US$120/day including fishing. Ask for Sam at the Balboa Yacht Club.

PEARL ISLANDS

It is a longer trip by launch, some 75 km, to the **Pearl Islands**, visited mostly by sea-anglers for the Pacific mackerel, red snapper, corvina, sailfish, marlin, and other species which teem in the waters around. High mountains rise from the sea, but there is a little fishing village on a shelf of land at the water's edge. There was much pearl fishing in colonial days. **Contadora**, one of the smallest Pearl Islands, has become quite famous since its name became associated with a Central American peace initiative. It was also where the Shah of Iran was exiled, in a house called Puntalara, after the Iranian Revolution. Contadora is popular with Canadian, Spanish and Italian holidaymakers and is

becoming crowded, built up and consequently not as peaceful as it once was. Beautiful beaches with crystal-clear water. Good skin-diving and sailing, 3-hr boat trip. Beware the sharks.

● **Accommodation & places to eat** Contadora has *Hotel de Villas*, T 250-4030, and the very luxurious chalet complex **L3** *Caesar Park Contadora Resort and Casino*, Spanish-owned, nice location on beach, T 250-4033, F 250-4000, in Panama City, T 269-5966, F 269-4721; *Gallo Nero*, run by German couple, Gerald and Sabine, restaurant good seafood esp lobster, pizza and pasta, by runway, reasonable prices; *Michael's*, opp *Gallo Nero*, good pizzas, ice cream; *Fonda Sagitario*, nearby, café, cheap; also a supermarket and a duty free shop.

● **Tour companies & travel agents** 1-day trip to Contadora on Sun, US$50 pp inc food and drinks. 3 day package tour, US$150 for 2, rec Argonaut Steamship Agency, C 55 No 7-82, Panama City, T 264-3459, runs launch cruises.

● **Transport Air** Return air ticket to **Contadora** from Paitilla, US$45 by Aeroperlas, T 269-4555 (extra flights at weekends, 15 mins, crowded). Paitilla-San Miguel, US$35 return, twice weekly. Mountain bike hire US$5/hr, by entrance to *Caesar Park*.

CERRO AZUL

About 40 km E of Panama City is **Cerro Azul**, a cooler highland area abutting Chagres National Park. At 850m elevation, the area has been developed as a weekend cottage resort. It is best visited by private car.

● **Accommodation** **A3** *Hostal Casa de Campo*, T 270-0018, F 226-0336, e-mail casa-camp@sinfo.net, formerly private residence, all rooms with bath, hot water, pool, jacuzzi, massage, scenic walks, holistic health activities, interesting flora, fauna, birding, lovely dining room, seniors, groups welcome; *Cabañas 4x4*, T 226-6206, F 226-7616, rustic cabins in forest setting, electricity 1800-2000 only; **B** *Mesón Tía Toya*, at El Castillo, T 232-5806, friendly country restaurant with nice porch for dining, also has good cottages for daily rental.

The Canal, Colón and the San Blas Islands

THE CANAL

The Panama Canal consists of an artificial, river-fed lake, Lago Gatún, across which ships sail after having been raised from sea level by the series of locks on either the Atlantic or the Pacific approach. They are then lowered by the locks on the opposite side. As the crow flies the distance across the isthmus is 55 km. From shore to shore the Canal is 67½ km, or 82 km (44.08 nautical miles) from deep water to deep water. It has been widened to 150m in most places. The trip normally takes 8 or 9 hrs for the 30 ships a day passing through. On the Atlantic side there is a normal variation of 30 cm between high and low tides, and on the Pacific of about 380 cm, rising sometimes to 640 cm.

From the Pacific, the Canal channel goes beneath the Puente de las Américas and passes Balboa. The waterway has to rise 16½m to the Lago **Miraflores**. The first stage of the process is the Miraflores Locks, 1½ km before the lake. A taxi to the Locks from the city, US$10. At the far end of the Lake, the Canal is raised again at the Pedro Miguel Locks, after which the 13 km Gaillard, or Culebra Cut is entered, a narrow rock defile leading to Lago Gatún. Opposite Miraflores Locks, there is a swing bridge. Gaillard Cut can be seen from Contractor's Hill, on the W side, reached by car (no buses) by turning right 3 km past Puente de las Américas, passing Cocolí, then turning as signed. The road beyond Cocolí goes on to Posa, where there are good views of the Locks, the cut and former Canal Zone buildings.

BARRO COLORADO

The largest section of the Canal is in Lago Gatún, the Canal's passage through which is 37 km. In the lake is **Barro Colorado** island, to which the animals fled as the basin slowly filled. It is now a biological reserve for scientific research. Visits can be arranged with the Smithsonian Institute in Ancón, US$22 including boat, audio-visual display and lunch; take a Gamboa Summit bus from next to Plaza 5 de Mayo (0600 and 0615) to the Dredging Division dock at Gamboa (US$0.65), from where the boat leaves. Trips go on Tues and Sat only for 15 people. Make arrangements with the Institute in Ancón, preferably the previous week to see if a space is available (the tours are booked up many months in advance). Individuals may be able to join a tour party. The excursion is highly recommended for seeing wildlife, especially monkeys. Visitors without permits will be turned away on arrival. For longer stays, write to the Director, Smithsonian Tropical Research Institute, Box 2072, Balboa, Panamá. Administration, T 227-6022; hours 0800-1145, 1315-1515. Tours also arranged by *Eco-Tours*, Panama City, T 263-3077, F 263-3089: Barro Colorado island is only seen from the water, but tourists walk a nature trail on the Gigante Peninsula, which is also part of the national park.

GATUN LOCKS

10 km SW of Colón are the **Gatún Locks** (*Esclusas de Gatún*) and their neat attendant town. The observation point here (open 1000-1630) is perhaps the best spot in the Canal Area for photographing the passage of ships. (Bus from Colón to Gatún Locks US$0.75.) The most magnificent of the Canal's locks, Gatún integrates all three lock 'steps' on the Atlantic side,

raising or lowering ships to the 26m level of the Lake in one operation. The flights are in duplicate to allow ships to be passed in opposite directions simultaneously. Passage of the Locks takes about 1 hr. The road forks after crossing the Lock: the left-hand branch crosses the Chagres River by bridge just downstream from the graceful Gatún Dam, which was the largest earth dam in the world when constructed in 1906. Enough water must be impounded in the reservoir during the rainy season to operate the locks throughout the 3-4 month dry season, since a single ship's transit can use up to 50 million gallons. (A high level reservoir, Lago Alajuela, formerly Madden Lake, feeds the lake and maintains its level; see below.) Opposite the power plant is the *Tarpon Club* (T 443-5316/5216 – owned by the same family as the posh *Tropic Star Lodge* in Piñas), a fishing club which has a very nice restaurant, disco and bar; good place to rent boats for a cruise around the Lake. A short distance further S is an attractive lakeside picnic area and small boat launching area. The partly-paved road goes on down the lake to Escobal and Cuipo through lovely scenery (good birding); no hotels in Cuipo but plenty of buses to/from Colón (US$1.60, 2 hrs; US$0.25 to the Locks).

Tours

Most people are surprised by the Canal. Few foresee that the scenery is so beautiful, and it is interesting to observe the mechanics of the passage. *Eco-Tours de Panamá* (T and F numbers under Panama City **Travel Agencies**) offer a day-long full transit through the canal on a luxury yacht for US$109. *Agencia Giscomes*, T 264-0111, also offers trips through the canal every 2nd and 4th Sat (or Sun) of the month, leaves at 0730, US$80. Also *Mia Travel*, T 263-8044, do a complete yacht transit of the Canal every Fri and Sat, provided they have 20 passengers, cost US$99 adult, US$79 children. It takes 8 hrs with lunch and snacks included. Partial boat trips are also offered on the canal, through Miraflores locks as far as Pedro Miguel locks. They go about twice monthly (eg *Argo Tours*, T 228-4348, F 228-1234, every Sat from pier 17, Balboa, US$45, children under 12 US$35, refreshments and snacks on sale); enquire at any travel agent. Otherwise since the Panama City-Colón train is not running (except to Summit on Sun, US$2 return), travellers should take a bus to the Miraflores Locks (open 0900-1700, best between 0900-1000 for photos and 1430-1800 for viewing only) to see shipping. Try to find out when large boats, particularly cruise liners, are in transit. The viewing gallery and a good brochure are free. A detailed model of the canal, formerly in the Department of Transport at Ancón, has been moved here and there is also a free slide show given throughout the day, with explanations in Spanish and English. About 250m past the entrance to the Locks is a road (left) to the filtration plant and observatory, behind which is a picnic area and viewing point. Orange bus from Panama City to Miraflores Locks leaves from the bus station next to Plaza 5 de Mayo (direction Paraíso), 20 mins, US$0.35. Ask driver to let you off at the stop for 'Esclusas de Miraflores', from where it's a 10-min walk to the Locks. Taxi to the Locks, US$10/hr. Another good way to see the Panama Canal area is to rent a car, or, if you have done well at the casinos, by air: Aerotours, T 262-8710, fly Piper J3 Cub trips, 30 mins US$60 pp, full coast to coast, 2 hrs, US$200.

The very best way to see the Canal is by boat: it is possible to traverse the canal as a linehandler (no experience necessary) on a yacht; the journey takes 2 days. Note that more boats pass the canal from N to S than the other way around. Yachts are allowed into the canal on Tues and Thur only. The yacht owners need 4-line handlers. Go to the Panama Canal Yacht Club in Colón, or the Yacht Clubs in Cristóbal (downstairs from the building next to the Wharf), or in Balboa a couple of days before, and ask people hanging

around the bar. The Balboa Club offers good daily lunch special. Good place to watch canal traffic. 50m right of the Club is a small white booth which has a list of boat departures for the next day; ask here if you can go to the dock and take the motor boat which shuttles out to yachts preparing for passage. Ask to speak to captains from the launch and see if they'll let you 'transit'. At Cristóbal you can approach the boats directly at their moorings. They have to book their passage through the canal 48 hrs in advance and are subject to a hefty fine if they default through lack of line handlers. However, don't expect too much, there may be many others with the same idea – see bulletin board at Balboa Club – and at times less than one private boat a week goes through the Canal.

LAGO ALAJUELA

It is a 2-hr drive through picturesque jungle to Lago Alajuela (formerly Madden Dam, E of the Canal). The lake, used to generate electricity as well as to maintain the level of Lago Gatún, covers 5,027 ha and is incorporated within the Chagres National Park. The drive runs from Balboa along the Gaillard Highway and near the Canal. Beyond Fort Clayton there is a fine view of the Miraflores and Pedro Miguel locks. Beyond Pedro Miguel town a road branches off to the left to Summit (Las Cumbres), where there are experimental gardens containing tropical plants from all over the world (closed Mon) and a good, small zoo containing native wildlife. In Las Cumbres the restaurant *La Hacienda* serves native dishes. (The trip to Summit may be made by train on Sun or buses marked Gamboa, every 1-1½ hrs, from bus station next to Plaza 5 de Mayo, US$0.45, 1½ hr journey; the Paraíso bus will also take you to the Miraflores and Pedro Miguel locks.) The road to Lago Alajuela (37 km) crosses the Las Cruces trail (an old cannon marks the spot), and beyond is deep jungle. If walking the trail, take machete and compass. Halfway along the

Las Cruces trail (1¼ hrs) a gravel track, the Plantation Rd, turns left, emerging after 1¼ hrs more on the Gamboa Highway 1½ km N of Summit. A large area of rain forest between Lago Gatún and Lago Alajuela has been set aside as **Parque Nacional Soberanía** (trails for walking). The Park has an information centre at the Summit Garden. A novel place to stay in the region is the **C** *Cabañas Flotantes* in the Chagres River, thatched cabins moored between Lago Alajuela and the Canal. For further information call *Panama Paradise*, T 269-9860.

COLON AND CRISTOBAL

Landfall on the Caribbean side for the passage of the Canal is made at the twin cities of Cristóbal and Colón, the one merging into the other almost imperceptibly and both built on Manzanillo Island at the entrance of the Canal; the island has now been connected with the mainland. Colón was founded in 1852 as the terminus of the railway across the isthmus; Cristóbal came into being as the port of entry for the supplies used in building the Canal.

At **Cristóbal** ships usually dock at Pier No 9, 5 mins from the shops of Colón. Vehicles are always waiting at the docks for those who want to visit Colón and other places.

Places of interest

Colón (*pop* 122,500) was originally called Aspinwall, after one of the founders of the transisthmian railway. The French-influenced **Cathedral** at C 5 y Av Herrera has an attractive altar and good stained glass windows, open 1400-1745 daily. The *Washington Hotel*, on the seafront at the N end of the town, is the most historic structure and is worth a look. The original wooden hotel was built in 1850 for employees of the Railroad Company; President Taft ordered a new fireproof hotel to be built in 1912 and the old one was later razed. Although remodelled a number of times, today's building, with its broad verandahs, waving palms, splendid chandelier, plush carpets and casino, still conjures up a past age; the a/c cafeteria provides an excellent view of ships waiting to enter the Canal. Next door is the **Casa de Lesseps**, home of the Suez Canal's chief engineer during the 1880s. Across from the *Washington* is the Old Stone Episcopal Church, built in 1865 for the railway workers; it was then the only Protestant church in Colombia (of which Panamá was a province). Running N through the centre of Colón is the palm-lined Av Central, with many statues (including one of Columbus and the Indian Girl, a gift from the Empress of France); the public market is at the corner of C 11 but holds little of interest. Front St (Av del Frente), facing the Bahía de Limón, has many old wooden buildings with wide verandahs. This is the main commercial street and is quite active but has lost its past splendour; the famous Bazar Francés closed in 1990, the curio shops are unnoteworthy and the railway station stands virtually deserted except for the movement of a few freight trains. Nevertheless, there is talk of declaring the whole of Colón a Free Zone, the authorities are moving to give the city new housing and employment (residential estates like 'Rainbow City' and 'Puerto Escondido' are being extended on the landward side to relocate entire neighbourhoods of slums), and the demands on Cristóbal's busy port facilities (200 million tons of cargo a year) continue to increase. It is to be hoped that if these plans are realized, Colón may become a pleasant place again.

The main reason to come to Colón is to shop at the present **Zona Libre** (Free Zone), the second-largest in the world, an extensive compound of international stores and warehouses established in 1949 and surrounded by a Berlin-like wall. Businessmen and tourists from all over Latin America come here to place orders for the (mostly bulk) merchandise on offer, or to arrange duty-free importation of bulk goods for re-export to neighbouring countries after packaging.

Colón

Not to Scale, Rough Sketch

Hotels:
1. Andros
2. Carlton
3. Pensión Acrópolis
4. Washington
5. YMCA

Individual items can be bought at some stores, which theoretically must be mailed out of the country or sent in-bond to Tocumen airport before you leave (allow a day for delivery and check-in 2 hrs early to pick up the goods); or you can try smuggling them out! Bargain hard for good prices, but most items are almost as competitively priced in Panama City. Several banks provide exchange facilities. A passport or official ID must be shown to gain entry to the Zone, which is open Mon-Fri 0800-1700 (a few places retail on Sat am, but not many). If with your own car, pay a minder US$1 to watch it while in the Zone, very necessary.

The 30-min beach drive around Colón's perimeter is pleasant and cool in the evening; despite the slums at the S end there are some nice homes along the E shore of the peninsula. Permission from the Port Authority security officer is required to enter the port area, where agents for all the world's great shipping lines are located in colonial Caribbean-style buildings dating from 1914. Almost lost in a forest of containers is the *Cristóbal Yacht Club* (T 441-5881), whose open-air restaurant and historically decorated bar offer very good food (seafood and Chinese); this is the place to enquire about sailing boat charters to the San Blas Islands or shorter trips aboard visiting yachts.

Excursions

A well-paved road branches off the Transisthmus Highway at Sabanitas, 10 km E of Colón, and runs NE along the coast for 34 km to the historic Spanish garrison port of Portobelo (see below), founded in 1519 on the protected bay in which Columbus sought shelter in 1502. The rocky Costa Arriba is very attractive, with a number of lovely white-sand beaches (crowded at weekends). María Chiquita (14 km) has a bathing pavilion, toilets, bar and restaurant managed by the government tourist bureau; a local speciality is *saos*, Jamaican-style pig's feet cooked with lime and chillies, sold from roadside stalls. 3 km further on is Playa Langosta, also with swimming facilities, bar and restaurant. There are plenty of small restaurants along this road serving fresh seafood. A group of people can rent a coastal boat at Puerto Pilón (US$100-150 a day) for an adventurous ride to Portobelo, seas are often rough, take precautions. In Buenavista, just before entering Portobelo, a cannon marks the spot where Henry Morgan landed for his devastating 15-day sack of the town in 1668.

Local information
● **Warning**
Do not go to the city alone. Mugging, even in daylight, is a real threat in both Colón and Cristóbal. We have received repeated warnings of robbery in Colón, often within 5 mins of arrival. The two main streets and some of the connecting ones are guarded by armed Panama Public Force men; you are strongly recommended not to leave their range of sight. One traveller recommends having a few dollars handy, so that "muggers are less likely to strip you for more".

● **Accommodation**
A1 *Washington*, Av del Frente Final, T 441-9662, art deco style, guarded enclave, clean, good restaurant, good view of ships entering the canal, there is also a small casino.

B *Carlton*, C 10 y Av Meléndez, T 445-0744, is the next best hotel.

C *Andros*, Av Herrera, between Calles 9 y 10, T 441-0477/7923, modern, clean, fan or a/c, bath, TV, good restaurant, cafetería; **C** *Sotelo*, C 10 y 11 con Av Guerrero, T 441-7542, also has a casino.

D *Pensión Plaza*, Av Central, T 441-3216, is clean, cheap.

E *Pensión Acrópolis*, Av Amador Guerrero y C 11, opp *Sotelo*, T 441-1456, shared bath. If destitute try the Salvation Army.

● **Places to eat**
See above for *Cristóbal Yacht Club*. *VIP Club*, C 11 y Av del Frente, T 441-3563, popular with visiting businessmen and port officials; *Panamá* and *Antonio*, both cnr Av Herrera y C 11, unremarkable but decent. **For Caribbean food**: *Restaurant Teresa*, Av Amador Guerrero y C 12; *La Cabaña*, Av Central y C 8. Hotels *Washington*, *Carlton* and *Andros* have good restaurants. *YMCA* restaurant, Av Bolívar between Calles 11 y 12, mostly Chinese menu, comparatively expensive. Several fast food outlets, eg *KFC*, Paseo Centenario nr C 7.

● **Banks & money changers**
Chase Manhattan Bank; **Citibank**; **Banco Nacional de Panamá**; **Caja de Ahorros**; **Lloyds Bank** agency in Colón Free Zone, at Av Santa Isabel y C 14, T 445-2177. Open 0800-1300, Mon to Fri.

● **Entertainment**
Cinemas: *Teatro Lido*, across from YMCA on Bolívar, and *Teatro Rex*, C 5 and Av Central.

● **Post & telecommunications**
Post Office: in Cristóbal Administration Building, on corner of Av Bolívar and C 9.

Telecommunications: Intel.

● **Sports**
Clubs: golf (18 holes) at *Brazos Brook Country Club*. Rotary Club, weekly lunches.

● **Transport**
Local Taxis: tariffs vary but not expensive, US$5-7/hr, US$50-80/day. Car rental and taxis on Front St facing C 11; most drivers speak some English and can advise on 'no-go' areas. Avis has two offices.

Air To Paitilla domestic airport in Panama City: former US France Field AFB has replaced Colón's old airstrip as the busy local airport, on mainland E of city, taxi under US$1 but bargain. Aeroperlas has many flights daily Mon-Fri in each direction; US$50 return. The above flights are hectic with Free Zone executives, no reservation system so allow plenty of time or plan to stay the night in Colón.

Buses Bus station on Front St and C 12. Express (a/c) US$1.75, and regular buses, US$1.25, daily to **Panama City** every 20 min, less frequent at weekends, US$1.75-2.25, about 2 hrs. Hourly to **Portobelo** daily, US$2, 1 hr.

Sea Shipping a vehicle: all ships leave from Coco Solo Wharf; to South America, see page 1220.

PORTOBELO

'Beautiful Port' was the northern terminus of the Camino Real, where Peruvian treasure carried on mule trains across the Isthmus from Panama City was stored in fortified warehouses until the periodic arrival of the Spanish Armada, the famed Fairs where the wealth of the New World was exchanged for goods and supplies from Europe. So much material changed hands that the 1637 Fair (described by Englishman Thomas Gage) took 30 days for the loading and unloading to be completed. In the Royal **Contaduría** or Customs House bars of gold and silver were piled up like firewood. Such riches could hardly fail to attract foreign corsairs; Portobelo was one of Francis Drake's favourite targets but also his downfall; he died here of dysentery in 1596 and was buried in a lead-lined coffin in the bay off Isla Drake. By the beginning of the 17th century several stone *castillos* (Santiago, San Gerónimo and San Fernando) had been built of coral stone quarried nearby to protect the harbour. Attacks continued, however, until in 1740 the treasure fleets were rerouted around the Horn and the Portobelo Fairs ended. The fortifications were rebuilt after Vernon's attack in 1744 but they were no longer seriously challenged, leaving the fortresses visible today. The largest, the aptly-named 'Iron Castle', was largely dismantled during Canal construction (its stones form the breakwaters at the N entrance to the Canal), but there are many other interesting ruined fortresses, walls, rows of cannon and remains of the town's 120 houses and public buildings to be seen standing along the foreshore amid the present-day village (population 5,850). (Note that Fuerte San Lorenzo and the nearby beach of La Huerta can only be reached by boat.) The Contaduría (1630) was recently restored, with similar plans in place for the Plaza, Hospital Chapel and the Fernández House.

In **San Felipe Church** (1776) is the 17th century, cocobolo-wood statue of the Black Christ, about whose origin there are many legends. One tells of how it was found by fishermen floating in the sea during an epidemic of cholera in the town. It was brought ashore and immediately the epidemic began to wane. Another says that the life-size image was on its way to Cartagena when the ship put in to Portobelo to buy supplies; after being thwarted five times by contrary weather to leave port, the crew decided the statue wished to remain in Panamá, it was thrown overboard, floated ashore and was rescued by the locals.

Local festivals

The Black Christ's miraculous reputation is celebrated each 21 Oct, when purple-clad pilgrims come from all over the country and the statue is paraded through the town at 1800 on a flower- and candle-covered platform carried by 80 men (who take 3 steps forward and 2 steps back to musical accompaniment); feasting and dancing till dawn follow the solemn procession.

Other *fiestas* in the Portobelo region (eg New Year's Eve, Carnival, Patron Saint's Day 20 Mar) are opportunities to experience the *Congos*. Unlike the dance of the same name found elsewhere on the Caribbean coast, the *Congo* here is the name given both to the main, male participants and a slowly enfolding ritual which lasts from Epiphany (6 Jan) to Easter. Among the various explanations of its symbolism are elements of the people's original African religions, their capture into slavery, their conversion to Catholicism and mockery of the colonial Spaniards. Members of the audience are often 'imprisoned' in a makeshift palisade and have to pay a 'ransom' to be freed. IPAT now has an office in Portobelo (T 448-2060) and can provide guides, schedules of *Congos* and other performances, and comprehensive information about the many local points of interest, including the surrounding 4,850-ha Portobelo National Park, scuba diving sites (superb) and renting a boat to visit secluded beaches nearby.

Local information
● Accommodation
D *Aquatic Park*, on road towards Colón, dormitory accommodation, expensive; **D** *Divers Haven*, friendly, US owner, safe parking, somewhat run down.

● Places to eat
El Hostal del Rey, corner of central park, good meals and value; *Restaurant-Bar Los Cañones*, T 448-2032; *La Torre*, T 448-2039, on main road 2 km before the town, good food; a number of small *fondas* serving coconut rice with fresh shrimps, Caribbean food (spicy) with octopus or fish, or *fufú* (fish soup cooked with coconut milk and vegetables).

● Transport
Buses from Colón, every hour from 0700 from the bus station on Front St y C 13, 1 hr, US$2; María Chiquita, 40 min, US$0.80. Portobelo can be visited from Panama City in a day without going into Colón by taking an early bus as far as the Sabanitas turnoff (US$1) and waiting for a Colón-Portobelo service (US$1).

ISLA GRANDE

A narrow gravel road (being extended by the US military but 4WD rec at present, limited bus service) continues on NE from Portobelo to Isla Grande, Nombre de Dios (25 km) and Palenque. Scuba diving offered at several places along the road. It passes through Garrote and La Guaira (**D** *Cabañas Montecarlo*, T 441-2054), from where *pangas* can be hired (US$1) at the car park to cross to **Isla Grande**, a favourite with international visitors because of its relaxed lifestyle, fishing, scuba diving and snorkelling, windsurfing and dazzling white palm-fringed beaches. The island's 300 black inhabitants make a living from fishing and coconut cultivation, and a powerful French-built lighthouse crowns the small island's northern point. There are a number of colourful African-tinged

festivals held here throughout the year, particularly on 24 June, 16 July and the pre-Lenten Carnival with *Congos*.

● Accommodation
Popular on holidays and dry season weekends, make reservations in advance, prices often double during high season. **A3** *Isla Grande*, T 264-3046, F 264-0646, bungalows scattered along an excellent sandy beach; boat, snorkel and jet ski hire, restaurant, minizoo (toucans, crocodiles, monkeys, etc), reduced tariffs on weekdays, rec; **B** *Posada Villa Ensueño*, T 268-2926/1445, good café/bar; **B** *La Cholita*, similar prices; **B** *Candy Rose*, **C** *Cabañas Jackson*, T 441-6172, many huts/bungalows available; **C** *Posada Guayaco*. All have bars and simple restaurants, *Candy Rose* serves drinks with a special octopus cooked in coconut milk.

NOMBRE DE DIOS

The beautiful, deserted mainland beaches continue as the 'road' heads E to **Nombre de Dios**. The historic town (1520) near the present village was once the thriving trading port which first hosted the famed Fairs, located at the end of the stone-paved Camino Real from the capital. By the 1550s more than half the trade between Spain and its colonies was passing through its lightly-defended harbour, but in 1594 the decision was made to move operations to the more-sheltered site of Portobelo. The Camino Real was diverted and Nombre de Dios was already dying when Drake captured and burnt it 2 years later, so that William Dampier could describe the site some years later as 'only a name ... everything is covered by the Jungle with no sign that it was ever populated'. Excavations have taken place, revealing the Spanish town, parts of the Camino Real, a broken cannon and other objects (most now in the National Museum). The modern village has few facilities (no hotel), but a beautiful beach can be enjoyed by those few who get this far. A *cayuco* (US$3 pp, 12 mins) can be taken to Playa Damas, an unusual beach where alternating patches of red and white sand resemble a chess board; the beach is owned by an amateur ecologist who has built some rustic huts and a campsite (*Costa El Oro*, T 263-5955) on a small island here, he also offers expert guidance on local fishing and diving spots.

The track staggers on as far as Cuango, a few kilometres E of **Palenque**, another unspoilt hamlet with a good beach where very rudimentary huts are being built for visitors. Locals eagerly await the road's eventual extension through a succession of seaside villages to the Golfo de San Blas opposite El Porvenir, the capital of the Kuna Indian's self-governed *comarca* of San Blas or 'Kuna Yala' (Kuna Earth). If a good road is built, tropical fishing villages like Miramar and Palmira, with their welcoming people, white-sand beaches, offshore reefs and crystal-clear waters will become wonderful resorts.

CAMINO REAL

Although little of the Camino Real remains, its two branches from Madden Lake/Lago Alajuela across the mountains to Nombre de Dios (30 km) and Portobelo can still be hiked. The trail starts at the old manganese mining zone (Mina 1, on the dirt road that runs from the Transístmica to a little way up the Río Boquerón). Buses run occasionally from the Transístmica to Salamanca, roughly where the Río Boquerón empties into Madden Lake. The trail follows the Río Boquerón up to the continental divide and the Río Nombre de Dios down the northern watershed to the coast near the present-day town. This historic trek is easy for anyone with reasonable fitness, as one can drive to entry and exit points. Guides are not really necessary, the rivers are beautiful (and carry little water in the dry season) and the jungle almost untouched; the trail is straightforward and rises only to 330m at the divide. Allow about 3 days for the Boquerón-Nombre de Dios trek. The trail to Portobelo branches off the above at the Río Diablo or Río Longue. After you leave the Boquerón you will need to navigate by compass. The Diablo takes the trekker higher into the divide (700m) than the Longue (the route the treasure-laden

mules followed, 350m) and the terrain is more broken; both lead to the Río Cascajal (higher reaches are strewn with large boulders), which descends to the Caribbean. The highest point in the region, Cerro Brujo (979m), is passed en route. There are jaguars in this forested refuge, but they are unlikely to present any danger to hikers. The Cascajal reaches the road about 1 km E of Portobelo. The Boquerón-Portobelo hike is more demanding than the other and takes 4 days maximum, a good machete is essential, solitude is guaranteed for at least 2 days.

To the S and E of the Camino Real are the rivers of the Chagres system which flow into Lago Alajuela. Some of these are now being exploited for rafting. Check with tourist agencies in Panama City.

WEST OF COLON

From Colón the Caribbean **Costa Abajo**, stretching W of the Canal, can also be visited. The road leaves Colón through new housing developments (on the left is the modern city of Margarita) and runs 10 km SW to the Gatún Locks (see under **The Canal** above).

The N road branch at Gatún follows Limón Bay through a well-preserved forest reserve to Fort Sherman, running beside the remnants of the French Canal excavations (most of their work on the Atlantic side is now below the Lake while the Pacific excavations were incorporated into the US construction). Fort Sherman is heavily-forested military property and a guard at the gate may issue you with a pass; since it is also the US Army's Jungle and Guerrilla Warfare Training Center it is advisable not to court any unpleasant surprises by leaving the road, which is gravel and well signposted (no public transport) for the 10 km to **Fuerte San Lorenzo**.

FUERTE SAN LORENZO

Perched on a cliff-top promontory overlooking the mouth of the Río Chagres with great views of the coast, San Lorenzo is one of the oldest and best-preserved Spanish fortifications in the Americas. Construction had begun the year before Drake launched a 23-ship attack on the post (1596) and proceeded up the Chagres in an unsuccessful attempt to reach Panamá City. Morgan fought a bloody 11-day battle to take the fort as a prelude to his decisive swoop on Panamá Viejo in 1671. Although new defences were then built, they were unable to prevent British Admiral Edward Vernon's successful attack in 1740 (one of Vernon's cannon with the GR monogram can still be seen). Engineer Hernández then spent 7 years strengthening the garrison (1760-67), but the threat to San Lorenzo gradually receded as Spanish galleons were diverted to the Cape Horn route and the era of the freebooters approached its end. The last Royalist soldiers left the fort in 1821 as Colombia declared its independence from Spain. The earliest artillery sheds can be seen on the lower cliff level but most of the bulwarks, arched stone rooms and lines of cannon are 18th century. The site recently underwent an extensive UNESCO renovation programme and is well worth a visit. There is a picnic area and a tiny beach is accessible by a steep path down the cliff. Take insect repellent.

There is no crossing of the Chagres at San Lorenzo; to continue down the **Costa Abajo** one must return to the Gatún Dam and take the gravel road along the W side of the river, which winds its way through pristine forest to the coastal village of Piña and its kilometre-long beach. The road runs W along a steep and rocky shore punctured by many small coves to Nuevo Chagres and Palmas Bellas, quiet fishing resorts in coconut palm groves, but with few facilities. 4WD is required to continue to Río Indio and Miguel de la Borda, where the road comes to an end. The villages beyond, including historic Río Belén where one of Columbus' ships was abandoned in 1502, remain accessible only by sea.

SAN BLAS ISLANDS

An interesting trip can be made to the San Blas (or Las Mulatas) archipelago, which has 365 islands ranging in size from tiny ones with a few coconut palms to islands on which hundreds of Cuna Indians live. About 50 are inhabited. The islands, off the Caribbean coast E of Colón, vary in distance from the shore from 100m to several kilometres and are strung out along the coast for over 200 km from the Gulf of San Blas to the Colombian border.

The Cuna (Kuna, or Tule) are the most sophisticated and politically organized of the country's three major groups. They run the San Blas Territory virtually on their own terms, with internal autonomy and, uniquely among Panama's Indians, send their representative to the National Assembly. Each community is presided over by a *sáhila* (or chief). The Cuna have their own language, but Spanish is widely spoken. The women wear gold nose and ear-rings, and costumes with unique designs based on local themes, geometric patterns, stylized fauna and flora, and pictorial representations of current events or political propaganda. They are outside the Panamanian tax zone and have negotiated a treaty perpetuating their long-standing trade with small craft from Colombia. Many men work on the mainland, but live on the islands.

Photographers need plenty of small change, as the set price for a Cuna to pose is US$0.25. *Molas* (decorative handsewn appliqué for blouse fronts) cost upwards of US$10 each (also obtainable in many Panama City and Colón shops). You can also try the San Blas perfume, Kantule, similarly available in city shops.

There are about 20 airports in the San Blas Islands and province, but most are 'larger' than the islands or places on which they are built. They include: El Porvenir, Carti, Río Sidra, Río Azúcar, Narganá, Corazón, Río Tigre, Playón Chico, Tupile, Tikankiki, Alligandi, Achutupu (also known as Uaguitupu)

Mamitupu, Ogobsucum, Ustupu, Mansucum, Mulatupu, Tubuala, Calidonia, Puerto Obaldía. You can be dropped off at any island or village and discuss your return with the pilot. It is probably not a wise idea since most of the islands may have nice-looking beaches, but no drinking water or food.

Local festivals

IPAT lists the following *fiestas* in the San Blas islands: Feb, anniversary of the Tule Revolution, at Playón Chico, Tupile, Ailigandi and Ustupu; 19 Mar, *fiesta patronal* on Narganá; 8 July, anniversary of *Inakiña* on Mulatupo; 29-31 July, *fiesta patronal* on Fulipe; 20 Aug, Charles Robinson anniversary on Narganá; 3 Sept, anniversary of Nele-Kantule on Ustupo; 11 Sept, anniversary of Yabilikiña on Tuwala. All involve dances, games, meals and speeches and are traditional, except those on Narganá, which have a stronger western element (but also typical dancing and food).

Local information
● Accommodation

Any travel agent in Panama can book a San Blas tour. A 1-night stay in the vicinity of El Porvenir costs US$120 inc food and lodging at the *Hotel Hanay Kantule* (also spelt *Anai Katule*) on Wichibwala, T 220-0746. You have to get up early for the return flight. Other hotels in the Porvenir area inc *San Blas*, T 262-1606/5410, on Nalunega Island (two daily tours inc in the price), and *Residencial Turístico Yeri*, T 262-3402; the *Hanay Kantule* charges US$55 pp a night, all others US$27, inc food. For the *Hanay*, ask for Israel Fernández on arrival at El Porvenir. One of the agents which will handle bookings is *Chadwicks*, see **Balboa** above.

Hotels and lodges are being opened on the islands off the Caribbean coast. These include, from W to E: *Sugtupu Hotel* in the Cartí-Sugtupu community (from the coast of Cartí a road runs inland to the Pan-American Highway at **El Llano** – see page 1211). **A3** *Kuanidup*, some 7 huts on the island, good food, lovely beaches, no electricity, bathrooms in the centre of the island. At Narganá there is a basic hotel,

F, and one restaurant, *El Caprichito*, good crab dishes. **L3** *Kwadule*, nr Corazón de Jesús and Narganá, owned by the Noveys, very nice restaurant/bar over the reef, some cabins built over the water, with bath. A short canoe ride from Narganá is Isla Tigre, a very traditional island. Further E again, reached from Playón Chico, is the **L2** *Iskardup Ecoresort* (T 269-6017, F 269-1604), with cabins, bar, restaurant, solar power, package tours inc trips to mainland and 'junjogging'(!). In the Ailigandi community is *La Palmera* hotel, restaurant and bar. Another rec trip is to *Dolphin Lodge*, owned by a Cuna Indian family on the island of Uaguitupu, for US$139 inc air fare, meals and overnight stay (bookings through *Eco-Tours*, T 263-3077, F 263-3089). These last two are about half way along the coast between El Porvenir and the Colombian border.

● Transport

Air Two companies fly the routes from Paitilla airport, Transpasa, T 226-0932/0843 (a couple of 6-seater Cessnas) and Ansa, who no longer take passengers, T 226-7891/6881 (twin-engined Islanders). The most popular destination is El Porvenir (other airports are listed above), on the N side of the Golfo de San Blas, where tourists are picked up by boat to go to a neighbouring island, about 20 mins ride. One way fares to the islands are US$25 to El Porvenir and US$40 to Puerto Obaldía. All other airport fares are scaled in between (price includes a 5% sales tax). You must take your passport because every month or so a hijack attempt to Colombia is made. All flights leave between 0600 and 0630, Mon-Sat, returning 0800-0830. Evening and Sun flights must be booked privately.

Sea There are occasional boats to the San Blas islands from Colón, but there is no scheduled service and the trip can be rough. One ship that goes from time to time is the *Almirante*, try to find the captain, Figueres Cooper, who charges US$30 for the trip. The port captain's office at Coco Solo may have information on boat departures, T 441-5231 or 445-1055, although most boats are 'not keen on being landed with potentially stranded gringos'. Alternatively, go to Portobelo (see above) and try for a boat from there, 9 hrs to El Porvenir.

The 'Interior'

C ROSS THE Puente de las Américas for the most
densely-populated rural quarter of the country, a
Panama that is in great contrast to the cosmopolitan
capital and the Canal: colonial towns, a variety of agricultural
zones, traditional crafts and music, Pacific beaches and
beautiful mountain landscapes with some good walking. The
Pan-American Highway traverses this region, known generally
to Panamanians as 'El Interior' (though the term can refer to
any area outside the capital), en route to Costa Rica.

PANAMA CITY TO COSTA RICA

The Pan-American Highway runs westwards from Panama City through Concepción to the Costa Rican border (489 km),
and is well graded and completely paved.
A main branch road turns S from Divisa
to Chitre, Los Santos and Las Tablas (see
below under **Azuero Peninsula**).

THE CANAL TO DIVISA

Leaving Panama City, the Inter-American
Highway crosses the **Puente de las Américas** over the Canal at the Pacific entrance.
The bridge was built between 1958 and
1962 by the US to replace the ferry crossing. It is 1,653m long and with the road
surface 117m above the seaway, more than
high enough to allow all ships to pass
under it. It has 3 lanes, a 4-lane approach
from Panama City and a pedestrian pavement all the way (muggings have occurred on the bridge in broad daylight,
so be careful!). Lane changes are frequent

during busy hours and vaguely indicated.
Be observant. It is the only way for vehicles
to cross the canal. Buses run to a *mirador*
on the far side of the bridge from the city.

Where the road W crosses the savannas, there are open pastures and fields
where clumps of beautiful trees, including mangoes and palms, alternate with
grass. In the W, acacia and teak plantings
are often seen. Watch for typical 'living
fences', whose posts sprout in the humid
climate. New growth is periodically har-
vested for additional posts.

LA CHORRERA

The first place you reach, 13 km from
Panama City, is the small town of **Arraiján**
(*pop* 6,600). Another 21 km by 4-lane highway (toll US$0.50) takes you to **La Chor-
rera** (*pop* 37,000); an interesting store,
Artes de las Américas, has items in wood,
etc. A branch road (right) leads 1½ km to
El Chorro, the waterfall from which the
town takes its name. On 20 km, among

hills, is the old town of Capira; good food next to Shell station run by Chinese. The Highway passes through the orange groves of Campana (where a 10-km road climbs to **Altos de Campana National Park**; several trails, rangers will advise; lodging at ranger station is possible, 5 km up the road), and then twists down to Río Sajalices (bathing) and the low-level plains. Good views on the road to the summit of Cerro Campana. 10 km up a side road, 2 km before the village of Chicá is a colony of retired North Americans, including Richard Freeley from the USA. He appreciates visitors.

● **Accommodation D** Hotel Clolysa, safe parking; **E** Pensión Arco Iris, without bath, fan, clean, partial walls between rooms, hourly rentals; similar, but more expensive and 'better' looking is a pensión across the street and a couple of blocks towards Panama City.

SAN CARLOS AND BEACHES

At Bejuco, 5 km E of Chame, there is a turn off for Punta Chame, at the end of a 28 km peninsula, with a white-sand beach, a few houses, and a hotel/restaurant. At low tide the sand is alive with legions of small pink crabs. From here there is a splendid view NE to Taboga Island and the entrance to the Canal in the distance. Food is prepared by the beach and there are several bars. A pick-up runs between the highway and the beach, US$1.

Beyond Chame are two beaches: **Nueva Gorgona** where the beach is about 3-4 km long, waves increase in size from W to E, and there is a well-stocked grocery store. The other is **Playa Coronado**, the most popular in Panama, even so it is rarely crowded. Homeowners from Playa Coronado have installed a checkpoint at the turning, unaffiliated with the police station opposite. Be polite, but do not be deterred from using the public beach.

● **Accommodation & places to eat B** Gorgona Hayes, T 223-7775, with pleasant pool, fountain, tennis court, restaurant, good; **B** Cabañas de Playa Gorgona, T 269-2433, cheaper, with kitchenettes, barbecue grills, pool, shade,

hammocks, on the ocean, prices rise at weekend. Restaurant El Prado, on the beach.

10 km beyond Playa Coronado is the town of **San Carlos**, near the sea; good river and sea-bathing (beware jelly fish and do not bathe in the estuarine lake). Not many restaurants in San Carlos, but there are plenty of shops where food can be bought.

Beyond San Carlos is the Río Mar beach, with the **A3** Río Mar, T 223-0192, which has a good seafood restaurant.

● **Transport** Minibus Panama City-San Carlos, frequent from 0615, US$3.50, San Carlos-David, US$10.

EL VALLE

5 km on, a road (right) leads after a few kilometres to a climb through fine scenery to the summit of Los Llanitos (792m), and then down 200m to a mountain-rimmed plateau (7 by 5½ km) on which is comparatively cool **El Valle**, a small summer resort; direct bus from Panama City US$3.50, or US$1 from San Carlos. 4 km before El Valle is a parking spot with fine views of the village, waterfall nearby. Soapstone carvings of animals, straw birds, painted gourds, carved wood tableware, pottery and molas are sold in the famous Sun market, which is very popular with Panamanians and tourists. There is also a colourful flower market. Gold coloured frogs can be seen in the area, and there are trees with square-shaped trunks, near Hotel Campestre. The orchid nursery has a small zoo and Panama's best-known petroglyphs can be seen near the town. This is one of many good walks in the vicinity (ask directions); another is to the cross in the hills to the W of town. The town has no real centre; everyone cycles.

● **Accommodation B** Hotel Campestre, T 993-6146/221-9602, F 226-4069, lunch from US$5.95; **B** Cabañas Las Mozas, T 993-6071, offers Cocina Arabe; **B** Cabañas Potosí, T 993-6181; **D** El Greco Motel, C Central, T 993-6149; **E** Pensión Niña Dalia, no towels or soap, will look after bags; private houses nearby rent rooms, **F** with meals; accommodation hard to find at weekends.

We leave Panamá Province at La Ermita and enter Coclé, whose large tracts of semi-arid land are used for cattle raising.

SANTA CLARA AND ANTON

Santa Clara, with its famous beach, 115 km from Panama City, is the usual target for motorists with *cabañas* at the beach, fishing, launches for hire, and riding. The beach is about 20 mins walk from the Pan-American Highway. There are *cabañas* to rent, the principal centre is *Cabañas Las Sirenas*, T 232-5841, F 232-5842, each costing US$77/day for 5 people, US$110 for 7 (minimum 2 nights), in an attractive landscaped environment.

About 13 km beyond is **Antón** (*pop* 5,100): it has a special local type of *manjar blanco*. There is a crucifix here which is reputed to be miraculous.

- **Accommodation & places to eat** D *Hotel Rivera*, with bath and a/c, cheaper without bath, a/c or fan, clean, Km 131, T 997-2245; across the Pan-American Highway is E *Pensión/Restaurant Panamá*, friendly, clean, safe, a/c; E *Chung*, on Highway, moderately-priced food.

PENONOME

On 20 km is the capital of Coclé: **Penonomé** (*pop* 10,715), an old town even when the Spaniards arrived. An advanced culture here, revealed by archaeologists was overwhelmed by volcanic eruption (things found are in Panama City, in the American Museum of Natural History in New York, and in the **Museo Conte de Penonomé** here, open Tues-Sat 0900-1200, 1400-1700, Sun 0900-1200, T 997-8490). University and Mercado de Artesanato on Highway. The town is frequently the lunch stop for motorists making the whole-day trip from Panama City to the western border.

- **Accommodation and places to eat** C *Dos Continentes*, Av JD Arosemena, T 997-2325, with shower, a/c, pool, restaurant; E *Pensión Dos Reales*, C Juan Vásquez, basic, mosquitos, noisy; E *Pensión Los Pinos*, on left of Highway to Panama City, with bath and fan (D with a/c); E *Pensión Ramírez*, with bath, C Juan

Arosemena nr church and Parque, no sign but look for black lanterns on wall, good value. Also, good basic restaurant, *Cielo Mar*, will let you sling a hammock free; *Mac Aro*, on Juan Arosemena, good for light meals, takeaway, English spoken.

Just under 1 km N of Penonomé is Balneario Las Mendozas, on street of the same name, an excellent river pool for bathing in deep water. Further up the Río Zaratí, also known as the Santa María, is La Angostura where the river dives down a canyon; dirt access road usually suitable for ordinary cars. There are copper and gold mining activities in this area and further N beyond La Pintada, where a new 35 km road has been built to Coclecito on the Caribbean side of the Continental Divide. The operating mining company is also involved in conservation work including reforestation near La Angostura. Northeast of Penonomé is Churuquita Grande (camping possible near river with waterfall and swimming hole); Feria de la Naranja last weekend of Jan, inauguration and dancing on Sat, big day on Sun which includes colourful parade and huge displays of fruit. Further inland, an excellent purpose-built lodge for walkers and ecotourists has been opened: *Posada del Cerro Viejo*, Apdo 543-9A, Chiguirí Arriba, Coclé, T 223-4553, F 264-4858; it offers guided treks on foot or mule, including through the mountains to El Valle, or across the isthmus to the Atlantic coast, the final stage being done by dugout.

24 km W of Penonomé is El Caño, and 3½ km from the main road is the **Parque Arqueológico del Caño** with a small museum, some excavations (several human skeletons found in the burial site), and standing stones (entrance charge US$1, open Tues-Fri 0900-1600, Sat-Sun 1030-1300, closed Mon, T 962-4183).

A further 7 km along the Panamerican Highway is **Natá** (*pop* 5,150), one of the oldest towns in Panama, if not the Americas (1520). The early colonists fought constant Indian attacks led by Urracá. The

Iglesia de Santiago Apóstol (1522) is impressive, with some interesting wood carvings. It is sadly rundown now; donations gratefully received for restoration work in progress. Around the plaza are other colonial buildings.

AGUADULCE

10 km beyond we enter the sugar area and come to **Aguadulce** (*pop* 14,800), a prosperous supply centre (bus from Panamá, US$6); local pottery for sale; cane fields, tomato-processing plants and *salinas* nearby.

- **Accommodation** C *El Interamericano*, on Pan-American Highway, T 997-4363, with bath, a/c, TV, balcony, clean rooms, swimming pool; **D** pp *Pensión Sarita*, T 997-4437, and others (it may be possible to sleep by the fire station).

17 km beyond Aguadulce, just after the large Santa Rosa sugar plantation, a road leads off right to the mountain spa of **Calobre** (31 km); the hot springs are, however, a good hour's drive away, on a very rough road; grand mountain scenery. (Bus Panama City-Aguadulce, US$5.)

AZUERO PENINSULA

6 km after the Calobre turnoff is the crossroads town of **Divisa**, 214 km from the capital. (The town itself is 1 km N of the Highway.) From here a major paved road branches off S into the **Azuero Peninsula**, one of the earliest parts of Panamá to be settled. Despite recent road paving in the S and E, many of the peninsula's small towns are still remote and preserve much of their 400-year-old colonial traditions, costumes and substantial white churches.

Local festivals Most towns of any size on the Peninsula have annual Carnivals (the 4 days before Ash Wednesday) but Las Tablas' is especially picturesque and popular with visitors; accommodation is in short supply at this time throughout the region.

CHITRE

After passing through **Parita** (*pop* 6,600), whose church dates from 1556, our road reaches (37 km) the cattle centre of **Chitré** (*pop* 34,400), capital of Herrera Province and the best base for exploration. The Cathedral (1578) is imposing and beautifully preserved. The small **Museo de Herrera** on C Manuel Correa, has interesting historical exhibits, open Tues-Sat 0830-1200, 1300-1600; Sun 0900-1200, US$0.35. The town is known primarily for its red clay pottery, especially roofing and floor tiles which are exported, and for its woven mats and carpets. The IPAT tourist office is in the Ministerio de Comercio e Industria building on the main road out to Los Santos; very friendly but no English spoken, details on the Peninsula's many festivals and points of interest, open Mon-Fri, 0830-1200, 1245-1630.

Excursions

There are some nice beaches close to Chitré served by local buses (20 min, US$0.90); eg Playas Monagre and El Rompio and at Punta Agallito, where many migratory birds congregate and are studied at the Humboldt Ecological Station. Along the swampy coast just to the N is the 8,000-ha **Sariguа National Park**, established in 1984 to preserve the distinctive tropical desert and mangrove margins of the Bahía de Parita; ancient artefacts have been unearthed within the park's boundaries; the precolombian site of Monegrillo is considered very significant but there is little for the non-specialist to appreciate.

2 km W of Chitré is **La Arena**, the centre for Panamanian pottery. The Christmas festivities here, 22-25 Dec, are worth seeing, with music, dancing, bull running in the *plaza de toros* and cock fights (popular all over Panamá). Tourist agencies in Panama City can arrange whirlwind shopping tours to La Arena. Bus from Chitré; 5 mins, US$0.30, taxi US$1.50.

Local festivals

Fiesta de San Juan Bautista, 24 June; the district's founding (1848) is celebrated with colourful parades and historical events each 19 October.

Local information

● **Accommodation**

D *El Prado*, Av Herrera 4260, opp Cathedral, T 996-4620, clean and modern, quiet, well run, a/c, parking, upstairs restaurant, rec; **D-E** *Santa Rita*, C M Correa y Av Herrera, T 996-4610, nr main plaza, clean, large rooms, modern, cheaper rooms have fans and cold water, restaurant, good value.

E *Pensión Central*, next to *El Prado*, with bath, clean and friendly, comfortable but noisy and overpriced. Plenty of eating places nr the Plaza and in the *mercado* (beside the Cathedral); **E** *Pensión Colombia*, C Manuel Correa nr museum (3 blocks from Plaza), T 996-1856, fans and private baths, good budget value.

● **Transport**

Buses Chitré is the transport hub of the peninsula but has no central bus terminal; most buses leave from different points around the Cathedral. To **Panama City** (250 km), regular departures by several companies, 4 hrs, US$7.25. To **Divisa**, 30 mins, US$1.30; same fare and time to **Las Tablas**. To **Tonosí**, 3 hrs, US$4.15; to **Santiago**, 1½ hrs, US$2.50. Daily flights (except Sun) to the capital with Chitreana de Aviación, US$27.50 – these also serve Los Santos, Guararé and Las Tablas; taxi to the small airport US$1.50 (maximum).

LOS SANTOS

Los Santos (*pop* 9,000), only 4 km across the Río La Villa from Chitré in Los Santos province, is an old, charming town with a fine 18th century church (San Anastacio) containing many images. The first call for Independence came from here; the interesting **Museo de la Nacionalidad** on the Plaza Bolívar is in the lovely house where the Declaration was signed on 10 November 1821, entrance charge US$0.25.

Local festivals The 4-day Feast of Corpus Christi (40 days after Easter) is celebrated in Los Santos with one of the country's most famous and popular festivals, medieval dances, skits and costumes galore, a glorious distillation of the Peninsula's uniquely-strong Spanish roots and well worth attending. The *Feria de Azuero* is held at the end of April (variable date). 'Little Devil' (*diablito*) and other masks featuring prominently in these *fiestas* are the local handicraft speciality and may be purchased from many stalls or workshops around town (also in Parita).

● **Accommodation C** *La Villa de Los Santos*, T 996-8201, a/c caravans, with swimming pool and good restaurant; **E** *Pensión Deportiva*, no single rooms, private showers.

The main road continues 22 km SE through agricultural country to the tiny town of **Guararé** (*pop* 700), notable only for its folkloric museum, the **Museo Manuel Zárate** 2 blocks behind the church, T 996-2535, where examples of Azuero's many traditional costumes, masks and crafts are exhibited in a turn-of-the-century house. There is also a wealth of traditional dance, music and singing contests during the annual National Festival of *La Mejorana* (24 Sept). Two hotels: *Eida* and *Guararé*.

LAS TABLAS

Las Tablas (6 km further, *pop* 22,140) is capital of Los Santos province and the Peninsula's second-largest city, 67 km from the Divisa turnoff. The central Iglesia de Santa Librada with its gold-leaf altar and majestic carvings, is one of the finest churches in this part of Panamá and is now a National Historic Monument. Lacking other outstanding points of interest (except perhaps El Pausilipo, former home of thrice-President Porras – known to Panamanians as 'the great man' – and in the process of being turned into a museum), Las Tablas is nevertheless widely-known for its *Fiesta de Santa Librada* and incorporated *Fiesta de la Pollera*. The *pollera* is a ruffled, intricately-embroidered off-the-shoulder dress based on colonial fashions and now the national costume of Panamá; *polleras* are made in a number of villages near Las Tablas (eg La Tiza, El Cocal, San

José), the most beautiful coming from Santo Domingo (5 km E); another high-quality manufacturing centre is La Enea, a small village close to Guararé.

Excursions The lovely and unspoilt beach of El Uverito is about 10 km to the E of town but has no public transport; taxi US$4.50. A paved road also runs to the port of Mensabé.

Local festivals *Fiesta de la Pollera* (19-23 July).

● **Accommodation** C *Oria*, Via Santo Domingo, T 994-6315, out of town; **D** *Piamonte*, Av Belisario Porras, T 994-6372, a/c only; **E** *Pensión Mariela*, opp, basic, run down; **E** *Pensión Marta*, dirty, unfriendly noisy and overpriced.

● **Places to eat** Some eating places around the church but not a lot of variety.

● **Sports Swimming pool**: nr National Guard barracks, US$0.25, not friendly, not rec.

● **Buses** From Chitré, buses leave when full, 30 mins, US$1.20. To **Panama City**, several daily, 4½ hrs, US$7; to **Santo Domingo**, 10 min, US$0.40; to **Tonosí**, 2½ hrs, US$4.25. Last bus from Los Santos to Las Tablas at 1800.

SOUTH OF LAS TABLAS

Smaller, badly-paved roads fan out from Las Tablas to the beaches along the S coast and the small hill villages in the interior. A circular tour around the eastern mountain range can be done by continuing S to Pocrí and Pedasí (42 km), then W to Tonosí, all with their ancient churches and lack of spectacular sights, but typical of the Azuero Peninsula. Another 57-km paved road runs directly over the hills from Las Tablas to Tonosí, good as far as the small tropical village of Flores (no hotel).

PEDASI

A peaceful colonial town, the municipal library, near the church (in front of a service station) has many old volumes. Beautiful empty beaches (beware dangerous cross-currents when swimming) and crystal-clear seas are 3 km away. The local festival is *Patronales de San Pablo* (29 June). **E** *Pensión Moscoso*, with shower, good,

friendly, only place in town, meals arranged by owner at nearby bar. Buses from Las Tablas leave when full, US$2.65, 1½ hrs, bumpy trip. Most things hereabouts, it seems, are run by the Moscoso clan, including a charming wildfowl reserve near the beach, with storks and herons. Offshore between Pocrí and Pedasí is **Isla Iguana**, a wildlife sanctuary protecting the island's bird life, reptiles and forest; the IPAT office in Chitré can arrange a tour with knowledgeable naturalist René Chan who lives locally.

The road onwards is quite good as far as **Cañas** (no hotel), running near the Pacific coast for a short distance, with a string of lovely coves and sandy beaches accessible by rough tracks. 10 km before Cañas, a small sign points to the black-sand beach of **Playa Venado**, a surfer's paradise down a long dirt road (being improved); there are *cabañas* for rent (US$10 pp) plenty of idyllic camping spots and a small basic restaurant; one bus a day from Las Tablas at 1300, about 2 hrs, US$3.20, return at 0700. Playa Venado can be busy at weekends. **Tonosí** has the **D** *Pensión Boamy*, with a/c, **E** with bath, a restaurant, gas station, chemist and a few basic shops. A branch road goes a few kilometres further S to Cambutal; little reason to detour here as the beaches are a long way out and difficult to get to. The main inland road turns back N following the Río Tonosí, crosses a saddle between the two mountain ranges occupying the centre of the Peninsula (picturesque views of forested Cerro Quema, 950m), and arrives at **Macaracas**, another attractive but unremarkable colonial town, from where two paved roads return to Los Santos and Chitré (35 km).

● **Transport** No direct bus Pedasí-Tonosí; Pedasí-Cañas at 1500, US$1 (returns 0700); Cañas-Tonosí 1/day. Tonosí-Las Tablas, 4 a day between 0700 and 1300, US$2, 1½ hrs, leave when full; a milk truck leaves Tonosí at 0700 for Chitré, via Cañas, Puerto Venado, Pedasí and Las Tablas, takes passengers, returns 1230. Bus Tonosí-Chitré via Macaracas, 4 a day before

1100, 3 hrs, US$4, mostly good, paved road. Hitching is very difficult in this area.

OCU

About 45 km W of Chitré is **Ocú** (*pop* 2,750), another old colonial town with a gracefully curving 16th century church, whose inhabitants celebrate quite a few notable *fiestas* throughout the year with traditional dress, music, masks and dancing, eg San Sebastián, the district's patron saint, costumed folklore groups, 19-24 Jan; the *Festival del Manito* at the Assumption (15 Aug). Straight from medieval Spain, and well-worth witnessing, are the festivities of *Matrimonio Campesino, El Penitente de la Otra Vida* and *El Duelo del Tamarindo*. IPAT tourist offices (Panama City, David, Santiago, Chitré) are best informed about dates and details. Ocú is also known for its woven hats, which are cheaper than elsewhere in Panamá.

● **Accommodation** E *Posada San Sebastián*, on the plaza, fans, clean bathrooms, patio, charming

● **Transport** Ocú can be reached directly from the Pan-American Highway (19 km) by a paved turnoff S just past the Río Conaca bridge (11 km W of Divisa); *colectivos* run from here for US$0.80. Alternatively, a mostly gravel road runs W from Parita along the Río Parita valley, giving good views of the fertile agricultural landscapes of the northern Peninsula. Several buses a day from Chitré, 1 hr, US$1.75, and minibuses on to Panama City, US$7. For those with limited time, a representative glimpse of the countryside and villages could be had by taking a bus from Chitré to Pesé, Los Pozos or Las Minas, all in the foothills of the western range, and then another bus to Ocú; staying the night and taking another bus on to Santiago to return to the Panama City-David highway.

The central mountains effectively cut off the western side of the Pensinsula from the more developed eastern half. Only one road down from the Highway, a gruelling gravel/dirt ribbon which staggers from near Santiago as far S as the village of Arenas (80 km) before giving up in the face of the surrounding scrubby mountain slopes. Eastward from here the

Peninsula reaches its highest point at Cerro Hoya (1,559m); no roads penetrate either to the coast or into the mountains, ensuring solitude for the **Cerro Hoya National Park**, which protects most of the SW tip.

DIVISA TO DAVID

SANTIAGO

The road from Divisa to Santiago, the next town, 37 km, runs across the Province of Veraguas, the only one which has seaboards on both oceans. It is very dry in the summer. **Santiago** (*pop* 32,560), capital of the Province, is well inland; one of the oldest towns in the country, in a grain-growing area (very good – and cheap – *chácaras*, macramé bags adopted by male peasants from the Indians as a convenient carryall for lunch, a file for sharpening the machete, and other necessities in the fields, are sold in the market here). Santiago is the mid-point rest stop for cross-country buses. 18 km N is **San Francisco**; it has a wonderful old church with wooden images, altar pieces and pulpit. Adjacent to the church is a swimming pool.

● **Accommodation In Santiago**: C *Gran David*, on Pan-American Highway, T 998-4510, a/c, TV, cheaper with black and white TV, **E** with fan, all rooms have bath, clean, pool, good inexpensive restaurant, rec; C *Piramidal* on Pan-Am Highway, T 998-4483, a/c, TV, shower, clean, quiet, good pool, rec; C *Roselas Apartotel*, Vía San Francisco, T 998-7269, apartments with kitchen, a/c, hot water, clean, friendly, safe parking for motorcycles. **D** *Santiago*, C 2 nr the Cathedral, T 998-4824, clean, with a/c, TV and shower, cheaper with shared bath, rec. *Pensiones* on Av Central: **E** *Jigoneva*, No 2038, basic, friendly; **E** *Central*, next door, basic, all rooms with shower, Chinese owner; *Continental*, next door, friendly, basic, shared bath. Swimming pool nr town centre.

● **Transport** Buses from Penonomé, US$4, from Aguadulce, US$2.50; Panama City-David buses stop outside *Hotel Piramidal*; bus to David from here US$6.

West of Santiago is the turn-off to **La Atalaya**, site of a major pilgrimage and festival in honour of a miraculous statue of Christ, and home of the Instituto Jesús Nazareno, an important agricultural school for rural boys (open to visitors on Sun). Further on is La Mesa, with a beautiful, white colonial church. The old, bad road through **Soná** (43 km, *pop* 5,000) in a deep fertile valley to **Guabalá**, near Remedios the country's largest stock-raising centre, has been replaced by a direct paved highway from Santiago to Guabalá. This saves a couple of hours. From Guabalá to David is 92 km.

About 17 km W of Guabalá is **Las Lajas**, take turn-off at San Félix. Las Lajas has good, wide beaches (no facilities, two bars, costly shade for cars – shark-infested waters and strong waves, nearest accommodation in David or Santiago). To get there take a bus from David to the turn off (US$2.50), then walk 3 km to the town, from where it is 10 km to the beach (taxis only, US$5).

About 10 km E of David is the small town of **Chiriquí**. A new paved road through Gualaca leads N to the mountains and over the divide to Chiriquí Grande, see page 1209.

DAVID

David (*pop* 102,400), capital of Chiriquí Province (*pop* 368,023), a hot and humid city, rich in timber, coffee, cacao, sugar, rice, bananas and cattle, is the third city of the Republic. It was founded in colonial times and has kept its traditions intact while modernizing itself. 24-hr Shell station at Av Cincuentenario y C C Norte; other service stations at E entrance to Pan-American Highway.

Places of interest

The attractive town has a fine central plaza, Parque Cervantes, with the colonial style Iglesia de San José on its W side. The bell tower in Barrio Bolívar was built separately as a defence against Indian attacks. Palacio Municipal, opp *Hotel Nacional* on Av and C Central.

Museums Museo José de Obaldía, C 8 Este, No 5067 y C A Norte, 4 blocks from Plaza, historical and art museum in house of the founder of Chiriquí province, open Tues-Sat 0900-1600, US$0.25.

Local festivals

Major week-long international fair and fiesta in mid-March.

Excursions

A few kilometres N of David is *Balneario Majagua*, where you can swim in a river under a waterfall; cold drinks for sale. There is another bathing place on the right 10 km further on. Take a Dolega or Boquete bus and ask the driver to let you out. Also, starting from David, white water rafting trips are made on the Río Chiriquí reached after a 2 hour ride into the mountains. Except in the early months of the year when the waters are low, grade III and IV rides can be made. Contact the Chiriquí River Rafting Co, T 236-5217 (Panama). There is also rafting on the neighbouring Río Chiriquí Viejo.

Local information

● **Accommodation**

B *Fiesta*, on Pan-American Highway, T 775-5454, good pool (US$2 for non-residents).

C *Nacional*, C Central, T 775-2221, clean rooms, good restaurant, small gaming room, major renovations in 1997.

D *Iris* on Parque Cervantes T 775-2251, with bath and fan (a/c more), rec; **D** *Saval*, C D Norte between Cincuentenario y Ave 1 Este, T 775-3543, a/c, small restaurant, clean and friendly.

E *Pensión Clark*, Av Francisco Clark, T 774-3452, bath, N of bus terminal; **E** *Pensión Costa Rica*, Av 5 Este, C A Sur, T 775-1241, with shower, **D** with a/c, **F**, in small, noisier rooms, toilet and fan, basic, clean, safe, and friendly, good value; **E** pp *Pensión Fanita*, Manuel J Posa between Calles 5 y 6, with bath and a/c, cheaper without a/c, not clean noisy, hourly rentals; *Pensión y Restaurante Canton*, C Central, Av 4-6 Este, opp supermarket, fan, good beds, but security not good; **F** *Pensión Rocío No 2*, with shower, big rooms with partition walls, good value restaurant. Most cheap hotels are on Av 5 Este.

David

To Boquete

To Panama City

Carretera Panamericana

Not to Scale

Stadium

Avenida Obaldía

Calle H Norte

Calle F Norte

Calle D Norte

Calle B Norte

Calle Central

Palacio Municipal

Parque Cervantes

Museum

Calle B Sur

Calle D Sur

Calle F Sur

Carretera Panamericana

Avenida 8 Oeste

Avenida 2 Oeste

Avenida Central

Avenida Cincuentenario (2 Este)

Avenida 3 de Noviembre (4 Este)

To Paso Canoas

Hotels:
1. Nacional
2. Pensión Costa Rica & Tracopa Buses to San José
3. Saval

Calle Feria

N

To Airport

● **Places to eat**

Las Cacerolas, Av Obaldía behind Super Barú, just off Pan American Highway, self-service, clean, fresh Panamanian dishes all day, cheap, highly rec; *Mariscos Daiquirí*, Av Central, Calle C Sur, fish and seafood, not cheap, but good; *Jimar*, corner of Calle C Norte and Av Bolívar, good value; *Las Brisas*, Av Obaldía, good steaks; *Las Vegas*, opp *Hotel Nacional*, steaks and pastas; *Parrillada El Portal*, C A Sur, Av 5 E, good; *El Portal Valle de la Luna*, C A Sur, nr *Pensión Costa Rica*, good food; *Restaurant Bar Bon Jour*, just outside town towards Boquete, very pleasant, steaks and pizzas good; *El Steak House*, Pan-American Highway W of Av Obaldía, good Chinese, moderate prices. Many around central plaza (*Parque*, *don Pedro*, *Pollo Riko*, all a/c); *Oasis*, 2 blocks W of Parque, good, reasonable prices; *Café Don Dicky*, Calle C Norte nr Av Domingo Díaz, better than it looks, Pizza House round corner. *América* in bus station, 0500-2400, others opp and of

varying quality in municipal market, Av Obaldía, nr Av 3 de Noviembre, 4 blocks N of plaza.

● **Banks & money changers**

Citibank on Plaza, only Citibank TCs; **Banco del Istmo**, Av 2 Este between C B Norte and C Central, for Visa cash advances and changes Bank of America TCs; **Banco Nacional de Panamá**, 0800-1330 (generally very convenient, but officious guards have been known to turn away neatly-dressed travellers wearing shorts), changes Amex TCs, 1% commission plus US$0.10 tax/cheque; **Banco General**, 1 block from main plaza, changes TCs, no commission, Visa ATM; **Banco de París**, C Central between Av 2 and 3, changes Amex TCs, no commission; **Caja de Ahorro** (Caja Pronto), for Mastercard and Amex T/Cs.

● **Embassies & consulates**

Costa Rican Consulate: Av 2 Oriente entre Calles D y G, diagonal a la Provedora Barú, T 774-1923. Consul is Juan Flores Badilla.

● **Entertainment**
Cinema: *Plaza* cinema, by Parque Cervantes.
Discotheque: *Metropolitan*, plays salsa.

● **Laundry**
Cisne Blanca, Av 3 Oriente, Mon-Sat 0700-1800. Laundry next to *Pensión Costa Rica*, US$2 a load, wash and dry.

● **Post & telecommunications**
Post Office: C C Norte, 1 block from Parque Cervantes.

Telecommunications: Intel, C C Norte, telex and long-distance telephone, open daily 0900-2030.

● **Tourist offices**
Beside the church, in the blue building, T 775-4120, not much information, Mon-Fri 0830-1630. Sr Oscar Renán Ortega, owner of *Viajes 4 Tours*, Vía Belisario Porras, T 775-1397, F 775-4652, specializes in local information.

● **Useful addresses**
Immigration office: C C Sur nr Av Central, T 775-4515, Mon-Fri 0800-1530.

● **Transport**
Local Bus: urban buses US$0.20; taxis US$0.65 in city. **Car hire**: Budget, T 775-5597; Hertz, T 775-6828; Mike's, T 775-4963; Fecar, T 775-3246, reasonable. If wishing to rent a 4WD vehicle for Volcán Barú, do so in David.

Air Several Aeroperlas flights a day from Panama City, US$55 one way. Also to Bocas del Toro and Changuinola, both US$22.50 one way. New frequent service to San José, Costa Rica, about US$90; enquire at Aeroperlas desk in Panama City.

Buses Bus to **Panama City**: apart from Ticabus (David terminal, Av Obaldía No 6308, C K, T 775-3358), ordinary buses, US$11 (7 hrs), every hour from 'Piquera de David' terminal on Av Balboa, Panama City, 0700 to 1300, 1½ hourly till 1900, plus express buses at midnight, 5½ hrs, US$15. Purchase express tickets during the day as they frequently sell out nearer departure time. All regional and long distance buses leave David from the bus terminal at the end of Av 2 Este/Cincuentenario, 200m N of Av Obaldía, except that Tracopa, T 775-0585, have buses to San José, with a stop at San Isidro, at 0830 and 1230 (8 hrs to San José), US$18 both destinations, from Av 5 Este, C A Sur next to *Pensión Costa Rica*. Boarding Tracopa buses here can be chaotic as tickets are only sold once the bus has arrived, and then people start clamouring for

seats immediately. An alternative way to Panama City is to Santiago (US$7) and then to Panama City (US$7). Regular minibus to **Boquete** from bus station (US$1.40) 1 hr. Frequent *'frontera'* buses to **Paso Canoas**, US$1.50, 1½ hrs. To **Volcán**, 1½ hrs, US$2.30, every 15 mins, 0700-1800; **Chiriquí Grande**, 3 hrs, US$7, 1½ hourly intervals 0630-1600. To **Cerro Punto**, 2¼ hrs, US$3.

BOQUETE

A well-paved road climbs gently N from David into the cool highlands around Volcán Barú, passing (10 km) a waterfall with a swimming hole at its base, open-air restaurant/bar and space for wild camping. It passes through Dolega (swimming pool, notable carnival 4 days before Ash Wednesday) before reaching (35 km) the popular mountain resort of **Boquete**, at 1,060m, in the valley of the Río Caldera, with the slopes of the Volcán Barú to the W. It enjoys a spring-like climate the year round: the mingling of Atlantic and Pacific winds creates an atmospheric oddity called the *bajareque* (literally 'falling down'), a fine mist or moisture always in the air, which combined with the black volcanic soil, creates highly fertile conditions. Around is a beautiful panorama of coffee plantations, orange groves, strawberry fields, and gardens which grow the finest flowers and vegetables in the country. The town has many attractions: good lodging and facilities, fishing, riding, and mountain climbing, and not too expensive. Prettier than the main plaza is Parque de las Madres, with fountains, flower beds, a monument to motherhood and a children's playground. The fair ground E of the river is the site for the *Feria de las Flores y el Café*, held each year mid-Jan (the dates are variable, it has been held in April). Accommodation is difficult to find during the Feria. The cemetery is worth a visit (see map). There is a panoramic view from the 'Bienvenidos a Boquete' arch at the *Coffee Bean Restaurant* (see below).

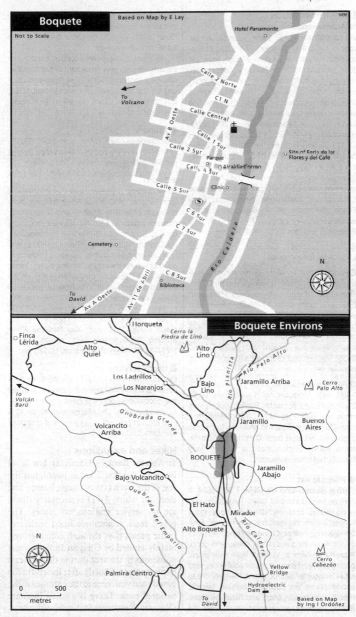

Boquete

Based on Map by E Lay

Not to Scale

M96

Hotel Panamonte

Calle 2 Norte

C1 N

To Volcano

Calle Central

Av B Oeste

Calle 1 Sur

Calle 2 Sur

Site of Feria de las Flores y del Café

Parque

Calle 3 Sur

Alcaldia/Correo

Clinico

Calle 5 Sur

C 6 Sur

Río Caldera

C 7 Sur

Cemetery

C 8 Sur

Av 11 de Abril

Av A Oeste

Biblioteca

To David

N

Boquete Environs

Finca Lérida

Horqueta

Cerro la Piedra de Lino

Alto Quiel

Alto Lino

Los Ladrillos

Río Palo Alto

Jaramillo Arriba

Cerro Palo Alto

Los Naranjos

Bajo Lino

Río Planista

To Volcán Barú

Quebrada Grande

Jaramillo

Buenos Aires

Volcancito Arriba

BOQUETE

Bajo Volcancito

Jaramillo Abajo

Quebrada del Emporio

El Hato

Mirador

N

Río Caldera

Alto Boquete

Cerro Cabezón

0   500
metres

Palmira Centro

Yellow Bridge

Hydroelectric Dam

To David

Based on Map by Ing I Ordóñez

Local information

● Accommodation

A2 *La Montaña y El Valle*, Jaramillo Arriba, opp *El Explorador Cafetería*, T/F 720-2211, e-mail montana@chiriqui.com. 2½ km from San Juan Bautista church in Boquete (pass church, turn right at fork, cross river, turn left at intersection, then follow signs), 2 deluxe cottages in 2½ ha (with kitchen, hot water, spacious), fine views gourmet take-away kitchen, also camping US$7 for 2; **A2** *Panamonte*, T 720-1327/4, with bath, some with kitchen, dinner costs US$13.50 and is highly rec, popular, garden boasts over 200 varieties of orchid, very attractive surroundings, run by the Collins family (Swedish/American), horse hire US$3/hr, guides available (ask about hot springs, Los Pozos de Caldera, see **Excursions** below, and Finca Lérida, see under Volcán Barú below; other excursions also available, such as the Río Monte Ecological Tour, ask for maps of the area).

B *Villa Lorena Cabañas*, T720-1848, US$50/day for 4 people.

C *Fundadores*, T 720-1298, restaurant, beautiful place with stream running through; **C** *Pensión Topas*, T 720-1005, opened 1996, with bath (one room without bath **D**), garden with view of Volcán Barú, pool, good breakfasts, run by Schöb family (artist/anthropologist), tours arranged; **C** *Rebequet*, T 720-1365, excellent rooms around a garden, with bath, TV and fridge, kitchen and eating area for guests' use, popular, rec.

D *Pensión Marilós*, Av a Este y C 6 Sur, T 720-1380, opp *Rebequet*, with bath (one single **E** without bath), hot water, English spoken, very clean and well run, motorcycle parking, rec, often full but will permit sharing, tours also organized, will store bags; **D** *Pensión Victoria*, main plaza, English-speaking owner, very friendly, has small restaurant.

● Places to eat

Coffee Bean/Grano de Café, T 720-1624, a café on road 3 km S of town, fantastic views, good snacks, book exchange, formerly had a lioness, T-shirts still available, very friendly, English-speaking owner; *Chinesse Food*, yes that's its name, on Parque Central, cheap and good; *Pizzeria Volcánica*, ½ block from main plaza, good pizzas and pasta at reasonable prices; opp is *La Conquista*, delicious trout. Plenty of cheap eating places eg *Lourdes*, outside terrace, friendly, good value, *Mary* and *Túnel* on plaza, *Rocío*, ½ block away, good value. Near the

bank, on main street are a French and a Mexican restaurant. Excellent patisserie on Av 11 de Abril, close to the church; on same avenue is *Pub Café*, nice atmosphere.

45 mins' walk from Boquete (past *Hotel Panamonte*) is a new restaurant *El Explorador*, beautiful location, picnic area, children's playground, hammocks etc, entrance to area, US$1, but free to restaurant (excellent local food, breakfast and dinner).

● Laundry

Econopronto, Av Central, 50m from church, closed Sun and lunchtimes. *Lavomático Benny*, just S of church, very friendly, US$1 to wash.

● Sports

River rafting: father-and-son team Héctor and Iann Sánchez of *Chiriquí River Rafting*, both bilingual, offer 4-hr Class III and IV trips with modern equipment on Río Chiriquí from Caldera, nr Boquete, to Gualaca on Fortuna-Chiriquí Grande highway, April-Dec, US$90 pp, and also can arrange lodging, transport to starting-point or vehicle delivery to landing point. During dry season, Dec-April, they arrange trips on Río Chiriquí Viejo (Class III/IV Technical) parallel to Costa Rican border from Breñón, nr Río Sereno, to Paso Canoas. Panama office T 236-5218, e-mail hsanchez@panama.c-com.net; in Boquete T 720-2112; rec. Also *Panama River Rafting*, Sr Graciano Cruz, speaks English, T 774-1230, offers shorter trips, US$75 pp.

● Useful services

On the main street, Av 11 de Abril, or Fundadores, are Banco Nacional (cashes TCs, as will the cooperative opp the bank on the plaza), farmacia, cinema, *Dejud* supermarket; on Av A Este are the post office, market and church of San Juan Bautista.

Hikes and excursions

To **Volcán Barú** (3,475m), 21 km W of Boquete, the first 7 km is paved, but the rest of the track is very rough, bumpy and steep for which 4WD is necessary (there are no service stations en route). The paved road, sometimes lined with aromatic pines, goes through coffee groves, mainly tended by Guaymí Indians, most numerous in the area during the year-end harvest season. Shortly after the end of the paved road you come to the entrance to the national park. There is a small Inrenare (National Resources Institute) office here, not always manned, and there is also an office on the southern outskirts of town, near the Colegio Franciscano, at which information is available. The track winds up from the office through impressive, tall cloud forest, thick with hanging creepers, lichen and bromeliads. The steep cuttings are carpeted with a glorious array of ferns and colourful flowers; many birds can be seen, including bee-sized hummingbirds and wild turkeys, also squirrels. The perfume from the flowers, especially in the wet season when there are many more blooms, is magnificent.

As the road rises, increasingly steeply, wonderful views appear, of the Boquete valley, the Río Caldera running through a steep gorge, and the misty plain beyond stretching to the sea (best seen in the early morning with the rising sun behind). About three-quarters of the way up there is a crater on the left, with a sign leading to a mirador, about a 15 mins' walk.

At the summit the jungle is replaced by a forest of TV and radio aerials, in fenced-off enclosures. A short path leads to a small cross and a trigonometric point, from which there are the best views all around, of dusty craters and the valley of Volcán, Bambito and Cerro Punta below. The barren, dusty slopes contrast spectacularly with the dark green forest, with wisps of mist and cloud clinging to the treetops. Sometimes horizontal rainbows can be seen in the haze, formed in the *bajareque* drizzle. There are many mini-craters around the main summit, with dwarf vegetation, lichens and orchids.

There is a makeshift campsite in a small grove of bushes on the left of the road before the final summit. From the cross there is a path down to the main crater where there is also plenty of flat ground for camping (local hikers say it is safer in groups). There is no running water – take plenty for the climb as well as for camping. Previous campers have badly littered the camping area and the graffiti is appalling. Take back everything you bring with you. After about 1100 you

will probably have the place to yourself; it is very quiet and atmospheric. The path that leads down from the cross branches right towards Volcán (no water on this path until you are out of the woods, at least 2½ hrs).

In a suitable vehicle it takes about 2 hrs to the top (depending on the weather), or from the park office, 4½-6 hrs hike up, 3 hrs down. A guide to the summit is not necessary, but Gonzalo Miranda and Generoso Rodríguez, neither trained guides, but both very knowledgeable and willing, take visitors to the summit, and to other sites, fix a price beforehand. T 720-1165 (Generoso's home, he speaks some English) or 720-1261, his office, or leave a message with Frank, who speaks good English, at *Pensión Marilós*. 'Zona Urbana' minibuses go virtually to the end of the asphalt. Vehicles belonging to Intel, the cable and telephone companies, often go up to the summit. They are not allowed to take passengers officially, but drivers may give you a lift if you start walking from their office in Boquete before 0800. They are also very friendly and like a chat. A taxi to the end of the paved road costs US$4. Hiking from the summit back to Boquete takes 6 hrs.

Mrs Inga Collins of *Hostal Panamonte* will give permission to visit her *Finca Lérida*, on the slopes of Barú volcano (ask at the hotel's front desk); there are many trails in the cloud forest where quetzales have been seen and bell birds heard. Entrance to the Finca costs US$1.50 pp. 'Zona Urbana' minibuses run to the Finca.

Other attractions include: *Café Ruiz*, on the northern edge of Boquete, a small factory known for its premium-grade roasted coffees which welcomes visitors for a free guided tour (Don José Ruiz speaks English), explaining the whole process from harvesting to selecting only the green beans; T 720-1392/1432. Los Ladrillos, a few kilometres further up the Caldera valley, is a small area of basalt cliffs with octagonal fingers of rock in clusters, similar to Northern Ireland's

Giant's Causeway. Beyond is Horqueta, a picturesque hillside area of coffee groves, with a roadside waterfall and banks of pink impatiens; beautiful views to the S.

15 km before Boquete is a turn off E to Caldera (14 km), from where a 25-30 mins walk leads to **Los Pozos de Caldera**, a well-known series of hot springs said to be good for rheumatism sufferers. No facilities, they are on land belonging to the Collins family (*Hotel Panamonte* in Boquete), who ask only that visitors and campers leave the area clean and litter-free. There is one bus a day from David to Caldera and there are pick-ups from the main road to the village.

A recommended half-day walk is across the suspension bridge in Boquete, then take a righthand fork winding steeply uphill. After about 30 mins the paved road gives way to gravel; keep going to a crossroads (10 mins) where you take the righthand fork, heading due S. (For a view of the Pacific continue straight on from the crossroads for 5 mins.) The righthand fork continues with the river on your right and sweeping hillsides to your left. Eventually you rejoin the main road, turning right along an avenue lined with pine trees. The road winds down and across a big yellow bridge by a dam. After an exposed, flat stretch you meet the main road into Boquete from David; from here it is 30 mins back to town and a well-deserved stop at the *Grano de Café*.

West of David After David, a dirt road turns off to the left to **Las Palmas**, a pleasant orange-growing village which welcomes tourists. Just before the village is a waterfall where a single column of water falls into a pool, delightful for swimming and camping.

The Pan-American Highway undergoing widening to a modern divided highway, goes through cattle land from David 26 km W to **La Concepción** (*pop* 11,900), often called Bugaba, which is the name of the district, by the locals. It is an important agricultural shipping point also widely-known for its hand-made saddles. There are several fair hotels (eg *Rico*, C 2 Oriente and the Highway; and *Caribe*, Av 1 Sur), but better accommodation in Volcán, Cerro Punta or David; a local *fiesta*, La Candelaria, is held at the end of January. Buses depart from the main plaza, called 'El Parque', old fashioned and picturesque, every 20 mins to Volcán (US$1.65), David (US$0.50), and Paso Canoas (US$0.75). *Lee Chang Hermanos* stores recommended for food, supplies, auto parts. Fill up before going to Volcán if lead-free petrol required.

CHIRIQUI HIGHLANDS

La Concepción is the gateway to the **Tierras Altas** (Highlands) **of Chiriquí**, an area bounded on the N by the Cordillera and on the W by the Costa Rican border, a prosperous agricultural region known for vegetables, flowers, superb coffees, and the Brown Swiss and Holstein dairy herds that thrive in the cool highland pastures. Less tourist-oriented than Boquete, the area is a bird-watchers' mecca and popular with residents of Panama City wishing to cool off for a few days. It has a wide variety of accommodation. Daytime temperatures are spring-like; evenings and nights chilly. Some days can be rather windy in the dry season. Mornings are especially clear and beautiful year-round. Travellers entering Panama from the N should consider a visit before pushing on to Panama City, 500 km on.

LA CONCEPCION TO VOLCAN

There is a very good paved road, rising 1,600m in 32 km, to Volcán. From Cuesta de Piedra, a turning to the right will take you to the canyons of the Macho de Monte, a rather small river which has worn very deep and narrow gorges. Further on, on the left, is the Mirador Alan Her, with good views from the purpose-built tower (US$0.10 unless you've bought something in the snackbar) to the sea, and on a clear day, the Punto Burica peninsula which marks the Panamá-Costa Rica frontier. On sale are very good local cheeses, especially the mozzarella. Near Volcán, excellent wood carvings at *Artes Cruz*; Don Cruz speaks English, will make charming souvenirs to order; they will be ready on your return trip.

VOLCAN

A rapidly growing farming town, with nurseries growing ferns for export, the *Café Volcán Barú* plant, and a small factory owned by the Swiss Bérard family producing excellent European-style sausages, pickled and smoked meats, including Panamanian *tasajo* (smoked jerky). San Benito school is noted for hardwood furniture and hand-painted ceramics; Bro Ælred will let you browse through his warehouse full of English books from the now-closed Canal Zone libraries and take away what you will; also visit *Cerámica Beija-Flor* run by local women who market their own wares. Southwest of town is the **Las Lagunas** nature reserve with two beautiful lakes; abundant aquatic and other birdlife, high vehicles or 4WD required in wet season. La Fuente park has playing fields, spring-fed swimming hole (source of Río Gariche) excellent for children (US$0.25). Volcán is a good jumping-off place for the 6-12 hr ascent of the Volcán Barú. Climbers frequently climb the W side, camp overnight at the summit, and descend to Boquete in the morning. See details under Boquete. Guides can be arranged in Volcán; climbers do get lost; time lost from a wrong turning on the track can result in being caught in an inhospitable spot at nightfall.

● **Accommodation NB** Price categories shown for cottages are for 1 or 2 persons, but most accommodate larger groups for the same price or slightly more. **A3** *Altozano*, Caizán Rd 2 km from main road, T 771-4076, charming new cottages for 1-6 people on secluded farm, full kitchen and bath, good hot water, fireplaces, good views, American owner Sr David will recommend guides, arrange tours, climbs of Cerro Punta or Volcán Barú, provide information in

Spanish, English, French, rec; *Las Huacas*, main street at W end of town, T 771-4363, nice cottages, hot water, clubhouse, elaborate gardens, interesting aviaries, English spoken; *Cabañas Dr Esquivel*, T 771-4770, several large houses in a compound on the road behind *Supermercado Bérard*, friendly; **C** *Hotel Don Tavo*, main street, T 771-4258, new, private baths, hot water, restaurant, clean, friendly, rec; *Hotel Dos Rios*, T 771-4271, older wooden building (upper floor rooms quieter), restaurant, bar (Sr Goyo speaks English), garden with stream, private baths, hot water unreliable; *Cabañas Reina*, signed from main road, T 771-4338 self-contained units with a kitchen in lawn setting; *Valle la Luna*, signed from main road, T 771-4225, older cabins; **D** *Motel California*, on main street, T 771-4272, friendly Croatian owner speaks English, clean private baths, hot water, larger units for up to 7, US$45, restaurant, bar, quiet, good; **D** *Cabañas Señorial*, main street at entrance to town, T 771-4239, basic, OK; **E** *El Oasis*, behind restaurant, C La Fuente, T 771-4644, bar can be noisy; *Cabañas Morales*, Nueva California, T 771-4435.

● **Places to eat** Plenty of cheap eating places, inc pizzerías; good fish brought from coast daily, *Marisquería El Pacífico*, main road E of main intersection, rec.

● **Entertainment Discos**: weekend discos at *Eruption* and *Kalahari*, rustic, good places to meet local youth.

The road divides at the police station in Volcán; the right branch continues N to Bambito and Cerro Punta (22 km), following the Chiriquí Viejo river valley up the NW foothills of Volcán Barú. Many roadside stands selling fresh vegetables and *chicha*, a fruit drink made from wild raspberries or fresh strawberries in season. At tiny **Bambito** is the luxurious **A2** *Hotel Bambito*, T 771-4265, F 771-4207, indoor pool, spa, conference room, good but expensive restaurant, tennis courts, motor-scooter rental, horse-riding – the lot! Very good bargains can be negotiated here in the off-season.

CERRO PUNTA

At the end of the road (buses from David via La Concepción and Volcán, 2¼ hrs, US$3.25), is **Cerro Punta** (*alt* 2,130m), in a beautiful valley which is the heart of a vegetables and flower-growing zone, and a region of dairy and racehorse farms. It is sometimes called 'Little Switzerland' because of its Alpine-style houses and the influence of Swiss and former-Yugoslav settlers; there is a settlement called Nueva Suiza just S of town. The countryside, full of orchids and rainbows, is beautiful, though economic pressures push the fields ever higher up the hillsides at the cost of the wooded areas. Many fine walks in the crisp mountain air. Continue through Cerro Punta to follow the main street as it curves to the left. Haras Cerro Punto (topiary initials clipped in the hedge) and Haras Carinthia (name visible on stable roof) are well known thoroughbred farms who will usually receive visitors and guide them round. Further on is the small bridge at Bajo Grande; the right fork will lead to *Respingo*, where there is a small forest ranger station. Here, as well as the end of the paved road – where the Fernández brothers, for a negotiated price will arrange to meet and guide you at the edge of the **Volcán Barú National Park** – in the early morning, quetzales can be seen.

Continuing along this road is the starting point of the 8 hrs' hike (minimum), mostly downhill after an initial climb, to Boquete (the track is clear in places and there are a few signs showing the direction and time – ambitious – to Boquete); the last part is down the Río Caldera canyon. It is easier in the dry season, Dec-April. Don't hike alone, take a machete and sufficient provisions for 2 days in case of mishap, wear ankle boots, and notify someone before leaving and on arrival. This hike is also recommended for bird watching. **Parque la Amistad** is another park, 6.8 km from the centre of Cerro Punta (signposted at road junction), the last section to the park office for 4WD only. (4WD taxis are available in town; drivers will arrange to park your car in a safe place; negotiate hourly price: US$8/hr for 2 passengers is official.) It has been open since 1991, with 2 trails,

good for bird watching, including quetzales (US$2 pp). Young staff of the AMISCONDE conservation office on the street leading to La Amistad Park give very interesting information about the ecology of the area. Boris Justavino speaks some English. Nature buffs should also visit Los Quetzales reserve inside Parque La Amistad. See under **Accommodation**.

● **Accommodation A2** *Cabañas Los Quetzales*, T 771-2182, F 771-2226, at Guadalupe, a true forest hideaway, 3 self-contained cabins, baths, hot water, no electricity, on a spectacular cloud forest reserve at 2,020m, inside Parque La Amistad, nearly 100 bird species, inc quetzales, visible from porches, streams, trout hatchery, primeval forest, 4WD only, bit of a hike from parking area, but worth it, owner Carlos Alfaro, fluent English, can arrange transport or daily cook; **C** *Hotel Cerro Punta*, T 771-2020, with 8 simple rooms and a quite good restaurant, just before the turning to La Amistad; *Hotel Los Quetzales*, T 771-2182, F 771-2226, Guadalupe, 10 basic rooms with baths, same owners as *Cabañas Los Quetzales*.

● **Banks & money changers** Banco Nacional and Banco de Istmo, Mon-Fri 0800-1500, Sat 0800-1200, both change dollar TCs.

● **Laundry** *Lavamático Volcán*, main road opp *Jardín Alegría* dancehall. Service only US$2.50 wash, dry and fold, reliable, Doña Miriam will have washing ready when promised.

● **Post & telecommunications** Ironmongers/hardware store *Ferremax*, main road opp police station, sends and receives international fax (771-4461), 0700-1200, 1400-1800, US$1.50/page plus telephone charge, and e-mail (ferremax@pananet.com), US$2/message; English spoken. International telephone at Intel office, main road opp police station. Phone service inside Panama at payphones outside Intel and in post office (quieter surroundings, small surcharge).

FRONTIER WITH COSTA RICA – RIO SERENO

From the fork at the police station in Volcán, the left branch loops 48 very scenic km W, climbing over the Cerro Pando, and passing through beautiful cattle country and coffee plantations to the Costa Rican frontier. Los Pozos, an area of small thermal pools, is a good campsite, but only accessible by 4WD vehicles and hard to find. Enquire at Volcán. At Río Colorado, *Beneficio Café Durán*, a coffee processing plant whose delicious aroma of fermenting pulp and drying beans will announce its proximity from kilometres away, is hospitable to visitors. Approaching the village, large installations from the era of military government, now abandoned, are visible on the right. The village of **Río Sereno**, with its Panamanian businesses centered around the plaza, and the Costa Rican along a street right on the border, has the air of a cowboy town. Numerous vendors' stalls, especially Sun during coffee harvest, when Indian workers and families shop. Costa Rican shops, selling leather goods, crafts, clothing, gladly accept US$ at current rates. Several good eating places; *Bar Universal* recommended for platters of fried chicken with plantain chips (family atmosphere, Sr Elí friendly and helpful). For river rafting trips on Río Chiriquí Viejo, see **River Rafting**, page 1200. **D** *Hotel Los Andes*, good. This is a minor international crossing post with uncertain hours and the probability that visa applications and tourist cards will be out-of-stock (better to arrange at *Paso Canoas*); frequent bus service dawn to dusk to and from David (US$4) via Volcán (US$2.65), but a chancy crossing for private vehicles. If you have the time to spare, worth a try. From Río Sereno, a recently paved road runs S along the border to Paso Canoas (about 2 hrs). Travellers unable to cross with private vehicles at Río Sereno can cross there. Customs and immigration officials at Río Sereno are unconcerned about local pedestrians or small purchases crossing in either direction.

LA CONCEPCIÓN TO THE FRONTIER

30 km from La Concepción is **Paso Canoas** on the Costa Rican border.

FRONTIER WITH COSTA RICA – PASO CANOAS

A busy border town, with many shops and outdoor stalls. Many good eating places, especially open-front restaurants opposite Costa Rican customs. Informally crossing back and forth among shops and business areas is easy, but travellers intending to leave one country for the other must submit to formalities before proceeding.

● **Panamanian immigration**
Panamanian customs are open 24 hrs – remember Panama is 1 hr ahead of Costa Rica. However, the Costa Rican side is open 0700-1200, 1400-1800, 1900-2200 Panama time. For those who need tourist cards, they are sold (if not out of stock) at the tourist office near immigration for US$2, free maps of Panama available here. No other charges are made, but an onward ticket and/or proof of adequate funds may be requested.

● **Accommodation**
E *Palace*, clean bathroom, basic. There is a reasonable restaurant at the border.

● **Exchange**
Money changers on the Panamanian side will change colones into dollars at a good rate (the bank on the Costa Rican side does not buy colones for dollars; the Banco Nacional de Panama on the other side cashes TCs, rates slightly better than money changers, also has Visa ATM).

● **Transport**
Regular buses run to David for US$1.50, 1½ hrs. If you are there at the right time, ask if Ticabus has space to Panama City – US$10.

Trains Chiriquí Railway Passenger service Puerto Armuelles-Progreso (half away to Paso Canoas), twice a day each way, 2 hrs, US$1. There is also a 'Finca Train', 4 decrepit, converted banana trucks, leaving at 1500 for the banana *fincas*, returning, by a different route, at 1800. No charge for passengers. Minibuses also leave all day for the *fincas*.

PUERTO ARMUELLES

Due S of Paso Canoas, on a good road, is **Puerto Armuelles** (*pop* 12,975), the port through which all the bananas grown in the area are exported. Puerto Armuelles on the Pacific and Almirante and Chiriquí Grande (Bocas del Toro) are the only ports in Panama outside the Canal area at which ocean-going vessels habitually call and anchor in deep water close inshore; there is now an oil transit pipeline across the isthmus between Puerto Armuelles and Chiriquí Grande. Bus from David, every 15 mins 0500-2000, 2½ hrs, US$3.

● **Accommodation** C *Kokos Place*, T 770-7049; **E** *Pensión Balboa*, on waterfront, pleasant; **E** *Pensión Trébol*, 1 block from waterfront. Plenty of cheap eating places, eg *Enrique's*, Chinese, good; *Club Social*, on water, ask any taxi, chicken and rice dishes.

The North-Western Caribbean Coast

DIFFERENT AGAIN, Panama's Caribbean, banana-growing region has historical links with Columbus' 4th voyage and with black slaves imported to work the plantations. Ports of varying age and activity lie on the Laguna de Chiriquí, all linked by ferry. Here is an alternative land route to Costa Rica.

LAGUNA DE CHIRIQUÍ TO COSTA RICA

Across the Cordillera from David, on the Caribbean side, is the important banana growing region which extends from **Almirante** NW across the border to Costa Rica. In the 1940-1950 period, disease virtually wiped out the business and plantations were converted to *abacá* and cacao. Resistant strains of banana were developed and have now all but replaced *abacá* and cacao. Thriving banana plantations are throughout this area on the mainland owned by Cobanat, a subsidiary of Standard Fruit (Dole, Chiquita, etc). Around 20 million boxes of bananas are exported annually to Europe alone from Almirante, where, if you must, there are places to stay, **D-E** *San Francisco*, a/c or fan, small dark rooms, overpriced; **D-E** *Hong Kong*, with fan, or more expensive with a/c, restaurant; **E** *Albergue Bahía*, T 778-9211, clean, friendly owner, will store belongings; **E** *Pensión Colón*, basic nice rooms, friendly owner.

ISLA COLON AND BOCAS DEL TORO

Across the bay are a number of islands, the most important of which is Isla Colón, which used to be a major banana producer, but this did not revive with the mainland plantations. Its main sources of income now are fishing and tourism, centred on **Bocas del Toro** on the SE tip of the island. Bocas del Toro deserves a visit (*Fiesta del Mar* end Sept/early Oct): peaceful, quiet, English spoken by most of the black population. The protected bay offers all forms of watersport and diving (snorkelling gear for hire at *Las Brisas*, US$5 a day), beautiful sunrises and sunsets, and, on land, tropical birds, butterflies, red frogs and other wildlife. Do not go to deserted stretches of beach alone. Excursions can be made to the islands of the archipelago (Bastimentos – see below, Carenero, Solarte), to Isla del Cisne, a bird sanctuary, and to the beautiful Islas Zapatillas, for beaches and fishing. At **Bastimentos** is a National Marine Park: on this island and on Isla Colón are turtle nesting grounds, whose protection is being improved. Colón also has a cave of long-beaked white bats, which fly out at dusk (tour, US$10, plus US$5 for lunch on beach). You can walk to the cave, a pleasant day there and back, but ask locals for directions and advice on safety. If hiring a boat, try to arrange it the day before, US$5/hr not including petrol, 4 hrs min, can take 5 people. Note that many of the names relate to Columbus' landfall here on his fourth voyage in Oct 1502 (Carenero was where he careened his ships, Bastimentos where he took on supplies, etc). The area has a rich buccaneering past, too.

Between Almirante and the Costa Rica border is **Changuinola** with an airstrip.

50 km to the SE of Almirante is **Chiriquí Grande** which has a road connection with the rest of the country (see below) but none to Almirante. There are understood to be plans for one but nothing has been done. (See below for all **Transport** details.)

NB A devastating earthquake struck NW Panamá and SE Costa Rica on 21 April 1991. The area is now recovering and reconstruction is proceeding. An island in the bay which sank during the earthquake now shows as a patch of shallow turquoise water. Also, this region is subject to very heavy rainfall from daily afternoon downpours to violent tropical storms. Normally, only from Jan to Mar is there much respite.

Local information
● **Accommodation**
At Bocas del Toro: **C-D** *Las Brisas*, on the sea (formerly *Botel Thomas*), T 757-9428, F 757-9257, Apdo 5, Bocas del Toro, wooden building on stilts, with bath and fan, restaurant, bicycle, snorkel and canoe hire, good but cockroaches and thin walls; **D** *Bahía*, T 757-9626, building formerly the HQ of the United Fruit Company, nice cafeteria, laundry.

At Bastimentos: **E** *Pensión Bastimentos*, friendly, fan, hot water, shared bathroom, restaurant – seafood speciality, laundry service, tours; *Calypso Club*, breakfast US$2.50, dinners from US$3.50, room and hammocks for rent, boat trips to the National Marine Park arranged. Rooms may also be arranged through Gabriel.

At Changuinola: **D** *Changuinola*, T 758-8681, nr airport; **D** *Carol*, T 758-8731, 100m from bus station, with bath, a/c, restaurant next door same ownership; restaurant *El Caribe*, nr airport, rec; also nightclubs (*54* best), cinema and theatre.

At Chiriquí Grande: **D** *Pensión Emperador*, T 757-9656, overlooking wharf, clean, friendly, balcony; **E** *Hotel Buena Vista*, does breakfasts, friendly, shared bath, mice; **F** pp *Osiris*, fan, basic but OK, awful food; **E** *Pensión Guillerma*, both are further away from the port's 24-hr generator so may be quieter, basic, shared bath (latter has noisy bar downstairs), take a flashlight, power only from 1800-2400; **E** *Hotel Fuente*, with bath, 1 block from waterfront next to *panadería*, friendly, clean, best in town, no sign, just ask.

● **Places to eat**
At Bocas del Toro: *Las Delicias*, good food (also has rooms above, T 757-9318); *El Lorito*, also good, and a good Chinese, with take-away, on the main street, rec; *Don Chico's Restaurant* does a mean *casado* for US$2 and a great lemon pie; bar by public dock very active, especially at weekends; *Red Lobster*, opp *Las Brisas*, same owners, small, very friendly, good food and cheap; *Todo Tropical*, opp police station, good seafood, American owned, you are invited to draw on the walls; *Pomodoro*, on C 3, good Italian, great atmosphere and music, reasonably priced; *Rapido Sub*, good sandwiches.

At Chiriquí Grande: *Mama Gina*, next to ferry dock, good; *Dallys*, popular, to right of wharf, and *Café*, also good.

● **Banks & money changers**
Banco Nacional de Panamá, Av F, between C1/C2, Bocas del Toro, open Mon-Fri 0800-1500, Sat 0900-1200. At Changuinola: Banco del Istmo, open till 1500 weekdays, 1200 Sats, changes Amex TCs and cash advances on Visa and Mastercard.

● **Sports**
Diving: there are several places in the Bocas del Toro archipelago popular for diving. On Isla Colón, **A1** *Mangrove Inn Eco-Dive Resort*, T/F 757-9594, restaurant, office in Bocas del Toro, C 3 (Mangrove Roots Shop), with several good locations near the resort for tank diving and for snorkelling in the clear waters around Mangrove Point. Their dive shop, *Turtle Divers*, has equipment for sale and rent and arranges courses and excursions. They also have underwater photo equipment. Also in Bocas del Toro

town is *Bocas Dive Shop*, C 3, similar services, 2 dives US$35. Three neighbouring islands are also visited.

● **Transport**

Air Bocas del Toro and Changuinola can be reached by Aeroperlas from Paitilla Airport (US$42-47 one-way) and David. To David, 0800 Mon-Fri. Fare Changuinola-Bocas del Toro, US$8 one way.

Trains The banana railways provide links between Guabito on the Costa Rican frontier, Changuinola and Almirante. No passenger trains although passage can be negotiated with officials. Schedules and fares should be checked with the Chiriquí Land Company, T Almirante 758-3215.

Buses There is a road from Changuinola to Almirante (buses every 30 mins till 2000, 30 mins, US$1). Bus to San José leaves Changuinola 1000 daily US$7, 6-7 hrs, one stop for refreshments but many police checks.

From Chiriquí Grande in Bocas del Toro there is a spectacular road over the mountains, mostly paved but some rough stretches and some earthquake damage under repair, passing through virgin rain forest, the Cricamola Indian Reservation and the Fortuna hydroelectric plant, to Gualaca and finally Chiriquí on the Pan-American Highway E of David (the turn off is 10 km E of David, just after the Río Chiriquí bridge). Bus to David from Chiriquí Grande hourly to 1700 daily, 3 hrs, US$7. Bus Panama City to Changuinola via Chiriquí Grande, ferry to Almirante, then road, departs Panama City from C 30 between Hotels *Dos Mares* and *Soloy* at 0500, not on Mon; leaves Changuinola from *Tropicana* restaurant opp Banco Nacional, 0645, 19 hrs, US$22.

Boat Water taxis from Almirante to Bocas del Toro daily from 0700 till 1430, except Wed, 30 mins minimum, US$3. Water taxi Bocas del Toro direct to Chiriquí Grande, US$10, and from Almirante to Chiriquí Grande, frequent, 1½ hrs, US$10.

Vehicle ferry ('Palanga') from Almirante to Chiriquí daily (except Mon) at 0800, US$40/car, and US$4/adult, 5 hrs if lucky; ferry Chiriquí Grande-Almirante daily (except Mon), 1330. The car ferry calls at Bocas del Toro Fri and Sun at 0900 and, on the return trip, at 1700 back to Almirante.

To Bocas del Toro by canoe with outboard motor, US$10, or US$15 for 2. Hire boats or water taxis in Bocas del Toro to Bastimentos and the other islands. If going on to Costa Rica from

Bocas, get the first water taxi for connections at Sixaola. There is reported to be a ferry between Bocas de Toro and Colón at the weekends, US$22, but we await full information.

At the continental divide (Km 56 from Pan-American Highway) there is a good restaurant, *Mary's*, buses stop here. On the southern side of the Fortuna Reserve is **B** *Finca La Suiza*, T 774-3117, F Quadrifoglio, David (507) 774-4030, owned by a Swiss couple, Herbert Brüllmann and Monika Kohler, excellent for birdwatching on forest trails, very good food, comfortable accommodation with bath and hot water, breakfast US$3.50, dinner US$8.50. To get there from Gualaca: pass the sign to Los Planes (16.4 km) and the turning to Chiriquicito; 300m after this junction is the sign for the Fortuna Reserve, 1 km beyond the sign is the gate to the *Finca* on the right. From Chiriquí Grande, the entrance is 1 km on the David side of *Restaurant Mary*. There are basic rest stops with views of both oceans 20.5 and 22.5 km S of the continental divide. There is a 10m waterfall 3 km S of the divide. Going N from the continental divide to Chiriquí Grande is a cyclist's delight — good road, spectacular views, little traffic and downhill all the way.

FRONTIER WITH COSTA RICA – GUABITO

● **Panamanian immigration**

The border at Sixaola-Guabito is open 0800-1800 Panama time. Advance clocks 1 hr entering Panama. Formalities for entry/exit for each country are performed at either end of the banana train bridge which crosses the frontier. Just a short walk over the bridge; onward ticket may not be asked for on the Costa Rican side.

Entering Panama If you need a visa or tourist card, best to obtain it in San José. Entry charge normally US$0.75 (receipt given) although if you already have a visa you may not be charged, 30 days given if you already have a visa, 5 days' entry card if not, US$2 (extensions at Changuinola airport immigration, opens 0830 – 5 passport photos, photographer nearby charges US$7 for 6).

● **Accommodation**

No accommodation in **Guabito**, but if seeking cheap accommodation, cross border as early as possible in order to get as far as Almirante (US$1 by bus).

● **Transport**

The bus to and from Changuinola to the frontier is marked 'Las Tablas', US$0.75, 30 mins (every 30 mins until 1700), or colectivo taxi, US$1.25 pp (private taxi US$10). Bus to San José, Costa Rica, at 1000 and 1600, US$8, or to Puerto Viejo, US$6.

Darién and how to get to Colombia

THE PAN-AMERICAN Highway ends at Yaviza; from there, if you want to cross by land to South America, it's on foot through the jungles of Darién. Alternative routes to Colombia are also given.

BY LAND

The Pan-American Highway runs E 60 km from Panama City to the sizeable town of **Chepo**. There are no hotels or *pensiones* in Chepo, but if you are stuck there, ask at the fire station, they will be able to find a place for you. There is a document check in Chepo and at one or two other places. From Chepo the Highway has been completed as far as Yaviza (225 km); it is gravel from Chepo until the last 30 km which are of earth (often impassable in rainy season).

From **El Llano**, 18 km E of Chepo, a road goes N to the Caribbean coast. After 27 km it passes the *Nusagandi Nature Lodge* in the Pemansky Nature Park. The Lodge is in Cuna territory, in an area of mostly primary forest. Visits can be arranged through Centro de Aventuras, Parque Urracá, Panama City, T 225-8946, F 227-6477. The coast is reached at Cartí, 20 km from Nusagandi. From here there is access to the San Blas Archipelago.

35 km E of Chepo it crosses the new Lago Bayano dam by bridge (the land to the N of the Highway as far as Cañazas is the **Reserva Indígena del Bayano**). Lago Bayano dam supplies a significant amount of Panama's electricity, and has

been a source of friction with the Cuna Indians who occupy the land around the lake and especially above in the catchment area. However, it was hoped that a new Indigenous *Comarca*, to be created in 1996, will confirm the Indian title to the land and set up conservation measures.

● **Buses** From Piquera bus terminal in Panama City, buses leave every 2 hrs 0630-1430 for **Pacora**, US$0.80, **Chepo**, US$1.60, **Cañitas**, 4 hrs, US$3.10, **Arretí**, 6 hrs, US$9, **Metetí** and **Canglón**, 8 hrs, US$11.20. Beyond, to **Yaviza**, in the dry season only, Jan-April, US$15, 10 hrs minimum. Plenty of pick-ups run on the last stretch to Yaviza, eg about 3 hrs from Metetí to Yaviza.

DARIEN

East of Chepo is known as Darién, which is over a third of the area of Panama and almost undeveloped. Most villages are accessible only by air or river and on foot.

At the end of 1992, Panama and Colombia revealed a plan to build a road through the Darién Gap which includes environmental protection. Construction had been halted in the 1970s by a lawsuit filed by US environmental groups who feared deforestation, soil erosion, endangerment of indigenous groups and the

Cautions and general notes on crossing the Darién gap

In planning your trip by land or along the coast to Colombia, remember there are strict rules on entry into Colombia and you must aim for either Turbo or Buenaventura to obtain your entry stamp. Failure to do this will almost certainly involve you in significant fines, accusations of illegal entry, or worse in Colombia. Also, do not enter Darién without first obtaining full details of which areas to avoid because of the activities of drug traffickers, bandits and guerrilla groups, mostly from Colombia, but operating on both sides of the border. **Latest information from Colombia (mid 1997) is that armed groups, hostile to travellers including tourists, are particularly active in the NW corner of Colombia which includes the area on the Colombian side of the border. If information has not improved before you set out to cross Darién by land either way, you are advised not to go.**

The New Tribes Mission, after the kidnap of 3 missionaries, has withdrawn its staff from the area and therefore one of a traveller's main sources of assistance has disappeared.

1. The best time to go is in the dry months (Jan-mid April); in the wet season (from May) it is only rec for the hardy.
2. Travel with a reliable companion or two.
3. Talk to knowledgeable locals for the best advice. Hire at least one Indian guide, but do it through the village *corregidor*, whose involvement may add to the reliability of the guides he selects. (Budget up to US$8/day for the guide and his food. Negotiate with the chief, but do not begrudge the cost.)
4. Travel light and move fast. The journey as described below takes about 7 days to Turbo.
5. Maps of the Darién area can be purchased from the Ministro de Obras Públicas, Instituto Geográfico Nacional Tommy Guardia, in Panama City (US$4, reported to contain serious mistakes). Information is also available from Asociación de Conservación de la Naturaleza, C 53, Bella Vista, Panamá City.

threat of foot-and-mouth disease reaching the USA. Of course, the more people who walk the Darién Gap, the greater the pressure for building a road link. Consider, therefore, the environmental implications of crossing between Panama and Colombia just for the sake of it. The Darién Gap road linking Panama with Colombia will not be open for many years, though, so the usual way of getting to Colombia is by sea or air. It is possible to go overland, but the journey is in fact more expensive than going by air.

THE LAND ROUTE

The main villages (Yaviza, Púcuro, Paya and Cristales) have electricity, radios and cassette decks, canned food is available in Yaviza, Pinogana, Unión de Chocó,

Púcuro and Paya (but no gasoline), only the Emberá-Wunan (Chocó) and Cuna women retain traditional dress. Organized jungle tours to Cuna Indians, Emberá-Wunan Indians and the Río Bayano costing from US$65 to over US$300 can be purchased through *Mar Go Tours*, Aptdo 473, Balboa.

The bus service from Panama City (see above) has its problems, the road is bad and may be washed out after rains. Find out before you leave how far you can get. Alternatively there is an irregular boat to Yaviza, about once a week, US$12 including meals, leaving from the harbour by the market in the old city, information from Muelle Fiscal, C 13 next to the Mercado Público. The only sleeping accommodation is the deck (take a hammock)

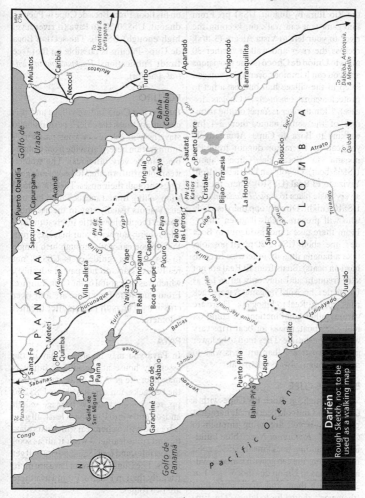

and there is one primitive toilet for about 120 people. The advertised travel time is 16 hrs, but it can take as much as 2 days.

YAVIZA/EL REAL

Another possibility is to fly to La Palma (see page 1219) and take the much shorter boat trip to Yaviza, or direct to El Real (3 a week, US$68 return), which is about 10 km from Yaviza. There is only one hotel at **Yaviza** (**E** *Tres Américas*, pay in *Casa Indira* shop next door, take mosquito coils – nowhere to hang a net, basic, noisy, meals available but not very sanitary); there is a TB clinic and a hospital. Crossing the river in Yaviza costs US$0.25. From Yaviza it is an easy 1-2 hrs' walk to **Pinogana** (small and primitive), where you have to cross the Río Tuira by dugout, US$1 pp. From Pinogana you can walk on, keeping the river to your left to Vista Alegre (3 hrs), recross the river and walk a further 30 mins to **Unión de Chocó** (some provisions and you can hammock overnight; you can sleep in the village hall but use a net to protect against *vinchucas* – Chagas disease). 1 km upriver is Yape, on the tributary of the same name, then 3-4 hrs walking to Boca de Cupe. Alternatively you can go by motor dugout from Pinogana to Boca de Cupe (about US$65/boat). Or you can take a boat from Yaviza to **El Real** (US$10), where there is a very basic place to stay, *El Nazareno*, for US$10 a night. Directly opp there is a lady who will prepare meals if given notice. From there take a motor dugout to Boca de Cupe, about US$15-20 pp (if possible, take a banana dugout, otherwise bargain hard on boats). Boats from El Real are not very frequent and may only go as far as Unión de Chocó or Pinogana. A jeep track runs from El Real to Pinogana. There are various other combinations of going on foot or by boat, prices for boat trips vary widely, so negotiate. They tend to be lower going downstream than up. It is wise to make payment always on arrival.

BOCA DE CUPE

Stay the night at **Boca de Cupe** with a family; food and cold beer on sale here (last possibility if you are going through to Colombia); *Restaurant Nena* (blue building near landing dock) meals US$2, good information. You can go with Emberá-Wunan Indians to Unión de Chocó, stay 1 or 2 days with them and share some food (they won't charge for lodging). The Emberá-Wunan are very friendly and shy, better not to take pictures. In Boca de Cupe get your exit stamp (though you may be told to get it at Púcuro) and keep your eye on your luggage. Lodging in Boca de Cupe for US$12.50 with Antonio (son of María who helped many hikers crossing Darién, but who died in 1989). Don Ramón will prepare meals for US$2 and let you sleep

on his floor. From Boca de Cupe to Púcuro, dugout, US$20-50, to Paya (if river level high enough) US$80. The section Boca de Cupe-Púcuro is possible on foot (see Bradt Publications' *Backpacking in Central America*).

PUCURO

Púcuro is a Cuna Indian village and it is customary to ask the chief's permission to stay (he will ask to see your passport – immigration here, if arriving from Colombia, can be very officious). The women wear colourful ornamented *molas* and gold rings through their noses. There is a small shop selling tinned meats, salted biscuits etc. Visitors usually stay in the assembly house. People show little interest in travellers there; stop with your luggage. From Púcuro you can walk through lush jungle to Paya, 6 hrs (guide costs US$20, not really necessary, do not pay in advance), which was the capital of the Cuna Empire. From Púcuro to Paya there are four river crossings. The path is clear after the first kilometre.

PAYA

In **Paya** you may be able to stay in the assembly house at the village, but it is mandatory to go 2 km away eastwards to the barracks. You can stay there, US$2.50 pp, rec (passport check, baggage search and, on entry into Panama at least, all gear is treated with a chemical which eats plastic and ruins leather – wash it off as soon as possible), and for US$2-2.50 you will get meals. The Cuna Indians in Paya are more friendly than in Púcuro. From Paya there are two routes.

Route 1

From Paya, the next step is a 4-6 hrs' walk to **Palo de las Letras**, the frontier stone, where you enter Los Katios, one of Colombia's National Parks (see below). The path is not difficult, but frequently blocked up to the frontier. From there you go down until you reach the left bank of the Río Tulé (in 3 hrs, no water between these points), you follow it downstream, which involves seven crossings (at the third crossing the trail almost disappears, so walk along the river bed – if possible – to the next crossing). If any of these watercourses are dry, watch out for snakes. About 30 mins after leaving this river you cross a small creek; 45 mins further on is the abandoned camp of the Montadero, near where the Tulé and Pailón rivers meet to form the Río Cacarica. Cross the Cacarica and follow the trail to the Inderena (Colombian National Parks) hut at **Cristales** (7 hrs from Palo de las Letras). Guides Paya-Cristales (they always go in pairs), US$55. If you insist on walking beyond Montadero, a machete, compass and fishing gear (or extra food) are essential; the path is so overgrown that it is easier, when the river is low, to walk and swim down it (Cristales is on the left bank, so perhaps it would be better to stick to this side). The rangers at Cristales (friendly) may sell you food, will let you sleep at the hut, cook, and will take you, or arrange a dugout to **Bijao** (or Viajado), 2 hrs, for around US$120 per boat. The rangers are often not there and there is no village nearby, so arrive prepared. It is possible to walk to Bijao down the right (W) bank of the Río Cacarica (heavy going). From the bend to the E of the river the path improves and it is 1 hr to Bijao. At Bijao ask for the Inderena station, where you can eat and sleep (floor space, or camp). From Bijao a motor dugout runs to **Travesía** (also called Puerto América) for US$30 pp (2-3 hrs), from where motorboats go to Turbo for US$6 to US$10 (in scheduled boat – if it stops; if not it'll cost you about US$130 to hire a boat). Bijao and Travesía have been reported as expensive and anti-gringo. Once again, there is a walking route S to Limón (2 hrs) and E to La Tapa (30 mins). A cargo boat may be caught from here to Turbo (price unknown). One *residencial* and a shop in Travesía. The last section from Travesía down the Atrato goes through an area full of birdlife, humming birds, kingfishers,

herons, etc, and 'screamers', about the size of turkeys and believed to be unique to the Atrato valley. The river enters the Great Atrato swamp and thence to the Bahía de Colombia. Turbo is on the opposite coast.

On arrival in Turbo, you must go to the DAS office at Postadero Naval, Cra 13 between Cs 101 and 102 (open 0800-1630), to get your entrance stamp. If you fail to do this, you will have to wait until Cartagena, or elsewhere, and then explain yourself in great detail to DAS and quite likely be fined. If you arrive at the weekend and the DAS is closed, make sure you obtain a letter or document from the police in Turbo that states when you arrived in Colombia. The problems with this route are mostly on the Colombian side, where route finding is difficult, the undergrowth very difficult to get through, and the terrain steep. Any rain adds greatly to the difficulties, though equally, when the water is low, boats need more pole assistance, and the cost increases.

If you are coming into Panama from Colombia by these routes, and you have difficulty in obtaining entry stamps at Púcuro or Boca de Cupe, obtain a document from an official en route stating when you arrived in Panama. This may be equally hard to get. Then go to the Oficina Nacional de Migración in Panama City (who may send you to the port immigration) and explain the problem. One traveller reports hearing of several arrests of travellers caught without their entry stamp. Many of these 'illegals' stay arrested for weeks. It may help to be able to prove that you have sufficient money to cover your stay in Panama.

The **Katios National Park** (**Warning**: entry by motorized vehicle is prohibited), extending in Colombia to the Panamanian border, can be visited with mules from the Inderena headquarters in Sautatá (rangers may offer free accommodation, very friendly). In the park is the Tilupo waterfall, 125m high; the water cascades down a series of rock staircases, surrounded by orchids and fantastic plants. Also in the park are the Alto de la Guillermina, a mountain behind which is a strange forest of palms called 'mil pesos', and the Ciénagas de Tumaradó, with red monkeys, waterfowl and alligators.

Route 2

The second route is a stenuous hike up the Río Paya valley through dense jungle (machete country) for about 16 hrs to the last point on the Paya (fill up with water), then a further 3 hrs to the continental divide where you cross into Colombia. Down through easier country (3-4 hrs) brings you to **Unguía** (accommodation, restaurants) where motor boats are available to take you down the Río Tarena, out into the Gulf of Urabá, across to Turbo. This trip should not be taken without a guide, though you may be lucky and find an Indian, or a group of Indians making the journey and willing to take you along. They will appreciate a gift when you arrive in Unguía. Hazards include blood-sucking ticks, the inevitable mosquitoes and, above all, thirst.

There are many other possible routes from Panama crossing the land frontier used by locals. Most involve river systems and are affected by water levels. There are few tracks and no reliable maps. We have heard of successful crossings using the Ríos Salaqui and Balsas, and a land route Jaqué-Jurado-Riosucio. Good guides and serious planning are essential.

HEALTH ADVICE

Dr Richard Dawood, author of *Travellers' Health: How to Stay Healthy Abroad*, and photographer Anthony Dawton, crossed the Darién Gap at the end of the wet season (Nov). We are pleased to include Dr Dawood's health recommendations for such a journey.

Heat

Acclimatization to a hot climate usually takes around 3 weeks. It is more difficult in humid climates than in dry ones, since sweat cannot evaporate easily, and when high humidity persists through the night as well, the body has no respite. (In desert conditions, where the temperature falls at night, adaptation is much easier.) Requirements for salt and water increase dramatically under such conditions. We had to drink 12 litres/day to keep pace with our own fluid loss on some parts of the trip.

We were travelling under extreme conditions, but it is important to remember that the human thirst sensation is not an accurate guide to true fluid requirements. In hot countries it is always essential to drink beyond the point of thirst quenching, and to drink sufficient water to ensure that the urine is consistently pale in colour.

Salt losses also need to be replaced. Deficiency of salt, water, or both, is referred to as heat exhaustion; lethargy, fatigue, and headache are typical features, eventually leading to coma and death. Prevention is the best approach, and we used the pre-salted water regime pioneered by Colonel Jim Adam and followed by the British Army; salt is added to all fluids, one quarter of a level teaspoon (approx 1 gram) per pint – to produce a solution that is just below the taste theshold. Salt tablets, however, are poorly absorbed, irritate the stomach and may cause vomiting; plenty of pre-salted fluid should be the rule for anyone spending much time outdoors in the tropics. (Salted biscuits are recommended by Darién travellers.)

Sun

Overcast conditions in the tropics can be misleading. The sun's rays can be fierce, and it is important to make sure that all exposed skin is constantly protected with a high factor sun screen – preferably waterproof for humid conditions. This was especially important while we were travelling by canoe. A hat was also essential.

Food and water

Diarrhoea can be annoying enough in a

luxurious holiday resort with comfortable sanitary facilities. The inconvenience under jungle conditions would have been more than trivial, however, with the added problem of coping with further fluid loss and dehydration.

Much caution was therefore needed with food hygiene. We carried our own supplies, which we prepared carefully ourselves: rather uninspiring camping fare, such as canned tuna fish, sardines, pasta, dried soup, biscuits and dried fruit. In the villages, oranges, bananas and coconuts were available. The freshly baked bread was safe, and so would have been the rice.

We purified our water with 2% tincture of iodine carried in a small plastic dropping bottle, 4 drops to each litre – more when the water is very turbid – wait 20 mins before drinking. This method is safe and effective, and is the only suitable technique for such conditions. (Another suggestion from Peter Ovenden is a water purifying pump based on a ceramic filter. There are several on the market, Peter used a Katadyn. It takes about a minute to purify a litre of water. When the water is cloudy, eg after rain, water pumps are less effective and harder work. Take purification tablets as back up – Ed.) It is also worth travelling with a suitable antidiarrhoeal medication such as Arret.

Malaria

Chloroquine resistant malaria is present in the Darién area, so appropriate antimalarial medication is essential. We took Paludrine, two tablets daily, and chloroquine, two tablets weekly. Free advice on antimalarial medication for all destinations is available from the Malaria Reference Laboratory, T 0891 600 350 in the UK. An insect repellent is also essential, and so are precautions to avoid insect bites.

Insects

Beside malaria and yellow fever, other insect-borne diseases such as dengue fever and leishmaniasis may pose a risk. The old fashioned mosquito net is ideal if you have to sleep outdoors, or in a room that is not mosquito-proof. Mosquito nets for hammocks are widely available in Latin America. An insecticide spray is valuable for clearing your room of flying insects before you go to sleep, and mosquito coils that burn through the night giving off an insecticidal vapour, are also valuable.

Ticks

It is said that ticks should be removed by holding a lighted cigarette close to them, and we had an opportunity to put this old remedy to the test. We duly unwrapped a pack of American duty-frees that we had preserved carefully in plastic just for such a purpose, as our Indian guides looked on in amazement, incredulous that we should use these prized items for such a lowly purpose. The British Army expedition to Darién in 1972 carried 60,000 cigarettes among its supplies, and one wonders if they were for this purpose! The cigarette method didn't work, but caused much amusement. (Further discussion with the experts indicates that the currently favoured method is to ease the tick's head gently away from the skin with tweezers.) New advice from Dr Hollins of Stockbridge, England is that cigarettes are definitely a no-no since it roasts the tick but leaves the mouthpiece in the skin. In the jungle, this could lead to a dangerous tropical ulcer. Ticks breathe through small openings in the skin. Smoothing with oil or vaseline will kill the tick and release the mouthparts. So too will alcohols. When removing, don't pull straight – the best way to break off the head – but gently and firmly twist to left or right while pulling to dislodge the barbs. Use tweezers, as close to the tiny head as possible.

Vaccinations

A yellow fever vaccination certificate is required from all travellers arriving from infected areas, and vaccination is advised for personal protection.

Immunization against hepatitis A (see **Health information** in the Horizons) and typhoid are strongly advised.

Attacks by dogs are relatively common: the new rabies vaccine is safe and effective, and carrying a machete for the extra purpose of discouraging animals is advised.

In addition, all travellers should be protected against tetanus, diptheria and polio.

You can get some food along the way, but take enough for at least 5 days. Do take, though, a torch/flashlight, and a bottle of rum (or similar!) for the ranger at Cristales and useful items for others who give help and information. Newspapers are of interest to missionaries etc. A compass can save your life in the remoter sections if you are without a guide – getting lost is the greatest danger according to the rangers. It is highly recommended to travel in the dry season only, when there is no mud and fewer mosquitoes. A hammock can be very useful. If you have time, bargains can be found, but as pointed out above, costs of guides and water transport are steadily increasing. Buying pesos in Panama is recommended as changing dollars when you enter Colombia will be at poor rates. You will need small denomination dollar notes on the trip.

Taking a motorcycle through Darién is not an endeavour to be undertaken lightly, and cannot be recommended. The late Ed Culberson (who, in 1986 after two unsuccessful attempts, was the first to accomplish the feat) wrote: 'Dry season passage is comparatively easy on foot and even with a bicycle. But it simply cannot be done with a standard sized motorcycle unless helped by Indians at a heavy cost in dollars ... It is a very strenuous, dangerous adventure, often underestimated by motorcyclists, some of whom have come to untimely ends in the jungle.' Culberson's account of his journey (in the Oct 1986 issue of *Rider* and in a book, *Obsessions Die Hard*, published 1991 by Teakwood Press, 160 Fiesta Drive, Kissimmee, Fla, USA, 34743, T (407) 348-7330), makes harrowing reading, not least his

encounter with an emotionally unstable police official in Bijao; the 46-km 'ride' from Púcuro to Palo de las Letras took 6 days with the help of six Indians (at US$8 a day each). Two riders were caught in an early start of rains in 1991 and barely escaped with their machines.

Not to be outdone, crossing by bicycle has been successfully completed.

BY SEA

The new ferry service, that commenced in Dec 1994, from Colón to Cartagena, Colombia was suspended in Nov 1996. The reasons are not clear, and hopes are expressed in Panama and Colombia that it will be restarted in the near future. The service was much appreciated by our readers both for its quality and its convenience for travellers with and without vehicles. At the time of writing, information was available at: Torre Banco Unión, p 4, Zona 7, Apdo 8379, F 263-3326, T 263-3323 (Panamá), T 441-6311 (Colón).

There are about two boats a week from Colón for San Andrés Island, Colombia, from which there are connections with Cartagena; the *Johnny Walker* takes 30 hrs, but the service is very irregular and travellers have sometimes waited over a week in vain. There are (contraband) boats from Coco Solo, Colón, to the Guajira Peninsula, Colombia. 3-day journey, uncomfortable, and entirely at your own risk; captains of these boats are reluctant to carry travellers (and you may have to wait days for a sailing – the customs officials will let you sleep in the wind-shadow of their office, will watch your luggage and let you use the sanitary facilities). A passenger travelling in a contraband boat had some problems in the DAS office about getting an entrance stamp: they wanted official papers from the boat's captain showing that he brought him in. You have to bargain for your fare on these boats. Accommodation is a little primitive. For shipping a vehicle now to Colombia, see below.

PUERTO OBALDIA

Boats also leave, irregularly, from the Coco Solo wharf in Colón (minibus from C 12, 15 mins, US$0.80, taxi US$4) for **Puerto Obaldía**, via the San Blas Islands. These are small boats and give a rough ride in bad weather, cost around US$30 pp, take your own food, water and shade; with stops, 2-4 days. There are flights with Ansa (T 226-7891/6881) and Transpasa (T 226-0932/0843) at 0600-0630 from Paitilla, Panama City to Puerto Obaldía daily except Sun for US$40 single (book well in advance). There are also flights with Aerotaxi and Saansa. Puerto Obaldía is a few kilometres from the Colombian border. There are *expresos* (speedboats) from Puerto Obaldía (after clearing Customs) to Capurganá, and then another on to Acandí (**F** *Hotel Central*, clean, safe; **G** *Hotel Pilar*, safe). From Acandí you can go on to Turbo, on the Gulf of Urabá, no fixed schedule (you cannot get to Turbo in the same day, take shade and drinks and be prepared for seasickness). From Turbo, Medellín can be reached by road. Walk from Puerto Obaldía to Zapzurro, just beyond the frontier, for a dugout to Turbo, US$10, where you must get your Colombia entry stamp. It seems that most of the boats leaving Puerto Obaldía for Colombian ports are contraband boats. One traveller obtained an unnecessary visa (free) from the Colombian consul in Puerto Obaldía which proved to be useful in Colombia where soldiers and police took it to be an entry stamp.

● **Accommodation** There is a good *pensión* in Puerto Obaldía: **E** *Residencia Cande*, nice and clean, which also serves very good meals for US$1.50, book in advance for meals.

● **Useful services** Also in Puerto Obaldía are shops, Colombian consulate, Panamanian immigration, but nowhere to change TCs until well into Colombia (not Turbo); changing cash is possible. (**NB** Arriving in Puerto Obaldía you have to pass through the military control for baggage search, immigration – proof of funds and onward ticket asked for, and malaria control.)

CAPURGANA (COLOMBIA)

Alternatively one can get from Puerto Obaldía to Acandí on the Colombian side of the border, either by walking 9 hrs or by hiring a dugout or a launch to Capurganá (US$60), thence another launch at 0715, 1 hr, US$3. Several hotels in **Capurganá**, **B** *Calypso*, also with a Medellín number for reservations, 250-3921, **D** *Náutico*, **E** *Uvita*, clean, safe, **E** *Al Mar*. There are cheaper *pensiones* and you can camp near the beach. Good snorkelling. There is a Panamanian consul in Capurganá (Roberto) who issues Panamanian visas. There are Twin Otter flights to Medellín. To walk to Capurganá takes 4 hrs, guide recommended (they charge US$10); first to go to La Miel (2 hrs), then to Zapzurro (20 mins), where there are shops and cabins for rent, then 1-1½ hrs to Capurganá. Most of the time the path follows the coast, but there are some hills to cross (which are hot – take drinking water). From Acandí a daily boat is scheduled to go at 0800 to Turbo (US$9, 3 hrs). Take pesos, if possible, to these Colombian places, the rate of exchange for dollars is poor.

On the Pacific side, there is another possible route to Colombia. Although not quick, it is relatively straightforward (spoken Spanish is essential). Take a bus from Panama (Plaza 5 de Mayo) to **Metetí**, 50 km from Yaviza (**F** *Hospedaje Feliz*, basic 'box' rooms), the junction for transport to **Puerto Quimba**, where boats can be taken to La Palma. Alternatively, take a bus to **Santa Fe**, which is 100 km short of Yaviza and off to the S, a rough but scenic 6-8 hrs (US$8, 3 a day, check times). In Santa Fe it is possible to camp near the national guard post (no *pensiones*). Then hitch a ride on a truck (scarce), or walk 2 hrs to the Río Sabanas at Puerto Lardo (11 km) where you must take a dugout or launch to La Palma, or hire one (US$5, 2 hrs; also reached by boat from Yaviza, US$3, 8 hrs – bank changes TCs in La Palma). **La Palma** is the capital of Darién; it has one *pensión* (friendly,

English-speaking owners, **F**, pricey, with cooking and laundry facilities, or see if you can stay with the *guardia*). There are daily Aeroperlas flights from Panama City to La Palma, US$31, and to Jaqué, US$37 3 days a week; also to Yaviza 3 days a week, but check with the airline Parsa, T 226-3883/3803. They have an office at the Paitilla airport in Panama City. It is not clear if you can get a plane from La Palma to Jaqué, but there are boats. **Jaqué** is on the Pacific coast, near Puerto Piña, 50 km N of the Colombian border. At **Bahía Piña** is the *Tropic Star Lodge*, T 264-5549, where a luxury fishing holiday may be enjoyed on the sea and in the jungle for over US$1,000 a week. (Information from *Hotel El Panamá*.) Bahía Piña has a 700m runway, used mainly by the expensive fishing resort.

Alternatively, at the Muelle Fiscal in Panama City (next to the main waterfront market, near C 13), ask for a passenger boat going to Jaqué. The journey takes 18 hrs, is cramped and passengers cook food themselves, but costs only US$12. Jaqué (*pop* 1,000) is only reached by sea or air (the airstrip is used mostly by the wealthy who come for sport fishing); there are small stores with few fruit and vegetables, a good *comedor*, one *hospedaje*, **F** *Hospedaje Chauela*, clean, basic, friendly (but it is easy to find accommodation with local families, and camping is possible anywhere on the beautiful 4 km beach. The guard post is open every day and gives exit stamps. Canoes from Jaqué go to Jurado (US$20, 4½ hrs) or Bahía Solano (US$45, 160 km, with two overnight stops) in Chocó. The first night is spent in Jurado (where the boat's captain may put you up and the local military commander may search you out of curiosity). There are flights from Jurado to Turbo, but it is possible to get 'stuck' in Jurado for several days. Bahía Solano is a deep-sea fishing resort with an airport and *residencias*. Flights from Bahía Solano go to Quibdó, connecting to Cali, or Medellín (all flights have to be booked in

advance; the town is popular with Colombian tourists). On this journey, you sail past the lush, mountainous Pacific coast of Darién and Chocó, with its beautiful coves and beaches, and you will see a great variety of marine life.

NB It is not easy to get a passage to any of the larger Colombian ports as the main shipping lines rarely take passengers. Those that do are booked up well in advance. The Agencias Panamá company, Muelle 18, Balboa, represents Delta Line and accepts passengers to Buenaventura. Anyone interested in using the Delta Line ships should book a passage before arriving in Panama. The only easy way of getting to Colombia is to fly (see **Air Services** in **Information for travellers**).

Shipping agencies do not have the authority to charge passages. Many travellers think they can travel as crew on cargo lines, but this is not possible because Panamanian law requires all crew taken on in Panama to be Panamanian nationals.

Colombia officially demands an exit ticket from the country. If you travel by air the tickets should be bought outside Panama and Colombia, which have taxes on all international air tickets. If you buy air tickets from IATA companies, they can be refunded. Copa tickets can be refunded in Cartagena (C Santos de Piedra 3466 – takes 4 days), Barranquilla – 2 days, Cali or Medellín. Refunds in pesos only. Copa office in Panama City, Av Justo Arosemena y C 39, T 227-5000.

SHIPPING A VEHICLE

The easiest way to ship a vehicle from Panama to Colombia was the *Crucero Express* ferry which has, unfortunately been suspended (see **By Sea** above). First, enquire if this option has been restored. Failing that, taking a vehicle to Colombia, Venezuela or Ecuador is not easy or cheap. The best advice is to shop around the agencies in Panama City or Colón to see what is available when you want to go.

Both local and international lines take vehicles, and sometimes passengers, but schedules and prices are very variable. To **Colombia**, agents include: Sudamericana de Vapores, T 229-3844, Cristóbal-Buenaventura, Boyd Steamship Corporation, T 263- 6311, Balboa-Buenaventura or Guayaquil. To Barranquilla: Vicente Simones, T Colón 195-1262, beeper 270-0000, code 700283, will arrange all paperwork for US$25: car passage US$800, motorcycle US$50, plus US$50/passenger, no accommodation on ship other than hammock space, take food and drink for a week (even though voyage should be 3 days). To Cartagena, Captain Newball, Edif Los Cristales, p 3, C 38 y Av Cuba, Panama City. On the same route Central American Lines sail once a week, agent in Panama, T Colón 441-2880, Panama City 236-1036. Also, Geminís Shipping Co SA, Apdo Postal No 3016, Zona Libre de Colón, Rep de Panamá, T 441-6269/6959, F 441-6571. Mr Ricardo Gil was helpful and reliable. If sending luggage separately, make enquiries at Tocumen airport, eg Tampa, T 238-4439.

One alternative is to try to ship on one of the small freighters that occasionally depart from Coco Solo Wharf in Colón for Turbo in Colombia, which allow you to travel with your car. Obviously there is a considerable element of risk involved (suspect cargo, crews and seaworthiness), though the financial cost is lower than on a regular line.

Once you have a bill of lading, have it stamped by a Colombian consulate. Note that the Colombian consul in Colón will only stamp a bill of lading if the carrier is going to Cartagena or Barranquilla. The consulate also provides tourist cards. They require proof, in the form of a letter from your Embassy (or the Embassy representing your country in Panama) that you do not intend to sell the car in Colombia, though this requirement is usually dispensed with. Then go to the customs office in Panama City (C 80 and 55) to have the vehicle cleared for export.

After that the vehicle details must be removed from your passport at the customs office at the port of departure. In Colón the customs office is behind the post office; in Cristóbal, at the entrance to the port on your left. The utmost patience is needed for this operation as regulations change frequently.

Some small freighters go only to intermediate ports such as San Andrés, and it is then necessary to get another freighter to Cartagena. Navieras Mitchell ship cars regularly to San Andrés and Barranquilla. Office at Coco Solo Wharf, T 441-6942. You may have to wait up to a week in San Andrés to make the onward connection. From Colón to San Andrés takes 2 days and from San Andrés to Cartagena takes 3 days. There are two boats plying regularly between Colón (Pier 3) and San Andrés that are big enough for vans, but there is no schedule; they leave when they finish loading. There are also two regular boats between San Andrés and Cartagena; each stays in port about 15 days, but it can be longer. Shipping companies on San Andrés know that they have a monopoly, so take care when dealing with them and do not believe all they tell you.

Customs formalities at the Colombian end will take 1-3 days to clear (customs officials do not work at weekends). Make sure the visa you get from the Colombian consulate in Colón is *not* a 15 day non-extendable transit visa, but a regular tourist visa, because it is difficult to get an extension of the original visa. Clearance from the Colombian consul at the Panamanian port of embarkation may reduce the bureaucracy when you arrive in Colombia, but it will cost you US$10. In Colombia you have to pay US$15/cu m for handling, as well as other document charges. An agent can reduce the aggravation but neither the waiting time, nor the cost (they charge US$55-70/day). Get as much help as possible inside the port; outside they only want your money, in Buenaventura at least. It is understood that Cartagena is much more efficient (and therefore less expensive) as far as paperwork is concerned. Apparently the delays and redtape at either end of the passage to Colombia may be reduced if you have a *Carnet de Passages*. The *Carnet* will exempt you from the bond of 10% of the vehicle's value.

To **Ecuador**: TNE (Transportes Navieros Ecuatorianos, T 269-2022) ship vehicles to Guayaquil; agent in Cristóbal, Agencia Continental SA, T 445-1818. Another agent rec in Cristóbal: Wilford & McKay, in front of *La Fortuna* restaurant, 2 blocks from the bus station, contact Sr Rosas or María del Carmen, T 445-0461. Customs agents cost US$60 in Colón, US$120 in Guayaquil; 12 days from starting arrangements in Panama to leaving Guayaquil docks. Seek advice on paperwork from the Ecuadorean consul in Panama. Barwil (T Panama City 263-7755, Colón 441-5533) will ship vehicles to Arica, **Chile**, rec.

It is also possible to ship a vehicle to **Venezuela**, from Cristóbal usually to La Guaira, but Puerto Cabello is possible. Agents include: Cia Transatlántica España, T 269-6300, to La Guaira. Also Barwil Agencies, T 263-7755 (see above). Also Vencaribe (a Venezuelan line), agent in Cristóbal: Associated Steamship, T 252-1258 (Panamá), T 445-0461 (Cristóbal). There are several agencies in Colón/Cristóbal across the street from the Chase Manhattan Bank and next door to the YMCA building. Formalities before leaving can be completed through a travel agency – recommended is Continental Travel Agency, at the *Hotel Continental*, T 263-6162 – Rosina Wong was very helpful.

Warning The contents of your vehicle are shipped at your own risk – generally considered to be a high one! Anything loose, tools, seat belts, etc, is liable to disappear, or to be swapped for an inferior replacement (eg spare tyre). One reader who escaped theft had chained two padlocked, wooden boxes to the car seats.

AIR-FREIGHTING A VEHICLE

Most people ship their vehicles from Panama to South America by sea but some find air-freighting much more convenient. Generally it is faster and avoids many of the unpleasant customs hassles, but is more expensive. Prices vary considerably. The major carriers, if they permit it on a regular commercial flight, tend to charge more than the cargo lines and independents. Prices and availability change from month to month depending on the demand by regular commercial shippers. You are generally not allowed to accompany the vehicle. For Copa Cargo, T 238-4414, Tocumen airport, talk to Otto Littman. Varig will ship vehicles to Brazil (Rio), Buenos Aires or Santiago de Chile.

Taking a motorcycle from Panama to Colombia can only be done on a cargo flight. Drain oil and gasoline, and remove battery before loading; the bike goes in with just an inch to spare so you must expect a scratch or two. Insist on loading the bike yourself. Having bought your passenger ticket, and checked your bike in at the carrier's office, go to customs in Paitilla airport (see page 1172) with your entry permit and freight papers, and pay US$4.20 to have the stamp cancelled in your passport. You may have to take your airweighbill to the Colombian Consulate for stamping 3 hrs before flight time. Allow 2 days in Panama. Retrieving the bike in Colombia, although costing very little (US$10 approx), will take from 0900 to 1630 for paperwork (or up to 2 days if there are any peculiarities in your documents).

Information for travellers

BEFORE TRAVELLING

ENTRY REQUIREMENTS
● Documents
Visitors must have a passport, together with a tourist card (issued for 30 days and renewable for another 60 in the Immigration Office, Panama City, see below) or a visa (issued for 30 days, extendable to 90 days in Panama). Tourist cards are available at borders, from Panamanian consulates, Ticabus or airlines. According to the Panamanian consulate in London, to enter Panama you must have an onward flight ticket, travel agent confirmation of same, or, if entering by land, sufficient funds to cover your stay (US$550, or US$330 if you have an onward ticket). 'Sufficient funds' do not have to be in cash; credit cards and TCs accepted. At Puerto Obaldía (Darién), both an onward ticket and funds are asked for. Once in Panama, you cannot get a refund for an onward flight ticket unless you have another exit ticket. Copa tickets can be refunded at any office in any country (in the currency of that country), but it can take 5 days to get your money back in Panama compared with 2 days in San José, Costa Rica. **Customs at Paso Canoas**, at the border with Costa Rica, have been known to run out of tourist cards. If not entering Panama at the main entry points (Tocumen airport, Paso Canoas), expect more complicated arrangements.

Neither visas nor tourist cards are required by nationals of Austria, Chile, Costa Rica, El Salvador, Finland, Germany, Honduras, Spain, Switzerland and the UK. US citizens may enter on a tourist card obtained at port of entry.

Citizens of the following countries need a visa which is free: the Netherlands, Norway, Denmark, Colombia and Mexico. Before visiting Panama it is advisable to enquire at a Panamanian consulate whether you need a visa stamped in your passport, or whether a tourist card will suffice.

A visa costing the local equivalent of US$10 must be obtained by all other nationals. These can be purchased with minimum delay by citizens of countries, not named above, in Central and South America, the EU, the Caribbean Islands, Australia, New Zealand, Canada, Japan, Israel, Dominican Republic and some others. However, visas for citizens of many African, Eastern European and Asian countries require authorization from Panama, which takes 3-5 days (this includes Hong Kong, India, Poland, the former Soviet republics, and also Cuba and South Africa).

30-day tourist cards can be renewed for another 60 days; requirements are 2 passport photos. A ticket out of the country, a letter explaining why you wish to extend your stay, and proof of sufficient funds may be asked for. There are similar requirements for renewing a visa but including two photocopies of the original visa. Renewals are obtainable from Dirección de Migración y Naturalización. Tourists who stay more than 30 days will require an exit visa, obtainable from Migración on presentation of a 'Paz y Salvo' tax-compliance slip obtained previously from Hacienda y Tesoro, Av Perú, C 35, or provincial offices.

● **Representation overseas**

UK, 40 Hertford St, London W1Y 7TG, T 0171-409-2255, F 0171-493-4499, open 1000-1200, 1400-1600. There are embassies/consulates in most European countries, throughout the Americas, and selected countries elsewhere.

● **Tourist information**

See under Panama City for address of IPAT, Instituto Panameño de Turismo. In USA: Laura Haayen, 1110 Brickell Ave, Suite 103, Miami, FL 33131, T (305) 579-2001, F 579-0910.

HEALTH

No particular precautions are necessary. Water in Panama City and Colón is safe to drink. In smaller towns, it is best to drink boiled or bottled water to avoid minor problems caused by indifferently maintained municipal distribution systems. Yellow fever vaccination is recommended before visiting Darién. Malaria prophylaxis for that area is highly recommended. It is currently very difficult to obtain chloroquine in Panama; stock up before arrival. In fact, stock up with all medicines, they are very costly in Panama. Tampons are available in larger towns at the same price as in UK. Hospital treatment is also expensive; insurance underwritten by a US company would be of great help.

MONEY

● **Currency**

The unit of currency in Panama is the Balboa (B/.), but Panama is one of the few countries in the world which issues no paper money; US banknotes are used exclusively. There are 'silver' coins of 50c (called a *peso*), 25c (called *cinco reales* or *cuara*, from US 'quarter'), 10c, nickel of 5c (called a *real*) and copper of 1c. All coins are used interchangeably with US equivalents, which are the same in size and composition. There is great reluctance in Panama to accept US$50 and US$100 dollar notes because of counterfeiting. Do not be offended if asked to produce ID and sign a register when spending them. Easier to use US$20, 10, 5 and 1 notes. You can take in or out any amount of foreign or Panamanian currency. If travelling N remember that US dollar notes, especially smaller denominations, are useful in all Central American countries and may be difficult to obtain in the other republics. Having a supply of US$5 and US$1 notes greatly facilitates border crossings and traffic problems in Central America where 'fees' and 'instant fines' can become exorbitant if you only have a US$20 note.

● **ATMs**

Visa ATMs are available at branches of Telered (T 001-800-111-0016 if card is lost or stolen). Mastercard/Cirrus ATMs are available at Caja de Ahorros offices and others in the Pronto system. See under **Banks & money changers**, Panama City, for other ATMs and for credit card phone numbers. For Western Union, T 269-1055.

● **Cost of living**

Living is costly, although food is much the same price as in Costa Rica. US military personnel buy their supplies at low prices in special stores. These facilities are not available to tourists. The annual average increase in consumer prices fluctuates in line with US trends.

GETTING THERE

BY AIR

● **From Europe**

British Airways, American, Delta, Continental or Virgin Atlantic from London to Miami, then by American, Copa, or LAB to Panama City. Iberia (Madrid via Miami), KLM (from Amsterdam).

● **From USA**

New York City, Continental direct, or American via Miami, Taca, change planes in El Salvador, or Lacsa, change planes in San José; from Los Angeles, Aviateca (4 stops), Eva Airlines (direct) or Lacsa (via San José); from Houston, Continental, Taca. American flies from Washington and Chicago via Miami. For other US cities, connections are made in Miami.

● **From Latin America**

From Central America, Copa, Lacsa (to San José, to connect with its Central American network and Los Angeles/Mexico/Miami/New Orleans/San Juan-Puerto Rico routes), Taca (inc to Belize) and Nica. There are no direct flights to Tegucigalpa, only Lacsa with connection in San José or Taca in San Salvador, but Copa flies direct to San Pedro Sula. Copa also flies to Havana, Kingston and Santo Domingo. From Mexico, AeroPerú/Servivensa, Copa, LAB, or connections with Lacsa via San José, or Taca via San Salvador. From South America, Lacsa (Barranquilla, Caracas, Lima, Santiago de Chile), Copa (Barranquilla, Bogotá, Caracas, Cartagena, Cali, Lima, Medellín, Quito, Guayaquil). **NB** One-way tickets are not available from Colombia to Panama, on SAM, or Copa, but a refund on an unused return portion is possible, less 17% taxes, on SAM. To Bogotá direct with Avianca and Aces, be at airport very early because it can leave before time; also to Cali with Intercontinental. To Guayaquil and Quito, Continental and Tame. Cubana and Tame fly direct to and from Havana once a week. Other carriers are Air Europa (to Cartagena), Lloyd Aéreo Boliviano, SAM, AeroPerú.

CUSTOMS

Even if you only change planes in Panama you must have the necessary papers for the airport officials. The Panamanian Customs are strict; drugs without a doctor's prescription are confiscated. Books deemed 'subversive' are no longer confiscated.

● Duty free allowance

Cameras, binoculars, etc, 500 cigarettes or 500 grams of tobacco and 3 bottles of alcoholic drinks for personal use are taken in free. **NB** Passengers leaving Panama by land are *not* entitled to any duty-free goods, which are delivered only to ships and aircraft.

ON ARRIVAL

● Clothing

Light weight tropical type clothes for men, light cotton or linen dresses for women, for whom the wearing of trousers is quite OK. The dry season, Jan-April, is the pleasantest time. Heaviest rainfall is in Oct and November.

● Hours of business

Government departments, 0800-1200, 1230-1630 (Mon to Fri). Banks: open and close at different times, but are usually open all morning, often on Sat. Shops and most private enterprises: 0700 or 0800-1200 and 1400-1800 or 1900 every day, inc Sat.

Business interests are concentrated in Panama City and Colón.

● Official time

GMT minus 5 hrs.

● Tipping

In restaurants: 10% of bill. Porters, 15 cents/item, but US$1 would be expected for assistance at the airport. Cloakroom, 25 cents. Hairdressers, 25 cents. Cinema usherettes, nothing. Taxi drivers don't expect tips, but see **Taxis** under Panama City.

● Voltage

US-style 110 volt, 60 Hz AC throughout the country. 220 volt is occasionally available in homes and hotels.

● Weights and measures

Both metric and the US system are used.

ON DEPARTURE

● Airport tax

An airport exit tax of US$20 has to be paid by all passengers (cash only). There is a 5.5% tax on air tickets purchased in Panama.

FOOD AND DRINK

● Food

The staple of Panamanian food is white rice, grown not in paddies but on dry land, and usually served at every meal, often with the addition of chicken, shrimp, vegetables, etc. Meat is usually fried (*frita*) or braised (*guisada*), rarely grilled. Beef is common, but poor in quality. Pork, chicken and fish are usually to be preferred.

Best hors d'oeuvre is *carimañola*, cooked mashed yuca wrapped round a savoury filling of chopped seasoned fried pork and fried a golden brown. The traditional stew, *sancocho*, made from chicken, yuca, dasheen, cut-up corn on the cob, plantain, potatoes, onions, flavoured with salt, pepper and coriander. *Ropa vieja*, shredded beef mixed with fried onions, garlic, tomatoes and green peppers and served with white rice, baked plantain or fried yuca. *Sopa borracha*, a rich sponge cake soaked in rum and garnished with raisins and prunes marinated in sherry. Panama is famous for its seafood: lobsters, corvina, red snapper (called *pargo rojo* in Panama, *huachinango* in Mexico), shrimp, tuna, etc. Piquant *ceviche* is usually corvina or shellfish seasoned with tiny red and yellow peppers, thin slices of onion and marinated in lemon juice; it is served very cold and has a bite. *Arroz con coco y tití* is rice with coconut and tiny dried shrimp. Plain coconut rice is also delicious. For low budget try *comida corriente* or *del día* (US$1.50 or so). Corn (maize) is eaten in various forms, depending on season, eg *tamales* (or *bollos*), made of corn meal mash filled with cooked chicken or pork, olives and prunes. Unlike Central American *tortillas*, the Panamanian version is a thick, fried corn-meal cake, usually served for breakfast. *Empanadas*, toothsome meat or sweetened fruit pies are made from wheat flour, fried crisp. Plantain, used as a vegetable, appears in various forms. A fine dessert is made from green plantain flour served with coconut cream. Other desserts are *arroz con cacao*, chocolate rice pudding;

buñuelos de viento, a puffy fritter served with syrup; *sopa de gloria*, sponge cake soaked in cooked cream mixture with rum added; *guanábana* ice cream is made from sweet ripe soursop.

GETTING AROUND

AIR TRANSPORT

Aeroperlas, the local airline which operates most domestic flights, is safe and reasonable, but service is basic. Paid ticket required to confirm reservations, as locals tend to make reservations they neither use nor cancel. Flights reported fully-booked in advance very often have seats available; show up 1-2 hrs early and register on Lista de Espera. Booking through travel agents recommended. Ticket counter and security personnel sometimes poorly trained. The main terminal at Paitilla airport has inadequate seating and neither baggage handlers, long-distance payphone for calling ahead, nor taxi rank. Arrange in advance to be picked up on arrival, especially in the evening and in the rainy season. Luggage pick-up is outdoors, wet and disorganized, but claim checks are verified.

There are local flights to most parts of Panama by the airlines Ansa, Aeroperlas, Parsa, Transpasa, Chitreana and Aerotaxi. On all internal flights passengers must present their identity documents, declare their own weight, in pounds (not kilos or stone) and have their luggage weighed. As excess baggage charges are frequent, ask if it is cheaper to ship excess as air freight (*carga*) on the same flight.

OTHER LAND TRANSPORT

● **Roads**

Speed limit on the Inter-American Highway is 90 kmph (but 60 is more realistic when planning a day's driving); the toll stretch (US$0.60) between Chame and Panama City has a 100 kmph limit. Observe 40 kmph speed zones in villages. Most streets have no lighting, many hotel signs are unlit, etc, so try to be at your destination before dusk (about 1830 Jan, 1800 July). Even driving at night in Panama City is unadvisable. Right turn against a red light is legal in cities if no vehicles are approaching from the left. If charged with a traffic violation, you should receive a document stipulating the infraction; fines to be paid to Dirección Nacional de Tránsito y Transporte Terrestre (Dpto de Infracciones Menores, Panama City, T 262-5687). In general, Panamanian highway police are helpful and

approachable, but some Spanish is an advantage. If you *have* committed an infraction, accept the ticket and pay it later. Fines are less than in Europe or the US. If you are sure an unscrupulous minor traffic policeman is harassing you, speak English and insist firmly but courteously that you be given a ticket or released. It is not recommended, or necessary to offer cash.

● **Local buses**

Most of the long distance buses are small 'mini' buses, normally modern and comfortable. They are more expensive than elsewhere in Central America, but nevertheless good value and recommended. Slower 'regular' buses run in some areas and better 'express' buses with a/c operate between Panama City and Colón.

● **Motoring**

Coming in by road from Costa Rica, passengers and vehicle (car or motorcycle) are given 30 days at the frontier. US$1 is payable for fumigation, US$3 for minibus. Exit calls for 4 papers which cost US$4.20 (obtainable, as are extensions for entry permits, from Customs in Paitilla airport). Taking a car with Panamanian plates to Costa Rica requires a lot of paperwork, eg proof of ownership, proof that the vehicle has not been stolen, etc. A travel agency eg Chadwick's in Balboa, will arrange this for you, for US$30. Rental cars are not allowed out of the country; they are marked by special license plates. Super grade gasoline (called *super*) costs about US$1.90/US gallon (3.78 litres); unleaded available in larger towns. Low octane (*regular* or *normal*) costs about US$1.80; diesel about US$1.30. Station attendants do not expect tips. For motorcyclists, note that a crash helmet must be worn. **NB** You may not take dogs into Panama by car, though they may be flown or shipped in if they have general health and rabies certificates; dogs and cats now have to spend 40 days in quarantine after entry.

NB It used to be virtually impossible for a tourist to sell a car in Panama unless he /she can show (with help from the Consulate) that he/she needed the money for a fare home. Recent reports (4/93 and 7/95) suggest that the whole procedure is now a lot easier. The vendor needs a document stating that the car has been sold, obtainable from a notary/lawyer. It is a great help if you have arranged for the Panamanian Embassy in San José to issue a Factura Consular from which the stated value of the car is used to calculate the import taxes payable. Taxes have to be paid by the buyer and if the title of the car is still in the seller's name, the buyer needs a similar document to be able to arrange all the paperwork at the Aduana/Customs. You have to authorize the buyer to pay the taxes for you by means of this document. A helpful address, both for finding potential buyers, and for the paperwork, is: Fernie and Co Shipping Agency, Sr Pérez, Panama City, English spoken. Another helpful office with English-speaking staff is in the same building as the Diablo Heights supermarket (in the street across the railway from the main entry of Albrook air base), which deals with license plates, transfer of titles. A great many US service personnel use this facility. There is a bulletin board outside. Your embassy will give you advice. At present, Japanese second hand cars are the most popular.

COMMUNICATIONS

● **Language**
Spanish (hard to understand), but English is widely understood. The older generation of West Indian immigrants speak Wari-Wari, a dialect of English incomprehensible to other English speakers, but the origin of much Panamanian Spanish slang. Indians in rural areas use their own languages, though many are bilingual.

● **Newspapers**
La Prensa is the major local daily newspaper, others are *La Estrella de Panamá*, *La República*, *El Universal*, *El Panamá América*, *Crítica Libre* and *El Siglo*. *Colón News* (weekly – Spanish and English). The imported *Miami Herald* and *USA Today* are widely available in the capital.

● **Postal services**
Great care should be taken to address all mail as 'Panama' or 'RP' (Republic of Panama). Mail addressed to the 'Panama Canal Zone' is likely to be returned to sender. Air mail takes 3-10 days, sea mail 3-5 weeks from Britain. Rates (examples) for air mail (up to 15 grams) are as follows: Central, North and South America and Caribbean, 35c; Europe, 45c up to 10 grams, 5c for every extra 5 grams; Africa, Asia, Oceania, 60c. Parcels to Europe can only be sent from the post office in the El Dorado shopping centre in Panama City (bus from C 12 to Tumba Muerto).

Post offices, marked with blue and yellow signs, are the only places permitted to sell stamps.

● **Telephone services**
The radio station at Gatún is open to commercial traffic; such messages are handled through the Government telegraph offices. The telegraph and cable companies are given under the towns in which they operate. **Telex** is available at the airport, the cable companies and many hotels. Rate for a 3-min call to Britain is US$14.40, and US$4.80 for each minute more. **Telephone** calls can be made between the UK and Panama any time, day or night. Collect calls are possible. Person to person calls, for the first 3 mins, cost (reduced rate in brackets): Central America US$5.50-10, depending on country (US$4.05-8); USA US$6-9, depending on zone (US$4.50-7.50); Canada US$9-12 (US$7.50-9); Mexico US$7.50 (US$6); Caribbean US$6-12, depending on island (US$7.50-8.25); South America US$8-12, depending on country (US$6-9); Europe US$12-16 (US$12, fax US$8/min); Israel US$15; Japan US$15 (US$12); Australia, New Zealand US$15 (US$12). For AT & T dial 109. For SPRINT (collect calls only) T 115 and MCI T 108. BT Chargecard calls to the UK can be made through the local operator.

Inter-continental contact by satellite is laid on by the Pan-American Earth Satellite Station. The local company is Intercomsa.

HOLIDAYS AND FESTIVALS

● **Holidays**
1 Jan: New Year's Day; 9 Jan: National Mourning; Shrove Tuesday: Carnival. Good Friday; 1 May: Labour Day (Republic), 15 Aug: Panama City only (O); 1 Nov: National Anthem Day (O); 2 Nov: All Souls (O); 3 Nov: Independence Day; 4 Nov: Flag Day (O); 5 Nov: Independence Day (Colón only), 10 Nov: First Call of Independence; 28 Nov: Independence from Spain; 8 Dec: Mothers' Day; 25 Dec: Christmas Day.

O=Official holiday, when banks and government offices close. On the rest – national holidays – business offices close too. Occasional others are added at short notice.

School holidays are Dec-Mar when holiday areas are busy; make reservations in advance.

● **Festivals**
The *fiestas* in the towns are well worth seeing. That of Panama City at Carnival time, held on the 4 days before Shrove Tuesday, is the best (book hotels and car hire in advance at this time). During carnival women who can afford it wear the *pollera* dress, with its 'infinity of diminutive gathers and its sweeping skirt finely embroidered', a shawl folded across the shoulders, velvet slippers, tinkling pearl and polished fish-scale hair ornaments (called *templeques* from their quivering motion) in spirited shapes and colours. The men wear a *montuno* outfit: round straw hats, embroidered blouses and trousers

sometimes to below the knee only, and carry the *chácara*, or small purse.

At the Holy Week ceremonies at Villa de Los Santos the farces and acrobatics of the big devils – with their debates and trials in which the main devil accuses and an angel defends the soul – the dance of the 'dirty little devils' and the dancing drama of the Montezumas are all notable. The ceremonies at Pesé (nr Chitré) are famous all over Panama. For other festivals in this region, see under the **Azuero Peninsula**, page 1192. At Portobelo, nr Colón, there is a procession of little boats in the canals of the city. See under Portobelo for the *Congos*, page 1184.

There are, too, the folk-tunes and dances. The music is cheerful, combining the rhythms of Africa with the melodic tones and dance-steps of Andalusia, to which certain characteristics of the Indian pentatonic scale have been added. The *tamborito* is the national dance. Couples dance separately and the song – which is sung by the women only, just as the song part of the *mejorana* or *socavón* is exclusively for male voices – is accompanied by the clapping of the audience and three kinds of regional drums. The *mejorana* is danced to the music of native guitars and in the interior are often heard the laments known as the *gallo* (rooster), *gallina* (hen), *zapatero* (shoemaker), or *mesano*. Two other dances commonly seen at *fiestas* are the *punto*, with its promenades and foot tapping, and the *cumbia*, of African origin, in which the dancers carry lighted candles and strut high.

Bullfights are an important part of rural fairs, as are rodeo events. The bulls are not killed in Panama.

The Ngöbe-Bugle (Guaymí) Indians of Chiriquí province meet around 12 Feb to transact tribal business, hold feasts and choose mates by tossing balsa logs at one another; those unhurt in this contest, known as Las Balserías, are viewed as heroes and are said to be regarded as promising suitors.

FURTHER READING

● **History**
For the history of the Canal, see David McCullough's *The Path Between the Seas*. For the era of military rule, John Dinges, *Our Man in Panamá*. Graham Greene's *Getting to Know the General* (Torrijos) is subjective and, as such, is not historically reliable, but is worth reading. John Le Carré's recent *Tailor of Panamá* is a cynical but entertaining view of Panama City society. Manuel Noriega has written *America's Prisoner* (Random House).

ACKNOWLEDGEMENTS

For a thorough review of a significant proportion of this chapter, we should like to extend our warmest thanks to David Fishlow, resident in Panama. We are also most grateful to Peter Pollard for updating the chapter, to Winston Johnson of the Panamanian Consulate, London, and to Andreas Siraa (USA).

Section 4

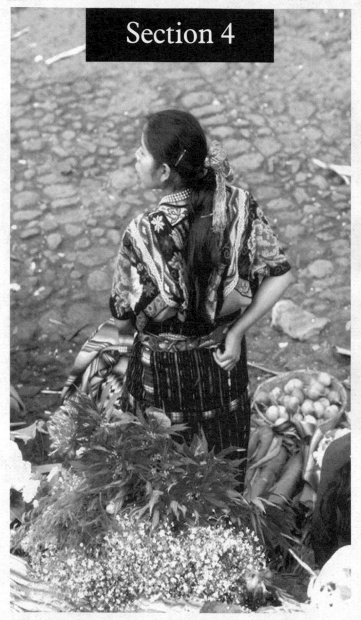

Rounding up

ACKNOWLEDGEMENTS

We are very grateful to all travellers who have written to us over the last year. Nimrod Abiram, Rishon le-Zion, Israel (Mex, Els, Hon); Felix Adank, Bern, Switzerland (Mex, Cub); Pierre Allard, Montreal, Canada (Pan); Jimmy Anderson, Malmö, Sweden (Mex.Gua); Regina and Larry Aragon, Palo Alto, USA (Mex); Mauricio Arias, (Cos); Debra Askanase, Jamaica Plain, USA (Mex, Gua); Pierre Atlan, Paris, France (Cub, Mex, Bel, Gua, Hon, Nic, Cos, Pan); Oliver Auras and Sandra Schweigert, Ettlingen, Germany (Mex, Gua); Yamir Avraham and Helga Noorman, Israel and The Netherlands (Col, Cos, Nic); Didier Bazin, Saint Chamond, France (Cub); Fritz Bechinger, Wingst, Germany (Gua); Lis Beck and Jakob Bergendorff, Kobenhavn, Denmark (Mex, Gua); Tali Ben-Ari, Herzeliya, israel (Mex, Gua); Patricia Bernet, Binningen, Switzerland (Gua, Mex, Bel, Hon), Silvia Besner, Nurnberg, Germany (Nic); Grahan Birch and Susan Smith, St Helens, UK (Cub, Mex); Alexander Bolle, Dortmund, Germany (Hon); David and Susan Brady, Leeds, England (Mex, Gua, Hon, Nic, Cos, Pan); Allesandro Brutti, Verona, Italy (Mex, Gua); Arnaldo Buch, Bogota, Colombia (Gua); Jurg Buhler and Christine Blauer, Winterthur, Switzerland (Per, Bol, Col, Mex, Gua); Russell Burrows, Mexico, (Mex).

Arnaldo Cabrera, Santa Clara, Cuba (Cub); John Carlisle, Kassel, Germany (Bel); Enrica Casanova, Bologna, Italy (Mex); Anna-Christina Carlson, Toronto, Canada (Mex, Gua); Aanon Clausen, Lions Bay, Canada (Mex, Bel, Gua, Nic, Pan, Col); Nicholas Couis, Northampton, England (Mex); Nicholas Couis, Northampton, England (Mex); Eithne Courtney and John Lane, Co Limerick, Ireland (Mex, Hon, Gua, Nic, Pan, Cos); Rob Craig, Lincolnwood, USA (Mex); Richard Crosfield, Madrid, Spain (Mex); Sharon Davies, Newtown, UK (Mex, Gua, Hon, Els), Christopher Davies, USA (Cos); Suzanne DiGiacomo, Logan, Utah USA (Hon, Gua, Bel, Mex); Tchau Dina, (Cos); Ditte Dossing, Homlebaek, Denmark (Mex, Gua, Col); Roy Downey, Willits, California, USA (Cos); Marianne Dume, Rodgan, Germany (Gua, Del, Hon, Nic, Pan); Axel Ebert, Muelheim, Germany (Cub, Mex, Gua), G Edwin Olsen, Ponte Vedra, USA (Gua, Mex, Hon); John Eyberg, El Paso, USA (Pan, Mex); Elad Faltin, Israel (Gua, Mex, Hon, Col); Jesse Ferris, Rosh Pinna, Israel (Mex.Bel), Rolf Ditsch, Aalen, Germany (Hon, Nic, Cos); Louise Foster, Pensacola, USA (Bel); Paul Foulkes-Arellano, León, Mexico (Mex); Sarah Fullerton, Calgary, Canada (Cos); Margarita Gonzales, Santiago, Chile (Mex); Wytze van Goor, Zwolla, The Netherlands (Cos); Cees de Gruyter and Gerdi ter Heegde, (Mex, Gua, Hon, Nic, Cos); J S Haggett, Yeovil, UK (Mex, Gua, Hon, Bel); Dr Bibi Hahn and Frank Elsen, Frankfurt and Wiesbaden, Germany (Mex); Mick Hamilton, Cheltenham, Australia (Mex, Cub); Steve Harris and Claire Bonnet, London, UK (Gua); Aviv Hassidov, Kfar-Saba, Israel (Cos); Marc Heim, Nyon, Switzerland (Pan, Cos, Nic, Hon, Gua, Mex); Paxton Hogg, Portland, USA (Mex); Aurelia Holliman, Deer Harbour, USA (Mex).

Barbara Jakisch, Munich, Germany (Mex); Nick James, Canberra, Australia (Mex, Gua, Bel); Marie Javins, New York, USA (Gua, Hon, Nic, Cos, Pan); Wil Jore, Galsmeer, Holland (Cos); Alexander Jurk, Hamburg, Germany (Gua, Bel,

Hon); Alan Juszyuski, Rehovot, Israel (Hon, Cos); Shirley & Alon Kadouri, Tel Aviv, Israel (Mex, Gua); Christina Kaiser, Austria (Mex, Gua, Hon); Tracey Keatman, Stone, UK (Cos, Nic, Hon, Gua, Bel, Mex); Verena Kiehn and Christoph Rathje, Hamburg, Germany (Mex, Gua, Bel); Piet Koene, Canada (Mex, Gua); Martin Kohchanski, London, UK (Mex); Grundula Kroel, Berlin, Germany (Hon, Gua); Andreas Kucher, Schorndorf, Germany (Mex, Gua, Bel, Els, Hon, Nic, Cos); Monique Leibovitch and Michael R Stone, Castlecrag, Australia (Mex); Florence Leon, Woodcliff Lake, USA (Mex, Bel); E Lew, San Francisco, USA (Mex); Gerlinde, Leyrer, Muhlhausen, Germany (Mex, Gua); Eva Lindenlaub and Ulrich Burmeister, Hamburg, Germany (Mex); Anja van der Lindne and Rob van der Kar, Tilburg, The Netherlands (Hon); Barry Lloyd, Newcastle upon Tyne. UK (Mex, Bra, Cos); Chuck Locher and Nancy Blackstock, Richmond, USA (Ven, Gui, Gua, Mex); Silvio Lorenzatto, Villaguay, Argentina (Nic, Hon, Gua); Lois Lragen, Texas, USA (Mex); Carey Luff, Woodinville, USA (Mex); Imk Luuk, Berlin, Germany (Mex, Gua); Sue Lyons, Costa Rica (Cub); James Maas, Panama (Pan); B MacGregor, Costa Rica (Cos); Eric Malfit, Tournon, France (Mex, Gua); Dagny Margrethe Oren, Honefoss, Norway (Pan, Hon, Gua); Katherine Maris, Charleston, USA (Cos); C G McKenzie, Bedford, UK (Mex, Hon, Gua); Rowland Mead, Leighton Buzzard, UK (Cos); Claire Mortimer, Exeter, UK (Hon, Bel, Mex, Gua); Kevin Murphy, Jegucigalpa, Honduras (Gua); Efrat Nativ, Jerusalem, Israel (Gua, Mex); Hugo Nielsen, Odense, Denmark (Gua); Heidi Nissen, Aergadkeabing, Denmark (Mex, Gua, Hon, Cos); D Nordman, Bowser, Canada (Gua, Mex, Hon, Els, Nic, Cos, Pan).

Yiftah Offer, Kfar Masarik, Israel (Mex, , Gua, Bel, Hon); Rebecca Omwanda, (Nic); Gabrielle Pauze, Quetzaltenago, Guatemala (Mex, Gua); Leo and Roma Pedersen, Midway, Canada (Mex); Linda Peregrine, Texas, USA (Mex); Gerald Petersen, Sparks, USA (Mex); Monika Pfaffelhuber, Freising, Germany (Mex, Gua); Mikko Pirinen, Tampere, Finland (Cos, Hon, Bel, Mex); Nigel Potter, La Paz, Honduras (Hon); Nathalie Pouliot and Juan Carlos, Quebec, Canada (Mex); Fernando Prati, Buenos Aires, Argentina (Mex, Bel, Gua, Hon, Cos,

Pan); Ann Rabin, California, USA (Mex); Silvia Ravaioli, Ravanna, Italy (Mex, Gua, Cos, Nic, Hon); Alan Reeve, Effingham, UK (Mex, Cos, Nic, Hon, Chi); Werner, Richter, Gerasdorf bei Wein, Austria (Hon, Mex); Lupi Roberto, Gordevio, Switzerland (Gua); Tiernan Roe, Mullingar, Ireland (Gua, Mex); Dalia Rosin and Riky Grunewald, (Mex, Gua, Hon, Cos); Andrea Rossbach, Osnabrüor, Germany (Mex, Gua, Bel, Hon, Cos); Lutz Rothermel, Magdeburg, Denmark (Mex); Yoav Rubenstein and Tal Benoudiz, Jerusalem, Israel (Mex, Gua, Hon, Cos, Pan).

Gunther Schafer, Herbertingen, Germany (Gua, Bel, Els, Hon, Nic, Cos, Pan); Britta Scheunemann and Stefan Bock, Bonn, Germany (Mex, Gua, Hon, Per); Ralph Schmarje, Phoenix, Arizona USA (Mex); Claudia Schreier, Lug, Switzerland (Cos, Bel); Chris Sharp, Vermont, USA (Hon, Mex, Gua, Els); Chris Sharp, Williston, Vermont USA (Mex, Bel, Gua); Karin Sieber, Ostermundigen, Switzerland (Cos); Bobby Singh, Honduras (Hon); Bruno Skorepa, Langenlebarn, Austria (Pan); Joris Smets and Vanessa Vandenberghe, Brechem, Belgium (Ecu, Per, Mex, Gua); Christine Somieski and Volker Betz, Gilching and Gauting, Germany (Mex, Gua, Hon); Angelika Straus, Munich, Germany (Cos); Anouk Studer, Lausanne, Switzerland (Cos); Andreas Terch and Silvia Dianello, Birsfelden, Switzerland (Hon, Cos, Bel); Penelope Thiebaut and Alexandre Megret, Perros Guirec, France (Pan, Cos); Karl Thieloke, Frieburg, Germany (Gua, Hon); Beatrix Trojer, Vienna, Austria (Mex); Gisela Vogl, Munich, Germany (Gua); J M Watts, Spalding, UK (Gua, Hon, Nic, Cos); Rolf Werckenthien, Waldkirch, Germany (Gua, Cos); Anne Wexlberger, Nurnberg, Germany (Nic, Gua); Lisa Williams, Castlemaine, Australia (Hin, Gua, Mex); Asa Winfridsson, Stokholm, Sweded (Nic, Cos); Rolf Wreckenthien, Waldkirch, Germany (Mex); Ralf Wyrwinski and Jorg Ohlhaver, Geesthacht and Buxtehude, Germany (Gua, Mex, Bel, Hon); Margarit and Ryal Yaffe, Ramat-Gan, Israel (Gua); Sabine Verhelst and Wim Pannecoucke, Brugge, Belgium (Cub); Björn Zeller, Niedereschach, Germany (Hon); Helmut Zettl, Ebergassing, Austira (Mex, Bel, Gua); Jan Zomer, Rijnsburg, The Netherlands (Gua, Els, Nic, Cos).

Advertisers

Writing to us

Many people write to us - with corrections, new information, or simply comments. If you want to let us know something, we would be delighted to hear from you. Please give us as precise Information as possible, quoting the edition and page number of the Handbook you are using and send as early in the year as you can. Your help will be greatly appreciated, especially by other travellers. In return we will send you details about our special guidebook offer.

For hotels and restaurants, please let us know:

- each establishment's name, address, phone and fax number
- number of rooms, whether a/c or air-cooled, attached (clean?) bathroom
- location - how far from the station or bus stand, or distance (walking time) from a prominent landmark
- if it's not already on one of our maps, can you place it?
- your comments - either good or bad - as to why it is distinctive
- tariff cards
- local transport used

For places of interest:

- location
- entry, camera charge
- access - by whatever means of transport is most approriate, eg time of main buses or trains to and from the site, journey time, fare
- facilities - nearby drinks stalls, restaurants, for the disabled
- any problems, eg steep climb, wildlife, unofficial guides
- opening hours
- site guides

CLIMATIC TABLES

The following tables have been very kindly furnished by Mr R K Headland. Each weather station is given with its altitude in metres (m). Temperatures (Centigrade) are given as averages for each month; the first line is the maximum and the second the minimum. The third line is the average number of wet days encountered in each month.

MEXICO AND CENTRAL AMERICA

	Jan	Feb	Mar	Apr	May	Jun	Jul	Aug	Sep	Oct	Nov	Dec
Acapulco, Mexico	29	31	31	31	32	32	32	32	31	31	31	31
3m	21	21	21	22	23	24	24	24	24	23	22	21
	0	0	0	0	2	9	7	7	12	6	1	0
Guatemala City	23	25	27	28	29	27	26	26	26	24	23	22
1490m	11	12	14	14	16	16	16	16	16	15	14	13
	2	2	2	5	8	20	17	16	17	13	6	2
Havana	26	27	28	29	30	31	31	32	31	29	27	26
49m	18	18	19	21	22	23	24	24	24	23	21	19
	6	4	4	4	7	10	9	10	11	11	7	6
Managua,	30	30	30	32	32	31	31	31	31	31	30	30
Nicaragua	23	24	26	28	27	26	26	25	26	24	24	24
46m	0	0	0	0	6	12	11	12	15	16	4	1
Mérida, Mexico	28	29	32	33	34	33	33	33	32	31	29	28
22m	17	17	19	21	22	23	23	23	23	22	19	18
	4	2	1	2	5	10	11	12	13	7	3	3
Mexico City	19	21	24	25	26	24	23	23	23	21	20	19
2309m	6	6	8	11	12	13	12	12	12	10	8	6
	2	1	2	6	9	14	19	18	17	8	3	2
Monterrey, 20	22	24	29	31	33	32	33	30	27	22	18	
Mexico	9	11	14	17	20	22	22	22	21	18	13	10
538m	3	3	3	4	4	4	4	3	8	5	4	4
Panama City	31	31	32	32	31	30	30	31	30	30	29	30
36m	21	21	22	23	23	23	23	23	23	22	22	23
	4	2	1	6	15	16	15	15	15	16	18	12
San José	24	24	26	27	27	27	26	26	27	26	25	24
Costa Rica	14	14	15	16	16	16	16	16	16	15	15	15
1172m	1	0	1	4	17	20	18	19	20	22	14	4
San Salvador	30	31	32	32	31	30	30	30	29	29	29	29
700m	16	16	17	19	19	19	18	18	19	18	17	16
	0	3	2	5	12	20	21	20	18	14	4	1
Tegucigalpa,	25	27	29	30	30	28	28	28	29	27	26	25
Honduras	14	14	15	16	18	19	17	17	17	17	16	15
935m	4	2	1	3	14	18	10	10	17	16	8	4

TEMPERATURE CONVERSION TABLE

°C	°F	°C	°F
1	34	26	79
2	36	27	81
3	38	28	82
4	39	29	84
5	41	30	86
6	43	31	88
7	45	32	90
8	46	33	92
9	48	34	93
10	50	35	95
11	52	36	97
12	54	37	99
13	56	38	100
14	57	39	102
15	59	40	104
16	61	41	106
17	63	42	108
18	64	43	109
19	66	44	111
20	68	45	113
21	70	46	115
22	72	47	117
23	74	48	118
24	75	49	120
25	77	50	122

The formula for converting °C to °F is:
$$°C \times 9 \div 5 + 32 = °F$$

WEIGHTS AND MEASURES

Metric

Weight
1 Kilogram (Kg) = 2.205 pounds
1 metric ton = 1.102 short tons

Length
1 millimetre (mm) = 0.03937 inch
1 metre = 3.281 feet
1 kilometre (km) = 0.621 mile

Area
1 heactare = 2.471 acres
1 square km = 0.386 sq mile

Capacity
1 litre = 0.220 imperial gallon
       = 0.264 US gallon

Volume
1 cubic metre (m³) = 35.31 cubic feet
                   = 1.31 cubic yards

British and US

Weight
1 pound (lb) = 454 grams
1 short ton (2,000lbs) = 0.907 m ton
1 long ton (2,240lbs) = 1.016 m tons

Length
1 inch = 25.417 millimetres
1 foot (ft) = 0.305 metre
1 mile = 1.609 kilometres

Area
1 acre = 0.405 hectare
1 sq mile = 2.590 sq kilometre

Capacity
1 imperial gallon = 4.546 litres
1 US gallon = 3.785 litres

Volume
1 cubic foot (cu ft) = 0.028 m³
1 cubic yard (cu yd) = 0.765 m³

NB 5 imperial gallons are approximately equal to 6 US gallons

The manzana, used in Central America, is about 0.7 hectare (1.73 acres).

Index

1244